Teacher Edition

HOLT McDOUGAL

Modern Chemistry

Sarquis • Sarquis

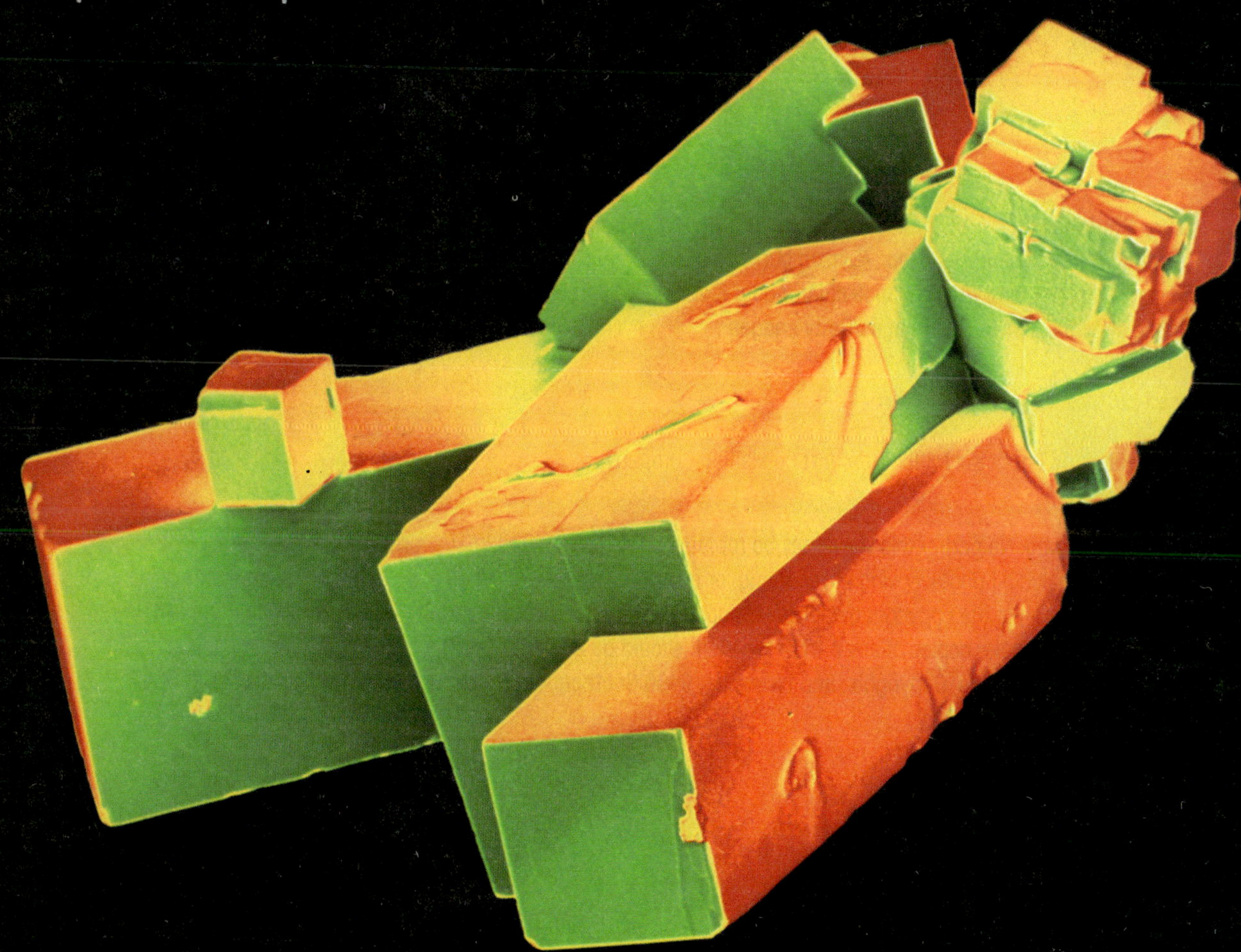

HOLT McDOUGAL

HOUGHTON MIFFLIN HARCOURT

Cover Photo Credits: Salt crystal ©Dr. Jeremy Burgess/Photo Researchers, Inc.; Bunsen burner flame ©Martyn F. Chillmaid/Photo Researchers, Inc.; Bunsen burner base ©Yoav Levy/Phototake Inc./Alamy; periodic chart, matches ©Science Photo Library/Corbis; molecular model ©Wayne Calabrese/Photonica/Getty Images; beaker ©Corbis Yellow/Corbis; snowflake ©Kallista Images/Getty Images

2015 Printing

Printed in the U.S.A.

ISBN 978-0-547-63634-4

9 10 0868 20 19 18 17 16 15

4500520215 D E F G

What's New for ©2012 . . .

Updated Student & Teacher Edition

- Increased Student Accessibility
- Differentiated Instruction in the Teacher Edition
- New 4-step Instructional Model used to organize the Teacher Edition

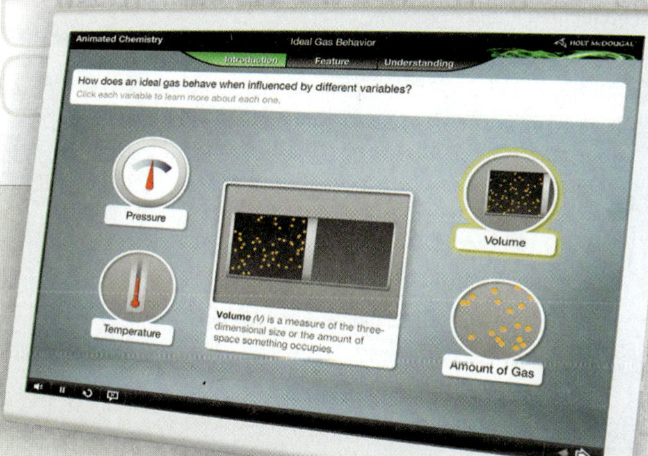

Innovative Technology

- Why It Matters videos
- Virtual Labs
- Animated Chemistry
- Interactive Review Games

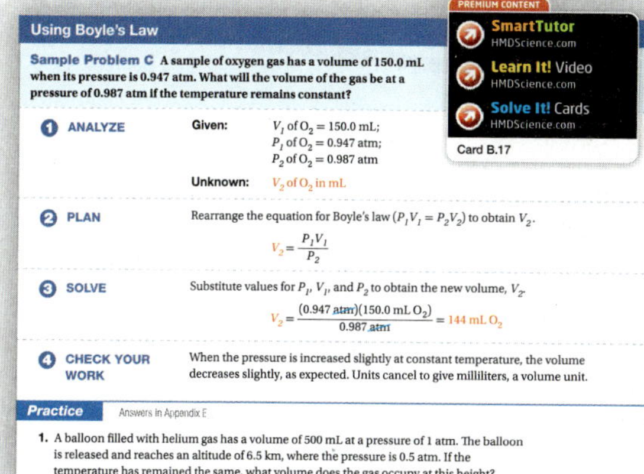

Using Boyle's Law

PREMIUM CONTENT
SmartTutor HMDScience.com
Learn It! Video HMDScience.com
Solve It! Cards HMDScience.com
Card B.17

Sample Problem C **A sample of oxygen gas has a volume of 150.0 mL when its pressure is 0.947 atm. What will the volume of the gas be at a pressure of 0.987 atm if the temperature remains constant?**

1 ANALYZE Given: V_1 of O_2 = 150.0 mL; P_1 of O_2 = 0.947 atm; P_2 of O_2 = 0.987 atm

Unknown: V_2 of O_2 in mL

2 PLAN Rearrange the equation for Boyle's law ($P_1V_1 = P_2V_2$) to obtain V_2.

$$V_2 = \frac{P_1V_1}{P_2}$$

3 SOLVE Substitute values for P_1, V_1, and P_2 to obtain the new volume, V_2.

$$V_2 = \frac{(0.947\ \text{atm})(150.0\ \text{mL}\ O_2)}{0.987\ \text{atm}} = 144\ \text{mL}\ O_2$$

4 CHECK YOUR WORK When the pressure is increased slightly at constant temperature, the volume decreases slightly, as expected. Units cancel to give milliliters, a volume unit.

Practice Answers in Appendix E

1. A balloon filled with helium gas has a volume of 500 mL at a pressure of 1 atm. The balloon is released and reaches an altitude of 6.5 km, where the pressure is 0.5 atm. If the temperature has remained the same, what volume does the gas occupy at this height?

Stronger Problem-Solving Support

- Revised Sample Problems
- Learn It! Video tutorials
- Solve It! Cards

The Standard by which all Chemistry programs are compared

Modern Chemistry presents a balanced and engaging approach to conceptual and problem-solving instruction. Many improvements have been made to the program to make the content accessible to more students.

A Friendlier Student Edition

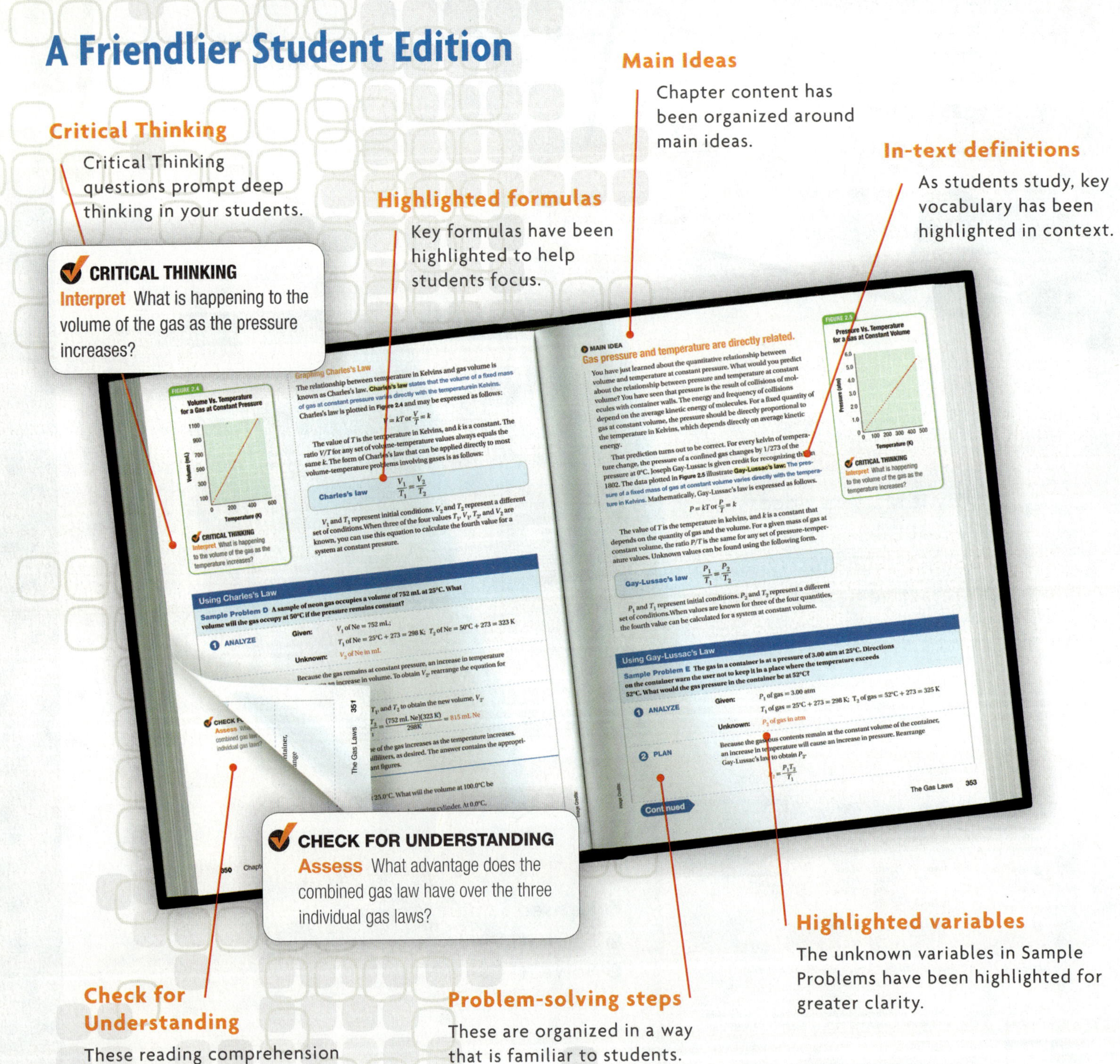

Critical Thinking

Critical Thinking questions prompt deep thinking in your students.

Highlighted formulas

Key formulas have been highlighted to help students focus.

Main Ideas

Chapter content has been organized around main ideas.

In-text definitions

As students study, key vocabulary has been highlighted in context.

Check for Understanding

These reading comprehension questions help reinforce the important points of the section.

Problem-solving steps

These are organized in a way that is familiar to students.

Highlighted variables

The unknown variables in Sample Problems have been highlighted for greater clarity.

ACKNOWLEDGMENTS, continued

Richard S. Treptow, Ph.D.
Professor of Chemistry
Department of Chemistry and Physics
Chicago State University
Chicago, Illinois

Barry Tucker
Chemistry Teacher
Colerain High School
Cincinnati, Ohio

Martin Van Dyke, Ph.D.
Chemistry Professor, Emeritus
Front Range Community College
Westminster, Colorado

Joseph E. Vitt, Ph.D.
Associate Professor
Chemistry Department
University of South Dakota
Vermillion, South Dakota

Verne Weidler, Ph.D.
Professor of Chemistry, Retired
Science and Engineering
Black Hawk College
Kewanee, Illinois

Dale Wheeler, Ph.D.
Associate Professor of Chemistry
A. R. Smith Department of Chemistry
Appalachian State University
Boone, North Carolina

David Wilson, Ph.D.
Professor Emeritus
Chemistry Department
Vanderbilt University
Nashville, Tennessee

Candace Woodside
Science Teacher
Winton Woods High School
Forest Park, Ohio

Charles M. Wynn, Sr., Ph.D.
Professor of Chemistry
Department of Physical Sciences
Eastern Connecticut State University
Willimantic, Connecticut

ACKNOWLEDGMENTS

Contributing Writers

Lisa Saunders Baugh, Ph.D.
Senior Chemist
Chemical Sciences Laboratory
ExxonMobil Research & Engineering Company
Corporate Strategic Research
Annandale, New Jersey

Robert Davisson
Science Writer
Albuquerque, New Mexico

Seth Madej
Writer/Producer
Pittsburgh, Pennsylvania

Jim Metzner
Executive Producer
Pulse of the Planet Radio Series
Jim Metzner Productions, Inc.
Accord, New York

Jay A. Young, Ph.D.
Chemical Safety Consultant
Silver Spring, Maryland

Inclusion Specialists

Joan Altobelli
Special Education Director
Austin Independent School District
Austin, Texas

John A. Solorio
Multiple Technologies Lab Facilitator
Austin Independent School District
Austin, Texas

Reviewers

Eric V. Anslyn, Ph.D.
Professor
Department of Chemistry and Biochemistry
University of Texas at Austin
Austin, Texas

George F. Atkinson, Ph.D.
Professor of Chemistry
Department of Chemistry
University of Waterloo
Waterloo, Ontario, Canada

Sonal S.D. Blumenthal, Ph.D.
Life Science Consultant
Austin, Texas

G. Lynn Carlson, Ph.D.
Senior Lecturer Emeritus
Department of Chemistry
University of Wisconsin—Parkside
Kenosha, Wisconsin

Scott A. Darveau, Ph.D.
Associate Professor
Department of Chemistry
University of Nebraska at Kearney
Kearney, Nebraska

Cassandra T. Eagle, Ph.D.
Professor of Chemistry
Department of Chemistry
Appalachian State University
Boone, North Carolina

Linda Gaul, Ph.D., M.P.H.
Epidemiologist
Infectious Disease Epidemiology and Surveillance
Department of State Health Services
Austin, Texas

Pamela Gollhofer
Science Teacher
Princeton High School
Cincinnati, Ohio

Hima Joshi, Ph.D.
Department of Chemistry
University of San Diego
San Diego, California

Doris Ingram Lewis, Ph.D.
Professor of Chemistry
Suffolk University
Boston, Massachusetts

Gary E. Mueller, Ph.D.
Associate Professor
Department of Nuclear Engineering
University of Missouri
Rolla Rolla, Missouri

Daniel B. Murphy, Ph.D.
Professor Emeritus of Chemistry
Department of Chemistry
Herbert H. Lehman College
City University of New York
Bronx, New York

R. Thomas Myers, Ph.D.
Professor Emeritus of Chemistry
Kent State University
Kent, Ohio

Keith B. Oldham, Ph.D.
Professor of Chemistry
Trent University
Peterborough, Ontario, Canada

Brian L. Pagenkopf, Ph.D.
Assistant Professor
Department of Chemistry and Biochemistry
University of Texas at Austin
Austin, Texas

Stanford Peppenhorst, Ed.D.
Chemistry Teacher
Germantown High School
Germantown, Tennessee

Charles Scaife, Ph.D.
Professor of Chemistry, Emeritus
Union College
Schenectady, New York

Peter Sheridan, Ph.D.
Professor
Department of Chemistry and Biochemistry
Colgate University
Hamilton, New York

Larry Stookey, P.E.
Physics and Chemistry Teacher
Antigo High School
Antigo, Wisconsin

David C. Taylor, Ph.D.
Professor of Chemistry
Department of Chemistry
Slippery Rock University
Slippery Rock, Pennsylvania

... is now more Accessible than ever.

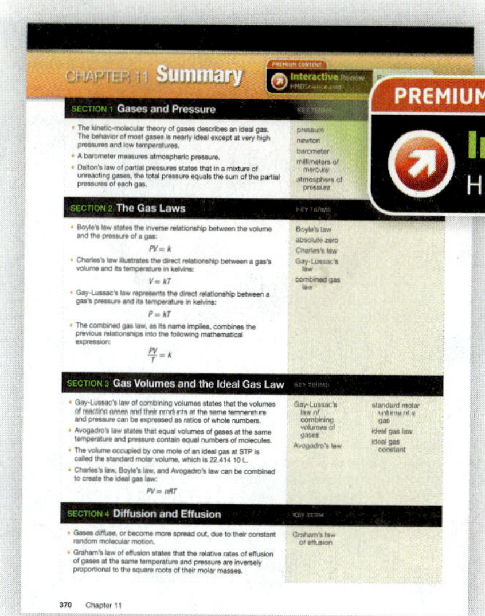

CHAPTER 11 Summary

PREMIUM CONTENT Interactive Review HMDScience.com

SECTION 1 Gases and Pressure — KEY TERMS

- The kinetic-molecular theory of gases describes an ideal gas. The behavior of most gases is nearly ideal except at very high pressures and low temperatures.
- A barometer measures atmospheric pressure.
- Dalton's law of partial pressures states that in a mixture of unreacting gases, the total pressure equals the sum of the partial pressures of each gas.

Key terms: pressure, newton, barometer, millimeters of mercury, atmosphere of pressure

SECTION 2 The Gas Laws — KEY TERMS

- Boyle's law states the inverse relationship between the volume and the pressure of a gas:

$$PV = k$$

- Charles's law illustrates the direct relationship between a gas's volume and its temperature in kelvins:

$$V = kT$$

- Gay-Lussac's law represents the direct relationship between a gas's pressure and its temperature in kelvins:

$$P = kT$$

- The combined gas law, as its name implies, combines the previous relationships into the following mathematical expression:

$$\frac{PV}{T} = k$$

Key terms: Boyle's law, absolute zero, Charles's law, Gay-Lussac's law, combined gas law

SECTION 3 Gas Volumes and the Ideal Gas Law — KEY TERMS

- Gay-Lussac's law of combining volumes states that the volumes of reacting gases and their products at the same temperature and pressure can be expressed as ratios of whole numbers.
- Avogadro's law states that equal volumes of gases at the same temperature and pressure contain equal numbers of molecules.
- The volume occupied by one mole of an ideal gas at STP is called the standard molar volume, which is 22.414 10 L.
- Charles's law, Boyle's law, and Avogadro's law can be combined to create the ideal gas law:

$$PV = nRT$$

Key terms: Gay-Lussac's law of combining volumes of gases, Avogadro's law, standard molar volume of a gas, ideal gas law, ideal gas constant

SECTION 4 Diffusion and Effusion — KEY TERM

- Gases *diffuse*, or become more spread out, due to their constant random molecular motion.
- Graham's law of effusion states that the relative rates of effusion of gases at the same temperature and pressure are inversely proportional to the square roots of their molar masses.

Key term: Graham's law of effusion

370 Chapter 11

PREMIUM CONTENT

Interactive Review
HMDScience.com

Review Games
Concept Maps

Chapter Summary

Even the chapter summary has been significantly redesigned to be more accessible and useful to students. Features include:

- Section-level summaries
- Section-level key terms
- Interactive Review Games and Concept Map links

Interactive Reader

The hugely popular Interactive Reader is now available for Modern Chemistry! Designed for struggling students, the Interactive Reader features all of the essential content, written below grade level and with additional learning support.

Interactive Reader
HOLT MCDOUGAL
Modern Chemistry
Sarquis • Sarquis

Prokaryotic cells lack a nucleus and most internal structures of eukaryotic cells.

Word and Formula Equations

1. The first step in writing a chemical equation is to identify the facts about a reaction that are known. It is often useful to represent these facts using a word equation. A **word equation** is an equation in which the reactants and products are written down in words.

   For example, when methane burns in air, it combines with oxygen to produce carbon dioxide and water vapor. To turn this information into a word equation, first identify the reactants and the products.

   REACTANTS: methane, oxygen
   PRODUCTS: carbon dioxide, water

   List the reactants on the left side of the equation and the products on the right side of the equation. Then draw an arrow pointing from the reactants to the products.

   methane + oxygen → carbon dioxide + water
   (reactant, reactant, yields, product, product)

   The result is a word equation. This equation reads "methane and oxygen react to yield carbon dioxide and water."

TIP Word equations are descriptions of a reaction. They do not tell you anything about the quantities of the substances.

PRACTICE

Write a word equation for each chemical reaction.

A. Solid calcium reacts with solid sulfur to produce solid calcium sulfide.

B. Hydrogen gas reacts with fluorine gas to produce hydrogen fluoride gas.

250 CHAPTER 8

New and Improved Teacher Edition with . . .

New Instructional Model

Enhanced Teacher Edition wrap is organized around an instructional model that includes:

Focus and Motivate
Plan and Prepare
Teach
Assess and Reteach

Why It Matters

Each chapter begins with new **Why It Matters** videos that help students connect chemistry subjects to the world around them.

Labs

The Teacher Edition wrap outlines all program labs that are relevant to the chapter. These labs are all accessed online or on the Lab Generator. **QuickLabs** are also available in the Student Edition.

CHAPTER 11

Chapter Overview

Section 1 reintroduces the kinetic-molecular theory of gases, defines pressure in terms of force, explains how pressure is measured, and defines and converts units of pressure.

Section 2 presents gas laws that express simple mathematical relationships among the pressure, temperature, volume, and quantity of gases.

Section 3 develops the relationships among the volume, mass, and number of particles of a gas and presents the ideal gas law.

Section 4 demonstrates the relationship between the mass of gas particles and their rate of effusion.

▼ Focus and Motivate

Activate Prior Knowledge

Students may need a review of the following concepts:

- states and physical properties of matter
- scientific notation and significant figures
- writing and balancing chemical equations
- stoichiometric calculations
- the relationship between temperature and particle motion

About the Image

Hot-air balloons are the oldest form of human flight. The density of the gas inside the balloon decreases as it is heated. This causes the balloon to become buoyant and "float" on top of the air.

Why It Matters

Students can access the videos online and find other helpful resources at HMDScience.com.

340 Chapter 11

CHAPTER 11
Gases

SECTION 1
Gases and Pressure
SECTION 2
The Gas Laws
SECTION 3
Gas Volumes and the Ideal Gas Laws
SECTION 4
Diffusion and Effusion

ONLINE Chemistry
HMDScience.com

ONLINE LABS include:
Mass and Density of Air at Different Pressures
Boyle's Law
Molar Volume of a Gas
Generating and Collecting O_2
Generating and Collecting H_2
Testing for Dissolved Oxygen

PREMIUM CONTENT
Why It Matters Video
HMDScience.com
Gases

Lab Preview

The following labs and demonstrations support the concepts presented in this chapter.

LABS
Mass and Density of Air at Different Pressures
Boyle's Law (Core Skill)
Molar Volume of a Gas (Core Skill)
Generating and Collecting O_2
Generating and Collecting H_2
Testing for Dissolved Oxygen

QUICKLAB
Diffusion

PROBEWARE LAB
Pressure-Volume Relationships: Understanding Boyle's Law

DEMONSTRATIONS
Relating Pressure to Area
Unbalanced Force of Atmospheric Pressure

Lab Preview

The following labs and demonstrations support the concepts presented in this chapter.

LABS
Mass and Density of Air at Different Pressures
Boyle's Law (Core Skill)
Molar Volume of a Gas (Core Skill)
Generating and Collecting O_2
Generating and Collecting H_2
Testing for Dissolved Oxygen

QUICKLAB
Diffusion

PROBEWARE LAB
Pressure-Volume Relationships: Understanding Boyle's Law

DEMONSTRATIONS
Relating Pressure to Area
Unbalanced Force of Atmospheric Pressure

Stronger instructional support

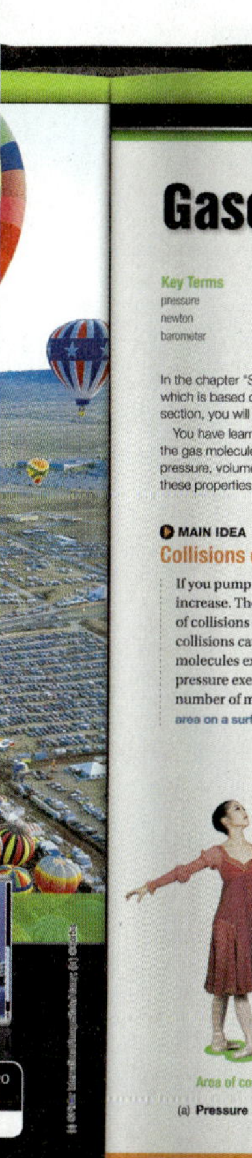

Gases and Pressure

SECTION 1

Main Ideas

- Collisions of air molecules generate pressure.
- Pressure depends on force and area.
- The total pressure of a gas mixture is the sum of the pressures of the gases in it.

Key Terms

pressure	millimeters of mercury	partial pressure
newton	atmosphere of pressure	Dalton's law of partial pressures
barometer	pascal	

In the chapter "States of Matter," you read about the kinetic-molecular theory, which is based on the idea that particles of matter are always in motion. In this section, you will study the implications of the kinetic-molecular theory of gases.

You have learned that the temperature of a gas is related to the kinetic energy of the gas molecules. Now you will learn about other properties of gases, including pressure, volume, and amount of gas present, and about the relationships among these properties.

VIRGINIA STANDARDS

CH.5 The student will investigate and understand that the phases of matter are explained by kinetic theory and forces of attraction between particles. Key concepts include:
CH.5.a pressure, temperature, and volume.
CH.5.b partial pressure and gas laws.

MAIN IDEA

Collisions of air molecules generate pressure.

If you pump air into an automobile tire, the pressure in the tire will increase. The pressure increase is caused by the increase in the number of collisions of molecules of air with the inside walls of the tire. The collisions cause an outward push, or force, against the inside walls. Gas molecules exert pressure on any surface with which they collide. The pressure exerted by a gas depends on volume, temperature, and the number of molecules present. **Pressure (P)** is defined as the force per unit area on a surface. The equation defining pressure is shown in **Figure 1.1**.

FIGURE 1.1

Pressure and Area of Contact Because force is constant, the pressure the ballet dancer exerts against the floor depends on the area of contact.

$$\text{Pressure} = \frac{\text{Force}}{\text{Area}}$$

Area of contact = 325 cm^2 (a) $\text{Pressure} = \frac{500\ \text{N}}{325\ \text{cm}^2} = 1.5\ \text{N/cm}^2$

Area of contact = 13 cm^2 (b) $\text{Pressure} = \frac{500\ \text{N}}{13\ \text{cm}^2} = 38.5\ \text{N/cm}^2$

Area of contact = 6.5 cm^2 (c) $\text{Pressure} = \frac{500\ \text{N}}{6.5\ \text{cm}^2} = 77\ \text{N/cm}^2$

Gases 341

Differentiated Instruction

BELOW LEVEL

Have students do a "jigsaw" activity to introduce this chapter. Divide the class into groups of 3–4 students and give each group a number. Divide Section 1 of this chapter into 3 or 4 parts, and name them "A," "B," "C," etc. Give each student in a group a letter designation in addition to their group number. For example, a student might be designated as "1A." Have the "A" students from all groups discuss and determine the major concepts within part A of the section. The "B" students will do the same with part B, and so on. Allow about 15 minutes for discussion. Then, have students report back to their original, numbered group, teaching the group what their designated part of the section had to say.

SECTION 1

Plan and Prepare ▼

Objectives

Upon completion of this section, students should be able to do the following:

- Define pressure, give units of pressure, and describe how pressure is measured.
- State the standard conditions of temperature and pressure and convert units of pressure.
- Use Dalton's law of partial pressures to calculate partial pressures and total pressures.

Classroom Catalyst

Have students make a list of gases. Ask them to separate the list into elements, compounds, and mixtures. Students can share these lists with the class by putting them on the board.

Teach ▼

Misconception Alert!

Students frequently think that the gas laws apply to real gases. Remind students that the gas laws are abstractions that apply to ideal gases and that they apply to real gases only as an approximation. Discuss the properties that prevent real gases from acting like ideal gases. Remind students of the ways in which real gases deviate from ideal behavior.

TEACH FROM VISUALS

FIGURE 1.1 Point out to students that the amount of force in each image remains the same. Only the surface area where the dancer's feet contact the floor changes.

Gases 341

Section Openers

Each section begins with learning objectives and a motivating "Classroom Catalyst" activity.

Strong Teaching Support

Point-of-use teaching support is provided throughout the chapter, including Misconception Alert!, Teach from Visuals, and Reading Toolkit features.

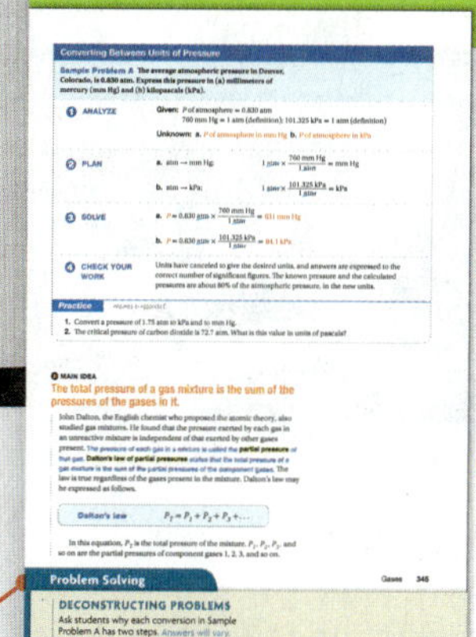

Differentiated Instruction

New differentiated instruction materials have been added to assist teachers with a wide range of student needs. Categories include:

Below Level
English Learners
Pre-AP
Inclusion

Problem-Solving Support

Teachers are provided with additional problem-solving strategies to help students solve chemistry problems.

Technology to inspire and engage

Nothing captures students' interest and facilitates meaningful learning like technology. Many highly effective technology learning tools have been added to ***Modern Chemistry*** to accomplish just that.

All Online!

Animated Chemistry

Students access chemistry concepts and principles in a meaningful way with dozens of high-quality animations and simulations.

Diffusion

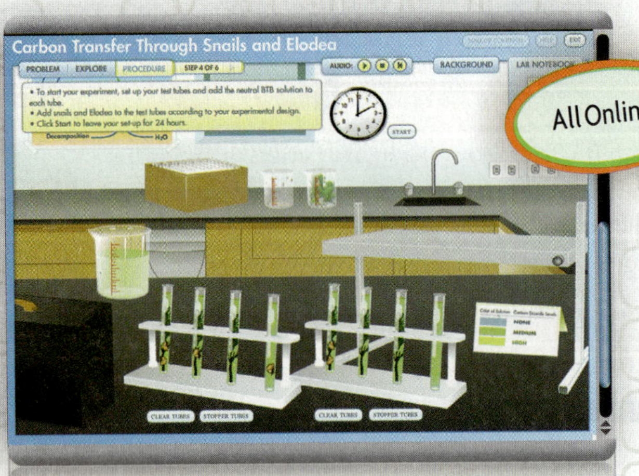

All Online!

Virtual Labs

Virtual Labs take students beyond the classroom to explore experiments not performed in a typical school laboratory setting.

All Online!

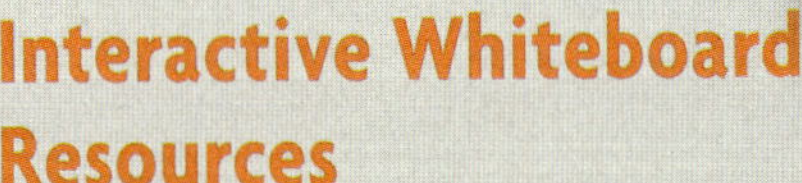

Interactive Whiteboard Resources

Key teaching visuals have been adapted specifically for interactive whiteboard use, allowing teachers to take advantage of this exciting technology.

Interactive Review Games

Nothing encourages students to study and review more than a game! These newly designed online review games help make chemistry more fun than ever.

Available to you online at HMDScience.com

Why It Matters

All Online!

Captivate student interest and boost real-world relevance with these short chapter introductory videos.

All Online!

WebLinks

Hand-selected resource links bring the BEST of the internet to the classroom. No longer will you have to spend endless hours scouring the internet for great resources—we've done all the work!

Teaching Visuals

Key illustrations and diagrams from the text are provided in a digital format so that you can display them on a whiteboard or projector.

Interactive Reader Audio

A full audio version of the Interactive Reader makes content more accessible for auditory learners, reluctant readers, and English Learners.

In addition, Modern Chemistry still offers the following popular technology features:

PowerPresentations Use these pre-designed lectures, or edit them to make your own customized presentations.

Chapter Summaries Audio These are available in English and Spanish.

Approach Problem Solving in NEW ways

Problem solving commonly stumps even the best students. ***Modern Chemistry*** has added new problem-solving support resources to help students master the fundamentals of chemistry problem solving.

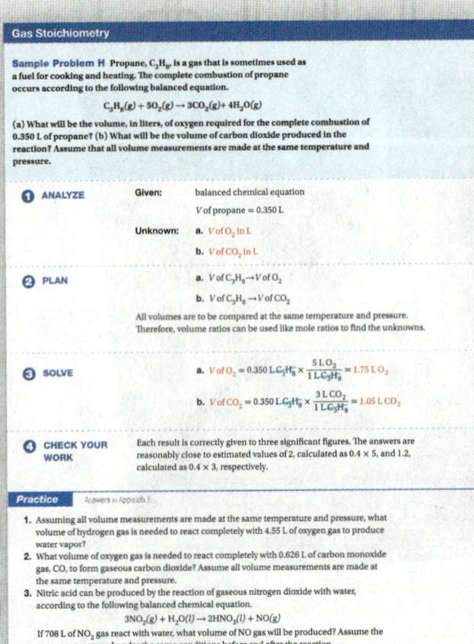

Gas Stoichiometry

Sample Problem H **Propane, C_3H_8, is a gas that is sometimes used as a fuel for cooking and heating. The complete combustion of propane occurs according to the following balanced equation.**

$$C_3H_8(g) + 5O_2(g) \rightarrow 3CO_2(g) + 4H_2O(g)$$

(a) What will be the volume, in liters, of oxygen required for the complete combustion of 0.350 L of propane? (b) What will be the volume of carbon dioxide produced in the reaction? Assume that all volume measurements are made at the same temperature and pressure.

1 ANALYZE

Given: balanced chemical equation

V of propane = 0.350 L

Unknown: a. V of O_2 in L

b. V of CO_2 in L

2 PLAN

a. V of $C_3H_8 \rightarrow V$ of O_2

b. V of $C_3H_8 \rightarrow V$ of CO_2

All volumes are to be compared at the same temperature and pressure. Therefore, volume ratios can be used like mole ratios to find the unknowns.

3 SOLVE

a. $V \text{ of } O_2 = 0.350 \text{ L } C_3H_8 \times \frac{5 \text{ L } O_2}{1 \text{ L } C_3H_8} = 1.75 \text{ L } O_2$

b. $V \text{ of } CO_2 = 0.350 \text{ L } C_3H_8 \times \frac{3 \text{ L } CO_2}{1 \text{ L } C_3H_8} = 1.05 \text{ L } CO_2$

4 CHECK YOUR WORK

Each result is correctly given to three significant figures. The answers are reasonably close to estimated values of 2, calculated as 0.4×5, and 1.2, calculated as 0.4×3, respectively.

Practice Answers in Appendix E

1. Assuming all volume measurements are made at the same temperature and pressure, what volume of hydrogen gas is needed to react completely with 4.55 L of oxygen gas to produce water vapor?
2. What volume of oxygen gas is needed to react completely with 0.626 L of carbon monoxide gas, CO, to form gaseous carbon dioxide? Assume all volume measurements are made at the same temperature and pressure.
3. Nitric acid can be produced by the reaction of gaseous nitrogen dioxide with water, according to the following balanced chemical equation.

$$3NO_2(g) + H_2O(l) \rightarrow 2HNO_3(l) + NO(g)$$

If 708 L of NO_2 gas react with water, what volume of NO gas will be produced? Assume the gases are measured under the same conditions before and after the reaction.

Revised Sample Problems

Major improvements have been made to the textbook Sample Problems to help boost student understanding. These include highlighting unknown variables, improved step references, and more.

Solve It! Cards

Printable cards help students master the core strategies to solve nearly any chemistry problem.

PREMIUM CONTENT

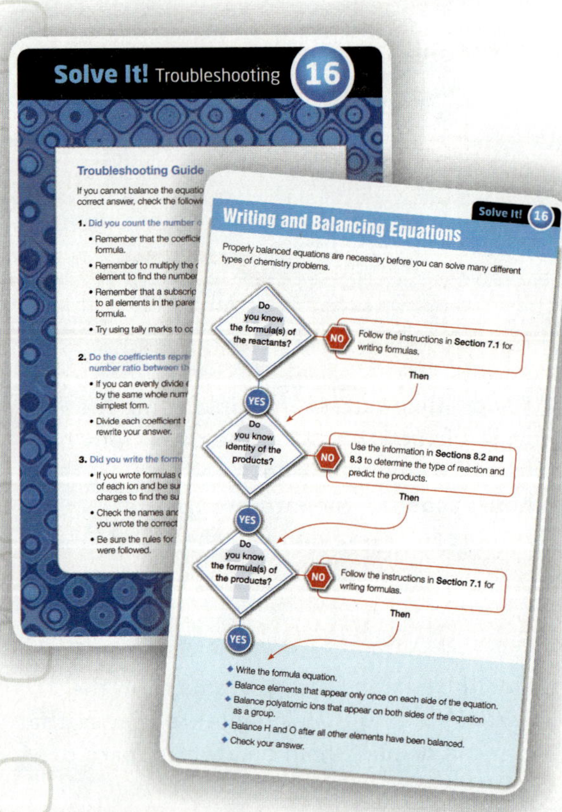

Learn It! Videos

Videos of master chemistry tutors guide students through the most challenging chemistry problems.

PREMIUM CONTENT

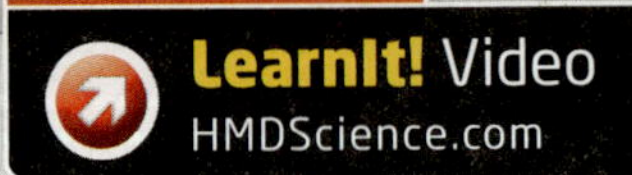

... with superior Problem-Solving support

TE Problem-Solving Support

The Teacher Edition includes additional problem-solving support strategies to help teachers guide students through a particular set of problems.

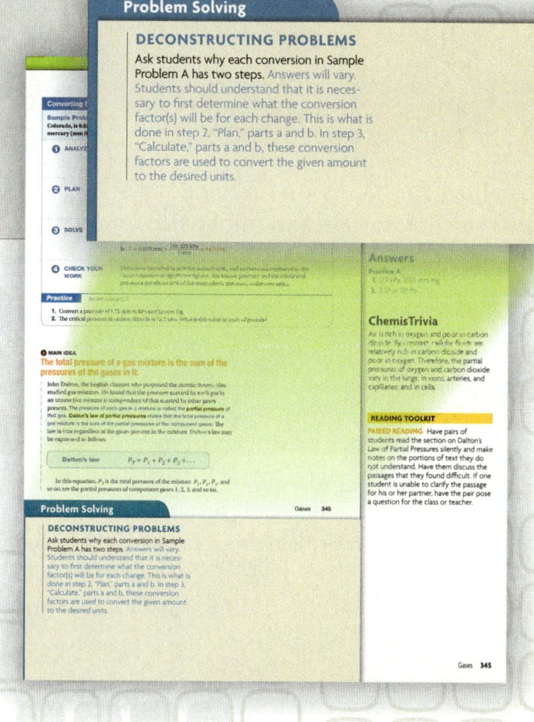
Problem Solving

DECONSTRUCTING PROBLEMS

Ask students why each conversion in Sample Problem A has two steps. Answers will vary. Students should understand that it is necessary to first determine what the conversion factor(s) will be for each change. This is what is done in step 2, "Plan," parts a and b. In step 3, "Calculate," parts a and b, these conversion factors are used to convert the given amount to the desired units.

Math Skills and Equations

A NEW Math Skills Handbook and Chemistry Equations appendix has been added for students who need extra math support.

APPENDIX C

Math Skills Handbook and Chemistry Equations

Scientific Notation

Positive exponents Many quantities that scientists deal with often have very large or very small values. For example, the speed of light is about 300 000 000 m/s, and the ink required to make the dot over an *i* in this textbook has a mass of about 0.000 000 001 kg. Obviously, it is cumbersome to work with numbers such as these. We avoid this problem by using a method based on powers of the number 10.

$$10^0 = 1$$
$$10^1 = 10$$
$$10^2 = 10 \times 10 = 100$$
$$10^3 = 10 \times 10 \times 10 = 1000$$
$$10^4 = 10 \times 10 \times 10 \times 10 = 10\,000$$
$$10^5 = 10 \times 10 \times 10 \times 10 \times 10 = 100\,000$$

The number of zeros determines the power to which 10 is raised, or the *exponent* of 10. For example, the speed of light, 300 000 000 m/s, can be expressed as 3×10^8 m/s. In this case, the exponent of 10 is 8.

Negative exponents For numbers less than one, we note the following:

$$10^{-1} = \frac{1}{10} = 0.1$$
$$10^{-2} = \frac{1}{10 \times 10} = 0.01$$
$$10^{-3} = \frac{1}{10 \times 10 \times 10} = 0.001$$
$$10^{-4} = \frac{1}{10 \times 10 \times 10 \times 10} = 0.0001$$
$$10^{-5} = \frac{1}{10 \times 10 \times 10 \times 10 \times 10} = 0.000\,01$$

The value of the negative exponent equals the number of places the decimal point must be moved to be to the right of the first nonzero digit (in these cases, the digit 1). Numbers that are expressed as a number between 1 and 10 multiplied by a power of 10 are said to be in *scientific notation*. For example, 5 943 000 000 is 5.943×10^9 when expressed in scientific notation, and 0.000 083 2 is 8.32×10^{-5} when expressed in scientific notation.

Interactive Demonstrations and Sample Problem Sets

Interactive Demonstrations Students hone their problem-solving skills through two modes of interactive problem-solving demonstrations, See How It's Done and Try It Yourself.

Sample Problem Sets Additional practice sets are provided for each type of Sample Problem.

Graphing

Smart Grapher The simple, clean graphing engine can be used to graph any data set. Use it as a stepping stone before exposing your students to more complex or sophisticated graphing tools.

Bringing Inquiry into your classroom with a robust lab suite

QuickLabs

QuickLabs allow for hands-on learning with simple, everyday materials and minimal planning.

Virtual Labs

Virtual Labs give students a lab experience without any need for materials, set-up, or advance planning. Many feature lab scenarios that are difficult to perform in the classroom.

Additional Lab Tools

Lab Generator This customizable database of chemistry labs is searchable by topic, difficulty level, duration, or standard.

Materials Lists are available for each chapter.

The Right Lab Option for Your Classroom

A broad range of lab types provides a wealth of options for hands-on learning, from core skills to open inquiry.

- **New S.T.E.M. Labs** bring the application of science, technology, engineering, and mathematics into your chemistry classroom.
- **New Open Inquiry Labs** introduce your students to a true inquiry-based lab experience.
- **Core Skill Labs** teach students how to apply chemistry techniques in the lab.
- **Probeware Labs** utilize calculator and data-probe techniques.
- **Forensics Labs** add excitement to your lab program through real-world scenarios.

Quick Labs are found in the textbook and online. All other labs are available online.

Assessing for **Mastery**

SECTION 4 FORMATIVE ASSESSMENT

Reviewing Main Ideas

1. Compare diffusion with effusion.
2. State Graham's law of effusion.
3. What are standard conditions for gas measurements?
4. Estimate the molar mass of a gas that effuses at 1.6 times the effusion rate of carbon dioxide.
5. List the following gases in orger of increasing average molecular velocity at 25 C: H_2O, He,HCO, BrF, and NO_2.
6. Why can you calculate the total pressure of a mixture of gases by adding together the partial pressures of the component gases?

Critical Thinking

7. **ANALYZING INFORMATION** An unknown gas effuses at one-half the speed of oxygen. What is the molar mass of the unknown? The gas is known to be either HBr or HI. Which gas is it?

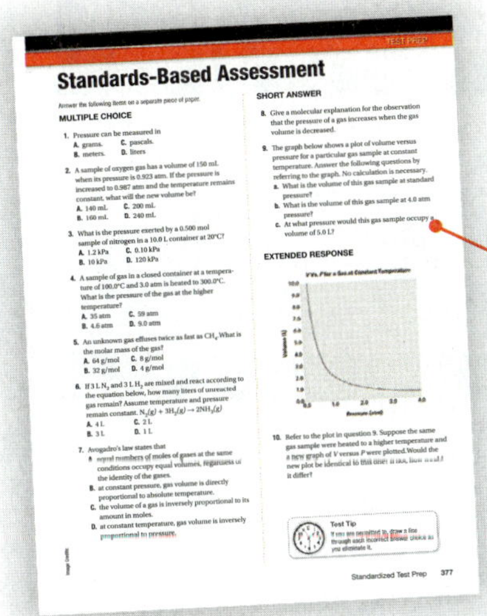

TEST PREP

Standards-Based Assessment

Answer the following items on a separate piece of paper.

MULTIPLE CHOICE

1. Pressure can be measured in
   A. grams. C. pascals.
   B. meters. D. liters
2. A sample of oxygen gas has a volume of 150 mL when its pressure is 0.923 atm. If the pressure is increased to 0.987 atm and the temperature remains constant, what will the new volume be?
   A. 140 mL C. 200 mL
   B. 160 mL D. 240 mL
3. What is the pressure exerted by a 0.500 mol sample of nitrogen in a 10.0 L container at 20°C?
   A. 1.2 kPa C. 0.10 kPa
   B. 10 kPa D. 120 kPa
4. A sample of gas in a closed container at a temperature of 100.0°C and 3.0 atm is heated to 300.0°C. What is the pressure of the gas at the higher temperature?
   A. 35 atm C. 59 atm
   B. 4.6 atm D. 9.0 atm
5. An unknown gas effuses twice as fast as CH_4. What is the molar mass of the gas?
   A. 64 g/mol C. 8 g/mol
   B. 32 g/mol D. 4 g/mol
6. If 3 L N_2 and 3 L H_2 are mixed and react according to the equation below, how many liters of unreacted gas remain? Assume temperature and pressure remain constant. $N_2(g) + 3H_2(g) \rightarrow 2NH_3(g)$
   A. 4 L C. 2 L
   B. 3 L D. 1 L
7. Avogadro's law states that
   A. equal numbers of moles of gases at the same conditions occupy equal volumes, regardless of the identity of the gases.
   B. at constant pressure, gas volume is directly proportional to absolute temperature.
   C. the volume of a gas is inversely proportional to its amount in moles.
   D. at constant temperature, gas volume is inversely proportional to pressure.

SHORT ANSWER

8. Give a molecular explanation for the observation that the pressure of a gas increases when the gas volume is decreased.
9. The graph below shows a plot of volume versus pressure for a particular gas sample at constant temperature. Answer the following questions by referring to the graph. No calculation is necessary.
   a. What is the volume of this gas sample at standard pressure?
   b. What is the volume of this gas sample at 4.0 atm pressure?
   c. At what pressure would this gas sample occupy a volume of 5.0 L?

EXTENDED RESPONSE

V Vs. P for a Gas at Constant Temperature

10. Refer to the plot in question 9. Suppose the same gas sample were heated to a higher temperature and a new graph of V versus P were plotted. Would the new plot be identical to this one? [illegible] it differ?

Test Tip
If you are permitted to, draw a line through each incorrect answer choice as you eliminate it.

Standardized Test Prep 377

Assessment Options

Ongoing Formative Assessment The **Critical Thinking** and **Check for Understanding** questions can be used as formative assessment, to diagnose trouble spots for students as you work through the section content.

Section Formative Assessment Formative assessment, provided with each section in the Student Edition, includes Reviewing Main Ideas and Critical Thinking.

Section Quizzes There are quizzes available online for each section.

Chapter Tests A and B Each chapter has two tests, **General** and **Advanced**, which you can edit directly or customize in **ExamView**. Students can take a version of the Chapter Test online and be directed to resources to help complete their learning.

Alternative Assessment Alternative Assessment features are woven throughout the Teacher Edition wrap.

Standards-Based Assessment Every chapter in the Student Edition concludes with a Standards-Based Assessment to prepare students for standardized tests.

ExamView Banks

ExamView Banks are now comprehensive, and include questions from the section quizzes and chapter tests. You can use the questions in these banks with clickers, and can customize your own tests.

Assessment and Remediation

Existing assessment instruments have been repurposed into an online assessment and remediation engine. This engine provides students with prescriptive remediation and re-assessment to determine mastery.

Pacing Guide

Today's chemistry classroom often requires a flexible curriculum. The Pacing Guide below shows a number of ways to adapt the program to your teaching schedule. This Guide can be further adapted, allowing you to mix and match or compress the material so that you can spend more time on select topics, or to allow for special projects and activities.

- **Basic** gives more time for the foundations of chemistry, especially mathematical problem-solving, with less emphasis on some advanced topics from later in the course.
- **General** follows a moderate pace through both the foundational material and the higher-level topics found later in the course.
- **Advanced** moves quickly through foundations of chemistry, to provide additional time for advanced topics.
- **Heavy Lab/Activity** indicates ways to streamline "lecture" time to provide hands-on experience for about a third of the blocks in the school year. (Note: even this approach does not cover all of the labs and activities that are available with the Modern Chemistry program.)

Numbers indicate class periods recommended for the material within each chapter.

	BASIC	GENERAL	ADVANCED	HEAVY LAB/ ACTIVITY
CHAPTER 1 Matter and Change	**6**	**6**	**5**	**6**
Section 1.1 Chemistry Is a Physical Science	1	1	1	1
Section 1.2 Matter and Its Properties	1	1	1	1
Section 1.3 Elements	1	1	1	1
Lab Experiments	1	1	1	1
Chapter Review and Assessment	2	2	1	2
CHAPTER 2 Measurements and Calculations	**7**	**7**	**5**	**8**
Section 2.1 Scientific Method	1	1	1	1
Section 2.2 Units of Measurement	1	1	1	1
Section 2.3 Using Scientific Measurements	2	2	1	1
Lab Experiments	1	1	1	3
Chapter Review and Assessment	2	2	1	2
CHAPTER 3 Atoms: The Building Blocks of Matter	**8**	**8**	**7**	**7**
Section 3.1 The Atom: From Philosophical Idea to Scientific Theory	1	1	1	1
Section 3.2 The Structure of the Atom	2	2	1	1
Section 3.3 Counting Atoms	2	2	2	2
Lab Experiments	1	1	1	1
Chapter Review and Assessment	2	2	2	2
CHAPTER 4 Arrangement of Electrons in Atoms	**9**	**8**	**7**	**7**
Section 4.1 The Development of a New Atomic Model	1	1	1	1
Section 4.2 The Quantum Model of the Atom	2	2	1	1
Section 4.3 Electron Configurations	3	2	2	2
Lab Experiments	1	1	1	1
Chapter Review and Assessment	2	2	2	2
CHAPTER 5 The Periodic Law	**8**	**8**	**8**	**7**
Section 5.1 History of the Periodic Table	1	1	1	1
Section 5.2 Electron Configuration and the Periodic Table	2	2	2	1
Section 5.3 Electron Configuration and Periodic Properties	2	2	2	2
Lab Experiments	1	1	1	1
Chapter Review and Assessment	2	2	2	2

Numbers indicate class periods recommended for the material within each chapter.

	BASIC	GENERAL	ADVANCED	HEAVY LAB/ ACTIVITY
CHAPTER 6 Chemical Bonding	12	11	11	9
Section 6.1 Introduction to Chemical Bonding	1	1	1	1
Section 6.2 Covalent Bonding and Molecular Compounds	2	2	2	2
Section 6.3 Ionic Bonding and Ionic Compounds	2	2	2	1
Section 6.4 Metallic Bonding	1	1	1	1
Section 6.5 Molecular Geometry	3	2	2	1
Lab Experiments	1	1	1	1
Chapter Review and Assessment	2	2	2	2
CHAPTER 7 Chemical Formulas and Chemical Compounds	10	9	9	10
Section 7.1 Chemical Names and Formulas	2	2	2	2
Section 7.2 Oxidation Numbers	1	1	1	1
Section 7.3 Using Chemical Formulas	2	2	2	2
Section 7.4 Determining Chemical Formulas	2	1	1	1
Lab Experiments	1	1	1	2
Chapter Review and Assessment	2	2	2	2
CHAPTER 8 Chemical Equations and Reactions	8	7	7	8
Section 8.1 Describing Chemical Reactions	2	2	2	2
Section 8.2 Types of Chemical Reactions	2	1	1	1
Section 8.3 Activity Series of the Elements	1	1	1	1
Lab Experiments	1	1	1	2
Chapter Review and Assessment	2	2	2	2
CHAPTER 9 Stoichiometry	11	8	8	8
Section 9.1 Introduction to Stoichiometry	3	2	2	2
Section 9.2 Ideal Stoichiometric Calculations	3	2	2	2
Section 9.3 Limiting Reactants and Percentage Yield	2	1	1	1
Lab Experiments	1	1	1	1
Chapter Review and Assessment	2	2	2	2
CHAPTER 10 States of Matter	10	9	10	9
Section 10.1 The Kinetic-Molecular Theory of Matter	1	1	1	1
Section 10.2 Liquids	1	1	1	1
Section 10.3 Solids	1	1	1	1
Section 10.4 Changes of State	3	2	3	1
Section 10.5 Water	1	1	1	0
Lab Experiments	1	1	1	3
Chapter Review and Assessment	2	2	2	2
CHAPTER 11 Gases	11	9	10	9
Section 11.1 Gases and Pressure	1	1	1	1
Section 11.2 The Gas Laws	3	2	2	2
Section 11.3 Gas Volumes and the Ideal Gas Law	3	2	3	1
Section 11.4 Diffusion and Effusion	1	1	1	0
Lab Experiments	1	1	1	3
Chapter Review and Assessment	2	2	2	2

Numbers indicate class periods recommended for the material within each chapter.

	BASIC	GENERAL	ADVANCED	HEAVY LAB/ ACTIVITY
CHAPTER 12 **Solutions**	10	8	8	9
Section 12.1 Types of Mixtures	1	1	1	1
Section 12.2 The Solution Process	3	2	2	1
Section 12.3 Concentration of Solutions	3	2	2	2
Lab Experiments	1	1	1	3
Chapter Review and Assessment	2	2	2	2
CHAPTER 13 **Ions in Aqueous Solutions and Colligative Properties**	7	6	6	5
Section 13.1 Compounds in Aqueous Solutions	2	1	1	1
Section 13.2 Colligative Properties of Solutions	2	2	2	1
Lab Experiments	1	1	1	1
Chapter Review and Assessment	2	2	2	2
CHAPTER 14 **Acids and Bases**	8	8	8	7
Section 14.1 Properties of Acids and Bases	1	1	1	1
Section 14.2 Acid-Base Theories	2	2	2	1
Section 14.3 Acid-Base Reactions	2	2	2	1
Lab Experiments	1	1	1	2
Chapter Review and Assessment	2	2	2	2
CHAPTER 15 **Acid-Base Titration and pH**	8	6	6	7
Section 15.1 Aqueous Solutions and the Concept of pH	2	1	1	1
Section 15.2 Determining pH and Titrations	3	2	2	2
Lab Experiments	1	1	1	2
Chapter Review and Assessment	2	2	2	2
CHAPTER 16 **Reaction Energy**	7	6	7	8
Section 16.1 Thermochemistry	3	2	2	2
Section 16.2 Driving Force of Reactions	1	1	2	1
Lab Experiments	1	1	1	3
Chapter Review and Assessment	2	2	2	2
CHAPTER 17 **Reaction Kinetics**	6	6	6	7
Section 17.1 The Reaction Process	1	1	1	1
Section 17.2 Reaction Rate	2	2	2	1
Lab Experiments	1	1	1	3
Chapter Review and Assessment	2	2	2	2
CHAPTER 18 **Chemical Equilibrium**	6	8	9	8
Section 18.1 The Nature of Chemical Equilibrium	1	1	1	1
Section 18.2 Shifting Equilibrium	1	1	2	1
Section 18.3 Equilibria of Acids, Bases, and Salts	0	2	2	1
Section 18.4 Solubility Equilibrium	1	1	1	1
Lab Experiments	1	1	1	2
Chapter Review and Assessment	2	2	2	2

Numbers indicate class periods recommended for the material within each chapter.

	BASIC	GENERAL	ADVANCED	HEAVY LAB/ ACTIVITY
CHAPTER 19 Oxidation-Reduction Reactions	**9**	**7**	**7**	**7**
Section 19.1 Oxidation and Reduction	2	1	1	1
Section 19.2 Balancing Redox Equations	3	2	2	1
Section 19.3 Oxidizing and Reducing Agents	1	1	1	1
Lab Experiments	1	1	1	2
Chapter Review and Assessment	2	2	2	2
CHAPTER 20 Electrochemistry	**6**	**6**	**6**	**7**
Section 20.1 Introduction to Electrochemistry	1	1	1	1
Section 20.2 Voltaic Cells	1	1	1	1
Section 20.3 Electrolytic Cells	1	1	1	1
Lab Experiments	1	1	1	2
Chapter Review and Assessment	2	2	2	2
CHAPTER 21 Nuclear Chemistry	**10**	**9**	**9**	**7**
Section 21.1 The Nucleus	1	1	1	1
Section 21.2 Radioactive Decay	3	2	2	1
Section 21.3 Nuclear Radiation	2	2	2	1
Section 21.4 Nuclear Fission and Nuclear Fusion	1	1	1	1
Lab Experiments	1	1	1	1
Chapter Review and Assessment	2	2	2	2
CHAPTER 22 Organic Chemistry	**0**	**8**	**9**	**8**
Section 22.1 Organic Compounds	0	1	1	1
Section 22.2 Hydrocarbons	0	2	2	1
Section 22.3 Functional Groups	0	1	1	1
Section 22.4 Organic Reactions	0	1	2	1
Lab Experiments	0	1	1	2
Chapter Review and Assessment	0	2	2	2
CHAPTER 23 Biological Chemistry	**0**	**9**	**9**	**9**
Section 23.1 Carbohydrates and Lipids	0	2	2	1
Section 23.2 Amino Acids and Proteins	0	2	2	1
Section 23.3 Metabolism	0	1	1	1
Section 23.4 Nucleic Acids	0	1	1	1
Lab Experiments	0	1	1	3
Chapter Review and Assessment	0	2	2	2
Total	**177**	**177**	**177**	**177**

Safety in Your Laboratory

Direct students to the section "Safety in the Chemistry Laboratory" in the *Student Edition* front-matter pages. This section includes a key to the safety icons used within the laboratory program.

Risk Assessment

MAKING YOUR LABORATORY A SAFE PLACE TO WORK AND LEARN

Concern for safety must begin before any activity in the classroom and before students enter the lab. A careful review of the facilities should be a basic part of preparation for each school term. You should investigate the physical environment, identify any safety risks, and inspect your work areas for compliance with safety regulations.

The review of the lab should be thorough, and all safety issues must be addressed immediately. Keep a file of your review, and add to the list each year. This will allow you to continue to raise the standard of safety in your lab and classroom.

Many classroom experiments, demonstrations, and other activities are classics that have been used for years. This familiarity may lead to a comfort that can obscure inherent safety concerns. Review all experiments, demonstrations, and activities for safety concerns before presenting them to the class. Identify and eliminate potential safety hazards.

1. **Identify the Risks**
   Before introducing any activity, demonstration, or experiment to the class, analyze it and consider what could possibly go wrong. Carefully review the list of materials to make sure they are safe. Inspect the equipment in your lab or classroom to make sure it is in good working order. Read the procedures to make sure they are safe. Record any hazards or concerns you identify.

2. **Evaluate the Risks**
   Minimize the risks you identified without sacrificing learning. Remember that no activity you perform in the lab or classroom is worth risking injury. Thus, extremely hazardous activities, or those that violate your school's policies, must be eliminated. For activities that present smaller risks, analyze each risk carefully to determine its likelihood. If the pedagogical value of the activity does not outweigh the risks, the activity must be eliminated.

3. **Select Controls to Address Risks**
   Even low-risk activities require controls to eliminate or minimize the risks. Make sure that in devising controls you do not substitute an equally or more hazardous alternative. Some control methods include the following:
   - Explicit verbal and written warnings may be added or posted.
   - Equipment may be rebuilt or relocated, have parts replaced, or be replaced entirely by safer alternatives.
   - Risky procedures may be eliminated.
   - Activities may be changed from student activities to teacher demonstrations.

4. **Implement and Review Selected Controls**
   Controls do not help if they are forgotten or not enforced. The implementation and review of controls should be as systematic and thorough as the initial analysis of safety concerns in the lab and laboratory activities.

SOME SAFETY RISKS AND PREVENTATIVE CONTROLS

The following list describes several possible safety hazards and controls that can be implemented to resolve them. This list is not complete, but it can be used as a starting point to identify hazards in your laboratory.

IDENTIFIED RISK	PREVENTATIVE CONTROL
Facilities and equipment	
Lab tables are in disrepair, room is poorly lighted and ventilated, faucets and electrical outlets do not work or are difficult to use because of their location.	Work surfaces should be level and stable. There should be adequate lighting and ventilation. Water supplies, drains, and electrical outlets should be in good working order. Any equipment in a dangerous location should not be used; it should be relocated or rendered inoperable.
Wiring, plumbing, and air circulation systems do not work or do not meet current specifications.	Specifications should be kept on file. Conduct a periodic review of all equipment, and document compliance. Damaged fixtures must be labeled as such and must be repaired as soon as possible.
Eyewash fountains and safety showers are presented, but no one knows anything about their specifications.	Ensure that eyewash fountains and safety showers meet the requirements of the ANSI standard (Z358.1).
Eyewash fountains are checked and cleaned once at the beginning of the school year. No records are kept of routine checks and maintenance on the safety showers and eyewash fountains.	Flush eyewash fountains for 5 minutes every month to remove any bacteria or other organisms from the pipes. Test safety showers (measure flow in gallons per min.) and eyewash fountains every 6 months and keep records of the test results.
Labs are conducted in multipurpose rooms, and equipment from other courses remains accessible.	Only items necessary for a given activity should be available to students. All equipment should be locked away when not in use.
Students are permitted to enter or work in the lab without teacher supervision.	Lock all laboratory rooms whenever teacher is not present. Supervising teachers must be trained in lab safety and emergency procedures.
Safety equipment and emergency procedures	
Fire and other emergency drills are infrequent, and no records or measurements are made of the results of the drills.	Always carry out critical reviews of fire or other emergency drills. Be sure that plans include alternate routes. Don't wait until an emergency to find the flaws in your plans.
Emergency evacuation plans do not include instructions for securing the lab in the event of an evacuation during a lab activity.	Plan actions in case of emergency: establish what devices should be turned off, which escape route to use, and where to meet outside the building.
Fire extinguishers are in out-of-the-way locations, not on the escape route.	Place fire extinguishers near escape routes so that they will be of use during an emergency.
Fire extinguishers are not maintained. Teachers are not trained to use them.	Document regular maintenance of fire extinguishers. Train supervisory personnel in the proper use of extinguishers. Instruct students not to use an extinguisher but to call for a teacher.

IDENTIFIED RISK	PREVENTATIVE CONTROL
Safety equipment and emergency procedures (continued)	
Teachers in labs and neighboring classrooms are not trained in CPR or first aid.	Teachers should receive training for first aid safety. The American Red Cross and other groups offer training. Certifications should be kept current with refresher courses.
Teachers are not aware of their legal responsibilities in case of an injury or accident.	Review your faculty handbook for your responsibilities regarding safety in the classroom and laboratory. Contact the legal counsel for your school district to find out the extent of their support and any rules, regulations, or procedures you must follow.
Emergency procedures are not posted. Emergency numbers are kept only at the switchboard or main office. Instructions are given verbally only at the beginning of the year.	Emergency procedures should be posted at all exits and near all safety equipment. Emergency numbers should be posted at all phones, and a script should be provided for the caller to use. Emergency procedures must be reviewed periodically, and students should be reminded of them at the beginning of each activity.
Spills are handled on a case-by-case basis and are cleaned up with whatever materials happen to be on hand.	Have the appropriate equipment and materials available for cleaning up; replace them before expiration dates. Make sure students know to alert you to spilled chemicals, blood, and broken glass.
Work habits and environment	
Safety gear is used only for activities involving chemicals or hot plates.	Aprons and goggles should be worn in the lab at all times. Long hair, loose clothing, and loose jewelry should be secured.
There is no dress code established for the laboratory; students are allowed to wear sandals or open-toed shoes.	Open-toed shoes should never be worn in the laboratory. Do not allow any footwear in the lab that does not cover feet completely.
Students are required to wear safety gear but teachers and visitors are not.	Everyone must wear safety gear while in the lab. Keep extra equipment on hand for visitors.
Safety is emphasized at the beginning of the term but is not mentioned later in the year.	Safety must be the first priority in all lab work. Students should be warned of risks and instructed in emergency procedures for each activity.
There is no assessment of students' knowledge and attitudes regarding safety.	Conduct frequent safety quizzes. Only students with perfect scores should be allowed to work in the lab.
You work alone during your preparation period to organize the day's labs.	Never work alone in a science laboratory or in a storage area.
Safety inspections are conducted irregularly and are not documented. Teachers and administrators are unaware of what documentation will be necessary in case of a lawsuit.	Safety reviews should be frequent and regular. All reviews should be documented, and improvements must be implemented immediately. Contact legal counsel for your district to make sure your procedures will protect you in case of a lawsuit.

IDENTIFIED RISK	PREVENTATIVE CONTROL
Purchasing, storing, and using chemicals	
The storeroom is too crowded, so you decide to keep some equipment on the lab benches.	Do not store reagents or equipment on lab benches. Keep shelves organized. Never place reactive chemicals (in bottles, beakers, flasks, wash bottles, etc.) near the edges of a lab bench.
You prepare solutions from concentrated stock to save money.	Reduce risks by ordering diluted instead of concentrated substances.
You purchase plenty of chemicals to be sure that you won't run out or to save money.	Purchase chemicals in class-size quantities. Do not purchase or have on hand more than one year's supply of each chemical.
You don't generally read labels on chemicals when preparing solutions for a lab, because you already know about a chemical.	Read each chemical label for stated hazards. Know the precautions and first aid procedures that apply to all chemicals and reagents for the specified lab. Make sure the chemical's label also contains this information, in case someone else has to deal with that chemical in an emergency.
You never read the Material Safety Data Sheets (MSDSs) that come with your chemicals.	Always read the Material Safety Data Sheet (MSDS) for a chemical before using it and follow the precautions described. File and organize MSDSs for all chemicals where they can be found easily in case of an emergency.
The main stockroom contains chemicals that haven't been used for years.	Do not leave unused chemicals on lab shelves for more than one week, or in the stockroom for more than one year. Dispose of, or use up, any leftover chemicals.
No extra precautions are taken when flammable liquids are dispensed from their containers.	When transferring flammable liquids from bulk containers, ground the container, and before transferring to a smaller metal container, ground both containers.
Students are told to put their broken glass and solid chemical wastes in the trash can.	Have separate containers for trash, for broken glass, and for different categories of hazardous chemical wastes.
You store chemicals alphabetically instead of by hazard class. Chemicals are stored without consideration of possible emergencies (fire, earthquake, flood, etc.), which could compound the hazard.	Use MSDSs to determine which chemicals are incompatible. Store chemicals by the hazard class indicated on the MSDS. Store chemicals that are incompatible with common fire-fighting media like water (such as alkali metals) or carbon dioxide (such as alkali and alkaline-earth metals) under conditions that eliminate the possibility of a reaction with water or carbon dioxide if it is necessary to fight a fire in the storage area.
Corrosives are kept above eye level, out of reach from any unauthorized person.	Always store corrosive chemicals on shelves below eye level. Remember, fumes from many corrosives can destroy metal cabinets and shelving.
Chemicals are kept on the stockroom floor on the days that they will be used so that they are easy to find.	Never store chemicals or other materials on floors or in the aisles of the laboratory or storeroom, even for a few minutes.

HOLT McDOUGAL

Modern Chemistry

Sarquis • Sarquis

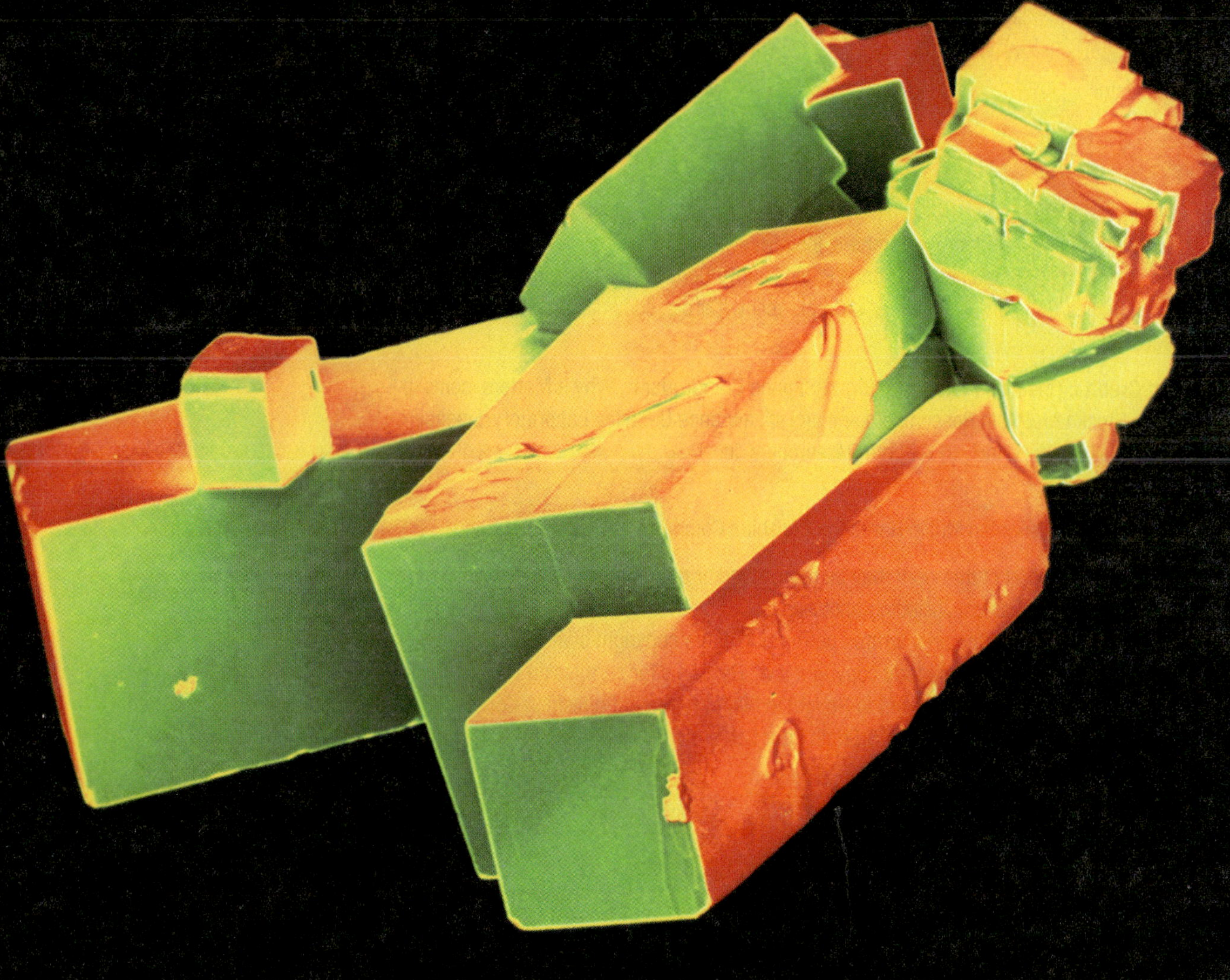

HOLT McDOUGAL

HOUGHTON MIFFLIN HARCOURT

AUTHORS

Mickey Sarquis
Professor and Director, Center for Chemistry Education
Department of Chemistry and Biochemistry
Miami University
Middletown, OH

Jerry L. Sarquis, Ph.D.
Professor
Department of Chemistry and Biochemistry
Miami University
Middletown, OH

Cover Photo Credits: Salt crystal ©Dr. Jeremy Burgess/Photo Researchers, Inc.; Bunsen burner flame ©Martyn F. Chillmaid/Photo Researchers, Inc.; Bunsen burner base ©Yoav Levy/Phototake Inc./Alamy; periodic chart, matches ©Science Photo Library/Corbis; molecular model ©Wayne Calabrese/Photonica/Getty Images; beaker ©Corbis Yellow/Corbis; snowflake ©Kallista Images/Getty Images

Master Art Credits: Chemistry Explorers: (bg) ©Simone Brandt/Alamy; Why It Matters icons: (l) ©Maximilian Stock Ltd./Photo Researchers, Inc.; (c) ©Lawrence Berkeley Laboratory/Science Source/Photo Researchers, Inc.; (r) ©Photo Researchers, Inc.

Printed in the U.S.A.

ISBN 978-0-547-58663-2

1 2 3 4 5 6 7 8 9 10 XXX 20 19 18 17 16 15 14 13 12 11

4500000000 A B C D E F G

Holt McDougal

MODERN CHEMISTRY

Yes, it's educational. No, it's not boring.

Student One-Stop

With this convenient DVD, you can carry your textbook in your pocket, along with printable copies of the interactive reader, labs, and study worksheets. Enjoy animations, virtual experiences, and more—without the need to carry a heavy textbook.

Online Chemistry

You can access all program resources at HMDScience.com. In addition to your textbook, you'll find enhanced analysis tools, interesting Web links, and exciting review games. Get your hands on interactive simulations, animations, videos, and a variety of lab activities.

Textbook

Explore the world around you with pages of colorful photos, helpful illustrations, detailed Sample Problems, and hands-on activities using everyday materials. Learn how chemistry concepts are connected to your everyday life.

Online Chemistry

PREMIUM CONTENT

Bring chemistry to life through animations.

PREMIUM CONTENT

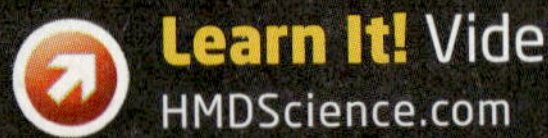

Strengthen your problem-solving skills in two ways:

- Videos with tips
- Printable skills cards

PREMIUM CONTENT

Review Games
Concept Maps

HMDScience.com

PREMIUM CONTENT

Why It Matters Video
HMDScience.com

Explore engaging application-focused videos.

Look for links throughout your book!

Labs Online

QuickLabs

Encounter key concepts in your classroom with QuickLabs. They're right in your book!

Open Inquiry Labs

Drive the lab activity—you make decisions about what to research and how to do it.

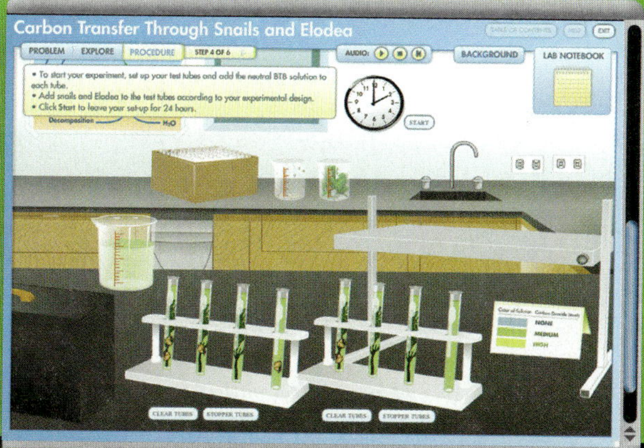

STEM Labs

Explore technology and engineering through hands-on projects.

Core Skill Labs

Practice hands-on skills and techniques.

Probeware Labs

Integrate data-collection technology into your labs.

Forensics Labs

Investigate practical applications of chemistry, such as crime scene analysis.

CONTENTS

CHAPTER 1 | MATTER AND CHANGE 2

1 Chemistry Is a Physical Science 3
2 Matter and Its Properties 6
3 Elements 16

Cross-Disciplinary Connection Secrets of the Cremona Violins 15
Why It Matters Superconductors 18
Math Tutor Converting SI Units 21

STANDARDS-BASED ASSESSMENT 25

CHAPTER LABS ONLINE Mixture Separation

HMDScience.com
Go online for the full complement of labs.

CHAPTER 2 | MEASUREMENTS AND CALCULATIONS 26

1 Scientific Method 27
2 Units of Measurement 31
3 Using Scientific Measurements 42

Why It Matters Models in Chemistry 30
QuickLab Density of Pennies 37
Chemistry Explorers Classical Ideas About Matter 41
Math Tutor Scientific Notation 56

STANDARDS-BASED ASSESSMENT 61

CHAPTER LABS ONLINE
Percentage of Water In Popcorn
Accuracy and Precision in Measurements
The Sports Shop Theft

HMDScience.com
Go online for the full complement of labs.

CHAPTER 3 ATOMS: THE BUILDING BLOCKS OF MATTER 62

1	The Atom: From Philosophical Idea to Scientific Theory	63
2	The Structure of the Atom	68
3	Counting Atoms	73
Careers in Chemistry	Physical Chemist	66
QuickLab	Constructing a Model	67
Chemistry Explorers	Discovery of Element 43	77
Math Tutor	Conversion Factors	84
	STANDARDS-BASED ASSESSMENT	89
CHAPTER LABS ONLINE	Conservation of Mass	

HMDScience.com

Go online for the full complement of labs.

CHAPTER 4 ARRANGEMENT OF ELECTRONS IN ATOMS 90

1	The Development of a New Atomic Model	91
2	The Quantum Model of the Atom	98
3	Electron Configurations	105
Why It Matters	Fireflies	96
QuickLab	The Wave Nature of Light: Interference	100
Chemistry Explorers	The Noble Decade	108
Math Tutor	Weighted Averages and Atomic Mass	117
	STANDARDS-BASED ASSESSMENT	123
CHAPTER LABS ONLINE	Flame Tests	

HMDScience.com

Go online for the full complement of labs.

CHAPTER 5 | THE PERIODIC LAW 124

1	History of the Periodic Table	125
2	Electron Configuration and the Periodic Table	130
3	Electron Configuration and Periodic Properties	142
QuickLab	Designing Your Own Periodic Table	128
Careers in Chemistry	Materials Scientist	137
Math Tutor	Writing Electron Configurations	157
	STANDARDS-BASED ASSESSMENT	163

CHAPTER LABS ONLINE
The Mendeleev Lab of 1869
Exploring the Periodic Table
Reactivity of Halide Atoms

HMDScience.com
Go online for the full complement of labs.

CHAPTER 6 | CHEMICAL BONDING 164

1	Introduction to Chemical Bonding	165
2	Covalent Bonding and Molecular Compounds	168
3	Ionic Bonding and Ionic Compounds	180
4	Metallic Bonding	185
5	Molecular Geometry	187
Chemistry Explorers	Ultrasonic Toxic-Waste Destroyer	170
Careers in Chemistry	Computational Chemist	194
Math Tutor	Drawing Lewis Structures	198
	STANDARDS-BASED ASSESSMENT	205

CHAPTER LABS ONLINE
Conductivity as an Indicator of Bond Type
Chemical Bonds
Types of Bonding in Solids

HMDScience.com
Go online for the full complement of labs.

CHAPTER 7 CHEMICAL FORMULAS AND CHEMICAL COMPOUNDS 206

1 Chemical Names and Formulas 207
2 Oxidation Numbers 220
3 Using Chemical Formulas 225
4 Determining Chemical Formulas 233

Careers in Chemistry Pharmacist 222
Why It Matters Mass Spectrometry: Identifying Molecules 224
Math Tutor Calculating Percentage Composition 238

STANDARDS-BASED ASSESSMENT 245

CHAPTER LABS ONLINE
Test for Fe(II) and Fe(III)
Water of Hydration
Determining the Empirical Formula of Magnesium Oxide

HMDScience.com
Go online for the full complement of labs.

CHAPTER 8 CHEMICAL EQUATIONS AND REACTIONS 246

1 Describing Chemical Reactions 247
2 Types of Chemical Reactions 262
3 Activity Series of the Elements 271

Why It Matters Carbon Monoxide Catalyst 261
Why It Matters Fluoridation and Tooth Decay 269
QuickLab Balancing Equations Using Models 270
Why It Matters Combustion Synthesis 274
Math Tutor Balancing Chemical Equations 275

STANDARDS-BASED ASSESSMENT 281

CHAPTER LABS ONLINE
Blueprint Paper
Evidence for a Chemical Change
Extraction of Copper From Its Ore

HMDScience.com
Go online for the full complement of labs.

CHAPTER 9 | STOICHIOMETRY 282

1	Introduction to Stoichiometry	283
2	Ideal Stoichiometric Calculations	288
3	Limiting Reactants and Percentage Yield	296
Careers in Chemistry	Chemical Technician	284
Chemistry Explorers	The Case of Combustion	286
QuickLab	Limiting Reactants in a Recipe	300
Math Tutor	Using Mole Ratios	303
	STANDARDS-BASED ASSESSMENT	309
CHAPTER LABS ONLINE	Stoichiometry and Gravimetric Analysis	

HMDScience.com
Go online for the full complement of labs.

CHAPTER 10 | STATES OF MATTER 310

1	The Kinetic-Molecular Theory of Matter	311
2	Liquids	315
3	Solids	319
4	Changes of State	324
5	Water	331
Why It Matters	Surface Melting	328
Math Tutor	Calculations Using Enthalpies of Fusion	334
	STANDARDS-BASED ASSESSMENT	339
CHAPTER LABS ONLINE	Viscosity of Liquids Evaporation and Ink Solvents "Wet" Dry Ice	

HMDScience.com
Go online for the full complement of labs.

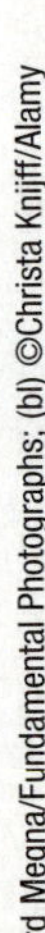

CHAPTER 11 | GASES 340

1	Gas and Pressure	341
2	The Gas Laws	349
3	Gas Volumes and the Ideal Gas Law	358
4	Diffusion and Effusion	366
Why It Matters	The Gas Laws and Scuba Diving	348
Chemistry Explorers	Chemistry's First Law	356
Why It Matters	Automobile Air Bags	360
QuickLab	Diffusion	367
Math Tutor	Algebraic Rearrangements of Gas Laws	369
	STANDARDS-BASED ASSESSMENT	377
CHAPTER LABS ONLINE	Boyle's Law Testing for Dissolved Oxygen Diffusion	

HMDScience.com

Go online for the full complement of labs.

CHAPTER 12 | SOLUTIONS 378

1	Types of Mixtures	379
2	The Solution Process	385
3	Concentration of Solutions	396
QuickLab	Observing Solutions, Suspensions, and Colloids	383
Careers in Chemistry	Environmental Chemist	386
Cross-Disciplinary Connection	Artificial Blood	395
Math Tutor	Calculating Solution Concentration	403
	STANDARDS-BASED ASSESSMENT	409
CHAPTER LABS ONLINE	Separation of Pen Inks by Paper Chromatography Effect of Temperature on Solubility of a Salt The Untimely Death	

HMDScience.com

Go online for the full complement of labs.

CHAPTER 13 **IONS IN AQUEOUS SOLUTIONS AND COLLIGATIVE PROPERTIES** 410

1 Compounds in Aqueous Solutions 411
2 Colligative Properties of Solutions 422

Chemistry Explorers The Riddle of Electrolysis 420
Why It Matters Water Purification by Reverse Osmosis 429
Math Tutor Boiling and Freezing Points of Solutions 433

STANDARDS-BASED ASSESSMENT 439

CHAPTER LABS ONLINE
Testing Water for Ions
Colored Precipitates
Diffusion and Cell Membranes

HMDScience.com
Go online for the full complement of labs.

CHAPTER 14 **ACIDS AND BASES** 440

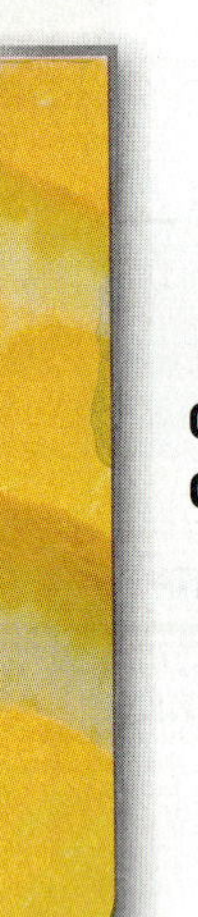

1 Properties of Acids and Bases 441
2 Acid-Base Theories 452
3 Acid-Base Reactions 457

QuickLab Household Acids and Bases 446
Cross-Disciplinary Connection Acid Water—A Hidden Menace 451
Cross-Disciplinary Connection It's a Bitter Pill 458
Math Tutor Writing Equations for Ionic Reactions 464

STANDARDS-BASED ASSESSMENT 469

CHAPTER LABS ONLINE
Is It an Acid or a Base?
Effects of Acid Rain on Plants

HMDScience.com
Go online for the full complement of labs.

CHAPTER 15 **ACID-BASE TITRATION AND PH** 470

1 Aqueous Solutions and the Concept of pH 471
2 Determining pH and Titrations 483

Cross-Disciplinary Connection Liming Streams 482
QuickLab Testing the pH of Rainwater 486
Careers in Chemistry Analytical Chemist 488
Math Tutor Using Logarithms and pH 494

STANDARDS-BASED ASSESSMENT 499

CHAPTER LABS ONLINE
Wetlands Acid Spill
Acid-Base Titration
Determination of Acetic Acid in Vinegar

HMDScience.com
Go online for the full complement of labs.

CHAPTER 16 | REACTION ENERGY 500

1	Thermochemistry	501
2	Driving Force of Reactions	516
Why It Matters	Self-Heating Meals	515
Why It Matters	Diamonds Are Forever?	519
Math Tutor	Hess's Law	521
	STANDARDS-BASED ASSESSMENT	527

CHAPTER LABS ONLINE
Evaluating Fuels
Calorimetry and Hess's law
Energy in Foods

HMDScience.com
Go online for the full complement of labs.

CHAPTER 17 | REACTION KINETICS 528

1	The Reaction Process	529
2	Reaction Rate	536
Why It Matters	Explosives	540
QuickLab	Factors Influencing Reaction Rate	546
Why It Matters	Catalytic Converters	547
Math Tutor	Writing Rate Laws	548
	STANDARDS-BASED ASSESSMENT	553

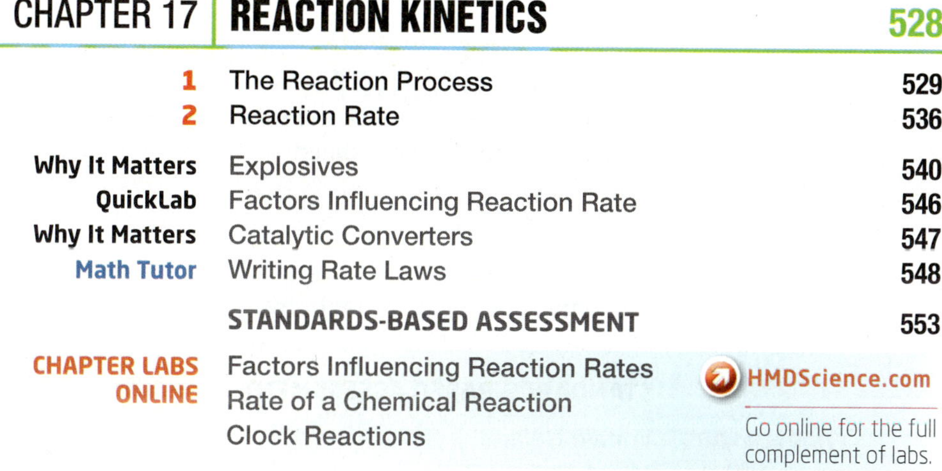

CHAPTER LABS ONLINE
Factors Influencing Reaction Rates
Rate of a Chemical Reaction
Clock Reactions

HMDScience.com
Go online for the full complement of labs.

CHAPTER 18 | CHEMICAL EQUILIBRIUM 554

1	The Nature of Chemical Equilibrium	555
2	Shifting Equilibrium	564
3	Equilibria of Acids, Bases, and Salts	571
4	Solubility Equilibrium	579
Chemistry Explorers	Fixing the Nitrogen Problem	562
Cross-Disciplinary Connection	Blood Buffers	575
Math Tutor	Determining Equilibrium Constants	587
	STANDARDS-BASED ASSESSMENT	593

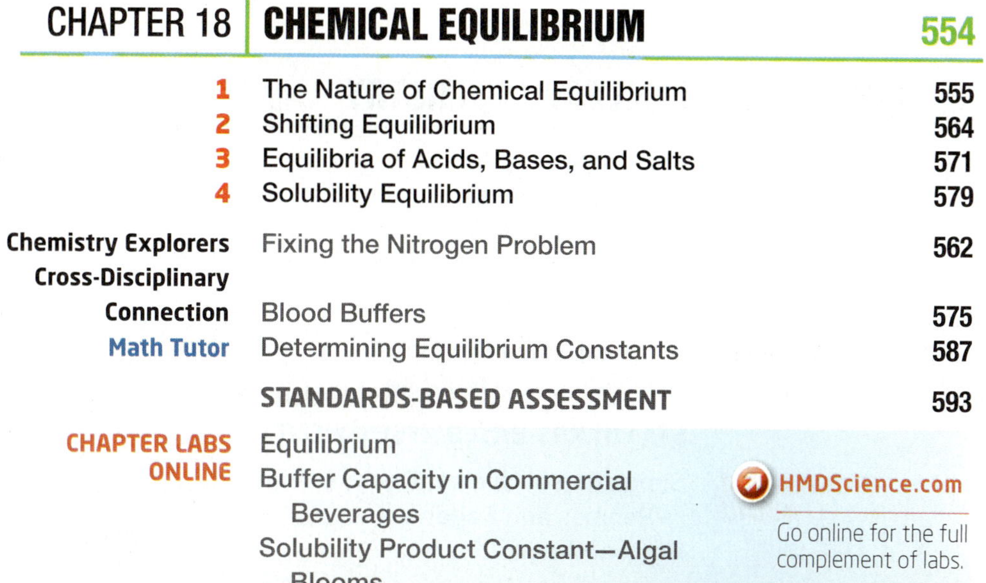

CHAPTER LABS ONLINE
Equilibrium
Buffer Capacity in Commercial Beverages
Solubility Product Constant—Algal Blooms

HMDScience.com
Go online for the full complement of labs.

(tr) ©Charles D. Winters; (cr) ©Steven Puetzer/Photographer's Choice/Getty Images; (br) ©Altrendo Travel/Getty Images

CHAPTER 19 | OXIDATION-REDUCTION REACTIONS 594

1 Oxidation and Reduction 595
2 Balancing Redox Equations 601
3 Oxidizing and Reducing Agents 606

Why It Matters Photochromic Lenses 598
Why It Matters Skunk-Spray Remedy 600
QuickLab Redox Reactions 608
Math Tutor Balancing Redox Equations 610

STANDARDS-BASED ASSESSMENT 615

CHAPTER LABS ONLINE
Rust Race
Reduction of Manganese in Permanganate Ion

HMDScience.com
Go online for the full complement of labs.

CHAPTER 20 | ELECTROCHEMISTRY 616

1 Introduction to Electrochemistry 617
2 Voltaic Cells 620
3 Electrolytic Cells 629

Why It Matters Fuel-Cell Cars 628
Why It Matters Sodium Production by Electrolysis 633
Math Tutor Calculating Cell Potentials 634

STANDARDS-BASED ASSESSMENT 639

CHAPTER LABS ONLINE
Voltaic Cells
Micro-Voltaic Cells

HMDScience.com
Go online for the full complement of labs.

CHAPTER 21 | NUCLEAR CHEMISTRY 640

1 The Nucleus 641
2 Radioactive Decay 645
3 Nuclear Radiation 653
4 Nuclear Fission and Nuclear Fusion 657

Cross-Disciplinary Connection Quarks 642
Chemistry Explorers An Unexpected Finding 660
Math Tutor Calculating with Half-Life 662

STANDARDS-BASED ASSESSMENT 667

CHAPTER LABS ONLINE
Simulation of Nuclear Decay Using Pennies and Paper
Radioactivity

HMDScience.com
Go online for the full complement of labs.

CHAPTER 22 ORGANIC CHEMISTRY 668

1 Organic Compounds 669
2 Hydrocarbons 674
3 Functional Groups 688
4 Organic Reactions 693

Chemistry Explorers The Beginnings of Organic Chemistry 673
Careers in Chemistry Petroleum Engineer 678
Why It Matters Carbon Allotropes 683
Math Tutor Calculating Empirical Formulas 698

STANDARDS-BASED ASSESSMENT 705

CHAPTER LABS ONLINE
Carbon
A Cloth of Many Colors
Polymers and Toy Balls
The Slime Challenge

HMDScience.com
Go online for the full complement of labs.

CHAPTER 23 BIOLOGICAL CHEMISTRY 706

1 Carbohydrates and Lipids 707
2 Amino Acids and Proteins 712
3 Metabolism 722
4 Nucleic Acids 726

Chemistry Explorers Charles Drew and Blood Transfusions 718
Careers in Chemistry Forensic Chemist 730
Math Tutor Interpretation of the Genetic Code 732

STANDARDS-BASED ASSESSMENT 737

CHAPTER LABS ONLINE
Casein Glue
Measuring the Iron Content of Cereal
The Murder and The Blood Sample
Measuring the Release of Energy from Sucrose

HMDScience.com
Go online for the full complement of labs.

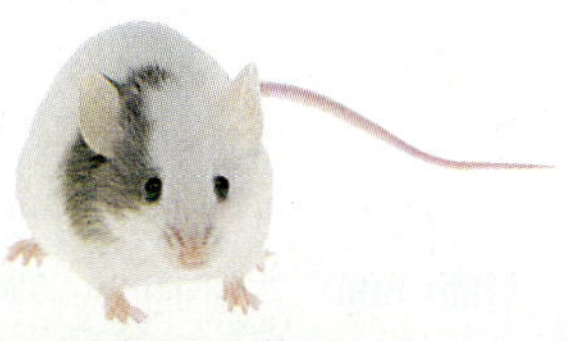

SAMPLE PROBLEMS AND MATH TUTORS

CHAPTER 1 **MATTER AND CHANGE**

Math Tutor Converting SI Units 21

CHAPTER 2 **MEASUREMENTS AND CALCULATIONS**

Sample Problems

- **A** Density 37
- **B** Conversion Factors 39
- **C** Percentage Error 43
- **D** Significant Figures 45
- **E** Significant Figures 48
- **F** Solving Problems Using the Four-Step Approach 52

Math Tutor Scientific Notation 56

CHAPTER 3 **ATOMS: THE BUILDING BLOCKS OF MATTER**

Sample Problems

- **A** Subatomic Particles 75
- **B** Gram/Mole Conversions 80
- **C** Gram/Mole Conversions 81
- **D** Conversions with Avogadro's Number 82
- **E** Conversions with Avogadro's Number 82

Math Tutor Conversion Factors 84

CHAPTER 4 **ARRANGEMENT OF ELECTRONS IN ATOMS**

Sample Problems

- **A** Electron Configurations 107
- **B** Electron Configurations 115
- **C** Electron Configurations 116

Math Tutor Weighted Averages and Atomic Mass 117

CHAPTER 5 **THE PERIODIC LAW**

Sample Problems

- **A** The Periodic Table and Electron Configurations 135
- **B** The Periodic Table and Electron Configurations 138
- **C** The Periodic Table and Electron Configurations 140
- **D** The Periodic Table and Electron Configurations 140
- **E** Atomic Radius 144
- **F** Periodic Trends in Ionization Energy 148
- **G** Periodic Trends in Electronegativity 155

Math Tutor Writing Electron Configurations 157

CHAPTER 6 **CHEMICAL BONDING**

Sample Problems

- **A** Classifying Bonds 167
- **B** Electron-Dot Notation 174
- **C** Lewis Structures 175
- **D** Lewis Structures 178
- **E** VSEPR Theory and Molecular Geometry 188
- **F** VSEPR Theory and Molecular Geometry 191

Math Tutor Drawing Lewis Structures 198

CHAPTER 7 **CHEMICAL FORMULAS AND CHEMICAL COMPOUNDS**

Sample Problems

- **A** Writing Formulas for Ionic Compounds 211
- **B** Naming Ionic Compounds 213
- **C** Writing Formulas for Ionic Compounds 215
- **D** Naming Binary Molecular Compounds 217
- **E** Oxidation Numbers 221
- **F** Formula Mass 226
- **G** Molar Mass 227
- **H** Molar Mass as a Conversion Factor 228
- **I** Molar Mass as a Conversion Factor 229
- **J** Percentage Composition 231
- **K** Percentage Composition 231
- **L** Empirical Formulas 234
- **M** Empirical Formulas 235
- **N** Molecular Formulas 236

Math Tutor Calculating Percentage Composition 238

CHAPTER 8 **CHEMICAL EQUATIONS AND REACTIONS**

Sample Problems

- **A** Writing Word, Formula, and Balanced Chemical Equations 253
- **B** Writing Word, Formula, and Balanced Chemical Equations 254
- **C** Writing Word, Formula, and Balanced Chemical Equations 258
- **D** Balancing Chemical Equations 259
- **E** Balancing Chemical Equations 259
- **F** Activity Series 273

Math Tutor Balancing Chemical Equations 275

CHAPTER 9 **STOICHIOMETRY**

Sample Problems

- **A** Stoichiometric Calculations Using Mole Ratios 289
- **B** Stoichiometric Calculations Using Mole Ratios 290
- **C** Stoichiometric Calculations Using Mole Ratios 291
- **D** Stoichiometric Calculations Using Mole Ratios 293
- **E** Stoichiometric Calculations Using Mole Ratios 294
- **F** Limiting Reactant 297
- **G** Limiting Reactant 298
- **H** Percentage Yield 301

Math Tutor Using Mole Ratios 303

CHAPTER 10 **STATES OF MATTER**

Sample Problems

- **A** Using Molar Enthalpy of Vaporization 333

Math Tutor Calculations Using Enthalpies of Fusion 334

CHAPTER 11 **GASES**

Sample Problems

A Converting Between Units of Pressure 345
B Calculating Partial Pressures 347
C Using Boyle's Law 350
D Using Charles's Law 352
E Using Gay-Lussac's Law 353
F Using the Combined Gas Law 355
G Calculating with Avogadro's Law 361
H Gas Stoichiometry 362
I Using the Ideal Gas Law 365
J Graham's Law of Effusion 368
Math Tutor Algebraic Rearrangements of Gas Laws 369

CHAPTER 12 **SOLUTIONS**

Sample Problems

A Calculating with Molarity 398
B Calculating with Molarity 398
C Calculating with Molarity 399
D Calculating with Molality 401
E Calculating with Molality 402
Math Tutor Calculating Solution Concentration 403

CHAPTER 13 **IONS IN AQUEOUS SOLUTIONS AND COLLIGATIVE PROPERTIES**

Sample Problems

A Calculating Moles of Dissolved Ions 412
B Writing Net Ionic Equations 416
C Calculating Freezing-Point Depression 425
D Calculating Molal Concentration 425
E Calculating Boiling-Point Elevation 427
F Freezing-Point Depression of Electrolytes 430
Math Tutor Boiling and Freezing Points of Solutions 433

CHAPTER 14 **ACIDS AND BASES**

Math Tutor Writing Equations for Ionic Reactions 464

CHAPTER 15 **ACID-BASE TITRATION AND PH**

Sample Problems

A Calculating Hydronium and Hydroxide Concentrations 474
B Calculating pH 477
C Calculating pH 478
D Calculating Hydronium Concentration Using pH 479
E Calculating Hydronium and Hydroxide Concentrations 480
F Calculating the Molarity of an Acid Solution 492
Math Tutor Using Logarithms and pH 494

CHAPTER 16 **REACTION ENERGY**

Sample Problems

A Specific Heat 503
B Enthalpy of Reaction 511
C Enthalpy of Formation 514
D Calculating Free-Energy Change 520
Math Tutor Hess's Law 521

CHAPTER 17 **REACTION KINETICS**

Sample Problems

A Energy Diagrams 534
B Determining Rate Law and Rate Constant 542
C Determining Rate Law and Rate Constant 543
D Determining Rate-Determining Step and Rate Law 545
E Determining Effects on Reaction Rate 545
Math Tutor Writing Rate Laws 548

CHAPTER 18 **CHEMICAL EQUILIBRIUM**

Sample Problems

A Equilibrium Constant 560
B Solubility Product Constant 582
C Calculating Solubility 583
D Precipitation Calculations 585
Math Tutor Determining Equilibrium Constants 587

CHAPTER 19 **OXIDATION-REDUCTION REACTIONS**

Sample Problems

A Balancing Equations for Redox Reactions 604
Math Tutor Balancing Redox Equations 610

CHAPTER 20 **ELECTROCHEMISTRY**

Sample Problems

A Calculating Cell Potentials 627
Math Tutor Calculating Cell Potentials 634

CHAPTER 21 **NUCLEAR CHEMISTRY**

Sample Problems

A Balancing Nuclear Reactions 644
B Calculating with Half-Life 649
Math Tutor Calculating With Half-Life 662

CHAPTER 22 **ORGANIC CHEMISTRY**

Sample Problems

A Naming Alkanes 679
B Naming Alkenes 684
Math Tutor Calculating Empirical Formulas 698

CHAPTER 23 **BIOLOGICAL CHEMISTRY**

Math Tutor Interpretation of the Genetic Code 732

FEATURE ARTICLES

Chemistry EXPLORERS

CHAPTER		
2	Classical Ideas About Matter	41
3	Discovery of Element 43	77
4	The Noble Decade	108
9	The Case of Combustion	286
11	Chemistry's First Law	356
13	The Riddle of Electrolysis	420
18	Fixing the Nitrogen Problem	562
21	An Unexpected Finding	660
22	The Beginnings of Organic Chemistry	673
23	Charles Drew and Blood Transfusions	718

CROSS-DISCIPLINARY CONNECTION

CHAPTER		
1	Secrets of the Cremona Violins	15
12	Artificial Blood	395
14	Acid Water—A Hidden Menace	451
	It's a Bitter Pill	458
15	Liming Streams	482
18	Blood Buffers	575
21	Quarks	642

CAREERS IN CHEMISTRY

CHAPTER		
3	Physical Chemist	66
5	Materials Scientist	137
6	Computational Chemist	194
7	Pharmacist	210
9	Chemical Technician	284
12	Environmental Chemist	386
15	Analytical Chemist	488
22	Petroleum Engineer	678
23	Forensic Chemist	730

WHY IT MATTERS

CHAPTER		
1	Superconductors	18
2	Models in Chemistry	34
4	Fireflies	96
6	Ultrasonic Toxic-Waste Destroyer	170
7	Mass Spectrometry: Identifying Molecules	224
8	Carbon Monoxide Catalyst	261
	Fluoridation and Tooth Decay	269
	Combustion Synthesis	274
10	Surface Melting	328
11	The Gas Laws and Scuba Diving	348
	Automobile Air Bags	360
13	Water Purification by Reverse Osmosis	429
16	Self-Heating Meals	515
	Diamonds Are Forever?	519
17	Explosives	540
	Catalytic Converters	547
19	Photochromic Lenses	598
	Skunk-Spray Remedy	600
20	Fuel-Cell Cars	628
	Sodium Production by Electrolysis	671
22	Carbon Allotropes	683

QuickLAB

CHAPTER		
2	Density of Pennies	37
3	Constructing a Model	67
4	The Wave Nature of Light: Interference	100
5	Designing Your Own Periodic Table	128
8	Balancing Equations Using Models	270
9	Limiting Reactants in a Recipe	300
11	Diffusion	367
12	Observing Solutions, Suspensions, and Colloids	383
14	Household Acids and Bases	446
15	Testing the pH of Rainwater	486
17	Factors Influencing Reaction Rate	546
19	Redox Reactions	608

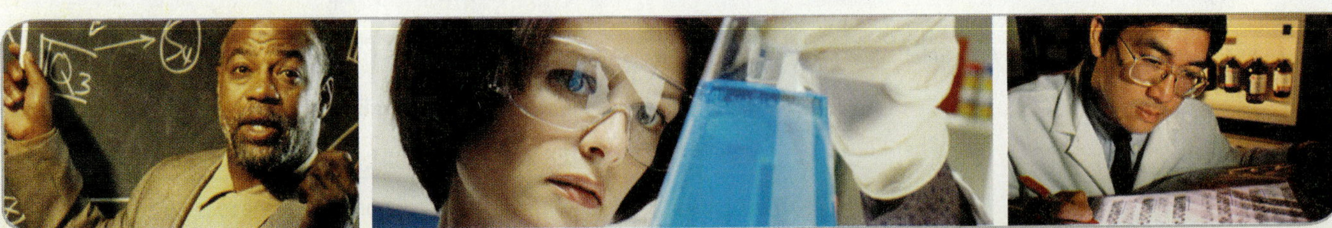

REFERENCE

APPENDIX A **ELEMENTS HANDBOOK** R2

GROUP 1 **ALKALI METALS** R4

APPLICATION *TECHNOLOGY*
Sodium Vapor Lighting R4
APPLICATION *HEALTH*
Electrolyte Balance in the Body R5

GROUP 2 **ALKALINE-EARTH METALS** R8

APPLICATION *TECHNOLOGY*
Fireworks R10
APPLICATION *HEALTH*
Calcium: An Essential Mineral in the Diet R12
Magnesium: An Essential Mineral in the Diet R12

GROUPS 3-12 **TRANSITION METALS** R14

APPLICATION *GEOLOGY*
Gemstones and Color R17
APPLICATION *TECHNOLOGY*
Alloys R18
APPLICATION *THE ENVIRONMENT*
Mercury Poisoning R21
APPLICATION *HEALTH*
Elements in the Body R22
Role of Iron R23

GROUP 13 **BORON FAMILY** R24

APPLICATION *TECHNOLOGY*
Aluminum R26
Aluminum Alloys R27

GROUP 14 **CARBON FAMILY** R28

APPLICATION *CHEMICAL INDUSTRY*
Carbon and the Reduction of Iron Ore R30
Carbon Dioxide R31
Carbon Monoxide R31
APPLICATION *BIOCHEMISTRY*
Carbon Dioxide and Respiration R32
APPLICATION *THE ENVIRONMENT*
Carbon Monoxide Poisoning R34
APPLICATION *BIOCHEMISTRY*
Macromolecules R35
APPLICATION *CHEMICAL INDUSTRY*
Silicon and Silicates R41
Silicones R41
APPLICATION *TECHNOLOGY*
Semiconductors R42

GROUP 15 **NITROGEN FAMILY** R44

APPLICATION *BIOLOGY*
Plants and Nitrogen R46
APPLICATION *CHEMICAL INDUSTRY*
Fertilizers R47

GROUP 16 **OXYGEN FAMILY** R48

APPLICATION *CHEMICAL INDUSTRY*
Oxides R50
APPLICATION *THE ENVIRONMENT*
Ozone R52
APPLICATION *CHEMICAL INDUSTRY*
Sulfuric Acid R53

GROUP 17 **HALOGEN FAMILY** R54

APPLICATION *THE ENVIRONMENT*
Chlorine in Water Treatment R56
Fluoride and Tooth Decay R57

APPENDIX B **REFERENCE TABLES** R58

APPENDIX C **MATH SKILLS HANDBOOK AND CHEMISTRY EQUATIONS** R68

APPENDIX D **PROBLEM BANK** R84

APPENDIX E **SELECTED ANSWERS** R119

GLOSSARY R127

INDEX R148

SAFETY IN THE CHEMISTRY LABORATORY

Any chemical can be dangerous if it is misused. Always follow the instructions for the experiment. Pay close attention to the safety notes. Do not do anything differently unless told to do so by your teacher.

Chemicals, even water, can cause harm. The challenge is to know how to use chemicals correctly. To make sure you are using chemicals correctly, follow the rules stated below, pay attention to your teacher's directions, and obey the cautions on chemical labels and in an experiment's procedure.

Specific experiments will use a system of Safety Symbols to highlight specific types of precautions. No matter what Safety Symbols an experiment may contain, the following safety rules apply any time you are in the lab.

BEFORE YOU BEGIN

1. **Read the entire activity before entering the lab.** Be familiar with the instructions before beginning an activity. Do not start an activity until you have asked your teacher to explain any parts of the activity that you do not understand.

2. **Student-designed procedures or inquiry activities must be approved by your teacher before you attempt the procedures or activities.**

3. **Wear the right clothing for lab work.** Before beginning work, roll up loose sleeves, and put on any required personal protective equipment as directed by your teacher. If your hair is longer than where the bottom of a shirt collar would be, tie your hair back. Avoid loose clothing or any kind of jewelry that could knock things over, catch on fire, get caught in moving parts, contact electrical connections, or absorb chemical solutions. In addition, chemical fumes may react with and ruin some jewelry, such as pearl jewelry. Wear pants rather than shorts or skirts. Nylon and polyester fabrics burn and melt more readily than cotton does. Protect your feet from chemical spills and falling objects. Do not wear open-toed shoes, sandals, or canvas shoes in the lab. Do not apply cosmetics in the lab. Some hair care products and nail polish are highly flammable.

4. **Do not wear contact lenses in the lab.** Even though you will be wearing safety goggles, chemicals could get between contact lenses and your eyes and could cause irreparable eye damage. If your doctor requires that you wear contact lenses instead of glasses, then you should wear eye-cup safety goggles—similar to goggles worn for underwater swimming—in the lab. Ask your doctor or your teacher how to use eye-cup safety goggles to protect your eyes.

5. **Know the location and usage of all safety and emergency equipment used in the lab.** Know proper fire-drill procedures and the location of all fire exits. Ask your teacher where the nearest eyewash stations, safety blankets, safety shower, fire extinguisher, first-aid kit, and chemical spill kit are located. Be sure that you know how to operate the equipment safely.

WHILE YOU ARE WORKING

6. **Always wear a lab apron and safety goggles.** Wear these items even if you are not working on an activity. Labs contain chemicals that can damage your clothing, skin, and eyes. Keep the strings of your lab apron tied. If your safety goggles cloud up or are uncomfortable, ask your teacher for help. Lengthening the strap slightly or washing the goggles with soap and warm water may relieve the problem.

7. **NEVER work alone in the lab.** Work in the lab only when supervised by your teacher. Do not leave assembled equipment unattended.

8. **Perform only activities specifically assigned by your teacher and no others.** Use only materials and equipment listed in the activity or authorized by your teacher. Steps in a procedure should be performed only as described in the activity or as approved by your teacher.

9. **Keep your work area neat and uncluttered.** Have only books and other materials that are needed to conduct the activity in the lab. Keep backpacks, purses, and other items in your desk, locker, or other designated storage areas.

10. **Always heed safety symbols and cautions listed in activities, listed on handouts, posted in the room, provided on chemical labels, and given verbally by your teacher.** Be aware of the potential hazards of the required materials and procedures, and follow all precautions indicated.

11. **Be alert, and walk with care in the lab.** Be aware of others near you and your equipment.

12. **Do not take food, drinks, chewing gum, or tobacco products into the lab.**

13. **Use extreme caution when working with hot plates and other heating devices.** Keep your head, hands, hair, and clothing away from the flame or heating area. Remember that metal surfaces connected to the heated area will become hot by conduction. Use tongs when heating containers and never hold or touch them. Gas burners should be lit only with a spark lighter, not with matches. Make sure that all heating devices and gas valves are turned off before you leave the lab. Never leave a heating device unattended when it is in use. Metal, ceramic, and glass items may not look hot when they are. Allow all items to cool before storing.

14. **Remember glass breaks easy and can cause serious cuts.** Check the condition of any glassware before and after using it. Inform your teacher of any broken, chipped, or cracked glassware, because it should not be used. Handle all glassware with care. To protect your hands, wear heavy cloth gloves or wrap toweling around the glass and the tubing, stopper, or cork, and gently push in the glass. Do not pick up broken glass with your bare hands. Dispose of broken glass appropriately.

15. **Exercise caution when working with electrical equipment.** Do not use electrical equipment with frayed or twisted wires. Be sure that your hands are dry before using electrical equipment. Do not let electrical cords dangle from work stations. Dangling cords can cause you to trip and can cause an electrical shock. The area under and around electrical equipment should be dry; cords should not lie in puddles of spilled liquid. In dryer weather, be careful of static electrical discharges that may occur when you touch metal objects. Not only can these hurt, but also they can sometimes short out electrical circuits.

16. **Do not fool around in the lab.** Take your lab work seriously, and behave appropriately in the lab. Lab equipment and apparatus are not toys; never use lab time or equipment for anything other than the intended purpose. Be aware of the safety of your classmates as well as your safety at all times.

WORKING WITH CHEMICALS

17. **NEVER taste chemicals or allow them to contact your skin.** Keep your hands away from your face and mouth, even if you are wearing gloves.

18. **Do not inhale fumes directly.** When instructed to smell a substance, use your hand to wave the fumes toward your nose, and inhale gently.

19. **Read chemical labels.** Follow the instructions and safety precautions stated on the labels.

20. **If you are working with flammable liquids, use only small amounts.** Be sure no one else is using a lit Bunsen burner or is planning to use one when you are working with flammable liquids, because the fumes can ignite.

21. For all chemicals, take only what you need. However, if you do happen to take too much and have some left over, DO NOT put it back in the bottle. If somebody accidentally puts a chemical into the wrong bottle, the next person to use it will have a contaminated sample. Ask your teacher what to do with any leftover chemicals.

22. NEVER take any chemicals out of the lab. (This is another one that you should already know. You probably know the remaining rules also, but read them anyway.)

EMERGENCY PROCEDURES

23. Follow standard fire-safety procedures. If your clothing catches on fire, do not run; STOP—DROP—AND ROLL. If another student's clothes catch on fire, keep them from running and wrap them in the fire blanket provided in your lab to smother the flames. While doing so, call to your teacher. In case of fire, alert your teacher and leave the lab according to instructions.

24. Report any accident, incident, or hazard— no matter how trivial—to your teacher immediately. Any incident involving bleeding, burns, fainting, nausea, dizziness, chemical exposure, or ingestion should also be reported immediately to the school nurse or to a physician. If you have a close call, tell your teacher so that you and your teacher can find a way to prevent it from happening again.

25. Report all spills to your teacher immediately. Call your teacher rather than trying to clean a spill yourself. Your teacher will tell you whether it is safe for you to clean up the spill; if it is not safe, your teacher will know how to clean up the spill.

26. If you spill a chemical on your skin, wash the chemical off in the sink and call your teacher. If you spill a solid chemical onto your clothing, brush it off carefully without scattering it onto somebody else, and call your teacher. If you get liquid on your clothing, wash it off right away by using the faucet at the sink, and call your teacher. Rinse your skin for 10-15 minutes. If the spill is on your pants or something else that will not fit under the sink faucet, use the safety shower. Remove the pants or other affected clothing while you are under the shower, and call your teacher. (It may be temporarily embarrassing to remove pants or other clothing in front of your classmates, but failure to flush the chemical off your skin could cause permanent damage.)

27. If you get a chemical in your eyes, walk immediately to the eyewash station, turn it on, and lower your head so your eyes are in the running water. Hold your eyelids open with your thumbs and fingers, and roll your eyeballs around. You have to flush your eyes continuously for at least 15 minutes. Call your teacher while you are doing this.

WHEN YOU ARE FINISHED

28. Clean your work area at the conclusion of each lab period as directed by your teacher. Broken glass, chemicals, and other waste products should be disposed of in separate, special containers. Dispose of waste materials as directed by your teacher. Put away all material and equipment according to your teacher's instructions. Report any damaged or missing equipment or materials to your teacher.

29. Wash your hands with soap and hot water after each lab period. To avoid contamination, wash your hands at the conclusion of each lab period, and before you leave the lab.

A FINAL REMINDER

30. Whether or not the lab instructions remind you, ALL OF THESE RULES APPLY ALL OF THE TIME!

SAFETY SYMBOLS

To highlight specific types of precautions, the following symbols are used throughout the lab program. Remember that no matter what safety symbols you see in the textbook, all 30 of the lab safety rules previously described should be followed at all times.

EYE PROTECTION

- Wear safety goggles in the lab at all times.
- Know how to use the eyewash station. If chemicals get into your eyes, flush your eyes (including under the eyelids) with running water at the eyewash station for at least 15 minutes. Use your thumb and fingers to hold your eyelids open and, roll your eyeball around. While doing so, ask another student to notify your teacher.

CLOTHING PROTECTION

- Wear an apron or lab coat at all times in the lab.
- Tie back long hair, secure loose clothing, and remove loose jewelry so that they do not knock over equipment or come into contact with hazardous materials.

HAND SAFETY

- Wear protective gloves when working with chemicals.
- Use a hot mitt or tongs to handle equipment that may be hot.

GLASSWARE SAFETY

- Inspect glassware before use; do not use chipped or cracked glassware.
- Never place glassware, containers of chemicals, or anything else near the edges of a lab bench or table.

CHEMICAL SAFETY

- Never return unused chemicals to the original container. Take only what you need.
- Label the beakers and test tubes you use with the chemicals they contain.
- Never transfer substances by sucking on a pipet or straw; use a suction device.
- Do not mix any chemicals unless specifically instructed to do so by your teacher.
- If a chemical spills on the floor or lab bench, tell your teacher, and wait for instructions before cleaning it up yourself.

CAUSTIC SUBSTANCE SAFETY

- Do not pour water into a strong acid or base. The mixture can produce heat and can splatter.

HEATING SAFETY

- Avoid using open flames. If possible, work only with hot plates having an on/off switch and an indicator light.
- When heating a chemical in a test tube, point the open end of the test tube away from yourself and others.

HYGIENE CARE

- Keep your hands away from your face and mouth while you work in the lab.
- Do not eat or drink any food from laboratory containers.
- Wash your hands thoroughly before you leave the lab.

WASTE DISPOSAL

- Help protect our environment by following the instructions for proper disposal.

SAFETY USING MSDS

Do you help with the housekeeping at home? Do you clean your bathtub? Do you use a commercial product intended just for that purpose? Or bleach, or powdered cleanser? It is important to know that you should never mix bleach and powdered cleanser together—doing so results in a chemical reaction that releases poisonous chlorine gas. The vapor from the reaction could do very serious damage to your lungs.

One important thing that you can take away from chemistry class is how to safely use all of the many chemicals in the world around you. Most of us don't think much about chemical safety when we're in our own homes, or in a place that we think of as "safe," like a school. However, hazardous chemicals are sometimes found in the most ordinary places.

WHAT IS AN MSDS?

Because there are dangerous chemicals all around us, chemical manufacturers are required to provide an *MSDS* for all their products sold in the United States. MSDS stands for Material Safety Data Sheet. Such sheets are lists of safety information and procedures for handling chemicals. These can range from household products like vinegar, soap, and baking soda, to some extremely powerful and dangerous chemicals. They are based on guidelines from the U.S. Department of Labor's Occupational Safety and Health Administration (OSHA). A hypothetical example of an MSDS is provided on the next page. It's for a compound you probably know very well.

WHAT KINDS OF INFORMATION DOES AN MSDS GIVE?

There are many different types of information on an MSDS. Some of the information is meant for emergency responders, like firefighters and emergency medical professionals. There are, however, many things in an MSDS that you need to know to be successful with your chemistry laboratory experiments. These sheets should be kept handy at all times when using chemicals. It's also important to read your lab experiment in advance and look up the MSDS for any chemicals to be used. Study the hypothetical example of an MSDS on the following page. Does this seem like a dangerous chemical? Do you recognize the chemical?

WHAT DO THE COLORED LOGOS ON AN MSDS MEAN?

OSHA requires all chemical manufacturers to label hazardous substances with specific types of information. Many companies use either the National Fire Prevention Association (NFPA) format or the Hazardous Materials Information Systems (HMIS) format. An example of each logo is shown below. The logos use the same color and number designations, but slightly different ways of presenting them. A zero indicates that no hazard exists, while a 4 indicates an extreme hazard. Always look for hazard labels on bottles of chemicals before you use the chemicals.

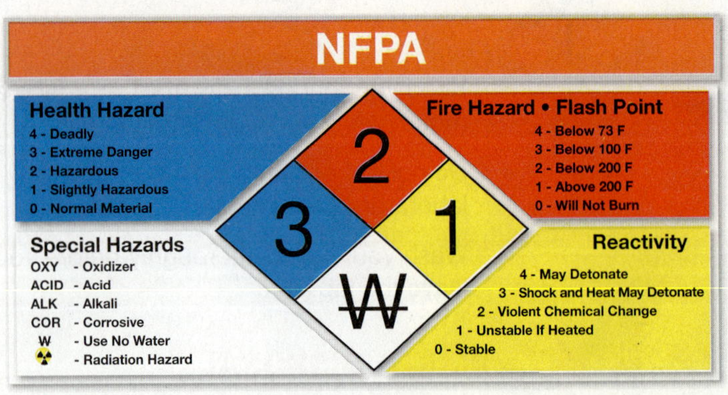

HMIS

Health	2
Flammability	4
Reactivity	4
PPE	D

SAMPLE MSDS (HYPOTHETICAL)

MEGACHEM CORPORATION, INC.
222 Oxygen Ave, City, State, 55555 (555) 555-5555

MATERIAL SAFETY DATA SHEET (MSDS)

MSDS #: 6.00 Revised: X/XX/XXXX

SECTION 1 | Product Identification

Dihydrogen monoxide

SECTION 2 | Composition and Ingredients

Dihydrogen monoxide
Synonyms: hydrogen oxide; agua; water
CAS No. N/A
Red: Fire/Explosive: 0 **Blue:** Health: 2
Yellow: Reactivity: 1 **White:** Special: OXY

SECTION 3 | Physical and Chemical Properties

Boiling point (760 mm Hg): 100°C (212°F)
Melting point: 0°C (32°F)
Specific gravity (H_2O = 1): 1
Vapor pressure - 100°C (212°F) 760 mm Hg - 0°C (32°F) 17.5 mm Hg
Solubility in water (% by wt.): 100%
% Volatiles by volume: 100%
Evap. rate: 750-3000 mm/yr (as measured by U.S. Weather Service)
Appearance and Odor: Clear liquid; No odor

SECTION 4 | Hazards Identification

Clear, colorless, odorless liquid.
Inhalation can result in asphyxiation.
High temperature fumes can cause severe burns to exposed body areas.
Prolonged skin immersion may result in digital vasoconstriction.
In solid form, can cause decreased resistance to hypothermia.

SECTION 5 | First Aid Measures

Seek medical attention for further treatment following first aid.
If inhaled, remove to fresh air; if not effective, apply artificial respiration and oxygen.
Inhalation may result in injury or death.
If skin contact is prolonged, cease immersion immediately; use soft, absorptive materials to dry affected areas.

SECTION 6 | Fire Fighting and Explosion Measures

Flash Point: Not applicable
Auto-ignition Temperature: Not applicable
Flammable limits in air (% by Vol.): Not applicable
Extinguishing Media: Do not use water to extinguish, this will only increase difficulty.
Special fire fighting procedures: Not applicable
Unusual Fire and Explosion Hazard: Explosive vaporization can occur in sealed containers after rapidly increasing temperature.

SECTION 7 | Accidental Spill or Release Measures

Restrict unprotected individuals from area.
Use absorptive materials to contain and soak up spill.
No neutralizing chemicals required.

SECTION 8 | Personal Protection and Exposure Measures

Avoid prolonged contact with eyes, skin, or clothing, particularly at temperatures above 100°C or below 0°C.
Wear chemical-splash goggles and chemical-resistant apron when working at high temperatures.
Insulated garments/gloves must be worn during exposure to solid or vaporous forms at temperatures above 100°C or below 0°C, respectively.
Exposure guidelines: Not available

SECTION 9 | Handling and Storage

Do not store in metal containers for prolonged periods.
Do not heat in closed container that is not pressure-sealed.
Do not store in open container for prolonged periods, as compound will evaporate.
Compound expands when freezing.
Do not inhale liquid.
Contact with many soluble compounds will result in complete dissolution.

SECTION 10 | Stability and Reactivity

Conditions contributing to instability: Generally stable except when exposed to high temperatures or electrical current.
Incompatibility: Rapid temperature increase can occur when added to strong acids or bases. Reaction with sodium metal can result in fire or explosion.
Hazardous decomposition products: Hydrogen - Highly flammable and explosive gas.
Oxygen - Supports rapid combustion.
Conditions contributing to hazardous polymerization: None
Forms solutions readily.

SECTION 11 | Toxicological Information

Acute effects: Harmful liquid if inhaled or skin contact in excess of 100°C
Chronic effects: Oxidation of metals
Target organs: Respiratory system
Commonly found in tumor cells.
Accumulates in vesicles formed from contact with compound at temperatures exceeding 100°C.

SECTION 12 | Ecological Information

Organism exposure to either extreme amounts of compound or prolonged evaporation of compound may result in injury or death.

SECTION 13 | Transportation Information

Shipping name: Dihydrogen monoxide; Liquid
Hazard class: Not regulated

SECTION 14 | Disposal Information

May be safely disposed of down sink or drain.
Disposal of excessive amounts may be subject to local, state, or federal regulations.

SECTION 15 | Regulatory Information

Not regulated

SECTION 16 | Other

This Material Safety Data Sheet (MSDS) is provided as a guideline only. MegaChem Corp., Inc. does not accept or assume any responsibility or liability for use, handling, storage, transportation, or disposal of this product, as these are beyond the control of MegaChem Corp., Inc. FOR THESE REASONS MEGACHEM CORPORATION, INC. EXPRESSLY DISAVOWS ALL KNOWLEDGE OR LIABILITY FOR LOSS, DAMAGE, OR EXPENSES RESULTING FROM THIS PRODUCT.

STUDY SKILLS HANDBOOK

Secrets for Success in Chemistry xxix

Study Strategies

Concept Maps xxxiv

Simple Outlines xxxvii

Cornell Notes xxxviii

K/W/L Strategy xxxix

Sequencing/Pattern Puzzles xl

Other Learning Strategies xli

Cooperative Learning Techniques xliii

Secrets for Success in Chemistry

Some people are gifted scholars and naturally pick up the skills that enable them to be successful in their studies. Most of us, however, have to *learn* the study habits that will help us succeed. No two people learn in exactly the same way, so each of us has to find what works best for us.

You may have heard teachers use terms like *visual, auditory,* and *kinesthetic* when talking about learning styles. These terms are a fancy way of saying that a person learns best when *seeing* something, *hearing* something, or *doing* something hands-on. Most people actually learn in multiple styles, although they may favor one method over others.

The last thing you probably want to hear is that you have to study. You are not alone. Not many people actually *like* to study. What a surprise! You may have asked, “Why do I even need to take chemistry? I'm not going to be a scientist.” The answer to that question is that you need chemistry because *everything* is chemistry. Every single thing around you, including you, is made up of atoms, molecules, and chemical compounds. Everything a person does has something to do with chemistry, from deciding what cleanser scrubs the bathtub best, to choosing what motor oil makes the car run smoothly in winter, or what toothpaste gives the whitest smile. With all these decisions that depend on chemistry, wouldn't you like to know more about it?

Chemistry is a subject that builds on the knowledge that you start accumulating from the first day of class. Imagine what it would be like if you tried writing a novel before learning the entire alphabet. The farther behind you fall at the beginning, the more likely you are to have trouble understanding things the rest of the course. So, the best thing to do is to get it right the first time!

You may have asked, “Why do I even need to take chemistry? I'm not going to be a scientist.” The answer to that question is that *everything* is chemistry.

A textbook is one of the many tools you will use in order to be successful in class. This handbook will provide a number of additional useful tips, tricks, and skills—you might say study *secrets*—that can help you a lot in chemistry. However, they only help if you actually *use* them!

SECRET 1: READ THE BOOK.

No matter how useful your chemistry book may be for holding up the shelf in your locker, it is virtually impossible to pass the class if you don't take it out, open it up, and actually see what is inside. It was not meant to be just a heavy burden in your backpack. It was written to help you to learn chemistry. Here are some tips to put it to the best use:

1. Read the assigned pages *before* you come to class. That way, you'll have a better idea of what the lecture is about.
2. Keep some note cards with you when you read. When you have a question, write it down on one side of a card. When you find the answer or your teacher explains it to you, write the answer on the other side of the card. You may even add diagrams or sketches that help to explain things. There you have it! An instant flashcard! Now you have a useful study tool to help you review a concept that you had a little trouble understanding.
3. Find a good place to study. Some people will tell you to find a quiet place, free from distractions, and that is what works best for them. If you're like many people, though, if a place is *too* quiet, you will *look* for distractions. Look at this realistically. If you study in front of the television, you *will* watch the television. If you study in a room where there are *video games*, and you happen to love video games, you will be distracted. However, there is nothing wrong with some quiet music while you study, if it helps you relax.
4. Use the Main Ideas in the section openers as a guide. These show you what is most important for you to focus on in each chapter. If you have looked at those carefully, you're one step ahead of the game.

SECRET 2: PAY ATTENTION IN CLASS.

The more actively you take part in things, the less bored and sleepy you will be. Sleep at night or on your vacation.

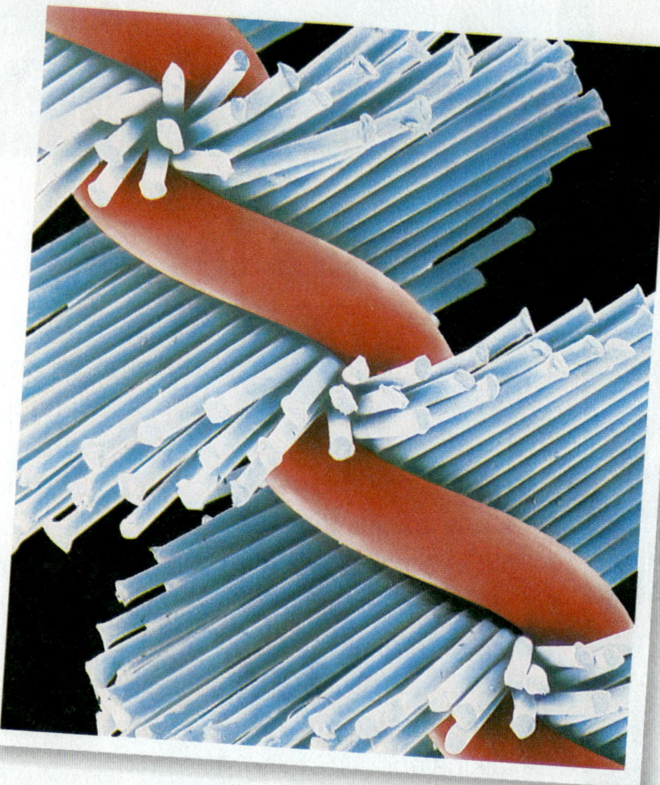

SECRET 3: WORK THE SAMPLE AND PRACTICE PROBLEMS.

For better or worse, problem-solving is a big part of chemistry. Practicing problem-solving skills will be a major part of successfully passing the class.

1. The Sample Problems in the textbook will take you step-by-step through the process, teaching you how to solve them as you go.
2. The solutions to these problems are given in the book. Try covering them up, and then using them to check your work when you finish.
3. The Practice Problems given right after the Sample Problems are there to reinforce what you just learned. The more you do something, the more it will stay in your memory. Practice is what helps you actually *learn* something, rather than just temporarily memorizing it for a test and then forgetting it when you need it later.
4. The problems in the Chapter Review are similar to the Sample Problems. If you can apply the things you learned in the Sample and Practice Problems to the ones in the Review, then you really know the concepts.

5. Plugging numbers into a calculator can be a great tool, but when something goes wrong, it's hard to see where you might have made a mistake. Use the four step problem-solving format: *Analyze, Plan, Solve,* and *Check Your Work.* These will organize your work and help you to better understand the process of solving the problem.
6. If you work on a problem for 15 minutes or more and are still having trouble with it, make note of it so that you can ask your teacher or a friend who understands it for help. Then move on. Otherwise, you may just become frustrated and give up.
7. Always check your answer to see if it makes sense. Is the number realistic when you look back at what you were asked to find? Does your final answer have the correct unit of measurement? Were you supposed to convert something from one unit to another somewhere along the way? Taking a few moments to check these things will not only make you sure that you have the correct answer, it will also help you keep from making the same mistakes over and over again.
8. Write a problem on one side of a note card and the solution on the other. Use the problem cards to periodically practice solving that type of problem.

SECRET 4: DO YOUR HOMEWORK.

You would be amazed at the difference it makes in your chemistry grade when you actually *do* your homework and turn it in on time. And it's important that you do *your own* homework. Friends may seem wonderful when they let you copy their homework in the morning, but they are not doing you any favors. If *they* did the work, *you* have not learned anything. Would you want to go to a doctor who copied someone else's work in school? Would you want to fly in an airplane designed by an engineer who had received all the answers from a friend? Think about it.

1. As soon as possible after class, review your notes, and do your homework. This is the best time, when things are still fairly fresh in your mind. If you wait too long, what you learned in class will fade away. You also will be tired and thus more likely to become frustrated and give up. At this time in your life, one of the most important things you can do is to make the most of your education. It will definitely pay off in your future.
2. Define the key terms, even if they have not been assigned. Take your note-cards and put a term on one side and the definition on the other side. If the key term refers to a scientific equation, put the term on one side of the card and the equation on the other side.

SECRET 5: TAKE NOTES IN CLASS.

Paying attention in class is great, but it is not enough! Very few people have perfect recall, and you can't expect to remember everything. If you don't take notes as you go along, you will forget things. Unless your teacher requires you to take notes in a specific way, there are a number of techniques you can try. Try several and see which one works best for you.

1. Bring paper and pen or pencil. It's pretty hard to take notes without them and your friends eventually will get tired of loaning them to you.
2. Bring your book and follow along in the chapter as your teacher lectures. Add page numbers to your notes so that you can find things again later.
3. Use highlighting markers or colored pens to differentiate between different types of information. It will help keep your notes more organized, and it makes note-taking a little more interesting.

4. Add diagrams or simple sketches to illustrate a concept. This will help you understand it better and also remember it later on, especially if you are mainly a visual learner.
5. It is impossible to write down every single thing a teacher says. If you try to do this, you'll just fall behind and aggravate the teacher and your peers by constantly asking them to wait or to repeat things. Focus on the main ideas and add the details later.
6. Use abbreviations and develop your own shorthand way of writing. Don't put in every *if, and, the,* or *but.*
7. Review your notes as soon as possible after class. Definitely do it within 24 to 48 hours; otherwise, it will fade from your mind. Use your note cards and write down questions that arise as you review. Ask the teacher about them the next time you are in class. Again, now you have a flashcard!
8. Create a note-taking co-op with your classmates. Each person can make copies of their notes and share them. Others may have picked up on concepts that you missed, and you may have notes that others missed. Together, you can have it all.
9. With your teacher's permission, record the lecture. Listen to the recording later and fill in any gaps in your class notes. Label recordings so that you know what subject each covers.
10. See the descriptions of Simple Outlines and Cornell Notes in this Handbook for additional note-taking suggestions.

SECRET 6: START PREPARING FOR A TEST THE DAY YOU START A TOPIC.

Just because you may have been able to wait until the night before the test to study in the past, skim through the chapter quickly, and then pass the test, doesn't mean it will work for you forever. Each year there is more to learn, and the concepts are at a higher level of understanding. If you don't review and practice things as you go along, there will be too much material by the time of the test. You also will not have the time to get enough help.

1. Break it down! It is easier to do a big task in small pieces. Look through your notes for 10 to 15 minutes and read a few pages of the chapter each night. By doing this, you will not have to learn new material the night before an exam.

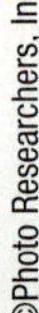

2. Ask the teacher for specific things you need to memorize for the test. Don't try to memorize everything. If you have consistently reviewed the material, you will be more likely to remember it. If you haven't looked at it since the day you first saw it, you will have too much to re-learn the night before the exam.
3. Use your flashcards. These address topics that you had questions about, and going over them will help you remember those questions. Again, don't think it's a waste of your time to make flashcards. Simply making the flashcards will help you better remember material, even if you don't look at them ever again.
4. Study with a friend and test one another with the flashcards. You could try to set some goals to make things more interesting. For example, see which one of you could answer the questions or do the problems on ten flashcards in a row first. This could make studying more fun.
5. Do the review questions in the book, even if they weren't assigned. Test questions often come from the Section and Chapter Reviews. If you do them a few days in advance of the test, you can check with the teacher for the answers to see what you need to spend more time on.
6. Take online quizzes. They are often made up of questions in the test bank and may well reappear on the test. These can help you to pinpoint areas where you're having trouble, so you can get help.
7. Some people, especially if they are in a note-taking co-op, find it beneficial to rewrite and reorganize their notes before a test, to make studying easier. In many cases, this can also refresh your memory and be a review in itself.
8. Get enough sleep. At your age, when you sleep is when your body is growing, building new bone and muscle, and doing general maintenance and repair. You actually require *more* than 8 hours of sleep a day while these things are going on. If you don't let your body and your brain rest, build, and repair, *things won't work right.*
9. Eat right. Your car won't run if it doesn't get the right fuel, and your body won't either. Save the junk food for a reward after the test. You'll certainly deserve it after all the hard work you've put into studying.

SECRET 7: BE PRACTICAL WHEN YOU TAKE A TEST.

There are skills that can help you be more successful when you take the test. Some of them are common sense things that your mom probably told you a million times until you stopped listening. Pay close attention to the phrase *common sense.* Common means that a lot of people know about it (not just your mom) and it will benefit you to pay attention.

1. When test day comes, bring a pen and/or pencil to class. Teachers don't accept answers transmitted by telepathy.
2. Ask the teacher if you may use scratch paper to work problems out.
3. If it's permitted, bring a calculator to help speed up doing the math on problems. But don't let it take the place of a step-by-step approach, because you might miss an important step. Calculators are only as good as the data you put into them.
4. Dress comfortably. Although the school is unlikely to allow you to wear your pajamas in class, you're bound to have a favorite pair of jeans and shirt that don't scratch, pinch, ride up, or cause other discomfort.
5. Once you are given the test, look over the whole thing first, before you start.
6. Read the directions. Some teachers occasionally like to give tests that have directions like the following, just to see if you are paying attention: "Sign your name on your paper, wait two minutes, then turn it in. Grin at everyone as you walk back to your seat. Do this and you'll get an A."
7. Start with the questions you're sure you know the answers to, then go back and work on the harder ones. Doing the easier questions first may spark your memory and help you to answer the ones you skipped.
8. Remember your problem-solving skills and check to make sure your answers make sense.

Concept Maps

Making concept maps can help you decide what material in a chapter is important and how to efficiently learn that material. A concept map presents key ideas, meanings, and relationships for the concepts being studied. It can be thought of as a visual road map of the chapter. Learning happens efficiently when you use concept maps because you work with only the key ideas and how they fit together.

The concept map shown as **Map A** was made from vocabulary terms in the chapter, "Matter and Change." Vocabulary terms are generally labels for concepts, and concepts are generally nouns. In a concept map, linking words are used to form propositions that connect concepts and give them meaning in context. For example, on the map below, "matter is described by physical properties" is a proposition.

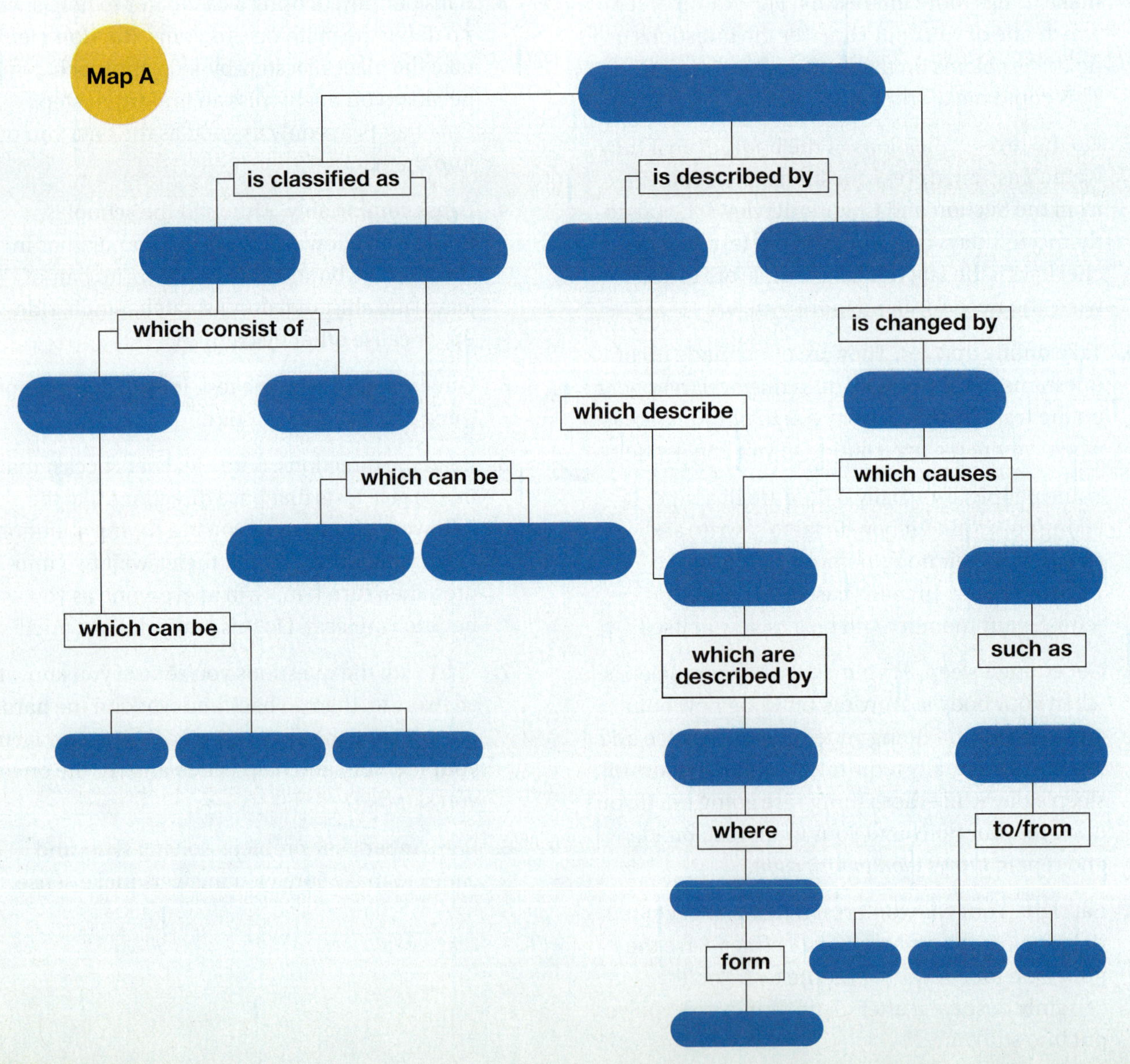

Studies show that people are better able to remember materials presented visually. In a concept map, you can see the relationships among many ideas.

The more concept maps you make, the better you will become at constructing them. Soon you may find that organizing them becomes second nature. You may even develop your own system of shapes, lines, and colors to emphasize different types of information contained in your concept maps. For example, you may decide to place all vocabulary terms in ovals, main ideas in squares, and clarifying examples in triangles. You could draw solid lines between concepts and terms that are very related and dotted lines between those that are only slightly related.

The great thing about concept maps is that they allow you the freedom to organize material in a way that makes sense to you.

To Make a Concept Map

1. **List all the important concepts.** We'll use some concepts from Section 2 of the chapter "Matter and Change."

matter	mixture
compound	pure substance
element	
homogeneous mixture	
heterogeneous mixture	

From this list, group similar concepts together. For example, one way to group these concepts would be into two groups—one that is related to mixtures and one that is related to pure substances.

mixture	pure substance
heterogeneous mixture	compound
homogeneous mixture	element

2. **Select a main concept for the map.**
We will use *matter* as the main concept for this map.

3. **Build the map by placing the concepts according to their importance under the main concept, *matter.***
One way of arranging the concepts is shown in **Map B.** (This map is continued on the next page.)

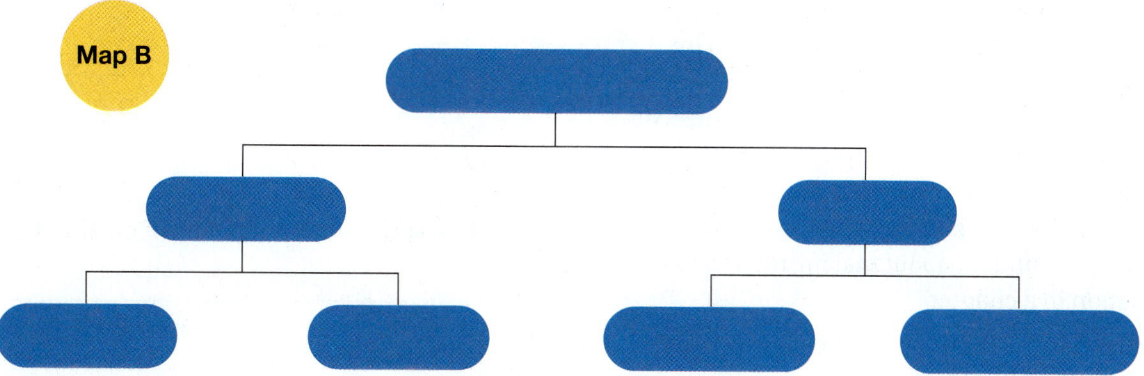

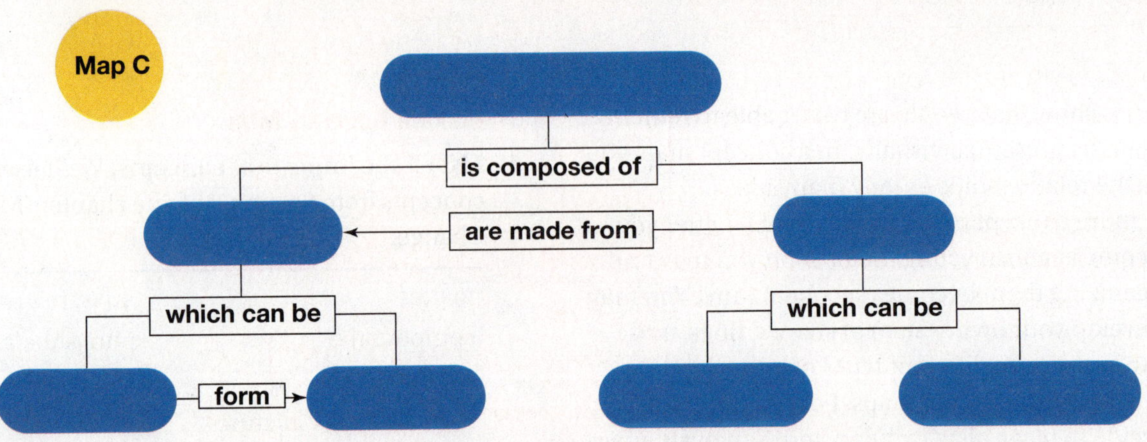

4. **Add linking words to give meaning to the arrangement of concepts.**

When adding the links, be sure that each proposition makes sense. To distinguish concepts from links, place your concepts in circles, ovals, or rectangles, as shown in the maps. Then make cross-links. Cross-links are made of propositions and lines connecting concepts across the map. Links that apply in only one direction are indicated with an arrowhead.

Map C is a finished map covering the main ideas listed in Step 1. Making maps might seem difficult at first, but the process forces you to think about the meanings and relationships among the concepts. If you do not understand those relationships, you can get help early on.

Practice mapping by making concept maps about topics you know. For example, if you know a lot about a particular sport, such as basketball, or if you have a particular hobby, such as playing a musical instrument, you can use that topic to make a practice map. By perfecting your skills with information that you know very well, you will begin to feel more confident about making maps from the information in a chapter.

Remember, the time you devote to mapping will pay off when it is time to review for an exam.

PRACTICE

1. Classify each of the following as either a concept or linking word(s).

   a. classification ____________

   b. is classified as ____________

   c. forms ____________

   d. is described by ____________

   e. reaction ____________

   f. reacts with ____________

   g. metal ____________

   h. defines ____________

2. Write three propositions from the information in **Map A.**

   ____
   ____
   ____

3. List two cross-links shown on **Map C.**

   ____
   ____
   ____

Simple Outlines

Outlining is a skill that is useful in many different subject areas. An outline can help you quickly identify the major concepts of a topic, along with key supporting details or examples. Your textbook layout was designed to help you set up a simple outline. Each section has a title, main ideas, and examples that support the main ideas. Under each example are additional details that help to explain the concept more fully.

Here is a simple outline based on the sections in the chapter "Matter and Change:"

I. Chemistry Is a Physical Science

II. Matter and Its Properties

III. Elements

Adding in the Main Ideas, subheadings, definitions, examples, and supporting information from the textbook can easily make this outline more detailed. A sample from the beginning of the section is shown below.

I. Chemistry is a Physical Science (Section Title)

A. Chemistry is the study of matter and its processes. (Main Idea)

B. There are several branches of chemistry. (Main Idea)

1. organic chemistry
2. inorganic chemistry
3. physical chemistry
4. analytical chemistry
5. biochemistry

Cornell Notes

The Cornell note-taking system was developed in the 1950's by Walter Pauk, while he was teaching at Cornell University. The method is now widely recommended and is used by schools and colleges all over the world due to its effectiveness as a study tool. Make things easier by setting up or printing out a note-taking template in advance.

Here is a template that can be used for taking notes with the Cornell system:

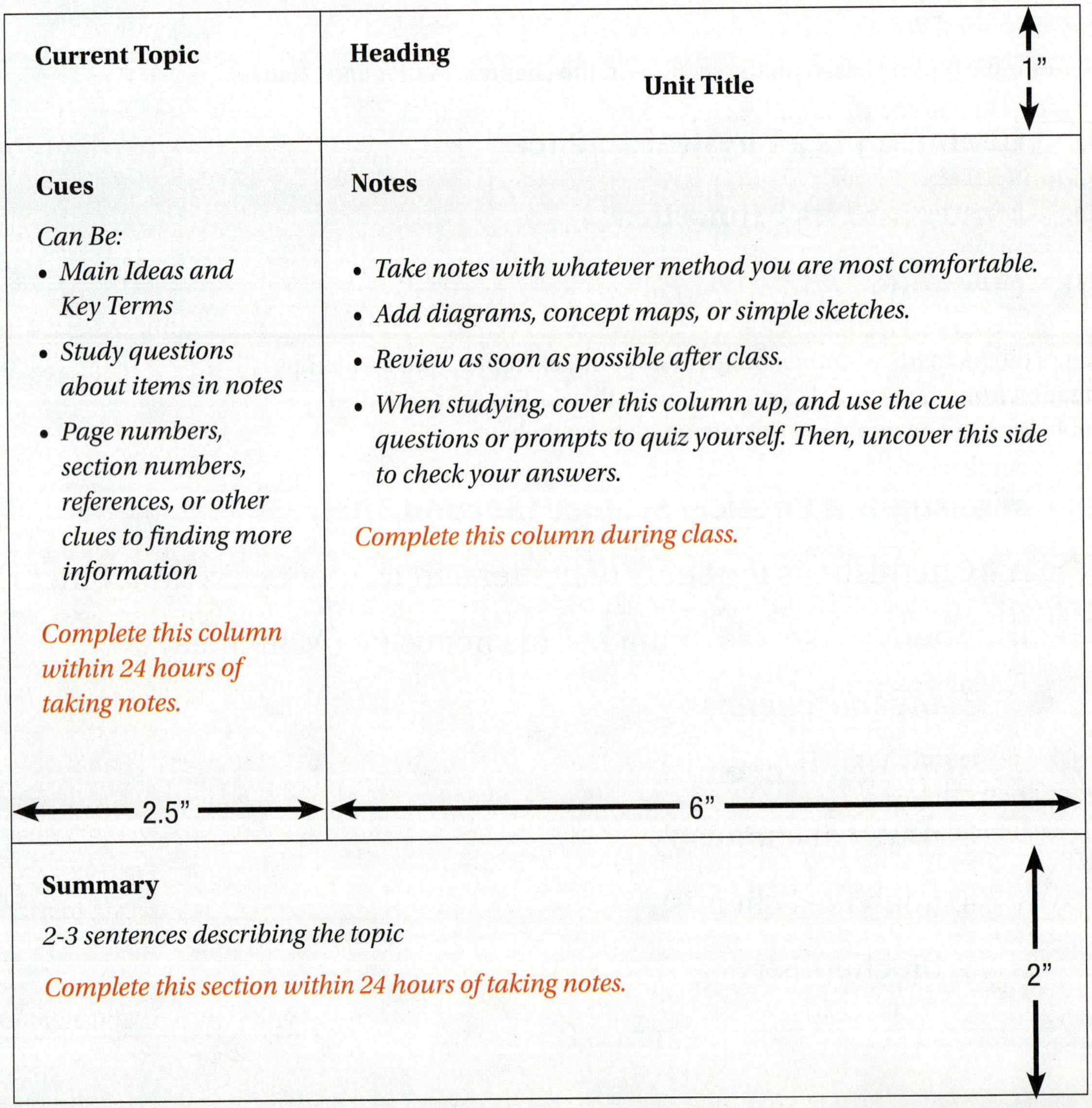

Current Topic	**Heading** **Unit Title** (1")
Cues *Can Be:* • *Main Ideas and Key Terms* • *Study questions about items in notes* • *Page numbers, section numbers, references, or other clues to finding more information* *Complete this column within 24 hours of taking notes.* ← 2.5" →	**Notes** • *Take notes with whatever method you are most comfortable.* • *Add diagrams, concept maps, or simple sketches.* • *Review as soon as possible after class.* • *When studying, cover this column up, and use the cue questions or prompts to quiz yourself. Then, uncover this side to check your answers.* *Complete this column during class.* ← 6" →
Summary *2-3 sentences describing the topic* *Complete this section within 24 hours of taking notes.* (2")	

K/W/L Strategy

The K/W/L strategy stands for "what I *Know*—what I *Want* to know—what I *Learned*." You start by brainstorming about the subject matter before reading the assigned material. Relating new ideas and concepts to those you have learned previously will help you better understand and apply the new knowledge you obtain. The main ideas throughout your textbook are ideal for using the K/W/L strategy.

1. **Read the main ideas.** You may also want to scan additional headings, highlighted terms, and equations before reading.
2. **Divide a sheet of paper into three columns, and label the columns "What I Know," "What I Want to Know," and "What I Learned."**
3. **Brainstorm what you know about the information in the objectives, and write these ideas in the first column.** Because this chart is designed primarily to help you integrate your own knowledge with new information, it is not necessary to write complete sentences.
4. **Think about what you want to know about the information in the objectives, and write these ideas in the second column.** Include information from both the section objectives and any other objectives your teacher has given you.
5. **While reading the section or afterwards, use the third column to write down the information you learned.** While reading, pay close attention to any information about the topics you wrote in the "What I Want to Know" column. If you do not find all of the answers you are looking for, you may need to reread the section or reference a second source. Be sure to ask your teacher if you still cannot find the information after reading the section a second time. It is also important to review your brainstormed ideas when you have completed reading the section. Compare your ideas in the first column with the information you wrote down in the third column.

If you find that some of your brainstormed ideas are incorrect, cross them out. It is extremely important to identify and correct any misconceptions you had prior to reading before you begin studying for your test.

The example below shows a K/W/L strategy a student may have written while studying about the different types of matter.

What I Know	What I Want to Know	What I Learned
• a gas has no definite shape or volume • a liquid has no definite shape, but has definite volume • a solid has definite shape and volume • a mixture is a combination of substances • a pure substance has only one component	• how gas, liquid, and solid states depend on the movements of particles • how mixtures and pure substances are different at the particle level	• molecules in solid and liquid states are close together, but are far apart in gas state • molecules in solid state have fixed positions, but molecules in liquid and gas states can flow • mixtures are combinations of pure substances • pure substances have fixed compositions and definite properties

Sequencing / Pattern Puzzles

You can use pattern puzzles to help you remember sequential information. Pattern puzzles are not just a tool for memorization. They also promote a greater understanding of a variety of chemical processes, from the steps in solving a mass-mass stoichiometry problem to the procedure for making a solution of specified molarity.

1. **Write down the steps of a process in your own words.** For an example, we will use the process for converting the amount of a substance in moles to mass in grams. (See Sample Problem B in the chapter, "Atoms: The Building Blocks of Matter.") On a sheet of notebook paper, write down one step per line, and do not number the steps. Also, do not copy the process straight from your textbook. Writing the steps in your own words promotes a more thorough understanding of the process. You may want to divide longer steps into two or three shorter steps.

• List the given and unknown information.
• Look at the periodic table to determine the molar mass of the substance.
• Write the correct conversion factor to convert moles to grams.
• Multiply the amount of substance by the conversion factor.
• Solve the equation and check your answer.

2. **Cut the sheet of paper into strips with only one step per strip of paper.** Shuffle the strips of paper so that they are out of sequence. Alternatively, you can write each step on a separate note card, and then shuffle the note cards.

• Look at the periodic table to determine the molar mass of the substance.
• Solve the equation and check your answer.
• List the given and unknown information.
• Multiply the amount of substance by the conversion factor.
• Write the correct conversion factor to convert moles to grams.

3. **Place the strips (or note cards) in their proper sequence.** Confirm the order of the process by checking your text or your class notes.

• List the given and unknown information.
• Look at the periodic table to determine the molar mass of the substance.
• Write the correct conversion factor to convert moles to grams.
• Multiply the amount of substance by the conversion factor.
• Solve the equation and check your answer.

Pattern puzzles are especially helpful when you are studying for your chemistry tests. Before tests, use your puzzles to practice sequencing and to review the steps of chemistry processes. You and a classmate can also take turns creating your own pattern puzzles of different chemical processes and putting each other's puzzles in the correct sequence. Studying with a classmate in this manner will help make studying fun and will enable you to help each other.

Other Learning Strategies

BRAINSTORMING

Brainstorming is a strategy that helps you recognize and evaluate the knowledge you already have before you start reading. It works well individually or in groups. When you brainstorm, you start with a central term or idea, then quickly list all the words, phrases, and other ideas that you think are related to it.

Because there are no "right" or "wrong" answers, you can use the list as a basis for classifying terms, developing a general explanation, or speculating about new relationships. For example, you might brainstorm a list of terms related to the word *element.* The list might include gold, metals, chemicals, silver, carbon, oxygen, and water. As you read the textbook, you might decide that some of the terms you listed are not elements. Later, you might use that information to help you distinguish between elements and compounds.

BUILDING / INTERPRETING VOCABULARY

Using a dictionary to look up the meanings of prefixes and suffixes as well as word origins and meanings helps you build your vocabulary and interpret what you read. If you know the meaning of prefixes like kilo- (one thousand) and milli- (one thousandth), you have a good idea what kilograms, kilometers, milligrams, and millimeters are and how they are different.

Knowledge of prefixes, suffixes, and word origins can help you understand the meaning of new words. For example, if you know the suffix -protic comes from the same word as proton, it will help you understand what monoprotic and polyprotic acids are.

READING HINTS

Reading hints help you identify and bookmark important charts, tables, and illustrations for easy reference. For example, you may want to use a self-adhesive note to bookmark the periodic table in your book so you can easily locate it and use it for reference as you study different aspects of chemistry and solve problems involving elements and compounds.

INTERPRETING GRAPHIC SOURCES OF INFORMATION

Charts, tables, photographs, diagrams, and other illustrations are graphic, or visual, sources of information. The labels and captions, together with the illustrations, help you make connections between the words and the ideas presented in the text.

READING RESPONSE LOGS

Keeping a reading response log helps you interpret what you read and gives you a chance to express your reactions and opinions about what you have read. Draw a vertical line down the center of a piece of paper. In the left-hand column, write down or make notes about passages you read to which you have reactions, thoughts, feelings, questions, or associations. In the right-hand column, write what those reactions, thoughts, feelings, questions, or associations are.

COMPARING AND CONTRASTING

Comparing and contrasting is a strategy that helps you note similarities and differences between two or more objects or events. When you determine similarities, you are comparing. When you determine differences, you are contrasting.

You can use comparing and contrasting to help you classify objects or properties, differentiate between similar concepts, and speculate about new relationships. For example, as you read the chapter, "Matter and Change," you might begin to make a table in which you compare and contrast metals, nonmetals, and metalloids. As you continue to learn about these substances you can add to your table, giving you a better understanding of the similarities and differences among elements.

IDENTIFYING CAUSE AND EFFECT

Identifying causes and effects as you read helps you understand the material and builds logical reasoning skills. An effect is an event or the result of some action. A cause is the reason the event or action occurred. Signal words, such as *because, so, since, therefore, as a result,* and *depends on,* indicate a cause-and-effect relationship. You can use arrows to show cause and effect. For example, you might write this cause-and-effect relationship as you read the chapter on gases: At constant pressure, increase in temperature (cause) → increase in gas volume (effect).

MAKING A PREDICTION GUIDE

A prediction guide is a list of statements about which you express your opinions and then try to justify them based on your current knowledge. After reading the material, you re-evaluate your opinions in light of what you learned. Using prediction guides helps you assess your knowledge, identify assumptions you may have that could lead to mistaken conclusions, and form an idea of expected results. Here are some suggestions for how to make a prediction guide.

1. **Start with the statements your teacher writes on the board or you find listed in your textbook.** For example, look at the five statements from Dalton's atomic theory in your textbook, in the chapter "Atoms: The Building Blocks of Matter."
2. **Decide whether you think each statement is true or false.** Discuss the reasons why you think so and write it all down. If someone disagrees with your conclusion, write down the reasons why.
3. **After reading the section or listening to a lecture, re-evaluate your opinion of each statement.** Discuss why your opinion changed or remained the same. Find passages in the text that account for the change of reinforcement of your opinions. For example, you might have agreed with all five statements from Dalton's theory before reading the text. Then, after reading about atoms and subatomic particles, you might have changed your opinion about the first statement.

COOPERATIVE LEARNING TECHNIQUES

READING WITH A PARTNER

Reading with a partner can help you understand what you read and point out where you need more study.

1. **First read the text silently by yourself and take notes.** Use self-adhesive notes to mark those parts of the text that you do not understand. For example, you might have difficulty with some of the material about quantum numbers, while another student might not understand electron configurations.
2. **Work with a partner to discuss the passages each of you marked.** Take turns listening and trying to clarify the difficult passages for each other. Together, study the related tables and illustrations and explain how they relate to the text.
3. **Work together to formulate questions for class discussion or for your teacher to answer.** Make note of the complications you both encountered and bring questions to your teacher.

USING L.I.N.K.

The L.I.N.K. strategy stands for **L**ist, **I**nquire, **N**otes, **K**now. It is similar to the K/W/L strategy, but you work as a class or in groups.

1. **Brainstorm all the words, phrases, and ideas associated with a term your teacher provides.** Volunteers can keep track of contributions on the board or on a separate sheet of paper.
2. **Have your teacher direct you in a class or group discussion about the words and ideas listed.** Now is the time to ask your teacher and other students for clarification of the listed ideas.
3. **At the end of the discussion, make notes about everything you can remember.** Look over your notes to see if you have left anything out.
4. **See what you now know about the given concept based on the discussion.** Consider if what you now know is different from what you previously believed.

SUMMARIZING/PAIRED SUMMARIZING

A summary is a brief statement of main ideas or important concepts. Making a summary of what you have read provides you with a way to review what you have learned, see what information needs further clarification, and make connections to material previously studied. Paired summarizing helps strengthen your ability to read, listen, and understand. It is especially useful when a section of text has several subdivisions, each dealing with different concepts.

1. **First read the material silently by yourself.**
2. **Then you and your partner take turns being the "listener" and the "speaker."** The speaker summarizes the material for the listener, who does not interrupt until the speaker has finished. If necessary, the speaker may consult the text, and the listener may ask for clarification. The listener then states any inaccuracies or omissions made by the speaker.
3. **Work together to refine the summary.** Make sure the summary states the important ideas in a clear and concise manner.

DISCUSSING IDEAS

Discussing ideas with someone else before you read is a strategy that can help you broaden your knowledge base and decide what concepts to focus on. Discussing ideas after you have read a section or chapter can help you check your understanding, clarify difficult concepts, and speculate about new ideas.

Matter and Change

① Core Instruction

Chapter Resources

- The Teacher's Edition wrap has extensive teaching support for every lesson, including Misconception Alerts, Teach from Visuals, Demonstrations, Teaching Tips, Differentiated Instruction, and Problem Solving support.
- Several additional presentation tools are available online for every chapter, including Animated Chemistry features and Visual Concepts.
- You can open your lesson with the Why It Matters Video: Chemistry Matters.

Section	Instruction	Labs and Demonstrations Go Online for Materials Lists and Solutions Lists.
1.1	■ **Textbook:** Chemistry Is a Physical Science **Teaching Visuals:** Top Eight Chemicals Made in the United States **PowerPresentations**	
1.2	■ **Textbook:** Matter and Its Properties **Teaching Visuals:** Water in Three States • Comparison of Physical and Chemical Properties • Classifying Matter • Electrolysis of Water • Evidence of a Chemical Change • Pure Substances • Types of Mixtures • Properties of Matter • Examples of Mixtures • Grades of Chemical Purity **PowerPresentations**	■ **Demonstration:** Conductivity of Water ■ **Demonstration:** Particle Energy ■ **Demonstration:** Homogeneous vs. Heterogeneous Mixtures ■ **Lab:** Mixture Separation (Core Skill)
1.3	■ **Textbook:** Elements **Animated Chemistry:** The Organization of the Periodic Table **Teaching Visuals:** Regions of the Periodic Table • Element Names • Symbols and the Symbols' Origins **PowerPresentations**	■ **Demonstration:** Metals and Non-Metals

2 Support and Intervention

- **Interactive Reader** (English and Spanish)
- **Study Guide**
- **Interactive Review:** Review Games, Concept Maps, and Section Self-Checks
- **Scientific Reasoning Skill Builder**

3 Specialized Support

- **Chapter Summary Audio Files**
- **Interactive Reader Audio Files**
- **Differentiated Instruction:** Inclusion, Below Level, and English Learners (TE wrap)

Enrichment and Challenge

- **Differentiated Instruction:** Pre-AP (TE wrap)
- **Cross-Disciplinary Connection:** Secrets of the Cremona Violins (SE)
- **WebLinks**

Assessment

- **Section Formative Assessments** (SE)
- **Section Quizzes**
- **Chapter Review** (SE)
- **Chapter Tests A and B**
- **Alternative Assessment** (TE wrap)
- **Online Assessment and Remediation**
- **ExamView Banks**

Where do I find it?

		PRINT	DVD	ONLINE
1	Animated Chemistry		■	■
	Demonstrations (TE wrap)	■		■
	Interactive Whiteboard		■	■
	Labs		■	■
	PowerPresentations		■	■
	QuickLabs	■	■	■
	Teaching Visuals		■	■
	Textbook	■	■	■
	Visual Concepts		■	■
	Why It Matters Videos		■	■
2	Interactive Demos		■	■
	Interactive Reader	■	■	■
	Interactive Reviews		■	■
	Learn It! Videos		■	■
	Sample Problem Sets		■	■
	Scientific Reasoning Skill Builder		■	■
	Smart Grapher Tool		■	■
	Solve It! Cards		■	■
	Study Guide		■	■
3	Chapter Summary Audio Files		■	■
	Differentiated Instruction (TE wrap)	■		
	Interactive Reader Audio Files		■	■

CHAPTER 1

Chapter Overview

Section 1 defines the field of chemistry and distinguishes between different branches of chemistry.

Section 2 defines matter and contrasts major physical and chemical changes that matter can undergo. This section also outlines the basic form of a chemical equation and describes how matter is classified.

Section 3 introduces the periodic table as a classification scheme for the elements with descriptions of metals, nonmetals, and metalloids.

▼ Focus and Motivate

Activate Prior Knowledge

This text assumes that students have some prior background in the physical sciences. Therefore, terms such as *energy, atom, element, compound, proton, neutron,* and *electron* should be familiar to them.

About the Image

Tartaric acid is an organic acid found naturally in some fruits, including bananas, pineapples, and grapes. Tartaric acid has a sour taste and is added to candies and soft drinks to create tartness. A form of tartaric acid is also used to make cream of tartar, which is used as a thickening agent in many foods.

Why It Matters

Students can access the videos online and find other helpful resources at **HMDScience.com**.

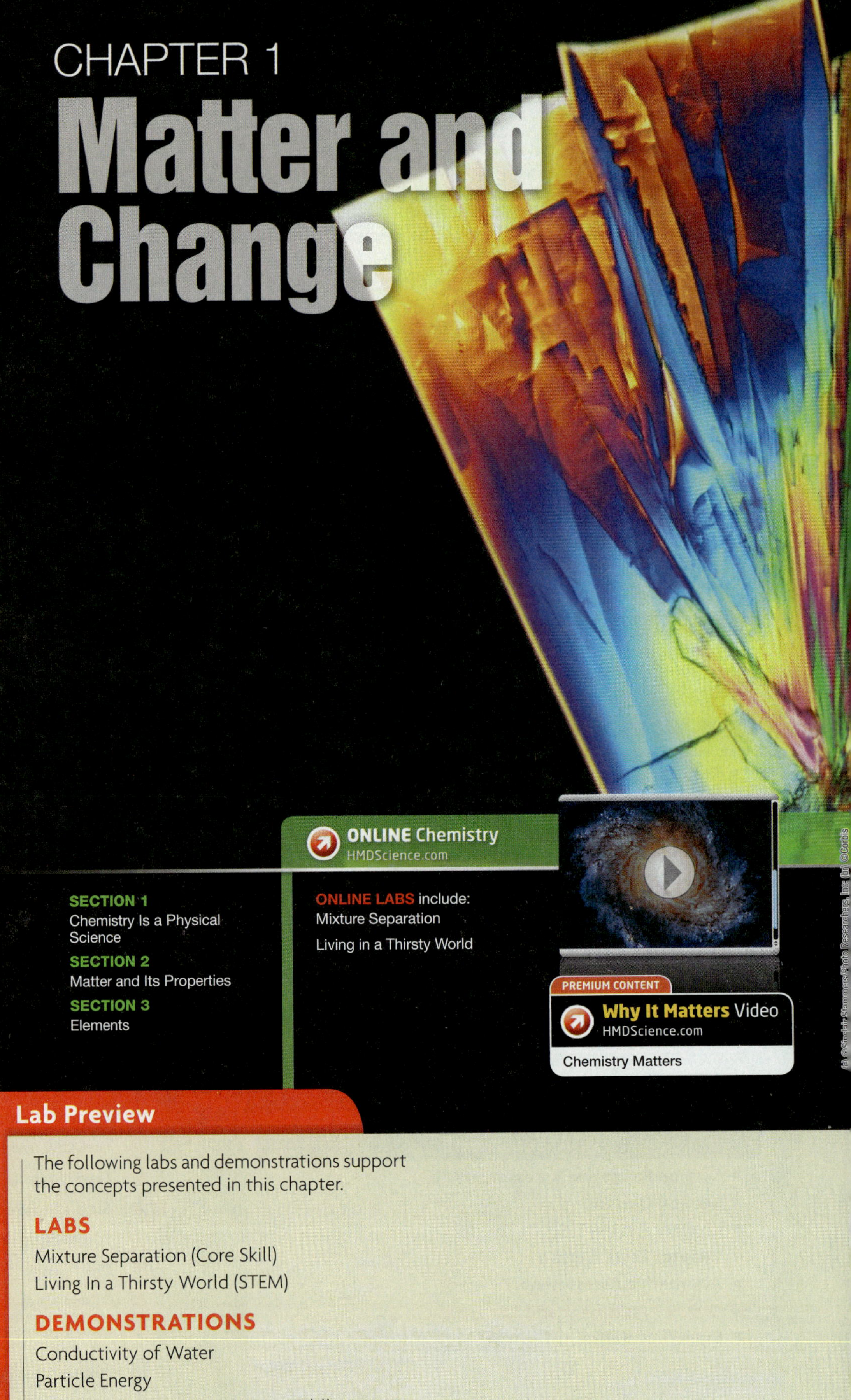

Lab Preview

The following labs and demonstrations support the concepts presented in this chapter.

LABS

Mixture Separation (Core Skill)

Living In a Thirsty World (STEM)

DEMONSTRATIONS

Conductivity of Water

Particle Energy

Homogeneous vs. Heterogeneous Mixtures

Metals and Non-Metals

Chemistry Is a Physical Science

SECTION 1

Main Ideas

- Chemistry is the study of matter and its processes.
- There are several branches of chemistry.

Key Terms

chemistry
chemical

The natural sciences were once divided into two broad categories: the biological sciences and the physical sciences. The biological sciences focus mainly on living things. The physical sciences focus mainly on nonliving things. However, because we now know that both living and nonliving matter consist of chemical structures, chemistry is central to all the sciences, and there are no longer distinct divisions between the biological and physical sciences.

MAIN IDEA

Chemistry is the study of matter and its processes.

Chemistry is the study of the composition, structure, and properties of matter, the processes that matter undergoes, and the energy changes that accompany these processes. Chemistry deals with questions such as: What is a material's makeup? How does a material change when heated, cooled, or mixed with other materials and why does this behavior occur? Chemists answer these kinds of questions during their work.

Instruments like those shown in **Figure 1.1** are routinely used in chemistry to extend our ability to observe and make measurements. They make it possible, for example, to look at microstructures—things too tiny to be seen with the unaided eye. The scanning tunneling microscope reveals tiny structures by beaming extremely small particles called electrons at materials. When the electrons hit a material, they scatter and produce a pattern that shows the material's microstructure.

FIGURE 1.1

Scientific Observations

(a) A balance is an instrument used to measure the mass of materials.

(b) A sample of DNA placed in a scanning tunneling microscope produces an image showing the contours of the DNA's surface.

Differentiated Instruction

BELOW LEVEL

Have students choose one of the branches of chemistry to look up online. Provide students with magazines, scissors, and glue sticks or tape. Ask them to construct a collage with any images they can find that are related to their chosen branch of chemistry.

SECTION 1

Plan and Prepare

Objectives

- Define chemistry.
- List examples of the branches of chemistry.
- Compare and contrast basic research, applied research, and technological development.

Classroom Catalyst

Have students consider all of the objects in their classroom that are related to the study of chemistry. Bring different materials, such as plastics, fabrics, fertilizer, clothes, cooking oil, motor oil, nail polish, nail polish remover, aspirin, and vitamins to class to help initiate discussion. Have students consider their daily activities. How many of these activities have something to do with chemistry?

Teach

TEACH FROM VISUALS

FIGURE 1.1 Use this figure to remind students that there are limits to the ability of our senses to make measurements. Instruments extend our senses and allow us to make quantitative measurements. Try to get students to recognize the benefits of making observations that include measurements.

READING TOOLKIT

K/W/L Students probably have preconceptions about chemistry. Have them list what they know about chemistry. Then have them list what they want to know about it. After they have completed Section 1, have them look at their lists and write down what they have learned about chemistry. Also, have them write down any new questions that they may have after reading the section.

▼ Teach *continued*

Teaching Tip

- Students should know that there are no clear-cut divisions that separate one kind of chemist from another. Just as doctors specialize in a certain type of medicine, chemists too have more specialized fields of study, but these fields often overlap.
- Have students bring in articles from news magazines and other periodicals showing chemistry in action. Photography magazines are one good source. Students are often surprised at the number of industries that rely in some way on basic chemical knowledge.

Misconception Alert!

Students often think of chemicals as artificial, or unnatural. You want them to understand that all matter—living and nonliving, natural or artificial—has a chemical basis. Ask students to try naming anything that they think is not made of at least one chemical.

Invisible rays called X-rays can also be used to determine microstructures. The patterns that appear can be analyzed to reveal the arrangement of atoms, molecules, or other particles that make up the material. By learning about microstructures, chemists can explain the behavior of macrostructures—the visible things all around you.

MAIN IDEA

There are several branches of chemistry.

Chemistry includes many different branches of study and research. The following are six main areas of study. But like the biological and physical sciences, these branches often overlap.

1. *Organic chemistry*—the study of most carbon-containing compounds
2. *Inorganic chemistry*—the study of non-organic substances, many of which have organic fragments bonded to metals (organometallics)
3. *Physical chemistry*—the study of the properties and changes of matter and their relation to energy
4. *Analytical chemistry*—the identification of the components and composition of materials
5. *Biochemistry*—the study of substances and processes occurring in living things
6. *Theoretical chemistry*—the use of mathematics and computers to understand the principles behind observed chemical behavior and to design and predict the properties of new compounds

In all areas of chemistry, scientists work with chemicals. **A chemical is any substance that has a definite composition.** For example, consider the material called sucrose, or cane sugar. It has a definite composition in terms of the atoms that compose it. It is produced by certain plants in the chemical process of photosynthesis. Sucrose is a chemical. Carbon dioxide, water, and countless other substances are chemicals as well.

Knowing the properties of chemicals allows chemists to find suitable uses for them. For example, researchers have synthesized new substances, such as artificial sweeteners and synthetic fibers. The reactions used to make these chemicals can often be carried out on a large scale to make new consumer products such as flavor enhancers and fabrics.

Basic Research

Basic research is carried out for the sake of increasing knowledge, such as how and why a specific reaction occurs and what the properties of a substance are. Chance discoveries can be the result of basic research. The properties of Teflon™, for example, were first discovered by accident. A researcher named Roy Plunkett was puzzled by the fact that a gas cylinder used for an experiment appeared to be empty even though the measured mass of the cylinder clearly indicated there was something inside. Plunkett cut the cylinder open and found a white solid. Through basic research, Plunkett's research team determined the nonstick properties, molecular structure, and chemical composition of the new material.

Differentiated Instruction

PRE-AP

Challenge students to choose one of the six branches of chemistry to explore in more depth. Students should research the education needed for a chemist in their chosen branch of chemistry, along with the practical applications related to it. Have students write a job description, such as might be found online or in a professional journal, and then exchange descriptions with a partner. Ask them to write a letter of interest for the position described by their partner, presenting their applicable education and professional experience.

Applied Research

Applied research is generally carried out to solve a problem. For example, when certain refrigerants escape into the upper atmosphere, they damage the ozone layer, which helps block harmful ultraviolet rays from reaching the surface of Earth. In response to concerns that this atmospheric damage could pose health problems, chemists have developed new refrigerants. In applied research, researchers are driven not by curiosity or a desire to know but by a desire to solve a specific problem.

CHECK FOR UNDERSTANDING

Apply Would testing a new drug to find if it is an effective treatment for a disease be considered basic research or applied research? Explain your answer.

Technological Development

Technological development typically involves the production and use of products that improve our quality of life. Examples include computers, catalytic converters for cars, and biodegradable materials.

Technological applications often lag far behind the discoveries that are eventually used in technologies. For example, nonstick cookware, a technological application, was developed well after the accidental discovery of Teflon. When it was later discovered that the Teflon coating on cookware often peeled off, a new challenge arose. Using applied research, scientists were then able to improve the bond between the Teflon and the metal surface of the cookware so that it did not peel.

Basic research, applied research, and technological development often overlap. Discoveries made in basic research may lead to applications that can result in new technologies. For example, knowledge of crystals and light that was gained from basic research was used to develop lasers. It was then discovered that pulses of light from lasers can be sent through optical fibers, like the ones shown in **Figure 1.2.** Today, telephone messages and cable television signals are carried quickly over long distances using fiber optics.

FIGURE 1.2

Applying Research The chemical structure of the material in an optical fiber gives it the property of total internal reflection. This property, which allows these fibers to carry light, was discovered through basic and applied research. The use of this property to build networks by sending data on light pulses is the technological development of fiber optics.

SECTION 1 FORMATIVE ASSESSMENT

Reviewing Main Ideas

1. Explain what chemistry is.
2. Name six branches of study in chemistry.
3. Compare and contrast basic research, applied research, and technological development.

Critical Thinking

4. **INFERRING RELATIONSHIPS** Scientific and technological advances are constantly changing how people live and work. Discuss a change you have observed in your lifetime that has made life easier or more enjoyable for you.

Answers to Section Assessment

1. Chemistry is the study of the composition, structure, and properties of matter and the changes matter undergoes.
2. Organic chemistry, inorganic chemistry, physical chemistry, analytical chemistry, biochemistry, and theoretical chemistry
3. Basic research is conducted for the sake of knowledge only and not to meet practical goals. Applied research is conducted to meet goals defined by specific needs. Technology employs existing knowledge to make life easier or more convenient.
4. Answers will vary. Students may mention technological improvements in devices such as "smart" phones that send texts, email and access the internet, mp3 players, and digital cameras that take photos and record HD video. Scientific advancements may include improvements in health care, food science, and pollution control.

Classroom Discussion

Survey students to find out if anyone has a friend or relative who works in the field of chemistry. Invite these people to speak to the class and describe their work. Encourage students to bring questions to class regarding the level of chemistry education the speaker needed to work in his or her field. Assign students the task of collecting items for a "Chemistry Careers" bulletin board. Award extra credit to students who find information on chemistry careers that are not within the traditional "scientist" role.

Misconception Alert!

Students often think that science and technology are the same. Science includes knowledge in its major disciplines, such as biology, chemistry, and physics. Technology is the application of that knowledge for practical purposes.

Check for Understanding

Answer: Testing a new drug to find if it is an effective treatment for a disease would be considered applied research, since the test is done to try to solve a problem.

Assess and Reteach ▼

Assess Use the Formative Assessment on this page to evaluate student mastery of the section.

Reteach For students who need additional instruction, download the Section Study Guide.

Response to Intervention To reassess students' mastery, use the Section Quiz, available to print or to take directly online at **HMDScience.com**.

SECTION 2

Plan and Prepare

Objectives

Upon completion of this section, students should be able to do the following:

- Distinguish between the physical properties and chemical properties of matter.
- Classify changes of matter as physical or chemical.
- Explain the gas, liquid, and solid states in terms of particles.
- Explain how the law of conservation of energy applies to changes in matter.
- Distinguish between a mixture and a pure substance.

Classroom Catalyst

Determine the mass of a deflated balloon. Then blow up the balloon, tie it, and find its new mass. Because the balloon increases in mass, the matter in the balloon must have mass. Point out to students that matter does not need to be visible to us and that it may be made of particles that we cannot see.

Teach

Teaching Tip

Ask students to consider the following questions: Which is heavier, a pound of lead or a pound of feathers? What does a pound represent? What happens to the matter of an astronaut who is in microgravity? Divide the class into small groups to design a tool that could be used to weigh something aboard the space shuttle. Use the Internet to find out how NASA really does it.

TEACH FROM VISUALS

FIGURE 2.1 Have students compare the models shown. Point out that chemists have different ways of representing the structures of substances. The diamond model is a ball-and-stick representation. Sucrose is shown as a space-fill model. Inform students that they will see both types throughout this book.

SECTION 2

Main Ideas

- Atoms are the building blocks of matter.
- All substances have characteristic properties.
- Matter can be a pure substance or a mixture.

Matter and Its Properties

Key Terms

mass	physical change	chemical reaction
matter	change of state	reactant
atom	solid	product
element	liquid	mixture
compound	gas	homogeneous
extensive property	plasma	solution
intensive property	chemical property	heterogeneous
physical property	chemical change	pure substance

All things are made up of matter, but exactly what is matter? What characteristics, or properties, make matter what it is? In this section, you will learn the answers to these questions.

Explaining what matter is involves finding properties that all matter has in common. That may seem difficult, given that matter takes so many different forms. For the moment, just consider one example of matter—a rock. The first thing you might notice is that the rock takes up space. In other words, it has *volume*. Volume is the amount of three-dimensional space an object occupies. All matter has volume. All matter also has a property called mass. **Mass is a measure of the amount of matter.** Mass is the measurement you make using a balance. **Matter can thus be defined as anything that has mass and takes up space.** These two properties are the general properties of all matter.

MAIN IDEA

Atoms are the building blocks of matter.

Matter comes in many forms. The fundamental building blocks of matter are atoms and molecules. These particles make up elements and compounds. **An atom is the smallest unit of an element that maintains the chemical identity of that element. An element is a pure substance that cannot be broken down into simpler, stable substances and is made of one type of atom.** Carbon is an element and contains one kind of atom. The model of diamond in **Figure 2.1a** consists of carbon atoms.

FIGURE 2.1

Atoms as Building Blocks Both elements and compounds are made of atoms, as shown in these models of diamond and table sugar.

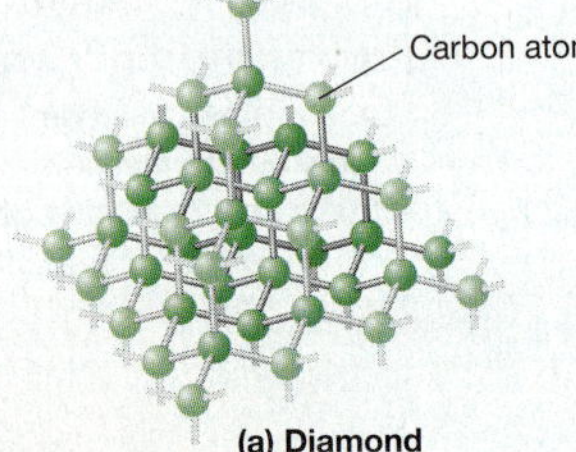

(a) Diamond

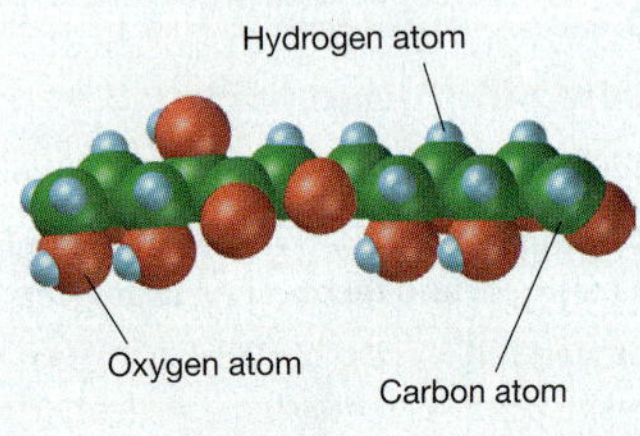

(b) Sucrose (table sugar)

Differentiated Instruction

ENGLISH LEARNERS

Offer students the following suggestion to help guide their reading on physical and chemical properties. Fold a large piece of paper in half vertically. Fold the paper in half the other way, to form two columns and two rows on the paper. Label the left-hand side "Physical" and the right-hand side "Chemical." Students should fill in the upper row with examples of physical and chemical properties. They should fill in the lower row with physical and chemical changes. A few classic examples should help them remember the difference between the two.

INCLUSION

Provide students with labeled pictures of an atom, an element, and a compound. Prepare a concept map that shows the relationships between these images. Include empty squares large enough to fit the labeled pictures. For example: A [blank square] --> is made of two or more kinds of [blank square] --> which are made up of only one kind of [blank square]. Have students place the pictures in the appropriate spots on the chart. Check their placement. When correct, have them tape or paste the pictures in place.

A **compound** is a substance that can be broken down into simple stable substances. Each compound is made from the atoms of two or more elements that are chemically bonded. Sucrose, in **Figure 2.1b**, is an example of a compound. It is made of three elements: carbon, hydrogen, and oxygen. The atoms are chemically bonded to form a molecule. You will learn more about the particles that make up compounds when you study chemical bonding. For now, you can think of a *molecule* as the smallest unit of an element or compound that retains all of the properties of that element or compound.

MAIN IDEA

All substances have characteristic properties.

Every substance, whether it is an element or a compound, has characteristic properties. Chemists use properties to distinguish between substances and to separate them. Most chemical investigations are related to or depend on the properties of substances.

A property may be a characteristic that defines an entire group of substances. That property can be used to classify an unknown substance as a member of that group. For example, many elements are classified as metals. The distinguishing property of metals is that they conduct electricity well. Therefore, if an unknown element is tested and found to conduct electricity well, it is a metal.

Properties can help reveal the identity of an unknown substance. However, conclusive identification usually cannot be made based on only one property. Comparisons of several properties can be used together to establish the identity of an unknown. Properties are either intensive or extensive. **Extensive properties** depend on the amount of matter that is present. Such properties include volume, mass, and the amount of energy in a substance. In contrast, **intensive properties** do not depend on the amount of matter present. Such properties include the melting point, boiling point, density, and ability to conduct electricity and to transfer energy as heat. Intensive properties are the same for a given substance regardless of how much of the substance is present. For example, iron melts at 1538°C regardless of whether or not you have 20 g or 20 kg of it. Properties can also be grouped into two general types: physical properties and chemical properties.

Physical Properties and Physical Changes

A **physical property** is a characteristic that can be observed or measured without changing the identity of the substance. We commonly use physical properties to describe a substance. Examples of physical properties are melting point and boiling point. For example, water melts from ice to liquid at 0°C (273 K or 32°F). Liquid water, as shown in **Figure 2.2**, boils to vapor at 100°C (373 K or 212°F). Density is also another physical property. Water's density at 4°C (277 K or 39°F) is about 1000 kg/m^3. Unlike most substances, the density of water decreases when it freezes to become ice. As a result, a pond or lake that freezes in the winter does so from the top down, enabling some fish to survive in the water at the bottom.

FIGURE 2.2

Physical Properties Water boils at 100°C. This is an example of a physical property.

CRITICAL THINKING

Classify Is the boiling point of water an extensive or an intensive property? Explain.

Teaching Tip

Students may be confused regarding the use of the term *molecule*, because all compounds are not made of molecules. It is not necessary to get into the details now, as this will be discussed later.

Demonstration

CONDUCTIVITY OF WATER

- Using **two clear drinking glasses,** fill one with **tap water** and the other with **completely dissolved salt water.** The two look the same, but are different. Tell students that a difference in properties may not be immediately obvious, so we use instruments to measure differences that we may not be able to see.
- Show students the difference in electrical conductivity between the two liquids by using a **handheld ohmmeter.** Set the ohmmeter to 200K range and insert both electrodes in the tap water about an inch apart from each other, noting the measurement. Then do the same with the salt water. Explain that the two different readings reveal that the liquids have different electrical conductivities. This demonstration shows students that differences in properties are not always obvious without using an instrument to measure the properties.

READING TOOLKIT

DISCUSSION Have students read about physical and chemical properties and changes. Then have them choose items in the classroom and classify the properties of each item, giving justification for each classification.

BELOW LEVEL

Read students the following paragraph:

Amy was making a salad for dinner. First, she cut up the carrots and tore the lettuce. The dressing she was making required her to mix oil and vinegar in a jar. She was unsure what to do with the food scraps. She thought about grinding them in the garbage disposal. But then she remembered she could put them in the compost pile to decompose.

Students should look at each underlined phrase and state whether it is an example of a physical or a chemical change. Physical change: cut carrots, tore lettuce, mixed oil and vinegar, ground scraps; chemical change: decompose. Challenge students to write their own short paragraphs involving physical and chemical changes.

Critical Thinking

Answer: Since water boils at the same temperature regardless of how much water is in the sample, the boiling point of water is an intensive property.

▼ Teach *continued*

Teaching Tip

Present different properties to students and have them determine whether they are *intensive* or *extensive* properties. Density, conductivity, and melting and boiling points are examples of intensive properties. Energy absorbed, volume, and mass are extensive properties. Compare the two types of properties by heating 100 mL and 400 mL of water. Both will boil at the same temperature (intensive), but the 400-mL sample will absorb more energy (extensive) and will therefore take longer to reach the boiling point. Ask students to predict which beaker will return to room temperature first.

TEACH FROM VISUALS

FIGURE 2.3 Help students recognize the differences between the states of matter at the macroscopic and microscopic levels. They will see illustrations throughout this book showing micromodels for systems that explain the macrophenomena they observe. Point out that ice floats on water because it is less dense. The model for ice shows that its structure is less dense than that of the liquid.

Demonstration

PARTICLE ENERGY

You can easily model the amount of energy a substance can have by putting **marbles** in a **plastic cup** or **plastic beaker.** The intensity with which you shake the beaker represents the energy of the particles and is demonstrated by how much the marbles move. With very little shaking, the marbles merely vibrate in their positions, like the particles of a solid. With moderate shaking, the marbles move relative to one another but stay inside the container (as in a liquid). With vigorous shaking, the marbles have enough energy to escape the container (as with a gas).

A change in a substance that does not involve a change in the identity of the substance is called a **physical change.** Examples of physical changes include grinding, cutting, melting, and boiling a material. These types of changes do not change the identity of the substance present.

States of Matter

Melting and boiling are part of an important class of physical changes called changes of state. As the name suggests, a **change of state** is a physical change of a substance from one state to another. The three common states of matter are solid, liquid, and gas. **Figure 2.3** shows the differences between the three states of matter at the molecular level.

Matter in the **solid** state has definite volume and definite shape. For example, a piece of quartz or coal keeps its size and its shape, regardless of the container it is in. Solids have this characteristic because the particles in them are packed together in relatively fixed positions. The particles are held close together by the strong attractive forces between them, and only vibrate about fixed points. The amount of attraction varies with different solids. This accounts for some solids being more easily compressible.

FIGURE 2.3

Modeling States of Matter
Models for water in three states. The molecules are close together in the solid and liquid states but far apart in the gas state. The molecules in the solid state are relatively fixed in position, but those in the liquid and gas states can flow around each other.

Differentiated Instruction

PRE-AP

Plasma is often called the "fourth state of matter." Have students choose one aspect of plasma to research on the Internet. Aspects to cover could include (but are not limited to): the scientific discovery of plasma, examples of plasma in space, examples of plasma on Earth (in the lab or natural), or implications of the designation of plasma as a different state of matter. Students should create a slide presentation or a simulation about their plasma topic and present it to the class.

Matter in the liquid state has a definite volume but an indefinite shape. A liquid assumes the shape of its container. For example, a given quantity of liquid water takes up a definite amount of space, but the water takes the shape of its container. Liquids have this characteristic because the particles in them are close together but can move past one another. The particles in a liquid move more rapidly than those in a solid. This causes them to overcome the strong attractive forces between them and flow.

Matter in the gas state has neither definite volume nor definite shape. For example, a given quantity of helium expands to fill any size container and takes the shape of the container. All gases have this characteristic because they are composed of particles that move very rapidly and are at great distances from one another compared with the particles of liquids and solids. At these great distances, the attractive forces between gas particles have a lesser effect than they do at the small distances between particles of liquids and solids.

An important fourth state of matter is plasma. **Plasma is a high-temperature physical state of matter in which atoms lose most of their electrons, particles that make up atoms.** Plasma is found in fluorescent bulbs.

Melting, the change from solid to liquid, is an example of a change of state. Boiling is a change of state from liquid to gas. Freezing, the opposite of melting, is the change from a liquid to a solid. A change of state does not affect the identity of the substance. For example, when ice melts to liquid water or when liquid water boils to form water vapor, the same substance, water, is still present. The water has simply changed state, but it has not turned into a different compound. Only the distances and interactions between the particles that make up water have changed.

Chemical Properties and Chemical Changes

Physical properties can be observed without changing the identity of the substance, but properties of the second type—chemical properties—cannot. **A chemical property relates to a substance's ability to undergo changes that transform it into different substances.** Chemical properties are easiest to see when substances react to form new substances. For example, the ability of charcoal (carbon) to burn in air is a chemical property. When charcoal burns, it combines with oxygen in air to become carbon dioxide gas. After the chemical change, the amounts of the original substances, carbon and oxygen, are not less than before. They simply have recombined to form different substances with different properties. **Figure 2.4** shows how a chemical property of a substance known as Benedict's solution is used to test for sugars in urine.

A change in which one or more substances are converted into different substances is called a chemical change or chemical reaction. The substances that react in a chemical change are called the reactants. The substances that are formed by the chemical change are called the products. In the case of burning charcoal, carbon and oxygen are the reactants in a combustion, or burning, reaction. Carbon dioxide, a gas, and ashes are the products, which are clearly different from the reactants.

FIGURE 2.4

Chemical Properties Because Benedict's solution possesses certain chemical properties, a test strip containing it is used to test for the presence of sugar in urine. The test strip is dipped into the sample. The test strip is then matched to a color scale to determine the sugar level in the urine.

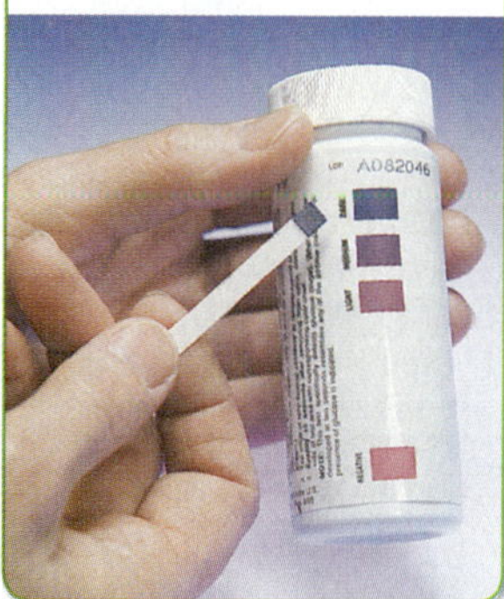

ChemisTrivia

Along with the three common states of matter, there are several more. The ultra-dense matter in a neutron star is unlike a solid, a liquid, or a gas. Other forms of matter, such as the Bose-Einstein condensate, can be created at low temperatures when several atoms occupy the same quantum state.

Classroom Discussion

Have students brainstorm about chemical changes with which they are familiar. Food digestion and rusting are two common examples.

PRE-AP

Tell students that the image on the first page of the chapter depicts crystals of tartaric acid. In addition to the uses listed in the caption, tartaric acid is sometimes added to foods as an antioxidant. Have students find out what the term *oxidation* means in relation to foods. As an antioxidant food additive, what function does tartaric acid serve?

Tartaric acid acts as an antioxidant by preventing foods such as fruits and some vegetables from turning brown (oxidizing).

Ask students to name at least one other chemical change that is a form of oxidation, from their research.

Rusting iron is the most common example of oxidation.

▼ Teach *continued*

Teaching Tip

Make students aware that *most* physical and chemical changes involve some transfer of energy. The body uses energy from the chemical reactions that break down food. Weather involves a transfer of energy to evaporate or condense water in the atmosphere. Therefore, the study of matter also involves the study of energy.

TEACH FROM VISUALS

FIGURE 2.5 This figure gives students the opportunity to read descriptions of the physical and chemical properties of substances found in the chemical literature. Have students identify aspects of this figure that signify a chemical change. Ask students to verify that the substances produced have properties different from those of the reactants. Tell students that mercury is both volatile and poisonous. The decomposition of mercury oxide should never be attempted outside the classroom or without teacher supervision.

Check for Understanding

Answer: When a substance dissolves, that is a physical change. When a gas is produced, however, a chemical change is occurring. This action involves both a physical AND a chemical change.

FIGURE 2.5

Chemical Changes When mercury(II) oxide is heated, it decomposes to form oxygen gas and mercury (which can be seen on the side of the test tube). Decomposition is a chemical change that can be observed by comparing the properties of mercury(II) oxide, mercury, and oxygen.

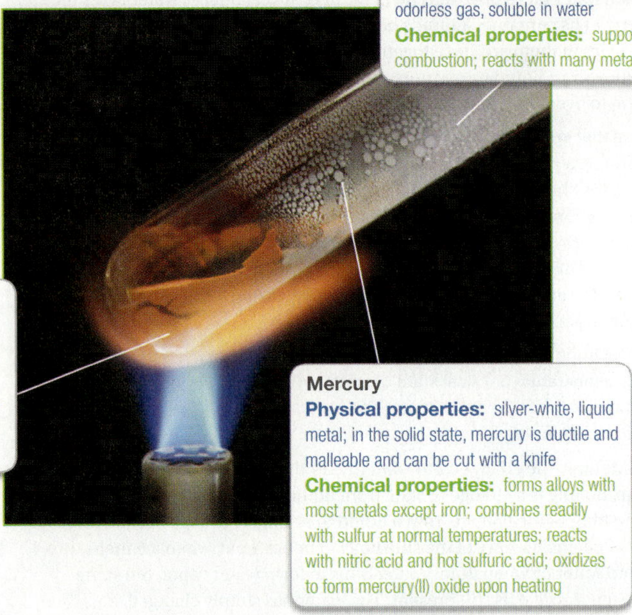

Oxygen
Physical properties: colorless, odorless gas, soluble in water
Chemical properties: supports combustion; reacts with many metals

Mercury(II) oxide
Physical properties: bright red or orange-red, odorless crystalline solid, almost insoluble in water
Chemical properties: decomposes when exposed to light or at 500°C to form mercury and oxygen gas

Mercury
Physical properties: silver-white, liquid metal; in the solid state, mercury is ductile and malleable and can be cut with a knife
Chemical properties: forms alloys with most metals except iron; combines readily with sulfur at normal temperatures; reacts with nitric acid and hot sulfuric acid; oxidizes to form mercury(II) oxide upon heating

Chemical reactions are normally written with arrows and plus signs. These stand for the words *yields* and *plus*, respectively. For example, to describe the decomposition of the mercury compound shown in **Figure 2.5,** we'd write it as follows:

$$\text{mercury(II) oxide} \longrightarrow \text{mercury} + \text{oxygen}$$

In other words, mercury(II) oxide *yields* mercury *plus* oxygen.

Although chemical reactions form products whose properties can differ greatly from those of the reactants, they do not affect the total amount of matter present before and after a reaction. The law of conservation of mass is always followed in chemical reactions.

✓ CHECK FOR UNDERSTANDING

Explain An antacid tablet is dropped into a glass of water and dissolves. The tablet fizzes, and bubbles of gas rise to the surface. Is this a physical change or a chemical change? Explain your answer.

Energy and Changes in Matter

When physical or chemical changes occur, energy is always involved. The energy can take several different forms, such as heat or light. Sometimes heat provides enough energy to cause a physical change, as in the melting of ice, and sometimes heat provides enough energy to cause a chemical change, as in the decomposition of water vapor to form oxygen gas and hydrogen gas. But the boundary between physical and chemical changes isn't always so clear. For example, although most chemists would consider the dissolving of sucrose in water to be a physical change, many chemists would consider the dissolving of table salt in water to be a chemical change. The boundaries can sometimes be confusing!

Differentiated Instruction

ENGLISH LEARNERS

Have students create a chart that lists examples of chemical changes and physical changes. Students can draw pictures that represent each example. Ask the students to label each picture with each type of change and the identity of each substance before and after the change has taken place. Students may use the textbook, reference books, and the Internet to complete their charts.

INCLUSION

Ask students to brainstorm examples of physical or chemical changes. Answers may include change in color, melting, freezing, change in shape, boiling, emission of heat, flames, change in odor. Write their answers on the board. Now ask students which changes indicate that energy is somehow involved. Boiling, emission of heat, flames. Circle these items on the board. Explain to students that while energy is most obviously involved in these examples, energy is actually involved in all chemical or physical changes in some way.

Accounting for all the energy present before and after a change is not a simple process. But scientists who have done such experimentation are confident that the total amount of energy remains the same. Although energy can be absorbed or released in a change, it is not destroyed or created. It simply assumes a different form. This is the law of conservation of energy.

MAIN IDEA

Matter can be a pure substance or a mixture.

Matter exists in an enormous variety of forms. Any sample of matter, however, can be classified either as a pure substance or as a mixture. The composition of a pure substance is the same throughout and does not vary from sample to sample. A pure substance can be an element or a compound. Mixtures, in contrast, contain more than one substance. They can vary in composition and properties from sample to sample and sometimes from one part of a sample to another part of the same sample. All matter, whether it is a pure substance or a mixture, can be classified in terms of uniformity of composition and properties of a given sample. **Figure 2.6** illustrates the overall classification of matter into elements, compounds, and mixtures.

Mixtures

You deal with mixtures every day. Nearly every object around you, including most things you eat and drink and even the air you breathe, is a mixture. Mixtures can be very simple or very complex, and they can have some unique properties.

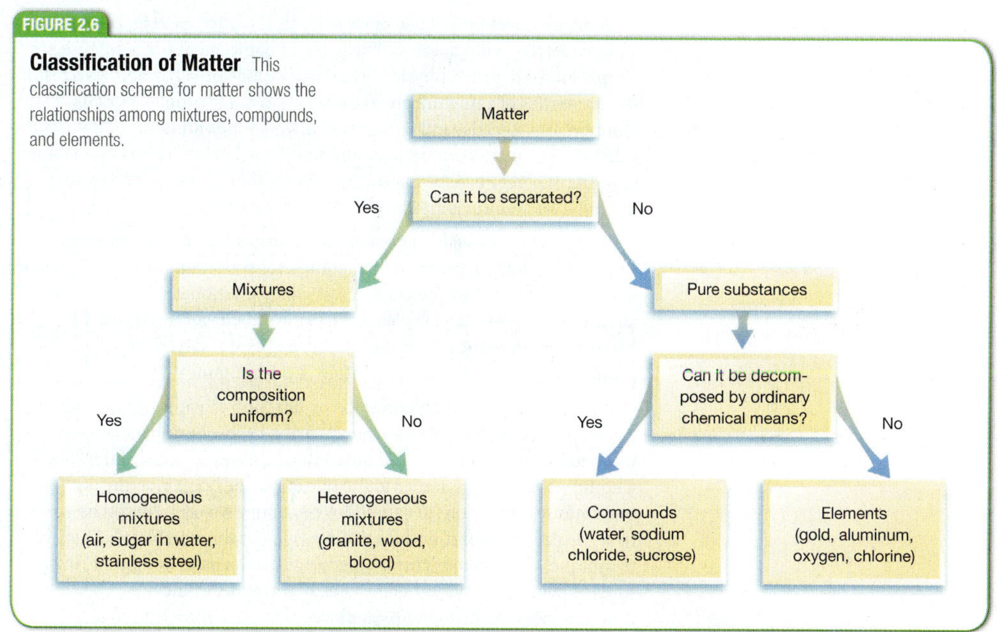

FIGURE 2.6

Classification of Matter This classification scheme for matter shows the relationships among mixtures, compounds, and elements.

Demonstration

HOMOGENEOUS VS. HETEROGENEOUS MIXTURES

Have students bring in **examples of matter** that represent heterogeneous and homogeneous mixtures. **Granite** and **milk** are two common heterogeneous mixtures; different components of these mixtures have different physical properties. A solution—such as a **soft drink**—and a **metallic alloy** are both examples of a homogeneous mixture. The physical properties in a homogeneous mixture are the same regardless of how the mixture is divided. Students might enjoy a study of **frosted cupcakes** (a heterogeneous mixture) and soft drinks (a homogeneous mixture).

TEACH FROM VISUALS

FIGURE 2.6 Have students carefully examine this chart. Have them use the chart by asking them to classify examples of matter they have brought to class. Ask students where atoms and molecules would fit into this scheme. You may also want pairs of students to brainstorm about other examples for each type of matter listed on the chart.

BELOW LEVEL

Have students create flashcards for compounds, elements, heterogeneous mixtures, and homogeneous mixtures. Each card should include information and examples for that category. For example, a flashcard for Homogeneous Mixtures would have the answers shown in blue:

Category: Homogeneous Mixture

Type of matter: Mixture

Properties of the category: Uniform composition

Examples: air, sugar in water, salt water

Encourage students to think of other examples from their real lives, as well as examples from the text, and then add them to their flashcards.

▼ Teach *continued*

TEACH FROM VISUALS

FIGURE 2.7 Either physical or chemical properties can be used to separate components in a mixture. Ask students whether the examples in this figure are being separated based on their physical properties or their chemical properties. All of the methods in this figure are using physical means to separate mixtures.

READING TOOLKIT

VOCABULARY BUILDING Point out the Greek prefixes in the words *homogeneous* and *heterogeneous*: *homo-* means "same," and *hetero-* means "different." Help students use this information to develop definitions such as the following: "A homogeneous mixture is one that has the same proportion of components throughout; a heterogeneous mixture is one that is not uniform throughout." Invite students to list word pairs that have these prefixes, such as *homonym* and *heteronym*, and look up their meanings.

Teaching Tip

This is a good time to review with students the information found in *Safety in the Chemistry Laboratory* at the front of the Student Edition. You may also wish to review the *Merck Index*, the *CRC Handbook of Chemistry and Physics*, *Lange's Handbook of Chemistry*, or other reference materials that you have available in the laboratory. It is important that students take responsibility for knowing the hazards of chemicals in the classroom.

Critical Thinking

Answer: The mixtures are heterogenous because they are not uniform throughout, as demonstrated by the separation of the mixtures into different components using the methods shown in the photos.

FIGURE 2.7

Separating Mixtures

(a) Filtration Barium chromate can be separated from the solution in the beaker using filtration.

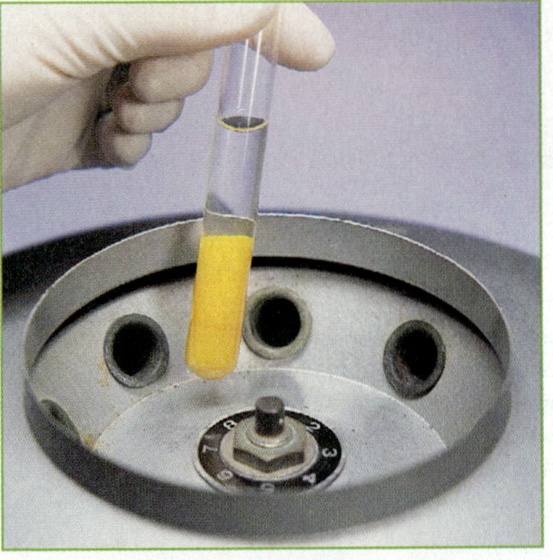

(b) Using a Centrifuge A centrifuge can be used to separate certain solid components. The centrifuge spins rapidly, which causes the solids to settle to the bottom of the test tube.

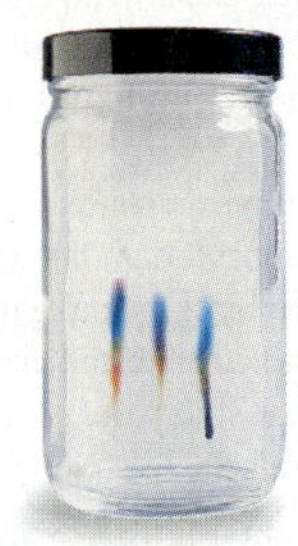

(c) Chromatography The components of an ink can be separated using paper chromatography.

CRITICAL THINKING

Classify Would the mixtures shown in the photos be defined as homogeneous or heterogeneous? Explain.

A mixture is a blend of two or more kinds of matter, each of which retains its own identity and properties. The parts, or components, of a mixture are simply mixed together physically and can usually be separated. As a result, the properties of a mixture are a combination of the properties of its components. Because mixtures can contain various amounts of different substances, a mixture's composition must be specified. This is often done in terms of percentage by mass or by volume. For example, a mixture might be 5% sodium chloride and 95% water by mass.

Mixtures that are uniform in composition are said to be homogeneous. They have the same proportion of components throughout. **Homogeneous mixtures are also called solutions.** A salt-water solution is an example of such a mixture. **Mixtures that are not uniform throughout are said to be heterogeneous.** For example, in a mixture of clay and water, heavier clay particles concentrate near the bottom of the container.

Some mixtures can be separated by filtration or vaporized to separate the different components. In **Figure 2.7a**, the yellow barium compound is trapped by the filter paper, but the solution passes through. If the solid in a liquid-solid mixture settles to the bottom of the container, the liquid can be carefully poured off (decanted). A centrifuge **(Figure 2.7b)** can be used to separate some solid-liquid mixtures, such as those in blood. Another technique, called paper chromatography, can be used to separate mixtures of dyes or pigments because the different substances move at different rates on the paper **(Figure 2.7c)**.

Differentiated Instruction

ENGLISH LEARNER

Many terms that students will encounter in this chapter and throughout the course may be especially difficult for students who are learning English as they are studying chemistry. In particular, the names of some of the items of equipment used in chemistry labs will be unfamiliar. Be sure to have photographs, diagrams, or examples of the equipment used in the labs that the students are doing. Illustrations of the equipment mentioned in the text will also give students a reference point.

BELOW LEVEL

Give students small samples of table salt and sand. Have students examine the two samples with magnifiers. Ask them if salt crystals appear to be the same throughout the sample. Yes; they are little cubes. Explain that salt is a pure substance called a compound and can only be separated by chemical means. Ask students how sand appears when viewed through the magnifier. It looks like small particles of different colors, shapes, and sizes. Explain that sand is made up of many different substances. Therefore, sand is a mixture.

Pure Substances

A pure substance has a fixed composition. Pure substances are always homogeneous. They differ from mixtures in the following ways:

1. *Every sample of a given pure substance has exactly the same characteristic properties.* All samples of a pure substance have the same characteristic physical and chemical properties. These properties are so specific that they can be used to identify the substance. In contrast, the properties of a mixture depend on the relative amounts of the mixture's components.
2. *Every sample of a pure substance has exactly the same composition.* All samples of a pure substance have the same makeup. For example, pure water is always 11.2% hydrogen and 88.8% oxygen by mass.

Pure substances are either compounds or elements. A compound can be decomposed, or broken down, into two or more simpler compounds or elements by a chemical change. Water is made of hydrogen and oxygen chemically bonded to form a single substance. Water can be broken down into hydrogen and oxygen through electrolysis, as shown in **Figure 2.8a**.

Sucrose is made of carbon, hydrogen, and oxygen. Sucrose breaks down under intense heating, to produce carbon and water (**Figure 2.8b**). This is of particular delight to anyone with a sweet tooth!

FIGURE 2.8

Decomposition of Compounds

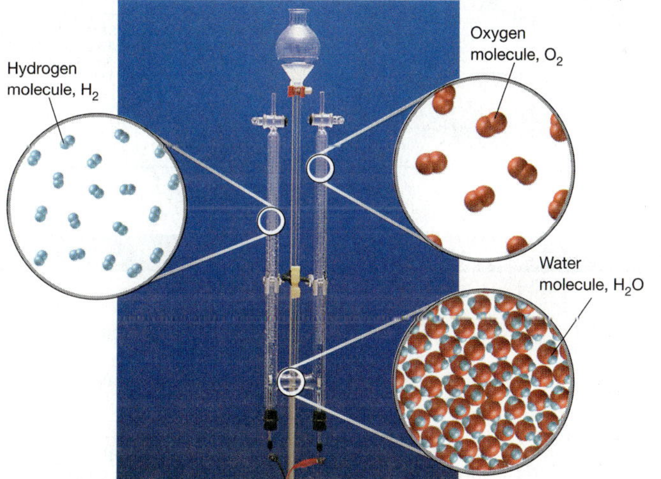

(a) Separation by Electrolysis Passing an electric current through water causes the compound to break down into the elements hydrogen and oxygen, which differ in composition from water.

(b) Decomposition by Heating When sucrose is heated, it caramelizes. When it is heated to a high enough temperature, it breaks down completely into carbon and water.

TEACH FROM VISUALS

FIGURE 2.8 Two very different reactions are shown, but they are both decomposition reactions. Ask students how they know that a chemical reaction has taken place in each photograph. Students should recognize that gases are produced during the electrolysis of water, while there is a color change in the oxidation of sugar. Point out to students that hydrogen gas differs chemically from oxygen gas even though they look the same. Use this illustration to reinforce the definitions of *atoms*, *molecules*, and *compounds*. Students should also note that two states of matter are represented in the electrolysis experiment.

PRE-AP

Think-Pair-Share: Fill some clear containers with samples of mixtures and other containers with samples of pure substances. Place each container at a different, numbered station around the room. Have students silently rotate through the stations, recording which samples they believe are mixtures and which are pure substances.

When all students have rotated through all stations, have each student choose a partner with whom to share and compare their findings. Allow several minutes for them to share, and then ask partners to revisit those stations they decided were mixtures. This time, have them record which samples they believe are homogeneous and which are heterogeneous.

When all partners have recorded their findings, write the numbers of the stations on the board. Have one student from each pair write their findings for each station beside the corresponding number. Go through the list one item at a time, and ask other students to raise their hands if they have different answers. Call on one or two students per item to explain the reasoning they used to arrive at their conclusion.

▼ Teach *continued*

TEACH FROM VISUALS

FIGURE 2.9 Establishing standards for chemical purity is the mission of the American Chemical Society Committee on Analytical Reagents. This group compiles the data and publishes the tests to determine if a manufactured chemical meets specifications for purity. Show students labels from stockroom reagents of different grades. Allow students to look through your chemical supply catalog for the listing of reagent grades provided by that distributor. Have them compare prices for different grades of the same chemical. Note that the names of grades in this table can vary by chemical manufacturer.

▼ Assess and Reteach

Assess Use the Formative Assessment on this page to evaluate student mastery of the section.

Reteach For students who need additional instruction, download the Section Study Guide.

Response to Intervention To reassess students' mastery, use the Section Quiz, available to print or to take directly online at **HMDScience.com**.

FIGURE 2.9

SOME GRADES OF CHEMICAL PURITY

Increasing purity ↑
Primary standard reagents
ACS (American Chemical Society–specified reagents)
USP (United States Pharmacopoeia standards)
CP (chemically pure; purer than technical grade)
NF (National Formulary specifications)
FCC (Food Chemical Code specifications)
Technical (industrial chemicals)

Laboratory Chemicals and Purity

The chemicals in laboratories are generally treated as if they are pure. However, all chemicals have some impurities. The purity ranking of the grades can vary with different agencies, as seen in **Figure 2.9.** For some chemicals, the USP grade may specify higher purity than the CP grade. For other chemicals, the opposite may be true. However, the primary standard reagent grade is always purer than the technical grade for the same chemical.

Chemists need to be aware of the kinds of impurities in a reagent because these impurities could affect the results of a reaction. The chemical manufacturer must ensure that the standards set for that reagent by the American Chemical Society (A.C.S.) are met. Reading and understanding the labels placed on chemicals, like those shown in **Figure 2.10,** is a crucial skill for chemists.

FIGURE 2.10

Chemical Purity The labeling on this bottle lists the grade of the reagent **(a)** and the percentages of impurities for that grade **(b)**. What grade is this chemical?

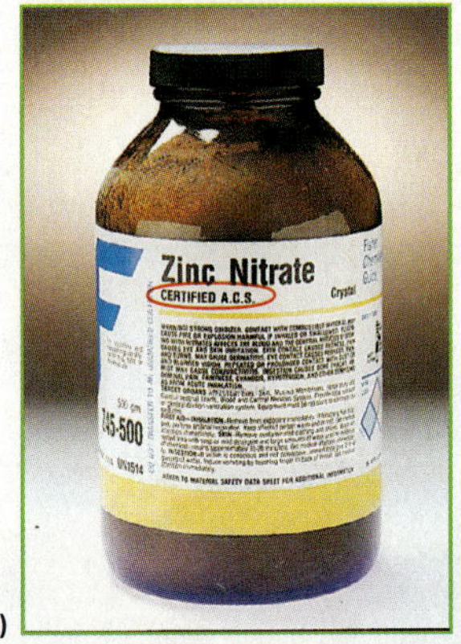

(a)

(b)

$Zn(NO_3)_2 \bullet 6H_2O$ F.W. 297.47

Certificate of Actual Lot Analysis	
Acidity (as HNO_3)	0.008%
Alkalies and Earths	0.02%
Chloride (Cl)	0.005%
Insoluble Matter	0.001%
Iron (Fe)	0.0002%
Lead (Pb)	0.001%
Phosphate (PO_4)	0.0002%
Sulfate (SO_4)	0.002%

Store separately from and avoid contact with combustible materials. Keep container closed and in a cool, dry place. Avoid contact with skin, eyes and clothing.

LOT NO. 917356

FL-02-0588 CAS 10196-18-6

SECTION 2 FORMATIVE ASSESSMENT

Reviewing Main Ideas

1. a. What is the main difference between physical properties and chemical properties?
   b. Give an example of each.
2. Classify each of the following as either a physical change or a chemical change.
   a. tearing a sheet of paper
   b. melting a piece of wax
   c. burning a log
3. How do you decide whether a sample of matter is a solid, a liquid, or a gas?
4. Contrast mixtures with pure substances.

Critical Thinking

5. **ANALYZING INFORMATION** Compare the composition of sucrose purified from sugar cane with the composition of sucrose purified from sugar beets. Explain your answer.

Answers to Section Assessment

1. a. Physical properties can be observed without changing the identity of the substance; chemical properties are observed by changing the substance into different substances.
   b. Physical: color, size, boiling point, etc.; chemical: burning of coal, rusting of iron, etc.
2. a. physical
   b. physical
   c. chemical
3. You can compare the sample with the characteristic properties of solids, liquids, and gases. If the sample has a fixed shape, it is a solid. If its volume changes to fill the volume of different containers, then it is a gas. If neither condition applies, the sample is a liquid.
4. Mixtures contain two or more substances blended together and generally can be separated. Pure substances have a fixed composition.
5. The compositions are identical. Sucrose is a compound, so it must have a definite composition no matter what its source is.

Cross-Disciplinary Connection S.T.E.M.

Secrets of the Cremona Violins

What are the most beautiful-sounding of all violins? Most professionals will pick the instruments created in Cremona, Italy, between the 16th and 18th centuries. At that time, Antonio Stradivari, members of the Guarneri family, and other designers created instruments of extraordinary sound that have yet to be matched. The craftsmen were notoriously secretive about their techniques, but based on 20 years of research, Dr. Joseph Nagyvary, a professor of biochemistry at Texas A&M University, thinks he has discovered the key to the violins' sound hidden in the chemistry of their materials.

According to Dr. Nagyvary, instruments made by Stradivari are nearly free of the shrill, high-pitched noises produced by modern violins. Generally, violin makers attribute this to the design of the instrument, but Dr. Nagyvary traces it to a different source. In Stradivari's day, wood for the violins was transported by floating it down a river from the mountains to Venice, where it was stored in seawater. Dr. Nagyvary first theorized that the soaking process could have removed ingredients from the wood that made it inherently noisy. Images taken with a scanning electron microscope showed a slimy fungus growing on the wood. Dr. Nagyvary's experiments revealed that the fungus released enzymes that destroyed a structural material in the plants, called hemicellulose. Attempting to reproduce the effects of seawater, Dr. Nagyvary soaks all his wood in a "secret" solution. One of his favorite ingredients is a cherry-and-plum puree, which contains an enzyme called pectinase. The pectinase softens the wood, making it resonate more freely.

"The other key factor in a violin's sound," says Dr. Nagyvary, "is the finish, which is the filler and the varnish covering the instrument. Most modern finishes are made from rubbery materials, which limit the vibrations of the wood." Modern analysis has revealed that the Cremona finish was different: it was a brittle mineral microcomposite of a very sophisticated nature. According to historical accounts, all violin makers, including Stradivari, procured their varnishes from the local drugstore chemist, and they didn't even know what they were using! Dr. Nagyvary and his co-workers have identified most of the key ingredients of the Cremona finish.

Many new violins made from the treated wood and replicated finish have been made, and their sound has been analyzed by modern signal analyzers. These violins have been favorably compared with authentic Stradivari violins.

Dr. Nagyvary and his violin

A number of expert violinists have praised the sound of Dr. Nagyvary's instruments, but some violin makers remain skeptical of the chemist's claims. They insist that it takes many years to reveal just how good a violin is. In the meantime, almost everyone agrees that the art and science of violin making are still epitomized by the instruments of Cremona.

Questions

1. According to Dr. Nagyvary, what are two factors that are believed to have created the unique sound of the Stradivari violins?
2. What technology did Dr. Nagyvary use in his experiments to recreate the violins?
3. Use the library or Internet resources to find additional information about the Cremona violin makers. Who were some of the other instrument makers during the time period in which Stradivari was alive? Were other stringed instruments made by these artisans? What are the estimated present-day values of instruments made during this period in Cremona?

Cross-Disciplinary Connection

Classroom Discussion

This story is a good example of how chemistry plays a fundamental role in other areas of study. Dr. Nagyvary's study of biochemistry and interest in music led him to investigate the origin and nature of the famous Stradivari sound. Students may be surprised to learn that modern technology has not been able to duplicate the effect created by the violinmakers of Cremona. This story is also a good example of the concept of reverse engineering. Reverse engineering is an attempt to duplicate a product already in existence.

Answers

1. One factor was the soaking in seawater of the wood used to make the violins and the introduction of microbes and minerals into the wood. Another factor was the varnish used to create the finish on the violins.
2. Dr. Nagyvary used a scanning electron microscope to study the water-soaked wood. He also performed experiments to identify the substance released by the fungus and the substance's effect on the wood.
3. Student answers will vary. Other important Cremona violinmakers were the members of the Amati and Guarneri families. Other instruments made by members of these families include the viola and the violoncello. Present-day values of these instruments can reach up to several million dollars.

SECTION 3

▼ Plan and Prepare

Objectives

Upon completion of this section, students should be able to do the following:

- Use the periodic table to name elements, given their symbols.
- Use a periodic table to write the symbols of elements, given their names.
- Describe the arrangement of the periodic table.
- List the characteristics that distinguish metals, nonmetals, and metalloids.

Classroom Catalyst

This might be a good time to make copies of the *Teaching Visuals* periodic table (found online) for each student for use during class and tests. Use these periodic tables or the large table in the room to get students to practice locating particular elements on the table.

▼ Teach

TEACH FROM TABLES

FIGURE 3.1 Have students use the *CRC Handbook of Chemistry and Physics* to find the language of origin (or meaning) for each of the older names listed in the table.

stibium—Latin
cuprum—Latin
aurum—Latin
ferrum—Latin
plumbum—Latin
hydrargyrum—Latin
kalium—Latin
argentum—Latin
natrium—Latin
stannum—Latin
wolfram—German

SECTION 3

Main Ideas

- The periodic table organizes elements by their chemical properties.
- Some elements are metals.
- Some elements are nonmetals or metalloids.

Elements

Key Terms

group
family
period
metal
nonmetal
metalloid

As you have read, elements are pure substances that cannot be decomposed by chemical changes. The elements serve as the building blocks of matter. Each element has characteristic properties. The elements are organized into groups based on similar chemical properties. This organization of elements is the *periodic table*, which is shown in **Figure 3.2** on the next page.

MAIN IDEA

The periodic table organizes elements by their chemical properties.

Each small square of the periodic table shows the symbol for an element and its atomic number. For example, the first square, at the upper left, represents element 1, hydrogen, which has the symbol H. As you look through the table, you will see many familiar elements, including iron, sodium, neon, silver, copper, aluminum, sulfur, and lead. You can often relate an element's symbol to its English name. Some symbols come from the element's older name, which was often in Latin. Still others come from German. For example, the symbol W for tungsten comes from its German name, wolfram. **Figure 3.1** lists some elements and their older names.

FIGURE 3.1

ELEMENTS WITH SYMBOLS BASED ON OLDER NAMES

Modern name	Symbol	Older name
Antimony	Sb	stibium
Copper	Cu	cuprum
Gold	Au	aurum
Iron	Fe	ferrum
Lead	Pb	plumbum
Mercury	Hg	hydrargyrum
Potassium	K	kalium
Silver	Ag	argentum
Sodium	Na	natrium
Tin	Sn	stannum
Tungsten	W	wolfram

Differentiated Instruction

INCLUSION

Involve active learners by using a deck of playing cards to show the organization of the periodic table. Before class, sort the cards so that you have only one of each number value, but a mixture of suits. For example: choose the ace of spades for the number one, and then the two of clubs, three of hearts, and four of diamonds. Continue in the same order of suits until you have one card of each number value. Use a jack for 11, a queen for 12, and a king for 13. Label these face cards with the appropriate numbers using small pieces of masking tape. Spread the cards face up. Ask students to arrange the cards in order by number. Once they have done so, ask them to examine the cards closely to see if there is any other pattern besides the numerical one. Students should answer that there is a repeating pattern of suits. Next, ask students to keep the cards in numerical order but arrange them in multiple rows, so that all cards forming a single suit fall into one column. Show them a periodic table and explain that the table is arranged in a similar fashion according to the characteristics of the elements.

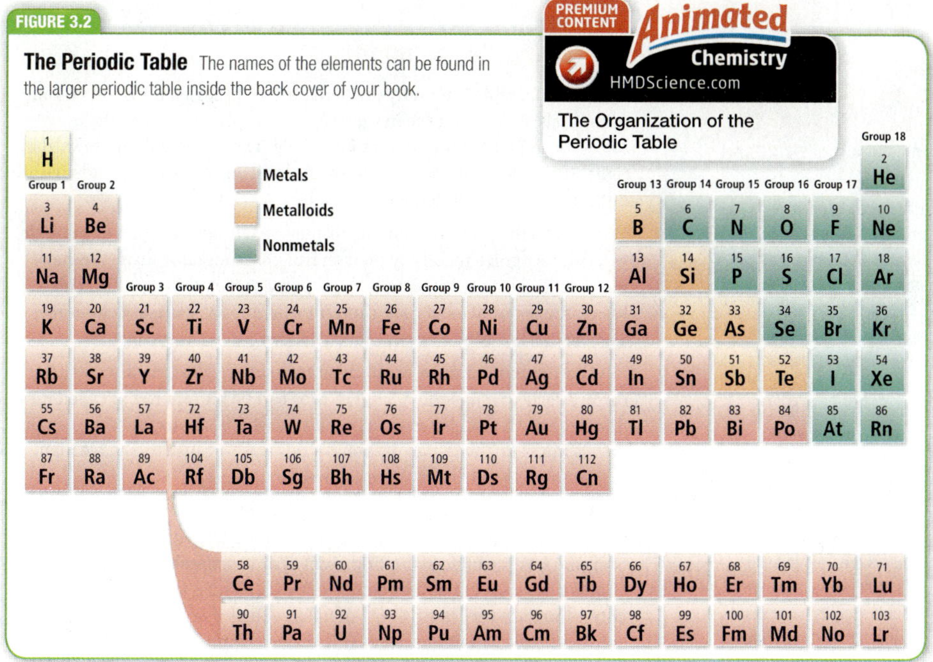

FIGURE 3.2

The Periodic Table The names of the elements can be found in the larger periodic table inside the back cover of your book.

The vertical columns of the periodic table are called groups, or families. Notice that they are numbered from 1 to 18 from left to right. Each group contains elements with similar chemical properties. For example, the elements in Group 2 are beryllium, magnesium, calcium, strontium, barium, and radium. All of these elements are reactive metals with similar abilities to bond to other kinds of atoms. The two major categories of elements are metals and nonmetals. Metalloids have properties intermediate between those of metals and nonmetals.

The horizontal rows of elements in the periodic table are called periods. Physical and chemical properties change somewhat regularly across a period. Elements that are close to each other in the same period tend to be more similar than elements that are farther apart. For example, in Period 2, the elements lithium and beryllium, in Groups 1 and 2, respectively, are somewhat similar in properties. However, their properties are very different from the properties of fluorine.

The two sets of elements placed below the periodic table make up what are called the lanthanide series and the actinide series. These metallic elements fit into the table just after elements 57 and 89. They are placed below the table to keep the table from being too wide.

There is a section in the back of this book called the *Elements Handbook* (Appendix A) which covers some elements in greater detail. You will use information from the handbook to complete the questions in the *Using the Handbook* sections in the chapter reviews.

Teaching Tip

Have students memorize the names and symbols of the first 36 elements. Quiz them on sets of 12 each week for three weeks. This exercise will help students prepare for writing formulas and balancing equations later in the text. They will also learn names of other common elements with frequent use throughout the course.

Teaching Tip

Assign each student a different element to research. Alternatively, have an "element of the day," when a particular element, its properties, and its position on the periodic table are highlighted.

TEACH FROM TABLES

FIGURE 3.2 The periodic table is included here to give students a context for the discussion of elements. Be sure students recognize the difference between the vertical columns (groups, or families) and the horizontal rows (periods) on the periodic table. Point out that the members of the same group have very similar chemical properties. Tell students that the elements at the base of the table are placed there for convenience. Placing them in the correct sequence makes the table very wide. Use the periodic table to point out that there are many more metals than there are nonmetals. Summarize the differences between the properties of metals and those of nonmetals.

BELOW LEVEL

Give students colored pencils and a black and white copy of the periodic table, printed on heavy paper or cardstock. Have students color-code metals, nonmetals, metalloids, and hydrogen in the same manner as **Figure 3.2**. Students may shade each category in the color of their choice, being certain that the shading is light enough to still read the information. Students should include a color key to their sheet to indicate what each colored section represents. Have students keep their tables for reference.

Review with students the definition of *element*. Have them brainstorm a list of substances that they think are elements. Then have them use Section 3 to confirm whether each of the substances on their list is an element and to devise a classification system for elements.

▼ Teach *continued*

TEACH FROM VISUALS

FIGURE 3.3 Use this figure to show how the properties of metals often determine how they are used, and explain that this is an example of the link between science and technology. Have students brainstorm about other uses of metals that depend on their physical or chemical properties.

Misconception Alert!

Students often think that all "metals" are the same. Because they are familiar with rusting as a corrosive property of iron, they may think that all metals rust. Make sure they understand that the definition and characteristics of metals are based on their functional properties and not just their appearance.

WHY IT MATTERS

Superconductors S.T.E.M.

Any metal becomes a better conductor of electrical energy as its temperature decreases. In 1911, scientists discovered that when mercury is cooled to about −269°C, it loses all resistance and becomes a superconductor. Scientists have long tried to find a material that would superconduct at temperatures above −196°C, the boiling point of liquid nitrogen. In 1987, scientists discovered ceramic materials that became superconductors when cooled only to −183°C. These "high-temperature" superconductors are used to build very powerful electromagnets. Ceramic electromagnets are used in medical magnetic resonance imaging (MRI) machines and in high-efficiency electric motors and generators.

MAIN IDEA

Some elements are metals.

The periodic table is broadly divided into two main sections: metals and nonmetals. As you can see in **Figure 3.2** on the previous page, the metals are at the left and in the center of the table. The nonmetals are toward the right. Some elements, such as boron and silicon, show characteristics of both metals and nonmetals.

Some of the properties of metals may be familiar to you. For example, you can recognize metals by their shininess, or metallic luster. Perhaps the most important characteristic property of metals is the ease with which they conduct electricity and transfer energy. **Thus, a metal is an element that is a good electrical conductor and a good heat conductor.**

At room temperature, most metals are solids. Most metals also have the property of *malleability,* that is, they can be hammered or rolled into thin sheets. Metals also tend to be *ductile,* which means that they can be drawn into a fine wire. Metals behave this way because they have high *tensile strength,* the ability to resist breaking when pulled.

Although all metals conduct electricity well, metals also have very diverse properties. Mercury is a liquid at room temperature, whereas tungsten has the highest melting point of any element. The metals in Group 1 are so soft that they can be cut with a knife, yet others, such as chromium, are very hard. Some metals, such as manganese and bismuth, are very brittle, yet others, such as iron and copper, are very malleable and ductile. Most metals have a silvery or grayish white *luster*. Two exceptions are gold and copper, which are yellow and reddish brown, respectively. **Figure 3.3** shows three examples of metals: gold, copper, and aluminum.

FIGURE 3.3

Characteristic Properties of Metals

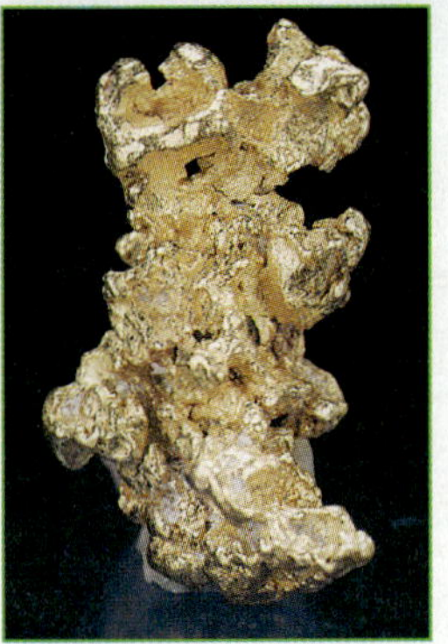

(a) Gold has a low reactivity, which is why it may be found in nature in relatively pure form.

(b) Copper is used in wiring because it is ductile and conducts electrical energy.

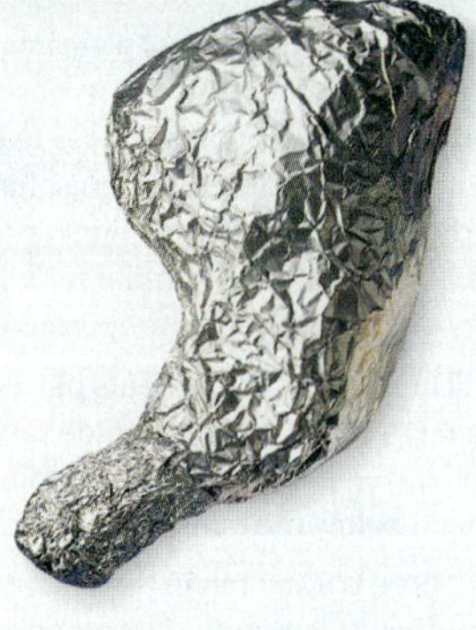

(c) Aluminum is malleable. It can be rolled into foil that is used for wrapping food.

Differentiated Instruction

PRE-AP

Have students open their textbooks to the *Elements Handbook* in Appendix A. Allow them 15–20 minutes to examine the properties of the various groups of elements. Permit them to keep their books open for reference, and begin a new version of a classic traveling game. Explain to students that you will start off the game, and then it will continue with them, in an order around the classroom that you determine. Tell students that the game has to do with the properties of the elements, and will follow the periodic table in order of atomic number. Begin the game by saying, "I'm doing an experiment and I'm going to use some hydrogen to make some...water molecules." The first student to play would then respond by saying, "I'm going to do an experiment and I'm going to use some hydrogen to make some water molecules, and some helium to...Sample answer: fill a balloon. Game play will continue from student to student, with each one repeating what the preceding players have said and adding on a new element and item that includes it.

Copper, shown in **Figure 3.3b,** has a characteristic reddish color and a metallic luster. It is found naturally in minerals such as chalcopyrite and malachite. Pure copper melts at 1083°C and boils at 2567°C. It can be readily drawn into fine wire, pressed into thin sheets, and formed into tubing. Copper conducts electricity with little loss of energy. Copper remains unchanged in pure, dry air at room temperature. When heated, it reacts with oxygen in air. It also reacts with sulfur and the elements in Group 17 of the periodic table. The green coating on a piece of weathered copper comes from the reaction of copper with oxygen, carbon dioxide, and sulfur compounds. Copper is also an essential mineral in the human diet.

CHECK FOR UNDERSTANDING
Mercury is a metal that is liquid at room temperature. Using the Elements Handbook (Appendix A) as a reference, are there any non-metals that are liquids at room temperature?

MAIN IDEA

Some elements are nonmetals or metalloids.

Many nonmetals are gases at room temperature. These include nitrogen, oxygen, fluorine, and chlorine. One nonmetal, bromine, is a liquid. The solid nonmetals include carbon, phosphorus, selenium, sulfur, and iodine. These solids tend to be brittle rather than malleable and ductile. Some nonmetals are illustrated in **Figure 3.4**.

Low conductivity can be used to define nonmetals. **A nonmetal is an element that is a poor conductor of heat and electricity.** If you look at the periodic table, you will see that there are fewer nonmetals than metals.

Phosphorus, shown in **Figure 3.4c,** is one of five solid nonmetals. Pure phosphorus is known in two common forms. Red phosphorus is a dark red powder that melts at 597°C. White phosphorus is a waxy solid that melts at 44°C. Because it ignites in air at room temperature, white phosphorus is stored under water. Phosphorus is too reactive to exist in pure form in nature. It is present in huge quantities in phosphate rock, where it is combined with oxygen and calcium. All living things contain phosphorus.

FIGURE 3.4

Nonmetallic Elements

(a) Carbon (b) Sulfur (c) Phosphorus (d) Iodine

Teaching Tip

The properties of the elements are discussed in greater detail in the *Elements Handbook* in Appendix A. Students can look over the transition-metal section to find out more about copper. Group 15 covers phosphorus, and Group 14 includes a section on the properties of semiconductors.

Demonstration

METALS AND NONMETALS

Show students an array of **metals** and **nonmetals.** Possible examples would be a **helium balloon** (nonlatex), **sulfur, copper wire, graphite, brass candle-stick.** Ask students to describe the properties of each item. Working as a class, you and the students should arrange the examples into two groups: metals and nonmetals.

Check for Understanding

Answer: Bromine is a liquid at room temperature.

▼ Assess and Reteach

Assess Use the Formative Assessment on this page to evaluate student mastery of the section.

Reteach For students who need additional instruction, download the Section Study Guide.

Response to Intervention To reassess students' mastery, use the Section Quiz, available to print or to take directly online at **HMDScience.com**.

FIGURE 3.5

Noble Gases Some noble gases are used to make lighted signs of various colors.

The elements in Group 18 of the periodic table are the noble gases. These elements are generally unreactive, although some can be made to form compounds, such as xenon hexafluoroplatinate. Low reactivity makes the noble gases very different from the other families of elements. Group 18 elements are gases at room temperature. Neon, argon, krypton, and xenon are all used to make lighted signs, like the one in **Figure 3.5.**

As you look from left to right on the periodic table, you can see that the metalloids are found between the metals and the nonmetals. **A metalloid is an element that has some characteristics of metals and some characteristics of nonmetals.** All metalloids are solids at room temperature. They tend to be less malleable than metals but not as brittle as nonmetals. Some metalloids, such as antimony, have a somewhat metallic luster.

Metalloids tend to be semiconductors of electricity. That is, their ability to conduct electricity is intermediate between that of metals and that of nonmetals. Metalloids are used in the solid state circuitry found in desktop computers, digital watches, televisions, and radios.

SECTION 3 FORMATIVE ASSESSMENT

Reviewing Main Ideas

1. Use the periodic table to write the names for the following elements: O, S, Cu, Ag.
2. Use the periodic table to write the symbols for the following elements: iron, nitrogen, calcium, mercury.
3. Which elements are most likely to undergo the same kinds of reactions, those in a group or those in a period?
4. Describe the main differences between metals, nonmetals, and metalloids.

Critical Thinking

5. **INFERRING CONCLUSIONS** If you find an element in nature in its pure elemental state, what can you infer about the element's chemical reactivity? How can you tell whether that element is a metal or a nonmetal?

Answers to Section Assessment

1. oxygen, sulfur, copper, silver
2. Fe, N, Ca, Hg
3. Elements in a group have similar chemical properties and will therefore undergo the same types of reactions.
4. Metals tend to be shiny, malleable, ductile, and good conductors of heat and electricity. Nonmetals tend to be brittle and poor conductors of heat and electricity. Metalloids tend to be intermediate in properties between metals and nonmetals and are therefore semiconductors of electricity.
5. The element is relatively unreactive. If it were reactive, it would have combined with other elements, such as oxygen in the air, to form compounds. If it is shiny, malleable, and ductile, a good conductor of electrical energy, and can transfer energy as heat well, it is probably a metal. If it is a nonconductor, it is probably a nonmetal.

Math Tutor

Converting SI Units

SI units of measurement are based on multiples of 10, making them much easier to work with mathematically than the unrelated units of the U.S. standard measurements like ounces, pounds, feet, and gallons. Most calculations with SI units can be converted from one unit to another simply by moving the decimal point.

For example, look at the illustration below.

10^3 m	10^2 m	10^1 m	10^0 m	10^{-1} m	10^{-2} m	10^{-3} m
kilo	hecto	deka	Base Unit	deci	centi	milli
king	harry	drools	ugly	dark	chocolate	milk

To convert the SI base unit for distance, meters, to centimeters, the decimal point is simply moved 2 spaces to the right. One meter is equal to 100 centimeters.

Problem-Solving TIPS

- Make note of the unit that is given at the beginning of the problem and check to see if the answer you are seeking is given in the same or a different unit.
- Is the unit given at the beginning an SI base unit, or does it have a prefix?
- If you are converting from a smaller unit to a larger unit, the decimal point will move to the left.
- If you are converting from a larger unit to a smaller unit, the decimal point will move to the right.
- The number of places you move the decimal point is equal to the power of 10 that is indicated by the prefix.
- If you are converting from a unit with a prefix back to a base unit, start with the prefix unit. Make note of the power of 10 of that prefix in the table in your text.
- Check your final unit to see if it makes sense in terms of the answer sought. For example, if you are measuring the length of a tabletop, an answer in tens of kilometers would not be appropriate.

Sample

How many liters are there in 9.844 mL?

The prefix *milli* has a power of 10 of −3. It is therefore smaller than the base unit of liters. Because you are converting from a smaller unit (mL) to a larger unit (L), move the decimal point 3 places to the left:
9.844 mL = 0.009844 L

Convert 0.35543 km into meters.

The power of 10 for the prefix *kilo* is 3. It is therefore a larger value than the base unit of meters. To convert from a larger unit (km) to a smaller unit (m), move the decimal point 3 places to the right:
0.35543 km = 355.43 m

Teaching Tip

A calculator gives results with as many digits as are available in the calculator display. However, a calculation cannot increase the certainty of the measurements used in the calculation. So, tell your students to follow the rules listed when they use a calculator. Remind students that in order to avoid accumulation of large rounding errors, they should not round after individual steps. Tell students that they should wait until they have finished the entire calculation.

CHAPTER 1 Summary

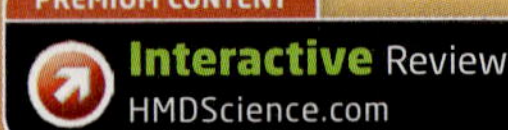

Review Games
Concept Maps

SECTION 1 Chemistry Is a Physical Science

- Chemistry is the study of the composition, structure, and properties of matter and the changes that matter undergoes.
- A chemical is any substance that has a definite composition or is used or produced in a chemical process.
- Basic research is carried out for the sake of increasing knowledge. Applied research is carried out to solve practical problems. Technological development involves the use of existing knowledge to make life easier.

KEY TERMS

chemistry
chemical

SECTION 2 Matter and Its Properties

- All matter has mass and takes up space. Mass is one measure of the amount of matter.
- Chemical properties refer to a substance's ability to undergo changes that alter its composition and identity.
- An element is composed of one kind of atom. Compounds are made from two or more elements in fixed proportions.
- All substances have characteristic properties that enable chemists to tell the substances apart and to separate the substances.
- Physical changes do not involve changes in identity of a substance.
- The three major states of matter are solid, liquid, and gas. Changes of state, such as melting and boiling, are physical changes.
- In a chemical change—or a chemical reaction—the identity of the substance changes.
- Energy changes accompany physical and chemical changes. Energy may be released or absorbed, but it is neither created nor destroyed.
- Matter can be classified into mixtures and pure substances.

KEY TERMS

mass
matter
atom
element
compound
extensive property
intensive property
physical property
physical change
change of state
solid
liquid
gas
plasma
chemical property
chemical change
chemical reaction
reactant
product
mixture
homogeneous
solution
heterogeneous
pure substance

SECTION 3 Elements

- Each element has a unique symbol. The periodic table shows the elements organized by their chemical properties. Columns on the table represent groups or families of elements that have similar chemical properties. Properties vary across the rows, or periods.
- The elements can be classified as metals, nonmetals, metalloids, and noble gases. These classes occupy different areas of the periodic table. Metals tend to be shiny, malleable, and ductile and tend to be good conductors. Nonmetals tend to be brittle and tend to be poor conductors.
- Metalloids are intermediate in properties between metals and nonmetals, They are semiconductors. The noble gases are generally unreactive.

KEY TERMS

group
family
period
metal
nonmetal
metalloid

CHAPTER 1 Review

SECTION 1

Chemistry Is a Physical Science

 REVIEWING MAIN IDEAS

1. What is chemistry?
2. What branch of chemistry is most concerned with the study of carbon compounds?
3. What is meant by the word *chemical,* as used by scientists?
4. In which of the six branches of chemistry would a scientist be working if he or she were doing the following:
   a. investigating energy relationships for various reactions
   b. comparing properties of alcohols with those of sugars
   c. studying reactions that occur during the digestion of food
5. Identify each of the following as an example of either basic research, applied research, or technological development:
   a. A new type of refrigerant that is less damaging to the environment is developed.
   b. A new element is synthesized in a particle accelerator.
   c. A computer chip is redesigned to increase the speed of the computer.

SECTION 2

Matter and Its Properties

 REVIEWING MAIN IDEAS

6. a. What is mass?
   b. What is volume?
7. How does the composition of a pure compound differ from that of a mixture?
8. a. Define property.
   b. How are properties useful in classifying materials?
9. What is the difference between extensive properties and intensive properties?
10. a. Define chemical property.
    b. List two examples of chemical properties.
11. Distinguish between a physical change and a chemical change.
12. a. How does a solid differ from a liquid?
    b. How does a liquid differ from a gas?
    c. How is a liquid similar to a gas?
    d. What is a plasma?
13. What is meant by a change in state?
14. Identify the reactants and products in the following reaction:
    potassium + water ⟶
    potassium hydroxide + hydrogen
15. Suppose different parts of a sample material have different compositions. What can you conclude about the material?

SECTION 3

Elements

 REVIEWING MAIN IDEAS

16. What is the significance of the vertical columns of the periodic table? What is the significance of the horizontal rows?
17. Compare the physical properties of metals, nonmetals, metalloids, and noble gases, and describe where in the periodic table each of these kinds of elements is located.
18. Suppose element X is a poor conductor of electricity and breaks when hit with a hammer. Element Z is a good conductor of electricity and heat. In what area of the periodic table does each element most likely belong?
19. Use the periodic table to write the names of the elements that have the following symbols, and identify each as a metal, nonmetal, metalloid, or noble gas.
    a. K
    b. Ag
    c. Si
    d. Na
    e. Hg
    f. He

Review Answers

1. the study of the composition, structure, and properties of matter and the changes that matter undergoes
2. organic chemistry
3. a substance that has a definite composition
4. a. physical
   b. organic
   c. biochemical
5. a. applied research, b. basic research
   c. technological development
6. a. a measure of an amount of matter
   b. a measure of an amount of space
7. The proportions of elements in a pure compound are fixed.
8. a. A property is any characteristic of a substance or material.
   b. Properties are useful for classifying unknown materials as members of known groups or subgroups of substances or for identifying substances directly.

9. Extensive properties depend on the amount of matter that is present. Intensive properties do not.
10. a. A chemical property describes a substance's ability to undergo changes that alter its identity.
    b. Examples include the ability of coal to burn and the ability of iron to rust.
11. A physical change does not involve a change in a substance's identity; a chemical change converts one substance into other substances.
12. a. A solid has a definite volume and a definite shape, whereas a liquid has a definite volume but takes the shape of its container.
    b. A gas has neither a definite volume nor a definite shape, but a liquid has a definite volume.
    c. Liquids and gases take the shape of the container.
    d. A plasma is a high-temperature physical state of matter in which atoms lose their electrons.
13. a change of a substance from one state of matter to another
14. Reactants are potassium and water; products are potassium hydroxide and hydrogen.
15. It must be a mixture.
16. Elements with similar properties are placed in the same vertical columns. Properties vary from left to right along the rows.
17. Metals (at left and center of table) are good heat conductors and electrical conductors. Nonmetals (at right of table) tend to be poor conductors. Metalloids (between metals and nonmetals) are intermediate in properties and are semiconductors. Noble gases (at extreme right) are generally unreactive.
18. X is probably a nonmetal on the right side of the table. Z is a metal on the left side or in the middle of the table.
19. a. potassium, metal
    b. silver, metal
    c. silicon, metalloid
    d. sodium, metal
    e. mercury, metal
    f. helium, noble gas

20. may be malleable and ductile and a good conductor of energy as heat

21. a. 14, 2 **c.** 6, 4
b. 18, 3 **d.** 2, 6

22. a. a property that can be observed or measured without changing the identity of the substance
b. Examples include color, odor, length, size, and melting point.

23. Compounds can be separated into elements by chemical means. Elements cannot be separated into simpler substances by chemical means.

24. a. physical, because the wood remains wood
b. chemical, because the milk changes composition, as signified by the change in flavor
c. physical, because the butter remains butter

25. A molecule is the smallest unit of a substance that keeps all of the physical and chemical properties of that substance. An element is composed of molecules that can be single atoms or can be more than one of the same kind of atom. A compound is composed of two or more elements, so a molecule of a compound is made up of two or more different kinds of atoms.

26. Answers will vary. Physical properties include shape, texture, state of matter, and taste. Chemical properties could not be observed unless a chemical change was attempted.

27. A mixture; the lemon juice, water, and sugar are not chemically combined.

28. a. Chemical; the physical appearance does not change, but the process of heating the material produces a gas and changes its reactivity.
b. Compound; the original solid material is observed to break down and form a gas and a different solid. A compound could be broken down by heating. An element cannot be broken down by heating.

29. a. Breaking an egg is a physical change, because the chemical nature of the egg has not been affected.
b. Cooking an egg is a chemical change, because the chemical properties of the egg are changed by the transfer of energy as heat.

20. An unknown element is shiny and is found to be a good conductor of electricity. What other properties would you predict for it?

21. Use the periodic table to identify the group numbers and period numbers of the following elements:
a. carbon, C
b. argon, Ar
c. chromium, Cr
d. barium, Ba

Mixed Review

 **REVIEWING MAIN IDEAS**

22. a. Define physical property.
b. List two examples of physical properties.

23. How can you tell the difference between an element and a compound?

24. Identify each of the following as either a physical change or a chemical change. Explain your answers.
a. A piece of wood is sawed in half.
b. Milk turns sour.
c. Melted butter solidifies in the refrigerator.

25. Write a brief paragraph that shows that you understand the following terms and the relationships between them: *atom, molecule, compound,* and *element.*

26. Pick an object you can see right now. List three of the object's physical properties that you can observe. Can you also observe a chemical property of the object? Explain your answer.

CRITICAL THINKING

27. Interpreting Concepts One way to make lemonade is to start by combining lemon juice and water. To make the lemonade taste better you could add some sugar. Is your lemonade-sugar combination classified as a compound or a mixture? Explain your answer.

28. Analyzing Results A pure white, solid material that looks like table salt releases gas when heated under certain conditions. There is no change in the appearance of the solid, but the reactivity of the material changes.
a. Did a chemical or physical change occur? How do you know?
b. Was the original material an element or a compound?

29. Interpreting Concepts
a. Is breaking an egg an example of a physical or chemical change? Explain your answer.
b. Is cooking an egg an example of a physical or chemical change? Explain your answer.

USING THE HANDBOOK

30. Review the information on trace elements in the *Elements Handbook* (Appendix A).
a. What are the functions of trace elements in the body?
b. What transition metal plays an important role in oxygen transport throughout the body?
c. What two Group 1 elements are part of the electrolyte balance in the body?

RESEARCH AND WRITING

31. Research any current technological product of your choosing. Find out about its manufacture and uses. Also find out about the basic research and applied research that made its development possible.

32. Investigate current and proposed technological applications of superconductors. Find out which of these applications have been successfully tested or are already in use.

ALTERNATIVE ASSESSMENT

33. During a 1 h period, make a list of all the changes that you see around you and that involve matter. Note whether each change seems to be a physical change or a chemical change. Give reasons for your answers.

34. Make a concept map using at least 15 terms from the vocabulary lists. An introduction to concept mapping is found in the *Study Skills Handbook* of this book.

30. a. Trace elements are minerals that are essential for normal body function.
b. iron
c. sodium, potassium

31. Student reports will vary. You can use the scoring rubric on the **HMDScience.com** website to set criteria for evaluating student reports.

32. Student reports will vary. Superconductors are currently used in magnetic resonance imaging (MRI), MAGLEV transportation systems, and electrical power production. Scientists are researching the use of superconductors to make computers process information at increasingly faster speeds. Superconducting radiation detectors and superconducting light detectors are also being developed for space research applications.

33. Students should be able to correctly categorize most of the changes on the basis of whether new substances are being formed (chemical changes) or are not being formed (physical changes).

34. See the criteria for evaluating concept maps on the **HMDScience.com** website.

Standards-Based Assessment

Answer the following items on a separate piece of paper.

MULTIPLE CHOICE

1. Magnesium reacts with hydrochloric acid to produce magnesium chloride and hydrogen gas. The reactants in this reaction are
A. magnesium and magnesium chloride.
B. hydrochloric acid and hydrogen gas.
C. magnesium and hydrochloric acid.
D. magnesium chloride and hydrogen gas.

2. Matter that has a definite shape and a definite volume is
A. a liquid. **C.** a solid.
B. an element. **D.** a gas.

3. We know that air is a mixture and not a compound because
A. it can be heated to a higher temperature.
B. it can be compressed to a smaller volume.
C. it is colorless.
D. its composition can vary.

4. Matter can be defined as anything that
A. has weight.
B. has mass and volume.
C. is uniform throughout.
D. exhibits both chemical and physical properties.

5. Which of the following is best classified as a homogeneous mixture?
A. pizza **C.** hot tea
B. blood **D.** copper wire

6. A compound differs from a mixture in that a compound
A. contains only one element.
B. varies in chemical composition depending on the sample size.
C. has a definite composition by mass of the elements that the compound contains.
D. can be classified as either heterogeneous or homogeneous.

7. Which of the following is *not* a physical state of matter?
A. solid **C.** element
B. gas **D.** liquid

8. Three of the following must contain two or more kinds of atoms. Which one does *not* contain two or more kinds of atoms?
A. element
B. compound
C. homogeneous mixture
D. heterogeneous mixture

9. Which of the following symbols does *not* match the element name given?
A. Al, aluminum
B. Co, copper
C. K, potassium
D. P, phosphorus

SHORT ANSWER

10. Give three examples of mixtures, and tell whether each one is homogeneous or heterogeneous. Give three examples of compounds.

11. In trying to identify a sample of a pure substance, we observe the following properties. Tell whether each one is a chemical property or a physical property.
A. Its mass is 124.3 g.
B. It is a shiny solid at room temperature.
C. It is easily etched by nitric acid.
D. It melts when heated to 670°C.
E. It is 31.7 centimeters long.
F. It is a good heat conductor.
G. It burns in air.
H. It is a good conductor of electrical energy.

EXTENDED RESPONSE

12. Describe the difference between a chemical change and a physical change. Give one example of each kind of change.

13. Describe general properties of metals, nonmetals, and metalloids.

Test Tip
Remember that if you can eliminate two of the four answer choices, your chances of choosing the correct answer choice will double.

STANDARDS-BASED ASSESSMENT

To give students practice under more realistic testing conditions, give them 60 minutes to answer all of the questions in this Standardized Test Preparation.

Test Answers

1. C
2. C
3. D
4. B
5. C
6. C
7. C
8. A
9. B
10. Answers may vary.
11. Observations C and G are chemical properties; the others are physical properties.
12. In a chemical change, one or more substances are converted into different substances. A physical change does not involve a change in the identity of the substance or substances present. Student examples of each kind of change will vary.
13. metals: shiny; good conductors of heat; good conductors of electricity; malleable or ductile; most are solids at room temperature

    nonmetals: poor conductors of heat; poor conductors of electricity; many are gases at room temperature; those that are solids are brittle rather than malleable or ductile

    metalloids: properties intermediate between those of metals and nonmetals; less malleable than metals but not as brittle as solid nonmetals; most are semiconductors of electricity

Measurements and Calculations

① Core Instruction

Chapter Resources

- The Teacher's Edition wrap has extensive teaching support for every lesson, including Misconception Alerts, Teach from Visuals, Demonstrations, Teaching Tips, Differentiated Instruction, and Problem Solving support.
- Several additional presentation tools are available online for every chapter, including Animated Chemistry features and Visual Concepts.
- You can open your lesson with the Why It Matters Video: Measurements and Calculations.

Section	Instruction	Labs and Demonstrations Go Online for Materials Lists and Solutions Lists.
2.1	■ **Textbook:** Scientific Method **Teaching Visuals:** Scientific Method **PowerPresentations**	■ **Demonstration:** Qualitative vs. Quantitative Observations ■ **Lab:** Laboratory Procedures (Core Skill) ■ **Lab:** Hit and Run (Forensics) ■ **Demonstration:** Water Molecule Model
2.2	■ **Textbook:** Units of Measurement **Teaching Visuals:** Using Conversion Factors • Densities of Some Familiar Materials • SI Conversions • SI Base Units; Mass vs. Volume for Lead Samples • SI Prefixes • SI Base Units • Conservation of Energy in a Chemical Reaction **PowerPresentations**	■ **QuickLab:** Density of Pennies ■ **Demonstration:** Mass vs. Weight ■ **Demonstration:** Density of Raisins and Bubbles ■ **Lab:** The Parking Lot Collision (Forensics) ■ **Lab:** Measure for Measure (Open Inquiry)
2.3	■ **Textbook:** Using Scientific Measurements **Animated Chemistry:** Accuracy and Precision **Teaching Visuals:** Accuracy and Precision • Reporting Measurements Using Significant Figures • Direct Proportion • Inverse Proportion • Rules for Using Significant Figures in Calculations • Rules for Determining the Number of Significant Figures • Rules for Making Calculations with Significant Figures • Rules for Rounding • Scientific Notation with Significant Figures • Rules for Calculations with Numbers in Scientific Notation **PowerPresentations**	■ **Demonstration:** Volume and Significant Figures ■ **Lab:** Percentage of Water in Popcorn ■ **Lab:** Analyzing Graphs and Establishing Relationships (Probeware) ■ **Lab:** Accuracy and Precision in Measurements (Core Skill) ■ **Lab:** Specific Heat ■ **Lab:** The Sports Shop Theft (Forensics)

2 Support and Intervention

- **Interactive Reader** (English and Spanish)
- **Study Guide**
- **Interactive Review:** Review Games, Concept Maps, and Section Self-Checks
- **Scientific Reasoning Skill Builder**
- **Learn It! Videos**
- **Solve It! Cards**
- **Interactive Demos**
- **Sample Problem Sets**

3 Specialized Support

- **Chapter Summary Audio Files**
- **Interactive Reader Audio Files**
- **Differentiated Instruction:** Inclusion, Below Level, and English Learners (TE wrap)

Enrichment and Challenge

- **Differentiated Instruction:** Pre-AP (TE wrap)
- **Why It Matters:** Models in Chemistry (SE)
- **Chemistry Explorers:** Classical Ideas About Matter (SE)
- **WebLinks**

Assessment

- **Section Formative Assessments** (SE)
- **Section Quizzes**
- **Chapter Review** (SE)
- **Chapter Tests A and B**
- **Alternative Assessment** (TE wrap)
- **Online Assessment and Remediation**
- **ExamView Banks**

Where do I find it?

		PRINT	DVD	ONLINE
1	Animated Chemistry		■	■
1	Demonstrations (TE wrap)	■		■
1	Interactive Whiteboard		■	■
1	Labs		■	■
1	PowerPresentations		■	■
1	QuickLabs	■	■	■
1	Teaching Visuals		■	■
1	Textbook	■	■	■
1	Visual Concepts		■	■
1	Why It Matters Videos		■	■
2	Interactive Demos		■	■
2	Interactive Reader	■	■	■
2	Interactive Reviews		■	■
2	Learn It! Videos		■	■
2	Sample Problem Sets		■	■
2	Scientific Reasoning Skill Builder		■	■
2	Smart Grapher Tool		■	■
2	Solve It! Cards		■	■
2	Study Guide		■	■
3	Chapter Summary Audio Files		■	■
3	Differentiated Instruction (TE wrap)	■		
3	Interactive Reader Audio Files		■	■

CHAPTER 2

Chapter Overview

Section 1 covers the scientific method and its component activities, such as observing, collecting data, formulating and testing hypotheses, and theorizing.

Section 2 presents SI units of measurement, the concepts of mass and density, and the use of conversion factors.

Section 3 describes accuracy and precision, percentage error, the use of significant figures and scientific notation, and steps to use in solving problems.

▼ Focus and Motivate

Activate Prior Knowledge

Students may need a review of the following concepts:

- the nature of mass and matter

About the Image

A Bose-Einstein condensate is considered a fifth state of matter, along with solids, liquids, gases, and plasma. Despite vastly different properties, all these states of matter have something in common. They are made of particles that can be analyzed quantitatively. Quantitative measurements are fundamental to chemistry.

Why It Matters

Students can access the video online and find other helpful resources at **HMDScience.com**.

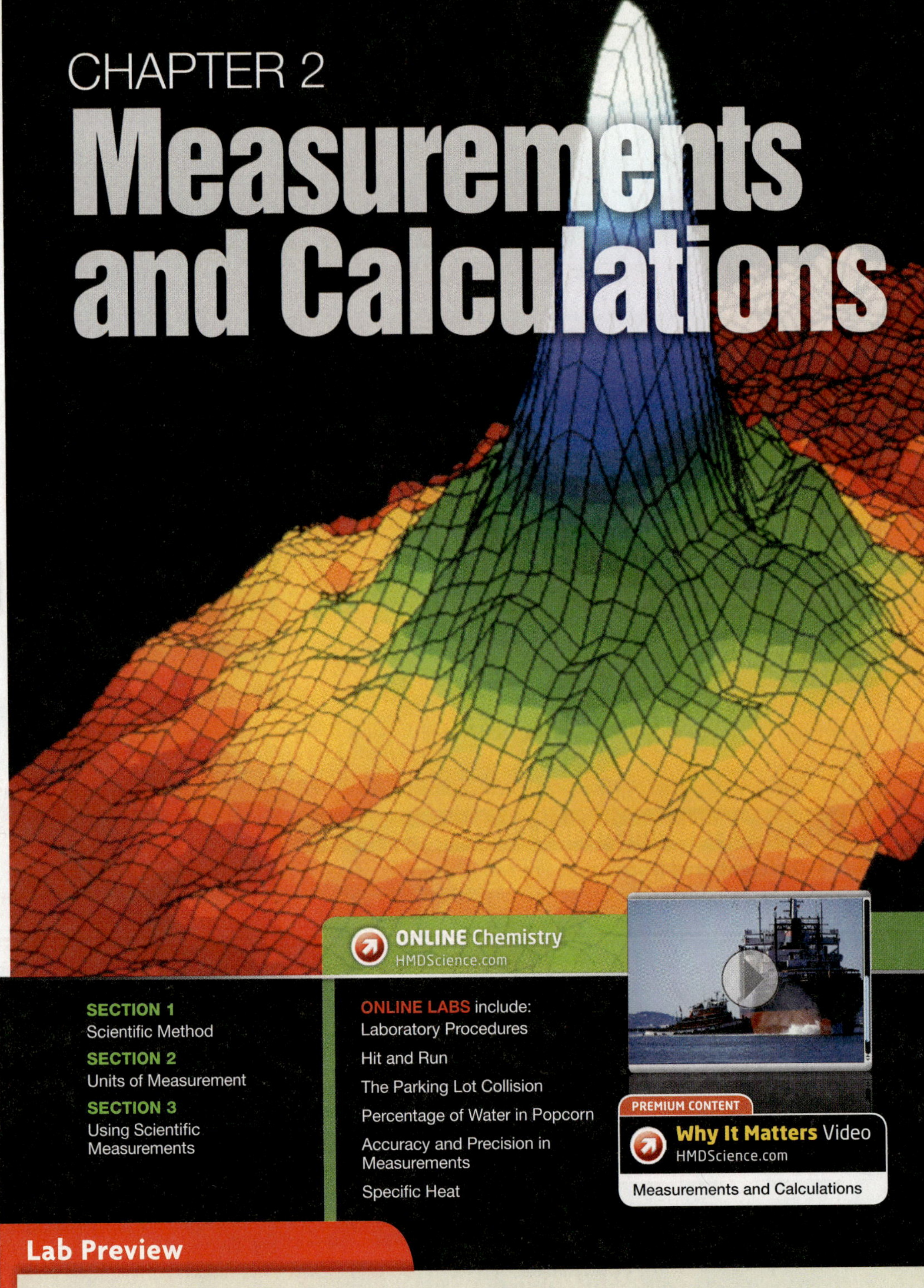

Lab Preview

These labs and demonstrations support the concepts presented in this chapter.

CHAPTER LABS

Laboratory Procedures (Core Skill)
Hit and Run (Forensics)
The Parking Lot Collision (Forensics)
Measure For Measure (Open Inquiry)
Analyzing Graphs and Establishing Relationships (Probeware)
Accuracy and Precision in Measurements (Core Skill)
Specific Heat (Core Skill)
The Sports Shop Theft (Forensics)

QUICKLAB

Density of Pennies

DEMONSTRATIONS

Qualitative vs. Quantitative Observations
Water Molecule Model
Mass vs. Weight
Density of Raisins and Bubbles
Volume and Significant Figures

SECTION 1

Scientific Method

Key Terms
scientific method
system
hypothesis
model
theory

SECTION 1

Main Ideas

- Observation includes making measurements and collecting data.
- Hypotheses are testable statements.
- Modeling ideas helps to form theories.

Sometimes progress in science comes about through accidental discoveries. Most scientific advances, however, result from carefully planned investigations. The process researchers use to carry out their investigations is often called the scientific method. The **scientific method** is a logical approach to solving problems by observing and collecting data, formulating hypotheses, testing hypotheses, and formulating theories that are supported by data.

MAIN IDEA

Observation includes making measurements and collecting data.

Observing is the use of the senses to obtain information. Observation often involves making measurements and collecting data. The data may be descriptive (qualitative) or numerical (quantitative) in nature. Numerical information, such as the fact that a sample of copper ore has a mass of 25.7 grams, is *quantitative*. Non-numerical information, such as the fact that the sky is blue, is *qualitative*.

Experimenting involves carrying out a procedure under controlled conditions to make observations and collect data. To learn more about matter, chemists study systems. The students in **Figure 1.1** are doing an experiment to test the effects absorbed water has on popcorn. A **system** is a specific portion of matter in a given region of space that has been selected for study during an experiment or observation. When you observe a reaction in a test tube, the test tube and its contents form a system.

FIGURE 1.1

Observation in an Experiment Students observe whether the volume of popped corn is greater when the kernels have been soaked in water prior to popping or when they have not.

Plan and Prepare

Objectives

Upon completion of this section, students should be able to do the following:

- Describe the purpose of the scientific method.
- Distinguish between qualitative and quantitative observations.
- Describe the differences between hypotheses, theories, and models.

Classroom Catalyst

Ask students what steps a detective might take in solving a case that is under investigation in your area. Write students' suggestions on the board. Compare these steps with those involved in solving other problems, such as how to determine the best route from their home to school. There should be similarities.

Teach

Misconception Alert!

The term *scientific method* may lead students to think that there is a single, unique sequence of steps that is always used in science. Point out that the scientific method is a general approach to problem solving and that the order of the steps may vary with the problem. Also emphasize that the independent verification of findings by other scientists is what lends credibility to scientific discoveries.

Demonstration

QUALITATIVE VS. QUANTITATIVE OBSERVATIONS

Ask students to observe an unlit **candle.** Record their observations on the board. Use a **match** to light the candle, and record students' observations as the candle burns. Have students determine which observations are qualitative and which are quantitative.

Differentiated Instruction

PRE-AP

While studying the material in this lesson, Ask students if they like to watch television shows about detectives or crime scene investigators. Answers will vary. Some should respond with a "Yes." Ask students to write a paragraph explaining why criminal investigators find information given by "trained observers" to be more reliable than that given by ordinary citizens. In their paragraph, have them explain what is meant by "trained observer" and how this might also apply to scientific investigations. Student responses will vary, but should indicate that a trained observer is someone who has learned what sort of details are important to notice and tells only what the facts are. It is important for scientists to also be factual and objective, rather than just speculating on what they think happened.

▼ Teach *continued*

TEACH FROM VISUALS

FIGURE 1.2 Have students decide whether the hypothesis proposed in the caption is valid, based on the results in the graph.

Ask students to predict how the data might look for a 75% phosphorus plot. Ask them to draw a conclusion from the data shown regarding the best percentage of phosphorus to use on these plants. Using 25% gives about the same results as using 50%. Using 25% would be more economical.

Class Discussion

Discuss generalizations that play a role in everyday life. For example, ask students what they observe each time they drop a heavy object. Ask how repeated observations have led them to the generalization that objects fall. Have students propose other real-life examples of making generalizations.

Misconception Alert!

Before discussing the scientific method and theories, ask students what they think a *theory* is. Students may believe that a theory is simply an idea or a guess. Explain that scientists use the term *theory* when discussing a scientific explanation or hypothesis that has been repeatedly verified over a long period of time and has accurately predicted results in many experiments. Make students aware that much of the public conflict on a range of issues can be traced to the mistaken idea that scientific theories are ideas or hunches, rather than the well-supported and proven work of scientists.

Critical Thinking

Answer: Answers will vary. Sample answer: If phosphorus stimulates the growth of corn plants, then corn plants treated with phosphorus should grow faster than corn plants under the same conditions that have not been treated with phosphorus.

FIGURE 1.2

Formulating Hypotheses A graph of data can show relationships between variables. In this case, the graph shows data collected during an experiment to determine the effect of phosphorus fertilizer compounds on plant growth.

CRITICAL THINKING

Predict Outcomes How would you finish this hypothesis: *If* phosphorus stimulates corn-plant growth, *then*...?

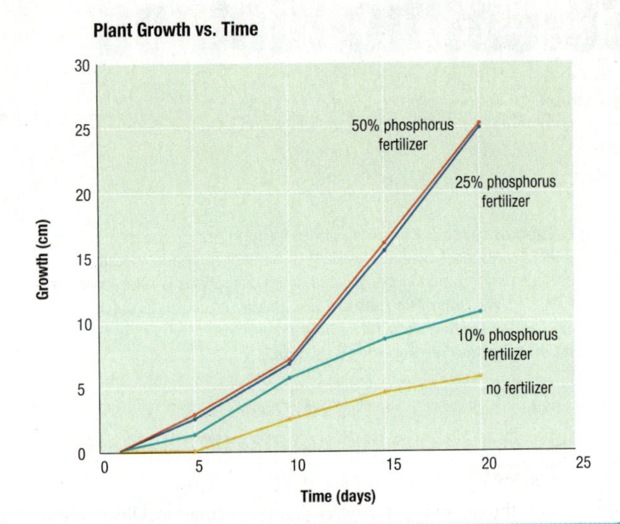

MAIN IDEA

Hypotheses are testable statements.

As scientists examine and compare the data from their experiments, they attempt to find relationships and patterns—in other words, they make generalizations based on the data. Generalizations are statements that apply to a range of information. To make generalizations, data are sometimes organized in tables and analyzed using statistics or other mathematical techniques, often with the aid of graphs and a computer.

Scientists use generalizations about the data to formulate a **hypothesis,** or testable statement. The hypothesis serves as a basis for making predictions and for carrying out further experiments. Hypotheses are often drafted as "if-then" statements. The "then" part of the hypothesis is a prediction that is the basis for testing by experiment. **Figure 1.2** shows data collected to test a hypothesis.

Controls and Variables

Testing a hypothesis requires experimentation that provides data to support or refute a hypothesis or theory. During testing, the experimental conditions that remain constant are called *controls*, and any condition that changes is called a *variable*. Any change observed is usually due to the effects of the variable. If testing reveals that the predictions were not correct, the hypothesis on which the predictions were based must be discarded or modified.

Differentiated Instruction

BELOW LEVEL

Students may be familiar with the idea of a hypothesis but be unsure of how to identify one. Most students have probably been taught that a hypothesis is in the "if...then" form. Provide students with a list of sample hypotheses, both in the "if...then" form and in other forms. Encourage students to rewrite any hypothesis not written in an "if...then" form.

FIGURE 1.3

The Scientific Method The scientific method is not a single, fixed process. Scientists may repeat steps many times before there is sufficient evidence to formulate a theory. You can see that each stage represents a number of different activities.

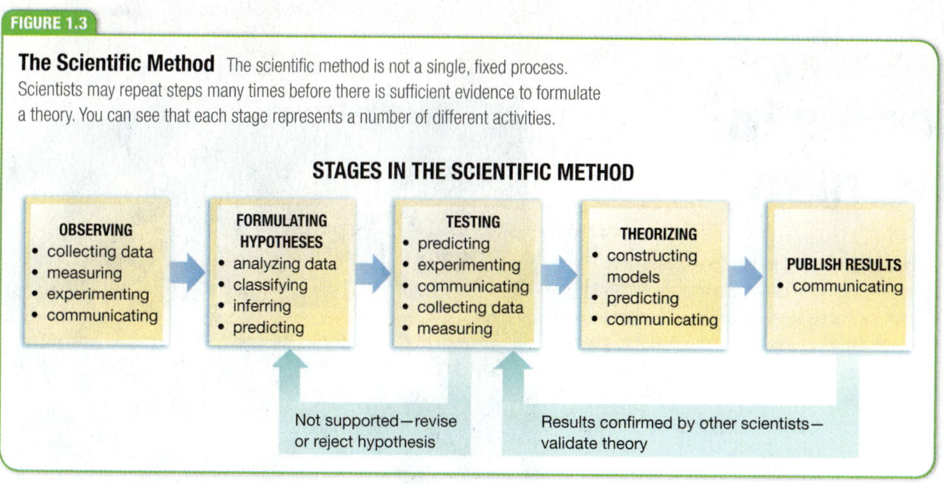

MAIN IDEA

Modeling ideas helps to form theories.

When the data from experiments show that the predictions of the hypothesis are successful, scientists typically try to explain the phenomena they are studying by constructing a model. **A model in science is more than a physical object; it is often an explanation of how phenomena occur and how data or events are related.** Models may be visual, verbal, or mathematical. One important model in chemistry is the atomic model of matter, which states that matter is composed of tiny particles called atoms.

If a model successfully explains many phenomena, it may become part of a theory. The atomic model is a part of the atomic theory, which you will study in the chapter "Atoms: The Building Blocks of Matter." **A theory is a broad generalization that explains a body of facts or phenomena.** Theories are considered successful if they can predict the results of many new experiments. Examples of the important theories you will study in chemistry are kinetic-molecular theory and collision theory. **Figure 1.3** shows where theorizing fits in the scheme of the scientific method.

SECTION 1 FORMATIVE ASSESSMENT

Reviewing Main Ideas

1. What is the scientific method?
2. Which of the following are quantitative?
   a. The liquid floats on water.
   b. The metal is malleable.
   c. The liquid has a temperature of 55.6°C.
3. How do hypotheses and theories differ?
4. How are models related to theories and hypotheses?

Critical Thinking

5. **INTERPRETING CONCEPTS** Suppose you had to test how well two types of soap work. Describe your experiment by using the terms *control* and *variable*.

Assess and Reteach

Assess Use the Formative Assessment on this page to evaluate student mastery of the section.

Reteach For students who need additional instruction, download the Section Study Guide.

Response to Intervention To reassess students' mastery, use the Section Quiz available to print or to take directly online at **HMDScience.com**.

Answers to Section Assessment

1. a logical approach to solving problems by observing and collecting data, formulating hypotheses, testing hypotheses, and formulating theories supported by data
2. c
3. A hypothesis is a testable statement that serves as a basis for making predictions and for carrying out further experiments. A theory is a broad generalization that explains a body of facts or phenomena.
4. A useful model is usually proposed after a hypothesis is shown to be correct. A model that successfully explains many phenomena may become part of a theory.
5. Answers may vary. Each trial in the experiment should involve using the two types of soap under the same set of conditions. Controlled variables might include water temperature or type of soil or grease to be cleaned.

Demonstration

WATER MOLECULE MODEL
Tell students that they will use paper and pencil to determine the geometry of molecules when they learn VSEPR theory. For now, write the formula for water on the board. Then draw the molecule on the board as a linear structure: H–O–H. Next, use a **molecular model kit** to assemble a water molecule. Have students compare the structure on the board with the molecular model. Ask them what they can conclude from this demonstration. Students should recognize that water is not a linear molecule. In this case, building a model provides an accurate representation of the three-dimensional structure of the molecule. Ask, "What would lead scientists to hypothesize that the water molecule is not linear?" evidence from experiments; observations of how water behaves

Class Discussion

Point out that computer models are a virtual means of understanding objects and events in the real world. Ask students to consider the differences between real life and any virtual online life they may have experienced. Then ask, "What are some of the risks of basing conclusions about the real world on virtual models?" The virtual models aren't real. Because the models exist in a computer, they do not react to events in the real world, and they cannot access the real world except for the information scientists provide them. The best way for scientists to improve their confidence in their models and conclusions is to provide the computers with as much data as possible.

Answers

1. Models must correctly explain evidence and predict observations and outcomes of further experiments. Models that are not based on observations do not explain those observations and are not scientifically valid, because they do not explain the real world.
2. Using more observations and measurements would improve the accuracy of a model.

Models in Chemistry

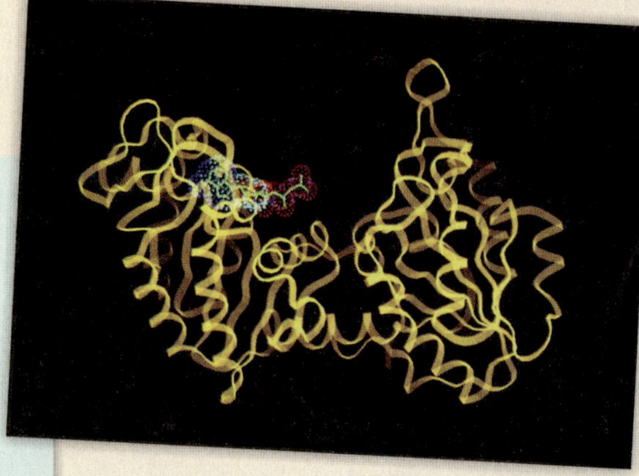

Seeing is believing, as the saying goes—but much of science deals with objects and events that cannot be seen. Models help explain the unseen, from the structures of far-off galaxies to the probable look and feel of subatomic particles. Models, however, must be based on observations. And how exactly do you model something as small as atoms or molecules?

Scientists have grappled with this problem for centuries. The atomic theory was developed by scientists, who observed the behavior of visible matter and then developed hypotheses to account for that behavior. Atoms simply seemed the most likely explanation. At first, atoms were modeled as tiny billiard balls. Then, as physicists and chemists discovered more and more about atoms, the atomic models became increasingly complex, until they included nuclei and electron clouds. Much still remains unknown. While the drawings in this book can give you some idea of what atoms and molecules look like, and they can be useful for predicting how the atoms and molecules will react under certain conditions, these models are far from perfect.

Today, however, supercomputers are creating very detailed atomic models that, although only two-dimensional, are unsurpassed in their ability to help scientists make predictions about molecular behavior in chemical reactions. Scientists feed information about the chemical behavior of a molecule into the supercomputer, which produces the model. The scientists can then manipulate the model's orientation and the conditions under which it exists. They can even highlight certain parts of the model at different times to study different things about the molecule. In this manner, they can test hypotheses about matter and how it behaves in a way that they can see and discuss.

Computer modeling can be especially useful for studying the complex molecules found in living organisms. For example, in 2010, two scientists at the University of Houston used computers to build a three-dimensional model of an enzyme linked to both Alzheimer's disease and cancer.

The enzyme is known as phosphoglycerate kinase, or PGK. The scientists used supercomputers to create a simulation that allowed them to change PGK's cellular environment. One thing they found was that the enzyme was 15 times more active when the cell's interior was crowded. Now, other researchers will probably have a better chance of figuring out how to control the enzyme so it doesn't have such serious effects.

Yet, while these new modeling techniques promise scientists models of hitherto unknown detail, one thing is worth remembering. Like all the atomic models before them, these models are still only our best guess of the unknown using empirical evidence, i.e., evidence we can see. Also, even though the model of atoms as tiny billiard balls may have proven to be too limiting a picture, thinking of models as being "right" or "wrong" misses the point of building them. Good models are not always the ones that turn out to be the "right" models. Good models are any models that help explain things we see and help us make predictions.

Questions

1. Why must all models be based on empirical observations and measurements?
2. How can scientists improve the accuracy of their computer models?

Units of Measurement

SECTION 2

Main Ideas

- Scientists worldwide use SI measurements.
- Prefixes added to SI base units indicate larger or smaller quantities.
- SI base units combine to form derived units.
- Conversion factors change one unit to another.

Key Terms

quantity
SI
weight
derived unit
volume
density
conversion factor
dimensional analysis

Measurements are quantitative information. A measurement is more than just a number, even in everyday life. Suppose a chef wrote a recipe, listing quantities such as 1 salt, 3 sugar, and 2 flour. Cooks could not use the recipe without more information. They would need to know whether the numbers 1, 3, and 2 represented teaspoons, tablespoons, cups, ounces, grams, or some other unit for salt, sugar, and flour, respectively.

Measurements *represent* quantities. **A quantity is something that has magnitude, size, or amount.** A quantity is not the same as a measurement. For example, the quantity represented by a teaspoon is volume. The teaspoon is a unit of measurement, while volume is a quantity. A teaspoon is a measurement standard in this country. Units of measurement compare what is to be measured with a previously defined size. Nearly every measurement is a number plus a unit. The choice of unit depends on the quantity being measured.

Many centuries ago, people sometimes marked off distances in the number of foot lengths it took to cover the distance. But this system was unsatisfactory because the number of foot lengths used to express a distance varied with the size of the measurer's foot. Once there was agreement on a standard for foot length, confusion as to the actual length was eliminated. It no longer mattered who made the measurement, as long as the standard measuring unit was correctly applied.

MAIN IDEA

Scientists worldwide use SI measurements.

Scientists all over the world have agreed on a single measurement system called Le Système International d'Unités, abbreviated SI. This system was adopted in 1960 by the General Conference on Weights and Measures. SI now has seven base units, and most other units are derived from these seven. Some non-SI units are still commonly used by chemists and are also used in this book.

SI units are defined in terms of standards of measurement. The standards are objects or natural phenomena that are of constant value, easy to preserve and reproduce, and practical in size. International organizations monitor the defining process. In the United States, the National Institute of Standards and Technology (NIST) plays the main role in maintaining standards and setting style conventions. For example, numbers are written in a form that is agreed upon internationally. The number seventy-five thousand is written 75 000, not 75,000, because the comma is used in other countries to represent a decimal point.

Differentiated Instruction

PRE-AP

Have each student imagine that he or she, along with other passengers, has become shipwrecked on an island. With no chance of rescue, the castaways decide to start a new country and elect him or her president. One of the first tasks of the president is to divide up the land among the people in a way that is fair to all. But, the president realizes he or she has nothing to use for taking measurements and so has to come up with a new measuring system.

On a sheet of paper, have students answer the following questions: 1) What will you call your unit of measurement? 2) Why would it be important to use a consistent standard of measurement? 3) What factors would be important as a basis for your measurement? Students should see that using a standard measurement would ensure that the land is parceled out equally. The basis for this measurement should be something that did not change greatly under different conditions, something that would last.

SECTION 2

Plan and Prepare ▼

Objectives

Upon completion of this section, students should be able to do the following:

- Distinguish between a quantity, a unit, and a measurement standard.
- Name and use SI units for length, mass, time, volume, and density.
- Distinguish between mass and weight.
- Perform density calculations.
- Transform a statement of equality into a conversion factor.

Classroom Catalyst

Ask students whether they would be breaking the speed limit in a 40 mi/h zone if they were traveling at 60 km/h. Explain that there are about 0.62 miles in one kilometer. Lead students to conclude that mi/h and km/h measure the same quantity using different units.

Teach ▼

Teaching Tip

It is important to emphasize the difference between a *quantity* and a *unit* and how each is represented. The Sample Problems throughout the text show both at various stages in the development of the solution to the problem. If students do not have a firm grasp of the difference, they will become confused.

READING TOOLKIT

BRAINSTORMING Write the words *qualitative* and *quantitative* on the board. Review the difference between qualitative (descriptive) and quantitative (numerical) data as described in Section 1. Have students brainstorm to come up with examples of each type of data. Invite two volunteers to write students' contributions in a list under each word. Have students revise and/or add to their lists as they read Section 2.

▼ Teach *continued*

TEACH FROM TABLES

FIGURE 2.1 Discuss each SI base unit, making sure students understand what each column and row in the table represents. The first five units will be the most important in their study of chemistry.

Draw attention to the following possible source of confusion for students. The letter *m* is used in three ways—in roman (plain) type, m, as the abbreviation for *meter* and *milli-*, and italicized, *m*, as the quantity symbol for *mass*.

Teaching Tip

Negative exponents represent inverses of numbers, not negative values. For example, 10^{-3} indicates $1/10^3$, 1/1000, or 0.001.

MAIN IDEA

Prefixes added to SI base units indicate larger or smaller quantities.

The seven SI base units and their standard abbreviated symbols are listed in **Figure 2.1**. All the other SI units can be derived from these seven fundamental units.

Prefixes added to the names of SI base units are used to represent quantities that are larger or smaller than the base units. **Figure 2.2** lists SI prefixes using units of length as examples. For example, the prefix *centi-*, abbreviated *c*, represents an exponential factor of 10^{-2}, which equals 1/100. Thus, 1 centimeter, 1 cm, equals 0.01 m, or 1/100 of a meter.

Mass

As you learned in the chapter "Matter and Change," mass is a measure of the quantity of matter. The SI standard unit for mass is the kilogram. The standard for mass defined in **Figure 2.1** is used to calibrate balances all over the world. A kilogram is about 2.2 pounds.

FIGURE 2.1

SI BASE UNITS

Quantity	Quantity symbol	Unit name	Unit abbreviation	Defined standard
Length	*l*	meter	m	the length of the path traveled by light in a vacuum during a time interval of 1/299 792 458 of a second
Mass	*m*	kilogram	kg	the unit of mass equal to the mass of the international prototype of the kilogram
Time	*t*	second	s	the duration of 9 192 631 770 periods of the radiation corresponding to the transition between the two hyperfine levels of the ground state of the cesium-133 atom
Temperature	*T*	kelvin	K	the fraction 1/273.16 of the thermodynamic temperature of the triple point of water
Amount of substance	*n*	mole	mol	the amount of substance of a system which contains as many elementary entities as there are atoms in 0.012 kilogram of carbon-12
Electric current	*I*	ampere	A	the constant current which, if maintained in two straight parallel conductors of infinite length, of negligible circular cross section, and placed 1 meter apart in vacuum, would produce between these conductors a force equal to 2×10^{-7} newton per meter of length
Luminous intensity	I_v	candela	cd	the luminous intensity, in a given direction, of a source that emits monochromatic radiation of frequency 540×10^{12} hertz and that has a radiant intensity in that direction of 1/683 watt per steradian

Differentiated Instruction

BELOW LEVEL

Using **Figure 2.1**, ask students to give examples of units they have used to express some of the familiar quantities listed. Students can draw pictures that represent the quantities or find pictures in magazines. Ask the students to label each picture with the name of the quantity, a familiar unit used to represent it, and the SI base unit used to represent it.

The gram, g, which is 1/1000 of a kilogram, is more useful for measuring masses of small objects, such as flasks and beakers. One gram is about the mass of a paper clip. For even smaller objects, such as tiny quantities of chemicals, the milligram, mg, is often used. One milligram is 1/1000 of a gram, or 1/1 000 000 of a kilogram.

Mass Versus Weight

Mass is often confused with weight. Remember, mass is a measure of the amount of matter. **Weight** is a measure of the gravitational pull on matter. Mass is determined by comparing the mass of an object with a set of standard masses on two sides of a balance. When the masses on each are the same, the sides balance. Unlike weight, mass does not depend on gravity. Thus, weight changes as gravitational force changes, while mass does not change.

Mass is measured on instruments such as a balance, and weight is typically measured on a spring scale. Taking weight measurements involves reading the amount that an object pulls down on a spring. As the force of Earth's gravity on an object increases, the object's weight increases. The weight of an object on the Moon is about one-sixth of its weight on Earth.

CHECK FOR UNDERSTANDING

Apply The gravity on the Moon is 1/6 of Earth's gravity. What would your weight be on the moon? Would your mass on the Moon be different from your mass on Earth? Explain.

FIGURE 2.2

SI PREFIXES

Prefix	Unit abbreviation	Exponential factor	Meaning	Example
tera	T	10^{12}	1 000 000 000 000	1 terameter (Tm) = 1×10^{12} m
giga	G	10^{9}	1 000 000 000	1 gigameter (Gm) = 1×10^{9} m
mega	M	10^{6}	1 000 000	1 megameter (Mm) = 1×10^{6} m
kilo	k	10^{3}	1000	1 kilometer (km) = 1000 m
hecto	h	10^{2}	100	1 hectometer (hm) = 100 m
deka	da	10^{1}	10	1 dekameter (dam) = 10 m
		$\mathbf{10^{0}}$	**1**	**1 meter (m)**
deci	d	10^{-1}	1/10	1 decimeter (dm) = 0.1 m
centi	c	10^{-2}	1/100	1 centimeter (cm) = 0.01 m
milli	m	10^{-3}	1/1000	1 millimeter (mm) = 0.001 m
micro	μ	10^{-6}	1/1 000 000	1 micrometer (μm) = 1×10^{-6} m
nano	n	10^{-9}	1/1 000 000 000	1 nanometer (nm) = 1×10^{-9} m
pico	p	10^{-12}	1/1 000 000 000 000	1 picometer (pm) = 1×10^{-12} m
femto	f	10^{-15}	1/1 000 000 000 000 000	1 femtometer (fm) = 1×10^{-15} m
atto	a	10^{-18}	1/1 000 000 000 000 000 000	1 attometer (am) = 1×10^{-18} m

INCLUSION

Kinesthetic learners may benefit from this activity. Provide groups of students with several common objects or photos of common objects. Have each student use **Figure 2.1** and **Figure 2.2** to determine the best unit for measuring the length of each object, and have each explain why that unit was chosen. Have the group come to a consensus for each object. Repeat the activity for units of mass. To help students visualize the base units, have a 1-kg mass and a meterstick available.

Demonstration

MASS VS. WEIGHT

Use a **triple-beam balance** to determine the mass in grams of a **fishing weight** or some other small object. Then use a **spring scale** to determine the weight in newtons of the same object. Ask students what determined the result in each case. The mass measurement is a comparison of the mass of the object and the masses built into the balance. The weight measurement is determined by the force of gravity on the object. Ask students what would happen if the same experiment were repeated on another planet. They should conclude that the mass would not change but the weight would.

READING TOOLKIT

VOCABULARY BUILDING Students are probably familiar with many of the prefixes listed in **Figure 2.2.** Write each prefix on the board as a column heading. Have students list as many different measurement words as they can that begin with each of the prefixes. Help students identify similarities and differences among terms based on these prefixes.

Check for Understanding

Answer: Your weight on the Moon would be 1/6 your weight on Earth, because weight is based on the force of gravity. Your mass on the Moon would be the same as your mass on Earth, because mass does not change with location.

▼ Teach *continued*

TEACH FROM VISUALS

FIGURE 2.3 Have students use markings on the ruler to determine the width of the foil shown in the photo. Informally prepare them for the concept of uncertainty, which is introduced in Section 3, by asking them how sure they are of the measured value.

TEACH FROM TABLES

FIGURE 2.4 Students should focus on the difference between the symbol for the quantity and the unit abbreviation.

ChemisTrivia

The metric system—the forerunner of SI—was first used in France in the late 18th century, around the time of the French Revolution. The revolutionaries embraced the system and wanted to standardize the number of days per month as 30, which is divisible by 10. There was even a movement to increase the number of days per week from seven to ten.

FIGURE 2.3

Metric Length The meter is the SI unit of length, but the centimeter is often used to measure smaller distances. What is the length in cm of the rectangular piece of aluminum foil shown?

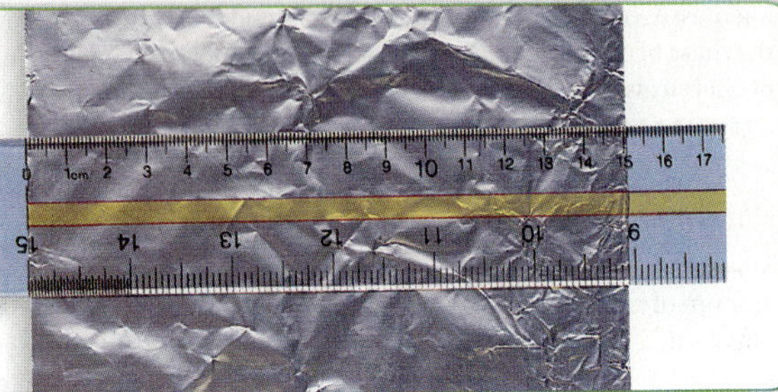

Length

The SI standard unit for length is the meter. A distance of 1 m is about the width of an average doorway. To express longer distances, the kilometer, km, is used. One kilometer equals 1000 m. To express shorter distances, the centimeter, as shown **Figure 2.3**, is often used. The centimeter is about the size of a paper clip. From **Figure 2.2**, on the previous page, you can see that one centimeter equals 1/100 of a meter.

MAIN IDEA

SI base units combine to form derived units.

Many SI units are combinations of the quantities shown in **Figure 2.1**. Combinations of SI base units form **derived units.** Derived units are produced by multiplying or dividing standard units. For example, area, a derived unit, is length times width. If both length and width are expressed in meters, the area unit equals meters times meters, or square meters, abbreviated m^2. Some derived units are shown in **Figure 2.4**. The last column of **Figure 2.4** shows the combination of fundamental units used to obtain derived units. **Figure 2.5**, on the next page, shows a speedometer measuring speed, another example of a derived unit.

FIGURE 2.4

DERIVED SI UNITS

Quantity	Quantity symbol	Unit	Unit abbreviation	Derivation
Area	A	square meter	m^2	length × width
Volume	V	cubic meter	m^3	length × width × height
Density	D	kilograms per cubic meter	$\frac{kg}{m^3}$	$\frac{\text{mass}}{\text{volume}}$
Molar mass	M	kilograms per mole	$\frac{kg}{mol}$	$\frac{\text{mass}}{\text{amount of substance}}$
Molar volume	V_m	cubic meters per mole	$\frac{m^3}{mol}$	$\frac{\text{volume}}{\text{amount of substance}}$
Energy	E	joule	J	force × length

Differentiated Instruction

ENGLISH LEARNERS

Explain to students what a mnemonic is and how they are often used as memory aids. Most students should have heard or used one in the past. Tell them that the most commonly used of the metric prefixes are *kilo-*, *hecto-*, *deca-*, *deci-*, *centi-*, and *milli-*. Provide students with a 3" X 5" note card and ask them to create a flashcard with their own mnemonic for remembering these units. It will help them with metric conversions if they also include either the letter *b* or the letter *u* in between deca- and deci-, to represent the base unit.

Sample: King Henry Drinks Ugly Dark Colored Muck

Some combination units are given their own names. For example, pressure expressed in base units is the following:

$$kg/m{\bullet}s^2$$

The name *pascal*, Pa, is given to this combination. You will learn more about pressure in the chapter "Gases." Prefixes can also be added to express derived units. For example, area can be expressed in cm^2, square centimeters, or mm^2, square millimeters.

Volume

Volume is the amount of space occupied by an object. The derived SI unit of volume is cubic meters, m^3. One cubic meter is equal to the volume of a cube whose edges are 1 m long. Such a large unit is inconvenient for expressing the volume of materials in a chemistry laboratory. Instead, a smaller unit, the cubic centimeter, cm^3, is often used. There are 100 centimeters in a meter, so a cubic meter contains 1 000 000 cm^3.

$$1\ m^3 \times \frac{100\ cm}{1\ m} \times \frac{100\ cm}{1\ m} \times \frac{100\ cm}{1\ m} = 1\ 000\ 000\ cm^3$$

When chemists measure the volumes of liquids and gases, they often use a non-SI unit called the liter. The liter is equivalent to one cubic decimeter. Thus, a liter, L, is also equivalent to 1000 cm^3. Another non-SI unit, the milliliter, mL, is used for smaller volumes. There are 1000 mL in 1 L. Because there are also 1000 cm^3 in a liter, the two units—milliliter and cubic centimeter—are interchangeable. **Figure 2.6** shows some of these different volume measurements.

FIGURE 2.6

Comparing Liquid Volumes One liter contains 1000 mL of liquid, and 1 mL is equivalent to 1 cm^3. A small perfume bottle contains about 15 mL of liquid. There are about 5 mL in 1 teaspoon. The volumetric flask (far left) and graduated cylinder (far right) are used for measuring liquid volumes in the lab.

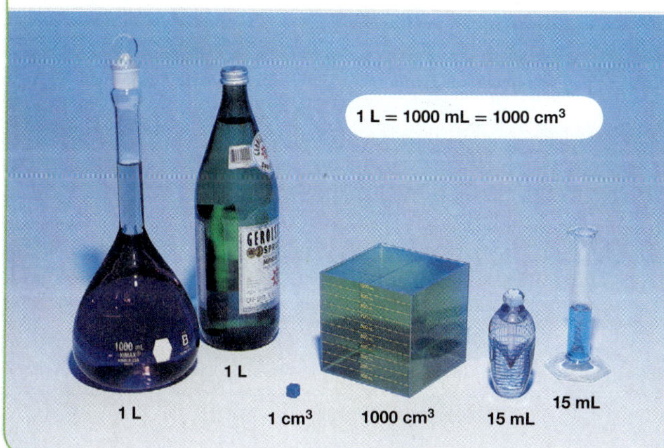

FIGURE 2.5

Using Derived Units to Measure Speed The speed that registers on a speedometer represents distance traveled per hour.

CRITICAL THINKING

Apply What derived SI units are used to express speed?

Misconception Alert!

Draw models of cubes on the board or display some three-dimensional models of cubes to help students with spatial relationships. Students often make errors in comparing related cubic units. For example, students know that there are 1000 mm in 1 m. They may then incorrectly assume that there are 1000 mm^3 ($10^3\ mm^3$) in 1 m^3 instead of the $10^9\ mm^3$ that are actually present ($10^3\ mm \times 10^3\ mm \times 10^3\ mm = 10^9\ mm^3$). Draw a model for this cube so students can see why a cube with lengths of 1000 mm per side has a volume of $1 \times 10^9\ mm^3$. Both the numerical value and the unit must be cubed.

Teaching Tip

The conversion factor $\frac{100^3\ cm^3}{1\ m^3}$ is simply the cube of the conversion factor $\frac{100\ cm}{1\ cm}$. This is a good opportunity to point out to students that a conversion factor raised to any power is still a valid conversion factor.

Demonstration

DENSITY OF RAISINS AND BUBBLES

Before beginning the discussion on density, fill a **large beaker** or **graduated cylinder** nearly full with **cold club soda** or seltzer. Add about a dozen **raisins.** The raisins will rise to the surface. They will then sink, only to rise again. This pattern will be repeated over and over. Have students attempt to explain what is occurring. Raisins are more dense than soda water, so raisins sink. However, gas bubbles are less dense than soda water, and they rise. When the bubbles attach to a raisin, the raisin-bubbles system is less dense than the soda water, and the raisin rises. At the surface, the bubbles escape, and the more-dense raisin falls until more bubbles attach to it.

Critical Thinking

Answer: Speed is generally expressed in the derived units of kilometers per hour or miles per hour.

BELOW LEVEL

Dealing with units of measurement can be one of the most confusing issues in chemistry for students. Provide students with a blank table and have them construct a reference table like **Figure 2.4.** Have students leave extra spaces at the bottom for adding in the derived units they will encounter as they progress through chemistry. Ask students if they know what a derived unit is and to give an example. The pascal (pa) is a derived unit used for pressure. 1 pascal (Pa) = 1 N/m^2 = $kg/m{\bullet}s^2$

▼ Teach continued

Application

Most substances and materials expand with an increase in temperature. Students have probably seen sidewalks designed with cracks or spaces between the squares to prevent the sidewalk from breaking or buckling when it expands in hot weather. Bridges and large buildings also are designed to allow for expansion and contraction.

ChemisTrivia

Heavy cream is actually lighter, or less dense, than light cream or milk, upon which it floats. The illusion of greater density is created by the thicker consistency of heavy cream.

TEACH FROM VISUALS

FIGURE 2.7 Students should make the connection between what they see in the photograph and the order of numerical values for density in **Figure 2.8.** The numerical relationship dictates what floats. For the substances in the photo, the density values are as follows:

$Hg = 13.6\ g/cm^3$

$H_2O = 1.0\ g/cm^3$

$Cu = 8.92\ g/cm^3$

Ask students whether ice would sink or float in a graduated cylinder filled with gasoline. Ice sinks in gasoline.

Critical Thinking

Answer: The diamond would float between the copper shot and the water.

FIGURE 2.7

Relative Densities Density is the ratio of mass to volume. Both water and copper shot float on mercury because they are less dense than mercury.

CRITICAL THINKING

Explain Using **Figure 2.8,** explain where a diamond would be in the layers in the graduated cylinder in **Figure 2.7.**

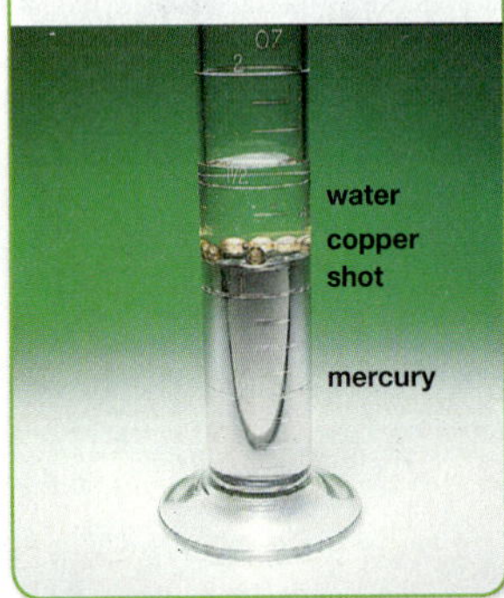

Density

A piece of cork is lighter than a piece of lead of the same size. Liquid mercury, as shown in **Figure 2.7,** is heavier than water. In other words, different substances contain different masses per volume. This property is called density. **Density is the ratio of mass to volume, or mass divided by volume.** Density is expressed by the equation

Density $$density = \frac{mass}{volume} \quad \text{or} \quad D = \frac{m}{V}$$

The quantity m is mass, V is volume, and D is density.

The SI unit for density is derived from the base units for mass and volume—the kilogram and the cubic meter, respectively—and can be expressed as kilograms per cubic meter, kg/m^3. This unit is inconveniently large for the density measurements you will make in the laboratory. You will often see density expressed in grams per cubic centimeter, g/cm^3, or grams per milliliter, g/mL. The densities of gases are generally reported either in kilograms per cubic meter, kg/m^3, or in grams per liter, g/L.

Density is a characteristic physical property of a substance. It does not depend on the size of a sample because as the mass of a sample increases, its volume increases proportionately. The ratio of mass to volume is constant. Therefore, density is one property that can help to identify a substance. **Figure 2.8** shows the densities of some common materials. As you can see, cork has a density of only 0.24 g/cm^3, which is less than the density of liquid water. Because cork is less dense than water, it floats on water. Lead, on the other hand, has a density of 11.35 g/cm^3. The density of lead is greater than that of water, so lead sinks in water.

Note that **Figure 2.8** specifies the temperatures at which the densities were measured. That is because density varies with temperature. Most objects expand as temperature increases, thereby increasing in volume. Because density is mass divided by volume, density usually decreases with increasing temperature.

FIGURE 2.8

DENSITIES OF SOME FAMILIAR MATERIALS

Solids	Density at 20°C (g/cm^3)	Liquids	Density at 20°C (g/mL)
cork	0.24*	gasoline	0.67*
butter	0.86	ethyl alcohol	0.791
ice	0.92†	kerosene	0.82
sucrose	1.59	turpentine	0.87
bone	1.85*	water	0.998
diamond	3.26*	sea water	1.025**
copper	8.92	milk	1.031*
lead	11.35	mercury	13.6

† measured at 0°C
* typical density
** measured at 15°C

Differentiated Instruction

PRE-AP

Have students select five liquids from **Figure 2.8.** Ask them to imagine that the five liquids are mixed in a large container and then poured into a graduated cylinder, such as the one shown in **Figure 2.7.** Have students predict what will happen as time passes. Students should realize that the liquids will separate based on their densities, with the liquid having the highest density settling to the bottom of the graduated cylinder.

QuickLAB DENSITY OF PENNIES

MATERIALS
- balance
- 100 mL graduated cylinder
- 40 pennies dated before 1982
- 40 pennies dated after 1982
- water

SAFETY

Wear safety goggles and an apron.

PROCEDURE

1. Using the balance, determine the mass of the 40 pennies minted prior to 1982. Repeat this measurement two more times. Average the results of the three trials to determine the average mass of the pennies.
2. Repeat step 1 with the 40 pennies minted after 1982.
3. Pour about 50 mL of water into the 100 mL graduated cylinder. Record the exact volume of the water. Add the 40 pennies minted before 1982. CAUTION: Add the pennies carefully so that no water is splashed out of the cylinder. Record the exact volume of the water and pennies. Repeat this process two more times. Determine the volume of the pennies for each trial. Average the results of those trials to determine the average volume of the pennies.
4. Repeat step 3 with the 40 pennies minted after 1982.
5. Review your data for any large differences between trials that could increase the error of your results. Repeat those measurements.
6. Use the average volume and average mass to calculate the average density for each group of pennies.
7. Compare the calculated average densities with the density of copper, listed in **Figure 2.8.**

DISCUSSION

1. Why is it best to use the results of three trials rather than a single trial for determining the density?
2. How did the densities of the two groups of pennies compare? How do you account for any difference?
3. Use the results of this investigation to formulate a hypothesis about the composition of the two groups of pennies. How could you test your hypothesis?

Density

Sample Problem A **A sample of aluminum metal has a mass of 8.4 g. The volume of the sample is 3.1 cm³. Calculate the density of aluminum.**

1 ANALYZE

Given: mass (m) = 8.4 g
volume (V) = 3.1 cm³

Unknown: density (D)

2 PLAN

$$\text{density} = \frac{\text{mass}}{\text{volume}}$$

3 SOLVE

$$\text{density} = \frac{8.4\text{ g}}{3.1\text{ cm}^3} = 2.7\text{ g/cm}^3$$

Problem Solving

DECONSTRUCTING PROBLEMS

Remind students that they can rearrange an equation to solve for an unknown. For example, if the values for density and volume are known, then the equation for density can be rewritten to solve for mass. To do this, start with the equation for density:

$$density = mass \div volume$$

Multiply both sides of the equation by the volume. When each side of the equation is multiplied by the same value, the equation is still correct.

So, on the right side of the equation, volume over volume equals one, so it cancels out, leaving:

$$density \times volume = mass$$

or

$$mass = density \times volume.$$

QuickLab

Students should make a data table to record their results.

- 40 pre-1982 pennies: mass for each of three trials, average mass, volume for each of three trials, average volume, calculated average density
- 40 post-1982 pennies: mass for each of three trials, average mass, volume for each of three trials, average volume, calculated average density

Pennies minted before 1982 were made of an alloy composed of 95% copper and 5% zinc. Pennies made since 1982 have a zinc center covered with a thin layer of copper and are 97.6% zinc and 2.4% copper.

DISCUSSION

1. The amount by which the result will be affected by a measurement error is decreased.
2. The post-1982 pennies have a lower density. The composition of the pre- and post-1982 pennies differs, resulting in differing masses.
3. Hypotheses will vary. Students should know that pennies contain copper. Research should show that they also contain zinc. Students could find the densities of copper and zinc and conclude that the less-dense pennies contain more zinc and less copper because zinc is less dense than copper.

Application

Carbon dioxide gas can be used to put out a fire because it is more dense than oxygen and thus sinks, blocking out oxygen from the fire.

▼ Teach continued

Answers

Practice A

1. 2.75 g/cm^3
2. 1.14 g
3. 5.60 mL

Classroom Practice

A-1 What is the density of a sample of ore that has a mass of 74.0 g and occupies 20.3 cm^3?

Answer: 3.65 g/cm^3

A-2 Find the volume of a sample of wood that has a mass of 95.1 g and a density of 0.857 g/cm^3.

Answer: 111 cm^3

NOTE: Students should not have to deal with significant figures in calculations until Section 3.

Class Discussion

Ask students to name examples of how conversion factors can be used in everyday life. An example would be using a vehicle's mileage conversion factor (number of miles/gallon) to estimate how much gasoline it would take for a trip of a certain length.

Teaching Tip

Help students understand that an equality statement is the basis for most conversion factors. Refer to **Figure 2.2** and have students write three equalities based on the table. Then have students express those equalities as ratios. For example, $1 \text{ kg} = 1 \times 10^3 \text{ g}$.

$$\frac{1 \times 10^3 \text{ g}}{\text{kg}} \text{ or } \frac{1 \text{ kg}}{1 \times 10^3 \text{ g}}$$

CHECK YOUR WORK The answer has two significant figures to match the number of significant figures in the given values. The units are correct for density.

Practice Answers in Appendix E

1. What is the density of a block of marble that occupies 310. cm^3 and has a mass of 853 g?
2. Diamond has a density of 3.26 g/cm^3. What is the mass of a diamond that has a volume of 0.351 cm^3?
3. What is the volume of a sample of liquid mercury that has a mass of 76.2 g, given that the density of mercury is 13.6 g/mL?

MAIN IDEA

Conversion factors change one unit to another.

A **conversion factor** is a ratio derived from the equality between two different units that can be used to convert from one unit to the other. For example, suppose you want to know how many quarters there are in a certain number of dollars. To figure out the answer, you need to know how quarters and dollars are related. There are four quarters per dollar and one dollar for every four quarters. Those facts can be expressed as ratios in four conversion factors.

$$\frac{4 \text{ quarters}}{1 \text{ dollar}} = 1 \quad \frac{1 \text{ dollar}}{4 \text{ quarters}} = 1 \quad \frac{0.25 \text{ dollar}}{1 \text{ quarter}} = 1 \quad \frac{1 \text{ quarter}}{0.25 \text{ dollar}} = 1$$

Notice that each conversion factor equals 1. That is because the two quantities divided in any conversion factor are equivalent to each other—as in this case, where 4 quarters equal 1 dollar. Because conversion factors are equal to 1, they can be multiplied by other factors in equations without changing the validity of the equations. You can use conversion factors to solve problems through dimensional analysis. **Dimensional analysis** is a mathematical technique that allows you to use units to solve problems involving measurements. When you want to use a conversion factor to change a unit in a problem, you can set up the problem in the following way.

$$\text{quantity sought} = \text{quantity given} \times \text{conversion factor}$$

For example, to determine the number of quarters in 12 dollars, you would carry out the unit conversion that allows you to change from dollars to quarters.

$$\text{number of quarters} = 12 \text{ dollars} \times \text{conversion factor}$$

Next, you need to decide which conversion factor gives you an answer in the desired unit. In this case, you have dollars and you want quarters. To eliminate dollars, you must divide the quantity by dollars. Therefore, the conversion factor in this case must have dollars in the denominator and quarters in the numerator: 4 quarters/1 dollar.

Problem Solving

REALITY CHECK

Encourage students to check their answers when they use a conversion factor. Using the example in the book, ask them to look at how many quarters they begin with. Have students assume that they start with 8 quarters. When they use a conversion factor of 4 quarters to 1 dollar, they should realize that the number of dollars must be less than the number of quarters. Point out that they should be aware of whether the quantity sought should be smaller or larger than the quantity known.

Thus, you would set up the calculation as follows:

$$? \text{ quarters} = 12 \text{ dollars} \times \text{conversion factor}$$

$$= 12 \text{ dollars} \times \frac{4 \text{ quarters}}{1 \text{ dollar}} = 48 \text{ quarters}$$

Notice that the dollars have divided out, leaving an answer in the desired unit—quarters.

Suppose you had guessed wrong and used 1 dollar/4 quarters when choosing which of the two conversion factors to use. You would have an answer with entirely inappropriate units.

$$? \text{ quarters} = 12 \text{ dollars} \times \frac{1 \text{ dollar}}{4 \text{ quarters}} = \frac{3 \text{ dollars}^2}{\text{quarter}}$$

It is always best to begin with an idea of the units you will need in your final answer. When working through the Sample Problems, keep track of the units needed for the unknown quantity. Check your final answer against what you've written as the unknown quantity.

Deriving Conversion Factors

You can derive conversion factors if you know the relationship between the unit you have and the unit you want. For example, from the fact that *deci-* means "1/10," you know that there is 1/10 of a meter per decimeter and that each meter must have 10 decimeters. Thus, from the equality 1 m = 10 dm, you can write the following conversion factors relating meters and decimeters.

$$\frac{1 \text{ m}}{10 \text{ dm}} \quad \text{and} \quad \frac{0.1 \text{ m}}{\text{dm}} \quad \text{and} \quad \frac{10 \text{ dm}}{\text{m}}$$

The following sample problem illustrates an example of deriving conversion factors to make a unit conversion. In this book, when there is no digit shown in the denominator, you can assume the value is 1.

Conversion Factors

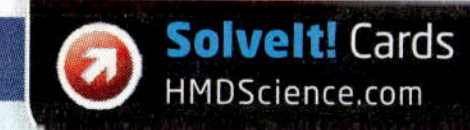

Sample Problem B **Express a mass of 5.712 grams in milligrams and in kilograms.**

1 ANALYZE

Given: 5.712 g

Unknown: mass in mg and mass in kg

The equality that relates grams to milligrams is

1 g = 1000 mg

2 PLAN

The possible conversion factors that can be written from this equality are

$$\frac{1000 \text{ mg}}{\text{g}} \quad \text{and} \quad \frac{1 \text{ g}}{1000 \text{ mg}}$$

Continued

Alternative Assessment

Give students a calendar, and ask them what conversion factors would be used to convert days to months, months to weeks, and so on. You could also use an egg carton and ask about conversions involving the unit *dozen*, or show a picture of shoes in a closet and ask about conversions involving the unit *pair*. Ask students to think of other examples of such conversion factors.

Classroom Practice

B-1 Express a time period of exactly 1.00 day in terms of seconds. Have students begin by writing out all of the equalities needed to solve this problem.

Answers: 1 day = 24 hours
1 hour = 60 minutes
1 minute = 60 seconds
86 400 s

B-2 How many centigrams are there in 6.25 kg?

Answer: 625 000 cg

ALTERNATIVE APPROACHES

Point out to students that most of the conversions in chemistry involve the same prefixes in the metric system. Encourage students to create a number line of the different metric prefixes to make their conversions quicker and easier. They could include everything from *pico-* to *giga-* and write the multiplication factors on the number line. This concept is illustrated in greater detail in the *Math Tutor* found at the end of the chapter, "Matter and Change".

▼ Teach *continued*

Answers

Practice B

1. 1645 cm, 0.01645 km
2. 0.000 014 g

▼ Assess and Reteach

Assess Use the Formative Assessment on this page to evaluate student mastery of the section.

Reteach For students who need additional instruction, download the Section Study Guide.

Response to Intervention To reassess students' mastery, use the Section Quiz available to print or to take directly online at **HMDScience.com**.

3 SOLVE

To derive an answer in mg, you'll need to multiply 5.712 g by 1000 mg/g.

$$5.712\ \cancel{g} \times \frac{1000\ \text{mg}}{\cancel{g}} = 5712\ \text{mg}$$

The kilogram problem is solved similarly.

$$1\ \text{kg} = 1000\ \text{g}$$

Conversion factors representing this equality are

$$\frac{1\ \text{kg}}{1000\ \text{g}} \text{ and } \frac{1000\ \text{g}}{\text{kg}}$$

To derive an answer in kg, you'll need to multiply 5.712 g by 1 kg/1000 g.

$$5.712\ \cancel{g} \times \frac{1\ \text{kg}}{1000\ \cancel{g}} = 0.005712\ \text{kg}$$

4 CHECK YOUR WORK

The first answer makes sense because milligrams is a smaller unit than grams, and therefore there should be more milligrams. The second answer makes sense because kilograms is a larger unit than grams, and therefore there should be fewer kilograms.

Practice Answers in Appendix E

1. Express a length of 16.45 m in centimeters and in kilometers.
2. Express a mass of 0.014 mg in grams.

SECTION 2 FORMATIVE ASSESSMENT

Reviewing Main Ideas

1. Why are standards needed for measured quantities?
2. Label each of the following measurements by the quantity each represents. For instance, a measurement of 10.6 kg/m^3 represents density.
   - **a.** 5.0 g/mL
   - **b.** 37 s
   - **c.** 47 J
   - **d.** 39.56 g
   - **e.** 25.3 cm^3
   - **f.** 325 ms
   - **g.** 500 m^2
   - **h.** 30.23 mL
   - **i.** 2.7 mg
   - **j.** 0.005 L
3. Complete the following conversions.
   - **a.** 10.5 g = ____ kg
   - **b.** 1.57 km = ____ m
   - **c.** 3.54 µg = ____ g
   - **d.** 3.5 mol = ____ µmol
   - **e.** 1.2 L = ____ mL
   - **f.** 358 cm^3 = ____ m^3
   - **g.** 548.6 mL = ____ cm^3
4. Write conversion factors for each equality.
   - **a.** 1 m^3 = 1 000 000 cm^3
   - **b.** 1 in. = 2.54 cm
   - **c.** 1 µg = 0.000 001 g
   - **d.** 1 Mm = 1 000 000 m
5. **a.** What is the density of an 84.7 g sample of an unknown substance if the sample occupies 49.6 cm^3?
   b. What volume would be occupied by 7.75 g of this same substance?

Critical Thinking

6. **INFERRING CONCLUSIONS** A student converts grams to milligrams by multiplying by the conversion factor $\frac{1\ \text{g}}{1000\ \text{mg}}$. Is the student performing this calculation correctly?

Answers to Section Assessment

1. There must be agreement on meaning and size of units. Standards for units must be unchanging to avoid confusion and ambiguity.
2. **a.** density
   b. time
   c. energy
   d. mass
   e. volume
   f. time
   g. area
   h. volume
   i. mass
   j. volume
3. **a.** 0.0105 kg
   b. 1570 m
   c. 0.000 003 54 g
   d. 3 500 000 µmol
   e. 1200 mL
   f. 0.000 358 m^3
   g. 548.6 cm^3
4. **a.** 1 m^3/1 000 000 cm^3 and 1 000 000 cm^3/m^3
   b. 1 in./2.54 cm and 2.54 cm/in.
   c. 1 µg/0.000 001 g and 0.000 001 g/µg
   d. 1 Mm/1 000 000 m and 1 000 000 m/Mm
5. **a.** 1.71 g/cm^3
   b. 4.53 cm^3
6. The method the student is using is incorrect. It gives the nonsense units $\frac{g^2}{mg}$. A correct method would be to multiply by $\frac{1000\ \text{mg}}{1\ \text{g}}$.

Chemistry EXPLORERS

Classical Ideas About Matter

The Greeks were among the many ancient peoples who sought to understand the nature of matter. One group of Greek philosophers, called the *atomists*, believed that matter could be broken down into pieces of a minute size. These pieces, called *atoms* or *atomos*, which means "indivisible," possessed intrinsic, unchanging qualities. Another group of Greeks believed that matter could be divided an infinite number of times and could be changed from one type of matter into another.

Between 500 and 300 BCE, the Greek philosophers Leucippus and Democritus formulated the ideas that the atomists held. Leucippus and Democritus believed that all atoms were essentially the same but that the properties of all substances arose from the unique characteristics of their atoms. For example, solids, such as most metals, were thought to have uneven, jagged atoms. Because the atoms were rough, they could stick together and form solids. Similarly, water was thought to have atoms with smooth surfaces, which would allow the atoms to flow past one another. Though atomists did not have the same ideas about matter that we have today, they did believe that atoms were constantly in motion, even in objects that appeared to be solid.

Some Greek philosophers who studied matter between 700 and 300 BCE described matter in a way that differed from the way atomists described it. They attempted to identify and describe a fundamental substance from which all other matter was formed. Thales of Miletus (640–546 BCE) was among the first to suggest the existence of a basic element. He chose water, which exists as liquid, ice, and steam. He interpreted water's changeability to mean that water could transform into any other substance. Other philosophers suggested that the basic element was air or fire. Empedokles (ca. 490–ca. 430 BCE) focused on four elements: earth, air, fire, and water. He thought that these elements combined in various proportions to make all known matter.

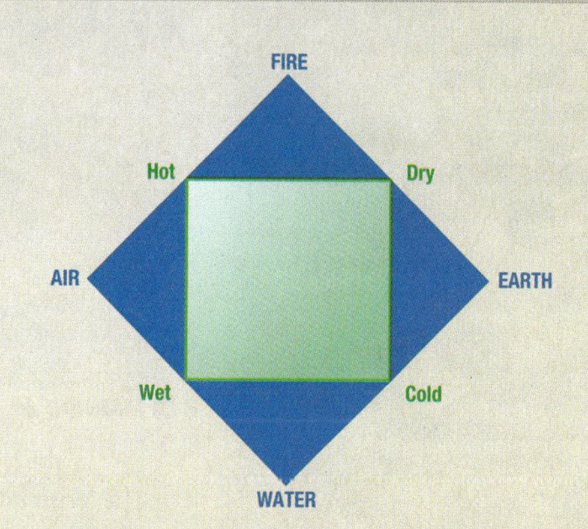

This diagram shows Aristotle's belief about the relationship between the basic elements and properties.

Aristotle (384–322 BCE), a student of Plato, elaborated on the earlier ideas about elements. He argued that in addition to the four elements that make up all matter, there were four basic properties: hot, cold, wet, and dry. In Aristotle's view, the four elements could each have two of the basic properties. For example, water was wet and cold, while air was wet and hot. He thought that one element could change into another element if its properties were changed.

For more than 2,000 years, Aristotle's classical ideas dominated scientific thought. It was not until the 1700s that the existence of atoms was shown experimentally and that the incredible intuition of the atomists was realized.

Questions

1. In Aristotle's system of elements, fire opposes water. Why do you think Aristotle chose this relationship?
2. Use the ideas of the atomists to describe the atoms of the physical phases of matter—solid, liquid, and gas.

Answers

1. Fire can be extinguished with water, so it is easy to assume that they cannot exist together. Also, their properties seem to be in opposition. Fire seems hot and dry, whereas water is typically wet and cold.
2. Solid atoms would be rough and irregularly shaped, because they stick together. Liquid atoms would be smooth but would still have an irregular shape, because they flow even though they are still held together. Gas atoms would be the most regularly shaped, because they do not stick together.

SECTION 3

▼ Plan and Prepare

Objectives

Upon completion of this section, students should be able to do the following:

- Distinguish between accuracy and precision.
- Determine the number of significant figures in measurements.
- Perform mathematical operations involving significant figures.
- Convert measurements into scientific notation.
- Distinguish between inversely and directly proportional relationships.

Classroom Catalyst

Students are often able to understand precision if they think of measurement instruments. Distribute some scientific equipment catalogs among the students, and have them look at the specifications for electronic balances. They can see how measuring instruments vary in precision. Ask students to discuss using a beaker to measure volume compared to using a graduated cylinder. Which is more precise?

▼ Teach

READING TOOLKIT

PAIRED SUMMARIZING Pair students together and have them silently read the section on Accuracy and Precision. Choose one of the pair to be the "reteller" and the other to be the "listener." First, have the reteller summarize the selection for the listener, who does not interrupt until the reteller has finished, or if there is a portion of the summary that requires clarification. Let the reteller consult the text during his or her summary. Next, have the listener state any inaccuracies or omissions. Finally, have the students work together to refine the summary. Students then alternate roles as they read the sections on Significant Figures, Scientific Notation, and Using Sample Problems. Use students' summaries to generate a summary for the class.

SECTION 3

Main Ideas

- Accuracy is different from precision.
- Significant figures are those measured precisely, plus one estimated digit.
- Scientific notation is used to express very large or very small numbers.
- Sample problems are guides to solving similar types of problems.
- Variables that are directly proportional increase or decrease by the same factor.
- Quantities are inversely proportional if one decreases in value when the other increases.

Using Scientific Measurements

Key Terms

accuracy
precision
percentage error
significant figures
scientific notation
directly proportional
inversely proportional

If you have ever measured something several times, you know that the results can vary. In science, for a reported measurement to be useful, there must be some indication of its reliability or uncertainty.

MAIN IDEA

Accuracy is different from precision.

The terms *accuracy* and *precision* mean the same thing to most people. However, in science their meanings are quite distinct. **Accuracy refers to the closeness of measurements to the correct or accepted value of the quantity measured. Precision refers to the closeness of a set of measurements of the same quantity made in the same way.** Thus, measured values that are accurate are close to the accepted value. Measured values that are precise are close to one another but not necessarily close to the accepted value.

Figure 3.1 on the facing page can help you visualize the difference between precision and accuracy. Several darts thrown separately at a dartboard may land in various positions, relative to the bull's-eye and to one another. The closer the darts land to the bull's-eye, the more accurately they were thrown. The closer they land to one another, the more precisely they were thrown. Thus, the set of results shown in **Figure 3.1a** is both accurate and precise: the darts are close to the bull's-eye and close to each other. In **Figure 3.1b**, the set of results is inaccurate but precise: the darts are far from the bull's-eye but close to each other. In **Figure 3.1c**, the set of results is both inaccurate and imprecise: the darts are far from the bull's-eye and far from each other. Notice also that the darts are not evenly distributed around the bull's-eye, so the set, even considered on average, is inaccurate. In **Figure 3.1d**, the set on average is accurate compared with the third case, but it is imprecise. That is because the darts are distributed evenly around the bull's-eye but are far from each other.

Percentage Error

The accuracy of an individual value or of an average experimental value can be compared quantitatively with the correct or accepted value by calculating the percentage error. **Percentage error is calculated by subtracting the accepted value from the experimental value, dividing the difference by the accepted value, and then multiplying by 100.**

Differentiated Instruction

INCLUSION

The terms *accuracy* and *precision* may be difficult for some students to fully understand. For students who are kinesthetic learners, you may want to play a quick game of "pin the tail on the donkey." Game pieces can be made and stuck onto the image of the donkey using tape to avoid having blind-folded students handle pins. Discuss how well students did in terms of accuracy and precision.

FIGURE 3.1

Comparing Precision and Accuracy

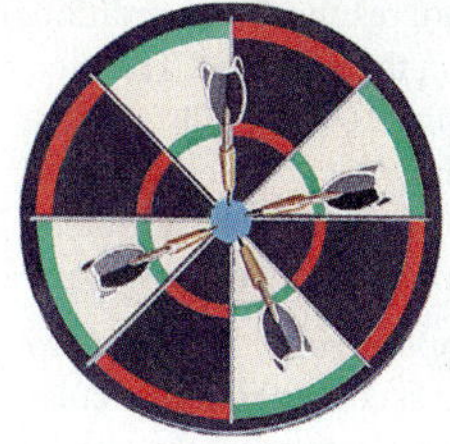

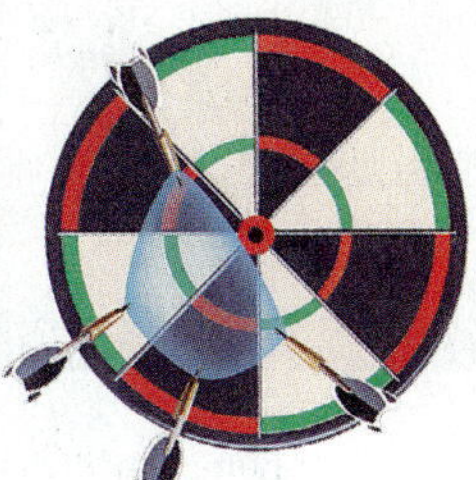
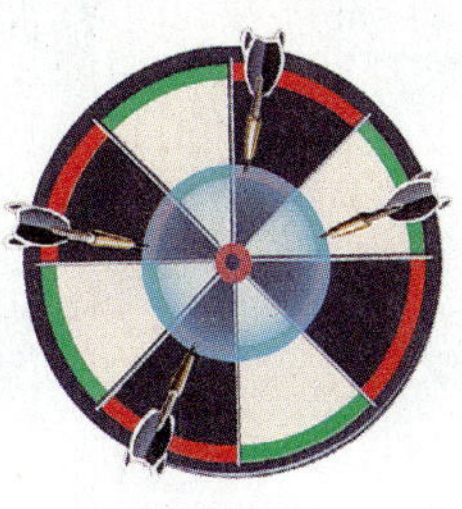

(a) Darts within small area = High precision

Area centered on bull's-eye = High accuracy

(b) Darts within small area = High precision

Area far from bull's-eye = Low accuracy

(c) Darts within large area = Low precision

Area far from bull's-eye = Low accuracy

(d) Darts within large area = Low precision

Area centered around bull's-eye = High accuracy (on average)

Percentage Error

$$\textit{Percentage error} = \frac{\textit{Value}_{experimental} - \textit{Value}_{accepted}}{\textit{Value}_{accepted}} \times 100$$

Percentage error has a negative value if the accepted value is greater than the experimental value. It has a positive value if the accepted value is less than the experimental value. The following sample problem illustrates the concept of percentage error.

Percentage Error

Sample Problem C A student measures the mass and volume of a substance and calculates its density as 1.40 g/mL. The correct, or accepted, value of the density is 1.30 g/mL. What is the percentage error of the student's measurement?

 **SOLVE**

$$\textit{Percentage error} = \frac{\textit{Value}_{experimental} - \textit{Value}_{accepted}}{\textit{Value}_{accepted}} \times 100$$

$$= \frac{1.40 \text{ g/mL} - 1.30 \text{ g/mL}}{1.30 \text{ g/mL}} \times 100 = 7.7\%$$

Practice Answers in Appendix E

1. What is the percentage error for a mass measurement of 17.7 g, given that the correct value is 21.2 g?
2. A volume is measured experimentally as 4.26 mL. What is the percentage error, given that the correct value is 4.15 mL?

Problem Solving

DECONSTRUCTING PROBLEMS

Have students look at the equation for percentage error. Ask students why they must subtract the accepted value from the experimental value. Be sure that students understand that when they are calculating percentage error, they are comparing the value they got (by experimenting or calculating) to a known value that has already been accepted as being accurate.

TEACH FROM VISUALS

FIGURE 3.1 Help students analyze the four dartboard situations. Use the illustration to compare and contrast various situations in terms of precision and accuracy. An additional example might be a pitcher's throws during a baseball game. Have students relate pitching results that have varying degrees of precision and accuracy.

Misconception Alert!

The term *precision* is often misunderstood as meaning the same thing as *accuracy*. Make sure students understand what precision is, and take time to reinforce the concept throughout the course.

Classroom Practice

C-1 The actual density of a certain material is 7.44 g/cm^3. A student measures the density of the same material as 7.30 g/cm^3. What is the percentage error of the measurement?

Answer: −1.9%

Class Discussion

Have students consider examples of precision and accuracy. For example, assume two technicians independently measure the density of a new substance. Technician A records values of 2.000, 1.999, and 2.001 g/mL. Technician B records values of 2.5, 2.9, and 2.7 g/mL. The correct value is found to be 2.701 g/mL. Students should be able to explain that A's results are more precise because they are closer together, and B's results are more accurate because they are closer to the correct value.

Answers

Practice C

1. −17%
2. 2.7%

▼ Teach *continued*

TEACH FROM VISUALS

FIGURE 3.2 Divide the class into groups of three or four. Provide each group with a set of the same objects and a metric ruler. Each group should have the same objects, but the rulers should vary somewhat in precision. Have the groups measure the lengths of the objects and compare their measurements with those of other groups. Ask them to note any trends in the measurements related to the precision of the rulers.

Application

The use of plus-or-minus notation corresponds closely to the use of the expression "give or take." For example, saying that the height of the ceiling is "10 feet, give or take a foot," is the same as expressing the height as 10 ft ± 1 ft. Have students come up with examples of other expressions.

Critical Thinking

Answer: The hundredths digit (6) is uncertain.

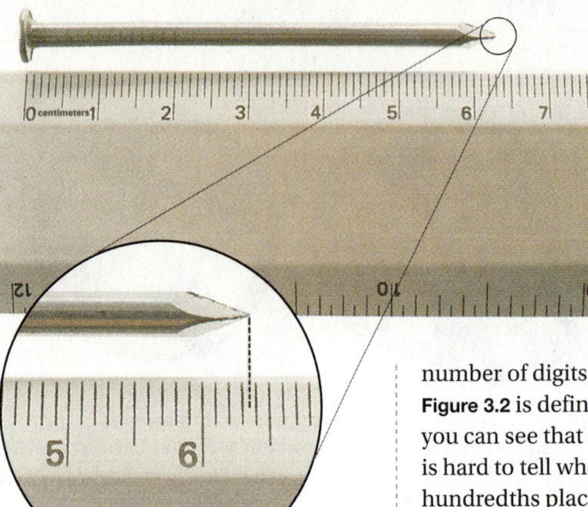

FIGURE 3.2

Significant Figures The length of this nail is between 6.3 cm and 6.4 cm.

CRITICAL THINKING

Apply Suppose you record the nail's length as 6.36 cm. Which part of this measurement is uncertain?

Significant Figures

Error in Measurement

Some error or uncertainty always exists in any measurement. The skill of the measurer places limits on the reliability of results. The conditions of measurement also affect the outcome. The measuring instruments themselves place limitations on precision. Some balances can be read more precisely than others. The same is true of rulers, graduated cylinders, and other measuring devices.

When you use a properly calibrated measuring device, you can be almost certain of a particular number of digits in a reading. For example, you can tell that the nail in **Figure 3.2** is definitely between 6.3 and 6.4 cm long. Looking more closely, you can see that the value is halfway between 6.3 and 6.4 cm. However, it is hard to tell whether the value should be read as 6.35 cm or 6.36 cm. The hundredths place is thus somewhat uncertain. Simply leaving it out would be misleading because you do have *some* indication of the value's likely range. Therefore, you would estimate the value to the final questionable digit, perhaps reporting the length of the nail as 6.36 cm. You might include a plus-or-minus value to express the range, for example, 6.36 cm ± 0.01 cm.

MAIN IDEA

Significant figures are those measured precisely, plus one estimated digit.

In science, measured values are reported in terms of significant figures. **Significant figures** in a measurement consist of all the digits known with certainty plus one final digit, which is somewhat uncertain or is estimated. For example, in the reported nail length of 6.36 cm discussed above, the last digit, 6, is uncertain. All the digits, including the uncertain one, are significant, however. All contain information and are included in the reported value. Thus, the term *significant* does not mean *certain*. In any correctly reported measured value, the final digit is significant but not certain. Insignificant digits are never reported. As a chemistry student, you will need to use and recognize significant figures when you work with measured quantities and report your results, and when you evaluate measurements reported by others.

Determining the Number of Significant Figures

When you look at a measured quantity, you need to determine which digits are significant. That process is very easy if the number has no zeros, because all the digits shown are significant. For example, in a number reported as 3.95, all three digits are significant. The significance of zeros in a number depends on their location, however. You need to learn and follow several rules involving zeros. After you have studied the rules in **Figure 3.3**, use them to express the answers in the sample problem that follows.

Problem Solving

REALITY CHECK

The most common mistakes that students make when working with significant figures are

1. Reporting all of the digits given in the calculator readout instead of rounding
2. Not including significant zeros that fall to the right of the decimal point, at the end of a number, for example 2.2560
3. Reporting all leading zeros as significant, for example, 0.005. This number has only one significant figure, 5.

Referencing these common mistakes made in significant figures, ask students if they can draw any "real world" analogies to them.

Example, students may draw the comparison between using all the numbers in a calculator display to answering a question with the correct but also unnecessary or misleading information.

FIGURE 3.3

RULES FOR DETERMINING SIGNIFICANT ZEROS

Rule	Examples
1. Zeros appearing between nonzero digits are significant.	a. 40.7 L has three significant figures. b. 87 009 km has five significant figures.
2. Zeros appearing in front of all nonzero digits are not significant.	a. 0.095 897 m has five significant figures. b. 0.0009 kg has one significant figure.
3. Zeros at the end of a number and to the right of a decimal point are significant.	a. 85.00 g has four significant figures. b. 9.000 000 000 mm has 10 significant figures.
4. Zeros at the end of a number but to the left of a decimal point may or may not be significant. If a zero has not been measured or estimated but is just a placeholder, it is not significant. A decimal point placed after zeros indicates that they are significant.	a. 2000 m may contain from one to four significant figures, depending on how many zeros are placeholders. **For measurements given in this text, assume that 2000 m has one significant figure.** b. 2000. m contains four significant figures, indicated by the presence of the decimal point.

Significant Figures

PREMIUM CONTENT

SolveIt! Cards
HMDScience.com

Sample Problem D **How many significant figures are in each of the following measurements?**

a. 28.6 g
b. 3440. cm
c. 910 m
d. 0.046 04 L
e. 0.006 700 0 kg

 **SOLVE**

Determine the number of significant figures in each measurement using the rules listed in **Figure 3.3.**

a. 28.6 g
There are no zeros, so all three digits are significant.

b. 3440. cm
By rule 4, the zero is significant because it is immediately followed by a decimal point; there are 4 significant figures.

c. 910 m
By rule 4, the zero is not significant; there are 2 significant figures.

d. 0.046 04 L
By rule 2, the first two zeros are not significant; by rule 1, the third zero is significant; there are 4 significant figures.

e. 0.006 700 0 kg
By rule 2, the first three zeros are not significant; by rule 3, the last three zeros are significant; there are 5 significant figures.

Continued

TEACH FROM TABLES

FIGURE 3.3 After going over each of the rules and examples listed in the figure, have students determine the number of significant figures in other values containing zeros. Have them state the rule used in each case. For example, 0.0023 has two significant figures (Rule 2), 70 000. has five (Rule 4), and 6.200 has four (Rule 3).

Classroom Practice

D-1 How many significant figures are there in the measured value 91.0020 m?

Answer: 6

D-2 Express the value of "exactly 15 cm" to three significant figures.

Answer: 15.0 cm

D-3 What is the number of significant figures in 0.092010 kg? Which rules did you apply?

Answer: 5; Rules 1, 2, and 3

TAKING IT FURTHER

Final zeros in a whole number may or may not be significant, depending on the instrument used to make the measurements. For example, suppose the distance between two cities was determined using an instrument that measured to the nearest meter. The length was measured at 540 m. All three of these digits are significant. However, if the instrument used to measure the distance only measured to the nearest hundred meters, then the 5 is the only figure that is significant. For each example, have students provide a scenario which would change the number of significant digits.

Example, in c., if a decimal point appeared after the zero, all three digits would be significant.

▼ Teach continued

Alternative Assessment

Write several numbers on the board. After each number, write the number of digits to which the number is to be rounded. Have students carry out each rounding and justify each answer.

Misconception Alert!

Students typically have difficulty in rounding numbers that are exactly halfway between two numbers. Use examples to show that these numbers are rounded to the nearest even number. Students may also be confused in rounding numbers that contain a 5 but to which the odd/even rule does not apply. For example, the number 1.651 rounded to two digits is 1.7, not 1.6; the fact that 6 is even is irrelevant, given that the number is closer to 1.7 than it is to 1.6.

Answers

Practice D

1. a. 5
   b. 6
   c. 4
   d. 1
   e. 5
   f. 6
2. a. 7000 cm
   b. 7000. cm
   c. 7000.00 cm

Practice Answers in Appendix E

1. Determine the number of significant figures in each of the following.
   a. 804.05 g
   b. 0.014 403 0 km
   c. 1002 m
   d. 400 mL
   e. 30 000. cm
   f. 0.000 625 000 kg
2. Suppose the value "seven thousand centimeters" is reported to you. How should the number be expressed if it is intended to contain the following?
   a. 1 significant figure
   b. 4 significant figures
   c. 6 significant figures

Rounding

When you perform calculations involving measurements, you need to know how to handle significant figures. This is especially true when you are using a calculator to carry out mathematical operations. The answers given on a calculator can be derived results with more digits than are justified by the measurements.

Suppose you used a calculator to divide a measured value of 154 g by a measured value of 327 mL. Each of these values has three significant figures. The calculator would show a numerical answer of 0.470948012. The answer contains digits not justified by the measurements used to calculate it. Such an answer has to be rounded off to make its degree of certainty match that in the original measurements. The answer should be 0.471 g/mL.

The rules for rounding are shown in **Figure 3.4**. The extent of rounding required in a given case depends on whether the numbers are being added, subtracted, multiplied, or divided.

FIGURE 3.4

RULES FOR ROUNDING NUMBERS

If the digit following the last digit to be retained is:	then the last digit should:	Example (rounded to three significant figures)
greater than 5	be increased by 1	42.68 g ⟶ 42.7 g
less than 5	stay the same	17.32 m ⟶ 17.3 m
5, followed by nonzero digit(s)	be increased by 1	2.7851 cm ⟶ 2.79 cm
5, not followed by nonzero digit(s), and preceded by an odd digit	be increased by 1	4.635 kg ⟶ 4.64 kg (because 3 is odd)
5, not followed by nonzero digit(s), and the preceding significant digit is even	stay the same	78.65 mL ⟶ 78.6 mL (because 6 is even)

Differentiated Instruction

BELOW LEVEL

Ask students how old they are. Then have them explain how the ages they gave are examples of rounding. Students should realize that when a student says that he or she is 15 years old, that person is rounding his or her age to a whole number. Point out that if two students are 15 years old, one student is probably older than the other.

INCLUSION

Practice rounding by playing *Rounding Bingo*. Prepare cards for each student, with answers to rounding problems in place of bingo numbers. Numbers must be mixed up and varied from card to card. Call out a question (or draw a slip of paper with the statement on it out of a box) such as: "What is 46.77, rounded to three significant figures?" The first student who finds the correct answer on their card calls out "Bingo!"

Addition or Subtraction with Significant Figures

Consider two mass measurements, 25.1 g and 2.03 g. The first measurement, 25.1 g, has one digit to the right of the decimal point, in the tenths place. There is no information on possible values for the hundredths place. That place is simply blank and cannot be assumed to be zero. The other measurement, 2.03 g, has two digits to the right of the decimal point. It provides information up to and including the hundredths place.

Suppose you were asked to add the two measurements. Simply carrying out the addition would result in an answer of $25.1\ g + 2.03\ g = 27.13\ g$. That answer suggests there is certainty all the way to the hundredths place. However, that result is not justified because the hundredths place in 25.1 g is completely unknown. The answer must be adjusted to reflect the uncertainty in the numbers added.

When adding or subtracting decimals, the answer must have the same number of digits to the right of the decimal point as there are in the measurement having the fewest digits to the right of the decimal point. When you compare the two values 25.1 g and 2.03 g, the measurement with the fewest digits to the right of the decimal point is 25.1 g. It has only one such digit. Following the rule, the answer must be rounded so that it has no more than one digit to the right of the decimal point. The answer should therefore be rounded to 27.1 g.

When working with whole numbers, the answer should be rounded so that the final significant digit is in the same place as the leftmost uncertain digit. For example, $5400 + 365 = 5800$.

Multiplication and Division with Significant Figures

Suppose you calculated the density of an object that has a mass of 3.05 g and a volume of 8.47 mL. The following division on a calculator will give a value of 0.360094451.

$$density = \frac{mass}{volume} = \frac{3.05\ g}{8.47\ mL} = 0.360094451\ g/mL$$

The answer must be rounded to the correct number of significant figures. The values of mass and volume used to obtain the answer have only three significant figures each. The degree of certainty in the calculated result is not justified. *For multiplication or division, the answer can have no more significant figures than are in the measurement with the fewest number of significant figures.* In the calculation just described, the answer, 0.360094451 g/mL, would be rounded to three significant figures to match the significant figures in 8.47 mL and 3.05 g. The answer would thus be 0.360 g/mL.

CHECK FOR UNDERSTANDING

Analyze Suppose you measure the classroom once using a piece of rope you know to be 10 m long and again with a measuring tape marked in m, cm, and mm. You then take the average of the two measurements. Which would determine the number of significant figures in your answer? Explain your answer.

Teaching Tip

For answers to problems in this textbook involving both types of calculations (multiplication/division and addition/subtraction), all calculations of one type were carried out and rounded before switching to calculations of the other type (whose results were also rounded). The more commonly used method is to use all available figures, both significant and insignificant, during intermediate calculations and to round to the correct number of significant figures only when reporting the final result. If an intermediate calculation needs to be reported, it should be rounded for only reporting purposes. The rounded number should not be used in any further calculations. Significant digits in calculations are important only when reporting a number. Be sure to explain to students which method you want them to follow.

Check for Understanding

Answer: The measurement made with the rope would determine the number of significant figures. Because the rope is not marked with smaller units of measurement, it cannot measure as accurately. The least accurate measurement—the one made using the rope—determines the number of significant figures in the answer.

▼ Teach *continued*

Classroom Practice

E-1 Find the volume of a cube that is 3.23 cm on each edge.

Answer: 33.7 cm^3

E-2 What is the sum of 67.14 kg and 8.2 kg?

Answer: 75.3 kg

E-3 Calculate the density of a 17.982 g object that occupies 4.13 cm^3.

Answer: 4.35 g/cm^3

Class Discussion

An example of a simple conversion factor that is not exact is the conversion of time from days to years. Because the year is defined by one revolution of Earth around the sun, it is not an exact value. We generally use 365 days for a year, but a year has 365.25 days if five significant figures are used.

Answers

Practice E

1. 2.156 g
2. 85.6 cm
3. 1.00 μm^2
4. 440 g

Significant Figures

Sample Problem E **Carry out the following calculations. Express each answer to the correct number of significant figures.**

a. 5.44 m − 2.6103 m
b. 2.4 g/mL × 15.82 mL

SOLVE

Carry out each mathematical operation. Follow the rules in **Figures 3.3** and **3.4** for determining significant figures and for rounding.

a. The answer is rounded to 2.83 m, because for subtraction there should be two digits to the right of the decimal point, to match 5.44 m.

b. The answer is rounded to 38 g, because for multiplication there should be two significant figures in the answer, to match 2.4 g/mL.

Practice

1. What is the sum of 2.099 g and 0.05681 g?
2. Calculate the quantity 87.3 cm − 1.655 cm.
3. Calculate the area of a rectangular crystal surface that measures 1.34 μm by 0.7488 μm. (Hint: Recall that *area* = *length* × *width* and is measured in square units.)
4. Polycarbonate plastic has a density of 1.2 g/cm^3. A photo frame is constructed from two 3.0 mm sheets of polycarbonate. Each sheet measures 28 cm by 22 cm. What is the mass of the photo frame?

Conversion Factors and Significant Figures

Earlier in this chapter, you learned how conversion factors are used to change one unit to another. Such conversion factors are typically exact. That is, there is no uncertainty in them. For example, there are exactly 100 cm in a meter. If you were to use the conversion factor 100 cm/m to change meters to centimeters, the 100 would not limit the degree of certainty in the answer. Thus, 4.608 m could be converted to centimeters as follows.

$$4.608 \text{ m} \times \frac{100 \text{ cm}}{\text{m}} = 460.8 \text{ cm}$$

The answer still has four significant figures. Because the conversion factor is considered exact, the answer would not be rounded. Most exact conversion factors are defined, rather than measured, quantities.

Counted numbers also produce conversion factors of unlimited precision. For example, if you counted that there are 10 test tubes for every student, that would produce an exact conversion factor of 10 test tubes/student. There is no uncertainty in that factor.

Problem Solving

TAKE IT FURTHER

Provide students with problems that involve both converting units and performing calculations to arrive at an answer with the correct number of significant figures. For example, ask students to add 10.8 cm and 102 mm or divide 274.1 grams by 0.025 L to get the density in g/mL.

MAIN IDEA

Scientific notation is used to express very large or very small numbers.

In scientific notation, numbers are written in the form $M \times 10^n$, where the factor M is a number greater than or equal to 1 but less than 10, and n is a whole number. For example, to put the quantity 65 000 km in scientific notation and show the first two digits as significant, you would write:

$$6.5 \times 10^4 \text{ km}$$

Writing the *M* factor as 6.5 shows that there are exactly two significant figures. If, instead, you intended the first three digits in 65 000 to be significant, you would write 6.50×10^4 km. When numbers are written in scientific notation, only the significant figures are shown.

Suppose you are expressing a very small quantity, such as the length of a flu virus. In ordinary notation this length could be 0.000 12 mm. That length can be expressed in scientific notation as follows.

$$0.000\,12 \text{ mm} = 1.2 \times 10^{-4} \text{ mm}$$

Move the decimal point four places to the right, and multiply the number by 10^{-4}.

1. Determine *M* by moving the decimal point in the original number to the left or the right so that only one nonzero digit remains to the left of the decimal point.
2. Determine *n* by counting the number of places that you moved the decimal point. If you moved it to the left, *n* is positive. If you moved it to the right, *n* is negative.

Mathematical Operations Using Scientific Notation

1. *Addition and subtraction* These operations can be performed only if the values have the same exponent (*n* factor). If they do not, adjustments must be made to the values so that the exponents are equal. Once the exponents are equal, the *M* factors can be added or subtracted. The exponent of the answer can remain the same, or it may then require adjustment if the *M* factor of the answer has more than one digit to the left of the decimal point. Consider the example of the addition of 4.2×10^4 kg and 7.9×10^3 kg. We can make both exponents either 3 or 4. The following solutions are possible.

$$\begin{array}{r} 4.2 \quad \times 10^4 \text{ kg} \\ +0.79 \times 10^4 \text{ kg} \\ \hline 4.99 \times 10^4 \text{ kg rounded to } 5.0 \times 10^4 \text{ kg} \end{array}$$

or

$$\begin{array}{r} 7.9 \times 10^3 \text{ kg} \\ +42 \quad \times 10^3 \text{ kg} \\ \hline 49.9 \times 10^3 \text{ kg} = 4.99 \times 10^4 \text{ kg rounded to } 5.0 \times 10^4 \text{ kg} \end{array}$$

Note that the units remain kg throughout.

Demonstration

VOLUME AND SIGNIFICANT FIGURES
Measure the length, width, and thickness in centimeters of a small, regular **rectangular prism or cube** (such as a die) that will not float in water. Record each value to one decimal place. Multiply the three values to obtain the volume. Do not round the value obtained. Then submerge the object in a measured amount of **water** in a **graduated cylinder**. Read the new volume in the cylinder. Subtract the final volume measurement from the initial measurement to obtain the volume of the object. The actual value will not match the unrounded result of the original calculation. Point out that there cannot be a net gain in significant information simply as a result of calculation. A calculation result cannot be more precise than the numbers used to generate it.

Teaching Tip

See the Math Tutor at the end of this chapter for more information on using scientific notation in calculations.

ALTERNATIVE APPROACHES

Remind students that moving the decimal point to the left results in a positive exponent. Moving the decimal place to the right results in a negative exponent. Have students explain the reason for this. Point out that by moving the decimal point to the left, the number becomes smaller. This is balanced by increasing the value of the exponent. For example, moving the decimal two places to the left makes the number smaller by a factor of 100. As an example, show how to change 100 to 1 by moving the decimal two places to the left. However, the positive exponent of 2 (10^2) indicates that this smaller number (1) is now multiplied by 100. Therefore, 100 written in scientific notation is 1×10^2. As a result, the value of the number has not changed, only the way in which it is written.

▼ Teach *continued*

TEACH FROM VISUALS

FIGURE 3.5 Emphasize that the number displayed on the calculator is expressed in scientific notation. If possible, use a calculator designed for use on an overhead projector to demonstrate the technique of working with numbers in scientific notation. Be sure students with calculators that use different keystrokes know how to work with scientific notation on their particular calculators.

FIGURE 3.5

Significant Figures and Calculators When you use a scientific calculator to work problems in scientific notation, don't forget to express the value on the display to the correct number of significant figures and show the units when you write the final answer.

5.44 [EE] 7 [÷] 8.1 [EE] 4 [ENTER]
671.6049383
rounded to 6.7×10^2 g/mol

5.44 [EXP] 7 [÷] 8.1 [EXP] 4 [=]
671.6049383
rounded to 6.7×10^2 g/mol

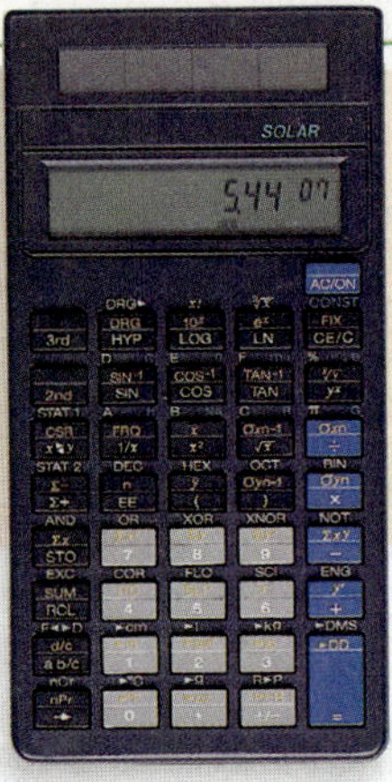

2. *Multiplication* The *M* factors are multiplied, and the exponents are added algebraically.

   Consider the multiplication of 5.23×10^6 µm by 7.1×10^{-2} µm.

$$\begin{aligned}(5.23 \times 10^6\ \mu\text{m})(7.1 \times 10^{-2}\ \mu\text{m}) &= (5.23 \times 7.1)(10^6 \times 10^{-2})\\ &= 37.133 \times 10^4\ \mu\text{m}^2 \text{ (adjust to two significant digits)}\\ &= 3.7 \times 10^5\ \mu\text{m}^2\end{aligned}$$

   Note that when length measurements are multiplied, the result is area. The unit is now μm^2.

3. *Division* The *M* factors are divided, and the exponent of the denominator is subtracted from that of the numerator. The calculator keystrokes for this problem are shown in **Figure 3.5**.

$$\begin{aligned}\frac{5.44 \times 10^7\ \text{g}}{8.1 \times 10^4\ \text{mol}} &= \frac{5.44}{8.1} \times 10^{7-4}\ \text{g/mol}\\ &= 0.6716049383 \times 10^3 \text{ (adjust to two significant digits)}\\ &= 6.7 \times 10^2\ \text{g/mol}\end{aligned}$$

   Note that the unit for the answer is the ratio of grams to moles.

MAIN IDEA

Sample problems are guides to solving similar types of problems.

Learning to analyze and solve such problems requires practice and a logical approach. In this section, you will review a process that can help you analyze problems effectively. Most sample problems in this book are organized by four basic steps to guide your thinking in how to work out the solution to a problem.

Problem Solving

REALITY CHECK

The most common error that students make in entering numbers in scientific notation can be illustrated as follows. Many students enter 5.44×10^7 as 5.44, followed by ×, then 10, then EE, and then 7. Of course, this gives 5.44×10^8. Students need to be warned that the EE button already *includes* the "× 10." Another common error is pressing the "−" (for subtract) button when they are trying to change the sign of a quantity, especially to get a negative exponent, as in 3.4×10^{-3}.

Step 1. Analyze

The first step in solving a quantitative word problem is to read the problem carefully at least twice and to analyze the information in it. Note any important descriptive terms that clarify or add meaning to the problem. Identify and list the data given in the problem. Also identify the unknown—the quantity you are asked to find.

Step 2. Plan

The second step is to develop a plan for solving the problem. The plan should show how the information given is to be used to find the unknown. In the process, reread the problem to make sure you have gathered all the necessary information. It is often helpful to draw a picture that represents the problem. For example, if you were asked to determine the volume of a crystal given its dimensions, you could draw a representation of the crystal and label the dimensions. This drawing would help you visualize the problem.

Decide which conversion factors, mathematical formulas, or chemical principles you will need to solve the problem. Your plan might suggest a single calculation or a series of them involving different conversion factors. Once you understand how you need to proceed, you may wish to sketch out the route you will take, using arrows to point the way from one stage of the solution to the next. Sometimes you will need data that are not actually part of the problem statement. For instance, you'll often use data from the periodic table.

Step 3. Solve

The third step involves substituting the data and necessary conversion factors into the plan you have developed. At this stage you calculate the answer, cancel units, and round the result to the correct number of significant figures. It is very important to have a plan worked out in step 2 before you start using the calculator. All too often, students start multiplying or dividing values given in the problem before they really understand what they need to do to get an answer.

Step 4. Check Your Work

Examine your answer to determine whether it is reasonable. Use the following methods, when appropriate, to carry out the evaluation.

1. Check to see that the units are correct. If they are not, look over the setup. Are the conversion factors correct?
2. Make an estimate of the expected answer. Use simpler, rounded numbers to do so. Compare the estimate with your actual result. The two should be similar.
3. Check the order of magnitude in your answer. Does it seem reasonable compared with the values given in the problem? If you calculated the density of vegetable oil and got a value of 54.9 g/mL, you should know that something is wrong. Oil floats on water.

Teaching Tip

Sample Problems are presented in a series of steps to model how students should approach problems. All too often, students pull numbers from the problems and wonder if they should multiply or divide without thinking about the problem statement. Emphasize problem analysis when working through examples in class. Once students learn to analyze problems successfully, they can drop the formality of the four steps. For many students, this stage in their learning may take the full year. Refer students to Appendix C in their text for a discussion of how to use Sample Problems when studying.

Differentiated Instruction

BELOW LEVEL

Give students a blank problem-solving template to use when working problems. Use the sample problem in the text as a guide to constructing the template. Be sure to include important hints. A sample template might include the following:

Analyze (Read the problem; identify the values that are given and those that you are trying to find; give the units for each value.):

Given -

Unknown -

Plan (What equations and conversion factors might you need to work this problem?)

Solve (Substitute given values for the variables in the equation; calculate your answer)

Check Your Work (Try putting your answer into the equation with one of the Given values; solve to see if you get the other Given value. Look back at the Unknown and make certain that your answer has the correct unit.).

Have students use this template every time they work a problem, so that they will internalize and become comfortable with this process.

▼ Teach *continued*

Alternative Assessment

Ask students to explain each step involved in problem solving. Then have students work at the board, perhaps in competing teams, to solve practice problems according to the analyze, plan, compute, and evaluate sequence of steps. Have the students constructively critique one another's solution strategies and setups.

Classroom Practice

F-1 Calculate the density of a liquid, given that 41.4 mL of it has a mass of 58.24 g.

Answer: 1.41 g/mL

F-2 How many kilometers are there in 6.2×10^7 cm?

Answer: 6.2×10^2 km

F-3 How many hours are there in exactly 3 weeks?

Answer: 504 hours

Answers

Practice F

1. 9.69 mL
2. 1.67 g/cm^3
3. 5.12×10^{11} mm
4. 5.2×10^3 s

Therefore, its density is less than water. So, the value obtained should be less than 1.0 g/mL.

4. Be sure that the answer given for any problem is expressed using the correct number of significant figures.

Look over the following quantitative Sample Problem. Notice how the four-step approach is used, and then apply the approach yourself in solving the practice problems that follow.

PREMIUM CONTENT
Learn It! Video HMDScience.com
Solve It! Cards HMDScience.com

Solving Problems Using the Four-Step Approach

Sample Problem F **Calculate the volume of a sample of aluminum that has a mass of 3.057 kg. The density of aluminum is 2.70 g/cm^3.**

1 ANALYZE

Given: mass = 3.057 kg, density = 2.70 g/cm^3

Unknown: volume of aluminum

2 PLAN

The density unit in the problem is g/cm^3, and the mass given in the problem is expressed in kg. Therefore, in addition to using the density equation, you will need a conversion factor representing the relationship between grams and kilograms.

$$1000 \text{ g} = 1 \text{ kg}$$

Also, rearrange the density equation to solve for volume.

$$density = \frac{mass}{volume} \quad \text{or} \quad D = \frac{m}{V}$$

$$V = \frac{m}{D}$$

3 SOLVE

$$V = \frac{3.057 \text{ kg}}{2.70 \text{ g/cm}^3} \times \frac{1000 \text{ g}}{\text{kg}} = 1132.222\ldots \text{ cm}^3 \text{ (calculator answer)}$$

The answer should be rounded to three significant figures.

$$V = 1.13 \times 10^3 \text{ cm}^3$$

4 CHECK YOUR WORK

The unit of volume, cm^3, is correct. An order-of-magnitude estimate would put the answer at over 1000 cm^3.

$$\frac{3}{2} \times 1000$$

The correct number of significant figures is three, which matches that in 2.70 g/cm^3.

Practice Answers in Appendix E

1. What is the volume, in milliliters, of a sample of helium that has a mass of 1.73×10^{-3} g, given that the density is 0.178 47 g/L?
2. What is the density of a piece of metal that has a mass of 6.25×10^5 g and is 92.5 cm × 47.3 cm × 85.4 cm?
3. How many millimeters are there in 5.12×10^5 kilometers?
4. A clock gains 0.020 second per minute. How many seconds will the clock gain in exactly six months, assuming exactly 30 days per month?

Problem Solving

DECONSTRUCTING PROBLEMS

Until students become used to working problems in a step-by-step manner, it will help if you lead them through the process. Make sure that students do not have their textbooks open, and then write Sample Problem F on the board. Ask students what the problem is asking them to find. Write the correct answer on the board. volume Next, ask students to identify the given values and write those answers on the board. mass and density of aluminum Have students take a closer look at the two given values. Ask if students notice anything about the units for these two values. Answers will vary. Students should indicate that while one given value indicates mass in grams, the other uses kilograms. Ask students what conversion factor will be needed to change kilograms to grams. Have them identify what equation will be needed to solve the problem. *density = mass/volume* Have students rearrange the density equation to solve for volume. Finally, have students outline the steps they would take to solve the problem. Have them make certain they have the correct units on their final answer.

MAIN IDEA

Variables that are directly proportional increase or decrease by the same factor.

Two quantities are directly proportional to each other if dividing one by the other gives a constant value. For example, if the masses and volumes of different samples of aluminum are measured, the masses and volumes will be directly proportional to each other. As the masses of the samples increase, their volumes increase by the same factor, as you can see from the data. Doubling the mass doubles the volume. Halving the mass halves the volume.

When two variables, x and y, are directly proportional to each other, the relationship can be expressed as $y \propto x$, which is read as "y is *proportional* to x." The general equation for a directly proportional relationship between the two variables can also be written as follows.

$$\frac{y}{x} = k$$

The value of k is a constant called the proportionality constant. Written in this form, the equation expresses an important fact about direct proportion: the ratio between the variables remains constant. Note that using the mass and volume values in **Figure 3.6** gives a mass-volume ratio that is constant (neglecting measurement error). The equation can be rearranged into the following form.

$$y = kx$$

The equation $y = kx$ may look familiar to you. It is the equation for a special case of a straight line. If two variables related in this way are graphed versus one another, a straight line, or linear plot that passes through the origin, results. The data for aluminum from **Figure 3.6** are graphed in **Figure 3.7**. The mass and volume of a pure substance are directly proportional to each other. Consider mass to be y and volume to be x. The constant ratio, k, for the two variables is density. The slope of the line reflects the constant density, or mass-volume ratio.

FIGURE 3.6

MASS-VOLUME DATA FOR ALUMINUM AT 20°C

Mass (g)	Volume (cm^3)	$\frac{m}{V}$ (g/cm^3)
54.7	20.1	2.72
65.7	24.4	2.69
83.5	30.9	2.70
96.3	35.8	2.69
105.7	39.1	2.70

FIGURE 3.7

Mass vs. Volume The graph of mass versus volume shows a relationship of direct proportion. Notice that the line is extrapolated to pass through the origin.

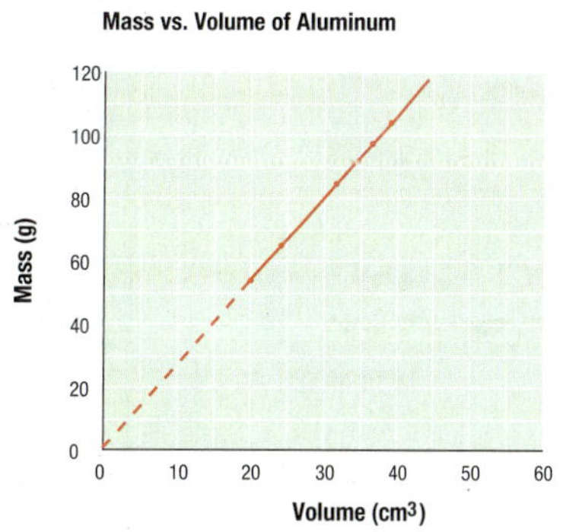

TEACH FROM VISUALS

FIGURE 3.7 Have each student choose a mass of aluminum that is not listed in **Figure 3.6** but lies on the line shown on the graph. Have the students use the graph to find the corresponding volume. Students should then be able to calculate the density of aluminum for their chosen samples and compare these values with those in **Figure 3.6.**

Misconception Alert!

Students may make the common error of thinking that all linear plots represent direct proportions. Point out that only straight lines that pass through the origin (0, 0) represent direct proportions. You can illustrate that fact by drawing a linear graph that does not pass through the origin and then showing that the ratio for the two variables does not remain constant.

Differentiated Instruction

ENGLISH LEARNERS

Although students have not yet studied the gas laws at this point, a balloon can help them understand direct and indirect proportionality. Show students an inflated balloon with a tied neck. Explain that *directly proportional* means that as one value increases, the other one increases—or that as one value decreases, the other decreases. *Inversely proportional* means that as one value increases, the other decreases—or that as one decreases, the other increases. Ask what would happen to the volume (or size) of the balloon if it was carried from a cool, air-conditioned building out into a hot, muggy summer day. volume will increase Ask students if volume and temperature are directly or inversely proportional. directly proportional Then ask what would happen to the volume of the balloon if someone gently sat on it. volume will decrease Sitting on a balloon also changes its pressure. How does the pressure change? pressure increases Are volume and pressure directly proportional or inversely proportional? Explain. They are inversely proportional; as the volume decreases the pressure increases.

▼ Teach *continued*

TEACH FROM TABLES

FIGURE 3.8 Use the table to show that the products of the two variables—pressure and volume—remain essentially equal, which is the criterion for an inverse relationship. Have students attempt to plot the values before they look at **Figure 3.9** on the next page, which displays the correct plot.

For aluminum, this value is 2.70 g/cm^3 at 20°C. Notice also that the plotted line passes through the origin (0,0). All directly proportional relationships produce linear graphs that pass through the origin.

MAIN IDEA

Quantities are inversely proportional if one decreases in value when the other increases.

Two quantities are **inversely proportional** to each other if their product is constant. An example of an inversely proportional relationship is that between speed of travel and the time required to cover a fixed distance. The greater the speed, the less time that is needed to go a certain fixed distance. Doubling the speed cuts the required time in half. Halving the speed doubles the required time.

When two variables, x and y, are inversely proportional to each other, the relationship can be expressed as follows.

$$y \propto \frac{1}{x}$$

This is read "y is *proportional* to 1 divided by x." The general equation for an inversely proportional relationship between the two variables can be written in the following form.

$$xy = k$$

In the equation, k is the proportionality constant. If x increases, y must decrease by the same factor to keep the product constant.

When the temperature of a sample of nitrogen is kept constant, the volume (V) of the gas sample decreases as the pressure (P) increases, as shown in **Figure 3.8**. Note that $P \times V$ gives a reasonably constant value. Thus, P and V are inversely proportional to each other. The graph of this data is shown in **Figure 3.9**. A graph of variables that are inversely proportional produces a curve called a *hyperbola*.

FIGURE 3.8

PRESSURE-VOLUME DATA FOR NITROGEN AT CONSTANT TEMPERATURE

Pressure (kPa)	Volume (cm^3)	$P \times V$
100	500	50 000
150	333	50 000
200	250	50 000
250	200	50 000
300	166	49 800
350	143	50 100
400	125	50 000
450	110	49 500

Differentiated Instruction

BELOW LEVEL

If students are struggling to understand the abstract concept of inverse proportionality, give them a visual image to associate with it. Draw a picture of a see-saw on the board. Write the letter representing one variable on one end of the see-saw and the second variable on the other end of the see-saw. When one person on a see-saw goes up, the other person has to go down. When the first person goes down, the second goes up. Each person's position is always the inverse, or opposite, of the other person's. Tell students to apply this "see-saw rule" to problems in which they are asked to determine direct or inverse proportionality. If they increase the value of one variable by doubling it, does the other variable double in value as well (that end of the see-saw goes up), or does it decrease by half (the other end of the see-saw goes down)? It decreases by half.

FIGURE 3.9

Volume vs. Pressure The graph of volume versus pressure shows an inversely proportional relationship. The curve is called a hyperbola. Note the difference between the shape of this graph and that of the graph in **Figure 3.7.**

CRITICAL THINKING

Apply For this graph, if $V \propto 1/x$, what does x represent?

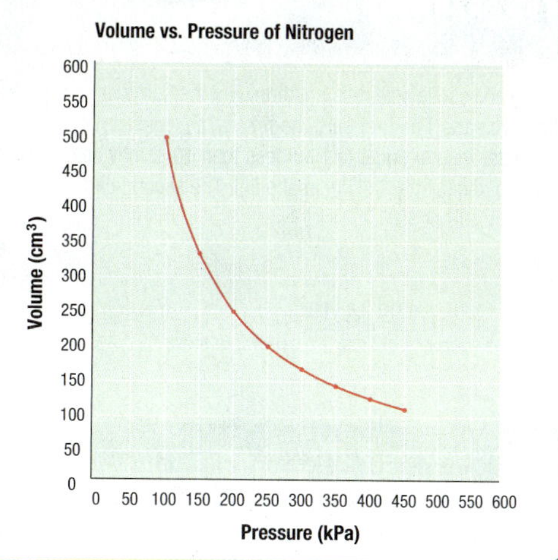

Assess and Reteach ▼

Assess Use the Formative Assessment on this page to evaluate student mastery of the section.

Reteach For students who need additional instruction, download the Section Study Guide.

Response to Intervention To reassess students' mastery, use the Section Quiz available to print or to take directly online at **HMDScience.com**.

SECTION 3 FORMATIVE ASSESSMENT

Reviewing Main Ideas

1. The density of copper is listed as 8.94 g/cm^3. Two students each make three density determinations of samples of the substance. Student A's results are 7.3 g/mL, 9.4 g/mL, and 8.3 g/mL. Student B's results are 8.4 g/cm^3, 8.8 g/cm^3, and 8.0 g/cm^3. Compare the two sets of results in terms of precision and accuracy.

2. Determine the number of significant figures.
   a. 6.002 cm
   b. 0.0020 m
   c. 10.0500 g
   d. 7000 kg
   e. 7000. kg

3. Round 2.6765 to two significant figures.

4. Carry out the following calculations.
   a. 52.13 g + 1.7502 g
   b. 12 m × 6.41 m
   c. $\frac{16.25\text{ g}}{5.1442\text{ mL}}$

5. Perform the following operations. Express each answer in scientific notation.
   a. $(1.54 \times 10^{-2}\text{ g}) + (2.86 \times 10^{-1}\text{ g})$
   b. $(7.023 \times 10^{9}\text{ g}) - (6.62 \times 10^{7}\text{ g})$
   c. $(8.99 \times 10^{-4}\text{ m}) \times (3.57 \times 10^{4}\text{ m})$
   d. $\frac{2.17 \times 10^{-3}\text{ g}}{5.002 \times 10^{4}\text{ mL}}$

6. Write the following numbers in scientific notation.
   a. 560 000
   b. 33 400
   c. 0.000 4120

7. A student measures the mass of a beaker filled with corn oil. The mass reading averages 215.6 g. The mass of the beaker is 110.4 g.
   a. What is the mass of the corn oil?
   b. What is the density of the corn oil if its volume is 114 cm^3?

8. Calculate the mass of gold that occupies 5.0×10^{-3} cm^3. The density of gold is 19.3 g/cm^3.

9. What is the difference between a graph representing data that are directly proportional and a graph of data that are inversely proportional?

Critical Thinking

10. **APPLYING CONCEPTS** The mass of a liquid is 11.50 g, and its volume is 9.03 mL. How many significant figures should its density value have? Explain the reason for your answer.

Answers to Section Assessment

1. Student B's results are more precise and more accurate.
2. **a.** 4
   b. 2
   c. 6
   d. 1
   e. 4
3. 2.7
4. **a.** 53.88 g
   b. 77 m^2
   c. 3.159 g/mL
5. **a.** 3.01×10^{-1} g
   b. 6.967×10^{9} g
   c. 3.21×10^{1} m^2
   d. 4.32×10^{-8} g/mL
6. **a.** 5.6×10^{5}
   b. 3.34×10^{4}
   c. 4.120×10^{-4}
7. **a.** 105.2 g
   b. 0.923 g/cm^3
8. 9.6×10^{-2} g
9. directly proportional: straight line that passes through the origin; inversely proportional: hyperbola
10. The density value should have three significant figures, because 9.03 mL has only three significant figures.

Answers

1. a. 7.45×10^{-5} g
   b. 5.984102×10^{6} nm
2. a. -9.11×10^{3}
   b. 8.25×10^{-2}

Math Tutor | Scientific Notation

Any value expressed in scientific notation, whether large or small, has two parts. The first part, the *first factor*, consists of a number greater than or equal to 1 but less than 10. It may have any number of digits after the decimal point. The second part consists of a power of 10.

$$6.02 \times 10^{23}$$

first factor: 6.02; power of ten: 10^{23}; exponent: 23

To write the first part, move the decimal point to the right or the left so that there is only one nonzero digit to the left of the decimal point. The second part is written as an exponent, which is determined by counting the number of places the decimal point must be moved. If it is moved to the right, the exponent is negative. If it is moved to the left, the exponent is positive.

Problem-Solving TIPS

- In addition and subtraction, all values must first be converted to numbers that have the same exponent of 10. The result is the sum or the difference of the first factors, multiplied by the same exponent of 10. Finally, the result should be rounded to the correct number of significant figures and expressed in scientific notation.
- In multiplication, the first factors are multiplied and the exponents of 10 are added.
- In division, the *first factors* of the numbers are divided, and the exponent of 10 in the denominator is subtracted from the exponent of 10 in the numerator.

Sample Problems

Write 299 800 000 m/s in scientific notation.

The decimal must move to the left 8 places, which indicates a positive exponent.

299 800 000. m/s
8 7 6 5 4 3 2 1

The value in scientific notation is 2.998×10^{8} m/s.

Solve the following equation and write the answer in scientific notation.

$(3.1 \times 10^{3})(5.21 \times 10^{4})$

Multiply the first factors, and then add the exponents of 10.

$(3.1 \times 5.21) \times 10^{(3+4)} = 16 \times 10^{7} = 1.6 \times 10^{8}$

Practice

1. Rewrite the following numbers in scientific notation.
   a. 0.0000745 g
   b. 5984102 nm
2. Solve the following equations, and write the answers in scientific notation.
   a. $1.017 \times 10^{3} - 1.013 \times 10^{4}$
   b. $\dfrac{9.27 \times 10^{4}}{11.24 \times 10^{5}}$

CHAPTER 2 Summary

Review Games
Concept Maps

SECTION 1 Scientific Method

- The scientific method is a logical approach to solving problems that lend themselves to investigation.
- A hypothesis is a testable statement that serves as the basis for predictions and further experiments.
- A theory is a broad generalization that explains a body of known facts or phenomena.

KEY TERMS

scientific method
system
hypothesis
model
theory

SECTION 2 Units of Measurement

- The result of nearly every measurement is a number and a unit.
- The SI system of measurement is used in science. It has seven base units: the meter (length), kilogram (mass), second (time), kelvin (temperature), mole (amount of substance), ampere (electric current), and candela (luminous intensity).
- Weight is a measure of the gravitational pull on matter.
- Derived SI units include the square meter (area) and the cubic meter (volume).
- Density is the ratio of mass to volume.
- Conversion factors are used to convert from one unit to another.

KEY TERMS

quantity
SI
weight
derived unit
volume
density
conversion factor
dimensional analysis

SECTION 3 Using Scientific Measurements

- Accuracy refers to the closeness of a measurement to the correct or accepted value. Precision refers to the closeness of values for a set of measurements.
- Percentage error is the difference between the experimental and the accepted value that is divided by the accepted value and then multiplied by 100.
- The significant figures in a number consist of all digits known with certainty plus one final digit, which is uncertain.
- After addition or subtraction, the answer should be rounded so that it has no more digits to the right of the decimal point than there are in the measurement that has the smallest number of digits to the right of the decimal point. After multiplication or division, the answer should be rounded so that it has no more significant figures than there are in the measurement that has the fewest number of significant figures.
- Exact conversion factors are completely certain and do not limit the number of digits in a calculation.
- A number written in scientific notation is of the form $M \times 10^n$, in which M is greater than or equal to 1 but less than 10, and n is an integer.
- Two quantities are directly proportional to each other if dividing one by the other yields a constant value. Two quantities are inversely proportional to each other if their product has a constant value.

KEY TERMS

accuracy
precision
percentage error
significant figures
scientific notation
directly proportional
inversely proportional

CHAPTER REVIEW

Review Answers

1. Quantitative information is numerical; qualitative information is non-numerical.
2. a testable statement that serves as a basis for making predictions and carrying out further experiments
3. **a.** a visual, verbal, or mathematical explanation of how phenomena occur and data are related
   b. A model, if it is successful, may become part of a theory. A theory is much broader than a model.
4. to have universal agreement and avoid confusion
5. A quantity, such as volume or mass, is something with magnitude, size, or amount. A unit, such as liter or gram, compares what is to be measured to a previously defined size.
6. meter, length; kilogram, mass; second, time; kelvin, temperature; mole, amount of substance; ampere, electric current; candela, luminous intensity
7. **a.** 1000 or 10^3
   b. $\frac{1}{100}$ or 10^{-2}
   c. 1 000 000 or 10^6
   d. $\frac{1}{1\,000\,000}$ or 10^{-6}
   e. $\frac{1}{1000}$ or 10^{-3}
8. **a.** meter
   b. millimeter or centimeter
   c. kilometer
   d. micrometer
9. **a.** kilogram
   b. gram
   c. gram
10. Fundamental units must be unvarying, but day length depends on Earth's rotation rate, which is not constant.
11. **a.** a unit that can be obtained from combinations of fundamental units
    b. the square meter (m^2)
12. **a.** cubic meter, cubic centimeter
    b. liter = 1000 cm^3; milliliter is equal to 1 cm^3

CHAPTER 2 Review

SECTION 1

Scientific Method

REVIEWING MAIN IDEAS

1. How does quantitative information differ from qualitative information?
2. What is a hypothesis?
3. **a.** What is a model in the scientific sense?
   b. How does a model differ from a theory?

SECTION 2

Units of Measurement

REVIEWING MAIN IDEAS

4. Why is it important for a measurement system to have an international standard?
5. How does a quantity differ from a unit? Use two examples to explain the difference.
6. List the seven SI base units and the quantities they represent.
7. What is the numerical equivalent of each of the following SI prefixes?
   a. kilo-
   b. centi-
   c. mega-
   d. micro-
   e. milli-
8. Identify the SI unit that would be most appropriate for expressing the length of the following.
   a. width of a gymnasium
   b. length of a finger
   c. distance between your town and the closest border of the next state
   d. length of a bacterial cell
9. Identify the SI unit that would be most appropriate for measuring the mass of each of the following objects.
   a. table
   b. coin
   c. a 250 mL beaker
10. Explain why the second is not defined by the length of the day.
11. **a.** What is a derived unit?
    b. What is the SI-derived unit for area?
12. **a.** List two SI-derived units for volume.
    b. List two non-SI units for volume, and explain how they relate to the cubic centimeter.
13. **a.** Why are the units that are used to express the densities of gases different from those used to express the densities of solids or liquids?
    b. Name two units for density.
    c. Why is the temperature at which density is measured usually specified?
14. **a.** Which of the solids listed in **Figure 2.8** will float on water?
    b. Which of the liquids will sink in milk?
15. **a.** Define *conversion factor*.
    b. Explain how conversion factors are used.

PRACTICE PROBLEMS

16. What is the volume, in cubic meters, of a rectangular solid that is 0.25 m long, 6.1 m wide, and 4.9 m high?
17. Find the density of a material, given that a 5.03 g sample occupies 3.24 mL. (Hint: See Sample Problem A.)
18. What is the mass of a sample of material that has a volume of 55.1 cm^3 and a density of 6.72 g/cm^3?
19. A sample of a substance that has a density of 0.824 g/mL has a mass of 0.451 g. Calculate the volume of the sample.
20. How many grams are in 882 μg? (Hint: See Sample Problem B.)
21. Calculate the number of milliliters in 0.603 L.
22. The density of gold is 19.3 g/cm^3.
    a. What is the volume, in cubic centimeters, of a sample of gold that has a mass of 0.715 kg?
    b. If this sample of gold is a cube, what is the length of each edge in centimeters?
23. **a.** Find the number of kilometers in 92.25 m.
    b. Convert the answer in kilometers to centimeters.

13. **a.** Smaller units are used because gases are less dense.
    b. g/cm^3, g/L
    c. Temperature affects volume.
14. **a.** cork, butter, ice
    b. mercury
15. **a.** a ratio that is derived from the equality between different units that can be used to convert from one unit to another unit
    b. The unit to be changed is multiplied by a conversion factor that has the desired unit in the numerator and the unit to be canceled in the denominator.
16. 7.5 m^3
17. 1.55 g/mL
18. 3.70×10^2 g
19. 0.547 mL
20. 8.82×10^{-4} g
21. 6.03×10^2 mL
22. **a.** 37.0 cm^3
    b. 3.33 cm
23. **a.** 9.225×10^{-2} km
    b. 9.225×10^3 cm

SECTION 3

Using Scientific Measurements

 REVIEWING MAIN IDEAS

24. Compare accuracy and precision.

25. a. Write the equation that is used to calculate percentage error.
    b. Under what condition will percentage error be negative?

26. How is the average for a set of values calculated?

27. What is meant by a mass measurement expressed in this form: 4.6 g ± 0.2 g?

28. Suppose a graduated cylinder were not correctly calibrated. How would this affect the results of a measurement? How would it affect the results of a calculation using this measurement?

29. Round each of the following measurements to the number of significant figures indicated.
    a. 67.029 g to three significant figures
    b. 0.15 L to one significant figure
    c. 52.8005 mg to five significant figures
    d. 3.174 97 mol to three significant figures

30. State the rules governing the number of significant figures that result from each of the following operations.
    a. addition and subtraction
    b. multiplication and division

31. What is the general form for writing numbers in scientific notation?

32. a. By using x and y, state the general equation for quantities that are directly proportional.
    b. For two directly proportional quantities, what happens to one variable when the other variable increases?

33. a. State the general equation for quantities, x and y, that are inversely proportional.
    b. For two inversely proportional quantities, what happens to one variable when the other increases?

34. Arrange in the correct order the following four basic steps for finding the solution to a problem: check your work, analyze, solve, and plan.

PRACTICE PROBLEMS

35. A student measures the mass of a sample as 9.67 g. Calculate the percentage error, given that the correct mass is 9.82 g. (Hint: See Sample Problem C.)

36. A handbook gives the density of calcium as 1.54 g/cm^3. Based on lab measurements, what is the percentage error of a density calculation of 1.25 g/cm^3?

37. What is the percentage error of a length measurement of 0.229 cm if the correct value is 0.225 cm?

38. How many significant figures are in each of the following measurements? (Hint: See Sample Problem D.)
    a. 0.4004 mL
    b. 6000 g
    c. 1.000 30 km
    d. 400. mm

39. Calculate the sum of 6.078 g and 0.3329 g.

40. Subtract 7.11 cm from 8.2 cm. (Hint: See Sample Problem E.)

41. What is the product of 0.8102 m and 3.44 m?

42. Divide 94.20 g by 3.167 22 mL.

43. Write the following numbers in scientific notation.
    a. 0.000 673 0
    b. 50 000.0
    c. 0.000 003 010

44. The following numbers are in scientific notation. Write them in ordinary notation.
    a. 7.050×10^3 g
    b. $4.000\,05 \times 10^7$ mg
    c. $2.350\,0 \times 10^4$ mL

45. Perform the following operation. Express the answer in scientific notation and with the correct number of significant figures.
    0.002115 m × 0.0000405 m

46. A sample of a certain material has a mass of 2.03×10^{-3} g. Calculate the volume of the sample, given that the density is 9.133×10^{-1} g/cm^3. Use the four-step method to solve the problem. (Hint: See Sample Problem F.)

24. Accuracy refers to the closeness of measurements to the correct or accepted value. Precision refers to the closeness of a set of measurements to one another.

25. a. $\% \text{ error} = \dfrac{value_{exp.} - value_{acc.}}{value_{accepted}} \times 100$
    b. if the experimental value is lower than the accepted value

26. by adding the values and dividing by the number of values

27. between 4.4 and 4.8 g

28. It would introduce error in the measurement and any subsequent calculations.

29. a. 67.0 g
    b. 0.2 L
    c. 52.800 mg
    d. 3.17 mol

30. a. The answer must have the same number of digits to the right of the decimal point as there are in the measurement that has the fewest digits to the right of the decimal point.
    b. The answer can have no more significant figures than are in the measurement with the fewest number of significant figures.

31. $M \times 10^n$, where M is greater than or equal to 1 but less than 10 and n is a whole number

32. a. $y/x = k$, or $y = kx$
    b. It increases by the same factor.

33. a. $xy = k$
    b. It decreases by the same factor.

34. analyze, plan, solve, check your work

35. −1.5%

36. −19%

37. 2%

38. a. four
    b. one
    c. six
    d. three

39. 6.411 g

40. 1.1 cm

41. 2.79 m^2

42. 29.74 g/mL

43. a. 6.730×10^{-4}
    b. $5.000\,00 \times 10^4$
    c. 3.010×10^{-6}

44. a. 7050 g
    b. 40 000 500 mg
    c. 23 500 mL

45. 8.57×10^{-8} m^2

46. 2.22×10^{-3} cm^3

47. rewritten numbers: 1.006×10^2 kg, 9.64×10^1 kg; final answer: 4.2 kg

48. 1.4×10^6 m^3

49. 1.43 g/cm^3

50. 9.47×10^{-4} g; 9.47×10^{-7} kg

51. −13.5%

52. Li = 1.47×10^7 pm^3
Na = 2.70×10^7 pm^3
K = 5.44×10^7 pm^3
Rb = 6.39×10^7 pm^3
Cs = 7.80×10^7 pm^3
Fr = 8.24×10^7 pm^3

53. 1.34×10^8 Na atoms

54. a. 1.01 g/cm^3

b. 4%

55. SI is the modern, more-simplified form of the metric system that has seven base units as its foundation. The older metric system was based on standards for length, time, capacity (volume), and mass. Use of SI in the United States allows a greater marketability for this country's goods and services throughout the world.

56. ISO, which is the International Standards Organization in Geneva, Switzerland, promotes international uniformity of standards in the technical fields.

57. Density data for some metals are found in Appendix A. The following metals are suggested for this activity: Zn, Fe, W, Mg, Cr, and Pb.

58. a. 15 Calories (fat)/2 g (fat) = 8 Cal (fat)/g (fat)

b. 0.6 kg

c. 2×10^6 μg

d. One; the value 2 g limits the number of significant figures for these data.

CHAPTER REVIEW

Mixed Review

47. A man finds that he has a mass of 100.6 kg. He goes on a diet, and several months later he finds that he has a mass of 96.4 kg. Express each number in scientific notation, and calculate the number of kilograms the man has lost by dieting.

48. A large office building is 1.07×10^2 m long, 31 m wide, and 4.25×10^2 m high. What is its volume?

49. An object has a mass of 57.6 g. Find the object's density, given that its volume is 40.25 cm^3.

50. A lab worker measures the mass of some sucrose as 0.947 mg. Convert that quantity to grams and to kilograms.

51. A student calculates the density of iron as 6.80 g/cm^3 by using lab data for mass and volume. A handbook reveals that the correct value is 7.86 g/cm^3. What is the percentage error?

USING THE HANDBOOK

52. Find the table of properties for Group 1 elements in the *Elements Handbook* (Appendix A). Calculate the volume of a single atom of each element listed in the table by using the equation for the volume of a sphere.

$$\frac{4}{3}\pi \cdot r^3$$

53. Use the radius of a sodium atom from the *Elements Handbook* (Appendix A) to calculate the number of sodium atoms in a row 5.00 cm long. Assume that each sodium atom touches the ones next to it.

54. a. A block of sodium that has the measurements 3.00 cm × 5.00 cm × 5.00 cm has a mass of 75.5 g. Calculate the density of sodium.

b. Compare your calculated density with the value in the properties table for Group 1 elements. Calculate the percentage error for your density determination.

RESEARCH AND WRITING

55. How does the metric system, which was once a standard for measurement, differ from SI? Why was it necessary for the United States to change to SI?

56. What are ISO 9000 standards? How do they affect industry on an international level?

ALTERNATIVE ASSESSMENT

57. Performance Obtain three metal samples from your teacher. Determine the mass and volume of each sample. Calculate the density of each metal from your measurement data. (Hint: Consider using the water displacement technique to measure the volume of your samples.)

58. Use the data from the Nutrition Facts label below to answer the following questions:

a. Use the data given on the label for grams of fat and calories from fat to construct a conversion factor that has the units calories per gram.

b. Calculate the mass in kilograms for 20 servings of the food.

c. Calculate the mass of protein in micrograms for one serving of the food.

d. What is the correct number of significant figures for the answer in item a? Why?

Nutrition Facts
Serving Size ¾ cup (30g)
Servings Per Container About 14

Amount Per Serving	Corn Crunch	with ½ cup skim milk
Calories	120	160
Calories from Fat	15	20
	% Daily Value**	
Total Fat 2g*	3%	3%
Saturated Fat 0g	0%	0%
Cholesterol 0mg	0%	1%
Sodium 160mg	7%	9%
Potassium 65mg	2%	8%
Total Carbohydrate 25g	8%	10%
Dietary Fiber 3g		
Sugars 3g		
Other Carbohydrate 11g		
Protein 2g		

*Amount in Cereal. A serving of cereal plus skim milk provides 2g fat, less 5mg cholesterol, 220mg sodium, 270mg potassium, 31g carbohydrate (19g sugars) and 6g protein.

**Percent Daily Values are based on a 2,000 calorie diet. Your daily values may be higher or lower depending on your calorie needs:

	Calories	2,000	2,500
Total Fat	Less than	65g	80g
Sat Fat	Less than	20g	25g
Cholesterol	Less than	300mg	300mg
Sodium	Less than	2,400mg	2,400mg
Potassium		3,500mg	3,500mg
Total Carbohydrate		300g	375g
Dietary Fiber		25g	30g

60 Chapter 2

Standards-Based Assessment

Answer the following items on a separate piece of paper.

MULTIPLE CHOICE

1. Which of the following masses is the largest?
   A. 0.200 g
   B. 0.020 kg
   C. 20.0 mg
   D. 2000 µg

2. Which of the following measurements contains three significant figures?
   A. 200 mL **C.** 20.2 mL
   B. 0.02 mL **D.** 200.0 mL

3. A theory differs from a hypothesis in that a theory
   A. cannot be disproved.
   B. always leads to the formation of a law.
   C. has been subjected to experimental testing.
   D. represents an educated guess.

4. All measurements in science
   A. must be expressed in scientific notation.
   B. have some degree of uncertainty.
   C. are both accurate and precise.
   D. must include only those digits that are known with certainty.

5. When numbers are multiplied or divided, the answer can have no more
   A. significant figures than are in the measurement that has the smallest number of significant figures.
   B. significant figures than are in the measurement that has the largest number of significant figures.
   C. digits to the right of the decimal point than are in the measurement that has the smallest number of digits to the right of the decimal point.
   D. digits to the right of the decimal point than are in the measurement that has the largest number of digits to the right of the decimal point.

6. Which of the following is not part of the scientific method?
   A. making measurements
   B. introducing bias
   C. making an educated guess
   D. analyzing data

7. The accuracy of a measurement
   A. is how close it is to the true value.
   B. does not depend on the instrument used to measure the object.
   C. indicates that the measurement is also precise.
   D. is something that scientists rarely achieve.

8. A measurement of 23 465 mg converted to grams equals
   A. 2.3465 g. **C.** 234.65 g.
   B. 23.465 g. **D.** 0.23465 g.

9. A metal sample has a mass of 45.65 g. The volume of the sample is 16.9 cm^3. The density of the sample is
   A. 2.7 g/cm^3. **C.** 0.370 g/cm^3.
   B. 2.70 g/cm^3. **D.** 0.37 g/cm^3.

SHORT ANSWER

10. A recipe for 18 cookies calls for 1 cup of chocolate chips. How many cups of chocolate chips are needed for 3 dozen cookies? What kind of proportion, direct or indirect, did you use to answer this question?

11. Which of the following statements contain exact numbers?
    A. There are 12 eggs in a dozen.
    B. The accident injured 21 people.
    C. The circumference of the Earth at the equator is 40 000 km.

EXTENDED RESPONSE

12. You have decided to test the effects of five garden fertilizers by applying some of each to separate rows of radishes. What is the variable you are testing? What factors should you control? How will you measure and analyze the results?

13. Around 1150, King David I of Scotland defined the inch as the width of a man's thumb at the base of the nail. Discuss the practical limitations of this early unit of measurement.

Test Tip

Carefully read questions that ask for the one choice that is not correct. Often these questions include words such as *is not, except,* or *all but.*

STANDARDS-BASED ASSESSMENT

To give students practice under more realistic testing conditions, give them 60 minutes to answer all of the questions in this Standardized Test Preparation.

Test Answers

1. B
2. C
3. C
4. B
5. A
6. B
7. A
8. B
9. B
10. 2 cups; direct proportion
11. Statements A and B contain exact numbers.
12. The type of fertilizer is the variable being tested. Control factors are the types of radishes, the amount of water and the amount of sunshine. One control row should be planted under the same control factors but with no fertilizer. There are at least four things that could be used to determine the results: size, quantity, appearance, and taste. Analysis might include bar graphs of each of these measurements for each of the five fertilizer types and the no-fertilizer control row.
13. A unit must be defined in a way that does not depend on the circumstances of the measurement. Not every thumbnail is the same size.

Atoms: The Building Blocks of Matter

① Core Instruction

Chapter Resources

- The Teacher's Edition wrap has extensive teaching support for every lesson, including Misconception Alerts, Teach from Visuals, Demonstrations, Teaching Tips, Differentiated Instruction, and Problem Solving support.
- Several additional presentation tools are available online for every chapter, including Animated Chemistry features and Visual Concepts.
- You can open your lesson with the Why It Matters Video: Atoms.

Section	Instruction	Labs and Demonstrations Go Online for Materials Lists and Solutions Lists.
3.1	■ **Textbook:** The Atom: From Philosophical Idea to Scientific Theory **Teaching Visuals:** Law of Conservation of Mass • Law of Multiple Proportions **PowerPresentations**	■ **QuickLab:** Constructing a Model
3.2	■ **Textbook:** The Structure of the Atom **Teaching Visuals:** Gold Foil Experiment • Gold Foil Experiment on the Atomic Level • Properties of Subatomic Particles **PowerPresentations**	■ **Demonstration:** Cathode-Ray Tube ■ **Lab:** Studying What You Can't See (Open Inquiry)
3.3	■ **Textbook:** Counting Atoms **Animated Chemistry:** Avogadro's Number **Teaching Visuals:** Solving Mole Problems • Determining the Mass from the Amount in Moles **PowerPresentations**	■ **Demonstration:** Average Beaker Mass ■ **Lab:** Conservation of Mass (Core Skill)

2 Support and Intervention

- **Interactive Reader** (English and Spanish)
- **Study Guide**
- **Interactive Review:** Review Games, Concept Maps, and Section Self-Checks
- **Scientific Reasoning Skill Builder**
- **Learn It! Videos**
- **Solve It! Cards**
- **Interactive Demos**
- **Sample Problem Sets**

3 Specialized Support

- **Chapter Summary Audio Files**
- **Interactive Reader Audio Files**
- **Differentiated Instruction:** Inclusion, Below Level, and English Learners (TE wrap)

Enrichment and Challenge

- **Differentiated Instruction:** Pre-AP (TE wrap)
- **Careers in Chemistry:** Physical Chemist (SE)
- **WebLinks**

Assessment

- **Section Formative Assessments** (SE)
- **Section Quizzes**
- **Chapter Review** (SE)
- **Chapter Tests A and B**
- **Alternative Assessment** (TE wrap)
- **Online Assessment and Remediation**
- **ExamView Banks**

Where do I find it?

	Resource	PRINT	DVD	ONLINE
1	Animated Chemistry		■	■
1	Demonstrations (TE wrap)	■		■
1	Interactive Whiteboard		■	■
1	Labs		■	■
1	PowerPresentations		■	■
1	QuickLabs	■	■	■
1	Teaching Visuals		■	■
1	Textbook	■	■	■
1	Visual Concepts		■	■
1	Why It Matters Videos		■	■
2	Interactive Demos		■	■
2	Interactive Reader	■	■	■
2	Interactive Reviews		■	■
2	Learn It! Videos		■	■
2	Sample Problem Sets		■	■
2	Scientific Reasoning Skill Builder		■	■
2	Smart Grapher Tool		■	■
2	Solve It! Cards		■	■
2	Study Guide		■	■
3	Chapter Summary Audio Files		■	■
3	Differentiated Instruction (TE wrap)	■		
3	Interactive Reader Audio Files		■	■

CHAPTER 3

Chapter Overview

Section 1 covers the history and development of atomic theory, from Democritus to Dalton to the modern era.

Section 2 covers the experiments that led to the discovery of the electron and the nucleus, and the principal properties of these subatomic particles.

Section 3 outlines the manner in which the number of atoms of an element and the number of an atom's subatomic particles can be expressed and measured.

▼ Focus and Motivate

Activate Prior Knowledge

Students may need a review of the following concepts:

- characteristics of matter
- calculations and units

About the Image

An atom is the smallest particle of an element that retains the chemical properties of that element. Scientists uncovered the structure of the atom without ever seeing one. Eventually, scientists were able to see atoms with the help of electron microscopes. This image, made by a scanning-tunneling microscope (STM), shows C-60 fullerene molecules as bright, sharp peaks rising above a surface of gold atoms, shown as rows. Scientists still cannot make images of the even smaller particles that make up an atom.

Why It Matters

Students can access the video online and find other helpful resources at **HMDScience.com**.

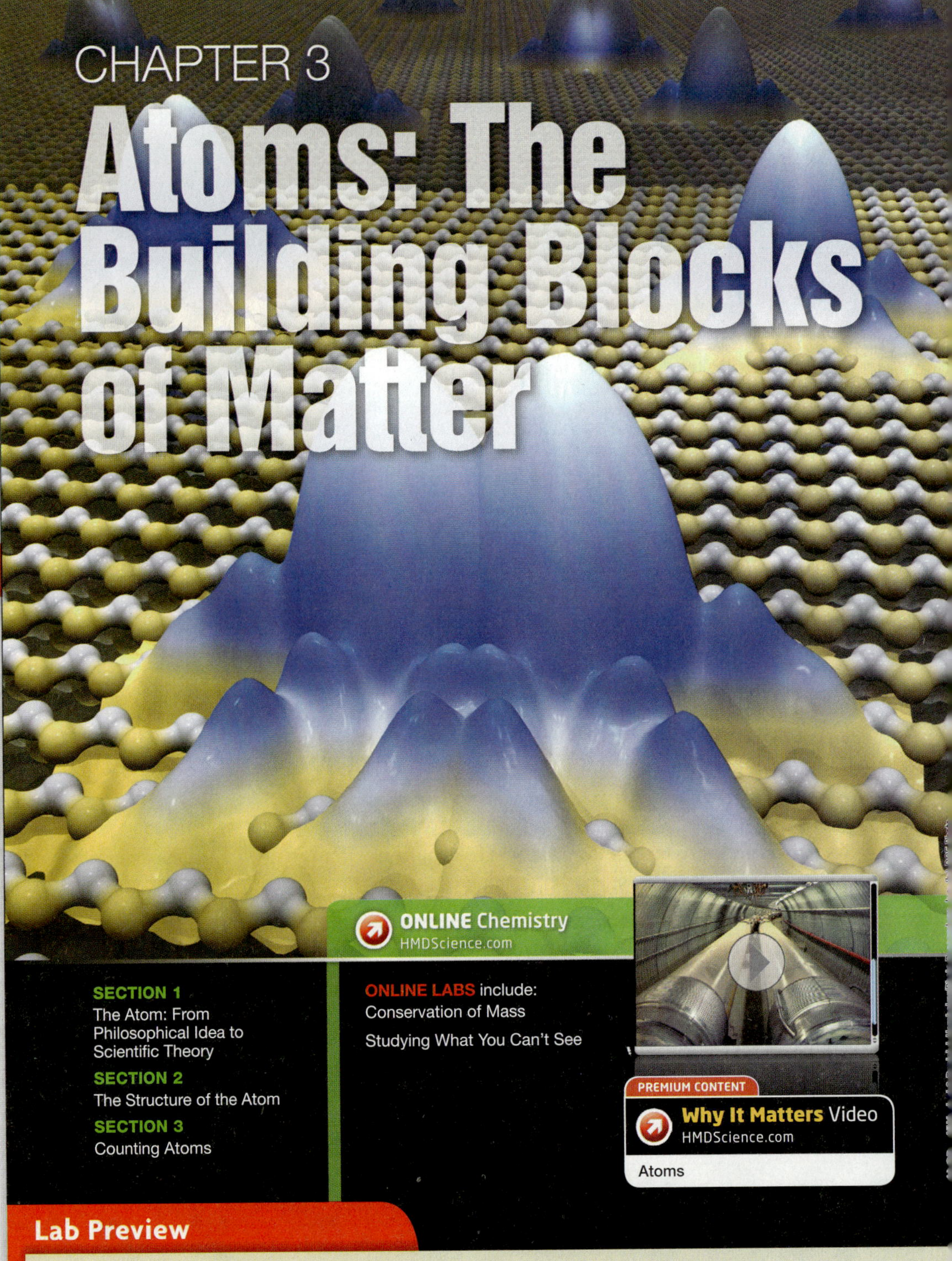

CHAPTER 3

Atoms: The Building Blocks of Matter

ONLINE Chemistry
HMDScience.com

SECTION 1
The Atom: From Philosophical Idea to Scientific Theory

SECTION 2
The Structure of the Atom

SECTION 3
Counting Atoms

ONLINE LABS include:
Conservation of Mass
Studying What You Can't See

PREMIUM CONTENT
Why It Matters Video
HMDScience.com
Atoms

Lab Preview

The following labs and demonstrations support the concepts presented in this chapter.

LABS

Conservation of Mass (Core Skill)

Studying What You Can't See (Open Inquiry)

QUICKLAB

Constructing a Model

DEMONSTRATIONS

Cathode-Ray Tube

Average Beaker Mass

The Atom: From Philosophical Idea to Scientific Theory

SECTION 1

Main Ideas

- Three basic laws describe how matter behaves in chemical reactions.
- Compounds contain atoms in whole-number ratios.
- Atoms can be subdivided into smaller particles.

Key Terms

law of conservation of mass
law of definite proportions
law of multiple proportions

When you crush a lump of sugar, you can see that it is made up of many smaller particles of sugar. You may grind these particles into a very fine powder, but each tiny piece is still sugar. Now suppose you dissolve the sugar in water. The tiny particles seem to disappear completely. Even if you look at the sugar-water solution through a powerful microscope, you cannot see any sugar particles. Yet if you were to taste the solution, you'd know that the sugar is still there. Observations like these led early philosophers to ponder the fundamental nature of matter. Is it continuous and infinitely divisible, or is it divisible only until a basic, invisible particle that cannot be divided further is reached?

The particle theory of matter was supported as early as 400 BCE by certain Greek thinkers, such as Democritus. He called nature's basic particle an *atom*, based on the Greek word meaning "indivisible." Aristotle was part of the generation that succeeded Democritus. His ideas had a lasting impact on Western civilization, and he did not believe in atoms. He thought that all matter was continuous, and his opinion was accepted for nearly 2000 years. Neither the view of Aristotle nor that of Democritus was supported by experimental evidence, so each remained under speculation until the eighteenth century. Then scientists began to gather evidence favoring the atomic theory of matter.

MAIN IDEA

Three basic laws describe how matter behaves in chemical reactions.

Virtually all chemists in the late 1700s accepted the modern definition of an element as a substance that cannot be further broken down by ordinary chemical means. They also assumed that these elements combined to form compounds that have different physical and chemical properties than those of the elements that make them. What troubled them, however, was the understanding of just exactly how the different substances could combine with one another to form new ones, what we know as *chemical reactions*. Most historians date the foundation of modern chemistry to this time when scientists finally began to ascribe rules to how matter interacts.

Differentiated Instruction

ENGLISH LEARNERS

K.T.L. Have students construct a table with three columns, labeled K, T, and L, respectively. Prior to beginning the chapter, have the students fill in the first two columns with the following: "What I **K**now for sure about atoms," and "What I **T**hink I know about atoms." At the conclusion of the chapter, have students to complete the table with "What I **L**earned about atoms." Also ask if they want to revise any of their initial ideas.

SECTION 1

Plan and Prepare ▼

Objectives

Upon completion of this section, students should be able to do the following:

- Explain the laws of conservation of mass, the law of definite proportions, and the law of multiple proportions.
- Summarize the five essential points of Dalton's atomic theory.
- Explain the relationship between Dalton's atomic theory and the laws of conservation of mass, definite proportions, and multiple proportions.

Classroom Catalyst

An opinion is an unsupported idea; a theory uses reason to explain observations and experimental data. Write the following two statements on the board: "Young people should not smoke," and "Smoking at an early age may make it more difficult to quit smoking later." Have students determine which statement is an opinion and which is a theory. Which is similar to Aristotle's statements?

Teach ▼

Application

Have students think of examples of evidence that invisible particles exist. Possible examples include perfume diffusing across a room or the sensation caused by wind.

READING TOOLKIT

INTERPRETING VOCABULARY Show students the derivation of the word *atom* from its Greek roots.

a-: not; *tomos*: cutting

Ask them what concept of matter is conveyed by that meaning. Explain that the concept, which originated in ancient Greece, is that matter can be subdivided into parts only as small as an elemental particle: the atom.

▼ Teach *continued*

TEACH FROM VISUALS

FIGURE 1.1 Be sure to make the point that no matter how few sodium chloride crystals one inspects, the mass percentage of sodium and chloride remains unchanged. This is an example of the law of definite proportions.

Teaching Tip

The ability of scientists to divide atoms into protons, neutrons, and electrons and then to further divide protons and neutrons into quarks is an example of why atoms are no longer considered indivisible.

READING TOOLKIT

VOCABULARY BUILDING Have students write *the law of conservation of mass, the law of definite proportions,* and *the law of multiple proportions,* each on a separate index card. Then have the students read the definition for each law. Finally, have them write a definition for each law in their own words. Have students work in pairs. One student holds up the definition while the other student tries to identify the law.

FIGURE 1.1

Table Salt Crystals Each of the salt crystals shown here contains exactly 39.34% sodium and 60.66% chlorine by mass.

In the 1790s, the study of matter was revolutionized by a new emphasis on the quantitative analysis of chemical reactions. Aided by improved balances, investigators began to accurately measure the masses of the elements and compounds they were studying. This led to the discovery of several basic laws. One of these laws was the **law of conservation of mass,** which states that mass is neither created nor destroyed during ordinary chemical reactions or physical changes. This discovery was soon followed by the assertion that, regardless of where or how a pure chemical compound is prepared, it is composed of a fixed proportion of elements. For example, sodium chloride, also known as ordinary table salt, as shown in **Figure 1.1**, *always* consists of 39.34% by mass of the element sodium, Na, and 60.66% by mass of the element chlorine, Cl. The fact that a chemical compound contains the same elements in exactly the same proportions by mass regardless of the size of the sample or source of the compound is known as the **law of definite proportions.**

It was also known that two elements sometimes combine to form more than one compound. For example, the elements carbon and oxygen form two compounds, carbon dioxide and carbon monoxide. Consider samples of each of these compounds, each containing 1.00 g of carbon. In carbon dioxide, 2.66 g of oxygen combine with 1.00 g of carbon. In carbon monoxide, 1.33 g of oxygen combine with 1.00 g of carbon. The ratio of the masses of oxygen in these two compounds is 2.66 to 1.33, or 2 to 1. This illustrates the **law of multiple proportions:** If two or more different compounds are composed of the same two elements, then the ratio of the masses of the second element combined with a certain mass of the first element is always a ratio of small whole numbers.

MAIN IDEA

Compounds contain atoms in whole-number ratios.

In 1808, an English schoolteacher named John Dalton proposed an explanation that encompassed all these laws. He reasoned that elements were composed of atoms and that only whole numbers of atoms can combine to form compounds. His theory can be summed up by the following statements.

1. All matter is composed of extremely small particles called atoms.
2. Atoms of an element are identical in size, mass, and other properties; atoms of different elements differ in size, mass, and other properties.
3. Atoms cannot be subdivided, created, or destroyed.
4. Atoms of different elements combine in simple whole-number ratios to form chemical compounds.
5. In chemical reactions, atoms are combined, separated, or rearranged.

Dalton's atomic theory explains the law of conservation of mass through the concept that chemical reactions involve merely the combination, separation, or rearrangement of atoms and that during reactions atoms are not subdivided, created, or destroyed. **Figure 1.2**, on the next page, illustrates this idea for the formation of carbon monoxide from carbon and oxygen.

Differentiated Instruction

INCLUSION

Use this activity to motivate and engage visual learners. Ask students to pair up. Then assign each pair one of the five principles of Dalton's Theory. Have student pairs write their principle on a sheet of paper, then draw a model or describe an example that explains or defines it. Students can show their understanding of the concept by presenting their examples to the class or to a small group of other student pairs, each with a different principle. The papers may then be displayed on a classroom bulletin board.

FIGURE 1.2

Atoms and the Law of Conservation of Mass

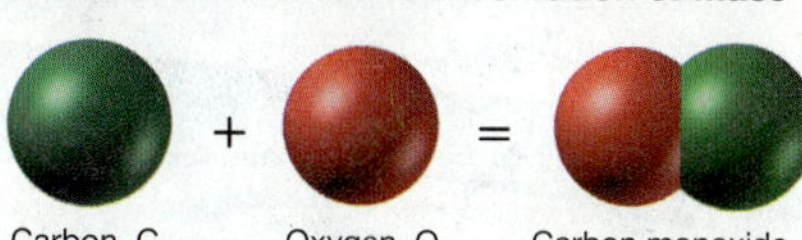

(a) An atom of carbon, C, and an atom of oxygen, O, can combine chemically to form a molecule of carbon monoxide, CO. The mass of the CO molecule is equal to the mass of the C atom plus the mass of the O atom.

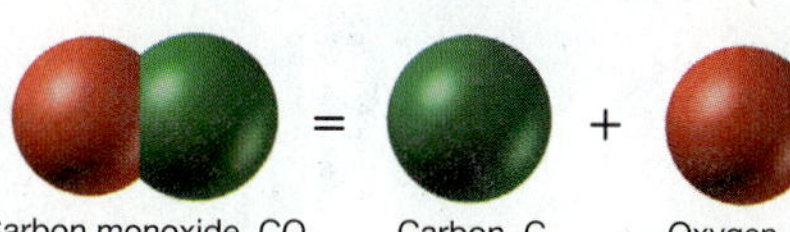

(b) The reverse holds true in a reaction in which a CO molecule is broken down into its elements.

FIGURE 1.3

Law of Multiple Proportions

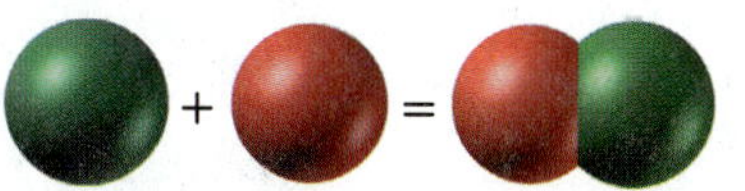

(a) CO molecules are always composed of one C atom and one O atom.

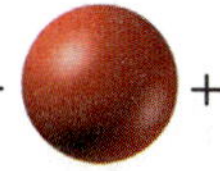

(b) CO_2 molecules are always composed of one C atom and two O atoms. Note that a molecule of carbon dioxide contains twice as many oxygen atoms as does a molecule of carbon monoxide.

Figure 1.3 illustrates how Dalton's atomic theory explained the other laws. The law of definite proportions results from the fact that a given chemical compound always contains the same combinations of atoms. As for the law of multiple proportions, in the case of the carbon oxides, the 2-to-1 ratio of oxygen masses results because carbon dioxide always contains twice as many atoms of oxygen (per atom of carbon) as does carbon monoxide.

MAIN IDEA

Atoms can be subdivided into smaller particles.

By relating atoms to the measurable property of mass, Dalton turned Democritus's *idea* into a *scientific theory* that could be tested by experiment. But not all aspects of Dalton's atomic theory have proven to be correct. For example, today we know that atoms are divisible into even smaller particles (although the law of conservation of mass still holds true for chemical reactions). And, as you will see in Section 3, we know that a given element can have atoms with different masses. Atomic theory has not been discarded—only modified! The important concepts that (1) all matter is composed of atoms and that (2) atoms of any one element differ in properties from atoms of another element remain unchanged.

TEACH FROM VISUALS

FIGURE 1.2 Point out to students that the number of oxygen atoms and the number of carbon atoms are the same before and after each reaction shown. This is an illustration of the law of conservation of mass.

FIGURE 1.3 The mass of oxygen in a molecule of carbon dioxide is twice the mass of oxygen in a molecule of carbon monoxide. This is an illustration of the law of multiple proportions. Have students draw analogies from the world around them. For example, a bicycle has a frame and two wheels, and a tricycle has a frame and three wheels. The ratio of wheels of a bicycle to those of a tricycle is always 2:3, a ratio of small whole numbers.

Figures 1.2 and **1.3** also illustrate the law of definite proportions. (Each type of molecule is always composed of the same ratio of atoms.)

Teaching Tip

Scientists now know that all atoms of a given element do not necessarily have the same mass. In nature, most elements consist of various *isotopes*, atoms with the same number of protons but a different number of neutrons.

PRE-AP

Challenge students to tell you what they know about subatomic particles. Some will list only protons, neutrons, and electrons. Others may know about quarks, leptons, and anti-matter particles. Quarks, which make up protons and neutrons, come in six "flavors." Combinations of quarks are known as hadrons. Leptons include electrons and several types of neutrinos. Little is known about anti-matter; only one anti-matter particle, the positron, has so far been discovered. Interested students can learn more and share their research with the class.

Answers

1. physics and mathematics
2. The electrons of surface atoms are detected by STM.

Physical Chemist

Physical chemists focus on understanding the physical properties of atoms and molecules. They are driven by a curiosity of what makes things work at the level of atoms, and they enjoy being challenged. In addition to chemistry, they study mathematics and physics extensively. Laboratory courses involving experience with electronics and optics are typically part of their training. Often, they enjoy working with instruments and computers. Physical chemists can be experimentalists or theoreticians. They use sophisticated instruments to make measurements or high-powered computers to perform intensive calculations. The instruments used include lasers, electron microscopes, nuclear magnetic resonance spectrometers, mass spectrometers, and particle accelerators. Physical chemists work in industry, government laboratories, research institutes, and academic institutions. Because physical chemists work on a wide range of problems, taking courses in other science disciplines is important.

Scanning Tunneling Microscopy

For years, scientists have yearned for the ability to "see" individual atoms. Because atoms are so small, this had been nothing more than a dream. Now, the scanning tunneling microscope, STM, gives scientists the ability to look at individual atoms. It was invented in 1981 by Gerd Binnig and Heinrich Rohrer, scientists working for IBM in Zurich, Switzerland. They shared the 1986 Nobel Prize in physics for their discovery.

The basic principle of STM is based on the current that exists between a metallic needle that is sharpened to a single atom, the probe, and a conducting sample. As the probe passes above the surface of the sample at a distance of one or two atoms, electrons can "tunnel" from the needle tip to the sample's surface. The probe moves across, or "scans," the surface of the sample. When the probe comes close to the electrons of an individual atom, a signal is produced. A weaker signal is produced between atoms. These signals build a topographical (hill and valley) "map" of conducting and nonconducting regions. The resulting map shows the position and spacing of atoms.

This STM image shows a "corral" of iron atoms on a copper surface.

Surface chemistry is a developing subdiscipline in physical chemistry, and STM is an important tool in the field. Scientists use STM to study surface reactions, such as those that take place in catalytic converters. Other areas of research in which STM is useful include semiconductors and microelectronics. Usually, STM is used with materials that conduct, but it has also been used to study biological molecules, such as DNA.

One innovative application of STM is the ability to position individual atoms. The figure shows the result of moving individual atoms. First, iron atoms were placed on a copper surface. Then, individual iron atoms were picked up by the probe and placed in position. The result is a "quantum corral" of 48 iron atoms on the surface of copper. The diameter of the corral is about 14 nm.

Questions

1. In addition to chemistry, what kinds of courses are important for a student interested in a physical chemistry career?
2. What part of an atom is detected by STM?

QuickLAB CONSTRUCTING A MODEL

QUESTION

How can you construct a model of an unknown object by (1) making inferences about an object that is in a closed container and (2) touching the object without seeing it?

PROCEDURE

Record all of your results in a data table.

1. Your teacher will provide you with a can that is covered by a sock sealed with tape. Without unsealing the container, try to determine the number of objects inside the can as well as the mass, shape, size, composition, and texture of each object. To do this, you may carefully tilt or shake the can. Record your observations in a data table.
2. Remove the tape from the top of the sock. Do *not* look inside the can. Put one hand through the opening, and make the same observations as in step 1 by handling the objects. To make more-accurate estimations, practice estimating the sizes and masses of some known objects outside the can. Then compare your estimates of these objects with actual measurements using a metric ruler and a balance.

DISCUSSION

1. Scientists often use more than one method to gather data. How was this illustrated in the investigation?
2. Of the observations you made, which were qualitative and which were quantitative?
3. Using the data you gathered, draw a model of the unknown object(s) and write a brief summary of your conclusions.

MATERIALS

- can covered by a sock sealed with tape
- one or more objects that fit in the container
- metric ruler
- balance

SAFETY

Wear safety goggles and an apron.

SECTION 1 FORMATIVE ASSESSMENT

Reviewing Main Ideas

1. List the five main points of Dalton's atomic theory.
2. What chemical laws can be explained by Dalton's theory?

Critical Thinking

3. **ANALYZING INFORMATION** Three compounds containing potassium and oxygen are compared. Analysis shows that for each 1.00 g of O, the compounds have 1.22 g, 2.44 g, and 4.89 g of K, respectively. Show how these data support the law of multiple proportions.

Answers to Section Assessment

1. The five main points of Dalton's theory are listed in Section 1.
2. The laws of conservation of mass, definite proportions, and multiple proportions can be explained by Dalton's theory.
3. Comparing the K/O mass ratios gives $2.44/1.22 = 2$; $4.89/2.44 = 2$; and $4.89/1.22 = 4$. These data support the law of multiple proportions because the three compounds have small, whole-number, mass ratios: 2, 2, and 4, respectively.

QuickLab

Students will make inferences about what is inside the can, based on both indirect and direct observations. Remind students not to look inside the container because scientists must draw conclusions without being able to "see" the answer. Do not place anything in the can that can spill, drip, or harm students.

DISCUSSION

1. Scientists use both indirect and direct observations to gather data. In step 1, observations were made without contact with the objects themselves. These observations were indirect. In step 2, students made direct observations by touching the objects. Between the two types of observations, students could get a good idea of the identity of the objects.
2. Determinations of the mass, size, and number of objects are quantitative. Shape, material, and texture determinations are qualitative.
3. Answers will vary.

Assess and Reteach ▼

Assess Use the Formative Assessment on this page to evaluate student mastery of the section.

Reteach For students who need additional instruction, download the Section Study Guide.

Response to Intervention To reassess students' mastery, use the Section Quiz available to print or to take directly online at **HMDScience.com**.

SECTION 2

▼ Plan and Prepare

Objectives

Upon completion of this section, students should be able to do the following:

- Summarize the observed properties of cathode rays that led to the discovery of the electron.
- Summarize the experiment carried out by Rutherford and his coworkers that led to the discovery of the nucleus.
- List the properties of protons, neutrons, and electrons.
- Define *atom*.

Classroom Catalyst

Show students two different shapes made from identical pieces of a toy construction set. Demonstrate how even though the two shapes look different, the characteristics of their various parts are the same. The same is true for the atom. Though atoms of different elements display different properties, isolated subatomic particles have the same properties, regardless of their source. As technology improved, scientists learned to isolate the parts of atoms that display similar properties. For example, the cathode-ray tube led to the isolation of a subatomic particle, the electron.

▼ Teach

TEACH FROM VISUALS

FIGURE 2.1 Alert students to the difference between the flow of electrons, or the cathode ray, and the conventional direction of electric current. The figure depicts a cathode ray, created by electrons, flowing from the negatively-charged cathode to the positively-charged anode. The electric current flows from the anode to the cathode.

SECTION 2

Main Ideas

- Atoms contain positive and negative particles.
- Atoms have small, dense, positively-charged nuclei.
- A nucleus contains protons and neutrons.
- The radii of atoms are expressed in picometers.

The Structure of the Atom

Key Terms
atom
nuclear force

Although John Dalton thought atoms were indivisible, investigators in the late 1800s proved otherwise. As scientific advances allowed a deeper exploration of matter, it became clear that atoms are actually composed of smaller particles and that the number and arrangement of these particles within an atom determine that atom's chemical properties. **Therefore, today we define an atom as the smallest particle of an element that retains the chemical properties of that element.**

All atoms consist of two regions. The *nucleus* is a very small region located at the center of an atom. In every atom, the nucleus is made up of at least one positively charged particle called a *proton* and usually one or more neutral particles called *neutrons*. Surrounding the nucleus is a region occupied by negatively charged particles called *electrons*. This region is very large compared with the size of the nucleus. Protons, neutrons, and electrons are referred to as *subatomic particles*.

MAIN IDEA

Atoms contain positive and negative particles.

The first discovery of a subatomic particle came in the late 1800s. At that time, many experiments were performed in which electric current was passed through various gases at low pressures. (Gases at atmospheric pressure don't conduct electricity well.) These experiments were carried out in glass tubes, like the one shown in **Figure 2.1**, that had been hooked up to a vacuum pump. Such tubes are known as *cathode-ray tubes*.

FIGURE 2.1

Structure of a Cathode-Ray Tube Particles pass through the tube from the *cathode*, the metal disk connected to the negative terminal of the voltage source, to the *anode*, the metal disk connected to the positive terminal.

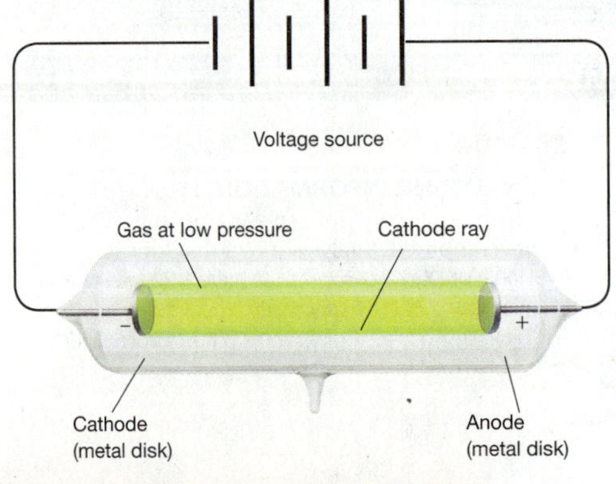

Cathode Rays and Electrons

Investigators noticed that when current was passed through the tube, the surface of the tube directly opposite the cathode glowed. They hypothesized that the glow was caused by a stream of particles, which they called a cathode ray. The ray traveled from the cathode to the anode when current was passed through the tube. Experiments devised to test this hypothesis revealed the following observations:

1. Cathode rays were deflected by a magnetic field in the same manner as a wire carrying electric current, which was known to have a negative charge (see **Figure 2.2** on the next page).
2. The rays were deflected away from a negatively charged object.

Differentiated Instruction

PRE-AP

Have students construct an acrostic using the word "electron." Their final acrostic must have eight statements related to atomic structure; each one beginning with one of the letters in the assigned word. Sample statements might be: **E**very type of matter is made up of atoms; **L**ittle electrons don't weigh much; **E**lectrons have a negative electric charge, and so on.

These observations led to the hypothesis that the particles that compose cathode rays are negatively charged. This hypothesis was strongly supported by a series of experiments carried out in 1897 by the English physicist Joseph John Thomson. In one investigation, he was able to measure the ratio of the charge of cathode-ray particles to their mass. He found that this ratio was always the same, regardless of the metal used to make the cathode or the nature of the gas inside the cathode-ray tube. Thomson concluded that all cathode rays must be composed of identical negatively charged particles, which were named electrons.

FIGURE 2.2

Finding Negative Particles Holding a magnet near a cathode-ray tube (attached to a vacuum pump) causes negatively-charged particles in the beam to be deflected.

Cathode

Anode

Charge and Mass of the Electron

Cathode rays have identical properties regardless of the element used to produce them. Therefore, it was concluded that electrons are present in atoms of all elements. Thus, cathode-ray experiments provided evidence that atoms are divisible and that one of the atom's basic constituents is the negatively charged electron. Thomson's experiment also revealed that the electron has a very large charge-to-mass ratio. In 1909, experiments conducted by the American physicist Robert A. Millikan measured the charge of the electron. Scientists used this information and the charge-to-mass ratio of the electron to determine that the mass of the electron is about one two-thousandth the mass of the simplest type of hydrogen atom, which is the smallest atom known. More-accurate experiments conducted since then indicate that the electron has a mass of 9.109×10^{-31} kg, or 1/1837 the mass of the simplest type of hydrogen atom.

Based on what was learned about electrons, two other inferences were made about atomic structure.

1. Because atoms are electrically neutral, they must contain a positive charge to balance the negative electrons.
2. Because electrons have so much less mass than atoms, atoms must contain other particles that account for most of their mass.

Thomson proposed a model for the atom that is called the *plum pudding model* (after the English dessert). He believed that the negative electrons were spread evenly throughout the positive charge of the rest of the atom. This arrangement is like seeds in a watermelon: the seeds are spread throughout the fruit but do not contribute much to the overall mass. However, shortly thereafter, new experiments disproved this model. Still, the plum pudding model was an important step forward in our modern understanding of the atom, as it represents the first time scientists tried to incorporate the then-revolutionary idea that atoms were not, strictly speaking, indivisible.

CHECK FOR UNDERSTANDING

Analyze Why is it necessary to use experiments such as those of J.J. Thomson and Robert A. Millikan to infer information about electrons?

ChemisTrivia

Inside conventional computer monitors or televisions, a cathode ray constantly undergoes deflections that result from the varying magnetic field within the tube. The ray strikes a coated screen, where a luminescent image is created.

Demonstration

CATHODE-RAY TUBE

If you have a **cathode-ray tube** such as the one pictured in **Figure 2.2,** use it to demonstrate the rays and their deflection by a **magnet.** Follow the instructions that accompany the tube and the power supply. Keep students 3 m away from the apparatus, wear **goggles,** and have students wear goggles. Do not touch the terminals or the tube while the power supply is on. Keep magnets away from the ends of the tube.

Teaching Tip

Millikan's oil-drop experiment did not measure the mass of an electron directly, but rather the charge of an electron. Using the charge determined by Millikan's experiment and the charge-to-mass ratio of an electron determined by Thomson's experiment, scientists were able to calculate the mass of an electron.

ChemisTrivia

The ratio of the mass of an electron to that of a proton is roughly equivalent to the mass of a house cat to that of an elephant.

ENGLISH LEARNERS

Using clip art, construct a concept cartoon. The cartoon should be a single square containing pictures of several characters, each with a thought or speech bubble over their head. These speech bubbles should contain various statements, true and false, about how scientists discovered electrons. Begin your presentation with the question, "How did scientists discover the existence of electrons?"

First, allow students several minutes to look over the cartoon individually and decide which statements they agree with. Then, ask each student to pair up with another student and discuss their choices.

To conclude, give students a second concept cartoon with blank speech bubbles. Tell students to develop their own cartoon based on the question, "How did scientists discover the existence of the nucleus of an atom?"

Check for Understanding

Answer: Answers will vary. A sample answer might be: It is necessary to observe the behavior of electrons in experiments such as these because electrons themselves are far too small to see.

▼ Teach *continued*

READING TOOLKIT

PREDICTION GUIDES Write the following statements on the chalkboard:

- An atom cannot be broken down into smaller parts.
- An atom is the same throughout.
- An atom is made up of several different, smaller parts.

Ask students their opinions of these statements. Have them discuss their opinions and try to justify them. Save a list of the opinions for discussion after completing Section 2.

TEACH FROM VISUALS

FIGURE 2.3 Have students explain what is happening in the figure. Students should realize that **Figure 2.3a** shows merely the setup of the Rutherford foil experiment and that **Figure 2.3b** shows the results.

Teaching Tip

If an atom were the size of a large football stadium, the nucleus would be approximately the size of a marble. This model suggests that the atom is mostly empty space. Ask students to consider how many alpha particles passed through the gold foil in the Rutherford experiment compared with the number deflected.

Check for Understanding

Answer: Rutherford expected the particles to pass through.

CHECK FOR UNDERSTANDING

Explain What did Rutherford expect to happen when he fired alpha particles at the gold foil?

MAIN IDEA

Atoms have small, dense, positively charged nuclei.

More detail of the atom's structure was provided in 1911 by New Zealander Ernest Rutherford and his associates Hans Geiger and Ernest Marsden. The scientists bombarded a thin piece of gold foil with fast-moving *alpha particles,* which are positively charged particles with about four times the mass of a hydrogen atom. Geiger and Marsden assumed that mass and charge were uniformly distributed throughout the atoms of the gold foil, as one would expect from the plum pudding model. They expected the alpha particles to pass through with only a slight deflection, and for the vast majority of the particles, this was the case. However, when the scientists checked for the possibility of wide-angle deflections, they were shocked to find that roughly 1 in 8000 of the alpha particles had actually been deflected back toward the source (see **Figure 2.3**). As Rutherford later exclaimed, it was "as if you had fired a 15-inch [artillery] shell at a piece of tissue paper and it came back and hit you."

After thinking about the startling result for a few months, Rutherford finally came up with an explanation. He reasoned that the deflected alpha particles must have experienced some powerful force within the atom. And he figured that the source of this force must occupy a very small amount of space because so few of the total number of alpha particles had been affected by it. He concluded that the force must be caused by a very densely packed bundle of matter with a positive electric charge. Rutherford called this positive bundle of matter the nucleus (see **Figure 2.4** on the next page).

Rutherford had discovered that the volume of a nucleus was very small compared with the total volume of an atom. In fact, if the nucleus were the size of a marble, then the size of the atom would be about the size of a football field. But where were the electrons? This question was not answered until Rutherford's student, Niels Bohr, proposed a model in which electrons surrounded the positively charged nucleus as the planets surround the sun. Bohr's model is discussed in a later chapter.

FIGURE 2.3

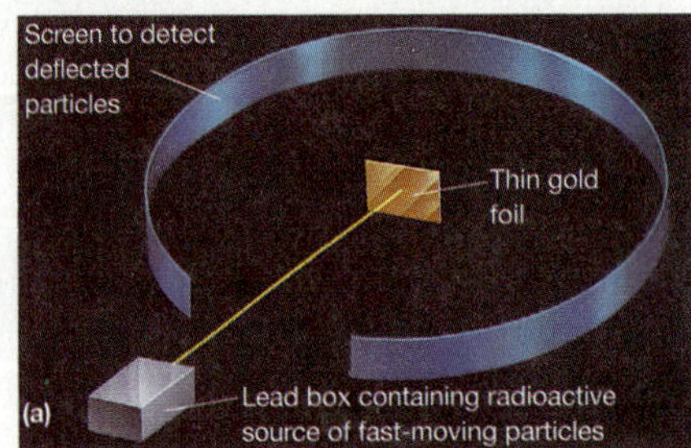

a) Geiger and Marsden bombarded a thin piece of gold foil with a narrow beam of alpha particles.

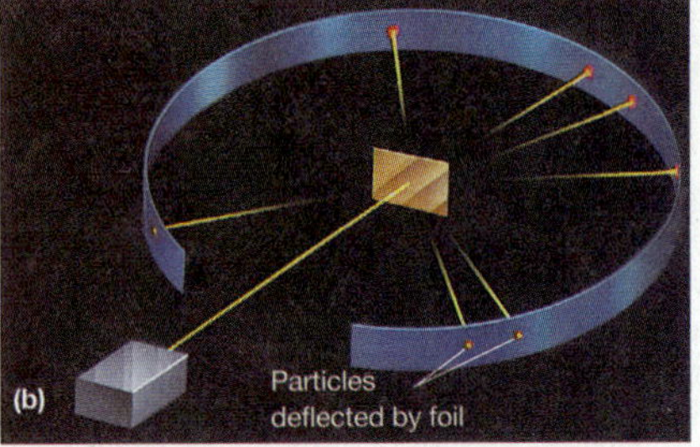

b) Some of the particles were deflected by the gold foil back toward their source.

Differentiated Instruction

BELOW LEVEL

Start a "chain-letter" note and send it around the room. At the top of the page, write the question, "How would you describe an atom?" Below that, write the following instructions: Add a sentence about atoms to the chain, then pass it on to the next student in the room. Your sentence must be brand new. You may not copy or re-state someone else's sentence. Skip a few lines, and then write the first sentence yourself, as follows:

1. An atom is the smallest part of an element that still has the properties of that element.

Tell the class that they must keep the chain letter going, and that if they do a good job, you will copy the final chain letter for each student to keep. Each student will need to read the statements that have been written before them, so that they will not duplicate them. Since the chain is being passed in order around the room, you should be able to tell afterwards who is struggling with the chapter.

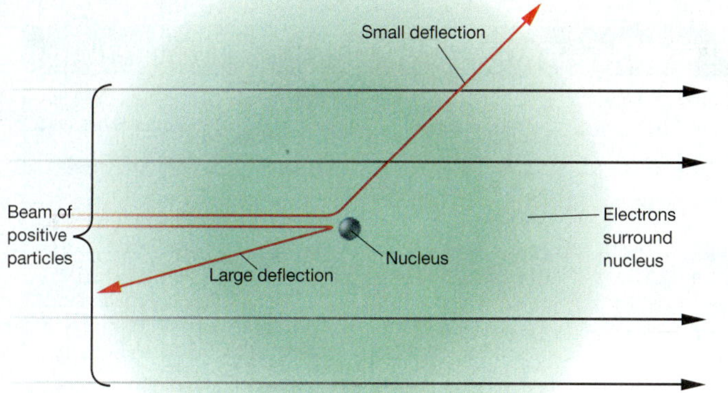

FIGURE 2.4

Finding the Nucleus Rutherford reasoned that each atom in the gold foil contained a small, dense, positively charged nucleus surrounded by electrons. A small number of the alpha particles directed toward the foil were deflected by the tiny nucleus (red arrows). Most of the particles passed through undisturbed (black arrows).

MAIN IDEA

A nucleus contains protons and neutrons.

Except for the nucleus of the simplest type of hydrogen atom (discussed in the next section), all atomic nuclei are made of two kinds of particles, protons and neutrons. A proton has a positive charge equal in magnitude to the negative charge of an electron. Atoms are electrically neutral because they contain equal numbers of protons and electrons. A neutron is electrically neutral.

The simplest hydrogen atom consists of a single-proton nucleus with a single electron moving about it. A proton has a mass of 1.673×10^{-27} kg, which is 1836 times greater than the mass of an electron and 1836/1837, or virtually all, of the mass of the simplest hydrogen atom. All atoms besides the simplest hydrogen atom also have neutrons. The mass of a neutron is 1.675×10^{-27} kg—slightly larger than that of a proton.

The nuclei of atoms of different elements differ in their number of protons and, therefore, in the amount of positive charge they possess. Thus, the number of protons determines that atom's identity. Physicists have identified other subatomic particles, but particles other than electrons, protons, and neutrons have little effect on the chemical properties of matter. **Figure 2.5** on the next page summarizes the properties of electrons, protons, and neutrons.

Forces in the Nucleus

Generally, particles that have the same electric charge repel one another. Therefore, we would expect a nucleus with more than one proton to be unstable. However, when two protons are extremely close to each other, there is a strong attraction between them. In fact, as many as 83 protons can exist close together to help form a stable nucleus. A similar attraction exists when neutrons are very close to each other or when protons and neutrons are very close together. **These short-range proton-neutron, proton-proton, and neutron-neutron forces hold the nuclear particles together and are referred to as nuclear forces.**

Problem Solving

TAKE IT FURTHER

Have students calculate the mass of an electron, based on a proton having a mass 1836 times greater than the mass of an electron. Have them compare their answers to an accepted value for the mass of an electron.

TEACH FROM VISUALS

FIGURE 2.4 Explain to students that the size of the nucleus and the number of deflected alpha particles have been exaggerated for emphasis. In reality, the nucleus occupies much less space in an atom than indicated here. In Rutherford's experiment, almost all of the alpha particles passed undisturbed through the atoms composing the foil.

ChemisTrivia

The forces holding the nucleus together, when unleashed, provide the energy associated with nuclear power or the detonation of an atomic weapon.

Alternative Assessment

Have students build a timeline for the major events in the development of the modern atomic theory. Start with events in the text. Award extra credit for events not mentioned in the text that contribute to a more complete chronology.

READING TOOLKIT

PREDICTION GUIDES Have students revisit their opinions from the beginning of the section. Have them discuss whether their opinions have changed or remain the same. Have them cite passages in the text that account for their decisions.

▼ Assess and Reteach

Assess Use the Formative Assessment on this page to evaluate student mastery of the section.

Reteach For students who need additional instruction, download the Section Study Guide.

Response to Intervention To reassess students' mastery, use the Section Quiz available to print or to take directly online at **HMDScience.com**.

FIGURE 2.5

PROPERTIES OF SUBATOMIC PARTICLES

Particle	Symbols	Relative electric charge	Mass number	Relative mass (u*)	Actual mass (kg)
Electron	e^-, ${}^{0}_{-1}e$	−1	0	0.000 5486	9.109×10^{-31}
Proton	p^+, ${}^{1}_{1}H$	+1	1	1.007 276	1.673×10^{-27}
Neutron	$n°$, ${}^{1}_{0}n$	0	1	1.008 665	1.675×10^{-27}

*1 u (unified atomic mass unit) = $1.660\ 5402 \times 10^{-27}$ kg

MAIN IDEA

The radii of atoms are expressed in picometers.

It is convenient to think of the region occupied by the electrons as an electron cloud—a cloud of negative charge. The radius of an atom is the distance from the center of the nucleus to the outer portion of this electron cloud. Because atomic radii are so small, they are expressed using a unit that is more convenient for the sizes of atoms. This unit is the picometer. The abbreviation for the picometer is *pm* ($1\ \text{pm} = 10^{-12}\ \text{m} = 10^{-10}\ \text{cm}$). To get an idea of how small a picometer is, consider that 1 cm is the same fractional part of 10^3 km (about 600 mi) as 100 pm is of 1 cm. Atomic radii range from about 40 to 270 pm. By contrast, the nuclei of atoms have much smaller radii, about 0.001 pm. Nuclei also have incredibly high densities, about 2×10^8 metric tons/cm^3.

SECTION 2 FORMATIVE ASSESSMENT

Reviewing Main Ideas

1. Define each of the following:
- **a.** atom
- **b.** electron
- **c.** nucleus
- **d.** proton
- **e.** neutron

2. Describe one conclusion made by each of the following scientists that led to the development of the current atomic theory:
- **a.** Thomson
- **b.** Millikan
- **c.** Rutherford

3. Compare the three subatomic particles in terms of location in the atom, mass, and relative charge.

4. Why are cathode-ray tubes, like the one in **Figure 2.1**, connected to a vacuum pump?

Critical Thinking

5. EVALUATING IDEAS Nuclear forces are said to hold protons and neutrons together. What is it about the composition of the nucleus that requires the concept of nuclear forces?

72 Chapter 3

Answers to Section Assessment

1. a. the smallest particle of an element that retains all of the chemical properties of that element

b. a negatively charged subatomic particle located outside the nucleus

c. the positively charged, dense central portion of an atom that contains nearly all the atom's mass but takes up a very small fraction of its volume

d. the subatomic particle of the nucleus that has a positive charge equal in magnitude to the negative charge of the electron

e. the electrically neutral subatomic particle found in atomic nuclei

2. a. concluded that electrons were found in all atoms

b. confirmed the negative charge of the electron and helped determine a possible mass

c. determined that most of the mass of an atom is found in the nucleus and that the nucleus occupies very little space within an atom

3. Electrons surround the nucleus and have a negative charge and small mass relative to protons and neutrons. In the central nucleus, protons and neutrons comprise most of an atom's mass. Protons have a positive charge; neutrons have no charge.

4. because charges will flow through gases only at very low pressures

5. As shown by Rutherford, the protons and neutrons are packed very close together. However, like-charged particles repel each other, so the protons would not be expected to be close to other protons. The forces that prevent protons from repelling each other are the nuclear forces.

Counting Atoms

Key Terms

atomic number
isotope
mass number
nuclide
unified atomic mass unit
average atomic mass
mole
Avogadro's number
molar mass

SECTION 3

Main Ideas

- All atoms of an element must have the same number of protons, but not neutrons.
- Atomic mass is a relative measure.
- Average atomic mass is a weighted value.
- A relative mass scale makes counting atoms possible.

Consider neon, Ne, the gas used in many illuminated signs. Neon is a minor component of the atmosphere. In fact, dry air contains only about 0.002% neon. And yet there are about 5×10^{17} atoms of neon present in each breath you inhale. In most experiments, atoms are much too small to be measured individually. Chemists can analyze atoms quantitatively, however, by knowing fundamental properties of the atoms of each element. In this section, you will be introduced to some of the basic properties of atoms. You will then discover how to use this information to count the number of atoms of an element in a sample with a known mass. You will also become familiar with the *mole*, a special unit used by chemists to express amounts of particles, such as atoms and molecules.

MAIN IDEA

All atoms of an element must have the same number of protons, but not neutrons.

All atoms contain the same particles. Yet all atoms are not the same. Atoms of different elements have different numbers of protons. Atoms of the same element all have the same number of protons. The **atomic number** (Z) of an element is the number of protons of each atom of that element.

Look at a periodic table. In most, an element's atomic number is indicated above its symbol, and the elements are placed in order of increasing atomic number. Hydrogen, H, is at the upper left of the table and has an atomic number of 1. All atoms of the element hydrogen have one proton. Next in order is helium, He, which has two protons. Lithium, Li, has three protons (see **Figure 3.1**); beryllium, Be, has four protons; and so on. The atomic number identifies an element. If the number of protons in the nucleus of an atom were to change, that atom would become a different element.

Isotopes

But just because all hydrogen atoms, for example, have only a single proton, it doesn't mean they all have the same number of neutrons, or even any neutrons at all. In fact, three types of hydrogen atoms are known. The most common type of hydrogen is sometimes called *protium*. It accounts for 99.9885% of the hydrogen atoms found on Earth, and its nucleus consists of only a single proton. Another type of hydrogen, *deuterium*, accounts for 0.0115% of Earth's hydrogen atoms; its nucleus has one proton and one neutron. The third form of hydrogen, *tritium*, has one proton and two neutrons in its nucleus. Tritium is radioactive so it is not very common at all on Earth; however, it is still hydrogen.

FIGURE 3.1

Atomic Numbers The atomic number in this periodic table entry reveals that an atom of lithium has three protons in its nucleus.

3
Li
Lithium
6.941
$[He]2s^1$

Differentiated Instruction

BELOW LEVEL

Construct a two-column table on the board or on a computer. Title the first column "Statement" and title the second column "How Can You Find Out." In each row of column one, write a statement related to the content of this section. For example, your first statement might be: "The atoms of each element have a specific number of protons." If you wish, you can use the Main Idea headings from the textbook for your statements. Under each statement, write four options: agree, disagree, it depends on_____, and not sure. Create a check box for each opinion. Allow students four to five minutes to look over and respond to the statements individually, by checking their opinion in the first column and by filling out the second column. Next, split the class up into small groups of three or four students, and have them share their opinions. Monitor the groups to encourage appropriate discussion.

SECTION 3

Plan and Prepare

Objectives

Upon completion of this section, students should be able to do the following:

- Explain what isotopes are.
- Define *atomic number* and *mass number*, and describe how they apply to isotopes.
- Given the identity of a nuclide, determine its numbers of protons, neutrons, and electrons.
- Define *mole*, *Avogadro's number*, and *molar mass*, and state how all three are related.

Classroom Catalyst

Have students consider a familiar example of a weighted average. For instance, if a student's semester grade depends 60% on exam scores and 40% on laboratory explorations, then the student's exam scores count more heavily toward his or her final grade. Hand out sample exam scores and laboratory scores, and have students determine the weighted average of the two. In this section, students will learn that the atomic mass of an element is a weighted average of the masses of the naturally occurring isotopes of that element.

Teach

Misconception Alert!

Emphasize that the identity of the atom is determined by the number of protons, not the number of electrons or neutrons. The numbers of electrons and neutrons can each vary and the atom will still be of the same element. But if the number of protons changes, then the atom becomes an atom of a different element.

TEACH FROM VISUALS

FIGURE 3.1 Have students identify the atomic number, atomic mass, and chemical symbol for different elements on the periodic table. Have them deduce the number of electrons from the atomic number for neutral atoms.

▼ Teach *continued*

TEACH FROM VISUALS

FIGURE 3.2 Note that the only difference between the hydrogen isotopes is in their number of neutrons.

TEACH FROM TABLES

FIGURE 3.3 How are hydrogen's isotopes different from one another? They have different numbers of neutrons. How does this information alter Dalton's atomic theory? Atoms of a single element do not always have the same mass, as Dalton suggested. Hydrogen is the only element whose isotopes have names. Isotopes of other elements are identified by their mass numbers.

Teaching Tip

The mass numbers of the stable ten isotopes of tin are 112, 114, 115, 116, 117, 118, 119, 120, 122, and 124.

ChemisTrivia

The name *deuterium* is derived from the Greek word "deuteros" meaning "second," and *tritium* is from the Greek word "tritos" meaning "third." Both isotopes have applications in nuclear chemistry. Deuterium is used to help control fission reactions. Tritium is used in nuclear bombs.

FIGURE 3.2

Three Isotopes of Hydrogen The nuclei of different isotopes of the same element have the same number of protons but different numbers of neutrons.

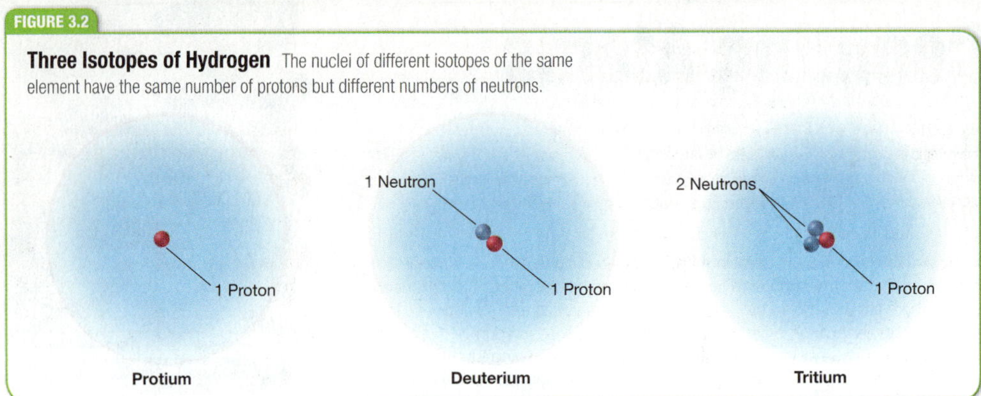

Protium, deuterium, and tritium are isotopes of hydrogen. **Isotopes are atoms of the same element that have different masses.** The isotopes of a particular element all have the same number of protons and electrons but different numbers of neutrons. In all three isotopes of hydrogen, shown in **Figure 3.2**, the positive charge of the single proton is balanced by the negative charge of the electron. Most of the elements consist of mixtures of isotopes. Tin has 10 stable isotopes, for example—the most of any element.

The atoms in any sample of an element you may find most likely will be a mixture of several isotopes in various proportions. The detection of these isotopes and determination of their relative proportions has become extremely precise. So precise that scientists can determine where some elements come from by measuring the percentages of different isotopes in a sample.

Mass Number

Identifying an isotope requires knowing both the name or atomic number of the element and the mass of the isotope. **The mass number is the total number of protons and neutrons that make up the nucleus of an isotope.** The three isotopes of hydrogen described earlier have mass numbers 1, 2, and 3, as shown in **Figure 3.3**.

FIGURE 3.3

MASS NUMBERS OF HYDROGEN ISOTOPES

	Atomic number (number of protons)	Number of neutrons	Mass number (protons + neutrons)
Protium	1	0	$1 + 0 = 1$
Deuterium	1	1	$1 + 1 = 2$
Tritium	1	2	$1 + 2 = 3$

Differentiated Instruction

INCLUSION

Many students benefit from having a concrete idea for understanding abstract concepts. Invite these students to think of an analogy for isotopes, using car models. Students should recognize that a car model comes in different colors and with different interior features. All cars of the same model are the same kind of car, but they have differences, just as all atoms of the same isotope are the same element, but have differences. Also, point out that pennies minted before 1983 were solid copper, whereas those minted in 1983 and thereafter have a zinc core. Have students explain how these pennies can also serve as a model for isotopes. Students should recognize that the same coin can have different compositions, just as the same kind of atom can have different numbers of neutrons in its nucleus.

Identifying Isotopes

There are two methods for specifying isotopes. In the first, the mass number appears with a hyphen after the name of the element. Tritium, for example, is written as hydrogen-3. We call this method *hyphen notation.* The uranium isotope with mass number 235, commonly used as fuel for nuclear power plants, is known as uranium-235. The second method shows the composition of a nucleus using the isotope's *nuclear symbol.* So uranium-235 is shown as $^{235}_{92}U$. The superscript indicates the mass number (protons + neutrons). The subscript indicates the atomic number (number of protons). The number of neutrons is found by subtracting the atomic number from the mass number.

mass number − atomic number = number of neutrons
235 (protons + neutrons) − 92 protons = 143 neutrons

Figure 3.4 gives the names, symbols, and compositions of the isotopes of hydrogen and helium. **Nuclide** is a general term for a specific isotope of an element.

FIGURE 3.4

ISOTOPES OF HYDROGEN AND HELIUM

Isotope	Nuclear symbol	Number of protons	Number of electrons	Number of neutrons
Hydrogen-1 (protium)	$^{1}_{1}H$	1	1	0
Hydrogen-2 (deuterium)	$^{2}_{1}H$	1	1	1
Hydrogen-3 (tritium)	$^{3}_{1}H$	1	1	2
Helium-3	$^{3}_{2}He$	2	2	1
Helium-4	$^{4}_{2}He$	2	2	2

Sub-Atomic Particles

Sample Problem A **How many protons, electrons, and neutrons are there in an atom of chlorine-37?**

1 ANALYZE

Given: name and mass number of chlorine-37

Unknown: numbers of protons, electrons, and neutrons

2 PLAN

atomic number = number of protons = number of electrons
mass number = number of neutrons + number of protons

Continued

Problem Solving

DECONSTRUCTING PROBLEMS

Some students may find it helpful to solve this type of problem stepwise.

1. The atomic number found on a periodic table is equal to the number of protons.
2. The number of protons equals the number of electrons.
3. The mass number (protons + neutrons) minus the atomic number (protons) equals the number of neutrons.

TEACH FROM TABLES

FIGURE 3.4 Explain the meaning of the two numbers associated with an isotope's nuclear symbol. The number on the bottom is the number of protons (the atomic number). For a neutral atom, the number of protons equals the number of electrons. The number on the top is the sum of the protons and the neutrons (the mass number). Have students determine the number of protons, neutrons, and electrons for some other elements.

Misconception Alert!

Many students confuse mass number with average atomic mass. Emphasize that the mass number is the mass of one *particular* atom, and average atomic mass is the average mass of a group of atoms of the same element.

Demonstration

AVERAGE BEAKER MASS

Record the mass of **ten empty 100-mL beakers.** Calculate the average beaker mass. Use this value as an analogy to average atomic mass.

▼ Teach continued

Classroom Practice

A-1 How many protons, electrons, and neutrons make up an atom of carbon-13?

Answer: 6 protons, 6 electrons, 7 neutrons

A-2 Write the nuclear symbol for oxygen-16.

Answer: $^{16}_{8}O$

A-3 Write the hyphen notation for the element whose atoms have 7 electrons and 9 neutrons.

Answer: nitrogen-16

Answers

Practice A

1. 35 protons, 35 electrons, 45 neutrons
2. $^{13}_{6}C$
3. phosphorus-30

Teaching Tip

You may wish to point out that 1 u is equal to $1.660\ 540 \times 10^{-27}$ kg or $1.660\ 540 \times 10^{-24}$ g.

Sub-Atomic Particles (continued)

3 SOLVE

The mass number of chlorine-37 is 37. Consulting the periodic table reveals that chlorine's atomic number is 17. Therefore we know that

$$\text{atomic number} = \text{number of protons} = \text{number of electrons} = 17 \text{ protons and } 17 \text{ electrons}$$

$$\text{number of neutrons} = \text{mass number} - \text{atomic number} = 37 - 17 = 20 \text{ neutrons}$$

An atom of chlorine-37 is made up of 17 electrons, 17 protons, and 20 neutrons.

4 CHECK YOUR WORK

The number of protons in a neutral atom equals the number of electrons. The sum of the protons and neutrons equals the given mass number (17 + 20 = 37).

Practice Answers in Appendix E

1. How many protons, electrons, and neutrons make up an atom of bromine-80?
2. Write the nuclear symbol for carbon-13.
3. Write the hyphen notation for the isotope with 15 electrons and 15 neutrons.

MAIN IDEA

Atomic mass is a relative measure.

Masses of atoms expressed in grams are very small. As we shall see, an atom of oxygen-16, for example, has a mass of 2.656×10^{-23} g. For most chemical calculations it is more convenient to use *relative* atomic masses. As you learned when you studied scientific measurement, scientists use standards of measurement that are constant and are the same everywhere. In order to set up a relative scale of atomic mass, one atom has been arbitrarily chosen as the standard and assigned a mass value. The masses of all other atoms are expressed in relation to this standard.

The standard used by scientists to compare units of atomic mass is the carbon-12 atom, which has been arbitrarily assigned a mass of exactly 12 unified atomic mass units, or 12 u. **One unified atomic mass unit, or 1 u, is exactly 1/12 the mass of a carbon-12 atom.** The atomic mass of any other atom is determined by comparing it with the mass of the carbon-12 atom. The hydrogen-1 atom has an atomic mass of *about* 1/12 that of the carbon-12 atom, or about 1 u. The precise value of the atomic mass of a hydrogen-1 atom is 1.007 825 u. An oxygen-16 atom has about 16/12 (or 4/3) the mass of a carbon-12 atom. Careful measurements show the atomic mass of oxygen-16 to be 15.994 915 u. The mass of a magnesium-24 atom is found to be slightly less than twice that of a carbon-12 atom. Its atomic mass is 23.985 042 u.

Differentiated Instruction

BELOW LEVEL

Use people's ages to help students understand the concept of relative atomic mass. Write down the names and ages of the students in class. Then ask who is the youngest. Point out that all the students were compared, and one was chosen as a reference point or standard. In the case of relative atomic mass, carbon-12 was chosen as the standard to which all the other elements are compared.

Some additional examples of the atomic masses of the naturally occurring isotopes of several elements are given in **Figure 3.5** on the next page. Isotopes of an element may occur naturally, or they may be made in the laboratory (*artificial isotopes*). *Although isotopes have different masses, they do not differ significantly in their chemical behavior.*

The masses of subatomic particles can also be expressed on the atomic mass scale (see **Figure 2.5**). The mass of the electron is 0.000 548 6 u, that of the proton is 1.007 276 u, and that of the neutron is 1.008 665 u. Note that the proton and neutron masses are close, but not equal, to 1 u. You have learned that the mass number is the total number of protons and neutrons that make up the nucleus of an atom. You can now see that the mass number and relative atomic mass of a given nuclide are quite close to each other. They are not identical, because the proton and neutron masses deviate slightly from 1 u and the atomic masses include electrons. Also, as you will read in a later chapter, a small amount of mass is changed to energy in the creation of a nucleus from its protons and neutrons.

Chemistry EXPLORERS

Discovery of Element 43

The discovery of element 43, technetium, is credited to Carlo Perrier and Emilio Segrè, who artificially produced it in 1937. However, scientists have found minute traces of technetium in the Earth's crust that result from the fission of uranium. Astronomers have also discovered technetium in S-type stars.

MAIN IDEA

Average atomic mass is a weighted value.

Most elements occur naturally as mixtures of isotopes, as indicated in **Figure 3.5** (see next page). Scientists determine the average mass of a sample of an element's isotopes by determining the percentages of each of the isotopes and then giving the proper weight to each value. **Average atomic mass** is the weighted average of the atomic masses of the naturally occurring isotopes of an element. Unlike atomic number, average atomic mass is a statistical calculation. Different samples of the same element can differ in their relative abundance of isotopes.

The following is an example of how to calculate a *weighted average*. Suppose you have a box containing two sizes of marbles. If 25% of the marbles have masses of 2.00 g each and 75% have masses of 3.00 g each, how is the weighted average calculated? You could count the number of each type of marble, calculate the total mass of the mixture, and divide by the total number of marbles. If you had 100 marbles, the calculations would be as follows:

$$25 \text{ marbles} \times 2.00 \text{ g} = 50 \text{ g}$$
$$75 \text{ marbles} \times 3.00 \text{ g} = 225 \text{ g}$$

Adding these masses gives the total mass of the marbles.

$$50 \text{ g} + 225 \text{ g} = 275 \text{ g}$$

Dividing the total mass by 100 gives an average marble mass of 2.75 g.

A simpler method is to multiply the mass of each marble by the decimal fraction representing its percentage in the mixture. Then add the products.

$$25\% = 0.25 \qquad 75\% = 0.75$$
$$(2.00 \text{ g} \times 0.25) + (3.00 \text{ g} \times 0.75) = 2.75 \text{ g}$$

Misconception Alert!

Many students do not understand that the mass of a nucleus is less than the sum of the masses of the protons and neutrons making up the nucleus. The difference is due to the binding energy that holds the nucleus together.

ChemisTrivia

Isotope abundances are measured very precisely using an instrument called a *mass spectrometer*. High-energy electrons collide with an atom, knocking away one of its electrons and giving the particle a positive charge. The charged particle is directed through a magnetic field. The isotopes of an element are separated from each other because they have the same charge but different masses. The particles with greater mass are deflected less than those of less mass. The data collected gives both the mass of the particles and their percentage abundance in the sample.

Problem Solving

ALTERNATIVE APPROACHES

Use the example of grades to help explain weighted averages to students. Give them these data:

Score	Number with score
95	4 students
91	6 students
86	6 students
83	1 student
88	8 students
62	3 students

Have them calculate the class average. 86.25

TEACH FROM TABLES

FIGURE 3.5 Point out to students that the average atomic mass of an element is often closest to the atomic mass of the most abundant isotope.

Alternative Assessment

Follow the example on this page to confirm the average atomic mass of hydrogen, carbon, oxygen, copper, and uranium using the percentage abundances and isotope masses listed in **Figure 3.5.**

READING TOOLKIT

SEQUENCING After students have read the text on relating mass and numbers of atoms to themselves, ask them to discuss the relationships illustrated in **Figure 3.7.** Have them work in pairs to write in their own words the steps they would follow to change from one expression to the other. Ask for volunteers to list the steps on the board.

FIGURE 3.5

ATOMIC MASSES AND ABUNDANCES OF SEVERAL NATURALLY OCCURRING ISOTOPES

Isotope	Mass number	Percentage natural abundance	Atomic mass (u)	Average atomic mass of element (u)
Hydrogen-1 Hydrogen-2	1 2	99.9885 0.0115	1.007 825 2.014 102	1.007 94
Carbon-12 Carbon-13	12 13	98.93 1.07	12 (by definition) 13.003 355	12.0107
Oxygen-16 Oxygen-17 Oxygen-18	16 17 18	99.757 0.038 0.205	15.994 915 16.999 132 17.999 160	15.9994
Copper-63 Copper-65	63 65	69.15 30.85	62.929 601 64.927 794	63.546
Cesium-133	133	100	132.905 447	132.905
Uranium-234 Uranium-235 Uranium-238	234 235 238	0.0054 0.7204 99.2742	234.040 945 235.043 922 238.050 784	238.029

Calculating Average Atomic Mass

The average atomic mass of an element depends on both the mass and the relative abundance of each of the element's isotopes. For example, naturally occurring copper consists of 69.15% copper-63, which has an atomic mass of 62.929 601 u, and 30.85% copper-65, which has an atomic mass of 64.927 794 u. The average atomic mass of copper can be calculated by multiplying the atomic mass of each isotope by its relative abundance (expressed in decimal form) and adding the results.

$$0.6915 \times 62.929\,601\ \text{u} + 0.3085 \times 64.927\,794\ \text{u} = 63.55\ \text{u}$$

The calculated average atomic mass of naturally occurring copper is 63.55 u.

The average atomic mass is included for the elements listed in **Figure 3.5.** As illustrated in the table, most atomic masses are known to four or more significant figures. *In this book, an element's atomic mass is usually rounded to two decimal places before it is used in a calculation.*

MAIN IDEA

A relative mass scale makes counting atoms possible.

The relative atomic mass scale makes it possible to know how many atoms of an element are present in a sample of the element with a measurable mass. Three very important concepts—the mole, Avogadro's number, and molar mass—provide the basis for relating masses in grams to numbers of atoms.

Problem Solving

DECONSTRUCTING PROBLEMS

Point out that the percentages themselves are not used in calculating an average atomic mass. Rather, the percentages must be converted to decimal form. Be sure that students understand that 100% is represented as 1 in decimal form. Likewise, 69.15% is represented as 0.6915 in decimal form. Have students practice writing percentages as decimals for values in **Figure 3.5.**

The Mole

The mole is the SI unit for amount of substance. **A mole (abbreviated mol) is the amount of a substance that contains as many particles as there are atoms in exactly 12 g of carbon-12.** The mole is a counting unit, just like a dozen is. We don't usually buy 12 or 24 ears of corn; we order one dozen or two dozen. Similarly, a chemist may want 1 mol of carbon, or 2 mol of iron, or 2.567 mol of calcium. In the sections that follow, you will see how the mole relates to masses of atoms and compounds.

Avogadro's Number

The number of particles in a mole has been experimentally determined in a number of ways. The best modern value is $6.022\ 141\ 79 \times 10^{23}$. This means that exactly 12 g of carbon-12 contains $6.022\ 141\ 79 \times 10^{23}$ carbon-12 atoms.

The number of particles in a mole is known as Avogadro's number, named for the nineteenth-century Italian scientist Amedeo Avogadro, whose ideas were crucial in explaining the relationship between mass and numbers of atoms. **Avogadro's number—$6.022\ 141\ 79 \times 10^{23}$—is the number of particles in exactly one mole of a pure substance.** For most purposes, Avogadro's number is rounded to 6.022×10^{23}.

To get a sense of how large Avogadro's number is, consider the following: If every person living on Earth (6.8 billion people) worked to count the atoms in one mole of an element, and if each person counted continuously at a rate of one atom per second, it would take about 3 million years for all the atoms to be counted.

Molar Mass

An alternative definition of *mole* is the amount of a substance that contains Avogadro's number of particles. Can you calculate the approximate mass of one mole of helium atoms? You know that a mole of carbon-12 atoms has a mass of exactly 12 g and that a carbon-12 atom has an atomic mass of 12 u. The atomic mass of a helium atom is 4.00 u, which is about one-third the mass of a carbon-12 atom. It follows that a mole of helium atoms will have about one-third the mass of a mole of carbon-12 atoms. Thus, one mole of helium has a mass of about 4.00 g.

The mass of one mole of a pure substance is called the molar mass of that substance. Molar mass is usually written in units of g/mol. The molar mass of an element is numerically equal to the atomic mass of the element in unified atomic mass units (which can be found in the periodic table). For example, the molar mass of lithium, Li, is 6.94 g/mol, while the molar mass of mercury, Hg, is 200.59 g/mol (rounding each value to two decimal places). The molar mass of an element contains one mole of atoms. For example, 4.00 g of helium, 6.94 g of lithium, and 200.59 g of mercury all contain a mole of atoms. **Figure 3.6** shows molar masses of three common elements.

FIGURE 3.6

Molar Mass Shown is approximately one molar mass of each of three elements.

(a) carbon (graphite)

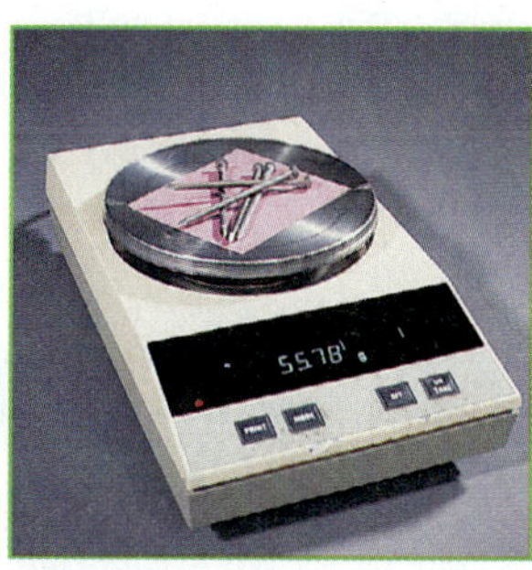

(b) iron (nails)

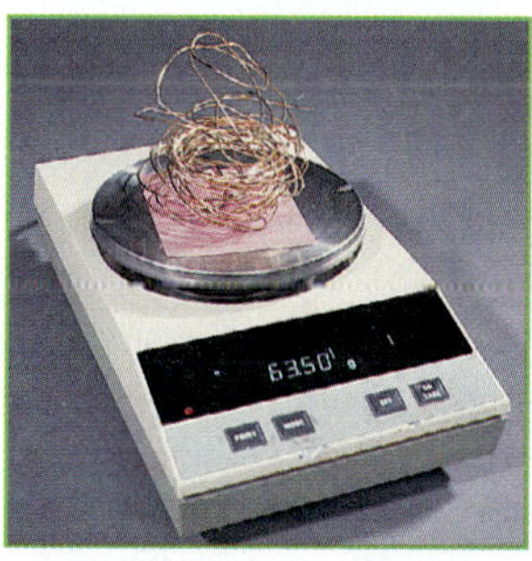

(c) copper (wire)

Classroom Discussion

Have students decide whether single moles of all materials have the same mass. Divide students into groups of four to develop an answer and an example. Then have one person from each group report the answer and example to the class.

Alternative Assessment

Have students determine the molar masses of different elements on the periodic table. The answer will be equal to the average atomic mass, expressed in g/mol. One may also calculate the molar mass of a compound; the molar mass of water is 18.02 g/mol, for example.

Misconception Alert!

It is easy to confuse the terms *atomic mass* and *molar mass*. Although they are often the same number, *atomic mass* is the mass of one atom, expressed in u, and *molar mass* is the mass of one mole of particles, expressed in g/mol.

Differentiated Instruction

BELOW LEVEL

Point out that the mole is a unit that stands for a specific number of items. Have students work in small groups to create a list of units that stand for a specific number of items. To get them started, point out that they would know exactly how many apples you had if you said you had a dozen. However, they would have no idea of how many apples you had if you said a bagful of apples. What are some other units that specify an exact number of items?

Possible counting units include a couple (2), a trio (3), a half-dozen (6), a baker's dozen (13), a gross (144), and a ream (500).

List all the counting units on the board and then add "a mole" to the bottom and write out the number in non-scientific notation, 602 214 179 000 000 000 000 000.

▼ Teach *continued*

Teaching Tip

The technique of using conversion factors (see the Math Tutor at the end of this chapter) can be extended to a more general case, called *unit analysis*. Using the example in the text, we see that 4.00 g He is equivalent to 1 mol He. The conversion factors possible are $\frac{4.00 \text{ g He}}{1 \text{ mol He}}$ or $\frac{1 \text{ mol He}}{4.00 \text{ g He}}$. If we choose the first conversion factor and treat the units as algebraic quantities, the units "mol He" will cancel and the unit "g He" remains, which tells us we have correctly solved the problem.

Classroom Practice

B-1 What is the mass in grams of 3.6 mol of the element carbon, C?

Answer: 43 g

B-2 What is the mass in grams of 0.733 mol of the element sulfur, S?

Answer: 23.5 g

FIGURE 3.7

Relating Mass to the Number of Atoms The diagram shows the relationship between mass in grams, amount in moles, and number of atoms of an element in a sample.

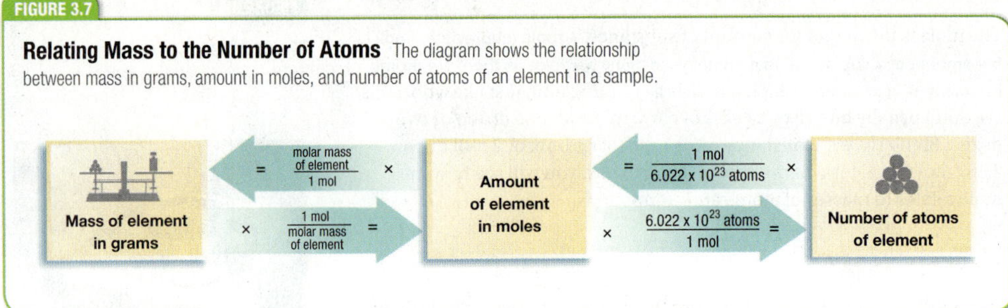

Gram/Mole Conversions

Chemists use molar mass as a conversion factor in chemical calculations. For example, the molar mass of helium is 4.00 g He/mol He. To find how many grams of helium there are in two moles of helium, multiply by the molar mass.

$$2.00 \text{ mol He} \times \frac{4.00_{\text{g}} \text{ He}}{1 \text{ mol He}} = 8.00 \text{ g He}$$

Figure 3.7 shows how to use molar mass, moles, and Avogadro's number to relate mass in grams, amount in moles, and number of atoms of an element.

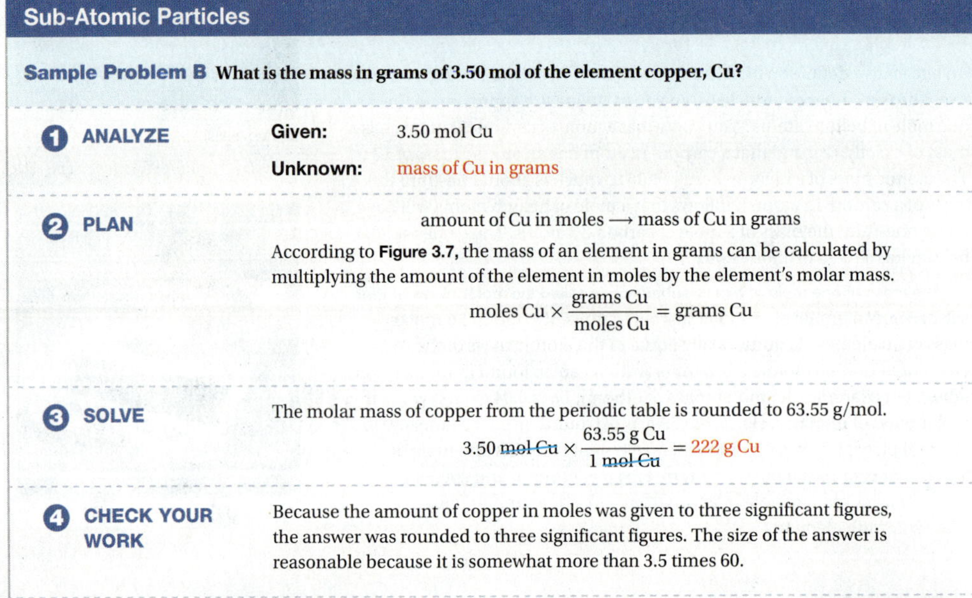

Sub-Atomic Particles

Sample Problem B **What is the mass in grams of 3.50 mol of the element copper, Cu?**

1 ANALYZE

Given: 3.50 mol Cu

Unknown: mass of Cu in grams

2 PLAN

amount of Cu in moles ⟶ mass of Cu in grams

According to **Figure 3.7**, the mass of an element in grams can be calculated by multiplying the amount of the element in moles by the element's molar mass.

$$\text{moles Cu} \times \frac{\text{grams Cu}}{\text{moles Cu}} = \text{grams Cu}$$

3 SOLVE

The molar mass of copper from the periodic table is rounded to 63.55 g/mol.

$$3.50 \text{ mol Cu} \times \frac{63.55 \text{ g Cu}}{1 \text{ mol Cu}} = 222 \text{ g Cu}$$

4 CHECK YOUR WORK

Because the amount of copper in moles was given to three significant figures, the answer was rounded to three significant figures. The size of the answer is reasonable because it is somewhat more than 3.5 times 60.

Continued

Problem Solving

TAKE IT FURTHER

Students can try to solve problems dealing with the mass in grams of a given number of moles of a binary compound. For example, ask students to calculate the mass in grams of 1.60 mol of NaCl (93.6 g) and 0.620 mol of MgO (24.8 g).

Sub-Atomic Particles (continued)

Practice Answers in Appendix E

1. What is the mass in grams of 2.25 mol of the element iron, Fe?
2. What is the mass in grams of 0.375 mol of the element potassium, K?
3. What is the mass in grams of 0.0135 mol of the element sodium, Na?
4. What is the mass in grams of 16.3 mol of the element nickel, Ni?

Gram/Mole Conversions

PREMIUM CONTENT

Learn It! Video HMDScience.com

Solve It! Cards HMDScience.com

Sample Problem C **A chemist produced 11.9 g of aluminum, Al. How many moles of aluminum were produced?**

1 ANALYZE

Given: 11.9 g Al

Unknown: amount of Al in moles

2 PLAN

mass of Al in grams ⟶ amount of Al in moles

As shown in **Figure 3.7**, amount in moles can be obtained by *dividing* mass in grams by molar mass, which is mathematically the same as *multiplying* mass in grams by the *reciprocal* of molar mass.

$$\text{grams Al} \times \frac{\text{moles Al}}{\text{grams Al}} = \text{moles Al}$$

3 SOLVE

The molar mass of aluminum from the periodic table is rounded to 26.98 g/mol.

$$11.9 \text{ g Al} \times \frac{1 \text{ mol Al}}{26.98 \text{ g Al}} = 0.441 \text{ mol Al}$$

4 CHECK YOUR WORK

The answer is correctly given to three significant figures. The answer is reasonable because 11.9 g is somewhat less than half of 26.98 g.

Practice Answers in Appendix E

1. How many moles of calcium, Ca, are in 5.00 g of calcium?
2. How many moles of gold, Au, are in 3.60×10^{-5} g of gold?
3. How many moles of zinc, Zn, are in 0.535 g of zinc?

DECONSTRUCTING PROBLEMS

Point out that Sample Problem C is the reverse of Sample Problem B. The former involves converting grams to moles, while the latter involves converting moles to grams. Emphasize that the same chemical concepts are used in both types of problems. The only difference is found in setting up the conversion factor to make sure that the units cancel properly. Have students compare the conversion factors used in the two sample problems. Students should recognize that the conversion factors are the inverse of one another.

Teaching Tip

Avogadro's number is a counting unit, just as a pair of gloves is equal to two gloves or a ream of paper is equal to 500 sheets. We typically use Avogadro's number as the "counting unit" for atoms and molecules. By definition, 1 mole of anything has 6.022×10^{23} items; 1 mole of C atoms, 1 mole of water molecules, or even 1 mole of students would all have 6.022×10^{23} atoms, molecules, or students, respectively. The atomic masses listed in the periodic table represent the average mass in u for one atom or the mass in grams of 1 mole of atoms.

Answers

Practice B

1. 126 g Fe
2. 14.7 g K
3. 0.310 g Na
4. 957 g Ni

Classroom Practice

C-1 How many moles of copper, Cu, are in 3.22 g of copper?

Answer: 0.0507 mol

C-2 How many moles of lithium, Li, are in 2.72×10^{-4} g of lithium?

Answer: 3.92×10^{-5} mol

Answers

Practice C

1. 0.125 mol Ca
2. 1.83×10^{-7} mol Au
3. 8.18×10^{-3} mol Zn

Teach *continued*

Classroom Practice

D-1 How many moles of carbon, C, are in 2.25×10^{22} atoms of carbon?

Answer: 0.0374 mol

D-2 How many moles of oxygen, O, are in 2 000 000 atoms of oxygen?

Answer: 3×10^{-18} mol

D-3 How many atoms of sodium, Na, are in 3.80 mol of sodium?

Answer: 2.29×10^{24} atoms

E-1 What is the mass in grams of 5.0×10^{9} atoms of neon, Ne?

Answer: 1.7×10^{-13} g

E-2 How many atoms of carbon, C, are in 0.020 g of carbon?

Answer: 1.0×10^{21} atoms

E-3 What mass of silver, Ag, contains the same number of atoms as 10.0 g of boron, B?

Answer: 99.8 g

Answers

Practice D

1. 2.49×10^{-12} mol Pb
2. 4.2×10^{-21} mol Sn
3. 1.66×10^{24} atoms Al

Check for Understanding

Answer: Answers will vary. A correct response might be: Using Avogadro's number in calculations is necessary when you need to find the number of atoms.

CHECK FOR UNDERSTANDING

Describe Although using the mole unit of measurement is often preferable for doing calculations to using Avogadro's number, at other times, using Avogadro's number is necessary. Describe a circumstance under which this is true.

Conversions with Avogadro's Number

Avogadro's number can be used to find the number of atoms of an element from the amount in moles or to find the amount of an element in moles from the number of atoms. While these types of problems are less common in chemistry than converting between amount in moles and mass in grams, they are useful in demonstrating the meaning of Avogadro's number. Note that in these calculations, Avogadro's number is expressed in units of atoms per mole.

Conversions with Avogadro's Number

PREMIUM CONTENT **Solve It! Cards** HMDScience.com

Sample Problem D **How many moles of silver, Ag, are in 3.01×10^{23} atoms of silver?**

1 ANALYZE

Given: 3.01×10^{23} atoms of Ag

Unknown: amount of Ag in moles

2 PLAN

number of atoms of Ag ⟶ amount of Ag in moles

From **Figure 3.7**, we know that number of atoms is converted to amount in moles by dividing by Avogadro's number. This is equivalent to multiplying numbers of atoms by the reciprocal of Avogadro's number.

$$\text{Ag atoms} \times \frac{\text{moles Ag}}{\text{Avogadro's number of Ag atoms}} = \text{moles Ag}$$

3 SOLVE

$$3.01 \times 10^{23}\ \text{Ag atoms} \times \frac{1\ \text{mol Ag}}{6.022 \times 10^{23}\ \text{Ag atoms}} = 0.500\ \text{mol Ag}$$

4 CHECK YOUR WORK

The answer is correct—units cancel correctly and the number of atoms is one-half of Avogadro's number.

Practice Answers in Appendix E

1. How many moles of lead, Pb, are in 1.50×10^{12} atoms of lead?
2. How many moles of tin, Sn, are in 2500 atoms of tin?
3. How many atoms of aluminum, Al, are in 2.75 mol of aluminum?

Conversions with Avogadro's Number

Sample Problem E **What is the mass in grams of 1.20×10^{8} atoms of copper, Cu?**

1 ANALYZE

Given: 1.20×10^{8} atoms of Cu

Unknown: mass of Cu in grams

Continued

Problem Solving

REALITY CHECK

Students may not use the correct conversion factor. When working with Avogadro's number, this mistake can be very apparent. For example, have students invert the conversion factor used in Sample Problem D. The result would be a huge number. Considering that the problem asks for the number of moles, this huge number would indicate that a mistake was made.

Conversions with Avogadro's Number (continued)

2 PLAN number of atoms of Cu ⟶ amount of Cu in moles ⟶ mass of Cu in grams

As indicated in **Figure 3.7,** the given number of atoms must first be converted to amount in moles by dividing by Avogadro's number. Amount in moles is then multiplied by molar mass to yield mass in grams.

$$\text{Cu atoms} \times \frac{\text{moles Cu}}{\text{Avogadro's number of Cu atoms}} \times \frac{\text{grams Cu}}{\text{moles Cu}} = \text{grams Cu}$$

3 SOLVE The molar mass of copper from the periodic table is rounded to 63.55 g/mol.

$$1.20 \times 10^8 \text{ Cu atoms} \times \frac{1 \text{ mol Cu}}{6.022 \times 10^{23} \text{ Cu atoms}} \times \frac{63.55 \text{ g Cu}}{1 \text{ mol Cu}} = 1.27 \times 10^{-14} \text{ g Cu}$$

4 CHECK YOUR WORK Units cancel correctly to give the answer in grams. The size of the answer is reasonable—108 has been divided by about 1024 and multiplied by about 102.

Practice

1. What is the mass in grams of 7.5×10^{15} atoms of nickel, Ni?
2. How many atoms of sulfur, S, are in 4.00 g of sulfur?
3. What mass of gold, Au, contains the same number of atoms as 9.0 g of aluminum, Al?

SECTION 3 FORMATIVE ASSESSMENT

Reviewing Main Ideas

1. Explain each of the following:
   a. atomic number
   b. mass number
   c. relative atomic mass
   d. average atomic mass
   e. mole
   f. Avogadro's number
   g. molar mass
   h. isotope
2. Determine the number of protons, electrons, and neutrons in each of the following isotopes:
   a. sodium-23
   b. calcium-40
   c. $^{64}_{22}Cu$
   d. $^{108}_{47}Ag$
3. Write the nuclear symbol and hyphen notation for each of the following isotopes:
   a. mass number of 28 and atomic number of 14
   b. 26 protons and 30 neutrons
4. To two decimal places, what is the relative atomic mass and the molar mass of the element potassium, K?
5. Determine the mass in grams of the following:
   a. 2.00 mol N
   b. 3.01×10^{23} atoms Cl
6. Determine the amount in moles of the following:
   a. 12.15 g Mg
   b. 1.50×10^{23} atoms F

Critical Thinking

7. **ANALYZING DATA** Beaker A contains 2.06 mol of copper, and Beaker B contains 222 grams of silver. Which beaker contains the larger mass? Which beaker has the larger number of atoms?

Answers

Practice E

1. 7.3×10^{-7} g Ni
2. 7.51×10^{22} atoms S
3. 66 g Au

Assess and Reteach ▼

Assess Use the Formative Assessment on this page to evaluate student mastery of the section.

Reteach For students who need additional instruction, download the Section Study Guide.

Response to Intervention To reassess students' mastery, use the Section Quiz available to print or to take directly online at **HMDScience.com**.

Answers to Section Assessment

1. a. the number of protons in the nucleus of an atom of that element
   b. the total number of protons and neutrons in a nucleus
   c. the mass of an atom given in atomic mass units
   d. the weighted average of the masses of the naturally occurring isotopes of an element
   e. the amount of a substance that contains a number of particles equal to the number of atoms in exactly 12 g of carbon-12
   f. the number of particles in exactly one mole of a pure substance
   g. the mass of one mole of a pure substance, usually given in units of g/mol
   h. an atom that has the same number of protons as another atom but a different number of neutrons
2. a. 11 protons, 11 electrons, 12 neutrons
   b. 20 protons, 20 electrons, 20 neutrons
   c. 29 protons, 29 electrons, 35 neutrons
   d. 47 protons, 47 electrons, 61 neutrons
3. a. $^{28}_{14}Si$, silicon-28
   b. $^{56}_{26}Fe$, iron-56
4. 39.10 u, 39.10 g/mol
5. a. 28.0 g N
   b. 17.7 g Cl
6. a. 0.5000 mol Mg
   b. 0.249 mol F
7. Beaker B; Both beakers contain the same number of atoms.

Answers

1. a. 2.25 g
   b. 59 300 L
2. a. 7.2×10^1 μg
   b. 3.98×10^3 km

Math Tutor Conversion Factors

Most calculations in chemistry require that all measurements of the same quantity (mass, length, volume, temperature, and so on) be expressed in the same unit. To change the units of a quantity, you can multiply the quantity by a conversion factor. With SI units, such conversions are easy because units of the same quantity are related by multiples of 10, 100, 1000, or 1 million. Suppose you want to convert a given amount in milliliters to liters. You can use the relationship 1 L = 1000 mL. From this relationship, you can derive the following conversion factors.

$$\frac{1000 \text{ mL}}{1 \text{ L}} \text{ and } \frac{1 \text{ L}}{1000 \text{ mL}}$$

The correct strategy is to multiply the given amount (in mL) by the conversion factor that allows milliliter units to cancel out and liter units to remain. Using the second conversion factor will give you the units you want.

These conversion factors are based on an exact definition (1000 mL = 1 L exactly), so significant figures do not apply to these factors. The number of significant figures in a converted measurement depends on the certainty of the measurement you start with.

Sample Problem

A sample of aluminum has a mass of 0.087 g. What is the sample's mass in milligrams?

Based on SI prefixes, you know that 1 g = 1000 mg. Therefore, the possible conversion factors are

$$\frac{1000 \text{ mg}}{1 \text{ g}} \text{ and } \frac{1 \text{ g}}{1000 \text{ mg}}$$

The first conversion factor cancels grams, leaving milligrams.

$$0.087 \text{ g} \times \frac{1000 \text{ mg}}{1 \text{ g}} = 87 \text{ mg}$$

Notice that the values 0.087 g and 87 mg each have two significant figures.

A sample of a mineral has 4.08×10^{-5} mol of vanadium per kilogram of mass. How many micromoles of vanadium per kilogram does the mineral contain?

The prefix *micro-* specifies $\frac{1}{1\,000\,000}$ or 1×10^{-6} of the base unit.
So, 1 μmol = 1×10^{-6} mol. The possible conversion factors are

$$\frac{1\ \mu\text{mol}}{1 \times 10^{-6} \text{ mol}} \text{ and } \frac{1 \times 10^{-6} \text{ mol}}{1\ \mu\text{mol}}$$

The first conversion factor will allow moles to cancel and micromoles to remain.

$$4.08 \times 10^{-5} \text{ mol} \times \frac{1\ \mu\text{mol}}{1 \times 10^{-6} \text{ mol}} = 40.8\ \mu\text{mol}$$

Notice that the values 4.08×10^{-5} mol and 40.8 μmol each have three significant figures.

Practice

1. Express each of the following measurements in the units indicated.
   a. 2250 mg in grams
   b. 59.3 kL in liters
2. Use scientific notation to express each of the following measurements in the units indicated.
   a. 0.000 072 g in micrograms
   b. 3.98×10^6 m in kilometers

84 Chapter 3

CHAPTER 3 Summary

Review Games
Concept Maps

SECTION 1 The Atom: From Philosophical Idea to Scientific Theory

- The idea of atoms has been around since the time of the ancient Greeks. In the nineteenth century, John Dalton proposed a scientific theory of atoms that can still be used to explain properties of most chemicals today.
- Matter and its mass cannot be created or destroyed in chemical reactions.
- The mass ratios of the elements that make up a given compound are always the same, regardless of how much of the compound there is or how it was formed.
- If two or more different compounds are composed of the same two elements, then the ratio of the masses of the second element combined with a certain mass of the first element can be expressed as a ratio of small whole numbers.

KEY TERMS

law of conservation of mass
law of definite proportions
law of multiple proportions

SECTION 2 The Structure of the Atom

- Cathode-ray tubes supplied evidence of the existence of electrons, which are negatively charged subatomic particles that have relatively little mass.
- Rutherford found evidence for the existence of the atomic nucleus by bombarding gold foil with a beam of positively charged particles.
- Atomic nuclei are composed of protons, which have an electric charge of +1, and (in all but one case) neutrons, which have no electric charge.
- Atomic nuclei have radii of about 0.001 pm (pm = picometers; 1 pm × 10^{-12} m), and atoms have radii of about 40–270 pm.

KEY TERMS

atom
nuclear forces

SECTION 3 Counting Atoms

- The atomic number of an element is equal to the number of protons of an atom of that element.
- The mass number is equal to the total number of protons and neutrons that make up the nucleus of an atom of that element.
- The unified atomic mass unit (u) is based on the carbon-12 atom and is a convenient unit for measuring the mass of atoms. It equals 1.660 540 × 10^{-24} g.
- The average atomic mass of an element is found by calculating the weighted average of the atomic masses of the naturally occurring isotopes of the element.
- Avogadro's number is equal to approximately 6.022 × 10^{23}. A sample that contains a number of particles equal to Avogadro's number contains a mole of those particles.

KEY TERMS

atomic number
isotope
mass number
nuclide
unified atomic mass unit
average atomic mass
mole
Avogadro's number
molar mass

Review Answers

1. **a.** Because all chemical reactions are only the rearrangements of atoms, mass is neither created nor destroyed in such changes.
   b. Atoms of each element have their own characteristic mass, so compounds consisting of these atoms always have the same composition by mass.
   c. Only whole atoms combine in chemical compounds, so different compounds between the same two elements must result from the combination of different whole numbers of atoms.
2. 5 mass units; 13 mass units
3. **a.** the smallest particle of an element that retains the chemical properties of that element
   b. the nucleus and the surrounding region of electrons
4. An electron is negatively charged, has a mass approximately 1/2000 that of a hydrogen atom, has a fixed charge-to-mass ratio, and is present in atoms of all elements.
5. His model had most of the mass in the nucleus. He bombarded gold atoms with positively charged particles; most went straight through the atom, but some were deflected and a few bounced back.
6. the atomic number
7. **a.** atoms of an element that have the same number of protons but a different number of neutrons
   b. They have the same number of protons and electrons.
   c. They have different numbers of neutrons.
8.

Isotope	Protons	Electrons	Neutrons
Si-28	14	14	14
Si-29	14	14	15
Si-30	14	14	16

9. **a.** its number of protons
   b. the total number of protons and neutrons in an isotope
   c. atomic = 1, mass = 2
10. any isotope of any element
11. **a.** helium-4 **b.** oxygen-16 **c.** potassium-39
12. **a.** carbon-12 **b.** exactly 12 u
13. **a.** 4 u **b.** 54 u

CHAPTER 3 Review

SECTION 1

The Atom: From Philosophical Idea to Scientific Theory

REVIEWING MAIN IDEAS

1. Explain each of the following in terms of Dalton's atomic theory:
   a. the law of conservation of mass
   b. the law of definite proportions
   c. the law of multiple proportions

2. According to the law of conservation of mass, if element A has an atomic mass of 2 mass units and element B has an atomic mass of 3 mass units, what mass would be expected for compound AB? for compound A_2B_3?

SECTION 2

The Structure of the Atom

REVIEWING MAIN IDEAS

3. **a.** What is an atom?
   b. What two regions make up all atoms?

4. Describe at least four properties of electrons that were determined based on the experiments of Thomson and Millikan.

5. Summarize Rutherford's model of the atom, and explain how he developed this model based on the results of his famous gold-foil experiment.

6. What number uniquely identifies an element?

SECTION 3

Counting Atoms

REVIEWING MAIN IDEAS

7. **a.** What are isotopes?
   b. How are the isotopes of a particular element alike?
   c. How are they different?

8. Copy and complete the following table concerning the three isotopes of silicon, Si. (Hint: See Sample Problem A.)

Isotope	Number of protons	Number of electrons	number of neutrons
Si-28			
Si-29			
Si-30			

9. **a.** What is the atomic number of an element?
   b. What is the mass number of an isotope?
   c. In the nuclear symbol for deuterium, ^2_1H, identify the atomic number and the mass number.

10. What is a nuclide?

11. Use the periodic table and the information that follows to write the hyphen notation for each isotope described.
    a. atomic number = 2, mass number = 4
    b. atomic number = 8, mass number = 16
    c. atomic number = 19, mass number = 39

12. **a.** What nuclide is used as the standard in the relative scale for atomic masses?
    b. What is its assigned atomic mass?

13. What is the atomic mass of an atom if its mass is approximately equal to the following?
    a. $\frac{1}{3}$ that of carbon-12
    b. 4.5 times as much as carbon-12

14. **a.** What is the definition of a *mole*?
    b. What is the abbreviation for *mole*?
    c. How many particles are in one mole?
    d. What name is given to the number of particles in a mole?

15. **a.** What is the molar mass of an element?
    b. To two decimal places, write the molar masses of carbon, neon, iron, and uranium.

16. Suppose you have a sample of an element.
    a. How is the mass in grams of the element converted to amount in moles?
    b. How is the mass in grams of the element converted to number of atoms?

14. **a.** the number of particles equal to the number of atoms in exactly 12 g of carbon-12
    b. mol
    c. 6.022×10^{23}
    d. Avogadro's number
15. **a.** the mass of one mole of atoms of that element
    b. 12.01 g/mol, 20.18 g/mol, 55.85 g/mol, 238.03 g/mol
16. **a.** divide by molar mass
    b. divide by molar mass, then multiply by Avogadro's number
17. **a.** 6.94 g **b.** 27.0 g **c.** 40.1 g **d.** 55.8 g **e.** 12.01 g **f.** 107.9 g
18. **a.** 1.000 mol **b.** 0.5000 mol **c.** 1.57×10^3 mol **d.** 2.81×10^{-13} mol
19. 39.95 u
20. 10.00 u
21. **a.** 9.03×10^{23} atoms
    b. 4.068×10^{24} atoms
    c. 1.50×10^{23} atoms

86 Chapter 3

PRACTICE PROBLEMS

17. What is the mass in grams of each of the following? (Hint: See Sample Problems B and E.)
- **a.** 1.00 mol Li
- **b.** 1.00 mol Al
- **c.** 1.00 molar mass Ca
- **d.** 1.00 molar mass Fe
- **e.** 6.022×10^{23} atoms C
- **f.** 6.022×10^{23} atoms Ag

18. How many moles of atoms are there in each of the following? (Hint: See Sample Problems C and D.)
- **a.** 6.022×10^{23} atoms Ne
- **b.** 3.011×10^{23} atoms Mg
- **c.** 3.25×10^5 g Pb
- **d.** 4.50×10^{-12} g O

19. Three isotopes of argon occur in nature—$^{36}_{18}Ar$, $^{38}_{18}Ar$, and $^{40}_{18}Ar$. Calculate the average atomic mass of argon to two decimal places, given the following relative atomic masses and abundances of each of the isotopes: argon-36 (35.97 u; 0.337%), argon-38 (37.96 u; 0.063%), and argon-40 (39.96 u; 99.600%).

20. Naturally occurring boron is 80.20% boron-11 (atomic mass = 11.01 u) and 19.80% of some other isotopic form of boron. What must the atomic mass of this second isotope be in order to account for the 10.81 u average atomic mass of boron? (Write the answer to two decimal places.)

21. How many atoms are there in each of the following?
- **a.** 1.50 mol Na
- **b.** 6.755 mol Pb
- **c.** 7.02 g Si

22. What is the mass in grams of each of the following?
- **a.** 3.011×10^{23} atoms F
- **b.** 1.50×10^{23} atoms Mg
- **c.** 4.50×10^{12} atoms Cl
- **d.** 8.42×10^{18} atoms Br
- **e.** 25 atoms W
- **f.** 1 atom Au

23. Determine the number of atoms in each of the following:
- **a.** 5.40 g B
- **b.** 0.250 mol S
- **c.** 0.0384 mol K
- **d.** 0.025 50 g Pt
- **e.** 1.00×10^{-10} g Au

Mixed Review

REVIEWING MAIN IDEAS

24. Determine the mass in grams of each of the following:
- **a.** 3.00 mol Al
- **b.** 2.56×10^{24} atoms Li
- **c.** 1.38 mol N
- **d.** 4.86×10^{24} atoms Au
- **e.** 6.50 mol Cu
- **f.** 2.57×10^8 mol S
- **g.** 1.05×10^{18} atoms Hg

25. Copy and complete the following table concerning the properties of subatomic particles.

Particle	Symbol	Mass number	Actual mass	Relative charge
Electron				
Proton				
Neutron				

26. a. How is a unified atomic mass unit (u) related to the mass of one carbon-12 atom?
b. What is the relative atomic mass of an atom?

27. a. What is the nucleus of an atom?
b. Who is credited with the discovery of the atomic nucleus?
c. Identify the two kinds of particles that make up the nucleus.

28. How many moles of atoms are there in each of the following?
- **a.** 40.1 g Ca
- **b.** 11.5 g Na
- **c.** 5.87 g Ni
- **d.** 150 g S
- **e.** 2.65 g Fe
- **f.** 0.007 50 g Ag
- **g.** 2.25×10^{25} atoms Zn
- **h.** 50 atoms Ba

29. State the law of multiple proportions, and give an example of two compounds that illustrate the law.

30. What is the approximate atomic mass of an atom if its mass is
- **a.** 12 times that of carbon-12?
- **b.** $\frac{1}{2}$ that of carbon-12?

31. What is an electron?

26. a. $1\ u = \frac{1}{12}$ the mass of a carbon-12 atom
b. the mass of an atom as it compares with the mass of a carbon-12 atom

27. a. central portion of the atom containing most of the mass
b. Ernest Rutherford
c. protons and neutrons

28. a. 1.00 mol **b.** 0.500 mol **c.** 0.100 mol **d.** 4.7 mol **e.** 0.0474 mol **f.** 6.95×10^{-5} mol **g.** 37.4 mol **h.** 8.30×10^{-23} mol

29. If two or more compounds are composed of the same two elements, then the ratio of the masses of the second element combined with a certain mass of the first element is always a ratio of small whole numbers; CO and CO_2 are examples.

30. a. 144 u **b.** 6 u

31. a negatively-charged particle of small mass found outside the nucleus

22. a. 9.500 g **b.** 6.05 g **c.** 2.65×10^{-10} g **d.** 1.12×10^{-3} g **e.** 7.6×10^{-21} g **f.** 3×10^{-22} g

23. a. 3.01×10^{23} atoms
b. 1.51×10^{23} atoms
c. 2.31×10^{22} atoms
d. 7.872×10^{19} atoms
e. 3.06×10^{11} atoms

24. a. 80.9 g **b.** 29.5 g **c.** 19.3 g **d.** 1.59×10^3 g **e.** 413 g **f.** 8.24×10^9 g **g.** 3.50×10^{-4} g

25.

Particle	Symbol	Mass no.	Actual mass	Relative charge
Electron	$^{0}_{-1}e$, e^-	0	9.109×10^{-31} kg	−1
Proton	$^{1}_{1}H$, p^+	1	1.673×10^{-27} kg	+1
Neutron	$^{1}_{0}n$, n^0	1	1.675×10^{-27} kg	0

32. Using carbon and oxygen: The law of definite proportions states that any amount of CO will contain a constant percentage by mass of C and O. The law of multiple proportions accounts for the difference between the oxygen : carbon mass ratio in the two compounds. The oxygen : carbon mass ratio in carbon dioxide is twice the ratio in carbon monoxide.

33. a. from the anode to the cathode
 b. positive

34. The density of the nucleus is 9×10^{12} times the density of osmium, or 9 trillion times as dense.

35. a. amount of O_2 present
 b. CO poisoning, because CO binds to hemoglobin more strongly than O_2 does
 c. CO produced by a heating system cannot be adequately ventilated.

Refer to the **HMDScience** website for appropriate scoring rubrics for items 36–39. Look for these points in each report:

36. Chadwick bombarded beryllium-9 with alpha particles to obtain carbon-12 and a single neutron.

37. Avogadro's work with gases

38. the wave nature of electrons; quantum theory; an essential tool in the study of science

39. Students' reports should mention elements and compounds commonly used in nuclear medicine.

40. Answers will vary.

41. 12 in each isotope

CHAPTER REVIEW

CRITICAL THINKING

32. **Organizing Ideas** Using two chemical compounds as an example, describe the difference between the law of definite proportions and the law of multiple proportions.

33. **Constructing Models** As described in Section 2, the structure of the atom was determined from observations made in painstaking experimental research. Suppose a series of experiments revealed that when an electric current is passed through gas at low pressure, the surface of the cathode-ray tube opposite the anode glows. In addition, a paddle wheel placed in the tube rolls from the anode toward the cathode when the current is on.
 a. In which direction do particles pass through the gas?
 b. What charge do the particles possess?

34. **Analyzing Data** Osmium is the element with the greatest density, 22.58 g/cm^3. How does the density of osmium compare to the density of a typical nucleus of 2×10^8 metric tons/cm^3? (1 metric ton = 1000 kg)

USING THE HANDBOOK

35. Group 14 of the *Elements Handbook* (Appendix A) describes the reactions that produce CO and CO_2. Review this section to answer the following:
 a. When a fuel burns, what determines whether CO or CO_2 will be produced?
 b. What happens in the body if hemoglobin picks up CO?
 c. Why is CO poisoning most likely to occur in homes that are well sealed during cold winter months?

RESEARCH AND WRITING

36. Prepare a report on the series of experiments conducted by Sir James Chadwick that led to the discovery of the neutron.

37. Write a report on the contributions of Amedeo Avogadro that led to the determination of the value of Avogadro's number.

38. Trace the development of the electron microscope, and cite some of its many uses.

39. The study of atomic structure and the nucleus produced a new field of medicine called *nuclear medicine*. Describe the use of radioactive tracers to detect and treat diseases.

ALTERNATIVE ASSESSMENT

40. Observe a cathode-ray tube in operation, and write a description of your observations.

41. **Performance Assessment** Using colored clay, build a model of the nucleus of each of carbon's three naturally occurring isotopes: carbon-12, carbon-13, and carbon-14. Specify the number of electrons that would surround each nucleus.

88 Chapter 3

Standards-Based Assessment

Answer the following items on a separate piece of paper.

MULTIPLE CHOICE

1. A chemical compound always has the same elements in the same proportions by mass regardless of the source of the compound. This is a statement of
   A. the law of multiple proportions.
   B. the law of isotopes.
   C. the law of definite proportions.
   D. the law of conservation of mass.

2. An important result of Rutherford's experiments with gold foil was to establish that
   A. atoms have mass.
   B. electrons have a negative charge.
   C. neutrons are uncharged particles.
   D. the atom is mostly empty space.

3. Which subatomic particle has a charge of +1?
   A. electron
   B. neutron
   C. proton
   D. meson

4. Which particle has the least mass?
   A. electron
   B. neutron
   C. proton
   D. All have the same mass.

5. Cathode rays are composed of
   A. alpha particles.
   B. electrons.
   C. protons.
   D. neutrons.

6. The atomic number of an element is the same as the number of
   A. protons.
   B. neutrons.
   C. protons + electrons.
   D. protons + neutrons.

7. How many neutrons are present in an atom of tin that has an atomic number of 50 and a mass number of 119?
   A. 50
   B. 69
   C. 119
   D. 169

8. What is the mass of 1.50 mol of sodium, Na?
   A. 0.652 g
   B. 0.478 g
   C. 11.0 g
   D. 34.5 g

9. How many moles of carbon are in a 28.0 g sample?
   A. 336 mol
   B. 72.0 mol
   C. 2.33 mol
   D. 0.500 mol

SHORT ANSWER

10. Which atom has more neutrons, potassium-40 or argon-40?

11. What is the mass of 1.20×10^{23} atoms of phosphorus?

EXTENDED RESPONSE

12. Cathode rays emitted by a piece of silver and a piece of copper illustrate identical properties. What is the significance of this observation?

13. A student believed that she had discovered a new element and named it mythium. Analysis found it contained two isotopes. The composition of the isotopes was 19.9% of atomic mass 10.013 and 80.1% of atomic mass 11.009. What is the average atomic mass, and do you think mythium was a new element?

Test Tip
Choose the best possible answer for each question, even if you think there is another possible answer that is not given.

STANDARDS-BASED ASSESSMENT

To give students practice under more realistic testing conditions, give them 60 minutes to answer all of the questions in this Standardized Test Preparation.

Test Answers

1. C
2. D
3. C
4. A
5. B
6. A
7. B
8. D
9. C
10. Argon-40 has 22 neutrons (40 – 18 = 22), and potassium-40 has 21 neutrons (40 – 19 = 21).
11. 6.17 g
12. All cathode rays are the same, regardless of their source. Therefore, the particles responsible for the cathode rays must be present in all atoms. The particles are electrons.
13. When the average atomic mass is calculated, it is 10.811. Because the atomic mass is the same as the atomic mass of boron, mythium was not a new element.

Arrangement of Electrons in Atoms

① Core Instruction

Chapter Resources

- The Teacher's Edition wrap has extensive teaching support for every lesson, including Misconception Alerts, Teach from Visuals, Demonstrations, Teaching Tips, Differentiated Instruction, and Problem Solving support.
- Several additional presentation tools are available online for every chapter, including Animated Chemistry features and Visual Concepts.
- You can open your lesson with the Why It Matters Video: Atoms.

Section	Instruction	Labs and Demonstrations Go Online for Materials Lists and Solutions Lists.
4.1	**Textbook:** The Development of a New Atomic Model **Animated Chemistry:** Energy Levels of an Atom **Teaching Visuals:** Electromagnetic Spectrum • Wavelength and Frequency • Photoelectric Effect • Hydrogen's Line-Emission Spectrum • Photon Emission and Absorption **PowerPresentations**	**Demonstration:** Wavelength and Frequency **Demonstration:** Photoelectric Effect **Demonstration:** Emission Spectra
4.2	**Textbook:** The Quantum Model of the Atom **Animated Chemistry:** Energy Levels of an Atom **Teaching Visuals:** Shapes of *s*, *p*, and *d* Orbitals • Electrons Accommodated in Energy Levels and Sublevels • Quantum Numbers of the First 30 Atomic Orbitals **PowerPresentations**	**QuickLab:** The Wave Nature of Light: Interference **Lab:** Flame Tests **Demonstration:** Magnetic Fields of Electrons **Lab:** Balloon Orbitals (STEM)
4.3	**Textbook:** Electron Configurations **Teaching Visuals:** Relative Energies of Orbitals • Writing Electron Configurations • Relative Energies of Orbitals • Orbital Notation for Three Noble Gases • Orbital Notation for Argon and Potassium **PowerPresentations**	

② Support and Intervention

- **Interactive Reader** (English and Spanish)
- **Study Guide**
- **Interactive Review:** Review Games, Concept Maps, and Section Self-Checks
- **Scientific Reasoning Skill Builder**
- **Learn It! Videos**
- **Solve It! Cards**
- **Interactive Demos**
- **Sample Problem Sets**

③ Specialized Support

- **Chapter Summary Audio Files**
- **Interactive Reader Audio Files**
- **Differentiated Instruction:** Inclusion, Below Level, and English Learners (TE wrap)

Enrichment and Challenge

- **Differentiated Instruction:** Pre-AP (TE wrap)
- **Chemistry Explorers:** The Noble Decade (SE)
- **WebLinks**

Assessment

- **Section Formative Assessments** (SE)
- **Section Quizzes**
- **Chapter Review** (SE)
- **Chapter Tests A and B**
- **Alternative Assessment** (TE wrap)
- **Online Assessment and Remediation**
- **ExamView Banks**

Where do I find it?

	Resource	PRINT	DVD	ONLINE
1	Animated Chemistry		■	■
1	Demonstrations (TE wrap)	■		■
1	Interactive Whiteboard		■	■
1	Labs		■	■
1	PowerPresentations		■	■
1	QuickLabs	■	■	■
1	Teaching Visuals		■	■
1	Textbook	■	■	■
1	Visual Concepts		■	■
1	Why It Matters Videos		■	■
2	Interactive Demos		■	■
2	Interactive Reader	■	■	■
2	Interactive Reviews		■	■
2	Learn It! Videos		■	■
2	Sample Problem Sets		■	■
2	Scientific Reasoning Skill Builder		■	■
2	Smart Grapher Tool		■	■
2	Solve It! Cards		■	■
2	Study Guide		■	■
3	Chapter Summary Audio Files		■	■
3	Differentiated Instruction (TE wrap)	■		
3	Interactive Reader Audio Files		■	■

CHAPTER 4

Chapter Overview

Section 1 describes the principles of electromagnetic radiation and the development of Bohr's model of the atom.

Section 2 describes the location of electrons around the nucleus from a wave-mechanical, or quantum, perspective using quantum numbers.

Section 3 discusses the rules used to determine the electron configurations of the elements and introduces electron configuration notations.

▼ Focus and Motivate

Activate Prior Knowledge

Students may need a review of the following concepts:

- inverse proportions
- the mass of electrons

About the Image

An electron is not confined to a specific orbital around the nucleus. Rather, electrons can move to orbitals that are either closer to or farther from the nucleus. As they move down to orbitals closer to the nucleus, electrons emit energy in the form of light. Consequently, the emission of light is fundamentally related to the behavior of electrons.

Why It Matters

Students can access the video online and find other helpful resources at **HMDScience.com**.

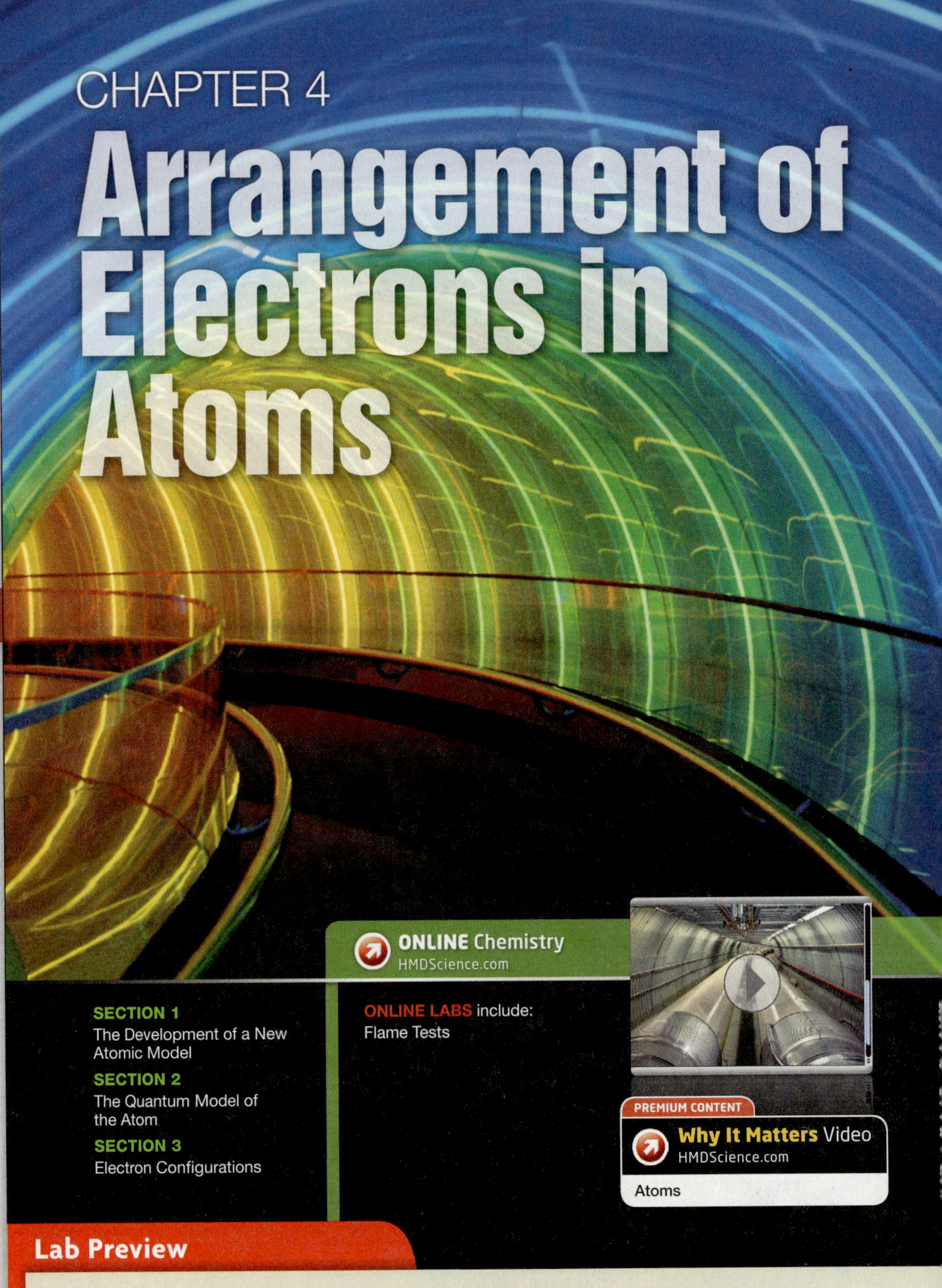

CHAPTER 4

Arrangement of Electrons in Atoms

ONLINE Chemistry
HMDScience.com

SECTION 1
The Development of a New Atomic Model

SECTION 2
The Quantum Model of the Atom

SECTION 3
Electron Configurations

ONLINE LABS include:
Flame Tests

PREMIUM CONTENT

Why It Matters Video
HMDScience.com

Atoms

Lab Preview

The following labs and demonstrations support the concepts presented in this chapter.

LABS

Flame Tests (Core Skill)
Balloon Orbitals (STEM)

QUICKLABS

The Wave Nature of Light: Interference

DEMONSTRATIONS

Wavelength and Frequency
Photoelectric Effect
Emission Spectra
Magnetic Fields of Electrons

The Development of a New Atomic Model

SECTION 1

Main Ideas

- Light has characteristics of both particles and waves.
- When certain frequencies of light strike a metal, electrons are emitted.
- Electrons exist only in very specific energy states for atoms of each element.
- Bohr's model of the hydrogen atom explained electron transition states.

Key Terms

electromagnetic radiation	photoelectric effect	excited state
electromagnetic spectrum	quantum	line-emission spectrum
wavelength	photon	continuous spectrum
frequency	ground state	

The Rutherford model of the atom was an improvement over previous models, but it was incomplete. It did not explain how the atom's negatively charged electrons are distributed in the space surrounding its positively charged nucleus. After all, it was well known that oppositely charged particles attract each other. So what prevented the negative electrons from being drawn into the positive nucleus?

In the early twentieth century, a new atomic model evolved as a result of investigations into the absorption and emission of light by matter. The studies revealed a relationship between light and an atom's electrons. This new understanding led directly to a revolutionary view of the nature of energy, matter, and atomic structure.

MAIN IDEA

Light has characteristics of both particles and waves.

Before 1900, scientists thought light behaved solely as a wave. This belief changed when it was later discovered that light also has particle-like characteristics. Still, many of light's properties can be described in terms of waves. A quick review of these wavelike properties will help you understand the basic theory of light as it existed at the beginning of the twentieth century.

The Wave Description of Light

Visible light is a kind of **electromagnetic radiation,** which is a form of energy that exhibits wavelike behavior as it travels through space. Other kinds of electromagnetic radiation include X-rays, ultraviolet and infrared light, microwaves, and radio waves. Together, all the forms of electromagnetic radiation form the **electromagnetic spectrum.** The electromagnetic spectrum is represented in **Figure 1.1** on the next page. All forms of electromagnetic radiation move at a constant speed of 3.00×10^8 meters per second (m/s) through a vacuum and at slightly slower speeds through matter. Because air is mostly empty space, the value of 3.00×10^8 m/s is also light's approximate speed through air.

The significant feature of wave motion is its repetitive nature, which can be characterized by the measurable properties of wavelength and frequency. **Wavelength** (λ) is the distance between corresponding points on adjacent waves. The unit for wavelength is a distance unit.

Differentiated Instruction

BELOW LEVEL

Have students list several types of electromagnetic radiation found in their homes. Students are likely to mention microwaves and radio waves based on the information in the text.

Point out that other kinds of electromagnetic radiation are also present, including ultraviolet waves from the sun and visible light. Emphasize that visible light is only a small portion of the electromagnetic spectrum. We need special devices to see or detect any form of electromagnetic radiation other than visible light. For example, point out that night-vision goggles enable a person to detect infrared waves. A radio enables a person to detect radio waves.

SECTION 1

Plan and Prepare ▼

Objectives

Upon completion of this section, students should be able to do the following:

- Explain the mathematical relationship among the speed, wavelength, and frequency of electromagnetic radiation.
- Discuss the dual wave-particle nature of light.
- Discuss the significance of the photoelectric effect and the line-emission spectrum of hydrogen to the development of the atomic model.
- Describe the Bohr model of the hydrogen atom.

Classroom Catalyst

Ask students if they agree with Rutherford's view that an atom has protons and neutrons at the center of a sphere of almost empty space. Explain that Rutherford's model was an important development but that additional research led to changes in the model. Bohr envisioned the electrons outside the nucleus orbiting in the same way that the planets orbit the sun. The problem with this model is that the electrons and the nucleus are oppositely charged. The tug of the electrostatic force between electron and nucleus would inevitably pull the electrons into the nucleus.

Teach ▼

Misconception Alert!

Show students a slide or picture of the planets. Explain that even though many people think that the organization of electrons in an atom is similar to the organization of the planets in a solar system, the two situations are quite different. The elliptical *orbits* in which planets travel are constant. *Orbitals* vary in shape and represent probable locations of electrons rather than paths on which electrons travel.

▼ Teach *continued*

TEACH FROM VISUALS

FIGURE 1.2 In each water wave, the wavelength is shown as the distance between the crest of one wave and the crest of the next wave. However, students should realize that wavelength is the distance between *any* two corresponding points on adjacent waves. Frequency refers to the number of waves that pass a given point in a specific time. Have students imagine that they are watching waves at the beach. If the waves begin to break more frequently on the beach and their speed remains the same, then the frequency of the waves is increasing and the distance between the wave crests is decreasing.

Demonstration

WAVELENGTH AND FREQUENCY

Have two students hold a **coiled spring** along the floor or a tabletop. Ask one of the students to begin moving the spring back and forth so that a wave pattern forms. How does the wavelength change when the student moves the spring back and forth with greater frequency? The wavelength decreases.

READING TOOLKIT

BRAINSTORMING Have students brainstorm a list of different types of waves. Invite students to speculate about how the different types of waves are similar and how they are different.

Critical Thinking

Answer: Wave A has the greater wavelength. The distance from wave crest to wave crest is longer than for Wave B. Wave B has the greater frequency. Because the crests are closer together, more waves will pass the post in one second than with Wave A.

FIGURE 1.1

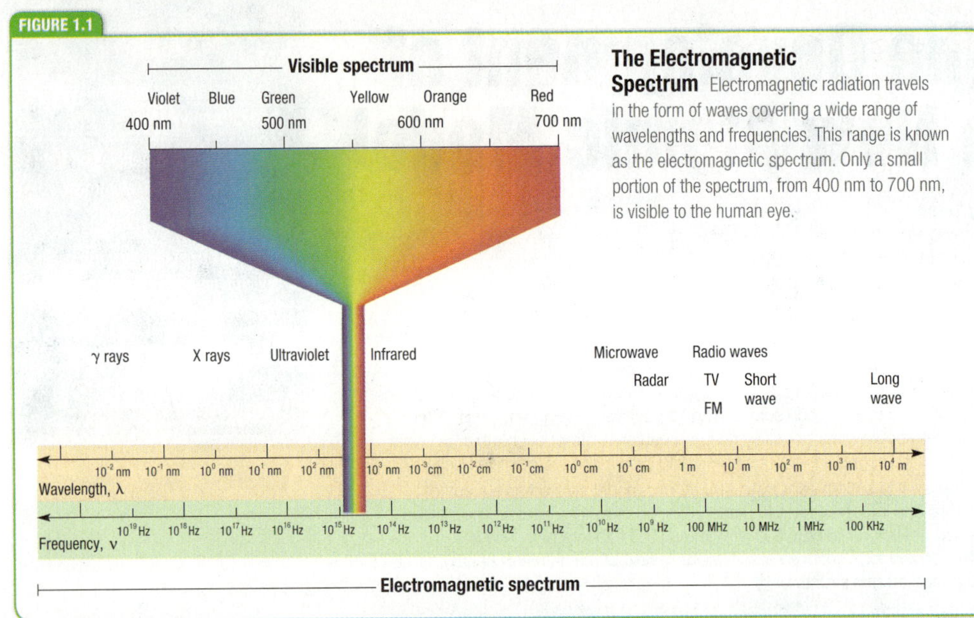

The Electromagnetic Spectrum Electromagnetic radiation travels in the form of waves covering a wide range of wavelengths and frequencies. This range is known as the electromagnetic spectrum. Only a small portion of the spectrum, from 400 nm to 700 nm, is visible to the human eye.

Depending on the type of electromagnetic radiation, it may be expressed in meters, centimeters, or nanometers, as shown in **Figure 1.1**.

Frequency (*ν*) **is defined as the number of waves that pass a given point in a specific time, usually one second.** Frequency is expressed in waves/second. One wave/second is called a hertz (Hz), named for Heinrich Hertz, who was a pioneer in the study of electromagnetic radiation. **Figure 1.2** illustrates the properties of wavelength and frequency for a familiar kind of wave, a wave on the surface of water. Frequency and wavelength are mathematically related to each other.

FIGURE 1.2

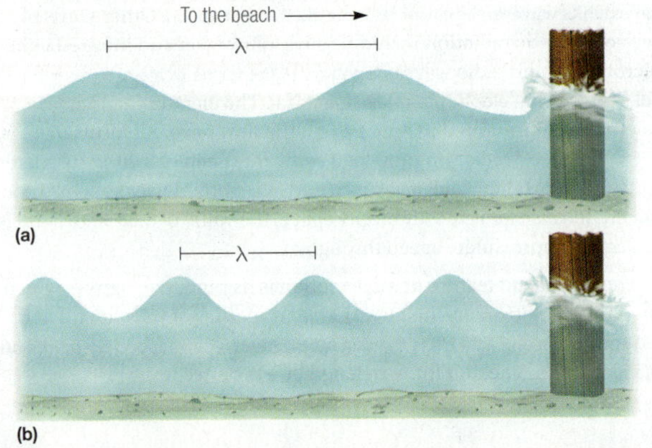

Wavelength and Frequency The distance between two corresponding points on one of these water waves, such as from crest to crest, is the wave's wavelength, λ. We can measure the wave's frequency, *ν*, by observing how often the water level rises and falls at a given point, such as at the post.

CRITICAL THINKING
Analyze Which waves have a greater wavelength, those in (a) or those in (b)? Which have the greater frequency? Explain each answer.

Problem Solving

REALITY CHECK

Use the values for frequency in **Figure 1.1** to show students the importance of units when comparing values. For example, point out that 1 MHz equals 1,000,000 Hz. Therefore, 100 MHz equals 10^8 Hz. Replacing 100 MHz with 10^8 Hz would clarify any misunderstanding that the frequency of a wavelength suddenly increases at this point.

Ask students to convert 10 MHz to Hz. 10^7 Hz

Then ask students to convert 1 MHz to Hz. 10^6 Hz

Have students find the conversion factor for converting KHz to Hz and then use this conversion factor to convert 100 KHz to Hz. 1000; 10^5 Hz

For electromagnetic radiation, the mathematical relationship between frequency and wavelength is written as follows:

$$c = \lambda \nu$$

In the equation, c is the speed of light (in m/s), λ is the wavelength of the electromagnetic wave (in m), and ν is the frequency of the electromagnetic wave (in s^{-1}). Because c is the same for all electromagnetic radiation, the product $\lambda\nu$ is a constant. Consequently, as the wavelength of light decreases, its frequency increases, and vice versa.

MAIN IDEA

When certain frequencies of light strike a metal, electrons are emitted.

In the early 1900s, scientists conducted two experiments involving interactions of light and matter that could not be explained by the wave theory of light. One experiment involved a phenomenon known as the photoelectric effect. **The photoelectric effect refers to the emission of electrons from a metal when light shines on the metal,** as illustrated in **Figure 1.3**.

The mystery of the photoelectric effect involved the frequency of the light striking the metal. For a given metal, no electrons were emitted if the light's frequency was below a certain minimum—regardless of the light's intensity. Light was known to be a form of energy, capable of knocking loose an electron from a metal. But the wave theory of light predicted that light of any frequency could supply enough energy to eject an electron. Scientists couldn't explain why the light had to be of a minimum frequency in order for the photoelectric effect to occur.

FIGURE 1.3

The Photoelectric Effect Electromagnetic radiation strikes the surface of the metal, rejecting electrons from the metal and causing an electric current.

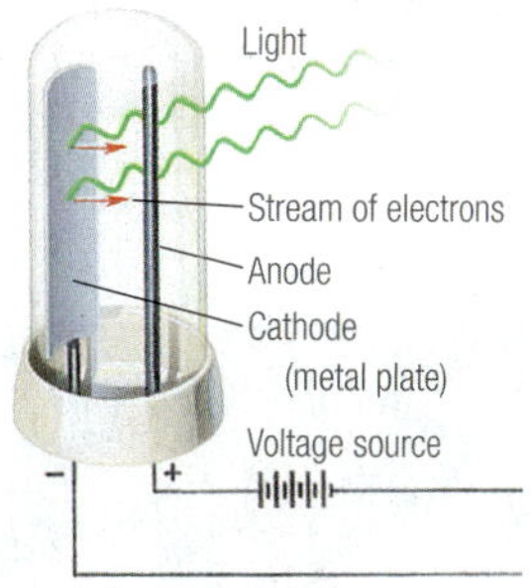

Light
Stream of electrons
Anode
Cathode (metal plate)
Voltage source
−
+

The Particle Description of Light

The explanation of the photoelectric effect dates back to 1900, when German physicist Max Planck was studying the emission of light by hot objects. He proposed that a hot object does not emit electromagnetic energy continuously, as would be expected if the energy emitted were in the form of waves. Instead, Planck suggested that the object emits energy in small, specific packets called quanta. **A quantum of energy is the minimum quantity of energy that can be lost or gained by an atom.** Planck proposed the following relationship between a quantum of energy and the frequency of radiation.

Quantum of Energy $E = h\nu$

In the equation, E is the energy, in joules, of a quantum of radiation, ν is the frequency, in s^{-1}, of the radiation emitted, and h is a fundamental physical constant now known as Planck's constant; $h = 6.626 \times 10^{-34}\ J \bullet s$.

In 1905, Albert Einstein expanded on Planck's theory by introducing the radical idea that electromagnetic radiation has a dual wave-particle nature. Light exhibits many wavelike properties, but it can also be thought of as a stream of particles. Each particle carries a quantum of energy.

Analogy

If you were throwing balls at milk bottles to try to knock them over to win a prize at a carnival, would you choose to throw 3 baseballs or 12 table-tennis balls? You would choose the baseballs, because each table-tennis ball would not have enough energy to knock over a milk bottle. Similarly, because of the photoelectric effect, an electron remains bound to a metal unless a single photon with the required minimum energy hits the metal with enough energy to eject the electron.

Application

The photoelectric effect causes electrons to be ejected from the surface of a metal when light of high enough frequency hits the metal's surface. This phenomenon is utilized in electric-eye door openers, light meters, and photovoltaic cells.

Demonstration

PHOTOELECTRIC EFFECT

To demonstrate the photoelectric effect, use **different colors of LED keychain lights** and **phosphorescent paper** (such as that used for "glow In the dark" items). When low-energy light is used, such as red, no phosphorescence is observed. But when using blue, UV, or white light, the phosphorescent paper glows.

Differentiated Instruction

INCLUSION

Have developmentally delayed students draw and color a rainbow on poster board. Have the students label each color of the visible spectrum with its approximate frequency or range of frequencies. In addition, have the students give examples of living things that can detect parts of the electromagnetic spectrum that humans cannot detect. For example, many birds such as penguins and homing pigeons can see a portion of the ultraviolet range.

▼ Teach continued

Misconception Alert!

It is easy for students to confuse an *emission* spectrum with an *absorption* spectrum. The spectra presented in this section are emission spectra because they show the frequencies at which light is emitted, or given off, from excited electrons in atoms. In an absorption spectrum, the frequencies shown are those of light that is absorbed, or taken in, by electrons in atoms. The energy absorbed excites the electrons to higher energy states.

Teaching Tip

Much information can be derived from a single line in an atomic-emission spectrum. The fact that a single color is produced proves that electrons are moving from a higher energy level to a lower energy level, and that the difference in energy between the two levels is always the same.

Demonstration

EMISSION SPECTRA

If your school has **gas discharge tubes** and a **power supply,** have students view the individual lines of emission spectra through **spectroscopes.** Students can also use a **CD** as a diffraction grating to observe different light sources. White light gives off all of the colors of visible light, but other lights, such as mercury vapor or sodium vapor, may show only a few lines.

Teaching Tip

A rainbow is a familiar example of a continuous spectrum. Sunlight contains a continuous range of colors (frequencies, wavelengths) of light.

Einstein called these particles photons. A **photon** is a particle of electromagnetic radiation having zero mass and carrying a quantum of energy. The energy of a photon depends on the frequency of the radiation.

$$E_{photon} = h\nu$$

Einstein explained the photoelectric effect by proposing that electromagnetic radiation is absorbed by matter only in whole numbers of photons. In order for an electron to be ejected from a metal surface, the electron must be struck by a single photon possessing at least the minimum energy required to knock the electron loose. According to the equation $E_{photon} = h\nu$, this minimum energy corresponds to a minimum frequency. If a photon's frequency is below the minimum, then the electron remains bound to the metal surface. Electrons in different metals are bound more or less tightly, so different metals require different minimum frequencies to exhibit the photoelectric effect.

MAIN IDEA

Electrons exist only in very specific energy states for every atom of each element.

When current is passed through a gas at low pressure, the potential energy of the gas atoms increases. The lowest energy state of an atom is its **ground state**. A state in which an atom has a higher potential energy than it has in its ground state is an **excited state.** There are many possible excited states, each with a unique energy, but only one ground state energy for atoms of a given element. When an excited atom returns to its ground state or a lower energy excited state, it gives off the energy it gained in the form of electromagnetic radiation. The production of colored light in neon signs, as shown in **Figure 1.4**, is a familiar example of this process.

FIGURE 1.4

Light Emission Excited neon atoms emit light when electrons in higher energy levels fall back to the ground state or to a lower-energy excited state.

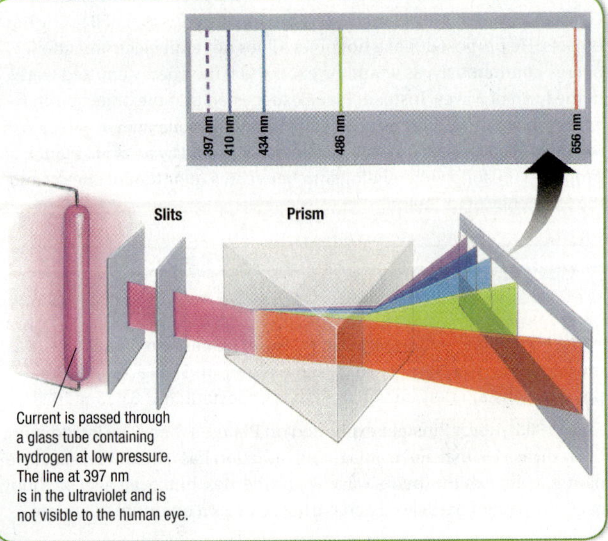

FIGURE 1.5

Emission-Line Spectra Excited hydrogen atoms emit a pinkish glow, as is shown in this diagram. When the visible portion of the emitted light is passed through a prism, it is separated into specific wavelengths that are part of hydrogen's emission-line spectrum. The line at 397 nm is in the ultraviolet and is not visible to the human eye.

Problem Solving

TAKE IT FURTHER

Have students use both equations, $c = \lambda\nu$ and $E = h\nu$, to solve a problem. For example, ask students to calculate the frequency and energy of blue light that has a wavelength of 400 nm.

By rearranging the first equation, the frequency of the blue light equals the speed of light (3.00×10^8 m•s^{-1}) divided by the wavelength in meters (4.0×10^{-7} m), which equals 7.50×10^{14} s^{-1}.
Substituting 7.50×10^{14} s^{-1} for the frequency into the second equation, which involves Planck's constant (6.62×10^{-34} J•s), yields an energy of:
$(6.62 \times 10^{-34}$ J•s$)(7.50 \times 10^{-14}$ s$^{-1})$
$= 4.96 \times 10^{-19}$ J.

FIGURE 1.6

Explaining Energy-Levels A series of specific wavelengths of emitted light makes up hydrogen's emission-line spectrum. The letters below the lines label hydrogen's various energy-level transitions. Niels Bohr's model of the hydrogen atom provided an explanation for these transitions.

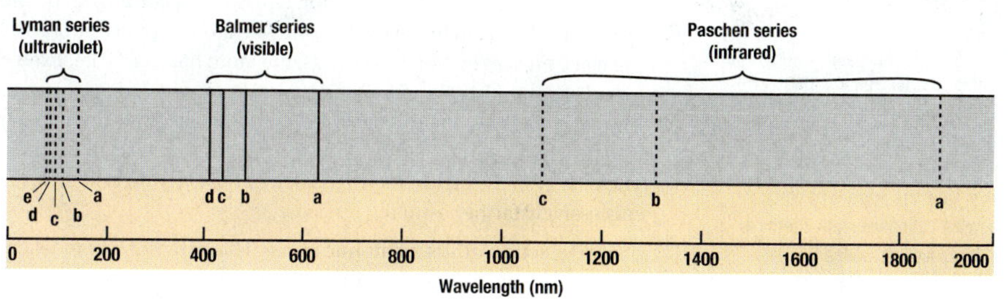

When investigators passed electric current through a vacuum tube containing hydrogen gas at low pressure, they observed the emission of a characteristic pinkish glow. **When a narrow beam of the emitted light was shined through a prism, it was separated into four specific colors of the visible spectrum. The four bands of light were part of what is known as hydrogen's emission-line spectrum.** The production of hydrogen's emission-line spectrum is illustrated in **Figure 1.5** (on the previous page). Additional series of lines were discovered in the ultraviolet and infrared regions of hydrogen's emission-line spectrum. The wavelengths of some of the spectral series are shown in **Figure 1.6.** They are known as the Lyman, Balmer, and Paschen series, after their discoverers.

Classical theory predicted that the hydrogen atoms would be excited by whatever amount of energy was added to them. **Scientists had thus expected to observe the emission of a continuous range of frequencies of electromagnetic radiation, that is, a continuous spectrum.** Why had the hydrogen atoms given off only specific frequencies of light? Attempts to explain this observation led to an entirely new atomic theory called *quantum theory.*

Whenever an excited hydrogen atom falls to its ground state or to a lower-energy excited state, it emits a photon of radiation. The energy of this photon ($E_{photon} = h\nu$) is equal to the difference in energy between the atom's initial state and its final state, as illustrated in **Figure 1.7.** The fact that hydrogen atoms emit only specific frequencies of light indicated that the energy differences between the atoms' energy states were fixed. This suggested that the electron of a hydrogen atom exists only in very specific energy states.

In the late nineteenth century, a mathematical formula that related the various wavelengths of hydrogen's emission-line spectrum was discovered. The challenge facing scientists was to provide a model of the hydrogen atom that accounted for this relationship.

FIGURE 1.7

Mathematical Model of Energy States When an excited atom with energy E_2 falls back to energy E_1, it releases a photon that has energy $E_2 - E_1 = E_{photon} = h\nu$.

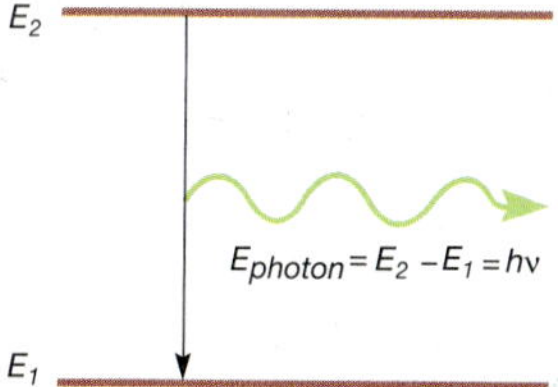

TEACH FROM VISUALS

FIGURE 1.5 When we observe a hydrogen lamp, our brains combine the different colors of its spectrum and perceive a single color. The visible lines of the hydrogen spectrum are a result of electron transitions from higher energy levels to the second energy level. Other electron transitions produce light of longer wavelengths (in the infrared region) and light of shorter wavelengths (in the ultraviolet region), none of which are visible.

FIGURE 1.6 Have students confirm that the four lines in the Balmer series are the same four lines shown in **Figure 1.5.** Why don't we see the lines of the Lyman or Paschen series in **Figure 1.5**? They are outside the visible portion of the electromagnetic spectrum.

ChemisTrivia

The emission spectrum of each element is unique. Emission spectra are used to identify unknown samples and to determine the relative composition of stars.

Teaching Tip

The *Elements Handbook* (Appendix A) features the different colors that are emitted by several different elements (see sections Group 1, Group 2, and Group 15) and displays an emission spectrum for strontium (see section Group 2).

ALTERNATIVE APPROACHES

Inform students that a Swedish mathematician named Johan Rydberg developed an equation $1/\lambda = 1.0974 \times 10^7\ m^{-1} (1/n_1^2 - 1/n_2^2)$ to explain the emission-line spectra of hydrogen and other elements. Have students use his equation, and $c = \lambda\nu$ and $E = h\nu$, to calculate the energy of light emitted by an electron moving from the second energy level (n_1) to the fourth energy level (n_2) in a hydrogen atom ($+4.08 \times 10^{-19}$ J). Point out that the positive value indicates that energy must be supplied to move the electron to a higher energy level. Ask students to find an alternative approach to solving this problem. Students can use the formula $E_n = -2.178 \times 10^{-18}/n^2$ J to calculate the energy of an electron in a particular energy level (n). They can then calculate the difference in energy between the two levels. The answer should agree with the value calculated using the Rydberg equation.

▼ Teach *continued*

Analogy

Expand on the ladder rung analogy. If you slip from a low rung (lower-energy excited state) and fall to the ground (ground state), you won't be hurt badly. But if you fall from a high rung (higher-energy excited state), you hit the ground with more kinetic energy. The energy change is greater from the excited-state rung at the top of the ladder to the ground than from the first rung to the ground. Point out to students that the rung analogy has limitations; unlike the rungs on a ladder, the "rungs" (energy levels) in an atom are not evenly spaced.

Teaching Tip

Bohr used classic Newtonian mechanics to study the angular momentum and radius of the electron around the nucleus. In the next section, students will see how *quantum mechanics* allows a more complete description of atomic structure.

Alternative Assessment

This section continues the discussion of atomic structure. Have students revise their chronology of current atomic theory to include Bohr and give reasons for his inclusion.

WHY IT MATTERS

Fireflies S.T.E.M.

What kinds of reactions produce light? In this chapter, you are learning how excited atoms can produce light. In parts of the United States, summer is accompanied by the appearance of fireflies, or lightning bugs. What makes them glow? A bioluminescent chemical reaction that involves luciferin, luciferase (an enzyme), adenosine triphosphate (ATP), and oxygen takes place in the firefly and produces the characteristic yellow-green glow. Unlike most reactions that produce light, bioluminescent reactions do not generate energy in the form of heat.

MAIN IDEA

Bohr's model of the hydrogen atom explained electron transition states.

The puzzle of the hydrogen-atom spectrum was solved in 1913 by the Danish physicist Niels Bohr. He proposed a hydrogen-atom model that linked the atom's electron to photon emission. According to the model, the electron can circle the nucleus only in allowed paths, or *orbits*. When the electron is in one of these orbits, the atom has a definite, fixed energy. The electron—and therefore the hydrogen atom—is in its lowest energy state when it is in the orbit closest to the nucleus. This orbit is separated from the nucleus by a large empty space where the electron cannot exist. The energy of the electron is higher when the electron is in orbits that are successively farther from the nucleus.

The electron orbits, or atomic energy levels, in Bohr's model can be compared to the rungs of a ladder. When you are standing on a ladder, your feet are on one rung or another. The amount of potential energy that you possess corresponds to standing on the first rung, the second rung, and so forth. Your energy cannot correspond to standing between two rungs because you cannot stand in midair. In the same way, an electron can be in one orbit or another, but not in between.

How does Bohr's model of the hydrogen atom explain the observed spectral lines? While in a given orbit, the electron is neither gaining nor losing energy. It can, however, move to a higher-energy orbit by gaining an amount of energy equal to the difference in energy between the higher-energy orbit and the initial lower-energy orbit. When a hydrogen atom is in an excited state, its electron is in one of the higher-energy orbits. When the electron falls to a lower energy level, a photon is emitted, and the process is called *emission*. The photon's energy is equal to the energy difference between the initial higher energy level and the final lower energy level. Energy must be added to an atom in order to move an electron from a lower energy level to a higher energy level. This process is called *absorption*. Absorption and emission of radiation in Bohr's model of the hydrogen atom are illustrated in **Figure 1.8**. The energy of each absorbed or emitted photon corresponds to a particular frequency of emitted radiation, $E_{photon} = h\nu$.

Based on the different wavelengths of the hydrogen emission-line spectrum, Bohr calculated the allowed energy levels for the hydrogen atom. He then related the possible energy-level changes to the lines in the hydrogen emission-line spectrum. The five lines in the Lyman series, for example, were shown to be the result of electrons dropping from energy levels E_6, E_5, E_4, E_3, and E_2 to the ground-state energy level E_1.

FIGURE 1.8

Absorption and Emission (a) Absorption and (b) emission of a photon by a hydrogen atom according to Bohr's model. The frequencies of light that can be absorbed and emitted are restricted because the electron can only be in orbits corresponding to the energies E_1, E_2, E_3, and so forth.

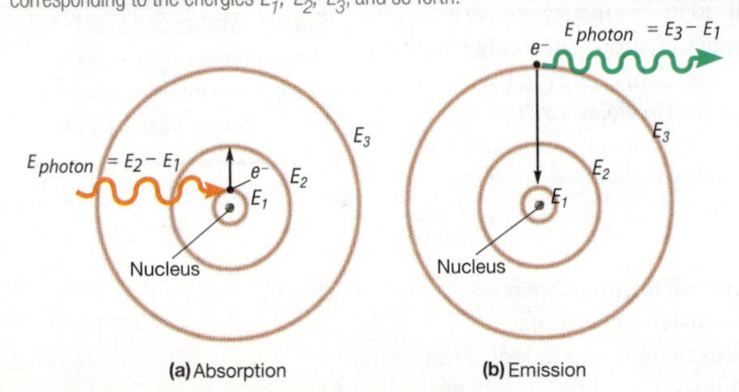

Differentiated Instruction

INCLUSION

Use an active demonstration to involve kinesthetic and visual learners. Locate a place in or near your school where there are stairs (at least 4 stairs high). Have a student stand on one of the stairs. Then ask the student to move from one stair to another. Each time the student moves up or down a stair, ask students to explain whether the move is analogous to **Figure 1.8a** or **Figure 1.8b.** Also ask the class to relate the student's moves in terms of the energy changes associated with an electron moving between orbits. Moving up a stair is analogous to Figure 1.8a; moving up a level requires an input of energy (from the photon that is absorbed), as does moving up a stair. Conversely, moving down a stair is analogous to Figure 1.8b.

FIGURE 1.9

Electron Energy Transitions This energy-state diagram for a hydrogen atom shows some of the energy transitions for the Lyman, Balmer, and Paschen spectral series. Bohr's model of the atom accounted mathematically for the energy of each of the transitions shown.

CRITICAL THINKING

Explain Why might spectra of atoms with more than one electron be difficult to explain using Bohr's model?

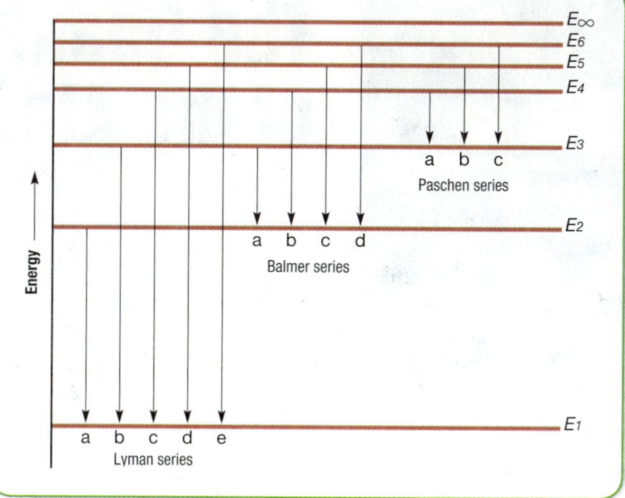

Bohr's calculated values agreed with the experimentally observed values for the lines in each series. The origins of three of the series of lines in hydrogen's emission-line spectrum are shown in **Figure 1.9.**

Bohr's model of the hydrogen atom explained observed spectral lines so well that many scientists concluded that the model could be applied to all atoms. It was soon recognized, however, that Bohr's approach did not explain the spectra of atoms with more than one electron. Nor did Bohr's theory explain the chemical behavior of atoms.

SECTION 1 FORMATIVE ASSESSMENT

Reviewing Main Ideas

1. What was the major shortcoming of Rutherford's model of the atom?
2. Write and label the equation that relates the speed, wavelength, and frequency of electromagnetic radiation.
3. Define the following:
   - **a.** electromagnetic radiation
   - **b.** wavelength
   - **c.** frequency
   - **d.** quantum
   - **e.** photon
4. What is meant by the dual wave-particle nature of light?
5. Describe Bohr's model of the hydrogen atom.

Critical Thinking

6. **INTERPRETING GRAPHICS** Use the diagram in **Figure 1.9** to answer the following:
   - **a.** Characterize each of the following as absorption or emission: an electron moves from E_2 to E_1; an electron moves from E_1 to E_3; and an electron moves from E_6 to E_3.
   - **b.** Which energy-level change above emits or absorbs the highest energy? the lowest energy?

TEACH FROM VISUALS

FIGURE 1.9 Ask students to refer to **Figure 1.9.** Have students describe the energy transition of an electron that would emit the most energy as light. Students should identify an electron that moves directly from E_6 to E_1.

Critical Thinking

Answer: Bohr's model does not take into account the interactions multiple electrons would have with one another.

Assess and Reteach ▼

Assess Use the Formative Assessment on this page to evaluate student mastery of the section.

Reteach For students who need additional instruction, download the Section Study Guide.

Response to Intervention To reassess students' mastery, use the Section Quiz, available to print or to take directly online at **HMDScience.com**.

Answers to Section Assessment

1. It did not explain how negative electrons fill the space surrounding a positive nucleus.
2. $c = \lambda\nu$, where
   c = speed
   λ = wavelength
   ν = frequency
3. **a.** a form of energy that exhibits wavelike behavior as it travels through space
   b. the distance between corresponding points on adjacent waves
   c. the number of waves that pass a given point in a specified amount of time, usually 1 s
   d. a finite quantity of energy gained or lost by an atom
   e. a quantum of light
4. Depending on the experiment devised to observe it, the behavior of light can be described in terms of waves or in terms of particles.
5. Bohr's model depicts a hydrogen nucleus with a single electron circling the nucleus at a specific radius in a path called an orbit. The electron exists in one of only a finite number of allowed orbits.
6. **a.** E_2 to E_1, emission; E_1 to E_3, absorption; E_6 to E_3, emission
   b. highest energy, E_1 to E_3; lowest energy, E_6 to E

SECTION 2

▼ Plan and Prepare

Objectives

Upon completion of this section, students should be able to do the following:

- Discuss Louis de Broglie's role in the development of the quantum model of the atom.
- Compare and contrast Bohr's model and the quantum model of the atom.
- Explain how the Heisenberg uncertainty principle and the Schrödinger wave equation led to the idea of atomic orbitals.
- List the four quantum numbers and describe their significance.
- Relate the number of sublevels corresponding to each of an atom's main energy levels, the number of orbitals per sublevel, and the number of orbitals per main energy level.

Classroom Catalyst

Write down some fake student addresses. Use the format of street name, house/apartment number, and ZIP Code. These items describe the location of their residence. How many students have the same ZIP Code? How many live on the same street? How many have the same house number? Create a unique address for each student. In the same way that no two houses have the same address, no two electrons in an atom have the same set of four quantum numbers. In this section, students will learn how to use the quantum-number code to describe the properties of electrons in atoms.

▼ Teach

TEACH FROM VISUALS

FIGURE 2.1 Diffraction and interference are two traits common to all waves. For example, water waves coming from two nearby sources will create diffraction and interference patterns. This could be demonstrated using a wave figure if one is available.

SECTION 2

Main Ideas

- Electrons have wave-like properties.
- The speed and position of an electron cannot be measured simultaneously.
- Orbitals indicate probable electron locations.
- Quantum numbers describe atomic orbitals.

The Quantum Model of the Atom

Key Terms

Heisenberg uncertainty principle
quantum theory
orbital
quantum number
principal quantum number
angular momentum quantum number
magnetic quantum number
spin quantum number

To the scientists of the early twentieth century, Bohr's model of the hydrogen atom contradicted common sense. Why did hydrogen's electron exist around the nucleus only in certain allowed orbits with definite energies? Why couldn't the electron exist in a limitless number of orbits with slightly different energies? To explain why atomic energy states are quantized, scientists had to change the way they viewed the nature of the electron.

MAIN IDEA

Electrons have wave-like properties.

The investigations into the photoelectric effect and hydrogen's emission line spectrum revealed that light could behave as both a wave and a particle. Could electrons have a dual wave-particle nature as well? In 1924, the French scientist Louis de Broglie asked himself this very question. And the answer that he proposed led to a revolution in our basic understanding of matter.

De Broglie pointed out that in many ways the behavior of electrons in Bohr's quantized orbits was similar to the known behavior of waves. For example, scientists at the time knew that any wave confined to a space can have only certain frequencies. De Broglie suggested that electrons be considered waves confined to the space around an atomic nucleus. It followed that the electron waves could exist only at specific frequencies. And according to the relationship $E = h\nu$, these frequencies corresponded to specific energies—the quantized energies of Bohr's orbits.

Other aspects of de Broglie's hypothesis that electrons have wavelike properties were soon confirmed by experiments. Investigators demonstrated that electrons, like light waves, can be bent, or diffracted. *Diffraction* refers to the bending of a wave as it passes by the edge of an object or through a small opening. Diffraction experiments and other investigations also showed that electron beams, like waves, can interfere with each other. *Interference* occurs when waves overlap (see the Quick Lab in this section). This overlapping results in a reduction of energy in some areas and an increase of energy in others. The effects of diffraction and interference can be seen in **Figure 2.1**, on the next page.

Differentiated Instruction

PRE-AP

De Broglie's hypothesis came about partly by combining two equations that were well known at the time. Planck suggested that $E = hc/\lambda$; Einstein suggested that matter and energy are conserved, $E = mc^2$, where m is mass and c is the speed of light. Have students set these two energy equations equal to one another and substitute velocity, v, for c to see what happens to the combined equations. The equation becomes $\lambda = h/mv$. This equation suggests that anything with both mass and velocity has a corresponding wavelength. Ask students to explain why everyday objects do not emit wavelength. These objects have very large masses compared to electrons. As a result, the mv term for them would be very large, and their wavelengths would be too small to be observed.

FIGURE 2.1

Interference Patterns Bright areas correspond to areas of increased energy, while dark areas indicate areas of decreased energy.

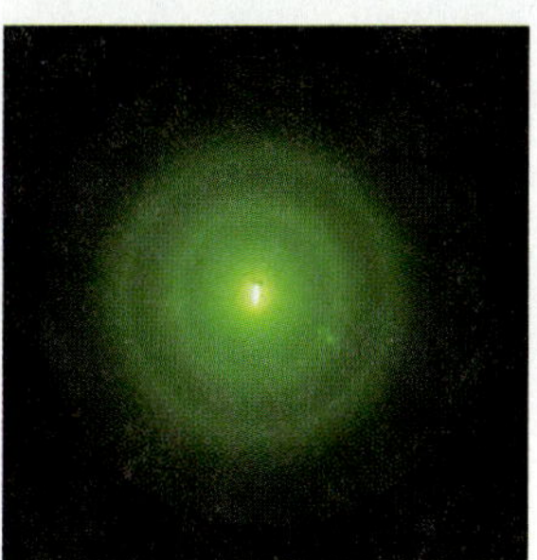

(a) Diffraction pattern produced by a beam of electrons passed through a substance.

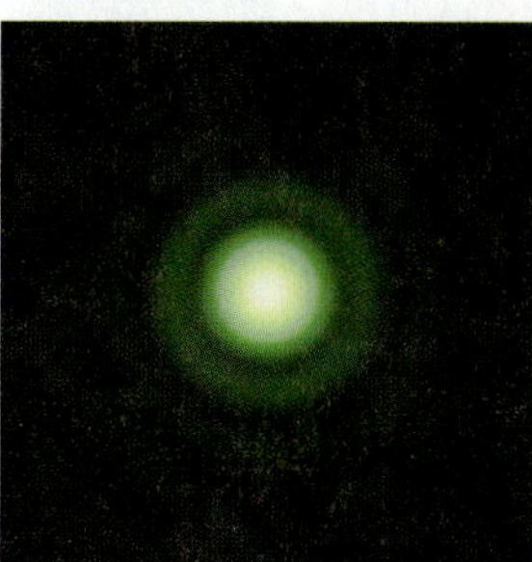

(b) Diffraction pattern for a beam of visible light passed through a tiny aperture.

CRITICAL THINKING

Apply How did evidence of diffraction and interference indicate that electrons behave like waves of light?

MAIN IDEA

The speed and position of an electron cannot be measured simultaneously.

The idea of electrons having a dual wave-particle nature troubled scientists. If electrons are both particles and waves, then where are they in the atom? To answer this question, we must consider a proposal first made in 1927 by the German theoretical physicist Werner Heisenberg.

Heisenberg's idea involved the detection of electrons. Electrons are detected by their interaction with photons. Because photons have about the same energy as electrons, any attempt to locate a specific electron with a photon knocks the electron off its course. As a result, there is always a basic uncertainty in trying to locate an electron (or any other particle). **The Heisenberg uncertainty principle states that it is impossible to determine simultaneously both the position and velocity of an electron or any other particle.** This was a difficult idea for scientists to accept at the time, but it is now fundamental to our understanding of light and matter.

MAIN IDEA

Orbitals indicate probable electron locations.

In 1926, the Austrian physicist Erwin Schrödinger used the hypothesis that electrons have a dual wave-particle nature to develop an equation that treated electrons in atoms as waves. Unlike Bohr's theory, which assumed quantization as a fact, quantization of electron energies was a natural outcome of Schrödinger's equation. Only waves of specific energies, and therefore frequencies, provided solutions to the equation. Along with the uncertainty principle, the Schrödinger wave equation laid the foundation for modern quantum theory. **Quantum theory describes mathematically the wave properties of electrons and other very small particles.**

Teaching Tip

Help students understand the meaning of the Heisenberg uncertainty principle by verbally "walking through" the definition in the book, while defining or clarifying each of the terms in the definition. For example: *The* **Heisenberg uncertainty principle** *states (says) that it is impossible (cannot be done) to determine (figure out) simultaneously (at the same time) both the position (where it is) and velocity (how fast it's moving and in what direction) of an electron or any other particle (within an atom).* Then ask students to summarize the meaning of the principle using these more familiar words. The Heisenberg uncertainty principle says that you cannot figure out at the same time, where an electron or any other particle is within an atom, and how fast and in what direction it's moving. You can figure out one or the other, but not both, at any one time.

Critical Thinking

Answer: Because diffraction occurs when waves interfere with each other, and interference occurs when waves overlap.

ENGLISH LEARNER

The Heisenberg uncertainty principle can be difficult for students to understand. Ask them to imagine a mouse running through a dark house. If they hear the mouse and point a flashlight at it, the mouse will turn and run in a different direction. The result is similar when you use light to try to observe an electron. The light's effect on the electron makes it impossible to know the electron's exact location and velocity at the same time.

▼ Teach *continued*

QuickLab

Both light and electrons exhibit wavelike properties during experiments that test for wave properties. Interference is one property of waves. This activity duplicates a historic experiment that tested both light and electrons for interference.

DISCUSSION

1. Most students should observe light and dark rings around the edge of the hole illuminated on the screen. These light and dark patterns are a result of interference.
2. Light has wavelike properties.

Analogy

Ask students to imagine the propeller of an airplane. They can be certain of its position as long as it has no kinetic energy, that is, as long as it is not moving. But as the propeller begins to move, it seems to take a different shape—that of a disk—and its position at any one instant is less certain. Electrons are much smaller and move much more quickly, creating even greater uncertainty. Like the propeller taking the shape of a disk, the electron is no longer considered to be at a single point in space, but rather it is thought of as a *cloud*. The mathematical solution to the Schrödinger equation established the different possible regions in space (orbitals) that electrons could occupy. These regions are summarized using quantum numbers.

QuickLAB THE WAVE NATURE OF LIGHT: INTERFERENCE

MATERIALS
- scissors
- manila folders
- thumbtack
- masking tape
- aluminum foil
- white poster board or cardboard
- flashlight

SAFETY

Wear safety goggles and an apron.

QUESTION

Does light show the wave property of interference when a beam of light is projected through a pinhole onto a screen?

PROCEDURE

Record all your observations.

1. To make the pinhole screen, cut a 20 cm × 20 cm square from a manila folder. In the center of the square, cut a 2 cm square hole. Cut a 7 cm × 7 cm square of aluminum foil. Using a thumbtack, make a pinhole in the center of the foil square. Tape the aluminum foil over the 2 cm square hole, making sure the pinhole is centered as shown in the diagram.
2. Use white poster board to make a projection screen 35 cm × 35 cm.
3. In a dark room, center the light beam from a flashlight on the pinhole. Hold the flashlight about 1 cm from the pinhole. The pinhole screen should be about 50 cm from the projection screen, as shown in the diagram. Adjust the distance to form a sharp image on the projection screen.

DISCUSSION

1. Did you observe interference patterns on the screen?
2. As a result of your observations, what do you conclude about the nature of light?

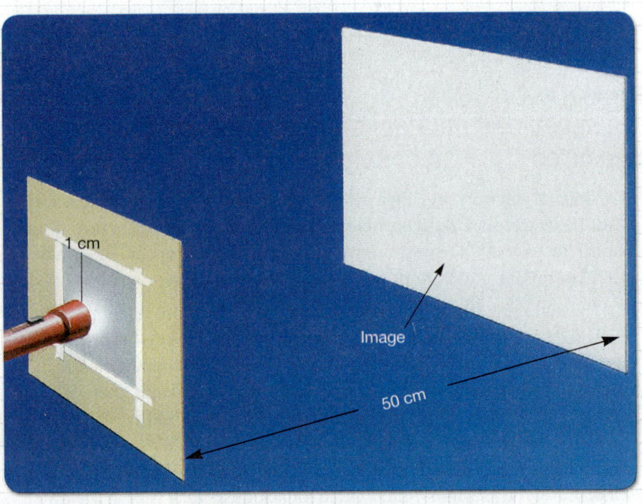

Solutions to the Schrödinger wave equation are known as wave functions. Based on the Heisenberg uncertainty principle, the early developers of quantum theory determined that wave functions give only the *probability* of finding an electron at a given place around the nucleus. Thus, electrons do not travel around the nucleus in neat orbits, as Bohr had postulated. Instead, they exist in certain regions called orbitals. **An orbital is a three-dimensional region around the nucleus that indicates the probable location of an electron.** **Figure 2.2**, on the next page, illustrates two ways of picturing one type of atomic orbital. As you will see later in this section, atomic orbitals have different shapes and sizes.

Differentiated Instruction

INCLUSION

Visually impaired students may have difficulty relating to analogies for the electron cloud such as spinning propellers, which depend on understanding the appearance of an object while it is not moving versus while it is moving. Instead, suggest that these students think of a large flock of noisy birds, such as blackbirds. Listening to the birds, you can tell that they are all flying together in a certain area, but you cannot pinpoint where each bird is within that area while they are moving, because the sounds all blend together.

FIGURE 2.2

Atomic Orbitals Two ways of showing a simple atomic orbital are presented.

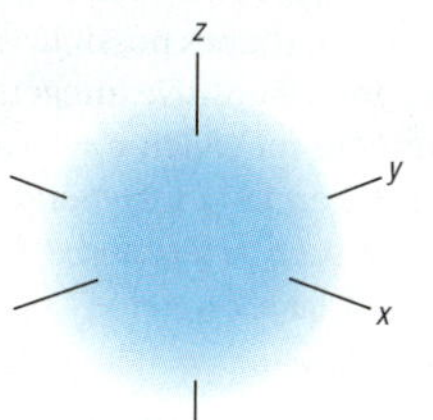

(a) In this atomic orbital model, the probability of finding the electron is proportional to the density of the cloud.

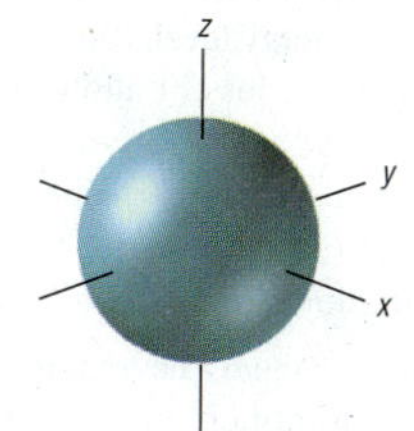

(b) An orbital can also be depicted as a surface within which the electron can be found a certain percentage of the time, conventionally 90%.

MAIN IDEA

Quantum numbers describe atomic orbitals.

According to the Schrödinger equation, electrons in atomic orbitals also have quantized energies. Unlike in the Bohr atomic model, therefore, an electron's energy level is not the only characteristic of an orbital.

To describe orbitals accurately, scientists use quantum numbers. **Quantum numbers** specify the properties of atomic orbitals and the properties of electrons in orbitals. The first three quantum numbers result from solutions to the Schrödinger equation. They indicate the main energy level, the shape, and the orientation of an orbital. The fourth, the spin quantum number, describes a fundamental state of the electron that occupies the orbital.

Principal Quantum Number

The **principal quantum number,** symbolized by n, indicates the main energy level occupied by the electron. Values of n are positive integers only—1, 2, 3, and so on. As n increases, the electron's energy and its average distance from the nucleus increase, as shown in **Figure 2.3**. For example, an electron for which $n = 1$ occupies the first, or lowest, main energy level and is located closest to the nucleus. An electron for which $n = 2$ occupies the second energy level and is further from the nucleus.

More than one electron can have the same n value. These electrons are said to be in the same electron *shell*. The total number of orbitals in a given shell, or main energy level, is equal to n^2.

FIGURE 2.3

The Principle Quantum Number The main energy levels of an atom are represented by the principal quantum number, n.

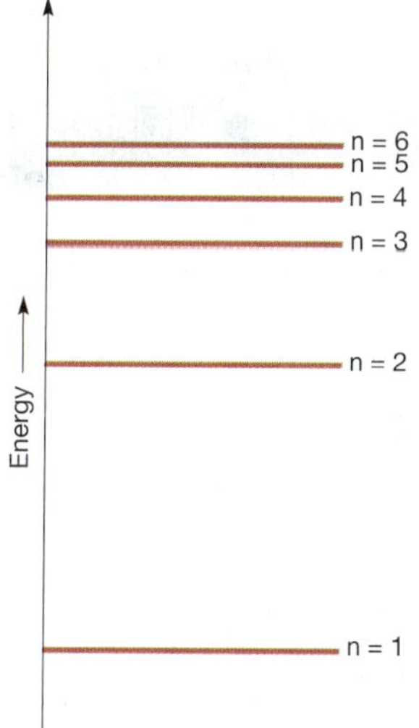

PRE-AP

As an introduction to how electrons occupy energy levels, inform students that each main energy level can hold only a certain number of electrons. Once that energy is filled, an electron must occupy the next higher energy level. The maximum number of electrons in any one energy level is equal to $2n^2$. Have students calculate the maximum number of electrons that can be found in the seven main energy levels (2, 8, 18, 32, 50, 72, and 98, respectively). Point out that the last three energy levels are not completely filled.

TEACH FROM VISUALS

FIGURE 2.2 Remind students that these images represent electron densities in three dimensions.

FIGURE 2.3 Each n value, or energy level, is one possible location for electrons around the nucleus. Emphasize that electrons can have energies corresponding only to those energies associated with values of n. The principal quantum number, n, also indicates the general distance of an electron to the nucleus. Electrons farther from the nucleus have greater energies and thus greater values of n.

Misconception Alert!

Although the word *orbital* is used to describe the location of electrons, electrons do not actually occur in planetlike orbits. In the quantum model, orbitals are actually electron clouds, or most likely locations for electrons. Students often cling to Bohr's model, which suggests that an orbiting electron moves at a specific radius, like a planet does. Help students move away from Bohr's model toward the quantum model.

Alternative Assessment

At this point, students can complete their chronology of the building of current atomic theory. Suggest that they put a new chronology on a concept map that also contains the experiments or ideas used to make each step: isolating different subatomic particles, locating each particle, discovering the nature of electrons, and so on.

▼ Teach *continued*

TEACH FROM TABLES

FIGURE 2.4 Emphasize that the values of *l* and the letters *s*, *p*, *d*, and *f* are synonymous for the names of differently shaped orbitals. Be sure students are aware of the general orbital shapes, which are shown in **Figure 2.5.**

Teaching Tip

Distinguish between the concepts of *sublevel* and *orbital*. An orbital is a single allowed location for atomic electrons. It is described by specific values of *n*, *m*, and *l*, and it is capable of holding a maximum of two electrons of opposite spin states, according to the Pauli exclusion principle. A sublevel includes *all* the similarly shaped orbitals in a particular main energy level. In other words, for a given value of *n*, a sublevel consists of all orbitals with the same value of *l*.

Answers to In-Text Questions

- The *p* sublevel in the third main energy level is designated 3*p*.
- There are two other sublevels in the third main energy level, 3*s* and 3*d* .

FIGURE 2.4

ORBITAL LETTER DESIGNATIONS

ℓ	Letter
0	*s*
1	*p*
2	*d*
3	*f*

Angular Momentum Quantum Number

Except at the first main energy level, orbitals of different shapes exist for a given value of *n*. These are known as *sublevels*. **The angular momentum quantum number, symbolized by ℓ, indicates the shape of the orbital.** For a specific main energy level, the number of orbital shapes possible is equal to *n*. The values of ℓ allowed are zero and all positive integers less than or equal to $n - 1$. For example, orbitals for which $n = 2$ can have one of two shapes corresponding to $\ell = 0$ and $\ell = 1$. Depending on its value of ℓ, an orbital is assigned a letter, such as *s*, *p*, and *d*. Orbital letter designations for values of ℓ are given in **Figure 2.4.**

As shown in **Figure 2.5a** on the next page, *s* orbitals are spherical, *p* orbitals have dumbbell shapes, and *d* orbitals are more complex. (The *f* orbital shapes are even more complex.) In the first energy level, $n = 1$, there is only one sublevel possible—an *s* orbital. As mentioned, the second energy level, $n = 2$, has two sublevels—the *s* and *p* orbitals. The third energy level, $n = 3$, has three sublevels—the *s*, *p*, and *d* orbitals. The fourth energy level, $n = 4$, has four sublevels—the *s*, *p*, *d*, and *f* orbitals. In an *n*th main energy level, there are *n* sublevels.

Each atomic orbital is designated by the principal quantum number followed by the letter of the sublevel. For example, the 1*s* sublevel is the *s* orbital in the first main energy level, while the 2*p* sublevel is the set of three *p* orbitals in the second main energy level. On the other hand, a 4*d* orbital is part of the *d* sublevel in the fourth main energy level. How would you designate the *p* sublevel in the third main energy level? How many other sublevels are in the third main energy level with this one?

Magnetic Quantum Number

Atomic orbitals can have the same shape but different orientations around the nucleus. **The magnetic quantum number, symbolized by *m*, indicates the orientation of an orbital around the nucleus.** Values of *m* are whole numbers, including zero, from $-\ell$ to $+\ell$. Because an *s* orbital is spherical and is centered around the nucleus, it has only one possible orientation. This orientation corresponds to a magnetic quantum number of $m = 0$. There is therefore only one *s* orbital in each *s* sublevel.

As shown in **Figure 2.5b** on the next page, the lobes of a *p* orbital extend along the *x*, *y*, or *z* axis of a three-dimensional coordinate system. There are therefore three *p* orbitals in each *p* sublevel, designated as p_x, p_y, and p_z orbitals. The three *p* orbitals occupy different regions of space and those regions are related to values of $m = -1$, $m = 0$, and $m = +1$.

There are five different *d* orbitals in each *d* sublevel, as shown in **Figure 2.5c** on the next page. For the *d* orbital, the five different orientations, including one with a different shape, correspond to values of $m = -2$, $m = -1$, $m = 0$, $m = +1$, and $m = +2$. There are seven different *f* orbitals in each *f* sublevel. (The *f* orbitals are not shown in **Figure 2.5.**)

Differentiated Instruction

BELOW LEVEL

Have students form pairs and use the following figures to explain what the first two quantum numbers indicate. Have them use **Figure 2.3** to explain the principal quantum number, *n*, and use **Figure 2.5** to explain the angular momentum number, *l*. Students should describe *n* as the quantum number that indicates the principal energy level in which an electron is located and *l* as the quantum number that describes the shape of the electron's orbital.

FIGURE 2.5

a. Orbital Shapes
The orbitals *s*, *p*, and *d* have different shapes. Each of the orbitals shown occupies a different region of space around the nucleus.

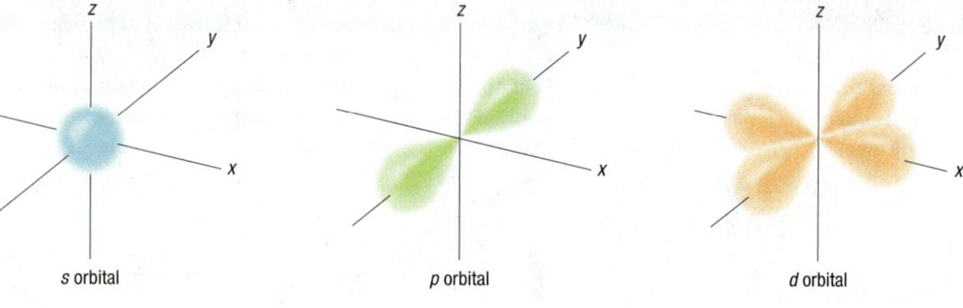

b. Three Orientations of *p* Orbitals
The subscripts *x*, *y*, and *z* indicate the three different orientations of *p* orbitals. The intersection of the *x*, *y*, and *z* axes indicates the location of the center of the nucleus.

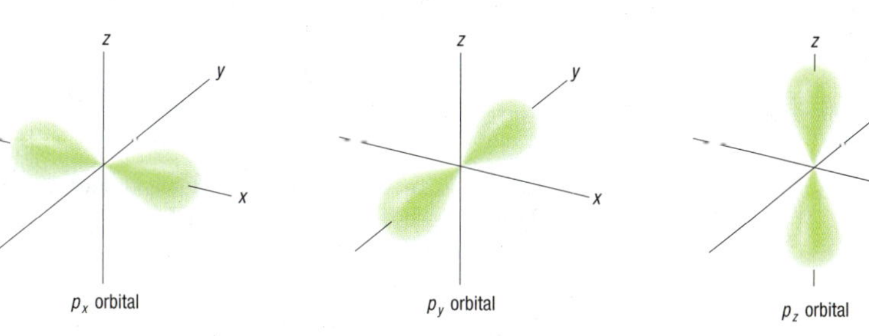

c. Five Orientations of *d* Orbitals
Four of the *d* orbitals have the same shape but different orientations. The fifth has a different shape and a different orientation. Each orbital occupies a different region of space.

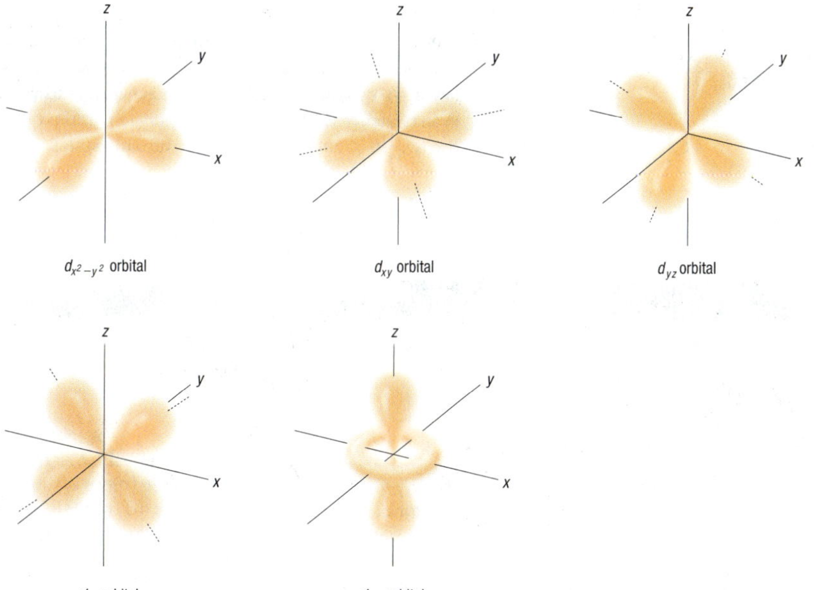

TEACH FROM VISUALS

FIGURE 2.5b Use three rulers at right angles to help students visualize the three-dimensional nature of the *x*, *y*, *z* coordinate system.

Teaching Tip

The number of different possible values for the magnetic quantum number determines the number of orbitals in a particular sublevel. For example, when $l = 1$, m can equal –1, 0, or 1. These three possible values for m indicate that there are three different orbitals (each oriented differently around the nucleus) in the sublevel corresponding to $l = 1$. These three orbitals are known as *p* orbitals. More specifically, they are the p_x, p_y, and p_z orbitals, as shown in **Figure 2.5b.**

Demonstration

MAGNETIC FIELDS OF ELECTRONS

Hold **two bar magnets** parallel to each other. If the north ends of both magnets point in the same direction, the magnets will repel each other. If the north end of one magnet faces the south end of the other magnet, then the magnets will attract each other. In this analogy, the magnets represent the magnetic fields around two electrons. For the two electrons to coexist in the same orbital, their spin quantum numbers must be different.

BELOW LEVEL

Inform students that they will learn how electrons fill the *s*, *p*, and *d* sublevels in the next section. For now, point out that each sublevel can hold different numbers of electrons, depending on the number of orbitals in the sublevel. Emphasize that an orbital in any sublevel can hold a maximum of two electrons. Then have students refer to **Figure 2.5a**. Have students count the number of orbitals in each sublevel. Point out that an *s* sublevel has only one orbital. With only one orbital, the *s* sublevel can hold only 2 electrons. Then have students refer to **Figure 2.5b** and identify how many orbitals a *p* sublevel can have. three orbitals, shown as p_x, p_y, and p_z Ask students to identify the maximum number of electrons in the *p* sublevel. 3 orbitals × 2 electrons per orbital = 6 electrons Finally, have students refer to **Figure 2.5c** and identify the maximum number of electrons in a *d* sublevel. 10

▼ Teach *continued*

TEACH FROM TABLES

FIGURE 2.6 Have students use the table to determine the number of electrons each sublevel can hold and the number of electrons that may be contained in a given main energy level.

Check for Understanding

Answer: Answers will vary. Sample answers might be: "They are too far apart;" They are too small;" or "They are all negative and will push each other away."

▼ Assess and Reteach

Assess Use the Formative Assessment on this page to evaluate student mastery of the section.

Reteach For students who need additional instruction, download the Section Study Guide.

Response to Intervention To reassess students' mastery, use the Section Quiz, available to print or to take directly online at **HMDScience.com**.

FIGURE 2.6

QUANTUM NUMBER RELATIONSHIPS IN ATOMIC STRUCTURE

Principal quantum number: main energy level (n)	Sublevel in main energy level (n sublevels)	Number of orbitals per sublevel	Number of orbitals per main energy level (n^2)	Number of electrons per sublevel	Number of electrons per main energy level ($2n^2$)
1	*s*	1	1	2	2
2	*s* *p*	1 3	4	2 6	8
3	*s* *p* *d*	1 3 5	9	2 6 10	18
4	*s* *p* *d* *f*	1 3 5 7	16	2 6 10 14	32

As you can see in **Figure 2.6**, the total number of orbitals in a main energy level increases with the value of n. In fact, the number of orbitals at each main energy level equals the square of the principal quantum number, n^2.

CHECK FOR UNDERSTANDING

Analyze With all of an atom's electrons spinning rapidly through the orbitals, half of them spinning in the opposite direction, why don't they collide?

Spin Quantum Number

An electron in an orbital behaves in some ways like Earth spinning on an axis. The electron exists in one of two possible spin states, which creates a magnetic field. To account for the magnetic properties of the electron, theoreticians of the early twentieth century created the spin quantum number. **The spin quantum number has only two possible values—(+1/2, −1/2)—which indicate the two fundamental spin states of an electron in an orbital.** A single orbital can hold a maximum of two electrons, but the two electrons must have opposite spin states.

SECTION 2 FORMATIVE ASSESSMENT

Reviewing Main Ideas

1. Define the following:
  a. main energy levels
  b. quantum numbers

2. a. List the four quantum numbers.
  b. What general information about atomic orbitals is provided by the quantum numbers?

3. Describe briefly what specific information is given by each of the four quantum numbers.

Critical Thinking

4. INFERRING RELATIONSHIPS What are the possible values of the magnetic quantum number m for f orbitals? What is the maximum number of electrons that can exist in 4f orbitals?

Answers to Section Assessment

1. a. quantized levels of increasing energy, specified by the quantum number n, at which atomic orbitals can exist
  b. numbers used to specify the energy, location, shape, and orientation of atomic orbitals, as well as the spins of electrons in these orbitals

2. a. principal, n; angular momentum, l; magnetic, m; and spin (+1/2 or −1/2)
  b. the distance of an orbital to the nucleus, the energy, shape, and orientation of the orbital, and the spin of the electrons in the orbital

3. The principal quantum number, n, describes the energy of the orbital as well as the orbital's distance to the nucleus. The angular momentum quantum number, l, signifies the shape of the orbital. The magnetic quantum number, m, indicates the orientation of an orbital. The spin quantum number indicates which of an electron's two fundamental states within an orbital an electron is in.

4. The seven values of m are −3, −2, −1, 0, +1, +2, +3. 14

SECTION 3

Electron Configurations

Key Terms

electron configuration
Aufbau principle
Pauli exclusion principle
Hund's rule
noble gas
noble-gas configuration

SECTION 3

Main Ideas

- Electrons fill in the lowest-energy orbitals first.
- There are three ways to indicate electron configuration.
- No electrons can occupy a higher-energy sublevel until the sublevel below it is filled.

The quantum model of the atom improves on the Bohr model because it describes the arrangements of electrons in atoms other than hydrogen. **The arrangement of electrons in an atom is known as the atom's electron configuration.** Because atoms of different elements have different numbers of electrons, a unique electron configuration exists for the atoms of each element. Like all systems in nature, electrons in atoms tend to assume arrangements that have the lowest possible energies. The lowest-energy arrangement of the electrons for each element is called the element's *ground-state electron configuration*. A few simple rules, combined with the quantum number relationships discussed in Section 2, allow us to determine these ground-state electron configurations.

MAIN IDEA

Electrons fill in the lowest-energy orbitals first.

To build up electron configurations for the ground state of any particular atom, first the energy levels of the orbitals are determined. Then electrons are added to the orbitals, one by one, according to three basic rules. (Remember that real atoms are not built up by adding protons and electrons one at a time.)

The first rule shows the order in which electrons occupy orbitals. **According to the Aufbau principle, an electron occupies the lowest-energy orbital that can receive it.** **Figure 3.1** shows the atomic orbitals in order of increasing energy. The orbital with the lowest energy is the 1*s* orbital. In a ground-state hydrogen atom, the electron is in this orbital. The 2*s* orbital is the next highest in energy, then the 2*p* orbitals. Beginning with the third main energy level, $n = 3$, the energies of the sublevels in different main energy levels begin to overlap.

Note in the figure, for example, that the 4*s* sublevel is lower in energy than the 3*d* sublevel. Therefore, the 4*s* orbital is filled before any electrons enter the 3*d* orbitals. (Less energy is required for two electrons to pair up in the 4*s* orbital than for those two electrons to occupy a 3*d* orbital.) Once the 3*d* orbitals are fully occupied, which sublevel will be occupied next?

FIGURE 3.1

Atomic Sublevels The order of increasing energy for atomic sublevels is shown on the vertical axis. Each individual box represents an orbital.

Plan and Prepare

Objectives

Upon completion of this section, students should be able to do the following:

- List the total number of electrons needed to fully occupy each main energy level.
- State the Aufbau principle, the Pauli exclusion principle, and Hund's rule.
- Describe the electron configurations for the atoms of any element using orbital notation, electron-configuration notation, and, when appropriate, noble-gas notation.

Classroom Catalyst

Write an electron configuration—such as that of carbon, $1s^22s^22p^2$—on the board. Explain that an electron configuration describes the arrangement of electrons in an atom. For example, in carbon's electron configuration, the integers indicate the main energy level (or principal quantum number, *n*) of each orbital occupied by electrons. The letters indicate the shape (or angular momentum quantum number, *l*) of the occupied orbitals. The superscripts identify the number of electrons in each sublevel.

Teach

READING TOOLKIT

PAIRED READING Have students read the section and mark with self-adhesive notes the passages they do not understand. Be sure students study all tables and figures to help clarify the relevant passages. After reading, pair up students and have the pairs discuss those passages that were difficult. For the passages that cannot be clarified by the pairs, have students ask questions for later class discussion or teacher explanation.

Answer to In-Text Question

- The 4*p* orbitals will begin to fill after the 3*d* orbitals are fully occupied.

Differentiated Instruction

INCLUSION

Point out that the Aufbau principle is a key to understanding how electrons fill orbitals. Be sure students understand that an electron will occupy the 4*s* sublevel before the 3*d* sublevel. Visual learners will benefit from a visual aid for understanding this principle. Have students place the edge of a ruler along the bottom of the box representing the 4*s* orbital in **Figure 3.1.** They should see that the five boxes representing the 3*d* orbitals are above the ruler, indicating that they have a higher energy level. Have students use the ruler to determine which sublevel electrons will first occupy according to the Aufbau principle –5*s* or 4*p*. 4*p*; The 4*p* orbitals will begin to fill after the 3*d* orbitals are fully occupied.

▼ Teach *continued*

TEACH FROM VISUALS

FIGURE 3.2 The significance of the Pauli exclusion principle is that two electrons can occupy the same orbital, but they must have opposite spins states. The arrows distinguish the two electrons in an orbital.

Analogy

Hund's rule can be compared to the way students would arrange themselves on a school bus after a muddy game of soccer. Each student will try to have his or her own seat until all the seats are filled. Only then will students begin to double up. In a like manner, each orbital in a sublevel will hold one electron until all of the sublevel's orbitals are half-filled. Only then will orbitals begin accepting second, higher energy electrons.

Teaching Tip

Emphasize the relationship between orbital diagrams and electron configurations. Write an orbital diagram on the board and show how the number of arrows corresponds to the superscripts in an electron configuration. When students begin to feel comfortable with electron configurations, organize a friendly competition between different groups. Have students from each group go to the board, then give them an element. The first group member who puts the correct electron configuration on the board earns a point for his or her group.

Answer to In-Text Question

- The maximum number of unpaired electrons in a *d* sublevel is five.

FIGURE 3.2

Pauli Exclusion Principle According to the Pauli exclusion principle, an orbital can hold two electrons of opposite spin states. In this electron configuration of a helium atom, each arrow represents one of the atom's two electrons. The direction of the arrow indicates the electron's spin state.

The second rule reflects the importance of the spin quantum number. **According to the Pauli exclusion principle, no two electrons in the same atom can have the same set of four quantum numbers.** The principal, angular momentum, and magnetic quantum numbers specify the energy, shape, and orientation of an orbital. The two values of the spin quantum number reflect the fact that for two electrons to occupy the same orbital, they must have opposite spin states (see **Figure 3.2**).

The third rule requires placing as many unpaired electrons as possible in separate orbitals in the same sublevel. In this way, electron-electron repulsion is minimized so that the electron arrangements have the lowest energy possible. **According to Hund's rule, orbitals of equal energy are each occupied by one electron before any orbital is occupied by a second electron, and all electrons in singly occupied orbitals must have the same spin state.** Applying this rule shows, for example, that one electron will enter each of the three *p* orbitals in a main energy level before a second electron enters any of them. This is illustrated in **Figure 3.3**. What is the maximum number of unpaired electrons in a *d* sublevel?

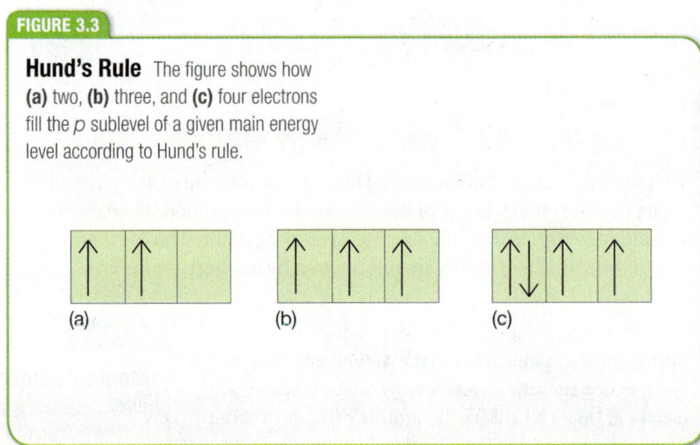

FIGURE 3.3

Hund's Rule The figure shows how **(a)** two, **(b)** three, and **(c)** four electrons fill the *p* sublevel of a given main energy level according to Hund's rule.

MAIN IDEA

There are three ways to indicate electron configuration.

Three methods, or notations, are used to indicate electron configurations. Two of these notations will be discussed for the first-period elements, hydrogen and helium, on the following page. The third notation is used mostly with elements of the third period and higher and will be discussed later in this section.

In a ground-state hydrogen atom, the single electron is in the lowest-energy orbital, the 1*s* orbital. The electron can be in either one of its two spin states. Helium has two electrons, which are paired in the 1*s* orbital.

Problem Solving

DECONSTRUCTING PROBLEMS

Have students draw five boxes similar to those shown in **Figure 3.3.** Tell them that the boxes represent the five orbitals in the 4*d* sublevel. Ask students to use Hund's rule to show how the following number of electrons fills these five orbitals: 3, 5, 8, and 10. Be sure that students do not pair electrons until each orbital has two electrons. Ask students what would happen if there were 11 electrons. The eleventh electron would occupy the 5*p* orbital. Students can verify this by referring to **Figure 3.1.**

Orbital Notation

In orbital notation, an unoccupied orbital is represented by a line, ___, with the orbital's name written underneath the line. An orbital containing one electron is represented as $\underline{\uparrow}$. An orbital containing two electrons is represented as $\underline{\uparrow\downarrow}$, showing the electrons paired and with opposite spin states. The lines are labeled with the principal quantum number and sublevel letter. For example, the orbital notations for hydrogen and helium are written as follows:

$$\text{H}\ \underset{1s}{\underline{\uparrow}} \qquad \text{He}\ \underset{1s}{\underline{\uparrow\downarrow}}$$

Electron-Configuration Notation

Electron-configuration notation eliminates the lines and arrows of orbital notation. Instead, the number of electrons in a sublevel is shown by adding a superscript to the sublevel designation. The hydrogen configuration is represented by $1s^1$. The superscript indicates that one electron is present in hydrogen's $1s$ orbital. The helium configuration is represented by $1s^2$. Here the superscript indicates that there are two electrons in helium's $1s$ orbital.

Electron Configurations

Sample Problem A **The electron configuration of boron is $1s^22s^22p^1$. How many electrons are present in an atom of boron? What is the atomic number for boron? Write the orbital notation for boron.**

SOLVE

The number of electrons in a boron atom is equal to the sum of the superscripts in its electron-configuration notation: $2 + 2 + 1 = 5$ electrons. The number of protons equals the number of electrons in a neutral atom. So we know that boron has 5 protons and thus has an atomic number of 5. To write the orbital notation, first draw the lines representing orbitals.

$$\underset{1s}{\underline{\quad}}\ \underset{2s}{\underline{\quad}}\ \underbrace{\underline{\quad}\ \underline{\quad}\ \underline{\quad}}_{2p}$$

Next, add arrows showing the electron locations. The first two electrons occupy $n = 1$ energy level and fill the $1s$ orbital.

$$\underset{1s}{\underline{\uparrow\downarrow}}\ \underset{2s}{\underline{\quad}}\ \underbrace{\underline{\quad}\ \underline{\quad}\ \underline{\quad}}_{2p}$$

The next three electrons occupy the $n = 2$ main energy level. Two of these occupy the lower-energy $2s$ orbital. The third occupies a higher-energy p orbital.

$$\underset{1s}{\underline{\uparrow\downarrow}}\ \underset{2s}{\underline{\uparrow\downarrow}}\ \underbrace{\underline{\uparrow}\ \underline{\quad}\ \underline{\quad}}_{2p}$$

Practice Answers in Appendix E

1. The electron configuration of nitrogen is $1s^22s^22p^3$. How many electrons are in a nitrogen atom? What is the atomic number of nitrogen? Write the orbital notation for nitrogen.
2. The electron configuration of fluorine is $1s^22s^22p^5$. What is the atomic number of fluorine? How many of its p orbitals are filled?

Classroom Practice

A-1 The electron configuration of carbon is $1s^22s^22p^2$. How many electrons are present in carbon? What is the atomic number of carbon?

Answers: 6, 6

A-2 Write the electron configuration of the element sulfur, which has an atomic number of 16.

Answer: $1s^22s^22p^63s^23p^4$

Answers

Practice A

1. 7, 7, $\underset{1s}{\underline{\uparrow\downarrow}}\ \underset{2s}{\underline{\uparrow\downarrow}}\ \underbrace{\underline{\uparrow}\ \underline{\uparrow}\ \underline{\uparrow}}_{2p}$
2. 9, 2

Teaching Tip

Tell students that the order in which the three $2p$ orbitals are filled is not important.

REALITY CHECK

Students can check their orbital notations by counting the number of arrows they have drawn and comparing them with the total number of electrons in the atom. The two numbers must be the same. Be sure that they also apply Aufbau's principle, Pauli's exclusion principle, and Hund's rule to check that the arrows have been both placed and drawn correctly.

Classroom Discussion

This feature outlines the progression of scientific activity that uncovered the noble gases, which made up a whole new group in the periodic table. Ask students if there are other examples—even outside the scientific world—in which several discoveries are made after a single person had a new insight. Examples within the scientific world may include the discoveries of the lanthanides and actinides or of the subatomic particles. Discuss the importance of using scientific literature to report findings in this process of discovery. Sharing information is important because different people have different talents. One investigator may be diligent in the laboratory and obtain clear results. Another may be better suited to reflect on the meaning of the results.

Chemistry EXPLORERS

The Noble Decade

By the late nineteenth century, the science of chemistry had begun to be organized. In 1860, the First International Congress of Chemistry established the field's first standards. And Dmitri Mendeleev's periodic table of elements gave chemists across the globe a systematic understanding of matter's building blocks. But many important findings—including the discovery of a family of rare, unreactive gases that were unlike any substances known at the time—were yet to come.

Cross-Disciplinary Correspondence

In 1888, the British physicist Lord Rayleigh encountered a small but significant discrepancy in the results of one of his experiments. In an effort to redetermine the atomic mass of nitrogen, he measured the densities of several samples of nitrogen gas. Each sample had been prepared by a different method. All samples that had been isolated from chemical reactions exhibited similar densities. But the densities were about one-tenth of a percent less dense than the nitrogen isolated from air, which at the time was believed to be a mixture of nitrogen, oxygen, water vapor, and carbon dioxide.

Rayleigh was at a loss to explain his discovery. Finally, in 1892, he published a letter in *Nature* magazine to appeal to his colleagues for an explanation. A month later, he received a reply from a Scottish chemist named William Ramsay. Ramsay related that he too had been stumped by the density difference between chemical and atmospheric nitrogen. Rayleigh decided to report his findings to the Royal Society.

A Chemist's Approach

With Rayleigh's permission, Ramsay attempted to remove all known components from a sample of air and to analyze what, if anything, remained. Having removed water vapor, carbon dioxide, and oxygen from the air, Ramsay repeatedly passed the sample over hot magnesium. The nitrogen reacted with the magnesium to form solid magnesium nitride. As a result, all of the then-known components of air were removed. What remained was a minuscule portion of a mysterious gas.

Ramsay tried to cause the gas to react with chemically active substances, such as hydrogen, sodium, and caustic soda, but the gas remained unaltered. He decided to name this new atmospheric component *argon* (Greek for "inert" or "idle").

SEPTEMBER 29, 1892 — *NATURE*

LETTERS TO THE EDITOR.

[*The Editor does not hold himself responsible for opinions expressed by his correspondents. Neither can he undertake to return, or to correspond with the writers of, rejected manuscripts intended for this or any other part of* NATURE. *No notice is taken of anonymous communications.*]

Density of Nitrogen.

I AM much puzzled by some recent results as to the density of *nitrogen*, and shall be obliged if any of your chemical readers can offer suggestions as to the cause. According to two methods of preparation I obtain quite distinct values. The relative difference, amounting to about $\frac{1}{1000}$ part, is small in itself; but it lies entirely outside the errors of experiment, and can only be attributed to a variation in the character of the gas...

Is it possible that the difference is independent of impurity, the nitrogen itself being to some extent in a different (dissociated) state?...

RAYLEIGH.

Terling Place, Witham, September 24.

This excerpt from Lord Rayleigh's letter was originally published in Nature magazine in 1892.

Periodic Problems

Rayleigh and Ramsay were sure that they had discovered a new element, which created a problem. Their calculations indicated that argon had an atomic mass of about 40. However, as it appeared in 1894, the periodic table had no space for such an element. The elements with atomic masses closest to that of argon were chlorine and potassium. Unfortunately, the chemical properties of the families of each of these elements were completely dissimilar to those of the strange gas.

In 1893, Scottish chemist William Ramsay isolated a previously unknown component of the atmosphere.

Groups / Periods	III b	IV b	V b	VI b	VII b	VIII b	I b	II b	III a	IV a	V a	VI a	VII a	0	I a	II a
1															H	He
2															Li	Be
3									B	C	N	O	F	Ne	Na	Mg
4									Al	Si	P	S	Cl	Ar	K	Ca
5	Sc	Ti	V	Cr	Mn	Fe Co Ni	Cu	Zn	Ga	Ge	As	Se	Br	Kr	Rb	Sr
6	Y	Zr	Nb	Mo	Tc	Ru Rh Pd	Ag	Cd	In	Sn	Sb	Te	I	Xe	Cs	Ba
7	La	Hf	Ta	W	Re	Os Ir Pt	Au	Hg	Tl	Pb	Bi	Po	At	Rn	Fr	Ra
8	Ac															
	Transition elements								Main-group elements							

This version of the periodic table shows how it looked after the discovery of the noble gases. The placement of the Group 1 and 2 elements at the far right of the table clearly illustrates how the noble gases fit in between the chlorine family and the potassium family of elements. The 0 above the noble-gas family indicates the zero valency of the gases.

Ramsay contemplated argon's lack of reactivity. He knew that Mendeleev had created the periodic table on the basis of valence, or the number of atomic partners an element bonds with in forming a compound. Because Ramsay could not cause argon to form any compounds, he assigned it a valence of zero. And because the valence of the elements in the families of both chlorine and potassium was one, perhaps argon fit in between them.

Ramsay's insight that argon merited a new spot between the halogen family and the alkali metal family on the periodic table was correct. And as Ramsay would soon confirm, his newly discovered gas was indeed one of a previously unknown family of elements.

New Neighbors

In 1895, Ramsay isolated a light, inert gas from a mineral called *cleveite*. Physical analysis revealed that the gas was the same as one that had been identified in the sun in 1868—helium. Helium was the second zero-valent element found on Earth, and its discovery made chemists aware that the periodic table had been missing an entire column of elements.

Over the next three years, Ramsay and his assistant, Morris Travers, identified three more inert gases present in the atmosphere: neon (Greek for "new"), krypton ("hidden"), and xenon ("stranger"). Finally in 1900, German chemist Friedrich Ernst Dorn discovered radon, the last of the new family of elements known today as the *noble gases*. For his discovery, Ramsay received the Nobel Prize in 1904.

Questions

1. What evidence led Ramsay to report that the mysterious gas was inert?
2. What property of argon caused Ramsay to propose a new column in the periodic table?

Alternative Assessment

Some students may be interested in mythology and its relationship to early alchemy. Have these students find out which names of elements on the periodic table have their origins in mythology. Then, have them give a brief report to the class.

Answers

1. Ramsay tried to make the unknown gas react with other chemically reactive substances, but no chemical change occurred.
2. The other elements of similar atomic weight reacted with other substances and had been assigned a combining tendency (valence) of 1. Because argon did not react, it was assigned a valence of 0 and placed between Cl and K.

▼ Teach *continued*

TEACH FROM VISUALS

FIGURE 3.4 Students can also use the periodic table to determine the order in which orbitals are filled. Use the first three rows of the table as examples.

TEACH FROM TABLES

FIGURE 3.5 Use the Table to help students understand the applications of Aufbau's principle, Pauli's exclusion principle, and Hund's rule. Have students explain how the electron configuration for lithium demonstrates Aufbau's principle. Students should recognize that the third electron must occupy the lowest energy level available (2*s*) rather than a higher one such as a 2*p* orbital. Ask how the Table demonstrates Pauli's exclusion principle. Students can point to any filled orbital and show that it can hold two electrons of opposite spin. Finally, have students explain how the Table illustrates Hund's rule. Students can point to nitrogen where the orbital notation shows that an electron must occupy an empty orbital before pairing up with another electron. In addition, the 2*p* orbital notation for nitrogen shows that unpaired electrons must have the same spin state.

Critical Thinking

Answer: Answers will vary. Sample answer: Because electrons move in a "cloud" around an atom's nucleus, their energy levels start to overlap at the 3rd orbital. Electrons fill the levels that have the least energy first. This overlap causes the 4*s* level to be lower in energy than the 3rd level and electrons will fill it before they fill the 3rd level.

MAIN IDEA

No electrons can occupy a higher-energy sublevel until the energy sublevel below it is filled.

In the first-period elements, hydrogen and helium, electrons occupy the orbital of the first main energy level. **Figure 3.4** provides a pattern to help you remember the order in which orbitals are filled according to the Aufbau principle. The ground-state configurations in **Figure 3.5** illustrate how the Aufbau principle, the Pauli exclusion principle, and Hund's rule are applied to atoms of elements in the second period.

FIGURE 3.4

The Aufbau Principle Follow the diagonal arrows from the bottom of one column to the top of the next to get the order in which atomic orbitals are filled according to the Aufbau principle.

CRITICAL THINKING

Interpret Review the statement of the Aufbau principle given at the beginning of this section, then study Figure 3.4 carefully. Based on your understanding of the two, explain in your own words why electrons fill atomic orbitals in this seemingly unusual order.

According to the Aufbau principle, after the 1*s* orbital is filled, the next electron occupies the *s* sublevel in the second main energy level. Thus, lithium, Li, has a configuration of $1s^22s^1$. The electron occupying the 2*s* level of a lithium atom is in the atom's highest, or outermost, occupied level. The *highest-occupied energy level* is the electron-containing main energy level with the highest principal quantum number. The two electrons in the 1*s* sublevel of lithium are no longer in the outermost main energy level. They have become *inner-shell electrons*, which are electrons that are not in the highest-occupied energy level.

The fourth electron in an atom of beryllium, Be, must complete the pair in the 2*s* sublevel because this sublevel is of lower energy than the 2*p* sublevel. With the 2*s* sublevel filled, the 2*p* sublevel, which has three vacant orbitals of equal energy, can be occupied. One of the three *p* orbitals is occupied by a single electron in an atom of boron, B. Two of the three *p* orbitals are occupied by unpaired electrons in an atom of carbon, C. And all three *p* orbitals are occupied by unpaired electrons in an atom of nitrogen, N. Hund's rule applies here, as is shown in the orbital notations in **Figure 3.5**.

According to the Aufbau principle, the next electron must pair with another electron in one of the 2*p* orbitals rather than enter the third main energy level. The Pauli exclusion principle allows the electron to pair with one of the electrons occupying the 2*p* orbitals as long as the spins of the paired electrons are opposite. Thus, atoms of oxygen, O, have the configuration $1s^22s^22p^4$. Oxygen's orbital notation is shown in **Figure 3.5**.

Two 2*p* orbitals are filled in fluorine, F, and all three are filled in neon, Ne. Atoms such as those of neon, which have the *s* and *p* sublevels of their highest occupied level filled with eight electrons, are said to have an *octet* of electrons. Examine the periodic table inside the back cover of the text. Notice that neon is the last element in the second period.

Problem Solving

ALTERNATIVE APPROACH

To help students understand and visualize the various rules for filling the electron orbitals, place five beakers on a counter. Label them 1*s*, 2*s*, $2p_x$, $2p_y$, and $2p_z$. Place 10 unsharpened pencils in another beaker. Have a student take the pencils and place them in the labeled beakers to show how the orbitals fill. Inform the student how many electrons the atom contains. As each pencil is placed in a beaker, ask the student to explain what rule is being applied. For example, if the student has six pencils (electrons) to place, the student should place the first pencil in the beaker labeled 1*s* (the Aufbau principle), the second pencil pointing in the opposite direction (the Pauli exclusion principle) in the same beaker, the third pencil in the beaker labeled 2*s*, the fourth pencil pointing in the opposite direction in the same beaker, the fifth pencil in the beaker labeled $2p_x$ and the last pencil pointing in the same direction as the fifth pencil in the beaker labeled $2p_y$ (Hund's rule).

FIGURE 3.5

ELECTRON CONFIGURATIONS OF ATOMS OF SECOND-PERIOD ELEMENTS SHOWING TWO NOTATIONS

Name	Symbol	Orbital notation 1s	2s	2p			Electron-configuration notation
Lithium	Li	↑↓	↑	—	—	—	$1s^22s^1$
Beryllium	Be	↑↓	↑↓	—	—	—	$1s^22s^2$
Boron	B	↑↓	↑↓	↑	—	—	$1s^22s^22p^1$
Carbon	C	↑↓	↑↓	↑	↑	—	$1s^22s^22p^2$
Nitrogen	N	↑↓	↑↓	↑	↑	↑	$1s^22s^22p^3$
Oxygen	O	↑↓	↑↓	↑↓	↑	↑	$1s^22s^22p^4$
Fluorine	F	↑↓	↑↓	↑↓	↑↓	↑	$1s^22s^22p^5$
Neon	Ne	↑↓	↑↓	↑↓	↑↓	↑↓	$1s^22s^22p^6$

Elements of the Third Period

After the outer octet is filled in neon, the next electron enters the *s* sublevel in the $n = 3$ main energy level. Thus, atoms of sodium, Na, have the configuration $1s^22s^22p^63s^1$. Compare the configuration of a sodium atom with that of an atom of neon in **Figure 3.5.** Notice that the first 10 electrons in a sodium atom have the same configuration as a neon atom, $1s^22s^22p^6$. In fact, the first 10 electrons in an atom of each of the third-period elements have the same configuration as neon. This similarity allows us to use a shorthand notation for the electron configurations of the third-period elements.

Noble-Gas Notation

Neon is a member of the Group 18 elements. **The Group 18 elements (helium, neon, argon, krypton, xenon, and radon) are called the noble gases.** To simplify sodium's notation, the symbol for neon, enclosed in square brackets, is used to represent the complete neon configuration: $[Ne] = 1s^22s^22p^6$. This allows us to write sodium's electron configuration as $[Ne]3s^1$, which is called sodium's *noble-gas notation.* **Figure 3.6,** on the next page, shows the electron configuration of each of the third-period elements using noble-gas notation.

The last element in the third period is argon, Ar, which is a noble gas. As in neon, the highest-occupied energy level of argon has an octet of electrons, $[Ne]3s^23p^6$. In fact, each noble gas other than He has an electron octet in its highest energy level. **A noble-gas configuration refers to an outer main energy level occupied, in most cases, by eight electrons.**

Differentiated Instruction

ENGLISH LEARNER

Point out that the term *noble* is used to describe a person of high birth, rank, or title such as a king or prince. Consequently, the term *noble* is associated with someone being above or removed from the common people. Ask students to suggest a reason why the noble gases are so named. Students may suggest that the noble gases are unique in that they are in some way above or removed from the other elements. Inform students that they will learn how the noble gases are unique in terms of their chemical reactivity.

TEACH FROM VISUALS

FIGURE 3.5 Have students compare the information provided by orbital notation to the noble-gas notation in **Figure 3.6** on the next page). Orbital notation indicates each orbital and its electrons. Noble-gas notation shows an electron configuration in an abbreviated manner, specifying the arrangements of only the electrons in the outer shell.

Then, have students refer to **Figure 3.6** to draw the orbital notations for the 3*p* electrons in phosphorus. Students should draw three boxes, each containing an arrow pointing upward. Draw a box representing the 3*s* orbital and place two arrows to show the two electrons with opposite spin in this orbital. Ask students which elements in Period 3 can have this orbital notation. Students can identify any element in Period 3 except sodium.

Misconception Alert!

To prevent students from developing the misconception that an atom changes its identity when it gains or loses an electron, have them explain why the sodium atom does not become a neon atom when it loses its 3*s* electron even though they both have the same electron configuration. Students should recognize that an atom's identity depends on its number of protons, or atomic number.

▼ Teach *continued*

Teaching Tip

Teachers should emphasize that in writing out electron configurations, it is acceptable to group together all occupied orbitals having the same value of *n*, even though this is not the usual order of filling. In other words, it is acceptable to write 3*d* before 4*s*, as is done in **Figure 3.7**, and 4*f* before 5*d* before 6*s*.

FIGURE 3.6

ELECTRON CONFIGURATIONS OF ATOMS OF THIRD-PERIOD ELEMENTS

Name	Symbol	Atomic number	Number of electrons in sublevels 1s	2s	2p	3s	3p	Noble-gas notation
Sodium	Na	11	2	2	6	1		*[Ne]$3s^1$
Magnesium	Mg	12	2	2	6	2		[Ne]$3s^2$
Aluminum	Al	13	2	2	6	2	1	[Ne]$3s^23p^1$
Silicon	Si	14	2	2	6	2	2	[Ne]$3s^23p^2$
Phosphorus	P	15	2	2	6	2	3	[Ne]$3s^23p^3$
Sulfur	S	16	2	2	6	2	4	[Ne]$3s^23p^4$
Chlorine	Cl	17	2	2	6	2	5	[Ne]$3s^23p^5$
Argon	Ar	18	2	2	6	2	6	[Ne]$3s^23p^6$

*[Ne] = $1s^22s^22p^6$

Elements of the Fourth Period

The electron configurations of atoms in the fourth-period elements are shown in **Figure 3.7** (on the next page). The period begins by filling the 4*s* orbital, the empty orbital of lowest energy. The first element in the fourth period is potassium, K, which has the electron configuration [Ar]$4s^1$. The next element is calcium, Ca, which has the electron configuration [Ar]$4s^2$.

With the 4*s* sublevel filled, the 4*p* and 3*d* sublevels are the next available vacant orbitals. **Figure 3.1** (on the first page of this section) shows that the 3*d* sublevel is lower in energy than the 4*p* sublevel. Therefore, the five 3*d* orbitals are next to be filled. A total of 10 electrons can occupy the 3*d* orbitals. These are filled successively in the 10 elements from scandium (atomic number 21) to zinc (atomic number 30).

Scandium, Sc, has the electron configuration [Ar]$3d^14s^2$. Titanium, Ti, has the configuration [Ar]$3d^24s^2$. And vanadium, V, has the configuration [Ar]$3d^34s^2$. Up to this point, three electrons with the same spin have been added to three separate *d* orbitals, as required by Hund's rule.

Surprisingly, chromium, Cr, has the electron configuration [Ar]$3d^54s^1$. Not only did the added electron go into the fourth 3*d* orbital, but an electron also moved from the 4*s* orbital into the fifth 3*d* orbital, leaving the 4*s* orbital with a single electron. Chromium's electron configuration is contrary to what is expected according to the Aufbau principle. However, in reality the [Ar]$3d^54s^1$ configuration is of lower energy than a [Ar]$3d^44s^2$ configuration. For chromium, having six orbitals with unpaired electrons is a more stable arrangement than having four unpaired electrons in the 3*d* orbitals and forcing two electrons to pair up in the 4*s* orbital. On the other hand, for tungsten, W, which is in the same group as chromium, having four electrons in the 5*d* orbitals and two electrons paired in the 6*s* orbital is the most stable arrangement. There is no simple explanation for such deviations from the expected order given in **Figure 3.4**.

Differentiated Instruction

PRE-AP

Point out to students that the 3*d* sublevel jumps from having 3 electrons to 5 and from having 8 electrons to 10. Ask students to explain the reason for this observation, which is sometimes called *d*-block contraction. Students should be aware that half-filled and filled orbitals in the 3*d* sublevel result in stability for these elements.

Manganese, Mn, has the electron configuration [Ar]$3d^5 4s^2$. The added electron goes to the 4s orbital, completely filling this orbital while leaving the 3d orbitals still half-filled. Beginning with the next element, electrons continue to pair in the d orbitals. Thus, iron, Fe, has the configuration [Ar]$3d^6 4s^2$; cobalt, Co, has the configuration [Ar]$3d^7 4s^2$; and nickel, Ni, has the configuration [Ar]$3d^8 4s^2$. Next is copper, Cu, in which an electron moves from the 4s orbital to pair with the electron in the fifth 3d orbital. The result is an electron configuration of [Ar]$3d^{10} 4s^1$—the lowest-energy configuration for Cu. As with Cr, there is no simple explanation for this deviation from the expected order.

In atoms of zinc, Zn, the 4s sublevel is filled to give the electron configuration [Ar]$3d^{10} 4s^2$. In atoms of the next six elements, electrons add one by one to the three 4p orbitals. According to Hund's rule, one electron is added to each of the three 4p orbitals before electrons are paired in any 4p orbital.

FIGURE 3.7

ELECTRON CONFIGURATION OF ATOMS OF ELEMENTS IN THE FOURTH PERIOD

Name	Symbol	Atomic number	Number of electrons in sublevels above 2p: 3s	3p	3d	4s	4p	Noble-gas notation
Potassium	K	19	2	6		1		*[Ar]$4s^1$
Calcium	Ca	20	2	6		2		[Ar]$4s^2$
Scandium	Sc	21	2	6	1	2		[Ar]$3d^1 4s^2$
Titanium	Ti	22	2	6	2	2		[Ar]$3d^2 4s^2$
Vanadium	V	23	2	6	3	2		[Ar]$3d^3 4s^2$
Chromium	Cr	24	2	6	5	1		[Ar]$3d^5 4s^1$
Manganese	Mn	25	2	6	5	2		[Ar]$3d^5 4s^2$
Iron	Fe	26	2	6	6	2		[Ar]$3d^6 4s^2$
Cobalt	Co	27	2	6	7	2		[Ar]$3d^7 4s^2$
Nickel	Ni	28	2	6	8	2		[Ar]$3d^8 4s^2$
Copper	Cu	29	2	6	10	1		[Ar]$3d^{10} 4s^1$
Zinc	Zn	30	2	6	10	2		[Ar]$3d^{10} 4s^2$
Gallium	Ga	31	2	6	10	2	1	[Ar]$3d^{10} 4s^2 4p^1$
Germanium	Ge	32	2	6	10	2	2	[Ar]$3d^{10} 4s^2 4p^2$
Arsenic	As	33	2	6	10	2	3	[Ar]$3d^{10} 4s^2 4p^3$
Selenium	Se	34	2	6	10	2	4	[Ar]$3d^{10} 4s^2 4p^4$
Bromine	Br	35	2	6	10	2	5	[Ar]$3d^{10} 4s^2 4p^5$
Krypton	Kr	36	2	6	10	2	6	[Ar]$3d^{10} 4s^2 4p^6$

*[Ar] = $1s^2 2s^2 2p^6 3s^2 3p^6$

Problem Solving

DECONSTRUCTING PROBLEMS

Ask students to draw the electron configuration for copper if the Aufbau principle were strictly followed. [Ar]$3d^9 4s^2$ Have students suggest a possible reason for this exception to Aufbau's principle. Students should recognize that the actual electron configuration of copper must have a lower energy state than the one predicted by the Aufbau principle.

TEACH FROM TABLES

FIGURE 3.7 Have students observe the situations in which an electron leaves an s orbital to create a half-filled or filled d sublevel. Explain that in each of these situations the electron configuration that results is the most stable configuration possible.

Demo Problems

1. Identify the element whose atoms have two electrons in the p sublevel of their second main energy level. What is the total number of electrons in the second main energy level of an atom of this element? Name the element in the third period that has the same number of electrons in its outermost main energy level as the element described in the first part of the problem.

Answers: carbon; 4; silicon

2. Identify the element whose atoms have five electrons in the p sublevel of their third main energy level. What is the total number of electrons in the third main energy level of an atom of this element? Name the element in the fourth period that has the same number of electrons in its outermost main energy level as the element described in the first part of the problem.

Answers: chlorine; 7; bromine

3. Which element does the noble-gas notation [Ne]$3s^1$ represent the electron configuration of? How many inner-shell electrons do its atoms contain?

Answers: sodium; 10

4. Write the noble-gas notation for aluminum. How many outer-shell electrons does an atom of aluminum contain? How many unpaired electrons does an atom of aluminum contain?

Answers: [Ne]$3s^2 3p^1$; 3; 1

▼ Teach *continued*

Classroom Practice

B-1 **a.** Write both the complete electron-configuration notation and the noble-gas notation for titanium, Ti.

b. How many electron-containing orbitals are in an atom of titanium? How many of these orbitals are filled? How many unpaired electrons are there in an atom of titanium?

Answers:

a. $1s^22s^22p^63s^23p^63d^24s^2$, $[Ar]3d^24s^2$

b. 12 (one 1*s* orbital, one 2*s* orbital, three 2*p* orbitals, one 3*s* orbital, three 3*p* orbitals, one 4*s* orbital, and two 3*d* orbitals); 10; 2

Elements of the Fifth Period

In the 18 elements of the fifth period, sublevels fill in a similar manner as in elements of the fourth period. However, they start at the 5*s* orbital instead of at the 4*s* orbital. Successive electrons are added first to the 5*s* orbital, then to the 4*d* orbitals, and finally to the 5*p* orbitals. This can be seen in **Figure 3.8.** There are occasional deviations from the predicted configurations here also. The deviations differ from those for fourth-period elements, but in each case the preferred configuration has the lowest possible energy.

FIGURE 3.8

ELECTRON CONFIGURATIONS OF ATOMS OF ELEMENTS IN THE FIFTH PERIOD

Name	Symbol	Atomic number	Number of electrons in sublevels above 3*d*					Noble-gas notation
			4*s*	4*p*	4*d*	5*s*	5*p*	
Rubidium	Rb	37	2	6		1		$*[Kr]5s^1$
Strontium	Sr	38	2	6		2		$[Kr]5s^2$
Yttrium	Y	39	2	6	1	2		$[Kr]4d^15s^2$
Zirconium	Zr	40	2	6	2	2		$[Kr]4d^25s^2$
Niobium	Nb	41	2	6	4	1		$[Kr]4d^45s^1$
Molybdenum	Mo	42	2	6	5	1		$[Kr]4d^55s^1$
Technetium	Tc	43	2	6	6	1		$[Kr]4d^65s^1$
Ruthenium	Ru	44	2	6	7	1		$[Kr]4d^75s^1$
Rhodium	Rh	45	2	6	8	1		$[Kr]4d^85s^1$
Palladium	Pd	46	2	6	10			$[Kr]4d^{10}$
Silver	Ag	47	2	6	10	1		$[Kr]4d^{10}5s^1$
Cadmium	Cd	48	2	6	10	2		$[Kr]4d^{10}5s^2$
Indium	In	49	2	6	10	2	1	$[Kr]4d^{10}5s^25p^1$
Tin	Sn	50	2	6	10	2	2	$[Kr]4d^{10}5s^25p^2$
Antimony	Sb	51	2	6	10	2	3	$[Kr]4d^{10}5s^25p^3$
Tellurium	Te	52	2	6	10	2	4	$[Kr]4d^{10}5s^25p^4$
Iodine	I	53	2	6	10	2	5	$[Kr]4d^{10}5s^25p^5$
Xenon	Xe	54	2	6	10	2	6	$[Kr]4d^{10}5s^25p^6$

$*[Kr] = 1s^22s^22p^63s^23p^63d^{10}4s^24p^6$

Problem Solving

DECONSTRUCTING PROBLEMS

Be sure that students remember that the values of *n* do not represent the order in which the electrons fill the sublevels. Remind students, for example, that the 4*s* sublevel usually fills before the 3*d* sublevel. Students may want to refer to **Figure 3.1** when writing electron configurations.

Electron Configurations

Sample Problem B

a. Write both the complete electron-configuration notation and the noble-gas notation for iron, Fe.

b. How many electron-containing orbitals are in an atom of iron? How many of these orbitals are completely filled? How many unpaired electrons are there in an atom of iron? In which sublevel are the unpaired electrons located?

SOLVE

a. The complete electron-configuration notation of iron is $1s^22s^22p^63s^23p^63d^64s^2$. The periodic table inside the back cover of the text reveals that $1s^22s^22p^63s^23p^6$ is the electron configuration of the noble gas argon, Ar. Therefore, as shown in **Figure 3.7**, iron's noble-gas notation is $[Ar]3d^64s^2$.

b. An iron atom has 15 orbitals that contain electrons. They consist of one 1*s* orbital, one 2*s* orbital, three 2*p* orbitals, one 3*s* orbital, three 3*p* orbitals, five 3*d* orbitals, and one 4*s* orbital. Eleven of these orbitals are filled, and there are four unpaired electrons. They are located in the 3*d* sublevel. The notation $3d^6$ represents:

Practice

Answers in Appendix E

1. **a.** Write both the complete electron-configuration notation and the noble-gas notation for iodine, I. How many inner-shell electrons does an iodine atom contain?
   b. How many electron-containing orbitals are in an atom of iodine? How many of these orbitals are filled? How many unpaired electrons are there in an atom of iodine?
2. **a.** Write the noble-gas notation for tin, Sn. How many unpaired electrons are there in an atom of tin?
   b. How many electron-containing *d* orbitals are there in an atom of tin? Name the element in the fourth period whose atoms have the same number of electrons in their highest energy levels that tin's atoms do.
3. **a.** Write the complete electron configuration for the element with atomic number 25. You may use the diagram shown in **Figure 3.2**.
   b. Identify the element described in item 3a.
4. **a.** How many orbitals are completely filled in an atom of the element with atomic number 18? Write the complete electron configuration for this element.
   b. Identify the element described in item 4a.

Elements of the Sixth Period

The sixth period consists of 32 elements. It is much longer than the periods that precede it in the periodic table. To build up electron configurations for elements of this period, electrons are added first to the 6*s* orbital in cesium, Cs, and barium, Ba. Then, in lanthanum, La, an electron is added to the 5*d* orbital.

ALTERNATIVE APPROACHES

Have students draw boxes representing the orbitals of the 4*f* and 5*d* sublevels. Instruct students that their diagrams must demonstrate that these sublevels are very close in energy with the 4*f* sublevel having a slightly lower energy. Students' diagrams should include seven boxes for the 4*f* sublevel and five boxes for the 5*d* sublevel. The boxes for the 4*f* sublevel should be slightly lower than those for the 5*d* boxes. Students can compare their diagrams to **Figure 3.1.**

Answers

Practice B

1. **a.** $1s^22s^22p^63s^23p^63d^{10}4s^24p^64d^{10}5s^25p^5$, $[Kr]4d^{10}5s^25p^5$, 46
   b. 27, 26, 1
2. **a.** $[Kr]4d^{10}5s^25p^2$, 2
   b. 10, germanium
3. **a.** $1s^22s^22p^63s^23p^63d^54s^2$
   b. manganese
4. **a.** 9, $1s^22s^22p^63s^23p^6$
   b. argon

▼ Teach *continued*

Classroom Practice

C-1 a. How many inner-shell electrons does an atom of silicon, Si, contain?

b. How many electron-containing orbitals are in an atom of silicon? How many of these orbitals are filled? How many unpaired electrons are there in an atom of silicon?

c. How many electron-containing p orbitals are there in an atom of silicon?

Answers:

a. 10 **b.** 8, 6, 2 **c.** 5

Answers

Practice C

1. **a.** $1s^22s^22p^63s^23p^63d^{10}4s^2 4p^64d^{10}5s^25p^66s^2$, $[Xe]6s^2$
   b. Be, Mg, Ca, Sr
2. **a.** $[Xe]4f^{14}5d^{10}6s^1$
   b. Au, Cs, Pt

▼ Assess and Reteach

Assess Use the Formative Assessment on this page to evaluate student mastery of the section.

Reteach For students who need additional instruction, download the Section Study Guide.

Response to Intervention To reassess students' mastery, use the Section Quiz, available to print or to take directly online at **HMDScience.com**.

With the next element, cerium, Ce, the $4f$ orbitals begin to fill, giving cerium atoms a configuration of $[Xe]4f^15d^16s^2$. In the next 13 elements, the $4f$ orbitals are filled. Next the $5d$ orbitals are filled and the period is completed by filling the $6p$ orbitals. Because the $4f$ and the $5d$ orbitals are very close in energy, numerous deviations from the simple rules occur as these orbitals are filled. The electron configurations of the sixth-period elements can be found in the periodic table inside the back cover of the text. The seventh period is incomplete and consists largely of synthetic elements.

Electron Configurations

Sample Problem C

a. Write both the complete electron-configuration notation and the noble-gas notation for a rubidium atom.

b. Identify the elements in the second, third, and fourth periods that have the same number of highest-energy-level electrons as rubidium.

SOLUTION

a. $1s^22s^22p^63s^23p^63d^{10}4s^24p^65s^1$, $[Kr]5s^1$

b. Rubidium has one electron in its highest energy level (the fifth). The elements with the same outermost configuration are, in the second period, lithium, Li; in the third period, sodium, Na; and in the fourth period, potassium, K.

Practice Answers in Appendix E

1. **a.** Write both the complete electron-configuration notation and the noble-gas notation for a barium atom.
   b. Identify the elements in the second, third, fourth, and fifth periods that have the same number of highest-energy-level electrons as barium.
2. **a.** Write the noble-gas notation for a gold atom.
   b. Identify the elements in the sixth period that have one unpaired $6s$ electron.

SECTION 3 FORMATIVE ASSESSMENT

Reviewing Main Ideas

1. **a.** What is an atom's electron configuration?
   b. What three principles guide the electron configuration of an atom?
2. What three methods are used to represent the arrangement of electrons in atoms?
3. What is an octet of electrons? Which elements contain an octet of electrons?
4. Write the complete electron-configuration notation, the noble-gas notation, and the orbital notation for the following elements:
   a. carbon **b.** neon **c.** sulfur
5. Identify the elements having the following electron configurations:
   a. $1s^22s^22p^63s^23p^3$
   b. $[Ar]4s^1$
   c. contains four electrons in its third and outer main energy level
   d. contains one set of paired and three unpaired electrons in its fourth and outer main energy level

Critical Thinking

6. **RELATING IDEAS** Write the electron configuration for the third-period elements Al, Si, P, S, and Cl. Is there a relationship between the group number of each element and the number of electrons in the outermost energy level?

Answers to Section Assessment

1. **a.** a description of the arrangement of an atom's electrons
   b. the Aufbau principle, Hund's rule, and the Pauli exclusion principle
2. orbital notation, electron-configuration notation, and noble-gas notation
3. An octet of electrons corresponds to filled s and p orbitals in an atom's highest main energy level. Noble gases (except helium, which has a filled outermost 1s orbital) contain octets.
4. **a.** $1s^22s^22p^2$, $[He]2s^22p^2$,
   ↑↓ (1s) ↑↓ (2s) ↑ ↑ __ (2p)
   b. $1s^22s^22p^6$, $[He]2s^22p^6$,
   ↑↓ (1s) ↑↓ (2s) ↑↓ ↑↓ ↑↓ (2p)
   c. $1s^22s^22p^63s^23p^4$, $[Ne]3s^23p^4$,
   ↑↓ (1s) ↑↓ (2s) ↑↓ ↑↓ ↑↓ (2p)
   ↑↓ (3s) ↑↓ ↑ ↑ (3p)
5. **a.** P **b.** K **c.** S **d.** As
6. In each case, the number of outermost energy-level electrons is equal to the group number minus 10.

Math Tutor

Weighted Averages and Atomic Mass

You have learned that the mass of a proton is about 1 u and that a neutron is only slightly heavier. Because atomic nuclei consist of whole numbers of protons and neutrons, you might expect that the atomic mass of an element would be very near a whole number. However, if you look at the periodic table, you will see that the atomic masses of many elements lie somewhere between whole numbers. In fact, the atomic masses listed on the table are *average* atomic masses. The atomic masses are averages because most elements occur in nature as a specific mixture of isotopes. For example, 75.76% of chlorine atoms have a mass of 34.969 u, and 24.24% have a mass of 36.966 u. If the isotopes were in a 1:1 ratio, you could simply add the masses of the two isotopes together and divide by 2. However, to account for the differing abundance of the isotopes, you must calculate a *weighted average*. For chlorine, the weighted average is 35.45 u. The following two examples demonstrate how weighted averages are calculated.

Sample Problem

A sample of naturally occurring silver consists of 51.839% Ag-107 (atomic mass 106.905 093 u) and 48.161% Ag-109 (atomic mass 108.904 756 u). What is the average atomic mass of silver?

To find average atomic mass, convert each percentage to a decimal equivalent and multiply by the atomic mass of the isotope.

$$0.518\,39 \times 106.905\,093 \text{ u} = 55.419 \text{ u}$$
$$\underline{0.481\,61 \times 108.904\,756 \text{ u} = 52.450 \text{ u}}$$
$$107.869 \text{ u}$$

Adding the masses contributed by each isotope gives an average atomic mass of 107.869 u. Note that this value for the average atomic mass of silver is very near the one given in the periodic table.

A sample of naturally occurring magnesium consists of 78.99% Mg-24 (atomic mass 23.985 042 u), 10.00% Mg-25 (atomic mass 24.985 837 u), and 11.01% Mg-26 (atomic mass 25.982 593 u). What is the average atomic mass of magnesium?

Again, convert each percentage to a decimal and multiply by the atomic mass of the isotope to get the mass contributed by each isotope.

$$0.7899 \times 23.985\,042 \text{ u} = 18.95 \text{ u}$$
$$0.1000 \times 24.985\,837 \text{ u} = 2.499 \text{ u}$$
$$\underline{0.1101 \times 25.982\,593 \text{ u} = 2.861 \text{ u}}$$
$$24.31 \text{ u}$$

Adding the masses contributed by each isotope gives an average atomic mass of 24.31 u.

Practice

1. Rubidium occurs naturally as a mixture of two isotopes, 72.17% Rb-85 (atomic mass 84.911 792 u) and 27.83% Rb-87 (atomic mass 86.909 186 u). What is the average atomic mass of rubidium?
2. The element silicon occurs as a mixture of three isotopes: 92.22% Si-28, 4.69% Si-29, and 3.09% Si-30. The atomic masses of these three isotopes are as follows: Si-28 = 27.976 926 u, Si-29 = 28.976 495 u, and Si-30 = 29.973 770 u.

   Find the average atomic mass of silicon.

MATH TUTOR

Answers

1. 85.47 u
2. 28.1 u

CHAPTER 4 Summary

Review Games
Concept Maps

SECTION 1 The Development of a New Atomic Model

- In the early twentieth century, light was determined to have a dual wave-particle nature.
- Quantum theory was developed to explain observations such as the photoelectric effect and the line-emission spectrum of hydrogen.
- Quantum theory states that electrons can exist only at specific atomic energy levels.
- When an electron moves from one main energy level to a main energy level of lower energy, a photon is emitted. The photon's energy equals the energy difference between the two levels.
- An electron in an atom can move from one main energy level to a higher main energy level only by absorbing an amount of energy exactly equal to the difference between the two levels.

KEY TERMS

electromagnetic radiation
electromagnetic spectrum
wavelength
frequency
photoelectric effect
quantum
photon
ground state
excited state
line-emission spectrum
continuous spectrum

SECTION 2 The Quantum Model of the Atom

- In the early twentieth century, electrons were determined to have a dual wave-particle nature.
- The Heisenberg uncertainty principle states that it is impossible to determine simultaneously the position and velocity of an electron or any other particle.
- Quantization of electron energies is a natural outcome of the Schrödinger wave equation, which describes the properties of an atom's electrons.
- An orbital, a three-dimensional region around the nucleus, shows the region in space where an electron is most likely to be found.
- The four quantum numbers that describe the properties of electrons in atomic orbitals are the principal quantum number, the angular momentum quantum number, the magnetic quantum number, and the spin quantum number.

KEY TERMS

Heisenberg uncertainty principle
quantum theory
orbital
quantum number
principal quantum number
angular momentum quantum number
magnetic quantum number
spin quantum number

SECTION 3 Electron Configurations

- The ground-state electron configuration of an atom can be written by using the Aufbau principle, Hund's rule, and the Pauli exclusion principle.
- Electron configurations can be depicted by using different types of notation. In this book, three types of notation are used: orbital notation, electron-configuration notation, and noble-gas notation.
- Electron configurations of some atoms, such as chromium, deviate from the predictions of the Aufbau principle, but the ground-state configuration that results is the configuration with the minimum possible energy.

KEY TERMS

electron configuration
Aufbau principle
Pauli exclusion principle
Hund's rule
noble gas
noble-gas configuration

Review Answers

1. **a.** Examples include gamma rays, X rays, ultraviolet light, visible light, infrared light, microwaves, and radio waves.
   b. 3.00×10^8 m/s
2. Light's wavelike properties include the measurable characteristics of frequency and wavelength as well as the ability to interfere and diffract. Light exhibits particle-like properties when it is absorbed and emitted by matter in phenomena such as the photoelectric effect, emission of light by hot objects, and the line-emission spectra of elements.
3. Frequency ranges from approximately 4.29×10^{14} to 7.50×10^{14} Hz. Wavelength ranges from 400 to 700 nm.
4. red, orange, yellow, green, blue, and violet
5. The wave theory could not explain the photoelectric effect or hydrogen's line-emission spectrum.
6. **a.** $c = \lambda\nu$, where λ is the wavelength, ν is the frequency, and c is the velocity

CHAPTER 4 Review

SECTION 1

The Development of a New Atomic Model

REVIEWING MAIN IDEAS

1. a. List five examples of electromagnetic radiation.
   b. What is the speed of all forms of electromagnetic radiation in a vacuum?

2. Prepare a two-column table. List the properties of light that can best be explained by the wave theory in one column. List those best explained by the particle theory in the second column. You may want to consult a physics textbook for reference.

3. What are the frequency and wavelength ranges of visible light?

4. List the colors of light in the visible spectrum in order of increasing frequency.

5. In the early twentieth century, what two experiments involving light and matter could not be explained by the wave theory of light?

6. a. How are the wavelength and frequency of electromagnetic radiation related?
   b. How are the energy and frequency of electromagnetic radiation related?
   c. How are the energy and wavelength of electromagnetic radiation related?

7. Which theory of light—the wave or particle theory—best explains the following phenomena?
   a. the interference of light
   b. the photoelectric effect
   c. the emission of electromagnetic radiation by an excited atom

8. Distinguish between the ground state and an excited state of an atom.

9. According to Bohr's model of the hydrogen atom, how is hydrogen's emission spectrum produced?

PRACTICE PROBLEMS

10. Determine the frequency of light whose wavelength is 4.257×10^{-7} cm.

11. Determine the energy in joules of a photon whose frequency is 3.55×10^{17} Hz.

12. Using the two equations $E = h\nu$ and $c = \lambda\nu$, derive an equation expressing E in terms of h, c, and λ.

13. How long would it take a radio wave whose frequency is 7.25×10^5 Hz to travel from Mars to Earth if the distance between the two planets is approximately 8.00×10^7 km?

14. Cobalt-60 is an artificial radioisotope that is produced in a nuclear reactor and is used as a gamma-ray source in the treatment of certain types of cancer. If the wavelength of the gamma radiation from a cobalt-60 source is 1.00×10^{-3} nm, calculate the energy of a photon of this radiation.

SECTION 2

The Quantum Model of the Atom

REVIEWING MAIN IDEAS

15. Describe two major shortcomings of Bohr's model of the atom.

16. a. What is the principal quantum number?
    b. How is it symbolized?
    c. What are shells?
    d. How does n relate to the number of electrons allowed per main energy level?

17. a. What information is given by the angular momentum quantum number?
    b. What are sublevels, or subshells?

18. For each of the following values of n, indicate the numbers and types of sublevels possible for that main energy level. (Hint: See **Figure 2.6.**)
    a. $n = 1$
    b. $n = 2$
    c. $n = 3$
    d. $n = 4$
    e. $n = 7$ (number only)

19. a. What information is given by the magnetic quantum number?
    b. How many orbital orientations are possible in each of the s, p, d, and f sublevels?
    c. Explain and illustrate the notation for distinguishing between the different p orbitals in a sublevel.

b. $E = h\nu$, where E is energy, h is Planck's constant, and ν is the frequency
c. $E = hc/\lambda$

7. a. wave theory
   b. particle theory
   c. particle theory

8. The ground state of an atom is the atom's lowest energy state. An excited state of an atom is any energy state that is higher in energy than the atom's ground state is.

9. According to Bohr, a line-emission spectrum is produced when an electron drops from a higher-energy orbit to a lower-energy orbit, emitting a photon. The photon's energy is equal to the difference in energy between the two levels.

10. 7.05×10^{16} Hz

11. 2.35×10^{-16} J

12. $E = hc/\lambda$

13. 267 s

14. 1.99×10^{-13} J

15. Bohr's model was valid only for a single-electron atom, and it did not explain the chemical nature of atoms.

16. a. the number used to specify the main energy level of an atom
    b. by the letter n
    c. all orbitals within the same main energy level
    d. The number of electrons allowed per main energy level is equal to $2n^2$.

17. a. The angular momentum quantum number indicates an orbital's shape.
    b. A sublevel, or subshell, consists of the orbitals that are within a given main energy level and share the same value of l. For example, an atom's 3d subshell consists of five d orbitals.

18. a. 1; s
    b. 2; s and p
    c. 3; s, p, and d
    d. 4; s, p, d, and f
    e. 7

19. a. the orientation of an orbital about the nucleus
    b. 1, 3, 5, and 7, respectively
    c. Subscripts are used to indicate the various orbital orientations possible in terms of an x, y, z, three-dimensional coordinate system centered on the nucleus. For example, p_x refers to a p orbital along the x-axis, p_y indicates a p orbital along the y-axis, and p_z indicates a p orbital along the z-axis.

CHAPTER REVIEW

20. a. The total number of possible orbitals in each main energy level is equal to n^2.

b. There are 9 orbitals in the third energy level and 25 orbitals in the fifth energy level.

21. a. The spin quantum number indicates the spin state of an electron in an orbital.

b. +1/2 and −1/2.

22. a. 2

b. 18

c. 32

d. Theoretically, $n = 6$ can contain 72 electrons.

e. Theoretically, $n = 7$ can contain 98 electrons.

23. Sketches should look like the *s* and *p* orbitals shown in **Figure 2.5a** or should show a line-circle and a line-dumbbell shape.

24. The 2*s* orbital has a higher energy than a 1*s* orbital does, and the distance of the electron from the nucleus is farther for a 2*s* orbital than for a 1*s* orbital.

25. The orientation of a $2p_x$ and a $2p_y$ orbital are at right angles to each other.

26. a. An electron occupies the lowest-energy orbital that can receive it.

b. In a multi-electron atom, the lowest-energy orbital is filled first. Electrons are then added to the orbital with the next lowest energy, and so on, until all of the electrons in the atom have been placed in orbitals.

27. a. Orbitals of equal energy are each occupied by one electron before any orbital is occupied by a second electron.

b. By placing as many single electrons as possible in separate orbitals in the same energy level, electron-electron repulsion is minimized and favorable lower-energy arrangements result.

28. a. No two electrons in the same atom can have the same four quantum numbers.

b. The two different values of the spin quantum number permit two electrons of opposite spin states to occupy the same orbital.

20. a. What is the relationship between n and the total number of orbitals in a main energy level?

b. How many total orbitals are contained in the third main energy level? in the fifth?

21. a. What information is given by the spin quantum number?

b. What are the possible values for this quantum number?

22. How many electrons could be contained in the following main energy levels with n equal to the number provided?

a. 1
b. 3
c. 4
d. 6
e. 7

PRACTICE PROBLEMS

23. Sketch the shape of an *s* orbital and a *p* orbital.

24. How does a 2*s* orbital differ from a 1*s* orbital?

25. How do a $2p_x$ and a $2p_y$ orbital differ?

SECTION 3

Electron Configurations

REVIEWING MAIN IDEAS

26. a. In your own words, state the Aufbau principle.

b. Explain the meaning of this principle in terms of an atom with many electrons.

27. a. In your own words, state Hund's rule.

b. What is the basis for this rule?

28. a. In your own words, state the Pauli exclusion principle.

b. What is the significance of the spin quantum number?

29. a. What is meant by the highest occupied energy level in an atom?

b. What are inner-shell electrons?

30. Determine the highest occupied energy level in the following elements:

a. He
b. Be
c. Al
d. Ca
e. Sn

31. Write the orbital notation for the following elements. (Hint: See Sample Problem A.)

a. P
b. B
c. Na
d. O

32. Write the electron-configuration notation for the element whose atoms contain the following number of electrons:

a. 3
b. 6
c. 8
d. 13

33. Given that the electron configuration for oxygen is $1s^22s^22p^4$, answer the following questions:

a. How many electrons are in each oxygen atom?

b. What is the atomic number of this element?

c. Write the orbital notation for oxygen's electron configuration.

d. How many unpaired electrons does oxygen have?

e. What is the highest occupied energy level?

f. How many inner-shell electrons does the atom contain?

g. In which orbital(s) are these inner-shell electrons located?

34. a. What are the noble gases?

b. What is a noble-gas configuration?

c. How does noble-gas notation simplify writing an atom's electron configuration?

35. Write the noble-gas notation for the electron configuration of each of the elements below. (Hint: See Sample Problem B.)

a. Cl
b. Ca
c. Se

36. a. What information is given by the noble-gas notation $[Ne]3s^2$?

b. What element does this represent?

37. Write both the complete electron-configuration notation and the noble-gas notation for each of the elements below. (Hint: See Sample Problem C.)

a. Na
b. Sr
c. P

29. a. The highest occupied energy level in an atom is the electron-containing main energy level that has the highest principal quantum number.

b. Inner-shell electrons are electrons that are not in the highest occupied energy level.

30. a. first main energy level ($n = 1$)

b. second main energy level ($n = 2$)

c. third main energy level ($n = 3$)

d. fourth main energy level ($n = 4$)

e. fifth main energy level ($n = 5$)

31. a. ↑↓ (1s) ↑↓ (2s) ↑↓ ↑↓ ↑↓ (2p) ↑↓ (3s) ↑ ↑ ↑ (3p)

b. ↑↓ (1s) ↑↓ (2s) ↑ __ __ (2p)

c. ↑↓ (1s) ↑↓ (2s) ↑↓ ↑↓ ↑↓ (2p) ↑ (3s)

38. Identify each of the following atoms on the basis of its electron configuration:
    a. $1s^22s^22p^1$
    b. $1s^22s^22p^5$
    c. $[Ne]3s^2$
    d. $[Ne]3s^23p^2$
    e. $[Ne]3s^23p^5$
    f. $[Ar]4s^1$
    g. $[Ar]3d^64s^2$

PRACTICE PROBLEMS

39. List the order in which orbitals generally fill, from the $1s$ to the $7p$ orbital.

40. Write the noble-gas notation for the electron configurations of each of the following elements:
    a. As
    b. Pb
    c. Lr
    d. Hg
    e. Sn
    f. Xe
    g. La

41. How do the electron configurations of chromium and copper contradict the Aufbau principle?

Mixed Review

 **REVIEWING MAIN IDEAS**

42. a. Which has a longer wavelength: green light or yellow light?
    b. Which has a higher frequency: an X ray or a microwave?
    c. Which travels at a greater speed: ultraviolet light or infrared light?

43. Write both the complete electron-configuration and noble-gas notation for each of the following:
    a. Ar
    b. Br
    c. Al

44. Given the speed of light as 3.00×10^8 m/s, calculate the wavelength of the electromagnetic radiation whose frequency is 7.500×10^{12} Hz.

45. a. What is the electromagnetic spectrum?
    b. What units can be used to express wavelength?
    c. What unit is used to express frequencies of electromagnetic waves?

46. Given that the electron configuration for phosphorus is $1s^22s^22p^63s^23p^3$, answer the following questions:
    a. How many electrons are in each atom?
    b. What is the atomic number of this element?
    c. Write the orbital notation for this element.
    d. How many unpaired electrons does an atom of phosphorus have?
    e. What is its highest occupied energy level?
    f. How many inner-shell electrons does the atom contain?
    g. In which orbital(s) are these inner-shell electrons located?

47. What is the frequency of a radio wave whose energy is 1.55×10^{-24} J per photon?

48. Write the noble-gas notation for the electron configurations of each of the following elements:
    a. Hf
    b. Sc
    c. Fe
    d. At
    e. Ac
    f. Zn

49. Describe the major similarities and differences between Schrödinger's model of the atom and the model proposed by Bohr.

50. When sodium is heated, a yellow spectral line whose energy is 3.37×10^{-19} J per photon is produced.
    a. What is the frequency of this light?
    b. What is the wavelength of this light?

51. a. What is an orbital?
    b. Describe an orbital in terms of an electron cloud.

CRITICAL THINKING

52. **Inferring Relationships** In the emission spectrum of hydrogen shown in **Figure 1.5**, each colored line is produced by the emission of photons with specific energies. Substances also produce absorption spectra when electromagnetic radiation passes through them. Certain wavelengths are absorbed. Using the diagram below, predict what the wavelengths of the absorption lines will be when white light (all of the colors of the visible spectrum) is passed through hydrogen gas.

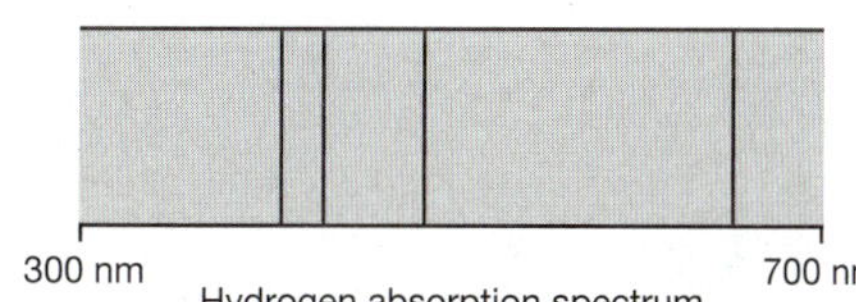

Hydrogen absorption spectrum

d. ↑↓ (1s) ↑↓ (2s) ↑↓ ↑ ↑ (2p)

32. a. $1s^22s^1$; b. $1s^22s^22p^2$; c. $1s^22s^22p^4$; d. $1s^22s^22p^63s^23p^1$

33. a. 8
    b. 8
    c. ↑↓ (1s) ↑↓ (2s) ↑↓ ↑ ↑ (2p)
    d. 2
    e. second main energy level ($n = 2$)
    f. 2
    g. the 1s orbital

34. a. The noble gases are the Group 18 elements: helium, neon, argon, krypton, xenon, and radon.
    b. A noble-gas configuration refers to an outer main energy level occupied, in most cases, by eight electrons.
    c. It allows one to abbreviate large portions of the configuration.

35. a. $[Ne]3s^23p^5$
    b. $[Ar]4s^2$
    c. $[Ar]3d^{10}4s^24p^4$

CHAPTER REVIEW

36. a. The notation indicates that in addition to having all of the electrons that would be contained by neon (10), the atom has two electrons in its 3s orbital.
    b. magnesium

37. a. $1s^22s^22p^63s^1$, $[Ne]3s^1$
    b. $1s^22s^22p^63s^23p^63d^{10}4s^24p^65s^2$, $[Kr]5s^2$
    c. $1s^22s^22p^63s^23p^3$, $[Ne]3s^23p^3$

38. a. boron
    b. fluorine
    c. magnesium
    d. silicon
    e. chlorine
    f. potassium
    g. iron

39. 1s, 2s, 2p, 3s, 3p, 4s, 3d, 4p, 5s, 4d, 5p, 6s, 4f, 5d, 6p, 7s, 5f, 6d, 7p

40. a. $[Ar]3d^{10}4s^24p^3$
    b. $[Xe]4f^{14}5d^{10}6s^26p^2$
    c. $[Rn]5f^{14}6d^17s^2$
    d. $[Xe]4f^{14}5d^{10}6s^2$
    e. $[Kr]4d^{10}5s^25p^2$
    f. $[Kr]4d^{10}5s^25p^6$
    g. $[Xe]5d^16s^2$

41. Electrons occupy the higher-energy 3d sublevel before filling the lower-energy 4s orbital. These unusual configurations result because they are the electron arrangements of minimum energy.

42. a. yellow light
    b. an X ray
    c. In a vacuum, both travel at the same speed, the speed of light.

43. a. $1s^22s^22p^63s^23p^6$, $[Ne]3s^23p^6$
    b. $1s^22s^22p^63s^23p^63d^{10}4s^24p^5$, $[Ar]3d^{10}4s^24p^5$
    c. $1s^22s^22p^63s^23p^1$, $[Ne]3s^23p^1$

44. 4.00×10^{-5} m (4.00×10^4 nm)

45. a. all the forms of electromagnetic radiation arranged according to increasing wavelength or frequency
    b. Any length unit is acceptable. Often, shorter wavelengths are measured in nanometers, and longer wavelengths are measured in centimeters or meters.
    c. hertz, Hz; one Hz equals one wave per second

46. a. 15
    b. 15
    c. ↑↓ (1s) ↑↓ (2s) ↑↓ ↑↓ ↑↓ (2p) ↑↓ (3s) ↑ ↑ ↑ (3p)
    d. 3

e. the third main energy level ($n = 3$)
f. 10
g. the 1s, 2s, and 2p orbitals

47. 2.34×10^9 Hz

48. a. $[Xe]4f^{14}5d^{2}6s^{2}$
b. $[Ar]3d^{1}4s^{2}$
c. $[Ar]3d^{6}4s^{2}$
d. $[Xe]4f^{14}5d^{10}6s^{2}6p^{5}$
e. $[Rn]6d^{1}7s^{2}$
f. $[Ar]3d^{10}4s^{2}$

49. Bohr's model worked only for the hydrogen atom, whereas Schrödinger's mathematical model applies to all atoms. The essential difference between the two models involves the issue of certainty. Bohr described definite orbits occupied by electron particles, whereas Schrödinger treated electrons as waves having a certain probability of being found in orbitals at various distances from the nucleus. The two models are similar in that both associate an electron's energy with its location relative to the nucleus. Also, the most probable location of an electron in hydrogen, according to Schrödinger, is at a distance from the nucleus exactly equal to that of Bohr's lowest-energy orbit.

50. a. 5.09×10^{14} Hz
b. 5.90×10^{-7} m (590. nm)

51. a. An orbital is a three-dimensional region about the nucleus where there is a high probability that a particular electron is located.
b. Orbitals are like clouds that show the region of probable electron locations. The sizes and shapes of electron clouds depend on the energies of the electrons that occupy them.

52. 656 nm, 486 nm, 434 nm, and 410 nm. Students might realize that these are the same frequencies of hydrogen's line-emission spectrum. Electronic transitions occur at the same frequencies whether an electron is absorbing energy and being excited or losing energy and emitting a photon.

53. 7.00×10^{-19} J

54. Electrons *a* and *b* are in the same orbital, because the only difference is the spin quantum number.

55. Possible: b. (All 4 quantum numbers follow rules.) Not possible: a (if $n = 2$, only $l = 0$ and $l = 1$ are allowed); c (if $l = 0$, only possible value of m is 0)

53. **Applying Models** In discussions of the photoelectric effect, the minimum energy needed to remove an electron from the metal is called the *threshold energy* and is a characteristic of the metal. For example, chromium, Cr, will emit electrons when the wavelength of the radiation is 284 nm or less. Calculate the threshold energy for chromium. (Hint: You will need to use the two equations that describe the relationships between wavelength, frequency, speed of light, and Planck's constant.)

54. **Analyzing Information** Four electrons in an atom have the four sets of quantum numbers given below. Which electrons are in the same orbital? Explain your answer.
a. 1, 0, 0, −__
b. 1, 0, 0, +__
c. 2, 1, 1, +__
d. 2, 1, 0, +__

55. **Relating Ideas** Which of the sets of quantum numbers below are possible? Which are impossible? Explain your choices.
a. 2, 2, 1, +__
b. 2, 0, 0, −__
c. 2, 0, 1, −__

USING THE HANDBOOK

56. Sections 1 and 2 of the *Elements Handbook* (Appendix A) contain information on an analytical test and a technological application for Group 1 and 2 elements. The test and application are based on the emission of light from atoms. Review these sections to answer the following:
a. What analytical technique utilizes the emission of light from excited atoms?
b. What elements in Groups 1 and 2 can be identified by this technique?
c. What types of compounds are used to provide color in fireworks?
d. What wavelengths within the visible spectrum would most likely contain emission lines for barium?

RESEARCH AND WRITING

57. Neon signs do not always contain neon gas. The various colored lights produced by the signs are due to the emission of a variety of low-pressure gases in different tubes. Research other kinds of gases used in neon signs, and list the colors that they emit.

58. Prepare a report about the photoelectric effect, and cite some of its practical uses. Explain the basic operation of each device or technique mentioned.

ALTERNATIVE ASSESSMENT

59. **Performance** A spectroscope is a device used to produce and analyze spectra. Construct a simple spectroscope, and determine the absorption spectra of several elemental gases. (Your teacher will provide you with the gas discharge tubes containing samples of different gases.)

56. a. flame tests
b. lithium, sodium, potassium, rubidium, cesium, calcium, strontium, and barium
c. chloride salts
d. those near 500 nm

57. Answers will vary depending on which gases students choose. One of the most common gases used or mixed with the red glow of neon is sodium, which appears yellow.

58. Be sure students focus on the movement of electrons, which results from photons striking the surface of metal. Photovoltaic solar cells may be mentioned as one device in which the moving electrons create an electric current. Many other answers are possible.

59. The spectroscope can be constructed with a long tube of black paper covered on one end with a slit, over which a diffraction grating is attached.

Standards-Based Assessment

Answer the following items on a separate piece of paper.

MULTIPLE CHOICE

1. Which of the following relationships is true?
   A. Higher-energy light has a higher frequency than lower-energy light does.
   B. Higher-energy light has a longer wavelength than lower-energy light does.
   C. Higher-energy light travels at a faster speed than lower-energy light does.
   D. Higher-frequency light travels at a slower speed than lower-energy light does.

2. The energy of a photon is greatest for
   A. visible light.
   B. ultraviolet light.
   C. infrared light.
   D. X-ray radiation.

3. What is the wavelength of radio waves that have a frequency of 88.5 MHz?
   A. 3.4 m   C. 0.30 m
   B. 8.9 nm   D. 300 nm

4. Which transition in an excited hydrogen atom will emit the longest wavelength of light?
   A. E_5 to E_1 C. E_3 to E_1
   B. E_4 to E_1 D. E_2 to E_1

5. Which of the following quantum numbers is often designated by the letters *s*, *p*, *d*, and *f* instead of by numbers?
   A. *n*   C. *m*
   B. *l*   D. *s*

6. Which quantum number is related to the shape of an orbital?
   A. *n*   C. *m*
   B. *l*   D. *s*

7. What is the maximum number of unpaired electrons that can be placed in a 3*p* sublevel?
   A. 1   C. 3
   B. 2   D. 4

8. What is the maximum number of electrons that can occupy a 3*s* orbital?
   A. 1   C. 6
   B. 2   D. 10

9. Which element has the noble-gas notation $[Kr]5s^24d^2$?
   A. Se   C. Zr
   B. Sr   D. Mo

SHORT ANSWER

10. When a calcium salt is heated in a flame, a photon of light with an energy of 3.2×10^{-19} J is emitted. On the basis of this fact and the table below, what color would be expected for the calcium flame?

Frequency, s^{-1}	7.1×10^{14}	6.4×10^{14}	5.7×10^{14}
Wavelength, nm	422	469	526
Color	violet	blue	green
Frequency, s^{-1}	5.2×10^{14}	4.8×10^{14}	4.3×10^{14}
Wavelength, nm	577	625	698
Color	yellow	orange	red

11. The electron configuration of sulfur is $1s^22s^22p^63s^23p^4$. Write the orbital notation for sulfur.

EXTENDED RESPONSE

12. Explain the reason for the hydrogen line-emission spectrum.

13. When blue light shines on potassium metal in a photocell, electrons are emitted. But when yellow light shines on the metal, no current is observed. Explain.

Test Tip
If time permits, take short mental breaks during the test to improve your concentration.

STANDARDS-BASED ASSESSMENT

To give students practice under more realistic testing conditions, give them 60 minutes to answer all of the questions in this Standardized Test Preparation.

Test Answers

1. A
2. D
3. A
4. D
5. B
6. B
7. C
8. B
9. C
10. The color will be orange. Converting energy into frequency gives 4.8×10^{14}, which corresponds to the frequency of orange light.
11. ↑↓ (1s) ↑↓ (2s) ↑↓ ↑↓ ↑↓ (2p)
    ↑↓ (3s) ↑↓ ↑ ↑ (3p)
12. Electrons in atoms can occupy orbitals of only specific energies. When an atom is excited, the electron is no longer in the ground state. When the electron returns to a lower energy level, light is emitted. Because only specific energies are allowed, certain wavelengths of light are emitted, giving rise to the individual lines in the spectrum.
13. Photons of blue light are higher energy than photons of yellow light. Electrons can be emitted only when a photon of sufficient energy strikes the surface of the metal. Therefore, the energy of blue light is greater than the threshold energy, but the energy of yellow light is not.

The Periodic Law

① Core Instruction

Chapter Resources

- **The Teacher's Edition wrap has extensive teaching support for every lesson, including Misconception Alerts, Teach from Visuals, Demonstrations, Teaching Tips, Differentiated Instruction, and Problem Solving support.**
- **Several additional presentation tools are available online for every chapter, including Animated Chemistry features and Visual Concepts.**
- **You can open your lesson with the Why It Matters Video: Periodic Law.**

Section	Instruction	Labs and Demonstrations Go Online for Materials Lists and Solutions Lists.
5.1	**Textbook:** History of the Periodic Table **Teaching Visuals:** Properties of Some Elements Predicted by Mendeleev • Predicted Versus Actual Properties for Three Elements • Periodicity of Atomic Numbers **PowerPresentations**	**Quick Lab:** Designing Your Own Periodic Table **Lab:** The Mendeleev Lab of 1869 (Core Skill)
5.2	**Textbook:** Electron Configuration and the Periodic Table **Teaching Visuals:** Periodic Table of the Elements • Relationship Between Periodicity and Electron Configurations • Blocks of the Periodic Table **PowerPresentations**	**Demonstration:** Comparing Reactivities of Alkaline-Earth Metals **Lab:** Reactivity of Halide Ions (Core Skill)
5.3	**Textbook:** Electron Configuration and Periodic Properties **Animated Chemistry:** Period Trends **Teaching Visuals:** Periodic Trends of Radii • Additional Periodic Trends • Electronegativity Versus Atomic Number • Summary of Periodic Trends • Melting Points and Boiling Points of Period 6 Elements **PowerPresentations**	**Lab:** Periodicity of Properties of Oxides (Core Skill) **Lab:** Exploring the Periodic Table (Core Skill)

2 Support and Intervention

- **Interactive Reader** (English and Spanish)
- **Study Guide**
- **Interactive Review:** Review Games, Concept Maps, and Section Self-Checks
- **Scientific Reasoning Skill Builder**
- **Learn It! Videos**
- **Solve It! Cards**
- **Interactive Demos**
- **Sample Problem Sets**

3 Specialized Support

- **Chapter Summary Audio Files**
- **Interactive Reader Audio Files**
- **Differentiated Instruction:** Inclusion, Below Level, and English Learners (TE wrap)

Enrichment and Challenge

- **Differentiated Instruction:** Pre-AP (TE wrap)
- **Careers in Chemistry:** Materials Scientist (SE)
- **WebLinks**

Assessment

- **Section Formative Assessments** (SE)
- **Section Quizzes**
- **Chapter Review** (SE)
- **Chapter Tests A and B**
- **Alternative Assessment** (TE wrap)
- **Online Assessment and Remediation**
- **ExamView Banks**

Where do I find it?

		PRINT	DVD	ONLINE
1	Animated Chemistry		■	■
	Demonstrations (TE wrap)	■		■
	Interactive Whiteboard		■	■
	Labs		■	■
	PowerPresentations		■	■
	QuickLabs	■	■	■
	Teaching Visuals		■	■
	Textbook	■	■	■
	Visual Concepts		■	■
	Why It Matters Videos		■	■
2	Interactive Demos		■	■
	Interactive Reader	■	■	■
	Interactive Reviews		■	■
	Learn It! Videos		■	■
	Sample Problem Sets		■	■
	Scientific Reasoning Skill Builder		■	■
	Smart Grapher Tool		■	■
	Solve It! Cards		■	■
	Study Guide		■	■
3	Chapter Summary Audio Files		■	■
	Differentiated Instruction (TE wrap)	■		
	Interactive Reader Audio Files		■	■

CHAPTER 5

Chapter Overview

Section 1 covers the work of Mendeleev and other chemists in developing the periodic table and explains how the periodic law is used to predict elements' physical and chemical properties.

Section 2 explains the relationship between electron configuration and the arrangement of elements in groups, blocks, and periods of the periodic table, as well as the elements' general properties.

Section 3 further explores the relationship between the periodic law and electron configuration, including trends in the properties of electron affinity, electronegativity, ionization energy, atomic radii, and ionic radii.

▼ Focus and Motivate

Activate Prior Knowledge

Students may need a review of the following concepts:

- structure of the atom, atomic number
- quantum numbers and atomic orbitals
- electron configurations

About the Image

A supernova is a huge stellar explosion involving an entire star. As a result of this explosion, a nebula forms, such as the one shown in this photo. Atoms of heavier elements form when a supernova explosion forms a nebula.

Why It Matters

Students can access the video online and find other helpful resources at **HMDScience.com**.

CHAPTER 5

The Periodic Law

SECTION 1
History of the Periodic Table

SECTION 2
Electron Configuration and the Periodic Table

SECTION 3
Electron Configuration and Periodic Properties

ONLINE Chemistry
HMDScience.com

ONLINE LABS include:
The Mendeleev Lab of 1869
Reactivity of Halide Ions
Periodicity of Properties of Oxides
Exploring the Periodic Table

PREMIUM CONTENT
Why It Matters Video
HMDScience.com
Periodic Law

Lab Preview

The following labs and demonstrations support the concepts presented in this chapter.

LABS

The Mendeleev Lab of 1869 (Core Skill)
Reactivity of Halide Ions (Core Skill)
Periodicity of Properties of Oxides (Core Skill)
Exploring the Periodic Table (Core Skill)

QUICKLAB

Designing Your Own Periodic Table

DEMONSTRATION

Comparing Reactivities of Alkaline-Earth Metals

History of the Periodic Table

Key Terms
periodic law
periodic table
lanthanide
actinide

SECTION 1

Main Ideas

- Mendeleev's periodic table grouped elements by their properties.
- Moseley arranged elements by their atomic numbers.
- Modern periodic tables arrange the elements by both atomic number and properties.

Imagine the confusion among chemists during the middle of the nineteenth century. By 1860, more than 60 elements had been discovered. Chemists had to learn the properties of these elements as well as those of the many compounds that they formed—a difficult task. And to make matters worse, there was no method for accurately determining an element's atomic mass or the number of atoms of an element in a particular chemical compound. Different chemists used different atomic masses for the same elements, resulting in different compositions being proposed for the same compounds. This made it nearly impossible for one chemist to understand the results of another.

In September 1860, a group of chemists assembled at the First International Congress of Chemists in Karlsruhe, Germany, to settle the issue of atomic mass as well as some other matters that were making communication difficult. At the Congress, Italian chemist Stanislao Cannizzaro presented a convincing method for accurately measuring the relative masses of atoms. Cannizzaro's method enabled chemists to agree on standard values for atomic mass and initiated a search for relationships between atomic mass and other properties of the elements.

MAIN IDEA

Mendeleev's periodic table grouped elements by their properties.

When the Russian chemist Dmitri Mendeleev heard about the new atomic masses discussed at Karlsruhe, he decided to include the new values in a chemistry textbook he was writing. In the book, Mendeleev hoped to organize the elements according to their properties. He went about this much as you might organize information for a research paper. He placed the name of each known element on a card, together with the atomic mass of the element and a list of its observed physical and chemical properties. He then arranged the cards according to various properties and looked for trends or patterns.

Mendeleev noticed that when the elements were arranged in order of increasing atomic mass, certain similarities in their chemical properties appeared at regular intervals. Such a repeating pattern is referred to as *periodic.* The second hand of a watch, for example, passes over any given mark at periodic, 60-second intervals. The circular waves created by a drop of water hitting a water surface, as shown in **Figure 1.1**, are also periodic.

FIGURE 1.1

Periodic Patterns The regularly spaced water waves represent a simple periodic pattern.

CRITICAL THINKING

Relate Why are regularly-spaced water waves referred to as a periodic pattern?

Differentiated Instruction

INCLUSION

To help visual learners understand the meaning of the periodic law, write the word *periodic* on the board. Ask students to brainstorm examples of phenomena that occur in a repeating or *periodic* pattern. Examples: the phases of the moon, tides, sine curves, and magazine publications Discuss the different examples and tell students to keep these in mind as you point out the arrangement of elements in the periodic table.

SECTION 1

Plan and Prepare

Objectives

Upon completion of this section, students should be able to do the following:

- Explain the roles of Mendeleev and Moseley in the development of the periodic table.
- Describe the modern periodic table.
- Explain how the periodic law can be used to predict the physical and chemical properties of elements.
- Describe how the elements belonging to a group of the periodic table are interrelated in terms of atomic number.

Classroom Catalyst

Project a visual of the periodic table or refer students to a periodic table displayed in your classroom. Ask students to share what they've learned previously about the periodic table. List their responses on the board to start a discussion of the periodic table.

Teach

Misconception Alert!

Explain to students that something does not need to vary uniformly in order to vary periodically. For example, although the spaces between the water waves shown in **Figure 1.1** are not equal, the waves spread in a periodic manner: as each wave spreads outward, it follows the same pattern as that of the preceding wave.

Critical Thinking

Answer: Patterns that repeat at regular intervals are periodic.

▼ Teach *continued*

TEACH FROM VISUALS

FIGURE 1.2 The illustration shows a representation of Mendeleev's original periodic table of the elements. Ask students to compare this arrangement with that of the modern periodic table. In Mendeleev's table, the periods are arranged vertically and the groups are arranged horizontally, which is the opposite of the modern periodic table's arrangement. Ask students how Mendeleev arranged the elements on the table. in order of increasing atomic mass Point out that part of Mendeleev's fame came from his ability to predict the properties of the missing elements Sc, Ga, and Ge.

ChemisTrivia

Surprisingly, Mendeleev never won a Nobel Prize; the monumental importance of his work was not recognized during his lifetime. In 1906, the year before his death, he was nominated for the Nobel Prize in chemistry but lost by one vote to Henri Moissan, who discovered fluorine.

FIGURE 1.2

Mendeleev's First Periodic Table In his first published periodic table, Mendeleev arranged the elements in vertical periods according to relative atomic mass. The atomic mass for each element is indicated by the number following the element's symbol. The unknown elements indicated by question marks at estimated atomic masses 45, 68, and 70 were later identified as scandium, Sc;gallium, Ga, and germanium, Ge.

но въ ней, мнѣ кажется, уже ясно выражается примѣнимость выставляемаго мною начала ко всей совокупности элементовъ, пай которыхъ извѣстенъ съ достовѣрностію. На этотъ разъ я и желалъ преимущественно найдти общую систему элементовъ. Вотъ этотъ опытъ:

			Ti=50	Zr=90	?=180.
			V=51	Nb=94	Ta=182.
			Cr=52	Mo=96	W=186.
			Mn=55	Rh=104,4	Pt=197,4
			Fe=56	Ru=104,4	Ir=198.
			Ni=Co=59	Pl=106,6	Os=199.
H=1			Cu=63,4	Ag=108	Hg=200.
	Be=9,4	Mg=24	Zn=65,2	Cd=112	
	B=11	Al=27,4	?=68	Ur=116	Au=197?
	C=12	Si=28	?=70	Sn=118	
	N=14	P=31	As=75	Sb=122	Bi=210
	O=16	S=32	Se=79,4	Te=128?	
	F=19	Cl=35,5	Br=80	I=127	
Li=7	Na=23	K=39	Rb=85,4	Cs=133	Tl=204
		Ca=40	Sr=87,6	Ba=137	Pb=207.
		?=45	Ce=92		
		?Er=56	La=94		
		?Yt=60	Di=95		
		?In=75,6	Th=118?		

а потому приходится въ разныхъ рядахъ имѣть различное измѣненіе разностей, чего нѣтъ въ главныхъ числахъ предлагаемой таблицы. Или же придется предполагать при составленіи системы очень много недостающихъ членовъ. То и другое мало выгодно. Мнѣ кажется притомъ, наиболѣе естественнымъ составить

Mendeleev created a table in which elements with similar properties were grouped together—a periodic table of the elements. His first periodic table, shown in **Figure 1.2**, was published in 1869. Note that Mendeleev placed iodine, I (atomic mass 127), after tellurium, Te (atomic mass 128). Although this contradicted the pattern of listing the elements in order of increasing atomic mass, it allowed Mendeleev to place tellurium in a group of elements with which it shares similar properties. Reading horizontally across Mendeleev's table, this group includes oxygen, O; sulfur, S; and selenium, Se. Iodine could also then be placed in the group it resembles chemically, which includes fluorine, F, chlorine, Cl, and bromine, Br.

Mendeleev's procedure left several empty spaces in his periodic table (see **Figure 1.2**). In 1871, the Russian chemist boldly predicted the existence and properties of the elements that would fill three of the spaces. By 1886, all three elements had been discovered. Today these elements are known as scandium, Sc, gallium, Ga; and germanium, Ge. Their properties are strikingly similar to those predicted by Mendeleev.

The success of Mendeleev's predictions persuaded most chemists to accept his periodic table and earned him credit as the discoverer of the periodic law. Two questions remained, however. (1) Why could most of the elements be arranged in the order of increasing atomic mass, but a few could not? (2) What was the reason for chemical periodicity?

Differentiated Instruction

BELOW LEVEL

To emphasize that the modern periodic table arranges elements according to increasing atomic numbers rather than atomic masses, have students examine the atomic numbers on the periodic table to see if they can spot a pattern. Then have them do the same with atomic masses. Students will find that Ar and K, Co and Ni, and Te and I are reversed in terms of atomic mass but that all elements are in order in terms of atomic number.

MAIN IDEA

Moseley arranged elements by their atomic numbers.

The first question was not answered until more than 40 years after Mendeleev's first periodic table was published. In 1911, the English scientist Henry Moseley, who was working with Ernest Rutherford, examined the spectra of 38 different metals. When analyzing his data, Moseley discovered a previously unrecognized pattern. The elements in the periodic table fit into patterns better when they were arranged in increasing order according to nuclear charge, or the number of protons in the nucleus. Moseley's work led to both the modern definition of atomic number and the recognition that atomic number, not atomic mass, is the basis for the organization of the periodic table.

Moseley's discovery was consistent with Mendeleev's ordering of the periodic table by properties rather than strictly by atomic mass. For example, according to Moseley, tellurium, with an atomic number of 52, belongs before iodine, which has an atomic number of 53. Today, **Mendeleev's principle of chemical periodicity is correctly stated in what is known as the periodic law: The physical and chemical properties of the elements are periodic functions of their atomic numbers.** In other words, when the elements are arranged in order of increasing atomic number, elements with similar properties appear at regular intervals.

MAIN IDEA

Modern periodic tables arrange the elements by both atomic number and properties.

The periodic table has undergone extensive change since Mendeleev's time. Chemists have discovered new elements and, in more recent years, synthesized new ones in the laboratory. Each of the more than 40 new elements, however, can be placed in a group of other elements with similar properties. **The periodic table is an arrangement of the elements in order of their atomic numbers so that elements with similar properties fall in the same column, or group.**

The Noble Gases

Perhaps the most significant addition to the periodic table came with the discovery of the noble gases. In 1894, English physicist John William Strutt (Lord Rayleigh) and Scottish chemist Sir William Ramsay discovered argon, Ar, a gas in the atmosphere that had previously escaped notice because of its total lack of chemical reactivity. Back in 1868 another noble gas, helium, He, had been discovered as a component of the sun. In 1895, Ramsay showed that helium also exists on Earth.

In order to fit argon and helium into the periodic table, Ramsay proposed a new group (see **Figure 1.3**). He placed this group between the groups now known as Group 17 (the fluorine family) and Group 1 (the lithium family). In 1898, Ramsay discovered two more noble gases, krypton, Kr, and xenon, Xe. The final noble gas, radon, Rn, was discovered in 1900 by the German scientist Friedrich Ernst Dorn.

FIGURE 1.3

Noble Gases The noble gases, also known as the Group 18 elements, are all rather unreactive. As you will read, the reason for this low reactivity also accounts for the special place occupied by the noble gases in the periodic table.

			2 He
7 N	8 O	9 F	10 Ne
15 P	16 S	17 Cl	18 Ar
33 As	34 Se	35 Br	36 Kr
51 Sb	52 Te	53 I	54 Xe
83 Bi	84 Po	85 At	86 Rn

ChemisTrivia

Remind students that scientists are constantly looking for order in the universe. Early chemists searched for ways to organize the elements before the establishment of the periodic table, but no one was able to discern the relationships among the elements. German chemist Julius Lothar Meyer arranged the elements by their atomic volume and produced findings similar to those of Mendeleev. Meyer published his findings in 1870, one year after Mendeleev published his.

TEACH FROM VISUALS

FIGURE 1.3 Explain that materials referred to as reactive (or active) undergo chemical reactions easily or quickly. Ask students to explain the meaning of *unreactive*. Materials of low reactivity undergo few chemical changes. When they do react, they do so with difficulty, and often only after the addition of energy. The noble gases are either unreactive (helium, neon, argon) or have very low reactivity (xenon, krypton, radon).

READING TOOLKIT

READING HINT Have students place bookmarks at **Figure 2.3,** The Periodic Table of the Elements, in the next section. Encourage students to familiarize themselves with the information listed in the table and to make frequent reference to this table as they read the rest of the chapter.

ENGLISH LEARNERS

Have students read the two questions posed in the last paragraph on the preceding page. Then ask them if the text on this page answers only one question or both. Students should not have any difficulty recognizing from the opening sentence of the next paragraph that the text provides an answer to the first question. All the elements are arranged in order in a periodic table based on their atomic numbers. However, the text on this page does not explain the second question. Tell students that they must know more about atomic structure (valence electrons) before they can fully answer the second question. This point is made in the last sentence of this section.

▼ Teach *continued*

ChemisTrivia

- Helium was discovered in 1868 by Pierre Janssen as he was studying a solar eclipse. However, helium was not accepted as an element until William Ramsay discovered that it also exists on Earth.
- Radon is the heaviest noble gas. Its isotopes are radioactive, making radon the only gas that is radioactive at normal temperatures and pressures.

Application

The noble gases are used in making lighted signs and displays. Neon is a colorless, odorless, and tasteless gas. But it emits reddish-orange light when its electrons are excited, such as with the application of a high voltage. True neon signs are reddish orange. Other colors in "neon" signs are obtained by using different gases.

QuickLab

In this activity, students will formulate their own periodic table. Assign letters or numbers to all or some of the elements. Then, write down chemical and physical characteristics of each element, and have students organize the "unknown" elements according to their properties. Students may organize their elements in a manner similar to the modern periodic table, or they may develop less orthodox styles.

DISCUSSION

1. **a.** Atomic numbers were not discovered until about 45 years later.
   b. Refer to the periodic table.
2. Answers may vary.
3. Answers may vary.

The Lanthanides

The next step in the development of the periodic table was completed in the early 1900s. It was then that the puzzling chemistry of the lanthanides was finally understood. The **lanthanides** are the 14 elements with atomic numbers from 58 (cerium, Ce) to 71 (lutetium, Lu). Because these elements are so similar in chemical and physical properties, the process of separating and identifying them was a tedious task that required the effort of many chemists.

The Actinides

Another major step in the development of the periodic table was the discovery of the actinides. The **actinides** are the 14 elements with atomic numbers from 90 (thorium, Th) to 103 (lawrencium, Lr). The lanthanides and actinides belong in Periods 6 and 7, respectively, of the periodic table, between the elements of Groups 3 and 4. To save space, the lanthanides and actinides are usually set off below the main portion of the periodic table.

QuickLAB DESIGNING YOUR OWN PERIODIC TABLE

MATERIALS

- index cards

QUESTION

Can you design your own periodic table using information similar to that available to Mendeleev?

PROCEDURE

1. Write down the information available for each element on separate index cards. The following information is appropriate: a letter of the alphabet (A, B, C, etc.) to identify each element; atomic mass; state; density; melting point; boiling point; and any other readily observable physical properties. Do not write the name of the element on the index card, but keep a separate list indicating the letter you have assigned to each element.
2. Organize the cards for the elements in a logical pattern as you think Mendeleev might have done.

DISCUSSION

1. Keeping in mind that the information you have is similar to that available to Mendeleev in 1869, answer the following questions.
   a. Why are atomic masses given instead of atomic numbers?
   b. Can you identify each element by name?
2. How many groups of elements, or families, are in your periodic table? How many periods, or series, are in the table?
3. Predict the characteristics of any missing elements. When you have finished, check your work using your separate list of elements and a periodic table.

Differentiated Instruction

PRE-AP

Emphasize that argon was difficult to detect because of its lack of chemical reactivity. Point out that this chemical property is characteristic of noble gases. As a result, noble gases do not normally react to form compounds. In 1962, Neil Bartlett synthesized the first chemical compound of a noble gas. Since then, numerous compounds of noble gases have been reported. Ask students to identify one such compound and locate information on why scientists are trying to produce such compounds. For example, compounds of xenon may be useful as anesthetic compounds because the gas does not have any negative effects on the body.

Periodicity

Periodicity with respect to atomic number can be observed in any group of elements in the periodic table. For example, consider the noble gases of Group 18. The first noble gas is helium, He. Helium has an atomic number of 2. The elements following helium in atomic number have completely different properties until the next noble gas, neon, Ne, is reached. Neon has an atomic number of 10. The remaining noble gases in order of increasing atomic number are argon (Ar, atomic number 18), krypton (Kr, atomic number 36), xenon (Xe, atomic number 54), and radon (Rn, atomic number 86). Thus, the differences in atomic number between successive noble gases are 8, 8, 18, 18, and 32, as shown in **Figure 1.4.**

Also shown in **Figure 1.4** are atomic-number differences between the elements of Group 1. These elements are all solid, silvery metals. As you can see, the differences in atomic number between the Group 1 metals follow the same pattern as the differences in atomic number between the noble gases: 8, 8, 18, 18, and 32.

Starting with the first member of Groups 13–17, a similar periodic tern is repeated. The atomic number of each successive element is 8, 18, 18, and 32 higher than the atomic number of the element above it. In Section 2, you will see that the second mystery presented by Mendeleev's periodic table—the reason for periodicity—is explained by the arrangement of the electrons around the nucleus.

FIGURE 1.4

Patterns in the Periodic Table In each of Groups 1 and 18, the differences between the atomic numbers of successive elements are 8, 8, 18, 18, and 32, respectively. Groups 2 and 13–17 follow a similar pattern.

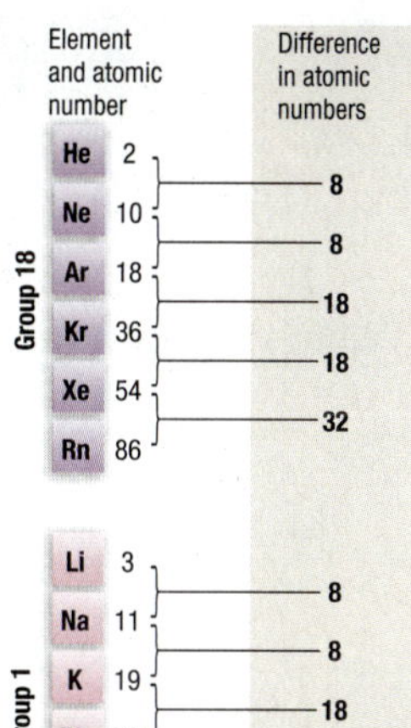

SECTION 1 FORMATIVE ASSESSMENT

Reviewing Main Ideas

1. **a.** Who is credited with developing a method that led to the determination of standard relative atomic masses?
   b. Who discovered the periodic law?
   c. Who established atomic numbers as the basis for organizing the periodic table?
2. State the periodic law.
3. Name three sets of elements that have been added to the periodic table since Mendeleev's time.
4. How do the atomic numbers of the elements within each of Groups 1, 2, and 13–18 of the periodic table vary? (Refer to **Figure 1.4** as a guide.)

Critical Thinking

5. **RELATING IDEAS** Why are elements' atomic masses not in strict increasing order in the periodic table, even though the properties of the elements are similar? For example, by atomic mass, tellurium, Te, should be in group 17, and iodine, I, should be in Group 16, but grouping by properties has Te in Group 16 and I in Group 17.

Assess and Reteach ▼

Assess Use the Formative Assessment on this page to evaluate student mastery of the section.

Reteach For students who need additional instruction, download the Section Study Guide.

Response to Intervention To reassess students' mastery, use the Section Quiz, available to print or to take directly online at **HMDScience.com**.

Answers to Section Assessment

1. **a.** Cannizzaro
   b. Mendeleev
   c. Moseley
2. The physical and chemical properties of the elements are periodic functions of their atomic numbers.
3. the noble gases, the lanthanides, and the actinides
4. In Groups 1, 2, and 18, the differences between the atomic numbers of successive elements are 8, 8, 18, 18, and 32, respectively. In Groups 13–17, the differences are 8, 18, 18, and 32, respectively.
5. The periodic table is arranged by atomic number, not atomic mass. Atomic mass is a weighted average of all of the naturally occurring isotopes of an element. A few elements have a higher atomic mass than does the element one atomic number higher, because those elements have disproportionately large heavy-isotope abundances.

SECTION 2

▼ Plan and Prepare

Objectives

Upon completion of this section, students should be able to do the following:

- Describe the relationship between electrons in sublevels and the length of each period of the periodic table.
- Locate and name the four blocks of the periodic table. Explain the reasons for these names.
- Discuss the relationship between group configurations and group numbers.
- Describe the locations in the periodic table and the general properties of the alkali metals, the alkaline-earth metals, the halogens, and the noble gases.

Classroom Catalyst

Ask students to name as many properties shared by elements of the same group in the periodic table as they can. Keep track of the characteristics by listing them on the board. For example, a good starting point would be to note the antiseptic characteristics of the halogens Cl, Br, and I. Then ask students to describe what they already know about an element by looking at its position in the periodic table. List students' responses on the board and have them identify any noticeable trends.

▼ Teach

TEACH FROM TABLES

FIGURE 2.1 Review with students the rules for governing electron configurations. The Aufbau principle states that an electron occupies the lowest energy orbital that can receive it. For example, the 4*s* sublevel is lower in energy than the 3*d* sublevel. Therefore, the 4*s* sublevel will fill before any electrons enter the 3*d* orbitals. Once the 3*d* orbitals are fully occupied, the 4*p* sublevel will start to fill.

SECTION 2

Main Ideas

The period of an element is determined by its electron configuration.

Electron Configuration and the Periodic Table

Key Terms

alkali metals
alkaline-earth metals
transition elements
main-group elements
halogens

The Group 18 elements of the periodic table (the noble gases) undergo few chemical reactions. This stability results from the gases' special electron configurations. Helium's highest occupied level, the 1*s* orbital, is completely filled with electrons. And the highest occupied levels of the other noble gases contain stable octets. Generally, the electron configuration of an atom's highest occupied energy level governs the atom's chemical properties.

MAIN IDEA

The period of an element is determined by its electron configuration.

While the elements are arranged vertically in the periodic table in groups that share similar chemical properties, they are also organized horizontally in rows, or *periods*. (There are a total of seven periods of elements in the modern periodic table.) As can be seen in **Figure 2.1**, the length of each period is determined by the number of electrons that can occupy the sublevels being filled in that period.

FIGURE 2.1

RELATIONSHIP BETWEEN PERIOD LENGTH AND SUBLEVELS BEING FILLED IN THE PERIODIC TABLE

Period number	Number of elements in period	Sublevels in order of filling
1	2	1*s*
2	8	2*s* 2*p*
3	8	3*s* 3*p*
4	18	4*s* 3*d* 4*p*
5	18	5*s* 4*d* 5*p*
6	32	6*s* 4*f* 5*d* 6*p*
7	32	7*s* 5*f* 6*d* 7*p*

Differentiated Instruction

PRE-AP

You may want to preview electron dot notation (Lewis structures) here. If you do so, emphasize that dot notation is normally used only for the *s*-block (Groups 1 and 2) and *p*-block (Groups 13–18) elements. Explain that dot notation for Groups 3–12 would generally not be useful because their outer electron orbits do not fill up as those of the other elements do.

In the first period, the 1*s* sublevel is being filled. The 1*s* sublevel can hold a total of two electrons. Therefore, the first period consists of two elements—hydrogen and helium. In the second period, the 2*s* sublevel, which can hold two electrons, and the 2*p* sublevel, which can hold six electrons, are being filled. Consequently, the second period totals eight elements. Similarly, filling of the 3*s* and 3*p* sublevels accounts for the eight elements of the third period. Filling 3*d* and 4*d* sublevels in addition to the *s* and *p* sublevels adds 10 elements to both the fourth and fifth periods. Therefore, each of these periods totals 18 elements. Filling 4*f* sublevels in addition to *s, p,* and *d* sublevels adds 14 elements to the sixth period, which totals 32 elements. And as new elements are created, the 25 named elements in Period 7 could, in theory, be extended to 32.

The period of an element can be determined from the element's electron configuration. For example, arsenic, As, has the electron configuration [Ar]$3d^{10}4s^24p^3$. The 4 in $4p^3$ indicates that arsenic's highest occupied energy level is the fourth energy level. Arsenic is thus in the fourth period in the periodic table. The period and electron configuration for each element can be found in the periodic table (on the next two pages). Based on the electron configurations of the elements, the periodic table can be divided into four blocks, the *s, p, d,* and *f* blocks. This division is illustrated in **Figure 2.2.** The name of each block is determined by whether an *s, p, d,* or *f* sublevel is being filled in successive elements of that block.

FIGURE 2.2

Sublevel Blocks Based on the electron configurations of the elements, the periodic table can be subdivided into four sublevel blocks.

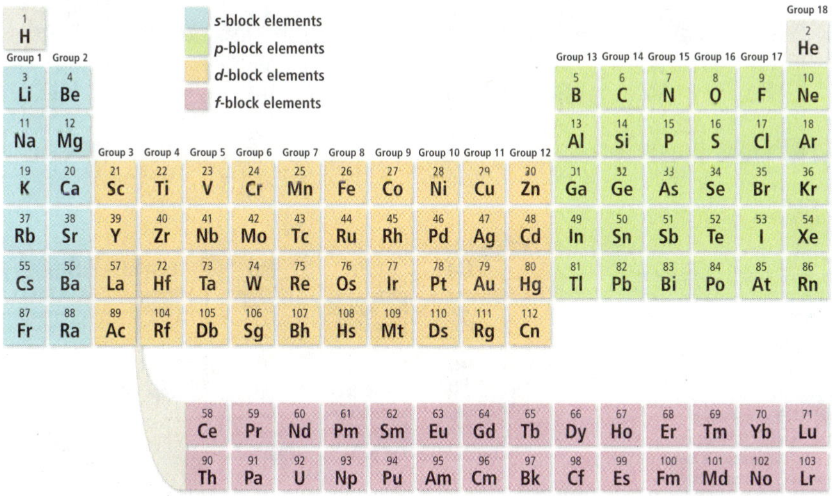

s-block elements
p-block elements
d-block elements
f-block elements

Group 1	Group 2	Group 3	Group 4	Group 5	Group 6	Group 7	Group 8	Group 9	Group 10	Group 11	Group 12	Group 13	Group 14	Group 15	Group 16	Group 17	Group 18
1 H																	2 He
3 Li	4 Be											5 B	6 C	7 N	8 O	9 F	10 Ne
11 Na	12 Mg											13 Al	14 Si	15 P	16 S	17 Cl	18 Ar
19 K	20 Ca	21 Sc	22 Ti	23 V	24 Cr	25 Mn	26 Fe	27 Co	28 Ni	29 Cu	30 Zn	31 Ga	32 Ge	33 As	34 Se	35 Br	36 Kr
37 Rb	38 Sr	39 Y	40 Zr	41 Nb	42 Mo	43 Tc	44 Ru	45 Rh	46 Pd	47 Ag	48 Cd	49 In	50 Sn	51 Sb	52 Te	53 I	54 Xe
55 Cs	56 Ba	57 La	72 Hf	73 Ta	74 W	75 Re	76 Os	77 Ir	78 Pt	79 Au	80 Hg	81 Tl	82 Pb	83 Bi	84 Po	85 At	86 Rn
87 Fr	88 Ra	89 Ac	104 Rf	105 Db	106 Sg	107 Bh	108 Hs	109 Mt	110 Ds	111 Rg	112 Cn						

58 Ce	59 Pr	60 Nd	61 Pm	62 Sm	63 Eu	64 Gd	65 Tb	66 Dy	67 Ho	68 Er	69 Tm	70 Yb	71 Lu
90 Th	91 Pa	92 U	93 Np	94 Pu	95 Am	96 Cm	97 Bk	98 Cf	99 Es	100 Fm	101 Md	102 No	103 Lr

Classroom Discussion

Have students write electron configurations for magnesium, calcium, fluorine, and chlorine. Then have them check their answers by looking up the configurations in **Figure 2.3**. Ask students to compare properties of the four elements and discuss their observations. Magnesium and calcium each have two valence electrons, and they share similar chemical properties. Fluorine and chlorine, with s^2p^5 outer-shell configurations, also have similar properties. Ask students to choose other elements from the same group and to make observations about their chemical properties based on electron configurations.

TEACH FROM TABLES

FIGURE 2.2 Ask students to work in pairs. One student should randomly select an element from the periodic table. Then, ask the other student to identify the highest occupied energy level for that element. This activity will acquaint students with the arrangement of the periods in the periodic table. For example, if a student chooses Pb (lead), then the other student should recognize that Pb is in Period 6, and therefore the highest occupied energy level is the sixth energy level. Be sure students recognize how the lanthanides and actinides fit into the periodic table.

INCLUSION

Involve visual learners by asking students to locate helium (He) in **Figure 2.3.** On the board, draw 4 concentric circles, with the two outermost circles placed close together. Write the symbol for helium inside the inner circle. Use the other circles to represent the energy levels. To represent the electrons, place 2 x's on the second circle from the center, 2 x's on the third circle, and 6 x's on the outermost circle. Point out that as a member of Period 1, helium has only one energy level, containing two electrons in the 1s sublevel. Point out that neon (Ne) has eight electrons in its highest occupied energy level, shown as 2*s* and 2*p*. Ask students to identify the number of electrons in each of these sublevels. Students should recognize that the *s* sublevel can hold only two electrons, regardless of the energy level. The remaining six electrons occupy the 2*p* sublevel. Ask students to do the same for argon (Ar), which has three energy levels. Students should recognize that each *s* sublevel and each *p* sublevel contains the same number of electrons, even though these sublevels are found in different energy levels.

▼ Teach *continued*

Teaching Tip

Explain that not all periodic tables have the information in each block organized in the same way. Some tables have the atomic number in a corner, and some have it under the element's name.

Application

To help students connect the symbols of the elements with the elements they represent, have them locate examples of metals, metalloids, nonmetals, and noble gases in the periodic table. Then show them samples or pictures of several elements, or ask them to bring in their own pictures from magazines or the internet. Ask students to form generalizations about the properties shared by groups of elements.

TEACH FROM TABLES

FIGURE 2.3 Discuss with students all of the information available from the periodic table, including atomic number, symbol, name, atomic mass, group, electron configuration, and whether the element is a metal, nonmetal, metalloid, or noble gas. Also point out the positions of the actinide and lanthanide series. Explain that these elements are found at the base of the table for convenience, to keep the table from being too wide. Ask students to sketch how large the periodic table would need to be to accommodate these elements in place. Point out that the periodic table is often shown with only the atomic number, element symbol, and atomic mass in each box.

FIGURE 2.3

The Periodic Table of the Elements In the modern periodic table, the elements are arranged by atomic number and form vertical groups and horizontal periods.

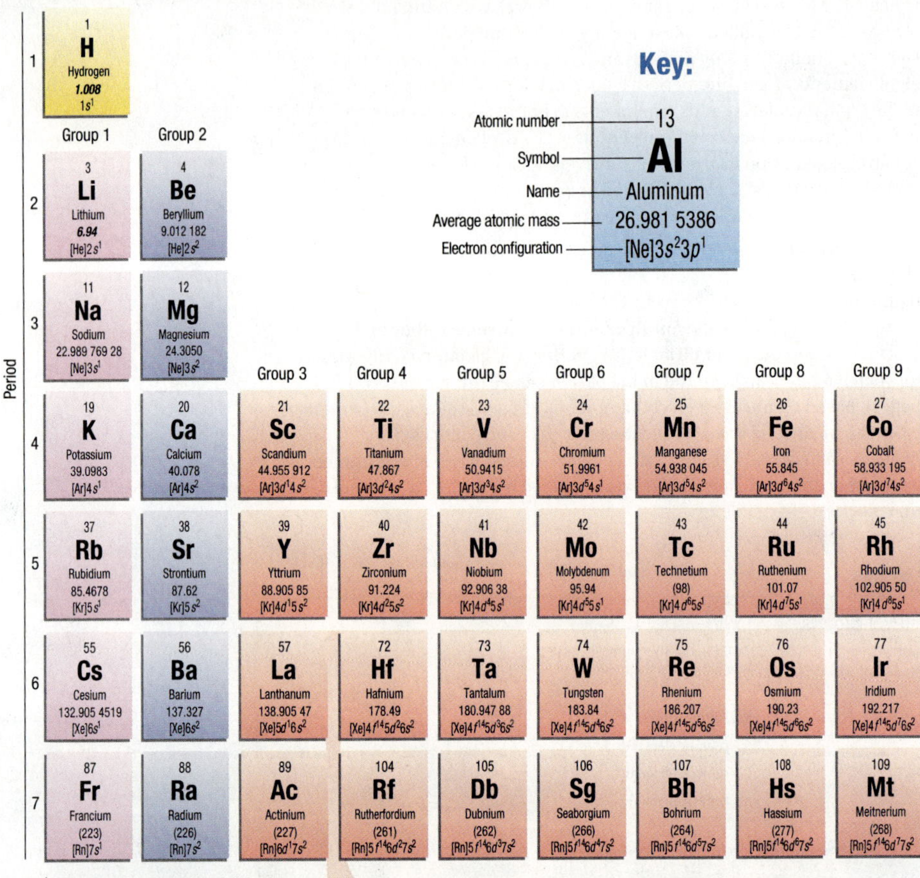

* The systematic names and symbols for elements greater than 112 will be used until the approval of trivial names by IUPAC.

58 Ce Cerium 140.116 $[Xe]4f^15d^16s^2$	59 Pr Praseodymium 140.907 65 $[Xe]4f^36s^2$	60 Nd Neodymium 144.242 $[Xe]4f^46s^2$	61 Pm Promethium (145) $[Xe]4f^56s^2$	62 Sm Samarium 150.36 $[Xe]4f^66s^2$
90 Th Thorium 232.038 06 $[Rn]6d^27s^2$	91 Pa Protactinium 231.035 88 $[Rn]5f^26d^17s^2$	92 U Uranium 238.028 91 $[Rn]5f^36d^17s^2$	93 Np Neptunium (237) $[Rn]5f^46d^17s^2$	94 Pu Plutonium (244) $[Rn]5f^67s^2$

Elements whose average atomic masses appear bolded and italicized are recognized by the International Union of Pure and Applied Chemistry (IUPAC) to have several stable isotopes. Thus, the average atomic mass for each of these elements is officially expressed as a range of values. A range of values expresses that the average atomic mass of a sample of one of these elements is not a constant in nature but varies depending on the physical, chemical, and nuclear history of the material in which the sample is found. However, the values in this table are appropriate for everyday calculations. A value given in parentheses is not an average atomic mass but is the mass number of that element's most stable or most common isotope.

Differentiated Instruction

INCLUSION

Use a game to involve kinesthetic learners. Ask students to refer to **Figure 2.3** and create questions for a game called "Name that Element." For example, a student may create a question such as, "Name an element in Group 15 that has four occupied energy levels." Se Another question might be: "Name two elements that are found in Group 2 that have more than five occupied energy levels." Ba and Ra

Hydrogen
Semiconductors (also known as metalloids)

Metals
Alkali metals
Alkaline-earth metals
Transition metals
Other metals

Nonmetals
Halogens
Noble gases
Other nonmetals

Group 10	Group 11	Group 12	Group 13	Group 14	Group 15	Group 16	Group 17	Group 18
								2 **He** Helium 4.002 602 $1s^2$
			5 **B** Boron 10.81 [He]$2s^22p^1$	6 **C** Carbon 12.011 [He]$2s^22p^2$	7 **N** Nitrogen 14.007 [He]$2s^22p^3$	8 **O** Oxygen 15.999 [He]$2s^22p^4$	9 **F** Fluorine 18.998 4032 [He]$2s^22p^5$	10 **Ne** Neon 20.1797 [He]$2s^22p^6$
			13 **Al** Aluminum 26.981 5386 [Ne]$3s^23p^1$	14 **Si** Silicon 28.085 [Ne]$3s^23p^2$	15 **P** Phosphorus 30.973 762 [Ne]$3s^23p^3$	16 **S** Sulfur 32.06 [Ne]$3s^23p^4$	17 **Cl** Chlorine 35.45 [Ne]$3s^23p^5$	18 **Ar** Argon 39.948 [Ne]$3s^23p^6$
28 **Ni** Nickel 58.6934 [Ar]$3d^84s^2$	29 **Cu** Copper 63.546 [Ar]$3d^{10}4s^1$	30 **Zn** Zinc 65.409 [Ar]$3d^{10}4s^2$	31 **Ga** Gallium 69.723 [Ar]$3d^{10}4s^24p^1$	32 **Ge** Germanium 72.63 [Ar]$3d^{10}4s^24p^2$	33 **As** Arsenic 74.921 60 [Ar]$3d^{10}4s^24p^3$	34 **Se** Selenium 78.96 [Ar]$3d^{10}4s^24p^4$	35 **Br** Bromine 79.904 [Ar]$3d^{10}4s^24p^5$	36 **Kr** Krypton 83.798 [Ar]$3d^{10}4s^24p^6$
46 **Pd** Palladium 106.42 [Kr]$4d^{10}$	47 **Ag** Silver 107.8682 [Kr]$4d^{10}5s^1$	48 **Cd** Cadmium 112.411 [Kr]$4d^{10}5s^2$	49 **In** Indium 114.818 [Kr]$4d^{10}5s^25p^1$	50 **Sn** Tin 118.710 [Kr]$4d^{10}5s^25p^2$	51 **Sb** Antimony 121.760 [Kr]$4d^{10}5s^25p^3$	52 **Te** Tellurium 127.60 [Kr]$4d^{10}5s^25p^4$	53 **I** Iodine 126.904 47 [Kr]$4d^{10}5s^25p^5$	54 **Xe** Xenon 131.293 [Kr]$4d^{10}5s^25p^6$
78 **Pt** Platinum 195.084 [Xe]$4f^{14}5d^96s^1$	79 **Au** Gold 196.966 569 [Xe]$4f^{14}5d^{10}6s^1$	80 **Hg** Mercury 200.59 [Xe]$4f^{14}5d^{10}6s^2$	81 **Tl** Thallium 204.38 [Xe]$4f^{14}5d^{10}6s^26p^1$	82 **Pb** Lead 207.2 [Xe]$4f^{14}5d^{10}6s^26p^2$	83 **Bi** Bismuth 208.980 40 [Xe]$4f^{14}5d^{10}6s^26p^3$	84 **Po** Polonium (209) [Xe]$4f^{14}5d^{10}6s^26p^4$	85 **At** Astatine (210) [Xe]$4f^{14}5d^{10}6s^26p^5$	86 **Rn** Radon (222) [Xe]$4f^{14}5d^{10}6s^26p^6$
110 **Ds** Darmstadtium (271) [Rn]$5f^{14}6d^97s^1$	111 **Rg** Roentgenium (272) [Rn]$5f^{14}6d^{10}7s^1$	112 **Cn** Copernicium (285) [Rn]$5f^{14}6d^{10}7s^2$	113 **Uut*** Ununtrium (284) [Rn]$5f^{14}6d^{10}7s^27p^1$	114 **Uuq*** Ununquadium (289) [Rn]$5f^{14}6d^{10}7s^27p^2$	115 **Uup*** Ununpentium (288) [Rn]$5f^{14}6d^{10}7s^27p^3$	116 **Uuh*** Ununhexium (292) [Rn]$5f^{14}6d^{10}7s^27p$	117 **Uus*** Ununseptium (294) [Rn]$5f^{14}6d^{10}7s^27p$	118 **Uuo*** Ununoctium (294) [Rn]$5f^{14}6d^{10}7s^27p$

The discoveries of elements with atomic numbers 113–118 have been reported but not fully confirmed.

63 **Eu** Europium 151.964 [Xe]$4f^76s^2$	64 **Gd** Gadolinium 157.25 [Xe]$4f^75d^16s^2$	65 **Tb** Terbium 158.925 35 [Xe]$4f^96s^2$	66 **Dy** Dysprosium 162.500 [Xe]$4f^{10}6s^2$	67 **Ho** Holmium 164.930 32 [Xe]$4f^{11}6s^2$	68 **Er** Erbium 167.259 [Xe]$4f^{12}6s^2$	69 **Tm** Thulium 168.934 21 [Xe]$4f^{13}6s^2$	70 **Yb** Ytterbium 173.04 [Xe]$4f^{14}6s^2$	71 **Lu** Lutetium 174.967 [Xe]$4f^{14}5d^16s^2$
95 **Am** Americium (243) [Rn]$5f^77s^2$	96 **Cm** Curium (247) [Rn]$5f^76d^17s^2$	97 **Bk** Berkelium (247) [Rn]$5f^97s^2$	98 **Cf** Californium (251) [Rn]$5f^{10}7s^2$	99 **Es** Einsteinium (252) [Rn]$5f^{11}7s^2$	100 **Fm** Fermium (257) [Rn]$5f^{12}7s^2$	101 **Md** Mendelevium (258) [Rn]$5f^{13}7s^2$	102 **No** Nobelium (259) [Rn]$5f^{14}7s^2$	103 **Lr** Lawrencium (262) [Rn]$5f^{14}6d^17s^2$

Teaching Tip

Properties and uses of Group 1 and Group 2 elements are further discussed in the *Elements Handbook* (Appendix A).

TEACH FROM TABLES

FIGURE 2.3 Point out that even the modern periodic table, as shown in **Figure 2.3**, contains gaps, just as Mendeleev's chart did over 100 years ago. Ask students to suggest possible reasons why there are blank spaces where elements 113 and 115 should be. Tell students that these synthetic elements have not yet been discovered (synthesized) and officially recognized.

Classroom Discussion

Show students a multiplication table. Ask them to explain how the table is similar to a periodic table. Students should recognize that the multiplication table, like a periodic table, organizes the information so that periodic properties are displayed. For example, the values increase by the same order of magnitude as you go down a column—2, 4, 6, 8, etc. Ask students what would happen if the numbers in the left column were rearranged. Students should recognize that the multiplication table would no longer have periodic properties. Point out that the same change would happen to a periodic table if the periods were not arranged the way they are.

BELOW LEVEL

Have students work in groups and use blank note cards to create element flash cards. Each card should have an element name on the front and a key on the back that includes the atomic number, symbol, properties, and an example of a common substance containing the element. Each member of a student group can be responsible for one or two of the element groups or periods. Students may use the cards to study the elements or line them up on a desk to represent groups and periods of the periodic table.

▼ Teach *continued*

Demonstration

COMPARING REACTIVITIES OF ALKALINE-EARTH METALS

Place **10 mL of water** into each of **two test tubes.** Add two drops of **phenolphthalein** to each tube. To one test tube, add a 5 cm piece of freshly sanded **magnesium ribbon** rolled into a coil. To the second test tube, add a piece of **calcium** about the size of half a pea. Magnesium will react very slowly, forming hydrogen gas bubbles and turning the water-phenolphthalein solution light pink. Calcium is more reactive. It will fizz and turn the water-phenolphthalein solution dark pink. The equations for these reactions are as follows:

$Mg + 2H_2O \longrightarrow Mg(OH)_2 + H_2$

$Ca + 2H_2O \longrightarrow Ca(OH)_2 + H_2$

Safety Wear **goggles** and **lab coat** at all times.

Disposal Combine all liquids, neutralize with **1 M HCl** to a pH between 5 and 9, and pour down the drain. Solid hydroxides may be dried and put in the trash. DO NOT put Ca metal in the trash; react any that is left over with water, and then neutralize and pour down the drain.

Classroom Discussion

Compare the reactivity of the alkali metals with that of the alkaline-earth metals. The alkali metals react with water to form hydrogen and are even more reactive than the alkaline-earth metals.

Teaching Tip

The *n* in a group notation is also equal to the period number.

ChemisTrivia

Hydrogen and helium are the simplest and most abundant elements. Hydrogen makes up 76% of the mass of the universe, and helium makes up 23%.

FIGURE 2.4

Group 1: Alkali Metals

(a) Like other alkali metals, potassium reacts strongly with water.

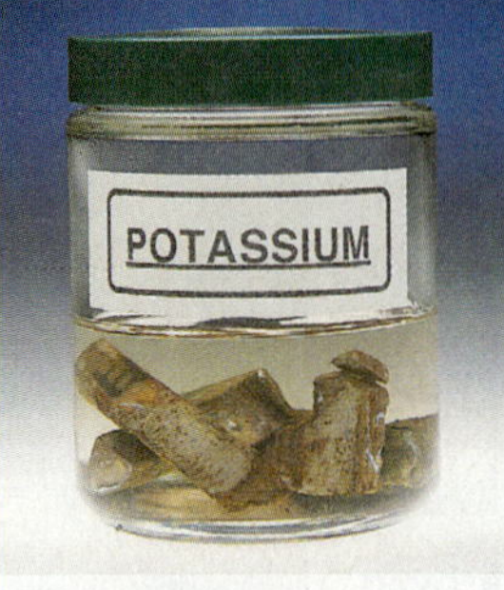

(b) Potassium must be stored in kerosene or oil to prevent it from reacting with moisture in the air.

The *S*-Block Elements: Groups 1 and 2

The elements of the *s*-block are chemically reactive metals. The Group 1 metals are more reactive than those of Group 2. The outermost energy level in an atom of each Group 1 element contains a single s electron. For example, the configurations of lithium and sodium are [He]$2s^1$ and [Ne]$3s^1$, respectively. As you will learn in Section 3, the ease with which the single electron is lost helps make the Group 1 metals extremely reactive. Using *n* for the number of the highest occupied energy level, the outer, or group, configurations of the Group 1 and 2 elements are written ns^1 and ns^2, respectively. For example, the configuration of Na is [Ne]$3s^1$, so the group configuration is written ns^1, where $n = 3$.

The elements of Group 1 of the periodic table (lithium, sodium, potassium, rubidium, cesium, and francium) are known as the **alkali metals.** In their pure state, all of the alkali metals have a silvery appearance and are soft enough to cut with a knife. However, because they are so reactive, alkali metals are not found in nature as free elements. They combine vigorously with most nonmetals. And they react strongly with water to produce hydrogen gas and aqueous solutions of substances known as alkalis. Because of their extreme reactivity with air or moisture, alkali metals are usually stored in kerosene. Proceeding down the column, the elements of Group 1 melt at successively lower temperatures.

The elements of Group 2 of the periodic table (beryllium, magnesium, calcium, strontium, barium, and radium) are called the **alkaline-earth metals.** Atoms of alkaline-earth metals contain a pair of electrons in their outermost *s* sublevel. Consequently, the group configuration for Group 2 is ns^2. The Group 2 metals are harder, denser, and stronger than the alkali metals. They also have higher melting points. Although they are less reactive than the alkali metals, the alkaline-earth metals are also too reactive to be found in nature as free elements.

FIGURE 2.5

Group 2: Alkaline-Earth Metals

(a) Calcium, an alkaline-earth metal, is too reactive to be found in nature in its pure state.

(b) Instead, it exists in compounds, such as in the minerals that make up marble.

Differentiated Instruction

ENGLISH LEARNERS

Be sure that students understand how the electron configuration for lithium (Li) can include the symbol for helium (He). Explain that instead of writing the complete electron configuration for lithium, the part that is identical to that of helium can be represented by the symbol for helium, placed inside brackets. Therefore, [He]$2s^1$ and $1s^22s^1$ are equivalent. Have students refer to the periodic table, and ask them what they notice about all the shorthand notations for electron configurations. They all represent noble gases.

Hydrogen and Helium

Before discussing the other blocks of the periodic table, let's consider two special cases in the classification of the elements—hydrogen and helium. Hydrogen has an electron configuration of $1s^1$, but despite the ns^1 configuration, it does not share the same properties as the elements of Group 1. Although it is located above the Group 1 elements in many periodic tables, hydrogen is a unique element, with properties that do not closely resemble those of any group.

Like the Group 2 elements, helium has an ns^2 group configuration. Yet it is part of Group 18. Because its highest occupied energy level is filled by two electrons, helium possesses special chemical stability, exhibiting the unreactive nature of a Group 18 element. By contrast, the Group 2 metals have no special stability; their highest occupied energy levels are not filled because each metal has an empty available p sublevel.

CHECK FOR UNDERSTANDING

Apply Which is more important in determining an element's group: the electron configuration or the element's properties? Explain.

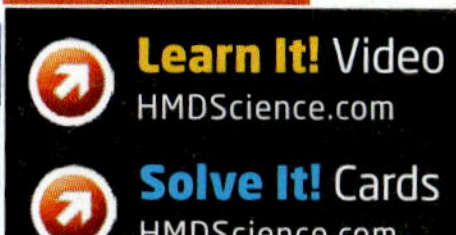

The Periodic Table and Electron Configurations

Sample Problem A (a) Without looking at the periodic table, identify the group, period, and block in which the element that has the electron configuration [Xe]$6s^2$ is located. (b) Without looking at the periodic table, write the electron configuration for the Group 1 element in the third period. Is this element likely to be more reactive or less reactive than the element described in (a)?

SOLVE

a. The element is in Group 2, as indicated by the group configuration of ns^2. It is in the sixth period, as indicated by the highest principal quantum number in its configuration, 6. The element is in the s-block.

b. In a third-period element, the highest occupied energy level is the third main energy level, $n = 3$. The $1s$, $2s$, and $2p$ sublevels are completely filled (see **Figure 2.1**). A Group 1 element has a group configuration of ns^1, which indicates a single electron in its highest s sublevel. Therefore, this element has the following configuration:

$$1s^22s^22p^63s^1 \quad \text{or} \quad [\text{Ne}]3s^1$$

Because it is in Group 1 (the alkali metals), this element is likely to be more reactive than the element described in (a), which is in Group 2 (the alkaline-earth metals).

Practice Answers in Appendix E

1. Without looking at the periodic table, identify the group, period, and block in which the element that has the electron configuration [Kr]$5s^1$ is located.
2. **a.** Without looking at the periodic table, write the group configuration for the Group 2 elements.
   b. Without looking at the periodic table, write the complete electron configuration for the Group 2 element in the fourth period.
   c. Refer to **Figure 2.3** to identify the element described in (b). Then, write the element's noble-gas notation.

Problem Solving

DECONSTRUCTING PROBLEMS

Explain that the symbols of the noble gases in brackets are merely an abbreviated way to indicate electron configuration. An analogy may help students understand this concept. Point out that secretaries sometimes take dictation in a system called *shorthand* that uses symbols to represent words. This allows them to write quickly while someone is talking. Ask students for another example of abbreviations in daily life. Sample answer: using abbreviations while texting on a cell phone

Classroom Practice

A-1 Without looking at the periodic table, give the group, period, and block in which the element with the electron configuration [Rn]$7s^1$ is located.

Answers: Group 1, seventh period, s-block

A-2

a. Without looking at the periodic table, give the group, period, and block in which the element with the electron configuration [He]$2s^2$ is located.

b. How does the reactivity of the element described in (a) compare with the reactivity of the element with the electron configuration [He]$2s^1$?

Answers

a. Group 2, second period, s-block

b. Both elements are in the same period, but the element described in (a) is in Group 2 and the element described in (b) is in Group 1. Therefore, the element in (b) is probably more reactive.

Answers

Practice A

1. Group 1, fifth period, s-block
2. **a.** ns^2
   b. $1s^22s^22p^63s^23p^64s^2$
   c. Ca, [Ar]$4s^2$

Check for Understanding

Answer: The properties are more important. For both hydrogen and helium, it is the properties rather than the electron configuration that determine the group. If electron configuration were the main factor, hydrogen would be in Group 1 and helium would be in Group 2. Instead, hydrogen is not part of a group due to its unique properties, and helium is part of Group 18 because of its chemical stability.

▼ Teach *continued*

Teaching Tip

Properties and uses of transition metals are further discussed in the *Elements Handbook* in Appendix A.

TEACH FROM VISUALS

FIGURE 2.7 The transition elements fill *s* and *d* orbitals with electrons at the same time, which leads to the variety of oxidation states that are characteristic of transition metals. The series of 10 groups exists as a transition from the highly reactive metals to the less reactive metals.

Application

Jewelry is made from alloys of gold, silver, and platinum because of the softness of these metals in their pure state. Sterling silver is an alloy containing 7.5% copper.

READING TOOLKIT

SUMMARIZING As students read each passage about a group of elements, have them make connections to what they learned about quantum numbers and electron configurations. Ask for volunteers to summarize each passage for the class, including how to solve problems. Then have the class, as listeners, ask for clarification of parts of the summary. All students may consult the text during the clarification process.

Check for Understanding

Answer: Answers will vary. A sample answer would be that as you move from left to right across the *d*-block in the periodic table, the properties of the elements transition from those of metals to those of nonmetals.

FIGURE 2.6

Group 3: Electron Configuration The diagram shows the electron configuration of scandium, Sc, the Group 3 element of the fourth period. In general, the $(n–1)d$ sublevel in Groups 3–12 is occupied by electrons after the ns sublevel is filled.

The *d*-Block Elements: Groups 3–12

For energy level n, there are n possible sublevels, so the d sublevel first appears when $n = 3$. This $3d$ sublevel is slightly higher in energy than the $4s$ sublevel, so these are filled in the order $4s3d$ (see **Figure 2.6**). This order of filling is also seen for higher values of n. Each d sublevel consists of five orbitals with a maximum of two electrons each, or up to 10 electrons possible in each d sublevel. In addition to the two ns electrons of Group 2, atoms of the Group 3 elements each have one electron in the d sublevel of the $(n–1)$ energy level. The group configuration for Group 3 is therefore $(n–1)d^1ns^2$. Atoms of the Group 12 elements have 10 electrons in the d sublevel plus two electrons in the ns sublevel. The group configuration for Group 12 is $(n–1)d^{10}ns^2$.

Some deviations from orderly d sublevel filling occur in Groups 4–11. As a result, elements in these d-block groups, unlike those in s-block and p-block groups, do not necessarily have identical outer electron configurations. For example, in Group 10, nickel, Ni, has the electron configuration $[Ar]3d^84s^2$. Palladium, Pd, has the configuration $[Kr]4d^{10}5s^0$. And platinum, Pt, has the configuration $[Xe]4f^{14}5d^96s^1$. Notice, however, that in each case the sum of the outer s and d electrons is equal to the group number.

The d-block elements are metals with typical metallic properties and are often referred to as **transition elements.** They are good conductors of electricity and have a high luster. They are typically less reactive than the alkali metals and the alkaline-earth metals. Some are so nonreactive that they do not easily form compounds and exist in nature as free elements. Palladium, platinum, and gold are among the least reactive of all the elements. Some d-block elements are shown in **Figure 2.7.**

CHECK FOR UNDERSTANDING

Explain The word *transition* refers to change. What would be a reasonable explanation for referring to the d-block elements as transition elements?

FIGURE 2.7

Transition Elements

Mercury

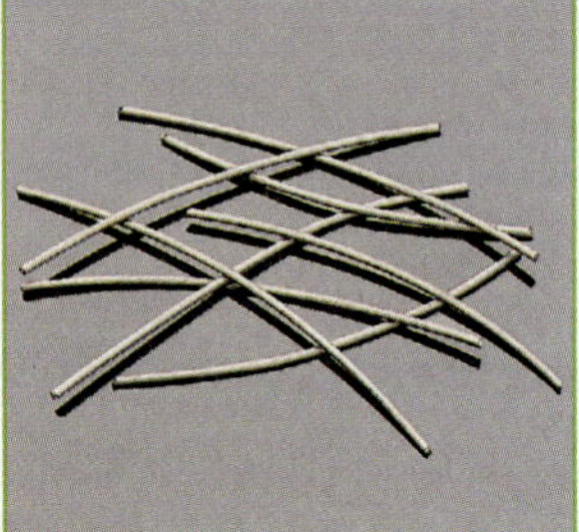

Tungsten

Vanadium

Differentiated Instruction

ENGLISH LEARNERS

Have students define the word *transition*. Perhaps they can use it to describe any issues they faced in making the transition to a new culture. Then ask the students what the significance of this term might be with reference to the transition elements. Have students locate these elements on a periodic table. Students should recognize that on a periodic table, the transition elements are between the metals on the left and the nonmetals on the right. As a result, moving across these elements may represent a transition from the metals to the nonmetals. Point out that the word *transition* was first used by a chemist in 1921 to describe a series of elements undergoing changes in an inner energy level of electrons.

S.T.E.M.

Materials Scientist

Almost everything we use or wear is composed of materials. Materials can include metals, ceramics, polymers, semiconductors, and composites. Metals are good conductors of heat and electricity. They are strong but deformable. Ceramics are compounds that are typically made up of both metals and nonmetals. Usually, ceramics are insulators and are resistant to high temperatures. Examples of products that contain ceramics are dishes, building materials, bone and tooth replacements, and high-speed communications equipment. Polymers are generally organic compounds and have very large molecular structures. Polymer products include toys, storage containers, paints, and biomedical items; plastics (polymers) are everywhere. The electrical properties of semiconductors are between those of conductors and insulators. Computers, calculators, and cell phones are just a few examples of products that use semiconductors. Composites, such as ceramics and polymers, are found in flooring, tiles, bicycles, space shuttles, and insulation.

Materials science includes the study of the processing, structure, properties, and performance of materials. Processing involves manufacturing the material from its raw components. Structure refers to the arrangement of the material's components, from an atomic to a macro scale. Understanding the structure helps materials scientists develop new materials that have desirable properties. Typical properties of interest are mechanical, such as tensile strength or hardness; electrical, such as conductivity or resistivity; magnetic, such as magnetic susceptibility; optical, such as refractive index; thermal, such as heat capacity or thermal conductivity; and environmental, such as corrosion behavior. Performance testing and analysis ensures that the product has the desired properties. Because a property or a structural characterization of a material closely depends on the processing used, evaluation often improves the process used to make the material.

Materials scientists study the microstructure of materials testing how they behave under various conditions.

Careers in Materials Science

Materials scientists go by many different titles, such as process or production engineers, research scientists, metallurgists, polymer scientists, ceramic engineers, plant managers, and quality control engineers. They are employed in industries such as transportation, electronics, aerospace, and biomedical engineering or work for research laboratories, the government, or universities. Materials scientists also help determine what materials should be used in products based on desired properties, help synthesize new materials, and help produce these materials efficiently.

Because of the interdisciplinary nature of this field, many kinds of programs, disciplines, or majors can prepare a person for a career in materials science. An undergraduate degree in materials science and engineering, chemistry, physics, or engineering can lead to a career in this field. Many materials scientists obtain a more advanced degree, such as a master's degree in materials science and engineering or a doctorate (Ph.D.) in chemistry, physics, or engineering.

The materials field is exciting and expanding. The ability to create materials to meet specific needs is just starting to be realized, and many say we are living in the Materials Age.

Questions

1. Choose a product you might use in your daily life. Discuss the materials that compose the product and the properties that those materials give the product.
2. Find a profile of a materials scientist or engineer, and describe what that scientist or engineer does.

Alternative Assessment

Have students select a subtopic in one of the categories of materials: metals, ceramics, polymers, semiconductors, or composites. Instruct them to research this subtopic and to discuss what advances there have been in this area of materials science. For example, students might discuss how the properties of plastics have changed since plastics were first introduced in the 1960s.

Answers

1. Answers may vary. Graphite tennis rackets, which are made of a graphite composite material, are one example. The graphite material is lightweight yet strong. The frames of newer rackets are injected with polyurethane foam, which helps to absorb vibrations and the shock of impact. Ultralight bicycles, which are extremely durable and have frames made of titanium and carbon fibers, are a second example. The frame consists of titanium tubes that are reinforced by an internal network of carbon fibers.
2. Answers may vary.

▼ Teach *continued*

Classroom Practice

B-1 Without looking at the periodic table, identify the period, block, and group in which the element with the electron configuration [Ar]$3d^{10}4s^{1}$ is located. Consult the periodic table to identify this element and the other elements in its group.

Answers: fourth period, *d*-block, Group 11; Cu; other elements: Ag, Au

Answers

Practice B

1. fourth period, *d*-block, Group 10
2. $4d^{10}5s^{2}$

Teaching Tip

- Remind students that Groups 13–16 are known by the top member of each group, i.e., the boron family, carbon family, nitrogen family, and oxygen family.
- Although they are not specifically indicated by the definition given, hydrogen and helium are also considered main-group elements.
- Point out that the main-group elements have traditionally also been called the *representative elements*.

Teaching Tip

Properties and uses of elements in Groups 13–17 are further discussed in the *Elements Handbook* in Appendix A.

The Periodic Table and Electron Configurations

Sample Problem B **An element has the electron configuration [Kr]$4d^{5}5s^{1}$. Without looking at the periodic table, identify the period, block, and group in which this element is located. Then, consult the periodic table to identify this element and the others in its group.**

 **SOLVE**

The number of the highest occupied energy level is 5, so the element is in the fifth period. There are five electrons in the *d* sublevel, which means that it is incompletely filled. The *d* sublevel can hold 10 electrons. Therefore, the element is in the d-block. For *d*-block elements, the number of electrons in the *ns* sublevel (1) plus the number of electrons in the $(n–1)d$ sublevel (5) equals the group number, 6. This Group 6 element is molybdenum. The others in Group 6 are chromium, tungsten, and seaborgium.

Practice Answers in Appendix E

1. Without looking at the periodic table, identify the period, block, and group in which the element that has the electron configuration [Ar]$3d^{8}4s^{2}$ is located.
2. Without looking at the periodic table, write the outer electron configuration for the Group 12 element in the fifth period.

The *p*-Block Elements: Groups 13–18

The *p*-block elements consist of all the elements of Groups 13–18 except helium. Electrons add to a *p* sublevel only after the *s* sublevel in the same energy level is filled. Therefore, atoms of all *p*-block elements contain two electrons in the *ns* sublevel. **The *p*-block elements together with the *s*-block elements are called the main-group elements.** For Group 13 elements, the added electron enters the *np* sublevel, giving a group configuration of $ns^{2}np^{1}$. Atoms of Group 14 elements contain two electrons in the *p* sublevel, giving $ns^{2}np^{2}$ for the group configuration. This pattern continues in Groups 15–18. In Group 18, the stable noble-gas configuration of $ns^{2}np^{6}$ is reached. The relationships among group numbers and electron configurations for all the groups are summarized in **Figure 2.8**, on the next page.

For atoms of *p*-block elements, the total number of electrons in the highest occupied level is equal to the group number minus 10. For example, bromine is in Group 17. It has $17 - 10 = 7$ electrons in its highest energy level. Because atoms of *p*-block elements contain two electrons in the *ns* sublevel, we know that bromine has five electrons in its outer *p* sublevel. The electron configuration of bromine is [Ar]$3d^{10}4s^{2}4p^{5}$.

The properties of elements of the *p*-block vary greatly. At its right-hand end, the *p*-block includes all of the *nonmetals* except hydrogen and helium. All six of the *metalloids* (boron, silicon, germanium, arsenic, antimony, and tellurium) are also in the *p*-block. At the left-hand side and bottom of the block, there are eight *p*-block metals. The locations of the nonmetals, metalloids, and metals in the *p*-block are shown with distinctive colors in **Figure 2.3.**

Problem Solving

ALTERNATIVE APPROACHES

Have students work problems such as those shown in Sample Problem B in reverse. Tell students to refer to a periodic table and select an element. Then have them write a question that tests the concept covered in Sample Problem B. For example, a student may select sulfur (S). The student could then write either of the following questions.

1. Without looking at a periodic table, write the outer electron configuration for the element with three energy levels that is found in Group 16.
2. Identify the period and block in which this element is located.

Students should then exchange their questions with others and answer them.

FIGURE 2.8

RELATIONSHIPS AMONG GROUP NUMBERS, BLOCKS, AND ELECTRON CONFIGURATIONS

Group number	Group configuration	Block	Comments
1, 2	$ns^{1,2}$	*s*	One or two electrons in *ns* sublevel
3–12	$(n-1)d^{1-10}ns^{0-2}$	*d*	Sum of electrons in *ns* and $(n-1)d$ levels equals group number
13–18	ns^2np^{1-6}	*p*	Number of electrons in *np* sublevel equals group number minus 12

The elements of Group 17 (fluorine, chlorine, bromine, iodine, and astatine) are known as the halogens (See **Figure 2.9**). The halogens are the most reactive nonmetals. They react vigorously with most metals to form salts. As you will see, the reactivity of the halogens is based on the presence of seven electrons in their outer energy levels—one electron short of the stable noble-gas configuration. Fluorine and chlorine are gases at room temperature, bromine is a reddish liquid, and iodine is a dark purple solid. Astatine is a synthetic element prepared in very small quantities. Most of its properties are estimated, although it is known to be a solid.

The metalloids, or semiconducting elements, are located between nonmetals and metals in the *p*-block. They are mostly brittle solids with some properties of metals and some of nonmetals. The metalloid elements have electrical conductivity intermediate between that of metals, which are good conductors, and nonmetals, which are nonconductors.

The metals of the *p*-block are generally harder and denser than the *s*-block alkaline-earth metals, but softer and less dense than the *d*-block metals. With the exception of bismuth, these metals are sufficiently reactive to be found in nature only in the form of compounds. Once obtained as free metals, however, they are stable in the presence of air.

FIGURE 2.9

The Halogens Fluorine, chlorine, bromine, and iodine are members of Group 17 of the periodic table, also known as the halogens. Locate the halogens in the *p*-block of the periodic table.

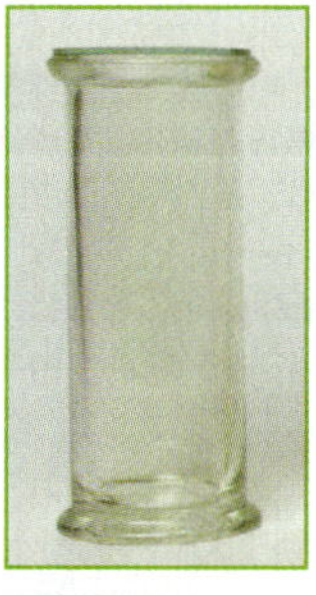

Fluorine

Chlorine

Bromine

Iodine

TEACH FROM TABLES

FIGURE 2.8 Point out that in atoms of the *p*-block elements, the number of outer *s* and *p* electrons is equal to the last digit in the group number. Point out also that *n* represents the principal quantum number for the outermost occupied energy level. The superscripts given in this table represent the possible ranges.

Teaching Tip

Students are generally surprised by the metallic appearance of metalloids. Emphasize that despite their similar appearances, metals are good conductors of electricity, while metalloids are semiconductors.

Teaching Tip

The chemistry of semiconductors is further discussed with Group 14 in the *Elements Handbook* in Appendix A.

Application

Many students will recognize the term *halogen* from halogen light bulbs in cars and flashlights. Others may recognize the term *halite*, which is derived from halogen. Halite is the name given to sodium chloride found in nature.

Differentiated Instruction

PRE-AP

Astatine was first synthesized in 1940 by scientists at the University of California. A cyclotron was used to change bismuth-209 into astatine-211. Because astatine is radioactive, it decays into other elements. As a result, only about 25 grams of astatine are believed to exist in nature. Have students research this element. They can explore how the cyclotron was used to create the element and how the small amount of astatine found in nature is produced.

▼ Teach *continued*

Classroom Practice

C-1 Without referring to the periodic table, write the outer electron configuration for the Group 16 element in the third period. Then name the element and characterize it as a metal, nonmetal, or metalloid.

Answers: $3s^23p^4$; S, nonmetal

Answers

Practice C

1. **a.** $3s^23p^5$
   b. chlorine, nonmetal
2. **a.** fourth period, *p*-block, Group 15
   b. arsenic, metalloid

ChemisTrivia

All members of the lanthanide series have an oxidation state of +3 in their compounds and share similar chemical properties.

The Periodic Table and Electron Configurations

Sample Problem C **Without looking at the periodic table, write the outer electron configuration for the Group 14 element in the second period. Then, name the element and identify it as a metal, nonmetal, or metalloid.**

SOLVE

The group number is higher than 12, so the element is in the *p*-block. The total number of electrons in the highest occupied *s* and *p* sublevels is therefore equal to the group number minus 10 ($14 - 10 = 4$). Two electrons are in the *s* sublevel, so two electrons must also be present in the 2*p* sublevel, which means that the outer electron configuration is $2s^22p^2$. The element is carbon, C, which is a nonmetal.

Practice Answers in Appendix E

1. **a.** Without looking at the periodic table, write the outer electron configuration for the Group 17 element in the third period.
   b. Name the element described in (a), and identify it as a metal, nonmetal, or metalloid.
2. **a.** Without looking at the periodic table, identify the period, block, and group of an element that has the electron configuration $[Ar]3d^{10}4s^24p^3$.
   b. Name the element described in (a), and identify it as a metal, nonmetal, or metalloid.

The *f*-Block Elements: Lanthanides and Actinides

In the periodic table, the *f*-block elements are wedged between Groups 3 and 4 in the sixth and seventh periods. The position of these inner transition elements reflects the fact that they involve the filling of the 4*f* sublevel. With seven 4*f* orbitals to be filled with two electrons each, there are a total of 14 *f*-block elements between lanthanum, La, and hafnium, Hf, in the sixth period. The lanthanides are shiny metals similar in reactivity to the Group 2 alkaline-earth metals.

There are also 14 *f*-block elements, the actinides, between actinium, Ac, and element 104, Rf, in the seventh period. In these elements the 5*f* sublevel is being filled with 14 electrons. The actinides are all radioactive. The first four actinides (thorium, Th, through neptunium, Np) have been found naturally on Earth. The remaining actinides are known only as laboratory-made elements.

The Periodic Table and Electron Configurations

Sample Problem D **The electron configurations of atoms of four elements are written below. Name the block and group in which each of these elements is located in the periodic table. Then, use the periodic table to name each element. Identify each element as a metal, nonmetal, or metalloid.**

Finally, describe whether each element has high reactivity or low reactivity.

a. $[Xe]4f^{14}5d^96s^1$ **c.** $[Ne]3s^23p^6$
b. $[Ne]3s^23p^5$ **d.** $[Xe]4f^66s^2$

Continued

Problem Solving

ALTERNATIVE APPROACHES

Have students work problems such as those shown in Sample Problem C in reverse. Tell students to refer to a periodic table and select an element. Then have them write a question that tests the concept covered in Sample Problem C. For example, a student may select silicon (Si). The student could then write either of the following questions.

1. Without looking at a periodic table, write the outer electron configuration for the metalloid in Period 3.
2. To which block does this element belong?

Students should then exchange their questions with others and answer them.

 **SOLVE**

a. The 4*f* sublevel is filled with 14 electrons. The 5*d* sublevel is partially filled with nine electrons. Therefore, this element is in the *d*-block. The element is the transition metal platinum, Pt, which is in Group 10 and has a low reactivity.

b. The incompletely filled *p* sublevel shows that this element is in the *p*-block. A total of seven electrons are in the *ns* and *np* sublevels, so this element is in Group 17, the halogens. The element is chlorine, Cl, and is highly reactive.

c. This element has a noble-gas configuration and thus is in Group 18 in the *p*-block. The element is argon, Ar, which is a nonreactive nonmetal and a noble gas.

d. The incomplete 4*f* sublevel shows that the element is in the *f*-block and is a lanthanide. Group numbers are not assigned to the *f*-block. The element is samarium, Sm. All of the lanthanides are reactive metals.

Practice Answers in Appendix E

1. For each of the following, identify the block, period, group, group name (where appropriate), element name, element type (metal, nonmetal, or metalloid), and relative reactivity (high or low):
   a. $[He]2s^22p^5$ **b.** $[Ar]3d^{10}4s^1$

SECTION 2 FORMATIVE ASSESSMENT

Reviewing Main Ideas

1. To illustrate the relationship between the elements' electron configurations and their placement in the periodic table, into what four blocks can the periodic table be divided?
2. What name is given to each of the following groups of elements in the periodic table?
   a. Group 1
   b. Group 2
   c. Groups 3–12
   d. Group 17
   e. Group 18
3. What are the relationships between group configuration and group number for elements in the *s*, *p*, and *d*-blocks?
4. Without looking at the periodic table, write the outer electron configuration for the Group 15 element in the fourth period.
5. Without looking at the periodic table, identify the period, block, and group of the element that has the electron configuration $[Ar]3d^74s^2$.

Critical Thinking

6. **APPLYING MODELS** Period 7 contains elements in the *s, p, d,* and *f*-blocks. Suppose that there were a Period 8 and it contained elements in the "g" block, where "g" had the angular momentum quantum number $\ell = 4$. If a hypothetical element in Period 8 had an atomic number of 120, into what group in the periodic table would the element fit, and what properties might it have (assuming it does not radioactively decay)?

Answers to Section Assessment

1. *s*, *p*, *d*, and *f*-blocks
2. **a.** alkali metals
   b. alkaline-earth metals
   c. transition metals
   d. halogens
   e. noble gases
3. See Figure 2.8.
4. $3d^{10}4s^24p^3$
5. fourth period, *d*-block, Group 9
6. An element that had the atomic number 120 would be in Group 2 and would have properties similar to the properties of the other alkaline-earth metals. For example, the element would be metallic, would have a high melting point, and could be less reactive than alkali metals.

Classroom Practice

D-1 For each of the following electron configurations, locate the corresponding element in the periodic table by determining its block, period, and group. Then use the periodic table to name the element, and predict whether it is likely to be of high or low reactivity.

a. $[He]2s^22p^3$
b. $[Xe]4f^{14}5d^{10}6s^1$
c. $[Rn]7s^1$
d. $[Ar]3d^{10}4s^24p^5$

Answers:

a. *p*-block, second period, Group 15; nitrogen, low reactivity
b. *d*-block, sixth period, Group 11; gold, low reactivity
c. *s*-block, seventh period, Group 1; francium, high reactivity
d. *p*-block, fourth period, Group 17; bromine, high reactivity

Answers

Practice D

1. **a.** *p*-block, second period, Group 17, halogens, fluorine, nonmetal, high reactivity
   b. *d*-block, fourth period, Group 11, transition elements, copper, metal, low reactivity

Assess and Reteach

Assess Use the Formative Assessment on this page to evaluate student mastery of the section.

Reteach For students who need additional instruction, download the Section Study Guide.

Response to Intervention To reassess students' mastery, use the Section Quiz, available to print or to take directly online at **HMDScience.com**.

SECTION 3

▼ Plan and Prepare

Objectives

Upon completion of this section, students should be able to do the following:

- Define *atomic* and *ionic radii*, *ionization energy*, *electron affinity*, and *electronegativity*.
- Compare the periodic trends of atomic radii, ionization energy, and electronegativity, and state the reasons for these variations.
- Define *valence electrons*, and state how many are present in atoms of each main-group element.
- Compare the atomic radii, ionization energies, and electronegativities of the *d*-block elements with those of the main-group elements.

Classroom Catalyst

Begin with a discussion of the term *trends*. Ask students to define a trend and to describe some trends they observe, such as trends in fashion, behavior, color, design, and foods. Discuss how trends are used for classification. Ask students how this idea applies to trends they will observe in the arrangement of elements in the periodic table.

▼ Teach

TEACH FROM VISUALS

FIGURE 3.1 Emphasize that the measurement shown in **Figure 3.1** is the distance between two identical nuclei, and that it must be divided by two to yield the approximate radius of the atom. Point out that there is no firm agreement on exact values for atomic radii, because of the various methods used to make the measurements and because the atom has no fixed boundary.

SECTION 3

Main Ideas

- Atomic radii are related to electron configuration.
- Removing electrons from atoms to form ions requires energy.
- Adding electrons to atoms to form ions also requires energy.
- When atoms become ions, their radii change.
- Only the outer electrons are involved in forming compounds.
- Atoms have different abilities to capture electrons.
- The properties of d-block metals do not vary much.

Electron Configuration and Periodic Properties

Key Terms

atomic radius	ionization energy	anion
ion	electron affinity	valence electron
ionization	cation	electronegativity

So far, you have learned that the elements are arranged in the periodic table according to their atomic number and that there is a rough correlation between the arrangement of the elements and their electron configurations. In this section, the relationship between the periodic law and electron configurations will be further explored.

MAIN IDEA

Atomic radii are related to electron configuration.

Ideally, the size of an atom is defined by the edge of its orbital. However, this boundary is fuzzy and varies under different conditions. Therefore, the conditions under which the atom exists must be specified to estimate its size. One way to express an atom's radius is to measure the distance between the nuclei of two identical atoms that are chemically bonded together and then divide this distance by two. **Atomic radius** may be defined as one-half the distance between the nuclei of identical atoms that are bonded together. This can be seen in **Figure 3.1** on the next page.

PREMIUM CONTENT
Animated Chemistry
HMDScience.com
Period Trends (Interaction)

Period Trends

Figure 3.2 gives the atomic radii of the elements, and **Figure 3.3** (on the next spread) presents this information graphically. Note that there is a gradual decrease in atomic radii across the second period from lithium, Li, to neon, Ne. *The trend to smaller atoms across a period is caused by the increasing positive charge of the nucleus.* As electrons add to *s* and *p* sublevels in the same main energy level, they are gradually pulled closer to the more highly charged nucleus. This increased pull results in a decrease in atomic radii. The attraction of the nucleus is somewhat offset by repulsion among the increased number of electrons in the same outer energy level. As a result, the difference in radii between neighboring atoms in each period grows smaller, as shown in **Figure 3.2.**

Group Trends

Examine the atomic radii of the Group 1 elements in **Figure 3.2.** Notice that the radii of the elements increase as you read down the group.

Differentiated Instruction

BELOW LEVEL

Draw a two-column table on the board and title it "Trends in the Periodic Table." Label the left column head "Period Trends" and the right column head "Group Trends." Have students copy the table and fill in the rows as they read the selections on Atomic Radii, Ionization Energy, Electron Affinity, Ionic Radii, Valence Electrons, and Electronegativity. When students have finished reading Section 3, ask them to volunteer information to complete the table on the board.

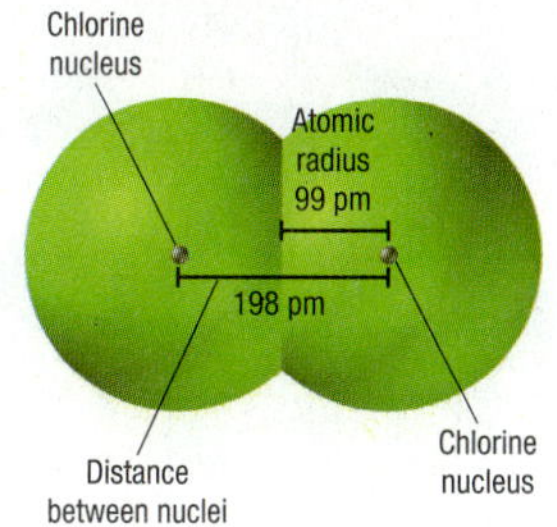

FIGURE 3.1

Atomic Radii One method of determining atomic radius is to measure the distance between the nuclei of two identical atoms that are bonded together in an element or compound and then divide this distance by two. The atomic radius of a chlorine atom, for example, is 100 picometers (pm).

As electrons occupy sublevels in successively higher main energy levels farther from the nucleus, the sizes of the atoms increase. *In general, the atomic radii of the main-group elements increase down a group.*

Now examine the radii of the Group 13 elements. Although gallium, Ga, follows aluminum, Al, it has a slightly smaller atomic radius than does aluminum. This is because gallium, unlike aluminum, is preceded in its period by the 10 *d*-block elements. The expected increase in gallium's radius caused by the filling of the fourth main-energy level is outweighed by a shrinking of the electron cloud caused by a nuclear charge that is considerably higher than that of aluminum.

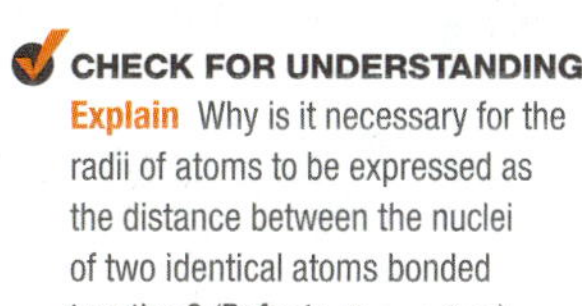

CHECK FOR UNDERSTANDING

Explain Why is it necessary for the radii of atoms to be expressed as the distance between the nuclei of two identical atoms bonded together? (Refer to **Figure 3.1**.)

FIGURE 3.2

Decreasing Radii Atomic radii decrease from left to right across a period and increase down a group. Values are given in picometers (pm).

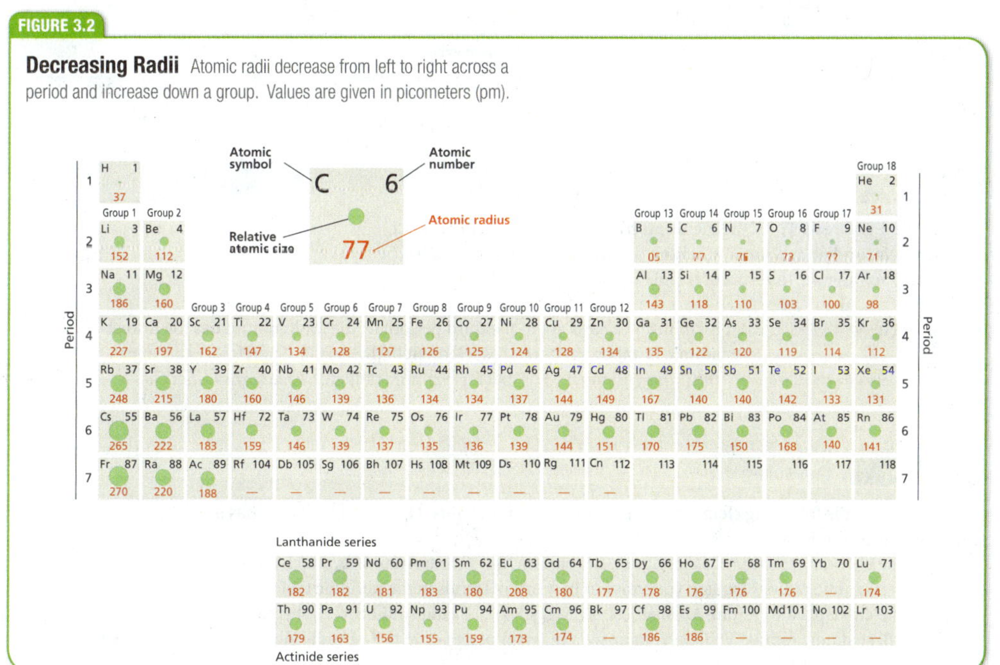

Teaching Tip

Summaries of group trends for Groups 1–17 can be found in the *Elements Handbook* in Appendix A.

TEACH FROM TABLES

FIGURE 3.2 Have students refer to **Figure 3.2,** and ask if they observe anything unusual about the trend involving atomic radii as they scan from right to left across a period. Students should observe that the atomic radii of the elements in Periods 4, 5, and 6 first decrease and then increase slightly before decreasing again. Explain that this is the result of the way in which the sublevels of the transition elements fill.

ChemisTrivia

French physicist Jean-Baptiste Perrin produced a close estimate for the size of an atom in 1908, based on an equation suggested by Albert Einstein in 1905.

Check for Understanding

Answer: It is necessary to express the radii in this manner because the location of the nucleus is stable, but the edges of orbitals are "fuzzy" and change according to the conditions.

PRE-AP

Have students compare the atomic radii of sodium (Na) and cesium (Cs) in **Figure 3.2.** Students should readily see that cesium has a larger atomic radius. Because cesium also has more protons and electrons than sodium, it has a greater effective nuclear charge than sodium. This difference should negate the increase in size caused by the addition of energy levels. Yet, a cesium atom is significantly larger than a sodium atom. Ask students to explain this, based on electron shielding.

▼ Teach *continued*

Classroom Practice

E-1 Which of the elements Li, Rb, K, and Na has the smallest atomic radius, and which has the largest?

Answers: Li, Rb

E-2 Which of the elements O, Se, S, and Po has the smallest atomic radius, and which has the largest?

Answers: O, Po

Answers

Practice E

1. Li; F
2. All of the elements are in Group 2. Of the four, barium has the highest atomic number and is farthest down the group. Therefore, barium has the largest atomic radius, because atomic radii increase down a group.
3. All of the elements are in Period 3. Of the four, silicon has the largest atomic number and therefore is the farthest to the right on the periodic table. Therefore, silicon has the smallest atomic radius, because atomic radii decrease *from left to right* across a period.

FIGURE 3.3

Periodic Trends The plot of atomic radius versus atomic number shows period and group trends.

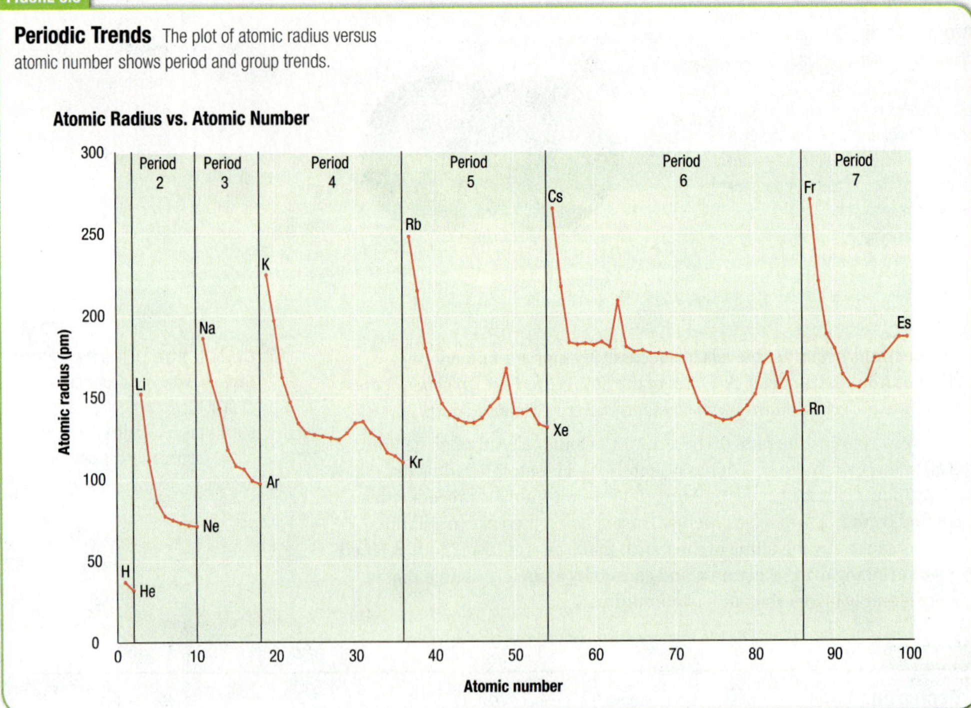

Atomic Radius

Sample Problem E **Of the elements magnesium, Mg, chlorine, Cl, sodium, Na, and phosphorus, P, which has the largest atomic radius? Explain your answer in terms of trends in the periodic table.**

SOLVE All of the elements are in the third period. Of the four, sodium has the lowest atomic number and is the first element in the period. Therefore, sodium has the largest atomic radius, because atomic radii decrease across a period.

Practice Answers in Appendix E

1. Which of the following elements has the largest atomic radius: Li, O, C, or F? Which has the smallest atomic radius?
2. Of the elements calcium, Ca, beryllium, Be, barium, Ba, and strontium, Sr, which has the largest atomic radius? Explain your answer in terms of trends in the periodic table.
3. Of the elements aluminum, Al, magnesium, Mg, silicon, Si, and sodium, Na, which has the smallest atomic radius? Explain your answer in terms of trends in the periodic table.

Problem Solving

TAKE IT FURTHER

Have students identify the blocks in which all the elements in Sample Problem E are located on a periodic table. They should recognize that only *s*- and *p*-block elements are included. Have students explain why *d*- and *f*-block elements are not included. Students should recognize that *d*- and *f*-block elements cause variations in the general trend of decrease in atomic radii as you move across a period This can be clearly seen in **Figure 3.3.** Ask students to identify how the graphs in **Figure 3.3** show this effect of *d*- and *f*-block elements on the periodic trend of atomic radii. Students should observe that the graphs for Periods 4–7 do not show a progressive trend as do the graphs for Periods 1–3.

MAIN IDEA

Removing electrons from atoms to form ions requires energy.

An electron can be removed from an atom if enough energy is supplied. Using A as a symbol for an atom of any element, the process can be expressed as follows.

$$A + \text{energy} \rightarrow A^+ + e^-$$

The A^+ represents an ion of element A with a single positive charge, referred to as a 1+ ion. An **ion** is an atom or group of bonded atoms that has a positive or negative charge. Sodium, for example, forms an Na^+ ion. Any process that results in the formation of an ion is referred to as **ionization.**

To compare the ease with which atoms of different elements give up electrons, chemists compare ionization energies. The energy required to remove one electron from a neutral atom of an element is the **ionization energy, IE (or first ionization energy, IE_1).** To avoid the influence of nearby atoms, measurements of ionization energies are made on isolated atoms in the gas phase. **Figure 3.4** gives the first ionization energies for the elements in kilojoules per mole (kJ/mol). **Figure 3.5**, on the next page, presents this information graphically.

FIGURE 3.4

Ionization Energy In general, first ionization energies increase across a period and decrease down a group. Values are given in KJ/mol.

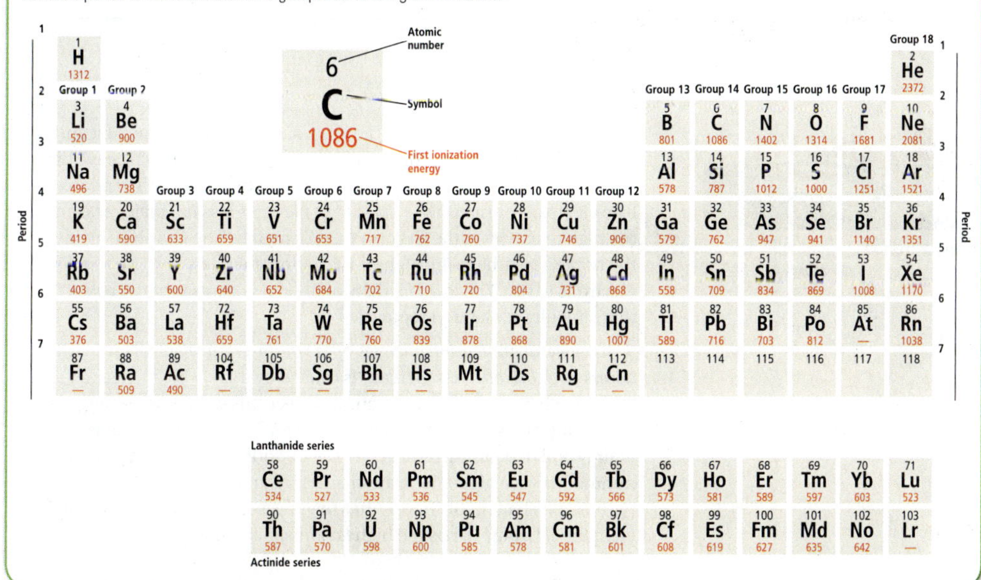

Misconception Alert!

Make sure students understand that ionization energy concerns only the *loss* of electrons. Students may be confused by the way in which electron loss is represented ($A + \text{energy} \longrightarrow A^+ + e^-$), because the electron appears to be added on the right side of the equation—especially because ions can have positive and negative charges. Also, many students mistakenly think atoms should become more negative (as on a number line) as they lose electrons. List the number of protons and electrons for some atoms and their accompanying ions. Show how the charges add to give a neutral or charged particle.

TEACH FROM TABLES

FIGURE 3.4 Ask students to identify the group in **Figure 3.4** that has the largest ionization energies. See if they can explain the reason why the noble gases have the highest ionization energy. Then ask them to explain why Group 1 elements have the lowest ionization energies. Be sure they recognize that hydrogen is not part of the Group 1 elements.

Differentiated Instruction

INCLUSION

To involve kinesthetic learners, have students develop a skit to show what happens when an atom becomes an ion, as shown by the word equation on this page. For example, a student can serve as a model of a Group 1 atom by holding a sign that says "electron." Another student can be a model for the energy that removes the electron and places it on a desk. The second student then replaces the "electron" sign with one that says "+." Ask the class how the same student can represent both the atom and the ion.

The Periodic Law 145

▼ Teach continued

TEACH FROM VISUALS

FIGURE 3.5 Remind students that each line segment on the graph represents a different period from the periodic table. Reading the graphs in **Figure 3.5** can be a challenge for many students because of all the information that is included. Students may find it helpful to read this graph by using paper to cover portions of it, so that only one period is shown at a time. They should readily see that ionization energies generally increase as you move across any period, with the noble gas in that period having the highest ionization energy.

FIGURE 3.5

Ionization Energy Plot of first ionization energy, IE_1, versus atomic number. As atomic number increases, both the period and the group trends become less pronounced.

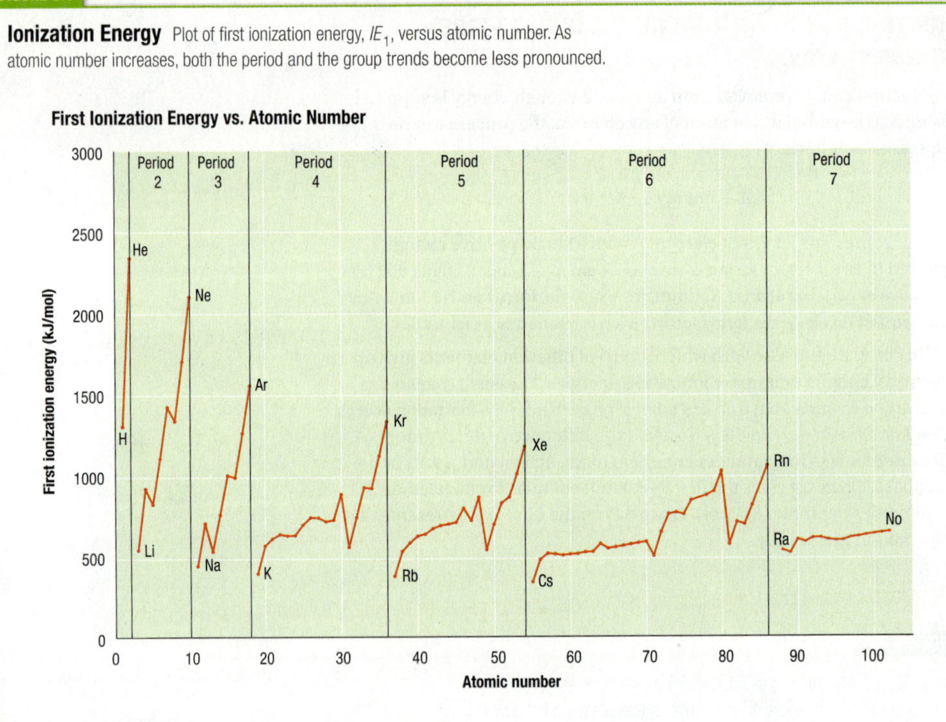

Period Trends

In **Figures 3.4** and **3.5**, examine the ionization energies for the first and last elements in each period. You can see that the Group 1 metals have the lowest first ionization energies in their respective periods. Therefore, they lose electrons most easily. This ease of electron loss is a major reason for the high reactivity of the Group 1 (alkali) metals. The Group 18 elements, the noble gases, have the highest ionization energies. They do not lose electrons easily. The low reactivity of the noble gases is partly based on this difficulty of electron removal.

In general, ionization energies of the main-group elements increase across each period. This increase is caused by increasing nuclear charge. A higher charge more strongly attracts electrons in the same energy level. Increasing nuclear charge is responsible for both increasing ionization energy and decreasing radii across the periods. Note that, in general, nonmetals have higher ionization energies than metals do. In each period, the element of Group 1 has the lowest ionization energy and the element of Group 18 has the highest ionization energy.

Differentiated Instruction

PRE-AP

To have students comprehend the magnitude of the changes in ionization energy, have them use **Figure 3.5** to calculate how many times greater the ionization energies are in each of the following pairs of elements: neon vs. lithium (neon is about 4 times greater); argon vs. sodium (argon is about 3 times greater); and xenon vs. rubidium (xenon is more than 2 times greater).

Group Trends

Among the main-group elements, ionization energies generally decrease down the groups. Electrons removed from atoms of each succeeding element in a group are in higher energy levels, farther from the nucleus. Therefore, they are removed more easily. Also, as atomic number increases going down a group, more electrons lie between the nucleus and the electrons in the highest occupied energy levels. This partially shields the outer electrons from the effect of the nuclear charge. Together, these influences overcome the attraction of the electrons to the increasing nuclear charge.

Removing Electrons from Positive Ions

With sufficient energy, electrons can be removed from positive ions as well as from neutral atoms. The energies for removal of additional electrons from an atom are referred to as *the second ionization energy* (IE_2), *third ionization energy* (IE_3), and so on. **Figure 3.6** shows the first five ionization energies for the elements of the first, second, and third periods. You can see that the second ionization energy is always higher than the first, the third is always higher than the second, and so on.

FIGURE 3.6

IONIZATION ENERGIES (IN KJ/MOL) FOR ELEMENTS OF PERIODS 1–3

	Period 1		Period 2							
	H	He	Li	Be	B	C	N	O	F	Ne
IE_1	1312	**2372**	520	900	801	1086	1402	1314	1681	2081
IE_2		5250	**7298**	1757	2427	2353	2856	3388	3374	3952
IE_3			11 815	**14 849**	3660	4621	4578	5300	6050	6122
IE_4				21 007	**25 026**	6223	7475	7469	8408	9370
IE_5					32 827	**37 830**	9445	10 990	11 023	12 178
			Period 3							
			Na	Mg	Al	Si	P	S	Cl	Ar
IE_1			496	738	578	787	1012	1000	1251	1521
IE_2			**4562**	1451	1817	1577	1903	2251	2297	2666
IE_3			6912	**7733**	2745	3232	2912	3361	3822	3931
IE_4			9544	10 540	**11 578**	4356	4957	4564	5158	5771
IE_5			13 353	13 628	14 831	**16 091**	6274	7013	6540	7238

TEACH FROM TABLES

FIGURE 3.6 Point out to students that the entries in the first column indicate the first through fifth ionization energies, respectively. Have students compare the highlighted ionization-energy values with the values immediately above them. Explain that a relatively large amount of energy is required to ionize *any* atom or ion that has a noble gas configuration. This fact is further evidence of the stability of an octet of electrons in the outer energy level of an atom or ion.

▼ Teach *continued*

Classroom Practice

F-1 In each of the following pairs of elements, choose the element that has the higher first ionization energy.

- **a.** Ca and Ba
- **b.** Ca and Br
- **c.** Ca and K
- **d.** Ca and Mg

Answers: **a.** Ca **b.** Br **c.** Ca **d.** Mg

F-2 State in words the general trends in ionization energies down a group and across a period of the periodic table.

Answer: In general, ionization energies decrease down a group and increase across a period.

Answers

Practice F

1. **a.** Q is in the *p*-block, R is in the *s*-block, T is in the *p*-block, and X is in the *p*-block.
   b. Q and R, and X and T are in the same period. Q and T are in the same group.
   c. Q would have the highest ionization energy, and R would have the lowest.
   d. R
   e. R

Check for Understanding

Answer: Answers will vary. A sample answer might be, "As negatively-charged electrons are removed, there are fewer to counter the positively-charged nucleus. The positive charge of the nucleus will then have a stronger attraction for those remaining electrons."

CHECK FOR UNDERSTANDING

Explain Explain in your own words what is meant by the italicized words in the text that state, "*each successive electron removed from an ion feels an increasingly stronger effective nuclear charge.*"

This is because as electrons are removed in successive ionizations, fewer electrons remain within the atom to shield the attractive force of the nucleus. *Thus, each successive electron removed from an ion feels an increasingly stronger effective nuclear charge (the nuclear charge minus the electron shielding).*

The first ionization energies in **Figure 3.6** show that removing a single electron from an atom of a Group 18 element is more difficult than removing an electron from atoms of other elements in the same period. This special stability of the noble-gas configuration also applies to ions that have noble-gas configurations. Notice in **Figure 3.6** the large increases between the first and second ionization energies of lithium, Li, and between the second and third ionization energies of beryllium, Be. Even larger increases in ionization energy exist between the third and fourth ionization energies of boron, B, and between the fourth and fifth ionization energies of carbon, C. In each case, the jump in ionization energy occurs when an ion assumes a noble-gas configuration. For example, the removal of one electron from a lithium atom ([He]$2s^1$) leaves the helium noble-gas configuration. The removal of four electrons from a carbon atom ([He]$2s^22p^2$) also leaves the helium configuration. This trend continues across the entire periodic system.

Periodic Trends in Ionization Energy

Sample Problem F **Consider two main-group elements, A and B. Element A has a first ionization energy of 419 kJ/mol. Element B has a first ionization energy of 1000 kJ/mol. Decide if each element is more likely to be in the *s*-block or *p*-block. Which element is more likely to form a positive ion?**

 **SOLVE**

Element A has a very low ionization energy, which means that atoms of A lose electrons easily. Therefore, element A is most likely to be an s-block metal, because ionization energies increase across the periods.

Element B has a very high ionization energy, which means that atoms of B have difficulty losing electrons. Element B would most likely lie at the end of a period in the p-block.

Element A is more likely to form a positive ion, because it has a much lower ionization energy than element B does.

Practice Answers in Appendix E

1. Consider four hypothetical main-group elements, Q, R, T, and X, that have the outer electron configurations indicated below. Then, answer the questions that follow.

   Q: $3s^23p^5$ R: $3s^1$ T: $4d^{10}5s^25p^5$ X: $4d^{10}5s^25p^1$

   a. Identify the block location of each hypothetical main-group element.
   b. Which of these elements are in the same period? Which are in the same group?
   c. Which element would you expect to have the highest first ionization energy? Which would have the lowest first ionization energy?
   d. Which element would you expect to have the highest second ionization energy?
   e. Which of the elements is most likely to form a 1+ ion?

Problem Solving

DECONSTRUCTING PROBLEMS

Ask students which electrons they must examine when working with problems involving ionization energies.

Students must recognize that such problems involve only the electrons in the sublevel found in the highest energy level.

For example, in Practice Problem 1 on this page, *Q*, *T*, and *X* all contain electrons in a *p* sublevel. However, the electrons in the *p* sublevel of *Q* are closest to the nucleus, resulting in a higher ionization energy. Therefore, *Q* has the ionization energy. Also be sure that students recognize that not all the energy levels are shown.

MAIN IDEA

Adding electrons to atoms to form ions also requires energy.

Neutral atoms can also acquire electrons. **The energy change that occurs when an electron is acquired by a neutral atom is called the atom's electron affinity.** Most atoms release energy when they acquire an electron.

$$A + e^- \rightarrow A^- + \text{energy}$$

On the other hand, some atoms must be "forced" to gain an electron by the addition of energy.

$$A + e^- + \text{energy} \rightarrow A^-$$

The quantity of energy absorbed would be represented by a positive number, but ions produced in this way are very unstable and hence the electron affinity for them is very difficult to determine. An ion produced in this way will be unstable and will lose the added electron spontaneously.

Figure 3.7 shows the electron affinity in kilojoules per mole for the elements. Positive electron affinities, because they are so difficult to determine with any accuracy, are denoted in **Figure 3.7** by "(0)." **Figure 3.8,** on the next page, presents these data graphically.

Period Trends

Among the elements of each period, the halogens (Group 17) gain electrons most readily. This is shown in **Figure 3.7** by the large negative values of halogens' electron affinities and is a major reason for the high reactivity levels of Group 17 elements. In general, as electrons add to the same p sublevel of atoms with increasing nuclear charge, electron affinities become more negative across each period within the p-block.

FIGURE 3.7

Periodic Table of Electron Affinities (kJ/mol) The values listed in parentheses in this periodic table of electron affinities are approximate. Electron affinity is estimated to be −50 kJ/mol for each of the lanthanides and 0 kJ/mol for each of the actinides.

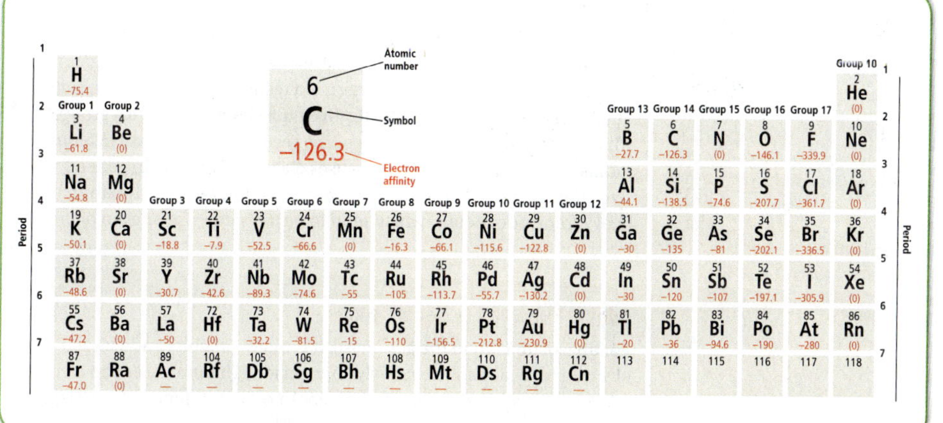

Teaching Tip

Students will remember the meaning of electron affinity more easily if they understand the meaning of the word *affinity*. Ask students to name things they might have an affinity for, such as foods, movies, sports, music, cars, and so forth.

Misconception Alert!

Many students have difficulty understanding that energy given off is denoted as a negative value, whereas energy absorbed is denoted as a positive value. Have students think of energy as a balance in a bank account. When money is put in, the balance increases because of a gain (positive change). When money is spent, the balance decreases because of a loss (negative change).

TEACH FROM TABLES

FIGURE 3.7 Have students refer to the two word equations at the top of the page in the student textbook and also to **Figure 3.7.** Ask them which elements in the periodic table would be represented by the second equation, which shows that energy must be supplied to add an electron to the atom. Have students explain their choice of elements.

▼ Teach *continued*

Teaching Tip

To help students understand positive and negative electron affinities, use the analogy of buying and selling. Those atoms that really need another electron to complete an octet (for example, Cl) will pay a lot for it (or expend a large amount of energy). Atoms that don't need another electron but that have space in their orbital (such as Na) would only pay a small amount. Atoms that already have a small amount of stability in their filled *s* sublevel (such as Mg) and those with total stability (such as Ne) would expect to be paid to take on another electron.

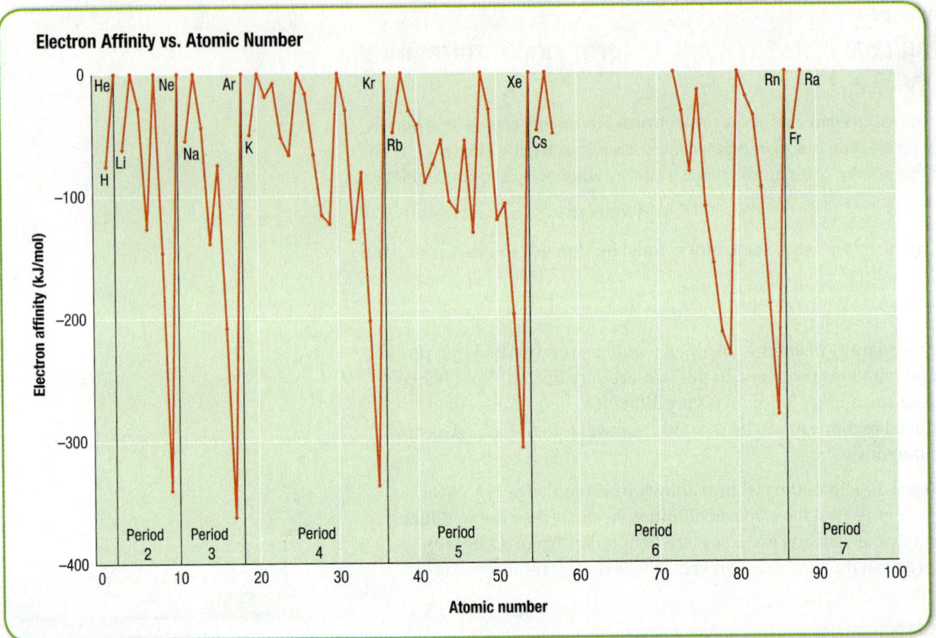

FIGURE 3.8

Electron Affinity and Atomic Numbers The plot of electron affinity versus atomic number shows that most atoms release energy when they acquire an electron, as indicated by negative values.

An exception to this trend occurs between Groups 14 and 15. Compare the electron affinities of carbon ([He]$2s^22p^2$) and nitrogen ([He]$2s^22p^3$). Adding an electron to a carbon atom gives a half-filled *p* sublevel. This occurs more easily than forcing an electron to pair with another electron in an orbital of the already half-filled *p* sublevel of a nitrogen atom.

Group Trends

Trends for electron affinities within groups are not as regular as trends for ionization energies. As a general rule, electrons are added with greater difficulty down a group. This pattern is a result of two competing factors. The first is a slight increase in effective nuclear charge down a group, which increases electron affinities. The second is an increase in atomic radius down a group, which decreases electron affinities. In general, the size effect predominates. But there are exceptions, especially among the heavy transition metals, which tend to be the same size or even decrease in radius down a group.

Adding Electrons to Negative Ions

For an isolated ion in the gas phase, it is more difficult to add a second electron to an already negatively charged ion. Therefore, second electron affinities are all positive. Certain *p*-block nonmetals tend to form negative ions that have noble gas configurations. The halogens do so by adding one electron. For example, chlorine has the configuration [Ne]$3s^23p^5$.

Differentiated Instruction

BELOW LEVEL

Be sure that students understand that the negative values in **Figure 3.8** indicate that energy is released when an atom gains an electron. Have them describe what happens in each period when moving from the Group 17 element to the Group 18 element (noble gas).

Students should recognize that the electron affinity suddenly increases, reflecting the fact that energy must be supplied to add an electron to a noble gas.

An atom of chlorine achieves the configuration of the noble gas argon by adding an electron to form the ion Cl^- ([Ne]$3s^23p^6$). Adding another electron is so difficult that Cl^{2-} never occurs. Atoms of Group 16 elements are present in many compounds as 2− ions. For example, oxygen ([He]$2s^22p^4$) achieves the configuration of the noble gas neon by adding two electrons to form the ion O^{2-}([He]$2s^22p^6$).

MAIN IDEA

When atoms become ions, their radii change.

Figure 3.9 shows the radii of some of the most common ions of the elements. Positive and negative ions have specific names.

A positive ion is known as a cation. The formation of a cation by the loss of one or more electrons always leads to a decrease in atomic radius, because the removal of the highest-energy-level electrons results in a smaller electron cloud. Also, the remaining electrons are drawn closer to the nucleus by its unbalanced positive charge.

A negative ion is known as an anion. The formation of an anion by the addition of one or more electrons always leads to an increase in atomic radius. This is because the total positive charge of the nucleus remains unchanged when an electron is added to an atom or an ion. So the electrons are not drawn to the nucleus as strongly as they were before the addition of the extra electron. The electron cloud also spreads out because of greater repulsion between the increased number of electrons.

Period Trends

Within each period of the periodic table, the metals at the left tend to form cations, and the nonmetals at the upper right tend to form anions. Cationic radii decrease across a period, because the electron cloud shrinks due to the increasing nuclear charge acting on the electrons in the same main energy level.

FIGURE 3.9

Periodic Table of Ionic Radii (pm) The ionic radii of the ions most common in chemical compounds are shown. Cations are smaller, and anions are larger than the atoms from which they are formed.

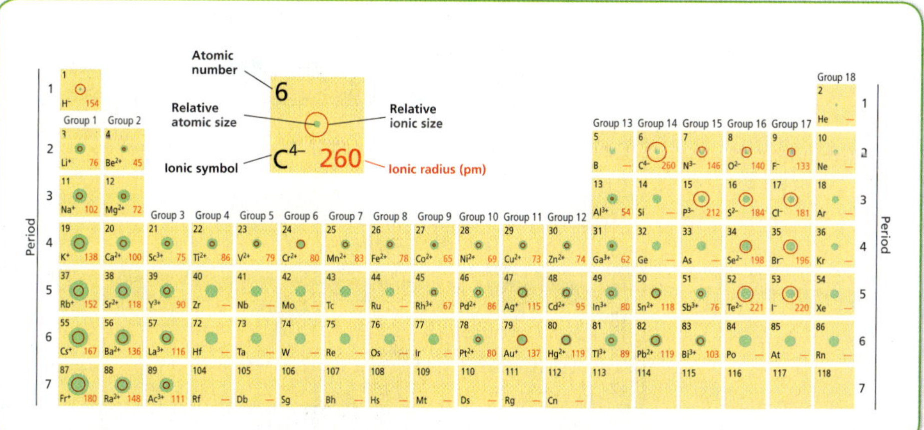

TEACH FROM TABLES

FIGURE 3.9 Have students compare the size of the ions with the size of the atoms from which they were formed. For example, the atomic radius of the sodium atom is 186 pm, while the ionic radius of Na^+ is 102 pm. Have students compare atomic and ionic radii of several other elements. Ask them to compare and explain the size differences of cations and anions. Ask what general trends they observe. In general, cations are smaller than the atoms from which they are formed, while anions are larger.

INCLUSION

Have visual learners focus on the information for each element that is shown as a green dot and a red circle. Ask students what the change in size of the red circle represents. This change indicates what happens to the size of an atom when it becomes an ion.

Next, ask students to explain why the red circles are smaller than the green dots for the Group 1 metals. Metal atoms, such as those in Group 1, form cations that are smaller than their original atoms, while non-metals form anions that are larger than their original atoms.

Have students contrast this with what is shown for the Group 15 halogens.

The Periodic Law 151

▼ Teach *continued*

Teaching Tip

To help students identify valence electrons in electron configurations, have them underline the largest Arabic numeral as often as it occurs and then add the superscripts together. For example, the electron configuration for Cl would have two underlined terms: $1s^22s^22p^6\underline{3s^23p^5}$. The number of valence electrons is 2 + 5, or 7. Calcium's electron configuration has 1 underlined term: $1s^22s^22p^63s^23p^6\underline{4s^2}$ There are two valence electrons.

TEACH FROM TABLES

FIGURE 3.10 As students study the table, have them focus on the reactivity or stability of the elements in relation to the elements' positions in the periodic table. Ask why elements in the same group tend to react similarly. They have the same valence electron configuration. Also, point out to students that for an element in the *s*-block or the *p*-block (Group 1, 2, or 13–18), the number of valence electrons is equal to the sum of the superscripts in the element's group configuration.

Starting with Group 15, in which atoms assume stable noble-gas configurations by gaining three electrons, anions are more common than cations. Anionic radii decrease across each period for the elements in Groups 15–18. The reasons for this trend are the same as the reasons that cationic radii decrease from left to right across a period.

Group Trends

The outer electrons in both cations and anions are in higher energy levels as one reads down a group. Thus, just as there is a gradual increase of atomic radii down a group, there is also a gradual increase of ionic radii.

MAIN IDEA

Only the outer electrons are involved in forming compounds.

Chemical compounds form because electrons are lost, gained, or shared between atoms. The electrons that interact in this manner are those in the highest energy levels. These are the electrons most subject to the influence of nearby atoms or ions. The electrons available to be lost, gained, or shared in the formation of chemical compounds are referred to as **valence electrons.** Valence electrons are often located in incompletely filled main-energy levels. For example, the electron lost from the 3*s* sublevel of Na to form Na^+ is a valence electron.

For main-group elements, the valence electrons are the electrons in the outermost *s* and *p* sublevels. The inner electrons are in filled energy levels and are held too tightly by the nucleus to be involved in compound formation. The Group 1 and Group 2 elements have one and two valence electrons, respectively, as shown in **Figure 3.10.** The elements of Groups 13–18 have a number of valence electrons equal to the group number minus 10. In some cases, both the *s* and *p* sublevel valence electrons of the *p*-block elements are involved in compound formation **(Figure 3.10)**. In other cases, only the electrons from the *p* sublevel are involved.

FIGURE 3.10

VALENCE ELECTRONS IN MAIN-GROUP ELEMENTS

Group number	Group configuration	Number of valence electrons
1	ns^1	1
2	ns^2	2
13	ns^2p^1	3
14	ns^2p^2	4
15	ns^2p^3	5
16	ns^2p^4	6
17	ns^2p^5	7
18	ns^2p^6	8

Differentiated Instruction

BELOW LEVEL

Be sure that students understand the difference between electronegativity and electron affinity. Point out that both properties tend to decrease as you move down a group and increase as you move across a period. However, the similarity ends there. To demonstrate the difference between these properties, ask two students to hold on to opposite ends of a meter stick. Ask one student to pull on the meter stick. Ask the class which student represents an atom with the higher electronegativity. Students should identify the student pulling on the meter stick, because electronegativity is a measure of an atom's attraction for an electron when the atom is bonded to another atom. Now ask the two students to move apart. Have a third student move between them. Point out that the moving student represents an electron. Have one of the original students grab and hold on to the moving student. Ask the class which student represents an atom with higher electron affinity. The student who grabbed the other student represents an atom with greater electron affinity, which represents the measure of a neutral atom's ability to attract an electron.

MAIN IDEA

Atoms have different abilities to capture electrons.

Valence electrons hold atoms together in chemical compounds. In many compounds, the negative charge of the valence electrons is concentrated closer to one atom than to another. This uneven concentration of charge has a significant effect on the chemical properties of a compound. It is therefore useful to have a measure of how strongly one atom attracts the electrons of another atom within a compound.

Linus Pauling, one of America's most famous chemists, devised a scale of numerical values reflecting the tendency of an atom to attract electrons. **Electronegativity** **is a measure of the ability of an atom in a chemical compound to attract electrons from another atom in the compound.** The most electronegative element, fluorine, is arbitrarily assigned an electronegativity of four. Other values are then calculated in relation to this value.

Period Trends

As shown in **Figure 3.11**, *electronegativities tend to increase across each period, although there are exceptions.* The alkali and alkaline-earth metals are the least electronegative elements. In compounds, their atoms have a low attraction for electrons. Nitrogen, oxygen, and the halogens are the most electronegative elements. Their atoms attract electrons strongly.

FIGURE 3.11

Periodic Table of Electronegativities Shown are the electronegativities of the elements according to the Pauling scale. The most-electronegative elements are located in the upper right of the *p*-block. The least-electronegative elements are located in the lower left of the *s*-block.

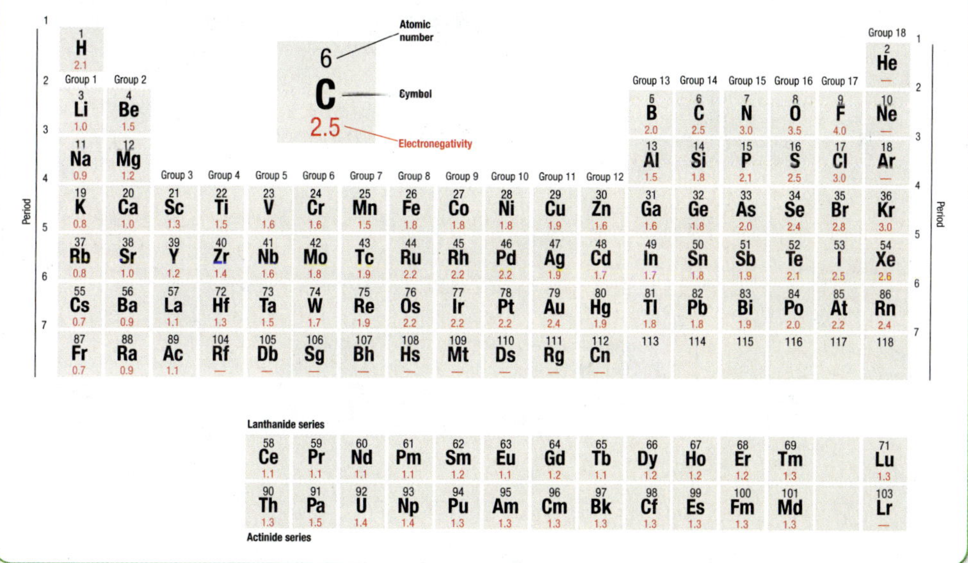

Period	Group 1	Group 2	Group 3	Group 4	Group 5	Group 6	Group 7	Group 8	Group 9	Group 10	Group 11	Group 12	Group 13	Group 14	Group 15	Group 16	Group 17	Group 18
1	1 H 2.1																	2 He —
2	3 Li 1.0	4 Be 1.5											5 B 2.0	6 C 2.5	7 N 3.0	8 O 3.5	9 F 4.0	10 Ne —
3	11 Na 0.9	12 Mg 1.2											13 Al 1.5	14 Si 1.8	15 P 2.1	16 S 2.5	17 Cl 3.0	18 Ar —
4	19 K 0.8	20 Ca 1.0	21 Sc 1.3	22 Ti 1.5	23 V 1.6	24 Cr 1.6	25 Mn 1.5	26 Fe 1.8	27 Co 1.8	28 Ni 1.8	29 Cu 1.9	30 Zn 1.6	31 Ga 1.6	32 Ge 1.8	33 As 2.0	34 Se 2.4	35 Br 2.8	36 Kr 3.0
5	37 Rb 0.8	38 Sr 1.0	39 Y 1.2	40 Zr 1.4	41 Nb 1.6	42 Mo 1.8	43 Tc 1.9	44 Ru 2.2	45 Rh 2.2	46 Pd 2.2	47 Ag 1.9	48 Cd 1.7	49 In 1.7	50 Sn 1.8	51 Sb 1.9	52 Te 2.1	53 I 2.5	54 Xe 2.6
6	55 Cs 0.7	56 Ba 0.9	57 La 1.1	72 Hf 1.3	73 Ta 1.5	74 W 1.7	75 Re 1.9	76 Os 2.2	77 Ir 2.2	78 Pt 2.2	79 Au 2.4	80 Hg 1.9	81 Tl 1.8	82 Pb 1.8	83 Bi 1.9	84 Po 2.0	85 At 2.2	86 Rn 2.4
7	87 Fr 0.7	88 Ra 0.9	89 Ac 1.1	104 Rf —	105 Db —	106 Sg —	107 Bh —	108 Hs —	109 Mt —	110 Ds —	111 Rg —	112 Cn —	113	114	115	116	117	118

Series															
Lanthanide series	58 Ce 1.1	59 Pr 1.1	60 Nd 1.1	61 Pm 1.1	62 Sm 1.2	63 Eu 1.1	64 Gd 1.2	65 Tb 1.1	66 Dy 1.2	67 Ho 1.2	68 Er 1.2	69 Tm 1.3		71 Lu 1.3
Actinide series	90 Th 1.3	91 Pa 1.5	92 U 1.4	93 Np 1.4	94 Pu 1.3	95 Am 1.3	96 Cm 1.3	97 Bk 1.3	98 Cf 1.3	99 Es 1.3	100 Fm 1.3	101 Md 1.3		103 Lr —

Teaching Tip

Note that electronegativity is a property of atoms in compounds and thus differs from electron affinity and ionization energy, which are properties of isolated atoms.

ChemisTrivia

- In general, metals are less electronegative than nonmetals.
- Electronegativity can be related to the size of the atom. The smaller the atom in a family, the greater its electronegativity. A small atom has a stronger force of attraction for its own electrons and for other atoms' electrons.

TEACH FROM TABLES

FIGURE 3.11 Have students compare **Figure 3.11** with **Figure 3.4** and **Figure 3.7**. What general trends do they observe? Electronegativity follows the same periodic trend as ionization energy and electron affinity: values generally decrease or remain about the same down a group and, with some exceptions, increase across a period.

▼ Teach *continued*

Classroom Practice

G-1 Explain why elements with high electron affinities are also the most electronegative.

Answer: Electron affinity and electronegativity measure an atom's ability to attract electrons—both its own (electron affinity) and those of other atoms (electronegativity).

Check for Understanding

Answer: Helium, neon, and argon are smaller than the other noble gases, and their electrons are closer to the nucleus. This means that the electrons are held more tightly by the attractive forces of the nucleus. The three larger noble gases have orbitals farther away from the nucleus. Since the attractive force of the nucleus decreases with distance, the larger noble gases have valence electrons that are not held so strongly.

CHECK FOR UNDERSTANDING

Compare The text states that some noble gases "do not form compounds and therefore cannot be assigned electronegativities." How can some of them form compounds, while others do not?

Electronegativities tend to either decrease down a group or remain about the same. The noble gases are unusual in that some of them do not form compounds and therefore cannot be assigned electronegativities. When a noble gas does form a compound, its electronegativity is rather high, similar to the values for the halogens. The combination of the period and group trends in electronegativity results in the highest values belonging to the elements in the upper right of the periodic table. The lowest values belong to the elements in the lower left of the table. These trends are shown graphically in **Figure 3.12.**

MAIN IDEA

The properties of *d*-block metals do not vary much.

The properties of the *d*-block elements (which are all metals) vary less and with less regularity than those of the main-group elements. This trend is indicated by the curves in **Figures 3.3** and **3.5,** which flatten where the *d*-block elements fall in the middle of Periods 4–6.

Recall that atoms of the *d*-block elements contain from zero to two electrons in the *s* orbital of their highest occupied energy level and one to ten electrons in the *d* sublevel of the next-lower energy level.

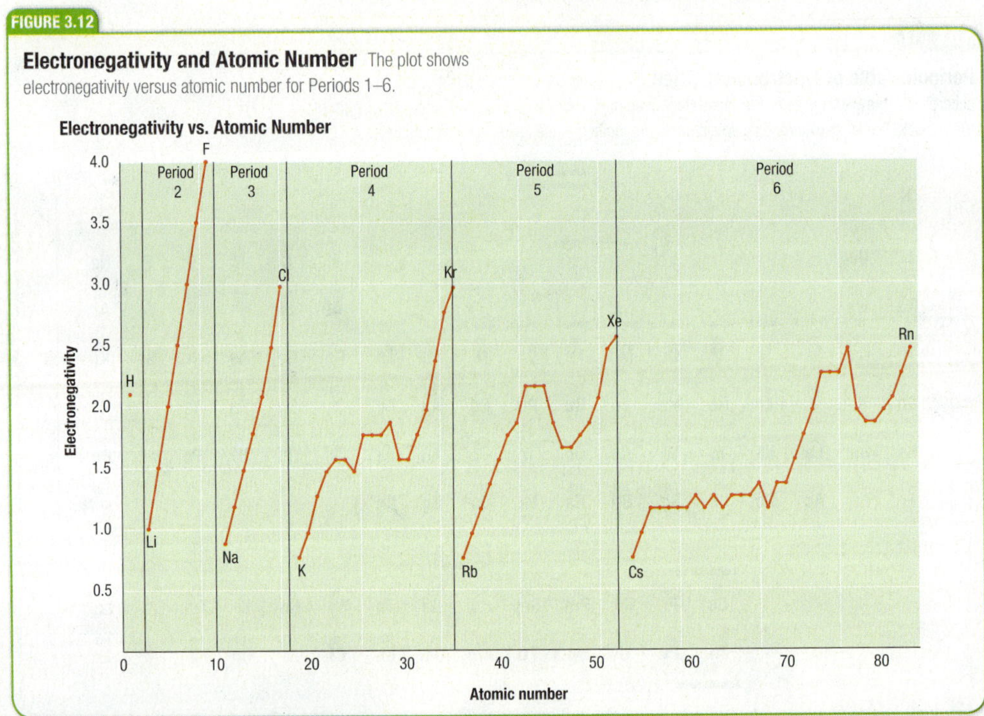

FIGURE 3.12

Electronegativity and Atomic Number The plot shows electronegativity versus atomic number for Periods 1–6.

Problem Solving

DECONSTRUCTING PROBLEMS

Emphasize the importance of reading the problem carefully and understanding what is being asked. For example, in Sample Problem G, the student is asked to identify the element with the highest electronegativity. Point out that the first step that students should take is to focus on the term *highest electronegativity*. Once they are sure that they know what is being asked, then the students can identify the element that has the greatest attraction for a shared electron.

Periodic Trends in Electronegativity

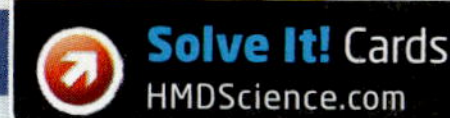

Sample Problem G Of the elements gallium, Ga, bromine, Br, and calcium, Ca, which has the highest electronegativity? Explain your answer in terms of periodic trends.

SOLVE All of these elements are in the fourth period. Bromine has the highest atomic number and is farthest to the right in the period. Therefore, bromine should have the highest electronegativity because electronegativity increases across the periods.

Practice Answers in Appendix E

1. Consider five hypothetical main-group elements, E, G, J, L, and M, that have the outer electron configurations shown at the top of the next page.

   $E = 2s^22p^5$ $G = 4d^{10}5s^25p^5$ $J = 2s^22p^2$

   $L = 5d^{10}6s^26p^5$ $M = 2s^22p^4$

   a. Identify the block location for each element. Then, determine which elements are in the same period and which are in the same group.
   b. Which element would you expect to have the highest electron affinity? Which would you expect to form a 1− ion? Which should have the highest electronegativity?
   c. Compare the ionic radius of the typical ion formed by the element G with the radius of the atom from which the ion was formed.
   d. Which element(s) contain seven valence electrons?

Therefore, electrons in both the *ns* sublevel and the $(n–1)d$ sublevel are available to interact with their surroundings. As a result, electrons in the incompletely filled *d* sublevels are responsible for many characteristic properties of the *d*-block elements.

Atomic Radii

The atomic radii of the *d*-block elements generally decrease across the periods. However, this decrease is less than that for the main-group elements, because the electrons added to the $(n–1)d$ sublevel shield the outer electrons from the nucleus.

Also, note in **Figure 3.3** that the radii dip to a low and then increase slightly across each of the four periods that contain *d*-block elements. As the number of electrons in the *d* sublevel increases, the radii increase because of repulsion among the electrons.

In the sixth period, the *f*-block elements fall between lanthanum (Group 3) and hafnium (Group 4). Because of the increase in atomic number that occurs from lanthanum to hafnium, the atomic radius of hafnium is actually slightly less than that of zirconium, Zr, the element immediately above it. The radii of elements following hafnium in the sixth period vary with increasing atomic number in the usual manner.

Alternative Assessment

Provide each student with a copy of the periodic table. Have students compare the atomic radii, ionic energies, and electronegativities of the *d*- and *f*-block elements with those of the main-group elements. Have students draw arrows indicating the periodic trends they observe.

Answers

Practice G

1. **a.** All are in the *p*-block. E, J, and M are in the same period, and E, G, and L are in the same group.
   b. E should have the highest electron affinity; E, G, and L are most likely to form 1− ions; E should have the highest electronegativity.
   c. The ionic radius would be larger.
   d. E, G, and L

ChemisTrivia

The exact size of an atom is hard to determine, mainly because the electrons do not follow well-defined orbits. As a result, one way to determine the size of an atom is to determine its bond radius, or half the distance between the centers of the nuclei for two atoms that are bonded together.

▼ Teach *continued*

READING TOOLKIT

PRE-READING Inform students that before reading a section of the text, they may wish to skim for highlighted key terms, and write down the terms with their definitions. For example, a student may want to write down a definition of ionization energy before reading about the *d*- and *f*-block elements.

▼ Assess and Reteach

Assess Use the Formative Assessment on this page to evaluate student mastery of the section.

Reteach For students who need additional instruction, download the Section Study Guide.

Response to Intervention To reassess students' mastery, use the Section Quiz, available to print or to take directly online at **HMDScience.com**.

Ionization Energy

As they do for the main-group elements, ionization energies of the *d*-block and *f*-block elements generally increase across the periods. In contrast to the decrease down the main groups, however, the first ionization energies of the *d*-block elements generally increase down each group. This is because the electrons available for ionization in the outer *s* sublevels are less shielded from the increasing nuclear charge by electrons in the incomplete $(n–1)d$ sublevels.

Ion Formation and Ionic Radii

Among all atoms of the *d*-block and *f*-block elements, electrons in the highest occupied sublevel are always removed first. For the *d*-block elements, this means that although newly added electrons occupy the *d* sublevels, the first electrons to be removed are those in the outermost level. For example, iron, Fe, has the electron configuration $[Ar]3d^64s^2$. First, it loses two 4*s* electrons to form Fe^{2+} ($[Ar]3d^6$). Fe^{2+} can then lose a 3*d* electron to form Fe^{3+} ($[Ar]3d^5$).

Most *d*-block elements commonly form 2+ ions in compounds. Some, such as iron and chromium, also commonly form 3+ ions. The Group 3 elements form only ions with a 3+ charge. Copper forms 1+ and 2+ ions, and silver usually forms only 1+ ions. As expected, the cations have smaller radii than the atoms do. Comparing 2+ ions across the periods shows a decrease in size that parallels the decrease in atomic radii.

Electronegativity

The *d*-block elements all have electronegativities between 1.1 and 2.54. Only the active metals of Groups 1 and 2 have lower electronegativities. The *d*-block elements also follow the general trend for electronegativity values to increase as radii decrease, and vice versa. The *f*-block elements all have similar electronegativities, which range from 1.1 to 1.5.

SECTION 3 FORMATIVE ASSESSMENT

Reviewing Main Ideas

1. State the general period and group trends among main-group elements with respect to each of the following properties:
   a. atomic radii
   b. first ionization energy
   c. electron affinity
   d. ionic radii
   e. electronegativity
2. a. In general, how do the periodic properties of the *d*-block elements compare with those of the main-group elements?
   b. Explain the comparison made in (a).
3. For each main-group element, what is the relationship between its group number and the number of valence electrons that the group members have?

Critical Thinking

4. **RELATING IDEAS** Graph the general trends (left to right and top to bottom) in the second ionization energy (IE_2) of an element as a function of its atomic number, over the range Z = 1–20. Label the minima and maxima on the graph with the appropriate element symbol.

Answers to Section Assessment

1. a. generally decreases across periods and increases down groups
   b. generally increases across periods and decreases down groups
   c. generally increases across periods among Groups 13–17 and decreases down groups, but many exceptions are observed
   d. generally decreases across periods and increases down groups
   e. gradually increases across periods and either decreases or remains about the same down groups
2. a. They vary less and with less regularity than main-group elements do
   b. The difference is generally attributed to the presence of electrons in incompletely filled *d* sublevels in atoms of the *d*-block elements
3. For Groups 1 and 2, the number of valence electrons is equal to the group number. For Groups 13–18, the number of valence electrons is equal to the group number minus 10.
4. Student graphs should look like the following:

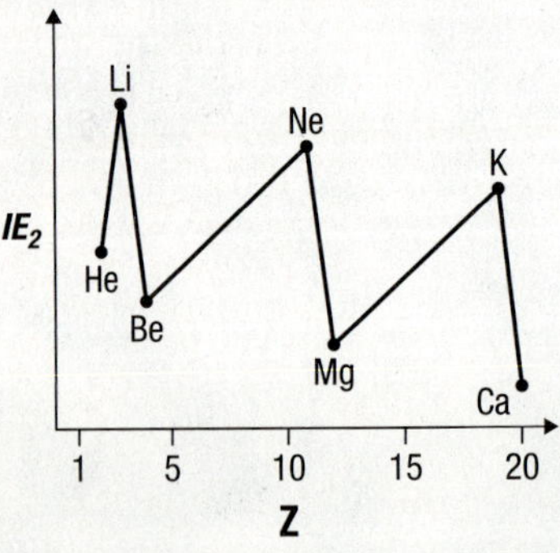

Math Tutor — Writing Electron Configurations

The arrangement of elements in the periodic table reflects the arrangement of electrons in an atom. Each period begins with an atom that has an electron in a new energy level and with the exception of the first period, each period ends with an atom that has a filled set of *p* orbitals.

To write the electron configuration of an element, you must fill the sublevels in order of increasing energy. If you follow the arrows in either of the two types of mnemonics shown below, you will get correct configurations for most elements.

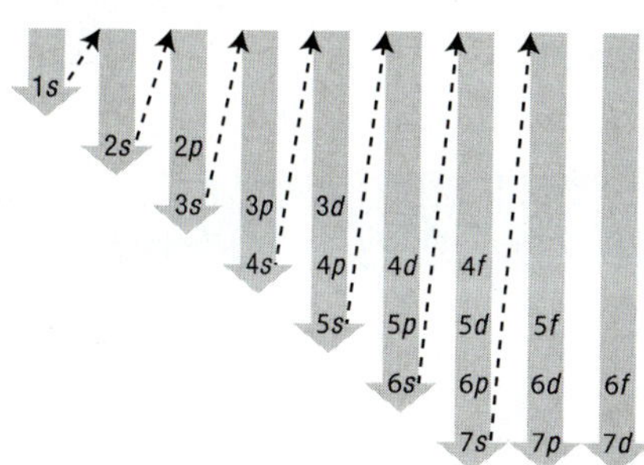

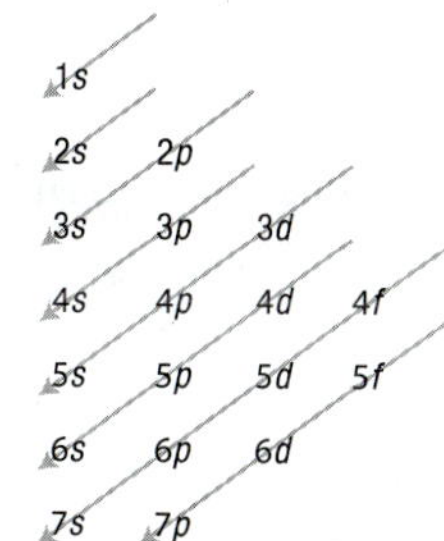

You also need to know how many orbitals are in each sublevel and that each orbital can contain two electrons of opposite spins. As shown in the following table, the sublevels *s, p, d,* and *f* have 1, 3, 5, and 7 available orbitals, respectively.

SUBLEVEL	*s*	*p*	*d*	*f*
No. of orbitals	1	3	5	7
No. of electrons	2	6	10	14

Sample Problem

Write the full electron configuration for phosphorus.

The atomic number of phosphorus is 15, so a phosphorus atom has 15 protons and electrons. Assign each of the 15 electrons to the appropriate sublevels. The final sublevel can be unfilled and will contain the number of valence electrons.

$$\underline{1s^2}\quad \underline{2s^2}\quad \underline{2p^6}\quad \underline{3s^2}\quad \underline{3p^3}$$
$$2e^- + 2e^- + 6e^- + 2e^- + 3e^- = 15e^-$$

So, the full electron configuration of phosphorus is $1s^22s^22p^63s^23p^3$.

Practice

Answers in Appendix E

1. Write full electron configurations for the following elements.
   - **a.** aluminum
   - **b.** neon
   - **c.** tin
   - **d.** potassium
2. Use noble gas symbols to write shorthand electron configurations for the following elements.
   - **a.** silicon
   - **b.** rubidium
   - **c.** antimony
   - **d.** arsenic

MATH TUTOR

Answers

1. **a.** $1s^22s^22p^63s^23p^1$
   b. $1s^22s^22p^6$
   c. $1s^22s^22p^63s^23p^63d^{10}4s^24p^64d^{10}5s^25p^2$
   d. $1s^22s^22p^63s^23p^64s^1$
2. **a.** $[Ne]3s^23p^2$
   b. $[Kr]5s^1$
   c. $[Kr]4d^{10}5s^25p^3$
   d. $[Ar]3d^{10}4s^24p^3$

CHAPTER 5 Summary

PREMIUM CONTENT
Interactive Review HMDScience.com
Review Games
Concept Maps

SECTION 1 History of the Periodic Table

- The periodic law states that the physical and chemical properties of the elements are periodic functions of their atomic numbers.
- The periodic table is an arrangement of the elements in order of their atomic numbers so that elements with similar properties fall in the same column.
- The columns in the periodic table are referred to as groups.

KEY TERMS

periodic law
periodic table
lanthanide
actinide

SECTION 2 Electron Configuration and the Periodic Table

- The rows in the periodic table are called periods.
- Many chemical properties of the elements can be explained by the configurations of the elements' outermost electrons.
- The noble gases exhibit unique chemical stability because their highest occupied levels have an octet of electrons, ns^2np^6 (with the exception of helium, whose stability arises from its highest occupied level being completely filled with two electrons, $1s^2$).
- Based on the electron configurations of the elements, the periodic table can be divided into four blocks: the *s*-block, the *p*-block, the *d*-block, and the *f*-block.

KEY TERMS

alkali metals
alkaline-earth metals
transition elements
main-group elements
halogens

SECTION 3 Electron Configuration and Periodic Properties

- The groups and periods of the periodic table display general trends in the following properties of the elements: electron affinity, electronegativity, ionization energy, atomic radius, and ionic radius.
- The electrons in an atom that are available to be lost, gained, or shared in the formation of chemical compounds are referred to as valence electrons.
- In determining the electron configuration of an ion, the order in which electrons are removed from the atom is the reverse of the order given by the atom's electron-configuration notation.

KEY TERMS

atomic radius
ion
ionization
ionization energy
electron affinity
cation
anion
valence electron
electronegativity

Review Answers

1. a. Cannizzaro developed a standard method for measuring atomic masses, which allowed chemists to search for periodic trends among elements.
   b. Mendeleev organized elements according to increasing atomic mass and noticed that similar properties appeared periodically.
   c. Moseley discovered that nuclear charge (i.e., atomic number), not atomic mass, should be the basis for organizing the periodic table.
2. The physical and chemical properties of the elements are periodic functions of their atomic numbers.
3. Groups of elements exhibit similar chemical and physical properties and behavior.
4. a. Generally, the configurations of the outermost electron shells of elements within the same group are the same. There are a number of exceptions to this rule, however, among the transition elements.
   b. Their outer shells are completely filled.

CHAPTER 5 Review

SECTION 1

History of the Periodic Table

REVIEWING MAIN IDEAS

1. Describe the contributions made by the following scientists to the development of the periodic table:
   a. Stanislao Cannizzaro
   b. Dmitri Mendeleev
   c. Henry Moseley
2. State the periodic law.
3. How is the periodic law demonstrated within the groups of the periodic table?

SECTION 2

Electron Configuration and the Periodic Table

REVIEWING MAIN IDEAS

4. a. How do the electron configurations within the same group of elements compare?
   b. Why are the noble gases relatively unreactive?
5. What determines the length of each period in the periodic table?
6. What is the relationship between the electron configuration of an element and the period in which that element appears in the periodic table?
7. a. What information is provided by the specific block location of an element?
   b. Identify, by number, the groups located within each of the four block areas.
8. a. Which elements are designated as the alkali metals?
   b. List four of their characteristic properties.
9. a. Which elements are designated as the alkaline-earth metals?
   b. How do their characteristic properties compare with those of the alkali metals?
10. a. Write the group configuration notation for each *d*-block group.
    b. How do the group numbers of those groups relate to the number of outer *s* and *d* electrons?
11. What name is sometimes used to refer to the entire set of *d*-block elements?
12. a. What types of elements make up the *p*-block?
    b. How do the properties of the *p*-block metals compare with those of the metals in the *s*- and *d*-blocks?
13. a. Which elements are designated as the halogens?
    b. List three of their characteristic properties.
14. a. Which elements are metalloids?
    b. Describe their characteristic properties.
15. Which elements make up the *f*-block in the periodic table?
16. a. What are the main-group elements?
    b. What trends can be observed across the various periods within the main-group elements?

PRACTICE PROBLEMS

17. Write the noble-gas notation for the electron configuration of each of the following elements, and indicate the period in which each belongs.
    a. Li c. Cu e. Sn
    b. O d. Br
18. Without looking at the periodic table, identify the period, block, and group in which the elements with the following electron configurations are located. (Hint: See Sample Problem A.)
    a. $[Ne]3s^23p^4$
    b. $[Kr]4d^{10}5s^25p^2$
    c. $[Xe]4f^{14}5d^{10}6s^26p^5$
19. Based on the information given below, give the group, period, block, and identity of each element described. (Hint: See Sample Problem B.)
    a. $[He]2s^2$
    b. $[Ne]3s^1$
    c. $[Kr]5s^2$
    d. $[Ar]4s^2$
    e. $[Ar]3d^54s^1$
20. Without looking at the periodic table, write the expected outer electron configuration for each of the following elements. (Hint: See Sample Problem C.)
    a. Group 7, fourth period
    b. Group 3, fifth period
    c. Group 12, sixth period

5. The length of a period is determined by the total number of electrons that can fill the outer sublevels of the elements of that period.
6. An element's period corresponds to its highest occupied main energy level.
7. a. the type of sublevel being filled in successive elements of that block
   b. *s*-block: Groups 1 and 2; *p*-block: Groups 13–18 (except for He); *d*-block: Groups 3–12 (except for the *f*-block elements); *f*-block: those elements of the sixth and seventh periods between Groups 3 and 4
8. a. the Group 1 elements
   b. The Group 1 elements are extremely reactive. They react vigorously with water, they are silvery in appearance, and each is soft enough to be cut with a knife.
9. a. the Group 2 elements
   b. The Group 2 elements are harder, denser, and stronger than the Group 1 elements. They also have higher melting points. Group 2 elements are less reactive than Group 1 elements.
10. a. Group 3: $(n-1)d^1ns^2$
    Group 4: $(n-1)d^2ns^2$
    Group 5: $(n-1)d^3ns^2$
    Group 6: $(n-1)d^5ns^1$ for Cr and Mo
    $(n-1)d^4ns^2$ for W and Sg
    Group 7: $(n-1)d^5ns^2$
    Group 8: $(n-1)d^6ns^2$
    Group 9: $(n-1)d^7ns^2$
    Group 10: $(n-1)d^8ns^2$
    Group 11: $(n-1)d^{10}ns^1$
    Group 12: $(n-1)d^{10}ns^2$
    b. The group number equals the sum of the outer *s* and *d* electrons.
11. the transition elements
12. a. The *p*-block consists of nonmetals at the right, metalloids in the middle, and metals at the left.
    b. The *p*-block metals are generally harder and more dense than the *s*-block metals but softer and less dense than the *d*-block metals.
13. a. the Group 17 elements
    b. The halogens are the most-reactive nonmetals; they react vigorously with most metals to form salts. They are also among the most electronegative elements.
14. a. B, Si, Ge, As, Sb, Te
    b. The metalloids are mostly brittle solids with electrical conductivities intermediate between those of metals (good conductors) and nonmetals (nonconductors).
15. the lanthanides and the actinides
16. a. the elements of the *s* and *p*-blocks (plus hydrogen and helium)
    b. decrease in atomic size, increase in ionization energy, increase in electron affinity, decrease in cationic size, decrease in anionic size, increase in electronegativity
17. a. $[He]2s^1$, second period
    b. $[He]2s^22p^4$, second period
    c. $[Ar]3d^{10}4s^1$, fourth period
    d. $[Ar]3d^{10}4s^24p^5$, fourth period
    e. $[Kr]4d^{10}5s^25p^2$, fifth period
18. a. third period, *p*-block, Group 16
    b. fifth period, *p*-block, Group 14
    c. sixth period, *p*-block, Group 17
19. a. Group 2, second period, *s*-block, Be
    b. Group 1, third period, *s*-block, Na
    c. Group 2, fifth period, *s*-block, Sr
    d. Group 2, fourth period, *s*-block, Ca
    e. Group 6, fourth period, *d*-block, Cr
20. a. $3d^54s^2$, b. $4d^15s^2$, c. $4f^{14}5d^{10}6s^2$

21. a. p-block, third period, Group 13, Al, metal, high reactivity
b. p-block, fourth period, Group 18, noble gases, Kr, nonmetal, low reactivity
c. d-block, fifth period, Group 11, Ag, metal, low reactivity
d. f-block, sixth period, between Groups 3 and 4, Ce, metal, high reactivity

22. a. one half the distance between the nuclei of two bonded identical atoms
b. They decrease.
c. As electrons are added to s and p sublevels in the same main energy level, the increasing positive charge of the nucleus pulls electrons closer to the nucleus, resulting in decreasing atomic radii.

23. a. They generally increase.
b. Down a group, the outer electrons of each element occupy comparable sublevels in successively higher main energy levels farther from the nucleus.

24. a. a charged atom or a charged group of bonded atoms
b. any process that results in the formation of an ion
c. the energy required to remove one electron from a neutral atom of an element
d. the energy required to remove an electron from a 1+ ion

25. a. They increase across a period and decrease down a group.
b. Across a period, the increasing nuclear charge attracts electrons in the same energy level more strongly and makes them more difficult to remove. Down a group, the electrons to be removed from each successive element are farther from the nucleus in increasingly higher energy levels and are thus more easily removed.

26. a. the energy taken in or given off when an electron is added to an atom
b. Electron affinity values are either negative or positive. A negative sign indicates that energy is given off; a positive sign indicates that energy is taken in.

27. a. A cation is a positive ion, and an anion is a negative ion.

CHAPTER REVIEW

21. Identify the block, period, group, group name (where appropriate), element name, element type, and relative reactivity for the elements with the following electron configurations. (Hint: See Sample Problem D.)
a. $[Ne]3s^23p^1$
b. $[Ar]3d^{10}4s^24p^6$
c. $[Kr]4d^{10}5s^1$
d. $[Xe]4f^15d^16s^2$

SECTION 3

Electron Configuration and Periodic Properties

REVIEWING MAIN IDEAS

22. a. What is meant by *atomic radius*?
b. What trend is observed among the atomic radii of main-group elements across a period?
c. Explain this trend.

23. a. What trend is observed among the atomic radii of main-group elements down a group?
b. Explain this trend.

24. Define each of the following terms:
a. ion
b. ionization
c. first ionization energy
d. second ionization energy

25. a. How do the first ionization energies of main-group elements vary across a period and down a group?
b. Explain the basis for each trend.

26. a. What is electron affinity?
b. What signs are associated with electron affinity values, and what is the significance of each sign?

27. a. Distinguish between a cation and an anion.
b. How does the size of each compare with the size of the neutral atom from which it is formed?

28. a. What are valence electrons?
b. Where are such electrons located?

29. For each of the following groups, indicate whether electrons are more likely to be lost or gained in compound formation, and give the number of such electrons typically involved.
a. Group 1
b. Group 2
c. Group 13
d. Group 16
e. Group 17
f. Group 18

30. a. What is electronegativity?
b. Why is fluorine special in terms of electronegativity?

31. Identify the most- and least-electronegative groups of elements in the periodic table.

PRACTICE PROBLEMS

32. Of cesium, Cs, hafnium, Hf, and gold, Au, which element has the smallest atomic radius? Explain your answer in terms of trends in the periodic table. (Hint: See Sample Problem E.)

33. a. Distinguish between the first, second, and third ionization energies of an atom.
b. How do the values of successive ionization energies compare?
c. Why does this occur?

34. Without looking at the electron affinity table, arrange the following elements in order of *decreasing* electron affinities: C, O, Li, Na, Rb, and F.

35. a. Without looking at the ionization energy table, arrange the following elements in order of decreasing first ionization energies: Li, O, C, K, Ne, and F.
b. Which of the elements listed in (a) would you expect to have the highest second ionization energy? Why?

36. a. Which of the following cations is least likely to form: Sr^{2+}, Al^{3+}, K^{2+}?
b. Which of the following anions is least likely to form: I^-, Cl^-, O^{2-}?

37. Which element is the most electronegative among C, N, O, Br, and S? Which group does it belong to? (Hint: See Sample Problem G.)

38. The two ions K^+ and Ca^{2+} each have 18 electrons surrounding the nucleus. Which would you expect to have the smaller radius? Why?

160 Chapter 5

b. Cations are always smaller than the atoms from which they are formed; anions are always larger.

28. a. Valence electrons are atomic electrons available to be lost, gained, or shared in the formation of chemical compounds.
b. Valence electrons are located in an atom's outermost energy level.

29. a. lost, 1
b. lost, 2
c. lost, 3
d. gained, 2
e. gained, 1
f. neither lost nor gained, 0

30. a. Electronegativity is the ability of an atom in a chemical compound to attract electrons from other atoms.
b. Fluorine is the most electronegative element and is arbitrarily assigned an electronegativity of 4.0. The values for all other elements are assigned in relation to this value.

31. Most-electronegative: Group 17, least-electronegative: Group 1

32. Gold; atomic radii decrease across a period, and gold is farthest to the right in the sixth period, in which all 3 elements are found.

33. a. First ionization energy is the energy required to remove one electron from an

Mixed Review

REVIEWING MAIN IDEAS

39. Without looking at the periodic table, identify the period, block, and group in which each of the following elements is located.
  a. $[Rn]7s^1$
  b. $[Ar]3d^24s^2$
  c. $[Kr]4d^{10}5s^1$
  d. $[Xe]4f^{14}5d^96s^1$

40. a. Which elements are designated as the noble gases?
  b. What is the most significant property of these elements?

41. Which of the following does not have a noble-gas configuration: Na^+, Rb^+, O^{2-}, Br^- Ca^+, Al^{3+}, S^{2-}?

42. a. How many groups are in the periodic table?
  b. How many periods are in the periodic table?
  c. Which two blocks of the periodic table make up the main-group elements?

43. Write the noble-gas notation for the electron configuration of each of the following elements, and indicate the period and group in which each belongs.
  a. Mg
  b. P
  c. Sc
  d. Y

44. Use the periodic table to describe the chemical properties of the following elements:
  a. fluorine, F
  b. xenon, Xe
  c. sodium, Na
  d. gold, Au

45. For each element listed below, determine the charge of the ion that is most likely to be formed and the identity of the noble gas whose electron configuration is thus achieved.

a. Li	**e.** Mg	**i.** Br
b. Rb	**f.** Al	**j.** Ba
c. O	**g.** P	
d. F	**h.** S	

46. Describe some differences between the *s*-block metals and the *d*-block metals.

47. Why do the halogens readily form 1–ions?

48. Identify which trends in the diagrams below describe atomic radius, ionization energy, electron affinity, and electronegativity.

49. The electron configuration of argon differs from those of chlorine and potassium by one electron each. Compare the reactivity of these three elements.

atom, which is neutral. Second ionization energy is the energy required to remove an electron from a 1+ ion. Third ionization energy is the energy required to remove an electron from a 2+ ion.
  b. Each successive ionization energy is larger than the preceding one.
  c. Each successive electron must be removed from a particle with a greater positive charge.

34. In order of decreasing electron affinities, the elements are F, O, C, Li, Na, and Rb.

35. a. Ne, F, O, C, Li, K
  b. Li and K would have the highest second ionization energies, because in both cases the second electron must come from a completely filled noble-gas electron configuration. Of the two, Li would have the higher second ionization energy, because the Li^+ ion is smaller than the K^+ ion.

36. a. K^{2+}, **b.** O^{2-}

37. O; Group 16

38. Ca^{2+}; because of the greater attraction that its 20 protons exert on the 18 electrons

39. a. seventh period, *s*-block, Group 1
  b. fourth period, *d*-block, Group 4
  c. fifth period, *d*-block, Group 11
  d. sixth period, *d*-block, Group 10

40. a. the Group 18 elements
  b. They are very unreactive.

41. Ca^+

42. a. 18; **b.** 7; **c.** the *s* and *p*-blocks

43. a. $[Ne]3s^2$, third period, Group 2
  b. $[Ne]3s^23p^3$, third period, Group 15
  c. $[Ar]3d^14s^2$, fourth period, Group 3
  d. $[Kr]4d^15s^2$, fifth period, Group 3

44. a. It is a highly reactive nonmetal in Group 17, Period 2. It needs one electron to achieve a noble gas configuration, which explains its high electron affinity. It has a high ionization energy, and thus the formation of positive ions is not likely. Fluorine is the most electronegative element.
  b. It is a nonmetal of low reactivity in Group 18, Period 5. It has a filled outer energy level, so there is little tendency to lose, gain, or share electrons. It has the highest ionization energy of the elements in the fifth period.
  c. It is a highly reactive metal in Group 1, Period 3. It has a low first ionization energy, because losing an electron to form Na^+ gives it a noble gas configuration. It has a low electron affinity and a low electronegativity.
  d. It is a metal of fairly low reactivity in Group 11, Period 6. Its ionization energy is relatively low, so it forms positive ions.

45. a. 1^+, He	**f.** 3+, Ne
b. 1+, Kr	**g.** 3−, Ar
c. 2−, Ne	**h.** 2−, Ar
d. 1−, Ne	**i.** 1−, Kr
e. 2+, Ne	**j.** 2+, Xe

46. The *d*-block metals are harder, denser, and less reactive, and except for mercury, they have higher melting points than *s*-block metals do.

47. In doing so, they achieve a noble-gas configuration.

48. ionization energy, electron affinity, electronegativity: diagram a; atomic radius: diagram b

49. Chlorine and potassium are reactive elements, whereas argon is unreactive. Chlorine readily gains one electron to achieve the configuration of argon, and potassium readily loses one electron to achieve the argon configuration.

50.

			4 Δ		
		9 Λ			12 γ
13 β					
				23 ε	

51. 5

52. 8

53. From left to right, the elements are organized according to their atomic numbers. Elements are organized into families or columns according to their properties. The elements exhibit increasingly nonmetallic behavior from left to right across the table. Their physical states suggest that melting points and boiling points also increase from left to right.

54. Na is a liquid at 97.8°C.
K is a liquid at 63.25°C.
Rb is a liquid at 38.89°C.
Cs is a liquid at 28.5°C.
Fr is a liquid at 27°C.
Hg is a liquid at −38.8°C.
Ga is a liquid at 29.77°C.
N as N_2 is a gas at −195.8°C.
P is a liquid at 44.1°C.
O as O_2 is a gas at −182.962°C.
F as F_2 is a gas at −188.14°C.
Cl as Cl_2 is a gas at −34.6°C.
Br as Br_2 is a gas at 58.78°C.

55. a. Cr^{3+}, violet or green; Cr^{6+}, yellow or orange
b. rubies
c. copper, blue; cadmium, yellow; cobalt, pink; zinc, white; nickel, green
d. Gold, silver, platinum, palladium, iridium, rhodium, ruthenium, osmium; they have low reactivity.

56. Possible responses include Friedrich Dorn's discovery of radon in 1900, Moseley's determination of the nuclear charge (i.e., atomic number) of each element by 1913, the discovery of the lanthanides by 1913, the synthesis in 1940 of the first element beyond uranium (neptunium) in the periodic table by Philip Abelson and Edwin McMillan, the creation of plutonium in 1941 by Seaborg, and the synthesis of element 109 in Germany in 1982.

CHAPTER REVIEW

CRITICAL THINKING

As a member on the newly-inhabited space station Alpha, you are given the task of organizing information on newly discovered elements as it comes in from the laboratory. To date, five elements have been discovered and have been assigned names and symbols from the Greek alphabet. An analysis of the new elements has yielded the following data:

Element name	Atomic no.	Atomic mass	Properties
Epsilon ε	23	47.33	nonmetal, very reactive, produces a salt when combined with a metal, gaseous state
Beta β	13	27.01	metal, very reactive, soft solid, low melting point
Gamma γ	12	25.35	nonmetal, gaseous element, extremely unreactive
Delta Δ	4	7.98	nonmetal, very abundant, forms compounds with most other elements
Lambda Λ	9	16.17	metal, solid state, good conductor, high luster, hard and dense

50. Applying Models Create a periodic table based on the properties of the five new elements.

51. Predicting Outcomes Using your newly created periodic table, predict the atomic number of an element with an atomic mass of 11.29 that has nonmetallic properties and is very reactive.

52. Predicting Outcomes Predict the atomic number of an element having an atomic mass of 15.02 that exhibits metallic properties but is softer than lambda and harder than beta.

53. Analyzing Information Analyze your periodic table for trends, and describe those trends.

USING THE HANDBOOK

54. Review the boiling point and melting point data in the tables of the *Elements Handbook* (Appendix A). Make a list of the elements that exist as liquids or gases at the boiling point of water, 100°C.

55. Because transition metals have vacant *d* orbitals, they form a greater variety of colored compounds than do the metals of Groups 1 and 2. Review the section of the *Elements Handbook* (Appendix A) on transition metals, and answer the following:
a. What colors are exhibited by chromium in its common oxidation states?
b. What gems contain chromium impurities?
c. What colors are often associated with the following metal ions: copper, cadmium, cobalt, zinc, and nickel?
d. What transition elements are considered noble metals? What are the characteristics of a noble metal?

RESEARCH AND WRITING

56. Prepare a report tracing the evolution of the current periodic table since 1900. Cite the chemists involved and their major contributions.

57. Write a report describing the contributions of Glenn Seaborg toward the discovery of many of the actinide elements.

ALTERNATIVE ASSESSMENT

58. Construct your own periodic table or obtain a poster that shows related objects, such as fruits or vegetables, in periodic arrangement. Describe the organization of the table and the trends it illustrates. Use this table to make predictions about your subject matter.

57. Reports should mention Seaborg's various roles in the syntheses of curium (element 96) in 1944, californium (element 98) in 1950, mendelevium (element 101) in 1955, and nobelium (element 102) in 1958.

58. Student examples may vary, but should include isolated trends arranged in a periodic manner—by columns and rows, as in the periodic table of the elements.

Standards-Based Assessment

Answer the following items on a separate piece of paper.

MULTIPLE CHOICE

1. In the modern periodic table, elements are arranged according to
A. decreasing atomic mass.
B. Mendeleev's original model.
C. increasing atomic number.
D. when they were discovered.

2. Group 17 elements, the halogens, are the most reactive of the nonmetal elements because they
A. require only one electron to fill their outer energy level.
B. have the highest ionization energies.
C. have the largest atomic radii.
D. are the farthest to the right in the periodic table.

3. The periodic law states that
A. the chemical properties of elements can be grouped according to periodicity.
B. the properties of the elements are functions of atomic mass.
C. all elements in the same group have the same number of valence electrons.
D. all elements with the same number of occupied energy levels must be in the same group.

4. As you move left to right across Period 3 from Mg to Cl, the energy needed to remove an electron from an atom
A. generally increases.
B. generally decreases.
C. does not change.
D. varies unpredictably.

5. Which of the following elements has the highest electronegativity?
A. oxygen
B. hydrogen
C. fluorine
D. carbon

6. The noble gases have
A. high ionization energies.
B. high electron affinities.
C. large atomic radii.
D. a tendency to form both cations and anions.

7. Which electron configuration is *not* correct?
A. O^{2-} $[He]2s^22p^6$
B. Mg^{2+} $[He]2s^22p^6$
C. V^{3+} $[Ar]3d^2$
D. Al^{3+} $[Ar]2s^22p^6$

8. Which two elements are more likely to have the same charge on their ions?
A. Se and As
B. Sn and Si
C. Ca and Rb
D. I and Xe

9. Using only the periodic table, choose the list that ranks the elements Sr, Te, Kr, Ru, and Cs in order of increasing ionization energy.
A. Sr < Te < Ru < Cs < Kr
B. Te < Ru < Sr < Cs < Kr
C. Cs < Sr < Ru < Te < Kr
D. Kr < Cs < Sr < Ru < Te

SHORT ANSWER

10. The second ionization energies for the elements S–Ti are listed in a scrambled order below. Assign the correct IE_2 value to each element. (Hint: S has IE_2 = 2251 kJ/mol, and Ti has IE_2 = 1310 kJ/mol.) Explain your reasoning.

IE_2 values (kJ/mol): 2666, 2297, 3051, 1235, 2251, 1310, and 1145

11. What group most commonly forms 2– ions? Explain your reasoning.

EXTENDED RESPONSE

12. An ordered list of atomic radii for 14 consecutive elements is shown below. Without using **Figure 3.2**, make a graph of these atomic radii versus the element's atomic number. Explain your reasoning.

Atomic radii (pm): 75, 73, 72, 71, 186, 160, 143, 118, 110, 103, 100, 98, 227, and 197

Test Tip
If you are short on time, quickly scan the unanswered questions to see which might be easiest to answer.

STANDARDS-BASED ASSESSMENT

To give students practice under more realistic testing conditions, give them 60 minutes to answer all of the questions in this Standardized Test Preparation.

Test Answers

1. C
2. A
3. A
4. A
5. C
6. A
7. D
8. B
9. C
10. S: 2251 kJ/mol; Cl: 2297 kJ/mol; Ar: 2666 kJ/mol; K: 3051 kJ/mol; Ca: 1145 kJ/mol; Sc: 1235 kJ/mol; Ti: 1310 kJ/mol. For the second ionization, the general trend is for increasing IE_2 across the period in Groups 2–18, with Group 1 having the highest IE_2. IE_2 decreases going down a group.
11. Group 16 most commonly forms 2– ions, because these elements require only two more electrons to fill their shell (obtain a noble-gas configuration).

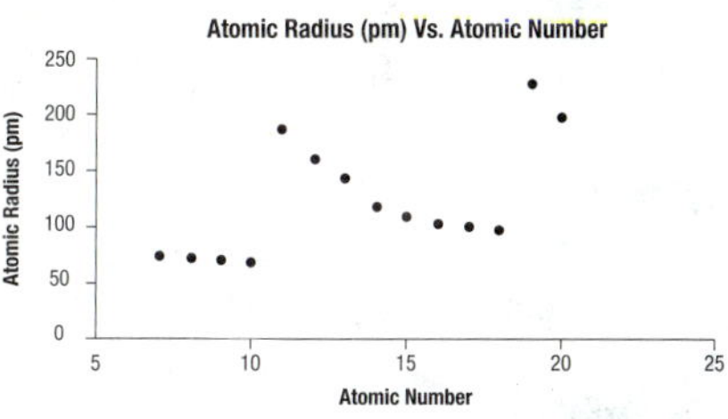

12. There are eight numbers between the first and second minimum; therefore, these eight elements must either be the second or third period. There are four numbers before the first maximum; hence, these four numbers must be elements in the second row because the first row contains only two elements (H and He). Therefore, the eight elements must be in the third period. The first atomic radius listed must correspond to atomic number 7, which is N. Students' graphs should look like the graph above:

Chemical Bonding

1 Core Instruction

Chapter Resources

- The Teacher's Edition wrap has extensive teaching support for every lesson, including Misconception Alerts, Teach from Visuals, Demonstrations, Teaching Tips, Differentiated Instruction, and Problem Solving support.
- Several additional presentation tools are available online for every chapter, including Animated Chemistry features and Visual Concepts.
- You can open your lesson with the Why It Matters Video: Chemical Bonding.

Section	Instruction	Labs and Demonstrations Go Online for Materials Lists and Solutions Lists.
6.1	■ **Textbook:** Introduction to Chemical Bonding **Animated Chemistry:** Types of Bonds **Teaching Visuals:** Predicting Bond Character from Electronegativity Differences • Electronegativity Differences for Hydrogen Halides **PowerPresentations**	
6.2	■ **Textbook:** Covalent Bonding and Molecular Compounds **Teaching Visuals:** Formation of a Covalent Bond • Bond Length and Stability • Lewis Structures of the Second Period Elements • Electron-Dot Notation • Drawing Lewis Structures with Many Atoms • Bond Energies and Bond Lengths for Single Bonds **PowerPresentations**	■ **Lab:** Conductivity as an Indicator of Bond Type (Core Skill)
6.3	■ **Textbook:** Ionic Bonding and Ionic Compounds **Teaching Visuals:** Ionic vs. Covalent Bonding • NaCl and CsCl Crystal Lattices • Melting and Boiling Points of Compounds • How to Identify Ionic Compounds **PowerPresentations**	■ **Lab:** Chemical Bonds (Core Skill)
6.4	■ **Textbook:** Metallic Bonding **Teaching Visuals:** Properties of Substances with Metallic, Ionic, and Covalent Bonds **PowerPresentations**	■ **Lab:** Types of Bonding in Solids (Core Skill)
6.5	■ **Textbook:** Molecular Geometry **Teaching Visuals:** Molecular Shapes with Three Electron Pairs Around Central Atom • Molecular Shape Affects Polarity • Geometry of Hybrid Orbitals • Predicting Polarity • Hydrogen Bonding Between Water Molecules • VSEPR and Molecular Geometry • Comparing Ionic and Molecular Substances • Comparing Dipole-Dipole Forces **PowerPresentations**	■ **Lab:** Repulsion Compulsion (Open Inquiry)

Find all of your resources online at HMDScience.com.

2 Support and Intervention

- **Interactive Reader** (English and Spanish)
- **Study Guide**
- **Interactive Review:** Review Games, Concept Maps, and Section Self-Checks
- **Scientific Reasoning Skill Builder**
- **Learn It! Videos**
- **Solve It! Cards**
- **Interactive Demos**
- **Sample Problem Sets**

3 Specialized Support

- **Chapter Summary Audio Files**
- **Interactive Reader Audio Files**
- **Differentiated Instruction:** Inclusion, Below Level, and English Learners (TE wrap)

Enrichment and Challenge

- **Differentiated Instruction:** Pre-AP (TE wrap)
- **Why It Matters:** Ultrasonic Toxic-Waste Destroyer (SE)
- **WebLinks**

Assessment

- **Section Formative Assessments** (SE)
- **Section Quizzes**
- **Chapter Review** (SE)
- **Chapter Tests A and B**
- **Alternative Assessment** (TE wrap)
- **Online Assessment and Remediation**
- **ExamView Banks**

Where do I find it?

	Resource	PRINT	DVD	ONLINE
1	Animated Chemistry		■	■
1	Demonstrations (TE wrap)	■		■
1	Interactive Whiteboard		■	■
1	Labs		■	■
1	PowerPresentations		■	■
1	QuickLabs	■	■	■
1	Teaching Visuals		■	■
1	Textbook	■	■	■
1	Visual Concepts		■	■
1	Why It Matters Videos		■	■
2	Interactive Demos		■	■
2	Interactive Reader	■	■	■
2	Interactive Reviews		■	■
2	Learn It! Videos		■	■
2	Sample Problem Sets		■	■
2	Scientific Reasoning Skill Builder		■	■
2	Smart Grapher Tool		■	■
2	Solve It! Cards		■	■
2	Study Guide		■	■
3	Chapter Summary Audio Files		■	■
3	Differentiated Instruction (TE wrap)	■		
3	Interactive Reader Audio Files		■	■

CHAPTER 6

Chapter Overview

Section 1 defines chemical bonding and uses electronegativity values to contrast polar-covalent, nonpolar-covalent, and ionic bonding.

Section 2 covers the characteristics of covalent bonding, including the relationship between bond length and bond strength, and the use of Lewis structures.

Section 3 covers the characteristics of ionic bonding.

Section 4 covers the characteristics of metallic bonding and the resulting properties of metals.

Section 5 covers theories of molecular geometry and discusses how the geometry of molecules affects intermolecular attraction.

▼ Focus and Motivate

Activate Prior Knowledge

Students may need a review of the following concepts:

- boiling points
- electron configurations and orbital notation
- ion formation and electronegativity

About the Image

This computer model of adenosine monophosphate clearly shows how chemical bonds join atoms. The computer model also provides a sense of the three-dimensional structure of the compound.

Why It Matters

Students can access the video online and find other helpful resources at **HMDScience.com**.

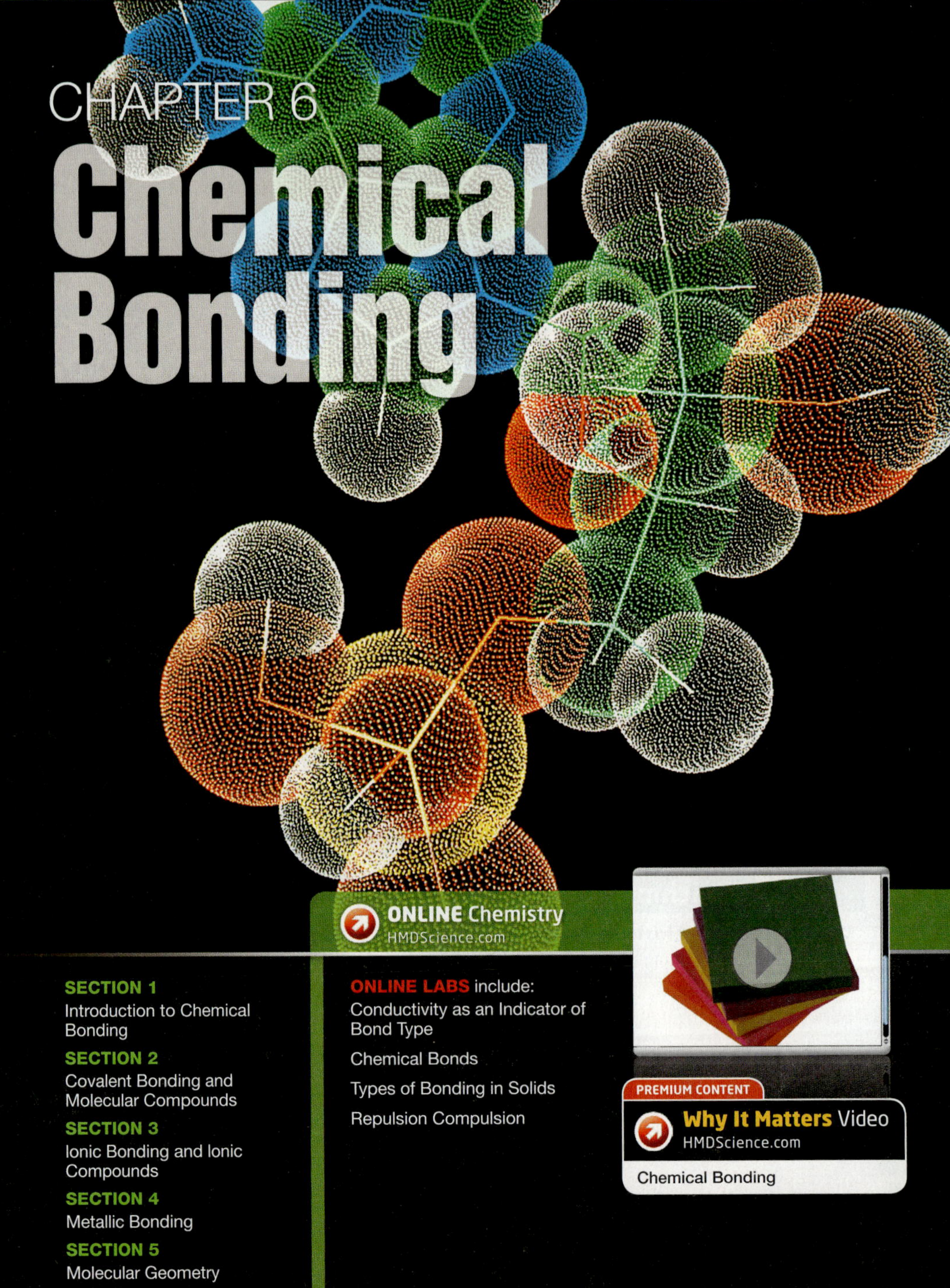

Lab Preview

The following labs support the concepts presented in this chapter.

LABS

Conductivity as an Indicator of Bond Type (Core Skill)

Chemical Bonds (Core Skill)

Types of Bonding in Solids (Core Skill)

Repulsion Compulsion (Open Inquiry)

SECTION 1

Main Ideas

Atoms form compounds by gaining, losing, or sharing electrons.

Introduction to Chemical Bonding

Key Terms

chemical bond
ionic bonding
covalent bonding
nonpolar-covalent bond
polar
polar-covalent bond

Atoms seldom exist as independent particles in nature. The oxygen you breathe, the water you drink, and nearly all other substances consist of combinations of atoms that are held together by chemical bonds. **A chemical bond is a mutual electrical attraction between the nuclei and valence electrons of different atoms that binds the atoms together.**

Why are most atoms chemically bonded to each other? As independent particles, most atoms are at relatively high potential energy. Nature, however, favors arrangements in which potential energy is minimized. Most atoms are less stable existing by themselves than when they are combined. By bonding with each other, atoms decrease in potential energy, creating more stable arrangements of matter.

MAIN IDEA

Atoms form compounds by gaining, losing, or sharing electrons.

When atoms bond, their valence electrons are redistributed in ways that make the atoms more stable. The way in which the electrons are redistributed determines the type of bonding. As discussed in the chapter "The Periodic Law," main-group metals tend to lose electrons to form positive ions, or *cations*, and nonmetals tend to gain electrons to form negative ions, or *anions*. **Chemical bonding that results from the electrical attraction between cations and anions is called ionic bonding.** In purely ionic bonding, atoms completely give up electrons to other atoms, as illustrated in **Figure 1.1** on the next page. In contrast to atoms joined by ionic bonding, atoms joined by covalent bonding share electrons. **Covalent bonding results from the sharing of electron pairs between two atoms** (see **Figure 1.1**). In a purely covalent bond, the shared electrons are "owned" equally by the two bonded atoms.

Ionic or Covalent?

Bonding between atoms of different elements is rarely purely ionic or purely covalent. It usually falls somewhere between these two extremes, depending on how strongly the atoms of each element attract electrons. Recall that electronegativity is a measure of an atom's ability to attract electrons. The degree to which bonding between atoms of two elements is ionic or covalent can be estimated by calculating the difference in the elements' electronegativities (see **Figure 1.2** on the next page).

Types of Bonds

Differentiated Instruction

BELOW LEVEL

Tell students they will examine a variety of chemical bonds. Emphasize the importance of understanding how each bond forms. As they read this chapter, have them work in pairs to explain what is happening in terms of bonding. They can use **Figures 1.1** and **1.2** to compare ionic and covalent bonding, and **Figure 1.3** to compare nonpolar- and polar-covalent bonding. For further details, they can consult **Figures 2.1**, **2.2**, and **2.3** for covalent bonding; **Figures 3.2**, **3.3**, and **3.5** for ionic bonding; and **Figure 4.1** for metallic bonding.

SECTION 1

Plan and Prepare ▼

Objectives

Upon completion of this section, students should be able to do the following:

- Define *chemical bond*.
- Explain why most atoms form chemical bonds.
- Differentiate ionic and covalent bonding.
- Explain why most chemical bonding is neither purely ionic nor purely covalent.
- Classify bonding type according to electronegativity differences.

Classroom Catalyst

Have students imagine getting onto a crowded elevator. As people squeeze into the confined space, they come in contact with each other. Many people will experience a sense of being too close together and wanting to push others away from them. Likewise, when atoms get close enough, their outer electrons repel each other. However, unlike in the elevator analogy, each atom's outer electrons are also strongly attracted to the nuclei of the surrounding atoms. The degree to which these outer electrons are attracted to other atoms determines the kind of chemical bonding that occurs between the atoms. Have students consider how many electrons exist in the outer energy levels of the atoms of various elements.

Teach ▼

Classroom Discussion

Emphasize the word *seldom* in the opening sentence on this page. Point out that some atoms *do* exist as independent particles in nature. Ask students to provide examples of atoms that exist as individual particles. Students can mention any of the noble gases. Have them explain why these atoms can exist as individual particles.

▼ Teach *continued*

TEACH FROM VISUALS

FIGURE 1.1 Have students recognize the fundamental difference between ionic and covalent bonding. In ionic bonding, large numbers of oppositely charged ions come together because of electrical attraction. (Be sure students identify the cations and the anions.) In covalent bonding, two atoms join by sharing one or more of their valence electrons. The shared electrons are simultaneously attracted to both atomic nuclei.

Some students will notice the changes in sizes for atoms A and B and ions A and B. Have students discuss what they know about atomic radii and ionic radii.

Misconception Alert!

Electronegativity difference is only a general guide for determining bonding type. For example, the electronegativity difference between boron and fluorine is 2.0. Yet scientists know through experimentation that boron trifluoride, BF_3, is a covalently bonded compound.

Classroom Practice

A-1 Ask students to complete the following chart:

Elements bonded	Electro-negativity difference	Bond type	More-negative atom
a. C & H	0.4		
b. C & S	0.0		
c. O & H	1.4		
d. Na & Cl	2.1		
e. Cs & S	1.8		

Answer:

a. polar-covalent; C
b. nonpolar-covalent; same electronegativity
c. polar-covalent; O
d. ionic; Cl
e. ionic; S

FIGURE 1.1

Ionic Bonding and Covalent Bonding In ionic bonding, many atoms transfer electrons. The resulting positive and negative ions combine due to mutual electrical attraction. In covalent bonding, atoms share electron pairs to form independent molecules.

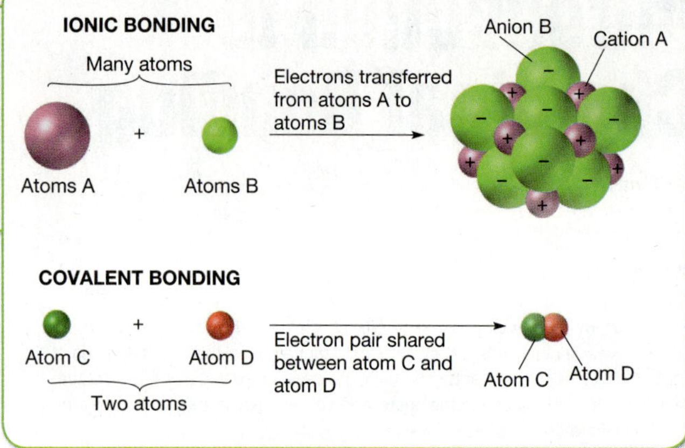

FIGURE 1.2

Bonding and Electronegativity Differences in electronegativities reflect the character of bonding between elements. The electronegativity of the less-electronegative element is subtracted from that of the more-electronegative element. The greater the electronegativity difference, the more ionic is the bonding.

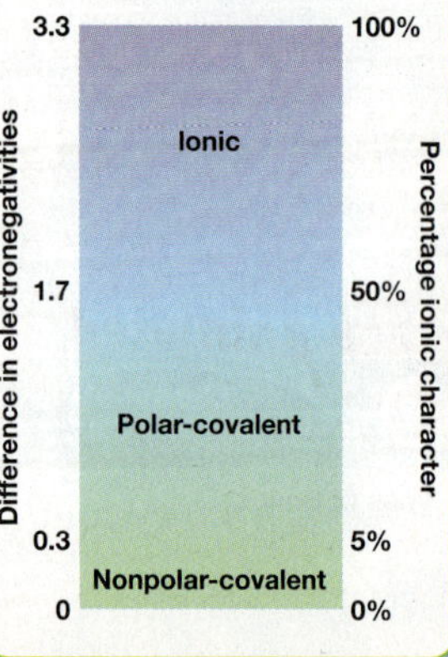

For example, the electronegativity difference between fluorine, F, and cesium, Cs, is 4.0 − 0.7 = 3.3. So, according to **Figure 1.2**, cesium-fluorine bonding is ionic. Fluorine atoms, which are highly electronegative, gain valence electrons, causing the atoms to become anions. Cesium atoms, which are less electronegative, lose valence electrons, causing the atoms to become cations.

Bonding between atoms with an electronegativity difference of 1.7 or less has an ionic character of 50% or less. These compounds are typically classified as covalent. Bonding between two atoms of the same element is completely covalent. Hydrogen, for example, exists in nature not as isolated atoms, but as pairs of atoms held together by covalent bonds. The hydrogen-hydrogen bond is a **nonpolar-covalent bond,** a covalent bond in which the bonding electrons are shared equally by the bonded atoms, resulting in a balanced distribution of electrical charge. Bonds having 0% to 5% ionic character, corresponding to electronegativity differences of roughly 0 to 0.3, are generally considered nonpolar-covalent bonds. In bonds with significantly different electronegativities, the electrons are more strongly attracted by the more-electronegative atom. Such bonds are **polar,** meaning that they have an uneven distribution of charge. Covalent bonds having 5% to 50% ionic character, corresponding to electronegativity differences of 0.3 to 1.7, are classified as polar. A **polar-covalent bond** is a covalent bond in which the bonded atoms have an unequal attraction for the shared electrons.

Nonpolar- and polar-covalent bonds are compared in **Figure 1.3**, which illustrates the electron density distribution in hydrogen-hydrogen and hydrogen-chlorine bonds. The electronegativity difference between chlorine and hydrogen is 3.0 − 2.1 = 0.9, indicating a polar-covalent bond. The electrons in this bond are closer to the more-electronegative chlorine atom than to the hydrogen atom. Thus, the chlorine end of the bond has a partial negative charge, indicated by the symbol $\delta-$. The hydrogen end of the bond then has an equal partial positive charge, $\delta+$.

Differentiated Instruction

BELOW LEVEL

Be sure that students understand the basis for the difference in the electronegativities of two bonded atoms. For example, review why chlorine has a higher electronegativity value than hydrogen. Students should expect that these two atoms will form a polar covalent bond based on their atomic structures. With a greater effective nuclear charge, a chlorine atom attracts the shared pair of electrons with a greater force. Point out that the process of calculating differences in electronegativity values to determine bond type is simply faster than analyzing atomic structures. Have students use atomic structures to determine the type of bond that forms between potassium (K) and bromine (Br) and between two Br atoms. Then have students check electronegativity differences to confirm their answers. Students should note that because K has only one valence electron and Br has seven valence electrons, the two atoms form an ionic bond. The electronegativity difference between these two atoms (2.8 − 0.8 = 2.0) confirms this answer. Two Br atoms form a nonpolar-covalent bond.

FIGURE 1.3

Electron Density Comparison of the electron density in **(a)** a nonpolar, hydrogen-hydrogen bond and **(b)** a polar, hydrogen-chlorine bond. Because chlorine is more electronegative than hydrogen, the electron density in the hydrogen-chlorine bond is greater around the chlorine atom.

CRITICAL THINKING

Explain Why is the density of the electron cloud greater around the chlorine atom in the polar hydrogen-chlorine bond?

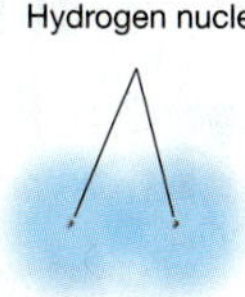

(a) Nonpolar-covalent bond

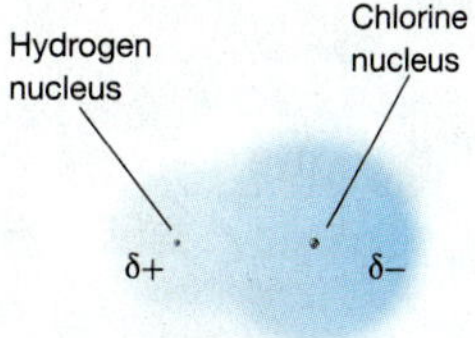

(b) Polar-covalent bond

Classifying Bonds

Sample Problem A **Use electronegativity differences and Figure 1.2 to classify bonding between sulfur, S, and the following elements: hydrogen, H; cesium, Cs; and chlorine, Cl. In each pair, which atom will be more negative?**

SOLVE From the Periodic Table of Electronegativities in the chapter "The Periodic Law," we know that the electronegativity of sulfur is 2.5. The electronegativities of hydrogen, cesium, and chlorine are 2.1, 0.7, and 3.0, respectively. In each pair, the atom with the larger electronegativity will be the more-negative atom.

Bonding between sulfur and	Electronegativity difference	Bond type	More-negative atom
hydrogen	$2.5 - 2.1 = 0.4$	polar-covalent	sulfur
cesium	$2.5 - 0.7 = 1.8$	ionic	sulfur
chlorine	$3.0 - 2.5 = 0.5$	polar-covalent	chlorine

Practice Answers in Appendix E

Use electronegativity differences and **Figure 1.2** to classify bonding between chlorine, Cl, and the following elements: calcium, Ca; oxygen, O; and bromine, Br. Indicate the more-negative atom in each pair.

SECTION 1 FORMATIVE ASSESSMENT

Reviewing Main Ideas

1. What is the main distinction between ionic and covalent bonding?
2. How is electronegativity used in determining the ionic or covalent character of the bonding between two elements?
3. What type of bonding would be expected between the following atoms?
   a. Li and F
   b. Cu and S
   c. I and Br
4. List the three pairs of atoms referred to in the previous question in order of increasing ionic character of the bonding between them.

Critical Thinking

5. **INTERPRETING CONCEPTS** Compare the following two pairs of atoms: Cu and Cl; I and Cl.
   a. Which pair would have a bond with a greater percent ionic character?
   b. In which pair would Cl have the greater negative charge?
6. **INFERRING RELATIONSHIPS** The isolated K atom is larger than the isolated Br atom.
   a. What type of bond is expected between K and Br?
   b. Which ion in the compound KBr is larger?

Answers

Practice A

Bonding between chlorine and:

calcium; oxygen; bromine

Electronegativity difference:

$3.0 - 1.0 = 2.0$

$3.5 - 3.0 = 0.5$

$3.0 - 2.8 = 0.2$

Bond type:

ionic

polar-covalent

nonpolar-covalent

More-negative atom:

chlorine; oxygen; chlorine

Critical Thinking

Answer: The density of chlorine's electron cloud is greater because chlorine is much more electronegative than hydrogen and draws the electrons closer to its nucleus.

Assess and Reteach ▼

Assess Use the Formative Assessment on this page to evaluate student mastery of the section.

Reteach For students who need additional instruction, download the Section Study Guide.

Response to Intervention To reassess students' mastery, use the Section Quiz, available to print or to take directly online at **HMDScience.com**.

Answers to Section Assessment

1. Ionic bonding involves the electrical attraction between large numbers of anions and cations. Covalent bonding involves the sharing of electron pairs between two atoms.
2. A large difference in electronegativity between two atoms in a bond will result in ionic bonding. A small difference in electronegativity between two atoms will result in covalent bonding.
3. **a.** ionic
   b. polar-covalent
   c. nonpolar-covalent
4. I and Br, Cu and S, Li and F
5. electronegativities: Cu = 1.9, Cl = 3.0, I = 2.5 differences in electronegativity: CuCl = 1.1 and ICl = 0.5
   a. CuCl has the greater percent ionic character.
   b. The chlorine in CuCl has greater negative partial charge than the chlorine in ICl. There is a greater difference in electronegativities between Cu and Cl; therefore, there is a greater separation of charge between Cu and Cl than between I and Cl.
6. **a.** Electronegativity for Br = 2.8 and for K = 0.8. The difference between the electronegativities is 2.0; thus, an ionic bond is expected between K and Br.
   b. Br^- is larger than K^+. Because an ionic bond is expected between the two, Br atom becomes Br^- and K atom becomes K^+. According to the Periodic Table of Ionic Radii, Br^- is larger than K^+.

SECTION 2

▼ Plan and Prepare

Objectives

Upon completion of this section, students should be able to do the following:

- Define *molecule* and *molecular formula.*
- Explain the relationships among potential energy, distance between approaching atoms, bond length, and bond energy.
- State the octet rule.
- List the six basic steps used in writing Lewis structures.
- Explain how to determine Lewis structures for molecules containing single bonds, multiple bonds, or both.
- Explain why scientists use resonance structures to represent some molecules.

Classroom Catalyst

Have students consider what happens if a soccer ball is rolled toward a ditch. The ball rolls down the near slope of the ditch, passes the bottom of the ditch, and rolls partway up the opposite slope. It then rolls back down, passes the bottom, and rolls partway up the near side of the ditch. The ball continues moving in this pattern, each time rolling to a lesser height, until it eventually comes to rest in the bottom of the ditch. At this point, the ball's gravitational potential energy is at a minimum. The formation of a covalent bond between two atoms is like the ball in the ditch. The atoms alternately attract and repel each other until they reach a distance (or bond length) at which their potential energy is minimized.

SECTION 2

Main Ideas

- Covalent bonds form from shared electrons.
- Bond lengths and energy vary from molecule to molecule.
- Atoms tend to form bonds to follow the octet rule.
- Dots placed around an element's symbol can represent valence electrons.
- Electron-dot notations can represent compounds.
- Some atoms can share multiple pairs of electrons.
- Resonance structures show hybrid bonds.
- Some compounds are networks of bonded atoms.

Covalent Bonding and Molecular Compounds

Key Terms

molecule
molecular compound
chemical formula
molecular formula
bond energy
electron-dot notation
Lewis structure
structural formula
single bond
multiple bond
resonance

Many chemical compounds, including most of the chemicals that are in living things and are produced by living things, are composed of molecules. **A molecule is a neutral group of atoms that are held together by covalent bonds.** A single molecule of a chemical compound is an individual unit capable of existing on its own. It may consist of two or more atoms of the same element, as in oxygen, or two or more different atoms, as in water or sugar (see **Figure 2.1** below). **A chemical compound whose simplest units are molecules is called a molecular compound.**

The composition of a compound is given by its chemical formula. **A chemical formula indicates the relative numbers of atoms of each kind in a chemical compound by using atomic symbols and numerical subscripts.** The chemical formula of a molecular compound is referred to as a molecular formula. **A molecular formula shows the types and numbers of atoms combined in a single molecule of a molecular compound.** The molecular formula for water, for example, is H_2O. A single water molecule consists of one oxygen atom joined by separate covalent bonds to two hydrogen atoms. A molecule of oxygen, O_2, is an example of a diatomic molecule. A *diatomic molecule* contains only two atoms.

FIGURE 2.1

Covalently Bonded Molecules The models for **(a)** water, **(b)** oxygen, and **(c)** sucrose, or table sugar, represent a few examples of the many molecular compounds in and around us. Atoms within molecules may form one or more covalent bonds.

(a) Water molecule, H_2O

(b) Oxygen molecule, O_2

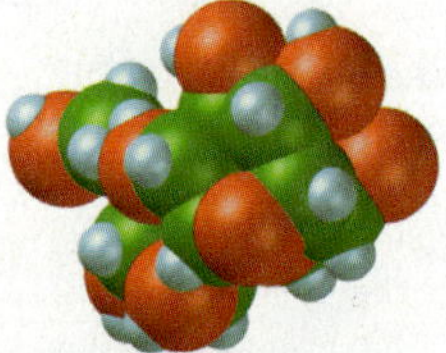

(c) Sucrose molecule, $C_{12}H_{22}O_{11}$

▼ Teach

TEACH FROM VISUALS

FIGURE 2.1 Have students carefully examine the atoms involved in these molecules. Point out that all the atoms are nonmetals and that the oxygen and carbon atoms can each form more than one bond. The ability of atoms to form more than one covalent bond allows the formation of extremely large molecules.

Differentiated Instruction

ENGLISH LEARNERS

Be sure students understand that the term *molecular* applies only to covalent compounds. Place a list of formulas of both ionic and molecular compounds on the board. Examples might include KCl, H_2S, MgO, CH_4, and Cl_2. Ask students to identify the molecules in the list. Remind them that they can use electronegativity differences to determine whether the bond is covalent or ionic.

FIGURE 2.2

Potential Energy Changes during the Formation of a Hydrogen-Hydrogen Bond **(a)** The separated hydrogen atoms do not affect each other. **(b)** Potential energy decreases as the atoms are drawn together by attractive forces. **(c)** Potential energy is at a minimum when attractive forces are balanced by repulsive forces. **(d)** Potential energy increases when repulsion between like charges outweighs attraction between opposite charges.

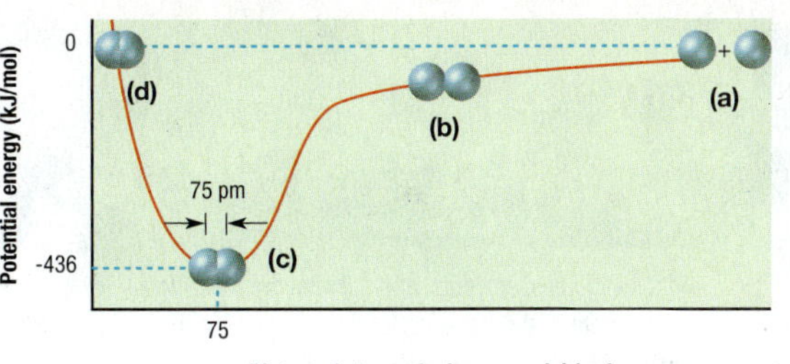

MAIN IDEA

Covalent bonds form from shared electrons.

As you read in Section 1, nature favors chemical bonding because most atoms have lower potential energy when they are bonded to other atoms than they have when they are independent particles. In the case of covalent bond formation, this idea is illustrated by a simple example, the formation of a hydrogen-hydrogen bond.

Picture two isolated hydrogen atoms separated by a distance large enough to prevent them from influencing each other. At this distance, the overall potential energy of the atoms is arbitrarily set at zero, as shown in part (a) of **Figure 2.2**.

Now consider what happens if the hydrogen atoms approach each other. Each atom has a nucleus containing a single positively charged proton. The nucleus of each atom is surrounded by a negatively charged electron in a spherical 1*s* orbital. As the atoms near each other, their charged particles begin to interact. As shown in **Figure 2.3**, the approaching nuclei and electrons are *attracted* to each other, which corresponds to a *decrease* in the total potential energy of the atoms. At the same time, the two nuclei *repel* each other and the two electrons *repel* each other, which results in an *increase* in potential energy.

The relative strength of attraction and repulsion between the charged particles depends on the distance separating the atoms. When the atoms first "sense" each other, the electron-proton attraction is stronger than the electron-electron and proton-proton repulsions. Thus, the atoms are drawn to each other and their potential energy is lowered, as shown in part (b) of **Figure 2.2**.

The attractive force continues to dominate and the total potential energy continues to decrease until, eventually, a distance is reached at which the repulsion between the like charges equals the attraction of the opposite charges. This is shown in part (c) of **Figure 2.2**. At this point, which is represented by the bottom of the valley in the curve, potential energy is at a minimum and a stable hydrogen molecule forms. A closer approach of the atoms, shown in part (d) of **Figure 2.2**, results in a sharp rise in potential energy as repulsion becomes increasingly greater than attraction.

FIGURE 2.3

Attractive and Repulsive Forces The arrows indicate the attractive and repulsive forces between the electrons (shown as electron clouds) and nuclei of two hydrogen atoms. Attraction between particles corresponds to a decrease in potential energy of the atoms, while repulsion corresponds to an increase.

CRITICAL THINKING

Explain How do covalently-bonded compounds stay together if both the nuclei and the electrons of the atoms involved repel each other?

Both nuclei repel each other, as do both electron clouds.

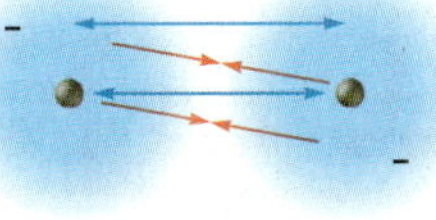

The nucleus of one atom attracts the electron cloud of the other atom, and vice versa.

TEACH FROM VISUALS

FIGURE 2.2 Ask students why the potential energy of the atoms increases as the atoms get very close to, or far from, each other. Have students consider the attraction between the electrons and the nuclei, as well as the repulsion between the two nuclei and between the two electrons.

TEACH FROM VISUALS

FIGURE 2.3 Have students prepare a table of information about the forces between two hydrogen nuclei. The table should have three headings: Atomic Particles Involved; Type of Force; and Effect on Potential Energy. Then have students write a summary of the information on their table. For example, students may write that the proton-proton interaction between the two nuclei is a repulsive force that increases potential energy.

Critical Thinking

Answer: Although the nuclei repel one another and the electron clouds repel one another, the positive charges of the nuclei are still attracted to the negative electron clouds of the other molecule(s).

BELOW LEVEL

Have students silently read the paragraphs on this page and the following textbook page (excluding the *Why It Matters* feature). Lead a discussion about the features of the graph in **Figure 2.2** that correspond to the changes in potential energy described in the text. You may wish to highlight these features on an overhead transparency as you discuss them. Have students make notes on their own copies of the graph.

Classroom Discussion

Have students assess the benefits and drawbacks of Professor Hoffmann's device. One possible benefit includes reducing the amount of toxic wastes in the environment. Two possible drawbacks are that this method requires considerable energy and that it would not remove all toxins from waste.

Alternative Assessment

Have students research the existing methods used to dispose of toxic wastes in your region.

Answers

1. The use of ultrasonic waves allows organic pollutants (and some inorganic wastes) to react and be broken down into non-harmful substances without having to create bulk high-temperature or high-pressure conditions. Therefore, this procedure is safer to use and more friendly to the environment than are more common methods, such as combustion (as in incinerators). This process also has the potential to be cheaper than combustion methods.
2. The ultrasound waves generate bubbles in the water, a process called *cavitation*. A second ultrasound breaks these bubbles. The internal pressure of these bubbles is extremely high and causes the temperature of the water right around the bubbles to reach about 5000°C. Hence, the hot spots in the water are localized, and the temperature of the bulk water remains low.

WHY IT MATTERS

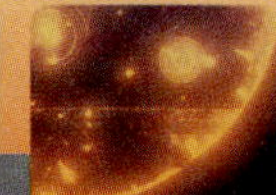

S.T.E.M.

Ultrasonic Toxic-Waste Destroyer

Paints, pesticides, solvents, and sulfides are just a few components of the 3 million tons of toxic waste that flow out of U.S. factories every year. Some of this waste ends up in groundwater and contaminates our streams and drinking water.

Eliminating hazardous waste is a constant challenge. Unfortunately, today's disposal methods often damage the environment as much as they help it. Incinerators burning certain wastes, for example, produce dioxins, one of the most dangerous class of toxins known.

Finding new methods to destroy toxic waste is a puzzle. Michael Hoffmann, a professor of environmental chemistry at the California Institute of Technology, thinks that part of the solution lies in sound-wave technology.

According to Hoffmann, cavitation is the key to eliminating certain chemical wastes from polluted water. Cavitation occurs when the pressure in water is made to fluctuate from slightly above to slightly below normal, causing bubbles. The bubbles are unstable and collapse, creating tiny areas of extremely high pressure and heat. The pressure inside a collapsing bubble can be 1000 times greater than normal, and the temperature reaches about 5000°C—just a bit cooler than the surface of the sun. These conditions are harsh enough to combust most toxic-waste compounds in the water, breaking them down into harmless components.

Hoffmann has employed a device that uses ultrasound—sound waves at frequencies just above the range of human hearing—to create cavitation in polluted water. As water flows between two panels that generate ultrasound at different frequencies, the ultrasonic waves generated by one panel form cavitation bubbles. An instant later, the ultrasound produced by the other panel collapses the bubbles. The intense pressure and heat generated break down toxic compounds into innocuous substances, such as carbon dioxide, chloride ions, and hydrogen ions.

"With ultrasound," says Hoffmann, "we can harness frequencies…of about 16 kilohertz up to 1 megahertz, and different…compounds are destroyed more readily at one frequency versus another. So by appropriately applying a particular frequency range, we can destroy a very broad range of chemical compounds."

The device destroys simple toxins in a few minutes and other toxins in several hours. To be destroyed completely, some compounds must first form intermediate chemicals, and then be treated again. To be sure the waste is totally removed, scientists use sophisticated tracking methods to trace what happens to every single molecule of the toxin.

The ultrasound toxic-waste destroyer treats about 10% of all types of waste, eliminating both organic and inorganic compounds, such as hydrogen cyanide, TNT, and many pesticides. While the device cannot destroy complex mixtures of compounds, such as those found in raw sewage, it does have many advantages over current technologies. Aside from having no harmful environmental side effects, ultrasonic waste destruction is cheaper and simpler than the process of combustion.

Questions

1. How does Dr. Hoffmann's ultrasound device benefit society?
2. Briefly explain why the bulk temperature of the water remains low (at room temperature).

MAIN IDEA

Bond lengths and energy vary from molecule to molecule.

In **Figure 2.2**, the bottom of the valley in the curve represents the balance between attraction and repulsion in a stable covalent bond. At this point, the electrons of each hydrogen atom of the hydrogen molecule are shared between the nuclei. As shown below in **Figure 2.4**, the molecule's electrons can be pictured as occupying overlapping orbitals, moving about freely in either orbital.

The bonded atoms vibrate a bit, but as long as their potential energy remains close to the minimum, they are covalently bonded to each other. The distance between two bonded atoms at their minimum potential energy, that is, the average distance between two bonded atoms, is the *bond length*. The bond length of a hydrogen-hydrogen bond is 75 pm.

In forming a covalent bond, the hydrogen atoms release energy as they change from isolated individual atoms to parts of a molecule. The amount of energy released equals the difference between the potential energy at the zero level (separated atoms) and that at the bottom of the valley (bonded atoms) in **Figure 2.2**. The same amount of energy must be added to separate the bonded atoms. **Bond energy** is the energy required to break a chemical bond and form neutral isolated atoms. Scientists usually report bond energies in kilojoules per mole (kJ/mol), which indicates the energy required to break one mole of bonds in isolated molecules. For example, 436 kJ of energy is needed to break the hydrogen-hydrogen bonds in one mole of hydrogen molecules and form two moles of separated hydrogen atoms.

The energy relationships described here for the formation of a hydrogen-hydrogen bond apply generally to all covalent bonds. However, bond lengths and bond energies vary with the types of atoms that have combined. Even the energy of a bond between the same two types of atoms varies somewhat, depending on what other bonds the atoms have formed. These facts should be considered when examining the data in **Figure 2.5** on the next page. The first three columns in the table list bonds, bond lengths, and bond energies of atoms in specific diatomic molecules. The last three columns give average values of specified bonds in many different compounds.

CHECK FOR UNDERSTANDING

Apply Does electronegativity play a role in the formation of covalent bonds? Explain.

FIGURE 2.4

Overlapping Orbitals The orbitals of the hydrogen atoms in a hydrogen molecule overlap, allowing each electron to feel the attraction of both nuclei. The result is an increase in electron density between the nuclei.

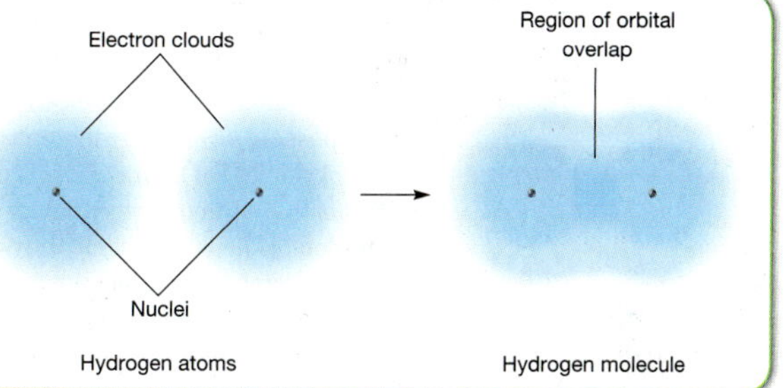

TEACH FROM VISUALS

FIGURE 2.4 The electron of an isolated hydrogen atom exists mostly within a predictable radius of the nucleus. Have students describe how the location of the electrons differs in a hydrogen molecule. The electrons spend more time in between the hydrogen nuclei, resulting in an increased electron density there.

ChemisTrivia

A microwave oven works by bathing food with radiation that has a frequency of about 3 GHz. This radiation rotates the water molecules, generating energy as heat and thereby cooking the food.

Teaching Tip

Be sure that students understand that longer bonds tend to be weaker. Bond strength is reflected by the amount of energy needed to break a bond, or the bond energy.

Check for Understanding

Answer: Electronegativity still plays a role in covalent bonding. Because the differences in electronegativity between covalently-bonded atoms are much smaller than in other types of bonds, the atoms tend to share the electrons, rather than transfer them from one to the other.

Differentiated Instruction

INCLUSION

Involve kinesthetic learners in a demonstration to better understand the relationship between bonds and energy. Have two students hold hands, imagining that this represents a chemical bond joining two atoms. Now ask another student to "break the bond" by unclasping the hands between the two students. Point out that the student used energy to break the bond. Emphasize that energy is always required to break a chemical bond. Ask students to explain what happens to the energy when a bond forms.

▼ Teach *continued*

TEACH FROM TABLES

FIGURE 2.5 Students can see a clear relationship between bond length and bond strength by plotting a graph with bond length on the *x*-axis and bond energy on the *y*-axis. Even without the graph, they may see that the bond length decreases as the strength of the bond—as represented by bond energy—increases.

Also, students should understand that the bonds, bond lengths, and bond energies in the first three columns of the table correspond to specific diatomic molecules. The bonds listed in the fourth column exist in many different molecules, and their lengths and energies vary from molecule to molecule. The bond lengths and bond energies in the fifth and sixth columns are average values for the bonds specified in the fourth column.

FIGURE 2.5

BOND LENGTHS AND BOND ENERGIES FOR SELECTED COVALENT BONDS

Bond	Average bond length (pm)	Average bond energy (kJ/mol)	Bond	Average bond length (pm)	Average bond energy (kJ/mol)
H—H	75	436	C—C	154	346
F—F	142	159	C—N	147	305
Cl—Cl	199	243	C—O	143	358
Br—Br	229	193	C—H	109	418
I—I	266	151	C—Cl	177	327
H—F	92	569	C—Br	194	285
H—Cl	127	432	N—N	145	163
H—Br	141	366	N—H	101	386
H—I	161	299	O—H	96	459

All individual hydrogen atoms contain a single, unpaired electron in a 1*s* atomic orbital. When two hydrogen atoms form a molecule, they share electrons in a covalent bond. As **Figure 2.6** shows, sharing electrons allows each atom to have the stable electron configuration of helium, $1s^2$. This tendency for atoms to achieve noble-gas configurations by bonding covalently extends beyond the simple case of a hydrogen molecule.

FIGURE 2.6

Bond Length and Stability By sharing electrons in overlapping orbitals, each hydrogen atom in a hydrogen molecule experiences the effect of a stable $1s^2$ configuration.

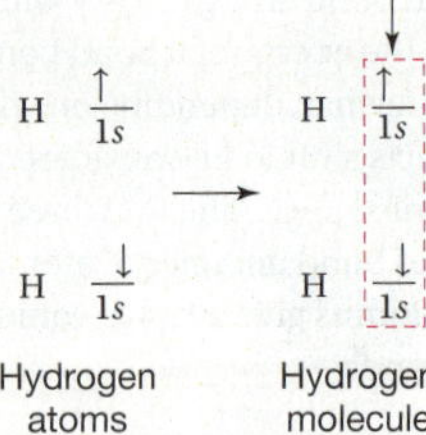

MAIN IDEA

Atoms tend to form bonds to follow the octet rule.

Unlike other atoms, the noble-gas atoms exist independently in nature. They possess a minimum of energy existing on their own because of the special stability of their electron configurations. This stability results from the fact that, with the exception of helium and its two electrons in a completely filled outer shell, the noble-gas atoms' outer *s* and *p* orbitals are completely filled by a total of eight electrons. Other main-group atoms can effectively fill their outermost *s* and *p* orbitals with electrons by sharing electrons through covalent bonding.

Differentiated Instruction

BELOW LEVEL

Have students refer to the classroom's periodic table and examine the electron configurations of the noble gases. Ask them to compare these electron configurations to those of the Group 17 elements. Have students describe the chemical behavior of the halogens using the octet rule. Students should see that the halogens react according to the octet rule to obtain one additional electron. Be sure that students do not develop the misconception that a halogen turns into a noble gas as a result of obtaining one electron. Make the point that only their electron configurations are the same once a halogen has reacted. In other words, the two atoms are *isoelectronic*.

Such bond formation follows the *octet rule:* Chemical compounds tend to form so that each atom, by gaining, losing, or sharing electrons, has an octet of electrons in its highest occupied energy level.

Let's examine how the bonding in a fluorine molecule illustrates the octet rule. An independent fluorine atom has seven electrons in its highest energy level ([He]$2s^22p^5$). Like hydrogen atoms, fluorine atoms bond covalently with each other to form diatomic molecules, F_2. When two fluorine atoms bond, each atom shares one of its valence electrons with its partner. The shared electron pair effectively fills each atom's outermost energy level with an octet of electrons, as illustrated in **Figure 2.7a**. **Figure 2.7b** shows another example of the octet rule, in which the chlorine atom in a molecule of hydrogen chloride, HCl, achieves an outermost octet by sharing an electron pair with an atom of hydrogen.

FIGURE 2.7

Octet Rule

(a) By sharing valence electrons in overlapping orbitals, each atom in a fluorine molecule feels the effect of neon's stable configuration, [He]$2s^22p^6$. **(b)** In a hydrogen chloride molecule, the hydrogen atom effectively fills its $1s$ orbital with two electrons, while the chlorine atom experiences the stability of an outermost octet of electrons.

(a)

F	↑↓ 1s	↑↓ 2s	↑↓ ↑↓ ↑ 2p	→	F	↑↓ 1s	↑↓ 2s	↑↓ ↑↓ ↑ 2p
F	↑↓ 1s	↑↓ 2s	↑↓ ↑↓ ↓ 2p		F	↑↓ 1s	↑↓ 2s	↑↓ ↑↓ ↓ 2p
	Fluorine atoms					Fluorine molecule		

Bonding electron pair in overlapping orbitals

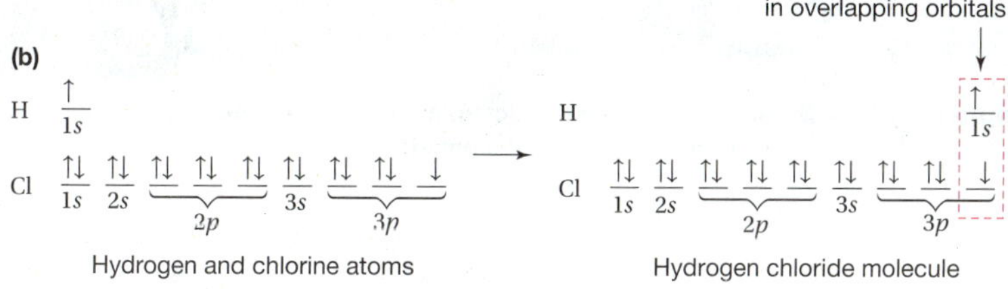

Exceptions to the Octet Rule

Most main-group elements tend to form covalent bonds according to the octet rule. However, there are exceptions. As you have seen, hydrogen forms bonds in which it is surrounded by only two electrons. Boron, B, has just three valence electrons ([He]$2s^22p^1$). Because electron pairs are shared in covalent bonds, boron tends to form bonds in which it is surrounded by six electrons. In boron trifluoride, BF_3, for example, the boron atom is surrounded by its own three valence electrons plus one from each of the three fluorine atoms bonded to it. Other elements can be surrounded by *more* than eight electrons when they combine with the highly electronegative elements fluorine, oxygen, and chlorine. In these cases of *expanded valence*, bonding involves electrons in *d* orbitals as well as in *s* and *p* orbitals. Examples of compounds that have an expanded valence include PCl_5 and SF_6, as shown in **Figure 5.4** (in Section 5).

TEACH FROM VISUALS

FIGURE 2.7 Have students look closely at the hydrogen chloride molecule. Point out that overlapping orbitals can occur between electrons in different energy levels. In this example, an electron from the first energy level of hydrogen forms a bond with an electron in the third energy level of chlorine.

PRE-AP

Point out that BF_3 easily attracts another molecule that has an unbonded electron pair, such as NH_3. The bond formed between these molecules is called a *coordinate covalent bond*. Have students provide other examples of coordinate covalent bonds. Have them draw a dot diagram (Lewis structure) to show how these bonds form. As an introduction to using Lewis structures to determine molecule shape, have students draw Lewis structures to show the expanded valences of PF_5 and SF_6. Students will study molecular geometry later in the chapter.

BELOW LEVEL

Ask students to use **Figure 2.7** as a guide to show how two chlorine atoms form a nonpolar-covalent bond. Students should recognize that two electrons from the same energy level and sublevel (*3p*) are involved in the overlapping orbitals.

▼ Teach *continued*

Classroom Practice

B-1 Write the electron-dot notation for the following elements:

a. phosphorus
b. silicon
c. sulfur
d. chlorine
e. xenon

Answers

a. ·P̈:
b. ·Ṡi·
c. :S̈:
d. :C̈l:
e. :Ẍe:

Teaching Tip

Students may question the value of placing dots to represent the valence electrons of an atom. Point out that electron-dot notations can help them understand how atoms will bond and can be useful in understanding molecular structure, as they will see in the last section of this chapter.

FIGURE 2.8

Writing Electron-Dot Notations To write an element's electron-dot notation, determine the element's number of valence electrons. Then place a corresponding number of dots around the element's symbol, as shown.

Number of valence electrons	Electron-dot notation	Example
1	X·	Na·
2	·X·	·Mg·
3	·Ẋ·	·Ḃ·
4	·Ẋ· (with dot below)	·Ċ· (with dot below)
5	·Ẋ:	·Ṅ:
6	:Ẋ:	:Ȯ:
7	:Ẍ:	:F̈:
8	:Ẍ:	:N̈e:

MAIN IDEA

Dots placed around an element's symbol can represent valence electrons.

Covalent bond formation usually involves only the electrons in an atom's outermost energy levels, or the atom's valence electrons. To keep track of these electrons, it is helpful to use electron-dot notation. **Electron-dot notation** is an electron-configuration notation in which only the valence electrons of an atom of a particular element are shown, indicated by dots placed around the element's symbol. The inner-shell electrons are not shown. For example, the electron-dot notation for a fluorine atom (electron configuration [He]$2s^2 2p^5$) may be written as follows.

In general, an element's number of valence electrons can be determined by adding the superscripts of the element's noble-gas notation. In this book, the electron-dot notations for elements with 1–8 valence electrons are written as shown in **Figure 2.8.**

Electron-Dot Notation

PREMIUM CONTENT

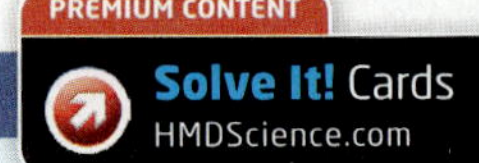

Sample Problem B **a. Write the electron-dot notation for hydrogen.**
b. Write the electron-dot notation for nitrogen.

SOLVE

a. A hydrogen atom has only one occupied energy level, the $n = 1$ level, which contains a single electron. Therefore, the electron-dot notation for hydrogen is written as follows.

H.

b. The group notation for nitrogen's family of elements is ns^2np^3, which indicates that nitrogen has five valence electrons. Therefore, the electron-dot notation for nitrogen is written as follows.

·Ṅ:

MAIN IDEA

Electron-dot notations can represent compounds.

Electron-dot notation can also be used to represent molecules. For example, a hydrogen molecule, H_2, is represented by combining the notations of two individual hydrogen atoms, as follows.

H:H

Problem Solving

DECONSTRUCTING PROBLEMS

When drawing an electron-dot notation, students may look only at the last sublevel. For example, a student may be asked to draw the electron-dot notation for bromine. The electron configuration is written as [Ar]$3d^{10}4s^24p^5$. Some students may then proceed to place five dots around Br. Be sure that students recognize the reason why they should place seven dots around Br.

The pair of dots represents the shared electron pair of the hydrogen-hydrogen covalent bond. For a molecule of fluorine, F_2, the electron-dot notations of two fluorine atoms are combined.

Here, too, the pair of dots between the two symbols represents the shared pair of a covalent bond. In addition, each fluorine atom is surrounded by three pairs of electrons that are not shared in bonds. An *unshared pair*, also called a *lone pair*, is a pair of electrons that is not involved in bonding and that belongs exclusively to one atom.

The pair of dots representing a shared pair of electrons in a covalent bond is often replaced by a long dash. According to this convention, hydrogen and fluorine molecules are represented as follows.

H—H   :F—F:

These representations are all Lewis structures, formulas in which atomic symbols represent nuclei and inner-shell electrons, dot-pairs or dashes between two atomic symbols represent electron pairs in covalent bonds, and dots adjacent to only one atomic symbol represent unshared electrons. It is common to write Lewis structures that show only the electrons that are shared, using dashes to represent the bonds. **A structural formula indicates the kind, number, arrangement, and bonds but not the unshared pairs of the atoms in a molecule.** For example, F—F and H—Cl are structural formulas.

The Lewis structures (and therefore the structural formulas) for many molecules can be drawn if one knows the composition of the molecule and which atoms are bonded to each other. The following sample problem illustrates the basic steps for writing Lewis structures. The molecule described in this problem contains bonds with single, shared electron pairs. **A single covalent bond, or a single bond, is a covalent bond in which one pair of electrons is shared between two atoms.**

Lewis Structures

Sample Problem C **Draw the Lewis structure of iodomethane, CH_3I.**

 **SOLVE**

1. *Determine the type and number of atoms in the molecule.*
   The formula shows one carbon atom, one iodine atom, and three hydrogen atoms.
2. *Write the electron-dot notation for each type of atom in the molecule.*
   Carbon is from Group 14 and has four valence electrons. Iodine is from Group 17 and has seven valence electrons. Hydrogen has one valence electron.

Continued

Classroom Practice

C-1 Draw the Lewis structure for each of the following compounds:

a. H_2O **c.** CH_3OH
b. CH_4 **d.** HCl

Answers

a. H:Ö:H (with two unshared pairs on O)
b. H:C:H with H above and H below C
c. H:C:Ö:H with H above and H below C, two unshared pairs on O
d. H:Cl: with three unshared pairs on Cl

Teaching Tip

Some students might derive Lewis structures more easily by representing the valence electrons from each atom in the molecule or ion with a different symbol. Emphasize, however, that this is only an intermediate representation, and that the other symbols should then be converted to dots. For example,

H×H or H:H

:F:×F× (with × for the second F's electrons) or :F:F:

DECONSTRUCTING PROBLEMS

Emphasize the importance of following the step-by-step instructions in Sample Problem C. For example, ask students what effect removing step 3 of Sample Problem C (on the next page) would have on drawing the Lewis structure for this molecule. Students would have no way of checking whether the number of electrons used in the final step equals the number of electrons that were available. As a result, a student may fail to place the three unshared pairs of electrons around I.

Chemical Bonding 175

▼ Teach continued

Answers

Practice C

1. 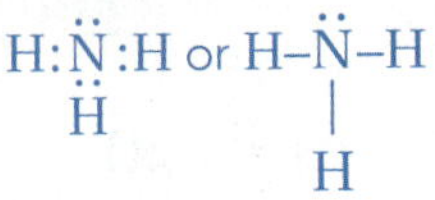 H:N̈:H or H–N̈–H (with H below N)
2.  H:S̈:H or H–S̈–H
3. 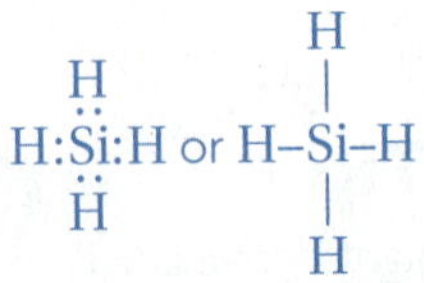 H:Si:H or H–Si–H (with H above and below Si)
4. 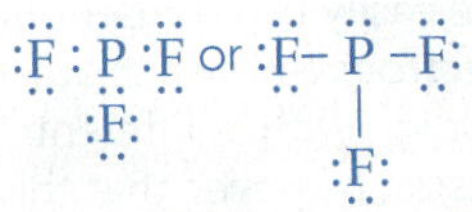 :F̈:P̈:F̈: or :F̈–P̈–F̈: (with :F̈: below P)

Lewis Structures (continued)

3. *Determine the total number of valence electrons available in the atoms to be combined.*

C	$1 \times 4e^- =$	$4e^-$
I	$1 \times 7e^- =$	$7e^-$
3H	$3 \times 1e^- =$	$3e^-$
		$14e^-$

4. *Arrange the atoms to form a skeleton structure for the molecule. If carbon is present, it is the central atom. Otherwise, the least-electronegative atom is central (except for hydrogen, which is never central). Then connect the atoms by electron-pair bonds.*

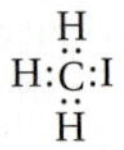

H:C:I (with H above and below C)

5. *Add unshared pairs of electrons to each nonmetal atom (except hydrogen) such that each is surrounded by eight electrons.*

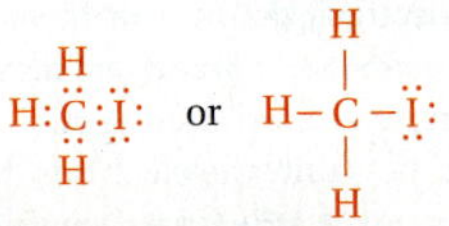

H:C:Ï: or H–C–Ï: (with H above and below C)

6. *Count the electrons in the structure to be sure that the number of valence electrons used equals the number available. Be sure the central atom and other atoms besides hydrogen have an octet.* There are eight electrons in the four covalent bonds and six electrons in the three unshared pairs, giving the correct total of 14 valence electrons.

Practice

1. Draw the Lewis structure for ammonia, NH_3.
2. Draw the Lewis structure for hydrogen sulfide, H_2S.
3. Draw the Lewis structure for silane, SiH_4.
4. Draw the Lewis structure for phosphorus trifluoride, PF_3.

MAIN IDEA

Some atoms can share multiple pairs of electrons.

Atoms of some elements, especially carbon, nitrogen, and oxygen, can share more than one electron pair. A double covalent bond, or simply a *double bond*, is a covalent bond in which two pairs of electrons are shared between two atoms. A double bond is shown either by two side-by-side pairs of dots or by two parallel dashes. All four electrons in a double bond "belong" to both atoms. In ethene, C_2H_4, for example, two electron pairs are simultaneously shared by two carbon atoms.

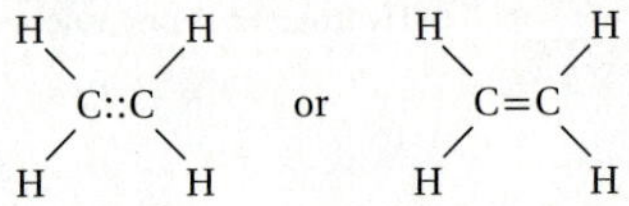

H₂C::CH₂ or H₂C=CH₂ (each carbon bonded to two H)

Differentiated Instruction

INCLUSION

Tactile learners may benefit from creating models to understand how a double bond forms. For example, have students develop a model to show the covalent bonds that form in CO_2. Be sure that they follow the steps in Sample Problem C. Students can use paper circles labeled with the element's symbol to represent the atoms, small candies for electrons, and toothpicks for covalent bonds. The final model should show a double bond between the carbon and each oxygen atom. Each oxygen atom must also have two unshared pairs of electrons. For added enrichment, have students pair up and discuss with their partners how their models demonstrate the octet rule.

A triple covalent bond, or simply a *triple bond,* is a covalent bond in which three pairs of electrons are shared between two atoms. For example, elemental nitrogen, N_2, like hydrogen and the halogens, normally exists as diatomic molecules. In this case, however, each nitrogen atom, which has five valence electrons, acquires three electrons to complete an octet by sharing three pairs of electrons with its partner. This is illustrated in the Lewis structure and the formula structure for N_2, as shown below.

:N:::N: or   :N≡N:

Figure 2.9 represents nitrogen's triple bond through orbital notation. Like the single bonds in hydrogen and halogen molecules, the triple bond in nitrogen molecules is nonpolar.

Carbon forms a number of compounds containing triple bonds. For example, the compound ethyne, C_2H_2, contains a carbon-carbon triple bond.

H:C:::C:H   or   H−C≡C−H

Double and triple bonds are referred to as multiple bonds, or multiple covalent bonds. Double bonds in general have greater bond energies and are shorter than single bonds. Triple bonds are even stronger and shorter. **Figure 2.10** compares average bond lengths and bond energies for some single, double, and triple bonds.

In writing Lewis structures for molecules that contain carbon, nitrogen, or oxygen, one must remember that multiple bonds between pairs of these atoms are possible. (A hydrogen atom, on the other hand, has only one electron and therefore always forms a single covalent bond.) The need for a multiple bond becomes obvious if there are not enough valence electrons to complete octets by adding unshared pairs. Sample Problem D on the next page shows how to deal with this situation.

FIGURE 2.9

Forming Triple Bonds In a molecule of nitrogen, N_2, each nitrogen atom is surrounded by six shared electrons plus one unshared pair of electrons. Thus, each nitrogen atom follows the octet rule in forming a triple covalent bond.

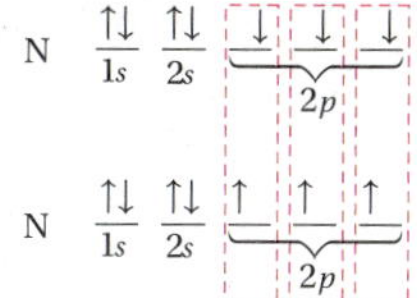

Nitrogen molecule

CHECK FOR UNDERSTANDING

Explain Although silicon is in the same periodic group and shares many properties with carbon, it has a significantly greater bond length. Explain why this would make carbon a better building block than silicon for living organisms.

FIGURE 2.10

BOND LENGTHS AND BOND ENERGIES FOR SINGLE AND MULTIPLE COVALENT BONDS

Bond	Average bond length (pm)	Average bond energy (kJ/mol)	Bond	Average bond length (pm)	Average bond energy (kJ/mol)
C−C	154	346	C−O	143	358
C=C	134	612	C=O	120	732
C≡C	120	835	C≡O	113	1072
C−N	147	305	N−N	145	163
C=N	132	615	N=N	125	418
C≡N	116	887	N≡N	110	945

TEACH FROM TABLES

FIGURE 2.10 Once again, have students observe the relationship between bond length and bond energy. In general, stronger bonds (those with greater bond energies) are shorter bonds.

Teaching Tip

The C=O bond energy in carbon dioxide is 799 kJ/mol, which is much stronger than the average C=O bond energy. However, it is still weaker than a C≡O triple bond.

Check for Understanding

Answer: Since carbon has a shorter bond length, its compounds will tend to be stronger and more stable.

BELOW LEVEL

Have students compare the average bond energies of single, double, and triple bonds between C and O. To help them understand these differences, ask two students to hold one another's hand. Have another two students hold both of their hands together. Ask the class which pair of students would require more energy to separate. Have students imagine what would happen to the energy required if the students were holding three pairs of hands together.

▼ Teach *continued*

Classroom Practice

D-1 Determine the Lewis structure for each of the following molecules:

a. O_2 **c.** C_2H_2

b. C_2H_4

Answers

a. $\ddot{\underset{..}{O}}::\ddot{\underset{..}{O}}$ **c.** H:C:::C:H

b.
```
H  H
¨  ¨
C::C
¨  ¨
H  H
```

ChemisTrivia

Formaldehyde, the molecule mentioned in Sample Problem D, is believed to cause cancer. Because it kills bacteria, formaldehyde was once used to preserve animals in biology labs. Now, however, safer chemicals are used.

Answers

Practice D

1. $\ddot{\underset{..}{O}}=C=\ddot{\underset{..}{O}}$
2. H–C≡N:

Lewis Structures

Sample Problem D **Draw the Lewis structure for methanal, CH_2O, which is also known as formaldehyde.**

SOLVE

1. *Determine the number of atoms of each element present in the molecule.* The formula shows one carbon atom, two hydrogen atoms, and one oxygen atom.
2. *Write the electron-dot notation for each type of atom.* Carbon is from Group 14 and has four valence electrons. Oxygen, which is in Group 16, has six valence electrons. Hydrogen has only one electron.

$\cdot\dot{\underset{\cdot}{C}}\cdot \quad :\dot{\underset{..}{O}}: \quad H\cdot$

3. *Determine the total number of valence electrons available in the atoms to be combined.*

$$\begin{array}{ll} \textbf{C} & \mathbf{1 \times 4}e^- = \mathbf{4}e^- \\ \textbf{O} & \mathbf{1 \times 6}e^- = \mathbf{6}e^- \\ \textbf{2H} & \mathbf{2 \times 1}e^- = \underline{\mathbf{2}e^-} \\ & \qquad\qquad \mathbf{12}e^- \end{array}$$

4. *Arrange the atoms to form a skeleton structure for the molecule, and connect the atoms by electron-pair bonds.*

```
  H
  ¨
H:C:O
  ¨
```

5. *Add unshared pairs of electrons to each nonmetal atom (except hydrogen) such that each is surrounded by eight electrons.*

```
  H
  ¨  ..
H:C:O:
  ¨  ¨
```

6a. *Count the electrons in the Lewis structure to be sure that the number of valence electrons used equals the number available.* The structure above has six electrons in covalent bonds and eight electrons in four lone pairs, for a total of 14 electrons. The structure has two valence electrons too many.

6b. *If too many electrons have been used, subtract one or more lone pairs until the total number of valence electrons is correct. Then move one or more lone electron pairs to existing bonds between non-hydrogen atoms until the outer shells of all atoms are completely filled.* Subtract the lone pair of electrons from the carbon atom. Then move one lone pair of electrons from the oxygen to the bond between carbon and oxygen to form a double bond.

```
  H                H
  ¨  ..            |  ..
H:C::O     or    H−C=O
     ¨                ¨
```

There are eight electrons in covalent bonds and four electrons in lone pairs, for a total of 12 valence electrons.

Practice

1. Draw the Lewis structure for carbon dioxide, CO_2.
2. Draw the Lewis structure for hydrogen cyanide, which contains one hydrogen atom, one carbon atom, and one nitrogen atom.

Problem Solving

DECONSTRUCTING PROBLEMS

Point out that the first five steps of Sample Problems C and D are the same. However, in Sample Problem D, the sixth and final step has been divided into two smaller steps indicated by 6a and 6b. Have students explain why this division was necessary to arrive at the correct Lewis structure for the molecule. Students should recognize that if too many electrons have been used in step 6, then steps 6a and 6b are necessary, indicating that multiple bonds are likely needed.

MAIN IDEA

Resonance structures show hybrid bonds.

Some molecules and ions cannot be represented adequately by a single Lewis structure. One such molecule is ozone, O_3, which can be represented by either of the following Lewis structures.

$$\ddot{\text{O}}=\ddot{\text{O}}-\ddot{\text{O}}: \quad \text{or} \quad :\ddot{\text{O}}-\ddot{\text{O}}=\ddot{\text{O}}$$

Notice that each structure indicates that the ozone molecule has two types of O—O bonds, one single and one double. Chemists once speculated that ozone split its time existing as one of these two structures, constantly alternating, or "resonating," from one to the other. Experiments, however, revealed that the oxygen-oxygen bonds in ozone are identical. Therefore, scientists now say that ozone has a single structure that is the average of these two structures. Together the structures are referred to as resonance structures or resonance hybrids. **Resonance** refers to bonding in molecules or ions that cannot be correctly represented by a single Lewis structure. To indicate resonance, a double-headed arrow is placed between a molecule's resonance structures.

$$\ddot{\text{O}}=\ddot{\text{O}}-\ddot{\text{O}}: \longleftrightarrow :\ddot{\text{O}}-\ddot{\text{O}}=\ddot{\text{O}}$$

MAIN IDEA

Some compounds are networks of bonded atoms.

The covalent compounds that you have read about so far consist of many identical molecules held together by forces acting between the molecules. (You will read more about these intermolecular forces in Section 5.) There are many covalently bonded compounds that do not contain individual molecules, but instead can be pictured as continuous, three-dimensional networks of bonded atoms. You will read more about covalently bonded networks in the chapter "Chemical Formulas and Chemical Compounds."

SECTION 2 FORMATIVE ASSESSMENT

Reviewing Main Ideas

1. Define the following:
   a. bond length
   b. bond energy
2. State the octet rule.
3. How many pairs of electrons are shared in the following types of covalent bonds?
   a. a single bond
   b. a double bond
   c. a triple bond
4. Draw the Lewis structures for the following molecules:
   a. IBr
   b. CH_3Br
   c. C_2HCl
   d. $SiCl_4$
   e. OF_2

Critical Thinking

5. **APPLYING MODELS** Compare the molecules H_2NNH_2 and HNNH. Which molecule has the stronger N—N bond?

Teaching Tip

Lewis structures assume that electrons are found only between the two atoms in a bond. However, sometimes electrons are *delocalized*, which means that they are distributed over three or more atoms. In such cases, Lewis structures do not clearly model the location of the electrons in the bond unless resonance structures are used.

ChemisTrivia

Diamond, the hardest material known, is actually made of many carbon atoms that are bonded together with single bonds. A diamond crystal is an example of a covalent network.

Assess and Reteach

Assess Use the Formative Assessment on this page to evaluate student mastery of the section.

Reteach For students who need additional instruction, download the Section Study Guide.

Response to Intervention To reassess students' mastery, use the Section Quiz, available to print or to take directly online at **HMDScience.com**.

Answers to Section Assessment

1. a. the distance at which two covalently bonded atoms minimize their potential energy
   b. the energy required to break a chemical bond and form neutral, isolated atoms (in the gas phase)
2. Chemical compounds tend to form so that each atom gains, loses, or shares electrons until an octet of electrons exists in its highest occupied energy level.
3. a. one
   b. two
   c. three
4. a. :I:Br:
   b. 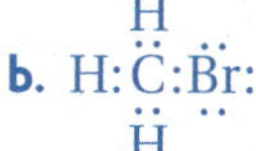
   c. H:C:::C:Cl
   d. :Cl:Si:Cl: (with Cl above and below Si)
   e. :F:O:F:
5. Draw the Lewis structures. HNNH has a double N—N bond, and H_2NNH_2 has a single N—N bond. Therefore, HNNH has the stronger N—N bond.

SECTION 3

▼ Plan and Prepare

Objectives

Upon completion of this section, students should be able to do the following:

- Compare and contrast a chemical formula for a molecular compound with one for an ionic compound.
- Discuss the arrangements of ions in crystals.
- Define *lattice energy* and explain its significance.
- List and compare the distinctive properties of ionic compounds and molecular compounds.
- Draw the Lewis structure for a polyatomic ion given the identity of the atoms combined and other appropriate information.

Classroom Catalyst

Use plastic, interlocking building blocks to demonstrate the difference between ionic and covalent bonding. Assemble a number of blocks so that all sides of the object created are flush. This is a model of a molecule—the atoms are bonded to create an individual unit capable of existing on its own. Assemble a number of blocks so that pieces of the various blocks are jutting out of the sides of the object created. This represents a small portion of the ionic arrangement within an ionic compound. The pieces of blocks jutting out represent cations and anions, which attract more ions (more blocks) to create a large array of packed ions. The result is a huge aggregate of ions that have minimized their potential energy through electrical attraction (as opposed to electron sharing).

▼ Teach

Critical Thinking

Answer: Most ionic compounds exist as crystalline solids.

SECTION 3

Main Ideas

- Ionic bonds form from attractions between positive and negative ions.
- Differences in attraction strength give ionic and molecular compounds different properties.
- Multiple atoms can bond covalently to form a single ion.

Ionic Bonding and Ionic Compounds

Key Terms

ionic compound
formula unit
lattice energy
polyatomic ion

Most of the rocks and minerals that make up Earth's crust consist of positive and negative ions held together by ionic bonding. A familiar example of an ionically bonded compound is sodium chloride, or common table salt, which is found in nature as rock salt. A sodium ion, Na^+, has a charge of 1+. A chloride ion, Cl^-, has a charge of 1−. There is an electrical force of attraction between oppositely charged ions. In sodium chloride, these ions combine in a one-to-one ratio—Na^+Cl^-—so that each positive charge is balanced by a negative charge. The chemical formula for sodium chloride is usually written simply as NaCl.

An ionic compound is composed of positive and negative ions that are combined so that the numbers of positive and negative charges are equal. Most ionic compounds exist as crystalline solids (see **Figure 3.1**). A crystal of any ionic compound is a three-dimensional network of positive and negative ions mutually attracted to one another. As a result, in contrast to a molecular compound, an ionic compound is not composed of independent, neutral units that can be isolated and examined. The chemical formula of an ionic compound merely represents the simplest ratio of the compound's combined ions that gives electrical neutrality.

The chemical formula of an ionic compound shows the ratio of the ions present in a sample of any size. **A formula unit is the simplest collection of atoms from which an ionic compound's formula can be written.** For example, one formula unit of sodium chloride, NaCl, is one sodium cation plus one chloride anion. (In the naming of a monatomic anion, the ending of the element's name becomes *-ide*.)

The ratio of ions in a formula unit depends on the charges of the ions combined. For example, to achieve electrical neutrality in the ionic compound calcium fluoride, two fluoride anions, F^-, each with a charge of 1−, must balance the 2+ charge of each calcium cation, Ca^{2+}. Therefore, the formula of calcium fluoride is CaF_2.

FIGURE 3.1

Ionic Compounds Sodium chloride (common table salt) is an ionic compound.

CRITICAL THINKING
Explain How is the structure of sodium chloride typical of ionic compounds?

MAIN IDEA

Ionic bonds form from attractions between positive and negative ions.

Electron-dot notation can be used to demonstrate the changes that take place in ionic bonding. Ionic compounds do not ordinarily form by the combination of isolated ions, but consider for a moment a sodium atom and a chlorine atom approaching each other. The two atoms are neutral and have one and seven valence electrons, respectively.

$Na\cdot$	$:\ddot{\underset{\cdot\cdot}{Cl}}\cdot$
Sodium atom	Chlorine atom

We have already seen that atoms of sodium and the other alkali metals readily lose one electron to form cations. And we have seen that atoms of chlorine and the other halogens readily gain one electron to form anions.

Differentiated Instruction

PRE-AP

Have students write the formula units for the following ionic compounds: calcium oxide (CaO), calcium chloride ($CaCl_2$), potassium chloride (KCl), and potassium oxide (K_2O). Tell students that they can check the electron configurations of these elements on a periodic table. Have students explain why each of these ionic compounds is electrically neutral.

The combination of sodium and chlorine atoms to produce one formula unit of sodium chloride can thus be represented as follows.

$$\underset{\text{Sodium atom}}{\text{Na}\cdot} + \underset{\text{Chlorine atom}}{:\ddot{\underset{..}{\text{Cl}}}\cdot} \longrightarrow \underset{\text{Sodium cation}}{\text{Na}^+} + \underset{\text{Chloride anion}}{:\ddot{\underset{..}{\text{Cl}}}:^-}$$

The transfer of an electron from the sodium atom to the chlorine atom transforms each atom into an ion with a noble-gas configuration. In the combination of calcium with fluorine, two fluorine atoms are needed to accept the two valence electrons given up by one calcium atom.

$$\underset{\text{Calcium atom}}{\cdot\text{Ca}\cdot} + \underbrace{:\ddot{\underset{..}{\text{F}}}\cdot + :\ddot{\underset{..}{\text{F}}}\cdot}_{\text{Fluorine atoms}} \longrightarrow \underset{\text{Calcium cation}}{\text{Ca}^{2+}} + \underbrace{:\ddot{\underset{..}{\text{F}}}:^- + :\ddot{\underset{..}{\text{F}}}:^-}_{\text{Fluoride anions}}$$

Characteristics of Ionic Bonding

Recall that nature favors arrangements in which potential energy is minimized. In an ionic crystal, ions minimize their potential energy by combining in an orderly arrangement known as a *crystal lattice* (see **Figure 3.2**). The attractive forces at work within an ionic crystal include those between oppositely charged ions and those between the nuclei and electrons of adjacent ions. The repulsive forces include those between like-charged ions and those between electrons of adjacent ions. The distances between ions and their arrangement in a crystal represent a balance among all these forces. Sodium chloride's crystal structure is shown in **Figure 3.3** below.

FIGURE 3.2

Ions and Electrical Forces The ions in an ionic compound lower their potential energy by forming an orderly, three-dimensional array in which the positive and negative charges are balanced. The electrical forces of attraction between oppositely charged ions extend over long distances, causing a large decrease in potential energy.

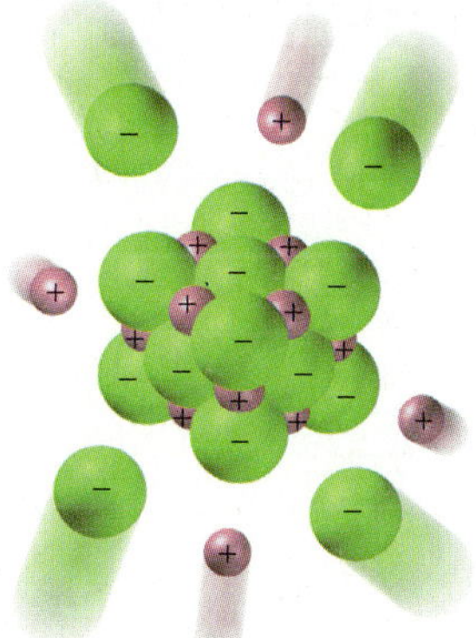

FIGURE 3.3

Crystal Structure of NaCl Two models of the crystal structure of sodium chloride are shown.

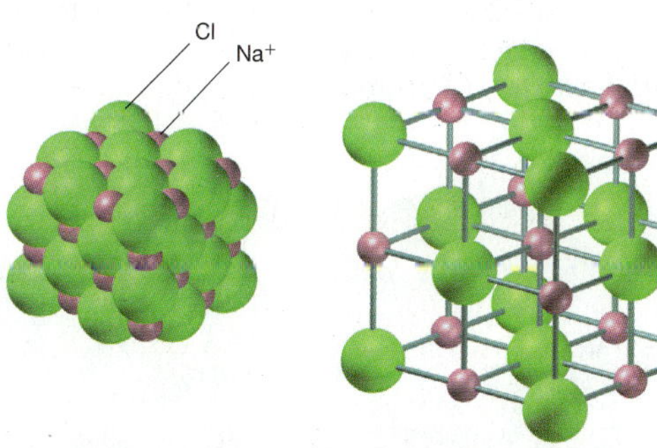

(a) To illustrate the ions' actual arrangement, the sodium and chloride ions are shown with their electron clouds just touching.

(b) In an expanded view, the distances between ions have been exaggerated in order to clarify the positioning of the ions in the structure.

TEACH FROM VISUALS

FIGURE 3.2 Emphasize that an ion in an ionic crystal is surrounded by ions of opposite charge. It is impossible to say that an ion "belongs" more to one of its neighbors than it does to another. The models of sodium chloride in **Figure 3.3** below and **Figure 3.4** on the next page help illustrate this.

Misconception Alert!

Remind students that the chemical formulas for ionic compounds represent the simplest formula of the compound, as opposed to the formulas for molecules, which represent separate molecules that are each a discrete group of atoms.

READING TOOLKIT

INTERPRETING VOCABULARY Have students carefully read the equation showing how calcium and fluorine form an ionic bond. Ask students to identify the terms they have learned that are related to this equation. Possible answers include valence electron, Lewis structure, cation, anion, ionic bond, and chemical reaction.

BELOW LEVEL

Be sure students do not think that a 1:1 ratio between cation and anion can be found only when each has a single charge, either 1+ or 1−. Have students draw Lewis structures for magnesium (Mg) and sulfur (S). Then have students follow the format shown in the text for calcium and fluorine to indicate how magnesium and sulfur form an ionic bond. Students should recognize that a cation with a 2+ charge can form an ionic bond with an anion in a 1:1 ratio. Point out that this results in electrical neutrality.

▼ Teach continued

TEACH FROM VISUALS

FIGURE 3.4 Have students look at the portion of sodium chloride's crystal arrangement from the perspective of the chloride ion, which is surrounded by six sodium ions. Then have them consider the perspective of a sodium ion, which is surrounded by six chloride ions. Ask students to deduce the ratio of sodium ions to chloride ions in sodium chloride. one-to-one

Teaching Tip

Students are often confused about the difference in signs of bond energies **(Figure 2.10)** and lattice energies **(Figure 3.6).** The lattice energy describes the energies associated with the *formation* of bonds, whereas the bond energy describes the energies associated with the *breaking* of bonds. The bonded atoms are *more stable* than the separate ones. The larger the *magnitude* of the lattice energy or the bond energy, the more stable the bonding.

FIGURE 3.4

Crystal Structure of NaCl The figure shows the ions that most closely surround a chloride anion and a sodium cation within the crystal structure of NaCl.

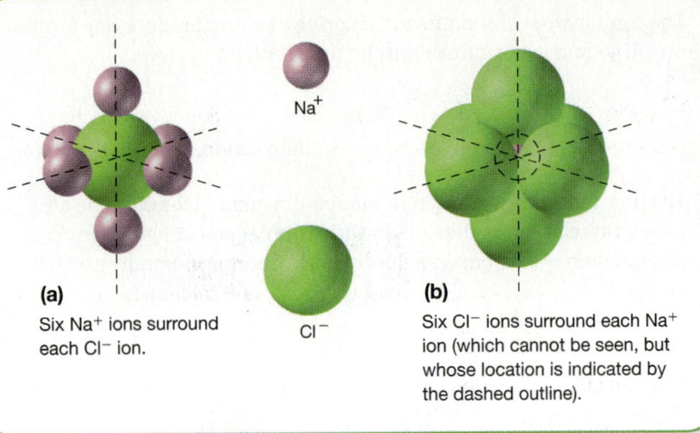

Figure 3.4 shows the crystal structure of sodium chloride in greater detail. Within the arrangement, each sodium cation is surrounded by six chloride anions. At the same time, each chloride anion is surrounded by six sodium cations. Attraction between the adjacent, oppositely charged ions is much stronger than repulsion by other ions of the same charge, which are farther away.

The three-dimensional arrangements of ions and the strengths of attraction between them vary with the sizes and charges of the ions and the numbers of ions of different charges. For example, in calcium fluoride, there are two anions for each cation. Each calcium cation is surrounded by eight fluoride anions. At the same time, each fluoride ion is surrounded by four calcium cations, as shown in **Figure 3.5.**

To compare bond strengths in ionic compounds, chemists compare the amounts of energy released when separated ions in a gas come together to form a crystalline solid. **Lattice energy** is the energy released when one mole of an ionic crystalline compound is formed from gaseous ions. Lattice energy values for a few common ionic compounds are shown in **Figure 3.6** (on the next page). The negative energy values indicate that energy is *released* when the crystals are formed.

FIGURE 3.5

Crystal Structure of CaF_2 In the crystal structure of calcium fluoride, CaF_2, each calcium cation is surrounded by eight fluoride anions, and each fluoride ion is surrounded by four calcium cations. This is the closest possible packing of the ions in which the positive and negative charges are balanced.

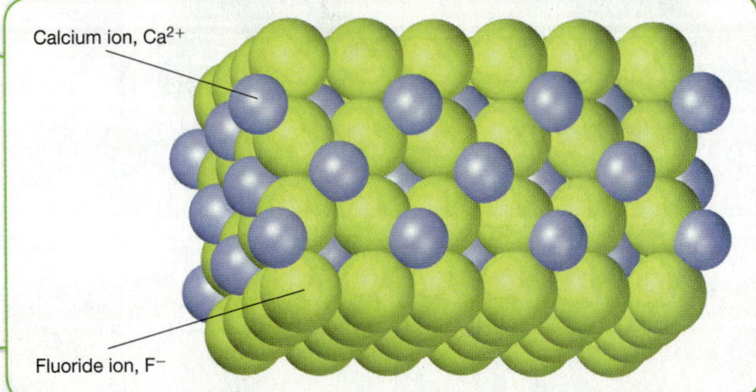

Differentiated Instruction

PRE-AP

The formation of an ionic compound involves both endothermic and exothermic processes. For example, removing an electron is an endothermic process (ionization energy). In contrast, the formation of a crystal lattice is an exothermic process. Several lattice energies are listed in **Figure 3.6** on the next page. Have students research the steps in the formation of an ionic bond and describe the energy changes that occur at each step. Suggest that they provide quantitative information about a specific ionic compound.

MAIN IDEA

Differences in attraction strength give ionic and molecular compounds different properties.

The force that holds ions together in ionic compounds is a very strong overall attraction between positive and negative charges. In a molecular compound, the covalent bonds of the atoms making up each molecule are also strong. But the forces of attraction *between* molecules are much weaker than the forces among formula units in ionic bonding. This difference in the strength of attraction between the basic units of molecular and ionic compounds gives rise to different properties in the two types of compounds.

The melting point, boiling point, and hardness of a compound depend on how strongly its basic units are attracted to each other. Because the forces of attraction between individual molecules are not very strong, many molecular compounds melt at low temperatures. In fact, many molecular compounds are already completely gaseous at room temperature. In contrast, the ions in ionic compounds are held together by strong attractive forces, so ionic compounds generally have higher melting and boiling points than do molecular compounds.

Ionic compounds are hard but brittle. Why? In an ionic crystal, even a slight shift of one row of ions relative to another causes a large buildup of repulsive forces, as shown in **Figure 3.7**. These forces make it difficult for one layer to move relative to another, causing ionic compounds to be hard. If one layer is moved, however, the repulsive forces make the layers part completely, causing ionic compounds to be brittle.

In the solid state, the ions cannot move, so the compounds are not electrical conductors. In the molten state, ionic compounds are electrical conductors because the ions can move freely to carry electrical current. Many ionic compounds can dissolve in water. When they dissolve, their ions separate from each other and become surrounded by water molecules. These ions are free to move through the solution, so such solutions are electrical conductors. Other ionic compounds do not dissolve in water, however, because the attractions between the water molecules and the ions cannot overcome the attractions between the ions.

FIGURE 3.6

LATTICE ENERGIES OF SOME COMMON IONIC COMPOUNDS

Compound	Lattice energy (kJ/mol)
NaCl	−787.5
NaBr	−751.4
CaF_2	−2634.7
LiCl	−861.3
LiF	−1032
MgO	−3760
KCl	−715

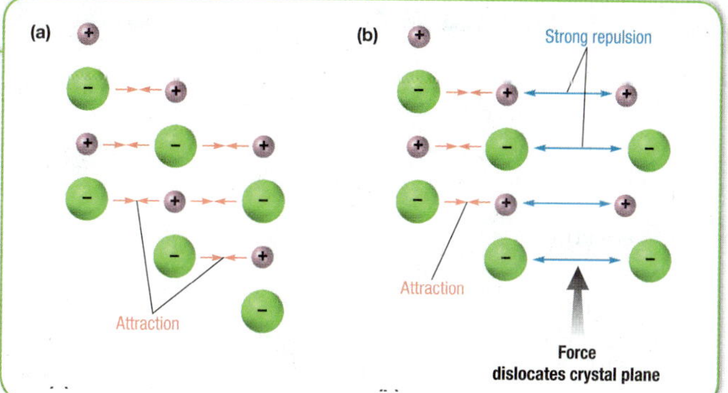

FIGURE 3.7

Ionic Properties **(a)** The attraction between positive and negative ions in a crystalline ionic compound causes layers of ions to resist motion.
(b) When struck with sufficient force, the layers shift so that ions of the same charge approach each other, causing repulsion. As a result, the crystal shatters along the planes.

Teaching Tip

Lattice energies are listed as negative values to indicate that energy is given off when the gaseous ions come together to form the ionic crystal.

TEACH FROM TABLES

FIGURE 3.6 The lattice energy must be overcome in order for an ionic compound to dissolve in water. Have students form a hypothesis about which two ionic compounds listed in the table are the least soluble in water. MgO and CaF_2

READING TOOLKIT

COMPARING AND CONTRASTING Have students use the paragraphs on this page as a starting point for a chart comparing and contrasting covalent and ionic bonding. Have students reread Sections 1, 2, and 3 to help them complete their charts. Suggest that they incorporate the highlighted terms in these sections as well as any other relevant information.

BELOW LEVEL

Ask students to diagram the differences in the arrangement of particles in a substance in the solid, liquid, and gas states. By doing so, students should more easily recognize that energy is required to move the particles apart as a solid turns into a liquid and then into a gas. The more strongly the particles are attracted to one another, the more energy is required to move them apart. As a result, ionic compounds have higher melting points and boiling points than covalent compounds.

▼ Teach *continued*

Misconception Alert!

Many students forget that although polyatomic ions are involved in ionic bonding, the ions themselves are held together by covalent bonding. For example, the atoms in the ammonium *ion* are held together by covalent bonding, but ammonium ions and chloride ions are held together by ionic bonding to form the *compound* ammonium chloride. Therefore, we call ammonium chloride an ionic compound.

Check for Understanding

Answer: It is necessary to add or subtract electrons to account for electrons lost or gained when the ion formed.

▼ Assess and Reteach

Assess Use the Formative Assessment on this page to evaluate student mastery of the section.

Reteach For students who need additional instruction, download the Section Study Guide.

Response to Intervention To reassess students' mastery, use the Section Quiz, available to print or to take directly online at **HMDScience.com**.

MAIN IDEA

Multiple atoms can bond covalently to form a single ion.

Certain atoms bond covalently with each other to form a group of atoms that has both molecular and ionic characteristics. **A charged group of covalently bonded atoms is known as a polyatomic ion.** Polyatomic ions combine with ions of opposite charge to form ionic compounds. The charge of a polyatomic ion results from an excess of electrons (negative charge) or a shortage of electrons (positive charge). For example, an ammonium ion, a common positively charged polyatomic ion, contains one nitrogen atom and four hydrogen atoms and has a single positive charge. Its formula is NH_4^+, sometimes written as $[NH_4]^+$ to show that the group of atoms *as a whole* has a charge of 1+. The seven protons in the nitrogen atom plus the four protons in the four hydrogen atoms give the ammonium ion a total positive charge of 11+. An independent nitrogen atom has seven electrons, and four independent hydrogen atoms have a total of four electrons. When these atoms combine to form an ammonium ion, one of their electrons is lost, giving the polyatomic ion a total negative charge of 10−.

CHECK FOR UNDERSTANDING
Why is it necessary to add or subtract electrons from the total number of valence electrons for polyatomic ions?

Lewis structures for the ammonium ion and some common negative polyatomic ions—the nitrate, sulfate, and phosphate ions—are shown below. To find the Lewis structure for a polyatomic ion, follow the steps of Sample Problem D, with the following exception. If the ion is negatively charged, add to the total number of valence electrons a number of electrons corresponding to the ion's negative charge. If the ion is positively charged, subtract from the total number of valence electrons a number of electrons corresponding to the ion's positive charge.

$\left[\begin{array}{c} H \\ H:\ddot{N}:H \\ H \end{array}\right]^+$ $\left[\begin{array}{c} :\ddot{O}: \\ \ddot{N}::\ddot{O} \\ :\ddot{O}: \end{array}\right]^-$ $\left[\begin{array}{c} :\ddot{O}: \\ :\ddot{O}:\ddot{S}:\ddot{O}: \\ :\ddot{O}: \end{array}\right]^{2-}$ $\left[\begin{array}{c} :\ddot{O}: \\ :\ddot{O}:\ddot{P}:\ddot{O}: \\ :\ddot{O}: \end{array}\right]^{3-}$

Ammonium ion Nitrate ion Sulfate ion Phosphate ion

SECTION 3 FORMATIVE ASSESSMENT

Reviewing Main Ideas

1. Give two examples of an ionic compound.
2. Use electron-dot notation to demonstrate the formation of ionic compounds involving the following:
   a. Li and Cl
   b. Ca and I
3. Distinguish between ionic and molecular compounds in terms of the basic units that make up each.
4. Compound B has lower melting and boiling points than compound A. At the same temperature, compound B vaporizes faster than compound A. If one of these compounds is ionic and the other is molecular, which would you expect to be molecular? ionic? Explain your reasoning.

Critical Thinking

5. **ANALYZING DATA** The melting points for the compounds Li_2S, Rb_2S, and K_2S are 900°C, 530°C, and 840°C, respectively. List these three compounds in order of increasing lattice energy.

Answers to Section Assessment

1. Two possible examples are sodium chloride, NaCl, and magnesium chloride, $MgCl_2$.
2. a. $Li\cdot + :\ddot{Cl}: \longrightarrow Li^+ + :\ddot{Cl}:^-$ (LiCl)
   b. $Ca\cdot + :\ddot{I}: + :\ddot{I}: \longrightarrow Ca^{2+} + :\ddot{I}:^- + :\ddot{I}:^-$ (CaI_2)
3. Ionic compounds consist of positive and negative ions bound together by electrical attraction. Molecular compounds are groups of atoms held together by covalent bonding, or the sharing of electrons.
4. Compound B is probably a molecular substance; compound A is probably ionic. The intermolecular attractions that hold molecules together are weaker than ionic attraction, resulting in lower melting and boiling points in molecular substances.
5. Rb_2S, K_2S, Li_2S

Metallic Bonding

SECTION 4

Main Ideas

Metal electrons move freely in empty, overlapping orbitals.

Key Terms
metallic bonding
malleability
ductility

Chemical bonding is different in metals than it is in ionic, molecular, or covalent-network compounds. This difference is reflected in the unique properties of metals. They are excellent electrical conductors in the solid state—much better conductors than even molten ionic compounds. This property is due to the highly mobile valence electrons of the atoms that make up a metal. Such mobility is not possible in molecular compounds, in which valence electrons are localized in electron-pair bonds between neutral atoms. Nor is it possible in solid ionic compounds, in which electrons are bound to individual ions that are held in place in crystal structures.

MAIN IDEA

Metal electrons move freely in empty, overlapping orbitals.

The highest energy levels of most metal atoms are occupied by very few electrons. In *s*-block metals, for example, one or two valence electrons occupy the outermost orbital, and all three outermost *p* orbitals, which can hold a total of six electrons, are vacant. In addition to completely vacant outer *p* orbitals, *d*-block metals also possess many vacant *d* orbitals in the energy level just below their highest energy level.

Within a metal, the vacant orbitals in the atoms' outer energy levels overlap. This overlapping of orbitals allows the outer electrons of the atoms to roam freely throughout the entire metal. The electrons are *delocalized,* which means that they do not belong to any one atom but move freely about the metal's network of empty atomic orbitals. These mobile electrons form a *sea of electrons* around the metal atoms, which are packed together in a crystal lattice (see **Figure 4.1**). The chemical bonding that results from the attraction between metal atoms and the surrounding sea of electrons is called **metallic bonding.**

Metallic Properties

The freedom of electrons to move in a network of metal atoms accounts for the high electrical and thermal conductivity characteristic of all metals. In addition, metals are both strong absorbers and reflectors of light. Because they contain many orbitals separated by extremely small energy differences, metals can absorb a wide range of light frequencies. This absorption of light results in the excitation of the metal atoms' electrons to higher energy levels. However, in metals the electrons immediately fall back down to lower levels, emitting energy in the form of light at a frequency similar to the absorbed frequency. This re-radiated (or reflected) light is responsible for the metallic appearance or luster of metal surfaces.

FIGURE 4.1

Crystal Structure of Solid Sodium The model shows a portion of the crystal structure of solid sodium. The atoms are arranged so that each sodium atom is surrounded by eight other sodium atoms. The atoms are relatively fixed in position, while the electrons are free to move throughout the crystal, forming an electron sea.

Differentiated Instruction

ENGLISH LEARNERS

Have students copy the crystal structure shown in **Figure 4.1** on a piece of paper. Then ask them to add the sea of electrons to the crystal structure. Be sure that students understand that their drawings must show how electrons can freely move about the metal atoms. One way would be to draw a squiggly line that connects the outer portions of all the atoms.

SECTION 4

Plan and Prepare

Objectives

Upon completion of this section, students should be able to do the following:

- Describe the electron-sea model of metallic bonding, and explain why metals are good electrical conductors.
- Explain why metal surfaces are shiny.
- Explain why metals are malleable and ductile but ionic-crystalline compounds are not.

Classroom Catalyst

Place a sample of sodium chloride or magnesium chloride and a sample of mossy zinc on the tabletop. Hit both with a hammer. (Use eye protection, and make sure students are at a sufficient distance from the samples to avoid the possibility of salt fragments getting in their eyes. You may want to put the salt in a plastic bag before you hit it.) The salt is brittle and shatters. The zinc will just flatten, because it is malleable. The malleability of metal is a property that results from metallic bonding.

Teach

Teaching Tip

Because electrons are delocalized and mobile, they can move from the region around one nucleus to the region around another. This allows for the conductivity of heat and electricity.

▼ Teach *continued*

Analogy

Metallically bonded atoms can be compared to ping-pong balls floating on the surface of a swimming pool, which represents the electron sea. In the same way that the ping-pong balls can move freely relative to one another on the surface of the water, the nuclei of metals can move freely relative to one another in all directions in the electron sea. Two characteristic properties of metals—malleability and ductility—are a result of this arrangement.

TEACH FROM TABLES

FIGURE 4.3 Have students describe what happens to the enthalpies of vaporization as they move across a period and explain what this means in terms of bond strength. Students should relate the increased enthalpy of vaporization to stronger metallic bonds.

▼ Assess and Reteach

Assess Use the Formative Assessment on this page to evaluate student mastery of the section.

Reteach For students who need additional instruction, download the Section Study Guide.

Response to Intervention To reassess students' mastery, use the Section Quiz, available to print or to take directly online at **HMDScience.com**.

FIGURE 4.2

Shaping Metals Unlike ionic crystalline compounds, most metals are malleable. This property allows iron, for example, to be shaped into useful tools.

Most metals are also easy to form into desired shapes. Two important properties related to this characteristic are malleability and ductility (see **Figure 4.2**). **Malleability** is the ability of a substance to be hammered or beaten into thin sheets. **Ductility** is the ability of a substance to be drawn, pulled, or extruded through a small opening to produce a wire. The malleability and ductility of metals are possible because metallic bonding is the same in all directions throughout the solid. When struck, one plane of atoms in a metal can slide past another without encountering resistance or breaking bonds. By contrast, recall from Section 3 that shifting the layers of an ionic crystal causes the bonds to break and the crystal to shatter.

Metallic Bond Strength

Metallic bond strength varies with the nuclear charge of the metal atoms and the number of electrons in the metal's electron sea. Both of these factors are reflected in a metal's *enthalpy of vaporization*. The amount of energy as heat required to vaporize the metal is a measure of the strength of the bonds that hold the metal together. The enthalpy of vaporization is defined as the amount of energy absorbed as heat when a specified amount of a substance vaporizes at constant pressure. Some enthalpies of vaporization for metals are given in **Figure 4.3**.

FIGURE 4.3

ENTHALPIES OF VAPORIZATION OF SOME METALS (kJ/mol)

Period	Element		
Second	Li 147	Be 297	
Third	Na 97	Mg 128	Al 294
Fourth	K 77	Ca 155	Sc 333
Fifth	Rb 76	Sr 137	Y 365
Sixth	Cs 64	Ba 140	La 402

SECTION 4 FORMATIVE ASSESSMENT

Reviewing Main Ideas

1. Describe the electron-sea model of metallic bonding.
2. What is the relationship between metallic bond strength and enthalpy of vaporization?
3. Explain why most metals are malleable and ductile but ionic crystals are not.

Critical Thinking

4. **ORGANIZING IDEAS** Explain why metals are good electrical conductors.

186 Chapter 6

Answers to Section Assessment

1. Metallic bonding is generally viewed as the result of the mutual sharing of many electrons by many atoms. Each atom contributes its valence electrons to a region surrounding the atoms. These electrons are then free to move about the mostly vacant outer orbitals of all the metal atoms. The mobile electrons are often referred to as an *electron sea*.
2. In general, the higher the enthalpy of vaporization, the stronger the metallic bonding.
3. Metallic bonding is not directional but is uniform throughout the solid. One group of atoms can slide past another group of atoms amid the electron sea without breaking any attractions. Ionic crystals are held together by strong electrical attraction between oppositely charged ions. Moving one plane of ions relative to another requires breaking this attraction.
4. A metal is a good electrical conductor because its valence electrons are delocalized and move freely among the metal's network of empty valence orbitals. Therefore, the electrons can move from one end of the metal to the other end; that is, the metal conducts electricity.

Molecular Geometry

SECTION 5

Main Ideas

- Negative particles repel and move away from each other.
- Multiple orbitals can combine to form hybrid orbitals.
- Weak forces exist between molecules.

Key Terms

VSEPR theory	hybrid orbitals	hydrogen bonding
hybridization	dipole	London dispersion forces

The properties of molecules depend not only on the bonding of atoms but also on molecular geometry—the three-dimensional arrangement of a molecule's atoms in space. The polarity of each bond, along with the geometry of the molecule, determines *molecular polarity*, or the uneven distribution of molecular charge. As you will read, molecular polarity strongly influences the forces that act *between* molecules in liquids and solids.

A chemical formula reveals little information about a molecule's geometry. After performing many tests designed to reveal the shapes of various molecules, chemists developed two different, equally successful theories to explain certain aspects of their findings. One theory accounts for molecular bond angles. The other is used to describe the orbitals that contain the valence electrons of a molecule's atoms.

MAIN IDEA

Negative particles repel and move away from each other.

As shown in **Figure 5.1**, diatomic molecules, like those of hydrogen, H_2, and hydrogen chloride, HCl, must be linear because they consist of only two atoms. To predict the geometries of more-complicated molecules, one must consider the locations of all electron pairs surrounding the bonded atoms. This is the basis of VSEPR theory.

The abbreviation VSEPR stands for "valence-shell, electron-pair repulsion," referring to the repulsion between pairs of valence electrons of the atoms in a molecule. **VSEPR theory** states that repulsion between the sets of valence-level electrons surrounding an atom causes these sets to be oriented as far apart as possible. How does the assumption that electrons in molecules repel each other account for molecular shapes? For now, let us consider only molecules with no unshared valence electron pairs on the central atom.

Let's examine the simple molecule BeF_2. The beryllium atom forms a covalent bond with each fluorine atom and does not follow the octet rule. It is surrounded by only the two electron pairs that it shares with the fluorine atoms.

$$:\ddot{\underset{..}{F}}:Be:\ddot{\underset{..}{F}}:$$

According to VSEPR theory, the shared pairs will be as far away from each other as possible. As shown in **Figure 5.2a** on the next page, the distance between electron pairs is maximized if the bonds to fluorine are on opposite sides of the beryllium atom, 180° apart. Thus, all three atoms lie on a straight line. The molecule is linear.

FIGURE 5.1

Linear Molecules Ball-and-stick models illustrate the linearity of diatomic molecules.

(a) Hydrogen, H_2

(a) A hydrogen molecule is represented by two identical balls (the hydrogen atoms) joined by a solid bar (the covalent bond).

(b) Hydrogen chloride, HCl

(b) A hydrogen chloride molecule is composed of dissimilar atoms, but it is still linear.

Differentiated Instruction

ENGLISH LEARNERS

Be sure that students understand the difference between shared and unshared pairs of electrons. Have them draw the Lewis structure for HCl. Ask them how many shared pairs are present in this molecule. Then ask them to identify how many unshared pairs of electrons are present in HCl.

SECTION 5

Plan and Prepare

Objectives

Upon completion of this section, students should be able to do the following:

- Explain VSEPR theory.
- Predict the shapes of molecules or polyatomic ions using VSEPR theory.
- Explain how the shapes of molecules are accounted for by hybridization theory.
- Describe dipole-dipole forces, hydrogen bonding, induced dipoles, and London dispersion forces and their effects on properties such as boiling points and melting points.
- Explain what determines the polarity of molecules.

Classroom Catalyst

Ask students to name as many geometric shapes as they can. Write each one on the board. Start the list by writing down *square*. Next to this list, write some of the geometric shapes listed in **Figure 5.4.** Tell students that these geometric shapes are used to describe molecules.

Teach

TEACH FROM VISUALS

FIGURE 5.1 Students should realize that in the ball-and-stick representations in this textbook, all atoms are drawn the same size. Relative atomic and ionic sizes are shown only in space-filling models.

▼ Teach *continued*

TEACH FROM VISUALS

FIGURE 5.2 Give students four nails, clay, and a protractor to duplicate the models shown. Have them arrange two of the nails so that the nails touch each other and the nail heads are as far apart as possible. They can use the clay to hold the nails in place. Then have them measure the angle between the nail heads. Repeat using three and four nails.

Teaching Tip

The central atom of a molecule or polyatomic ion usually is the one with the lowest electronegativity. The more electronegative atoms are generally around the outside of a molecule or polyatomic ion, so they share electrons with fewer other atoms. Note, however, that H is never a central atom, because it can bond to only one other atom.

Teaching Tip

Exceptions of the type shown in Sample Problem E (where the central atom has *fewer* than eight electrons) are common for Group 2 and Group 13 elements. Group 2 elements in covalent compounds commonly have only four valence electrons (two bonds); BeF_2 in **Figure 5.2a** is an example of such an exception. Group 13 elements in covalent compounds commonly have only six valence electrons (three bonds); BF_3 in **Figure 5.2b** is an example of such an exception.

FIGURE 5.2

Molecular Geometry Ball-and-stick models show the shapes of molecules according to VSEPR theory.

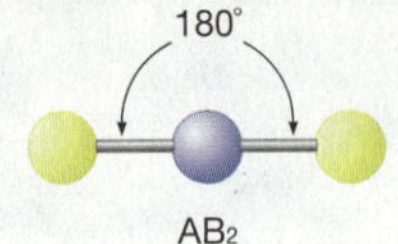

AB_2

(a) Beryllium fluoride, BeF_2

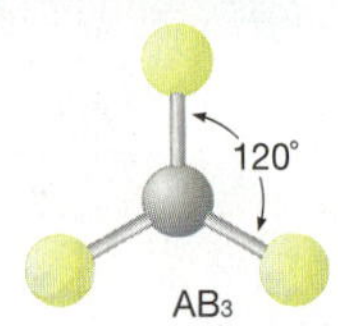

AB_3

(b) Boron trifluoride, BF_3

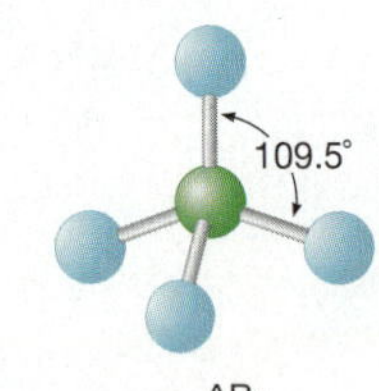

AB_4

(c) Methane, CH_4

If we represent the central atom in a molecule by the letter A and the atoms bonded to the central atom by the letter B, then according to VSEPR theory, BeF_2 is an example of an AB_2 molecule, which is linear. Can you determine what an AB_3 molecule looks like? The three A—B bonds stay farthest apart by pointing to the corners of an equilateral triangle, giving 120° angles between the bonds. This trigonal-planar geometry is shown in **Figure 5.2b** for the AB_3 molecule boron trifluoride, BF_3.

The central atoms in AB_4 molecules follow the octet rule by sharing four electron pairs with B atoms, for a total of eight shared electrons. The distance between electron pairs is maximized if each A—B bond points to one of four corners of a tetrahedron. This geometry is shown in **Figure 5.2c** for the AB_4 molecule methane, CH_4. The same figure shows that in a tetrahedral molecule, each of the bond angles formed by the A atom and any two of the B atoms is equal to 109.5°.

The shapes of various molecules are summarized in the table on the next spread (**Figure 5.4**). B can represent a single type of atom, a group of identical atoms, or a group of different atoms in the same molecule. The shape of the molecule will still be based on the forms given in the table. However, different sizes of B groups distort the bond angles, making some bond angles larger or smaller than those given in the table.

PREMIUM CONTENT

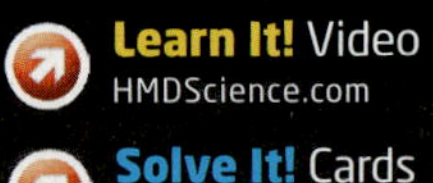
Learn It! Video
HMDScience.com

Solve It! Cards
HMDScience.com

VSEPR Theory and Molecular Geometry

Sample Problem E **Use VSEPR theory to predict the molecular geometry of boron trichloride, BCl_3.**

SOLVE

First write the Lewis structure for BCl_3. Boron is in Group 13 and has three valence electrons.

$\cdot\dot{B}\cdot$

Chlorine is in Group 17, so each chlorine atom has seven valence electrons.

$:\ddot{\underset{\cdot\cdot}{Cl}}\cdot$

The total number of available valence electrons is therefore $24e^-$ ($3e^-$ from boron and $21e^-$ from chlorine). The following Lewis structure uses all $24e^-$.

:Cl:
:Cl:B:Cl:

This molecule is an exception to the octet rule because in this case B forms only three bonds. Boron trichloride is an AB_3 type of molecule. Therefore, according to VSEPR theory, it should have trigonal-planar geometry.

Practice Answers in Appendix E

1. Use VSEPR theory to predict the molecular geometry of the following molecules:
   a. HI **b.** CBr_4 **c.** CH_2Cl_2

Problem Solving

DECONSTRUCTING PROBLEMS

Emphasize that VSEPR theory is based upon Lewis structures. Therefore, students must be sure to draw the correct Lewis structure for each atom and then show how these Lewis structures combine to form the molecule. Students may find it helpful to follow the six steps outlined in Sample Problem C earlier in this chapter to draw the Lewis structure for BCl_3.

VSEPR Theory and Unshared Electron Pairs

Ammonia, NH_3, and water, H_2O, are examples of molecules in which the central atom has both shared and unshared electron pairs (see **Figure 5.4** on the next page for their Lewis structures). How does VSEPR theory account for the geometries of these molecules?

The Lewis structure of ammonia shows that in addition to the three electron pairs it shares with the three hydrogen atoms, the central nitrogen atom has one unshared pair of electrons.

$$\begin{matrix} & \ddot{} & \\ H: & N & :H \\ & \ddot{H} & \end{matrix}$$

VSEPR theory postulates that the lone pair occupies space around the nitrogen atom just as the bonding pairs do. Thus, as in an AB_4 molecule, the electron pairs maximize their separation by assuming the four corners of a tetrahedron. Lone pairs do occupy space, but our description of the observed shape of a molecule refers to the *positions of atoms only.* Consequently, as shown in **Figure 5.3a,** the molecular geometry of an ammonia molecule is that of a pyramid with a triangular base. The general VSEPR formula for molecules such as ammonia is AB_3E, where E represents the unshared electron pair.

A water molecule has two unshared electron pairs. It is an AB_2E_2 molecule. Here, the oxygen atom is at the center of a tetrahedron, with two corners occupied by hydrogen atoms and two by the unshared pairs (**Figure 5.3b**). Again, VSEPR theory states that the lone pairs occupy space around the central atom but that the actual shape of the molecule is determined by the positions of the atoms only. In the case of water, this results in a "bent," or angular, molecule. In **Figure 5.3b,** the bond angles in ammonia and water are somewhat less than the 109.5° bond angles of a perfectly tetrahedral molecule, because the unshared electron pairs repel electrons more strongly than do bonding electron pairs.

FIGURE 5.3

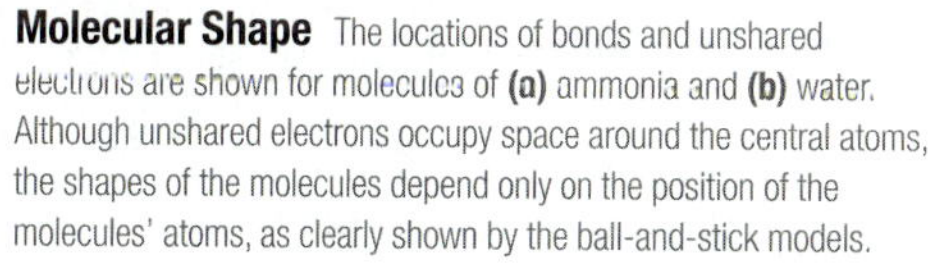

Molecular Shape The locations of bonds and unshared electrons are shown for molecules of **(a)** ammonia and **(b)** water. Although unshared electrons occupy space around the central atoms, the shapes of the molecules depend only on the position of the molecules' atoms, as clearly shown by the ball-and-stick models.

CRITICAL THINKING

Explain Why would unshared electrons affect the geometry of a molecule?

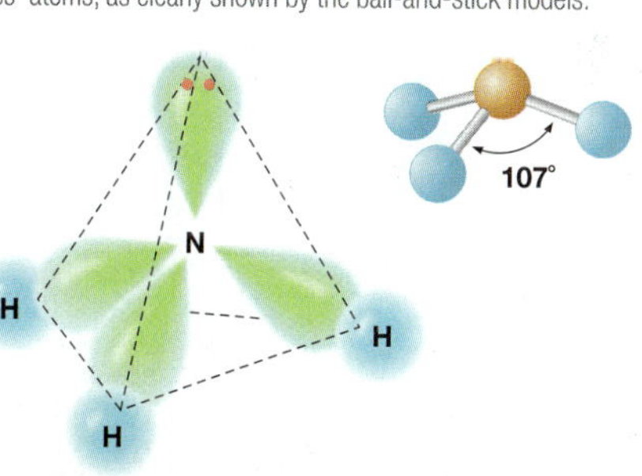

(a) Ammonia, NH_3

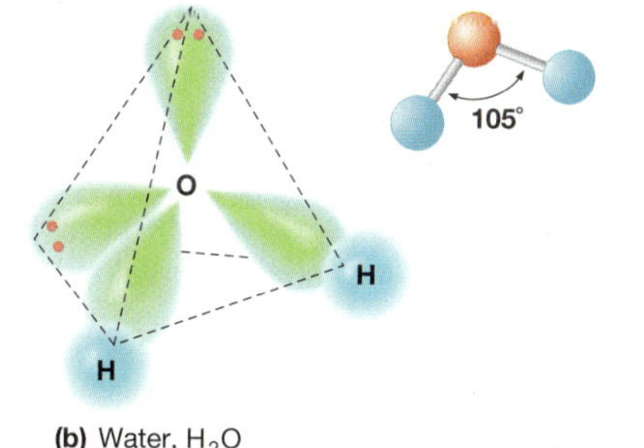

(b) Water, H_2O

Classroom Practice

E-1 Use VSEPR theory to predict the molecular geometry of the following molecules:

a. CCl_4

b. HCN

c. $SiBr_4$

Answers:

1. **a.** tetrahedral
   b. linear
   c. tetrahedral

Answers

Practice E

1. **a.** linear
   b. tetrahedral
   c. tetrahedral

TEACH FROM VISUALS

FIGURE 5.3 Inform students that a pair of unshared electrons will take up more space than a pair of electrons in a bond will. As a result, pairs of unshared electrons play a significant role in determining the geometry of a molecule, despite the fact that only atoms are taken into account when we visualize the shape of a molecule.

Critical Thinking

Answer: Unshared electrons affect the geometry of the molecule because they still have negative charges that will repel other electrons.

Differentiated Instruction

PRE-AP

As **Figure 5.3** illustrates, the geometry of a water molecule is bent. Have students investigate what the consequence would be if a water molecule had a linear shape. Students should recognize that the shape of the molecule is responsible for hydrogen bonding, an intermolecular force that accounts for many of the unusual properties of water.

▼ Teach *continued*

TEACH FROM TABLES

FIGURE 5.4 You may want to return to the use of nails and clay to illustrate the molecular shapes in this table. Once students can visualize how the electron pairs repel one another, the three-dimensional geometry is more straightforward.

Teaching Tip

It might be useful to point out that AB_2E structures are similar to AB_3 structures, but with an unshared electron pair in place of one of the bonds. Similarly, AB_3E and AB_2E_2 structures are similar to AB_4 structures, but with one and two unshared electron pairs, respectively, in place of bonds. This will help students to recognize the hybridizations later in the chapter: sp^2 for AB_3 and AB_2E; sp^3 for AB_4, AB_3E, and AB_2E_2. The molecule types AB_5 and AB_6 do not follow the octet rule. These two types of structures involve expanded valence shells and sp^3d and sp^3d^2 orbitals.

Figure 5.4 also includes an example of an AB_2E type molecule. This type of molecule results when a central atom forms two bonds and retains one unshared electron pair.

Finally, in VSEPR theory, double and triple bonds are treated in the same way as single bonds. And polyatomic ions are treated similarly to molecules. (Remember to consider *all* of the electron pairs present in any ion or molecule.) Thus, Lewis structures and **Figure 5.4** can be used together to predict the shapes of polyatomic ions as well as molecules with double or triple bonds.

FIGURE 5.4

VSEPR THEORY AND MOLECULAR GEOMETRY

	Molecular shape	Atoms bonded to central atom	Lone pairs of electrons	Type of molecule	Formula example	Lewis structure
Linear	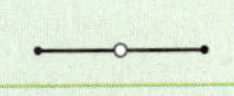	2	0	AB_2	BeF_2	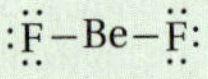 :F̤̈–Be–F̤̈:
Trigonal-planar	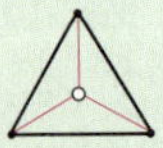	3	0	AB_3	BF_3	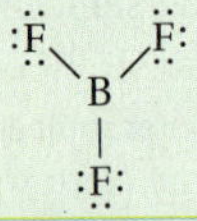
Bent or Angular	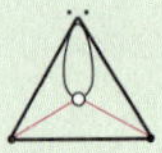	2	1	AB_2E	ONF	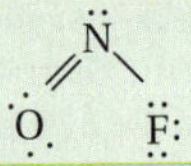
Tetrahedral	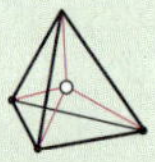	4	0	AB_4	CH_4	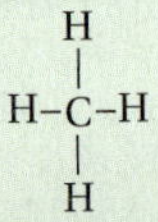
Trigonal-pyramidal	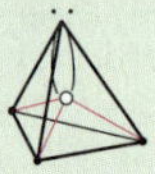	3	1	AB_3E	NH_3	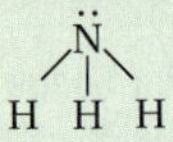
Bent or Angular	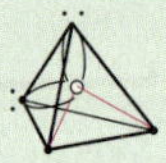	2	2	AB_2E_2	H_2O	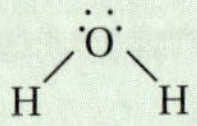
Trigonal-bipyramidal	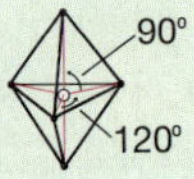 90° 120°	5	0	AB_5	PCl_5	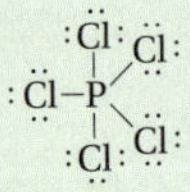
Octahedral	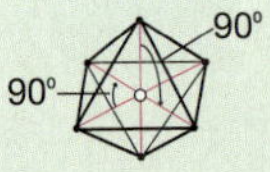 90° 90°	6	0	AB_6	SF_6	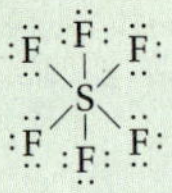

Differentiated Instruction

INCLUSION

Engage tactile and visual learners by making molecular modeling kits available to them. Demonstrate how three-dimensional models can be made from two-dimensional images, such as those in **Figure 5.4**. Ask students to model each of the geometric structure types in **Figure 5.4.** Have them show each model to you before continuing on to the next one. If commercial modeling kits are not available, models can be constructed with marshmallows and pretzel sticks.

VSEPR Theory and Molecular Geometry

Sample Problem F

a. Use VSEPR theory to predict the shape of a molecule of carbon dioxide, CO_2.
b. Use VSEPR theory to predict the shape of a chlorate ion, ClO_3^-.

 **SOLVE**

a. The Lewis structure of carbon dioxide shows two carbon-oxygen double bonds and no unshared electron pairs on the carbon atom. To simplify the molecule's Lewis structure, we represent the covalent bonds with lines instead of dots.

$$\ddot{\underset{\cdot\cdot}{O}}=C=\ddot{\underset{\cdot\cdot}{O}}$$

This is an AB_2 molecule, which is linear.

b. The Lewis structure of a chlorate ion shows three oxygen atoms and an unshared pair of electrons surrounding a central chlorine atom. Again, lines are used to represent the covalent bonds.

$$\left[\begin{array}{ccc} & \ddot{Cl} & \\ / & | & \backslash \\ :\ddot{\underset{\cdot\cdot}{O}} & :\underset{\cdot\cdot}{O}: & \ddot{\underset{\cdot\cdot}{O}}: \end{array}\right]^-$$

The chlorate ion is an AB_3E type. It has trigonal-pyramidal geometry, with the three oxygen atoms at the base of the pyramid and the chlorine atom at the top.

Practice
Answers in Appendix E

1. Use VSEPR theory to predict the molecular geometries of the molecules whose Lewis structures are given below.
   a. $:\ddot{\underset{\cdot\cdot}{F}}-\ddot{\underset{\cdot\cdot}{S}}-\ddot{\underset{\cdot\cdot}{F}}:$ **b.** $:\ddot{\underset{\cdot\cdot}{Cl}}-\ddot{P}(-\ddot{\underset{\cdot\cdot}{Cl}}:)-\ddot{\underset{\cdot\cdot}{Cl}}:$

MAIN IDEA

Multiple orbitals can combine to form hybrid orbitals.

VSEPR theory is useful for explaining the shapes of molecules. However, it does not reveal the relationship between a molecule's geometry and the orbitals occupied by its bonding electrons. To explain how the orbitals become rearranged when an atom forms covalent bonds, a different model is used. This model is called **hybridization**, which is the mixing of two or more atomic orbitals of similar energies on the same atom to produce new hybrid atomic orbitals of equal energies. Methane, CH_4, provides a good example of how hybridization is used to explain the geometry of molecular orbitals. The orbital notation for a carbon atom shows that it has four valence electrons, two in the $2s$ orbital and two in the $2p$ orbitals.

$$\text{C} \quad \underset{1s}{\uparrow\downarrow} \quad \underset{2s}{\uparrow\downarrow} \quad \underbrace{\uparrow \;\; \uparrow \;\; \_}_{2p}$$

Problem Solving

TAKE IT FURTHER

Challenge students by pointing out that H_2S, CO_2 and H_2O all consist of three atoms. Yet, only CO_2 is linear, while H_2O and H_2S are bent. Ask students to explain. Students should realize that while CO_2 is an AB_2 type of molecule, H_2O and H_2S are AB_2E_2 types. Have them refer to **Figure 5.4** to check the relationship between the type of molecule and molecular geometry.

Classroom Practice

F-1 Use VSEPR theory to predict the shape of the each of the following molecules and ions:

a. AsF_5
b. SeF_6
c. CF_4
d. NO_3^-

Answer:
a. trigonal-bipyramidal
b. octahedral
c. tetrahedral
d. trigonal-planar

Answers

Practice F

1. a. bent or angular
b. trigonal-pyramidal

Teaching Tip

Neither Lewis structures nor VSEPR theory can explain why the two unpaired valence electrons in carbon result in four bonds of equal energy. Hybridization theory explains that the two electrons in carbon's $2s$ orbital are also used for bonding, allowing all four valence electrons around carbon to form covalent bonds.

▼ Teach *continued*

Misconception Alert!

The labeling of hybrid orbitals is different from that used for electron configurations. The superscripts in hybrid orbitals refer to the number of orbitals of that particular type that are involved in the orbital blending. The superscripts in electron configurations refer to the number of electrons in that type of orbital.

TEACH FROM VISUALS

FIGURE 5.6 Be sure students do not think that the three molecules in the figure have the same molecular geometry. Have students determine each type of molecule and its molecular geometry. Students should realize that CH_4 is an AB_4 type of molecule (tetrahedron), NH_3 is an AB_3E type (triangular pyramid), and H_2O is an AB_2E_2 type (bent).

FIGURE 5.5

Hybridization of Carbon The sp^3 hybridization of carbon's outer orbitals combines one *s* and three *p* orbitals to form four sp^3 hybrid orbitals. Whenever hybridization occurs, the resulting hybrid orbitals are at an energy level between the levels of the orbitals that have combined.

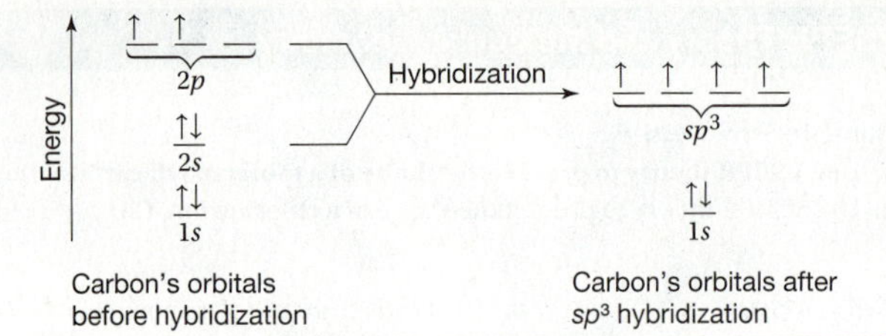

We know from experiments that a methane molecule has tetrahedral geometry. How does carbon form four equivalent, tetrahedrally arranged covalent bonds by orbital overlap with four other atoms?

Two of carbon's valence electrons occupy the 2*s* orbital, and two occupy the 2*p* orbitals. Recall that the 2*s* orbital and the 2*p* orbitals have different shapes. To achieve four equivalent bonds, carbon's 2*s* and three 2*p* orbitals *hybridize* to form four new, identical orbitals called sp^3 orbitals. The superscript 3 indicates that three *p* orbitals were included in the hybridization; the superscript 1 on the *s* is understood. The sp^3 orbitals all have the same energy, which is greater than that of the 2*s* orbital but less than that of the 2*p* orbitals, as shown in **Figure 5.5.**

Hybrid orbitals are orbitals of equal energy produced by the combination of two or more orbitals on the same atom. The number of hybrid orbitals produced equals the number of orbitals that have combined. Bonding with carbon sp^3 orbitals is shown in **Figure 5.6a** for a molecule of methane.

Hybridization also explains the bonding and geometry of many molecules formed by Group 15 and 16 elements. The sp^3 hybridization of a nitrogen atom ($[He]2s^22p^3$) yields four hybrid orbitals—one orbital containing a pair of electrons and three orbitals that each contain an unpaired electron. Each unpaired electron is capable of forming a single bond, as shown for ammonia in **Figure 5.6b.** Similarly, two of the four sp^3 hybrid orbitals of an oxygen atom ($[He]2s^22p^4$) are occupied by two electron pairs and two are occupied by unpaired electrons. Each unpaired electron can form a single bond, as shown for water in **Figure 5.6c.**

FIGURE 5.6

Hybrid Orbitals Bonds formed by the overlap of the 1*s* orbitals of hydrogen atoms and the sp^3 orbitals of **(a)** carbon, **(b)** nitrogen, and **(c)** oxygen. For the sake of clarity, only the hybrid orbitals of the central atoms are shown.

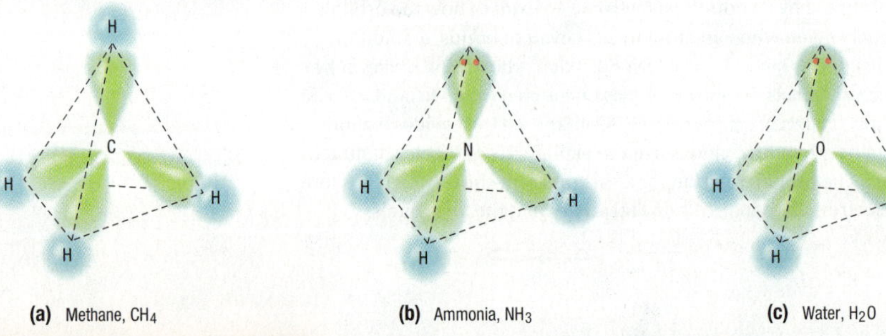

(a) Methane, CH_4 **(b)** Ammonia, NH_3 **(c)** Water, H_2O

Differentiated Instruction

PRE-AP

Point out that there are more hybrid orbitals than those described on this page and listed in **Figure 5.7.** Explain that these additional hybrid orbitals involve the *d* sublevel. Have students compile a table summarizing the various types of hybrid orbitals. Their table should include the following information: name of molecule, molecular formula, type of molecule (AB_4E, etc.), molecular geometry, and type of hybridization.

FIGURE 5.7

GEOMETRY OF HYBRID ORBITALS

Atomic orbitals	Type of hybridization	Number of hybrid orbitals	Geometry
s, *p*	*sp*	2	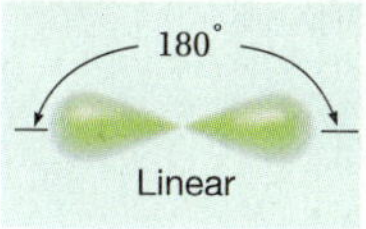 180° Linear
s, *p*, *p*	sp^2	3	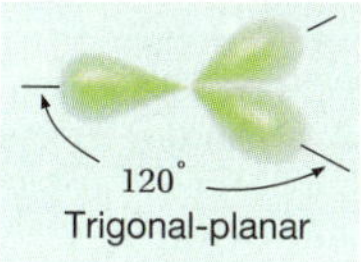 120° Trigonal-planar
s, *p*, *p*, *p*	sp^3	4	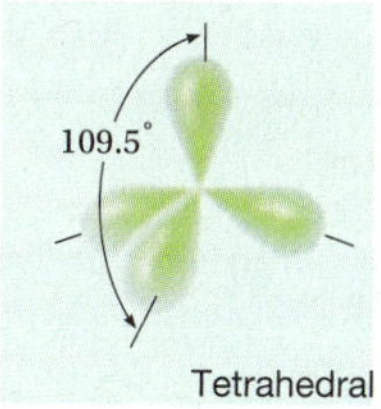 109.5° Tetrahedral

The linear geometry of molecules such as beryllium fluoride, BeF_2, is made possible by hybridization involving the *s* orbital and one available empty *p* orbital to yield *sp* hybrid orbitals. The trigonal-planar geometry of molecules such as boron fluoride, BF_3, is made possible by hybridization involving the *s* orbital, one singly occupied *p* orbital, and one empty *p* orbital to yield sp^2 hybrid orbitals (see **Figure 5.7**).

MAIN IDEA

Weak forces exist between molecules.

As a liquid is heated, the kinetic energy of its particles increases. At the boiling point, the energy is sufficient to overcome the force of attraction between the liquid's particles. The particles pull away from each other and enter the gas phase. Boiling point is therefore a good measure of the force of attraction between particles of a liquid. The higher the boiling point, the stronger the forces between particles.

The forces of attraction between molecules are known as *intermolecular forces.* Intermolecular forces vary in strength but are generally weaker than bonds that join atoms in molecules, ions in ionic compounds, or metal atoms in solid metals. Compare the boiling points of the metals and ionic compounds in **Figure 5.8** (on the next page) with those of the molecular substances listed. Note that the values for ionic compounds and metals are much higher than those for molecular substances.

Teaching Tip

The number of orbitals involved in hybridization determines the geometry of a molecule. There must be space around the atom for every hybrid orbital; each orbital will be as far as possible from every other orbital.

READING TOOLKIT

INTERPRETING VOCABULARY Point out the meanings of the prefixes *inter-* and *intra-*.

inter-: between or among; together

intra-: within; inside

Explain that molecules are affected by both *intermolecular* forces and *intramolecular* forces. Intermolecular forces are those between molecules. The attraction between the positive part of one polar molecule and the negative part of another is an intermolecular force. Intramolecular forces are those within the molecule. A covalent bond within a molecule is an intramolecular force. Ask students to list other examples of inter- and intramolecular forces. Also have students brainstorm a list of other words that use these prefixes and their definitions.

ENGLISH LEARNERS

Make copies of the following paragraph for students to read. Have them pay particular attention to the underlined terms. Ask them to correct any mistakes. You may want to point out that no underlined term is used correctly in this paragraph.

Intermolecular forces (Metallic bonds) are responsible for metallic solids such as a silver spoon or a gold necklace. Ionic bonds (Covalent bonds) are responsible for the forces of attraction between the hydrogen and oxygen atoms in a water molecule. The force of attraction between two water molecules is an example of a covalent bond (intermolecular force). The high boiling and melting points of ionic compounds are the result of intermolecular forces (ionic bonds).

▼ Teach continued

Teaching Tip

Remind students that boiling point is a measure of the force of attraction between molecules in covalent compounds, between ions in ionic compounds, and between atoms in metals.

TEACH FROM TABLES

FIGURE 5.8 Have students use the boiling points in this table to assess the relative strengths of the forces of attraction at work in molecular, ionic, and metallic substances.

Misconception Alert!

Some might infer from the table on this page that covalent bonding involves the weakest force of attraction. In fact, covalent bonding involves the strongest force of attraction—as evidenced by the fact that boiling a diamond is more difficult than boiling any metal. The attraction that must be overcome to boil a molecular compound is the *intermolecular attraction*, not covalent bonding.

CAREERS IN CHEMISTRY

Computational Chemist S.T.E.M.

Computational chemistry is the study of molecules, their properties, and the interactions between them, using mathematical equations that are based on the laws of quantum mechanics and which describe the motion of the electrons. Today, widely-available software packages exist that allow chemists to solve these equations for molecules under study.

Computational chemists combine their expertise in mathematics, their computer skills, and their love of chemistry. Computational chemistry has been used in industry to aid in the discovery of new pharmaceutical drugs and new catalysts. Computational chemists are employed in all areas of chemistry and work closely with experimental chemists.

FIGURE 5.8

BOILING POINTS AND BONDING TYPES

Bonding type	Substance	bp (1 atm, °C)
Nonpolar-covalent (molecular)	H_2	−253
	O_2	−183
	Cl_2	−34
	Br_2	59
	CH_4	−164
	CCl_4	77
	C_6H_6	80
Polar-covalent (molecular)	PH_3	−88
	NH_3	−33
	H_2S	−61
	H_2O	100
	HF	20
	HCl	−85
	ICl	97
Ionic	NaCl	1413
	MgF_2	2239
Metallic	Cu	2567
	Fe	2750
	W	5660

Molecular Polarity and Dipole-Dipole Forces

The strongest intermolecular forces exist between polar molecules. Polar molecules act as tiny dipoles because of their uneven charge distribution. A **dipole** is created by equal but opposite charges that are separated by a short distance. The direction of a dipole is from the dipole's positive pole to its negative pole. A dipole is represented by an arrow with a head pointing toward the negative pole and a crossed tail situated at the positive pole. The dipole created by a hydrogen chloride molecule, which has its negative end at the more electronegative chlorine atom, is indicated as follows.

H—Cl

The negative region in one polar molecule attracts the positive region in adjacent molecules, and so on throughout a liquid or solid. The forces of attraction between polar molecules are known as *dipole-dipole forces*. These forces are short-range forces, acting only between nearby molecules. The effect of dipole-dipole forces is reflected, for example, by the significant difference between the boiling points of iodine chloride, I—Cl, and bromine, Br—Br. The boiling point of polar iodine chloride is 97°C, whereas that of nonpolar bromine is only 59°C. The dipole-dipole forces responsible for the relatively high boiling point of ICl are illustrated schematically in **Figure 5.9** (on the next page).

Differentiated Instruction

INCLUSION

Visual learners may benefit from this demonstration of polarity. Point out the two opposite poles of a magnet. Ask why a magnet can be considered to have polarity. Students should recognize that a magnet has equal but opposite magnetic fields separated by a short distance. Use two magnets to show dipole-dipole forces. Bring the north pole of one magnet close to the south pole of the other. Compare the attractive forces between the magnets to the attractive forces between the oppositely charged ends of polar molecules.

FIGURE 5.9

Dipole-Dipole Forces Ball-and-stick models illustrate the dipole-dipole forces between molecules of iodine chloride, ICl. In each molecule, the highly electronegative chlorine atom has a partial negative charge, leaving each iodine atom with a partial positive charge. Consequently, the negative and positive ends of neighboring molecules attract each other.

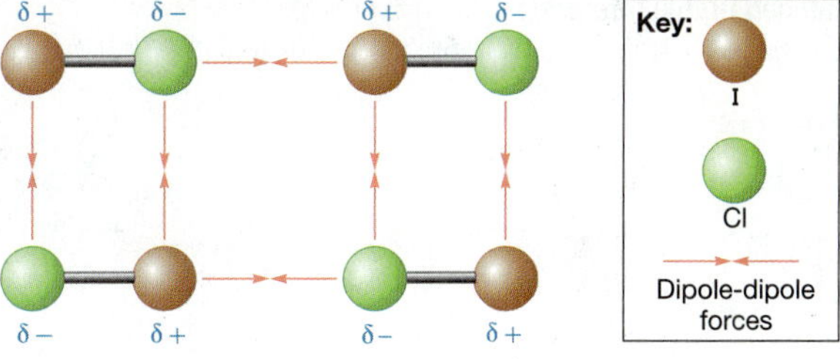

The polarity of diatomic molecules such as ICl is determined by just one bond. For molecules containing more than two atoms, molecular polarity depends on both the polarity and the orientation of each bond. A molecule of water, for example, has two hydrogen-oxygen bonds in which the more-electronegative oxygen atom is the negative pole of each bond. Because the molecule is bent, the polarities of these two bonds combine to make the molecule highly polar, as shown in **Figure 5.10.** An ammonia molecule is also highly polar because the dipoles of the three nitrogen-hydrogen bonds are additive, combining to create a net molecular dipole. In some molecules, individual bond dipoles cancel one another, causing the resulting molecular polarity to be zero. Carbon dioxide and carbon tetrachloride are molecules of this type.

A polar molecule can *induce* a dipole in a nonpolar molecule by temporarily attracting its electrons. The result is a short-range intermolecular force that is somewhat weaker than the dipole-dipole force. The force of an induced dipole accounts for the solubility of nonpolar O_2 in water. The positive pole of a water molecule attracts the outer electrons

FIGURE 5.10

Bond Polarities (a) The bond polarities in a water or an ammonia molecule are additive, causing the molecule as a whole to be polar. **(b)** In molecules of carbon tetrachloride and carbon dioxide, the bond polarities extend equally and symmetrically in different directions, canceling each other's effect and causing each molecule as a whole to be nonpolar.

CRITICAL THINKING

Explain What explanation can you give for the fact that the boiling point of H_2O is significantly higher than the boiling point of either H_2 (g) or O_2 (g) alone?

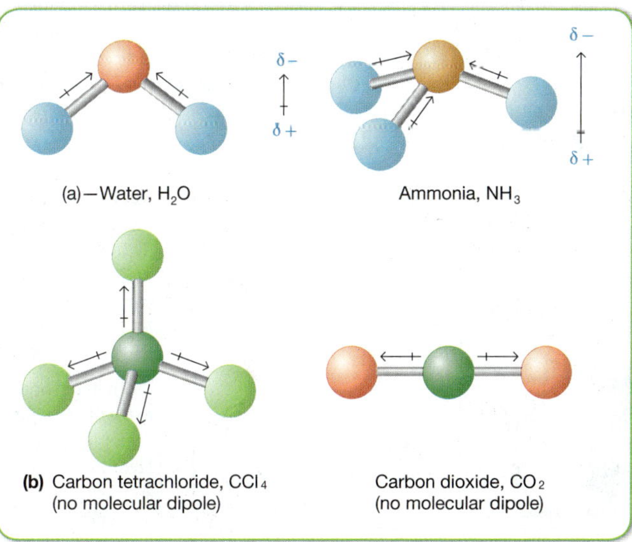

TEACH FROM VISUALS

FIGURE 5.10 Emphasize to students that a large difference in electronegativities between the atoms in a molecule does not necessarily mean that the molecule will be polar. Dipoles within a molecule can cancel each other out, resulting in a nonpolar molecule, as in carbon tetrachloride. Polarity is a result of both the existence of polar covalent bonds and the nature of the molecule's geometry.

Critical Thinking

Answer: Water has a higher boiling point than either hydrogen gas or oxygen gas because water is polar. Dipole-dipole forces are the strongest type of intermolecular force, and therefore take more energy to break.

BELOW LEVEL

Have students explain these statements.

1. A molecule can be nonpolar even if the bonds between its atoms are polar.

Students can use Figure 5.10b to show that the symmetrical distribution of atoms around the central molecule results in a nonpolar molecule, even though the bonds are polar.

2. A linear molecule can be either nonpolar or polar.

Students can use H_2 or CO_2 (see Figure 5.10b) to show that a linear molecule can be nonpolar. They can use HCl as an example of a linear, polar molecule.

3. Two identical atoms can never form a polar molecule.

Students should realize that the electronegativity difference between two identical atoms is zero, resulting in a nonpolar molecule.

▼ Teach *continued*

Misconception Alert!

Many students think of hydrogen bonding as a separate type of intermolecular force. In fact, it is a particularly strong dipole-dipole force.

ChemisTrivia

Hydrogen bonds are responsible for holding DNA in its helical shape.

Answer to In-Text Question

H_2S boils at a much lower temperature than does H_2O. This is explained by the fact that oxygen is so electronegative that hydrogen bonding occurs between H_2O molecules.

FIGURE 5.11

Dipole-Induced Dipole Interaction The positive pole of a water molecule causes a temporary change in the electron distribution of an oxygen molecule. The negative pole induced in the oxygen molecule is then attracted to the positive pole of the water molecule.

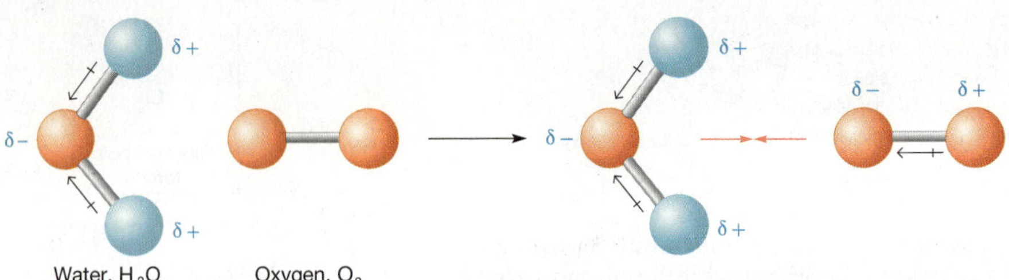

of an adjacent oxygen molecule. The oxygen molecule, then, has an induced negative pole on the side toward the water molecule and an induced positive pole on the opposite side. The result is an attraction to the water molecule, as shown in **Figure 5.11.**

Hydrogen Bonding

Some hydrogen-containing compounds, such as hydrogen fluoride (HF), water (H_2O), and ammonia (NH_3), have unusually high boiling points. This is explained by the presence of a particularly strong type of dipole-dipole force. In compounds containing H—F, H—O, or H—N bonds, the large electronegativity differences between hydrogen atoms and fluorine, oxygen, or nitrogen atoms make the bonds connecting them highly polar. This gives the hydrogen atom a positive charge that is almost half as large as that of a proton. Moreover, the small size of the hydrogen atom allows the atom to come very close to an unshared pair of electrons on an adjacent molecule. **The intermolecular force in which a hydrogen atom that is bonded to a highly electronegative atom is attracted to an unshared pair of electrons of an electronegative atom in a nearby molecule is known as hydrogen bonding.**

FIGURE 5.12

Hydrogen Bonding Space-filling models illustrate hydrogen bonding between water molecules. The dotted lines indicate the attraction between electronegative oxygen atoms and electropositive hydrogen atoms of neighboring molecules.

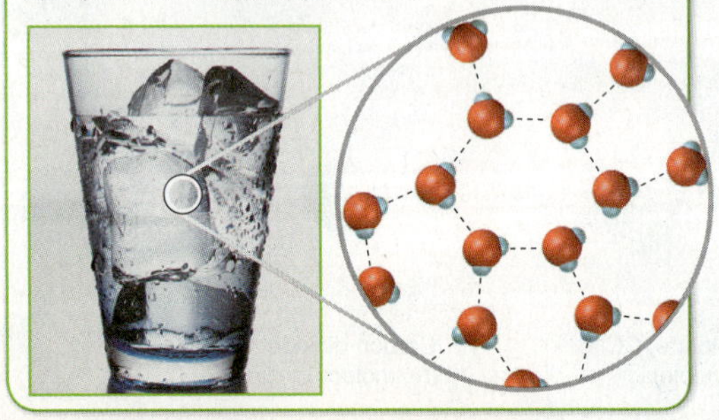

Hydrogen bonds are usually represented by dotted lines connecting the hydrogen-bonded hydrogen to the unshared electron pair of the electronegative atom to which it is attracted, as illustrated for water in **Figure 5.12.** The effect of hydrogen bonding can be seen by comparing the boiling points in **Figure 5.8.** Look at phosphine, PH_3, compared with hydrogen-bonded ammonia, NH_3. How does hydrogen sulfide, H_2S, compare with hydrogen-bonded water, H_2O?

In living organisms, hydrogen bonds play an extremely important role: that of stabilizing the structure of deoxyribonucleic acid (DNA). Hydrogen bonds are individually very weak, but the sum of millions of these bonds forms a very strong force holding two DNA strands together.

Differentiated Instruction

INCLUSION

Help students visualize the strength of hydrogen bonding by doing this simple activity designed to benefit kinesthetic learners. Have students place a quarter in a beaker containing some ethanol. After a minutes, have students pour off the ethanol and use a paper towel to dry the quarter. Tell students to avoid touching the coin with their fingers. Have students use a dropper to see how many water drops they can get on the coin. Point out that hydrogen bonding is responsible for the surprising number of drops that can remain on the coin. Mention that oils from fingers can affect the results. Some students may be interested in pursuing the interaction between polar molecules (water) and nonpolar molecules (oils).

FIGURE 5.13

Temporary Dipoles When an instantaneous, temporary dipole develops in a helium atom, it induces a dipole in a neighboring atom.

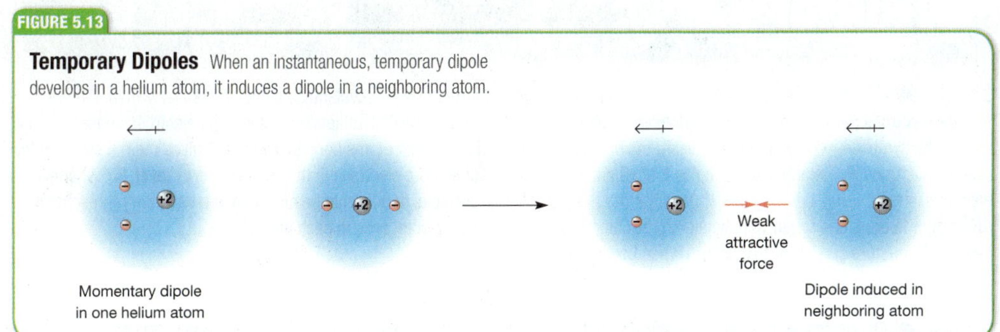

London Dispersion Forces

Even noble-gas atoms and molecules that are nonpolar experience a weak intermolecular attraction. In any atom or molecule—polar or nonpolar—the electrons are in continuous motion. As a result, at any instant, the electron distribution may be slightly uneven. The momentary, uneven charge creates a positive pole in one part of the atom or molecule and a negative pole in another. This temporary dipole can then induce a dipole in an adjacent atom or molecule. The two are held together for an instant by the weak attraction between the temporary dipoles, as illustrated in **Figure 5.13.** The intermolecular attractions resulting from the constant motion of electrons and the creation of instantaneous dipoles are called **London dispersion forces,** after Fritz London, who first proposed their existence in 1930.

London forces act between all atoms and molecules. But they are the *only* intermolecular forces acting among noble-gas atoms and nonpolar molecules. This fact is reflected in the low boiling points of the noble gases and nonpolar molecular compounds listed in **Figure 5.8.** Because London forces are dependent on the motion of electrons, their strength increases with the number of electrons in the interacting atoms or molecules. In other words, London forces increase with increasing atomic or molar mass. This trend can be seen by comparing the boiling points of the gases helium, He, and argon, Ar; hydrogen, H_2, and oxygen, O_2; and chlorine, Cl_2, and bromine, Br_2.

SECTION 5 FORMATIVE ASSESSMENT

Reviewing Main Ideas

1. What two theories can be used to predict molecular geometry?
2. Draw the Lewis structure and predict the molecular geometry of the following molecules:
   a. SO_2 **b.** CI_4 **c.** BCl_3
3. What factors affect the geometry of a molecule?
4. Explain what is meant by sp^3 hybridization.
5. What type of intermolecular force contributes to the high boiling point of water? Explain.

Critical Thinking

6. **INFERRING RELATIONSHIPS** What experimental property directly correlates with the strength of the intermolecular forces? Briefly explain your answer.

Misconception Alert!

Some students might think that a molecule experiences either dipole-dipole forces or London dispersion forces with another molecule. In fact, *all* molecules experience London dispersion forces. In polar molecules, London dispersion forces are insignificant relative to dipole-dipole forces.

Assess and Reteach ▼

Assess Use the Formative Assessment on this page to evaluate student mastery of the section.

Reteach For students who need additional instruction, download the Section Study Guide.

Response to Intervention To reassess students' mastery, use the Section Quiz, available to print or to take directly online at **HMDScience.com**.

Answers to Section Assessment

1. VSEPR theory and hybridization theory
2. **a.** $:\ddot{O}::\ddot{S}:\ddot{O}:$
   bent or angular

   b. (Lewis structure of CI_4: C bonded to four I atoms, each with lone pairs)
   tetrahedral

   c. (Lewis structure of BCl_3: B bonded to three Cl atoms, each with lone pairs)
   trigonal-planar
3. Factors include the number of bonds formed by each atom in the molecule, the number of lone pairs of electrons on the atoms, and the hybridization of some of the atoms' orbitals.
4. One *s* orbital and three *p* orbitals combine to form four hybrid orbitals of equal energy.
5. Hydrogen bonding is responsible for water's high boiling point. In general, boiling point is a measure of the amount of energy required to overcome intermolecular attractions. Hydrogen bonding, a particularly strong dipole-dipole force, causes a powerful attraction between water molecules, which results in a high boiling point.
6. The boiling point of a molecule is directly correlated to the strength of the intermolecular forces. The boiling point is the temperature at which a molecule goes from the liquid state to the gaseous state. In the gaseous state, all the intermolecular forces are essentially broken. The stronger the intermolecular forces, the more energy needed to break the intermolecular forces, and the higher the boiling point.

Math Tutor | Drawing Lewis Structures

Drawing Lewis dot structures can help you understand how valence electrons participate in bonding. Dots are placed around the symbol of an element to represent the element's valence electrons. For example, carbon has four valence electrons, and its Lewis dot structure is usually written as $\cdot\dot{\text{C}}\cdot$ (with a dot below). An atom of fluorine has seven valence electrons. Fluorine's Lewis dot structure can be written as $:\ddot{\text{F}}:$ (with a dot below). When Lewis structures for covalently bonded atoms are written, the dots may be placed as needed to show the electrons shared in each bond. Most atoms bond in a way that gives them a stable octet of *s* and *p* electrons in the highest energy level. So, whenever possible, dots should be arranged in a way that represents a stable octet around each atom.

Problem-Solving TIPS

- Hydrogen is an exception to the octet rule, because hydrogen has only one electron and becomes stable with two electrons.
- Some elements, such as boron, can bond without achieving an octet, because they have three or fewer electrons to share.

Sample Problem

Draw the Lewis dot structure for a molecule of sulfur dichloride, SCl_2.

First, write the electron dot notation for each atom.

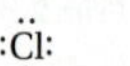

$:\ddot{\text{Cl}}\cdot$ $:\ddot{\text{Cl}}\cdot$ $:\dot{\text{S}}:$

Next, determine the total number of valence electrons in the atoms.

S	$1 \times 6e^-$	=	$6e^-$
2Cl	$2 \times 7e^-$	=	$14e^-$
	Total e^-	=	$20e^-$

Arrange the atoms to form a skeleton structure for the molecule, and place electron pairs between atoms to represent covalent bonds. You can predict the arrangement of atoms by figuring out how many covalent bonds each atom must form in order to achieve a stable octet. Each chlorine atom, which has 7 valence electrons, must form a single covalent bond. Sulfur, which has 6 valence electrons, must form two covalent bonds. The only possible structure is Cl—S—Cl.

Finally, insert dots representing the remaining electrons (16 in this case), in order to give each atom an octet.

$:\ddot{\underset{\cdot\cdot}{\text{Cl}}}:\ddot{\underset{\cdot\cdot}{\text{S}}}:\ddot{\underset{\cdot\cdot}{\text{Cl}}}:$

Practice

1. Draw the electron dot notations for a silicon atom and a strontium atom.
2. Draw Lewis structures for hydrogen sulfide, H_2S, and formic acid, HCO_2H.

Answers

1. a. $\cdot\dot{\underset{\cdot}{\text{Si}}}\cdot$

   b. $\text{Sr}\cdot$ (with a dot above)

2. a. $\text{H}:\underset{\cdot\cdot}{\ddot{\text{S}}}$ with H above S

   b. $\text{H}:\overset{:\text{O}:}{\ddot{\text{C}}}\,:\underset{\cdot\cdot}{\ddot{\text{O}}}:\text{H}$

Review Answers

1. A chemical bond is a link between atoms resulting from the mutual attraction of their nuclei and electrons.
2. The three major types of chemical bonding are ionic, covalent, and metallic. In *ionic bonding*, large numbers of oppositely charged ions join because of mutual electrical attraction. In *covalent bonding*, atoms join by sharing electron pairs. In *metallic bonding*, atoms join through an attraction to a sea of valence electrons.
3. In general, the greater the electronegativity difference between two atoms, the more ionic is the bond between them.
4. a. *Polar* refers to bonds that have an uneven distribution of charge.

   b. In a polar-covalent bond, there is an unequal attraction for the electron pair, resulting in one of the bonded atoms possessing a partial negative charge and the other atom possessing a partial positive charge. In a nonpolar-covalent bond, the electron pair is shared equally by the bonded atoms.
5. In general, atoms will form a chemical bond if their potential energy is lowered by doing so.
6.

Elements bonded	Electronegativity difference	Bond type	More negative atom
a. H & I	0.4	polar-covalent	I
b. S & O	1.0	polar-covalent	O
c. K & Br	2.0	ionic	Br
d. Si & Cl	1.2	polar-covalent	Cl
e. K & Cl	2.2	non-polar-covalent	S
f. Se & S	0.1	non-polar-covalent	S
g. C & H	0.4	polar-covalent	C

7. K and Cl, K and Br, Si and Cl, S and O, H and I, C and H, Se and S
8. a. Cl $\underset{1s}{\uparrow\downarrow}$ $\underset{2s}{\uparrow\downarrow}$ $\underset{2p}{\uparrow\downarrow\ \uparrow\downarrow\ \uparrow\downarrow}$ $\underset{3s}{\uparrow\downarrow}$ $\underset{3p}{\uparrow\downarrow\ \uparrow\downarrow\ \uparrow}$

   Cl $\underset{1s}{\uparrow\downarrow}$ $\underset{2s}{\uparrow\downarrow}$ $\underset{2p}{\uparrow\downarrow\ \uparrow\downarrow\ \uparrow\downarrow}$ $\underset{3s}{\uparrow\downarrow}$ $\underset{3p}{\uparrow\downarrow\ \uparrow\downarrow\ \_\downarrow}$

→

198 Chapter 6

CHAPTER 6 Summary

Review Games
Concept Maps

SECTION 1 Introduction to Chemical Bonding

- Most atoms are chemically bonded to other atoms. The three major types of chemical bonding are ionic, covalent, and metallic.
- In general, atoms of metals bond ionically with atoms of nonmetals, atoms of metals bond metallically with each other, and atoms of nonmetals bond covalently with each other.

KEY TERMS

chemical bond	nonpolar-covalent bond
ionic bonding	polar
covalent bonding	polar-covalent bond

SECTION 2 Covalent Bonding and Molecular Compounds

- Atoms in molecules are joined by covalent bonds. In a covalent bond, two atoms share one or more pairs of electrons.
- The octet rule states that many chemical compounds tend to form bonds so that each atom shares or has eight electrons in its highest occupied energy level.
- Bonding within many molecules and ions can be indicated by a Lewis structure. Molecules or ions that cannot be correctly represented by a single Lewis structure are represented by resonance structures.

KEY TERMS

molecule	Lewis structure
molecular compound	structural formula
chemical formula	single bond
molecular formula	multiple bond
bond energy	resonance
electron-dot notation	

SECTION 3 Ionic Bonding and Ionic Compounds

- An ionic compound is a three-dimensional network of positive and negative ions mutually attracted to one another.
- Ionic compounds tend to be harder and more brittle and have higher boiling points than materials containing only covalently bonded atoms.

KEY TERMS

ionic compound
formula unit
lattice energy
polyatomic ion

SECTION 4 Metallic Bonding

- The "electron sea" formed in metallic bonding gives metals their properties of high electrical and thermal conductivity, malleability, ductility, and luster.

KEY TERMS

metallic bonding
malleability
ductility

SECTION 5 Molecular Geometry

- VSEPR theory is used to predict the shapes of molecules based on the fact that electron pairs strongly repel each other.
- Hybridization theory is used to predict the shapes of molecules, based on the fact that orbitals within an atom can mix to form orbitals of equal energy.
- Intermolecular forces include dipole-dipole forces and London dispersion forces. Hydrogen bonding is a special case of dipole-dipole forces.

KEY TERMS

VSEPR theory
hybridization
hybrid orbitals
dipole
hydrogen bonding
London dispersion forces

↑↓ ↑↓ ↑↓↑↓↑↓ ↑↓ ↑↓↑↓↑
$1s$ $2s$ $2p$ $3s$ $3p$

↑↓ ↑↓ ↑↓↑↓↑↓ ↑↓ ↑↓↑↓ ↓
$1s$ $2s$ $2p$ $3s$ $3p$

b. O ↑↓ ↑↓ ↑↓↑ ↑ ($1s$ $2s$ $2p$) ↑↓ ↑↓ ↑↓↑ ↑ ($1s$ $2s$ $2p$)

→

O ↑↓ ↑↓ ↑↓ ↓ ↓ ($1s$ $2s$ $2p$) ↑↓ ↑↓ ↑↓ ↓ ↓ ($1s$ $2s$ $2p$)

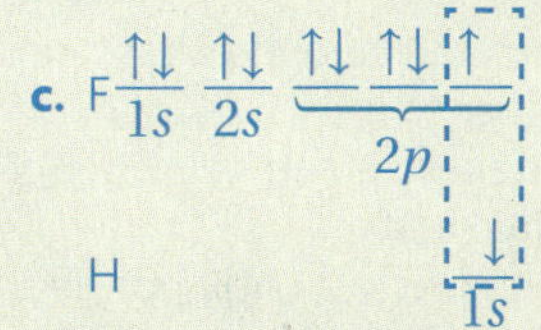

9. Bonding is stronger between the ions in sodium chloride because its lattice energy is greater (more negative). Greater lattice energy indicates stronger ionic bonding.

10. A molecule is a neutral group of two or more atoms—usually nonmetals—held together by covalent bonds.

11. a. Bond length, the distance at which potential energy is at a minimum, is determined by balancing the forces of attraction and repulsion between atoms in a covalent bond.

b. In general, higher bond energies correspond to shorter bond lengths.

12. The electrons in a covalent bond occupy overlapping orbitals; each electron is free to occupy either of the orbitals, but both are more likely to be in the space between the nuclei of the bonded atoms.

13. a pair of electrons that is not involved in bonding but instead belongs exclusively to one atom

14. A noble-gas configuration corresponds to a set of outer *s* and *p* orbitals that is completely filled with a total of eight electrons. These eight outer electrons are referred to as an octet. Atoms that possess a noble-gas configuration are very stable because the potential energy of their electrons is relatively low. The octet rule states that elements will gain, lose, or share electrons to form a noble-gas configuration.

15. a. 1 **b.** 7 **c.** 2 **d.** 6 **e.** 3 **f.** 5 **g.** 4

16. The least-electronegative atom is usually the central atom (except for hydrogen, which is never central). If carbon is present, however, it is usually the central atom, regardless of what other atoms are in the molecule.

17. A single bond involves one electron pair, as in the bond between hydrogen and oxygen in water, H_2O. A double bond involves two electron pairs, as in the bond between the carbon and oxygen atoms in a molecule of carbon dioxide, CO_2. A triple bond involves three electron pairs, as in the bond between carbon and nitrogen in hydrogen cyanide, HCN.

18. A multiple bond is needed when there are not enough valence electrons to complete octets by adding unshared pairs

19. a. Li· **b.** ·Ca· **c.** :C̤̈l: **d.** :Ö: **e.** ·Ċ· **f.** ·P̤: **g.** ·Al· **h.** :S̈:

20. a. $Na^{\cdot} + Na^{\cdot} + :\ddot{S}: \longrightarrow Na^{+} + Na^{+} + :\ddot{S}:^{2-}$ (Na_2S)

b. $\cdot Ca^{\cdot} + :\dot{O}: \longrightarrow Ca^{2+} + :\ddot{O}:^{2-}$ (CaO)

CHAPTER REVIEW

c. ·A· + ·Al· + :S: + :S: + :S: ⟶
Al^{3+} + Al^{3+} + $:S:^{2-}$ + $:S:^{2-}$ + $:S:^{2-}$
(Al_2S_3)

21 a.
```
    :F:
:F: C :F:
    :F:
```
d.
```
     :Br:
:Br: Si :Br:
     :Br:
```
b.
```
H:Se:H
```
e.
```
  H
H:C:Cl:
  H
```
c.
```
:I:N:I:
   :I:
```

22. sp^2 hybrid orbitals

23. a. :O::O: b. :N:::N: c. :C:::O:

d. :O:S::O: ⟷ :O::S:O:

24 a. $[:O:H]^-$

b.
```
[   H        ]-          [   H       ]-
[ H:C: C ::O ]    ⟷      [ H:C: C :O: ]
[   H :O:    ]           [   H  :O:   ]
```

c.
```
[ :O: Br :O: ]-
[    :O:     ]
```

25. a. An ionic compound is composed of cations and anions such that the total positive and negative charges are equal.

b. Most ionic compounds occur naturally as crystalline solids.

26. a. the simplest collection of atoms from which an ionic compound's formula can be established

b. one calcium ion, Ca^{2+}, and two fluoride ions, F^-

27. a. the energy released when one mole of an ionic crystalline compound is formed from gaseous ions

b. The greater the lattice energy, the stronger the ionic bonding.

28. a. Ionic compounds have higher melting and boiling points than molecular compounds and do not vaporize at room temperature.

b. The differences in the properties of ionic and molecular compounds are due to differences in how strongly the compound's basic units are held together.

c. hardness, brittleness, electrical conductivity in the molten state

29. a. a charged group of covalently bonded atoms

b. Some common examples of polyatomic anions include the nitrate ion, NO_3^-, the ammonium ion, NH_4^+, the sulfate ion, SO_4^{2-}, and the phosphate ion, PO_4^{3-}.

c. Polyatomic ions combine with ions of opposite charge to form ionic compounds.

30. a. Metals are better heat conductors than ionic or molecular compounds. In the solid state, metals are more easily deformed and are better electrical conductors than solid ionic or molecular compounds. Unlike ionic and molecular compounds, metals are also shiny in appearance.

b. Metals are good electrical conductors because of the presence of highly mobile electrons within the bonding networks of their atoms.

CHAPTER 6 Review

SECTION 1

Introduction to Chemical Bonding

REVIEWING MAIN IDEAS

1. What is a chemical bond?
2. Identify and define the three major types of chemical bonding.
3. What is the relationship between electronegativity and the ionic character of a chemical bond?
4. a. What is the meaning of the term polar, as applied to chemical bonding?
   b. Distinguish between polar-covalent and nonpolar-covalent bonds.
5. In general, what determines whether atoms will form chemical bonds?

PRACTICE PROBLEMS

6. Determine the electronegativity difference, the probable bond type, and the more-electronegative atom with respect to bonds formed between the following pairs of atoms. (Hint: See Sample Problem A.)
   a. H and I
   b. S and O
   c. K and Br
   d. Si and Cl
   e. K and Cl
   f. Se and S
   g. C and H
7. List the bonding pairs described in item 6 in order of increasing covalent character.
8. Use orbital notation to illustrate the bonding in each of the following molecules:
   a. chlorine, Cl_2
   b. oxygen, O_2
   c. hydrogen fluoride, HF
9. The lattice energy of sodium chloride, NaCl, is −787.5 kJ/mol. The lattice energy of potassium chloride, KCl, is −715 kJ/mol. In which compound is the bonding between ions stronger? Why?

SECTION 2

Covalent Bonding and Molecular Compounds

REVIEWING MAIN IDEAS

10. What is a molecule?
11. a. What determines bond length?
    b. In general, how are bond energies and bond lengths related?
12. Describe the general location of the electrons in a covalent bond.
13. As applied to covalent bonding, what is meant by an unshared or lone pair of electrons?
14. Describe the octet rule in terms of noble-gas configurations and potential energy.
15. Determine the number of valence electrons in an atom of each of the following elements:
    a. H
    b. F
    c. Mg
    d. O
    e. Al
    f. N
    g. C
16. In a Lewis structure, which atom is usually the central atom?
17. Distinguish between single, double, and triple covalent bonds by defining each and providing an illustration of each type.
18. For Lewis structures, how is the need for multiple bonds generally determined?

PRACTICE PROBLEMS

19. Use electron-dot notation to illustrate the number of valence electrons present in one atom of each of the following elements. (Hint: See Sample Problem B.)
    a. Li
    b. Ca
    c. Cl
    d. O
    e. C
    f. P
    g. Al
    h. S

20. Use electron-dot structures to demonstrate the formation of ionic compounds involving the following elements:
    a. Na and S
    b. Ca and O
    c. Al and S

21. Draw Lewis structures for each of the following molecules. (Hint: See Sample Problem D.)
    a. contains one C and four F atoms
    b. contains two H and one Se atom
    c. contains one N and three I atoms
    d. contains one Si and four Br atoms
    e. contains one C, one Cl, and three H atoms

22. Determine the type of hybrid orbitals formed by the boron atom in a molecule of boron fluoride, BF_3.

23. Draw Lewis structures for each of the following molecules. Show resonance structures, if they exist.
    a. O_2
    b. N_2
    c. CO
    d. SO_2

24. Draw Lewis structures for each of the following polyatomic ions. Show resonance structures, if they exist.
    a. OH^-
    b. $H_3C_2O_2^-$
    c. BrO_3^-

SECTION 3

Ionic Bonding and Ionic Compounds

REVIEWING MAIN IDEAS

25. a. What is an ionic compound?
    b. In what form do most ionic compounds occur?

26. a. What is a formula unit?
    b. What are the components of one formula unit of CaF_2?

27. a. What is lattice energy?
    b. In general, what is the relationship between lattice energy and the strength of ionic bonding?

28. a. In general, how do ionic and molecular compounds compare in terms of melting points, boiling points, and ease of vaporization?
    b. What accounts for the observed differences in the properties of ionic and molecular compounds?
    c. Cite three physical properties of ionic compounds.

29. a. What is a polyatomic ion?
    b. Give two examples of polyatomic ions.
    c. In what form do such ions often occur in nature?

SECTION 4

Metallic Bonding

 REVIEWING MAIN IDEAS

30. a. How do the properties of metals differ from those of both ionic and molecular compounds?
    b. What specific property of metals accounts for their unusual electrical conductivity?

31. What properties of metals contribute to their tendency to form metallic bonds?

32. a. What is metallic bonding?
    b. How can the strength of metallic bonding be measured?

SECTION 5

Molecular Geometry

 REVIEWING MAIN IDEAS

33. a. How is the VSEPR theory used to classify molecules?
    b. What molecular geometry would be expected for F_2 and HF?

34. According to the VSEPR theory, what molecular geometries are associated with the following types of molecules?
    a. AD_2
    b. AB_3
    c. AB_4
    d. AB_5
    e. AB_6

35. Describe the role of each of the following in predicting molecular geometries:
    a. unshared electron pairs
    b. double bonds

31. Most contain sparsely populated outermost orbitals, they have low ionization energies, and they have low electronegativities.

32. a. Metallic bonding results from the attraction between metal atoms and a sea of surrounding electrons.
    b. A metal's enthalpy of vaporization is a measure of the strength of its bonding.

33. a. According to VSEPR theory, the shape of a molecule is classified based on the number of bonding electron pairs and lone pairs that surround the central atom.
    b. Both molecules are linear.

34. a. linear
    b. trigonal-planar
    c. tetrahedral
    d. trigonal-bipyramidal
    e. octahedral

35. a. Unshared electron pairs occupy space, but they are not part of the visualized molecular geometry.
    b. Double (and triple) bonds are treated the same as single bonds.

36. a. Hybrid orbitals are identically shaped orbitals of equal energy that are produced by the mixing of two or more atomic orbitals of similar, but not identical, energies on the same atom.
    b. The number of hybrid orbitals produced is always equal to the number of atomic orbitals that have combined.

37. a. Intermolecular forces are the forces of attraction between molecules.
    b. Intermolecular forces are weaker than the forces involved in ionic and metallic bonding.
    c. The strongest intermolecular forces occur between polar molecules.

38. The larger the difference in electronegativities of the atoms in the bond, the greater the polarity of that bond.

39. a. Dipole-dipole forces are the forces of attraction between polar molecules.
    b. The overall polarity of a molecule is determined by the polarity of the molecule's individual bonds as well as the orientation of the bonds with respect to one another.

40. a. An induced dipole is an instantaneous dipole that is produced in a nonpolar molecule when the molecule's electrons are momentarily attracted by a polar molecule.
    b. Induced dipoles account for the solubility of nonpolar compounds, such as oxygen, in polar compounds, such as water.

41. a. Hydrogen bonding is a particularly strong dipole-dipole force that occurs among molecules containing hydrogen atoms and highly electronegative atoms, such as those of N, O, and F.
    b. Because of the large electronegativity difference between H and F, N, or O, an atom of hydrogen has a positive charge that is almost half as large as that of a proton. This, coupled with the small size of the hydrogen atom, results in a very strong dipole-dipole attraction.

42. London dispersion forces are intermolecular forces resulting from the creation of induced dipoles.

43. a. trigonal-pyramidal
    b. bent or angular
    c. bent or angular

44. The carbon atom contains four valence electrons, two in the 2*s* and two in the 2*p* orbitals. Hybridization of the 2*s* orbital and the three 2*p* orbitals creates four sp^3 hybrid orbitals, each of which can bond with a hydrogen atom to form four covalent bonds.

45. The direction of the dipole is toward

a. F **c.** Br
b. Cl **d.** I

46. a. nonpolar **d.** nonpolar
b. polar **e.** polar
c. polar **f.** polar

47. a. polar **d.** polar
b. nonpolar **e.** nonpolar
c. nonpolar

48. a. :C̤̈l:S̤̈:C̤̈l: bent or angular
d. H:N̈:H with :C̤̈l: below; trigonal-pyramidal
b. :Ï:P̈:Ï: with :Ï: below; trigonal-pyramidal
e. :C̤̈l:Si:C̤̈l: with :C̤̈l: above and :B̤̈r: below; tetrahedral
c. :C̤̈l:Ö:C̤̈l: bent or angular
f. Ö::N̈:C̤̈l: bent or angular

49. a. $[$:Ö:N::Ö: with :Ö: below$]^-$ trigonal-planar
c. $[$:Ö:S:Ö: with :Ö: above and below$]^{2-}$ tetrahedral
b. $[$H:N:H with H above and below$]^+$ tetrahedral
d. $[$:Ö:C̤̈l:Ö:$]^-$ bent or angular

50. d, c, a, b

51. a. tetrahedral
b. linear
c. trigonal-pyramidal

52. a. metals and nonmetals
b. nonmetals only
c. metals only

53. The energies of the atoms increase and the atoms become less stable.

54.
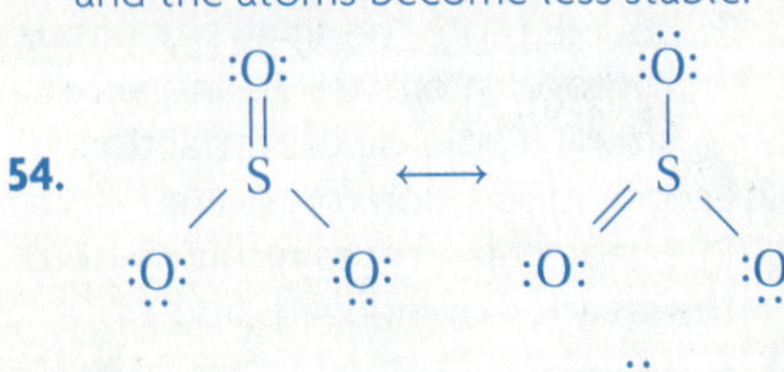
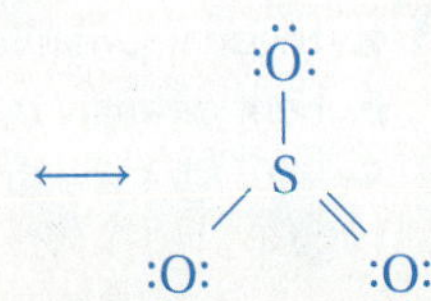

55. a. In ionic bonding, valence electrons of the atoms of the less-electronegative element are donated entirely to the atoms of the more-electronegative element. In covalent bonding, valence electrons are shared between the bonded atoms.

b. A molecular compound consists of individual units able to exist on their own. An ionic compound consists of an arrangement of a large number of ions. There is no discrete, independent particle in an ionic compound.

c. An ionic compound is held together by electrical attraction between ions. A metal is held together by the sharing by atoms of a sea of mobile valence electrons.

56. a. .He˙ **b.** :C̤̈l: **c.** :Ö: **d.** .P̤: **e.** .B˙

57.

```
    H
    |
H–C–O–H
    |
    H
```


36. a. What are hybrid orbitals?
b. What determines the number of hybrid orbitals produced by the hybridization of an atom?

37. a. What are intermolecular forces?
b. In general, how do these forces compare in strength with those in ionic and metallic bonding?
c. What types of molecules have the strongest intermolecular forces?

38. What is the relationship between electronegativity and the polarity of a chemical bond?

39. a. What are dipole-dipole forces?
b. What determines the polarity of a molecule?

40. a. What is meant by an induced dipole?
b. What is the everyday importance of this type of intermolecular force?

41. a. What is hydrogen bonding?
b. What accounts for its extraordinary strength?

42. What are London dispersion forces?

PRACTICE PROBLEMS

43. According to the VSEPR theory, what molecular geometries are associated with the following types of molecules?
a. AB_3E
b. AB_2E_2
c. AB_2E

44. Use hybridization to explain the bonding in methane, CH_4.

45. For each of the following polar molecules, indicate the direction of the resulting dipole:
a. H–F
b. H–Cl
c. H–Br
d. H–I

46. Determine whether each of the following bonds would be polar or nonpolar:
a. H–H
b. H–O
c. H–F
d. Br–Br
e. H–Cl
f. H–N

47. On the basis of individual bond polarity and orientation, determine whether each of the following molecules would be polar or nonpolar:
a. H_2O
b. I_2
c. CF_4
d. NH_3
e. CO_2

48. Draw a Lewis structure for each of the following molecules, and then use the VSEPR theory to predict the molecular geometry of each:
a. SCl_2
b. PI_3
c. Cl_2O
d. NH_2Cl
e. $SiCl_3Br$
f. ONCl

49. Draw a Lewis structure for each of the following polyatomic ions, and then use VSEPR theory to determine the geometry of each:
a. NO_3^-
b. NH_4^+
c. SO_4^{2-}
d. ClO_2^-

Mixed Review

REVIEWING MAIN IDEAS

50. Arrange the following pairs from strongest to weakest attraction:
a. polar molecule and polar molecule
b. nonpolar molecule and nonpolar molecule
c. polar molecule and ion
d. ion and ion

51. Determine the geometry of the following molecules:
a. CCl_4
b. $BeCl_2$
c. PH_3

52. What types of atoms tend to form the following types of bonding?
a. ionic
b. covalent
c. metallic

53. What happens to the energy level and stability of two bonded atoms when they are separated and become individual atoms?

54. Draw the three resonance structures for sulfur trioxide, SO_3.

55. a. How do ionic and covalent bonding differ?
b. How does an ionic compound differ from a molecular compound?
c. How does an ionic compound differ from a metal?

56. Write the electron-dot notation for each of the following elements:
a. He
b. Cl
c. O
d. P
e. B

57. Write the structural formula for methanol, CH_3OH.

58. How many K^+ and S^{2-} ions would be in one formula unit of the ionic compound formed by these ions?

59. Explain metallic bonding in terms of the sparsely populated outermost orbitals of metal atoms.

60. Explain the role of molecular geometry in determining molecular polarity.

61. How does the energy level of a hybrid orbital compare with the energy levels of the orbitals from which it was formed?

62. Aluminum's enthalpy of vaporization is 284 kJ/mol. Beryllium's enthalpy of vaporization is 224 kJ/mol. In which element is the bonding stronger between atoms?

63. Determine the electronegativity difference, the probable bonding type, and the more-electronegative atom for each of the following pairs of atoms:
a. Zn and O
b. Br and I
c. S and Cl

64. Draw the Lewis structure for each of the following molecules:
a. PCl_3
b. CCl_2F_2
c. CH_3NH_2

65. Draw the Lewis structure for $BeCl_2$. (Hint: Beryllium atoms do not follow the octet rule.)

66. Draw a Lewis structure for each of the following polyatomic ions and determine their geometries:
a. NO_2^-
b. NO_3^-
c. NH_4^+

67. Why do most atoms tend to be chemically bonded to other atoms?

CRITICAL THINKING

68. **Inferring Relationships** The length of a bond varies depending on the type of bond formed. Predict and compare the lengths of the carbon-carbon bonds in the following molecules. Explain your answer. (Hint: See Figure 2.10)

```
 H  H         H  H
 |  |         |  |
H–C–C–H     H–C=C–H      H–C≡C–H
 |  |
 H  H
```

C_2H_6 C_2H_4 C_2H_2

69. Why does F generally form covalent bonds with great polarity?

70. Explain what is wrong with the following Lewis structures, and then correct each one.

a. H–H–S̈:

```
      :O:
       ||   ..
b. H– C =O–H
            ..
```

```
      :Cl:
       ||
c.     N
      /  \
   :Cl    Cl:
```

71. Ionic compounds tend to have higher boiling points than covalent substances do. Both ammonia, NH_3, and methane, CH_4, are covalent compounds, yet the boiling point of ammonia is 130°C higher than that of methane. What might account for this large difference?

USING THE HANDBOOK

72. Figure 4.1 shows a model for a body-centered cubic crystal. Review the Properties tables for all of the metals in the *Elements Handbook* (Appendix A). What metals exist in body-centered cubic structures?

58. two potassium cations, K^+, and one sulfide anion, S^{2-}

59. Vacant orbitals in the outer energy levels of the metal's atoms overlap and are occupied by electrons from adjacent atoms.

60. Although a particular bond in a molecule may be polar, it is the arrangement of all the polar bonds in space—or molecular geometry—that determines whether a molecule is polar.

61. It lies between the energy levels of the orbitals from which it was made.

62. aluminum

63.

Elements bonded	Electro-negativity difference	Bond type	More-negative atom
a. Zn & O	1.9	ionic	O
b. Br & I	0.3	polar-covalent	Br
c. S & Cl	0.5	polar-covalent	Cl

CHAPTER REVIEW

64. a. :C̤l̈:P̤̈:C̤l̈: with :C̤l̈: below P
c. H:C:N:H with H above C and H H below

b. :F̤̈:C:C̤l̈: with :Cl: above C and :F: below C

65. a. :C̤l̈:Be:C̤l̈:

66. a. $[:\ddot{O}::\ddot{N}:\ddot{O}:]^-$ bent or angular
c. $[H:\ddot{N}:H]^+$ with H above and H below N — tetrahedral

b. $[:\ddot{O}:\ N::\ddot{O}:]^-$ with :O: above N — trigonal-planar

67. Most atoms are bonded to other atoms in nature because bonding lowers their potential energy.

68. The carbon-carbon triple bond in C_2H_2 is the strongest of the bonds. Therefore, it is the shortest because stronger bonds are shorter bonds. The carbon-carbon single bond in C_2H_6 is the weakest of the bonds, so it is the longest. From **Figure 2.5**, students should surmise that the lengths of the single, double, and triple carbon-carbon bonds are about 154 pm, 134 pm, and 120 pm, respectively.

69. F has the highest electronegativity and therefore has the greatest attraction for the electrons it shares in a covalent bond.

70. a. Hydrogen is never a central atom. The second hydrogen atom has two single bonds and can have only one single bond. The total number of valence electrons is wrong. Correct structure:

```
 H
 |
:S–H
 ..
```

b. The octet rule is not followed for the carbon atom or for the central oxygen atom. Correct structure:

```
   :O:
    ||
H– C –Ö–H
       ..
```

c. The top chlorine atoms contain too many electrons. Correct structure:

```
:C̈l– N̈ –C̈l:
      |
     :Cl:
```

71. Because of its shape (tetrahedral), methane is a nonpolar molecule. As a result, CH_4 molecules are not strongly attracted to one another. In contrast, ammonia is a polar molecule. As a result, NH_3 molecules are attracted to one another. Therefore, it takes more energy to separate ammonia molecules and change ammonia to a gas than to separate methane molecules.

72. Lithium, sodium, potassium, rubidium, cesium, barium, and radium are listed as bcc.

73. The electrons in metals require very little energy to enter the conduction band, which is a set of overlapping orbitals. Thus, electrons can move freely through a metal with a small, applied voltage.

Refer to the **HMDScience.com** web site for appropriate scoring rubrics for items 74–77. Look for the following points in each report:

74. a. Students should mention Dr. Pauling's role in establishing the electronegativity scale and in discovering the hydrogen bond. For this work, Dr. Pauling received a Nobel Prize.

b. Some scientists criticize Pauling for having been an advocate of something as trendy as vitamin supplements. Be sure students examine real scientific data, rather than political responses, to make their decision.

75. Students should discuss some properties of metalloids.

76. Answers may vary. Proteins are another type of substance that can have disulfide bridges.

77. Answers may vary.

78. Students might use either physical or chemical properties to distinguish between these substances. Ionic substances will be solid at room temperature, eliminating water. They will not conduct electricity, eliminating Cu. And they will be composed of more than one type of atom, eliminating C. Ionic solids are brittle and have high melting points.

79. Students' answers may vary greatly. Some possible responses include plastics *(covalent)*, paper *(covalent)*, wood *(covalent)*, dishes *(ionic or covalent)*, cookware *(metallic)*, and cloth *(covalent)*.

CHAPTER REVIEW

73. Group 14 of the *Elements Handbook* (Appendix A) contains a discussion of semiconductors and the band theory of metals. How does this model explain the electrical conductivity of metals?

RESEARCH AND WRITING

74. Prepare a report on the work of Linus Pauling.

a. Discuss his work on the nature of the chemical bond.

b. Linus Pauling was an advocate of the use of vitamin C as a preventative for colds. Evaluate Pauling's claims. Determine if there is any scientific evidence that indicates whether vitamin C helps prevent colds.

75. Covalently bonded solids, such as silicon, an element used in computer components, are harder than pure metals. Research theories that explain the hardness of covalently bonded solids and their usefulness in the computer industry. Present your findings to the class.

76. Natural rubber consists of long chains of carbon and hydrogen atoms covalently bonded together. When Charles Goodyear accidentally dropped a mixture of sulfur and rubber on a hot stove, the energy from the stove joined these chains together to make vulcanized rubber (named for Vulcan, the Roman god of fire). The carbon-hydrogen chains in vulcanized rubber are held together by two sulfur atoms that form covalent bonds between the chains. These covalent bonds are commonly called disulfide bridges. Explore other molecules that have such disulfide bridges. Present your findings to the class.

77. Searching for the perfect artificial sweetener—great taste with no Calories—has been the focus of chemical research for some time. Molecules such as sucralose, aspartamine, and saccharine owe their sweetness to their size and shape. One theory holds that any sweetener must have three sites that fit into the proper taste buds on the tongue. This theory is appropriately known as the "triangle theory." Research artificial sweeteners to develop a model to show how the triangle theory operates.

ALTERNATIVE ASSESSMENT

78. Devise a set of criteria that will allow you to classify the following substances as ionic or non-ionic: $CaCO_3$, Cu, H_2O, NaBr, and C (graphite). Show your criteria to your instructor.

79. **Performance Assessment** Identify 10 common substances in and around your home, and indicate whether you would expect these substances to contain ionic, covalent, or metallic bonds.

204 Chapter 6

Standards-Based Assessment

Answer the following items on a separate piece of paper.

MULTIPLE CHOICE

1. A chemical bond results from the mutual attraction of the nuclei for
   A. electrons.
   B. neutrons.
   C. protons.
   D. dipoles.

2. A polar covalent bond is likely to form between two atoms that
   A. are similar in electronegativity.
   B. are of similar size.
   C. differ in electronegativity.
   D. have the same number of electrons.

3. The Lewis structure of HCN contains
   A. one double bond and one single bond.
   B. one triple bond and one single bond.
   C. two single bonds.
   D. two double bonds.

4. According to VSEPR theory, the molecular geometry for CH_3^+ is
   A. tetrahedral.
   B. trigonal-pyramidal.
   C. bent or angular.
   D. None of the above

5. Which molecule contains a double bond?
   A. $COCl_2$
   B. C_2H_6
   C. CF_4
   D. SF_2

6. Which molecule is polar?
   A. CCl_4
   B. CO_2
   C. SO_3
   D. none of these

7. What is the hybridization of the carbon atoms in C_2H_2?
   A. *sp*
   B. sp^2
   C. sp^3
   D. The carbon atoms do not hybridize in C_2H_2.

8. Which of the following compounds is predicted to have the highest boiling point?
   A. HCl
   B. CH_3COOH (Note: The two oxygen atoms bond to the carbon.)
   C. Cl_2
   D. SO_2

9. An unknown substance is an excellent electrical conductor in the solid state and is malleable. What type of chemical bonding does this substance exhibit?
   A. ionic bonding
   B. molecular bonding
   C. metallic bonding
   D. cannot determine from the information given

SHORT RESPONSE

10. What does the hybridization model help explain?

11. Explain why ionic crystals are brittle.

EXTENDED RESPONSE

12. Naphthalene, $C_{10}H_8$, is a nonpolar molecule and has a boiling point of 218°C. Acetic acid, CH_3CO_2H, is a polar molecule and has a boiling point of 118°C. Which substance has the stronger intermolecular forces? Briefly explain your answer.

13. Describe and explain the potential energy changes that occur during the formation of a covalent bond.

Test Tip
When several questions refer to the same graph, table, drawing, or passage, answer the questions you are sure of first.

STANDARDS-BASED ASSESSMENT

To give students practice under more realistic testing conditions, give them 60 minutes to answer all of the questions in this Standardized Test Preparation.

Test Answers

1. A
2. C
3. B
4. D
5. A
6. D
7. A
8. B
9. C
10. Hybridization explains how the orbitals of an atom become re-arranged when the atom forms covalent bonds.
11. Ionic crystals are brittle because shifting of the layers of ions results in large repulsive forces that cause the layers to part completely.
12. Naphthalene has the stronger intermolecular forces even though it is nonpolar, because its boiling point is higher than that of acetic acid. Boiling point is directly correlated to strength of intermolecular forces; the stronger the intermolecular forces, the more energy needed to break all the intermolecular forces, and therefore the higher the boiling point. Naphthalene is so large that its dispersion forces are greater than the sum of the dispersion forces and hydrogen bonding in acetic acid.
13. There is a repulsive region at small bond distances, a minimum well at an intermediate bond distance, and an asymptotic region at large bond distances. The repulsive region is due to the repulsion between the two positive nuclei at distances where the nuclei are close to each other. The asymptotic region is where the atoms are far apart and therefore do not interact with each other. The potential energy decreases as the atoms come closer together and are attracted to each other. The minimum well is the region where the attractive forces are balanced by the repulsive forces. This distance is the equilibrium bond length.

Chemical Formulas and Chemical Compounds

① Core Instruction

Chapter Resources

- **The Teacher's Edition wrap has extensive teaching support for every lesson, including Misconception Alerts, Teach from Visuals, Demonstrations, Teaching Tips, Differentiated Instruction, and Problem Solving support.**
- **Several additional presentation tools are available online for every chapter, including Animated Chemistry features and Visual Concepts.**
- **You can open your lesson with the Why It Matters Video: Formulas and Compounds.**

Section	Instruction	Labs and Demonstrations Go Online for Materials Lists and Solutions Lists.
7.1	**Textbook: Chemical Names and Formulas** **Teaching Visuals:** Common Monatomic Ions • Polyatomic Ions • Writing the Formula of an Ionic Compound • Naming Compounds with Polyatomic Ions • Prefixes for Naming Covalent Compounds • Understanding Formulas for Polyatomic Ionic Compounds **PowerPresentations**	**Lab:** The Formula For Delicious (Open Inquiry)
7.2	**Textbook: Oxidation Numbers** **Teaching Visuals:** Common Oxidation States of Nonmetals **PowerPresentations**	**Demonstration:** Oxidation States **Lab:** Test for Fe(II) and Fe(III) (Core Skill)
7.3	**Textbook: Using Chemical Formulas** **Animated Chemistry:** Formula Mass and Molar Mass **Teaching Visuals:** Working Practice Problems • Mole-Mass Calculations • Converting Between Amount in Moles and Number of Particles • Converting Between Mass, Amount, and Number of Particles • Calculating Molar Masses for Ionic Compounds • Percentage Composition of Iron Oxides • Percentage Composition Calculations **PowerPresentations**	**Lab:** Water of Hydration (Core Skill)
7.4	**Textbook: Determining Chemical Formulas** **Teaching Visuals:** Empirical and Actual Formulas • Comparing Empirical and Molecular Formulas • Lab Technique: Heating Setup for a Crucible **PowerPresentations**	**Lab:** Determining the Empirical Formula of Magnesium Oxide (Core Skill)

2 Support and Intervention

- **Interactive Reader** (English and Spanish)
- **Study Guide**
- **Interactive Review:** Review Games, Concept Maps, and Section Self-Checks
- **Scientific Reasoning Skill Builder**
- **Learn It! Videos**
- **Solve It! Cards**
- **Interactive Demos**
- **Sample Problem Sets**

3 Specialized Support

- **Chapter Summary Audio Files**
- **Interactive Reader Audio Files**
- **Differentiated Instruction:** Inclusion, Below Level, and English Learners (TE wrap)

Enrichment and Challenge

- **Differentiated Instruction:** Pre-AP (TE wrap)
- **Why It Matters:** Mass Spectrometry: Identifying Molecules (SE)
- **WebLinks**

Assessment

- **Section Formative Assessments** (SE)
- **Section Quizzes**
- **Chapter Review** (SE)
- **Chapter Tests A and B**
- **Alternative Assessment** (TE wrap)
- **Online Assessment and Remediation**
- **ExamView Banks**

Where do I find it?

		PRINT	DVD	ONLINE
1	Animated Chemistry		■	■
1	Demonstrations (TE wrap)	■		■
1	Interactive Whiteboard		■	■
1	Labs		■	■
1	PowerPresentations		■	■
1	QuickLabs	■	■	■
1	Teaching Visuals		■	■
1	Textbook	■	■	■
1	Visual Concepts		■	■
1	Why It Matters Videos		■	■
2	Interactive Demos		■	■
2	Interactive Reader	■	■	■
2	Interactive Reviews		■	■
2	Learn It! Videos		■	■
2	Sample Problem Sets		■	■
2	Scientific Reasoning Skill Builder		■	■
2	Smart Grapher Tool		■	■
2	Solve It! Cards		■	■
2	Study Guide		■	■
3	Chapter Summary Audio Files		■	■
3	Differentiated Instruction (TE wrap)	■		
3	Interactive Reader Audio Files		■	■

CHAPTER 7

Chapter Overview

Section 1 describes the naming of binary ionic and molecular compounds.

Section 2 describes the way oxidation numbers are assigned and the Stock system of naming compounds.

Section 3 describes how to calculate formula masses, molar masses, and percentage compositions.

Section 4 describes how to determine chemical formulas from percentage compositions and empirical data.

▼ Focus and Motivate

Activate Prior Knowledge

Students may need a review of the following concepts:

- laws of multiple and definite proportions
- conversions between mass in grams and amount in moles
- electronegativity
- bonding in polyatomic ions

About the Image

Although compounds display a wide variety of properties, such as color, each compound has its own chemical name and formula.

Why It Matters

Students can access the video online and find other helpful resources at **HMDScience.com**.

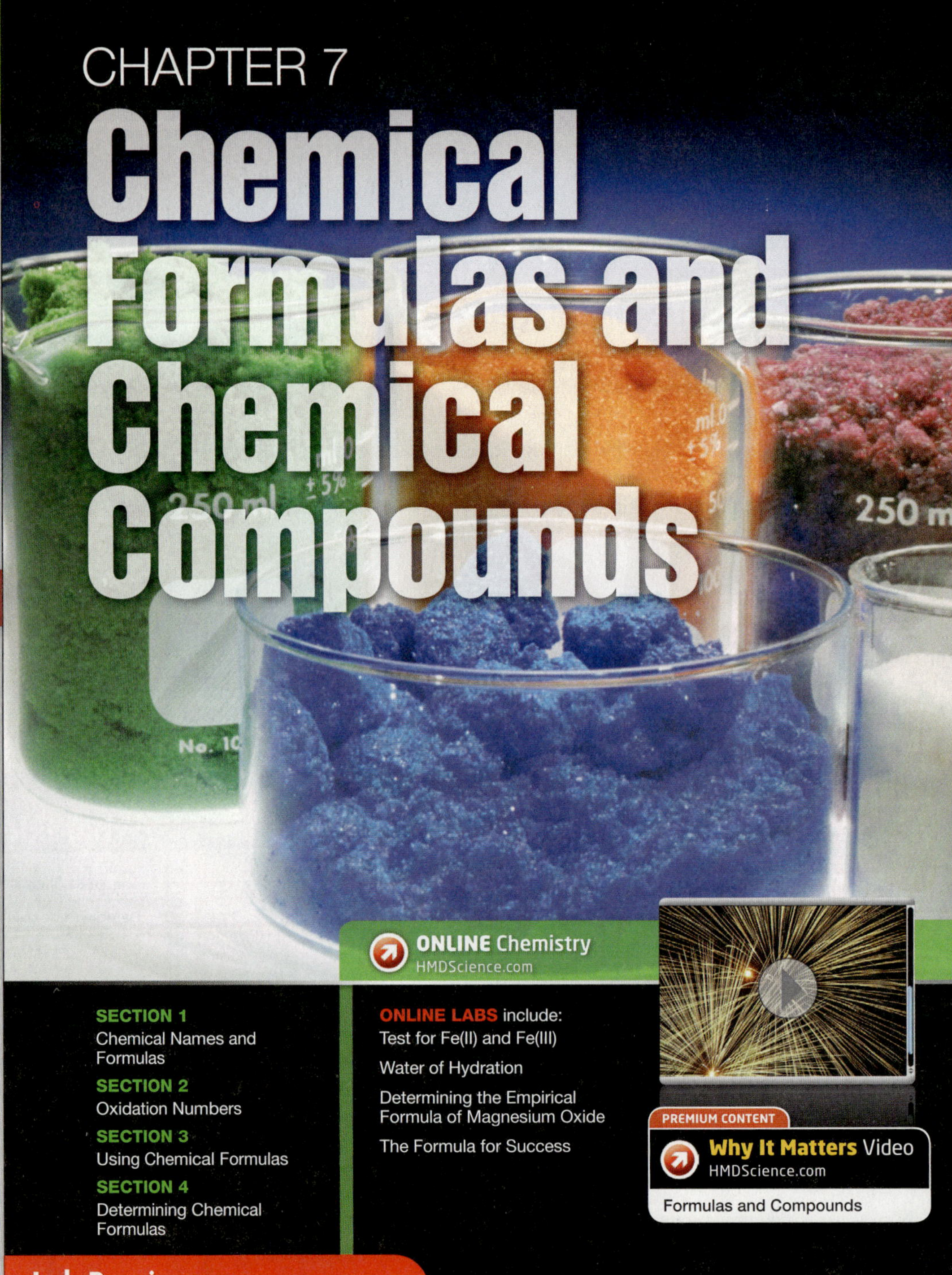

SECTION 1 Chemical Names and Formulas

SECTION 2 Oxidation Numbers

SECTION 3 Using Chemical Formulas

SECTION 4 Determining Chemical Formulas

ONLINE LABS include:

Test for Fe(II) and Fe(III)

Water of Hydration

Determining the Empirical Formula of Magnesium Oxide

The Formula for Success

PREMIUM CONTENT

Why It Matters Video
HMDScience.com

Formulas and Compounds

Lab Preview

The following labs and demonstrations support the concepts presented in this chapter.

LABS

Test for Fe(II) and Fe(III) (Core Skill)

Water of Hydration (Core Skill)

Determining the Empirical Formula of Magnesium Oxide (Core Skill)

The Formula for Success (Open Inquiry)

DEMONSTRATION

Oxidation States

Chemical Names and Formulas

Key Terms
monatomic ion
binary compound
nomenclature
oxyanion
salt

SECTION 1

Main Ideas

- Formulas tell the number and kinds of atoms in a compound.
- Monatomic ions are made of only one type of atom.
- Binary compounds contain atoms of two elements.
- Some covalent compounds are a network with no single molecules.
- Acids are solutions of water and a special type of compound.

The total number of natural and synthetic chemical compounds runs in the millions. For some of these substances, certain common names remain in everyday use. For example, calcium carbonate is better known as limestone, and sodium chloride is usually referred to simply as table salt. And everyone recognizes dihydrogen monoxide by its popular name, water.

Unfortunately, common names usually give no information about chemical composition. To describe the atomic makeup of compounds, chemists use systematic methods for naming compounds and writing chemical formulas. In this chapter, you will be introduced to some of the rules used to identify simple chemical compounds.

MAIN IDEA

Formulas tell the number and kinds of atoms in a compound.

Recall that a chemical formula indicates the relative number of atoms of each kind in a chemical compound. For a molecular compound, the chemical formula reveals the number of atoms of each element contained in a single molecule of the compound, as shown below for the hydrocarbon octane. (*Hydrocarbons* are molecular compounds composed solely of carbon and hydrogen.)

C_8H_{18}

Subscript indicates that there are 8 carbon atoms in a molecule of octane.

Subscript indicates that there are 18 hydrogen atoms in a molecule of octane.

Unlike a molecular compound, an ionic compound consists of a lattice of positive and negative ions held together by mutual attraction. The chemical formula for an ionic compound represents one formula unit—the simplest ratio of the compound's positive ions (cations) and its negative ions (anions). The chemical formula for aluminum sulfate, an ionic compound consisting of aluminum cations and polyatomic sulfate anions, is written as shown on the next page.

Differentiated Instruction

BELOW LEVEL

Ask students what they notice about the following chemical formulas: CH_4, CO_2, and CS_2. Students should recognize that a subscript is not used in a chemical formula when only one atom of the element is present.

SECTION 1

Plan and Prepare

Objectives

Upon completion of this section, students should be able to do the following:

- Explain the significance of a chemical formula.
- Determine the formula of an ionic compound formed between two given ions.
- Name an ionic compound given its formula.
- Using prefixes, name a binary molecular compound from its formula.
- Write the formula of a binary molecular compound given its name.

Classroom Catalyst

Write the formula for a binary molecular compound, such as carbon tetrachloride, CCl_4, and the formula for a binary ionic compound, such as magnesium chloride, $MgCl_2$, on the board. Have students guess the name of each compound based on its formula. Ask what kind of information they can discern from the formulas. Then ask them to guess which of the represented compounds is molecular and which is ionic. Explain that chemical formulas form the basis of the language of chemistry and reveal much information about the substances they represent.

Teach

Teaching Tip

The subscripts in the chemical formula for a compound reveal the ratio of atoms that make up the compound.

Application

Tell students that caffeine is a molecule that contains eight carbon atoms, ten hydrogen atoms, four nitrogen atoms, and two oxygen atoms. Ask them to write the chemical formula.

The formula is $C_8H_{10}N_4O_2$.

Teach *continued*

Classroom Discussion

Write the formula for aluminum sulfate on the board. Also write $Al_2S_3O_{12}$. Ask students to compare the number of atoms of each element in the two formulas. Ask why, then, if both formulas contain the same number of atoms of each element, it is incorrect to write the formula as $Al_2S_3O_{12}$. Students should recognize that without the parentheses around the polyatomic ion, the formula does not show that the elements in the ion act as a unit.

Teaching Tip

This text uses the convention of writing ion charges with the number preceding the sign, $n+$ and $n-$; this is done to distinguish ion charges from oxidation numbers, introduced later in this chapter, which are written as $+n$ and $-n$.

READING TOOLKIT

SUMMARIZING Have students read about how to name and write formulas for ionic and covalent compounds in Sections 1 and 2. After reading each topic, have volunteers summarize each process for the rest of the class. Have students ask for clarification of anything they do not understand once each summary is completed.

Check for Understanding

Answer: A good answer would be the following: The characteristic of atoms that determines whether they will exchange valence electrons or share them is their electronegativity. If the atoms have fairly equivalent electronegativities, then they will share the valence electrons. If there is a significant difference, then the atom with the greater electronegativity will pull valence electrons away from the atom that has the lower electronegativity.

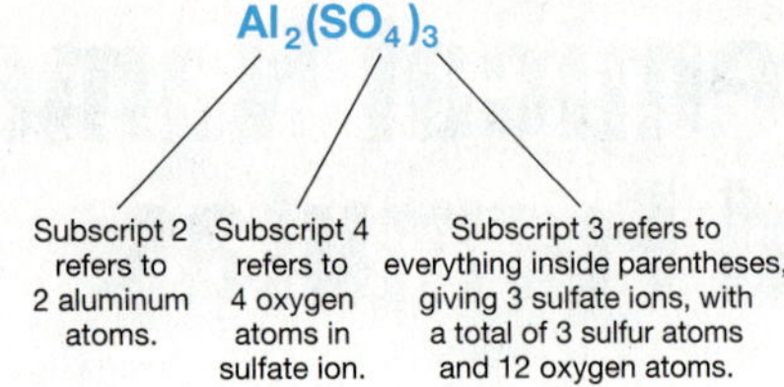

Note how the parentheses are used. They surround the polyatomic anion to identify it as a unit. The subscript 3 refers to the entire unit. Notice also that there is no subscript written next to the symbol for sulfur. When there is no subscript written next to an atom's symbol, the value of the subscript is understood to be 1.

MAIN IDEA

Monatomic ions are made of only one type of atom.

CHECK FOR UNDERSTANDING
Describe What characteristic of atoms determines whether they will exchange valence electrons (form an ionic compound) or share them (form a covalent compound)? Describe how this happens. Refer to the chapter "Chemical Bonding" for help.

By gaining or losing electrons, many main-group elements form ions with noble-gas configurations. For example, Group 1 metals lose one electron to give 1+ cations, such as Na^+. Group 2 metals lose two electrons to give 2+ cations, such as Mg^{2+}. **Ions formed from a single atom are known as monatomic ions.** The nonmetals of Groups 15, 16, and 17 gain electrons to form anions. For example, in ionic compounds nitrogen forms the 3− anion, N^{3-}. The three added electrons plus the five outermost electrons in nitrogen atoms give a completed outermost octet. Similarly, the Group 16 elements oxygen and sulfur form 2− anions, and the Group 17 halogens form 1− anions.

Not all main-group elements readily form ions, however. Rather than gain or lose electrons, atoms of carbon and silicon form covalent bonds in which they share electrons with other atoms. Other elements tend to form ions that do not have noble-gas configurations. For instance, it is difficult for the Group 14 metals tin and lead to lose four electrons to achieve a noble-gas configuration. Instead, they tend to lose the two electrons in their outer *p* orbitals but retain the two electrons in their outer *s* orbitals to form 2+ cations. (Tin and lead can also form molecular compounds in which all four valence electrons are involved in covalent bonding.)

Elements from the *d*-block form 2+, 3+, or, in a few cases, 1+ or 4+ cations. Many *d*-block elements form two ions of different charges. For example, copper forms 1+ and 2+ cations. Iron and chromium each form 2+ cations as well as 3+ cations. And vanadium forms 2+, 3+, and 4+ cations.

Examples of Cations

K^+
Potassium cation

Mg^{2+}
Magnesium cation

Naming Monatomic Ions

Monatomic cations are identified simply by the element's name, as illustrated by the examples at left. Naming monatomic anions is slightly more complicated. First, the ending of the element's name is dropped. Then the ending *-ide* is added to the root name, as illustrated by the examples on the next page.

Differentiated Instruction

BELOW LEVEL

On the board, write Iron (Fe). Beneath it, write 26 + (protons). Beneath that, write 26 − (electrons). Draw a line beneath the two and add them, showing students that the sum of the two is zero. Explain that an atom of iron has no electric charge because the positive charges of the protons and the negative charges of the electrons cancel each other out. Then ask students what would happen if an iron atom lost two electrons. Erase the 26 − (electrons) and replace it with 24 − (electrons). Add the protons and electrons again, showing the students that when there are two fewer electrons, the iron atom becomes an ion with a charge of +2. Follow the same procedure a second time, using oxygen, and show students what happens when oxygen gains two electrons. Finally, give students a list of common ions. Have them partner with another student and write beside each ion whether it gained or lost electrons and how many, based on its charge.

The names and symbols of the common monatomic cations and anions are organized according to their charges in **Figure 1.1**. The names of many of the ions in the table include Roman numerals. These numerals are part of the *Stock system* of naming chemical ions and elements. You will read more about the Stock system and other systems of naming chemicals later in this chapter.

Examples of Anions

Element	Anion
F Fluor*ine*	F^- Fluor*ide* anion
N Nitro*gen*	N^{3-} Nitr*ide* anion

FIGURE 1.1

SOME COMMON MONATOMIC IONS

Main-group elements

1+		2+		3+			
lithium	Li^+	beryllium	Be^{2+}	aluminum	Al^{3+}		
sodium	Na^+	magnesium	Mg^{2+}				
potassium	K^+	calcium	Ca^{2+}				
rubidium	Rb^+	strontium	Sr^{2+}				
cesium	Cs^+	barium	Ba^{2+}				
1–		**2–**		**3–**			
fluoride	F^-	oxide	O^{2-}	nitride	N^{3-}		
chloride	Cl^-	sulfide	S^{2-}	phosphide	P^{3-}		
bromide	Br^-						
iodide	I^-						

***d*-Block elements and others with multiple ions**

1+		2+		3+		4+	
copper(I)	Cu^+	vanadium(II)	V^{2+}	vanadium(III)	V^{3+}	vanadium(IV)	V^{4+}
silver	Ag^+	chromium(II)	Cr^{2+}	chromium(III)	Cr^{3+}	tin(IV)	Sn^{4+}
		manganese(II)	Mn^{2+}	iron(III)	Fe^{3+}	lead(IV)	Pb^{4+}
		iron(II)	Fe^{2+}	cobalt(III)	Co^{3+}		
		cobalt(II)	Co^{2+}				
		nickel(II)	Ni^{2+}				
		copper(II)	Cu^{2+}				
		zinc	Zn^{2+}				
		cadmium	Cd^{2+}				
		tin(II)	Sn^{2+}				
		mercury(II)	Hg^{2+}				
		lead(II)	Pb^{2+}				

TEACH FROM TABLES

FIGURE 1.1 Point out to students that the columns of 1+ and 2+ cations of the main-group elements in this table correspond to the columns of the Group 1 and Group 2 elements in the periodic table. The similarity of the contents and ordering of the columns results from the fact that these main-group elements have only one or two electrons in their outermost energy levels and tend to lose those electrons to form 1+ and 2+ cations, respectively.

Teaching Tip

Suggest to students that they may find flash cards helpful for learning the monatomic ions that many elements form. Each flash card could have the name of the element written on one side and the symbol(s) for the ion(s) that the element commonly forms written on the other side. For example, a card for tin would feature "tin" on one side and "Sn^{2+}, Sn^{4+}" on the other side.

ENGLISH LEARNERS

Have students open their textbooks to this page and look at the table. Explain the meaning of the Roman numerals used for some of the monatomic ions. Tell students that certain elements can lose different numbers of electrons, and the Roman numerals indicate how many electrons were lost. Then, ask them if they can describe the difference between the iron(II) cation and the iron(III) cation. The Stock system of nomenclature will be described later in this chapter.

▼ Teach *continued*

Application

Metallic aluminum, such as that used in house siding, is highly reactive. However, aluminum combines with oxygen from the air and rapidly develops a thin coating of aluminum oxide, Al_2O_3. This oxide is unreactive and serves as a protective coating on the outside of aluminum siding, preventing further reaction with the aluminum beneath.

ChemisTrivia

Although aluminum oxide is one of the most common compounds on Earth, pure aluminum was one of the rarest and most precious metals on Earth for centuries. The extreme stability of aluminum oxide made the process of extracting aluminum from its oxide difficult. It was not until the development of modern extraction processes, such as the Hall process, that aluminum could be produced cheaply and in large quantities.

Check for Understanding

Answer: A good answer might be the following: Use the tables of oxidation numbers to find the charges on the different ions. Write down the symbols for the two elements with the oxidation numbers as superscripts. Take the oxidation number for the positive ion, remove the plus sign, and use that as the subscript for the negative ion. Then take the oxidation number for the negative ion, remove the minus sign, and use that for the positive ion's subscript.

CAREERS IN CHEMISTRY

Pharmacist S.T.E.M.

Pharmacists work in many areas of healthcare. Traditionally, they have dispensed medications in pharmacies. Today, pharmacists work with other health professionals to develop and implement customized drug treatment plans. They advise medical professionals on the side effects of and interactions between medicines. Increasingly, pharmacists are working in nontraditional settings, such as in managed-care companies, pharmaceutical companies, and governmental agencies. In these settings, pharmacists establish drug guidelines, conduct drug reviews, and assist in the research and development of new drugs.

CHECK FOR UNDERSTANDING

Describe In your own words, describe how to determine the subscripts of a binary ionic compound by using the oxidation numbers of the ions.

MAIN IDEA

Binary compounds contain atoms of two elements.

Compounds composed of two elements are known as binary compounds. In a binary ionic compound, the total numbers of positive charges and negative charges must be equal. Therefore, the formula for such a compound can be written given the identities of the compound's ions. For example, magnesium and bromine combine to form the ionic compound magnesium bromide. Magnesium, a Group 2 metal, forms the Mg^{2+} cation. Note that the $^{2+}$ in Mg^{2+} is written as a superscript. Bromine, a halogen, forms the Br^- anion when combined with a metal. In each formula unit of magnesium bromide, two Br^- anions are required to balance the 2+ charge of the Mg^{2+} cation. The compound's formula must therefore indicate one Mg^{2+} cation and two Br^- anions. The symbol for the cation is written first.

Ions combined: Mg^{2+}, Br^-, Br^- *Chemical formula:* $MgBr_2$

Note that the $_2$ in Br_2 is written as a subscript. The charges of the ions are not included in the formula. This is usually the case when writing formulas for binary ionic compounds.

As an aid for determining subscripts in formulas for ionic compounds, the positive and negative charges can be "crossed over." Crossing over is a method of balancing the charges between ions in an ionic compound. For example, the formula for the compound formed by the aluminum ion, Al^{3+}, and the oxide ion, O^{2-}, is determined as follows.

1. *Write the symbols for the ions side by side. Write the cation first.*

$$Al^{3+} \quad O^{2-}$$

2. *Cross over the charges by using the absolute value of each ion's charge as the subscript for the other ion.*

$$Al_2^{3+} \quad O_3^{2-}$$

3. *Check the subscripts and divide them by their largest common factor to give the smallest possible whole-number ratio of ions. Then write the formula.*

Multiplying the charge by the subscript shows that the charge on two Al^{3+} cations $(2 \times 3+ = 6+)$ equals the charge on three O^{2-} anions $(3 \times 2- = 6-)$. The largest common factor of the subscripts is 1. The correct formula is therefore written as follows.

$$Al_2O_3$$

Naming Binary Ionic Compounds

The nomenclature, or naming system, of binary ionic compounds involves combining the names of the compound's positive and negative ions. The name of the cation is given first, followed by the name of the anion. For most simple ionic compounds, the ratio of the ions is not indicated in the compound's name, because it is understood based on the relative charges of the compound's ions.

Differentiated Instruction

BELOW LEVEL

Because some elements can form more than one cation, many students find naming a compound from its formula more difficult than writing the formula from its name. For example, students may name FeO as iron oxide, forgetting that there are two iron cations. Students may also forget to change the name of a nonmetal that forms an anion. For example, they may name FeS as iron sulfur. Have students work in pairs, taking turns writing formulas for ionic compounds and asking their partner to name the compound.

The naming of a simple binary ionic compound is illustrated below for aluminum chloride. Notice that the known relative charges of each ion make specifying ratios in the name unnecessary.

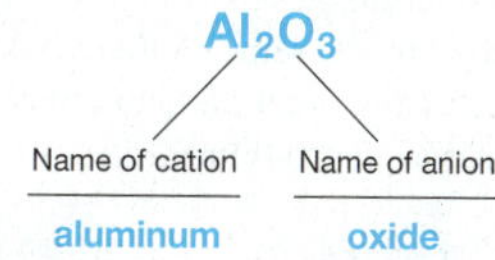

Writing Formulas For Ionic Compounds

Sample Problem A **Write the formulas for the binary ionic compounds formed between the following elements:**

a. zinc and iodine **b. zinc and sulfur**

 **SOLVE**

Write the symbols for the ions side by side. Write the cation first.

a. Zn^{2+} I^{-}

b. Zn^{2+} S^{2-}

Cross over the charges to give subscripts.

a. Zn_1^{2+} I_2^{-}

b. Zn_2^{2+} S_2^{2-}

Check the subscripts, and divide them by their largest common factor to give the smallest possible whole-number ratio of ions. Then write the formula.

a. The subscripts are mathematically correct because they give equal total charges of $1 \times 2+ = 2+$ and $2 \times 1- = 2-$. The largest common factor of the subscripts is 1.

The smallest possible whole-number ratio of ions in the compound is therefore 1:2.

The subscript 1 is not written, so the formula is ZnI_2.

b. The subscripts are mathematically correct because they give equal total charges of $2 \times 2+ = 4+$ and $2 \times 2- = 4-$. The largest common factor of the subscripts is 2.

The smallest whole-number ratio of ions in the compound is therefore 1:1.

The correct formula is ZnS.

Practice Answers in Appendix E

1. Write formulas for the binary ionic compounds formed between the following elements:
   - **a.** potassium and iodine
   - **b.** magnesium and chlorine
   - **c.** sodium and sulfur
   - **d.** aluminum and sulfur
   - **e.** aluminum and nitrogen
2. Name the binary ionic compounds indicated by the following formulas:
   - **a.** AgCl
   - **b.** ZnO
   - **c.** $CaBr_2$
   - **d.** SrF_2
   - **e.** BaO
   - **f.** $CaCl_2$

Classroom Practice

A-1 Write the formula for the binary ionic compound formed between each of the following pairs of elements:

a. magnesium and iodine
b. potassium and sulfur
c. aluminum and chlorine
d. zinc and bromine
e. cesium and sulfur
f. strontium and oxygen
g. calcium and nitrogen

Answers

a. MgI_2
b. K_2S
c. $AlCl_3$
d. $ZnBr_2$
e. Cs_2S
f. SrO
g. Ca_3N_2

A-2 Name the following binary ionic compounds:

a. BaF_2
b. CaO
c. AgF
d. CdO
e. K_3N
f. NaI
g. $AlBr_3$

Answers

a. barium fluoride
b. calcium oxide
c. silver fluoride
d. cadmium oxide
e. potassium nitride
f. sodium iodide
g. aluminum bromide

Answers

Practice A

1. **a.** KI
   b. $MgCl_2$
   c. Na_2S
   d. Al_2S_3
   e. AlN
2. **a.** silver chloride
   b. zinc oxide
   c. calcium bromide
   d. strontium fluoride
   e. barium oxide
   f. calcium chloride

Problem Solving

ALTERNATIVE APPROACHES

Show students the "crisscross" method for writing the formula of a binary ionic compound. In this method, the superscript that represents the charge on one atom is crossed so that it becomes the subscript of the other atom. The same exchange is done with the other superscript, thus resulting in the name "crisscross." Show students how this is done by writing the ions Mg^{2+} and N^{3-} on the board and then showing how the superscripts are crisscrossed to get the formula, Mg_3N_2. Be sure that students recognize that if a cation with a 1+ charge or an anion with a 1− charge is involved, then the superscript 1 is not written as a subscript in the chemical formula when it is crisscrossed.

▼ Teach *continued*

ChemisTrivia

Cations of different charge formed by the same element were once named using the Latin or Greek name of the element and the suffixes *-ous* for the ion of lower charge and *-ic* for the ion of higher charge. For example, the iron(II) ion and the iron(III) ion were formerly called the *ferrous* ion and the *ferric* ion, respectively. The copper(I) ion and the copper(II) ion were called the *cuprous* ion and the *cupric* ion. The endings did not correspond to the actual charge for all such elements, which led to confusion. As a result, the system is no longer commonly advocated today.

TEACH FROM VISUALS

FIGURE 1.2 Students should note that although the two substances shown are made up of the same two elements, they are different compounds because the elements are present in different proportions. Have students interpret the Stock system names for the two compounds.

The Stock System of Nomenclature

Some elements, such as iron, form two or more cations with different charges. To distinguish the ions formed by such elements, scientists use the Stock system of nomenclature. It is useful for distinguishing two different compounds formed by the same elements, as the lead oxides in **Figure 1.2.** This system uses a Roman numeral to indicate an ion's charge. The numeral in parentheses is placed *immediately* after the metal name.

Fe^{2+}	Fe^{3+}
iron(II)	iron(III)

Names of metals that commonly form only one cation do *not* include a Roman numeral.

Na^{+}	Ba^{2+}	Al^{3+}
sodium	barium	aluminum

No element forms more than one monatomic anion.

Naming a binary ionic compound according to the Stock system is illustrated below.

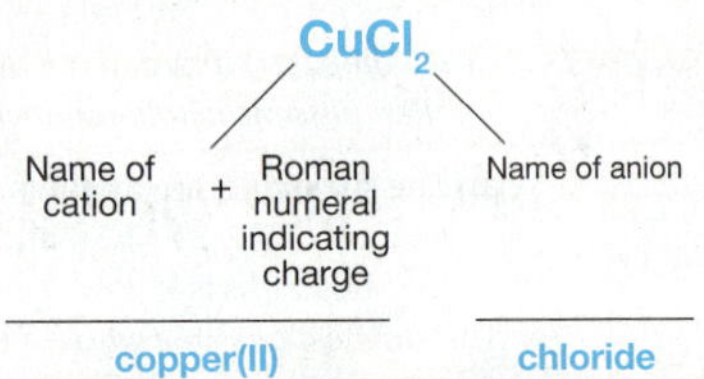

FIGURE 1.2

Different Cations of a Metal Different cations of the same metal form different compounds even when they combine with the same anion.

Differentiated Instruction

PRE-AP

Although an element usually forms only one monatomic anion, this element can form more than one cation. For example, chlorine normally forms an anion with a 1− charge, but is listed on some periodic tables with positive charges ranging from 1+ to 7+. Have students research how elements such as chlorine that usually form an anion can also form more than one cation.

Naming Ionic Compounds

Sample Problem B **Write the formula and give the name for the compound formed by the ions Cr^{3+} and F^-.**

 **SOLVE**

Write the symbols for the ions side by side. Write the cation first.

$$Cr^{3+} \quad F^-$$

Cross over the charges to give subscripts.

$$Cr_1^{3+} \quad F_3^-$$

Check the subscripts, and write the formula.

The subscripts are correct because they give charges of $1 \times 3+ = 3+$ and $3 \times 1- = 3-$. The largest common factor of the subscripts is 1, so the smallest whole-number ratio of the ions is 1:3. The formula is therefore CrF_3. As **Figure 1.1** shows, chromium forms more than one ion. Therefore, the name of the 3+ chromium ion must be followed by a Roman numeral indicating its charge. The compound's name is chromium(III) fluoride.

Practice Answers in Appendix E

1. Write the formula and give the name for the compounds formed between the following ions:
   - **a.** Cu^{2+} and Br^-
   - **b.** Fe^{2+} and O^{2-}
   - **c.** Pb^{2+} and Cl^-
   - **d.** Hg^{2+} and S^{2-}
   - **e.** Sn^{2+} and F^-
   - **f.** Fe^{3+} and O^{2-}
2. Give the names for the following compounds:
   - **a.** CuO
   - **b.** CoF_3
   - **c.** SnI_4
   - **d.** FeS

Compounds Containing Polyatomic Ions

Figure 1.3 on the next page lists some common polyatomic ions. Most are negatively charged and most are **oxyanions**—polyatomic ions that contain oxygen. Some elements can combine with oxygen to form more than one type of oxyanion. For example, nitrogen can form NO_3^- or NO_2^-. The name given a compound containing such an oxyanion depends on the number of oxygen atoms in the oxyanion. The name of the ion with the greater number of oxygen atoms ends in *-ate*. The name of the ion with the smaller number of oxygen atoms ends in *-ite*.

NO_2^-	NO_3^-
nitrite	nitrate

Problem Solving

DECONSTRUCTING PROBLEMS

Provide students with the formulas for various ionic compounds. Include some formulas that are written incorrectly, such as Ca_2O and KS_2. Have students check whether each formula is correct by determining whether the compound is neutral. For example, Ca_2O is incorrect because $2 \times 2+$ (the charge on Ca) $= 4+$, and $1 \times 2-$ (the charge on O) $= 2-$, resulting in a net charge of 2+.

Classroom Practice

B-1 Write the formula and give the name for the compound formed between each of the following pairs of ions:

- **a.** Cu^+ and O^{2-}
- **b.** Fe^{3+} and S^{2-}
- **c.** Cu^{2+} and Cl^-
- **d.** Sn^{2+} and Cl^-
- **e.** Hg^{2+} and O^{2-}
- **f.** Sn^{4+} and S^{2-}
- **g.** V^{2+} and F^-
- **h.** V^{3+} and Br^-

Answers:

- **a.** Cu_2O, copper(I) oxide
- **b.** Fe_2S_3, iron(III) sulfide
- **c.** $CuCl_2$, copper(II) chloride
- **d.** $SnCl_2$, tin(II) chloride
- **e.** HgO, mercury(II) oxide
- **f.** SnS_2, tin(IV) sulfide
- **g.** VF_2, vanadium(II) fluoride
- **h.** VBr_3, vanadium(III) bromide

B-2 Give the names for the following compounds:

- **a.** CoI_2
- **b.** HgI_2
- **c.** PbS_2
- **d.** $CuBr_2$

Answers:

- **a.** cobalt(II) iodide
- **b.** mercury(II) iodide
- **c.** lead(IV) sulfide
- **d.** copper(II) bromide

Answers

Practice B

1. **a.** $CuBr_2$, copper(II) bromide
   b. FeO, iron(II) oxide
   c. $PbCl_2$, lead(II) chloride
   d. HgS, mercury(II) sulfide
   e. SnF_2, tin(II) fluoride
   f. Fe_2O_3, iron(III) oxide
2. **a.** copper(II) oxide
   b. cobalt(III) fluoride
   c. tin(IV) iodide
   d. iron(II) sulfide

▼ Teach *continued*

TEACH FROM TABLES

FIGURE 1.3 Point out that the atoms composing polyatomic ions are held together by covalent bonds. These ions can therefore be modeled with Lewis dot structures. Have students construct such structures for various polyatomic ions in the table.

Application

Hypochlorites are often used in laundry bleaches and in swimming pool disinfectants. The hypochlorite ion reacts with water to produce hypochlorous acid (HClO) which, like elemental chlorine, effectively kills bacteria.

FIGURE 1.3

SOME POLYATOMIC IONS

1+		2+			
ammonium	NH_4^+	dimercury*	Hg_2^{2+}		

1–		2–		3–	
acetate	CH_3COO^-	carbonate	CO_3^{2-}	arsenate	AsO_4^{3-}
bromate	BrO_3^-	chromate	CrO_4^{2-}	phosphate	PO_4^{3-}
chlorate	ClO_3^-	dichromate	$Cr_2O_7^{2-}$		
chlorite	ClO_2^-	hydrogen phosphate	HPO_4^{2-}		
cyanide	CN^-	oxalate	$C_2O_4^{2-}$		
dihydrogen phosphate	$H_2PO_4^-$	peroxide	O_2^{2-}		
hydrogen carbonate (bicarbonate)	HCO_3^-	sulfate	SO_4^{2-}		
hydrogen sulfate	HSO_4^-	sulfite	SO_3^{2-}		
hydroxide	OH^-				
hypochlorite	ClO^-				
nitrate	NO_3^-				
nitrite	NO_2^-				
perchlorate	ClO_4^-				
permanganate	MnO_4^-				

*The mercury(I) cation exists as two Hg^+ ions joined together by a covalent bond and is written as Hg_2^{2+}.

Sometimes, an element can form more than two types of oxyanions. In this case, the prefix *hypo-* is given to an anion that has one fewer oxygen atom than the -ite anion. The prefix *per-* is given to an anion that has one more oxygen atom than the -ate anion. This nomenclature is illustrated by the four oxyanions formed by chlorine.

ClO^-	ClO_2^-	ClO_3^-	ClO_4^-
hypochlorite	chlorite	chlorate	perchlorate

Compounds containing polyatomic ions are named in the same manner as binary ionic compounds. The name of the cation is given first, followed by the name of the anion. For example, the two compounds formed with silver by the nitrate and nitrite anions are named *silver nitrate*, $AgNO_3$, and *silver nitrite*, $AgNO_2$, respectively. When multiples of a polyatomic ion are present in a compound, the formula for the polyatomic ion is enclosed in parentheses.

Differentiated Instruction

INCLUSION

Drawing Lewis structures can be especially useful for visual learners. Draw for students the Lewis structure for a chlorate ion. Use the structure to show that the atoms of a polyatomic ion are covalently bonded to one another but, as a unit, form an ion.

Writing Formulas for Ionic Compounds

Sample Problem C **Write the formula for tin(IV) sulfate.**

SOLVE

Write the symbols for the ions side by side. Write the cation first.

$$Sn^{4+} \quad SO_4^{2-}$$

Cross over the charges to give subscripts. Add parentheses around the polyatomic ion if necessary.

$$Sn_2^{4+} \quad (SO_4)_4^{2-}$$

Check the subscripts and write the formula.
The total positive charge is $2 \times 4+ = 8+$. The total negative charge is $4 \times 2- = 8-$. The charges are equal. The largest common factor of the subscripts is 2, so the smallest whole-number ratio of ions in the compound is 1:2. The correct formula is therefore $Sn(SO_4)_2$.

Practice

1. Write formulas for the following ionic compounds:
   a. sodium iodide
   b. calcium chloride
   c. potassium sulfide
   d. lithium nitrate
   e. copper(II) sulfate
   f. sodium carbonate
   g. calcium nitrite
   h. potassium perchlorate
2. Give the names for the following compounds:
   a. Ag_2O
   b. $Ca(OH)_2$
   c. $KClO_3$
   d. NH_4OH
   e. $Fe_2(CrO_4)_3$
   f. KClO

Naming Binary Molecular Compounds

Unlike ionic compounds, molecular compounds are composed of individual covalently bonded units, or molecules. Chemists use two nomenclature systems to name binary molecules. The newer system is the Stock system for naming molecular compounds, which requires an understanding of oxidation numbers. This system will be discussed in Section 2.

The old system of naming molecular compounds is based on the use of prefixes. For example, the molecular compound CCl_4 is named carbon *tetra*chloride. The prefix *tetra-* indicates that four chloride atoms are present in a single molecule of the compound. The two oxides of carbon, CO and CO_2, are named carbon *mon*oxide and carbon *di*oxide, respectively. These prefix-based names are often the most widely-recognized names for some molecular compounds. However, either naming system is acceptable, unless specified otherwise.

Classroom Practice

C-1 Write formulas for the following ionic compounds:

a. copper(II) nitrate
b. potassium iodide
c. sodium hydroxide
d. ammonium acetate
e. calcium carbonate

Answers: **a.** $Cu(NO_3)_2$
b. KI
c. NaOH
d. NH_4CH_3COO
e. $CaCO_3$

C-2 Give the names of the following compounds:

a. Ag_2S
b. $NaMnO_4$
c. $Ba(OH)_2$
d. NH_4NO_3
e. $Fe(ClO)_2$

Answers: **a.** silver sulfide
b. sodium permanganate
c. barium hydroxide
d. ammonium nitrate
e. iron(II) hypochlorite

Answers

Practice C

1. a. NaI
   b. $CaCl_2$
   c. K_2S
   d. $LiNO_3$
   e. $CuSO_4$
   f. Na_2CO_3
   g. $Ca(NO_2)_2$
   h. $KClO_4$
2. a. silver oxide
   b. calcium hydroxide
   c. potassium chlorate
   d. ammonium hydroxide
   e. iron(III) chromate
   f. potassium hypochlorite

Problem Solving

DECONSTRUCTING PROBLEMS

Point out that the process of writing the formulas for ionic compounds with polyatomic ions is the same as the process for writing formulas for binary ionic compounds. The only difference is that students must remember to place the polyatomic ion in parentheses if it is present in the formula more than once.

▼ Teach *continued*

Alternative Assessment

After reviewing the meanings of the various numerical prefixes, carry out a drill concerning their uses by calling out formulas and asking students to use the prefixes to name the compounds. You may wish to have students work together in teams in TV-quiz-show fashion.

Teaching Tip

Many college texts do not address the naming of binary molecular compounds using the Stock system. Instead, they adhere solely to the prefix system to identify such compounds.

Misconception Alert!

Students often think that, like an ionic formula, a correctly written molecular formula shows the simplest ratio of atoms in the compound that the formula represents. However, a molecular formula represents the actual numbers of individual atoms in a molecule of the compound. Thus, the subscripts in such formulas are not always reduced to the smallest possible ratio. For example, the molecular formulas for ethyne (acetylene) and benzene are C_2H_2 and C_6H_6, respectively. Reducing the subscripts to the smallest possible ratios would produce CH in these two cases, although the compounds are completely different.

FIGURE 1.4

NUMERICAL PREFIXES

Number	Prefix
1	mono-
2	di-
3	tri-
4	tetra-
5	penta-
6	hexa-
7	hepta-
8	octa-
9	nona-
10	deca-

In these names, the prefix *mon-* (from *mono-*) indicates one oxygen atom, and the prefix *di-* indicates two oxygen atoms. The prefixes used to specify the number of atoms in a molecule are listed in **Figure 1.4.**

The rules for the prefix system of nomenclature of binary molecular compounds are as follows.

1. The element that has the smaller group number is usually given first. If both elements are in the same group, the element whose period number is greater is given first. The element is given a prefix only if it contributes more than one atom to a molecule of the compound.
2. The second element is named by combining (a) a prefix indicating the number of atoms contributed by the element, (b) the root of the name of the element, and (c) the ending *-ide*. With few exceptions, the ending *-ide* indicates that a compound contains only two elements.
3. The *o* or *a* at the end of a prefix is usually dropped when the word following the prefix begins with another vowel. For example, one would write *monoxide* and *pentoxide* instead of *mono-oxide* and *penta-oxide*.

The prefix system is illustrated below.

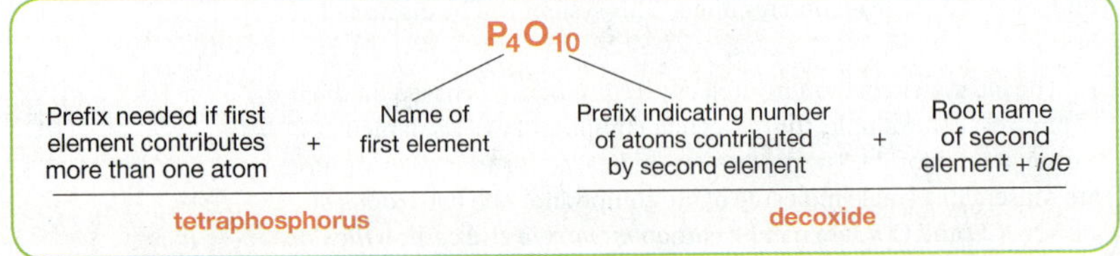

In general, the order of nonmetals in binary compound names and formulas is C, P, N, H, S, I, Br, Cl, O, and F.

Differentiated Instruction

ENGLISH LEARNERS

To help students become familiar with the prefixes used to name molecules, provide some common examples of words with prefixes, such as *monopoly*, *diverge*, *triathlon*, *pentagon*, and *octane*. Ask students to select two terms and explain how the prefixes in these words are similar to those used to name chemical compounds. For example, a *pentagon* is a structure with five sides, while the prefix *penta-* in chemical nomenclature indicates the presence of five atoms in a molecule.

FIGURE 1.5

BINARY COMPOUNDS OF NITROGEN AND OXYGEN

Formula	Prefix-system name
N_2O	dinitrogen monoxide
NO	nitrogen monoxide
NO_2	nitrogen dioxide
N_2O_3	dinitrogen trioxide
N_2O_4	dinitrogen tetroxide
N_2O_5	dinitrogen pentoxide

The prefix system is illustrated further in **Figure 1.5**, which lists the names of the six oxides of nitrogen. Note the application of rule 1, for example, in the name *nitrogen dioxide* for NO_2. No prefix is needed with *nitrogen* because only one atom of nitrogen is present in a molecule of NO_2. On the other hand, according to rule 2, the prefix *di-* in *dioxide* is needed to indicate the presence of two atoms of oxygen. Take a moment to review the prefixes in the other names in **Figure 1.5**.

CHECK FOR UNDERSTANDING

Explain You have learned several ways to name compounds. Explain why it is necessary to have so many different methods of nomenclature.

PREMIUM CONTENT

SolveIt! Cards
HMDScience.com

Naming Binary Molecular Compounds

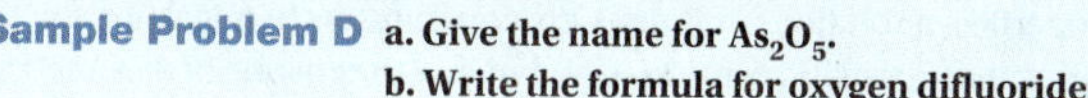

Sample Problem D **a. Give the name for As_2O_5.**
b. Write the formula for oxygen difluoride.

SOLVE

a. A molecule of the compound contains two arsenic atoms, so the first word in the name is *diarsenic*. The five oxygen atoms are indicated by adding the prefix *pent-* to the word *oxide*. The complete name is *diarsenic pentoxide*.

b. The first symbol in the formula is that for oxygen. Oxygen is first in the name because it is less electronegative than fluorine. Since there is no prefix, there must be only one oxygen atom. The prefix *di-* in *difluoride* shows that there are two fluorine atoms in the molecule. The formula is OF_2.

Practice Answers in Appendix E

1. Name the following binary molecular compounds:
   - **a.** SO_3
   - **b.** ICl_3
   - **c.** PBr_5
2. Write formulas for the following compounds:
   - **a.** carbon tetraiodide
   - **b.** phosphorus trichloride
   - **c.** dinitrogen trioxide

Problem Solving

TAKE IT FURTHER

Ask students to use prefixes to give the scientific name for water (dihydrogen monoxide) and for hydrogen peroxide, H_2O_2 (dihydrogen dioxide).

Teaching Tip

It is common practice to omit the prefix *mono-* when naming the second element of a binary molecular compound. For example, nitrogen monoxide, NO, is frequently referred to as nitrogen oxide. One exception to this practice is carbon monoxide, in which the prefix is never omitted.

Classroom Practice

D-1 Name the following binary molecular compounds:

a. PF_5
b. XeF_4
c. CCl_4

Answers: a. phosphorus pentafluoride
b. xenon tetrafluoride
c. carbon tetrachloride

D-2 Write formulas for the following compounds:

a. carbon dioxide
b. dinitrogen pentoxide
c. sulfur hexafluoride

Answers: a. CO_2
b. N_2O_5
c. SF_6

Answers

Practice D

1. **a.** sulfur trioxide
   b. iodine trichloride
   c. phosphorus pentabromide
2. **a.** CI_4
   b. PCl_3
   c. N_2O_3

Check for Understanding

Answer: A good answer would be the following: For most compounds, the compound's name indicates to chemists what type of compound it is. In the case of binary molecular compounds, there are two methods of naming them, because many scientists are used to the older method.

▼ Teach *continued*

TEACH FROM TABLES

FIGURE 1.6 Ask students to identify what is similar about the formulas of all the acids shown in the table. All contain the symbol for hydrogen. Point out that most common acidic substances contain hydrogen. Ask students to familiarize themselves with the formulas of a few of the most common acids, such as hydrochloric acid, sulfuric acid, nitric acid, phosphoric acid, carbonic acid, and acetic acid.

Teaching Tip

In diluting concentrated acids, it is important never to add water to acid because the water, being less dense, tends to remain on top, where it becomes hot and may boil and spatter.

MAIN IDEA

Some covalent compounds are a network with no single molecules.

Some covalent compounds do not consist of individual molecules. Instead, each atom is joined to all its neighbors in a covalently bonded, three-dimensional network. There are no distinct units in these compounds, just as there are no such units in ionic compounds. The subscripts in a formula for a covalent-network compound indicate the smallest whole-number ratio of the atoms in the compound. Naming such compounds is similar to naming molecular compounds. Some common examples are given below.

SiC	SiO_2	Si_3N_4
silicon carbide	silicon dioxide	trisilicon tetranitride

MAIN IDEA

Acids are solutions of water and a special type of compound.

An *acid* is a distinct type of molecular compound. Most acids used in the laboratory can be classified as either binary acids or oxyacids. *Binary acids* are acids that consist of two elements, usually hydrogen and one of the halogens— fluorine, chlorine, bromine, iodine. *Oxyacids* are acids that contain hydrogen, oxygen, and a third element (usually a nonmetal).

Acids were first recognized as a specific class of compounds based on their properties in solutions of water. Consequently, in chemical nomenclature, the term *acid* usually refers to a solution in water of one of these special compounds rather than to the compound itself. For example, *hydrochloric acid* refers to a water solution of the molecular compound hydrogen chloride, HCl. Some common binary and oxyacids are listed in **Figure 1.6. Figure 1.7** shows some common laboratory acids.

Many polyatomic ions are produced by the loss of hydrogen ions from oxyacids. A few examples of the relationship between oxyacids and oxyanions are shown below.

sulfuric acid	H_2SO_4	sulfate	SO_4^{2-}
nitric acid	HNO_3	nitrate	NO_3^-
phosphoric acid	H_3PO_4	phosphate	PO_4^{3-}

FIGURE 1.6

COMMON BINARY ACIDS AND OXYACIDS

HF	hydrofluoric acid	HNO_2	nitrous acid	$HClO$	hypochlorous acid
HCl	hydrochloric acid	HNO_3	nitric acid	$HClO_2$	chlorous acid
HBr	hydrobromic acid	H_2SO_3	sulfurous acid	$HClO_3$	chloric acid
HI	hydriodic acid	H_2SO_4	sulfuric acid	$HClO_4$	perchloric acid
H_3PO_4	phosphoric acid	CH_3COOH	acetic acid	H_2CO_3	carbonic acid

Differentiated Instruction

PRE-AP

Tell students that both diamond and graphite are covalent networks made of carbon atoms covalently bonded to one another. Have students research how the carbon atoms are bonded to one another in both of these compounds. Have students explain why diamond is hard, while graphite is soft.

FIGURE 1.7

Common Acids Some common laboratory acids are nitric acid, hydrochloric acid, and sulfuric acid. Acids should always be handled with care and according to instructions. They can burn holes in skin or clothing.

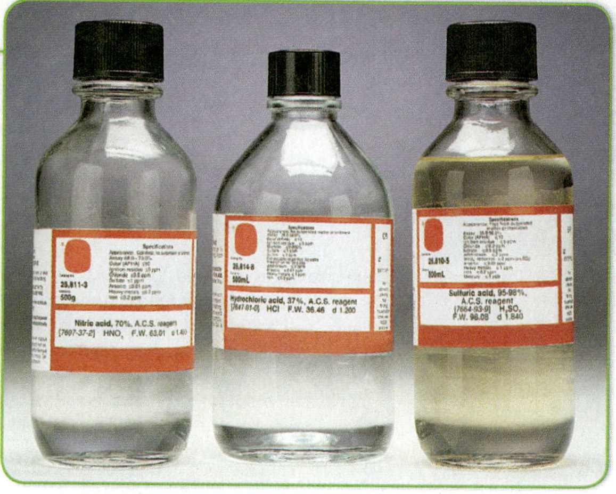

An ionic compound composed of a cation and the anion from an acid is often referred to as a **salt**. Table salt, NaCl, contains the anion from hydrochloric acid. Calcium sulfate, $CaSO_4$, is a salt containing an anion from sulfuric acid. Some salts contain anions in which one or more hydrogen atoms from the acid are retained. Such anions are named by adding the word *hydrogen* or the prefix *bi-* to the anion name. The best known such anion comes from carbonic acid, H_2CO_3.

HCO_3^-
hydrogen carbonate ion
bicarbonate ion

SECTION 1 FORMATIVE ASSESSMENT

Reviewing Main Ideas

1. What is the significance of a chemical formula?
2. Write formulas for the compounds formed between the following:
   a. aluminum and bromine
   b. sodium and oxygen
   c. magnesium and iodine
   d. Pb^{2+} and O^{2-}
   e. Sn^{2+} and I^-
   f. Fe^{3+} and S^{2-}
   g. Cu^{2+} and NO_3^-
   h. NH_4^+ and SO_4^{2-}
3. Name the following compounds by using the Stock system:
   a. NaI c. CaO e. CuBr
   b. MgS d. K_2S f. $FeCl_2$
4. Write formulas for each of the following compounds:
   a. sodium hydroxide e. carbon diselenide
   b. lead(II) nitrate f. acetic acid
   c. iron(II) sulfate g. chloric acid
   d. diphosphorus trioxide h. sulfurous acid

Critical Thinking

5. **RELATING IDEAS** Draw the Lewis structure, give the name, and predict VSEPR geometry of SCl_2.

TEACH FROM VISUALS

FIGURE 1.7 Review the formulas for each of the three acids pictured. Point out that all of these acids are extremely corrosive and potentially dangerous. Ask students to discuss laboratory safety principles they should use in working with such acids.

Assess and Reteach

Assess Use the Formative Assessment on this page to evaluate student mastery of the section.

Reteach For students who need additional instruction, download the Section Study Guide.

Response to Intervention To reassess students' mastery, use the Section Quiz, available to print or to take directly online at **HMDScience.com**.

Answers to Section Assessment

1. It indicates the types and numbers of atoms or ions present in a formula unit or molecule of a compound.
2. a. $AlBr_3$
   b. Na_2O
   c. MgI_2
   d. PbO
   e. SnI_2
   f. Fe_2S_3
   g. $Cu(NO_3)_2$
   h. $(NH_4)_2SO_4$
3. a. sodium iodide
   b. magnesium sulfide
   c. calcium oxide
   d. potassium sulfide
   e. copper(I) bromide
   f. iron(II) chloride
4. a. NaOH e. CSe_2
   b. $Pb(NO_3)_2$ f. CH_3COOH
   c. $FeSO_4$ g. $HClO_3$
   d. P_2O_3 h. H_2SO_3
5. :S̤̈ – C̤̈l:
   |
   :C̤l:
   sulfur dichloride, bent or angular

SECTION 2

▼ Plan and Prepare

Objectives

Upon completion of this section, students should be able to do the following:

- List the rules for assigning oxidation numbers.
- Give the oxidation number for each element in the formula of a chemical compound.
- Name binary molecular compounds using oxidation numbers and the Stock system.

Classroom Catalyst

Remind students that it is possible to determine the charge of an ion in an ionic compound given the charges of the other ions present in the compound. For example, ask students to determine the charge on the bromide ion in the compound NaBr given that Na^+ has a 1+ charge. The total charge is 0, so Br- must have a charge of 1- in order to balance the 1+ charge of Na+. Explain that, in similar fashion, numbers called oxidation numbers can be assigned to atoms in order to keep track of electron distributions in molecular as well as ionic compounds. Point out that the system is based on electronegativity. Explain that in this section, students will learn how to use oxidation numbers in compounds and polyatomic ions.

▼ Teach

Misconception Alert!

Students often confuse oxidation numbers with charges. Remind them that charges are physically real characteristics but oxidation numbers are simply artificial "bookkeeping" devices to keep track of overall electron distribution. Oxidation numbers are not actual physical characteristics of atoms.

SECTION 2

Main Ideas

- Specific rules are used to assign oxidation numbers.
- Many nonmetals have multiple oxidation numbers.

Oxidation Numbers

Key Terms
oxidation number
oxidation state

The charges on the ions composing an ionic compound reflect the electron distribution of the compound. **In order to indicate the general distribution of electrons among the bonded atoms in a molecular compound or a polyatomic ion, oxidation numbers, also called oxidation states, are assigned to the atoms composing the compound or ion.** Unlike ionic charges, oxidation numbers do not have an exact physical meaning. In fact, they are quite arbitrary in some cases. However, oxidation numbers are useful in naming compounds, in writing formulas, and in balancing chemical equations. And, as is discussed in the chapter "Chemical Equations and Reactions", they are helpful in studying certain reactions.

MAIN IDEA

Specific rules are used to assign oxidation numbers.

As a general rule in assigning oxidation numbers, shared electrons are assumed to belong to the more electronegative atom in each bond. More specific rules for determining oxidation numbers are provided by the following guidelines.

1. The atoms in a pure element have an oxidation number of zero. For example, the atoms in pure sodium, Na, oxygen, O_2, phosphorus, P_4, and sulfur, S_8, all have oxidation numbers of zero.
2. The more-electronegative element in a binary molecular compound is assigned the number equal to the negative charge it would have as an anion. The less-electronegative atom is assigned the number equal to the positive charge it would have as a cation.
3. Fluorine has an oxidation number of -1 in all of its compounds because it is the most electronegative element.
4. Oxygen has an oxidation number of -2 in almost all compounds. Exceptions include when it forms peroxides, such as H_2O_2, in which its oxidation number is -1, and when it forms compounds with fluorine, such as OF_2, in which its oxidation number is $+2$.
5. Hydrogen has an oxidation number of $+1$ in all compounds containing elements that are more electronegative than it; it has an oxidation number of -1 in compounds with metals.
6. The algebraic sum of the oxidation numbers of all atoms in a neutral compound is equal to zero.
7. The algebraic sum of the oxidation numbers of all atoms in a polyatomic ion is equal to the charge of the ion.
8. Although rules 1 through 7 apply to covalently bonded atoms, oxidation numbers can also be assigned to atoms in ionic compounds.

Differentiated Instruction

BELOW LEVEL

The nine guidelines for assigning oxidation numbers can seem overwhelming to many students. Have students take a piece of paper and cover all but the first guideline on this page. Have them write Guideline 1 at the top of the paper. Then ask them to read the guideline carefully and write the guideline in their own words on the paper. For example, a student may write, "The atoms in all pure elements have a zero oxidation number." Have students repeat this process until they have finished all nine guidelines.

9. A monatomic ion has an oxidation number equal to the charge of the ion. For example, the ions Na+, Ca^{2}+, and Cl– have oxidation numbers of +1, +2, and −1, respectively.

Let's examine the assignment of oxidation numbers to the atoms in two molecular compounds, hydrogen fluoride, HF, and water, H_2O. Both compounds have polar-covalent bonds. In HF, the fluorine atom should have an oxidation number of −1 (see Rule 3 on the previous page). Rule 5 tells us that hydrogen should have an oxidation number of +1. This makes sense because fluorine is more electronegative than hydrogen, and in a polar-covalent bond, shared electrons are assumed to belong to the more-electronegative element. For water, Rules 4 and 5 tell us that the oxidation number of oxygen should be −2, and the oxidation number of each hydrogen atom should be +1. Again, oxygen is more electronegative than hydrogen, so the shared electrons are assumed to belong to oxygen.

Because the sum of the oxidation numbers of the atoms in a compound must satisfy Rule 6 or 7 of the guidelines on the previous page, it is often possible to assign oxidation numbers when they are not known. This is illustrated in Sample Problem E.

Oxidation Numbers

Sample Problem E **Assign oxidation numbers to each atom in the following compounds or ions:**

a. UF_6

b. H_2SO_4

c. ClO_3^-

a. Start by placing known oxidation numbers above the appropriate elements. From the guidelines, we know that fluorine always has an oxidation number of −1.

Multiply known oxidation numbers by the appropriate number of atoms, and place the totals underneath the corresponding elements. There are six fluorine atoms, 6 × −1 = −6.

The compound UF_6 is molecular. According to the guidelines, the sum of the oxidation numbers must equal zero. The total of positive oxidation numbers is therefore +6.

Divide the total calculated oxidation number by the appropriate number of atoms. There is only one uranium atom in the molecule, so it must have an oxidation number of +6.

Continued

Demonstration

OXIDATION STATES

In advance, prepare a **0.0004 M $KMnO_4$** solution by dissolving 0.06 g of solute in **1 L of water.** Also prepare a **0.1 M $NaHSO_3$** solution by dissolving 1.0 g of solute in **100 mL water.** You will also need **1 M solutions of HCl and NaOH.**

Use a **graduated cylinder** to place 20 mL of the $KMnO_4$ solution in each of **four 50-mL beakers.** Place the beakers on an **overhead projector.** Point out that all the beakers contain Mn^{7+} in MnO_4^- (violet). For a control, add nothing to the first beaker. To the second, use **two droppers** to add 48 drops of the HCl solution and 8 drops of the $NaHSO_3$ solution. The pale pink color is the result of production of Mn^{2+}. To the third beaker, use a **third dropper** to add 4 drops of the $NaHSO_3$ solution. An orange color, characteristic of Mn^{4+} (in MnO_2), should result. To the fourth beaker, add 64 drops of NaOH solution and 1 drop of $NaHSO_3$ solution. The green color of Mn^{6+} (in MnO_4^{2-}) should result. Too little $NaHSO_3$ will produce a blue color and too much will produce orange, so you may need to make slight adjustments in the amount added.

Safety The solutions will stain the skin. Wear **gloves**, an **apron**, and **goggles**.

Disposal Combine all solutions, adjust the pH to between 8 and 10, and then pour them down the drain.

Problem Solving

DECONSTRUCTING PROBLEMS

Ask students why there are two sets of oxidation numbers, one below and the other above the symbol UF_6. Students should recognize that the bottom set of numbers represents the total charge on all the atoms of the compound. Emphasize that this set of oxidation numbers must equal zero.

▼ Teach *continued*

Classroom Practice

E-1 Assign oxidation numbers to each atom in the following compounds or ions:

a. $KClO_4$
b. SO_3^{2-}
c. NF_3
d. CO_2
e. NO_3^-
f. NH_4Cl

Answers:

a. +1, +7, −2
b. +4, −2
c. +3, −1
d. +4, −2
e. +5, −2
f. −3, +1, −1

Answers

Practice E

1. a. +1, −1
   b. +4, −1
   c. +3, −1
   d. +4, −2
   e. +1, +5, −2
   f. +1, −1
   g. +5, −2
   h. +1, +5, −2
   i. +5, −2
   j. +2, −1

Oxidation Numbers (continued)

$$\overset{+6\,-1}{UF_6}$$
$$+6\;-6$$

b. Oxygen and sulfur are each more electronegative than hydrogen, so hydrogen has an oxidation number of +1. Oxygen is not combined with a halogen, nor is H_2SO_4 a peroxide. Therefore, the oxidation number of oxygen is −2. Place these known oxidation numbers above the appropriate symbols. Place the total of the oxidation numbers underneath.

$$\overset{+1\;\;-2}{H_2SO_4}$$
$$+2\;-8$$

The sum of the oxidation numbers must equal zero, and there is only one sulfur atom in each molecule of H_2SO_4. Because $(+2) + (-8) = -6$, the oxidation number of each sulfur atom must be +6.

c. To assign oxidation numbers to the elements in ClO_3^-, proceed as in parts (a) and (b). Remember, however, that the total of the oxidation numbers should equal the overall charge of the anion, 1−. The oxidation number of a single oxygen atom in the ion is −2. The total oxidation number due to the three oxygen atoms is −6. For the chlorate ion to have a 1− charge, chlorine must be assigned an oxidation number of +5.

$$\overset{+5\,-2}{ClO_3^-}$$
$$+5\;-6$$

Practice

1. Assign oxidation numbers to each atom in the following compounds or ions:

a. HCl	**e.** HNO_3	**h.** $HClO_3$
b. CF_4	**f.** KH	**i.** N_2O_5
c. PCl_3	**g.** P_4O_{10}	**j.** $GeCl_2$
d. SO_2		

MAIN IDEA

Many nonmetals have multiple oxidation numbers.

As shown in **Figure 2.1**, many nonmetals can have more than one oxidation number. (A more extensive list of oxidation numbers is given in Appendix Table B-15.) These numbers can sometimes be used in the same manner as ionic charges to determine formulas. Suppose, for example, you want to know the formula of a binary compound formed between sulfur and oxygen. From the common +4 and +6 oxidation states of sulfur, you could expect that sulfur might form SO_2 or SO_3. Both are known compounds. Of course, a formula must represent facts. Oxidation numbers alone cannot be used to prove the existence of a compound.

Differentiated Instruction

BELOW LEVEL

Have students explain how the formula SO_2 is derived if the oxidation number of sulfur is +4. Have them do the same for SO_3 when the oxidation number for sulfur is 6^+. If students use the "crisscross" method, be sure that they reduce the subscripts to the lowest whole-number ratio. For example, the "crisscross" method using the oxidation number of +4 for S would give the formula S_2O_4, which is then reduced to SO_2.

FIGURE 2.1

COMMON OXIDATION NUMBERS OF SOME NONMETALS THAT HAVE VARIABLE OXIDATION STATES*		
Group 14	carbon	−4, +2, +4
Group 15	nitrogen phosphorus	−3, +1, +2, +3, +4, +5 −3, +3, +5
Group 16	sulfur	−2, +4, +6
Group 17	chlorine bromine iodine	−1, +1, +3, +5, +7 −1, +1, +3, +5, +7 −1, +1, +3, +5, +7

*In addition to the values shown, atoms of each element in its pure state are assigned an oxidation number of zero.

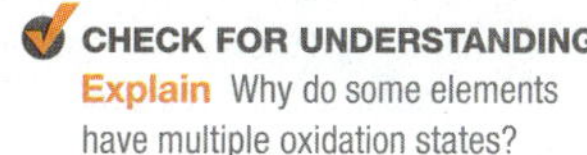
CHECK FOR UNDERSTANDING
Explain Why do some elements have multiple oxidation states?

In Section 1, we introduced the use of Roman numerals to denote ionic charges in the Stock system of naming ionic compounds. The Stock system is actually based on oxidation numbers, and it can be used as an alternative to the prefix system for naming binary molecular compounds. In the prefix system, for example, SO_2 and SO_3 are named sulfur dioxide and sulfur trioxide, respectively. Their names according to the Stock system are sulfur(IV) oxide and sulfur(VI) oxide. The international body that governs nomenclature has endorsed the Stock system, which is more practical for complicated compounds. Prefix-based names and Stock-system names are still used interchangeably for many simple compounds, however. A few additional examples of names in both systems are given below.

	Prefix system	Stock system
PCl_3	phosphorus trichloride	phosphorus(III) chloride
PCl_5	phosphorus pentachloride	phosphorus(V) chloride
N_2O	dinitrogen monoxide	nitrogen(I) oxide
NO	nitrogen monoxide	nitrogen(II) oxide
PbO_2	lead dioxide	lead(IV) oxide
Mo_2O_3	dimolybdenum trioxide	molybdenum(III) oxide

SECTION 2 FORMATIVE ASSESSMENT

Reviewing Main Ideas

1. Assign oxidation numbers to each atom in the following compounds or ions:
   a. HF
   b. CI_4
   c. H_2O
   d. PI_3
   e. CS_2
   f. Na_2O_2
   g. H_2CO_3
   h. NO_2^-
   i. SO_4^{2-}
2. Name each of the following binary molecular compounds according to the Stock system:
   a. CI_4
   b. SO_3
   c. As_2S_3
   d. NCl_3

Critical Thinking

3. **DRAWING CONCLUSIONS** Determine the oxidation numbers for iron oxide, Fe_3O_4. (Recall that oxidation numbers are integers.)

Teaching Tip

In practical chemistry, the prefix system is still much more commonly used than the Stock system for naming binary molecular compounds.

Classroom Discussion

Have students compare the Stock system with the older prefix system of naming binary molecular compounds. Students should discuss the advantages of each system. For example, they might point out the convenience of using easily recognizable prefixes, such as *mono-*, *di-*, and *tri-*, in the prefix system and the more informative and less ambiguous nature of the Roman numerals used in the Stock system. Encourage students to offer and discuss their own ideas for naming such compounds.

Check for Understanding

Answer: Some elements have multiple oxidation states because, depending on conditions, they can gain or lose different numbers of valence electrons.

Assess and Reteach ▼

Assess Use the Formative Assessment on this page to evaluate student mastery of the section.

Reteach For students who need additional instruction, download the Section Study Guide.

Response to Intervention To reassess students' mastery, use the Section Quiz, available to print or to take directly online at **HMDScience.com**.

Answers to Section Assessment

1. a. +1, −1
   b. +4, −1
   c. +1, −2
   d. +3, −1
   e. +4, −2
   f. +1, −1
   g. +1, +4, −2
   h. +3, −2
   i. +6, −2
2. a. carbon(IV) iodide
   b. sulfur(VI) oxide
   c. arsenic(III) sulfide
   d. nitrogen(III) chloride
3. The oxidation number for oxygen is −2. Therefore, Fe must have mixed oxidation numbers. One of the iron atoms in the compound has an oxidation number of +2, and the other two iron atoms have an oxidation number of +3.

WHY IT MATTERS

Classroom Discussion

Use this feature after discussing molecular formulas. Remind students that mass spectrometry can help determine the molecular formula versus the empirical formula. Because the molecular mass can be determined from the spectrum, the molecular formula can be obtained.

Alternative Assessment

Have students research the two scientists who won the 2002 Nobel Prize for their work on mass spectrometry. Have students give two examples of ways that the scientists' methods have been used in the field of medicine.

Answers

1. Fragments are sorted and separated by electric and magnetic fields that change the path of the fragments according to the fragments' mass-to-charge ratio. Molecules, which lack a net charge, do not respond significantly in this way to electric and magnetic fields.
2. Scientists are now able to use mass spectrometry to study large molecules such as nucleic acids and proteins.

WHY IT MATTERS

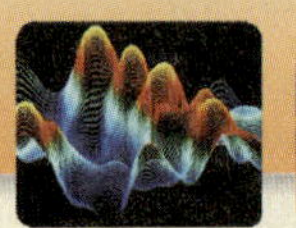

Mass Spectrometry: Identifying Molecules

S.T.E.M

Tests for locating oil deposits in the ground and detecting dioxins in our food supply are commonly performed today. These tests can be performed by using a technique known as *mass spectrometry*. Mass spectrometry is now used in many fields, such as medicine, chemistry, forensic science, and astronomy.

What is mass spectrometry? It is the most accurate technique available to measure the mass of an individual molecule or atom. Knowing the molecular mass is an essential part of identifying an unknown compound and determining the structure of a molecule of the compound. As the diagram of a mass spectrometer shows, the molecules in a gaseous sample are converted into ions. The ions then are separated and sorted according to their mass-to-charge ratio by a combination of electric and magnetic fields. The fields cause the ions' trajectories to change based on the ions' masses and charges. Then, the sorted ions are detected, and a mass spectrum is obtained. The mass spectrum is a graph of relative intensity (related to the number of ions detected) versus mass-to-charge ratio. Mass spectrometry uses a very small sample size (10^{-12} g) to obtain results.

The resulting spectrum is like a puzzle. It contains numerous peaks that correspond to fragments of the initial molecule. The largest peak (parent peak) corresponds to the molecular mass of the molecular ion. By analyzing the peaks, scientists can determine the identity and structure of a compound. Computers are used to help interpret the spectrum and identify the molecule by using online spectral database libraries.

Mass spectrometry has been an essential tool for scientists since its invention in the early 1900s. But its use was limited to small molecules from which ion creation was easy. Large biological molecules could not be studied, because they would break down or decompose during conventional ion-formation techniques. In the late 1980s, two groups developed ion-formation methods that are used today in commercial mass spectrometers. John Fenn (Virginia Commonwealth University) developed electrospray ionization mass spectrometry, and Koichi Tanaka (Shimadzu Corporation, Japan) developed matrix-assisted laser desorption ionization (MALDI) mass spectrometry. In 2002, both scientists received the Nobel Prize in chemistry for their work. Their methods opened the field to the study of large molecules, allowing scientists to use mass spectrometry to study the structure of macromolecules, such as nucleic acids and steroids, and to identify the sequence of proteins.

Questions

1. Why is it necessary to convert the sample into ions in the mass spectrometer?
2. How have recent developments in mass spectrometry contributed to the field of medicine?

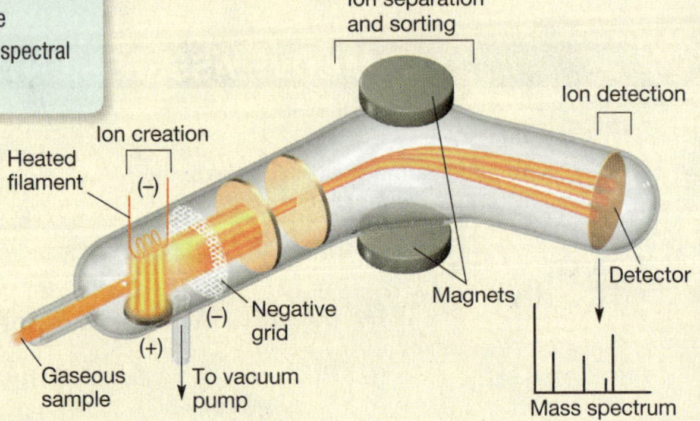

Scientists use mass spectrometers to identify and study the structure of molecules.

Using Chemical Formulas

SECTION 3

Main Ideas

- Formula mass is the sum of the average atomic masses of a compound's elements.
- The molar mass of a compound is numerically equal to its formula mass.
- Molar mass is used to convert from moles to grams.
- Percent composition is the number of grams in one mole of a compound.

Key Terms
formula mass
percentage composition

As you have seen, a chemical formula indicates the elements as well as the relative number of atoms or ions of each element present in a compound. Chemical formulas also allow chemists to calculate a number of characteristic values for a given compound. In this section, you will learn how to use chemical formulas to calculate the *formula mass*, the *molar mass*, and the *percentage composition* by mass of a compound.

MAIN IDEA

Formula mass is the sum of the average atomic masses of a compound's elements.

In an earlier chapter, we saw that hydrogen atoms have an average atomic mass of 1.007 94 u and that oxygen atoms have an average atomic mass of 15.9994 u. Like individual atoms, molecules, formula units, or ions have characteristic average masses. For example, we know from the chemical formula H_2O that a single water molecule is composed of exactly two hydrogen atoms and one oxygen atom. The mass of a water molecule is found by adding the masses of the three atoms in the molecule. (In the calculation, the average atomic masses have been rounded to two decimal places.)

average atomic mass of H: 1.01 u
average atomic mass of O: 16.00 u

$$2 \text{ H atoms} \times \frac{1.01 \text{ u}}{\text{H atom}} = 2.02 \text{ u}$$

$$1 \text{ O atom} \times \frac{16.00 \text{ u}}{\text{O atom}} = 16.00 \text{ u}$$

average mass of H_2O molecule = 18.02 u

The mass of a water molecule can be correctly referred to as a *molecular mass*. The mass of one NaCl formula unit, on the other hand, is not a molecular mass, because NaCl is an ionic compound. The mass of *any* unit represented by a chemical formula, whether the unit is a molecule, a formula unit, or an ion, is known as the formula mass. The **formula mass** of any molecule, formula unit, or ion is the sum of the average atomic masses of all atoms represented in its formula.

Differentiated Instruction

BELOW LEVEL

Have students prepare a table with two columns. They should label one column *Molecular Mass* and the other column *Formula Mass*. Have them write formulas for five compounds that are correctly placed under each label. Students should recognize that only the formulas for covalent compounds can be placed under *Molecular Mass*, while the formulas for both ionic and covalent compounds can be placed under *Formula Mass*.

SECTION 3

Plan and Prepare

Objectives

Upon completion of this section, students should be able to do the following:

- Calculate the formula mass or molar mass of any given compound.
- Use molar mass to convert between mass in grams and amount in moles of a chemical compound.
- Calculate the number of molecules, formula units, or ions in a given molar amount of a chemical compound.
- Calculate the percentage composition of a given chemical compound.

Classroom Catalyst

Write a common chemical formula, such as the formula for water, on the board. Then hold up or pass around a model of a water molecule. Have students identify the number of atoms of hydrogen and oxygen in one water molecule. Ask students how they think they might calculate the mass of a water molecule, given the atomic masses of hydrogen and oxygen. Explain that in this section, they will learn how to carry out these and other calculations for any compound.

Teach

Misconception Alert!

Students often mistakenly think that the subscripts in a compound's formula reveal a mass ratio. Point out that the subscripts actually reveal an atom ratio and a mole ratio. A mass ratio can be obtained by converting amounts in moles to masses in grams.

Teaching Tip

Atomic masses are rounded to two decimal places for all calculations in this book.

▼ Teach continued

Classroom Practice

F-1 Find the formula mass of each of the following:

a. Na_2SO_3
b. $HClO_3$
c. MnO_4^-
d. C_2H_6O

Answers:
a. 126.05 u
b. 84.46 u
c. 118.94 u
d. 46.08 u

Answers

Practice F

1. **a.** 98.09 u
b. 164.10 u
c. 94.97 u
d. 95.21 u

The procedure illustrated for calculating the formula mass of a water molecule can be used to calculate the mass of any unit represented by a chemical formula. In each of the problems that follow, the atomic masses from the periodic table in the back of the book have been rounded to two decimal places.

Formula Mass

Sample Problem F **Find the formula mass of potassium chlorate, $KClO_3$.**

SOLVE The mass of a formula unit of $KClO_3$ is found by summing the masses of one K atom, one Cl atom, and three O atoms. The required atomic masses can be found in the periodic table in the back of the book. In the calculation, each atomic mass has been rounded to two decimal places.

$$1 \text{ K atom} \times \frac{39.10 \text{ u}}{\text{K atom}} = 39.10 \text{ u}$$

$$1 \text{ Cl atom} \times \frac{35.45 \text{ u}}{\text{Cl atom}} = 35.45 \text{ u}$$

$$3 \text{ O atoms} \times \frac{16.00 \text{ u}}{\text{O atom}} = 48.00 \text{ u}$$

$$\text{formula mass of } KClO_3 = 122.55 \text{ u}$$

Practice Answers in Appendix E

1. Find the formula mass of each of the following:
   a. H_2SO_4
   b. $Ca(NO_3)_2$
   c. PO_4^{3-}
   d. $MgCl_2$

Formula Mass and Molar Mass (Animation)

MAIN IDEA

The molar mass of a compound is numerically equal to its formula mass.

In an earlier chapter, you learned that the molar mass of a substance is equal to the mass in grams of one mole, or approximately 6.022×10^{23} particles, of the substance. For example, the molar mass of pure calcium, Ca, is 40.08 g/mol because one mole of calcium atoms has a mass of 40.08 g.

The molar mass of a compound is calculated by adding the masses of the elements present in a mole of the molecules or formula units that make up the compound. For example, one mole of water molecules contains exactly two moles of H atoms and one mole of O atoms.

Problem Solving

TAKE IT FURTHER

Ask students to explain why Sample Problem F cannot be written as "Find the molecular mass of potassium chlorate, $KClO_3$." Students should recognize that $KClO_3$ is an ionic compound, consisting of a metal cation and a polyatomic anion. Molecular mass applies only to molecules, not to ionic compounds

DECONSTRUCTING PROBLEMS

Have students carefully read the *Solution* to Sample Problem G. Ask them to what types of chemical substances the term *mole* is applied. Students should recognize that *mole* applies to atoms, N and O, ions, Ba^{2+} and NO^{3-}, and compounds. $Ba(NO_3)_2$

Rounded to two decimal places, a mole of hydrogen atoms has a mass of 1.01 g, and a mole of oxygen atoms has a mass of 16.00 g. The molar mass of water is calculated as follows.

$$2 \text{ mol H} \times \frac{1.01 \text{ g H}}{\text{mol H}} = 2.02 \text{ g H}$$

$$1 \text{ mol O} \times \frac{16.00 \text{ g O}}{\text{mol O}} = 16.00 \text{ g O}$$

$$\text{molar mass of } H_2O = 18.02 \text{ g/mol}$$

Figure 3.1 shows a mole of water as well as a mole of several other substances.

You may have noticed that *a compound's molar mass is numerically equal to its formula mass.* For instance, in Sample Problem F the formula mass of $KClO_3$ was found to be 122.55 u. Therefore, because molar mass is numerically equal to formula mass, we know that the molar mass of $KClO_3$ is 122.55 g/mol.

FIGURE 3.1

Molar Mass Every compound has a characteristic molar mass. Shown here are one mole each of nitrogen (in balloon), water (in graduated cylinder), cadmium sulfide, CdS (yellow substance), and sodium chloride, NaCl (white substance).

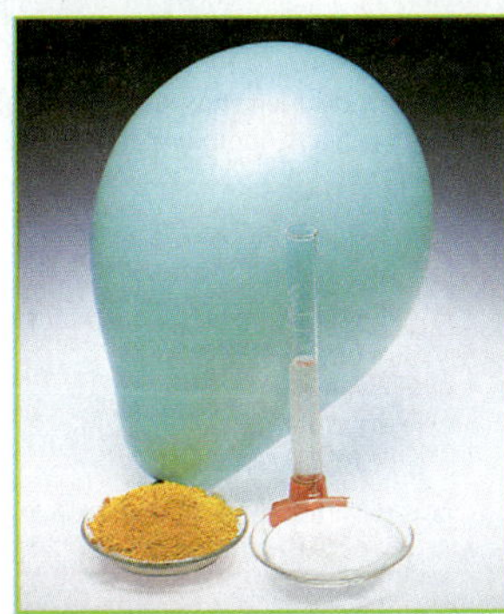

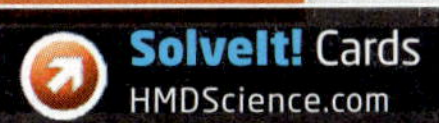

PREMIUM CONTENT

SolveIt! Cards HMDScience.com

Molar Mass

Sample Problem G **What is the molar mass of barium nitrate, $Ba(NO_3)_2$?**

SOLVE One mole of barium nitrate contains exactly one mole of Ba^{2+} ions and two moles of NO_3^- ions. The two moles of NO_3^- ions contain two moles of N atoms and six moles of O atoms. Therefore, the molar mass of $Ba(NO_3)_2$ is calculated as follows.

$$1 \text{ mol Ba} \times \frac{137.33 \text{ g Ba}}{\text{mol Ba}} = 137.33 \text{ g Ba}$$

$$2 \text{ mol N} \times \frac{14.01 \text{ g N}}{\text{mol N}} = 28.02 \text{ g N}$$

$$6 \text{ mol O} \times \frac{16.00 \text{ g O}}{\text{mol O}} = 96.00 \text{ g O}$$

$$\text{molar mass of } Ba(NO_3)_2 = 261.35 \text{ g/mol}$$

Practice Answers in Appendix E

1. How many moles of atoms of each element are there in one mole of the following compounds?
   a. Al_2S_3
   b. $NaNO_3$
   c. $Ba(OH)_2$
2. Find the molar mass of each of the compounds listed in item 1.

Differentiated Instruction

BELOW LEVEL

Place the formulas for both a covalent compound ($C_6H_{12}O_6$) and an ionic compound (Na_3PO_4) on the board. Ask students for which compound(s) they can calculate the molecular mass, $C_6H_{12}O_6$ formula mass, both compounds, and molar mass. both compounds

TEACH FROM VISUALS

FIGURE 3.1 Point out that the same number of formula units is present for each substance, despite the large differences in volume. Ask students how many formula units there are for each substance. 6.022×10^{23}

Classroom Practice

G-1 Determine the number of moles of atoms of each element in one mole of the following compounds:

a. K_2SO_4
b. $(NH_4)_2CrO_4$

Answers:

a. 2 mol K, 1 mol S, 4 mol O
b. 2 mol N, 8 mol H, 1 mol Cr, 4 mol O

G-2 Calculate the molar mass of each of the compounds listed in the preceding sample problem.

Answers:

a. 174.27 g/mol
b. 152.10 g/mol

Answers

Practice G

1. a. 2 mol Al, 3 mol S
   b. 1 mol Na, 1 mol N, 3 mol O
   c. 1 mol Ba, 2 mol O, 2 mol H
2. a. 150.17 g/mol
   b. 85.00 g/mol
   c. 171.35 g/mol

▼ Teach *continued*

TEACH FROM VISUALS

FIGURE 3.2 Have students formulate different general types of questions that can be answered by means of the relationships illustrated. For example, they might formulate questions such as: "How many moles of a substance are found in a given mass of the substance?" or "What is the mass in grams of a given number of moles of a substance?" Then have them use the diagram to explain how the question can be answered.

Teaching Tip

Remind students that the subscripts in a compound's chemical formula reveal a molar ratio of the elements composing the compound. The subscript next to a particular element therefore indicates how many moles of atoms of an element there are in one mole of the compound.

Classroom Practice

H-1 What is the mass in grams of 3.04 mol of ammonia vapor, NH_3?

Answer: 51.8 g

H-2 Calculate the mass of 0.257 mol of calcium nitrate, $Ca(NO_3)_2$.

Answer: 42.2 g

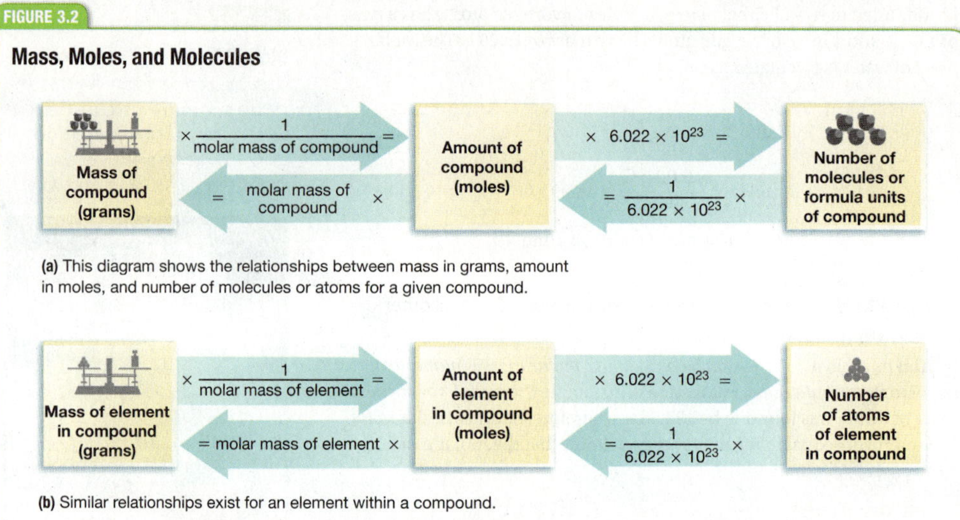

(a) This diagram shows the relationships between mass in grams, amount in moles, and number of molecules or atoms for a given compound.

(b) Similar relationships exist for an element within a compound.

MAIN IDEA

Molar mass is used to convert from moles to grams.

The molar mass of a compound can be used as a conversion factor to relate an amount in moles to a mass in grams for a given substance. Recall that molar mass usually has the units of grams per mole. To convert a known amount of a compound in moles to a mass in grams, multiply the amount in moles by the molar mass.

$$\text{amount in moles} \times \text{molar mass (g/mol)} = \text{mass in grams}$$

Conversions of this type for elements and compounds are summarized above in **Figure 3.2.** Becoming familiar with this process now will help you a great deal, as mass-to-mole and mole-to-mass conversions will be widely used in future chapters.

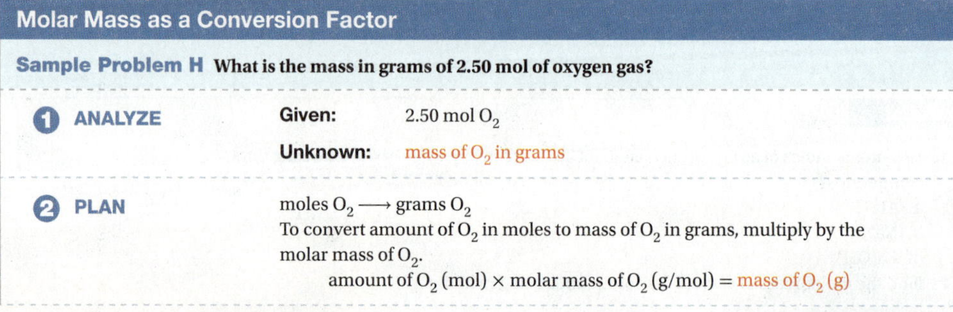

Molar Mass as a Conversion Factor

Sample Problem H **What is the mass in grams of 2.50 mol of oxygen gas?**

1 ANALYZE

Given: 2.50 mol O_2

Unknown: mass of O_2 in grams

2 PLAN

moles $O_2 \longrightarrow$ grams O_2

To convert amount of O_2 in moles to mass of O_2 in grams, multiply by the molar mass of O_2.

$$\text{amount of } O_2 \text{ (mol)} \times \text{molar mass of } O_2 \text{ (g/mol)} = \text{mass of } O_2 \text{ (g)}$$

Continued

Differentiated Instruction

ENGLISH LEARNERS

Ask students to describe something they have in terms of quantity. For example, one student may say that he has 100 CDs while another has 20 pairs of shoes. Point out that in chemistry, amount is a quantity whose unit is the mole. For example, a chemist may say that she has 2 moles of a compound.

BELOW LEVEL

The units for molar mass are included in the equation shown for using molar mass as a conversion factor. Have students plug in the units for amount in moles (m) and for mass in grams (g) in this equation. Students should see how the mole units cancel, leaving only grams in the answer.

Molar Mass as a Conversion Factor (continued)

3 SOLVE

First, the molar mass of O_2 must be calculated.

$$2 \text{ mol O} \times \frac{16.00 \text{ g O}}{\text{mol O}} = 32.00 \text{ g (mass of one mole of } O_2)$$

The molar mass of O_2 is therefore 32.00 g/mol. Now do the calculation shown in step 2.

$$2.50 \text{ mol } O_2 \times \frac{32.00 \text{ g } O_2}{\text{mol } O_2} = 80.0 \text{ g } O_2$$

4 CHECK YOUR WORK

The answer is correctly given to three significant figures and is close to an estimated value of 75 g (2.50 mol × 30 g/mol).

To convert a known mass of a compound in grams to an amount in moles, the mass must be divided by the molar mass. Or you can invert the molar mass and multiply so that units are easily canceled.

$$\text{mass in grams} \times \frac{1}{\text{molar mass (g/mol)}} = \text{amount in moles}$$

PREMIUM CONTENT

Learn It! Video HMDScience.com

Solve It! Cards HMDScience.com

Molar Mass as a Conversion Factor

Sample Problem I **Ibuprofen, $C_{13}H_{18}O_2$, is the active ingredient in many nonprescription pain relievers. Its molar mass is 206.31 g/mol.**

a. If the tablets in a bottle contain a total of 33 g of ibuprofen, how many moles of ibuprofen are in the bottle?
b. How many molecules of ibuprofen are in the bottle?
c. What is the total mass in grams of carbon in 33 g of ibuprofen?

1 ANALYZE

Given: 33 g of $C_{13}H_{18}O_2$, molar mass 206.31 g/mol

Unknown:
a. moles $C_{13}H_{10}O_2$
b. molecules $C_{13}H_{18}O_2$
c. total mass of C

2 PLAN

a. grams ⟶ moles
To convert mass of ibuprofen in grams to amount of ibuprofen in moles, multiply by the inverted molar mass of $C_{13}H_{18}O_2$.

$$\text{g } C_{13}H_{18}O_2 \times \frac{1 \text{ mol } C_{13}H_{18}O_2}{206.31 \text{ g } C_{13}H_{18}O_2} = \text{mol } C_{13}H_{18}O_2$$

b. moles ⟶ molecules
To find the number of molecules of ibuprofen, multiply amount of $C_{13}H_{18}O_2$ in moles by Avogadro's number.

$$\text{mol } C_{13}H_{18}O_2 \times \frac{6.022 \times 10^{23} \text{ molecules}}{\text{mol}} = \text{molecules } C_{13}H_{18}O_2$$

Continued

Classroom Practice

1-1 How many moles of compound are there in each of the following?

a. 3.82 g SO_2
b. 4.15×10^{-3} g $C_6H_{12}O_6$
c. 77.1 g Cl_2

Answers:
a. 0.0596 mol
b. 2.30×10^{-5} mol
c. 1.09 mol

1-2 How many molecules are there in each of the samples listed in the preceding sample problem?

Answers:
a. 3.59×10^{22} molecules
b. 1.39×10^{19} molecules
c. 6.56×10^{23} molecules

ChemisTrivia

Drugs, such as ibuprofen, tend to be given several different names. The actual chemical name is rarely used. Instead, a generic name is used. That name is often replaced by specific brand names created by various companies that manufacture and sell the drug. Mixtures of different active substances can also occur in the same medication, which is itself given its own brand name. $C_{13}H_{18}O_2$ is marketed generically under the name ibuprofen and also under several specific brand names. The process of drug nomenclature is regulated by the Food and Drug Administration.

Problem Solving

DECONSTRUCTING PROBLEMS

In any problem involving conversions, students must recognize the necessity of correctly setting up the conversion factor. To illustrate this point, have students invert the conversion factor used in step 2a so that the unit *g* is in the numerator and the unit *mol* is in the denominator. Ask students why this conversion factor (g/mol) cannot be used in this example. Students should recognize that the conversion factor must be set up so that the units *g* cancel, leaving the unit *mol* in the answer.

▼ Teach *continued*

Application

The percentage composition of any pure substance is always constant, whatever the source or sample size. Therefore, percentage composition is an identifying characteristic of any substance. For that reason, percentage composition is used by investigators in many different fields—from analytical chemistry to criminal forensics—to determine the identity of unknown materials.

Answers

Practice I

1. a. 0.0499 mol
   b. 61 mol
2. a. 1.53×10^{23} molecules
   b. 2.20×10^{23} molecules
3. 1170 g

Molar Mass as a Conversion Factor (continued)

c. moles $C_{13}H_{18}O_2 \longrightarrow$ moles C $\longrightarrow$ grams C

To find the mass of carbon present in the ibuprofen, the two conversion factors needed are the amount of carbon in moles per mole of $C_{13}H_{18}O_2$ and the molar mass of carbon.

$$\text{mol } C_{13}H_{18}O_2 \times \frac{13 \text{ mol C}}{\text{mol } C_{13}H_{18}O_2} \times \frac{12.01 \text{ g C}}{\text{mol C}} = \text{g C}$$

3 SOLVE

a. $33 \text{ g } C_{13}H_{18}O_2 \times \frac{1 \text{ mol } C_{13}H_{18}O_2}{206.31 \text{ g } C_{13}H_{18}O_2} = 0.16 \text{ mol } C_{13}H_{18}O_2$

b. $0.16 \text{ mol } C_{13}H_{18}O_2 \times \frac{6.022 \times 10^{23} \text{ molecules}}{\text{mol}} = 9.6 \times 10^{22} \text{ molecules } C_{13}H_{18}O_2$

c. $0.16 \text{ mol } C_{13}H_{18}O_2 \times \frac{13 \text{ mol C}}{\text{mol } C_{13}H_{18}O_2} \times \frac{12.01 \text{ g C}}{\text{mol C}} = 25 \text{ g C}$

The bottle contains 0.16 mol of ibuprofen, which is 9.6×10^{22} molecules of ibuprofen.

The sample of ibuprofen contains 25 g of carbon.

4 CHECK YOUR WORK

Checking each step shows that the arithmetic is correct, significant figures have been used correctly, and units have canceled as desired.

Practice Answers in Appendix E

1. How many moles of compound are there in the following?
   a. 6.60 g $(NH_4)_2SO_4$
   b. 4.5 kg $Ca(OH)_2$
2. How many molecules are there in the following.
   a. 25.0 g H_2SO_4
   b. 125 g of sugar, $C_{12}H_{22}O_{11}$
3. What is the mass in grams of 6.25 mol of copper(II) nitrate?

MAIN IDEA

Percent composition is the number of grams in one mole of a compound.

It is often useful to know the percentage by mass of a particular element in a chemical compound. For example, suppose the compound potassium chlorate, $KClO_3$, were to be used as a source of oxygen. It would be helpful to know the percentage of oxygen in the compound. To find the mass percentage of an element in a compound, one can divide the mass of the element in a sample of the compound by the total mass of the sample, and then multiply this value by 100.

$$\frac{\text{mass of element in sample of compound}}{\text{mass of sample of compound}} \times 100 = \begin{matrix}\text{\% element in} \\ \text{compound}\end{matrix}$$

Differentiated Instruction

BELOW LEVEL

Give each student an individually-sized bag of chocolate candies with brightly-colored shell coatings. Have them count the total number of candies in the bag and then sort the candies according to color. They should then count and write down how many candies of each color the bag contains. Say: "If your bag contained a total number of 20 candies and 5 of the candies are red, you could find out what percentage of the candies in the bag are red by dividing 5 by 20 and then multiplying the answer by 100." The answer is 25%. Say: "Chemists use a similar method to find out what percentage of the mass of a compound is made up of a particular element. You can find this using the equation given in your text." Demonstrate how to do this with a simple compound, such as water. Then give students a short list of 2-3 simple compounds. Have them continue to find the percentage of each color of candy and to then use the same process to find the percentage of each element in each compound.

The mass percentage of an element in a compound is the same regardless of the sample's size. Therefore, a simpler way to calculate the percentage of an element in a compound is to determine how many grams of the element are present in one mole of the compound. Then divide this value by the molar mass of the compound and multiply by 100.

$$\frac{\text{mass of element in 1 mol of compound}}{\text{molar mass of compound}} \times 100 = \text{\% element in compound}$$

The percentage by mass of each element in a compound is known as the **percentage composition** of the compound.

Percentage Composition

Sample Problem J **Find the percentage composition of copper(I) sulfide, Cu_2S.**

1 ANALYZE

Given: formula, Cu_2S

Unknown: percentage composition of Cu_2S

2 PLAN

formula ⟶ molar mass ⟶ mass percentage of each element

The molar mass of the compound must be found. Then the mass of each element present in one mole of the compound is used to calculate the mass percentage of each element.

3 SOLVE

$$2 \text{ mol Cu} \times \frac{63.55 \text{ g Cu}}{\text{mol Cu}} = 127.1 \text{ g Cu}$$

$$1 \text{ mol S} \times \frac{32.07 \text{ g S}}{\text{mol S}} = 32.07 \text{ g S}$$

$$\text{molar mass of } Cu_2S = 159.2 \text{ g}$$

$$\frac{127.1 \text{ g Cu}}{159.2 \text{ g } Cu_2S} \times 100 = 79.85\% \text{ Cu}$$

$$\frac{32.07 \text{ g S}}{159.2 \text{ g } Cu_2S} \times 100 = 20.15\% \text{ S}$$

4 CHECK YOUR WORK

A good check is to see if the results add up to about 100%. (Because of rounding, the total may not always be exactly 100%.)

Percentage Composition

Sample Problem K **As some salts crystallize from a water solution, they bind water molecules in their crystal structure. Sodium carbonate forms such a *hydrate*, in which 10 water molecules are present for every formula unit of sodium carbonate. Find the mass percentage of water in sodium carbonate decahydrate, Na_2CO_3•$10H_2O$, which has a molar mass of 286.19 g/mol.**

Continued

Classroom Practice

J-1 Calculate the percentage composition of sodium nitrate, $NaNO_3$.

Answers: 27.05% Na, 16.48% N, 56.47% O

J-2 Calculate the percentage composition of silver sulfate, Ag_2SO_4.

Answers: 69.19% Ag, 10.28% S, 20.52% O

Problem Solving

TAKE IT FURTHER

Ask students to calculate the percent composition of copper(II) chloride and compare it to that of copper(I) chloride. Be sure students base their calculations on 1 mol Cu and 1 mol Cl.

▼ Teach *continued*

Classroom Practice

K-1 What is the mass percentage of water in the hydrate $CuSO_4 \bullet 5H_2O$?

Answer: 36.08%

K-2 Zinc chloride, $ZnCl_2$, is 52.02% chlorine by mass.

a. What mass of chlorine is contained in 80.3 g of $ZnCl_2$?

b. How many moles of Cl is this?

Answers: **a.** 41.8 g
b. 1.18 mol

Answers

Practice K

1. **a.** 74.51% Pb, 25.49% Cl
   b. 52.55% Ba, 10.72% N, 36.73% O
2. 43.85% H_2O
3. 96.0 g O; 6.00 mol O

▼ Assess and Reteach

Assess Use the Formative Assessment on this page to evaluate student mastery of the section.

Reteach For students who need additional instruction, download the Section Study Guide.

Response to Intervention To reassess students' mastery, use the Section Quiz, available to print or to take directly online at **HMDScience.com**.

Percentage Composition (continued)

1 ANALYZE

Given: chemical formula, $Na_2CO_3 \bullet 10H_2O$
molar mass of $Na_2CO_3 \bullet 10H_2O$

Unknown: mass percentage of H_2O

2 PLAN

chemical formula $\longrightarrow$ mass H_2O per mole of $Na_2CO_3 \bullet 10H_2O \longrightarrow$ % water

The mass of water per mole of sodium carbonate decahydrate must first be found. This value is then divided by the mass of one mole of $Na_2CO_3 \bullet 10H_2O$.

3 SOLVE

One mole of $Na_2CO_3 \bullet 10H_2O$ contains 10 mol H_2O. As noted earlier, the molar mass of H_2O is 18.02 g/mol. The mass of 10 mol H_2O is calculated as follows.

$$10 \text{ mol } H_2O \times \frac{18.02 \text{ g } H_2O}{\text{mol } H_2O} = 180.2 \text{ g } H_2O$$

$$\text{mass of } H_2O \text{ per mole of } Na_2CO_3 \bullet 10H_2O = 180.2 \text{ g}$$

The molar mass of $Na_2CO_3 \bullet 10H_2O$ is 286.19 g/mol, so we know that 1 mol of the hydrate has a mass of 286.19 g. The mass percentage of 10 mol H_2O in 1 mol $Na_2CO_3 \bullet 10H_2O$ can now be calculated.

$$\text{mass percentage of } H_2O \text{ in } Na_2CO_3 \bullet 10H_2O = \frac{180.2 \text{ g } H_2O}{286.19 \text{ g } Na_2CO_3 \bullet 10H_2O} \times 100$$
$$= 62.97\% \ H_2O$$

4 CHECK YOUR WORK

Checking shows that the arithmetic is correct and that units cancel as desired.

Practice Answers in Appendix E

1. Find the percentage compositions of the following:
   a. $PbCl_2$ **b.** $Ba(NO_3)_2$
2. Find the mass percentage of water in $ZnSO_4 \bullet 7H_2O$.
3. Magnesium hydroxide is 54.87% oxygen by mass. How many grams of oxygen are in 175 g of the compound? How many moles of oxygen is this?

SECTION 3 FORMATIVE ASSESSMENT

Reviewing Main Ideas

1. Determine both the formula mass and molar mass of ammonium carbonate, $(NH_4)_2CO_3$.
2. How many moles of atoms of each element are there in one mole of $(NH_4)_2CO_3$?
3. What is the mass in grams of 3.25 mol $Fe_2(SO_4)_3$?
4. How many molecules of aspirin, $C_9H_8O_4$, are there in a 100.0 mg tablet of aspirin?
5. Calculate the percentage composition of $(NH_4)_2CO_3$.

Critical Thinking

6. **RELATING IDEAS** A sample of hydrated copper (II) sulfate ($CuSO_4 \bullet nH_2O$) is heated to 150°C and produces 103.74 g anhydrous copper (II) sulfate and 58.55 g water. How many moles of water molecules are present in 1.0 mol of hydrated copper (II) sulfate?

Answers to Section Assessment

1. formula mass = 96.11 u; molar mass = 96.11 g/mol
2. 2 mol N, 8 mol H, 1 mol C, 3 mol O
3. 1.30×10^3 g
4. 3.342×10^{20} molecules
5. 29.15% N, 8.407% H, 12.50% C, 49.94% O
6. 5 mol H_2O

Determining Chemical Formulas

Key Terms
empirical formula

SECTION 4

Main Ideas

- Empirical formulas show the whole number ratio of elements in a compound.
- Molecular formulas give the types and numbers of atoms in a compound.

When a new substance is synthesized or is discovered, it is analyzed quantitatively to reveal its percentage composition. From these data, the empirical formula is then determined. **An empirical formula consists of the symbols for the elements combined in a compound, with subscripts showing the smallest whole-number mole ratio of the different atoms in the compound.** For an ionic compound, the formula unit is usually the compound's empirical formula. For a molecular compound, however, the empirical formula does not necessarily indicate the actual numbers of atoms present in each molecule. For example, the empirical formula of the gas diborane is BH_3, but the molecular formula is B_2H_6. In this case, the number of atoms given by the molecular formula corresponds to the empirical ratio multiplied by two.

MAIN IDEA

Empirical formulas show the whole number ratio of elements in a compound.

To determine a compound's empirical formula from its percentage composition, begin by converting percentage composition to a mass composition. Assume that you have a 100.0 g sample of the compound. Then calculate the amount of each element in the sample. For example, the percentage composition of diborane is 78.1% B and 21.9% H. Therefore, 100.0 g of diborane contains 78.1 g of B and 21.9 g of H.

Next, convert the mass composition of each element to a composition in moles by dividing by the appropriate molar mass.

$$78.1 \text{ g B} \times \frac{1 \text{ mol B}}{10.81 \text{ g B}} = 7.22 \text{ mol B}$$

$$21.9 \text{ g H} \times \frac{1 \text{ mol H}}{1.01 \text{ g H}} = 21.7 \text{ mol H}$$

These values give a mole ratio of 7.22 mol B to 21.7 mol H. However, this is not a ratio of smallest whole numbers. To find such a ratio, divide each number of moles by the smallest number in the existing ratio.

$$\frac{7.22 \text{ mol B}}{7.22} : \frac{21.7 \text{ mol H}}{7.22} = 1 \text{ mol B} : 3.01 \text{ mol H}$$

Differentiated Instruction

PRE-AP

Place several formulas on the board and ask students to identify the empirical formulas. Examples can include H_2O, H_2O_2, C_6H_6, O_2, H_2SO_4, $C_6H_{12}O_6$, and $C_2H_{10}O$. Have students show the empirical formulas for any that are not written as such.

$H_2O_2 \rightarrow HO$; $C_6H_6 \rightarrow CH$; $C_6H_{12}O_6 \rightarrow CH_2O$

SECTION 4

Plan and Prepare

Objectives

Upon completion of this section, students should be able to do the following:

- Define *empirical formula*, and explain how the term applies to ionic and molecular compounds.
- Determine an empirical formula from either a percentage or a mass composition.
- Explain the relationship between the empirical formula and the molecular formula of a given compound.
- Determine a molecular formula from an empirical formula.

Classroom Catalyst

Show the students models of molecules in which the numbers of the various types of atoms differ but the ratios are the same, for example, NO_2 and N_2O_4. Have them compare and contrast the molecules, and lead them to the conclusion that the ratios are equal but the numbers of atoms differ. This will help prepare the class for the concept of empirical formula.

Teach

READING TOOLKIT

VOCABULARY BUILDING Have students look up the meaning of the word *empirical* in the dictionary. Have them use the definition to explain where information is obtained about an empirical formula. Their explanations should reflect that empirical formulas are determined from experimental data.

▼ Teach *continued*

Classroom Practice

L-1 A compound is analyzed and found to contain 36.70% potassium, 33.27% chlorine, and 30.03% oxygen. What is the empirical formula of the compound?

Answer: $KClO_2$

L-2 Determine the empirical formula of the compound that contains 17.15% carbon, 1.44% hydrogen, and 81.41% fluorine.

Answer: CHF_3

Because of rounding or experimental error, a compound's mole ratio sometimes consists of numbers close to whole numbers instead of exact whole numbers. In this case, the differences from whole numbers may be ignored and the nearest whole number taken. Thus, diborane contains atoms in the ratio 1 B : 3 H. The compound's empirical formula is BH_3.

Sometimes mass composition is known instead of percentage composition. To determine the empirical formula in this case, convert mass composition to composition in moles. Then calculate the smallest whole-number mole ratio of atoms. This process is shown in Sample Problem M.

Empirical Formulas

Sample Problem L **Quantitative analysis shows that a compound contains 32.38% sodium, 22.65% sulfur, and 44.99% oxygen. Find the empirical formula of this compound.**

1 ANALYZE

Given: percentage composition: 32.38% Na, 22.65% S, and 44.99% O

Unknown: empirical formula

2 PLAN

percentage composition ⟶ mass composition ⟶ composition in moles ⟶ smallest whole-number mole ratio of atoms

3 SOLVE

Mass composition (mass of each element in 100.0 g sample): 32.38 g Na, 22.65 g S, 44.99 g O

Composition in moles:

$$32.38 \text{ g Na} \times \frac{1 \text{ mol Na}}{22.99 \text{ g Na}} = 1.408 \text{ mol Na}$$

$$22.65 \text{ g S} \times \frac{1 \text{ mol S}}{32.07 \text{ g S}} = 0.7063 \text{ mol S}$$

$$44.99 \text{ g O} \times \frac{1 \text{ mol O}}{16.00 \text{ g O}} = 2.812 \text{ mol O}$$

Smallest whole-number mole ratio of atoms:
The compound contains atoms in the ratio 1.408 mol Na : 0.7063 mol S : 2.812 mol O. To find the smallest whole-number mole ratio, divide each value by the smallest number in the ratio.

$$\frac{1.408 \text{ mol Na}}{0.7063} : \frac{0.7063 \text{ mol S}}{0.7063} : \frac{2.812 \text{ mol O}}{0.7063} = 1.993 \text{ mol Na} : 1 \text{ mol S} : 3.981 \text{ mol O}$$

Rounding each number in the ratio to the nearest whole number yields a mole ratio of 2 mol Na : 1 mol S : 4 mol O. The empirical formula of the compound is Na_2SO_4.

4 CHECK YOUR WORK

Calculating the percentage composition of the compound based on the empirical formula determined in the problem reveals a percentage composition of 32.37% Na, 22.58% S, and 45.05% O. These values agree reasonably well with the given percentage composition.

Differentiated Instruction

BELOW LEVEL

Ask students to give examples of objects that are counted by different units, such as dozens, hours, or moles. Students can draw pictures of the items or find pictures on the internet. Ask the students to label each picture with its name, the unit used to count the objects, and the amount of individual parts equivalent to one unit.

Empirical Formulas

Sample Problem M **Analysis of a 10.150 g sample of a compound known to contain only phosphorus and oxygen indicates a phosphorus content of 4.433 g. What is the empirical formula of this compound?**

1 ANALYZE

Given: sample mass = 10.150 g

phosphorus mass = 4.433 g

Unknown: empirical formula

2 PLAN

Mass composition ⟶ composition in moles ⟶ smallest whole-number ratio of atoms

3 SOLVE

The mass of oxygen is found by subtracting the phosphorus mass from the sample mass.

sample mass − phosphorus mass = 10.150 g − 4.433 g = 5.717 g

Mass composition: 4.433 g P, 5.717 g O

Composition in moles:

$$4.433 \text{ g P} \times \frac{1 \text{ mol P}}{30.97 \text{ g P}} = 0.1431 \text{ mol P}$$

$$5.717 \text{ g O} \times \frac{1 \text{ mol O}}{16.00 \text{ g O}} = 0.3573 \text{ mol O}$$

Smallest whole-number mole ratio of atoms:

$$\frac{0.1431 \text{ mol P}}{0.1431} : \frac{0.3573 \text{ mol O}}{0.1431}$$

$$1 \text{ mol P} : 2.497 \text{ mol O}$$

The number of O atoms is not close to a whole number. But if we multiply each number in the ratio by 2, then the number of O atoms becomes 4.994 mol, which is close to 5 mol. The simplest whole-number mole ratio of P atoms to O atoms is 2 : 5. The compound's empirical formula is P_2O_5.

4 CHECK YOUR WORK

The arithmetic is correct, significant figures have been used correctly, and units cancel as desired. The formula is reasonable because +5 is a common oxidation state of phosphorus.

Practice Answers in Appendix E

1. A compound is found to contain 63.52% iron and 36.48% sulfur. Find its empirical formula.
2. Find the empirical formula of a compound found to contain 26.56% potassium, 35.41% chromium, and the remainder oxygen.
3. Analysis of 20.0 g of a compound containing only calcium and bromine indicates that 4.00 g of calcium are present. What is the empirical formula of the compound formed?

Classroom Practice

M-1 A 60.00 g sample of tetraethyllead, a gasoline additive, is found to contain 38.43 g lead, 17.83 g carbon, and 3.74 g hydrogen. Find its empirical formula.

Answer: PbC_8H_{20}

M-2 A 170.00 g sample of an unidentified compound contains 29.84 g sodium, 67.49 g chromium, and 72.67 g oxygen. What is the compound's empirical formula?

Answer: $Na_2Cr_2O_7$

Teaching Tip

Point out to students that the decimals 0.33, 0.67, 0.25, 0.75, and 0.20 are equivalent (to two decimal places) to the fractions $\frac{1}{3}$, $\frac{2}{3}$, $\frac{1}{4}$, $\frac{3}{4}$, and $\frac{1}{5}$, and that a number ending in one of these decimals is converted to a whole number when it is multiplied by the denominator of the corresponding fraction. Remind students that they must multiply each number in the mole ratio by the same factor in order to avoid changing the mole ratio.

Answers

Practice M

1. FeS
2. $K_2Cr_2O_7$
3. $CaBr_2$

Problem Solving

DECONSTRUCTING PROBLEMS

Have students look closely at Step 3 in Sample Problem L. An assumption is made that there are 100 grams of the compound. Point out that percentage composition for all the elements in a compound must add up to 100%. Therefore, students can assume that 100 grams of a compound are present and change the percentages to grams. For example, in Practice Problem 1 on this page, 100 grams of the compound would consist of 63.52 g iron and 36.48 g sulfur.

▼ Teach continued

Teaching Tip

The subscripts in an empirical formula can be obtained by dividing all the subscripts of the corresponding molecular formula by the same whole number.

Alternative Assessment

Have students explain how it is possible to derive the empirical formula from a molecular formula but not be able to derive the molecular formula from an empirical formula. Students should recognize that in the first case, you can reduce the subscripts in the molecular formula to whole-number ratios. However, in the second case, you need to know the multiple to apply it to the empirical formula and change it to the molecular formula.

MAIN IDEA

Molecular formulas give the types and numbers of atoms in a compound.

Remember that the *empirical formula* contains the smallest possible whole numbers that describe the atomic ratio. The *molecular formula* is the actual formula of a molecular compound. An empirical formula may or may not be a correct molecular formula. For example, diborane's empirical formula is BH_3. Any multiple of BH_3, such as B_2H_6, B_3H_9, B_4H_{12}, and so on, represents the same ratio of B atoms to H atoms. The molecular compounds ethene, C_2H_4, and cyclopropane, C_3H_6, also share an identical atomic ratio (2 H:1 C), yet they are very different substances. How is the correct formula of a molecular compound found from an empirical formula?

The relationship between a compound's empirical formula and its molecular formula can be written as follows.

$$x(\text{empirical formula}) = \text{molecular formula}$$

The number represented by x is a whole-number multiple indicating the factor by which the subscripts in the empirical formula must be multiplied to obtain the molecular formula. (The value of x is sometimes 1.) The formula masses have a similar relationship.

$$x(\text{empirical formula mass}) = \text{molecular formula mass}$$

To determine the molecular formula of a compound, you must know the compound's formula mass. For example, experimentation shows the formula mass of diborane to be 27.67 u. The formula mass for the empirical formula, BH_3, is 13.84 u. Dividing the experimental formula mass by the empirical formula mass gives the value of x for diborane.

$$x = \frac{27.67\ \text{u}}{13.84\ \text{u}} = 2.000$$

The molecular formula of diborane is therefore B_2H_6.

$$2(BH_3) = B_2H_6$$

Recall that a compound's molecular formula mass is numerically equal to its molar mass, so a compound's molecular formula can also be found given the compound's empirical formula and its molar mass.

Molecular Formulas

Sample Problem N **In Sample Problem M, the empirical formula of a compound of phosphorus and oxygen was found to be P_2O_5. Experimentation shows that the molar mass of this compound is 283.89 g/mol. What is the compound's molecular formula?**

1 ANALYZE

Given: empirical formula

Unknown: molecular formula

Continued

Differentiated Instruction

BELOW LEVEL

Ask students why problems involving the determination of a molecular formula from an empirical formula do not involve ionic compounds. Students should know that molecular formulas do not apply to ionic compounds. Students should recall that ionic compounds are expressed in formula units, which already show the simplest whole number ratio.

Molecular Formulas (continued)

2 PLAN

$$x(\text{empirical formula}) = \text{molecular formula}$$

$$x = \frac{\text{molecular formula mass}}{\text{empirical formula mass}}$$

3 SOLVE

Molecular formula mass is numerically equal to molar mass. Thus, changing the g/mol unit of the compound's molar mass to u yields the compound's molecular formula mass.

$$\text{molecular molar mass} = 283.89 \text{ g/mol}$$
$$\text{molecular formula mass} = 283.89 \text{ u}$$

The empirical formula mass is found by adding the masses of each of the atoms indicated in the empirical formula.

$$\text{mass of phosphorus atom} = 30.97 \text{ u}$$
$$\text{mass of oxygen atom} = 16.00 \text{ u}$$
$$\text{empirical formula mass of } P_2O_5 = 2 \times 30.97 \text{ u} + 5 \times 16.00 \text{ u} = 141.94 \text{ u}$$

Dividing the experimental formula mass by the empirical formula mass gives the value of x. The formula mass is numerically equal to the molar mass.

$$x = \frac{283.89 \text{ u}}{141.94 \text{ u}} = 2.0001$$

The compound's molecular formula is therefore P_4O_{10}.

$$2 \times (P_2O_5) = P_4O_{10}$$

4 CHECK YOUR WORK

Checking the arithmetic shows that it is correct.

Practice Answers in Appendix E

1. Determine the molecular formula of the compound with an empirical formula of CH and a formula mass of 78.110 u.
2. A sample of a compound with a formula mass of 34.00 u is found to consist of 0.44 g H and 6.92 g O. Find its molecular formula.

SECTION 4 FORMATIVE ASSESSMENT

Reviewing Main Ideas

1. A compound contains 36.48% Na, 25.41% S, and 38.11% O. Find its empirical formula.
2. Find the empirical formula of a compound that contains 53.70% iron and 46.30% sulfur.
3. Analysis of a compound indicates that it contains 1.04 g K, 0.70 g Cr, and 0.86 g O. Find its empirical formula.
4. If 4.04 g of N combine with 11.46 g O to produce a compound with a formula mass of 108.0 u, what is the molecular formula of this compound?

Critical Thinking

5. **RELATING IDEAS** A compound containing sodium, chlorine, and oxygen is 25.42% sodium by mass. A 3.25 g sample gives 4.33×10^{22} atoms of oxygen. What is the empirical formula?

Answers to Section Assessment

1. Na_2SO_3
2. Fe_2S_3
3. K_2CrO_4
4. N_2O_5
5. $NaClO_2$

Classroom Practice

N-1 The empirical formula for trichloroisocyanuric acid, the active ingredient in many household bleaches, is OCNCl. The molar mass of this compound is 232.41 g/mol. What is the molecular formula of trichloroisocyanuric acid?

Answer: $O_3C_3N_3Cl_3$

N-2 Determine the molecular formula of a compound with an empirical formula of NH_2 and a formula mass of 32.06 u.

Answer: N_2H_4

Answers

Practice N

1. C_6H_6
2. H_2O_2

Assess and Reteach

Assess Use the Formative Assessment on this page to evaluate student mastery of the section.

Reteach For students who need additional instruction, download the Section Study Guide.

Response to Intervention To reassess students' mastery, use the Section Quiz, available to print or to take directly online at **HMDScience.com**.

Answers

1. 43.38% Na, 11.33% C, 45.29% O
2. 61.13% I

Math Tutor | Calculating Percentage Composition

Chemists can analyze an unknown substance by determining its percentage composition by mass. Percentage composition is determined by finding the mass of each element in a sample of the substance as a percentage of the mass of the whole sample. The results of this analysis can then be compared with the percentage composition of known compounds to determine the probable identity of the unknown substance. Once you know a compound's formula, you can determine its percentage composition by mass.

Sample Problem

Determine the percentage composition of potassium chlorate, $KClO_3$.

First, calculate the molar mass of $KClO_3$. The formula shows you that one mole of $KClO_3$ consists of 1 mol K atoms, 1 mol Cl atoms, and 3 mol O atoms. Thus, the molar mass of $KClO_3$ is molar mass K + molar mass Cl + 3(molar mass O) = 39.10 g K + 35.45 g Cl + 3(16.00 g O).

$$\text{molar mass } KClO_3 = 122.55 \text{ g}$$

The percentage composition of $KClO_3$ is determined by calculating the percentage of the total molar mass contributed by each element.

$$\frac{\text{mass of element in 1 mol of compound}}{\text{molar mass of compound}} \times 100 = \% \text{ element in compound}$$

$$\% \text{ K in } KClO_3 = \frac{39.10 \text{ g K}}{122.55 \text{ g } KClO_3} \times 100 = 31.91\%$$

$$\% \text{ Cl in } KClO_3 = \frac{35.45 \text{ g Cl}}{122.55 \text{ g } KClO_3} \times 100 = 28.93\%$$

$$\% \text{ O in } KClO_3 = \frac{48.00 \text{ g O}}{122.55 \text{ g } KClO_3} \times 100 = 39.17\%$$

Determine the percentage of nitrogen in ammonium sulfate, $(NH_4)_2SO_4$.

Even though you want to find the percentage of only one element, you must calculate the molar mass of $(NH_4)_2SO_4$. To do that, examine the formula to find the number of moles of each element in the compound. The two ammonium groups, indicated by $(NH_4)_2$, contain 2 mol N and 8 mol H per mole of $(NH_4)_2SO_4$. The sulfate group, SO_4, contains 1 mol S and 4 mol O per mole of $(NH_4)_2SO_4$.

$$\begin{aligned} 2 \text{ mol N} = 2 \times 14.01 \text{ g} &= 28.02 \text{ g} \\ 8 \text{ mol H} = 8 \times 1.01 \text{ g} &= 8.08 \text{ g} \\ 1 \text{ mol S} = 1 \times 32.07 &= 32.07 \text{ g} \\ 4 \text{ mol O} = 4 \times 16.00 &= 64.00 \text{ g} \\ \text{molar mass } (NH_4)_2SO_4 &= 132.17 \text{ g} \end{aligned}$$

Now, you can determine the percentage of nitrogen in the compound as follows.

$$\% \text{ N in } (NH_4)_2SO_4 = \frac{28.02 \text{ g N}}{132.17 \text{ g } (NH_4)_2SO_4} \times 100 = 21.20\%$$

Practice

1. What is the percentage composition of sodium carbonate, Na_2CO_3?
2. What is the percentage of iodine in zinc iodate, $Zn(IO_3)_2$?

CHAPTER 7 Summary

PREMIUM CONTENT
Interactive Review HMDScience.com
Review Games
Concept Maps

SECTION 1 Chemical Names and Formulas

- A positive monatomic ion is identified simply by the name of the appropriate element. A negative monatomic ion is named by dropping parts of the ending of the element's name and adding *-ide* to the root.
- The charge of each ion in an ionic compound may be used to determine the simplest chemical formula for the compound.
- Binary compounds are composed of two elements.
- Binary ionic compounds are named by combining the names of the positive and negative ions.
- The old system of naming binary molecular compounds uses prefixes. The new system, known as the *Stock system*, uses oxidation numbers.

KEY TERMS

monatomic ion
binary compound
nomenclature
oxyanion
salt

SECTION 2 Oxidation Numbers

- Oxidation numbers are useful in naming compounds, in writing formulas, and in balancing chemical equations.
- Compounds containing elements that have more than one oxidation state are named by using the Stock system.
- Stock-system names and prefix-system names are used interchangeably for many molecular compounds.
- Oxidation numbers of each element in a compound may be used to determine the compound's simplest chemical formula.
- By knowing oxidation numbers, we can name compounds without knowing whether they are ionic or molecular.

KEY TERMS

oxidation number
oxidation state

SECTION 3 Using Chemical Formulas

- Formula mass, molar mass, and percentage composition can be calculated from the chemical formula for a compound.
- The percentage composition of a compound is the percentage by mass of each element in the compound.
- Molar mass is used as a conversion factor between amount in moles and mass in grams of a given compound or element.

KEY TERMS

formula mass
percentage composition

SECTION 4 Determining Chemical Formulas

- An empirical formula shows the simplest whole-number ratio of atoms in a given compound.
- Empirical formulas indicate how many atoms of each element are combined in the simplest unit of a chemical compound.
- A molecular formula can be found from the empirical formula if the molar mass is measured.

KEY TERMS

empirical formula

Review Answers

1. a. ions formed from a single atom
   b. Na^+, Mg^{2+}, and Cl^-.
2. The nitrate ion, NO_3^-, has one more oxygen atom than the nitrite ion, NO_2^- does.
3. a. K^+ d. Cl^-
   b. Ca^{2+} e. Ba^{2+}
   c. S^{2-} f. Br^-
4. a. Na^+, 1+ d. N^{3-}, 3−
   b. Al^{3+}, 3+ e. Fe^{2+}, 2+
   c. Cl^-, 1− f. Fe^{3+}, 3+
5. a. potassium ion (or potassium cation)
   b. magnesium ion (or magnesium cation)
   c. aluminum ion (or aluminum cation)
   d. chloride ion (or chloride anion)
   e. oxide ion (or oxide anion)
   f. calcium ion (or calcium cation)
6. a. NaI d. BaF_2
   b. CaS e. Li_2O
   c. $ZnCl_2$
7. a. potassium chloride
   b. calcium bromide
   c. lithium oxide
   d. magnesium chloride
8. a. CrF_2, chromium(II) fluoride
   b. NiO, nickel(II) oxide
   c. Fe_2O_3, iron(III) oxide
9. The less electronegative element is written first.
10. a. carbon dioxide
    b. carbon tetrachloride
    c. phosphorus pentachloride
    d. selenium hexafluoride
    e. diarsenic pentoxide
11. a. CBr_4 c. P_4O_{10}
    b. SiO_2 d. As_2S_3
12. Binary acids (HCl and HBr) contain two elements, usually hydrogen and a halogen. Oxyacids (H_2SO_4 and HNO_3) contain hydrogen, oxygen, and a third element.
13. a. ionic compound with a cation and the anion from an acid
    b. NaCl and $MgSO_4$.
14. a. hydrofluoric acid
    b. hydrobromic acid
    c. nitric acid
    d. sulfuric acid
    e. phosphoric acid
15. a. H_2SO_3 e. $HClO_4$
    b. $HClO_3$ f. H_2CO_3
    c. HCl g. CH_3COOH
    d. HClO
16. a. NaF e. $AlBr_3$
    b. CaO f. Li_3N
    c. K_2S g. FeO
    d. $MgCl_2$

CHAPTER 7 Review

SECTION 1

Chemical Names and Formulas

REVIEWING MAIN IDEAS

1. a. What are monatomic ions?
   b. Give three examples of monatomic ions.
2. How does the chemical formula for the nitrite ion differ from the chemical formula for the nitrate ion?
3. Using only the periodic table, write the symbol of the ion most typically formed by each of the following elements:
   a. K d. Cl
   b. Ca e. Ba
   c. S f. Br
4. Write the formula for and indicate the charge on each of the following ions:
   a. sodium ion
   b. aluminum ion
   c. chloride ion
   d. nitride ion
   e. iron(II) ion
   f. iron(III) ion
5. Name each of the following monatomic ions:
   a. K^+ d. Cl^-
   b. Mg^{2+} e. O^{2-}
   c. Al^{3+} f. Ca^{2+}
6. Write formulas for the binary ionic compounds formed between the following elements. (Hint: See Sample Problem A.)
   a. sodium and iodine
   b. calcium and sulfur
   c. zinc and chlorine
   d. barium and fluorine
   e. lithium and oxygen
7. Give the name of each of the following binary ionic compounds. (Hint: See Sample Problem B.)
   a. KCl c. Li_2O
   b. $CaBr_2$ d. $MgCl_2$
8. Write the formulas for and give the names of the compounds formed by the following ions:
   a. Cr^{2+} and F^-
   b. Ni^{2+} and O^{2-}
   c. Fe^{3+} and O^{2-}
9. What determines the order in which the component elements of binary molecular compounds are written?
10. Name the following binary molecular compounds according to the prefix system. (Hint: See Sample Problem D.)
    a. CO_2 d. SeF_6
    b. CCl_4 e. As_2O_5
    c. PCl_5
11. Write formulas for each of the following binary molecular compounds. (Hint: See Sample Problem D.)
    a. carbon tetrabromide
    b. silicon dioxide
    c. tetraphosphorus decoxide
    d. diarsenic trisulfide
12. Distinguish between binary acids and oxyacids, and give two examples of each.
13. a. What is a salt?
    b. Give two examples of salts.
14. Name each of the following acids:
    a. HF d. H_2SO_4
    b. HBr e. H_3PO_4
    c. HNO_3
15. Give the molecular formula for each of the following acids:
    a. sulfurous acid
    b. chloric acid
    c. hydrochloric acid
    d. hypochlorous acid
    e. perchloric acid
    f. carbonic acid
    g. acetic acid

PRACTICE PROBLEMS

16. Write formulas for each of the following compounds:
    a. sodium fluoride
    b. calcium oxide
    c. potassium sulfide
    d. magnesium chloride
    e. aluminum bromide
    f. lithium nitride
    g. iron(II) oxide

17. Name each of the following ions:

a. NH_4^+
b. ClO_3^-
c. OH^-
d. SO_4^{2-}
e. NO_3^-
f. CO_3^{2-}
g. PO_4^{3-}
h. CH_3COO^-
i. HCO_3^-
j. CrO_4^{2-}

18. Write the formula and charge for each of the following ions:

a. ammonium ion
b. acetate ion
c. hydroxide ion
d. carbonate ion
e. sulfate ion
f. phosphate ion
g. copper(II) ion
h. tin(II) ion
i. iron(III) ion
j. copper(I) ion
k. mercury(I) ion
l. mercury(II) ion

SECTION 2

Oxidation Numbers

REVIEWING MAIN IDEAS

19. Name each of the following ions according to the Stock system:

a. Fe^{2+}
b. Fe^{3+}
c. Pb^{2+}
d. Pb^{4+}
e. Sn^{2+}
f. Sn^{4+}

20. Name each of the binary molecular compounds in item 11 by using the Stock system.

21. Write formulas for each of the following compounds:

a. phosphorus(III) iodide
b. sulfur(II) chloride
c. carbon(IV) sulfide
d. nitrogen(V) oxide

22. **a.** What are oxidation numbers?
b. What useful functions do oxidation numbers serve?

PRACTICE PROBLEMS

23. Name each of the following ionic compounds by using the Stock system:

a. NaCl
b. KF
c. CaS
d. $Co(NO_3)_2$
e. $FePO_4$
f. Hg_2SO_4
g. $Hg_3(PO_4)_2$

24. Assign oxidation numbers to each atom in the following compounds. (Hint: See Sample Problem E.)

a. HI
b. PBr_3
c. GeS_2
d. KH
e. As_2O_5
f. H_3PO_4

25. Assign oxidation numbers to each atom in the following ions. (Hint: See Sample Problem E.)

a. NO_3^-
b. ClO_4^-
c. PO_4^{3-}
d. $Cr_2O_7^{2-}$
e. CO_3^{2-}

SECTION 3

Using Chemical Formulas

REVIEWING MAIN IDEAS

26. **a.** Define *formula mass.*
b. In what unit is formula mass expressed?

27. What is meant by the molar mass of a compound?

PRACTICE PROBLEMS

28. Determine the formula mass of each of the following compounds or ions. (Hint: See Sample Problem F.)

a. glucose, $C_6H_{12}O_6$
b. calcium acetate, $Ca(CH_3COO)_2$
c. the ammonium ion, NH_4^+
d. the chlorate ion, ClO_3^-

29. Determine the number of moles of each type of monatomic or polyatomic ion in one mole of the following compounds. For each polyatomic ion, determine the number of moles of each atom present in one mole of the ion.

a. KNO_3
b. Na_2SO_4
c. $Ca(OH)_2$
d. $(NH_4)_2SO_3$
e. $Ca_3(PO_4)_2$
f. $Al_2(CrO_4)_3$

17. a. ammonium ion
b. chlorate ion
c. hydroxide ion
d. sulfate ion
e. nitrate ion
f. carbonate ion
g. phosphate ion
h. acetate ion
i. hydrogen carbonate ion (or bicarbonate ion)
j. chromate ion

18. a. NH_4^+, 1+
b. CH_3COO^-, 1−
c. OH^-, 1−
d. CO_3^{2-}, 2−
e. SO_4^{2-}, 2−
f. PO_4^{3-}, 3−
g. Cu^{2+}, 2+
h. Sn^{2+}, 2+
i. Fe^{3+}, 3+
j. Cu^+, 1+
k. Hg_2^{2+}, 2+
l. Hg^{2+}, 2+

19. a. iron(II) ion
b. iron(III) ion
c. lead(II) ion
d. lead(IV) ion
e. tin(II) ion
f. tin(IV) ion

20. a. carbon(IV) bromide
b. silicon(IV) oxide
c. phosphorus(V) oxide
d. arsenic(III) sulfide

21. a. PI_3
b. SCl_2
c. CS_2
d. N_2O_5

22. a. numbers assigned to either bonded atoms in molecular compounds or polyatomic ions, that indicate the general distribution of electrons
b. They aid in naming compounds, writing formulas, balancing chemical equations, and studying chemical reactions.

23. a. sodium chloride
b. potassium fluoride
c. calcium sulfide
d. cobalt(II) nitrate
e. iron(III) phosphate
f. mercury(I) sulfate
g. mercury(II) phosphate

24. a. +1, −1
b. +3, −1
c. +4, −2
d. +1, −1
e. +5, −2
f. +1, +5, −2

25. a. +5, −2
b. +7, −2
c. +5, −2
d. +6, −2
e. +4, −2

26. a. the sum of the average atomic masses of all atoms represented in the formula of a molecule, of a formula unit, or of an ion
b. u

27. the mass in grams of 1 mol of the basic particles in a compound—it is numerically equal to formula mass

28. a. 180.18 u
b. 158.18 u
c. 18.05 u
d. 83.45 u

29. a. 1 mol K^+, 1 mol NO_3^-; 1 mol N, 3 mol O
b. 2 mol Na^+, 1 mol SO_4^{2-}; 1 mol S, 4 mol O
c. 1 mol Ca^{2+}, 2 mol OH^-; 1 mol O, 1 mol H
d. 2 mol NH_4^+, 1 mol SO_3^{2-}; 1 mol N, 4 mol H, 1 mol S, 3 mol O
e. 3 mol Ca^{2+}, 2 mol PO_4^{3-}; 1 mol P, 4 mol O
f. 2 mol Al^{3+}, 3 mol CrO_4^{2-}; 1 mol Cr, 4 mol O

30. a. 101.11 g/mol
   b. 142.05 g/mol
   c. 74.10 g/mol
   d. 116.17 g/mol
   e. 310.18 g/mol
   f. 401.96 g/mol

31. a. 0.250 mol
   b. 2.752 mol
   c. 0.3627 mol

32. a. 39.34% Na, 60.66% Cl
   b. 63.50% Ag, 8.25% N, 28.26% O
   c. 41.68% Mg, 54.86% O, 3.46% H

33. 36.07% H_2O

34. percentage composition, mass composition, and composition by moles

35. *x*(empirical formula) = molecular formula, where *x* is a multiple of the subscripts in the molecular formula

36. $AgNO_3$

37. C_2H_6O

38. $C_4H_8O_4$

39. C_3H_6

40. $C_6H_8O_7$

41. a. lithium bromide
   b. tin(II) nitrate
   c. iron(II) chloride
   d. magnesium oxide
   e. potassium hydroxide
   f. iron(III) oxide
   g. silver nitrate
   h. iron(II) hydroxide
   i. chromium(II) fluoride

42. a. 58.44 g   c. 259.4 g
   b. 36.04 g   d. 163 g

43. a. 207.29 u, 207.29 g/mol
   b. 264.36 u, 264.36 g/mol
   c. 654.98 u, 654.98 g/mol
   d. 89.57 u, 89.57 g/mol

44. a. AlF_3 d. CoS
   b. MgO   e. $SrBr_2$
   c. V_2O_5 f. SO_3

45. 1 Fe, 3 C, 5 H, 7 O; 8.62%

46. a. nitrous acid; +1, +3, −2
   b. sulfurous acid; +1, +4, −2
   c. carbonic acid; +1, +4, −2
   d. hydriodic acid; +1, −1

47. a. 30.88% Na, 47.62% Cl, 21.49% O
   b. 2.46% H, 39.07% S, 58.47% O
   c. 48.63% C, 8.18% H, 43.19% O
   d. 11.28% Be, 88.72% Cl

30. Determine the molar mass of each compound listed in item 29. (Hint: See Sample Problem G.)

31. Determine the number of moles of compound in each of the following samples. (Hint: See Sample Problem I.)
a. 4.50 g H_2O
b. 471.6 g $Ba(OH)_2$
c. 129.68 g $Fe_3(PO_4)_2$

32. Determine the percentage composition of each of the following compounds. (Hint: See Sample Problem J.)
a. NaCl
b. $AgNO_3$
c. $Mg(OH)_2$

33. Determine the percentage by mass of water in the hydrate $CuSO_4 \bullet 5H_2O$. (Hint: See Sample Problem K.)

SECTION 4

Determining Chemical Formulas

REVIEWING MAIN IDEAS

34. What three types of information are used to find an empirical formula from percentage composition data?

35. What is the relationship between the empirical formula and the molecular formula of a compound?

PRACTICE PROBLEMS

36. Determine the empirical formula of a compound containing 63.50% silver, 8.25% nitrogen, and 28.25% oxygen. (Hint: See Sample Problem L.)

37. Determine the empirical formula of a compound found to contain 52.11% carbon, 13.14% hydrogen, and 34.75% oxygen.

38. What is the molecular formula of the molecule that has an empirical formula of CH_2O and a molar mass of 120.12 g/mol?

39. A compound with a formula mass of 42.08 u is found to be 85.64% carbon and 14.36% hydrogen by mass. Find its molecular formula.

Mixed Review

REVIEWING MAIN IDEAS

40. Chemical analysis shows that citric acid contains 37.51% C, 4.20% H, and 58.29% O. What is the empirical formula for citric acid?

41. Name each of the following compounds by using the Stock system:
a. LiBr
b. $Sn(NO_3)_2$
c. $FeCl_2$
d. MgO
e. KOH
f. Fe_2O_3
g. $AgNO_3$
h. $Fe(OH)_2$
i. CrF_2

42. What is the mass in grams of each of the following samples?
a. 1.000 mol NaCl
b. 2.000 mol H_2O
c. 3.500 mol $Ca(OH)_2$
d. 0.625 mol $Ba(NO_3)_2$

43. Determine the formula mass and molar mass of each of the following compounds:
a. XeF_4
b. $C_{12}H_{24}O_6$
c. Hg_2I_2
d. CuCN

44. Write the chemical formulas for the following compounds:
a. aluminum fluoride
b. magnesium oxide
c. vanadium(V) oxide
d. cobalt(II) sulfide
e. strontium bromide
f. sulfur trioxide

45. How many atoms of each element are contained in a single formula unit of iron(III) formate, $Fe(CHO_2)_3 \bullet H_2O$? What percentage by mass of the compound is water?

46. Name each of the following acids, and assign oxidation numbers to the atoms in each:
a. HNO_2
b. H_2SO_3
c. H_2CO_3
d. HI

47. Determine the percentage composition of the following compounds:
a. NaClO
b. H_2SO_3
c. C_2H_5COOH
d. $BeCl_2$

48. Name each of the following binary compounds:
a. MgI_2
b. NaF
c. CS_2
d. N_2O_4
e. SO_2
f. PBr_3
g. $CaCl_2$
h. AgI

49. Assign oxidation numbers to each atom in the following molecules and ions:
a. CO_2
b. NH_4^+
c. MnO_4^-
d. $S_2O_3^{2-}$
e. H_2O_2
f. P_4O_{10}
g. OF_2

50. A 175.0 g sample of a compound contains 56.15 g C, 9.43 g H, 74.81 g O, 13.11 g N, and 21.49 g Na. What is the compound's empirical formula?

CRITICAL THINKING

51. **Analyzing Information** Sulfur trioxide is produced in the atmosphere through a reaction of sulfur dioxide and oxygen. Sulfur dioxide is a primary air pollutant. Analyze the formula for sulfur trioxide. Then, use your analysis to list all of the chemical information that you can.

52. **Analyzing Data** In the laboratory, a sample of pure nickel was placed in a clean, dry, weighed crucible. The crucible was heated so that the nickel would react with the oxygen in the air. After the reaction appeared complete, the crucible was allowed to cool and the mass was determined. The crucible was reheated and allowed to cool. Its mass was then determined again to be certain that the reaction was complete. The following data were collected:

Mass of crucible	= 30.02 g
Mass of nickel and crucible	= 31.07 g
Mass of nickel oxide and crucible	= 31.36 g

Determine the following information based on the data given above:

Mass of nickel	=
Mass of nickel oxide	=
Mass of oxygen	=

Based on your calculations, what is the empirical formula for the nickel oxide?

USING THE HANDBOOK

53. Review the common reactions of Group 1 metals in the *Elements Handbook* (Appendix A), and answer the following questions:
a. Some of the Group 1 metals react with oxygen to form superoxides. Write the formulas for these compounds.
b. What is the charge on each cation for the formulas that you wrote in (a)?
c. How does the charge on the anion vary for oxides, peroxides, and superoxides?

54. Review the common reactions of Group 2 metals in the *Elements Handbook* (Appendix A), and answer the following questions:
a. Some of the Group 2 metals react with oxygen to form oxides. Write the formulas for these compounds.
b. Some of the Group 2 metals react with oxygen to form peroxides. Write the formulas for these compounds.
c. Some of the Group 2 metals react with nitrogen to form nitrides. Write the formulas for these compounds.
d. Most Group 2 elements form hydrides. What is hydrogen's oxidation state in these compounds?

55. Review the analytical tests for transition metals in the *Elements Handbook* (Appendix A), and answer the following questions:
a. Determine the oxidation state of each metal in the precipitates shown for cadmium, zinc, and lead.
b. Determine the oxidation state of each metal in the complex ions shown for iron, manganese, and cobalt.
c. The copper compound shown is called a *coordination compound*. The ammonia shown in the formula exists as molecules that do not have a charge. Determine copper's oxidation state in this compound.

CHAPTER REVIEW

48. a. magnesium iodide
b. sodium fluoride
c. carbon disulfide
d. dinitrogen tetroxide
e. sulfur dioxide
f. phosphorus tribromide
g. calcium chloride
h. silver iodide

49. a. +4, −2
b. −3, +1
c. +7, −2
d. +2, −2
e. +1, −1
f. +5, −2
g. +2, −1

50. $C_5H_{10}O_5NNa$

51. The formula is SO_3, so the molecule contains one sulfur atom and three oxygen atoms. The oxidation numbers are +6 and −2, respectively.

52. mass of nickel = 1.05 g; mass of nickel oxide = 1.34 g; mass of oxygen = 0.29 g; empirical formula: NiO

53. a. KO_2, RbO_2, CsO_2
b. 1+
c. 2− in oxides, 1− in peroxides, 1− for the two oxygen atoms together in superoxides

54. a. MgO, BeO, CaO
b. SrO_2, BaO_2
c. Mg_3N_2, Be_3N_2, Ca_3N_2
d. −1

55. a. Cd = +2, Zn = +2, Pb = +2
b. Fe = +3, Mn = +7, Co = +2
c. Cu = +2

56. a. NO, NO_2, N_2O_3, N_2O_5, P_4O_{10}, As_2O_5, Sb_2O_5, Bi_2O_5

b. for NO, N = +2; for NO_2, N = +4; for N_2O_3, N = +3; for N_2O_5, N = +5

57. Answers will vary.

58. a. sodium bicarbonate, $NaHCO_3$

b. magnesium hydroxide, $Mg(OH)_2$

c. magnesium sulfate hepta-hydrate, $MgSO_4 \bullet 7H_2O$

d. calcium carbonate, $CaCO_3$

e. sodium hydroxide, NaOH

f. methanol, CH_3OH

59. Answers will vary.

60. NH_3 has a higher percentage of nitrogen than NH_4NO_3. Answers will vary.

CHAPTER REVIEW

56. Review the common reactions of Group 15 elements in the *Elements Handbook* (Appendix A), and answer the following questions:

a. Write formulas for each of the oxides listed for the Group 15 elements.

b. Determine nitrogen's oxidation state in the oxides listed in (a).

RESEARCH AND WRITING

57. Nomenclature Biologists who name newly discovered organisms use a system that is structured very much like the one used by chemists in naming compounds. The system used by biologists is called the *Linnaean system of binomial nomenclature*, after its creator, Carolus Linnaeus. Research this system in a biology textbook, and then note similarities and differences between the Linnaeus system and chemical nomenclature.

58. Common Chemicals Find out the systematic chemical name and write the chemical formula for each of the following common compounds:

a. baking soda
b. milk of magnesia
c. Epsom salts
d. limestone
e. lye
f. wood alcohol

ALTERNATIVE ASSESSMENT

59. Performance Assessment Your teacher will supply you with a note card that has one of the following formulas on it: $NaCH_3COO \bullet 3H_2O$, $MgCl_2 \bullet 6H_2O$, $LiC_2H_3O_2 \bullet 2H_2O$, or $MgSO_4 \bullet 7H_2O$. Design an experiment to determine the percentage of water by mass in the hydrated salt assigned to you. Be sure to explain what steps you will take to ensure that the salt is completely dry. If your teacher approves your design, obtain the salt and perform the experiment. What percentage of water does the salt contain?

60. Both ammonia, NH_3, and ammonium nitrate, NH_4NO_3, are used in fertilizers as a source of nitrogen. Which compound has the higher percentage of nitrogen? Research the physical properties of both compounds, and find out how each compound is manufactured and used. Explain why each compound has its own particular application. (Consider factors such as the cost of raw ingredients, the ease of manufacture, and shipping costs.)

244 Chapter 7

Standards-Based Assessment

Answer the following items on a separate piece of paper.

MULTIPLE CHOICE

1. Which of the following compounds does not contain a polyatomic ion?
   A. sodium carbonate
   B. sodium sulfate
   C. sodium sulfite
   D. sodium sulfide

2. The correct formula for ammonium phosphate is
   A. $(NH_4)_3PO_4$.
   B. $(NH_4)_2PO_4$.
   C. NH_4PO_4.
   D. $NH_4(PO_4)_2$.

3. When writing the formula for a compound that contains a polyatomic ion,
   A. write the anion's formula first.
   B. use superscripts to show the number of polyatomic ions present.
   C. use parentheses if the number of polyatomic ions is greater than 1.
   D. always place the polyatomic ion in parentheses.

4. The correct name for NH_4CH_3COO is
   A. ammonium carbonate.
   B. ammonium hydroxide.
   C. ammonium acetate.
   D. ammonium nitrate.

5. Which of the following is the correct formula for iron (III) sulfate?
   A. Fe_3SO_4
   B. $Fe_3(SO_4)_2$
   C. $Fe_2(SO_4)_3$
   D. $3FeSO_4$

6. The molecular formula for acetylene is C_2H_2. The molecular formula for benzene is C_6H_6. The empirical formula for both is
   A. CH.
   B. C_2H_2.
   C. C_6H_6.
   D. $(CH)_2$.

7. Which of the following shows the percentage composition of H_2SO_4?
   A. 2.5% H, 39.1% S, 58.5% O
   B. 2.1% H, 32.7% S, 65.2% O
   C. 28.6% H, 14.3% S, 57.1% O
   D. 33.3% H, 16.7% S, 50% O

8. Which of the following compounds has the highest percentage of oxygen?
   A. CH_4O
   B. CO_2
   C. H_2O
   D. Na_2CO_3

9. The empirical formula for a compound that is 1.2% H, 42.0% Cl, and 56.8% O is
   A. HClO.
   B. $HClO_2$.
   C. $HClO_3$.
   D. $HClO_4$.

SHORT ANSWER

10. When a new substance is synthesized or is discovered experimentally, the substance is analyzed quantitatively. What information is obtained from this typical analysis, and how is this information used?

11. An oxide of selenium is 28.8% O. Find the empirical formula. Assuming that the empirical formula is also the molecular formula, name the oxide.

EXTENDED RESPONSE

12. What is an empirical formula, and how does it differ from a molecular formula?

13. What are Stock system names based on?

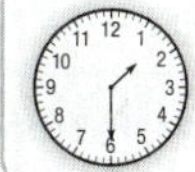

Test Tip
Whenever possible, highlight or underline numbers or words critical to answering a question correctly.

STANDARDS-BASED ASSESSMENT

To give students practice under more realistic testing conditions, give them 60 minutes to answer all of the questions in this Standardized Test Preparation.

Test Answers

1. D
2. A
3. C
4. C
5. C
6. A
7. B
8. C
9. C
10. The percentage composition is obtained and used to determine the substance's empirical formula.
11. SeO_2; selenium dioxide
12. The empirical formula is the simplest whole-number ratio of the atoms in a chemical formula. The molecular formula is the actual number of atoms of each element in a chemical formula. The two formulas differ by an integer factor.
13. The Stock system is based on the oxidation number of the cation.

Chemical Equations and Reactions

① Core Instruction

Chapter Resources

- **The Teacher's Edition wrap has extensive teaching support for every lesson, including Misconception Alerts, Teach from Visuals, Demonstrations, Teaching Tips, Differentiated Instruction, and Problem Solving support.**
- **Several additional presentation tools are available online for every chapter, including Animated Chemistry features and Visual Concepts.**
- **You can open your lesson with the Why It Matters Video: Equations and Reactions.**

Section	Instruction	Labs and Demonstrations Go Online for Materials Lists and Solutions Lists.
8.1	■ **Textbook:** Describing Chemical Reactions **Animated Chemistry:** Conservation (of Mass) in Reactions **Teaching Visuals:** Methane Combustion • Interpreting a Chemical Reaction • Elements that Normally Exist as Diatomic Molecules • Symbols Used in Chemical Equations **PowerPresentations**	■ **Demonstration:** Evidence of a Chemical Reaction ■ **Demonstration:** Electrolysis of Water ■ **Lab:** Blueprint Paper ■ **Lab:** Getting a Reaction (Open Inquiry)
8.2	■ **Textbook:** Types of Chemical Reactions **Teaching Visuals:** Determining Reaction Types • Identifying Reactions and Predicting Products **PowerPresentations**	■ **Demonstration:** Synthesis of a Base from a Metal Oxide ■ **Demonstration:** Double-Displacement Reactions ■ **QuickLab:** Balancing Equations Using Models ■ **Lab:** Evidence for a Chemical Change (Core Skill)
8.3	■ **Textbook:** Activity Series of the Elements **Teaching Visuals:** Activity Series of the Elements **PowerPresentations**	■ **Demonstration:** Activity Series of Metals ■ **Lab:** Simple Qualitative Analysis (Core Skill) ■ **Lab:** Extraction of Copper from Its Ore (Forensics) ■ **Lab:** Factors Affecting CO_2 Production in Yeast

② Support and Intervention

- **Interactive Reader** (English and Spanish)
- **Study Guide**
- **Interactive Review:** Review Games, Concept Maps, and Section Self-Checks
- **Scientific Reasoning Skill Builder**
- **Learn It! Videos**
- **Solve It! Cards**
- **Interactive Demos**
- **Sample Problem Sets**

③ Specialized Support

- **Chapter Summary Audio Files**
- **Interactive Reader Audio Files**
- **Differentiated Instruction:** Inclusion, Below Level, and English Learners (TE wrap)

Enrichment and Challenge

- **Differentiated Instruction:** Pre-AP (TE wrap)
- **Why It Matters:** Carbon Monoxide Catalyst (SE)
- **Why It Matters:** Combustion Synthesis (SE)
- **WebLinks**

Assessment

- **Section Formative Assessments** (SE)
- **Section Quizzes**
- **Chapter Review** (SE)
- **Chapter Tests A and B**
- **Alternative Assessment** (TE wrap)
- **Online Assessment and Remediation**
- **ExamView Banks**

Where do I find it?

	Resource	PRINT	DVD	ONLINE
1	Animated Chemistry		■	■
1	Demonstrations (TE wrap)	■		■
1	Interactive Whiteboard		■	■
1	Labs		■	■
1	PowerPresentations		■	■
1	QuickLabs	■	■	■
1	Teaching Visuals		■	■
1	Textbook	■	■	■
1	Visual Concepts		■	■
1	Why It Matters Videos		■	■
2	Interactive Demos		■	■
2	Interactive Reader	■	■	■
2	Interactive Reviews		■	■
2	Learn It! Videos		■	■
2	Sample Problem Sets		■	■
2	Scientific Reasoning Skill Builder		■	■
2	Smart Grapher Tool		■	■
2	Solve It! Cards		■	■
2	Study Guide		■	■
3	Chapter Summary Audio Files		■	■
3	Differentiated Instruction (TE wrap)	■		
3	Interactive Reader Audio Files		■	■

CHAPTER 8

Chapter Overview

Section 1 covers the writing and balancing of chemical equations and lists the information contained in an equation.

Section 2 describes five basic types of chemical reactions: synthesis, decomposition, single-displacement, double-displacement, and combustion.

Section 3 presents activity series for metals and the halogens and explains how they are used in writing chemical equations.

▼ Focus and Motivate

Activate Prior Knowledge

Students may need a review of the following concepts:

- energy in chemical reactions
- conservation of mass

About the Image

A fireworks display involves chemical reactions. The release of light and heat during a fireworks display is an indication that a chemical reaction is taking place.

Why It Matters

Students can access the video online and find other helpful resources at **HMDScience.com**.

Lab Preview

The following investigations support the concepts presented in this chapter.

LABS

Blueprint Paper
Evidence for a Chemical Change (Core Skill)
Simple Qualitative Analysis (Core Skill)
Extraction of Copper from Its Ore (Forensics)
Factors Affecting CO_2 Production in Yeast
Getting a Reaction (Open Inquiry)

QUICKLAB

Balancing Equations Using Models

DEMONSTRATIONS

Evidence of a Chemical Reaction
Electrolysis of Water
Synthesis of a Base from a Metal Oxide
Double-Displacement Reactions
Activity Series of Metals

Describing Chemical Reactions

SECTION 1

Main Ideas

- Chemical reactions have physical indicators.
- Chemical equations must satisfy the law of conservation of mass.
- Chemical equations show relative amounts, masses, and progression of chemical reactions.
- Chemical equations can be balanced with step-by-step inspection.

Key Terms

chemical equation	word equation
precipitate	formula equation
coefficient	reversible reaction

A *chemical reaction* is the process by which one or more substances are changed into one or more different substances. In any chemical reaction, the original substances are known as the *reactants* and the resulting substances are known as the *products*. According to the law of conservation of mass, the total mass of reactants must equal the total mass of *products* for any given chemical reaction.

Chemical reactions are described by chemical equations. **A chemical equation represents, with symbols and formulas, the identities and relative molecular or molar amounts of the reactants and products in a chemical reaction.** For example, the following chemical equation shows that the reactant ammonium dichromate yields the products nitrogen, chromium(III) oxide, and water.

$$(NH_4)_2Cr_2O_7(s) \longrightarrow N_2(g) + Cr_2O_3(s) + 4H_2O(g)$$

This strongly exothermic reaction is shown in **Figure 1.1.**

MAIN IDEA

Chemical reactions have physical indicators.

To know for certain that a chemical reaction has taken place requires evidence that one or more substances have undergone a change in identity. Absolute proof of such a change can be provided only by chemical analysis of the products. However, certain easily observed changes usually indicate that a chemical reaction has occurred.

1. *Evolution of energy as heat and light.* A change in matter that releases energy as both heat and light is strong evidence that a chemical reaction has taken place. For example, you can see in **Figure 1.1** that the decomposition of ammonium dichromate is accompanied by the evolution of energy as heat and light. And you can see evidence that a chemical reaction occurs between natural gas and oxygen if you burn gas for cooking in your house. Some reactions involve only heat or only light. But heat or light by itself is not necessarily a sign of chemical change, because many physical changes also involve either heat or light. However, heat and light are very strong indicators of a chemical change and should encourage you to investigate further.
2. *Color change.* A change in color is often an indication of a chemical reaction. Again, color change should not be the only physical indicator considered, because color changes can also be physical changes.

FIGURE 1.1

Evolution of Energy as Heat and Light The decomposition of ammonium dichromate proceeds rapidly, releasing energy as light and heat.

Differentiated Instruction

BELOW LEVEL

Take a sheet of paper and crumple it up. Ask students if this is a physical change or a chemical change. a physical change If there is confusion, ask if it is still a piece of paper. yes Point out that if it is still the same substance, then only a physical change has occurred. Next, smooth out the piece of paper and tear it into several pieces. Again, ask students if this is a physical change or a chemical change. responses should be as above Finally, take one of the torn pieces of paper, hold it over a clean, empty beaker, and set it alight with a match. Immediately drop the burning paper into the beaker and cover with a wire screen. Ask: Now, is it *still* a piece of paper? no Point out that the paper has become carbon and various gases. Ask: Is this a physical change or a chemical change? a chemical change Finally, write the words physical and chemical at the top of the board or on a projector. Ask students to brainstorm further examples of changes and categorize them as physical or chemical. Write their ideas under the appropriate columns.

SECTION 1

Plan and Prepare ▼

Objectives

Upon completion of this section, students should be able to do the following:

- List three observations that suggest that a chemical reaction has taken place.
- List three requirements for a correctly written chemical equation.
- Write a word equation and a formula equation for a given chemical reaction.
- Balance a formula equation by inspection.

Classroom Catalyst

Show students a sample of ammonium dichromate, $(NH_4)_2Cr_2O_7$, and then refer them to **Figure 1.1.** The photograph provides evidence that an exothermic chemical reaction is occurring. Encourage students to think about how they would convey to other scientists what is occurring in the photograph. Explain that a chemical equation is a shorthand way of communicating this information. A chemical equation packs a great deal of information into relatively few symbols.

Teach ▼

Classroom Discussion

Encourage students to think of chemical changes that they have observed in their everyday experience: hydrocarbons (gasoline, fuel oil) are oxidized, iron rusts, food spoils, leaves change color in fall, deposits form in pipes. Follow the discussion with the Demonstration on the next page, in which evidence of chemical change is observed.

▼ Teach *continued*

Demonstration

EVIDENCE OF A CHEMICAL REACTION

Place a small piece of **mossy zinc** in a **Petri dish** containing **0.1 M HCl.** Observe. When the reaction is complete, have students list the evidence of chemical change. Bubbles of H_2 form, and the Zn disappears or decreases in size.

Safety Wear **safety goggles** and a **lab apron.**

Disposal Treat the contents in the Petri dish with an excess of **1 M NaOH** in order to precipitate the Zn as $Zn(OH)_2$. Use **filter paper** to filter the products. Then wrap the precipitate in **paper** and put it in the trash. Neutralize the filtrate with **1 M acid** and pour down the drain.

TEACH FROM VISUALS

FIGURE 1.2 Have students write the formulas for the compounds mentioned in the caption to **Figure 1.2b.** Three compounds are named in the caption: $(NH_4)_2S$, $Cd(NO_3)_2$, and CdS. Have students examine the formulas of these compounds. Tell them that the second product is not mentioned in the caption. Ask students to look closely at the three formulas and use them to predict the name and formula of the other product. ammonium nitrate, NH_4NO_3

FIGURE 1.2

Evidence of Reaction As shown in the photos, the production of a gas and the formation of a precipitate are two strong indicators that a chemical reaction has occurred.

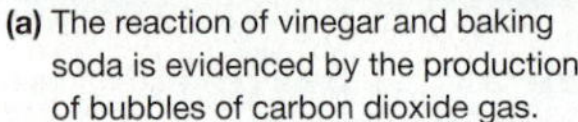

(a) The reaction of vinegar and baking soda is evidenced by the production of bubbles of carbon dioxide gas.

(b) When water solutions of ammonium sulfide and cadmium nitrate are combined, the yellow precipitate cadmium sulfide forms.

3. *Production of a gas.* The evolution of gas bubbles when two substances are mixed is often evidence of a chemical reaction. For example, bubbles of carbon dioxide gas form immediately when baking soda is mixed with vinegar, as shown in **Figure 1.2a.**
4. *Formation of a precipitate.* Many chemical reactions take place between substances that are dissolved in liquids. If a solid appears after two solutions are mixed, a reaction has likely occurred. **A solid that is produced as a result of a chemical reaction in solution and that separates from the solution is known as a precipitate.** A precipitate-forming reaction is shown in **Figure 1.2b.**

MAIN IDEA

Chemical equations must satisfy the law of conservation of mass.

A properly written chemical equation can summarize any chemical change. The following requirements will aid you in writing and reading chemical equations correctly.

1. *The equation must represent known facts.* All reactants and products must be identified, either through chemical analysis in the laboratory or from sources that give the results of experiments.
2. *The equation must contain the correct formulas for the reactants and products.* Remember what you've learned about symbols and formulas. Knowledge of the common oxidation states of the elements and of methods of writing formulas will enable you to write formulas for reactants and products if they are unavailable. Some elements are represented simply by their atomic symbols when they are in their elemental state. For example, iron is represented as Fe and carbon is represented as C. The symbols are not given any subscripts because the elements do not form definite molecular structures. Two exceptions are sulfur, which is usually written S_8, and phosphorus, which is usually written P_4. In these cases, the formulas reflect each element's unique atomic arrangement in its natural state.

Conservation (of Mass) in Reactions

Differentiated Instruction

BELOW LEVEL

Emphasize that if the chemical formulas for all the reactants and products are not written correctly, then it is impossible to write the correct chemical equation. Have students review writing chemical formulas for various substances. Be sure to include diatomic gases such as hydrogen (H_2) and oxygen (O_2), and ionic compounds containing polyatomic ions such as ammonium phosphate, $(NH_4)_3PO_4$.

FIGURE 1.3

ELEMENTS THAT NORMALLY EXIST AS DIATOMIC MOLECULES

Element	Symbol	Molecular formula	Physical state at room temperature
Hydrogen	H	H_2	gas
Nitrogen	N	N_2	gas
Oxygen	O	O_2	gas
Fluorine	F	F_2	gas
Chlorine	Cl	Cl_2	gas
Bromine	Br	Br_2	liquid
Iodine	I	I_2	solid

Also remember some elements, listed in **Figure 1.3**, exist primarily as diatomic molecules, such as H_2 and O_2. Each of these elements is represented in an equation by its molecular formula.

3. *The law of conservation of mass must be satisfied.* Atoms are neither created nor destroyed in ordinary chemical reactions. Thus, the same number of atoms of each element must appear on each side of a correct chemical equation. To balance numbers of atoms, add coefficients where necessary. **A coefficient is a small whole number that appears in front of a formula in a chemical equation.** Placing a coefficient in front of a formula specifies the relative number of moles of the substance. If no coefficient is written, it's assumed to be 1.

Writing Word Equations

The first step in writing a chemical equation is to identify the facts to be represented. **It is often helpful to write a word equation, an equation in which the reactants and products in a chemical reaction are represented by words.** A word equation has only qualitative (descriptive) meaning. It does not give the whole story because it does not give the quantities of reactants used or products formed.

Consider the reaction of methane, the principal component of natural gas, with oxygen. When methane burns in air, it combines with oxygen to produce carbon dioxide and water vapor. In the reaction, methane and oxygen are the reactants. Carbon dioxide and water are the products. The word equation for the reaction is written as follows:

$$\text{methane} + \text{oxygen} \longrightarrow \text{carbon dioxide} + \text{water}$$

The arrow, $\longrightarrow$, is read as *react to yield* or *yield* (also *produce* or *form*). So the equation above is read, "methane and oxygen react to yield carbon dioxide and water," or simply, "methane and oxygen yield carbon dioxide and water."

Classroom Discussion

Provide students with the formulas of the reactants in the demonstration reaction on the previous page, and have them predict the names and formulas of the products on the basis of their observations. Write a word equation for the reaction, and then write the appropriate formula equation, as follows.

$$\text{zinc} + \text{hydrochloric acid} \longrightarrow \text{hydrogen} + \text{zinc chloride};$$

$$Zn(s) + 2HCl(aq) \longrightarrow H_2(g) + ZnCl_2(aq)$$

TEACH FROM TABLES

FIGURE 1.3 Have students prepare a table similar to **Figure 1.3** that includes the element name, symbol, and chemical formula for each of the noble gases. Be sure students understand why these gases are written as monatomic molecules.

BELOW LEVEL

Emphasize that once the correct chemical formula has been written, the subscripts cannot be changed. Placing the correct coefficient in front of a formula is the only way to show that the law of conservation of mass is obeyed.

As an example, write the formula for water on the board. Point out that a chemical reaction involving water produces two oxygen atoms. Ask students how they would show how the water molecule supplies the two oxygen atoms. by placing a 2 in front of H_2O: $2H_2O$

Emphasize that H_2O cannot be changed to H_2O_2. Point out that these are two different compounds with very different properties. Whereas H_2O is taken internally, H_2O_2 is the formula for hydrogen peroxide, a strong oxidizing agent that can only be applied externally to prevent bacterial infections in cuts.

▼ Teach continued

Classroom Discussion

Point out that the same elements are always present on both sides of every chemical equation. For example, both sides of the equation on this page include C, H, and O. Ask students what actually happens to the atoms of the elements during a chemical reaction if the same ones are always present in both the reactants and products. Students should understand that a chemical reaction involves a rearrangement of the atoms. Point out how carbon is bonded to hydrogen in CH_4, which is a reactant. Then point out that carbon is bonded to oxygen in CO_2, which is a product. Ask students what must happen to the bonds between the atoms of reactants and products during a chemical reaction. Students should recognize that bonds are broken to separate the atoms in the reactant(s), and then new bonds form to make the product(s).

Writing Formula Equations

The next step in writing a correct chemical equation is to replace the names of the reactants and products with appropriate symbols and formulas. Methane is a molecular compound composed of one carbon atom and four hydrogen atoms. Its chemical formula is CH_4. Recall that oxygen exists in nature as diatomic molecules; it is therefore represented as O_2. The correct formulas for carbon dioxide and water are CO_2 and H_2O, respectively.

A formula equation represents the reactants and products of a chemical reaction by their symbols or formulas. The formula equation for the reaction of methane and oxygen is written as follows:

$$CH_4(g) + O_2(g) \longrightarrow CO_2(g) + H_2O(g) \text{ (not balanced)}$$

The *g* in parentheses after each formula indicates that the corresponding substance is in the gaseous state. Like a word equation, a formula equation is a qualitative statement. It gives no information about the amounts of reactants or products.

Writing Balanced Equations

A formula equation meets two of the three requirements for a correct chemical equation. It represents the facts and shows the correct symbols and formulas for the reactants and products. To complete the process of writing a correct equation, the law of conservation of mass must be taken into account. The relative amounts of reactants and products represented in the equation must be adjusted so that the numbers and types of atoms are the same on both sides of the equation. This process is called *balancing an equation* and is carried out by inserting coefficients. Once it is balanced, a formula equation is a correctly written chemical equation.

Look again at the formula equation for the reaction of methane and oxygen.

$$CH_4(g) + O_2(g) \longrightarrow CO_2(g) + H_2O(g) \text{ (not balanced)}$$

To balance the equation, begin by counting atoms of elements that are combined with atoms of other elements and that appear only once on each side of the equation. In this case, we could begin by counting either carbon or hydrogen atoms. Usually, the elements hydrogen and oxygen are balanced only after balancing all other elements in an equation. (You will read more about the rules of balancing equations later in the chapter.) Thus, we begin by counting carbon atoms.

Inspecting the formula equation reveals that there is one carbon atom on each side of the arrow. Therefore, carbon is already balanced in the equation. Counting hydrogen atoms reveals that there are four hydrogen atoms in the reactants but only two in the products. Two additional hydrogen atoms are needed on the right side of the equation. They can be added by placing the coefficient 2 in front of the chemical formula H_2O.

$$CH_4(g) + O_2(g) \longrightarrow CO_2(g) + 2H_2O(g) \text{ (partially balanced)}$$

Differentiated Instruction

ENGLISH LEARNERS

Point out that the chemical equation at the bottom of this page is labeled as being "partially balanced." Ask students what they think the term partially balanced means. Students should recognize that only some of the atoms (C and H) have been balanced, whereas others (O) are yet to be balanced. Ask students what it means when the word *partially* is no longer used, so that a chemical equation is considered balanced.

A coefficient multiplies the number of atoms of each element indicated in a chemical formula. Thus, $2H_2O$ represents *four* H atoms and *two* O atoms. To add two more hydrogen atoms to the right side of the equation, one may be tempted to change the subscript in the formula of water so that H_2O becomes H_4O. However, this would be a mistake because changing the subscripts of a chemical formula changes the *identity* of the compound. H_4O is not a product in the combustion of methane. In fact, there is no such compound. One must use only coefficients to change the relative number of atoms in a chemical equation because coefficients change the numbers of atoms without changing the identities of the reactants or products.

Now consider the number of oxygen atoms. There are four oxygen atoms on the right side of the arrow in the partially balanced equation. Yet there are only two oxygen atoms on the left side of the arrow. One can increase the number of oxygen atoms on the left side to four by placing the coefficient 2 in front of the molecular formula for oxygen. This results in a correct chemical equation, or *balanced formula equation,* for the burning of methane in oxygen.

$$CH_4(g) + 2O_2(g) \longrightarrow CO_2(g) + 2H_2O(g)$$

This reaction is further illustrated in **Figure 1.4.** As you study the molecular models, consider carefully the effects associated with changing the subscripts in formulas and those associated with changing coefficients. Also, be patient. Balancing equations is a skill that takes practice, and any chemist will admit to it being sometimes extremely complex.

CHECK FOR UNDERSTANDING

Discuss Why are formula equations, using symbols and numbers, used more commonly in chemistry than word equations?

FIGURE 1.4

Chemical Equations

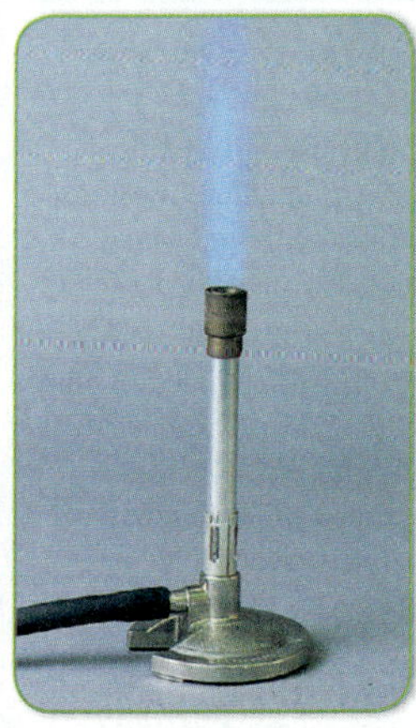

(a) In a Bunsen burner, methane combines with oxygen in the air to form carbon dioxide and water vapor.

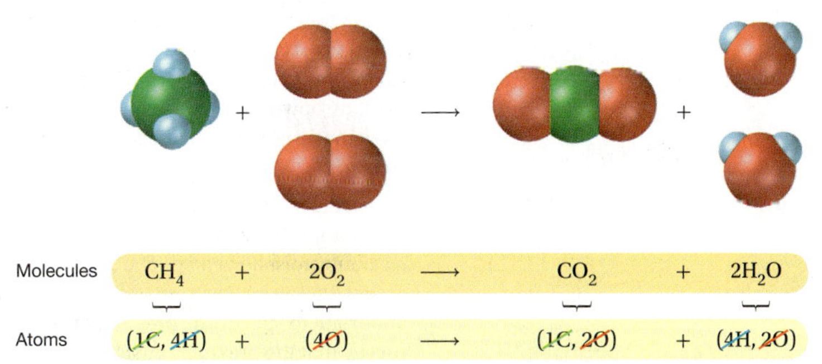

(b) The reaction is represented by both a molecular model and a balanced equation. Each shows that the number of atoms of each element in the reactants equals the number of atoms of each element in the products.

Classroom Discussion

Stress that the formulas for all reactants and products in a chemical equation must be written correctly and that each pure substance has only one chemical formula. To make this point clear, write the balanced equation for the formation of NaCl from the elements.

$$2Na + Cl_2 \longrightarrow 2NaCl$$

Now show what would happen if the formula for salt were incorrectly written as Na_2Cl.

$$4Na + Cl_2 \longrightarrow 2Na_2Cl$$

To demonstrate that this equation is not valid, have students determine the oxidation numbers for the reactants and the products. Students will see that the oxidation numbers do not add up to zero for the product, as required.

Teaching Tip

Although the equation for the combustion of methane on this page shows that three moles of reactants produce three moles of products, this is coincidental. Conservation laws apply to the reactants and products of chemical reactions in terms of grams and atoms, but not in terms of moles or molecules. It is more common for the number of moles of reactants and products in a reaction to differ.

Check for Understanding

Answer: Formula equations are used more often because word equations would be too long and unwieldy for practical use.

BELOW LEVEL

Have students explain how **Figure 1.4** shows that a chemical reaction can rearrange atoms while still obeying the law of conservation of mass. The molecular models clearly show how the atoms have been rearranged as bonds are broken in the reactants and new bonds form in the products. Students should point out that the number of atoms for each element is equal on both sides of the chemical equation.

INCLUSION

Ask tactile learners how they could use a deck of cards to show how mass is conserved while atoms are rearranged in a chemical reaction. After dealing out the cards to the players, the deck can be shuffled and a new hand dealt. The players will receive a different hand, but all the cards will still be present.

▼ Teach *continued*

TEACH FROM TABLES

FIGURE 1.5 Point out to students that the table summarizes the symbols needed to incorporate the maximum amount of information into a chemical equation. Encourage students to refer to it often until they know its contents. Emphasize that the last five symbols represent conditions that are often necessary to make a reaction occur.

Teaching Tip

Although a catalyst speeds up a reaction, it does not appear as a reactant in the equation because it can be recovered unchanged after the reaction.

FIGURE 1.5

SYMBOLS USED IN CHEMICAL EQUATIONS

Symbol	Explanation
$\longrightarrow$	"Yields"; indicates result of reaction
$\rightleftarrows$	Used in place of a single arrow to indicate a reversible reaction
(s)	A reactant or product in the solid state; also used to indicate a precipitate
$\downarrow$	Alternative to (s), but used only to indicate a precipitate
(l)	A reactant or product in the liquid state
(aq)	A reactant or product in an aqueous solution (dissolved in water)
(g)	A reactant or product in the gaseous state
$\uparrow$	Alternative to (g), but used only to indicate a gaseous product
$\xrightarrow{\Delta}$ or $\xrightarrow{\text{heat}}$	Reactants are heated
$\xrightarrow{2\text{ atm}}$	Pressure at which reaction is carried out, in this case 2 atm
$\xrightarrow{\text{Pressure}}$	Pressure at which reaction is carried out exceeds normal atmospheric pressure
$\xrightarrow{0^{\circ}\text{C}}$	Temperature at which reaction is carried out, in this case 0°C
$\xrightarrow{MnO_2}$	Formula of catalyst, in this case manganese dioxide, used to alter the rate of the reaction

Additional Symbols Used in Chemical Equations

Figure 1.5 above summarizes the symbols commonly used in chemical equations. As you can see, some things can be shown in different ways. For example, sometimes a gaseous product is indicated by an arrow pointing upward, $\uparrow$, instead of (g). A downward arrow, $\downarrow$, is often used to show the formation of a precipitate during a reaction in solution.

The conditions under which a reaction takes place are often indicated by placing information above or below the reaction arrow. The word *heat,* which is symbolized by a Greek capital delta (Δ), indicates that the reactants must be heated. The specific temperature at which a reaction occurs may also be written over the arrow. For some reactions, it is important to specify the pressure at which the reaction occurs or to specify that the pressure must be above normal. Many reactions are speeded up and can take place at lower temperatures in the presence of a *catalyst.* A catalyst is a substance that changes the rate of a chemical reaction but can be recovered unchanged. To show that a catalyst is present, the formula for the catalyst or the word *catalyst* is written over the reaction arrow.

Differentiated Instruction

BELOW LEVEL

Have students practice using the symbols in **Figure 1.5.** Tell them that they can use letters to represent reactants and products. For example, ask them to write the chemical equation that shows how a solid and a liquid produce a gas when heated.

A correct answer would be:

$A(s) + B(l) \xrightarrow{\text{heat}} C(g)$.

Encourage students to see that there may be multiple ways to write the same equation.

In the example given, the word "heat" above the arrow can be replaced by the symbol Δ, and (g) can be replaced by the symbol $\uparrow$.

In many reactions, as soon as the products begin to form, they immediately begin to react with each other and re-form the reactants. In other words, the reverse reaction also occurs. The reverse reaction may occur to a greater or lesser degree than the original reaction, depending on the specific reaction and the conditions. **A reversible reaction is a chemical reaction in which the products re-form the original reactants.** The reversibility of a reaction is indicated by writing two arrows pointing in opposite directions. For example, the reversible reaction between iron and water vapor is written as follows:

$$3Fe(s) + 4H_2O(g) \rightleftarrows Fe_3O_4(s) + 4H_2(g)$$

With an understanding of all the symbols and formulas used, it is possible to translate a chemical equation into a sentence. Consider the following equation:

$$2HgO(s) \xrightarrow{\Delta} 2Hg(l) + O_2(g)$$

Translated into a sentence, this equation reads, "When heated, solid mercury(II) oxide yields liquid mercury and gaseous oxygen."

It is also possible to write a chemical equation from a sentence describing a reaction. Consider the sentence, "Under pressure and in the presence of a platinum catalyst, gaseous ethene and hydrogen form gaseous ethane." This sentence can be translated into the following equation:

$$C_2H_4(g) + H_2(g) \xrightarrow{\text{pressure, Pt}} C_2H_6(g)$$

Throughout this chapter we will often include the symbols for physical states (*s*, *l*, *g*, and *aq*) in balanced formula equations. You should be able to interpret these symbols when they are used and to supply them when the necessary information is available.

Writing Word, Formula, and Balanced Chemical Equations

Sample Problem A **Write word and formula equations for the chemical reaction that occurs when solid sodium oxide is added to water at room temperature and forms sodium hydroxide (dissolved in the water). Include symbols for physical states in the formula equation. Then balance the formula equation to give a balanced chemical equation.**

 **SOLVE**

The word equation must show the reactants, sodium oxide and water, to the left of the arrow. The product, sodium hydroxide, must appear to the right of the arrow.

sodium oxide + water ⟶ sodium hydroxide

The word equation is converted to a formula equation by replacing the name of each compound with the appropriate chemical formula. To do this requires knowing that sodium has an oxidation state of +1, that oxygen usually has an oxidation state of −2, and that a hydroxide ion has a charge of 1−.

$$Na_2O + H_2O \longrightarrow NaOH \text{ (not balanced)}$$

Adding symbols for the physical states of the reactants and products and the coefficient 2 in front of NaOH produces a balanced chemical equation.

$$Na_2O(s) + H_2O(l) \longrightarrow 2NaOH(aq)$$

Problem Solving

DECONSTRUCTING PROBLEMS

Have students interpret what the symbols in the balanced equation represent. Students should explain that sodium oxide is a solid that reacts with water to produce sodium hydroxide, which dissolves in water to form an aqueous solution.

Classroom Practice

A-1 Write word and balanced chemical equations for each of the following chemical reactions. Include symbols for physical states when indicated.

a. Hydrogen peroxide in an aqueous solution decomposes to produce oxygen and water.

b. Solid copper metal reacts with aqueous silver nitrate to produce solid silver metal and aqueous copper nitrate.

c. Solid zinc metal reacts with aqueous copper sulfate to produce solid copper metal and aqueous zinc sulfate.

Answers:

a. hydrogen peroxide ⟶ oxygen + water; $2H_2O_2(aq) \longrightarrow O_2(g) + 2H_2O(l)$

b. copper + silver nitrate ⟶ silver + copper nitrate; $Cu(s) + 2AgNO_3(aq) \longrightarrow 2Ag(s) + Cu(NO_3)_2(aq)$

c. zinc + copper sulfate ⟶ copper + zinc sulfate; $Zn(s) + CuSO_4(aq) \longrightarrow Cu(s) + ZnSO_4(aq)$

▼ Teach *continued*

Classroom Practice

B-1 Translate the following equations into sentences:

a. $2ZnO(s) + C(s) \longrightarrow 2Zn(s) + CO_2(g)$

b. $Na_2O(s) + 2CO_2(g) + H_2O(g) \longrightarrow 2NaHCO_3(s)$

Answers:

a. Solid zinc oxide and solid carbon react to produce solid zinc metal and carbon dioxide gas.

b. Solid sodium oxide reacts with carbon dioxide gas and water vapor to produce solid sodium hydrogen carbonate (also called *sodium bicarbonate*).

Answers

Practice B

1. a. calcium + sulfur ⟶ calcium sulfide; $8Ca(s) + S_8(s) \longrightarrow 8CaS(s)$

b. hydrogen + fluorine ⟶ hydrogen fluoride; $H_2(g) + F_2(g) \longrightarrow 2HF(g)$

c. aluminum + zinc chloride ⟶ zinc + aluminum chloride; $2Al(s) + 3ZnCl_2(aq) \longrightarrow 3Zn(s) + 2AlCl_3(aq)$

2. a. Liquid carbon disulfide reacts with oxygen gas to produce carbon dioxide gas and sulfur dioxide gas.

b. Aqueous solutions of sodium chloride and silver nitrate react to produce aqueous sodium nitrate and a precipitate of silver chloride.

3. $N_2H_4(l) + O_2(g) \longrightarrow N_2(g) + 2H_2O(l)$

Writing Word, Formula, and Balanced Chemical Equations

Sample Problem B **Translate the following chemical equation into a sentence:**

$$BaCl_2(aq) + Na_2CrO_4(aq) \longrightarrow BaCrO_4(s) + 2NaCl(aq)$$

SOLVE Each reactant is an ionic compound and is named according to the rules for such compounds. Both reactants are in aqueous solution. One product is a precipitate and the other remains in solution. The equation is translated as follows: Aqueous solutions of barium chloride and sodium chromate react to produce a precipitate of barium chromate plus sodium chloride in aqueous solution.

Practice Answers in Appendix E

1. Write word and balanced chemical equations for the following reactions. Include symbols for physical states when indicated.
   a. Solid calcium reacts with solid sulfur to produce solid calcium sulfide.
   b. Hydrogen gas reacts with fluorine gas to produce hydrogen fluoride gas. (Hint: See **Figure 1.3.**)
   c. Solid aluminum metal reacts with aqueous zinc chloride to produce solid zinc metal and aqueous aluminum chloride.
2. Translate the following chemical equations into sentences:
   a. $CS_2(l) + 3O_2(g) \longrightarrow CO_2(g) + 2SO_2(g)$
   b. $NaCl(aq) + AgNO_3(aq) \longrightarrow NaNO_3(aq) + AgCl(s)$
3. Hydrazine, N_2H_4, is used as rocket fuel. Hydrazine reacts violently with oxygen to produce gaseous nitrogen and water. Write the balanced chemical equation.

MAIN IDEA

Chemical equations show relative amounts, masses, and progression of chemical reactions.

Chemical equations are very useful in doing quantitative chemical work. The arrow in a balanced chemical equation is like an equal sign. And the chemical equation as a whole is similar to an algebraic equation in that it expresses an equality. Let's examine some of the quantitative information revealed by a chemical equation.

1. *The coefficients of a chemical reaction indicate relative, not absolute, amounts of reactants and products.* A chemical equation usually shows the smallest numbers of atoms, molecules, or ions that will satisfy the law of conservation of mass in a given chemical reaction.

   Consider the equation for the formation of hydrogen chloride from hydrogen and chlorine.

$$H_2(g) + Cl_2(g) \longrightarrow 2HCl(g)$$

The equation indicates that 1 molecule of hydrogen reacts with 1 molecule of chlorine to produce 2 molecules of hydrogen chloride, resulting in the following molecular ratio of reactants and products.

$$1 \text{ molecule } H_2 : 1 \text{ molecule } Cl_2 : 2 \text{ molecules } HCl$$

Problem Solving

DECONSTRUCTING PROBLEMS

Help students write the word equation from the chemical equation by breaking down the process into two steps. Tell students that they can begin by writing the name of each compound under its formula. For example, a student would write "barium chloride" under $BaCl_2$. Students can then put together the name along with any symbol associated with the formula. For example, "an aqueous solution of barium chloride reacts with ...."

ALTERNATIVE APPROACHES

Have students work the solutions shown for converting moles to grams in reverse. For example, ask them to convert 2.02 g H_2 to mol H_2. Be sure students recognize that they must invert the conversion factor in each case to solve the problems. Students can easily verify their answers by checking the values for moles given in the text.

This ratio shows the smallest possible relative amounts of the reaction's reactants and products. To obtain larger relative amounts, we simply multiply each coefficient by the same number. For example, we could multiply each by a factor of 20. Thus, 20 molecules of hydrogen would react with 20 molecules of chlorine to yield 40 molecules of hydrogen chloride. The reaction can also be considered in terms of amounts in moles: 1 mol of hydrogen molecules reacts with 1 mol of chlorine molecules to yield 2 mol of hydrogen chloride molecules.

2. *The relative masses of the reactants and products of a chemical reaction can be determined from the reaction's coefficients.* Recall that an amount of an element or compound in moles can be converted to a mass in grams by multiplying by the appropriate molar mass. We know that 1 mol of hydrogen reacts with 1 mol of chlorine to yield 2 mol of hydrogen chloride. The relative masses of the reactants and products are calculated as follows.

$$1\ \cancel{\text{mol } H_2} \times \frac{2.02\text{ g } H_2}{\cancel{\text{mol } H_2}} = 2.02\text{ g } H_2$$

$$1\ \cancel{\text{mol } Cl_2} \times \frac{70.90\text{ g } Cl_2}{\cancel{\text{mol } Cl_2}} = 70.90\text{ g } Cl_2$$

$$2\ \cancel{\text{mol HCl}} \times \frac{36.46\text{ g HCl}}{\cancel{\text{mol HCl}}} = 72.92\text{ g HCl}$$

The chemical equation shows that 2.02 g of hydrogen will react with 70.90 g of chlorine to yield 72.92 g of hydrogen chloride.

3. *The reverse reaction for a chemical equation has the same relative amounts of substances as the forward reaction.* Because a chemical equation is like an algebraic equation, the equality can be read in either direction. Reading the hydrogen chloride formation equation, we can see that 2 molecules of hydrogen chloride break down to form 1 molecule of hydrogen plus 1 molecule of chlorine. Similarly, 2 mol (72.92 g) of hydrogen chloride yield 1 mol (2.02 g) of hydrogen and 1 mol (70.90 g) of chlorine. **Figure 1.6** summarizes the above ideas.

FIGURE 1.6

Interpreting Chemical Equations This representation of the reaction of hydrogen and chlorine to yield hydrogen chloride shows several ways to interpret the quantitative information of a chemical reaction.

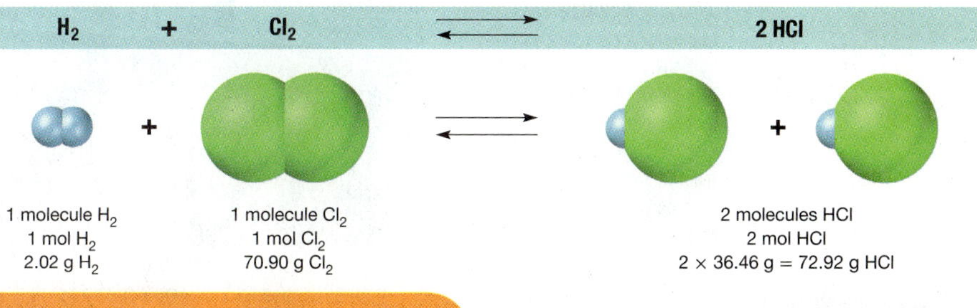

Teaching Tip

Mass ratios are derived by multiplying mole ratios by the molar mass of each substance.

TEACH FROM VISUALS

FIGURE 1.6 Have students explain how **Figure 1.6** illustrates the law of conservation of mass. Students should add the masses of the reactants and see that their combined masses equal the combined masses of the products.

Differentiated Instruction

ENGLISH LEARNERS

Be sure students understand the difference between *relative* and *absolute*. Give them two statements.

(1) Paul is older than Maria.

(2) Paul is 16 years old.

Ask students to explain the difference between these statements. Point out that the first statement describes a relative age. Ask students what information it provides. In this case, no one can tell the age of either person, but only that Paul is older than Maria.

The second statement describes an absolute age. Ask students what information this statement provides. In this case, everyone knows Paul's age. Ask students to write a sentence that uses ages in both absolute and relative terms. An example is, "Paul is 16 years old and is two years younger than Maria." In this case, Paul's age is an absolute age, whereas Maria's age is a relative age.

▼ Teach *continued*

TEACH FROM VISUALS

FIGURE 1.7 Although students have not yet learned that equal volumes of gases under the same conditions of temperature and pressure contain the same number of molecules, they are likely to understand intuitively that the 2:1 ratio of volumes of H_2 to O_2 shown in the photograph confirms the ratio found in the balanced equation.

Demonstration

ELECTROLYSIS OF WATER

Using a **graduated cylinder,** put 300 mL of **0.01 M aqueous Na_2SO_4** in a **500-mL beaker.** Add 1 mL of **bromothymol blue** and stir. Fill **two small test tubes** with the colored solution from the beaker, and carefully invert the test tubes into the solution. Do not introduce any air bubbles into the test tubes. Immerse a **9 V battery** into the solution and position it upright in the center of the beaker. Put the open mouth of one test tube over each terminal of the battery.

Students will observe that twice as much H_2 as O_2 is produced. Relate this observation to the balanced chemical equation. (Note: the solution at the anode—where O_2 is produced—turns yellow because of the presence of H_3O^+ ions; the solution at the cathode turns blue because of the presence of OH^- ions.)

Safety Wear **safety goggles** and a **lab apron.**

Disposal Pour the liquid down the drain. Dry the battery, put tape over the terminals, and save it for reuse.

We have seen that a chemical equation provides useful quantitative information about a chemical reaction. However, there is also important information that is *not* provided by a chemical equation. For instance, an equation gives no indication of whether a reaction will actually occur. A chemical equation can be written for a reaction that may not even take place. Some guidelines about the types of simple reactions that can be expected to occur are given in later sections. And later chapters provide additional guidelines for other types of reactions. In all these guidelines, it is important to remember that experimentation forms the basis for confirming that a particular chemical reaction will occur.

In addition, chemical equations give no information about the speed at which reactions occur or about how the bonding between atoms or ions changes during the reaction. These aspects of chemical reactions are discussed in the chapter "Reaction Kinetics."

MAIN IDEA

Chemical equations can be balanced with step-by-step inspection.

Most of the equations in the remainder of this chapter can be balanced by inspection. The following procedure demonstrates how to master balancing equations by inspection using a step-by-step approach. The equation for the decomposition of water (see **Figure 1.7**) will be used as an example.

1. *Identify the names of the reactants and the products, and write a word equation.* The word equation for the reaction shown in **Figure 1.7** is written as follows.

$$\text{water} \longrightarrow \text{hydrogen} + \text{oxygen}$$

2. *Write a formula equation by substituting correct formulas for the names of the reactants and the products.* We know that the formula for water is H_2O. And recall that both hydrogen and oxygen exist as diatomic molecules. Therefore, their correct formulas are H_2 and O_2, respectively.

$$H_2O(l) \longrightarrow H_2(g) + O_2(g) \text{ (not balanced)}$$

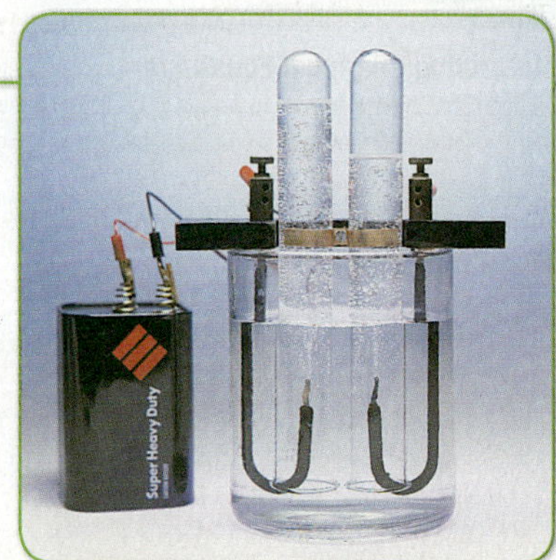

FIGURE 1.7

Decomposition of Water When an electric current is passed through water that has been made slightly conductive, the water molecules break down to yield hydrogen (in tube at right) and oxygen (in tube at left). Bubbles of each gas are evidence of the reaction. Note that twice as much hydrogen as oxygen is produced.

Differentiated Instruction

PRE-AP

Tell students that they may have to change a coefficient they first place in front of a formula. Use the following equation as an example.

$Fe + MgBr_2 \longrightarrow Fe_2Br_3 + Mg$

$4Fe + 3MgBr_2 \longrightarrow 2Fe_2Br_3 + 3Mg$

Point out that even though a balanced equation can be written for the reaction between iron and magnesium bromide, the reaction does not take place.

Tell students that in the last section of this chapter, they will learn how to identify whether a chemical reaction will or will not occur.

3. *Balance the formula equation according to the law of conservation of mass.* This last step is done by trial and error. Coefficients are changed and the numbers of atoms are counted on both sides of the equation. When the numbers of each type of atom are the same for both the products and the reactants, the equation is balanced. The trial-and-error method of balancing equations is made easier by the use of the following guidelines.
   - Balance the different types of atoms one at a time.
   - First balance the atoms of elements that are combined and that appear only once on each side of the equation.
   - Balance polyatomic ions that appear on both sides of the equation as single units. Look closely to see if these ions are enclosed in parentheses, and count the individual atoms accordingly.
   - Balance H atoms and O atoms after atoms of all other elements have been balanced.

The formula equation in our example shows that there are two oxygen atoms on the right and only one on the left. To balance oxygen atoms, the number of H_2O molecules must be increased. Placing the coefficient 2 before H_2O gives the necessary two oxygen atoms on the left.

$$2H_2O(l) \longrightarrow H_2(g) + O_2(g) \text{ (partially balanced)}$$

The coefficient 2 in front of H_2O has upset the balance of hydrogen atoms. Placing the coefficient 2 in front of hydrogen, H_2, on the right, gives an equal number of hydrogen atoms (4) on both sides of the equation.

$$2H_2O(l) \longrightarrow 2H_2(g) + O_2(g)$$

4. *Count atoms to be sure that the equation is balanced.* Make sure that equal numbers of atoms of each element appear on both sides of the arrow.

$$2H_2O(l) \longrightarrow 2H_2(g) + O_2(g)$$
$$(4H + 2O) = (4H) + (2O)$$

Occasionally at this point, the coefficients do not represent the smallest possible whole-number ratio of reactants and products. When this happens, the coefficients should be divided by their greatest common factor in order to obtain the smallest possible whole-number coefficients.

Balancing chemical equations by inspection becomes easier as you gain experience. Learn to avoid the most common mistakes: (1) writing incorrect chemical formulas for reactants or products and (2) trying to balance an equation by changing subscripts. Remember that subscripts cannot be added, deleted, or changed. Eventually, you will probably be able to skip writing the word equation and each separate step. You may even may develop several "tricks" of your own for deciding how best to deal with certain compounds and polyatomic ions. Remember, there is no one, singular way to go about balancing a chemical equation, so you should not be afraid to use a method you feel works best for you. However, *do not* leave out the final step of counting atoms to be sure the equation is balanced.

CHECK FOR UNDERSTANDING

Discuss Why should subscripts not be changed when balancing chemical equations?

Alternative Assessment

Have students use **Figure 1.6** as a model for making a chart for the formation of NH_3 from H_2 and N_2. Have them draw representations of the molecules of reactants and products, and then have them calculate the number of molecules and moles of each reactant and product. Ask them to show that mass is conserved.

Teaching Tip

Tell students that occasionally they will see fractional coefficients in balanced chemical equations, such as some thermochemical equations. Remind them that the fractions in these equations represent the number of moles, not the number of atoms or molecules.

READING TOOLKIT

READING HINT As students read through the remainder of this section, have them use the examples of balanced and unbalanced chemical equations on the following pages to help understand the difference between the two.

Check for Understanding

Answer: Subscripts indicate how many atoms of a particular element are in a compound. Changing them would change the chemical formula itself.

Problem Solving

REALITY CHECK

Students can construct a table to use as they try to balance an equation. The table should show the number of atoms of each element in the reactants on the left and the number of atoms of each element in the products on the right. For example, the table below summarizes the partially-balanced equation shown on this page.

	Reactants		Products	
Elements	H	O	H	O
Number of atoms	4	2	2	2

This table clearly shows that the oxygen atoms are balanced, but that the hydrogen atoms still need to be balanced. Ask students to construct a table that verifies that the equation is balanced.

▼ Teach *continued*

Classroom Practice

C-1 Write word, formula, and balanced chemical equations for each of the following reactions:

a. Nitrogen dioxide gas reacts with water to form aqueous nitric acid and nitrogen monoxide gas.

b. Solid potassium chlorate decomposes to form solid potassium chloride and oxygen gas.

Answers:

a. nitrogen dioxide + water ⟶ nitric acid + nitrogen monoxide; $NO_2(g) + H_2O(l) \longrightarrow HNO_3(aq) + NO(g)$; $3NO_2(g) + H_2O(l) \longrightarrow 2HNO_3(aq) + NO(g)$

b. potassium chlorate ⟶ potassium chloride + oxygen; $KClO_3(s) \longrightarrow KCl(s) + O_2(g)$; $2KClO_3(s) \longrightarrow 2KCl(s) + 3O_2(g)$

Answers

Practice C

1. a. Word: magnesium + hydrochloric acid ⟶ magnesium chloride + hydrogen

Formula: $Mg + HCl \longrightarrow MgCl_2 + H_2$

Balanced: $Mg + 2HCl \longrightarrow MgCl_2 + H_2$

b. Word: nitric acid + magnesium hydroxide ⟶ magnesium nitrate + water

Formula:

$HNO_3(aq) + Mg(OH)_2(s) \longrightarrow Mg(NO_3)_2(aq) + H_2O(l)$

Balanced:

$2HNO_3(aq) + Mg(OH)_2(s) \longrightarrow Mg(NO_3)_2(aq) + 2H_2O(l)$

2. $Ca(s) + 2H_2O(l) \longrightarrow Ca(OH)_2(aq) + H_2(g)$

Writing Word, Formula, and Balanced Chemical Equations

Sample Problem C **The reaction of zinc with aqueous hydrochloric acid produces a solution of zinc chloride and hydrogen gas. This reaction is shown in Figure 1.8. Write a balanced chemical equation for the reaction.**

1 ANALYZE *Write the word equation.*

zinc + hydrochloric acid ⟶ zinc chloride + hydrogen

2 PLAN *Write the formula equation.*

$Zn(s) + HCl(aq) \longrightarrow ZnCl_2(aq) + H_2(g)$ (not balanced)

3 SOLVE *Adjust the coefficients.* Note that chlorine and hydrogeneach appear only once on each side of the equation. We balance chlorine first because it is combined on both sides of the equation. Also, recall from the guidelines on the previous page that hydrogen and oxygen are balanced only after all other elements in the reaction are balanced. To balance chlorine, we place the coefficient 2 before HCl. Two molecules of hydrogen chloride also yield the required two hydrogen atoms on the right. Finally, note that there is one zinc atom on each side in the formula equation. Therefore, no further coefficients are needed.

$Zn(s) + 2HCl(aq) \longrightarrow ZnCl_2(aq) + H_2(g)$

4 CHECK YOUR WORK *Count atoms to check balance.*

$Zn(s) + 2HCl(aq) \longrightarrow ZnCl_2(aq) + H_2(g)$

(1Zn) + (2H + 2Cl) = (1Zn + 2Cl) + (2H)

The equation is balanced.

FIGURE 1.8

Reacting Zinc with HCl Solid zinc reacts with hydrochloric acid to form aqueous zinc chloride and hydrogen gas.

Practice Answers in Appendix E

1. Write word, formula, and balanced chemical equations for each of the following reactions:
   - **a.** Solid magnesium and aqueous hydrochloric acid react to produce aqueous magnesium chloride and hydrogen gas.
   - **b.** Aqueous nitric acid reacts with solid magnesium hydroxide to produce aqueous magnesium nitrate and water.
2. Solid calcium metal reacts with water to form aqueous calcium hydroxide and hydrogen gas. Write a balanced chemical equation for this reaction.

Problem Solving

TAKE IT FURTHER

To emphasize the importance of writing the correct chemical formula for every compound involved in a reaction, have students rewrite a formula equation in Sample Problem C, substituting H for H_2. Then ask students to balance this equation. Have them compare their balanced equation to the one given in Sample Problem C. Students should see that writing an incorrect formula will lead to an incorrect answer.

Balancing Chemical Equations

Sample Problem D **Solid aluminum carbide, Al_4C_3, reacts with water to produce methane gas and solid aluminum hydroxide. Write a balanced chemical equation for this reaction.**

 **SOLVE**

The reactants are aluminum carbide and water. The products are methane and aluminum hydroxide. The formula equation is written as follows.

$$Al_4C_3(s) + H_2O(l) \longrightarrow CH_4(g) + Al(OH)_3(s) \text{ (not balanced)}$$

Begin balancing the formula equation by counting either aluminum atoms or carbon atoms. (Remember that hydrogen and oxygen atoms are balanced last.) There are four Al atoms on the left. To balance Al atoms, place the coefficient 4 before $Al(OH)_3$ on the right.

$$Al_4C_3(s) + H_2O(l) \longrightarrow CH_4(g) + 4Al(OH)_3(s) \text{ (partially balanced)}$$

Now balance the carbon atoms. With three C atoms on the left, the coefficient 3 must be placed before CH_4 on the right.

$$Al_4C_3(s) + H_2O(l) \longrightarrow 3CH_4(g) + 4Al(OH)_3(s) \text{ (partially balanced)}$$

Balance oxygen atoms next because oxygen, unlike hydrogen, appears only once on each side of the equation. There is one O atom on the left and 12 O atoms in the four $Al(OH)_3$ formula units on the right. Placing the coefficient 12 before H_2O balances the O atoms.

$$Al_4C_3(s) + 12H_2O(l) \longrightarrow 3CH_4(g) + 4Al(OH)_3(s)$$

This leaves the hydrogen atoms to be balanced. There are 24 H atoms on the left. On the right, there are 12 H atoms in the methane molecules and 12 in the aluminum hydroxide formula units, totaling 24 H atoms. The H atoms are balanced.

$$Al_4C_3(s) \quad + \quad 12H_2O(l) \quad \longrightarrow \quad 3CH_4(g) \quad + \quad 4Al(OH)_3(s)$$

$$(\cancel{4Al} + \cancel{3C}) + (\cancel{24H} + \cancel{12O}) \quad = \quad (\cancel{3C} + \cancel{12H}) + (\cancel{4Al} + \cancel{12H} + \cancel{12O})$$

The equation is balanced.

Balancing Chemical Equations

Sample Problem E **Aluminum sulfate and calcium hydroxide are used in a water-purification process. When added to water, they dissolve and react to produce two insoluble products, aluminum hydroxide and calcium sulfate. These products settle out, taking suspended solid impurities with them.** Write a balanced chemical equation for the reaction.

 **SOLVE**

Each of the reactants and products is an ionic compound. Recall that the formulas of ionic compounds are determined by the charges of the ions composing each compound. The formula reaction is thus written as follows.

$$Al_2(SO_4)_3 + Ca(OH)_2 \longrightarrow Al(OH)_3 + CaSO_4 \text{ (not balanced)}$$

Continued

DECONSTRUCTING PROBLEMS

Tell students that they should not balance an equation by starting with the first element on the left side and then working through each element in order. For example, point out that in Sample Problem D, O was balanced before H, even though H appears first in H_2O. Leaving H for last is often a good practice to follow when balancing chemical equations.

REALITY CHECK

Point out that every compound in the equation in Sample Problem E contains a polyatomic ion. Remind students that they should treat a polyatomic ion as a unit when balancing an equation. For example, a student should evaluate the formula $Ca(OH)_2$ as having two OH− polyatomic ions, not as has having two O atoms and two H atoms. Be sure students understand how this is done for each polyatomic ion that is part of the equation being balanced in Sample Problem E.

Classroom Practice

D-1 Write balanced chemical equations for each of the following reactions.

a. When aqueous solutions of sulfuric acid and barium chloride are mixed, barium sulfate precipitates from an aqueous solution of hydrochloric acid.

b. Aluminum sulfate, an ingredient used in water treatment, is made by the reaction of solid aluminum oxide with aqueous sulfuric acid. In addition to aqueous aluminum sulfate, water is also produced.

Answers:

a. $H_2SO_4(aq) + BaCl_2(aq) \longrightarrow 2HCl(aq) + BaSO_4(s)$

b. $Al_2O_3(s) + 3H_2SO_4(aq) \longrightarrow Al_2(SO_4)_3(aq) + 3H_2O(l)$

E-1 The white paste that some life-guards rub on their noses to prevent sunburn contains the active ingredient zinc oxide. Zinc oxide is made by reacting solid zinc sulfide with oxygen gas. Sulfur dioxide gas is also produced. Write a balanced chemical equation for this reaction.

Answer: $2ZnS(s) + 3O_2(g) \longrightarrow 2ZnO(s) + 2SO_2(g)$

▼ Teach *continued*

Alternative Assessment

Provide students with a challenging unbalanced chemical equation, for example, $Li(s) + Al_2(SO_4)_3(aq) \longrightarrow Li_2SO_4(aq) + Al(s)$. Ask them to outline the steps they use in balancing the equation and to explain their reasoning.

Answers

Practice E

1. a. $2Na(s) + Cl_2(g) \longrightarrow 2NaCl(s)$
   b. $Cu(s) + 2AgNO_3(aq) \longrightarrow Cu(NO_3)_2(aq) + 2Ag(s)$
   c. $Fe_2O_3(s) + 3CO(g) \longrightarrow 2Fe(s) + 3CO_2(g)$

▼ Assess and Reteach

Assess Use the Formative Assessment on this page to evaluate student mastery of the section.

Reteach For students who need additional instruction, download the Section Study Guide.

Response to Intervention To reassess students' mastery, use the Section Quiz, available to print or to take directly online at **HMDScience.com**.

Balancing Chemical Equations (continued)

There is one Ca atom on each side of the equation, so the calcium atoms are already balanced. There are two Al atoms on the left and one Al atom on the right. Placing the coefficient 2 in front of $Al(OH)_3$ produces the same number of Al atoms on each side of the equation.

$$Al_2(SO_4)_3 + Ca(OH)_2 \longrightarrow 2Al(OH)_3 + CaSO_4 \text{ (partially balanced)}$$

Next, checking SO_4^{2-} ions shows that there are three SO_4^{2-} ions on the left side of the equation and only one on the right side. Placing the coefficient 3 before $CaSO_4$ gives an equal number of SO_4^{2-} ions on each side.

$$Al_2(SO_4)_3 + Ca(OH)_2 \longrightarrow 2Al(OH)_3 + 3CaSO_4 \text{ (partially balanced)}$$

There are now three Ca atoms on the right, however. By placing the coefficient 3 in front of $Ca(OH)_2$, we once again have an equal number of Ca atoms on each side. This last step also gives six OH^- ions on both sides of the equation.

$$Al_2(SO_4)_3(aq) + 3Ca(OH)_2(aq) \longrightarrow 2Al(OH)_3(s) + 3CaSO_4(s)$$

$$(2Al + 3SO_4^{2-}) + (3Ca + 6OH^-) = (2Al + 6OH^-) + (3Ca + 3SO_4^{2-})$$

The equation is balanced.

Practice

1. Write balanced chemical equations for each of the following reactions:
   a. Solid sodium combines with chlorine gas to produce solid sodium chloride.
   b. When solid copper reacts with aqueous silver nitrate, the products are aqueous copper(II) nitrate and solid silver.
   c. In a blast furnace, the reaction between solid iron(III) oxide and carbon monoxide gas produces solid iron and carbon dioxide gas.

SECTION 1 FORMATIVE ASSESSMENT

Reviewing Main Ideas

1. Describe the differences between word equations, formula equations, and chemical equations.
2. Write word and formula equations for the reaction in which aqueous solutions of sulfuric acid and sodium hydroxide react to form aqueous sodium sulfate and water.
3. Translate the following chemical equations into sentences:
   a. $2K(s) + 2H_2O(l) \longrightarrow 2KOH(aq) + H_2(g)$
   b. $2Fe(s) + 3Cl_2(g) \longrightarrow 2FeCl_3(s)$
4. Write the word, formula, and chemical equations for the reaction between hydrogen sulfide gas and oxygen gas that produces sulfur dioxide gas and water vapor.

Critical Thinking

5. **INTEGRATING CONCEPTS** The reaction of vanadium(II) oxide with iron(III) oxide results in the formation of vanadium(V) oxide and iron(II) oxide. Write the balanced chemical equation.

Answers to Section Assessment

1. A word equation is qualitative; it uses words to represent the reactants and products in a chemical reaction. A formula equation is also qualitative; it uses chemical symbols or formulas, but it does not reveal the ratios of the reactants and products. A chemical equation is a balanced formula equation.
2. sulfuric acid + sodium hydroxide $\longrightarrow$ sodium sulfate + water; $H_2SO_4(aq) + NaOH(aq) \longrightarrow Na_2SO_4(aq) + H_2O(l)$ (formula equation)
3. a. Solid potassium metal reacts with (liquid) water to form aqueous potassium hydroxide and hydrogen gas.
   b. Solid iron metal reacts with chlorine gas to produce solid iron(III) chloride.
4. hydrogen sulfide + oxygen $\longrightarrow$ sulfur dioxide + water vapor; $H_2S(g) + O_2(g) \longrightarrow SO_2(g) + H_2O(g)$; $2H_2S(g) + 3O_2(g) \longrightarrow 2SO_2(g) + 2H_2O(g)$
5. $2VO + 3Fe_2O_3 \longrightarrow V_2O_5 + 6FeO$

WHY IT MATTERS

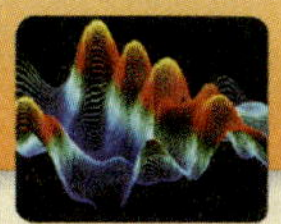
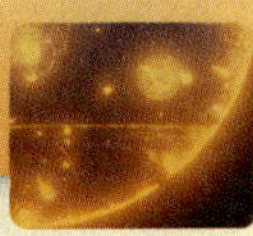

Carbon Monoxide Catalyst

S.T.E.M.

Colorless, odorless, and deadly, carbon monoxide, "the silent killer," causes the deaths of hundreds of Americans every year. When fuel does not burn completely in a combustion process, carbon monoxide is produced. Often this occurs in a malfunctioning heater, furnace, or fireplace. When the carbon monoxide is inhaled, it bonds to the hemoglobin in the blood, leaving the body oxygen-starved. Before people realize a combustion device is malfunctioning, it's often too late.

$$O_2Hb + CO \longrightarrow COHb + O_2$$

Carbon monoxide, CO, has almost 200 times the affinity to bind with the hemoglobin, Hb, in the blood as oxygen. This means that hemoglobin will bind to carbon monoxide rather than oxygen in the body. If enough carbon monoxide is present in the blood, it can be fatal.

Carbon monoxide poisoning can be prevented by installing filters that absorb the gas. After some time, however, filters become saturated, and then carbon monoxide can pass freely into the air. The best way to prevent carbon monoxide poisoning is not just to filter out the gas, but to eliminate it completely.

The solution came to research chemists at NASA who were working on a problem with a space-based laser. In order to operate properly, NASA's space-based carbon dioxide laser needed to be fed a continuous supply of CO_2. This was necessary because as a byproduct of its operation, the laser degraded some of the CO_2 into carbon monoxide and oxygen. To address this problem, NASA scientists developed a catalyst made of tin oxide and platinum that oxidized the waste carbon monoxide back into carbon dioxide. The NASA scientists then realized that this catalyst had the potential to be used in many applications here on Earth, including removing carbon monoxide from houses and other buildings.

Typically, a malfunctioning heater circulates the carbon monoxide it produces through its air intake system back into a dwelling space. Installing the catalyst in the air intake would oxidize any carbon monoxide to nontoxic carbon dioxide before it reentered the room.

"The form of our catalyst is a very thin coating on some sort of a support, or substrate as we call it," says NASA chemist David Schryer. "And that support, or substrate, can be any one of a number of things. The great thing about a catalyst is that the only thing that matters about it is its surface. So a catalyst can be incredibly thin and still be very effective."

The idea of using catalysts to oxidize gases is not a new one. Catalytic converters in cars oxidize carbon monoxide and unburned hydrocarbons to minimize pollution. Many substances are oxidized into new materials for manufacturing purposes. But both of these types of catalytic reactions occur at very high temperatures. NASA's catalyst is special, because it's able to eliminate carbon monoxide at room temperature.

According to David Schryer, low-temperature catalysts constitute a whole new class of catalysts with abundant applications for the future.

Questions

1. How did NASA's research on the space-based carbon dioxide laser result in a benefit for consumers?
2. According to the chemical reaction, if there are 4.5 mol of oxygenated hemoglobin present in an excess of carbon monoxide, how many moles of hemoglobin would release oxygen and bind to carbon monoxide? Explain your answer.

WHY IT MATTERS

Misconception Alert!

Students may think that all effects of carbon monoxide are undesirable. The gas has some important useful applications. It is used to reduce metallic ores to pure metals. It is also an important component of several industrial fuels.

Answers

1. Developing a tin oxide and platinum catalyst to oxidize the carbon monoxide byproduct of the laser provided the technology to reduce the effects of harmful carbon monoxide gas in homes.
2. The reaction shows that for every mole of oxygenated hemoglobin present, one mole of CO bound to hemoglobin would be produced, assuming CO is in excess. Therefore, 4.5 mol oxygenated hemoglobin would release 4.5 mol O_2 and bind to 4.5 mol CO.

Teaching Tip

More information on CO poisoning can be found in Group 14 of the *Elements Handbook* (Appendix A).

SECTION 2

▼ Plan and Prepare

Objectives

Upon completion of this section, students should be able to do the following:

- Define and give general equations for *synthesis*, *decomposition*, *single-displacement*, and *double-displacement* reactions.
- Classify a reaction as a synthesis, decomposition, single-displacement, double-displacement, or combustion reaction.
- List three kinds of synthesis reactions and six kinds of decomposition reactions.
- List four kinds of single-displacement reactions and three kinds of double-displacement reactions.
- Predict the products of simple reactions given the reactants.

Classroom Catalyst

Start off with the message that so many chemical reactions can occur or are occurring that it would be impossible to predict their products if we could not place many of them into categories. Then begin with an introductory discussion of synthesis reactions.

▼ Teach

Classroom Discussion

Describe synthesis reactions, and then have students name examples. Students may mention the formation of rust from iron and oxygen or the formation of water when hydrogen and oxygen gases are ignited. Emphasize that in synthesis reactions, elements or compounds combine to form a new compound.

READING TOOLKIT

READING ORGANIZER Have students read the section and then organize what they have learned in a concept map, starting with *Reaction Types*. They should list each type of reaction, describe it, and provide examples.

SECTION 2

Main Ideas

- Substances are combined in synthesis reactions.
- Substances are broken down in decomposition reactions.
- One element replaces another in single-displacement reactions.
- In double-displacement reactions, two compounds exchange ions.
- Combustion reactions involve oxygen.

Types of Chemical Reactions

Key Terms

synthesis reaction
decomposition reaction
electrolysis
single-displacement reaction
double-displacement reaction
combustion reaction

Thousands of known chemical reactions occur in living systems, in industrial processes, and in chemical laboratories. Often it is necessary to predict the products formed in one of these reactions. Memorizing the equations for so many chemical reactions would be a difficult task. It is therefore more useful and realistic to classify reactions according to various similarities and regularities. This general information about reaction types can then be used to predict the products of specific reactions.

There are several ways to classify chemical reactions, and none are entirely satisfactory. The classification scheme described in this section provides an introduction to five basic types of reactions: synthesis, decomposition, single-displacement, double-displacement, and combustion reactions. In later chapters, you will be introduced to categories that are useful in classifying other types of chemical reactions.

MAIN IDEA

Substances are combined in synthesis reactions.

In a **synthesis reaction,** also known as a composition reaction, two or more substances combine to form a new compound. This type of reaction is represented by the following general equation:

$$A + X \longrightarrow AX$$

A and X can be elements or compounds. AX is a compound. The following examples illustrate several kinds of synthesis reactions.

Reactions of Elements with Oxygen and Sulfur

One simple type of synthesis reaction is the combination of an element with oxygen to produce an *oxide* of the element. Almost all metals react with oxygen to form oxides. For example, when a thin strip of magnesium metal is placed in an open flame, it burns with bright white light. When the metal strip is completely burned, only a fine white powder of magnesium oxide is left. This chemical reaction, shown in **Figure 2.1** on the next page, is represented by the following equation:

$$2Mg(s) + O_2(g) \longrightarrow 2MgO(s)$$

Differentiated Instruction

BELOW LEVEL

Ask students if they have to help put away the clean dishes at home. Many should say they do. Then, ask if they put them into the cabinets all mixed up together, or if there are certain places for certain types of dishes. There are particular places for each type of dish. Next, ask them if they put away silverware into the drawer mixed together. Most should say that they sort the silverware into a tray by type. Explain to the class that when they sort dishes or silverware by categories like this, they are making these items easier to find and use. Explain to students that we classify chemical reactions for a similar reason. There are millions of different chemical reactions that can be grouped or classified into categories or types. By knowing which type of reaction you are dealing with, you can work with the reactions more easily.

The other Group 2 elements react in a similar manner, forming oxides with the formula MO, where M represents the metal. The Group 1 metals form oxides with the formula M_2O, for example, Li_2O. The Group 1 and Group 2 elements react similarly with sulfur, forming *sulfides* with the formulas M_2S and MS, respectively. Examples of these types of synthesis reactions are shown below.

$$16Rb(s) + S_8(s) \longrightarrow 8Rb_2S(s)$$

$$8Ba(s) + S_8(s) \longrightarrow 8BaS(s)$$

Some metals, such as iron, combine with oxygen to produce two different oxides.

$$2Fe(s) + O_2(g) \longrightarrow 2FeO(s)$$

$$4Fe(s) + 3O_2(g) \longrightarrow 2Fe_2O_3(s)$$

In the product of the first reaction, iron is in an oxidation state of +2. In the product of the second reaction, iron is in an oxidation state of +3. The particular oxide formed depends on the conditions surrounding the reactants. Both oxides are shown below in **Figure 2.2.**

Nonmetals also undergo synthesis reactions with oxygen to form oxides. Sulfur, for example, reacts with oxygen to form sulfur dioxide. And when carbon is burned in air, carbon dioxide is produced.

$$S_8(s) + 8O_2(g) \longrightarrow 8SO_2(g)$$

$$C(s) + O_2(g) \longrightarrow CO_2(g)$$

In a limited supply of oxygen, carbon monoxide is formed.

$$2C(s) + O_2(g) \longrightarrow 2CO(g)$$

Hydrogen reacts with oxygen to form dihydrogen monoxide, better known as water.

$$2H_2(g) + O_2(g) \longrightarrow 2H_2O(g)$$

FIGURE 2.1

Synthesis Reaction of Magnesium and Oxygen

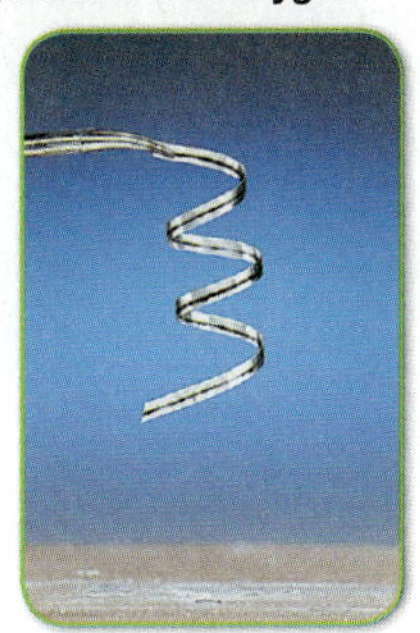

(a) Magnesium, Mg, pictured here, undergoes a synthesis reaction with oxygen, O_2.

(b) The reaction produced magnesium oxide, MgO.

FIGURE 2.2

Synthesis Reactions of Iron and Oxygen Iron (Fe) and oxygen (O_2) combine to form two different oxides: FeO and Fe_2O_3.

(a) iron(II) oxide, FeO

(b) iron(III) oxide, Fe_2O_3

TEACH FROM VISUALS

FIGURE 2.1 In synthesis reactions, the reactants and the products are usually quite different in appearance and in properties. Here, shiny, silver-colored magnesium metal and gaseous oxygen react to form the white ionic solid magnesium oxide.

Teaching Tip

Students are probably familiar with the characteristic appearance of many metallic elements. With the exceptions of copper and gold, most metals are silver in color. But students may not be as familiar with the appearance of compounds synthesized from metals, many of which are ionic salts. Provide students with references that describe physical and chemical properties of inorganic compounds so that they can become familiar with these compounds.

PRE-AP

An example of a synthesis reaction that chemists call a *condensation reaction* is sometimes referred to in biological systems as *dehydration synthesis*. Have students describe these reactions and explain why they are called dehydration synthesis reactions. Students should include the dehydration synthesis of three types of organic molecules: proteins, carbohydrates, and lipids.

▼ Teach *continued*

Demonstration

SYNTHESIS OF A BASE FROM A METAL OXIDE

Use a **dropper** to add a few drops of **phenolphthalein** solution to 25 mL of **water** in a **50-mL beaker,** and place the beaker on an **overhead projector.** Add approximately **0.005 g of calcium oxide.** After students have noted that the phenolphthalein has turned pink, indicating the presence of OH^- ions, ask them to interpret the results and write the equation for the synthesis.

$CaO + H_2O \longrightarrow Ca(OH)_2$

Safety Wear **safety goggles** and a **lab apron.**

Disposal Pour the solution down the drain.

Reactions of Metals with Halogens

Most metals react with the Group 17 elements, the halogens, to form either ionic or covalent compounds. For example, Group 1 metals react with halogens to form ionic compounds with the formula MX, where M is the metal and X is the halogen. Examples of this type of synthesis reaction include the reactions of sodium with chlorine and potassium with iodine.

$$2Na(s) + Cl_2(g) \longrightarrow 2NaCl(s)$$

$$2K(s) + I_2(g) \longrightarrow 2KI(s)$$

Group 2 metals react with the halogens to form ionic compounds with the formula MX_2.

$$Mg(s) + F_2(g) \longrightarrow MgF_2(s)$$

$$Sr(s) + Br_2(l) \longrightarrow SrBr_2(s)$$

The halogens undergo synthesis reactions with many different metals. Fluorine in particular is so reactive that it combines with almost all metals. For example, fluorine reacts with sodium to produce sodium fluoride. Similarly, it reacts with cobalt to form cobalt(III) fluoride and with uranium to form uranium(VI) fluoride.

$$2Na(s) + F_2(g) \longrightarrow 2NaF(s)$$

$$2Co(s) + 3F_2(g) \longrightarrow 2CoF_3(s)$$

$$U(s) + 3F_2(g) \longrightarrow UF_6(g)$$

Sodium fluoride, NaF, is added to municipal water supplies in trace amounts to provide fluoride ions, which help to prevent tooth decay in the people who drink the water. Cobalt(III) fluoride, CoF_3, is a strong fluorinating agent. And natural uranium is converted to uranium(VI) fluoride, UF_6, as the first step in the production of uranium for use in nuclear power plants.

FIGURE 2.3

Calcium Hydroxide Calcium hydroxide, a base, can be used to *neutralize* hydrochloric acid in your stomach. The chapter "Acids and Bases" describes neutralization reactions in more detail.

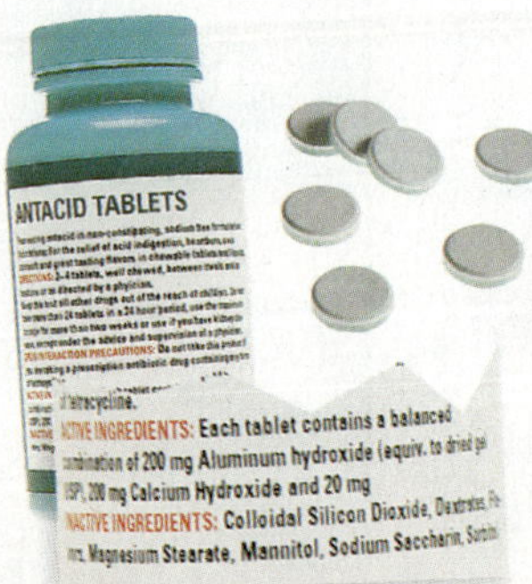

Synthesis Reactions with Oxides

Active metals are highly reactive metals. Oxides of active metals react with water to produce metal hydroxides. Calcium oxide, CaO, also known as lime or quicklime, is manufactured in large quantities. The addition of water to lime to produce $Ca(OH)_2$, which is also known as slaked lime, is a crucial step in the setting of cement.

$$CaO(s) + H_2O(l) \longrightarrow Ca(OH)_2(s)$$

Calcium hydroxide also is an ingredient in some stomach antacids, as shown in **Figure 2.3.** In the stomach, it reacts with hydrochloric, neutralizing its effects. These *neutralization* reactions are dealt with in more detail in the chapter on acids and bases.

Many oxides of nonmetals in the upper-right portion of the periodic table react with water to produce oxyacids. For example, sulfur dioxide, SO_2, reacts with water to produce sulfurous acid.

Differentiated Instruction

BELOW LEVEL

Point out to students that the Group 1 metals react with the halogens to form compounds with the general formula MX while the Group 2 metals form compounds with the general formula MX_2. This happens because the halogens can each accept just one electron. Group 1 metals have one valence electron to donate, while Group 2 metals have two electrons to donate, so two halogen ions are needed to form a stable compound.

$$SO_2(g) + H_2O(l) \longrightarrow H_2SO_3(aq)$$

In air polluted with SO_2, sulfurous acid further reacts with oxygen to form sulfuric acid, one of the main ingredients in *acid precipitation*, known more familiarly as *acid rain*.

$$2H_2SO_3(aq) + O_2(g) \longrightarrow 2H_2SO_4(aq)$$

Certain metal oxides and nonmetal oxides react with each other in synthesis reactions to form salts. For example, calcium sulfite is formed by the reaction of calcium oxide and sulfur dioxide.

$$CaO(s) + SO_2(g) \longrightarrow CaSO_3(s)$$

CHECK FOR UNDERSTANDING

Apply Using your knowledge of synthesis reactions, explain the relationship between air pollution and acid rain.

MAIN IDEA

Substances are broken down in decomposition reactions.

In a decomposition reaction, a single compound undergoes a reaction that produces two or more simpler substances. Decomposition reactions are the opposite of synthesis reactions and are represented by the following general equation.

$$AX \longrightarrow A + X$$

AX is a compound. A and X can be elements or compounds.

Most decomposition reactions take place only when energy in the form of electricity or heat is added. Examples of several types of decomposition reactions are given in the following sections.

Decomposition of Binary Compounds

The simplest kind of decomposition reaction is the decomposition of a binary compound into its elements. We have already examined one example of a decomposition reaction, the decomposition of water into hydrogen and oxygen. An electric current passed through water will decomposes it into its constituent elements. **The decomposition of a substance by an electric current is called electrolysis.**

$$2H_2O(l) \xrightarrow{\text{electricity}} 2H_2(g) + O_2(g)$$

Notice the word *electricity* above the reaction arrow.

Oxides of the less-active metals, which are located in the lower center of the periodic table, decompose into their elements when heated. Joseph Priestley, one of the founders of modern chemistry, discovered oxygen through such a decomposition reaction in 1774, when he heated mercury(II) oxide to produce mercury and oxygen.

$$2HgO(s) \xrightarrow{\Delta} 2Hg(l) + O_2(g)$$

This reaction is shown in **Figure 2.4** on the following page.

Classroom Discussion

If you performed the demonstration on electrolysis of water, remind students about their observations. Have them write the equation for the reaction, and be sure they recognize it as a decomposition reaction. Ask students if there is any relationship between this decomposition reaction and the reaction for the synthesis of water.

Teaching Tip

A reaction with only one reactant and more than one product is a decomposition reaction.

Check for Understanding

Answer: Pollutants, such as sulfur dioxide, are emitted into the atmosphere by a variety of sources. There, they undergo a series of synthesis reactions, first with water vapor and then with oxygen in the atmosphere, forming aid rain.

ENGLISH LEARNERS

To help students understand the meanings of the terms *synthesis* and *decomposition*, ask them what it means if something is synthetic. It is man-made. Expand on this by explaining that in synthesis reactions, chemicals in the reactants are being rearranged to make something new. Next, ask the class what it means when something decomposes. Most will answer that it is rotting. Once more, clarify for them that when something rots or decomposes, it is breaking down into the simpler compounds and elements that made up its structure. Finally, ask students how these two explanations could apply to using those terms to describe chemical reactions.

▼ Teach *continued*

ChemisTrivia

After hearing of the discovery of oxygen by Joseph Priestley in 1774, Antoine Laurent Lavoisier began his classic 12-day experiment to investigate the nature of burning. He heated mercury in air within a closed system for 12 days. Red mercury(II) oxide was formed—a synthesis reaction. Lavoisier continued his investigation by strongly heating the mercury(II) oxide until he had recovered the mercury and the oxygen—a decomposition reaction.

Classroom Discussion

Have students write equations for both the synthesis reaction and the decomposition reaction described above in ChemisTrivia.

Critical Thinking

Answer: The products of the decomposition of mercury (II) oxide are metallic mercury and oxygen gas.

FIGURE 2.4

Decomposition Reaction
When mercury(II) oxide (the red-orange substance in the bottom of the test tube) is heated, it decomposes into oxygen and metallic mercury, which can be seen as droplets on the inside wall of the test tube.

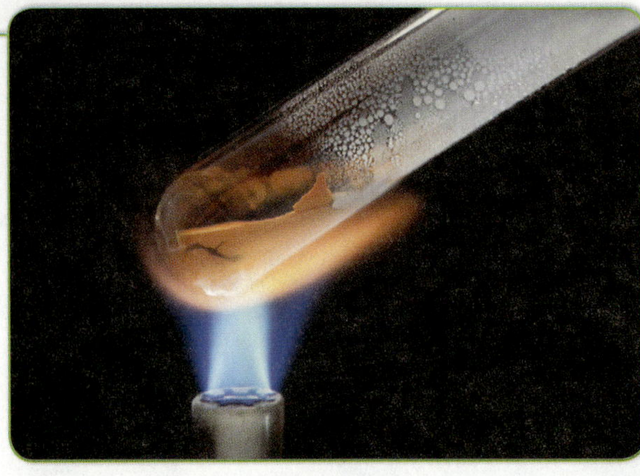

CRITICAL THINKING
Apply What are the products of this reaction?

Decomposition of Metal Carbonates

When a metal carbonate is heated, it breaks down to produce a metal oxide and carbon dioxide gas. For example, calcium carbonate decomposes to produce calcium oxide and carbon dioxide.

$$CaCO_3(s) \xrightarrow{\Delta} CaO(s) + CO_2(g)$$

Decomposition of Metal Hydroxides

All metal hydroxides except those containing Group 1 metals decompose when heated to yield metal oxides and water. For example, calcium hydroxide decomposes to produce calcium oxide and water.

$$Ca(OH)_2(s) \xrightarrow{\Delta} CaO(s) + H_2O(g)$$

Decomposition of Metal Chlorates

When a metal chlorate is heated, it decomposes to produce a metal chloride and oxygen. For example, potassium chlorate, $KClO_3$, decomposes in the presence of the catalyst $MnO_2(s)$ to produce potassium chloride and oxygen.

$$2KClO_3(s) \xrightarrow[MnO_2(s)]{\Delta} 2KCl(s) + 3O_2(g)$$

Decomposition of Acids

Certain acids decompose into nonmetal oxides and water. Carbonic acid is unstable and decomposes readily at room temperature to produce carbon dioxide and water.

$$H_2CO_3(aq) \longrightarrow CO_2(g) + H_2O(l)$$

When heated, sulfuric acid decomposes into sulfur trioxide and water.

$$H_2SO_4(aq) \xrightarrow{\Delta} SO_3(g) + H_2O(l)$$

Sulfurous acid, H_2SO_3, decomposes similarly.

Differentiated Instruction

BELOW LEVEL

Have students look carefully at the equations on this page. Point out that all of them are examples of decomposition reactions. However, only four of them have something else in common. Ask students to identify the common factor. Students should recognize the symbol used for heat (Δ), which indicates that four of the decomposition reactions require heat.

MAIN IDEA

One element replaces another in single-displacement reactions.

In a single-displacement reaction, also known as a replacement reaction, one element replaces a similar element in a compound. Many single-displacement reactions take place in aqueous solution. The amount of energy involved in this type of reaction is usually smaller than the amount involved in synthesis or decomposition reactions. Single-displacement reactions can be represented by the following general equations:

$$A + BX \longrightarrow AX + B$$

or

$$Y + BX \longrightarrow BY + X$$

A, B, X, and Y are elements. AX, BX, and BY are compounds.

Displacement of a Metal in a Compound by Another Metal

Aluminum is more active than lead. When solid aluminum is placed in aqueous lead(II) nitrate, $Pb(NO_3)_2(aq)$, the aluminum replaces the lead. Solid lead and aqueous aluminum nitrate are formed.

$$2Al(s) + 3Pb(NO_3)_2(aq) \longrightarrow 3Pb(s) + 2Al(NO_3)_3(aq)$$

Displacement of Hydrogen in Water by a Metal

The most-active metals, such as those in Group 1, react vigorously with water to produce metal hydroxides and hydrogen. For example, sodium reacts with water to form sodium hydroxide and hydrogen gas.

$$2Na(s) + 2H_2O(l) \longrightarrow 2NaOH(aq) + H_2(g)$$

Less-active metals, such as iron, react with steam to form a metal oxide and hydrogen gas.

$$3Fe(s) + 4H_2O(g) \longrightarrow Fe_3O_4(s) + 4H_2(g)$$

Displacement of Hydrogen in an Acid by a Metal

The more-active metals react with certain acidic solutions, such as hydrochloric acid and dilute sulfuric acid, replacing the hydrogen in the acid. The reaction products are a metal compound (a salt) and hydrogen gas. For example, when solid magnesium reacts with hydrochloric acid, as shown in **Figure 2.5**, the reaction products are hydrogen gas and aqueous magnesium chloride.

$$Mg(s) + 2HCl(aq) \longrightarrow H_2(g) + MgCl_2(aq)$$

Be careful as you study chemistry to remember that the term *salt* often has a wider definition than simply that of the table salt (sodium chloride) you put on food. Strictly speaking, a salt is any ionic compound formed in the neutralization of an acid by a base.

FIGURE 2.5

Single Displacement Reaction In this single-displacement reaction, the hydrogen in hydrochloric acid, HCl, is replaced by magnesium, Mg.

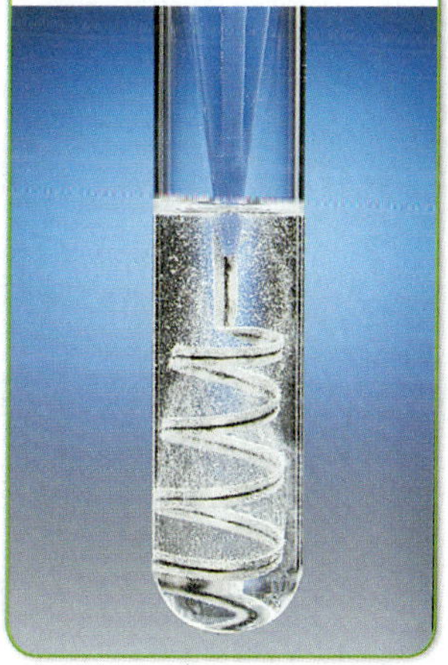

Classroom Practice

1. Write a balanced chemical equation for the heated decomposition of sulfurous acid.

Answer: $H_2SO_3(aq) \xrightarrow{\Delta} SO_2(g) + H_2O(l)$

READING TOOLKIT

PREDICTION GUIDES Review the opinions listed at the beginning of Section 1. Ask students whether their opinions are the same or have changed. Have them cite passages in the text that account for any changes.

BELOW LEVEL

Students can create "Reaction Flashcards" by labeling note cards with the different types of reactions discussed in the chapter. Students should write on one side of each card the name of a reaction type. On the other side, they should write specific examples of the reaction type, including the reactants and products of the reaction. Notes about patterns, trends, or similarities with other reactions can also be written on each card. The cards can be used as a study guide for individual study or for discussion in small groups.

▼ Teach *continued*

Demonstration

DOUBLE-DISPLACEMENT REACTIONS

Produce five products of different colors by mixing **0.1 M aqueous solutions of $SrCl_2$, Na_2SO_4, $CuSO_4$, NH_3, $MnCl_2$, Na_2CO_3, $FeCl_3$, KSCN, and a saturated solution of NaCl.** Use a **graduated cylinder** to mix 5 mL of the respective solutions according to the following scheme. If mixture number 3 does not turn green, add more NaCl solution.

Mixture
1. $SrCl_2$ and Na_2SO_4
2. $CuSO_4$ and NH_3
3. $CuSO_4$ and NaCl
4. $MnCl_2$ and Na_2CO_3
5. $FeCl_3$ and KSCN

Results	Color
1. $SrSO_4$ precipitate	white
2. tetraaminecopper(II) hydroxide	blue
3. chloro-copper complex	green
4. $MnCO_3$ precipitate	pink
5. $[Fe(SCN)]^{2+}$ complex ion	red

Have students write equations for the double-displacement reactions that occur in mixtures 1 and 4.

Safety Wear **safety goggles** and a **lab apron.**

Disposal Combine mixtures 1 and 4, and use **filter paper** to filter the result. Dry the solid and put it into the trash. Pour the filtrate down the drain. Combine mixtures 2, 3, and 5, and add sufficient **1 M H_2SO_4** to dissolve all copper-containing precipitates. Scour **six 6d iron nails** with **steel wool** until they are shiny. Immerse the nails in the solution. until all Cu has precipitated (overnight). Remove the nails and filter the solution.

Continued on the next page

Displacement of Halogens

In another type of single-displacement reaction, one halogen replaces another halogen in a compound. Fluorine is the most-active halogen. As such, it can replace any of the other halogens in their compounds. Each halogen is less active than the one above it in the periodic table. Therefore, in Group 17 each element can replace any element below it, but not any element above it. For example, while chlorine can replace bromine in potassium bromide, it cannot replace fluorine in potassium fluoride. The reaction of chlorine with potassium bromide produces bromine and potassium chloride, whereas the combination of fluorine and sodium chloride produces sodium fluoride and solid chlorine.

$$Cl_2(g) + 2KBr(aq) \longrightarrow 2KCl(aq) + Br_2(l)$$

$$F_2(g) + 2NaCl(aq) \longrightarrow 2NaF(aq) + Cl_2(g)$$

$$Br_2(l) + KCl(aq) \longrightarrow \text{no reaction}$$

MAIN IDEA

In double-displacement reactions, two compounds exchange ions.

In **double-displacement reactions,** the ions of two compounds exchange places in an aqueous solution to form two new compounds. One of the compounds formed is usually a precipitate, an insoluble gas that bubbles out of the solution, or a molecular compound, usually water. The other compound is often soluble and remains dissolved in solution. A double-displacement reaction is represented by the following general equation.

$$AX + BY \longrightarrow AY + BX$$

A, X, B, and Y in the reactants represent ions. AY and BX represent ionic or molecular compounds.

FIGURE 2.6

Double-Displacement Reaction

The double-displacement reaction between aqueous lead(II) nitrate, $Pb(NO_3)_2(aq)$, and aqueous potassium iodide, $KI(aq)$, yields the precipitate lead(II) iodide, $PbI_2(s)$.

Formation of a Precipitate

The formation of a precipitate occurs when the cations of one reactant combine with the anions of another reactant to form an insoluble or slightly soluble compound. For example, when an aqueous solution of potassium iodide is added to an aqueous solution of lead(II) nitrate, the yellow precipitate lead(II) iodide forms. This is shown in **Figure 2.6.**

$$2KI(aq) + Pb(NO_3)_2(aq) \longrightarrow PbI_2(s) + 2KNO_3(aq)$$

The precipitate forms as a result of the very strong attractive forces between the Pb^{2+} cations and the I^- anions. The other product is the water-soluble salt potassium nitrate, KNO_3. The potassium and nitrate ions do not take part in the reaction. They remain in solution as aqueous ions and therefore are often referred to as *spectator ions.* The guidelines that help identify which ions form a precipitate and which ions remain in solution are developed in a later chapter on ions in aqueous solutions.

Differentiated Instruction

ENGLISH LEARNERS

Describe the following scene to students.

A man and a woman are dancing when another man asks if he can dance with the woman. Another two couples are dancing when they switch partners.

Have students identify which sentence can be used to describe a single-replacement reaction (the men switching places) and which can be used to describe a double-replacement reaction (the partners switching places). Have students explain the reason for their choices.

Formation of a Gas

In some double-displacement reactions, one of the products is an insoluble gas that bubbles out of the mixture. For example, iron(II) sulfide reacts with hydrochloric acid to form hydrogen sulfide gas and iron(II) chloride.

$$FeS(s) + 2HCl(aq) \longrightarrow H_2S(g) + FeCl_2(aq)$$

Formation of Water

In some double-displacement reactions, a very stable molecular compound, such as water, is one of the products. For example, hydrochloric acid reacts with an aqueous solution of sodium hydroxide to yield aqueous sodium chloride and water.

$$HCl(aq) + NaOH(aq) \longrightarrow NaCl(aq) + H_2O(l)$$

MAIN IDEA

Combustion reactions involve oxygen.

In a **combustion reaction,** a substance combines with oxygen, releasing a large amount of energy in the form of light and heat. The burning of natural gas, propane, gasoline, and wood are also examples of combustion reactions. For example, the propane, C_3H_8, combustion results in the production of carbon dioxide and water vapor.

$$C_3H_8(g) + 5O_2(g) \longrightarrow 3CO_2(g) + 4H_2O(g)$$

The combustion of hydrogen, shown in **Figure 2.7**, produces water vapor.

$$2H_2(g) + O_2(g) \longrightarrow 2H_2O(g)$$

WHY IT MATTERS

Fluoridation and Tooth Decay

The main component of tooth enamel is a mineral called hydroxyapatite, $Ca_5(PO_4)_3OH$. Some foods contain acids or produce acids in the mouth, and acid dissolves tooth enamel, which leads to tooth decay.

One way to help prevent tooth decay is by using fluoride. Fluoride reacts with hydroxyapatite in a double-displacement reaction. It displaces the OH^- group in hydroxyapatite to produce fluorapatite, $Ca_5(PO_4)_3F$. Studies show that calcium fluorapatite is about 20% less soluble than hydroxyapatite in acid. Therefore, fluoride lowers the incidence of tooth decay.

FIGURE 2.7

Combustion Reaction of Hydrogen

(a) The candle supplies heat to the hydrogen and oxygen in the balloon.

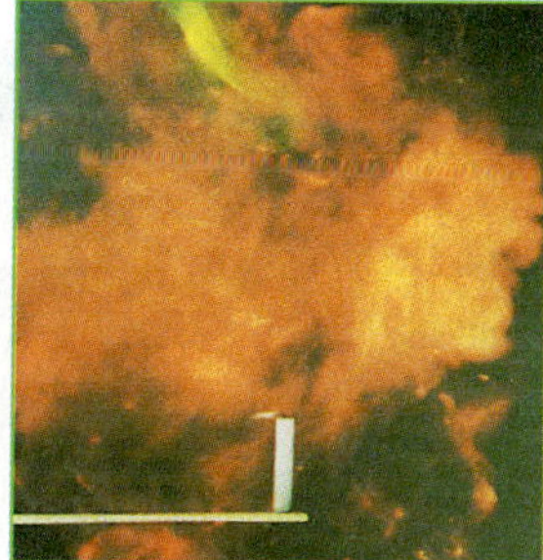

(b) The heat triggers the explosive combustion reaction.

CRITICAL THINKING

Explain In combustion reactions, substances combined with oxygen usually result in a fire or explosion. What remains afterwards is usually ash or fine particles, which often do not contain all of the elements found in the reactants. Explain what happens to the missing elements in terms of conservation of matter.

PRE-AP

Tell students that the complete combustion of a compound produces water and carbon dioxide. Ask them to write the balanced equation for the complete combustion of the octane (C_8H_{18}) in gasoline.

$2C_8H_{18} + 25O_2 \longrightarrow 18H_2O + 16CO_2$

Have students investigate whether the combustion of octane in a car's engine is complete.

Heat the nails and any precipitate from the filtration sufficiently to convert the copper precipitate and the copper on the nails to CuO. Cool and put the CuO and the nails in the trash. Treat the filtrate with sufficient **1 M NaOH** to bring the pH to 8 to 10. Heat to boiling, let cool, and filter. Dry the precipitate and put into the trash. Pour the filtrate down the drain.

TEACH FROM VISUALS

FIGURE 2.7 Have students explain how **Figure 2.7b** is similar to the Chapter Opener Image in terms of chemical reactions.

Both images indicate that a chemical reaction has occurred, as evidenced by the release of light and heat.

QuickLab

In the QuickLab on the next page, students will practice balancing chemical equations using gumdrops.

Critical Thinking

Answer: All of the elements found in the reactants are not found in the products of combustion reactions because they have been chemically converted to gaseous form and evaporated into the atmosphere.

Assess and Reteach

Assess Use the Formative Assessment on this page to evaluate student mastery of the section.

Reteach For students who need additional instruction, download the Section Study Guide.

Response to Intervention To reassess students' mastery, use the Section Quiz, available to print or to take directly online at **HMDScience.com**.

QuickLab

Models provide visual insights into the five types of reactions introduced in this chapter. Students can count model atoms as they balance equations. To avoid confusion, have students write down a key of the colors of the gumdrops representing each kind of atom. Do not be concerned with molecular geometry at this time.

Safety Make sure that students do not eat any of the gumdrops.

Answers

1. Group A: **a.** $H_2 + Cl_2 \longrightarrow 2HCl$
   b. $2Mg + O_2 \longrightarrow 2MgO$
   Group B: **a.** $H_2CO_3 \longrightarrow CO_2 + H_2O$
   b. $2KClO_3 \longrightarrow 2KCl + 3O_2$
   Group C: **a.** $Ca + 2H_2O \longrightarrow Ca(OH)_2 + H_2$
   b. $2KI + Br_2 \longrightarrow 2KBr + I_2$
   Group D: **a.** $AgNO_3 + NaCl \longrightarrow AgCl + NaNO_3$
   b. $FeS + 2HCl \longrightarrow FeCl_2 + H_2S$
   Group E: **a.** $CH_4 + 2O_2 \longrightarrow CO_2 + 2H_2O$
   b. $2CO + O_2 \longrightarrow 2CO_2$
2. Group A: $Ba(OH)_2$
   Group B: $H_2 + O_2$
   Group C: $H_2 + ZnCl_2$
   Group D: $K_2SO_4 + H_2O$
   Group E: $CO_2 + H_2O$
3. Group A: $BaO + H_2O \longrightarrow Ba(OH)_2$
   Group B: $2H_2O \longrightarrow 2H_2 + O_2$
   Group C: $Zn + 2HCl \longrightarrow ZnCl_2 + H_2$
   Group D: $H_2SO_4 + 2KOH \longrightarrow K_2SO_4 + 2H_2O$
   Group E: $C_3H_8 + 5O_2 \longrightarrow 3CO_2 + 4H_2O$
4. Group A: synthesis
   Group B: decomposition
   Group C: single displacement
   Group D: double displacement
   Group E: combustion

QuickLAB BALANCING EQUATIONS USING MODELS

QUESTION

How can molecular models and formula-unit ionic models be used to balance chemical equations and classify chemical reactions?

PROCEDURE

Examine the partial equations in Groups A–E. Using different-colored gumdrops to represent atoms of different elements, make models of the reactions by connecting the appropriate "atoms" with toothpicks. Use your models to (1) balance equations (a) and (b) in each group, (2) determine the products for reaction (c) in each group, and (3) complete and balance each equation (c). Finally, (4) classify each group of reactions by type.

Group A

a. $H_2 + Cl_2 \longrightarrow HCl$
b. $Mg + O_2 \longrightarrow MgO$
c. $BaO + H_2O \longrightarrow$ ______

Group B

a. $H_2CO_3 \longrightarrow CO_2 + H_2O$
b. $KClO_3 \longrightarrow KCl + O_2$
c. $H_2O \xrightarrow{\text{electricity}}$ ______

Group C

a. $Ca + H_2O \longrightarrow Ca(OH)_2 + H_2$
b. $KI + Br_2 \longrightarrow KBr + I_2$
c. $Zn + HCl \longrightarrow$ ______

Group D

a. $AgNO_3 + NaCl \longrightarrow AgCl + NaNO_3$
b. $FeS + HCl \longrightarrow FeCl_2 + H_2S$
c. $H_2SO_4 + KOH \longrightarrow$ ______

Group E

a. $CH_4 + O_2 \longrightarrow CO_2 + H_2O$
b. $CO + O_2 \longrightarrow CO_2$
c. $C_3H_8 + O_2 \longrightarrow$ ______

MATERIALS

- large and small gumdrops in at least four different colors
- toothpicks

SAFETY

Wear safety goggles and an apron.

SECTION 2 FORMATIVE ASSESSMENT

Reviewing Main Ideas

1. List five types of chemical reactions.
2. Classify each of the following reactions as a synthesis, decomposition, single-displacement, double-displacement, or combustion reaction:
   a. $N_2(g) + 3H_2(g) \longrightarrow 2NH_3(g)$
   b. $2Li(s) + 2H_2O(l) \longrightarrow 2LiOH(aq) + H_2(g)$
   c. $2NaNO_3(s) \longrightarrow 2NaNO_2(s) + O_2(g)$
   d. $2C_6H_{14}(l) + 19O_2(g) \longrightarrow 12CO_2(g) + 14H_2O(l)$
3. For each of the following reactions, identify the missing reactant(s) or products(s) and then balance the resulting equation. Note that each empty slot may require one or more substances.
   a. synthesis: ______ $\longrightarrow Li_2O$
   b. decomposition: $Mg(ClO_3)_2 \longrightarrow$ ______
   c. double displacement: $HNO_3 + Ca(OH)_2 \longrightarrow$ ______
   d. combustion: $C_5H_{12} + O_2 \longrightarrow$ ______
4. For each of the following reactions, write the missing product(s) and then balance the resulting equation. Identify each reaction by type.
   a. $Br_2 + KI \longrightarrow$ ______
   b. $NaClO_3 \xrightarrow{\Delta}$ ______
   c. $C_7H_{14} + O_2 \longrightarrow$ ______
   d. $CuCl_2 + Na_2S \longrightarrow$ ______

Critical Thinking

5. **INFERRING RELATIONSHIPS** In an experiment, an iron sample is oxidized to iron(III) oxide by oxygen, which is generated in the thermal decomposition of potassium chlorate. Write the two chemical reactions in the correct sequence.

Answers to Section Assessment

1. synthesis, decomposition, single-displacement, double-displacement, and combustion reactions
2. **a.** synthesis reaction
   b. single-displacement reaction
   c. decomposition reaction
   d. combustion reaction
3. **a.** $4Li + O_2 \longrightarrow 2Li_2O$
   b. $Mg(ClO_3)_2 \longrightarrow MgCl_2 + 3O_2$
   c. $2HNO_3 + Ca(OH)_2 \longrightarrow Ca(NO_3)_2 + 2H_2O$
   d. $C_5H_{12} + 8O_2 \longrightarrow 5CO_2 + 6H_2O$
4. **a.** $Br_2 + 2KI \longrightarrow 2KBr + I2$; single-displacement reaction
   b. $2NaClO_3 \xrightarrow{\Delta} 2NaCl + 3O_2$; decomposition reaction
   c. $2C_7H_{14} + 21O_2 \longrightarrow 14CO_2 + 14H_2O$; combustion reaction
   d. $CuCl_2 + Na_2S \longrightarrow 2NaCl + CuS$; double-displacement reaction
5. $2KClO_3 \xrightarrow{\Delta} 2KCl + 3O_2$; $4Fe + 3O_2 \longrightarrow 2Fe_2O_3$

Activity Series of the Elements

SECTION 3

Main Ideas

An activity series helps determine what substances will displace others in chemical reactions.

Key Term
activity series

The ability of an element to react is referred to as the element's *activity.* The more readily an element reacts with other substances, the greater its activity is. **An activity series is a list of elements organized according to the ease with which the elements undergo certain chemical reactions.** For metals, greater activity means a greater ease of *loss* of electrons, to form positive ions. For nonmetals, greater activity means a greater ease of *gain* of electrons, to form negative ions.

MAIN IDEA

An activity series helps determine what substances will displace others in chemical reactions.

The order in which the elements are listed is usually determined by single-displacement reactions. The most-active element, placed at the top in the series, can replace each of the elements below it from a compound in a single-displacement reaction. An element farther down can replace any element below it but not any above it. For example, in the discussion of single-displacement reactions in Section 2, it was noted that each halogen will react to replace any halogen listed below it in the periodic table. Therefore, an activity series for the Group 17 elements lists them in the same order, from top to bottom, as they appear in the periodic table. This is shown in **Figure 3.1** on the next page.

As mentioned in Section 1, the fact that a chemical equation can be written does not necessarily mean that the reaction it represents will actually take place. Activity series are used to help predict whether certain chemical reactions will occur. For example, according to the activity series for metals in **Figure 3.1**, aluminum replaces zinc. Therefore, we could predict that the following reaction does occur.

$$2Al(s) + 3ZnCl_2(aq) \longrightarrow 3Zn(s) + 2AlCl_3(aq)$$

Cobalt, however, cannot replace sodium. Therefore, we write the following:

$$Co(s) + 2NaCl(aq) \longrightarrow \text{no reaction}$$

It is important to remember that like many other aids used to predict the products of chemical reactions, activity series are based on experiment. The information that they contain is used as a general guide for predicting reaction outcomes.

Differentiated Instruction

BELOW LEVEL

Compare an activity series to a list of baseball players. Tell students that the list contains the names of five players arranged in order of decreasing batting averages. Place five randomly chosen names on the board, arranged in order of decreasing batting averages. Point out that only the third player on the list started the game because of his outstanding defensive play. Tell students, however, that the manager wants to substitute another hitter for the third player on the list when he comes to bat. Ask students which player the manager is most likely to choose as a replacement. Students should recognize that the manager is most likely to choose one of the two players whose names appear above that of the third player. These two players have a higher batting average. Ask students how this scenario relates to an activity series.

SECTION 3

Plan and Prepare ▼

Objectives

Upon completion of this section, students should be able to do the following:

- Explain the significance of an activity series.
- Use an activity series to predict whether a given reaction will occur and what the products will be.

Classroom Catalyst

Perform the following demonstration of an activity series.

Demonstration

ACTIVITY SERIES OF METALS

Label **four 50-mL beakers for each of the five cations** Al^{3+}, Zn^{2+}, Fe^{3+}, Cu^{2+}, and H^+. Add 15 mL of **0.1 M aqueous solutions of $Al(NO_3)_3$, $Zn(NO_3)_2$, $Fe(NO_3)_3$, $Cu(NO_3)_2$,** and **HCl** to the appropriate four beakers. To the $Al(NO_3)_3$ solutions, add **0.5 g pieces of Al, Zn, Fe,** and **Cu.** Do the same for the other four solutions. Record observations after 3 min, 30 min, and one day. Count the number of reactions for each metal and each cation. Have students use this information to develop an activity series.

Safety Wear **safety goggles, gloves,** and a **lab apron.**

Disposal Rinse off remaining metal pieces. Combine the rinses with the solutions and add **1 M aqueous NaOH** to bring the pH to approximately 10. Filter. Heat the precipitate sufficiently to convert any $Cu(OH)_2$ to CuO. Cool and put in the trash. Treat the filtrate with sufficient 1 M acid to bring the pH to between 6 and 8. Pour it down the drain.

Teach ▼

Teaching Tip

Students will relate the activity series to standard reduction potentials in another chapter.

▼ Teach continued

TEACH FROM TABLES

FIGURE 3.1 The table can be used to verify the results of the demonstration on the previous page. Encourage students to refer to the table until they become familiar with its contents. Point out that the activity series of the halogens is separate from the activity series of the metals.

Teaching Tip

Relate the order of activities of the halogens (all in Group 17) to their positions in the periodic table. The activities of the halogens decrease going down the group. To help students remember which direction is which in the activity series of the metals, remind them that the elements near the top include the very reactive metals at the left-hand side of the periodic table, whereas Ag, Pt, and Au, the metals at the bottom, are so unreactive that they are used for jewelry.

Such experimental observations are the basis for the activity series shown in **Figure 3.1**. For example, the activity series reflects the fact that some metals (potassium, for example) react vigorously with water and acids, replacing hydrogen to form new compounds. Other metals, such as iron or zinc, replace hydrogen in acids such as hydrochloric acid but react with water only when the water is hot enough to become steam. Nickel, however, will replace hydrogen in acids but will not react with steam at all. And gold will not react with individual acids or water, either as a liquid or as steam. If you look closely at the fairly unreactive metals in this activity series, you'll notice instantly that they represent the so-called precious metals that are very important to commerce. The ability of these metals to "stay intact" and not react with such things as water and acids, which are everywhere, should give you a clue as to why they have come to hold such great value by cultures all around the world.

FIGURE 3.1

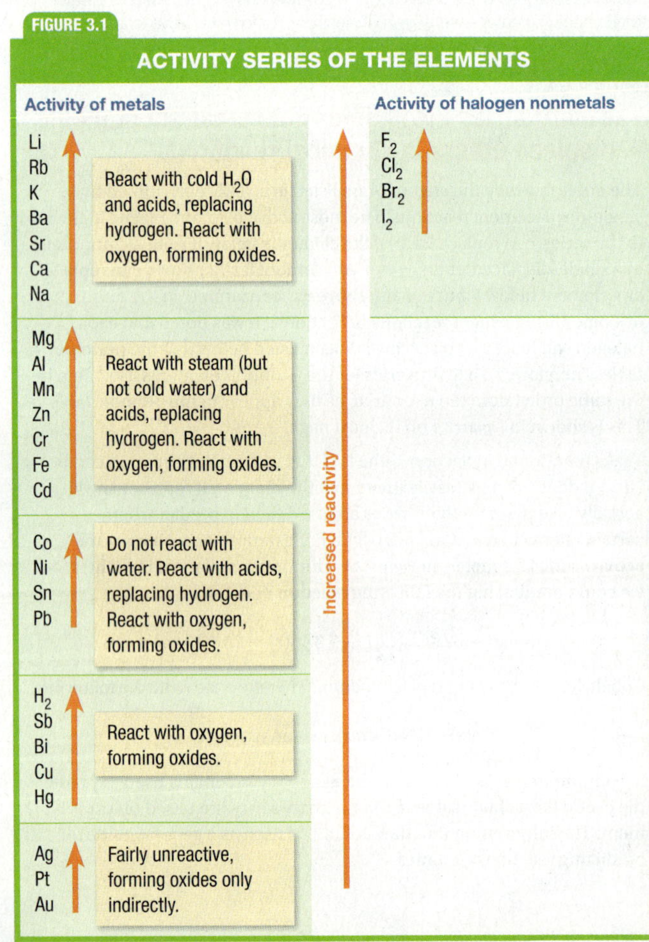

Problem Solving

PRE-AP

Have students identify the least reactive metal in **Figure 3.1.** As the text indicates, gold will not react with individual acids. However, gold will react with combinations of acids, such as a mixture of concentrated nitric and hydrochloric acids. Such a combination is called *aqua regia*.

Encourage students to investigate why gold reacts with this combination of acids. Ask students to also include information about the Hungarian chemist George de Hevesy, who used *aqua regia* to dissolve gold Nobel Prize medals to hide them from the Nazis during World War II.

PREMIUM CONTENT

Solve It! Cards HMDScience.com

Activity Series

Sample Problem F **Using the activity series shown in Figure 3.1, explain whether each of the possible reactions listed below will occur. For those reactions that will occur, predict what the products will be.**

a. $Zn(s) + H_2O(l) \xrightarrow{50°C}$ ______ **b.** $Sn(s) + O_2(g) \longrightarrow$ ______
c. $Cd(s) + Pb(NO_3)_2(aq) \longrightarrow$ ______ **d.** $Cu(s) + HCl(aq) \longrightarrow$ ______

SOLVE

a. This is a reaction between a metal and water at 50°C. Zinc reacts with water only when it is hot enough to be steam. Therefore, no reaction will occur.

b. Any metal more active than silver will react with oxygen to form an oxide. Tin is above silver in the activity series. Therefore, a reaction will occur, and the product will be a tin oxide, either SnO or SnO2.

c. An element will replace any element below it in the activity series from a compound in aqueous solution. Cadmium is above lead, and therefore a reaction will occur to produce lead, Pb, and cadmium nitrate, Cd(NO3)2.

d. Any metal more active than hydrogen will replace hydrogen from an acid. Copper is not above hydrogen in the series. Therefore, no reaction will occur.

Practice

Answers in Appendix F

1. Using the activity series shown in **Figure 3.1**, predict whether each of the possible reactions listed below will occur. For the reactions that will occur, write the products and balance the equation.
   a. $Cr(s) + H_2O(l) \longrightarrow$ ______ **c.** $Cd(s) + 2HBr(aq) \longrightarrow$ ______
   b. $Pt(s) + O_2(g) \longrightarrow$ ______ **d.** $Mg(s) +$ steam $\longrightarrow$ ______
2. Identify the element that replaces hydrogen from acids but cannot replace tin from its compounds.
3. According to **Figure 3.1**, what is the most-active transition metal?

SECTION 3 FORMATIVE ASSESSMENT

Reviewing Main Ideas

1. How is the activity series useful in predicting chemical behavior?
2. Based on the activity series, predict whether each of the following possible reactions will occur:
   a. $Ni(s) + H_2O(l) \longrightarrow$ ______
   b. $Br_2(l) + KI(aq) \longrightarrow$ ______
   c. $Au(s) + HCl(aq) \longrightarrow$ ______
   d. $Cd(s) + HCl(aq) \longrightarrow$ ______
   e. $Mg(s) + Co(NO_3)_2(aq) \longrightarrow$ ______
3. For each of the reactions in item 2 that will occur, write the products and balance the equation.

Critical Thinking

4. **PREDICTING OUTCOMES** A mixture contains cobalt metal, copper metal, and tin metal. This mixture is mixed with nickel nitrate. Which metals, if any, will react? Write the chemical equation for any reaction.

Answers to Section Assessment

1. It helps predict whether a chemical reaction will occur and what the product(s) of the reaction will be.
2. **a.** no **b.** yes **c.** no
   d. yes **e.** yes
3. **b.** $Br_2(l) + 2KI(aq) \longrightarrow 2KBr(aq) + I_2(s)$
   d. $Cd(s) + 2HCl(aq) \longrightarrow CdCl_2(aq) + H_2(g)$
   e. $Mg(s) + Co(NO_3)_2(aq) \longrightarrow Mg(NO_3)_2(aq) + Co(s)$
4. According to the activity series, only cobalt will react. Copper and tin will not react because they are below nickel in the activity chart.
   $Co + Ni(NO_3)_2 \longrightarrow Co(NO_3)_2 + Ni$

Classroom Practice

F-1 Using the activity series in **Figure 3.1**, predict whether each of the possible reactions listed below will occur. For reactions that will occur, write the products and balance the equation.

a. $MgCl_2(aq) + Zn(s) \longrightarrow$
b. $Al(s) + H_2O(g) \longrightarrow$
c. $Cd(s) + O_2(g) \longrightarrow$
d. $I_2(s) + KF(g) \longrightarrow$

Answers:
a. no
b. yes; $2Al(s) + 3H_2O(g) \longrightarrow Al_2O_3(s) + 3H_2(g)$
c. yes; $2Cd(s) + O_2(g) \longrightarrow 2CdO(s)$
d. no

Answers

Practice F

1. **a.** no
   b. no
   c. yes; $Cd(s) + 2HBr(aq) \longrightarrow CdBr_2(aq) + H_2(g)$
   d. yes; $Mg(s) + 2H_2O(g) \longrightarrow Mg(OH)_2(aq) + H_2(g)$
2. Pb
3. Mn

Assess and Reteach

Assess Use the Formative Assessment on this page to evaluate student mastery of the section.

Reteach For students who need additional instruction, download the Section Study Guide.

Response to Intervention To reassess students' mastery, use the Section Quiz, available to print or to take directly online at **HMDScience.com**.

Applications

Have students list different applications for advanced materials. Discuss the different types of compounds that make up these materials.

Teaching Strategy

In groups, have students research different advanced materials to determine the type of technique used to produce the material. Then, have the groups present the information about their materials to the class to compare.

Classroom Discussion

Materials scientists study both high-temperature methods and low-temperature methods of synthesizing materials. Have students discuss possible reasons that low-temperature methods might be advantageous.

Some possible reasons are that high temperatures can decompose reactants before they can react, high temperatures can decompose products, and high-temperature reactions are not as controllable. Therefore, a mixture of products can be produced or impurities can be produced.

Answers

1. The term *combustion* is used because once the mixture is ignited, the reaction is exothermic, giving off heat. The term *synthesis* is used because the heat wave that propagates through the mixture creates (or synthesizes) a new material.
2. During combustion synthesis, the temperature is very high and evenly spread, which gives a fast reaction time. These conditions force all particles of the starting material to be heated in the same manner, resulting in a more homogeneous product.

WHY IT MATTERS

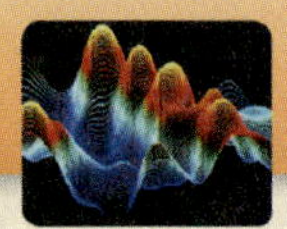
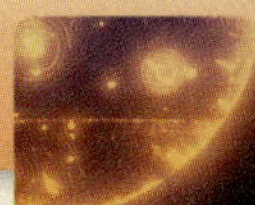

S.T.E.M.

Combustion Synthesis

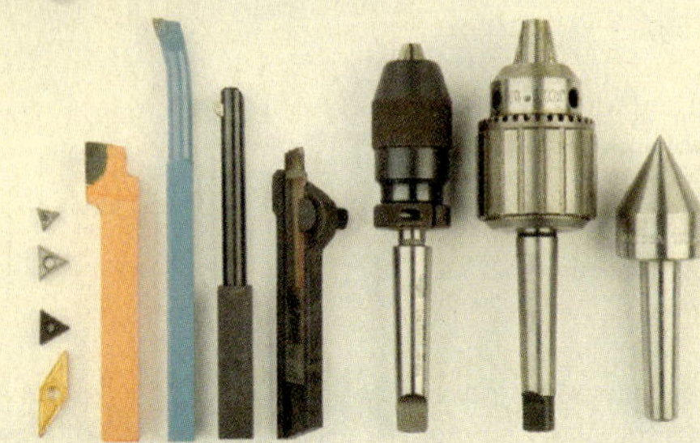

What do aerospace materials, cutting tools, catalytic materials, ceramic engine parts, ball bearings, high-temperature superconductors, hydrogen storage, and fuel cells have in common? They are made of ceramics, composites, and other advanced materials.

Conventional techniques used to make these materials consist of a high-temperature furnace, with temperatures ranging from 500°C to 2000°C, to supply the energy needed for the reaction to take place. Because these furnaces may reach only 2000°C, it may take minutes to hours to convert reactants to solid-state products, and the mixtures are heated unevenly. As a result, flaws can be introduced into the structures, which can cause stress points in the materials.

A different high-temperature technique is *combustion synthesis*, which generates its own energy to keep the reaction continuing. Once the reactant mixture is ignited, a heat wave moves through the sample, producing the solid-state product. The mixture can reach temperatures up to 4000°C, twice what is possible with conventional high-temperature furnaces. Combustion synthesis also allows reactions to be completed in just seconds. Hence, this technique produces the desired material faster and requires less supplied energy than conventional techniques do. In addition, the intense and quick heating produces materials that are chemically homogeneous. More than 500 compounds, such as lightweight and heat-resistant aerospace materials, are created by combustion synthesis.

In a typical combustion synthesis procedure, the reactant powders are mixed and then pressed into a cylindrical pellet. The pellet is ignited by an intense heat source, such as an electrically heated coil or a laser. Because the combustion-synthesis reaction is very exothermic, the reaction is self-propagating, and the process does not need any further input of energy. This type of self-propagation is called a *reaction wave*, in which the reaction propagates through the starting material in a self-sustained manner. Therefore, compared with conventional high-temperature methods, this technique is an energy-saving process. In addition, the high temperatures and short reaction times can produce materials that would not be synthesized under conventional conditions. Currently, scientists are studying reaction waves, including how they move through the initial mixtures. As scientists better understand the characteristics of combustion synthesis, they can refine the technique to be more useful in advanced materials production.

Questions

1. Why is this technique called *combustion synthesis*?
2. Why might this technique result in a more chemically homogeneous material?

Superconducting ceramics, like those used to make supercooled electromagnets, are formed using a combustion synthesis reaction.

Math Tutor | Balancing Chemical Equations

A chemical equation is a written expression of an actual chemical reaction in which certain atoms, ions, or molecules become rearranged in a specific way. Therefore, the equation must represent exactly what happens in the reaction.

Recall that atoms are never created or destroyed in chemical reactions. A balanced chemical equation shows that all of the atoms present in reactants are still present in products.

Problem-Solving TIPS

- First, identify reactants and products. (You may find it helpful to write a word equation first.)
- Using correct formulas and symbols, write an unbalanced equation for the reaction.
- Balance atoms one element at a time by inserting coefficients.
- Identify elements that appear in only one reactant and one product, and balance the atoms of those elements first.
- If a polyatomic ion appears on both sides of the equation, treat it as a single unit.
- Double-check to be sure that the number of atoms of each element is the same on both sides of the equation.

Sample

When an aqueous solution of ammonium sulfate, $(NH_4)_2SO_4(aq)$, is combined with an aqueous solution of silver nitrate, $AgNO_3(aq)$, a precipitate of solid silver sulfate, $Ag_2SO_4(s)$, forms, leaving ammonium nitrate, $NH_4NO_3(aq)$, in solution. Balance the equation for this reaction.

As before, first write an equation with correct formulas for all reactants and products.

$$(NH_4)_2SO_4(aq) + AgNO_3(aq) \longrightarrow NH_4NO_3(aq) + Ag_2SO_4(s)$$

If you compare the number of silver atoms on each side, you can see that the equation is not balanced. This equation may look very complex, but it is really fairly simple. In many reactions involving polyatomic ions such as sulfate, nitrate, and ammonium, the ions do not change. In the equation above, you can see that NO_3 is present on both sides, as are SO_4 and NH_4. You can balance the equation by treating the groups as if they were single atoms. To balance the NH_4 groups, place a 2 in front of NH_4NO_3. This gives you two ammonium groups on the left and two on the right. Now, because you have two nitrate groups on the right, place a 2 in front of $AgNO_3$ to give two nitrate groups on the left. Finally, check silver atoms and sulfate groups, and you find that they balance.

$$(NH_4)_2SO_4(aq) + 2AgNO_3(aq) \longrightarrow 2NH_4NO_3(aq) + Ag_2SO_4(s)$$

Practice

1. When propane burns completely in air, the reaction forms carbon dioxide and water vapor. Balance the equation for this reaction.

$$C_3H_8 + O_2 \longrightarrow CO_2 + H_2O$$

2. Balance the following chemical equations:
   a. $KI(aq) + Cl_2(g) \longrightarrow KCl(aq) + I_2(s)$
   b. $Al(s) + H_2SO_4(aq) \longrightarrow Al_2(SO_4)_3(aq) + H_2(g)$

Answers

1. $C_3H_8 + 5O_2 \longrightarrow 3CO_2 + 4H_2O$
2. a. $2KI(aq) + Cl_2(g) \longrightarrow 2KCl(aq) + I_2(s)$
   b. $2Al(s) + 3H_2SO_4(aq) \longrightarrow Al_2(SO_4)_3(aq) + 3H_2(g)$

CHAPTER SUMMARY

Review Answers

1. the evolution of energy, the production of a gas, the formation of a precipitate, and a color change
2. It must represent the known facts, contain the correct formulas for the reactants and products, and satisfy the law of conservation of mass.
3. **a.** a number that appears in front of a formula in a chemical equation.
   b. The number of atoms of each type in the formula is multiplied by the coefficient.
4. methane + oxygen $\longrightarrow$ carbon dioxide + water; $CH_4(g) + O_2(g) \longrightarrow CO_2(g) + H_2O(g)$; $CH_4(g) + 2O_2(g) \longrightarrow CO_2(g) + 2H_2O(g)$
5. the number of molecules, moles, and atoms of each element or compound composing the reactants and products as well as the mole ratios of the reactants to each other and to the products
6. They have only qualitative meaning; they do not express the relative quantities reactants or products.
7. **a.** a solution in water
   b. a substance that accelerates a chemical reaction but can be recovered unchanged
   c. a reaction in which the products re-form the original reactants
8. **a.** KOH
   b. $Ca(NO_3)_2$
   c. Na_2CO_3
   d. CCl_4
   e. $MgBr_2$
9. (1) Balance different types of atoms one at a time; (2) balance types of atoms that appear only once on each side first; (3) balance as single units any polyatomic ions that appear on both sides; (4) balance H and O last.

CHAPTER 8 Summary

Review Games
Concept Maps

SECTION 1 Describing Chemical Reactions

- Four observations that suggest a chemical reaction is taking place are the evolution of energy as heat and light, the production of gas, a change in color, and the formation of a precipitate.
- A balanced chemical equation represents, with symbols and formulas, the identities and relative amounts of reactants and products in a chemical reaction.

KEY TERMS
chemical equation
precipitate
coefficient
word equation
formula equation
reversible reaction

SECTION 2 Types of Chemical Reactions

- Synthesis reactions are represented by the general equation $A + X \longrightarrow AX$.
- Decomposition reactions are represented by the general equation $AX \longrightarrow A + X$.
- Single-displacement reactions are represented by the general equations $A + BX \longrightarrow AX + B$ and $Y + BX \longrightarrow BY + X$.
- Double-displacement reactions are represented by the general equation $AX + BY \longrightarrow AY + BX$.
- In a combustion reaction, a substance combines with oxygen, releasing energy in the form of heat and light.

KEY TERMS
synthesis reaction
decomposition reaction
electrolysis
single-displacement reaction
double-displacement reaction
combustion reaction

SECTION 3 Activity Series of the Elements

- Activity series list the elements in order of their chemical reactivity and are useful in predicting whether a chemical reaction will occur.
- Chemists determine activity series through experiments.

KEY TERMS
activity series

CHAPTER 8 Review

SECTION 1

Describing Chemical Reactions

REVIEWING MAIN IDEAS

1. List four observations that indicate that a chemical reaction may be taking place.
2. List the three requirements for a correctly written chemical equation.
3. a. What is meant by the term *coefficient* in relation to a chemical equation?
   b. How does the presence of a coefficient affect the number of atoms of each type in the formula that the coefficient precedes?
4. Give an example of a word equation, a formula equation, and a chemical equation.
5. What quantitative information is revealed by a chemical equation?
6. What limitations are associated with the use of both word and formula equations?
7. Define each of the following terms:
   a. aqueous solution
   b. catalyst
   c. reversible reaction
8. Write formulas for each of the following compounds:
   a. potassium hydroxide
   b. calcium nitrate
   c. sodium carbonate
   d. carbon tetrachloride
   e. magnesium bromide
9. What four guidelines are useful in balancing an equation?
10. How many atoms of each type are represented in each of the following?
    a. $3N_2$
    b. $2H_2O$
    c. $4HNO_3$
    d. $2Ca(OH)_2$
    e. $3Ba(ClO_3)_2$
    f. $5Fe(NO_3)_2$
    g. $4Mg_3(PO_4)_2$
    h. $2(NH_4)_2SO_4$
    i. $6Al_2(SeO_4)_3$
    j. $4C_3H_8$

PRACTICE PROBLEMS

11. Write the chemical equation that relates to each of the following word equations. Include symbols for physical states in the equation.
    a. solid zinc sulfide + oxygen gas $\longrightarrow$ solid zinc oxide + sulfur dioxide gas
    b. aqueous hydrochloric acid + aqueous barium hydroxide $\longrightarrow$ aqueous barium chloride + water
    c. aqueous nitric acid + aqueous calcium hydroxide $\longrightarrow$ aqueous calcium nitrate + water
12. Translate each of the following chemical equations into a sentence.
    a. $2ZnS(s) + 3O_2(g) \longrightarrow 2ZnO(s) + 2SO_2(g)$
    b. $CaH_2(s) + 2H_2O(l) \longrightarrow Ca(OH)_2(aq) + 2H_2(g)$
    c. $AgNO_3(aq) + KI(aq) \longrightarrow AgI(s) + KNO_3(aq)$
13. Balance each of the following:
    a. $H_2 + Cl_2 \longrightarrow HCl$
    b. $Al + Fe_2O_3 \longrightarrow Al_2O_3 + Fe$
    c. $Pb(CH_3COO)_2 + H_2S \longrightarrow PbS + CH_3COOH$
14. Identify and correct each error in the following equations, and then balance each equation.
    a. $Li + O_2 \longrightarrow LiO_2$
    b. $H_2 + Cl_2 \longrightarrow H_2Cl_2$
    c. $MgCO_3 \longrightarrow MgO_2 + CO_2$
    d. $NaI + Cl_2 \longrightarrow NaCl + I$
15. Write chemical equations for each of the following sentences:
    a. Aluminum reacts with oxygen to produce aluminum oxide.
    b. Phosphoric acid, H_3PO_4, is produced through the reaction between tetraphosphorus decoxide and water.
    c. Iron(III) oxide reacts with carbon monoxide to produce iron and carbon dioxide.
16. Carbon tetrachloride is used as an intermediate chemical in the manufacture of other chemicals. It is prepared in liquid form by reacting chlorine gas with methane gas. Hydrogen chloride gas is also formed in this reaction. Write the balanced chemical equation for the production of carbon tetrachloride. (Hint: See Sample Problems C and D.)

CHAPTER REVIEW

10. a. 6N
    b. 4H, 2O
    c. 4H, 4N, 12O
    d. 2Ca, 4O, 4H
    e. 3Ba, 6Cl, 18O
    f. 5Fe, 10N, 30O
    g. 12Mg, 8P, 32O
    h. 4N, 16H, 2S, 8O
    i. 12Al, 18Se, 72O
    j. 12C, 32H
11. a. $2ZnS(s) + 3O_2(g) \longrightarrow 2ZnO(s) + 2SO_2(g)$
    b. $2HCl(aq) + Ba(OH)_2(aq) \longrightarrow BaCl_2(aq) + 2H_2O(l)$
    c. $2HNO_3(aq) + Ca(OH)_2(aq) \longrightarrow Ca(NO_3)_2(aq) + 2H_2O(l)$
12. a. Solid zinc sulfide reacts with oxygen gas to form solid zinc oxide and sulfur dioxide gas.
    b. When solid calcium hydride is added to water, aqueous calcium hydroxide and hydrogen gas are formed.
    c. Aqueous silver nitrate mixed with aqueous potassium iodide produces a precipitate of silver iodide and aqueous potassium nitrate.
13. a. $H_2 + Cl_2 \longrightarrow 2HCl$
    b. $2Al + Fe_2O_3 \longrightarrow Al_2O_3 + 2Fe$
    c. $Pb(CH_3COO)_2 + H_2S \longrightarrow PbS + 2CH_3COOH$
14. a. LiO_2 is an incorrect formula; $4Li + O_2 \longrightarrow 2Li_2O$
    b. H_2Cl_2 is an incorrect formula; $H_2 + Cl_2 \longrightarrow 2HCl$
    c. MgO_2 is an incorrect formula, and the equation as written is not balanced; $MgCO_3 \longrightarrow MgO + CO_2$
    d. I is an incorrect formula for iodine; the equation is not balanced; $2NaI + Cl_2 \longrightarrow 2NaCl + I_2$
15. a. $4Al + 3O_2 \longrightarrow 2Al_2O_3$
    b. $P_4O_{10} + 6H_2O \longrightarrow 4H_3PO_4$
    c. $Fe_2O_3 + 3CO \longrightarrow 2Fe + 3CO_2$
16. $CH_4(g) + 4Cl_2(g) \longrightarrow CCl_4(l) + 4HCl(g)$
17. a. $2Mg + O_2 \longrightarrow 2MgO$
    b. $4Fe + 3O_2 \longrightarrow 2Fe_2O_3$
    c. $2Li + Cl_2 \longrightarrow 2LiCl$
    d. $Ca + I_2 \longrightarrow CaI_2$

18. (1) Synthesis: two or more substances combine to form a new substance;

$A + X \longrightarrow AX$

(2) Decomposition: a single compound undergoes a reaction that produces two or more simpler substances; $AX \longrightarrow A + X$

(3) Single-displacement: one element replaces another element in a compound; $A + BX \longrightarrow AX + B$ or

$Y + BX \longrightarrow BY + X$

(4) Double-displacement: the ions of two compounds exchange places in an aqueous solution to form two new compounds;

$AX + BY \longrightarrow BX + AY$

(5) Combustion: a substance combines with oxygen, releasing a large amount of energy in the form of light and heat; for example, $C_3H_8(g) + 5O_2(g) \longrightarrow 3CO_2(g) + 4H_2O(g)$

19. by the addition of energy in the form of electricity or heat

20. electrolysis

21. a. aqueous solutions

b. They generally involve less energy.

22. a. Sodium and oxygen react to form sodium oxide;

$4Na + O_2 \longrightarrow 2Na_2O$

b. Magnesium and fluorine combine to form magnesium fluoride;

$Mg + F_2 \longrightarrow MgF_2$

23. a. $2HgO \xrightarrow{\Delta} 2Hg + O_2$

b. $2H_2O(l) \xrightarrow{\text{electricity}} 2H_2(g) + O_2(g)$

c. $2Ag_2O \xrightarrow{\Delta} 4Ag + O_2$

d. $CuCl_2 \xrightarrow{\text{electricity}} Cu + Cl_2$

24. a. $Zn + Pb(NO_3)_2 \longrightarrow Pb + Zn(NO_3)_2$

b. $2Al + 3Hg(CH_3COO)_2 \longrightarrow 3Hg + 2Al(CH_3COO)_3$

c. $2Al + 3NiSO_4 \longrightarrow 3Ni + Al_2(SO_4)_3$

d. $2Na + 2H_2O \longrightarrow 2NaOH + H_2$

25. a. $AgNO_3(aq) + NaCl(aq) \longrightarrow NaNO_3(aq) + AgCl(s)$

b. $Mg(NO_3)_2(aq) + 2KOH(aq) \longrightarrow Mg(OH)_2(s) + 2KNO_3(aq)$

c. $3LiOH(aq) + Fe(NO_3)_3(aq) \longrightarrow Fe(OH)\ 3(s) + 3LiNO_3(aq)$

26. a. $CH_4 + 2O_2 \longrightarrow CO_2 + 2H_2O$

b. $2C_3H_6 + 9O_2 \longrightarrow 6CO_2 + 6H_2O$

c. $C_5H_{12} + 8O_2 \longrightarrow 5CO_2 + 6H_2O$

17. For each of the following synthesis reactions, identify the missing reactant(s) or product(s), and then balance the resulting equation.

a. $Mg + \_\_\_\_ \longrightarrow MgO$

b. $\_\_\_\_ + O_2 \longrightarrow Fe_2O_3$

c. $Li + Cl_2 \longrightarrow \_\_\_\_$

d. $Ca + \_\_\_\_ \longrightarrow CaI_2$

SECTION 2

Types of Chemical Reactions

REVIEWING MAIN IDEAS

18. Define and give general equations for the five basic types of chemical reactions.

19. How are most decomposition reactions initiated?

20. A substance is decomposed by an electric current. What is the name of this type of reaction?

21. a. In what environment do many single-displacement reactions commonly occur?

b. In general, how do single-displacement reactions compare with synthesis and decomposition reactions in terms of the amount of energy involved?

PRACTICE PROBLEMS

22. Complete each of the following synthesis reactions by writing both a word equation and a chemical equation.

a. sodium + oxygen ⟶ ____

b. magnesium + fluorine ⟶ ____

23. Complete and balance the equations for the following decomposition reactions:

a. $HgO \xrightarrow{\Delta}$

b. $H_2O(l) \xrightarrow{\text{electricity}}$

c. $Ag_2O \xrightarrow{\Delta}$

d. $CuCl_2 \xrightarrow{\text{electricity}}$

24. Complete and balance the equations for the following single-displacement reactions:

a. $Zn + Pb(NO_3)_2 \longrightarrow \_\_\_\_$

b. $Al + Hg(CH_3COO)_2 \longrightarrow \_\_\_\_$

c. $Al + NiSO_4 \longrightarrow \_\_\_\_$

d. $Na + H_2O \longrightarrow \_\_\_\_$

25. Complete and balance the equations for the following double-displacement reactions:

a. $AgNO_3(aq) + NaCl(aq) \longrightarrow \_\_\_\_$

b. $Mg(NO_3)_2(aq) + KOH(aq) \longrightarrow \_\_\_\_$

c. $LiOH(aq) + Fe(NO_3)_3(aq) \longrightarrow \_\_\_\_$

26. Complete and balance the equations for the following combustion reactions:

a. $CH_4 + O_2 \longrightarrow \_\_\_\_$

b. $C_3H_6 + O_2 \longrightarrow \_\_\_\_$

c. $C_5H_{12} + O_2 \longrightarrow \_\_\_\_$

27. Write and balance each of the following equations, and then identify each by type.

a. hydrogen + iodine ⟶ hydrogen iodide

b. lithium + hydrochloric acid ⟶ lithium chloride + hydrogen

c. sodium carbonate ⟶ sodium oxide + carbon dioxide

d. mercury(II) oxide ⟶ mercury + oxygen

e. magnesium hydroxide ⟶ magnesium oxide + water

28. Identify the compound that could undergo decomposition to produce the following products, and then balance the final equation.

a. magnesium oxide and water

b. lead(II) oxide and water

c. lithium chloride and oxygen

d. barium chloride and oxygen

e. nickel chloride and oxygen

29. In each of the following combustion reactions, identify the missing reactant(s), product(s), or both, and then balance the resulting equation.

a. $C_3H_8 + \_\_\_\_ \longrightarrow \_\_\_\_ + H_2O$

b. $\_\_\_\_ + 8O_2 \longrightarrow 5CO_2 + 6H_2O$

c. $C_2H_5OH + \_\_\_\_ \longrightarrow \_\_\_\_ + \_\_\_\_$

30. Complete and balance the equations for the following reactions, and then identify each by type.

a. zinc + sulfur ⟶ ____

b. silver nitrate + potassium iodide ⟶ ____

c. toluene, C_7H_8 + oxygen ⟶ ____

d. nonane, C_9H_{20} + oxygen ⟶ ____

SECTION 3

Activity Series of the Elements

REVIEWING MAIN IDEAS

31. a. What is meant by the *activity* of an element?

b. How does this description differ for metals and nonmetals?

27. a. $H_2 + I_2 \longrightarrow 2HI$; synthesis

b. $2Li + 2HCl \longrightarrow 2LiCl + H_2$; single displacement

c. $Na_2CO_3 \longrightarrow Na_2O + CO_2$; decomposition

d. $2HgO \longrightarrow 2Hg + O_2$; decomposition

e. $Mg(OH)_2 \longrightarrow MgO + H_2O$; decomposition

28. a. magnesium hydroxide; $Mg(OH)_2 \longrightarrow MgO + H_2O$

b. lead(II) hydroxide; $Pb(OH)_2 \longrightarrow PbO + H_2O$

c. lithium chlorate; $2LiClO_3 \longrightarrow 2LiCl + 3O_2$

d. barium chlorate; $Ba(ClO_3)_2 \longrightarrow BaCl_2 + 3O_2$

e. nickel chlorate; $Ni(ClO_3)_2 \longrightarrow NiCl_2 + 3O_2$

29. a. oxygen, carbon dioxide; $C_3H_8 + 5O_2 \longrightarrow 3CO_2 + 4H_2O$

b. pentane; $C_5H_{12} + 8O_2 \longrightarrow 5CO_2 + 6H_2O$

c. oxygen, carbon dioxide, water; $C_2H_5OH + 3O_2 \longrightarrow 2CO_2 + 3H_2O$

30. a. $Zn + S \longrightarrow ZnS$; synthesis

b. $AgNO_3 + KI \longrightarrow AgI + KNO_3$; double displacement

32. a. What is an activity series of elements?
b. What is the basis for the ordering of the elements in the activity series?

33. a. What chemical principle is the basis for the activity series of metals?
b. What is the significance of the distance between two metals in the activity series?

PRACTICE PROBLEMS

34. Based on the activity series of metals and halogens, in **Figure 3.1**, which element within each pair is more likely to replace the other in a compound?

a. K and Na
b. Al and Ni
c. Bi and Cr
d. Cl and F
e. Au and Ag
f. Cl and I
g. Fe and Sr
h. I and F

35. Using the activity series in **Figure 3.1**, predict whether each of the possible reactions listed below will occur. For the reactions that will occur, write the products and balance the equation.

a. $Ni(s) + CuCl_2(aq) \longrightarrow$ ______
b. $Zn(s) + Pb(NO_3)_2(aq) \longrightarrow$ ______
c. $Cl_2(g) + KI(aq) \longrightarrow$ ______
d. $Cu(s) + FeSO_4(aq) \longrightarrow$ ______
e. $Ba(s) + H_2O(l) \longrightarrow$ ______

36. Use the activity series in **Figure 3.1** to predict whether each of the following synthesis reactions will occur, and write the chemical equations for those predicted to occur.

a. $Ca(s) + O_2(g) \longrightarrow$ ______
b. $Ni(s) + O_2(g) \longrightarrow$ ______
c. $Au(s) + O_2(g) \longrightarrow$ ______

Mixed Review

REVIEWING MAIN IDEAS

37. Ammonia reacts with oxygen to yield nitrogen and water.

$$4NH_3(g) + 3O_2(g) \longrightarrow 2N_2(g) + 6H_2O(l)$$

Given this chemical equation, as well as the number of moles of the reactant or product indicated below, determine the number of moles of all remaining reactants and products.

a. 3.0 mol O_2
b. 8.0 mol NH_3
c. 1.0 mol N_2
d. 0.40 mol H_2O

38. Complete the following synthesis reactions by writing both the word and chemical equation for each:

a. potassium + chlorine $\longrightarrow$ ______
b. hydrogen + iodine $\longrightarrow$ ______
c. magnesium + oxygen $\longrightarrow$ ______

39. Use the activity series in **Figure 3.1** to predict which metal—Sn, Mn, or Pt—would be the best choice as a container for an acid.

40. Aqueous sodium hydroxide is produced commercially by the electrolysis of aqueous sodium chloride. Hydrogen and chlorine gases are also produced. Write the balanced chemical equation for the production of sodium hydroxide. Include the physical states of the reactants and products.

41. Balance each of the following:

a. $Ca(OH)_2 + (NH_4)_2SO_4 \longrightarrow CaSO_4 + NH_3 + H_2O$
b. $C_2H_6 + O_2 \longrightarrow CO_2 + H_2O$
c. $Cu_2S + O_2 \longrightarrow Cu_2O + SO_2$
d. $Al + H_2SO_4 \longrightarrow Al_2(SO_4)_3 + H_2$

42. Use the activity series in **Figure 3.1** to predict whether each of the following reactions will occur, and write the balanced chemical equations for those predicted to occur.

a. $Al(s) + O_2(g) \longrightarrow$ ______
b. $Pb(s) + ZnCl_2(s) \longrightarrow$ ______

43. Complete and balance the equations for the following reactions, and identify the type of reaction that each equation represents.

a. $(NH_4)_2S(aq) + ZnCl_2(aq) \longrightarrow$ ______ $+ ZnS(s)$
b. $Al(s) + Pb(NO_3)_2(aq) \longrightarrow$ ______
c. $Ba(s) + H_2O(l) \longrightarrow$ ______
d. $Cl_2(g) + KBr(aq) \longrightarrow$
e. $NH_3(g) + O_2(g) \xrightarrow{Pt} NO(g) + H_2O(l)$
f. $H_2O(l) \longrightarrow H_2(g) + O_2(g)$

44. Write and balance each of the following equations, and then identify each by type.

a. copper + chlorine $\longrightarrow$ copper(II) chloride
b. calcium chlorate $\longrightarrow$ calcium chloride + oxygen
c. lithium + water $\longrightarrow$ lithium hydroxide + hydrogen
d. lead(II) carbonate $\longrightarrow$ lead(II) oxide + carbon dioxide

c. $C_7H_8 + 9O_2 \longrightarrow 7CO_2 + 4H_2O$; combustion
d. $C_9H_{20} + 14O_2 \longrightarrow 9CO_2 + 10H_2O$; combustion

31. a. the element's ability to react
b. For metals, the ability to lose electrons; for nonmetals, the ability to gain them.

32. a. a set of elements listed according to the ease with which the elements undergo certain chemical reactions
b. Elements are usually listed in order of their tendency to undergo single-displacement reactions. An element can replace any element listed below it.

33. a. The activity series of metals is based on the ease with which metal atoms lose electrons to form ions in aqueous solution; the higher a metal is in the series, the more easily its atoms lose electrons and the greater its reactivity.
b. The greater the distance is, the greater the likelihood that one metal will replace the other in a reaction.

34. a. K **b.** Al **c.** Cr **d.** F **e.** Ag **f.** Cl **g.** Sr **h.** F

CHAPTER REVIEW

35. a. $Ni(s) + CuCl_2(aq) \longrightarrow NiCl_2(aq) + Cu(s)$
b. $Zn(s) + Pb(NO_3)_2(aq) \longrightarrow Zn(NO_3)_2(aq) + Pb(s)$
c. $Cl_2(g) + 2KI(aq) \longrightarrow 2KCl(aq) + I_2(s)$
d. no reaction
e. $Ba(s) + 2H_2O(l) \longrightarrow H_2(g) + Ba(OH)_2(s)$

36. a. $2Ca(s) + O_2(g) \longrightarrow 2CaO(s)$
b. $2Ni(s) + O_2(g) \longrightarrow 2NiO(s)$
c. no reaction

37. a. 4.0 mol NH_3, 2.0 mol N_2, and 6.0 mol H_2O
b. 6.0 mol O_2, 4.0 mol N_2, and 12.0 mol H_2O
c. 2.0 mol NH_3, 1.5 mol O_2, and 3.0 mol H_2O
d. 0.27 mol NH_3, 0.20 mol O_2, and 0.13 mol N_2

38. a. Potassium and chlorine react to form potassium chloride; $2K + Cl_2 \longrightarrow 2KCl$
b. Hydrogen and iodine react to produce hydrogen iodide; $H_2 + I_2 \longrightarrow 2HI$
c. Magnesium and oxygen react to produce magnesium oxide; $2Mg + O_2 \longrightarrow 2MgO$

39. Pt

40. $2NaCl(aq) + 2H_2O(l) \xrightarrow{\text{electricty}} 2NaOH(aq) + H_2(g) + Cl_2(g)$

41. a. $Ca(OH)_2 + (NH_4)_2SO_4 \longrightarrow CaSO_4 + 2NH_3 + 2H_2O$
b. $2C_2H_6 + 7O_2 \longrightarrow 4CO_2 + 6H_2O$
c. $2Cu_2S + 3O_2 \longrightarrow 2Cu_2O + 2SO_2$
d. $2Al + 3H_2SO_4 \longrightarrow Al_2(SO_4)_3 + 3H_2$

42. a. $4Al(s) + 3O_2(g) \longrightarrow 2Al_2O_3(s)$
b. no reaction

43. a. $(NH_4)_2S(aq) + ZnCl_2(aq) \longrightarrow 2NH_4Cl(aq) + ZnS(s)$; double-displacement reaction
b. $2Al(s) + 3Pb(NO_3)_2(aq) \longrightarrow 3Pb(s) + 2Al(NO_3)_3(aq)$; single-displacement reaction
c. $Ba(s) + 2H_2O(l) \longrightarrow Ba(OH)_2(s) + H_2(g)$; single-displacement reaction
d. $Cl_2(g) + 2KBr(aq) \longrightarrow 2KCl(aq) + Br_2(l)$; single-displacement reaction
e. $4NH_3(g) + 5O_2(g) \xrightarrow{pt} 4NO(g) + 6H_2O(l)$; combustion reaction
f. $2H_2O(l) \longrightarrow 2H_2(g) + O_2(g)$; decomposition reaction

44. a. $Cu(s) + Cl_2(g) \longrightarrow CuCl_2(s)$; synthesis reaction

b. $Ca(ClO_3)_2(s) \longrightarrow CaCl_2(s) + 3O_2(g)$; decomposition reaction

c. $2Li(s) + 2H_2O(l) \longrightarrow 2LiOH(aq) + H_2(g)$; single-displacement reaction

d. $PbCO_3(s) \longrightarrow PbO(s) + CO_2(g)$; decomposition reaction

45. 12.3 mol HCl

46. H_2O

47. a. $Pb(NO_3)_2(aq) + 2NaOH(aq) \longrightarrow Pb(OH)_2(s) + 2NaNO_3(aq)$

b. $C_{12}H_{22}O_{11}(l) + 12O_2(g) \longrightarrow 12CO_2(g) + 11H_2O(l)$

c. $2Al(OH)_3(s) + 3H_2SO_4(aq) \longrightarrow Al_2(SO_4)_3(aq) + 6H_2O(l)$

48. The most reactive metals are on the left side in Groups 1 and 2. These metals have one (Group 1) or two (Group 2) electrons in their outer energy level. The energy needed to lose these electrons and achieve a stable configuration is much less than the energy needed to gain electrons. The least reactive metals are in the lower right of the transition metal block. The *d* sublevel of the fifth energy level is more than half full in these metals. These metals are much more stable than metals on the left side of the periodic table.

49. Q is most reactive, followed by A, then Z, and then J.

50. a. $Rb_2O(s) + H_2O(l) \longrightarrow 2RbOH(aq)$

b. $2Cs(s) + I_2(s) \longrightarrow 2CsI(s)$

c. Both are synthesis reactions.

d. Solid rubidium oxide reacts with water to yield an aqueous solution of rubidium hydroxide. Solid cesium reacts with solid iodine to yield solid cesium iodide.

51. a. $2Ga(s) + 6HBr(aq) \longrightarrow 2GaBr_3(aq) + 3H_2(g)$

b. $4Ga(s) + 3O_2(g) \longrightarrow 2Ga_2O_3(s)$

c. The first reaction is a single-displacement reaction; the second reaction is a synthesis reaction.

d. Solid gallium reacts with hydrobromic acid to yield aqueous gallium bromide and hydrogen gas. Solid gallium reacts with oxygen gas to yield solid gallium oxide.

45. How many moles of HCl can be made from 6.15 mol H_2 and an excess of Cl_2?

46. What product is missing in the following equation?

$MgO + 2HCl \longrightarrow MgCl_2 +$ ______

47. Balance the following equations:

a. $Pb(NO_3)_2(aq) + NaOH(aq) \longrightarrow Pb(OH)_2(s) + NaNO_3(aq)$

b. $C_{12}H_{22}O_{11}(l) + O_2(g) \longrightarrow CO_2(g) + H_2O(l)$

c. $Al(OH)_3(s) + H_2SO_4(aq) \longrightarrow Al_2(SO_4)_3(aq) + H_2O(l)$

CRITICAL THINKING

48. Inferring Relationships Activity series are prepared by comparing single-displacement reactions between metals. Based on observations, the metals can be ranked by their ability to react. However, reactivity can be explained by the ease with which atoms of metals lose electrons. Using information from the activity series, identify the locations in the periodic table of the most reactive metals and the least reactive metals. Using your knowledge of electron configurations and periodic trends, infer possible explanations for the metals' reactivity and position in the periodic table.

49. Analyzing Results Formulate an activity series for the hypothetical elements A, J, Q, and Z by using the following reaction information:

$A + ZX \longrightarrow AX + Z$

$J + ZX \longrightarrow$ no reaction

$Q + AX \longrightarrow QX + A$

USING THE HANDBOOK

50. Find the common-reactions section for Group 1 metals in the *Elements Handbook* in Appendix A. Use this information to answer the following:

a. Write a balanced chemical equation for the formation of rubidium hydroxide from rubidum oxide.

b. Write a balanced chemical equation for the formation of cesium iodide.

c. Classify the reactions you wrote in (a) and (b).

d. Write word equations for the reactions you wrote in (a) and (b).

51. Find the common-reactions section for Group 13 in the *Elements Handbook* (Appendix A). Use this information to answer the following:

a. Write a balanced chemical equation for the formation of gallium bromide prepared from hydrobromic acid.

b. Write a balanced chemical equation for the formation of gallium oxide.

c. Classify the reactions you wrote in (a) and (b).

d. Write word equations for the reactions you wrote in (a) and (b).

RESEARCH AND WRITING

52. Trace the evolution of municipal water fluoridation. What advantages and disadvantages are associated with this practice?

53. Research how a soda-acid fire extinguisher works, and write the chemical equation for the reaction. Check your house and other structures for different types of fire extinguishers, and ask your local fire department to verify the effectiveness of each type of extinguisher.

ALTERNATIVE ASSESSMENT

54. Performance Assessment For one day, record situations that show evidence of a chemical change. Identify the reactants and the products, and determine whether there is proof of a chemical reaction. Classify each of the chemical reactions according to the common reaction types discussed in the chapter.

Visit **HMDScience.com** for appropriate scoring rubrics for items 52 and 53. Look for the following points in each report.

52. Students may discover that tin(II) fluoride and sodium fluoride harden tooth enamel when the fluoride ion participates in a double-displacement reaction with the principal constituent of tooth enamel, hydroxyapatite. $Ca_5(PO_4)_3OH$.

$Ca_5(PO_4)_3OH(aq) + NaF(aq) \longrightarrow Ca_5(PO_4)_3F(s) + NaOH(aq)$

Fluoroapatite is harder, stronger, and more resistant to bacterial attack than hydroxyapatite.

53. The soda-acid fire extinguisher has been generally replaced by extinguishers consisting of liquid CO_2. However, students can write the equation:

$H_2SO_4 + 2NaHCO_3 \longrightarrow 2CO_2 + Na_2SO_4 + 2H_2O$

54. Students may see evidence of chemical changes that are too complex to incorporate into a simple equation. Ask them to include the evidence. Students could summarize their findings in a chart.

Standards-Based Assessment

Answer the following items on a separate piece of paper.

MULTIPLE CHOICE

1. According to the law of conservation of mass, the total mass of the reacting substances is
   - **A.** always more than the total mass of the products.
   - **B.** always less than the total mass of the products.
   - **C.** sometimes more and sometimes less than the total mass of the products.
   - **D.** always equal to the total mass of the products.

2. To balance a chemical equation, you may adjust the
   - **A.** coefficients.
   - **B.** subscripts.
   - **C.** formulas of the products.
   - **D.** either the coefficients or the subscripts.

3. Which is the correct chemical equation for the following formula equation: $(NH_4)_2S \longrightarrow NH_3 + H_2S$?
   - **A.** $2(NH_4)_2S \longrightarrow 2NH_3 + H_2S_2$
   - **B.** $2(NH_4)_2S \longrightarrow 2NH_3 + H_2S$
   - **C.** $(NH_4)_2S \longrightarrow 2NH_3 + H_2S$
   - **D.** None of the above

4. Select the missing reactant(s) for the double-displacement reaction that produces PF_5 and $AsCl_3$.
   - **A.** PCl_5 and AsF_3
   - **B.** PCl_3 and AsF_5
   - **C.** PCl_3 and AsF_3
   - **D.** None of the above

5. Select the missing reactant for the following combustion reaction: 2 _____ $+ 15O_2 \longrightarrow 14CO_2 + 6H_2O$.
   - **A.** $C_{14}H_{12}$
   - **D.** $C_{14}H_{12}O_4$
   - **C.** C_7H_6
   - **D.** $C_7H_6O_2$

6. A mixture consists of Ag, Pb, and Fe metals. Which of these metals will react with $ZnCl_2$?
   - **A.** Ag(*s*)
   - **B.** Pb(*s*)
   - **C.** Fe(*s*)
   - **D.** None of these metals

7. Which of the following statements is true about the reaction $2F_2 + 2H_2O \longrightarrow 4HF + O_2$?
   - **A.** Two grams of O_2 are produced when 2 g F_2 reacts with 2 g H_2O.
   - **B.** Two moles of HF are produced when 1 mol F_2 reacts with 1 mol H_2O.
   - **C.** For every 2 mol O_2 produced, 6 mol HF are produced.
   - **D.** For every 1 mol H_2O that reacts, 2 mol O_2 are produced.

SHORT ANSWER

8. Determine the products and write a balanced equation for the reaction of solid magnesium and water.

9. A precipitation of iron(III) hydroxide is produced by reacting an aqueous solution of iron(III) chloride with an aqueous solution of sodium hydroxide. Write a balanced chemical equation.

EXTENDED RESPONSE

10. List the hypothetical metals A, E, M, and R in increasing order of reactivity by using the reaction data in the table below. The reaction of interest is of the form $C + ZX \longrightarrow CX + Z$. Explain your reasoning.

	AX	EX	MX	RX
A	_____	no reaction	reaction	no reaction
E	reaction	_____	reaction	reaction
M	no reaction	no reaction	_____	no reaction
R	reaction	no reaction	reaction	_____

11. Calcium hypochlorite, $Ca(OCl)_2$, is a bleaching agent produced from sodium hydroxide, calcium hydroxide, and chlorine. Sodium chloride and water are also produced in the reaction. Write the balanced chemical equation. If 2 mol NaOH react, how many moles of calcium hypochlorite can be produced?

Test Tip

Focus on one question at a time unless you are asked to refer to previous answers.

STANDARDS-BASED ASSESSMENT

To give students practice under more realistic testing conditions, give them 60 minutes to answer all of the questions in this Standardized Test Preparation.

Test Answers

1. D
2. A
3. C
4. A
5. D
6. D
7. B
8. $Mg(s) + 2H_2O(l) \longrightarrow Mg(OH)_2(aq) + H_2(g)$
9. $FeCl_3(aq) + 3NaOH(aq) \longrightarrow Fe(OH)_3(s) + 3NaCl(s)$
10. The metals in increasing order of reactivity are M, A, R, and E. M is the least reactive because it does not react with any of the other metals in a single-displacement reaction. A is the next least reactive because it will react in a single-displacement reaction with only M. E is the most reactive metal of the series because E will react in a single-displacement reaction with the other three metals.
11. The balanced chemical equation is $2NaOH + Ca(OH)_2 + 2Cl_2 \longrightarrow Ca(OCl)_2 + 2NaCl + 2H_2O$. If 2 mol NaOH react, then 1 mol $Ca(OCl)_2$ can be produced.

Stoichiometry

① Core Instruction

Chapter Resources

- **The Teacher's Edition wrap has extensive teaching support for every lesson, including Misconception Alerts, Teach from Visuals, Demonstrations, Teaching Tips, Differentiated Instruction, and Problem Solving support.**
- **Several additional presentation tools are available online for every chapter, including Animated Chemistry features and Visual Concepts.**
- **You can open your lesson with the Why It Matters Video: Stoichiometry.**

Section	Instruction	Labs and Demonstrations Go Online for Materials Lists and Solutions Lists.
9.1	**Textbook:** **Introduction to Stoichiometry** **Teaching Visuals:** Converting Between Amounts in Moles • Fuel-Oxygen Ratio • Stoichiometry Calculations • Solving Stoichiometry Problems **Power Presentations**	**Demonstration:** Mass Relationships in Chemical Reactions
9.2	**Textbook:** **Ideal Stoichiometric Calculations** **Teaching Visuals:** Stoichiometry Calculations • Solving Mass-Mass Stoichiometry Problems • Solving Stoichiometry Problems with Moles or Grams • Solving Various Types of Stoichiometry Problems • Solving Mass-Mass Problems • Solving Volume-Volume Problems • Solving Particle Problems • Diffusion **Power Presentations**	
9.3	**Textbook:** **Limiting Reactants and Percentage Yield** **Animated Chemistry:** Limiting Reactants **Teaching Visuals:** Lab Technique: Filtration Setup • Lab Technique: Folding Filter Paper • Solving Stoichiometry Problems **Power Presentations**	**Demonstration:** Limiting Reactant **QuickLab:** Limiting Reactants in a Recipe **Lab:** Stoichiometry and Gravimetric Analysis (Forensics) **Lab:** Stoichiometry (Open Inquiry)

2 Support and Intervention

- **Interactive Reader** (English and Spanish)
- **Study Guide**
- **Interactive Review:** Review Games, Concept Maps, and Section Self-Checks
- **Scientific Reasoning Skill Builder**
- **Learn It! Videos**
- **Solve It! Cards**
- **Interactive Demos**
- **Sample Problem Sets**

3 Specialized Support

- **Chapter Summary Audio Files**
- **Interactive Reader Audio Files**
- **Differentiated Instruction:** Inclusion, Below Level, and English Learners (TE wrap)

Enrichment and Challenge

- **Differentiated Instruction:** Pre-AP (TE wrap)
- **Chemistry Explorers:** The Case of Combustion (SE)
- **WebLinks**

Assessment

- **Section Formative Assessments** (SE)
- **Section Quizzes**
- **Chapter Review** (SE)
- **Chapter Tests A and B**
- **Alternative Assessment** (TE wrap)
- **Online Assessment and Remediation**
- **ExamView Banks**

Where do I find it?

		PRINT	DVD	ONLINE
1	Animated Chemistry		■	■
	Demonstrations (TE wrap)	■		■
	Interactive Whiteboard		■	■
	Labs		■	■
	PowerPresentations		■	■
	QuickLabs	■	■	■
	Teaching Visuals		■	■
	Textbook	■	■	■
	Visual Concepts		■	■
	Why It Matters Videos		■	■
2	Interactive Demos		■	■
	Interactive Reader	■	■	■
	Interactive Reviews		■	■
	Learn It! Videos		■	■
	Sample Problem Sets		■	■
	Scientific Reasoning Skill Builder		■	■
	Smart Grapher Tool		■	■
	Solve It! Cards		■	■
	Study Guide		■	■
3	Chapter Summary Audio Files		■	■
	Differentiated Instruction (TE wrap)	■		
	Interactive Reader Audio Files		■	■

CHAPTER 9

Chapter Overview

Section 1 defines mole ratio and introduces molar mass as a conversion factor in solving stoichiometry problems.

Section 2 demonstrates solutions to problems involving conversions from moles of *given* to moles of *unknown*, from moles to mass, from mass to moles, and from mass to mass.

Section 3 explains the concepts of limiting reactant and percentage yield and provides strategies for solving problems based on these concepts.

▼ Focus and Motivate

Activate Prior Knowledge

Students may need a review of the following concepts:

- coefficients in a chemical reaction
- molar mass
- composition stoichiometry problems

About the Image

The quantities involved in chemical reactions are described using stoichiometry. The term *stoichiometry* comes from the Greek words *stoicheion,* meaning "element," and *metron,* meaning "measure." The image shows the results of the double-replacement reaction between solutions of potassium iodide, KI, and lead nitrate, $Pb(NO_3)_2$:

$2KI(aq) + Pb(NO_3)_2(aq)\ 2KNO_3(aq) + PbI(s)$

Why It Matters

Students can access the video online and find other helpful resources at **HMDScience.com**.

Lab Preview

The following labs and demonstrations support the concepts presented in this chapter.

LABS

Stoichiometry and Gravimetric Analysis (Forensics)

Stoichiometry (Open Inquiry)

QUICKLAB

Limiting Reactants in a Recipe

DEMONSTRATIONS

Mass Relationships in Chemical Reactions

Limiting Reactant

Introduction to Stoichiometry

SECTION 1

Main Idea

Ratios of substances in chemical reactions can be used as conversion factors.

Key Terms

composition stoichiometry
reaction stoichiometry
mole ratio

Much of our knowledge of chemistry is based on the careful quantitative analysis of substances involved in chemical reactions. **Composition stoichiometry deals with the mass relationships of elements in compounds. Reaction stoichiometry involves the mass relationships between reactants and products in a chemical reaction.** Reaction stoichiometry, the subject of this chapter, is based on chemical equations and the law of conservation of mass. All reaction stoichiometry calculations start with a balanced chemical equation. This equation gives the relative numbers of moles of reactants and products.

MAIN IDEA

Ratios of substances in chemical reactions can be used as conversion factors.

The reaction stoichiometry problems in this chapter can be classified according to the information *given* in the problem and the information you are expected to find, the *unknown*. The *given* and the *unknown* may both be reactants, they may both be products, or one may be a reactant and the other a product. The masses are generally expressed in grams, but you will encounter both large-scale and microscale problems with other mass units, such as kg or mg. Stoichiometric problems are solved by using ratios from the balanced equation to convert the given quantity.

Problem Type 1: *Given* and *unknown* quantities are amounts in moles.

When you are given the amount of a substance in moles and asked to calculate the amount in moles of another substance in the chemical reaction, the general plan is

$$\begin{matrix}\text{amount of} \\ \textit{given}\text{ substance (mol)}\end{matrix} \longrightarrow \begin{matrix}\text{amount of} \\ \textit{unknown}\text{ substance (mol)}\end{matrix}$$

Problem Type 2: *Given* is an amount in moles and *unknown* is a mass that is often expressed in grams.

When you are given the amount in moles of one substance and asked to calculate the mass of another substance in the chemical reaction, the general plan is

$$\begin{matrix}\text{amount of} \\ \textit{given}\text{ substance} \\ \text{(mol)}\end{matrix} \longrightarrow \begin{matrix}\text{amount of} \\ \textit{unknown}\text{ substance} \\ \text{(mol)}\end{matrix} \longrightarrow \begin{matrix}\text{mass of} \\ \textit{unknown}\text{ substance} \\ \text{(g)}\end{matrix}$$

Differentiated Instruction

BELOW LEVEL

Review how molar mass is used to convert between the amount of a given substance (moles) and the mass of a substance (grams). Tell students that solving stoichiometry problems requires knowing how to make this conversion. Ask students which Problem Types shown on this page and the next will require using molar mass as a conversion. Students should identify Problem Types 2, 3, and 4.

SECTION 1

Plan and Prepare ▼

Objectives

Upon completion of this section, students should be able to do the following:

- Define *stoichiometry*.
- Describe the importance of the *mole ratio* in stoichio-metric calculations.
- Write a mole ratio relating two substances in a chemical equation.

Classroom Catalyst

Write on the board the equation for the reaction of Mg with HCl.

$$Mg(s) + 2HCl(aq) \longrightarrow MgCl_2(aq) + H_2(g)$$

Use it to help students realize that if they know the amount of one substance in a reaction, they can determine the amounts of all the other substances. Ask how many moles of H_2 are obtained from 2 mol HCl. Ask how many moles of Mg will react with 2 mol HCl. Double the moles of HCl, and ask about the moles of $MgCl_2$ and H_2 that would result. Finally, ask students how they might convert moles of these substances to masses.

Teach ▼

READING TOOLKIT

BRAINSTORMING Write the words *reactants* and *products* on the board. Have students brainstorm a list of measurements that a chemist might want to make in relation to reactants and products. Possible answers include mass and volume. Then have students compare and contrast differences in mass relation-ships of compounds versus those of reactants and products in a chemical reaction.

▼ Teach *continued*

Demonstration

MASS RELATIONSHIPS IN CHEMICAL REACTIONS

Use the reaction of Na_2CO_3 with HCl to trace mass relationships in a reaction and to set the stage for the concepts of limiting reagent and percentage yield.

$$Na_2CO_3(s) + 2HCl(aq) \longrightarrow 2NaCl(aq) + H_2O(l) + CO_2(g)$$

1. Use a **balance** to determine the mass of a **porcelain evaporating dish** to the nearest 0.01 g, and record the mass.
2. Add 1 g of **anhydrous Na_2CO_3**, and record the mass of the dish and salt to the nearest 0.01 g.
3. Use a **dropper** to add **1 M HCl** dropwise until the bubbling stops. Then add a little more HCl to make sure the reaction has gone to completion.
4. In a **fume hood,** place the evaporating dish on a piece of **wire gauze** on a **ring stand** over a **heat source.** Heat the dish until the liquid evaporates to dryness (heat gently to avoid spattering).
5. Record the mass of the dish and dried NaCl to the nearest 0.01 g.
6. Tell students to use the data to calculate the masses of Na_2CO_3 and NaCl.
7. Tell students to use molar mass as a conversion factor to find the moles of Na_2CO_3 and NaCl.
8. Save the results for use in Section 3.

Safety Wear **safety goggles** and a **lab apron.** Students should stand back 10 feet.

Disposal The NaCl may be washed down the drain.

Problem Type 3: *Given* is a mass in grams and *unknown* is an amount in moles.

When you are given the mass of one substance and asked to calculate the amount in moles of another substance in the chemical reaction, the general plan is

mass of *given* substance (g) ⟶ amount of *given* substance (mol) ⟶ amount of *unknown* substance (mol)

Problem Type 4: *Given* is a mass in grams and *unknown* is a mass in grams.

When you are given the mass of one substance and asked to calculate the mass of another substance in the chemical reaction, the general plan is

mass of *given* substance (g) ⟶ amount of *given* substance (mol) ⟶ amount of *unknown* substance (mol) ⟶ mass of *unknown* substance (g)

Mole Ratio

Solving any reaction stoichiometry problem requires the use of a mole ratio to convert from moles or grams of one substance in a reaction to moles or grams of another substance. **A mole ratio is a conversion factor that relates the amounts in moles of any two substances involved in a chemical reaction.** This information is obtained directly from the balanced chemical equation. Consider, for example, the chemical equation for the electrolysis of melted aluminum oxide to produce aluminum and oxygen.

$$2Al_2O_3(l) \longrightarrow 4Al(s) + 3O_2(g)$$

Recall from your study of equations and reactions that the coefficients in a chemical equation satisfy the law of conservation of matter and represent the relative amounts in moles of reactants and products. Therefore, 2 mol of aluminum oxide decompose to produce 4 mol of aluminum and 3 mol of oxygen gas. These relationships can be expressed in the following mole ratios.

$$\frac{2\text{ mol }Al_2O_3}{4\text{ mol Al}} \text{ or } \frac{4\text{ mol Al}}{2\text{ mol }Al_2O_3}$$

$$\frac{2\text{ mol }Al_2O_3}{3\text{ mol }O_2} \text{ or } \frac{3\text{ mol }O_2}{2\text{ mol }Al_2O_3}$$

$$\frac{4\text{ mol Al}}{3\text{ mol }O_2} \text{ or } \frac{3\text{ mol }O_2}{4\text{ mol Al}}$$

For the decomposition of aluminum oxide, the appropriate mole ratio is used as a conversion factor to convert a given amount in moles of one substance to the corresponding amount in moles of another substance.

CAREERS IN CHEMISTRY

Chemical Technician S.T.E.M.

Chemical technicians are highly skilled scientific professionals who bring valuable skills to the development of new products, the processing of materials, the management of hazardous waste, regulatory compliance, and many other aspects of getting products and services to the consumer. Chemical technicians must have a solid background in applied chemistry and mathematics and be highly skilled in laboratory methods. Earning an associate's degree in applied science or chemical technology is one good way to prepare for this career. Many chemical technicians have a bachelor's degree in chemical technology, chemistry, or other sciences.

Differentiated Instruction

BELOW LEVEL

Have students identify a mole ratio between a reactant and a product in the chemical equation given in the Demonstration. Possible answers include 1 mol Na_2CO_3 : 2 mol NaCl and 1 mol HCl : 1 mol NaCl. Be sure that students understand how the 2 : 2 mole ratio in the second example reduces to a 1 : 1 ratio.

To determine the amount in moles of aluminum that can be produced from 13.0 mol of aluminum oxide, the mole ratio needed is that of Al to Al_2O_3.

$$13.0 \text{ mol } Al_2O_3 \times \frac{4 \text{ mol Al}}{2 \text{ mol } Al_2O_3} = 26.0 \text{ mol Al}$$

Mole ratios are exact, so they do not limit the number of significant figures in a calculation. The number of significant figures in the answer is therefore determined only by the number of significant figures of any measured quantities in a particular problem.

Molar Mass

Recall that the molar mass is the mass, in grams, of one mole of a substance. The molar mass is the conversion factor that relates the mass of a substance to the amount in moles of that substance. To solve reaction stoichiometry problems, you will need to determine molar masses using the periodic table.

Returning to the previous example, the decomposition of aluminum oxide, the rounded masses from the periodic table are the following.

$1 \text{ mol } Al_2O_3 = 101.96 \text{ g}$ $\quad 1 \text{ mol Al} = 26.98 \text{ g}$ $\quad 1 \text{ mol } O_2 = 32.00 \text{ g}$

These molar masses can be expressed by the following conversion factors.

$$\frac{101.96 \text{ g } Al_2O_3}{1 \text{ mol } Al_2O_3} \text{ or } \frac{1 \text{ mol } Al_2O_3}{101.96 \text{ g } Al_2O_3}$$

$$\frac{26.98 \text{ g Al}}{1 \text{ mol Al}} \text{ or } \frac{1 \text{ mol Al}}{26.98 \text{ g Al}}$$

$$\frac{32.00 \text{ g } O_2}{1 \text{ mol } O_2} \text{ or } \frac{1 \text{ mol } O_2}{32.00 \text{ g } O_2}$$

To find the number of grams of aluminum equivalent to 26.0 mol of aluminum, the calculation would be as follows.

$$26.0 \text{ mol Al} \times \frac{26.98 \text{ g Al}}{1 \text{ mol Al}} = 701 \text{ g Al}$$

Teaching Tip

Have students explain why the second conversion factor shown for Al (1 mol Al / 26.98 g Al) cannot be used to find the number of grams of aluminum in the solution shown at the bottom of this page. Students should recognize that this conversion factor would not allow for the canceling of mol units to give an answer in g.

Assess and Reteach

Assess Use the Formative Assessment on this page to evaluate student mastery of the section.

Reteach For students who need additional instruction, download the Section Study Guide.

Response to Intervention To reassess students' mastery, use the Section Quiz, available to print or to take directly online at **HMDScience.com**.

SECTION 1 FORMATIVE ASSESSMENT

Reviewing Main Ideas

1. What is stoichiometry?
2. For each equation, write all possible mole ratios.
   a. $2HgO(s) \longrightarrow 2Hg(l) + O_2(g)$
   b. $4NH_3(g) + 6NO(g) \longrightarrow 5N_2(g) + 6H_2O(l)$
3. How is a mole ratio used in stoichiometry?

Critical Thinking

4. **RELATING IDEAS** What step must be performed before any stoichiometry problem is solved? Explain.

Answers to Section Assessment

1. the branch of chemistry that deals with the mass relationships of elements in compounds and the mass relationships between reactants and products in a chemical reaction
2. a. $\frac{2 \text{ mol HgO}}{2 \text{ mol Hg}}, \frac{2 \text{ mol HgO}}{1 \text{ mol } O_2}$, $\frac{2 \text{ mol Hg}}{2 \text{ mol HgO}}, \frac{2 \text{ mol Hg}}{1 \text{ mol } O_2}$, $\frac{1 \text{ mol } O_2}{2 \text{ mol HgO}}, \frac{1 \text{ mol } O_2}{2 \text{ mol Hg}}$

   b. $\frac{4 \text{ mol } NH_3}{6 \text{ mol NO}}, \frac{4 \text{ mol } NH_3}{5 \text{ mol } N_2}, \frac{4 \text{ mol } NH_3}{6 \text{ mol } H_2O}$, $\frac{6 \text{ mol NO}}{4 \text{ mol } NH_3}, \frac{6 \text{ mol NO}}{5 \text{ mol } N_2}, \frac{6 \text{ mol NO}}{6 \text{ mol } H_2O}$, $\frac{5 \text{ mol } N_2}{6 \text{ mol } H_2O}, \frac{5 \text{ mol } N_2}{6 \text{ mol NO}}, \frac{5 \text{ mol } N_2}{4 \text{ mol } NH_3}$, $\frac{6 \text{ mol } H_2O}{5 \text{ mol } N_2}, \frac{6 \text{ mol } H_2O}{6 \text{ mol NO}}, \frac{6 \text{ mol } H_2O}{4 \text{ mol } NH_3}$
3. A mole ratio is used to convert moles of one substance to moles of another substance.
4. The equation must be balanced. The coefficients of the balanced equation are necessary to relate the amount of one substance to another.

Teaching Strategy

Ask students to try to forget everything they know about combustion. Tell them that all they know about burning is what they can observe qualitatively. Then, have them read the feature and prepare to discuss it. Some suggested topics follow. Brief summaries of the topics are on the next page.

Classroom Discussion

1. A theory is useful as long as it can help explain new scientific evidence. Have students describe how the phlogiston theory was at first supported by new findings but later abandoned in favor of a new theory.
2. Have students describe what Rutherford named "phlogisticated air" and what Priestley called "dephlogisticated air."
3. Discuss the results of the experiment that Daniel Rutherford performed in 1772 in terms of what is known today.
4. Lavoisier burned a known mass of tin in a closed container. When he opened the container, he observed that air rushed in and that the tin had increased in mass. Discuss how this finding was critical in destroying the phlogiston theory.
5. Do you suppose that the new theory proposed by Lavoisier was immediately adopted by other scientists? Why or why not?

ChemisTrivia

Lavoisier's talented wife, Marie, assisted her husband with his research. She made drawings of apparatus for publications and translated chemical works from English into French for him.

Chemistry EXPLORERS

The Case of Combustion

People throughout history have transformed substances by burning them in air. Yet at the dawn of the scientific revolution, very little was known about the process of combustion. In attempting to explain this common phenomenon, chemists of the 18th century developed one of the first universally accepted theories in their field. But as one man would show, scientific theories do not always stand the test of time.

Changing Attitudes

Shunning the ancient Greek approach of logical argument based on untested premises, investigators of the 17th century began to understand the laws of nature by observing, measuring, and performing experiments on the world around them. However, this scientific method was incorporated into chemistry slowly. Although early chemists experimented extensively, most considered measurement to be unimportant. This viewpoint hindered the progress of chemistry for nearly a century.

A Flawed Theory

By 1700, combustion was assumed to be the decomposition of a material into simpler substances. People saw burning substances emitting smoke and energy as heat and light. To account for this emission, scientists proposed a theory that combustion depended on the emission of a substance called *phlogiston* (Greek, meaning "burned"), which appeared as a combination of energy as heat and light while the material was burning but which could not be detected beforehand.

The phlogiston theory was used to explain many chemical observations of the day. For example, a lit candle under a glass jar burned until the surrounding air became saturated with phlogiston, at which time the flame died because the air inside could not absorb more phlogiston.

A New Phase of Study

By the 1770s, the phlogiston theory had gained universal acceptance. At that time, chemists also began to experiment with air, which was generally believed to be an element.

Antoine Laurent Lavoisier helped establish chemistry as a science.

In 1772, when Daniel Rutherford found that a mouse kept in a closed container soon died, he explained the results based on the phlogiston theory. Like a burning candle, the mouse emitted phlogiston; when the air could hold no more phlogiston, the mouse died. Thus, Rutherford figured that the air in the container had become "phlogisticated air."

A couple of years later, Joseph Priestley obtained a reddish powder when he heated mercury in the air. He assumed that the powder was mercury devoid of phlogiston. But when he heated the powder, an unexpected result occurred: Metallic mercury, along with a gas that allowed a candle to burn, formed. Following the phlogiston theory, he believed this gas that supports combustion to be "dephlogisticated air."

Nice Try, But . . .

Antoine Laurent Lavoisier was a meticulous scientist. He realized that Rutherford and Priestley had carefully observed and described their experiments but had not measured the mass of anything. Unlike his colleagues, Lavoisier knew the importance of using a balance. He measured the masses of reactants and products and compared them. He observed that the total mass of the reactants equaled the total mass of the products. Based on these observations, which supported what would become known as the *law of conservation of mass*, Lavoisier endeavored to explain the results of Rutherford and Priestley.

Lavoisier put some tin in a closed vessel and weighed the entire system. He then burned the tin. When he opened the vessel, air rushed into it as if something had been *removed* from the air in the vessel during combustion. He then measured the mass of the burned metal and observed that this mass was greater than the mass of the original tin. Curiously, this increase in mass equaled the mass of the air that had rushed into the vessel. To Lavoisier, this change in mass did not support the idea of phlogiston escaping the burning material. Instead, it indicated that during combustion, part of the air reacted with the tin.

TABLE OF SIMPLE SUBSTANCES

Simple substances belonging to all the kingdoms of nature, which may be considered as the elements of bodies.

New Names	*Correspondent old Names*
Light - - -	*Light.*
Caloric - - -	*Heat. Principle or element of heat. Fire. Igneous fluid. Matter of fire and of heat.*
Oxygen - - -	*Dephlogisticated air. Empyreal air. Vital air, or Base of vital air.*
Azote - - -	*Phlogisticated air or gas. Mephitis, or its base.*
Hydrogen - -	*Inflammable air or gas, or the base of inflammable air.*

Lavoisier's concept of simple substances was published in his book **Elements of Chemistry** ***in 1789.***

After obtaining similar results by using various substances, Lavoisier concluded that air was not an element but a mixture composed principally of two gases, Priestley's "dephlogisticated air" (which Lavoisier renamed *oxygen*) and Rutherford's "phlogisticated air" (which was mostly nitrogen but had traces of other nonflammable atmospheric gases). When a substance burned, it chemically combined with oxygen, resulting in a product Lavoisier named an *oxide*. Lavoisier's theory of combustion persists today. He used the name *oxygen* because he thought that all acids contained oxygen. *Oxygen* means "acid former."

The Father of Chemistry

By emphasizing the importance of quantitative analysis, Lavoisier helped establish chemistry as a science. His work on combustion laid to rest the phlogiston theory and the theory that air is an element. He also explained why hydrogen burned in oxygen to form water, or hydrogen oxide. He later published one of the first chemistry textbooks, which established a common naming system of compounds and elements and helped unify chemistry worldwide. These accomplishments earned Lavoisier the reputation of being the father of chemistry.

Questions

1. Why does the mass of tin increase when tin is heated in air?
2. What was the composition of Priestley's "dephlogisticated air" and Rutherford's "phlogisticated air"?

Discussion Points

1. The phlogiston theory explained combustion and respiration. When Priestley could not explain his experimental results, he expanded the phlogiston theory to include dephlogisticated air. The quantitative experiments of Lavoisier showed that another interpretation of the evidence was more likely to explain combustion and respiration correctly.
2. "Phlogisticated air" is air from which oxygen has been removed. "Dephlogisticated air" is oxygen.
3. The mouse used up all of the oxygen and added CO_2 to the container.
4. According to the phlogiston theory, when a substance burns, it loses phlogiston to the air. The gain in mass of the burned tin and the presence of a partial vacuum are effects opposite those predicted by the phlogiston theory.
5. A well-established theory is not easily abandoned. It is natural for scientists to hang onto a theory until the evidence accumulated against it is overwhelming and verifiable.

Answers

1. Tin(IV) oxide, SnO_2, forms. The mass of the resulting tin(IV) oxide is equal to the original mass of the tin plus the mass of the oxygen with which the tin combined.
2. "Dephlogisticated air" is oxygen, and "phlogisticated air" is mostly nitrogen.

SECTION 2

▼ Plan and Prepare

Objectives

Upon completion of this section, students should be able to do the following:

- Calculate the amount in moles of a reactant or product from the amount in moles of a different reactant or product.
- Calculate the mass of a reactant or product from the amount in moles of a different reactant or product.
- Calculate the amount in moles of a reactant or product from the mass of a different reactant or product.
- Calculate the mass of a reactant or product from the mass of a different reactant or product.

Classroom Catalyst

Try this demonstration to relate moles of an acid to moles of base.

1. Set up **two burets,** one with 25–50 mL of **0.1 M NaOH** and the other with 25–50 mL of **0.1 M HCl.** Record the initial volumes of both solutions.
2. Let about 20 mL of acid flow from the HCl buret into a **125 mL Erlenmeyer flask.** Add a few drops of **phenolphthalein** to the flask.
3. Swirl the HCl flask while adding NaOH solution from the buret. Continue to add NaOH until the red color of phenolphthalein indicates that the neutralization reaction is complete.
4. Record the final volumes of both HCl and NaOH. Calculate each volume.
5. Compare the volumes of the two solutions. This determines the number of moles of acid in a solution when the number of moles of base are known. If the number of moles of acid in solution are known, the unknown number of moles of base can be determined.
6. Ask students to write an equation for the reaction of HCl and NaOH and write the mole ratio of HCl to NaOH.

Safety Wear **safety goggles** and a **lab apron.** Students should remain back at least 10 feet.

Disposal Combine liquids, adjust pH to 5–9, and pour down the drain.

SECTION 2

Main Ideas

- Balanced equations give amounts of reactants and products under ideal conditions.
- Mole-to-gram calculations require two conversion factors.
- Gram-to-mole conversions require the molar mass of the given substance and the mole ratio.
- Mass-to-mass calculations use the mole ratio and the molar masses of the given and unknown substances.

Ideal Stoichiometric Calculations

A balanced chemical equation is the key step in all stoichiometric calculations, because the mole ratio is obtained directly from it. Solving any reaction stoichiometry problem must begin with a balanced equation.

Chemical equations help us plan the amounts of reactants to use in a chemical reaction without having to run the reaction in the laboratory. The reaction stoichiometry calculations described in this chapter are theoretical. They tell us the amounts of reactants and products for a given chemical reaction under *ideal conditions*, in which all reactants are completely converted into products. However, many reactions do not proceed such that all reactants are completely converted into products. Theoretical stoichiometric calculations allow us to determine the maximum amount of product that could be obtained in a reaction when the reactants are not pure or when by-products are formed in addition to the expected products.

Solving stoichiometric problems requires practice. Practice by working the sample problems in the rest of this chapter. Using a logical, systematic approach will help you successfully solve these problems.

MAIN IDEA

Balanced equations give amounts of reactants and products under ideal conditions.

In these stoichiometric problems, you are asked to calculate the amount in moles of one substance that will react with or be produced from the given amount in moles of another substance. The plan for a simple mole conversion problem is

$$\text{amount of } \textit{given} \text{ substance (mol)} \longrightarrow \text{amount of } \textit{unknown} \text{ substance (mol)}$$

This plan requires one conversion factor—the stoichiometric mole ratio of the *unknown* substance to the *given* substance from the balanced equation. To solve this type of problem, simply multiply the *known* quantity by the appropriate conversion factor (see **Figure 2.1**).

$$\textit{given} \text{ quantity} \times \text{conversion factor} = \textit{unknown} \text{ quantity}$$

FIGURE 2.1

Mole-to-Mole Conversions This is a solution plan for problems in which the given and unknown quantities are expressed in moles.

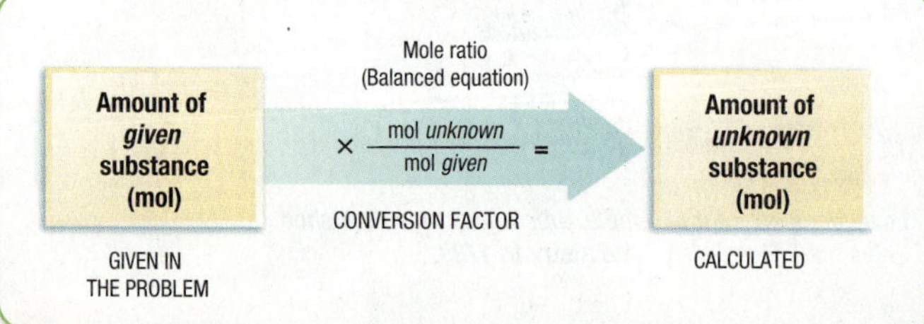

Differentiated Instruction

BELOW LEVEL

Ask students why a conversion factor is not used when converting the amount of a given substance to the amount of an unknown substance as shown on this page. Students should recognize that there is no need for a conversion factor because the mole (mol) is the unit for both substances. Emphasize that a conversion factor is required only when the unit in the known quantity is not the same as the unit in the unknown quantity.

Stoichiometric Calculations Using Mole Ratios

Sample Problem A **In a spacecraft, the carbon dioxide exhaled by astronauts can be removed by its reaction with lithium hydroxide, LiOH, according to the following chemical equation.**

$$CO_2(g) + 2LiOH(s) \longrightarrow Li_2CO_3(s) + H_2O(l)$$

How many moles of lithium hydroxide are required to react with 20 mol CO_2, the average amount exhaled by a person each day?

1 ANALYZE

Given: amount of CO_2 = 20 mol

Unknown: amount of LiOH (mol)

2 PLAN

amount of CO_2 (mol) ⟶ amount of LiOH (mol)

This problem requires one conversion factor—the mole ratio of LiOH to CO_2. The mole ratio is obtained from the balanced chemical equation. Because you are given moles of CO_2, select a mole ratio that will cancel mol CO_2 and give you mol LiOH in your final answer. The correct ratio has the following units.

$$\frac{\text{mol LiOH}}{\text{mol } CO_2}$$

This ratio cancels mol CO_2 and gives the units mol LiOH in the answer.

$$\text{mol } CO_2 \times \overbrace{\frac{\text{mol LiOH}}{\text{mol } CO_2}}^{\text{mol ratio}} = \text{mol LiOH}$$

3 SOLVE

Substitute the values in the equation in step 2, and compute the answer.

$$20 \text{ mol } CO_2 \times \frac{2 \text{ mol LiOH}}{1 \text{ mol } CO_2} = 40 \text{ mol LiOH}$$

4 CHECK YOUR WORK

The answer is written correctly with one significant figure to match the number of significant figures in the given 20 mol CO_2, and the units cancel to leave mol LiOH, which is the unknown. The balanced equation shows that twice the amount in moles of LiOH reacts with CO_2. Therefore, the answer should be 2 × 20 = 40.

Practice Answers in Appendix E

1. Ammonia, NH_3, is widely used as a fertilizer and as an ingredient in many household cleaners. How many moles of ammonia are produced when 6 mol of hydrogen gas react with an excess of nitrogen gas?
2. The decomposition of potassium chlorate, $KClO_3$, into KCl and O_2 is used as a source of oxygen in the laboratory. How many moles of potassium chlorate are needed to produce 15 mol of oxygen gas?

TEACH FROM VISUALS

FIGURE 2.1 This diagram is one of a series of visual models students can use when comparing the solution steps for the different problem types. Your teaching models may vary, but it is important that students see how similar these problem types are.

Teaching Tip

Do not underestimate the difficulties some students may have in understanding problem statements. Focus on analyzing problem statements as an important problem-solving technique. You may find it helpful to have students write down what is *given* and what is *unknown* before they begin a problem.

Classroom Practice

A-1 The elements lithium and oxygen react explosively to form lithium oxide, Li_2O. How many moles of lithium oxide will form if 2 mol of lithium react?

Answer: 1 mol Li_2O

A-2 The disinfectant hydrogen peroxide, H_2O_2, decomposes to form water and oxygen gas. How many moles of O_2 will result from the decomposition of 5 mol of hydrogen peroxide?

Answer: 2.5 mol O_2

Problem Solving

DECONSTRUCTING PROBLEMS

Write the following equation on the board.

$CO_2(g) + LiOH(s) \longrightarrow Li_2CO_3(s) + H_2O(l)$

Have students compare this equation to the one in Sample Problem A. Ask them to explain why the problem cannot be solved using the equation you placed on the board. Students must recognize that stoichiometry problems can be solved only from balanced equations.

▼ Teach *continued*

Answers

Practice A

1. 4 mol NH_3
2. 10. mol $KClO_3$

ChemisTrivia

Joseph Black (1728–1799) and his student Daniel Rutherford studied the redistribution of mass during the course of this reaction and its reverse: $CaCO_3(s) \longleftrightarrow CaO(s)$ and $CO_2(g)$. Their quantified findings laid the groundwork for modern stoichiometry.

TEACH FROM VISUALS

FIGURE 2.2 Have students set up a calculation scheme to show the units of each term and then cancel them to produce the result in grams.

Teaching Tip

Remind the students that the chemical equation must *always* be balanced before starting to work a reaction stoichiometry problem. This balanced equation gives the mole ratio between the *given* substance and the *unknown* substance that will always be required.

If the mass of the *unknown* is to be calculated in grams, then the molar mass of the unknown must be known.

Check for Understanding

Answer: A sample answer might be the following: A chemist requiring a specific amount of product for a given task would need to calculate how much reactant is needed to produce that amount of product.

MAIN IDEA

Mole-to-gram calculations require two conversion factors.

In these stoichiometric calculations, you are asked to calculate the mass (usually in grams) of a substance that will react with or be produced from a given amount in moles of a second substance. The plan for these mole-to-gram conversions is

amount of *given* substance (mol)	⟶	amount of *unknown* substance (mol)	⟶	mass of *unknown* substance (g)

This plan requires two conversion factors—the mole ratio of the *unknown* substance to the *given* substance and the molar mass of the *unknown* substance for the mass conversion. To solve this kind of problem, you simply multiply the known quantity, which is the amount in moles, by the appropriate conversion factors (see **Figure 2.2** on the next page).

CHECK FOR UNDERSTANDING

Explain Why might it be important for a chemist to be able to calculate, in advance, how much product a chemical reaction would yield?

Stoichiometric Calculations Using Mole Ratios

Sample Problem B **In photosynthesis, plants use energy from the sun to produce glucose, $C_6H_{12}O_6$, and oxygen from the reaction of carbon dioxide and water. What mass, in grams, of glucose is produced when 3.00 mol of water react with carbon dioxide?**

1 ANALYZE

Given: amount of H_2O = 3.00 mol

Unknown: mass of $C_6H_{12}O_6$ produced (g)

2 PLAN

You must start with a balanced equation.

$$6CO_2(g) + 6H_2O(l) \longrightarrow C_6H_{12}O_6(s) + 6O_2(g)$$

Given the amount in mol of H_2O, you need to get the mass of $C_6H_{12}O_6$ in grams. Two conversion factors are needed—the mole ratio of $C_6H_{12}O_6$ to H_2O and the molar mass of $C_6H_{12}O_6$.

$$\text{mol } H_2O \times \underbrace{\frac{\text{mol } C_6H_{12}O_6}{\text{mol } H_2O}}_{\text{mol ratio}} \times \underbrace{\frac{\text{g } C_6H_{12}O_6}{\text{mol } C_6H_{12}O_6}}_{\text{molar mass factor}} = \text{g } C_6H_{12}O_6$$

3 SOLVE

Use the periodic table to compute the molar mass of $C_6H_{12}O_6$.

$$C_6H_{12}O_6 = 180.18 \text{ g/mol}$$

$$3.00 \text{ mol } H_2O \times \frac{1 \text{ mol } C_6H_{12}O_6}{6 \text{ mol } H_2O} \times \frac{180.18 \text{ g } C_6H_{12}O_6}{1 \text{ mol } C_6H_{12}O_6} = 90.1 \text{ g } C_6H_{12}O_6$$

4 CHECK YOUR WORK

The answer is correctly rounded to three significant figures, to match those in 3.00 mol H_2O. The units cancel in the problem, leaving g $C_6H_{12}O_6$ as the units for the answer, which matches the unknown. The answer is reasonable because it is one-half of 180.

Problem Solving

DECONSTRUCTING PROBLEMS

When solving a stoichiometry problem, students should start by identifying the reactants and products. Point out that they should look for key words such as *produce*, as this word will indicate what the products are. In Sample Problem B, they can start by combining both a word equation and the chemical formula for glucose that is given.

carbon dioxide + water $\longrightarrow C_6H_{12}O_6$ + oxygen

Students can then replace the words with the correct chemical formulas before balancing the equation as shown on the next page.

$CO_2 + H_2O \longrightarrow C_6H_{12}O_6 + O_2$

FIGURE 2.2

Mole-to-Gram Conversions This is a solution plan for problems in which the given quantity is expressed in moles, and the unknown quantity is expressed in grams.

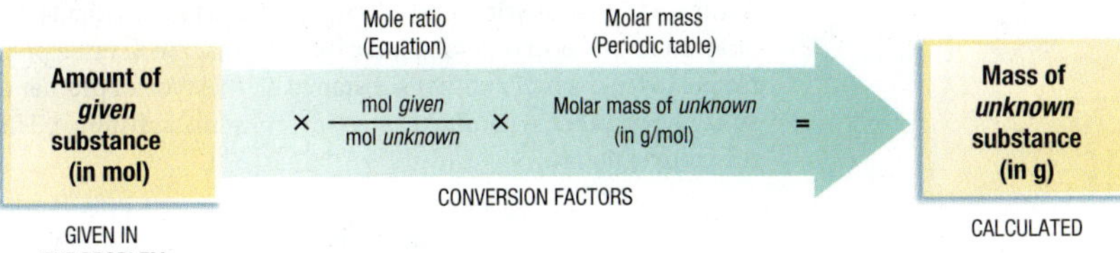

Stoichiometric Calculations Using Mole Ratios

Sample Problem C What mass of carbon dioxide, in grams, is needed to react with 3.00 mol H_2O in the photosynthetic reaction described in Sample Problem B?

1 ANALYZE

Given: amount of $H_2O = 3.00$ mol

Unknown: mass of CO_2 (g)

2 PLAN

The chemical equation from Sample Problem B is

$$6CO_2(g) + 6H_2O(l) \longrightarrow C_6H_{12}O_6(s) + 6O_2(g).$$

Two conversion factors are needed—the mole ratio of CO_2 to H_2O and the molar mass factor of CO_2.

3 SOLVE

$$\text{mol } H_2O \times \underbrace{\frac{\text{mol } CO_2}{\text{mol } H_2O}}_{\text{mol ratio}} \times \underbrace{\frac{\text{g } CO_2}{\text{mol } CO_2}}_{\text{molar mass factor}} = \text{g } CO_2$$

Use the periodic table to compute the molar mass of CO_2.

$CO_2 = 44.01$ g/mol

4 CHECK YOUR WORK

$$3.00 \text{ mol } H_2O \times \frac{6 \text{ mol } CO_2}{6 \text{ mol } H_2O} \times \frac{44.01 \text{ g } CO_2}{1 \text{ mol } CO_2} = 132 \text{ g } CO_2$$

The answer is rounded correctly to three significant figures to match those in 3.00 mol H_2O. The units cancel to leave g CO_2, which is the unknown. The answer is close to an estimate of 120, which is 3 × 40.

Practice Answers in Appendix E

1. When magnesium burns in air, it combines with oxygen to form magnesium oxide according to the following equation.

$$2Mg(s) + O_2(g) \longrightarrow 2MgO(s)$$

What mass in grams of magnesium oxide is produced from 2.00 mol of magnesium?

2. What mass of glucose can be produced from a photosynthesis reaction that occurs using 10 mol CO_2?

$$6CO_2(g) + 6H_2O(l) \longrightarrow C_6H_{12}O_6(aq) + 6O_2(g)$$

ALTERNATIVE APPROACHES

Point out that Sample Problems B and C use two conversion factors in a single step to convert mol to g. If students have difficulty setting up two conversion factors within a single mathematical manipulation, they can use two steps. For example, in Sample Problem C, students can first calculate the mol CO_2 produced from 3.00 mol H_2O. 3 mol CO_2 In the next step, students can use the molar mass conversion factor to convert the 3 mol CO_2 to the mass (g) of CO_2 produced.

Classroom Practice

B-1 When sodium azide is activated in an automobile airbag, nitrogen gas and sodium are produced according to the following equation:

$2NaN_3(s) \longrightarrow 2Na(s) + 3N_2(g)$

If 0.500 mol NaN_3 react, what mass in grams of nitrogen would result?

Answer: 21.0 g N_2

B-2 Carborundum, SiC, is a hard substance made by combining silicon dioxide with coke (C) as follows:

$SiO_2(s) + 3C(s) \longrightarrow SiC(s) + 2CO(g)$

What mass in grams of SiC is formed from the complete reaction of 2.00 mol of carbon?

Answer: 26.7 g SiC

C-1 Coal can be converted to methane gas by a process called coal gasification. The equation for the reaction is the following:

$2C(s) + 2H_2O(l) \longrightarrow CH_4(g) + CO_2(g)$

What mass in grams of carbon is required to react with water to form 1.00 mol CH_4?

Answer: 24.0 g C

C-2 Sulfur dioxide, SO_2, is an unwelcome result of burning soft coal in power plants. Some of the SO_2 ends up as sulfuric acid in acid rain. The net reaction is as follows:

$2SO_2(g) + O_2(g) + 2H_2O(l) \longrightarrow 2H_2SO_4(l)$

What mass in grams of SO_2 is needed to react with 37.50 mol O_2?

Answer: 4805 g SO_2

Answers

Practice C

1. 80.6 g MgO
2. 300 g $C_6H_{12}O_6$

▼ Teach *continued*

TEACH FROM VISUALS

FIGURE 2.3 Have students set up a generic calculation scheme showing the units of each term and cancel them to produce the result in moles.

Misconception Alert!

Some students use their calculators inefficiently when they have numbers that are multiplied in the denominator of fractions. For example, a student might calculate the problem

$$\frac{62 \times 70}{15 \times 35}$$

by dividing the product of the numerator by the product of the denominator. This requires that the products be written down. Show students that a number in the numerator is multiplied, and a number in the denominator is divided. The problem then becomes a single process of pressing the keys: 62 × 70 divided by 15 divided by 35 = 8.3

Teaching Tip

The text labels the factor used to convert from grams to moles as the *inverted molar mass*. If the mass of the *given* substance is known in grams, then the molar mass of the given substance must be known.

MAIN IDEA

Gram-to-mole conversions require the molar mass of the given substance and the mole ratio.

In these stoichiometric calculations, you are asked to calculate the amount in moles of one substance that will react with or be produced from a given mass of another substance. In this type of problem, you are starting with a mass (probably in grams) of some substance. The plan for this conversion is

mass of *given* substance (g)	⟶	amount of *given* substance (mol)	⟶	amount of *unknown* substance (mol)

This route requires two additional pieces of data: the molar mass of the *given* substance and the mole ratio. The molar mass is determined by using masses from the periodic table. We will follow a procedure much like the one used previously by using the units of the molar mass conversion factor to guide our mathematical operations. Because the known quantity is a mass, the conversion factor will need to be 1 mol divided by molar mass. This conversion factor cancels units of grams and leaves units of moles (see **Figure 2.3** below).

You should take time at this point to look at each type of stoichiometric conversion and make note that in every type, you must begin with a correctly balanced chemical equation. It is important to remember that without a balanced equation, you will not have an accurate molar ratio and will not be able to calculate the correct molar mass to use in your conversions.

If you are still struggling with balancing equations, it is highly recommended that you continue to practice the process. The skill of balancing chemical equations will be used continuously throughout the remainder of the course.

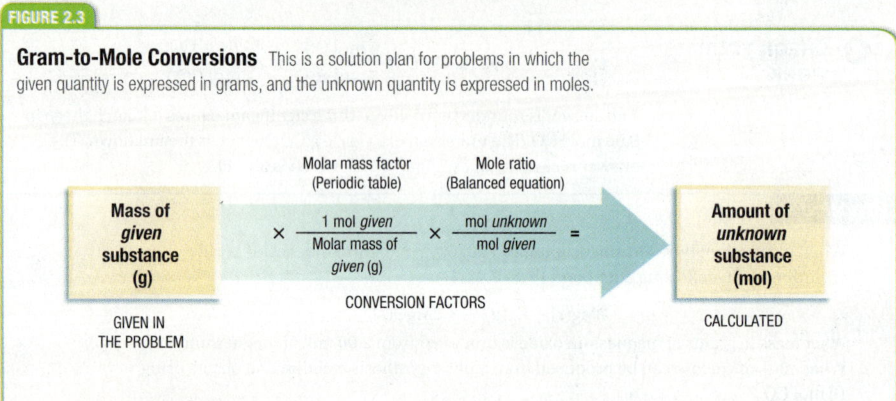

FIGURE 2.3

Gram-to-Mole Conversions This is a solution plan for problems in which the given quantity is expressed in grams, and the unknown quantity is expressed in moles.

Differentiated Instruction

BELOW LEVEL

Have students compare and contrast **Figure 2.2** and **Figure 2.3**. Students should recognize that the conversions are being reversed. In **Figure 2.2**, amount is converted to mass. In **Figure 2.3**, mass is converted to amount. Students will use the same concepts but must be aware of how to set up the conversion factors so that the units cancel correctly.

PREMIUM CONTENT

Learn It! Video
HMDScience.com

Solve It! Cards
HMDScience.com

Stoichiometric Calculations Using Mole Ratios

Sample Problem D **The first step in the industrial manufacture of nitric acid is the catalytic oxidation of ammonia.**

$$NH_3(g) + O_2(g) \longrightarrow NO(g) + H_2O(g) \text{ (unbalanced)}$$

The reaction is run using 824 g NH_3 and excess oxygen.

a. How many moles of NO are formed?

b. How many moles of H_2O are formed?

1 ANALYZE

Given: mass of NH_3 = 824 g

Unknown: **a.** amount of NO produced (mol)

b. amount of H_2O produced (mol)

2 PLAN

First, write the balanced chemical equation.

$$4NH_3(g) + 5O_2(g) \longrightarrow 4NO(g) + 6H_2O(g)$$

Two conversion factors are needed to solve part (a)—the molar mass factor for NH_3 and the mole ratio of NO to NH_3. Part (b) starts with the same conversion factor as part (a), but then the mole ratio of H_2O to NH_3 is used to convert to the amount in moles of H_2O. The first conversion factor in each part is the molar mass factor of NH_3.

$$\textbf{a. } g\ NH_3 \times \underset{\text{molar mass factor}}{\frac{1\ mol\ NH_3}{g\ NH_3}} \times \underset{\text{mol ratio}}{\frac{mol\ NO}{mol\ NH_3}} = mol\ NO$$

$$\textbf{b. } g\ NH_3 \times \underset{\text{molar mass factor}}{\frac{1\ mol\ NH_3}{g\ NH_3}} \times \underset{\text{mol ratio}}{\frac{mol\ H_2O}{mol\ NH_3}} = mol\ H_2O$$

3 SOLVE

Use the periodic table to compute the molar mass of NH_3.

$$1\ mol\ NH_3 = 17.04\ g/mol$$

$$\textbf{a. } 824\ \cancel{g\ NH_3} \times \frac{1\ \cancel{mol\ NH_3}}{17.04\ \cancel{g\ NH_3}} \times \frac{4\ mol\ NO}{4\ \cancel{mol\ NH_3}} = 48.4\ mol\ NO$$

$$\textbf{b. } 824\ \cancel{g\ NH_3} \times \frac{1\ \cancel{mol\ NH_3}}{17.04\ \cancel{g\ NH_3}} \times \frac{6\ mol\ H_2O}{4\ \cancel{mol\ NH_3}} = 72.5\ mol\ H_2O$$

4 CHECK YOUR WORK

The answers are correctly given to three significant figures. The units cancel in the two problems to leave mol NO and mol H_2O, respectively, which are the unknowns.

Practice Answers in Appendix E

Oxygen was discovered by Joseph Priestley in 1774 when he heated mercury(II) oxide to decompose it to form its constituent elements.

1. How many moles of mercury(II) oxide, HgO, are needed to produce 125 g of oxygen, O_2?
2. How many moles of mercury are produced?

Problem Solving

TAKE IT FURTHER

Sample Problem D states that an excess of oxygen is used. Have students explain what would happen if this reaction occurred in a situation where oxygen was not present in excess. Students should recognize that not all of the ammonia may react. Have students check was is meant by the term *limiting reagent*. The concept of limiting reactant is explained in the last section of this chapter.

Classroom Practice

D-1 Chlorine gas can be produced commercially by passing an electric current through a concentrated solution of sodium chloride (brine). The equation is as follows:

$$2NaCl(aq) + 2H_2O(l) \longrightarrow 2NaOH(aq) + Cl_2(g) + H_2(g)$$

a. If the brine contains 250 g NaCl, how many moles of Cl_2 can be produced?

b. How many moles of H_2 can be produced?

Answers:

a. 2.14 mol Cl_2

b. 2.14 mol H_2

D-2 The compound $PtCl_2(NH_3)_2$ is effective as a treatment for some cancers. It is synthesized by the reaction shown in the following equation.

$$K_2PtCl_4(aq) + 2NH_3(aq) \longrightarrow 2KCl(aq) + PtCl_2(NH_3)_2(aq)$$

a. How many moles of K_2PtCl_4 must react in order to produce 30.0 g $PtCl_2(NH_3)_2$?

b. How many moles of NH_3 are needed to produce 30.0 g $PtCl_2(NH_3)_2$?

Answers:

a. 0.100 mol K_2PtCl_4

b. 0.200 mol NH_3

Answers

Practice D

1. 7.81 mol HgO
2. 7.81 mol Hg

Stoichiometry 293

▼ Teach *continued*

Teaching Tip

The sum of the masses on the reactant side of an equation must equal the sum of the masses on the product side. Encourage students to use this fact as a verification strategy to determine if a problem is correctly solved.

TEACH FROM VISUALS

FIGURE 2.4 Again have students verify the process by means of a unit analysis, and encourage them to return to this figure and **Figures 2.2** and **2.3** whenever they are in doubt about how to proceed with a problem.

Alternative Assessment

Ask students to determine the mass in grams of sodium to add to 50 g of fluorine to make sodium fluoride, a substance that is added to drinking water to help stop tooth decay. Students should first work without calculators (estimate answers) and proceed according to the methods described in the sample problems. Provide these values as molar masses: Na = 23 g/mol, F = 19 g/mol.

Expected solution:

$2Na + F_2 \longrightarrow 2NaF$

$$50.\ g\ F_2 \times \frac{1\ mol\ F_2}{38\ g\ F_2} \times \frac{2\ mol\ Na}{1\ mol\ F_2} \times \frac{23\ g\ Na}{1\ mol\ Na} = 61\ g\ Na$$

FIGURE 2.4

Mass-to-Mass Conversions This is a solution plan for problems in which the given quantity is expressed in grams, and the unknown quantity is also expressed in grams.

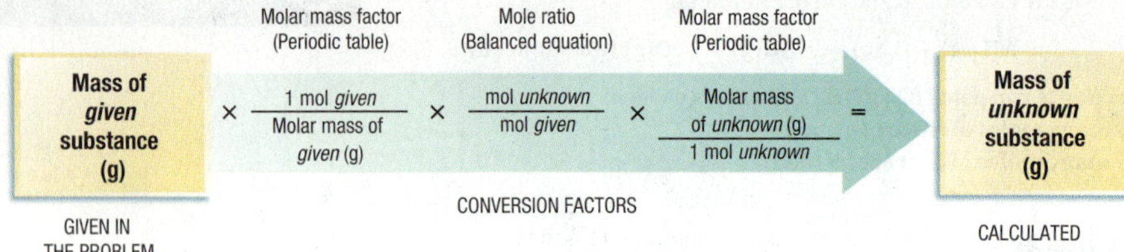

MAIN IDEA

Mass-to-mass calculations use the mole ratio and the molar masses of the given and unknown substances.

Mass-mass calculations are more practical than other mole calculations you have studied. You can never measure moles directly. You are generally required to calculate the amount in moles of a substance from its mass, which you can measure in the lab. Mass-mass problems can be viewed as the combination of the other types of problems. The plan for solving mass-mass problems is

$$\text{mass of } \textit{given} \text{ substance (g)} \longrightarrow \text{amount of } \textit{given} \text{ substance (mol)} \longrightarrow \text{amount of } \textit{unknown} \text{ substance (mol)} \longrightarrow \text{mass of } \textit{unknown} \text{ substance (g)}$$

Three additional pieces of data are needed to solve mass-mass problems: the molar mass of the *given* substance, the mole ratio, and the molar mass of the *unknown* substance (see **Figure 2.4** above).

Stoichiometric Calculations Using Mole Ratios

Sample Problem E **Tin(II) fluoride, SnF_2, is used in some toothpastes. It is made by the reaction of tin with hydrogen fluoride according to the following equation.**

$$Sn(s) + 2HF(g) \longrightarrow SnF_2(s) + H_2(g)$$

How many grams of SnF_2 are produced from the reaction of 30.00 g HF with Sn?

1 ANALYZE

Given: amount of HF = 3.00 g

Unknown: mass of SnF_2 produced (g)

2 PLAN

The conversion factors needed are the molar masses of HF and SnF_2 and the mole ratio of SnF_2 to HF.

$$g\ HF \times \underset{\text{molar mass factor}}{\frac{mol\ HF}{g\ HF}} \times \underset{\text{mol ratio}}{\frac{mol\ SnF_2}{mol\ HF}} \times \underset{\text{molar mass factor}}{\frac{g\ SnF_2}{mol\ SnF_2}} = g\ SnF_2$$

Continued

Problem Solving

DECONSTRUCTING PROBLEMS

Have students compare the flow diagram on this page with the flow diagrams that they encountered earlier in the chapter. Point out that the flow diagram on this page has four steps, while the earlier ones each have only three steps. Emphasize that no new concepts are being introduced. The only change is that three conversion factors, rather than two, are needed to solve mass-mass calculations.

3 SOLVE

Use the periodic table to compute the molar masses of HF and SnF_2.

$$1 \text{ mol HF} = 20.01 \text{ g}$$
$$1 \text{ mol } SnF_2 = 156.71 \text{ g}$$

$$30.00 \text{ g HF} \times \frac{1 \text{ mol HF}}{20.01 \text{ g HF}} \times \frac{1 \text{ mol } SnF_2}{2 \text{ mol HF}} \times \frac{156.71 \text{ g } SnF_2}{1 \text{ mol } SnF_2} = 117.5 \text{ g } SnF_2$$

4 CHECK YOUR WORK

The answer is correctly rounded to four significant figures. The units cancel to leave g SnF_2, which matches the unknown. The answer is close to an estimated value of 120.

Practice Answers in Appendix E

1. Laughing gas (nitrous oxide, N_2O) is sometimes used as an anesthetic in dentistry. It is produced when ammonium nitrate is decomposed according to the following reaction.

$$NH_4NO_3(s) \longrightarrow N_2O(g) + 2H_2O(l)$$

   a. How many grams of NH_4NO_3 are required to produce 33.0 g N_2O?
   b. How many grams of water are produced in this reaction?
2. When copper metal is added to silver nitrate in solution, silver metal and copper(II) nitrate are produced. What mass of silver is produced from 100. g Cu?
3. What mass of aluminum is produced by the decomposition of 5.0 kg Al_2O_3?

SECTION 2 FORMATIVE ASSESSMENT

Reviewing Main Ideas

1. Balance the following equation. Then, given the moles of reactant or product below, determine the corresponding amount in moles of each of the other reactants and products.

$$NH_3 + O_2 \longrightarrow N_2 + H_2O$$

   a. 4 mol NH_3 b. 4 mol N_2 c. 4.5 mol O_2
2. One reaction that produces hydrogen gas can be represented by the following unbalanced chemical equation:

$$Mg(s) + HCl(aq) \longrightarrow MgCl_2(aq) + H_2(g)$$

   a. What mass of HCl is consumed by the reaction of 2.50 moles of magnesium?
   b. What mass of each product is produced in part (a)?
3. Acetylene gas, C_2H_2, is produced as a result of the following reaction:

$$CaC_2(s) + 2H_2O(l) \longrightarrow C_2H_2(g) + Ca(OH)_2(aq)$$

   a. If 32.0 g CaC_2 are consumed in this reaction, how many moles of H_2O are needed?
   b. How many moles of each product would form?
4. When sodium chloride reacts with silver nitrate, silver chloride precipitates. What mass of AgCl is produced from 75.0 g $AgNO_3$?

Critical Thinking

5. **RELATING IDEAS** Carbon and oxygen react to form carbon monoxide: $2C + O_2 \longrightarrow 2CO$. What masses of carbon and oxygen are needed to make 56.0 g CO? Which law does this illustrate?

Classroom Practice

E-1 Sodium peroxide reacts vigorously with water in the following unbalanced equation:

$$Na_2O_2(s) + H_2O(l) \longrightarrow NaOH(aq) + O_2(g)$$

a. What mass of O_2 is produced when 50.0 g Na_2O_2 react with H_2O?

b. What mass in grams of water is needed to react completely with the Na_2O_2?

Answers:

a. 10.3 g O_2
b. 11.6 g H_2O

Answers

Practice E

1. **a.** 60.0 g NH_4NO_3
   b. 27.0 g H_2O
2. 339 g Ag
3. 2.6 kg Al

Assess and Reteach

Assess Use the Formative Assessment on this page to evaluate student mastery of the section.

Reteach For students who need additional instruction, download the Section Study Guide.

Response to Intervention To reassess students' mastery, use the Section Quiz, available to print or to take directly online at **HMDScience.com**.

Answers to Section Assessment

1. $4NH_3 + 3O_2 \longrightarrow 2N_2 + 6H_2O$
   a. 3 mol O_2, 2 mol N_2, 6 mol H_2O
   b. 8 mol NH_3, 6 mol O_2, 12 mol H_2O
   c. 6.0 mol NH_3, 3.0 mol N_2, 9.0 mol H_2O
2. a. 182 g HCl
   b. 238 g $MgCl_2$, 5.05 g H_2
3. a. 0.998 mol H_2O
   b. 0.499 mol C_2H_2, 0.499 mol $Ca(OH)_2$
4. 63.3 g AgCl
5. 24.0 g C and 32.0 g O_2; law of conservation of mass

SECTION 3

▼ Plan and Prepare

Objectives

Upon completion of this section, students should be able to do the following:

- Describe a method for determining which of two reactants is a limiting reactant.
- Calculate the amount in moles or mass in grams of a product, given the amounts in moles or masses in grams of two reactants, one of which is in excess.
- Distinguish between theoretical yield, actual yield, and percentage yield.
- Calculate percentage yield, given the actual yield and quantity of a reactant.

Classroom Catalyst

Use the game of musical chairs to illustrate the concepts of limiting reactant and excess reactant. Students will recognize the chairs as limiting and the participants as excess.

▼ Teach

Teaching Tip

Many students have difficulty solving limiting-reactant problems. If this is the case, omit this section for fundamental classes and spend more time on mass-to-mass problems.

Demonstration

LIMITING REACTANT

Display **12 bottles** and **10 bottle caps.** Bottles are in excess and caps are the limiting reactant. Refer to this demonstration as you proceed.

Critical Thinking

Answer: The carbon atoms are the limiting reactant. When molecules of CO_2 are formed, 5 molecules can be made, since there are 5 carbon atoms.

SECTION 3

Main Ideas

- One reactant limits the product of a reaction.
- Comparing the actual and theoretical yields helps chemists determine the reaction's efficiency.

Limiting Reactants and Percentage Yield

Key Terms

limiting reactant
excess reactant
theoretical yield
actual yield
percentage yield

In the laboratory, a reaction is rarely carried out with exactly the required amount of each of the reactants. In many cases, one or more reactants is present in excess; that is, there is more than the exact amount required to react.

MAIN IDEA

One reactant limits the product of a reaction.

Once one of the reactants is used up, no more product can be formed. The substance that is completely used up first in a reaction is called the limiting reactant. The **limiting reactant** is the reactant that limits the amount of the other reactant that can combine and the amount of product that can form in a chemical reaction. The substance that is not used up completely in a reaction is called the **excess reactant.** A limiting reactant may also be referred to as a *limiting reagent.*

PREMIUM CONTENT

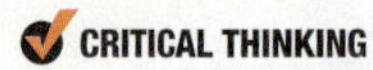

Limiting Reactants

Consider the reaction between carbon and oxygen:

$$C(s) + O_2(g) \longrightarrow CO_2(g)$$

According to the equation, one mole of carbon reacts with one mole of oxygen to form one mole of carbon dioxide. Suppose you could mix 5 mol C with 10 mol O_2 and allow the reaction to take place. **Figure 3.1** shows that there is more oxygen than is needed to react with the carbon. Carbon is the limiting reactant in this situation, and it limits the amount of CO_2 that is formed. Oxygen is the excess reactant, and 5 mol O_2 will be left over at the end of the reaction.

FIGURE 3.1

Limiting Reactants Carbon and oxygen always react in the same molar ratio to form carbon dioxide.

CRITICAL THINKING

Explain Which substance is the limiting reactant in this chemical reaction? Explain your answer.

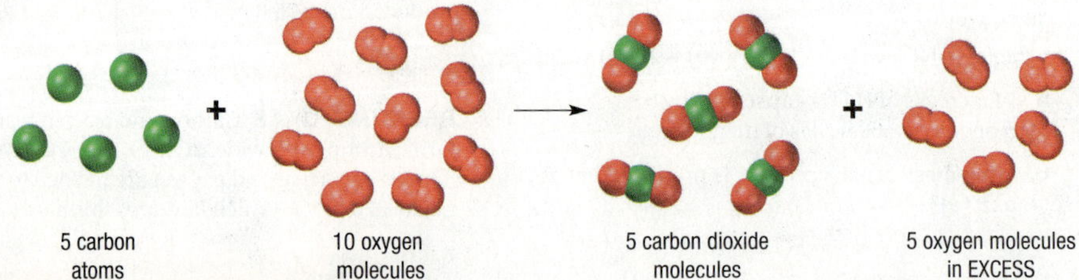

Differentiated Instruction

ENGLISH LEARNERS

Tell students that a reaction can involve three reactants that combine to form a single product. Write the following equation on the board.

$$A + B + C \longrightarrow D$$

Ask students: If B is the limiting reactant, how would you describe reactants A and C? Students should point out that reactants A and C are either present in sufficient amounts or present in excess.

Limiting Reactant

Sample Problem F **Silicon dioxide (quartz) is usually quite unreactive but reacts readily with hydrogen fluoride according to the following equation.**

$$SiO_2(s) + 4HF(g) \longrightarrow SiF_4(g) + 2H_2O(l)$$

If 6.0 mol HF are added to 4.5 mol SiO_2, which is the limiting reactant?

ANALYZE

Given: amount of HF = 6.0 mol
amount of SiO_2 = 4.5 mol

Unknown: limiting reactant

PLAN

Pick one of the products, in this case SiF_4. Use the given amounts of each reactant to calculate the amount of SiF_4 that could be produced from that reactant. Compare the amounts of SiF_4. The limiting reactant is the reactant that produces the smallest number of moles of SiF_4. The smallest amount of product is also the maximum amount that can be formed.

$$\text{mol HF} \times \frac{\text{mol SiF}_4}{\text{mol HF}} = \text{mol SiF}_4 \text{ produced} \qquad \text{mol SiO}_2 \times \frac{\text{mol SiF}_4}{\text{mol SiO}_2} = \text{mol SiF}_4 \text{ produced}$$

SOLVE

$$6.0 \text{ mol HF} \times \frac{1 \text{ mol SiF}_4}{4 \text{ mol HF}} = 1.5 \text{ mol SiF}_4 \text{ produced}$$

$$4.5 \text{ mol SiO}_2 \times \frac{1 \text{ mol SiF}_4}{1 \text{ mol SiO}_2} = 4.5 \text{ mol SiF}_4 \text{ produced}$$

Under ideal conditions, 6.0 mol HF can make 1.5 mol SiF_4, and 4.5 mol SiO_2 present can make 4.5 mol SiF_4. Because 1.5 mol SiF_4 is smaller than 4.5 mol SiF_4, the HF is the limiting reactant, and SiO_2 is the excess reactant.

CHECK YOUR WORK

From the balanced equation, we can see that the reaction requires four times the number of moles of HF as it does moles of SiO_2. Because the molar amount of HF that we have is less than four times the moles of SiO_2, our calculations clearly show that HF is the limiting reactant.

Practice

Answers in Appendix E

1. Some rocket engines use a mixture of hydrazine, N_2H_4, and hydrogen peroxide, H_2O_2, as the propellant. The reaction is given by the following equation.

$$N_2H_4(l) + 2H_2O_2(l) \longrightarrow N_2(g) + 4H_2O(g)$$

   a. Which is the limiting reactant in this reaction, when 0.750 mol N_2H_4 is mixed with 0.500 mol H_2O_2?
   b. How much of the excess reactant, in moles, remains unchanged?
   c. How much of each product, in moles, is formed?

Misconception Alert!

Students often mistakenly choose the reactant present in smaller amounts as the limiting reactant. Tell students that to determine the limiting reactant, they must factor in the coefficients of the reactants in the balanced equation.

Classroom Practice

F-1 Methanol, CH_3OH, is the simplest of the alcohols. It is synthesized by the reaction of hydrogen and carbon monoxide.

$$CO(g) + 2H_2(g) \longrightarrow CH_3OH$$

a. If 500 mol CO and 750 mol H_2 are present, which is the limiting reactant?

b. How many moles of the excess reactant remain unchanged?

c. How many moles of CH_3OH are formed?

Answers:
- **a.** H_2
- **b.** 125 mol CO
- **c.** 375 mol CH_3OH

Answers

Practice F

1. **a.** H_2O_2
   b. 0.500 mol N_2H_4
   c. 0.250 mol N_2, 1.00 mol H_2O

Problem Solving

DECONSTRUCTING PROBLEMS

Point out that the limiting reactant is always responsible for producing the smallest number of moles or the smallest number of grams of the product(s).

▼ Teach continued

Teaching Tip

In part c of Sample Problem G, emphasize that the balanced chemical equation cannot be used to calculate the amounts of substances that do *not* react, only the amounts that *do* react. The amount of the excess reactant left over must be determined as the difference between the amount originally present and the amount that reacts.

Classroom Practice

G-1 Aspirin, $C_9H_8O_4$, is synthesized by the reaction of salicylic acid, $C_7H_6O_3$, with acetic anhydride, $C_4H_6O_3$.

$$C_7H_6O_3 + C_4H_6O_3 \longrightarrow C_9H_8O_4 + CH_3COOH$$

a. When 20.0 g $C_7H_6O_3$ and 20.0 g $C_4H_6O_3$ react, which is the limiting reactant? How many moles of the excess reactant are used when the reaction is complete?

b. What mass in grams of aspirin is formed?

Answers:

a. $C_7H_6O_3$, 0.0725 mol
b. 26.1 g

Limiting Reactant

Sample Problem G **The black oxide of iron, Fe_3O_4, occurs in nature as the mineral magnetite. This substance can also be made in the laboratory by the reaction between red-hot iron and steam according to the following equation.**

$$3Fe(s) + 4H_2O(g) \longrightarrow Fe_3O_4(s) + 4H_2(g)$$

a. When 36.0 g H_2O are mixed with 67.0 g Fe, which is the limiting reactant?
b. What mass in grams of black iron oxide is produced?
c. What mass in grams of excess reactant remains when the reaction is completed?

1 ANALYZE

Given: mass of H_2O = 36.0 g
mass of Fe = 67.0 g

Unknown: limiting reactant
mass of Fe_3O_4, in grams
mass of excess reactant remaining

2 PLAN

a. First, convert both given masses in grams to amounts in moles. Then, calculate the number of moles of one of the products. Because the problem asks for the mass of Fe_3O_4 formed, we will calculate moles of Fe_3O_4. The reactant yielding the smaller number of moles of product is the limiting reactant.

$$\text{g Fe} \times \underbrace{\frac{\text{mol Fe}}{\text{g Fe}}}_{\text{molar mass factor}} \times \underbrace{\frac{\text{mol Fe}_3\text{O}_4}{\text{mol Fe}}}_{\text{mol ratio}} = \text{mol Fe}_3\text{O}_4$$

$$\text{g H}_2\text{O} \times \underbrace{\frac{\text{mol H}_2\text{O}}{\text{g H}_2\text{O}}}_{\text{molar mass factor}} \times \underbrace{\frac{\text{mol Fe}_3\text{O}_4}{\text{mol H}_2\text{O}}}_{\text{mol ratio}} = \text{mol Fe}_3\text{O}_4$$

b. To find the maximum mass of Fe_3O_4 that can be produced, we must use the amount of Fe_3O_4 in moles from the limiting reactant in a simple stoichiometric problem.

$$\text{mole Fe}_3\text{O}_4 \text{ from limiting reactant} \times \underbrace{\frac{\text{g Fe}_3\text{O}_4}{\text{mol Fe}_3\text{O}_4}}_{\text{molar mass factor}} = \text{g Fe}_3\text{O}_4 \text{ produced}$$

c. To find the amount of excess reactant remaining, we must first determine the amount of the excess reactant that is consumed. The calculated moles of the product (from the limiting reactant) is used to determine the amount of excess reactant that is consumed.

$$\text{mol product} \times \frac{\text{mol excess reactant}}{\text{mol product}} \times \frac{\text{g excess reactant}}{\text{mol excess reactant}} = \text{g excess reactant consumed}$$

The amount of excess reactant remaining can then be found by subtracting the amount consumed from the amount originally present.

$$\text{original g excess reactant} - \text{g excess reactant consumed} = \text{g excess reactant remaining}$$

Continued

Problem Solving

REALITY CHECK

Ask students to provide a recipe for a food they like. Ask them to select one ingredient and describe what would happen if it were a limiting reactant.

ALTERNATIVE APPROACHES

Have a student construct a triangle with mini marshmallows and toothpicks. Provide one bag of marshmallows and one box of toothpicks, and have the student determine how many triangles can be constructed from the materials present. To do this, the student will need to figure out which ingredient will run out first (the limiting factor). After checking the results, have the student share this demonstration with the class.

Limiting Reactant (continued)

SOLVE

a. Use the periodic table to determine the molar masses of H_2O, Fe, and Fe_3O_4. Then, determine how many mol Fe_3O_4 can be produced from each reactant.

1 mol H_2O = 18.02 g
1 mol Fe = 55.85 g
1 mol Fe_3O_4 = 231.55 g

$$67.0\ \text{g Fe} \times \frac{1\ \text{mol Fe}}{55.85\ \text{g Fe}} \times \frac{1\ \text{mol Fe}_3\text{O}_4}{3\ \text{mol Fe}} = 0.400\ \text{mol Fe}_3\text{O}_4$$

$$36.0\ \text{g H}_2\text{O} \times \frac{1\ \text{mol H}_2\text{O}}{18.02\ \text{g H}_2\text{O}} \times \frac{1\ \text{mol Fe}_3\text{O}_4}{4\ \text{mol H}_2\text{O}} = 0.499\ \text{mol Fe}_3\text{O}_4$$

Fe is the limiting reactant, because the given amount of Fe can make only 0.400 mol Fe_3O_4, which is less than the 0.499 mol Fe_3O_4 that the given amount of H_2O would produce.

b. $0.400\ \text{mol Fe}_3\text{O}_4 \times \frac{231.55\ \text{g Fe}_3\text{O}_4}{1\ \text{mol Fe}_3\text{O}_4} = 92.6\ \text{g Fe}_3\text{O}_4$

c. $0.400\ \text{mol Fe}_3\text{O}_4 \times \frac{4\ \text{mol H}_2\text{O}}{1\ \text{mol Fe}_3\text{O}_4} \times \frac{18.02\ \text{g H}_2\text{O}}{1\ \text{mol H}_2\text{O}} = 28.8\ \text{g H}_2\text{O consumed}$

$36.0\ \text{g H}_2\text{O} - 28.8\ \text{g H}_2\text{O consumed} = 7.2\ \text{g H}_2\text{O remaining}$

CHECK YOUR WORK

The mass of original reactants is 67.0 + 36.0 = 103.0 g; the mass of Fe_3O_4 + unreacted water is 92.6 g + 7.2 g = 99.8 g. The difference of 3.2 g is the mass of hydrogen that is produced with the Fe_3O_4.

Practice

Answers in Appendix E

1. Zinc and sulfur react to form zinc sulfide according to the following equation.

$$8\text{Zn}(s) + \text{S}_8(s) \longrightarrow 8\text{ZnS}(s)$$

   a. If 2.00 mol of Zn are heated with 1.00 mol of S_8, identify the limiting reactant.
   b. How many moles of excess reactant remain?
   c. How many moles of the product are formed?

2. Carbon reacts with steam, H_2O, at high temperatures to produce hydrogen and carbon monoxide.
   a. If 2.40 mol of carbon are exposed to 3.10 mol of steam, identify the limiting reactant.
   b. How many moles of each product are formed?
   c. What mass of each product is formed?

TAKE IT FURTHER

Ask students to evaluate the impact on Sample Problem G if the product were Fe_2O_3 and not Fe_3O_4. Students should recognize that the balanced equation would be different. ($2Fe + 3H_2O \longrightarrow Fe_2O_3 + 3H_2$) As a result, the mole ratios are different. Therefore, some of the conversion factors used in the problem would have to be changed. Have them identify which conversion factors must be changed.

Teaching Tip

Fe_3O_4 contains iron in both the +2 and +3 oxidation states. Its actual formula can be written as $Fe(II)Fe(III)_2O_4$.

Answers

Practice G

1. **a.** Zn
   b. 0.75 mol S8 remains
   c. 2.00 mol ZnS
2. **a.** carbon
   b. 2.40 mol H_2 and 2.40 mol CO
   c. 4.85 g H_2 and 67.2 g CO

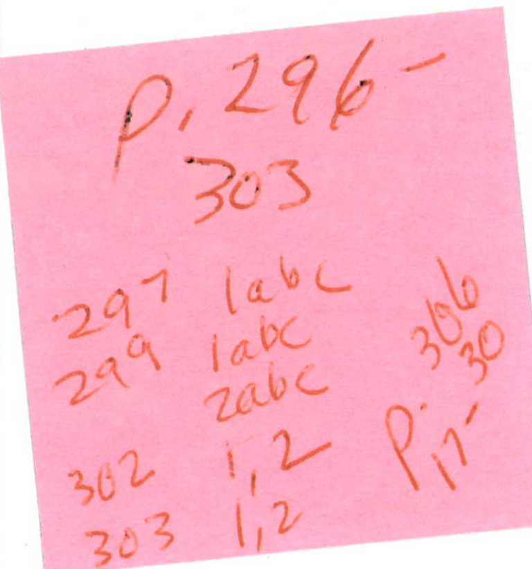

▼ Teach *continued*

QuickLab

Note: This activity should *not* be done in the chemistry lab. It can be done at home or in a home economics room at school.

BACKGROUND

Students soon realize that putting together the ingredients for a batch of cookies is analogous to measuring known masses of reactants for a chemical reaction. The yield from the recipe is 24 cookies. To increase the yield, the ingredients may be increased proportionally. Just as the number of cookies that can be produced is limited by the amounts of the ingredients available to use, the amount of product that can be obtained from a chemical reaction is limited by the amount of each reactant available to react.

DISCUSSION

1. **a.** 1 dozen eggs: 288 cookies; 24 tsp. of vanilla: 576 cookies; 82 tsp. of salt: 3936 cookies; 84 tsp. of baking soda: 4032 cookies; 3 cups of chocolate chips: 54 cookies; 11 cups of sugar: 528 cookies; 4 cups of brown sugar: 192 cookies; 4 sticks of margarine: 72 cookies

   b. chocolate chips

   c. 54 cookies

QuickLAB LIMITING REACTANTS IN A RECIPE

PROCEDURE

1. In the mixing bowl, combine the sugars and margarine together until smooth. (An electric mixer will make this process go much faster.)
2. Add the egg, salt, and vanilla. Mix well.
3. Stir in the baking soda, flour, and chocolate chips. Chill the dough for an hour in the refrigerator for best results.
4. Divide the dough into 24 small balls about 3 cm in diameter. Place the balls on an ungreased cookie sheet.
5. Bake at 350°F for about 10 minutes, or until the cookies are light brown.

Yield: 24 cookies

DISCUSSION

1. Suppose you are given the following amounts of ingredients:

   1 dozen eggs
   24 tsp. of vanilla
   1 lb. (82 tsp.) of salt
   1 lb. (84 tsp.) of baking soda
   3 cups of chocolate chips
   5 lb. (11 cups) of sugar
   2 lb. (4 cups) of brown sugar
   1 lb. (4 sticks) of margarine

   a. For each ingredient, calculate how many cookies could be prepared if all of that ingredient were consumed. (For example, the recipe shows that using 1 egg—with the right amounts of the other ingredients—yields 24 cookies. How many cookies can you make if the recipe is increased proportionately for 12 eggs?)

   b. To determine the limiting reactant for the new ingredients list, identify which ingredient will result in the fewest number of cookies.

   c. What is the maximum number of cookies that can be produced from the new amounts of ingredients?

MATERIALS

- 1/2 cup sugar
- 1/2 cup brown sugar
- 1 1/3 stick margarine (at room temperature)
- 1 egg
- 1/2 tsp. salt
- 1 tsp. vanilla
- 1/2 tsp. baking soda
- 1 1/2 cup flour
- 1 1/3 cup chocolate chips
- mixing bowl
- mixing spoon
- measuring spoons and cups
- cookie sheet
- oven preheated to 350°F

Differentiated Instruction

PRE-AP

Have students research how chemists increase the yield of a chemical reaction. One example involves the Haber process used to make ammonia, which is then used to make fertilizers. Point out the importance of fertilizers in growing food crops. To increase the percent yield, the Haber process involves very high temperature and pressure.

MAIN IDEA

Comparing the actual and theoretical yields helps chemists determine the reaction's efficiency.

The amounts of products calculated in the ideal stoichiometry problems in this chapter so far represent theoretical yields. The **theoretical yield** is the maximum amount of product that can be produced from a given amount of reactant. In most chemical reactions, the amount of product obtained is less than the theoretical yield. There are many reasons for this result. Reactants may contain impurities or may form by-products in competing side reactions. Also, in many reactions, all reactants are not converted to products. As a result, less product is produced than ideal stoichiometric calculations predict. The measured amount of a product obtained from a reaction is called the **actual yield** of that product.

Chemists are usually interested in the efficiency of a reaction. The efficiency is expressed by comparing the actual and theoretical yields. The **percentage yield** is the ratio of the actual yield to the theoretical yield, multiplied by 100.

Percentage Yield $= \frac{\text{actual yield}}{\text{theoretical yield}} \times 100$

CHECK FOR UNDERSTANDING

Explain Explain why it might be necessary for a chemist in industry to find out how efficient a chemical reaction is.

Percentage Yield

Sample Problem H **Chlorobenzene, C_6H_5Cl, is used in the production of many important chemicals, such as aspirin, dyes, and disinfectants. One industrial method of preparing chlorobenzene is to react benzene, C_6H_6, with chlorine, as represented by the following equation.**

$$C_6H_6(l) + Cl_2(g) \longrightarrow C_6H_5Cl(l) + HCl(g)$$

When 36.8 g C_6H_6 react with an excess of Cl_2, the actual yield of C_6H_5Cl is 38.8 g. What is the percentage yield of C_6H_5Cl?

1 ANALYZE

Given: mass of $C_6H_6 = 36.8$ g
mass of Cl_2 = excess
actual yield of $C_6H_5Cl = 38.8$ g

Unknown: percentage yield of C_6H_5Cl

2 PLAN

First do a mass-mass calculation to find the theoretical yield of C_6H_5Cl.

$$\text{g } C_6H_6 \times \underset{\text{molar mass factor}}{\frac{\text{mol } C_6H_6}{\text{g } C_6H_6}} \times \underset{\text{mol ratio}}{\frac{\text{mol } C_6H_5Cl}{\text{mol } C_6H_6}} \times \underset{\text{molar mass}}{\frac{\text{g } C_6H_5Cl}{\text{mol } C_6H_5Cl}} = \text{g } C_6H_5Cl \text{ (theoretical yield)}$$

Then the percentage yield can be found.

$$\text{percentage yield } C_6H_5Cl = \frac{\text{actual yield}}{\text{theoretical yield}} \times 100$$

Continued

Teaching Tip

A chemical reaction system is not as simple as the balanced equation implies. Competing side reactions may interfere with the production of the desired product.

Misconception Alert!

Students often think all reactions go to completion. They will learn in a future chapter that reversible reactions and equilibrium systems limit the masses of products in chemical reactions. Reintroduce the concept of percentage yield at that time.

Classroom Discussion

Discuss the results of the demonstration done at the beginning of the chapter in terms of percentage yield. The theoretical yield for a 2.000 g sample of sodium carbonate is calculated as follows.

$$2.000 \text{ g } Na_2CO_3 \times \frac{1 \text{ mol } Na_2CO_3}{105.99 \text{ g } Na_2CO_3} \times \frac{2 \text{ mol NaCl}}{1 \text{ mol } Na_2CO_3} \times \frac{58.44 \text{ g NaCl}}{1 \text{ mol NaCl}} = 2.205 \text{ g NaCl}$$

The actual yield is typically 2.100 g. Therefore,

$$\text{yield (\%)} = \frac{2.100 \text{ g}}{2.205 \text{ g}} \times 100 = 95.24\%$$

READING TOOLKIT

DISCUSSION Discuss with students the difference between *theoretical yield* and *actual yield*. Have them speculate about what factors might cause the actual yield to be less than the theoretical yield.

Check for Understanding

Answer: Chemists working in industry may need to calculate the efficiency of a process to determine whether the process is profitable.

▼ Teach continued

Classroom Practice

H-1 Huge quantities of sulfur dioxide are produced from zinc sulfide by means of the following reaction.

$2ZnS(s) + 3O_2(g) \longrightarrow 2ZnO(s) + 2SO_2(g)$

If the typical yield is 86.78%, what mass of SO_2 should be expected if 4897 g of ZnS are used?

Answer: 2794 g SO_2

Answers

Pratice H

1. 79.7%
2. 3.70 g Cu

▼ Assess and Reteach

Assess Use the Formative Assessment on this page to evaluate student mastery of the section.

Reteach For students who need additional instruction, download the Section Study Guide.

Response to Intervention To reassess students' mastery, use the Section Quiz, available to print or to take directly online at **HMDScience.com**.

3 SOLVE

Use the periodic table to determine the molar masses of C_6H_6 and C_6H_5Cl.

$$1 \text{ mol } C_6H_6 = 78.12 \text{ g}$$
$$1 \text{ mol } C_6H_5Cl = 112.56 \text{ g}$$

$$36.8 \text{ g } C_6H_6 \times \frac{1 \text{ mol } C_6H_6}{78.12 \text{ g } C_6H_6} \times \frac{1 \text{ mol } C_6H_5Cl}{1 \text{ mol } C_6H_6} \times \frac{112.56 \text{ g } C_6H_5Cl}{1 \text{ mol } C_6H_5Cl} = 53.0 \text{ g } C_6H_5Cl$$

(theoretical yield)

$$\text{percentage yield} = \frac{38.8 \text{ g}}{53.0 \text{ g}} \times 100 = 73.2\%$$

4 CHECK YOUR WORK

The answer is correctly rounded to three significant figures to match those in 36.8 g C_6H_6. The units have canceled correctly. The theoretical yield is close to an estimated value of 50 g (one-half of 100 g). The percentage yield is close to an estimated value of 80% (40/50 × 100).

Practice Answers in Appendix E

1. Methanol can be produced through the reaction of CO and H_2 in the presence of a catalyst.

$$CO(g) + 2H_2(g) \xrightarrow{\text{catalyst}} CH_3OH(l)$$

If 75.0 g of CO react to produce 68.4 g CH_3OH, what is the percentage yield of CH_3OH?

2. Aluminum reacts with excess copper(II) sulfate according to the reaction given below. If 1.85 g of Al react, and the percentage yield of Cu is 56.6%, what mass of Cu is produced?

$$Al(s) + CuSO_4(aq) \longrightarrow Al_2(SO_4)_3(aq) + Cu(s) \text{ (unbalanced)}$$

SECTION 3 FORMATIVE ASSESSMENT

Reviewing Main Ideas

1. Carbon disulfide burns in oxygen to yield carbon dioxide and sulfur dioxide according to the following chemical equation.

$$CS_2(l) + 3O_2(g) \longrightarrow CO_2(g) + 2SO_2(g)$$

   a. If 1.00 mol CS_2 reacts with 1.00 mol O_2, identify the limiting reactant.
   b. How many moles of excess reactant remain?
   c. How many moles of each product are formed?

2. Metallic magnesium reacts with steam to produce magnesium hydroxide and hydrogen gas.
   a. If 16.2 g Mg are heated with 12.0 g H_2O, what is the limiting reactant?
   b. How many moles of the excess reactant are left?
   c. How many grams of each product are formed?

3. Quicklime, CaO, can be prepared by roasting limestone, $CaCO_3$, according to the following reaction.

$$CaCO_3(s) \xrightarrow{\Delta} CaO(s) + CO_2(g).$$

When 2.00×10^3 g $CaCO_3$ are heated, the actual yield of CaO is 1.05×10^3 g. What is the percentage yield?

Critical Thinking

4. **ANALYZING DATA** A chemical engineer calculated that 15.0 mol H_2 was needed to react with excess N_2 to prepare 10.0 mol NH_3. But the actual yield is 60.0%. Write a balanced chemical equation for the reaction. Is the amount of H_2 needed to make 10.0 mol NH_3 more than, the same as, or less than 15 mol? How many moles of H_2 are needed?

Answers to Section Assessment

1. **a.** O_2 is the limiting reactant.
   b. 0.667 mol CS_2 remains.
   c. 0.333 mol CO_2, 0.667 mol SO_2
2. **a.** H_2O is the limiting reactant.
   b. 0.334 mol Mg remains
   c. 19.4 g $Mg(OH)_2$, 0.673 g H_2
3. 93.8%
4. $N_2(g) + 3H_2(g) \longrightarrow 2NH_3(g)$;
   More H_2 is needed because only 60.0% is converted to ammonia; 25.0 mol of H_2

Math Tutor | Using Mole Ratios

An unbalanced chemical equation tells you what substances react and what products are produced. A balanced chemical equation gives you even more information. It tells you how many atoms, molecules, or ions react and how many atoms, molecules, or ions are produced. The coefficients in a balanced equation represent the relative amounts in moles of reactants and products. Using this information, you can set up a mole ratio. A mole ratio is a conversion factor that relates the amounts in moles of any two substances involved in a chemical reaction.

Problem-Solving TIPS

- When solving stoichiometric problems, always start with a balanced chemical equation.
- Identify the amount known from the problem (in moles or mass).
- If you are given the mass of a substance, use the molar mass factor as a conversion factor to find the amount in moles. If you are given the amount in moles of a substance, use the molar mass factor as a conversion factor to find the mass.

Sample Problem

If 3.61 g of aluminum reacts completely with excess $CuCl_2$, what mass of copper metal is produced? Use the balanced equation below.

$$2Al(s) + 3CuCl_2(aq) \longrightarrow 2AlCl_3(aq) + 3Cu(s)$$

You know the mass of aluminum that reacts. If you convert that mass to moles, you can apply the mole ratio of aluminum to copper in this reaction to find the moles of copper produced.

$$\text{mol Al} = 3.61\ \cancel{\text{g Al}} \times \frac{1\ \text{mol Al}}{26.98\ \cancel{\text{g Al}}} = 0.134\ \text{mol Al}$$

$$\cancel{\text{mol Al}} \times \frac{3\ \text{mol Cu}}{2\ \cancel{\text{mol Al}}} = \text{mol Cu}$$

$$0.134\ \cancel{\text{mol Al}} \times \frac{3\ \text{mol Cu}}{2\ \cancel{\text{mol Al}}} = 0.201\ \text{mol Cu}$$

Then, convert moles of Cu to mass of Cu by applying the following factor:

$$\text{mol Cu} \times \frac{\text{molar mass Cu}}{1\ \text{mol Cu}} = \text{mass Cu, or } 0.201\ \text{mol Cu} \times \frac{63.55\ \text{g Cu}}{1\ \text{mol Cu}} = 12.8\ \text{g Cu}$$

Practice

1. If 12.24 moles of O_2 react with excess SO_2, how many moles of SO_3 are formed? Use the balanced equation below.

$$2SO_2(g) + O_2(g) \longrightarrow 2SO_3(g)$$

2. If 78.50 g $KClO_3$ decomposes, what mass of O_2 is produced? Use the balanced equation below.

$$2KClO_3(s) \longrightarrow 2KCl(s) + 3O_2(g)$$

MATH TUTOR

Answers

1. 24.48 mol SO_3
2. 30.75 g O_2

CHAPTER 9 Summary

Review Games
Concept Maps

SECTION 1 Introduction to Stoichiometry

- Reaction stoichiometry involves the mass relationships between reactants and products in a chemical reaction.
- Relating one substance to another requires expressing the amount of each substance in moles.
- A mole ratio is the conversion factor that relates the amount in moles of any two substances in a chemical reaction. The mole ratio is derived from the balanced equation.
- Amount of a substance is expressed in moles, and mass of a substance is expressed by using mass units such as grams, kilograms, or milligrams.
- Mass and amount of substance are quantities, whereas moles and grams are units.
- A balanced chemical equation is necessary to solve any stoichiometric problem.

KEY TERMS

composition stoichiometry
reaction stoichiometry
mole ratio

SECTION 2 Ideal Stoichiometric Calculations

- In an ideal stoichiometric calculation, the mass or the amount of any reactant or product can be calculated if the balanced chemical equation and the mass or amount of any other reactant or product is known.

SECTION 3 Limiting Reactants and Percentage Yield

- In actual reactions, the reactants may be present in proportions that differ from the stoichiometric proportions required for a complete reaction in which all of each reactant is converted to product.
- The limiting reactant controls the maximum possible amount of product formed.
- For many reactions, the quantity of a product is less than the theoretical maximum for that product. Percentage yield shows the relationship between the theoretical yield and actual yield for the product of a reaction.

KEY TERMS

limiting reactant
excess reactant
theoretical yield
actual yield
percentage yield

304 Chapter 9

CHAPTER 9 Review

SECTION 1

Introduction to Stoichiometry

REVIEWING MAIN IDEAS

1. a. Explain the concept of mole ratio as used in reaction stoichiometry problems.
   b. What is the source of this ratio?

2. For each of the following balanced chemical equations, write all possible mole ratios:
   a. $2Ca + O_2 \longrightarrow 2CaO$
   b. $Mg + 2HF \longrightarrow MgF_2 + H_2$

PRACTICE PROBLEMS

3. Given the chemical equation $Na_2CO_3(aq) + Ca(OH)_2 \longrightarrow 2NaOH(aq) + CaCO_3(s)$, determine to two decimal places the molar masses of all substances involved. Then, write the molar masses as conversion factors.

SECTION 2

Ideal Stoichiometric Calculations

REVIEWING MAIN IDEAS

4. a. What is molar mass?
   b. What is its role in reaction stoichiometry?

PRACTICE PROBLEMS

5. Hydrogen and oxygen react under a specific set of conditions to produce water according to the following: $2H_2(g) + O_2(g) \longrightarrow 2H_2O(g)$.
   a. How many moles of hydrogen would be required to produce 5.0 mol of water?
   b. How many moles of oxygen would be required? (Hint: See Sample Problem A.)

6. a. If 4.50 mol of ethane, C_2H_6, undergo combustion according to the unbalanced equation $C_2H_6 + O_2 \longrightarrow CO_2 + H_2O$, how many moles of oxygen are required?
   b. How many moles of each product are formed?

7. Sodium chloride is produced from its elements through a synthesis reaction. What mass of each reactant would be required to produce 25.0 mol of sodium chloride?

8. In a blast furnace, iron(III) oxide is used to produce iron by the following (unbalanced) reaction:
   $$Fe_2O_3(s) + CO(g) \longrightarrow Fe(s) + CO_2(g)$$
   a. If 4.00 kg Fe_2O_3 are available to react, how many moles of CO are needed?
   b. How many moles of each product are formed?

9. Methanol, CH_3OH, is an important industrial compound that is produced from the following (unbalanced) reaction: $CO(g) + H_2(g) \longrightarrow CH_3OH(g)$. What mass of each reactant would be needed to produce 100.0 kg of methanol? (Hint: See Sample Problem E.)

10. During lightning flashes, nitrogen combines with oxygen in the atmosphere to form nitrogen monoxide, NO, which then reacts further with O_2 to produce nitrogen dioxide, NO_2.
    a. What mass of NO_2 is formed when NO reacts with 384 g O_2?
    b. How many grams of NO are required to react with this amount of O_2?

11. As early as 1938, the use of NaOH was suggested as a means of removing CO_2 from the cabin of a spacecraft according to the following (unbalanced) reaction: $NaOH + CO_2 \longrightarrow Na_2CO_3 + H_2O$.
    a. If the average human body discharges 925.0 g CO_2 per day, how many moles of NaOH are needed each day for each person in the spacecraft?
    b. How many moles of each product are formed?

12. The double-replacement reaction between silver nitrate and sodium bromide produces silver bromide, a component of photographic film.
    a. If 4.50 mol of silver nitrate react, what mass of sodium bromide is required?
    b. What mass of silver bromide is formed?

13. In a soda-acid fire extinguisher, concentrated sulfuric acid reacts with sodium hydrogen carbonate to produce carbon dioxide, sodium sulfate, and water.
    a. How many moles of sodium hydrogen carbonate would be needed to react with 150.0 g of sulfuric acid?
    b. How many moles of each product would be formed?

CHAPTER REVIEW

1. a. A mole ratio is a conversion factor that relates the number of moles of any two substances involved in a chemical reaction.
   b. Mole ratios are obtained from a balanced chemical equation.
2. a. $\frac{2 \text{ mol Ca}}{1 \text{ mol } O_2}, \frac{2 \text{ mol Ca}}{2 \text{ mol CaO}}$
   $\frac{1 \text{ mol } O_2}{2 \text{ mol Ca}}, \frac{1 \text{ mol } O_2}{2 \text{ mol CaO}}$
   $\frac{2 \text{ mol CaO}}{2 \text{ mol Ca}}, \frac{2 \text{ mol CaO}}{1 \text{ mol } O_2}$
   b. $\frac{1 \text{ mol Mg}}{2 \text{ mol HF}}, \frac{1 \text{ mol Mg}}{1 \text{ mol } MgF_2}, \frac{1 \text{ mol Mg}}{1 \text{ mol } H_2}$
   $\frac{2 \text{ mol HF}}{1 \text{ mol Mg}}, \frac{2 \text{ mol HF}}{1 \text{ mol } MgF_2}, \frac{2 \text{ mol HF}}{1 \text{ mol } H_2}$
   $\frac{1 \text{ mol } MgF_2}{1 \text{ mol Mg}}, \frac{1 \text{ mol } MgF_2}{2 \text{ mol HF}}, \frac{1 \text{ mol } MgF_2}{2 \text{ mol } H_2}$
   $\frac{1 \text{ mol } H_2}{1 \text{ mol Mg}}, \frac{1 \text{ mol } H_2}{2 \text{ mol HF}}, \frac{1 \text{ mol } H_2}{1 \text{ mol } HgF_2}$
3. $\frac{105.99 \text{ g } Na_2CO_3}{1 \text{ mol } Na_2CO_3}, \frac{1 \text{ mol } Na_2CO_3}{105.99 \text{ g } Na_2CO_3}$
   $\frac{74.10 \text{ g } Ca(OH)_2}{1 \text{ mol } Ca(OH)_2}, \frac{1 \text{ mol } Ca(OH)_2}{74.10 \text{ g } Ca(OH)_2}$
   $\frac{40.00 \text{ g NaOH}}{1 \text{ mol NaOH}}, \frac{1 \text{ mol NaOH}}{40.00 \text{ g NaOH}}$
   $\frac{100.09 \text{ g } CaCO_3}{1 \text{ mol } CaCO_3}, \frac{1 \text{ mol } CaCO_3}{100.09 \text{ g } CaCO_3}$
4. a. the mass in grams of one mole of a substance
   b. the conversion factor that relates the mass of a substance to the number of moles of that substance
5. a. 5.0 mol H_2 b. 2.5 mol O_2
6. a. 15.8 mol O_2
   b. 9.00 mol CO_2, 13.5 mol H_2O
7. 575 g Na, 886 g Cl_2
8. a. 75.1 mol CO
   b. 50.1 mol Fe, 75.1 mol CO_2
9. 8.739×10^4 g CO, 1.261×10^4 g H_2
10. a. 1.10×10^3 g NO_2
    b. 720. g NO
11. a. 42.04 mol NaOH
    b. 21.02 mol Na_2CO_3, 21.02 mol H_2O
12. a. 463 g NaBr b. 845 g AgBr
13. a. 3.058 mol $NaHCO_3$
    b. 3.058 mol CO_2, 1.529 mol Na_2SO_4, 3.058 mol H_2O

14. a. $H_2SO_4 + 2NaOH \longrightarrow Na_2SO_4 + 2H_2O$
b. 37 g H_2SO_4
c. 53 g Na_2SO_4, 14 g H_2O

15. a. 0.0104 mol $Cu(NO_3)_2$
b. 0.0104 mol Cu, 0.0209 mol $AgNO_3$

16. a. 13.5 kg $C_9H_8O_4$
b. 7.66 kg $C_4H_6O_3$
c. 4.29 L $HC_2H_3O_2$

17. Ideal stoichiometry calculations do not account for factors that can affect the relative amounts of reactants needed or products produced in chemical reactions; they deal with the amounts of reactants or products under ideal conditions. Real stoichiometry calculations account for actual conditions.

18. The limiting reactant is the reactant that controls the amount of product formed in a chemical reaction. The excess reactant is the substance that is not used up completely in a reaction.

19. a. The theoretical yield is the maximum amount of product that can be produced from a given amount of reactant. The actual yield is the measured amount obtained.
b. Actual yield is usually less than theoretical yield.

20. The percentage yield is the ratio of the actual yield to the theoretical yield multiplied by 100.

21. Reactions often do not go to completion, impure reactants produce less product than expected, competing side reactions may consume some of the reactants, and some of the product may be lost when it is purified.

22. a. HCl is the limiting reactant.
b. Zn is the limiting reactant.
c. $Fe(OH)_3$ is the limiting reactant.

23. a. 0.5 mol excess NaOH
b. 1.0 mol excess HCl
c. 0.5 mol excess H_2SO_4

24. a. 2.0 mol NaCl, 2.0 mol H_2O
b. 2.5 mol $ZnCl_2$, 2.5 mol H_2
c. 2.0 mol $Fe_2(SO_4)_3$, 12 mol H_2O

25. a. Cu is the limiting reactant.
b. 0.50 mol $AgNO_3$
c. 2.50 mol $Cu(NO_3)_2$, 5.00 mol Ag
d. 469 g $Cu(NO_3)_2$, 539 g Ag

14. Sulfuric acid reacts with sodium hydroxide according to the following:

$$H_2SO_4 + NaOH \longrightarrow Na_2SO_4 + H_2O$$

a. Balance the equation for this reaction.
b. What mass of H_2SO_4 would be required to react with 0.75 mol NaOH?
c. What mass of each product is formed by this reaction? (Hint: See Sample Problem B.)

15. Copper reacts with silver nitrate through single replacement.
a. If 2.25 g of silver are produced from the reaction, how many moles of copper(II) nitrate are also produced?
b. How many moles of each reactant are required in this reaction? (Hint: See Sample Problem D.)

16. Aspirin, $C_9H_8O_4$, is produced through the following reaction of salicylic acid, $C_7H_6O_3$, and acetic anhydride, $C_4H_6O_3$: $C_7H_6O_3(s) + C_4H_6O_3(l) \longrightarrow C_9H_8O_4(s) + HC_2H_3O_2(l)$.
a. What mass of aspirin (kg) could be produced from 75.0 mol of salicylic acid?
b. What mass of acetic anhydride (kg) would be required?
c. At 20°C, how many liters of acetic acid, $HC_2H_3O_2$, would be formed? The density of $HC_2H_3O_2$ is 1.05 g/mL.

SECTION 3

Limiting Reactants and Percentage Yield

REVIEWING MAIN IDEAS

17. Distinguish between ideal and real stoichiometric calculations.

18. Distinguish between the limiting reactant and the excess reactant in a chemical reaction.

19. a. Distinguish between the theoretical yield and actual yield in stoichiometric calculations.
b. How does the value of the theoretical yield generally compare with the value of the actual yield?

20. What is the percentage yield of a reaction?

21. Why are actual yields usually less than calculated theoretical yields?

PRACTICE PROBLEMS

22. Given the reactant amounts specified in each chemical equation, determine the limiting reactant in each case:

a. $HCl + NaOH \longrightarrow NaCl + H_2O$
2.0 mol, 2.5 mol

b. $Zn + 2HCl \longrightarrow ZnCl_2 + H_2$
2.5 mol, 6.0 mol

c. $2Fe(OH)_3 + 3H_2SO_4 \longrightarrow Fe_2(SO_4)_3 + 6H_2O$
4.0 mol, 6.5 mol

(Hint: See Sample Problem F.)

23. For each reaction specified in Problem 22, determine the amount in moles of excess reactant that remains. (Hint: See Sample Problem G.)

24. For each reaction specified in Problem 22, calculate the amount in moles of each product formed.

25. a. If 2.50 mol of copper and 5.50 mol of silver nitrate are available to react by single replacement, identify the limiting reactant.
b. Determine the amount in moles of excess reactant remaining.
c. Determine the amount in moles of each product formed.
d. Determine the mass of each product formed.

26. Sulfuric acid reacts with aluminum hydroxide by double replacement.
a. If 30.0 g of sulfuric acid react with 25.0 g of aluminum hydroxide, identify the limiting reactant.
b. Determine the mass of excess reactant remaining.
c. Determine the mass of each product formed. Assume 100% yield.

27. The energy used to power one of the Apollo lunar missions was supplied by the following overall reaction: $2N_2H_4 + (CH_3)_2N_2H_2 + 3N_2O_4 \longrightarrow 6N_2 + 2CO_2 + 8H_2O$. For the phase of the mission when the lunar module ascended from the surface of the moon, a total of 1200. kg N_2H_4 was available to react with 1000. kg $(CH_3)_2N_2H_2$ and 4500. kg N_2O_4.
a. For this portion of the flight, which of the allocated components was used up first?
b. How much water, in kilograms, was put into the lunar atmosphere through this reaction?

26. a. H_2SO_4 is the limiting reactant.
b. 9.05 g excess $Al(OH)_3$
c. 34.9 g $Al_2(SO_4)_3$, 11.0 g H_2O

27. a. N_2O_4 was used up first.
b. 2.350×10^3 kg H_2O

28. Calculate the indicated quantity for each of the various chemical reactions given:
   a. theoretical yield = 20.0 g, actual yield = 15.0 g, percentage yield = ?
   b. theoretical yield = 1.0 g, percentage yield = 90.0%, actual yield = ?
   c. theoretical yield = 5.00 g, actual yield = 4.75 g, percentage yield = ?
   d. theoretical yield = 3.45 g, percentage yield = 48.0%, actual yield = ?

29. The percentage yield for the reaction
$$PCl_3 + Cl_2 \longrightarrow PCl_5$$
is 83.2%. What mass of PCl_5 is expected from the reaction of 73.7 g PCl_3 with excess chlorine?

30. The Ostwald process for producing nitric acid from ammonia consists of the following steps:
$4NH_3(g) + 5O_2(g) \longrightarrow 4NO(g) + 6H_2O(g)$
$2NO(g) + O_2(g) \longrightarrow 2NO_2(g)$
$3NO_2(g) + H_2O(g) \longrightarrow 2HNO_3(aq) + NO(g)$
If the yield in each step is 94.0%, how many grams of nitric acid can be produced from 5.00kg of ammonia?

Mixed Review

REVIEWING MAIN IDEAS

31. Magnesium is obtained from sea water. $Ca(OH)_2$ is added to sea water to precipitate $Mg(OH)_2$. The precipitate is filtered and reacted with HCl to produce $MgCl_2$. The $MgCl_2$ is electrolyzed to produce Mg and Cl_2. If 185.0 g of magnesium are recovered from 1000. g $MgCl_2$, what is the percentage yield for this reaction?

32. Phosphate baking powder is a mixture of starch, sodium hydrogen carbonate, and calcium dihydrogen phosphate. When mixed with water, phosphate baking powder releases carbon dioxide gas, causing a dough or batter to bubble and rise.
$2NaHCO_3(aq) + Ca(H_2PO_4)_2(aq) \longrightarrow Na_2HPO_4(aq) + CaHPO_4(aq) + 2CO_2(g) + 2H_2O(l)$
If 0.750 L CO_2 is needed for a cake, and each kilogram of baking powder contains 168 g of $NaHCO_3$, how many grams of baking powder must be used to generate this amount of CO_2? The density of CO_2 at baking temperature is about 1.20 g/L.

33. Coal gasification is a process that converts coal into methane gas. If this reaction has a percentage yield of 85.0%, what mass of methane can be obtained from 1250 g of carbon?
$$2C(s) + 2H_2O(l) \longrightarrow CH_4(g) + CO_2(g)$$

34. If the percentage yield for the coal gasification process is increased to 95%, what mass of methane can be obtained from 2750 g of carbon?

35. Builders and dentists must store plaster of Paris, $CaSO_4 \bullet \frac{1}{2}H_2O$, in airtight containers to prevent it from absorbing water vapor from the air and changing to gypsum, $CaSO_4 \bullet 2H_2O$. How many liters of water vapor evolve when 2.00 kg of gypsum are heated at 110°C to produce plaster of Paris? At 110°C, the density of water vapor is 0.574 g/L.

36. Gold can be recovered from sea water by reacting the water with zinc, which is refined from zinc oxide. The zinc displaces the gold in the water. What mass of gold can be recovered if 2.00 g of ZnO and an excess of sea water are available?
$2ZnO(s) + C(s) \longrightarrow 2Zn(s) + CO_2(g)$
$2Au^{3+}(aq) + 3Zn(s) \longrightarrow 3Zn^{2+}(aq) + 2Au(s)$

CRITICAL THINKING

37. **Relating Ideas** The chemical equation is a good source of information concerning a reaction. Explain the relationship between the actual yield of a reaction product and the chemical equation of the product.

38. **Analyzing Results** Very seldom are chemists able to achieve a 100% yield of a product from a chemical reaction. However, the yield of a reaction is usually important because of the expense involved in producing less product. For example, when magnesium metal is heated in a crucible at high temperatures, the product magnesium oxide, MgO, is formed. Based on your analysis of the reaction, describe some of the actions that you would take to increase your percentage yield. The reaction is as follows:
$$2Mg(s) + O_2(g) \longrightarrow 2MgO(s)$$

CHAPTER REVIEW

28. a. 75.0% b. 0.90 g
c. 95.0% d. 1.66 g
29. 93.2 g PCl_5
30. 1.02×10^4 g HNO_3
31. 72.46%
32. 10.2 g baking powder
33. 710. g CH_4
34. 1750 g CH_4
35. 547 L water vapor
36. 3.23 g Au
37. The chemical equation shows the theoretical yield of product to be expected under ideal conditions. Because it is rare for a reaction to meet ideal conditions, the actual yield is usually less than the yield predicted by the equation.
38. To ensure that all magnesium is converted to MgO, I would use pure oxygen, not air, to carry out the reaction, because Mg could react with N_2 in air to form Mg_3N_2. The pure oxygen should be in excess.

CHAPTER REVIEW

39. A percentage yield greater than 100% is not possible, because the actual yield can never be greater than the theoretical yield—the yield predicted by the chemical equation. A calculated percentage yield greater than 100% may result if the product is not dry or contains impurities such as unreacted reactant or the product of a competing reaction.

40. A smoldering campfire is not getting enough oxygen to produce the products of complete combustion, CO_2 and H_2O. Blowing on the smoldering fire may increase the amount of oxygen to the stoichiometric amount and cause the fire to burn completely.

41. a. 2.62×10^2 kg C
    b. 3.91×10^3 kg Fe_3C

42. a. 56.7 g Al_2O_3
    b. Because the reaction occurs on the surface of the metal, 30 g Al will not react completely, thereby reducing the yield.

43. a. 168.8 g CO_2
    b. 323.4 g $MgCO_3$
    c. 99.9 g $Ca_3(PO_4)_2$

44. Refer to the One-Stop Planner for appropriate scoring rubrics. Be sure that students include information about Germany's need for nitrogen compounds for the manufacture of explosives prior to World War I. A reasonable yield of ammonia could be obtained only at high pressures. (The reaction also is carried out at high temperature in the presence of a catalyst. The high temperature actually diminishes the yield but allows the reaction to occur more rapidly. Likewise, the catalyst does not improve the yield but allows the reaction to reach equilibrium more rapidly. While high temperature and the use of a catalyst do not improve the yield, they are necessary to make the process commercially feasible.)

45. As students begin to mix pigments experimentally, warn them to keep track of how much of each pigment they are using. For each color mixed, have students develop a quasi equation whose coefficients indicate the proportions of water and primary pigments used in compounding the color.

39. **Analyzing Results** In the lab, you run an experiment that appears to have a percentage yield of 115%. Propose reasons for this result. Can an actual yield ever exceed a theoretical yield? Explain your answer.

40. **Relating Ideas** Explain the stoichiometry of blowing air on a smoldering campfire to keep the coals burning.

USING THE HANDBOOK

41. The steel-making process described in the Transition Metal section of the *Elements Handbook* (Appendix A) shows the equation for the formation of iron carbide. Use this equation to answer the following questions:
    a. If 3.65×10^3 kg of iron is used in a steel-making process, what is the minimum mass of carbon needed to react with all of the iron?
    b. What is the theoretical mass of iron carbide that is formed?

42. The reaction of aluminum with oxygen to produce a protective coating for the metal's surface is described in the discussion of aluminum in Group 13 of the *Elements Handbook* (Appendix A). Use this equation to answer the following questions:
    a. What mass of aluminum oxide would theoretically be formed if a 30.0 g piece of aluminum foil reacted with excess oxygen?
    b. Why would you expect the actual yield from this reaction to be far less than the mass you calculated in item (a)?

43. The reactions of oxide compounds to produce carbonates, phosphates, and sulfates are described in the section on oxides in Group 16 of the *Elements Handbook* (Appendix A). Use those equations to answer the following questions:
    a. What mass of CO_2 is needed to react with 154.6 g MgO?
    b. What mass of magnesium carbonate is produced?
    c. When 45.7 g P_4O_{10} is reacted with an excess of calcium oxide, what mass of calcium phosphate is produced?

RESEARCH AND WRITING

44. Research the history of the Haber process for the production of ammonia. What was the significance of this process in history? How is this process related to the discussion of reaction yields in this chapter?

ALTERNATIVE ASSESSMENT

45. **Performance** Just as reactants combine in certain proportions to form a product, colors can be combined to create other colors. Artists do this all the time to find just the right color for their paintings. Using poster paint, determine the proportions of primary pigments used to create the following colors. Your proportions should be such that anyone could mix the color perfectly.

46. **Performance** Write two of your own sample problems that are descriptions of how to solve a mass-mass problem. Assume that your sample problems will be used by other students to learn how to solve mass-mass problems.

46. Allow students to choose any two chemical reactions that they know or find in the text. The completed sample problems should include a statement of the problem and the four elements of the solution as developed in Sample Problem E.

Standards-Based Assessment

Answer the following items on a separate piece of paper.

MULTIPLE CHOICE

1. In stoichiometry, chemists are mainly concerned with
   A. the types of bonds found in compounds.
   B. mass relationships in chemical reactions.
   C. energy changes occurring in chemical reactions.
   D. the speed with which chemical reactions occur.

2. Assume ideal stoichiometry in the reaction $CH_4 + 2O_2 \longrightarrow CO_2 + 2H_2O$. If you know the mass of CH_4, you can calculate
   A. only the mass of CO_2 produced.
   B. only the mass of O_2 reacting.
   C. only the mass of $CO_2 + H_2O$ produced.
   D. the mass of O_2 reacting and $CO_2 + H_2O$ produced.

3. Which mole ratio for the equation $6Li + N_2 \longrightarrow 2Li_3N$ is incorrect?
   A. $\frac{6 \text{ mol Li}}{2 \text{ mol } N_2}$ C. $\frac{2 \text{ mol } Li_3N}{1 \text{ mol } N_2}$
   B. $\frac{1 \text{ mol } N_2}{6 \text{ mol Li}}$ D. $\frac{2 \text{ mol } Li_3N}{6 \text{ mol Li}}$

4. For the reaction below, how many moles of N_2 are required to produce 18 mol NH_3?
   $$N_2 + 3H_2 \longrightarrow 2NH_3$$
   A. 4.5 C. 18
   B. 9.0 D. 36

5. What mass of NaCl can be produced by the reaction of 0.75 mol Cl_2?
   $$2Na + Cl_2 \longrightarrow 2NaCl$$
   A. 0.75 g C. 44 g
   B. 1.5 g D. 88 g

6. What mass of CO_2 can be produced from 25.0 g $CaCO_3$ given the decomposition reaction
   $$CaCO_3 \longrightarrow CaO + CO_2$$
   A. 11.0 g C. 25.0 g
   B. 22.0 g D. 56.0 g

7. If a chemical reaction involving substances A and B stops when B is completely used up, then B is referred to as the
   A. excess reactant. C. limiting reactant.
   B. primary reactant. D. primary product.

8. If a chemist calculates the maximum amount of product that could be obtained in a chemical reaction, he or she is calculating the
   A. percentage yield.
   B. mole ratio.
   C. theoretical yield.
   D. actual yield.

9. What is the maximum number of moles of $AlCl_3$ that can be produced from 5.0 mol Al and 6.0 mol Cl_2?
   $$2Al + 3Cl_2 \longrightarrow 2AlCl_3$$
   A. 2.0 mol $AlCl_3$ C. 5.0 mol $AlCl_3$
   B. 4.0 mol $AlCl_3$ D. 6.0 mol $AlCl_3$

SHORT ANSWER

10. Why is a balanced equation necessary to solve a mass-mass stoichiometry problem?

11. What data are necessary to calculate the percentage yield of a reaction?

EXTENDED RESPONSE

12. A student makes a compound in the laboratory and reports an actual yield of 120%. Is this result possible? Assuming that all masses were measured correctly, give an explanation.

13. Benzene, C_6H_6, is reacted with bromine, Br_2, to produce bromobenzene, C_6H_5Br, and hydrogen bromide, HBr, as shown below. When 40.0 g of benzene are reacted with 95.0 g of bromine, 65.0 g of bromobenzene are produced.
    $$C_6H_6 + Br_2 \longrightarrow C_6H_5Br + HBr$$
    a. Which compound is the limiting reactant?
    b. What is the theoretical yield of bromobenzene?
    c. What is the reactant in excess, and how much remains after the reaction is completed?
    d. What is the percentage yield?

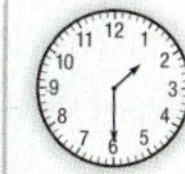

Test Tip
Choose an answer to a question based on both information that you already know and information that is presented in the question.

STANDARDS-BASED ASSESSMENT

To give students practice under more realistic testing conditions, give them 60 minutes to answer all of the questions in this Standardized Test Preparation.

Test Answers

1. B
2. D
3. A
4. B
5. D
6. A
7. C
8. C
9. B
10. The coefficients of the balanced equation are needed for the mole-mole ratio that is necessary to solve stoichiometric problems involving two different substances.
11. the theoretical yield and the actual yield of the product
12. The product was impure, so the mass contained the product and other substances. For example, if NaCl is made from HCl and NaOH but is not dried, the mass of NaCl can include water, which would result in a yield greater than 100%.
13. a. benzene;
    b. 80.4 g of bromobenzene;
    c. bromine, 13.2 g;
    d. 80.8%

States of Matter

① Core Instruction

Chapter Resources

- The Teacher's Edition wrap has extensive teaching support for every lesson, including Misconception Alerts, Teach from Visuals, Demonstrations, Teaching Tips, Differentiated Instruction, and Problem Solving support.
- Several additional presentation tools are available online for every chapter, including Animated Chemistry features and Visual Concepts.
- You can open your lesson with the Why It Matters Video: States of Matter.

Section	Instruction	Labs and Demonstrations Go Online for Materials Lists and Solutions Lists.
10.1	■ **Textbook:** The Kinetic-Molecular Theory of Matter **Power Presentations**	■ **Demonstration:** Compressibility of Gases
10.2	■ **Textbook:** Liquids **Teaching Visuals:** Diffusion **Power Presentations**	
10.3	■ **Textbook:** Solids **Teaching Visuals:** Comparing Relative Volumes for a Solid, Liquid, and Gas • Unit Cells • Mercury in Three States • Sodium as a Solid, Liquid, and Gas **Power Presentations**	■ **Demonstration:** Diffusion of Liquids ■ **Demonstration:** Evaporation ■ **Lab:** Viscosity of Liquids (Core Skill) ■ **Lab:** Evaporation and Ink Solvents (Forensics)
10.4	■ **Textbook:** Changes of State **Animated Chemistry:** Kinetic-Molecular Theory **Teaching Visuals:** Liquid-Vapor Equilibrium System • Changes of State • Measuring the Vapor Pressure of a Liquid • Molar Enthalpy Versus Temperature for Water • Molar Enthalpies and Entropies of Fusion and Vaporization **Power Presentations**	■ **Demonstration:** Changes of State in Ice and Liquid Water ■ **Lab:** "Wet" Dry Ice (Core Skill) ■ **Lab:** Constructing a Heating/Cooling Curve (Core Skill)
10.5	■ **Textbook:** Water **Teaching Visuals:** Ice and Water • Heating Curve for Water • Phase Diagram for H_2O • Phase Diagram for CO_2 • Temporary Dipoles **Power Presentations**	

② Support and Intervention

- **Interactive Reader** (English and Spanish)
- **Study Guide**
- **Interactive Review:** Review Games, Concept Maps, and Section Self-Checks
- **Scientific Reasoning Skill Builder**
- **Learn It! Videos**
- **Solve It! Cards**
- **Interactive Demos**
- **Sample Problem Sets**

③ Specialized Support

- **Chapter Summary Audio Files**
- **Interactive Reader Audio Files**
- **Differentiated Instruction:** Inclusion, Below Level, and English Learners (TE wrap)

Enrichment and Challenge

- **Differentiated Instruction:** Pre-AP (TE wrap)
- **WebLinks**

Assessment

- **Section Formative Assessments** (SE)
- **Section Quizzes**
- **Chapter Review** (SE)
- **Chapter Tests A and B**
- **Alternative Assessment** (TE wrap)
- **Online Assessment and Remediation**
- **ExamView Banks**

Where do I find it?

	Resource	PRINT	DVD	ONLINE
1	Animated Chemistry		■	■
1	Demonstrations (TE wrap)	■		■
1	Interactive Whiteboard		■	■
1	Labs		■	■
1	PowerPresentations		■	■
1	QuickLabs	■	■	■
1	Teaching Visuals		■	■
1	Textbook	■	■	■
1	Visual Concepts		■	■
1	Why It Matters Videos		■	■
2	Interactive Demos		■	■
2	Interactive Reader	■	■	■
2	Interactive Reviews		■	■
2	Learn It! Videos		■	■
2	Sample Problem Sets		■	■
2	Scientific Reasoning Skill Builder		■	■
2	Smart Grapher Tool		■	■
2	Solve It! Cards		■	■
2	Study Guide		■	■
3	Chapter Summary Audio Files		■	■
3	Differentiated Instruction (TE wrap)	■		
3	Interactive Reader Audio Files		■	■

CHAPTER 10

Chapter Overview

Section 1 introduces the kinetic-molecular theory of matter and explains how the theory accounts for certain physical properties of ideal gases, which differ from real gases.

Section 2 uses the kinetic-molecular theory to describe properties of liquids and explain changes of state involving liquids.

Section 3 describes the properties of solids, contrasts them with liquid properties, and explains them on the basis of the kinetic-molecular theory.

Section 4 covers changes of state and the factors that determine them.

Section 5 covers the structure, physical properties, and changes of state of water.

▼ Focus and Motivate

Activate Prior Knowledge

Students may need a review of the following concepts:

- the properties of matter
- density
- covalent and ionic bonding

About the Image

Water is the only substance on Earth that exists in nature as a solid, liquid, and gas. As a solid, water molecules form crystals, such as those that make up an icicle. The total three-dimensional arrangement of these molecules within an icicle is its crystal structure.

Why It Matters

Students can access the video online and find other helpful resources at **HMDScience.com**.

CHAPTER 10

States of Matter

SECTION 1 The Kinetic-Molecular Theory of Matter
SECTION 2 Liquids
SECTION 3 Solids
SECTION 4 Changes of State
SECTION 5 Water

ONLINE Chemistry
HMDScience.com

ONLINE LABS include:
Viscosity of Liquids
Evaporation and Ink Solvents
"Wet" Dry Ice
Constructing a Heating/Cooling Curve

PREMIUM CONTENT
Why It Matters Video
HMDScience.com
States of Matter

Lab Preview

The following labs and demonstrations support the concepts presented in this chapter.

LABS

Viscosity of Liquids (Core Skill)
Evaporation and Ink Solvents (Forensics)
"Wet" Dry Ice (Core Skill)
Constructing a Heating/Cooling Curve (Core Skill)

DEMONSTRATIONS

Compressibility of Gases
Diffusion of Liquids
Evaporation
Changes of State in Ice and Liquid Water

The Kinetic-Molecular Theory of Matter

Key Terms
kinetic-molecular theory
ideal gas
elastic collision
diffusion
effusion
real gas

SECTION 1

Main Ideas

- The kinetic-molecular theory explains the constant motion of gas particles.
- The kinetic-molecular theory explains the physical properties of gases.
- Real gases do not behave according to the kinetic-molecular theory.

In the chapter "Matter and Change," you read that matter exists on Earth in the forms of solids, liquids, and gases. Although it is not usually possible to observe individual particles directly, scientists have studied large groups of these particles as they occur in solids, liquids, and gases.

In the late nineteenth century, scientists developed the kinetic-molecular theory of matter to account for the behavior of the atoms and molecules that make up matter. **The kinetic-molecular theory is based on the idea that particles of matter are always in motion.** The theory can be used to explain the properties of solids, liquids, and gases in terms of the energy of particles and the forces that act between them. In this section, you will study the theory as it applies to gas molecules.

MAIN IDEA

The kinetic-molecular theory explains the constant motion of gas particles.

The kinetic-molecular theory can help you understand the behavior of gas molecules and the physical properties of gases. The theory provides a model of what is called an ideal gas. **An ideal gas is a hypothetical gas that perfectly fits all the assumptions of the kinetic-molecular theory.**

The kinetic-molecular theory of gases is based on the following five assumptions:

1. *Gases consist of large numbers of tiny particles that are far apart relative to their size.* These particles, usually molecules or atoms, typically occupy a volume that is about 1000 times greater than the volume occupied by an equal number of particles in the liquid or solid state. Thus, molecules of gases are much farther apart than molecules of liquids or solids. Most of the volume occupied by a gas is empty space, which is the reason that gases have a lower density than liquids and solids do. This also explains the fact that gases are easily compressed.
2. *Collisions between gas particles and between particles and container walls are elastic collisions.* **An elastic collision is one in which there is no net loss of total kinetic energy.** Kinetic energy is transferred between two particles during collisions. However, the total kinetic energy of the two particles remains the same as long as temperature is constant.

Differentiated Instruction

INCLUSION

Kinesthetic learners will benefit from acting out a model of the states of matter. Have the class stand in place and wiggle their arms. Then ask them to walk slowly around the room, brushing gently against each other as they do so. Finally, ask students to get as far away as possible from one another. Tell them to return to their seats and explain how they just demonstrated the three states of matter. Students should understand that wiggling their arms while remaining in place represents the particles of a solid, brushing against one another represents the particles of a liquid, and moving as far apart as possible represents the particles of a gas. Emphasize that the particles in all three states of matter are always in motion. Point out that the kinetic-molecular theory describes the behavior of these particles.

SECTION 1

Plan and Prepare ▼

Objectives

Upon completion of this section, students should be able to do the following:

- State the kinetic-molecular theory of matter, and describe how it explains certain properties of matter.
- List the five assumptions of the kinetic-molecular theory of gases. Define the terms ideal gas and real gas.
- Describe each of the following characteristic properties of gases: expansion, density, fluidity, compressibility, diffusion, and effusion.
- Describe the conditions under which a real gas deviates from "ideal" behavior.

Classroom Catalyst

Open a bottle of strong-smelling perfume or dilute ammonia solution in the middle of the classroom. Ask students to raise a hand when they first detect the odor of the vapor. Ask them to try to explain this event in terms of the motion of molecules.

Safety Be sure no one breathes the fumes directly from or close to the bottle.

Teach ▼

Classroom Discussion

You may choose to begin this chapter by discussing the fundamental physical properties of gases and then introducing the kinetic-molecular theory of gases. Compare and contrast ideal and real gases, and discuss other instances in which real and ideal situations exist. For example, an ideal car might be completely energy-efficient, but a real car loses energy through friction and unburned fuel. Ideal situations are important models but rarely, if ever, exist in real life.

▼ Teach continued

TEACH FROM VISUALS

FIGURE 1.1 Have students relate the assumptions of the kinetic-molecular theory of gases to the figure. Point out that the large size of the particles relative to the space involved is not realistic but is necessary in the illustration so that the particles can be seen.

Demo Problem

Have students use the formula for KE to explain why a truck has more kinetic energy than a car, even when they are moving at the same speed. Then have students explain why two gas particles at the same temperature but with different masses must move at different speeds. Refer to the formula for KE to show students that if the mass (m) is smaller, then the speed (v^2) must be greater, so that the kinetic energy is the same between the two gas particles.

Misconception Alert!

Ask students to give examples of a fluid. Answers will most likely include liquids such as water and juice. Point out that gases are also considered fluids. Have students explain why.

FIGURE 1.1

Elastic Collisions Gas particles travel in a straight-line motion until they collide with each other or the walls of their container.

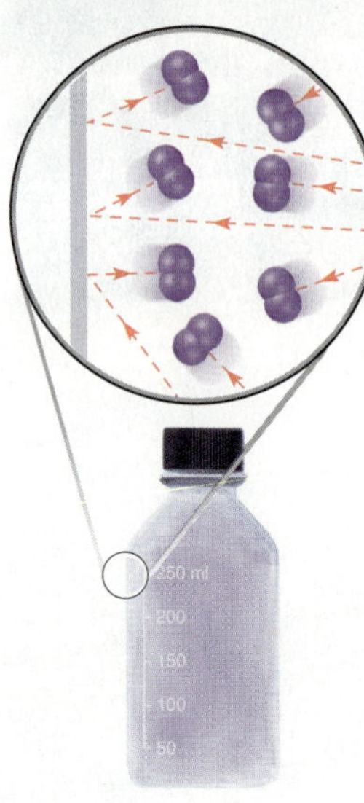

3. *Gas particles are in continuous, rapid, random motion. They therefore possess kinetic energy, which is energy of motion.* Gas particles move in all directions, as shown in **Figure 1.1.** The kinetic energy of the particles overcomes the attractive forces between them, except near the temperature at which the gas condenses and becomes a liquid.
4. *There are no forces of attraction between gas particles.* You can think of ideal gas molecules as behaving like small billiard balls. When they collide, they do not stick together but immediately bounce apart.
5. *The temperature of a gas depends on the average kinetic energy of the particles of the gas.* The kinetic energy of any moving object, including a particle, is given by the following equation:

Kinetic Energy $$KE = \frac{1}{2}mv^2$$

In the equation, m is the mass of the particle and v is its speed. Because all the particles of a specific gas have the same mass, their kinetic energies depend only on their speeds. The average speeds and kinetic energies of gas particles increase with an increase in temperature and decrease with a decrease in temperature.

All gases at the same temperature have the same average kinetic energy. Therefore, at the same temperature, lighter gas particles, such as hydrogen molecules, have higher average speeds than do heavier gas particles, such as oxygen molecules.

MAIN IDEA

The kinetic-molecular theory explains the physical properties of gases.

The kinetic-molecular theory applies only to ideal gases. Although ideal gases do not actually exist, many gases behave nearly ideally if pressure is not very high and temperature is not very low. As you will see, the kinetic-molecular theory accounts for the physical properties of gases.

Expansion

Gases do not have a definite shape or volume. They completely fill any container in which they are enclosed, and take its shape. A gas transferred from a one-liter vessel to a two-liter vessel will expand to fill the larger volume. The kinetic-molecular theory explains these facts. According to the theory, gas particles move rapidly in all directions (assumption 3), with no significant attraction between them (assumption 4).

Fluidity

Because the attractive forces between gas particles are insignificant (assumption 4), gas particles glide easily past one another. This ability to flow causes gases to behave as liquids do. Because liquids and gases flow, they are both referred to as *fluids.*

Differentiated Instruction

INCLUSION

Use the following activity to help developmentally-delayed students understand the expansion of gases. Give each student a balloon, and have the students inflate their balloons. Remind students that air is a mixture of different gases, such as nitrogen and oxygen. Ask students how inflating a balloon illustrates the expansion of gases.

Students should realize that the gas particles expanded, causing the balloon to inflate.

Have students allow the gases to escape from the balloon. Ask students to explain what happened to the gas particles. Students should explain that the gas particles moved even farther apart as they expanded to fill the room.

Low Density

The density of a gaseous substance at atmospheric pressure is about 1/1000 the density of the same substance in the liquid or solid state. The reason is that the particles are so much farther apart in the gaseous state (assumption 1).

Compressibility

During compression, the gas particles, which are initially very far apart (assumption 1), are crowded closer together. The volume of a given sample of a gas can be greatly decreased. Steel cylinders containing gases under pressure are widely used in industry. When they are full, such cylinders may contain more than 100 times as many particles of gas as nonpressurized containers of the same size could contain.

Diffusion and Effusion

Gases spread out and mix with one another, even without being stirred. If the stopper is removed from a container of ammonia in a room, ammonia gas will mix uniformly with the air and spread throughout the room. The random and continuous motion of the ammonia molecules (assumption 3) carries them throughout the available space. **Such spontaneous mixing of the particles of two substances caused by their random motion is called diffusion.**

Gases diffuse readily into one another and mix together due to the rapid motion of the molecules and the empty space between the molecules. The gas molecules in each of the two flasks in **Figure 1.2a** continuously move about in separate flasks because the stopcock is closed. When the stopcock is open, the gas molecules continuously diffuse back and forth from one flask to the other through the opening in the stopcock, as shown in **Figure 1.2b.**

Diffusion is a process by which particles of a gas spread out spontaneously and mix with other gases. **In contrast, effusion is a process by which gas particles pass through a tiny opening.**

FIGURE 1.2

Diffusion Gases diffuse readily into one another. The space between the molecules allows different gases to mix together easily.

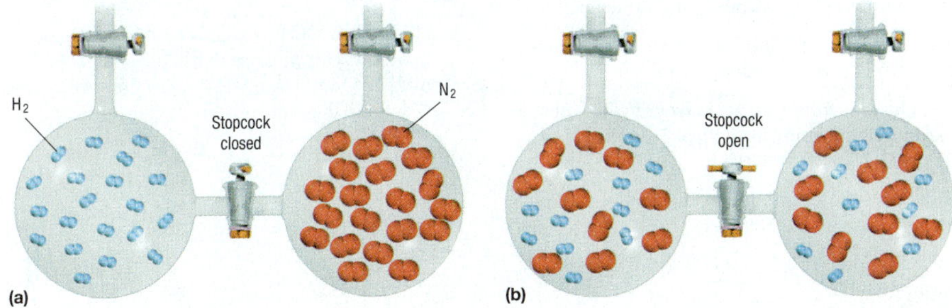

Demo Problem

Point out that oil floats on water because oil has a lower density than water. Tell students that the density of cooking oil is about 0.930 g/cm^3. Have them use the information about the low density of gases to calculate what the density of this oil should be if it were a gas at atmospheric pressure.

Answer:
$0.930\ g/cm^3 \times 1/1000 = 0.000930\ g/cm^3$

Demonstration

COMPRESSIBILITY OF GASES

Use **two balloons** to demonstrate the compressibility of gases. Fill one balloon with **water** and the other balloon with **air**. Be careful not to over-inflate the balloon with air; it must remain compressible. Try to compress both balloons between your two hands. Have students explain why the balloon filled with water is not as compressible as the balloon filled with air. Students should explain that water is more dense than air and thus harder to compress.

PRE-AP

Have students research Graham's laws regarding the behavior of gases.

Graham's law of diffusion explains how two gases mix. The law also states that the rate at which gases diffuse is inversely proportional to the square root of their densities.

Graham's law of effusion explains the rate at which a gas escapes through a pinhole into a vacuum. This law states that the rate of effusion of a gas is inversely proportional to the square root of either the density or the molar mass of the gas. Have students select two gases and show how Graham's laws apply to their behavior.

▼ Teach *continued*

Critical Thinking

Answer: If a gas is compressed enough it changes to a liquid.

▼ Assess and Reteach

Assess Use the Formative Assessment on this page to evaluate student mastery of the section.

Reteach For students who need additional instruction, download the Section Study Guide.

Response to Intervention To reassess students' mastery, use the Section Quiz, available to print or to take directly online at **HMDScience.com**.

FIGURE 1.3

Real Gases

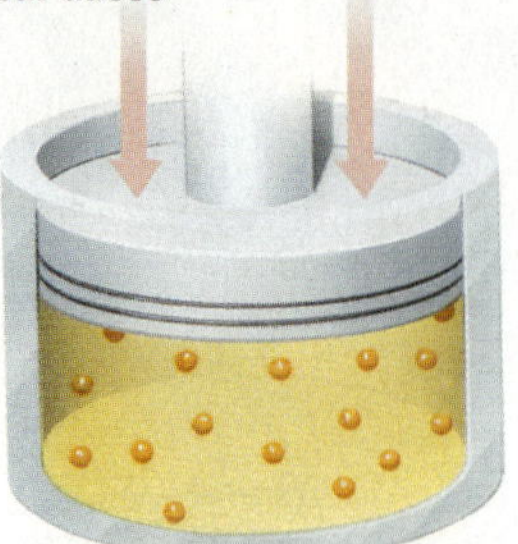

(a) Gas molecules in a car engine cylinder expand to fill the cylinder.

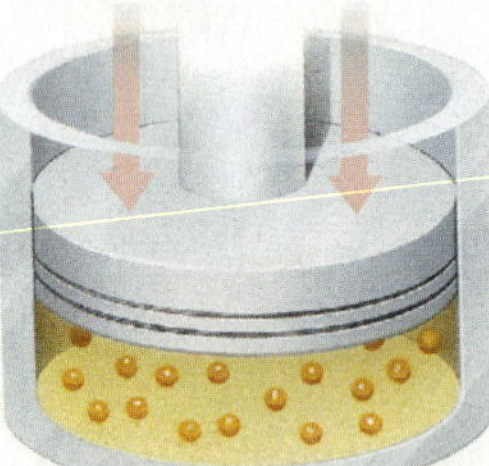

(b) As pressure is exerted on them, the gas molecules move closer together, reducing their volume.

CRITICAL THINKING

Describe What will eventually happen to a gas if it is compressed enough?

The rates of effusion of different gases are directly proportional to the velocities of their particles. Because of this proportionality, molecules of low mass effuse faster than molecules of high mass.

MAIN IDEA

Real gases do not behave according to the kinetic-molecular theory.

Because particles of gases occupy space and exert attractive forces on each other, all real gases deviate to some degree from ideal gas behavior. **A real gas is a gas that does not behave completely according to the assumptions of the kinetic-molecular theory.** At very high pressures and low temperatures, the gas particles will be closer together and their kinetic energy will be insufficient to completely overcome the attractive forces. At such conditions, the gas is most likely to behave like a non-ideal gas. These conditions are illustrated in **Figure 1.3.**

The kinetic-molecular theory is more likely to hold true for gases whose particles have little attraction for each other. The noble gases, such as helium, He, and neon, Ne, show essentially ideal gas behavior over a wide range of temperatures and pressures. The particles of these gases are monatomic and thus nonpolar. The particles of gases, such as nitrogen, N_2, and hydrogen, H_2, are nonpolar diatomic molecules. The behavior of these gases most closely approximates that of the ideal gas under certain conditions. The more polar the molecules of a gas are, the greater the attractive forces between them and the more the gas will deviate from ideal gas behavior. For example, highly polar gases, such as ammonia (NH_3) and water vapor, deviate from ideal behavior to a larger degree than nonpolar gases.

SECTION 1 FORMATIVE ASSESSMENT

Reviewing Main Ideas

1. Use the kinetic-molecular theory to explain the following properties of gases: expansion, fluidity, low density, compressibility, and diffusion.
2. Describe the conditions under which a real gas is most likely to behave ideally.
3. Which of the following gases would you expect to deviate significantly from ideal behavior: He, O_2, H_2, H_2O, N_2, HCl, or NH_3?
4. How does the kinetic-molecular theory explain the pressure exerted by gases?
5. What happens to gas particles when a gas is compressed?
6. What happens to gas particles when a gas is heated?

Critical Thinking

7. **DRAWING CONCLUSIONS** Molecules of hydrogen escape from Earth, but molecules of oxygen and nitrogen are held to the surface and remain in the atmosphere. Explain.

Answers to Section Assessment

1. Expansion: gas particles move rapidly in all directions without significant attraction between them. Fluidity: attractive forces between gas particles are too weak to hold the particles in a rigid structure. Low density and compressibility: gas particles are farther apart than they are in any other state. Diffusion: gas particles are in continuous and random motion.
2. Under high temperature and low pressure, real gases approach ideal gas behavior.
3. H_2O, NH_3, and HCl, because they are polar.
4. Pressure exerted by gases is caused by collisions of the gas molecules with the walls of the container.
5. They are pushed closer together.
6. They move more rapidly, increasing their average kinetic energy.
7. The lower mass of hydrogen molecules means that they are traveling at higher speeds, so fewer of them remain captured by gravity.

Liquids

SECTION 2

Main Idea

The intermolecular forces of liquids determine their properties.

Key Terms

fluid	capillary action	evaporation
surface tension	vaporization	freezing

When you think of Earth's oceans, lakes, and rivers and the many liquids you use every day, it is hard to believe that liquids are the *least* common state of matter in the universe. Liquids are less common than solids and gases because a substance can exist in the liquid state only within a relatively narrow range of temperatures and pressures. In this section, you will examine the properties of the liquid state and compare them with those of the solid state and the gas state. These properties will be discussed in terms of the kinetic-molecular theory.

MAIN IDEA

The intermolecular forces of liquids determine their properties.

A liquid can be described as a form of matter that has a definite volume and takes the shape of its container. The properties of liquids can be understood by applying the kinetic-molecular theory.

As in a gas, particles in a liquid are in constant motion. However, the particles in a liquid are closer together than the particles in a gas are. Therefore, the attractive forces between particles in a liquid are more effective than those between particles in a gas. This attraction between liquid particles is caused by intermolecular forces, such as dipole-dipole forces, London dispersion forces, and hydrogen bonding.

Liquids are more ordered than gases because of the stronger intermolecular forces and the lower mobility of the liquid particles. According to the kinetic-molecular theory of liquids, the particles are not bound together in fixed positions, but move about constantly. This particle mobility explains why liquids and gases are referred to as fluids. **A fluid is a substance that can flow and therefore take the shape of its container.** Most liquids naturally flow downhill because of gravity. However, some liquids can flow in other directions as well. For example, liquid helium near absolute zero is able to flow uphill.

Relatively High Density

At normal atmospheric pressure, most substances are hundreds of times denser in a liquid state than in a gaseous state. This higher density is a result of the close arrangement of liquid particles. Most substances are only slightly less dense (about 10%) in a liquid state than in a solid state, however. Water is one of the few substances that becomes less dense when it solidifies, as will be discussed further in Section 5.

At the same temperature and pressure, different liquids can differ greatly in density. **Figure 2.1** shows some liquids and solids with different densities. The densities differ to such an extent that the liquids form layers.

FIGURE 2.1

Density Solids and liquids of different densities are shown. The densest materials are at the bottom. The least dense are at the top. (Dyes have been added to the liquids to make the layers more visible.)

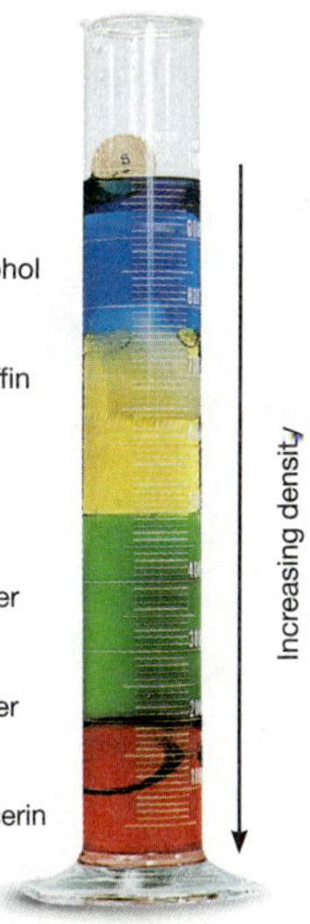

Differentiated Instruction

INCLUSION

Show students a closed, colorless container of soft drink. Ask them how they are able to tell that the container is filled with a liquid. Lead them to the idea that liquids have definite volume but take the shape of their container. Contrast these properties with those of gases, which have neither fixed shape nor fixed volume.

Plan and Prepare

Objectives

Upon completion of this section, students should be able to do the following:

- Describe the motion of particles in liquids and the properties of liquids according to the kinetic-molecular theory.
- Discuss the process by which liquids can change into a gas. Define *vaporization*.
- Discuss the process by which liquids can change into a solid. Define *freezing*.

Classroom Catalyst

To help visual learners understand the kinetic-molecular theory of liquids, have them create diagrams to show how intermolecular forces are established between the molecules of a liquid. Be sure that students include an example of each type of intermolecular force mentioned in the text. Provide students with the following three liquids to diagram: HCl (dipole-dipole forces), H_2O (hydrogen bonding), and C_6H_{14} (London dispersion forces).

Teach

READING TOOLKIT

Write the words *liquid* and *solid* on the board. Have students brainstorm all the words, phrases, and ideas that they associate with liquids and solids. Have a volunteer write students' contributions on the board. Then, have students develop a list of physical properties of liquids and solids. After the discussion, have students make notes of everything that they remember.

TEACH FROM VISUALS

FIGURE 2.1 Have students consult references to obtain quantitative density information on some of the layered materials. Have them compare these values to the order of layering in the column.

▼ **Teach** *continued*

Teaching Tip

Ask students what evidence they have that solid water (ice) is less dense than liquid water. Ice floats on water.

Application

Automobile brakes function because brake fluid, like other liquids, is essentially incompressible. Foot pressure on the brake pedal applies pressure to the master cylinder, and the pressure is transmitted throughout the braking system by the fluid.

ChemisTrivia

Emphasize the low compressibility of liquids by pointing out that even in the deep oceans at 4 km depth, where pressures are 40 MPa, there is only a 1.8% decrease in the volume of water.

Demonstration

DIFFUSION OF LIQUIDS

The experiment in **Figure 2.2** can readily be demonstrated on an **overhead projector** by placing a few drops of **liquid food coloring or ink** at various points on the surface of **water** in a **petri dish.**

Relative Incompressibility

When liquid water at 20°C is compressed by a pressure of 1000 atm, its volume decreases by only 4%. Such behavior is typical of all liquids and is similar to the behavior of solids. In contrast, a gas under a pressure of 1000 atm would have only about 1/1000 of its volume at normal atmospheric pressure. Liquids are much less compressible than gases because liquid particles are more closely packed together. Like gases, liquids can transmit pressure equally in all directions.

Ability to Diffuse

As described in Section 1, gases diffuse and mix with other gas particles. Liquids also diffuse and mix with other liquids, as shown in **Figure 2.2.** Any liquid gradually diffuses throughout any other liquid in which it can dissolve. The constant, random motion of particles causes diffusion in liquids, as it does in gases. Yet diffusion is much slower in liquids than in gases because liquid particles are closer together. Also, the attractive forces between the particles of a liquid slow their movement. As the temperature of a liquid is increased, diffusion occurs more rapidly. The reason is that the average kinetic energy, and therefore the average speed of the particles, is increased.

Surface Tension

A property common to all liquids is **surface tension,** a force that tends to pull adjacent parts of a liquid's surface together, thereby decreasing surface area to the smallest possible size. Surface tension results from the attractive forces between particles of a liquid. The higher the force of attraction, the higher the surface tension.

FIGURE 2.2

Diffusion of Liquids Like gases, the two liquids in this beaker diffuse over time. The green liquid food coloring from the drop will eventually form a uniform solution with the water.

Differentiated Instruction

ENGLISH LEARNERS

Students may have difficulty understanding the concepts of density, compressibility, and diffusion as they relate to liquids. Have students look at the molecular models shown in **Figure 2.2** . Work with students to help them explain why liquids display these three properties. Students can explain the relative high density of liquids by pointing out that the models show that the particles of a liquid are relatively close together. Therefore, there are many particles (mass) in a relatively small area (volume). The models also show that there are tiny spaces between the molecules, allowing for a small degree of compressibility. **Figure 2.2** also shows that the liquid molecules have diffused so that the water molecules and dye molecules are mixed.

Water has a higher surface tension than most liquids. This is due in large part to the hydrogen bonds water molecules can form with each other. The molecules at the surface of the water are a special case. They can form hydrogen bonds with the other water molecules beneath them and beside them, but not with the molecules in the air above them. As a result, the surface water molecules are drawn together and toward the body of the liquid, creating a high surface tension. Surface tension causes liquid droplets to take on a spherical shape because a sphere has the smallest possible surface area for a given volume. An example of this phenomenon is shown in **Figure 2.3.**

Capillary action, the attraction of the surface of a liquid to the surface of a solid, is a property closely related to surface tension. A liquid will rise quite high in a very narrow tube and will wet the tube if a strong attraction exists between the liquid molecules and the molecules that make up the surface of the tube. This attraction tends to pull the liquid molecules upward along the surface and against the pull of gravity. This process continues until the attractive forces between the liquid molecules and the surface of the tube are balanced by the weight of the liquid. Capillary action can occur between water molecules and paper fibers, as shown in **Figure 2.4.** Capillary action is at least partly responsible for the transportation of water from the roots of a plant to its leaves. The same process is responsible for the concave liquid surface, called a *meniscus,* that forms in a test tube or graduated cylinder.

Evaporation and Boiling

The process by which a liquid or solid changes to a gas is **vaporization.** Evaporation is a form of vaporization. **Evaporation** is the process by which particles escape from the surface of a nonboiling liquid and enter the gas state.

FIGURE 2.3

Surface Tension As a result of surface tension, liquids form roughly spherical drops. The net attractive forces between the particles pull the molecules on the surface of the drop inward. The molecules are pulled very close together, which minimizes the surface area.

Attractions on a typical molecule in a liquid

Attractions on a surface molecule

FIGURE 2.4

Polar Attraction

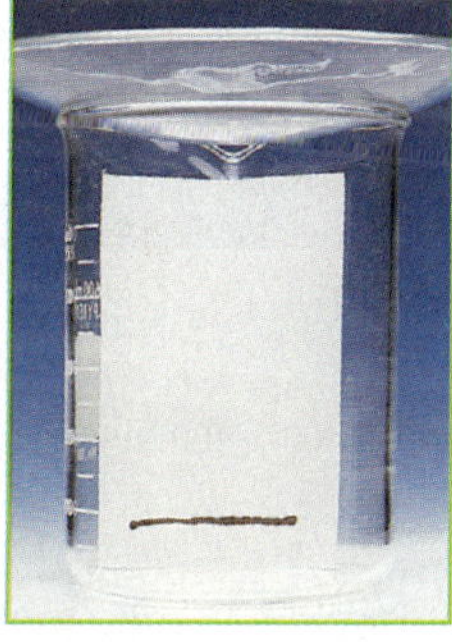

(a) Water-soluble ink is placed near the bottom of a piece of chromatography paper in shallow water.

(b) The ink has separated and has risen up the paper. These actions are the result of specific properties of water molecules.

CRITICAL THINKING

Apply Using the principles of capillary action, describe why water-soluble ink rises up the chromatography paper, which is set into a small amount of water.

PRE-AP

Have students investigate the cohesion-tension theory that explains how water molecules can move from the roots to the tops of giant trees, such as redwoods and sequoias. Be sure students include information about the roles of water potential, hydrogen bonding, and adhesion in this theory.

ChemisTrivia

Capillary action and other known factors, such as root pressure, account for most plants' ability to deliver groundwater to their highest branches. However, even if the known mechanisms all act together, they do not completely explain how very tall trees are able to accomplish this task.

Demonstration

EVAPORATION

Pour some **hot water** into a **beaker.** Cover the beaker with a cool **watch glass.** Have students observe what happens and attempt to account for it.

Safety Be careful handling the hot water and beaker.

Teaching Tip

There are some liquids, such as mercury, whose cohesive forces are much greater than their adhesive forces. Because of mercury's strong cohesive forces, mercury does not "climb" up the walls of a glass container to form a concave meniscus in the way that water does. Instead, mercury forms a convex meniscus.

Critical Thinking

Answer: As the paper absorbs the water in the bottom of the beaker, the water moves upward, drawing the dissolved ink with it. The water and the paper attract the various types of molecules found in the ink in different ways, causing the pigments to separate.

States of Matter 317

▼ Teach continued

Alternative Assessment

Have students draw a simple outline or concept map that illustrates the relationships between evaporation, boiling, and vaporization, and have them include examples. The outlines or concept maps should show vaporization as the top entry, with evaporation and boiling listed as types of vaporization.

▼ Assess and Reteach

Assess Use the Formative Assessment on this page to evaluate student mastery of the section.

Reteach For students who need additional instruction, download the Section Study Guide.

Response to Intervention To reassess students' mastery, use the Section Quiz, available to print or to take directly online at **HMDScience.com**.

FIGURE 2.5

Evaporation Liquid bromine, Br_2, evaporates near room temperature. The resulting brownish-red gas diffuses into the air above the surface of the liquid.

A small amount of liquid bromine was added to the bottle shown in **Figure 2.5.** Within a few minutes, the air above the liquid bromine turned brownish-red because some bromine molecules escaped from the surface of the liquid. These molecules became gas molecules, or bromine vapor, which mixed with the air. A similar phenomenon occurs if you apply perfume to your wrist. Within seconds, you become aware of the perfume's fragrance. Scent molecules evaporate from your skin and diffuse through the air, where your nose detects them.

Evaporation occurs because the particles of a liquid have different kinetic energies. Particles with higher-than-average energies move faster. Some surface particles with higher-than-average energies can overcome the intermolecular forces that bind them to the liquid. They can then escape into the gas state.

Evaporation is a crucial process in nature. Evaporation removes fresh water from the surface of the ocean, leaving behind a higher concentration of salts. In tropical areas, evaporation occurs at a higher rate, causing the surface water to be saltier. All water that falls to Earth in the form of rain and snow previously evaporated from oceans, lakes, and rivers. Evaporation of perspiration plays an important role in keeping you cool. Perspiration, which is mostly water, cools you by absorbing body heat when it evaporates. Energy as heat is absorbed from the skin, causing the cooling effect.

Boiling is the change of a liquid to bubbles of vapor that appear throughout the liquid. Boiling differs from evaporation, as you will see in Section 4.

Formation of Solids

When a liquid is cooled, the average energy of its particles decreases. If the energy is low enough, attractive forces pull the particles into an even more orderly arrangement. The substance then becomes a solid. **The physical change of a liquid to a solid by removal of energy as heat is called freezing or solidification.** Perhaps the best-known example of freezing is the change of liquid water to solid water, or ice, at 0°C. Another familiar example is the solidification of paraffin at room temperature. All liquids freeze, although not necessarily at temperatures you normally encounter. Ethanol, for example, freezes near −114°C.

SECTION 2 FORMATIVE ASSESSMENT

Reviewing Main Ideas

1. Describe the liquid state according to the kinetic-molecular theory.
2. List the properties of liquids.
3. How does the kinetic-molecular theory explain the following properties of liquids: (a) relatively high density, (b) ability to diffuse, and (c) ability to evaporate?
4. Explain why liquids in a test tube form a meniscus.
5. Compare vaporization and evaporation.

Critical Thinking

6. **INTERPRETING CONCEPTS** The evaporation of liquid water from the surface of Earth is an important step in the water cycle. How do water molecules obtain enough kinetic energy to escape into the gas state?

Answers to Section Assessment

1. Liquid particles are held close together by intermolecular forces, but they are in constant motion because of their kinetic energy.
2. Liquids have definite volume, take the shape of their container, can flow, have relatively high density, are relatively incompressible, can diffuse, and have surface tension.
3. a. Intermolecular forces hold particles close together.
   b. Liquid particles are in constant motion.
   c. Some particles have enough kinetic energy to escape into the gas state.
4. If the liquid is attracted to the glass, it is pulled upward into the test tube creating a concave surface. This effect is called capillary action, and the surface is called a meniscus. (If the liquid is not attracted to the glass, it is pushed downward in the test tube, and the surface becomes convex.)
5. Vaporization is any change to the gas state. Evaporation is a type of vaporization in which particles from the surface of a nonboiling liquid escape into the gas state.
6. Water molecules absorb energy from the sun. When enough energy is absorbed the water molecules can leave the liquid to become gas molecules.

SECTION 3

Solids

Key Terms

crystalline solid
crystal
amorphous solid
melting
melting point
supercooled liquid
crystal structure
unit cell

Main Ideas

- The particles in a solid hold relatively fixed positions.
- Crystal particles are arranged in a 3-dimensional lattice.
- The particles in amorphous solids are not arranged in a regular pattern.

The common expression "solid as a rock" suggests something that is hard or unyielding and has a definite shape and volume. In this section you will examine the properties of solids and compare them with those of liquids and gases. The properties of solids are explained in terms of the kinetic-molecular theory, as are the other states of matter.

MAIN IDEA

The particles in a solid hold relatively fixed positions.

The particles of a solid are more closely packed than those of a liquid or gas. Intermolecular forces between particles are thus much more effective in solids. All interparticle attractions, such as dipole-dipole attractions, London dispersion forces, and hydrogen bonding, exert stronger effects in solids than in the corresponding liquids or gases. Attractive forces tend to hold the particles of a solid in relatively fixed positions, with only vibrational movement around fixed points. Because the motions of the particles are restricted in this way, solids are more ordered than liquids and are much more ordered than gases. The importance of order and disorder in physical and chemical changes will be discussed in the chapter "Reaction Energy." Compare the physical appearance and molecular arrangement of the element in **Figure 3.1** in solid, liquid, and gas form.

CRITICAL THINKING

Analyze Analyze the pictures below and describe in detail what each picture is showing.

FIGURE 3.1

States of Matter

Particles of sodium metal in three different states are shown.

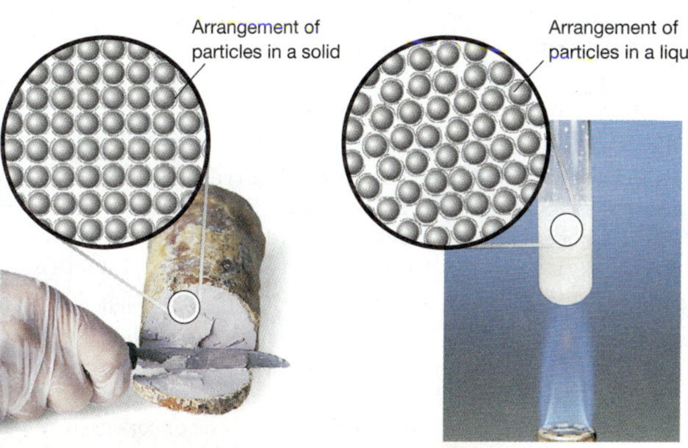

Differentiated Instruction

BELOW LEVEL

Have students summarize the kinetic-molecular theory by preparing a table with two columns. Ask students to label one column *Kinetic Energy* and the second column *Arrangement of Particles*. Have them write *Solid*, *Liquid*, and *Gas* down the left side of the table. Students should then complete the table to describe how these three states of matter differ with respect to their kinetic energy and the arrangement of their particles.

SECTION 3

Plan and Prepare ▼

Objectives

Upon completion of this section, students should be able to do the following:

- Describe the motion of particles in solids and the properties of solids according to the kinetic-molecular theory.
- Distinguish between the two types of solids.
- Describe the different types of crystal symmetry. Define *crystal structure* and *unit cell*.

Classroom Catalyst

Mix up a small amount of plaster of Paris according to package directions. Pour the mixture onto a piece of cardboard, and allow it to harden. Ask students to compare the mixture before it hardens to the product after it hardens. Student observations should include differences between the plaster of Paris as a fluid and the plaster of Paris as a solid.

Teach ▼

TEACH FROM VISUALS

FIGURE 3.1 Have students compare the movement of particles in this figure with the movement of people at a crowded football or soccer game. The people in the stands, like the particles in the solid, have very limited movement. The people walking in front of the stands, like the particles in a liquid, are somewhat limited but have more freedom of movement. The players on the field are similar to particles in a gas; they have more kinetic energy, and few limitations are placed on their locations.

Critical Thinking

Answer: The first image shows the closely-packed molecular structure of a solid. The second shows the loosely-organized particles of a liquid. The final image shows the fast-moving, widely-spaced particles in a gas.

Classroom Discussion

Ask students which properties of amorphous materials are like those of solids and which are like those of liquids. The ability of amorphous materials to have a definite shape is like that of a solid; the ability for amorphous materials to be transformed into a different shape is like that of a liquid. Point out that amorphous substances are sometimes classified as supercooled liquids rather than solids. Have students debate which of the two classifications is more appropriate.

Teaching Tip

Make students aware that melting point and freezing point have the same value for any given material.

TEACH FROM VISUALS

FIGURE 3.2 Have students note the arrangement of the positive sodium ions and negative chloride ions in the crystal. Have students use a hand lens to examine several grains of table salt and compare the shape of these crystals to the shape of the crystal in the figure.

There are two types of solids: crystalline solids and amorphous solids. **Most solids are crystalline solids—they consist of crystals. A crystal is a substance in which the particles are arranged in an orderly, geometric, repeating pattern.** Noncrystalline solids, including glass and plastics, are called amorphous solids. **An amorphous solid is one in which the particles are arranged randomly.** The two types of solids will be discussed in more detail later in this section.

Definite Shape and Volume

Unlike liquids and gases, solids can maintain a definite shape without a container. In addition, crystalline solids are geometrically regular. Even the fragments of a shattered crystalline solid have distinct geometric shapes that reflect their internal structure. Amorphous solids maintain a definite shape, but they do not have the distinct geometric shapes of crystalline solids. For example, glass can be molded into any shape. If glass is shattered, the fragments can have a variety of irregular shapes.

The volume of a solid changes only slightly with a change in temperature or pressure. Solids have definite volume because their particles are packed closely together. There is very little empty space into which the particles can be compressed. Crystalline solids generally do not flow, because their particles are held in relatively fixed positions.

Definite Melting Point

Melting is the physical change of a solid to a liquid by the addition of energy as heat. The temperature at which a solid becomes a liquid is its melting point. At this temperature, the kinetic energies of the particles within the solid overcome the attractive forces holding them together. The particles can then break out of their positions in crystalline solids, which have definite melting points. In contrast, amorphous solids, such as glass and plastics, have no definite melting point. They have the ability to flow over a range of temperatures. Therefore, amorphous solids are sometimes classified as **supercooled liquids, which are substances that retain certain liquid properties even at temperatures at which they appear to be solid.** These properties exist because the particles in amorphous solids are arranged randomly, much like the particles in a liquid. Unlike the particles in a true liquid, however, the particles in amorphous solids are not constantly changing their positions.

High Density and Incompressibility

In general, substances are most dense in the solid state. Solids tend to be slightly denser than liquids and much denser than gases. The higher density results from the fact that the particles of a solid are more closely packed than those of a liquid or a gas. Solid hydrogen is the least dense solid; its density is about 1/320 that of the densest element, osmium, Os.

Solids are generally less compressible than liquids. For practical purposes, solids can be considered incompressible. Some solids, such as wood and cork, may *seem* compressible, but they are not. They contain pores that are filled with air. When subjected to intense pressure, the pores are compressed, not the solid matter in the wood or cork itself.

FIGURE 3.2

Crystal Lattice of Sodium Chloride

(a) This is a scanning electron micrograph (SEM) of sodium chloride crystals.

Sodium ion, Na^+

Chloride ion, Cl^-

(b) The crystal structure of sodium chloride is made up of individual unit cells represented regularly in three dimensions. Here, one unit cell is outlined in red.

Differentiated Instruction

ENGLISH LEARNERS

Encourage English learners to look closely at the first two sentences under *High Density and Incompressibility*. Ask: What do the words "tend to" imply about the comparative densities of solids and liquids? "Tend to" implies that for most substances, the particles in a solid are closer together (more dense) than those in a liquid or gas, but this may not be true for all substances. Tell students that water is an example of a substance for which this statement is not true. You can demonstrate this by placing an ice cube in a beaker of water. Ask: Why does the ice cube float? Unlike most substances, solid water (ice) is less dense than liquid water. As a result, ice floats in water.

FIGURE 3.3

Crystal Systems in Minerals Shown are the seven basic crystal systems and representative crystals of each.

Fluorite
Cubic

Chalcopyrite
Tetragonal

Emerald
Hexagonal

Calcite
Trigonal

Aragonite
Orthorhombic

Azurite
Monoclinic

Rhodonite
Triclinic

Low Rate of Diffusion

If a zinc plate and a copper plate are clamped together for a long time, a few atoms of each metal will diffuse into the other. This observation shows that diffusion does occur in solids. The rate of diffusion is millions of times faster in liquids than in solids, however.

MAIN IDEA

Crystal particles are arranged in a 3-dimensional lattice.

Crystalline solids exist either as single crystals or as groups of crystals fused together. **The total three-dimensional arrangement of particles of a crystal is called a crystal structure.** The arrangement of particles in the crystal can be represented by a coordinate system called a lattice. **The smallest portion of a crystal lattice that shows the three-dimensional pattern of the entire lattice is called a unit cell.** Each crystal lattice contains many unit cells packed together. **Figure 3.2** (on the previous page) shows the relationship between a crystal lattice and its unit cell. A crystal and its unit cells can have any one of seven types of symmetry. This fact enables scientists to classify crystals by their shape. Diagrams and examples of each type of crystal symmetry are shown in **Figure 3.3.**

Alternative Assessment

Provide photographs or examples of various minerals that exhibit a definite crystalline form. Ask students to try to identify the type of basic crystal system in each.

ChemisTrivia

Diffusion welding is a process that is used to join two solids; the metals are subjected to high temperatures. The high temperatures cause the metal atoms at the interface to diffuse into one another. Diffusion welding is used in the aerospace industry to make rockets.

PRE-AP

Fluorite is a halide mineral composed of calcium fluoride, CaF_2. As shown in **Figure 3.3,** fluorite has cubic symmetry. Ask students to show how ionic bonding occurs in CaF_2 and then use this as a basis for building a model of a fluorite crystal. Tell students that their model should show how unit cells are combined to form the lattice. Students should show a cubic structure in which Ca is connected to eight F ions, and each F ion is surrounded by four Ca ions.

▼ Teach *continued*

TEACH FROM TABLES

FIGURE 3.4 Point out that general trends in melting point can be determined, but that ranges overlap.

ChemisTrivia

Glasslike materials can be made from combinations of metals. The alloys take on amorphous forms when they are melted, formed into thin films, and cooled rapidly. The "metallic glasses" are strong, flexible, and resistant to corrosion.

READING TOOLKIT

INTERPRETING VOCABULARY Ask students what they think of when they hear the term *network*. They may mention television networks or networked computers. Elicit from students that a network consists of many individual parts joined as a unit. Covalent network crystals form giant molecules, or *macromolecules*.

FIGURE 3.4

MELTING AND BOILING POINTS OF REPRESENTATIVE CRYSTALLINE SOLIDS

Type of substance	Formula	Melting point (°C)	Boiling point at 1 atm (°C)
Ionic	$NaCl$ MgF_2	801 1266	1413 2239
Covalent network	$(SiO_2)_x$ C_x (diamond)	1610 3500	2230 3930
Metallic	Hg Cu Fe W	−39 1083 1535 3410	357 2567 2750 5660
Covalent molecular (nonpolar)	H_2 O_2 CH_4 CCl_4 C_6H_6	−259 −218 −182 −23 −6	−253 −183 −164 77 80
Covalent molecular (polar)	NH_3 H_2O	−78 0	−33 100

Binding Forces in Crystals

Crystal structures can also be described in terms of the types of particles in the crystals and the types of chemical bonding between the particles. According to this method of classification, there are four types of crystals. These types are listed in **Figure 3.4.** Refer to this table as you read the following discussion.

1. *Ionic crystals.* The ionic crystal structure consists of positive and negative ions arranged in a regular pattern. The ions can be monatomic or polyatomic. Generally, ionic crystals form when Group 1 or Group 2 metals combine with Group 16 or Group 17 nonmetals or nonmetallic polyatomic ions. The strong binding forces between the positive and negative ions in the crystal structure give the ionic crystals certain properties. For example, these crystals are hard and brittle, have high melting points, and are good insulators.
2. *Covalent network crystals.* In covalent network crystals, each atom is covalently bonded to its nearest neighboring atoms. The covalent bonding extends throughout a network that includes a very large number of atoms. Three-dimensional covalent network solids include diamond, C_x, quartz, $(SiO_2)_x$ (see **Figure 3.5** on the next page), silicon carbide, $(SiC)_x$, and many oxides of transition metals. Such solids are essentially giant molecules. The subscript x in these formulas indicates that the component within the parentheses extends indefinitely. The network solids are nearly always very hard and brittle. They have rather high melting points and are usually nonconductors or semiconductors.

Differentiated Instruction

INCLUSION

Show the class samples to help visual learners understand the differences between the four types of crystals. Use salt for an ionic crystal, graphite for a covalent network solid, aluminum foil for a metallic crystal, and rock candy for a covalent molecular crystal. As you hold up each sample, have students review the features of the crystal. For example, as you hold up the salt, students should describe it in terms of sodium cations, chloride anions, ionic bonds, unit cell arrangement, and lattice formation.

3. *Metallic crystals.* The metallic crystal structure consists of metal cations surrounded by a sea of delocalized valence electrons. The electrons come from the metal atoms and belong to the crystal as a whole. This explains the high electrical conductivity of metals.

4. *Covalent molecular crystals.* The crystal structure of a covalent molecular substance consists of covalently bonded molecules held together by intermolecular forces. If the molecules are nonpolar—for example, hydrogen, H_2, methane, CH_4, and benzene, C_6H_6—then there are only weak London dispersion forces between molecules. In a polar covalent molecular crystal—for example, water, H_2O, and ammonia, NH_3—molecules are held together by dispersion forces, by somewhat stronger dipole-dipole forces, and sometimes by even stronger hydrogen bonding. The forces that hold polar or nonpolar molecules together in the structure are much weaker than the covalent chemical bonds between the atoms within each molecule. Covalent molecular crystals thus have low melting points. They are easily vaporized, are relatively soft, and are good insulators. Ice crystals, the most familiar molecular crystals, are discussed in Section 5.

FIGURE 3.5

Covalent Network Crystals

Covalent network crystals include three-dimensional network solids, such as this quartz, $(SiO_2)_x$, shown here with its three-dimensional atomic structure.

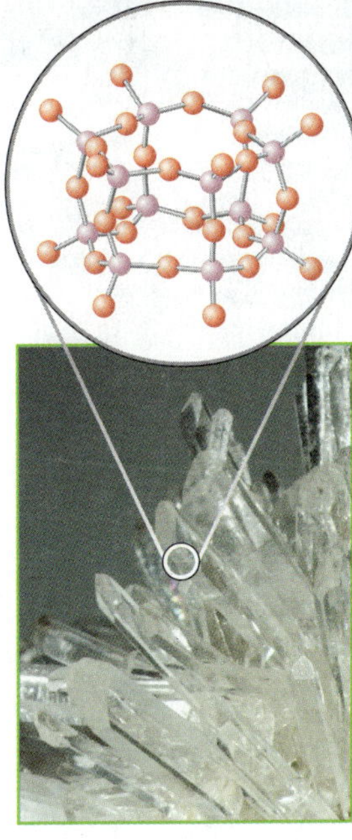

MAIN IDEA

The particles in amorphous solids are not arranged in a regular pattern.

The word *amorphous* comes from the Greek for "without shape." Unlike the atoms that form crystals, the atoms that make up amorphous solids, such as glasses and plastics, are not arranged in a regular pattern.

Glasses are made by cooling certain molten materials in a way that prevents them from crystallizing. The properties that result make glasses suitable for many uses, including windows, light bulbs, transformer cores, and optical fibers that carry telephone conversations.

Plastics, another type of amorphous solid, are easily molded at high temperatures and pressures. They are used in many structural materials.

Other, more recently created amorphous solids have been placed in many important applications. Amorphous semiconductors are used in electronic devices, including solar cells, copiers, laser printers, and flat-panel displays for computer monitors and television screens.

SECTION 3 FORMATIVE ASSESSMENT

Reviewing Main Ideas

1. Describe the solid state according to the kinetic-molecular theory.
2. What is the difference between an amorphous solid and a crystalline solid?
3. Account for each of the following properties of solids: (a) the definite volume, (b) the relatively high density, (c) the extremely low rate of diffusion.
4. Compare and contrast the four types of crystals.
5. Why do crystalline solids shatter into regularly-shaped fragments when broken?

Critical Thinking

6. **RELATING IDEAS** Explain why ionic crystals melt at much higher temperatures than typical covalent molecular crystals.

ChemisTrivia

Both cotton candy and candle wax are amorphous solids.

Assess and Reteach ▼

Assess Use the Formative Assessment on this page to evaluate student mastery of the section.

Reteach For students who need additional instruction, download the Section Study Guide.

Response to Intervention To reassess students' mastery, use the Section Quiz, available to print or to take directly online at **HMDScience.com**.

Answers to Section Assessment

1. Solids consist of closely packed particles held together by intermolecular forces; these particles are able to move back and forth about fixed positions.
2. The particles in an amorphous solid are arranged randomly; those in a crystalline solid are in an orderly, geometric, repeating pattern.
3. a. Particles are packed closely together.
   b. Particles are packed closely together.
   c. Particles are in relatively fixed positions and are unable to flow.
4. Ionic crystals have a regular arrangement of charged particles, melt at a high temperature, are brittle, and are good insulators. Covalent network crystals have a large number of atoms covalently bonded to one another, melt at a high temperature, and tend to be nonconductors or semiconductors. Metallic crystals have metal cations surrounded by a sea of delocalized valence electrons and are good conductors. Covalent molecular crystals have covalently bonded molecules held together by intermolecular forces, have low melting points, and are good insulators.
5. No matter what its particle size, any crystalline solid has a distinct geometric shape that reflects its internal structure.
6. Ionic crystals are held together by the very strong attractive forces between ions of opposite charge. The hydrogen bonding, dipole-dipole forces, and London dispersion forces that hold covalent molecular crystals together are much weaker and more easily overcome.

SECTION 4

▼ Plan and Prepare

Objectives

Upon completion of this section, students should be able to do the following:

- Explain the relationship between equilibrium and changes of state.
- Interpret phase diagrams.
- Explain what is meant by equilibrium vapor pressure.
- Describe the processes of boiling, freezing, melting, and sublimation.

Classroom Catalyst

Break a golf-ball-sized piece of dry ice into small pieces. Use tongs and a funnel to put the chips inside a deflated balloon. Tie the opening shut. As the dry ice sublimes, the balloon will inflate. Ask students to try to explain what is happening.

Safety Do not touch the dry ice.

▼ Teach

TEACH FROM TABLES

FIGURE 4.1 Have students list additional examples of each change of state shown in the table. Answers will vary and could include butter softening (melting), solid air freshener disappearing (sublimation), molten lava hardening (freezing), rain evaporating (vaporization), clouds forming (condensation), ice spraying from a CO_2 fire extinguisher (deposition).

READING TOOLKIT

READING ORGANIZER As students read this section, have them create a concept map that shows what happens during changes of state. Concept maps should include terms such as *evaporation, condensation, boiling point, freezing point, sublimation*, and *deposition*, as well as indicating where energy is absorbed or released. Ask students to compare their concept maps to **Figure 4.6** and to make revisions as needed.

SECTION 4

Main Ideas

- Substances in equilibrium change back and forth between states at equal speeds.
- A liquid boils when it has absorbed enough energy to evaporate.
- Freezing occurs when a substance loses enough heat energy to solidify.
- Under certain conditions, water can exist in all three phases at the same time.

Changes of State

Key Terms

phase
condensation
equilibrium
equilibrium vapor pressure
volatile liquid
boiling
boiling point
molar enthalpy of vaporization
freezing
freezing point
molar enthalpy of fusion
sublimation
deposition
phase diagram
triple point
critical point
critical temperature
critical pressure

Matter on Earth can exist in any of three states—gas, liquid, or solid—and can change from one state to another. **Figure 4.1** lists the possible changes of state. In this section, you will examine these changes of state and the factors that cause them.

MAIN IDEA

Substances in equilibrium change back and forth between states at equal speeds.

Some liquid chemical substances, such as rubbing alcohol, have an odor that is very easily detected. This is because some molecules at the upper surface of the liquid have enough energy to overcome the attraction of neighboring molecules, leave the liquid phase, and evaporate. **A phase is any part of a system that has uniform composition and properties.** In a closed bottle of rubbing alcohol, gas molecules under the cap strike the liquid surface and reenter the liquid phase through *condensation.* **Condensation is the process by which a gas changes to a liquid.** A gas in contact with its liquid or solid phase is often called a *vapor.*

If the temperature of the liquid remains constant and the cap remains closed, the rate at which molecules move from the liquid to vapor remains constant. Near the beginning of the evaporation process, very few molecules are in the gas phase, so the rate of condensation is very low.

FIGURE 4.1

POSSIBLE CHANGES OF STATE

Change of state	Process	Example
Solid ⟶ liquid	melting	ice ⟶ water
Solid ⟶ gas	sublimation	dry ice ⟶ CO_2 gas
Liquid ⟶ solid	freezing	water ⟶ ice
Liquid ⟶ gas	vaporization	liquid bromine ⟶ bromine vapor
Gas ⟶ liquid	condensation	water vapor ⟶ water
Gas ⟶ solid	deposition	water vapor ⟶ ice

Differentiated Instruction

INCLUSION

Students often equate equilibrium with equality. To help kinesthetic learners understand the concept of equilibrium, divide the class so that a few more students are on one side of the classroom than on the other side. Tell one student from each side to exchange places. Then have two students from each side do the same. Point out that the class is said to be in equilibrium because the two opposing changes occur at equal rates. Students should notice that at equilibrium there is a different number of particles (students) on either side. Therefore, an equilibrium can be established without having an equality. Ask the class to upset the equilibrium by having more students move to one side. Finally, tell the class to separate so that there is an equal number of students on both sides. Again have students exchange places to demonstrate what happens in an equilibrium. Point out that an equilibrium may be established when there is an equality or the same number of particles on either side.

FIGURE 4.2

Liquid-Vapor Equilibrium A liquid-vapor equilibrium develops in a closed system.

(a) At first there is only liquid present, but molecules are beginning to evaporate.

(b) Evaporation continues at a constant rate. Some vapor molecules are beginning to condense to liquid.

(c) Equilibrium has been reached between the rate of condensation and the rate of evaporation.

As more liquid evaporates, the increasing number of gas molecules causes the rate of condensation to increase, until the rate of condensation equals the rate of evaporation, and a state of equilibrium is established (see **Figure 4.2**). **Equilibrium is a dynamic condition in which two opposing changes occur at equal rates in a closed system.** Even though molecules are constantly moving between liquid and gas phases, there is no net change in the amount of substance in either phase.

Equilibrium Vapor Pressure of a Liquid

Vapor molecules in equilibrium with a liquid in a closed system exert a pressure proportional to the concentration of molecules in the vapor phase. **The pressure exerted by a vapor in equilibrium with its corresponding liquid at a given temperature is called the equilibrium vapor pressure of the liquid.**

The increase in equilibrium vapor pressure with increasing temperature can be explained in terms of the kinetic-molecular theory for the liquid and gaseous states. Increasing the temperature of a liquid increases the average kinetic energy of the liquid's molecules. This increases the number of molecules that have enough energy to escape from the liquid phase into the vapor phase. The resulting increased evaporation rate increases the number of molecules in the vapor phase, which in turn increases the equilibrium vapor pressure.

Every liquid has a specific equilibrium vapor pressure at a given temperature. The stronger these attractive forces are, the smaller is the percentage of liquid particles that can evaporate at any given temperature. A low percentage of evaporation results in a low equilibrium vapor pressure. **Volatile liquids, which are liquids that evaporate readily,** have **relatively weak forces of attraction between their particles.**

Misconception Alert!

Because of the unchanging numbers of particles involved in an equilibrium, students often think that equilibrium is static, or involves no changes. Point out and periodically remind them that equilibrium is a dynamic condition in which two opposing processes continue to occur.

TEACH FROM VISUALS

FIGURE 4.2 Have students explain why an equilibrium could not be reached if the flask shown in the figure were not sealed with a stopper. Students should realize that the gas particles would escape. The rate of condensation would not equal the rate of evaporation.

PRE-AP

Ask students how they would demonstrate that an ionic compound that has been melted is a nonvolatile liquid. Students may describe a process in which an ionic compound is heated in a flask, such as the one shown in **Figure 4.2.** The solid is heated until it completely liquefies. The flask is then sealed and observed for any evidence of evaporation occurring inside the flask.

ENGLISH LEARNERS

To help English learners understand the concepts of equilibrium vapor pressure and volatility, place the following figure on the board:

Substance	Vapor Pressure at 25°C
bromine	0.3 atm
water	0.03 atm
ethyl alcohol	0.08 atm
diethyl ether	0.7 atm

Have students rank these liquids in decreasing order of volatility. Have students explain the reason for their order. Students should generate the following list: diethyl ether, bromine, ethyl alcohol, water. The more volatile the liquid is, the higher the vapor pressure.

▼ Teach continued

Misconception Alert!

Students often assume that boiling indicates that a large amount of energy in the form of heat has been added to the liquid. Point out that reducing atmospheric pressure reduces the energy needed for boiling to occur, resulting in a lower boiling point. For example, water under near-vacuum conditions can boil at 25°C, but that water would not be able to cook an egg because cooking depends on the temperature, not on whether the liquid is boiling.

Teaching Tip

Explain to students that at high elevations, where atmospheric pressures are lower than at sea level, a cooking liquid boils at a lower temperature and foods take longer to cook.

Ether is a typical volatile liquid. Nonvolatile liquids, such as molten ionic compounds, do not evaporate readily and have relatively strong attractive forces between their particles.

MAIN IDEA

A liquid boils when it has absorbed enough energy to evaporate.

Equilibrium vapor pressures can be used to explain and define the concept of **boiling,** which is the conversion of a liquid to a vapor within the liquid as well as at its surface.

If the temperature of the liquid is increased, the equilibrium vapor pressure also increases. The **boiling point** of a liquid is the temperature at which the equilibrium vapor pressure of the liquid equals the atmospheric pressure. The lower the atmospheric pressure is, the lower the boiling point is.

At boiling point, all of the energy absorbed is used to evaporate the liquid, and the temperature remains constant as long as the pressure does not change. If the pressure above the liquid being heated is increased, the temperature of the liquid will rise until the vapor pressure equals the new pressure and the liquid boils once again. A pressure cooker is sealed so that steam pressure builds up over the surface of the boiling water inside. The boiling temperature of the water increases, resulting in shorter cooking times. A device called a *vacuum evaporator* causes boiling at lower-than-normal temperatures. Vacuum evaporators used to prepare evaporated and sweetened condensed milk remove water from milk and sugar solutions. Under reduced pressure, the water boils away at a temperature low enough to avoid scorching the milk or sugar.

At normal atmospheric pressure (1 atm, 760 torr, or 101.3 kPa), water boils at exactly 100°C. This is the *normal* boiling point of water.

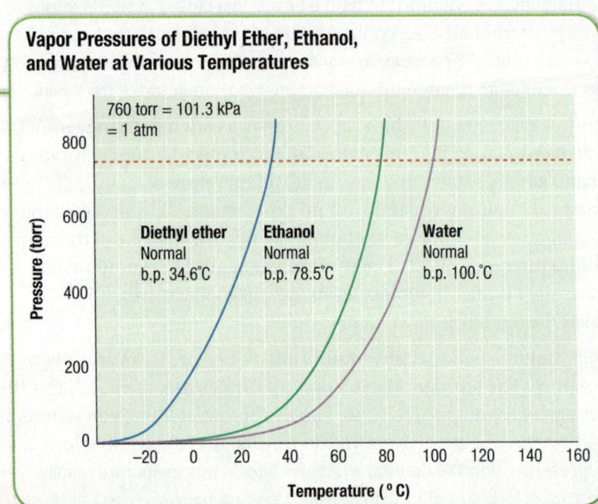

FIGURE 4.3

Boiling Point The vapor pressure of any liquid increases as its temperature increases. A liquid boils when its vapor pressure equals the pressure of the atmosphere.

Differentiated Instruction

BELOW LEVEL

For twenty-four hours, have students keep a "Phase Change Diary" in which they write down phase changes they observe occurring around them. Sample observations: seeing condensation form on the outside of a cold drink; boiling water to cook pasta For each phase change, have them describe the starting substance and the final substance, the circumstance in which the phase change occurred, and the name of the phase change. Have them refer to **Figure 4.6** for help naming the different phase changes they observe.

FIGURE 4.4

Energy Distribution The number of molecules in a liquid with various kinetic energies is represented at two different temperatures.

CRITICAL THINKING
Analyze Look at the graph, and describe what is happening in the shaded area at the lower right.

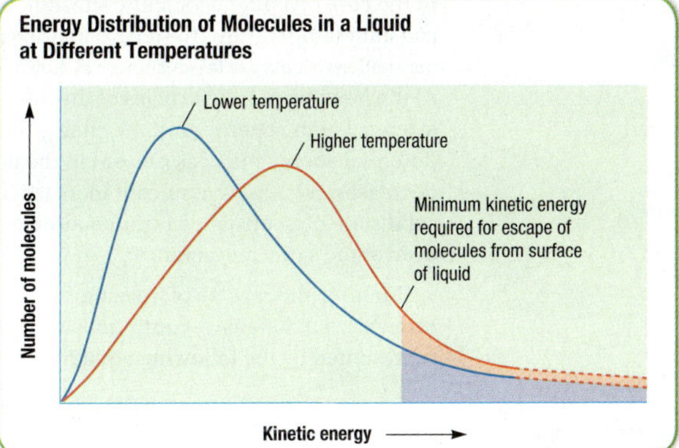

Figure 4.3 (see previous page) shows that the normal boiling point of each liquid occurs when its equilibrium vapor pressure equals 760 torr. Energy must be added continuously in order to keep a liquid boiling. The temperature of a liquid and its vapor at the boiling point remains constant despite the continuous addition of energy. The added energy is used to overcome the attractive forces between molecules of the liquid during the liquid-to-gas change and is stored in the vapor as potential energy.

Molar Enthalpy of Vaporization

The amount of energy as heat that is needed to vaporize one mole of liquid at the liquid's boiling point at constant pressure is called the liquid's **molar enthalpy of vaporization,** ΔH_v. Molar enthalpy of vaporization measures the attraction between particles of the liquid. The stronger the attraction is, the more energy is required to overcome it, resulting in a higher molar enthalpy of vaporization. Each liquid has a characteristic molar enthalpy of vaporization. Liquid water's molar enthalpy of vaporization is very high, due to its extensive hydrogen bonding, This makes water an effective cooling agent. When water evaporates, the escaping molecules carry away with them a great deal of energy as heat. **Figure 4.4** shows the distribution of the kinetic energies of molecules in a liquid at two different temperatures. At higher temperatures, a greater portion of the surface molecules have the kinetic energy required to escape and become vapor.

MAIN IDEA

Freezing occurs when a substance loses enough heat energy to solidify.

The physical change of a liquid to a solid is called **freezing.** Freezing involves a loss of energy in the form of heat by the liquid.

$$\text{liquid} \rightarrow \text{solid} + \text{energy}$$

Application

Energy is given off during freezing of a liquid. This fact is used to protect developing citrus fruits during a frost. Water is sprayed onto the trees. As the water freezes, it gives off energy that is absorbed by the fruit, protecting it from freezing.

Classroom Discussion

Ask students to explain how it is possible for boiling water and the steam produced to be at the same temperature, even though energy is absorbed during the boiling process. Students should indicate their understanding that temperature reflects kinetic energy only.

Critical Thinking

Answer: The shaded area of the graph represents the small number of molecules that have the minimum amount of kinetic energy needed for evaporation to take place.

PRE-AP

The energy required to vaporize a given amount of a substance can be calculated by using the following formula: energy required for vaporization = mass of substance (g) × molar mass (mol/g) × molar enthalpy of vaporization (kJ/mol).

Tell students that the molar enthalpy of vaporization for water is 40.79 kJ/mol. Have students calculate how much energy as heat must be transferred to change 100 grams of water into a vapor. (226 kJ) Have students compare this value to the energy required to vaporize 100 grams of lead, whose molar enthalpy of vaporization is 178 kJ/mol. (85.9 kJ) Ask students to explain why less energy is needed to vaporize 100 grams of lead compared to 100 grams of water. Students should explain that the metallic bonds between lead atoms require less energy to break. As a result, lead requires less energy as heat to change from a solid into a liquid. Be sure that students understand that equal amounts of water and lead are being compared.

▼ Teach continued

Demonstration

CHANGES OF STATE IN ICE AND LIQUID WATER

Half fill a **250-mL beaker** with an **ice**-and-**water** mixture. Place the beaker on a **hot plate.** While stirring the mixture with a **glass rod,** place a **thermometer** in the beaker and measure and record the ice-water temperature initially and at roughly 1 min intervals throughout the melting process. Continue to do so for the pure liquid water that results and then for the boiling water that is produced. Have students use **graph paper** to plot the temperature data on the vertical axis versus the time data on the horizontal axis. Then have them interpret the results. The temperature will remain at 0°C throughout the melting period. Then the liquid will increase in temperature to 100°C at boiling and will remain at that temperature as long as liquid water still remains. The absorbed energy is converted to potential energy to provide the enthalpies of fusion and vaporization during the changes of state.

Safety Be careful using heat sources and working with the hot water.

Classroom Discussion

Have students explain why the temperature does not increase as a solid is melting. Be sure that students understand that the average kinetic energy of the particles is not increasing.

WHY IT MATTERS

Surface Melting S.T.E.M.

Freezing of water and melting of ice are phase changes that are familiar to all of us. Yet physicists and chemists have only recently begun to understand the basic aspects of these phase changes, through experimental and theoretical studies of a phenomenon known as surface melting. Experimental studies in the mid-1980s confirmed that the rigid surface arrangements of metals can become increasingly disordered several degrees below the melting point of the metal, forming a "quasi-liquid layer." Many different techniques have now shown that ice also has such a fluid surface layer just a few molecules thick. This surface melting of ice might explain observations as diverse as the origin of lightning, the unique shapes of snowflakes, and ice skating.

In the case of a pure crystalline substance, this change occurs at constant temperature. The normal **freezing point** is the temperature at which the solid and liquid are in equilibrium at 1 atm (760 torr, or 101.3 kPa) pressure. At the freezing point, particles of the liquid and the solid have the same average kinetic energy, and the energy lost during freezing is the potential energy that was present in the liquid. At the same time energy decreases, there is a significant increase in particle order, because the solid state of a substance is much more ordered than the liquid state, even at the same temperature.

Melting, the reverse of freezing, also occurs at constant temperature. As a solid melts, it continuously absorbs energy as heat, as represented by the following equation.

$$\text{solid} + \text{energy} \longrightarrow \text{liquid}$$

For pure crystalline solids, the melting point and freezing point are the same. At equilibrium, melting and freezing proceed at equal rates. The following general equilibrium equation can be used to represent these states.

$$\text{solid} + \text{energy} \rightleftarrows \text{liquid}$$

At normal atmospheric pressure, the temperature of a system containing ice and liquid water will remain at 0.°C as long as both ice and water are present, no matter what the surrounding temperature. Adding energy in the form of heat to such a system shifts the equilibrium to the right. That shift increases the proportion of liquid water and decreases that of ice. Only after all the ice has melted will the addition of energy increase the temperature of the system.

Molar Enthalpy of Fusion

The amount of energy as heat required to melt one mole of solid at the solid's melting point is the solid's **molar enthalpy of fusion,** ΔH_f. The energy absorbed increases the solid's potential energy as its particles are pulled apart, overcoming the attractive forces holding them together. At the same time, there is a significant decrease in particle order as the substance makes the transformation from solid to liquid. Similar to the molar enthalpy of vaporization, the magnitude of the molar enthalpy of fusion depends on the attraction between the solid particles.

Sublimation and Deposition

At sufficiently low temperature and pressure conditions, a liquid cannot exist. Under such conditions, a solid substance exists in equilibrium with its vapor instead of its liquid, as represented by the following equation.

$$\text{solid} + \text{energy} \rightleftarrows \text{vapor}$$

The change of state from a solid directly to a gas is known as **sublimation.** The reverse process is called **deposition,** the change of state from a gas directly to a solid. Among the common substances that sublime at ordinary temperatures are dry ice (solid CO_2) and iodine.

Differentiated Instruction

ENGLISH LEARNERS

Point out that fusion is a scientific term for melting. Tell students that the molar enthalpy of fusion for ice is 6.01 kJ/mol. Have students calculate how much energy is required to melt 0.5 mol of ice. 3 kJ

PRE-AP

Have students design and carry out an experiment to determine the molar enthalpy of fusion for ice. Students can use a polystyrene foam cup as a calorimeter and calculate the energy transferred as heat to melt a known amount of ice. Have students calculate the percent error in their experiment. Encourage students to identify possible sources of error.

Ordinary ice sublimes slowly at temperatures lower than its melting point (0.°C). This explains how a thin layer of snow can eventually disappear, even if the temperature remains below 0.°C. Sublimation occurs in frost-free refrigerators when the temperature in the freezer compartment is periodically raised to cause any ice that has formed to sublime. A blower then removes the water vapor that has formed. The formation of frost on a cold surface is a familiar example of deposition.

MAIN IDEA

Under certain conditions, water can exist in all three phases at the same time.

A phase diagram is a graph of pressure versus temperature that shows the conditions under which the phases of a substance exist. A phase diagram also reveals how the states of a system change with changing temperature or pressure.

Figure 4.5 shows the phase diagram for water over a range of temperatures and pressures. Note the three curves, AB, AC, and AD. Curve AB indicates the temperature and pressure conditions at which ice and water vapor can coexist at equilibrium. Curve AC indicates the temperature and pressure conditions at which liquid water and water vapor coexist at equilibrium. Similarly, curve AD indicates the temperature and pressure conditions at which ice and liquid water coexist at equilibrium. Because ice is less dense than liquid water, an increase in pressure lowers the melting point. (Most substances have a positive slope for this curve.) Point A is the triple point of water. **The triple point of a substance indicates the temperature and pressure conditions at which the solid, liquid, and vapor of the substance can coexist at equilibrium.** Point C is the critical point of water. **The critical point of a substance indicates the critical temperature and critical pressure. The critical temperature (t_c) is the temperature above which the substance cannot exist in the liquid state.**

FIGURE 4.5

Phase Diagram This phase diagram shows the relationships between the physical states of water and its pressure and temperature.

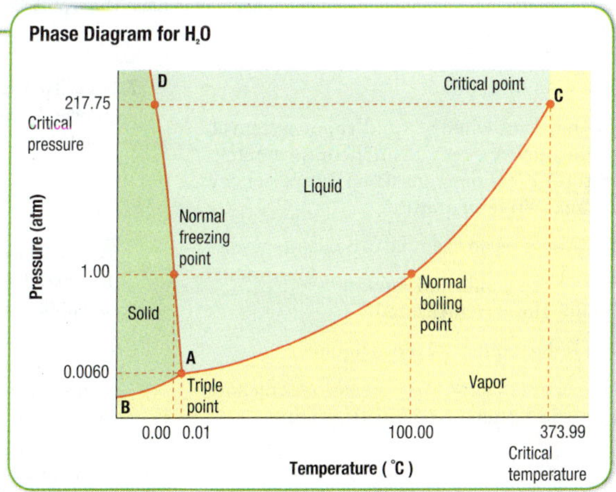

TEACH FROM VISUALS

FIGURE 4.5 Ensure students understand a phase diagram, its information, and its purpose by having them interpret the diagram. Give them several sets of temperature and pressure values, having them find the state in which water exists under each set of conditions. Another strategy is to give students either a temperature or a pressure value and have them find the corresponding temperature or pressure at which a certain phase change occurs, if it occurs at all.

Application

The sublimation of ice into water vapor accounts for the fact that wet clothing hung outside on a clothesline eventually dries, even if the temperature is below freezing.

READING TOOLKIT

DISCUSSION Have students silently read the section on phase diagrams. Lead a discussion of the diagram's important features that are mentioned in the text. As you discuss these features, highlight them on a projector or whiteboard. Have students make notes on their own copies of a phase diagram.

PRE-AP

Provide students with a phase diagram for carbon dioxide. Ask them to compare the phase diagrams for carbon dioxide and water and describe any similarities and differences. Have students explain the significance of the slope of the curve between the solid and liquid phases for carbon dioxide. Students should recognize that the positive slope indicates that solid carbon dioxide is denser than the liquid. Have students also interpret the phase diagram for carbon dioxide to explain why the solid sublimes. Students should notice the unusally high triple point, which occurs at around 5 atm. At 1 atm, solid carbon dioxide will sublime at −78°C, meaning that liquid carbon dioxide cannot exist under STP conditions.

▼ Teach *continued*

TEACH FROM VISUALS

FIGURE 4.6 Have students select one term describing a phase change in the figure. Ask students to describe what happens during that phase change according to the kinetic-molecular theory.

▼ Assess and Reteach

Assess Use the Formative Assessment on this page to evaluate student mastery of the section.

Reteach For students who need additional instruction, download the Section Study Guide.

Response to Intervention To reassess students' mastery, use the Section Quiz, available to print or to take directly online at **HMDScience.com**.

FIGURE 4.6

Changes of State Solids, liquids, and gases can undergo various changes of state. The changes shown in green are exothermic, and those shown in blue are endothermic.

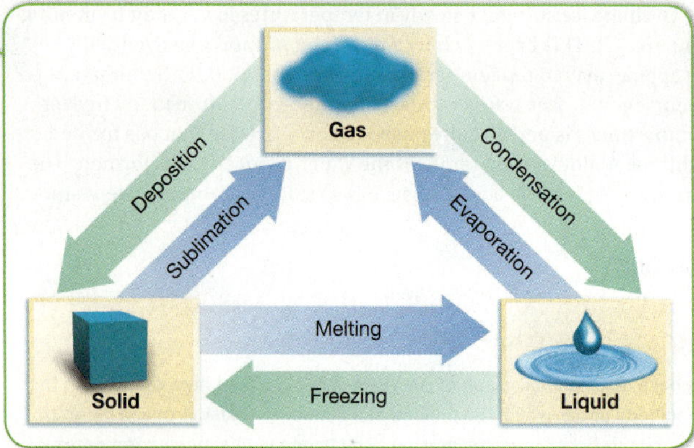

The critical temperature of water is 373.99°C. Above this temperature, water cannot be liquefied, no matter how much pressure is applied. The **critical pressure** (P_c) is the lowest pressure at which the substance can exist as a liquid at the critical temperature. The critical pressure of water is 217.75 atm.

The phase diagram in **Figure 4.5** on the previous page indicates the normal boiling point and the normal freezing point of water. It also shows how boiling point and freezing point change with pressure. As shown by the slope of line AD, ice melts at a higher temperature with decreasing pressure. Below the triple point, the temperature of sublimation decreases with decreasing pressure. **Figure 4.6** summarizes the changes of state of solids, liquids, and gases.

SECTION 4 FORMATIVE ASSESSMENT

Reviewing Main Ideas

1. What is equilibrium?
2. What happens when a liquid-vapor system at equilibrium experiences an increase in temperature? What happens when it experiences a decrease in temperature?
3. What would be an example of deposition?
4. What is the equilibrium vapor pressure of a liquid? How is it measured?
5. What is the boiling point of a liquid?
6. In the phase diagram for water, what is meant by the triple point and the critical point?

Critical Thinking

7. **INTERPRETING GRAPHICS** Refer to the phase diagram for water (**Figure 4.5**) to answer the following questions.
   a. Describe all the changes a sample of solid water would undergo when heated from −10°C to its critical temperature at a pressure of 1.00 atm.
   b. Describe all the changes a sample of water vapor would undergo when cooled from 110°C to 5°C at a pressure of 1.00 atm.
   c. At approximately what pressure will water be a vapor at 0°C?
   d. Within what range of pressures will water be a liquid at temperatures above its normal boiling point?

Answers to Section Assessment

1. a dynamic condition in which two opposing changes occur at equal rates in a closed system
2. During a temperature increase, the system shifts toward formation of more vapor, absorbing energy and counteracting the temperature increase. During a temperature decrease, the system shifts toward formation of more liquid, releasing energy and counteracting the effect of the temperature decrease.
3. frost forming on a cold surface
4. pressure exerted by a vapor in equilibrium with its corresponding liquid at a given temperature; it is measured by introducing a liquid into an evacuated flask, allowing enough liquid to evaporate to reach equilibrium, and then measuring the increase in gas pressure.
5. the temperature at which equilibrium vapor pressure equals atmospheric pressure
6. triple point: temperature and pressure conditions under which ice, liquid water, and water vapor all exist together at equilibrium; critical point: temperature above which water cannot exist in the liquid state and the lowest pressure at which water can exist as a liquid at that temperature
7. a. It would warm as a solid to 0°C, melt to a liquid at 0°C, heat up as a liquid to 100°C, boil, and then heat up as a vapor.
   b. It would cool as a gas from 110°C to 100°C, condense to a liquid at 100°C, and then continue to cool as a liquid to 5°C.
   c. at pressures less than roughly 0.006 atm
   d. within 1.00 atm and 217.75 atm

SECTION 5

Main Ideas

- The properties of water in all phases are determined by its structure.
- The molar enthalpy of water determines many of its physical characteristics.

Water

Water is a familiar substance in all three physical states: solid, liquid, and gas. On Earth, water is by far the most abundant liquid. Oceans, rivers, and lakes cover about 75% of Earth's surface. Significant quantities of water are also frozen in glaciers. Water is an essential component of all organisms; 70% to 90% of the mass of living things is water. The chemical reactions of most life processes take place in water, and water is frequently a reactant or product in such reactions. In order to better understand the importance of water, let us take a closer look at its structure and its properties.

MAIN IDEA

The properties of water in all phases are determined by its structure.

Water molecules consist of two atoms of hydrogen and one atom of oxygen united by polar-covalent bonds. Research shows that a water molecule is bent. The structure can be represented as follows.

$$\underset{\text{H}\quad 105^\circ \quad \text{H}}{\ddot{\text{O}}}$$

The angle between the two hydrogen-oxygen bonds is about 105°. This is close to the angle expected for sp^3 hybridization of the oxygen-atom orbitals.

The molecules in solid or liquid water are linked by hydrogen bonding. The number of linked molecules decreases with increasing temperature, because increases in kinetic energy make hydrogen bond formation difficult. Nevertheless, there are usually from four to eight molecules per group in liquid water, as shown in **Figure 5.1**. If it were not for these molecular groups, water would be a gas at room temperature. Nonpolar molecules, such as methane, CH_4, that are similar in size and mass to water molecules do not undergo hydrogen bonding. Such substances are gases at room temperature.

Ice consists of water molecules in the hexagonal arrangement shown in **Figure 5.2** on the next page. The empty spaces between molecules in this pattern account for the relatively low density of ice. As ice is heated, the increased energy of the molecules causes them to move and vibrate more vigorously. When the melting point is reached, the energy of the molecules is so great that the rigid open structure of the ice crystals breaks down, and ice turns into liquid water.

Figures 5.1 and **Figure 5.2** also show that the hydrogen bonds between molecules of liquid water at 0°C are fewer and more disordered than those between molecules of ice at the same temperature. Because the rigid open structure of ice has broken down, water molecules can crowd closer together. Thus, liquid water is denser than ice.

FIGURE 5.1

Liquid Water Within the water molecule, oxygen and hydrogen are covalently bonded to each other. Hydrogen bonds hold the molecules together in groups.

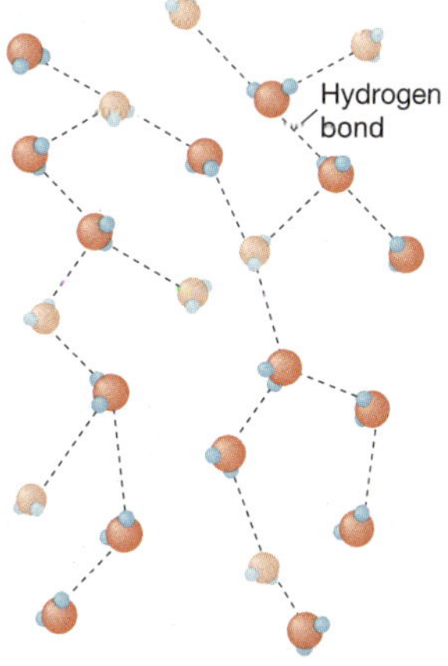

Differentiated Instruction

PRE-AP

Have students review VSEPR theory to explain why CO_2 is linear while H_2O is bent. Be sure that students remember how to draw the Lewis structures for each molecule and recognize the effect of unshared electron pairs on molecular geometry. From the Lewis structures, students should recognize that CO_2 has two electron pairs around the carbon, which results in a linear structure. H_2O has four electron pairs around the oxygen, two bonding and two non-bonding, which results in a bent structure.

SECTION 5

Plan and Prepare ▼

Objectives

Upon completion of this section, students should be able to do the following:

- Describe the structure of a water molecule.
- Discuss the physical properties of water and explain how they are determined by the structure of water.
- Calculate the amount of energy absorbed or released when a quantity of water changes state.

Classroom Catalyst

Show students a model of a water molecule. Ask them to think about how the molecule's structure would affect the properties of water. Remind them to think in terms of hydrogen bonding.

Teach ▼

Misconception Alert!

Students sometimes think that any bond involving hydrogen is a hydrogen bond. Remind them that an intramolecular bond, such as the bond that exists between a hydrogen atom and an oxygen atom within a water molecule, is a covalent bond. True hydrogen bonds are intermolecular attractions between a hydrogen atom on one molecule and a highly electronegative atom on another molecule.

▼ Teach *continued*

Classroom Discussion

Have students discuss the importance of the properties of water in relation to life. For example, they might discuss the significance of water being liquid over such a wide range of temperatures so that many areas of Earth are habitable. Also encourage students to bring in newspaper and magazine articles and pictures that focus on the importance of water in daily life.

Alternative Assessment

Provide a wide assortment of materials (such as plastic foam balls, gumdrops, toothpicks, springs, tape, and dowels), and have groups of students make models that illustrate the process by which liquid water molecules break away from ice crystals during melting. The models should reflect the arrangements typical of sets of water molecules in both states. Have groups compare their models and discuss any differences.

FIGURE 5.2

Solid Water Ice contains the same types of bonding as liquid water. However, the structure of the hydrogen bonding is much more rigid and open than it is in liquid water.

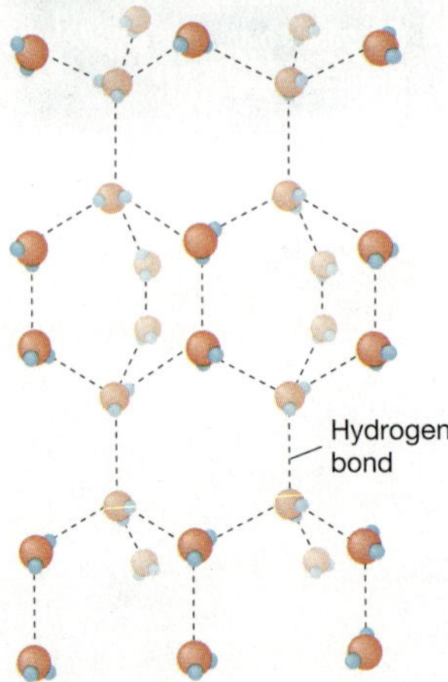

As the liquid water is warmed from 0°C, the water molecules crowd still closer together. Water molecules are as tightly packed as possible at 3.98°C. At temperatures above 3.98°C, the increasing kinetic energy of the water molecules causes them to overcome molecular attractions. The molecules move farther apart as the temperature continues to rise. As the temperature approaches the boiling point, groups of liquid water molecules absorb enough energy to break up into separate molecules. Because of hydrogen bonding between water molecules, a high kinetic energy is needed, causing water's boiling point to be relatively high (100°C) compared to other liquids that have similar molar masses.

MAIN IDEA

The molar enthalpy of water determines many of its physical characteristics.

At room temperature, pure liquid water is transparent, odorless, tasteless, and almost colorless. Any observable odor or taste is caused by impurities, such as dissolved minerals, liquids, or gases.

As shown by its phase diagram in **Figure 4.5** (in Section 4), water freezes and ice melts at 0°C at a pressure of 1 atm (101.3 kPa). The molar enthalpy of fusion of ice is 6.009 kJ/mol. That value is relatively large compared with the molar enthalpy of fusion of other solids. As you have read, water has the unusual property of expanding in volume as it freezes, because its molecules form an open rigid structure. As a result, ice at 0°C has a density of only about 0.917 g/cm^3, but liquid water at 0°C has a density of 0.999 84 g/cm^3.

This lower density explains why ice floats in liquid water. The insulating effect of floating ice is particularly important in the case of large bodies of water. If ice were more dense than liquid water, it would sink to the bottom of lakes and ponds, where it would be less likely to melt completely. The water of such bodies of water in temperate climates would eventually freeze solid, killing nearly all the living things in it.

Under a pressure of 1 atm (101.3 kPa), water boils at 100°C. At this temperature, water's molar enthalpy of vaporization is 40.79 kJ/mol. Both the boiling point and the molar enthalpy of vaporization of water are quite high compared with those of nonpolar substances of comparable molecular mass, such as methane. The values are high because of the strong hydrogen bonding that must be overcome for boiling to occur. The high molar enthalpy of vaporization makes water useful for household steam-heating systems. The steam (vaporized water) stores a great deal of energy as heat. When the steam condenses in radiators, great quantities of energy are released. In living organisms, the high molar enthalpy of vaporization helps them to resist dehydration when sources of water intake are restricted and provides a large degree of evaporative cooling to carry excess heat away from their bodies. This property especially allows warm-blooded organisms to better regulate their internal temperatures, reduce cell death from water loss, and maintain homeostasis.

Problem Solving

TAKE IT FURTHER

Have students explain why the enthalpy of vaporization for water in Sample Problem A is significantly greater than the enthalpy of fusion. Students should realize that fusion involves breaking only some of the hydrogen bonds between the water molecules in ice so that the groups of molecules can freely move past one another. In contrast, vaporization requires that all the hydrogen bonds be broken to produce individual vapor molecules.

Using Molar Enthalpy of Vaporization

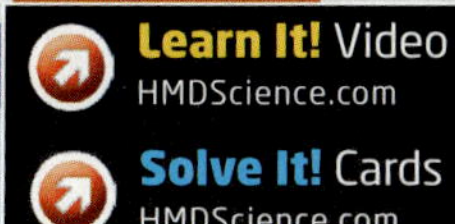

Sample Problem A **How much energy is absorbed when 47.0 g of ice melts at STP? How much energy is absorbed when this same mass of liquid water boils?**

1 ANALYZE

Given: mass of $H_2O(s) = 47.0$ g
mass of $H_2O(l) = 47.0$ g
molar enthalpy of fusion of ice = 6.009 kJ/mol
molar enthalpy of vaporization = 40.79 kJ/mol

Unknown: energy absorbed when ice melts; energy absorbed when liquid water boils

2 PLAN

First, convert the mass of water from grams to moles.

$$47.0 \text{ g } H_2O \times \frac{1 \text{ mol } H_2O}{18.02 \text{ g } H_2O} = 2.61 \text{ mol } H_2O$$

Then, use the molar enthalpy of fusion of a solid to calculate the amount of energy absorbed when the solid melts. Multiply the number of moles by the amount of energy needed to melt one mole of ice at its melting point (the molar enthalpy of fusion of ice). Using the same method, calculate the amount of energy absorbed when water boils by using the molar enthalpy of vaporization.

amount of substance (mol) × molar enthalpy of fusion or vaporization (kJ/mol) = energy (kJ)

3 SOLVE

$2.61 \text{ mol} \times 6.009 \text{ kJ/mol} = 15.7$ kJ (on melting)
$2.61 \text{ mol} \times 40.79 \text{ kJ/mol} = 106$ kJ (on vaporizing or boiling)

4 CHECK YOUR WORK

Units have canceled correctly. The answers have the proper number of significant digits and are reasonably close to estimated values of 18 (3 × 6) and 120 (3 × 40), respectively.

Practice Answers in Appendix E

1. What quantity of energy is released when 506 g of liquid water freezes?
2. What mass of steam is required to release 4.97×10^5 kJ of energy on condensation?

SECTION 5 FORMATIVE ASSESSMENT

Reviewing Main Ideas

1. Why is a water molecule polar?
2. How is the structure of water responsible for some of water's unique characteristics?
3. Describe the arrangement of molecules in liquid water and in ice.
4. Why does ice float? Why is this phenomenon important?
5. Why is ice less dense than liquid water?
6. Is more energy required to melt one gram of ice at 0°C or to boil one gram of water at 100°C? How do you know?

Critical Thinking

7. **RELATING IDEAS** Why is exposure to steam dangerous?

Classroom Practice

A-1 Find the mass of liquid water required to absorb 5.23×10^4 kJ of energy on boiling.
Answer: 2.31×10^4 g

A-2 How much energy is absorbed when 16.3 g of ice melts?
Answer: 5.44 kJ

A-3 Calculate the quantity of energy released when 783 g of steam condenses.
Answer: 1.77×10^3 kJ

Answers

Practice A

1. 169 kJ
2. 2.19×10^5 g

Assess and Reteach ▼

Assess Use the Formative Assessment on this page to evaluate student mastery of the section.

Reteach For students who need additional instruction, download the Section Study Guide.

Response to Intervention To reassess students' mastery, use the Section Quiz, available to print or to take directly online at **HMDScience.com**.

Answers to Section Assessment

1. Because of the bent (angular) shape of the molecule, the large electronegativity difference between oxygen and hydrogen atoms results in overall polarity of the molecule.
2. The structure allows for hydrogen bonding, resulting in the formation of molecular groups that produce a high enthalpy of fusion, boiling point, and enthalpy of vaporization.
3. There are intermolecular hydrogen bonds in both. The liquid usually has 4 to 8 molecules per group. In the solid, all the molecules are arranged in a hexagonal structure.
4. Ice floats because it is less dense than liquid water. When a lake freezes, less-dense ice forms only on the surface. The solid top layer insulates the liquid water beneath it, preventing a total freeze, which would kill most living things in the lake.
5. The regular hydrogen bonding pattern in ice leads to an open structure with significant empty space between molecules. The hydrogen bonds in liquid water are fewer and more disordered, allowing the molecules in the liquid to crowd closer together.
6. Boiling requires more energy. We know this because the molar enthalpy of vaporization of water is greater than its molar enthalpy of fusion.
7. The high enthalpy of vaporization of water means that a great quantity of energy is released as heat when the steam condenses on contact with the skin. Steam burns can be very severe.

Answers

1. 11.65 kJ/mol
2. 74.7 kJ

Math Tutor: Calculations Using Enthalpies of Fusion

When one mole of a liquid freezes to a solid, energy is released as attractive forces between particles pull the disordered particles of the liquid into a more orderly crystalline solid. When the solid melts to a liquid, the solid must absorb the same quantity of energy in order to separate the particles of the crystal and overcome the attractive forces opposing separation. This quantity of energy used to melt or freeze one mole of a substance at its melting point is called its molar enthalpy of fusion, ΔH_f.

Problem-Solving TIPS

- The enthalpy of fusion of a substance can be given as either joules per gram or kilojoules per mole.
- *Molar* enthalpy of fusion is most commonly used in calculations.
- The enthalpy of fusion is the energy absorbed or given off as heat when a substance melts or freezes at the melting point of the substance.
- There is no net change in temperature as the change of state occurs.

Samples

7.30 kJ of energy is required to melt 0.650 mol of ethylene glycol ($C_2H_6O_2$) at its melting point. Calculate the molar enthalpy of fusion, ΔH_f, of ethylene glycol and the energy absorbed.

$$\text{molar enthalpy of fusion} = \Delta H_f = \frac{\text{energy absorbed}}{\text{moles of substance}}$$

$$\Delta H_{f,\ ethylene\ glycol} = \frac{7.30\ \text{kJ}}{0.065\ \text{mol}} = 11.2\frac{\text{kJ}}{\text{mol}}$$

Determine the quantity of energy that will be needed to melt 2.50×10^5 kg of iron at its melting point, 1536°C. The ΔH_f of iron is 13.807 kJ/mol.

To calculate the number of moles of iron, use the equation below.

$$\text{moles of substance} = \frac{\text{mass of substance}}{\text{molar mass of substance}}$$

Next, use the following equation for energy as heat absorbed.

$$\text{energy absorbed} = \Delta H_f \times \text{moles of substance}$$

Now, substitute the calculation for moles of substance, and solve.

$$\text{energy absorbed} = \Delta H_f \times \frac{\text{grams of substance}}{\text{molar mass of substance}}$$

$$= 13.807\frac{\text{kJ}}{\text{mol}} \times \frac{2.50 \times 10^8\ \text{g Fe}}{55.847\ \text{g Fe/mol Fe}}$$

$$\text{energy absorbed} = 6.18 \times 10^7\ \text{kJ}$$

Practice

Answers in Appendix E

1. Calculate the molar enthalpy of fusion of silver if 1.940 mol of silver requires 22.60 kJ of energy to change from a solid to a liquid at its melting point, 961°C.
2. What quantity of energy in kJ must be absorbed by 6.47 mol of solid acetic acid, $C_2H_4O_2$, to melt it at its melting point, 16.7°C? The ΔH_f for acetic acid is 11.54 kJ/mol.

CHAPTER 10 Summary

PREMIUM CONTENT
Interactive Review HMDScience.com
Review Games
Concept Maps

SECTION 1 The Kinetic-Molecular Theory of Matter

- The kinetic-molecular theory of matter can be used to explain the properties of gases, liquids, and solids.
- The kinetic-molecular theory of gases describes a model of an ideal gas.
- Gases consist of large numbers of tiny, fast-moving particles that are far apart relative to their size.

KEY TERMS

kinetic-molecular theory
ideal gas
elastic collision
diffusion
effusion
real gas

SECTION 2 Liquids

- The particles of a liquid are closer together and more ordered than those of a gas and are less ordered than those of a solid.
- Liquids have a definite volume and a fairly high density, and they are relatively incompressible. Like gases, liquids can flow and thus are considered to be fluids.

KEY TERMS

fluid
surface tension
capillary action
vaporization
evaporation
freezing

SECTION 3 Solids

- The particles of a solid are not nearly as free to move about as those of a liquid or a gas are.
- Solids have a definite shape and may be crystalline or amorphous. They have a definite volume and are generally nonfluid.
- A crystal structure is the total three-dimensional array of points that describes the arrangement of the particles of a crystal.
- Unlike crystalline solids, amorphous solids do not have a highly ordered structure or a regular shape.

KEY TERMS

crystalline solid
crystal
amorphous solid
melting
melting point
supercooled liquid
crystal structure
unit cell

SECTION 4 Changes of State

- A liquid in a closed system will gradually reach a liquid-vapor equilibrium as the rate at which molecules condense equals the rate at which they evaporate.
- When two opposing changes occur at equal rates in the same closed system, the system is said to be in dynamic equilibrium.

KEY TERMS

phase
condensation
equilibrium
equilibrium vapor pressure
volatile liquid
boiling
boiling point
molar enthalpy of vaporization
freezing
freezing point
molar enthalpy of fusion
sublimation
deposition
phase diagram
triple point
critical point
critical temperature
critical pressure

SECTION 5 Water

- Water is a polar covalent compound.
- The structure and the hydrogen bonding in water are responsible for its relatively high melting point, molar enthalpy of fusion, boiling point, and molar enthalpy of vaporization.

CHAPTER REVIEW

Review Answers

1. Particles of matter are always in motion.
2. An ideal gas is a hypothetical gas that fits perfectly all the assumptions of the kinetic theory.
3. Gases consist of large numbers of tiny particles that are far apart in comparison to their size. The particles of a gas are in constant rapid motion. All collisions between gas particles and between particles and container walls are elastic collisions. There are no forces of attraction between gas particles. The average kinetic energy of gas particles determines the temperature of the gas.
4. The molecules of gases are much farther apart.
5. The average speed and kinetic energy of gas molecules increase as temperature increases and decrease as temperature decreases.
6. **a.** the spontaneous mixing of the particles of two substances due to their random motion
   b. the speeds of the gas particles
7. a substance that flows and conforms to the shape of its container
8. a force that tends to pull adjacent parts of a liquid's surface together, decreasing surface area
9. Water that falls to Earth evaporates from oceans and lakes. Evaporating perspiration cools the body.
10. maintain a definite shape (are nonfluid), because of relatively fixed arrangement of particles; have definite volume, because of close packing; have definite melting points, because of kinetic energies needed to overcome attractive forces; have high densities, because of close packing; are incompressible, because of close packing; have a low rate of diffusion, because of low mobility of particles
11. rubber, glass, plastics, synthetic fibers
12. ionic: ionically bonded positive and negative ions in a regular pattern; covalent network: single atoms covalently bonded to nearest neighbors in extensive pattern; metallic: positive metal cations surrounded by negative valence electrons that belong to the crystal as a whole and are attracted to the cations; covalent molecular: covalently bonded molecules held together by London dispersion forces, dipole-dipole forces, or hydrogen bonding
13. **a.** 350 torr **b.** 500 torr **c.** 375 torr
14. **a.** change of state directly from solid to gas
    b. dry ice, iodine
15. the temperature at which solid and liquid are in equilibrium at 1 atm pressure
16. The stronger the attractive forces, the lower the percentage of particles that can escape to the vapor phase and the lower the equilibrium vapor pressure.
17. The higher the atmospheric pressure is, the higher the boiling point is. The liquid must be heated to a higher temperature to allow the equilibrium vapor pressure to equal atmospheric pressure.
18. The greater the attraction, the greater the energy required to overcome it and the higher the molar enthalpy of fusion.
19. **a.** 2264 J/g **b.** 333.5 J/g
20. 84.3 kJ/mol
21. **a.** 0.277 mol **b.** 15.5 kJ

CHAPTER 10 Review

SECTION 1

The Kinetic-Molecular Theory of Matter

 REVIEWING MAIN IDEAS

1. What idea is the kinetic-molecular theory based on?
2. What is an ideal gas?
3. State the five basic assumptions of the kinetic-molecular theory.
4. How do gases compare with liquids and solids in terms of the distance between their molecules?
5. What is the relationship between the temperature, speed, and kinetic energy of gas molecules?
6. **a.** What is diffusion?
   b. What factors affect the rate of diffusion of one gas through another?

SECTION 2

Liquids

 REVIEWING MAIN IDEAS

7. What is a fluid?
8. What is surface tension?
9. Give two reasons why evaporation is a crucial process in nature.

SECTION 3

Solids

 REVIEWING MAIN IDEAS

10. List six properties of solids, and explain each in terms of the kinetic-molecular theory of solids.
11. List four common examples of amorphous solids.
12. List and describe the four types of crystals in terms of the nature of their component particles and the type of bonding between them.

SECTION 4

Changes of State

 REVIEWING MAIN IDEAS

13. Using **Figure 4.3,** estimate the approximate equilibrium vapor pressure of each of the following at the specified temperature.
    a. water at 80°C
    b. diethyl ether at 20°C
    c. ethanol at 60°C
14. **a.** What is sublimation?
    b. Give two examples of common substances that sublime at ordinary temperatures.
15. What is meant by the normal freezing point of a substance?
16. Explain how the attractive forces between the particles in a liquid are related to the equilibrium vapor pressure of that liquid.
17. Explain the relationship between atmospheric pressure and the actual boiling point of a liquid.
18. Explain the relationship between the molar enthalpy of fusion of a solid and the strength of attraction between that solid's particles.

PRACTICE PROBLEMS

19. **a.** The molar enthalpy of vaporization for water is 40.79 kJ/mol. Express this enthalpy of vaporization in joules per gram.
    b. The molar enthalpy of fusion for water is 6.009 kJ/mol. Express this enthalpy of fusion in joules per gram.
20. Calculate the molar enthalpy of vaporization of a substance, given that 0.433 mol of the substance absorbs 36.5 kJ of energy when it is vaporized.
21. Given that a substance has a molar mass of 259.0 g/mol and a 71.8 g sample of the substance absorbs 4.307 kJ when it melts,
    a. calculate the number of moles in the sample.
    b. calculate the molar enthalpy of fusion.

22. **a.** Calculate the number of moles in a liquid sample of a substance that has a molar enthalpy of fusion of 3.811 kJ/mol, given that the sample releases 83.2 kJ when it freezes.
b. Calculate the molar mass of this substance if the mass of the sample is 5519 g.

SECTION 5

Water

REVIEWING MAIN IDEAS

23. Describe the structure of a water molecule.

24. List at least eight physical properties of water.

PRACTICE PROBLEMS

25. Which contains more molecules of water: 5.00 cm^3 of ice at 0°C or 5.00 cm^3 of liquid water at 0.°C? How many more? What is the ratio of the numbers of molecules in these two samples?

26. **a.** What volume and mass of steam at 100.°C and 1.00 atm would release the same amount of energy during condensation as 100. cm^3 of liquid water would release during freezing?
b. What do you note, qualitatively, about the relative volumes and masses of steam and liquid water required to release the same amount of heat? (Hint: See Sample Problem A.)

Mixed Review

REVIEWING MAIN IDEAS

27. Find the molar enthalpy of vaporization for a substance, given that 3.21 mol of the substance absorbs 28.4 kJ of energy as heat when the substance changes from a liquid to a gas.

28. Water's molar enthalpy of fusion is 6.009 kJ/mol. Calculate the amount of energy as heat required to melt 7.95×10^5 g of ice.

29. A certain substance has a molar enthalpy of vaporization of 31.6 kJ/mol. How much of the substance is in a sample that requires 57.0 kJ to vaporize?

30. Given that water has a molar enthalpy of vaporization of 40.79 kJ/mol, how many grams of water could be vaporized by 0.545 kJ?

31. Calculate the amount of energy released as heat by the freezing of 13.3 g of a liquid substance, given that the substance has a molar mass of 82.9 g/mol and a molar enthalpy of fusion of 4.60 kJ/mol.

32. What volume and mass of steam at 100.°C and 760. torr would release the same amount of energy as heat during condensation as 65.5 cm^3 of liquid water would release during freezing?

33. The following liquid-vapor system is at equilibrium at a given temperature in a closed system.

$$\text{liquid} + \text{energy} \rightleftharpoons \text{vapor}$$

Suppose the temperature is increased, and equilibrium is established at the higher temperature. How does the final value of each of the following compare with its initial value? (In each case, answer either higher, lower, or the same.)
a. the rate of evaporation
b. the rate of condensation
c. the final concentration of vapor molecules
d. the final number of liquid molecules

34. Given a sample of water at any point on curve AB in **Figure 4.5**, what effect would each of the following changes have on that sample?
a. adding energy at constant pressure
b. decreasing the volume at constant temperature
c. removing energy at constant pressure
d. increasing the volume at constant temperature

35. Using the phase diagram for CO_2, describe all the phase changes that would occur when CO_2 is heated from −100°C to −10°C at a constant pressure of 6 atm.

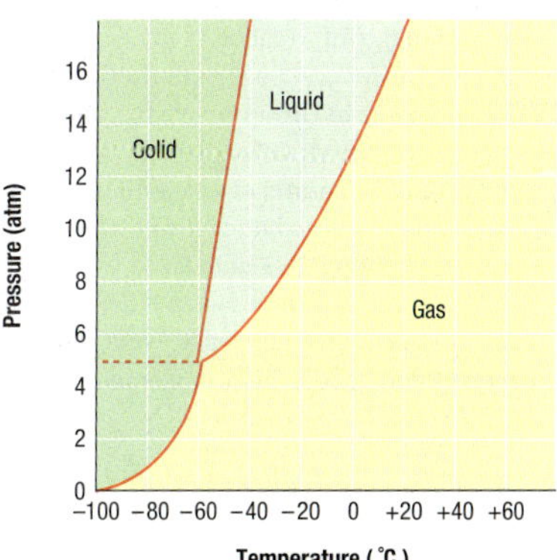

CHAPTER REVIEW

22. a. 21.8 mol **b.** 253 g/mol
23. Two atoms of H are joined to the same O atom by polar covalent bonds at an angle of about 105°.
24. at room temperature, a transparent, tasteless, odorless, nearly colorless liquid; freezing point, 0°C at 1 atm; molar enthalpy of fusion, 6.009 kJ/mol; expands during freezing; maximum density at about 4°C; boiling point at 1 atm, 100°C; molar enthalpy of vaporization, 40.79 kJ/mol
25. liquid water; 1.4×10^{22} more molecules; 1.09:1.00 ratio
26. a. 5.0 L, 14.7 g
b. A larger volume but a smaller mass of steam is required.
27. 8.85 kJ/mol
28. 2.65×10^5 kJ
29. 1.80 mol
30. 0.241 g
31. 0.738 kJ
32. 16.4 L, 9.63 g
33. a. higher **c.** higher
b. higher **d.** lower
34. a. More solid would sublime.
b. More vapor would deposit.
c. More vapor would deposit.
d. More solid would vaporize.
35. At 6 atm and −100.°C, CO_2 is a solid and remains so until about −60°C, when it melts. At about −45°C, the liquid boils.

36. The energy being removed is a loss of potential energy resulting from attracting particles moving closer together, not a loss of kinetic energy that would be reflected in the temperature.

37. Adding energy as heat to an ice-water system pushes the equilibrium to the right. Removing energy shifts it to the left. If both ice and liquid are present, adding or removing energy is reflected in the change of state (which involves potential energy), rather than in a change of kinetic energy.

38. The pressure could be decreased, which would cause the system to try to reduce the imposed stress by having the liquid take a less dense form. This would cause the liquid's volume to increase as it became a solid. The diagram shows that a movement into the solid region of the graph would occur at the lower pressure.

39. a. It changes from solid directly to gas (sublimes).
 b. Yes, liquid exists only at pressures higher than the triple point pressure (the dashed line). This pressure is about 5 atm.

40. a. calcium and strontium
 b. The model would show all atoms to be of the same size.
 c. Group 1: Li, Na, K, Rb, and Cs; Group 2: Ba and Ra

41. Answers may vary. Refer to HMDScience.com for the appropriate scoring rubric.

42. Answers may vary. Refer to HMDScience.com for the appropriate scoring rubric.

43. Answers may vary. Check students' lists for accuracy.

44. Answers may vary. Remind students to follow all safety cautions and disposal guidelines.

CHAPTER REVIEW

CRITICAL THINKING

36. **Interpreting Concepts** During the freezing of a substance, energy is being removed from that substance. Yet the temperature of the liquid-solid system remains constant. Explain this phenomenon.

37. **Applying Models** At normal atmospheric pressure, the temperature of an ice-water system remains at 0°C as long as both ice and liquid water are present, regardless of the surrounding temperature. Explain why this occurs.

38. **Predicting Outcomes** Given a sample of water at any point on curve AD in **Figure 4.5,** how could more of the liquid water in that sample be converted into a solid without changing the temperature? Explain your reasoning.

39. **Interpreting Diagrams** Refer to the phase diagram in question 35.
 a. Explain what happens when solid CO_2 ("dry ice") warms up to room temperature at normal atmospheric pressure.
 b. Is there a pressure below which liquid CO_2 cannot exist? Estimate that pressure from the graph.

USING THE HANDBOOK

40. The *Elements Handbook* (Appendix A) contains a table of properties for each group that includes information on the crystal structures of the elements. Most metals crystallize in one of three lattice arrangements: body-centered cubic, face-centered cubic, or hexagonal close-packed. **Figure 3.2** shows a model of the face-centered cubic lattice for sodium chloride. Use this figure and the information in the *Elements Handbook* (Appendix A) to answer the following.
 a. What elements in Group 2 have the same lattice structure as sodium chloride?
 b. How would the model of an element in a face-centered cubic lattice differ from the compound shown in **Figure 3.2**?
 c. The body-centered cubic lattice is the least-efficient packing structure of the metals. What elements in Groups 1 and 2 show this arrangement?

RESEARCH AND WRITING

41. Ceramics are formed from silicates found in the soil. Artists use them to create pottery, but engineers and scientists have created ceramics with superconductive properties. Investigate the growing field of superconductive ceramics.

42. Liquid crystals are substances that possess the combined properties of both liquids and crystals. Write a report on these substances and the various uses we are finding for them.

ALTERNATIVE ASSESSMENT

43. Compile separate lists of crystalline and amorphous solids found in your home. Compare your lists with those of your classmates.

44. Design an experiment to grow crystals of various safe, common household materials. Record the conditions under which each type of crystal is best grown.

338 Chapter 10

Standards-Based Assessment

Answer the following items on a separate piece of paper.

MULTIPLE CHOICE

1. Surface tension is
   A. skin on the surface of a liquid.
   B. the tendency of the surface of liquids to decrease the area.
   C. the spontaneous mixing of two substances.
   D. the same as vapor pressure.

2. Pure liquids boil at higher temperatures under high pressures than they do under low pressures, because
   A. the molecules of liquid are closer together under higher pressures.
   B. it takes a higher temperature for the vapor pressure to equal the higher external pressure.
   C. the molecules of vapor are farther apart under higher pressures.
   D. the vapor diffuses more rapidly at higher pressures.

3. The formation of frost is an example of
   A. condensation.
   B. evaporation.
   C. deposition.
   D. melting point.

4. A graph that shows the pressure and temperature conditions under which the phases of a substance exist is called
   A. a phase diagram.
   B. a vapor pressure curve.
   C. a unit cell.
   D. the kinetic-molecular theory of matter.

5. Water boils at 100°C. Ethanol boils at 78.5°C. Which of the following statements is true?
   A. Water has the higher vapor pressure at 78.5°C.
   B. Ethanol has the higher vapor pressure at 78.5°C.
   C. Both have the same vapor pressure at 78.5°C.
   D. Vapor pressure is not related to boiling point.

6. Which of the following is not a property of typical solids?
   A. definite melting point
   B. high density
   C. easily compressible
   D. low rate of diffusion

7. The kinetic-molecular theory states that ideal gas molecules
   A. are in constant, rapid, random motion.
   B. have mass and take up space.
   C. exert forces of attraction and repulsion on each other.
   D. have high densities compared with liquids and solids.

SHORT ANSWER

8. Using this graph of vapor pressures of substances at various temperatures, estimate the boiling point of ethanol at an applied (external) pressure of 300 torr.

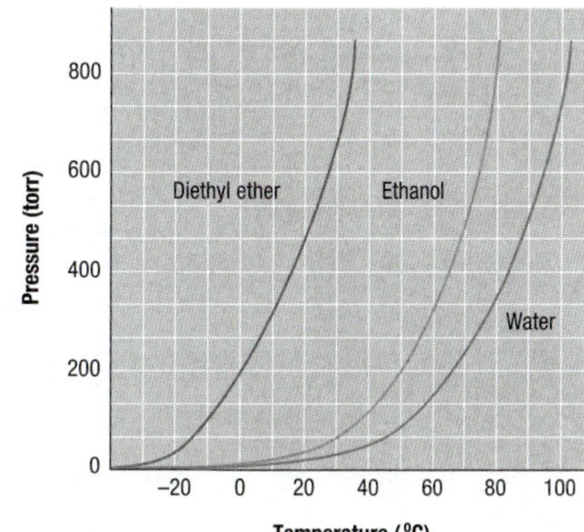

9. It is found that 60.0 J of energy are required to melt 15 g of a substance. The molar mass of the substance is 120 g/mol. Calculate the enthalpy of fusion of the substance in kilojoules per mole.

EXTENDED RESPONSE

10. Describe how a pressure cooker works.

11. What is meant by the statement that a liquid and its vapor in a closed container are in a state of dynamic equilibrium?

Test Tip

Test questions are not necessarily arranged in order of increasing difficulty. If you are unable to answer a question, mark it and move on to other questions.

STANDARDS-BASED ASSESSMENT

To give students practice under more realistic testing conditions, give them 60 minutes to answer all of the questions in this Standardized Test Preparation.

Test Answers

1. B
2. B
3. C
4. A
5. B
6. C
7. A
8. 60°C. Students should be able to read the graph to within 5 degrees.
9. 0.48 kJ/mol
10. In the sealed cooker, steam pressure builds up in the space above the boiling water. At this higher pressure, the water boils at a higher temperature. Like all chemical reactions, the cooking of the food takes place more rapidly at this higher temperature, so cooking times are decreased.
11. At a given temperature, molecules are continually leaving the surface at a constant rate of evaporation. Molecules of the vapor striking the surface can rejoin the liquid at a constant rate of condensation. When there are enough molecules in the vapor, the rate of condensation equals the rate of evaporation. At this point, molecules are entering and leaving the liquid at the same rate, so no net change in the amount of either phase is observed. This is a condition of dynamic equilibrium.

Gases

① Core Instruction

Chapter Resources

- The Teacher's Edition wrap has extensive teaching support for every lesson, including Misconception Alerts, Teach from Visuals, Demonstrations, Teaching Tips, Differentiated Instruction, and Problem Solving support.
- Several additional presentation tools are available online for every chapter, including Animated Chemistry features and Visual Concepts.
- You can open your lesson with the Why It Matters Video: Gases.

Section	Instruction	Labs and Demonstrations Go Online for Materials Lists and Solutions Lists.
11.1	■ **Textbook:** Gases and Pressure **Teaching Visuals:** Relationship Between Pressure, Force, and Area • Mercury Barometer • Gas Mixtures and Dalton's Law • Particle Model for a Gas Collected Over Water • Units of Pressure • Water-Vapor Pressure • Vapor Pressure of Water at Various Temperatures • Vapor Pressures of Diethyl Ether, Ethanol, and Water at Various Temperatures **Power Presentations**	■ **Demonstration:** Relating Pressure to Area ■ **Demonstration:** Unbalanced Force of Atmospheric Pressure ■ **Lab:** Mass and Density of Air at Different Pressures (Core Skill)
11.2	■ **Textbook:** The Gas Laws **Teaching Visuals:** Volume Versus Pressure for a Gas at Constant Temperature • Volume Versus Temperature for a Gas at Constant Pressure • Pressure Versus Temperature for a Gas at Constant Volume • Boyle's Law Relationship • Reciprocal of Volume vs. Pressure • Charles's Law Relationship • Gay-Lussac's Law Relationship **Power Presentations**	■ **Lab:** Boyle's Law (Core Skill) ■ **Lab:** Pressure-Volume Relationships: Understanding Boyle's Law (Probeware)
11.3	■ **Textbook:** Gas Volumes and the Ideal Gas Law **Animated Chemistry:** Ideal Gas Behavior **Teaching Visuals:** Avogadro's Law • Finding Volume of Unknown • Gas Law Calculations • Summary of the Basic Gas Laws • Deviation of Real Gases from Ideal Behavior • Numerical Values of the Gas Constant **Power Presentations**	■ **Lab:** Molar Volume of a Gas (Core Skill) ■ **Lab:** Generating and Collecting O_2 (Core Skill) ■ **Lab:** Generating and Collecting H_2 (Core Skill) ■ **Lab:** Testing for Dissolved Oxygen (Core Skill)
11.4	■ **Textbook:** Diffusion and Effusion **Teaching Visuals:** Graham's Law • Energy Distribution of Gas Molecules at Different Temperatures **Power Presentations**	■ **QuickLab:** Diffusion ■ **Lab:** Why Are The Fish Dying? (Open Inquiry)

② Support and Intervention

- **Interactive Reader** (English and Spanish)
- **Study Guide**
- **Interactive Review:** Review Games, Concept Maps, and Section Self-Checks
- **Scientific Reasoning Skill Builder**
- **Learn It! Videos**
- **Solve It! Cards**
- **Interactive Demos**
- **Sample Problem Sets**

③ Specialized Support

- **Chapter Summary Audio Files**
- **Interactive Reader Audio Files**
- **Differentiated Instruction:** Inclusion, Below Level, and English Learners (TE wrap)

Enrichment and Challenge

- **Differentiated Instruction:** Pre-AP (TE wrap)
- **Why It Matters:** The Gas Laws and Scuba Diving (SE)
- **Chemistry Explorers:** Chemistry's First Law (SE)
- **WebLinks**

Assessment

- **Section Formative Assessments** (SE)
- **Section Quizzes**
- **Chapter Review** (SE)
- **Chapter Tests A and B**
- **Alternative Assessment** (TE wrap)
- **Online Assessment and Remediation**
- **ExamView Banks**

Where do I find it?

	Resource	PRINT	DVD	ONLINE
1	Animated Chemistry		■	■
1	Demonstrations (TE wrap)	■		■
1	Interactive Whiteboard		■	■
1	Labs		■	■
1	PowerPresentations		■	■
1	QuickLabs	■	■	■
1	Teaching Visuals		■	■
1	Textbook	■	■	■
1	Visual Concepts		■	■
1	Why It Matters Videos		■	■
2	Interactive Demos		■	■
2	Interactive Reader	■	■	■
2	Interactive Reviews		■	■
2	Learn It! Videos		■	■
2	Sample Problem Sets		■	■
2	Scientific Reasoning Skill Builder		■	■
2	Smart Grapher Tool		■	■
2	Solve It! Cards		■	■
2	Study Guide		■	■
3	Chapter Summary Audio Files		■	■
3	Differentiated Instruction (TE wrap)	■		
3	Interactive Reader Audio Files		■	■

CHAPTER 11

Chapter Overview

Section 1 reintroduces the kinetic-molecular theory of gases, defines pressure in terms of force, explains how pressure is measured, and defines and converts units of pressure.

Section 2 presents gas laws that express simple mathematical relationships among the pressure, temperature, volume, and quantity of gases.

Section 3 develops the relationships among the volume, mass, and number of particles of a gas and presents the ideal gas law.

Section 4 demonstrates the relationship between the mass of gas particles and their rate of effusion.

▼ Focus and Motivate

Activate Prior Knowledge

Students may need a review of the following concepts:

- states and physical properties of matter
- scientific notation and significant figures
- writing and balancing chemical equations
- stoichiometric calculations
- the relationship between temperature and particle motion

About the Image

Hot-air balloons are the oldest form of human flight. The density of the gas inside the balloon decreases as it is heated. This causes the balloon to become buoyant and "float" on top of the air.

Why It Matters

Students can access the videos online and find other helpful resources at **HMDScience.com**.

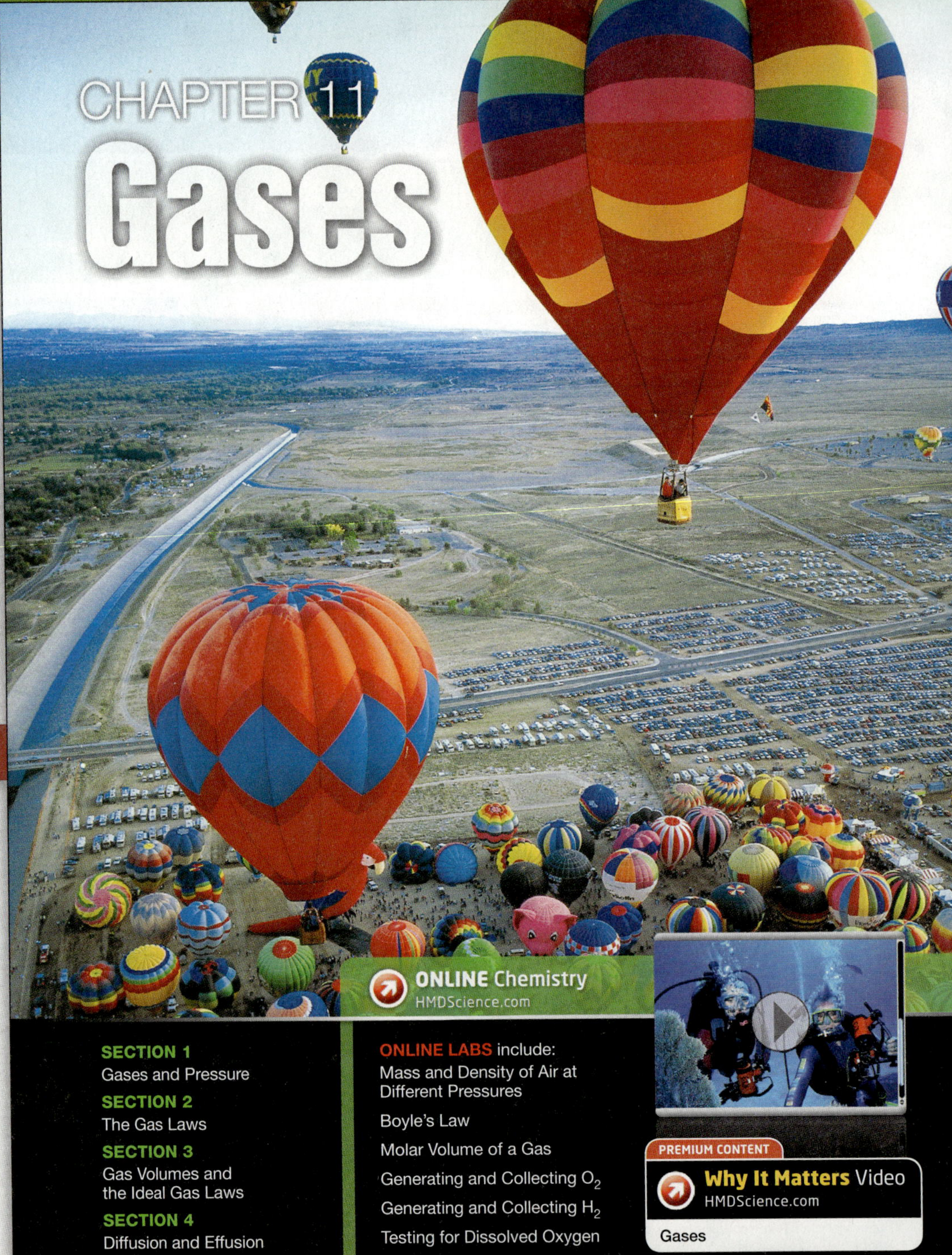

SECTION 1
Gases and Pressure

SECTION 2
The Gas Laws

SECTION 3
Gas Volumes and the Ideal Gas Laws

SECTION 4
Diffusion and Effusion

ONLINE LABS include:
Mass and Density of Air at Different Pressures
Boyle's Law
Molar Volume of a Gas
Generating and Collecting O_2
Generating and Collecting H_2
Testing for Dissolved Oxygen

PREMIUM CONTENT
Why It Matters Video
HMDScience.com
Gases

Lab Preview

The following labs and demonstrations support the concepts presented in this chapter.

LABS

Mass and Density of Air at Different Pressures
Boyle's Law (Core Skill)
Molar Volume of a Gas (Core Skill)
Generating and Collecting O_2 (Core Skill)
Generating and Collecting H_2 (Core Skill)
Testing for Dissolved Oxygen (Core Skill)
Pressure-Volume Relationships: Understanding Boyle's Law (Probeware)
Why Are The Fish Dying? (Open Inquiry)

QUICKLAB

Diffusion

DEMONSTRATIONS

Relating Pressure to Area
Unbalanced Force of Atmospheric Pressure

SECTION 1

Gases and Pressure

Key Terms

pressure
newton
barometer
millimeters of mercury
atmosphere of pressure
pascal
partial pressure
Dalton's law of partial pressures

SECTION 1

Main Ideas

- Collisions of air molecules generate pressure.
- Pressure depends on force and area.
- The total pressure of a gas mixture is the sum of the pressures of the gases in it.

In the chapter "States of Matter," you read about the kinetic-molecular theory, which is based on the idea that particles of matter are always in motion. In this section, you will study the implications of the kinetic-molecular theory of gases.

You have learned that the temperature of a gas is related to the kinetic energy of the gas molecules. Now you will learn about other properties of gases, including pressure, volume, and amount of gas present, and about the relationships among these properties.

MAIN IDEA

Collisions of air molecules generate pressure.

If you pump air into an automobile tire, the pressure in the tire will increase. The pressure increase is caused by the increase in the number of collisions of molecules of air with the inside walls of the tire. The collisions cause an outward push, or force, against the inside walls. Gas molecules exert pressure on any surface with which they collide. The pressure exerted by a gas depends on volume, temperature, and the number of molecules present. **Pressure** (P) is defined as the force per unit area on a surface. The equation defining pressure is shown in **Figure 1.1**.

FIGURE 1.1

Pressure and Area of Contact Because force is constant, the pressure the ballet dancer exerts against the floor depends on the area of contact.

$$\text{Pressure} = \frac{\text{Force}}{\text{Area}}$$

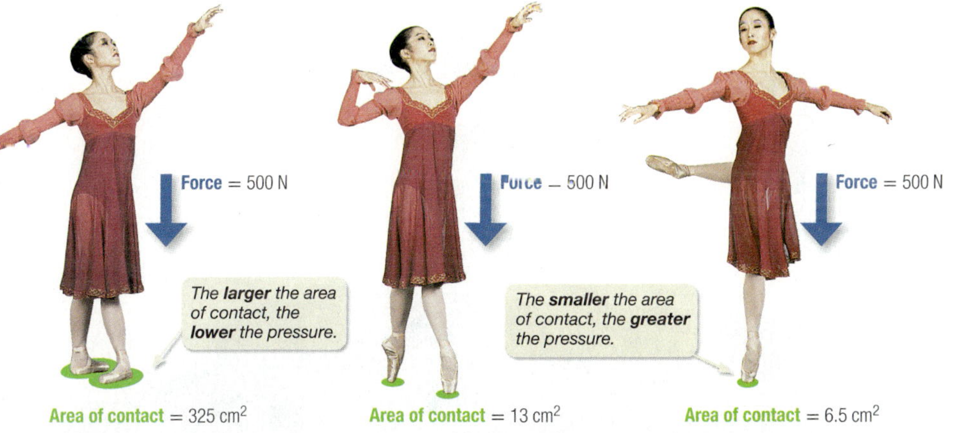

(a) $\text{Pressure} = \frac{500\ \text{N}}{325\ \text{cm}^2} = 1.5\ \text{N/cm}^2$ (b) $\text{Pressure} = \frac{500\ \text{N}}{13\ \text{cm}^2} = 38.5\ \text{N/cm}^2$ (c) $\text{Pressure} = \frac{500\ \text{N}}{6.5\ \text{cm}^2} = 77\ \text{N/cm}^2$

Differentiated Instruction

BELOW LEVEL

Have students do a *jigsaw* activity to introduce this chapter. Divide the class into groups of 3–4 students and give each group a number. Divide Section 1 of this chapter into 3 or 4 parts, and name them *A, B, C*, etc. Give each student in a group a letter designation in addition to their group number. For example, a student might be designated as *1A*. Have the *A* students from all groups discuss and determine the major concepts within part A of the section. The *B* students will do the same with part B, and so on. Allow about 15 minutes for discussion. Then, have students report back to their original, numbered group, teaching the group what their designated part of the section had to say.

SECTION 1

Plan and Prepare

Objectives

Upon completion of this section, students should be able to do the following:

- Define pressure, give units of pressure, and describe how pressure is measured.
- State the standard conditions of temperature and pressure and convert units of pressure.
- Use Dalton's law of partial pressures to calculate partial pressures and total pressures.

Classroom Catalyst

Have students make a list of gases. Ask them to separate the list into elements, compounds, and mixtures. Students can share these lists with the class by putting them on the board.

Teach

Misconception Alert!

Students frequently think that the gas laws apply to real gases. Remind students that the gas laws are abstractions that apply to ideal gases and that they apply to real gases only as an approximation. Discuss the properties that prevent real gases from acting like ideal gases. Remind students of the ways in which real gases deviate from ideal behavior.

TEACH FROM VISUALS

FIGURE 1.1 Point out to students that the amount of force in each image remains the same. Only the surface area where the dancer's feet contact the floor changes.

▼ Teach *continued*

Demonstration

RELATING PRESSURE TO AREA
Place a **wooden block** with three different dimensions on a slab of **modeling clay.** Add sufficient **weights** to force the block into the clay by a noticeable amount. Remove the block, and measure the depth of the impression. Using the same weights, repeat the process with a different-sized side of the block. Repeat the process with the third side. Ask students what their measurements and observations imply about pressure.

TEACH FROM VISUALS

FIGURE 1.2 Ask students to explain why airplanes that fly at high altitudes have pressurized cabins.

Classroom Discussion

Ask students: "If an airplane that flies at high altitudes must be pressurized, does a submarine that travels deep beneath the sea also need to be pressurized?" Answers will vary widely. If necessary, explain that because submarines do not have to be as lightweight as airplanes, they are made of more rigid materials and can maintain an internal pressure of 1 atm.

Check for Understanding

Answer: The sharp object provides greater pressure.

MAIN IDEA

Pressure depends on force and area.

The SI unit for force is the newton, (N). **The newton is the force that will increase the speed of a one-kilogram mass by one meter per second each second that the force is applied.** At Earth's surface, gravity has an acceleration of 9.8 m/s^2. Consider a ballet dancer with a mass of 51 kg, as shown in **Figure 1.1** (on the previous page). A mass of 51 kg exerts a force of 500 N (51 kg × 9.8 m/s^2) on Earth's surface. No matter how the dancer stands, she exerts the same force—500 N—against the floor. But the pressure exerted against the floor depends on the area of contact.

When the dancer rests her weight on the soles of both feet, as shown in **Figure 1.1a**, the area of contact with the floor is about 325 cm^2. The pressure, or force per unit area, when she stands in this manner is 500 N/325 cm^2, or roughly 1.5 N/cm^2. When she stands on her toes, as in **Figure 1.1b**, the total area of contact with the floor is only 13 cm^2. The pressure exerted is then equal to 500 N/13 cm^2—roughly 38 N/cm^2. And when she stands on one toe, as in **Figure 1.1c**, the pressure exerted is twice that, or about 77 N/cm^2. Thus, the same force applied to a smaller area results in a greater pressure.

CHECK FOR UNDERSTANDING
Explain Why is it easier to pop a balloon with a sharp object than by squeezing it between your hands? Use the term "pressure" in your explanation.

Atmospheric Pressure

The atmosphere—the shell of air surrounding Earth—exerts pressure. **Figure 1.2** shows that atmospheric pressure at sea level is about equal to the weight of a 1.03 kg mass per square centimeter of surface, or 10.1 N/cm^2. The pressure of the atmosphere can be thought of as caused by the weight of the gases that compose the atmosphere. The atmosphere contains about 78% nitrogen, 21% oxygen, and 1% other gases, including argon and carbon dioxide. Atmospheric pressure is the sum of the individual pressures of the various gases in the atmosphere.

FIGURE 1.2

Atmospheric Pressure Air molecules collide with Earth's surface, creating pressure.

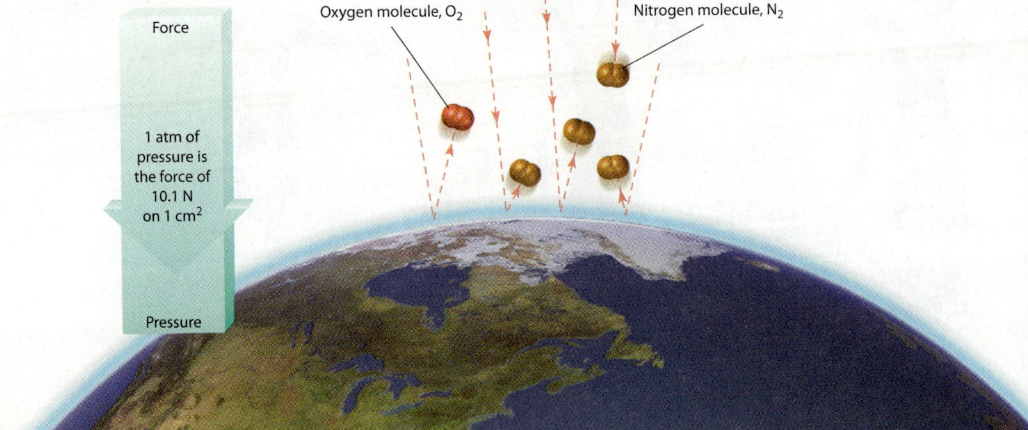

Differentiated Instruction

INCLUSION
For visual and kinesthetic learners, use either a hot plate and some popcorn in a package that expands as the kernels pop or a microwave and a package of microwaveable popcorn. Before popping the corn, ask students to predict what they will see. The bag will expand or "get bigger." Tell students that this expansion is a result of the pressure from the kernels bouncing against the inside of the bag, just as gas molecules bounce off of surfaces and each other. Relate this to the kinetic-molecular theory.

The Barometer

A **barometer** is a device used to measure atmospheric pressure. The first type of barometer, illustrated in **Figure 1.3**, was introduced by Evangelista Torricelli during the early 1600s. Torricelli wondered why water pumps could raise water to a maximum height of only about 34 feet. He thought that the height must depend somehow on the weight of water compared with the weight of air. He reasoned that liquid mercury, which is about 14 times as dense as water, could be raised only 1/14 as high as water. To test this idea, Torricelli sealed a long glass tube at one end and filled it with mercury. Holding the open end with his thumb, he inverted the tube into a dish of mercury without allowing any air to enter the tube. When he removed his thumb, the mercury column in the tube dropped to a height of about 30 in. (760 mm) above the surface of the mercury in the dish, just as he predicted.

FIGURE 1.3

Torricelli's Barometer Torricelli discovered that the pressure of the atmosphere supports a column of mercury about 760 mm above the surface of the mercury in the dish.

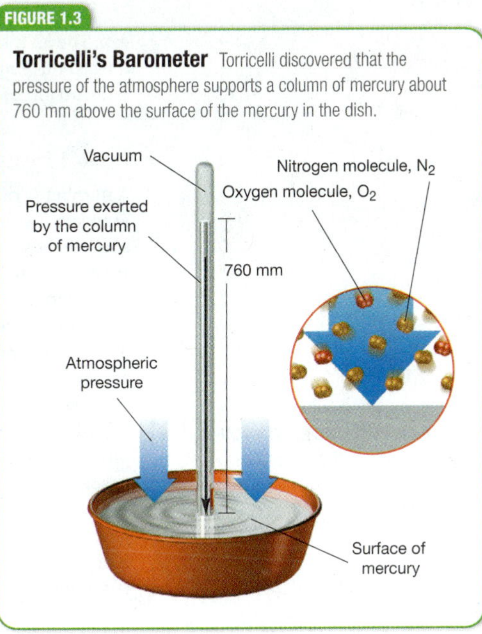

How a Barometer Works

The space above the mercury in the tube of a barometer is nearly a vacuum. The mercury in the tube pushes downward because of gravitational force. The column of mercury in the tube is stopped from falling beyond a certain point because the atmosphere exerts a pressure on the surface of the mercury outside the tube. This pressure is transmitted through the fluid mercury and is exerted upward on the column of mercury.

The exact height of the mercury in the tube depends on the atmospheric pressure, or force per unit area. The pressure is measured in terms of the mercury column's height in the barometer tube.

From experiments like Torricelli's, it is known that at sea level at 0°C, the average pressure of the atmosphere can support a 760 mm column of mercury. The atmospheric pressure at any given place depends on the elevation and the weather conditions. If the atmospheric pressure is greater than the average at sea level, the height of the mercury column in a barometer will be greater than 760 mm. If the atmospheric pressure is less, the height of the mercury column will be less than 760 mm.

Using a Manometer

All gases exert pressure. A device called a manometer can be used to measure the pressure of an enclosed gas sample (see **Figure 1.4**). The difference in the height of mercury in the two arms of the U-tube is a measure of the oxygen gas pressure in the container.

FIGURE 1.4

Measuring the Pressure of a Gas Sample In the manometer below, the pressure of the oxygen gas in the flask pushes on the mercury column.

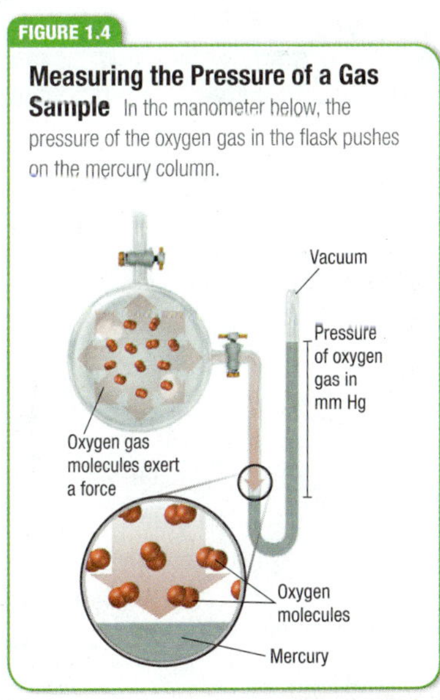

Demonstration

UNBALANCED FORCE OF ATMOSPHERIC PRESSURE

Demonstrate in an experiment a case of unbalanced force of atmospheric pressure. Use a clean, **1-gal metal container.** Pour about **50 mL of water** into the container, and set the container on a **hot plate** with the screw cap off. When the water inside the container begins to boil, remove the container from the hot plate and immediately screw the cap on tightly. Discuss with students why the container collapses as it cools.

Safety Wear **goggles** throughout the demonstration. To prevent rupture of the can, do not heat a sealed can or seal the can while it is on the hot plate. Use a **thermal mitt** when handling the hot container or putting on the cap.

ChemisTrivia

Torricelli served as secretary and companion to Galileo during the last three months of Galileo's life. It was Galileo who suggested the problem of measuring air pressure to Torricelli.

Alternative Assessment

In terms of pressure, have students explain why shoes with small-diameter heels are often not allowed on a gymnasium floor.

READING TOOLKIT

BRAINSTORMING Write the words *pressure* and *force* on the board. Ask students to volunteer words and phrases that they associate with each or both of these terms. Write their associations on the board under the relevant term. Guide the discussion toward having students recognize the relationship between these words in the scientific sense.

BELOW LEVEL

Have students create a folded study aid for keeping the gas laws and their equations straight. They should first glue a sheet of notebook paper to one side of a sheet of colored card stock. They next should fold the outer edges of the card stock inward along their length, with the notebook paper on the inside of the folds. The folded study aid should now resemble two window shutters that open in the center. Using a ruler, students should divide each shutter into three sections, one above the other. On each shutter "door," students should write the name of one of the gas laws. Then, inside the shutter for a particular gas law, students should state that gas law and give the equation for solving problems with that law.

▼ Teach *continued*

Teaching Tip

Several units of pressure are presented in this book. This was done to familiarize students with all of them, because various chemistry publications use different units. The units mm Hg and torr are gradually being phased out by many scientists in favor of the SI unit, the pascal, and its derivative, the kilopascal.

Teaching Tip

Do not confuse STP (0°C and 1 atm) with the thermodynamic standard state conditions (25°C and 1 atm), which will be used in the chapter "Reaction Energy."

Alternative Assessment

The following chart shows changes in air pressure in relation to altitude above Earth's surface. Have students graph these data. Then, discuss the relationship shown between altitude and atmospheric pressure.

Altitude (km)	Percent of sea level pressure
0	100
5.6	50
16.2	10
31.2	1
48.1	0.1
65.1	0.01
79.2	0.001

Check for Understanding

Answer: 760 mm is the height of a column of mercury under average atmospheric pressure at sea level.

Consider a can filled with air. The atmosphere exerts a pressure on the can. The air inside the can pushes outward and balances the atmosphere's inward-pushing force. If a vacuum pump removes the air from the can, the outward force is removed, and the atmospheric pressure crushes the can.

Units of Pressure

A number of different units are used to measure pressure. Because atmospheric pressure is often measured by a mercury barometer, pressure can be expressed in terms of the height of a mercury column. **Thus, the common unit of pressure is millimeters of mercury, symbolized mm Hg.** A pressure of 1 mm Hg is also called 1 torr to honor Torricelli for his invention of the barometer. The average atmospheric pressure at sea level at 0°C is 760 mm Hg. Pressures are often measured in units of atmospheres. **One atmosphere of pressure (atm) is defined as being exactly equivalent to 760 mm Hg.** In SI, pressure is expressed in derived units called pascals. The unit is named for Blaise Pascal, a French mathematician and philosopher who studied pressure during the seventeenth century. **One pascal (Pa) is defined as the pressure exerted by a force of one newton (1 N) acting on an area of one square meter.** In many cases, it is more convenient to express pressure in kilopascals (kPa). The standard atmosphere (1 atm) is equal to $1.013\ 25 \times 10^5$ Pa, or 101.325 kPa. Several pressure units and common uses for them are summarized in **Figure 1.5.**

✔ CHECK FOR UNDERSTANDING
Apply Why is 760 mm of mercury equal to 1 atmosphere?

Standard Temperature and Pressure

To compare gas volumes, one must know the temperature and pressure at which they are measured. *For purposes of comparison, scientists have agreed on standard conditions of 1 atm pressure and 0°C.* These conditions are called standard temperature and pressure, abbreviated STP.

FIGURE 1.5

UNITS OF PRESSURE

Unit	Symbol	Definition/relationship	Application
pascal	Pa	SI pressure unit $1\ \text{Pa} = \frac{1\ \text{N}}{\text{m}^2}$	scientific (kPa)
millimeter of mercury	mm Hg	pressure that supports a 1 mm mercury column in a barometer	blood pressure monitors
torr	torr	1 torr = 1 mm Hg	vacuum pumps
atmosphere	atm	average atmospheric pressure at sea level and 0°C 1 atm = 760 mm Hg = 760 torr $= 1.013\ 25 \times 10^5$ Pa = 101.325 kPa	atmospheric pressure
pounds per square inch	psi	$1\ \text{psi} = 6.892\ 86 \times 10^3$ Pa 1 atm = 14.700 psi	tire gauges

Differentiated Instruction

PRE-AP

Have students go to the National Oceanic and Atmospheric Administration's (NOAA) national buoy system website. Students should select five buoys in an area.

Have students construct a table giving the data from each of their selected buoys. Ask students to take the atmospheric pressure readings and convert them to kilopascals, using the four-step method of problem-solving illustrated in the sample problems.

ENGLISH LEARNERS

Explain to students that there are different units of measurement for pressure because different people, at different times and in different countries, devised their own units for their own purposes. Although many have adopted the SI units of pascals and kilopascals, the other units are still in use. Have students do research on the Internet to determine which of these or other units is most commonly used in their country of origin.

Converting Between Units of Pressure

Sample Problem A **The average atmospheric pressure in Denver, Colorado, is 0.830 atm. Express this pressure in (a) millimeters of mercury (mm Hg) and (b) kilopascals (kPa).**

1 ANALYZE

Given: P of atmosphere = 0.830 atm
760 mm Hg = 1 atm (definition); 101.325 kPa = 1 atm (definition)

Unknown: **a.** P of atmosphere in mm Hg **b.** P of atmosphere in kPa

2 PLAN

a. atm → mm Hg; $1\ \text{atm} \times \frac{760\ \text{mm Hg}}{1\ \text{atm}} = \text{mm Hg}$

b. atm → kPa; $1\ \text{atm} \times \frac{101.325\ \text{kPa}}{1\ \text{atm}} = \text{kPa}$

3 SOLVE

a. $P = 0.830\ \text{atm} \times \frac{760\ \text{mm Hg}}{1\ \text{atm}} = 631\ \text{mm Hg}$

b. $P = 0.830\ \text{atm} \times \frac{101.325\ \text{kPa}}{1\ \text{atm}} = 84.1\ \text{kPa}$

4 CHECK YOUR WORK

Units have canceled to give the desired units, and answers are expressed to the correct number of significant figures. The known pressure and the calculated pressures are about 80% of the atmospheric pressure, in the new units.

Practice Answers in Appendix E

1. Convert a pressure of 1.75 atm to kPa and to mm Hg.
2. The critical pressure of carbon dioxide is 72.7 atm. What is this value in units of pascals?

MAIN IDEA

The total pressure of a gas mixture is the sum of the pressures of the gases in it.

John Dalton, the English chemist who proposed the atomic theory, also studied gas mixtures. He found that the pressure exerted by each gas in an unreactive mixture is independent of that exerted by other gases present. The pressure of each gas in a mixture is called the **partial pressure** of that gas. **Dalton's law of partial pressures** states that the total pressure of a gas mixture is the sum of the partial pressures of the component gases. The law is true regardless of the gases present in the mixture. Dalton's law may be expressed as follows.

Dalton's law $P_T = P_1 + P_2 + P_3 + \ldots$

In this equation, P_T is the total pressure of the mixture. P_1, P_2, P_3, and so on are the partial pressures of component gases 1, 2, 3, and so on.

Problem Solving

DECONSTRUCTING PROBLEMS

Ask students why each conversion in Sample Problem A has two steps. Answers will vary. Students should understand that it is necessary to first determine what the conversion factor(s) will be for each change. This is what is done in step 2, **Plan**, parts a and b. In step 3, **Solve**, parts a and b, these conversion factors are used to convert the given amount to the desired units.

Classroom Practice

A-1 A weather report gives a current atmospheric pressure reading of 745.8 mm Hg. Express this reading in the following units:

a. atmospheres
b. torrs
c. kilopascals

Answers
a. 0.9813 atm
b. 745.8 torr
c. 99.43 kPa

Answers

Practice A
1. 177 kPa, 1330 mm Hg
2. 7.37×10^6 Pa

ChemisTrivia

Air is rich in oxygen and poor in carbon dioxide. By contrast, cellular fluids are relatively rich in carbon dioxide and poor in oxygen. Therefore, the partial pressures of oxygen and carbon dioxide vary in the lungs; in veins, arteries, and capillaries; and in cells.

READING TOOLKIT

PAIRED READING Have pairs of students read the section on Dalton's Law of Partial Pressures silently and make notes on the portions of text they do not understand. Have them discuss the passages that they found difficult. If one student is unable to clarify the passage for his or her partner, have the pair pose a question for the class or teacher.

▼ Teach *continued*

Application

Dalton's law of partial pressures has important applications for people who work at high altitudes, such as mountain climbers and pilots. For example, at an altitude of about 10 000 m (higher than Mount Everest), air pressure is about one-third of an atmosphere. The partial pressure of oxygen at this altitude is 0.3 atm × 0.21 (percentage of O_2 in air) × 760 mm Hg, or less than 50 mm Hg. By comparison, humans require a partial pressure of oxygen in their alveolar blood of about 100 mm Hg. Thus, respiration cannot occur normally at 10 000 m, and an outside source of oxygen is needed in order for people to survive at that elevation.

Demo Problem

1. Calculate the partial pressure in millimeters of mercury exerted by the four main gases in air at 760 mm Hg: nitrogen, oxygen, argon, and carbon dioxide. Their abundance by volume is 78.08%, 20.95%, 0.934%, and 0.035%, respectively.

Answers

N_2: 593.4 mm Hg

O_2: 159.2 mm Hg

Ar: 7.10 mm Hg

CO_2: 0.27 mm Hg

Critical Thinking

Answer: The water will be pushed down into the bowl.

FIGURE 1.6

Collecting Gas by Displacement
Hydrogen can be collected by water displacement by reacting zinc with sulfuric acid. The hydrogen gas produced displaces the water in the gas-collecting bottle to the right. It now also contains some water vapor.

CRITICAL THINKING

Infer As the gas accumulates in the collecting bottle, what will happen to the water it displaces?

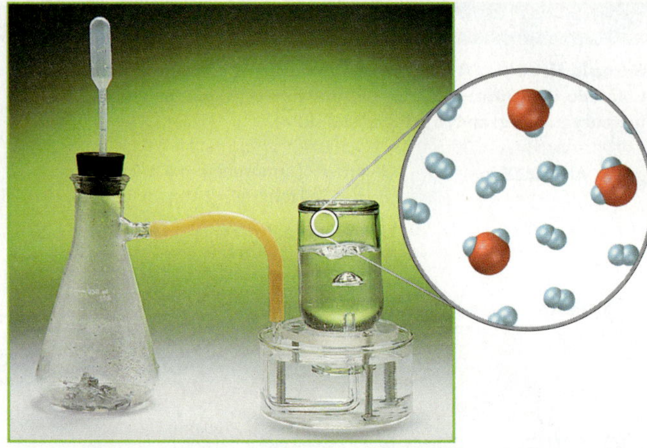

Dalton's Law and the Kinetic-Molecular Theory

You can understand Dalton's law in terms of the kinetic-molecular theory. Each of the rapidly moving particles of gases in a mixture has an equal chance to collide with the container walls. Therefore, each gas exerts a pressure independent of that exerted by the other gases present. The total pressure is the result of the total number of collisions per unit of wall area in a given time.

Vapor Pressure of Water

Gases produced in the laboratory are often collected over water, as shown in **Figure 1.6.** The gas produced by the reaction displaces the water, which is more dense, in the collection bottle. You need to apply Dalton's law of partial pressures in calculating the pressures of gases collected in this way. A gas collected by water displacement is not pure but is always mixed with water vapor. That is because water molecules at the liquid surface evaporate and mix with the gas molecules. In a closed system, water vapor, like other gases, exerts a pressure known as *vapor pressure*.

Suppose you wished to determine the total pressure of the gas and water vapor inside a collection bottle. You would raise the bottle until the water levels inside and outside the bottle were the same. At that point, the total pressure inside the bottle would be the same as the atmospheric pressure, P_{atm}. According to Dalton's law of partial pressures, the following is true:

$$P_{atm} = P_{gas} + P_{H_2O}$$

To calculate the partial pressure of the dry gas collected, you would read the atmospheric pressure, P_{atm}, from a barometer in the laboratory. Subtract the vapor pressure of the water at the given temperature from the total pressure. The vapor pressure of water varies with temperature. You need to look up the value of P_{H_2O} at the temperature of the experiment in a standard reference table (see Appendix B).

Differentiated Instruction

PRE-AP

Have students write a hypothesis predicting whether the water will stop the reaction in **Figure 1.6** from occurring. As the water gradually dilutes the sulfuric acid, the reaction will diminish and stop. Student hypotheses can be referenced at a later date, when students study solutions.

Calculating Partial Pressure

Sample Problem B **Oxygen gas from the decomposition of potassium chlorate, $KClO_3$, was collected by water displacement. The barometric pressure and the temperature during the experiment were 731.0 torr and 20.0°C, respectively. What was the partial pressure of the oxygen collected?**

1 ANALYZE

Given: $P_T = P_{atm} = 731.0$ torr

$P_{H_2O} = 17.5$ torr (vapor pressure of H_2O at 20.0°C; **Table B-8** in App. B)

$P_{atm} = P_{O_2} + P_{H_2O}$

Unknown: P_{O_2} in torr

2 PLAN

The partial pressure of the collected oxygen is found by subtracting the partial pressure of water vapor from the atmospheric pressure, according to Dalton's law of partial pressures.

$$P_{O_2} = P_{atm} - P_{H_2O}$$

3 SOLVE

Substituting values for P_{atm} and P_{H_2O} gives P_{O_2}.

$$P_{O_2} = 731.0 \text{ torr} - 17.5 \text{ torr} = 713.5 \text{ torr}$$

4 CHECK YOUR WORK

As expected, the oxygen partial pressure is less than atmospheric pressure. It is reasonably close to an estimated value of 713, calculated as 730 − 17.

Practice Answers in Appendix E

1. Some hydrogen gas is collected over water at 20.0°C. The levels of water inside and outside the gas-collection bottle are the same. The partial pressure of hydrogen is 742.5 torr. What is the barometric pressure at the time the gas is collected?

SECTION 1 FORMATIVE ASSESSMENT

Reviewing Main Ideas

1. Define *pressure.*
2. What units are used to express pressure measurements?
3. What are standard conditions for gas measurements?
4. Convert the following pressures to pressures in standard atmospheres:
   a. 151.98 kPa
   b. 456 torr
5. A sample of nitrogen gas is collected over water at a temperature of 23.0°C. What is the pressure of the nitrogen gas if atmospheric pressure is 785 mm Hg?
6. Why can you calculate the total pressure of a mixture of gases by adding together the partial pressures of the component gases?

Critical Thinking

7. **EVALUATING METHODS** Clean rooms used for sterile biological research are sealed and operate at slightly above atmospheric pressure. Explain why.
8. **INFERRING RELATIONSHIPS** Explain why helium-filled balloons deflate over time faster than air-filled balloons do.

Answers to Section Assessment

1. Pressure is force per unit area.
2. Pressure is measured in Pa, kPa, mm Hg, atm, torr, or psi.
3. 0°C and 1 atm pressure
4. **a.** 1.4999 atm
   b. 0.600 atm
5. 764 mm Hg
6. The pressure that each gas exerts is independent of the pressures exerted by the other gases.
7. Although the rooms are sealed, there will still be small leaks. Air effusing outward hinders microbes from entering clean rooms.
8. The average velocity of helium molecules is higher than that of the molecules of any gas found in air, so helium molecules escape through the pores in the balloon more quickly.

Classroom Practice

B-1 A student has stored 100.0 mL of neon gas over water on a day when the temperature is 27.0°C. If the barometer in the room reads 743.3 mm Hg, what is the pressure of the neon gas in its container?

Answer: 716.6 mm Hg

Answers

Practice B

1. 760.0 torr

Assess and Reteach

Assess Use the Formative Assessment on this page to evaluate student mastery of the section.

Reteach For students who need additional instruction, download the Section Study Guide.

Response to Intervention To reassess students' mastery, use the Section Quiz, available to print or to take directly online at **HMDScience.com**.

WHY IT MATTERS

Teaching Tip

Tell students that they will learn about Henry's Law in greater detail when they study solutions.

ChemisTrivia

Divers suffering from decompression sickness are treated on land by repressurization in a hyperbaric chamber. Divers are also discouraged from air travel within 24 hours after diving, because airline cabins are typically not fully pressurized to 1 atm (sea level). This reduced air pressure during a flight can lead to symptoms associated with decompression sickness.

Answers

1. The total pressure of a gas mixture is equal to the sum of the partial pressures of the gases in the mixture. To reduce the partial pressure of oxygen, one must increase the pressure of another gas. The helium concentration is increased because helium does not have the same effects on divers as nitrogen does.
2. Carbon monoxide is toxic. Although slightly elevated levels of CO may not be dangerous at sea level, the partial pressure of CO in the diver's lungs will increase by 100% of the initial CO pressure for every 33 ft a diver descends. As a result, the concentration of CO in the blood will increase. Thus, the toxicity threshold for CO can be reached more quickly during a dive than under normal conditions.

WHY IT MATTERS S.T.E.M.

The Gas Laws and Scuba Diving

An understanding of Dalton's law and Henry's law is essential to safe scuba diving. Dalton's law states that the total pressure of a gas mixture is equal to the sum of the partial pressures of the component gases. Henry's law predicts that the solubility of a gas in a liquid is a direct function of the partial pressure of that gas.

For every 33 ft of sea water that a diver descends, he or she feels one additional atmosphere of pressure because of the increasing weight of water overhead. Most divers use compressed air tanks to breathe underwater. The air in these tanks, which contains approximately 78% nitrogen and 21% oxygen, is the same as the air that we breathe. Once the compressed air enters the diver's lungs, it is subjected to the pressure caused by the water. The increase in the air pressure leads to an increase in the partial pressures of the nitrogen and oxygen in air, as predicted by Dalton's law. Henry's law predicts that this increase in partial pressures will increase the solubility of nitrogen and oxygen in the diver's bloodstream.

The increase in the partial pressure of oxygen is not problematic under typical diving conditions, because a diver's body can metabolize the extra oxygen that is present in the bloodstream. The body does not metabolize nitrogen, however, so it can accumulate in a diver's body during a dive. The extra nitrogen can affect the nerve cells of the diver, causing *nitrogen narcosis.* Divers suffering from nitrogen narcosis become disoriented and experience symptoms similar to intoxication. This impairment of a diver's judgment can be very dangerous. To decrease the probability of contracting nitrogen narcosis, divers can use gas mixtures that contain less nitrogen than compressed air does.

Dissolved nitrogen can also be harmful if a diver ascends too quickly. As Henry's law predicts, nitrogen becomes less soluble in the blood as the pressure decreases. This decrease in solubility causes nitrogen to leave the diver's tissues and blood. Normally, the excess nitrogen is discharged through the lungs.

In order to dive safely, scuba divers must be aware of some of the basic gas laws.

However, if the diver comes up too rapidly, the nitrogen will form bubbles in the tissues and veins. This condition is known as *decompression sickness*, or "the bends." If the bubbles block blood flow, a wide range of effects, including severe joint pain, may occur. For this reason, divers are very careful to ascend slowly after diving.

At extreme depths, even the increased pressure of oxygen becomes a problem for scuba divers. Although oxygen is necessary for life, extended exposure to large concentrations of oxygen can result in *oxygen toxicity.* This condition can cause damage to the lungs and nervous system. Divers can avoid oxygen toxicity by breathing gas mixtures that contain more helium and less oxygen than compressed air does.

Questions

1. Why is the concentration of helium increased in some gas mixtures that divers breathe in order to reduce the partial pressure of oxygen?
2. Although carbon monoxide, CO, is normally present in trace quantities in air, compressed air scuba tanks that are filled improperly can contain elevated levels of CO. Why is this particularly dangerous for divers?

The Gas Laws

SECTION 2

Main Ideas

- Gas volume and pressure are indirectly proportional.
- Gas volume and temperature are directly related.
- Gas pressure and temperature are directly related.
- Gas pressure, temperature, and volume are interrelated.

Key Terms

Boyle's law
absolute zero
Charles's law
Gay-Lussac's law
combined gas law

Scientists have been studying physical properties of gases for hundreds of years. In 1662, Robert Boyle discovered that gas pressure and volume are related mathematically. The observations of Boyle and others led to the development of the gas laws. The gas laws are simple mathematical relationships among the volume, temperature, pressure, and amount of a gas.

MAIN IDEA

Gas volume and pressure are indirectly proportional.

Robert Boyle discovered that doubling the pressure on a sample of gas at constant temperature reduces its volume by one-half. Reducing the pressure on a gas by one-half allows the volume of the gas to double. As one variable increases, the other decreases. **Figure 2.1** shows that as the volume of gas in the syringe decreases, the pressure of the gas increases.

You can use the kinetic-molecular theory to understand why this pressure-volume relationship holds. The pressure of a gas is caused by moving molecules hitting the container walls. Suppose the volume of a container is decreased, but the same number of gas molecules is present at the same temperature. There will be more molecules per unit volume. The number of collisions with a given unit of wall area per unit time will increase as a result. Therefore, pressure will also increase.

FIGURE 2.1

Volume and Pressure The volume of gas in the syringe shown in **(a)** is reduced when the plunger is pushed down. The gas pressure in **(b)** is increased as the volume is reduced, because the molecules collide more frequently with the walls of the container in the smaller volume.

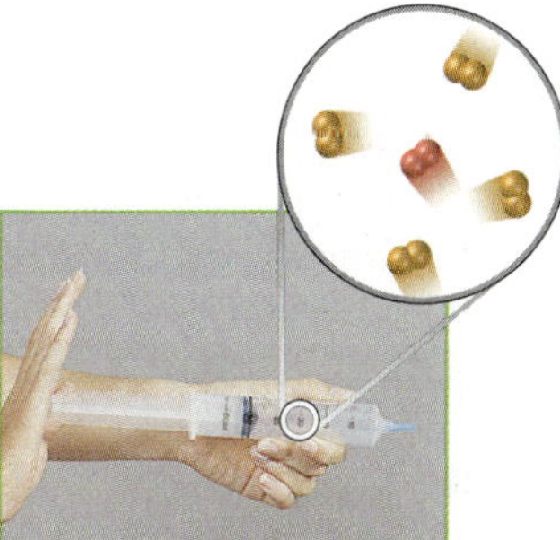

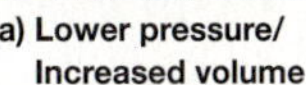

(a) Lower pressure/ Increased volume

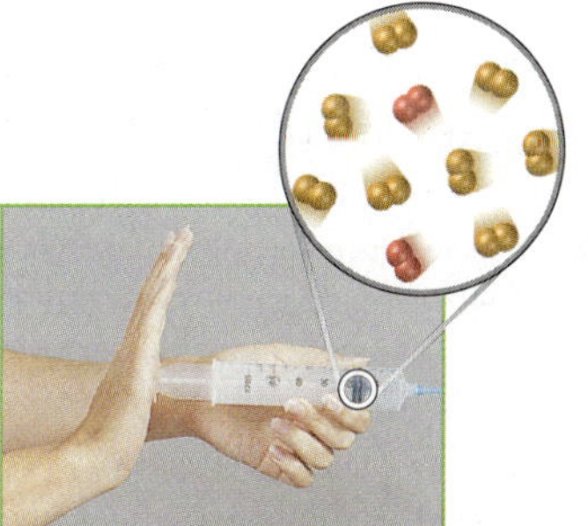

(b) Higher pressure/ Decreased volume

SECTION 2

Plan and Prepare ▼

Objectives

Upon completion of this section, students should be able to do the following:

- Use the kinetic-molecular theory to explain the relationship among gas volume, temperature, and pressure.
- Use Boyle's law to calculate volume-pressure changes at constant temperature.
- Use Charles's Law to calculate volume-temperature changes at constant pressure.
- Use Gay-Lussac's law to calculate pressure-temperature changes at constant volume.
- Use the combined gas law to calculate volume-temperature-pressure changes.

Classroom Catalyst

Place a marshmallow under a bell jar. Tell students that the marshmallow is mostly air. Use a vacuum pump to reduce the pressure in the bell jar. Students will observe that the marshmallow increases in size as the pressure in the bell jar decreases. Help students infer that the volume and pressure of a gas are related.

Teach ▼

READING TOOLKIT

IDENTIFYING CAUSE AND EFFECT As students read this section, have them identify reading signal words and phrases that indicate a cause-and-effect relationship among temperature, pressure, and volume of gases, such as "causes," "as a result," "if... then," and "depends on." Have student pairs write cause-and-effect statements to summarize the relationships shown in the graphs.

Differentiated Instruction

BELOW LEVEL

Give students paper on which has been printed empty "cartoon" boxes. Have them draw an original cartoon illustrating how the pressure and volume of a gas are related to one another. When their cartoons are completed, post them around the classroom and take the class on a "tour." Have each student explain how his or her cartoon depicts the topic.

ENGLISH LEARNERS

Divide packages of stick-on notes into sets of approximately 10–15 sheets, keeping them stuck together into smaller pads.

Show students a teacher-made example of a flip book. Stick figures are great! Have students create their own flip book, illustrating Boyle's Law.

▼ Teach *continued*

Misconception Alert!

Students often are unclear about whether gas law references to pressure refer to pressure exerted *by* the gas or pressure exerted *on* the gas. Point out that in most cases the two quantities are the same. In **Figure 2.1** on the previous page, for example, the pressure exerted by the syringe on the gas is matched by the pressure exerted by the gas on the syringe.

ChemisTrivia

Robert Boyle was the first person to collect a gas for study and analysis and to determine that a gas is compressible. This discovery led Boyle to conclude that a gas must be composed of separate particles separated by empty space.

Classroom Practice

C-1 The piston of an internal combustion engine compresses 450 mL of gas. The final pressure is 15 times greater than the initial pressure. What is the final volume of the gas, assuming constant temperature? (Treat "15 times" as a pure number, with unlimited significant figures.)

Answer: 30.0 mL

C-2 A helium-filled balloon contains 125 mL of gas at a pressure of 0.974 atm. What volume will the gas occupy at standard pressure?

Answer: 122 mL

Answers

Practice C

1. 1000 mL He

Critical Thinking

Answer: The gas volume is decreasing as the pressure is increasing.

FIGURE 2.2

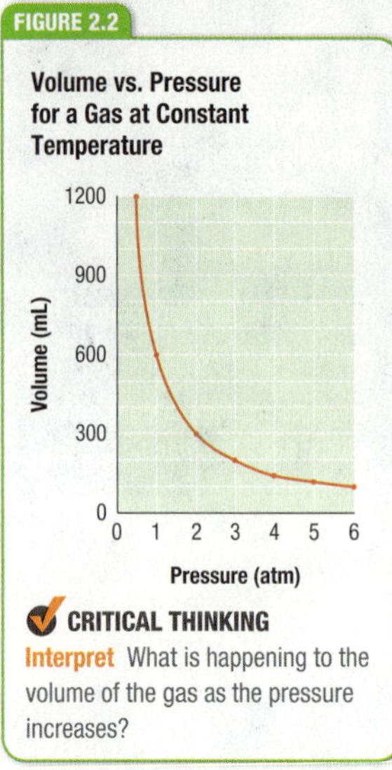

CRITICAL THINKING

Interpret What is happening to the volume of the gas as the pressure increases?

Graphing Boyle's Law

Plotting the values of volume versus pressure for a gas at constant temperature gives a curve like that in **Figure 2.2.** The general volume-pressure relationship that is illustrated is called Boyle's law. **Boyle's law states that the volume of a fixed mass of gas varies inversely with the pressure at constant temperature.**

Mathematically, Boyle's law can be expressed as follows:

$$PV = k$$

P is the pressure, V is the volume, and k is a constant. Since P and V vary inversely, their product remains the same. The inverse relationship between changes of pressure and volume can be expressed as shown below.

Boyle's law $$P_1V_1 = P_2V_2$$

P_1 and V_1 represent initial conditions, and P_2 and V_2 represent a different set of conditions. Given three of the four values P_1, V_1, P_2, and V_2, you can use this equation to calculate the fourth value for a system at constant temperature.

Using Boyle's Law

Sample Problem C **A sample of oxygen gas has a volume of 150.0 mL when its pressure is 0.947 atm. What will the volume of the gas be at a pressure of 0.987 atm if the temperature remains constant?**

1 ANALYZE

Given: V_1 of O_2 = 150.0 mL
P_1 of O_2 = 0.947 atm
P_2 of O_2 = 0.987 atm

Unknown: V_2 of O_2 in mL

2 PLAN

Rearrange the equation for Boyle's law ($P_1V_1 = P_2V_2$) to obtain V_2.

$$V_2 = \frac{P_1V_1}{P_2}$$

3 SOLVE

Substitute values for P_1, V_1, and P_2 to obtain the new volume, V_2.

$$V_2 = \frac{(0.947\ \text{atm})(150.0\ \text{mL } O_2)}{0.987\ \text{atm}} = 144\ \text{mL } O_2$$

4 CHECK YOUR WORK

When the pressure is increased slightly at constant temperature, the volume decreases slightly, as expected. Units cancel to give milliliters, a volume unit.

Practice Answers in Appendix E

1. A balloon filled with helium gas has a volume of 500 mL at a pressure of 1 atm. The balloon is released and reaches an altitude of 6.5 km, where the pressure is 0.5 atm. If the temperature has remained the same, what volume does the gas occupy at this height?

Problem Solving

DECONSTRUCTING PROBLEMS

To obtain unknown and given values, read the problem sentence carefully. To identify unknown(s), look for the question being asked. What will the volume of the gas be? Since that volume is the one being sought, that must be V_2. The volume and pressure with which the problem begins are V_1 and P_1, and the new pressure that is being applied to the gas will be P_2.

MAIN IDEA

Gas volume and temperature are directly related.

Balloonists, such as those in the photo at the beginning of this chapter, are making use of a physical property of gases: if pressure is constant, gases expand when heated. When the temperature increases, the volume of a fixed number of gas molecules must increase if the pressure is to stay constant. At the higher temperature, the gas molecules move faster. They collide with the walls of the container more frequently and with more force. The volume of a flexible container must then increase in order for the pressure to remain the same.

The quantitative relationship between volume and temperature was discovered by the French scientist Jacques Charles in 1787. Charles's experiments showed that all gases expand to the same extent when heated through the same temperature interval. Charles found that the volume changes by 1/273 of the original volume for each Celsius degree, at constant pressure and an initial temperature of 0°C. For example, raising the temperature to 1°C causes the gas volume to increase by 1/273 of the volume it had at 0°C. If the temperature is increased by 273°C, the volume increases by 273/273 of the original; that is, the volume doubles. The same regularity of volume change occurs if a gas is cooled at constant pressure, as the balloons in **Figure 2.3** show.

The Kelvin temperature scale is a scale that starts at a temperature corresponding to −273.15°C. That temperature is the lowest one possible. The temperature −273.15°C is referred to as **absolute zero** and is given a value of zero in the Kelvin scale. This fact gives the following relationship between the two temperature scales.

$$K = 273.15 + °C$$

For calculations in this book, 273.15 is rounded off to 273.

FIGURE 2.3

The Relationship between Temperature and Volume

(a) Air-filled balloons are supercooled with liquid nitrogen.

(b) The balloons collapse.

(c) The balloons expand when the air inside warms up.

CRITICAL THINKING

Explain Use the kinetic-molecular theory to explain what happens to the balloons.

Differentiated Instruction

INCLUSION

Have tactile learners blow up a balloon to the size of a softball. Place the balloon in a freezer for an hour. After an hour, take out the balloon and have the students record any changes in the size of the balloon. Have the students indicate what factor caused the change in the balloon. Additionally, have the students indicate what might cause the balloon to "regain" its original size.

Misconception Alert!

Students may wonder about the fact that temperature measurement has a lowest possible value (0 K), but no maximum value. Discuss with them the relationship between temperature and particle motion.

Critical Thinking

Answer: As the molecules of air cool, they lose energy and their speed slows, causing fewer collisions. Fewer collisions means less pressure and a reduction in volume.

▼ Teach *continued*

Teaching Tip

The value of the constant k in Charles's law differs from one situation to another. Its value depends on the amount of gas present and the temperature of the gas. The fact that it is called a constant does not mean that it has the same value in all situations.

Classroom Practice

Assume constant pressure in the following problem:

D-1 A balloon filled with oxygen gas occupies a volume of 5.5 L at 25°C. What volume will the gas occupy at 100.0°C?

Answer: 6.9 L

Answers

Practice D

1. 941 mL
2. 91°C

Misconception Alert!

Students may think that the size of one unit is the same for all temperature scales. The size of a kelvin is exactly the same as the size of a Celsius degree, but the Fahrenheit unit is a different size. One Fahrenheit unit is five-ninths the size of a Celsius unit.

Critical Thinking

Answer: As the temperature increases, the volume of the gas increases.

FIGURE 2.4

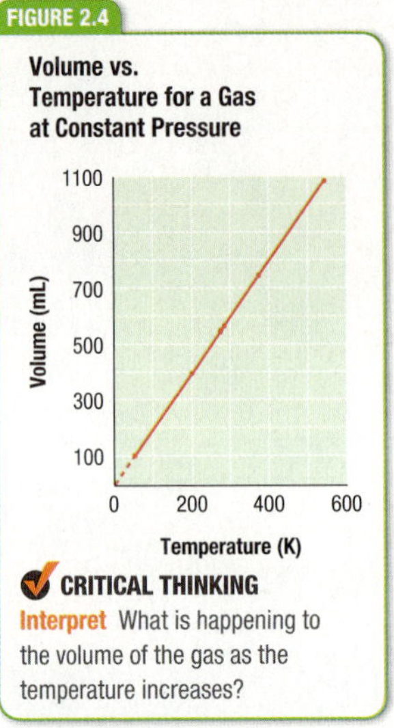

CRITICAL THINKING

Interpret What is happening to the volume of the gas as the temperature increases?

Graphing Charles's Law

The relationship between temperature in Kelvins and gas volume is known as Charles's law. **Charles's law states that the volume of a fixed mass of gas at constant pressure varies directly with the temperature in Kelvins.** Charles's law is plotted in **Figure 2.4** and may be expressed as follows:

$$V = kT \text{ or } \frac{V}{T} = k$$

The value of T is the temperature in Kelvins, and k is a constant. The ratio V/T for any set of volume-temperature values always equals the same k. The form of Charles's law that can be applied directly to most volume-temperature problems involving gases is as follows:

Charles's law $$\frac{V_1}{T_1} = \frac{V_2}{T_2}$$

V_1 and T_1 represent initial conditions and V_2 and T_2 represent a different set of conditions. When three of the four values T_1, V_1, T_2, and V_2 are known, you can use this equation to calculate the fourth value for a system at constant pressure.

Using Charles's Law

Sample Problem D **A sample of neon gas occupies a volume of 752 mL at 25°C. What volume will the gas occupy at 50°C if the pressure remains constant?**

1 ANALYZE

Given: V_1 of Ne = 752 mL

T_1 of Ne = 25°C + 273 = 298 K; T_2 of Ne = 50°C + 273 = 323 K

Unknown: V_2 of Ne in mL

2 PLAN

Because the gas remains at constant pressure, an increase in temperature will cause an increase in volume. To obtain V_2, rearrange the equation for Charles's law.

3 SOLVE

Substitute values for V_1, T_1, and T_2 to obtain the new volume, V_2.

$$V_2 = \frac{(752 \text{ mL Ne})(323 \text{ K})}{298 \text{ K}} = 815 \text{ mL Ne}$$

4 CHECK YOUR WORK

As expected, the volume of the gas increases as the temperature increases. Units cancel to yield milliliters, as desired. The answer contains the appropriate number of significant figures.

Practice Answers in Appendix E

1. A sample of neon gas has a volume of 752 mL at 25.0°C. What will be the volume at 100.0°C if pressure is constant?
2. A sample of nitrogen gas is contained in a piston with a freely moving cylinder. At 0.0°C, the volume of the gas is 375 mL. To what temperature must the gas be heated to occupy a volume of 500.0 mL?

Problem Solving

REALITY CHECK

In sample problem D and other gas law problems, students may forget initially to change degrees Celsius to Kelvins. Remind students to look carefully at their temperature values. If the values are low, up to 100 or so, urge them to recheck to make sure they have made the correct conversion.

MAIN IDEA

Gas pressure and temperature are directly related.

You have just learned about the quantitative relationship between volume and temperature at constant pressure. What would you predict about the relationship between pressure and temperature at constant volume? You have seen that pressure is the result of collisions of molecules with container walls. The energy and frequency of collisions depend on the average kinetic energy of molecules. For a fixed quantity of gas at constant volume, the pressure should be directly proportional to the temperature in Kelvins, which depends directly on average kinetic energy.

That prediction turns out to be correct. For every kelvin of temperature change, the pressure of a confined gas changes by 1/273 of the pressure at 0°C. Joseph Gay-Lussac is given credit for recognizing this in 1802. The data plotted in Figure 2.5 illustrate **Gay-Lussac's law:** The pressure of a fixed mass of gas at constant volume varies directly with the temperature in Kelvins. Mathematically, Gay-Lussac's law is expressed as follows.

$$P = kT \text{ or } \frac{P}{T} = k$$

The value of T is the temperature in kelvins, and k is a constant that depends on the quantity of gas and the volume. For a given mass of gas at constant volume, the ratio P/T is the same for any set of pressure-temperature values. Unknown values can be found using the following form.

Gay-Lussac's law $$\frac{P_1}{T_1} = \frac{P_2}{T_2}$$

P_1 and T_1 represent initial conditions, and P_2 and T_2 represent a different set of conditions. When values are known for three of the four quantities, the fourth value can be calculated for a system at constant volume.

FIGURE 2.5

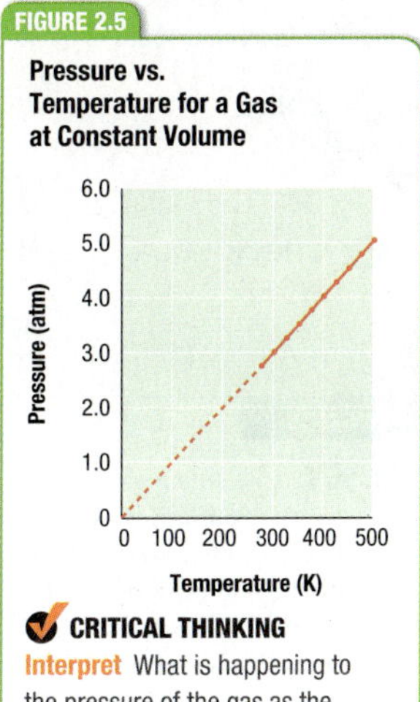

CRITICAL THINKING

Interpret What is happening to the pressure of the gas as the temperature increases?

Using Gay-Lussac's Law

Sample Problem E **The gas in a container is at a pressure of 3.00 atm at 25°C. Directions on the container warn the user not to keep it in a place where the temperature exceeds 52°C. What would be the gas pressure in the container at 52°C?**

1 ANALYZE

Given: P_1 of gas = 3.00 atm

T_1 of gas = 25°C + 273 = 298 K; T_2 of gas = 52°C + 273 = 325 K

Unknown: P_2 of gas in atm

2 PLAN

Because the gaseous contents remain at the constant volume of the container, an increase in temperature will cause an increase in pressure. Rearrange Gay-Lussac's law to obtain P_2.

$$P_2 = \frac{P_1 T_2}{T_1}$$

Continued

Teaching Tip

Remind students that temperature calculations with the gas laws must always be done with absolute temperatures (in K); the temperature can then be converted to other desired units, such as degrees Celsius (°C).

Classroom Discussion

Ask students what happens to the pressure in a tire as an automobile is driven 100 km on a hot day (assume constant volume). Discuss the heating that takes place in the tire as a result of friction between the tire and the highway, and the increase in pressure that results because of more rapidly moving air molecules.

Classroom Practice

E-1 A gas cylinder at room temperature (20.0°C) is thrown into an incinerator where the temperature reaches 500.0°C. If the gas inside the container was initially at a pressure of 1.0 atm, what pressure did it reach inside the incinerator? Assume the gas was at constant volume and the container did not explode.

Answer: 2.6 atm

Critical Thinking

Answer: As the temperature increases, the pressure of the gas increases.

Differentiated Instruction

BELOW LEVEL

Give students a 3" × 5" note card and a ruler. Have them construct a table with the names of the gas laws in the first column and the equation for each gas law in the second column. Allow them to use this study guide both in class and on assessments.

PRE-AP

Ask students to silently think about the following question: "Why do fish in shallow ponds sometimes asphyxiate during summer heat waves?" Then, ask students to pick a partner and share their ideas. Have each pair of partners write the answers to the following: (1) What did the two of you decide was the reason the fish died? (2) Show the relationship between the cause of the death of the fish and Gay-Lussac's Law.

▼ Teach continued

Answers

Practice E

1. 1.30 atm
2. 1.29 atm
3. 219°C

Teaching Tip

The combined gas law can appear overwhelming to students who have difficulty with math skills. Verify that students possess the algebraic skills necessary to solve for any one of the six variables expressed in the equation. Write the combined gas law on the board. Then have students solve for each variable in terms of the other variables.

Check for Understanding

Answer: The combined gas law gives you the mathematical advantage of being able to solve for any of the variables, using only one equation.

Using Gay-Lussac's Law (continued)

3 SOLVE Substitute values for P_1, T_1, and T_2 to obtain the new volume, P_2.

$$P_2 = \frac{(3.00\ \text{atm})(325\ \cancel{\text{K}})}{298\ \cancel{\text{K}}} = 3.27\ \text{atm}$$

4 CHECK YOUR WORK As expected, a temperature increase at constant volume causes the pressure of the contents in the container to increase. Units cancel correctly. The answer contains the proper number of significant figures. It is close to an estimated value of 3.25, calculated as $(3 \times 325)/300$.

Practice

1. At 120.0°C, the pressure of a sample of nitrogen is 1.07 atm. What will the pressure be at 205°C, assuming constant volume?
2. At 122°C the pressure of a sample of nitrogen gas is 1.07 atm. What will the pressure be at 205°C, assuming constant volume?
3. A sample of helium gas has a pressure of 1.20 atm at 22°C. At what Celsius temperature will the helium reach a pressure of 2.00 atm, assuming constant volume?

MAIN IDEA

Gas pressure, temperature, and volume are interrelated.

A gas sample often undergoes changes in temperature, pressure, and volume all at the same time. When this happens, three variables must be dealt with at once. Boyle's law, Charles's law, and Gay-Lussac's law can be combined into a single expression that is useful in such situations. **The combined gas law expresses the relationship between pressure, volume, and temperature of a fixed amount of gas.** The combined gas law can be expressed as follows:

$$\frac{PV}{T} = k$$

In the equation, k is constant and depends on the amount of gas. The combined gas law can also be written as follows:

Combined gas law $$\frac{P_1V_1}{T_1} = \frac{P_2V_2}{T_2}$$

The subscripts in the equation above indicate two different sets of conditions, and T represents the temperature in Kelvins.

From this expression, any value can be calculated if the other five are known. Note that each of the gas laws can be obtained from the combined gas law when the proper variable is constant. For example, Boyle's law is obtained when the temperature is constant. Because $T_1 = T_2$, T_1 and T_2 will cancel out on both sides of the combined gas law equation, giving Boyle's law.

$$P_1V_1 = P_2V_2$$

CHECK FOR UNDERSTANDING

Assess What advantage does the combined gas law have over the three individual gas laws?

Differentiated Instruction

BELOW LEVEL

Have students create a folded study aid for keeping the gas laws and their equations straight. Students should first glue a sheet of notebook paper to a sheet of colored card stock. Once the glue has dried, fold the outer edges of the card stock inward along the long sides, with the notebook paper on the inside. The folded study aid should now resemble two window shutters that open in the center. Using a ruler, students should divide each shutter into three sections, one above the other. Now, the folded study aid should look like six smaller window shutters that open in the center. On each shutter "door," students should write the name of one of the gas laws. Then, opening the shutter for a particular gas law, students should state that gas law and give the equation for solving problems with that law. Writing the laws and their equations again will help students retain that information. Students can then use the folded study aid to quiz themselves or to help them prepare for assessments.

Using the Combined Gas Law

Sample Problem F **A helium-filled balloon has a volume of 50.0 L at 25°C and 1.08 atm. What volume will it have at 0.855 atm and 10.0°C?**

1 ANALYZE

Given: V_1 of He = 50.0 L

T_1 of He = 25°C + 273 = 298 K; T_2 of He = 10°C + 273 = 283 K

P_1 of He = 1.08 atm; P_2 of He = 0.855 atm

Unknown: V_2 of He

2 PLAN

Because the gas remains at constant pressure, an increase in temperature will cause an increase in volume. To obtain V_2, rearrange the equation for Charles's law.

$$\frac{P_1V_1}{T_1} = \frac{P_2V_2}{T_2} \rightarrow V_2 = \frac{P_1V_1T_2}{P_2T_1}$$

3 SOLVE

Substitute the known values to obtain the new volume, V_2.

$$V_2 = \frac{(1.08\ \text{atm})(50.0\ \text{L He})(283\ \text{K})}{(0.855\ \text{atm})(298\ \text{K})} = 60.0\ \text{L He}$$

4 CHECK YOUR WORK

Here the pressure decreases much more than the temperature decreases. As expected, the net result of the two changes gives an increase in the volume, from 50.0 L to 60.0 L. Units cancel appropriately. The answer is correctly expressed to three significant figures. It is also reasonably close to an estimated value of 50, calculated as (50 × 300)/300.

Practice Answers in Appendix E

1. The volume of a gas is 27.5 mL at 22.0°C and 0.974 atm. What will the volume be at 15.0°C and 0.993 atm?
2. A 700.0 mL gas sample at STP is compressed to a volume of 200.0 mL, and the temperature is increased to 30.0°C. What is the new pressure of the gas in Pa?

SECTION 2 FORMATIVE ASSESSMENT

Reviewing Main Ideas

1. Relate the effect of temperature and pressure on a gas to the model of a gas given by the kinetic-molecular theory.
2. A sample of helium gas has a volume of 200.0 mL at 0.960 atm. What pressure, in atmospheres, is needed to reduce the volume at constant temperature to 50.0 mL?
3. A sample of nitrogen gas occupies 1.55 L at 27.0°C and 1.00 atm. What will the volume be at −100.0°C and the same pressure?
4. A gas occupies 2.0 m^3 at 100.0 K and exerts a pressure of 100.0 kPa. What volume will the gas occupy if the temperature is increased to 400.0 K and the pressure is increased to 200.0 kPa?

Critical Thinking

5. **ANALYZING RESULTS** A student has the following data: V_1 = 822 mL, T_1 = 75°C, and T_2 = −25°C. He calculates V_2 and gets −274 mL. Is this value correct? Explain why or why not.
6. **APPLYING MODELS** Explain Charles's law in terms of the kinetic-molecular theory.

Answers to Section Assessment

1. As the temperature of gas molecules increases, the speeds of the gas molecules increase. A gas can be compressed to a smaller volume, so as the pressure of gas molecules in a container increases, the gas molecules move closer together.
2. 3.84 atm
3. 0.89 L
4. 4.0 m^3
5. No; the volume cannot be negative. The temperatures must be converted into Kelvins for the calculation.
6. Gas particles at higher temperatures will have a higher average kinetic energy. This means that their molecular speeds will be higher. Therefore, the volume of the gas must be larger in order to maintain constant pressure, because each molecule is colliding with the wall more frequently and with greater force.

Classroom Practice

F-1 The volume of a gas at 27.0°C and 0.200 atm is 80.0 mL. What volume will the same gas sample occupy at standard conditions?

Answer: 14.6 mL

F-2 A gas occupying 75 mL at standard conditions is heated to 17°C while the pressure is reduced to 0.97 atm. What is the new volume occupied by the gas?

Answer: 82 mL

Answers

Practice F

1. 26.3 mL
2. 3.94 x 10^5 Pa, or 394 kPa

Assess and Reteach ▼

Assess Use the Formative Assessment on this page to evaluate student mastery of the section.

Reteach For students who need additional instruction, download the Section Study Guide.

Response to Intervention To reassess students' mastery, use the Section Quiz, available to print or to take directly online at **HMDScience.com**.

Teaching Tip

The term *empirical* refers to data or conclusions derived from experimental evidence. For example, an empirical formula is a formula derived from experimental evidence.

ChemisTrivia

The mid to late 1600s were marked by great events. One year before Torricelli's significant discovery, Galileo died in Italy, blind and convicted of heresy by the Inquisition for insisting that Earth revolved around the sun. Isaac Newton was born, and England entered into a terrible civil war. Within twenty years, Robert Boyle published his findings, and London was ravaged by both the plague and what became known as "the great London fire."

Chemistry EXPLORERS

Chemistry's First Law

The notion that "nature abhors a vacuum"—meaning that there is no such thing as "empty space"—was proposed by the ancient Greek philosopher Aristotle, whose word was unchallenged for nearly 2000 years. Then, in the mid 1600s, a new breed of thinkers known as *natural philosophers*—what we now know as "scientists"—began testing the long-held assumption that all space must contain matter. These investigations were some of the earliest experiments with gases, and they led to the discovery of the first empirical principle of chemistry, Boyle's law.

Overturning an Ancient Assumption

The first scientist to demonstrate the existence of a vacuum was Evangelista Torricelli. In 1643, he showed that when a glass tube that was 3 ft. long and about 1 in. in diameter was sealed at one end, filled with mercury, and inverted in a container full of mercury, the mercury in the tube fell to a height of about 30 in. above the level of mercury in the container. Some thinkers remained skeptical, but it was generally accepted that the space between the mercury and the sealed end of the tube was indeed a vacuum.

Torricelli then turned his attention to how the mercury in the glass tube of his apparatus was supported. The fact that liquids exert a pressure on objects immersed in them inspired him to hypothesize that a "sea of air" surrounded Earth. He further hypothesized that the air exerted pressure on the mercury in the container and thus supported the mercury in the column.

Support for the New Theory

Although the idea of an atmosphere that has weight and exerts a pressure on the objects within it seems obvious today, it was a radical theory at the time. To test the effects of the atmosphere, Robert Boyle, one of the period's great scientists, had his talented assistant, Robert Hooke, create a piece of equipment that would revolutionize the study of air. The apparatus was an improved version of a pump designed by the German experimenter Otto von Guericke; the pump had a large receptacle in which a partial vacuum could be created.

Boyle placed Torricelli's setup, known today as a barometer, in the receptacle of the pump and observed the mercury column as he reduced the pressure around it. The height of the mercury decreased as the pressure surrounding the mercury in the container dropped, strongly supporting Torricelli's atmospheric theory.

Using Hooke's pump, Boyle performed additional studies that verified the idea that air exerted pressure and had weight. Boyle's experiments also led to the important conclusion that air was elastic: that is, it could expand and contract. Boyle discovered the fundamental law that bears his name during an investigation into air's elasticity.

An Ingenious Experiment

In response to a criticism of his findings, Boyle performed an experiment to show that air could be compressed to a pressure greater than that of the atmosphere. First, he prepared a glass J-tube with the short end sealed off and the long end left open. Then, he poured mercury into the tube, making sure that the levels in the two ends were the same. He then let air travel freely between the ends to ensure that each column was at atmospheric pressure.

Then, Boyle poured more mercury into the long end of the tube until it was about 30 in. above the level of mercury in the short end. He observed that the volume of the trapped air was halved. He continued to add mercury until the total pressure on the trapped air was about 4 times that of the atmosphere. Noting that the air had been compressed to a volume about one-fourth of what it originally was, Boyle discovered the inverse relationship between air's pressure and volume.

A Long-Standing Contribution

Boyle went on to show that the relationship between air pressure and volume, $P \propto 1/V$ (at constant temperature), held not only when the gas was compressed but also when it was allowed to expand. Future investigators would show that the law is a principle that applies to gases in general. Along with the findings of other researchers, such as Jacques Charles, Joseph Gay-Lussac, and Amadeo Avogadro, Boyle's discovery led chemists to the famous ideal gas law, $PV = nRT$, which serves as a starting point in the study of chemistry today.

Questions

1. Why was it necessary for Boyle to seal one end of his J-tube?
2. What would have happened if Boyle had allowed the temperature of the trapped air sample to change as he added mercury to the tube?

We can measure the difference between the atmospheric pressure on a mountaintop and the atmospheric pressure at sea level thanks to the work of Torricelli and Boyle.

Application

Boyle's law can be used to explain how a plunger opens a clogged drain. As the plunger is pushed down, the volume of air in the plunger decreases, and the pressure increases. Increased pressure is transferred throughout any water in the drain, and this pressure is applied to the clog, dislodging it.

Teaching Tip

The symbol $\propto$ means "proportional to."

Classroom Discussion

Have students compare Boyle's work with tubes and mercury to their drinking a beverage through a straw.

Answers

1. If both ends were open, no air would be trapped. In other words, the amount of gas would not be kept constant. Gas would escape, so its pressure would not change.
2. The temperature change would also have contributed to the volume change, so Boyle would not have been able to interpret the relationship between volume and pressure.

SECTION 3

▼ Plan and Prepare

Objectives

Upon completion of this section, students should be able to do the following:

- State the law of combining volumes.
- State Avogadro's law and explain its significance.
- Define standard volume of a gas and use it to calculate masses and volumes.
- State the ideal gas law.
- Using the ideal gas law, calculate pressure, volume, temperature, or amount of gas when the other three quantities are known.

Classroom Catalyst

Have students write balanced chemical equations for the two reactions described on this page. Ask them to compare the balanced equation with the expressions on the page. They should notice that the balancing coefficients are the same as the volume in liters of the gases in each reaction.

▼ Teach

ChemisTrivia

When Gay-Lussac made his discovery involving volume relationships in chemical reactions, chemists had not accepted the atomic theory, nor did they know the correct composition of substances. Therefore, they could not have written chemical equations. Work such as that of Gay-Lussac and Avogadro made it possible to write chemical equations as we do today.

READING TOOLKIT

READING HINT As students read through the sections, have them use **Figures 3.1, 3.2,** and **3.3** to help them understand the relationships among volume, mass, number of moles, and number of molecules in a gas sample.

SECTION 3

Main Ideas

- Gases react in whole-number ratios.
- Equal volumes of gases under the same conditions contain equal numbers of molecules.
- All gases have a volume of 22.4 L under standard conditions.
- In a chemical equation, the coefficients can indicate moles, molecules, or volume.
- Pressure, volume, and temperature are related to the number of moles of a gas.
- The ideal gas law relates pressure to volume to temperature.

Gas Volumes and the Ideal Gas Law

Key Terms

Gay-Lussac's law of combining volumes of gases
Avogadro's law
standard molar volume of a gas
ideal gas law
ideal gas constant

In this section, you will study the relationships between the volumes of gases that react with each other. You will also learn about the relationship between molar amount of gas and volume, and a single gas law that unifies all the basic gas laws into a single equation.

MAIN IDEA

Gases react in whole-number ratios.

In the early 1800s, French chemist Joseph Gay-Lussac studied gas volume relationships involving a chemical reaction between hydrogen and oxygen. He observed that 2 L of hydrogen can react with 1 L of oxygen to form 2 L of water vapor at constant temperature and pressure.

hydrogen gas	+	oxygen gas	→	water vapor
2 L (2 volumes)		1 L (1 volume)		2 L (2 volumes)

In other words, this reaction shows a simple and definite 2 : 1 : 2 relationship between the volumes of the reactants and the product. Two volumes of hydrogen react with 1 volume of oxygen to produce 2 volumes of water vapor. The 2 : 1 : 2 relationship for this reaction applies to any proportions for volume—for example, 2 mL, 1 mL, and 2 mL; 600 L, 300 L, and 600 L; or 400 cm^3, 200 cm^3, and 400 cm^3.

Gay-Lussac also noticed simple and definite proportions by volume in other reactions of gases, such as in the reaction between hydrogen gas and chlorine gas.

hydrogen gas	+	chlorine gas	→	hydrogen chloride gas
2 L (2 volumes)		1 L (1 volume)		2 L (2 volumes)

In 1808, in what is known today as Gay-Lussac's law of combining volumes of gases; the scientist summarized the results of his experiments by stating that at constant temperature and pressure, the volumes of gaseous reactants and products can be expressed as ratios of small whole numbers. This simple observation, combined with the insight of Avogadro, provided more understanding of how gases react and combine with each other.

Differentiated Instruction

ENGLISH LEARNERS

Have students make a concept map using cards. Rather than constructing the concept map on paper, have them write the major concepts on cards and then arrange the cards to show the connections. For example, some of their concept cards for this section might include *STP, Volume, Reactants, Products, Moles, Molecules,* and so forth.

MAIN IDEA

Equal volumes of gases under the same conditions contain equal numbers of molecules.

Recall an important point of Dalton's atomic theory: atoms are indivisible. Dalton also thought that the particles of gaseous elements exist in the form of isolated single atoms. He believed that one atom of one element always combines with one atom of another element to form a single particle of the product. However, some of the volume relationships observed by Gay-Lussac could not be accounted for by Dalton's theory. For example, in reactions such as the formation of water vapor, mentioned on the preceding page, it would seem that the oxygen atoms involved would have to divide into two parts.

In 1811, Avogadro found a way to explain Gay-Lussac's simple ratios of combining volumes without violating Dalton's idea of indivisible atoms. He did this by rejecting Dalton's idea that reactant elements are always in monatomic form when they combine to form products. He reasoned that these molecules could contain more than one atom. **Avogadro's law** **states that equal volumes of gases at the same temperature and pressure contain equal numbers of molecules.** **Figure 3.1** illustrates Avogadro's law. It follows that at the same temperature and pressure, the volume of any given gas varies directly with the number of molecules. Avogadro's law also indicates that gas volume is directly proportional to the amount of gas, at a given temperature and pressure, as shown in the following equation:

Here, n is the amount of gas, in moles, and k is a constant.

Avogadro's law $V = kn$

Avogadro's reasoning applies to the combining volumes for the reaction of hydrogen and oxygen to form water vapor. Dalton had guessed that the formula of water was HO, because this formula seemed to be the most likely formula for such a common compound. But Avogadro's reasoning established that water must contain twice as many H atoms as O atoms, consistent with the formula H_2O. As shown below, the coefficients in a chemical reaction involving gases indicate the relative numbers of molecules, the relative numbers of moles, and the relative volumes.

$2H_2(g)$	+ $O_2(g)$	→ $2H_2O(g)$
2 molecules	1 molecule	2 molecules
2 mol	1 mol	2 mol
2 volumes	1 volume	2 volumes

The simplest hypothetical formula for oxygen indicated two oxygen atoms, which turns out to be correct. The simplest possible molecule of water indicated two hydrogen atoms and one oxygen atom per molecule, which is also correct. Experiments eventually showed that all elements that are gases near room temperature, except the noble gases, normally exist as diatomic molecules.

FIGURE 3.1

Avogadro's Law

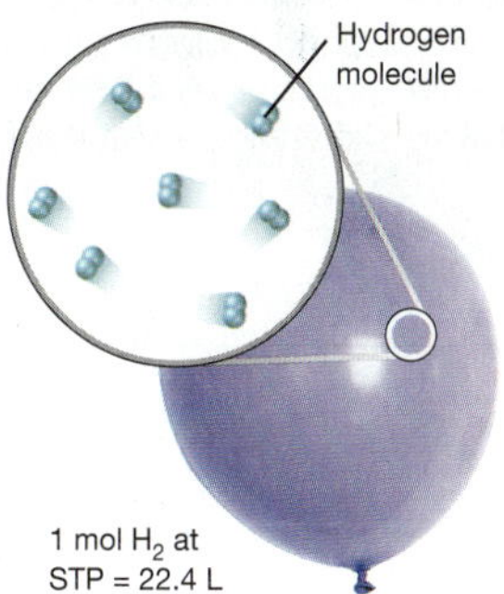

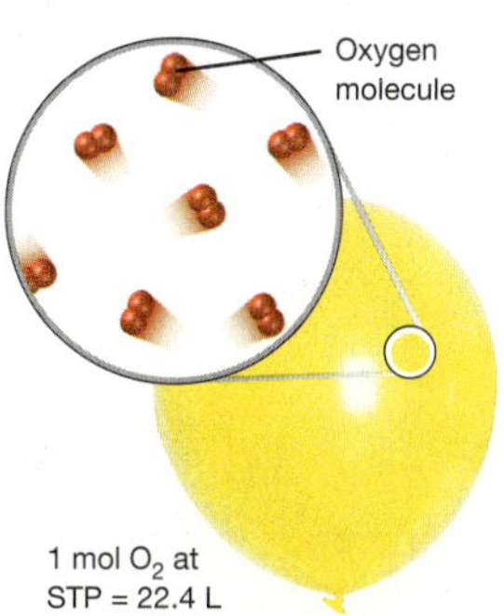

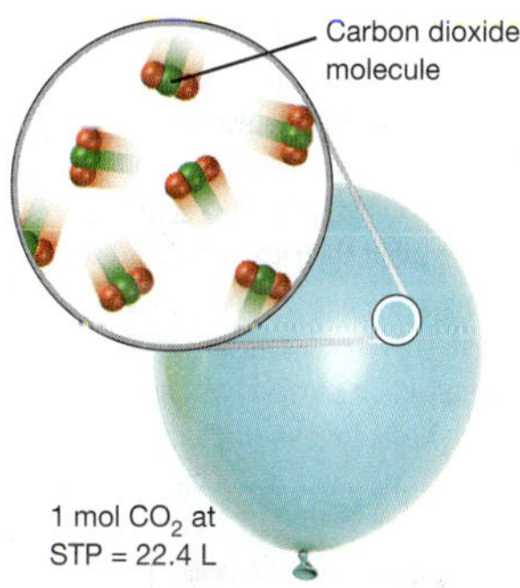

CRITICAL THINKING

Conclude By observing the figures above, what statement could you make about what these three gases at STP have in common?

TEACH FROM VISUALS

FIGURE 3.1 Ask students to compare the masses of the balloons, which contain the same number of particles. Establish that the masses of equal volumes are in the same ratio as the molecular mass of each substance. This knowledge is important later in the section.

Misconception Alert!

Students may think that because the molecules shown in the figures are drawn large, the volume of gas depends on the volume of the molecules. Remind students that in reality, gas molecules are very far apart at ordinary temperatures and pressures and that the sizes of the molecules themselves are inconsequential when compared to the total volume of the gas.

Teaching Tip

You may want to remind students of the common diatomic elements: H_2, N_2, O_2, F_2, Cl_2, Br_2, and I_2.

Critical Thinking

Answer: Responses will vary. A correct response should be that all three gases occupy the same volume (22.4 L) at STP.

INCLUSION

Give students cards with the major concepts printed on one side. Have students with learning disabilities paraphrase those concepts and write them in their own words on the opposite sides of the cards.

▼ Teach *continued*

TEACH FROM VISUALS

FIGURE 3.2 Ask students to draw a representation of the reaction of hydrogen and oxygen in the same style as **Figure 3.2.** Use both diagrams to help students understand that if equal volumes of gases under the same conditions contain the same number of molecules, then the reverse is also true—equal numbers of molecules will occupy the same volume under the same conditions. Thus, it is possible to represent "one volume" with a single molecule.

Demo Problem

1. Ozone, O_3, can be formed from diatomic oxygen by the following reaction.

$$3O_2(g) \rightarrow 2O_3(g)$$

Both gases are measured at the same temperature and pressure.

   a. How many molecules of ozone are formed from the reaction of 24 oxygen molecules?

   b. How many liters of ozone are formed from 12 L of oxygen?

Answer: **a.** 16 molecules O_3, **b.** 8 L O_3

2. How many liters of chlorine at STP will react with 35 L O_2 at STP? Use the following reaction.

$$2Cl_2(g) + 7O_2(g) \rightarrow 2Cl_2O_7(l)$$

Answer: 10 L Cl_2

Alternative Assessment

Challenge students to find or construct containers having a volume of 22.4 L.

A cubic box whose volume is 22.4 L would measure 22 400 cm³. The cubed root of this value is the length needed for each side: about 28.2 cm (or 11.1 in.). Students may also find or construct non-cubic containers that have a volume of 22.4 L.

FIGURE 3.2

Avogadro's Law Hydrogen molecules combine with chlorine molecules in a 1:1 volume ratio to produce two volumes of hydrogen chloride. Avogadro's law thus demonstrates that hydrogen and chlorine gases are diatomic.

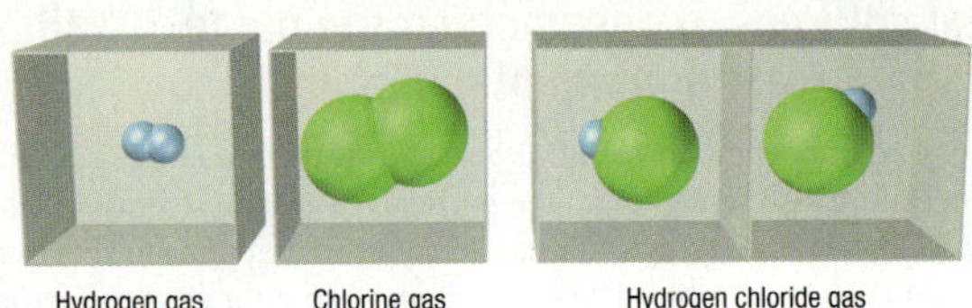

Consider the reaction of hydrogen and chlorine to produce hydrogen chloride, illustrated in **Figure 3.2.** According to Avogadro's law, equal volumes of hydrogen and chlorine contain the same number of molecules. Avogadro's idea of diatomic gases applies to this reaction also. He concluded that the hydrogen and chlorine components must each consist of two or more atoms joined together. The simplest assumption was that hydrogen and chlorine molecules are composed of two atoms each. That assumption leads to the following balanced equation for the reaction of hydrogen with chlorine.

$H_2(g)$	+	$Cl_2(g)$	$\rightarrow$	$2HCl(g)$
1 volume		1 volume		2 volumes
1 molecule		1 molecule		2 molecules

The simplest hypothetical formula for hydrogen chloride, HCl, indicates that the molecule contains one hydrogen atom and one chlorine atom. Given the ratios of the combined volumes, the simplest formulas for hydrogen and chlorine must be H_2 and Cl_2, respectively.

WHY IT MATTERS

Automobile Air Bags S.T.E.M.

Since the late 1980s, air bags have been offered as a safety feature in cars to minimize injuries in the event of a high-speed collision. Modern automobile air bags use a series of very rapid chemical reactions to inflate the bag. When a collision is detected by sensors, an igniter triggers decomposition of solid sodium azide, Na_3N, to form N_2 gas. The hazardous sodium metal that also forms reacts with KNO_3 to form Na_2O, also producing additional N_2. Finally, the highly reactive Na_2O is removed by reaction with SiO_2 to form harmless silicate glass. This entire sequence of reactions occurs to inflate the air bag with nitrogen gas in as few as 40 milliseconds (0.04 s) after a collision is detected by sensors.

MAIN IDEA

All gases have a volume of 22.4 L under standard conditions.

Recall that one mole of a molecular substance contains a number of molecules equal to Avogadro's constant (6.022×10^{23}). One mole of oxygen, O_2, contains 6.022×10^{23} diatomic oxygen molecules and has a mass of 31.9988 g. One mole of helium, a monatomic gas, contains the same number of helium atoms and has a mass of 4.002 602 g.

According to Avogadro's law, one mole of any gas will occupy the same volume as one mole of any other gas at the same temperature and pressure, despite mass differences. **The volume occupied by one mole of a gas at STP is known as the standard molar volume of a gas. It has been found to be 22.414 10 L.** For calculations in this book, we use 22.4 L as the standard molar volume.

Knowing the volume of a gas, you can use 1 mol/22.4 L as a conversion factor to find the number of moles, and therefore the mass, of a given volume of a given gas at STP. You can also use the molar volume of a gas to find the volume, at STP, of a known number of moles or a known mass of a gas.

Differentiated Instruction

PRE-AP

Draw or use clip art to create a concept cartoon for students about standard molar volume of gases. Have several different characters in the cartoon, all with blank speech or thought bubbles. Students should fill in the speech bubbles with statements that show their understanding of standard molar volume. For example, cartoons might have children at a birthday party looking at balloons, or scuba divers filling tanks.

Calculating with Avogadro's Law

Sample Problem G **a. What volume does 0.0685 mol of gas occupy at STP?**
b. What quantity of gas, in moles, is contained in 2.21 L at STP?

 **SOLVE**

a. Multiply the amount in moles by the conversion factor, $\frac{22.4 \text{ L}}{1 \text{ mol}}$.

$$V = 0.0685 \text{ mol} \times \frac{22.4 \text{ L}}{1 \text{ mol}} = 1.53 \text{ L}$$

b. Multiply the volume in liters by the conversion factor, $\frac{1 \text{ mol}}{22.4 \text{ L}}$.

$$\text{Moles} = 2.21 \text{ L} \times \frac{1 \text{ mol}}{22.4 \text{ L}} = 0.0987 \text{ mol}$$

Practice Answers in Appendix E

1. At STP, what is the volume of 7.08 mol of nitrogen gas?
2. A sample of hydrogen gas occupies 14.1 L at STP. How many moles of the gas are present?

MAIN IDEA

In a chemical equation, the coefficients can indicate moles, molecules, or volume.

You can apply the discoveries of Gay-Lussac and Avogadro to calculate the stoichiometry of reactions involving gases. For gaseous reactants or products, the coefficients in chemical equations not only indicate molar amounts and mole ratios but also reveal volume ratios, assuming conditions remain the same. For example, consider the reaction of carbon monoxide with oxygen to give carbon dioxide.

$2CO(g)$	+	$O_2(g)$	→	$2CO_2(g)$
2 molecules		1 molecule		2 molecules
2 mol		1 mol		2 mol
2 volumes		1 volume		2 volumes

The possible volume ratios can be expressed in the following ways.

a. $\frac{2 \text{ volumes CO}}{1 \text{ volume } O_2}$ or $\frac{1 \text{ volume } O_2}{2 \text{ volumes CO}}$

b. $\frac{2 \text{ volumes CO}}{2 \text{ volumes } CO_2}$ or $\frac{2 \text{ volumes } CO_2}{2 \text{ volumes CO}}$

c. $\frac{1 \text{ volume } O_2}{2 \text{ volumes } CO_2}$ or $\frac{2 \text{ volumes } CO_2}{1 \text{ volume } O_2}$

BELOW LEVEL

Provide students with a list of balanced chemical equations with writing space underneath each. Work the first few together, using the example in the text above. Have students circle or highlight the coefficient for each reactant and product. If there are any without coefficients, have students write a "1" in the appropriate spot. Beneath the equation, as in the example, have students list how many molecules, moles, and volumes each coefficient represents for that reactant or product. Have students complete the equations on their own.

Classroom Practice

G-1 You are planning an experiment that requires 0.0580 mol of nitrogen monoxide gas, NO. What volume would you need at STP?

Answer: 1.30 L

Answers

Practice G

1. 159 L N_2
2. 0.629 mol H_2

Classroom Discussion

If room temperature is 25°C, the molar volume will be 24.5 L at 1 atm pressure. You may want to have students use Charles's law to determine this room-temperature volume of a mole of gas.

Misconception Alert!

Students may think that the relationship between volume and moles is true for solid and liquid substances as well. Point out that Avogadro's law applies only to gases.

▼ Teach *continued*

Classroom Practice

H-1 Xenon gas reacts with fluorine gas to produce the compound xenon hexafluoride, XeF_6. Write the balanced equation for this reaction. If a researcher needs 3.14 L of XeF_6 for an experiment, what volumes of xenon and fluorine should be reacted? Assume all volumes are measured under the same conditions of temperature and pressure.

Answer: $Xe(g) + 3F_2(g) \longrightarrow XeF_6(g)$; 3.14 L of Xe and 9.42 L of F_2

Misconception Alert!

Students may believe that volume-volume calculations are possible only if all reactants and products are gases. However, volume-volume ratio calculations are applicable even if other substances in the reaction are not gases.

Answers

Practice H

1. 9.10 L H_2
2. 0.313 L O_2
3. 236 L NO

Gas Stoichiometry

Sample Problem H **Propane, C_3H_8, is a gas that is sometimes used as a fuel for cooking and heating. The complete combustion of propane occurs according to the following balanced equation.**

$$C_3H_8(g) + 5O_2(g) \longrightarrow 3CO_2(g) + 4H_2O(g)$$

(a) What will be the volume, in liters, of oxygen required for the complete combustion of 0.350 L of propane? (b) What will be the volume of carbon dioxide produced in the reaction? Assume that all volume measurements are made at the same temperature and pressure.

1 ANALYZE

Given: balanced chemical equation

V of propane = 0.350 L

Unknown: **a.** V of O_2 in L

b. V of CO_2 in L

2 PLAN

a. V of $C_3H_8 \rightarrow V$ of O_2

b. V of $C_3H_8 \rightarrow V$ of CO_2

All volumes are to be compared at the same temperature and pressure. Therefore, volume ratios can be used like mole ratios to find the unknowns.

3 SOLVE

a. $V \text{ of } O_2 = 0.350 \text{ L } C_3H_8 \times \frac{5 \text{ L } O_2}{1 \text{ L } C_3H_8} = 1.75 \text{ L } O_2$

b. $V \text{ of } CO_2 = 0.350 \text{ L } C_3H_8 \times \frac{3 \text{ L } CO_2}{1 \text{ L } C_3H_8} = 1.05 \text{ L } CO_2$

4 CHECK YOUR WORK

Each result is correctly given to three significant figures. The answers are reasonably close to estimated values of 2, calculated as 0.4 × 5, and 1.2, calculated as 0.4 × 3, respectively.

Practice Answers in Appendix E

1. Assuming all volume measurements are made at the same temperature and pressure, what volume of hydrogen gas is needed to react completely with 4.55 L of oxygen gas to produce water vapor?
2. What volume of oxygen gas is needed to react completely with 0.626 L of carbon monoxide gas, CO, to form gaseous carbon dioxide? Assume all volume measurements are made at the same temperature and pressure.
3. Nitric acid can be produced by the reaction of gaseous nitrogen dioxide with water, according to the following balanced chemical equation.

$$3NO_2(g) + H_2O(l) \longrightarrow 2HNO_3(l) + NO(g)$$

If 708 L of NO_2 gas react with water, what volume of NO gas will be produced? Assume the gases are measured under the same conditions before and after the reaction.

Problem Solving

REALITY CHECK

Before beginning a problem of this type, students should write down the equation on their paper as one of their pieces of given data. Have students pay close attention to the coefficients in the equation, as these numbers will be used in the conversion factors of their calculations. One way to emphasize this would be to have students highlight or circle the coefficients in the equation and write a "1" before formulas that do not have a coefficient.

MAIN IDEA

Pressure, volume, and temperature are related to the number of moles of a gas.

You have learned about equations describing the relationships between two or three of the four variables—pressure, volume, temperature, and moles—needed to describe a gas sample. All the gas laws you have learned thus far can be combined into a single equation. The **ideal gas law** is the mathematical relationship among pressure, volume, temperature, and the number of moles of a gas. It is the equation of state for an ideal gas, because the state of a gas can be defined by its pressure, volume, temperature, and number of moles. It is stated as shown below, where R is a constant.

Ideal gas law $PV = nRT$

The ideal gas law reduces to Boyle's law, Charles's law, Gay-Lussac's law, or Avogadro's law when the appropriate variables are held constant.

The number of molecules or moles present will always affect at least one of the other three quantities. The collision rate of molecules per unit area of container wall depends on the number of molecules present. If the number of molecules is increased for a sample at constant volume and temperature, the collision rate increases. Therefore, the pressure increases, as shown by the model in **Figure 3.3a.** Consider what would happen if the pressure and temperature were kept constant while the number of molecules increased. According to Avogadro's law, the volume would increase. As **Figure 3.3b** shows, an increase in volume keeps the pressure constant at constant temperature. Increasing the volume keeps the collision rate per unit of wall area constant.

FIGURE 3.3

The Ideal Gas Law

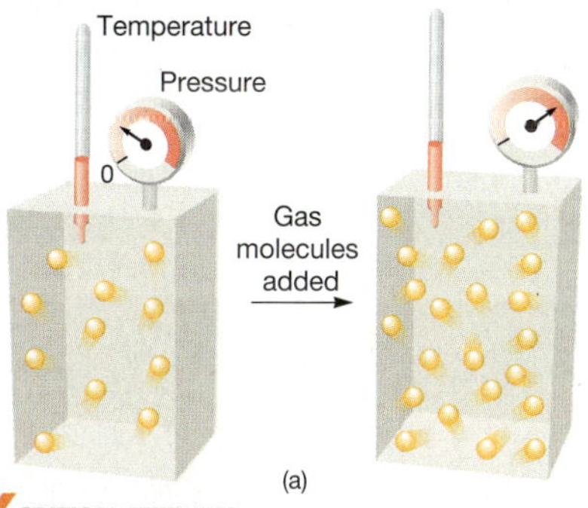

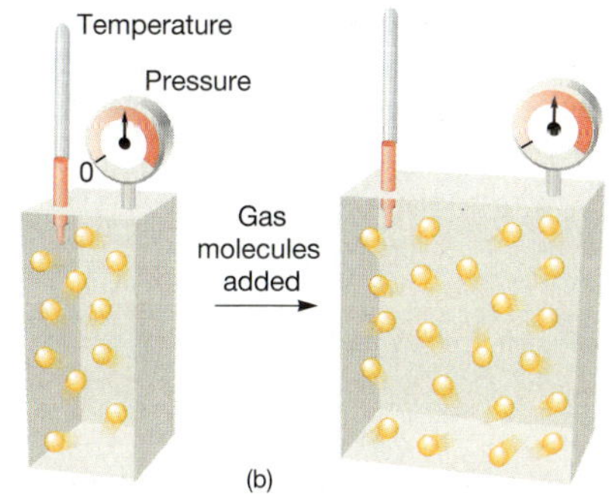

CRITICAL THINKING

Analyze When volume and temperature are constant, and the number of molecules increases, what happens to the gas pressure?

Analyze When pressure and temperature are constant, and the number of molecules increases, what happens to the gas volume?

Teaching Tip

The ideal gas law is not a magic expression. It is a combination of all the gas laws students have learned so far. The gas constant combines all of the proportionality constants of the individual relationships (Boyle's law, Charles's law, Avogadro's law) into a single value.

Classroom Discussion

Ask students to discuss whether there is such a thing as a mole of air. Remind them that air is not a substance but a mixture. A mole of air can be defined as an Avogadro's number of particles of the gas mixture that makes up air. Ask students if it would be possible to determine the volume of a mole of air, and have them explain their conclusions. A mole of air occupies 22.4 L at STP, just as any pure gas would. All of the components of air behave as ideal gases at ordinary temperatures and pressures; therefore, the mixture would also behave as an ideal gas.

Critical Thinking

Answers: (a) The gas pressure increases. **(b)** The volume increases.

Differentiated Instruction

PRE-AP

Challenge students to construct a model of a hot-air balloon. Make it a competition. Size, materials, and launch conditions should be standardized (only tissue paper, for example), but design might vary. Students should be allowed to use only air, not helium. Methods for heating the air would have to be approved in advance by the teacher. For lighter materials, a hand-held hair dryer can be used as the heat source. Heavier materials may require a propane-burning launcher. Plans for building such a launcher can be found on the Internet, but these should not be used without adequate supervision and safety measures. Models should include some method of measuring air temperature and volume, both before launch and once the balloon is afloat. Using the measurements taken and the ideal gas law, students should be able to show empirically why their balloons rose or not.

▼ Teach *continued*

Teaching Tip

Remind students that they can convert a proportionality

$y \propto x$

to an equality by multiplying by a constant:

$y = kx$

TEACH FROM TABLES

FIGURE 3.4 Have students compare the values of R shown in the table to reinforce the idea that the value 0.0821 L•atm/(mol•K) can be used only with measurements that match these units. Measurements with different units must be converted, or another value of R must be used.

ChemisTrivia

Although students will continue to use 22.4 L as standard molar volume at STP, true molar volume varies according to how much a gas deviates from the ideal. The following list shows values for specific gases.

H_2	22.42 L
N_2	22.40 L

To three significant figures, these values still round off to 22.4 L. Other common gases deviate further from the ideal because of interactions among the molecules. Note the following molar volumes.

CO_2	22.26 L
NH_3	22.08 L

Check for Understanding

Answer: The variable n does not change units because it always represents the number of moles of the gas, and thus is always in units of "mol." Pressure (P), temperature (T), and volume (V) could be measured in various units, while R is a constant whose value depends on the chosen units for the variables.

MAIN IDEA

The ideal gas law relates pressure to volume to temperature.

In the equation representing the ideal gas law, the constant R is known as the ideal gas constant. Its value depends on the units chosen for pressure, volume, and temperature. Measured values of P, V, T, and n for a gas at near-ideal conditions can be used to calculate R. Recall that the volume of one mole of an ideal gas at STP (1 atm and 273.15 K) is 22.414 10 L. Substituting these values and solving the ideal gas law equation for R gives the following.

$$R = \frac{PV}{nT} = \frac{(1\ \text{atm})\,(22.414\ 10\ \text{L})}{(1\ \text{mol})\,(273.15\ \text{K})} = 0.082\ 057\ 84\ \frac{\text{L•atm}}{\text{mol•K}}$$

CHECK FOR UNDERSTANDING
Identify What variable in the ideal gas law does not change units?

This calculated value of R is usually rounded to 0.0821 L • atm/(mol•K). Use this value in ideal gas law calculations when the volume is in liters, the pressure is in atmospheres, and the temperature is in kelvins. See **Figure 3.4** for the value of R when other units for n, P, V, and T are used.

Finding *P*, *V*, *T*, or *n* from the Ideal Gas Law

The ideal gas law can be applied to determine the existing conditions of a gas sample when three of the four variables, P, V, T, and n, are known. It can also be used to calculate the molar mass or density of a gas sample.

Be sure to match the units of the known quantities and the units of R. In this book, you will be using R = 0.0821 L•atm/(mol•K). Your first step in solving any ideal gas law problem should be to check the known values to be sure you are working with the correct units. If necessary, you must convert volumes to liters, pressures to atmospheres, temperatures to kelvins, and masses to numbers of moles before using the ideal gas law.

FIGURE 3.4

NUMERICAL VALUES OF GAS CONSTANT, *R*

Units of *R*	Numerical value of *R*	Unit of *P*	Unit of *V*	Unit of *T*	Unit of *n*
$\frac{\text{L•mm Hg}}{\text{mol•K}}$	62.4	mm Hg	L	K	mol
$\frac{\text{L•atm}}{\text{mol•K}}$	0.0821	atm	L	K	mol
$\frac{\text{J}}{\text{mol•K}}$*	8.314	Pa	m^3	K	mol
$\frac{\text{L•kPa}}{\text{mol•K}}$	8.314	kPa	L	K	mol

Note: 1 L•atm = 101.325 J; 1 J = 1 Pa•m^3
*SI units

Differentiated Instruction

PRE-AP

Have students close and put away their textbooks. Give them a sheet of paper printed with the gas laws. Using these, have them derive the ideal gas law, showing all of their work. This exercise can be extended by asking them to substitute the values for STP and the volume for one mole of an ideal gas at STP (22.414 L), and then derive the value of the ideal gas constant (R). Again, be certain that they show all of their work, using the four-step problem-solving strategy.

Using the Ideal Gas Law

PREMIUM CONTENT

Learn It! Video
HMDScience.com

Solve It! Cards
HMDScience.com

Sample Problem I **What is the pressure in atmospheres exerted by a 0.500 mol sample of nitrogen gas in a 10.0 L container at 298 K?**

1 ANALYZE

Given: V of $N_2 = 10.0$ L

n of $N_2 = 0.500$ mol

T of $N_2 = 298$ K

Unknown: P of N_2 in atm

2 PLAN

$n, V, T \rightarrow P$

The gas sample undergoes no change in conditions. Therefore, the ideal gas law can be rearranged and used to find the pressure as follows:

$$P = \frac{nRT}{V}$$

3 SOLVE

$$P = \frac{(0.500\ \cancel{\text{mol}})\left(\dfrac{0.0821\ \cancel{\text{L}} \cdot \text{atm}}{\cancel{\text{mol}} \cdot \cancel{\text{K}}}\right)(298\ \cancel{\text{K}})}{10.0\ \cancel{\text{L}}} = 1.22\ \text{atm}$$

4 CHECK YOUR WORK

All units cancel correctly to give the result in atmospheres. The answer is properly limited to three significant figures. It is also close to an estimated value of 1.5, computed as $(0.5 \times 0.1 \times 300)/10$.

Practice

Answers in Appendix E

1. What pressure, in atmospheres, is exerted by 0.325 mol of hydrogen gas in a 4.08 L container at 35°C?
2. A gas sample occupies 8.77 L at 20°C. What is the pressure, in atmospheres, given that there are 1.45 mol of gas in the sample?

SECTION 3 FORMATIVE ASSESSMENT

Reviewing Main Ideas

1. State Avogadro's law, and explain its significance.
2. What volume (in milliliters) at STP will be occupied by 0.0035 mol of methane, CH_4?
3. State the ideal gas law equation, and tell what each term means.
4. What would be the units for R if P is in pascals, T is in kelvins, V is in liters, and n is in moles?
5. A 4.44 L container holds 15.4 g of oxygen at 22.55°C. What is the pressure?
6. A tank of hydrogen gas has a volume of 22.9 L and holds 14.0 mol of the gas at 12°C. What is the pressure of the gas in atmospheres?

Critical Thinking

7. **ANALYZING DATA** Nitrous oxide is sometimes used as a source of oxygen gas:

$$2N_2O(g) \rightarrow 2N_2(g) + O_2(g)$$

What volume of each product will be formed from 2.22 L N_2O? At STP, what is the density of the product gases when they are mixed?

Answers to Section Assessment

1. The law states that equal volumes of gases at the same temperature and pressure contain equal numbers of molecules. The significance is that at the same temperature and pressure, the volume of any given gas varies directly with the number of molecules.
2. 78 mL
3. $PV = nRT$; pressure, volume, number of moles, constant, and temperature
4. The units would be L•Pa/(K•mol).
5. 2.63 atm
6. 14.3 atm
7. 2.22 L N_2 and 1.11 L O_2; 1.31 g/L

Classroom Practice

I-1 A 2.07 L cylinder contains 2.88 mol of helium gas at 22°C. What is the pressure in atmospheres of the gas in the cylinder?

Answer: 33.7 atm

Answers

Practice I

1. 2.01 atm
2. 3.98 atm

READING TOOLKIT

SEQUENCING After students read and study the sample problem, ask them to outline the process as a series of general steps. Have a volunteer list the steps on the board.

Assess and Reteach ▼

Assess Use the Formative Assessment on this page to evaluate student mastery of the section.

Reteach For students who need additional instruction, download the Section Study Guide.

Response to Intervention To reassess students' mastery, use the Section Quiz, available to print or to take directly online at **HMDScience.com**.

SECTION 4

▼ Plan and Prepare

Objectives

Upon completion of this section, students should be able to do the following:

- Describe the process of diffusion.
- State Graham's law of effusion.
- State the relationship between the average molecular velocities of two gases and their molar masses.

Classroom Catalyst

Ask students to assume that the perfume bottle in **Figure 4.1** stands open in a room where the air is perfectly still. Ask them to speculate on what will happen as time passes.

▼ Teach

Teaching Tip

If students have difficulty understanding the relationship in the last paragraph, the following might help:

$$(KE)_A = \tfrac{1}{2}m_A v_A^2$$

$$(KE)_B = \tfrac{1}{2}m_B v_B^2$$

At the same temperature,

$$(KE)_A = (KE)_B$$

so

$$\tfrac{1}{2}m_A v_A^2 = \tfrac{1}{2}m_B v_B^2$$

The value of m_A (the mass of an individual molecule of gas A) is proportional to M_A (the molar mass of gas A), so

$$\tfrac{1}{2}M_A v_A^2 = \tfrac{1}{2}M_B v_B^2$$

Critical Thinking

Answer: Answers will vary. The different molecules will mix and be more evenly distributed among each other.

SECTION 4

Main Idea

The rates of effusion and diffusion for gases depend on the velocities of their molecules.

Diffusion and Effusion

Key Term

Graham's law of effusion

The constant motion of gas molecules causes them to spread out to fill any container in which they are placed. The gradual mixing of two or more gases due to their spontaneous, random motion is known as diffusion, illustrated in **Figure 4.1.** *Effusion* is the process whereby the molecules of a gas confined in a container randomly pass through a tiny opening in the container. In this section, you will learn how effusion can be used to estimate the molar mass of a gas.

MAIN IDEA

The rates of effusion and diffusion for gases depend on the velocities of their molecules.

The rates of effusion and diffusion depend on the relative velocities of gas molecules. The velocity of a gas varies inversely with the square root of its molar mass. Lighter molecules move faster than heavier molecules at the same temperature.

Recall that the average kinetic energy of the molecules in any gas depends only on the temperature and equals $\frac{1}{2}mv^2$. For two different gases, A and B, at the same temperature, the following relationship is true:

$$\tfrac{1}{2}M_A v_A^2 = \tfrac{1}{2}M_B v_B^2$$

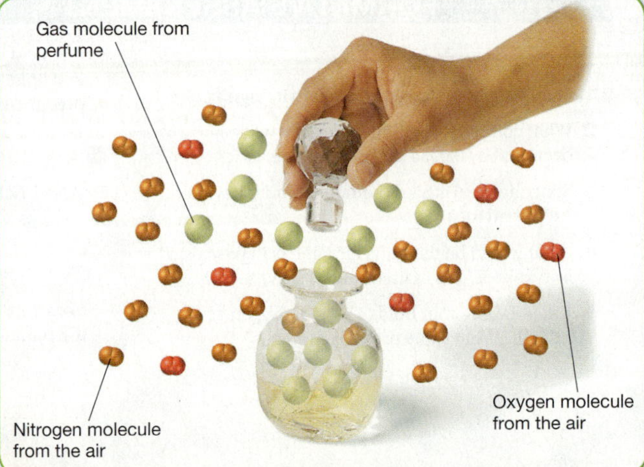

FIGURE 4.1

Diffusion When a bottle of perfume is opened, some of its molecules diffuse into the air and mix with the molecules of the air. At the same time, molecules from the air, such as nitrogen and oxygen, diffuse into the bottle and mix with the gaseous scent molecules.

CRITICAL THINKING

Deduce As diffusion occurs, what would you expect to see happen to the different molecules in the figure at the right?

Differentiated Instruction

BELOW LEVEL

Using cartooning frames, have students illustrate the principles of diffusion and effusion.

PRE-AP

Have students use the drawing and custom animation tools within presentation software to construct animated slides illustrating diffusion and effusion. With the animation tools, only one slide each is needed to illustrate the two principles.

From the equation relating the kinetic energy of two different gases at the same conditions, one can derive an equation relating the rates of effusion of two gases with their molecular mass. This equation is shown below.

$$\frac{\text{rate of effusion of } A}{\text{rate of effusion of } B} = \frac{\sqrt{M_B}}{\sqrt{M_A}}$$

In the mid-1800s, the Scottish chemist Thomas Graham studied the effusion and diffusion of gases. The above equation is a mathematical statement of some of Graham's discoveries. It describes the rates of effusion. It can also be used to find the molar mass of an unknown gas. **Graham's law of effusion** states that the rates of effusion of gases at the same temperature and pressure are inversely proportional to the square roots of their molar masses.

QuickLAB DIFFUSION

QUESTION

Do different gases diffuse at different rates?

PROCEDURE

Record all of your results in a data table.

1. Outdoors or in a room separate from the one in which you will carry out the rest of the investigation, pour approximately 10 mL of the household ammonia into one of the 250 mL beakers, and cover it with a watch glass. Pour roughly the same amount of perfume or cologne into the second beaker. Cover it with a watch glass also.
2. Take the two samples you just prepared into a large, draft-free room. Place the samples about 12 to 15 ft apart and at the same height. Position someone as the observer midway between the two beakers. Remove both watch glass covers at the same time.
3. Note whether the observer smells the ammonia or the perfume first. Record how long this takes. Also, record how long it takes the vapor of the other substance to reach the observer. Air the room after you have finished.

DISCUSSION

1. What do the times that the two vapors took to reach the observer show about the two gases?
2. What factors other than molecular mass (which determines diffusion rate) could affect how quickly the observer smells each vapor?

MATERIALS

- household ammonia
- perfume or cologne
- two 250 mL beakers
- two watch glasses
- 10 mL graduated cylinder
- clock or watch with second hand

SAFETY

Wear safety goggles and an apron.

Ammonia

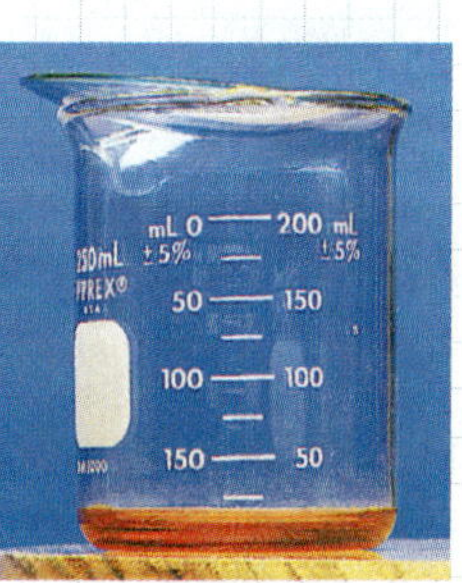

Perfume

Demo Problem

1. At 25°C, the average velocity of oxygen molecules is 420 m/s. What is the average velocity of helium molecules at the same temperature?

   Answer: 1200 m/s
2. At a certain temperature, hydrogen molecules move at an average velocity of 1.84×10^3 m/s. Estimate the molar mass of a gas whose molecules have an average velocity of 312 m/s.

   Answer: 70 g/mol

QuickLab

Students should make a data figure to record their results.

Students should record the following:

- the identity of the two materials
- the location of each material relative to the observer
- the distance from each sample to the observer
- the time in seconds until the observer detects each material

(If the air is quite still, the observer will detect the ammonia first.)

Safety Ammonia vapors are very irritating to human tissue. Be sure students do not breathe concentrated vapors. Before performing this activity, survey students to determine whether any of them have asthma or allergies to perfumes.

Disposal Combine all liquids, dilute tenfold with water, and pour down the drain.

DISCUSSION

1. Ammonia molecules diffuse more rapidly than perfume-scent molecules do.
2. concentration, vapor pressure, air currents, and the sensitivity of the observer to the two odors

▼ Teach *continued*

Classroom Practice

J-1 Nitrogen effuses through a pinhole 1.7 times as fast as another gaseous element at the same conditions. Estimate the other element's molar mass, and determine its probable identity.

Answer: 81 g/mol, krypton

Answers

Practice J

1. CO_2 will effuse about 0.9 times as fast as HCl
2. 160 g/mol
3. about 235 m/s

▼ Assess and Reteach

Assess Use the Formative Assessment on this page to evaluate student mastery of the section.

Reteach For students who need additional instruction, download the Section Study Guide.

Response to Intervention To reassess students' mastery, use the Section Quiz, available to print or to take directly online at **HMDScience.com**.

Graham's Law of Effusion

Sample Problem J **Compare the rates of effusion of hydrogen and oxygen at the same temperature and pressure.**

1 ANALYZE

Given: identities of two gases, H_2 and O_2

Unknown: relative rates of effusion

2 PLAN

molar mass ratio → ratio of rates of effusion

The ratio of the rates of effusion of two gases at the same temperature and pressure can be found from Graham's Law.

$$\frac{\text{rate of effusion of A}}{\text{rate of effusion of B}} = \frac{\sqrt{M_B}}{\sqrt{M_A}}$$

3 SOLVE

$$\frac{\text{rate of effusion of } H_2}{\text{rate of effusion of } O_2} = \frac{\sqrt{M_{O_2}}}{\sqrt{M_{H_2}}} = \frac{\sqrt{32.00\text{ g/mol}}}{\sqrt{2.02\text{ g/mol}}} = \sqrt{\frac{32.00\text{ g/mol}}{2.02\text{ g/mol}}} = 3.98$$

Hydrogen effuses 3.98 times faster than oxygen.

4 CHECK YOUR WORK

The result is correctly reported to three significant figures. It is also approximately equivalent to an estimated value of 4, calculated as $\sqrt{32}/\sqrt{2}$.

Practice Answers in Appendix E

1. Compare the rate of effusion of carbon dioxide with that of hydrogen chloride at the same temperature and pressure.
2. A sample of hydrogen effuses through a porous container about 9 times faster than an unknown gas. Estimate the molar mass of the unknown gas.
3. If a molecule of neon gas travels at an average of 400. m/s at a given temperature, estimate the average speed of a molecule of butane gas, C_4H_{10}, at the same temperature.

SECTION 4 FORMATIVE ASSESSMENT

Reviewing Main Ideas

1. Compare diffusion with effusion.
2. State Graham's law of effusion.
3. Estimate the molar mass of a gas that effuses at 1.6 times the effusion rate of carbon dioxide.
4. Determine the molecular mass ratio of two gases whose rates of effusion have a ratio of 16 : 1.
5. List the following gases in order of increasing average molecular velocity at 25°C: H_2O, He, HCl, BrF, and NO_2.

Critical Thinking

6. **ANALYZING INFORMATION** An unknown gas effuses at one-half the speed of oxygen. What is the molar mass of the unknown? The gas is known to be either HBr or HI. Which gas is it?

Answers to Section Assessment

1. Effusion is the process by which gas molecules under pressure pass through a tiny opening. Diffusion is the mixing of two gases by random molecular motion.
2. The law states that the rates of effusion of gases at the same temperature and pressure are inversely proportional to the square roots of their molar masses.
3. 17 g/mol
4. 256 : 1
5. The gases should be listed in order of decreasing molecular mass: BrF, NO_2, HCl, H_2O, He.
6. molar mass = 128 g/mol. The gas is HI.

Math Tutor

Algebraic Rearrangements of Gas Laws

When you solve problems in chemistry, it's usually a bad idea to just start entering numbers into a calculator. Instead, doing a little pencil-and-paper work beforehand will help you eliminate errors. When using the gas laws, you do not need to memorize all of the equations because they are easily derived from the equation for the combined gas law.

Study the table below. In each of Boyle's, Charles's, and Gay-Lussac's laws, one of the quantities—*T*, *P*, or *V*—does not change. By simply eliminating that factor from the equation, you obtain the equation for one particular gas law.

The conditions stated in the problem should make clear which factors change and which are held constant. This information will tell you which law's equation to use.

GAS LAW	HELD CONSTANT	CANCELLATION	RESULT
combined gas law	none	$\frac{P_1V_1}{T_1} = \frac{P_2V_2}{T_2}$	$\frac{P_1V_1}{T_1} = \frac{P_2V_2}{T_2}$
Boyle's law	temperature	$\frac{P_1V_1}{\cancel{T_1}} = \frac{P_2V_2}{\cancel{T_2}}$	$P_1V_1 = P_2V_2$
Charles's law	pressure	$\frac{\cancel{P_1}V_1}{T_1} = \frac{\cancel{P_2}V_2}{T_2}$	$\frac{V_1}{T_1} = \frac{V_2}{T_2}$
Gay-Lussac's law	volume	$\frac{P_1\cancel{V_1}}{T_1} = \frac{P_2\cancel{V_2}}{T_2}$	$\frac{P_1}{T_1} = \frac{P_2}{T_2}$

Sample Problem

A cylinder of nitrogen gas has a volume of 35.00 L at a pressure of 11.50 atm. What pressure will the nitrogen have if the contents of the cylinder are allowed to flow into a sealed reaction chamber whose volume is 140.0 L, and if the temperature remains constant?

1 ANALYZE Start with the combined gas law, and cancel the temperature, which does not change.

$$\frac{P_1V_1}{\cancel{T_1}} = \frac{P_2V_2}{\cancel{T_2}}; P_1V_1 = P_2V_2$$

You want to know the new pressure in the chamber, so solve for P_2.

$$\frac{P_1V_1}{V_2} = \frac{P_2\cancel{V_2}}{\cancel{V_2}}; \frac{P_1V_1}{V_2} = P_2$$

2 SOLVE The resulting equation to use in solving the problem is

$$P_2 = \frac{P_1V_1}{V_2} = \frac{(11.50 \text{ atm})(35.00 \text{ L})}{140.0 \text{ L}} = 2.875 \text{ atm.}$$

Practice Answers in Appendix E

1. A sample of gas has a pressure P_1 at a temperature T_1. Write the equation that you would use to find the temperature, T_2, at which the gas has a pressure of P_2.
2. An ideal gas occupies a volume of 785 mL at a pressure of 0.879 atm. What volume will the gas occupy at the pressure of 0.994 atm?

Answers

1. $T_2 = \frac{P_2T_1}{P_1}$
2. 694 mL

CHAPTER 11 Summary

PREMIUM CONTENT
Interactive Review HMDScience.com
Review Games
Concept Maps

SECTION 1 Gases and Pressure

- The kinetic-molecular theory of gases describes an ideal gas. The behavior of most gases is nearly ideal except at very high pressures and low temperatures.
- A barometer measures atmospheric pressure.
- Dalton's law of partial pressures states that in a mixture of unreacting gases, the total pressure equals the sum of the partial pressures of each gas.

KEY TERMS

- pressure
- newton
- barometer
- millimeters of mercury
- atmosphere of pressure
- pascal
- partial pressure
- Dalton's law of partial pressures

SECTION 2 The Gas Laws

- Boyle's law states the inverse relationship between the volume and the pressure of a gas:

$$PV = k$$

- Charles's law illustrates the direct relationship between a gas's volume and its temperature in kelvins:

$$V = kT$$

- Gay-Lussac's law represents the direct relationship between a gas's pressure and its temperature in kelvins:

$$P = kT$$

- The combined gas law, as its name implies, combines the previous relationships into the following mathematical expression:

$$\frac{PV}{T} = k$$

KEY TERMS

- Boyle's law
- absolute zero
- Charles's law
- Gay-Lussac's law
- combined gas law

SECTION 3 Gas Volumes and the Ideal Gas Law

- Gay-Lussac's law of combining volumes states that the volumes of reacting gases and their products at the same temperature and pressure can be expressed as ratios of whole numbers.
- Avogadro's law states that equal volumes of gases at the same temperature and pressure contain equal numbers of molecules.
- The volume occupied by one mole of an ideal gas at STP is called the standard molar volume, which is 22.414 10 L.
- Charles's law, Boyle's law, and Avogadro's law can be combined to create the ideal gas law:

$$PV = nRT$$

KEY TERMS

- Gay-Lussac's law of combining volumes of gases
- Avogadro's law
- standard molar volume of a gas
- ideal gas law
- ideal gas constant

SECTION 4 Diffusion and Effusion

- Gases diffuse, or become more spread out, due to their constant random molecular motion.
- Graham's law of effusion states that the relative rates of effusion of gases at the same temperature and pressure are inversely proportional to the square roots of their molar masses.

KEY TERM

- Graham's law of effusion

370 Chapter 11

CHAPTER 11 Review

SECTION 1

Gases and Pressure

REVIEWING MAIN IDEAS

1. State the assumptions that the kinetic-molecular theory makes about the characteristics of gas particles.
2. What is an ideal gas?
3. a. Why does a gas in a closed container exert pressure?
   b. What is the relationship between the area a force is applied to and the resulting pressure?
4. a. Why does a column of mercury in a tube that is inverted in a dish of mercury have a height of about 760 mm at sea level?
   b. The density of water is approximately 1/13.5 the density of mercury. What height would be maintained by a column of water inverted in a dish of water at sea level?
   c. What accounts for the difference in the heights of the mercury and water columns?
5. a. Identify three units used to express pressure.
   b. Convert one atmosphere to millimeters of mercury.
   c. What is a pascal?
   d. What is the SI equivalent of one standard atmosphere of pressure?
6. a. Explain what is meant by the partial pressure of each gas within a mixture of gases.
   b. How do the partial pressures of gases in a mixture affect each other?

PRACTICE PROBLEMS

7. If the atmosphere can support a column of mercury 760 mm high at sea level, what height of a hypothetical liquid whose density is 1.40 times the density of mercury could be supported?
8. Convert each of the following into a pressure reading expressed in torrs.
   a. 1.25 atm
   b. 2.48×10^{-3} atm
   c. 4.75×10^{4} atm
   d. 7.60×10^{6} atm
9. Convert each of the following into the unit specified.
   a. 125 mm Hg into atmospheres
   b. 3.20 atm into pascals
   c. 5.38 kPa into millimeters of mercury
10. Three of the primary components of air are carbon dioxide, nitrogen, and oxygen. In a sample containing a mixture of only these gases at exactly 1 atm, the partial pressures of carbon dioxide and nitrogen are given as $P_{CO_2} = 0.285$ torr and $P_{N_2} = 593.525$ torr. What is the partial pressure of oxygen?
11. A gas sample is collected over water at a temperature of 35.0°C when the barometric pressure reading is 742.0 torr. What is the partial pressure of the dry gas?

SECTION 2

The Gas Laws

REVIEWING MAIN IDEAS

12. How are the volume and pressure of a gas at constant temperature related?
13. Explain why pressure increases as a gas is compressed into a smaller volume.
14. How are the absolute temperature and volume of a gas at constant pressure related?
15. How are the pressure and absolute temperature of a gas at constant volume related?
16. Explain Gay-Lussac's law in terms of the kinetic-molecular theory.
17. State the combined gas law.

PRACTICE PROBLEMS

18. Use Boyle's law to solve for the missing value in each of the following:
   a. $P_1 = 350.0$ torr, $V_1 = 200.0$ mL, $P_2 = 700.0$ torr, $V_2 = ?$
   b. $V_1 = 2.4 \times 10^5$ L, $P_2 = 180$ mm Hg, $V_2 = 1.8 \times 10^3$ L, $P_1 = ?$
19. Use Charles's law to solve for the missing value in each of the following:
   a. $V_1 = 80.0$ mL, $T_1 = 27°C$, $T_2 = 77°C$, $V_2 = ?$
   b. $V_1 = 125$ L, $V_2 = 85.0$ L, $T_2 = 127°C$, $T_1 = ?$
   c. $T_1 = -33°C$, $V_2 = 54.0$ mL, $T_2 = 160.0°C$, $V_1 = ?$

Review Answers

1. Particles of matter are always in motion. These particles are tiny and far apart relative to their size. They do not attract one another, and their collisions are elastic. The temperature of the gas depends on the average kinetic energy of the particles.
2. An ideal gas is a theoretical gas that fits perfectly all assumptions of the kinetic-molecular theory.
3. a. The moving molecules of the gas hit the container walls.
   b. The same force applied to a smaller area results in a greater pressure.
4. a. The pressure exerted by the mercury in the tube equals that exerted by the atmosphere, which, at sea level, is equal to the pressure exerted by a column of mercury that is approximately 760 mm in height.
   b. 10.3 m, or about 34 ft
   c. Mercury is 13.5 times as dense as water, so it exerts 13.5 times the pressure as a comparable column of water.

5. a. millimeters of mercury (mm Hg), torrs (torr), atmospheres (atm), pascals (Pa), and pounds per square inch (psi)
   b. 1 atm = 760 mm Hg
   c. the pressure exerted by a force of one newton (N) acting on an area of 1 m^2; 1 Pa = 1 N/m^2
   d. 1.01325×10^5 Pa, or 101.325 kPa
6. a. the pressure that each gas exerts in the mixture of gases
   b. They are independent of one another.
7. 543 mm
8. a. 950. torr
   b. 1.88 torr
   c. 3.61×10^7 torr
   d. 5.78×10^9 torr
9. a. 0.164 atm
   b. 3.24×10^5 Pa
   c. 40.4 mm Hg
10. 166.190 torr
11. 699.8 torr
12. They are inversely related.
13. The molecules are closer together and strike a unit area of the walls of the container more often.
14. They are directly proportional.
15. They are directly proportional.
16. Gas particles at higher temperatures will have higher average kinetic energy. This means that at constant volume they will collide with a unit area of their container wall more often, thus exerting more pressure.
17. $\frac{P_1V_1}{T_1} = \frac{P_2V_2}{T_2}$, or $PV/T = k$
18. a. 100.0 mL
   b. 1.4 mm Hg
19. a. 93.3 mL
   b. 588 K or 315°C
   c. 29.9 mL

20. 121 K or −152°C
21. 142 mL
22. 0.360 atm
23. 3.41 L
24. 127°C
25. 38.8 kPa
26. a. 225.0 mL
b. 1800. mL
27. 6.05×10^5 mL
28. 540 K or 267°C
29. 260 K or −13°C
30. −16°C
31. 243 L
32. −43°C
33. 9.98 m^3/day
34. a. It applies only to gases measured under the same temperature and pressure.
b. The volume varies directly with the number of molecules.
35. a. As long as temperature and pressure are the same, the volume ratios will be the same as the mole ratios.
b. Volume ratios are valid only when the volumes of all gases being compared are measured under the same temperature and pressure. Volume ratios also apply only to gases.
36. a. If temperature and pressure remain constant, the volume varies directly with the number of moles present.
b. $V = kn$, where V is volume, n is the number of moles, and k is a proportionality constant
37. At STP, 22.4 L of any gas contains one mole of molecules. The mass of 22.4 L of gas is therefore equal to the molar mass of that gas.
38. a. when three of the four variables P, V, T, and n are known
b. The units of volume, temperature, and pressure must match those of the gas constant used.
39. a. $PV = nRT$
b. It relates pressure, volume, temperature, and number of moles of any gas under any set of conditions at which the gas behaves as an ideal gas.

CHAPTER REVIEW

20. A sample of air has a volume of 140.0 mL at 67°C. At what temperature would its volume be 50.0 mL at constant pressure?

21. The pressure exerted on a 240.0 mL sample of hydrogen gas at constant temperature is increased from 0.428 atm to 0.724 atm. What will the final volume of the sample be?

22. A sample of hydrogen at 47°C exerts a pressure of 0.329 atm. The gas is heated to 77°C at constant volume. What will its new pressure be?

23. A sample of gas at 47°C and 1.03 atm occupies a volume of 2.20 L. What volume would this gas occupy at 107°C and 0.789 atm?

24. The pressure on a gas at −73°C is doubled, but its volume is held constant. What will the final temperature be in degrees Celsius?

25. A flask containing 155 cm^3 of hydrogen was collected under a pressure of 22.5 kPa. What pressure would have been required for the volume of the gas to have been 90.0 cm^3, assuming the same temperature?

26. A gas has a volume of 450.0 mL. If the temperature is held constant, what volume would the gas occupy if the pressure were
a. doubled? (Hint: Express P_2 in terms of P_1.)
b. reduced to one-fourth of its original value?

27. A sample of oxygen that occupies 1.00×10^6 mL at 575 mm Hg is subjected to a pressure of 1.25 atm. What will the final volume of the sample be if the temperature is held constant?

28. To what temperature must a sample of nitrogen at 27°C and 0.625 atm be taken so that its pressure becomes 1.125 atm at constant volume?

29. A gas has a volume of 1.75 L at −23°C and 150.0 kPa. At what temperature would the gas occupy 1.30 L at 210.0 kPa?

30. A gas at 7.75×10^4 Pa and 17°C occupies a volume of 850.0 cm^3. At what temperature, in degrees Celsius, would the gas occupy 720.0 cm^3 at 8.10×10^4 Pa?

31. A meteorological balloon contains 250.0 L He at 22°C and 740.0 mm Hg. If the volume of the balloon can vary according to external conditions, what volume would it occupy at an altitude at which the temperature is −52°C and the pressure is 0.750 atm?

32. The balloon in the previous problem will burst if its volume reaches 400.0 L. Given the initial conditions specified in that problem, determine at what temperature, in degrees Celsius, the balloon will burst if its pressure at that bursting point is 0.475 atm.

33. The normal respiratory rate for a human being is 15.0 breaths per minute. The average volume of air for each breath is 505 cm^3 at 20.0°C and 9.95×10^4 Pa. What is the volume of air at STP that an individual breathes in one day? Give your answer in cubic meters.

SECTION 3

Gas Volumes and the Ideal Gas Law

REVIEWING MAIN IDEAS

34. a. What are the restrictions on the use of Gay-Lussac's law of combining volumes?
b. At the same temperature and pressure, what is the relationship between the volume of a gas and the number of molecules present?

35. a. In a balanced chemical equation, what is the relationship between the molar ratios and the volume ratios of gaseous reactants and products?
b. What restriction applies to the use of the volume ratios in solving stoichiometry problems?

36. According to Avogadro,
a. what is the relationship between gas volume and number of moles at constant temperature and pressure?
b. what is the mathematical expression denoting this relationship?

37. What is the relationship between the number of molecules and the mass of 22.4 L of different gases at STP?

38. a. In what situations is the ideal gas law most suitable for calculations?
b. When using this law, why do you have to pay particular attention to units?

39. a. Write the equation for the ideal gas law.
b. What relationship is expressed in the ideal gas law?

372 Chapter 11

PRACTICE PROBLEMS

40. Suppose a 5.00 L sample of O_2 at a given temperature and pressure contains 1.08×10^{23} molecules. How many molecules would be contained in each of the following at the same temperature and pressure?
a. 5.0 L H_2
b. 5.0 L CO_2
c. 10.0 L NH_3

41. How many moles are contained in each of the following at STP?
a. 22.4 L N_2
b. 5.60 L Cl_2
c. 0.125 L Ne
d. 70.0 mL NH_3

42. Find the mass, in grams, of each of the following at STP.
a. 11.2 L H_2
b. 2.80 L CO_2
c. 15.0 mL SO_2
d. 3.40 cm^3 F_2

43. Find the volume, in liters, of each of the following at STP.
a. 8.00 g O_2
b. 3.50 g CO
c. 0.0170 g H_2S
d. 2.25×10^5 kg NH_3

44. Acetylene gas, C_2H_2, undergoes combustion to produce carbon dioxide and water vapor. If 75.0 L CO_2 is produced,
a. how many liters of C_2H_2 are required?
b. what volume of H_2O vapor is produced?
c. what volume of O_2 is required?

45. Assume that 5.60 L H_2 at STP reacts with excess CuO according to the following equation:

$$CuO(s) + H_2(g) \rightarrow Cu(s) + H_2O(g)$$

Make sure the equation is balanced before beginning your calculations.
a. How many moles of H_2 react?
b. How many moles of Cu are produced?
c. How many grams of Cu are produced?

46. If 29.0 L of methane, CH_4, undergoes complete combustion at 0.961 atm and 140°C, how many liters of each product would be present at the same temperature and pressure?

47. If air is 20.9% oxygen by volume,
a. how many liters of air are needed for complete combustion of 25.0 L of octane vapor, C_8H_{18}?
b. what volume of each product is produced?

48. Methanol, CH_3OH, is made by causing carbon monoxide and hydrogen gases to react at high temperature and pressure. If 4.50×10^2 mL CO and 8.25×10^2 mL H_2 are mixed,
a. which reactant is present in excess?
b. how much of that reactant remains after the reaction?
c. what volume of CH_3OH is produced, assuming the same pressure?

49. Calculate the pressure, in atmospheres, exerted by each of the following:
a. 2.50 L HF containing 1.35 mol at 320.0 K
b. 4.75 L NO_2 containing 0.86 mol at 300.0 K
c. 5.50×10^4 mL CO_2 containing 2.15 mol at 57°C

50. Calculate the volume, in liters, occupied by each of the following:
a. 2.00 mol H_2 at 300.0 K and 1.25 atm
b. 0.425 mol NH_3 at 37°C and 0.724 atm
c. 4.00 g O_2 at 57°C and 0.888 atm

51. Determine the number of moles of gas contained in each of the following:
a. 1.25 L at 250.0 K and 1.06 atm
b. 0.80 L at 27°C and 0.925 atm
c. 7.50×10^2 mL at −50.0°C and 0.921 atm

52. Find the mass of each of the following.
a. 5.60 L O_2 at 1.75 atm and 250.0 K
b. 3.50 L NH_3 at 0.921 atm and 27°C
c. 125 mL SO_2 at 0.822 atm and −5°C

SECTION 4

Diffusion and Effusion

REVIEWING MAIN IDEAS

53. Describe in your own words the process of diffusion.

54. At a given temperature, what factor determines the rates at which different molecules undergo diffusion and effusion?

55. Ammonia, NH_3, and alcohol, C_2H_6O, are released together across a room. Which will you smell first?

CHAPTER REVIEW

40. a. 1.08×10^{23} molecules H_2
b. 1.08×10^{23} molecules CO_2
c. 2.16×10^{23} molecules NH_3
41. a. 1.00 mol N_2
b. 0.250 mol Cl_2
c. 5.58×10^{-3} mol Ne
d. 3.13×10^{-3} mol NH_3
42. a. 1.01 g H_2
b. 5.50 g CO_2
c. 0.0429 g SO_2
d. 5.77×10^{-3} g F_2
43. a. 5.60 L O_2
b. 2.80 L CO
c. 0.0112 L H_2S
d. 2.96×10^8 L NH_3
44. a. 37.5 L C_2H_2
b. 37.5 L H_2O
c. 93.8 L O_2
45. a. 0.250 mol H_2
b. 0.250 mol Cu
c. 15.9 g Cu
46. 29.0 L CO_2, 58.0 L H_2O vapor
47. a. 1.50×10^3 L of air
b. 200 L CO_2, 225 L H_2O vapor
48. a. CO
b. 37 mL CO
c. 413 mL CH_3OH
49. a. 14.2 atm
b. 4.5 atm
c. 0.777 atm
50. a. 39.4 L H_2
b. 14.9 L NH_3
c. 3.81 L O_2
51. a. 0.0646 mol
b. 0.030 mol
c. 0.0377 mol
52. a. 15.3 g O_2
b. 2.23 g NH_3
c. 0.299 g SO_2
53. Answers should include the idea that gas molecules that are initially concentrated in one area will spread evenly throughout the space available to them.
54. At the same temperature, heavier molecules have a lower average velocity than lighter molecules. Thus, heavier molecules diffuse and effuse more slowly than lighter molecules. The rate varies inversely with the square root of the molar mass.
55. Both travel by diffusion. Ammonia, whose mass is lower, travels faster.

56. a. $\frac{\text{rate } H_2}{\text{rate } N_2} = 3.72$

b. $\frac{\text{rate } F_2}{\text{rate } Cl_2} = 1.37$

57. $\frac{\text{velocity } H_2}{\text{velocity Ne}} = 3.16$

58. 341 m/s
59. 0.54 atm
60. 2.18 L
61. 313 mL
62. 0.660 atm
63. 579°C
64. 299 K
65. 7940 torr
66. 4.00×10^8 L
67. 64 g/mol
68. 0.839 g
69. 97.2 L
70. CO diffuses approximately 1.7 times as fast as SO_3.
71. 27.9 g/mol
72. 0.0395 mol He
73. 3.67 L, 45.1 g/mol
74. a. An increase in one variable is accompanied by a corresponding decrease in the other variable.
b. An increase in one variable is accompanied by a corresponding increase in the second variable.
75. If all gases behaved ideally at all conditions, the individual gas particles would never exert the attractive forces on one another that are needed to form liquids or solids.
76. Both the pressure exerted by the column of mercury in the tube and the pressure exerted by the atmosphere on the surface of mercury in the dish can be thought of as acting on the imaginary surface of the mercury in the tube that is level with the surface of the mercury in the dish. Because both forces are acting on the same surface, the size of the surface is not a factor in determining the eventual pressures.
77. a. The combined gas law applies when a sample of gas changes from one set of *P*, *V*, and *T* conditions to another. It assumes that the molar quantity of gas does not change.
b. The ideal gas law applies to any situation in which you must determine *P*, *V*, *T*, or *n*, given any three of the four variables.

PRACTICE PROBLEMS

56. Quantitatively compare the rates of effusion for the following pairs of gases at the same temperature and pressure:
a. hydrogen and nitrogen
b. fluorine and chlorine

57. What is the ratio of the average velocity of hydrogen molecules to that of neon atoms at the same temperature and pressure?

58. At a certain temperature and pressure, chlorine molecules have an average velocity of 324 m/s. What is the average velocity of sulfur dioxide molecules under the same conditions?

Mixed Review

REVIEWING MAIN IDEAS

59. A mixture of three gases, A, B, and C, is at a total pressure of 6.11 atm. The partial pressure of gas A is 1.68 atm; that of gas B is 3.89 atm. What is the partial pressure of gas C?

60. A child receives a balloon filled with 2.30 L of helium from a vendor at an amusement park. The temperature outside is 311 K. What will the volume of the balloon be when the child brings it home to an air-conditioned house at 295 K? Assume that the pressure stays the same.

61. A sample of argon gas occupies a volume of 295 mL at 36°C. What volume will the gas occupy at 55°C, assuming constant pressure?

62. A sample of carbon dioxide gas occupies 638 mL at 0.893 atm and 12°C. What will the pressure be at a volume of 881 mL and a temperature of 18°C?

63. At 84°C, a gas in a container exerts a pressure of 0.503 atm. Assuming the size of the container has not changed, at what temperature in Celsius degrees would the pressure be 1.20 atm?

64. A weather balloon at Earth's surface has a volume of 4.00 L at 304 K and 755 mm Hg. If the balloon is released and the volume reaches 4.08 L at 728 mm Hg, what is the temperature?

65. A gas has a pressure of 4.62 atm when its volume is 2.33 L. If the temperature remains constant, what will the pressure be when the volume is changed to 1.03 L? Express the final pressure in torrs.

66. At a deep-sea station that is 200 m below the surface of the Pacific Ocean, workers live in a highly pressurized environment. How many liters of gas at STP must be compressed on the surface to fill the underwater environment with 2.00×10^7 L of gas at 20.0 atm? Assume that temperature remains constant.

67. An unknown gas effuses at 0.850 times the effusion rate of nitrogen dioxide, NO_2. Estimate the molar mass of the unknown gas.

68. A container holds 265 mL of chlorine gas, Cl_2. If the gas sample is at STP, what is its mass?

69. Suppose that 3.11 mol of carbon dioxide is at a pressure of 0.820 atm and a temperature of 39°C. What is the volume of the sample, in liters?

70. Compare the rates of diffusion of carbon monoxide, CO, and sulfur trioxide, SO_3.

71. A gas sample that has a mass of 0.993 g occupies 0.570 L. Given that the temperature is 281 K and the pressure is 1.44 atm, what is the molar mass of the gas?

72. How many moles of helium gas would it take to fill a balloon with a volume of 1000.0 cm^3 when the temperature is 32°C and the atmospheric pressure is 752 mm Hg?

73. A gas sample is collected at 16°C and 0.982 atm. If the sample has a mass of 7.40 g and a volume of 3.96 L, find the volume of the gas at STP and the molar mass.

CRITICAL THINKING

74. Applying Models
a. Why do we say the graph in **Figure 2.2** illustrates an inverse relationship?
b. Why do we say the data plotted in **Figure 2.4** indicate a direct relationship?

75. Inferring Conclusions If all gases behaved as ideal gases under all conditions of temperature and pressure, solid or liquid forms of these substances would not exist. Explain.

78. According to Avogadro's law, equal volumes of gases under the same conditions of pressure and temperature contain equal numbers of molecules. It follows that the volume of a gas is proportional to the number of molecules present under the same conditions of *P* and *T*, $V \propto n$, or $V = kn$. Gay-Lussac did not know of moles and molecules, but he observed that at constant *T* and *P*, volumes of gaseous reactants and products can be expressed in small, whole-number ratios. Today, we know the exact composition of most common substances. Therefore, we can write balanced chemical equations for a reaction by using a set of whole numbers as balancing coefficients to represent the relative numbers of molecules involved in the reaction. In a reaction, a ratio between the number of molecules of two components can be represented as a ratio of the balancing coefficients—simple whole numbers. If these components are gases under the same conditions, we know that volumes are proportional to the number of molecules. Therefore, the volumes will be in simple whole-number ratios, just as the numbers of molecules are.

76. Relating Ideas Pressure is defined as force per unit area. Yet Torricelli found that the diameter of the barometer dish and the surface area of contact between the mercury in the tube and in the dish did not affect the height of mercury that was supported. Explain this seemingly inconsistent observation in view of the relationship between pressure and surface area.

77. Evaluating Methods In solving a problem, what types of conditions involving temperature, pressure, volume, or number of moles would allow you to use
a. the combined gas law?
b. the ideal gas law?

78. Evaluating Ideas Gay-Lussac's law of combining volumes holds true for relative volumes at any proportionate size. Use Avogadro's law to explain why this proportionality exists.

79. Interpreting Graphics The graph below shows velocity distribution curves for the same gas under two different conditions, A and B. Compare the behavior of the gas under conditions A and B in relation to each of the following:
a. temperature
b. average kinetic energy
c. average molecular velocity
d. gas volume
e. gas pressure

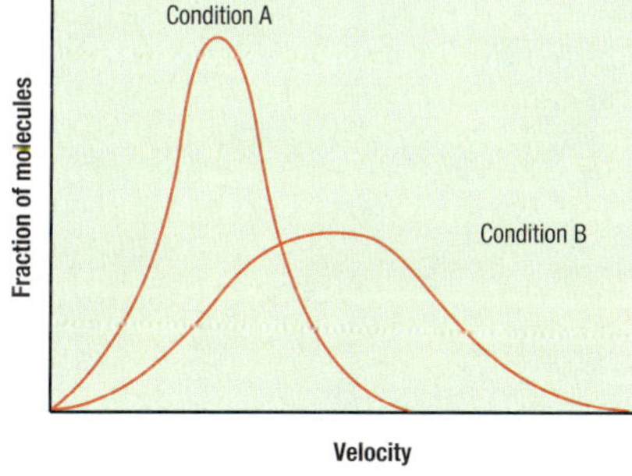

80. Interpreting Concepts The diagrams below represent equal volumes of four different gases.

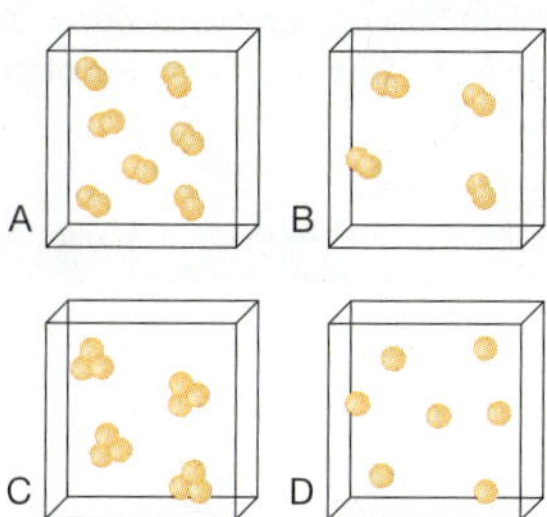

Use the diagrams to answer the following questions:
a. Are these gases at the same temperature and pressure? How do you know?
b. If the molar mass of gas B is 38 g/mol and that of gas C is 46 g/mol, which gas sample is denser?
c. To make the densities of gas samples B and C equal, which gas should expand in volume?
d. If the densities of gas samples A and C are equal, what is the relationship between their molar masses?

RESEARCH AND WRITING

81. Design and conduct a meteorological study to examine the interrelationships among barometric pressure, temperature, humidity, and other weather variables. Prepare a report explaining your results.

82. Conduct library research on attempts made to approach absolute zero and on the interesting properties that materials exhibit near that temperature. Write a report on your findings.

83. How do scuba divers use the laws and principles that describe the behavior of gases to their advantage? What precautions do they take to prevent the bends?

84. Explain the processes involved in the liquefaction of gases. Name some substances that are gases under normal room conditions and that are typically used in the liquid form. Explain why this is so.

79. a. The temperature is greater for B.
b. The average kinetic energy is greater for B.
c. The average molecular velocity is greater for B.
d. There is not enough information to tell.
e. There is not enough information to tell.

80. a. No; if the gases were at the same temperature and pressure, all of the boxes would contain the same number of molecules.
b. gas C
c. gas C
d. The molar mass of gas A is less than that of gas C, because it takes more molecules of A in the same space to equal the density of C.

81. Student answers may vary. Factors that could be discussed include barometric pressure, temperature, humidity, wind speed and direction, and forms of precipitation, such as rain, snow, sleet, and hail.

CHAPTER REVIEW

82. Student answers may vary. Factors that could be discussed include the kinetic-molecular theory and other interpretations of temperature, low temperatures that have been achieved by various techniques (within a few billionths of one kelvin of absolute zero), the microkelvin refrigerator, laser cooling, and perhaps the thermodynamic impossibility of achieving absolute zero.

83. Student answers may vary. Discussion should include the effects of pressure on lung capacity, the necessity of breathing more highly compressed gas when diving to greater depths, and the greater solubility of gases in the blood at these increased pressures. The bends are caused when the diver swims too quickly to the surface. The resulting rapid decompression causes dissolved gases to be released too quickly, causing extreme pain and sometimes death. To avoid the bends, divers either surface very slowly, or enter a compression chamber where the pressure is released very gradually.

84. Student answers may vary. The most obvious processes to be mentioned are cooling below the boiling point at constant pressure and raising the pressure at constant temperature. Other processes are adiabatic expansion (allowing a gas to expand so quickly that no energy as heat enters the system) and use of the Joule-Thompson effect (the effect that occurs when a highly compressed nonideal gas expands into a region of lower pressure, as in an air conditioner). Some substances that are gases under room conditions are typically used in the liquid form, usually to save storage space. Some examples are (1) hydrogen, H_2, for use in fuel cells and in combustion engines; (2) carbon dioxide, CO_2, most of which is used to carbonate soft drinks; (3) natural gas (a mixture of hydrocarbons), principally for use in combustion applications, (4) nitrogen, N_2, used for many cooling applications, and (5) liquefied propane, C_3H_8, and butane, C_4H_{10}, used in many ways, such as home heating and in cigarette lighters.

85. Student answers may vary. Significant points to be mentioned are (1) Gay-Lussac's observation that volumes of gases involved in any chemical reaction, measured at the same temperature and pressure, are always in the ratio of small integers; (2) Avogadro's explanation of this observation by suggesting that (a) a mole of any substance contains the same number of molecules as a mole of any other substance and (b) a mole of any gas occupies the same volume as a mole of any other gas at the same volume and pressure. Avogadro explained remaining discrepancies by proposing that some gaseous elements are diatomic and that some gaseous compounds have formulas containing unequal numbers of atoms (e.g., H_2O, not HO).

86. nitrogen, oxygen, fluorine, and chlorine (also, hydrogen and the noble gases, which are not discussed in the *Elements Handbook*: Appendix A)

87. nitrogen, oxygen, ethylene, ammonia, propylene, and chlorine

88. a. $Ba(s) + 2H_2O(l) \longrightarrow Ba(OH)_2(aq) + H_2(g)$

b. $2Cs(s) + 2HCl(aq) \longrightarrow 2CsCl(aq) + H_2(g)$

c. $2Ga(s) + 6HF(aq) \longrightarrow 2GaF_3(aq) + 3H_2(g)$

d. 61.8 g Ba

e. 120 g Cs, 32.9 g HCl

89. a. The oxidation number of oxygen in oxides is −2, in peroxides it is −1, and in superoxides it is −1/2, or written as O_2^-.

b. 15.8 g Na_2O_2

90. Student answers may vary. Most tire gauges use units of pounds per square inch. A tire gauge measures the pressure in excess of atmospheric pressure. For this reading, the gauge pressure is often denoted "psig." The absolute pressure of the gas is found by adding the atmospheric pressure (14.70 psi at normal atmospheric pressure) to the gauge reading.

91. Student answers may vary. Answers will probably involve smelling various odors, such as perfume, the odor of baking or cooking, perspiration odor, etc. Some students might comment on the role that odor plays in the overall sensation of taste.

CHAPTER REVIEW

85. Write a summary describing how Gay-Lussac's work on combining volumes relates to Avogadro's study of gases. Explain how certain conclusions about gases followed logically from consideration of the work of both scientists.

USING THE HANDBOOK

86. Review the melting point data in the properties tables for each group of the *Elements Handbook* (Appendix A). What elements on the periodic table exist as gases at room temperature?

87. Review in the *Elements Handbook* (Appendix A) the listing of the top 10 chemicals produced in the United States. Which of the top 10 chemicals are gases?

88. Most elements from Groups 1, 2, and 13 will react with water, acids, or bases to produce hydrogen gas. Review the common reactions information in the *Elements Handbook* (Appendix A) and answer the following questions:

a. What is the equation for the reaction of barium with water?

b. What is the equation for the reaction between cesium and hydrochloric acid?

c. What is the equation for the reaction of gallium with hydrofluoric acid?

d. What mass of barium would be needed to react with excess water to produce 10.1 L H_2 at STP?

e. What masses of cesium and hydrochloric acid would be required to produce 10.1 L H_2 at STP?

89. Group 1 metals react with oxygen to produce oxides, peroxides, or superoxides. Review the equations for these common reactions in the *Elements Handbook* (Appendix A), and answer the following:

a. How do oxides, peroxides, and superoxides differ?

b. What mass of product will be formed from a reaction of 5.00 L O_2 with excess sodium? The reaction occurs at 27°C and 1 atm.

ALTERNATIVE ASSESSMENT

90. The air pressure of car tires should be checked regularly for safety reasons and for prevention of uneven tire wear. Find out the units of measurement on a typical tire gauge, and determine how gauge pressure relates to atmospheric pressure.

91. During a typical day, record every instance in which you encounter the diffusion or effusion of gases (for example, when smelling perfume).

92. Performance Qualitatively compare the molecular masses of various gases by noting how long it takes you to smell them from a fixed distance. Work only with materials that are not dangerous, such as flavor extracts, fruit peels, and onions.

93. Performance Design an experiment to gather data to verify the ideal gas law. If your teacher approves of your plan, carry it out. Illustrate your data with a graph, and determine if the data are consistent with the ideal gas law.

92. Student answers may vary. Some answers might even include library or Web searches to learn the identity of various odors and confirm relative molecular masses.

93. Student answers may vary. Reasonable experimental design will keep one or more variables constant and measure the interdependence of the other two, perhaps representing these effects graphically.

Standards-Based Assessment

Answer the following items on a separate piece of paper.

MULTIPLE CHOICE

1. Pressure can be measured in
   A. grams. **C.** pascals.
   B. meters. **D.** liters

2. A sample of oxygen gas has a volume of 150 mL when its pressure is 0.923 atm. If the pressure is increased to 0.987 atm and the temperature remains constant, what will the new volume be?
   A. 140 mL **C.** 200 mL
   B. 160 mL **D.** 240 mL

3. What is the pressure exerted by a 0.500 mol sample of nitrogen in a 10.0 L container at 20°C?
   A. 1.2 kPa **C.** 0.10 kPa
   B. 10 kPa **D.** 120 kPa

4. A sample of gas in a closed container at a temperature of 100.0°C and 3.0 atm is heated to 300.0°C. What is the pressure of the gas at the higher temperature?
   A. 35 atm **C.** 59 atm
   B. 4.6 atm **D.** 9.0 atm

5. An unknown gas effuses twice as fast as CH_4. What is the molar mass of the gas?
   A. 64 g/mol **C.** 8 g/mol
   B. 32 g/mol **D.** 4 g/mol

6. If 3 L N_2 and 3 L H_2 are mixed and react according to the equation below, how many liters of unreacted gas remain? Assume temperature and pressure remain constant.
   $N_2(g) + 3H_2(g) \rightarrow 2NH_3(g)$
   A. 4 L **C.** 2 L
   B. 3 L **D.** 1 L

7. Avogadro's law states that
   A. equal numbers of moles of gases at the same conditions occupy equal volumes, regardless of the identity of the gases.
   B. at constant pressure, gas volume is directly proportional to absolute temperature.
   C. the volume of a gas is inversely proportional to its amount in moles.
   D. at constant temperature, gas volume is inversely proportional to pressure.

SHORT ANSWER

8. Give a molecular explanation for the observation that the pressure of a gas increases when the gas volume is decreased.

9. The graph below shows a plot of volume versus pressure for a particular gas sample at constant temperature. Answer the following questions by referring to the graph. No calculation is necessary.
   a. What is the volume of this gas sample at standard pressure?
   b. What is the volume of this gas sample at 4.0 atm pressure?
   c. At what pressure would this gas sample occupy a volume of 5.0 L?

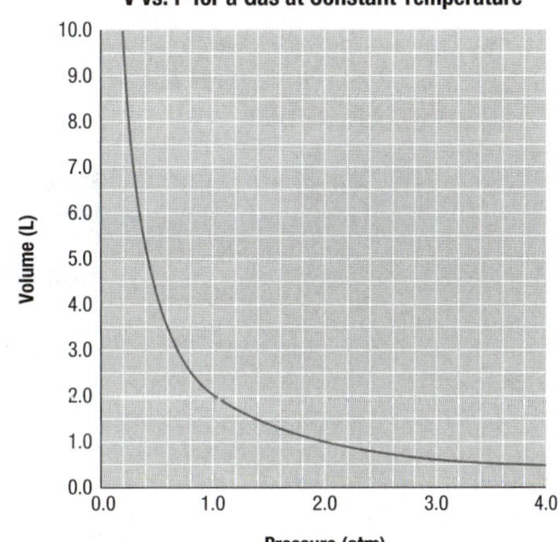

EXTENDED RESPONSE

10. Refer to the plot in question 9. Suppose the same gas sample were heated to a higher temperature, and a new graph of *V* versus *P* were plotted. Would the new plot be identical to this one? If not, how would it differ?

Test Tip
If you are permitted to, draw a line through each incorrect answer choice as you eliminate it.

STANDARDS-BASED ASSESSMENT

To give students practice under more realistic testing conditions, give them 60 minutes to answer all of the questions in this Standardized Test Preparation.

Test Answers

1. C
2. A
3. D
4. B
5. D
6. C
7. A
8. The molecules are closer together, so the frequency of collisions per unit volume increases.
9. **a.** 2.0 L
   b. 0.5 L
   c. 0.4 atm
10. The plot would not be identical to this one. It would have a similar shape, but would appear higher on the graph. This is because at any pressure, the volume would be higher at the higher temperature.

Solutions

1 Core Instruction

Chapter Resources

- The Teacher's Edition wrap has extensive teaching support for every lesson, including Misconception Alerts, Teach from Visuals, Demonstrations, Teaching Tips, Differentiated Instruction, and Problem Solving support.
- Several additional presentation tools are available online for every chapter, including Animated Chemistry features and Visual Concepts.
- You can open your lesson with the Why It Matters Video: Solutions.

Section	Instruction	Labs and Demonstrations Go Online for Materials Lists and Solutions Lists.
12.1	**Textbook:** Types of Mixtures **Animated Chemistry:** Solution Dilution **Teaching Visuals:** Particle Model for a Solution • Fresh Water Versus Salt Water • Particle Models for Gold and Gold Alloy • Particle Model for a Suspension • Electrical Conductivity of Solutions • Properties of Solutions, Colloids, and Suspensions **PowerPresentations**	**Demonstration:** Volume of Solutions **QuickLab:** Observing Solutions, Suspensions, and Colloids **Lab:** Separation of Pen Inks by Paper Chromatography (Core Skill) **Lab:** A Close Look at Soaps and Detergents (Core Skill) **Lab:** The Counterfeit Drugs (Forensics) **Lab:** The Athletic Rivals (Forensics)
12.2	**Textbook:** The Solution Process **Teaching Visuals:** Mass of Solute Added Versus Mass of Solute Dissolved • Models for Miscible and Immiscible Solutions • Hydrogen Bonding Between a Solute and a Solvent • Particle Model for Soluble and Insoluble Substances • Solubility vs. Temperature • Predicting Solubility • Energy Changes in the Solution Process • Solubility of Common Compounds • Solubility Versus Temperature for Some Solid Solutes **PowerPresentations**	**Demonstration:** Solution Equilibrium **Demonstration:** Seeding a Supersaturated Solution **Demonstration:** Cold Water vs. Hot Water **Lab:** Effect of Temperature on Solubility of a Salt (Probeware) **Lab:** Allergic to Color (STEM)
12.3	**Textbook:** Concentration of Solutions **Teaching Visuals:** Preparing 1.000 L of a 0.5000 M Solution • Calculating Molarity Given Mass of Solute and Volume of Solution • Moles Solute vs. Volume • Making a Molal Solution • Calculating Mass of Solute Given Molarity and Volume of Solution • Measures of Concentration • Concentration Units **PowerPresentations**	**Lab:** The Fast Food Arson (Forensics) **Lab:** The Untimely Death (Forensics) **Lab:** Testing Reaction Combinations of H_2 and O_2 (Core Skill)

2 Support and Intervention

- **Interactive Reader** (English and Spanish)
- **Study Guide**
- **Interactive Review:** Review Games, Concept Maps, and Section Self-Checks
- **Scientific Reasoning Skill Builder**
- **Learn It! Videos**
- **Solve It! Cards**
- **Interactive Demos**
- **Sample Problem Sets**

3 Specialized Support

- **Chapter Summary Audio Files**
- **Interactive Reader Audio Files**
- **Differentiated Instruction:** Inclusion, Below Level, and English Learners (TE wrap)

Enrichment and Challenge

- **Differentiated Instruction:** Pre-AP (TE wrap)
- **Cross-Disciplinary Connection:** Artificial Blood (SE)
- **WebLinks**

Assessment

- **Section Formative Assessments** (SE)
- **Section Quizzes**
- **Chapter Review** (SE)
- **Chapter Tests A and B**
- **Alternative Assessment** (TE wrap)
- **Online Assessment and Remediation**
- **ExamView Banks**

Where do I find it?

		PRINT	DVD	ONLINE
1	Animated Chemistry		■	■
	Demonstrations (TE wrap)	■		■
	Interactive Whiteboard		■	■
	Labs		■	■
	PowerPresentations		■	■
	QuickLabs	■	■	■
	Teaching Visuals		■	■
	Textbook	■	■	■
	Visual Concepts		■	■
	Why It Matters Videos		■	■
2	Interactive Demos		■	■
	Interactive Reader	■	■	■
	Interactive Reviews		■	■
	Learn It! Videos		■	■
	Sample Problem Sets		■	■
	Scientific Reasoning Skill Builder		■	■
	Smart Grapher Tool		■	■
	Solve It! Cards		■	■
	Study Guide		■	■
3	Chapter Summary Audio Files		■	■
	Differentiated Instruction (TE wrap)	■		
	Interactive Reader Audio Files		■	■

CHAPTER 12

Chapter Overview

Section 1 outlines characteristics that distinguish solutions from suspensions and colloids.

Section 2 covers the physical and chemical factors that affect solubility.

Section 3 presents concentration expressed as molarity and molality with calculations.

▼ Focus and Motivate

Activate Prior Knowledge

Students may need a review of the following concepts:

- properties and types of mixtures
- electronegativity
- molecular polarity and intermolecular forces
- mass and mole relationships

About the Image

The liquid in the beaker is a solution, which is a homogeneous mixture of two or more substances in a single phase.

Why It Matters

Students can access the video online and find other helpful resources at **HMDScience.com**.

Lab Preview

The following labs and demonstrations support the concepts presented in this chapter.

LABS

Separation of Pen Inks by Paper Chromatography (Core Skill)

A Close Look at Soaps and Detergents

The Counterfeit Drugs (Forensics)

The Athletic Rivals (Forensics)

Effect of Temperature on Solubility of a Salt (Probeware)

The Fast Food Arson (Forensics)

The Untimely Death (Forensics)

Testing Reaction Combinations of H_2 and O_2

Allergic to Color (STEM)

QUICKLAB

Observing Solutions, Suspensions, and Colloids

DEMONSTRATIONS

Volume of Solutions

Solution Equilibrium

Seeding a Supersaturated Solution

Cold Water vs. Hot Water

Types of Mixtures

SECTION 1

Main Ideas

- Solutions are homogeneous mixtures.
- The particles in a suspension are large.
- Colloids have particles of intermediate size.
- Electrolytes are ionic solutions that conduct electricity.

Key Terms

soluble, solution, solvent, solute, suspension, colloid, electrolyte, nonelectrolyte

It is easy to determine that some materials are mixtures because you can see their component parts. For example, soil is a mixture of substances, including small rocks and decomposed animal and plant matter. You can see this by picking up some soil in your hand and looking at it closely. Milk, on the other hand, does not appear to be a mixture, but in fact it is. Milk is composed principally of fats, proteins, milk sugar, and water. If you look at milk under a microscope, it will look something like **Figure 1.1a.** You can see round lipid (fat) droplets that measure from 1 to 10 μm in diameter. Irregularly shaped casein (protein) particles that are about 0.2 μm wide can also be seen. Both milk and soil are examples of ***heterogeneous mixtures*** because their composition is not uniform.

Salt (sodium chloride) and water form a ***homogeneous mixture***. The sodium and chloride ions are interspersed among the water molecules, and the mixture appears uniform throughout, as illustrated in **Figure 1.1b.**

MAIN IDEA

Solutions are homogeneous mixtures.

Suppose a sugar cube is dropped into a glass of water. You know from experience that the sugar will dissolve. Sugar is described as "soluble in water." By **soluble** we mean capable of being dissolved. As it dissolves, a sugar lump gradually disappears as sugar molecules leave the surface of their crystals and mix with water molecules. Eventually all the sugar molecules become uniformly distributed among the water molecules, as indicated by the equally sweet taste of any part of the mixture. All visible traces of the solid sugar are gone. Such a mixture is called a solution. A **solution** is a homogeneous mixture of two or more substances uniformly dispersed throughout a single phase.

FIGURE 1.1

Heterogeneous and Homogeneous Mixtures

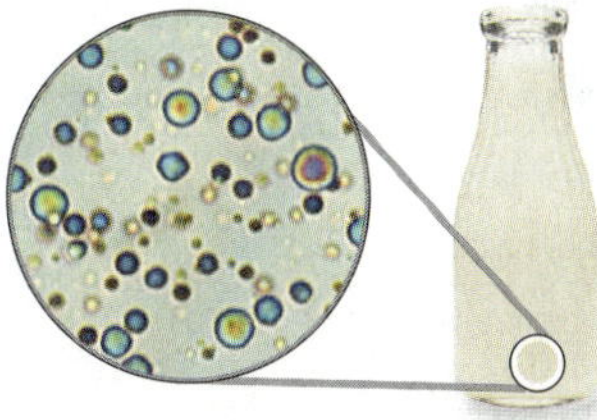

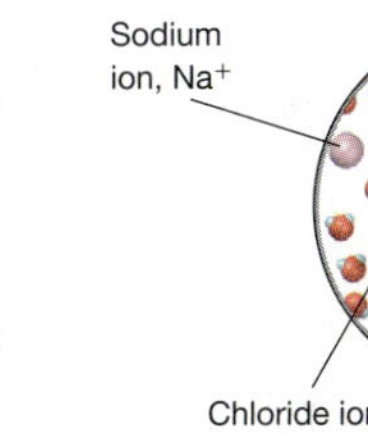

(a) Milk is a heterogeneous mixture that consists of visible particles in a nonuniform arrangement.

(b) Salt water is an example of a homogeneous mixture. Ions and water molecules are in a random arrangement.

Differentiated Instruction

INCLUSION

To help visual learners understand why milk is a heterogeneous mixture, show the class a glass of milk. Be sure to use a clear glass so that students can see the milk. Have students explain why they cannot tell if milk is a homogeneous or heterogeneous mixture. Students should point out that there is no way of telling if the milk's composition is uniform to determine if milk is a homogeneous or heterogeneous mixture. Slowly add some white vinegar to the milk until clumps appear. Filter the mixture to trap the solids, which are known as the *curds*. The liquid is called the *whey*. Inform students that the vinegar reacted with the casein (proteins) in the milk to form a precipitate. Point out that the nonuniform distribution of the particles, such as casein, make milk a heterogeneous mixture.

SECTION 1

Plan and Prepare ▼

Objectives

Upon completion of this section, students should be able to do the following:

- Distinguish between heterogeneous and homogeneous mixtures.
- List three different solute-solvent combinations.
- Compare the properties of suspensions, colloids, and solutions.
- Distinguish between electrolytes and nonelectrolytes.

Classroom Catalyst

Bring two samples of dirt to class. One sample should contain small rocks, and the other should contain a few rocks that are much larger. It should be obvious to students that it is easier to use a sieve to separate the large rocks from their dirt sample than it is to separate the small rocks from their dirt sample. In this section, students will be looking at different types of mixtures, all of which are classified by the size of the particles in them.

Teach ▼

READING TOOLKIT

BRAINSTORMING Define the term *solution*. Have students brainstorm a list of common solutions. Then have them use Section 1 and other resources to confirm or deny the items on their lists, giving reasons why each item is or is not a solution. Though familiar with many water-based solutions, students may be surprised to learn that air, a mixture of gases, and brass, a mixture of solids, are also solutions.

TEACH FROM VISUALS

FIGURE 1.1 Students should note that the microscopic view of milk does not show its chemical constituents like the solution on the right does. The globules represent lipids and proteins, large organic molecules that are too complex to show in this small view.

▼ Teach *continued*

TEACH FROM VISUALS

FIGURE 1.2 Students should note that the particle models represent the homogeneous nature of solutions. Use these models to establish the difference between solutes composed of electrolytes and solutes composed of nonelectrolytes. Ask students which of these two solutions would conduct electricity.

Classroom Discussion

Ask students to list common solvents found in their homes. Examples include water, kerosene, mineral oil, turpentine, paint remover, and nail polish remover.

Demonstration

VOLUME OF SOLUTIONS

Obtain **four 100-mL graduated cylinders,** and fill each with one of the following substances: **50 mL of 95% ethanol, 50 mL of distilled water, 50 mL of sucrose,** and **50 mL of hot water (≈ 70°C).** Ask students to predict the volume of the solution made from 50 mL of ethanol and 50 mL of water. Ask them to make the same prediction about the volumes of the solution made from 50 mL of 95% ethanol and 50 mL of water and the solution made from 50 mL of sucrose and 50 mL of hot water. The ethanol-water solution should be about 92 mL, and the sucrose-water solution should be about 75 mL.

Safety Ethanol is flammable. Limit the amount in the room to 100 mL. Make sure there are no sources of ignition in the room.

Disposal All liquids may be poured down the drain.

FIGURE 1.2

Solutes and Solvents The solute in a solution can be a solid, liquid, or gas.

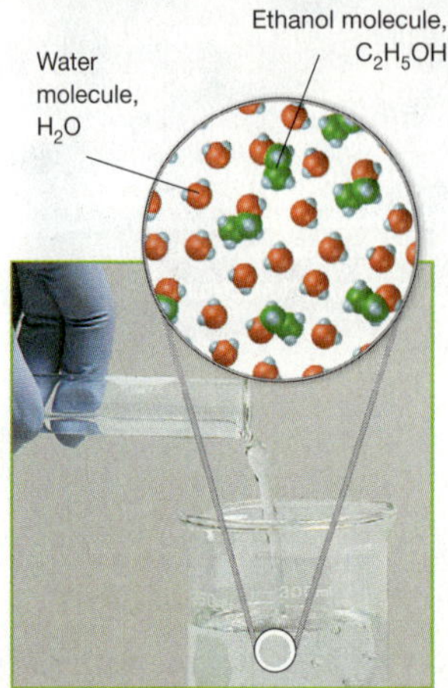

(a) The ethanol-water solution is made from a liquid solute in a liquid solvent.

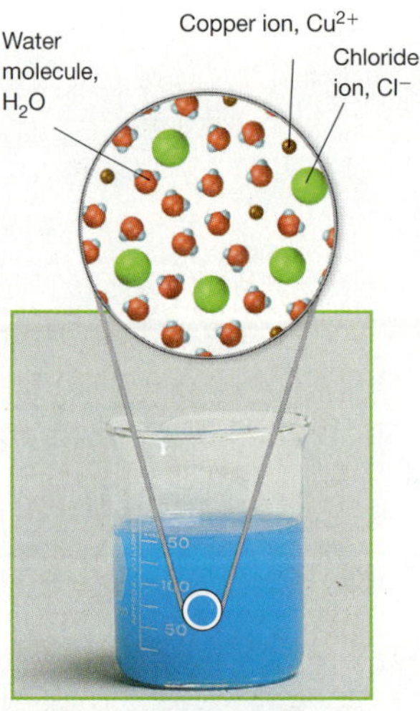

(b) The copper(II) chloride–water solution is made from a solid solute in a liquid solvent. Note that the composition of each solution is uniform.

Components of Solutions

In a solution, atoms, molecules, or ions are thoroughly mixed, resulting in a mixture that has the same composition and properties throughout. In the simplest type of solution, such as a sugar-water solution, the particles of one substance are randomly mixed with the particles of another substance. **The dissolving medium in a solution is called the solvent, and the substance dissolved in a solution is called the solute.** The solute is generally designated as that component of a solution that is of lesser quantity. In the ethanol-water solution shown in **Figure 1.2,** ethanol is the solute and water is the solvent. Occasionally, these terms have little meaning. For example, in a 50%-50% solution of ethanol and water, it would be difficult and unnecessary to say which is the solvent and which the solute.

In a solution, the dissolved solute particles are so small that they cannot be seen. They remain mixed with the solvent indefinitely, as long as the existing conditions remain unchanged. If the solutions in **Figure 1.2** are poured through filter paper, both the solute and the solvent will pass through the paper. The solute-particle dimensions are those of atoms, molecules, and ions—which range from about 0.01 to 1 nm in diameter.

Types of Solutions

Solutions may exist as gases, liquids, or solids. Some possible solute-solvent combinations of gases, liquids, and solids in solutions are summarized in **Figure 1.3.** Note each has a defined solvent and solute.

Many alloys, such as brass (made from zinc and copper) and sterling silver (made from silver and copper), are solid solutions in which the atoms of two or more metals are uniformly mixed. By properly choosing the proportions of each metal in the alloy, many desirable properties can be obtained. For example, alloys can have more strength and greater resistance to corrosion than the pure metals. Pure gold (24K), for instance, is too soft to use in jewelry. Alloying it with silver and copper greatly increases its strength and hardness while retaining its appearance and corrosion resistance. **Figure 1.4** (on the next page) shows a comparison between pure gold and a gold alloy. 14-karat gold is a solution because the gold, silver, and copper are evenly mixed at the atomic level.

FIGURE 1.3

SOME SOLUTE-SOLVENT COMBINATIONS FOR SOLUTIONS

Solute state	Solvent state	Example
gas	gas	oxygen in nitrogen
gas	liquid	carbon dioxide in water
liquid	liquid	alcohol in water
liquid	solid	mercury in silver and tin (dental amalgam)
solid	liquid	sugar in water
solid	solid	copper in nickel (Monel™ alloy)

Differentiated Instruction

INCLUSION

To help visual learners distinguish between solute and solvent, dissolve some copper(II) chloride crystals in water to make a blue-green solution. Next, use a straw to blow into a beaker of water. Ask students to first identify the solute and the solvent in each solution, then describe the difference between the solute-solvent states of the two solutions. Dissolving copper(II) chloride crystals in water is a solid solute in a liquid solvent, while blowing carbon dioxide into water is a gas solute in a liquid solvent.

ENGLISH LEARNERS

Students may have difficulty distinguishing the words *solute*, *solvent*, and *solution*, since all three begin with the same syllable. Suggest that students sketch a diagram in their notebooks to which they can refer as needed. Their diagrams should show a container of liquid with a spoonful of sugar or salt being added. Label each part of diagram with the appropriate word.

FIGURE 1.4

Pure Gold vs. Gold Alloy Pure gold is too soft to use in jewelry. Alloying it with other metals increases its strength and hardness, while retaining its appearance and corrosion resistance.

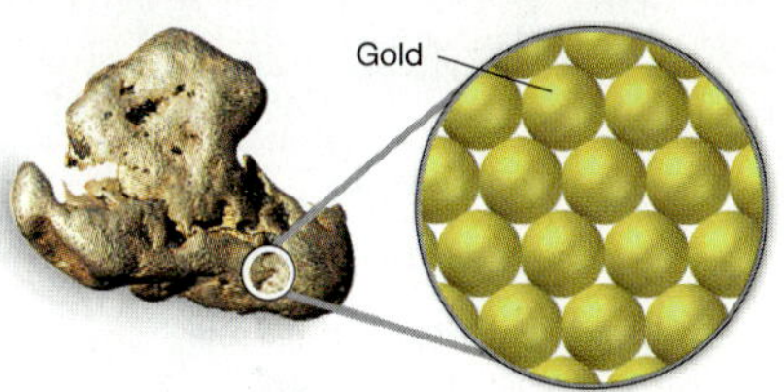

(a) 24-karat gold is pure gold.

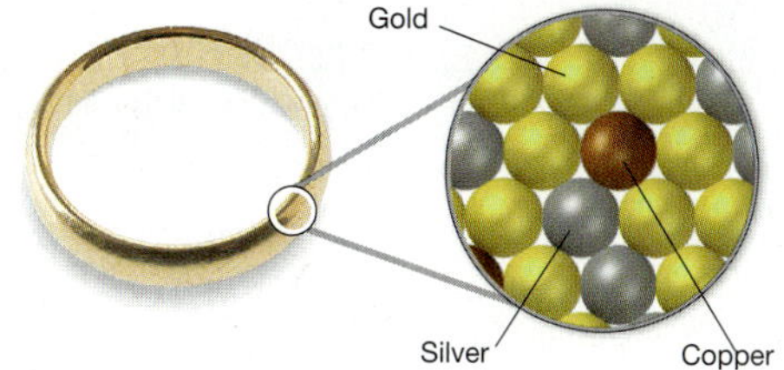

(b) 14-karat gold is an alloy of gold with silver and copper. 14-karat gold is 14/24, or 58.3%, gold.

MAIN IDEA

The particles in a suspension are large.

If the particles in a solvent are so large that they settle out unless the mixture is constantly stirred or agitated, the mixture is called a suspension. Think of a jar of muddy water. If left undisturbed, particles of soil collect on the bottom of the jar. The soil particles are denser than the solvent, water. Gravity pulls them to the bottom of the container. Particles over 1000 nm in diameter—1000 times as large as atoms, molecules, or ions—form suspensions. The particles in suspension can be separated from heterogeneous mixtures by passing the mixture through a filter.

MAIN IDEA

Colloids have particles of intermediate size.

Particles that are intermediate in size between those in solutions and suspensions form mixtures known as colloidal dispersions, or simply colloids. Particles between 1 nm and 1000 nm in diameter may form colloids. After large soil particles settle out of muddy water, the water is often still cloudy because colloidal particles remain dispersed in the water. If the cloudy mixture is poured through a filter, the colloidal particles will pass through the filter, and the mixture will remain cloudy. The particles in a colloid are small enough to be suspended throughout the solvent by the constant movement of the surrounding molecules. The colloidal particles make up the *dispersed phase,* and water is the *dispersing medium.* Many common things you use regularly, such as milk, hair spray, and photographic film, are colloids. Similar to solutions, colloids can be classified according to their dispersed phase and dispersed medium. For example, a solid might be dispersed in a liquid, as is the case with many paints, or a gas might be dispersed in a liquid, as is the case with foams such as whipped cream. The different types of colloids have common names you may recognize. For example, an *emulsion* is a liquid in a liquid, like milk. And clouds and fog, liquids dispersed in gas, are *liquid aerosols.* **Figure 1.5** on the next page lists these different types of colloids and gives some examples of each one.

TEACH FROM TABLES

FIGURE 1.3 Have students identify specific, common examples of each type of solution. For example, the oxygen gas, dissolved in water, upon which fish depend.

Misconception Alert!

Many students think solvents must be liquids. Use **Figure 1.3** to remind them that many solutions do not involve a liquid solvent. A common example is metal alloy, which is a solution of two metals. The metal in the greatest abundance is the solvent, and the other metals in the alloy are the solutes.

Application

Lecithin is a common emulsifying agent. Emulsions are mixtures that consist of colloidal-sized particles. The emulsifying agent causes the solutes and solvent to form a colloidal-type mixture. Lecithin is used in margarine, mayonnaise, chocolate, candy, baked goods, salad dressing, printing inks, soaps, and cosmetics.

Teaching Tip

Alloys are discussed in greater detail in the *Elements Handbook* in Appendix A.

INCLUSION

To help visual learners understand the properties of a colloid, show them a sample of gelatin. Point out that gelatin is an example of a colloid. Inform students that this colloid exists in the gel state. Heat a small sample of the gelatin in a test tube until it liquefies. Point out that the colloid is now in the sol state. Ask students how the sol can be transformed back into a gel. Students should suggest that the colloid be placed in a refrigerator to turn the sol back into a gel.

▼ Teach *continued*

ChemisTrivia

Thomas Graham, an English chemist, began the study of colloids in 1861. Because the first colloids were gelatin or glue, he used the Greek word *kolla*, meaning "glue," as the root for the name.

TEACH FROM TABLES

FIGURE 1.5 Have students think of common examples of different types of colloids. For example, shaving cream is a foam.

TEACH FROM TABLES

FIGURE 1.7 Be sure students notice that a major distinguishing characteristic of solutions, colloids, and suspensions is the size of their solute particles. Ask students to predict whether the components of a solution are separated with filter paper or a centrifuge.

Teaching Tip

Smog is a combination of a solid aerosol and a liquid aerosol—that is, it consists of both solid and liquid particles dispersed in gas.

FIGURE 1.5

CLASSES OF COLLOIDS

Class of colloid	Phases	Example
sol	solid dispersed in liquid	paints, mud
gel	solid network extending throughout liquid	gelatin
liquid emulsion	liquid dispersed in a liquid	milk, mayonnaise
foam	gas dispersed in liquid	shaving cream, whipped cream
solid aerosol	solid dispersed in gas	smoke, airborne particulate matter, auto exhaust
liquid aerosol	liquid dispersed in gas	fog, mist, clouds, aerosol spray
solid emulsion	liquid dispersed in solid	cheese, butter

FIGURE 1.6

Tyndall Effect A beam of light distinguishes a colloid from a solution. The particles in a colloid will scatter light, making the beam visible. The mixture of gelatin and water in the jar on the right is a colloid. The mixture of water and sodium chloride in the jar on the left is a true solution.

Tyndall Effect

Many colloids appear homogeneous because the individual particles cannot be seen. The particles are, however, large enough to scatter light. You have probably noticed that a headlight beam is visible from the side on a foggy night. Known as the *Tyndall effect*, this occurs when light is scattered by colloidal particles dispersed in a transparent medium. The Tyndall effect is a property that can be used to distinguish between a solution and a colloid, as demonstrated in **Figure 1.6.**

The distinctive properties of solutions, colloids, and suspensions are summarized in **Figure 1.7.** The individual particles of a colloid can be detected under a microscope if a bright light is cast on the specimen at a right angle. The particles, which appear as tiny specks of light, are seen to move rapidly in a random motion. This motion is due to collisions of rapidly moving molecules and is called *Brownian motion*, after its discoverer, Robert Brown. Brownian motion is not simply a casual curiosity for interesting lighting effects. In fact, it is one of the strongest macroscopic observations that science has for assuming matter is ultimately composed of particulate atoms and molecules. Only small, randomly moving particles could produce such effects.

FIGURE 1.7

PROPERTIES OF SOLUTIONS, COLLOIDS, AND SUSPENSIONS

Solutions	Colloids	Suspensions
Homogeneous	Heterogeneous	Heterogeneous
Particle size: 0.01–1 nm; can be atoms, ions, molecules	Particle size: 1–1000 nm, dispersed; can be aggregates or large molecules	Particle size: over 1000 nm, suspended; can be large particles or aggregates
Do not separate on standing	Do not separate on standing	Particles settle out
Cannot be separated by filtration	Cannot be separated by filtration	Can be separated by filtration
Do not scatter light	Scatter light (Tyndall effect)	May scatter light, but are not transparent

Differentiated Instruction

PRE-AP

Have students explain how the Tyndall effect is responsible for the blue color of the sky, blue eyes, a blue moon, and the opalescence of some gemstones. Students can also report on why physicists refer to this phenomenon as the *Rayleigh effect* rather than the Tyndall effect.

ENGLISH LEARNERS

Students can better recognize the meanings of words when they can find a way to tie their meanings in with the words themselves. The word *electrolyte* sounds like "electric light" —and an electrolyte will complete an electric circuit, allowing an electric light bulb to light.

QuickLAB: OBSERVING SOLUTIONS, SUSPENSIONS, AND COLLOIDS

PROCEDURE

1. Prepare seven mixtures, each containing 250 mL of water and one of the following substances.
   a. 12 g of sucrose
   b. 3 g of soluble starch
   c. 5 g of clay
   d. 2 mL of food coloring
   e. 2 g of sodium borate
   f. 50 mL of cooking oil
   g. 3 g of gelatin

   Making the gelatin mixture: Soften the gelatin in 65 mL of cold water, and then add 185 mL of boiling water.
2. Observe the seven mixtures and their characteristics. Record the appearance of each mixture after stirring.
3. Transfer to individual test tubes 10 mL of each mixture that does not separate after stirring. Shine a flashlight on each mixture in a dark room. Make note of the mixtures in which the path of the light beam is visible.

DISCUSSION

1. Using your observations, classify each mixture as a solution, suspension, or colloid.
2. What characteristics did you use to classify each mixture?

MATERIALS

- balance
- 7 beakers, 400 mL
- clay
- cooking oil
- flashlight
- gelatin, plain
- hot plate (to boil H_2O)
- red food coloring
- sodium borate ($Na_2B_4O_7 \bullet 10H_2O$)
- soluble starch
- stirring rod
- sucrose
- test-tube rack
- water

SAFETY

Wear safety goggles and an apron.

MAIN IDEA

Electrolytes are ionic solutions that conduct electricity.

Substances that dissolve in water are classified according to whether they yield molecules or ions in solution. When an ionic compound dissolves, the positive and negative ions separate from each other and are surrounded by water molecules. These solute ions are free to move, making it possible for an electric current to pass through the solution. A substance that dissolves in water to give a solution that conducts electric current is called an **electrolyte.** Sodium chloride, NaCl, is an electrolyte, as is any soluble ionic compound. Certain highly polar molecular compounds, such as hydrogen chloride, HCl, are also electrolytes because HCl molecules form the ions H_3O^+ and Cl^- when dissolved in water.

By contrast, a solution containing neutral solute molecules does not conduct electric current because it does not contain mobile, charged particles. A substance that dissolves in water to give a solution that does not conduct an electric current is called a **nonelectrolyte.** Sugar is a nonelectrolyte.

QuickLab

BACKGROUND

Three different types of mixtures—solutions, colloids, and suspensions—can be identified by using a beam of light to illustrate the Tyndall effect. If a mixture is transparent and the Tyndall effect is not seen, the mixture is a solution. If the mixture shows the Tyndall effect and does not settle, it is a colloid. If the mixture shows the Tyndall effect and settles, it is a suspension.

DISCUSSION

1. sucrose in water: solution; starch in water: colloid; clay in water: suspension; food coloring in water: solution; sodium borate in water: solution; cooking oil in water: suspension; gelatin in water: colloid
2. If a mixture is cloudy or displays the Tyndall effect, then it is either a colloid or a suspension. A suspension can be identified by its ability to settle out.

ChemisTrivia

In 1884, Svante Arrhenius nearly failed his doctoral exam by suggesting that copper chloride dissociates in water to form copper and chloride ions. He received his doctorate, but with the lowest possible grade. Nineteen years later, he was awarded the Nobel Prize for the same theory.

INCLUSION

Use an electrical conductivity apparatus to help visual learners understand the concepts of *solution*, *electrolyte*, and *conductivity*. Show that distilled water does not contain electrolytes, as evidenced by the light bulb not glowing when the apparatus is placed in the water. Dissolve a small amount of sodium chloride in the water and show students that electrolytes are present in solution. Discard the solution and repeat the procedure by adding a different solid or liquid substance to the distilled water. Write the chemical formula for each substance on the board and have students predict whether electrolytes will form in solution. Students should recognize that ionic compounds can produce electrolytes when dissolved in water.

▼ Teach *continued*

TEACH FROM VISUALS

FIGURE 1.8 As students inspect the figure on this page, ask them why aqueous solutions with electrolyte solutes conduct electricity and solutions with nonelectrolyte solutes do not.

Critical Thinking

Answer: In **Figure 1.8a**, the light bulb is lit; salt is ionic and polar, so salt conducts electricity. In **Figure 1.8b**, the light bulb is not lit; sugar is covalently bonded and non-polar, so sugar water does not conduct electricity. In **Figure 1.8c**, the light bulb is lit; HCl is ionic and polar, so an HCl-water solution conducts electricity.

▼ Assess and Reteach

Assess Use the Formative Assessment on this page to evaluate student mastery of the section.

Reteach For students who need additional instruction, download the Section Study Guide.

Response to Intervention To reassess students' mastery, use the Section Quiz, available to print or to take directly online at **HMDScience.com**.

FIGURE 1.8

Electrolytes and Nonelectrolytes

Chloride ion, Cl^-
Water molecule, H_2O
Sodium ion, Na^+
Sugar molecule, $C_{12}H_{22}O_{11}$
Water molecule, H_2O
Hydronium ion, H_3O^+
Water molecule, H_2O
Chloride ion, Cl^-

(a) Salt solution—electrolyte solute

(b) Sugar solution—nonelectrolyte solute

(c) Hydrochloric acid solution—electrolyte solute

CRITICAL THINKING

Analyze Observe the three solutions. Based on your analysis, explain what is happening in each part (a, b, and c).

Figure 1.8 shows an apparatus for testing the conductivity of solutions. Electrodes are attached to a power supply and make contact with the test solution. If the test solution provides a conducting path, the light bulb will glow. A nonconducting solution is like an open switch between the electrodes, and there is no current in the circuit. The light bulb glows brightly if a solution that is a good conductor is tested. For a moderately conductive solution, the light bulb is dim. If a solution is a poor conductor, the light bulb does not glow at all; such solutions contain solutes that are nonelectrolytes.

SECTION 1 FORMATIVE ASSESSMENT

Reviewing Main Ideas

1. Classify the following as either a heterogeneous or homogeneous mixture. Explain your answers.
a. orange juice **b.** tap water

2. a. What are substances called whose water solutions conduct electricity?
b. Why does a salt solution conduct electricity?
c. Why does a sugar-water solution not conduct electricity?

3. Make a drawing of the particles in an NaCl solution to show why this solution conducts electricity. Make a drawing of the particles in an NaCl crystal to show why pure salt does not conduct.

4. Describe one way to prove that a mixture of sugar and water is a solution and that a mixture of sand and water is not a solution.

5. Name the solute and solvent in the following:
a. 14-karat gold
b. corn syrup
c. carbonated, or sparkling, water

Critical Thinking

6. ANALYZING INFORMATION If you allow a container of sea water to sit in the sun, the liquid level gets lower and lower, and finally crystals appear. What is happening?

Answers to Section Assessment

1. a. heterogeneous; The pulp and aqueous components together constitute a suspension.
b. homogeneous; The water and solutes together constitute a solution.

2. a. electrolytes
b. A salt solution conducts electricity because mobile ions can move a charge from one point in the solution to another.
c. A sugar solution does not conduct electricity because there are no charged particles in the solution.

3. Student drawings should look similar to **Figure 1.8a,** showing ions dispersed in a solvent. The solid NaCl should show an orderly arrangement. The ions are not free to move.

4. Sand in water can settle or be filtered out, proving that it is not a solution. Dissolved sugar cannot be removed from water through settling or filtration; the water must be evaporated.

5.

	solvent	solute
a.	gold	silver, copper
b.	water	sugar
c.	water	carbon dioxide

6. Water (the solvent) is evaporating, leaving behind the dissolved salts (solutes) as solids.

The Solution Process

SECTION 2

Main Ideas

- Several factors affect dissolving.
- Solubility is a measure of how well one substance dissolves in another.
- A change in energy accompanies solution formation.

Key Terms

solution equilibrium	solubility	Henry's Law
saturated solution	hydration	effervescence
unsaturated solution	immiscible	solvated
supersaturated solution	miscible	enthalpy of solution

MAIN IDEA

Several factors affect dissolving.

If you have ever tried to dissolve sugar in iced tea, you know that temperature has something to do with how quickly a solute dissolves. What other factors affect how quickly you can dissolve sugar in iced tea?

Increasing the Surface Area of the Solute

Sugar dissolves as sugar molecules leave the crystal surface and mix with water molecules. The same is true for any solid solute in a liquid solvent: molecules or ions of the solute are attracted by the solvent.

Because the dissolution process occurs at the surface of the solute, it can be speeded up if the surface area of the solute is increased. Crushing sugar that is in cubes or large crystals increases its surface area. In general, the more finely divided a substance is, the greater the surface area per unit mass and the more quickly it dissolves. **Figure 2.1** shows a model of solutions that are made from the same solute but have different amounts of surface area exposed to the solvent.

FIGURE 2.1

Rates of Dissolution The rate at which a solid solute dissolves can be increased by increasing the surface area. A powdered solute has a greater surface area exposed to solvent particles and therefore dissolves faster than a solute in large crystals.

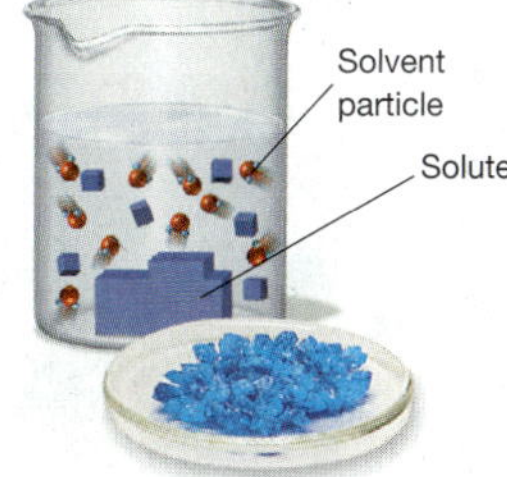

$CuSO_4 \cdot 5H_2O$ large crystals

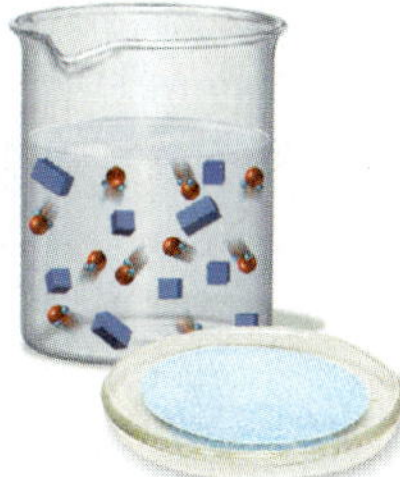

$CuSO_4 \cdot 5H_2O$ powdered (increased surface area)

Differentiated Instruction

BELOW LEVEL

Have students imagine that two people are drinking coffee together. One person adds two sugar cubes to his or her cup, while the other person adds two packets of powdered sugar. Ask students which person has to stir the coffee longer to dissolve the sugar. Have them explain the reasons for their answer.

INCLUSION

Help hands-on learners understand how surface area affects the solution process. Give students two sugar cubes and have them crush one of them. Tell students to place the cube in one beaker of water and the crushed sugar in another beaker of water. Have students stir both solutions gently. Have them compare the rates at which the sugar dissolves in each solution. Students' observations should help them understand how a greater surface area affects the solution process.

SECTION 2

Plan and Prepare ▼

Objectives

Upon completion of this section, students should be able to do the following:

- List and explain three factors that affect the rate at which a solid solute dissolves in a liquid solvent.
- Explain solution equilibrium, and distinguish among saturated, unsaturated, and supersaturated solutions.
- Explain the meaning of "like dissolves like" in terms of polar substances and nonpolar substances.
- List the three interactions that contribute to the enthalpy of solution, and explain how they combine to cause dissolution to be exothermic or endothermic.
- Compare the effects of temperature and pressure on solubility.

Classroom Catalyst

Obtain three pieces of iron(II) chloride of equal mass and shape, and three different beakers containing water. Add the $FeCl_2$ to one beaker, and mix the contents using a magnetic stirrer while introducing this lesson. Pulverize the $FeCl_2$, and let it sit in the second beaker. Add the last crystal to the third beaker, and allow it to stand still. Use the results of this demonstration to introduce the principles of this section.

Teach ▼

READING TOOLKIT

PREDICTION GUIDES Write the following statements on the board:

- The rate at which any substance dissolves varies with temperature.
- The solubility of any substance varies with temperature.
- The solubility of any substance varies with pressure.

Ask students for their opinions of each statement. Then have them discuss their opinions, giving reasons based on knowledge and/or experience. Keep a list of the opinions for discussion at the end of the section.

▼ Teach *continued*

Demonstration

SOLUTION EQUILIBRIUM

Add enough **sugar** to a **glass of iced tea** so that an excess settles to the bottom of the glass. Students should observe whether any sugar on the bottom dissolves after you stir the tea thoroughly. Ask students to describe the relationship between a saturated solution and solution equilibrium. Ask them to predict what will happen to the solution equilibrium if the solution is heated or cooled.

TEACH FROM VISUALS

FIGURE 2.2 Students should recognize that although the system appears stable, there is activity at the particle level.

CAREERS IN CHEMISTRY

Environmental Chemist S.T.E.M.

What happens to all of our chemical waste, such as household cleaners and shampoos that we rinse down the drain, industrial smoke, and materials that have not been removed in water treatment plants? Environmental chemists investigate the sources and effects of chemicals in all parts of the environment. Then, chemists also devise acceptable ways to dispose of chemicals. This may involve conducting tests to determine whether the air, water, or soil is contaminated; developing programs to help remove contamination; designing new production processes to reduce the amounts of waste produced; handling regulation and compliance issues; and advising on safety and emergency responses. Environmental chemists must understand and use many other disciplines, including biology, geology, and ecology.

Agitating a Solution

Very close to the surface of a solute, the concentration of dissolved solute is high. Stirring or shaking helps to disperse the solute particles and bring fresh solvent into contact with the solute surface. Thus, the effect of stirring is similar to that of crushing a solid—contact between the solvent and the solute surface is increased.

Heating a Solvent

You probably have noticed that sugar and other materials dissolve more quickly in warm water than in cold water. As the temperature of the solvent increases, solvent molecules move faster, and their average kinetic energy increases. Therefore, at higher temperatures, collisions between the solvent molecules and the solute are more frequent and of higher energy than at lower temperatures. This separates and disperses the solute molecules.

MAIN IDEA

Solubility is a measure of how well one substance dissolves in another.

If you add spoonful after spoonful of sugar to tea, eventually no more sugar will dissolve. For every combination of solvent with a solid solute at a given temperature, there is a limit to the amount of solute that can be dissolved. The point at which this limit is reached for any solute-solvent combination is difficult to predict precisely and depends on the nature of the solute, the nature of the solvent, and the temperature.

The following model describes why there is a limit. When solid sugar is added to water, sugar molecules leave the solid surface and move about at random. Some of these dissolved molecules may collide with the crystal and remain there (recrystallize). As more solid dissolves, these collisions become more frequent. Eventually, molecules are returning to the crystal at the same rate at which they are going into solution, and a dynamic equilibrium is established between dissolution and crystallization. Ionic solids behave similarly, as shown in **Figure 2.2.**

Solution equilibrium is the physical state in which the opposing processes of dissolution and crystallization of a solute occur at equal rates.

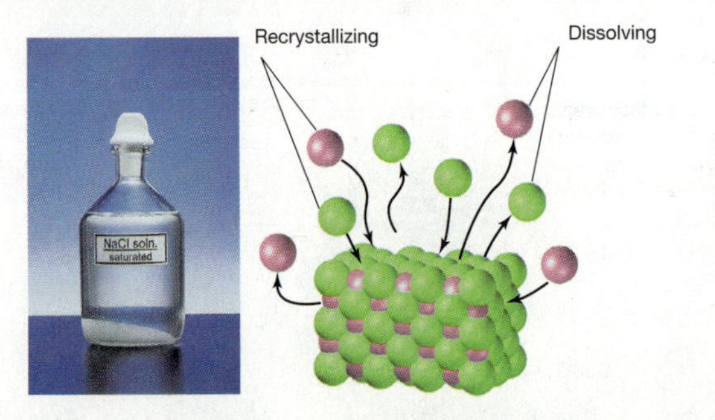

FIGURE 2.2

Solution Equilibrium A saturated solution in a closed system is at equilibrium. The solute is recrystallizing at the same rate that it is dissolving, even though it appears that there is no activity in the system.

Differentiated Instruction

PRE-AP

A solution equilibrium can also be established across a semipermeable membrane, such as the one surrounding a cell. Have students research the *Gibbs-Donnan effect*. This effect explains how the charged particles in solution establish an electrical gradient across a semipermeable membrane. Be sure that students explain how impermeable charged particles, such as large anions found in the blood, affect the equilibrium.

FIGURE 2.3

Saturation Point The graph shows the range of solute masses that will produce an unsaturated solution. Once the saturation point is exceeded, the system will contain undissolved solute.

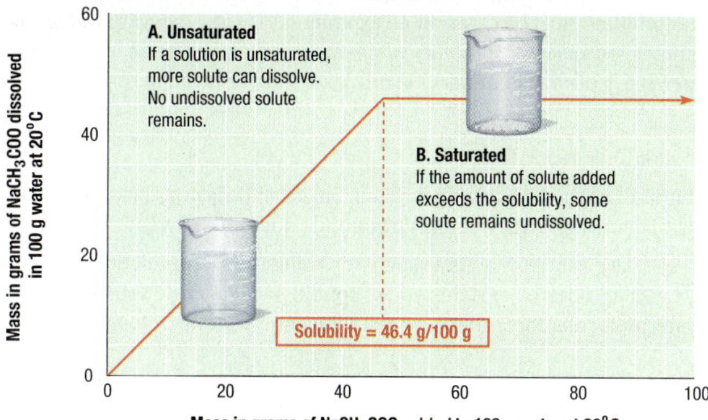

Saturated Versus Unsaturated Solutions

A solution that contains the maximum amount of dissolved solute is described as a saturated solution. How can you tell that the $NaCH_3COO$ solution pictured in **Figure 2.3** is saturated? If more sodium acetate is added to the solution, it falls to the bottom and does not dissolve because an equilibrium has been established between ions leaving and entering the solid phase. If more water is added to the saturated solution, then more sodium acetate will dissolve in it. At 20°C, 46.4 g of $NaCH_3COO$ is the maximum amount that will dissolve in 100 g of water. **A solution that contains less solute than a saturated solution under the existing conditions is an unsaturated solution.**

Supersaturated Solutions

When a saturated solution of a solute whose solubility increases with temperature is cooled, the excess solute usually comes out of solution, leaving the solution saturated at the lower temperature. But sometimes, if the solution is left to cool undisturbed, the excess solute does not separate and a supersaturated solution is produced. **A supersaturated solution is a solution that contains more dissolved solute than a saturated solution contains under the same conditions.** A supersaturated solution may remain unchanged for a long time if it is not disturbed, but once crystals begin to form, the process continues until equilibrium is reestablished at the lower temperature. An example of a supersaturated solution is one prepared from a saturated solution of sodium thiosulfate, $Na_2S_2O_3$, or sodium acetate, $NaCH_3COO$. Solute is added to hot water until the solution is saturated, and the hot solution is filtered. The filtrate is left to stand undisturbed as it cools. Dropping a small crystal of the solute into the supersaturated solution ("seeding") or disturbing the solution causes a rapid formation of crystals by the excess solute.

TEACH FROM VISUALS

FIGURE 2.3 Students should notice that solutions can be unsaturated over a range of solute masses. However, once the saturation point is reached, excess solute remains undissolved unless the temperature of the system changes.

Teaching Tip

Point out that the formula for sodium acetate is written several ways.

$NaC_2H_3O_2$
CH_3COONa
$NaCH_3COO$

Demonstration

SEEDING A SUPERSATURATED SOLUTION

The seeding of a supersaturated solution is a very effective demonstration. **Test tubes containing a supersaturated solution of sodium thiosulfate (100 g/100 mL), $Na_2S_2O_3$,** can be reused year after year. Several hours before performing the demonstration, heat the test tube until the solute is all dissolved. Allow the solution to stand undisturbed until it has cooled to room temperature before seeding the supersaturated solution with a **small crystal of $Na_2S_2O_3$.** It is suggested that you prepare several test tubes, as the solution occasionally crystallizes when it is cooled. It might be necessary occasionally to filter the warm solution to remove dust particles that can initiate crystallization.

BELOW LEVEL

Use mini-marshmallows to explain the concepts of *unsaturated*, *saturated*, and *supersaturated*. Use a half-full beaker of marshmallows to represent an unsaturated solution. Have students explain how to represent a saturated solution and then an unsaturated solution. Students should indicate that a beaker full of marshmallows represents a saturated solution. Pushing down on the marshmallows so that more can be added would represent a supersaturated solution.

▼ Teach *continued*

TEACH FROM TABLES

FIGURE 2.4 Have students use this table to decide whether the solubility increases or decreases when temperature increases. Most students believe that increasing the temperature will increase the solubility of any solute in a solvent. Use this table to find examples in which the solubility of a solute decreases with increased temperature.

Demonstration

COLD WATER VS. HOT WATER

Get **two 600-mL beakers.** Fill one beaker with **cold water.** Fill the other beaker with **hot water.** The cold water is clear, and the warm water is cloudy with small bubbles. You can prove that the cloudiness is caused by small bubbles and not by solid impurities because as the beaker sits, the bubbles rise to the top. If the cloudiness were due to solid impurities, they would sink to the bottom of the beaker.

Solubility Values

The solubility of a substance is the amount of that substance required to form a saturated solution with a specific amount of solvent at a specified temperature. The solubility of sugar, for example, is 204 g per 100. g of water at 20.°C. The temperature must be specified because solubility varies with temperature. For gases, the pressure must also be specified. Solubilities must be determined experimentally and can vary widely, as shown in **Figure 2.4.** Solubility values are usually given as grams of solute per 100. g of solvent or per 100. mL of solvent at a given temperature.

"Like Dissolves Like"

Lithium chloride is soluble in water, but gasoline is not. Gasoline mixes with benzene, C_6H_6, but lithium chloride does not. Why?

"Like dissolves like" is a rough but useful rule for predicting solubility. The "like" referred to is the type of bonding—polar or nonpolar—and the intermolecular forces between the solute and solvent molecules.

FIGURE 2.4

SOLUBILITY OF SOLUTES AS A FUNCTION OF TEMPERATURE (IN g SOLUTE/100 g H_2O)

	Temperature (°C)					
Substance	0	20	40	60	80	100
$AgNO_3$	122	216	311	440	585	733
$Ba(OH)_2$	1.67	3.89	8.22	20.94	101.4	—
$C_{12}H_{22}O_{11}$	179	204	238	287	362	487
$Ca(OH)_2$	0.189	0.173	0.141	0.121	—	0.07
$Ce_2(SO_4)_3$	20.8	10.1	—	3.87	—	—
KCl	28.0	34.2	40.1	45.8	51.3	56.3
KI	128	144	162	176	192	206
KNO_3	13.9	31.6	61.3	106	167	245
LiCl	69.2	83.5	89.8	98.4	112	128
Li_2CO_3	1.54	1.33	1.17	1.01	0.85	0.72
NaCl	35.7	35.9	36.4	37.1	38.0	39.2
$NaNO_3$	73	87.6	102	122	148	180
CO_2 (gas at SP)	0.335	0.169	0.0973	0.058	—	—
O_2 (gas at SP)	0.00694	0.00537	0.00308	0.00227	0.00138	0.00

Differentiated Instruction

BELOW LEVEL

Have students use **Figure 2.4** to review unsaturated, saturated, and supersaturated solutions. Ask students to work in pairs. One student should make up a question, such as, "How would you make an unsaturated solution of LiCl if the temperature of the water is 80°C?" The other student should respond by saying that less than 112 g LiCl must be dissolved in 100 g H_2O at this temperature. Students should then reverse roles. Encourage each student to make up three questions about solutions.

FIGURE 2.5

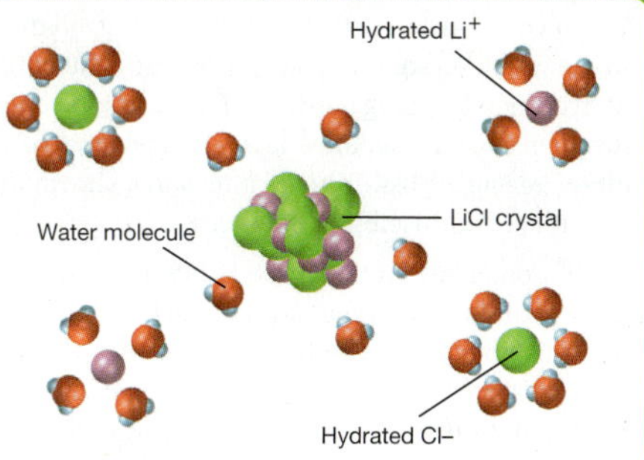

Hydration When LiCl dissolves, the ions are hydrated. The attraction between ions and water molecules is strong enough that each ion in solution is surrounded by water molecules.

Dissolving Ionic Compounds in Aqueous Solution

The polarity of water molecules plays an important role in the formation of solutions of ionic compounds in water. The slightly charged parts of water molecules attract the ions in the ionic compounds and surround them to keep them separated from the other ions in the solution. Suppose we drop a few crystals of lithium chloride into a beaker of water. At the crystal surface, water molecules come into contact with Li^+ and Cl^- ions. The positive ends of the water molecules are attracted to Cl^- ions, while the negative ends are attracted to Li^+ ions. The attraction between water molecules and the ions is strong enough to draw the ions away from the crystal surface and into solution, as illustrated in **Figure 2.5.** **This solution process with water as the solvent is referred to as hydration.** The ions are said to be *hydrated.* As hydrated ions diffuse into the solution, other ions are exposed and drawn away from the crystal surface by the solvent. The entire crystal gradually dissolves, and hydrated ions become uniformly distributed in the solution.

When crystallized from aqueous solutions, some ionic substances form crystals that incorporate water molecules. These crystalline compounds, known as *hydrates,* retain specific ratios of water molecules, as shown in figure **Figure 2.6,** and are represented by formulas such as $CuSO_4 \bullet 5H_2O$. Heating the crystals of a hydrate can drive off the water of hydration and leave the anhydrous salt. When a crystalline hydrate dissolves in water, the water of hydration returns to the solvent. The behavior of a solution made from a hydrate is no different from the behavior of one made from the anhydrous form. Dissolving either results in a system containing hydrated ions and water.

Nonpolar Solvents

Ionic compounds are generally not soluble in nonpolar solvents such as carbon tetrachloride, CCl_4, and toluene, $C_6H_5CH_3$. The nonpolar solvent molecules do not attract the ions of the crystal strongly enough to overcome the forces holding the crystal together.

Would you expect lithium chloride to dissolve in toluene? No, LiCl is not soluble in toluene. LiCl and $C_6H_5CH_3$ differ widely in bonding, polarity, and intermolecular forces.

FIGURE 2.6

Hydrate Hydrated copper(II) sulfate has water as part of its crystal structure. Heating releases the water and produces the anhydrous form of the substance, which has the formula $CuSO_4$.

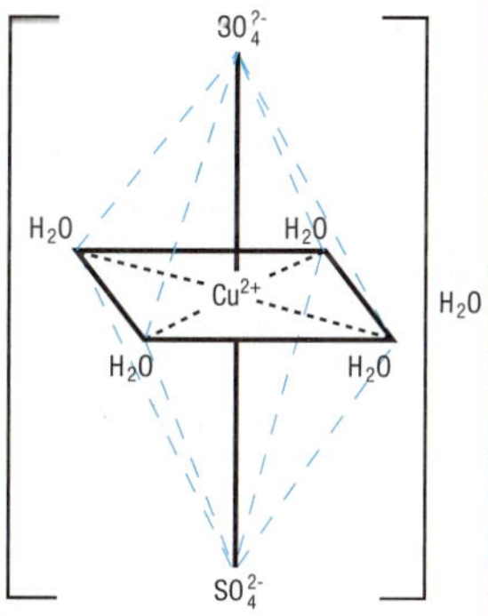

TEACH FROM VISUALS

FIGURE 2.5 Students should notice that the orientation of the water molecules changes depending on which ion they surround. Ask students what kind of forces are represented in this model. ion-dipole interactions

TEACH FROM VISUALS

FIGURE 2.6 Have students decide whether the water in hydrates is a solute or a solvent. Point out that four water molecules are part of the octahedral complex held in place by shared pairs from H_2O in coordinate covalent bonds. The fifth water molecule is attracted to the octahedral complex by dipole interactions. Two sulfate ions are shown even though each is also bound to another copper ion in the extended array for this crystal.

PRE-AP

Ask students how they would determine the percent by mass of water in a hydrated compound such as $CuSO_4 \bullet 5H_2O$. Students should suggest a procedure that involves measuring the mass of the compound and then heating it until all the water of hydration has evaporated. Using the difference between the masses of the compound both before and after heating provides the data needed to calculate the percent by mass of water in the compound.

▼ Teach *continued*

TEACH FROM VISUALS

FIGURES 2.7 and 2.8 Point out that the terms *phase* and *state* are not synonyms. **Figure 2.7** shows a two-phase system with both phases in the liquid state. The saturated solution shown in **Figure 2.2** is also a two-phase system, but the phases are in two different states—solid and liquid. Have students identify the forces that exist between the molecules shown in **Figure 2.7** and **Figure 2.8.**

Alternative Assessment

Have students draw a picture of the dissolution process. Make sure they include the breakup of the solute and the new attraction formed between solute and solvent.

Teaching Tip

If you wish to carry out a demonstration similar to **Figure 2.7** to show that hydrocarbons and water are immiscible, you may wish to add a drop of food coloring (soluble in water) to help distinguish the layers.

Check for Understanding

Answer: oil-and-vinegar salad dressing

FIGURE 2.7

Immiscibility
Toluene and water are immiscible. The components of this system exist in two distinct phases.

Toluene
Water
Insoluble and immiscible

✔ CHECK FOR UNDERSTANDING
Apply Give an example of an everyday mixture that is immiscible.

Liquid Solutes and Solvents

When you shake a bottle of salad dressing, oil droplets become dispersed in the water. As soon as you stop shaking the bottle, the strong attraction of hydrogen bonding between the water molecules squeezes out the oil droplets, forming separate layers. **Liquids that are not soluble in each other are immiscible.** Toluene and water, shown in **Figure 2.7,** are another example of immiscible substances.

Nonpolar substances, such as fats, oils, and greases, are generally quite soluble in nonpolar liquids, such as carbon tetrachloride, toluene, and gasoline. The only attractions between the nonpolar molecules are London forces, which are quite weak. The intermolecular forces existing in the solution are therefore very similar to those in pure substances. Thus, the molecules can mix freely with one another.

Liquids that dissolve freely in one another in any proportion are said to be miscible. Benzene and carbon tetrachloride are miscible. The nonpolar molecules of these substances exert no strong forces of attraction or repulsion, so the molecules mix freely. Ethanol and water, shown in **Figure 2.8,** also mix freely, but for a different reason. The —OH group on an ethanol molecule is somewhat polar. This group can form hydrogen bonds with water as well as with other ethanol molecules. The intermolecular forces in the mixture are so similar to those in the pure liquids that the liquids are mutually soluble in all proportions.

Gasoline is a solution composed mainly of nonpolar hydrocarbons and is also an excellent solvent for fats, oils, and greases. The major intermolecular forces acting between the nonpolar molecules are weak London forces.

Ethanol is intermediate in polarity between water and carbon tetrachloride. It is not as good as water as a solvent for polar or ionic substances. Sodium chloride is only slightly soluble in ethanol. On the other hand, ethanol is a better solvent than water for less-polar substances because the molecule has a nonpolar region.

FIGURE 2.8

Miscibility

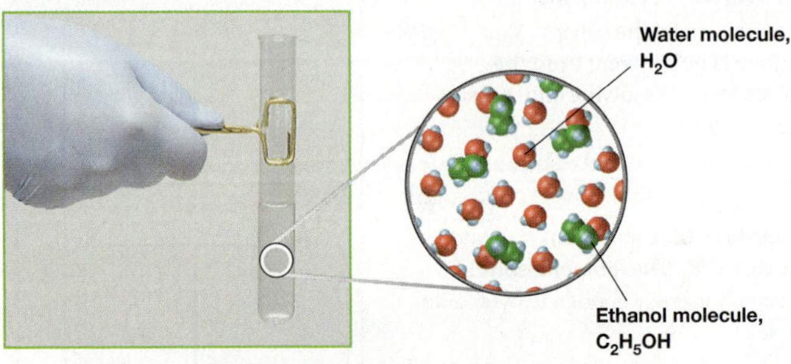

(a) Water and ethanol are miscible. The components of this system exist in a single phase with a uniform arrangement.

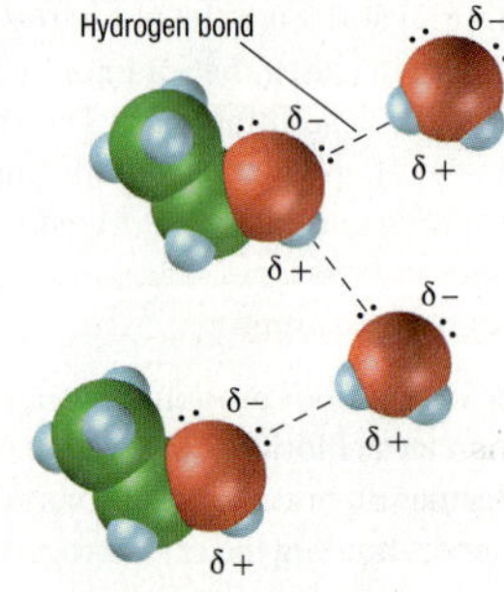

(b) Hydrogen bonding between the solute and solvent enhances the solubility of ethanol in water.

Differentiated Instruction

INCLUSION

Ask learning-disabled students to fold a piece of paper in half to form two columns. Label one half of the paper "Polar Compounds" and the other half of the paper "Nonpolar Compounds." Students can list various compounds under each heading. Compounds and their polarity can be found in the textbook or other reference books. To reinforce the concept, discuss whether combinations of various compounds would be miscible or immiscible in each other.

Effects of Pressure on Solubility

Changes in pressure have very little effect on the solubilities of liquids or solids in liquid solvents. However, increases in pressure increase gas solubilities in liquids.

When a gas is in contact with the surface of a liquid, gas molecules can enter the liquid. As the amount of dissolved gas increases, some molecules begin to escape and reenter the gas phase. An equilibrium is eventually established between the rates at which gas molecules enter and leave the liquid phase. As long as this equilibrium is undisturbed, the solubility of the gas in the liquid is unchanged at a given pressure.

$$\text{gas} + \text{solvent} \rightleftharpoons \text{solution}$$

Increasing the pressure of the solute gas above the solution puts stress on the equilibrium. Molecules collide with the liquid surface more often. The increase in pressure is partially offset by an increase in the rate of gas molecules entering the solution. In turn, the increase in the amount of dissolved gas causes an increase in the rate at which molecules escape from the liquid surface and become vapor. Eventually, equilibrium is restored at a higher gas solubility. An increase in gas pressure causes the equilibrium to shift so that more molecules are in the liquid phase.

Henry's Law

Henry's law, named after the English chemist William Henry, states: The solubility of a gas in a liquid is directly proportional to the partial pressure of that gas on the surface of the liquid. Henry's law applies to gas-liquid solutions at constant temperature.

Recall that when a mixture of ideal gases is confined in a constant volume at a constant temperature, each gas exerts the same pressure it would exert if it occupied the space alone. Assuming that the gases do not react in any way, each gas dissolves to the extent it would dissolve if no other gases were present.

In carbonated beverages, the solubility of CO_2 is increased by increasing the pressure. At the bottling plant, carbon dioxide gas is forced into the solution of flavored water at a pressure of 5–10 atm. The gas-in-liquid solution is then sealed in bottles or cans. When the cap is removed, the pressure is reduced to 1 atm, and some of the carbon dioxide escapes as gas bubbles. The rapid escape of a gas from a liquid in which it is dissolved is known as **effervescence**. This is shown in **Figure 2.9.**

FIGURE 2.9

Partial Pressure

(a) There are no gas bubbles in the unopened bottle of soda because the pressure of CO_2 applied during bottling keeps the carbon dioxide gas dissolved in the liquid.

(b) When the cap on the bottle is removed, the pressure of CO_2 on the liquid is reduced, and CO_2 can escape from the liquid. The soda effervesces when the bottle is opened and the pressure is reduced.

Application

When scuba divers remain underwater at high pressures for a long period of time, more nitrogen dissolves in their blood, as described by Henry's law. This can lead to a state called *nitrogen narcosis*, which causes sleepiness and poor judgment that can lead to serious accidents and death.

Henry's law also provides an explanation for "the bends." After being underwater for a long time, a diver will have more gases dissolved in the blood. The diver must pause during the ascent to allow the dissolved gas to come out of solution slowly and to be exhaled. If the ascent is too fast, the gas can come out of solution while flowing through blood vessels and block essential blood vessels, causing extreme pain, paralysis, or even death.

TEACH FROM VISUALS

FIGURE 2.9 Have students squeeze an unopened 2-L bottle of soda the next time they have a chance. They will find that the plastic bottle seems firm. This is due to the pressure of the liquid-gas system pushing out on the bottle. When opened, the bottle seems "softer" due to the drop in pressure. The decreased pressure also allows some of the dissolved gas to come out of solution.

BELOW LEVEL

Inform students that champagne, unlike wine, continues to ferment inside the bottle. Fermentation produces carbon dioxide gas. Ask students why the cork is secured to a bottle of champagne with a wire, but a wire is not placed over the cork in a bottle of wine. Students should realize that as more carbon dioxide forms inside the champagne, the pressure of the gas increases and could cause the cork to pop.

▼ Teach *continued*

TEACH FROM VISUALS

FIGURES 2.10 and 2.11 Have students interpret the data in the three graphs. SO_2 is more soluble at 30°C. Ask students how the solubility of different substances is affected by an increase in temperature. Have them identify the saturation point on each graph for any given temperature.

Application

Sodium nitrite and sodium nitrate are used as preservatives in meat to prevent bacterial growth. However, large doses can be unhealthy. Have students explain why meat that is boiled contains fewer nitrates and nitrites.

Teaching Tip

Hot sodas tend to "fizz" more than cold ones. Have students explain this tendency in terms of solubility and temperature. Gases are less soluble in liquid at high temperature, so they escape more readily when the pressure is released.

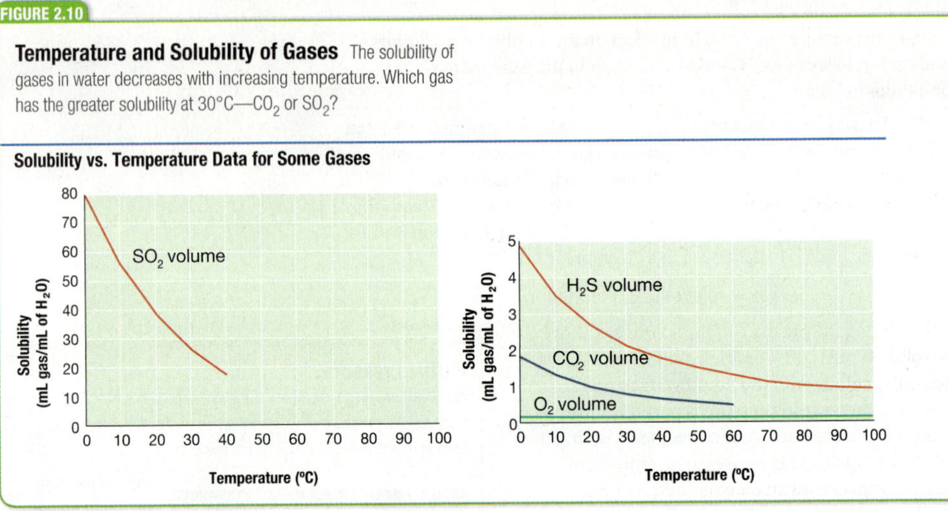

FIGURE 2.10

Temperature and Solubility of Gases The solubility of gases in water decreases with increasing temperature. Which gas has the greater solubility at 30°C—CO_2 or SO_2?

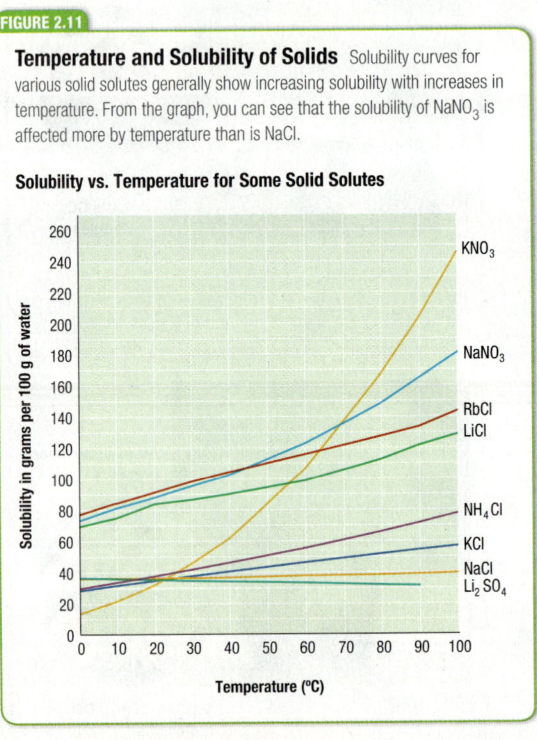

FIGURE 2.11

Temperature and Solubility of Solids Solubility curves for various solid solutes generally show increasing solubility with increases in temperature. From the graph, you can see that the solubility of $NaNO_3$ is affected more by temperature than is NaCl.

Effects of Temperature on Solubility

First, let's consider gas solubility. Increasing the temperature usually decreases gas solubility. As the temperature increases, the average kinetic energy of the molecules in solution increases. A greater number of solute molecules are able to escape from the attraction of solvent molecules and return to the gas phase. At higher temperatures, therefore, equilibrium is reached with fewer gas molecules in solution, and gases are generally less soluble, as shown in **Figure 2.10**.

The effect of temperature on the solubility of solids in liquids is more difficult to predict. Often, increasing the temperature increases the solubility of solids. However, an equivalent temperature increase can result in a large increase in solubility for some solvents and only a slight change for others.

Compare the effect of temperature on the solubility of NaCl (**Figure 2.11**) with the effect of temperature on the solubility of potassium nitrate, KNO_3 (**Figure 2.4**). About 14 g of potassium nitrate dissolves in 100 g of water at 0°C. The solubility of potassium nitrate increases by more than 150 g KNO_3 per 100 g H_2O when

Differentiated Instruction

PRE-AP

The regions found above and below each solubility curve in **Figure 2.11** represent supersaturated and unsaturated solutions, respectively. Ask students to describe the type of solution represented by any point above a solubility curve. For example, have students identify the point on the solubility curve for $NaNO_3$ represented by the values 40°C and 200 grams. Students should recognize that this value represents a supersaturated solution. Then ask students which type of solution is represented by any point found below a solubility curve. Students should recognize that values below a solubility curve represent an unsaturated solution.

the temperature is raised to 80°C. Under similar circumstances, the solubility of sodium chloride increases by only about 2 g NaCl per 100 g H_2O. Sometimes, solubility of a solid *decreases* with an increase in temperature. For example, between 0°C and 60.°C the solubility of cerium sulfate, $Ce_2(SO_4)_3$, decreases by about 17 g/100 g.

MAIN IDEA

A change in energy accompanies solution formation.

The formation of a solution is accompanied by an energy change. If you dissolve some potassium iodide, KI, in water, you will find that the outside of the container feels cold to the touch. But if you dissolve some sodium hydroxide, NaOH, in the same way, the outside of the container feels hot. The formation of a solid-liquid solution can apparently either absorb energy (KI in water) or release energy as heat (NaOH in water).

During solution formation, changes occur in the forces between solvent and solute particles. Before dissolving begins, solvent and solute molecules are held to one another by intermolecular forces (solvent-solvent or solute-solute). Energy is required to separate each from their neighbors. **A solute particle that is surrounded by solvent molecules is said to be solvated. The net amount of energy absorbed as heat by the solution when a specific amount of solute dissolves in a solvent is the enthalpy of solution.** **Figure 2.12** should help you understand this process better. From the model you can see that the enthalpy of solution is negative (energy is released) when the sum of attractions from Steps 1 and 2 is less than Step 3. The enthalpy of solution is positive (energy is absorbed) when the sum of attractions from Steps 1 and 2 is greater than Step 3.

FIGURE 2.12

Enthalpy of Solution The graph shows the changes in the enthalpy that occur during the formation of a solution. How would the graph differ for a system with an endothermic heat of solution?

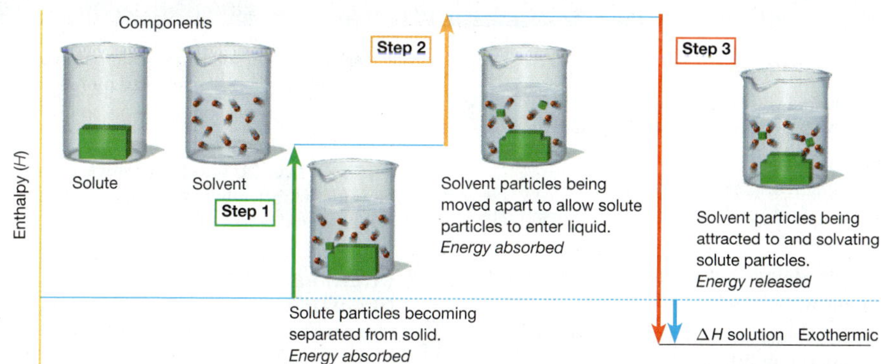

INCLUSION

To help kinesthetic learners understand the enthalpy of solutions, ask eight students to form two groups of four students each. Have the students in each group hold hands. Give one group a sign labeled *solute*, and the other group a sign labeled *solvent*. Have one student in the solute group take the sign and leave the group to represent a solute particle separating from a solid. Point out that energy is required to overcome the intermolecular force and separate the solute particle. Next have a student in the solvent group take the sign and leave the group. Relate this student's action to how energy is required to separate solvent particles. Finally, have the two individual students join hands to represent a solvated solute particle. Point out that solvation releases energy. The quantity of energy released during solvation determines whether the solution process is exothermic or endothermic.

Application

Hot packs and cold packs depend on exothermic and endothermic heats of solution, respectively. Bring in a cold pack to demonstrate.

Teaching Tip

The enthalpy of solution for ionic compounds can be found by subtracting the enthalpy of hydration from the lattice energy. The lattice energy represents the energy required to break the solute-solute attraction. The enthalpy of hydration represents both the solvent-solvent attraction being broken and the solvent-solute attraction being formed. In a subsequent chapter, students will learn how to use Hess's law to prove this.

READING TOOLKIT

PREDICTION GUIDES Review the list of opinions developed at the beginning of this section. Ask students whether their opinions have changed or are the same. Have students cite passages in the text that account for the change or reinforcement of their opinions.

▼ Teach *continued*

TEACH FROM TABLES

FIGURE 2.13 Ask students how dissolving $AgNO_3$ in water would affect the temperature. The temperature of the solution would decrease.

▼ Assess and Reteach

Assess Use the Formative Assessment on this page to evaluate student mastery of the section.

Reteach For students who need additional instruction, download the Section Study Guide.

Response to Intervention To reassess students' mastery, use the Section Quiz, available to print or to take directly online at **HMDScience.com**.

FIGURE 2.13

ENTHALPIES OF SOLUTION (kJ/MOL SOLUTE AT 25°C)

Substance	Enthalpy of solution	Substance	Enthalpy of solution
$AgNO_3(s)$	+22.59	$KOH(s)$	−57.61
$CH_3COOH(l)$	−1.51	$MgSO_4(s)$	+15.9
$HCl(g)$	−74.84	$NaCl(s)$	+3.88
$HI(g)$	−81.67	$NaNO_3(s)$	+20.50
$KCl(s)$	+17.22	$NaOH(s)$	−44.51
$KClO_3(s)$	+41.38	$NH_3(g)$	−30.50
$KI(s)$	+20.33	$NH_4Cl(s)$	+14.78
$KNO_3(s)$	+34.89	$NH_4NO_3(s)$	+25.69

You know that heating decreases the solubility of a gas, so dissolution of gases is exothermic. How do the values for the enthalpies of solution in **Figure 2.13** support this idea of exothermic solution processes for gaseous solutes?

In the gaseous state, molecules are so far apart that there are virtually no intermolecular forces of attraction between them. Therefore, the solute-solute interaction has little effect on the enthalpy of a solution of a gas. Energy is released when a gas dissolves in a liquid because attraction between solute gas and solvent molecules outweighs the energy needed to separate solvent molecules.

SECTION 2 FORMATIVE ASSESSMENT

Reviewing Main Ideas

1. Why would you expect a packet of sugar to dissolve faster in hot tea than in iced tea?
2. **a.** Explain how you would prepare a saturated solution of sugar in water.
   b. How would you then make it a supersaturated solution?
3. Explain why ethanol will dissolve in water and carbon tetrachloride will not.
4. When a solute molecule is solvated, is energy released or absorbed?
5. If a warm bottle of soda and a cold bottle of soda are opened, which will effervesce more and why?

Critical Thinking

6. **PREDICTING OUTCOMES** You get a small amount of lubricating oil on your clothing. Which would work better to remove the oil—water or toluene? Explain your answer.
7. **INTERPRETING CONCEPTS** A commercial "fizz saver" pumps helium under pressure into a soda bottle to keep gas from escaping. Will this keep CO_2 in the soda bottle? Explain your answer.

Answers to Section Assessment

1. The particles in hot tea move faster than in iced tea. Therefore, there are more collisions between the tea and sugar molecules at the surface of the sugar grains, and sugar molecules leave the surface of the grains faster in hot tea than in cold tea.
2. **a.** Continually add sugar to hot water until undissolved grains remain at the bottom of the container. This is a saturated solution of sugar and water.
   b. Filter the hot solution to remove any seed crystals. Set the saturated solution aside until it cools to room temperature. Once it cools, it will be supersaturated.
3. Ethanol and water are each polar molecules. The negatively charged region of the ethanol molecules is attracted to the positively charged region of the water molecules, and vice versa. Carbon tetrachloride is nonpolar and will not form a strong enough attraction to water molecules to dissolve.
4. Intermolecular attraction brings the solvent and solute molecules together. Energy is released in this process.
5. The warm bottle will effervesce more because the gas will be less soluble in the warmer bottle of soda.
6. toluene; Because oil and toluene are nonpolar, they will dissolve in each other.
7. It will not keep CO_2 from escaping from solution; Henry's law states that it is the partial pressure of the same gas both above and within the solution that keeps that gas in solution. Increased pressure of only helium will have no effect on the solubility of CO_2.

Cross-Disciplinary Connection S.T.E.M.

Artificial Blood

A patient lies bleeding on a stretcher. The doctor leans over to check the patient's wounds and barks an order to a nearby nurse: "Get him a unit of artificial blood, stat!" According to Dr. Peter Keipert, Program Director of Oxygen Carriers Development at Alliance Pharmaceutical Corp., this scenario may soon be commonplace thanks to a synthetic mixture that can perform one of the main functions of human blood—transporting oxygen.

The hemoglobin inside red blood cells collects oxygen in our lungs, transports it to all the tissues of the body, and then takes carbon dioxide back to the lungs. Dr. Keipert's blood substitute accomplishes the same task, but it uses nonpolar chemicals called *perfluorocarbons* instead of hemoglobin to transport the oxygen. The perfluorocarbons are carried in a water-based saline solution, but because nonpolar substances and water do not mix well, a bonding chemical called a *surfactant* is added to hold the mixture together. The perfluorocarbons are sheared into tiny droplets and then coated with the bonding molecules. One end of these molecules attaches to the perfluorocarbon and the other end attaches to the water, creating a milky emulsion. The blood-substitute mixture, called Oxygent™, is administered to a patient in the same way regular blood is. The perfluorocarbons are eventually exhaled through the lungs in the same way other products of respiration are.

Oxygent only functions to carry gases to and from tissues; it cannot clot or perform any of the immune-system functions that blood does. Still, the substitute has several advantages over real blood. Oxygent has a shelf life of more than a year. Oxygent also eliminates many of the risks associated with blood transfusions. Because the substitute can dissolve larger amounts of oxygen than real blood can, smaller amounts of the mixture are needed.

$C_8F_{17}Br$ belongs to a class of compounds called perfluorocarbons.

Oxygent is currently being tested in surgical patients.

"Once this product is approved and has been demonstrated to be safe and effective in elective surgery, I think you will see its use spread into the emergency, critical-care arena," says Dr. Keipert. "A patient who has lost a lot of blood and is currently being resuscitated with normal fluids, like saline solutions, would be given Oxygent as an additional oxygen-delivery agent in the emergency room."

Questions

1. How would the approval of Oxygent benefit the medical community?
2. How do scientists prevent the nonpolar perfluorocarbons in Oxygent from separating from the water?

Cross-Disciplinary Connection

Background

This article is an example of how molecules with specific properties to fulfill specific needs are researched and developed.

Point out that Dr. Keipert uses a surfactant as a "bridge molecule" to enable the nonpolar perfluorocarbons to "mix" with the polar saline solution.

Classroom Discussion

Have students find out more about the different functions performed by blood. How many of these functions are performed by Dr. Keipert's new blood?

Answers

1. Using Oxygent would allow patients needing large amounts of blood to get a better oxygen carrier in a smaller volume of mixture.
2. A surfactant is added to hold the mixture together.

SECTION 3

▼ Plan and Prepare

Objectives

Upon completion of this section, students should be able to do the following:

- Given the mass of solute and volume of solvent, calculate the concentration of a solution.
- Given the concentration of a solution, determine the amount of solute in a given amount of solution.
- Given the concentration of a solution, determine the amount of solution that contains a given amount of solute.

Classroom Catalyst

Fill four different test tubes with different concentrations of potassium permanganate. Students can see how the color of the solution varies with the concentration. Tell students that permanganate ions in solution absorb light in the visible range. Light reflected in the purple and red range makes the solution appear purple. The greater the concentration, the more purple the solution appears. Tell students that color alone is a qualitative measure of concentration. Light absorption by colored solutions can be used to make a quantitative determination of concentration.

▼ Teach

Misconception Alert!

Most students have a vague notion that the terms *weak acid* and *dilute acid* mean the same thing. In fact, a *dilute* acid means any acid with a low concentration. That an acid is *weak* has nothing to do with concentration but describes the nature of the acid molecule and its ability to donate protons. Therefore, it is possible to have a *dilute* solution of *strong* acid or a *concentrated* solution of *weak* acid.

SECTION 3

Main Ideas

- Molarity is moles of solute per liter of solution.
- Molality is moles of solute per kilogram of solvent.

Concentration of Solutions

Key Terms

concentration molarity molality

The concentration of a solution is a measure of the amount of solute in a given amount of solvent or solution. Some medications are solutions of drugs—a one-teaspoon dose at the correct concentration might cure the patient, while the same dose in the wrong concentration might kill the patient.

In this section, we introduce two different ways of expressing the concentrations of solutions: molarity and molality.

Sometimes, solutions are referred to as "dilute" or "concentrated," but these are not very definite terms. "Dilute" just means that there is a relatively small amount of solute in a solvent. "Concentrated," on the other hand, means that there is a relatively large amount of solute in a solvent. Note that these terms are unrelated to the degree to which a solution is saturated. A saturated solution of a substance that is not very soluble might be very dilute.

PREMIUM CONTENT Animated Chemistry HMDScience.com

Solution Dilution

MAIN IDEA

Molarity is moles of solute per liter of solution.

Molarity is the number of moles of solute in one liter of solution. To relate the molarity of a solution to the mass of solute present, you must know the molar mass of the solute. For example, a "one molar" solution of sodium hydroxide, NaOH, contains one mole of NaOH in every liter of solution. The symbol for molarity is M, and the concentration of a one-molar solution of sodium hydroxide is written as 1 M NaOH.

One mole of NaOH has a mass of 40.0 g. If this quantity of NaOH is dissolved in enough water to make exactly 1.00 L of solution, the solution is a 1 M solution. If 20.0 g of NaOH, which is 0.500 mol, is dissolved in enough water to make 1.00 L of solution, a 0.500 M NaOH solution is produced. This relationship between molarity, moles, and volume may be expressed in the following ways.

Molarity (*M*)

$$\text{molarity} = \frac{\text{amount of solute (mol)}}{\text{volume of solution (L)}}$$

$$= \frac{0.500 \text{ mol NaOH}}{1.00 \text{ L}}$$

$$= 0.500 \text{ M NaOH}$$

If twice the molar mass of NaOH, 80.0 g, is dissolved in enough water to make 1 L of solution, a 2 M solution is produced. The molarity of any solution can be calculated by dividing the number of moles of solute by the number of liters of solution.

Differentiated Instruction

ENGLISH LEARNERS

Open a can of frozen orange juice and follow the directions to make a drinkable solution. Have students use the terms *dilute* and *concentrated* to explain what happens when water is added to the frozen orange juice. Students should say that adding water dilutes the concentrated juice so that fewer solutes are present in the same volume of solvent.

Note that a 1 M solution is *not* made by adding 1 mol of solute to 1 L of *solvent*. In such a case, the final total volume of the solution might not be 1 L. Instead, 1 mol of solute is first dissolved in less than 1 L of solvent. Then the resulting solution is carefully diluted with more solvent to bring the *total volume* to 1 L, as shown in **Figure 3.1.** The following sample problem will show you how molarity is often used.

FIGURE 3.1

Preparing a 0.5000 M Solution The preparation of a 0.5000 M solution of $CuSO_4 \bullet 5H_2O$ starts with calculating the mass of solute needed.

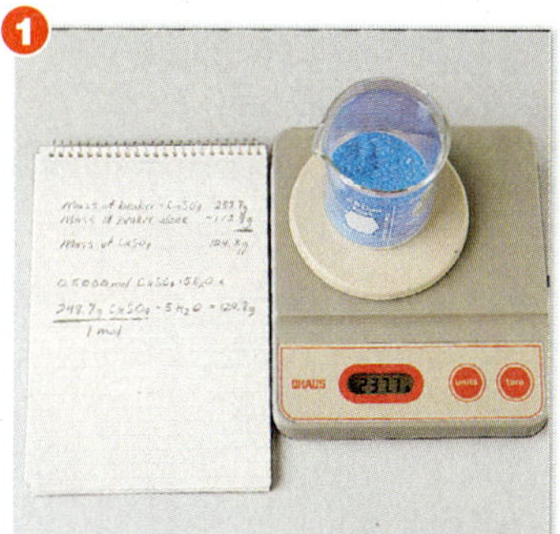

1 Start by calculating the mass of $CuSO_4 \bullet 5H_2O$ needed. Making a liter of this solution requires 0.5000 mol of solute. Convert the moles to mass by multiplying by the molar mass of $CuSO_4 \bullet 5H_2O$. This mass is calculated to be 124.8 g.

2 Add some solvent to the solute to dissolve it, and then pour it into a 1.0-L volumetric flask.

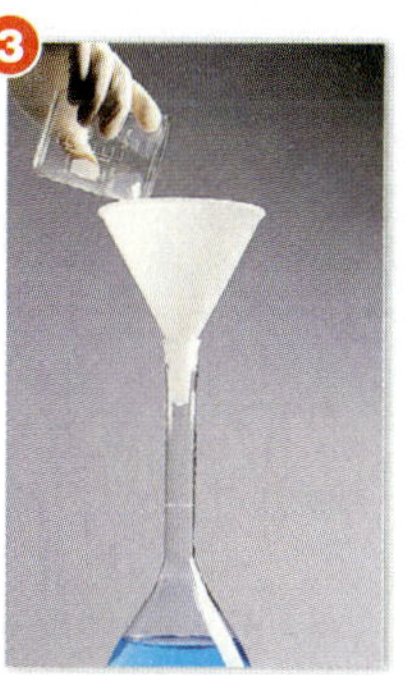

3 Rinse the weighing beaker with more solvent to remove all the solute, and pour the rinse into the flask. Add water until the volume of the solution nears the neck of the flask.

4 Put the stopper in the flask, and swirl the solution thoroughly.

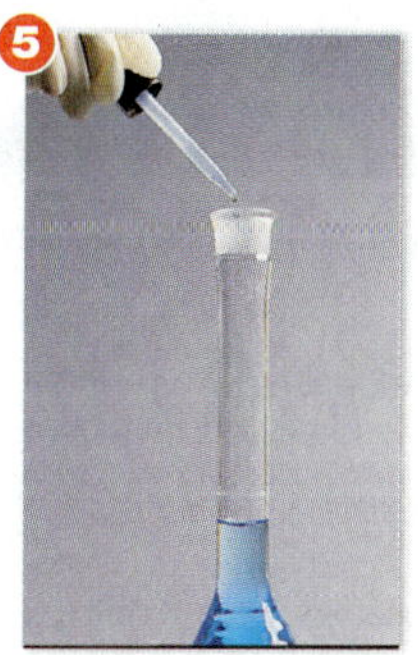

5 Carefully fill the flask to the 1.0-L mark with water.

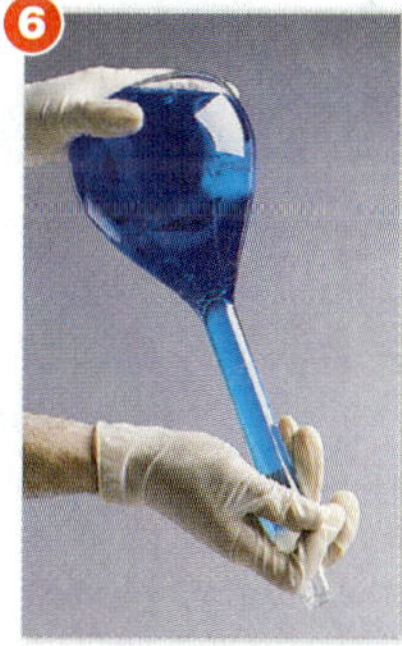

6 Restopper the flask, and invert it at least 10 times to ensure complete mixing.

7 The resulting solution has 0.5000 mol of solute dissolved in 1.000 L of solution, which is a 0.5000 M concentration.

Alternative Assessment

Have students prepare a flowchart or concept map that describes how to prepare a solution of specified molarity. In future laboratories, take the time to have students prepare their own solutions using this flowchart.

Misconception Alert!

Some students will believe that the amount of a solution is proportional to the molar concentration. Remind them that the molar concentration of a solution is independent of the volume.

INCLUSION

To help visual learners understand why a volumetric flask is used to make the 0.5000 M solution in **Figure 3.1,** fill a 1-L Erlenmeyer flask with water to the 1-L mark. Then pour the water into a volumetric flask. Have students determine if the water fills the volumetric flask to the 1.0-L mark.

▼ Teach *continued*

Classroom Practice

A-1 **a.** What is the molarity of 2.00 L of solution that is made from 14.6 g of NaCl?

b. What is the molarity of hydrochloric acid that contains 10.0 g of HCl in 250. mL of solution?

Answers:

a. 0.125 M

b. 1.10 M

B-1 **a.** How many moles of NaCl are in 1.25 L of 0.330 M NaCl?

b. How many moles of HCl exist in 500. mL of 0.50 M solution of HCl?

Answers:

a. 0.413 mol

b. 0.25 mol

Calculating with Molarity

Sample Problem A **You have 3.50 L of solution that contains 90.0 g of sodium chloride, NaCl. What is the molarity of that solution?**

1 ANALYZE

Given: solute mass = 90.0 g NaCl
solution volume = 3.50 L

Unknown: molarity of NaCl solution

2 PLAN

Molarity is the number of moles of solute per liter of solution. The solute is described in the problem by mass, not the amount in moles. You need one conversion (grams to moles of solute) using the inverted molar mass of NaCl to arrive at your answer.

$$\text{grams of solute} \longrightarrow \text{number of moles of solute} \longrightarrow \text{molarity}$$

$$\text{g NaCl} \times \frac{\text{mol NaCl}}{\text{g NaCl}} = \text{mol NaCl}$$

$$\frac{\text{amount of solute (mol)}}{V\,\text{solution (L)}} = \text{molarity of solution (M)}$$

3 SOLVE

You will need the molar mass of NaCl.
NaCl = 58.44 g/mol

$$90.0\ \cancel{\text{g NaCl}} \times \frac{1\ \text{mol NaCl}}{58.44\ \cancel{\text{g NaCl}}} = 1.54\ \text{mol NaCl}$$

$$\frac{1.54\ \text{mol NaCl}}{3.50\ \text{L of solution}} = 0.440\ \text{M NaCl}$$

4 CHECK YOUR WORK

Because each factor involved is limited to three significant digits, the answer should have three significant digits—which it does. The units cancel correctly to give the desired moles of solute per liter of solution, which is molarity.

Calculating with Molarity

Sample Problem B **You have 0.8 L of a 0.5 M HCl solution. How many moles of HCl does this solution contain?**

1 ANALYZE

Given: volume of solution = 0.8 L
concentration of solution = 0.5 M HCl

Unknown: moles of HCl in a given volume

2 PLAN

The molarity indicates the moles of solute that are in one liter of solution. Given the volume of the solution, the number of moles of solute can then be found.

concentration (mol of HCl/L of solution) × volume (L of solution) = mol of HCl

Continued

Problem Solving

TAKE IT FURTHER

Ask students how they would change Sample Problem A if the question read, "You have 350 mL of solution that contains 90.0 g of sodium chloride, NaCl." Students must be aware that molarity is expressed in terms of liters. Therefore, they must convert 350 mL to 0.350 L when solving the problem.

Calculating with Molarity (continued)

3 SOLVE

$$\frac{0.5\ \text{mol HCl}}{1.0\ \cancel{\text{L of solution}}} \times 0.8\ \cancel{\text{L of solution}} = 0.4\ \text{mol HCl}$$

4 CHECK YOUR WORK

The answer is correctly given to one significant digit. The units cancel correctly to give the desired unit, mol. There should be less than 0.5 mol HCl, because less than 1 L of solution was used.

Calculating with Molarity

Sample Problem C **To produce 40.0 g of silver chromate, you will need at least 23.4 g of potassium chromate in solution as a reactant. All you have on hand is 5 L of a 6.0 M K_2CrO_4 solution. What volume of the solution is needed to give you the 23.4 g K_2CrO_4 needed for the reaction?**

1 ANALYZE

Given: volume of solution = 5 L
concentration of solution = 6.0 M K_2CrO_4
mass of solute = 23.4 g K_2CrO_4
mass of product = 40.0 g Ag_2CrO_4

Unknown: volume of K_2CrO_4 solution in L

2 PLAN

The molarity indicates the moles of solute that are in 1 L of solution. Given the mass of solute needed, the amount in moles of solute can then be found. Use the molarity and the amount, in moles, of K_2CrO_4 to determine the volume of K_2CrO_4 that will provide 23.4 g.

grams of solute ⟶ moles solute
moles solute and molarity ⟶ liters of solution needed

3 SOLVE

To get the moles of solute, you'll need to calculate the molar mass of K_2CrO_4.

$$1\ \text{mol}\ K_2CrO_4 = 194.2\ \text{g}\ K_2CrO_4$$

$$23.4\ \cancel{\text{g}\ K_2CrO_4} \times \frac{1\ \text{mol}\ K_2CrO_4}{194.2\ \cancel{\text{g}\ K_2CrO_4}} = 0.120\ \text{mol}\ K_2CrO_4$$

$$6.0\ \text{M}\ K_2CrO_4 - \frac{0.120\ \text{mol}\ K_2CrO_4}{x\ \text{L}\ K_2CrO_4\ \text{soln}}$$

$$x = 0.020\ \text{L}\ K_2CrO_4\ \text{of solution}$$

4 CHECK YOUR WORK

The answer is correctly given to two significant digits. The units cancel correctly to give the desired unit, liters of solution.

Practice Answers in Appendix E

1. What is the molarity of a solution composed of 5.85 g of potassium iodide, KI, dissolved in enough water to make 0.125 L of solution?
2. How many moles of H_2SO_4 are present in 0.500 L of a 0.150 M H_2SO_4 solution?
3. What volume of 3.00 M NaCl is needed for a reaction that requires 146.3 g of NaCl?

DECONSTRUCTING PROBLEMS

Point out that not all the information given in a problem may be used. For example, in Sample Problem C, students do not need to use the volume of solution (5 L of potassium chromate) in their calculations. First, students need to calculate the number of moles of K_2CrO_4 to be added as a reactant. Then students must use the formula for molarity to determine the volume of the 6.0 M solution that contains this number of moles.

Classroom Practice

C-1 **a.** What is the molarity of a solution composed of 6.25 g of HCl in 0.300 L of solution?

b. How many moles of KI are present in 0.250 L of a 2.30 M solution?

c. What volume of a 0.500 M solution of HBr is needed for a reaction that requires 32.5 g of HBr?

Answers:

a. 0.571 M
b. 0.575 mol
c. 0.803 L

Answers

Practice C

1. 0.282 M KI
2. 0.0750 mol
3. 0.834 L

▼ Teach *continued*

Teaching Tip

Have students consider what happens to the denominator in the expression for molality as the amount of solute increases. There is no change. Then have students consider what happens to the denominator in the expression for molarity as the amount of solute increases. Because it involves the combined volume of solute and solvent, the denominator could change as the amount of solute increases.

TEACH FROM VISUALS

FIGURE 3.2 Have students compare and contrast this procedure with that shown in **Figure 3.1.** Be sure students can convert between the mass of solute and the molality of a solute. Emphasize that in the preparation shown, 1000 mL of H_2O is equivalent to 1 kg of H_2O. A balance should be used to measure 1-kg quantities of solvents.

Teaching Tip

Remind students that water is the most common solvent, and that such solutions are called *aqueous solutions*. When a problem does not identify the solvent, they should assume that it is water.

MAIN IDEA

Molality is moles of solute per kilogram of solvent.

Molality is the concentration of a solution expressed in moles of solute per kilogram of solvent. A solution that contains 1 mol of solute, sodium hydroxide, NaOH, for example, dissolved in exactly 1 kg of solvent is a "one molal" solution. The symbol for molality is *m*, and the concentration of this solution is written as 1 *m* NaOH.

One mole of NaOH has a molar mass of 40.0 g, so 40.0 g of NaOH dissolved in 1 kg of water results in a one-molal NaOH solution. If 20.0 g of NaOH, which is 0.500 mol of NaOH, is dissolved in exactly 1 kg of water, the concentration of the solution is 0.500 *m* NaOH.

molality (*m*)

$$\text{molality} = \frac{\text{moles solute}}{\text{mass of solvent (kg)}}$$

$$\frac{0.500 \text{ mol NaOH}}{1 \text{ kg } H_2O} = 0.500\ m \text{ NaOH}$$

If 80.0 g of sodium hydroxide, which is 2 mol, is dissolved in 1 kg of water, a 2.00 *m* solution of NaOH is produced. The molality of any solution can be found by dividing the number of moles of solute by the mass in kilograms of the solvent in which it is dissolved. Note that if the amount of solvent is expressed in grams, the mass of solvent must be converted to kilograms by multiplying by the following conversion factor:

$$1 \text{ kg}/1000 \text{ g}$$

Figure 3.2 shows how a 0.5000 *m* solution of $CuSO_4 \bullet 5H_2O$ is prepared, in contrast with the 0.5000 M solution in **Figure 3.1.**

FIGURE 3.2

Preparation of a 0.5000 *m* Solution The preparation of a 0.5000 *m* solution of $CuSO_4 \bullet 5H_2O$ also starts with the calculation of the mass of solute needed.

1

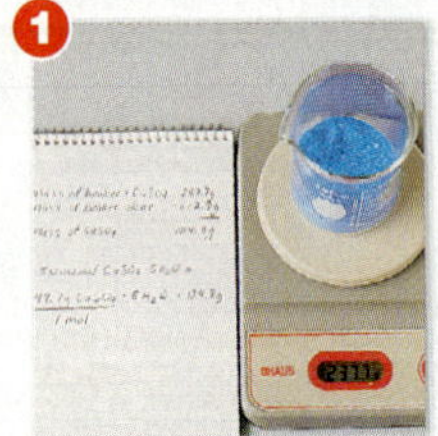

Calculate the mass of $CuSO_4 \bullet 5H_2O$ needed. Making this solution will require 0.5000 mol of $CuSO_4 \bullet 5H_2O$ per kilogram of solvent (1000 g). This mass is calculated to be 124.8 g.

2

Add 1.000 kg of solvent to the solute in the beaker. Because the solvent is water, 1.000 kg will equal 1000 mL.

3

Mix thoroughly.

4

The resulting solution has 0.5000 mol of solute dissolved in 1.000 kg of solvent.

Differentiated Instruction

PRE-AP

Students will commonly encounter molarity in their study of chemistry, but they will rarely encounter molality. Have students research the use of molality in physical chemistry, especially with respect to colligative properties such as freezing point depression and boiling point elevation.

ENGLISH LEARNERS

Be sure to point out the difference between the terms *molarity* and *molality*. Have students make special note of these two terms, the single letter that is different between them, and their specific meanings.

Concentrations are expressed as molalities when studying properties of solutions related to vapor pressure and temperature changes. Molality is used because it does not change with changes in temperature. Below is a comparison of the equations for molarity and molality.

Molarity (M) $\text{molarity} = \frac{\text{amount of A (mol)}}{\text{volume of solution (L)}}$

Molality (m) $\text{molality} = \frac{\text{amount of A (mol)}}{\text{mass of solvent (kg)}}$

PREMIUM CONTENT

Solve It! Cards
HMDScience.com

Calculating with Molality

Sample Problem D **A solution was prepared by dissolving 17.1 g of sucrose (table sugar, $C_{12}H_{22}O_{11}$) in 125 g of water. Find the molal concentration of this solution.**

1 ANALYZE

Given: solute mass = 17.1 g $C_{12}H_{22}O_{11}$
solvent mass = 125 g H_2O

Unknown: molal concentration of $C_{12}H_{22}O_{11}$

2 PLAN

To find molality, you need moles of solute and kilograms of solvent. The given grams of sucrose must be converted to moles. The mass in grams of solvent must be converted to kilograms.

$$\text{mol } C_{12}H_{22}O_{11} = \frac{\text{g } C_{12}H_{22}O_{11}}{\text{molar mass } C_{12}H_{22}O_{11}}$$

$$\text{kg } H_2O = \text{g } H_2O \times \frac{1 \text{ kg}}{1000 \text{ g}}$$

$$\text{molality } C_{12}H_{22}O_{11} = \frac{\text{mol } C_{12}H_{22}O_{11}}{\text{kg } H_2O}$$

3 SOLVE

Use the periodic table to compute the molar mass of $C_{12}H_{22}O_{11}$.
$C_{12}H_{22}O_{11}$ = 342.34 g/mol

$$17.1 \text{ g } C_{12}H_{22}O_{11} \times \frac{1 \text{ mol } C_{12}H_{22}O_{11}}{342.34 \text{ g } C_{12}H_{22}O_{11}} = 0.0500 \text{ mol } C_{12}H_{22}O_{11}$$

$$\frac{125 \text{ g } H_2O}{1000 \text{ g/kg}} = 0.125 \text{ kg } H_2O$$

$$\frac{0.0500 \text{ mol } C_{12}H_{22}O_{11}}{0.125 \text{ kg } H_2O} = 0.400\ m\ C_{12}H_{22}O_{11}$$

4 CHECK YOUR WORK

The answer is correctly given to three significant digits. The unit mol solute/kg solvent is correct for molality.

Problem Solving

DECONSTRUCTING PROBLEMS

Be sure that students recognize that both molarity and molality problems involve working with moles. Emphasize, however, that molarity involves the volume of the solution (moles/liter of solution) while molality involves the mass of the solvent (moles solute/kg solvent).

Alternative Assessment

Have students construct a concept map that includes these terms: *miscible, immiscible, soluble, insoluble, saturated, unsaturated, concentration, molarity, molality, dilute,* and *concentrated.*

READING TOOLKIT

SEQUENCING/PATTERN PUZZLES

Have student pairs list the steps for solving molarity and molality problems on a sheet of paper, one step per line without numbering the steps. Encourage students to write the steps in their own words, dividing longer steps into two or three shorter steps if necessary.

When students have finished, have them cut their sheets of paper into strips with only one step per strip. Direct students to shuffle the strips so they are out of order. Have them trade strips with their partners and place the strips in the proper sequence. Students can confirm the order of the process by checking the text or their class notes.

▼ Teach *continued*

Classroom Practice

D-1 What is the molality of a solution composed of 13.0 g NaCl dissolved in 500. g of water?

Answer: 0.445 *m*

E-2 How many grams of NaCl are needed to prepare a 1.0 *m* solution using 250 g of solvent?

Answer: 15 g

Answers

Practice E

1. 22.0 *m* acetone
2. 3.13 g CH_3OH

▼ Assess and Reteach

Assess Use the Formative Assessment on this page to evaluate student mastery of the section.

Reteach For students who need additional instruction, download the Section Study Guide.

Response to Intervention To reassess students' mastery, use the Section Quiz, available to print or to take directly online at **HMDScience.com**.

Calculating with Molality

Sample Problem E **A solution of iodine, I_2, in carbon tetrachloride, CCl_4, is used when iodine is needed for certain chemical tests. How much iodine must be added to prepare a 0.480 *m* solution of iodine in CCl_4 if 100.0 g of CCl_4 is used?**

1 ANALYZE

Given: molality of solution = 0.480 $m\ I_2$
mass of solvent = 100.0 g CCl_4

Unknown: mass of solute

2 PLAN

Your first step should be to convert the grams of solvent to kilograms. The molality gives you the moles of solute, which can be converted to the grams of solute using the molar mass of I_2.

3 SOLVE

Use the periodic table to compute the molar mass of I_2.
$I_2 = 253.8$ g/mol

$$100.0\ \text{g}\ CCl_4 \times \frac{1\ \text{kg}}{1000\ \text{g}\ CCl_4} = 0.100\ \text{kg}\ CCl_4$$

$$0.480\ m = \frac{x\ \text{mol}\ I_2}{0.1\ \text{kg}\ H_2O} \qquad x = 0.0480\ \text{mol}\ I_2$$

$$0.0480\ \text{mol}\ I_2 \times \frac{253.\ \text{g}\ I_2}{\text{mol}\ I_2} = 12.2\ \text{g}\ I_2$$

4 CHECK YOUR WORK

The answer has three significant digits and the units for mass of I_2.

Practice

1. What is the molality of acetone in a solution composed of 255 g of acetone, $(CH_3)_2CO$, dissolved in 200 g of water?
2. What quantity, in grams, of methanol, CH_3OH, is required to prepare a 0.244 *m* solution in 400 g of water?

SECTION 3 FORMATIVE ASSESSMENT

Reviewing Main Ideas

1. What quantity represents the ratio of the number of moles of solute for a given volume of solution?
2. We dissolve 5.00 grams of sugar, $C_{12}H_{22}O_{11}$, in water to make 1.000 L of solution. What is the concentration of this solution expressed as a molarity?

Critical Thinking

3. **ANALYZING DATA** You evaporate all of the water from 100 mL of NaCl solution and obtain 11.3 grams of NaCl. What was the molarity of the NaCl solution?
4. **RELATING IDEAS** Suppose you know the molarity of a solution. What additional information would you need to calculate the molality of the solution?

Answers to Section Assessment

1. molarity
2. The solution is 0.0146 M.
3. 1.93 M NaCl
4. the density of the solution

Math Tutor

Calculating Solution Concentration

You can use the relationship below to calculate the concentration in molarity of any solution.

$$\text{molarity of solution (M)} = \frac{\text{moles of solute (mol)}}{\text{volume of solution (L)}}$$

Suppose you dissolve 20.00 g of NaOH in some water and dilute the solution to a volume of 250.0 mL (0.2500 L). You don't know the molarity of this solution until you know how many moles of NaOH were dissolved. The number of moles of a substance can be found by dividing the mass of the substance by the mass of 1 mol (molar mass) of the substance.

The molar mass of NaOH is 40.00, so the number of moles of NaOH dissolved is

$$20.00 \text{ g NaOH} \times \frac{1 \text{ mol NaOH}}{40.00 \text{ g NaOH}} = 0.5000 \text{ mol NaOH}$$

Now you know that the solution has 0.5000 mol NaOH dissolved in 0.2500 L of solution, so you can calculate molarity.

$$\text{molarity of NaOH} \times \frac{\text{mol NaOH}}{\text{L solution}} = \frac{0.5000 \text{ mol NaOH}}{0.2500 \text{ L solution}}$$

$$= 2.000 \text{ mol/L} = 2.000 \text{ M NaOH}$$

Problem-Solving TIPS

- Remember that balances measure mass and not moles, so you often have to convert between mass and moles of solute when making or using solutions.

Sample Problem

A 0.5000 L volume of a solution contains 36.49 g of magnesium chloride, $MgCl_2$. What is the molarity of the solution?

You know the volume of the solution, but you need to find the number of moles of the solute $MgCl_2$ by the following conversion:

$$\text{mass } MgCl_2 \times \frac{1 \text{ mol } MgCl_2}{\text{molar mass } MgCl_2} = \text{mol } MgCl_2$$

$$36.49 \text{ g } MgCl_2 \times \frac{1 \text{ mol } MgCl_2}{95.20 \text{ g } MgCl_2} = 0.3833 \text{ mol } MgCl_2$$

Now you can calculate mol $MgCl_2$ per liter of solution (molarity).

$$\frac{0.3833 \text{ mol } MgCl_2}{0.5000 \text{ L soultion}} = 0.7666 \text{ M } MgCl_2$$

Practice

1. What is the molarity of a solution that contains 0.0350 mol of sodium sulfate, Na_2SO_4, dissolved in 50.0 mL of solution?
2. What is the molarity of a solution that contains 45.00 g of cadmium nitrate, $Cd(NO_3)_2$, dissolved in 400.0 mL of solution?

MATH TUTOR

Answers

1. 0.700 M Na_2SO_4
2. 0.4758 M $Cd(NO_3)_2$

CHAPTER 12 Summary

Review Games
Concept Maps

SECTION 1 Types of Mixtures

- Solutions are homogeneous mixtures.
- Mixtures are classified as solutions, suspensions, or colloids, depending on the size of the solute particles in the mixture.
- The dissolved substance is the solute. Solutions that have water as a solvent are aqueous solutions.
- Solutions can consist of solutes and solvents that are solids, liquids, or gases.
- Suspensions settle out upon standing. Colloids do not settle out, and they scatter light that is shined through them.
- Most ionic solutes and some molecular solutes form aqueous solutions that conduct an electric current. These solutes are called electrolytes.
- Nonelectrolytes are solutes that dissolve in water to form solutions that do not conduct electric currents.

KEY TERMS

soluble
solution
solvent
solute
suspension
colloid
electrolyte
nonelectrolyte

SECTION 2 The Solution Process

- A solute dissolves at a rate that depends on the surface area of the solute, how vigorously the solution is mixed, and the temperature of the solvent.
- The solubility of a substance indicates how much of that substance will dissolve in a specified amount of solvent under certain conditions.
- The solubility of a substance depends on the temperature.
- The solubility of gases in liquids increases with increases in pressure.
- The solubility of gases in liquids decreases with increases in temperature.
- The overall energy absorbed as heat by the system when a specified amount of solute dissolves during solution formation is called the enthalpy of solution.

KEY TERMS

solution equilibrium
saturated solution
unsaturated solution
supersaturated solution
solubility
hydration
immiscible
miscible
Henry's law
effervescence
solvated
enthalpy of solution

SECTION 3 Concentration of Solutions

- Two useful expressions of concentration are molarity and molality.
- The molar concentration of a solution represents the ratio of moles of solute to liters of solution.
- The molal concentration of a solution represents the ratio of moles of solute to kilograms of solvent.

KEY TERMS

concentration
molarity
molality

404 Chapter 12

CHAPTER 12 Review

SECTION 1

Types of Mixtures

 REVIEWING MAIN IDEAS

1. a. What is the Tyndall effect?
   b. Identify one example of this effect.
2. Given an unknown mixture consisting of two or more substances, explain how you could determine whether that mixture is a true solution, a colloid, or a suspension.
3. Explain why a suspension is considered a heterogeneous mixture.
4. Does a solution have to involve a liquid? Explain your answer.
5. What is the difference between an electrolyte and a nonelectrolyte?

SECTION 2

The Solution Process

 REVIEWING MAIN IDEAS

6. a. What is solution equilibrium?
   b. What factors determine the point at which a given solute-solvent combination reaches equilibrium?
7. a. What is a saturated solution?
   b. What visible evidence indicates that a solution is saturated?
   c. What is an unsaturated solution?
8. a. What is meant by the solubility of a substance?
   b. What condition(s) must be specified when expressing the solubility of a substance?
9. a. What rule of thumb is useful for predicting whether one substance will dissolve in another?
   b. Describe what the rule means in terms of various combinations of polar and nonpolar solutes and solvents.
10. a. How does pressure affect the solubility of a gas in a liquid?
    b. What law is a statement of this relationship?
    c. If the pressure of a gas above a liquid is increased, what happens to the amount of the gas that will dissolve in the liquid, if all other conditions remain constant?
    d. Two bottles of soda are opened. One is a cold bottle and the other is at room temperature. Which system will show more effervescence and why?
11. Based on **Figure 2.11**, determine the solubility of each of the following in grams of solute per 100 g H_2O.
    a. $NaNO_3$ at 10°C
    b. KNO_3 at 60°C
    c. NaCl at 50°C
12. Based on **Figure 2.11**, at what temperature would each of the following solubility levels be observed?
    a. 50 g KCl in 100 g H_2O
    b. 100 g $NaNO_3$ in 100 g H_2O
    c. 60 g KNO_3 in 100 g H_2O
13. The enthalpy of solution for $AgNO_3$ is +22.8 kJ/mol.
    a. Write the equation that represents the dissolution of $AgNO_3$ in water.
    b. Is the dissolution process endothermic or exothermic? Is the crystallization process endothermic or exothermic?
    c. As $AgNO_3$ dissolves, what change occurs in the temperature of the solution?
    d. When the system is at equilibrium, how do the rates of dissolution and crystallization compare?
    e. If the solution is then heated, how will the rates of dissolution and crystallization be affected? Why?
    f. How will the increased temperature affect the amount of solute that can be dissolved?
    g. If the solution is allowed to reach equilibrium and is then cooled, how will the system be affected?
14. What opposing forces are at equilibrium in the sodium chloride system shown in **Figure 2.2**?

SECTION 3

Concentration of Solutions

 REVIEWING MAIN IDEAS

15. On which property of solutions does the concept of concentration rely?

Review Answers

1. a. The Tyndall effect is the scattering of light by colloidal particles dispersed in a transparent medium.
   b. The visibility of a headlight beam on a foggy night is an example of this effect.
2. Shine a beam of light through the mixture. If it is a solution, light scattering will not be observed. If it is a colloid, the light will be scattered. A suspension will settle out.
3. A suspension consists of particles that are large enough to be viewed under a microscope.
4. No, a solution is any homogeneous mixture and can be, for instance, gas/gas or solid/solid.
5. An electrolyte is a solute that dissolves in water to produce a solution that conducts electric current, and a nonelectrolyte is a solute that does not.

6. a. Solution equilibrium is the state in which the opposing processes of the dissolution and crystallization of a solute occur at equal rates.
   b. The factors that determine the equilibrium point are the nature of the solute, the nature of the solvent, and the temperature. In the case of a gaseous solution, pressure is also a factor.
7. a. A saturated solution is one that contains the maximum possible amount of dissolved solute at solution equilibrium under the existing conditions.
   b. A residual quantity of undissolved solute remains in contact with a saturated solution.
   c. An unsaturated solution contains less solute than a saturated solution under the same conditions.
8. a. The solubility of a substance is the amount of that substance dissolved at solution equilibrium in a specific amount of solvent at a specified temperature.
   b. Temperature and pressure (for gases) must be specified.
9. a. The rule of thumb for predicting solubility is "like dissolves like."
   b. In general, the rule means that polar substances dissolve in polar solvents, and nonpolar substances dissolve in nonpolar solvents.
10. a. The solubility of a gas in a liquid is directly proportional to its pressure above the liquid.
    b. Henry's law states this relationship.
    c. If the pressure above the gas increases, the amount of gas that can dissolve will increase.
    d. The soda at room temperature will effervesce more than the cold soda. The gas is less soluble in the warmer solvent.
11. a. about 84 g per 100 g solvent
    b. about 105 g per 100 g solvent
    c. about 36 g per 100 g solvent
12. a. 70°C
    b. 40°C
    c. 40°C

13. a. $AgNO_3(s) + 22.8 \text{ kJ/mol} \xrightarrow{H_2O} AgNO_3(aq)$
   b. The dissolution process is endothermic; crystallization is exothermic.
   c. The temperature drops as silver nitrate dissolves.
   d. At equilibrium, the rates of dissolution and crystallization are equal.
   e. The rate of dissolution will initially increase at a faster pace than the rate of crystallization because the dissolution process is endothermic and will serve to reduce the stress placed on the system.
   f. The amount will increase if additional solute is available.
   g. The rate of crystallization will increase to relieve the stress, so the solubility of the solute will then decrease.
14. dissolution and recrystallization
15. the fact that solute is distributed evenly throughout the solvent
16. mol/L (moles of solute per liter of solution)
17. a. Molarity would be used when it is important to know the number of moles of solute in a given volume of solution.
   b. Molality is preferred when it is important to know the relative numbers of solute and solvent particles independent of temperature changes.
18. No; the total volume of the solution may be different after the solute is dissolved in the solvent.
19. a. (1) 106 g/mol
   (2) 0.167 M
   b. 0.953 M NH_4Br
20. a. (1) H_2SO_4
   (2) H_2O
   (3) 343 g
   b. 1140 g
21. 0.143 mol NaOH
22. a. 132.1 g/mol
   b. 4.000 M
23. a. to determine the molar mass of $AgNO_3$
   b. 169.9 g/mol
   c. 1000 mL

16. In what units is molarity expressed?

17. Under what circumstances might we prefer to express solution concentrations in terms of
   a. molarity?
   b. molality?

18. If you dissolve 2.00 mol KI in 1.00 L of water, will you get a 2.00 M solution? Explain.

PRACTICE PROBLEMS

19. a. Suppose you wanted to dissolve 106 g of Na_2CO_3 in enough H_2O to make 6.00 L of solution.
   (1) What is the molar mass of Na_2CO_3?
   (2) What is the molarity of this solution?
   b. What is the molarity of a solution of 14.0 g NH_4Br in enough H_2O to make 150 mL of solution?

20. a. Suppose you wanted to produce 1.00 L of a 3.50 M aqueous solution of H_2SO_4.
   (1) What is the solute?
   (2) What is the solvent?
   (3) How many grams of solute are needed to make this solution?
   b. How many grams of solute are needed to make 2.50 L of a 1.75 M solution of $Ba(NO_3)_2$?

21. How many moles of NaOH are contained in 65.0 mL of a 2.20 M solution of NaOH in H_2O? (Hint: See Sample Problem B.)

22. A solution is made by dissolving 26.42 g of $(NH_4)_2SO_4$ in enough H_2O to make 50.00 mL of solution.
   a. What is the molar mass of $(NH_4)_2SO_4$?
   b. What is the molarity of this solution?

23. Suppose you wanted to find out how many milliliters of 1.0 M $AgNO_3$ are needed to provide 169.9 g of pure $AgNO_3$.
   a. What is the first step in solving the problem?
   b. What is the molar mass of $AgNO_3$?
   c. How many milliliters of solution are needed?

24. a. Balance this equation:
   $H_3PO_4 + Ca(OH)_2 \longrightarrow Ca_3(PO_4)_2 + H_2O$
   b. What mass of each product results if 750 mL of 6.00 M H_3PO_4 reacts according to the equation?

25. How many milliliters of 0.750 M H_3PO_4 are required to react with 250 mL of 0.150 M $Ba(OH)_2$ if the products are barium phosphate and water?

26. 75.0 mL of an $AgNO_3$ solution reacts with enough Cu to produce 0.250 g of Ag by single displacement. What is the molarity of the initial $AgNO_3$ solution if $Cu(NO_3)_2$ is the other product?

27. Determine the number of grams of solute needed to make each of the following molal solutions:
   a. a 4.50 *m* solution of H_2SO_4 in 1.00 kg H_2O
   b. a 1.00 *m* solution of HNO_3 in 2.00 kg H_2O

28. A solution is prepared by dissolving 17.1 g of sucrose, $C_{12}H_{22}O_{11}$, in 275 g of H_2O.
   a. What is the molar mass of sucrose?
   b. What is the molality of that solution?

29. How many kilograms of H_2O must be added to 75.5 g of $Ca(NO_3)_2$ to form a 0.500 *m* solution?

30. A solution made from ethanol, C_2H_5OH, and water is 1.75 *m* ethanol. How many grams of C_2H_5OH are contained per 250. g of water?

Mixed Review

REVIEWING MAIN IDEAS

31. Na_2SO_4 is dissolved in water to make 450 mL of a 0.250 M solution.
   a. What is the molar mass of Na_2SO_4?
   b. How many moles of Na_2SO_4 are needed?

32. Citric acid is one component of some soft drinks. Suppose that 2.00 L of solution are made from 150. mg of citric acid, $C_6H_8O_7$.
   a. What is the molar mass of citric acid?
   b. What is the molarity of citric acid in the solution?

33. Suppose you wanted to know how many grams of KCl would be left if 350 mL of a 2.0 M KCl solution were evaporated to dryness.
   a. What is the molar mass of KCl?
   b. How would heating the solution affect the mass of KCl remaining?
   c. How many grams of KCl would remain?

24. a. $2H_3PO_4 + 3Ca(OH)_2 \longrightarrow Ca_3(PO_4)_2 + 6H_2O$
   b. 698 g calcium phosphate and 243 g water
25. 33.3 mL
26. 0.0309 M
27. a. 441 g
   b. 126 g
28. a. 342 g
   b. 0.182 *m*
29. 0.920 kg
30. 20.2 g
31. a. 142.01 g/mol
   b. 0.113 mol
32. a. 192.1 g/mol
   b. 3.90×10^{-4} M
33. a. 74.6 g/mol
   b. not at all
   c. 53 g

34. Sodium metal reacts violently with water to form NaOH and release hydrogen gas. Suppose that 10.0 g of Na react completely with 1.00 L of water and the final solution volume is 1.00 L.

a. What is the molar mass of NaOH?
b. Write a balanced equation for the reaction.
c. What is the molarity of the NaOH solution formed by the reaction?

35. In cars, ethylene glycol, $C_2H_6O_2$, is used as a coolant and antifreeze. A mechanic fills a radiator with 6.5 kg of ethylene glycol and 1.5 kg of water.

a. What is the molar mass of ethylene glycol?
b. What is the molality of the water in the solution?

36. Plot a solubility graph for $AgNO_3$ from the following data, with grams of solute (by increments of 50) per 100 g of H_2O on the vertical axis and with temperature in °C on the horizontal axis.

Grams solute per 100 g H_2O	Temperature (°C)
122	0
216	30
311	40
440	60
585	80
733	100

a. How does the solubility of $AgNO_3$ vary with the temperature of the water?
b. Estimate the solubility of $AgNO_3$ at 35°C, 55°C, and 75°C.
c. At what temperature would the solubility of $AgNO_3$ be 275 g per 100 g of H_2O?
d. If 100 g of $AgNO_3$ were added to 100 g of H_2O at 10°C, would the resulting solution be saturated or unsaturated? What would occur if 325 g of $AgNO_3$ were added to 100 g of H_2O at 35°C?

37. If a saturated solution of KNO_3 in 100 g of H_2O at 60°C is cooled to 20°C, approximately how many grams of the solute will precipitate out of the solution? (Use **Figure 2.4.**)

38. a. Suppose you wanted to dissolve 294.3 g of H_2SO_4 in 1.000 kg of H_2O.
(1) What is the solute?
(2) What is the solvent?
(3) What is the molality of this solution?

b. What is the molality of a solution of 63.0 g HNO_3 in 0.250 kg H_2O?

ALTERNATIVE ASSESSMENT

39. Predicting Outcomes You have been investigating the nature of suspensions, colloids, and solutions and have collected the following observational data on four unknown samples. From the data, infer whether each sample is a solution, suspension, or colloid.

DATA TABLE 1 *Samples*

Sample	Color	Clarity (clear or cloudy)	Settle out	Tyndall effect
1	green	clear	no	no
2	blue	cloudy	yes	no
3	colorless	clear	no	yes
4	white	cloudy	no	yes

Based on your inferences in Data Table 1, you decide to conduct one more test of the particles. You filter the samples and then reexamine the filtrate. You obtain the data found in Data Table 2. Infer the classifications of the filtrate based on the data in Data Table 2.

DATA TABLE 2 *Filtrate of Samples*

Sample	Color	Clarity (clear or cloudy)	On filter paper	Tyndall effect
1	green	clear	nothing	no
2	blue	cloudy	gray solid	yes
3	colorless	clear	none	yes
4	colorless	clear	white solid	no

CHAPTER REVIEW

34. a. 40.0 g/mol
b. $2Na + 2H_2O \longrightarrow 2NaOH + H_2$
c. 0.435 M

35. a. 62.1 g/mol
b. 13 *m*

36. Graphs should accurately match data shown. A good range for the *y*-axis is 0 to 800 g. The *x*-axis range should be 0 to 100°C.
a. Solubility increases with increasing temperature.
b. at 35°C, 250 g per 100 g solvent; at 55°C, 380 g per 100 g solvent; at 75°C, 540 g per 100 g solvent
c. This solubility would be observed at about 35°C.
d. The resulting solution would be unsaturated; The solution would be saturated.

37. 74.4 g

38. a. (1) H_2SO_4
(2) H_2O
(3) 3.000 *m*
b. 4.00 *m*

39.

DATA TABLE 1
sample 1 = solution
sample 2 = suspension
sample 3 = colloid
sample 4 = colloid

DATA TABLE 2
sample 1 = solution
sample 2 = colloid
sample 3 = colloid
sample 4 = suspension

40. a. It is lightweight and strong, resists corrosion, and has good conductivity properties.

b. copper and tin

c. copper and zinc

d. any alloy of iron with less than 2.5% carbon

e. pure iron, carbon, and cementite—an iron carbide

41. a. 500 ppm

b. 2.5 times the limit

42. Students will discover that molecules of emulsifying agents contain a polar center and a nonpolar center.

43. Usually, the information regarding sugar will be given in units of grams per amount of drink. Have students convert the mass of sugar to moles of sugar, which will result in the units of mole per liter, or molarity.

44. Answers may vary. At some point, students will need to convert from mass of solute to moles of solute. The number of grams in one mole of copper sulfate pentahydrate is 90 g more than the molar mass of copper sulfate anhydrous.

CHAPTER REVIEW

40. Review the information on alloys in the *Elements Handbook* (Appendix A).

a. Why is aluminum such an important component of alloys?

b. What metals make up bronze?

c. What metals make up brass?

d. What is steel?

e. What is the composition of the mixture called *cast iron*?

41. **Table 5A** of the *Elements Handbook* (Appendix A) contains carbon monoxide concentration data expressed as parts per million (ppm). The OSHA (Occupational Safety and Health Administration) limit for worker exposure to CO is 200 ppm for an eight-hour period.

a. At what concentration do harmful effects occur in less than one hour?

b. By what factor does the concentration in item (a) exceed the maximum limit set by OSHA?

RESEARCH AND WRITING

42. Find out about the chemistry of emulsifying agents. How do these substances affect the dissolution of immiscible substances such as oil and water? As part of your research on this topic, find out why eggs are an emulsifying agent for baking mixtures.

ALTERNATIVE ASSESSMENT

43. Make a comparison of the electrolyte concentration in various brands of sports drinks. Using the labeling information for sugar, calculate the molarity of sugar in each product or brand. Construct a poster to show the results of your analysis of the product labels.

44. Write a set of instructions on how to prepare a solution that is 1 M $CuSO_4$, using $CuSO_4{\bullet}5H_2O$ as the solute. How do the instructions differ if the solute is anhydrous $CuSO_4$? Your instructions should include a list of all materials needed.

Standards-Based Assessment

Answer the following items on a separate piece of paper.

MULTIPLE CHOICE

1. Water is an excellent solvent because
   A. it is a covalent compound.
   B. it is a nonconductor of electricity.
   C. its molecules are quite polar.
   D. it is a clear, colorless liquid.

2. Two liquids are likely to be immiscible if
   A. both have polar molecules.
   B. both have nonpolar molecules.
   C. one is polar and the other is nonpolar.
   D. one is water and the other is methyl alcohol, CH_3OH.

3. The solubility of a gas in a liquid would be increased by
   A. the addition of an electrolyte.
   B. the addition of an emulsifier.
   C. agitation of the solution.
   D. an increase in its partial pressure.

4. Which of the following types of compounds is most likely to be a strong electrolyte?
   A. a polar compound
   B. a nonpolar compound
   C. a covalent compound
   D. an ionic compound

5. A saturated solution can become supersaturated under which of the following conditions?
   A. It contains electrolytes.
   B. The solution is heated and then allowed to cool.
   C. More solvent is added.
   D. More solute is added.

6. Molarity is expressed in units of
   A. moles of solute per liter of solution.
   B. liters of solution per mole of solute.
   C. moles of solute per liter of solvent.
   D. liters of solvent per mole of solute.

7. What mass of NaOH is contained in 2.5 L of a 0.010 M solution?
   A. 0.010 g
   B. 1.0 g
   C. 2.5 g
   D. 0.40 g

8. Which one of the following statements is false?
   A. Gases are generally more soluble in water under high pressures than under low pressures.
   B. As temperature increases, the solubilities of some solids in water increase and the solubilities of other solids in water decrease.
   C. Water dissolves many ionic solutes because of its ability to hydrate ions in solution.
   D. Many solids dissolve more quickly in a cold solvent than in a warm solvent.

SHORT ANSWER

9. Several experiments are carried out to determine the solubility of cadmium iodide, CdI_2, in water. In each experiment, a measured mass of CdI_2 is added to 100 g of water at 25°C and the mixture is stirred. Any undissolved CdI_2 is then filtered off and dried, and its mass is determined. Results for several such experiments are shown in the table below. What is the solubility of CdI_2 in water at this temperature?

Mass of CdI_2 added, g	Mass of undissolved CdI_2 recovered, g
17.9	0.0
38.2	0.0
53.6	0.0
79.3	0.0
93.6	7.4
104.3	18.1

EXTENDED RESPONSE

10. Explain why oil and water do not mix.

11. Write a set of instructions on how to prepare a solution that is 0.100 M KBr, using solid KBr (molar mass 119 g/mol) as the solute. Your instructions should include a list of all materials and equipment needed.

Test Tip

Allow a few minutes at the end of the test-taking period to check for careless mistakes, such as marking two answers for a single question.

STANDARDS-BASED ASSESSMENT

To give students practice under more realistic testing conditions, give them 60 minutes to answer all of the questions in this Standardized Test Preparation.

Test Answers

1. C
2. C
3. D
4. D
5. B
6. A
7. B
8. D
9. 86.2 g
10. Water is polar, and oil is nonpolar. When the two are combined, the strong hydrogen bonding between water molecules squeezes out the oil droplets, forming separate layers. Simply citing the rule of thumb that "like dissolves like" is not an acceptable explanation.
11. Student answers should summarize the steps in **Figure 3.1**, using 11.9 g of KBr in a 1.00-L volumetric flask (or values proportional to these).

Ions in Aqueous Solutions and Colligative Properties

① Core Instruction

Chapter Resources

- The Teacher's Edition wrap has extensive teaching support for every lesson, including Misconception Alerts, Teach from Visuals, Demonstrations, Teaching Tips, Differentiated Instruction, and Problem Solving support.
- Several additional presentation tools are available online for every chapter, including Animated Chemistry features and Visual Concepts.
- You can open your lesson with the Why It Matters Video: Colligative Properties.

Section	Instruction	Labs and Demonstrations Go Online for Materials Lists and Solutions Lists.
13.1	■ **Textbook:** Compounds in Aqueous Solution **Animated Chemistry:** Precipitation Reactions **Teaching Visuals:** Dissociation of NaCl • Soluble and Insoluble Ionic Compounds • Particle Model for the Formation of a Precipitate • Writing a Net Ionic Equation • Models for Strong, Weak, and Nonelectrolytes • General Solubility Guidelines • Solubility Rules for Some Common Ionic Compounds	■ **Demonstration:** A Precipitation Reaction ■ **Lab:** Testing Water for Ions (Core Skill) ■ **Lab:** Reacting Ionic Species in Aqueous Solution (Core Skill) ■ **Lab:** Colored Precipitates (Core Skill) ■ **Lab:** Solubility and Chemical Fertilizers (Forensics)
13.2	■ **Textbook:** Colligative Properties of Solutions **Teaching Visuals:** Vapor Pressures of Pure Water and an Aqueous Solution • Osmotic Pressure • Colligative Properties Graph • Molal Freezing-Point Depressions • Solute Effects on the Vapor Pressure of a Pure Solvent **PowerPresentations**	■ **Demonstration:** The Process of Osmosis ■ **Lab:** Diffusion and Cell Membranes ■ **Lab:** The Heat Is On! (STEM)

2 Support and Intervention

- **Interactive Reader** (English and Spanish)
- **Study Guide**
- **Interactive Review:** Review Games, Concept Maps, and Section Self-Checks
- **Scientific Reasoning Skill Builder**
- **Learn It! Videos**
- **Solve It! Cards**
- **Interactive Demos**
- **Sample Problem Sets**

3 Specialized Support

- **Chapter Summary Audio Files**
- **Interactive Reader Audio Files**
- **Differentiated Instruction:** Inclusion, Below Level, and English Learners (TE wrap)

Enrichment and Challenge

- **Differentiated Instruction:** Pre-AP (TE wrap)
- **Chemistry Explorers:** The Riddle of Electrolysis (SE)
- **WebLinks**

Assessment

- **Section Formative Assessments** (SE)
- **Section Quizzes**
- **Chapter Review** (SE)
- **Chapter Tests A and B**
- **Alternative Assessment** (TE wrap)
- **Online Assessment and Remediation**
- **ExamView Banks**

Where do I find it?

	Resource	PRINT	DVD	ONLINE
1	Animated Chemistry		■	■
1	Demonstrations (TE wrap)	■		■
1	Interactive Whiteboard		■	■
1	Labs		■	■
1	PowerPresentations		■	■
1	QuickLabs	■	■	■
1	Teaching Visuals		■	■
1	Textbook	■	■	■
1	Visual Concepts		■	■
1	Why It Matters Videos		■	■
2	Interactive Demos		■	■
2	Interactive Reader	■	■	■
2	Interactive Reviews		■	■
2	Learn It! Videos		■	■
2	Sample Problem Sets		■	■
2	Scientific Reasoning Skill Builder		■	■
2	Smart Grapher Tool		■	■
2	Solve It! Cards		■	■
2	Study Guide		■	■
3	Chapter Summary Audio Files		■	■
3	Differentiated Instruction (TE wrap)	■		
3	Interactive Reader Audio Files		■	■

CHAPTER 13

Chapter Overview

Section 1 describes the dissociation of ionic compounds and the ionization of some molecular compounds when they dissolve in water, distinguishes between strong and weak electrolytes, shows how precipitation reactions occur, and describes methods of writing ionic equations for precipitation reactions.

Section 2 describes, both descriptively and mathematically, boiling-point elevation and freezing-point depression. The mechanism of osmosis and the cause of osmotic pressure are described.

▼ Focus and Motivate

Activate Prior Knowledge

Students may need a review of the following concepts:

- bonding and structure in both ionic and covalent compounds
- writing and interpreting chemical formulas
- dissolution, molarity and molality

About the Image

Ionic compounds in aqueous solution can react to form different ionic compounds that can come out of solution under the correct conditions. The fragile formations in the image are naturally-occurring crystals of the mineral cyanotrichite ($Cu_4Al_2SO_4(OH)_{12} \cdot 2H_2O$), composed of hydrous copper aluminum sulfate. Cyanotrichite crystals form in hidden cavities underground, as water evaporates from solutions of ionic compounds. Although not a copper ore, it is associated with copper mines and is a favorite of collectors.

Why It Matters

Students can access the video online and find other helpful resources at **HMDScience.com**.

CHAPTER 13

Ions in Aqueous Solutions and Colligative Properties

ONLINE Chemistry
HMDScience.com

SECTION 1
Compounds in Aqueous Solutions

SECTION 2
Colligative Properties of Solutions

ONLINE LABS include:
Testing Water for Ions
Reacting Ionic Species in Aqueous Solution
Colored Precipitates
Diffusion and Cell Membranes
Solubility and Chemical Fertilizers

PREMIUM CONTENT
Why It Matters Video
HMDScience.com
Colligative Properties

Lab Preview

The following labs and demonstrations support the concepts presented in this chapter.

LABS

Testing Water for Ions (Core Skill)
Reacting Ionic Species in Aqueous Solution (Core Skill)
Colored Precipitates (Core Skill)
Solubility and Chemical Fertilizers (Forensics)
Diffusion and Cell Membranes
The Heat Is On! (STEM)

DEMONSTRATIONS

A Precipitation Reaction
The Process of Osmosis

Compounds in Aqueous Solutions

SECTION 1

Main Ideas

- Ions separate from each other when ionic compounds are dissolved in water.
- A molecular compound ionizes in a polar solvent.
- An electrolyte's strength depends on how many dissolved ions it contains.

Key Terms

dissociation
net ionic equation
spectator ions
ionization
hydronium ion
strong electrolyte
weak electrolyte

As you have learned, solid compounds can be ionic or molecular. In an ionic solid, a crystal structure is made up of charged particles held together by ionic attractions. In a molecular solid, molecules are composed of covalently bonded atoms. The solid is held together by noncovalent, intermolecular forces. When they dissolve in water, ionic compounds and molecular compounds behave differently.

MAIN IDEA

Ions separate from each other when ionic compounds are dissolved in water.

When a compound that is made of ions dissolves in water, the ions separate from one another, as shown in **Figure 1.1.** This separation of ions that occurs when an ionic compound dissolves is called **dissociation.** For example, dissociation of sodium chloride and calcium chloride in water can be represented by the following equations. (As usual, (*s*) indicates a solid species, and (*aq*) indicates a species in an aqueous solution. Note that each equation is balanced for charge as well as for atoms.)

$$NaCl(s) \xrightarrow{H_2O} Na^+(aq) + Cl^-(aq)$$

$$CaCl_2(s) \xrightarrow{H_2O} Ca^{2+}(aq) + 2Cl^-(aq)$$

Notice the number of ions produced per formula unit in the equations above. One formula unit of sodium chloride gives two ions in solution, whereas one formula unit of calcium chloride gives three ions in solution.

FIGURE 1.1

Dissociation When NaCl dissolves in water, the ions separate as they leave the crystal.

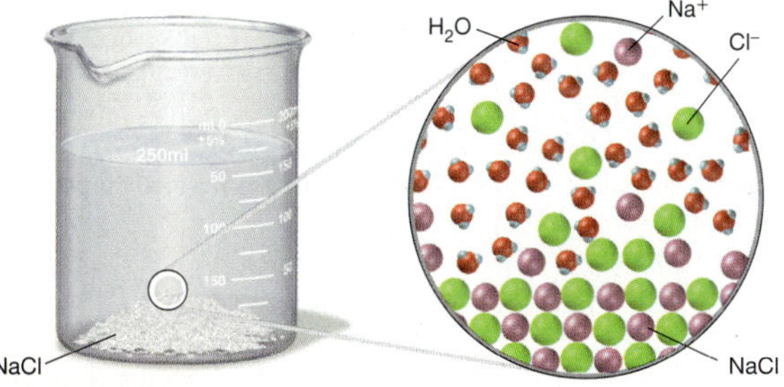

Differentiated Instruction

ENGLISH LEARNERS

Have students look up the meaning of the word *dissociation.* Ask them to include the word in a sentence. Then have students compare their use of the word to the scientific definition. Students should recognize that both contexts use dissociation to mean a separation. Point out that in chemistry, dissociation refers to the separation of ions as the ionic compound dissolves.

SECTION 1

Plan and Prepare

Objectives

Upon completion of this section, students should be able to do the following:

- Write equations for the dissolution of soluble ionic compounds in water.
- Predict whether a precipitate will form when solutions of soluble ionic compounds are combined, and write net ionic equations for precipitation reactions.
- Compare dissociation of ionic compounds with ionization of molecular compounds.
- Draw the structure of the hydronium ion, and explain why it is used to represent the hydrogen ion in solution.
- Distinguish between strong electrolytes and weak electrolytes.

Classroom Catalyst

Display a colored crystalline salt, such as $CuSO_4 \bullet 5H_2O$, in its solid form alongside a large beaker or flask containing an aqueous solution of the same salt. Ask students to compare the composition and arrangement of particles in the crystals with those in the solution.

Teach

READING TOOLKIT

DISCUSSION Have students read Section 1, then discuss these questions:

- How can you predict if a certain compound will form a precipitate?
- How do you write a net ionic equation?
- How is dissociation different from ionization?
- What compounds are strong electrolytes? Why?

▼ Teach *continued*

Classroom Practice

A-1 Write the equation for the dissolution of magnesium chlorate in water. How many moles of ions are produced for every 1 mol of magnesium chlorate dissolved?

Answer: $Mg(ClO_3)_2(s) \xrightarrow{H_2O} Mg^{2+}(aq) + 2ClO_3^-(aq)$; 3 mol

A-2 Write the equation for the dissolution of NH_4NO_3 in water. If 3.5 mol NH_4NO_3 are dissolved, how many moles of each type of ion are produced? How many total moles of ions are produced?

Answer: $NH_4NO_3(s) \xrightarrow{H_2O} NH_4^+(aq) + NO_3^-(aq)$; 3.5 mol of each ion, 7.0 mol total ions

Answers

Practice A

1. a. $NH_4Cl(s) \xrightarrow{H_2O} NH_4^+(aq) + Cl^-(aq)$; 1 mol NH_4^+, 1 mol Cl^-, 2 mol ions

   b. $Na_2S(s) \xrightarrow{H_2O} 2Na^+(aq) + S^{2-}(aq)$; 2 mol Na^+, 1 mol S^{2-}, 3 mol ions

   c. $Ba(NO_3)_2(s) \xrightarrow{H_2O} Ba^{2+}(aq) + 2NO_3^-(aq)$; 0.5 mol Ba^{2+}, 1 mol NO_3^-, 1.5 mol ions

Assuming 100% dissociation, a solution that contains 1 mol of sodium chloride contains 1 mol of Na^+ ions and 1 mol of Cl^- ions. In this book, you can assume 100% dissociation for all soluble ionic compounds. The dissociation of NaCl can be represented as follows.

$$\underset{1\text{ mol}}{NaCl(s)} \xrightarrow{H_2O} \underset{1\text{ mol}}{Na^+(aq)} + \underset{1\text{ mol}}{Cl^-(aq)}$$

A solution that contains 1 mol of calcium chloride contains 1 mol of Ca^{2+} ions and 2 mol of Cl^- ions—a total of 3 mol of ions.

$$\underset{1\text{ mol}}{CaCl_2(s)} \xrightarrow{H_2O} \underset{1\text{ mol}}{Ca^{2+}(aq)} + \underset{2\text{ mol}}{2Cl^-(aq)}$$

Calculating Moles of Dissolved Ions

Sample Problem A **Write the equation for the dissolution of aluminum sulfate, $Al_2(SO_4)_3$, in water. How many moles of aluminum ions and sulfate ions are produced by dissolving 1 mol of aluminum sulfate? What is the total number of moles of ions produced by dissolving 1 mol of aluminum sulfate?**

1 ANALYZE

Given: amount of solute = 1 mol $Al_2(SO_4)_3$

solvent identity = water

Unknown: **a.** moles of aluminum ions and sulfate ions

b. total number of moles of solute ions produced

2 PLAN

The coefficients in the balanced dissociation equation will reveal the mole relationships, so you can use the equation to determine the number of moles of solute ions produced.

$$Al_2(SO_4)_3(s) \xrightarrow{H_2O} 2Al^{3+}(aq) + 3SO_4^{2-}(aq)$$

3 SOLVE

a. 1 mol $Al_2(SO_4)_3 \longrightarrow$ 2 mol Al^{3+} + 3 mol SO_4^{2-}

b. 2 mol Al^{3+} + 3 mol SO_4^{2-} = 5 mol of solute ions

4 CHECK YOUR WORK

The equation is correctly balanced. Because one formula unit of $Al_2(SO_4)_3$ produces 5 ions, 1 mol of $Al_2(SO_4)_3$ produces 5 mol of ions.

Practice Answers in Appendix E

1. Write the equation for the dissolution of each of the following in water, and then determine the number of moles of each ion produced as well as the total number of moles of ions produced.
   a. 1 mol ammonium chloride
   b. 1 mol sodium sulfide
   c. 0.5 mol barium nitrate

Problem Solving

TAKE IT FURTHER

Ask students why H_2O is placed above the arrow in the chemical equation rather than being included as either a reactant or product. Students should recognize that H_2O is not involved in the reaction because its chemical composition remains unchanged. Point out that the water molecules are responsible for the dissociation of aluminum sulfate and that they surround the aluminum cations and sulfate anions as part of the solvation process.

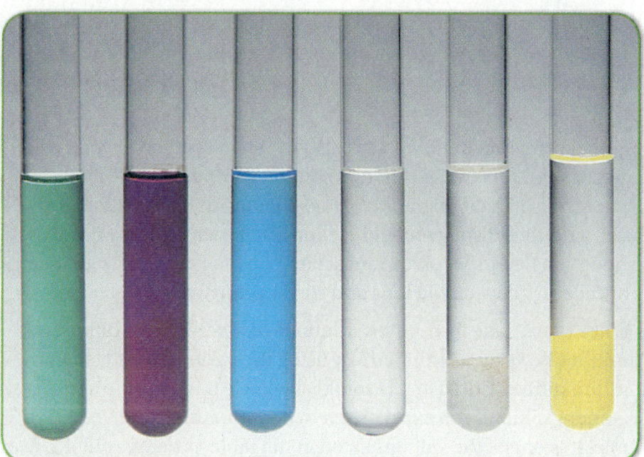

FIGURE 1.2

Solubility of Ionic Compounds Ionic compounds can be soluble or insoluble in water. $NiCl_2$, $KMnO_4$, $CuSO_4$, and $Pb(NO_3)_2$ are soluble in water. AgCl and CdS are insoluble in water.

Precipitation Reactions

Precipitation Reactions

Although no ionic compound is completely insoluble, compounds of very low solubility can be considered insoluble for most practical purposes. Some examples of ionic compounds that are soluble and insoluble in water are shown in **Figure 1.2.** It is difficult to write solubility rules that cover all possible conditions. However, we can write some general guidelines to help predict whether a compound made of a certain combination of ions is soluble. These general solubility guidelines are given in **Figure 1.3.**

By looking at the table you can tell that most sodium compounds are soluble. Sodium carbonate, Na_2CO_3, is soluble because it contains sodium. Its dissociation equation is as follows.

$$Na_2CO_3(s) \xrightarrow{H_2O} 2Na^+(aq) + CO_3^{2-}(aq)$$

FIGURE 1.3

GENERAL SOLUBILITY GUIDELINES
1. Sodium, potassium, and ammonium compounds are soluble in water.
2. Nitrates, acetates, and chlorates are soluble.
3. Most chlorides are soluble, except those of silver, mercury(I), and lead. Lead(II) chloride is soluble in hot water.
4. Most sulfates are soluble, except those of barium, strontium, lead, calcium, and mercury.
5. Most carbonates, phosphates, and silicates are insoluble, except those of sodium, potassium, and ammonium.
6. Most sulfides are insoluble, except those of calcium, strontium, sodium, potassium, and ammonium.

Differentiated Instruction

BELOW LEVEL

Have students practice using the solubility guidelines in **Figure 1.3** to predict whether an ionic compound is soluble. Provide examples that are not shown in **Figure 1.2.** Possibilities include $NaNO_3$ (soluble), HgCl (insoluble), $BaSO_4$ (insoluble), K_3PO_4 (soluble), and $(NH_4)_2S$ (soluble).

TEACH FROM VISUALS

FIGURE 1.2 Have students find the guidelines in **Figure 1.3** that apply to the compounds in **Figure 1.2.**

READING TOOLKIT

BRAINSTORMING Write the word *precipitation* on the board. Ask students to list words or phrases that relate to precipitation. Have them use their list, the chapter overview, and objectives for Section 1 to devise a hypothesis about the chemical definition of precipitation.

Misconception Alert!

Until now, most of the ionic compounds that students have studied have been highly soluble in water. Students therefore may have the impression that high solubility in water is a characteristic of ionic compounds. Use **Figure 1.2** and **Figure 1.3** to dispel that perception.

TEACH FROM TABLES

FIGURE 1.3 Emphasize that no ionic compound is entirely insoluble in water. Some ionic compounds are just considered insoluble because their solubility is less than 0.1 g/100 g water. Also, students will learn later in this chapter that no matter how insoluble an ionic compound may be, it is still an electrolyte because the amount that *does* dissolve in water completely dissociates. This is why most tap water, which contains very small amounts of ions from the dissociation of "insoluble" carbonates or phosphates of magnesium and calcium, conducts electricity.

▼ Teach *continued*

Demonstration

A PRECIPITATION REACTION

Dissolve **13 g $SrCl_2 \bullet 6H_2O$** in 100 mL of **water** in a **flask** to make a 0.5 *m* solution. In an identical **flask**, dissolve **7 g anhydrous Na_2SO_4** in 100 mL of **water** to give a 0.5 *m* solution. Exhibit the two flasks, and tell students what is in each flask. Have them write ionic equations for the dissociation of each salt. Pour the contents of one flask into the other flask, and point out the white precipitate that forms. Using the solubility guidelines in **Table 1.3** to identify the precipitate, $SrSO_4$, have students write a full ionic equation for the reaction.

Safety Wear an **apron** and **goggles.** Have students wear goggles and a lab apron, or keep students at a distance of at least 10 ft.

Disposal Filter the solution to remove the precipitate, and wash the filtrate down the drain with plenty of water. Dry the solid in air, and put it in the trash.

Teaching Tip

Make sure that students understand that they cannot write a dissociation equation for an insoluble ionic compound because an ionic compound that does not dissolve in water cannot dissociate in water.

Is calcium phosphate, $Ca_3(PO_4)_2$, soluble or insoluble? According to **Figure 1.3,** most phosphates are insoluble. Calcium phosphate is not one of the exceptions listed, so it is insoluble. Dissociation equations cannot be written for insoluble compounds.

The information in **Figure 1.3** is also useful in predicting what will happen if solutions of two different soluble compounds are mixed. If the mixing results in a combination of ions that forms an insoluble compound, a double-displacement reaction and precipitation will occur. Precipitation occurs when the attraction between the ions is greater than the attraction between the ions and surrounding water molecules.

Will a precipitate form when solutions of ammonium sulfide and cadmium nitrate are combined? By using the table, you can tell that cadmium nitrate, $Cd(NO_3)_2$, is soluble because it is a nitrate and all nitrates are soluble. You can also tell that ammonium sulfide, $(NH_4)_2S$, is soluble. It is one of the sulfides listed in the table as being soluble. Their dissociation equations are as follows.

$$(NH_4)_2S(s) \xrightarrow{H_2O} 2NH_4^+(aq) + S^{2-}(aq)$$

$$Cd(NO_3)_2(s) \xrightarrow{H_2O} Cd^{2+}(aq) + 2NO_3^-(aq)$$

FIGURE 1.4

Precipitation Ammonium sulfide is a soluble compound that dissociates in water to form NH_4^+ and S^{2-} ions. Cadmium nitrate is a soluble compound that dissociates in water to form NO_3^- and Cd^{2+} ions. Precipitation of cadmium sulfide occurs when the two solutions are mixed.

Differentiated Instruction

INCLUSION

Help visual learners understand what happens at the ionic level when a precipitate forms. Challenge students to look closely at the models shown on the left side of **Figure 1.4.** Have them describe what happens to each of the ions as the compound dissociates.

Be sure students notice that, in the case of $(NH_4)_2S$, the NH^{+4} cations are solvated, while the S_{2-} anions are not. When $Cd(NO_3)_2$ dissociates, the NO^{-4} anions are solvated, but the Cd^{2+} cations are not. Students should then recognize that a precipitate can occur between Cd^{2+} ions and S^{2-} anions as shown on the right side of **Figure 1.4.**

The two possible products of a double-displacement reaction between $(NH_4)_2S$ and $Cd(NO_3)_2$ are ammonium nitrate, NH_4NO_3, and cadmium sulfide, CdS. The question marks indicate that the states are unknown.

$$(NH_4)_2S(aq) + Cd(NO_3)_2(aq) \longrightarrow 2NH_4NO_3(?) + CdS(?)$$

To decide whether a precipitate can form, you must know the solubilities of these two compounds. Consulting **Figure 1.3**, you can see that NH_4NO_3 is soluble in water. However, CdS is insoluble. You can therefore predict that when solutions of ammonium sulfide and cadmium nitrate are combined, ammonium nitrate will not precipitate and cadmium sulfide will. As illustrated in **Figure 1.4**, on the previous page, crystals of CdS form when the solutions are mixed. In the following equation, the designations (*aq*) and (*s*) show that $NH_4NO_3(aq)$ remains in solution and CdS(*s*) precipitates.

$$(NH_4)_2S(aq) + Cd(NO_3)_2(aq) \longrightarrow 2NH_4NO_3(aq) + CdS(s)$$

Net Ionic Equations

Reactions of ions in aqueous solution are usually represented by net ionic equations rather than formula equations. **A net ionic equation includes only those compounds and ions that undergo a chemical change in a reaction in an aqueous solution.** They do not include any ions or substances that do not actually participate in the chemical reaction. To write a net ionic equation, you first convert the chemical equation into an overall ionic equation. All soluble ionic compounds are shown as dissociated ions in solution. The precipitates are shown as solids. The precipitation of cadmium sulfide described previously can be shown by the following overall ionic equation.

$$Cd^{2+}(aq) + 2NO_3^-(aq) + 2NH_4^+(aq) + S^{2-}(aq) \longrightarrow CdS(s) + 2NO_3^-(aq) + 2NH_4^+(aq)$$

Notice that the aqueous ammonium ion, $NH_4^+(aq)$, and the aqueous nitrate ion, $NO_3^-(aq)$, appear on both sides of this equation. Therefore, they have not undergone any chemical change and are still present in their original form. **Ions that do not take part in a chemical reaction and are found in solution both before and after the reaction are spectator ions.**

To convert an ionic equation into a net ionic equation, the spectator ions are canceled on both sides of the equation. Eliminating the NH_4^+ and NO_3^- ions from the overall ionic equation above gives the following net ionic equation.

$$Cd^{2+}(aq) + S^{2-}(aq) \longrightarrow CdS(s)$$

This net ionic equation applies not only to the reaction between $(NH_4)_2S$ and $Cd(NO_3)_2$ but also to *any* reaction in which a precipitate of cadmium sulfide forms when the ions are combined in solution. For example, it is also the net ionic equation for the precipitation of CdS when $CdSO_4$ and H_2S react.

CHECK FOR UNDERSTANDING
Interpret In your own words, state why it is helpful to write net ionic equations for chemical reactions.

Demo Problem

1. Have students reduce the full ionic equation they wrote for the demonstration on the previous page to its net form by eliminating spectator ions.

Answer: $Sr^{2+}(aq) + SO_4^{2-}(aq) \longrightarrow SrSO_4(s)$

Misconception Alert!

Students sometimes view balancing ionic equations and writing net ionic equations as strictly mathematical operations. Encourage students to recognize the physical reality of ions as reactive particles that form new substances by examining **Figure 1.4** together as a class.

Alternative Assessment

Have students manipulate physical models of ionic reactions. Have them eliminate spectator ions and isolate the ions that combine. Ask the class to develop a verbal description of what is taking place in each ionic reaction.

Check for Understanding

Answer: A good answer might be: Net ionic equations are important because they focus only on the substances that are reacting and ignore those substances that don't actually participate in the reaction.

ENGLISH LEARNERS

Have students explain how spectators at a sporting event, such as a football game or soccer match, can be compared to spectator ions. Students should explain that in both cases, the spectators are only observers and do not directly participate in what is happening.

▼ Teach *continued*

Classroom Practice

B-1 A solution of strontium chloride is added to a solution of potassium sulfate. Write the net ionic equation for any reaction that takes place.

Answer:
$Sr^{2+}(aq) + SO_4^{2-}(aq) \longrightarrow SrSO_4(s)$

B-2 A solution of sodium sulfide is combined with a solution of iron(II) nitrate. Write the net ionic equation for any reaction that occurs.

Answer: $Fe^{2+}(aq) + S^{2-}(aq) \longrightarrow FeS(s)$

Teaching Tip

Point out that the reactions in Practice problems (1) and (3) have the same net ionic equation.

Answers

Practice B

1. Yes;
   $Ba^{2+}(aq) + SO_4^{2-}(aq) \longrightarrow BaSO_4(s)$
2. No
3. Yes; Na^+ and Cl^-;
   $Ba^{2+}(aq) + SO_4^{2-}(aq) \longrightarrow BaSO_4(s)$
4. $Ni^{2+}(aq) + S^{2-}(aq) \longrightarrow NiS(s)$

Writing Net Ionic Equations

PREMIUM CONTENT

Learn It! Video
HMDScience.com

Solve It! Cards
HMDScience.com

Sample Problem B **Identify the precipitate that forms when aqueous solutions of zinc nitrate and ammonium sulfide are combined. Write the equation for the possible double-displacement reaction. Then write the formula equation, overall ionic equation, and net ionic equation for the reaction.**

1 ANALYZE

Given: identity of reactants: zinc nitrate and ammonium sulfide reaction medium: aqueous solution

Unknown:
a. equation for the possible double-displacement reaction
b. identity of the precipitate
c. formula equation
d. overall ionic equation
e. net ionic equation

2 PLAN

Write the possible double-displacement reaction between $Zn(NO_3)_2$ and $(NH_4)_2S$. Use **Figure 1.3** to determine if any of the products are insoluble and will precipitate. Write a formula equation and an overall ionic equation, and then cancel the spectator ions to produce a net ionic equation.

3 SOLVE

a. The equation for the possible double-displacement reaction is as follows.

$$Zn(NO_3)_2(aq) + (NH_4)_2S(aq) \longrightarrow ZnS(?) + 2NH_4NO_3(?)$$

b. **Figure 1.3** reveals that because it is not soluble, zinc sulfide is a precipitate. Ammonium nitrate is soluble according to the table.

c. The formula equation is as follows.

$$Zn(NO_3)_2(aq) + (NH_4)_2S(aq) \longrightarrow ZnS(s) + 2NH_4NO_3(aq)$$

d. The overall ionic equation is as follows.

$$Zn^{2+}(aq) + 2NO_3^-(aq) + 2NH_4^+(aq) + S^{2-}(aq) \longrightarrow ZnS(s) + 2NH_4^+(aq) + 2NO_3^-(aq)$$

e. The ammonium and nitrate ions appear on both sides of the equation as spectator ions. The net ionic equation is as follows.

$$Zn^{2+}(aq) + S^{2-}(aq) \longrightarrow ZnS(s)$$

Practice Answers in Appendix E

1. Will a precipitate form if solutions of potassium sulfate and barium nitrate are combined? If so, write the net ionic equation for the reaction.
2. Will a precipitate form if solutions of potassium nitrate and magnesium sulfate are combined? If so, write the net ionic equation for the reaction.
3. Will a precipitate form if solutions of barium chloride and sodium sulfate are combined? If so, identify the spectator ions and write the net ionic equation.
4. Write the net ionic equation for the precipitation of nickel(II) sulfide.

Problem Solving

REALITY CHECK

Ask students what process is being illustrated when a formula equation is changed into an overall ionic equation. dissociation Then ask students what process is being illustrated when an overall ionic equation is changed into a net ionic equation. precipitation

MAIN IDEA

A molecular compound ionizes in a polar solvent.

Some molecular compounds can also form ions in solution. Usually such compounds are polar. **Ions are formed from solute molecules by the action of the solvent in a process called ionization.** The more general meaning of this term is the creation of ions where there were none. Note that *ionization* is different from *dissociation*. When an ionic compound dissolves, the ions that were already present separate from one another. When a molecular compound dissolves and ionizes in a polar solvent, ions are formed where none existed in the undissolved compound. Like all ions in aqueous solution, the ions formed by such a molecular solute are hydrated. The energy released as heat during the hydration of the ions provides the energy needed to break the covalent bonds.

In general, the extent to which a solute ionizes in solution depends on the strength of the bonds within the molecules of the solute and the strength of attraction between the solute and solvent molecules. If the strength of a bond within the solute molecule is weaker than the attractive forces of the solvent molecules, then the covalent bond of the solute breaks and the molecule is separated into ions. Hydrogen chloride, HCl, is a molecular compound that ionizes in aqueous solution. It contains a highly polar bond. The attraction between a polar HCl molecule and the polar water molecules is strong enough to break the HCl bond, forming hydrogen ions and chloride ions.

$$HCl \xrightarrow{H_2O} H^+(aq) + Cl^-(aq)$$

The Hydronium Ion

Many molecular compounds contain a hydrogen atom bonded by a polar covalent bond. Some of these compounds ionize in an aqueous solution to release H^+. The H^+ ion attracts other molecules or ions so strongly that it does not normally exist alone. The ionization of hydrogen chloride in water is better described as a chemical reaction in which a proton is transferred directly from HCl to a water molecule, where it becomes covalently bonded to oxygen and forms H_3O^+.

$$H_2O(l) + HCl(g) \longrightarrow H_3O^+(aq) + Cl^-(aq)$$

This process is represented in **Figure 1.5. The H_3O^+ ion is known as the hydronium ion.** The reaction of the H^+ ion to form the hydronium ion produces much of the energy needed to ionize a molecular solute.

FIGURE 1.5

Ionization When hydrogen chloride gas dissolves in water, it ionizes to form an H^+ ion and a Cl^- ion. The H^+ ion immediately bonds to a water molecule, forming a hydronium ion. The aqueous solution of hydrogen chloride is called hydrochloric acid.

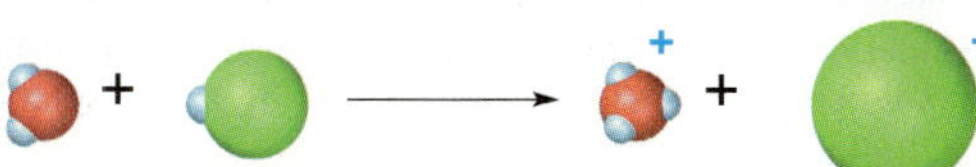

Teaching Tip

Polar molecules ionize in aqueous solution because each end of a polar molecule has a partial charge that is attracted to the oppositely charged end of a water molecule, which is also polar.

ChemisTrivia

Experimental evidence shows that protons are hydrated by more than one water molecule. The actual formula of the hydronium ion can be represented by $H^+\bullet(H_2O)_n$, where *n* varies from about 3 to about 5 depending on the temperature and concentration of the solution.

TEACH FROM VISUALS

FIGURE 1.5 Be sure students are not confused by the apparent conflict between the equation on the page, which uses H^+, and this figure, which uses H_3O^+. One reason the notation H_3O^+ is used is to avoid suggesting that free protons, in the form of hydrogen atoms that have lost an electron, can be found in aqueous solutions. Another reason is to emphasize that hydrogen ions exist in hydrated form. Experienced chemists often use $H^+(aq)$ with the understanding that it is hydrated.

Differentiated Instruction

BELOW LEVEL

Write the following two equations on the board.

$NaBr(s) \longrightarrow Ba^+(aq) + Br^-(aq)$

$HBr(g) \longrightarrow H^+(aq) + Br^-(aq)$

Ask students to identify each equation as either a dissociation process or an ionization process. Have them explain the reason for their choice.

Students should identify the first equation as a dissociation process, because NaBr is an ionic compound that dissociates into individual ions during the solution process. The second equation is an ionization process because HBr is a molecular compound that forms ions in solution.

▼ Teach *continued*

TEACH FROM VISUALS

FIGURE 1.6 Have students look back at the solubility guidelines in **Figure 1.3** to name another compound that is insoluble but, like AgCl, is considered to be a strong electrolyte. Possible responses might include mercury(I) chloride or barium sulfate. Use this apparent contradiction to reinforce the idea that, even if a compound is nearly insoluble, the part that does dissolve is dissociated.

Teaching Tip

A soluble ionic compound is a strong electrolyte. Most molecular compounds are nonelectrolytes; those that ionize in water are electrolytes.

FIGURE 1.6

Electrolytes Strong electrolytes, such as NaCl, yield only ions when they dissolve in aqueous solution. Weak electrolytes, such as HF, exist as both ions and unionized molecules in aqueous solution. Nonelectrolytes, such as sucrose, $C_{12}H_{22}O_{11}$, do not form any ions in aqueous solution.

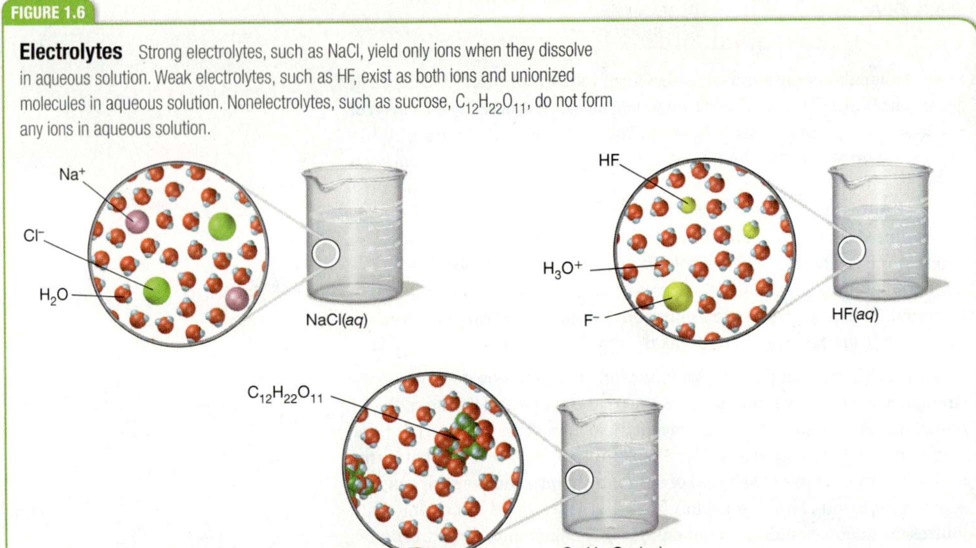

MAIN IDEA

An electrolyte's strength depends on how many dissolved ions it contains.

Substances that yield ions and conduct an electric current in solution are electrolytes. Substances that do not yield ions and do not conduct an electric current in solution are non-electrolytes. Hydrogen chloride is one of a series of compounds composed of hydrogen and the members of Group 17 (known as the halogens). The hydrogen halides are all molecular compounds with single polar-covalent bonds. All are gases, all are very soluble in water, and all are electrolytes. Hydrogen chloride, hydrogen bromide, and hydrogen iodide strongly conduct an electric current in an aqueous solution. However, hydrogen fluoride only weakly conducts an electric current at the same concentration. The strength with which substances conduct an electric current is related to their ability to form ions in solution, as shown in **Figure 1.6.**

Strong Electrolytes

Hydrogen chloride, hydrogen bromide, and hydrogen iodide are 100% ionized in dilute aqueous solution. **A strong electrolyte is any compound whose dilute aqueous solutions conduct electricity well; this is due to the presence of all or almost all of the dissolved compound in the form of ions.** Hydrogen chloride, hydrogen bromide, and hydrogen iodide are all acids in aqueous solution. These acids, several other acids, and all soluble ionic compounds are strong electrolytes.

Differentiated Instruction

PRE-AP

Have students explain the relative conductivities of HF, HCl, HBr, and HI in terms of their covalent bond strengths and with respect to the role of hydrogen bonding. Students should recognize that the extent of hydrogen bonding in HF is the main reason this molecule does not ionize as readily as the other hydrogen halides. As a result, it does not produce many electrolytes.

INCLUSION

Engage students with attention deficit disorder by having them actively create models. Have students draw models of any of the compound formulas listed in the chapter. Students can use colored markers or pencils to draw models of the compounds similar to those depicted in **Figure 1.6.** The models should be clearly labeled to show understanding of the composition of the formula. Students could also use colored clay to make three-dimensional models of the compound formulas.

The distinguishing feature of strong electrolytes is that to whatever extent they dissolve in water, they yield only ions. For example, some strong electrolytes, such as NaCl, may be highly soluble in water and form ions in solution.

Weak Electrolytes

Some molecular compounds form aqueous solutions that contain dissolved ions and some dissolved molecules that are not ionized. Hydrogen fluoride, HF, dissolves in water to give an acidic solution known as hydrofluoric acid. However, the hydrogen-fluorine bond is much stronger than the bonds between hydrogen and the other halogens. When hydrogen fluoride dissolves, some molecules ionize. But the reverse reaction—the transfer of H^+ ions back to F^- ions to form hydrogen fluoride molecules—also takes place.

$$HF(aq) + H_2O(l) \rightleftarrows H_3O^+(aq) + F^-(aq)$$

Thus, the concentration of dissolved intact HF is much greater than the concentration of H_3O^+ and F^- ions.

Hydrogen fluoride is an example of a weak electrolyte. **A weak electrolyte is any compound whose dilute aqueous solutions conduct electricity poorly; this is due to the presence of a small amount of the dissolved compound in the form of ions.** This is in contrast to a nonelectrolyte, such as the molecular compound sucrose, which dissolves but does not produce any ions in solution. Another example of a weak electrolyte is acetic acid, CH_3COOH. Only a small percentage of the acetic acid molecules ionize in aqueous solution.

$$CH_3COOH(aq) + H_2O(l) \rightleftarrows CH_3COO^-(aq) + H_3O^+(aq)$$

The description of an electrolyte as strong or weak must not be confused with concentrated or dilute. Strong and weak electrolytes differ in the *degree of ionization or dissociation.* Concentrated and dilute solutions differ in the *amount of solute dissolved* in a given quantity of a solvent. Hydrochloric acid is always a strong electrolyte. This is true even in a solution that is 0.000 01 M—a very dilute solution. By contrast, acetic acid is always considered a weak electrolyte, even in a 10 M solution—a very concentrated solution.

SECTION 1 FORMATIVE ASSESSMENT

Reviewing Main Ideas

1. Write the equation for the dissolution of $Sr(NO_3)_2$ in water. How many moles of strontium ions and nitrate ions are produced by dissolving 0.5 mol of strontium nitrate?
2. Will a precipitate form if solutions of magnesium acetate and strontium chloride are combined?
3. What determines whether a molecular compound will be ionized in a polar solvent?
4. Explain why HCl is a strong electrolyte and HF is a weak electrolyte.

Critical Thinking

5. **PREDICTING OUTCOMES** For each of the following pairs, tell which solution contains the larger total concentration of ions.
   a. 0.10 M HCl and 0.05 M HCl
   b. 0.10 M HCl and 0.10 M HF
   c. 0.10 M HCl and 0.10 M $CaCl_2$

Classroom Discussion

Have students explain how molecular compounds can be strong electrolytes, weak electrolytes, or nonconductors.

Assess and Reteach ▼

Assess Use the Formative Assessment on this page to evaluate student mastery of the section.

Reteach For students who need additional instruction, download the Section Study Guide.

Response to Intervention To reassess students' mastery, use the Section Quiz, available to print or to take directly online at **HMDScience.com**.

Answers to Section Assessment

1. $Sr(NO_3)_2(s) \xrightarrow{H_2O} Sr^{2+}(aq) + 2NO_3^-(aq)$; 0.5 mol of Sr^{2+} ions and 1 mol of NO_3^- ions
2. No. The salts that could potentially form, magnesium chloride and strontium acetate, are soluble.
3. If the attraction of polar solvent molecules is stronger than a covalent bond in the solute, the molecule will break into ions.
4. HCl is essentially 100% ionized in water solution. HF is only slightly ionized because its covalent bond is strong.
5. a. 0.10 M HCl; HCl is a strong acid, so the HCL in solution is completely converted to $H_3O^+(aq)$ and $Cl^-(aq)$. The HCl solution with the higher concentration would have more ions.
   b. 0.10 M HCl; HF is a weak acid, so only some of the HF molecules ionize.
   c. 0.10 M $CaCl_2$; In 0.10 M solution, HCl forms 0.10 M H_3O^+ and 0.10 M Cl^- for a total ion concentration of 0.20 M. $CaCl_2$ is a soluble ionic salt that forms 0.10 M Ca^{2+} and 0.20 M Cl^- to give a total ion concentration of 0.30 M.

Application

Many common products are made by using electrolysis. For example, cookware, sporting goods, and building materials contain anodized aluminum. During the process of anodizing, the surface of the aluminum is oxidized to produce aluminum oxide, Al_2O_3. The aluminum oxide provides a protective barrier against corrosion and is a harder material than aluminum metal is. A second process, called electrodeposition, is used to coat metal items with another metal. Gold- and silver-plated jewelry is produced by electrodeposition. The application of a voltage to a solution containing silver or gold ions causes silver or gold metal to electrodeposit onto the cathode in the electrochemical cell.

Chemistry EXPLORERS

The Riddle of Electrolysis

Historical Perspective

When Michael Faraday performed his electrochemical experiments, little was known about the relationship between matter and electricity. Chemists were still debating the existence of atoms, and the discovery of the electron was more than 50 years in the future. Combining his talents in electrical and chemical investigation, Faraday pointed researchers to the intimate connection between chemical reactions and electricity while setting the stage for the development of a new branch of chemistry.

Electrifying Experiments

In 1800, Italian physicist Alessandro Volta introduced his *voltaic pile,* better known as the battery. The stack of alternating zinc and silver disks provided scientists with a source of electric current for the first time.

That same year, chemists discovered a new phenomenon using Volta's device. They immersed the two poles of a battery at different locations in a container of water. The current caused the water to decompose into its elemental components, with hydrogen evolving at the positive pole of the battery and oxygen evolving at the negative pole. Similar experiments using solutions of certain solids dissolved in water resulted in the decomposition of the solids, with the two products of the solids' breakdown also evolving at opposite poles of the battery. This electrochemical decomposition was later named *electrolysis.*

The Roots of Electrolytic Theory

The discovery of electrolysis led two pioneering chemists to ponder the connection between chemical forces and electricity. One of the chemists was Humphry Davy, who thought that chemical bonding must be driven by the same forces that drive electrical attractions.

The Swedish chemist Jöns Jacob Berzelius took Davy's idea a step further. He postulated that matter consisted of combinations of "electropositive" and "electronegative" substances, classifying the parts by the pole at which they accumulated during electrolysis.

These ideas inspired two early electrolytic theories, each of which ultimately proved incorrect but contributed to our present understanding of the phenomenon. The *contact theory* proposed that electrolytic current was due merely to the contact of the battery's metals with the electrolytic solution. The *chemical theory,* on the other hand, attributed the current to undefined changes in the solution's components.

Chlorine being produced by electrolysis.

Faraday Provides a Spark

Although Michael Faraday is best remembered for his work in electromagnetism, he began his career as Humphry Davy's laboratory assistant at the Royal Institution in London and went on to be the professor of chemistry there for over 30 years. In the 1830s, Faraday devised several ingenious experiments to determine whether the current in an electrolytic solution is dependent solely on the contact of the battery's poles with the solution. In a typical setup, one of the poles was separated from the solution, and electricity was permitted to enter the solution by way of a spark. In all cases, Faraday observed current in the electrolytic cell despite one or both of the poles not being in direct contact with the electrolytic solution. In 1833, he made the hypothesis that the process of electrolysis was due to the intrinsic properties of the metals in solution and the effect of current on these properties.

Although the battery's poles were, in fact, later shown to play a part in the current, Faraday had established the active role of the electrolytic solution in electrolysis. And in realizing that electricity affected the chemical nature of the solution, he anticipated the ideas of oxidation and reduction despite that the concepts of electrons and ions were unknown at the time.

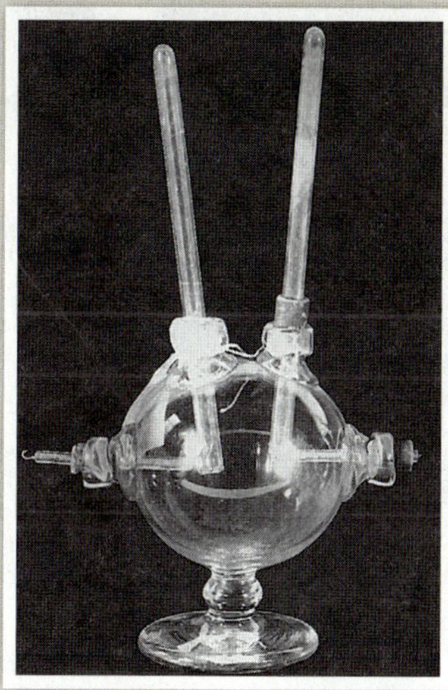

Michael Faraday used this instrument in his studies of electrolysis.

Faraday's Legacy

Faraday continued to study the role of the electrolytic solution, or electrolyte, as he named it, in electrolysis. He also coined most of the other modern terms of electrolysis, including *electrode, ion, anode, cathode, anion,* and *cation.* These investigations culminated in the discovery of his basic laws of electrolysis.

Electrolytic processes are used every day for such things as depositing a thin layer of a superior metal (like gold or silver) over a metal of lower quality (such as iron or brass), extracting pure metals from impure ones and refining them. These processes are known as *electroplating, electrofining,* and *electrometallurgy.*

Still valid, these principles put electrolysis on a quantitative footing, leading to our current understanding of the phenomenon. They also bolstered the atomic theory, which was still seriously contested by many chemists at the time. And perhaps most important, Faraday's experiments inspired his successors to further clarify the chemical nature of solutions. This ultimately led to Svante Arrhenius's theory of electrolytic dissociation and the evolution of a new division in the chemical field, known today as *physical chemistry.*

Questions

1. To which scientist does this feature give the most credit for the initial understanding of the basic nature of electrolysis? Briefly summarize his contributions in this area.
2. How are amounts of hydrogen and oxygen gas made from the electrolytic decomposition of water related to the chemical formula of water?

Classroom Discussion

Ask students to explain why electrolysis might be used to coat a sheet of iron with another metal, such as zinc. Students should be able to infer that other metals may protect iron from substances in the air that may cause the iron to rust. Zinc electroplated onto iron objects produces materials that are galvanized. Try to find a piece of galvanized steel so that students can view its appearance.

Teaching Tip

Electrolysis can be defined as the use of an electric current to bring about a chemical change.

Answers

1. Michael Faraday; he established that the metals in the electrolytic solution played an active role in the electrolysis process; he also realized that electricity affected the chemical nature of the solution. Faraday's laws of electrolysis helped support the atomic theory.
2. This electrolytic process breaks water into its constituent elements, hydrogen and oxygen. The relative volumes of hydrogen and oxygen depend on the relative numbers of moles (or molecules) of these elements that come from water.

SECTION 2

▼ Plan and Prepare

Objectives

Upon completion of this section, students should be able to do the following:

- List four colligative properties, and explain why they are classified as colligative properties.
- Calculate freezing-point depression, boiling-point elevation, and solution molality of nonelectrolyte solutions.
- Calculate the expected changes in freezing point and boiling point of an electrolyte solution.
- Discuss causes of the differences between expected and experimentally observed colligative properties of electrolyte solutions.

Classroom Catalyst

Demonstrate that NaCl lowers the freezing point of water. At the beginning of class, fill two containers with the same amount of ice. Add a large handful of rock salt to one of the containers, and mix the solution. During class, observe the containers and note the rate at which the ice melts in both containers. Ask students to explain why the ice mixed with NaCl melts faster.

▼ Teach

TEACH FROM VISUALS

FIGURE 2.1 Before students read the caption, have them interpret the graph to tell how the solution curve differs from the normal curve of pure water and how the boiling and freezing points have changed. Have them check their conclusions against the caption information.

SECTION 2

Main Ideas

- Lowering vapor pressure depends on nonelectrolyte solute concentration.
- A solution with a nonelectrolyte solute will have a lower freezing point than the pure solvent.
- A solution with a nonelectrolyte solute will have a higher boiling point than the pure solvent.
- Osmotic pressure is determined by the concentration of dissolved solute particles.
- The total molality of all dissolved particles determines changes in colligative properties.

Colligative Properties of Solutions

Key Terms

colligative properties
nonvolatile substance
molal freezing-point constant, K_f
freezing point depression, Δt_f
molal boiling-point constant, K_b
boiling-point elevation, Δt_b
semipermeable membrane
osmosis
osmotic pressure

The presence of solutes affects the properties of the solutions. Some of these properties are not dependent on the nature of the dissolved substance but only on how many dissolved particles are present. **Properties that depend on the concentration of solute particles but not on their identity are called colligative properties.** In calculations involving some colligative properties, the concentration is given in terms of molality, m.

MAIN IDEA

Lowering vapor pressure depends on nonelectrolyte solute concentration.

The boiling point and freezing point of a solution differ from those of the pure solvent. The graph in **Figure 2.1** shows that a nonvolatile solute raises

FIGURE 2.1

Vapor Pressure Lowering Vapor pressure as a function of temperature is shown for a pure solvent and for a solution of a nonvolatile solute in that solvent. The vapor pressure of the solution is lower than the vapor pressure of the pure solvent. This can be seen by noting the decrease in pressure between the pure solvent and the solution at the temperature that is the boiling point of the pure solvent. The solute thus reduces the freezing point and elevates the boiling point.

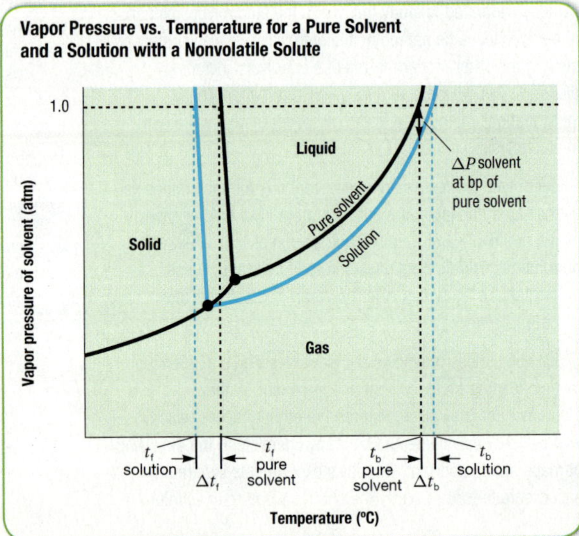

Differentiated Instruction

BELOW LEVEL

Have students review how molality is calculated. For example, ask them to calculate the molality of a solution that contains 80.0 g NaOH dissolved in 2 kg of water. 1 m

FIGURE 2.2

Vapor Pressure Lowering: Pure Solvent vs Solution

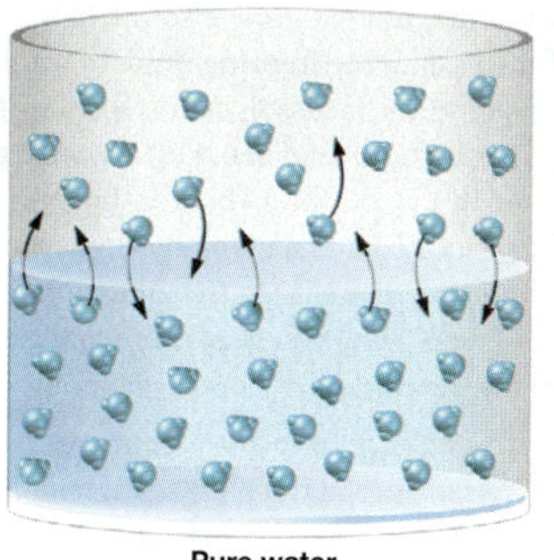

Pure water

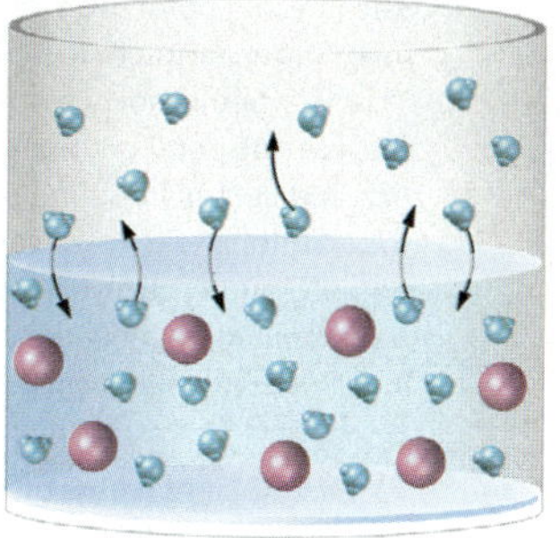

Aqueous solution of nonvolatile solute

Used to represent $C_{12}H_{22}O_{11}$, sucrose

Used to represent H_2O, water

CRITICAL THINKING

Compare Compare and contrast the two images and explain how they relate to vapor pressure lowering.

the boiling point and lowers the freezing point. A **nonvolatile substance** is one that has little tendency to become a gas under existing conditions.

To understand why a nonvolatile solute changes the boiling point and freezing point, you must consider equilibrium vapor pressure. Vapor pressure is the pressure caused by molecules in the gas phase that are in equilibrium with the liquid phase. Experiments show that the vapor pressure of a solvent containing a nonvolatile solute is lower than the vapor pressure of the pure solvent at the same temperature, as shown in **Figure 2.2**. As the number of solute particles increases in a given volume of solution, the proportion of solvent (water) molecules decreases. Fewer water molecules will be available to escape from the liquid. As a result, the tendency of water molecules to leave the solution and enter the vapor phase decreases. Thus, the vapor pressure of the solution is less than the vapor pressure of pure water.

Nonelectrolyte solutions of the same molality have the same concentration of particles. Equally dilute molal solutions of any nonelectrolyte solutes in the same solvent lower the vapor pressure equally. For example, a 1 *m* aqueous solution of the nonelectrolyte glucose, $C_6H_{12}O_6$, lowers the vapor pressure of water by 5.5×10^{-4} atm at 25°C. A 1 *m* solution of sucrose, $C_{12}H_{22}O_{11}$, another nonelectrolyte, also lowers the vapor pressure by 5.5×10^{-4} atm. Because vapor-pressure lowering depends on the concentration of a nonelectrolyte solute and is independent of solute identity, it is a colligative property.

Refer to the graph in **Figure 2.1**. Because the vapor pressure has been lowered, the solution remains liquid over a larger temperature range. This lowers the freezing point and raises the boiling point. It follows that changes in boiling point and freezing point also depend on the concentration of solute and are therefore colligative properties.

TEACH FROM VISUALS

FIGURE 2.2 Emphasize that in order for vapor pressure of the pure water to be compared with that of an aqueous solution, the temperatures of both solutions must be identical.

In this diagram, the water molecules are portrayed in a single color to emphasize the interactions between solvent and solute.

READING TOOLKIT

READING ORGANIZER Students can use two-column notes to help them distinguish between main ideas and details. Have students label a blank sheet of notebook paper with the title "Colligative Properties." Then have them divide their papers into two columns. In the left-hand column, have them write the four colligative properties discussed in Section 2 (vapor-pressure lowering, freezing-point depression, boiling-point elevation, and osmotic pressure). In the right-hand column, direct students to write the definition, an example, and other details for each property.

Teaching Tip

Point out that both nonelectrolytes and electrolytes affect colligative properties. However, because the effects are different, electrolytes will be discussed later in the chapter.

Critical Thinking

Answer: The image on the left shows a pure solvent in vapor pressure equilibrium. The image on the right shows a solution containing a nonvolatile solute. The image of the pure substance shows more molecules having escaped from solution than in the image of the solution on the right. The two images illustrate that a solution containing a nonvolatile solute will have lowered vapor pressure.

ENGLISH LEARNERS

Use the following flowchart to help students understand colligative properties by showing them cause-and-effect relationships:

increased number of solute particles ⟶ fewer solvent molecules at surface of the solution ⟶ fewer solvent molecules escape to form vapor ⟶ vapor pressure decreases ⟶ solution remains liquid over a longer temperature range ⟶ lower freezing point and higher boiling point.

▼ Teach continued

ChemisTrivia

Some animals are able to survive freezing temperatures by producing antifreezes, substances that lower the freezing point of a liquid. In many freeze-tolerant insects, the antifreezes are alcohols and sugars. Glucose (a sugar) and glycerol (an alcohol) have been shown to serve as antifreezes in some reptiles, including box turtles, painted turtles, and—to a limited extent—garter snakes. Some animals, such as certain species of fish in the Antarctic, have antifreeze proteins and glycoproteins. These antifreezes function not by affecting colligative properties based only on the concentration of particles, as discussed in this chapter, but rather by inhibiting the growth of ice crystals.

TEACH FROM TABLES

FIGURE 2.3 Ask students which solvents have the greatest freezing-point depression constants. Point out that the table emphasizes that freezing-point depression is entirely a function of the solvent and has nothing to do with the nonvolatile, nonelectrolyte solute used (at dilute concentrations and under ordinary conditions of temperature and pressure). Solutes are not mentioned on this table.

Check for Understanding

Answer: Answers may vary. Homemade ice cream is usually formed when a metal container holding the liquid ice cream mixture is submerged in a mixture of ice and rock salt and then agitated. The relationship to freezing point depression is seen in the concentration of salt to ice in the external mixture. The more salt that is added to the ice, the more the freezing point is lowered. As a result, the temperature of the internal mixture is also lowered, causing the ice cream to freeze.

MAIN IDEA

A solution with a nonelectrolyte solute will have a lower freezing point than the pure solvent.

The freezing point of a 1 m solution of any nonelectrolyte solute in water is found by experiment to be 1.86°C lower than the freezing point of water. That is, when 1 mol of a nonelectrolyte solute is dissolved in 1 kg of water, the freezing point of the solution is −1.86°C instead of 0.00°C. When 2 mol of a nonelectrolyte solute is dissolved in 1 kg of water, the freezing point of the solution is −3.72°C. This is 2 × (−1.86°C). In fact, for any concentration of a nonelectrolyte solute in water, the decrease in freezing point can be estimated by using the value of −1.86°C/m. This value, called the **molal freezing-point constant (K_f)** is the freezing-point depression of the solvent in a 1-molal solution of a nonvolatile, nonelectrolyte solute.

Each solvent has its own characteristic molal freezing-point constant. The values of K_f for some common solvents are given in **Figure 2.3.** These values are most accurate for dilute solutions at 1 atmosphere of pressure. Some variations are introduced in the value of K_f at other pressures and with more-concentrated solutions. The table also shows the values of a related quantity called K_b, which you will study next.

CHECK FOR UNDERSTANDING

Interpret In your own words, describe the process by which ice cream is made at home and explain how the process relates to freezing-point depression.

As stated earlier, the freezing point of a solution containing 1 mol of a nonelectrolyte solute in 1 kg water is 1.86°C lower than the normal freezing point of water. The **freezing-point depression, Δt_f**, is the difference between the freezing points of the pure solvent and a solution of a nonelectrolyte in that solvent, and it is directly proportional to the molal concentration of the solution. As shown by the previous example, if the molal concentration is doubled, the freezing-point depression is doubled. Freezing-point depression can be calculated by the following equation.

Freezing-Point Depression $\Delta t_f = K_f m$

K_f is expressed as °C/m, m is expressed in mol solute/kg solvent (molality), and Δt_f is expressed in °C. Sample Problems C and D show how this relationship can be used to determine the freezing-point depression and molal concentration of a solution.

FIGURE 2.3

MOLAL FREEZING-POINT AND BOILING-POINT CONSTANTS

Solvent	Normal f.p. (°C)	Molal f.p. constant, K_f (°C/m)	Normal b.p. (°C)	Molal b.p. constant, K_b (°C/m)
Acetic acid	16.6	−3.90	117.9	3.07
Camphor	178.8	−39.7	207.4	5.61
Ether	−116.3	−1.79	34.6	2.02
Naphthalene	80.2	−6.94	217.7	5.80
Phenol	40.9	−7.40	181.8	3.60
Water	0.00	−1.86	100.0	0.51

Differentiated Instruction

INCLUSION

Check the Internet for a recipe for making ice cream using a re-sealable plastic bag. Kinesthetic learners will not only enjoy the product of their work but also see a practical application of colligative properties. The salt added to the ice lowers the freezing point so that the ingredients can freeze and form ice cream.

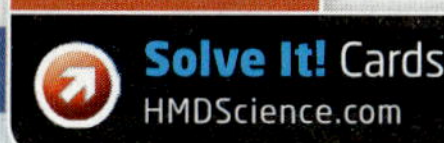

Calculating Freezing-Point Depression

Sample Problem C **What is the freezing-point depression of water in a solution of 17.1 g of sucrose, $C_{12}H_{22}O_{11}$, in 200. g of water? What is the actual freezing point of the solution?**

1 ANALYZE

Given: solute mass and chemical formula = 17.1 g $C_{12}H_{22}O_{11}$

solvent mass and identity = 200. g water

Unknown: **a.** freezing-point depression

b. freezing point of the solution

2 PLAN

Find the molal freezing-point constant, K_f, for water in **Figure 2.3.** To use the equation for freezing-point depression, $\Delta t_f = K_f m$, you need to determine the molality of the solution.

$$\text{mass of solute (g)} \times \frac{1 \text{ mol solute}}{\text{molar mass of solute (g)}} = \text{amount of solute (mol)}$$

$$\frac{\text{amount of solute (mol)}}{\text{mass of solvent (g)}} \times \frac{1000 \text{ g water}}{1 \text{ kg water}} = \text{molality}$$

$$\Delta t_f = K_f m$$

$$\text{f.p. solution} = \text{f.p. solvent} + \Delta t_f$$

3 SOLVE

$$17.1 \text{ g } C_{12}H_{22}O_{11} \times \frac{1 \text{ mol } C_{12}H_{22}O_{11}}{342.34 \text{ g } C_{12}H_{22}O_{11}} = 0.0500 \text{ mol } C_{12}H_{22}O_{11}$$

$$\frac{0.0500 \text{ mol } C_{12}H_{22}O_{11}}{200. \text{ g water}} \times \frac{1000 \text{ g water}}{\text{kg water}} = \frac{0.250 \text{ mol } C_{12}H_{22}O_{11}}{\text{kg water}} = 0.250\ m$$

a. $\Delta t_f = 0.250\ m \times (-1.86°\text{C}/m) = -0.465°\text{C}$

b. f.p. solution = 0.000°C + (−0.465°C) = −0.465°C

Calculating Molal Concentration

Sample Problem D **A water solution containing an unknown quantity of a nonelectrolyte solute is found to have a freezing point of −0.23°C. What is the molal concentration of the solution?**

1 ANALYZE

Given: freezing point of solution = −0.23°C

Unknown: molality of the solution

2 PLAN

Water is the solvent, so you will need the value of K_f, the molal-freezing-point constant for water, from **Figure 2.3.** The Δt_f for this solution is the difference between the f.p. of water and the f.p. of the solution. Use the equation for freezing-point depression to calculate molality.

$$\Delta t_f = \text{f.p. of solution} - \text{f.p. of pure solvent}$$

$$\Delta t_f = K_f m \qquad \text{Solve for molality, } m.$$

$$m = \frac{\Delta t_f}{K_f}$$

Classroom Practice

C-1 Determine the freezing point of a water solution of fructose, $C_6H_{12}O_6$, made by dissolving 58.0 g of fructose in 185 g of water.

Answer: −3.24°C

C-2 Calculate the molality of a solution of 39.2 g of urea, H_2NCONH_2, in 485 g of pure acetic acid. Determine the freezing point of this solution.

Answer: 1.35 *m*; 11.4°C

D-1 Determine the molal concentration of a solution of ethylene glycol, $HOCH_2CH_2OH$, in water if the solution's freezing point is −6.40°C. What mass of ethylene glycol would you dissolve in 500 g of water to prepare such a solution?

Answer: 3.44 *m*; 107 g ethylene glycol

Problem Solving

DECONSTRUCTING PROBLEMS

Be sure students see that a conversion factor was used in Sample Problem C to convert 200 g to kg as required to calculate the molality of the solution. Students may also benefit by analyzing the individual steps used to solve the problem:

grams ⟶ moles ⟶ molality ⟶ freezing-point depression ⟶ actual freezing point.

▼ Teach continued

Application

A common antifreeze is a solution of ethylene glycol, $HOCH_2CH_2OH$, a relatively nonvolatile liquid substance, combined with dissolved dyes and corrosion inhibitors. This coolant solution provides not only a lower freezing point but also a higher boiling point as compared with plain water. Car manufacturers recommend that people leave the coolant mixture in the engine year round. A typical coolant mixture is 50% water and 50% ethylene glycol by volume. This mixture contains 1.116 kg of ethylene glycol per 1.000 kg of water, which is a 17.98 *m* solution. Ethylene glycol has a density of 1.1135 g/mL at 20°C, compared with water's 0.998 g/mL at 20°C. The theoretical boiling point of this solution is 109.2°C, or 229.6°F. The theoretical freezing point of this solution is −33.4°C, or −28.1°F.

Answers

Practice D

1. −0.426°C
2. 0.175 *m*
3. −118.1°C
4. a. −9.0°C
   b. 4.8 *m*

Calculating Molal Concentration (continued)

3 SOLVE

$$\Delta t_f = -0.23°C - 0.00°C = -0.23°C$$

$$m = \frac{-0.23°C}{-1.86°C/m} = 0.12\ m$$

4 CHECK YOUR WORK As shown by the unit cancellation, the answer gives the molality, as desired. The answer is properly limited to two significant digits.

Practice Answers in Appendix E

1. A solution consists of 10.3 g of the nonelectrolyte glucose, $C_6H_{12}O_6$, dissolved in 250. g of water. What is the freezing-point depression of the solution?
2. In a laboratory experiment, the freezing point of an aqueous solution of glucose is found to be −0.325°C. What is the molal concentration of this solution?
3. If 0.500 mol of a nonelectrolyte solute are dissolved in 500.0 g of ether, what is the freezing point of the solution?
4. The freezing point of an aqueous solution that contains a nonelectrolyte is −9.0°C.
   a. What is the freezing-point depression of the solution?
   b. What is the molal concentration of the solution?

MAIN IDEA

A solution with a nonelectrolyte solute will have a higher boiling point than the pure solvent.

As discussed previously, the boiling point of a liquid is the temperature at which the vapor pressure of the liquid is equal to the prevailing atmospheric pressure. Therefore, a change in the vapor pressure of the liquid will cause a corresponding change in the boiling point. In other words, if the vapor pressure is lowered, the boiling point is raised. If the vapor pressure is increased, the boiling point decreases. The vapor pressure of a solution containing a nonvolatile solute is lower than the vapor pressure of the pure solvent. This means that more energy as heat will be required to raise the vapor pressure of the solution to equal the atmospheric pressure. Thus, the boiling point of a solution is higher than the boiling point of the pure solvent.

The **molal boiling-point constant (K_b)** is the boiling-point elevation of the solvent in a 1-molal solution of a nonvolatile, nonelectrolyte solute. The boiling-point elevation of a 1-molal solution of any nonelectrolyte solute in water has been found by experiment to be 0.51°C. Thus, the molal boiling-point constant for water is 0.51°C/*m*.

For different solvents, the molal boiling-point constants have different values. Some other values for K_b are included in **Figure 2.3**. Like the freezing-point constants, these values are most accurate for dilute solutions.

The **boiling-point elevation, Δt_b,** is the difference between the boiling points of the pure solvent and a nonelectrolyte solution of that solvent, and it is directly proportional to the molal concentration of the solution.

Problem Solving

TAKE IT FURTHER

Remind students that water is the solvent in Sample Problem D. Ask students to identify the solvents in **Figure 2.3** that would have a freezing point lower than −0.23°C if the same nonelectrolyte were added in the same molal concentration (0.12 *m*) to each of the solvents listed in the table.

Given that m = 0.12, students should solve for ΔT_f by substituting the K_f value for each solvent from **Figure 2.3.** Students may recognize that only ether on **Figure 2.3** has a K_f value lower than that for water. Therefore, ether would be the only solvent in the table that does not have a lower freezing point than water under these conditions.

Boiling-point elevation can be calculated by the following equation.

Boiling-Point Elevation $\Delta t_b = K_b m$

When K_b is expressed in °C/m and m is expressed in mol of solute/kg of solvent, Δt_b is the boiling-point elevation in °C.

Calculating Boiling-Point Elevation

Sample Problem E **What is the boiling-point elevation of a solution made from 20.1 g of a nonelectrolyte solute and 400.0 g of water? The molar mass of the solute is 62.0 g.**

1 ANALYZE

Given: solute mass = 20.1 g

solute molar mass = 62.0 g

solvent mass and identity = 400.0 g of water

Unknown: boiling-point elevation

2 PLAN

Find the molal boiling-point constant, K_b, for water in **Figure 2.3.** To use the equation for boiling-point elevation, $\Delta t_b = K_b m$, you need to determine the molality of the solution.

$$\text{mass of solute (g)} \times \frac{\text{1 mol solute}}{\text{molar mass solute (g)}} = \text{amount of solute (mol)}$$

$$\frac{\text{amount of solute (mol)}}{\text{mass of solvent (g)}} \times \frac{\text{1000 g water}}{\text{1 kg water}} = \text{molality}$$

$$\Delta t_b = K_b m$$

3 SOLVE

$$20.1 \text{ g of solute} \times \frac{\text{1 mol solute}}{\text{62.0 g of solute}} = 0.324 \text{ mol of solute}$$

$$\frac{\text{0.324 mol of solute}}{\text{400.0 g water}} \times \frac{\text{1000 g water}}{\text{1 kg water}} = 0.810 \frac{\text{mol solute}}{\text{kg water}} = 0.810\ m$$

$$\Delta t_b = 0.51\text{°C}/m \times 0.810\ m = 0.41\text{°C}$$

Practice

1. A solution contains 50.0 g of sucrose, $C_{12}H_{22}O_{11}$, a nonelectrolyte, dissolved in 500.0 g of water. What is the boiling-point elevation?
2. A solution contains 450.0 g of sucrose, $C_{12}H_{22}O_{11}$, a nonelectrolyte, dissolved in 250.0 g of water. What is the boiling point of the solution?
3. If the boiling-point elevation of an aqueous solution containing a nonvolatile electrolyte is 1.02°C, what is the molality of the solution?
4. The boiling point of an aqueous solution containing a nonvolatile electrolyte is 100.75°C.
   a. What is the boiling-point elevation?
   b. What is the molality of the solution?

Classroom Practice

E-1 What is the boiling point of a solution of 25.0 g of 2-butoxyethanol (butyl cellosolve), $HOCH_2CH_2OC_4H_9$, in 68.7 g of ether?

Answer: 40.8°C

E-2 What mass of glycerol, $CH_2OHCHOHCH_2OH$, must be dissolved in $1.00 \times 10_3$ g of water in order to have a boiling point of 104.5°C at standard pressure?

Answer: 810 g

Answers

Practice E

1. 0.15°C
2. 102.7°C
3. 2.0 m
4. a. 0.75°C
   b. 1.5 m

DECONSTRUCTING PROBLEMS

Students may benefit by analyzing the individual steps used in Sample Problem E: grams ⟶ moles ⟶ molality ⟶ freezing point elevation. Have them compare these steps to those followed in Sample Problem C. Students should recognize that the first three steps in these two sample problems are the same. Only the last step is different, depending on whether the problem involves freezing-point depression or boiling-point elevation.

▼ Teach *continued*

TEACH FROM VISUALS

FIGURE 2.4 Make sure the students understand that osmosis stops because the column of water in (b) is now high enough to exert a pressure equal to the osmotic pressure. Point out that if a piston were used to apply pressure to the solution side of the tube in (a), osmosis would stop when the piston applied a pressure equal to the osmotic pressure. If this applied pressure were greater than the osmotic pressure, reverse osmosis would occur and the height of the pure water side would rise.

Classroom Discussion

Ask students to explain osmosis using a mental model based on a theoretical model of how semipermeable membranes work. From a molecule's viewpoint, a membrane is like a wire fence or a net—little structural material and lots of openings. Water molecules are able to pass through these openings freely. Large solute molecules cannot get through the holes but are able to block the passage of many water molecules. Meanwhile, water molecules from the other side are still passing through freely.

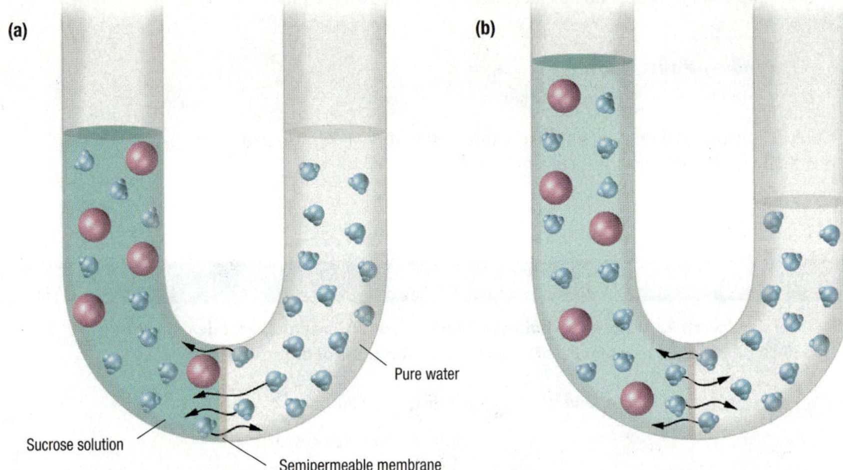

FIGURE 2.4

Osmotic Pressure **(a)** When pure water and an aqueous sucrose solution are separated by a semipermeable membrane, the net movement of water molecules through the membrane is from the pure water side into the aqueous solution. **(b)** The level of the solution rises until pressure exerted by the height of the solution equals the osmotic pressure, at which point no net movement of water molecules occurs.

MAIN IDEA

Osmotic pressure is determined by the concentration of dissolved solute particles.

Figure 2.4 illustrates another colligative property. In the figure, an aqueous sucrose solution is separated from pure water by a semipermeable membrane. **A semipermeable membrane allows the passage of some particles while blocking the passage of others.** The level of the sucrose solution will rise until a certain height is reached. What causes the level of the solution to rise?

The semipermeable membrane allows water molecules, but not sucrose molecules, to pass through. The sucrose molecules on the solution side allow fewer water molecules to strike the membrane than to strike on the pure water side in the same amount of time. Thus, the rate at which water molecules leave the pure water side is greater than the rate at which they leave the solution. This causes the level of the solution to rise. The level rises until the pressure exerted by the height of the solution is large enough to force water molecules back through the membrane from the solution at a rate equal to that at which they enter from the pure water side.

The movement of solvent through a semipermeable membrane from the side of lower solute concentration to the side of higher solute concentration is osmosis. Osmosis occurs whenever two solutions of different concentrations are separated by a semipermeable membrane. **Osmotic pressure is the external pressure that must be applied to stop osmosis.** In the example given above, osmosis caused the level of the solution to rise until the height of the solution provided the pressure necessary to stop osmosis. Because osmotic pressure is dependent on the concentration of solute particles and not on the type of solute particles, it

Differentiated Instruction

PRE-AP

Have students research how reverse osmosis operates to obtain drinking water from seawater. This process is known as desalination. The process of reverse osmosis is used to purify water because it removes many contaminants at relatively low cost. The osmosis process can be reversed by applying a pressure greater than the osmotic pressure to an aqueous solution. This causes the water, but not the dissolved solutes, to flow from the solution through the semipermeable membrane. Encourage students to include information about specific desalination plants. Possibilities include the Hadera seawater desalination plant in Israel, which is the largest in the world. The largest municipal desalination plant in the United States is in Sarasota, Florida.

is a colligative property. The greater the concentration of a solution, the greater the osmotic pressure of the solution.

Regulation of osmosis is vital to the life of a cell because cell membranes are semipermeable. Cells lose water and shrink when placed in a solution of higher concentration. They gain water and swell when placed in a solution of lower concentration. In vertebrates, cells are protected from swelling and shrinking by blood and lymph that surround the cells. Blood and lymph are equal in concentration to the concentration inside the cell.

MAIN IDEA

The total molality of all dissolved particles determines changes in colligative properties.

Early investigators were puzzled by experiments in which certain substances depressed the freezing point or elevated the boiling point of a solvent more than expected. For example, a 0.1 *m* solution of sodium chloride, NaCl, lowers the freezing point of the solvent nearly twice as much as a 0.1 *m* solution of sucrose. A 0.1 *m* solution of calcium chloride, $CaCl_2$, lowers the freezing point of the solvent nearly three times as much as a 0.1 *m* solution of sucrose. The effect on boiling points is similar.

To understand why this is so, contrast the behavior of sucrose with that of sodium chloride in aqueous solutions. Sugar is a nonelectrolyte. Each sucrose molecule dissolves to produce only one particle in solution, so 1 mol of sucrose dissolves to produce only 1 mol of particles in solution. NaCl, however, is a strong electrolyte. Each mole of NaCl dissolves to produce 2 mol of particles in solution: 1 mol of sodium ions and 1 mol of chloride ions. **Figure 2.5** compares the production of particles in solution for three different solutes. As you can see, electrolytes produce more than 1 mol of solute particles for each mole of compound dissolved.

WHY IT MATTERS

Water Purification by Reverse Osmosis S.T.E.M.

The process of reverse osmosis is used to purify water because it removes many contaminants at relatively low cost. The osmosis process can be reversed by applying a pressure greater than the osmotic pressure to an aqueous solution. This causes the water, but not the dissolved solutes, to flow from the solution through the semipermeable membrane. The largest municipal desalination plant in the United States is in Sarasota, Florida. It treats salt water by reverse osmosis to produce more than 12 million gallons of fresh water per day. Other applications include the desalination of sea water on ocean-going vessels and wastewater purification.

FIGURE 2.5

Colligative Properties Compare the number of particles produced per formula unit for these three solutes. Colligative properties depend on the total concentration of particles.

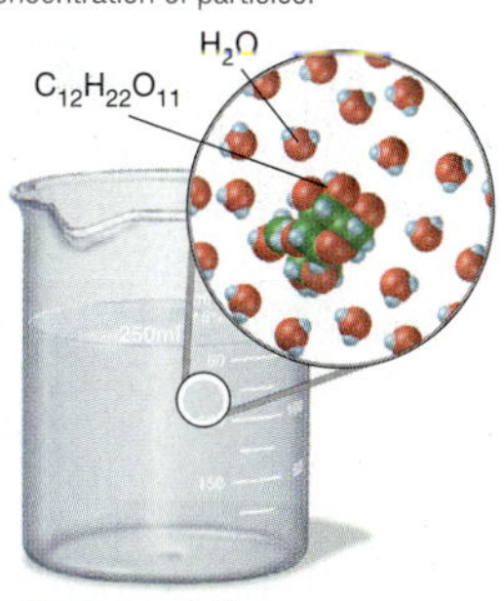

Sucrose solution

$C_{12}H_{22}O_{11} \xrightarrow{H_2O} C_{12}H_{22}O_{11}(aq)$

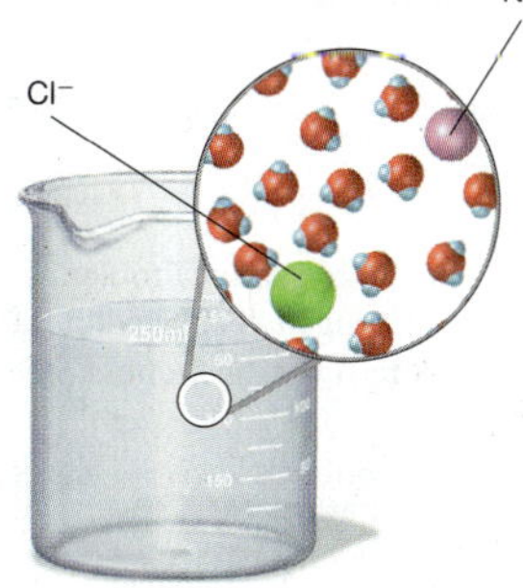

Sodium chloride solution

$NaC \xrightarrow{H_2O} Na^+(aq) + Cl^-(aq)$

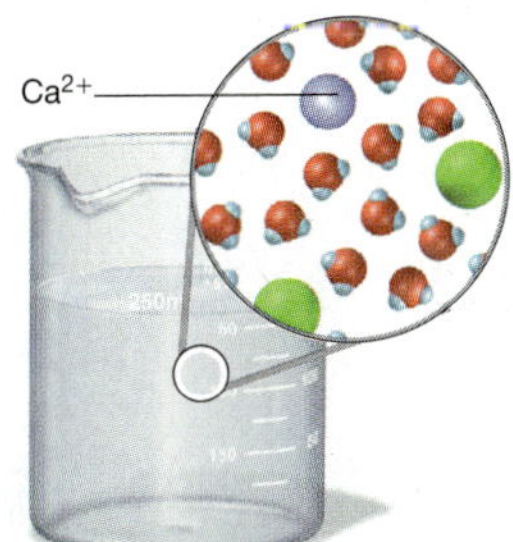

Calcium chloride solution

$CaCl_2 \xrightarrow{H_2O} Ca^{2+}(aq) + 2Cl^-(aq)$

Demonstration

THE PROCESS OF OSMOSIS

Dissolve **350 g of sucrose** in **500 mL of water** in a **1 L beaker.** Soak a 30-cm length of **dialysis tubing** in **distilled water** until completely softened. (The dialysis tubing should have a diameter of 21 mm or 27 mm when filled with distilled water.) Rub the softened tubing between your hands until the sides no longer stick to each other. Tie a tight knot in one end of the tubing, and return it to the water. Fill the tubing to overflowing with distilled water. Tie the open end tightly, excluding air bubbles. Submerge the sausage-shaped tube in the sugar solution, and have students observe the conditions of the tube and sugar solution immediately and again in 20 minutes, after the tube has shrunk noticeably. Observe the setup again the next day. Much of the water inside the dialysis tubing will have diffused into the solution by osmosis, leaving the tube shriveled. Have students explain what took place at the molecular level. As an option, show that the volume of the sugar solution increased.

Safety Wear an **apron** and **goggles.**
Disposal Wash all liquids down the drain, and dispose of tubing in the trash.

TEACH FROM VISUALS

FIGURE 2.5 Challenge students to use the figure to explain why calcium chloride is often used instead of sodium chloride to melt snow and ice from slick roads and sidewalks.

BELOW LEVEL

Have students predict whether copper(II) chloride will have the same effect as NaCl or $CaCl_2$ on colligative properties. Students should write the equation for the dissociation of copper(II) chloride: $CuCl_2(s) \longrightarrow Cu^{2+}(aq) + 2Cl^-(aq)$. Therefore, 1 mol of Cu^{2+} cations and 2 mol of Cl^- anions are produced. Students should recognize that copper(II) chloride and calcium chloride have the same effect on colligative properties.

▼ Teach continued

Classroom Practice

F-1 What is the expected boiling point of a 1.70 *m* solution of sodium sulfate in water?

Answer: 102.6°C

F-2 A water solution contains 42.9 g of calcium nitrate dissolved in 500. g of water. Calculate the freezing point of the solution.

Answer: −2.92°C

Alternative Assessment

Have students determine the salt concentration required to prevent 500 mL of an aqueous solution from freezing when placed in a freezer overnight. A 0.9 *m* NaCl solution has a freezing point of approximately −3°C, or 27°F. A 1.9 *m* NaCl solution has a freezing point of approximately −7°C, or 19°F. Make sure the students use a plastic container large enough to allow for ice expansion if their solution does freeze.

Calculated Values for Electrolyte Solutions

Remember that colligative properties depend on the total concentration of solute particles regardless of their identity. The changes in colligative properties caused by electrolytes will be proportional to the total molality of all dissolved particles, not to formula units. For the same molal concentrations of sucrose and sodium chloride, you would expect the effect on colligative properties to be twice as large for sodium chloride as for sucrose. What about barium nitrate, $Ba(NO_3)_2$? Each mole of barium nitrate yields 3 mol of ions in solution.

$$Ba(NO_3)_2(s) \longrightarrow Ba^{2+}(aq) + 2NO_3^-(aq)$$

You would expect a $Ba(NO_3)_2$ solution of a given molality to lower the freezing point of its solvent three times as much as a nonelectrolytic solution of the same molality.

Freezing-Point Depression of Electrolytes

Sample Problem F **What is the expected change in the freezing point of water in a solution of 62.5 g of barium nitrate, $Ba(NO_3)_2$, in 1.00 kg of water?**

1 ANALYZE

Given: solute mass and formula = 62.5 g $Ba(NO_3)_2$

solvent mass and identity = 1.00 kg water

$\Delta t_f = K_f m$

Unknown: expected freezing-point depression

2 PLAN

The molality can be calculated by converting the solute mass to moles and then dividing by the number of kilograms of solvent. That molality is in terms of formula units of $Ba(NO_3)_2$ and must be converted to molality in terms of dissociated ions in solution. It must be multiplied by the number of moles of ions produced per mole of formula unit. This adjusted molality can then be used to calculate the freezing-point depression.

$$\frac{\text{mass of solute (g)}}{\text{mass of solvent (kg)}} \times \frac{\text{1 mass solute}}{\text{molar mass solute (g)}} = \text{molality of solution}\left(\frac{\text{mol}}{\text{kg}}\right)$$

$$\text{molality of solution}\left(\frac{\text{mol}}{\text{kg}}\right) \times \text{molality conversion}\left(\frac{\text{mol ions}}{\text{mol}}\right) \times K_f\left(\frac{°\text{C} \bullet \text{kg } H_2O}{\text{mol ions}}\right)$$
$$= \text{expected freezing-point depression (°C)}$$

This problem is similar to Sample Problem E, except that the solute is ionic rather than a nonionizing molecular solute. The number of particles in solution will therefore equal the number of ions of the solute.

3 SOLVE

$$\frac{62.5 \text{ g } Ba(NO_3)_2}{1.00 \text{ kg } H_2O} \times \frac{\text{mol } Ba(NO_3)_2}{261.35 \text{ g } Ba(NO_3)_2} = \frac{0.239 \text{ mol } Ba(NO_3)_2}{\text{kg } H_2O}$$

Continued

Differentiated Instruction

INCLUSION

Cooperative work groups can help students with learning disabilities. Have students work in pairs. Each student should write the name and formula for an ionic compound. Encourage students to use polyatomic ions as part of their formulas. The two students should then share their formulas and compare the effect of their compounds on colligative properties. If the students select one compound as having a greater effect, be sure they explain their reasoning.

Freezing-Point Depression of Electrolytes (continued)

$Ba(NO_3)_2(s) \longrightarrow Ba^{2+}(aq) + 2NO_3^-(aq)$

Each formula unit of barium nitrate yields three ions in solution.

$$\frac{0.239 \text{ mol } Ba(NO_3)_2}{\text{kg } H_2O} \times \frac{3 \text{ mol ions}}{\text{mol } Ba(NO_3)_2} \times \frac{-1.86°C \bullet \text{kg } H_2O}{\text{mol ions}} = -1.33°C$$

4 CHECK YOUR WORK

The units cancel properly to give the desired answer in °C. The answer is correctly given to three significant digits. The mass of the solute is approximately one–fourth its molar mass and would give 0.75 mol of ions in the 1 kg of solvent, so the estimated answer of 0.75 × (−1.86°C) = 1.4°C supports our computation.

Practice Answers in Appendix E

1. What is the expected freezing-point depression for a solution that contains 2.0 mol of magnesium sulfate dissolved in 1.0 kg of water?
2. What is the expected boiling-point elevation of water for a solution that contains 150 g of sodium chloride dissolved in 1.0 kg of water?
3. The freezing point of an aqueous sodium chloride solution is −0.20°C. What is the molality of the solution?

Actual Values for Electrolyte Solutions

It is important to remember that the values just calculated are only *expected* values. As stated earlier, a 0.1 *m* solution of sodium chloride lowers the freezing point *nearly* twice as much as a 0.1 *m* solution of sucrose. The actual values of the colligative properties for all strong electrolytes are *almost* what would be expected based on the number of particles they produce in solution. Some specific examples are given in **Figure 2.6.** The freezing-point depression of a compound that produces two ions per formula unit is almost twice that of a nonelectrolytic solution. The freezing-point depression of a compound that produces three ions per formula unit is almost three times that of a nonelectrolytic solution.

FIGURE 2.6

MOLAL FREEZING-POINT DEPRESSIONS FOR AQUEOUS SOLUTIONS OF IONIC SOLUTES

Solute	Concentration (*m*)	Δt_f, observed (°C)	Δt_f, nonelectrolyte solution (°C)	$\frac{\Delta t_f\text{, observed}}{\Delta t_f\text{, nonelectrolyte solution (°C)}}$
KCl	0.1	−0.345	−0.186	1.85
	0.01	−0.0361	−0.0186	1.94
	0.001	−0.00366	−0.00186	1.97
$MgSO_4$	0.1	−0.225	−0.186	1.21
	0.01	−0.0285	−0.0186	1.53
	0.001	−0.00338	−0.00186	1.82
$BaCl_2$	0.1	−0.470	−0.186	2.53
	0.01	−0.0503	−0.0186	2.70
	0.001	−0.00530	−0.00186	2.84

Problem Solving

DECONSTRUCTING PROBLEMS

Have students list the steps that are involved in Sample Problem F.

Students should develop a list similar to the following:

1. Convert grams of solute to moles.
2. Calculate the molality of the solution.
3. Write the ionic equation for the dissociation process.
4. Determine the molality of the solution in terms of the number of moles of ions produced.
5. Substitute values into the formula to calculate the freezing-point depression.

Answers

Practice F

1. −7.4°C
2. 2.6°C
3. 0.054 *m* NaCl

TEACH FROM TABLES

FIGURE 2.6 Make sure students understand that the expected values of

$$\frac{\Delta t_f\text{, observed}}{\Delta t_f\text{, nonelectrolyte solution}}$$

would be 2 for KCl and $MgSO_4$ and 3 for $BaCl_2$ according to calculations based on number of particles in solution. These values get closer to their predicted values as the solutions are less concentrated.

READING TOOLKIT

PAIRED SUMMARIZING Pair students together and have them silently re-read this section, "Electrolytes and Colligative Properties." Ask one of the pair to be the "reteller" and the other the "listener." Have the reteller summarize the selection for the listener. The reteller may consult the text during his or her summary. The listener should then state any inaccuracies or omissions. Encourage the students to work together to refine the summary for use as a study guide.

▼ Teach *continued*

Misconception Alert!

Students may think that adding salt to a pot of cooking water raises the boiling point and causes food to cook faster. As a practical example, a cook might add about 30 g (about $1\frac{1}{2}$ tbsp) of NaCl to 5 L of water to cook pasta. This 5-L solution contains 1.0 mol of ions, so its ion concentration is 0.2 *m*. At best, such a solution would have a boiling point about 0.1°C higher than that of pure water, hardly enough to make a difference in cooking time. Raising the boiling point from 100°C to 102°C would require almost 600 g (1.3 lb) of salt in 5 L of water.

▼ Assess and Reteach

Assess Use the Formative Assessment on this page to evaluate student mastery of the section.

Reteach For students who need additional instruction, download the Section Study Guide.

Response to Intervention To reassess students' mastery, use the Section Quiz, available to print or to take directly online at **HMDScience.com**

FIGURE 2.7

Freezing Point Depression

The salts applied to icy roads lower the freezing point of water and melt the ice.

Look at the values given for KCl solutions in **Figure 2.6**, on the previous page. The freezing-point depression of a 0.1 *m* KCl solution is only 1.85 times greater than that of a nonelectrolyte solution. However, as the concentration decreases, the freezing-point depression comes closer to the value that is twice that of a nonelectrolyte solution (see **Figure 2.7**).

The differences between the expected and calculated values are caused by the attractive forces that exist between dissociated ions in aqueous solution. The attraction between the hydrated ions in the solution is small compared with those in the crystalline solid. However, forces of attraction do interfere with the movements of the aqueous ions. Only in very dilute solutions is the average distance between the ions large enough and the attraction between ions small enough for the solute ions to move about almost completely freely.

Peter Debye and Erich Hückel introduced a theory in 1923 to account for this attraction between ions in dilute aqueous solutions. According to this theory, the attraction between dissociated ions of ionic solids in dilute aqueous solutions is caused by an ionic atmosphere that surrounds each ion. This means that each ion is, on average, surrounded by more ions of opposite charge than of like charge. A cluster of hydrated ions can act as a single unit rather than as individual ions. Thus, the effective total concentration is less than expected, based on the number of ions known to be present.

Ions of higher charge attract other ions very strongly. They therefore cluster more and have lower effective concentrations than ions with smaller charge. For example, ions formed by $MgSO_4$ have charges of 2^+ and 2^-. Ions formed by KCl have charges of 1^+ and 1^-. Note in **Figure 2.6** that $MgSO_4$ in a solution does not depress the freezing point as much as the same concentration of KCl.

SECTION 2 FORMATIVE ASSESSMENT

Reviewing Main Ideas

1. What colligative properties are displayed by each of the following situations?
   a. Antifreeze is added to a car's cooling system to prevent freezing when the air temperature is below 0°C.
   b. Ice melts on sidewalks after salt has been spread on them.
2. Two moles of a nonelectrolyte solute are dissolved in 1 kg of an unknown solvent. The solution freezes at 7.8°C *below* its normal freezing point. What is the molal freezing-point constant of the unknown solvent? Suggest a possible identity of the solvent.
3. If two solutions of equal amounts in a U-tube are separated by a semipermeable membrane, will the level of the more-concentrated solution or the less-concentrated solution rise?
4. a. Calculate the expected freezing-point depression of a 0.200 *m* KNO_3 solution.
   b. Will the value you calculated match the actual freezing-point depression for this solution? Why or why not?

Critical Thinking

5. **INFERRING RELATIONSHIPS** The freezing-point depressions of aqueous solutions A, B, and C are −2.3°C, −1.2°C, and −4.1°C, respectively. Predict the order of the boiling-point elevations of these solutions, from lowest to highest. Explain your ranking.

Answers to Section Assessment

1. a. freezing-point depression
   b. freezing-point depression
2. −3.9°C/*m*; acetic acid
3. the more-concentrated solution
4. a. −0.744°C
   b. No. At this concentration, clustering of ions will cause the freezing-point depression to be less than expected.
5. Solution B < Solution A < Solution C (lowest to highest); For a given solution, the freezing point depression and the boiling point elevation depend only on the solute concentration. Because the freezing point of solution B is depressed the least, that solution must have the lowest solute concentration, so its boiling point would be elevated the least. Similarly, the freezing point of solution C is depressed the most, so solution C must have the highest solute concentration and thus the highest boiling point elevation.

Math Tutor — Boiling and Freezing Points of Solutions

The presence of a nonvolatile solute causes the freezing point of a solution to be lower and the boiling point to be higher than those of the pure solvent. The freezing-point depression, Δt_f, is the amount that the freezing point is lowered. It is calculated by using the formula $\Delta t_f = K_f m$. The boiling-point elevation, Δt_b, is the amount that the boiling point is elevated. It is found by using the equation $\Delta t_b = K_b m$. To determine Δt_f or Δt_b, you need to know its *molal* concentration, m (moles of solute per kilogram of solvent). You also need to know the molal freezing-point constant, K_f, or the molal boiling-point constant, K_b. The values for K_f and K_b depend on the solvent and are given in **Figure 2.3.** When these equations are used for electrolytes, the molality represents the total number of moles of ions in solution.

Problem-Solving TIPS

- Make sure that you find the molal concentration, not the molar concentration.
- For electrolytes, calculate the total number of moles of ions in solution.

Sample Problem

What is the theoretical boiling point of a solution of 247 g of potassium chloride, KCl, dissolved in 2.90 kg of water? Potassium chloride is a strong electrolyte.

First, determine the molality of the KCl that dissolved.

$$\text{mass of solute (g)} \times \frac{1 \text{ mol solute}}{\text{molar mass of solute (g)}} = \text{amount of solute (mol)}$$

$$247 \text{ g KCl} \times \frac{1 \text{ mol KCl}}{74.55 \text{ g KCl}} = 3.31 \text{ mol KCl}$$

$$\text{molality KCl}(m) = \frac{\text{mol solute particles}}{\text{mass of solvent (kg)}} = \frac{3.31 \text{ mol KCl}}{2.90 \text{ kg } H_2O} = 1.14\ m \text{ KCl}$$

Because KCl is an electrolyte, the total moles of ions in solution must now be determined. The equation $KCl(s) \longrightarrow K^+(aq) + Cl^-(aq)$ shows that 1 mol KCl will yield 2 mol of ions.

To find the total molality of particles in solution, multiply the molality of the solute by the moles of ions produced by the dissociation: $2 \times 1.14\ m$ KCl $= 2.28\ m$.

Next, use the equation $\Delta t_b = K_b m$, where K_b for water is $0.51°C/m$ and the value for m is 2.28.

$$\Delta t_b = (0.51°C/m)(2.28\ m) = 1.16°C$$

The new boiling point is equal to the sum of the boiling point of the solvent and Δt_b.

$$\text{boiling point of solution} = 100°C + 1.16°C = 101.16°C$$

Practice

1. What is the freezing point of a solution containing 28.0 g of the strong electrolyte calcium chloride, $CaCl_2$, dissolved in 295 g of water?
2. What is the boiling point of a solution composed of 850 g of ethylene glycol, $C_2H_6O_2$, mixed with 1100 g of water?

MATH TUTOR

Answers

1. −4.77°C
2. 106.3°C

CHAPTER SUMMARY

Review Answers

1. 2 mol; 3 mol
2. **a.** soluble, **b.** soluble, **c.** insoluble **d.** insoluble, **e.** insoluble, **f.** soluble, **g.** soluble, **h.** insoluble, **i.** insoluble, **j.** soluble
3. an equation that includes only those compounds and ions that are involved in a chemical change in aqueous solution
4. **a.** the formation of ions from solute molecules by the action of the solvent

   b. In dissociation, ions of an ionic compound separate from each other. In ionization, ions form where none existed in the undissolved compound.
5. **a.** A strong electrolyte exists almost entirely as ions in dilute aqueous solution to whatever extent the solute dissolves in water. A weak electrolyte dissolves in water but ionizes only to a slight extent.

   b. Answers may include that hydrogen chloride and aluminum chloride are strong electrolytes and hydrogen fluoride and acetic acid are weak electrolytes.
6. the extent to which a compound forms ions when dissolved
7. *Strong* and *weak* refer to the extent to which the solute is dissociated or ionized. *Dilute* and *concentrated* refer to the quantity of solute dissolved in a given quantity of solvent.
8. **a.** $KI(s) \xrightarrow{H_2O} K^+(aq) + I^-(aq)$

   b. $NaNO_3(s) \xrightarrow{H_2O} Na+(aq) + NO_3^-(aq)$

   c. $MgCl_2(s) \xrightarrow{H_2O} Mg^2+(aq) + 2Cl^-(aq)$

   d. $Na_2SO_4(s) \xrightarrow{H_2O} 2Na^+(aq) + SO_4^{2-}(aq)$
9. **a.** 1 mol K^+, 1 mol I^-; 2 mol ions

   b. 1 mol Na^+, 1 mol NO_3^-; 2 mol ions

   c. 1 mol Mg^{2+}, 2 mol Cl^-; 3 mol ions

   d. 2 mol Na^+, 1 mol SO_4^{2-}; mol ions

CHAPTER 13 Summary

Review Games
Concept Maps

SECTION 1 Compounds in Aqueous Solutions

- The separation of ions that occurs when an ionic solid dissolves is called dissociation.
- When two different ionic solutions are mixed, a precipitate may form if ions from the two solutions react to form an insoluble compound.
- A net ionic equation for a reaction in aqueous solution includes only compounds and ions that change chemically in the reaction. Spectator ions are ions that do not take part in such a reaction.
- Formation of ions from molecular compounds is called ionization. A molecular compound may ionize in an aqueous solution if the attraction of the polar water molecules is strong enough to break the polar-covalent bonds of the solute molecules.
- An H_3O^+ ion is called a hydronium ion.
- All, or almost all, of a dissolved strong electrolyte exists as ions in an aqueous solution, whereas a relatively small amount of a dissolved weak electrolyte exists as ions in an aqueous solution.

KEY TERMS

dissociation
net ionic equation
spectator ions
ionization
hydronium ion
strong electrolyte
weak electrolyte

SECTION 2 Colligative Properties of Solutions

- Colligative properties of solutions depend only on the total number of solute particles present. Boiling-point elevation, freezing-point depression, vapor-pressure lowering, and osmotic pressure are colligative properties.
- The molal boiling-point and freezing-point constants are used to calculate boiling-point elevations and freezing-point depressions of solvents containing nonvolatile solutes.
- Electrolytes have a greater effect on the freezing and boiling points of solvents than nonelectrolytes do.
- Except in very dilute solutions, the values of colligative properties of electrolyte solutions are less than expected because of the attraction between ions in solution.

KEY TERMS

colligative properties
nonvolatile substance
molal freezing-point constant, K_f
freezing-point depression, Δt_f
molal boiling-point constant, K_b
boiling-point elevation, Δt_b
semipermeable membrane
osmosis
osmotic pressure

CHAPTER 13 Review

SECTION 1

Compounds in Aqueous Solutions

REVIEWING MAIN IDEAS

1. How many moles of ions are contained in 1 L of a 1 M solution of KCl? of $Mg(NO_3)_2$?

2. Use **Figure 1.3** to predict whether each of the following compounds is considered soluble or insoluble:
   a. KCl
   b. $NaNO_3$
   c. AgCl
   d. $BaSO_4$
   e. $Ca_3(PO_4)_2$
   f. $Pb(ClO_3)_2$
   g. $(NH_4)_2S$
   h. $PbCl_2$ (in cold water)
   i. FeS
   j. $Al_2(SO_4)_3$

3. What is a net ionic equation?

4. a. What is ionization?
   b. Distinguish between ionization and dissociation.

5. a. Define and distinguish between strong electrolytes and weak electrolytes.
   b. Give two examples of each type.

6. What determines the strength of a solute as an electrolyte?

7. Distinguish between the use of the terms *strong* and *weak* and the use of the terms *dilute* and *concentrated* when describing electrolyte solutions.

PRACTICE PROBLEMS

8. Write the equation for the dissolution of each of the following ionic compounds in water. (Hint: See Sample Problem A.)
   a. KI c. $MgCl_2$
   b. $NaNO_3$ d. Na_2SO_4

9. For the compounds listed in the previous problem, determine the number of moles of each ion produced as well as the total number of moles of ions produced when 1 mol of each compound dissolves in water.

10. Write the equation for the dissolution of each of the following in water, and then indicate the total number of moles of solute ions formed.
    a. 0.50 mol strontium nitrate
    b. 0.50 mol sodium phosphate

11. Using **Figure 1.3**, write the balanced chemical equation, write the overall ionic equation, identify the spectator ions and possible precipitates, and write the net ionic equation for each of the following reactions. (Hint: See Sample Problem B.)
    a. mercury(II) chloride (aq) + potassium sulfide $(aq) \longrightarrow$
    b. sodium carbonate (aq) + calcium chloride $(aq) \longrightarrow$
    c. copper(II) chloride (aq) + ammonium phosphate $(aq) \longrightarrow$

12. Identify the spectator ions in the reaction between KCl and $AgNO_3$ in an aqueous solution.

13. Copper(II) chloride and lead(II) nitrate react in aqueous solutions by double displacement. Write the balanced chemical equation, the overall ionic equation, and the net ionic equation for this reaction. If 13.45 g of copper(II) chloride react, what is the maximum amount of precipitate that could be formed?

SECTION 2

Colligative Properties of Solutions

REVIEWING MAIN IDEAS

14. How does the presence of a nonvolatile solute affect each of the following properties of the solvent in which the solute is dissolved?
    a. vapor pressure
    b. freezing point
    c. boiling point
    d. osmotic pressure

15. Using **Figure 2.1** as a guide, make a graph of vapor pressure versus temperature that shows the comparison of pure water, a solution with x concentration of solute, and a solution with $2x$ concentration of solute. What is the relationship between Δt_f for the x solution and Δt_f for the $2x$ solution?

CHAPTER REVIEW

10. a. $Sr(NO_3)_2(s) \xrightarrow{H_2O} Sr^{2+}(aq) + 2NO_3^-(aq)$
1.50 mol ions
b. $Na_3PO_4(s) \xrightarrow{H_2O} 3Na^+(aq) + PO_4^{3-}(aq)$
2.00 mol ions

11. a. $HgCl_2(aq) + K_2S(aq) \longrightarrow HgS(s) + 2KCl(aq)$
$Hg^{2+}(aq) + 2Cl^-(aq) + 2K+(aq) + S^{2-}(aq) \longrightarrow HgS(s) + 2K^+(aq) + 2Cl^-(aq)$
spectator ions: Cl^- and K^+;
precipitate: HgS
$Hg^{2+}(aq) + S^{2-}(aq) \longrightarrow HgS(s)$
b. $Na_2CO_3(aq) + CaCl_2(aq) \longrightarrow 2NaCl(aq) + CaCO_3(s)$
$2Na^+(aq) + CO_3^{2-}(aq) + Ca^{2+}(aq) + 2Cl^-(aq) \longrightarrow CaCO_3(s) + 2Na^+(aq) + 2Cl^-(aq)$
spectator ions: Na^+ and Cl^-;
precipitate: $CaCO_3$
$Ca^{2+}(aq) + CO_3^{2-}(aq) \longrightarrow CaCO_3(s)$
c. $3CuCl_2(aq) + 2(NH_4)_3PO_4(aq) \longrightarrow Cu_3(PO_4)_2(s) + 6NH4Cl(aq)$
$3Cu^{2+}(aq) + 6Cl^-(aq) + 6NH_4^+(aq) + 2PO_4^{3-}(aq) \longrightarrow Cu_3(PO_4)_2(s) + 6NH_4^+(aq) + 6Cl^-(aq)$
spectator ions: NH_4^+ and Cl^-;
precipitate: $Cu_3(PO_4)_2$
$3Cu^{2+}(aq) + 2PO_4^{3-}(aq) \longrightarrow Cu_3(PO_4)_2(s)$

12. K^+ and NO_3^-

13. $CuCl_2(aq) + Pb(NO_3)_2(aq) \longrightarrow Cu(NO_3)_2(aq) + PbCl_2(s)$
$Cu^{2+}(aq) + 2Cl^-(aq) + Pb^{2+}(aq) + 2NO_3^-(aq) \longrightarrow$
$Cu^{2+}(aq) + 2NO_3^-(aq) + PbCl_2(s)$
$Pb^{2+}(aq) + 2Cl^-(aq) \longrightarrow PbCl_2(s)$
27.82 g $PbCl_2$

14. a. lowers the vapor pressure,
b. lowers the freezing poing,
c. raises the boiling, point,
d. increases the osmotic pressure

15. Δt_f for $2x$ concentration of solute is twice that for x concentration of solute.

16. a. Water from the less concentrated solution passes through the membrane by osmosis into the more-concentrated solution.
    b. when the added pressure resulting from the height of the solution equals the osmotic pressure
    c. There is no net movement.

17. a. A nonvolatile electrolyte will lower the freezing point or raise the boiling point more than a nonelectrolyte at the same concentration will.
    b. One mole of a nonelectrolyte produces 1 mol of particles in solution. A mole of a nonvolatile electrolyte produces more than 1 mol of ions in solution.

18. The difference is caused by attractive forces between the ions in solution.

19. a. −2.79°C c. −1.05°C
    b. −0.93°C

20. a. 0.500 *m* c. 4.50 *m*
    b. 2.00 *m*

21. a. −0.826°C
    b. −0.826°C

22. 334 g $C_2H_4(OH)_2$

23. −5.07°C/*m*

24. 165.2°C

25. a. 1.3°C c. 0.060°C
    b. 0.0091°C

26. a. 0.49 *m* solute c. 5.5 *m* solute
    b. 3.0 *m* solute

27. a. −3.72°C c. −5.58°C
    b. −5.58°C

28. −0.11°C

29. −12.0°C

30. 101.2°C

31. 0.64 *m* KI

32. 0.475 *m* $Ba(NO_3)_2$

33. −0.930°C

34. −5.58°C; Because of forces of attraction between them, the ions cluster together somewhat.

CHAPTER REVIEW

16. a. Why does the level of the more-concentrated solution rise when two solutions of different concentrations are separated by a semipermeable membrane?
b. When does the level of the solution stop rising?
c. When the level stops rising, what is the net movement of water molecules across the membrane?

17. a. Compare the effects of nonvolatile electrolytes with the effects of nonvolatile nonelectrolytes on the freezing and boiling points of solvents in which they are dissolved.
b. Why are such differences observed?

18. Why does the actual freezing-point depression of an electrolytic solution differ from the freezing-point depression calculated on the basis of the concentration of particles?

PRACTICE PROBLEMS

19. Determine the freezing-point depression of H_2O in each of the following solutions. (Hint: See Sample Problem C.)
a. 1.50 *m* solution of $C_{12}H_{22}O_{11}$ (sucrose) in H_2O
b. 171 g of $C_{12}H_{22}O_{11}$ in 1.00 kg H_2O
c. 77.0 g of $C_{12}H_{22}O_{11}$ in 400. g H_2O

20. Given the following freezing-point depressions, determine the molality of each solution of an unknown nonelectrolyte in water. (Hint: See Sample Problem D.)
a. −0.930°C
b. −3.72°C
c. −8.37°C

21. A solution contains 20.0 g of $C_6H_{12}O_6$ (glucose) in 250. g of water.
a. What is the freezing-point depression of the solvent?
b. What is the freezing point of the solution?

22. How many grams of antifreeze, $C_2H_4(OH)_2$, would be required per 500. g of water to prevent the water from freezing at a temperature of −20.0°C?

23. Pure benzene, C_6H_6, freezes at 5.45°C. A solution containing 7.24 g $C_2Cl_4H_2$ in 115 g of benzene (specific gravity = 0.879) freezes at 3.55°C. Based on these data, what is the molal freezing-point constant for benzene?

24. If 1.500 g of a solute that has a molar mass of 125.0 g were dissolved in 35.00 g of camphor, what would be the resulting freezing point of the solution?

25. Determine the boiling-point elevation of H_2O in each of the following solutions. (Hint: See Sample Problem E.)
a. 2.5 *m* solution of $C_6H_{12}O_6$ (glucose) in H_2O
b. 3.20 g $C_6H_{12}O_6$ in 1.00 kg H_2O
c. 20.0 g $C_{12}H_{22}O_{11}$ (sucrose) in 500. g H_2O

26. Given the following boiling points, determine the molality of each water solution.
a. 100.25°C
b. 101.53°C
c. 102.805°C

27. Given 1.00 *m* aqueous solutions of each of the following electrolytic substances, determine the expected change in the freezing point of the solvent. (Hint: See Sample Problem F.)
a. KI
b. $CaCl_2$
c. $Ba(NO_3)_2$

28. What is the expected change in the freezing point of water for a 0.015 *m* aqueous solution of $AlCl_3$?

29. What is the expected freezing point of a solution containing 85.0 g NaCl dissolved in 450. g of water?

30. Determine the expected boiling point of a solution made by dissolving 25.0 g of barium chloride in 0.150 kg of water.

31. The change in the boiling point of water for an aqueous solution of potassium iodide is 0.65°C. Determine the molal concentration of potassium iodide.

32. The freezing point of an aqueous solution of barium nitrate is −2.65°C. Determine the molal concentration of barium nitrate.

33. Calculate the expected freezing point of a solution containing 1.00 kg H_2O and 0.250 mol NaCl.

34. Experimental data for a 1.00 *m* MgI_2 aqueous solution indicate an actual change in the freezing point of water of −4.78°C. Find the expected change in the freezing point of water. Suggest a possible reason for the discrepancy between the experimental and expected values.

436 Chapter 13

Mixed Review

REVIEWING MAIN IDEAS

35. Given 0.01 *m* aqueous solutions of each of the following, arrange the solutions in order of increasing change in the freezing point of the solution.
a. NaI
b. $CaCl_2$
c. K_3PO_4
d. $C_6H_{12}O_6$ (glucose)

36. What is the molal concentration of an aqueous calcium chloride solution that freezes at −2.43°C?

37. a. Write the balanced formula equation that shows the possible products of a double-displacement reaction between calcium nitrate and sodium chloride.
b. Using **Figure 1.3**, determine whether there is a precipitate.
c. Does this reaction occur?

38. Write a balanced equation to show what occurs when hydrogen bromide dissolves and reacts with water. Include a hydronium ion in the equation.

39. Write the equation for the dissolution of each of the following in water, and then indicate the total number of moles of solute ions formed.
a. 0.275 mol of potassium sulfide
b. 0.15 mol of aluminum sulfate

40. Calculate the expected change in the boiling point of water in a solution made up of 131.2 g of silver nitrate, $AgNO_3$, in 2.00 kg of water.

41. Nitrous acid, HNO_2, is a weak electrolyte. Nitric acid, HNO_3, is a strong electrolyte. Write equations to represent the ionization of each in water. Include the hydronium ion, and show the appropriate kind of arrow in each equation.

42. Find the boiling point of an aqueous solution containing a nonelectrolyte that freezes at −6.51°C.

43. Write a balanced equation for the dissolution of sodium carbonate, Na_2CO_3, in water. Find the number of moles of each ion produced when 0.20 mol of sodium carbonate dissolves. Then, find the total number of moles of ions.

44. Given the reaction below and the information in **Figure 1.3**, write the net ionic equation for the reaction.

potassium phosphate (*aq*) + lead(II) nitrate (*aq*)

45. Find the expected freezing point of a water solution that contains 268 g of aluminum nitrate, $Al(NO_3)_3$, in 8.50 kg of water.

CRITICAL THINKING

46. Applying Models
a. You are conducting a freezing-point determination in the laboratory by using an aqueous solution of KNO_3. The observed freezing point of the solution is −1.15°C. Using a pure water sample, you recorded the freezing point of the pure solvent on the same thermometer as 0.25°C. Determine the molal concentration of KNO_3. Assume that there are no forces of attraction between ions.
b. You are not satisfied with the result in part (a) because you suspect that you should not ignore the effect of ion interaction. You take a 10.00 mL sample of the solution. After carefully evaporating the water from the solution, you obtain 0.415 g KNO_3. Determine the actual molal concentration of KNO_3 and the percentage difference between the concentration observed in the freezing-point determination and the actual concentration of KNO_3. Assume that the solution's density is 1.00 g/mL.

47. Analyzing Information The observed freezing-point depression for electrolyte solutions is sometimes less than the calculated value. Why does this occur? Is the difference greater for concentrated solutions or dilute solutions?

48. Analyzing Information The osmotic pressure of a dilute solution can be calculated as follows:

$\pi = MRT$
π = osmotic pressure
M = concentration in moles per liter
R = ideal gas constant
T = absolute temperature of the solution

How does the osmotic-pressure equation compare with the ideal gas law?

CHAPTER REVIEW

35. d, a, b, c
36. 0.435 *m* $CaCl_2$
37. a. $Ca(NO_3)_2(aq) + 2NaCl(aq) \longrightarrow CaCl_2(aq) + 2NaNO_3(aq)$
b. No precipitate forms.
c. No reaction occurs.
38. $HBr(g) + H_2O(l) \longrightarrow H_3O^+(aq) + Br^-(aq)$
39. a. $K_2S(s) \xrightarrow{H_2O} 2K^+(aq) + S^{2-}(aq)$
0.825 mol solute ions
b. $Al_2(SO_4)_3(s) \xrightarrow{H_2O} 2Al^{3+}(aq) + 3SO_4^{2-}(aq)$
0.75 mol solute ions
40. 0.39°C
41. $HNO_2(aq) + H_2O(l) \rightleftharpoons H_3O^+(aq) + NO_2^-(aq)$
$HNO_3(aq) + H_2O(l) \longrightarrow H_3O^+(aq) + NO_3^-(aq)$
42. 101.8°C
43. $Na_2CO_3(s) \xrightarrow{H_2O} 2Na^+(aq) + CO_3^{2-}(aq)$
0.40 mol Na^+; 0.20 mol CO_3^{2-};
0.60 mol solute ions
44. $3Pb^{2+}(aq) + 2PO_4^{3-}(aq) \longrightarrow Pb_3(PO_4)_2(s)$
45. −1.10°C
46. a. 0.376 *m*
b. 0.410 *m*; −8.29%
47. There are attractive forces between ions. The attractive forces are greater for concentrated solutions.
48. In the equation $\pi = MRT$, the variable *M* stands for molarity, which is expressed as a concentration in moles per liter. So, M = number of moles per unit volume = n/V. Substituting n/V into the equation gives
$\pi = \frac{nRT}{V}$
or $\pi V = nRT$, which is identical to the ideal gas law except for π, which represents osmotic pressure.

49. a. $2Al(s) + 2OH^-(aq) + 2H_2O(l) \longrightarrow 2AlO_2^-(aq) + 3H_2(g)$
$2Al(s) + 6H^+(aq) \longrightarrow 2Al^{3+}(aq) + 3H_2(g)$
$2Al(s) + 3Cl_2(g) \longrightarrow 2AlCl_3(s)$
$4Al(s) + 3O_2(g) \longrightarrow 2Al_2O_3(s)$
b. formation of the halide and oxide; because there are no spectator ions

50. a. $Sn(s) + O_2(g) \longrightarrow SnO_2(s)$
$Sn(s) + 2H^+(aq) \longrightarrow Sn^{2+}(aq) + H_2(g)$
$Sn(s) + 2Cl_2(g) \longrightarrow SnCl_4(s)$
b. formation of the halide and oxide; because there are no spectator ions

51. Student answers will vary but should include environmental problems that result from salt and salt substitutes.

52. Answers will vary but should include how electrolytes work in the body and the health problems that can occur when a body has an imbalance of electrolytes.

53. Student answers will vary depending on the concentrations of the solutions. The mixture with the lowest freezing point should be the one with the highest concentration of ethylene glycol.

54. Student answers will vary but should include the concentration of the salt solution that will freeze the ice-cream mixture.

55. Student answers will depend on the solutions provided but they should identify the solutions that conduct electricity as electrolytes and those that do not conduct as nonelectrolytes.

56. Student answers may vary but should include that for equal molar solutions, the number of moles of solute particles will be greater in the electrolyte solutions than in the nonelectrolyte solutions. As a result, the electrolyte solutions will lower the freezing point more than the nonelectrolyte solutions will. The experiment should be designed around this concept, and students should measure freezing points of the solutions.

CHAPTER REVIEW

USING THE HANDBOOK

49. Common reactions for Group 13 elements are found in the *Elements Handbook* (Appendix A). Review this material, and answer the following:
  a. Write net ionic equations for each of the example reactions listed under "Common Reactions" for Group 13.
  b. Which reactions did not change when written in net ionic form? Why?

50. Common reactions for Group 14 elements are found in the *Elements Handbook* (Appendix A). Review this material, and answer the following:
  a. Write net ionic equations for each of the example reactions listed under "Common Reactions" for Group 14.
  b. Which reactions did not change when written in net ionic form? Why?

RESEARCH AND WRITING

51. Find out how much salt a large northern city, such as New York City or Chicago, uses on its streets in a typical winter. What environmental problems result from this use of salt? What substitutes for salt are being used to melt ice and snow?

52. Research the role of electrolytes and electrolytic solutions in your body. Find out how electrolytes work in the functioning of nerves and muscles. What are some of the health problems that can arise from an imbalance of electrolytes in body fluids?

ALTERNATIVE ASSESSMENT

53. Performance Determine the freezing point of four different mixtures of water and ethylene glycol (use commercial antifreeze). What mixture has the lowest freezing point?

54. Performance Find the optimum mixture of salt and ice for reducing the temperature of the chilling bath for an ice-cream freezer. Use your data to write a set of instructions on how to prepare the chilling bath for making ice cream.

55. Performance Using a low-voltage dry cell, assemble a conductivity apparatus. Secure several unknown aqueous solutions of equal molality from your instructor, and use the apparatus to distinguish the electrolytes from the nonelectrolytes. Among those identified as electrolytes, rank their relative strengths as conductors from good to poor.

56. Performance Using equal volumes of the unknown solutions from the preceding activity, explain how you could use the freezing-point depression concept to distinguish the electrolytes from the nonelectrolytes. Explain how you could determine the number of ions contained per molecule among the solutes identified as electrolytes. Design and conduct an experiment to test your theories.

438 Chapter 13

Standards-Based Assessment

Answer the following items on a separate piece of paper.

MULTIPLE CHOICE

1. Acetic acid is a weak electrolyte because it
   A. is miscible with water.
   B. forms hydronium and hydroxide ions in aqueous solution.
   C. lowers the freezing point of water.
   D. ionizes only slightly in aqueous solution.

2. Which of the following solutions would contain the highest concentration of hydronium ions, H_3O^+?
   A. 0.10 M HCl
   B. 0.10 M HF
   C. 0.10 M CH_3COOH
   D. 0.10 M NaCl

3. Which of the following is the best representation of the precipitation reaction that occurs when aqueous solutions of sodium carbonate and calcium chloride are mixed?
   A. $Na^+(aq) + Cl^-(aq) \longrightarrow 2NaCl(s)$
   B. $2Na^+(aq) + CO_3^{2-}(aq) + Ca^{2+}(aq) + 2Cl^-(aq) \longrightarrow CaCO_3(s) + 2NaCl(s)$
   C. $Ca^{2+}(aq) + CO_3^{2-}(aq) \longrightarrow CaCO_3(s)$
   D. No precipitation reaction occurs.

4. Which of the following is *not* a colligative property?
   A. molality
   B. vapor-pressure lowering
   C. boiling-point elevation
   D. osmotic pressure

5. Solution A contains 0.1 mol of sucrose, $C_{12}H_{22}O_{11}$, dissolved in 500 g of water. Solution B contains 0.1 mol of sodium chloride, NaCl, in 500 g of water. Which of the following statements about these solutions is true?
   A. Both solutions have the same vapor pressure.
   B. Solution A would boil at a higher temperature than solution B would.
   C. Solution A would freeze at a higher temperature than solution B would.
   D. Both solutions would boil at the same temperature.

The table below shows the freezing points of solutions of three nonvolatile solutes, X, Y, and Z, in water. Refer to the table to answer items 6 and 7. The K_f for water is $-1.86°C/m$.

Solute	Solute (mol)	Water (g)	Freezing point (°C)
X	1.00	1000	−5.58
Y	1.00	1000	−1.86
Z	1.00	1000	−3.72

6. Which of the following statements is *not* true?
   A. All three solutes are nonelectrolytes.
   B. Solute X could be $Ca(NO_3)_2$.
   C. Solute Y could be sucrose.
   D. Solute Z could be KCl.

7. Which of the solutions described in the table would have the highest boiling point?
   A. the solution of solute X
   B. the solution of solute Y
   C. the solution of solute Z
   D. All three solutions would have the same boiling point.

SHORT ANSWER

8. An aqueous solution of an unknown quantity of a nonelectrolyte solute is found to have a freezing point of −0.58°C. What is the molal concentration of the solution?

9. Give the names and formulas of two strong electrolytes.

EXTENDED RESPONSE

10. Write the formula equation, the overall ionic equation, and the net ionic equation for the precipitation reaction that occurs when solutions of zinc chloride, $ZnCl_2$, and sodium sulfide, Na_2S, are mixed.

11. Distinguish between dissociation and ionization. Write one chemical equation to illustrate each of these terms.

Test Tip
Before choosing an answer to a question, try to answer the question without looking at the answer choices on the test.

STANDARDS-BASED ASSESSMENT

To give students practice under more realistic testing conditions, give them 60 minutes to answer all of the questions in this Standardized Test Preparation.

Test Answers

1. D
2. A
3. C
4. A
5. C
6. A
7. A
8. 0.31 *m*
9. Answers will vary. Any strong acid, any strong base, or any soluble ionic compound are acceptable answers. Weak acids, weak bases, or insoluble ionic compounds are not acceptable.
10. formula:
    $ZnCl_2(aq) + Na_2S(aq) \longrightarrow ZnS(s) + 2NaCl(aq)$
    overall ionic:
    $Zn^{2+}(aq) + 2Cl^-(aq) + 2Na^+(aq) + S^{2-}(aq) \longrightarrow ZnS(s) + 2Na^+(aq) + 2Cl^-(aq)$
    Net ionic:
    $Zn^{2+}(aq) + S^{2+}(aq) \longrightarrow ZnS(s)$
11. Dissociation is the separation of ions that occurs when an ionic compound dissolves. Examples will vary. Two possibilities are
    $Na_2SO_4(s) \xrightarrow{H_2O} 2Na^+(aq) + SO_4^{2-}(aq)$
    $CrCl_3(s) \xrightarrow{H_2O} Cr^{3+}(aq) + 3Cl^-(aq)$
    Ionization is the creation of ions from solute molecules by the action of the solvent. Examples will vary. Two possibilities are
    $HCl(g) + H_2O(l) \longrightarrow H_3O^+(aq) + Cl^-(aq)$
    $HF(g) + H_2O(l) \rightleftarrows H_3O^+(aq) + F^-(aq)$

Acids and Bases

① Core Instruction

Chapter Resources

- The Teacher's Edition wrap has extensive teaching support for every lesson, including Misconception Alerts, Teach from Visuals, Demonstrations, Teaching Tips, Differentiated Instruction, and Problem Solving support.
- Several additional presentation tools are available online for every chapter, including Animated Chemistry features and Visual Concepts.
- You can open your lesson with the Why It Matters Video: Acids and Bases.

Section	Instruction	Labs and Demonstrations Go Online for Materials Lists and Solutions Lists.
14.1	**Textbook:** Properties of Acids and Bases **Teaching Visuals:** Relationship of $[H_3O^+]$ to $[OH^-]$ • Names of Acids • Common Aqueous Acids and Bases • Some Strong Acids and Some Weak Acids • Some Strong Bases and Some Weak Bases **PowerPresentations**	**Demonstration:** Color Change of Phenolphthalien **QuickLab:** Household Acids and Bases **Demonstration:** Strength and Conductivity **Lab:** Is It an Acid or a Base? (Core Skill)
14.2	**Textbook:** Acid-Base Theories **Teaching Visuals:** Monoprotic and Diprotic Acids • Acid-Base Definitions **PowerPresentations**	
14.3	**Textbook:** Acid-Base Reactions **Animated Chemistry:** Neutralization Reactions **Teaching Visuals:** Oxyacids of Chlorine • Neutralization Reactions • Conjugate Acid-Base Pairs • Relative Strengths of Acids and Bases **PowerPresentations**	**Lab:** Effects of Acid Rain on Plants (Forensics) **Lab:** I've Got A Secret (Open Inquiry)

Find all of your resources online at HMDScience.com.

2 Support and Intervention

- **Interactive Reader** (English and Spanish)
- **Study Guide**
- **Interactive Review:** Review Games, Concept Maps, and Section Self-Checks
- **Scientific Reasoning Skill Builder**

3 Specialized Support

- **Chapter Summary Audio Files**
- **Interactive Reader Audio Files**
- **Differentiated Instruction:** Inclusion, Below Level, and English Learners (TE wrap)

Enrichment and Challenge

- **Differentiated Instruction:** Pre-AP (TE wrap)
- **Cross-Disciplinary Connection:** Acid Water—A Hidden Menace (SE)
- **WebLinks**

Assessment

- **Section Formative Assessments** (SE)
- **Section Quizzes**
- **Chapter Review** (SE)
- **Chapter Tests A and B**
- **Alternative Assessment** (TE wrap)
- **Online Assessment and Remediation**
- **ExamView Banks**

Where do I find it?

		PRINT	DVD	ONLINE
1	Animated Chemistry		■	■
	Demonstrations (TE wrap)	■		■
	Interactive Whiteboard		■	■
	Labs		■	■
	PowerPresentations		■	■
	QuickLabs	■	■	■
	Teaching Visuals		■	■
	Textbook	■	■	■
	Visual Concepts		■	■
	Why It Matters Videos		■	■
2	Interactive Demos		■	■
	Interactive Reader	■	■	■
	Interactive Reviews		■	■
	Learn It! Videos		■	■
	Sample Problem Sets		■	■
	Scientific Reasoning Skill Builder		■	■
	Smart Grapher Tool		■	■
	Solve It! Cards		■	■
	Study Guide		■	■
3	Chapter Summary Audio Files		■	■
	Differentiated Instruction (TE wrap)	■		
	Interactive Reader Audio Files		■	■

CHAPTER 14

Chapter Overview

Section 1 describes acids and bases, defines Arrhenius acids and bases, introduces acid-base nomenclature, and characterizes strong and weak acids and bases.

Section 2 describes two more acid-base theories: the Brønsted-Lowry and Lewis theories.

Section 3 explains acid-base reactions in aqueous solutions.

▼ Focus and Motivate

Activate Prior Knowledge

Students may need a review of the following concepts:

- chemical bonding
- writing chemical formulas
- writing and balancing chemical equations and the activity series
- properties of solutions
- ions in aqueous solution

About the Image

Many of the foods we eat, such as lemons, are acidic. The acid found in lemons is citric acid. Lemons have a high concentration of citric acid as compared to most other fruits, which gives them a particularly sour taste. The total amount of citric acid in a lemon can account for as much as 8% of its dry weight.

Why It Matters

Students can access the video online and find other helpful resources at **HMDScience.com**.

CHAPTER 14

Acids and Bases

SECTION 1
Properties of Acids and Bases

SECTION 2
Acid-Base Theories

SECTION 3
Acid-Base Reactions

ONLINE LABS include:
Is It an Acid or a Base?
Effects of Acid Rain on Plants

PREMIUM CONTENT

Why It Matters Video
HMDScience.com

Acids and Bases

Lab Preview

The following labs and demonstrations support the concepts presented in this chapter.

LABS

Is It an Acid or a Base?
Effects of Acid Rain on Plants (Forensics)
I've Got a Secret (Open Inquiry)

QUICKLAB

Household Acids and Bases

DEMONSTRATIONS

Color Change of Phenolphthalein
Strength and Conductivity

Properties of Acids and Bases

SECTION 1

Main Ideas

- Acids are identified by their properties.
- Some acids are useful in industry.
- The properties of bases differ from those of acids.
- Arrhenius acids and bases produce ions in solution.

Key Terms

binary acid
oxyacid
Arrhenius acid
Arrhenius base
strong acid
weak acid

How many foods can you think of that are sour? Chances are that almost all the foods you thought of, like those in **Figure 1.1a,** owe their sour taste to an acid. Sour milk contains *lactic acid*. Vinegar, which can be produced by fermenting juices, contains *acetic acid*. *Phosphoric acid* gives a tart flavor to many carbonated beverages. Most fruits contain some kind of acid. Lemons, oranges, grapefruits, and other citrus fruits contain *citric acid*. Apples contain *malic acid*, and grape juice contains *tartaric acid*.

Many substances known as bases are commonly found in household products, such as those in **Figure 1.1b.** Household ammonia is an ammonia-water solution that is useful for all types of general cleaning. Sodium hydroxide, NaOH, known by the common name *lye*, is present in some commercial cleaners. Milk of magnesia is a suspension in water of magnesium hydroxide, $Mg(OH)_2$, which is not very water-soluble. It is used as an antacid to relieve discomfort caused by excess hydrochloric acid in the stomach. Aluminum hydroxide, $Al(OH)_3$, and sodium hydrogen carbonate, $NaHCO_3$, are also bases commonly found in antacids.

FIGURE 1.1

Common Acids and Bases

(a) Fruits and fruit juices contain acids such as citric acid and ascorbic acid. Carbonated beverages contain benzoic acid, phosphoric acid, and carbonic acid.

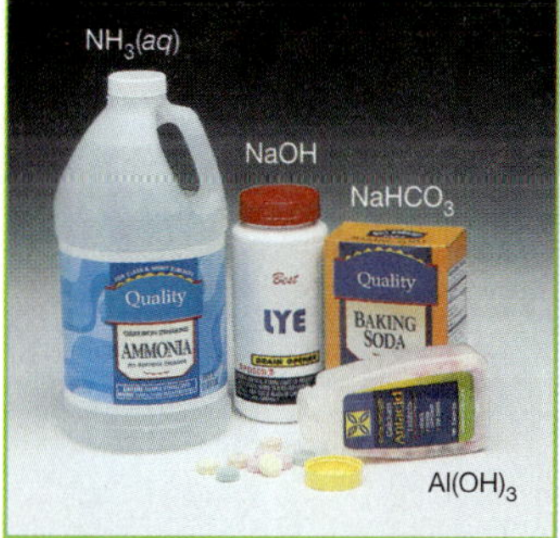

(b) Many household cleaners contain bases such as ammonia and sodium hydroxide. Antacids contain bases such as aluminum hydroxide.

Differentiated Instruction

ENGLISH LEARNERS

Point out that the prefix *anti-* means "opposed to" or "against". Show the class an antacid product. Point out that people take antacids when they have an upset stomach caused by the presence of excess hydrochloric acid. Have students explain why the term *antacid* is an appropriate name for this consumer product. Students should explain that the name indicates that the product will work against stomach acid.

SECTION 1

Plan and Prepare ▼

Objectives

Upon completion of this section, students should be able to do the following:

- List five general properties of aqueous acids and bases.
- Name common binary acids and oxyacids, given their chemical formulas.
- List five acids commonly used in industry and the laboratory, and give two properties of each.
- Define *acid* and *base* according to Arrhenius's theory of ionization.
- Explain the differences between strong and weak acids and bases.

Classroom Catalyst

Before class, pour 200 mL of water into each of two 400 mL beakers. Add a few drops of ammonia solution to the water in one beaker and a few drops of hydrochloric acid to the water in the other beaker. Stir each. At the beginning of class, test the contents of each beaker with pH paper. Help students conclude that although the contents look the same, the solutions in the two beakers have different properties. Save the solutions for the Color Change of Phenolphthalein Demonstration.

Teach ▼

TEACH FROM VISUALS

FIGURE 1.1 Ask students how they can find out the names of some of the acids that are present in a packaged beverage, such as a soft drink or a fruit drink. See how many names of acids they can recognize on the labels of various commercial drink products. Point out that not all acids present may be listed separately. For example, orange juice contains citric and ascorbic acids, but these names may not be listed.

▼ Teach *continued*

TEACH FROM VISUALS

FIGURE 1.2 Introduce an acid-base indicator as a substance that is one color in an acid and a different color in a base. Demonstrate the effect shown in the figure using vinegar and other acids and bases. Use a variety of indicators to show that various indicators have different colors in acids and bases.

Demonstration

COLOR CHANGE OF PHENOLPHTHALEIN

Tell students that one of the **two beakers** from the Classroom Catalyst demonstration contained a **weak solution of ammonia** and the other a **weak solution of hydrochloric acid**. Add a drop of **phenolphthalein** solution to each beaker. Students will note that the indicator turns pink in the ammonia solution (base) and remains colorless in the acidic solution. If students have trouble seeing the difference in color, hold the beakers in front of sheets of **white paper**.

Safety Wear **goggles** and a **lab apron.**

Disposal Solutions may be poured down the drain.

Classroom Discussion

Ask students to predict which metals will react with acids and which metals will not react with acids, based on their position in the activity series.

FIGURE 1.2

Acid Indicator A strip of pH paper dipped into vinegar turns red, showing that vinegar is an acid.

MAIN IDEA

Acids are identified by their properties.

Acids were first recognized as a distinct class of compounds because of the common properties of their aqueous solutions. These properties are listed below.

1. *Aqueous solutions of acids have a sour taste.* Taste, however, should NEVER be used as a test to evaluate any chemical substance. Many acids, especially in concentrated solutions, are corrosive; that is, they destroy body tissue and clothing. Many are also poisons.
2. *Acids change the color of acid-base indicators.* When pH paper is used as an indicator, the paper turns certain colors in acidic solution. This reaction is demonstrated in **Figure 1.2.**
3. *Some acids react with active metals and release hydrogen gas, H_2.* Recall that metals can be ordered in terms of an activity series. Metals above hydrogen in the series undergo single-displacement reactions with certain acids. Hydrogen gas is formed as a product, as shown by the reaction of barium with sulfuric acid.

$$Ba(s) + H_2SO_4(aq) \longrightarrow BaSO_4(s) + H_2(g)$$

4. *Acids react with bases to produce salts and water.* When chemically equivalent amounts of acids and bases react, the three properties just described disappear because the acid is "neutralized." The reaction products are water and an ionic compound called a *salt*.
5. *Acids conduct electric current.* Some acids completely separate into ions in water and are strong electrolytes. Other acids are weak electrolytes.

Acid Nomenclature

A binary acid is an acid that contains only two different elements: hydrogen and one of the more electronegative elements. Many common inorganic acids are binary acids. The hydrogen halides—HF, HCl, HBr, and HI—are all binary acids. Names for some binary acids are given in **Figure 1.3.**

FIGURE 1.3

NAMES OF BINARY ACIDS

Formula	Acid name	Molecule name
HF	hydrofluoric acid	hydrogen fluoride
HCl	hydrochloric acid	hydrogen chloride
HBr	hydrobromic acid	hydrogen bromide
HI	hydriodic acid	hydrogen iodide
H_2S	hydrosulfuric acid	hydrogen sulfide

Differentiated Instruction

BELOW LEVEL

To help students understand how acids and bases react, write the following chemical equations on the board:

$HCl(aq) + NaOH(aq) \longrightarrow NaCl(aq) + H_2O(l)$ (double-replacement reaction)

$HCl(aq) \longrightarrow H^+(aq) + Cl^-(aq)$ (ionization)

$NaOH(aq) \longrightarrow Na^+(aq) + Cl^-(aq)$ (dissociation)

Then write the following list of chemical terms on the board:

ionization

double-replacement reaction

dissociation

Have students match each chemical equation with the correct descriptive term. Have them explain the reasons for their choices.

In pure form, each compound listed in the table is a gas. Aqueous solutions of these compounds are known by the acid names. Specific rules for naming binary compounds are listed below.

Binary Acid Nomenclature

1. The name of a binary acid begins with the prefix *hydro-*.
2. The root of the name of the second element follows this prefix.
3. The name then ends with the suffix *-ic*.

An oxyacid is an acid that is a compound of hydrogen, oxygen, and a third element, usually a nonmetal. Nitric acid, HNO_3, is an oxyacid. The structures of two other oxyacids are shown in **Figure 1.4.** Oxyacids are one class of ternary acids, which are acids that contain three different elements. Usually, the elements in an oxyacid formula are written as one or more hydrogen atoms followed by a polyatomic anion. But as you can see from the structures, the H atoms are bonded to O atoms. The names of oxyacids follow a pattern, and the names of their anions are based on the names of the acids. Some common oxyacids and their anions are given in **Figure 1.5.** Many of these names should be familiar to you.

FIGURE 1.4

Oxyacid Structure Although the chemical formula shows hydrogen atoms and a polyatomic ion, notice that the hydrogens are bonded to the oxygen in an oxyacid.

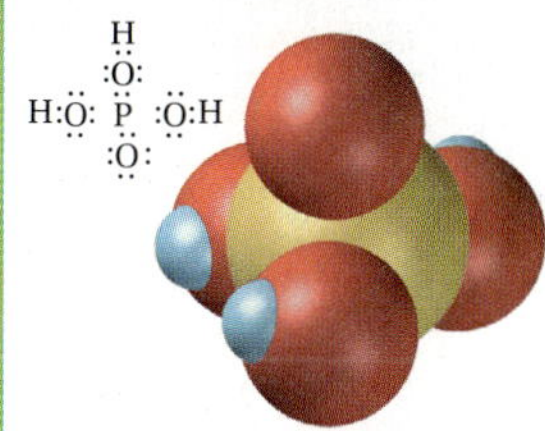

(a) Structure of H_3PO_4

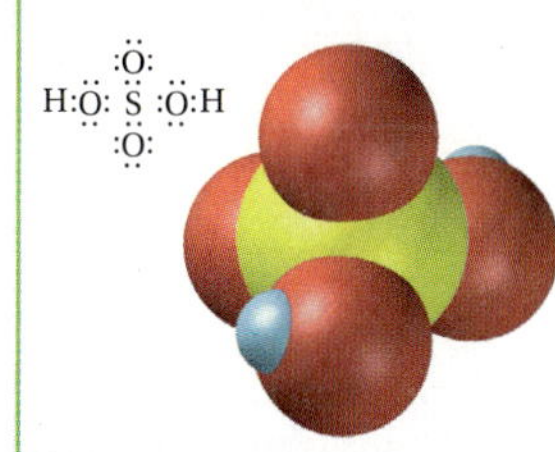

(b) Structure of H_2SO_4

FIGURE 1.5

NAMES OF COMMON OXYACIDS AND OXYANIONS

Formula	Acid name	Anion
CH_3COOH	acetic acid	CH_3COO^-, acetate
H_2CO_3	carbonic acid	CO_3^{2-}, carbonate
$HClO$	hypochlorous acid	ClO^-, hypochlorite
$HClO_2$	chlorous acid	ClO_2^-, chlorite
$HClO_3$	chloric acid	ClO_3^-, chlorate
$HClO_4$	perchloric acid	ClO_4^-, perchlorate
HIO_3	iodic acid	IO_3^-, iodate
HNO_2	nitrous acid	NO_2^-, nitrite
HNO_3	nitric acid	NO_3^-, nitrate
H_3PO_3	phosphorous acid	PO_3^{3-}, phosphite
H_3PO_4	phosphoric acid	PO_4^{3-}, phosphate
H_2SO_3	sulfurous acid	SO_3^{2-}, sulfite
H_2SO_4	sulfuric acid	SO_4^{2-}, sulfate

PRE-AP

As the *oxidation state* of the central atom in an oxyacid increases, the strength of the acid increases significantly. An atom with a higher oxidation state has a greater tendency to draw electrons towards itself. Therefore, in an oxyacid, an increase in the oxidation state of the central atom makes the oxygen atom even more electronegative. As a result, the O-H bond becomes more polar and thus more prone to form ions. This increases the strength of the oxyacid.

Have students find data on the oxyacids of H, Cl, and O to verify this correlation between oxidation state and the strength of an oxyacid.

Teaching Tip

The names of oxyanions match those of the corresponding oxyacids in a systematic way, as shown below.

Name of oxyacid		Name of oxyanion	
prefix	**suffix**	**prefix**	**suffix**
hypo-	-ous	hypo-	-ite
none	-ous	*none*	-ite
none	-ic	*none*	-ate
per-	-ic	per-	-ate

ChemisTrivia

Certain acids, such as hydrocyanic acid, HCN, are considered to be *pseudobinary* acids and are named according to binary naming rules.

TEACH FROM TABLES

FIGURE 1.5 Ask students to suggest a general rule that relates the name of *-ic* and *-ous* acids to the anions that the acids produce.

Demo Problems

1. Name each of the following binary acids:
   a. H_2Se
   b. H_2Te

Answers:
   a. hydroselenic acid
   b. hydrotelluric acid

2. Use the relationships shown in **Figure 1.5** to name the following oxyacids:
   a. HIO
   b. HIO_4

Answers:
   a. hypoiodous acid
   b. periodic acid

▼ Teach *continued*

Teaching Tip

- Pure sulfuric acid is a colorless, dense, and viscous liquid. The United States produces more sulfuric acid than any other chemical each year. Its use in manufacturing is so widespread that its annual production is an indicator of the health of the economy.
- The chemical formula for acetic acid is written as CH_3COOH, following the convention used by organic chemists. This formula emphasizes that the acidic hydrogen is part of the carboxylic acid functional group. In the formulas of other, more complicated organic acids, the acidic hydrogens are listed first. For example, ascorbic acid, which has two ionizable hydrogens, is written as $H_2C_6H_6O_6$. The structural formulas of carboxylic acids will be introduced in the chapter "Organic Chemistry".

ChemisTrivia

Sulfuric and nitric acids are the major acidic components of acid precipitation (acid rain).

MAIN IDEA

Some acids are useful in industry.

The properties of acids make them important chemicals both in the laboratory and in industry. Sulfuric acid, nitric acid, phosphoric acid, hydrochloric acid, and acetic acid are all common industrial acids.

Sulfuric Acid

Sulfuric acid is the most commonly produced industrial chemical in the world. More than 37 million metric tons of it are made each year in the United States alone. Sulfuric acid is used in large quantities in petroleum refining and metallurgy as well as in the manufacture of fertilizer. It is also essential to a vast number of industrial processes, including the production of metals, paper, paint, dyes, detergents, and many chemical raw materials. Sulfuric acid is the acid used in automobile batteries.

Because it attracts water, concentrated sulfuric acid is an effective dehydrating (water-removing) agent. It can be used to remove water from gases with which it does not react. Sugar and certain other organic compounds are also dehydrated by sulfuric acid. Skin contains organic compounds that are attacked by concentrated sulfuric acid, which can cause serious burns.

Nitric Acid

Pure nitric acid is a volatile, unstable liquid. Dissolving the acid in water makes the acid more stable. Solutions of nitric acid are widely used in industry. Nitric acid also stains proteins yellow. The feather in **Figure 1.6** was stained by nitric acid. The acid has a suffocating odor, stains skin, and can cause serious burns. It is used in making explosives, many of which are nitrogen-containing compounds. It is also used to make rubber, plastics, dyes, and pharmaceuticals. Initially, nitric acid solutions are colorless; however, upon standing, they gradually become yellow because of slight decomposition to brown nitrogen dioxide gas.

FIGURE 1.6

Nitric Acid and Proteins Concentrated nitric acid stains a feather yellow.

Differentiated Instruction

INCLUSION

To help visual learners see the dehydrating property of sulfuric acid, have them check the Internet for a video that shows what happens when sulfuric acid is added to sugar. Be sure that students understand that the sugar is a carbohydrate or hydrated carbon that consists of C, H, and O. The sulfuric acid dehydrates the sugar by removing the H and O to form water, leaving behind a column of black, carbon residue.

Phosphoric Acid

Phosphorus, along with nitrogen and potassium, is an essential element for plants and animals. The bulk of phosphoric acid produced each year is used directly for manufacturing fertilizers and animal feed. Dilute phosphoric acid has a pleasant but sour taste and is not toxic. It is used as a flavoring agent in beverages and as a cleaning agent for dairy equipment. Phosphoric acid is also important in the manufacture of detergents and ceramics.

Hydrochloric Acid

The stomach produces HCl to aid in digestion. Industrially, hydrochloric acid is important for "pickling" iron and steel. Pickling is the immersion of metals in acid solutions to remove surface impurities. This acid is also used in industry as a general cleaning agent, in food processing, in the activation of oil wells, in the recovery of magnesium from sea water, and in the production of other chemicals.

Concentrated solutions of hydrochloric acid, commonly referred to as *muriatic acid*, can be found in hardware stores. It is used to maintain the correct acidity in swimming pools and to clean masonry.

Acetic Acid

Pure acetic acid is a clear, colorless, and pungent-smelling liquid known as *glacial acetic acid*. This name is derived from the fact that pure acetic acid has a freezing point of 17°C. It can form crystals in a cold room. The fermentation of certain plants produces vinegars containing acetic acid. White vinegar contains 4% to 8% acetic acid.

Acetic acid is important industrially in synthesizing chemicals used in the manufacture of plastics. It is a raw material in the production of food supplements—for example, lysine, an essential amino acid. Acetic acid is also used as a fungicide.

MAIN IDEA

The properties of bases differ from those of acids.

How do bases differ from acids? You can answer this question by comparing the following properties of bases with those of acids.

1. *Aqueous solutions of bases taste bitter.* You may have noticed this fact if you have ever gotten soap, a basic substance, in your mouth. As with acids, taste should NEVER be used to test a substance to see if it is a base. Many bases are caustic; they attack the skin and tissues, causing severe burns.
2. *Bases change the color of acid-base indicators.* As **Figure 1.7** shows, an indicator will be a different color in a basic solution than it would be in an acidic solution.

FIGURE 1.7

Base Indicator pH paper turns blue in the presence of this solution of sodium hydroxide.

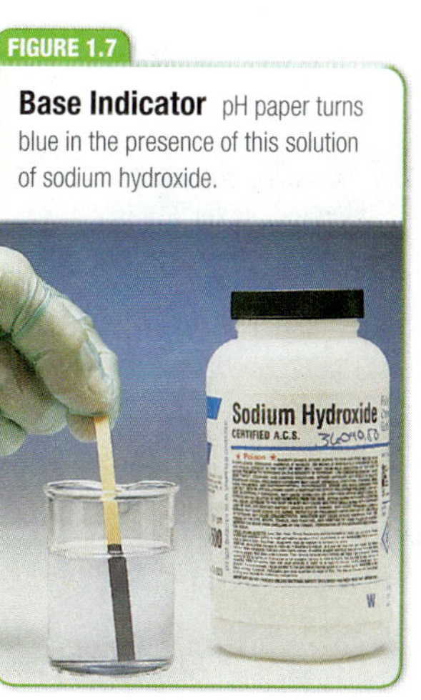

Application

- The phosphate ion, the anion of phosphoric acid, is used in the body to make many critical biochemical compounds. For example, it is used in making nucleotides from which DNA and RNA are made. It is also an important part of compounds such as adenosine triphosphate (ATP), which provides energy for cells.
- Much of the industrial acetic acid produced is used in the manufacture of vinyl acetate, which in turn is used in the synthesis of polyvinyl acetate. Polyvinyl acetate is used in adhesives, coatings, and sealants. However, a quarter of all industrial acetic acid produced is used for the synthesis of cellulose acetate, which is used for coatings and films.

Teaching Tip

Solutions of HCl(*aq*) give off fumes of HCl(*g*), which can cause severe chemical burns and irritation of human tissue. HCl(*aq*) should be used only with adequate ventilation.

Classroom Discussion

Discuss the role of hydrochloric acid in the digestion of foods. Point out how excess acid contributes to the discomfort known as indigestion. Explain how the stomach secretes a mucous layer, which protects it from being damaged by the hydrochloric acid it produces.

ENGLISH LEARNERS

Emphasize that in chemistry, minor differences in words can convey specific information about a substance. Have students review and then explain the basis for naming the three acids mentioned on this page.

Students should identify phosphoric acid and acetic acid as oxyacids. The names are derived from the polyatomic anion (phosphate and acetate, respectively) by changing the *-ate* ending of the polyatomic anion to the *-ic* ending for the acid. In contrast, hydrochloric acid is named according to the rules for binary acids.

▼ Teach *continued*

QuickLab

Products containing acids and bases are commonly found in the kitchen at home. Occasionally these products consist of an acid or a base that is simply mixed with water, such as vinegar or household ammonia. In most cases, the acid or base is a part of a more complex mixture, such as a soft drink or dishwashing liquid.

Safety Wear goggles, gloves, and a lab apron. Avoid skin contact with the items to be tested. Caution students never to taste any materials in the lab. Turn off the hot plate when not in use. Use thermal gloves when handling hot glassware. Never hold or touch glassware with your hands while heating it or while it is cooling.

Disposal Place all solids in the trash. Pour all liquids down the drain.

DISCUSSION

1. Most cleaning products are basic or neutral.
2. Acidic food products taste tart or sour. Basic food products taste bitter. Of the food products listed, only baking soda is basic.
3. Consumer warning labels about the acidity or basicity of food products will probably not be found. Most cleaning products have warning labels; a caustic warning indicates a strongly basic substance that can cause burns.

Teaching Tip

Instead of boiling the red cabbage, you could use a blender to mix the cabbage with water. Pour the blended liquid through a colander. Juice that is not used immediately should be frozen and stored. (If stored without freezing, the juice soon develops a very strong smell.)

3. *Dilute aqueous solutions of bases feel slippery.* You encounter this property of aqueous bases whenever you wash with soap.
4. *Bases react with acids to produce salts and water.* The properties of a base disappear with the addition of an equivalent amount of an acid. It could also be said that "neutralization" of the base occurs when these two substances react to produce a salt and water.
5. *Bases conduct electric current.* Like acids, bases form ions in aqueous solutions and are thus electrolytes.

QuickLAB HOUSEHOLD ACIDS AND BASES

QUESTION

Which of the household substances are acids, and which are bases?

PROCEDURE

Record all your results in a data table.

1. To make an acid-base indicator, extract juice from red cabbage. First, cut up some red cabbage and place it in a large beaker. Add enough water so that the beaker is half full. Then, bring the mixture to a boil. Let it cool, and then pour off and save the cabbage juice. This solution is an acid-base indicator.
2. Assemble foods, beverages, and cleaning products to be tested.
3. If the substance being tested is a liquid, pour about 5 mL into a small beaker. If it is a solid, place a small amount into a beaker, and moisten it with about 5 mL of water.
4. Add a drop or two of the red cabbage juice to the solution being tested, and note the color. The solution will turn red if it is acidic and green if it is basic.

DISCUSSION

1. Are the cleaning products acids, bases, or neither?
2. What are acid/base characteristics of foods and beverages?
3. Did you find consumer warning labels on basic or acidic products?

MATERIALS

- dishwashing liquid, dishwasher detergent, laundry detergent, laundry stain remover, fabric softener, and bleach
- mayonnaise, baking powder, baking soda, white vinegar, cider vinegar, lemon juice, soft drinks, mineral water, and milk
- fresh red cabbage
- hot plate
- beaker, 500 mL or larger
- beakers, 50 mL
- spatula
- tap water
- tongs

SAFETY

Wear safety goggles, gloves and an apron.

Red cabbage, which contains an anthocyanin pigment, can be made into an acid-base indicator.

Differentiated Instruction

BELOW LEVEL

Have students compare the five properties of bases to the five properties of acids. Then ask students to prepare flash cards, each containing a statement describing acids, bases, or both. For example, a student may write "feels slippery" or "conducts electricity." The student should show the card to another student, who must identify the substance.

MAIN IDEA

Arrhenius acids and bases produce ions in solution.

Svante Arrhenius, a Swedish chemist who lived from 1859 to 1927, understood that aqueous solutions of acids and bases conducted electric current. Arrhenius therefore theorized that acids and bases must produce ions in solution. An **Arrhenius acid** is a chemical compound that increases the concentration of hydrogen ions, H^+, in aqueous solution. In other words, an acid will ionize in solution, increasing the number of hydrogen ions present. An **Arrhenius base** is a substance that increases the concentration of hydroxide ions, OH^-, in aqueous solution. Some bases are ionic hydroxides. These bases dissociate in solution to release hydroxide ions into the solution. Other bases are substances that react with water to remove a hydrogen ion, leaving hydroxide ions in the solution.

Aqueous Solutions of Acids

The acids described by Arrhenius are molecular compounds with ionizable hydrogen atoms. Their water solutions are known as *aqueous acids.* All aqueous acids are electrolytes.

Because acid molecules are sufficiently polar, water molecules attract one or more of their hydrogen ions. Negatively charged anions are left behind. As explained in a previous chapter, the hydrogen ion in aqueous solution is best represented as H_3O^+, the hydronium ion. The ionization of an HNO_3 molecule is shown by the following equation. **Figure 1.8** also shows how the hydronium ion forms when nitric acid reacts with water.

$$HNO_3(l) + H_2O(l) \longrightarrow H_3O^+(aq) + NO_3^-(aq)$$

Similarly, ionization of a hydrogen chloride molecule in hydrochloric acid can be represented in the following way.

$$HCl(g) + H_2O(l) \longrightarrow H_3O^+(aq) + Cl^-(aq)$$

FIGURE 1.8

Arrhenius Acids Arrhenius's observations form the basis of a definition of acids. Arrhenius acids, such as the nitric acid shown here, produce hydronium ions in aqueous solution.

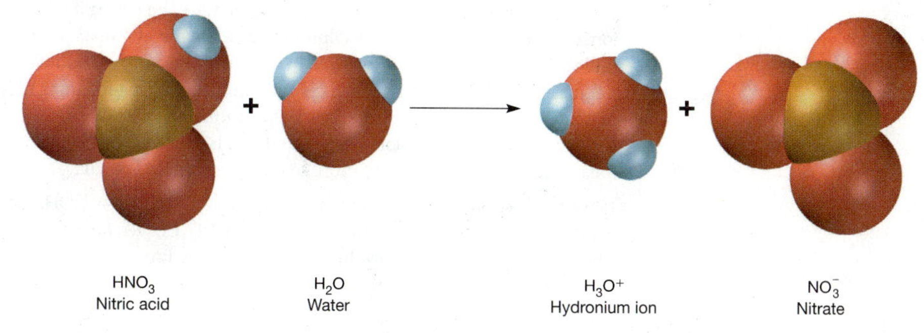

ChemisTrivia

Some hydrangea flowers can act as acid-base indicators. The color of these flowers depends upon the acidity of the soil in which the plants are growing, as seen in the photo on the first page of the chapter, "Acid-Base Titration and pH". The flowers contain an anthocyanin pigment that is sensitive to changes in acidity and basicity. The red cabbage used in the QuickLab in this section also contains an antho-cyanin pigment.

Classroom Discussion

To emphasize the role of polarity in the ionization of acids, ask students why a nonpolar molecule, such as methane, (CH_4) is so much less likely to ionize than is hydrogen chloride (HCl).

TEACH FROM VISUALS

FIGURE 1.8 Have students demonstrate an understanding of the proton-transfer reaction by using electron-dot formulas to explain how a proton bonds with a water molecule to yield a hydronium ion.

PRE-AP

Have students explain how aqueous solutions of H_2SO_4, H_3PO_4, and HNO_3 differ from one another. Students should point out that the polyatomic anions produced in aqueous solution are different in each case. However, the important difference is the number of hydronium ions each acid can produce. Nitric acid produces only one hydronium ion, sulfuric acid can produce two, and phosphoric acid can produce three. Inform students that they will learn about polyprotic acids later in this section.

▼ Teach *continued*

TEACH FROM TABLES

FIGURE 1.9 Ask students to explain why double arrows are used in the weak-acid equations.

Demonstration

STRENGTH AND CONDUCTIVITY

To make sure that students understand the relationship between acid and base strength and electrical conductivity, test a variety of solutions with a **battery-powered conductivity set.** For the solutions, use **beakers** containing the same concentrations of **strong and weak acids** and **strong and weak bases.** Have students note the conductivity of each solution tested and, from that information, infer the strength of the acid or base tested.

Safety Wear **goggles** and a **lab apron.** Avoid skin contact with the solutions to be tested. Use a conductivity set with leads long enough that students can read the results without getting close to the solutions.

Disposal Combine liquids, adjust the pH to a range from 5 to 9, and pour the solution down the drain.

FIGURE 1.9

COMMON AQUEOUS ACIDS

Strong acids	Weak acids
$HI + H_2O \longrightarrow H_3O^+ + I^-$	$HSO_4^- + H_2O \rightleftharpoons H_3O^+ + SO_4^{2-}$
$HClO_4 + H_2O \longrightarrow H_3O^+ + ClO_4^-$	$H_3PO_4 + H_2O \rightleftharpoons H_3O^+ + H_2PO_4^-$
$HBr + H_2O \longrightarrow H_3O^+ + Br^-$	$HF + H_2O \rightleftharpoons H_3O^+ + F^-$
$HCl + H_2O \longrightarrow H_3O^+ + Cl^-$	$CH_3COOH + H_2O \rightleftharpoons H_3O^+ + CH_3COO^-$
$H_2SO_4 + H_2O \longrightarrow H_3O^+ + HSO_4^-$	$H_2CO_3 + H_2O \rightleftharpoons H_3O^+ + HCO_3^-$
$HClO_3 + H_2O \longrightarrow H_3O^+ + ClO_3^-$	$H_2S + H_2O \rightleftharpoons H_3O^+ + HS^-$
	$HCN + H_2O \rightleftharpoons H_3O^+ + CN^-$
	$HCO_3^- + H_2O \rightleftharpoons H_3O^+ + CO_3^{2-}$

Strength of Acids

A **strong acid** is one that ionizes completely in aqueous solution. A strong acid is a strong electrolyte. Perchloric acid, $HClO_4$, hydrochloric acid, HCl, and nitric acid, HNO_3, are examples of strong acids. In water, 100% of the acid molecules are ionized. The strength of an acid depends on the polarity of the bond between hydrogen and the element to which it is bonded and the ease with which that bond can be broken. Acid strength increases with increasing polarity and decreasing bond energy.

An acid that releases few hydrogen ions in aqueous solution is a **weak acid.** The aqueous solution of a weak acid contains hydronium ions, anions, and dissolved acid molecules. Hydrocyanic acid is an example of a weak acid. In aqueous solution, both the ionization of HCN and the reverse reaction occur simultaneously. In a 1 M solution of HCN there will be only two H^+ ions and two CN^- ions out of 100,000 molecules. The other 99,998 molecules remain as HCN.

$$HCN(aq) + H_2O(l) \rightleftharpoons H_3O^+(aq) + CN^-(aq)$$

Common aqueous acids are listed in **Figure 1.9.** Each strong acid ionizes completely in aqueous solution to give up one hydrogen ion per molecule. Notice that the number of hydrogen atoms in the formula does not indicate acid strength. Molecules with multiple hydrogen atoms may not readily give them up. The fact that phosphoric acid has three hydrogen atoms per molecule does not mean that it is a strong acid. None of these ionize completely in solution, so phosphoric acid is weak.

Organic acids, which contain the acidic carboxyl group—COOH, are generally weak acids. For example, acetic acid, CH_3COOH, ionizes slightly in water to give hydronium ions and acetate ions, CH_3COO^-.

$$CH_3COOH(aq) + H_2O(l) \rightleftharpoons H_3O^+(aq) + CH_3COO^-(aq)$$

Differentiated Instruction

INCLUSION

To help visual and kinesthetic learners understand the difference between a strong acid and a weak acid, have six students form three pairs by holding hands. One student in each pair should hold a sign labeled H^+, and the other student should hold a sign labeled Cl^-. Have another nine students form three groups of three students each, holding hands. Two students in each group should hold a sign labeled H^+, while the remaining student in each group should hold a sign labeled S^{2-}. Have the HCl groups illustrate why they represent a strong acid. All three students holding the H^+ labels should separate from the other students. Then have the H_2S groups illustrate how they are a weak acid. Only one student holding an H^+ label should separate from the other students.

A molecule of acetic acid contains four hydrogen atoms. However, only one of the hydrogen atoms is ionizable. The hydrogen atom in the carboxyl group in acetic acid is the one that is "acidic" and forms the hydronium ion. This acidic hydrogen can be seen in the structural diagram in **Figure 1.10**.

FIGURE 1.10

Acetic Acid Acetic acid contains four hydrogen atoms, but only one of them is "acidic" and forms the hydronium ion in solution.

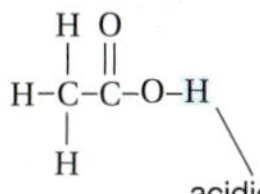

```
H O
| ||
H-C-C-O-H
|        \
H         acidic hydrogen
```

Aqueous Solutions of Bases

Most bases are ionic compounds containing metal cations and the hydroxide anion, OH^-. Because these bases are ionic, they dissociate when dissolved in water. When a base completely dissociates in water to yield aqueous OH^- ions, the solution is referred to as strongly basic. Sodium hydroxide, NaOH, is a common laboratory base. It is water-soluble and dissociates as shown by the equation below.

$$NaOH(s) \xrightarrow{H_2O} Na^+(aq) + OH^-(aq)$$

As you will remember from learning about the periodic table, Group 1 elements are the alkali metals. This group gets its name from the fact that the hydroxides of Li, Na, K, Rb, and Cs all form alkaline (basic) solutions.

Not all bases are ionic compounds. A base commonly used in household cleaners is ammonia, NH_3, which is molecular. Ammonia is a base because it produces hydroxide ions when it reacts with water molecules, as shown in the equation below.

$$NH_3(aq) + H_2O(l) \rightleftarrows NH_4^+(aq) + OH^-(aq)$$

Strength of Bases

As with acids, the strength of a base also depends on the extent to which the base dissociates, or adds hydroxide ions to the solution. For example, potassium hydroxide, KOH, is a strong base because it completely dissociates into its ions in dilute aqueous solutions.

$$KOH(s) \xrightarrow{H_2O} K^+(aq) + OH^-(aq)$$

Strong bases are strong electrolytes, just as strong acids are strong electrolytes. **Figure 1.11** lists some strong bases.

CHECK FOR UNDERSTANDING

Differentiate What is the difference between the strength and the concentration of an acid or base?

FIGURE 1.11

COMMON AQUEOUS ACIDS

Strong bases	Weak bases
$Ca(OH)_2 \longrightarrow Ca^{2+} + 2OH^-$	$NH_3 + H_2O \rightleftarrows NH_4^+ + OH^-$
$Sr(OH)_2 \longrightarrow Sr^{2+} + 2OH^-$	$C_6H_5NH_2 + H_2O \rightleftarrows C_6H_5NH_3^+ + OH^-$
$Ba(OH)_2 \longrightarrow Ba^{2+} + 2OH^-$	
$NaOH \longrightarrow Na^+ + OH^-$	
$KOH \longrightarrow K^+ + OH^-$	
$RbOH \longrightarrow Rb^+ + OH^-$	
$CsOH \longrightarrow Cs^+ + OH^-$	

TEACH FROM VISUALS

FIGURE 1.10 Discuss why only one hydrogen in the acetic acid molecule is easily ionized. Contrast acetic acid with phosphoric acid. There are four hydrogen atoms in acetic acid, only one of which is ionizable. There are three hydrogen atoms in phosphoric acid, all of which are ionizable.

Teaching Tip

For aqueous weak acids and bases, a small fraction of molecules ionize to form ions in solution. Because the reverse reaction is favored, most of the molecules do not ionize.

Classroom Discussion

Have students examine the equation that shows the reaction between ammonia and water. Ask the class how NH_3 has "room" to accept another H^+ (proton) that is donated by H_2O to form the ammonium cation. Students can draw the Lewis structure for ammonia to see that it has an unshared electron pair. A proton can form a covalent bond with this unshared pair of electrons.

Check for Understanding

Answer: The strength of an acid or base depends on the extent to which it ionizes in solution. The concentration depends on the amount of the acid or base that is in the solution.

INCLUSION

Use the following activity to help students identify common acids and bases. Ask students to use product labels from vinegar products, citrus products, and other household products to identify acids used as ingredients. Using **Figure 1.9,** students can classify those acids as strong or weak. Ask students to use product labels from soaps, cleaning agents, and other household products to identify bases used as ingredients. Using **Figure 1.11,** students can classify those bases as strong or weak. Students may create two charts showing the products containing acids and bases along with their classification as strong or weak.

▼ Teach continued

TEACH FROM VISUALS

FIGURE 1.12 Ask students to list other *d*-block metals that would behave in a manner similar to that of copper.

READING TOOLKIT

COMPARING When students have finished reading this section, have them construct a chart to compare acids with bases in terms of physical properties, chemical properties, ions in solution, and strength.

▼ Assess and Reteach

Assess Use the Formative Assessment on this page to evaluate student mastery of the section.

Reteach For students who need additional instruction, download the Section Study Guide.

Response to Intervention To reassess students' mastery, use the Section Quiz, available to print or to take directly online at **HMDScience.com**.

FIGURE 1.12

Insoluble Hydroxides The hydroxides of most *d*-block metals are nearly insoluble in water, as is shown by the gelatinous precipitate, copper(II) hydroxide, $Cu(OH)_2$, in the beaker on the right.

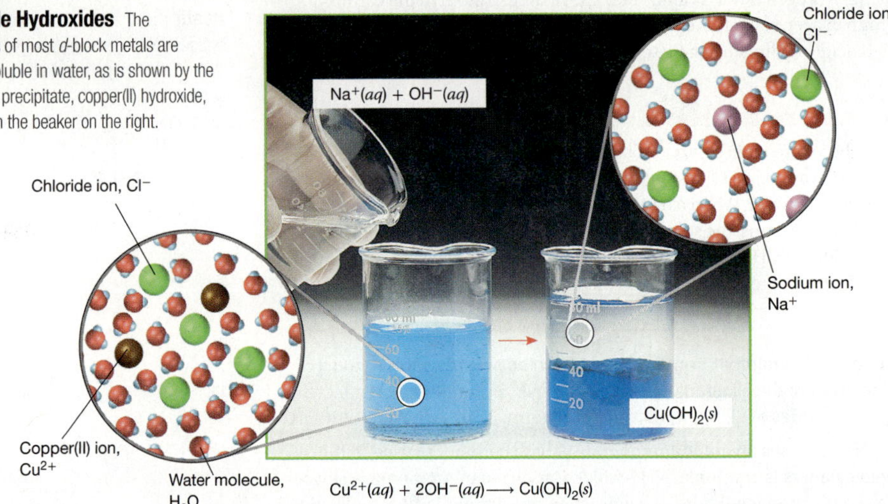

Bases that are not very soluble do not produce a large number of hydroxide ions when added to water. Some metal hydroxides, such as $Cu(OH)_2$, are not very soluble in water, as seen in **Figure 1.12.** They cannot produce strongly alkaline solutions. The alkalinity of aqueous solutions depends on the concentration of OH^- ions in solution. It is unrelated to the number of hydroxide ions in the undissolved compound.

Now consider ammonia, which is highly soluble but is a weak electrolyte. The concentration of OH^- ions in an ammonia solution is relatively low. Ammonia is therefore a *weak base*. Many organic compounds that contain nitrogen atoms are also weak bases. For example, codeine, $C_{18}H_{21}NO_3$, a pain reliever and common cough suppressant found in prescription cough medicine, is a weak base.

SECTION 1 FORMATIVE ASSESSMENT

Reviewing Main Ideas

1. **a.** What are five general properties of aqueous acids?
   b. Name some common substances that have one or more of these properties.
2. Name the following acids: a. HBrO b. $HBrO_3$.
3. **a.** What are five general properties of aqueous bases?
   b. Name some common substances that have one or more of these properties.
4. **a.** Why are strong acids also strong electrolytes?
   b. Is every strong electrolyte also a strong acid?

Critical Thinking

5. **RELATING IDEAS** A classmate states, "All compounds containing H atoms are acids, and all compounds containing OH groups are bases." Do you agree? Give examples.

Answers to Section Assessment

1. **a.** sour taste; react with metals to give off H_2; change color of indicator; react with bases to produce salts and water; are electrolytes
   b. vinegar; many soft drinks; sour milk; fruits and fruit juices; muriatic acid
2. **a.** hypobromous acid **b.** bromic acid
3. **a.** bitter taste; slippery feel; change color of indicator; react with acids to produce salts and water; are electrolytes
   b. household ammonia; milk of magnesia; antacids; lye
4. **a.** Strong acids ionize completely in aqueous solution.
   b. No; materials other than acids can ionize in aqueous solution.
5. Only compounds containing H atoms that ionize are acids, and only compounds that dissociate or ionize to produce hydroxide ions are bases. HCl is an acid, but NH_3 is not; NaOH and NH_3 are bases. CH_3OH is not a base or an acid. Many other examples are possible.

CROSS-DISCIPLINARY CONNECTION S.T.E.M.

Acid Water—A Hidden Menace

Many people are unaware of the pH of the tap water in their home until they are confronted with such phenomena as a blue ring materializing around a porcelain sink drain, a water heater suddenly giving out, or tropical fish that keep dying. Each of these events could be due to acidic water. Acidic water can also cause the amount of lead in the water to rise.

The possibility of lead poisoning from home water supplies is a concern. Many older homes still have lead pipes in their plumbing, though most modern homes use copper piping. Copper pipe joints, however, are often sealed with lead-containing solder. Highly acidic water can leach out both the lead from the solder joints and copper from the pipes themselves, which turns the sink drain blue. In addition, people who are in the habit of filling their tea kettles and coffee pots in the morning without letting the tap run awhile first could be adding copper and lead ions to their tea or coffee.

Lead poisoning is of particular concern in young children. The absorption rate of lead in the intestinal tract of a child is much higher than in that of an adult, and lead poisoning can permanently impair a child's rapidly growing nervous system. The good news is that lead poisoning and other effects of acidic water in the home can be easily prevented by following these tips:

1. Monitor the pH of your water on a regular basis, especially if you have well water. This can easily be done with pH test kits (see photograph) that are sold in hardware or pet stores—many tropical fish are intolerant of water with a pH that is either too high (basic) or too low (acidic). The pH of municipal water supplies is already regulated, but regularly checking your water's pH yourself is a good idea.
2. In the morning, let your water tap run for about half a minute before you fill your kettle or drink the water. If the water is acidic, the first flush of water will have the highest concentration of lead and copper ions.
3. Install an alkali-injection pump, a low-cost, low-maintenance solution that can save your plumbing and lessen the risk of lead poisoning from your own water supply. The pump injects a small amount of an alkali (usually potassium carbonate or sodium carbonate) into your water-pressure tank each time your well's pump starts. This effectively neutralizes the acidity of your water.

Questions

1. What is the source of lead contamination in water in the home?
2. Does the use of copper water pipes ensure that your household water is free from lead?
3. Why does lead poisoning affect children more severely than it affects adults?

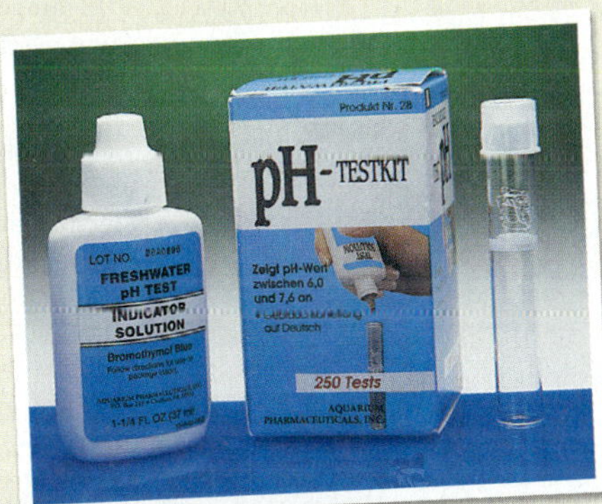

The pH of your home's water supply can be easily monitored using a test kit, such as the one shown here.

451

CROSS-DISCIPLINARY CONNECTION

Obtain a simple pH test kit or pH paper. Have students test the school's water supply. Then have them take home a piece of pH paper to test their water at home. If any students have well water, have them compare the pH they obtain to see how much variation exists among local wells. Note whether there are differences between all results obtained by students.

Alternative Assessment

Have students research the various devices presently available to improve the quality of water in homes. Their findings could be presented in the form of an oral or written report or as a poster showing pictures and diagrams of available equipment and how it functions.

Answers

1. lead water pipes or lead in the solder used with copper water pipes
2. no, because the solder used with older copper pipes can contain lead
3. Children absorb lead more readily than adults do, and children's rapidly growing nervous systems can be permanently impaired.

SECTION 2

▼ Plan and Prepare

Objectives

Upon completion of this section, students should be able to do the following:

- Define and recognize *Brønsted-Lowry acids* and *bases*.
- Define a *Lewis acid* and a *Lewis base*.
- Name compounds that are acids under the Lewis definition but are not acids under the Brønsted-Lowry definition.

Classroom Catalyst

Show students an action photo of a person, and ask each student to list three terms that describe that person. Make a master list of the terms. Point out that, although the person has been described in many different ways—appearance, vocation, attitude—he or she is still the same person. Point out that the same acid or base can also be described differently based on the criteria.

▼ Teach

Misconception Alert!

Have students examine the equations on this page. They may have difficulty recognizing how the positive charges on the hydronium and ammonium ions are distributed. Point out that brackets are used with both ions to show that the charge is distributed over the whole ion and is not localized on any one hydrogen atom.

SECTION 2

Main Ideas

- Brønsted-Lowry acids and bases donate or accept protons.
- A Lewis acid or base accepts or donates a pair of electrons.

Acid-Base Theories

Key Terms

Brønsted-Lowry acid
Brønsted-Lowry base
Brønsted-Lowry acid-base reaction
monoprotic acid
polyprotic acid
diprotic acid
triprotic acid
Lewis acid
Lewis base
Lewis acid-base reaction

For most uses, scientists found the Arrhenius definition of acids and bases to be adequate. However, as scientists further investigated acid-base behavior, they found that some substances acted as acids or bases when they were not in a water solution. Because the Arrhenius definition requires that the substances be aqueous, the definitions of acids and bases had to be revised.

MAIN IDEA

Brønsted-Lowry acids and bases donate or accept protons.

In 1923, the Danish chemist J. N. Brønsted and the English chemist T. M. Lowry independently expanded the Arrhenius acid definition. **A Brønsted-Lowry acid is a molecule or ion that is a proton donor.** Because H^+ is a proton, all acids as defined by Arrhenius donate protons to water and are Brønsted-Lowry acids as well. Substances other than molecules, such as certain ions, can also donate protons. Such substances are not Arrhenius acids but are included in the category of Brønsted-Lowry acids.

Hydrogen chloride acts as a Brønsted-Lowry acid when it reacts with ammonia. The HCl transfers protons to NH_3 much as it does in water.

$$HCl + NH_3 \longrightarrow NH_4^+ + Cl^-$$

A proton is transferred from the hydrogen chloride molecule, HCl, to the ammonia molecule, NH_3. The ammonium ion, NH_4^+, is formed. Electron-dot formulas show the similarity of this reaction to the reaction of HCl with water.

$$H{:}\underset{..}{\ddot{Cl}}{:} + H{:}\underset{\underset{H}{..}}{\ddot{O}}{:} \longrightarrow \left[H{:}\underset{\underset{H}{..}}{\ddot{O}}{:}H\right]^+ + {:}\underset{..}{\ddot{Cl}}{:}^-$$

$$H{:}\underset{..}{\ddot{Cl}}{:} + H{:}\underset{\underset{H}{..}}{\ddot{N}}{:}H \longrightarrow \left[H{:}\underset{\underset{H}{..}}{\overset{\overset{H}{..}}{N}}{:}H\right]^+ + {:}\underset{..}{\ddot{Cl}}{:}^-$$

In both reactions, hydrogen chloride is a Brønsted-Lowry acid.

Differentiated Instruction

BELOW LEVEL

Draw the Lewis structure for the ammonium ion on the board. Have students explain how this polyatomic ion can be considered a Brønsted-Lowry acid. Students should explain that a proton can be removed from the ammonium ion, leaving an unshared pair of electrons and forming ammonia.

Have students explain how the last equation at the bottom of this page should be rewritten to show the ammonium ion acting as a Brønsted-Lowry acid. The last equation should be rewritten in reverse, showing the ammonium ion and hydroxide ion as the reactants and not the products.

FIGURE 2.1

Brønsted-Lowry Acid-Base Reactions Hydrogen chloride gas escapes from a hydrochloric acid solution and combines with ammonia gas that has escaped from an aqueous ammonia solution. The resulting cloud is solid ammonium chloride that is dispersed in air.

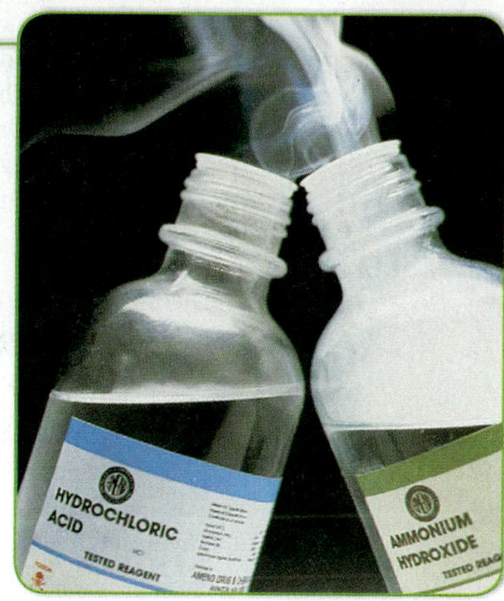

Water can also act as a Brønsted-Lowry acid. Consider, for example, the following reaction, in which the water molecule donates a proton to the ammonia molecule.

$$H_2O(l) + NH_3(aq) \rightleftharpoons NH_4^+(aq) + OH^-(aq)$$

$$\mathrm{H{:}\ddot{\underset{\cdot\cdot}{O}}{:}\atop H} + \mathrm{H{:}\ddot{\underset{\cdot\cdot}{N}}{:}H\atop H} \rightleftharpoons \left[\mathrm{H{:}\ddot{\underset{\cdot\cdot}{N}}{:}H}\right]^+ + \left[{:}\ddot{\underset{\cdot\cdot}{O}}{:}\ \mathrm{H}\right]^-$$

A Brønsted-Lowry base is a molecule or ion that is a proton acceptor. In the reaction between hydrochloric acid and ammonia, ammonia accepts a proton from the hydrochloric acid. It is a Brønsted-Lowry base. The Arrhenius hydroxide bases, such as NaOH, are not, strictly speaking, Brønsted-Lowry bases. Instead, it is the OH^- ion produced in solution that is the Brønsted-Lowry base. It is the species that can accept a proton.

In a Brønsted-Lowry acid-base reaction, protons are transferred from one reactant (the acid) to another (the base). Figure 2.1 shows the reaction between the Brønsted-Lowry acid HCl and the Brønsted-Lowry base NH_3.

Monoprotic and Polyprotic Acids

An acid that can donate only one proton (hydrogen ion) per molecule is known as a monoprotic acid. Perchloric acid, $HClO_4$, hydrochloric acid, HCl, and nitric acid, HNO_3, are all monoprotic. The following equation shows how a molecule of the monoprotic acid HCl donates a proton to a water molecule. The HCl ionizes to form H_3O^+ ions and Cl^- ions. The Cl^- has no hydrogens to lose, so HCl has only one ionization step.

$$HCl(g) + H_2O(l) \longrightarrow H_3O^+(aq) + Cl^-(aq)$$

INCLUSION

To help tactile learners understand the Brønsted-Lowry definitions of acids and bases, make a large sign labeled proton. Give it to a student while saying "Acid." Ask the student what he or she should say upon receiving the proton. The student should say "Base." Have the student pass the sign to another student. As they do so, each student should shout out how they are acting in terms of Brønsted-Lowry acids and bases.

TEACH FROM VISUALS

FIGURE 2.1 Ask students to explain why the Arrhenius definition of acids and bases cannot be used to explain the chemical reaction shown in the figure. Students should explain that the chemical reaction shown in the figure is between gases and because the Arrhenius definition of acids and bases involves only aqueous solutions, it cannot be used.

Teaching Tip

Students have difficulty with the idea that whether a compound is a Brønsted-Lowry acid or base depends on the specific reaction. For example, water can act as an acid (proton donor) or a base (proton acceptor):

water as an acid

$$\underset{A_1}{H_2O} + \underset{B_2}{NH_3} \rightleftharpoons \underset{B_1}{OH^-} + \underset{A_2}{NH_4^+}$$

water as a base

$$\underset{B_1}{H_2O} + \underset{A_2}{HCl} \rightleftharpoons \underset{A_1}{H_3O^+} + \underset{B_2}{Cl^-}$$

This can be emphasized by having them label the acid-base pairs A_1/B_1 and A_2/B_2. More examples are given in the next section.

Classroom Discussion

Clarify the relationships among the terms *monoprotic*, *polyprotic*, *binary*, and *ternary*. For example, ask whether all binary acids are also monoprotic or have students give examples of polyprotic acids that are also binary. Examples could include hydrosulfuric acid (H_2S), a binary acid that is diprotic.

READING TOOLKIT

VOCABULARY BUILDING Explain that the suffix *-protic* is related to the word *proton.* Have students use their knowledge of the prefixes *mono-*, *bi-*, *tri-*, and *poly-* to develop definitions for the terms monoprotic acid, biprotic acid, triprotic acid, and polyprotic acid.

▼ Teach *continued*

Misconception Alert!

It is not unusual for an equation such as the following to be written for a polyprotic acid.

$$H_3PO_4 + 3H_2O \longrightarrow 3H_3O^+ + PO_4^{3-}$$

Such a representation may lead students to think that the phosphoric acid molecule loses all three protons at the same time. Ask students why this assumption is incorrect. Students should answer that because phosphoric acid is a polyprotic acid, ionization occurs in stages.

ChemisTrivia

Sulfuric acid is one of the most important industrial chemicals that is produced on a large scale. Although its major use is in the manufacture of fertilizers, it is also widely used in making dyes and pigments, detergents, pharmaceuticals, and rayon fabric. It is also used to clean metals and petroleum products as they are refined. Because of its ionization properties, it is used as the electrolyte in automobile batteries, where it is often referred to as "battery acid."

Critical Thinking

Answer: Answers may vary. A correct response would be that it is not possible to have a Brønsted-Lowry acid without a Brønsted-Lowry base, because the acid donates a proton and a base accepts it.

A polyprotic acid is an acid that can donate more than one proton per molecule. Sulfuric acid, H_2SO_4, and phosphoric acid, H_3PO_4, are examples of polyprotic acids. The ionization of a polyprotic acid occurs in stages. The acid loses its hydrogen ions one at a time. Sulfuric acid ionizes in two stages. In its first ionization, sulfuric acid is a strong acid. It is completely converted to hydrogen sulfate ions, HSO_4^-.

$$H_2SO_4(l) + H_2O(l) \longrightarrow H_3O^+(aq) + HSO_4^-(aq)$$

The hydrogen sulfate ion is itself a weak acid. It establishes the following equilibrium in solution.

$$HSO_4^-(aq) + H_2O(l) \rightleftarrows H_3O^+(aq) + SO_4^{2-}(aq)$$

All stages of ionization of a polyprotic acid occur in the same solution. Sulfuric acid solutions therefore contain H_3O^+, HSO_4^-, and SO_4^{2-} ions. Note that in sulfuric acid solutions, there are many more hydrogen sulfate and hydronium ions than there are sulfate ions.

Sulfuric acid is the type of polyprotic acid that can donate two protons per molecule, and it is therefore known as a diprotic acid. Ionizations of a monoprotic acid and a diprotic acid are shown in **Figure 2.2.**

FIGURE 2.2

Monoprotic and Diprotic Acids Hydrochloric acid, HCl, is a strong monoprotic acid. A dilute HCl solution contains hydronium ions and chloride ions. Sulfuric acid, H_2SO_4, is a strong diprotic acid. A dilute H_2SO_4 solution contains hydrogen sulfate ions from the first ionization, sulfate ions from the second ionization, and hydronium ions from both ionizations.

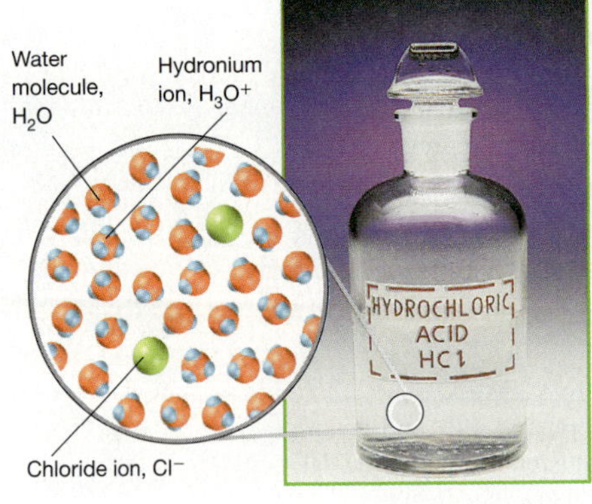

$$HCl + H_2O \longrightarrow H_3O^+ + Cl^-$$

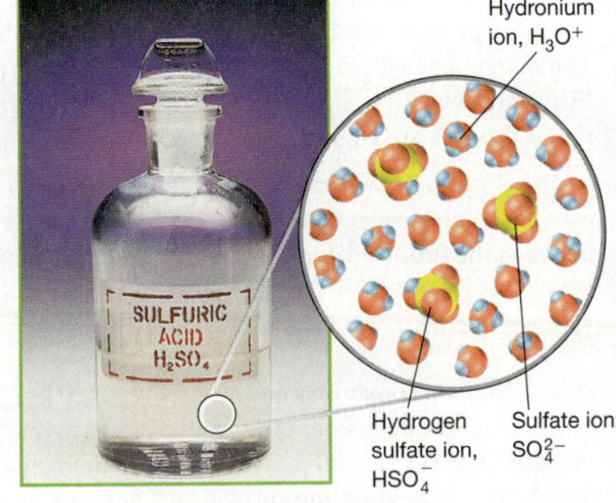

$$H_2SO_4 + H_2O \longrightarrow H_3O^+ + HSO_4^-$$
$$HSO_4^- + H_2O \rightleftarrows H_3O^+ + SO_4^{2-}$$

✓ CRITICAL THINKING

Explain Using the Brønsted-Lowry definition, is it possible to have an acid without an accompanying base?

Differentiated Instruction

ENGLISH LEARNERS

To help students understand polyprotic acids, use the skeletal structural formula for glucose to draw a hexagon on the board. Inform students that this structure represents a monosaccharide, which is the building block of carbohydrates. Ask them to explain how a disaccharide is built when two monosacharides are combined. Relate the prefix *di-* to its meaning in diprotic acids. Then have students do the same for a trisaccharide and a polysaccharide. Finally, ask students to explain why diprotic and triprotic acids, but not monoprotic acids, can be considered polyproprotic acids. Diprotic and triprotic acids are polyprotic because they donate more than one proton per molecule, whereas monoprotic acids only donate one proton and therefore are not considered polyprotic by definition.

Phosphoric acid is the type of polyprotic acid known as a **triprotic acid**—an acid able to donate three protons per molecule.
The equations for these reactions are shown below.

$$H_3PO_4(aq) + H_2O(l) \rightleftharpoons H_3O^+(aq) + H_2PO_4^-(aq)$$

$$H_2PO_4^-(aq) + H_2O(l) \rightleftharpoons H_3O^+(aq) + HPO_4^{2-}(aq)$$

$$HPO_4^{2-}(aq) + H_2O(l) \rightleftharpoons H_3O^+(aq) + PO_4^{3-}(aq)$$

A solution of phosphoric acid contains H_3O^+, H_3PO_4, $H_2PO_4^-$, HPO_4^{2-}, and PO_4^{3-}. As with most polyprotic acids, the concentration of ions formed in the first ionization is the greatest. There are lesser concentrations of the respective ions from each succeeding ionization. Phosphoric acid is a weak acid in each step of its ionization.

MAIN IDEA

A Lewis acid or base accepts or donates a pair of electrons.

The Arrhenius and Brønsted-Lowry definitions describe most acids and bases. Both definitions assume that the acid contains or produces hydrogen ions. A third acid classification, based on bonding and structure, includes, as acids, substances that do not contain hydrogen at all. This definition of acids was introduced in 1923 by G. N. Lewis, the American chemist whose name was given to electron-dot structures. Lewis's definition emphasizes the role of electron pairs in acid-base reactions. A **Lewis acid** is an atom, ion, or molecule that accepts an electron pair to form a covalent bond.

The Lewis definition is the broadest of the three acid definitions you have read about so far. It applies to any species that can accept an electron pair to form a covalent bond with another species. A bare proton (hydrogen ion) is a Lewis acid in reactions in which it forms a covalent bond, as shown below.

$$H^+(aq) + :NH_3(aq) \longrightarrow [H\text{–}NH_3]^+(aq) \text{ or } [NH_4]^+(aq)$$

The formula for a Lewis acid need not include hydrogen. Even a silver ion can be a Lewis acid, accepting electron pairs from ammonia to form covalent bonds.

$$Ag^+(aq) + 2:NH_3(aq) \longrightarrow [H_3N\text{–}Ag\text{–}NH_3]^+(aq) \text{ or } [Ag(NH_3)_2]^+$$

Any compound in which the central atom has three valence electrons and forms three covalent bonds can react as a Lewis acid. It does so by accepting a pair of electrons to form a fourth covalent bond, completing an electron octet. Boron trifluoride, for example, is an excellent Lewis acid. It forms a fourth covalent bond with many molecules and ions. Its reaction with a fluoride ion is shown below.

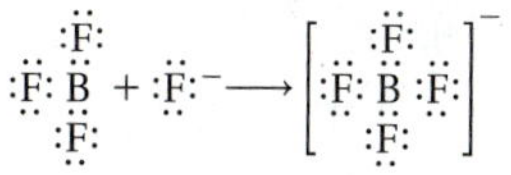

$$:\ddot{F}:\ddot{B}(:\ddot{F}:)_2 + :\ddot{F}:^- \longrightarrow [BF_4]^-$$

$$BF_3(aq) + F^-(aq) \longrightarrow BF_4^-(aq)$$

Teaching Tip

Students sometimes think that the number of H atoms in the formula is an indication of whether the acid is strong or weak. Emphasize that this is not the case. Work with students to identify a weak diprotic acid, a strong diprotic acid, a strong monoprotic acid, and a weak monoprotic acid.

Classroom Discussion

Have the class explain why the $H^+(aq)$ shown reacting with NH_3 can be considered a Brønsted-Lowry acid, and a Lewis acid, but not an Arrhenius acid. The $H^+(aq)$ donates a proton, making it a Brønsted-Lowry acid; it accepts an electron pair to form a covalent bond with ammonia, making it a Lewis acid. However, $H^+(aq)$ forms the ammonium ion and does not increase the concentration of hydrogen ions in aqueous solution when it reacts with ammonia. Therefore, it does not fit the definition of an Arrhenius acid.

PRE-AP

Most substances act as Lewis acids to complete an electron octet, as shown by the reaction of boron trifluoride. However, compounds containing elements lower than Period 2 can act as Lewis acids by the expansion of their valence shell. An example is stannic chloride, $SnCl_4$. Have students explain how this compound acts as a Lewis acid through valence shell expansion as evidenced by the presence of 12 valence electrons in $SnCl_4$. Students should explain that although the valence shell of the Sn atom is filled with an octet of electrons, it has two empty *d*-orbitals which can each accept a pair of electrons, thus allowing $SnCl_4$ to act as a Lewis acid.

▼ Teach *continued*

Teaching Tip

The three definitions of acids and bases are not mutually exclusive. The Lewis definition is the most inclusive. The Lewis definition of acids and bases is most commonly used for nonaqueous reactions, particularly those encountered in organic chemistry.

▼ Assess and Reteach

Assess Use the Formative Assessment on this page to evaluate student mastery of the section.

Reteach For students who need additional instruction, download the Section Study Guide.

Response to Intervention To reassess students' mastery, use the Section Quiz, available to print or to take directly online at **HMDScience.com**.

FIGURE 2.3

ACID-BASE DEFINITIONS

Type	Acid	Base
Arrhenius	H^+ or H_3O^+ producer	OH^- producer
Brønsted-Lowry	proton (H^+) donor	proton (H^+) acceptor
Lewis	electron-pair acceptor	electron-pair donor

The Lewis definition of acids can apply to species in any phase. For example, boron trifluoride is a Lewis acid in the gas-phase combination with ammonia.

$$BF_3 + :NH_3 \longrightarrow F_3B:NH_3$$

A **Lewis base** is an atom, ion, or molecule that donates an electron pair to form a covalent bond. An anion is a Lewis base in a reaction in which it forms a covalent bond by donating an electron pair. In the example of boron trifluoride reacting with the fluoride anion, F^- donates an electron pair to boron trifluoride. F^- acts as a Lewis base.

$$BF_3(aq) + :\ddot{F}:^-(aq) \longrightarrow BF_4^-(aq)$$

A **Lewis acid-base reaction** is the formation of one or more covalent bonds between an electron-pair donor and an electron-pair acceptor.

Note that although the three acid-base definitions differ, many compounds may be categorized as acids or bases according to all three descriptions. For example, ammonia is an Arrhenius base because OH^- ions are created when ammonia is in solution, it is a Brønsted-Lowry base because it accepts a proton in an acid-base reaction, and it is a Lewis base in all reactions in which it donates its lone pair to form a covalent bond. A comparison of the three acid-base definitions is given in **Figure 2.3.**

SECTION 2 FORMATIVE ASSESSMENT

Reviewing Main Ideas

1. Label each reactant in the reaction below as a proton donor or a proton acceptor and as acidic or basic.

$$H_2CO_3 + H_2O \rightleftharpoons HCO_3^- + H_3O^+$$

2. For the reaction below, label each reactant as an electron pair acceptor or electron pair donor and as a Lewis acid or a Lewis base.

$$AlCl_3 + Cl^- \longrightarrow AlCl_4^-$$

Critical Thinking

3. **ANALYZING INFORMATION** For the following three reactions, identify the reactants that are Arrhenius bases, Brønsted-Lowry bases, and/or Lewis bases. State which type(s) of bases each reactant is. Explain your answers.
   a. $NaOH(s) \longrightarrow Na^+(aq) + OH^-(aq)$
   b. $HF(aq) + H_2O(l) \longrightarrow F^-(aq) + H_3O^+(aq)$
   c. $H^+(aq) + NH_3(aq) \longrightarrow NH_4^+(aq)$

Answers to Section Assessment

1. H_2CO_3: proton donor, acidic; H_2O: proton acceptor, basic
2. $AlCl_3$: electron pair acceptor, Lewis acid; Cl^-: electron pair donor, Lewis base
3. a. NaOH, an Arrhenius base
   b. H_2O, a Brønsted-Lowry and Lewis base
   c. NH_3, a Brønsted-Lowry and Lewis base

SECTION 3

Acid-Base Reactions

Key Terms
conjugate base
conjugate acid
amphoteric
neutralization
salt

Main Ideas

- Brønsted-Lowry reactions involve conjugate acid-base pairs.
- Some substances act as either acids or bases.
- Neutralization reactions produce water and a salt.

In the previous sections, you learned about three acid-base theories: Arrhenius, Brønsted-Lowry, and Lewis. The Brønsted-Lowry theory is especially useful for describing acid-base reactions that take place in aqueous solutions. This section will use the Brønsted-Lowry description to explore reactions between acids and bases.

MAIN IDEA

Brønsted-Lowry reactions involve conjugate acid-base pairs.

The Brønsted-Lowry definitions of acids and bases provide a basis for studying proton-transfer reactions. Suppose that a Brønsted-Lowry acid gives up a proton; the remaining ion or molecule can re-accept that proton and can act as a base. Such a base is known as a conjugate base. **Thus, the species that remains after a Brønsted-Lowry acid has given up a proton is the conjugate base of that acid.** For example, the fluoride ion is the conjugate base of hydrofluoric acid.

$$\underset{\text{acid}}{HF(aq)} + H_2O(l) \rightleftharpoons \underset{\text{conjugate base}}{F^-(aq)} + H_3O^+(aq)$$

In this reaction, the water molecule is a Brønsted-Lowry base. It accepts a proton from HF to form H_3O^+, which is an acid. The hydronium ion is the conjugate acid of water. **The species that is formed when a Brønsted-Lowry base gains a proton is the conjugate acid of that base.**

$$HF(aq) + \underset{\text{base}}{H_2O(l)} \rightleftharpoons F^-(aq) + \underset{\text{conjugate acid}}{H_3O^+(aq)}$$

In general, Brønsted-Lowry acid-base reactions are equilibrium systems meaning that both the forward and reverse reactions occur. They involve two acid-base pairs, known as conjugate acid-base pairs.

$$\underset{\text{acid}_1}{HF(aq)} + \underset{\text{base}_2}{H_2O(l)} \rightleftharpoons \underset{\text{base}_1}{F^-(aq)} + \underset{\text{acid}_2}{H_3O^+(aq)}$$

The subscripts designate the two conjugate acid-base pairs: (1) HF and F^- and (2) H_3O^+ and H_2O. In every conjugate acid-base pair, the acid has one more proton than its conjugate base.

Differentiated Instruction

BELOW LEVEL

To help students understand conjugate acids and bases, have them copy the last equation on this page. Then have them write this equation in reverse, directly beneath the other equation. Be sure that they place $F^-(aq)$ below $HF(aq)$ and $H_3O^+(aq)$ below $H_2O(l)$. By looking at the bottom (reverse) equation, students should see that $F^-(aq)$ acts as a base by accepting a proton from $H_3O^+(aq)$. Therefore, $F^-(aq)$ is a base, known as a conjugate base, formed by the ionization of the acid $HF(aq)$.

SECTION 3

Plan and Prepare

Objectives

Upon completion of this section, students should be able to do the following:

- Describe a conjugate acid, a conjugate base, and an amphoteric compound.
- Explain the process of neutralization.
- Define *acid rain*, give examples of compounds that can cause acid rain, and describe effects of acid rain.

Classroom Catalyst

Ask students for their ideas about the meaning of the word *neutralization*. How is the term used in everyday life? How is it likely to apply to discussion of acids and bases?

Teach

Teaching Tip

The terms *conjugate acid* and *conjugate base* are typically reserved for products of a reaction. The terms *acid* and *base* are generally reserved for reactants. The labels "acid_1" and "base_1" are arbitrary. In the equation shown for the reaction of HF and H_2O, HF could have been assigned acid_2, and H_2O could have been assigned base_1. What is important is that the conjugate pairs have the same subscript.

▼ Teach *continued*

Classroom Discussion

Have students read the explanations on this page and make sure they understand how HCl and $HClO_4$ are classified as *strong* or *stronger acids*, how H_2O can be classified as a *stronger base*, and how Cl^-, H_3O^+, and ClO_4^- can be classified as *weak* or *weaker bases*.

Alternative Assessment

Have students produce an illustration to show that the stronger an acid is, the weaker its conjugate base, and the stronger a base is, the weaker its conjugate acid. One possibility is to list several conjugate acids in order of decreasing strength and place the label *Acid Strength* along the side with an arrow pointing upward. The conjugate bases can be listed in order of increasing strength on the other side and labeled *Base Strength* with an arrow pointing downward. If students draw such a table, they can compare theirs to **Figure 3.1**.

Cross-Disciplinary Connection

"It's a Bitter Pill" S.T.E.M.

Have you ever wondered about the origin of the saying, "It's a bitter pill to swallow"? This saying is used to describe a situation that is difficult to accept. Many medications contain bases, and a bitter taste is a property of bases. So, many medications actually have a bitter taste. If you look at the chemical formulas of the components of medications, you will see that they often contain nitrogen. One such component is caffeine, which acts as a stimulant on the central nervous and respiratory systems. Its molecular formula is $C_8H_{10}O_2N_4$. Like ammonia, caffeine has basic properties because it has a nitrogen that can accept a proton.

Strength of Conjugate Acids and Bases

The extent of the reaction between a Brønsted-Lowry acid and base depends on the relative strengths of the acids and bases involved. Consider the following example. Hydrochloric acid is a strong acid. It gives up protons readily. Therefore, the Cl^- ion has little tendency to attract and retain a proton. Consequently, the Cl^- ion is an extremely weak base.

$HCl(g)$	+	$H_2O(l)$	$\longrightarrow$	$H_3O^+(aq)$	+	$Cl^-(aq)$
stronger acid		stronger base		weaker acid		weaker base

This observation leads to an important conclusion: *the stronger an acid is, the weaker its conjugate base; the stronger a base is, the weaker its conjugate acid.*

Using Strength to Predict Reactions

This concept allows strengths of different acids and bases to be compared to predict the outcome of a reaction. As an example, consider the reaction of perchloric acid, $HClO_4$, and water.

$HClO_4(aq)$	+	$H_2O(l)$	$\longrightarrow$	$H_3O^+(aq)$	+	$ClO_4^-(aq)$
stronger acid		stronger base		weaker acid		weaker base

The hydronium ion is too weak an acid to compete successfully with perchloric acid in donating a proton; $HClO_4$ is the stronger acid. In this reaction, the perchlorate ion, ClO_4^-, and H_2O are both bases. Because $HClO_4$ is a very strong acid, ClO_4^- is an extremely weak base. Therefore, H_2O competes more strongly than ClO_4^- to acquire a proton. The reaction proceeds such that the stronger acid reacts with the stronger base to produce the weaker acid and base.

Now consider a comparable reaction between water and acetic acid.

$CH_3COOH(aq)$ +	$H_2O(l)$	$\longleftarrow$	$H_3O^+(aq)$	+ $CH_3COO^-(aq)$
weaker acid	weaker base		stronger acid	stronger base

The H_3O^+ ion concentration in this solution is much lower than it was in the $HClO_4$ solution because acetic acid is a weak acid. The CH_3COOH molecule does not compete successfully with the H_3O^+ ion in donating protons to a base. The acetate ion, CH_3COO^-, is a stronger base than H_2O. Therefore, the H_2O molecule does not compete successfully with the CH_3COO^- ion in accepting a proton. The H_3O^+ ion is the stronger acid, and the CH_3COO^- ion is the stronger base. Thus, the reverse reaction (to the left) is more favorable.

Note that in the reactions for both perchloric acid and acetic acid, the favored direction is toward the weaker acid and the weaker base. This observation leads to a second important general conclusion: *proton-transfer reactions favor the production of the weaker acid and the weaker base.* For an acid-base reaction to form products completely, the reactants must be much stronger as acids and bases than the products.

Differentiated Instruction

BELOW LEVEL

Have students complete the following table of relative strengths of conjugate acids and bases.

Formula	Description	Formula	Description
HNO_3	strong acid	NO_3^-	weaker base
HS^-	weak acid	S^{2-}	stronger base
HCO_3^-	weak acid	CO_3^{2-}	stronger base
H_2O	weaker acid	OH^-	strong base
HCl	stronger acid	Cl^-	weak base
PO_4^{3-}	stronger base	HPO_4^{2-}	weak acid

The table in **Figure 3.1** shows that a very strong acid, such as $HClO_4$, has a very weak conjugate base, ClO_4^-. The strongest base listed in the table, the hydride ion, H^-, has the weakest conjugate acid, H_2. In aqueous solutions, all of the strong acids are 100% ionized, forming hydronium ions along with their anion. The acids below hydronium ion in **Figure 3.1** do not ionize 100% in water. Water will react as an acid if a very strong base, such as hydride ion, is present.

FIGURE 3.1

RELATIVE STRENGTHS OF ACIDS AND BASES

Conjugate acid	Formula	Conjugate base	Formula
hydriodic acid*	HI	iodide ion	I^-
perchloric acid*	$HClO_4$	perchlorate ion	ClO_4^-
hydrobromic acid*	HBr	bromide ion	Br^-
hydrochloric acid*	HCl	chloride ion	Cl^-
sulfuric acid*	H_2SO_4	hydrogen sulfate ion	HSO_4^-
chloric acid*	$HClO_3$	chlorate ion	ClO_3^-
nitric acid*	HNO_3	nitrate ion	NO_3^-
hydronium ion	H_3O^+	water	H_2O
chlorous acid	$HClO_2$	chlorite ion	ClO_2^-
hydrogen sulfate ion	HSO_4^-	sulfate ion	SO_4^{2-}
phosphoric acid	H_3PO_4	dihydrogen phosphate ion	$H_2PO_4^-$
hydrofluoric acid	HF	fluoride ion	F^-
acetic acid	CH_3COOH	acetate ion	CH_3COO^-
carbonic acid	H_2CO_3	hydrogen carbonate ion	HCO_3^-
hydrosulfuric acid	H_2S	hydrosulfide ion	HS^-
dihydrogen phosphate ion	$H_2PO_4^-$	hydrogen phosphate ion	HPO_4^{2-}
hypochlorous acid	$HClO$	hypochlorite ion	ClO^-
ammonium ion	NH_4^+	ammonia	NH_3
hydrogen carbonate ion	HCO_3^-	carbonate ion	CO_3^{2-}
hydrogen phosphate ion	HPO_4^{2-}	phosphate ion	PO_4^{3-}
water	H_2O	hydroxide ion	OH^-
ammonia	NH_3	amide ion†	NH_2^-
hydrogen	H_2	hydride ion†	H^-

Increasing acid strength (↑)

Increasing base strength (↓)

* Strong acids

† Strong bases

PRE-AP

Students will explore the subject of amphoteric compounds by focusing on acids and bases. Point out that the term *amphoteric* can be applied to other types of compounds. For example, an amino acid can be considered an amphoteric compound because it contains both an acidic functional group and a basic functional group. Have students consider the amphoteric nature of proteins in terms of their chemical structure. Point out that blood proteins serve as powerful buffers to control the pH of plasma.

TEACH FROM TABLES

FIGURE 3.1 Ask students to choose a strong conjugate acid, a weak conjugate acid, a strong conjugate base, and a weak conjugate base from those listed in the table. For each selection, have them write an equation that involves water. In each equation, students should label the weaker acid, the weaker base, the stronger acid, and the stronger base. Reinforce the concept that in all cases, the species that are present in the greatest amount after reaction are the weaker acid and the weaker base.

Classroom Discussion

To emphasize the amphoteric character of water, ask students to identify the conjugate acid and conjugate base in the reaction of two water molecules with each other. In the reaction of two water molecules, $H_2O + H_2O \longrightarrow H_3O^+ + OH^-$, one water molecule donates a proton and acts as an acid, while the other water molecule accepts a proton and acts as a base. The conjugate acid is H_3O^+ and the conjugate base is OH^-.

▼ Teach *continued*

TEACH FROM VISUALS

FIGURE 3.2 Ask students to draw the electron-dot structure of the hydride ion, H^- (as in the calcium hydride reacting in the image.) Have them explain why the hydride ion acts as such a strong base based on that structure. The hydride ion consists of two electrons and a proton and is a strong proton acceptor. Also have students explain how water behaves as an acid in the reaction. Water readily gives up a proton and as such, acts as an acid.

Teaching Tip

The reaction between calcium hydride and water can be represented as a net ionic equation to show more clearly the proton transfer that takes place:

$$\underset{\text{base}_1}{H^-(aq)} + \underset{\text{acid}_2}{H_2O(l)} \longrightarrow \underset{\text{base}_2}{OH^-(aq)} + \underset{\text{acid}_1}{H_2(g)}$$

TEACH FROM VISUALS

FIGURE 3.3 Ask students to consider the molecular structures in the figure as "contests for electrons." Have them choose which atoms or groups of atoms are likely to be winners in this contest and which are likely to be losers. Use this analogy to reinforce their understanding of the differences in acid strength among the four acids. In a covalent bond, the more attracted electrons are to one atom than to the other, the easier it is to break the bond. In the case of the oxyacids of chlorine, as the number of oxygen atoms bonded to the chlorine atom increases, the pull of electrons from the O–H bond increases. So, the acids become stronger because the O–H bond becomes weaker.

Check for Understanding

Answer: $Ca(OH)_2$ (conjugate base); 2 H_2 (conjugate acid)

FIGURE 3.2

Water as a Base Calcium hydride, CaH_2, reacts vigorously with water to produce hydrogen gas. Water acts as a base in this reaction because it is in a very strong acid.

CHECK FOR UNDERSTANDING
Identify Identify the conjugate acid and base in the reaction of calcium hydride with water.

MAIN IDEA

Some substances act as either acids or bases.

You have probably noticed that water can be either an acid or a base. **Any species that can react as either an acid or a base is described as amphoteric.** For example, consider the first ionization of sulfuric acid, in which water acts as a base.

$$\underset{\text{acid}_1}{H_2SO_4(aq)} + \underset{\text{base}_2}{H_2O(l)} \longrightarrow \underset{\text{acid}_2}{H_3O^+(aq)} + \underset{\text{base}_1}{HSO_4^-(aq)}$$

Water is acting as a base in the reaction shown in **Figure 3.2.**

However, water acts as an acid in the following reaction.

$$\underset{\text{base}_1}{NH_3(g)} + \underset{\text{acid}_2}{H_2O(l)} \rightleftarrows \underset{\text{acid}_1}{NH_4^+(aq)} + \underset{\text{base}_2}{OH^-(aq)}$$

Thus, water can act as either an acid or a base and is amphoteric. Such a substance acts as either an acid or a base depending on the strength of the acid or base with which it is reacting—if it's a stronger acid than the substance, the substance will act as a base. If, however, it's a stronger base than the substance, the substance will act as an acid.

FIGURE 3.3

O—H Bonds and Acid Strength Each oxyacid of chlorine contains one chlorine atom and one hydrogen atom. They differ in the number of oxygen atoms they contain. The effect of the changing O—H bond polarity can be seen in the increasing acid strength from hypochlorous acid to perchloric acid.

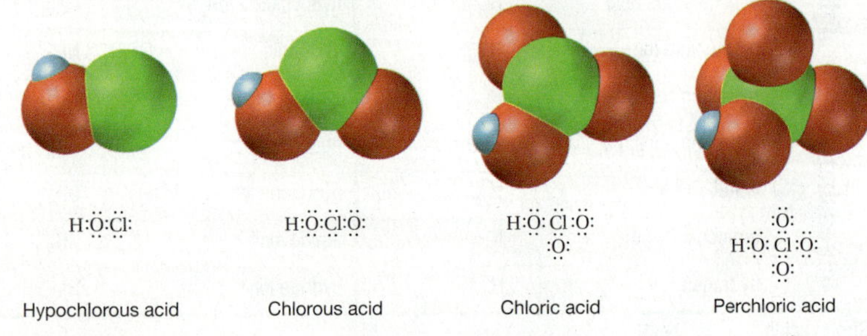

Differentiated Instruction

PRE-AP

Some metal oxides, such as aluminum oxide, are amphoteric. Aluminum oxide can act as a base by accepting a proton from hydrochloric acid to form aluminum chloride and water. Aluminum oxide can also act as an acid by reacting with sodium hydroxide to form complex ions, such as sodium tetrahydroxoaluminate. Have students illustrate the amphoteric nature of a metal oxide.

–OH in a Molecule

Molecular compounds containing –OH groups can be acidic or amphoteric. The covalently bonded –OH group in an acid is referred to as a *hydroxyl group*. For the compound to be acidic, a water molecule must be able to attract a hydrogen atom from a hydroxyl group. This occurs more easily when the O–H bond is very polar. Any feature of a molecule that increases the polarity of the O–H bond increases the acidity of a molecular compound. The small, more-electronegative atoms of nonmetals at the upper right in the periodic table form compounds with acidic hydroxyl groups. All oxyacids are molecular electrolytes that contain one or more of these O–H bonds. Such compounds include chloric and perchloric acids.

Figure 3.3 (on the previous page) shows the electron-dot formulas of the four oxyacids of chlorine. Notice that all of the oxygen atoms are bonded to the chlorine atom. Each hydrogen atom is bonded to an oxygen atom. Aqueous solutions of these molecules are acids because the O–H bonds are broken as the hydrogen is pulled away by water molecules.

The behavior of a compound is affected by the number of oxygen atoms bonded to the atom connected to the –OH group. The larger the number of such oxygen atoms is, the more acidic the compound is. The electronegative oxygen atoms draw electron density away from the O–H bond and make it more polar. For example, chromium forms three different compounds containing –OH groups, as shown below.

basic	*amphoteric*	*acidic*
$Cr(OH)_2$	$Cr(OH)_3$	H_2CrO_4
chromium(II) hydroxide	chromium(III) hydroxide	chromic acid

Notice that as the number of oxygen atoms increases, so does the acidity of the compound.

Consider also the compounds shown in **Figure 3.4.** In acetic acid, but not in ethanol, a second oxygen atom is bonded to the carbon atom connected to the –OH group. That explains why acetic acid is acidic but ethanol is not, even though the same elements form each compound.

MAIN IDEA

Neutralization reactions produce water and a salt.

There are many common examples of acidic compounds reacting with basic compounds, each neutralizing the other. Sodium bicarbonate, $NaHCO_3$, and tartaric acid, $H_2C_4H_4O_6$, are two components in baking powder. When water is added, the two compounds produce carbon dioxide. The escaping carbon dioxide causes foods, such as biscuits, to rise. Another example is an antacid soothing an overly acidic stomach by neutralizing the stomach acid.

FIGURE 3.4

Polarity and Acids

(a) CH_3COOH
Acetic acid is acidic. The second oxygen atom on the carbon draws electron density away from the –OH group, making the O–H bond more polar.

(b) C_2H_5OH
Ethanol is essentially neutral. It has no second oxygen atom, so the O–H bond is less polar than in acetic acid, and is a much weaker acid.

Neutralization Reactions

Classroom Discussion

Ask students to write the net ionic equation for the reaction between HCl and NaOH. Ask them what the net ionic equation tells about the specific acid and specific base used in a neutralization reaction. The acid completely ionizes to produce H_3O^+ and the base completely dissociates to form OH^-, which yields water molecules and results in neutralization.

TEACH FROM VISUALS

FIGURE 3.4 Draw the structure of formic acid, and ask students to predict whether it is more or less acidic than acetic acid. Formic acid is more acidic than acetic acid.

Misconception Alert!

Students are likely to be confused about the naming of the –OH group as both *hydroxide* and *hydroxyl*. Make sure they understand that *hydroxide* refers to a charged polyatomic ion that may be combined with a positive ion in an ionic compound. The *hydroxyl* group is covalently bonded to another atom, often carbon.

BELOW LEVEL

To help students understand neutralization reactions, place the following table on the board.

Compound	Chemical Formula	Chemical Reaction
Aluminum hydroxide	$Al(OH)_3$	$Al(OH)_3(s) + 3HCl(aq) \longrightarrow AlCl_3(aq) + 3H_2O(l)$
Calcium carbonate	$CaCO_3$	$CaCO_3(s) + 2HCl(aq) \longrightarrow CaCl_2(aq) + H_2O(l) + CO_2(g)$
Magnesium carbonate	$MgCO_3$	$MgCO_3(s) + 2HCl(aq) \longrightarrow MgCl_2(aq) + H_2O(l) + CO_2(g)$
Magnesium hydroxide	$Mg(OH)_2$	$Mg(OH)_2(s) + 2HCl(aq) \longrightarrow MgCl_2(aq) + 2H_2O(l)$
Sodium bicarbonate	$NaHCO_3$	$NaHCO_3(aq) + HCl(aq) \longrightarrow NaCl(aq) + H_2O(l) + CO_2(g)$

Inform students that the compounds listed are the active ingredients in various brands of antacid products. Ask students to examine the table and describe what the compounds all have in common. Students should notice that each compound reacts with HCl, the acid secreted by the stomach, to produce a salt, water, and in some cases, carbon dioxide gas. As a result, all the compounds reduce the concentration of hydrogen ions in the stomach.

▼ Teach continued

Classroom Discussion

Ask students to describe situations in which neutralization might have important everyday applications. Answers may include the neutralization of a chemical spill on a highway or in a factory, the use of an antacid to treat an upset stomach, or the treatment of soil that is either too acidic or basic.

TEACH FROM VISUALS

FIGURE 3.5 Ask students to describe in as many different ways as possible how this illustration shows that the properties of HCl and NaOH have been neutralized.

Alternative Assessment

Explain to students that the initial steps in the formation of acid rain take place when fuels that contain sulfur impurities are burned. Nitrogen and oxygen from the air also react when the fuel is burned. Ask students to write a series of related chemical equations that begin with elemental sulfur, nitrogen, and oxygen. The series should end with oxides of sulfur and nitrogen reacting with water in the air to form the corresponding acids.

Teaching Tip

See the Math Tutor at the end of this chapter for more information on writing net ionic equations.

Strong Acid-Strong Base Neutralization

An acid-base reaction occurs in aqueous solution between hydrochloric acid, a strong acid that completely ionizes to produce H_3O^+, and sodium hydroxide, a strong base that completely dissociates to produce OH^-. The formula equation for this reaction is written as follows.

$$HCl(aq) + NaOH(aq) \longrightarrow NaCl(aq) + H_2O(l)$$

In an aqueous solution containing 1 mol of sodium hydroxide, NaOH dissociates as represented by the following equation.

$$NaOH(aq) \longrightarrow Na^+(aq) + OH^-(aq)$$

A solution containing 1 mol of hydrochloric acid ionizes as represented by the following equation.

$$HCl(aq) + H_2O(l) \longrightarrow H_3O^+(aq) + Cl^-(aq)$$

If the two solutions are mixed, as in **Figure 3.5**, a reaction occurs between the aqueous H_3O^+ and OH^- ions. Notice that sodium chloride, NaCl, and water are produced. The overall ionic equation is shown below.

$$H_3O^+(aq) + Cl^-(aq) + Na^+(aq) + OH^-(aq) \longrightarrow Na^+(aq) + Cl^-(aq) + 2H_2O(l)$$

FIGURE 3.5

Neutralization When aqueous hydrochloric acid, HCl, reacts with aqueous sodium hydroxide, NaOH, the reaction produces aqueous sodium chloride, NaCl. Ions that are present in each solution are represented by the models.

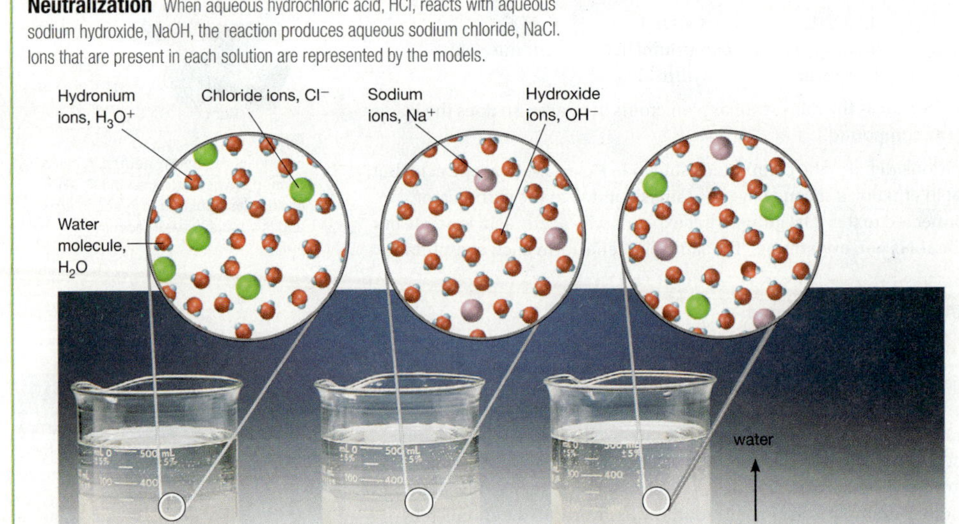

Differentiated Instruction

INCLUSION

Visually-impaired students might have difficulty following the sequence of events in **Figure 3.5.** Make the sequence more visible by using a larger model. Have four students serve in place of the models shown in this figure. Each student should hold one of the following signs, written large: Na^+, OH^-, H_3O^+, and Cl^-. Have several other students surround these four students. Ask the class what these students represent. water molecules Then have the four students holding signs interact to show what happens during a neutralization reaction. Expand the activity to show what happens when the molar ratios of acid and base are not equal. For example, add more acid by having students holding H_3O^+ and Cl^- signs join the original four students. The class should see that when a reaction occurs this time, not all the H_3O^+ ions have been neutralized by OH^- ions.

Because they appear on both sides of the overall ionic equation, Na^+ and Cl^- are spectator ions. The only participants in the reaction are the hydronium ion and the hydroxide ion, as shown in the following net ionic equation.

$$H_3O^+(aq) + OH^-(aq) \longrightarrow 2H_2O(l)$$

There are equal numbers of H_3O^+ and OH^- ions in this reaction, and they are fully converted to water. **In aqueous solutions, neutralization is the reaction of hydronium ions and hydroxide ions to form water molecules.**

Notice that water is not the only product of a neutralization. A salt is also produced. **A salt is an ionic compound composed of a cation from a base and an anion from an acid.**

Acid Rain

Many industrial processes produce gases such as NO, NO_2, CO_2, SO_2, and SO_3. These compounds can dissolve in atmospheric water to produce acidic solutions that fall to the ground in the form of rain or snow. For example, sulfur from the burning of oil and coal forms sulfur dioxide, SO_2. The SO_2 is then converted to SO_3, sulfur trioxide, which reacts with water in the atmosphere to produce sulfuric acid, as shown below.

$$SO_3(g) + H_2O(l) \longrightarrow H_2SO_4(aq)$$

Rainwater is normally slightly acidic, but sometimes rain is very acidic and is called *acid rain*. **Figure 3.6** shows a forest that was damaged by severe acid rain. Acid rain can erode statues and affect ecosystems, such as water environments and forests. In the 1970s, scientists found that acid rain was causing the fish populations in some lakes and streams to decline. When fish are completely eliminated from lakes and streams because of acid rain, the biodiversity of the ecosystem decreases. Because of amendments to the Clean Air Act in 1990, a limit was set on the amount of SO_2 that power plants are permitted to emit. This limit has decreased but not eliminated acid rain in the United States.

FIGURE 3.6

Acid Precipitation Acid precipitation causes extensive environmental damage.

SECTION 3 FORMATIVE ASSESSMENT

Reviewing Main Ideas

1. Complete and balance the equations for the following acid-base reactions:
   a. $H_2CO_3 + Sr(OH)_2 \longrightarrow$
   b. $HClO_4 + NaOH \longrightarrow$
   c. $HBr + Ba(OH)_2 \longrightarrow$
   d. $NaHCO_3 + H_2SO_4 \longrightarrow$
2. Consider the equation for acetic acid plus water.
   $$CH_3COOH + H_2O \longrightarrow CH_3COO^- + H_3O^+$$
   a. Refer to **Figure 3.1** to compare the strengths of the two acids in the equation. Do the same for the two bases.
   b. Determine which direction—forward or reverse—is favored in the reaction.

Critical Thinking

3. **INFERRING RELATIONSHIPS** Explain how the presence of several oxygen atoms in a compound containing an —OH group can make the compound acidic.

Answers to Section Assessment

1. a. $H_2CO_3 + Sr(OH)_2 \longrightarrow SrCO_3 + 2H_2O$
   b. $HClO_4 + NaOH \longrightarrow NaClO_4 + H_2O$
   c. $2HBr + Ba(OH)_2 \longrightarrow BaBr_2 + 2H_2O$
   d. $2NaHCO_3 + H_2SO_4 \longrightarrow Na_2SO_4 + 2H_2O + 2CO_2$
2. a. H_3O^+ is the stronger acid; CH_3COO^- is the stronger base.
   b. The reverse reaction is favored.
3. Oxygen atoms draw electron density away from the O—H bond, making it more polar (more easily broken).

Classroom Discussion

Ask students to identify as many issues involving acid rain as possible. Answers should include not only the harmful effects produced by acid rain, but also the economic disruptions that result when efforts are made to reduce acid rain. They should also include the problems of identifying the effects of acid rain and the uncertainties involved in large-scale environmental issues.

READING TOOLKIT

DISCUSSION After students read the selection, "Acid Rain", lead a discussion in which students volunteer what they know about its effects on the environment. Discuss how neutralization reactions might play a role in reducing acid rain.

Assess and Reteach

Assess Use the Formative Assessment on this page to evaluate student mastery of the section.

Reteach For students who need additional instruction, download the Section Study Guide.

Response to Intervention To reassess students' mastery, use the Section Quiz, available to print or to take directly online at **HMDScience.com**.

Answers

1. **Formula equation:**
$CuSO_4(aq) + Na_2S(aq) \longrightarrow Na_2SO_4(aq) + CuS(s)$

Full ionic equation:
$Cu^{2+}(aq) + SO_4^{2-}(aq) + 2Na^+(aq) + S^{2-}(aq) \longrightarrow 2Na^+(aq) + SO_4^{2-}(aq) + CuS(s)$

Net ionic equation:
$Cu^{2+}(aq) + S^{2-}(aq) \longrightarrow CuS(s)$

2. **Full ionic equation:**
$Cd^{2+}(aq) + 2Cl^-(aq) + 2Na^+(aq) + CO_3^{2-}(aq) \longrightarrow 2Na^+(aq) + 2Cl^-(aq) + CdCO_3(s)$

Net ionic equation:
$Cd^{2+}(aq) + CO_3^{2-}(aq) \longrightarrow CdCO_3(s)$

Math Tutor — Writing Equations for Ionic Reactions

Many chemical reactions that occur in water solutions are reactions involving ions. Soluble ionic compounds dissociate into ions when they dissolve, and some molecular compounds, including acids, ionize when they dissolve. An ionic equation represents the species actually present more accurately than an equation that uses full formulas.

Problem-Solving TIPS

- All dissolved substances in ionic reactions are dissociated into ions. Therefore, soluble ionic compounds are shown as the separated ions in the full ionic equation. Strong acids and bases are also shown as the separated ions in the full ionic equation because they are 100% ionized.
- Ions that do not take part in the reaction are called *spectator ions.* In other words, spectator ions stay in solution and will be labeled "(*aq*)" on both sides of the equation. Eliminating spectator ions reduces the "clutter" of the full ionic equation and produces a net ionic equation that shows only the species that actually react.

Sample Problem

Write the net ionic equation for the reaction of aqueous ammonium sulfate and aqueous barium nitrate to produce a precipitate of barium sulfate. The balanced formula equation is $(NH_4)_2SO_4(aq) + Ba(NO_3)_2(aq) \longrightarrow 2NH_4NO_3(aq) + BaSO_4(s)$

Rewrite the equation in full ionic form; because ammonium sulfate and barium nitrate are soluble, they are written as separated ions:

$$2NH_4^+(aq) + SO_4^{2-}(aq) + Ba^{2+}(aq) + 2NO_3^-(aq) \longrightarrow 2NH_4^+(aq) + 2NO_3^-(aq) + BaSO_4(s)$$

Eliminating spectator ions, NH_4^+ and NO_3^-, yields the net ionic equation:

$$SO_4^{2-}(aq) + Ba^{2+}(aq) \longrightarrow BaSO_4(s)$$

Write full and net ionic equations for the reaction that occurs when hydrochloric acid solution is combined with silver nitrate solution.

Hydrochloric acid is a strong acid, so it is completely ionized in solution. Silver nitrate is a soluble ionic compound, so its ions are separated in solution. Although most chlorides are soluble, silver chloride is not, so silver chloride will precipitate. The balanced formula equation is

$$HCl(aq) + AgNO_3(aq) \longrightarrow AgCl(s) + HNO_3(aq)$$

The full ionic equation is

$$H_3O^+(aq) + Cl^-(aq) + Ag^+(aq) + NO_3^-(aq) \longrightarrow H_3O^+(aq) + NO_3^-(aq) + AgCl(s)$$

Eliminate spectator ions to obtain the net ionic equation:

$$Cl^-(aq) + Ag^+(aq) \longrightarrow AgCl(s)$$

Practice

Answers in Appendix E

1. Aqueous copper(II) sulfate reacts with aqueous sodium sulfide to produce a black precipitate of copper(II) sulfide. Write the formula equation, the full ionic equation, and the net ionic equation for this reaction.
2. Write full and net ionic equations for the reaction that occurs when a solution of cadmium chloride, $CdCl_2$, is mixed with a solution of sodium carbonate, Na_2CO_3. Cadmium carbonate is insoluble.

CHAPTER 14 Summary

Review Games
Concept Maps

SECTION 1 Properties of Acids and Bases

KEY TERMS

binary acid
oxyacid
Arrhenius acid
Arrhenius base
strong acid
weak acid

- Acids have a sour taste and react with active metals. Acids change the colors of acid-base indicators, react with bases to produce salts and water, and conduct electricity in aqueous solutions.
- Bases have a bitter taste, feel slippery to the skin in dilute aqueous solutions, change the colors of acid-base indicators, react with acids to produce salts and water, and conduct electricity in aqueous solution.
- An Arrhenius acid contains hydrogen and ionizes in aqueous solution to form hydrogen ions. An Arrhenius base produces hydroxide ions in aqueous solution.
- The strength of an Arrhenius acid or base is determined by the extent to which the acid or base ionizes or dissociates in aqueous solutions.

SECTION 2 Acid-Base Theories

KEY TERMS

Brønsted-Lowry acid
Brønsted-Lowry base
Brønsted-Lowry acid-base reaction
monoprotic acid
polyprotic acid
diprotic acid
triprotic acid
Lewis acid
Lewis base
Lewis acid-base reaction

- A Brønsted-Lowry acid is a proton donor. A Brønsted-Lowry base is a proton acceptor.
- A Lewis acid is an electron-pair acceptor. A Lewis base is an electron-pair donor.
- Acids are described as monoprotic, diprotic, or triprotic depending on whether they can donate one, two, or three protons per molecule, respectively, in aqueous solutions. Polyprotic acids include both diprotic and triprotic acids.

SECTION 3 Acid-Base Reactions

KEY TERMS

conjugate base
conjugate acid
amphoteric
neutralization
salt

- In every Brønsted-Lowry acid-base reaction, there are two conjugate acid-base pairs.
- A strong acid has a weak conjugate base; a strong base has a weak conjugate acid.
- Proton-transfer reactions favor the production of the weaker acid and weaker base.
- The acidic or basic behavior of a molecule containing –OH groups depends on the electronegativity of other atoms in the molecule and on the number of oxygen atoms bonded to the atom that is connected to the –OH group.
- A neutralization reaction produces water and an ionic compound called a salt.
- Acid rain can create severe ecological problems.

Review Answers

1. Both acids and bases change the color of indicators and are electrolytes. Acids taste sour, react with active metals to release $H_2(g)$, and react with bases to form a salt and water. Bases taste bitter, feel slippery, and react with acids to form salt and water.
2. **a.** Binary acids consist of hydrogen and a more electronegative element. They are named using the prefix *hydro-*, followed by the root name of the second element and the suffix *-ic*. Oxyacids consist of hydrogen, oxygen, and a third element (usually a nonmetal). Oxyacid names follow a systematic pattern. Acids whose name ends in *-ic* have one more oxygen atom than do acids whose name has an *-ous* suffix. For example, nitric acid is HNO_3, and nitrous acid is HNO_2. Acids whose name contains the prefix *hypo-* and the suffix *-ous* have one fewer oxygen atom than the corresponding acid whose name does not contain the *hypo-* prefix. For example, hypochlorous acid is HClO, and chlorous acid is $HClO_2$.

Acids whose name begins with *per-* and ends with *-ic* have one more oxygen atom that the corresponding acid whose name does not have the *per-* prefix. For example, perchloric acid is $HClO_4$, and chloric acid is $HClO_3$.

   b. Answers will vary;. examples of binary acids: HF, HCl, and HBr; examples of oxyacids: $HClO_3$, HNO_3, and H_2SO_4.
3. Sulfuric acid, H_2SO_4, is the most common acid, is a dehydrating agent, is used to make fertilizers, and is used in petroleum refining, metallurgy, and automobile batteries. Phosphoric acid, H_3PO_4, is used in making fertilizers, cleaners, and animal feed and as a flavoring agent. Nitric acid, HNO_3, is a volatile, unstable liquid that stains proteins yellow. It is used to make fertilizers, explosives, rubber, plastics, dyes, and drugs. Hydrochloric acid, HCl, also called *muriatic acid*, is used as a cleaning agent, in food processing, to pickle iron, and in activating oil wells. Hydrochloric acid is also produced in the stomach to aid digestion. Acetic acid, CH_3COOH, is an organic acid. It is a clear, colorless liquid produced by fermentation of cereal grains and fruit juices. It is found in household vinegar and is used to make plastics, food supplements, and fungicides.
4. HCl(*g*) consists of covalently bonded molecules that do not ionize. Nonpolar solvent molecules do not attract HCl molecules to cause them to be ionized.
5. **a.** Strong acids ionize 100% in dilute aqueous solution; weak acids ionize much less than 100%.
   b. examples of strong acids: HCl and HNO_3; examples of weak acids: HF and H_3PO_4
6. The strength of an acid depends on the degree of ionization, not on the amount of hydrogen in the molecule. HCl ionizes completely. H_3PO_4 ionizes only slightly.
7. **a.** concentration of OH^- ions in solution
   b. Answers will vary. For example, NaOH(*aq*) is a strong base; $NH_3(aq)$ is a weak base.
8. **a.** hydrochloric acid
   b. hydrosulfuric acid

CHAPTER REVIEW

9. a. nitric acid **c.** chloric acid
b. sulfurous acid **d.** nitrous acid

10. a. HF **b.** HI

11. a. $HBrO_4$ **b.** $HClO_2$ **c.** H_3PO_4 **d.** HClO

12. Monoprotic acids (HCl) can donate only one proton per molecule; diprotic acids (H_2SO_4) can donate two protons per molecule; and triprotic acids(H_3PO_4) can donate three protons per molecule.

13. The Lewis definition is the broadest. Any substance defined as an Arrhenius or Brønsted-Lowry acid is also an acid as defined by the Lewis theory. The reverse is not always true.

14. a. $H_2SO_4(l) + H_2O(l) \longrightarrow H_3O^+(aq) + HSO_4(aq)$;
$HSO_4(aq) + H_2O(l) \leftrightarrows H_3O^+(aq) + SO_4^{2}(aq)$

b. The degree of ionization in the first stage is much greater than that in the second.

15. a. $HCl(aq) + KOH(aq) \longrightarrow KCl(aq) + H_2O(l)$

b. $H_3O^+(aq) + Cl(aq) + K^+(aq) + OH(aq) \longrightarrow K^+(aq) + Cl(aq) + 2H_2O(l)$

c. $H_3O^+(aq) + OH(aq) \longrightarrow 2H_2O(l)$

16. a. $H_3PO_4(aq) + 3NaOH(aq) \longrightarrow Na_3PO_4(aq) + 3H_2O(l)$

b. $3H_3O^+(aq) + PO_4^3(aq) + 3Na^+(aq) + 3OH(aq) \longrightarrow 3Na^+(aq) + PO_4^3(aq) + 6H_2O(l)$

c. $H_3O^+(aq) + OH(aq) \longrightarrow 2H_2O(l)$ (Cancellation of spectator ions gives $3H_3O^+(aq) + 3OH(aq) \longrightarrow 6H_2O(l)$. Then divide out the common factor of 3 to give the net ionic equation with the smallest integer coefficients.)

17. a. $Zn(s) + 2HCl(aq) \longrightarrow ZnCl_2(aq) + H_2(g)$; $Zn(s) + 2H_3O^+(aq) \longrightarrow Zn^{2+}(aq) + H_2(g) + 2H_2O(l)$

b. $2Al(s) + 3H_2SO_4(aq) \longrightarrow Al_2(SO_4)_3(aq) + 3H_2(g)$;
$2Al(s) + 6H_3O^+(aq) \longrightarrow 2Al^{3+}(aq) + 3H_2(g) + 6H_2O(l)$

18. $Ca(s) + 2HCl(aq) \longrightarrow CaCl_2(aq) + H_2(g)$; $Ca(s) + 2H_3O^+(aq) \longrightarrow Ca^{2+}(aq) + H_2(g) + 2H_2O(l)$

19. a. A conjugate base remains after an acid has given up a proton. For example,
$HF + H_2O \longrightarrow H_3O^+ + F^-$
acid: HF; conjugate base: F^-

b. A conjugate acid is what forms when a proton is added to a base. For example, H_3O^+ is the conjugate acid of the base in H_2O.

20. a. The stronger an acid is, the weaker its conjugate base is.

b. The stronger a base is, the weaker its conjugate acid is.

21. a. Production of the weaker acid and weaker base is favored.

b. It depends on the relative strengths of the acids and bases involved. For an acid-base reaction to approach completion, the reactants must be much stronger acids and bases than the products are.

22. a. the term describes a species that can react as either an acid or a base

b. Answers will vary, may include $H_2PO_4^-$ is the conjugate base of H_3PO_4 and can act as an acid to further ionize to HPO_4^{2-}.

23. a. acid: CH_3COOH, conjugate base: CH_3COO^-; base: H_2O, conjugate acid: H_3O^+

CHAPTER 14 Review

SECTION 1

Properties of Acids and Bases

 REVIEWING MAIN IDEAS

1. Compare the general properties of acids with the general properties of bases.

2. a. Distinguish between binary acids and oxyacids in terms of their component elements and the systems used in naming them.
   b. Give three examples of each type of acid.

3. Identify and describe the characteristic properties of five common acids used in industry. Give some examples of the typical uses of each.

4. Although $HCl(aq)$ exhibits properties of an Arrhenius acid, pure HCl gas and HCl dissolved in a nonpolar solvent exhibit none of the properties of an Arrhenius acid. Explain why.

5. a. What distinguishes strong acids from weak acids?
   b. Give two examples each of strong acids and weak acids.

6. H_3PO_4, which contains three hydrogen atoms per molecule, is a weak acid, whereas HCl, which contains only one hydrogen atom per molecule, is a strong acid. Explain why.

7. a. What determines the strength of an Arrhenius base?
   b. Give one example each of an aqueous solution of a strong base and an aqueous solution of a weak base.

PRACTICE PROBLEMS

8. Name each of the following binary acids:
   a. HCl
   b. H_2S

9. Name each of the following oxyacids:
   a. HNO_3 c. $HClO_3$
   b. H_2SO_3 d. HNO_2

10. Write formulas for the following binary acids:
    a. hydrofluoric acid
    b. hydriodic acid

11. Write formulas for the following oxyacids:
    a. perbromic acid
    b. chlorous acid
    c. phosphoric acid
    d. hypochlorous acid

SECTION 2

Acid-Base Theories

 REVIEWING MAIN IDEAS

12. Distinguish between a monoprotic, a diprotic, and a triprotic acid. Give an example of each.

13. Which of the three acid definitions is the broadest? Explain.

PRACTICE PROBLEMS

14. a. Write the balanced equations that describe the two-step ionization of sulfuric acid in a dilute aqueous solution.
    b. How do the degrees of ionization in the two steps compare?

15. Dilute $HCl(aq)$ and $KOH(aq)$ are mixed in chemically equivalent quantities. Write the following:
    a. formula equation for the reaction
    b. overall ionic equation
    c. net ionic equation

16. Repeat item 15, but mix $H_3PO_4(aq)$ and $NaOH(aq)$.

17. Write the formula equation and net ionic equation for each of the following reactions:
    a. $Zn(s) + HCl(aq) \longrightarrow$
    b. $Al(s) + H_2SO_4(aq) \longrightarrow$

18. Write the formula equation and net ionic equation for the reaction between $Ca(s)$ and $HCl(aq)$.

SECTION 3

Acid-Base Reactions

 REVIEWING MAIN IDEAS

19. Define and give an equation to illustrate each of the following substances:
    a. a conjugate base
    b. a conjugate acid

20. a. What is the relationship between the strength of an acid and the strength of its conjugate base?
b. What is the relationship between the strength of a base and the strength of its conjugate acid?

21. a. What trend is there in the favored direction of proton-transfer reactions?
b. What determines the extent to which a proton-transfer reaction occurs?

22. a. What is meant by the term *amphoteric?*
b. Give an example of a substance or ion that has amphoteric characteristics.

23. For each reaction listed, identify the proton donor or acid and the proton acceptor or base. Label each conjugate acid-base pair.
a. $CH_3COOH(aq) + H_2O(l) \rightleftarrows H_3O+(aq) + CH_3COO-(aq)$
b. $HCO_3^-(aq) + H_2O(l) \rightleftarrows H_2CO_3(aq) + OH^-(aq)$
c. $HNO_3 + SO_4^{2-} \longrightarrow HSO_4^- + NO_3^-$

24. Using the information given in **Figure 3.1**, determine the following relative to HF, H_2S, HNO_3, and CH_3COOH:
a. strongest acid
b. weakest acid
c. strongest conjugate base among the four conjugate bases produced by the acids listed
d. weakest conjugate base among the four conjugate bases produced by the acids listed

25. Explain why the conjugate base of a strong acid is a weak base and the conjugate acid of a strong base is a weak acid.

PRACTICE PROBLEMS

26. Complete the following neutralization reactions. Balance each reaction, and then write the overall ionic and net ionic equation for each.
a. $HCl(aq) + NaOH(aq) \longrightarrow$
b. $HNO_3(aq) + KOH(aq) \longrightarrow$
c. $Ca(OH)_2(aq) + HNO_3(aq) \longrightarrow$
d. $Mg(OH)_2(aq) + HCl(aq) \longrightarrow$

27. Write the formula equation, the overall ionic equation, and the net ionic equation for the neutralization reaction involving aqueous solutions of H_3PO_4 and $Mg(OH)_2$. Assume that the solutions are sufficiently dilute so that no precipitates form.

28. Write the balanced chemical equation for each of the following reactions between water and the non-metallic oxide to form an acid.
a. $CO_2(g) + H_2O(l) \longrightarrow$
b. $SO_3(g) + H_2O(l) \longrightarrow$
c. $N_2O_5(g) + H_2O(l) \longrightarrow$

29. Write the formula equation, the overall ionic equation, and the net ionic equation for a neutralization reaction that would form each of the following salts.
a. $RbClO_4$ c. $CaCl_2$
b. $BaSO_4$ d. K_2SO_4

30. Zinc reacts with 100.0 mL of 6.00 M cold, aqueous sulfuric acid through single replacement.
a. How many grams of zinc sulfate can be produced?
b. How many liters of hydrogen gas could be released at STP?

31. A 211 g sample of barium carbonate, $BaCO_3$, reacts with a solution of nitric acid to give barium nitrate, carbon dioxide and water. If the acid is present in excess, what mass and volume of dry carbon dioxide gas at STP will be produced?

32. A seashell that is composed largely of calcium carbonate reacts with a solution of HCl. As a result, 1500 mL of dry CO_2 gas at STP is produced. The other products are $CaCl_2$ and H_2O.
a. How many grams of $CaCO_3$ are consumed in the reaction?
b. What volume of 2.00 M HCl solution is used in this reaction?

33. *Acid precipitation* is the term generally used to describe rain or snow that is more acidic than it normally is. One cause of acid precipitation is the formation of sulfuric and nitric acids from various sulfur and nitrogen oxides produced in volcanic eruptions, forest fires, and thunderstorms. In a typical volcanic eruption, for example, 3.50×10^8 kg SO_2 may be produced. If this amount of SO_2 were converted to H_2SO_4 according to the two-step process given below, how many kilograms of H_2SO_4 would be produced from such an eruption?

$$SO_2 + \frac{1}{2}O_2 \longrightarrow SO_3$$
$$SO_3 + H_2O \longrightarrow H_2SO_4$$

b. acid: H_2O, conjugate base: OH^-; base: HCO_3^-, conjugate acid: H_2CO_3
c. acid: HNO_3, conjugate base: NO_3^-; base: SO_4^{2-}, conjugate acid: HSO_4^-

24. a. HNO_3 **b.** H_2S **c.** HS^- **d.** NO_3^-

25. Strong acids and bases readily ionize or dissociate in solution. For a strong acid to remain ionized, the conjugate base and conjugate acid, respectively, must be too weak to compete successfully with the strong acid or the strong base.

26. a. $HCl(aq) + NaOH(aq) \longrightarrow NaCl(aq) + H_2O(l)$;
$H_3O^+(aq) + Cl^-(aq) + Na^+(aq) + OH^-(aq) \longrightarrow Na^+(aq) + Cl^-(aq) + 2H_2O(l)$;
$H_3O^+(aq) + OH^-(aq) \longrightarrow 2H_2O(l)$

b. $HNO_3(aq) + KOH(aq) \longrightarrow KNO_3(aq) + H_2O(l)$;
$H_3O^+(aq) + NO_3^-(aq) + K^+(aq) + OH^-(aq) \longrightarrow K^+(aq) + NO_3^-(aq) + 2H_2O(l)$;
$H_3O^+(aq) + OH^-(aq) \longrightarrow 2H_2O(l)$

c. $Ca(OH)_2(aq) + 2HNO_3(aq) \longrightarrow Ca(NO_3)_2(aq) + 2H_2O(l)$

CHAPTER REVIEW

$Ca_2^+(aq) + 2OH^-(aq) + 2H_3O^+(aq) + 2NO_3^-(aq) \longrightarrow Ca_2^+(aq) + 2NO_3^-(aq) + 4H_2O(l)$;
$H_3O^+(aq) + OH^-(aq) \longrightarrow 2H_2O(l)$

d. $Mg(OH)_2(aq) + 2HCl(aq) \longrightarrow MgCl_2(aq) + 2H_2O(l)$;
$Mg_2^+(aq) + 2OH^-(aq) + 2H_3O^+(aq) + 2Cl^-(aq) \longrightarrow Mg_2^+(aq) + 2Cl^-(aq) + 4H_2O(l)$;
$H_3O^+(aq) + OH^-(aq) \longrightarrow 2H_2O(l)$

27. $2H_3PO_4(aq) + 3Mg(OH)_2(aq) \longrightarrow Mg_3(PO_4)_2(aq) + 6H_2O(l)$;
$6H_3O^+(aq) + 2PO_4^{3-}(aq) + 3Mg_2^+(aq) + 6OH^-(aq) \longrightarrow 3Mg_2^+(aq) + 2PO_4^{3-}(aq) + 12H_2O(l)$;
$H_3O^+(aq) + OH^-(aq) \longrightarrow 2H_2O(l)$

28. a. $CO_2(g) + H_2O(l) \longrightarrow H_2CO_3(aq)$
b. $SO_3(g) + H_2O(l) \longrightarrow H_2SO_4(aq)$
c. $N_2O_5(g) + H_2O(l) \longrightarrow 2HNO_3(aq)$

29. a. $RbOH(aq) + HClO_4(aq) \longrightarrow RbClO_4(aq) + H_2O(l)$;
$Rb^+(aq) + OH^-(aq) + H_3O^+(aq) + ClO_4^-(aq) \longrightarrow Rb^+(aq) + ClO_4^-(aq) + 2H_2O(l)$;
$H_3O^+(aq) + OH^-(aq) \longrightarrow 2H_2O(l)$

b. $Ba(OH)_2(aq) + H_2SO_4(aq) \longrightarrow BaSO_4(s) + 2H_2O(l)$;
$Ba^{2+}(aq) + 2OH^-(aq) + 2H_3O^+(aq) + SO_4^{2-}(aq) \longrightarrow BaSO_4(s) + 4H_2O(l)$;
$Ba_2^+(aq) + 2OH^-(aq) + 2H_3O^+(aq) + SO_4^{2-}(aq) \longrightarrow BaSO_4(s) + 4H_2O(l)$ (There are no spectator ions, so the net ionic equation is the same as the overall ionic equation.)

c. $Ca(OH)_2(aq) + 2HCl(aq) \longrightarrow CaCl_2(aq) + 2H_2O(l)$;
$Ca^{2+}(aq) + 2OH^-(aq) + 2H_3O^+(aq) + 2Cl^-(aq) \longrightarrow Ca_2^+(aq) + 2Cl^-(aq) + 4H_2O(l)$;
$H_3O^+(aq) + OH^-(aq) \longrightarrow 2H_2O(l)$ (Cancellation of spectator ions gives $2H_3O^+(aq) + 2OH^-(aq) \longrightarrow 4H_2O(l)$; divide out the common factor of 2 to give the net ionic equation with the smallest integer coefficients.)

d. $2KOH(aq) + H_2SO_4(aq) \longrightarrow K_2SO_4(aq) + 2H_2O(l)$;
$2K^+(aq) + 2OH^-(aq) + 2H_3O^+(aq) + SO_4^{2-}(aq) \longrightarrow 2K^+(aq) + SO_4^{2-}(aq) + 4H_2O(l)$;
$H_3O^+(aq) + OH^-(aq) \longrightarrow 2H_2O(l)$

30. a. 96.9 g $ZnSO_4$ **b.** 13.4 L H_2

31. 47.1 g CO_2, 24.0 L CO_2

32. a. 6.7 g $CaCO_3$ **b.** 0.067 L (or 67 mL)

33. 5.36×10^8 kg H_2SO_4

34. a. $HNO_3(aq) + LiOH(aq) \longrightarrow LiNO_3(aq) + H_2O(l)$

b. $H_3O^+(aq) + NO_3^-(aq) + Li^+(aq) + OH^-(aq) \longrightarrow Li^+(aq) + NO_3^-(aq) + 2H_2O(l)$

c. $H_3O^+(aq) + OH^-(aq) \longrightarrow 2H_2O(l)$

35. $Mg(s) + 2HCl(aq) \longrightarrow MgCl_2(aq) + H_2(g)$

36. $H_3PO_4(aq) + H_2O(l) \leftrightarrows H_3O^+(aq) + H_2PO_4^-(aq)$; greatest degree of ionization

$H_2PO_4^-(aq) + H_2O(l) \leftrightarrows H_3O^+(aq) + HPO_4^{2-}(aq)$; less ionization

$HPO_4^{2-}(aq) + H_2O(l) \leftrightarrows H_3O^+(aq) + PO_4^{3-}(aq)$; least ionization

37. a. hydrofluoric acid; **b.** CH_3COOH **c.** H_3PO_3; **d.** perchloric acid; **e.** phosphoric acid; **f.** HBr; **g.** hypochlorous acid; **h.** carbonic acid; **i.** H_2SO_4

38. Answers will vary. Should include examples of acids that do not contain oxygen (HCl or HBr). They should discuss how acids are defined, including ways that narrow or broaden the definition and that do not require oxygen in the acid.

39. a. Oxides of nonmetals are acidic.

b. Acid anhydrides are oxide compounds that react with water to form acids.

c. The following are possible responses: B_2O_3, CO_2, N_2O_5, P_4O_{10}, SO_3, SeO_3, TeO_3, Cl_2O, I_2O_5.

d. Basic oxides are the dehydrated forms of the hydroxides of reactive metals (Groups 1 and 2). Basic oxides form metal hydroxides when reacted with water.

40. a. Basic oxides come from elements on the far left of the table. Elements in the metalloid region of the table form amphoteric oxides. Nonmetals form acidic oxides. Oxide character within a group is related to metallic character within a group.

b. Reactions of CO_2 with excess NaOH will produce Na_2CO_3. Reactions of CO_2 with a limited amount of NaOH (less than the mole ratio) will result in the production of $NaHCO_3$.

41. Sulfuric acid is involved in many technical and manufacturing processes. Typically, the more highly industrialized a country is, the greater the amount of sulfuric acid consumed by that country in the course of its everyday industrial activities. Thus, sulfuric acid production can serve as a measure of the degree of industrialization and economic activity of a country.

42. Refer to **HMDScience.com** for appropriate scoring rubrics. Answers should include an explanation of how buffers cause solutions to be resistant to changes in acidity or basicity.

43. Answers will vary.

44. Answers should include $CaCO_3$, $NaHCO_3$, $Mg(OH)_2$, and $Al(OH)_3$.

45. Check the design of experiments before students proceed.

CHAPTER REVIEW

Mixed Review

REVIEWING MAIN IDEAS

34. Suppose that dilute $HNO_3(aq)$ and $LiOH(aq)$ are mixed in chemically equivalent quantities. Write the following for the resulting reaction:
- **a.** formula equation
- **b.** overall ionic equation
- **c.** net ionic equation

35. Write the balanced chemical equation for the reaction between hydrochloric acid and magnesium metal.

36. Write equations for the three-step ionization of phosphoric acid, H_3PO_4. Compare the degree of ionization for the three steps.

37. Name or give the molecular formula for each of the following acids:
- **a.** HF
- **b.** acetic acid
- **c.** phosphorous acid
- **d.** $HClO_4$
- **e.** H_3PO_4
- **f.** hydrobromic acid
- **g.** HClO
- **h.** H_2CO_3
- **i.** sulfuric acid

CRITICAL THINKING

38. Analyzing Conclusions In the 18th century, Antoine Lavoisier experimented with oxides, such as CO_2 and SO_2. He observed that they formed acidic solutions. His observations led him to infer that to exhibit acidic behavior, a substance must contain oxygen. However, today that inference is known to be incorrect. Provide evidence to refute Lavoisier's conclusion.

USING THE HANDBOOK

39. Group 16 of the *Elements Handbook* (Appendix A) contains a section covering the acid-base chemistry of oxides. Review this material, and answer the following questions:
- **a.** What types of compounds form acidic oxides?
- **b.** What is an acid anhydride?
- **c.** What are three examples of compounds that are classified as acid anhydrides?
- **d.** What types of compounds form basic oxides? Why are they basic oxides?

40. a. Look at Table 7A in the *Elements Handbook* (Appendix A). What periodic trends regarding the acid-base character of oxides do you notice?

b. How is the nature of the product affected by the concentrations of the reactants?

RESEARCH AND WRITING

41. Explain how sulfuric acid production serves as a measure of a country's economy. Write a report on your findings.

42. Performance Conduct library research to find out about the buffering of solutions. Include information on why solutions are buffered and what kinds of materials are used as buffers. Write a brief report on your findings.

43. Research how to determine whether the soil around your house is acidic or basic using pH paper obtained from your teacher. Write a brief description of what you should do, then follow the directions and test the soil. Find one type of plant that would grow well in the type of soil around your home and one that would not grow well.

ALTERNATIVE ASSESSMENT

44. Antacids are designed to neutralize excess hydrochloric acid secreted by the stomach during digestion. Carbonates, bicarbonates, and hydroxides are the active ingredients in the most widely used antacids. These ingredients act to drive the neutralization reactions. Examine the labels of several common antacids, and identify the active ingredients.

45. Design an experiment that compares three brands of antacids in terms of the speed of symptom relief and amount of acid neutralized.

468 Chapter 14

Standards-Based Assessment

Answer the following items on a separate piece of paper.

MULTIPLE CHOICE

1. Which of the following is *not* a characteristic of an acid?
A. An acid changes the color of an indicator.
B. An acid has a bitter taste.
C. An acid ionizes in water.
D. An acid produces hydronium ions in water.

2. When an acid reacts with an active metal,
A. the hydronium ion concentration increases.
B. the metal forms anions.
C. hydrogen gas is produced.
D. carbon dioxide gas is produced.

3. Which of the following is a Brønsted-Lowry base?
A. an electron pair donor
B. an electron pair acceptor
C. a proton donor
D. a proton acceptor

4. Which acid is the most commonly produced industrial chemical?
A. hydrochloric acid
B. acetic acid
C. nitric acid
D. sulfuric acid

5. Which of the following is a conjugate pair?
A. H^+ and OH^-
B. NH_2 and NH_4^+
C. HCl and Cl^-
D. H_2SO_4 and SO_4^{2-}

6. What is the formula for acetic acid?
A. CH_3COOH
B. HNO_3
C. $HClO_4$
D. HCN

7. Which of the following species is the conjugate acid of another species in the list?
A. PO_4^{3-}
B. H_3PO_4
C. H_2O
D. $H_2PO_4^-$

8. Identify the salt that forms when a solution of H_2SO_4 is titrated with a solution of $Ca(OH)_2$.
A. calcium sulfate
B. calcium hydroxide
C. calcium oxide
D. calcium phosphate

9. Which of the following statements is true for the reaction below?

$$HF(aq) + HPO_4^{2-}(aq) \rightleftharpoons F^-(aq) + H_2PO_4^-(aq)$$

A. HF is the base.
B. HPO_4^{2-} is the acid.
C. F^- is the conjugate base.
D. $H_2PO_4^-$ is the conjugate base.

SHORT ANSWER

10. How does a strong acid differ from a weak acid? Give one example of each.

11. Identify the conjugate acid-base pairs in the following reaction:

$$HClO_2(aq) + NH_3(aq) \rightleftharpoons ClO_2^-(aq) + NH_4^+(aq)$$

EXTENDED RESPONSE

12. Phosphoric acid, H_3PO_4, has three hydrogen atoms and is classified as a triprotic acid. Acetic acid, CH_3COOH, has four hydrogen atoms and is classified as a monoprotic acid. Explain the difference, and justify your explanation by drawing the Lewis structure for both acids.

13. Write the full equation, ionic equation, and net ionic equation for the neutralization reaction between ammonia and sulfuric acid. Identify the spectator ion(s).

Test Tip
Double check (with a calculator, if permitted) all mathematical computations involved in answering a question.

STANDARDS-BASED ASSESSMENT

To give students practice under more realistic testing conditions, give them 60 minutes to answer all of the questions in this Standardized Test Preparation.

Test Answers

1. B
2. C
3. D
4. D
5. C
6. A
7. B
8. A
9. C
10. A strong acid is 100% ionized; a weak acid is less than 100% ionized. Possible strong acids are HCl, HI, HBr, HNO_3, H_2SO_4, $HClO_4$, and $HClO_3$. With very few exceptions, any other acid will be a weak acid.
11. $HClO_2(aq)$ $acid_1$, $ClO_2^-(aq)$ $base_1$; $NH_3(aq)$ $base_2$, $NH_4^+(aq)$ $acid_2$
12. Each of the H atoms in phosphoric acid is attached to an oxygen atom and can ionize. Only one of the H atoms in acetic acid is attached to an oxygen atom and can be ionized. The three H atoms bonded to C do not ionize; thus, acetic acid is a monoprotic acid.

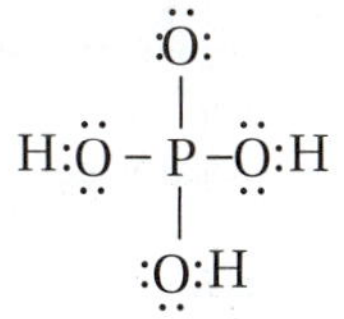

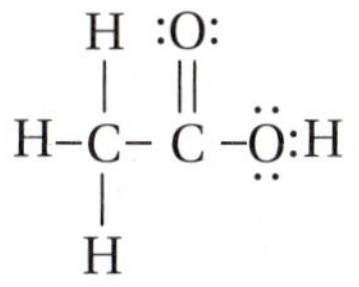

```
        :Ö:
         |
  H:Ö – P –Ö:H
         |
       :O:H

     H  :O:
     |  ||
  H–C– C –Ö:H
     |
     H
```

13. $2NH_3(aq) + H_2SO_4(aq) \longrightarrow (NH_4)_2SO_4(aq)$;
$2NH_3(aq) + 2H_3O^+(aq) + SO_4^{2-}(aq) \longrightarrow 2NH_4^+(aq) + SO_4^{2-}(aq) + 2H_2O(l)$;
$2NH_3(aq) + 2H_3O^+(aq) \longrightarrow 2NH_4^+(aq) + 2H_2O(l)$;
SO_4^{2-} is the spectator ion.

Acid-Base Titration and pH

① Core Instruction

Chapter Resources

- The Teacher's Edition wrap has extensive teaching support for every lesson, including Misconception Alerts, Teach from Visuals, Demonstrations, Teaching Tips, Differentiated Instruction, and Problem Solving support.
- Several additional presentation tools are available online for every chapter, including Animated Chemistry features and Visual Concepts.
- You can open your lesson with the Why It Matters Video: Acids and Bases.

Section	Instruction	Labs and Demonstrations Go Online for Materials Lists and Solutions Lists.
15.1	■ **Textbook:** **Aqueous Solutions and the Concept of pH** **Teaching Visuals:** pH Values at Specified $[H_3O^+]$ • Some Strong Acids and Some Weak Acids • $[H_3O^+]$, $[OH^-]$, pH, and pOH of Solutions • Approximate pH Range of Common Materials • Concentrations and K_w • Using Logarithms in pH Calculations • pH of Strong and Weak Acids and Bases **PowerPresentations**	■ **Demonstration:** Comparing Concentrations ■ **Demonstration:** The pH of Common Materials ■ **Lab:** Hydronium Ion Concentration and pH (Core Skill) ■ **Lab:** Wetlands Acid Spill (Forensics) ■ **Lab:** To Grow or Not To Grow (Open Inquiry)
15.2	■ **Textbook:** **Determining pH and Titrations** **Animated Chemistry:** Titration **Teaching Visuals:** pH Values of Some Common Materials • Color Ranges of Indicators • Titration Curve for a Strong Acid and a Strong Base • Titration Curve for a Weak Acid and a Strong Base • Performing a Titration, Part 1 • Performing a Titration, Part 2 • Transition Ranges of Some Indicators **PowerPresentations**	■ **Demonstration:** Natural Indicators ■ **Demonstration:** pH Change in an Acid-Base Titration ■ **Demonstration:** Reading a Meniscus ■ **QuickLab:** Testing the pH of Rainwater ■ **Lab:** How Much Calcium Carbonate Is in an Eggshell? (Core Skill) ■ **Lab:** Acid-Base Titration (Probeware) ■ **Lab:** Titration with an Acid and a Base (Core Skill) ■ **Lab:** Determination of Acetic Acid in Vinegar (Core Skill) ■ **Lab:** Determination of Vitamin C in Fruit Juices (Core Skill) ■ **Lab:** How Effective Are Antacids? (Core Skill) ■ **Lab:** Shampoo Chemistry (Core Skill) ■ **Lab:** How Do Pollutants Affect a Lake? (Forensics)

2 Support and Intervention

- **Interactive Reader** (English and Spanish)
- **Study Guide**
- **Interactive Review:** Review Games, Concept Maps, and Section Self-Checks
- **Scientific Reasoning Skill Builder**
- **Learn It! Videos**
- **Solve It! Cards**
- **Interactive Demos**
- **Sample Problem Sets**

3 Specialized Support

- **Chapter Summary Audio Files**
- **Interactive Reader Audio Files**
- **Differentiated Instruction:** Inclusion, Below Level, and English Learners (TE wrap)

Enrichment and Challenge

- **Differentiated Instruction:** Pre-AP (TE wrap)
- **Cross-Disciplinary Connection:** Liming Streams (SE)
- **WebLinks**

Assessment

- **Section Formative Assessments** (SE)
- **Section Quizzes**
- **Chapter Review** (SE)
- **Chapter Tests A and B**
- **Alternative Assessment** (TE wrap)
- **Online Assessment and Remediation**
- **ExamView Banks**

Where do I find it?

	Resource	PRINT	DVD	ONLINE
1	Animated Chemistry		■	■
1	Demonstrations (TE wrap)	■		■
1	Interactive Whiteboard		■	■
1	Labs		■	■
1	PowerPresentations		■	■
1	QuickLabs	■	■	■
1	Teaching Visuals		■	■
1	Textbook	■	■	■
1	Visual Concepts		■	■
1	Why It Matters Videos		■	■
2	Interactive Demos		■	■
2	Interactive Reader	■	■	■
2	Interactive Reviews		■	■
2	Learn It! Videos		■	■
2	Sample Problem Sets		■	■
2	Scientific Reasoning Skill Builder		■	■
2	Smart Grapher Tool		■	■
2	Solve It! Cards		■	■
2	Study Guide		■	■
3	Chapter Summary Audio Files		■	■
3	Differentiated Instruction (TE wrap)	■		
3	Interactive Reader Audio Files		■	■

CHAPTER 15

Chapter Overview

Section 1 covers the ionization of water and the equilibrium concentrations of H_3O^+ and OH^- in water and in aqueous solutions of acids and bases. The concept of pH is presented mathematically.

Section 2 explains how acid-base indicators work, how indicators and pH meters are used to determine the pH of a solution, and how titrations are used to measure the concentration or mass of a substance in a sample.

▼ Focus and Motivate

Activate Prior Knowledge

Students may need a review of the following concepts:

- stoichiometric calculations
- the nature of solutions
- ionization of solutes
- acids, bases, and neutralization reactions

About the Image

Hydrangeas come in a variety of colors, including white, pink, and blue. This variety of colors depends on compounds called indicators. Acids and bases change the color of indicators.

Why It Matters

Students can access the video online and find other helpful resources at **HMDScience.com**.

CHAPTER 15

Acid-Base Titration and pH

ONLINE Chemistry
HMDScience.com

SECTION 1
Aqueous Solutions and the Concept of pH

SECTION 2
Determining pH and Titrations

ONLINE LABS include:

Hydronium Ion Concentration and pH

Wetlands Acid Spill

How Much Calcium Carbonate Is in an Eggshell?

Titration with an Acid and a Base

Shampoo Chemistry

PREMIUM CONTENT
Why It Matters Video
HMDScience.com
Acids and Bases

Lab Preview

The following labs and demonstrations support the concepts in this chapter.

LABS

Hydronium Ion Concentration and pH (Core Skill)

Wetlands Acid Spill (Forensics)

How Much Calcium Carbonate Is in an Eggshell? (Core Skill)

Acid-Base Titration (Probeware)

Titration with an Acid and a Base (Core Skill)

Determination of Acetic Acid in Vinegar

Determination of Vitamin C in Fruit Juices

How Effective Are Antacids? (Core Skill)

Shampoo Chemistry (Core Skill)

How Do Pollutants Affect a Lake? (Forensics)

QUICKLAB

Testing the pH of Rainwater

DEMONSTRATIONS

Comparing Concentrations

The pH of Common Materials

Natural Indicators

pH Change in an Acid-Base Titration

Reading a Meniscus

Aqueous Solutions and the Concept of pH

SECTION 1

Main Ideas

- Self-ionization of water forms hydronium and hydroxide ions.
- The concentrations of hydronium and hydroxide ions determine pH and pOH.
- The sum of a solution's pH and pOH is always 14.

Key Terms

self-ionization of water
pH
pOH

MAIN IDEA

Self-ionization of water forms hydronium and hydroxide ions.

You have already seen that acids and bases form hydronium ions and hydroxide ions, respectively, in aqueous solutions. However, these ions formed from the solute are not the only such ions present in an aqueous solution. Hydronium ions and hydroxide ions are also provided by the solvent, water.

Self-Ionization of Water

Careful electrical conductivity experiments have shown that pure water is an extremely weak electrolyte. Water undergoes self-ionization, as shown in the model in **Figure 1.1.** In the **self-ionization of water,** two water molecules produce a hydronium ion and a hydroxide ion by transfer of a proton. The following equilibrium takes place.

$$H_2O(l) + H_2O(l) \rightleftharpoons H_3O^+(aq) + OH^-(aq)$$

Conductivity measurements show that concentrations of H_3O^+ and OH^- in pure water are each only 1.0×10^{-7} mol/L of water at 25°C.

FIGURE 1.1

Self-Ionization of Water Water undergoes self-ionization to a slight extent. A proton is transferred from one water molecule to another. A hydronium ion, H_3O^+, and a hydroxide ion, OH^-, are produced.

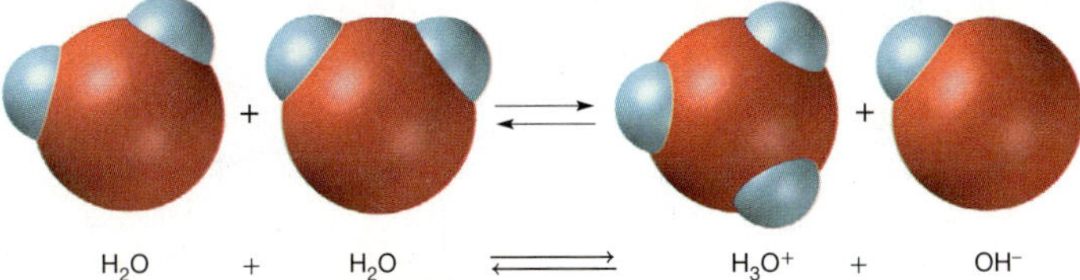

Differentiated Instruction

BELOW LEVEL

Relating concepts to one another can help students solidify their understanding of the vocabulary. Review the definition of *amphoteric substance,* and then ask students to explain this statement: "The equation for the self-ionization of water shows that water is an amphoteric substance." Students should explain that one of the two water molecules in the equation acts as a Brønsted-Lowry acid by donating a proton to form $OH^-(aq)$. The other acts as a Brønsted-Lowry base by accepting the proton to form $H_3O^+(aq)$.

SECTION 1

Plan and Prepare ▼

Objectives

Upon completion of this section, students should be able to do the following:

- Describe the self-ionization of water.
- Define *pH*, and give the pH of a neutral solution at 25°C.
- Explain and use the pH scale.
- Given $[H_3O^+]$ or $[OH^-]$, find pH.
- Given pH, find $[H_3O^+]$ or $[OH^-]$.

Classroom Catalyst

Have students view a model, board artwork, or overhead (with reaction not showing) representing the ionization of water, as shown in **Figure 1.1.** Ask them to describe what they think is taking place in this reaction.

Teach ▼

READING TOOLKIT

K/W/L Write the term *pH* on the board. Have students list what they know or think they know about pH. Then have them list what they want to know about pH and its relation to acids and bases. After they have read Section 1, have them look at their lists and write down what they have learned about the pH of acids and bases. Also have them write down any new questions that they have after reading the section.

TEACH FROM VISUALS

FIGURE 1.1 Ask students to compare their Classroom Catalyst responses with what they now know about this figure. Point out the charges on the ions.

Teaching Tip

In 5 000 L of pure water, less than one drop would be ionized.

▼ Teach *continued*

TEACH FROM TABLES

FIGURE 1.2 This table once again emphasizes the importance of specifying conditions when stating a measured quantity. Students should note the variation of K_w in the range from 0°C to 50°C and realize the importance of citing temperature.

Teaching Tip

Important relationships involving acidic, neutral, and basic solutions will be summarized in **Figure 1.7.** It is suggested that you emphasize the most important of these relationships now:

Acidic: $[H_3O^+] > [OH^-]$
Neutral: $[H_3O^+] = [OH^-]$
Basic: $[H_3O^+] < [OH^-]$

TEACH FROM VISUALS

FIGURE 1.3 Write the equations for the reactions shown in the figure to emphasize that H_3O^+ is produced in the reaction in part (a) and OH^- is produced in the reaction in part (b).

(a) $CO_2(g) + H_2O(l) \longrightarrow H_2CO_3(aq)$;
$H_2CO_3(aq) + H_2O(l) \rightleftarrows H_3O^+(aq) + HCO_3^-(aq)$

(b) $Na_2O_2(s) + 2H_2O(l) \longrightarrow 2Na^+(aq) + 2OH^-(aq) + H_2O_2(g)$

Ask students to speculate how $[OH^-]$ and $[H_3O^+]$ change as each reaction takes place.

FIGURE 1.2

K_W AT SELECTED TEMPERATURES

Temperature (°C)	K_w
0	1.2×10^{-15}
10	3.0×10^{-15}
25	1.0×10^{-14}
50	5.3×10^{-14}

There is a standard notation to show concentration in moles per liter. The formula of the particular ion or molecule is enclosed in brackets, [ ]. For example, the symbol $[H_3O^+]$ means "hydronium ion concentration in moles per liter," or "molar hydronium ion concentration." In water at 25°C, $[H_3O^+] = 1.0 \times 10^{-7}$ M and $[OH^-] = 1.0 \times 10^{-7}$ M.

The mathematical product of $[H_3O^+]$ and $[OH^-]$ remains constant in water and dilute aqueous solutions at constant temperature. This constant mathematical product is called the *ionization constant of water*, K_w, and is expressed by the following equation.

$$K_w = [H_3O^+][OH^-]$$

For example, in water and dilute aqueous solutions at 25°C, the following relationship is valid.

$$K_w = [H_3O^+][OH^-] = (1.0 \times 10^{-7})(1.0 \times 10^{-7}) = 1.0 \times 10^{-14}$$

The ionization of water increases as temperature increases. Therefore, the ion product, K_w, also increases as temperature increases, as shown in **Figure 1.2.** However, at any given temperature K_w is always a constant value. The value 1.0×10^{-14} is assumed to be constant within the ordinary range of room temperatures. In this chapter, you can assume that these conditions are present unless otherwise stated.

Neutral, Acidic, and Basic Solutions

Because the hydronium ion and hydroxide ion concentrations are the same in pure water, it is *neutral*. In fact, any solution in which $[H_3O^+] = [OH^-]$ is neutral. Recall that acids increase the concentration of H_3O^+ in aqueous solutions, as shown in **Figure 1.3a.** Solutions in which the $[H_3O^+]$ is greater than the $[OH^-]$ are *acidic*. Bases increase the concentration of OH^- in aqueous solutions, as shown in **Figure 1.3b.** In *basic* solutions, the $[OH^-]$ is greater than the $[H_3O^+]$.

FIGURE 1.3

Identifying Acids and Bases

(a) Addition of dry ice, carbon dioxide, to water increases the $[H_3O^+]$, which is shown by the color change of the indicator bromthymol blue to yellow. The white mist is formed by condensation of water vapor because the dry ice is cold.

(b) Addition of sodium peroxide to water increases the $[OH^-]$, which is shown by the color change of the indicator phenolphthalein to pink.

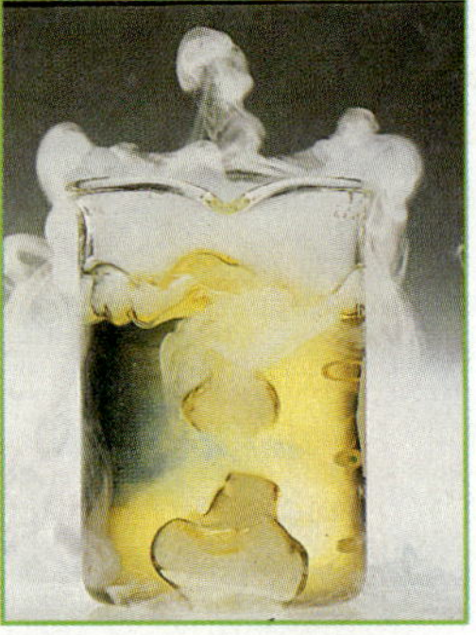

(a)

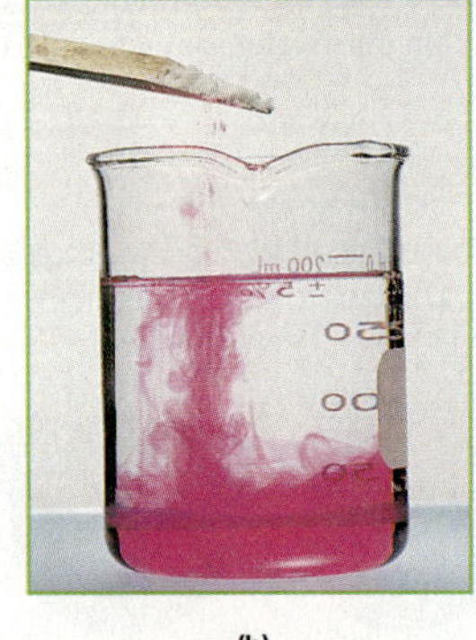

(b)

Differentiated Instruction

BELOW LEVEL

Have students review scientific notation by solving problems involving K_w. Ask students to work in pairs. One student should give a value for either $[H_3O^+]$ or $[OH^-]$. The other student should then calculate the unknown concentration and state whether the solution is acidic or basic. Be sure that students use only whole numbers at this point and do not give decimal values, such as 1.5×10^{-6}. Point out that they will learn how to deal with such values by using logarithms later in this section.

As stated earlier, the $[H_3O^+]$ and the $[OH^-]$ of a neutral solution at 25°C both equal 1.0×10^{-7} M. Therefore, if the $[H_3O^+]$ is increased to greater than 1.0×10^{-7} M, the solution becomes acidic. A solution containing 1.0×10^{-5} mol H_3O^+ ion/L at 25°C is acidic because 1.0×10^{-5} is greater than 1.0×10^{-7}. If the $[OH^-]$ is increased to greater than 1.0×10^{-7} M, the solution becomes basic. A solution containing 1.0×10^{-4} mol OH^- ions/L at 25°C is basic because 1.0×10^{-4} is greater than 1.0×10^{-7}.

Calculating $[H_3O^+]$ and $[OH^-]$

Recall that strong acids and bases are considered completely ionized or dissociated in weak aqueous solutions. A review of strong acids and bases is given in **Figure 1.4.** Because NaOH is a strong base, 1 mol of it will yield 1 mol of OH^- in an aqueous solution.

$$\underset{1\text{ mol}}{\mathrm{NaOH}(s)} \xrightarrow{\mathrm{H_2O}} \underset{1\text{ mol}}{\mathrm{Na^+}(aq)} + \underset{1\text{ mol}}{\mathrm{OH^-}(aq)}$$

Therefore, a 1.0×10^{-2} M NaOH solution has an $[OH^-]$ of 1.0×10^{-2} M, as shown by the following.

$$\frac{1.0 \times 10^{-2}\ \cancel{\text{mol NaOH}}}{1\text{ L solution}} \times \frac{1\text{ mol OH}^-}{1\ \cancel{\text{mol NaOH}}} = \frac{1.0 \times 10^{-2}\text{ mol OH}^-}{1\text{ L solution}}$$

$$= 1.0 \times 10^{-2}\text{ M OH}^-$$

Notice that the $[OH^-]$ is greater than 1.0×10^{-7} M. This solution is basic.

Because the K_w of an aqueous solution is a relatively constant 1.0×10^{-14} at ordinary room temperatures, the concentration of either ion can be determined if the concentration of the other ion is known. The $[H_3O^+]$ of this solution is calculated as follows.

$$K_w = [H_3O^+][OH^-] = 1.0 \times 10^{-14}$$

$$[H_3O^+] = \frac{1.0 \times 10^{-14}}{[OH^-]} = \frac{1.0 \times 10^{-14}}{1.0 \times 10^{-2}} = 1.0 \times 10^{-12}\text{ M}$$

The $[OH^-]$, 1.0×10^{-2} M, is greater than the $[H_3O^+]$, 1.0×10^{-12} M, as is true for all basic solutions.

Now consider a 2.0×10^{-4} M HCl solution. Because HCl is a strong acid, the $[H_3O^+]$ is 2.0×10^{-4} M, as shown by the following.

$$\underset{1\text{ mol}}{\mathrm{HCl}(g)} + \underset{1\text{ mol}}{\mathrm{H_2O}(l)} \longrightarrow \underset{1\text{ mol}}{\mathrm{H_3O^+}(aq)} + \underset{1\text{ mol}}{\mathrm{Cl^-}(aq)}$$

$$\frac{2.0 \times 10^{-4}\ \cancel{\text{mol HCl}}}{1\text{ L solution}} \times \frac{1\text{ mol H}_3\text{O}^+}{1\ \cancel{\text{mol HCl}}} = \frac{2.0 \times 10^{-4}\text{ mol H}_3\text{O}^+}{1\text{ L solution}}$$

$$= 2.0 \times 10^{-4}\text{ M H}_3\text{O}^+$$

Notice that the $[H_3O^+]$ is greater than 1.0×10^{-7} M. This solution is acidic. The $[OH^-]$ of this solution is calculated as follows.

$$K_w = [H_3O^+][OH^-] = 1.0 \times 10^{-14}$$

$$[OH^-] = \frac{1.0 \times 10^{-14}}{[H_3O^+]} = \frac{1.0 \times 10^{-14}}{2.0 \times 10^{-4}} = 5.0 \times 10^{-10}\text{ M}$$

The $[H_3O^+]$ is greater than the $[OH^-]$ for all acidic solutions.

FIGURE 1.4

COMMON STRONG ACIDS AND BASES

Strong Acids	Strong Bases
HCl	LiOH
HBr	NaOH
HI	KOH
$HClO_4$	RbOH
$HClO_3$	CsOH
HNO_3	$Ca(OH)_2$
H_2SO_4	$Sr(OH)_2$
	$Ba(OH)_2$

Teaching Tip

The convention for expressing equilibrium constants (for example, K_w) is to exclude units. This convention will be used here and in other chapters. The reason is that true equilibrium constants are activities, which are ratios of two concentrations and therefore are expressed without units. For dilute solutions, concentrations and activities are essentially the same, so that distinction will not be made in this text.

Teaching Strategy

It is helpful to correlate the common strong bases with the periodic table. These are the hydroxides of the Group 1 metals (formulas MOH) and of the heavier Group 2 metals (formulas $M(OH)_2$).

Teaching Tip

When an acid is added to a solution, the $[H_3O^+]$ increases. Because there is an excess of H_3O^+ ions, some of the H_3O^+ ions react with OH^- ions and reduce the $[OH^-]$. At 25°C, this process continues until $[H_3O^+][OH^-] = 1.0 \times 10^{-14}$.

ChemisTrivia

Not all alkaline-earth hydroxides are soluble, and therefore some do not produce a large concentration of hydroxide ions in water. This is why milk of magnesia—a suspension of $Mg(OH)_2$—can be consumed as an antacid or as a laxative.

Problem Solving

TAKE IT FURTHER

Have students calculate the $[OH^-]$ and $[H_3O^+]$ of a 1.0×10^{-3} M $Ca(OH)_2$ solution. Point out that calcium hydroxide is not very soluble in water. However, what does dissolve completely dissociates in aqueous solution. Therefore, $Ca(OH)_2$ produces a dilute solution of a strong base.

For every mol of $Ca(OH)_2$, 2 mol of OH^- ions are produced. As a result, in a 1.0×10^{-3} M $Ca(OH)_2$ solution, the $[OH^-] = 2.0 \times 10^{-3}$ M. Substituting this value into the K_w results in the $[H_3O^+] = 5.0 \times 10^{-12}$ M.

Ask students whether the solution is acidic or basic. Have them explain their choice.

The solution is basic, because the $[OH^-]$ is greater than the $[H_3O^+]$.

▼ Teach *continued*

Classroom Practice

A-1 Determine the $[H_3O^+]$ and $[OH^-]$ in a 0.01 M solution of $HClO_4$.

Answer: $[H_3O^+] = 1 \times 10^{-2}$ M; $[OH^-] = 1 \times 10^{-12}$ M

A-2 An aqueous solution of $Ba(OH)_2$ has a $[H_3O^+]$ of 1×10^{-11} M. What is the $[OH^-]$? What is the molarity of the solution?

Answer: $[OH^-] = 1 \times 10^{-3}$ M; 5×10^{-4} M $Ba(OH)_2$

Misconception Alert!

Students may have difficulty understanding that 1×10^{-5} is a smaller number than 1×10^{-2}. Have students write the decimal equivalents, 0.00001 and 0.01, to emphasize the difference between the two numbers.

Answers

Practice A

a. $[H_3O^+] = 1 \times 10^{-4}$ M; $[OH^-] = 1 \times 10^{-10}$ M

b. $[H_3O^+] = 1.0 \times 10^{-3}$ M; $[OH^-] = 1.0 \times 10^{-11}$ M

c. $[H_3O^+] = 3.3 \times 10^{-13}$ M; $[OH^-] = 3.0 \times 10^{-2}$ M

d. $[H_3O^+] = 5.0 \times 10^{-11}$ M; $[OH^-] = 2.0 \times 10^{-4}$ M

You may have realized that in order for K_w to remain constant, an increase in either the $[H_3O^+]$ or the $[OH^-]$ in an aqueous solution causes a decrease in the concentration of the other ion. Sample Problem A also shows calculation of the $[H_3O^+]$ and $[OH^-]$ of an acidic solution.

PREMIUM CONTENT

Learn It! Video
HMDScience.com

Solve It! Cards
HMDScience.com

Calculating Hydronium and Hydroxide Concentrations

Sample Problem A **A 1.0×10^{-4} M solution of HNO_3 has been prepared for a laboratory experiment. a. Calculate the $[H_3O^+]$ of this solution. b. Calculate the $[OH^-]$.**

1 ANALYZE

Given: Concentration of the solution $= 1.0 \times 10^{-4}$ M HNO_3

Unknown: **a.** $[H_3O^+]$ **b.** $[OH^-]$

2 PLAN

HNO_3 is a strong acid, which means that it is essentially 100% ionized in dilute solutions. One molecule of acid produces one hydronium ion. The concentration of the hydronium ions thus equals the concentration of the acid. Because the ion product, $[H_3O^+][OH^-]$, is a constant, $[OH^-]$ can easily be determined by using the value for $[H_3O^+]$.

a. $HNO_3(l) + H_2O(l) \longrightarrow H_3O^+(aq) + NO_3^-(aq)$ (assuming 100% ionization)

1 mol 1 mol 1 mol 1 mol

$$\text{molarity of } HNO_3 = \frac{\text{mol } HNO_3}{\text{1 L solution}}$$

$$\frac{\cancel{\text{mol } HNO_3}}{\text{L solution}} \times \frac{\text{1 mol } H_3O^+}{\cancel{\text{1 mol } HNO_3}} = \frac{\text{mol } H_3O^+}{\text{L solution}} = \text{molarity of } H_3O^+$$

b. $[H_3O^+][OH^-] = 1.0 \times 10^{-14}$

$$[OH^-] = \frac{1.0 \times 10^{-14}}{[H_3O^+]}$$

3 SOLVE

a. $$\frac{1.0 \times 10^{-4}\ \cancel{\text{mol } HNO_3}}{\text{1 L solution}} \times \frac{\text{1 mol } H_3O^+}{\cancel{\text{1 mol } HNO_3}} = \frac{1.0 \times 10^{-4}\ \text{M } H_3O^+}{\text{1 L solution}} = 1.0 \times 10^{-4}\ \text{M } H_3O^+$$

b. $$[OH^-] = \frac{1.0 \times 10^{-14}}{[H_3O^+]} = \frac{1.0 \times 10^{-14}}{1.0 \times 10^{-4}} = 1.0 \times 10^{-10}\ \text{M}$$

4 CHECK YOUR WORK

Because the $[H_3O^+]$, 1.0×10^{-4}, is greater than 1.0×10^{-7}, the $[OH^-]$ must be less than 1.0×10^{-7}. The answers are correctly expressed to two significant digits.

Practice Answers in Appendix E

1. Determine the hydronium and hydroxide ion concentrations in a solution that is:

a. 1×10^{-4} M HCl.

b. 1.0×10^{-3} M HNO_3.

c. 3.0×10^{-2} M NaOH.

d. 1.0×10^{-4} M $Ca(OH)_2$.

Problem Solving

DECONSTRUCTING PROBLEMS

Point out that the first step in calculating the $[H_3O^+]$ and $[OH^-]$ is to write the ionic equation for the dissociation or ionization process that the given solution undergoes. Looking at the mole ratios in the balanced equation will tell students the $[H_3O^+]$ or $[OH^-]$. As an example, write the ionic equation for the dissociation of barium hydroxide on the board: $Ba(OH)_2(s) \longrightarrow Ba^{2+}(aq) + 2OH^-(aq)$. Point out why the $[OH^-]$ will be twice that of the given molarity of the barium hydroxide solution.

MAIN IDEA

The concentrations of hydronium and hydroxide ions determine pH and pOH.

Expressing acidity or basicity in terms of the concentration of H_3O^+ or OH^- can be cumbersome because the values tend to be very small. A more convenient quantity, called pH, also indicates the hydronium ion concentration of a solution. The letters *pH* stand for the French words *pouvoir hydrogène*, meaning "hydrogen power." **The pH of a solution is defined as the negative of the common logarithm of the hydronium ion concentration, $[H_3O^+]$.** The pH is expressed by the following equation.

pH $$pH = -\log [H_3O^+]$$

The common logarithm of a number is the power to which 10 must be raised to equal the number. A neutral solution at 25°C has a $[H_3O^+]$ of 1×10^{-7} M. The logarithm of 1×10^{-7} is −7.0. The pH is determined as follows.

$$pH = -\log [H_3O^+] = -\log (1 \times 10^{-7}) = -(-7.0) = 7.0$$

The relationship between pH and $[H_3O^+]$ is shown on the scale in **Figure 1.5.**

Likewise, the pOH of a solution is defined as the negative of the common logarithm of the hydroxide ion concentration, $[OH^-]$.

pOH $$pOH = -\log [OH^-]$$

A neutral solution at 25°C has a $[OH^-]$ of 1×10^{-7} M and a pOH of 7.0.

Remember, the values of $[H_3O^+]$ and $[OH^-]$ are related by K_w. The negative logarithm of K_w at 25°C, 1×10^{-14}, is 14.0. Notice that the sum of the pH and the pOH of a neutral solution at 25°C is also equal to 14.0. The following relationship is true at 25°C.

$$pH + pOH = 14.0$$

CRITICAL THINKING

Explain **Figure 1.5** shows the pH scale with which most people are familiar. Can there be pH measurements above 14 or below zero? Explain.

FIGURE 1.5

The pH Scale As the concentration of hydronium ions increases, the solution becomes more acidic and the pH decreases. As the concentration of hydronium ions decreases, the solution becomes more basic and the pH increases.

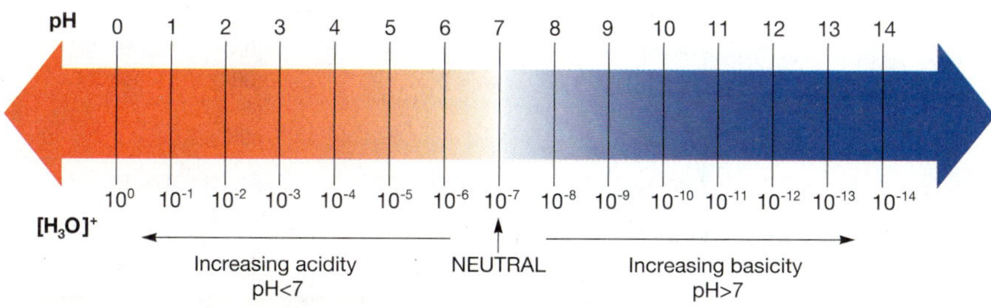

Differentiated Instruction

BELOW LEVEL

The term *logarithmic* may sound intimidating to some students. Point out that in this context the term simply means that the problem involves dealing with powers of 10. Emphasize that because pH is a logarithmic scale, each unit represents a ten-fold difference. For example, point out that the $[H_3O^+]$ in a solution with a pH of 3 is ten times greater than the $[H_3O^+]$ in a solution with a pH of 4. Ask students how the $[H_3O^+]$ in a solution with a pH of 3 compares to the $[H_3O^+]$ of a solution with a pH of 5.

The $[H_3O^+]$ in a solution with a pH of 3 is 10 × 10, or 100 times, greater than the $[H_3O^+]$ of a solution with a pH of 5.

Give students other pH values to calculate their relative H_3O^+ or OH^- concentrations.

Misconception Alert!

Some students have difficulty understanding that increasing $[H_3O^+]$ means decreasing pH. To emphasize the inverse relationship between pH and $[H_3O^+]$, use an analogy in which an increase in one number has an inverse effect on another number. For example, if a pizza is cut into 4 pieces, each piece is 1/4 of the pizza. If a pizza is cut into 8 pieces, then each piece is 1/8 of the pizza. The number 8 is bigger than 4, but 1/8 is smaller than 1/4.

Demonstration

COMPARING CONCENTRATIONS

You can reinforce the relationship between $[H_3O^+]$ and $[OH^-]$ in aqueous solution. Wrap a **meterstick** in **white paper.** Use a **marker** to divide each side into 14 equal intervals. Label one side $[H_3O^+]$, and number it from 100 M to 10^{-14} M. Starting at the same end, number the other side from 10^{-14} M to 10^0 M and label it $[OH^-]$. Have students pick concentrations of $[H_3O^+]$ on one side of the stick and read the corresponding concentrations of $[OH^-]$ on the other side of the stick. The paper can be changed to show the similar relationship between pH and pOH.

READING TOOLKIT

READING ORGANIZER Have students read the section under the Main Idea "The concentrations of hydronium and hydroxide ions determine pH and pOH." Then have them combine the information presented in **Figure 1.6** and the diagram of the pH scale (**Figure 1.5**) into a graphic display showing the pH of common substances.

Critical Thinking

Answer: Yes. Because pH is a mathematical construction, it can in theory be < 0 or > 14 (though these values may be rare or not possible in the real world). For instance, a 2 M HCl solution has 2 M H^+. Substituting into the equation shows that this solution has a negative pH:

$pH = -\log[H^+] = -\log[2] = -0.3$

▼ Teach *continued*

TEACH FROM TABLES

FIGURE 1.7 Point out the connections between the relationships that are true under all conditions and those that are true at 25°C. For example, in acidic solutions at 25°C, the pH is less than 7.0 and the pOH is greater than 7.0. This follows from the general condition that the pH is less than the pOH for acidic solutions. The text derives the relationships true for acidic solutions at 25°C. Go over the analogous calculations for basic solutions at 25°C.

Demonstration

THE pH OF COMMON MATERIALS

Prepare small samples of the following: **1 M NaOH in a dropper bottle, household ammonia, milk of magnesia, sea water, lake water, baking soda solution, distilled water, milk, rainwater, apple juice, orange juice, vinegar, lemon juice, and 1 M HCl in a dropper bottle.** Test each with **pH paper.** Place the strips on a clean **white plastic plate** and label each material. Have students observe the colors and estimate the pH of each material.

Safety Wear **goggles** and a **lab apron.**

Disposal Keep HCl and NaOH solutions for later use. Combine all other waste liquids, adjust the mixture's pH to between 5 and 9, and pour it down the drain.

FIGURE 1.6

APPROXIMATE pH RANGE OF SOME COMMON MATERIALS (AT 25°C)

Material	pH	Material	pH
Gastric juice	1.0–3.0	Bread	5.0–6.0
Lemons	1.8–2.4	Rainwater	5.5–5.8
Vinegar	2.4–3.4	Potatoes	5.6–6.0
Soft drinks	2.0–4.0	Milk	6.3–6.6
Apples	2.9–3.3	Saliva	6.5–7.5
Grapefruit	2.9–3.4	Pure water	7.0
Oranges	3.0–4.0	Blood	7.3–7.5
Cherries	3.2–4.7	Eggs	7.6–8.0
Tomatoes	4.0–4.4	Sea water	8.0–8.5
Bananas	4.5–5.7	Milk of magnesia	10.5

At 25°C the range of pH values of aqueous solutions generally falls between 0 and 14, as shown in **Figure 1.6.**

Suppose the $[H_3O^+]$ in a solution is greater than the $[OH^-]$, as is true for acidic solutions. For example, the pH of an acidic solution at 25°C with a $[H_3O^+]$ of 1×10^{-6} M is 6.0.

$$pH = -\log [H_3O^+] = -\log (1 \times 10^{-6}) = -(-6.0) = 6.0$$

FIGURE 1.7

$[H_3O^+]$, $[OH^-]$, pH, AND pOH OF SOLUTIONS

Solution	General condition	At 25°C
Neutral	$[H_3O^+] = [OH^-]$ pH = pOH	$[H_3O^+] = [OH^-] = 1 \times 10^{-7}$ M pH = pOH = 7.0
Acidic	$[H_3O^+] > [OH^-]$ pH < pOH	$[H_3O^+] > 1 \times 10^{-7}$ M $[OH^-] < 1 \times 10^{-7}$ M pH < 7.0 pOH > 7.0
Basic	$[H_3O^+] < [OH^-]$ pH > pOH	$[H_3O^+] < 1 \times 10^{-7}$ M $[OH^-] > 1 \times 10^{-7}$ M pH > 7.0 pOH < 7.0

Differentiated Instruction

INCLUSION

Help visual and kinesthetic learners understand the relationship between pH, $[H_3O^+]$, and $[OH^-]$ by carrying out the following activity. Give three students signs, one labeled $[H_3O^+]$, the second labeled $[OH^-]$, and the third with a greater than (>) sign. Ask the three students to stand in front of the class.

Have another student give either a pH value or a pOH value. The three students should then arrange themselves to display the correct relationship of the concentrations. Repeat the process until students understand the relationships. Ask which pH value the three students cannot represent. pH 7.0

The pH of this solution is less than 7. This is the case for all acidic solutions at 25°C. The following calculation shows that the pOH is greater than 7.0, as is true for all acidic solutions at 25°C.

$$pOH = 14.0 - pH = 14.0 - 6.0 = 8.0$$

Similar calculations show that the pH of a basic solution at 25°C is more than 7.0 and the pOH is less than 7.0. These and other relationships are listed in **Figure 1.7** (on the previous page). As the temperature changes, the exact values will change because the value of K_w changes. However, the relationship $pH + pOH = pK_w$ will remain the same.

MAIN IDEA

The sum of a solution's pH and pOH is always 14.

If either the $[H_3O^+]$ or pH of a solution is known, the other can be calculated. Because pH represents a logarithm, the number to the *left of the decimal* only locates the decimal point. It isn't included when counting significant figures. So there must be as many significant figures to the *right of the decimal* as there are in the number whose logarithm was found.

PREMIUM CONTENT

Solve It! Cards
HMDScience.com

Calculating pH

Sample Problem B **What is the pH of a 1.0×10^{-3} M NaOH solution?**

1 ANALYZE

Given: Identity and concentration of solution = 1.0×10^{-3} M NaOH

Unknown: pH of solution

2 PLAN

concentration of base $\longrightarrow$ concentration of OH^- $\longrightarrow$ concentration of H_3O^+ $\longrightarrow$ pH

NaOH is completely dissociated when it is dissolved in water. A 1.0×10^{-3} M NaOH solution therefore produces a $[OH^-]$ equal to 1.0×10^{-3} M. The ion product of $[H_3O^+]$ and $[OH^-]$ is a constant, 1.0×10^{-14}. By substitution, the $[H_3O^+]$ can be determined. The pH can then be calculated.

3 SOLVE

$$[H_3O^+][OH^-] = 1.0 \times 10^{-14}$$

$$[H_3O^+] = \frac{1.0 \times 10^{-14}}{[OH^-]} = \frac{1.0 \times 10^{-14}}{1.0 \times 10^{-3}} = 1.0 \times 10^{-11} \text{ M}$$

$$pH = -\log [H_3O^+] = -\log (1.0 \times 10^{-11}) = 11.00$$

4 CHECK YOUR WORK

The answer correctly indicates that NaOH forms a solution with pH > 7, which is basic.

Practice Answers in Appendix E

1. Determine the pH of the following solutions:
   a. 1×10^{-3} M HCl
   b. 1.0×10^{-5} M HNO_3
   c. 1×10^{-4} M NaOH
   d. 1.0×10^{-2} M KOH

ChemisTrivia

The Danish chemist Søren P. L. Sørensen introduced the pH scale in 1909 in order to simplify the expression of acidity and basicity by using a scale of positive numbers.

Classroom Practice

B-1 Determine the pH of a 1×10^{-4} M solution of HBr.

Answer: pH = 4.0

B-2 Determine the pH of a 5×10^{-4} M solution of $Ca(OH)_2$.

Answer: pH = 11.0

Answers

Practice B

1. **a.** pH = 3.0
   b. pH = 5.00
   c. pH = 10.0
   d. pH = 12.00

Problem Solving

DECONSTRUCTING PROBLEMS

Point out that all acidic and basic solutions in Sample Problem B and the Practice problems are given with a positive integer value of 1 or 1.0 times a power of ten. Be sure that students understand that this is the only situation where the pH is the positive value of the exponent used to express the H_3O^+ concentration. For example, the pH of a 1.0×10^{-6} HCl solution is 6.0, but the pH of a 2.5×10^{-7} M HCl solution is not 7.0.

Misconception Alert!

Because the pH scale is derived from logarithms, students may not realize the real meaning of a change in pH. Going down the scale, a change of one pH unit indicates a tenfold increase in $[H_3O^+]$ and a tenfold decrease in $[OH^-]$. From pH 7 to pH 0, $[H_3O^+]$ increases 10 000 000 times. From pH 14 to pH 0, $[H_3O^+]$ increases 10^{14} times, or 100 trillion times.

Teaching Tip

Some calculators may have different keys for the same function. For example, some calculators may have a (−) key instead of a +/− key or an EXP key instead of an EE key.

Classroom Practice

C-1 What is the pH of a solution whose $[H_3O^+] = 6.2 \times 10^{-9}$ M?

Answer: pH = 8.21

C-2 Determine the pH of a 7.4×10^{-4} M solution of NaOH.

Answer: pH = 10.87

Answers

Practice C

1. pH = 3.17
2. pH = 1.60
3. pH = 5.60
4. pH = 12.60

For example, a $[H_3O^+]$ value of 1×10^{-7} has *one* significant figure. Therefore, the pH, or −log, of this value must have one digit to the right of the decimal. Thus, pH = 7.0 has the correct number of significant figures.

Calculating pH from $[H_3O^+]$

You have already seen the simplest pH problems. In these problems, the $[H_3O^+]$ of the solution is an integral power of 10, such as 1 M or 0.01 M. The pH of this type of solution is the exponent of the hydronium ion concentration with the sign changed. For example, the pH of a solution in which $[H_3O^+]$ is 1×10^{-5} M is 5.0.

Using a Calculator to Calculate pH from $[H_3O^+]$

Most problems involve hydronium ion concentrations that are not equal to integral powers of 10. These problems require a calculator. Most scientific calculators have a "log" key. Consult the instructions for your particular calculator.

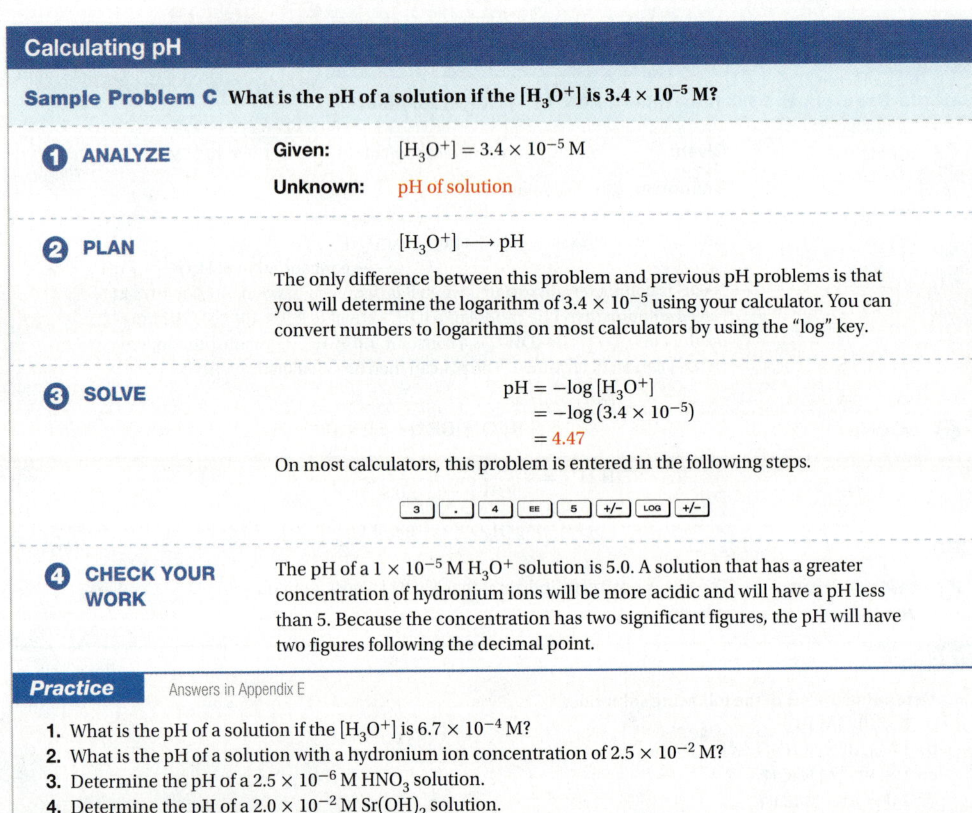

Calculating pH

Sample Problem C **What is the pH of a solution if the $[H_3O^+]$ is 3.4×10^{-5} M?**

1 ANALYZE

Given: $[H_3O^+] = 3.4 \times 10^{-5}$ M

Unknown: pH of solution

2 PLAN

$[H_3O^+] \longrightarrow \text{pH}$

The only difference between this problem and previous pH problems is that you will determine the logarithm of 3.4×10^{-5} using your calculator. You can convert numbers to logarithms on most calculators by using the "log" key.

3 SOLVE

$$\begin{aligned}\text{pH} &= -\log [H_3O^+] \\ &= -\log (3.4 \times 10^{-5}) \\ &= 4.47\end{aligned}$$

On most calculators, this problem is entered in the following steps.

3 . 4 EE 5 +/- LOG +/-

4 CHECK YOUR WORK

The pH of a 1×10^{-5} M H_3O^+ solution is 5.0. A solution that has a greater concentration of hydronium ions will be more acidic and will have a pH less than 5. Because the concentration has two significant figures, the pH will have two figures following the decimal point.

Practice Answers in Appendix E

1. What is the pH of a solution if the $[H_3O^+]$ is 6.7×10^{-4} M?
2. What is the pH of a solution with a hydronium ion concentration of 2.5×10^{-2} M?
3. Determine the pH of a 2.5×10^{-6} M HNO_3 solution.
4. Determine the pH of a 2.0×10^{-2} M $Sr(OH)_2$ solution.

Problem Solving

REALITY CHECK

Remind students that it is important to check the reasonableness of their answers. Tell them to evaluate the given concentration in terms of integral powers of ten. For example, if the given solution is 1.64×10^{-6} M HCl, then the value for H_3O^+ must be between 1×10^{-5} and 1×10^{-6}, or between pH 5.0 and 6.0. Because the number given (1.64) is greater than 1.5, the answer must be closer to pH 6.0. Students can verify this by using their calculators to see that the pH of this solution is 5.79, rounded to the correct number of significant figures.

DECONSTRUCTING PROBLEMS

Point out that Sample Problem D does not introduce any new concepts. It simply shows how to do the reverse of the operation in Sample Problem C, going from pH $\longrightarrow [H_3O^+]$ rather than going from $[H_3O^+] \longrightarrow$ pH as is done in Sample Problem C. The main difference is that students will need to calculate the antilog value rather than the log value.

An estimate of pH can be used to check your calculations. For example, suppose the $[H_3O^+]$ of a solution is 3.4×10^{-5} M. Because 3.4×10^{-5} lies between 1×10^{-4} and 1×10^{-5}, the pH of the solution must be between 4 and 5. Sample Problem C (on the previous page) continues the actual calculation of the pH value for a solution with $[H_3O^+] = 3.4 \times 10^{-5}$ M.

Calculating $[H_3O^+]$ and $[OH^-]$ from pH

You have now learned to calculate the pH of a solution, given its $[H_3O^+]$. Suppose you are given the pH of a solution instead. How can you determine its hydronium ion concentration?

You already know the following equation.

$$pH = -\log [H_3O^+]$$

Remember that the base of common logarithms is 10. Therefore, the antilog of a common logarithm is 10 raised to that number.

$$\log [H_3O^+] = -pH$$
$$[H_3O^+] = \text{antilog}(-pH)$$
$$[H_3O^+] = 10^{-pH}$$

The simplest cases are those in which pH values are integers. The exponent of 10 that gives the $[H_3O^+]$ is the negative of the pH. For an aqueous solution that has a pH of 2, for example, the $[H_3O^+]$ is equal to 1×10^{-2} M. Likewise, when the pH is 0, the $[H_3O^+]$ is 1 M because $10^0 = 1$. Sample Problem D shows how to convert a pH value that is a positive integer. Sample Problem E shows how to use a calculator to convert a pH that is not an integral number.

PREMIUM CONTENT

Solve It! Cards
HMDScience.com

Calculating Hydronium Concentration Using pH

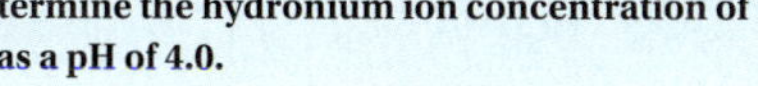

Sample Problem D **Determine the hydronium ion concentration of an aqueous solution that has a pH of 4.0.**

1 ANALYZE

Given: pH = 4.0

Unknown: $[H_3O^+]$

2 PLAN

$$pH \longrightarrow [H_3O+]$$

This problem requires that you rearrange the pH equation and solve for the $[H_3O^+]$. Because 4.0 has one digit to the right of the decimal, the answer must have one significant figure.

$$pH = -\log [H_3O^+]$$
$$\log [H_3O^+] = -pH$$
$$[H_3O^+] = \text{antilog}(-pH)$$
$$[H_3O^+] = 1 \times 10^{-pHw}$$

3 SOLVE

$$[H_3O^+] = 1 \times 10^{-pH} = 1 \times 10^{-4}\ M$$

4 CHECK YOUR WORK

A solution with a pH of 4.0 is acidic. The answer, 1×10^{-4} M, is greater than 1.0×10^{-7} M, which is correct for an acidic solution.

Differentiated Instruction

INCLUSION

To help students understand the role of pH in their daily lives, use ingredient labels from shampoos, antacids, and packaged foods to find household products that contain phosphates. In small groups, discuss the reasons manufacturers use phosphates in the products identified. Be sure to include products that use phosphates to control pH and to alter taste and texture. Categorize those products that use phosphates for the same purpose, and discuss the similarities and differences in how the products are used.

Classroom Practice

D-1 What are the $[H_3O^+]$ and $[OH^-]$ of a solution if its pH = 9.0?

Answer: $[H_3O^+] = 1 \times 10^{-9}$ M; $[OH^-] = 1 \times 10^{-5}$ M

D-2 The pH of a solution is 10.0. What is the concentration of hydroxide ions in the solution? If the solution is $Sr(OH)_2(aq)$, what is its molarity?

Answer: $[OH^-] = 1 \times 10^{-4}$ M; 5×10^{-5} M $Sr(OH)_2$

▼ Teach *continued*

Classroom Practice

E-1 The pH of a hydrochloric acid solution for cleaning tile is 0.45. What is the $[H_3O^+]$ in the solution?

Answer: $[H_3O^+] = 0.35$ M

E-2 A shampoo has a pH of 8.7. What are the $[H_3O^+]$ and $[OH^-]$ of the shampoo?

Answer: $[H_3O^+] = 2 \times 10^{-9}$ M; $[OH^-] = 5 \times 10^{-6}$ M

Answers

Practice E

1. $[H_3O^+] = 1 \times 10^{-5}$ M
2. $[H_3O^+] = 1 \times 10^{-12}$ M
3. $[H_3O^+] = 3.2 \times 10^{-2}$ M; $[OH^-] = 3.2 \times 10^{-13}$ M
4. $[H_3O^+] = 2.1 \times 10^{-4}$ M

Calculating Hydronium and Hydroxide Concentrations

Sample Problem E **The pH of a solution is measured and determined to be 7.52.**
a. What is the hydronium ion concentration?
b. What is the hydroxide ion concentration?
c. Is the solution acidic or basic?

1 ANALYZE

Given: pH of the solution = 7.52

Unknown: **a.** $[H_3O^+]$ **b.** $[OH^-]$ **c.** Is the solution acidic or basic?

2 PLAN

$$pH \longrightarrow [H_3O^+] \longrightarrow [OH^-]$$

This problem is very similar to previous pH problems. You will need to substitute values into the $pH = -\log [H_3O^+]$ equation and use a calculator. Once the $[H_3O^+]$ is determined, the ion-product constant $[H_3O^+][OH^-] = 1.0 \times 10^{-14}$ may be used to calculate $[OH^-]$.

3 SOLVE

a. $pH = -\log [H_3O^+]$

$\log [H_3O^+] = -pH$

$[H_3O^+] = \text{antilog}(-pH) = \text{antilog}(-7.52) = 1.0 \times 10^{-7.52} = 3.0 \times 10^{-8}\text{ M } H_3O^+$

On most calculators, this is entered in one of the following two ways.

[7] [.] [5] [2] [+/−] [2nd] [10^x] *or* [7] [.] [5] [2] [+/−] [2nd] [LOG]

b. $[H_3O^+][OH^-] = 1.0 \times 10^{-14}$

$$[OH^-] = \frac{1.0 \times 10^{-14}}{[H_3O^+]}$$

$$= \frac{1.0 \times 10^{-14}}{3.0 \times 10^{-8}} = 3.3 \times 10^{-7}\text{ M } OH^-$$

c. A pH of 7.52 is slightly greater than a pH of 7. This means that the solution is slightly basic.

4 CHECK YOUR WORK

Because the solution is slightly basic, a hydroxide ion concentration slightly larger than 10^{-7} M is predicted. A hydronium ion concentration slightly less than 10^{-7} M is also predicted. The answers agree with these predictions.

Practice

1. The pH of a solution is determined to be 5.0. What is the hydronium ion concentration of this solution?
2. The pH of a solution is determined to be 12.0. What is the hydronium ion concentration of this solution?
3. The pH of an aqueous solution is measured as 1.50. Calculate the $[H_3O^+]$ and the $[OH^-]$.
4. The pH of an aqueous solution is 3.67. Determine $[H_3O^+]$.

Problem Solving

DECONSTRUCTING PROBLEMS

As pointed out in the solution, Sample Problem E is very similar to previous problems. For example, both Sample Problem D and Sample Problem E involve pH calculations. Ask students to explain how Sample Problem E differs from Sample Problem D.

The pH in Sample Problem E is not an integral number, and the student must also calculate the OH^- concentration.

FIGURE 1.8

Solution	$[H_3O^+]$	$[OH^-]$	pH
RELATIONSHIP OF $[H_3O^+]$ TO $[OH^-]$ AND pH (AT 25°C)			
1.0×10^{-2} M KOH	1.0×10^{-12}	1.0×10^{-2}	12.00
1.0×10^{-2} M NH_3	2.4×10^{-11}	4.2×10^{-4}	10.63
Pure H_2O	1.0×10^{-7}	1.0×10^{-7}	7.00
1.0×10^{-3} M HCl	1.0×10^{-3}	1.0×10^{-11}	3.00
1.0×10^{-1} M CH_3COOH	1.3×10^{-3}	7.5×10^{-12}	2.87

pH Calculations and the Strength of Acids and Bases

So far, we have discussed the pH of solutions that contain only strong acids or strong bases. We must also consider weak acids and weak bases. **Figure 1.8** lists the $[H_3O^+]$, the $[OH^-]$, and the pH for several solutions.

KOH, the solute in the first solution listed, is a soluble ionic compound and a strong base. The molarity of a KOH solution directly indicates the $[OH^-]$, and the $[H_3O^+]$ can be calculated. Once the $[H_3O^+]$ is known, the pH can be calculated as in Sample Problem C. If the pH of this solution is measured experimentally, it will be the same as this calculated value. Methods for experimentally determining the pH of solutions will be presented in Section 2. Hydrochloric acid, HCl, is a strong acid, and similar calculations can be made for solutions that contain HCl.

Solutions of weak acids, such as acetic acid, CH_3COOH, present a different problem. The $[H_3O^+]$ cannot be calculated directly from the molar concentration because not all of the acetic acid molecules are ionized. The same problem occurs for weak bases such as ammonia, NH_3. The pH of these solutions must be measured experimentally. The $[H_3O^+]$ and $[OH^-]$ can then be calculated from the measured pH values.

SECTION 1 FORMATIVE ASSESSMENT

Reviewing Main Ideas

1. What is the concentration of hydronium and hydroxide ions in pure water at 25°C?
2. Why does the pH scale generally range from 0 to 14 in aqueous solutions?
3. Why does a pH of 7 represent a neutral solution at 25°C?
4. A solution contains 4.5×10^{-3} M HCl. Determine the following for the solution:
   a. $[H_3O^+]$ **b.** $[OH^-]$ **c.** pH
5. A $Ca(OH)_2$ solution has a pH of 8.0. Determine the following for the solution:
   a. $[H_3O^+]$ **b.** $[OH^-]$ **c.** $[Ca(OH)_2]$

Critical Thinking

6. **PREDICTING OUTCOMES** Arrange the following solutions in order from lowest to highest pH: 0.10 M HCl, 0.10 M H_2SO_4, and 0.10 M HF.

Answers to Section Assessment

1. $[H_3O^+] = 1.0 \times 10^{-7}$ M; $[OH^-] = 1.0 \times 10^{-7}$ M
2. For most water solutions, $[H_3O^+]$ usually falls between 1×10^0 M and 1×10^{-14} M.
3. For aqueous solutions, $[H_3O^+][OH^-] = 1 \times 10^{-14}$ M at 25°C. In neutral solutions, $[H_3O^+] = [OH^-]$, so they both equal 1×10^{-7} M, which is pH 7.
4. **a.** 4.5×10^{-3} M
   b. 2.2×10^{-12} M
   c. pH = 2.35
5. **a.** 1×10^{-8} M
   b. 1×10^{-6} M
   c. 5×10^{-7} M
6. 0.10 M H_2SO_4 < 0.10 M HCl < 0.10 M HF (H_2SO_4 is diprotic, strong; HCl is strong; HF is weak.)

TEACH FROM TABLES

FIGURE 1.8 Ask students why the concentrations of NH_3 and KOH are equal but the KOH solution has more than 20 times the concentration of OH^- ions. Likewise, the concentration of the acetic acid solution is 100 times the concentration of the HCl solution, yet they have nearly the same pH. Use these apparent discrepancies to emphasize the differences in degree of ionization between strong and weak acids and bases.

Teaching Tip

A real-life connection with the importance of pH can be found in the maintenance of blood pH within the human body and the behavior of the CO_2 and HCO_3^- equilibrium system. This is described with Group 14 of the *Elements Handbook* (Appendix A).

Assess and Reteach

Assess Use the Formative Assessment on this page to evaluate student mastery of the section.

Reteach For students who need additional instruction, download the Section Study Guide.

Response to Intervention To reassess students' mastery, use the Section Quiz, available to print or to take directly online at **HMDScience.com**.

CROSS-DISCIPLINARY CONNECTION

Teaching Tip

Point out that rainwater is not neutral (pH 7), because naturally-occurring carbon dioxide from the air reacts with water and forms carbonic acid. The pH of natural rainwater is about 5.6. The term *acid rain* refers to rain with a pH of less than 5.6, or rain that is more acidic than usual. The natural pH of specific bodies of water depends not only on the pH of the rain that falls, but also on the chemical composition of rocks and soil in the region.

ChemisTrivia

Bodies of water with the lowest pH values are located in the northeastern United States, where cities, dense populations, and power and industrial plants are concentrated. In addition, the prevailing wind direction brings pollutants that contribute to acid rain from the Midwest to the Northeast.

Classroom Discussion

Ask students why studies such as the one on liming Whetstone Brook must be carefully monitored. Responses may point out that too much lime may change an environment's pH too drastically for organisms that live there. Also, the studies must be monitored to see if factors other than the factor being tested remain constant. Point out that human activities are the main cause of acid rain. Ask students to identify as many activities as possible that contribute to this environmental problem. Any activity that releases oxides of sulfur, nitrogen, or carbon into the atmosphere is a contributing factor.

Answers

1. Calcium carbonate is a base, so it neutralizes the acid in the stream. This raises the pH of the water.
2. Nitrogen and sulfur, particularly their oxides, are responsible for acid deposition. Nitrogen and sulfur enter streams from acid rain. Acid rain occurs when the burning of fossil fuels releases these elements into the air, where they combine with moisture.

CROSS-DISCIPLINARY CONNECTION

Liming Streams

Scientists have documented many examples of the effect of acid deposition on aquatic organisms. One example involves the work of Dr. Ken Simmons, who investigated how acid rain affected rainbow trout in the waters of Whetstone Brook in north-central Massachusetts. He placed the trout in cages in the brook so that their behavior and survival could be monitored. Three days later, the trout were dead. Acid rain had lowered the pH level of the water to a point at which the trout simply could not survive.

Fish are affected by pH. It is a limiting factor for many aquatic species. As the pH decreases, physical stress occurs to the mucous membranes and gills of the fish. Their reproductive cycles become disrupted and their eggs don't hatch, or the baby fish, called *fry*, are born with physical defects. Many fish die from disease and loss of calcium and other electrolytes. The acidity of the precipitation can also cause aluminum and other metals to leach out of the rock and soil, posing a toxic threat to the organisms.

Dr. Simmons and other researchers carried out an experiment to decrease the acidity of the stream. They created a system to continuously add calcium carbonate, or *limestone*, in measured amounts to part of the brook. The limestone, a natural base which was ground into a powder, immediately reacted with the acid, raising the pH level of the water. The experiment lasted three years and managed to raise the average pH level of the stream from 5.97 to 6.54, which met the scientists' goal.

At that point, Dr. Simmons again tested rainbow trout in the waters of the Whetstone. This time, all the trout survived. Dr. Simmons seemed to have found a way to address one problem of acid rain. However, as Dr. Simmons warned, "We clearly don't view it as a solution. It's a band-aid approach." He was referring to the fact that he and other scientists had to design and construct a system to continuously add calcium carbonate to the water. Research eventually revealed that a single application of calcium carbonate sand to a stream can provide an effective, time-released solution to acid deposition for as long as 5 years.

Changes in stream pH from acid deposition do not affect all bodies of water equally. The geology and soils underlying the stream must be taken into consideration.

Streams, such as the Shenandoah River, that run through Virginia and West Virginia flow over natural limestone deposits. This alkaline rock formation tends to naturally neutralize the acid in rainwater, thereby increasing the stream's *acid neutralizing capacity* or ANC. Once the calcium ions react with the acid, the change in pH also converts any aluminum in the water to an inert compound that is no longer toxic to the fish.

Questions

1. Describe how calcium carbonate acts to decrease acidity.
2. What elements are responsible for acid deposition? How do they get into the water?

This scientist is testing pH in order to determine how to best neutralize the effects of acid rain.

SECTION 2

Determining pH and Titrations

Key Terms
acid-base indicators
transition interval
pH meter
titration
equivalence point
end point
standard solution
primary standard

SECTION 2

Main Ideas

- Indicators can determine pH, pOH, and strength.
- Titration is used to determine exact concentrations.
- A standard solution is used to titrate unknowns.

MAIN IDEA

Indicators can determine pH, pOH, and strength.

An approximate value for the pH of a solution can be obtained using acid-base indicators. **Acid-base indicators** are compounds whose colors are sensitive to pH. In other words, the color of an indicator changes as the pH of a solution changes.

Indicators change colors because they are either weak acids or weak bases. In solution, a weak-acid indicator (H*In*) can be represented by the equation below, which is modeled in **Figure 2.1**.

$$\mathrm{H}In \rightleftarrows \mathrm{H}^{+} + In^{-}$$

(In^{-} is the symbol of the anion part of the indicator.) Because the reaction is reversible, both H*In* and In^{-} are present. The colors displayed result from the fact that H*In* and In^{-} are different colors.

In acidic solutions, any In^{-} ions that are present act as Brønsted bases and accept protons from the acid. The indicator is then present in largely nonionized form, H*In*. The indicator has its acid-indicating color, as shown for litmus in **Figure 2.1**.

In basic solutions, the OH^{-} ions combine with the H^{+} ions produced by the indicator. The indicator molecules further ionize to offset the loss of H^{+} ions. The indicator is present largely in the form of its anion, In^{-}. The solution now displays the base-indicating color, which for litmus is blue.

FIGURE 2.1

Equilibrium in Indicators Basic solutions shift the equilibrium of litmus to the right. The ionized form, In^{-}, then predominates, and the litmus turns blue. Acidic solutions shift the equilibrium of the indicator litmus to the left. The nonionized form, H*In*, predominates, and the litmus turns red.

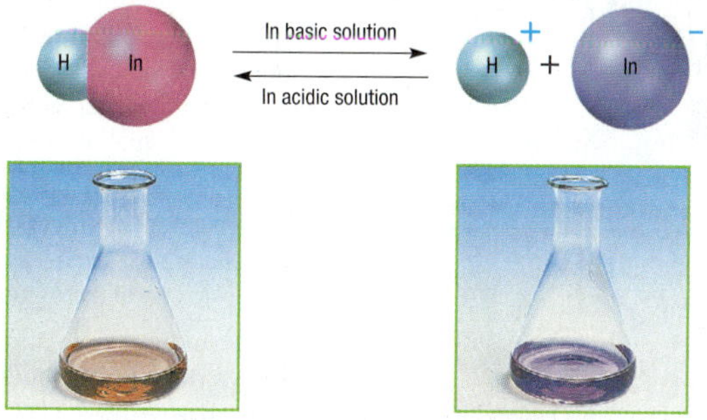

Plan and Prepare

Objectives

Upon completion of this section, students should be able to do the following:

- Describe how an acid-base indicator functions.
- Explain how to carry out an acid-base titration.
- Calculate the molarity of a solution from titration data.

Classroom Catalyst

The day before class, mix a few drops of **phenolphthalein** indicator with 20 mL of **distilled water.** Use this solution to write a message on a piece of **white paper.** Allow the paper to dry. To start the lesson, hang up the paper and spray the message with an **ammonia-based window cleaner.** Remind students that ammonia is a weak base. Ask them to speculate about the cause of the color change from colorless to pink.

Safety Wear **safety goggles** and a **lab apron.** Students should remain at least 3 m from the demonstration. Spray the cleaner away from the students.

Disposal Throw the paper into the trash.

Teach

Teaching Tip

Acid-base indicators are organic compounds that act as very weak Brønsted-Lowry acids and bases. They change color when they accept a proton from an acid or donate one to a base.

Classroom Discussion

During a political campaign, the term *litmus test* is often used in discussions about candidates or issues. Discuss with students the meaning of the term *litmus test* in the context of a political debate.

Differentiated Instruction

INCLUSION

Perform the following stage-magic trick of turning water into wine (or fruit juice) to help visual learners realize that indicators have practical applications. Fill a **glass** with **water.** Add a few grams of **sodium carbonate** (washing soda) to the water to make a slightly alkaline solution. Place a few drops of **phenolphthalein solution** in the bottom of a clean **wine or juice glass.** Pour the alkaline water into the wine glass to convert the phenolphthalein to its red form. Place a few drops of a **concentrated acid** in the bottom of a **third glass.** Pour the "wine" into this glass. The phenolphthalein converts back into its colorless form.

Explain to students how an indicator was used to perform this trick. Inform the class that, during the trick, the magician usually taps the edge of a glass of water with a wand and quickly pours the water into an empty wine glass. The water instantly changes into "red wine." Pouring the "wine" into a third container changes it back into water.

Safety Do not allow anyone to handle or taste the solutions.

▼ Teach *continued*

Misconception Alert!

Students who have used pH paper may believe that a single indicator should act in the same way. Emphasize that pH paper incorporates a mixture of several indicators to produce a continuous spectrum of color.

TEACH FROM VISUALS

FIGURE 2.2 Use pH paper to test the pH of tap water from different sources, bottled water, rainwater, and distilled water. Students may be surprised to learn that the pH of water can deviate markedly from pH 7. If the pH differs from 7, ask students to speculate about why it differs. Tap water that has been treated with lime (CaO) to reduce the concentration of Ca^{2+} and Mg^{2+} ions is likely to be basic—between pH 8 and pH 9. Water that is chlorinated is likely to have an acidic pH of 5 to 6 because of the formation of HCl. Even the pH of distilled water that has been left uncovered can deviate from 7 because CO_2 from the air dissolves in the water and forms carbonic acid, H_2CO_3.

Classroom Discussion

Look up the structures of some acid-base indicators. Ask students to identify possible sites of acid-base reactions. Some acid-base indicators have a carboxyl group (—COOH) or another group that can donate a proton to a base. Others have groups, such as an amino group ($—NH_2$) that can accept a proton from an acid.

FIGURE 2.2

pH of Common Materials The pH of a solution can be determined by comparing the color it turns pH paper with the scale of the paper. The colors of pH paper at various pH values are shown, as are the pH values for some common materials.

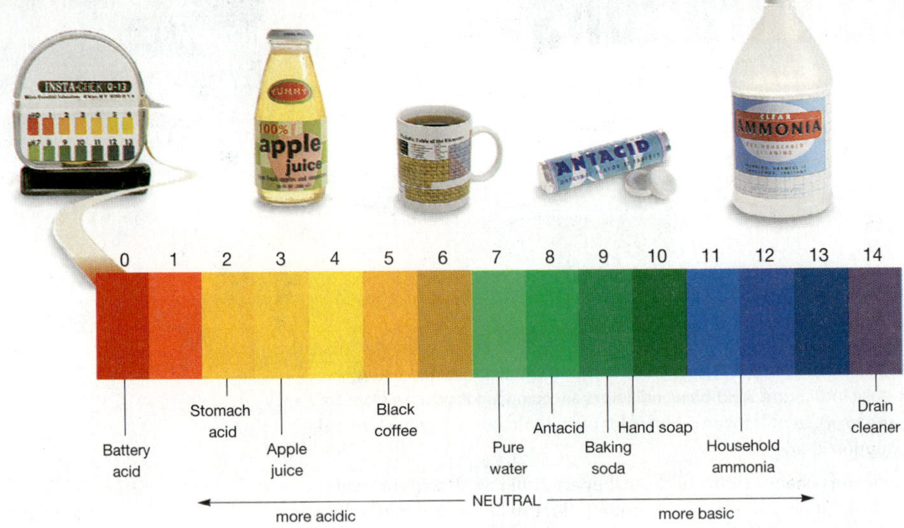

FIGURE 2.3

pH Meters A pH meter precisely measures the pH of a solution.

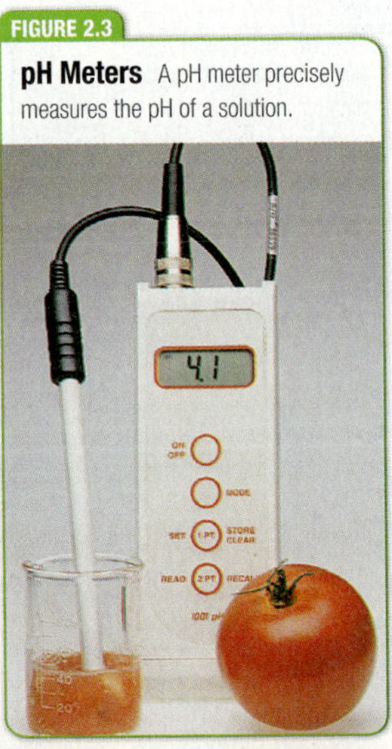

Indicators come in many different colors. The exact pH range over which an indicator changes color also varies. **The pH range over which an indicator changes color is called its transition interval.** **Figure 2.4** gives the color changes and transition intervals for a number of common indicators.

Different indicators change color at different pH values. The color depends on the relative amounts of H*In* and *In*⁻ at a given pH. Methyl red changes from red to yellow between pH 4.4 and 6.2. At pH 4.4, the indicator exists mostly as H*In* molecules, which appear red in the solution. Above pH 6.2, the indicator exists mostly as In^- ions, which appear yellow. A similar situation exists with other indicators. Phenol red at 6.4 or below is yellow as H*In*. Above 8.0, it is in the In^- form, which is red. In the transition interval, significant amounts of both forms are present, so the color is due to the mixture of H*In* and In^-.

Universal indicators are made by mixing several different indicators. Paper soaked in universal indicator solution is called pH paper. This paper can turn almost any color of the rainbow and provides a fairly accurate way of distinguishing the pH of solutions, as shown in **Figure 2.2.**

If a more precise value for the pH of a solution is needed, a pH meter, shown in **Figure 2.3**, should be used. **A pH meter determines the pH of a solution by measuring the voltage between the two electrodes that are placed in the solution.** The voltage changes as the hydronium ion concentration in the solution changes.

Differentiated Instruction

ENGLISH LEARNERS

Help students understand the meaning of transition interval by relating it to other transitions. Ask students to define the word *transition*. Have them describe transitions that they have experienced. A likely response may be the transition they experienced in adapting to a new culture, or to a new school. In fact, some students may say that they are still in a transition period. In this case, the transition has been occurring gradually.

Then ask students how this discussion relates to the transition interval for an indicator. Students should point out that a transition interval represents the range during which an indicator undergoes a change as it is exposed to a new environment.

FIGURE 2.4

COLOR RANGES OF VARIOUS INDICATORS USED IN TITRATIONS

Titration type	Indicator	Acid color	Transition color	Base color
Strong acid/ strong base	methyl red (4.4–6.2)			
	bromthymol blue (6.2–7.6)			
Strong acid/ weak base	methyl orange (3.1–4.4)			
	bromphenol blue (3.0–4.6)			
Weak acid/ strong base	phenolphthalein (8.0–10.0)			
	phenol red (6.4–8.0)			

Demonstration

NATURAL INDICATORS

Tea and the **juice from beets, carrots, and blueberries** are natural indicators. Natural indicators can also be made by boiling **rose petals** and **other vegetable sources** in **water** until the liquid turns dark. Decant the liquid and discard the sediment.

Add a few drops of **vinegar** to a natural indicator and observe what happens. Then add some household **ammonia solution.**

Safety Wear **safety goggles** and a **lab apron.** Students should remain at least 3 m from the demonstration.

Disposal Combine all waste liquids, adjust the mixture's pH to between 5 and 9, and pour it down the drain.

ChemisTrivia

The pH of gastric juice in the human stomach is about 2. The stomach produces hydrochloric acid, which helps digest food particles and kills bacteria that enter the stomach. Gastric juice is acidic enough to damage living tissue.

PRE-AP

Students can investigate how acid precipitation forms and how it affects the environment. Point out that two processes are mainly responsible. In some cases, hydrochloric acid is released directly into the atmosphere. But in most cases, reactions involving compounds such as nitrous oxides and sulfur dioxide that are released into the atmosphere are the main cause. Chemical reactions at Earth's surface or within the atmosphere can convert these pollutants into nitric acid and sulfuric acid. Because this conversion of gases into acidic pollutants takes several days, these substances can be transported hundreds of kilometers from their original source before coming to Earth as acid precipitation. Have students do research and then create a visual display, such as a poster, that illustrates acid precipitation formation and deposition.

▼ Teach *continued*

QuickLab

Students should create one data table to record data obtained in step 3 and step 4. Then, they should create a new data figure for data obtained in step 6. They should note the pH of each sample and the average pH. The pH of distilled water may be lower than 7.0 because of dissolved carbon dioxide.

Answers

1. 7.0 ± 0.2; may be lower because of dissolved carbon dioxide
2. 5.5–5.8; Dissolved CO_2 and other pollutants, such as sulfur dioxide, lower pH, so the pH will vary slightly according to the amount of dissolved CO_2 or pollutants.
3. Answers could include optical distortion, the fact that submerging the ruler raises the water level, the formation of a meniscus when the ruler is too close to the side of the jar, and the fact that the bottom of the jar may not be flat. You could use a calibrated rain gauge with markings on the glass to increase precision.
4. Answers will vary depending on results.
5. Answers will vary. If the pH is consistently below 5.5, you may have acid rain.

QuickLAB TESTING THE pH OF RAINWATER

MATERIALS
- rainwater
- distilled water
- 500 mL jars
- thin, transparent metric ruler (± 0.1cm)
- pH test paper: narrow range, ± 0.2–0.3, or pH meter

QUESTION

Do you have acid precipitation in your area?

PROCEDURE

Record all of your results in a data table.

1. Each time it rains, set out five clean jars to collect the rainwater. If the rain continues for more than 24 hours, put out new containers at the end of each 24-hour period until the rain stops. (The same procedure can be used with snow if the snow is allowed to melt before measurements are taken. You may need to use larger containers if a heavy snowfall is expected.)
2. After the rain stops or at the end of each 24-hour period, use a thin, plastic ruler to measure the depth of the water to the nearest 0.1 cm. Using the pH paper, test the water to determine its pH to the nearest 0.2 to 0.3.
3. Record the following:
   a. the date and time the collection started
   b. the date and time the collection ended
   c. the location where the collection was made (town and state)
   d. the amount of rainfall in centimeters
   e. the pH of the rainwater
4. Find the average pH of each collection that you have made for each rainfall, and record it in the data table.
5. Collect samples on at least five different days. The more samples you collect, the more informative your data will be.
6. For comparison, determine the pH of pure water by testing five samples of distilled water with pH paper. Record your results in a separate data table, and then calculate an average pH for distilled water.

DISCUSSION

1. What is the pH of distilled water?
2. What is the pH of normal rainwater? How do you explain any differences between the pH readings?
3. What are the drawbacks of using a ruler to measure the depth of collected water? How could you increase the precision of your measurement?
4. Does the amount of rainfall or the time of day the sample is taken have an effect on its pH? Try to explain any variability among samples.
5. What conclusion can you draw from this investigation? Explain how your data support your conclusion.

Differentiated Instruction

ENGLISH LEARNERS

The definition of the word *titration* is lengthy and may be difficult for students to comprehend. Have students open their textbooks to the Glossary and follow along as you break the definition into fragments, as shown below. Explain what is meant by each fragment, and provide an example for each, as shown.

(1) The controlled addition and measurement of the amount of a solution: 10 mL

(2) of known concentration: 0.50 M HCl

(3) required to react completely with a measured amount of a solution: 5 mL

(4) of unknown concentration: ? M NaOH

This breakdown should also prepare students for titration problems that require solving for the concentration of either an acid or a base.

MAIN IDEA

Titration is used to determine exact concentrations.

As you know, neutralization reactions occur between acids and bases. The OH^- ion acquires a proton from the H_3O^+ ion, forming two molecules of water. The following equation summarizes this reaction.

$$H_3O^+(aq) + OH^-(aq) \longrightarrow 2H_2O(l)$$

This equation shows that one mol of hydronium ions and one mol of hydroxide ions are chemically equivalent amounts. They combine in a one-to-one mole ratio. Neutralization occurs when hydronium ions and hydroxide ions are supplied in equal numbers by reactants, as shown in **Figure 2.5.**

One liter of a 0.10 M HCl solution contains 0.10 mol of hydronium ions. Now suppose that 0.10 mol of solid NaOH is added to 1 L of 0.10 M HCl solution. The NaOH dissolves and supplies 0.10 mol of hydroxide ions to the solution. HCl and NaOH are present in chemically equivalent amounts. Hydronium and hydroxide ions, which are present in equal numbers, combine until the product $[H_3O^+][OH^-]$ returns to the value of 1×10^{-14}. NaCl, the salt produced in the reaction, is the product of this neutralization of a strong acid and a strong base. The resulting solution is neutral.

Because acids and bases react, the progressive addition of an acid to a base (or a base to an acid) can be used to compare the concentrations of the acid and the base. **Titration** is the controlled addition and measurement of the amount of a solution of known concentration required to react completely with a measured amount of a solution of unknown concentration. Titration provides a sensitive means of determining the chemically equivalent amounts of acid and base.

CRITICAL THINKING

Assess From your own experiences, describe three everyday reasons to test for pH.

FIGURE 2.5

Neutralization The solution on the left turns pH paper red because it is acidic. The solution on the right turns pH paper blue because it is basic. When equal numbers of H_3O^+ and OH^- from the acidic and basic solutions react, the resulting solution is neutral. The neutral solution turns pH paper green.

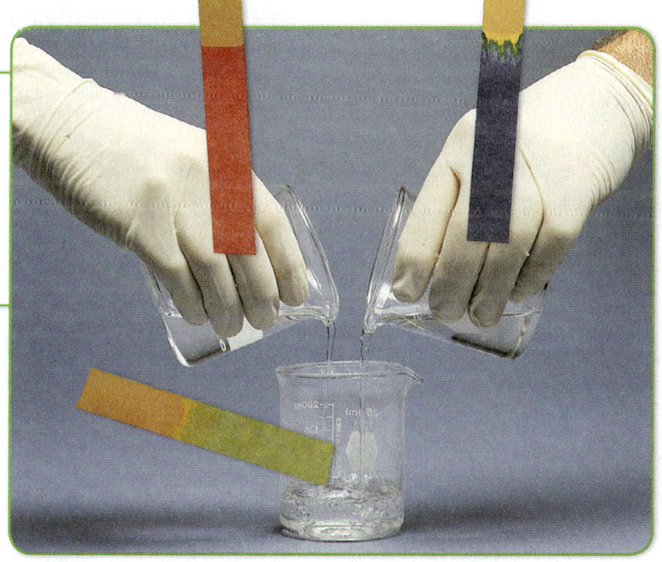

Teaching Tip

When a strong base, such as NaOH, is used to titrate a strong acid, such as HCl, or vice versa, the resulting solution is neutral at the point when the acid and base are stoichiometrically equivalent.

ChemisTrivia

In highly precise titrations, the quantity of acid or base needed to titrate the indicator itself must be taken into account.

READING TOOLKIT

READING HINT As students read through the section on titration, have them use **Figures 2.5, 2.6,** and **2.7** to help them understand and explain equivalence points and end points.

Check for Understanding

Answer: Possible answers include the following. Aquariums: Most aquatic organisms have a limited range of pH in which they can thrive. Swimming pools: The chlorine used to keep a swimming pool sanitized works best at a pH near 7.0. Soil testing: Many plants grow better in a particular pH. Testing the soil can help determine what to plant in a certain area.

Acid-Base Titration and pH 487

▼ Teach continued

ChemisTrivia

In contrast to most other indicators, litmus is a mixture of organic substances extracted from lichens that grow in coastal regions. Because it is a mixture, it has a fairly wide transition interval. Thus, litmus is less desirable as a titration indicator than indicators with sharper end points.

Misconception Alert!

Students may think that television commercials advertising "pH balanced" shampoos or skin creams mean that the ingredients of the products have been "balanced" to make the solution pH neutral. In reality, the product has been formulated to approximately the same pH as human hair or skin, so that it will not cause damage.

Teaching Tip

When weak acids or bases are titrated with strong acids or bases, the equivalence point occurs at a pH that differs from neutral in the direction of the strong component. If a strong acid titrates a weak base, the salt at the equivalence point is an acidic salt. If a strong base titrates a weak acid, the salt at the equivalence point is a basic salt.

CAREERS IN CHEMISTRY

Analytical Chemist S.T.E.M.

The primary job of an analytical chemist is to obtain information by making precise measurements. Analytical chemists often use sophisticated, state-of-the-art instruments to analyze for barely detectable amounts of materials. In addition to collecting data, analytical chemists must process the data and communicate their findings with others. These findings must be the result of careful and reproducible work, strict accountability, and control of the samples. Although analytical chemists work in all areas of chemistry, one important area is environmental chemistry, which involves analyzing air, water, and soil samples. The results of these tests are used by regulatory agencies such as the Environmental Protection Agency.

Equivalence Point

The point at which the two solutions used in a titration are present in chemically equivalent amounts is the equivalence point. Indicators and pH meters can be used to determine the equivalence point. The pH will change rapidly as the equivalence point is approached. If an indicator is used, it must change color over a range that includes the pH of the equivalence point, as shown in **Figure 2.6**. **The point in a titration at which an indicator changes color is called the end point of the indicator.**

Some indicators, such as litmus, change color at about pH 7. However, the color-change interval for litmus is broad, pH 5.5–8.0. This broad range makes it difficult to determine an accurate pH. Bromthymol blue is better because it has a smaller transition interval, pH 6.2–7.6 (see **Figure 2.4**). Indicators that undergo transition at about pH 7 are used to determine the equivalence point of strong-acid/strong-base titrations because the neutralization of strong acids with strong bases produces a salt solution with a pH of 7.

Indicators that change color at pH lower than 7 are useful in determining the equivalence point of strong-acid/weak-base titrations. Methyl orange is an example of this type. The equivalence point of a strong-acid/weak-base titration is acidic because the salt formed is itself a weak acid. Thus the salt solution has a pH lower than 7 at the equivalence point.

Indicators that change color at pH higher than 7 are useful in determining the equivalence point of weak-acid/strong-base titrations. Phenolphthalein is an example. These reactions produce salt solutions whose pH is greater than 7. This occurs because the salt formed is a weak base.

You may be wondering what type of indicator is used to determine the equivalence point of weak-acid/weak-base titrations. The surprising answer is "none at all." The pH at the equivalence point of a weak-acid/weak-base titration could be acidic, basic, or neutral, depending on the relative acid-base strengths. Because the pH value does not change dramatically as the equivalence point is approached, it is not practical to carry out weak-acid/weak-base titrations.

FIGURE 2.6

End Point Indicators change color at the end point of a titration with a base.

(a) Phenolphthalein turns pink at the end point.

(b) Methyl red turns red at the end point.

Differentiated Instruction

BELOW LEVEL

Students may think that the equivalence point always occurs at pH 7. Explain why the equivalence point can occur either at an acidic pH or at a basic pH by using a specific example. One possibility is a titration between a strong acid (HCl) and a weak base (NH_3).

Ask students why HCl is considered a strong acid. Student should point out that HCl ionizes completely to produce H^+ ions in aqueous solution. Then ask why NH_3 is considered a weak base. Students should explain that NH_3 reacts with water to produce relatively few OH^- ions. Ask students what salt is formed in this reaction between HCl and NH_3. NH_4Cl Have students explain why this salt is a weak acid. This salt can slightly ionize to produce ammonium ions that act as proton donors. Point out that this salt remains in solution at the equivalence point, causing the solution to have a pH value below 7.

FIGURE 2.7

Equivalence Points

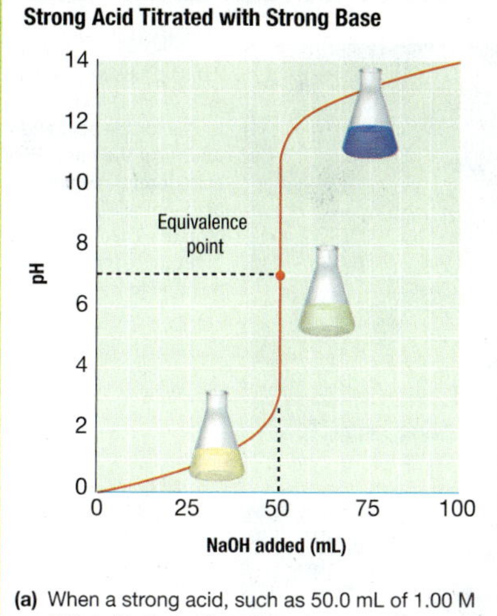

(a) When a strong acid, such as 50.0 mL of 1.00 M HCl, is titrated with a strong base, such as 1.00 M NaOH, the equivalence point occurs at pH 7.00.

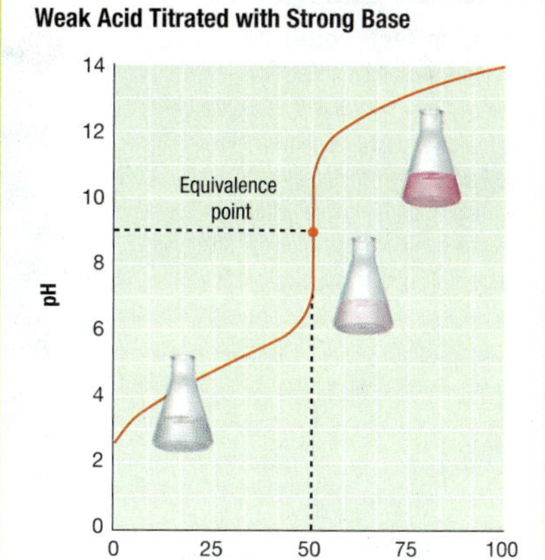

(b) When a weak acid, such as 50.0 mL of 1.00 M CH_3COOH, is titrated with a strong base, such as 1.00 M NaOH, the initial pH is higher and the equivalence point occurs at a pH above 7.00.

In a titration, successive additions of an aqueous base are made to a measured volume of an aqueous acid. As base is added, the pH changes from a lower numerical value to a higher one. The change in pH occurs slowly at first, then rapidly through the equivalence point, and then slowly again as the solution becomes more basic. Near the equivalence point, one drop can cause a pH change of 3 to 5 pH units! Typical pH curves for strong-acid/strong-base and weak-acid/strong-base titrations are shown in **Figure 2.7.**

MAIN IDEA

A standard solution is used to titrate unknowns.

Figure 2.8 on the following pages shows the proper method of carrying out a titration. If the concentration of one solution is known precisely, the concentration of the other solution in a titration can be calculated from the chemically equivalent volumes. The solution that contains the precisely known concentration of a solute is known as a **standard solution.** It is often called simply the "known" solution.

To be certain of the concentration of the known solution, that solution must first be compared with a solution of a primary standard. A **primary standard** is a highly purified solid compound used to check the concentration of the known solution in a titration. The known solution is prepared first to give approximately the desired concentration. The known solution concentration is then determined precisely by titrating a carefully measured quantity of the primary standard.

PRE-AP

Have students use the graphs in **Figure 2.7** to draw titration curves for the reactions between a strong acid and a weak base and between a weak acid and a weak base. Ask students to explain what happens at the equivalence point in each titration. Have them also explain the statement that the equivalence point is defined by the stoichiometry and not by the pH. Students should realize that equivalence is reached when enough titrant has been added to react exactly with all the acid or base being titrated.

TEACH FROM VISUALS

FIGURE 2.7 Emphasize that each equivalence point occurs at a pH that is halfway between the two points where the line curves. Also, the higher initial pH and the greater slope of the lower part of the curve in **Figure 2.7(b)** is typical of a weak acid-strong base titration.

Demonstration

pH CHANGE IN AN ACID-BASE TITRATION

Fill a **buret** with a **0.1 M NaOH solution.** Measure **25 mL of 0.1 M HCl** into a **beaker,** and place the probe of a **pH meter** into the solution. Record the pH of the solution. Slowly add NaOH from the buret, and record the amount of NaOH added and the pH as you continue. **Graph** the resulting titration curve, and point out the very large change in pH that results when one drop of NaOH is added at the equivalence point.

Safety Wear **safety goggles** and a **lab apron.**

Disposal Combine all liquids, adjust the mixture's pH to between 5 and 9, and pour it down the drain.

Misconception Alert!

For a given amount of a strong base titrated first by a strong and then by a weak acid of the same concentration, students may believe that it will take a larger volume of the weak acid to reach the equivalence point than the strong acid. This is not the case! The equivalence point relates moles of acid to moles of base. So the same number of moles of acid is present in 100. mL of 0.10 M weak acid as are in 100. mL of 0.10 M strong acid. The two cases differ in the pH at the equivalence point, 7.00 for the strong acid/strong base and > 7.00 for the weak acid/strong base.

▼ Teach *continued*

Misconception Alert!

Students may think that if a little indicator is good, then more is better and will make the color change more vivid. Remind them that indicators are themselves acids or bases. An indicator should be present in a quantity low enough that the amount of acid or base needed to change the color of the indicator is negligible. Also, with too much indicator, the end point is often less distinct than with a small amount.

Demonstration

READING A MENISCUS

For students who have trouble reading the volume in a buret to the nearest 0.01 mL, show them an effective way to locate the bottom of the meniscus. Add about 7 mL of **water** to a **buret.** To minimize problems with room lighting and reflections, use a **marker** to make a black line about 1 cm in width lengthwise down the center of a **white business card.** Hold the card at about a 45° angle behind the buret, with the black line perpendicular to the buret. When held correctly, the meniscus appears black and contrasts with the white background of the card. Read the meniscus at eye level to avoid parallax error. Refer students to the pre-lab procedure on volumetric analysis (online) for more information on using a buret and reading a measurement with a meniscus.

FIGURE 2.8

Titration Techniques Following is the proper method for carrying out an acid-base titration. To be sure you have an accurate value, you should repeat the titration until you have three results that agree within 0.05 mL. A standardized base solution is used in this procedure to determine the unknown concentration of an acid.

1

First set up two clean burets as shown. Decide which buret to use for the acid and which to use for the base. Rinse the acid buret three times with the acid that will be used in the titration. Then, rinse the base buret three times with the base solution to be used.

2

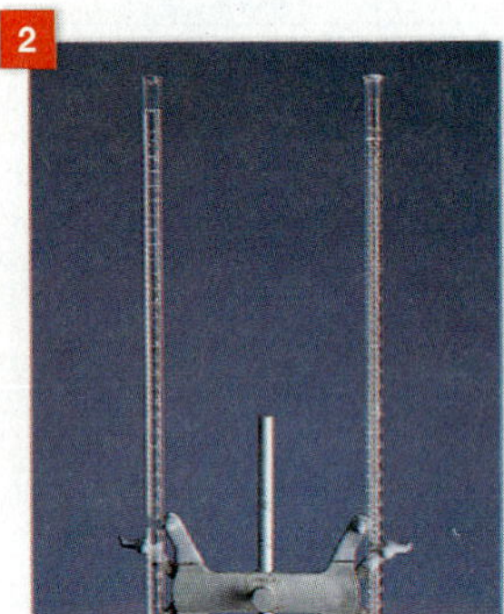

Fill the first buret to a point above the 0 mL calibration mark with the acid of unknown concentration.

3

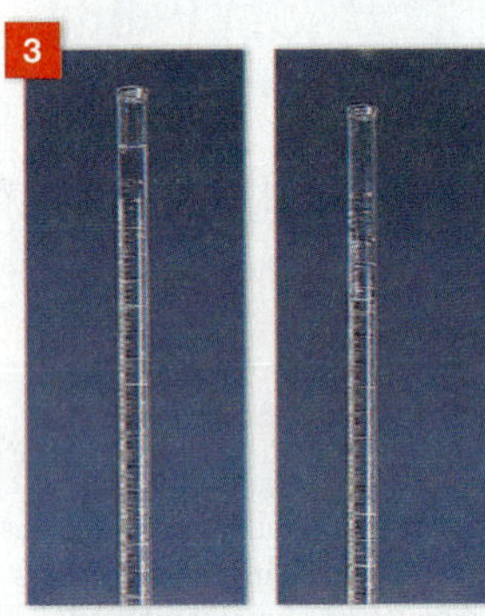

Release some acid from the buret to remove any air bubbles from the tip and to lower the volume to the calibrated portion of the buret.

4

Record the volume of the acid in the buret to the nearest 0.01 mL as the initial volume. Remember to read the volume at the bottom of the meniscus.

5

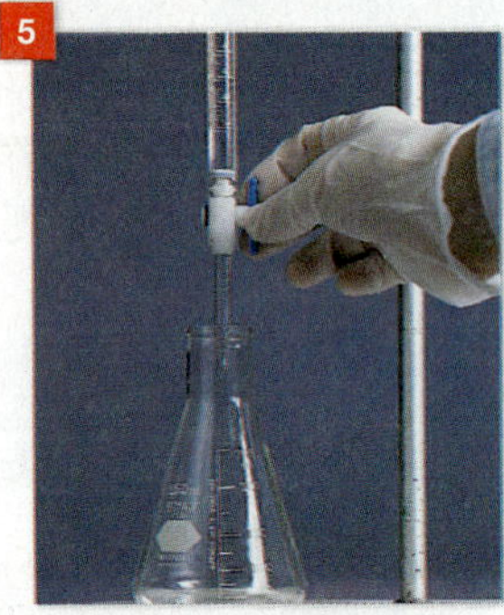

Allow approximately the volume of acid that was determined by your teacher or lab procedure to flow into a clean Erlenmeyer flask.

6

Subtract the initial volume reading on the buret from the final reading. This is the exact volume of the acid released into the flask. Record it to the nearest 0.01 mL.

7

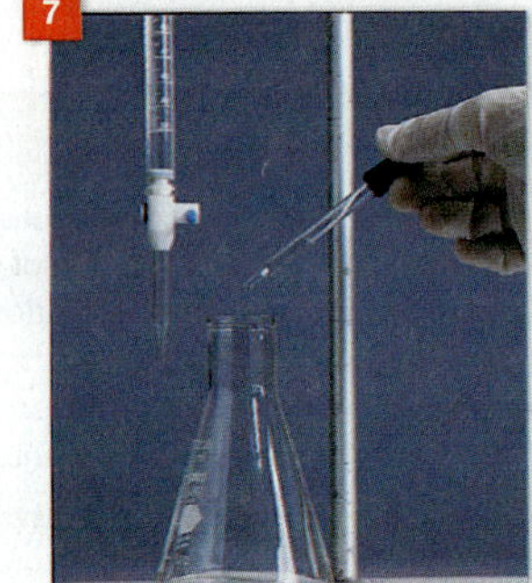

Add three drops of the appropriate indicator (in this case phenolphthalein) to the flask.

Differentiated Instruction

INCLUSION

Tactile and auditory learners may have difficulty understanding how to perform a titration by trying to read the captions and studying the illustrations in **Figure 2.8.** Ask two students to demonstrate the proper technique for carrying out a titration. Set up the titration apparatus with solutions of an acid and a base of known molarity. Have one student perform the steps as the other student reads the instructions.

8

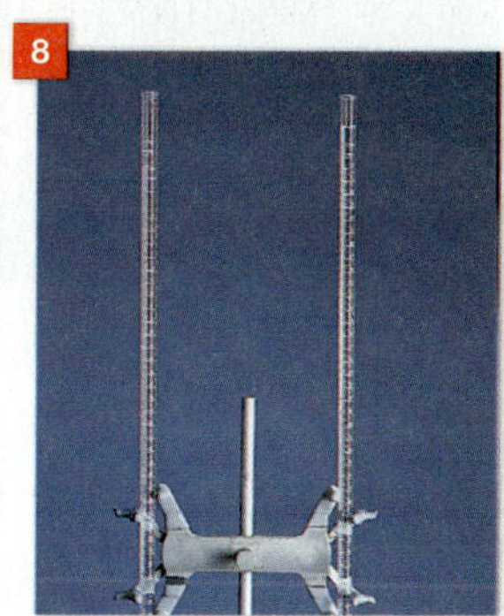

Fill the other buret with the standard base solution to a point above the calibration mark. The concentration of the standard base is known to a certain degree of precision because the base was previously titrated with an exact mass of solid acid, which is the primary standard.

9

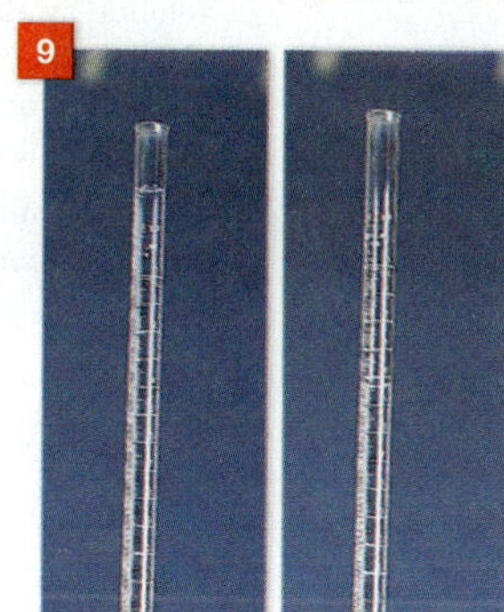

Release some base from the buret to remove any air bubbles and to lower the volume to the calibrated portion of the buret.

10

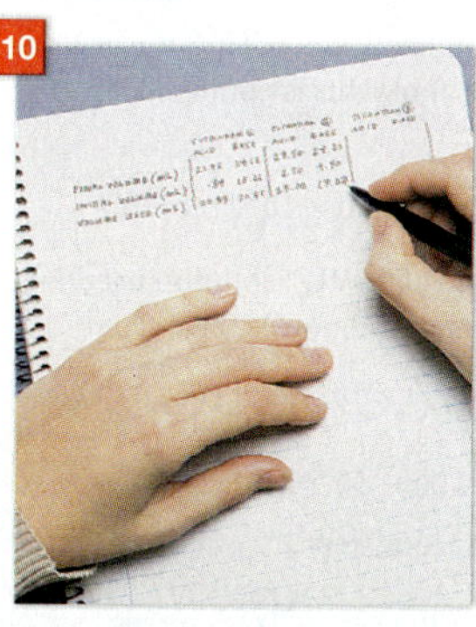

Record the volume of the base to the nearest 0.01 mL as your initial volume. Remember to read the volume at the bottom of the meniscus.

11

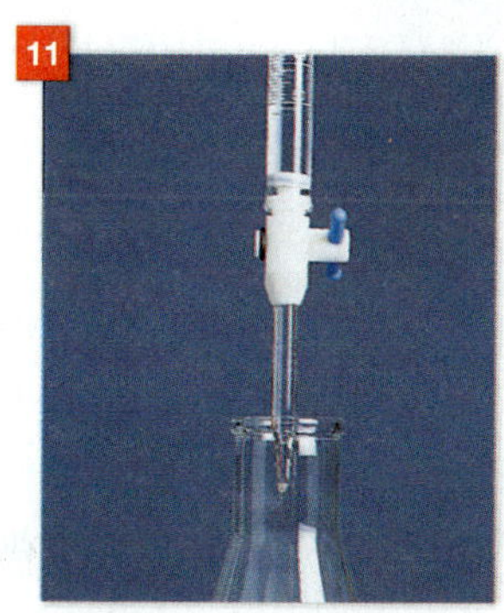

Place the Erlenmeyer flask under the base buret as shown. Notice that the tip of the buret extends into the mouth of the flask.

12

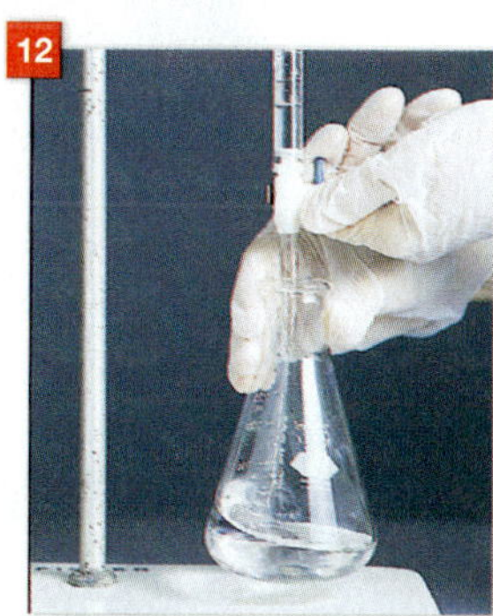

Slowly release base from the buret into the flask while constantly swirling the contents of the flask. The pink color of the indicator should fade with swirling.

13

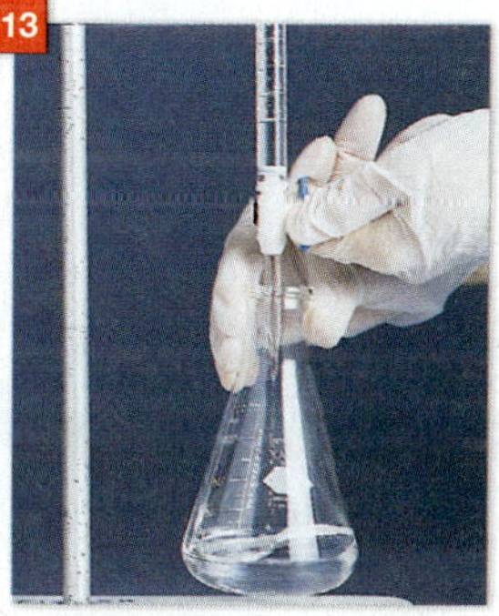

The titration is nearing the end point when the pink color stays for longer periods of time. At this point, add base drop by drop.

14

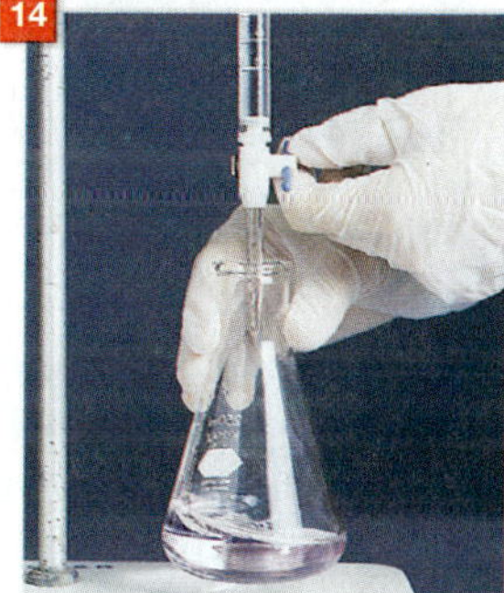

The equivalence point is reached when a very light pink color remains after 30 seconds of swirling.

15

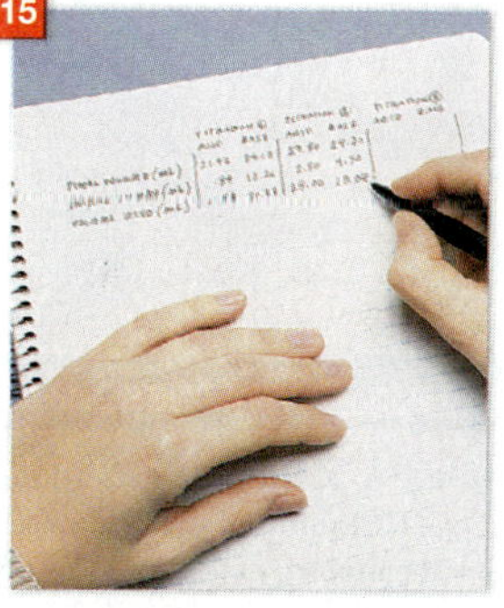

Subtract the initial volume reading on the buret from the final reading. This is the exact volume of the base released into the flask. Record it to the nearest 0.01 mL.

Teaching Tip

It is common to run a quick, imprecise titration in order to determine approximately where the end point will fall. Then in subsequent trials, students must titrate slowly only near the end point.

READING TOOLKIT

SEQUENCING/PATTERN PUZZLES

Have students silently read the previous page and this page. Then ask students to form pairs and to each list on a sheet of notebook paper the steps for carrying out an acid-base titration. One step should be listed per line, and the steps should not be numbered. Encourage students to write the steps in their own words and to divide longer steps into two or three shorter steps if necessary.

When students have finished, have them cut their sheets of paper into strips so that there is only one step per strip. Direct students to shuffle the strips so that the strips are out of order. Ask students to trade strips with their partners and to place their partner's strips in the proper sequence. Students can confirm the order of the process by checking with the text or their class notes.

Acid-Base Titration and pH 491

▼ Teach *continued*

Demo Problems

1. How many moles of HCl are in 31.15 mL of a 0.688 M solution?

Answer: 2.14×10^{-2} mol HCl

2. How many moles of NaOH would neutralize 20.0 mL of a 1.39 M solution of H_2SO_4?

Answer: 5.56×10^{-2} mol NaOH

3. How many milliliters of a 2.76 M KOH solution contain 0.0825 mol of KOH?

Answer: 29.9 mL

Classroom Practice

F-1 A 25.00 mL sample of a solution of RbOH is neutralized by 19.22 mL of a 1.017 M solution of HBr. What is the molarity of the RbOH solution?

Answer: 0.7819 M RbOH

F-2 If 29.96 mL of a solution of $Ba(OH)_2$ requires 16.08 mL of a 2.303 M solution of HNO_3 for complete titration, what is the molarity of the $Ba(OH)_2$ solution?

Answer: 0.6180 M $Ba(OH)_2$

F-3 You have a vinegar solution you believe to be 0.83 M. You are going to titrate 20.00 mL of it with a NaOH solution that you know to be 0.519 M. At what volume of added NaOH solution would you expect to see an end point?

Answer: 32 mL NaOH solution

The known solution can be used to determine the molarity of another solution by titration. Suppose 20.0 mL of 5.00×10^{-3} M NaOH is required to reach the end point in the titration of 10.0 mL of HCl of unknown concentration. How can these titration data be used to determine the molarity of the acidic solution?

Begin with the balanced neutralization reaction equation. From the equation, determine the chemically equivalent amounts of HCl and NaOH.

$$\underset{1\text{ mol}}{HCl(aq)} + \underset{1\text{ mol}}{NaOH(aq)} \longrightarrow \underset{1\text{ mol}}{NaCl(aq)} + \underset{1\text{ mol}}{H_2O(l)}$$

Calculate the number of moles of NaOH used in the titration.

$$\frac{5.00 \times 10^{-3}\text{ mol NaOH}}{1\text{ L}} \times \frac{1\text{ L}}{1000\text{ mL}} \times 20.0\text{ mL} = 1.00 \times 10^{-4}\text{ mol NaOH used}$$

Because 1 mol of NaOH is needed to neutralize 1 mol of HCl, the amount of HCl in the titration must be 1.00×10^{-4} mol. This is confirmed by the following equation.

$$1.00 \times 10^{-4}\text{ mol NaOH} \times \frac{1\text{ mol HCl}}{1\text{ mol NaOH}} = 1.00 \times 10^{-4}\text{ mol HCl}$$

This amount of acid must be in the 10.0 mL of the HCl solution used for the titration. The molarity of the HCl solution can now be calculated.

$$\frac{1.00 \times 10^{-4}\text{ mol HCl}}{10.0\text{ mL}} \times \frac{1000\text{ mL}}{1\text{ L}} = \frac{1.00 \times 10^{-2}\text{ mol HCl}}{1\text{ L}} = 1.00 \times 10^{-2}\text{ M HCl}$$

Sample Problem F illustrates the following four steps.

1. Start with the balanced equation for the neutralization reaction, and determine the chemically equivalent amounts of the acid and base.
2. Determine the moles of acid (or base) from the known solution used during the titration.
3. Determine the moles of solute of the unknown solution used during the titration.
4. Determine the molarity of the unknown solution.

PREMIUM CONTENT
SolveIt! Cards
HMDScience.com

Calculating the Molarity of an Acid Solution

Sample Problem F **In a titration, 27.4 mL of 0.0154 M $Ba(OH)_2$ is added to a 20.0 mL sample of HCl solution of unknown concentration until the equivalence point is reached. What is the molarity of the acid solution?**

 **ANALYZE**

Given: volume and concentration of known solution = 27.4 mL of 0.0154 M $Ba(OH)_2$; volume of unknown HCl solution = 20.0 mL

Unknown: molarity of acid solution

Continued

Problem Solving

ALTERNATIVE APPROACHES

Students can also use the following formula that applies at the equivalence point:

volume (base) × molarity (base) = volume (acid) × molarity (acid)

However, students must be careful not to use the molarity given in the problem without first looking at the formula for the acid or base. For example, in Sample Problem F, the base is $Ba(OH)_2$. Students must recognize that this base dissociates so that 2 mol of OH^- ions are formed for every mol of $Ba(OH)_2$ that dissociates. Therefore, the correct values to substitute in the equation above would be:

$$(27.4\text{ mL})(0.0308\text{ M}) = (20\text{ mL})(X\text{ M})$$

Solving for X in this equation yields 0.042196 or 4.22×10^{-2} M HCl, which agrees with the answer given in Sample Problem F. Point out that the molarity of the base used in the equation (0.0308 M) was calculated by multiplying the molarity of $Ba(OH)_2$ by 2 to account for the formation of 2 OH^- ions for every $Ba(OH)_2$ that dissociates.

Calculating the Molarity of an Acid Solution (continued)

 **PLAN**

1. balanced neutralization equation ⟶ chemically equivalent amounts

$$\underset{1\text{ mol}}{Ba(OH)_2} + \underset{2\text{ mol}}{2HCl} \longrightarrow \underset{1\text{ mol}}{BaCl_2} + \underset{2\text{ mol}}{2H_2O}$$

2. volume of known basic solution used (mL) ⟶ amount of base used (mol)

$$\frac{\text{mol } Ba(OH)_2}{1\ \cancel{L}} \times \cancel{mL} \text{ of } Ba(OH)_2 \text{ solution} \times \frac{1\ \cancel{L}}{1000\ \cancel{mL}} = \text{mol } Ba(OH)_2$$

3. moles of base used, mole ratio ⟶ moles of acid used from unknown solution

$$\cancel{\text{mol } Ba(OH)_2} \times \frac{2\text{ mol HCl}}{1\ \cancel{\text{mol } Ba(OH)_2}} \text{ in known solution} = \text{mol HCl in unknown solution}$$

4. volume of unknown, moles of solute in unknown ⟶ molarity of unknown

$$\frac{\text{amount of solute in unknown solution (mol)}}{\text{volume of unknown solution }(\cancel{mL})} \times \frac{1000\ \cancel{mL}}{1\text{ L}} \times \text{molarity of unknown solution}$$

 **SOLVE**

1. The mole ratio from the equation is 1 mol $Ba(OH)_2$ for every 2 mol HCl.
2. $\frac{0.0154\text{ mol } Ba(OH)_2}{1\ \cancel{L}} \times \frac{1\ \cancel{L}}{1000\ \cancel{mL}} \times 27.4\ \cancel{mL} = 4.22 \times 10^{-4}\text{ mol } Ba(OH)_2$
3. $4.22 \times 10^{-4}\ \cancel{\text{mol } Ba(OH)_2} \times \frac{2\text{ mol HCl}}{1\ \cancel{\text{mol } Ba(OH)_2}} = 8.44 \times 10^{-4}\text{ mol HCl}$
4. $\frac{8.44 \times 10^{-4}\text{ mol HCl}}{20.0\ \cancel{mL}} \times \frac{1000\ \cancel{mL}}{1\text{ L}} = \frac{4.22 \times 10^{-2}\text{ mol HCl}}{1\text{ L}} = 4.22 \times 10^{-2}\text{ M HCl}$

Practice Answers in Appendix E

1. A 15.5 mL sample of 0.215 M KOH solution required 21.2 mL of aqueous acetic acid solution in a titration experiment. Calculate the molarity of the acetic acid solution.
2. By titration, 17.6 mL of aqueous H_2SO_4 neutralized 27.4 mL of 0.0165 M LiOH solution. What was the molarity of the aqueous acid solution?

 SECTION 2 FORMATIVE ASSESSMENT

Reviewing Main Ideas

1. Name an appropriate indicator for titrating the following:
   a. a strong acid and a weak base
   b. a strong base and a weak acid
2. If 20.0 mL of 0.0100 M aqueous HCl is required to neutralize 30.0 mL of an aqueous solution of NaOH, determine the molarity of the NaOH solution.
3. Suppose that 20.0 mL of 0.010 M $Ca(OH)_2$ is required to neutralize 12.0 mL of aqueous HCl solution. What is the molarity of the HCl solution?

Critical Thinking

4. **PREDICTING OUTCOMES** Sketch the titration curve for 50.0 mL of 0.10 M NH_3 that is titrated with 0.10 M HCl.

Answers to Section Assessment

1. a. Methyl orange and bromphenol blue are possible answers.
   b. Phenolphthalein and phenol red are possible answers.
2. 6.67×10^{-3} M NaOH
3. 0.030 M HCl
4. pH (y-axis: 1, 4, 7, 10, 14); mL HCl (x-axis: 0, 20, 40, 60, 80); Equivalence point

Alternative Assessment

Have students write a balanced equation for the titration of H_2SO_3 with KOH. Ask them how they would prepare a 1.00 M standard solution of KOH and how many moles of KOH would react with each mole of H_2SO_3.

Sample answer:

a) $H_2SO_3 + 2KOH = K_2SO_3 + 2H_2O$

b) To prepare 1.00 M solution of KOH, I would dissolve 57g of KOH in 1 liter of solution.

c) It takes to 2 moles of KOH to react with each mole of H_2SO_3.

Answers

Practice F

1. 0.157 M CH_3COOH
2. 0.0128 M H_2SO_4

Assess and Reteach ▼

Assess Use the Formative Assessment on this page to evaluate student mastery of the section.

Reteach For students who need additional instruction, download the Section Study Guide.

Response to Intervention To reassess students' mastery, use the Section Quiz, available to print or to take directly online at **HMDScience.com**.

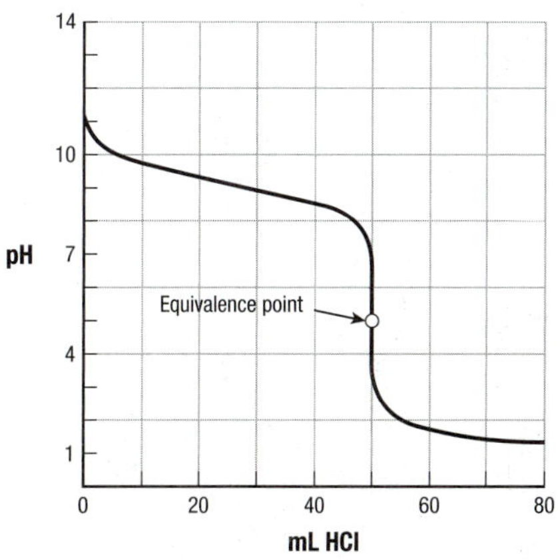

Answers

1. pH = 3.07
2. 8.9×10^{-5} M OH^-

Teaching Tip

With log calculations, rounding off intermediate steps can result in a difference in the final answer. Take this opportunity to remind students that intermediate results in a problem should not be rounded to the correct number of significant figures until the final result is obtained.

Math Tutor | Using Logarithms and pH

When you work with acids and bases, you often need to state the hydronium ion concentration, $[H_3O^+]$, of a solution. One simple way is to use the negative logarithm of $[H_3O^+]$. This quantity is called *pH*. For example, pure water has a $[H_3O^+]$ of 1.00×10^{-7} M. So, the pH of pure water is $-\log(1.00 \times 10^{-7}\text{ M}) = 7.00$. A solution of 0.1 M HCl has a pH of 1.00 or pH = $-\log(1 \times 10^{-1}) = 1.00$. The term *pOH* is also used for the negative logarithm of the hydroxide ion concentration, $[OH^-]$. The pOH of pure water is also 7.00.

Problem-Solving TIPS

- For pure water at 25°C, $[H_3O^+] = [OH^-] = 1.00 \times 10^{-7}$ M.
- The ionization constant of water, K_w, is the product of $[H_3O^+]$ and $[OH^-]$, so $K_w = [H_3O^+][OH^-] = (1.00 \times 10^{-7})(1.00 \times 10^{-7}) = 1.00 \times 10^{-14}$ at 25°C.
- If you know either $[H_3O^+]$ or $[OH^-]$, you can determine the other concentration.
- In terms of pH and pOH, pH + pOH = 14.00 for an aqueous solution at 25°C.
- Because pH calculations involve scientific notation and changes in signs, you should always check to see if answers make sense.

Sample Problem

What is the pH of a 0.0046 M solution of KOH?

KOH is completely dissociated into equal numbers of $K^+(aq)$ and $OH^-(aq)$. The concentration of OH^- is the same as the concentration of dissolved KOH, 0.0046 M. So, $[OH^-] = 4.6 \times 10^{-3}$ M, and pOH = $-\log(4.6 \times 10^{-3}\text{ M}) = 2.34$.

For an aqueous solution at 25°C, pH + pOH = 14.00, so pH + 2.34 = 14.00.

Therefore, the pH of 0.0046 M KOH solution = 14.00 − 2.34 = 11.66.

What is the hydronium ion concentration, $[H_3O^+]$, of a solution with a pH of 4.08? What is the pOH of the solution?

In this solution, $\log[H_3O^+] = -4.08$

$[H_3O^+] = \text{antilog}(-4.08) = 0.000\,083\text{ M} = 8.3 \times 10^{-5}$ M

The pOH of the solution is 14.00 − pH = 14.00 − 4.08 = 9.92.

Practice

Answers in Appendix E

1. What is the pH of a 0.000 85 M solution of nitric acid, HNO_3, which is a strong acid?
2. What is the hydroxide ion concentration of an aqueous solution that has a pH of 9.95?

CHAPTER 15 Summary

Review Games
Concept Maps

SECTION 1 Aqueous Solutions and the Concept of pH

- Pure water undergoes self-ionization to give 1.0×10^{-7} M H_3O^+ and 1.0×10^{-7} M OH^- at 25°C.
- $pH = -log[H_3O^+]$; $pOH = -log[OH^-]$; at 25°C, pH + pOH = 14.0.
- At 25°C, acids have a pH of less than 7, bases have a pH of greater than 7, and neutral solutions have a pH of 7.
- If a solution contains a strong acid or a strong base, the $[H_3O^+]$, $[OH^-]$, and pH can be calculated from the molarity of the solution. If a solution contains a weak acid or a weak base, the $[H_3O^+]$ and the $[OH^-]$ must be calculated from an experimentally measured pH.

KEY TERMS

self-ionization of water
pH
pOH

SECTION 2 Determining pH and Titrations

- The pH of a solution can be measured using either a pH meter or acid-base indicators.
- Titration uses a solution of known concentration to determine the concentration of a solution of unknown concentration.
- To determine the end point of a titration, one should choose indicators that change color over ranges that include the pH of the equivalence point.
- When the molarity and volume of a known solution used in a titration are known, then the molarity of a given volume of an unknown solution can be found.

KEY TERMS

acid-base indicators
transition interval
pH meter
titration
equivalence point
end point
standard solution
primary standard

Review Answers

1. Water undergoes self-ionization.
2. the concentration of the substance in molarity (moles per liter)
3. a. 1.0×10^{-7} M
   b. No, $[H_3O^+]$ increases with increasing temperature because the ionization of water increases.
4. a. The $[H_3O^+]$ is greater than the $[OH^-]$.
   b. The $[H_3O^+]$ is greater than 1.0×10^{-7} M.
5. a. the negative common logarithm of the hydronium ion concentration
   b. $pH = -\log [H_3O^+]$
   c. Answers will vary but may include that it is the power to which 10 must be raised to give the number. For example, the log of 10^7 is 7.
6. a. neutral
   b. basic
   c. neutral
   d. acidic
   e. neutral
   f. acidic
   g. basic
7. g, b, c, e, f, d, a, i, h
8. a. $[H_3O^+] = 3.0 \times 10^{-2}$ M; $[OH^-] = 3.3 \times 10^{-13}$ M
   b. $[H_3O^+] = 1.0 \times 10^{-10}$ M; $[OH^-] = 1.0 \times 10^{-4}$ M
   c. $[H_3O^+] = 5.0 \times 10^{-3}$ M; $[OH^-] = 2.0 \times 10^{-12}$ M
   d. $[H_3O^+] = 5.0 \times 10^{-13}$ M; $[OH^-] = 2.0 \times 10^{-2}$ M
9. a. 2.00
   b. 3.00
   c. 5.00
   d. 4.00
10. a. 8.00
    b. 5.00
    c. 12.00
    d. 7.00
11. a. 12.00
    b. 11.00
    c. 10.00
12. a. 4.70
    b. 6.33
    c. 2.42
13. a. 1×10^{-3}
    b. 1.0×10^{-7}
    c. 1×10^{-11}
    d. 1×10^{-5}
14. a. 1.0×10^{-7}
    b. 1.0×10^{-3}
    c. 1.0×10^{-10}
    d. 1.0×10^{-8}
15. a. 5.9×10^{-5} M
    b. 2.2×10^{-8} M
    c. 3.3×10^{-10} M

CHAPTER 15 Review

SECTION 1

Aqueous Solutions and the Concept of pH

REVIEWING MAIN IDEAS

1. Why is pure water a very weak electric conductor?
2. What does it mean when the formula of a particular ion or molecule is enclosed in brackets?
3. a. What is the $[H_3O^+]$ of pure water at 25°C?
   b. Is this true at all temperatures? Why or why not?
4. a. What is always true about the $[H_3O^+]$ value of acidic solutions?
   b. What is true about the $[H_3O^+]$ value of acidic solutions at 25°C?
5. a. Describe what is meant by the pH of a solution.
   b. Write the equation for determining pH.
   c. Explain and illustrate what is meant by the common logarithm of a number.
6. Identify each of the following solutions that are at 25°C as acidic, basic, or neutral:
   a. $[H_3O^+] = 1.0 \times 10^{-7}$ M
   b. $[H_3O^+] = 1.0 \times 10^{-10}$ M
   c. $[OH^-] = 1.0 \times 10^{-7}$ M
   d. $[OH^-] = 1.0 \times 10^{-11}$ M
   e. $[H_3O^+] = [OH^-]$
   f. pH = 3.0
   g. pH = 13.0
7. Arrange the following common substances in order of increasing pH:
   a. eggs
   b. apples
   c. tomatoes
   d. milk
   e. bananas
   f. potatoes
   g. lemons
   h. milk of magnesia
   i. sea water

PRACTICE PROBLEMS

8. Calculate the $[H_3O^+]$ and $[OH^-]$ for each of the following. (Hint: See Sample Problem A.)
   a. 0.030 M HCl
   b. 1.0×10^{-4} M NaOH
   c. 5.0×10^{-3} M HNO_3
   d. 0.010 M $Ca(OH)_2$
9. Determine the pH of each of the following solutions. (Hint: See Sample Problem B.)
   a. 1.0×10^{-2} M HCl
   b. 1.0×10^{-3} M HNO_3
   c. 1.0×10^{-5} M HI
   d. 1.0×10^{-4} M HBr
10. Given the following $[OH^-]$ values, determine the pH of each solution.
    a. 1.0×10^{-6} M
    b. 1.0×10^{-9} M
    c. 1.0×10^{-2} M
    d. 1.0×10^{-7} M
11. Determine the pH of each solution.
    a. 1.0×10^{-2} M NaOH
    b. 1.0×10^{-3} M KOH
    c. 1.0×10^{-4} M LiOH
12. Determine the pH of solutions with each of the following $[H_3O^+]$. (Hint: See Sample Problem C.)
    a. 2.0×10^{-5} M
    b. 4.7×10^{-7} M
    c. 3.8×10^{-3} M
13. Given the following pH values, determine the $[H_3O^+]$ for each solution. (Hint: See Sample Problem D.)
    a. 3.0
    b. 7.00
    c. 11.0
    d. 5.0
14. Given the following pH values, determine the $[OH^-]$ for each solution.
    a. 7.00
    b. 11.00
    c. 4.00
    d. 6.00
15. Determine $[H_3O^+]$ for solutions with the following pH values. (Hint: See Sample Problem E.)
    a. 4.23
    b. 7.65
    c. 9.48
16. A nitric acid solution is found to have a pH of 2.70. Determine each of the following:
    a. $[H_3O^+]$
    b. $[OH^-]$
    c. the number of moles of HNO_3 required to prepare 5.50 L of this solution
    d. the mass of HNO_3 in the solution in part (c)
    e. the milliliters of concentrated acid needed to prepare the solution in part (c) (Concentrated nitric acid is 69.5% HNO_3 by mass and has a density of 1.42 g/mL.)

496 Chapter 15

SECTION 2

Determining pH and Titrations

REVIEWING MAIN IDEAS

17. What is meant by the transition interval of an indicator?

18. Explain how changes in pH affect the color of an indicator.

19. a. Without using an indicator, how can you determine the equivalence point of a titration experiment or the pH of a solution?
b. What can be observed about the rate of change of the pH of a solution near the end point of a titration?

20. a. What is meant by the end point of a titration?
b. What is the role of an indicator in the titration process?
c. On what basis is an indicator selected for a particular titration experiment?

21. For each of the four possible types of acid-base titration combinations (strong-strong, strong-weak, etc.), indicate the approximate pH at the end point. Also name a suitable indicator for detecting that end point.

22. Use **Figures 2.7a** and **2.7b** to sketch the pH curve of a strong acid being titrated by a weak base.

23. An unknown solution is colorless when tested with phenolphthalein but causes the indicator phenol red to turn red. Use this information to find the approximate pH of this solution.

PRACTICE PROBLEMS

24. For each of the following acid-base titration combinations, determine the number of moles of the first substance listed that would be the chemically equivalent amount of the second substance.
a. NaOH with 1.0 mol HCl
b. HNO_3 with 0.75 mol KOH
c. $Ba(OH)_2$ with 0.20 mol HF
d. H_2SO_4 with 0.90 mol $Mg(OH)_2$

25. Suppose that 15.0 mL of 2.50×10^{-2} M aqueous H_2SO_4 is required to neutralize 10.0 mL of an aqueous solution of KOH. What is the molarity of the KOH solution? (Hint: See Sample Problem F.)

26. In a titration experiment, a 12.5 mL sample of 1.75×10^{-2} M $Ba(OH)_2$ just neutralized 14.5 mL of HNO_3 solution. Calculate the molarity of the HNO_3 solution.

Mixed Review

REVIEWING MAIN IDEAS

27. a. What is the $[OH^-]$ of a 4.0×10^{-4} M solution of $Ca(OH)_2$?
b. What is the $[H_3O^+]$ of the solution?

28. Given the following $[H_3O^+]$ values, determine the pH of each solution.
a. 1.0×10^{-7} M
b. 1.0×10^{-3} M
c. 1.0×10^{-12} M
d. 1.0×10^{-5} M

29. What is the $[H_3O^+]$ for a solution that has a pH of 6.0?

30. Suppose that a 5.0×10^{-5} M solution of $Ba(OH)_2$ is prepared. What is the pH of the solution?

31. a. Calculate the pH of a solution that has an $[H_3O^+]$ of 8.4×10^{-11} M.
b. Calculate the $[H_3O^+]$ of a solution that has a pH of 2.50.

32. a. What is the concentration of OH^- in a 5.4×10^{-5} M solution of magnesium hydroxide, $Mg(OH)_2$?
b. Calculate the concentration of H_3O^+ for this solution.

33. a. Calculate the molarity of H_3O^+ in a solution that has a pH of 8.90.
b. Calculate the concentration of OH^- for this solution.

34. What is the pH of a solution in which $[OH^-]$ equals 6.9×10^{-10} M?

35. In a titration, 25.9 mL of 3.4×10^{-3} M $Ba(OH)_2$ neutralized 16.6 mL of HCl solution. What is the molarity of the HCl solution?

36. Find the molarity of a $Ca(OH)_2$ solution given that 428 mL of the solution is neutralized in a titration by 115 mL of 6.7×10^{-3} M HNO_3.

37. Suppose that 10.1 mL of HNO_3 is neutralized by 71.4 mL of a 4.2×10^{-3} M solution of KOH in a titration. Calculate the concentration of the HNO_3 solution.

16. a. 2.0×10^{-3} M
b. 5.0×10^{-12} M
c. 1.1×10^{-2} mol HNO_3
d. 0.69 g HNO_3
e. 0.70 mL concentrated acid

17. the pH range over which an indicator changes color

18. An acid-base indicator is a weak acid or a weak base. In solution, it is in equilibrium with an ionized form that has a different color. The addition of H_3O^+ pushes the equilibrium in one direction, toward one color. An increase in OH^- pushes the equilibrium toward the other color.

19. a. by using a pH meter
b. A rapid change in pH occurs.

CHAPTER REVIEW

20. a. the point in a titration when an indicator changes color
b. to show a color change when the equivalence point is reached
c. Its transition interval must include the pH of the equivalence point.

21. Answers may vary. Sample answer: strong-acid/strong-base: pH about 7.0, litmus, phenolphthalein, methyl red, or bromthymol blue; strong-acid/weak-base: pH below 7, methyl orange or bromphenol blue; weak-acid/strong-base: pH above 7, phenolphthalein or phenol red; weak-acid/weak-base: pH either above or below 7, no satisfactory indicator

22. The graph should be similar in shape to those found in **Figure 2.7**, with the equivalence point below pH 7.

23. approximately 7 to 8

24. a. 1.0 mol NaOH
b. 0.75 mol HNO_3
c. 0.10 mol $Ba(OH)_2$
d. 0.90 mol H_2SO_4

25. 7.50×10^{-2} M KOH

26. 3.02×10^{-2} M HNO_3

27. a. 8.0×10^{-4} M
b. 1.3×10^{-11} M

28. a. 7.00
b. 3.00
c. 12.00
d. 5.00

29. 1×10^{-6} M

30. 10.00

31. a. 10.08
b. 3.2×10^{-3} M

32. a. 1.1×10^{-4} M
b. 9.3×10^{-11} M

33. a. 1.3×10^{-9} M
b. 7.9×10^{-6} M

34. 4.84

35. 1.1×10^{-2} M HCl

36. 9.0×10^{-4} M $Ca(OH)_2$

37. 3.0×10^{-2} M

38. The two sudden changes of pH at about 25 mL and 50 mL indicate a diprotic acid. The first change indicates the depletion of the first H^+ that dissociates, and the second change indicates the depletion of the second H^+. The pH ends near 13, which corresponds to that of a 0.1 M NaOH solution.

39. a. CO_2 and HCO_3^-

b. acidosis

c. Hyperventilation is rapid breathing for an extended period of time, which results in a reduction of CO_2 levels in the blood. To compensate, the equilibrium system of the blood shifts to favor the formation of CO_2, which reduces the H_3O^+ and causes the pH of the blood to rise.

40. The flexibility of healthy hair depends on the ability of the protein chains in the cuticle layer to shift. Scalp oils and a natural acid coating help protect hair. A shampoo with a basic pH can neutralize the acidic protective coating of the hair and can also help eliminate scalp oils.

41. Answers may vary. Ask students to document their sources of information. Generally, areas affected by acid rain are downwind from industrialized areas where sulfur and nitrogen oxides originate.

42. Answers may vary but should be fairly close in range. Remind students to use proper laboratory technique.

43. Answers may vary. Remind students to observe all lab safety precautions.

CRITICAL THINKING

38. Interpreting Graphics The following titration curve resulted from the titration of an unknown acid with 0.10 M NaOH. Analyze the curve. Make inferences related to the type of acidic solution titrated.

Titration of an Unknown Acid

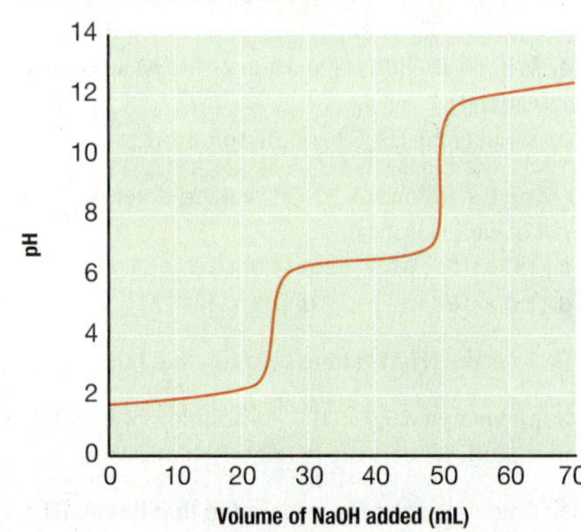

USING THE HANDBOOK

39. The normal pH of blood is about 7.4. When the pH shifts above or below that level, the results are acidosis or alkalosis. Review the section on blood pH in Group 14 of the *Elements Handbook* (Appendix A), and answer the following.

a. What chemical species keep H_3O^+ in blood at the appropriate pH?

b. What condition results when there is an excess of CO_2 in the blood?

c. What is hyperventilation and how does it affect blood pH?

RESEARCH AND WRITING

40. Examine the labels of at least five brands of shampoo. Note what is written there, if anything, regarding the pH of the shampoo. Do library research to find out why such pH ranges are chosen and why other ranges might be harmful to hair or eyes.

41. Acid rain is an environmental issue that crosses state and national boundaries. Conduct library research on this topic and write a brief report. Include a description of the areas in the United States affected by acid rain, and the geographical source of the sulfur and nitrogen oxides that are responsible for acid rain in each region.

ALTERNATIVE ASSESSMENT

42. Performance Use pH paper to determine the approximate pH of various brands of orange juice, which contains citric acid.

43. Performance Design and conduct an experiment to extract possible acid-base indicators from sources such as red cabbage, berries, and flower petals. Use known acidic, basic, and neutral solutions to test the action of each indicator that you are able to isolate.

Standards-Based Assessment

Answer the following items on a separate piece of paper.

MULTIPLE CHOICE

1. Distilled water contains
   A. H_2O.
   B. H_3O^+.
   C. OH^-.
   D. All of the above

2. What is the pH of a 0.0010 M HNO_3?
   A. 1.0
   B. 3.0
   C. 4.0
   D. 5.0

3. Which of the following solutions would have a pH value greater than 7?
   A. $[OH^-] = 2.4 \times 10^{-2}$ M
   B. $[H_3O^+] = 1.53 \times 10^{-2}$ M
   C. 0.0001 M HCl
   D. $[OH^-] = 4.4 \times 10^{-9}$ M

4. If the pH of a solution of the strong base NaOH is known, which property of the solution can be calculated?
   A. molar concentration
   B. $[OH^-]$
   C. $[H_3O^+]$
   D. All of the above

5. A neutral aqueous solution
   A. has a 7.0 M H_3O^+ concentration.
   B. contains neither hydronium ions nor hydroxide ions.
   C. has an equal number of hydronium ions and hydroxide ions.
   D. None of the above

6. Identify the salt that forms when a solution of H_2SO_4 is titrated with a solution of $Ca(OH)_2$.
   A. calcium sulfate
   B. calcium hydroxide
   C. calcium oxide
   D. calcium phosphate

7. The pH of a solution is 6.32. What is the pOH?
   A. 6.32
   B. 4.8×10^{-7}
   C. 7.68
   D. 2.1×10^{-8}

8. The K_w value for water can be affected by
   A. dissolving a salt in the solution.
   B. changes in temperature.
   C. changes in the hydroxide ion concentration.
   D. the presence of a strong acid.

9. Which of the pH levels listed below is the most acidic?
   A. pH = 1
   B. pH = 5
   C. pH = 9
   D. pH = 13

SHORT ANSWER

10. A solution has a pH of 4.75. What is the hydronium ion concentration? Is the solution acidic or basic?

11. A weak acid that is used as an indicator is added to a strong acid solution before titration of the strong acid with a strong base. Why doesn't the weak acid affect the value calculated for the concentration of the acid?

EXTENDED RESPONSE

12. The hydroxide ion concentration in a solution is 1.6×10^{-11} M. What are the $[H_3O^+]$, the pH, and the pOH of the solution?

13. Write the balanced equation and the net ionic equation that represent the reaction that takes place when milk of magnesia (magnesium hydroxide) reacts with hydrochloric acid in your stomach.

Test Tip
If you do not understand a question, try to reword it. But be careful not to change its meaning.

STANDARDS-BASED ASSESSMENT

To give students practice under more realistic testing conditions, give them 60 minutes to answer all of the questions in this Standardized Test Preparation.

Test Answers

1. D
2. B
3. A
4. D
5. C
6. A
7. C
8. B
9. A
10. $[H_3O^+] = 1.8 \times 10^{-5}$ M; acidic
11. A very small amount of indicator is added. Therefore, the amount of base required to neutralize the very small amount of the weak acid is not significant.
12. $[H_3O^+] = 6.3 \times 10^{-4}$; pH = 3.20; pOH = 10.80
13. $Mg(OH)_2(s) + 2HCl(aq) \longrightarrow MgCl_2(aq) + 2H_2O(aq)$; $Mg(OH)_2(s) + 2H_3O^+(aq) \longrightarrow Mg^{2+}(aq) + 4H_2O(aq)$

Reaction Energy

1 Core Instruction

Chapter Resources

- The Teacher's Edition wrap has extensive teaching support for every lesson, including Misconception Alerts, Teach from Visuals, Demonstrations, Teaching Tips, Differentiated Instruction, and Problem Solving support.
- Several additional presentation tools are available online for every chapter, including Animated Chemistry features and Visual Concepts.
- You can open your lesson with the Why It Matters Video: Equations and Reactions.

Section	Instruction	Labs and Demonstrations Go Online for Materials Lists and Solutions Lists.
16.1	▪ **Textbook:** Thermochemistry **Animated Chemistry:** Endothermic and Exothermic Reactions **Teaching Visuals:** Enthalpy Changes in an Exothermic Reaction • Enthalpy Changes in an Endothermic Reaction • Transfers of Energy for Different Types of Changes • Molar Heat Capacities of Elements and Compounds • Thermodynamic Data **PowerPresentations**	▪ **Demonstration:** Boiling Water in a Paper Cup ▪ **Demonstration:** Hess's Law ▪ **Lab:** Calorimetry and Hess's Law (Core Skill) ▪ **Lab:** Evaluating Fuels (Forensics) ▪ **Lab:** Energy in Foods (Probeware) ▪ **Lab:** A Burning Interest (STEM)
16.2	▪ **Textbook:** Driving Force of Reactions **Teaching Visuals:** Models for Low Entropy and High Entropy Systems • Calculations Involving Energy • Standard Entropy Changes for Some Reactions • Relating Enthalpy and Entropy Changes to Spontaneity **PowerPresentations**	

2 Support and Intervention

- **Interactive Reader** (English and Spanish)
- **Study Guide**
- **Interactive Review:** Review Games, Concept Maps, and Section Self-Checks
- **Scientific Reasoning Skill Builder**
- **Learn It! Videos**
- **Solve It! Cards**
- **Interactive Demos**
- **Sample Problem Sets**

3 Specialized Support

- **Chapter Summary Audio Files**
- **Interactive Reader Audio Files**
- **Differentiated Instruction:** Inclusion, Below Level, and English Learners (TE wrap)

Enrichment and Challenge

- **Differentiated Instruction:** Pre-AP (TE wrap)
- **Why It Matters:** Self-Heating Meals (SE)
- **WebLinks**

Assessment

- **Section Formative Assessments** (SE)
- **Section Quizzes**
- **Chapter Review** (SE)
- **Chapter Tests A and B**
- **Alternative Assessment** (TE wrap)
- **Online Assessment and Remediation**
- **ExamView Banks**

Where do I find it?

		PRINT	DVD	ONLINE
1	Animated Chemistry		■	■
	Demonstrations (TE wrap)	■		■
	Interactive Whiteboard		■	■
	Labs		■	■
	PowerPresentations		■	■
	QuickLabs	■	■	■
	Teaching Visuals		■	■
	Textbook	■	■	■
	Visual Concepts		■	■
	Why It Matters Videos		■	■
2	Interactive Demos		■	■
	Interactive Reader	■	■	■
	Interactive Reviews		■	■
	Learn It! Videos		■	■
	Sample Problem Sets		■	■
	Scientific Reasoning Skill Builder		■	■
	Smart Grapher Tool		■	■
	Solve It! Cards		■	■
	Study Guide		■	■
3	Chapter Summary Audio Files		■	■
	Differentiated Instruction (TE wrap)	■		
	Interactive Reader Audio Files		■	■

CHAPTER 16

Chapter Overview

Section 1 defines heat and temperature and explains enthalpy change, as well as enthalpies of reaction, formation, and combustion.

Section 2 explains how to use enthalpy, entropy, and free energy to predict whether a reaction will occur.

▼ Focus and Motivate

Activate Prior Knowledge

Students may need a review of the following concepts:

- conservation of energy
- bond energies
- kinetic theory of matter
- molar concentrations
- enthalpy of solution

About the Image

Chemists can determine the rate at which chemical reactions occur. Some reactions occur very quickly. An example is the thermite reaction, in which iron(III) oxide reacts with aluminum to produce molten iron.

Why It Matters

Students can access the video online and find other helpful resources at **HMDScience.com**.

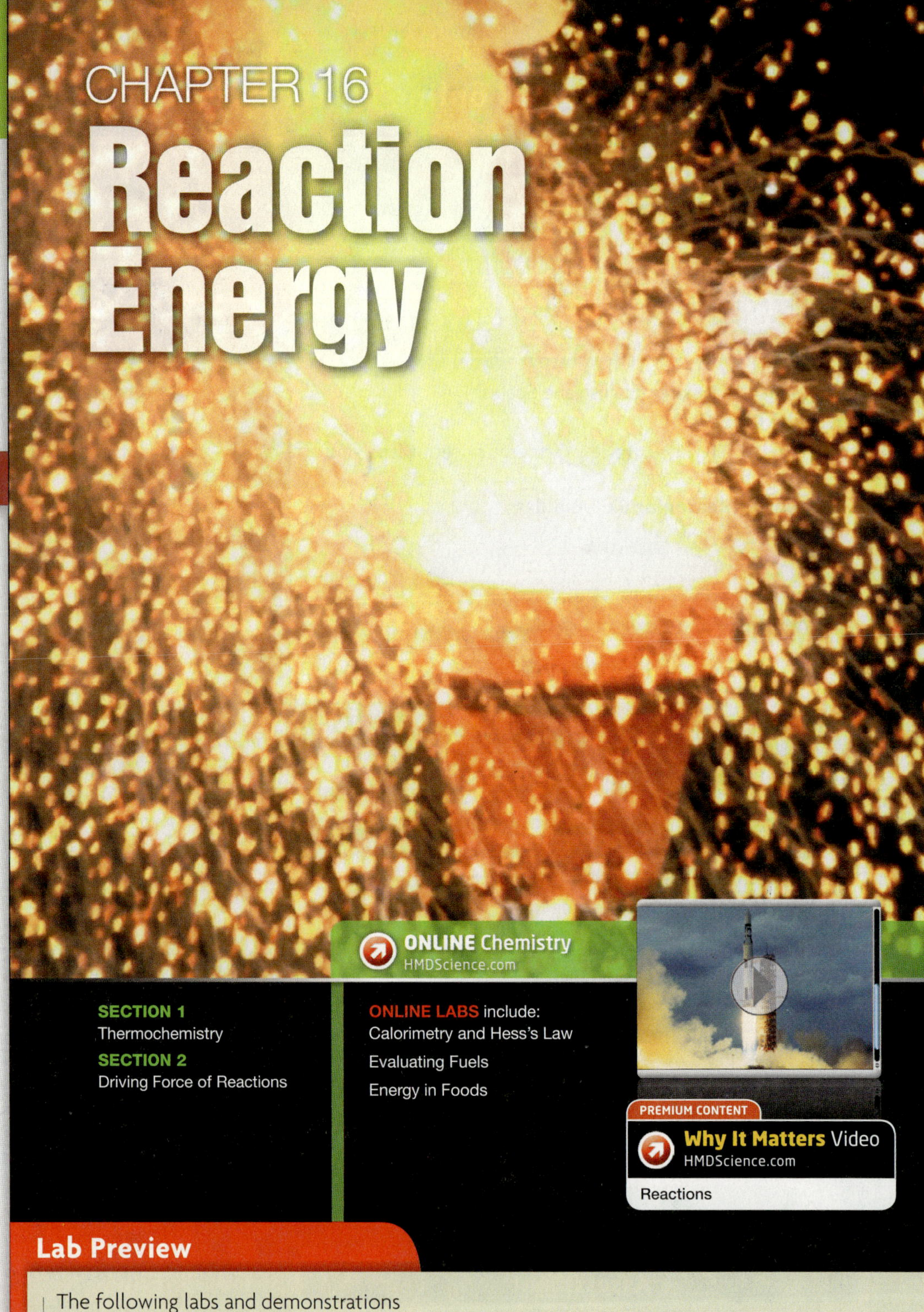

CHAPTER 16

Reaction Energy

ONLINE Chemistry
HMDScience.com

SECTION 1
Thermochemistry

SECTION 2
Driving Force of Reactions

ONLINE LABS include:
Calorimetry and Hess's Law
Evaluating Fuels
Energy in Foods

PREMIUM CONTENT
Why It Matters Video
HMDScience.com
Reactions

Lab Preview

The following labs and demonstrations support the concepts in this chapter.

LABS

Calorimetry and Hess's Law (Core Skill)
Evaluating Fuels (Forensics)
Energy in Foods (Probeware)
A Burning Interest (STEM)

DEMONSTRATIONS

Boiling Water in a Paper Cup
Hess's Law

Thermochemistry

Key Terms

thermochemistry
calorimeter
temperature
joule
heat
specific heat
enthalpy change
enthalpy of reaction
thermochemical equation
molar enthalpy of formation
enthalpy of combustion
Hess's law

Virtually every chemical reaction is accompanied by a change in energy. Chemical reactions usually absorb or release energy as heat. You learned in the chapter about changes in state, that energy is also absorbed or released in physical changes, such as melting a solid or condensing a vapor. **Thermochemistry is the study of the transfers of energy as heat that accompany chemical reactions and physical changes.**

SECTION 1

Main Ideas

- Temperature and heat are related but not identical.
- Energy transfer varies from reaction to reaction.
- Heat energy is transferred during a reaction.
- Enthalpy of formation is the energy change when elements form one mole of a compound.
- Exothermic compounds tend to be very stable.
- Enthalpy changes in combustion.
- Change in enthalpy is calculated using Hess's Law.
- Enthalpy of formation is the sum of its sub-reaction enthalpies.

MAIN IDEA

Temperature and heat are related but not identical.

The energy absorbed or released as heat in a chemical or physical change is measured in a calorimeter. In one kind of calorimeter, known quantities of reactants are sealed in a reaction chamber, which is immersed in a known quantity of water in an insulated vessel. Therefore, the energy given off (or absorbed) during the reaction is equal to the energy absorbed (or given off) by the known quantity of water. The amount of energy is determined from the temperature change of the known mass of surrounding water. The data collected from calorimetry experiments are temperature changes because energy cannot be measured directly; but temperature, which is affected by the transfer of energy as heat, is directly measurable. To see why this is so, let us look at the definitions of heat and temperature and at how temperature is measured.

Temperature is a measure of the average kinetic energy of the particles in a sample of matter. The greater the kinetic energy of the particles in a sample, the higher the temperature is and the hotter it feels. To assign a numerical value to temperature, it is necessary to define a temperature scale. For calculations in thermochemistry, we use the Celsius and Kelvin scales. Celsius and Kelvin temperatures are related by the following equation.

$$K = 273.15 + {}^\circ C$$

For most calculations in this book, 273.15 is rounded to 273.

The ability to measure temperature is thus based on energy transfer. The amount of energy transferred as heat is usually measured in joules. **A joule is the SI unit of heat as well as all other forms of energy.** The joule, abbreviated J, is derived from the units for force and length.

$$N \times m = \frac{kg \times m^2}{s^2}$$

Differentiated Instruction

BELOW LEVEL

Remind students that there are only seven SI units, which are used to derive other units, such as the joule. Show students how the joule is a derived unit. Have students identify the SI base unit for length. meter (m) Point out that the newton (N) is a derived unit for force: kg × m × s^{-2}. Ask students to show how the joule has the derived units kg × m^2 × s^{-2}. Students should multiply the SI unit for length (m) by the derived unit for newton (kg × m^2 × s^{-2}).

SECTION 1

Plan and Prepare ▼

Objectives

Upon completion of this section, students should be able to do the following:

- Define *temperature* and state the units in which it is measured.
- Define *heat* and state its units.
- Perform specific-heat calculations.
- Explain enthalpy change, enthalpy of reaction, enthalpy of formation, and enthalpy of combustion.
- Solve problems involving enthalpies of reaction, enthalpies of formation, and enthalpies of combustion.

Classroom Catalyst

Fill a **250-mL beaker** and a **10-mL graduated cylinder** with **hot water.** Ask a student to confirm that the water in both containers has the same temperature. Ask students which container they think can potentially release more energy as heat. Have them informally compare temperature and heat

Teach ▼

READING TOOLKIT

Write the terms heat and temperature on the board. Have students brainstorm all the words, phrases, and ideas that they associate with these terms. Have a volunteer write the students' contributions on the board. Lead a discussion about how the ideas on the board are related. As they read Section 1, have students add to the list and mark portions of the text that need clarification. After further class discussion, have students make notes of everything they remember about heat and temperature based on experience and the discussion..

▼ Teach *continued*

Teaching Tip

Scientists have different understandings of what *heat* is. To some scientists, heat is the *process of energy transfer* between substances because of a difference in their temperatures. To other scientists, heat is the *energy that is transferred* between substances because of a difference in their temperatures. Explain to students that they may encounter either understanding in a different science course.

Misconception Alert!

Students often misuse the terms *temperature* and *heat*. Be sure they understand that there is a difference. Temperature is a measure of the average kinetic energy of particles in a sample of matter. Heat is the energy that is transferred between samples of matter because of a difference in their temperatures.

TEACH FROM VISUALS

FIGURE 1.1 Use the figures to emphasize that terms such as *hot* and *cold* are not scientific terms. They do not have absolute meanings and can be used only as comparisons.

Demonstration

BOILING WATER IN A PAPER CUP

Place a **small paper cup** on **wire gauze** above a lit **Bunsen burner,** and watch the cup burn. Fill a **second paper cup** about half full of **water** and place it on the wire gauze above the Bunsen burner. The water will begin to boil in the cup, keeping the temperature of the cup below the combustion temperature of paper (233°C).

Safety Wear **safety goggles** and a **lab apron.** Have students stand back at least 2 m from the demonstration.

Disposal Pour any remaining water down the drain. Put used cups in the trash.

FIGURE 1.1

Transfer of Energy The direction of energy transfer as heat is determined by the temperature differences between the objects within a system. The energy is transferred as heat from the hotter brass bar to the cooler water. This energy transfer will continue until the bar and the water reach the same temperature.

Heat can be thought of as the energy transferred between samples of matter because of a difference in their temperatures. Energy transferred as heat always moves spontaneously from matter at a higher temperature to matter at a lower temperature. As shown in **Figure 1.1,** the temperature of the cool water in the beaker increases as energy flows into it. Likewise, the temperature of the hot brass bar decreases as energy flows away from it. When the temperature of the water equals the temperature of the brass bar, energy is no longer transferred as heat within the system.

MAIN IDEA

Energy transfer varies from reaction to reaction.

The quantity of energy transferred as heat during a temperature change depends on the nature of the material changing temperature, the mass of the material changing temperature, and the size of the temperature change. One gram of iron heated to 100.0°C and cooled to 50.0°C in a calorimeter transfers 22.5 J of energy to the surrounding water. But one gram of silver transfers 11.8 J of energy under the same conditions. The difference depends on the metals' differing capacities for absorbing this energy. A quantity called specific heat can be used to compare heat absorption capacities for different materials. **Specific heat is the amount of energy required to raise the temperature of one gram of a substance by one Celsius degree (1°C) or one kelvin (1 K) (because the sizes of the degree divisions on both scales are equal).** Values of specific heat can be given in units of joules per gram per Celsius degree, J/(g • °C), joules per gram per kelvin, J/(g • K), or calories per gram per Celsius degree, cal/(g • °C). **Figure 1.2** gives the specific heats of some common substances. Notice the extremely high specific heat of water, one of the highest of most common substances. This is why water plays such a crucial role in regulating temperature.

Differentiated Instruction

ENGLISH LEARNERS

To help students understand the concept of specific heat, have them make a list of the three units for specific heat given on this page:

J/(g • °C)
J/(g • K)
cal/(g • °C)

Next to each one, have students write the quantities that are involved.

J/(g • °C) energy, mass, temperature
J/(g • K) energy, mass, temperature
cal/(g • °C) energy, mass, temperature

Students should then see that these three quantities are used in problems involving specific heat, as they will learn in Sample Problem A.

FIGURE 1.2

SPECIFIC HEATS OF SOME COMMON SUBSTANCES AT 298.15 K

Substance	Specific heat J/(g•K)
Water (*l*)	4.18
Water (*s*)	2.06
Water (*g*)	1.87
Ammonia (*g*)	2.09
Benzene (*l*)	1.74
Ethanol (*l*)	2.44
Ethanol (*g*)	1.42
Aluminum (*s*)	0.897
Calcium (*s*)	0.647
Carbon, graphite (*s*)	0.709
Copper (*s*)	0.385
Gold (*s*)	0.129
Iron (*s*)	0.449
Mercury (*l*)	0.140
Lead (*s*)	0.129

Specific heat is measured under constant pressure conditions, so its symbol, c_p, has a subscripted p as a reminder. In the equation, c_p is the specific heat at a given pressure, q is the energy lost or gained, m is the mass of the sample, and ΔT represents the change in temperature.

$$c_p = \frac{q}{m \times \Delta T}$$

This equation can be rearranged to give an equation that can be used to find the quantity of energy gained or lost with a change in temperature.

Energy Lost or Gained $q = c_p \times m \times \Delta T$

Specific Heat

Sample Problem A **A 4.0-g sample of glass was heated from 274 K to 314 K, a temperature increase of 40. K, and was found to have absorbed 32 J of energy as heat.**

a. What is the specific heat of this type of glass?

b. How much energy will the same glass sample gain when it is heated from 314 K to 344 K?

Continued

Problem Solving

TAKE IT FURTHER

Point out that in Sample Problem A, energy as heat is transferred to the glass. Students should realize that ΔT will have a positive value, because energy as heat is being absorbed. Ask students what would happen if, in part b, the temperature decreased from 344 K to 314 K. Students should see that the glass will cool as energy as heat is transferred from the glass to the surroundings. This loss of energy as heat by the glass is shown by the negative value for joules (−24 J) when the problem is solved using a $-\Delta T$ (−30 K).

Application

The kilocalorie (or Calorie) is used to measure the energy content of foods. The number of Calories supplied by a certain amount of a food is determined by reacting the food with oxygen in a calorimeter and measuring the amount of energy released as heat.

TEACH FROM TABLES

FIGURE 1.2 Ask students what conclusions, if any, they can draw about the relationship between specific heat and state of matter as indicated in this table. Ask them what other patterns they can find between specific heat and other properties of the substances shown in the table.

Classroom Discussion

Discuss with students the ways in which the defining equation for specific heat can also be solved for mass (m), for temperature change (ΔT), or for initial or final temperature (T_i or T_f) in a reaction.

Misconception Alert!

Students often think that a temperature change, ΔT, expressed in kelvins is 273 units larger than the same change expressed in degrees Celsius. Remind them that the temperature *increment* of one kelvin is the same size change as a temperature increment of one °C, so ΔT is the same number whether expressed in °C or in K. You will probably need to illustrate this with numbers.

For instance, the change from 20°C to 60°C is ΔT = 60°C−20°C = +40°C; converting each temperature to kelvins, the change is from 293 K to 333 K, or ΔT = 333 K − 293 K = ±40 K. Specific heats are often tabulated in J/(g • °C), but the values are the same as those in **Figure 1.2** in J/(g • K).

▼ Teach *continued*

Classroom Practice

A-1 A piece of copper alloy with a mass of 85.0 g is heated from 30.°C to 45°C. In the process, it absorbs 523 J of energy as heat.

a. What is the specific heat of this copper alloy?

b. How much energy will the same sample lose if it is cooled from 45°C to 25°C?

Answers: a. 0.41 J/(g • K)

b. 7.0×10^2 J

A-2 The temperature of a 74-g sample of material increases from 15°C to 45°C when it absorbs 2.0 kJ of energy as heat. What is the specific heat of the material?

Answer: 0.90 J/(g • K)

Answers

Practice A

1. 0.14 J/(g • K)

2. 329 K

Specific Heat (continued)

1 ANALYZE

Given: $m = 4.0\ g$

$\Delta T = 40.K$

$q = 32\ J$

Unknown: **a.** c_p = in J/(g • K) and **b.** q when $\Delta T = 344\ K - 314\ K$

2 PLAN

a. The specific heat, c_p, of the glass is calculated using the equation given for specific heat.

$$c_p = \frac{q}{m \times \Delta T}$$

b. The rearranged specific heat equation is used to find the energy gained when the glass was heated.

$$q = c_p \times m \times \Delta T$$

3 SOLVE

a. $c_p = \frac{32\ J}{(4.0\ g)(40.K)} = 0.20\ J/(g \cdot K)$

b. $q = \frac{0.20\ J}{(g \cdot K)}(4.0\ g)(344\ K - 314\ K)$

$q = \frac{0.20\ J}{(g \cdot K)}(4.0\ g)(30\ K) = 24\ J$

4 CHECK YOUR WORK

The units combine or cancel correctly to give the specific heat in J/(g • K) and the energy in J.

Practice Answers in Appendix E

1. Determine the specific heat of a material if a 35-g sample absorbed 96 J as it was heated from 293 K to 313 K.
2. If 980 kJ of energy are added to 6.2 L of water at 291 K, what will the final temperature of the water be?

MAIN IDEA

Heat energy is transferred during a reaction.

The energy absorbed as heat during a chemical reaction at constant pressure is represented by ΔH. The H is the symbol for a quantity called *enthalpy*. It is not practical to talk just about enthalpy as a quantity, because we have no way to directly measure the enthalpy of a system. Only *changes* in enthalpy can be measured. The Greek letter Δ ("delta") stands for "change in." Therefore, ΔH is read as "change in enthalpy." **An enthalpy change is the amount of energy absorbed by a system as heat during a process at constant pressure.** The enthalpy change is always the difference between the enthalpies of the products and the reactants. The following equation expresses an enthalpy change for a reaction.

Enthalpy $\Delta H = H_{products} - H_{reactants}$

Differentiated Instruction

PRE-AP

Explain that the enthalpy change of a reaction is commonly recorded in the unit kJ/mol. Ask students to use the equation for specific heat to calculate the ΔH in kJ/mol for a neutralization reaction. Inform students that solutions of NaOH and HCl were mixed in a calorimeter. Give students the following information:

100 mL of 0.50 M NaOH; 100 mL of 0.50 M HCl;
T_i = 20°C; T_f = 23.5°C; C_p [water]: 4.18 J/(g • K)

Tell students to assume that 1 mL of both the HCl and NaOH solutions have masses of 1 g.

energy released as heat =
(200 g)[4.18 J/(g • K)](3.5 K) = 2926 J = 2.9 kJ

Because the reactants are present in a 1:1 stoichiometric ratio, the ΔH will be calculated per mol of NaOH or per mol of HCl.

100 mL of 0.50 M NaOH = 0.05 mol NaOH

100 mL of 0.50 M HCl = 0.05 mol HCl

2.9 kJ/0.05 mol = −58 kJ/mol

The increase in temperature indicates that energy was released as heat when the NaOH and HCl solutions were mixed. As a result, the ΔH value is negative.

The enthalpy of reaction is the quantity of energy transferred as heat during a chemical reaction. You can think of enthalpy of reaction as the difference between the stored energy of the reactants and the products. Enthalpy of reaction is sometimes called "heat of reaction."

Enthalpy of Reaction in Exothermic Reactions

If a mixture of hydrogen and oxygen is ignited, water will form and energy will be released explosively. The energy that is released comes from the reactants as they form products. Because energy is released, the reaction is *exothermic*, and the energy of the product, water, must be less than the energy of the reactants. The following chemical equation for this reaction shows that when 2 mol of hydrogen gas at room temperature are burned, 1 mol of oxygen gas is consumed and 2 mol of water vapor are formed.

$$2H_2(g) + O_2(g) \longrightarrow 2H_2O(g)$$

The equation does not tell you that energy is evolved as heat during the reaction. Experiments have shown that 483.6 kJ of energy are evolved when 2 mol of gaseous water are formed from its elements at 298.15 K.

Modifying the chemical equation to show the amount of energy as heat released during the reaction gives the following expression.

$$2H_2(g) + O_2(g) \longrightarrow 2H_2O(g) + 483.6 \text{ kJ}$$

This expression is an example of a thermochemical equation, an equation that includes the quantity of energy released or absorbed as heat during the reaction as written. In any thermochemical equation, we must always interpret the coefficients as *numbers of moles* and never as *numbers of molecules*. The quantity of energy released as heat in this or any other reaction depends on the amounts of reactants and products. The quantity of energy as heat released during the formation of water from H_2 and O_2 is proportional to the quantity of water formed. Producing twice as much water vapor would require twice as many moles of reactants and would release 2 × 483.6 kJ of energy as heat, as shown in the following thermochemical equation (which is simply the previous thermochemical equation, multiplied by two).

$$4H_2(g) + 2O_2(g) \longrightarrow 4H_2O(g) + 967.2 \text{ kJ}$$

Producing one-half as much water requires one-half as many moles of reactants and releases only one-half as much energy, or $\frac{1}{2} \times 483.6$ kJ. The thermochemical equation for this reaction is follows.

$$H_2(g) + \frac{1}{2}O_2(g) \longrightarrow H_2O(g) + 241.8 \text{ kJ}$$

Enthalpy of Reaction in Endothermic Reactions

The situation is reversed in an *endothermic* reaction—products have a larger enthalpy than reactants. The decomposition of water vapor is endothermic; it is the reverse of the reaction that forms water vapor. The amount of energy as heat absorbed by water molecules to form hydrogen and oxygen equals the amount of energy as heat released when the elements combine to form the water. The equation changes accordingly.

ENGLISH LEARNERS

Explain that the use of the prefix *thermo-* in the term *thermochemical equation* simply means that the equation includes information about energy changes. Have students supply other examples of the use of *thermo-* in chemistry. Possibilities include thermometer, thermodynamics, and thermochemistry. Have students define each term to see that energy is involved. For example, a thermometer measures the average kinetic energy of particles.

Classroom Discussion

Discussing thermochemical equations provides a good opportunity to review alternative interpretations that can be given to coefficients in a chemical equation. Ask students why fractional coefficients can be used when the coefficients represent moles but not when they represent molecules.

Teaching Tip

When chemical changes and changes of state occur at the same time, energy changes associated with both must be considered in determining total energy changes in the system.

Misconception Alert!

Phrases such as "at constant temperature" and "at constant pressure" are often misunderstood. Processes described using these phrases can involve changes in temperature or pressure. When such a process is complete, the products are brought back to the initial temperature and pressure. The change in enthalpy is the same as if the temperature and pressure had not changed during the process. So the phrase "at constant temperature and pressure" means only that the initial and final conditions are the same.

▼ Teach continued

Misconception Alert!

Emphasize that a negative value of ΔH does not indicate a negative energy value. No such condition exists, because any substance contains at least some particle kinetic energy. Review with students the meaning of negative values of ΔH.

TEACH FROM VISUALS

FIGURE 1.3 Demonstrate the relationship between the figure and the defining relationship for ΔH by replacing words in the figure with their mathematical equivalents wherever possible. For example, the label "Initial energy" can be replaced by $H_{reactants}$. Then the equation $\Delta H = H_{products} - H_{reactants}$ can be used to show how the sign of ΔH is obtained.

Critical Thinking

Answer: The negative change in enthalpy indicates that energy is released during the chemical reaction.

FIGURE 1.3

Enthalpy in Exothermic Reactions In an exothermic chemical reaction, the enthalpy change is negative because energy is released into the system as heat.

CRITICAL THINKING

Interpret Data What is the connection between the negative ΔH and the slope of the red line in the graph?

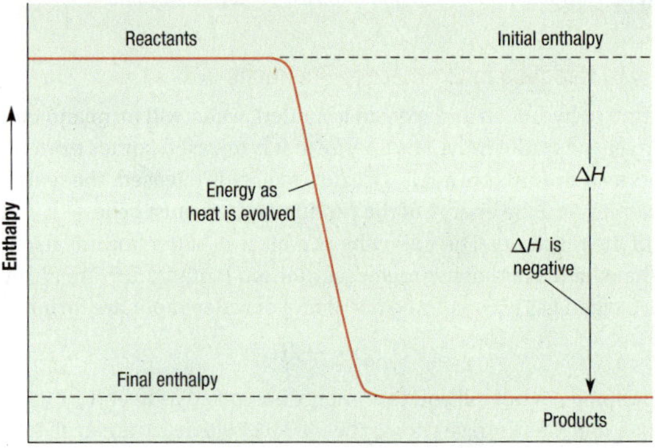

PREMIUM CONTENT

Animated Chemistry

HMDScience.com

Endothermic and Exothermic Reactions

So, for an endothermic reaction, enthalpy now appears on the reactant side of the thermochemical equation. However, it hasn't changed value.

$$2H_2O(g) + 483.6 \text{ kJ} \longrightarrow 2H_2(g) + O_2(g)$$

The physical states of reactants and products must always be included in thermochemical equations because they influence the overall amount of energy as heat gained or lost. For example, the energy needed to decompose water would be greater than 483.6 kJ if we started with ice, because extra energy would be needed to go from ice to liquid and then to vapor.

Thermochemical Equations

Thermochemical equations are usually written by designating the value of ΔH, rather than by writing the energy as a reactant or product. For an exothermic reaction, ΔH is always negative because the system loses energy. So, the thermochemical equation for the formation of 2 mol of gaseous water would be written as

$$2H_2(g) + O_2(g) \longrightarrow 2H_2O(g) \quad \Delta H = -483.6 \text{ kJ}$$

Figure 1.3 graphically shows the course of an exothermic reaction. The initial enthalpy of the reactants is greater than the final enthalpy of the products. This means energy as heat is evolved, or given off, during the reaction; this is described as a negative enthalpy change.

For an endothermic reaction, ΔH is always positive because the system gains energy. Thus, the endothermic decomposition of 2 mol of gaseous water has the following thermochemical equation.

$$2H_2O(g) \longrightarrow 2H_2(g) + O_2(g) \quad \Delta H = +483.6 \text{ kJ}$$

Problem Solving

REALITY CHECK

To help students understand the difference between positive and negative ΔH values, ask them to consider the two equations on this page. First, they should describe in words whether the reaction *requires* energy in order for the products to react, or *results* in energy being released with the reactants. Then have them rewrite the two equations so that the energy involved is shown as either a reactant or product.

Hydrogen and oxygen combining to form water results in energy being released:

$$2H_2(g) + O_2(g) \longrightarrow 2H_2O(g) + 483.6 \text{ kJ}$$

Energy is required for the decomposition of water into hydrogen and oxygen gas:

$$2H_2O(g) + 483.6 \text{ kJ} \longrightarrow 2H_2(g) + O_2(g)$$

FIGURE 1.4

Enthalpy in Endothermic Reactions In an endothermic chemical reaction, the enthalpy change is positive because energy is absorbed into the system as heat.

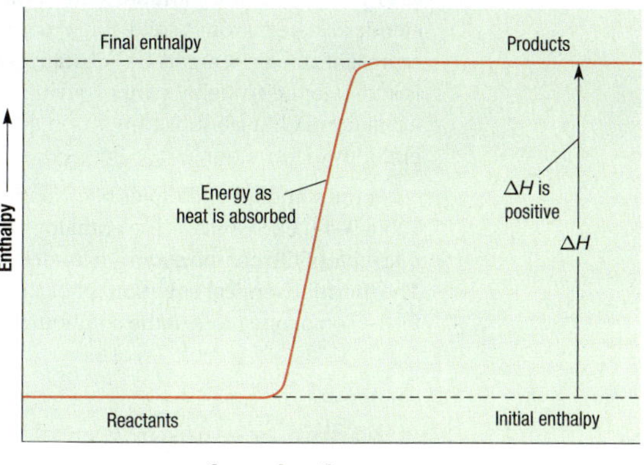

The course of an endothermic reaction is illustrated in **Figure 1.4.** Since energy as heat is absorbed, the enthalpy of the reactants is lower than the final enthalpy of the products, and ΔH is positive. In general, when looking at all thermochemical equations, consider the following.

1. The coefficients in a balanced thermochemical equation represent the numbers of *moles* of reactants and products and never the numbers of *molecules*. They can be fractions when necessary.
2. The physical state of the product or reactant involved in a reaction is an important factor and, therefore, must be included in the thermochemical equation.
3. The change in enthalpy represented by a thermochemical equation is directly proportional to the number of moles of substances undergoing a change. For example, if 2 mol of water are decomposed, twice as much enthalpy, 483.6 kJ, is needed than for the decomposition of 1 mol of water.
4. The value of the enthalpy change, ΔH, is usually not significantly influenced by changing temperature.

MAIN IDEA

Enthalpy of formation is the energy change when elements form one mole of a compound.

The formation of water from hydrogen and oxygen is a composition reaction—the formation of a compound from its elements in their standard form. Thermochemical data are often recorded as the enthalpies of such composition reactions. **The molar enthalpy of formation is the enthalpy change that occurs when one mole of a compound is formed from its elements in their standard state at 25°C and 1 atm.**

Classroom Discussion

Have students discuss the connection between the sign of ΔH and the increase or decrease of enthalpy in a reaction. Comparing the situation to investing can help identify similarities. If money is invested and a profit is made (taken in, as energy as heat is in an endothermic reaction), the new amount of money the investor has is greater (+) than the original amount. If money is lost (given out, as energy as heat is in an exothermic reaction), the new amount of money is less (−) than the original amount.

Differentiated Instruction

INCLUSION

To help visual and auditory learners understand the four statements to keep in mind when working with thermochemical equations, write the following on the board:

$$CaCl_2 + H_2O \longrightarrow CaO + 2HCl$$

Point out that this equation is balanced. However, it is not written correctly as a thermochemical equation. Ask students which statement (1–4) is violated by the equation you wrote on the board. the second statement

Next, write the following equation on the board:

$$C_{12}H_{22}O_{11}(s) + 12O_2(g) \longrightarrow 12CO_2(g) + 11H_2O(l) \quad \Delta H = -2226 \text{ kJ}$$

Then tell students that for 2 molecules of sucrose oxidized, the value of ΔH will be doubled. Ask students which statement (1–4) you just violated. the first statement

Finally tell students that for 2 moles of sucrose oxidized, only 1113 kJ of energy as heat will be released. Which statement (1–4) was violated in this case? the third statement

▼ Teach *continued*

Classroom Discussion

Present students with the following list of enthalpies of formation and ask them to comment on the stability of each of the substances listed.

$Al_2O_3(s)$	−1676.0 kJ/mol
$CaCO_3(s)$	−1206.92 kJ/mol
$NO(g)$	90.29 kJ/mol
$O_3(g)$	142.7 kJ/mol

Alternative Assessment

Ask students to draw inferences from each of the pairs of enthalpies of formation listed below. (All enthalpies of formation are in kJ/mol.)

C(*s*), diamond: 1.897
C(*s*), graphite: 0.0

$I_2(s)$: 0.0
$I_2(g)$: 62.43

P(*s*), white: 0.0
P(*s*), red: −17.46

$SO_2(g)$: −296.84
$SO_3(g)$: −395.77

Teaching Tip

Enthalpy of formation and enthalpy of combustion are sometimes called "heat of formation" and "heat of combustion," respectively. However, most chemists today use the term "enthalpy," rather than "heat," whenever possible, for accuracy.

To make comparisons meaningful, enthalpies of formation are given for the standard states of reactants and products—these are the states found at atmospheric pressure and, usually, room temperature (298.15 K). Thus, the standard state of water is liquid, not gas or solid. The standard state of iron is solid, not a molten liquid. To signify that a value represents measurements on substances in their standard states, a ^{0} sign is added to the enthalpy symbol, giving ΔH^0 for the standard enthalpy of a reaction. Adding a subscript *f*, as in ΔH_f^0, further indicates a standard enthalpy of formation.

Some standard enthalpies of formation are given in Appendix Table B–14. Each entry is the enthalpy of formation for the synthesis of *one mole* of the compound from its elements in their standard states. The thermochemical equation for each enthalpy of formation shows the formation of one mole of the compound from its elements.

MAIN IDEA

Exothermic compounds tend to be very stable.

If a large amount of energy as heat is released when a compound is formed, the compound has a large negative enthalpy of formation. Such compounds are very stable.

Elements in their standard states are defined as having $\Delta H_f^0 = 0$. The ΔH_f^0 of carbon dioxide is −393.5 kJ/mol of gas produced. Therefore, carbon dioxide is more stable than the elements from which it was formed. You can see in Appendix Table B–14 that the majority of the enthalpies of formation are negative.

Compounds with relatively positive values of enthalpies of formation, or only slightly negative values, are typically unstable. For example, hydrogen iodide, HI, is a colorless gas that decomposes somewhat when stored at room temperature. It has a relatively high positive enthalpy of formation of +26.5 kJ/mol. As it decomposes, violet iodine vapor, I_2, becomes visible throughout the container of the gas.

Compounds with a high positive enthalpy of formation are sometimes very unstable and may react or decompose violently. For example, ethyne (acetylene), C_2H_2 ($\Delta H_f^0 = +226.7$ kJ/mol), reacts violently with oxygen and must be stored in cylinders as a solution in acetone. Mercury fulminate, $HgC_2N_2O_2$, has a very large enthalpy of formation of +270 kJ/mol. Its instability makes it useful as a detonator for explosives.

MAIN IDEA

Enthalpy changes in combustion.

Combustion reactions produce a considerable amount of energy in the form of light and heat when a substance is combined with oxygen. **The enthalpy change that occurs during the complete combustion of one mole of a substance is called the enthalpy of combustion of the substance.** Enthalpy of combustion is defined in terms of *one mole of reactant*, whereas the enthalpy of formation is defined in terms of *one mole of product*.

Differentiated Instruction

BELOW LEVEL

To help students understand the relationship between stability and enthalpy of formation, place the following table on the board.

Compound	ΔH_f^0
$C_6H_6(l)$	+49.03
$HCl(g)$	−92.3
$MgO(s)$	−601.7
$AgN_3(s)$	+620.6
$NO_2(g)$	+33.2

Ask students to use the values for the enthalpies of formation to rank these compounds in increasing order of stability.
$AgN_3(s)$, $C_6H_6(l)$, $NO_2(g)$, $HCl(g)$, $MgO(s)$

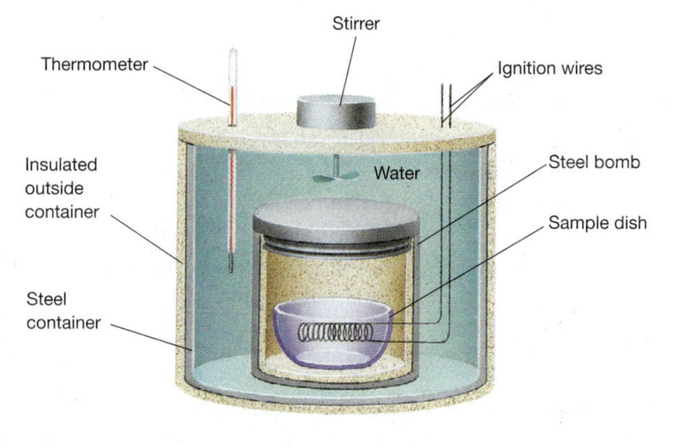

FIGURE 1.5

Combustion Calorimeter A weighed sample is ignited by an electric spark and burned in the sample dish in an atmosphere of pure oxygen. The energy generated by the combustion reaction warms the steel bomb and the water surrounding it. The thermometer measures the initial and final temperatures of the water, and this temperature change is then used to calculate the energy evolved by the reaction as heat.

CRITICAL THINKING

Deduce What is the relationship between calories as a measurement of heat energy and the Calories found in the food you eat?

All substances are in their standard states. The general enthalpy notation, ΔH, applies to enthalpies of reaction, but the addition of a subscripted c, ΔH_c, refers specifically to enthalpy of combustion. A list of enthalpies of combustion can be found in Appendix Table B-5. A combustion calorimeter is a common instrument used to determine enthalpies of combustion. **Figure 1.5** shows a fixed-volume calorimeter. A similar apparatus under constant pressure is used to obtain enthalpy measurements.

MAIN IDEA

Change in enthalpy is calculated using Hess's Law.

Thermochemical equations can be rearranged and added to give enthalpy changes for reactions not included in the data tables. **The basis for calculating enthalpies of reaction is known as Hess's law: The overall enthalpy change in a reaction is equal to the sum of enthalpy changes for the individual steps in the process.** The energy difference between reactants and products is independent of the route taken to get from one to the other. In fact, measured enthalpies of reaction can be combined to calculate enthalpies of reaction that are difficult or impossible to actually measure.

To demonstrate how to apply Hess's law, we will work through the calculation of the enthalpy of formation for the formation of methane gas from its elements. The calculation often takes several steps.

TEACH FROM VISUALS

FIGURE 1.5 Ask students to clarify the function of each of the following parts of the calorimeter: ignition wires, insulated outer container, water, stirrer, and thermometer.

Classroom Discussion

Write the following equation on the board: $22 + 4 - 9 + 16 + 7 - 8 = 32$ Ask students how the answer was calculated. Students should point out that the process was done stepwise. First, 22 and 4 were added, then 9 was subtracted, etc. Point out that this is how Hess's law operates. The overall enthalpy change is determined by calculating the enthalpy change for the individual steps that make up the entire process.

Critical Thinking

Answer: Calories are a measure of the amount of energy released to the body from the "burning" of the foods we eat.

PRE-AP

Ask students to use the equation for specific heat to calculate the ΔH_c in kJ/mol for ethanol when 1.75 g of ethanol, C_2H_5OH, are completely combusted. The temperature of 200 g of water in the calorimeter increases from 20.0°C to 75.0°C.

energy released as heat =

(200 g)[4.18 J/(g • K)](55 K) = 45980 J = 45.9 kJ

1.75 g × 1 mol/46.1 g = 0.038 mol

45.9 kJ/0.038 mol = 1208 kJ/mol

Tell students that the accepted value for the heat of combustion for ethanol is 1368 kJ/mol. Have them explain why their calculated value might be less than the accepted value. Students should point out that some energy as heat may have been lost to the atmosphere rather than to the water.

▼ Teach *continued*

Demonstration

HESS'S LAW

Write the following three equations on the board:

1. $NaOH + H_2O \longrightarrow Na^+ + OH^- + H_2O + energy_1$
2. $Na^+ + OH^- + H_3O^+ + Cl^- \longrightarrow 2H_2O + Na^+ + Cl^- + energy_2$
3. $NaOH + H_3O^+ + Cl^- \longrightarrow 2H_2O + Na^+ + Cl^- + energy_3$

Have students show that:
equation 1 + equation 2 = equation 3.

If equal numbers of moles are used, Hess's law applies, and $T_1 + T_2 = T_3$. For each of the following reactions, measure and record the temperature of the initial solution poured into a **plastic-foam cup;** then use a **thermometer** to measure and record the temperature of the final system after the second reactant has been added and dissolved by stirring with a **stirring rod.**

Reaction 1: 50 mL of **distilled water;** 1 g of **NaOH pellets**

Reaction 2: 25 mL of **1 M HCl;** 25 mL of **1 M NaOH**

Reaction 3: 50 mL of **1 M HCl;** 1 g of **NaOH pellets**

Compare $T_1 + T_2$ with T_3.

Safety Wear **safety goggles** and a **lab apron**. Have students stand at least 2 m from the demonstration. Use a **non-mercury thermometer.** Follow first-aid instructions on the label if acid or base gets in the eyes or on skin or clothing.

Disposal Rinse out the plastic-foam cups and put them in the trash. Combine all liquids, adjust the pH to between 5 and 9, and pour the mixture down the drain.

Our calculation will consider how methane gas, CH_4, forms from its elements, hydrogen gas and solid carbon (graphite), at 298.15 K (25°C).

$$C(s) + 2H_2(g) \longrightarrow CH_4(g) \quad \Delta H_f^0 = ?$$

In order to calculate the change in enthalpy for this reaction, we can use the combustion reactions of the elements, carbon and hydrogen, and of methane.

$$C(s) + O_2(g) \longrightarrow CO_2(g) \qquad \Delta H_c^0 = -393.5 \text{ kJ}$$
$$H_2(g) + \tfrac{1}{2}O_2(g) \longrightarrow H_2O(l) \qquad \Delta H_c^0 = -285.8 \text{ kJ}$$
$$CH_4(g) + 2O_2(g) \longrightarrow CO_2(g) + 2H_2O(l) \qquad \Delta H_c^0 = -890.8 \text{ kJ}$$

The general principles for combining thermochemical equations follow.

1. If a reaction is reversed, the sign of ΔH is also reversed.
2. Multiply the coefficients of the known equations so that, when added together, they give the desired thermochemical equation. Multiply the ΔH by the same factor as the corresponding equation.

In this case, we must reverse the combustion equation for methane, and remember to change the sign of ΔH from negative to positive. This will change the exothermic reaction to an endothermic one.

$$CO_2(g) + 2H_2O(l) \longrightarrow CH_4(g) + 2O_2(g) \quad \Delta H^0 = +890.8 \text{ kJ}$$

Now we notice that 2 moles of water are used as a reactant; therefore, 2 moles of water will be needed as a product. Remember, mass is conserved in chemical reactions. In the combustion reaction for hydrogen as it is written, it only produces one mole of water. We must multiply the coefficients of this combustion reaction and the value of ΔH by 2 in order to obtain the desired quantity of water.

$$2H_2(g) + O_2(g) \longrightarrow 2H_2O(l) \quad \Delta H_c^0 = 2(-285.8 \text{ kJ})$$

We are now ready to add the three equations together using Hess's law to give the enthalpy of formation of methane and the balanced equation.

$$C(s) + \cancel{O_2(g)} \longrightarrow \cancel{CO_2(g)} \qquad \Delta H_c^0 = -393.5 \text{ kJ}$$
$$2H_2(g) + \cancel{O_2(g)} \longrightarrow \cancel{2H_2O(l)} \qquad \Delta H_c^0 = 2(-285.8 \text{ kJ})$$
$$\cancel{CO_2(g)} + \cancel{2H_2O(l)} \longrightarrow CH_4(g) + \cancel{2O_2(g)} \qquad \Delta H^0 = +890.8 \text{ kJ}$$
$$C(s) + 2H_2(g) \longrightarrow CH_4(g) \qquad \Delta H_f^0 = -74.3 \text{ kJ}$$

Hess's law says that the enthalpy difference between reactants and products is independent of pathway. Therefore, any enthalpy of reaction may be calculated using enthalpies of formation for all the substances in the reaction of interest, without knowing anything else about how the reaction occurs. Mathematically, the overall equation for enthalpy change will be in the form of the equation shown below.

Total Enthalpy Change

$$\Delta H^0 = \text{sum of } [(\Delta H_f^0 \text{ of products}) \times (\text{mol of products})] - \text{sum of } [(\Delta H_f^0 \text{ of reactants}) \times (\text{mol of reactants})]$$

An example using Hess's law is shown in Sample Problem B.

Differentiated Instruction

BELOW LEVEL

Compare Hess's law to a football game. Emphasize that the law states that the pathway of the overall reaction is not important and only the initial and final conditions matter. Tell students that a team has the ball on their 20-yard line. A pass play is good for 25 yards, but the team was penalized 5 yards on the play. As a result, the team advances only to their 40-yard line, just as if the pass play had been good for only 20 yards, rather than 25 yards.

Enthalpy of Reaction

Sample Problem B **Calculate the enthalpy of reaction for the combustion of nitrogen monoxide gas, NO, to form nitrogen dioxide gas, NO_2, as given in the following thermochemical equation.**

$$NO(g) + \frac{1}{2}O_2(g) \longrightarrow NO_2(g)$$

Use the enthalpy of formation data in Appendix Table B–14. Solve by combining the known thermochemical equations. Verify the result by using the general equation for finding enthalpies of reaction from enthalpies of formation.

1 ANALYZE

Given: $\frac{1}{2}N_2(g) + \frac{1}{2}O_2(g) \longrightarrow NO(g) \quad \Delta H_f^0 = +90.29\text{ kJ}$

$\frac{1}{2}N_2(g) + O_2(g) \longrightarrow NO_2(g) \quad \Delta H_f^0 = +33.2\text{ kJ}$

Unknown: ΔH^0 for $NO(g) + \frac{1}{2}O_2(g) \longrightarrow NO_2(g)$

2 PLAN

ΔH can be found by adding all the ΔH values of the component reactions as specified in Hess's law. The desired equation has $NO(g)$ and $\frac{1}{2}O_2(g)$ as reactants and $NO_2(g)$ as the product.

$$NO(g) + \frac{1}{2}O_2(g) \longrightarrow NO_2(g)$$

We need an equation with NO as a reactant. Reversing the first reaction for the formation of NO from its elements and the sign of ΔH yields the following thermochemical equation.

$$NO(g) \longrightarrow \frac{1}{2}N_2(g) + \frac{1}{2}O_2(g) \quad \Delta H^0 = -90.29\text{ kJ}$$

The other equation should have NO_2 as a product, so we can retain the second equation for the formation of NO_2 from its elements as it stands.

$$\frac{1}{2}N_2(g) + O_2(g) \longrightarrow NO_2(g) \quad \Delta H_f^0 = +33.2\text{ kJ}$$

3 SOLVE

$$NO(g) \longrightarrow \frac{1}{2}N_2(g) + \frac{1}{2}O_2(g) \quad \Delta H^0 = -90.29\text{ kJ}$$

$$\frac{1}{2}N_2(g) + O_2(g) \longrightarrow NO_2(g) \quad \Delta H_f^0 = +33.2\text{ kJ}$$

$$NO(g) + \frac{1}{2}O_2(g) \longrightarrow NO_2(g) \quad \Delta H^0 = -57.1\text{ kJ}$$

Note the cancellation of the $\frac{1}{2}N_2(g)$ and the partial cancellation of the $O_2(g)$.

4 CHECK YOUR WORK

The unnecessary reactants and products cancel to give the desired equation. The general relationship between the enthalpy of a reaction and the enthalpies of formation of the reactants and products is described in the following word equation.

$$\Delta H^0 = \text{sum of } [(\Delta H_f^0 \text{ of products}) \times (\text{mol of products})] - \text{sum of } [(\Delta H_f^0 \text{ of reactants}) \times (\text{mol of reactants})]$$

Continued

Application

The equilibrium between nitrogen monoxide and nitrogen dioxide is of great interest to environmental chemists. The gases are involved in the production of photochemical smog in the atmosphere. Nitrogen monoxide is formed during the combustion of gasoline in internal-combustion engines and is converted to nitrogen dioxide in the atmosphere. The exact mechanism by which this change takes place, however, is unknown because the reaction $2NO + O_2 \longrightarrow 2NO_2$ occurs much too slowly to account for the change.

Problem Solving

ALTERNATIVE APPROACHES

The formulas for the compounds in Sample Problem B may make Hess's law confusing for some students to follow. Point out how this problem can be solved by substituting letters for the formulas in each equation.

Write the two given equations on the board. Under the first given equation, write:

$$\frac{1}{2}A + \frac{1}{2}B \longrightarrow C \text{ (equation 1)}$$

Under the second given equation, write:

$$\frac{1}{2}A + B \longrightarrow D \text{ (equation 2)}$$

Then write the equation for the reaction where the ΔH value must be calculated. Under this equation, write:

$$C + \frac{1}{2}B \longrightarrow D \text{ (equation 3)}$$

Ask students how equation 1 and equation 2 can be changed so that the result is equation 3. Students should reverse equation 1. Then the $\frac{1}{2}$A on each side cancel, and the Bs cancel so that only $\frac{1}{2}$B remains on the left side. Add equation 1 and equation 2 to get equation 3. Have students compare what they did with the letters to what is done with the equations in Sample Problem B.

▼ Teach continued

Classroom Practice

B-1 Calculate ΔH for the following reaction:

$2N_2(g) + 5O_2(g) \longrightarrow 2N_2O_5(g)$

Use the following data in your calculation:

$H_2(g) + \frac{1}{2}O_2(g) \longrightarrow H_2O(l)$ $\quad \Delta H_f^0 = -285.8$ kJ

$N_2O_5(g) + H_2O(l) \longrightarrow 2HNO_3(l)$ $\quad \Delta H^0 = -76.6$ kJ

$\frac{1}{2}N_2(g) + O_2(g) + H_2(g) \longrightarrow HNO_3(l)$ $\quad \Delta H_f^0 = -174.1$ kJ

Answer: 28.4 kJ

Answers

Practice B

1. −890.8 kJ
2. 2 kJ

Enthalpy of Reaction (continued)

To find the necessary sums, the ΔH_f^0 value for each reactant and each product must be multiplied by its respective coefficient in the desired equation. For the reaction of NO with O_2, applying this equation gives the following value for ΔH^0.

$$\Delta H^0 = \Delta H_f^0(NO_2) - [\Delta H_f^0(NO) + 0]$$
$$= +33.2 \text{ kJ/mol} - 90.29 \text{ kJ/mol} = -57.1 \text{ kJ}$$

Note that zero is the assigned value for the enthalpies of formation of elements in their standard states.

Practice Answers in Appendix E

1. Calculate the enthalpy of reaction for the combustion of methane gas, CH_4, to form $CO_2(g) + H_2O(l)$.
2. Carbon occurs in two distinct forms. It can be the soft, black material found in pencils and lock lubricants, called graphite, or it can be the hard, brilliant gem we know as diamond. Calculate ΔH^0 for the conversion of graphite to diamond for the following reaction.

$$C_{graphite}(s) \longrightarrow C_{diamond}(s)$$

The combustion reactions you will need follow.

$$C_{graphite}(s) + O_2(g) \longrightarrow CO_2(g) \quad \Delta H_c^0 = -394 \text{ kJ}$$
$$C_{diamond}(s) + O_2(g) \longrightarrow CO_2(g) \quad \Delta H_c^0 = -396 \text{ kJ}$$

MAIN IDEA

Enthalpy of formation is the sum of its sub-reaction enthalpies.

When carbon is burned in a limited supply of oxygen, carbon monoxide is produced. In this reaction, carbon is probably first oxidized to carbon dioxide. Then part of the carbon dioxide is reduced with carbon to give some carbon monoxide. Because these two reactions occur simultaneously and we get a mixture of CO and CO_2, it is not possible to directly measure the enthalpy of formation of CO(*g*) from C(*s*) and $O_2(g)$.

$$C(s) + \frac{1}{2}O_2(g) \longrightarrow CO(g) \qquad \Delta H_f^0 = ?$$

However, we do know the enthalpy of formation of carbon dioxide and the enthalpy of combustion of carbon monoxide.

$$C(s) + O_2(g) \longrightarrow CO_2(g) \qquad \Delta H_f^0 = -393.5 \text{ kJ/mol}$$
$$CO(g) + \frac{1}{2}O_2(g) \longrightarrow CO_2(g) \qquad \Delta H_c^0 = -283.0 \text{ kJ/mol}$$

We reverse the second equation because we need CO as a product. Adding gives the desired enthalpy of formation of carbon monoxide.

$$C(s) + O_2(g) \longrightarrow \cancel{CO_2(g)} \qquad \Delta H^0 = -393.5 \text{ kJ}$$
$$\cancel{CO_2(g)} \longrightarrow CO(g) + \cancel{\tfrac{1}{2}O_2(g)} \qquad \Delta H^0 = +283.0 \text{ kJ}$$
$$C(s) + \frac{1}{2}O_2(g) \longrightarrow CO(g) \qquad \Delta H_f^0 = -110.5 \text{ kJ}$$

Differentiated Instruction

ENGLISH LEARNERS

Have students write a sentence that explains the expression used for the enthalpy of formation, ΔH_f^0. One possible sentence is "The symbol Δ signifies change in the enthalpy, *H*, for a synthesis reaction (*f*) under conditions in which the substances were measured in their standard states (0)." Then ask students to do the same for the expression ΔH_c^0. Students should point out that the reaction in this case is a combustion process.

FIGURE 1.6

Enthalpy of a Two-Part Reaction This diagram shows the enthalpy of reaction for carbon dioxide, CO_2, and carbon monoxide, CO.

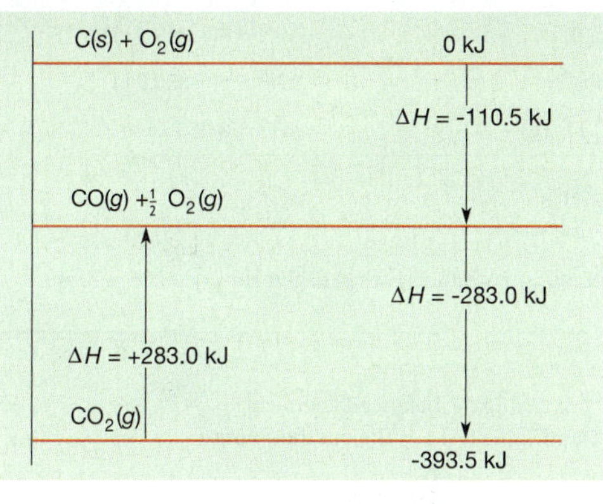

Look closely at **Figure 1.6.** This diagram is a model for a reaction that takes place in two distinct steps. If we plot the reactions based on their relative energy, you can see the relationship among the values obtained for the enthalpy of formation of carbon monoxide. The formation of CO_2 is plotted at a level corresponding to −393.5 kJ/mol. The diagram shows the reverse of the combustion reaction (+283.0 kJ/mol) is added to that level. From the diagram, you see the difference between the two. This represents the formation of CO. The value of this is −110.5 kJ/mol.

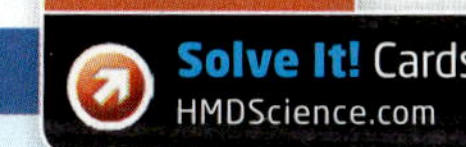

Enthalpy of Formation

Sample Problem C **Calculate the enthalpy of formation of pentane, C_5H_{12}, using the information on enthalpies of formation in Appendix Table B-14 and the information on enthalpies of combustion in Appendix Table B-5. Solve by combining the known thermochemical equations.**

1 ANALYZE

Given:

$C(s) + O_2(g) \longrightarrow CO_2(g)$ $\quad \Delta H_f^0 = -393.5 \text{ kJ}$

$H_2(g) + \frac{1}{2}O_2(g) \longrightarrow H_2O(l)$ $\quad \Delta H_f^0 = -285.8 \text{ kJ}$

$C_5H_{12}(g) + 8O_2(g) \longrightarrow 5CO_2(g) + 6H_2O(l)$ $\quad \Delta H_c^0 = -3535.6 \text{ kJ}$

Unknown: ΔH_f^0 for $5C(s) + 6H_2(g) \longrightarrow C_5H_{12}(g)$

Continued

TEACH FROM VISUALS

FIGURE 1.6 Ask students to explain in words how the graph illustrates Hess's law.

Classroom Discussion

Ask students to explain why the enthalpy of formation of carbon dioxide and the enthalpy of combustion of carbon monoxide can be measured, but the enthalpy of formation of carbon monoxide cannot be measured directly.

Problem Solving

DECONSTRUCTING PROBLEMS

Emphasize that no new concepts are introduced in Sample Problem C. The solution again is found by applying Hess's law. The only difference in Sample Problem C is that two multiplication factors are needed. Students will have to determine the integer to use in each equation so that the moles of substances cancel to leave what is required.

▼ Teach continued

Answers

Practice C

1. −125.4 kJ
2. +66.4 kJ
3. −296.1 kJ

▼ Assess and Reteach

Assess Use the Formative Assessment on this page to evaluate student mastery of the section.

Reteach For students who need additional instruction, download the Section Study Guide.

Response to Intervention To reassess students' mastery, use the Section Quiz, available to print or to take directly online at **HMDScience.com**.

2 PLAN Combine the given equations according to Hess's law. We need C_5H_{12} as a product, so we reverse the equation for combustion of C_5H_{12} and the sign for ΔH_c^0. Multiply the equation for formation of CO_2 by 5 to give 5C as a reactant. Multiply the equation for formation of H_2O by 6 to give $6H_2$ as a reactant.

3 SOLVE

$$5C(s) + \cancel{5O_2(g)} \longrightarrow \cancel{5CO_2(g)} \qquad \Delta H^0 = 5(-393.5\text{ kJ})$$

$$6H_2(g) + \cancel{3O_2(g)} \longrightarrow \cancel{6H_2O(l)} \qquad \Delta H^0 = 6(-285.8\text{ kJ})$$

$$\cancel{5CO_2(g)} + \cancel{6H_2O(l)} \longrightarrow C_5H_{12}(g) + \cancel{8O_2(g)} \qquad \Delta H^0 = +3535.6\text{ kJ}$$

$$5C(s) + 6H_2(g) \longrightarrow C_5H_{12}(g) \qquad \Delta H_f^0 = -146.7\text{ kJ}$$

4 CHECK YOUR WORK The unnecessary reactants and products cancel to give the correct equation.

Practice Answers in Appendix E

1. Calculate the enthalpy of formation of butane, C_4H_{10}, using the balanced chemical equation and information in Appendix Table B–5 and Table B–14. Write out the solution according to Hess's law.
2. Calculate the enthalpy of combustion of 1 mol of nitrogen, N_2, to form NO_2 using the balanced chemical equation and Appendix Table B–14.
3. Calculate the enthalpy of formation for sulfur dioxide, SO_2, from its elements, sulfur and oxygen. Use the balanced chemical equation and the following information.

$$S(s) + \frac{3}{2}O_2(g) \longrightarrow SO_3(g) \qquad \Delta H_c^0 = -395.2\text{ kJ}$$

$$2SO_2(g) + O_2(g) \longrightarrow 2SO_3(g) \qquad \Delta H^0 = -198.2\text{ kJ}$$

SECTION 1 FORMATIVE ASSESSMENT

Reviewing Main Ideas

1. What is meant by *enthalpy change*?
2. What is meant by *enthalpy of reaction*?
3. Describe the relationship between a compound's stability and its enthalpy of formation.
4. What is the importance of Hess's law to thermodynamic calculations?
5. How much energy would be absorbed as heat by 75 g of iron when heated from 295 K to 301 K?

Critical Thinking

6. **INTEGRATING CONCEPTS** Isooctane (C_8H_{18}) is a major component of gasoline.
   a. Using the following thermodynamic data, calculate the change in enthalpy for the combustion of 1.0 mol of isooctane.
   $$H_2(g) + \frac{1}{2}O_2(g) \longrightarrow H_2O(g)\ \Delta H^0 = -241.8\text{ kJ}$$
   $$C(s) + O_2(g) \longrightarrow CO_2(g)\ \Delta H^0 = -393.5\text{ kJ}$$
   $$8C(s) + 9H_2(g) \longrightarrow C_8H_{18}(l)\ \Delta H^0 = -224.13\text{ kJ}$$
   b. One gallon of isooctane has a mass of 2.6 kg. What is the change in enthalpy for the combustion of one gallon of this compound?

Answers to Section Assessment

1. Enthalpy change is the amount of enthalpy gained or lost by a system during a process at constant pressure.
2. The enthalpy of reaction is the quantity of energy released or absorbed as heat during a reaction.
3. The more negative the enthalpy of formation, the more stable the compound.
4. Hess's law provides a method of finding the value of ΔH for a given reaction by summing the discrete values of ΔH for other reactions that can be added to give that reaction. It allows one to determine the ΔH of a given reaction even if the ΔH of that reaction cannot be measured directly.
5. 2.0×10^2 J
6. a. Use Hess's law:
   $$9(H_2(g) = \tfrac{1}{2}O_2(g) \longrightarrow H_2O(g)) \qquad \Delta H^0 = 9(-241.8\text{ kJ})$$
   $$8(C(s) + O_2(g) \longrightarrow CO_2(g)) \qquad \Delta H^0 = 8(-393.5\text{ kj})$$
   $$C_8H_{18}(l) \longrightarrow 8C(s) + 9H_2(g) \qquad \Delta H^0 = +224.13\text{ kJ}$$
   $$C_8H_{18}(l) + \tfrac{25}{2}O_2(g) \longrightarrow 8CO_2(g) + 9H_2O(g) \qquad \Delta H^0 = -5100\text{ kJ}$$
   b. $\text{mols } C_8H_{18} = 2.6\text{ kg} \times \frac{10^3\text{ g}}{1\text{ g}} \times \frac{1\text{ mol}}{114.26\text{ g}} = 22.8\text{ mol}$
   $22.8\text{ mol} \times (-5100\text{ kJ/mol}) = -1.2 \times 10^5$ kJ for one gallon of C_8H_{18}

WHY IT MATTERS

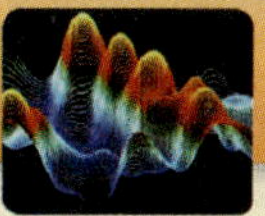
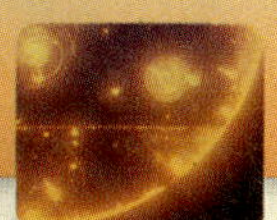

Self-Heating Meals

S.T.E.M.

Who would have thought that corrosion could be useful? The HeaterMeals Company did. This company uses the properties of saltwater corrosion to heat TV-type dinners, and now it is taking packaged foods to a new level of convenience.

HeaterMeals' products, as their name implies, come with a self-contained heat source. Each meal contains a package of food, a tray that holds a porous pouch containing powdered Na, Mg, and Fe, and a 2-oz pouch filled with salt water. When the salt water is poured into the tray with the porous pouch, it begins to vigorously corrode the metals. The sealed, precooked food package is then placed on top of the tray and returned to its box, where the temperature of the food package is raised by 100°F, heating the meal in 14 min. When disposed of, the package materials are nontoxic and biodegradeable.

Corrosion, the process by which a metal reacts with air or water, is usually an undesirable event, such as when iron corrodes to form rust. With HeaterMeals, however, the corrosion process is speeded up to produce an exothermic reaction—with the excess energy as the desired result.

According to Drew McLandrich, of the HeaterMeals Company, the idea for using self-heating metallic alloy powders has been around since the 1930s. "But," says McLandrich, "there really have been no significant uses of the product until the Desert Storm conflict, which led to the military's taking this technology and adopting it for field use so that soldiers could heat a meal-ready-to-eat (M.R.E.).

"We've made about 80 million heaters for the military in the last 10 years. Lately, we've been successfully marketing them to long-distance truck drivers. The product is in about 800 truck stops in 48 states."

The company has also developed other products using the controlled use of "supercorrosion." A hot beverage kit now exists for making a portable hot cup of coffee or a hot cup of tea or cocoa and the company is working on prototypes for a baby-bottle warmer.

Questions

1. How did the development of self-heating metallic alloy powders benefit the military?
2. If the temperature of 50.0 mL of water is raised from 25.0°C to 100.°C using the self-heating meal package, what is the change in the enthalpy of the magnesium reaction in this package?

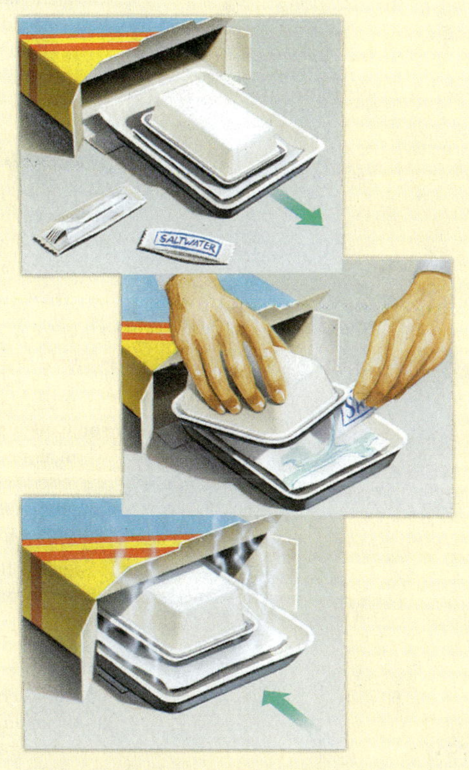

This product uses supercorrosion to give you a hot meal.

515

Teaching Tip

Many hot packs use enthalpy of solution, not enthalpy of reaction, to produce energy.

Classroom Discussion

Have students refer to earlier instruction concerning exothermic and endothermic reactions to think of possible ways in which the addition of water to a dry mixture could result in the release of energy as heat.

Ask students to name materials that they think are involved in the energy-producing reaction in the self-heating meals. Most of the energy is from the reaction of magnesium metal and water, producing magnesium hydroxide and hydrogen gas. Why are iron and sodium chloride added? Pure magnesium reacts with oxygen in the air, forming a coating of magnesium oxide, which prevents the metal from reacting with the water. Adding sodium chloride and iron prevents formation of the magnesium oxide coating.

ChemisTrivia

One mole of Mg (24.30 g), when mixed with water, produces enough energy to raise the temperature of 1 L of water from room temperature to 100°C.

Answers

1. The exothermic reaction that occurs when the alloy powders react with salt water provides the energy to warm a meal. The system is portable, which made it ideal for heating the meals of soldiers in the field.
2. The amount of energy absorbed by the water as heat is $(50.0 \text{ ml} \times \frac{1.0 \text{ g}}{1 \text{ ml}})[4.18 \text{ J}/(\text{g} \bullet \text{K})](75.0 \text{ K}) = 15.7 \text{ kJ}$. Therefore, the ΔH^0 for the magnesium reaction is -15.7 kJ.

SECTION 2

▼ Plan and Prepare

Objectives

Upon completion of this section, students should be able to do the following:

- Explain the relationship between enthalpy change and the tendency of a reaction to occur.
- Explain the relationship between entropy change and the tendency of a reaction to occur.
- Discuss the concept of free energy, and explain how the value of this quantity is calculated and interpreted.
- Describe the use of free energy change to determine the tendency of a reaction to occur.

Classroom Catalyst

Before class, make 9 M H_2SO_4 by slowly adding **100 mL concentrated H_2SO_4** to **100 mL H_2O** in a **500-mL beaker,** while stirring with a **glass stirring rod.** Cool to room temperature.

Caution Be careful when handling the concentrated acid. Use H_2SO_4 only with proper ventilation. In case of spills, first dilute with water. Then mop the spill with **wet cloths or a wet cloth mop** designated for spill cleanup while wearing **disposable gloves.**

In class, place **100 g of liquid water at 0°C** in a **plastic foam cup,** and use a **thermometer** to record its temperature. Add 100 mL of 9 M H_2SO_4 to the cup, and stir. After 1 min, measure and record the temperature. Repeat these steps for **100 g of crushed ice at 0°C in a plastic foam cup.**

Point out that the energy produced by dissolving H_2SO_4 in water causes the temperature in the first cup to increase, but the temperature in the second cup to decrease. Ask students to try to explain these results. Student explanations may include that energy as heat is used to break down the crystal structure of the ice in the second system. Entropy increases.

Safety Wear **goggles, lab apron, gloves,** and a **face shield.** Be sure that an operating **safety shower or eyewash station** is nearby. Use a non-mercury thermometer. Have students stand 5 m away from the demonstration area.

SECTION 2

Main Ideas

- Reactions generally move to a lower-energy state.
- Entropy measures randomness in a system.
- Free energy changes determine if a reaction is endothermic or exothermic.

Driving Force of Reactions

Key Terms

entropy   free energy   free energy change

The change in energy of a reaction system is one of two factors that allow chemists to predict whether a reaction will occur spontaneously and to explain how it occurs. The randomness of the particles in a system is the second factor affecting whether a reaction will occur spontaneously.

MAIN IDEA

Reactions generally move to a lower-energy state.

The great majority of chemical reactions in nature are exothermic. As these reactions proceed, energy is liberated and the products have less energy than the original reactants. The products are also more resistant to change, more stable, than the original reactants. In nature, reactions tend to proceed in a direction that leads to a lower energy state.

But can endothermic reactions, ones in which energy is absorbed and products are less stable than the original reactants, occur spontaneously? We might expect this only with the assistance of an outside influence, such as continued heating. However, some endothermic reactions *do* occur spontaneously. Thus, we can conclude that something other than enthalpy change must help determine whether a reaction will occur.

MAIN IDEA

Entropy measures randomness in a system.

A naturally occurring endothermic process is melting. An ice cube melts spontaneously at room temperature as energy is transferred from the warm air to the ice. The well-ordered arrangement of water molecules in the ice crystal is lost, and the less-ordered liquid phase of higher energy content is formed. A system that can go from one state to another without a decrease in enthalpy does so with an increase in entropy.

Look at the physical states of the reactants in the chemical equation for the decomposition of ammonium nitrate.

$$2NH_4NO_3(s) \longrightarrow 2N_2(g) + 4H_2O(l) + O_2(g)$$

On the left side are 2 mol of solid ammonium nitrate. The right side of the equation shows 3 mol of gaseous molecules plus 4 mol of a liquid. The arrangement of particles on the right side of the equation is more random than the arrangement on the left side of the equation and hence is less ordered. **Figures 2.1a** and **2.1b** show the reactant and products of this decomposition reaction.

Differentiated Instruction

BELOW LEVEL

Have students write a short summary in their own words of how enthalpy and entropy determine reaction tendency. Students should point out that a reaction tends to occur spontaneously if the products are more stable (have less energy) than the reactants. In this case, a decrease in enthalpy favors the reaction. A second factor that tends to make a reaction occur spontaneously is entropy. A reaction tends to occur spontaneously if there is an increase in entropy so that the products are less ordered than the reactants.

Decomposition and Entropy

When ammonium nitrate, NH_4NO_3, decomposes, the entropy of the reaction system increases as **(a)** one solid reactant becomes **(b)** three products: two gaseous and one liquid.

CRITICAL THINKING

Explain Why does adding energy to a system increase its entropy?

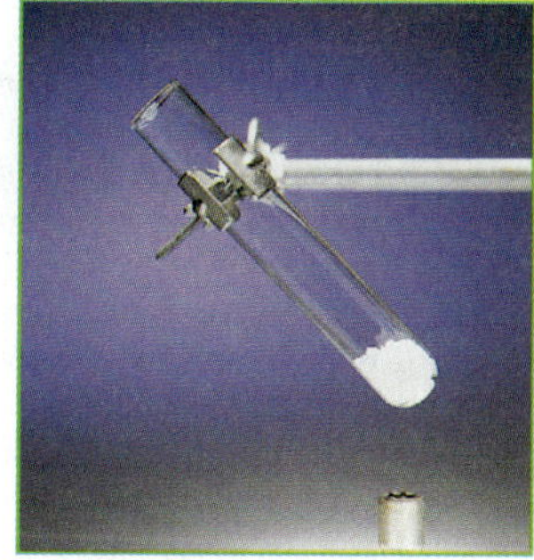

(a) The ammonium nitrate starts as a solid.

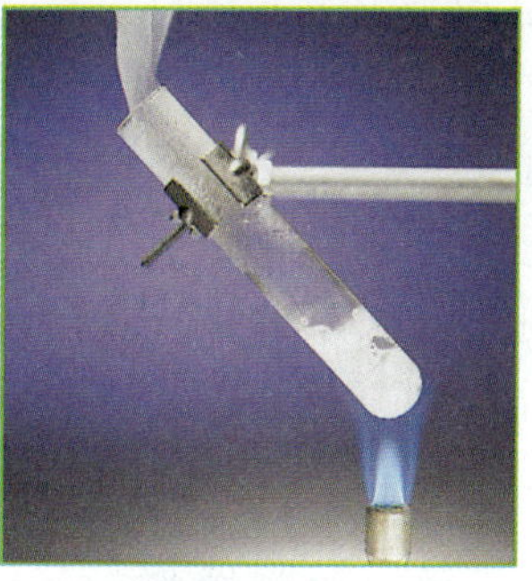

(b) It becomes two gaseous products and one liquid product.

There is a tendency in nature to proceed in a direction that increases the randomness of a system. A random system is one that lacks a regular arrangement of its parts. This tendency toward randomness is called entropy. **Entropy,** *S*, **can be defined in a simple qualitative way as a measure of the degree of randomness of the particles, such as molecules, in a system.** To understand the concept of entropy, consider solids, liquids, and gases. In a solid, the particles are fixed in position in their small regions of space, but they are vibrating back and forth. Even so, we can determine with fair precision the location of the particles. The degree of randomness is low, so the entropy is low. When the solid melts, the particles are still very close together, but they can move about somewhat. The system is more random, it is more difficult to describe the location of the particles, and the entropy is higher. When the liquid evaporates, the particles are moving rapidly and are much farther apart. Locating an individual particle is more difficult, the system is much more random, and the entropy of the gas is higher than that of the liquid. A general rule is that the entropy of liquids is greater than that of solids and the entropy of gases is greater than that of liquids. An exception to this rule is the entropy of liquid mercury which is much less than that of some solids.

The entropy of a pure crystalline solid at absolute zero is zero. As energy is added, the randomness of the molecular motion increases. Measurements of energy absorbed and calculations are used to determine the absolute entropy or standard molar entropy, and values are then recorded in tables. These molar values are reported as kJ/(mol • K). Entropy change, which can also be measured, is defined as the difference between the entropy of the products and the reactants. Therefore, an increase in entropy is represented by a positive value for ΔS, and a decrease in entropy is represented by a negative value for ΔS.

The process of forming a solution almost always involves an increase in entropy because there is an increase in randomness. This is true for mixing gases, dissolving a liquid in another liquid, and dissolving a solid in a liquid.

Teach ▼

Classroom Discussion

Have students list examples of increased randomness from their daily lives. Examples might include spilling a glass of milk or juice, dissolving salt or sugar in water, breaking ranks from some ordered formation (as in a marching band), and setting fire to a piece of paper.

Have students compare enthalpy and entropy, including the properties they measure, the symbols used to represent them, and the units associated with each. Emphasize that enthalpy is measured in energy units (J/mol or kJ/mol), but entropy is measured in energy and temperature units (J/(mol • K) or kJ/(mol • K)).

READING TOOLKIT

PAIRED READING Have students silently read Section 2 and mark any passages in the text that they do not understand with self-adhesive notes. Be sure students read all tables, figures, captions, and sample problems to help clarify the relevant passages. Next, divide students into pairs, and have each pair of students discuss the passages that were difficult. Ask them to create a list of questions to pose to the class about ideas that are still unclear after the discussion.

Critical Thinking

Answer: Answers will vary. A good answer could be: Adding energy to a system causes the particles to vibrate more quickly, moving around and bouncing further and further apart, which increases the randomness of their distribution.

ENGLISH LEARNERS

Students may have difficulty relating enthalpy and entropy to reaction tendency. In fact, they may think that only one of these factors is involved in a reaction at any one time. To help them understand what favors the tendency of a reaction to occur, use the symbols for both enthalpy and entropy to describe how they affect reaction tendency. Ask students whether a $+\Delta H$ or a $-\Delta H$ indicates if a reaction is likely to occur spontaneously. Have them explain the reason for their choice. Students should select $-\Delta H$ because a decrease in enthalpy leads to a more stable state. Then ask students whether a $+\Delta S$ or a $-\Delta S$ indicates if a reaction is likely to occur spontaneously. Students should select $+\Delta S$ because systems tend to move toward a more disordered state. Finally, ask students to describe a reaction that has both a $-\Delta H$ and a $+\Delta S$. Students should realize that both conditions favor a spontaneous reaction.

▼ Teach *continued*

TEACH FROM VISUALS

FIGURE 2.2 Have students compare the figures to students at a sporting event. Which situation is more like **(a)**: several students sitting in the bleachers watching a game, or those same students on the field, playing? Which situation is more like **(b)**?

Teaching Tip

Free energy emphasizes that neither enthalpy nor entropy is solely responsible for whether a reaction is spontaneous.

FIGURE 2.2

Mixtures and Entropy When a solid dissolves in a liquid, the entropy of the system increases.

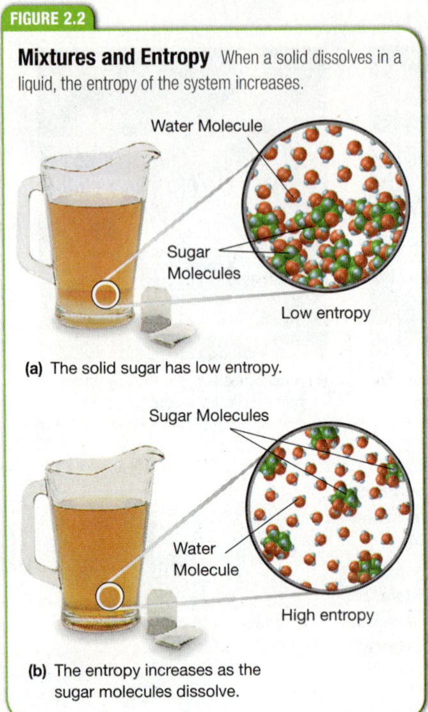

(a) The solid sugar has low entropy.

(b) The entropy increases as the sugar molecules dissolve.

Figure 2.2 illustrates the entropy change that takes place when solid sugar is dissolved in tea (an aqueous solution). In the sugar-water system shown in **Figure 2.2a,** the solid sugar has just been added to the tea, but most of it has not yet dissolved. The entropy is low because the majority of the sugar molecules are in one region at the bottom of the pitcher and the majority of the water molecules can be found everywhere else in the pitcher. After the sugar dissolves in the tea, shown in **Figure 2.2b,** the sugar molecules are thoroughly mixed throughout the tea solution. Sugar molecules and water molecules might be found anywhere in the solution, so the entropy, the randomness, of the system increases. This would give ΔS a positive value for this solid-liquid system. You can imagine the same series of events happening for a system of gases mixing with each other or a system of liquids mixing. In each case, ΔS would have a positive value once the solution was formed.

MAIN IDEA

Free energy changes determine if a reaction is endothermic or exothermic.

Processes in nature are driven in two directions: toward least enthalpy and toward greatest entropy. When these two oppose each other, the dominant factor determines the direction of change. As a way to predict which factor will dominate for a given system, a function has been defined to relate the enthalpy and entropy factors at a given temperature and constant pressure. This combined enthalpy-entropy function is called the **free energy,** *G*, of the system; it is also called Gibbs free energy. This function simultaneously assesses the tendencies for enthalpy and entropy to change. Natural processes proceed in the direction that lowers the free energy of a system.

Only the *change* in free energy can be measured. It can be defined in terms of changes in enthalpy and entropy. At a constant pressure and temperature, the **free-energy change,** ΔG, of a system is defined as the difference between the change in enthalpy, ΔH, and the product of the Kelvin temperature and the entropy change, which is defined as $T\Delta S$.

Free Energy Change $\Delta G^0 = \Delta H^0 - T\Delta S^0$

Note that this expression is for substances in their standard states. The product $T\Delta S$ and the quantities ΔG and ΔH have the same units, usually kJ. The units of ΔS for use in this equation are usually kJ/K. If $\Delta G < 0$, the reaction is spontaneous.

ΔH and ΔS in the free-energy equation can have positive or negative values. This leads to four possible combinations of terms.

Differentiated Instruction

PRE-AP

Use Gibbs free energy to show students how changes in temperature affect the tendency of a reaction. Give students the following information.

$2NO_2(g) \rightleftharpoons N_2O_4(g)$
$NO_2(g)$: brown gas
$N_2O_4(g)$: colorless gas
$\Delta H = -57.20$ kJ
$\Delta S = -175.83$ J/K

Tell students that both gases are present in a sealed tube at 100°C. At this temperature, the tube has a brown color. Have students use Gibbs free energy to explain why the tube becomes colorless as the temperature falls below 0°C. Students should see that positive temperature values result in a positive ΔG value. Only when the temperatures have negative values does the expression $-T\Delta S$ become a positive value. Therefore, the result is a negative ΔG value, which indicates that the reaction will proceed in the forward direction at these low temperatures. As a result, the colorless gas, N_2O_4, will be present in the tube.

Figure 2.3 shows that if ΔH is negative and ΔS is positive, then both terms on the right in the free energy equation are negative. Both factors contribute to the process being spontaneous. Therefore, ΔG will always be negative, and the reaction is definitely spontaneous. On the other hand, if ΔH is positive (endothermic process) and ΔS is negative (decrease in randomness), then the reaction, as written, is not spontaneous. When the enthalpy and entropy changes are operating in different directions, sometimes one will predominate and sometimes the other will predominate. There are reactions in which the enthalpy change is negative and the entropy change is negative. The enthalpy factor leads to a spontaneous process, but the negative entropy change opposes this. This is true in the following reaction. The entropy decreases because there is a decrease in moles of gas.

$$C_2H_4(g) + H_2(g) \longrightarrow C_2H_6(g)$$

There is a fairly large decrease in entropy, $\Delta S^0 = -0.1207\ kJ/(mol \bullet K)$. However, the reaction is strongly exothermic, with a $\Delta H^0 = -136.9\ kJ/mol$. The reaction proceeds because the enthalpy term predominates.

$$\Delta G^0 = \Delta H^0 - T\Delta S^0 = -136.9\ kJ/mol - 298\ K[-0.1207\ kJ/(mol \bullet K)]$$
$$= -100.9\ kJ/mol$$

We can contrast this with the common commercial process for the manufacture of syngas, a mixture of CO and H_2. (This gas mixture is the starting point for the synthesis of a number of large-volume commercial chemicals, such as methanol, CH_3OH.)

$$CH_4(g) + H_2O(g) \longrightarrow CO(g) + 3H_2(g)$$

This reaction is endothermic, with $\Delta H^0 = +206.1\ kJ/mol$ and $\Delta S^0 = +0.215\ kJ/(mol \bullet K)$, at standard conditions. The resulting ΔG is positive at room temperature. This tells us that the reaction will not occur at room temperature even though the entropy change is favorable.

$$\Delta G^0 = \Delta H^0 - T\Delta S^0 = +206.1\ kJ/mol - 298\ K[+0.215\ kJ/(mol \bullet K)]$$
$$= +142.0\ kJ/mol$$

FIGURE 2.3

RELATING ENTHALPY, ENTROPY, AND FREE-ENERGY CHANGES TO REACTION OCCURRENCE

ΔH	ΔS	ΔG
– value (exothermic)	+ value (more random)	always negative
– value (exothermic)	– value (less random)	negative at *lower* temperatures
+ value (endothermic)	+ value (more random)	negative at *higher* temperatures
+ value (endothermic)	– value (less random)	never negative

WHY IT MATTERS

Diamonds Are Forever? S.T.E.M.

Carbon occurs in different forms, two of which are graphite and diamond. Using thermodynamic data, the change in free energy for diamond converting to graphite under standard thermodynamic conditions is –3 kJ/mol. That is, since ΔG is negative for this reaction, diamond should spontaneously change to graphite at 25°C and 1 atm. So, why doesn't all of our diamond jewelry change to graphite? The reaction rate is too slow for this spontaneous change to be observed. Therefore, at 25°C and 1 atm, although diamonds are not "forever," they will last a very long time.

Application

Scientists have long studied the use of syngas (or synthesis gas) as a substitute for petroleum and natural gas because it can be made from coal, which is far more abundant than is either crude oil or natural gas. The practical problem thus far is that syngas has only about a third of the energy value of either natural product.

TEACH FROM TABLES

FIGURE 2.3 Select simple values for ΔH, T, and ΔS to illustrate why ΔG is always negative, never negative, or either positive or negative, depending on the temperature.

Demo Problems

Predict whether the value of ΔS for each of the following reactions will be greater than, less than, or equal to zero.

1. $3H_2(g) + N_2(g) \longrightarrow 2NH_3(g)$

Answer: $\Delta S < 0$

2. $2Mg(s) + O_2(g) \longrightarrow 2MgO(s)$

Answer: $\Delta S < 0$

3. $C_6H_{12}O_6(s) + 6O_2(g) \longrightarrow 6CO_2(g) + 6H_2O(g)$

Answer: $\Delta S > 0$

4. $KNO_3(s) \longrightarrow K^+(aq) + NO_3^-(aq)$

Answer: $\Delta S > 0$

Problem Solving

TAKE IT FURTHER

Have students determine at which temperature the reaction in Sample Problem D would proceed spontaneously in the forward direction. Students should realize that the value of $-T\Delta S$ must be greater than the positive ΔH value (176 kJ/mol) to produce a negative ΔG value. Any temperature greater than 618 K would result in a negative ΔT value, thus indicating that the reaction would proceed spontaneously in the forward direction.

▼ Teach *continued*

Classroom Practice

D-1 Calculate the value of ΔG^0 for the reaction below, given the values of ΔH^0 and ΔS^0. Will the reaction be spontaneous at 298 K?

$Cu_2S(s) + S(s) \longrightarrow 2CuS(s)$

$\Delta H^0 = -26.7$ kJ

$\Delta S^0 = -19.7$ J/(mol • K)

Answers: $\Delta G^0 = -20.8$ kJ/mol; yes

Answer

Practice D

1. above 333 K

▼ Assess and Reteach

Assess Use the Formative Assessment on this page to evaluate student mastery of the section.

Reteach For students who need additional instruction, download the Section Study Guide.

Response to Intervention To reassess students' mastery, use the Section Quiz, available to print or to take directly online at **HMDScience.com**.

Calculating Free Energy Change

Sample Problem D **For the reaction $NH_4Cl(s) \longrightarrow NH_3(g) + HCl(g)$, at 298.15 K, $\Delta H^0 = 176$ kJ/mol and $\Delta S^0 = 0.285$ kJ/(mol • K). Calculate ΔG^0, and tell whether this reaction is spontaneous in the forward direction at 298.15 K.**

1 ANALYZE

Given: $\Delta H^0 = 176$ kJ/mol at 298.15 K

$\Delta S^0 = 0.285$ kJ/(mol • K) at 298.15 K

Unknown: ΔG^0 at 298.15 K

2 PLAN

$\Delta S, \Delta H, T \rightarrow \Delta G$

The value of ΔG can be calculated according to the following equation.

3 SOLVE

$$\Delta G^0 = \Delta H^0 - T\Delta S^0$$

$$\Delta G^0 = 176 \text{ kJ/mol} - 298 \cancel{\text{K}} [0.285 \text{ kJ/(mol} \bullet \cancel{\text{K}})]$$

$$\Delta G^0 = 176 \text{ kJ/mol} - 84.9 \text{ kJ/mol}$$

$$\Delta G^0 = 91.1 \text{ kJ/mol}$$

4 CHECK YOUR WORK

The answer is reasonably close to an estimated value of 110, calculated as $200 - (300 \times 0.3)$. The positive value of ΔG shows that this reaction does not occur naturally at 298.15 K.

Practice Answers in Appendix E

1. For the vaporization reaction $Br_2(l) \longrightarrow Br_2(g)$, $\Delta H^0 = 31.0$ kJ/mol and $\Delta S^0 = 93.0$ J/(mol • K). At what temperature will this process be spontaneous?

SECTION 2 FORMATIVE ASSESSMENT

Reviewing Main Ideas

1. What kind of enthalpy change favors a spontaneous reaction?
2. What is entropy, and how does it relate to spontaneity of reactions?
3. List several changes that result in an entropy increase.
4. Define *free energy*, and explain how its change is calculated.
5. Explain the relationship between free-energy change and spontaneity of reactions.
6. In the reaction in Sample Problem D, why does the entropy increase?

Critical Thinking

7. **APPLYING MODELS** Most biological enzymes become denatured when they are heated and lose their ability to catalyze reactions. This process (original enzyme ⟶ denatured enzyme) is endothermic and spontaneous. Which structure, the original enzyme or the denatured enzyme, is more ordered? Explain your reasoning using thermodynamic concepts.

Answers to Section Assessment

1. a large negative change
2. Entropy is a measure of randomness. An increase in entropy favors a spontaneous reaction.
3. Answers may include dissolving a solid, changing state from solid to liquid or gas or from liquid to gas, and increasing the number of particles during the course of a reaction.
4. Free energy equals the difference between the change in enthalpy and the product of the Kelvin temperature multiplied by the change in entropy.
5. To be spontaneous, the free energy of a reaction must decrease.
6. One mole of solid is converted into two moles of gas.
7. Determine the sign of ΔS. The reaction is endothermic, and therefore ΔH is positive. The reaction is spontaneous, and therefore ΔG is negative. $\Delta G = \Delta H - T\Delta S$. Because $\Delta G < 0$ and $\Delta H > 0$, then ΔS must be positive. Entropy of the enzyme increases when the enzyme becomes denatured. Therefore, the original enzyme is more ordered than the denatured form.

Math Tutor Hess's Law

You may have seen a popular comic strip in which a little boy takes a long, twisting path between the school-bus stop and home. No matter which path the boy takes, the result is always the same: He goes from the bus stop to the door of his house. Hess's law covers a similar situation in thermochemistry. No matter which or how many steps occur in the process of changing one or more substances into one or more other substances, the overall change in enthalpy is always the same. Hess's law can be used, for example, to predict the enthalpy change, ΔH^0, of a reaction without actually carrying out the reaction.

Sample Problem

Determine ΔH for the burning of carbon disulfide in oxygen.

$$CS_2(l) + 3O_2(g) \longrightarrow CO_2(g) + 2SO_2(g);\ \Delta H^0 = ?$$

Use the following information:

$$C(s) + O_2(g) \longrightarrow CO_2(g) \qquad \Delta H_f^0 = -393.5\ \text{kJ/mol}$$

$$S(s) + O_2(g) \longrightarrow SO_2(g) \qquad \Delta H_f^0 = -296.8\ \text{kJ/mol}$$

$$C(s) + 2S(s) \longrightarrow CS_2(l) \qquad \Delta H_f^0 = 87.9\ \text{kJ/mol}$$

Rearrange the given equations in a way that will put the reactants of the above equation on the left and the products on the right.

1. $C(s) + O_2(g) \longrightarrow CO_2(g) \qquad \Delta H_f^0 = -393.5\ \text{kJ/mol}$

2. $2S(s) + 2O_2(g) \longrightarrow 2SO_2(g) \qquad \Delta H^0 = 2(-296.8\ \text{kJ})$

3. $CS_2(l) \longrightarrow C(s) + 2S(s) \qquad \Delta H^0 = -87.9\ \text{kJ}$

SUM: $CS_2(l) + 3O_2(g) \longrightarrow CO_2(g) + 2SO_2(g)$

Notice that equation 2 is double the original equation $S(s) + O_2(g) \longrightarrow SO_2(g)$. The reason for this is that $2SO_2$ are needed on the product side to match the $2SO_2$ in $CS_2(l) + 3O_2(g) \longrightarrow CO_2(g) + 2SO_2(g)$. The third equation is the reverse of the original, putting CS_2 on the reactant side of the final equation. The sign of ΔH is likewise reversed. The value of ΔH^0 is the sum of the ΔH^0 values for the three added equations.

$$\Delta H^0 = -393.5\ \text{kJ} + 2(-296.8\ \text{kJ}) + (-87.9\ \text{kJ})$$

$$\Delta H^0 = -1075.0\ \text{kJ}$$

Practice

Answers in Appendix E

1. Calculate ΔH^0 for the complete oxidation of sulfur to sulfur trioxide.

$$S(s) + \frac{3}{2}O_2(g) \longrightarrow SO_3(g)$$

Use the following information.

$$S(s) + O_2(g) \longrightarrow SO_2(g) \qquad \Delta H_f^0 = -296.8\ \text{kJ/mol}$$

$$SO_2(g) + \frac{1}{2}O_2(g) \longrightarrow SO_3(g) \qquad \Delta H_f^0 = -99.2\ \text{kJ/mol}$$

2. Calculate ΔH^0 for the reaction in which zinc sulfide ore is roasted to obtain zinc oxide.

$$ZnS(s) + \frac{3}{2}O_2(g) \longrightarrow ZnO(s) + SO_2(g)$$

Use the following information.

$$Zn(s) + \frac{1}{2}O_2(g) \longrightarrow ZnO(s) \qquad \Delta H_f^0 = -348.0\ \text{kJ/mol}$$

$$Zn(s) + S(s) \longrightarrow ZnS(s) \qquad \Delta H_f^0 = -203.0\ \text{kJ/mol}$$

$$S(s) + O_2(g) \longrightarrow SO_2(g) \qquad \Delta H_f^0 = -296.8\ \text{kJ/mol}$$

Answers

1. $\Delta H^0 = -396.0$ kJ
2. $\Delta H^0 = -441.8$ kJ

Teaching Tip

Tell students to pay attention to the physical state of a product or reactant involved in a reaction; substances in different states will have different characteristic enthalpies of formation.

Teaching Tip

Be sure students know that energy absorbed in a chemical reaction is directly proportional to the number of moles. To calculate the energy, they should multiply per-mole amounts by the number of moles actually involved.

CHAPTER 16 Summary

Review Games
Concept Maps

SECTION 1 Thermochemistry

- Thermochemistry is the study of the changes in energy that accompany chemical reactions and physical changes.
- A thermochemical equation is an equation that includes the quantity of energy released or absorbed as heat during the reaction as written.
- An enthalpy change is the amount of energy absorbed as heat by a system in a process carried out at constant pressure.
- The enthalpy of reaction is the enthalpy change that occurs during a chemical reaction.
- The enthalpy change is negative for exothermic reactions and positive for endothermic reactions.
- Compounds with highly negative enthalpies of formation tend to be stable; compounds with highly positive or only slightly negative enthalpies of formation tend to be unstable.
- The standard molar enthalpy of formation is the enthalpy change that occurs when one mole of a compound is formed from its elements in their standard states at 25°C and 1 atm.
- The enthalpy change that occurs in a combustion reaction is called the enthalpy of combustion.
- Enthalpies of reaction can be calculated by using enthalpies of formation of reactants and products.

KEY TERMS

thermochemistry
calorimeter
temperature
joule
heat
specific heat
enthalpy change
enthalpy of reaction
thermochemical equation
molar enthalpy of formation
enthalpy of combustion
Hess's law

SECTION 2 Driving Force of Reactions

- The tendency throughout nature is for a reaction to proceed in the direction that leads to a lower energy state.
- Entropy is a measure of the randomness of a system.
- Free-energy change combines the effects of entropy and enthalpy changes and temperature of a system, and it is a measure of the overall tendency toward natural change.
- A reaction is spontaneous if it is accompanied by a decrease in free energy. It is not spontaneous if there is an increase in free energy.

KEY TERMS

entropy
free energy
free-energy change

522 Chapter 16

CHAPTER 16 Review

SECTION 1

Thermochemistry

REVIEWING MAIN IDEAS

1. How does the enthalpy of the products of a reaction system compare with the enthalpy of the reactants when the reaction is
   a. endothermic?
   b. exothermic?

2. a. Distinguish between enthalpies of reaction, formation, and combustion.
   b. On what basis are enthalpies of formation and combustion defined?

3. Write the equation that can be used to calculate the enthalpy of reaction from enthalpies of formation.

4. What factors affect the value of ΔH in a reaction system?

5. State Hess's law. How is it used?

6. Describe a combustion calorimeter. What information can it give?

PRACTICE PROBLEMS

7. How much energy is needed to raise the temperature of a 55 g sample of aluminum from 22.4°C to 94.6°C? Refer to **Figure 1.2** for the specific heat of aluminum. (Hint: See Sample Problem A.)

8. If 3.5 kJ of energy are added to a 28.2 g sample of iron at 20°C, what is the final temperature of the iron in kelvins? Refer to **Figure 1.2** for the specific heat of iron.

9. You need 70.2 J to raise the temperature of 34.0 g of ammonia, $NH_3(g)$, from 23.0°C to 24.0°C. Calculate the specific heat of ammonia.

10. Calculate c_p for indium metal, given that 1.0 mol In absorbs 53 J while increasing in temperature from 297.5 K to 299.5 K.

11. For each equation listed below, determine the ΔH and type of reaction (endothermic or exothermic).
   a. $C(s) + O_2(g) \longrightarrow CO_2(g) + 393.51\text{ kJ}$
   b. $CH_4(g) + 2O_2(g) \longrightarrow CO_2(g) + 2H_2O(l) + 890.31\text{ kJ}$
   c. $CaCO_3(s) + 176\text{ kJ} \longrightarrow CaO(s) + CO_2(g)$
   d. $H_2O(g) \longrightarrow H_2O(l) + 44.02\text{ kJ}$

12. Rewrite each equation below with the ΔH value included with either the reactants or the products, and identify the reaction as endothermic or exothermic.
   a. $H_2(g) + O_2(g) \longrightarrow H_2O(l)$; $\Delta H^0 = -285.83\text{ kJ}$
   b. $2Mg(s) + O_2(g) \longrightarrow 2MgO(s)$; $\Delta H^0 = -1200\text{ kJ}$
   c. $I_2(s) \longrightarrow I_2(g)$; $\Delta H^0 = +62.4\text{ kJ}$
   d. $3CO(g) + Fe_2O_3(s) \longrightarrow 2Fe(s) + 3CO_2(g)$; $\Delta H^0 = -24.7\text{ kJ}$

13. Use Appendix Table B–14 to write the reaction illustrating the formation of each of the following compounds from its elements. Write the ΔH as part of each equation, and indicate the ΔH for the reverse reaction.
   a. $CaCl_2(s)$
   b. $C_2H_2(g)$ (ethyne, or acetylene)
   c. $SO_2(g)$

14. The reaction $2Fe_2O_3(s) + 3C(s) \longrightarrow 4Fe(s) + 3CO_2(g)$ is involved in the smelting of iron. Use ΔH_f values given in Appendix Table B–14 to calculate the enthalpy change during the production of 1 mol of iron.

15. Use enthalpy-of-formation data given in Appendix Table B–14 to calculate the enthalpy of reaction for each of the following. Solve each by combining the known thermochemical equations. Verify each result by using the general equation for finding enthalpies of reaction from enthalpies of formation. (Hint: See Sample Problem B.)
   a. $CaCO_3(s) \longrightarrow CaO(s) + CO_2(g)$
   b. $Ca(OH)_2(s) \longrightarrow CaO(s) + H_2O(g)$
   c. $Fe_2O_3(s) + 3CO(g) \longrightarrow 2Fe(s) + 3CO_2(g)$

16. For glucose, $C_6H_{12}O_6(s)$, $\Delta H_f = -1263\text{ kJ/mol}$. Calculate the enthalpy change when 1 mol of $C_6H_{12}O_6(s)$ combusts to form $CO_2(g)$ and $H_2O(l)$.

17. Calculate the standard enthalpies of reaction for combustion reactions in which ethane, C_2H_6, and benzene, C_6H_6, are the respective reactants and $CO_2(g)$ and $H_2O(l)$ are the products in each. Solve each by combining the known thermochemical equations using the ΔH_f values in Appendix Table B–14. Verify the result by using the general equation for finding enthalpies of reaction from enthalpies of formation.
   a. $C_2H_6(g) + O_2(g) \longrightarrow$
   b. $C_6H_6(l) + O_2(g) \longrightarrow$

CHAPTER REVIEW

Review Answers

1. a. The energy of the products is greater than the energy of the reactants.
   b. The energy of the products is less than the energy of the reactants.
2. a. ΔH is the quantity of energy absorbed or released during a chemical reaction. ΔH_f^0 is the enthalpy change that occurs when one mole of a compound is formed from its elements in their standard states at 25°C and 1 atm at room temperature. ΔH_c^0 is the enthalpy change that is produced by the complete combustion of one mole of a substance.
   b. The enthalpy of combustion is defined in terms of one mole of reactant. Enthalpy of formation is defined in terms of one mole of product.
3. $\Delta H^0 = \text{sum of } [(\Delta H_f^0 \text{ of products}) \times (\text{mol of products})] - \text{sum of } [(\Delta H_f^0 \text{ of reactants}) \times (\text{mol of reactants})]$
4. the change in the number of bonds breaking and forming and the strengths of these bonds as the reactants form products
5. Hess's law states that the change in enthalpy (or entropy) during a process is independent of the route taken. It is useful, for example, in calculating the enthalpy change during a reaction from the molar enthalpies of formation of the reactants and products.
6. A combustion calorimeter is a sturdy vessel inside which a substance can react with oxygen. The heat energy generated passes to water that is surrounding the reaction chamber. The temperature change of the water can be used to find the energy given off by the combustion reaction.
7. 3.6×10^3 J
8. 570 K
9. 2.06 J/(g • K)
10. 0.23 J/(g • K)
11. a. −393.51 kJ; exothermic
    b. −890.31 kJ; exothermic
    c. +176 kJ; endothermic
    d. −44.02 kJ; exothermic

12. a. $H_2(g) + \frac{1}{2}O_2(g) \longrightarrow H_2O(l) +$ 285.83 kJ; exothermic

b. $2Mg(s) + O_2(g) \longrightarrow 2MgO(s)$ + 1200 kJ; exothermic

c. $I_2(s)$ + 62.4 kJ $\longrightarrow I_2(g)$; endothermic

d. $3CO(g) + Fe_2O_3(s) \longrightarrow 2Fe(s) + 3CO_2(g)$ + 24.7 kJ; exothermic

13. a. $Ca(s) + Cl_2(g) \longrightarrow CaCl_2(g)$ + 795.4 kJ

$\Delta H_{reverse} = +795.4$ kJ

b. $2C(s) + H_2(g)$ + 228.2 kJ $\longrightarrow C_2H_2(g)$

$\Delta H_{reverse} = -228.2$ kJ

c. $S(s) + O_2(g) \longrightarrow SO_2(g)$ + 296.8 kJ

$\Delta H_{reverse} = +296.8$ kJ

14. $\Delta H = 117.6$ kJ

15. a. +179.2 kJ

b. +106.5 kJ

c. −23.5 kJ

16. −2813 kJ

17. a. −1560.6 kJ

b. −3267.5 kJ

18. −1367.4 kJ

19. decrease; −

20. It causes an increase in entropy.

21. a negative ΔH and a positive ΔS

22. At low temperatures, $T\Delta S$ is generally small in comparison with ΔH, so the sign of ΔH determines the sign of ΔG. At high temperatures, the $T\Delta S$ factor may be large enough to exceed the ΔH value and thereby allow the sign and magnitude of ΔS to dictate the spontaneity of the reaction.

23. $\Delta G = -345$ kJ; The reaction is spontaneous.

24. $\Delta G = 11$ kJ; The reaction is not spontaneous at 25°C, but it will become so at higher temperatures (greater than about 63°C).

25. $\Delta G = -41$ kJ; Yes, the reaction is spontaneous.

26. $\Delta G = -1.2$ kJ; Yes, the reaction is spontaneous.

27. a. 115 kJ/mol; not spontaneous

b. −135 kJ/mol; spontaneous

c. −623 kJ/mol; spontaneous

28. −394.40 kJ/mol; spontaneous

CHAPTER REVIEW

18. The enthalpy of formation of ethanol, C_2H_5OH, is −277.0 kJ/mol at 298.15 K. Calculate the enthalpy of combustion of one mole of ethanol, assuming that the products are $CO_2(g)$ and $H_2O(l)$. (Hint: See Sample Problem C.)

SECTION 2

Driving Force of Reactions

REVIEWING MAIN IDEAS

19. Would entropy increase or decrease for changes in state in which the reactant is a gas or liquid and the product is a solid? What sign would the entropy change have?

20. How does an increase in temperature affect the entropy of a system?

21. What combination of ΔH and ΔS values always produces a negative free-energy change?

22. Explain the relationship between temperature and the tendency for reactions to occur spontaneously.

PRACTICE PROBLEMS

23. A reaction has $\Delta H = -356$ kJ and $\Delta S = -36$ J/K. Calculate ΔG at 25°C to confirm that the reaction is spontaneous.

24. A reaction has $\Delta H = 98$ kJ and $\Delta S = 292$ J/K. Investigate the spontaneity of the reaction at room temperature. Would increasing the temperature have any effect on the spontaneity of the reaction?

25. A reaction has $\Delta H = -76$ kJ and $\Delta S = -117$ J/K. Calculate ΔG for the reaction at 298.15 K. Is the reaction spontaneous?

26. The gas-phase reaction of H_2 with CO_2 to produce H_2O and CO has $\Delta H = 11$ kJ and $\Delta S = 41$ J/K. Is the reaction spontaneous at 298.15 K? What is ΔG?

27. Based on the following values, compute ΔG values for each reaction and predict whether the reaction will occur spontaneously. (Hint: See Sample Problem D.)

a. $\Delta H = +125$ kJ, $T = 293$ K, $\Delta S = 0.0350$ kJ/K

b. $\Delta H = -85.2$ kJ, $T = 127$°C, $\Delta S = 0.125$ kJ/K

c. $\Delta H = -275$ kJ, $T = 773$ K, $\Delta S = 0.450$ kJ/K

28. The ΔS^0 for the reaction shown, at 298.15 K, is 0.003 00 kJ/(mol • K). Calculate the ΔG^0 for this reaction, and determine whether it will occur spontaneously at 298.15 K.

$$C(s) + O_2(g) \longrightarrow CO_2(g) + 393.51 \text{ kJ}$$

Mixed Review

REVIEWING MAIN IDEAS

29. When graphite reacts with hydrogen at 300 K, ΔH is −74.8 kJ and ΔS is −0.0809 kJ/K. Will this reaction occur spontaneously?

30. How might you change reaction conditions to induce an endothermic reaction that does not occur naturally?

31. The diagram below represents an interpretation of Hess's law for the following reaction.

$$Sn(s) + 2Cl_2(g) \longrightarrow SnCl_4(l)$$

Use the diagram to determine ΔH for each step and the net reaction.

$Sn(s) + Cl_2(g) \longrightarrow SnCl_2(s)$	$\Delta H = ?$
$SnCl_2(l) + Cl_2(g) \longrightarrow SnCl_4(s)$	$\Delta H = ?$
$Sn(s) + 2Cl_2(g) \longrightarrow SnCl_4(l)$	$\Delta H = ?$

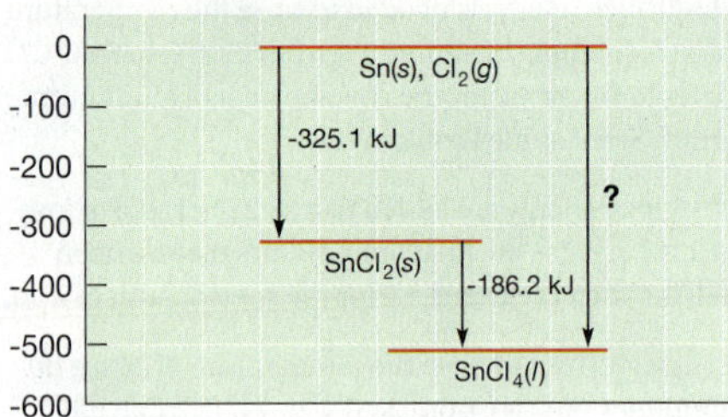

32. The standard enthalpy of formation for sulfur dioxide gas is −296.8 kJ/mol. Calculate the amount of energy given off in kJ when 30.0 g of $SO_2(g)$ is formed from its elements.

524 Chapter 16

33. The thermite reaction used in some welding applications has the following enthalpy and entropy changes at 298.15 K. Assuming ΔS and ΔH are constant, calculate ΔG at 448 K.

$$Fe_2O_3 + 2Al(s) \longrightarrow 2Fe(s) + Al_2O_3(s)$$

$$\Delta H^0 = -851.5 \text{ kJ}, \Delta S^0 = -38.5 \text{ J/K}$$

34. Rewrite each equation below with the ΔH value included in either the reactants or products, and identify the reaction as endothermic or exothermic.

a. $2SO_2(g) + O_2(g) \longrightarrow 2SO_3(g)$; $\Delta H = -197.8$ kJ

b. $2NO_2(g) \longrightarrow 2NO(g) + O_2(g)$; $\Delta H = +114.2$ kJ

c. $C_2H_4(g) + 3O_2(g) \longrightarrow 2CO_2(g) + 2H_2O(l)$; $\Delta H = -1411.0$ kJ

35. Calculate the change in enthalpy for the following reaction.

$$4FeO(s) + O_2(g) \longrightarrow 2Fe_2O_3(s)$$

Use the enthalpy-of-formation data listed in Appendix Table B-14.

36. The reaction to synthesize methanol (CH_3OH) industrially is

$$CO(g) + 2H_2(g) \longrightarrow CH_3OH(g).$$

The $\Delta H^0_{\text{reaction}} = -90.7$ kJ and the $\Delta S^0_{reaction} = -220.8$ J/K. At what temperatures is the reaction nonspontaneous?

37. What is the main characteristic of a calorimeter in a bomb calorimeter experiment, and why is this characteristic essential?

CRITICAL THINKING

38. Relating Ideas Given the entropy change for the first two reactions below, calculate the entropy change for the third reaction below.

$S_8(s) + 8O_2(s) \longrightarrow 8SO_2(g)$	$\Delta S = 89$ J/K
$2SO_2(s) + O_2(s) \longrightarrow 2SO_3(g)$	$\Delta S = -188$ J/K
$S_8(s) + 12O_2(s) \longrightarrow 8SO_3(g)$	$\Delta S = ?$

39. Interpreting Concepts Look at the two pictures below. Which picture appears to have more order? Why? Are there any similarities between the amount of order the marbles have and the entropy of particles?

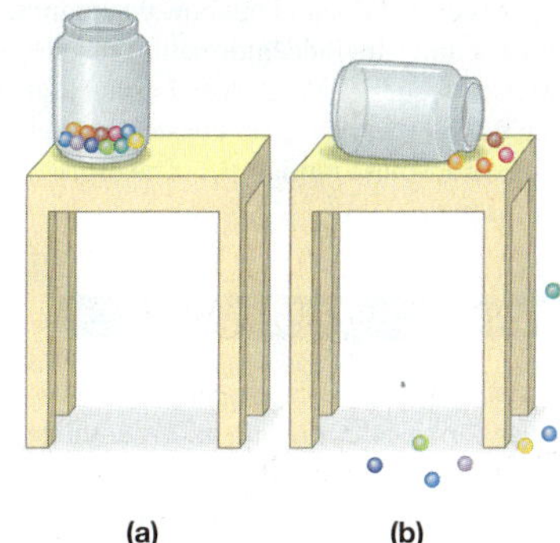

(a) (b)

40. Inferring Conclusions A reaction is endothermic and has a $\Delta H = 8$ kJ. This reaction occurs spontaneously at 25°C. What must be true about the entropy change?

41. Inferring Conclusions If both ΔH and ΔS are negative, how does temperature affect spontaneity?

42. Inferring Relationships If the reaction $X \longrightarrow Y$ is spontaneous, what can be said about the reaction $Y \longrightarrow X$?

43. Interpreting Concepts Absolute enthalpy cannot be determined; only change in energy can be measured. However, absolute entropy can be determined. Explain why an absolute entropy can be determined.

CHAPTER REVIEW

29. yes ($\Delta G = -50.53$ kJ)

30. If ΔS is positive, heat the system so that the second term $-T\Delta S$ causes ΔG to become negative, giving a spontaneous reaction.

31. $\Delta H = -325.1$ kJ, $\Delta H = -186.2$ kJ, $\Delta H = -511.3$ kJ

32. 139 kJ

33. −834.3 kJ

34. a. exothermic

$$2SO_2(g) + O_2(g) \longrightarrow 2SO_3(g) + 197.8 \text{ kJ}$$

b. endothermic

$$2NO_2(g) + 114.2 \text{ kJ} \longrightarrow 2NO(g) + O_2(g)$$

c. exothermic

$$C_2H_4(g) + 3O_2(g) \longrightarrow 2CO_2(g) + 2H_2O(l) + 1411.0 \text{ kJ}$$

35. −560.4 kJ

36. above 411 K

37. The calorimeter is a container whose main characteristic is the ability to insulate. The calorimeter must insulate so that the heat evolved from the reaction is absorbed by the water bath and recorded by the thermometer instead of being released to the environment.

38. −663 J/K

39. (a), because the marbles are ordered in the jar. The entropy of the particles increases when the arrangement of the particles becomes more random.

40. It must be positive, and of a value exceeding about 30 J/K.

41. The reaction will be spontaneous at a sufficiently low temperature and nonspontaneous at a sufficiently high temperature.

42. It is nonspontaneous.

43. Entropy is the measure of randomness in a system. At absolute zero, random motion stops; therefore, the entropy of a pure crystalline solid is zero at absolute zero. The randomness of the system increases as energy is added to the system, and by calculations, the absolute (standard molar) entropy can be determined.

44. In one joule, there are: 9.488×10^{-4} British thermal units (BTUs), 0.2390 calories, and 1.0 newton-meter.

45. Students' answers may vary but should include measuring the mass of the ice cube and using a known mass of room-temperature water. Students should measure the temperature of the water bath, place the ice cube into the water bath, and measure the temperature of the water bath after the ice cube melts, making sure that the water bath is stirred continuously. The calorimeter should be the large plastic-foam cup with a cover. Be sure students use safe procedures.

46. Students' answers may vary but should include measuring the mass of samples, heating them, and determining how much they increase the temperature of a known mass of water in a calorimeter. Be sure students use safe procedures and available materials. A calorimeter can easily be made from a foam cup.

47. Students' answers may vary but should include dissolving a known mass of sodium acetate in a known mass of water and measuring the resulting temperature change. Be sure students follow proper safety procedures, wear proper personal protective equipment, and follow chemical safety guidelines.

CHAPTER REVIEW

RESEARCH AND WRITING

44. Obtain information on alternative units of measure used to express values of energy as heat and other forms of energy. Also, find out how the quantities relate to SI units. Include information specifically on English units, such as the British thermal unit (BTU), and on typical BTU ratings of household appliances. Calculate how these ratings would be expressed in joules instead.

ALTERNATIVE ASSESSMENT

45. **Performance** Design a simple calorimeter investigation to determine the molar enthalpy of fusion of water. Use the following materials: a large plastic-foam cup with cover, a thermometer, a balance, water at room temperature, and an ice cube. Allow your teacher to review your design. Then carry out the investigation, and write a laboratory report including your calculations and a comparison of your quantitative results with known values. Try to account for any disagreements between the experimental and actual values.

46. **Performance** Design an experiment to measure the molar heat capacities of zinc and copper. If your teacher approves the design, obtain the materials needed and conduct the experiment. When you are finished, compare your experimental values with those from a chemical handbook or other reference source.

47. **Performance** Develop a procedure to measure the ΔH of the reaction shown below. If your teacher approves your procedure, test your procedure by measuring the ΔH value of the reaction. Determine the accuracy of your method by comparing your ΔH with the accepted ΔH value.

$$CH_3COONa(s) \longrightarrow Na^+(aq) + CH_3COO^-(aq)$$

526 Chapter 16

Standards-Based Assessment

Answer the following items on a separate piece of paper.

MULTIPLE CHOICE

1. Which of the following two conditions will favor a spontaneous reaction?
A. an increase in entropy and a decrease in enthalpy
B. an increase in both entropy and in enthalpy
C. a decrease in entropy and a decrease in enthalpy
D. a decrease in entropy and an increase in enthalpy

2. The gasification of coal is a method of producing methane by the following reaction.

$$C(s) + 2H_2(g) \longrightarrow CH_4(g) \qquad \Delta H = ?$$

Find ΔH by using the enthalpy changes in the following combustion reactions:

$$C(s) + O_2(g) \longrightarrow CO_2(g) \qquad \Delta H = -394 \text{ kJ}$$

$$H_2(g) + \frac{1}{2}O_2(g) \longrightarrow H_2O(l) \qquad \Delta H = -286 \text{ kJ}$$

$$CH_4(g) + 2O_2(g) \longrightarrow CO_2(g) + 2H_2O(l) \qquad \Delta H = -891 \text{ kJ}$$

A. 75 kJ
B. −75 kJ
C. 1856 kJ
D. −1856 kJ

3. Two metals of equal mass but different specific heats absorb the same amount of heat. Which metal undergoes the smaller change in temperature?
A. The metal with the higher specific heat.
B. The metal with the lower specific heat.
C. Both undergo the same change in temperature.
D. Cannot determine from the information given.

4. Which of the following processes has a negative ΔS?
A. evaporating 1 mol of a liquid
B. raising the temperature of 1 L of water from 295 K to 350 K
C. freezing of 1 mol of a liquid
D. none of the above

5. At a constant pressure, the following reaction is exothermic: $2NO_2(g) \longrightarrow N_2O_4(g)$. Which of the following statements is true about the reaction (as written)?
A. The reaction is always spontaneous.
B. The reaction is spontaneous at low temperatures, but not at high temperatures.
C. The reaction is spontaneous at high temperatures, but not at low temperatures.
D. The reaction is never spontaneous.

SHORT ANSWER

6. For a reaction in which a diatomic molecule dissociates into atoms, what are the signs of ΔS and ΔH? Explain your answer. You may use the reaction $N_2(g) \longrightarrow 2N(g)$ as an example of such a reaction.

EXTENDED RESPONSE

7. For certain molecules, enthalpies of formation can be determined from combustion data. Using the diagram below, calculate the enthalpy of formation (ΔH), of methane gas $CH_4(g)$, and the enthalpies for two of the combustion reactions listed below.

$$C(s) + O_2(g) \longrightarrow CO_2(g) \qquad \Delta H = -394 \text{ kJ}$$

$$H_2(g) + \frac{1}{2}O_2(g) \longrightarrow H_2O(l) \qquad \Delta H = ?$$

$$CH_4(g) + 2O_2(g) \longrightarrow CO_2(g) + 2H_2O(l) \quad \Delta H = ?$$

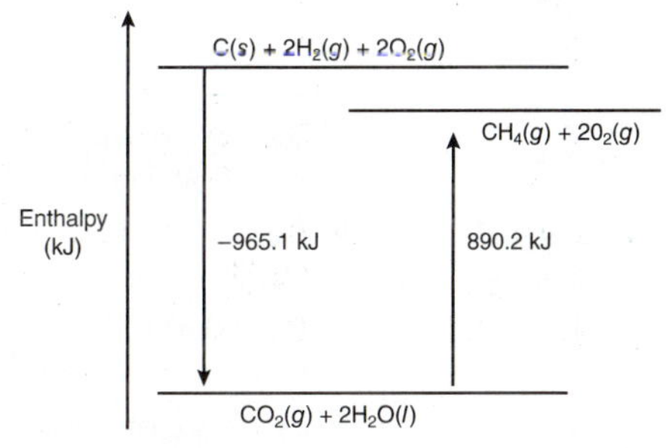

Test Tip
Always read the question before looking at the answer choices.

STANDARDS-BASED ASSESSMENT

To give students practice under more realistic testing conditions, give them 60 minutes to answer all of the questions in this Standardized Test Preparation.

Test Answers

1. A
2. B
3. A
4. C
5. B
6. ΔS is positive, because the reaction is producing more moles of gas than were originally present. Therefore, there is more randomness in the sample. ΔH is positive, because bonds are being broken and it takes energy to break a bond.
7. The formation reaction for $CH_4(g)$ is $C(s) + 2H_2(g) \longrightarrow CH_4(g)$.
From the graph,
ΔH for $H_2(g) + \frac{1}{2}O_2(g) \longrightarrow H_2O(l)$ is $[-965.1 \text{ kJ} - (-393.5 \text{ kJ})]/2 = -285.8 \text{ kJ}$.
The ΔH for $CH_4(g) + 2O_2(g) \longrightarrow CO_2(g) + 2H_2O(l)$ can be read directly from the graph and is −890.2 kJ. The enthalpy of formation for $CH_4(g)$ is −965.1 kJ + 890.2 kJ = −74.9 kJ.

Reaction Kinetics

① Core Instruction

Chapter Resources

- **The Teacher's Edition wrap has extensive teaching support for every lesson, including Misconception Alerts, Teach from Visuals, Demonstrations, Teaching Tips, Differentiated Instruction, and Problem Solving support.**
- **Several additional presentation tools are available online for every chapter, including Animated Chemistry features and Visual Concepts.**
- **You can open your lesson with the Why It Matters Video: Reaction Kinetics.**

Section	Instruction	Labs and Demonstrations Go Online for Materials Lists and Solutions Lists.
17.1	**Textbook:** The Reaction Process **Teaching Visuals:** Activation Energies • Possible Collision Orientations for the Reaction of H_2 and I_2 • Activation Energy Differences in Exothermic and Endothermic Reactions **PowerPresentations**	**Demonstration:** Effect of Orientation
17.2	**Textbook:** Reaction Rate **Animated Chemistry:** Catalysts **Teaching Visuals:** Activation Energies • Particle Collisions • Possible Collision Orientations for the Reaction of H_2 and I_2, • Concentration vs. Possible Collisions **PowerPresentations**	**Demonstration:** Temperature and Reaction Time **Demonstration:** Decomposition and Catalysts **QuickLab:** Factors Influencing Reaction Rates **Lab:** Rate of a Chemical Reaction (Core Skill) **Lab:** A Leaky Reaction (Forensics) **Lab:** Clock Reactions **Lab:** Reaction Action (Open Inquiry)

2 Support and Intervention

- **Interactive Reader** (English and Spanish)
- **Study Guide**
- **Interactive Review:** Review Games, Concept Maps, and Section Self-Checks
- **Scientific Reasoning Skill Builder**
- **Learn It! Videos**
- **Solve It! Cards**
- **Interactive Demos**
- **Sample Problem Sets**

3 Specialized Support

- **Chapter Summary Audio Files**
- **Interactive Reader Audio Files**
- **Differentiated Instruction:** Inclusion, Below Level, and English Learners (TE wrap)

Enrichment and Challenge

- **Differentiated Instruction:** Pre-AP (TE wrap)
- **Why It Matters:** Catalytic Converters (SE)
- **WebLinks**

Assessment

- **Section Formative Assessments** (SE)
- **Section Quizzes**
- **Chapter Review** (SE)
- **Chapter Tests A and B**
- **Alternative Assessment** (TE wrap)
- **Online Assessment and Remediation**
- **ExamView Banks**

Where do I find it?

		PRINT	DVD	ONLINE
1	Animated Chemistry		■	■
	Demonstrations (TE wrap)	■		■
	Interactive Whiteboard		■	■
	Labs		■	■
	PowerPresentations		■	■
	QuickLabs	■	■	■
	Teaching Visuals		■	■
	Textbook	■	■	■
	Visual Concepts		■	■
	Why It Matters Videos		■	■
2	Interactive Demos		■	■
	Interactive Reader	■	■	■
	Interactive Reviews		■	■
	Learn It! Videos		■	■
	Sample Problem Sets		■	■
	Scientific Reasoning Skill Builder		■	■
	Smart Grapher Tool		■	■
	Solve It! Cards		■	■
	Study Guide		■	■
3	Chapter Summary Audio Files		■	■
	Differentiated Instruction (TE wrap)	■		
	Interactive Reader Audio Files		■	■

CHAPTER 17

Chapter Overview

Section 1 uses collision theory and activation energy to describe the mechanisms by which chemical reactions take place.

Section 2 reviews the factors that influence the rate of a chemical reaction, shows how to describe the rate based on experimental data, and relates the reaction rate to the mechanism of the reaction.

▼ Focus and Motivate

Activate Prior Knowledge

Students may need a review of the following concepts:

- conservation of energy
- bond energies
- kinetic theory of matter
- molar concentrations
- enthalpy of solution

About the Image

A firefly produces a chemical reaction, called *bioluminescence*, that creates light. The light is produced when oxygen is added to other chemicals in the firefly's light organ, and is catalyzed by an enzyme called *luciferase*. The light goes out when the oxygen is no longer available. This results in the flashing appearance of a firefly on a summer evening.

Why It Matters

Students can access the video online and find other helpful resources at **HMDScience.com**.

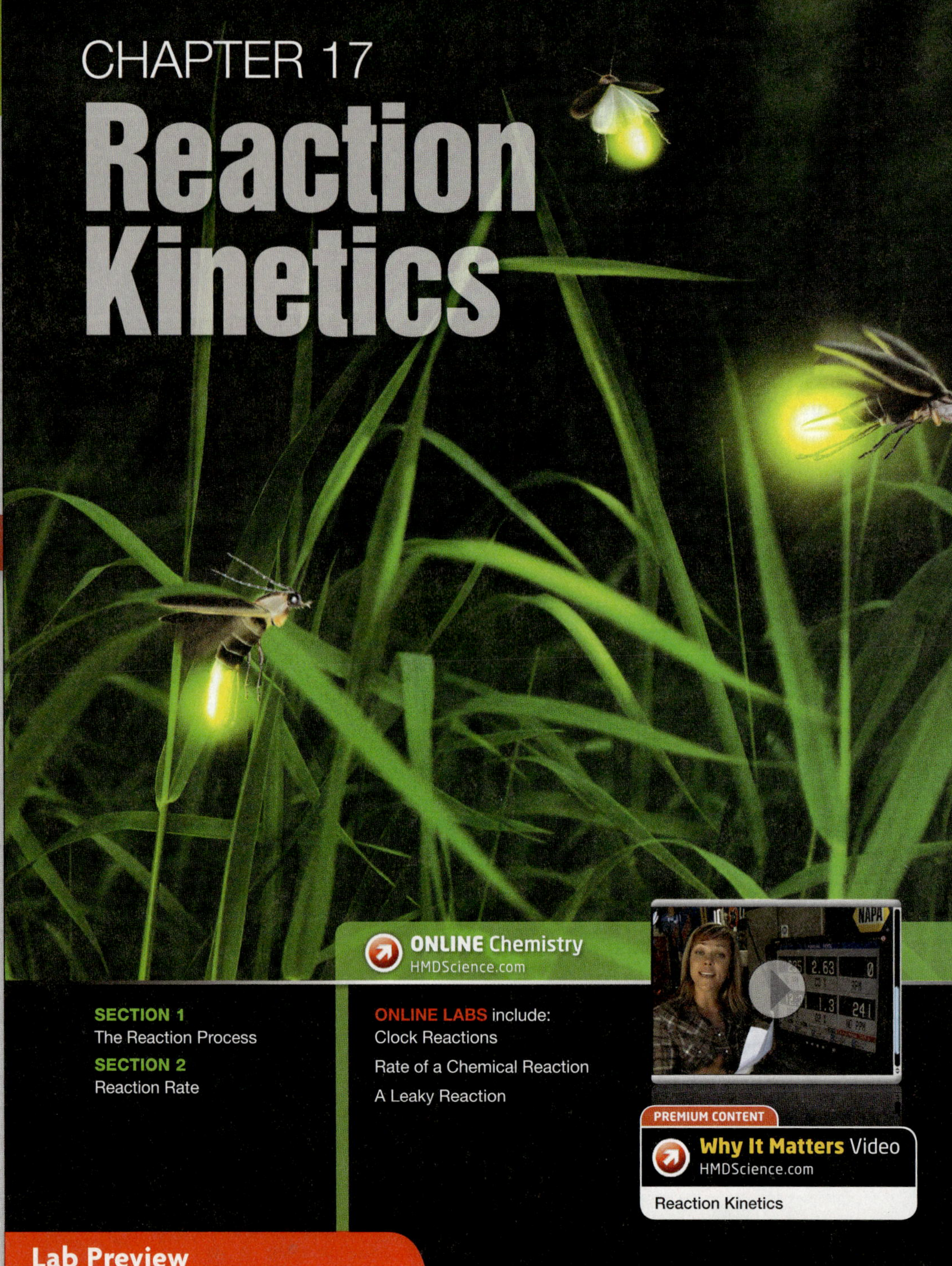

CHAPTER 17

Reaction Kinetics

ONLINE Chemistry
HMDScience.com

SECTION 1
The Reaction Process

SECTION 2
Reaction Rate

ONLINE LABS include:
Clock Reactions
Rate of a Chemical Reaction
A Leaky Reaction

PREMIUM CONTENT
Why It Matters Video
HMDScience.com
Reaction Kinetics

Lab Preview

The following labs and demonstrations support the concepts presented in this chapter.

LABS

Rate of a Chemical Reaction (Core Skill)
A Leaky Reaction (Forensics)
Clock Reactions
Reaction Action (Open Inquiry)

QUICKLAB

Factors Influencing Reaction Rates

DEMONSTRATIONS

Effect of Orientation
Temperature and Reaction Time
Decomposition and Catalysts

The Reaction Process

Key Terms

reaction mechanism
intermediate
homogenous reaction
collision theory
activation energy
activated complex

By studying many types of experiments, chemists have found that chemical reactions occur at widely differing rates. For example, in the presence of air, iron rusts very slowly, whereas the methane in natural gas burns rapidly. The speed of a chemical reaction depends on the energy pathway that a reaction follows and the changes that take place on the molecular level when substances interact. In this chapter, you will study the factors that affect how fast chemical reactions take place.

SECTION 1

Main Ideas

- Some reactions have intermediate steps.
- Molecular collisions need the right energy and orientation to react.
- Reactions occur only if there is enough energy.
- In a transition state, molecules break bonds and form new ones.

MAIN IDEA

Some reactions have intermediate steps.

If you mix aqueous solutions of HCl and NaOH, an extremely rapid neutralization reaction occurs, as shown in **Figure 1.1.**

$$H_3O^+(aq) + Cl^-(aq) + Na^+(aq) + OH^-(aq) \longrightarrow 2H_2O(l) + Na^+(aq) + Cl^-(aq)$$

The reaction is practically instantaneous; the rate is limited only by the speed with which the H_3O^+ and OH^- ions can diffuse through the water to meet each other. On the other hand, reactions between ions of the same charge and between molecular substances are not instantaneous. Negative ions repel each other, as do positive ions. The electron clouds of molecules also repel each other strongly at very short distances. Therefore, only ions or molecules with very high kinetic energy can overcome repulsive forces and get close enough to react. In this section, we will limit our discussion to reactions between molecules.

Colorless hydrogen gas consists of pairs of hydrogen atoms bonded together as diatomic molecules, H_2. Violet-colored iodine vapor is also diatomic, consisting of pairs of iodine atoms bonded together as I_2 molecules. A chemical reaction between these two gases at elevated temperatures produces hydrogen iodide, HI, a colorless gas. Hydrogen iodide molecules, in turn, tend to decompose and re-form hydrogen and iodine molecules, producing the violet gas shown in **Figure 1.2** on the next page. The following chemical equations describe these two reactions.

$$H_2(g) + I_2(g) \longrightarrow 2HI(g)$$

$$2HI(g) \longrightarrow H_2(g) + I_2(g)$$

Such equations indicate only which molecular species disappear as a result of the reactions and which species are produced. They do not show the **reaction mechanism,** the step-by-step sequence of reactions by which the overall chemical change occurs.

FIGURE 1.1

Instantaneous Reaction As NaOH solution is poured into HCl solution, a very rapid neutralization reaction occurs. Excess NaOH turns the phenolphthalein indicator pink.

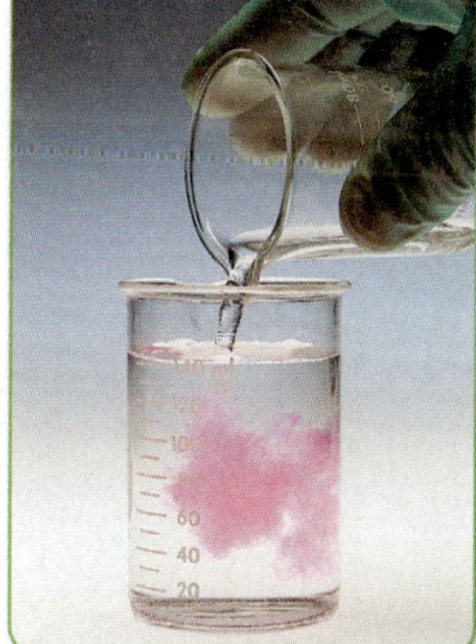

Differentiated Instruction

BELOW LEVEL

Use a baseball game or some other sporting event as an analogy to explain the concept of reaction mechanism. Write the score for a game on the board. Ask students how the score is similar to a chemical equation. Students should point out that both a score and a chemical equation tell you which teams played (the reactants) and the outcome (the products). Have students explain why the score is not like a reaction mechanism. Students should explain that the score tells the outcome but does not give any idea of the stepwise process that led up to the final result. Also, the team configurations do not change during the game—the same members are on each team when the game is over. Now ask students what additional information they need so that the baseball game is similar to a reaction mechanism. Students may suggest that a breakdown by inning would indicate the step-by-step sequence leading up to the final score. Students may even suggest that a breakdown of each batter's performance inning by inning would be comparable to a reaction mechanism.

SECTION 1

Plan and Prepare

Objectives

Upon completion of this section, students should be able to do the following:

- Explain the concept of reaction mechanism.
- Use the collision theory to interpret chemical reactions.
- Define *activated complex.*
- Relate activation energy to enthalpy of reaction.

Classroom Catalyst

Use a molecular model kit, or gumdrops and toothpicks, to illustrate the reaction between H_2 and I_2. Point out that the reaction $H_2 + I_2 \longrightarrow 2HI$ need not occur in a single step. Have students list reactions that might occur, such as the following:

(1) $H_2 \longrightarrow 2H$, $2H + I_2 \longrightarrow 2HI$; or
(2) $I_2 \longrightarrow 2I$, $2I + H_2 \longrightarrow 2HI$; or
(3) $I_2 \longrightarrow 2I$, $H_2 + I \longrightarrow HI + H$, $H + I \longrightarrow HI$

Teach

READING TOOLKIT

USING RATES Ask a student to read the definition of rate aloud. A rate represents a change over time. Then, have students give examples of different types of rates. Sample answers: heart rate; miles per hour Explain that some chemical reactions occur very rapidly or very slowly. Ask students to give examples of these. Sample answers: cooking food; rusting iron Discuss ways to make these reactions speed up or slow down.

Classroom Discussion

Ask students to identify intermediate species in the reaction between H_2 and I_2. Most chemical reactions involve two or more steps. Intermediate species form in one step of a reaction and are used as reactants in a later step.

▼ Teach *continued*

Application

Atmospheric chemists have unraveled the reaction mechanisms by which stratospheric ozone, O_3, is destroyed by chlorofluorocarbons (CFCs) released by human activities. The principle mechanism is the following:

(1) $Cl + O_3 \longrightarrow ClO + O_2$

(2) $2ClO \longrightarrow ClOOCl$

(3) $ClOOCl \longrightarrow ClOO + Cl$

(4) $ClOO \longrightarrow Cl + O_2$

In the atmosphere, CFCs are first broken down by sunlight, releasing free chlorine atoms. A free chlorine atom then causes an ozone molecule to break down. Note that a chlorine atom is regenerated each time the reaction mechanism occurs, making the atom available for the destruction of additional ozone molecules. Chemists have learned that even more complex reaction mechanisms may also be involved in the destruction of ozone by CFCs in the atmosphere.

Check for Understanding

Answer: Answers will vary. A good answer would be the following: A chemist in industry might need to know all of the steps that a reaction goes through in order to change reaction conditions to either maximize the product or speed up the reaction.

FIGURE 1.2

Intermediates Colorless hydrogen iodide gas, HI, decomposes into colorless hydrogen gas and violet iodine gas. Some of the hydrogen gas and iodine gas will reform HI.

Although only the net chemical change is directly observable for most chemical reactions, experiments can often be designed that suggest the probable sequence of steps in a reaction mechanism. Each reaction step is usually a simple process. The equation for each step represents the *actual* atoms, ions, or molecules that participate in that step. Even a reaction that appears from its balanced equation to be a simple process may actually be the result of several simple steps.

For many years, the formation of hydrogen iodide, as shown in **Figure 1.2**, was considered a simple one-step process. It was thought to involve the interaction of two molecules, H_2 and I_2, in the forward reaction and two HI molecules in the reverse reaction. Experiments eventually showed, however, that a direct reaction between H_2 and I_2 does not take place.

Alternative mechanisms for the reaction were proposed based on the experimental results. The steps in each reaction mechanism had to add together to give the overall equation. Note that two of the species in the mechanism steps—I and H_2I—do not appear in the net equation. **Species that appear in some steps but not in the net equation are known as intermediates.** (Notice that they cancel each other out in the following mechanisms.) The first possible mechanism has the following two-step pathway.

Step 1: $I_2 \rightleftharpoons 2I$

Step 2: $2I + H_2 \rightleftharpoons 2HI$

$I_2 + H_2 \rightleftharpoons 2HI$

The second possible mechanism has a three-step pathway.

Step 1: $I_2 \rightleftharpoons 2I$

Step 2: $I + H_2 \rightleftharpoons H_2I$

Step 3: $H_2I + I \rightleftharpoons 2HI$

$I_2 + H_2 \rightleftharpoons 2HI$

✓ **CHECK FOR UNDERSTANDING**

Propose Based on your knowledge of reaction mechanisms, propose at least one reason why a chemist working in industry might need to know all of the steps in a chemical reaction.

The reaction between hydrogen gas and iodine vapor to produce hydrogen iodide gas is an example of a homogeneous reaction, a reaction whose reactants and products exist in a single phase—in this case, the gas phase. This reaction system is also an example of a homogeneous chemical system, because all reactants and products in all intermediate steps are in the same phase.

MAIN IDEA

Molecular collisions need the right energy and orientation to react.

In order for reactions to occur between substances, their particles (molecules, atoms, or ions) must collide. Furthermore, these collisions must result in interactions. **The set of assumptions regarding collisions and reactions is known as collision theory.** Chemists use this theory to interpret many of their observations about chemical reactions.

Differentiated Instruction

INCLUSION

To help tactile learners understand reaction kinetics and the role of intermediates, ask five students to form a line. Give the first student two small balls of modeling clay. Use a different color of clay for each ball. Tell the class that one ball represents a molecule of H_2 gas and the other ball represents a molecule of I_2 gas. Tell the first student to give the two balls to the next student in line. The second student should take a small piece from one ball and stick it on the other ball. Repeat this process until the two balls get to the last student in line. Tell the class that the balls now represent two molecules of HI gas. Have the class explain what happened in terms of a reaction mechanism. Students should point out that the modeling activity took place over several intermediate steps, rather than in just a single action. Explain to students that the real reaction between hydrogen and iodine happens in a similar fashion.

Consider what might happen on a molecular scale in one step of a homogeneous reaction system. We will analyze a proposed first step in a hypothetical decomposition reaction.

$$AB + AB \rightleftharpoons A_2 + 2B$$

According to the collision theory, the two AB molecules must collide in order to react. Furthermore, they must collide with a favorable orientation and with enough energy to merge the valence electrons and disrupt the bonds of the AB molecules. If they do so, a reshuffling of bonds leads to the formation of the products, one A_2 molecule and two B atoms. An effective collision is modeled in **Figure 1.3a.**

If a collision is too gentle, the two molecules simply rebound from each other unchanged. This effect is illustrated in **Figure 1.3b.** Similarly, a collision in which the reactant molecules have an unfavorable orientation has little effect. The colliding molecules rebound without reacting. A collision that has poor orientation is shown in **Figure 1.3c.**

A chemical reaction produces new bonds that are formed between specific atoms in the colliding molecules. Unless the collision brings the correct atoms close together and in the proper orientation, the molecules will not react. For example, if a chlorine molecule collides with the oxygen end of a nitrogen monoxide molecule, the following reaction may occur.

FIGURE 1.3

Collision Patterns

Three possible collision patterns for AB molecules are shown. Not every collision produces a chemical reaction.

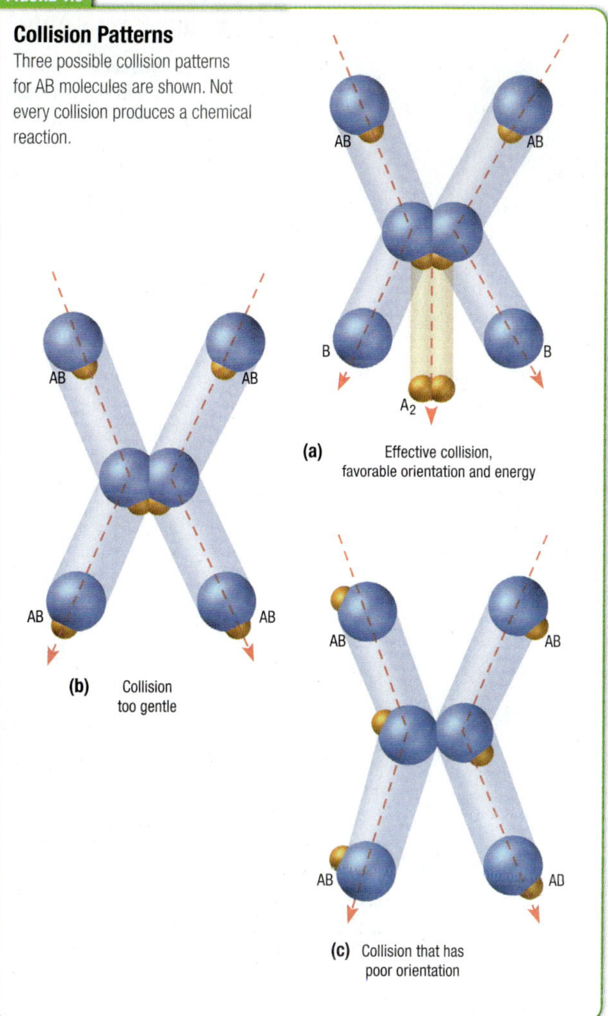

(a) Effective collision, favorable orientation and energy

(b) Collision too gentle

(c) Collision that has poor orientation

$$NO(g) + Cl_2(g) \longrightarrow NOCl(g) + Cl(g)$$

This reaction will not occur if the chlorine molecule strikes the nitrogen end of the molecule.

Thus, collision theory provides two reasons why a collision between reactant molecules may fail to produce a new chemical species: the collision is not energetic enough to supply the required energy, or the colliding molecules are not oriented in a way that enables them to react with each other.

TEACH FROM VISUALS

FIGURE 1.3 Explore with students how valence electrons in the AB molecules have an effect on the way a reaction will occur in case (a) and will not occur in cases (b) and (c).

Demonstration

EFFECT OF ORIENTATION

Using models from a **molecular model kit** or **gumdrops** and **toothpicks,** show students a variety of orientations in the collision of two HI molecules. Have students predict and explain why some orientations would be effective and others would not.

Teaching Tip

The kinetic energy of colliding particles can be converted into vibrational energy of the chemically bonded atoms. The bonds that have sufficient vibrational energy can then rupture, making possible the formation of new bonds.

READING TOOLKIT

BRAINSTORMING Have students read the sections about activation energy and the activated complex. Lead a discussion of the important features of the graphs shown in **Figures 1.4 and 1.5** (on the next two pages). Highlight these features visually (using an overhead projector or digital document projector) as you discuss them and students take notes. Then challenge student pairs to work through Sample Problem A by using their notes.

BELOW LEVEL

To help students understand collision theory, ask them to give examples of a collision they have seen. Students may describe a collision between two cars or between two football players. Tell students to think of an effective collision between two cars as a collision that results in damage to one or both cars. Ask students to explain how two cars may collide without experiencing an effective collision. Students may describe a situation in which the two cars were moving slowly. In other words, they did not have enough energy to cause any damage when they collided. Students may suggest that the two cars hit each other's bumpers and thus prevented any damage. In this case, the cars were not oriented in a way that could cause damage.

▼ Teach *continued*

TEACH FROM VISUALS

FIGURE 1.4 Ask students to explain how the height of the activation curve is related to the ease with which a reaction will occur. What would the activation curve look like for a very rapid reaction? Have students hypothesize about what would happen if an amount of energy less than E_a were supplied to the reactants in the reaction represented in this graph.

Classroom Discussion

Analyze with students the series of reactions involved in lighting a match, which is used to ignite paper, which is used to ignite kindling, which is used to ignite larger pieces of wood in a fireplace. Explain how energy released in each step is used to provide the activation energy needed in the next step.

Teaching Tip

ΔE is closely related to ΔH for a reaction. As students will learn in more advanced studies, these two terms actually differ by the amount of work done in the reaction.

MAIN IDEA

Reactions occur only if there is enough energy.

Consider the reaction for the formation of water from the diatomic gases oxygen and hydrogen according to the following equation:

$$2H_2(g) + O_2(g) \longrightarrow 2H_2O(l)$$

The enthalpy of formation is quite high: $\Delta H_f^0 = -285.8$ kJ/mol at 298.15 K. The free-energy change is also large: $\Delta G^0 = -237.1$ kJ/mol. Why, then, don't oxygen and hydrogen combine spontaneously and immediately to form water when they are mixed at room temperature?

FIGURE 1.4

Reaction Pathways The difference between the activation energies for the reverse and forward reactions of a reversible reaction equals the energy change in the reaction, ΔE. The quantity for ΔE is the same for both directions, but is negative for the exothermic direction and positive for the endothermic direction.

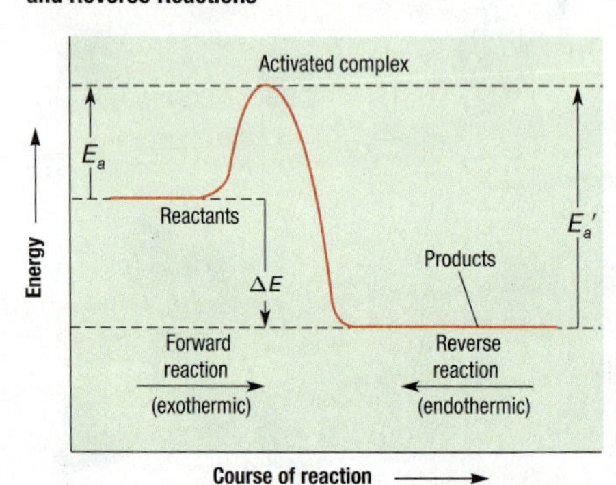

Hydrogen and oxygen gases exist as diatomic molecules. When the molecules approach each other, the electron clouds repel each other, so the molecules might not meet. For a reaction to occur, the colliding molecules must have enough kinetic energy to intermingle the valence electrons. In other words, the bonds of these molecular species must be broken in order for new bonds to be formed between oxygen and hydrogen atoms. Bond breaking is an endothermic process, and bond forming is exothermic. Even though the net process for forming water is exothermic, an initial input of energy is needed to overcome the repulsion forces that occur between reactant molecules when they are brought very close together. This initial energy input activates the reaction.

Once an exothermic reaction is started, the energy released is enough to sustain the reaction by activating other molecules. Thus, the reaction rate keeps increasing. It is limited only by the time required for reactant particles to acquire the energy and make contact. Energy from an outside source may start exothermic reactants along the pathway of reaction. A generalized reaction pathway for an exothermic reaction is shown as the forward reaction in **Figure 1.4.** The minimum amount of energy needed to activate this reaction is the activation energy represented by E_a. **Activation energy** is the minimum energy required to transform the reactants into an activated complex.

The reverse reaction, decomposition of water molecules, is endothermic, because the water molecules lie at an energy level lower than that of the hydrogen and oxygen molecules. The water molecules require a larger activation energy before they can decompose to re-form oxygen and hydrogen. The energy needed to activate an endothermic reaction is greater than that required for the original exothermic change and is represented by E_a' in **Figure 1.4.** The difference between E_a' and E_a is equal to the energy change in the reaction, ΔE. This energy change has the same numerical value for the forward reaction as it has for the reverse reaction, but with the opposite sign.

Problem Solving

TAKE IT FURTHER

Have each student construct a graph showing the reaction pathway for an endothermic reaction. Instruct them to include labels, especially the ΔE for the reaction. Their graphs should show that the energy level of the products is higher than the energy level of the reactants. Have students compare and contrast their graphs with **Figure 1.4.**

MAIN IDEA

In a transition state, molecules break bonds and form new ones.

When molecules collide, some of their high kinetic energy is converted into internal potential energy within the colliding molecules. If enough energy is converted, molecules with suitable orientation become activated. New bonds can then form. In this brief interval of bond breakage and bond formation, the collision complex is in a *transition state*. Some partial bonding exists in this transitional structure. **A transitional structure that results from an effective collision and that persists while old bonds are breaking and new bonds are forming is called an activated complex.**

Figure 1.5 graphically breaks down the reaction pathway of the formation of hydrogen iodide gas into three steps. Beginning with the reactants, H_2 and I_2, a certain amount of activation energy, E_{a1}, is needed to form the activated complex that leads to the formation of the intermediates H_2 and 2I. Then more activation energy, E_{a2}, is needed to form the activated complex leading to the intermediates H_2I and I. In order to arrive at the final product, 2HI, another increase in activation energy is necessary, as seen by the highest peak, labeled E_{a3}.

An activated complex is formed when an effective collision raises the internal energies of the reactants to their minimum level for reaction, as in **Figure 1.4** (see previous page). Both forward and reverse reactions go through the same activated complex. A bond broken in the activated complex for the forward reaction must be re-formed in the activated complex for the reverse reaction. Observe that an activated complex occurs at a high-energy position along the reaction pathway.

The kinetic-molecular theory states that the speeds and the kinetic energies of the molecules increase as the temperature increases. An increase in speed causes more collisions, which can cause an increase in the number of reactions. However, an increase in the reaction rate depends on more than simply the number of collisions, as **Figure 1.3** (earlier in the section) illustrates. The collisions between molecules must possess sufficient energy to form an activated complex, or a reaction will not take place. Raising the temperature of a reaction provides more molecules that have this activation energy and causes an increase in the reaction rate.

In its brief existence, the activated complex has partial bonding that is characteristic of both reactant and product. It may then re-form the original bonds and separate back into the reactant particles, or it may form new bonds and separate into product particles. The activated complex, unlike the relatively stable intermediate products, is a very short-lived molecular complex in which bonds are in the process of being broken and formed.

FIGURE 1.5

Activation Energy This energy profile graphically shows the formation of three activated complexes (*) during the gas-phase reaction $H_2 + I_2 \longrightarrow 2HI$.

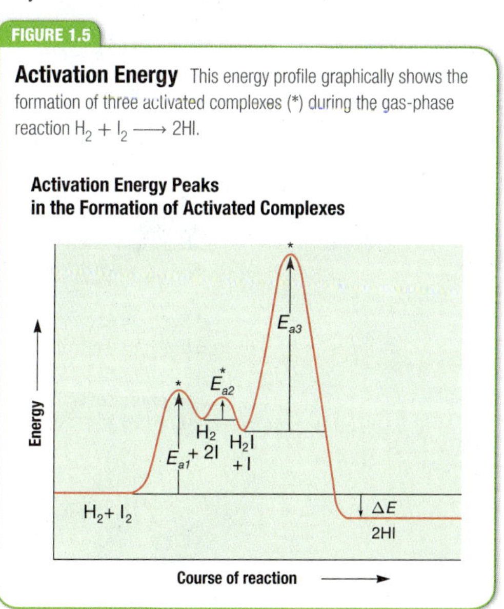

Differentiated Instruction

INCLUSION

Use an analogy of a person on an A-frame ladder to help students understand the factors that play a role in a reaction pathway. On the board, sketch a simple diagram of a person standing halfway up a tall ladder that has steps on both sides. Inform students that the person represents the reactants and that the ladder represents the energy involved in the reaction. Ask students the following questions: "What represents the potential energy of the reactants?" the place where the person is standing on the ladder "What represents the activation energy for the forward reaction?" the distance between where the person is standing and the top of the ladder "Where is the activated complex found?" at the top of the ladder

Tell students that the person climbs the ladder and then descends on the other side to the bottom. Then ask "What represents the potential energy of the products?" the ground "What represents the ΔE of the reaction?" the difference between the ground and where the person first stood on the ladder

TEACH FROM VISUALS

FIGURE 1.5 Use models to explore with students possible structures for activated complexes represented in the figure. Show how energy is required to form each of the activated complexes hypothesized.

Classroom Discussion

Ask students why the exact structure of an activated complex cannot be determined. Have them suggest improvements in technology that might make it possible to make such a determination.

Ask students to compare and contrast the graphs shown in **Figures 1.4** and **1.5.**

▼ Teach *continued*

Misconception Alert!

Because a reaction can go in either direction, students may have trouble distinguishing reactants from products. Make sure that students are not confused by the diagram in Sample Problem A.

Classroom Practice

A-1 Draw and label the energy diagram for a reaction in which $\Delta E = 30$ kJ/mol, and $E_a = 40$ kJ/mol. Place the reactants at energy level zero. Give values of $\Delta E_{forward}$, $\Delta E_{reverse}$, and E_a'.

Answers:

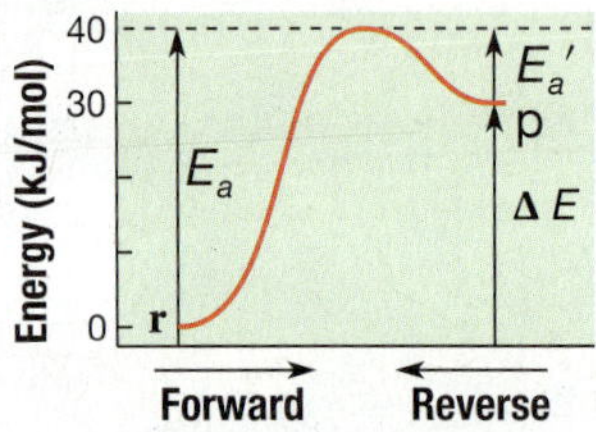

$\Delta E_{forward} = +30$ kJ/mol
$\Delta E_{reverse} = -30$ kJ/mol
$E_a' = 10$ kJ/mol

Answers

Practice A

1. a.

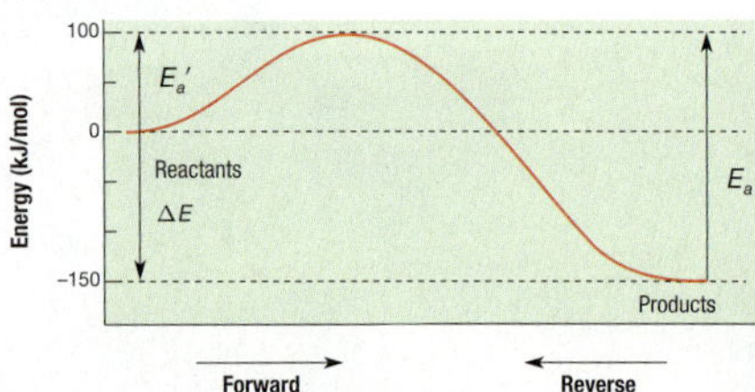

$\Delta E_{forward} = -150$ kJ/mol
$\Delta E_{reverse} = +150$ kJ/mol
$E_a = 100$ kJ/mol
$E_a' = 250$ kJ/mol

b. Exothermic; the energy of the reactants is greater than the energy of the products.

Energy Diagrams

Sample Problem A **Copy the energy diagram below, and label the reactants, products, ΔE, E_a, and E_a'. Determine the value of $\Delta E_{forward}$, $\Delta E_{reverse}$, E_a, and E_a'.**

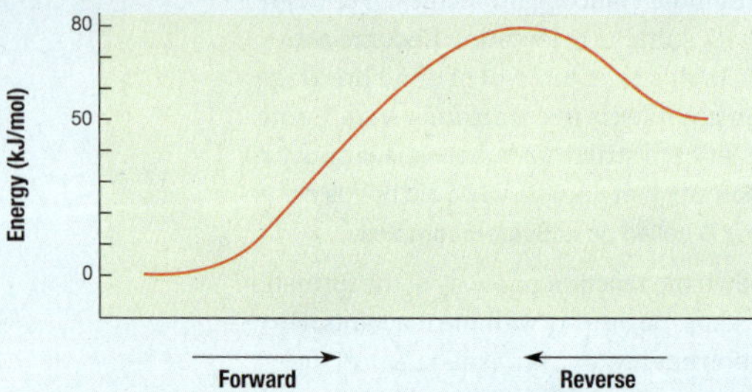

SOLVE

The energy level of reactants is always at the left-hand end of such a curve, and the energy level of products is always at the right-hand end. The energy change in the reaction, ΔE, is the difference between these two energy levels. The activation energy differs in the forward and reverse directions. It is the minimum energy needed to achieve effective reaction in either direction. As E_a, it is the difference between the reactant energy level and the peak in the curve. As E_a', it is the difference between the product energy level and the peak in the curve.

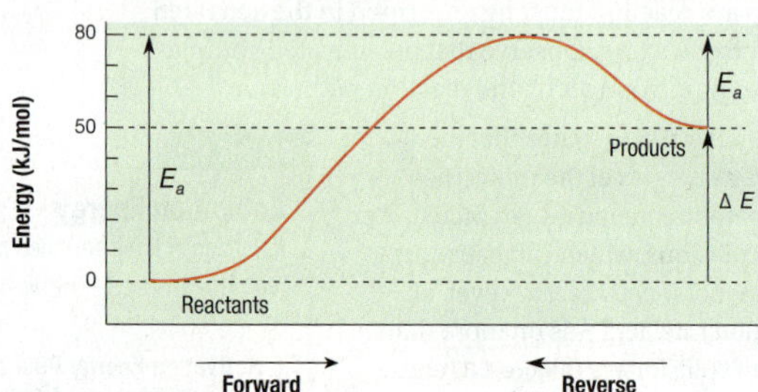

$\Delta E_{forward}$ = energy of products − energy of reactants
$\Delta E_{forward}$ = 50 kJ/mol − 0 kJ/mol = +50 kJ/mol

$\Delta E_{reverse}$ = energy of reactants − energy of products
$\Delta E_{reverse}$ = 0 kJ/mol − 50 kJ/mol = −50 kJ/mol

E_a = energy of activated complex − energy of reactants
E_a = 80 kJ/mol − 0 kJ/mol = 80 kJ/mol

E_a' = energy of activated complex − energy of products
E_a' = 80 kJ/mol − 50 kJ/mol = 30 kJ/mol

Continued

Problem Solving

REALITY CHECK

Point out to students that the graph in Sample Problem A shows that the products have a higher energy level than the reactants. Ask them to consider what that means in terms of energy in the reaction. Energy must have been supplied in order for the forward reaction to occur. As a result, the $\Delta E_{forward}$ should have a positive value. Ask them to think of an example of a reaction in which energy is added, and the products have more energy than the reactants. Answers will vary; one example is the reactions that make up photosynthesis. The same line of reasoning applies to the reverse reaction, in which case there is a decrease in energy in the products. This release of energy is shown by the negative value for the $\Delta E_{reverse}$. Have students think of an example in which the products have less energy than the reactants. Answers will vary; combustion of wood is one example.

Energy Diagrams (continued)

Practice Answers in Appendix E

1. **a.** Use the method shown in the sample problem to redraw and label the following energy diagram. Determine the value of $\Delta E_{forward}$, $\Delta E_{reverse}$, E_a, and E_a'.
   b. Is the forward reaction shown in the diagram exothermic or endothermic? Explain your answer.

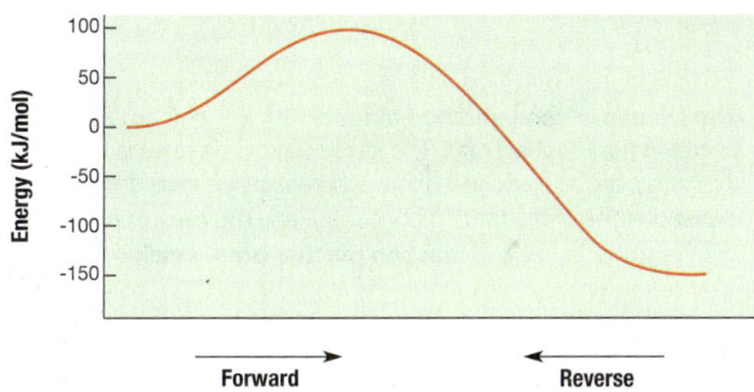

2. **a.** Draw and label an energy diagram similar to the one shown in the sample problem for a reaction in which E_a = 125 kJ/mol and E_a' = 86 kJ/mol. Place the reactants at energy level zero.
   b. Calculate the values of $\Delta E_{forward}$ and $\Delta E_{reverse}$.
   c. Is this reaction endothermic or exothermic? Explain your answer.
3. **a.** Draw and label an energy diagram for a reaction in which E_a = 154 kJ/mol and ΔE = 136 kJ/mol.
   b. Calculate the activation energy, E_a', for the reverse reaction.

2. a.

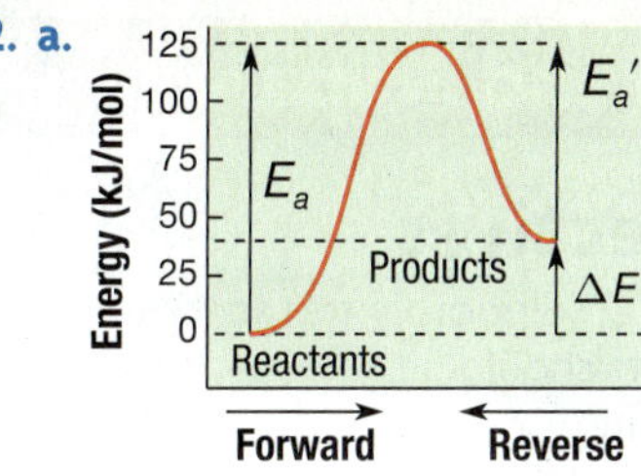

b. $\Delta E_{forward}$ = 39 kJ/mol
$\Delta E_{reverse}$ = −39 kJ/mol

c. Endothermic; the energy of the products is greater than the energy of the products.

3. a.

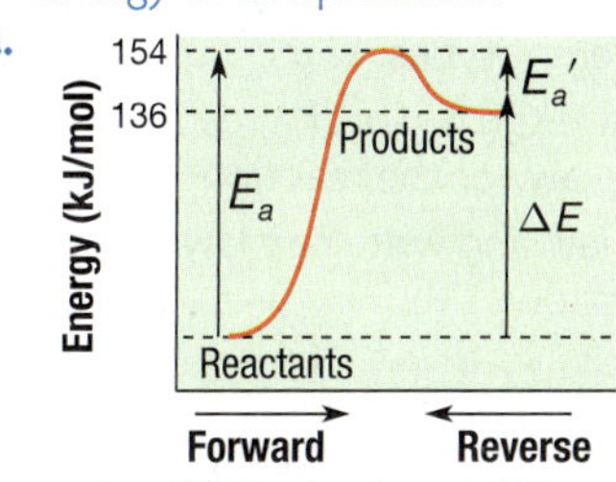

b. E_a (reverse) = 18 kJ/mol

Assess and Reteach ▼

Assess Use the Formative Assessment on this page to evaluate student mastery of the section.

Reteach For students who need additional instruction, download the Section Study Guide.

Response to Intervention To reassess students' mastery, use the Section Quiz, available to print or to take directly online at **HMDScience.com**.

SECTION 1 FORMATIVE ASSESSMENT

Reviewing Main Ideas

1. What is meant by *reaction mechanism*?
2. What factors determine whether a molecular collision produces a reaction?
3. What is activation energy?
4. What is an activated complex?
5. How is activation energy related to the energy of reaction?
6. What is the difference between an activated complex and an intermediate?
7. Explain why, even though a collision may have energy in excess of the activation energy, a reaction may not occur.

Critical Thinking

8. **ANALYZING INFORMATION** Which corresponds to the faster rate: a mechanism with a small activation energy or one with a large activation energy? Explain your answer.

Answers to Section Assessment

1. a sequence of steps by which a reaction occurs
2. A reaction will occur if the species involved in a collision have sufficient energy and if they are oriented correctly toward each other.
3. Activation energy is the minimum energy required to transform reactants into an activated complex.
4. An activated complex is a transitional structure that results from an effective collision and that persists while old bonds are breaking and new bonds are forming.
5. The difference between the activation energies of the forward and reverse reactions is the energy of the reaction.
6. In an activated complex, bonds are partially broken and partially formed, so the complex represents a maximum on the energy profile. An intermediate is a distinct molecular species that is formed in one step of a reaction mechanism and then reacts in a subsequent step; it represents a minimum in the energy profile.
7. For a reaction to occur, it is necessary that the collision be sufficiently energetic. The molecules must also have a favorable orientation at the time of collision. Not all molecules meet both of these requirements.
8. a mechanism that has a small activation energy, because more molecular collisions would exceed the smaller activation energy

SECTION 2

▼ Plan and Prepare

Objectives

Upon completion of this section, students should be able to do the following:

- Define *chemical kinetics,* and explain the two conditions necessary for chemical reactions to occur.
- Discuss the factors that influence reaction rate.
- Define *catalyst,* and discuss two different types.
- Relate the order of a reaction to the rate law for the reaction.
- Explain and write rate laws for chemical reactions.

Classroom Catalyst

Demonstrate the effect of surface area on the combustibility of **lycopodium powder.** (**Flour** can be used in place of lycopodium powder.) Place about 2 g of the powder on a **metal jar lid.** Remove any rubber or plastic from the lid. Attempt to set fire to the powder with a **laboratory burner.** The powder will not burn. Next, blow the powder into the flame of the burner using an **aspirator bulb.** The powder ignites with bursts of flame. Have the students try to explain the reason for the results.

Safety Wear **safety goggles** and a **laboratory apron.** Be sure all flammable and combustible materials are removed from the area. Be sure students are at least 3 m away.

Disposal Once the powder has stopped burning and the lid has cooled, put all materials in the trash.

▼ Teach

Application

Certain materials have practical applications because of their tendency not to react with other materials. For example, the noble gases are used as inert atmospheres to protect valuable historical documents and to prevent oxidation when welding metals.

SECTION 2

Main Ideas

- Several factors can influence reaction rates.
- Concentration and reaction rate are related.

Reaction Rate

Key Terms

reaction rate
chemical kinetics
heterogeneous reaction
catalyst
catalysis
homogeneous catalyst
heterogeneous catalyst
rate law
order
rate-determining step

The change in concentration of reactants per unit time as a reaction proceeds is called the reaction rate. The study of reaction rates is concerned with the factors that affect the rate and with the mathematical expressions that reveal the specific dependencies of the rate on concentration. **The area of chemistry that is concerned with reaction rates and reaction mechanisms is called chemical kinetics.**

MAIN IDEA

Several factors can influence reaction rates.

For reactions other than simple decompositions to occur, particles must come into contact in a favorable orientation and with enough energy for activation. Thus, the rate of a reaction depends on the collision frequency of the reactants and on the collision efficiency. Any change in reaction conditions that affects the collision frequency, the collision efficiency, or the collision energy affects the reaction rate. At least five important factors influence the rate of a chemical reaction.

Nature of Reactants

Substances vary greatly in their tendencies to react. For example, hydrogen combines vigorously with chlorine under certain conditions. Under the same conditions, it may react only weakly with nitrogen. Sodium and oxygen combine much more rapidly than iron and oxygen under similar conditions. Bonds are broken, and other bonds are formed in reactions. The rate of reaction depends on the particular reactants and bonds involved.

Surface Area

Gaseous mixtures and dissolved particles can mix and collide freely; therefore, reactions involving them can occur rapidly. In heterogeneous reactions, the reaction rate depends on the area of contact of the reaction substances. **Heterogeneous reactions involve reactants in two different phases.** These reactions can occur only when the two phases are in contact. Thus, the surface area of a solid reactant is an important factor in determining rate. An increase in surface area increases the rate of heterogeneous reactions.

Solid zinc reacts with aqueous hydrochloric acid to produce zinc chloride and hydrogen gas according to the following equation:

$$Zn(s) + 2HCl(aq) \rightarrow ZnCl_2(aq) + H_2(g)$$

Differentiated Instruction

PRE-AP

Have students calculate the surface area to volume ratio of four different cubes, measuring 1 cm, 2 cm, 3 cm, and 4 cm on a side. The volume of a cube equals length x width x height. The surface area of a cube equals 6 times the area of one surface.

For a cube 4 cm on each side, the volume would be 64 cm^3. For a cube 4 cm on each side, the surface area equals 96 cm^2. The ratio of surface area to volume for a 4-cm cube is 96/64 or 3/2.

Students should find that the surface area-to-volume ratio increases significantly as cube size decreases. Have students relate this observation to the effect of surface area on reaction rate.

This reaction occurs at the surface of the zinc solid. A cube of zinc measuring 1 cm on each edge presents only 6 cm^2 of contact area. The same amount of zinc in the form of a fine powder might provide a contact area thousands of times greater than the original area. Consequently, the reaction rate of the powdered solid is much faster.

A lump of coal burns slowly when kindled in air. The rate of burning can be increased by breaking the lump into smaller pieces, exposing more surface area. If the piece of coal is powdered and then ignited while suspended in air, it burns explosively. This is the cause of some explosions in coal mines.

Temperature

An increase in temperature increases the average kinetic energy of the particles in a substance; this can result in a greater number of effective collisions when the substance is allowed to react with another substance. If the number of effective collisions increases, the reaction rate will increase.

To be effective, the energy of the collisions must be equal to or greater than the activation energy. At higher temperatures, more particles possess enough energy to form the activated complex when collisions occur. Thus, a rise in temperature produces an increase in collision energy as well as in collision frequency.

Decreasing the temperature of a reaction system has the opposite effect. The average kinetic energy of the particles decreases, so they collide less frequently and with less energy, producing fewer effective collisions. Beginning near room temperature, the reaction rates of many common reactions roughly double with each 10 K (10°C) rise in temperature. This rule of thumb should be used with caution, however. The actual rate increase with a given rise in temperature must be determined experimentally.

Concentration

Pure oxygen has five times the concentration of oxygen molecules that air has at the same pressure; consequently, a substance that oxidizes in air oxidizes more vigorously in pure oxygen. For example, in **Figure 2.1,** the light produced when the lump of charcoal is burned in pure oxygen is much more intense than the light produced when the charcoal lump is heated in air until combustion begins. The oxidation of charcoal is a heterogeneous reaction system in which one reactant is a gas. The reaction rate depends not only on the amount of exposed charcoal surface but also on the concentration of the reacting species, O_2.

In homogeneous reaction systems, reaction rates depend on the concentration of the reactants. Predicting the mathematical relationship between rate and concentration is difficult, because most chemical reactions occur in a series of steps, and only one of these steps determines the reaction rate. If the number of effective collisions increases, the rate increases as well. In general, an increase in rate is expected if the concentration of one or more of the reactants is increased.

FIGURE 2.1

Concentration and Reaction Rate A greater concentration increases the number of effective collisions, so the reaction rate increases.

(a) Pure oxygen has five times the concentration of oxygen molecules compared to air, so the charcoal will burn more intensely.

(b) Air contains substances in addition to oxygen, so oxygen molecules have fewer chances to collide with the charcoal to react.

Demonstration

TEMPERATURE AND REACTION TIME

Demonstrate the effect of temperature on the rate at which an **effervescent tablet** reacts with water. Place **150 mL of water** in each of **three 250-mL beakers.** Use **ice water** in the first beaker, **water at room temperature** in the second beaker, and **hot water** in the third beaker. Record the temperature of the water in each beaker. Simultaneously add a tablet to each beaker and begin timing with a stopwatch. Record the amount of time needed for each tablet to dissolve completely. Construct a **graph** showing the relationship of temperature and reaction time.

TEACH FROM VISUALS

FIGURE 2.1 Ask students to discuss the role of the nitrogen in air when determining the rate at which carbon burns in the reaction depicted in part (b) of the figure.

READING TOOLKIT

PREDICTION GUIDES Write the following factors on the board:

- type of reactants
- presence of a catalyst
- surface area
- temperature
- concentration

Have students predict whether each of these factors has an effect on the rate at which a reaction occurs, and if so, how. Have a volunteer write students' predictions on the board. Return to these predictions when students finish the section. Have students cite passages to account for the change or reinforcement of their opinions about the effect of each factor on reaction rate.

INCLUSION

Some students may have trouble understanding the effect of temperature and concentration on reaction rate. Ask students to create a model showing how these two different factors each affect reaction rate.

For example, students may use their classmates to demonstrate the relationship. Students can move about the room when they are told that energy as heat is being added to the room. Students should then move faster to show that their average kinetic energy has increased. As a result of their increased kinetic energy, students are more likely to collide. The effect of concentration can be demonstrated by having more students move about the room.

▼ Teach *continued*

TEACH FROM VISUALS

FIGURE 2.2 Point out that the lines connecting the balls in the figure show each ball in the top row colliding with each ball in the bottom row. Thus, as the number of balls in one or both rows increases, the number of possible collisions also increases. If other factors remain constant, the ratio of effective collisions to total collisions remains the same. This means that, as total number of collisions increases, the total number of effective collisions also increases.

Application

In reality, increasing concentration does not always produce an increase in the reaction rate of a desired reaction. Higher reactant concentrations may make side reactions or competing reactions more of a problem, which may slow down the primary reaction. This problem is one faced by chemical engineers when they scale up a chemical process from a flask in a laboratory to a reactor in a chemical plant.

Critical Thinking

Answer: Answers will vary. A good answer might be the following: Catalysts in living things are called enzymes. In the human body, an important reaction that requires enzymes is the breakdown of hydrogen peroxide that accumulates in cells. Unless it is broken down, the hydrogen peroxide can damage or kill cells. Another reaction might be the breakdown of lactose, or milk sugar, by the enzyme lactase. This enables a person to digest milk. If a person's body stops producing lactase, the person is said to be lactose intolerant.

FIGURE 2.2

Collisions and Reaction Rates

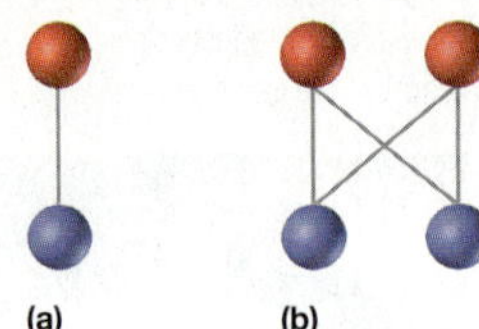

(a) (b)

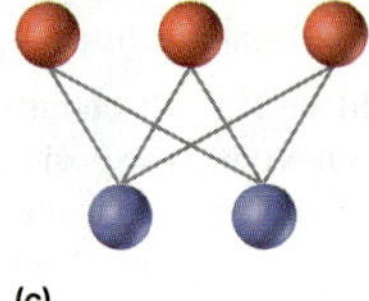

(c)

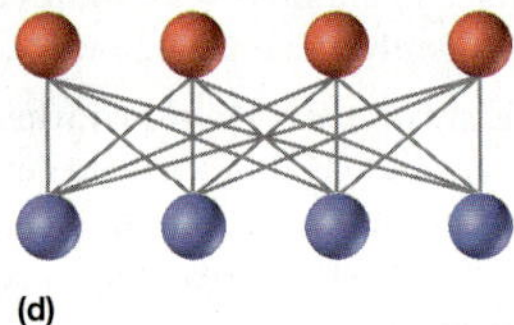

(d)

Consider the model depicted in **Figure 2.2.** In the system with only two molecules, shown in **Figure 2.2a,** only one collision can possibly occur. When there are four molecules in the system, as in **Figure 2.2b,** there can be four possible collisions. With temperature and pressure under constant conditions, as the number of molecules in the system increases, so does the total number of possible collisions between them. **Figures 2.2c** and **d** show a five- and eight-molecule system, allowing six and sixteen possible collisions, respectively. Lowering the concentration should have the opposite effect. The actual effect of concentration changes on reaction rate, however, must be determined experimentally.

FIGURE 2.3

Reaction Rate and Catalysts The reaction rate of the decomposition of hydrogen peroxide, H_2O_2, can be increased by using a catalyst. The catalyst used here is manganese dioxide, MnO_2, a black solid. A 30% H_2O_2 solution is added dropwise onto the MnO_2 in the beaker and rapidly decomposes to O_2 and H_2O. Both the oxygen and water appear as gases, because the energy released by the reaction causes much of the water to vaporize.

CRITICAL THINKING

Describe Research and describe at least two important chemical reactions in the human body that require catalysts.

Presence of Catalysts

Some chemical reactions proceed quite slowly. Sometimes their reaction rates can be increased dramatically by the presence of a catalyst. **A catalyst is a substance that changes the rate of a chemical reaction without itself being permanently consumed. The action of a catalyst is called catalysis.** The catalysis of the decomposition reaction of hydrogen peroxide by manganese dioxide is shown in **Figure 2.3.** A catalyst provides an alternative energy pathway or reaction mechanism in which the potential-energy barrier between reactants and products is lowered. Think of it as an extra push to get a cart over a bump before it will continue rolling down the hill on its own. The catalyst may be effective in forming an alternative activated complex that requires a lower activation energy—as suggested in the energy profiles of the decomposition of hydrogen peroxide, H_2O_2, shown on the next page in **Figure 2.4**—via the following equation:

$$2H_2O_2(l) \rightarrow O_2(g) + 2H_2O(l)$$

Catalysts do not appear among the final products of reactions they accelerate. They may participate in one step along a reaction pathway and be regenerated in a later step. In large, cost-sensitive reaction systems, catalysts are recovered and reused. **A catalyst that is in the same phase as all the reactants and products in a reaction system is called a homogeneous catalyst. When its phase is different from that of the reactants, it is called a heterogeneous catalyst.** Metals are often used as heterogeneous catalysts. The catalysis of many reactions is promoted by adsorption of reactants on the metal surfaces, which increases the concentration of the reactants. In the chapter "Biochemistry," you will learn about enzymes, biological catalysts to facilitate chemical reactions in living organisms.

Differentiated Instruction

PRE-AP

Students can research the enzyme lactase and learn how it relates to lactose intolerance. Have them report to the class about lactase as a catalyst, how lack of lactase makes a person lactose intolerant, and what people do to adjust to being lactose intolerant. If you have students who are lactose intolerant, they could speak about this condition to their classmates. Others may talk to a person who is lactose intolerant to gain a better understanding of this condition.

FIGURE 2.4

Reaction Pathways and Catalysts

A catalyst can reduce the activation energy for a chemical reaction.

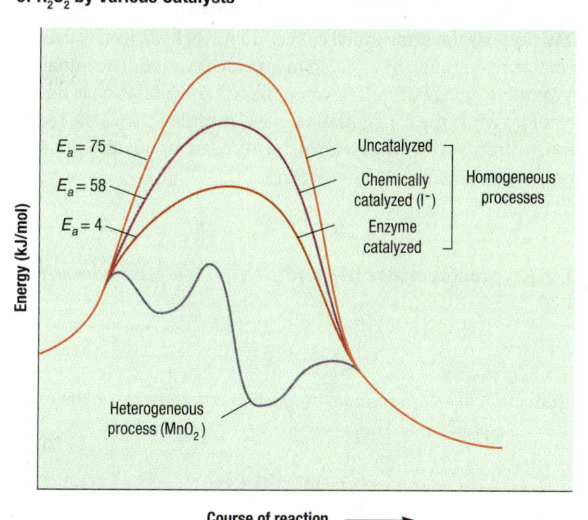

MAIN IDEA

Concentration and reaction rate are related.

The relationship between the rate of a reaction and the concentration of one reactant is determined experimentally by first keeping the concentrations of other reactants and the temperature of the system constant. Then the reaction rate is measured for various concentrations of the reactant in question. A series of such experiments reveals how the concentration of each reactant affects the reaction rate.

Hydrogen gas reacts with nitrogen monoxide gas at constant volume and at an elevated constant temperature, via the following equation.

$$2H_2(g) + 2NO(g) \longrightarrow N_2(g) + 2H_2O(g)$$

Four moles of reactant gases produce three moles of product gases; thus, the pressure of the system diminishes as the reaction proceeds. The rate of the reaction can, therefore, be determined by measuring the change of pressure in the vessel with time.

Suppose a series of experiments is conducted using the same initial concentration of nitrogen monoxide but different initial concentrations of hydrogen. The initial reaction rate is found to vary directly with the hydrogen concentration: doubling the concentration of H_2 doubles the rate, and tripling the concentration of H_2 triples the rate, and so on.

TEACH FROM VISUALS

FIGURE 2.4 Identify and compare the E_a values for the different reactions on this graph. Ask students why H_2O_2 is stored in brown plastic bottles. to protect it from ultraviolet (UV) light Point out that the amount of energy as heat released in the decomposition of H_2O_2 is the same regardless of the reaction pathway followed.

Demonstration

DECOMPOSITION AND CATALYSTS

Place **three petri dishes** on an **overhead projector.** Pour **10 mL of 3% H_2O_2** into each dish. To one dish, add several drops of **1 M KI solution.** To another dish, add **juice from a crushed turnip.** The juice contains the enzyme catalase. Add nothing to the third dish. Have students observe the results and compare them with what would be expected from the graph in **Figure 2.4.**

Safety Wear **goggles** and a **lab apron.**

Disposal Combine solutions; when bubbling stops, pour the mixture down the drain.

BELOW LEVEL

Have students give familiar examples of rates. Possible answers include the speed of a car in miles per hour, snowfall in inches per hour, wages earned in dollars per hour, heart rate in beats per minute, and speed of a race horse in meters per second. Ask students what all these rates have in common. a time value Then ask students how the rate of a chemical reaction could be expressed. Students must include values for both a substance and for time, such as moles of reactant used per second or volume of gas produced per minute.

▼ Teach *continued*

Misconception Alert!

Students may think that the rate law for a chemical reaction is determined solely by the coefficients in the equation for the reaction. Emphasize that the rate law for any particular reaction must be determined experimentally.

Teaching Tip

Symbolism is important in rate law problems, specifically the meaning of k and the use of brackets to represent molar concentrations.

Check for Understanding

Answer: Answers will vary. Good answers to this question might describe corrosion (rust), oxidation of metals (tarnish), or decomposition of once-living tissues (decay).

WHY IT MATTERS

Explosives S.T.E.M.

In a tiny fraction of a second, the reactions of explosives such as nitroglycerin, trinitrotoluene (TNT), and dynamite are over. These materials are primarily organic substances containing mostly carbon, hydrogen, oxygen, and nitrogen atoms held together by relatively weak bonds. When "set off," explosive materials experience rapid decomposition. The released elements immediately react to form gaseous N_2, CO, CO_2, and NO_2. The bonds in these small molecules are much stronger than those in the original explosive material, and so an enormous amount of energy is released. In addition, the sudden formation of gaseous material causes a tremendous increase in pressure that provides the force to demolish an unwanted building or break rocks for building roads.

We can represent this proportion mathematically. If R represents the reaction rate and $[H_2]$ is the concentration of hydrogen in moles per liter, the mathematical relationship between rate and concentration can be expressed as follows:

$$R \propto [H_2]$$

The $\propto$ is a symbol that is read "is proportional to."

Now suppose the same initial concentration of hydrogen is used, but the initial concentration of nitrogen monoxide is varied. The initial reaction rate is found to increase fourfold when the NO concentration is doubled and ninefold when the concentration of NO is tripled. Thus, the reaction rate varies directly with the square of the nitrogen monoxide concentration, as described by the following proportion:

$$R \propto [NO]^2$$

Because R is proportional to $[H_2]$ and to $[NO]^2$, it is proportional to their product:

$$R \propto [H_2][NO]^2$$

By introduction of an appropriate proportionality constant, k, the expression becomes an equality:

$$R = k[H_2][NO]^2$$

An equation that relates reaction rate and concentrations of reactants is called the **rate law** for the reaction. It is applicable for a specific reaction at a given temperature. A rise in temperature increases the reaction rates of most reactions. The value of k usually increases as the temperature increases, but the relationship between reaction rate and concentration almost always remains unchanged.

✓ CHECK FOR UNDERSTANDING

Describe The feature on this page, "Why It Matters: Explosives," describes why TNT and dynamite explosions occur very quickly. Describe a chemical reaction with a very slow reaction rate.

Using the Rate Law

The general form for the rate law is given by the following equation:

$$R = k[A]^n[B]^m$$

The reaction rate is represented by R, k is the specific rate constant, and [A] and [B] represent the molar concentrations of reactants. The respective powers to which the concentrations are raised are represented by n and m. The rate law is applicable for a specific reaction at a given set of conditions and must be determined from experimental data.

The power to which a reactant concentration is raised is called the **order** in that reactant. The value of n is said to be the order of the reaction with respect to [A], so the reaction is said to be "n^{th} order in A." Similarly, for the value of m, the reaction is said to be "m^{th} order in B." The orders, or powers, n and m, are usually small integers or zero.

Problem Solving

DECONSTRUCTING PROBLEMS

Understanding how to interpret a rate law from its mathematical expression can be a challenge for students. Have students use the rate law $R = k[H_2][NO]^2$ to state the order of the reaction. Students should say that the reaction is said to be first order in H_2 and second order in NO. Then ask students to write the rate law for a reaction, C + D ⟶ CD, that is third order in C and fourth order in D. $R = k[C]^3[D]^4$

An order of *one* for a reactant means that the reaction rate is directly proportional to the concentration of that reactant. An order of *two* means that the reaction rate is directly proportional to the *square* of the reactant. An order of *zero* means that the rate does not depend on the concentration of the reactant, *as long as some of the reactant is present.* The sum of all of the reactant orders is called the *order of the reaction*, or *overall order*. The overall order of the reaction is equal to the sum of the reactant orders, or $n + m$. Some examples of observed rate laws that have been derived experimentally are shown below. Some of these reactions involve nitrogen oxides, which are highly reactive gases that contribute to the formation of smog that can blanket an entire city, as shown in **Figure 2.5.**

$3NO(g) \rightarrow N_2O(g) + NO_2(g)$	$R = k[NO]^2$ second order in NO, second order overall
$NO_2(g) + CO(g) \rightarrow NO(g) + CO_2(g)$	$R = k[NO_2]^2$ second order in NO_2, zero order in CO, second order overall
$2NO_2(g) \rightarrow 2NO(g) + O_2(g)$	$R = k[NO_2]^2$ second order in NO_2, second order overall
$2H_2O_2(aq) \rightarrow 2H_2O(l) + O_2(g)$	$R = k[H_2O_2]$ first order in H_2O_2, first order overall

It is important to understand that the orders in the rate law *may* or *may not* match the coefficients in the balanced equation. These orders must be determined from experimental data.

Specific Rate Constant

The *specific rate constant* (k) is the proportionality constant relating the rate of the reaction to the concentrations of reactants. It is important to remember the following about the value of k:

1. Once the reaction orders (powers) are known, the value of k must be determined from experimental data.
2. The value of k is for a *specific reaction*; k has a different value for other reactions, even at the same conditions.
3. The units of k depend on the *overall order of the reaction.*
4. The value of k *does not change* for different concentrations of reactants or products. So, the value of k for a reaction remains the same throughout the reaction and does not change with time.
5. The value of k is for the reaction *at a specific temperature*; if we increase the temperature of the reaction, the value of k increases.
6. The value of k changes (becomes larger) if a *catalyst* is present.

FIGURE 2.5

Smog A cloud of polluted air, commonly known as smog, settles over a city. Smog is common in industrialized areas, where highly reactive gases and particulate matter are released into the air. The rate of the reaction that produces smog is determined by the amount of sunlight present.

Teaching Tip

Explain to students that reactions involving oxides of nitrogen are often used to illustrate reaction orders. This is because reactions involving these compounds have been studied extensively for their role in air pollution, and the data from these studies are readily available for further use by other scientists.

Differentiated Instruction

PRE-AP

Point out that the second equation given on this page shows that the reaction between $NO_2(g)$ and $CO(g)$ is zero order in CO. Zero order reactions usually involve a catalyst operating at maximum capacity and reactions involving multiple pathways where there is a rate-limiting step. Have students research such zero order reactions and explain why changes in reactant concentrations do not affect the reaction rate.

▼ Teach *continued*

Teaching Tip

For a chemical reaction, the value of k depends on both the temperature, T, and the activation energy, E_a. Remind students that the presence of a catalyst decreases the activation energy, and changing temperature alters the fraction of molecular collisions that exceed the activation energy.

Classroom Practice

B-1 In a study of the $2Mn_2O_7(aq) \longrightarrow 4Mn(s) + 7O_2(g)$ reaction, when the manganese heptoxide concentration was changed from 7.5×10^{-5} M to 1.5×10^{-4} M, the rate increased from 1.2×10^{-4} to 4.8×10^{-4}. Write the rate law for the reaction.

Answer: rate $= k[Mn_2O_7]^2$

B-2 For the reaction $A + B \longrightarrow C$, when the initial concentration of A was doubled from 0.100 M to 0.200 M, the rate changed from 4.0×10^{-5} to 16.0×10^{-5}. Find the rate law and the rate constant for this reaction.

Answers: rate $= k[A]^2$; rate constant $= 4.0 \times 10^{-3}$ M/s

Answers

Practice B

1. rate $= k[A]^2$
2. 27

Determining Rate Law and Rate Constant

Sample Problem B **Three experiments that have identical conditions were performed to measure the initial rate of the reaction**

$$2HI(g) \longrightarrow H_2(g) + I_2(g)$$

The results for the three experiments in which only the HI concentration was varied are as follows:

Experiment	[HI] (M)	Rate (M/s)
1	0.015	1.1×10^{-3}
2	0.030	4.4×10^{-3}
3	0.045	9.9×10^{-3}

Write the rate law for the reaction. Find the value and units of the specific rate constant, *k*.

1 ANALYZE The general rate law for this reaction has the form $R = k[HI]^n$. We need to deduce the value of the power n.

2 PLAN Find the ratio of the reactant concentrations between two experiments, such as 1 and 2, $\frac{[HI]_2}{[HI]_1}$. Then, see how the ratio of concentration affects the ratio of rates, $\frac{R_2}{R_1}$.

3 SOLVE Concentration ratio: $\frac{[HI]_2}{[HI]_1} = \frac{0.030 \text{ M}}{0.015 \text{ M}} = 2.0$; rate ratio: $\frac{R_2}{R_1} = \frac{4.4 \times 10^{-3} \text{ M/s}}{1.1 \times 10^{-3} \text{ M/s}} = 4.0$

Thus, when the concentration changes by a factor of 2, the rate changes by a factor of 4, or 2^2, so the rate law is $R = k[HI]^2$.

To find the value of k, we can rearrange the rate law and substitute known values for any one experiment. Do the following for Experiment 1:

$$k = \frac{R}{[HI]^2} = \frac{1.1 \times 10^{-3} \text{ M/s}}{(0.0015 \text{ M})^2} = 4.9 \text{ M}^{-1}\text{s}^{-1}$$

4 CHECK YOUR WORK By comparing items 1 and 3 in the table, we see that when [HI] is tripled, the rate changes by a factor of 9, or 3^2. This rate change confirms that the order is 2. The same value of k can be calculated from any other experiment. Thus, the rate law and k are correct.

Practice Answers in Appendix E

1. For the reaction $3A \longrightarrow C$, the initial concentration of A was 0.2 M and the reaction rate was 1.0 M/s. When [A] was doubled, the reaction rate increased to 4.0 M/s. Determine the rate law for the reaction.
2. The rate law for a reaction is found to be rate $= k[X]^3$. By what factor does the rate increase if [X] is tripled?

Problem Solving

REALITY CHECK

Have students use the data from Experiments 2 and 3 to write the rate law for the reaction in Sample Problem B. The data show that when [HI] is increased by a factor of 1.5 $\left(\frac{0.045}{0.030}\right)$, the rate is increased by a factor of 2.25 $\left(\frac{9.9 \times 10^{-3}}{4.4 \times 10^{-3}}\right)$. The rate therefore changes by a factor of 2.25, or 1.5^2. These calculations confirm that the rate law is $R = k[HI]^2$ and that the order is 2 in HI.

PREMIUM CONTENT

Solve It! Cards HMDScience.com

Determining Rate Law and Rate Constant

Sample Problem C **Three experiments were performed to measure the initial rate of the reaction**

$$A + B \rightarrow C$$

Conditions were identical in the three experiments, except that the concentrations of reactants varied. The results are as follows:

Experiment	[A] (M)	[B] (M)	Rate (M/s)
1	1.2	2.4	8.0×10^{-8}
2	1.2	1.2	4.0×10^{-8}
3	3.6	2.4	7.2×10^{-7}

Write the rate law for the reaction. Find the value and units of the specific rate constant, k.

1 ANALYZE The general rate law for this reaction has the form $R = k[A]^n[B]^m$. We need to calculate the values of the powers n and m.

2 PLAN Find the ratio of the reactant concentrations between two experiments that have the same [A] but different [B]. Then, see how this ratio affects the ratio of rates, $\frac{R_2}{R_1}$; this ratio of rates lets us find the value of m. A similar approach of comparing two experiments that have the same [B] but a different [A] lets us find the value of n.

3 SOLVE First compare Experiments 1 and 2, which have the same [A], to find m:

$$\text{Concentration ratio: } \frac{[B]_1}{[B]_2} = \frac{2.4\ M}{1.2\ M} = 2.0;\ \text{rate ratio: } \frac{R_1}{R_2} = \frac{8.0 \times 10^{-8}\ M/s}{4.0 \times 10^{-8}\ M/s} = 2.0$$

Thus, when the concentration of B changes by a factor of 2, the rate changes by a factor of 2, or 2^1. So, m is 1, and the reaction is first order in B.
Then, compare Experiments 1 and 3, which have the same [B], to find n.

$$\text{Concentration ratio: } \frac{[A]_3}{[A]_1} = \frac{3.6\ M}{1.2\ M} = 3.0;\ \text{rate ratio: } \frac{R_3}{R_1} = \frac{7.2 \times 10^{-7}\ M/s}{8.0 \times 10^{-8}\ M/s} = 9.0$$

Thus, when the concentration of A changes by a factor of 3, the rate changes by a factor of 9, or 3^2. So, n is 2, and the reaction is second order in A.
The rate law is $R = k[A]^2[B]$.
To find the value of k, we can rearrange the rate law and substitute known values for any one experiment. Do the following for Experiment 1:

$$k = \frac{R}{[A]^2[B]} = \frac{8.0 \times 10^{-8}\ M/s}{(1.2\ M)^2(2.4\ M)} = 2.3 \times 10^{-8}\ M^{-2}s^{-1}$$

4 CHECK YOUR WORK The same value of k can be calculated from the data for any other experiment. So, the rate law and the calculation of k are correct.

Classroom Practice

C-1 The reaction $CH_3NC(g) \longrightarrow CH_3CN(g)$ is first order. The rate of this reaction is 1.3×10^{-4} M/s when the reactant concentration is 0.040 M. Predict the rate when $[CH_3NC(g)] = 0.025$ M.

Answer: The rate changes by a factor of (0.025 M)/(0.040 M) = 0.625. Because the order is 1, the rate will change by the same factor. Therefore the new rate is $0.625 \times 1.3 \times 10^{-4}$ M/s $= 8.1 \times 10^{-5}$ M/s.

C-2 The following reaction is first order: $(CH_2)_3(g) \longrightarrow CH_2CHCH_3\ (g)$
What change in reaction rate would you expect if the pressure of $(CH_2)_3$ is doubled?

Answer: an increase by a factor of 2

DECONSTRUCTING PROBLEMS

Have students explain why the data from Experiments 2 and 3 cannot be used to determine the rate law in Sample Problem C. Students should observe that the concentrations of both reactants A and B change. Therefore, there are two variables that prohibit using the data from Experiments 2 and 3 to calculate the rate law. Students must be aware that the rate law can be determined only from experimental data in which the concentration of one reactant is held constant.

▼ Teach continued

Classroom Discussion

Rate-determining steps are common in many everyday events. For example, suppose that a series of five individuals are involved in filling an order at a fast-food restaurant. The order can be filled no more quickly than the slowest-moving person in the sequence. Ask students to think of similar examples of rate-determining steps they may be familiar with.

Teaching Tip

You cannot tell whether a reaction is a simple one-step reaction or a multistep reaction simply by looking at the equation for the reaction. Additional information is necessary to make that determination.

Misconception Alert!

In many reaction mechanisms, the first step is not the slowest one. The prediction of an acceptable rate law for such mechanisms is somewhat complex, and it will not be covered here.

Rate Laws and Reaction Pathway

The form of the rate law depends on the reaction mechanism. For a reaction that occurs in a *single step*, the reaction rate of that step is proportional to the product of the reactant concentrations, each of which is raised to its stoichiometric coefficient. For example, suppose one molecule of gas A collides with one molecule of gas B to form two molecules of substance C, according to the following equation:

$$A + B \rightarrow 2C$$

One particle of each reactant is involved in each collision. Thus, doubling the concentration of either reactant will double the collision frequency. It will also double the reaction rate *for this step*. Therefore, the rate for this step is directly proportional to the concentration of A and B. The rate law for this one-step forward reaction follows:

$$R_{forward} = k_{forward}[A][B]$$

Now suppose the reaction is reversible. In the reverse step, two molecules of C must decompose to form one molecule of A and one of B, or $2C \rightarrow A + B$.

Thus, the reaction rate for this reverse step is directly proportional to $[C] \times [C]$. The rate law for the reverse step is $R_{reverse} = k_{reverse}[C]^2$.

The power to which the molar concentration of each reactant is raised in the rate laws above corresponds to the coefficient for the reactant in the balanced chemical equation. Such a relationship holds *only* if the reaction follows a simple one-step path, that is, if the reaction occurs at the molecular level exactly as written in the chemical equation.

If a chemical reaction proceeds in a sequence of steps, the rate law is determined from the slowest step because it has the lowest rate. **This slowest-rate step is called the rate-determining step for the chemical reaction.**

FIGURE 2.6

Formation of Intermediate Species This diagram is a representation of Step 1 in the reaction of nitrogen dioxide and carbon monoxide. Notice the formation of the intermediate species NO_3 after two molecules of NO_2 collide.

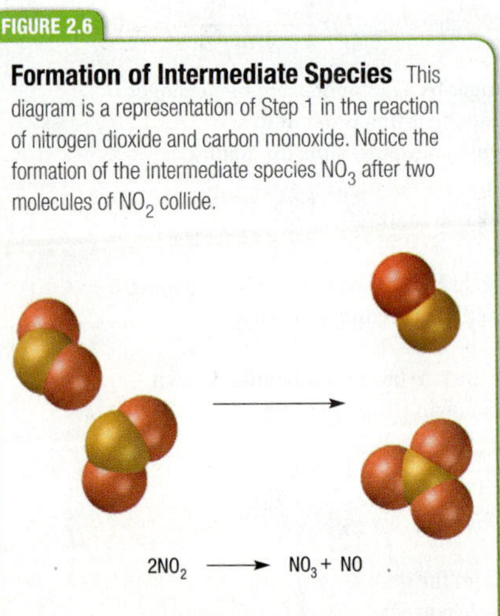

Consider the reaction of nitrogen dioxide and carbon monoxide.

$$NO_2(g) + CO(g) \rightarrow NO(g) + CO_2(g)$$

The reaction is believed to be a two-step process represented by the following mechanism:

Step 1: $NO_2 + NO_2 \rightarrow NO_3 + NO$ slow

Step 2: $NO_3 + CO \rightarrow NO_2 + CO_2$ fast

In the first step, shown in **Figure 2.6**, two molecules of NO_2 collide, forming the intermediate species NO_3. This molecule then collides with one molecule of CO and reacts quickly to produce one molecule each of NO_2 and CO_2. The first step is the slower of the two and is therefore the rate-determining step. We can write the rate law from this rate-determining step, which has two molecules of NO_2 as the reactants.

$$R = k[NO_2]^2$$

The rate law does not include [CO], because CO reacts after the rate-determining step and does not affect the rate.

Differentiated Instruction

BELOW LEVEL

Use funnels and sand to create a model of a rate-determining step for students. Attach a large-bore funnel to a ring stand. Place a beaker under the funnel. Pour one cup of sand into the funnel and record the time it takes for the sand to empty into the beaker. Repeat the process, but this time pour the sand into a small-bore funnel that is placed above the large-bore funnel. Ask students to identify the funnel that acts as the rate-determining step. small-bore funnel Next, ask students how the use of another large-bore funnel would affect the results. Students should recognize that the placement of the small-bore funnel in this model still determines the rate. Adding another large-bore funnel to the system will not affect the rate.

Determining Rate-Determining Step and Law and Rate Constant

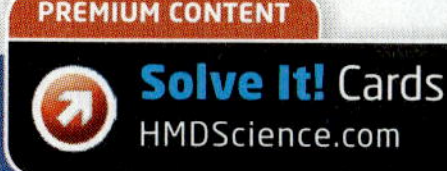

Sample Problem D **Nitrogen dioxide and fluorine react in the gas phase according to the following equation.**

$$2NO_2(g) + F_2(g) \rightarrow 2NO_2F(g)$$

A proposed mechanism for this reaction follows.

Step 1:	$NO_2 + F_2 \rightarrow NO_2F + F$	(slow)
Step 2:	$F + NO_2 \rightarrow NO_2F$	(fast)

Identify the rate-determining step, and write an acceptable rate law.

SOLVE

If we combine these two steps, the intermediate, F, cancels out and we are left with the original equation. The first step is the slower step and is considered the rate-determining step. We can write the rate law from this rate-determining step.

$$R = k[NO_2][F_2]$$

Determining Effects on Reaction Rate

Sample Problem E **A reaction involving reactants X and Y was found to occur by a one-step mechanism: $X + 2Y \rightarrow XY_2$. Write the rate law for this reaction, and then determine the effect of each of the following on the reaction rate:**

a. doubling the concentration of X

b. doubling the concentration of Y

c. using one-third the concentration of Y

SOLVE

Because the equation represents a single-step mechanism, the rate law can be written from the equation (otherwise, it could not be). The rate will vary directly with the concentration of X, which has an implied coefficient of 1 in the equation. And the rate will vary directly with the square of the concentration of Y, which has the coefficient of 2: $R = k[X][Y]^2$.

a. Doubling the concentration of X will double the rate ($R = k[2X][Y]^2$).

b. Doubling the concentration of Y will increase the rate fourfold ($R = k[X][2Y]^2$).

c. Using one-third the concentration of Y will reduce the rate to one-ninth of its original value ($R = k[X][\frac{1}{3}Y]^2$).

Practice Answers in Appendix E

1. The rate of a hypothetical reaction involving L and M is found to double when the concentration of L is doubled and to increase fourfold when the concentration of M is doubled. Write the rate law for this reaction.
2. At temperatures below 498 K, the following reaction takes place.

$$NO_2(g) + CO(g) \rightarrow CO_2(g) + NO(g)$$

Doubling the concentration of NO_2 quadruples the rate of CO_2 formed if the CO concentration is held constant. However, doubling the concentration of CO has no effect on the rate of CO_2 formation. Write a rate-law expression for this reaction.

Classroom Practice

D-1 The rate law for a single-step reaction that forms one product, C, is $R = k[A][B]^2$. Write the balanced reaction of A and B to form C.

Answer: $A + 2B \longrightarrow C$

E-1 The rate law of a reaction is found to be $R = k[X]^3$. By what factor does the rate increase if the concentration of X is tripled?

Answer: The rate will increase by a factor of 27.

E-2 The rate of reaction involving two reactants, X and Z, is found to double when the concentration of X is doubled and to quadruple when the concentration of Z is doubled. Write the rate law for this reaction.

Answer: $R = k[X][Z]^2$

Answers

Practice E

1. $R = k[L][M]^2$
2. $R = k[NO_2]^2$

Problem Solving

DECONSTRUCTING PROBLEMS

Tell students that the rate-determining step in Sample Problem D was used to write the rate law. For example, write the following reaction on the board.

$$2NO(g) + O_2(g) \longrightarrow 2NO_2(g)$$

Next, write a possible mechanism for this reaction on the board.

$NO + NO \longrightarrow N_2O_2$	fast
$N_2O_2 + O_2 \longrightarrow 2NO_2$	slow

Tell students that a rate law can be determined from the rate-determining step only if the sum of the stepwise mechanisms gives the balanced equation. Show that this requirement is met by canceling the N_2O_2 that appears on both sides of the equation.

$NO + NO \longrightarrow N_2O_2$	fast
$N_2O_2 + O_2 \longrightarrow 2NO_2$	slow

Therefore, the rate law can be determined from the rate-determining step.

$$R = k[O_2]$$

Point out that N_2O_2 is not included in the rate law because it is an intermediate and not a reactant.

▼ Teach *continued*

QuickLab

Students should prepare a data table to record their observations. The table should reflect a rate-influencing factor for each step of the procedure.

Safety Students must wear goggles and an apron during the investigation. Keep flammable and combustible materials away from the open flame of the Bunsen burner.

Disposal Combine all liquids and pour them down the drain. Save all metal strips for reuse, but if they are too corroded, put them in the trash. Put all other solids in the trash.

DISCUSSION

1. 1: the nature of the materials
   2: surface area of the metal
   3: concentration of the reactant
   4: the presence of a catalyst
2. 1: Mg reacts faster than Zn, which reacts faster than Cu; nature of reactants affects reaction rate
   2: steel wool reacts faster with oxygen than a paper clip does; increasing surface area increases rate of reaction
   3: Mg reacts faster with more concentrated vinegar; increased concentration increases reaction rate
   4: sugar reacts faster when covered with ash than without; catalysts increase rate of reaction

▼ Assess and Reteach

Assess Use the Formative Assessment on this page to evaluate student mastery of the section.

Reteach For students who need additional instruction, download the Section Study Guide.

Response to Intervention To reassess students' mastery, use the Section Quiz, available to print or to take directly online at **HMDScience.com**.

QuickLAB FACTORS INFLUENCING REACTION RATE

QUESTION

How do the type of reactants, surface area of reactants, concentration of reactants, and catalysts affect the rates of chemical reactions?

PROCEDURE

Remove all combustible material from the work area. Wear safety goggles and an apron. Record all your results in a data table.

1. Add 10 mL of vinegar to each of three test tubes. To one test tube, add a 3 cm piece of magnesium ribbon; to a second, add a 3 cm zinc strip; and to a third, add a 3 cm copper strip. (All metals should be the same width.) If necessary, polish the metals with sandpaper until they are shiny.
2. Using tongs, hold a paper clip in the hottest part of the burner flame for 30 s. Repeat with a ball of steel wool 2 cm in diameter.
3. To one test tube, add 10 mL of vinegar; to a second, add 5 mL of vinegar plus 5 mL of water; and to a third, add 2.5 mL of vinegar plus 7.5 mL of water. To each of the three test tubes, add a 3 cm piece of magnesium ribbon.
4. Using tongs, hold a sugar cube and try to ignite it with a match. Then try to ignite it in a burner flame. Rub paper ash on a second cube, and try to ignite it with a match.

DISCUSSION

1. What are the rate-influencing factors in each step of the procedure?
2. What were the results from each step of the procedure? How do you interpret each result?

MATERIALS

- Bunsen burner
- paper ash
- copper foil strip
- graduated cylinder, 10 mL
- magnesium ribbon
- matches
- paper clip
- sandpaper
- steel wool
- 2 sugar cubes
- white vinegar
- zinc strip
- 6 test tubes, 16 × 150 mm
- tongs

SECTION 2 FORMATIVE ASSESSMENT

Reviewing Main Ideas

1. What is studied in the branch of chemistry that is known as chemical kinetics?
2. List five important factors that influence the rate of chemical reactions.
3. What is a catalyst? Explain the effect of a catalyst on the rate of chemical reactions. How does a catalyst influence the activation energy required by a particular reaction?
4. What is meant by a rate law for a chemical reaction? Explain the conditions under which a rate law can be written from a chemical equation. When can a rate law not be written from a single step?

Critical Thinking

5. **RELATING IDEAS** Using the ideas of reaction kinetics, explain the purpose of food refrigeration.

Answers to Section Assessment

1. reaction rates and mechanisms
2. nature of reactants, surface area, concentration, temperature, presence of a catalyst
3. It increases the rate of a chemical reaction without itself being permanently consumed. It makes possible an alternative mechanism in which the activation energy is lower than it is without the catalyst.
4. It is an equation that relates reaction rate to concentrations of reactants. It can be written from a chemical equation if it is a single-step reaction. In a multistep reaction, the rate law must be obtained experimentally.
5. Foods decompose by slow chemical reactions caused by bacteria. One reason that keeping food at a lower temperature delays spoilage is that the rates of all reactions decrease when cooled.

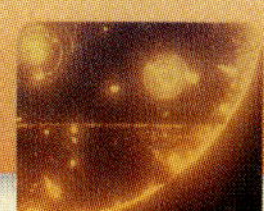

Catalytic Converters

S.T.E.M.

To see an important example of *heterogeneous catalysis,* you do not need to look any farther than the streets near your home. The *catalytic converter,* an important part of a vehicle's exhaust system, uses metal catalysts to reduce harmful gaseous pollutants.

In an automobile engine, hydrocarbon molecules in gasoline or diesel fuel undergo a combustion reaction with oxygen from air to make carbon dioxide, CO_2, and water. The correct stoichiometric ratio of fuel to oxygen is required for the fuel to be completely burned in the reaction. Additional reaction products are formed when not enough oxygen or excess oxygen is present. These products include carbon monoxide, CO, and NO_x compounds, such as nitric oxide, NO, and nitrogen dioxide, NO_2. There is also leftover unburned fuel, which is called a volatile organic compound (VOC).

The Clean Air Act, enacted in 1990, regulates automobile emissions of CO, NO_x, and VOCs. Without a catalytic converter, a car would release all of the by-products of incomplete combustion into the atmosphere. In addition to being harmful themselves, NO_x compounds, CO, and VOCs react with sunlight to make ozone, O_3. In the lower atmosphere, ozone is a major part of photochemical smog. NO_x gases can also mix with rainwater to produce acid rain.

Catalytic converters use precious metal catalysts to change the gases coming from the engine into less harmful gases. A combination of rhodium and platinum, and sometimes palladium, is used to convert nitrogen compounds back into N_2 and O_2. This combination also converts CO into CO_2 and converts VOCs into CO_2 and water. The catalysts need O_2 from the air and temperatures above approximately 500°F to work properly. The temperatures are achieved from the normal operation of the car engine. However, until the car engine reaches the temperatures needed for the catalysts to work, CO, NO_x, and VOCs will be released into the air by the automobile.

The interior structure of a catalytic converter is usually made of a ceramic honeycomb with a surface coating of metal catalyst particles. The honeycomb has many holes for the gases to pass through and provides a large surface area for the metal to be deposited on. A large surface area is needed to maximize the reactions that occur during heterogeneous catalysis, because the transformation of the gas molecules occurs at the surface of the metal.

Up to 90% of CO, NO_x, and VOCs are typically eliminated from automobile exhaust by a catalytic converter. Although catalytic converters are beneficial to our environment, they could still be improved. Catalysts that work at lower temperatures would reduce an automobile's emission during the first few minutes of operation. Other gases that are emitted by cars may also pose problems for the environment. Nitrous oxide, N_2O, can be formed from the incomplete reduction of NO_x in catalytic converters. Unlike the NO_x gases, N_2O can travel to the upper atmosphere, where it can destroy ozone. As a greenhouse gas, N_2O is more than 300 times more potent than CO_2.

Questions

1. Why do you think a heterogeneous catalyst is used instead of a homogeneous catalyst in a catalytic converter?
2. Nitrous oxide, N_2O, actually has beneficial uses, despite its role as a greenhouse gas. Can you name a beneficial use of N_2O?

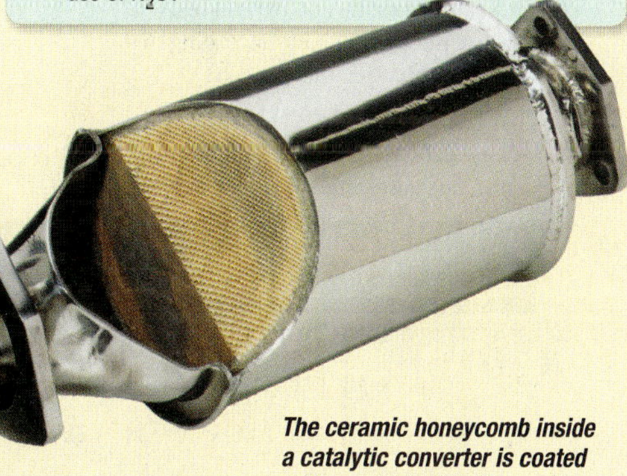

The ceramic honeycomb inside a catalytic converter is coated with a metal catalyst.

547

WHY IT MATTERS

Did You Know?

Prior to the 1980s, tetraethyl lead was added to most automobile gasoline as an anti-knock additive. However, the introduction of catalytic converters contributed to the phasing out of the additive because lead coated the surfaces of the converters, rendering the catalysts useless. Tetraethyl lead was also removed from gasoline because of lead emissions. Even small amounts of lead in the air can cause severe health problems.

Misconception Alert!

Ozone production is occasionally attributed to the photochemical dissociation of NO_2. Although this reaction does occur, the rate of the reaction is so slow in normal atmospheric conditions that a negligible amount of ozone is produced. For appreciable amounts of ozone to be produced, CO and VOCs must be added to the NO_x gases.

Answers

1. Heterogeneous catalysis involves reactants that are in two different phases, such as a solid catalyst and gas reactants. After the reaction is complete, it is much easier to separate the reactants from the catalyst if they are in different phases.
2. N_2O, also known as laughing gas, is frequently used as an anesthetic to calm dental patients.

Answers

1. $R = k[O_2][NO]_2$
2. $R = k[H_2]$; Students should observe that changing the concentration of C_2H_2 has no effect on the rate. The rate depends on only the concentration of hydrogen.

Math Tutor | Writing Rate Laws

Factors such as surface area and temperature affect the rate of reactions because they affect the frequency and energy of collisions between particles. The concentrations of reactants can also affect the frequency of collisions. If other factors are kept constant, the rates of most chemical reactions will be determined by the concentrations of reactants. Thus, it is possible to write an equation called a *rate law* that relates the rate of a reaction to the concentrations of reactants.

Sample Problem

Fluorine gas reacts with chlorine dioxide according to the following equation.

$$F_2(g) + 2ClO_2(g) \longrightarrow 2FClO_2(g)$$

Use the following experimental data to write a rate law for this reaction.

TRIAL	CONCENTRATION OF F_2	CONCENTRATION OF ClO_2	RATE (MOL/L•S)
1	0.10 M	0.10 M	1.1×10^{-3}
2	0.20 M	0.10 M	2.2×10^{-3}
3	0.10 M	0.20 M	2.2×10^{-3}
4	0.20 M	0.20 M	4.4×10^{-3}

To write the rate law, first examine the data to see how the rate of reaction changes as the concentrations of the reactants change.

- When $[F_2]$ doubles and $[ClO_2]$ remains constant, the rate of reaction doubles from 1.1×10^{-3} mol/L•s to 2.2×10^{-3} mol/L•s. So, the rate is directly proportional to $[F_2]$, or $R \propto [F_2]$.
- When $[ClO_2]$ doubles and $[F_2]$ remains constant, the rate of reaction also doubles from 1.1×10^{-3} mol/L•s to 2.2×10^{-3} mol/L•s. So, the rate is directly proportional to $[ClO_2]$, or $R \propto [ClO_2]$.
- Because rate is proportional to both $[F_2]$ and $[ClO_2]$, you can write the rate law $R = k[F_2][ClO_2]$. The data from Trial 4 help confirm the rate law, because when both $[F_2]$ and $[ClO_2]$ double, the rate increases by a factor of four, from 1.1×10^{-3} mol/L•s to 4.4×10^{-3} mol/L•s.

Practice

1. Nitrogen monoxide and oxygen react to produce nitrogen dioxide according to the following equation:

   $$O_2(g) + 2NO(g) \longrightarrow 2NO_2(g)$$

   Use the data in the following table to write a rate law for this reaction.

TRIAL	$[O_2]$	[NO]	REACTION RATE (MOL/L•S)
1	1.20×10^{-2} M	1.40×10^{-2} M	3.30×10^{-3}
2	2.40×10^{-2} M	1.40×10^{-2} M	6.60×10^{-3}
3	1.20×10^{-2} M	2.80×10^{-2} M	1.32×10^{-2}

2. Hydrogen reacts with ethyne, C_2H_2, to produce ethane, C_2H_6, as shown below:

   $$2H_2(g) + C_2H_2(g) \longrightarrow C_2H_6(g)$$

   Use the data in the following table to write a rate law for this reaction.

TRIAL	$[H_2]$	$[C_2H_2]$	REACTION RATE (MOL/L•MIN)
1	0.20 M	0.20 M	1.5×10^{-4}
2	0.40 M	0.20 M	3.0×10^{-4}
3	0.20 M	0.40 M	1.5×10^{-4}

CHAPTER 17 Summary

PREMIUM CONTENT
Interactive Review HMDScience.com
Review Games
Concept Maps

SECTION 1 The Reaction Process

- The step-by-step process by which an overall chemical reaction occurs is called the *reaction mechanism*.
- In order for chemical reactions to occur, the particles of the reactants must collide.
- Activation energy is needed to merge valence electrons and to loosen bonds sufficiently for molecules to react.
- An activated complex is formed when an effective collision between molecules of reactants raises the internal energy to the minimum level necessary for a reaction to occur.

KEY TERMS

reaction mechanism
intermediate
homogeneous reaction
collision theory
activation energy
activated complex

SECTION 2 Reaction Rate

- The rate of reaction is influenced by the following factors: nature of reactants, surface area, temperature, concentration of reactants, and the presence of catalysts.
- The rates at which chemical reactions occur can sometimes be experimentally measured and expressed in terms of mathematical equations called *rate laws*.
- Rate laws are determined by studying how reaction rate depends on concentration.

KEY TERMS

reaction rate
chemical kinetics
heterogeneous reaction
catalyst
catalysis
homogeneous catalyst
heterogeneous catalyst
rate law
order
rate-determining step

Review Answers

1. a. It is the set of assumptions regarding collisions and reactions between molecules.
   b. It must be energetic enough to supply the necessary activation energy, and the colliding molecules must be oriented in a way that favors their efficient interaction.
2. a. The reactant particles must undergo an effective collision that raises the internal energies of the reactants to their minimum level for reaction.
   b. at the maximum-energy position
3. The activation energy required for the endothermic change is greater by the amount of enthalpy of reaction of the system.
4. No; Most reactions take place in a sequence of step-wise processes. It would be virtually impossible for so many molecules to collide simultaneously in a single step.
5. $NO_2 + O \longrightarrow NO + O_2$
6. a.

$\Delta E_{forward} = +80$ kJ/mol
$\Delta E_{reverse} = -80$ kJ/mol
$E_a = 100$ kJ/mol
$E_a' = 20$ kJ/mol

b.

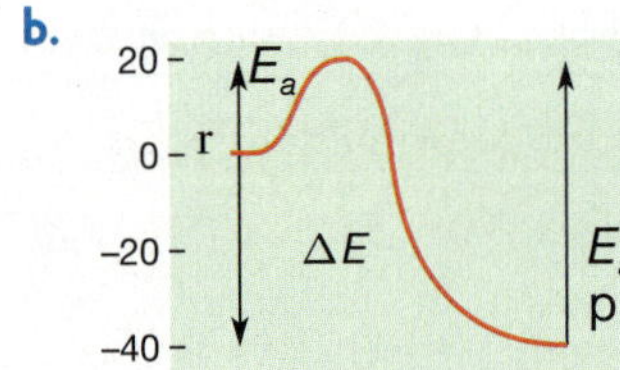

$\Delta E_{forward} = -40$ kJ/mol
$\Delta E_{reverse} = +40$ kJ/mol
$E_a = 20$ kJ/mol
$E_a' = 60$ kJ/mol

c.

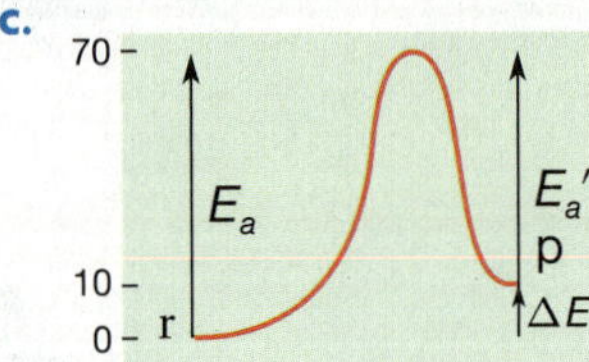

$\Delta E_{forward} = +10$ kJ/mol
$\Delta E_{reverse} = -10$ kJ/mol
$E_a = 70$ kJ/mol
$E_a' = 60$ kJ/mol

CHAPTER 17 Review

SECTION 1

The Reaction Process

REVIEWING MAIN IDEAS

1. a. What is the collision theory?
   b. According to this theory, what two conditions must be met for a collision between reactant molecules to be effective in producing new chemical species?
2. a. What condition must be met for an activated complex to result from the collision of reactant particles?
   b. Where, in terms of energy, does the activated complex occur along a typical reaction pathway?
3. In a reversible reaction, how does the activation energy required for the exothermic change compare with the activation energy required for the endothermic change?
4. Would you expect the following equation to represent the mechanism by which propane, C_3H_8, burns? Why or why not?

$$C_3H_8(g) + 5O_2(g) \longrightarrow 3CO_2(g) + 4H_2O(g)$$

5. The decomposition of nitrogen dioxide, $2NO_2 \longrightarrow 2NO + O_2$, occurs in a two-step sequence at elevated temperatures. The first step is $NO_2 \longrightarrow NO + O$. Predict a possible second step that, when combined with the first step, gives the complete reaction.

PRACTICE PROBLEMS

6. For each of the energy diagrams provided below, label the reactants, products, ΔE, E_a, and E_a'. Also determine the values of ΔE for the forward and reverse reactions, and determine the values of E_a and E_a'. (Hint: See Sample Problem A.)

(a)

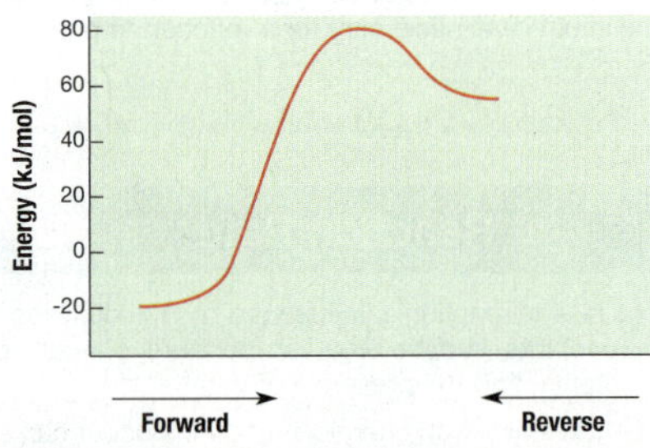

(b)

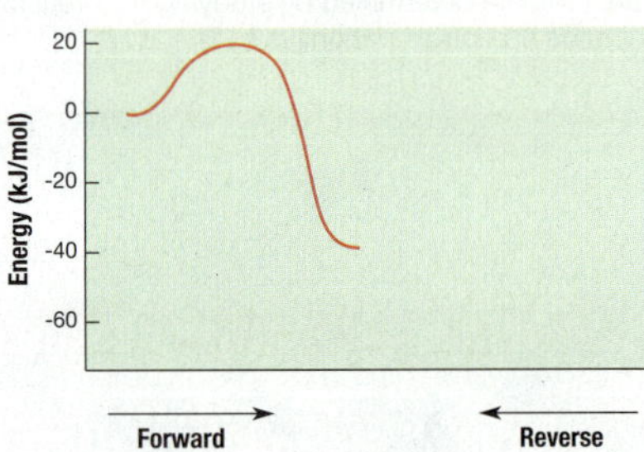

(c)

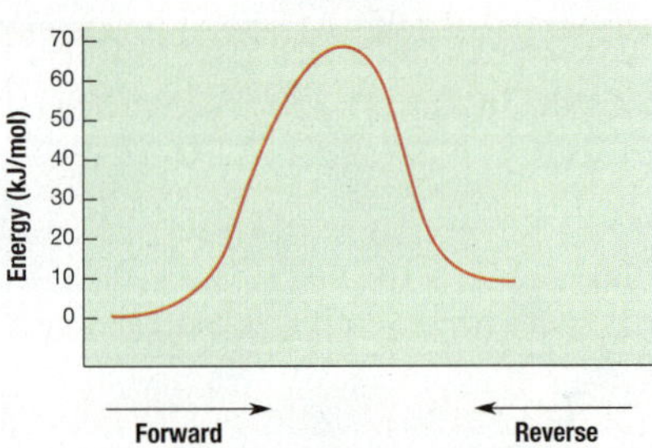

7. Draw and label energy diagrams that depict the following reactions, and determine all remaining values. Place the reactants at energy level zero.
   a. $\Delta E_{forward} = -10$ kJ/mol, $E_a' = 40$ kJ/mol
   b. $\Delta E_{forward} = -95$ kJ/mol, $E_a = 20$ kJ/mol
   c. $\Delta E_{reverse} = -40$ kJ/mol, $E_a' = 30$ kJ/mol

SECTION 2

Reaction Rate

REVIEWING MAIN IDEAS

8. Define the rate-determining step for a chemical reaction.

9. Write the general equation for the rate law, and label the various factors.

PRACTICE PROBLEMS

10. a. Determine the overall balanced equation for a reaction that has the following proposed mechanism, and write an acceptable rate law. (Hint: See Sample Problem C.)
    Step 1: $B_2 + B_2 \longrightarrow E_3 + D$ slow
    Step 2: $E_3 + A \longrightarrow B_2 + C_2$ fast
    b. Give the order of the reaction with respect to each reactant.
    c. What is the overall order of the reaction?

11. A reaction that involves reactants A and B is found to occur in the one-step mechanism: $2A + B \longrightarrow A_2B$. Write the rate law for this reaction, and predict the effect of doubling the concentration of either reactant on the overall reaction rate. (Hint: See Sample Problem C.)

12. A chemical reaction is expressed by the balanced chemical equation $A + 2B \longrightarrow C$. Three reaction-rate experiments yield the following data.

Experiment number	Initial [A]	Initial [B]	Initial rate of formation of C
1	0.20 M	0.20 M	2.0×10^{-4} M/min
2	0.20 M	0.40 M	8.0×10^{-4} M/min
3	0.40 M	0.40 M	1.6×10^{-3} M/min

   a. Determine the rate law for the reaction.
   b. Calculate the value of the specific rate constant.
   c. If the initial concentrations of both A and B are 0.30 M, at what initial rate is C formed?
   d. What is the order of the reaction with respect to A?
   e. What is the order of the reaction with respect to B?

Mixed Review

REVIEWING MAIN IDEAS

13. Draw and label energy diagrams that depict the following reactions, and determine all remaining values. Place the reactants at energy level zero.
    a. $\Delta E = +30$ kJ/mol $\quad E_a' = 20$ kJ/mol
    b. $\Delta E = -30$ kJ/mol $\quad E_a = 20$ kJ/mol

14. A particular reaction is found to have the following rate law:

$$R = k[A][B]^2$$

How is the rate affected by each of the following changes?
   a. The initial concentration of A is cut in half.
   b. The initial concentration of B is tripled.
   c. The concentration of A is doubled, but the concentration of B is cut in half.
   d. A catalyst is added.

15. For each of the following pairs, choose the substance or process that you would expect to react more rapidly.
    a. granulated sugar or powdered sugar
    b. zinc in HCl at 298.15 K or zinc in HCl at 320 K
    c. 5 g of thick platinum wire or 5 g of thin platinum wire

16. The following data relate to the reaction $A + B \longrightarrow C$. Find the order with respect to each reactant.

[A] (M)	[B] (M)	Rate (M/s)
0.08	0.06	0.012
0.08	0.03	0.006
0.04	0.06	0.003

7. a.
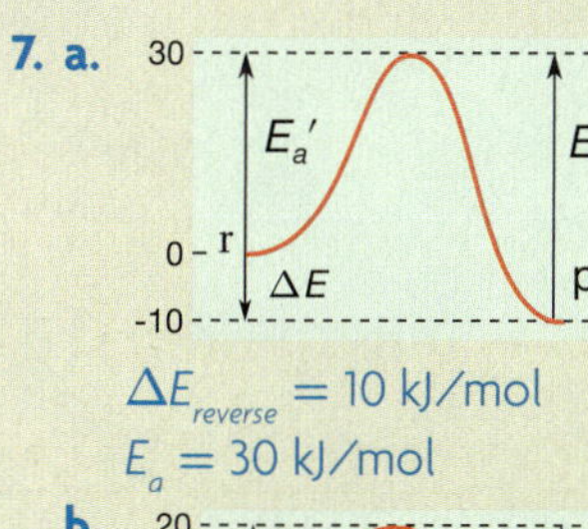

$\Delta E_{reverse} = 10$ kJ/mol
$E_a = 30$ kJ/mol

b.
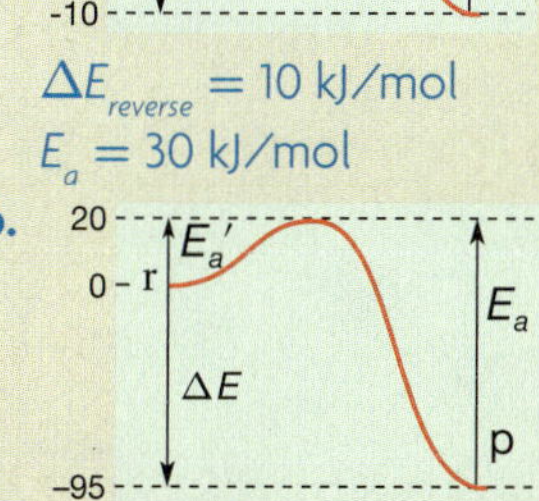

$\Delta E_{reverse} = 95$ kJ/mol
$E_a' = 115$ kJ/mol

c.
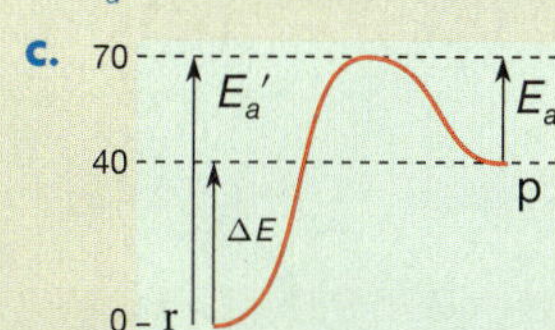

$\Delta E_{forward} = 40$ kJ/mol
$E_a = 70$ kJ/mol

8. It is the slowest step in a mechanism, and determines the overall reaction rate.

CHAPTER REVIEW

9. $R = k[A]^n[B]^m$, where R is the reaction rate; k is the rate constant; [A] and [B] are the molar concentrations of the reactants; n and m are the respective powers to which the concentration is raised. For each reactant, the power is called the *order* with respect to that reactant.

10. a. $A + B_2 \longrightarrow C_2 + D$; $R = k[B_2]^2$
    b. zero order in A, second order in B_2
    c. second order overall

11. $R = k[A]^2[B]$; doubling [A] increases the rate by a factor of 4; doubling [B] doubles the rate of the reaction.

12. a. $R = k[A][B]^2$
    b. 2.5×10^{-2} $M^{-2}min^{-1}$
    c. 6.8×10^{-4} M/min
    d. first order with respect to A
    e. second order with respect to B

13. a.
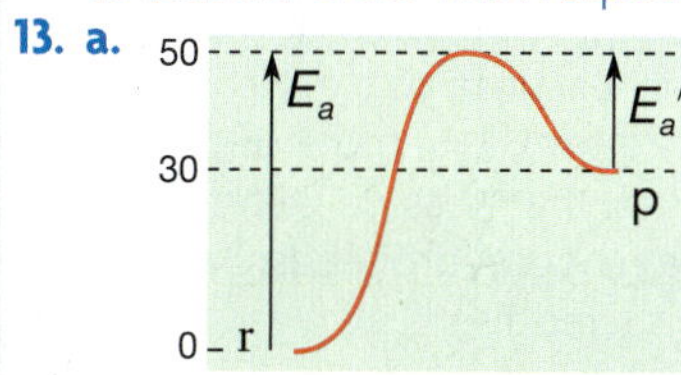

$E_a = 50$ kJ/mol

b.
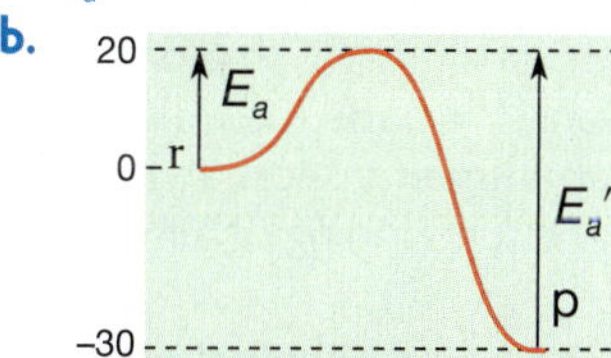

$E_a' = 50$ kJ/mol

14. a. If [A] is halved, the reaction rate is halved.
    b. If [B] is tripled, the reaction rate will increase by a factor of nine.
    c. If [A] is doubled and [B] is halved, the rate of the reaction will be halved.
    d. If the catalyst is specific for this reaction, the reaction will speed up.

15. a. powdered sugar
    b. zinc in HCl at 320 K
    c. thin platinum wire

16. first order in B (because rate is halved when concentration is halved); second order in A (because rate decreases by a factor of 4 when concentration is halved)

17. The formation of a single activated complex by the simultaneous collision of five molecules is highly improbable, and the reaction mechanisms must involve some sequence of simple steps.
18. a. It is the one by which the potential energy of the reactants is raised to the minimum level needed for effective collisions.
    b. The maximum-energy region is reached when the activated complex is formed.
19. The powdered nature of the dry materials provides large surface areas of contact for oxygen, so even a spark could initiate a very rapid reaction that could result in an explosion.
20. Measure the pressure of the reaction system. Because two moles of gas react to form one mole of gas product, the pressure will decrease as the reaction proceeds. Because NO_2 is a reddish brown gas and N_2O_4 is colorless, the change in color intensity can also be used.
21. Answers will vary. Some possible responses include the following: the metabolism of insects and reptiles and the functioning of air conditioning.
22. Designed experiments should include all appropriate safety cautions and controls.

CRITICAL THINKING

17. **Predicting Outcomes** The balanced equation for a rapid homogeneous reaction between two gases is as follows: $4A + B \longrightarrow 2C + 2D$. Because the simultaneous collision of four molecules of one reactant with one molecule of the other reactant is extremely improbable, what would you predict about the nature of the reaction mechanism for this reaction system?

18. **Evaluating Ideas**
    a. How can you justify calling the reaction pathway that is shown in **Figure 1.4** the minimum-energy pathway for reaction?
    b. What significance is associated with the maximum-energy region of this minimum-energy pathway?

19. **Applying Models** Explain why there is a danger of explosion in places such as coal mines, sawmills, and grain elevators, where large amounts of dry, powdered combustible materials are present.

20. **Evaluating Methods** What property would you measure to determine the reaction rate for the following reaction? Justify your choice.

$$2NO_2(g) \longrightarrow N_2O_4(g)$$

RESEARCH AND WRITING

21. Look for situations around your house in which processes are speeded up by an increase in temperature or slowed down by a decrease in temperature. Make a list, and discuss the different processes.

ALTERNATIVE ASSESSMENT

22. Boilers are sometimes used to heat large buildings. Deposits of $CaCO_3$, $MgCO_3$, and $FeCO_3$ can hinder the boiler operation. Aqueous solutions of hydrochloric acid are commonly used to remove these deposits. The general equation for the reaction is written below.

$$MCO_3(s) + 2H_3O^+(aq) \longrightarrow M^{2+}(aq) + 3H_2O(l) + CO_2(g)$$

In the equation, M stands for Ca, Mg, or Fe. Design an experiment to determine the effect of various HCl concentrations on the rates of this reaction. Present your design to the class.

552 Chapter 17

Standards-Based Assessment

Answer the following items on a separate piece of paper.

MULTIPLE CHOICE

1. The sequence of steps that occurs in a reaction process is called the
A. order of the reaction.
B. rate law.
C. overall reaction.
D. reaction mechanism.

2. To be effective, a collision requires
A. enough energy only.
B. favorable orientation only.
C. enough energy and a favorable orientation.
D. a reaction mechanism.

3. How does the energy of the activated complex compare with the energies of the reactants and products?
A. It is lower than both the energy of the reactants and the energy of the products.
B. It is lower than the energy of the reactants but higher than the energy of the products.
C. It is higher than the energy of the reactants but lower than the energy of the products.
D. It is higher than both the energy of the reactants and the energy of the products.

4. If a collision between molecules is very gentle, the molecules are
A. more likely to be oriented favorably.
B. less likely to be oriented favorably.
C. likely to react.
D. likely to rebound without reacting.

5. A species that changes the rate of a reaction but is neither consumed nor changed is
A. a catalyst.
B. an activated complex.
C. an intermediate.
D. a reactant.

6. A rate law relates
A. reaction rate and temperature.
B. reaction rate and concentration.
C. temperature and concentration.
D. energy and concentration.

7. In a graph of how energy changes with reaction progress, the activated complex appears at the
A. left end of the curve.
B. right end of the curve.
C. bottom of the curve.
D. peak of the curve.

8. The slowest step in a mechanism is called
A. the rate-determining step.
B. the uncatalyzed reaction.
C. the activation step.
D. None of the above

9. A certain reaction is zero order in reactant A and second order in reactant B. What happens to the reaction rate when the concentrations of both reactants are doubled?
A. The reaction rate remains the same.
B. The reaction increases by a factor of two.
C. The reaction rate increases by a factor of four.
D. The reaction rate increases by a factor of eight.

SHORT ANSWER

10. Two molecules collide but bounce apart unchanged. What two reasons could account for their failure to react?

11. Sketch a diagram that shows how the energy changes with the progress of an endothermic reaction. Label the curve "Reactants," "Products," and "Activated complex." On the same diagram, sketch a second curve to show the change caused by a catalyst.

EXTENDED RESPONSE

12. Suggest ways of measuring the concentration of a reactant or product in a reaction mixture.

13. Why are reaction orders not always equal to the coefficients in a balanced chemical equation?

Test Tip
Sometimes, only one part of a graph or table is needed to answer a question. In such cases, focus on only the information that is required to answer the question.

STANDARDS-BASED ASSESSMENT

To give students practice under more realistic testing conditions, give them 60 minutes to answer all of the questions in this Standardized Test Preparation.

Test Answers

1. D
2. C
3. D
4. D
5. A
6. B
7. D
8. A
9. C
10. They had insufficient energy for bonds to break, or they did not collide in a favorable orientation.
11. The humped curve should have a final plateau that is higher than its initial plateau. The second curve should share the same plateaus as the first but should also have a lower hump.
12. Answers may vary. Among the methods that might be suggested are observing a change in color intensity, removing samples and analyzing for one component, and measuring pressure change.
13. Reactions often occur by a multi-step mechanism. Reaction orders reflect the coefficients in the rate-determining step of such a mechanism, not the coefficients in the overall equation.

Chemical Equilibrium

① Core Instruction

Chapter Resources

- The Teacher's Edition wrap has extensive teaching support for every lesson, including Misconception Alerts, Teach from Visuals, Demonstrations, Teaching Tips, Differentiated Instruction, and Problem Solving support.
- Several additional presentation tools are available online for every chapter, including Animated Chemistry features and Visual Concepts.
- You can open your lesson with the Why It Matters Video: Acids and Bases.

Section	Instruction	Labs and Demonstrations Go Online for Materials Lists and Solutions Lists.
18.1	■ **Textbook:** The Nature of Chemical Equilibrium **Animated Chemistry:** Dynamic Equilibrium **Teaching Visuals:** Reaction Rate Over Time for an Equilibrium System • Determining K_{eq} for Reactions at Chemical Equilibrium • Equilibrium Constants **PowerPresentations**	■ **Demonstration:** Achieving Equilibrium
18.2	■ **Textbook:** Shifting Equilibrium **Teaching Visuals:** Temperature Changes Affect an Equilibrium System • Particle Model for the Common-Ion Effect **PowerPresentations**	■ **Demonstration:** The Common-Ion Effect ■ **Lab:** Equilibrium (Core Skill)
18.3	■ **Textbook:** Equilibria of Acids, Bases, and Salts **Teaching Visuals:** Buffered vs. Nonbuffered Solutions • Rate Comparison for $H_2(g) + I_2(g) = 2HI(g)$ • Equilibrium and pH Calculations • Neutralization Curve for a Weak Acid and Strong Base • Neutralization Curve for a Strong Acid and Weak Base **PowerPresentations**	■ **Lab:** Measuring K_a for Acetic Acid (Core Skill) ■ **Lab:** Buffer Capacity in Commercial Beverages (Probeware)
18.4	■ **Textbook:** Solubility Equilibrium **Teaching Visuals:** Equilibrium Calculations • Determining K_{sp} for Reactions at Chemical Equilibrium • Solubility Product Constants at 25°C **PowerPresentations**	■ **Lab:** Solubility Product Constant (Core Skill) ■ **Lab:** Solubility Product Constant—Algal Blooms (Forensics) ■ **Lab:** Striking A Balance (Open Inquiry)

2 Support and Intervention

- **Interactive Reader** (English and Spanish)
- **Study Guide**
- **Interactive Review:** Review Games, Concept Maps, and Section Self-Checks
- **Scientific Reasoning Skill Builder**
- **Learn It! Videos**
- **Solve It! Cards**
- **Interactive Demos**
- **Sample Problem Sets**

3 Specialized Support

- **Chapter Summary Audio Files**
- **Interactive Reader Audio Files**
- **Differentiated Instruction:** Inclusion, Below Level, and English Learners (TE wrap)

Enrichment and Challenge

- **Differentiated Instruction:** Pre-AP (TE wrap)
- **Chemistry Explorers:** Fixing the Nitrogen Problem (SE)
- **WebLinks**

Assessment

- **Section Formative Assessments** (SE)
- **Section Quizzes**
- **Chapter Review** (SE)
- **Chapter Tests A and B**
- **Alternative Assessment** (TE wrap)
- **Online Assessment and Remediation**
- **ExamView Banks**

Where do I find it?

		PRINT	DVD	ONLINE
1	Animated Chemistry		■	■
	Demonstrations (TE wrap)	■		■
	Interactive Whiteboard		■	■
	Labs		■	■
	PowerPresentations		■	■
	QuickLabs	■	■	■
	Teaching Visuals		■	■
	Textbook	■	■	■
	Visual Concepts		■	■
	Why It Matters Videos		■	■
2	Interactive Demos		■	■
	Interactive Reader	■	■	■
	Interactive Reviews		■	■
	Learn It! Videos		■	■
	Sample Problem Sets		■	■
	Scientific Reasoning Skill Builder		■	■
	Smart Grapher Tool		■	■
	Solve It! Cards		■	■
	Study Guide		■	■
3	Chapter Summary Audio Files		■	■
	Differentiated Instruction (TE wrap)	■		
	Interactive Reader Audio Files		■	■

CHAPTER 18

Chapter Overview

Section 1 defines reversible reactions; the state of equilibrium; and *K*, the equilibrium constant.

Section 2 describes how equilibria will shift in response to changes in concentration, pressure, and temperature; and discusses the common-ion effect.

Section 3 describes the equilibria of acids, bases, and salts; explains the acid ionization constant, K_a; and discusses buffering and hydrolysis.

Section 4 discusses solubility equilibria; and explains calculations involving the solubility product constant, K_{sp}, and precipitate formation.

▼ Focus and Motivate

Activate Prior Knowledge

Students may need a review of the following concepts:

- equilibrium
- Brønsted-Lowry acids and bases
- pH and self-ionization of water

About the Image

The formation of stalactites and stalagmites is the result of a reversible chemical reaction. Unlike reactions that go to completion, reversible reactions establish an equilibrium in which the rates of the forward and reverse reactions are equal.

Why It Matters

Students can access the video online and find other helpful resources at **HMDScience.com**.

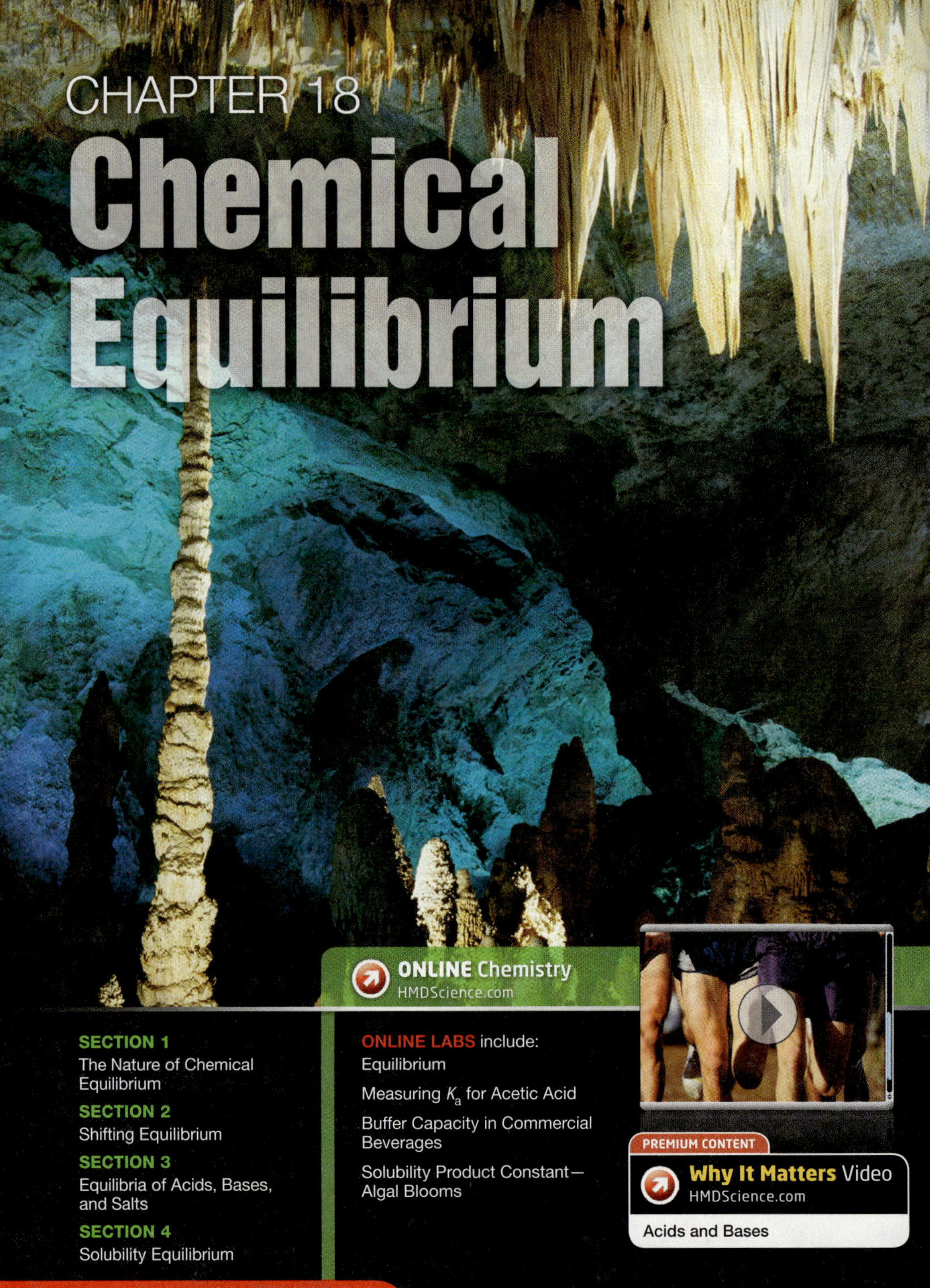

Lab Preview

The following labs and demonstrations support the concepts presented in this chapter.

LABS

Equilibrium (Core Skill)

Measuring K_a for Acetic Acid (Core Skill)

Buffer Capacity in Commercial Beverages (Probeware)

Solubility Product Constant (Core Skill)

Solubility Product Constant—Algal Blooms (Forensics)

Striking A Balance (Open Inquiry)

DEMONSTRATIONS

Achieving Equilibrium

The Common-Ion Effect

The Nature of Chemical Equilibrium

SECTION 1

Main Ideas

- All reactions are reversible under certain conditions.
- Some reactions favor products, and others reactants.
- In equilibrium, the concentrations of reactants and products remain constant.

Key Terms

reversible reaction
chemical equilibrium
equilibrium constant
chemical equilibrium expression

In systems that are in equilibrium, opposing processes occur at the same time and at the same rate. For example, when an excess of sugar is placed in water, some sugar molecules go into solution, and others remain undissolved. At equilibrium, molecules of sugar are crystallizing at the same rate that molecules from the crystal are dissolving. The rate of evaporation of a liquid in a closed vessel can eventually be equaled by the rate of condensation of its vapor. The resulting equilibrium vapor pressure is a characteristic of the liquid at the prevailing temperature. The preceding examples are physical equilibria. In this chapter, we will expand on the concept of equilibrium to include chemical reactions. You will learn how a system at equilibrium responds when equilibrium conditions are altered by changing concentration, pressure, and temperature.

MAIN IDEA

All reactions are reversible under certain conditions.

Theoretically, every reaction can proceed in two directions, forward and reverse. Thus, essentially all chemical reactions are considered to be reversible under suitable conditions. A chemical reaction in which the products can react to re-form the reactants is called a **reversible reaction.**

Mercury(II) oxide decomposes when heated.

$$2HgO(s) \xrightarrow{\Delta} 2Hg(l) + O_2(g)$$

Mercury and oxygen combine to form mercury(II) oxide when heated gently.

$$2Hg(l) + O_2(g) \xrightarrow{\Delta} 2HgO(s)$$

Figure 1.1 shows both of these reactions taking place. Suppose mercury(II) oxide is heated in a closed container from which neither the mercury nor the oxygen can escape. Once decomposition has begun, the mercury and oxygen released can recombine to form mercury(II) oxide again. Thus, both reactions can proceed at the same time. Under these conditions, the rate of the synthesis reaction will eventually equal that of the decomposition reaction. At equilibrium, mercury and oxygen will combine to form mercury(II) oxide at the same rate that mercury(II) oxide decomposes into mercury and oxygen. The amounts of mercury(II) oxide, mercury, and oxygen can then be expected to remain constant as long as these conditions persist: a state of dynamic equilibrium has been reached.

FIGURE 1.1

Reversible Reactions When heated, mercury(II) oxide decomposes into its elements, mercury and oxygen. Liquid mercury reacts with oxygen to re-form mercury(II) oxide. Together, these reactions represent a reversible chemical process.

CRITICAL THINKING

Relate What is the relationship between reversible reactions and photosynthesis? Explain the importance of this connection.

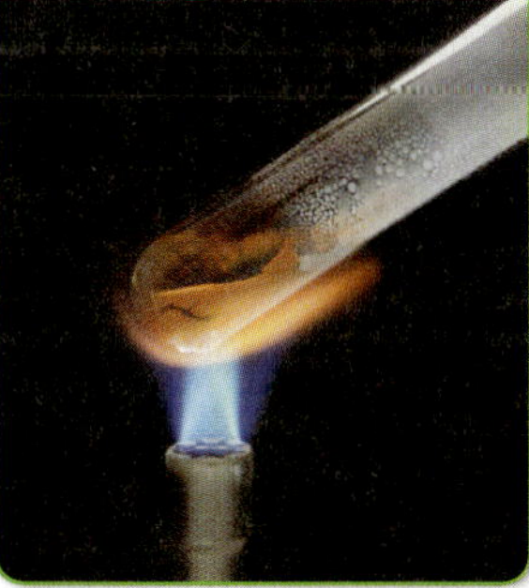

Differentiated Instruction

BELOW LEVEL

Point out that although every chemical reaction can be reversible, many of them go to completion in just the forward direction. Ask students why reactions that produce a gas or a precipitate go to completion rather than establishing a reversible reaction. Students should point out that the gas or precipitate is no longer available to react. All the products must be available to react with one another so that they can re-form the reactants. Students will learn more about reactions that go to completion in the next section of this chapter.

SECTION 1

Plan and Prepare ▼

Objectives

Upon completion of this section, students should be able to do the following:

- Define *chemical equilibrium*.
- Explain the nature of the equilibrium constant.
- Write chemical equilibrium expressions and solve calculations involving them.

Classroom Catalyst

Have students list two everyday processes that can easily be reversed, such as the freezing of water and the melting of ice, and two that cannot, such as the cooking of an egg or the lighting of a match. For the reversible processes, ask students to describe the conditions that favor the process going in a particular direction (for example, low temperature favors freezing, and high temperature favors melting). Use the student examples to introduce reversibility of processes and the concept that various conditions can favor a particular direction in a certain process.

Teach ▼

READING TOOLKIT

BRAINSTORMING Have students brainstorm a list of reactions that they think are reversible. Write their contributions on the board. Have students suggest potential applications of reversible reactions in industry and in daily life.

Critical Thinking

Answer: The reverse reaction of photosynthesis is cellular respiration. This is important because if the reaction could not reverse, photosynthetic organisms would not be able to break down and use the glucose formed in photosynthesis to have energy to live.

▼ Teach continued

Teaching Tip

A visible indication of an irreversible reaction in a solution includes the formation of a gas or insoluble product.

Application

The reaction that darkens some sunglasses when they are exposed to the ultraviolet radiation in sunlight is an example of a reversible reaction. When energy from sunlight is added, the forward reaction is favored, forming dark elemental silver from white silver chloride. When the glasses are not in sunlight, the reaction reverses.

Misconception Alert!

Students often think that the reaction process is no longer occurring in a reaction system that has reached equilibrium. Emphasize that at equilibrium, the forward and reverse reactions continue to occur, but at equal rates, so there is no net change in the amounts of reactants and products.

Check for Understanding

Answer: The term *dynamic equilibrium* is correct because although the balance between the forward and backward reaction rates is reached, the reactions continue to occur and do not just stop.

Dynamic Equilibrium

In such a state of dynamic equilibrium, both reactions continue, but there is no net change in the composition of the system. **A reversible chemical reaction is in chemical equilibrium when the rate of its forward reaction equals the rate of its reverse reaction and the concentrations of its products and reactants remain unchanged.** The chemical equation for the reaction at equilibrium is written using double arrows to indicate the overall reversibility of the reaction.

$$2HgO(s) \rightleftarrows 2Hg(l) + O_2(g)$$

MAIN IDEA

Some reactions favor products, and others reactants.

Many chemical reactions are reversible under ordinary conditions of temperature and concentration. They will reach a state of equilibrium unless at least one of the substances involved escapes or is removed from the reaction system. In some cases, however, the forward reaction is so predominant that essentially all reactants will react to form products. Here, the products of the forward reaction are favored, meaning that at equilibrium there is a much higher concentration of products than of reactants. Hence, we can say that the equilibrium "lies to the right," because products predominate, and products conventionally are written on the right side of a chemical equation. An example of such a system is the formation of sulfur trioxide from sulfur dioxide and oxygen.

$$2SO_2(g) + O_2(g) \rightleftarrows 2SO_3(g)$$

Notice that the equation is written showing an inequality of the two arrow lengths. The forward reaction is represented by the longer arrow to imply that the product is favored in this reaction.

CHECK FOR UNDERSTANDING

Explain The two terms *dynamic* and *equilibrium* seem to contradict each other at first. Dynamic means that changes are occurring, but equilibrium means that no overall change is happening. Given this, explain why the combination of the two, *dynamic equilibrium*, is correct.

In other cases, the forward reaction is barely under way when the rate of the reverse reaction becomes equal to that of the forward reaction, and equilibrium is established. In these cases, the amounts of reactants remain high, and the amounts of products are low. Here, we say that the equilibrium "lies to the left," because the reactants are the predominant species. An example of such a system is the acid-base reaction between carbonic acid and water.

$$H_2CO_3(aq) + H_2O(l) \rightleftarrows H_3O^+(aq) + HCO_3^-(aq)$$

In still other cases, both forward and reverse reactions occur to nearly the same extent before chemical equilibrium is established. Neither reaction is favored, and considerable concentrations of both reactants and products are present at equilibrium. An example is the dissociation of sulfurous acid in water.

$$H_2SO_3(aq) + H_2O(l) \rightleftarrows H_3O^+(aq) + HSO_3^-(aq)$$

Chemical reactions ordinarily are used to convert available reactants into more desirable products. Chemists try to convert as much of these reactants as possible into products. The extent to which reactants are converted to products is indicated by the numerical value of the equilibrium constant.

Differentiated Instruction

INCLUSION

This demonstration of the concept of dynamic equilibrium can be helpful for both tactile and visually-impaired learners. Have students work in pairs, and give each pair two small beakers. Have students label one beaker *reactants* and the other beaker *products.* Place 20 pennies in the reactant beaker. Ask students to use the pennies to model how a dynamic equilibrium is established that "lies to the right." Students should move most of the pennies to the product beaker. Once the products predominate, students should exchange one penny between the two beakers to show that a dynamic equilibrium has been established. Ask students to repeat the process to model a dynamic equilibrium that "lies to the left." Students should move most of the pennies to the reactant beaker and then exchange one penny between the two beakers. Finally, have students model a dynamic equilibrium in which neither the forward nor the reverse reaction is favored. Students should have an equal number of pennies in each beaker and swap equal numbers of pennies between beakers to model the dynamic equilibrium.

MAIN IDEA

In equilibrium, the concentrations of reactants and products remain constant.

Suppose two substances, A and B, react to form products C and D. In turn, C and D react to produce A and B. Under appropriate conditions, equilibrium occurs for this reversible reaction. This hypothetical equilibrium reaction is described by the following general equation.

$$nA + mB \rightleftarrows xC + yD$$

Initially, the concentrations of C and D are zero, and those of A and B are maximum. **Figure 1.2** shows that, over time, the rate of the forward reaction decreases as A and B are used up. Meanwhile, the rate of the reverse reaction increases as C and D are formed. When these two reaction rates become equal, equilibrium is established. The individual concentrations of A, B, C, and D undergo no further change if conditions remain the same.

After equilibrium is attained, the concentrations of products and reactants remain constant, so a ratio of their concentrations should also remain constant. The ratio of the mathematical product $[C]^x \times [D]^y$ to the mathematical product $[A]^n \times [B]^m$ for this reaction has a definite value at a given temperature. It is the equilibrium constant of the reaction and is designated by the letter *K*. The following equation describes the equilibrium constant for the hypothetical equilibrium system. The brackets ([ ]) indicate the concentration of each substance as expressed in mol/L. The superscripts are the coefficients of each substance in the balanced chemical equation.

Equilibrium Constant $$K = \frac{[C]^x[D]^y}{[A]^n[B]^m}$$

FIGURE 1.2

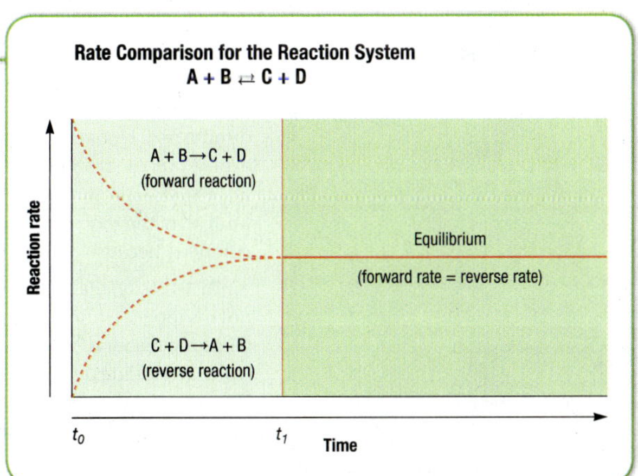

Equilibrium Reaction Systems Shown are reaction rates for the hypothetical equilibrium reaction system $A + B \rightleftarrows C + D$. From the time A and B are mixed together at t_0, the rate of the forward reaction declines and the rate of the reverse reaction increases until both forward and reverse reaction rates are equal at t_1, when the equilibrium condition begins.

TEACH FROM VISUALS

FIGURE 1.2 Point out to students that the graph of rate versus time becomes horizontal at equilibrium (slope = 0), which indicates that there is no further increase in the amount of products or decrease in the amount of reactants.

Classroom Discussion

Have students discuss the meaning of the general chemical equation shown on this page, including the symbols for coefficients. They should explain the use of the double arrow as an indication of equilibrium and describe what is meant by equilibrium in a reaction.

Demonstration

ACHIEVING EQUILIBRIUM

You will need **two 2-L plastic beakers** and **two 100-mL or 50-mL plastic beakers.** Fill one of the large beakers with **water.** Ask two students to assist you, and give each one a small beaker. Give them these instructions: "Fill your small beaker with as much water as you can by dipping it into your large beaker, and then pour the water into the other student's large beaker. Do this at the same time, and repeat for several cycles." Obviously, the first time, only one student can fill the small beaker. The second time, the student who started with the empty 2-L beaker will have a little water in the small beaker but will not be able to fill it. After several cycles, students will see that equilibrium has been achieved, and each person is transferring a full beaker of water each time. You may also perform an extension in which the two beakers used to transfer water are not the same size. Can equilibrium still be achieved?

ENGLISH LEARNERS

Write the general equation for an equilibrium reaction on the board. Have students explain what the letters *n*, *m*, *x*, and *y* represent. Students should recognize that these letters represent the coefficients indicating the moles or molecules of each substance involved in the reaction.

PRE-AP

Explain that **Figure 1.2** shows the rate comparison for a balanced equilibrium reaction. Have students draw a graph to show the rate comparison for a dynamic equilibrium that "lies to the right." Students should draw the graph so that the equilibrium point (horizontal line) lies closer to the reverse reaction. Have students draw a second graph to show the rate comparison for a dynamic equilibrium that "lies to the left." Students should draw the graph so that the equilibrium point lies closer to the forward reaction.

▼ Teach continued

Alternative Assessment

On the board, write several chemical equations representing equilibrium situations. Then, have students work singly or in small groups to write the equilibrium expression for each. Have students compare their results with those of other students or groups.

READING TOOLKIT

DECODING Have students write the equation for the formation of sulfur trioxide from a reaction between sulfur dioxide and oxygen.

$$2SO_2(g) + O_2(g) \longrightarrow 2SO_3(g)$$

Then have students put together the equilibrium expression for this reaction step by step as they read the definition of the equilibrium constant. For example, as they read "the equilibrium constant, *K*, is the ratio of the mathematical product of the concentrations of substances formed...," students should write the following:

$$K = \frac{[SO_3]^2}{[SO_2]^2[O_2]}$$

Teaching Tip

The higher the value of the equilibrium constant, the more the products are favored.

TEACH FROM VISUALS

FIGURE 1.3 Ask students whether the fact that the color has become constant means that the reaction has stopped. The forward and reverse reactions continue to occur at equal rates, so there are no further macroscopic changes.

The concentrations of substances on the right side of the chemical equation appear in the numerator of the ratio, with each concentration raised to a power equal to the coefficient of that substance in the balanced chemical equation. These substances are the products of the forward reaction. The concentrations of substances on the left side of the chemical equation are in the denominator of the ratio, with each concentration raised to a power equal to the coefficient of that substance in the balanced chemical equation. These substances are the reactants of the forward reaction. The constant *K* is independent of the initial concentrations. It is, however, dependent on the temperature of the system.

The Equilibrium Constant

The numerical value of *K* for a particular equilibrium system is obtained experimentally. The chemist must analyze the equilibrium mixture and determine the concentrations of all substances. The value of *K* for a given equilibrium reaction at a given temperature shows the extent to which the reactants are converted into the products of the reaction. If the value of *K* is small, the forward reaction occurs only very slightly before equilibrium is established, and the reactants are favored. A large value of *K* indicates an equilibrium in which the original reactants are largely converted to products. Only the concentrations of substances that can actually change are included in *K*. This means that *pure* solids and liquids are omitted, because their concentrations cannot change.

In general, then, the **equilibrium constant,** ***K***, is the ratio of the mathematical product of the concentrations of substances formed at equilibrium to the mathematical product of the concentrations of reacting substances. Each concentration is raised to a power equal to the coefficient of that substance in the chemical equation. The equation for *K* is referred to as the **chemical equilibrium expression.**

FIGURE 1.3

H_2, I_2, HI Equilibrium System The violet color of the reactant iodine gas, I_2, gives an indication of the progress of the reaction between hydrogen and iodine. Both H_2 (reactant) and HI (product) are colorless gases. The darker the purple color in the flask, the less I_2 gas reacted, so the more reactants remain.

The H_2, I_2, HI Equilibrium System

An excellent example of an equilibrium system occurs with the reaction between H_2 and I_2 vapor in a sealed flask at an elevated temperature. A typical look at this reaction can be seen in **Figure 1.3.** If the reaction were observed, its rate could be followed by making note of how quickly the violet color of the iodine vapor diminished. If colorless H_2 gas is present in excess, we might expect that the reaction would continue until all of the I_2 is used up. The violet color of the beaker would decrease in intensity until all of the iodine reacts. At that time, the beaker would be colorless, because both HI and the excess H_2 are colorless gases.

In actuality, the color fades to a constant intensity but does not disappear completely, because the reaction is reversible. Once the reaction between H_2 and I_2 reaches a certain point, hydrogen iodide decomposes to re-form hydrogen and iodine. The rate of this reverse reaction increases as the concentration of hydrogen iodide increases.

Differentiated Instruction

PRE-AP

Have students research chimney safety on the internet. If possible, students may want to interview a fireman or an insurance fire investigator. Students should report back to the class with a presentation that includes visuals. Presentations should cover knowledge of the periodic care of a chimney, information about the reversible reaction that causes soot, and the procedures used by chimney sweeps in order to keep chimneys functioning well. Students could also address other instances where practical applications of reversible reactions are used in everyday life.

The rate of the forward reaction decreases accordingly. The concentrations of hydrogen and iodine decrease as they react. As the rates of the opposing reactions become equal, equilibrium is established. The constant color achieved indicates that equilibrium exists among hydrogen, iodine, and hydrogen iodide. The net chemical equation for the reaction system at equilibrium follows.

$$H_2(g) + I_2(g) \rightleftarrows 2HI(g)$$

From this chemical equation, the following chemical equilibrium expression can be written. The concentration of HI is raised to the power of 2, because the coefficient of HI in the balanced chemical equation is 2.

$$K = \frac{[HI]^2}{[H_2][I_2]}$$

Chemists have carefully measured the concentrations of H_2, I_2, and HI in equilibrium mixtures at various temperatures. In some experiments, the flasks were filled with hydrogen iodide at known pressure. The flasks were held at fixed temperatures until equilibrium was established. In other experiments, hydrogen and iodine were the original substances. Experimental data, together with the calculated values for K, are listed in **Figure 1.4.** Experiments 1 and 2 began with hydrogen iodide. Experiments 3 and 4 began with hydrogen and iodine. Note the close agreement obtained for the numerical values of the equilibrium constant in all cases.

At 425°C, the equilibrium constant for this equilibrium reaction system has the average value of 54.34. This value for K is constant for any system of H_2, I_2, and HI at equilibrium at this temperature. If the calculation for K yields a different result, there must be a reason. Either the H_2, I_2, and HI system has not reached equilibrium or the system is not at 425°C.

The balanced chemical equation for an equilibrium system is necessary to write the expression for the equilibrium constant. The data in **Figure 1.4** show that the validity of this expression is confirmed when the actual values of the equilibrium concentrations of reactants and products are determined experimentally. The values of K are calculated from these concentrations. No information concerning the kinetics of the reacting systems is required.

FIGURE 1.4

TYPICAL EQUILIBRIUM CONCENTRATIONS OF H_2, I_2, AND HI IN MOL/L AT 425°C

Experiment	$[H_2]$	$[I_2]$	[HI]	$K = \frac{[HI]^2}{[H_2][I_2]}$
1	0.4953×10^{-3}	0.4953×10^{-3}	3.655×10^{-3}	54.46
2	1.141×10^{-3}	1.141×10^{-3}	8.410×10^{-3}	54.33
3	3.560×10^{-3}	1.250×10^{-3}	15.59×10^{-3}	54.62
4	2.252×10^{-3}	2.336×10^{-3}	16.85×10^{-3}	53.97

TEACH FROM TABLES

FIGURE 1.4 Tell students to cover the last column of the table and use a calculator to determine each value of K. In this way, students can discover on their own—and better appreciate—the surprising closeness of the four values of the equilibrium constant.

Teaching Tip

Remind students that the convention is not to include units in an equilibrium constant. Remind them that they followed this practice when using K_w.

BELOW LEVEL

Be sure students understand that for a given reaction system at a given temperature, the equilibrium expression is constant, although the equilibrium concentrations will not always be the same. Emphasize that it is the ratio of the concentrations that determines the equilibrium constant. To help students grasp this concept, write these fractions on the board: 1/2, 2/4, 4/8, 8/16, 16/32, and 32/64. Compare this to an equilibrium reaction. Point out that even though the numbers (concentrations) can change, the ratio (K value) is always the same.

▼ Teach *continued*

Misconception Alert!

Students often become confused by the use of the same letter of the alphabet to represent three different quantities: the rate constant, the equilibrium constant, and the Kelvin temperature. Point out that the first is represented by an italic lowercase *k*, the second by an italic uppercase *K*, and the third by a Roman uppercase K.

Teaching Tip

The equilibrium constant for a forward reaction is the mathematical inverse of the equilibrium constant for the corresponding reverse reaction.

Classroom Practice

A-1 At 25°C, an equilibrium mixture of gases contains 6.4×10^{-3} mol/L PCl_3, 2.5×10^{-2} mol/L Cl_2, and 4.0×10^{-3} mol/L PCl_5. What is the equilibrium constant for the following reaction?

$$PCl_5(g) \rightleftharpoons PCl_3(g) + Cl_2(g)$$

Answer: 4.0×10^{-2}

A-2 At equilibrium, a 2.0-L vessel contains 0.36 mol of H_2, 0.11 mol of Br, and 37 mol of HBr. What is the equilibrium constant for the reaction

$$H_2(g) + Br_2(g) \rightleftharpoons 2HBr(g)$$

at this temperature?

Answer: 3.5×10^4

Once the value of the equilibrium constant is known, the equilibrium-constant expression can be used to calculate concentrations of reactants or products at equilibrium. Suppose an equilibrium system at 425°C is found to contain 0.015 mol/L each of H_2 and I_2. To find the concentration of HI in this system, rearrange the chemical equilibrium expression as shown in the two equations that follow.

$$K = \frac{[HI]^2}{[H_2][I_2]}$$

$$[HI] = \sqrt{K[H_2][I_2]}$$

Using the known K value and the given concentrations for H_2 and I_2, if you solve the equation for [HI], you will observe the following result:

$$[HI] = \sqrt{0.015 \times 0.015 \times 54.34}$$

$$[HI] = 0.11 \text{ mol/L}$$

When calculating concentrations at equilibrium, always be sure to note the temperature at which the reaction is taking place. Values for K do change with changing temperature.

PREMIUM CONTENT
Solve It! Cards
HMDScience.com

Equilibrium Constant

Sample Problem A **An equilibrium mixture of N_2, O_2, and NO gases at 1500 *K* is determined to consist of 6.4×10^{-3} mol/L of N_2, 1.7×10^{-3} mol/L of O_2, and 1.1×10^{-5} mol/L of NO. What is the equilibrium constant for the system at this temperature?**

1 ANALYZE

Given: $[N_2] = 6.4 \times 10^{-3}$ mol/L

$[O_2] = 1.7 \times 10^{-3}$ mol/L

$[NO] = 1.1 \times 10^{-5}$ mol/L

Unknown: K

2 PLAN

The balanced chemical equation is $N_2(g) + O_2(g) \rightleftarrows 2NO(g)$.

The chemical equilibrium expression is $K = \frac{[NO]^2}{[N_2][O_2]}$.

3 SOLVE

Substitute the given values for the concentrations into the equilibrium expression.

$$K = \frac{(1.1 \times 10^{-5} \text{ mol/L})^2}{(6.4 \times 10^{-3} \text{ mol/L})(1.7 \times 10^{-3} \text{ mol/L})} = 1.1 \times 10^{-5}$$

Continued

Problem Solving

TAKE IT FURTHER

Have students calculate the value of the equilibrium constant for the reaction when it is written in the reverse order: $2NO(g) \rightleftharpoons N_2(g) + O_2(g)$. Students can use the concentrations given in Sample Problem A and solve for K by substituting in the following equilibrium expression.

$$K = \frac{[N_2][O_2]}{[NO]^2}$$

$$= \frac{(6.4 \times 10^{-3} \text{ mol/L})(1.7 \times 10^{-3} \text{ mol/L})}{(1.1 \times 10^{-5} \text{ mol/L})^2}$$

$$= 9.0 \times 10^4$$

Students can also use the reciprocal of the K value for the original reaction.

$$K = \frac{1}{1.1 \times 10^{-5}} = 9.0 \times 10^4$$

Ask students to explain the significance of the reverse reaction having a positive K value, while the forward reaction has a negative K value.

CHECK YOUR WORK

The value of *K* is small, which is consistent with more N_2 and O_2 being present at equilibrium than NO. The answer has the correct number of significant figures and is close to an estimated value of 8×10^{-6}, calculated as:

$$\frac{(1 \times 10^{-5})^2}{(6 \times 10^{-3})(2 \times 10^{-3})}$$

Practice Answers in Appendix E

1. At equilibrium, a mixture of N_2, H_2, and NH_3 gas at 500°C is determined to consist of 0.602 mol/L of N_2, 0.420 mol/L of H_2, and 0.113 mol/L of NH_3. What is the equilibrium constant for the reaction $N_2(g) + 3H_2(g) \rightleftarrows 2NH_3(g)$ at this temperature?
2. The reaction $AB_2C(g) \rightleftarrows B_2(g) + AC(g)$ reached equilibrium at 900 K in a 5.00-L vessel. At equilibrium, 0.084 mol of AB_2C, 0.035 mol of B_2, and 0.059 mol of AC were detected. What is the equilibrium constant at this temperature for this system? (Don't forget to convert amounts to concentrations.)
3. A reaction between gaseous sulfur dioxide and oxygen gas to produce gaseous sulfur trioxide takes place at 600°C. At that temperature, the concentration of SO_2 is found to be 1.50 mol/L, the concentration of O_2 is 1.25 mol/L, and the concentration of SO_3 is 3.50 mol/L. Using the balanced chemical equation, calculate the equilibrium constant for this system.

SECTION 1 FORMATIVE ASSESSMENT

Reviewing Main Ideas

1. What is meant by *chemical equilibrium*?
2. What is an equilibrium constant?
3. How does the value of an equilibrium constant relate to the relative quantities of reactants and products at equilibrium?
4. What is meant by a *chemical equilibrium expression*?
5. Hydrochloric acid, HCl, is a strong acid that dissociates completely in water to form H_3O^+ and Cl^-. Should the value of *K* for the reaction $HCl(aq) + H_2O(l) \rightleftarrows H_3O^+(aq) + Cl^-(aq)$ be 1×10^{-2}, 1×10^{-5}, or "very large"? Justify your answer.
6. Write the chemical equilibrium expression for the following reaction: $4HCl(g) + O_2(g) \rightleftarrows 2Cl_2(g) + 2H_2O(g)$
7. At equilibrium at 2500 K, [HCl] = 0.0625 mol/L and $[H_2] = [Cl_2] = 0.00450$ mol/L for the reaction $H_2(g) + Cl_2(g) \rightleftarrows 2HCl(g)$. Find the value of *K*.
8. An equilibrium mixture at 425°C is found to consist of 1.83×10^{-3} mol/L of H_2, 3.13×10^{-3} mol/L of I_2, and 1.77×10^{-2} mol/L of HI. Calculate the equilibrium constant, *K*, for the reaction $H_2(g) + I_2(g) \rightleftarrows 2HI(g)$.
9. For the reaction $H_2(g) + I_2(g) \rightleftarrows 2HI(g)$ at 425°C, calculate [HI], given $[H_2] = [I_2] = 4.79 \times 10^{-4}$ mol/L and $K = 54.3$.

Critical Thinking

10. **INFERRING RELATIONSHIPS** Use the data from Experiment 1 in **Figure 1.4** to calculate the value of *K* for the following reaction:

$$2HI(g) \rightleftarrows H_2(g) + I_2(g)$$

Do you see a relationship between the value you obtained and the value in the table?

Answers

Practice A

1. 0.286
2. 4.9×10^{-3}
3. 4.36

Assess and Reteach ▼

Assess Use the Formative Assessment on this page to evaluate student mastery of the section.

Reteach For students who need additional instruction, download the Section Study Guide.

Response to Intervention To reassess students' mastery, use the Section Quiz, available to print or to take directly online at **HMDScience.com**.

Answers to Section Assessment

1. The rates of forward and reverse chemical reactions are equal, and the concentrations of products and reactants do not change.
2. the ratio of the mathematical product of product concentrations to the mathematical product of the reactant concentrations, each raised to a power equal to the corresponding coefficient in the balanced chemical equation
3. The larger the value of *K* is, the larger the relative amount of products.
4. the expression of product and reactant concentrations that equal an equilibrium constant, *K*
5. very large, because virtually all of the reactants have formed products
6. $K = \frac{[Cl_2]^2[H_2O]^2}{[HCl]^4[O_2]}$
7. 190
8. 54.7
9. 3.53×10^{-3} mol/L
10. 1.836×10^{-2}; it is the inverse of the value of *K* given in **Figure 1.4.**

CHEMISTRY EXPLORERS

Both Haber and Bosch received the Nobel Prize in chemistry, Haber in 1918 and Bosch in 1931.

Classroom Discussion

Atmospheric nitrogen gas is relatively unreactive because the triple bond contained in N_2 is difficult to break. Ask students to explain why lightning is another way nitrogen is fixed. Student answers might include that the extremely high temperature of lightning can break the strong triple bond in the nitrogen molecule.

This story contains a good lesson regarding the scientific process. Ask students how Nernst contributed, even though his idea proved wrong.

Chemistry EXPLORERS

Fixing the Nitrogen Problem

Historical Perspective

Each year, the chemical industry synthesizes tons of nitrogenous fertilizers, increasing agricultural production around the globe. But prior to 1915, people had to rely solely on natural resources for fertilizer, and the dwindling supply of these materials caused widespread fear of world starvation. A crisis was averted, however, through the discovery of an answer to the "nitrogen problem," a term used at the time to describe the shortage of useful nitrogen despite its abundance in the atmosphere.

The Malthusian Threat

In 1798, Thomas Malthus published his famous "Essay on Population," a report predicting that the world's food supplies could not keep up with the growing human population and that famine, death, and misery were inevitable. Malthus's warning seemed to be echoed in the 1840s by the great Irish potato famine. In fact, the rest of Europe likely would have suffered serious food shortages as well had crop yields per acre not been increased through the use of fertilizers containing nitrogen.

Few living organisms can utilize the gas that forms 78% of the atmosphere; they need nitrogen that has been combined with other elements, or "fixed," to survive.

But soils often lack enough of the microorganisms that fix nitrogen for plants, so fertilizers containing usable nitrogen compounds are added. In 1898, two-thirds of the world's supply of these compounds came from Chile, where beds of sodium nitrate, or Chile saltpeter, were abundant. But, as the chemist William Crookes emphasized in his speech to the British Association that year, these reserves were limited; it was up to his colleagues to discover alternatives and prevent Malthus's dire forecast from coming true.

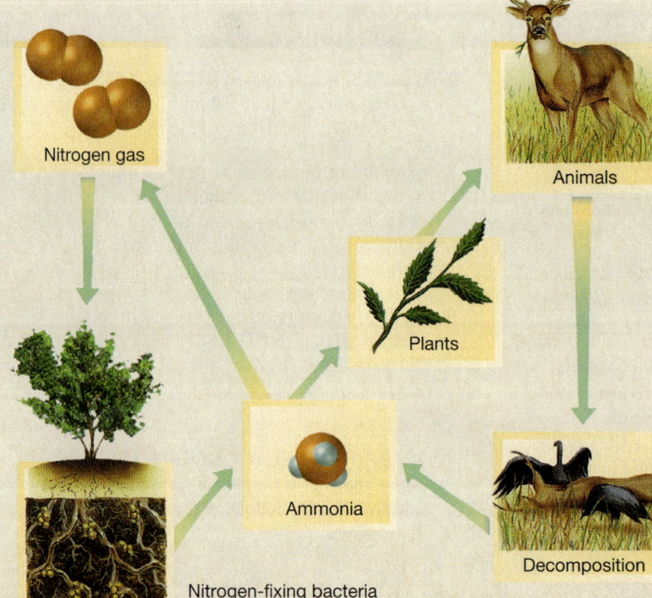

Nitrogen is released when living organisms die. It is also released from animal wastes and plant material. Some bacteria are able to break the bond holding the nitrogen molecule together, freeing the nitrogen atoms to combine with hydrogen to form ammonia. Plants can absorb the nitrogen in this form from the soil. Animals then benefit from the nitrogen by eating the plants.

562

The Haber-Nernst Controversy

As early as the 1890s, chemists had shown that ammonia, a practical source of fixed nitrogen, could be synthesized at high temperatures and at atmospheric pressure from elemental hydrogen and nitrogen. The problem was that the end product was present in such minute amounts that the process was not industrially practical.

In 1904, the German chemist Fritz Haber seemed to confirm this assessment. He tried reacting hydrogen and nitrogen at temperatures up to 1020°C using pure iron as well as other metals as a catalyst. He found that the amount of ammonia was a mere 0.005% to 0.012% at equilibrium.

Today, ammonia is produced on an industrial scale in plants like this one.

Haber had apparently closed the door on the synthesis of ammonia from its elements. But in 1906, Walther Nernst, using his new heat theorem, calculated the reaction's theoretical ammonia concentration at equilibria corresponding to several pressures. He found that his value at atmospheric pressure disagreed significantly with Haber's, and he publicly challenged Haber's values.

Haber was convinced that he was right. He ran the reaction at increased pressure to attain an amount of ammonia that could be measured more accurately.

Haber and his assistants confirmed their original findings, and Nernst later conceded a mathematical error. But more important, the new round of experiments indicated that a reasonable amount of ammonia might be attained at pressures of 200 atm (20,000 kPa) using a uranium or osmium catalyst.

Scaling Up

Large-scale equipment that could withstand such high pressures was unheard of at the time, and osmium and uranium were far too scarce to be cost-effective for industry. Nevertheless, in 1909, the German firm BASF bought the rights to Haber's findings and put its gifted chemical engineer Karl Bosch in charge of creating an industrial-scale system that would make the process profitable.

After nearly five years, Bosch and the company's chief chemist, Alwin Mittasch, succeeded in developing a suitable reactor that could handle the reaction's high pressures. They also discovered that a catalyst of iron containing small amounts of impurities was an effective replacement for the rare metals used by Haber.

An Eerie Epilogue

By September 1913, BASF was producing 20 metric tons of ammonia a day using the Haber-Bosch process. Eventually, enough ammonia was produced by the chemical industry to free Germany and the world of dependence on Chile saltpeter for fertilizer. Chemists had thwarted the Malthusian threat. Yet, the victory proved bittersweet; the new ammonia synthesis also became the basis for the production of nitric acid, used to make many of the explosives employed in the wars that rocked Europe and the rest of the globe in the first half of the twentieth century.

Questions

1. What is the major use for ammonia?
2. What did Haber find when he tried to synthesize ammonia at increased pressure?

Application

To reduce the amount of chemical fertilizers needed, agriculturists usually rotate crops, alternating a nitrogen-fixing legume crop, such as clover, beans, peas, or peanuts, with other crops. Nodules in the roots of legumes contain nitrogen-fixing bacteria that convert atmospheric nitrogen to ammonia. Recently, researchers at the University of Sydney, in Australia, have succeeded in adding nitrogen-fixing bacteria to the roots of wheat plants. Similar research is ongoing with other crops, such as corn and rice.

Teaching Tip

The Haber process for producing ammonia is dependent on the correct temperature, pressure, and catalyst.

Answers

1. as fertilizer
2. He found that a reasonable amount of ammonia could be produced from its elements at 200 atm.

SECTION 2

▼ Plan and Prepare

Objectives

Upon completion of this section, students should be able to do the following:

- Discuss the factors that disturb equilibrium.
- Discuss conditions under which reactions go to completion.
- Describe the common-ion effect.

Classroom Catalyst

A system at equilibrium is stressed by adding a reactant or product, changing the temperature, or changing the pressure. A new equilibrium is established, which counteracts the stress. Imagine people passing through a revolving door. The room on one side of the door holds 10 people, while the room on the other side holds 15 people. If a person moves from one side to the other, that room becomes overcrowded, stress is placed on the system, and the system is no longer in equilibrium. If another person moves in the opposite direction, then equilibrium is reestablished. As long as equal numbers of people move through the door from each side, equilibrium is maintained. Ask students how a chemical system in equilibrium would respond to removing one of the products. *Remind students that this is a thought experiment and should not be tried.*

▼ Teach

READING TOOLKIT

IDENTIFYING CAUSE AND EFFECT
Have students construct a three-column chart on the board titled *Shifting Equilibrium.* Label the first column *Cause,* the second column *Effect on Equilibrium,* and the third column *Effect on Equilibrium Constant.* List the three causes (changes in pressure, changes in concentration, and changes in temperature), and have students fill in the rest of the chart for each cause.

SECTION 2

Main Ideas

- Equilibrium shifts to relieve stress on the system.
- Some ionic reactions seem to go to completion.
- Common ions often produce precipitates.

Shifting Equilibrium

Key Term
common-ion effect

In systems that have attained chemical equilibrium, the relative amounts of reactants and products stay the same. But changes in pressure, concentration, or temperature can alter the equilibrium position and thereby change the relative amounts of reactants and products. By shifting an equilibrium in the desired direction, chemists can often improve the yield of the product they are seeking.

MAIN IDEA

Equilibrium shifts to relieve stress on the system.

In 1888, the French chemist Henri Louis Le Châtelier developed a principle that provides a means of predicting the influence of stress factors on equilibrium systems. Le Châtelier's principle states that *if a system at equilibrium is subjected to a stress, the equilibrium is shifted in the direction that tends to relieve the stress.* This principle is true for all dynamic equilibria, chemical as well as physical. Changes in pressure, concentration, and temperature illustrate Le Châtelier's principle.

Changes in Pressure

A change in pressure affects only equilibrium systems in which gases are involved. For changes in pressure to affect the system, the *total* number of moles of gas on the left side of the equation must be different from the *total* number of moles of gas on the right side of the equation.

Let us consider the Haber-Bosch process for the synthesis of ammonia. Note that there is a total of four molecules of gas on the reactant side of the equation and two molecules of gas on the product side of the equation.

$$N_2(g) + 3H_2(g) \rightleftarrows 2NH_3(g)$$

First, consider an increase in pressure as the applied stress. Can the system shift in a way that reduces the stress? Yes. An increase in pressure causes increases in the concentrations of all species. The system can reduce the number of molecules, and hence the total pressure, by shifting the equilibrium to the right. For each four molecules of reactants, nitrogen and hydrogen, there are two molecules of product, ammonia. By producing more NH_3, and using up N_2 and H_2, the system can reduce the total number of molecules. This leads to a decrease in pressure. Although the new equilibrium pressure is still higher than before, it is not as high as the pressure caused by the initial stress. Even though changes in pressure may shift the equilibrium position, they do not affect the value of the equilibrium constant.

Differentiated Instruction

PRE-AP

When Fritz Haber was developing the process for the synthesis of ammonia, he conducted experiments to determine how changes in temperature and pressure affected the equilibrium concentration of ammonia. Have students report on Haber's results and determine if his conclusion was valid based on the data he obtained. Ask students to prepare a table summarizing Haber's data for the class to analyze. Haber discovered that increasing the pressure shifted the equilibrium to produce more ammonia. For example, increasing the pressure from 300 atm to 500 atm at 400°C increased the percent by mass of ammonia produced at equilibrium from 48% to 61%. In contrast, raising the temperature shifted the equilibrium to reduce the amount of ammonia produced. For example, increasing the temperature from 400°C to 600°C at 300 atm reduced the mass percent of ammonia produced at equilibrium from 48% to 13%.

Ammonia produced in the Haber-Bosch process is continuously removed by condensing it to liquid ammonia. This condensation removes most of the product from the gas phase in which the reaction occurs. The resulting decrease in the partial pressure of NH_3 gas in the reaction vessel is a stress and is the same as a decrease in product concentration, which shifts the equilibrium to the right.

The introduction of an inert gas, such as helium, into the reaction vessel for the synthesis of ammonia increases the total pressure in the vessel. But it does not change the partial pressures of the reaction gases present. Therefore, increasing pressure by adding a gas that is not a reactant or a product *cannot* affect the equilibrium position of the reaction system.

Changes in Concentration

An increase in the concentration of a reactant is a stress on the equilibrium system. Consider the following hypothetical reaction.

$$A + B \rightleftarrows C + D$$

An increase in the concentration of A creates a stress. To relieve the stress, some of the added A reacts with B to form products C and D. The equilibrium is reestablished with a higher concentration of A than before the addition, but with a lower concentration of B. Similarly, an increase in the concentration of B drives the reaction to the right. An increase in the concentration of either C or D shifts the equilibrium to the left. A decrease in the concentration of C or D has the same effect on the position of the equilibrium as does an increase in the concentration of A or B; the equilibrium shifts to the right. **Figure 2.1** gives an example of such an instance by showing what effects an increase of N_2 has on the equilibrium in the Haber process.

Changes in concentration have no effect on the value of the equilibrium constant. Although concentrations of both reactants and products do change, the new concentrations give the same value of the equilibrium constant when equilibrium is reestablished.

Many chemical processes involve heterogeneous reactions in which reactants or products are in different phases. The concentrations of pure solids and liquids do not change, and by convention are not written in the equilibrium expression. Also, in a system involving acids and bases, when a solvent such as water is in an equilibrium equation, it is not included in the equilibrium expression. In an earlier chapter, the expression for K_w used this convention, and the concentration of water is not included in the expression. The reaction representing the self-ionization of water is

$$2H_2O(l) \rightleftarrows H_3O^+(aq) + OH^-(aq)$$

and the equation for K_w is $K_w = [H_3O^+][OH^-]$.

The following equation describes the equilibrium system established by the decomposition of solid calcium carbonate.

$$CaCO_3(s) \rightleftarrows CaO(s) + CO_2(g)$$

CHECK FOR UNDERSTANDING

Explain Why would increasing the pressure by using an inert gas not change the equilibrium of a reaction?

FIGURE 2.1

Concentration's Effect on Equilibrium

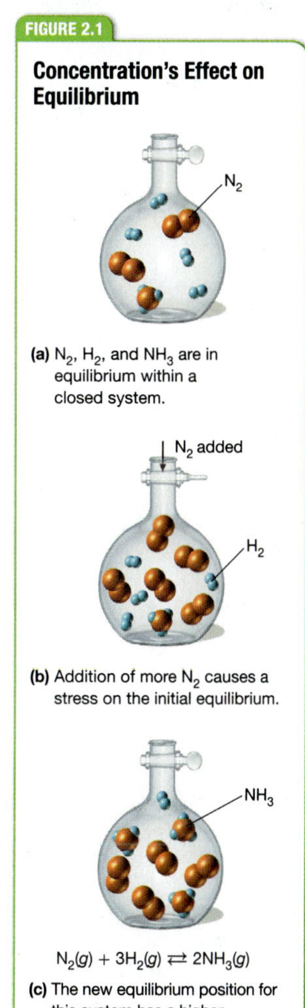

(a) N_2, H_2, and NH_3 are in equilibrium within a closed system.

(b) Addition of more N_2 causes a stress on the initial equilibrium.

$N_2(g) + 3H_2(g) \rightleftarrows 2NH_3(g)$

(c) The new equilibrium position for this system has a higher concentration of N_2, a lower concentration of H_2, and a higher concentration of NH_3 than initially.

Application

Le Châtelier's principle is applied in the bottling of carbonated soft drinks. Adding carbon dioxide to water produces carbonic acid in a reversible reaction:

$$H_2O(l) + CO_2(g) \rightleftarrows H_2CO_3(aq)$$

The beverages are bottled under increased pressure, placing stress on the equilibrium, which shifts to the right to reduce the stress on the system. When the bottle is opened, the pressure is reduced. The reaction is forced to the left, and CO_2 forms and comes out of solution.

Misconception Alert

Students generally master the concept that increases of pressure affect equilibrium, but they often misapply it to all pressure changes. In gaseous systems, the only situations affected by such imposed changes are those in which the total numbers of reactant molecules and product molecules differ. Also, only changes in the partial pressure of a gas taking part in the reaction cause a shift. The addition or removal of some other gas has no effect, even though it changes the total pressure.

Check for Understanding

Answer: A good answer would be that adding an inert gas will change the pressure of the system, but because it is neither a reactant nor a product, it cannot affect the reaction itself.

Problem Solving

TAKE IT FURTHER

Have students write the equilibrium expression for the following reaction. Solid phosphorus pentachloride decomposes to form phosphorus trichloride liquid and chlorine gas.

$$PCl_5(s) \rightleftarrows PCl_3(l) + Cl_2(g)$$

$$K = [Cl_2]$$

Next, ask students to write the equilibrium expression for the decomposition of solid iron(II) sulfate into solid iron(III) oxide, sulfur dioxide gas, and sulfur trioxide gas.

$$2FeSO_4(s) \rightleftarrows Fe_2O_3(s) + SO_2(g) + SO_3(g)$$

$$K = [SO_2][SO_3]$$

Misconception Alert!

Some students have difficulty differentiating between the concepts of equilibrium and equality. Refer back to the analogy used in the "Classroom Catalyst" for this section. The rooms on either side of the revolving door did not hold equal numbers of people, just as a reaction may favor one direction more than the other. As long as equal numbers of people are exchanged from side to side, so that neither side is under stress, the system maintains equilibrium.

Classroom Discussion

Point out that the final conditions established for an equilibrium reaction must take into account not only kinetics but also thermodynamics. Have students explain how this can be demonstrated in the Haber process. Students should recognize that a low temperature favors a shift in the equilibrium to the right, according to Le Châtelier's principle. However, a low temperature reduces the number of effective collisions needed to form ammonia from the reactants, according to the kinetic-molecular theory.

The products are a solid and a gas. Because both $CaCO_3$ and CaO are solids, they are not in the equilibrium constant expression. This leads to the following expression for the equilibrium constant.

$$K = [CO_2]$$

Carbon dioxide is the only substance in the system that appears in the equilibrium expression. Because the total number of moles of gas on the left side of the equation is different from the total number of moles on the right side of the equation, pressure changes will affect the equilibrium. High pressure favors the reverse reaction, which causes CO_2 molecules to react with the solid CaO to form solid $CaCO_3$. Low pressure favors the formation of CO_2 from the decomposition of $CaCO_3$. Because both CaO and $CaCO_3$ are solids, changing their amounts will not change the equilibrium concentration of CO_2.

Changes in Temperature

Reversible reactions are exothermic in one direction and endothermic in the other. Remember, equilibrium constants are for a given temperature, because changing the temperature changes the relative amounts of reactants and products.

Increasing the temperature is, in effect, the addition of energy in the form of heat. According to Le Châtelier's principle, the stress of the added heat will be lessened by shifting the equilibrium in the direction that removes heat (lowers the temperature). This means that energy must be absorbed so the reaction that is endothermic occurs until a new equilibrium is established. Likewise, the removal of energy as a result of lowering the temperature causes the exothermic reaction to take place.

The synthesis of ammonia by the Haber-Bosch process is exothermic, as indicated by the energy as heat shown on the product side of the equation.

$$N_2(g) + 3H_2(g) \rightleftarrows 2NH_3(g) + 92 \text{ kJ}$$

A high temperature favors the decomposition of ammonia, the endothermic reaction. But at low temperatures, the forward reaction is too slow to be commercially useful. The temperature used represents a compromise between kinetic and equilibrium requirements. It is high enough that equilibrium is established rapidly but low enough that the equilibrium concentration of ammonia is significant. Moderate temperature (about 500°C) and very high pressure (700–1000 atm) produce a satisfactory yield of ammonia.

The production of colorless dinitrogen tetroxide gas, N_2O_4, from dark red-brown NO_2 gas is also an exothermic reaction. **Figure 2.2** shows how temperature affects the equilibrium of this system. **Figure 2.2b** shows the NO_2/N_2O_4 equilibrium mixture at 25°C. When the temperature of the system is lowered to 0°C, the system experiences a stress (removal of energy as heat). To counteract this stress, the system shifts to the right, or in the direction of the exothermic reaction. This shift increases the amount of colorless N_2O_4 gas and decreases the amount of brown NO_2 gas, as shown in **Figure 2.2a.** Because more N_2O_4 is present, K is increased.

Problem Solving

DECONSTRUCTING PROBLEMS

Creating a table may help students to understand how various factors can shift an equilibrium. Write the following equation on the board.

$$2SO_2(g) + O_2(g) \rightarrow 2SO_3(g) \quad \Delta H = -198 \text{ kJ}$$

Have students make a three-column table. Tell them to label the left column *Change*, the middle column *Stress*, and the right column *Effect on Equilibrium.* Have them write the following give items under *Change.*

Change

$[SO_2]$ increased

$[O_2]$ decreased

$[SO_3]$ decreased

pressure increased

temperature increased

Have students complete the table based on Le Châtelier's principle.

FIGURE 2.2

Temperature Effects on Equilibrium Different temperatures can cause an equilibrium system to shift and seek a new equilibrium position.

(a) When energy as heat is taken away from the system, the exothermic reaction is favored, so more N_2O_4 is produced. N_2O_4 is colorless, so the bottle appears lighter.

0°C

(b) At increasing temperatures, more of the endothermic reaction can occur, so more of the brown NO_2 forms.

25°C

(c) At even higher temperatures, still more of the brown NO_2 forms, and the color in the bottle appears even darker.

100°C

$$2NO_2(g) \rightleftharpoons N_2O_4(g) + \text{energy as heat}$$
(brown) (colorless)

When the system is heated to 100°C, the added energy is the stress, and the equilibrium shifts to the left, or in the direction of the endothermic reaction. This shift decreases the amount of colorless N_2O_4 gas and increases the amount of brown NO_2 gas, as shown in **Figure 2.2c.** Because less N_2O_4 gas is present, K is decreased. The change in temperature changes the value of K. For any system in which the forward reaction is an exothermic reaction, increasing the temperature decreases the value of K.

For an endothermic reaction, such as the decomposition of calcium carbonate, energy as heat shows up on the reactant side of the equation.

$$556 \text{ kJ} + CaCO_3(s) \rightleftharpoons CaO(s) + CO_2(g)$$

An increase in temperature caused by adding energy to the system causes the value of K to increase and the equilibrium to shift to the right.

Catalysts speed up the rate of reactions. So what happens to equilibrium concentrations if a catalyst is present? Nothing! When a catalyst is added to an equilibrium system, it speeds up both the forward and reverse reactions. The equilibrium concentrations are achieved faster, but the concentrations and K remain the same.

MAIN IDEA

Some ionic reactions seem to go to completion.

Some reactions involving compounds formed by the chemical interaction of ions in solutions appear to go to completion in the sense that the ions are almost completely removed from solution. The extent to which reacting ions are removed from solution depends on the solubility of the compound formed and, if the compound is soluble, on the degree of ionization. Thus, a product that escapes as a gas, precipitates as a solid, or is only slightly ionized effectively removes from solution the bulk of the reacting ions that compose it.

Teaching Tip

When determining the effect of temperature change on an equilibrium, energy in the form of heat can be considered as if it is actually a reactant (in the endothermic direction) or a product (in the exothermic direction).

Alternative Assessment

On the board, write the following general equilibrium equation:

$$X(g) + 2Y(g) \rightleftharpoons Z(g) + \text{energy as heat}$$

Then, ask students to write how they think each of the imposed changes below will shift the equilibrium:

a. remove Z by continuous condensation (shift to the right)

b. introduce an inert gas (no shift)

c. decrease the volume of the container (shift to right)

d. add energy as heat (shift to left)

e. add extra Y (shift to right)

f. add a catalyst (no shift)

Differentiated Instruction

BELOW LEVEL

Be sure that students understand that energy is neither a reactant nor a product in any reaction. Ask students to identify the reactant in the equation on this page. $CaCO_3$ Then ask why the energy as heat is written as if it were a reactant. Its inclusion in chemical equations is simply a way of making it easier to apply Le Châtelier's principle. Point out that placing energy in the equation makes it easier to see where stress is placed when energy is added or when energy is removed.

▼ Teach *continued*

Application

Water softeners remove ions from "hard" water. The ions responsible for hardness are Ca^{2+} and Mg^{2+}. They react with soaps to produce precipitates (the bathtub ring). The Mg^{2+} and Ca^{2+} ions are replaced by Na^+ ions, which are on a resin inside the water softener. When the Na^+ ions on the resin are depleted, the resin can be regenerated with a concentrated NaCl solution. During regeneration, the Na^+ ions in solution can displace Mg^{2+} and Ca^{2+} ions on the resin. This represents a practical application of Le Châtelier's principle.

TEACH FROM VISUALS

FIGURE 2.3 Have students note the various species shown in the diagrams. Ask them to follow the precipitation process that is occurring and to describe it in terms of equilibrium principles.

Check for Understanding

Answer: Formation of a gas or precipitate would affect the equilibrium of a reaction. It would effectively remove some of the reactants, as the products are no longer able to participate in the reaction.

CHECK FOR UNDERSTANDING
Explain Why would formation of a gas or a precipitate stop a reversible reaction from remaining in equilibrium?

Formation of a Gas

Reactions that form a gas as a product are one example of reactions that go to completion. When a strong acid is added to an aqueous solution of baking soda, or sodium bicarbonate, carbon dioxide is formed. The net ionic equation shows that ions are removed.

$$H_3O^+ + HCO_3^- \rightarrow 2H_2O(l) + CO_2(g)$$

This reaction goes practically to completion because one of the products, CO_2, escapes as a gas if the container is open to the air.

Formation of a Precipitate

When solutions of sodium chloride and silver nitrate are mixed, a white precipitate of silver chloride immediately forms, as shown in **Figure 2.3.** The overall ionic equation for this reaction follows.

$$Na^+(aq) + Cl^-(aq) + Ag^+(aq) + NO_3^-(aq) \rightarrow Na^+(aq) + NO_3^-(aq) + AgCl(s)$$

If chemically equivalent amounts of the two solutes are mixed, only Na^+ ions and NO_3^- ions remain in solution in appreciable quantities. Almost all of the Ag^+ ions and Cl^- ions combine and separate from the solution as a precipitate of AgCl. The reason is that AgCl is only very slightly soluble in water. The solution is now a saturated solution of AgCl. Thus, the reaction effectively goes to completion, because an essentially insoluble product is formed.

FIGURE 2.3

Precipitate Formation When a clear sodium chloride solution is combined with a clear solution of silver nitrate, an insoluble white precipitate of silver chloride is formed.

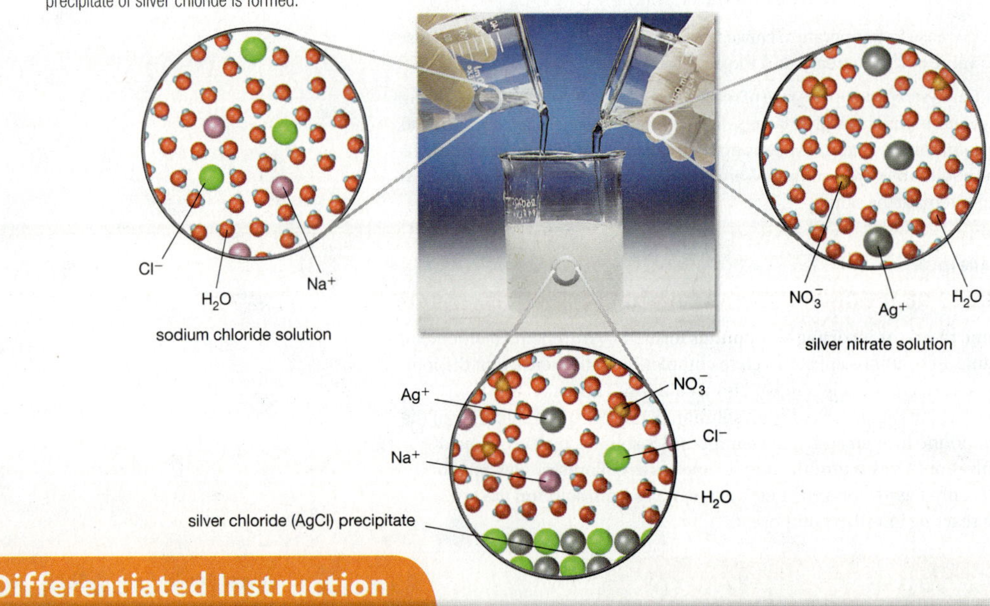

Differentiated Instruction

BELOW LEVEL

Ask students why an equilibrium expression cannot be written for either of the two reactions described on this page.

Students should recognize that neither reaction establishes a dynamic equilibrium. As a result, a *K* value cannot be determined for either reaction or for any reaction that goes to completion.

Formation of a Slightly Ionized Product

Neutralization reactions between H_3O^+ ions from aqueous acids and OH^- ions from aqueous bases result in the formation of water molecules, which are only slightly ionized. A reaction between HCl and NaOH illustrates this process. Aqueous HCl supplies H_3O^+ ions and Cl^- ions to the solution, and aqueous NaOH supplies Na^+ ions and OH^- ions, as shown in the following overall ionic equation:

$$H_3O^+(aq) + Cl^-(aq) + Na^+(aq) + OH^-(aq) \longrightarrow Na^+(aq) + Cl^-(aq) + 2H_2O(l)$$

Neglecting the spectator ions, the net ionic equation is as follows:

$$H_3O^+(aq) + OH^-(aq) \longrightarrow 2H_2O(l)$$

Because it is only slightly ionized, the water exists almost entirely as molecules. Thus, hydronium ions and hydroxide ions are almost entirely removed from the solution. The reaction effectively goes to completion because the product is only slightly ionized.

MAIN IDEA

Common ions often produce precipitates.

An equilibrium reaction may be driven in the desired direction by applying Le Châtelier's principle. Suppose hydrogen chloride gas is bubbled into a saturated solution of sodium chloride. Hydrogen chloride is extremely soluble in water, and it is completely ionized.

$$HCl(g) + H_2O(l) \longrightarrow H_3O^+(aq) + Cl^-(aq)$$

The equilibrium for a saturated solution of sodium chloride is described by the following equation.

$$NaCl(s) \rightleftarrows Na^+(aq) + Cl^-(aq)$$

As the hydrogen chloride dissolves in sufficient quantity, it increases the concentration of Cl^- ions in the solution, which is a stress on the equilibrium system. The system can compensate, according to Le Châtelier's principle, by combining some of the added Cl^- ions with an equivalent amount of Na^+ ions. This causes some solid NaCl to precipitate out, relieving the stress of added chloride. The new equilibrium has a greater concentration of Cl^- ions but a decreased concentration of Na^+ ions. However, the product of $[Na^+]$ and $[Cl^-]$ still has the same value as before. **This phenomenon, in which the addition of an ion common to two solutes brings about precipitation or reduced ionization, is an example of the common-ion effect.**

The common-ion effect is also observed when one ion species of a weak electrolyte is added in excess to a solution. Acetic acid, CH_3COOH, is such an electrolyte. A 0.1 M CH_3COOH solution is only about 1.3% ionized as hydronium ions and acetate ions, CH_3COO^-. The ionic equilibrium is shown by the following equation:

$$CH_3COOH(aq) + H_2O(l) \rightleftarrows H_3O^+(aq) + CH_3COO^-(aq)$$

Demonstration

THE COMMON-ION EFFECT

Demonstrate the example of the common-ion effect shown on this page. In advance, prepare a saturated NaCl solution by placing **50 g of sodium chloride** in a **beaker** containing **100 mL of water.** Stir, and let stand overnight. To ensure that saturation is reached, stir again the next morning and then allow the solution to settle. Some solid should remain in the bottom of the beaker. In class, show students the beaker of solution and then carefully pour off some of the liquid into a **large test tube.** Add **concentrated hydrochloric acid** dropwise, using a **dropper.**

Caution Be careful when handling the concentrated acid. In case of spills, first dilute with water. Then, while wearing **disposable gloves,** mop the spill with **wet cloths or a wet cloth mop** designated for spill cleanup.

Ask students to explain why solid NaCl precipitates. Student responses should mention the common-ion effect or Le Châtelier's principle.

Safety Wear **goggles, gloves,** and an **apron,** and do not allow students to stand too close.

Disposal Dilute with **tap water** and pour down the drain.

PRE-AP

Have students explain the following data.

solubility of Ag_2CrO_4 in pure water $= 1.3 \times 10^{-4}$ mol/L

solubility of Ag_2CrO_4 in 0.100 M $AgNO_3$ $= 9.0 \times 10^{-10}$ mol/L

The solubility of silver chromate is much less in a solution of silver nitrate, due to the common-ion effect. Here, Ag^+ is the common ion. Explain that the solubility of a solid is lower in a solution that contains ions present in the solid due to the common-ion effect.

▼ Teach *continued*

TEACH FROM VISUALS

FIGURE 2.4 Use molecular models to show students what is happening in the solutions. Have students explain what is happening in terms of the common-ion effect and Le Châtelier's principle.

Teaching Tip

The explanation for the basicity of a sodium acetate solution is given in Section 3.

▼ Assess and Reteach

Assess Use the Formative Assessment on this page to evaluate student mastery of the section.

Reteach For students who need additional instruction, download the Section Study Guide.

Response to Intervention To reassess students' mastery, use the Section Quiz, available to print or to take directly online at **HMDScience.com**.

FIGURE 2.4

Common-Ion Effect The solution of CH_3COOH on the left is combined with the solution of $NaCH_3COO$ in the center. Both contain the common ion CH_3COO^-. They produce the solution on the right, which is only slightly acidic due to the decreased ionization of the acid. The colors of the solutions are due to the addition of an acid-base indicator.

Addition of sodium acetate, $NaCH_3COO$ (an ionic salt soluble in water), to a solution containing acetic acid increases the acetate ion concentration. The equilibrium then shifts in the direction that uses up some of the added acetate ions in accordance with Le Châtelier's principle. More molecules of acetic acid are formed, and the concentration of hydronium ions is reduced. In general, the addition of a salt with an ion in common with the weak electrolyte reduces the ionization of the electrolyte. **Figure 2.4** shows a 0.25 M CH_3COOH solution on the left that has a pH of about 2.7. Mixing that with the 0.10 M $NaCH_3COO$ solution in the center produces the solution on the right, which has a pH of about 4.5, indicating lower $[H_3O^+]$ and thus lowered acetic acid ionization.

SECTION 2 FORMATIVE ASSESSMENT

Reviewing Main Ideas

1. Name three ways the chemical equilibrium can be disturbed.

2. Describe three situations in which ionic reactions go to completion.

3. Describe the common-ion effect.

4. Identify the common ion in each of the following situations.

a. 5 g of NaCl is added to a 2.0 M solution of HCl

b. 50 mL of 1.0 M $NaCH_3COO$ is added to 1.0 M CH_3COOH

c. 1 g of NH_4Cl is added to 100 mL of aqueous NH_3

5. Predict the effect that decreasing pressure would have on each of the following reaction systems at equilibrium.

a. $H_2(g) + Cl_2(g) \rightleftarrows 2HCl(g)$

b. $NH_4Cl(s) \rightleftarrows NH_3(g) + HCl(g)$

c. $2H_2O_2(aq) \rightleftarrows 2H_2O(l) + O_2(g)$

d. $3O_2(g) \rightleftarrows 2O_3(g)$

Critical Thinking

6. PREDICTING OUTCOMES Carbon dioxide and water react to form bicarbonate ion and hydronium ion. Hyperventilation (rapid breathing) causes more carbon dioxide to be exhaled than normal. How will hyperventilation affect the pH of blood? Explain.

Answers to Section Assessment

1. change in concentration, pressure, or temperature

2. formation of gas, a precipitate, or a slightly ionized product

3. The addition of an ion common to two solutes brings about precipitation or reduced ionization.

4. a. Cl^-

b. CH_3COO^-

c. NH_4^+

5. a. no effect

b. shift to the right

c. shift to the right

d. shift to the left

6. The pH will increase. Because carbon dioxide is being lost, bicarbonate ion and hydronium ion combine to replace the lost CO_2, so the solution becomes less acidic.

Equilibria of Acids, Bases, and Salts

SECTION 3

Main Ideas

- The ionization constant is a measure of acid and base strength in solution.
- Buffers resist changes in pH.
- Water reaches equilibrium at a very low level of ionization.
- Hydrolysis of anions and cations produces non-neutral solutions.

Key Terms
acid ionization constant
buffered solution
hydrolysis

MAIN IDEA

The ionization constant is a measure of acid and base strength in solution.

About 1.3% of the solute molecules in a 0.1 M acetic acid solution are ionized at room temperature. The remaining 98.7% of the acetic acid molecules, CH_3COOH, remain nonionized. Thus, the solution contains three species of particles in equilibrium: CH_3COOH molecules, H_3O^+ ions, and acetate ions, CH_3COO^-. From the equilibrium equation for the ionization of acetic acid, the equilibrium constant equation can be written.

$$CH_3COOH + H_2O \rightleftarrows H_3O^+ + CH_3COO^-$$

$$K = \frac{[H_3O^+][CH_3COO^-]}{[CH_3COOH][H_2O]}$$

Notice that the concentration of water is not included in the equilibrium expression. The reason is that water is the solvent, and water molecules greatly exceed the number of acetic acid molecules. Without introducing a measurable error, one can assume that the molar concentration of H_2O molecules remains constant in such a solution. Thus, because both K and $[H_2O]$ are constant, the product $K[H_2O]$ is constant.

$$K[H_2O] = \frac{[H_3O^+][CH_3COO^-]}{[CH_3COOH]}$$

The left side of the equation can be simplified by setting $K[H_2O] = K_a$.

$$K_a = \frac{[H_3O^+][CH_3COO^-]}{[CH_3COOH]}$$

The term K_a is called the **acid ionization constant.** The acid ionization constant, K_a, like the equilibrium constant, K, is constant for a specified temperature but has a new value for each new temperature.

The acid ionization constant for a weak acid represents a small value. To determine the numerical value of the ionization constant for acetic acid at a specific temperature, the equilibrium concentrations of H_3O^+ ions, CH_3COO^- ions, and CH_3COOH molecules must be known. The ionization of a molecule of CH_3COOH in water yields one H_3O^+ ion and one CH_3COO^- ion. These concentrations can therefore be found experimentally by measuring the pH of the solution.

Differentiated Instruction

BELOW LEVEL

Explain that the acid ionization constant is just an example of a specific equilibrium expression. The same rules for writing the equilibrium expression apply. For a weak acid, the K value shows the concentrations of the reactants and products at equilibrium as the weak acid ionizes. The subscript in the equilibrium constant, K_a, indicates that the value applies to the equilibrium expression of an acid. Have students predict what K_b represents. the equilibrium constant for a weak base

SECTION 3

Plan and Prepare ▼

Objectives

Upon completion of this section, students should be able to do the following:

- Explain the concept of acid ionization constants, and write acid ionization equilibrium expressions.
- Review the ionization constant of water.
- Explain buffering.
- Compare cation and anion hydrolysis.

Classroom Catalyst

Measure the pH of 0.10 M HCl and the pH of 0.10 M CH_3COOH. Compare the results. Ask students to try to explain the difference in the pH. Repeat this exercise with 0.10 M NaOH and 0.10 M NH_3 solution.

Teach ▼

ChemisTrivia

The phrase *acetic acid* comes from the Latin word *acetum*, which means "vinegar." Acetic acid is the acid that gives vinegar its sour taste.

READING TOOLKIT

READING ORGANIZER Have students read the section and then organize the ideas presented in the section in the form of a concept map. Concept maps should include ionization constants and hydrolysis reactions.

▼ **Teach** *continued*

Teaching Tip

Small equilibrium constants indicate equilibria that favor the reactants. Therefore, K_a values for weak acids, which are only partially dissociated, are all much less than 1.0.

TEACH FROM TABLES

FIGURE 3.1 Draw attention to the near constancy of K_a values for acetic acid. Ask students to note that the concentrations of both the hydronium ion (and, logically, the acetate ion) and acetic acid decrease as molarity decreases. Because both the numerator and the denominator of the equilibrium expression decrease, the overall ratio, K_a, remains the same.

FIGURE 3.1

IONIZATION OF ACETIC ACID

Molarity	% ionized	$[H_3O^+]$	$[CH_3COOH]$	K_a
0.100	1.33	0.00133	0.0987	1.79×10^{-5}
0.0500	1.89	0.000945	0.0491	1.82×10^{-5}
0.0100	4.17	0.000417	0.00958	1.81×10^{-5}
0.00500	5.86	0.000293	0.00471	1.82×10^{-5}
0.00100	12.6	0.000126	0.000874	1.82×10^{-5}

FIGURE 3.2

Buffered Solution

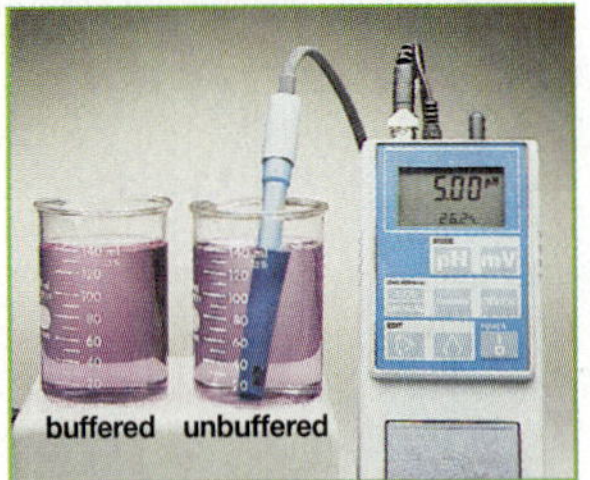

(a) The beaker on the left contains a buffered solution and an indicator and has a pH of about 5. The beaker on the right contains mostly water with a trace amount of acid and an indicator. The pH meter shows a pH of 5.00 for this solution.

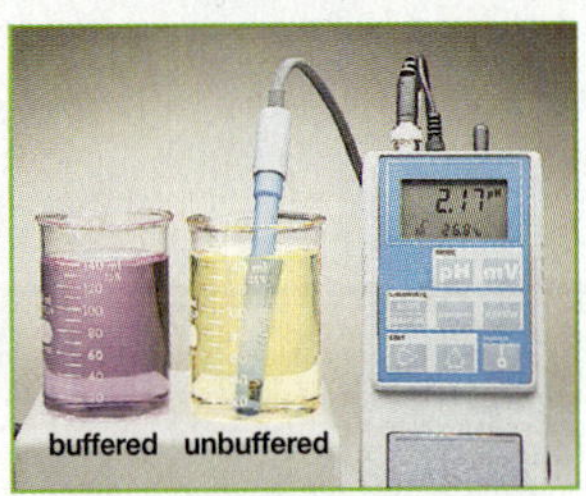

(b) After 5 mL of 0.10 M HCl is added to both beakers, the beaker on the left does not change color, indicating no substantial change in its pH. However, the beaker on the right undergoes a definite color change, and the pH meter shows a pH of 2.17.

Ionization data and constants for some dilute acetic acid solutions at 25°C are given in **Figure 3.1.** Notice that the numerical value of K_a is almost identical for each solution molarity shown. The numerical value of K_a for CH_3COOH at 25°C can be determined by substituting numerical values for concentration into the equilibrium equation.

$$K_a = \frac{[H_3O^+][CH_3COO^-]}{[CH_3COOH]}$$

At constant temperature, an increase in the concentration of CH_3COO^- ions through the addition of sodium acetate, $NaCH_3COO$, disturbs the equilibrium, as predicted by Le Châtelier's principle. This disturbance causes a decrease in $[H_3O^+]$ and an increase in $[CH_3COOH]$. Eventually, the equilibrium is reestablished with the *same* value of K_a. But there is a higher concentration of nonionized acetic acid molecules and a lower concentration of H_3O^+ ions than before the extra CH_3COO^- was added. Changes in the hydronium ion concentration affect pH. In this example, the reduction in $[H_3O^+]$ means an increase in the pH of the solution.

MAIN IDEA

Buffers resist changes in pH.

The solution just described contains both a weak acid, CH_3COOH, and a salt of the weak acid, $NaCH_3COO$. The solution can react with either an acid or a base. When small amounts of acids or bases are added, the pH of the solution remains nearly constant. The weak acid and the common ion, CH_3COO^-, act as a "buffer" against significant changes in the pH of the solution. **Because it can resist changes in pH, this solution is a buffered solution. Figure 3.2** shows how a buffered and an unbuffered solution react to the addition of an acid.

Suppose a small amount of acid is added to the acetic acid–sodium acetate solution. Acetate ions react with most of the added hydronium ions to form nonionized acetic acid molecules.

$$CH_3COO^-(aq) + H_3O^+(aq) \rightarrow CH_3COOH(aq) + H_2O(l)$$

The hydronium ion concentration and the pH of the solution remain practically unchanged.

Problem Solving

ALTERNATIVE APPROACHES

Tell students that the K_a value can be calculated by knowing just the concentration of a weak acid and its percent ionization. For example, tell students that 3.7% of a 0.100 M aqueous solution of lactic acid ionizes. The ionization of lactic acid is shown by the following equation.

$$HC_3H_5O_3(aq) \rightleftharpoons H^+(aq) + C_3H_5O^-(aq)$$

Have students find out how the K_a value is calculated from the information given. Students should set up the K_a expression and then calculate the concentration of $H^+(aq)$, based on the information that 3.7% of a 0.100 M aqueous solution ionizes.

$$[H^+] = 3.7 \times 10^{-3}\ M$$

This is also the concentration of $C_3H_5O^-(aq)$. Therefore, the K_a is calculated as follows.

$$K_a = \frac{(3.7 \times 10^{-3})(3.7 \times 10^{-3})}{0.10} = 1.4 \times 10^{-4}$$

Notice that the assumption is made that any change in $[HC_3H_5O_3(aq)]$ is insignificant in view of the very small percent ionization.

Suppose a small amount of a base is added to the original solution. The OH^- ions of the base react with and remove hydronium ions to form nonionized water molecules. Acetic acid molecules then ionize and mostly replace the hydronium ions neutralized by the added OH^- ions.

$$CH_3COOH(aq) + H_2O(l) \rightarrow H_3O^+(aq) + CH_3COO^-(aq)$$

The pH of the solution again remains practically unchanged.

A solution of a weak base containing a salt of the base behaves in a similar manner. The hydroxide ion concentration and the pH of the solution remain essentially constant with small additions of acids or bases. Suppose a base is added to an aqueous solution of ammonia that also contains ammonium chloride. Ammonium ions donate a proton to the added hydroxide ions to form nonionized water molecules.

$$NH_4^+(aq) + OH^-(aq) \rightarrow NH_3(aq) + H_2O(l)$$

If a small amount of an acid is added to the solution instead, hydroxide ions from the solution accept protons from the added hydronium ions to form nonionized water molecules. Ammonia molecules in the solution then ionize and mostly replace the hydroxide ions neutralized by added H_3O^+.

$$NH_3(aq) + H_2O(l) \rightarrow NH_4^+(aq) + OH^-(aq)$$

Buffer action has many important applications in chemistry and physiology. Human blood is naturally buffered to maintain a pH of between 7.3 and 7.5. This is essential, because large changes in pH would lead to serious disturbances of normal body functions. **Figure 3.3** shows an example of one of the many medicines buffered to prevent large and potentially damaging changes in pH.

FIGURE 3.3

Buffers Many consumer products are buffered to protect the body from potentially harmful pH changes.

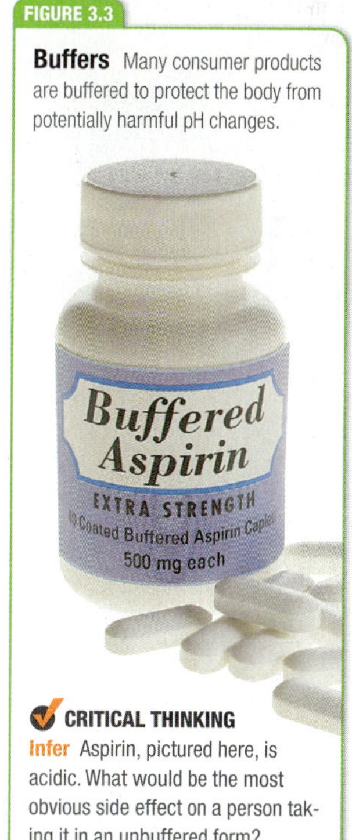

CRITICAL THINKING

Infer Aspirin, pictured here, is acidic. What would be the most obvious side effect on a person taking it in an unbuffered form?

MAIN IDEA

Water reaches equilibrium at a very low level of ionization.

In the chapter "Acid-Base Titration and pH," you learned that the self-ionization of water is an equilibrium reaction.

$$H_2O(l) + H_2O(l) \rightleftarrows H_3O^+(aq) + OH^-(aq)$$

Equilibrium is established with a very low concentration of H_3O^+ and OH^- ions. The expression for the equilibrium constant, $K_w = [H_3O^+][OH^-]$, is derived from the balanced chemical equation. The numerical value of K_w, obtained experimentally, is 1.0×10^{-14} at 25°C.

The self-ionization of water may seem inconsequential at first, since the percent of ionization is very low and the resulting product neutral; however, it has a major impact on the equilibrium achieved in the aqueous solutions of salts. Because salts dissociate into their constituent ions when dissolved, these ions can, and often do, interact with the ions produced by water's self-ionization. The result is a solution that can be acidic, basic, or neutral depending on how the equilibrium shifts to accommodate the ions.

Application

Aspirin, or acetylsalicylic acid, is often buffered because the acid it contains can irritate the stomach by lowering the pH of stomach fluids (or gastric juices). Buffering involves the use of the salts of a weak acid whose anion can combine with the extra H^+ that is produced by the aspirin.

Alternative Assessment

Have students examine the equations on this page and identify the conjugate Brønsted acids and bases in each. They should explain their reasoning in each case.

Teaching Tip

Remind students that the *ion product* constant for water is $K_w = [H_3O^+][OH^-]$.

Misconception Alert!

Students often think buffers *prevent* a change in pH. This is not true. Any time an acid or base is added to a solution, the pH changes. But a buffer minimizes the change because the buffer has two components—one to mostly neutralize any added acid, and the other to mostly neutralize any added base.

Critical Thinking

Answer: Answers will vary. Some students may answer that the person's pain will go away. A good answer would be that the acid in its unbuffered form would eventually increase acid in the person's stomach and cause damage to its lining.

DECONSTRUCTING PROBLEMS

Write the following general equation on the board.

$$OH^- + HX \longrightarrow X^- + H_2O$$

Use this equation to show how a buffer that contains a weak acid (HX) and its conjugate base (X^-) works to prevent a significant increase in pH when OH^- is added.

The weak acid ionizes: $HX \longrightarrow H^+ + X^-$

The H^+ then reacts with the added OH^-:

$$H^+ + OH^- \longrightarrow H_2O$$

The OH^- ions are replaced by the conjugate base (X^- anions) in solution. Explain how the same buffer works to prevent a significant decrease in pH when H^+ is added.

The weak acid ionizes: $HX \longrightarrow H^+ + X^-$

The X^- then reacts with the added H^+:

$$H^+ + X^- \longrightarrow HX$$

Point out that the added H^+ reacts with X^- to form a weak acid. The pH of a buffered solution actually depends on the ratio $[HX]/[X^-]$. The change in this ratio is very small, thus resulting in only a slight change in pH.

▼ Teach *continued*

Teaching Tip

The salt of a strong acid and a weak base is acidic. The salt of a strong base and a weak acid is basic. The salt of a strong acid and a strong base is neutral.

Misconception Alert!

Many students confuse hydrolysis and hydration. Point out that *hydrolysis* is a chemical reaction in which water molecules are changed to produce hydronium or hydroxide ions. *Hydration* is part of an aqueous solution process in which water surrounds solute particles.

MAIN IDEA

Hydrolysis of anions and cations produces non-neutral solutions.

Salts are formed during neutralization reactions between acids and bases. When a salt dissolves in water, it produces positive ions (cations) of the base from which it was formed and negative ions (anions) of the acid from which it was formed. Therefore, the solution might be expected to be neutral. The aqueous solutions of some salts, such as NaCl and KNO_3, are neutral, having a pH of 7. However, when sodium carbonate dissolves in water, the resulting solution turns red litmus paper blue, indicating a pH greater than 7. Ammonium chloride produces an aqueous solution that turns blue litmus paper red, indicating a pH less than 7. Salts formed from combining strong or weak acids and bases are shown in **Figure 3.4.**

The variation in pH values can be accounted for by examining the ions formed when each of these salts dissociates. If the ions formed are from weak acids or bases, they react chemically with the water molecules, and the pH of the solution will have a value other than 7. **A reaction between water molecules and ions of a dissolved salt is hydrolysis.** If the anions react with water, the process is anion hydrolysis and results in a more basic solution. If the cations react with water molecules, the process is cation hydrolysis and results in a more acidic solution.

Anion Hydrolysis

In the Brønsted sense, the anion of the salt is the conjugate base of the acid from which it was formed. It is also a proton acceptor. If the acid is weak, its conjugate base (the anion) will be strong enough to remove protons from some water molecules, proton donors, to form OH^- ions.

FIGURE 3.4

Hydrolysis The universal indicator shows that the pH of salt solutions varies, depending on the strength of the acid and the base that formed the salt.

(a) NaCl is formed from a strong acid and a strong base; the color of the indicator shows the pH is neutral.

(b) The indicator shows the pH of the sodium acetate solution is basic. This was formed from a strong base and a weak acid.

(c) The strong acid and weak base combination in ammonium chloride produces an acidic solution, as shown by the reddish tint of the indicator.

(d) The weak acid and weak base that form ammonium acetate are of comparable strength. A solution of ammonium acetate is essentially neutral.

Differentiated Instruction

INCLUSION

Help visual learners understand why some salts do not affect the pH of a solution. Pour some distilled water into a beaker and measure its pH. Dissolve some NaCl in the water and again measure its pH. Students should see that there has been no change in the pH value after the NaCl dissolved. Write the dissociation process for NaCl on the board.

$$NaCl(s) \longrightarrow Na^+(aq) + Cl^-(aq)$$

Point out that neither the cation nor the anion reacts with water. They are merely solvated.

An equilibrium is established in which the net effect of the anion hydrolysis is an increase in the hydroxide ion concentration, $[OH^-]$, of the solution.

The equilibrium equation for a typical weak acid in water, HA, forming hydronium ion and an anion, A^-, is as follows:

$$HA(aq) + H_2O(l) \rightleftarrows H_3O^+(aq) + A^-(aq)$$

From this equation, the generalized expression for K_a can be written. Note that as before, water does not appear in the general equilibrium equation.

$$K_a = \frac{[H_3O^+][A^-]}{[HA]}$$

The hydrolysis reaction between water and the anion, A^-, that is produced by the ionization of the weak acid, HA, is represented by the general equilibrium equation that follows:

$$A^-(aq) + H_2O(l) \rightleftarrows HA(aq) + OH^-(aq)$$

Neutral water has equal concentrations of H_3O^+ and OH^-. Since HA is a weak acid, the anion A^- has a strong attraction for protons. Adding A^- to water in effect attracts (removes) H_3O^+ in water to form HA. This causes OH^- to increase relative to H_3O^+ as represented in the equation above. The lower the value of K_a, the stronger the attraction A^- will have for protons and the larger the concentration of OH^-. In other words, the weaker the acid, HA, the stronger its conjugate base, A^-.

Aqueous solutions of sodium carbonate are strongly basic. The sodium ions, Na^+, in sodium carbonate do not undergo hydrolysis in aqueous solution, but the carbonate ions, CO_3^{2-}, react as a Brønsted base. A CO_3^{2-} anion acquires a proton from a water molecule to form the weak Brønsted acid, HCO_3^-, and the OH^- ion.

$$CO_3^{2-}(aq) + H_2O(l) \rightleftarrows HCO_3^-(aq) + OH^-(aq)$$

The OH^- ion concentration increases until equilibrium is established. Consequently, the H_3O^+ ion concentration decreases so that the product $[H_3O^+][OH^-]$ remains equal to the ionization constant, K_w, of water at the temperature of the solution. Thus, the pH is *higher* than 7, and the solution is basic.

Cation Hydrolysis

In the Brønsted sense, the cation of the salt is the conjugate acid of the base from which it was formed. It is also a proton donor. If the base is weak, the cation is an acid strong enough to donate a proton to a water molecule, a proton acceptor, to form H_3O^+ ions. An equilibrium is established in which the net effect of the cation hydrolysis is an increase in the hydronium ion concentration, $[H_3O^+]$, of the solution.

CROSS-DISCIPLINARY CONNECTION

Blood Buffers S.T.E.M.

Blood normally has a pH of 7.4. If the pH of blood in a human rises above 7.8 or falls below 7.0, this change in pH is usually fatal. The primary buffer in blood is the carbonic acid–bicarbonate ion system, $CO_2(g) + H_2O(l) \rightleftarrows H_2CO_3(aq) + HCO_3^-(aq)$. A condition called *respiratory acidosis* causes the pH to drop. It is the result of *hypoventilation*, or slowed breathing, the opposite of hyperventilation. Hypoventilation can be caused by congestive heart failure, pneumonia, or narcotics. Because breathing is slowed, carbon dioxide accumulates, and its concentration rises. This change causes a shift in the equilibrium to the right due to Le Châtelier's principle, and the blood becomes more acidic because of the higher concentration of carbonic acid.

CHECK FOR UNDERSTANDING

Explain In the Cross-Disciplinary feature, "Blood Buffers," above, *hypo*ventilation is described as the opposite of *hyper*ventilation. Based on information in the feature, explain why one treatment for hyperventilation is breathing with a paper bag placed over the mouth and nose.

ENGLISH LEARNERS

Explain anion hydrolysis in terms of a cause-and-effect relationship. First review the meaning of *cause and effect* and give a simple example. Then write the following equation on the board:

$$NaC_2H_3O_2(s) \longrightarrow Na^+(aq) + C_2H_3O^{-2}(aq)$$

Point out that water causes the dissociation of sodium acetate, which releases acetate anions into solution (the effect). Next, write the equation to show what happens when the acetate anions react with water.

$$C_2H_3O^{-2}(aq) + H_2O(l) \longrightarrow HC_2H_3O_2(aq) + OH^-(aq)$$

Point out that the hydrolysis of the anions (the cause) produces hydroxide ions in solution (the effect). As a result, a solution of sodium acetate is basic.

Alternative Assessment

Refer students to the *Names of Binary Acids* table and *Names of Common Oxyacids and Oxyanions* table in the chapter on acids and bases. Have students make cards with the formula of an acid or a base on each. Then, using an acid card and a base card, have them refer to the tables to predict whether the salt formed from a reaction between the acid and base will produce an acidic, basic, or neutral solution.

Classroom Discussion

Tell students that for any salt whose cation does not undergo hydrolysis and whose anion is the conjugate base of a weak acid, the aqueous solution will be basic. Help students understand this description by using KNO_2 as an example. Have students go through the statement slowly to explain it in terms of what happens to KNO_2 in solution. Students should explain that the K^+ cation is solvated but does not undergo hydrolysis, and that the NO_2^- anion is the conjugate base of the weak acid HNO_2.

Check for Understanding

Answer: The traditional treatment for hyperventilation is to have the person place an open paper bag over his/her nose and mouth and breathe in and out. In hypoventilation, too much carbon dioxide accumulates in the lungs. In hyperventilation, there is too much oxygen and not enough carbon dioxide. By breathing in and out into an open bag, a person exhales carbon dioxide and then breathes it in again, increasing the amount of CO_2 in the blood and reducing the amount of O_2

▼ Teach continued

TEACH FROM VISUALS

FIGURE 3.5 Remind students that pH increases with increasing basicity. Ask them to define *equivalence point*, which is the point at which the moles of base added are equal to the moles of acid in the sample. Point out that at the equivalence point, the solution is basic, because the acetate anion hydrolyzes in water to produce hydroxide ions. Ask students how this graph would differ from a graph for a titration of a strong acid with a strong base.

Misconception Alert!

Students often think that the equivalence point in a titration is the point at which pH equals 7. Point out that this is the case for strong acid–strong base titrations only. In general, the equivalence point is simply the point at which the numbers of moles of acid and base are equal.

ChemisTrivia

The region of the curve on either side of 2 is referred to as the "buffer region." Because both acetic acid and sodium acetate (the product of sodium hydroxide reacting with acetic acid) are present, this solution is a buffer solution. Only when the acetic acid is essentially all reacted does the pH change dramatically.

The following equilibrium equation for a typical weak base, B, is used to derive the generalized expression for K_b, the base dissociation constant.

$$B(aq) + H_2O(l) \rightleftarrows BH^+(aq) + OH^-(aq)$$

$$K_b = \frac{[BH^+][OH^-]}{[B]}$$

The hydrolysis between water and the cation, BH^+, from the dissociation of the weak base, B, is shown by the general equilibrium equation:

$$BH^+(aq) + H_2O(l) \rightleftarrows H_3O^+(aq) + B(aq)$$

In the forward reaction, the cation BH^+ donates a proton to the water molecule to form the hydronium ion. Because H_3O^+ ions are formed, the solution must become more acidic, as shown in the equation above. The extent of H_3O^+ ion formation depends on the relative strength of the base B. The weaker the base, the greater the concentration of H_3O^+ ions will be. Therefore, the weaker the base, the stronger its conjugate acid.

Ammonium chloride, NH_4Cl, dissociates in water to produce NH_4^+ ions and Cl^- ions. Chloride ions are the conjugate base of the strong acid HCl, so they do not hydrolyze in water. Ammonium ions, however, are the conjugate acid of a weak base, NH_3. Ammonium ions donate protons to water molecules. Equilibrium is established with an increased $[H_3O^+]$, so pH is *lower* than 7.

Hydrolysis in Acid-Base Reactions

Many assume that a neutralization reaction between an acid and a base always results in a neutral solution. However, this is not necessarily the case. Hydrolysis can help explain why the end point of a neutralization reaction can occur at a pH other than 7.

FIGURE 3.5

Neutralization Curve of a Weak Acid and Strong Base At point 1, only acetic acid is present. The pH depends on the weak acid alone. At 2, there is a mixture of CH_3COOH and CH_3COO^-. Adding NaOH changes the pH slowly. At point 3, all acid has been converted to CH_3COO^-. This hydrolyzes to produce a slightly basic solution. At 4, the pH is due to the excess OH^- that has been added.

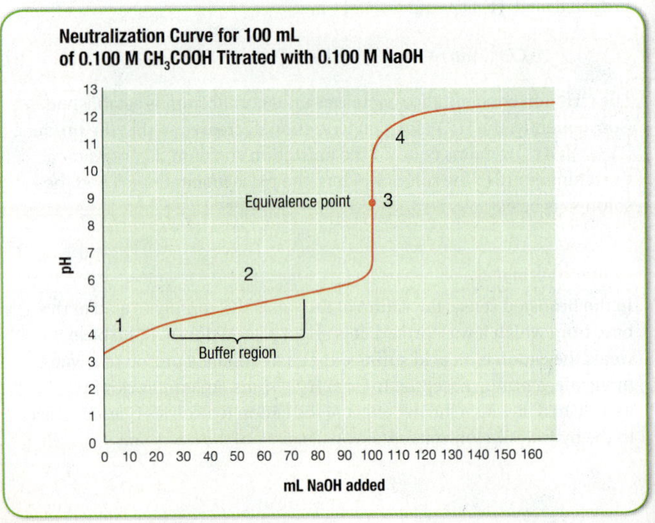

Differentiated Instruction

BELOW LEVEL

Explain cation hydrolysis in terms of a cause-and-effect relationship. Write the following equation on the board.

$$NH_4Cl(s) \longrightarrow NH_4^+(aq) + Cl^-(aq)$$

Point out that water causes the dissociation of ammonium chloride, which releases ammonium cations into solution (the effect).

Next, write the equation to show what happens when the ammonium cations react with water.

$$NH_4^+(aq) + H_2O(l) \longrightarrow NH_3(aq) + H_3O^+(aq)$$

Point out that the hydrolysis of the cations (the cause) produces hydronium ions in solution (the effect). As a result, a solution of ammonium chloride is acidic.

The hydrolysis properties of salts are determined by the relative strengths of the acids and bases from which the salts form. We can place these salts into four general categories: strong acid–strong base, strong acid–weak base, weak acid–strong base, and weak acid–weak base.

Salts of strong acids and strong bases produce neutral solutions because neither the cation of a strong base nor the anion of a strong acid hydrolyzes appreciably in aqueous solutions. An example of this is the reaction between HCl(*aq*), which is a strong acid, and NaOH(*aq*), which is a strong base. Neither the Na^+ cation of the strong base nor the Cl^- anion of the strong acid undergoes hydrolysis in water solutions. Therefore, aqueous solutions of NaCl are neutral. KNO_3 is the salt of the strong acid HNO_3 and the strong base KOH, and, in solution, also has a pH close to 7.

Aqueous solutions of salts formed from weak acids and strong bases are basic at the equivalence point (see **Figure 3.5**). Anions of the dissolved salt are hydrolyzed by the water molecules, and the pH of the solution is raised, indicating that the hydroxide-ion concentration has increased. Aqueous solutions of sodium acetate, $NaCH_3COO$, are basic. The acetate ions, CH_3COO^-, undergo hydrolysis because they are the anions of the weak acid acetic acid. The cations of the salt are from a strong base, NaOH, and do not hydrolyze, because NaOH is 100% dissociated.

Figure 3.6 shows that salts of strong acids and weak bases are acidic at the equivalence point. Cations of the dissolved salt are hydrolyzed in the water solvent, and the pH of the solution is lowered, indicating that the hydronium ion concentration has increased. In this case, the cations of the salt undergo hydrolysis because they are the positive ions from a weak base. The anions of the salt are the negative ions from a strong acid and do not hydrolyze appreciably. Ammonium chloride, NH_4Cl, is a salt that produces an acidic solution.

FIGURE 3.6

Neutralization Curve of a Strong Acid and a Weak Base At point 1 on the titration curve, only aqueous ammonia is present. The pH is determined by the base alone. At 2, there is a mixture of NH_3 and NH_4^+. Adding HCl changes the pH slowly. At point 3, all aqueous ammonia has been converted to NH_4^+. At 4, the pH is determined by the excess H_3O^+ that is being added.

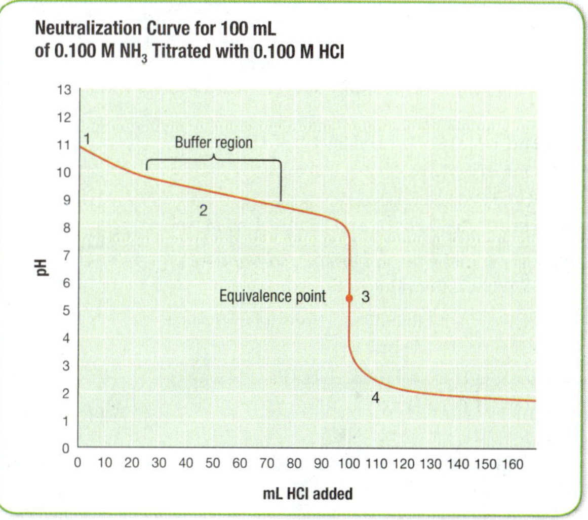

Problem Solving

TAKE IT FURTHER

At the equivalence point in this titration, all the original NH_3 is converted to NH_4^+. Have students assume that 100.0 mL of 0.050 M NH_3 are titrated with 0.10 M HCl. Ask students to calculate how many millimoles of NH_3 are in the solution. 5.0 mmol Have them calculate the volume of 0.10 M HCl that must be added to reach the equivalence point. 50 mL Have students explain their reasoning. Adding 50 mL of 0.10 M HCl supplies 5.0 mmol HCl, or the amount needed to react completely with the 5.0 mmol of NH_3 in solution.

TEACH FROM VISUALS

FIGURE 3.6 Ask students to compare this graph with **Figure 3.5.** Have them explain why the pH values at the equivalence points differ.

Classroom Discussion

Have students compare the results of hydrolysis of different salts to a tug-of-war. Have them visualize the different sides as "acid" and "base." Have them explain the results of a tug-of-war for salts of strong bases and strong acids, strong bases and weak acids, weak bases and strong acids, and weak bases and weak acids.

Chemical Equilibrium 577

▼ Teach *continued*

Teaching Tip

To predict the results of hydrolysis of the salt of a weak acid and a weak base, you must know the values of K_a and K_b for the acidic cation and basic anion, respectively.

▼ Assess and Reteach

Assess Use the Formative Assessment on this page to evaluate student mastery of the section.

Reteach For students who need additional instruction, download the Section Study Guide.

Response to Intervention To reassess students' mastery, use the Section Quiz, available to print or to take directly online at **HMDScience.com**.

Salts of weak acids and weak bases can produce either acidic, neutral, or basic aqueous solutions, depending on the salt dissolved. This is because both ions of the dissolved salt are hydrolyzed extensively. If both ions are hydrolyzed equally, the solution remains neutral. The ions in ammonium acetate, NH_4CH_3COO, hydrolyze equally, producing a neutral solution (see **Figure 3.4d** in this section).

In salts formed from a weak acid and weak base, the cation and anion both undergo hydrolysis. For example, when aluminum sulfide is placed in water, Al^{3+} reacts with OH^-, forming $Al(OH)_3$, and S^{2-} reacts with H^+, forming H_2S. The reaction is shown by the following chemical equation.

$$Al_2S_3(s) + 6H_2O(l) \longrightarrow 2Al(OH)_3(s) + 3H_2S(g)$$

Since $Al(OH)_3$ is a precipitate and H_2S is a gas, both leave the solution.

As you can see, there are several variations on neutralization reactions, each based on whether the reactants are strong or weak acids and bases. It is good practice to start your determination of the pH of one of these solutions by looking closely at the balanced equation for the reaction. By taking this first step and determining the strength or weakness of the reactants, you can make a generalized prediction of what the pH of the product solution will be at the equivalence point.

SECTION 3 FORMATIVE ASSESSMENT

Reviewing Main Ideas

1. What is meant by an *acid ionization constant*?
2. How is an acid ionization equilibrium expression written?
3. What is meant by the term *buffered solution*?
4. Which of the following combinations of solutions would form buffers when they are mixed?
   a. 50 mL of 1.0 M HCl and 50 mL of 1.0 M NaCl
   b. 25 mL of 0.5 M HNO_2 and 50 mL of 1.0 M $NaNO_2$
   c. 25 mL of 1.0 M HNO_2 and 25 mL of 1.0 M NaCl
5. What is meant by the *ion product constant* for water? What is the value of this constant?
6. For each of the following reactions, identify each conjugate acid-base pair.
   a. $H_2CO_3 + H_2O \rightleftarrows HCO_3^- + H_3O^+$
   b. $H_2O + H_2O \rightleftarrows H_3O^+ + OH^-$
   c. $H_2S + NH_3 \rightleftarrows HS^- + NH_4^+$
   d. $H_2PO_4^- + H_2O \rightleftarrows H_3PO_4 + OH^-$
7. What is hydrolysis? Compare cation and anion hydrolysis.
8. Which of the following ions hydrolyze in aqueous solution?
   a. NO_3^- **e.** CH_3COO^-
   b. F^- **f.** SO_4^{2-}
   c. NH_4^+ **g.** CO_3^{2-}
   d. K^+ **h.** PO_4^{3-}
9. Identify the following solutions as acidic, basic, or neutral.
   a. 0.5 M KI **c.** 0.25 M NH_4NO_3
   b. 0.10 M $Ba(OH)_2$ **d.** 0.05 M K_2CO_3
10. Identify the acid and base from which each of the following salts was formed.
   a. K_2CrO_4 **c.** CaF_2
   b. $Ca(CH_3COO)_2$ **d.** $(NH_4)_2SO_4$

Critical Thinking

11. **RELATING IDEAS** Describe how to make a buffer solution using a strong base and one other reagent.

Answers to Section Assessment

1. the equilibrium constant, K_a, for the reaction that produces hydronium ions
2. K_a equals the product of the concentration of the ions formed by the acid divided by the concentration of the nonionized acid.
3. a solution that contains a weak acid or base and a salt of that acid or base and that can resist changes in pH
4. b
5. the equilibrium constant for the self-ionization of water, K_w, which equals $[H_3O^+][OH^-] = 1.00 \times 10^{-14}$
6. **a.** H_2CO_3 and HCO_3^-; H_2O and H_3O^+
   b. H_2O and OH^-; H_2O and H_3O^+
   c. H_2S and HS^-; NH_3 and NH_4^+
   d. $H_2PO_4^-$ and H_3PO_4; H_2O and OH^-
7. Hydrolysis is the reaction between water molecules and ions of a dissolved salt. Cation hydrolysis produces H_3O^+ and an acidic solution; anion hydrolysis produces OH^- and a basic solution.
8. b, c, e, g, h
9. **a.** neutral **c.** acidic
   b. basic **d.** basic
10. **a.** H_2CrO_4, KOH
   b. CH_3COOH, $Ca(OH)_2$
   c. HF, $Ca(OH)_2$
   d. H_2SO_4, NH_3
11. Start with a weak acid. Add the strong base until half of the weak acid is neutralized. At that point, the other half of the weak acid remains. The rest has been converted to its salt. Thus, the solution is a buffer solution containing a weak acid and its salt.

SECTION 4

Solubility Equilibrium

Key Term
solubility product constant

Main Ideas

- The equilibrium product constant (K_{sp}) describes how soluble a substance is.
- Solubility of a slightly soluble salt is found using the solubility product constant.
- Solubility constants predict precipitate formation.
- K_{sp} cannot be used for solutions of soluble compounds.

Ionic solids dissolve in water until they are in equilibrium with their ions. An equilibrium expression can be written from the balanced chemical equation of the solid's dissociation. Concentrations of the ions can be determined from the balanced chemical equation and solubility data. The ion concentrations can then be used to determine the value of the equilibrium constant. The numerical value for the equilibrium constant can be used to predict whether precipitation occurs when solutions of various concentrations are combined.

MAIN IDEA

The equilibrium product constant (K_{sp}) describes how soluble a substance is.

A saturated solution contains the maximum amount of solute possible at a given temperature in equilibrium with an undissolved excess of the substance. A saturated solution is not necessarily a concentrated solution. The concentration can be low, if the solubility of the solute is low.

A general rule is often used to express solubilities qualitatively. By this rule, a substance is said to be *soluble* if the solubility is *greater than* 1 g per 100 g of water and slightly soluble if less than that. Even substances we have previously referred to as "insoluble" are slightly soluble. We will describe the degree of solubility with an equilibrium constant.

The equilibrium principles developed in this chapter apply to all saturated solutions of slightly soluble salts. Silver chloride is a slightly soluble salt. It reaches saturation when the Ag^+ and Cl^- concentrations are 1.3×10^{-5} M, or about 2×10^{-4} g of AgCl in 100 mL. When mixed, all ions in excess of this concentration eventually precipitate as AgCl.

Consider the equilibrium system in a saturated solution of silver chloride containing an excess of the solid AgCl. This system is represented by the following equilibrium equation.

$$AgCl(s) \rightleftarrows Ag^+(aq) + Cl^-(aq)$$

This is a heterogeneous reaction. Recall that the convention is to write its equilibrium expression without the solid species, AgCl. The resulting equilibrium expression is known as the solubility product constant, K_{sp}.

$$K_{sp} = [Ag^+][Cl^-]$$

The **solubility product constant** of a substance is the product of the molar concentrations of its ions in a saturated solution, each raised to the power that is the coefficient of that ion in the balanced chemical equation.

Problem Solving

REALITY CHECK

Be sure students understand that the solubility product constant is just another example of a specific equilibrium expression. Point out that the same rules for writing the equilibrium expression apply. In the case of a slightly soluble salt, the *K* value is written to show the concentrations of the ions in solution. Ask students why the concentration of the salt is not included in the solubility product constant. Students should recognize that as a solid, the salt concentration can be disregarded because it remains almost unchanged.

SECTION 4

Plan and Prepare

Objectives

Upon completion of this section, students should be able to do the following:

- Explain what is meant by *solubility product constants*, and calculate their values.
- Calculate solubilities using solubility product constants.
- Carry out calculations to predict whether precipitates will form when solutions are combined.

Classroom Catalyst

Show students unlabeled solutions of sodium hydroxide and copper(II) chloride. Ask them what they think is in each container. Then pour one solution into the other. A dark precipitate of $Cu(OH)_2$ will form. Ask students to think about what is occurring and how it is that ions are highly soluble in some combinations but only slightly soluble in others.

Teach

Misconception Alert!

Use of the term *insoluble* leads some students to think that certain substances do not dissolve at all. Point out that there are no completely insoluble substances—that is, no substances for which K_{sp} is truly equal to zero. However, some substances can be considered insoluble for practical purposes.

READING TOOLKIT

PAIRED SUMMARIZING Assign pairs of students to read this section. One member of the pair should concentrate on examples involving solubility calculations. The other member of the pair should do the same for precipitation calculations. Students should then explain to each other how to solve each kind of problem.

▼ **Teach** *continued*

Application

Low solubility might seem to be a drawback in terms of the usefulness of a substance; however, the extremely low solubility of a material may be the key to some of its uses. For example, the low solubility of barium sulfate makes it a good visualizing agent for X rays of the gastrointestinal tract.

Misconception Alert!

Students generally master the idea that the coefficients are to be used as exponents of concentration in the equilibrium expression. However, they often forget that the concentration values themselves must reflect the number of ions produced per formula unit. For example, if AB_2 produces a saturation concentration of 1×10^{-5} mol/L, the concentration of B^- will be twice that value, 2×10^{-5}, and that is the value that must be squared in the equilibrium expression.

Teaching Tip

The very small K_{sp} of AgCl tells us that only about 1.3×10^{-5} mol of AgCl dissolves in 1 L of solution. The volume occupied by this minute amount of solute is very small compared to the total volume of solution. This allows us to make the assumption that the solubility of a slightly soluble salt expressed in moles per liter of water is very nearly equal to moles per liter of solution.

Like all such equilibrium expressions, the solubility product constant is expressing an equilibrium and, in the case of AgCl, is equal to the product of the concentrations of its ions in solution. It depends on the form of the equilibrium expression.

For example, calcium fluoride is another slightly soluble salt. The equilibrium in a saturated CaF_2 solution is described by the equation.

$$CaF_2(s) \rightleftarrows Ca^{2+}(aq) + 2F^-(aq)$$

The solubility product constant has the following form.

$$K_{sp} = [Ca^{2+}][F^-]^2$$

Notice that K_{sp} is the product of the molar concentration of Ca^{2+} ions and the molar concentration of F^- ions squared, as required by the balanced chemical equilibrium expression.

The numerical value of K_{sp} can be determined from solubility data. These data indicate that a maximum of 1.9×10^{-4} g of AgCl can dissolve in 100 g of water at 25°C. One mole of AgCl has a mass of 143.32 g. The solubility of AgCl can therefore be expressed in moles per liter of water, which is very nearly equal to moles per liter of solution.

$$\frac{1.9 \times 10^{-4}\ \text{g AgCl}}{100\ \text{g}\ H_2O} \times \frac{1\ \text{g}\ H_2O}{1\ \text{mL}\ H_2O} \times \frac{1000\ \text{mL}}{1\ \text{L}} \times \frac{1\ \text{mol AgCl}}{143.32\ \text{g AgCl}} = 1.3 \times 10^{-5}\ \text{mol/L}$$

Silver chloride dissociates in solution, contributing equal numbers of Ag^+ and Cl^- ions. The ion concentrations in the saturated solution are therefore 1.3×10^{-5} mol/L.

$$[Ag^+] = 1.3 \times 10^{-5}$$
$$[Cl^-] = 1.3 \times 10^{-5}$$

and

$$K_{sp} = [Ag^+][Cl^-]$$
$$K_{sp} = (1.3 \times 10^{-5})(1.3 \times 10^{-5}) = 1.7 \times 10^{-10}$$

This result is the solubility product constant of AgCl at 25°C.

The solubility of CaF_2 is 8.6×10^{-3} g/100 g of water at 25°C. Expressed in moles per liter, as before, this concentration is 1.1×10^{-3} mol/L. CaF_2 dissociates in solution to yield twice as many F^- ions as Ca^{2+} ions. The ion concentrations in the saturated solution are 1.1×10^{-3} for the calcium ion and $2(1.1 \times 10^{-3})$, or 2.2×10^{-3}, for the fluoride ion. Note that at equilibrium at 25°C, $[Ca^{2+}]$ equals the solubility of 1.1×10^{-3} mol/L, but $[F^-]$ equals twice the solubility, or 2.2×10^{-3} mol/L. The number of moles of positive and negative ions per mole of compound must always be accounted for when using K_{sp} and solubilities.

$$K_{sp} = [Ca^{2+}][F^-]^2$$
$$K_{sp} = (1.1 \times 10^{-3})(2.2 \times 10^{-3})^2$$
$$K_{sp} = 5.3 \times 10^{-9}$$

Thus, the solubility product constant of CaF_2 is 5.3×10^{-9} at 25°C.

Problem Solving

DECONSTRUCTING PROBLEMS

Review how the dimensional analysis was set up to change the solubility of AgCl, given as 1.9×10^{-4} g/100g H_2O, to the molarity of AgCl.

The first conversion factor is used to change 100 g H_2O to 100 mL H_2O. Ask students why this conversion is necessary. Molarity is expressed in volume, not mass.

The second conversion factor is used to change 100 mL H_2O to L H_2O. Ask students why this conversion is necessary. The unit of volume for molarity is the liter.

The third conversion factor is used to change g AgCl to mol AgCl. Ask students why this conversion is necessary. Molarity equals moles/L.

Comparing Solubility and K_{sp}

It is difficult to measure very small concentrations of a solute with precision. For this reason, solubility data from different sources may report different values of K_{sp} for a substance. Thus, calculations of K_{sp} ordinarily should be limited to two significant figures. Representative values of K_{sp} at 25°C for some slightly soluble compounds are listed in **Figure 4.1.** Assume that all data used in K_{sp} calculations have been taken at 25°C unless otherwise specified.

At this point, you should note the difference between the solubility of a given solid and its solubility product constant. Remember that the *solubility product constant* is an equilibrium constant representing the product of the molar concentrations of its ions in a saturated solution. It has only one value for a given solid at a given temperature. It is not a value like an amount is a value. It is a product that is used as a guide for predicting quantitatively how systems respond to changes in order to reestablish equilibrium.

FIGURE 4.1

SOLUBILITY PRODUCT CONSTANTS, K_{SP}, AT 25°C

Salt	Ion product	K_{sp}	Salt	Ion product	K_{sp}
$AgCH_3COO$	$[Ag^+][CH_3COO^-]$	1.9×10^{-3}	$CuCl$	$[Cu^+][Cl^-]$	1.2×10^{-6}
$AgBr$	$[Ag^+][Br^-]$	5.0×10^{-13}	CuS	$[Cu^{2+}][S^{2-}]$	6.3×10^{-36}
Ag_2CO_3	$[Ag^+]^2[CO_3^{2-}]$	8.1×10^{-12}	FeS	$[Fe^{2+}][S^{2-}]$	6.3×10^{-18}
$AgCl$	$[Ag^+][Cl^-]$	1.8×10^{-10}	$Fe(OH)_2$	$[Fe^{2+}][OH^-]^2$	8.0×10^{-16}
AgI	$[Ag^+][I^-]$	8.3×10^{-17}	$Fe(OH)_3$	$[Fe^{3+}][OH^-]^3$	4.0×10^{-38}
Ag_2S	$[Ag^+]^2[S^{2-}]$	6.3×10^{-50}	HgS	$[Hg^{2+}][S^{2-}]$	1.6×10^{-52}
$Al(OH)_3$	$[Al^{3+}][OH^-]^3$	1.3×10^{-33}	$MgCO_3$	$[Mg^{2+}][CO_3^{2-}]$	3.5×10^{-8}
$BaCO_3$	$[Ba^{2+}][CO_3^{2-}]$	5.1×10^{-9}	$Mg(OH)_2$	$[Mg^{2+}][OH^-]^2$	1.8×10^{-11}
$BaSO_4$	$[Ba^{2+}][SO_4^{2-}]$	1.1×10^{-10}	MnS	$[Mn^{2+}][S^{2-}]$	2.5×10^{-13}
CdS	$[Cd^{2+}][S^{2-}]$	8.0×10^{-27}	$PbCl_2$	$[Pb^{2+}][Cl^-]^2$	1.6×10^{-5}
$CaCO_3$	$[Ca^{2+}][CO_3^{2-}]$	2.8×10^{-9}	$PbCrO_4$	$[Pb^{2+}][CrO_4^{2-}]$	2.8×10^{-13}
CaF_2	$[Ca^{2+}][F^-]^2$	5.3×10^{-9}	$PbSO_4$	$[Pb^{2+}][SO_4^{2-}]$	1.6×10^{-8}
$Ca(OH)_2$	$[Ca^{2+}][OH^-]^2$	5.5×10^{-6}	PbS	$[Pb^{2+}][S^{2-}]$	8.0×10^{-28}
$CaSO_4$	$[Ca^{2+}][SO_4^{2-}]$	9.1×10^{-6}	SnS	$[Sn^{2+}][S^{2-}]$	1.0×10^{-25}
$CoCO_3$	$[Co^{2+}][CO_3^{2-}]$	1.4×10^{-13}	$SrSO_4$	$[Sr^{2+}][SO_4^{2-}]$	3.2×10^{-7}
CoS	$[Co^{2+}][S^{2-}]$	4.0×10^{-21}	ZnS	$[Zn^{2+}][S^{2-}]$	1.6×10^{-24}

Differentiated Instruction

PRE-AP

Have students explain why CaF_2 is added to toothpaste to change the solubility of the mineral in tooth enamel. The mineral in tooth enamel is hydroxyapatite, $Ca_5(PO_4)_3OH$. This mineral is very soluble in acids, which form from the foods trapped between teeth. The fluoride from CaF_2 replaces the OH to produce hydroxyfluorite, $Ca_5(PO_4)_3F$. This mineral is much less soluble in acids because F^- is a weaker base than OH^-.

TEACH FROM TABLES

FIGURE 4.1 Have students compare the K_{sp} values shown. Direct their attention to the enormous ranges of solubility. Point out that exponents such as −52 are incredibly small numbers. The molar solubility of HgS ($K_{sp} = 1.6 \times 10^{-52}$), for example, is 1.3×10^{-26}. This means that only 5 ng (nanograms) would dissolve in the water contained in all of the world's oceans, 1.37×10^{15} L.

▼ Teach continued

Classroom Practice

B-1 What is the value of K_{sp} for tin(II) sulfide, given that its solubility is 5.2×10^{-12} g/100. g water?

Answer: 1.2×10^{-25}

(Emphasize that these K_{sp} values can be calculated from the solubility, even though they are given in **Figure 4.1.**)

B-2 Calculate the solubility product constant for calcium carbonate, given that it has a solubility of 5.3×10^{-3} g/L of water.

Answer: 2.8×10^{-9}

Answers

Practice B

1. 1.9×10^{-4}

   If students notice that the value differs from that in **Figure 4.1**, point out that the temperature given is different (20°C instead of 25°C), and that the solubility of $PbCl_2$ increases as the temperature increases.

2. 1.6×10^{-5}

Check for Understanding

Answer: Solubility is an amount, usually expressed in g/L. Since a solvent can, in general, hold more of a solute at higher temperatures, this amount can change with increased temperatures. However, since the solubility product constant represents the product of the molar concentrations of the ions in a saturated solution, the ratio of the ions in a given compound will not change, and temperature will not affect its value.

✓ CHECK FOR UNDERSTANDING

Explain In your own words, explain why the solubility of a compound is affected by temperature, but the solubility product constant is not.

On the other hand, the *solubility* of a substance is a value and not a product of values. Solubility is an equilibrium position that represents the amount of the solid required to form a saturated solution with a specific amount of solvent. It has an infinite number of possible values at a given temperature and is dependent on other conditions, such as the presence of a common ion. Another way to distinguish the two is that solubility speaks of the substance as a whole, while the solubility product constant deals with its constituent parts.

PREMIUM CONTENT

Solubility Product Constant

Sample Problem B Calculate the solubility product constant, K_{sp}, for copper(I) chloride, CuCl, given that the solubility of this compound at 25°C is 1.08×10^{-2} g/100. g H_2O.

1 ANALYZE

Given: solubility of CuCl = 1.08×10^{-2} g CuCl/100. g H_2O

Unknown: K_{sp}

2 PLAN

Start by converting the solubility of CuCl in g/100 g H_2O to mol/L. You will need the molar mass of CuCl to get moles CuCl from grams CuCl. Then use the solubility of the $[Cu^+]$ and $[Cl^-]$ ions in the K_{sp} expression and solve for K_{sp}.

$$\frac{\text{g CuCl}}{100\text{ g }H_2O} \times \frac{1\text{ g }H_2O}{1\text{ mL }H_2O} \times \frac{1000\text{ mL}}{1\text{ L}} \times \frac{1\text{ mol CuCl}}{\text{g CuCl}} = \text{solubility in mol/L}$$

$$CuCl(s) \rightleftarrows Cu^+(aq) + Cl^-(aq)$$

$$K_{sp} = [Cu^+][Cl^-]$$

$$[Cu^+] = [Cl^-] = \text{solubility in mol/L}$$

3 SOLVE

The molar mass of CuCl is 99.0 g/mol.

$$\text{solubility in mol/L} = \frac{1.08 \times 10^{-2}\text{ g CuCl}}{100.\text{ g }H_2O} \times \frac{1\text{ g }H_2O}{1\text{ mL}} \times \frac{1000\text{ mL}}{1\text{ L}} \times \frac{1\text{ mol CuCl}}{99.0\text{ g CuCl}} =$$

1.09×10^{-3} mol/L CuCl

$$[Cu^+] = [Cl^-] = 1.09 \times 10^{-3}\text{ mol/L}$$

$$K_{sp} = (1.09 \times 10^{-3})(1.09 \times 10^{-3}) = 1.19 \times 10^{-6}$$

4 CHECK YOUR WORK

The answer contains the proper number of significant figures and is close to the K_{sp} value given in **Figure 4.1.**

Practice Answers in Appendix E

1. Calculate the solubility product constant, K_{sp}, of lead(II) chloride, $PbCl_2$, which has a solubility of 1.0 g/100 g H_2O at 20°C.
2. A 5.0 gram sample of Ag_2SO_4 will dissolve in 1.0 L of water. Calculate the solubility product constant for this salt.

Problem Solving

ALTERNATIVE APPROACHES

Have students explain how the solution to Sample Problem B would change if the solubility of CuCl had been given in the units mol/L. There would not be any need to perform the dimensional analysis to convert the solubility from g/100 g H_2O to mol/L H_2O. The molarity values could be substituted directly into the solubility product expression to solve for the K_{sp}.

MAIN IDEA

Solubility of a slightly soluble salt is found using the solubility product constant.

Once known, the solubility product constant can be used to determine the solubility of a slightly soluble salt. Suppose you wish to know how many moles of barium carbonate, $BaCO_3$, can be dissolved in 1 L of water at 25°C. From **Figure 4.1**, K_{sp} for $BaCO_3$ has the numerical value 5.1×10^{-9}. The equilibrium equation is written as follows:

$$BaCO_3(s) \rightleftarrows Ba^{2+}(aq) + CO_3^{2-}(aq)$$

Given the value for K_{sp}, we can write the solubility equilibrium expression as follows:

$$K_{sp} = [Ba^{2+}][CO_3^{2-}] = 5.1 \times 10^{-9}$$

Therefore, $BaCO_3$ dissolves until the product of the molar concentrations of Ba^{2+} ions and CO_3^{2-} ions equals 5.1×10^{-9}. The solubility equilibrium equation shows that Ba^{2+} ions and CO_3^{2-} ions enter the solution in equal numbers as the salt dissolves. Thus, they have the same concentration. Let $[Ba^{2+}] = x$. Then $[CO_3^{2-}] = x$ also.

$$[Ba^{2+}][CO_3^{2-}] = K_{sp} = 5.1 \times 10^{-9}$$
$$(x)(x) = x^2 = 5.1 \times 10^{-9}$$
$$x = \sqrt{5.1 \times 10^{-9}}$$

The molar solubility of $BaCO_3$ is 7.1×10^{-5} mol/L.

Thus, the solution concentration is 7.1×10^{-5} M for Ba^{2+} ions and 7.1×10^{-5} M for CO_3^{2-} ions.

Calculating Solubility

Sample Problem C **Calculate the solubility of silver bromide, AgBr, in mol/L, using the K_{sp} value for this compound listed in Figure 4.1.**

1 ANALYZE

Given: $K_{sp} = 5.0 \times 10^{-13}$

Unknown: solubility of AgBr

2 PLAN

$$AgBr \rightleftarrows Ag^{+}(aq) + Br^{-}(aq)$$
$$K_{sp} = [Ag^{+}][Br^{-}]$$

$[Ag^{+}] = [Br^{-}]$, so let $[Ag^{+}] = x$ and $[Br^{-}] = x$

3 SOLVE

$$K_{sp} = [Ag^{+}][Br^{-}]$$
$$K_{sp} = x^2$$
$$x^2 = 5.0 \times 10^{-13}$$
$$x = \sqrt{5.0 \times 10^{-13}}$$

Solubility of AgBr $= \sqrt{5.0 \times 10^{-13}} = 7.1 \times 10^{-7}$ mol/L

4 CHECK YOUR WORK

The answer has the proper number of significant figures and is close to an estimated value of 7.0×10^{-7}, calculated as $\sqrt{4.9 \times 10^{-14}}$.

Continued

Alternative Assessment

Have students research the solubilities of various combinations of ions. Have them then prepare a chart in periodic-table form that illustrates useful generalizations regarding solubility. For example, the alkali metals form virtually all soluble compounds, and most alkaline earth metals form soluble compounds with nearly all anions except carbonates, phosphates, and fluorides. Have students compare charts and discuss any differences they notice.

DECONSTRUCTING PROBLEMS

Some students may mistakenly take $[Ag^{+}] = x$ and $[Br^{-}] = x$ and substitute $2x$ into the equilibrium expression to solve for the solubility of AgBr. Emphasize that the unknown concentrations of the ions are multiplied (x^2) and not added ($2x$).

▼ Teach continued

Classroom Practice

C-1 What is the solubility in mol/L of manganese(II) sulfide, MnS, given that its K_{sp} value is 2.5×10^{-13}?

Answer: 5.0×10^{-7} mol/L

C-2 Calculate the concentration of Zn^{2+} in a saturated solution of zinc sulfide, ZnS, given that K_{sp} of zinc sulfide equals 1.6×10^{-24}.

Answer: 1.3×10^{-12} mol/L

TEACH FROM VISUALS

FIGURE 4.2 Point out to students that cloudiness of a mixture of solutions, as well as the appearance of a solid in the bottom, is evidence of formation of a precipitate. Have them look at each picture and decide whether a precipitate has formed Precipitates form in (c), (d), and (e). Be sure students understand that a change of color does not indicate a precipitate if the solution remains clear. While this is the case in **(f)**, it may be hard to distinguish between a precipitate and a colored solution when the sample is so dark that one can not tell that it is clear. Alert students to the fact that there is no obvious settling as there is in **(c)**, **(d)**, and **(e)**.

Answers

Practice C

1. 8.9×10^{-14} mol/L
2. 5.7×10^{-4} mol/L

Calculating Solubility (continued)

Practice Answers in Appendix E

1. Calculate the solubility of cadmium sulfide, CdS, in mol/L, given the K_{sp} value listed in **Figure 4.1.**
2. Determine the concentration of strontium ions in a saturated solution of strontium sulfate, $SrSO_4$, if the K_{sp} for $SrSO_4$ is 3.2×10^{-7}.

MAIN IDEA

Solubility constants predict precipitate formation.

In an earlier example, $BaCO_3$ served as the source of both Ba^{2+} and CO_3^{2-} ions. Because each mole of $BaCO_3$ yields one mole of Ba^{2+} ions and one mole of CO_3^{2-} ions, the concentrations of the two ions were equal. However, the equilibrium condition does not require that the two ion concentrations be equal. Equilibrium will still be established so that the ion product $[Ba^{2+}][CO_3^{2-}]$ does not exceed the value of K_{sp} for the system.

Similarly, if the ion product $[Ca^{2+}][F^-]^2$ is less than the value of K_{sp} at a particular temperature, the solution is unsaturated. If the ion product is greater than the value for K_{sp}, CaF_2 precipitates. This precipitation reduces the concentrations of Ca^{2+} and F^- ions until equilibrium is established.

Suppose that unequal quantities of $BaCl_2$ and Na_2CO_3 are dissolved in water and the solutions are then mixed. If the ion product $[Ba^{2+}][CO_3^{2-}]$ exceeds the K_{sp} of $BaCO_3$, a precipitate of $BaCO_3$ forms. After precipitation, the ion concentrations are such that $[Ba^{2+}][CO_3^{2-}]$ equals the K_{sp}.

FIGURE 4.2

Precipitation Reactions

(a) Ag^+ and NO_3^- ions are soluble.

(b) Pb^{2+} and NO_3^- ions are soluble.

(c) Chromate, CrO_4^{2-}, and Ag^+ ions form a slightly soluble salt.

(d) Chromate, CrO_4^{2-}, and Pb^{2+} ions form a slightly soluble salt.

(e) Thiocyanate ions, SCN^-, form a slightly soluble salt with Ag^+ ions.

(f) Thiocyanate ions, SCN^-, form a soluble salt with Fe^{3+}.

Differentiated Instruction

ENGLISH LEARNERS

Students may have difficulty with the multiple meanings of the term *product*. Point out that as used here, product refers to a mathematical product—the result of multiplication—rather than the product of a reaction. *Ion product* simply refers to the value obtained when the concentrations of the ions are multiplied. Ask them how the ion product is calculated for a solution of $CaSO_4$. The ion product is calculated by multiplying [Ca][SO_4].

Substances differ greatly in their tendencies to form precipitates when mixed in moderate concentrations. The photos in **Figure 4.2** show the behavior of some anions in the presence of certain cations. Note that some of the combinations have produced precipitates and some have not. The solubility product can be used to predict whether a precipitate forms when two solutions are mixed.

Precipitation Calculations

Sample Problem D **Will a precipitate form if 20.0 mL of 0.010 M $BaCl_2$ is mixed with 20.0 mL of 0.0050 M Na_2SO_4?**

1 ANALYZE

Given: concentration of $BaCl_2$ = 0.010 M

volume of $BaCl_2$ = 20.0 mL

concentration of Na_2SO_4 = 0.0050 M

volume of Na_2SO_4 = 20.0 mL

Unknown: whether a precipitate forms

2 PLAN

The two possible new pairings of ions are NaCl and $BaSO_4$. Of these, only $BaSO_4$ is a slightly soluble salt. It will precipitate if the ion product $[Ba^{2+}][SO_4^{2-}]$ in the mixed solution exceeds K_{sp} for $BaSO_4$. From the list of solubility products in **Figure 4.2**, the K_{sp} is found to be 1.1×10^{-10}. The solubility equilibrium equation follows:

$$BaSO_4(s) \rightleftarrows Ba^{2+}(aq) + SO_4^{2-}(aq)$$

The solubility equilibrium expression is written as follows:

$$K_{sp} = [Ba^{2+}][SO_4^{2-}] = 1.1 \times 10^{-10}$$

First $[Ba^{2+}]$ and $[SO_4^{2-}]$ in the above solution must be found. Then the ion product is calculated and compared with the K_{sp}.

3 SOLVE

Calculate the mole quantities of Ba^{2+} and SO_4^{2-} ions.

$$0.020\ \cancel{L} \times \frac{0.010\ \text{mol}\ Ba^{2+}}{1\ \cancel{L}} = 0.000\ 20\ \text{mol}\ Ba^{2+}$$

$$0.020\ \cancel{L} \times \frac{0.0050\ \text{mol}\ SO_4^{2-}}{1\ \cancel{L}} = 0.000\ 10\ \text{mol}\ SO_4^{2-}$$

Calculate the total volume of solution containing Ba^{2+} and SO_4^{2-} ions.

$$0.020\ L + 0.020\ L = 0.040\ L$$

Calculate the Ba^{2+} and SO_4^{2-} ion concentrations in the combined solution.

$$\frac{0.000\ 20\ \text{mol}\ Ba^{2+}}{0.040\ L} = 5.0 \times 10^{-3}\ \text{mol/L}\ Ba^{2+}$$

$$\frac{0.000\ 10\ \text{mol}\ SO_4^{2-}}{0.040\ L} = 2.5 \times 10^{-3}\ \text{mol/L}\ SO_4^{2-}$$

Calculate the ion product.

$$[Ba^{2+}][SO_4^{2-}] = (5.0 \times 10^{-3})(2.5 \times 10^{-3}) = 1.2 \times 10^{-5}$$

The ion product, 1.2×10^{-5}, is greater than the value of K_{sp}, 1.1×10^{-10}, so precipitation occurs.

Problem Solving

ALTERNATIVE APPROACHES

To help students predict whether a precipitate will form, have them assign Q as the ion product. Tell them that if Q is greater than K_{sp}, precipitation occurs ($Q > K_{sp}$ = precipitation). If Q is less than K_{sp}, then there is no precipitation ($Q < K_{sp} \neq$ precipitation).

Teaching Tip

Most Na^+, K^+, NH_4^+, nitrate, acetate, sulfate, and halide salts are soluble. Most hydroxides, sulfides, carbonates, and phosphates are slightly soluble.

Misconception Alert!

Students often think simply in terms of solubility of a compound as a whole. They assume that the ratio of ions present in solution is always the same as that in the compound. When different solutions are mixed, however, the initial ion concentrations in the mixture depend on the concentrations in the components and on the relative volumes mixed. Point out this concept as you go over the Sample Problem on this page.

Classroom Practice

D-1 Will a precipitate form if 20 mL of 0.034 M NaCl and 15 mL of 0.083 M $CuNO_3$ are mixed?

Answer: Yes, CuCl precipitates.

D-2 Does a precipitate form if 100. mL of 0.0014 M $Ca(NO_3)_2$ and 200. mL of 0.00020 M Na_2SO_4 are mixed?

Answer: No, $CaSO_4$ does not precipitate.

Teach *continued*

Answers

Practice D

1. AgBr precipitates.
2. $PbCl_2$ does *not* precipitate.

Assess and Reteach

Assess Use the Formative Assessment on this page to evaluate student mastery of the section.

Reteach For students who need additional instruction, download the Section Study Guide.

Response to Intervention To reassess students' mastery, use the Section Quiz, available to print or to take directly online at **HMDScience.com**.

Precipitation Calculations (continued)

4 CHECK YOUR WORK The answer contains the appropriate number of significant figures and is close to an estimated value of 1×10^{-5}, calculated as $(5 \times 10^{-3})(2 \times 10^{-3})$; because $10^{-5} > 10^{-10}$, precipitation should occur.

Practice Answers in Appendix E

1. Does a precipitate form when 100. mL of 0.0025 M $AgNO_3$ and 150. mL of 0.0020 M NaBr solutions are mixed?
2. Does a precipitate form when 20. mL of 0.038 M $Pb(NO_3)_2$ and 30. mL of 0.018 M KCl solutions are mixed?

MAIN IDEA

K_{sp} cannot be used for solutions of soluble compounds.

The solubility product principle can be very useful when applied to solutions of slightly soluble substances. It *cannot* be applied to solutions of soluble substances. This is because the positive and negative ions attract each other, and this attraction becomes appreciable when the ions are close together. Sometimes it is necessary to consider two equilibria simultaneously. For example, if either ion hydrolyzes, the salt will be more soluble than predicted when only the solubility product constant is used. The solubility product is also sensitive to changes in solution temperature to the extent that the solubility of the dissolved substance is affected by such changes. All of these factors limit the conditions under which the solubility product principle can be applied.

SECTION 4 FORMATIVE ASSESSMENT

Reviewing Main Ideas

1. What is a solubility product constant? How are such constants determined?
2. How are solubility product constants used to calculate solubilities?
3. What is an ion product?
4. How are calculations to predict possible precipitation carried out?
5. What is the value of K_{sp} for Ag_2SO_4 if 5.40 g is soluble in 1.00 L of water?
6. Determine whether a precipitate will form if 20.0 mL of 1.00×10^{-7} M $AgNO_3$ is mixed with 20.0 mL of 2.00×10^{-9} M NaCl at 25°C.

Critical Thinking

7. **ANALYZING DATA** A solution is 0.20 M in each of the following: $Ca(NO_3)_2$, $Cr(NO_3)_3$, and $La(NO_3)_3$. Solid NaF is added to the solution until the $[F^-]$ of the solution is 1.0×10^{-4} M. Given the values of K_{sp} below, describe what will happen.

$CaF_2 = 3.9 \times 10^{-11}$

$CrF_3 = 6.6 \times 10^{-11}$

$LaF_3 = 4.0 \times 10^{-17}$

Answers to Section Assessment

1. the product of the molar concentrations of the ions in a saturated solution, each raised to a power that is the coefficient of that ion in the chemical equation; from careful measurements of ion solubilities
2. by using the solubility equilibrium equation, solving for an ion concentration, and then relating ion concentration to moles of solute
3. the product of the ion concentrations present in solution, each raised to the appropriate power
4. The ion product is calculated; if it exceeds the K_{sp}, then a precipitate will form.
5. 2.07×10^{-5}
6. The ion product of silver and chloride ions in the sample solution is less than the solubility product constant, so no precipitate will form.
7. CaF_2 and LaF_3 will precipitate. The ion product of those two salts is greater than the value of K_{sp} for the salts.

Math Tutor

Determining Equilibrium Constants

For a given temperature, you can write a mathematical equation that describes the equilibrium of a reaction in terms of concentration. The equation defines an equilibrium constant, *K*, as a function of the concentrations of products and reactants at equilibrium.

Consider an equilibrium process in which reactants A and B form products C and D.

$$nA + mB \rightleftarrows xC + yD$$

The terms *n*, *m*, *x*, and *y* are the coefficients of the balanced equation.

$$K = \frac{[C]^x[D]^y}{[A]^n[B]^m}$$

Problem-Solving TIPS

- Always use a balanced chemical equation to write an equilibrium-constant equation.
- To write an equation, place the product concentrations in the numerator and the reactant concentrations in the denominator. Raise each substance's concentration to the power equal to the substance's coefficient in the balanced chemical equation.
- The concentration of any solid or pure liquid that takes part in the reaction is left out, because these concentrations never change.

Sample Problem

Write an equation for the equilibrium constant of the reaction in which nitrogen monoxide changes to dinitrogen monoxide and nitrogen dioxide.

To write an equation for an equilibrium constant, you must start with a balanced chemical equation for the equilibrium reaction. By writing the formulas of the compounds mentioned in the description, you get the unbalanced equilibrium equation $NO(g) \rightleftarrows N_2O(g) + NO_2(g)$.

Balancing the equation requires a coefficient of 3 in front of NO, giving $3NO(g) \rightleftarrows N_2O(g) + NO_2(g)$. Next, write an equilibrium equation. Remember, each concentration in the equilibrium equation is raised to a power equal to its coefficient in the balanced chemical equation. The product concentrations, $[N_2O]$ and $[NO_2]$, are placed in the numerator. The coefficient of each of the products is 1, so the exponent of each concentration is 1. There is only one reactant, so its concentration, [NO], is written in the denominator. Its coefficient is 3 in the balanced chemical equation, so the concentration of NO is raised to the third power. The exponents with a value of 1 do not have to be written. The resulting equation is

$$K = \frac{[N_2O]^1[NO_2]^1}{[NO]^3} = \frac{[N_2O][NO_2]}{[NO]^3}$$

Practice

1. Write equations for the equilibrium constant of each of the following hypothetical reactions:
   a. $A(aq) + 2B(aq) \rightleftarrows AB_2(aq)$
   b. $2DE_2(g) \rightleftarrows D_2(g) + 2E_2(g)$
2. Use the equilibrium concentrations below to calculate the equilibrium constant for the following decomposition reaction:

$$2BrF_5(g) \rightleftarrows Br_2(g) + 5F_2(g)$$

$[BrF_5] = 0.000137$ mol/L, $[Br_2] = 0.00050$ mol/L, and $[F_2] = 0.0025$ mol/L

MATH TUTOR

Answers

1. **a.** $K = \frac{[AB_2]}{[A][B]^2}$

   b. $K = \frac{[D_2][E_2]^2}{[DE_2]^2}$

2. $K = 2.6 \times 10^{-9}$

CHAPTER 18 Summary

PREMIUM CONTENT
Interactive Review HMDScience.com
Review Games
Concept Maps

SECTION 1 The Nature of Chemical Equilibrium

KEY TERMS
- reversible reaction
- chemical equilibrium
- equilibrium constant
- chemical equilibrium expression

- A reaction system in which the forward and reverse reactions occur simultaneously and at the same rate is said to be at *equilibrium*. Both reactions continue, but there is no net change in the composition of the system.
- At equilibrium, the ratio of the product of the molar concentrations of substances formed to the product of the molar concentrations of reactants, each raised to the appropriate power, has a definite numerical value, K, which is the equilibrium constant at a given temperature.

SECTION 2 Shifting Equilibrium

KEY TERM
- common-ion effect

- According to Le Châtelier's principle, when a stress (a change in concentration, pressure, or temperature) is applied to a system at equilibrium, the equilibrium is shifted in the direction that relieves the stress.
- The common-ion effect is recognized when a solution containing ions, such as those of a reactant or a product in an equilibrium system, is added to the system. Le Châtelier's principle explains the response of the system to the stress.

SECTION 3 Equilibria of Acids, Bases, and Salts

KEY TERMS
- acid ionization constant
- buffered solution
- hydrolysis

- The equilibrium expression for the ionization constant of the weak acid HA follows:

$$K_a = \frac{[H_3O^+][A^-]}{[HA]}$$

- Salts formed from strong bases and weak acids produce aqueous solutions that are basic because of *anion hydrolysis*.
- Salts formed from strong acids and weak bases produce aqueous solutions that are acidic because of *cation hydrolysis*.
- Salts formed from strong acids and strong bases do not hydrolyze in water, and their solutions are neutral.
- Salts formed from weak acids and weak bases may produce neutral, acidic, or basic solutions, depending on the relative amounts of cation and anion hydrolysis.

SECTION 4 Solubility Equilibrium

KEY TERM
- solubility product constant

- Ions of salts that are slightly soluble form saturated aqueous solutions at low concentrations. The solubility equilibrium expression for such salts yields a constant—the solubility product constant, K_{sp}.

588 Chapter 18

CHAPTER 18 Review

SECTION 1

The Nature of Chemical Equilibrium

REVIEWING MAIN IDEAS

1. Describe and explain how the concentrations of A, B, C, and D change from the time when A and B are first combined to the point at which equilibrium is established for the reaction $A + B \rightleftarrows C + D$.

2. a. Write the general expression for an equilibrium constant based on the equation $nA + mB + \ldots \rightleftarrows xC + yD + \ldots$
   b. What information is provided by the value of K for a given equilibrium system at a specified temperature?

3. In general, which reaction is favored (forward or reverse) if the value of K at a specified temperature is
   a. very small?
   b. very large?

PRACTICE PROBLEMS

4. Determine the value of the equilibrium constant for each reaction given, assuming that the equilibrium concentrations are found to be those specified. (Concentrations are in mol/L.) (Hint: See Sample Problem A.)
   a. $A + B \rightleftarrows C$; $[A] = 2.0$; $[B] = 3.0$; $[C] = 4.0$
   b. $D + 2E \rightleftarrows F + 3G$; $[D] = 1.5$; $[E] = 2.0$; $[F] = 1.8$; $[G] = 1.2$
   c. $N_2(g) + 3H_2(g) \rightleftarrows 2NH_3(g)$; $[N_2] = 0.45$; $[H_2] = 0.14$; $[NH_3] = 0.62$

5. An equilibrium mixture at a specific temperature is found to consist of 1.2×10^{-3} mol/L HCl, 3.8×10^{-4} mol/L O_2, 5.8×10^{-2} mol/L H_2O, and 5.8×10^{-2} mol/L Cl_2 according to the following:
   $$4HCl(g) + O_2(g) \rightleftarrows 2H_2O(g) + 2Cl_2(g).$$
   Determine the value of the equilibrium constant for this system.

6. At 450°C, the value of the equilibrium constant for the following system is 6.59×10^{-3}. If $[NH_3] = 1.23 \times 10^{-4}$ M and $[H_2] = 2.75 \times 10^{-2}$ M at equilibrium, determine the concentration of N_2 at that point.
   $$N_2(g) + 3H_2(g) \rightleftarrows 2NH_3(g)$$

7. The value of the equilibrium constant for the reaction below is 40.0 at a specified temperature. What would be the value of that constant for the reverse reaction under the same conditions?
   $$H_2(g) + I_2(g) \rightleftarrows 2HI(g)$$

SECTION 2

Shifting Equilibrium

REVIEWING MAIN IDEAS

8. Predict whether each of the following pressure changes would favor the forward or reverse reaction.
   $$2NO(g) + O_2(g) \rightleftarrows 2NO_2(g)$$
   a. increased pressure
   b. decreased pressure

9. In heterogeneous reaction systems, what types of substances do not appear in the equilibrium constant expression? Why?

10. Explain the effect of a catalyst on an equilibrium system.

11. Predict the effect of each of the following on the indicated equilibrium system in terms of the direction of equilibrium shift (forward, reverse, or neither).
   $$H_2(g) + Cl_2(g) \rightleftarrows 2HCl(g) + 184 \text{ kJ}$$
   a. addition of Cl_2
   b. removal of HCl
   c. increased pressure
   d. decreased temperature
   e. removal of H_2
   f. decreased pressure
   g. addition of a catalyst
   h. increased temperature
   i. decreased system volume

12. How would the changes in (a) through (i) of item 11 affect the new equilibrium concentration of HCl and the value of K at the new equilibrium?

13. Explain why changes in the concentrations of the reactants and products at equilibrium have no effect on the value of the equilibrium constant.

Review Answers

1. At the start, A and B are at their maximum concentrations, and there is no C or D. As A and B react, their concentrations decrease, and those of C and D increase. The rate at which C and D combine increases, while the rate at which A and B combine decreases. Eventually, the two rates become equal, and equilibrium is established. The concentrations of A, B, C, and D then remain constant as long as conditions remain the same.
2. a. $K = \dfrac{[C]^x[D]^y \ldots}{[A]^n[B]^m \ldots}$
   b. the extent to which reactants are converted into products
3. a. reverse b. forward
4. a. 0.67 b. 0.52 c. 3.1×10^2
5. 1.4×10^{10}
6. 0.110 M
7. 0.0250
8. a. forward b. reverse
9. pure substances in the solid and liquid phases; because their concentrations are not changed by the addition or removal of quantities of these materials
10. It increases the rates of forward and reverse reactions equally, so the relative equilibrium amounts are not affected.
11. a. forward b. forward c. neither d. forward e. reverse f. neither g. neither h. reverse i. neither
12. [HCl] and K, respectively, would:
   a. increase, remain the same
   b. decrease, remain the same
   c. remain the same, remain the same
   d. increase, increase
   e. decrease, remain the same
   f. remain the same, remain the same
   g. remain the same, remain the same
   h. decrease, decrease
   i. remain the same, remain the same
13. Such changes cause the amounts of reactants and products to change, but the value of K, which is a ratio, is not changed.

CHAPTER REVIEW

14. What relative pressure (high or low) would result in the production of the maximum level of CO_2 according to the following equation? Why?

$$2CO(g) + O_2(g) \rightleftarrows 2CO_2(g)$$

15. What relative conditions (reactant concentrations, pressure, and temperature) would favor a high equilibrium concentration of the underlined substance in each of the following equilibrium systems?

a. $2CO(g) + O_2(g) \rightleftarrows \underline{2CO_2(g)} + 167\ kJ$

b. $Cu^{2+}(aq) + 4NH_3(aq) \rightleftarrows \underline{Cu(NH_3)_4^{2+}(aq)} + 42\ kJ$

c. $2HI(g) + 12.6\ kJ \rightleftarrows H_2(g) + \underline{I_2(g)}$

d. $4HCl(g) + O_2(g) \rightleftarrows 2H_2O(g) + \underline{2Cl_2(g)} + 113\ kJ$

e. $PCl_5(g) + 88\ kJ \rightleftarrows PCl_3(g) + \underline{Cl_2(g)}$

16. The reaction between hemoglobin, Hb, and oxygen, O_2, in red blood cells is responsible for transporting O_2 to body tissues. This process can be represented by the following equilibrium reaction:

$$Hb(aq) + O_2(g) \rightleftarrows HbO_2(aq)$$

What will happen to the concentration of oxygenated hemoglobin, HbO_2, at high altitude, where the pressure of oxygen is 0.1 atm instead of 0.2 atm, as it is at sea level?

17. What two factors determine the extent to which reacting ions are removed from solution?

18. Identify the three conditions under which ionic reactions can run to completion, and write an equation for each.

SECTION 3

Equilibria of Acids, Bases, and Salts

REVIEWING MAIN IDEAS

19. a. Write the ion product constant expression for water.

b. What is the value of this constant at 25°C?

20. List and distinguish between the four general categories of salts, based on their hydrolysis properties, and give an example of each.

21. Explain why the pH of a solution containing both acetic acid and sodium acetate is higher than that of a solution containing the same concentration of acetic acid alone.

22. The ionization constant, K_a, for acetic acid is 1.8×10^{-5} at 25°C. Explain the significance of this value.

23. a. From the development of K_a described in Section 3, show how you would express an ionization constant, K_b, for the weak base NH_3.

b. In this case, $K_b = 1.8 \times 10^{-5}$. What is the significance of this numerical value to equilibrium?

SECTION 4

Solubility Equilibrium

REVIEWING MAIN IDEAS

24. Explain why a saturated solution is not necessarily a concentrated solution.

25. What rule of thumb is used to distinguish between soluble and slightly soluble substances?

26. What is the relative ion concentration of an ionic substance typically involved in solubility equilibrium systems?

27. What is the relationship between K_{sp} and the product of the ion concentrations in terms of determining whether a solution of those ions is saturated?

PRACTICE PROBLEMS

28. The ionic substance EJ dissociates to form E^{2+} and J^{2-} ions. The solubility of EJ is 8.45×10^{-6} mol/L. What is the value of the solubility product constant? (Hint: See Sample Problem B.)

29. Calculate the solubility product constant K_{sp} for each of the following, based on the solubility information provided.

a. $BaSO_4 = 2.4 \times 10^{-4}$ g/100. g H_2O at 20°C

b. $Ca(OH)_2 = 0.173$ g/100. g H_2O at 20°C

30. Calculate the molar solubility of a substance MN that ionizes to form M^{2+} and N^{2-} ions, given that $K_{sp} = 8.1 \times 10^{-6}$. (Hint: See Sample Problem C.)

14. high pressure, because the forward reaction converts three gas molecules into two, relieving the stress imposed by the pressure increase

15. a. high reactant concentrations, high pressure, low temperature

b. high reactant concentrations, pressure not relevant, low temperature

c. high reactant concentrations, pressure not relevant, high temperature

d. high reactant concentrations, high pressure, low temperature

e. high reactant concentrations, low pressure, high temperature

16. The concentration of oxygenated hemoglobin will be less than it is at sea level.

17. solubility of the compound formed and degree of ionization

18. A gaseous product is formed:

$$H_3O^+(aq) + HCO_3^-(aq) \longrightarrow 2H_2O(l) + CO_2(g)$$

A precipitate is formed:

$$Ag^+(aq) + Cl^-(aq) \longrightarrow AgCl(s)$$

A slightly ionized product (a weak electrolyte) is formed:

$$H_3O^+(aq) + OH^-(aq) \longrightarrow 2H_2O(l)$$

19. a. $K_w = [H_3O^+][OH^-]$

b. $K_w = 1.0 \times 10^{-14}$

20. *Salts of strong acids and strong bases*: neither the cations nor the anions hydrolyze appreciably. Neutral aqueous solutions with a pH of 7 result. NaCl is an example.

Salts of weak acids and strong bases: the anions hydrolyze; the cations do not. Basic aqueous solutions result. $NaCH_3COO$ is an example.

Salts of strong acids and weak bases: the anions do not hydrolyze; the cations do. Acidic aqueous solutions result. NH_4Cl is an example.

Salts of weak acids and weak bases: both the cations and the anions hydrolyze. Aqueous solutions can be acidic, basic, or neutral. Neutral NH_4CH_3COO is one example.

21. Acetic acid is a weak electrolyte and slightly ionizes in water solution. Equilibrium is established between the acid molecules and the hydronium and acetate ions in the solution. Sodium acetate is an ionic salt that completely dissociates in water. When it is added to the acetic acid solution, the concentration of acetate ion is increased, shifting the equilibrium to the left to relieve the stress. This shift removes hydronium ions from the solution, making it higher in pH.

22. At equilibrium, the concentration of nonionized acetic acid is high, and the concentrations of hydronium and acetate ions are low. Acetic acid is a weak acid.

23. a. $K_b = \dfrac{[NH_4^+][OH^-]}{[NH_3]}$

b. K_b is small, so there are comparatively few ions at equilibrium. Ammonia is a weak base.

24. A saturated solution is at equilibrium and contains the maximum concentration of solute. But the actual concentration of dissolved solute may be high or low, depending on the solubility.

25. soluble: greater than 1 g/100 g water; slightly soluble: less than 1 g/100 g water

26. Ion concentration is very low.

31. Use the K_{sp} values given in **Figure 4.2** to evaluate the solubility of each of the following in moles per liter.
   a. AgBr
   b. CoS

32. Complete each of the following relative to the reaction that occurs when 25.0 mL of 0.0500 M $Pb(NO_3)_2$ is combined with 25.0 mL of 0.0400 M Na_2SO_4 if equilibrium is reached at 25°C.
   a. Write the solubility equilibrium equation at 25°C.
   b. Write the solubility equilibrium expression for the net reaction.

33. The ionic substance T_3U_2 ionizes to form T^{2+} and U^{3-} ions. The solubility of T_3U_2 is 3.8×10^{-10} mol/L. What is the value of the solubility product constant?

34. A solution of AgI contains 2.7×10^{-10} mol/L Ag^+. What is the maximum I^- concentration that can exist in this solution?

35. Calculate whether a precipitate will form if 0.35 L of 0.0044 M $Ca(NO_3)_2$ and 0.17 L of 0.000 39 M NaOH are mixed at 25°C. (See **Figure 4.2** for K_{sp} values.) (Hint: See Sample Problem D.)

36. Determine whether a precipitate will form if 1.70 g of solid $AgNO_3$ and 14.5 g of solid NaCl are dissolved in 200. mL of water to form a solution at 25°C.

37. If 2.50×10^{-2} g of solid $Fe(NO_3)_3$ is added to 100. mL of a 1.0×10^{-4} M NaOH solution, will a precipitate form?

Mixed Review

REVIEWING MAIN IDEAS

38. Calcium carbonate is only slightly soluble in water.
   a. Write the equilibrium equation for calcium carbonate in solution.
   b. Write the solubility product constant expression, K_{sp}, for the equilibrium in a saturated solution of $CaCO_3$.

39. Calculate the concentration of Hg^{2+} ions in a saturated solution of HgS(*s*). How many Hg^{2+} ions are in 1000 L of the solution?

40. Calculate the equilibrium constant, *K*, for the following reaction at 900°C.
$$H_2(g) + CO_2(g) \rightleftarrows H_2O(g) + CO(g)$$
The components were analyzed, and it was found that $[H_2] = 0.061$ mol/L, $[CO_2] = 0.16$ mol/L, $[H_2O] = 0.11$ mol/L, and $[CO] = 0.14$ mol/L.

41. A solution in equilibrium with solid barium phosphate is found to have a barium ion concentration of 5.0×10^{-4} M and a K_{sp} of 3.4×10^{-23}. Calculate the concentration of phosphate ion.

42. At 25°C, the value of *K* is 1.7×10^{-13} for the following reaction.
$$2N_2O(g) + O_2(g) \rightleftarrows 4NO(g)$$
It is determined that $[N_2O] = 0.0035$ mol/L and $[O_2] = 0.0027$ mol/L. Using this information, what is the concentration of NO(*g*) at equilibrium?

43. Tooth enamel is composed of the mineral hydroxyapatite, $Ca_5(PO_4)_3OH$, which has a K_{sp} of 6.8×10^{-37}. The molar solubility of hydroxyapatite is 2.7×10^{-5} mol/L. When hydroxyapatite is reacted with fluoride, the OH^- is replaced with the F^- ion on the mineral, forming fluorapatite, $Ca_5(PO_4)_3F$. (The latter is harder and less susceptible to cavities.) The K_{sp} of fluorapatite is 1×10^{-60}. Calculate the molar solubility of fluorapatite in water. Given your calculations, can you support the fluoridation of drinking water?

44. Determine whether a precipitate will form when 0.96 g Na_2CO_3 is combined with 0.20 g $BaBr_2$ in a 10. L solution ($K_{sp} = 2.8 \times 10^{-9}$).

45. For the formation of ammonia, the equilibrium constant is calculated to be 5.2×10^{-5} at 25°C. After analysis, it is determined that $[N_2] = 2.00$ M and $[H_2] = 0.80$ M. How many grams of ammonia are in the 10. L reaction vessel at equilibrium? Use the following equilibrium equation.
$$N_2(g) + 3H_2(g) \rightleftarrows 2NH_3(g)$$

CRITICAL THINKING

46. **Relating Ideas** Let *s* equal the solubility, in mol/L, of AB_2. In terms of *s*, what is the molar concentration of A? of B? What is the K_{sp} of AB_2?

CHAPTER REVIEW

31. a. 7.1×10^{-7} mol/L
   b. 6.3×10^{-11} mol/L

32. a. $PbSO_4(s) \rightleftarrows Pb^{2+}(aq) + SO_4^{2-}(aq)$
   b. $K_{sp} = [Pb^{2+}][SO_4^{2-}]$

33. 8.6×10^{-46}

34. 3.1×10^{-7} mol/L

35. No precipitate will form.

36. A precipitate of AgCl will form.

37. A precipitate of $Fe(OH)_3$ will form.

38. a. $CaCO_3(s) \rightleftarrows Ca^{2+}(aq) + CO_3^{2-}(aq)$
   b. $K_{sp} = [Ca^{2+}][CO_3^{2-}]$

39. 1.3×10^{-26} mol/L; 8 ions

40. 1.6

41. 5.2×10^{-7} mol/L

42. 8.7×10^{-6} mol/L

43. The solubility is 6.1×10^{-8} mol/L. The fluoridation produces a lowered solubility, which protects tooth enamel. Answers will vary as to the benefits of fluoridation.

44. A precipitate will form.

45. 1.2 g

46. [A] = s; [B] = 2s; $K_{sp} = 4s^3$

27. If the ion product is less than K_{sp}, the solution is unsaturated and precipitation will not occur. If the ion product is greater than K_{sp}, precipitation will occur until the ion concentrations decrease to equilibrium values.

28. 7.14×10^{-11}

29. a. 1.1×10^{-10}
   b. 5.06×10^{-5}

30. 2.8×10^{-3} mol/L

47. the reverse reaction

48. a. $CO_2(aq) + 2H_2O(l) \rightleftarrows H_3O^+(aq) + HCO_3^-(aq)$

b. During hyperventilation, the CO_2 concentration of the system is reduced. The reaction shifts to the left to compensate for the reduced CO_2 concentration.

c. The addition of acid shifts the reaction to the left, which results in a decrease of H_3O^+ to compensate for the addition of acid.

49. The Zn^{2+} concentration must be greater than 1.1×10^{-4} M.

50. Answers will vary.

51. Answers will vary.

52. Answers will vary.

CHAPTER REVIEW

47. Predicting Outcomes When gasoline burns in an automobile engine, nitric oxide is formed from oxygen and nitrogen. Nitric oxide is a major air pollutant. High temperatures, such as those found in a combustion engine, are needed for the following reaction:

$$N_2(g) + O_2(g) \rightleftarrows 2NO(g)$$

K for the reaction is 0.01 at 2000°C. If 4.0 mol of N_2, 0.1 mol of O_2, and 0.08 mol of NO are placed in a 1.0-L vessel at 2000°C, predict which reaction will be favored.

USING THE HANDBOOK

48. An equilibrium system helps maintain the pH of the blood. Review the material on the carbon dioxide-bicarbonate ion equilibrium system in Group 14 of the *Elements Handbook* (Appendix A), and answer the following.

a. Write the equation for the equilibrium system that responds to changes in H_3O^+ concentration.

b. Use Le Châtelier's principle to explain how hyperventilation affects this system.

c. How does this system maintain pH when acid is added?

49. The reactions used to confirm the presence of transition metal ions often involve the formation of precipitates. Review the analytical tests for the transition metals in the *Elements Handbook* (Appendix A). Use that information and **Figure 4.2** to determine the minimum concentration of Zn^{2+} needed to produce a precipitate that confirms the presence of Zn. Assume enough sulfide ion reagent is added to the unknown solution in the test tube to produce a sulfide ion concentration of 1.4×10^{-20} M.

RESEARCH AND WRITING

50. Find photos of several examples of stalagmites and stalactites in various caves. Investigate the equilibrium processes involved in the formation of stalagmites and stalactites.

51. Carry out library research on the use of catalysts in industrial processes. Explain what types of catalysts are used for specific processes, such as the Haber-Bosch process.

ALTERNATIVE ASSESSMENT

52. Research nitrogen narcosis in the library. What causes nitrogen narcosis, and how does it relate to Le Châtelier's principle?

Standards-Based Assessment

Answer the following items on a separate piece of paper.

MULTIPLE CHOICE

1. A chemical reaction is in equilibrium when
A. forward and reverse reactions have ceased.
B. the equilibrium constant equals 1.
C. forward and reverse reaction rates are equal.
D. No reactants remain.

2. Which change can cause the value of the equilibrium constant to change?
A. temperature
B. concentration of a reactant
C. concentration of a product
D. None of the above

3. Consider the following reaction:

$$2C(s) + O_2(g) \rightleftarrows 2CO(g)$$

The equilibrium constant expression for this reaction is
A. $\frac{[CO]^2}{[O_2]}$.
B. $\frac{[CO]^2}{[O_2][C]^2}$.
C. $\frac{2[CO]}{[O_2][2C]}$.
D. $\frac{[CO]}{[O_2]^2}$.

4. The solubility product of cadmium carbonate, $CdCO_3$, is 1.0×10^{-12}. In a saturated solution of this salt, the concentration of $Cd^{2+}(aq)$ ions is
A. 5.0×10^{-13} mol/L.
B. 1.0×10^{-12} mol/L.
C. 1.0×10^{-6} mol/L.
D. 5.0×10^{-7} mol/L.

5. Consider the following equation for an equilibrium system:

$$2PbS(s) + 3O_2(g) + C(s) \rightleftarrows 2Pb(s) + CO_2(g) + 2SO_2(g)$$

Which concentration(s) would be included in the denominator of the equilibrium constant expression?
A. $Pb(s)$, $CO_2(g)$, and $SO_2(g)$
B. $PbS(s)$, $O_2(g)$, and $C(s)$
C. $O_2(g)$, $Pb(s)$, $CO_2(g)$, and $SO_2(g)$
D. $O_2(g)$

6. If an exothermic reaction has reached equilibrium, then increasing the temperature will
A. favor the forward reaction.
B. favor the reverse reaction.
C. favor both the forward and reverse reactions.
D. have no effect on the equilibrium.

7. Le Châtelier's principle states that
A. at equilibrium, the forward and reverse reaction rates are equal.
B. stresses include changes in concentrations, pressure, and temperature.
C. to relieve stress, solids and solvents are omitted from equilibrium constant expressions.
D. chemical equilibria respond to reduce applied stress.

SHORT ANSWER

8. Describe the conditions that would allow you to conclusively determine that a solution is saturated. You can use only visual observation and cannot add anything to the solution.

9. The graph below shows the neutralization curve for 100 mL of 0.100 M acid with 0.100 M base. Which letter represents the equivalence point? What type of acid and base produced this curve?

EXTENDED RESPONSE

10. Explain how the same buffer can resist a change in pH when either an acid or a base is added. Give an example.

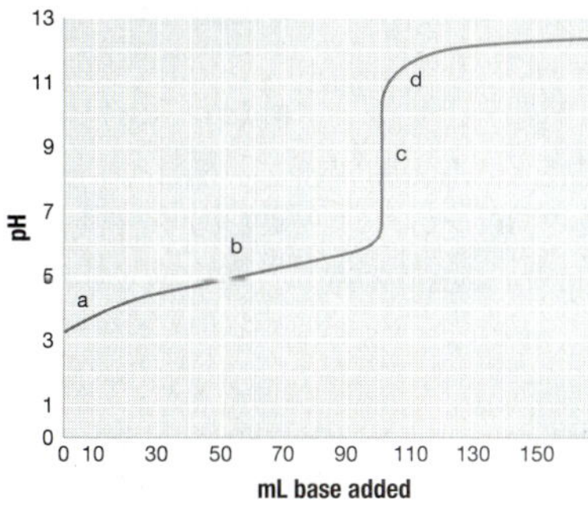

Test Tip
Keeping a positive attitude during any test will help you focus on the test and likely improve your score.

To give students practice under more realistic testing conditions, give them 60 minutes to answer all of the questions in this Standardized Test Preparation.

Test Answers

1. C
2. A
3. A
4. C
5. D
6. B
7. D
8. There would have to be some undissolved solid present in equilibrium with the solution. (The only way to determine for certain that a solution is saturated if no solid is present is to add more of the solid to see if it dissolves.)
9. c; weak acid and strong base
10. There are two components to all buffers, one to react with added acid and the other to react with added base. Examples will vary, but the components will include a weak acid and its salt, such as CH_3COOH and CH_3COONa, or a weak base and its salt, such as NH_3 and NH_4Cl.

Oxidation-Reduction Reactions

① Core Instruction

Chapter Resources

- The Teacher's Edition wrap has extensive teaching support for every lesson, including Misconception Alerts, Teach from Visuals, Demonstrations, Teaching Tips, Differentiated Instruction, and Problem Solving support.
- Several additional presentation tools are available online for every chapter, including Animated Chemistry features and Visual Concepts.
- You can open your lesson with the Why It Matters Video: Equations and Reactions.

Section	Instruction	Labs and Demonstrations Go Online for Materials Lists and Solutions Lists.
19.1	▪ **Textbook:** Oxidation and Reduction **Teaching Visuals:** Assigning Oxidation Numbers • Particle Model for a Redox Reaction • Rules for Assigning Oxidation Numbers **PowerPresentations**	▪ **Demonstration:** A Spontaneous Redox Reaction ▪ **Lab:** Oxidation-Reduction Reactions (Core Skill) ▪ **Lab:** Rust Race (Core Skill)
19.2	▪ **Textbook:** Balancing Redox Equations **Teaching Visuals:** Balancing Redox Equations Using the Half-Reaction Method **PowerPresentations**	▪ **Lab:** Reduction of Manganese in Permanganate Ion (Core Skill)
19.3	▪ **Textbook:** Oxidizing and Reducing Agents **Animated Chemistry:** Oxidizing and Reducing Agents **PowerPresentations**	▪ **QuickLab:** Redox Reactions

Find all of your resources online at HMDScience.com.

2 Support and Intervention

- **Interactive Reader** (English and Spanish)
- **Study Guide**
- **Interactive Review:** Review Games, Concept Maps, and Section Self-Checks
- **Scientific Reasoning Skill Builder**
- **Learn It! Videos**
- **Solve It! Cards**
- **Interactive Demos**
- **Sample Problem Sets**

3 Specialized Support

- **Chapter Summary Audio Files**
- **Interactive Reader Audio Files**
- **Differentiated Instruction:** Inclusion, Below Level, and English Learners (TE wrap)

Enrichment and Challenge

- **Why It Matters:** Skunk-Spray Remedy (SE)
- **WebLinks**

Assessment

- **Section Formative Assessments** (SE)
- **Section Quizzes**
- **Chapter Review** (SE)
- **Chapter Tests A and B**
- **Alternative Assessment** (TE wrap)
- **Online Assessment and Remediation**
- **ExamView Banks**

Where do I find it?

		PRINT	DVD	ONLINE
1	Animated Chemistry		■	■
	Demonstrations (TE wrap)	■		■
	Interactive Whiteboard		■	■
	Labs		■	■
	PowerPresentations		■	■
	QuickLabs	■	■	■
	Teaching Visuals		■	■
	Textbook	■	■	■
	Visual Concepts		■	■
	Why It Matters Videos		■	■
2	Interactive Demos		■	■
	Interactive Reader	■	■	■
	Interactive Reviews		■	■
	Learn It! Videos		■	■
	Sample Problem Sets		■	■
	Scientific Reasoning Skill Builder		■	■
	Smart Grapher Tool		■	■
	Solve It! Cards		■	■
	Study Guide		■	■
3	Chapter Summary Audio Files		■	■
	Differentiated Instruction (TE wrap)	■		
	Interactive Reader Audio Files		■	■

CHAPTER 19

Chapter Overview

Section 1 defines oxidation and reduction reactions and provides rules for determining oxidation numbers.

Section 2 presents guidelines for balancing redox equations by using the half-reaction method.

Section 3 describes the roles of the oxidizing agent and the reducing agent in a redox reaction.

▼ Focus and Motivate

Activate Prior Knowledge

Students may need a review of the following concepts:

- oxidation numbers
- balancing equations
- electronegativity
- the activity series

About the Image

The green patina on this building is the result of an oxidation-reduction reaction. The copper oxidizes in air to form the patina. At the same time, oxygen in the air is reduced.

Why It Matters

Students can access the video online and find other helpful resources at **HMDScience.com**.

Lab Preview

The following labs and demonstrations support the concepts presented in this chapter.

LABS

Oxidation-Reduction Reactions (Core Skill)

Rust Race (Core Skill)

Reduction of Manganese in Permanganate Ion (Core Skill)

QUICKLAB

Redox Reactions

DEMONSTRATION

A Spontaneous Redox Reaction

Oxidation and Reduction

Key Terms
oxidation
oxidized
reduction
reduced
oxidation-reduction reaction
redox reaction
half-reaction

SECTION 1

Main Ideas

- You can use rules to assign oxidation numbers.
- Oxidation occurs when valence electrons are lost.
- Reduction occurs when valence electrons are gained.
- Oxidation and reduction are paired reactions.

MAIN IDEA

You can use rules to assign oxidation numbers.

Oxidation-reduction reactions involve a transfer of electrons. Oxidation involves the loss of electrons, whereas reduction involves the gain of electrons. Reduction and oxidation half-reactions must occur simultaneously. These processes can be identified through the use of oxidation numbers (oxidation states). You became familiar with oxidation states and the rules for assigning oxidation numbers in a previous chapter. The rules to better understand reactions involving changing oxidation states are summarized in **Figure 1.1**.

FIGURE 1.1

RULES FOR ASSIGNING OXIDATION NUMBERS

Rule	Example
1. The oxidation number of any pure element is 0.	The oxidation number of Na(*s*) is 0.
2. The oxidation number of a monatomic ion equals the charge on the ion.	The oxidation number of Cl^- is −1.
3. The more electronegative element in a binary compound is assigned the number equal to the charge it would have if it were an ion.	The oxidation number of O in NO is −2.
4. The oxidation number of fluorine in a compound is always −1.	The oxidation number of F in LiF is −1.
5. Oxygen has an oxidation number of −2 unless it is combined with F, in which it is +1 or +2, or it is in a peroxide, in which it is −1.	The oxidation number of O in NO_2 is −2.
6 Hydrogen's oxidation state in most of its compounds is +1 unless it is combined with a metal, in which case it is −1.	The oxidation number of H in LiH is −1.
7. In compounds, Group 1 and 2 elements and aluminum have oxidation numbers of +1, +2, and +3, respectively.	The oxidation number of Ca in $CaCO_3$ is +2.
8. The sum of the oxidation numbers of all atoms in a neutral compound is 0.	The oxidation number of C in $CaCO_3$ is +4.
9. The sum of the oxidation numbers of all atoms in a polyatomic ion equals the charge of the ion.	The oxidation number of P in $H_2PO_4^-$ is +5.

Differentiated Instruction

BELOW LEVEL

Help students understand the definitions of *oxidation* and *reduction* by asking them what happens to the oxidation number of an atom or ion that undergoes oxidation. Students should recognize that oxidation involves the loss of electrons, which results in an increase in oxidation number. Point out that if a pure element is oxidized by losing an electron, its oxidation number increases from 0 to +1. Do the same for reduction. Students should recognize that reduction involves the gain of electrons, which results in a decrease in the oxidation number. Point out that if a pure element is reduced by gaining an electron, its oxidation number decreases from 0 to −1.

SECTION 1

Plan and Prepare

Objectives

Upon completion of this section, students should be able to do the following:

- Assign oxidation numbers to reactant and product species.
- Define *oxidation* and *reduction*.
- Explain what an oxidation-reduction reaction (redox reaction) is.

Classroom Catalyst

Quickly review oxidation numbers as previously presented, and then go immediately to **Figure 1.1.** Focus on each rule in turn, and ask students for additional examples. Emphasize that they should refer to **Figure 1.1** repeatedly until they memorize its contents.

Teach

Demonstration

A SPONTANEOUS REDOX REACTION

1. Add approximately **7 mL of 0.1 M KI** to a **100 mm petri dish,** and place the dish on an **overhead projector.**
2. Add **7 mL of 0.01 M $KMnO_4$** to the petri dish, and mix the solutions with a **stirring rod.**
3. Add a few drops of **1.0 M HCl** to the mixture, stir, and observe. (The purple color of $KMnO_4$ fades. An orange-brown precipitate of MnO_2 forms, and the solution develops the red-brown color of dissolved I_2.)

   Make sure students recognize the significance of the changes they observe.

Disposal Add 0.1 M KI to the $KMnO_4$ solution while stirring until all of the permanganate color is gone. Then add sufficient **0.1 M $Na_2S_2O_3$** while stirring to reduce all of the iodine to iodide. Adjust the pH to between 5 and 9, testing with a **pH meter** or **pH paper,** and pour the solution down the drain.

▼ Teach *continued*

TEACH FROM VISUALS

FIGURE 1.2 Point out to students that the figure illustrates how an element can exist in a number of different oxidation states. Reinforce this idea by asking students what oxidation numbers sulfur has in H_2S, S_8, SO_2, SO_4^{2-}, S_2O_3, and $S_2O_3^{2-}$. −2, 0, +4, +6, +3, +2

Application

Potassium dichromate, the orange solution in **Figure 1.2,** is used in some breath analyzers to estimate the level of alcohol in a person's bloodstream. When a person breathes into the dichromate solution, any ethanol present is oxidized by chromium, which has a +6 oxidation number. Chromium is reduced to a lower oxidation state that has a different color, such as the green color seen in Cr^{3+}. The color change can then be related to the amount of alcohol in the bloodstream.

ChemisTrivia

Transition-metal complexes show such dramatic color changes at different oxidation states because of variations of *d*-*d* transitions. Different oxidation numbers indicate different numbers of *d* valence electrons. This leads to different *d*-*d* transitions when the electrons are excited and hence different colors. For example, in Cr^{6+}, chromium no longer has any *d* electrons, so no *d*-*d* transitions can occur. The color changes in **Figure 1.2** are due to either slightly different ligand-ligand transitions or ligand-metal transitions, which are higher-lying excited states. Therefore, the color change is less significant between the two solutions where the metal has the same oxidation number.

Critical Thinking

Answer: Elements with multiple oxidation states are generally transition elements, located in the center of the periodic table.

FIGURE 1.2

Oxidation States of Chromium Compounds Chromium provides a very visual example of oxidation numbers. Different oxidation states of chromium have dramatically different colors. Solutions with the same oxidation state show less dramatic differences.

CRITICAL THINKING

Relate Examine the tables of ions and their oxidation numbers, **Figures 1.1** and **1.3,** in the chapter "Chemical Formulas and Chemical Compounds." Compare the elements that have multiple ions or oxidation states with the placement of those elements on the periodic table. What relationship is there between the ability to form multiple ions and where those elements are generally found on the periodic table?

FIGURE 1.3

Oxidation in NaCl Synthesis Sodium and chlorine react violently to form NaCl. The synthesis of NaCl from its elements illustrates the oxidation-reduction process.

MAIN IDEA

Oxidation occurs when valence electrons are lost.

Processes in which the atoms or ions of an element experience an increase in oxidation state are oxidation processes. The combustion of metallic sodium in an atmosphere of chlorine gas is shown in **Figure 1.3.** The sodium ions and chloride ions produced during this strongly exothermic reaction form a cubic crystal lattice in which sodium cations form ionic bonds to chloride anions. The chemical equation for this reaction is written as follows.

$$2Na(s) + Cl_2(g) \longrightarrow 2NaCl(s)$$

The formation of sodium ions illustrates an oxidation process because each sodium atom loses an electron to become a sodium ion. The oxidation state is represented by placing an oxidation number above the symbol of the atom and the ion.

$$\overset{0}{Na} \longrightarrow \overset{+1}{Na^+} + e^-$$

The oxidation state of sodium has changed from 0, its elemental state, to the +1 state of the ion (Rules 1 and 7, **Figure 1.1**). **A species whose oxidation number increases is oxidized.** The sodium atom is *oxidized* to a sodium ion.

Differentiated Instruction

BELOW LEVEL

Ask students why the Group 1 elements (alkali metals) form ions that have a +1 oxidation state and why the Group 2 elements (alkaline-earth metals) form ions that have a +2 oxidation state. Students should relate the oxidation state that is achieved to the number of valence electrons that are transferred to another atom in the formation of an ionic bond.

MAIN IDEA

Reduction occurs when valence electrons are gained.

Processes in which the oxidation state of an element decreases are reduction processes. Consider the behavior of chlorine in its reaction with sodium. Each chlorine atom accepts an electron and becomes a chloride ion. The oxidation state of chlorine decreases from 0 to −1 for the chloride ion (Rules 1 and 2, **Figure 1.1**).

$$\overset{0}{Cl_2} + 2e^- \longrightarrow 2\overset{-1}{Cl^-}$$

A species that undergoes a decrease in oxidation state is reduced. The chlorine atom is reduced to the chloride ion.

MAIN IDEA

Oxidation and reduction are paired reactions.

Electrons are released in oxidation and acquired in reduction. Therefore, for oxidation to occur during a chemical reaction, reduction must also occur. Furthermore, the number of electrons produced in oxidation must equal the number of electrons acquired in reduction. Recall that electrons are negatively charged and that for charge to be conserved, the number of electrons lost must equal the number of electrons gained. Mass is conserved in any chemical reaction. Therefore, like mass, the electrons exchanged during oxidation and reduction are conserved.

But why do we say a substance is *reduced* when it *gains* electrons? Remember, when electrons are gained, their negative electrical charge will cause the overall oxidation number to drop, that is, be reduced.

A transfer of electrons causes changes in the oxidation states of one or more elements. **Any chemical process in which elements undergo changes in oxidation number is an oxidation-reduction reaction. This name is often shortened to redox reaction.** An example of a redox reaction can be seen in **Figure 1.4,** in which copper is being oxidized and NO_3^- from nitric acid is being reduced. **The part of the reaction involving oxidation or reduction alone can be written as a half-reaction.** The overall equation for a redox reaction is the sum of two half-reactions. Because the number of electrons involved is the same for oxidation and reduction, they cancel each other out and do not appear in the overall chemical equation.

Equations for the reaction between nitric acid and copper illustrate the relationship between half-reactions and the overall redox reaction.

$$\overset{0}{Cu} \longrightarrow \overset{+2}{Cu^{2+}} + 2e^- \quad \text{(oxidation half-reaction)}$$

$$2\overset{+5\,-2}{NO_3^-} + 2e^- + 4\overset{+1}{H^+} \longrightarrow 2\overset{+4\,-2}{NO_2} + 2\overset{+1\,-2}{H_2O} \quad \text{(reduction half-reaction)}$$

$$\overset{0}{Cu} + 2\overset{+5}{NO_3^-} + 4H^+ \longrightarrow \overset{+2}{Cu^{2+}} + 2\overset{+4}{NO_2} + 2H_2O \quad \text{(redox reaction)}$$

Notice that electrons lost in oxidation appear on the product side of the oxidation half-reaction. Electrons are gained in reduction and appear as reactants in the reduction half-reaction.

FIGURE 1.4

Oxidation of Copper Copper is oxidized and nitrogen dioxide is produced when this penny is placed in a concentrated nitric acid solution.

ChemisTrivia

The term *oxidation* arose early in the history of chemistry, when scientists observed common combustion reactions in which an element was combined with oxygen. In all combustion reactions, electrons are lost by the burned element. In addition, when an element was separated from oxygen, as in the separation of a metal from its ore, the term *reduction* was used because a large amount of ore usually resulted in a much smaller amount of pure metal. Later, the terms *oxidation* and *reduction* came to be applied to any reaction in which electrons are lost and gained, respectively.

Misconception Alert!

Because both positive and negative charges arise in redox reactions, students may think that both positive and negative charges move from reactant to reactant. Use diagrams to show that only negatively-charged electrons move; positive charges arise when nuclear protons do not have enough electrons to neutralize them. For example, the Na^+ ion has a nuclear charge of +11 but has only 10 electrons. The Cl^- ion has a nuclear charge of +17 but has 18 electrons.

Teaching Tip

The acronym O.I.L. R.I.G. may help students remember the definitions of oxidation and reduction. **O.I.L.** stands for "**O**xidation **I**s **L**osing," and **R.I.G.** stands for "reduction is gaining."

INCLUSION

Help students understand oxidation and reduction by having students model the process. Have one student hold three signs, labeled *Na atom (oxidation state 0), electron,* and *Na ion (oxidation state +1)*. Have the student place the signs one over the other in the order given. Have another student hold two signs, labeled *Cl atom (oxidation state 0)* and *Cl ion (oxidation state −1)*. Have the two students stand slightly apart. Ask the students to rearrange the signs to model what happens during a redox reaction. The first student should take the *Na atom* sign and place it behind the other two signs, and then give the sign labeled *electron* to the other student. At this point, the sign labeled *Na ion (oxidation state +1)* will show. The other student should take the sign labeled *electron*, place it behind the other two signs, and move the *Cl atom* sign to the back so that the *Cl ion (oxidation state −1)* shows. The two students should then stand closer together. Have the class discuss what happened in terms of a redox reaction forming an ionic bond.

READING TOOLKIT

BRAINSTORMING Write the words *oxidation* and *reduction* on the board. In a class discussion, ask students to use prior knowledge to develop a definition for each term. Record the definitions so that they can be referenced later when the specific chemical meaning of each term is taught in the sections that follow.

▼ Teach *continued*

Application

Household bleach, sodium hypochlorite (NaOCl), removes stains from clothing through a redox reaction. The molecules that cause the stain are oxidized by OCl^-, and OCl^- is reduced to Cl^-.

$$\text{Stain molecules}(s) + OCl^-(aq) \longrightarrow \text{colorless molecules}(s) + Cl^-(aq)$$

For further discussion, ask students to determine the oxidation numbers of oxygen and chlorine in OCl^-.

Oxygen is more electronegative, so its oxidation number is −2, while chlorine's is +1.

Classroom Discussion

Instruct students to write the formulas of the reactants and products in the demonstration at the beginning of the section and to use **Figure 1.1** to determine the oxidation numbers of each atom. (It is not necessary to have performed the demonstration.) Ask students to interpret the changes in oxidation number in terms of oxidation and reduction. Ask them how many electrons are lost by one mole of the oxidized reactant and how many electrons are gained by one mole of the reduced reactant. Emphasize that just as many electrons are gained in reduction as are lost in oxidation. Therefore, the equation for the reaction must be balanced. Later, students will revisit this reaction and balance it.

WHY IT MATTERS

Photochromic Lenses S.T.E.M.

Photochromic eyeglasses darken when exposed to ultraviolet light and become transparent again in the absence of ultraviolet light. This process is the result of oxidation-reduction reactions. Silver chloride and copper(I) chloride are embedded in the lenses. The chloride ions absorb photons, and the silver chloride dissociates and forms chlorine atoms and silver atoms. The elemental silver darkens the lenses. Note that the chlorine ions are oxidized and the silver atoms are reduced. Then, the copper(I) ions reduce the chlorine atoms and form copper(II) ions. In the reverse process, the copper(II) ions oxidize the silver atoms back to the transparent silver ions.

Distinguishing Redox Reactions

Combining the half reactions gives a full picture of what occurs. Metallic copper reacts in nitric acid and in so doing one copper atom is oxidized from Cu to Cu^{2+} as two nitrogen atoms are reduced from a +5 oxidation state to a +4 oxidation state. Both atoms and electrons are conserved. This balanced chemical equation shows this.

$$3Cu + 8HNO_3 = 3Cu(NO_3)_2 + 2NO + 4H_2O$$

Remember, redox reactions are only those involving atoms that change oxidation states. If none of the atoms in a reaction change oxidation state, the reaction is *not* a redox reaction. For example, sulfur dioxide gas, SO_2, dissolves in water to form an acidic solution containing a low concentration of sulfurous acid, H_2SO_3.

$$\overset{+4\,-2}{SO_2} + \overset{+1\,-2}{H_2O} \longrightarrow \overset{+1\,+4\,-2}{H_2SO_3}$$

No atoms change oxidation states, so this is *not* a redox reaction.

When a solution of sodium chloride is added to a solution of silver nitrate, an ion-exchange reaction occurs and white silver chloride precipitates.

$$\overset{+1}{Na^+} + \overset{-1}{Cl^-} + \overset{+1}{Ag^+} + \overset{+5\,-2}{NO_3^-} \longrightarrow \overset{+1}{Na^+} + \overset{+5\,-2}{NO_3^-} + \overset{+1\,-1}{AgCl}$$

The oxidation state of each monatomic ion remains unchanged. Again, this reaction is *not* an oxidation-reduction reaction.

Redox Reactions and Covalent Bonds

Both the synthesis of NaCl from its elements and the reaction between copper and nitric acid involve ionic bonding. Substances with covalent bonds also undergo redox reactions. An oxidation number, unlike an ionic charge, has no physical meaning. That is, the oxidation number assigned to a particular atom is based on its electronegativity relative to the other atoms to which it is bonded in a given molecule; it is not based on any real charge on the atom. For example, an ionic charge of 1− results from the complete gain of one electron by an atom or other neutral species, whereas an oxidation state of −1 means an increased attraction for a bonding electron. A change in oxidation number does not require a change in actual charge.

When hydrogen burns in chlorine, a covalent bond forms from the sharing of two electrons. The two bonding electrons in the HCl molecule are not shared equally. Rather, the pair of electrons is more strongly attracted to the chlorine atom because of its higher electronegativity.

$$\overset{0}{H_2} + \overset{0}{Cl_2} \longrightarrow \overset{+1\,-1}{2HCl}$$

As specified by Rule 3 in **Figure 1.1**, chlorine in HCl is assigned an oxidation number of −1. Thus, the oxidation number for the chlorine atoms changes from 0, its oxidation number in the elemental state, to −1; chlorine atoms are reduced. As specified by Rule 1, the oxidation number of each hydrogen atom in the hydrogen molecule is 0. As specified by Rule 6, the oxidation state of the hydrogen atom in the HCl molecule is +1; the hydrogen atom is oxidized.

Differentiated Instruction

ENGLISH LEARNERS

Point out that oxidation numbers only provide a way to keep track of electrons in a redox reaction. For ionic compounds involving monatomic ions, keeping track of electrons is relatively easy. The oxidation number of the ion is equal to the ion charge. Emphasize, however, that oxidation number and ion charge are not the same. The former is an imaginary number, whereas the latter represents the actual charge on an ion. Ask students to explain what is meant by the term *imaginary*. Then have students use the covalent bond formed in HCl to explain why oxidation numbers are imaginary. Students should recognize that the oxidation numbers are assigned based on the unequal sharing of electrons. In the case of HCl, the shared electrons are attracted more toward the Cl atom, causing the atom to have a partial negative charge, represented by the oxidation number −1.

Thinking of Oxidation States

When you think of atoms changing oxidation states, don't think that either atom has totally lost or totally gained any electrons. In the case of the formation of hydrogen chloride, for example, hydrogen simply has donated a share of its bonding electron to the chlorine; it has not completely transferred that electron. The assignment of oxidation numbers allows an approximation of the electron distribution of a molecule. An element can have different oxidation numbers in different compounds. This difference in oxidation numbers can reveal the difference in electron distribution of the compounds.

Reactants and products in redox reactions are not limited to monatomic ions and uncombined elements. Elements in molecular compounds or polyatomic ions can also be oxidized and reduced if they have more than one nonzero oxidation state. An example of this is provided in the reaction between the copper penny and nitric acid in which the nitrate ion, NO_3^-, is converted to nitrogen dioxide, NO_2. Nitrogen is reduced in this reaction. Usually, we refer to the oxidation or reduction of the entire molecule or ion. Instead of saying that the nitrogen atom is reduced, we say the nitrate ion is reduced to nitrogen dioxide.

$$\cdots + \overset{+5}{N}O_3^- \longrightarrow \overset{+4}{N}O_2 + \cdots$$

SECTION 1 FORMATIVE ASSESSMENT

Reviewing Main Ideas

1. How are oxidation numbers assigned?
2. Label each of the following half-reactions as either an oxidation or a reduction half-reaction:
   a. $\overset{0}{Br_2} + 2e^- \longrightarrow 2\,\overset{-1}{Br^-}$
   b. $\overset{0}{Na} \longrightarrow \overset{+1}{Na^+} + e^-$
   c. $2\overset{-1}{Cl^-} \longrightarrow \overset{0}{Cl_2} + 2e^-$
   d. $\overset{0}{Cl_2} + 2e^- \longrightarrow 2\,\overset{-1}{Cl^-}$
   e. $\overset{+1}{Na^+} + e^- \longrightarrow \overset{0}{Na}$
   f. $\overset{0}{Fe} \longrightarrow \overset{+2}{Fe2+} + 2e^-$
   g. $\overset{+2}{Cu^{2+}} + 2e^- \longrightarrow \overset{0}{Cu}$
   h. $\overset{+3}{Fe^{3+}} + e^- \longrightarrow \overset{+2}{Fe^{2+}}$
3. Which of the following equations represent redox reactions?
   a. $2KNO_3(s) \longrightarrow 2KNO_2(s) + O_2(g)$
   b. $H_2(g) + CuO(s) \longrightarrow Cu(s) + H_2O(l)$
   c. $NaOH(aq) + HCl(aq) \longrightarrow NaCl(aq) + H_2O(l)$
   d. $H_2(g) + Cl_2(g) \longrightarrow 2HCl(g)$
   e. $SO_3(g) + H_2O(l) \longrightarrow H_2SO_4(aq)$
4. For each redox equation identified in the previous question, determine which element is oxidized and which is reduced.

Critical Thinking

5. **ANALYZING INFORMATION** Use the following equations for the redox reaction between Al^{3+} and Na to answer the questions below.

$$3\overset{0}{Na} \longrightarrow 3\overset{+1}{Na^+} + 3e^- \quad \text{(oxidation)}$$

$$\overset{+3}{Al^{3+}} + 3e^- \longrightarrow \overset{0}{Al} \quad \text{(reduction)}$$

$$3\overset{0}{Na} + \overset{+3}{Al^{3+}} \longrightarrow 3\overset{+1}{Na^+} + \overset{0}{Al} \quad \text{(redox reaction)}$$

   a. Explain how this reaction illustrates that charge is conserved in a redox reaction.
   b. Explain how this reaction illustrates that mass is conserved in a redox reaction.
   c. Explain why electrons do not appear as reactants or products in the combined equation.

Alternative Assessment

Place a small piece of magnesium ribbon in a petri dish on an overhead projector, and add enough 0.1 M HCl to cover the metal. Describe the nature of the reactants for the class. Allow students to observe the reaction, and then ask them to write the oxidation and reduction half-reactions and the complete redox equation.

Assess and Reteach

Assess Use the Formative Assessment on this page to evaluate student mastery of the section.

Reteach For students who need additional instruction, download the Section Study Guide.

Response to Intervention To reassess students' mastery, use the Section Quiz, available to print or to take directly online at **HMDScience.com**.

Answers to Section Assessment

1. See **Figure 1.1**.
2. a. reduction
   b. oxidation
   c. oxidation
   d. reduction
   e. reduction
   f. oxidation
   g. reduction
   h. reduction
3. a, b, and d
4. a. $\overset{-2}{O}$ is oxidized to $\overset{0}{O_2}$; $\overset{+5}{N}$ is reduced to $\overset{+3}{N}$
   b. $\overset{0}{H_2}$ is oxidized to $\overset{+1}{H}$; $\overset{2+}{Cu^{2+}}$ is reduced to $\overset{0}{Cu}$
   c. $\overset{0}{H_2}$ is oxidized to $\overset{+1}{H}$; $\overset{0}{Cl_2}$ is reduced to $\overset{-1}{C}$
5. a. Three electrons are lost in the oxidation half-reaction; three electrons are gained in the reduction process. The balanced equation has a charge of 3+ on both sides.
   b. There are 3 mol Na and 1 mol Al on both sides of the equation.
   c. The number of electrons lost equals the number of electrons gained, so they cancel out in the overall equation.

ChemisTrivia

In skunk spray, the pervasive odor similar to that of hydrogen sulfide comes from *mercaptans*, which are organic compounds that contain the functional group –SH. Ask students to look up in an organic chemistry textbook the structures of some other simple mercaptans and to explain how these compounds relate to H_2S.

Classroom Discussion

1. The article states that receptors in the nose are sensitive to sulfur in its low oxidation state but not to sulfur in its high oxidation state. Ask students to give examples of sulfur in both a low and a high oxidation state. Have them specify the oxidation number of sulfur in H_2S.
2. Have students explain the effect of the reaction with H_2O_2 on the oxidation states discussed in item 1.
3. Ask students if another reactant, such as Na_2O_2, could have been used instead of H_2O_2. They may realize that the choice of H_2O_2 was based partly on its availability and its harmlessness to animals and humans.

Answers

1. He learned that hydrogen peroxide can oxidize the compounds that cause the odor associated with hydrogen sulfide. He then thought of using hydrogen peroxide to safely neutralize the odor on a dog sprayed by a skunk.
2. Answers will vary, but the basic design must show that the ingredients in the package are kept separate until they are ready to be used. The packaging must also enable the ingredients to be mixed.

WHY IT MATTERS

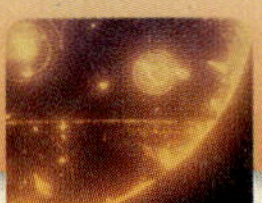

S.T.E.M.

Skunk-Spray Remedy

Have you ever given your pet a tomato juice bath to get rid of the smell of skunk spray on its coat? Chemistry has a much better way of conquering skunk spray.

Paul Krebaum, the inventor of a new "de-skunking" formula, says that while working as a materials engineer, he constantly had to deal with the less-than-pleasant smell of the hydrogen sulfide gas that was released from one of his experiments. Venting off the gas only partially solved the problem. A better solution would be to eliminate the smell entirely.

Mr. Krebaum rifled through his old chemistry books and found that hydrogen peroxide could oxidize these sulfur-containing compounds to much less smelly components. He immediately whipped up a hydrogen peroxide mixture, and it worked like a charm.

The equation below shows that hydrogen sulfide reacts with H_2O_2 to form sulfate compounds that do not have a bad odor.

$$2NaOH + 4H_2O_2 + H_2S \longrightarrow Na_2SO_4 + 6H_2O$$

"The receptors that are in your nose are sensitive to sulfur in its low oxidation state," says Mr. Krebaum. "However, they are not sensitive to sulfur in its high oxidation state."

Some time later, a friend of Mr. Krebaum's complained to him that a skunk had sprayed his pet. Because the odor in a skunk's spray also comes from compounds containing sulfur in a low oxidation state, Mr. Krebaum thought his solution might also work on this age-old problem. He mixed up a milder version to try out on the pet: 1 qt of a 3% hydrogen peroxide solution, $\frac{1}{4}$ cup of baking soda, and 1 tsp of liquid soap. His friend tried it out, and the result was one wet and unhappy—but much less smelly—pet.

Mr. Krebaum says that the hydrogen peroxide in the remedy actually oxidizes the compounds, while the baking soda reduces the acidity of the mixture and the soap helps to wash out the greasy skunk spray. This reaction can be seen in the following equation. The symbol *R* represents all the other elements in the sulfur-containing compound that are in skunk spray.

$$RSH + 3H_2O_2 + NaHCO_3 \longrightarrow RSO_3Na + 4H_2O + CO_2$$

The pet should be thoroughly washed with the mixture, and care should be taken to avoid the eyes. If the mixture is left on for a few minutes—long enough for the reaction to occur—and then rinsed away with tap water, the smell will disappear.

The formula does not bleach or cause any other negative side effects. Mr. Krebaum does have one warning: Mix the formula just before using it, because the mixture breaks down quickly. The reaction releases oxygen, so the formula should not be kept in a sealed container. Pressure will build up, and the lid could eventually blow off. For this reason, bottles of "Krebaum's Skunkinator" will not be appearing on drugstore shelves any time soon.

Questions

1. How did Paul Krebaum's research into the properties of H_2S result in a benefit to dog owners?
2. What are some possible packaging designs that Paul Krebaum could have used if he had wanted to sell his formula?

Skunk spray gets its odor from chemicals called mercaptans.

Balancing Redox Equations

SECTION 2

Main Idea

Oxidation and reduction reactions are balanced separately, then added together.

Equations for simple redox reactions can be balanced by inspection. Most redox equations, however, require more systematic methods. The equation-balancing process requires the use of oxidation numbers. In a balanced equation, both charge and mass are conserved. Although oxidation and reduction half-reactions occur together, their reaction equations are balanced separately and then combined to give the balanced redox-reaction equation.

MAIN IDEA

Oxidation and reduction reactions are balanced separately, then added together.

The *half-reaction method,* or ion-electron method, for balancing redox equations consists of seven steps. Oxidation numbers are assigned to all atoms and polyatomic ions to determine which species are part of the redox process. The oxidation and reduction equations are balanced separately for mass and charge. They are then added together to produce a complete balanced equation. These seven steps are applied to balance the reaction of hydrogen sulfide and nitric acid. Sulfuric acid, nitrogen dioxide, and water are the products of the reaction.

1. **Write the formula equation if it is not given in the problem. Then write the ionic equation.**

   Formula equation: $H_2S + HNO_3 \longrightarrow H_2SO_4 + NO_2 + H_2O$

   Ionic equation: $H_2S + H^+ + NO_3^- \longrightarrow 2H^+ + SO_4^{2-} + NO_2 + H_2O$

2. **Assign oxidation numbers. Delete substances containing only elements that do not change oxidation state.**

   $$\overset{+1\,-2}{H_2S} + \overset{+1}{H^+} + \overset{+5\,-2}{NO_3^-} \longrightarrow \overset{+1}{2H^+} + \overset{+6\,-2}{SO_4^{2-}} + \overset{+4\,-2}{NO_2} + \overset{+1\,-2}{H_2O}$$

   The sulfur changes oxidation state from −2 to +6. The nitrogen changes oxidation state from +5 to +4. The other substances are deleted.

   $$\overset{+1\,-2}{H_2S} + \overset{+5\,-2}{NO_3^-} \longrightarrow \overset{+6\,-2}{SO_4^{2-}} + \overset{+4\,-2}{NO_2}$$

   The remaining species are used in step 3.

Differentiated Instruction

INCLUSION

Learning-disabled and attention-deficit-disorder students can develop a study aid for understanding oxidation and reduction. Have them fold a piece of paper in half vertically. Label one side *Oxidation* and the other side *Reduction.* Students can fill each column with examples and descriptions of the appropriate change. For example, under *Oxidation,* they can write "loss of electrons," "increase in oxidation number," or "$\overset{0}{Na^0} \longrightarrow \overset{+1}{Na^{+1}}$."

SECTION 2

Plan and Prepare ▼

Objectives

Upon completion of this section, students should be able to do the following:

- Explain what must be conserved in redox equations.
- Balance redox equations by using the half-reaction method.

Classroom Catalyst

Students are already used to balancing equations by inspection and may resist the idea of following a procedure involving half-reactions. To emphasize the need for a systematic approach, write the equation for the reaction in the Spontaneous Redox Reaction demonstration (at the beginning of this chapter) on the board, and ask students to balance it.

$$MnO_4^- + I^- + H^+ \longrightarrow MnO_2 + I_2 + H_2O$$

The likely result will be

$$MnO_4^- + 2I^- + 4H^+ \longrightarrow MnO_2 + I_2 + 2H_2O$$

The equation is balanced as to mass but not balanced as to charge. Having made the point, use the half-reaction method to balance the equation.

The two half-reactions are

$$2MnO_4^- + 8H^+ + 6e^- \longrightarrow 2MnO_2 + 4H_2O$$

and

$$6I^- \longrightarrow 3I_2 + 6e^-$$

Teach ▼

Teaching Tip

Remind students that in redox reactions, the number of electrons lost in the oxidation half of the reaction should equal the number of electrons gained in the reduction half of the reaction. The net charge and number of ions must be the same on both sides of the balanced equation.

▼ Teach *continued*

Classroom Discussion

Ask students to think about the fact that hydrogen ions and hydroxide ions may be added to half-reactions when needed even when these ions are not specified in the equation. Reactions such as these occur in aqueous solutions in which both H^+ and OH^- are available.

READING TOOLKIT

SEQUENCING After students read this section, have them construct a flow chart or other visual graphic to represent the sequence they would follow to balance redox reactions.

3. Write the half-reaction for oxidation. In this example, the sulfur is being oxidized.

$$\overset{-2}{H_2S} \longrightarrow \overset{+6}{SO_4^{2-}}$$

- **Balance the atoms.** To balance the oxygen in this half-reaction, 4 water, H_2O, molecules must be added to the left side. This gives 10 extra hydrogen atoms on that side of the equation. Therefore, 10 hydrogen ions are added to the right side. In basic solution, OH^- ions and water may be used to balance atoms.

$$\overset{-2}{H_2S} + 4H_2O \longrightarrow \overset{+6}{SO_4^{2-}} + 10H^+$$

- **Balance the charge.** Electrons are added to the side having the greater positive net charge. The left side of the equation has no net charge; the right side has a net charge of 8+. For the charges to balance, each side must have the same net charge. Therefore, 8 electrons are added to the product side so that it has no charge and balances with the reactant side of the equation. Notice that the oxidation of sulfur from a state of −2 to +6 indicates a loss of 8 electrons.

$$\overset{-2}{H_2S} + 4H_2O \longrightarrow \overset{+6}{SO_4^{2-}} + 10H^+ + 8e^-$$

The oxidation half-reaction is now balanced.

4. Write the half-reaction for reduction. In this example, nitrogen is being reduced from a +5 state to a +4 state.

$$\overset{+5}{NO_3^-} \longrightarrow \overset{+4}{NO_2}$$

- **Balance the atoms.** One water, H_2O, molecule must be added to the product side of the reaction to balance the oxygen atoms. Therefore, two hydrogen ions must be added to the reactant side to balance the hydrogen atoms.

$$\overset{+5}{NO_3^-} + 2H^+ \longrightarrow \overset{+4}{NO_2} + H_2O$$

- **Balance the charge.** Electrons are added to the side having the greater positive net charge. The left side of the equation has a net charge of 1+. Therefore, 1 electron must be added to this side to balance the charge.

$$\overset{+5}{NO_3^-} + 2H^+ + e^- \longrightarrow \overset{+4}{NO_2} + H_2O$$

The reduction half-reaction is now balanced.

Problem Solving

DECONSTRUCTING PROBLEMS

Point out that if the oxidation numbers have been assigned correctly in step 2, then one species should be oxidized, as shown by an increase in its oxidation state. In this case, S is oxidized as evidenced by its oxidation number changing from -2 to +6 in step 3. Another species should be reduced, as shown by a decrease in its oxidation state. In this case, N is reduced as evidenced by its oxidation number changing from +5 to +4 in step 4.

5. **Conserve charge by adjusting the coefficients in front of the electrons so that the number lost in oxidation equals the number gained in reduction.** Write the ratio of the number of electrons lost to the number of electrons gained.

$$\frac{e^- \text{ lost in oxidation}}{e^- \text{ gained in reduction}} = \frac{8}{1}$$

This ratio is already in its lowest terms. If it were not, it would need to be reduced. Multiply the oxidation half-reaction by 1 (it remains unchanged) and the reduction half-reaction by 8. The number of electrons lost now equals the number of electrons gained.

$$1\left(H_2\overset{-2}{S} + 4H_2O \longrightarrow \overset{+6}{S}O_4^{2-} + 10H^+ + 8e^-\right)$$
$$8\left(\overset{+5}{N}O_3^- + 2H^- + e^- \longrightarrow \overset{+4}{N}O_2 + H_2O\right)$$

6. **Combine the half-reactions, and cancel out anything common to both sides of the equation.**

$$H_2\overset{-2}{S} + 4H_2O \longrightarrow \overset{+6}{S}O_4^{2-} + 10H^+ + 8e^-$$
$$8\overset{+5}{N}O_3^- + 16H^+ + 8e^- \longrightarrow 8\overset{+4}{N}O_2 + 8H_2O$$

$$8\overset{+5}{N}O_3^- + \overset{6}{\cancel{16}}H^+ + \cancel{8e^-} + H_2\overset{-2}{S} + \cancel{4H_2O} \longrightarrow$$
$$8\overset{+4}{N}O_2 + \overset{4}{\cancel{8}}H_2O + \overset{+6}{S}O_4^{2-} + \cancel{10H^+} + \cancel{8e^-}$$

Each side of the above equation has $10H^+$, $8e^-$, and $4H_2O$. These cancel each other out and do not appear in the balanced equation.

$$8\overset{+5}{N}O_3^- + H_2\overset{-2}{S} + 6H^+ \longrightarrow 8\overset{+4}{N}O_2 + 4H_2O + \overset{+6}{S}O_4^{2-}$$

7. **Combine ions to form the compounds shown in the original formula equation. Check to ensure that all other ions balance.** The NO_3^- ion appeared as nitric acid in the original equation. There are only 6 hydrogen ions to pair with the 8 nitrate ions. Therefore, 2 hydrogen ions must be added to complete this formula. If 2 hydrogen ions are added to the left side of the equation, 2 hydrogen ions must also be added to the right side of the equation.

$$8HNO_3 + H_2S \longrightarrow 8NO_2 + 4H_2O + SO_4^{2-} + 2H^+$$

The sulfate ion appeared as sulfuric acid in the original equation. The hydrogen ions added to the right side are used to complete the formula for sulfuric acid.

$$8HNO_3 + H_2S \longrightarrow 8NO_2 + 4H_2O + H_2SO_4$$

A final check must be made to ensure that all elements are correctly balanced.

FIGURE 2.1

Redox Titration As a $KMnO_4$ solution is titrated into an acidic solution of $FeSO_4$, deep purple MnO_4^- ions are reduced to colorless Mn^{2+} ions. When all Fe^{2+} ions are oxidized, MnO_4^- ions are no longer reduced to colorless Mn^{2+} ions. Thus, the first faint appearance of the MnO_4^- color indicates the end point of the titration.

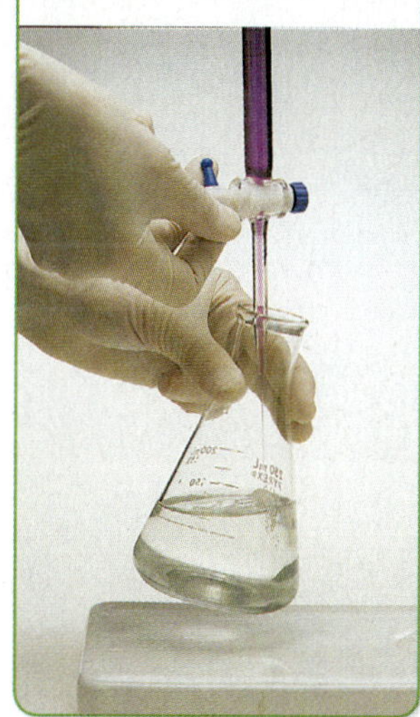

Teaching Tip

Although there is more than one procedure for balancing redox equations, only the half-reaction method is presented here. This method is the most useful because it can be applied to a wide range of reactions that occur in both acidic and basic solutions.

TEACH FROM VISUALS

FIGURE 2.1 This figure shows the experimental setup for performing the reaction upon which Sample Problem A (on the next page) is based. Draw students' attention to the deep purple color of the potassium permanganate in the buret and the colorless solution of iron(II) sulfate and sulfuric acid in the flask. As long as there are iron(II) ions available to be oxidized, the solution will remain colorless, but as soon as all the iron(II) ions are oxidized to iron(III), excess potassium permanganate will tinge the solution pink. It will begin to look more like the purple solution in the buret.

Differentiated Instruction

ENGLISH LEARNERS

Remind students that previously they balanced chemical equations by using the inspection method. In other words, they looked to determine how many atoms of each element were present on both sides of the equation. Point out that the process used to balance redox reactions shown here is called the half-reaction method. Have students explain why this term is used.

Students should recognize that the overall reaction is broken down into two half-reactions (oxidation and reduction), each half-reaction is balanced separately, and then the two half-reactions are combined to write the balanced equation.

▼ Teach continued

Teaching Tip

For reactions that take place in a basic solution, OH^- and H_2O are used to balance hydrogen and oxygen in redox half-reactions. To balance the oxygen, OH^- must be added to the reactant side of the reaction. Then, H_2O must be added to the product side of the reaction. For example, ClO^- ions react with CrO_2^- ions in a basic solution as follows.

oxidation:

$$1(CrO_2^- + 4OH^- \longrightarrow CrO_4^- + 2H_2O + 4e^-)$$

reduction:

$$2(ClO^- + H_2O + 2e^- \longrightarrow Cl^- + 2OH^-)$$

net:

$$CrO_2^- + 2ClO^- \longrightarrow CrO_4^- + 2Cl^-$$

Alternative Assessment

Instruct students to research the redox reactions that take place in the black-and-white photographic process and to write equations for their half-reactions and complete redox reactions.

Balancing Equations for Redox Reactions

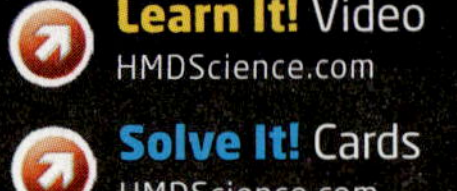

PREMIUM CONTENT

Learn It! Video HMDScience.com

Solve It! Cards HMDScience.com

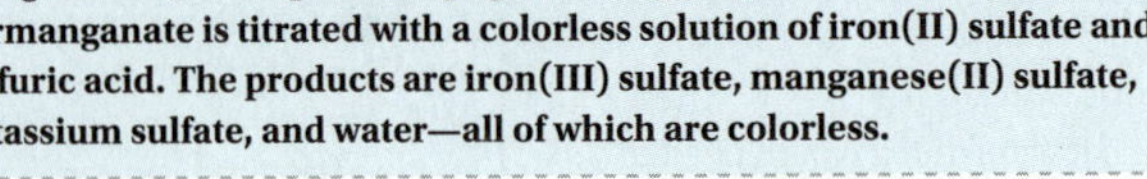

Sample Problem A **Write a balanced equation for the reaction shown in Figure 2.1 (on the previous page). A deep purple solution of potassium permanganate is titrated with a colorless solution of iron(II) sulfate and sulfuric acid. The products are iron(III) sulfate, manganese(II) sulfate, potassium sulfate, and water—all of which are colorless.**

SOLVE

1. *Write the formula equation if it is not given in the problem. Then write the ionic equation.*

$$KMnO_4 + FeSO_4 + H_2SO_4 \longrightarrow Fe_2(SO_4)_3 + MnSO_4 + K_2SO_4 + H_2O$$

$$K^+ + MnO_4^- + Fe^{2+} + SO_4^{2-} + 2H^+ + SO_4^{2-} \longrightarrow 2Fe^{3+} + 3SO_4^{2-} + Mn^{2+} + SO_4^{2-} + 2K^+ + SO_4^{2-} + H_2O$$

2. *Assign oxidation numbers to each element and ion. Delete substances containing an element that does not change oxidation state.*

$$\overset{+1}{K^+} + \overset{+7}{Mn}\overset{-2}{O_4^-} + \overset{+2}{Fe^{2+}} + \overset{+6}{S}\overset{-2}{O_4^{2-}} + 2\overset{+1}{H^+} + \overset{+6}{S}\overset{-2}{O_4^{2-}} \longrightarrow$$

$$2\overset{+3}{Fe^{3+}} + 3\overset{+6}{S}\overset{-2}{O_4^{2-}} + \overset{+2}{Mn^{2+}} + \overset{+6}{S}\overset{-2}{O_4^{2-}} + 2\overset{+1}{K^+} + \overset{+6}{S}\overset{-2}{O_4^{2-}} + \overset{+1}{H_2}\overset{-2}{O}$$

Only ions or molecules whose oxidation numbers change are retained.

$$\overset{+7}{Mn}\overset{-2}{O_4^-} + \overset{+2}{Fe^{2+}} \longrightarrow \overset{+3}{Fe^{3+}} + \overset{+2}{Mn^{2+}}$$

3. *Write the half-reaction for oxidation.* The iron shows the increase in oxidation number. Therefore, it is oxidized.

$$\overset{+2}{Fe^{2+}} \longrightarrow \overset{+3}{Fe^{3+}}$$

- *Balance the mass.* The mass is already balanced.
- *Balance the charge.*

$$\overset{+2}{Fe^{2+}} \longrightarrow \overset{+3}{Fe^{3+}} + e^-$$

4. *Write the half-reaction for reduction.* Manganese shows a change in oxidation number from +7 to +2. It is reduced.

$$\overset{+7}{MnO_4^-} \longrightarrow \overset{+7}{Mn^{2+}}$$

- *Balance the mass.* Water and hydrogen ions must be added to balance the oxygen atoms in the permanganate ion.

$$\overset{+7}{MnO_4^-} + 8H^+ \longrightarrow \overset{+7}{Mn^{2+}} + 4H_2O$$

- *Balance the charge.*

$$\overset{+7}{MnO_4^-} + 8H^+ + 5e^- \longrightarrow \overset{+7}{Mn^{2+}} + 4H_2O$$

5. *Adjust the coefficients to conserve charge.*

$$\frac{e^- \text{ lost in oxidation}}{e^- \text{ gained in reduction}} = \frac{1}{5}$$

$$5(Fe^{2+} \longrightarrow Fe^{3+} + e^-)$$

$$1(MnO_4^- + 8H^+ + 5e^- \longrightarrow Mn^{2+} + 4H_2O)$$

Continued

Problem Solving

TAKE IT FURTHER

Inform students that balancing redox reactions is more involved when they occur in either acidic or basic solutions. In acidic solutions, oxygen is balanced by using H_2O, and hydrogen is balanced by using H^+. In basic solutions, the same rules apply, but the equation is balanced as if H^+ were present. Have students identify a redox reaction that occurs in an acidic solution and show the steps that are used to balance it. Have them do the same for a redox reaction that occurs in a basic solution.

Balancing Equations for Redox Reactions (continued)

6. *Combine the half-reactions and cancel.*

$$5Fe^{2+} \longrightarrow 5Fe^{3+} + 5e^-$$
$$MnO_4^- + 8H^+ + 5e^- \longrightarrow Mn^{2+} + 4H_2O$$
$$MnO_4^- + 5Fe^{2+} + 8H^+ + \cancel{5e^-} \longrightarrow Mn^{2+} + 5Fe^{3+} + 4H_2O + \cancel{5e^-}$$

7. *Combine ions to form compounds from the original equation.* The iron(III) product appears in the original equation as $Fe_2(SO_4)_3$. Every iron(III) sulfate molecule requires two iron ions. Therefore, the entire equation must be multiplied by 2 to provide an even number of iron ions.

$$2(5Fe^{2+} + MnO_4^- + 8H^+ \longrightarrow 5Fe^{3+} + Mn^{2+} + 4H_2O)$$
$$10Fe^{2+} + 2MnO_4^- + 16H^+ \longrightarrow 10Fe^{3+} + 2Mn^{2+} + 8H_2O$$

The iron(II), iron(III), manganese(II), and 2 hydrogen ions in the original equation are paired with sulfate ions. Iron(II) sulfate requires 10 sulfate ions, and sulfuric acid requires 8 sulfate ions. To balance the equation, 18 sulfate ions must be added to each side. On the product side, 15 of these ions form iron(III) sulfate, and 2 of them form manganese(II) sulfate. That leaves 1 sulfate ion unaccounted for. The permanganate ion requires the addition of 2 potassium ions to each side. These 2 potassium ions form potassium sulfate on the product side of the reaction.

$$10FeSO_4 + 2KMnO_4 + 8H_2SO_4 \longrightarrow 5Fe_2(SO_4)_3 + 2MnSO_4 + K_2SO_4 + 8H_2O$$

Final inspection shows that atoms and charges are balanced.

Practice

Answers in Appendix E

1. Copper reacts with hot, concentrated sulfuric acid to form copper(II) sulfate, sulfur dioxide, and water. Write and balance the equation for this reaction.
2. Write and balance the equation for the reaction between nitric acid and potassium iodide. The products are potassium nitrate, iodine, nitrogen monoxide, and water.

SECTION 2 FORMATIVE ASSESSMENT

Reviewing Main Ideas

1. What two quantities are conserved in redox equations?
2. Why do we add H^+ and H_2O to some half-reactions and OH^- and H_2O to others?
3. Balance the following redox reaction:
$Na_2SnO_2 + Bi(OH)_3 \longrightarrow Bi + Na_2SnO_3 + H_2O$

Critical Thinking

4. **RELATING IDEAS** When heated, elemental phosphorus, P_4, produces phosphine, PH_3, and phosphoric acid, H_3PO_4. How many grams of phosphine are produced if 56 g P_4 have reacted?

Answers to Section Assessment

1. charge and mass
2. Because these reactions take place in aqueous solution, there are always some H^+ and OH^- ions present. In acidic solutions, excess H^+ ions are available. In basic solutions, excess OH^- ions are available.
3. $3Na_2SnO_2 + 2Bi(OH)_3 \longrightarrow 2Bi + 3Na_2SnO_3 + 3H_2O$
4. 38 g PH_3

Classroom Practice

A-1 The orange color of $K_2Cr_2O_7$ changes to the green color of the Cr^{3+} ion when an acidic solution of potassium dichromate is used in a breath analyzer to test for the presence of ethanol, C_2H_5OH. Write and balance the equation. $K_2Cr_2O_7$, HCl, and C_2H_5OH are the reactants; $CrCl_3$, CO_2, KCl, and H_2O are the products.

Answer:
$2K_2Cr_2O_7 + C_2H_5OH + 16HCl \longrightarrow 4CrCl_3 + 11H_2O + 2CO_2 + 4KCl$

Answers

Practice A

1. $Cu + 2H_2SO_4 \longrightarrow CuSO_4 + SO_2 + 2H_2O$
2. $8HNO_3 + 6KI \longrightarrow 6KNO_3 + 3I_2 + 2NO + 4H_2O$

Assess and Reteach

Assess Use the Formative Assessment on this page to evaluate student mastery of the section.

Reteach For students who need additional instruction, download the Section Study Guide.

Response to Intervention To reassess students' mastery, use the Section Quiz, available to print or to take directly online at **HMDScience.com**.

SECTION 3

▼ Plan and Prepare

Objectives

Upon completion of this section, students should be able to do the following:

- Relate chemical activity to oxidizing and reducing strength.
- Explain the concept of disproportionation.

Classroom Catalyst

Introduce definitions of *oxidizing agent* and *reducing agent* by labeling an empty box "electrons." Ask a student to take electrons (the box) from you. Point out that the student was the agent of your loss of electrons and that you were the agent of the student's gain of electrons. Introduce the term *oxidizing agent* by telling students that by causing you to lose electrons, the student is the oxidizing agent. You are the *reducing agent* because you caused the student to gain electrons.

▼ Teach

TEACH FROM TABLES

FIGURE 3.1 Encourage students to refer to the table until they master the definitions and concepts of oxidation and reduction. Ask students questions such as the following: Is the process oxidation or reduction when Br^- is converted to Br_2? oxidation Is Br^- an oxidizing or reducing agent? reducing Does Fe^{2+} gain or lose electrons when it is converted to Fe^{3+}? lose electrons When sodium reacts with chlorine, which is the oxidizing agent? chlorine

Check for Understanding

Answer: The more reactive an element is, the higher it appears in the activity series and the greater a reducing agent it is. The less reactive an element is, the lower it appears in the activity series and the greater an oxidizing agent it is.

SECTION 3

Main Ideas

- The more active an element is, the better it acts as an oxidizer or reducer.
- Some substances can be oxidizers and reducers in the same reaction.

Oxidizing and Reducing Agents

Key Terms
reducing agent
oxidizing agent
disproportionation

A reducing agent is a substance that has the potential to cause another substance to be reduced. Reducing agents lose electrons; they attain a more positive oxidation state during an oxidation-reduction reaction. Therefore, the reducing agent is the oxidized substance.

An oxidizing agent is a substance that has the potential to cause another substance to be oxidized. Oxidizing agents gain electrons and attain a more negative oxidation state during an oxidation-reduction reaction. The oxidizing agent is the reduced substance. **Figure 3.1** helps clarify the terms describing the oxidation-reduction process.

MAIN IDEA

The more active an element is, the better it acts as an oxidizer or reducer.

Different substances can be compared and rated by their relative potential as reducing and oxidizing agents. For example, the order of the elements in the activity series, seen in the chapter on chemical equations and reactions, is related to each element's tendency to lose electrons. Elements in this series lose electrons to the positively charged ions of any element below them in the series. The more active an element is, the greater its tendency to lose electrons and the better a reducing agent it is. The greater the distance is between two elements in the list, the more likely it is that a redox reaction will take place between them. These elements and some other familiar substances are arranged in **Figure 3.2** according to their activity as oxidizing and reducing agents.

CHECK FOR UNDERSTANDING
Describe In your own words, describe the relationship between the relative strength of oxidizing and reducing agents and their placement on the activity series table (given in the chapter "Chemical Equations and Reactions").

FIGURE 3.1

OXIDATION-REDUCTION TERMINOLOGY

Term	Change in oxidation number	Change in electron population
Oxidation	in a positive direction	loss of electrons
Reduction	in a negative direction	gain of electrons
Oxidizing agent	in a negative direction	gains electrons
Reducing agent	in a positive direction	loses electrons

Differentiated Instruction

BELOW LEVEL

Write the equation for the reaction between Na and Cl_2 on the board.

$2Na(s) + Cl_2(g) \longrightarrow 2NaCl(s)$

Have students assign oxidation numbers, and identify the substance oxidized, the substance reduced, and the reducing and oxidizing agents.

Students should recognize that the substance that is oxidized is the reducing agent because it supplies the electron that reduces the other substance. In turn, the substance that is reduced is the oxidizing agent because it "allows" the other substance to be oxidized by accepting the electron. The oxidation number for sodium ions is +1 and the oxidation number for chloride ions is −1.

The fluorine atom is the most highly electronegative atom. It is also the most active oxidizing agent. Because of its strong attraction for its own electrons, the fluoride ion is the weakest reducing agent. The negative ion of a strong oxidizing agent is a weak reducing agent.

The positive ion of a strong reducing agent is a weak oxidizing agent. As shown in **Figure 3.2,** Li atoms are strong reducing agents because Li is a very active metal. When Li atoms oxidize, they produce Li^+ ions, which are unlikely to reacquire electrons, so Li^+ ions are weak oxidizing agents.

The left column of each pair also shows the relative abilities of these metals to displace other metals from compounds. Zinc, for example, is above copper, so zinc is a more active reducing agent. It displaces copper ions from solutions of copper compounds, as shown in **Figure 3.3.** A copper(II) ion, however, is a more active oxidizing agent than a zinc ion.

Nonmetals and some important ions also are included in the series in **Figure 3.2.** Any reducing agent is oxidized by the oxidizing agents below it. Observe that F_2 displaces Cl^-, Br^-, and I^- ions from their solutions. Cl_2 displaces Br^- and I^- ions, and Br_2 displaces I^- ions. The equation for the displacement of Br^- by Cl_2 is as follows.

$$Cl_2 + 2Br^{-2}(aq) \longrightarrow 2Cl^-(aq) + Br_2$$

$$2\overset{-1}{Br^-} \longrightarrow \overset{0}{Br_2} + 2e^- \quad \text{(oxidation)}$$

$$\overset{0}{Cl_2} + 2e^- \longrightarrow 2\overset{-1}{Cl^-} \quad \text{(reduction)}$$

In every redox reaction, there is one reducing agent and one oxidizing agent. In the preceding example, Br^- is the reducing agent and Cl_2 is the oxidizing agent.

FIGURE 3.2

RELATIVE STRENGTH OF OXIDIZING AND REDUCING AGENTS

Reducing agents	Oxidizing agents
Li	Li^+
K	K^+
Ca	Ca^{2+}
Na	Na^+
Mg	Mg^{2+}
Al	Al^{3+}
Zn	Zn^{2+}
Cr	Cr^{3+}
Fe	Fe^{2+}
Ni	Ni^{2+}
Sn	Sn^{2+}
Pb	Pb^{2+}
H_2	H_3O^+
H_2S	S
Cu	Cu^{2+}
I^-	I_2
MnO_4^{2-}	MnO_4^-
Fe^{2+}	Fe^{3+}
Hg	Hg_2^{2+}
Ag	Ag^+
NO_2^-	NO_3^-
Br^-	Br_2
Mn^{2+}	MnO_2
SO_2	H_2SO_4 (conc.)
Cr^{3+}	$Cr_2O_7^{2-}$
Cl^-	Cl_2
Mn^{2+}	MnO_4^-
F^-	F_2

Increasing strength (reducing agents, upward) — Increasing strength (oxidizing agents, downward)

FIGURE 3.3

Reduction of Copper by Zinc

Zinc displaces copper ions from a copper(II) sulfate solution. Metallic copper precipitates.

CRITICAL THINKING

Analyze Examine **Figure 3.2** closely. Various oxidation states of iron (Fe) appear in both the top and bottom half and left and right columns of the table. What pattern becomes apparent when you compare the oxidation numbers in each case and iron's function as an oxidizing or reducing agent?

TEACH FROM TABLES

FIGURE 3.2 Point out that the strong reducing agents are those that easily give up electrons. Lithium easily gives up an electron to form the 1+ ion. Relate this fact to the electron configuration of lithium. The lost electron is the $2s^1$ electron; by losing it, lithium achieves the stable noble-gas configuration of helium. Point out that other Group 1 and 2 elements are near the top of the first column in this table. This should not be a surprise because students have already learned that these groups have low ionization energies. F^- is at the bottom of the column of reducing agents, so it is not a strong reducing agent, which means it has little tendency to give up an electron and become oxidized. Students should recall that fluorine has the highest electron affinity of any element. A reducing agent can reduce any species in the right-hand column that is below it. So, lithium readily reduces F_2 to form LiF.

Teaching Tip

The following polyatomic ions make excellent oxidizing agents because their central atoms have high oxidation numbers: IO_4^-, ClO_4^-, MnO_4^-, NO_3^-, CrO_4^{2-}, and $Cr_2O_7^{2-}$.

READING TOOLKIT

PAIRED READING Instruct students to form pairs and to silently read Section 3. As they read, have them place self-adhesive notes with check marks next to passages they understand and place notes with question marks next to passages they find confusing. Both readers should work together to understand all the passages. Have each pair create a list of questions to pose to the class.

Critical Thinking

Answer: Iron can easily act as both an oxidizing agent and a reducing agent because it has the ability to donate electrons (reducing) and it contains an extra orbital to accept electrons (oxidizing).

INCLUSION

Help students understand how to use an activity series to predict if a redox reaction will occur. Write the following on the board:

$Mg + Pb(NO_3)_2 \longrightarrow ?$

Have students use toothpicks and gumdrops of three different colors to build models of these substances. Ask students to use the activity series in **Figure 3.2** to predict if the reaction occurs and to rearrange the toothpicks and gumdrops if necessary. Students should rearrange the gumdrops to show that this redox reaction occurs.

Other possibilities to write on the board include:

$Ag + NaNO_3$ no redox reaction

$Zn + PbSO_4$ redox reaction

$Au + HCl$ no redox reaction

▼ Teach *continued*

QuickLab

In the decomposition of H_2O_2, the MnO_2 acts as a catalyst to speed up the normally slow reaction.

Safety Students should wear safety goggles and an apron. During the $CuCl_2$ experiment, the solution can get hot. Do not allow students to touch the beaker while the reaction is in progress.

Disposal Solids should be removed from the solutions and thrown away. Add 1.0 M NaOH to the solution to precipitate any remaining copper as solid $Cu(OH)_2$; discard the solid. Adjust the pH so that it is between 5 and 9 and dilute with a tenfold excess of water. Then pour the diluted solutions down the drain.

DISCUSSION

1. $2H_2O_2 \longrightarrow O_2 + 2H_2O$; $3CuCl_2 + 2Al \longrightarrow 2AlCl_3 + 3Cu$
2. Hydrogen peroxide was oxidized to oxygen and reduced to water. Evidence for the formation of O_2 was seen when a glowing splint burst into flames when placed in the reaction test tube. Copper(II) ions were reduced to copper metal, and aluminum metal was oxidized to Al(III) ions.

QuickLAB REDOX REACTIONS

PROCEDURE

Record your results in a data table.

1. Put 10 mL of hydrogen peroxide in a test tube, and add a small amount of manganese dioxide (equal to the size of about half a pea). What is the result?
2. Insert a glowing wooden splint into the test tube (see diagram). What is the result? If oxygen is produced, a glowing wooden splint inserted into the test tube will glow brighter.
3. Fill the 250 mL beaker halfway with the copper(II) chloride solution.
4. Cut foil into 2 cm × 12 cm strips.
5. Add the aluminum strips to the copper(II) chloride solution. Use a glass rod to stir the mixture, and observe for 12 to 15 minutes. What is the result?

DISCUSSION

1. Write balanced equations showing what happened in each of the reactions.
2. Write a conclusion for the two experiments.

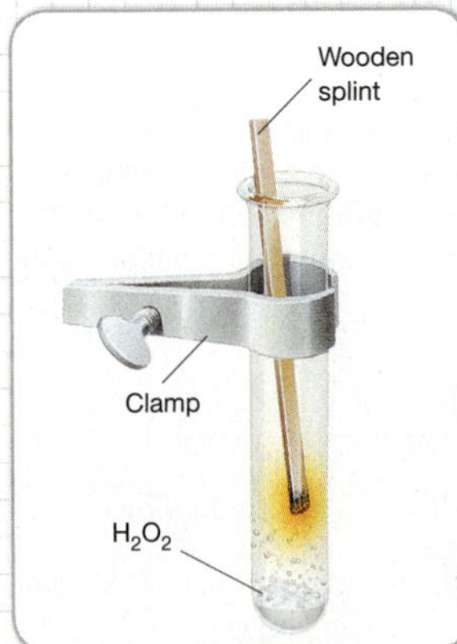

MATERIALS

- aluminum foil
- beaker, 250 mL
- 1 M copper(II) chloride solution, $CuCl_2$
- 3% hydrogen peroxide
- manganese dioxide
- metric ruler
- scissors
- test-tube clamp
- test tube, 16 × 150 mm
- wooden splint

SAFETY

Wear safety goggles and an apron.

MAIN IDEA

Some substances can be oxidizers and reducers in the same reaction.

Some substances can be both reduced and oxidized easily. For example, peroxide ions, O_2^{2-}, have a relatively unstable covalent bond between the two oxygen atoms. The electron-dot formula is written as follows.

$$[:\ddot{O}:\ddot{O}:]^{2-}$$

Each oxygen atom has an oxidation number of −1. The peroxide ion structure represents an intermediate oxidation state between O_2 and O^{2-}. Therefore, the peroxide ion is highly reactive.

Hydrogen peroxide, H_2O_2, is a covalent compound. It decomposes into water and molecular oxygen, as shown in the equation below.

$$2H_2\overset{-1}{O}_2 \longrightarrow 2H_2\overset{-2}{O} + \overset{0}{O}_2$$

Differentiated Instruction

ENGLISH LEARNERS

To help students understand what the term *disproportionation reaction* means, write the following equation on the board.

$$Cl_2(aq) + H_2O(l) \longleftrightarrow HOCl(aq) + H^+(aq) + Cl^-(aq)$$

Have students explain why this reaction is an example of a disproportionation reaction. Provide a hint by telling students to assign oxidation numbers and look for a substance that is oxidized and a substance that is reduced. Students should recognize that the oxidation number of Cl in Cl_2 is 0. This oxidation number changes from 0 to −1 in Cl^- and from 0 to +1 in HOCl. Therefore, Cl_2 has undergone both reduction and oxidation.

FIGURE 3.4

Disproportionation in Nature A bombardier beetle can repel large predators such as frogs with a chemical defense mechanism that uses the disproportionation of hydrogen peroxide.

Notice that in this reaction, hydrogen peroxide is both oxidized and reduced. Oxygen atoms that become part of gaseous oxygen molecules are oxidized. The oxidation number of these oxygen atoms increases from −1 to 0. Oxygen atoms that become part of water are reduced. The oxidation number of these oxygen atoms decreases from −1 to −2. **A process in which a substance acts as both an oxidizing agent and a reducing agent is called disproportionation.** A substance that undergoes disproportionation is both *self-oxidizing* and *self-reducing*.

The bombardier beetle defends itself by spraying its enemies with an unpleasant hot chemical mixture, as shown in **Figure 3.4.** The catalyzed disproportionation of hydrogen peroxide produces hot oxygen gas. This gas gives the insect an ability to eject irritating chemicals from its abdomen with explosive force.

SECTION 3 FORMATIVE ASSESSMENT

Reviewing Main Ideas

1. Describe the chemical activity of the alkali metals and of the halogens on the basis of oxidizing and reducing strength.
2. The photo on the right depicts two redox reactions. Both nails are in a sulfuric acid solution. Answer the following questions:
   a. When zinc is wrapped around an iron nail, is the iron or zinc oxidized?
   b. When copper is wrapped around an iron nail, is the iron or copper oxidized?
3. Would Cl_2 be reduced by I^-? Explain.
4. Which is the stronger oxidizing agent in each of the following pairs: Cu^{2+} or Al^{3+}, I_2 or S, F_2 or Li^+?
5. What is meant by *disproportionation*?

Critical Thinking

6. **ORGANIZING IDEAS** In general, where in the periodic table are the elements found that in elemental form are the strongest oxidizing agents? Explain.

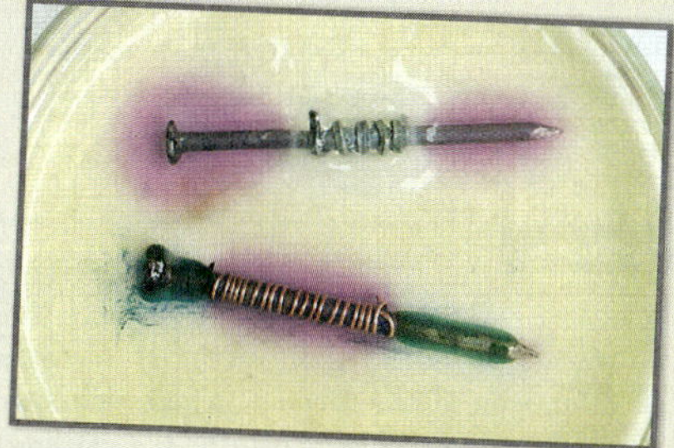

Answers to Section Assessment

1. The alkali metals are active reducing agents, while the halogens are active oxidizing agents.
2. a. zinc
   b. iron
3. Yes; Cl_2 is a stronger oxidizing agent than I_2.
4. Cu^{2+}, I_2, F_2
5. Disproportionation is a process by which a substance acts as both an oxidizing agent and a reducing agent and is self-oxidizing and self-reducing.
6. The strongest oxidizing agents contain elements that are located in the top right of the periodic table (excluding the noble gases). These elements have the highest electron affinity and therefore are the ones that most easily gain electrons.

Teaching Tip

Peroxides are the only compounds in which oxygen has the oxidation number −1 instead of −2. Sodium peroxide, Na_2O_2, is a common peroxide.

Assess and Reteach ▼

Assess Use the Formative Assessment on this page to evaluate student mastery of the section.

Reteach For students who need additional instruction, download the Section Study Guide.

Response to Intervention To reassess students' mastery, use the Section Quiz, available to print or to take directly online at **HMDScience.com**.

Answers

1. $2MnO_2 + NaClO_3 + 2NaOH \longrightarrow 2NaMnO_4 + NaCl + H_2O$
2. $N_2O + 2KClO + 2KOH \longrightarrow 2KCl + 2KNO_2 + H_2O$

Math Tutor — Balancing Redox Equations

A redox equation must conserve both mass and charge. So, to balance a redox equation, you must balance both atoms and charge (electrons). The problem-solving tips and sample below show how to balance an equation for a redox reaction in *basic* solution.

Problem-Solving TIPS

To balance redox equations for reactions in *basic* solution:

- Add OH^- and H_2O to balance oxygen and hydrogen in the redox half-reactions.
- Add OH^- ions to the side of the equation that needs oxygen atoms. Make sure you add enough OH^- ions so that the number of oxygen atoms added is twice the number needed.
- Then, add enough H_2O molecules to the other side of the equation to balance the hydrogen atoms.

Sample Problem

The following unbalanced equation represents a redox reaction that takes place in a basic solution containing KOH. Balance the redox equation.

$$Br_2(l) + KOH(aq) \longrightarrow KBr(aq) + KBrO_3(aq)$$

Write the full ionic equation, assign oxidation numbers, and eliminate species whose oxidation numbers do not change. The result is the following equation:

$$\overset{0}{Br_2} \longrightarrow \overset{-1}{Br^-} + \overset{+5}{Br}O_3^-$$

Divide this equation into half-reactions. Note that Br_2 is the reactant in both half-reactions.

Reduction: $Br_2 \longrightarrow Br^-$ Oxidation: $Br_2 \longrightarrow BrO_3^-$

Add H_2O and OH^- to balance atoms in basic solution. Then, add electrons to balance charge.

Reduction: $Br_2 + 2e^- \longrightarrow 2Br^-$ (no need to add H_2O or OH^-)

Oxidation: $12OH^- + Br_2 \longrightarrow 2BrO_3^- + 6H_2O + 10e^-$

To balance transferred electrons, you must multiply the reduction half-reaction by 5 so that both reactions have $10e^-$.

$$5 \times (Br_2 + 2e^- \longrightarrow 2Br^-) = 5Br_2 + 10e^- \longrightarrow 10Br^-$$

Combining the two half-reactions gives

$$5Br_2 + 12OH^- + Br_2 + 10e^- \longrightarrow 10Br^- + 2BrO_3^- + 6H_2O + 10e^-$$

Canceling common species gives

$$6Br_2 + 12OH^- \longrightarrow 10Br^- + 2BrO_3^- + 6H_2O$$

Returning the potassium ions to the equation gives

$$6Br_2 + 12KOH \longrightarrow 10KBr + 2KBrO_3 + 6H_2O, \text{ or } 3Br_2 + 6KOH \longrightarrow 5KBr + KBrO_3 + 3H_2O$$

Practice

1. Balance the following equation for a redox reaction that takes place in basic solution:
   $MnO_2(s) + NaClO_3(aq) + NaOH(aq) \longrightarrow NaMnO_4(aq) + NaCl(aq) + H_2O(l)$
2. Balance the following equation for a redox reaction that takes place in basic solution:
   $N_2O(g) + KClO(aq) + KOH(aq) \longrightarrow KCl(aq) + KNO_2(aq) + H_2O(l)$

610 Chapter 19

CHAPTER 19 Summary

Review Games
Concept Maps

SECTION 1 Oxidation and Reduction

- Oxidation numbers are assigned by the set of rules listed in **Figure 1.1.** Oxidation numbers are based on the distribution of electrons in a molecule.
- Oxidation-reduction reactions consist of two half-reactions that must occur simultaneously.
- Oxidation-reduction reactions are identified by examining the changes in the oxidation numbers of atoms in the reactants and products.
- Oxidation involves the loss of electrons, and reduction involves the gain of electrons.
- A species whose oxidation number increases is oxidized. A species whose oxidation number decreases is reduced.

KEY TERMS

oxidation
oxidized
reduction
reduced
oxidation-reduction reaction
redox reaction
half-reaction

SECTION 2 Balancing Redox Equations

- Charge and mass are conserved in a balanced redox equation.
- In the half-reaction method for balancing equations, the atoms and charge of oxidation and reduction equations are balanced separately. Then, they are combined to give a complete balanced equation.
- In a half-reaction, the charge on the reactant side must equal the charge on the product side, but these charges do not need to be zero.
- For the half-reaction method, the atoms in each half-reaction are balanced by adding H^+ ions and H_2O molecules in acidic solutions. If the solution is basic, OH^- ions and H_2O molecules are added to balance the atoms in each half-reaction.
- The number of electrons lost in the oxidation half-reaction must equal the number of electrons gained in the reduction half-reaction. The two half-reactions must be multiplied by appropriate factors to ensure that the same number of electrons are transferred.

SECTION 3 Oxidizing and Reducing Agents

- The substance that is *reduced* in redox reactions is the *oxidizing agent* because it *acquires* electrons from the substance that is oxidized.
- The substance that is *oxidized* in a redox reaction is the *reducing agent* because it *supplies* the electrons to the substance that is reduced.
- Strong reducing agents are substances that easily give up electrons.
- Disproportionation is a process in which a substance is both an oxidizing agent and a reducing agent.

KEY TERMS

reducing agent
oxidizing agent
disproportionation

Review Answers

1. a. Oxidation causes atoms or ions to attain a more positive oxidation state and lose e^-. Reduction causes atoms or ions to attain a more negative oxidation state and gain e^-.
   b. Answers will vary; oxidation: $Na \longrightarrow Na^+ + e^-$ reduction: $Cl_2 + 2e^- \longrightarrow 2Cl^-$
2. a, b, c, f, g, i
3.

Equation	Oxidized	Reduced
a	Na	Cl_2
b	C	O_2
c	$\overset{-2}{O}$	$\overset{+1}{H}$
f	$\overset{-2}{O}$	$\overset{+5}{Cl}$
g	H_2	Cl_2
i	Zn	Cu^{2+}

4. a. oxidation: $K \longrightarrow K^+ + e^-$
   b. reduction: $S + 2e^- \longrightarrow S^{2-}$
   c. oxidation: $Mg \longrightarrow Mg^{2+} + 2e^-$
   d. oxidation: $2F^- \longrightarrow F_2 + 2e^-$
   e. oxidation: $H_2 \longrightarrow 2H^+ + 2e^-$
   f. reduction: $O_2 + 4e^- \longrightarrow 2O^{2-}$
   g. reduction: $Fe^{3+} + e^- \longrightarrow Fe^{2+}$
   h. oxidation: $Mn^{2+} \longrightarrow MnO_4^- + 5e^-$
5. a. nonredox
   b. redox
   c. nonredox
6. Xe, XeF, XeF_2, $XeOF_2$, XeO_3, $CsXeF_8$
7. a. $\overset{0}{H_2}$
   b. $\overset{+1}{H_2}\overset{-2}{O}$
   c. $\overset{0}{Al}$
   d. $\overset{+2}{Mg}\overset{-2}{O}$
   e. $\overset{+3}{Al_2}\overset{-2}{S_3}$
   f. $\overset{+1}{H}\overset{+5}{N}\overset{-2}{O_3}$
   g. $\overset{+1}{H_2}\overset{+6}{S}\overset{-2}{O_4}$
   h. $\overset{+2}{Ca}(\overset{-2}{O}\overset{+1}{H})_2$
   i. $\overset{+2}{Fe}(\overset{+5}{N}\overset{-2}{O_3})_2$
   j. $\overset{0}{O_2}$
8. a. oxidation
   b. reduction
   c. reduction
   d. oxidation

CHAPTER 19 Review

SECTION 1

Oxidation and Reduction

REVIEWING MAIN IDEAS

1. a. Distinguish between the processes of oxidation and reduction.
   b. Write an equation to illustrate each process.
2. Which of the following are redox reactions?
   a. $2Na + Cl_2 \longrightarrow 2NaCl$
   b. $C + O_2 \longrightarrow CO_2$
   c. $2H_2O \longrightarrow 2H_2 + O_2$
   d. $NaCl + AgNO_3 \longrightarrow AgCl + NaNO_3$
   e. $NH_3 + HCl \longrightarrow NH_4^+ + Cl^-$
   f. $2KClO_3 \longrightarrow 2KCl + 3O_2$
   g. $H_2 + Cl_2 \longrightarrow 2HCl$
   h. $H_2SO_4 + 2KOH \longrightarrow K_2SO_4 + 2H_2O$
   i. $Zn + CuSO_4 \longrightarrow ZnSO_4 + Cu$
3. For each oxidation-reduction reaction in the previous question, identify what is oxidized and what is reduced.

PRACTICE PROBLEMS

4. Each of the following atom/ion pairs undergoes the oxidation number change indicated below. For each pair, determine whether oxidation or reduction has occurred, and then write the electronic equation indicating the corresponding number of electrons lost or gained.
   a. $K \longrightarrow K^+$
   b. $S \longrightarrow S^{2-}$
   c. $Mg \longrightarrow Mg^{2+}$
   d. $F^- \longrightarrow F_2$
   e. $H_2 \longrightarrow H^+$
   f. $O_2 \longrightarrow O^{2-}$
   g. $Fe^{3+} \longrightarrow Fe^{2+}$
   h. $Mn^{2+} \longrightarrow MnO_4^-$
5. Identify the following reactions as redox or nonredox:
   a. $2NH_4Cl(aq) + Ca(OH)_2(aq) \longrightarrow 2NH_3(aq) + 2H_2O(l) + CaCl_2(aq)$
   b. $2HNO_3(aq) + 3H_2S(g) \longrightarrow 2NO(g) + 4H_2O(l) + 3S(s)$
   c. $[Be(H_2O)_4]^2 + (aq) + H_2O(l) \longrightarrow H_3O + (aq) + [Be(H_2O)_3OH] + (aq)$
6. Arrange the following in order of increasing oxidation number of the xenon atom: $CsXeF_8$, Xe, XeF_2, $XeOF_2$, XeO_3, and XeF.
7. Determine the oxidation number of each atom indicated in the following:
   a. H_2
   b. H_2O
   c. Al
   d. MgO
   e. Al_2S_3
   f. HNO_3
   g. H_2SO_4
   h. $Ca(OH)_2$
   i. $Fe(NO_3)_2$
   j. O_2

SECTION 2

Balancing Redox Equations

REVIEWING MAIN IDEAS

8. Label the following half-reactions as either reduction or oxidation half-reactions.
   a. $H_2S \longrightarrow S + 2e^- + 2H^+$
   b. $SO_2 + 4e^- + 2H_2O \longrightarrow S + 4OH^-$
   c. $ClO_3^- + 6H^+ + 6e^- \longrightarrow Cl^- + 3H_2O$
   d. $Mn(CN)_6^{4-} \longrightarrow Mn(CN)_6^{3-} + e^-$
9. What are the oxidation states of the elements that changed oxidation states in the half-reactions in the above question?
10. Balance the equation for the following reaction in a basic solution. Give balanced equations for both half-reactions and a balanced equation for the overall reaction.
   $$KMnO_4 + NaIO_3 \longrightarrow MnO_2 + NaIO_4$$

PRACTICE PROBLEMS

11. For each requested step, use the half-reaction method to balance the oxidation-reduction equation below. (Hint: See Sample Problem A.)
   $$K + H_2O \longrightarrow KOH + H_2$$
   a. Write the ionic equation, and assign oxidation numbers to all atoms to determine what is oxidized and what is reduced.
   b. Write the equation for the reduction, and balance it for both atoms and charge.
   c. Write the equation for the oxidation, and balance it for both atoms and charge.
   d. Multiply the coefficients of the oxidation and reduction equations so that the number of electrons lost equals the number of electrons gained. Add the two equations.
   e. Add species as necessary to balance the overall formula equation.

9. a. S: −2 to 0
   b. S: +4 to 0
   c. C: +5 to −1
   d. Mn: +2 to +3
10. oxidation:
   $2OH^- + IO_3^- \longrightarrow IO_4^- + 2e^- + H_2O$
   reduction:
   $2H_2O + MnO_4^- + 3e^- \longrightarrow MnO_2 + 4OH^-$
   overall:
   $H_2O + 3NaIO_3 + 2KMnO_4 \longrightarrow 3NaIO_4 + 2MnO_2 + 2KOH$
11. a. $\overset{0}{K} + \overset{+1}{H_2}\overset{-2}{O} \longrightarrow \overset{+1}{K^+} + \overset{-2}{O}\overset{+1}{H^-} + \overset{0}{H_2}$
   b. $2H_2O + 2e^- \longrightarrow 2OH^- + H_2$
   c. $K \longrightarrow K^+ + e^-$
   d. $2H_2O + 2e^- \longrightarrow 2OH^- + H_2$
   $2(K \longrightarrow K^+ + 2e^-)$
   $2H_2O + 2K \longrightarrow 2OH^- + H_2 + 2K^+$
   e. $2H_2O + 2K \longrightarrow 2KOH + H_2$

12. Use the method in the previous problem to balance each of the reactions below.
    a. $HI + HNO_2 \longrightarrow NO + I_2 + H_2O$
    b. $FeCl_3 + H_2S \longrightarrow FeCl_2 + HCl + S$

13. Balance the equation for the reaction in which hot, concentrated sulfuric acid reacts with zinc to form zinc sulfate, hydrogen sulfide, and water.

SECTION 3

Oxidizing and Reducing Agents

 REVIEWING MAIN IDEAS

14. a. Identify the most active reducing agent among all common elements.
    b. Why are all of the elements in its group in the periodic table very active reducing agents?
    c. Identify the most active oxidizing agent among the common elements.

15. Use **Figure 3.1** to identify the strongest and weakest reducing agents among the substances listed within each of the following groupings:
    a. Ca, Ag, Sn, Cl^-
    b. Fe, Hg, Al, Br^-
    c. F^-, Pb, Mn^{2+}, Na

16. Use **Figure 3.1** to respond to each of the following:
    a. Would Al be oxidized by Ni^{2+}?
    b. Would Cu be oxidized by Ag^+?
    c. Would Pb be oxidized by Na^+?
    d. Would F_2 be reduced by Cl^-?
    e. Would Br_2 be reduced by Cl^-?

Mixed Review

REVIEWING MAIN IDEAS

17. Identify the following reactions as redox or nonredox:
    a. $Mg(s) + ZnCl_2(aq) \longrightarrow Zn(s) + MgCl_2(aq)$
    b. $2H_2(g) + OF_2(g) \longrightarrow H_2O(g) + 2HF(g)$
    c. $2KI(aq) + Pb(NO_3)_2(aq) \longrightarrow PbI_2(s) + 2KNO_3(aq)$
    d. $CaO(s) + H_2O(l) \longrightarrow Ca(OH)_2(aq)$
    e. $3CuCl_2(aq) + 2(NH_4)_3PO_4(aq) \longrightarrow 6NH_4Cl(aq) + Cu_3(PO_4)_2(s)$
    f. $CH_4(g) + 2O_2(g) \longrightarrow CO_2(g) + 2H_2O(g)$

18. Arrange the following in order of decreasing oxidation number of the nitrogen atom: N_2, NH_3, N_2O_4, N_2O, N_2H_4, and NO_3^-.

19. Balance the following redox equations:
    a. $SbCl_5 + KI \longrightarrow KCl + I_2 + SbCl_3$
    b. $Ca(OH)_2 + NaOH + ClO_2 + C \longrightarrow NaClO_2 + CaCO_3 + H_2O$

20. Balance the following equations in basic solution:
    a. $PbO_2 + KCl \longrightarrow KClO + KPb(OH)_3$
    b. $KMnO_4 + KIO_3 \longrightarrow MnO_2 + KIO_4$
    c. $K_2MnO_4 \longrightarrow MnO_2 + KMnO_4$

21. Balance the following equations in acidic solution:
    a. $MnO_4^- + Cl^- \longrightarrow Mn_2^+ + HClO$
    b. $NO_3^- + I_2 \longrightarrow IO_3^- + NO_2$
    c. $NO_2^- \longrightarrow NO + NO_3^-$

CRITICAL THINKING

22. **Interpreting Graphics** Given the activity table below, determine whether a reaction will occur or not. If the reaction will occur, give the products.

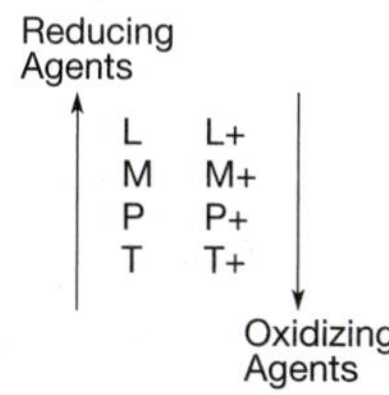

    a. L and M^+
    b. P and M^+
    c. P and T^+

23. **Drawing Conclusions** A substance has an element in one of its highest possible oxidation states. Is this substance more likely to be an oxidizing agent or a reducing agent? Explain your reasoning.

24. **Drawing Conclusions** Use **Figure 3.2** to decide if a redox reaction would occur between the two species, and if so, write the balanced equation. Explain your reasoning.
    a. Cl_2 and Br_2
    b. Sn^{2+} and Zn

25. **Drawing Conclusions** An element that disproportionates must have at least how many different oxidation states? Explain your reasoning.

12. a. $\overset{+1}{2H^+} + \overset{-1}{I^-} + \overset{+3\,-2}{NO_2^-} \longrightarrow \overset{+2\,-2}{NO} + \overset{0}{I_2} + \overset{+1\,-2}{H_2O}$

$2I^- \longrightarrow I_2 + 2e^-$

$2[NO^{2-} + e^- + 2H^+ \longrightarrow NO + H_2O]$

$2HI + 2HNO_2 \longrightarrow 2NO + I_2 + 2H_2O$

b. $\overset{+3}{Fe^{3+}} + \overset{-1}{3Cl^-} + \overset{+1\,-2}{H_2S} \longrightarrow \overset{+2}{Fe^{2+}} + \overset{-1}{2Cl^-} + \overset{1}{+H^+} + \overset{-1}{Cl^-} + \overset{0}{S}$

$2[Fe^{3+} + e^- \longrightarrow Fe^{2+}]$

$H_2S \longrightarrow S + 2e^- + 2H^+$

$2FeCl_3 + H_2S \longrightarrow 2FeCl_2 + 2HCl + S$

13. $\overset{1\,+6\,-2}{H_2SO_4} + \overset{0}{Zn} \longrightarrow \overset{+2\,+6\,-2}{ZnSO_4} + \overset{+1\,-2}{H_2S} + \overset{+1\,-2}{H_2O}$

$SO_4^{2-} + 10H^+ + 8e^- \longrightarrow H_2S + 4H_2O$

$4[Zn \longrightarrow Zn^{2+} + 2e^-]$

$4Zn + 5H_2SO_4 \longrightarrow 4ZnSO_4 + H_2S + 4H_2O$

14. a. lithium
    b. They all have weak attraction for their valence electrons and readily lose electrons to reduce other substances.
    c. fluorine

CHAPTER REVIEW

15. a. strongest: Ca, weakest: Cl^-
    b. strongest: Al, weakest: Br^-
    c. strongest: Na, weakest: F^-
16. a. yes
    b. yes
    c. no
    d. yes
    e. no
17. a. redox
    b. redox
    c. nonredox
    d. nonredox
    e. nonredox
    f. redox
18. NO_3^-, N_2O_4, N_2O, N_2, N_2H_4, NH_3
19. a. $SbCl_5 + 2KI \longrightarrow 2KCl + I_2 + SbCl_3$
    b. $Ca(OH)_2 + 4NaOH + 4ClO_2 + C \longrightarrow 4NaClO_2 + CaCO_3 + 3H_2O$
20. a. $PbO_2 + KCl + H_2O + KOH \longrightarrow KClO + KPb(OH)_3$
    b. $3KIO_3 + 2KMnO_4 + H_2O \longrightarrow 3KIO_4 + 2MnO_2 + 2KOH$
    c. $3K_2MnO_4 + 2H_2O \longrightarrow 2KMnO_4 + MnO_5 + 4KOH$
21. a. $5Cl^- + 2MnO_4^- + 11H^+ \longrightarrow 5HClO + 2Mn^{2+} + 3H_2O$
    b. $I_2 + 10NO_3^- + 8H^+ \longrightarrow 2IO_3^- + 10NO_2 + 4H_2O$
    c. $3NO_2^- + 2H^+ \longrightarrow NO_3^- + 2NO + H_2O$
22. a. reaction; products are L^+ and M
    b. no reaction
    c. reaction; products are P^+ and T
23. The substance is more likely to be an oxidizing agent. Oxidizing agents are reduced and therefore must gain electrons. A substance in its highest oxidation state gains electrons to lower its oxidation state.
24. a. No reaction; Both Cl_2 and Br_2 are oxidizing agents. There is no reducing agent available.
    b. There is a reaction between the two species. Sn^{2+} is the oxidizing agent, and Zn is the reducing agent.
    $Sn^{2+} + Zn \longrightarrow Zn^{2+} + Sn$
25. The element must have a minimum of three different oxidation states: the original state in the reactant, one state that is lower than the original (for reduction), and one state that is higher than the original (for oxidation).

26. a. All of them are redox reactions. In each case, aluminum metal is oxidized.

b.

Oxidized	Reduced
reaction 1: Al	H^+
reaction 2: Al	H^+
reaction 3: Al	N^{5+}
reaction 4: Al	Cl_2
reaction 5: Al	O_2

c. reaction 1: $2Al \longrightarrow 2Al^{3+} + 6e^-$
$6H^+ + 6e^- \longrightarrow 3H_2$
reaction 2: same as reaction 1
reaction 3: $Al \longrightarrow Al^{3+} + 3e^-$
$NO_3^- + 3e^- + 4H^+ \longrightarrow NO + 2H_2O$
reaction 4: $2Al \longrightarrow 2Al^{3+} + 6e^-$
$3Cl_2 + 6e^- \longrightarrow 6Cl^-$
reaction 5: $4Al \longrightarrow 4Al^{3+} + 12e^-$
$3O_2 + 12e^- \longrightarrow 6O^{2-}$

27. a. $4Al(s) + 3O_2(g) \longrightarrow 2Al_2O_3(s)$

b. See reaction 5 in answer 26(c).

c. The buildup of Al_2O_3 increases the electrical resistance of the wire at contact points with switches and outlets. This increased resistance generates sufficient heat to start a fire within the walls of a home.

28. Students' answers will vary, but should mention environmental issues and production costs.

29. Students' answers will vary. Examples of biological processes are photosynthesis, metabolism, and the transport of oxygen.

30. Oxygen is a good oxidizing agent; therefore, a good reducing agent needs to be added to the water to remove the oxygen. A reducing agent that is typically used is hydrazine, N_2H_4.

31. Students may not know all of the reactants and products involved. However, they should recognize evidence of some oxidation-reduction reactions. Ask them to include the evidence. Students can then research some of the reactions via the Internet.

CHAPTER REVIEW

USING THE HANDBOOK

26. Several reactions of aluminum are shown in the common reactions section for Group 13 of the *Elements Handbook* (Appendix A). Use these reactions to answer the following:

a. Which of the five reactions shown are oxidation-reduction reactions? How do you know?

b. For each redox reaction you listed in item **a,** identify what is oxidized and what is reduced.

c. Write half-reactions for each equation you listed in item **a.**

27. Aluminum is described in Group 13 of the *Elements Handbook* (Appendix A) as a self-protecting metal. This property of aluminum results from a redox reaction.

a. Write the redox equation for the oxidation of aluminum.

b. Write the half-reactions for this reaction, and show the number of electrons transferred.

c. What problems are associated with the buildup of aluminum oxide on electrical wiring made of aluminum?

RESEARCH AND WRITING

28. Oxidizing agents are used in the cleaning industry. Research three different oxidizing agents used in this area, and write a report on the advantages and disadvantages of these compounds.

29. Oxidizing and reducing agents play important roles in biological systems. Research the role of one of these agents in a biological process. Write a report describing the process and the role of oxidation and reduction.

ALTERNATIVE ASSESSMENT

30. Boilers are used to convert water to steam in electric power plants. Dissolved oxygen in the water promotes corrosion of the steel used in boiler parts. Explain how dissolved oxygen is removed from the water in boilers.

31. Performance For one day, record situations that show evidence of oxidation-reduction reactions. Identify the reactants and the products, and determine whether there is proof that a chemical reaction has taken place.

Standards-Based Assessment

Answer the following items on a separate piece of paper.

MULTIPLE CHOICE

1. In the following reaction, which species is reduced?
$$2K + Br_2 \longrightarrow 2K^+ + 2Br^-$$
   A. K
   B. Br_2
   C. All of the above
   D. None of the above

2. The oxidation number of the sulfur atom in the SO_4^{2-} ion is
   A. +2.
   B. −2.
   C. +6.
   D. +4.

3. A half-reaction
   A. involves a change in the oxidation state of an element.
   B. always contains H_2O molecules.
   C. always contains H^+ ions.
   D. All of the above

4. In the following reaction, which is the oxidizing agent?
$$AgNO_2 + Cl_2 + 2KOH \longrightarrow AgNO_3 + 2KCl + H_2O$$
   A. $AgNO_2$
   B. Cl_2
   C. KOH
   D. KCl

5. What are the oxidation states (in increasing order) of the element that undergoes disproportionation in the following reaction:
$$Cl_2 + H_2O \longrightarrow HCl + HOCl$$
   A. −1, 0, +2
   B. −1, 0, +1
   C. −2, −1, 0
   D. None of the above

6. Which reaction is a redox reaction?
   A. $Al_2O_3 + 6HCl \longrightarrow 2AlCl_3 + 3H_2O$
   B. $2HCO_3^- \longrightarrow CO_2 + CO_3^{2-} + H_2O$
   C. $SiBr_4 + 3H_2O \longrightarrow H_2SiO_3 + 4HBr$
   D. $H_2O + PbO_2 + NaOH + KCl \longrightarrow KClO + NaPb(OH)_3$

7. Arrange the following in order of increasing oxidation number of the sulfur atom: $S_2O_3^{2-}$, $S_4O_6^{2-}$, HSO_4^-, and H_2S.
   A. H_2S, $S_2O_3^{2-}$, $S_4O_6^{2-}$, HSO_4^-
   B. $S_2O_3^{2-}$, H_2S, $S_4O_6^{2-}$, HSO_4^-,
   C. H_2S, $S_2O_3^{2-}$, HSO_4^-, $S_4O_6^{2-}$
   D. HSO_4^-, $S_2O_3^{2-}$, $S_4O_6^{2-}$, H_2S

8. Which answer contains the correct information about the following reaction:
$$2Pb(NO_3)_2 \longrightarrow 2PbO + 4NO_2 + O_2$$
   A. This reaction is a decomposition reaction and not a redox reaction.
   B. This reaction is a redox reaction in which the lead is reduced and the oxygen is oxidized.
   C. This reaction is a disproportionation reaction.
   D. This reaction is a redox reaction in which the nitrogen is reduced and the oxygen is oxidized.

SHORT ANSWER

9. Determine the oxidation numbers for Cu in the superconductor $YBa_2Cu_3O_7$. Yttrium (Y) has an oxidation number of +3. (Cu does not have oxidation numbers greater than +3.) Give only integer oxidation numbers.

10. What is an oxidizing agent?

EXTENDED RESPONSE

11. B, F, K, and L are four unknown reducing agents that oxidize to singly charged cations. Using the following information, construct a table showing the relative strengths of the oxidizing and reducing agents. Data: F reduces K^+, B^+, and L^+. B^+ oxidizes K and F, but not L.

12. Balance the equation for the following reaction in basic solution:
$$ClO_2 \longrightarrow KClO_3 + KClO_2$$
Give the balanced equation for each half-reaction and for the overall reaction. Give the oxidizing agent and the reducing agent.

Test Tip
If you are short on time, quickly scan the unanswered questions to see which might be easiest to answer.

STANDARDS-BASED ASSESSMENT

To give students practice under more realistic testing conditions, give them 60 minutes to answer all of the questions in this Standardized Test Preparation.

Test Answers

1. B
2. C
3. A
4. B
5. B
6. D
7. A
8. D
9. The oxidation numbers for Y, Ba, and O are +3, +2, and −2, respectively. Therefore, the sum of the oxidation numbers for the three Cu atoms must be +7. Two Cu atoms must have a +2 oxidation state, and one Cu atom must have a +3 oxidation state.
10. An oxidizing agent is a species that causes another species to be oxidized in a redox reaction. An oxidizing agent is therefore reduced in a redox reaction.
11. ↑ (reducing agent strength increases upward; oxidizing agent strength increases downward ↓)

Reducing agents	Oxidizing agents
F	F^+
K	K^+
B	B^+
L	L^+

12. Oxidation half-reaction:
$2OH^- + ClO_2 \longrightarrow ClO_3^- + e^- + H_2O$
Reduction half-reaction:
$ClO_2 + e^- \longrightarrow ClO_2^-$
Overall reaction:
$2ClO_2 + 2KOH \longrightarrow KClO_3 + KClO_2 + H_2O$
This reaction is a disproportionation reaction; therefore, ClO_2 is both the reducing agent and the oxidizing agent.

Electrochemistry

① Core Instruction

Chapter Resources

- The Teacher's Edition wrap has extensive teaching support for every lesson, including Misconception Alerts, Teach from Visuals, Demonstrations, Teaching Tips, Differentiated Instruction, and Problem Solving support.
- Several additional presentation tools are available online for every chapter, including Animated Chemistry features and Visual Concepts.
- You can open your lesson with the Why It Matters Video: Electrochemistry.

Section	Instruction	Labs and Demonstrations Go Online for Materials Lists and Solutions Lists.
20.1	■ **Textbook:** Introduction to Electrochemistry **Teaching Visuals:** Ion Movement Through a Porous Barrier • Electron Pathway in an Electrochemical Cell **PowerPresentations**	■ **Demonstration:** Energy in an Electrochemical Cell ■ **Lab:** Electric Charge (Core Skill)
20.2	■ **Textbook:** Voltaic Cells **Animated Chemistry:** Voltaic Cell **Teaching Visuals:** Particle Models for Redox Reactions in Electrochemical Cells • Dry Cells • Fuel Cell • Mercury Cell • Galvanic Cell • Model of a Lead-Acid Storage Battery • Comparing Reduction Potentials of Various Metals • Standard Reduction Potentials • Standard Electrode Potentials **PowerPresentations**	■ **Demonstration:** Fruit Battery ■ **Lab:** Voltaic Cells (Core Skill) ■ **Demonstration:** Preventing Oxidation ■ **Lab:** Micro-Voltaic Cells (Probeware) ■ **Lab:** Store Charge (STEM)
20.3	■ **Textbook:** Electrolytic Cells **Teaching Visuals:** Comparison of Voltaic and Electrolytic Cells • Refining Copper Using an Electrolytic Cell • Hall-Héroult Process • Downs Cell **PowerPresentations**	■ **Demonstration:** An Electrolytic Cell ■ **Demonstration:** The Electrolysis of KI ■ **Lab:** Electroplating for Corrosion Protection (Core Skill)

Find all of your resources online at HMDScience.com.

② Support and Intervention

- **Interactive Reader** (English and Spanish)
- **Study Guide**
- **Interactive Review:** Review Games, Concept Maps, and Section Self-Checks
- **Scientific Reasoning Skill Builder**
- **Learn It! Videos**
- **Solve It! Cards**
- **Interactive Demos**
- **Sample Problem Sets**

③ Specialized Support

- **Chapter Summary Audio Files**
- **Interactive Reader Audio Files**
- **Differentiated Instruction:** Inclusion, Below Level, and English Learners (TE wrap)

Enrichment and Challenge

- **Differentiated Instruction:** Pre-AP (TE wrap)
- **Why It Matters:** Fuel-Cell Cars (SE)
- **WebLinks**

Assessment

- **Section Formative Assessments** (SE)
- **Section Quizzes**
- **Chapter Review** (SE)
- **Chapter Tests A and B**
- **Alternative Assessment** (TE wrap)
- **Online Assessment and Remediation**
- **ExamView Banks**

Where do I find it?

	Resource	PRINT	DVD	ONLINE
1	Animated Chemistry		■	■
	Demonstrations (TE wrap)	■		■
	Interactive Whiteboard		■	■
	Labs		■	■
	PowerPresentations		■	■
	QuickLabs	■	■	■
	Teaching Visuals		■	■
	Textbook	■	■	■
	Visual Concepts		■	■
	Why It Matters Videos		■	■
2	Interactive Demos		■	■
	Interactive Reader	■	■	■
	Interactive Reviews		■	■
	Learn It! Videos		■	■
	Sample Problem Sets		■	■
	Scientific Reasoning Skill Builder		■	■
	Smart Grapher Tool		■	■
	Solve It! Cards		■	■
	Study Guide		■	■
3	Chapter Summary Audio Files		■	■
	Differentiated Instruction (TE wrap)	■		
	Interactive Reader Audio Files		■	■

CHAPTER 20

Chapter Overview

Section 1 presents the general principles involved in electrochemical cells.

Section 2 explains voltaic cells, corrosion, and electrode potential.

Section 3 explains electrolytic cells, electrolysis, and real-world uses of electrolytic cells.

▼ Focus and Motivate

Activate Prior Knowledge

Students may need a review of the following concepts:

- electrons
- ion formation
- chemical equilibrium
- oxidation-reduction reactions

About the Image

Electrochemical reactions provide energy in all kinds of applications, including space exploration. The Mars Rover used solar panels to trap light energy, which was then stored in electrochemical batteries for later use.

Why It Matters

Students can access the video online and find other helpful resources at **HMDScience.com**.

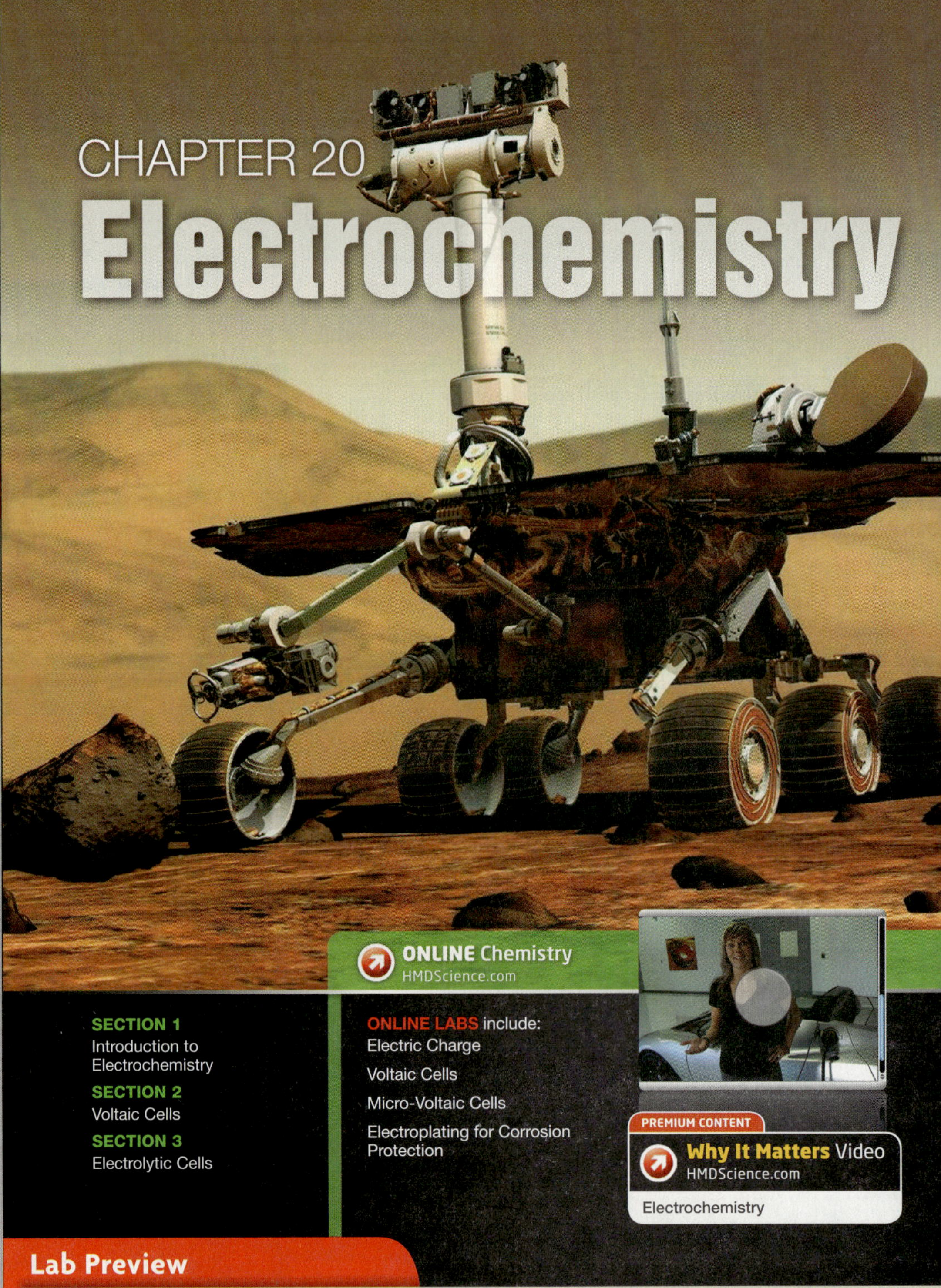

CHAPTER 20
Electrochemistry

SECTION 1 Introduction to Electrochemistry
SECTION 2 Voltaic Cells
SECTION 3 Electrolytic Cells

ONLINE Chemistry HMDScience.com

ONLINE LABS include:
Electric Charge
Voltaic Cells
Micro-Voltaic Cells
Electroplating for Corrosion Protection

PREMIUM CONTENT
Why It Matters Video HMDScience.com
Electrochemistry

Lab Preview

The following labs and demonstrations support the concepts in this chapter:

LABS

Electric Charge (Core Skill)
Voltaic Cells (Core Skill)
Micro-Voltaic Cells (Probeware)
Electroplating for Corrosion Protection (Core Skill)
Store Charge (STEM)

DEMONSTRATIONS

Energy in an Electrochemical Cell
Fruit Battery
Preventing Oxidation
An Electrolytic Cell
The Electrolysis of KI

SECTION 1

Main Idea

Electrochemical cells separate oxidation reactions from reduction reactions.

Introduction to Electrochemistry

Key Terms

electrochemistry
electrode
half-cell
anode
cathode

Oxidation-reduction reactions involve energy changes. Because these reactions involve electron transfer, the net *release* or net *absorption* of energy can occur in the form of electrical energy rather than as heat. This property allows for a great many practical applications of redox reactions. **The branch of chemistry that deals with electricity-related applications of oxidation-reduction reactions is called electrochemistry.**

MAIN IDEA

Electrochemical cells separate oxidation reactions from reduction reactions.

Oxidation-reduction reactions involve a transfer of electrons. If the two substances are in contact with one another, a transfer of energy as heat accompanies the electron transfer. In **Figure 1.1** a zinc strip is in contact with a copper(II) sulfate solution. The zinc strip loses electrons to the copper(II) ions in solution. Copper(II) ions accept the electrons and fall out of solution as copper atoms. As electrons are transferred between zinc atoms and copper(II) ions, energy is released as heat, as indicated by the rise in temperature.

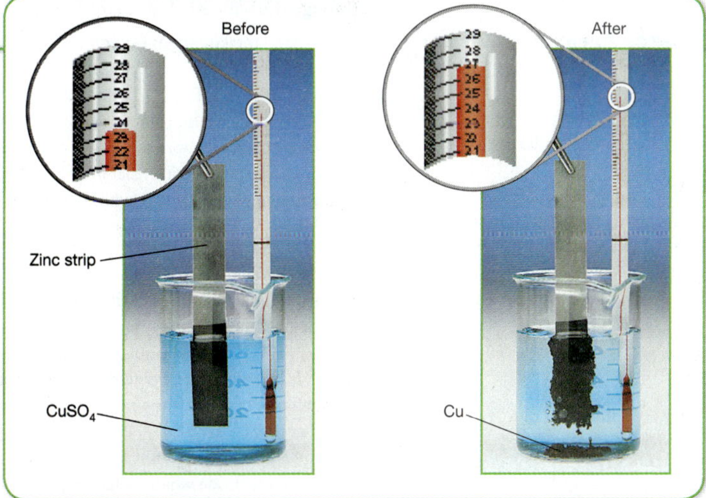

FIGURE 1.1

Temperature Change with Electron Transfer Energy as heat given off when electrons are transferred directly from Zn atoms to Cu^{2+} ions causes the temperature of the aqueous $CuSO_4$ solution to rise.

Differentiated Instruction

BELOW LEVEL

To help students feel more comfortable about studying electrochemistry, have them discuss the requirements of an electric circuit. Have the students list and discuss the different components of an electric circuit, and how those components are connected. If possible, obtain a battery and connect it to an LED.

ENGLISH LEARNERS

Even native English speakers are easily confused by some electrochemistry terms. Invite students to make flashcards for words and concepts unique to this chapter, such as anode, salt bridge, and half-cell.

SECTION 1

Plan and Prepare

Objectives

Upon completion of this section, students should be able to do the following:

- Identify parts of an electrochemical cell and their functions.
- Write electrode half-reactions for cathodes and anodes.

Classroom Catalyst

Note that in **Figure 1.1** an increase in temperature indicates that chemical energy in the form of heat is released. Perform the demonstration below.

Teach

Demonstration

ENERGY IN AN ELECTROCHEMICAL CELL

1. Fill a **porous cup** $\frac{3}{4}$ full with **0.1 M $CuSO_4$** solution. Place the porous cup in a **250 mL beaker.** Fill the beaker $\frac{3}{4}$ full with **0.1 M $ZnSO_4$** solution.
2. Place a polished **4 × 150 mm copper strip** in the $CuSO_4$ solution and a polished **4 × 150 mm zinc strip** in the $ZnSO_4$ solution.
3. Connect leads from a **voltmeter** to the two electrodes, and note the voltage.
4. Relate the voltage reading to the chemical energy observed in **Figure 1.1.**

Disposal Add **1 M NaOH** to the $ZnSO_4$ solution to precipitate $Zn(OH)_2$. Filter the solution, dry the precipitate, and put the solid in the trash. Adjust the pH of the filtrate to between 5 and 9, and pour the solution down drain. Scour **six 6d iron nails** with **steel wool** until they are shiny; immerse them in the $CuSO_4$ solution overnight. Remove the nails and filter the solution. Heat the nails and any precipitate to convert the copper to copper oxide. Let the nails cool, and put the copper oxide and nails in the trash. Pour the filtrate down the drain.

▼ Teach *continued*

Teaching Tip

Electrical energy is released by the spontaneous flow of electrons from a substance that has less affinity for electrons to a substance that has a greater affinity. The greater the difference in attraction, the greater the energy that is released.

Classroom Discussion

Use the electrochemical cell in the Demonstration on the previous page or the same cell illustrated in **Figure 1.2** as a basis for a discussion of the parts of a cell. Have students diagram the electrochemical process, answering your questions about where oxidation occurs, where reduction occurs, what happens to the electrons, and how charge neutrality is preserved. Introduce the terms *anode* and *cathode*, and identify them in relation to oxidation and reduction.

Teaching Tip

Emphasize that in an electrochemical cell, the anode is the electrode at which oxidation occurs and the cathode is the electrode at which reduction occurs. This correlation is always valid, even though the anode is sometimes positive (as in electrolytic cells) and sometimes negative (as in voltaic cells). As a memory aid, you can point out that anode and oxidation both begin with vowels, and cathode and reduction both begin with consonants.

Check for Understanding

Answer: Oxidation takes place at the anode. Reduction takes place at the cathode.

FIGURE 1.2

Electrochemical Cell

An electrochemical cell consists of two electrodes. Each electrode is in contact with an electrolyte; the electrode and the electrolyte make up a half-cell. The two electrodes are connected by a wire, and a porous barrier separates the two electrolytes.

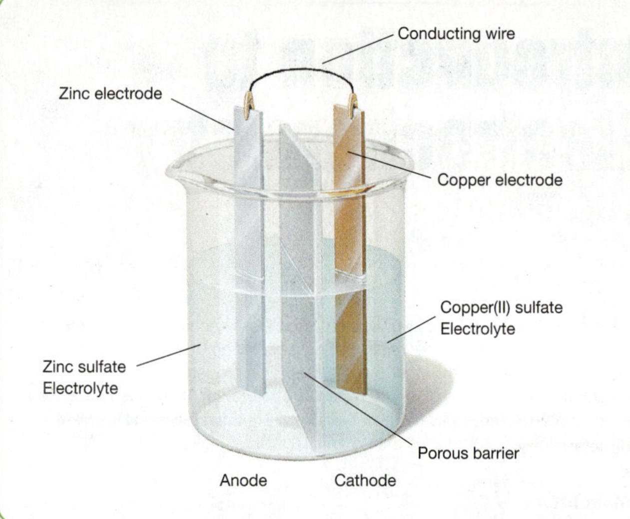

If, however, we separate the substance that is oxidized from the substance that is reduced, the electron transfer is accompanied by a transfer of electrical energy instead of energy as heat. One means of separating oxidation and reduction half-reactions is with a *porous barrier*, or *salt bridge*. This barrier prevents the metal atoms of one half-reaction from mixing with the ions of the other half-reaction. Ions in the two solutions can move through the porous barrier, which keeps a charge from building up on the electrodes. Electrons can be transferred from one side to the other through an external connecting wire. Electric current moves in a closed loop path, or *circuit*, so this movement of electrons through the wire is balanced by the movement of ions in solution.

CHECK FOR UNDERSTANDING

Identify In an electrochemical cell, at which electrode does oxidation take place? At which electrode does reduction take place?

Altering the system in **Figure 1.1** as just described would simply involve separating the copper and zinc, as shown in **Figure 1.2**. The Zn strip is in an aqueous solution of $ZnSO_4$. The Cu strip is in an aqueous solution of $CuSO_4$. Both solutions conduct electricity, because they are electrolytes. An **electrode** is a conductor used to establish electrical contact with a nonmetallic part of a circuit, such as an electrolyte. In **Figure 1.2**, the Zn and Cu strips are electrodes. A single electrode immersed in a solution of its ions is a **half-cell.**

The Half-Cells

In the half-cell that contains the Zn electrode in aqueous $ZnSO_4$ solution, the half-reaction is $Zn(s) \longrightarrow Zn^{2+}(aq) + 2e^-$. The Zn metal loses two electrons to form Zn^{2+} ions in solution, and therefore oxidation is taking place in this half-cell. The electrode where oxidation occurs is called the **anode.** In the half-cell that contains the Cu electrode in aqueous $CuSO_4$ solution, the half-reaction is $Cu^{2+}(aq) + 2e^- \longrightarrow Cu(s)$. In this half-reaction, the Cu^{2+} ions in solution gain electrons to become Cu solid; that is, reduction is taking place. The electrode where reduction occurs is called the **cathode.**

Differentiated Instruction

INCLUSION

To help students differentiate between cathodes and anodes, have three students serve as a model of an electric wire. Divide the remainder of the class into two groups: the anode and the cathode. All the anode students should hold a pen or pencil representing an electron and be clustered together at one end of the "wire." The cathode students should move around in a space representing the cathode "solution."

To start the simulation, the students on the cathode side should gather near their end of the "wire" as one student at the anode transfers a pencil (electron) to the "wire," which is then transferred by the wire to the cathode. The cathode student attaches to the "wire" by holding hands. The anode student who lost the electron starts to roam. This process is repeated until no more electrons are left to be transferred.

The Complete Cell

Recall that oxidation cannot occur separately from reduction. Both must occur in an electrochemical reaction. The two half-cells taken together make an electrochemical cell. In the Zn/Cu electrochemical cell, the electrons move from the Zn electrode through the wire and down the Cu electrode to the Cu^{2+} ions at the electrode-solution interface. The Cu^{2+} ions are reduced to solid Cu, and the resulting Cu atoms attach themselves to the surface of the Cu electrode. For this reaction, a charge is carried through the barrier by a combination of $Zn^{2+}(aq)$ ions moving from the anode to the cathode and the $SO_4^{2-}(aq)$ ions moving from the cathode to the anode.

An electrochemical cell may be represented by the following notation:

anode electrode |anode solution | |cathode solution | cathode electrode

The double line represents the salt bridge, or porous barrier, between the two half-cells. For the present cell, the cell notation is

$$Zn(s) \mid Zn^{2+}(aq) \mid\mid Cu^{2+}(aq) \mid Cu(s)$$

The electrochemical reaction can be found by adding the anode half-reaction to the cathode half-reaction. This overall (or net) reaction is the following redox reaction:

$$Zn(s) + Cu^{2+}(aq) \longrightarrow Zn^{2+}(aq) + Cu(s)$$

Although the two half-reactions occur at the same time, they occur at different places in the cell. Thus, for the reaction to proceed, electrons must pass through the wire that connects the two half-cells.

An electrochemical cell that consists of the Zn and Cu reaction described above is called the *Daniell Cell*, named for the English chemist John Frederick Daniell. The Daniell Cell can generate enough electricity to light up the light bulb shown in **Figure 1.3.** In electrochemical cells, either a chemical reaction produces electrical energy or an electric current produces a chemical change.

FIGURE1.3

The Daniell Cell The light bulb is powered by the reaction in this cell.

CRITICAL THINKING

Infer What would happen if the porous barrier was removed from between the two electrodes?

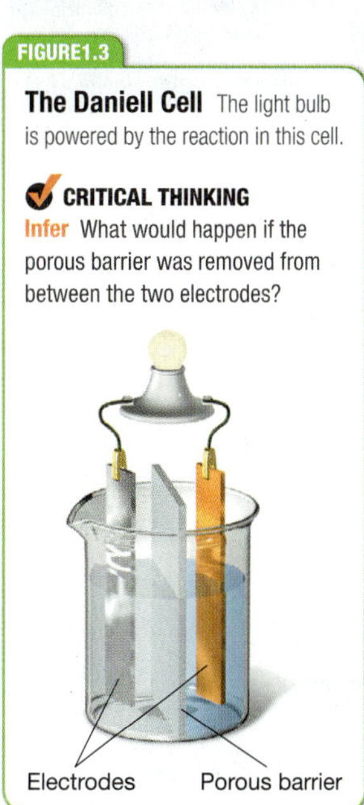

SECTION 1 FORMATIVE ASSESSMENT

Reviewing Main Ideas

1. Why is the use of a salt bridge or porous barrier necessary in an electrochemical cell?
2. Given the $Cu^{2+}(aq) \mid Cu(s)$ and $Mg^{2+}(aq) \mid Mg(s)$ half-reactions, where $Cu^{2+}(aq) \mid Cu(s)$ is the cathode reaction,
   a. write the overall reaction.
   b. write the cell notation.
3. Write the half-reaction in which $I^-(aq)$ changes to $I_2(s)$. Would this reaction occur at the anode or cathode?

Critical Thinking

4. **RELATING IDEAS** Is the net chemical result of an electrochemical cell a redox reaction? Explain your answer.

Answers to Section Assessment

1. A salt bridge (or porous barrier) is necessary to keep the two half-cells electrically balanced so that a charge does not build up in the cell and stop the electrochemical reaction prematurely. The salt bridge allows the passage of ions in the cell.
2. **a.** anode: $Mg(s) \longrightarrow Mg^{2+}(aq) + 2e^-$; cathode: $Cu^{2+}(aq) + 2e^- \longrightarrow Cu(s)$; overall: $Cu^{2+}(aq) + Mg(s) \longrightarrow Mg^{2+}(aq) + Cu(s)$
   b. $Mg(s) \mid Mg^{2+}(aq) \mid\mid Cu^{2+}(aq) \mid Cu(s)$
3. $2I^-(aq) \longrightarrow I_2(s) + 2e^-$. This reaction is an oxidation half-reaction and therefore occurs at the anode.
4. Yes; The two half-reactions that occur at the electrodes combine to form an overall redox reaction.

Classroom Discussion

Lead a discussion on the function of the porous barrier in an electrochemical cell. Help students by asking them to discuss what would happen if the barrier were removed. Students should understand that a cell can generate an electric current only if the oxidation and reduction halves of an overall redox reaction are isolated from each other. That way, the electrons being lost at the anode pass through an external wire, reaching the cathode, where reduction takes place.

ChemisTrivia

In 1836, John Daniell developed the Daniell Cell, which was the first battery to produce a constant electrical current over a long period of time. This invention was important for the operation of the electric telegraph.

Critical Thinking

Answer: If the barrier were removed from the cell, the ions from the two products of the two half-reactions would mix and current would not flow.

Assess and Reteach ▼

Assess Use the Formative Assessment on this page to evaluate student mastery of the section.

Reteach For students who need additional instruction, download the Section Study Guide.

Response to Intervention To reassess students' mastery, use the Section Quiz, available to print or to take directly online at **HMDScience.com**.

SECTION 2

▼ Plan and Prepare

Objectives

Upon completion of this section, students should be able to do the following:

- Describe the operation of voltaic cells, including dry cells, lead-acid batteries, and fuel cells.
- Identify conditions that lead to corrosion and ways to prevent corrosion.
- Describe the relationship between voltage and the movement of electrons.
- Calculate cell voltage/potentials from a figure of standard electrode potentials.

Classroom Catalyst

Have students get into groups and make a list of items that use batteries to run. Talk about the different types of batteries (alkaline, rechargeable, mercury, etc.). Have students list the advantages and disadvantages of the different types of batteries from a consumer point of view. Have a variety of commonly used batteries available for students to examine.

▼ Teach

READING TOOLKIT

DISCUSSION Have students read aloud or silently the sections in this chapter: Electrochemical Cells, Voltaic Cells, and Electrolytic Cells. Start a class discussion about scenarios that involve the use of electrochemistry in industry or daily life. Be sure to emphasize that electrochemical reactions are examples of redox reactions.

SECTION 2

Main Ideas

- Batteries and fuel cells are two types of voltaic cells.
- Exposure to water and oxygen causes iron to corrode.
- The electric potential of a voltaic cell depends on the strengths of the oxidizing and reducing agents.

Voltaic Cells

Key Terms

voltaic cell
reduction potential
electrode potential
standard electrode potential

Voltaic cells use spontaneous oxidation-reduction reactions to convert chemical energy into electrical energy. Voltaic cells are also called galvanic cells. The most common application of voltaic cells is in batteries.

MAIN IDEA

Batteries and fuel cells are two types of voltaic cells.

Figure 2.1 shows an example of a voltaic cell: the Zn || Cu electrochemical cell discussed in the previous section.

Electrons given up at the anode pass along the external connecting wire to the cathode. The movement of electrons through the wire must be balanced by the movement of ions in the solution. Thus, in **Figure 2.1**, sulfate ions in the $CuSO_4$ solution can move through the barrier into the $ZnSO_4$ solution.

The dry cells pictured in **Figure 2.2** are common sources of electrical energy. Like the wet cell previously described, dry cells are voltaic cells. The three most common types of dry cells are the zinc-carbon battery, the alkaline battery, and the mercury battery. They differ in the substances being oxidized and reduced.

FIGURE 2.1

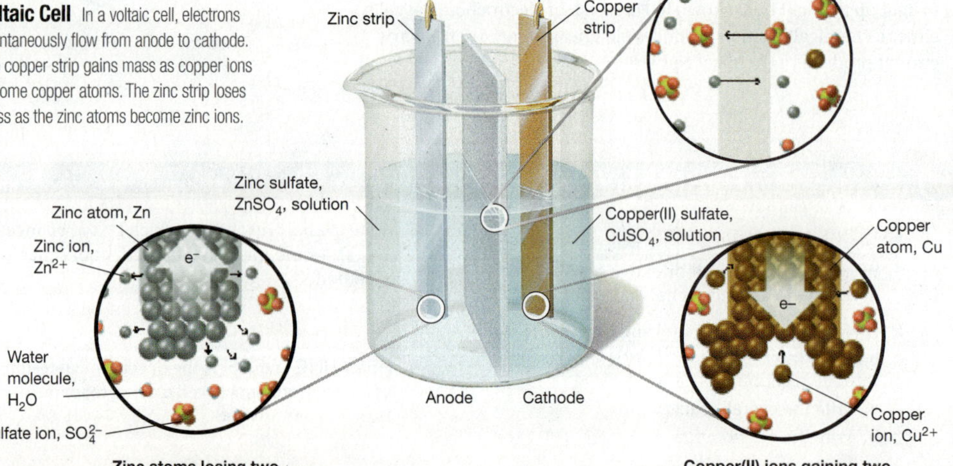

Voltaic Cell In a voltaic cell, electrons spontaneously flow from anode to cathode. The copper strip gains mass as copper ions become copper atoms. The zinc strip loses mass as the zinc atoms become zinc ions.

Differentiated Instruction

BELOW LEVEL

Students may be confused that the two half-reactions are separated even though they are in the same beaker. Draw the two half-cells in different beakers and then connect them by a salt bridge to help students see that the reactions are separate, but still connected. Explain the significance of the salt bridge. A salt bridge allows the ions to flow between the two half-cells so as to maintain a balance in charge. If no salt bridge is used, the charge difference would prevent the flow of electrons.

Zinc-Carbon Dry Cells

Batteries such as those used in flashlights are zinc-carbon dry cells. These cells consist of a zinc container, which serves as the anode, filled with a moist paste of MnO_2, carbon black, NH_4Cl, and $ZnCl_2$, as illustrated in **Figure 2.3a.** When the external circuit is closed, zinc atoms are oxidized at the negative electrode, or anode.

$$\overset{0}{Zn}(s) \longrightarrow \overset{+2}{Zn}{}^{2+}(aq) + 2e^-$$

Electrons move across the circuit and reenter the cell through the carbon rod. The carbon rod is the cathode or positive electrode. Here MnO_2 is reduced in the presence of H_2O according to the following half-reaction.

$$2\overset{+4}{Mn}O_2(s) + H_2O(l) + 2e^- \longrightarrow \overset{+3}{Mn}_2O_3(s) + 2OH^-(aq)$$

Alkaline Batteries

The batteries found in a portable compact disc player or other small electronic device are frequently alkaline dry cells. These cells do not have a carbon rod cathode, as in the zinc-carbon cell. The absence of the carbon rod allows them to be smaller. **Figure 2.3b** shows a model of an alkaline battery. This cell uses a paste of Zn metal and potassium hydroxide instead of a solid metal anode. The half-reaction at the anode is as follows.

$$\overset{0}{Zn}(s) + 2OH^-(aq) \longrightarrow \overset{+2}{Zn}(OH)_2(s) + 2e^-$$

The reduction half-reaction, the reaction at the cathode, is exactly the same as that for the zinc-carbon dry cell.

FIGURE 2.2

Batteries Many common batteries are simple voltaic dry cells.

Voltaic Cell

FIGURE 2.3

Zinc and Alkaline Dry Cells

CRITICAL THINKING

Distinguish What is the difference between a zinc-carbon dry cell and an alkaline battery?

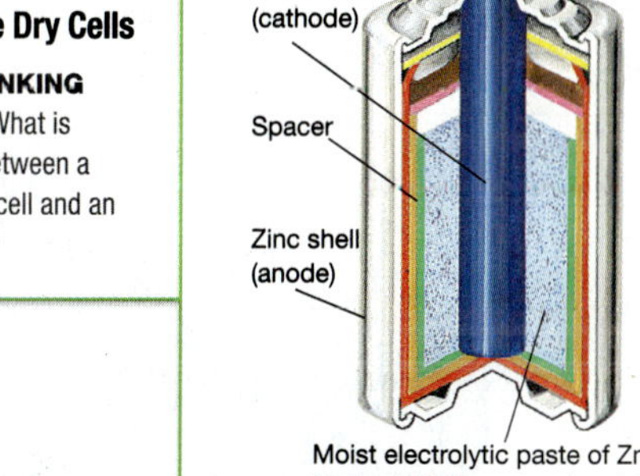

(a) Zinc Dry Cell In a zinc dry cell, zinc is oxidized to Zn^{2+} at the anode, and manganese(IV) is reduced to manganese(III) at the cathode.

(b) Alkaline Dry Cell KOH makes the electrolyte paste in this battery basic. Thus, it is called an alkaline dry cell.

Demonstration

FRUIT BATTERY

1. Obtain a **lemon, grapefruit,** or **apple,** and use a **knife** to slice it into six sections.
2. Cut **six Cu** and **six Zn strips,** each 1 cm × 10 cm, and clean each strip with **steel wool.**
3. Insert one Cu strip and one Zn strip through the skin of each section of fruit. The strips should be separated by at least 1 cm.
4. Lay the fruit sections side by side. Using **paper clips,** attach the copper strip in the first fruit section to the zinc strip in the second section. Continue this process until all six sections are connected.
5. Connect the free copper strip to one end of a **light-emitting diode** (LED) and the free zinc strip to the other end of the LED. The LED should glow brightly, which will be more visible if the room lights are dimmed.

Safety Do not eat the fruit. Wear **goggles** and a **lab apron.**

Disposal Mark the fruit "Unfit for Food Use," and throw it in the trash. Save the metal strips for reuse.

TEACH FROM VISUALS

FIGURE 2.3 Students could be questioned about the role of the carbon rod. Point out that inert materials often act as electrodes. These materials do not react, but they provide a surface on which an oxidation or reduction half-reaction can take place.

PRE-AP

Why are different types (compositions) of batteries used in different applications? How do use and price influence the kind of battery needed for a specific application? As a follow-up to the Classroom Catalyst, ask students why we do not run everything on batteries. Have students research how much energy is stored in one battery and the power requirements of a typical television. How many batteries would be needed to watch one hour of television on a 32-inch television set?

Critical Thinking

Answer: A zinc-carbon dry cell contains a carbon rod cathode, whereas an alkaline battery does not. Alkaline batteries also tend to be smaller in size than zinc-carbon dry cells.

▼ Teach *continued*

Application

We live in an increasingly wireless world. But although a wireless device can send and receive signals as just as a wired device can, it is useful only as long as its battery stays charged. Thus, battery technology is the limitation in many of today's small electronic devices, and major breakthroughs in energy storage are required to advance some of our favorite electronics.

ChemisTrivia

To contain as much potential energy as an average gasoline tank in a car, a hydrogen tank would need to be 3.26 times larger due to its lower energy density. However, fuel cells are more efficient than gasoline engines, resulting in less energy required to travel the same distance.

Critical Thinking

Answer: Fuel cells exhaust water, not carbon dioxide (a greenhouse gas) or carbon monoxide (a poisonous gas), as internal combustion engines do. Water would potentially have less of an impact on the environment than the gases emitted by internal combustion engines.

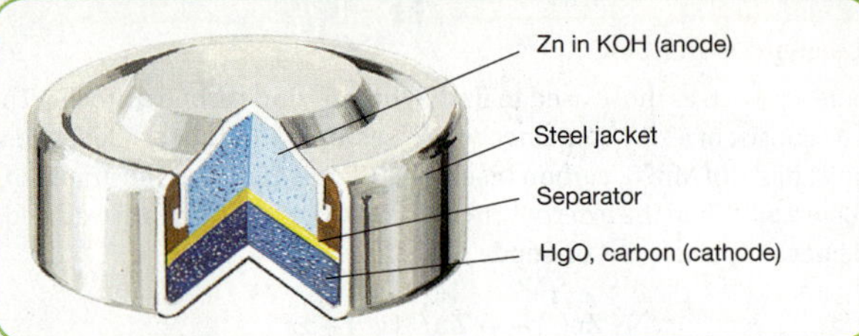

FIGURE 2.4

Mercury Batteries It is important that mercury batteries be recycled and not just discarded because mercury is a poisonous substance.

Mercury Batteries

The tiny batteries found in hearing aids, calculators, and camera flashes are mercury batteries, as shown in **Figure 2.4.** The anode half-reaction is identical to that found in the alkaline dry cell. However, the cathode, or reduction, half-reaction is different. The cathode half-reaction is described by the following equation.

$$\overset{+2}{Hg}O(s) + H_2O(l) + 2e^- \longrightarrow \overset{0}{Hg}(l) + 2OH^-(aq)$$

Fuel Cells

A fuel cell is a voltaic cell in which the reactants are being continuously supplied and the products are being continuously removed. Therefore, unlike a battery, a fuel cell could, in principle, work forever, changing chemical energy into electrical energy.

Fuel cells based on the reactions listed below and shown in **Figure 2.5** are used in the United States space program.

$$\text{Cathode: } O_2(g) + 2H_2O(l) + 4e^- \longrightarrow 4OH^-(aq)$$

$$\text{Anode: } 2H_2(g) + 4OH^-(aq) \longrightarrow 4e^- + 4H_2O(l)$$

$$\text{Net reaction: } 2H_2 + O_2 \longrightarrow 2H_2O$$

Fuel cells are very efficient and have very low emissions.

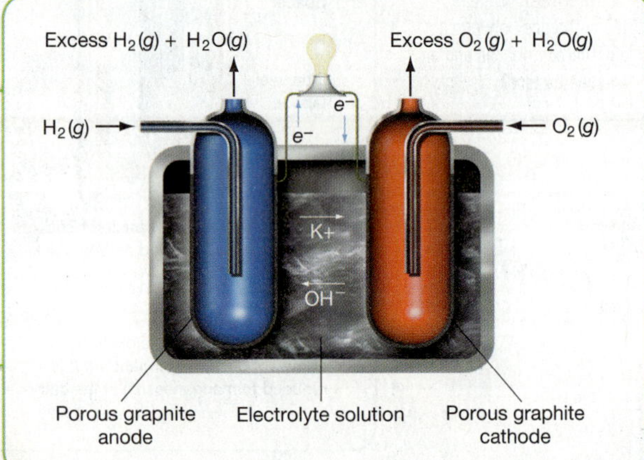

FIGURE 2.5

Fuel Cells The reactions in this fuel cell take place at carbon electrodes that contain metal catalysts. The water formed is removed as a gas.

CRITICAL THINKING

Analyze Why would a fuel cell have less of an impact on the environment than other types of cells?

Differentiated Instruction

INCLUSION

Help learning-disabled students with an activity to develop life skills related to batteries and how they work. Students can create a collage of different items that require batteries to operate. Pictures of many common items can be found in magazine and newspaper advertisements. Additionally, students could draw a diagram of a battery and label the negative and positive terminals. They could then examine a flashlight or other device and explain how to insert the batteries based on the markings on the device.

MAIN IDEA

Exposure to water and oxygen causes iron to corrode.

Corrosion is an electrochemical process that has a large economic impact. Approximately 20% of all the iron and steel produced is used to repair or replace corroded structures. One of the metals most commonly affected by corrosion is iron. Rust, hydrated iron(III) oxide, forms by the following overall reaction.

$$4Fe(s) + 3O_2(g) + xH_2O(l) \longrightarrow 2Fe_2O_3 \bullet xH_2O(s)$$

The amount of hydration of the iron oxide, noted by the coefficient x in the equation above, varies, and affects the color of the rust formed.

The mechanism for the corrosion of iron contains the following electrochemical reactions.

$$\text{Anode: } Fe(s) \longrightarrow Fe^{2+}(aq) + 2e^-$$

$$\text{Cathode: } O_2(g) + 2H_2O(l) + 4e^- \longrightarrow 4OH^-(aq)$$

The anode and cathode reactions occur at different regions of the metal surface. The electric circuit is completed by electron flow through the metal itself, which acts like the wire in an electrochemical cell. The water on the surface of the metal serves as the salt bridge. Thus, for corrosion to occur, water and oxygen must be present with the iron.

As shown in **Figure 2.6**, when the iron is exposed to water and oxygen, the iron metal at the anodic site is oxidized to Fe^{2+} ions. The electrons released at this site travel along the metal (like the wire of a cell) to the cathodic region, where oxygen is reduced. The Fe^{2+} ions travel along the moisture toward the cathodic regions. At the cathode, the Fe^{2+} ions are further oxidized to Fe^{3+} ions and form rust, which is hydrated iron oxide, $Fe_2O_3 \bullet xH_2O$.

$$2Fe^{2+}(aq) + (3 + x)H_2O(l) \longrightarrow Fe_2O_3 \bullet xH_2O(s) + 6H^+(aq) + 2e^-$$

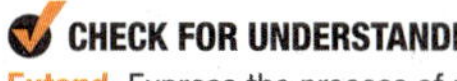

CHECK FOR UNDERSTANDING

Extend Express the process of rusting in electrochemical cell notation.

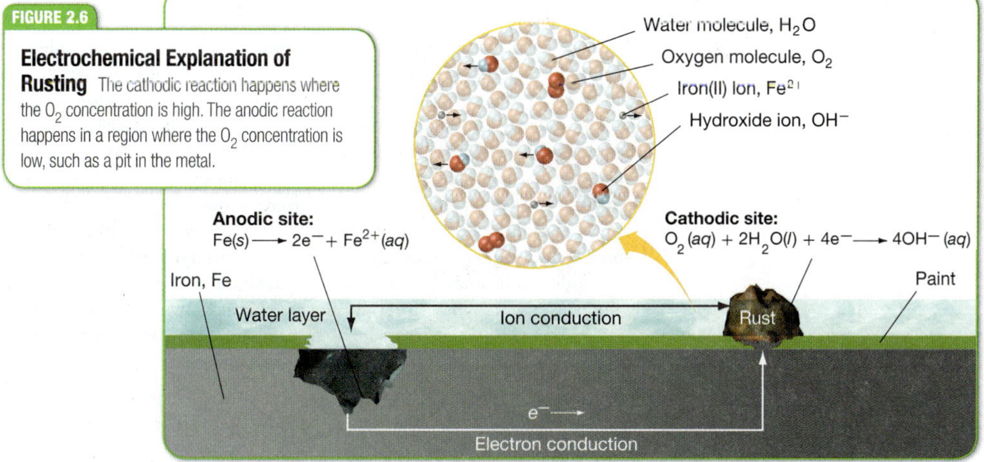

FIGURE 2.6 **Electrochemical Explanation of Rusting** The cathodic reaction happens where the O_2 concentration is high. The anodic reaction happens in a region where the O_2 concentration is low, such as a pit in the metal.

ChemisTrivia

British chemist Sir Humphry Davy (1778–1829) developed cathodic protection in 1824. The method was first used to control corrosion on British naval ships.

Application

Various everyday activities, from painting metal to sealing food in plastic wrap, are designed to prevent corrosion or oxidation. This protection is necessary because oxygen is a very powerful oxidizing agent and will accept electrons from many substances.

Demonstration

PREVENTING OXIDATION

Demonstrate why chefs often squeeze a lemon or lime over a salad containing freshly-cut apples. Cut an **apple** into sections. Soak half the sections in a **fruit juice** that contains vitamin C for 10 minutes. Placed both the soaked and unsoaked sections on separate **paper towels.** Have students observe both samples. Students should observe that the unsoaked sections turn brown as a result of oxidation. Vitamin C prevents oxidation.

Check for Understanding

Answer: Fe | Fe^{+2} (aq) || H_2O | $4OH^-$ (aq)

PRE-AP

Ask students how they could remove the rust from a screw so that they could unscrew it. Have them use the chemical equations in **Figure 2.6** as a starting point. Reacting rust with an acid, such as hydrochloric acid, will form iron cations. Ask students, if materials are always corroding, could we harness the energy released by corrosion to do useful work? No, because the half-reactions aren't separated. Also we don't want the materials to rust because their functionality is impacted.

▼ Teach continued

Application

Many metal structures, such as underground fuel tanks at gas stations, have a sacrificial anode.

Teaching Tip

The terms *voltage* and *volt* honor Italian physicist Alessandro Giuseppe Antonio Anastasio Volta (1745–1827). Volta produced the first electric battery by stacking copper and zinc disks in a pile, separating them by pieces of cloth soaked in salt water, and attaching a metal wire at each end. The battery he made was originally called a *voltaic pile*. Ask students to think about the activity of Cu and Zn and to determine which metal is oxidized and which is reduced. Zn is oxidized and Cu is reduced. Ask students to compare a volatic pile with the fruit battery made in the demonstration earlier in this section.

ChemisTrivia

Volta was also the first to derive the electromotive series—a list that ranks metals in order of their ability to generate electric current. He tested this ability by touching two metals to his tongue and rating the strength of the electric shock he received.

Analogy

Use water as an analogy to explain certain concepts in electricity. For example, current (amps) can be compared to water flow, or how much water passes by a certain point in a given time.

FIGURE 2.7

Sacrificial Anode The Alaskan pipeline is cathodically protected by a parallel zinc cable.

Preventing Corrosion

The presence of salt or high acidity speed the corrosion process, because the movement of electrons is facilitated by the extra ions present.

How can corrosion be prevented? One way, which makes use of electrochemical properties of metals, is to coat steel with zinc in a process called *galvanizing*. Zinc is more easily oxidized than iron; therefore, zinc will react before the iron is oxidized. This is called *cathodic protection*, and the more easily oxidized metal used is called a *sacrificial anode*.

The Alaskan oil pipeline, shown in **Figure 2.7**, is an example of steel that is cathodically protected. However, instead of coating, zinc is connected to the pipe by a wire. The zinc will oxidize before the iron in the steel does. As the zinc anode corrodes, it gives electrons to the cathode, the steel, and as the zinc anode does so, it prevents the steel from corroding. As the zinc dissolves, it needs to be replaced. As long as zinc metal that is able to corrode is present, the steel will be protected from corrosion.

MAIN IDEA

The electric potential of a voltaic cell depends on the strengths of the oxidizing and reducing agents.

In a voltaic cell, the oxidizing agent at the cathode pulls the electrons through the wire away from the reducing agent at the anode. The "pull," or driving force on the electrons, is called the *electric potential*. Electric potential, or voltage, is expressed in units of volts (V), which is the potential energy per unit charge. Current is the movement of the electrons and is expressed in units of amperes, or amps (A).

Electrical potential is analogous to gravitational potential. Just as water flows from a position of higher gravitational potential to a position of lower gravitational potential, electrons flow from higher electrical potential to lower electrical potential.

Electrode Potentials

Reconsider the voltaic cell shown in **Figure 2.1.** There are two electrodes, Zn and Cu. These two metals each have different tendencies for accepting electrons. **This tendency for the half-reaction of either copper or zinc to occur as a reduction half-reaction in an electrochemical cell can be quantified as a reduction potential.** There are two half-cells in **Figure 2.1:** a strip of zinc placed in a solution of $ZnSO_4$ and a strip of copper placed in a solution of $CuSO_4$. **The difference in potential between an electrode and its solution is known as electrode potential.** When these two half-cells are connected and the reaction begins, a difference in potential is observed between the electrodes. This potential difference, or voltage, is proportional to the energy required to move a certain electric charge between the electrodes. A voltmeter connected across the Zn||Cu voltaic cell measures a potential difference of about 1.10 V when the solution concentrations of Zn^{2+} and Cu^{2+} ions are each 1 M.

Differentiated Instruction

ENGLISH LEARNERS

Call students' attention to the names and terms in this section that you want them to know. Notable terms that may be tricky include *galvanizing* (coating steel with zinc, from the name Galvani), *cathodic* (relating to the cathode), and *potential* (the ability to do something).

The potential difference measured across the complete voltaic cell is easily measured and equals the sum of the electrode potentials for the two half-reactions. Individual electrode potential cannot be measured directly, because there can be no transfer of electrons unless both the anode and the cathode are connected to form a complete circuit. A relative value for the potential of a half-reaction can be determined by connecting it to a standard half-cell as a reference. This standard half-cell, shown in **Figure 2.8**, is called a standard hydrogen electrode, or SHE. It consists of a platinum electrode dipped into a 1.00 M acid solution surrounded by hydrogen gas at 1 atm pressure and 25°C. Other electrodes are ranked according to their ability to reduce hydrogen in the SHE.

The anodic reaction for the standard hydrogen electrode is described by the forward half-reaction in the following equilibrium equation.

$$\overset{0}{H_2}(g) \rightleftharpoons \overset{+1}{2H^+}(aq) + 2e^-$$

The cathodic half-reaction is the reverse. An arbitrary potential of 0.00 V is assigned to both of these half-reactions. **The potential of a half-cell under standard conditions measured relative to the standard hydrogen electrode is a standard electrode potential, E^0.** Electrode potentials are expressed as *potentials for reduction*, which provide a reliable indication of the tendency of a substance to be reduced. **Figure 2.9** shows how the SHE is used to find the electrode potentials of the zinc and copper half-cells. Half-reactions for some common electrodes and their standard electrode potentials are listed in **Figure 2.10** on the next page.

Effective oxidizing agents, such as Cu^{2+} and F_2, have positive E^0 values. Half-reactions with negative reduction potentials prefer oxidation over reduction. Effective reducing agents, such as Li and Zn, have negative E^0 values, indicating that the metal or other electrode is more willing to give up electrons than hydrogen.

When a half-reaction is written as an oxidation reaction, the sign of its electrode potential is reversed, as shown for the half-reactions for zinc.

$$Zn^{2+} + 2e^- \longrightarrow Zn \qquad E^0 = -0.76\ V$$
$$Zn \longrightarrow Zn^{2+} + 2e^- \qquad E^0 = +0.76\ V$$

The potential difference across the zinc/hydrogen cell is −0.76 V, so zinc is considered to have an electrode potential of −0.76. The negative number indicates that electrons flow from the zinc electrode, where zinc is oxidized, to the hydrogen electrode, reducing aqueous hydrogen ions.

FIGURE 2.8

Standard Hydrogen Electrode (SHE) A hydrogen electrode is the standard reference electrode for measuring electrode potentials. The electrode surface in contact with the solution is actually a layer of hydrogen adsorbed onto the surface of the platinum.

CRITICAL THINKING

Evaluate What is the advantage of using a standard electrode compared to all other electrodes?

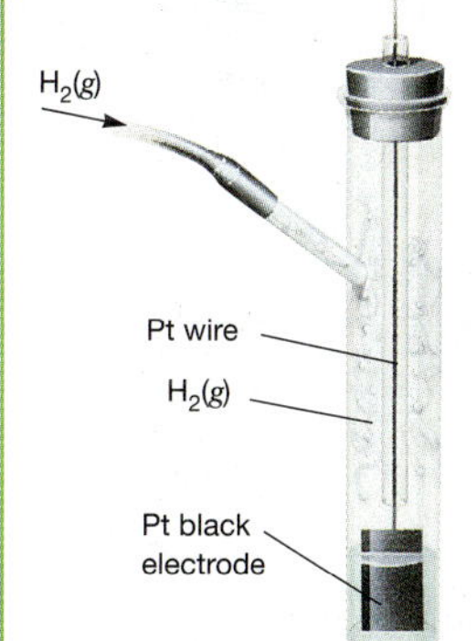

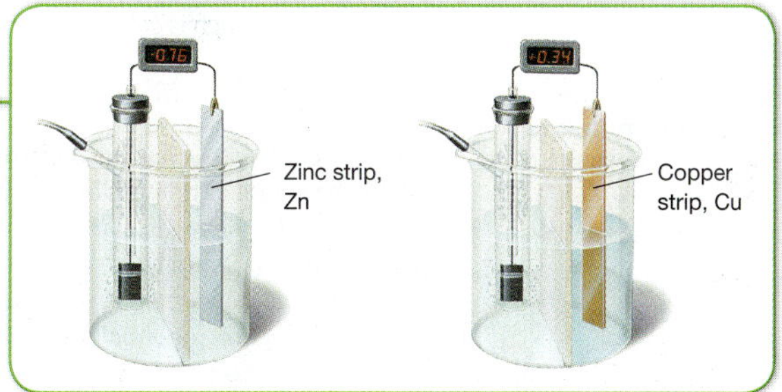

FIGURE 2.9

Finding Electrode Potentials The electrode potentials of zinc and copper half-cells are measured by coupling them with a standard hydrogen electrode.

Alternative Assessment

Provide students with diagrams of cells similar to the voltaic cells in **Figure 2.9** but with different metals as electrodes. Identify the metals from which the two electrodes are made and the electrolytes in each half-cell. Use metals listed in **Figure 2.10** on the next page. Ask students to indicate the direction of electron flow, the identity of the anode and the cathode, the half-reactions that occur, and the overall reaction with its E^0 value.

Teaching Tip

Standard conditions for electrochemical cells are a pressure of 1 atm and a concentration of solutions of 1 M at a specific temperature, which is typically 25°C.

Critical Thinking

Answer: Using a standard gives you a single reference by which other electrodes can be compared and provides a reliable method for measuring differences in electrode potentials.

PRE-AP

E^0 is a relative scale with a defined zero point. To emphasize the relative nature of the E^0 value, pick several half-reactions from **Figure 2.10** on the next page, including the SHE, and place them along a number line. Calculate the relative differences. Then redefine the series with a different reaction chosen as the zero point, and recalculate the differences to show that they are the same.

▼ Teach continued

TEACH FROM TABLES

FIGURE 2.10 Call attention to the change in the magnitude and sign of the E^0 values from the top to the bottom of the table. Ask students the significance of a high positive number for E^0 (effective oxidizing agent) and the significance of a large negative number (effective reducing agent). Relate the table to electronegativity values, activities, electron affinities, and ionization energies. Ask students questions about the reducing strengths of various metals in the table, and then ask them about oxidizing strengths.

Misconception Alert!

Students may see the positive and negative E^0 values and think they need a positive and negative value to create a voltaic cell. However, the difference in E^0 values determines if a reaction will occur or not, regardless of the relation of each half-reaction to the SHE.

Check for Understanding

Answer: Reversing the reaction changes the value of the number from positive to negative or from negative to positive, just as subtracting does.

FIGURE 2.10

STANDARD REDUCTION POTENTIALS

Half-cell reaction	Standard electrode potential, E^0 (in volts)	Half-cell reaction	Standard electrode potential, E^0 (in volts)
$F_2 + 2e^- \rightleftarrows 2F^-$	+2.87	$Fe^{3+} + 3e^- \rightleftarrows Fe$	−0.04
$MnO_4^- + 8H^+ + 5e^- \rightleftarrows Mn^{2+} + 4H_2O$	+1.49	$Pb^{2+} + 2e^- \rightleftarrows Pb$	−0.13
$Au^{3+} + 3e^- \rightleftarrows Au$	+1.42	$Sn^{2+} + 2e^- \rightleftarrows Sn$	−0.14
$Cl_2 + 2e^- \rightleftarrows 2Cl^-$	+1.36	$Ni^{2+} + 2e^- \rightleftarrows Ni$	−0.23
$Cr_2O_7^{2-} + 14H^+ + 6e^- \rightleftarrows 2Cr^{3+} + 7H_2O$	+1.33	$Co^{2+} + 2e^- \rightleftarrows Co$	−0.28
$MnO_2 + 4H^+ + 2e^- \rightleftarrows Mn^{2+} + 2H_2O$	+1.21	$Cd^{2+} + 2e^- \rightleftarrows Cd$	−0.40
$Br_2 + 2e^- \rightleftarrows 2Br^-$	+1.07	$Fe^{2+} + 2e^- \rightleftarrows Fe$	−0.41
$Hg^{2+} + 2e^- \rightleftarrows Hg$	+0.85	$S + 2e^- \rightleftarrows S^{2-}$	−0.51
$Ag^+ + e^- \rightleftarrows Ag$	+0.80	$Cr^{3+} + 3e^- \rightleftarrows Cr$	−0.74
$Hg_2^{2+} + 2e^- \rightleftarrows 2Hg$	+0.80	$Zn^{2+} + 2e^- \rightleftarrows Zn$	−0.76
$Fe^{3+} + e^- \rightleftarrows Fe^{2+}$	+0.77	$Al^{3+} + 3e^- \rightleftarrows Al$	−1.66
$MnO_4^- + e^- \rightleftarrows MnO_4^{2-}$	+0.56	$Mg^{2+} + 2e^- \rightleftarrows Mg$	−2.37
$I_2 + 2e^- \rightleftarrows 2I^-$	+0.54	$Na^+ + e^- \rightleftarrows Na$	−2.71
$Cu^{2+} + 2e^- \rightleftarrows Cu$	+0.34	$Ca^{2+} + 2e^- \rightleftarrows Ca$	−2.76
$Cu^{2+} + e^- \rightleftarrows Cu^+$	+0.16	$Ba^{2+} + 2e^- \rightleftarrows Ba$	−2.90
$S + 2H^+(aq) + 2e^- \rightleftarrows H_2S(aq)$	+0.14	$K^+ + e^- \rightleftarrows K$	−2.93
$2H^+(aq) + 2e^- \rightleftarrows H_2$	0.00	$Li^+ + e^- \rightleftarrows Li$	−3.04

A copper half-cell coupled with the standard hydrogen electrode gives a potential difference measurement of +0.34 V. This positive number indicates that $Cu^{2+}(aq)$ ions are more readily reduced than $H^+(aq)$ ions.

Standard electrode potentials can be used to predict if a redox reaction will occur spontaneously. A spontaneous reaction will have a positive value for E^0_{cell}, which is calculated using the following equation.

$$E^0_{cell} = E^0_{cathode} - E^0_{anode}$$

The half-reaction that has the more negative standard reduction potential will be the anode. Oxidation occurs at the anode, so the anode half-cell reaction will be the reverse of the reduction reaction found in **Figure 2.10.** Thus, the total potential of a cell is calculated by *subtracting* the standard reduction potential for the reaction at the anode (E^0_{anode}) from the standard reduction potential for the reaction at the cathode ($E^0_{cathode}$).

✓ CHECK FOR UNDERSTANDING

Compare How is subtracting the value the for the half-cell reaction at the anode the same as reversing the reaction?

Problem Solving

ALTERNATIVE APPROACHES

The equation for calculating the standard potential of a cell uses the standard reduction potential of both half-reactions because the subtraction of the anode reduction potential makes it an oxidation potential. Explain to students that as an alternative, you could flip the oxidation half-reaction and its standard reduction potential to become an oxidation potential—as shown previously in the text—and then add the potentials of the two half-reactions together.

REALITY CHECK

When students are calculating cell voltage, they should always end up with a positive number (assuming the cell is voltaic), signifying the cell has potential to do work.

Calculating Cell Potentials

PREMIUM CONTENT

Learn It! Video HMDScience.com

Solve It! Cards HMDScience.com

Sample Problem A **Write the overall cell reaction, and calculate the cell potential for a voltaic cell consisting of the following half-cells: an iron (Fe) electrode in a solution of $Fe(NO_3)_3$ and a silver (Ag) electrode in a solution of $AgNO_3$.**

1 ANALYZE

Given: A half-cell consists of $Fe(s)$ with $Fe(NO_3)_3(aq)$ and a second half-cell consists of $Ag(s)$ with $AgNO_3(aq)$.

Unknown: E^0_{cell}

2 PLAN

1. Look up E^0 for each half-reaction (written as reductions) in **Figure 2.10.**

   $Fe^{3+}(aq) + 3e^- \longrightarrow Fe(s)$ $E^0 = -0.04$ V $\quad Ag^+(aq) + e^- \longrightarrow Ag(s)$ $E^0 = +0.80$ V

2. Determine the cathode and anode.

   Fe in $Fe(NO_3)_3$ is the anode because it has a lower reduction potential than Ag. Ag in $Ag(NO_3)$ is therefore the cathode.

3 SOLVE

1. Determine the overall cell reaction. Multiply the Ag half-reaction by 3 so that the number of electrons lost in that half-reaction equals the number of electrons gained in the oxidation of iron. Reverse the iron half-reaction to be an oxidation half-reaction.

   $$3Ag^+(aq) + Fe(s) \longrightarrow 3Ag(s) + Fe^{3+}(aq)$$

2. Calculate the cell potential by $E^0_{cell} = E^0_{cathode} - E^0_{anode}$. Note that when a half-reaction is multiplied by a constant, the E^0 value is not multiplied by that constant but remains the same.

   $$E^0_{cell} = E^0_{cathode} - E^0_{anode} = +0.80\text{ V} - (-0.04\text{ V}) = +0.84\text{ V}$$

4 CHECK YOUR WORK

The calculated value for E^0_{cell} is positive, which confirms that it is a voltaic cell, as the problem states.

Practice Answers in Appendix E

1. For each pair of half-cells, determine the overall electrochemical reaction that proceeds spontaneously and the E^0 value.
   a. $Cr_2O_7^{2-}/Cr^{3+}$ and Ni^{2+}/Ni
   b. SHE and Fe^{2+}/Fe^{3+}

SECTION 2 FORMATIVE ASSESSMENT

Reviewing Main Ideas

1. What is a voltaic cell?
2. What is electrode potential, and how is it used to calculate information about an electrochemical cell?
3. Given the Na^+/Na and K^+/K half-cells, determine the overall electrochemical reaction that proceeds spontaneously and the E^0 value.
4. Given the MnO_2/Mn^{2+} and Cr^{3+}/Cr half-cells, determine the overall electrochemical reaction that occurs spontaneously and the E^0 value.

Critical Thinking

5. **EVALUATING IDEAS** A sacrificial anode is allowed to corrode. Why is the use of a sacrificial anode considered to be a way to prevent corrosion?

Answers to Section Assessment

1. A voltaic cell is one in which a spontaneous redox reaction produces electricity.
2. Electrode potential is the potential difference between an electrode and its solution; its magnitude measures the tendency for reduction half-reactions to occur.
3. $K + Na^+ \longrightarrow K^+ + Na$; $E^0 = +0.22$ V
4. $3MnO_2 + 12H^+ + 2Cr \longrightarrow 3Mn^{2+} + 6H_2O + 2Cr^{3+}$; $E^0 = +1.95$ V
5. The sacrificial anode oxidizes more easily than the structural metal. As it does so, it gives electrons to the structural metal, preventing it from oxidizing.

Teaching Tip

This discussion involves only 1 M solutions. In order to discuss cell potentials for solutions at concentrations other than 1 M, the Nernst equation must be used.

Answers

Practice A

1. **a.** $Cr_2O_7^{2-} + 14H^+ + 3Ni \longrightarrow 2Cr^{3+} + 3Ni^{2+} + 7H_2O$; $E^0 = +1.33\text{ V} - (-0.23\text{ V}) = +1.56$ V
   b. $2Fe^{3+} + H_2 \longrightarrow 2Fe^{2+} + 2H^+$; $E^0 = +0.77\text{ V} - 0.0\text{ V} = +0.77$ V

Assess and Reteach

Assess Use the Formative Assessment on this page to evaluate student mastery of the section.

Reteach For students who need additional instruction, download the Section Study Guide.

Response to Intervention To reassess students' mastery, use the Section Quiz, available to print or to take directly online at **HMDScience.com**.

Classroom Discussion

1. In groups, have students research the pilot fuel-cell cars from the major car companies. Have them use the Internet to determine the following items: fuel used, storage used, where is the car in the development cycle, and forecast of availability and cost. Then have each group present the information about the cars that they chose to research to the class.
2. Have students research the methods used in this country to produce hydrogen. Have them compare the different methods in terms of cost, environmental benefits, and feasibility.

Answers

1. If methanol or some other fuel is used to produce the hydrogen gas on board the car, there will be emissions from that other fuel. Even if the hydrogen reactant is stored in the car, one needs to know how the hydrogen gas was produced originally. Hydrogen gas can be produced using methanol, ethanol, natural gas, gasoline, or compressed or liquid hydrogen.
2. The hydrogen ions are produced at the anode. The hydrogen gas is oxidized to hydrogen ions; oxidation always occurs at the anode.

WHY IT MATTERS

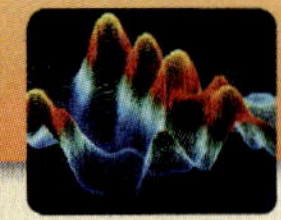
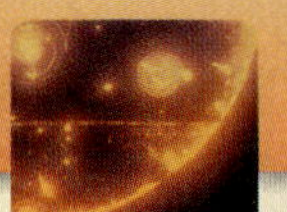

Fuel-Cell Cars

S.T.E.M.

The car of the future is quiet, has low emissions, and requires less maintenance than cars of today do. These are the promises of fuel-cell cars. The development of fuel-cell cars has been pushed by state and federal programs, legislation, and funding. There are a number of issues that need to be resolved before the large-scale manufacture of fuel-cell cars becomes feasible. These include the fuel-storage capacity of the car, and the fueling infrastructure.

The technology currently favored for automobiles is the proton-exchange membrane (PEM) fuel cell. The system works by combining hydrogen with oxygen taken from the outside air. The movement of the electrons (produced by a redox reaction) along an external route generates electricity, which is used eventually to turn the car wheels. The process is two to three times more efficient than that of the internal-combustion engine, and the only products are water and a moderate amount of energy as heat. In most cases, a traditional car battery is used to operate the car's electrical system.

In principle, fuel cells can run on any hydrogen-rich fuel. Several candidate fuels that can power fuel cells are being investigated: methanol, ethanol, natural gas, gasoline, and liquid or compressed hydrogen. If the fuel is not hydrogen gas, the engine needs to include a reformer that can convert the other fuel (such as methanol) to hydrogen.

The range of fuel-cell powered cars is limited by the amount of fuel that can be stored in the storage tank. Current storage technology can take the cars to 300 miles or more before requiring refueling. Researchers in this area are looking into carbon-adsorption systems, which are refrigerated and pressurized tanks that can store large amounts of hydrogen. Hydrogen is very combustible, but safe hydrogen tanks have been developed.

Eventually, fuel-cell cars such as this one may replace gasoline-powered cars.

So today, the experts do not have any more concern about the safety of hydrogen storage than they do about gasoline storage.

However, the landscape is not yet dotted with hydrogen refueling stations. Current experimental users such as governmental institutions must have their own hydrogen refueling stations. Auto companies say there needs to be a consumer infrastructure for the hydrogen fuel-cell cars before consumers will buy. On the other hand, possible developers of such hydrogen stations say that there needs to be a demand before the infrastructure can form.

The use of fuels such as methanol solves the storage and fuel infrastructure problem, because these fuels can be stored similar to the way gasoline is stored. Therefore, these fuels can be sold at current gasoline stations.

One should also consider the emissions and energy use involved in making and delivering the hydrogen fuel in addition to the emissions from the hydrogen fuel cell. Producing hydrogen fuel itself could involve substantial emissions. Even so, fuel-cell cars are still more efficient and have greater environmental benefits than the internal-combustion cars of today.

Currently, all major car companies are developing and researching fuel-cell cars. Most companies have prototype cars and some cars are in use by governmental institutions. Which type will ultimately succeed in the mass market is yet unknown. Experts agree, though, that for zero-emission cars, hydrogen is the only major fuel option that has been identified to date.

Questions

1. Fuel cells that use hydrogen as fuel produce water and moderate amounts of energy in the form of heat as the only emissions. What kinds of negative effects might cars that use hydrogen-rich fuels have on the environment?
2. In the PEM fuel cell, the hydrogen ions are produced at which electrode: the anode or cathode?

SECTION 3

Electrolytic Cells

SECTION 3

Main Ideas

- Nonspontaneous redox reactions occur in electrolytic cells.
- Electrolysis uses electrical energy to cause a nonspontaneous chemical reaction to occur.

Key Terms

electrolytic cell

electroplating

electrolysis

Some oxidation-reduction reactions do not occur spontaneously but can be driven by electrical energy. **If electrical energy is required to produce a redox reaction and bring about a chemical change in an electrochemical cell, it is an electrolytic cell.** Most commercial uses of redox reactions make use of electrolytic cells.

MAIN IDEA

Nonspontaneous redox reactions occur in electrolytic cells.

A comparison of electrolytic and voltaic cells can be seen in **Figure 3.1.** The voltaic cell shown has a copper cathode and a zinc anode. If a battery is connected so that the positive terminal contacts the copper electrode and the negative terminal contacts the zinc electrode, the electrons move in the opposite direction. The battery forces the cell to reverse its reaction; the zinc electrode becomes the cathode, and the copper electrode becomes the anode. The half-reaction at the anode, in which copper metal is oxidized, can be written as follows:

$$\overset{0}{Cu} \longrightarrow \overset{+2}{Cu}^{2+} + 2e^-$$

The reduction half-reaction of zinc at the cathode is written as follows:

$$\overset{+2}{Zn}^{2+} + 2e^- \longrightarrow \overset{0}{Zn}$$

FIGURE 3.1

Voltaic Versus Electrolytic Cells
The direction in which the electrons move reverses if a voltaic cell is connected to a direct current source to become an electrolytic cell.

CRITICAL THINKING
Analyze Can any voltaic cell become an electrolytic cell?

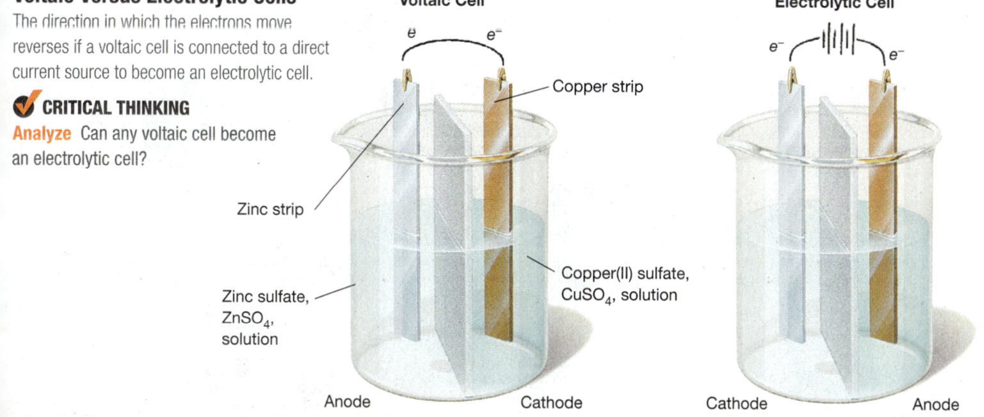

Differentiated Instruction

BELOW LEVEL

To help students see that voltaic cells and electrolytic cells are opposites of each other, ask students to create a figure comparing the two electrochemical processes. Be sure that students note whether energy is released or absorbed, if the reaction proceeds spontaneously or not, and whether the value of E^0 is positive or negative.

Plan and Prepare

Objectives

Upon completion of this section, students should be able to do the following:

- Describe the nature of electrolytic cells.
- Describe the process of electrolysis in the decomposition of water and in the production of metals.
- Explain the process of electroplating.
- Describe the chemistry of a rechargeable cell.

Classroom Catalyst

Tell students that electroplating of jewelry is a very common application of electrochemistry. Show them a demonstration of electroplating copper onto a zinc or iron electrode.

Teach

TEACH FROM VISUALS

FIGURE 3.1 Point out the change in identity of the anode and cathode between the two cells. Be sure students understand that the key difference between the voltaic cell and the electrolytic cell is that in the voltaic cell the reaction proceeds *spontaneously*, whereas the reaction in the electrolytic cell is *nonspontaneous* and must be driven by an external source of electric current, such as a battery. The diagram of the electrolytic cell in **Figure 3.1** uses the circuit-diagram symbol for a battery between the cathode and anode.

Critical Thinking

Answer: Yes. If you force current the opposite way through a voltaic cell, it will become an electrolytic cell.

▼ Teach *continued*

Demonstration

AN ELECTROLYTIC CELL

1. Place **300 mL of 0.1 M $CuSO_4$** solution in a **500-mL beaker.**
2. Connect one end of a **6-inch wire** to a **polished 4 × 150 mm copper strip** using an **alligator clip** and the other end to the positive terminal of a **battery**.
3. Connect one end of a second piece of 6-inch wire to a **polished 4 × 150 mm zinc (or iron) strip** using an **alligator clip** and the other end to the negative battery terminal.
4. Place the electrodes in the solution and let the experiment run for five minutes. Little bubbles should form on the copper electrode soon after it is placed in the solution. (If the electrodes are hooked up backwards, a black film will coat the electrode.)
5. After the electrodes are removed, the anode should be plated with copper.

Check for Understanding

Answer: Differences: 1) electrolytic cells are connected to an external power source; 2) nonspontaneous reactions occur in eletrolytic cells while spontaneous reactions occur in voltaic cells

CHECK FOR UNDERSTANDING
List State the two important differences between a voltaic and an electrolytic cell.

There are two main differences between voltaic and electrolytic cells.

1. Electrolytic cells are connected to a battery or other direct-current source. A voltaic cell is a source of electrical energy.
2. In an electrolytic cell, electrical energy from an external source causes *nonspontaneous* redox reactions. In a voltaic cell *spontaneous* redox reactions produce electricity. In an electrolytic cell, electrical energy turns to chemical energy; in a voltaic cell, the reverse occurs.

Electroplating

An electrolytic process in which a metal ion is reduced and a solid metal is deposited on a surface is called electroplating. An electroplating cell contains a solution of a salt of the plating metal, an object to be plated (the cathode), and a piece of the plating metal (the anode). A silver-plating cell contains a solution of a soluble silver salt and a silver anode. The cathode is the object to be plated. The silver anode is connected to the positive electrode of a battery or to some other source of direct current. The object to be plated is connected to the negative electrode.

Figure 3.2 shows silver being electroplated onto a bracelet. Silver ions are reduced at the cathode according to the following half-reaction and deposited as metallic silver when electrons flow through the circuit.

$$\overset{+1}{Ag^+} + e^- \longrightarrow \overset{0}{Ag}$$

At the anode, metallic silver is oxidized by the following half-reaction.

$$\overset{0}{Ag} \longrightarrow \overset{+1}{Ag^+} + e^-$$

In effect, silver is transferred from the anode to the cathode of the cell.

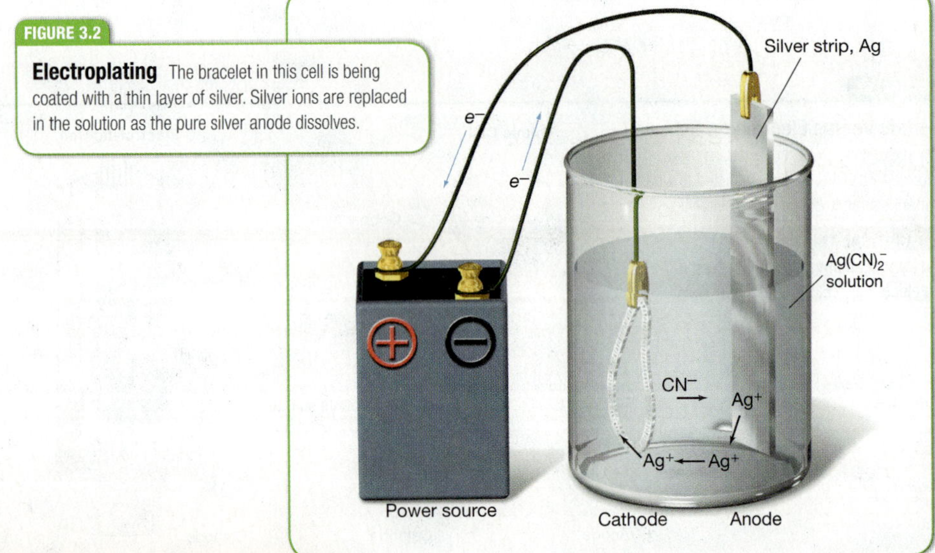

FIGURE 3.2

Electroplating The bracelet in this cell is being coated with a thin layer of silver. Silver ions are replaced in the solution as the pure silver anode dissolves.

Differentiated Instruction

PRE-AP

Because batteries are basically voltaic cells, challenge students to draw two connected cells with one acting as a voltaic cell supplying energy to the other acting as an electrolytic cell. Have students determine a viable set of half-reactions that would be appropriate and support their proposal with the proper chemical equations and cell potential calculations.

Rechargeable Cells

A rechargeable cell combines the oxidation-reduction chemistry of both voltaic cells and electrolytic cells. When a rechargeable cell converts chemical energy to electrical energy, it operates as a voltaic cell. But when the cell is recharged, it operates as an electrolytic cell, converting electrical energy to chemical energy.

The standard 12 V automobile battery, shown in **Figure 3.3**, is a set of six rechargeable cells. The anode in each cell is lead submerged in a solution of H_2SO_4. The anode half-reaction is described below.

$$Pb(s) + SO_4^{2-}(aq) \longrightarrow PbSO_4(s) + 2e^-$$

At the cathode, PbO_2 is reduced according to the following equation.

$$PbO_2(s) + 4H^+(aq) + SO_4^{2-}(aq) + 2e^- \longrightarrow PbSO_4(s) + 2H_2O(l)$$

The net oxidation-reduction reaction for the discharge cycle is:

$$Pb(s) + PbO_2(s) + 2H_2SO_4(aq) \longrightarrow 2PbSO_4(s) + 2H_2O(l)$$

A car's battery produces the electric energy needed to start its engine. Sulfuric acid, present as its ions, is consumed, and lead(II) sulfate accumulates as a white powder on the electrodes. Once the car is running, the half-reactions are reversed by a voltage produced by the alternator. The Pb, PbO_2, and H_2SO_4 are regenerated. A battery can be recharged as long as all reactants necessary for the electrolytic reaction are present, and all reactions are reversible.

The lead storage battery is one of the oldest types of rechargeable batteries. It is designed to deliver a high amount of current in a short period of time, as, for example, when an engine needs to be started. If the battery has been in use too long without being recharged by the alternator, it will not be able to deliver the starting current. In such cases, cars require a "jump start" from another source.

FIGURE 3.3

Rechargeable Batteries
The rechargeable cells of a car battery produce electricity from reactions between lead(IV) oxide, lead, and sulfuric acid.

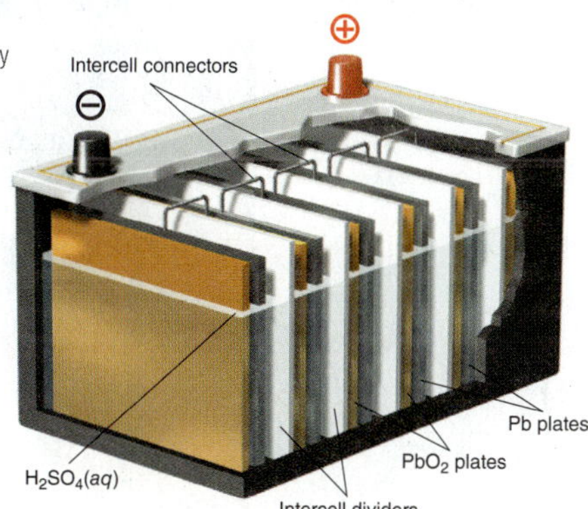

Classroom Discussion

Michael Faraday (1791–1867) described the following laws of electrolysis. Use them as an opportunity to extend students' understanding of the electrolytic process.

1. The mass of substance liberated at an electrode during electrolysis is proportional to the quantity of electricity driven through the solution.
2. The mass liberated by a given quantity of electricity is proportional to the atomic weight of the element liberated and inversely proportional to the valence of the element liberated.

In the first law, students can recognize that the amount of substance deposited at the cathode depends on the number of electrons available for reduction. The second law states that a heavy element with the same valence as a lighter one requires the same amount of electricity but produces a greater mass of product. In addition, elements with higher valences require more electrons to produce the same number of moles of product as elements with lower valences.

Application

Pennies minted in the United States prior to 1982 are 95% copper and 5% zinc, but by 1982 the copper in a penny became more valuable than its buying power. To prevent the practice of melting down coins for the metal they contain, the composition of the penny was changed. Post-1982 pennies consist of a zinc core (97.5%) electroplated with a layer of copper.

INCLUSION

Have students create a model of a rechargeable cell by using a large storage bin cover or tray and several table-tennis balls. Have two students hold the cover or tray to form a ramp with a slight tilt on a counter top. Have students hold the balls at the top of the ramp. When all the balls are held at the top of the ramp, the "cell" is charged. Have students release balls, one at a time, to simulate the cell releasing its energy. Then, have students gather the balls and hold them again at the top of the ramp to simulate recharging the cell.

▼ Teach continued

Demonstration

THE ELECTROLYSIS OF KI

1. Place a **petri dish** on an **overhead projector.** Add **20 mL of 0.1 M KI** solution.
2. Add a few drops of **phenolphthalein** and a few drops of **starch solution** to the KI solution.
3. Using **insulated leads**, attach **two electrodes** to a **9-V battery.**
4. Hold the electrodes in the KI solution. I_2 can be detected at the anode by the characteristic blue-black color of starch in the presence of I_2. H_2 bubbles can be detected at the cathode. OH^- ions can be detected near the cathode by the appearance of the pink color of phenolphthalein.
5. Students can use the above evidence to write the half-reactions that took place.
   Anode: $2I^-(aq) \longrightarrow I_2(aq) + 2e^-$
   Cathode: $2e^- + 2H_2O(l) \longrightarrow H_2(g) + 2OH^-(aq)$
6. Discuss the fact that the reaction did not proceed until the electrodes and battery were added. When students realize that this is a nonspontaneous reaction, have them trace the path of the electrons. Electrons are pumped from the anode, where I^- ions are oxidized, and forced through the external circuit to the cathode, where H^+ ions from the water are reduced to H_2.

Disposal Add sufficient **1 M $Na_2S_2O_3$** to reduce I_2, and pour the solution down the drain.

MAIN IDEA

Electrolysis uses electrical energy to cause a nonspontaneous chemical reaction to occur.

Electroplating and recharging a battery are examples of electrolysis. **Electrolysis** is the process of passing a current through a cell for which the cell potential is negative and causing an oxidation-reduction reaction to occur. That is, electrical energy is used to force a nonspontaneous chemical reaction to occur. For this cell reaction to occur, the external voltage must be greater than the potential that would be produced by the spontaneous reverse cell reaction.

Electrolysis is of great industrial importance. It is used to purify many metals from the ores in which they are found chemically combined in Earth's crust.

Electrolysis of Water

The electrolysis of water, shown in **Figure 3.4,** leads to the cell reaction in which water is broken down into its elements, H_2 and O_2. Recall that hydrogen gas and oxygen gas combine spontaneously to form water and are used to power fuel cells, which produce electricity. Therefore, the reverse process (electrolysis of water) is nonspontaneous and requires electrical energy. The two half-reactions occur at the anode and cathode.

$$\text{Anode: } 6H_2O(l) \longrightarrow 4e^- + O_2(g) + 4H_3O^+(aq)$$

$$\text{Cathode: } 4H_2O(l) + 4e^- \longrightarrow 2H_2(g) + 4OH^-(aq)$$

FIGURE 3.4

Electrolysis
Electrical energy from the battery is used to break down water. Hydrogen forms at the cathode (left tube), and oxygen forms at the anode (right tube).

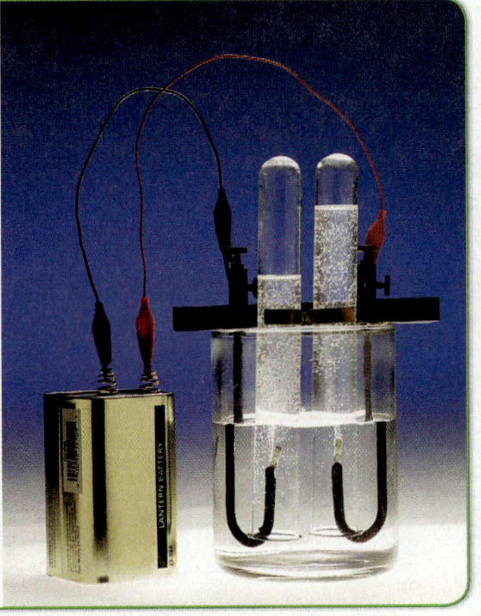

Differentiated Instruction

PRE-AP

Have students explore what happens when a salt is added to water to make an aqueous solution and then a potential is placed across the solution.

Have students investigate the following questions: What will happen? What species will evolve at each electrode? Does the nature of the salt matter?

What forms at each electrode is a function of the standard reduction potential of the ions in the salt relative to the two half-reactions of the electrolysis of water. Whichever half-reaction occurs more easily at each electrode (in other words, whichever yields the smallest required voltage) will occur.

Aluminum Production by Electrolysis

Aluminum is the most abundant metal in Earth's crust. It is a relatively reactive metal; therefore, in nature, it is found as its oxide in an ore called *bauxite.* Aluminum is now very useful commercially, but it was not until 1886 that a process to obtain pure aluminum metal was discovered. Charles M. Hall (from the United States) and Paul Héroult (from France) simultaneously, but independently, determined a practical method for producing aluminum; it is an electrolytic process called the Hall-Héroult process.

Bauxite ore contains not only aluminum oxide (Al_2O_3), but oxides of iron, silicon, and titanium. Therefore, the aluminum oxide (called alumina) must first be separated from the other compounds in the ore. The pure hydrated alumina ($Al_2O_3 \bullet nH_2O$) is obtained by treating bauxite with sodium hydroxide, which dissolves the alumina but does not dissolve the other compounds in the ore. The alumina solution is then separated from the remaining solid compounds and reprecipitated to obtain pure alumina. The purified alumina is dissolved in molten cryolite, Na_3AlF_6, at 970°C in an electrochemical cell, and the aluminum ions are reduced to aluminum metal. The liquid aluminum is denser than the molten cryolite and alumina; therefore, the molten aluminum metal settles to the bottom of the cell and is drained off periodically.

The electrolytic solution contains a large number of aluminum-containing ions, and the chemistry of the electrochemical reaction is not completely understood. Scientists still debate the exact species that participate in the half-reactions; but the overall cell reaction is

$$2Al_2O_3(l) + 3C(s) \longrightarrow 4Al(l) + 3CO_2(g),$$

where carbon is the anode and steel is the cathode in the cell.

The aluminum metal produced in this process is 99.5% pure. The Hall-Héroult process made the production of aluminum economically feasible. However, this process is the largest single user of electrical energy in the United States—nearly 5% of the national total. Recycling aluminum saves almost 95% of the cost of production. Aluminum recycling is one of the most economically worthwhile recycling programs that has been developed.

WHY IT MATTERS

Sodium Production by Electrolysis S.T.E.M.

Sodium is such a reactive metal that preparing it through a chemical process can be dangerous. Today, sodium is produced mainly by the electrolysis of molten sodium chloride. The melting point of sodium chloride is about 800°C; but mixing it with solid calcium chloride lowers the melting point to around 600°C. This mixture is introduced into an electrolytic cell called the Downs Cell to retrieve the sodium metal, and the lower melting point allows the cell to use less electrical energy to run.

CHECK FOR UNDERSTANDING

Distinguish Why is it so critical for people to recycle aluminum?

SECTION 3 FORMATIVE ASSESSMENT

Reviewing Main Ideas

1. Describe an electrolytic cell.
2. Explain the process of electroplating.
3. What is a rechargeable cell?
4. Give an example of how electrolytic cells are used in industry.

Critical Thinking

5. **APPLYING CONCEPTS** Copper ore contains zinc metal, which is oxidized along with Cu during the electrolytic purification process. However, the Zn^{2+} ions are not then reduced when the Cu^{2+} ions are reduced to Cu at the cathode to obtain purified copper metal. Explain how Zn can be oxidized with Cu, but their ions not be reduced together.

Answers to Section Assessment

1. In an electrolytic cell, electrical energy from an external source causes a nonspontaneous redox reaction to occur.
2. Electroplating is a process in which a metal ion is reduced and solid metal is deposited on a surface.
3. A rechargeable cell operates both as a voltaic and as an electrolytic cell. It operates as a voltaic cell when it converts chemical energy to electrical energy; when the cell is recharging, it operates as an electrolytic cell, converting electrical energy to chemical energy.
4. Sample answer: Electrolytic cells are used to drive a reaction that purifies aluminum metal from its ore.
5. The reduction half-reactions are $Zn^{2+} + 2e^- \longrightarrow Zn$ ($E^0 = -0.76$ V) and $Cu^{2+} + 2e^- \longrightarrow Cu$ ($E^0 = +0.34$ V). Zn oxidizes spontaneously; Cu needs 0.34 V to oxidize. However, Cu^{2+} is reduced spontaneously, whereas Zn^{2+} needs 0.76 V to be reduced. Thus, if the voltage applied to the cell is less than 0.76 V, then only Cu^{2+} will be reduced. Thus, only Cu will be plated out; Zn will stay in solution as Zn^{2+}.

Teaching Tip

Inform students that the cost of refining aluminum from recycled materials is between 5% and 10% of the cost of producing the same amount of aluminum from ore. As a result, aluminum scrap has considerable value, and aluminum recycling has been highly successful.

Classroom Discussion

To help students develop an appreciation for how fundamentally the Hall-Héroult process affects their lives, have them break up into small groups and brainstorm as many things that contain aluminium as they can. Then come together as a class and compile a list on the board.

Check for Understanding

Answer: Refining aluminum from ore requires a lot of energy and is very costly. Since aluminum can be recycled indefinitely with no quality loss, recycling is the most energy-efficient and cost effective way to obtain aluminum for new products.

Assess and Reteach ▼

Assess Use the Formative Assessment on this page to evaluate student mastery of the section.

Reteach For students who need additional instruction, download the Section Study Guide.

Response to Intervention To reassess students' mastery, use the Section Quiz, available to print or to take directly online at **HMDScience.com**.

Answers

1. $E^0_{cell} = 1.82$ V
2. $E^0_{cell} = 1.20$ V

Math Tutor

CALCULATING CELL POTENTIALS

You have learned that electrons are transferred in all oxidation-reduction reactions. Electrons from a substance being oxidized are transferred to another substance being reduced. A voltaic cell is a simple device that physically separates the oxidation reaction from the reduction reaction, thus forcing electrons released during oxidation to travel through a wire to reach the site of reduction. If a device, such as a light bulb or a motor, is placed in the circuit, the moving electrons can perform useful work. The device will continue to operate until the circuit is broken or the reaction ceases to occur spontaneously.

The potential (voltage) of a given voltaic cell depends on how strongly the oxidation process tends to give up electrons and how strongly the reduction process tends to take them. The greater these two combined tendencies, the higher the potential of the cell. Potentials have been measured for each half-reaction. In a voltaic cell, the process with the more negative reduction potential will proceed as the oxidation reaction at the anode of the cell. The more positive reaction will proceed as reduction at the cathode. The sample problem shows how to find the potential of a voltaic cell.

Problem-Solving TIPS

- In a voltaic cell, the process that has the more negative reduction potential will proceed as the oxidation reaction at the anode of the cell.

Sample Problem

Calculate the potential of a voltaic cell in which Hg^{2+} ions are reduced to Hg metal while Zn metal is oxidized to Zn^{2+} ions.

Reduction takes place at the cathode, so the cathode half-reaction is

$$Hg^{2+}(aq) + 2e^- \longrightarrow Hg(l)$$

Oxidation takes place at the anode, so the anode half-reaction is

$$Zn(s) \longrightarrow Zn^{2+}(aq) + 2e^-$$

To use the equation for cell potential, rewrite the anode half-reaction as a reduction reaction, $Zn^{2+}(aq) + 2e^- \longrightarrow Zn(s)$.

Use **Figure 2.10** in the current chapter to find the standard reduction potential for each half-reaction. Then, calculate the cell potential.

$$Hg^{2+}(aq) + 2e^- \longrightarrow Hg(l)\ E\ cathode\ 0 = +0.85\text{ V}$$

$$Zn^{2+}(aq) + 2e^- \longrightarrow Zn(s)\ E\ anode\ 0 = -0.76\text{ V}$$

$$E\ cell\ 0 = E\ cathode\ 0 - E\ anode\ 0 = +0.85\text{ V} - (-0.76\text{ V}) = 1.61\text{ V}$$

Practice

Answers in Appendix E

1. Calculate the potential of a voltaic cell in which aluminum metal is oxidized to Al^{3+} ions while Cu^{2+} ions are reduced to Cu^+ ions.
2. Calculate the potential of a cell in which the reaction is $Pb(s) + Br_2(l) \longrightarrow Pb^{2+}(aq) + 2Br^-(aq)$.

CHAPTER 20 Summary

Review Games
Concept Maps

SECTION 1 Introduction to Electrochemistry

- Electrochemistry is the branch of chemistry that deals with electricity-related applications of redox reactions.
- The electrode immersed in an electrolyte solution is a half-cell.
- The anode is the electrode where oxidation takes place. The cathode is the electrode where reduction occurs.
- The cell consists of electrodes connected by a wire along which the electron travels and a salt bridge (or porous barrier) through which ions transfer to balance the charge.
- An electrochemical cell is a system of electrodes and electrolytes in which either chemical reactions produce electrical energy or electric current produces chemical change.

KEY TERMS

electrochemistry
electrode
half-cell
anode
cathode

SECTION 2 Voltaic Cells

- A voltaic cell, sometimes called a galvanic cell, uses a spontaneous redox reaction to produce electrical energy. Examples of voltaic cells are batteries and fuel cells.
- Fuel cells are voltaic cells in which the reactants are continuously supplied and the products are continuously removed.
- The potential difference must be measured across a complete cell because no transfer of electrons can occur unless both the anode and cathode are connected to form a complete circuit. Thus, the standard electrode potential for a half-cell is measured against the standard hydrogen electrode (SHE).
- Standard reduction potentials, E^0, are stated as reduction half-reactions. Effective oxidizing agents have positive E^0 values, while effective reducing agents have negative E^0 values.
- A voltaic cell has an E^0_{cell} value that is positive.
- Corrosion occurs when iron is exposed to oxygen and water. One of the best methods to prevent corrosion is by the use of sacrificial anodes.

KEY TERMS

voltaic cell
reduction potential
electrode potential
standard electrode potential

SECTION 3 Electrolytic Cells

- Electrolytic cells are cells in which electrical energy from an external source causes a nonspontaneous reaction to occur.
- An electrolytic cell has an E^0_{cell} value that is negative.
- Electrolysis has great economic impact. Applications of electrolytic cells are electroplating of metallic surfaces, rechargeable batteries, aluminum production, and purification of metals.

KEY TERMS

electrolytic cell
electroplating
electrolysis

Review Answers

1. The electrode is Zn(*s*). The reaction is a reduction; therefore, it is a cathodic reaction.
2. The porous barrier allows the movement of charge by ion transfer from one half-cell to the other in an electrochemical cell.
3. **a.** $2Ag^+ + Co \longrightarrow 2Ag + Co^{2+}$; $Co(s) \mid Co^{2+}(aq) \parallel Ag^+(aq) \mid Ag(s)$

   b. $2Au^{3+} + 3Zn \longrightarrow 2Au + 3Zn^{2+}$; $Zn(s) \mid Zn^{2+}(aq) \parallel Au^{3+}(aq) \mid Au(s)$

   c. $Hg_2^{2+} + 2K \longrightarrow 2Hg + 2K^+$; $K(s) \mid K^+(aq) \parallel Hg^{2+}(aq) \mid Hg(s)$
4. An electrochemical cell consists of two electrodes in electrolyte solutions that are separated by a porous barrier or a salt bridge. The two electrodes are connected by a wire. Electrons travel from the anode through the wire down the cathode to the cathodic electrolyte solution. To balance the charge, ions travel between the two half-cells by way of the porous barrier or the salt bridge.
5. A voltaic cell is an electrochemical cell in which the reaction is spontaneous and generates electrical energy. Batteries and fuel cells are examples of voltaic cells.
6. A fuel cell can, in principle, supply electrical energy indefinitely without stopping to recharge, because its reactants are continuously supplied and its products are continuously removed.
7. The oxidation and reduction half-reactions occur spontaneously at different sites; therefore, they are half-cells and are voltaic. The two sites are connected by a metal conductor to move the electrons from one half-cell to the other. There are also electrolytes (the ions in the water) and a salt bridge (the water).

CHAPTER REVIEW

8. Answers may vary. The advantages of plating with another metal are that the coating is more durable than paint, and if a more easily oxidized metal is used, that metal will react before the coated metal does. One disadvantage of metal plating is if water gets behind the plating, corrosion can occur and may not be noticed. Advantages of a sacrificial anode are that it can be used for underground structures, where paint or plating cannot easily be done, and it is easy to replace the sacrificial anode when it has dissolved.
9. The half-reaction with a standard reduction potential of −0.42 V would be more likely to be an oxidation. The negative value indicates that the electrode will be an anode when coupled with a SHE.
10. Dry cells use a moist paste as the electrolyte, so they are drier than cells that use solutions.
11. a. a measure of the energy required to move a certain electric charge across the cell
    b. The potential difference is measured in volts by a voltmeter that is connected across the two electrodes.
12. The electrode potential (potential of a half-cell) cannot be measured directly. Therefore, an arbitrary potential of zero is assigned to the SHE half-cell, and the other half-cell potential can be measured against this reference.
13. a. The half-cell potential is an indication of the tendency of a substance to undergo reduction as compared to H^+.
    b. A large reduction potential means that there is a greater tendency for reduction and therefore the half-cell is less likely to undergo oxidation. Smaller potentials (or more negative potentials) mean there is a greater tendency for oxidation and less tendency for reduction.
14. Barium metal is being oxidized because it is the anode; therefore, one would observe the barium electrode dissolving. Tin ions are being reduced because they are present in the cathodic half-cell; thus, one would observe tin atoms depositing onto the tin metal electrode.

CHAPTER 20 Review

SECTION 1

Introduction to Electrochemistry

REVIEWING MAIN IDEAS

1. In the half-cell $Zn^{2+}(aq) + 2e^- \longrightarrow Zn(s)$, what is the electrode and is this half-reaction an anodic reaction or a cathodic reaction?
2. What role does the porous barrier play?
3. For each of the following pairs of half-cells, write the overall reaction and the cell notation. Assume the first half-cell given in each pair is the cathodic half-cell.
   a. Ag^+/Ag, Co^{2+}/Co
   b. Au^{3+}/Au, Zn^{2+}/Zn
   c. Hg^{2+}/Hg, K^+/K
4. Describe the components of an electrochemical cell and how the electrical charge travels through these components.

SECTION 2

Voltaic Cells

REVIEWING MAIN IDEAS

5. Describe a voltaic cell, and give two examples of a voltaic cell.
6. What is the essential advantage of a fuel cell over batteries in the generation of electrical energy?
7. Explain why corrosion is a voltaic cell.
8. Discuss the advantages and disadvantages of corrosion-prevention methods.
9. Which half reaction would more likely be an oxidation reaction: one with a standard reduction potential of −0.42 V, or one with a standard reduction potential of +0.42 V?
10. Why are dry-cell batteries called *dry cells*, even though their chemistry involves water?
11. a. Explain what is meant by the potential difference between the two electrodes in an electrochemical cell.
    b. How is this potential difference measured? What units are used?
12. The standard hydrogen electrode is assigned an electrode potential of 0.00 V. Explain why this voltage is assigned.
13. a. What information is provided by the standard reduction potential of a given half-cell?
    b. What does the relative value of the reduction potential of a given half-reaction indicate about its oxidation-reduction tendency?
14. When the cell $Ba(s) \mid Ba^{2+}(aq) \mid\mid Sn^{2+}(aq) \mid Sn(s)$ is running, what observations can be made?

PRACTICE PROBLEMS

15. For each of the following pairs of half-cells, determine the overall electrochemical reaction that proceeds spontaneously:
    a. Na^+/Na, Ni^{2+}/Ni
    b. F_2/F^-, S/H_2S
    c. Br_2/Br^-, Cr^{3+}/Cr
    d. MnO_4^-/Mn^{2+}, Co^{2+}/Co
16. Determine the values of E^0 for the cells in the previous problem.
17. Suppose chemists had chosen to make the $I_2 + 2e^- \longrightarrow 2I^-$ half-cell the standard electrode and had assigned it a potential of zero volts.
    a. What would be the E^0 value for the $Br_2 + 2e^- \longrightarrow 2Br^-$ half-cell?
    b. What would be the E^0 value for the $Al^{3+} + 3e^- \longrightarrow Al$ half-cell?
    c. How much change would be observed in the E^0 value for the reaction involving $Br_2 + I^-$ if the I_2 half-cell is the standard?
18. If a strip of Ni were dipped into a solution of $AgNO_3$, what would be expected to occur? Explain, using E^0 values and equations.

SECTION 3

Electrolytic Cells

REVIEWING MAIN IDEAS

19. What reaction happens at the cathode in an electrolysis process?
20. Explain why water cannot be used in the electrochemical cell during the production of aluminum.

15. a. $Ni^{2+}(aq) + 2Na(s) \longrightarrow Ni(s) + 2Na^+(aq)$
    b. $F_2(g) + H_2S(aq) \longrightarrow 2F^-(aq) + S(s) + 2H^+(aq)$
    c. $3Br_2(l) + 2Cr(s) \longrightarrow 6Br^-(aq) + 2Cr^{3+}(aq)$
    d. $2MnO_4^-(aq) + 16H^+(aq) + 5Co(s) \longrightarrow 2Mn^{2+}(aq) + 8H_2O(l) + 5Co^{2+}(aq)$
16. a. +2.48 V
    b. +2.73 V
    c. +1.81 V
    d. +1.77 V
17. a. +0.53 V
    b. −2.20 V
    c. no change
18. $Ni(s) + 2Ag^+(aq) \longrightarrow Ni^{2+}(aq) + 2Ag(s)$; $E^0 = 0.23\ V + 0.80\ V = +1.03\ V$; Nickel dissolves and solid silver forms.
19. The reduction reaction occurs at the cathode during an electrolysis process. Reduction always occurs at the cathode in all types of processes.

21. Calculate the voltage of a cell in which the overall reaction is the electrolysis of aqueous cadmium chloride into its elements.

22. According to electrochemical data, can Ni be plated onto a zinc metal object using a nickel nitrate solution? Explain.

23. Distinguish between a voltaic cell and an electrolytic cell in terms of the nature of the reaction involved.

24. a. What is electroplating?
 b. Identify the anode and cathode in such a process.

Mixed Review

REVIEWING MAIN IDEAS

25. Predict whether each of the following reactions will occur spontaneously as written by determining the E^0 value for potential reaction. Write and balance the overall equation for each reaction that does occur spontaneously.
 a. $Mg + Sn^{2+} \longrightarrow$
 b. $K + Al^{3+} \longrightarrow$
 c. $Li^{+} + Zn \longrightarrow$
 d. $Cu + Cl_2 \longrightarrow$

26. Why is it possible for alkaline batteries to be smaller than zinc-carbon dry cells?

27. Draw a diagram of a voltaic cell whose two half-reactions consist of Ag in $AgNO_3$ and Ni in $NiSO_4$. Identify the anode and cathode, and indicate the directions in which the electrons and ions are moving.

28. Can a solution of $Sn(NO_3)_2$ be stored in an aluminum container? Explain, using E^0 values.

29. A voltaic cell is made up of a cadmium electrode in a solution of $CdSO_4$ and a zinc electrode in a solution of $ZnSO_4$. The two half-cells are separated by a porous barrier.
 a. Which is the cathode, and which is the anode?
 b. In which direction are the electrons flowing?
 c. Write balanced equations for the two half-reactions, and write a net equation for the combined reaction.

30. Would the following pair of electrodes make a good battery? Explain.
 $Cd \longrightarrow Cd^{2+} + 2e^-$
 $Fe \longrightarrow Fe^{2+} + 2e^-$

31. a. What would happen if an aluminum spoon were used to stir a solution of $Zn(NO_3)_2$?
 b. Could a strip of Zn be used to stir a solution of $Al(NO_3)_3$? Explain, using E^0 values.

32. How do the redox reactions for each of the following types of batteries differ?
 a. zinc-carbon
 b. alkaline
 c. mercury

33. a. Why are some standard reduction potentials positive and some negative?
 b. Compare the E^0 value for a metal with the reactivity of that metal.

CRITICAL THINKING

34. **Applying Models** Explain how the oxidation-reduction chemistry of both the voltaic cell and the electrolytic cell are combined in the chemistry of rechargeable cells.

35. **Applying Ideas** In lead-acid batteries, such as your car battery, the degree of discharge of the battery can be determined by measuring the density of the battery fluid. Explain how this is possible.

36. **Applying Ideas** In lead-acid batteries, the battery cannot be recharged indefinitely. Explain why not.

37. **Interpreting Graphics** A voltaic cell is pictured below. Identify the species that is oxidized if current is allowed to flow.

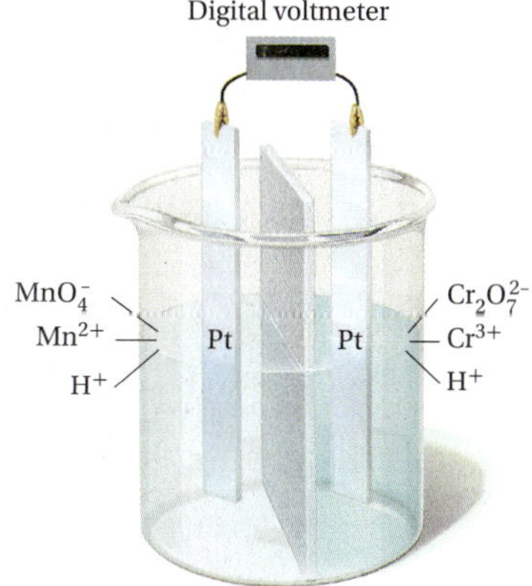

20. Water reduces more easily than aluminum ions do. Water has a larger reduction potential than aluminum ions have.

21. $Cd^{2+} + 2Cl^- \longrightarrow Cl_2 + Cd$;
 $-0.40 V - (+1.36 V) = -1.76 V$

22. In order for Ni to be plated onto a Zn object, the Zn object must be the cathode. The anode could be made of Ni. The half-reaction for the reduction of Ni is $Ni^{2+} + 2e^- \longrightarrow Ni$ ($E^0 = -0.23$ V). Ni can be plated onto the Zn cathode as long as the applied voltage is at least +0.23 V.

23. A voltaic cell contains a spontaneous reaction, and an electrolytic cell contains a nonspontaneous reaction.

24. a. Electroplating is an electrolytic process that deposits metal onto a surface.
 b. The object to be plated is the cathode, and the plating metal is the anode.

25. a. $E^0 = +2.23$ V; spontaneous;
 $Mg + Sn^{2+} \longrightarrow Mg^{2+} + Sn$
 b. $E^0 = +1.27$ V; spontaneous;
 $3K + Al^{3+} \longrightarrow 3K^+ + Al$
 c. $E^0 = -2.28$ V; nonspontaneous

CHAPTER REVIEW

 d. $E^0 = +1.02$ V; spontaneous;
 $Cu + Cl_2 \longrightarrow Cu^{2+} + 2Cl^-$

26. Alkaline batteries do not need carbon rods, as zinc-carbon dry cells do. Thus, alkaline batteries can be smaller than zinc-carbon dry cells.

27.

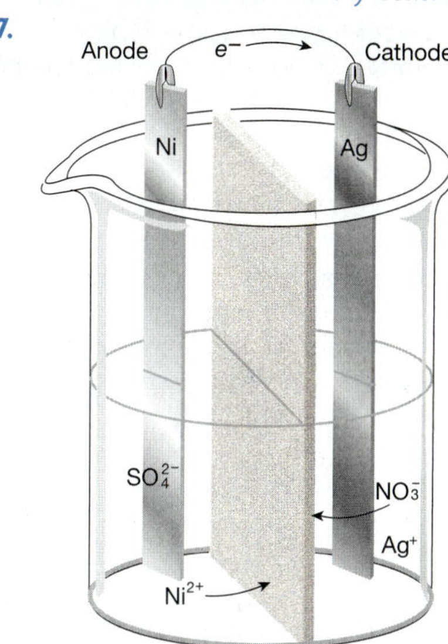

28. $E^0 = +1.52$ V; No, the aluminum container dissolves and solid Sn forms.

29. a. cathode: Cd, anode: Zn
 b. Electron flow is from Zn to Cd.
 c. $Zn \longrightarrow Zn^{2+} + 2e^-$;
 $Cd^{2+} + 2e^- \longrightarrow Cd$;
 Net: $Zn + Cd^{2+} \longrightarrow Zn^{2+} + Cd$

30. No; Fe and Cd are similar in activity; the cell voltage is +0.01 V.

31. a. $2Al + 3Zn^{2+} \longrightarrow 2Al^{3+} + 3Zn$;
 $E^0 = 1.66 V - 0.76 V = +0.90 V$;
 The spoon disintegrates and solid Zn forms.
 b. $2Al^{3+} + 3Zn \longrightarrow 2Al + 3Zn^{2+}$;
 $E^0 = -1.66 V + 0.76 V = -0.90 V$;
 Yes, no reaction would occur.

32. Zinc-carbon and alkaline batteries both have the following cathodic reaction:
 $2MnO_2 + H_2O + 2e^- \longrightarrow Mn_2O_3 + 2OH^-$
 The zinc-carbon battery has an anode in an aqueous environment; the alkaline battery has an anode in an alkaline environment.
 A mercury battery's anode is like an alkaline battery's anode, but a mercury battery's cathode reaction is:
 $HgO + H_2O + 2e^- \longrightarrow Hg + 2OH^-$

33. a. Positive E^0 values are for species that reduce more easily than H^+; negative E^0 values are for species that reduce less easily than H^+.

b. smaller E^0 value, more reactive

34. During the discharge cycle, spontaneous redox reactions typical of voltaic cells convert chemical energy to electrical energy. During the recharge cycle, electrical energy is converted to chemical energy through redox reactions characteristic of electrolytic cells.

35. Fully charged, a battery contains concentrated sulfuric acid. During discharge the acid is consumed as shown in this equation:

$$Pb + PbO_2 + 2H_2SO_4 \longrightarrow 2PbSO_4 + 2H_2O$$

Sulfuric acid is quite dense; as it is used up, the density of the fluid in the battery decreases. Therefore, a battery that is more charged will have fluid of a greater density than a battery that is less charged.

36. For batteries to be recharged, the reactants for the electrolytic reaction must be present and near the electrodes. In a lead-acid battery, the lead(II) sulfate is a powder that accumulates on the electrodes after being generated as the battery produces energy. This lead(II) sulfate is necessary as a reactant to recharge the battery. However, because it is a powder, some of the lead(II) sulfate is knocked off the electrodes during normal functioning. Thus, eventually, there is not enough lead(II) sulfate present on the electrode to recharge the battery.

37. Cr^{3+} is oxidized.

38. Aluminum oxide forms a hard, protective surface and therefore when iron is coated with aluminum oxide, the oxygen and water cannot reach the iron's surface. However, aluminum also acts as a sacrificial coating because it is more reactive than iron, as evidenced by the reduction potentials:

$Fe^{2+} + 2e^- \longrightarrow Fe$ ($E^0 = -0.41$ V) and

$Al^{3+} + 3e^- \longrightarrow Al$ ($E^0 = -1.66$ V).

39. Answers may vary. Students may not find information about the top three metals and production figures, but they should mention copper, silver, and gold as being important in electroplating.

USING THE HANDBOOK

38. Aluminum is described in Group 13 of the *Elements Handbook* (Appendix A) as a self-protecting metal, and can be used in preventing corrosion of iron structures. Using electrochemical data, explain how aluminum protects iron structures.

RESEARCH AND WRITING

39. Go to the library, and find out about the electroplating industry in the United States. What are the top three metals used for plating, and how many metric tons of each are used for electroplating each year in the United States?

40. Investigate the types of batteries being considered for electric cars. Write a report on the advantages and disadvantages of these types of batteries.

ALTERNATIVE ASSESSMENT

41. Performance Take an inventory of the types of batteries used in your home. Find out the voltage supplied by each battery and what electrochemical reaction each uses. Suggest why that electrochemical reaction is used in each case.

42. In our portable society, batteries have become a necessary power supply. As consumers, we want to purchase batteries that will last as long as possible. Advertisements tell us that some batteries last longer than others, but do they really? Design an investigation to answer the question. Is there a difference in longevity between the major brands of AA batteries? Add a cost-effectiveness component to your design.

43. When someone who has a silver filling in a tooth bites down on an aluminum gum wrapper, saliva acts as an electrolyte. The system is an electrochemical cell that produces a small jolt of pain. Explain what occurs, using half-cell reactions and E^0 values.

40. Answers may vary. Students should be sure to examine the environmental costs of developing and disposing of the batteries.

41. Students can make a table to display the data. Tables can be posted for other students to study.

42. Check the design of students' investigations before they begin.

43. The aluminum wrapper acts as the anode, and the filling acts as the cathode. The jolt of pain is caused by the voltage produced by the electrochemical cell. The half-reactions, stated as reductions, are:

$Al^{3+} + 3e^- \longrightarrow Al$;

$Ag^+ + e^- \longrightarrow Ag$;

$E^0_{cell} = +2.46$ V.

Standards-Based Assessment

Answer the following items on a separate piece of paper.

MULTIPLE CHOICE

1. The electrode at which reduction occurs is
   A. always the anode.
   B. always the cathode.
   C. either the anode or the cathode.
   D. always the half-cell.

2. Refer to the table of standard reduction potentials below. A voltaic cell contains a strip of zinc metal in a solution containing zinc ions in one half-cell. The second is a strip of tin metal in a solution containing tin ions. When this cell operates,
   A. Sn is oxidized and Zn^{2+} is reduced.
   B. Sn is reduced and Zn^{2+} is oxidized.
   C. Sn^{2+} is oxidized and Zn is reduced.
   D. Sn^{2+} is reduced and Zn is oxidized.

3. When a rechargeable cell is being recharged, the cell acts as a(n)
   A. fuel cell. **C.** voltaic cell.
   B. electrolytic cell. **D.** Leclanche cell.

4. Refer to the table of standard reduction potentials below. The standard potential of the cell $Sn | Sn^{2+} || Cr^{3+} | Cr$ is −0.60 V. What is the standard reduction potential of the Cr^{3+}/Cr electrode?
   A. +0.88 V **C.** −0.88 V
   B. +0.74 V **D.** −0.74 V

Half-cell reaction	Standard reduction potential, E^0 (in volts)
$Au^{3+} + 3e^- \rightleftharpoons Au$	+1.50
$Cu^{2+} + 2e^- \rightleftharpoons Cu$	+0.34
$Fe^{2+} + 2e^- \rightleftharpoons Fe$	−0.41
$Sn^{2+} + 2e^- \rightleftharpoons Sn$	−0.14
$Zn^{2+} + 2e^- \rightleftharpoons Zn$	−0.76
$Mg^{2+} + 2e^- \rightleftharpoons Mg$	−2.37

5. Refer to the table of reduction potentials above. Which metal, Zn or Au, can reduce Sn^{2+} ions to Sn metal when placed in an aqueous solution of Sn^{2+} ions?
   A. Zn
   B. Au
   C. Both Zn and Au can reduce Sn^{2+} ions.
   D. Neither Zn nor Au can reduce Sn^{2+} ions.

6. When silver is electroplated onto another metal, Ag^+ is
   A. oxidized at the anode.
   B. reduced at the anode.
   C. oxidized at the cathode.
   D. reduced at the cathode.

7. Which metal would best provide cathodic protection from corrosion for an iron bridge?
   A. Au
   B. Sn
   C. Cu
   D. Mg

SHORT ANSWER

8. In the production of aluminum by the Hall-Héroult process, is the aluminum metal produced at the cathode or the anode?

9. The reduction potential for nitric acid is 0.96 V (reduction half-reaction is $NO_3^- + 4H^+ + 3e^- \longrightarrow NO + 2H_2O$). If gold (Au) is placed in a beaker of 1 M nitric acid, will the gold dissolve?

EXTENDED RESPONSE

10. Given a voltaic cell consisting of a gold electrode in a gold nitrate solution in one half-cell and a zinc electrode in a zinc nitrate solution in the other half-cell, what occurs once the wire is connected to both electrodes?

11. If pure water is placed in a beaker with wires connected to a cathode and anode and electrical voltage is applied, will electrolysis of water occur? Explain your answer.

Test Tip
Remember that if you can eliminate two of the four answer choices, your chances of choosing the correct answer choice will double.

STANDARDS-BASED ASSESSMENT

To give students practice under more realistic testing conditions, give them 60 minutes to answer all of the questions in this Standardized Test Preparation.

Test Answers

1. B
2. D
3. B
4. D
5. A
6. D
7. D
8. Since the aluminum metal is produced by the reduction of Al^{3+} ions to aluminum metal, the metal is produced at the cathode. Reduction always occurs at the cathode.
9. The Au will not dissolve because its reduction potential is +1.50 V. Hence, for Au to be oxidized (dissolved), there needs to be at least 1.50 V from the reduction of nitric acid and there is only 0.96 V.
10. The gold ions are reduced and zinc is oxidized because gold has a higher reduction potential than zinc does. The zinc electrode dissolves as electrons travel from the anode through the wire down the gold electrode to the gold nitrate solution. As the gold ions are reduced, gold atoms are deposited onto the gold electrode, which is the cathode. To keep the charge balanced, nitrate ions move from the anode to the cathode through the porous barrier. Depending on the type of porous barrier, gold ions could move from the cathode to the anode to keep the charge balanced.
11. Significant electrolysis of water will not occur for pure water because it does not contain enough ions for current to flow. An electrolyte needs to be added. The electrolytes are not part of the half-cell reactions, but they are needed for the transfer of charge.

Nuclear Chemistry

① Core Instruction

Chapter Resources

- The Teacher's Edition wrap has extensive teaching support for every lesson, including Misconception Alerts, Teach from Visuals, Demonstrations, Teaching Tips, Differentiated Instruction, and Problem Solving support.
- Several additional presentation tools are available online for every chapter, including Animated Chemistry features and Visual Concepts.
- You can open your lesson with the Why It Matters Video: Atoms.

Section	Instruction	Labs and Demonstrations Go Online for Materials Lists and Solutions Lists.
21.1	■ **Textbook:** The Nucleus **Animated Chemistry:** Types of Radioactive Decay **Teaching Visuals:** Binding Energy per Nucleon • Band of Stability • Balancing Nuclear Equations • Radioactive Nuclide Emissions **PowerPresentations**	
21.2	■ **Textbook:** Radioactive Decay **Teaching Visuals:** Potassium-40 Half-Life Comparison • Uranium-238 Decay Series • Characteristics of Nuclear Particles and Rays • Rate of Decay • Half-Lives of Some Radioactive Isotopes **PowerPresentations**	■ **Lab:** Simulation of Nuclear Decay Using Pennies and Paper (Core Skill) ■ **Lab:** Radioactivity (Core Skill)
21.3	■ **Textbook:** Nuclear Radiation **Teaching Visuals:** Units Used in Measurements of Radioactivity • Effect of Whole-Body Exposure to a Single Dose of Radiation **PowerPresentations**	■ **Demonstration:** Detecting and Measuring Beta Radiation ■ **Lab:** Detecting Radioactivity (Core Skill)
21.4	■ **Textbook:** Nuclear Fission and Nuclear Fusion **Teaching Visuals:** Nuclear Chain Reaction • Nuclear Power Plant Model • Nuclear Fusion: Stellar Formation of Carbon-12 **PowerPresentations**	■ **Demonstration:** Modeling a Chain Reaction

Find all of your resources online at HMDScience.com.

2 Support and Intervention

- **Interactive Reader** (English and Spanish)
- **Study Guide**
- **Interactive Review:** Review Games, Concept Maps, and Section Self-Checks
- **Scientific Reasoning Skill Builder**
- **Learn It! Videos**
- **Solve It! Cards**
- **Interactive Demos**
- **Sample Problem Sets**

3 Specialized Support

- **Chapter Summary Audio Files**
- **Interactive Reader Audio Files**
- **Differentiated Instruction:** Inclusion, Below Level, and English Learners (TE wrap)

Enrichment and Challenge

- **Differentiated Instruction:** Pre-AP (TE wrap)
- **Chemistry Explorers:** An Unexpected Finding (SE)
- **WebLinks**

Assessment

- **Section Formative Assessments** (SE)
- **Section Quizzes**
- **Chapter Review** (SE)
- **Chapter Tests A and B**
- **Alternative Assessment** (TE wrap)
- **Online Assessment and Remediation**
- **ExamView Banks**

Where do I find it?

		PRINT	DVD	ONLINE
1	Animated Chemistry		■	■
	Demonstrations (TE wrap)	■		■
	Interactive Whiteboard		■	■
	Labs		■	■
	PowerPresentations		■	■
	QuickLabs	■	■	■
	Teaching Visuals		■	■
	Textbook	■	■	■
	Visual Concepts		■	■
	Why It Matters Videos		■	■
2	Interactive Demos		■	■
	Interactive Reader	■	■	■
	Interactive Reviews		■	■
	Learn It! Videos		■	■
	Sample Problem Sets		■	■
	Scientific Reasoning Skill Builder		■	■
	Smart Grapher Tool		■	■
	Solve It! Cards		■	■
	Study Guide		■	■
3	Chapter Summary Audio Files		■	■
	Differentiated Instruction (TE wrap)	■		
	Interactive Reader Audio Files		■	■

CHAPTER 21

Chapter Overview

Section 1 identifies the forces that affect the stability of the nucleus. This section also shows how to write balanced nuclear equations.

Section 2 outlines the different types of radioactive decay and demonstrates calculations involving the half-life of an isotope.

Section 3 surveys the penetrating ability of nuclear radiation and methods for detecting radiation. This section also describes some common applications of nuclear radiation.

Section 4 explains the difference between fission and fusion and discusses their uses and potential uses as energy sources.

▼ Focus and Motivate

Activate Prior Knowledge

Students may need a review of the following concepts:

- conservation of mass and energy
- atomic structure
- units of energy

About the Image

In addition to solids, liquids, and gases, plasma is another state of matter. Plasma consists of ionized particles. High-temperature plasmas generated by electric or magnetic fields are being studied as potential sources of fusion energy.

Why It Matters

Students can access the video online and find other helpful resources at **HMDScience.com**.

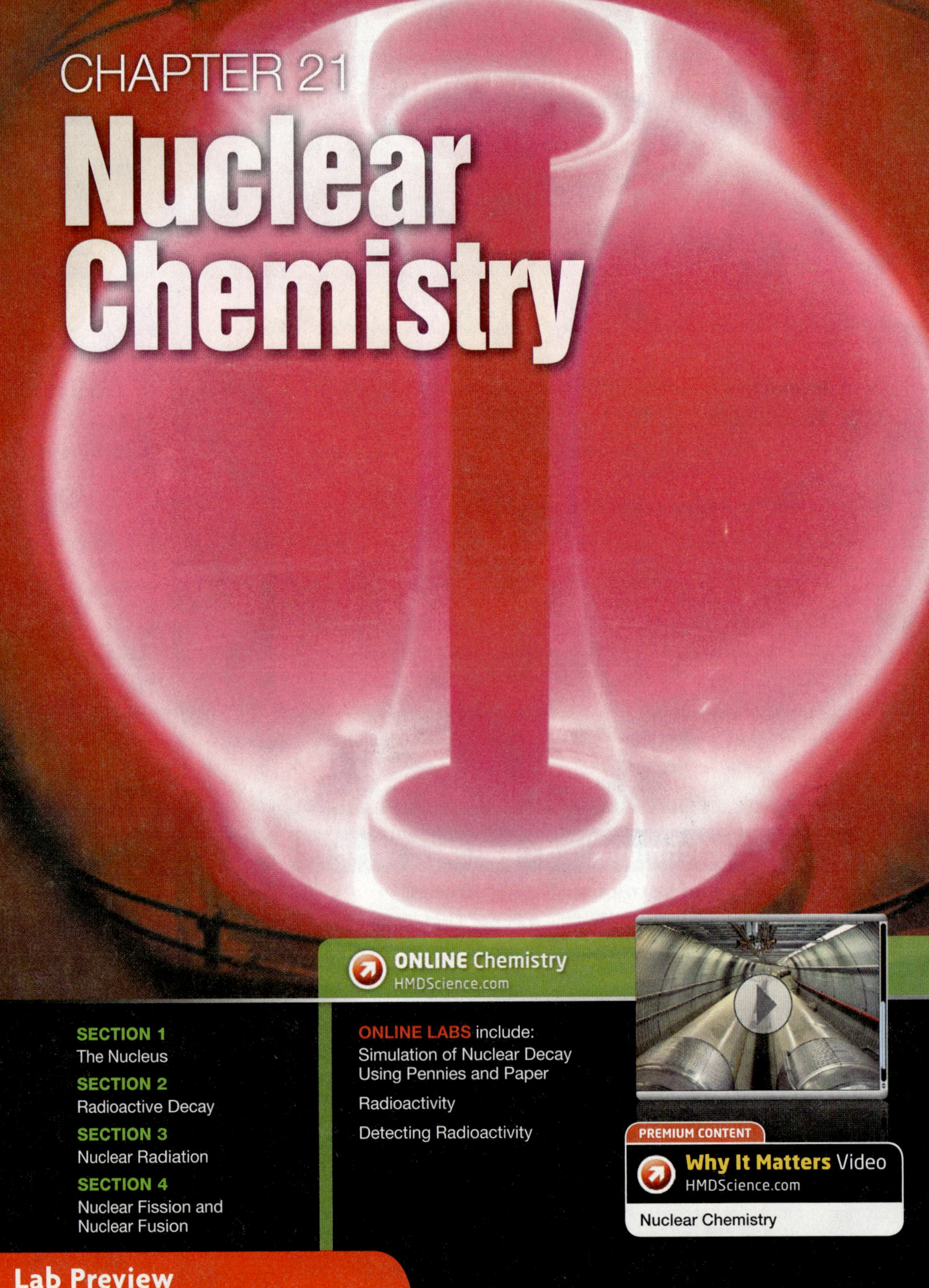

CHAPTER 21

Nuclear Chemistry

ONLINE Chemistry
HMDScience.com

SECTION 1
The Nucleus

SECTION 2
Radioactive Decay

SECTION 3
Nuclear Radiation

SECTION 4
Nuclear Fission and Nuclear Fusion

ONLINE LABS include:

Simulation of Nuclear Decay Using Pennies and Paper

Radioactivity

Detecting Radioactivity

PREMIUM CONTENT

Why It Matters Video
HMDScience.com

Nuclear Chemistry

Lab Preview

The following labs and demonstrations support concepts presented in this chapter.

LABS

Simulation of Nuclear Decay Using Pennies and Paper (Core Skill)

Radioactivity (Core Skill)

Detecting Radioactivity (Core Skill)

DEMONSTRATIONS

Detecting and Measuring Beta Radiation

Modeling a Chain Reaction

SECTION 1

The Nucleus

Key Terms

nucleon
nuclide
mass defect
nuclear binding energy
nuclear shell model
magic number
nuclear reaction
transmutation

Atomic nuclei are made of protons and neutrons, which are collectively called nucleons. In nuclear chemistry, an atom is referred to as a nuclide and is identified by the number of protons and neutrons in its nucleus. We identify nuclides in two ways. When a symbol such as $^{228}_{88}\text{Ra}$ is used, the superscript is the mass number and the subscript is the atomic number. The same nuclide can also be written as radium-228, where the mass number is written following the element name.

Main Ideas

- An atom's mass is less than the masses of its parts.
- Stable nuclides cluster over a range of neutron-proton ratios known as the band of stability.
- Nuclear reactions affect the nucleus of an atom.

MAIN IDEA

An atom's mass is less than the masses of its parts.

The mass of an atom is not equal to the total mass of an equal number of isolated parts. Consider a $^{4}_{2}\text{He}$ atom. The combined mass of two protons, two neutrons, and two electrons is calculated below.

$$\begin{aligned}
&\text{2 protons:} && (2 \times 1.007\,276\text{ u}) = 2.014\,552\text{ u}\\
&\text{2 neutrons:} && (2 \times 1.008\,665\text{ u}) = 2.017\,330\text{ u}\\
&\text{2 electrons:} && (2 \times 0.000\,548\,6\text{ u}) = \underline{0.001\,097\text{ u}}\\
&&&\text{total combined mass: } 4.032\,979\text{ u}
\end{aligned}$$

However, the atomic mass of a $^{4}_{2}\text{He}$ atom has been measured to be 4.002 602 u. The measured mass, 4.002 602 u, is 0.030 377 u *less* than the combined mass, 4.032 979 u, calculated above. **This difference between the mass of an atom and the sum of the masses of its particles is the mass defect.**

Nuclear Binding Energy

What causes the loss in mass? According to Albert Einstein's equation $E = mc^2$, mass can be converted to energy, and energy to mass. The mass defect is caused by the conversion of mass to energy upon formation of the nucleus. The mass units of the mass defect can be converted to energy units by using Einstein's equation. First, convert 0.030 377 u to kilograms to match the mass units for energy, $\text{kg} \bullet \text{m}^2/\text{s}^2$.

$$0.030\,377\text{ u} \times \frac{1.6605 \times 10^{-27}\text{ kg}}{1\text{ u}} = 5.0441 \times 10^{-29}\text{ kg}$$

The energy equivalent can now be calculated.

$$\begin{aligned}
E &= mc^2\\
E &= (5.0441 \times 10^{-29}\text{ kg})(3.00 \times 10^8\text{ m/s})^2\\
&= 4.54 \times 10^{-12}\text{ kg} \bullet \text{m}^2/\text{s}^2 = 4.54 \times 10^{-12}\text{ J}
\end{aligned}$$

This is the nuclear binding energy, the energy released when a nucleus is formed from nucleons. Think of it as the amount of energy needed to break apart the nucleus, or as a measure of the stability of a nucleus.

Differentiated Instruction

BELOW LEVEL

Have students use modeling clay to build six small balls representing 2 protons, 2 neutrons, and 2 electrons. The balls representing protons and neutrons should have about the same mass, but those representing electrons should be much less massive. Have students determine the mass of each individual particle and then of all six particles together. The sum of the individual masses should equal the total mass. Ask students to use their models to demonstrate mass defect. Students should remove a tiny piece from a ball representing a proton or a neutron and reweigh the six particles together. In this case, the total mass will be slightly less than the sum of the individual masses. Point out that the difference in masses represents the mass defect.

SECTION 1

Plan and Prepare ▼

Objectives

Upon completion of this section, students should be able to do the following:

- Explain what a nuclide is and describe the different ways nuclides can be represented.
- Define and relate the terms *mass defect* and *nuclear binding energy*.
- Explain the relationship between number of nucleons and stability of nuclei.
- Explain why nuclear reactions occur, and be able to balance a nuclear equation.

Classroom Catalyst

Compare chemical reactions with nuclear reactions. Nuclear reactions result in larger energy changes than chemical reactions. For example, deuterium, an isotope of hydrogen, is a potential fuel for fusion reactors. There is approximately 1 g of deuterium in 30 L of sea water. The fusion of deuterium in 30 L of sea water would produce as much energy as the combustion of about 9000 L of gasoline.

In chemical reactions, the elements are the same in the products and reactants, while in nuclear reactions one element is transformed into another element by the loss or gain of subatomic particles in the nucleus.

Teach ▼

READING TOOLKIT

BRAINSTORMING Ask students to find words and phrases that relate to *nuclear chemistry*. Record student responses. Encourage students to make a hypothesis about the definition of the phrase based on their responses.

Teaching Tip

Be sure students use isotopic atomic masses (not average atomic masses) when calculating the mass defect.

▼ Teach *continued*

TEACH FROM VISUALS

FIGURE 1.1 Turn this graph upside down, and ask students where a marble would rest if you were to let it roll along on the top of the graph. That resting point represents the greatest amount of binding energy per nucleon and thus the most stable nucleus.

ChemisTrivia

Figure 1.1 identifies iron as the most stable nucleus. The elements between hydrogen and iron are made during the lifetime of a star in a process called *fusion*, discussed later in this chapter. After most of the nuclear fuel has been used up, the star "dies." Many stars undergo a tremendous explosion called a *nova*. At the instant a nova occurs, the energy from the massive explosion produces the elements that are heavier than iron. So in a sense, we and all that surrounds us are forged in the furnaces of the stars.

Classroom Practice

1. Calculate nuclear binding energy of a $^{32}_{16}S$ atom. The measured atomic mass of $^{32}_{16}S$ is 31.972 070 u.

Answer: 4.36×10^{-11} J

2. Calculate nuclear binding energy per mole of $^{16}_{8}O$ atoms. The measured atomic mass of $^{16}_{8}O$ is 15.994 915 u.

Answer: 1.23×10^{13} J/mol

3. Calculate the binding energy per nucleon of a $^{55}_{25}Mn$ atom. The measured atomic mass of $^{55}_{25}Mn$ is 54.938 047 u.

Answer: 1.41×10^{-12} J/nucleon

Critical Thinking

Answer: Fe. It is slightly higher on the graph.

FIGURE 1.1

Binding Energy This graph shows the relationship between binding energy per nucleon and mass number. The binding energy per nucleon is a measure of the stability of a nucleus.

CRITICAL THINKING

Interpret Which nucleon has the greater binding energy, Fe or U?

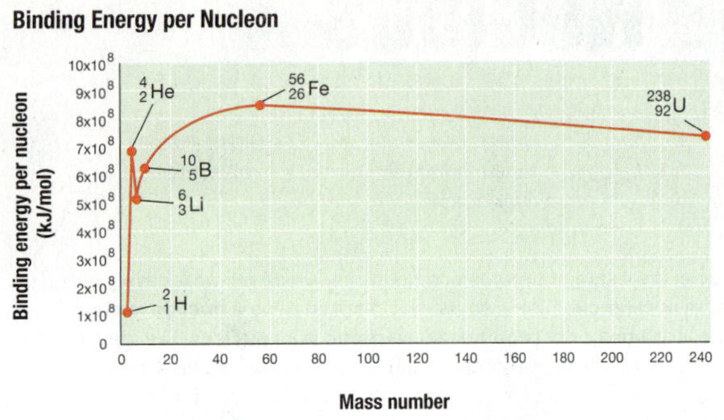

CROSS-DISCIPLINARY CONNECTION

Quarks S.T.E.M.

Many subatomic particles have been identified. Leptons and quarks are the elementary particles of matter. The electron is a lepton. Protons and neutrons are made of quarks. There are six types of quarks that differ in mass and charge. They are named *up, down, strange, charm, bottom,* and *top.* Protons consist of two *up* quarks and one *down* quark, and neutrons consist of two *down* quarks and one *up* quark. Although individual quarks have not been isolated, their existence explains the patterns of nuclear binding and decay.

Binding Energy per Nucleon

The binding energy per nucleon is used to compare the stability of different nuclides, as shown in **Figure 1.1.** The *binding energy per nucleon* is the binding energy of the nucleus divided by its number of nucleons. The higher the binding energy per nucleon, the more tightly the nucleons are held together. Elements with intermediate atomic masses have the greatest binding energies per nucleon and are therefore the most stable.

MAIN IDEA

Stable nuclides cluster over a range of neutron-proton ratios known as the band of stability.

Stable nuclides have certain characteristics. When the number of protons in stable nuclei is plotted against the number of neutrons, as shown in **Figure 1.2,** a belt-like graph is obtained. This stable nuclei cluster over a range of neutron-proton ratios is referred to as the *band of stability*. Among atoms having low atomic numbers, the most stable nuclei are those with a neutron-proton ratio of approximately 1:1. For example, $^{4}_{2}He$, a stable isotope of helium with two neutrons and two protons, has a neutron-proton ratio of 1:1. As the atomic number increases, the stable neutron-proton ratio increases to about 1.5:1. For example, $^{206}_{82}Pb$, with 124 neutrons and 82 protons, has a neutron-proton ratio of 1.51:1.

This trend can be explained by the relationship between the nuclear force and the electrostatic forces between protons. Protons in a nucleus repel all other protons through electrostatic repulsion, but the short range of the nuclear force allows them to attract only protons very close to them, as shown in **Figure 1.3.**

As the number of protons in a nucleus increases, the repulsive electrostatic force between protons increases faster than the nuclear force. More neutrons are required to increase the nuclear force and stabilize the nucleus. Beyond the atomic number 83, bismuth, the repulsive force of the protons is so great that no stable nuclides exist, because the protons push one another away.

Problem Solving

DECONSTRUCTING PROBLEMS

Point out to students that three steps must be followed to calculate the nuclear binding energy.

1. Determine the mass defect in u.
2. Convert the mass defect into energy (Joules), using the equation $E = mc^2$.
3. Express the value as energy per mole of atoms or as energy per nucleon.

FIGURE 1.2

Band of Stability The neutron-proton ratios of stable nuclides cluster together in a region known as the band of stability. As the number of protons increases, the ratio increases from 1:1 to about 1.5:1.

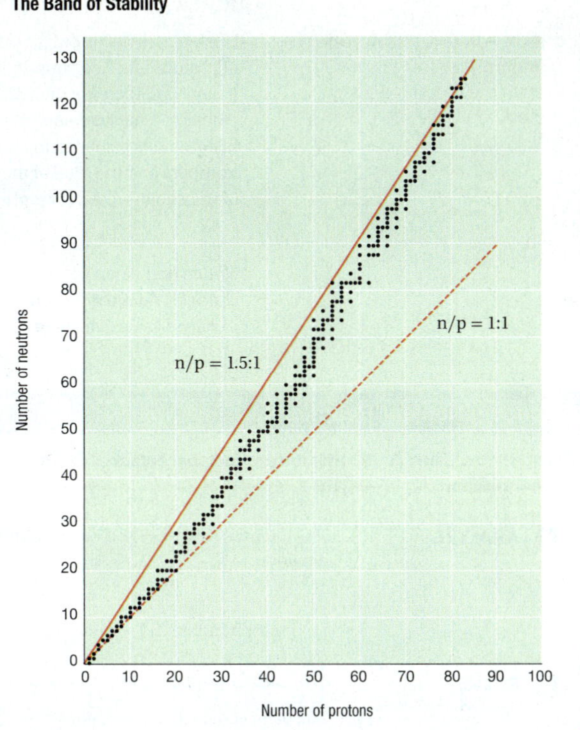

FIGURE 1.3

Competing Forces Proton A attracts proton B through the nuclear force, but repels it through the electrostatic force. Proton A mainly repels proton C through the electrostatic force, because the nuclear force reaches only a few nucleon diameters.

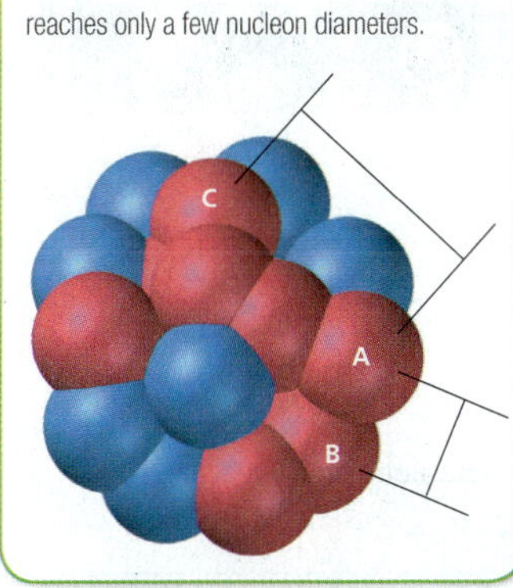

Stable nuclei tend to have even numbers of nucleons. Of the stable nuclides, more than half have even numbers of both protons and neutrons. Only five nuclides have odd numbers of both. This indicates that stability of a nucleus is greatest when the nucleons—like electrons—are paired.

The most stable nuclides are those having 2, 8, 20, 28, 50, 82, or 126 protons, neutrons, or total nucleons. This extra stability at certain numbers supports a theory that nucleons—like electrons—exist at certain energy levels. **According to the nuclear shell model, nucleons exist in different energy levels, or shells, in the nucleus. The numbers of nucleons that represent completed nuclear energy levels—2, 8, 20, 28, 50, 82, and 126—are called magic numbers.**

The nuclear shell model suggests that there might be an "island of stability" for elements that lie beyond uranium in the periodic table. The explanation is that although smaller nuclides may be quite unstable individually, once enough are assembled to fill an entire shell, those nuclides may be stable enough to stay together for minutes or even hours. Minutes and hours are a long time in the usually nanosecond lifetimes of the larger, laboratory-synthesized elements.

Teaching Tip

- The nuclear force is also referred to as the *strong nuclear force*.
- Nuclear stability is very complex. The n/p ratio serves only as a general guide to nuclear stability.

TEACH FROM VISUALS

FIGURE 1.3 Students should recognize that the positive charges of all the protons in the nucleus will make each proton repel all of the others. The nuclear force must overcome this proton-proton repulsion to hold the nucleus together. In small nuclei, the protons are close together, and therefore both repel each other through electrostatic forces and attract each other through the nuclear force. Relatively few neutrons are needed to increase the nuclear force enough to hold the nucleus together. As nuclei become larger, the protons become farther apart. Most of the protons are not close enough together to attract each other, and therefore only repel each other. More neutrons are needed to increase the nuclear force to stabilize the nucleus.

ChemisTrivia

The nuclear force is theoretically thought to be the result of the exchange of fundamental particles between nucleons. Interested students may want to further research fundamental particles and their connection to the nuclear force.

Differentiated Instruction

PRE-AP

Emphasize that the *magic numbers* mentioned in this section apply to either the number of protons or the number of electrons. Therefore, both helium-4 and lead-208 are stable. Point out that nuclei with even numbers of neutrons and protons are also more stable. Have students refer to a periodic table to compile a list of such stable nuclides. Possibilities include carbon-12, oxygen-16, and magnesium-24. Have students use the periodic table to identify the stable nuclide that has the magic number 126. bismuth-209

▼ Teach *continued*

Teaching Tip

- Consider using the *CRC Handbook for Chemistry and Physics* to construct sample nuclear reaction problems.
- When solving for the unknown, use the atomic number to determine the identity of an unknown atom or particle. If the atomic number is 1 or greater, it is an element; if the atomic number is 0, it is a neutron; if the atomic number is −1, it is an electron (beta particle).

Classroom Practice

A-1 ${}^{238}_{92}\text{U} \longrightarrow ? + {}^{234}_{90}\text{Th}$

Answer: ${}^{4}_{2}\text{He}$

A-2 ${}^{37}_{18}\text{Ar} + ? \longrightarrow {}^{37}_{17}\text{Cl}$

Answer: ${}^{-1}_{0}\text{e}$

Answers

Practice A

1. ${}^{253}_{99}\text{Es} + {}^{4}_{2}\text{He} \longrightarrow {}^{1}_{0}n + {}^{256}_{101}\text{Md}$
2. ${}^{142}_{61}\text{Pm} + {}^{-1}_{0}e \longrightarrow {}^{142}_{60}\text{Nd}$

Check for Understanding

Answer: In chemical reactions, atoms combine and break apart. Nuclear reactions involve the nuclei of atoms, in which atoms change identities. Atoms do not change identities in chemical reactions.

▼ Assess and Reteach

Assess Use the Formative Assessment on this page to evaluate student mastery of the section.

Reteach For students who need additional instruction, download the Section Study Guide.

Response to Intervention To reassess students' mastery, use the Section Quiz, available to print or to take directly online at **HMDScience.com**.

CHECK FOR UNDERSTANDING
Compare How does a nuclear reaction compare to a chemical reaction?

MAIN IDEA

Nuclear reactions affect the nucleus of an atom.

Unstable nuclei undergo spontaneous changes that change their numbers of protons and neutrons. In this process, they give off large amounts of energy and increase their stability. These changes are a type of nuclear reaction. **A nuclear reaction is a reaction that affects the nucleus of an atom.** In equations representing nuclear reactions, the total of the atomic numbers and the total of the mass numbers must be equal on both sides of the equation. An example is shown below.

$${}^{9}_{4}\text{Be} + {}^{4}_{2}\text{He} \rightarrow {}^{12}_{6}\text{C} + {}^{1}_{0}n$$

Notice that when the atomic number changes, the identity of the element changes. **A transmutation is a change in the identity of a nucleus as a result of a change in the number of its protons.**

PREMIUM CONTENT

Balancing Nuclear Reactions

Sample Problem A **Identify the product that balances the following nuclear reaction: ${}^{212}_{84}\text{Po} \rightarrow {}^{4}_{2}\text{He} + \underline{?}$**

1 ANALYZE The total mass number and atomic number must be equal on both sides of the equation.

$${}^{212}_{84}\text{Po} \rightarrow {}^{4}_{2}\text{He} + \underline{?}$$

mass number: $212 - 4 = 208$ atomic number: $84 - 2 = 82$

2 SOLVE The nuclide has a mass number of 208 and an atomic number of 82, ${}^{208}_{82}\text{Pb}$.

The balanced nuclear equation is ${}^{212}_{84}\text{Po} \rightarrow {}^{4}_{2}\text{He} + {}^{208}_{82}\text{Pb}$

Practice Answers in Appendix E

Using ${}^{1}_{0}n$ to represent a neutron and ${}_{-1}^{0}e$ to represent an electron, complete the following nuclear equations:

1. ${}^{253}_{99}\text{Es} + {}^{4}_{2}\text{He} \rightarrow {}^{1}_{0}n + \underline{?}$
2. ${}^{142}_{61}\text{Pm} + \underline{?} \rightarrow {}^{142}_{60}\text{Nd}$

SECTION 1 FORMATIVE ASSESSMENT

Reviewing Main Ideas

1. Define *mass defect.*
2. How is nuclear stability related to the neutron-proton ratio?
3. Complete and balance the following nuclear equations:
   a. ${}^{187}_{75}\text{Re} + \underline{?} \rightarrow {}^{187}_{75}\text{Re} + {}^{1}_{1}\text{H}$
   b. ${}^{9}_{4}\text{Be} + {}^{4}_{2}\text{He} \rightarrow \underline{?} + {}^{1}_{0}n$
   c. ${}^{22}_{11}\text{Na} + \underline{?} \rightarrow {}^{22}_{10}\text{Ne}$

Critical Thinking

4. **INTERPRETING GRAPHICS** Examine **Figure 1.2**, and predict whether ${}^{9}_{3}\text{Li}$ is a stable isotope of lithium. Explain your answer.

Answers to Section Assessment

1. the difference between the mass of an atom and the sum of the masses of its protons, neutrons, and electrons
2. A certain number of neutrons are needed to increase the nuclear force enough to hold a nucleus together. For small atoms, a stable neutron to proton ratio is 1 : 1; for large atoms, 1.5 : 1.
3. a. ${}^{2}_{1}\text{H}$ b. ${}^{12}_{6}\text{C}$ c. ${}^{0}_{-1}\text{e}$
4. ${}^{9}_{3}\text{Li}$ has 3 protons and 6 neutrons; it lies above the band of nuclear stability, so it is unstable.

Radioactive Decay

Key Terms

radioactive decay
nuclear radiation
radioactive nuclide
alpha particle
beta particle
positron
electron capture
gamma ray
half-life
decay series
parent nuclide
daughter nuclide
artificial transmutation
transuranium element

SECTION 2

Main Ideas

- Radioactive decay leads to more stable nucleons.
- Half-life is the time needed for one half of an amount of radioactive nuclei to decay.
- Radioactive nuclides become stable nuclides through a series of decays.
- Nuclides can become radioactive artificially.

In 1896, Henri Becquerel was studying the possible connection between light emission of some uranium compounds after exposure to sunlight and X-ray emission. He wrapped a photographic plate in a lightproof covering and placed a uranium compound on top of it. He then placed them in sunlight. The photographic plate was exposed even though it was protected from visible light, suggesting that it had been exposed by X rays. When he tried to repeat his experiment, cloudy weather prevented him from placing the experiment in sunlight. To his surprise, the plate was still exposed. This meant that sunlight was not needed to produce the rays that exposed the plate. The rays were produced by radioactive decay. **Radioactive decay** is the spontaneous disintegration of a nucleus into a slightly lighter nucleus, accompanied by emission of particles, electromagnetic radiation, or both. The radiation that exposed the plate was **nuclear radiation,** particles or electromagnetic radiation emitted from the nucleus during radioactive decay.

Uranium is a **radioactive nuclide,** an unstable nucleus that undergoes radioactive decay. Studies by Marie Curie and Pierre Curie found that of the elements known in 1896, only uranium and thorium were radioactive. In 1898, the Curies discovered two new radioactive metallic elements, polonium and radium. Since that time, many other radioactive nuclides have been identified. In fact, all of the nuclides beyond atomic number 83 are unstable and thus radioactive.

MAIN IDEA

Radioactive decay leads to more stable nucleons.

A nuclide's type and rate of decay depend on the nucleon content and energy level of the nucleus. Some common types of radioactive nuclide emissions are summarized in **Figure 2.1**.

Types of Radioactive Decay

FIGURE 2.1

RADIOACTIVE NUCLIDE EMISSIONS

Type	Symbol	Charge	Mass (u)
Alpha particle	$^{4}_{2}He$	2+	4.001 5062
Beta particle	$^{0}_{-1}\beta$	1−	0.000 5486
Positron	$^{0}_{+1}\beta$	1+	0.000 5486
Gamma ray	γ	0	0

Differentiated Instruction

ENGLISH LEARNERS

Students may be frustrated that there are multiple names for the same kind of particle. Remind students that although an alpha particle is a helium atom, it is not a regular helium atom. It is a "high-speed" helium atom. In the same manner, a beta particle is a "high-speed" electron that originated from the nucleus of the atom, not a regular electron that exists in the energy levels of the atom. Scientists give the particles different names to clarify the context—the multiple names help avoid confusion.

SECTION 2

Plan and Prepare ▼

Objectives

Upon completion of this section, students should be able to do the following:

- Define and relate the terms *radioactive decay* and *nuclear radiation.*
- Describe the different types of radioactive decay and their effects on the nucleus.
- Define the term *half-life,* and explain how it relates to the stability of a nucleus.
- Define and relate the terms *decay series, parent nuclide,* and *daughter nuclide.*
- Explain how artificial radioactive nuclides are made, and discuss their significance.

Classroom Catalyst

Place a transparency of the band of stability on the overhead projector. Ask the students to propose different ways for an unstable nucleus to get into the band of stability. An unstable nucleus can undergo alpha emission, beta emission, positron emission and electron capture. Show how each of the types of emission can lead to a more stable nucleus.

Teach ▼

TEACH FROM TABLES

FIGURE 2.1 Point out that a beta particle (an electron) and a positron have the same mass. Beta particle is the name given to an electron emitted from the nucleus.

READING TOOLKIT

SUMMARIZING Have students read about the types of radioactive decay. Have pairs of students use **Figure 2.1** to summarize the characteristics of each. Encourage students to find more characteristics of nuclear radiation.

▼ Teach *continued*

TEACH FROM VISUALS

FIGURES 2.2 AND 2.3 Point out that the total mass of the nucleus does not change in beta decay, but the atomic number does. However, during alpha decay, both the mass and atomic number change.

Show students where the nuclides given as examples lie relative to the band of stability in **Figure 1.2.**

Misconception Alert!

Students might be confused by the statement about beta particles, or electrons, being emitted from the nucleus. They will remember that electrons are outside the nucleus. Emphasize that there are no electrons in the nucleus. A beta particle, or electron, is emitted from the nucleus only when a neutron is converted to a proton.

ChemisTrivia

Conversion of a neutron into a proton and an electron and conversion of a proton into a neutron and a positron appear to violate the law of conservation of energy. To explain this, Wolfgang Pauli proposed that an undiscovered particle, a neutrino, is also emitted during these conversions. Neutrinos were not originally detected because they have no charge and negligible mass. The existence of neutrinos has since been confirmed. Most chemistry courses do not present the role of neutrinos, but they are fascinating particles. Perhaps some students would like to find out more about neutrinos for extra credit.

Check for Understanding

Answer: Because an alpha particle is a heavy particle; only large atoms could easily lose such a large particle.

FIGURE 2.2

Alpha Emission An alpha particle, identical to a helium nucleus, is emitted during the radioactive decay of some very heavy nuclei.

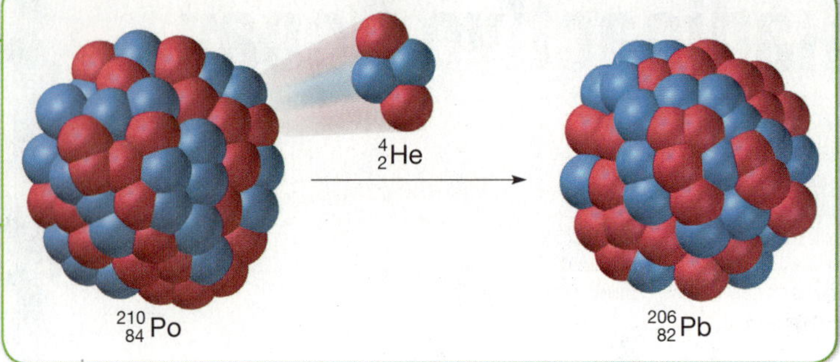

CHECK FOR UNDERSTANDING
Infer Why would alpha emission occur in only more massive nuclei?

Alpha Emission

An alpha particle (α) is two protons and two neutrons bound together and is emitted from the nucleus during some kinds of radioactive decay. Alpha particles are helium nuclei and have a charge of 2+. They are often represented with the symbol $^{4}_{2}He$. Alpha emission is restricted almost entirely to very heavy nuclei. In these nuclei, both the number of neutrons and the number of protons need to be reduced in order to increase the stability of the nucleus. An example of alpha emission is the decay of $^{210}_{84}Po$ into $^{206}_{82}Pb$, shown in **Figure 2.2.** The atomic number decreases by two, and the mass number decreases by four.

$$^{210}_{84}Po \longrightarrow \, ^{206}_{82}Pb + \, ^{4}_{2}He$$

FIGURE 2.3

Beta Emission Beta emission causes the transmutation of $^{14}_{6}C$ into $^{14}_{7}N$. Beta emission is a type of radioactive decay in which a neutron is converted to a proton with the emission of a beta particle.

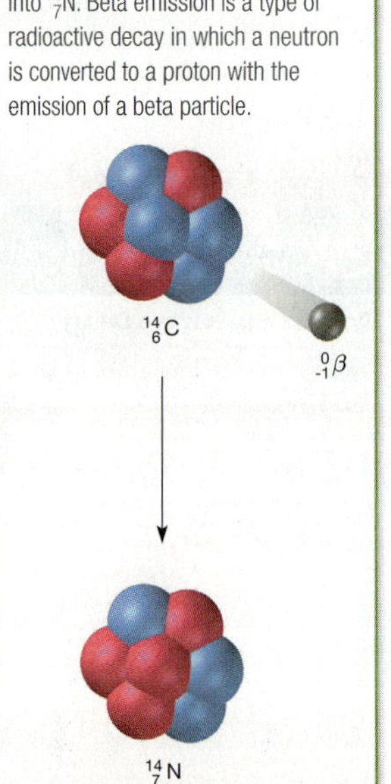

Beta Emission

Nuclides above the band of stability are unstable because their neutron/proton ratio is too large. To decrease the number of neutrons, a neutron can be converted into a proton and an electron. The electron is emitted from the nucleus as a beta particle. **A beta particle (β) is an electron emitted from the nucleus during some kinds of radioactive decay.**

$$^{1}_{0}n \longrightarrow \, ^{1}_{1}p + \, ^{0}_{-1}\beta$$

An example of beta emission, shown in **Figure 2.3**, is the decay of $^{14}_{6}C$ into $^{14}_{7}N$. Notice that the atomic number increases by one, and the mass number stays the same.

$$^{14}_{6}C \longrightarrow \, ^{14}_{7}N + \, ^{0}_{-1}\beta$$

Positron Emission

Nuclides below the band of stability are unstable because their neutron/proton ratio is too small. To decrease the number of protons, a proton can be converted into a neutron by emitting a positron. **A positron is a particle that has the same mass as an electron, but has a positive charge and is emitted from the nucleus during some kinds of radioactive decay.**

$$^{1}_{1}p \longrightarrow \, ^{1}_{0}n + \, ^{0}_{+1}\beta$$

Differentiated Instruction

BELOW LEVEL

Have students compare and contrast each of the following pairs:

helium atom, alpha particle

electron, beta particle

proton, positron

Students should point out that an alpha particle has the same particle composition as a helium atom, but is emitted from the nucleus of a radioactive atom. Unlike a helium atom, an alpha particle has a +2 charge. A beta particle is a "high-speed" electron originating from the nucleus of the atom—not an electron that orbits the nucleus. A proton is very large compared to a positron. A positron is the "opposite" or "antimatter" of an electron. If a proton and a positron get together, they annihilate each other, producing energy in the form of gamma rays. This is used in a *PET (positron emission tomography) scan.*

An example of positron emission is the decay of $^{38}_{19}K$ into $^{38}_{18}Ar$. Notice that the atomic number decreases by one, but the mass number stays the same.

$$^{38}_{19}K \longrightarrow ^{38}_{18}Ar + ^{0}_{+1}\beta$$

Electron Capture

Another type of decay for nuclides that have a neutron/proton ratio that is too small is electron capture. **In electron capture, an inner orbital electron is captured by the nucleus of its own atom.** The inner orbital electron combines with a proton, and a neutron is formed.

$$^{0}_{-1}e + ^{1}_{1}p \longrightarrow ^{1}_{0}n$$

An example of electron capture is the radioactive decay of $^{106}_{47}Ag$ into $^{106}_{46}Pd$. Just as in positron emission, the atomic number decreases by one, but the mass number stays the same.

$$^{106}_{47}Ag + ^{0}_{-1}e \longrightarrow ^{106}_{46}Pd$$

Gamma Emission

Gamma rays (γ) **are high-energy electromagnetic waves emitted from a nucleus as it changes from an excited state to a ground energy state.** The position of gamma rays in the electromagnetic spectrum is shown in **Figure 2.4.** The emission of gamma rays is another piece of evidence supporting the nuclear shell model. According to the nuclear shell model, gamma rays are produced when nuclear particles undergo transitions in nuclear-energy levels. This is similar to the emission of photons (light or X rays) when an electron drops to a lower energy level, which was covered in another chapter. Gamma emission usually occurs immediately following other types of decay, when other types of decay leave the nucleus in an excited state.

FIGURE 2.4

Gamma Rays in the EM Spectrum Gamma rays, like visible light, are a form of electromagnetic radiation. They have a shorter wavelength and are higher in energy than visible light.

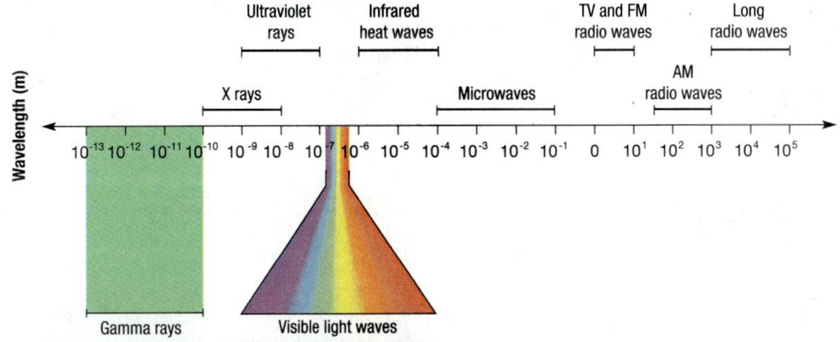

Problem Solving

DECONSTRUCTING PROBLEMS

Point out that nuclear equations are balanced, just as chemical equations are. Copy one of the nuclear equations shown on this page on the board. Have students explain how the equation is balanced. Students should recognize that the atomic masses, represented by the superscripts, are balanced. The charges, represented by the subscripts, are also balanced.

Teaching Tip

Because a beta particle has the same atomic number and mass number as an electron, students may be confused as to which symbol to use when solving for an unknown in a nuclear equation. Point out that if the unknown is a reactant, the nuclear reaction is electron capture, and the symbol e should be used. If the unknown is a product, then the reaction is beta emission, and the symbol β should be used.

Alternative Assessment

Determine whether each of the following nuclear reactions involves alpha decay, beta decay, positron emission, or electron capture.

1. $^{234}_{90}Th \longrightarrow ^{0}_{-1}\beta + ^{234}_{91}Pa$
   beta decay
2. $^{238}_{92}U \longrightarrow ^{4}_{2}He + ^{234}_{90}Th$
   alpha decay
3. $^{15}_{8}O \longrightarrow ^{0}_{+1}\beta + ^{15}_{7}N$
   positron emission
4. $^{22}_{11}Na + ^{0}_{-1}e \longrightarrow ^{22}_{10}Ne$
   electron capture

▼ Teach *continued*

TEACH FROM VISUALS

FIGURE 2.5 Point out that the graph shows what would happen to a sample of radium-226 starting now, represented by time zero. Have students use this graph to determine how much radium-226 would have been present 3198 years ago. Because 3198 years represents two half-lives, there would have been 80 mg of radium-226 present at that time.

TEACH FROM TABLES

FIGURE 2.6 Have students compare half-lives of the nuclei listed in this table. How many times faster does the polonium-214 nuclide decompose than potassium-40? The polonium nuclide decomposes almost instantaneously. The potassium nuclide decomposes in 1.3×10^9 years. Which nuclides are the most unstable? those with the shortest half-lives

Critical Thinking

Answer: Answers may vary. For example: If the oranges were radioactive nuclei having a half-life of one year, and you started with 50 oranges, then you would have only 25 after one year. After the next year, you would have 12 or 13, and so forth.

FIGURE 2.5

Half-Life The half-life of radium-226 is 1599 years. Half of the remaining radium-226 decays by the end of each additional half-life.

CRITICAL THINKING

Model Describe half-life using a bag of oranges, assuming each orange to be an individual atom.

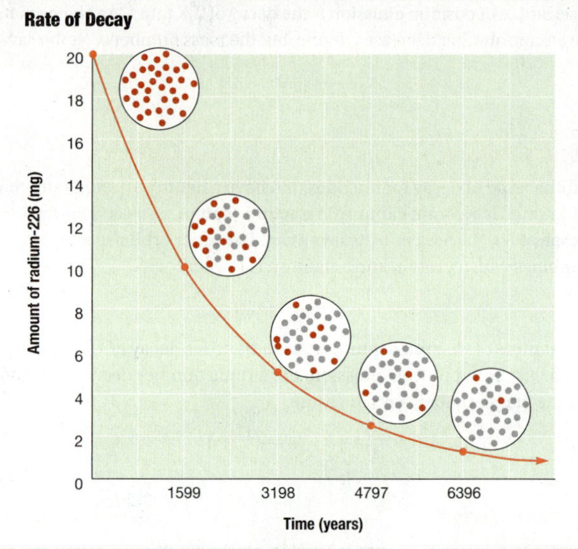

MAIN IDEA

Half-life is the time needed for one half of an amount of radioactive nuclei to decay.

No two radioactive isotopes decay at the same rate. **Half-life,** $t_{1/2}$, **is the time required for half the atoms of a radioactive nuclide to decay.** Look at the graph of the decay of radium-226 in **Figure 2.5.** Radium-226 has a half-life of 1599 years. Half of a given amount of radium-226 decays in 1599 years. In another 1599 years, half of the remaining radium-226 decays. This process continues until there is a negligible amount of radium-226. Each radioactive nuclide has its own half-life. More-stable nuclides decay slowly and have longer half-lives. Less-stable nuclides decay very quickly and have shorter half-lives, sometimes just a fraction of a second. Some representative radioactive nuclides, along with their half-lives, are given in **Figure 2.6.**

FIGURE 2.6

REPRESENTATIVE RADIOACTIVE NUCLIDES AND THEIR HALF-LIVES

Nuclide	Half-life	Nuclide	Half-life
$^{3}_{1}H$	12.32 years	$^{214}_{84}Po$	163.7 μs
$^{14}_{6}C$	5715 years	$^{218}_{84}Po$	3.0 min
$^{32}_{15}P$	14.28 days	$^{218}_{85}At$	1.6 s
$^{40}_{19}K$	1.3×10^9 years	$^{238}_{92}U$	4.46×10^9 years
$^{60}_{27}Co$	5.27 years	$^{239}_{94}Pu$	2.41×10^4 years

Differentiated Instruction

INCLUSION

Help kinesthetic learners understand the concept of half-life with this activity. Have all of the students stand. Then, have each of them flip a coin. Have those who flip "heads" sit down. Have those who remain standing flip their coins again. The students who flip "heads" this time should sit. Continue this process until one or no students remain standing. Because there is a 50 percent chance of flipping "heads" with each toss, this process simulates half-life. Ask the students to guess how many cycles it will take before all students are sitting down. You can estimate this by finding the power to which 2 is raised to give the number of students in your class. For example, if you have 35 students, it will probably take 5 cycles, since $2^5 = 32$. Greater meaning can be given to the figure on this page if you graph the number of students standing after each "half-life."

PREMIUM CONTENT

Learn It! Video
HMDScience.com

Solve It! Cards
HMDScience.com

Calculating with Half-Life

Sample Problem B **Phosphorus-32 has a half-life of 14.3 days. How many milligrams of phosphorus-32 remain after 57.2 days if you start with 4.0 mg of the isotope?**

1 ANALYZE

Given: original mass of phosphorus-32 = 4.0 mg
half-life of phosphorus-32 = 14.3 days
time elapsed = 57.2 days

Unknown: amount of phosphorus-32 remaining

2 PLAN

To determine the number of milligrams of phosphorus-32 remaining, we must first find the number of half-lives that have passed in the time elapsed. Then the amount of phosphorus-32 is determined by reducing the original amount by half for every half-life that has passed.

$$\text{number of half-lives} = \text{time elapsed (days)} \times \frac{\text{1 half-life}}{\text{14.3 days}}$$

amount of phosphorus-32 remaining =

$$\text{original amount of phosphorus-32} \times \frac{1}{2} \text{ for each half-life}$$

3 SOLVE

$$\text{number of half-lives} = 57.2 \text{ days} \times \frac{\text{1 half-life}}{\text{14.3 days}} = 4 \text{ half-lives}$$

$$\text{amount of phosphorus-32 remaining} = 4.0 \text{ mg} \times \frac{1}{2} \times \frac{1}{2} \times \frac{1}{2} \times \frac{1}{2} = 0.25 \text{ mg}$$

4 CHECK YOUR WORK

A period of 57.2 days is four half-lives for phosphorus-32. At the end of one half-life, 2.0 mg of phosphorus-32 remains; 1.0 mg remains at the end of two half-lives; 0.50 mg remains at the end of three half-lives; and 0.25 mg remains at the end of four half-lives.

Practice

Answers in Appendix E

1. The half-life of polonium-210 is 138.4 days. How many milligrams of polonium-210 remain after 415.2 days if you start with 2.0 mg of the isotope?
2. Assuming a half-life of 1599 years, how many years will be needed for the decay of $\frac{15}{16}$ of a given amount of radium-226?
3. The half-life of radon-222 is 3.824 days. After what time will one-fourth of a given amount of radon remain?
4. The half-life of cobalt-60 is 5.27 years. How many milligrams of cobalt-60 remain after 52.7 years if you start with 10.0 mg?
5. A sample contains 4.0 mg of uranium-238. After 4.46×10^9 years, the sample will contain 2.0 mg of uranium-238. What is the half-life of uranium-238?

Problem Solving

TAKE IT FURTHER

Divide students into three groups, and have each group make a poster to illustrate a decay series including the mode of decay, the product of decay, half-lives, and the final stable product. Have the first group illustrate uranium-235; the second group illustrate thorium-232; and the third group illustrate neptunium-237.

Teaching Tip

This method for calculating the amount of an isotope that remains works only for an integer number of half-lives.

Classroom Practice

B-1 The half-life of carbon-14 is 5715 years. How long will it be until only half of the carbon-14 in a sample remains?

Answer: 5715 years

B-2 The Environmental Protection Agency and health officials nationwide are concerned about the levels of radon gas in homes. The half-life of the radon-222 isotope is 3.8 days. If a sample of gas taken from a basement contains 4.38 μg of radon-222, how much radon will remain in the sample after 15.2 days?

Answer: 0.274 μg

B-3 Uranium–238 decays through alpha decay with a half-life of 4.46×10^9 years. How long would it take for 7/8 of a sample of uranium-238 to decay?

Answer: three half-lives, or 1.34×10^{10} years

Answers

Practice B

1. 0.25 mg
2. 6396 years
3. 7.648 days
4. 0.00977 mg
5. 4.46×10^9 years

▼ Teach *continued*

TEACH FROM VISUALS

FIGURE 2.7 Ensure that students understand the type of radioactive decay that converts one nuclide to another in this decay series. Have students write the nuclear equations for the different decay modes represented on this chart.

ChemisTrivia

- Have students locate radon in the U-238 decay series. Because it is a gas, radon formed by uranium decay inside Earth rises to the surface and into the atmosphere. This is the source of radon that can accumulate in buildings, as is discussed in the next section.
- The Curies discovered polonium and radium when the uranium ore they were studying was found to be more radioactive than would have been expected on the basis of its uranium content alone. Have the students locate polonium and radium in the U-238 decay series. Polonium and radium are present in some uranium ores because they are daughter nuclides of U-238.

MAIN IDEA

Radioactive nuclides become stable nuclides through a series of decays.

One nuclear reaction is not always enough to produce a stable nuclide. **A decay series is a series of radioactive nuclides produced by successive radioactive decay until a stable nuclide is reached. The heaviest nuclide of each decay series is called the parent nuclide. The nuclides produced by the decay of the parent nuclides are called daughter nuclides.** All naturally occurring nuclides with atomic numbers greater than 83 are radioactive and belong to one of three natural decay series. The parent nuclides are uranium-238, uranium-235, and thorium-232.

The transmutations of the uranium-238 decay series are charted in **Figure 2.7.** Locate the parent nuclide, uranium-238, on the chart. As the nucleus of uranium-238 decays, it emits an alpha particle. The mass number of the nuclide, and thus the vertical position on the graph, decreases by four. The atomic number, and thus the horizontal position, decreases by two. The daughter nuclide is an isotope of thorium.

$$^{238}_{92}\text{U} \rightarrow {}^{234}_{90}\text{Th} + {}^{4}_{2}\text{He}$$

FIGURE 2.7

Uranium-238 Decay Series This chart shows the transmutations that occur as $^{238}_{92}$U decays to the final, stable nuclide, $^{206}_{82}$Pb. Decay usually follows the solid arrows. The dotted arrows represent alternative routes of decay.

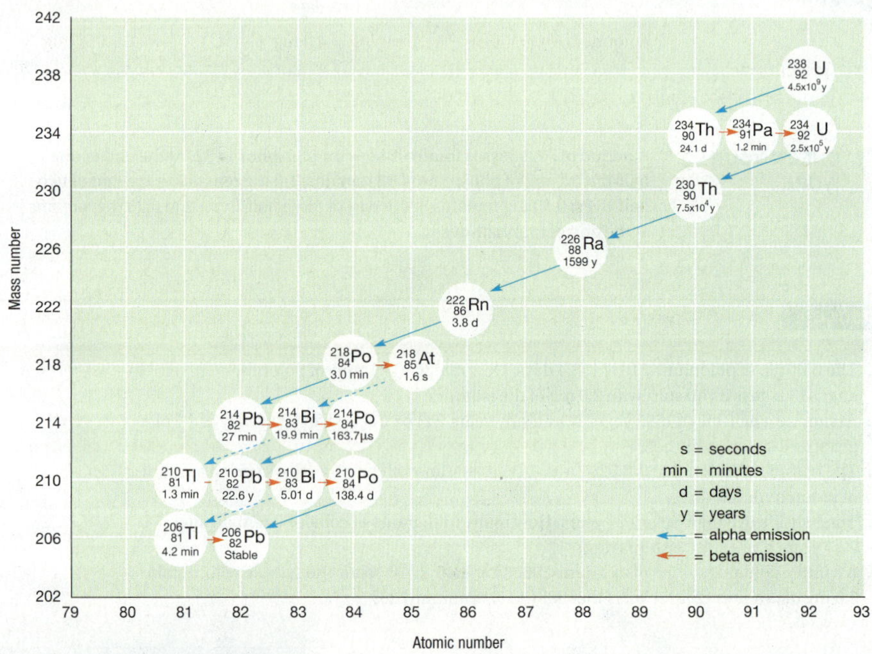

Problem Solving

DECONSTRUCTING PROBLEMS

Have students write out the equations so that they can see that mass is conserved. In alpha decay, the nucleus loses two protons and two neutrons and leaves behind a new element. In beta decay, the nucleus loses a high-speed electron. The radioactive elements can decay forward and backward in the periodic table.

The half-life of $^{234}_{90}Th$, about 24 days, is indicated on the chart. It decays by giving off beta particles. This increases its atomic number, and thus its horizontal position, by one. The mass number, and thus its vertical position, remain the same.

$$^{234}_{90}Th \longrightarrow ^{234}_{91}Pa + ^{0}_{-1}\beta$$

The remaining atomic number and mass number changes shown on the decay chart are also explained in terms of the particles given off. In the final step, $^{210}_{84}Po$ loses an alpha particle to form $^{206}_{82}Pb$. This is a stable, nonradioactive isotope of lead. Notice that $^{206}_{82}Pb$ contains 82 protons, a magic number. It contains the extra-stable nuclear configuration of a completed nuclear shell.

MAIN IDEA

Nuclides can become radioactive artificially.

Artificial radioactive nuclides are radioactive nuclides not found naturally on Earth. They are made by **artificial transmutations,** bombardment of nuclei with charged and uncharged particles. Because neutrons have no charge, they can easily penetrate the nucleus of an atom. However, positively charged alpha particles, protons, and other ions are repelled by the nucleus. Because of this repulsion, great quantities of energy are required to bombard nuclei with these particles. The necessary energy may be supplied by accelerating these particles in the magnetic or electrical field of a particle accelerator. **Figure 2.8** shows an example of an accelerator.

CHECK FOR UNDERSTANDING
Hypothesize The neutrons released by atoms are moving incredibly fast. Why do you think scientists found they needed to slow down these neutrons for them to produce artificial transmutations?

FIGURE 2.8

Particle Accelerator This is an aerial view of the Fermi International Accelerator Laboratory (Fermilab), in Illinois. The particle accelerators are underground. The Tevatron ring, the larger particle accelerator, has a circumference of 4 mi. The smaller ring (top left) is a new accelerator, the Main Injector.

ChemisTrivia

- Particle accelerators can be linear or circular. The linear accelerator at Stanford Linear Accelerator Center (SLAC) in Palo Alto, California, is 2 miles long. Scientists ride bicycles to get from one part of the accelerator to another.
- Seaborgium was officially accepted as the name for element 106 in 1997. It was named for Glenn Seaborg (1912–1999). Seaborg is the first person to have an element named for him while he was still alive.

Check for Understanding

Answer: The neutrons were moving so fast that they missed the atomic nuclei the scientists wanted them to hit. Slowing down the neutrons increased the chance of collision.

Differentiated Instruction

BELOW LEVEL

Have students work in pairs. One student should write a balanced chemical equation, while the other student writes a balanced nuclear equation. Working as a team, the students should compare and contrast the two equations. Students should recognize that both kinds of equations involve chemical elements, show the conservation of mass, and include reactants and products. Students should point out that the chemical equation represents a rearrangement of atoms, while the nuclear equation shows a transmutation of an atom of one element to an atom of a different element.

▼ Teach *continued*

ChemisTrivia

- The daughter of Marie and Pierre Curie, Iréne Joliot-Curie, and her husband, Frédéric Joliot-Curie, produced the first artificial radioactive nuclide in 1934 by bombarding Al-27 with an alpha particle to produce radioactive P-30 and a neutron.
- During the Chernobyl, Ukraine, accident in 1986, radioactive iodine-131, a product of the nuclear fission of uranium, was released into the atmosphere. In surrounding countries, children were given large doses of potassium iodide so that the radioactive I-131 that resulted from the accident would be less likely to be absorbed by the children's thyroid glands. Absorption of I-131 by the thyroid gland can cause thyroid cancer. Iodine-131 is also used for both diagnostic and therapeutic purposes for thyroid disease.

▼ Assess and Reteach

Assess Use the Formative Assessment on this page to evaluate student mastery of the section.

Reteach For students who need additional instruction, download the Section Study Guide.

Response to Intervention To reassess students' mastery, use the Section Quiz, available to print or to take directly online at **HMDScience.com**.

FIGURE 2.9

REACTIONS FOR THE FIRST PREPARATION OF SEVERAL TRANSURANIUM ELEMENTS

Atomic number	Name	Symbol	Nuclear reaction
93	neptunium	Np	${}^{238}_{92}U + {}^{1}_{0}n \rightarrow {}^{239}_{92}U$ ${}^{239}_{92}U \rightarrow {}^{239}_{93}Np + {}^{0}_{-1}\beta$
94	plutonium	Pu	${}^{238}_{93}Np \rightarrow {}^{238}_{94}Pu + {}^{0}_{-1}\beta$
95	americium	Am	${}^{239}_{94}Pu + 2{}^{1}_{0}n \rightarrow {}^{241}_{95}Am + {}^{0}_{-1}\beta$
96	curium	Cm	${}^{239}_{94}Pu + {}^{4}_{2}He \rightarrow {}^{242}_{96}Cm + {}^{1}_{0}n$
97	berkelium	Bk	${}^{241}_{95}Am + {}^{4}_{2}He \rightarrow {}^{243}_{97}Bk + 2{}^{1}_{0}n$
98	californium	Cf	${}^{242}_{96}Cm + {}^{4}_{2}He \rightarrow {}^{245}_{98}Cf + {}^{1}_{0}n$
99	einsteinium	Es	${}^{238}_{92}U + 15{}^{1}_{0}n \rightarrow {}^{253}_{99}Es + 7{}^{0}_{-1}\beta$
100	fermium	Fm	${}^{238}_{92}U + 17{}^{1}_{0}n \rightarrow {}^{255}_{100}Fm + 8{}^{0}_{-1}\beta$
101	mendelevium	Md	${}^{253}_{99}Es + {}^{4}_{2}He \rightarrow {}^{256}_{101}Md + {}^{1}_{0}n$
102	nobelium	No	${}^{246}_{96}Cm + {}^{12}_{6}C \rightarrow {}^{254}_{102}No + 4{}^{1}_{0}n$
103	lawrencium	Lr	${}^{252}_{98}Cf + {}^{10}_{5}B \rightarrow {}^{258}_{103}Lr + 4{}^{1}_{0}n$

FIGURE 2.10

Manufactured Elements Artificial transmutations filled the gaps in the periodic table, shown in red, and extended the periodic table with the transuranium elements, shown in blue.

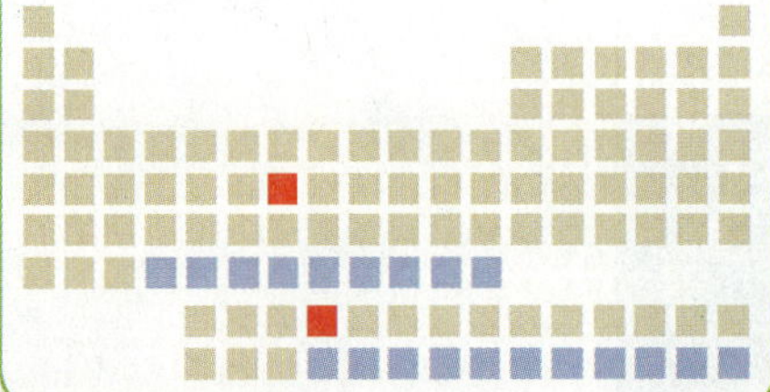

Artificial Radioactive Nuclides

Radioactive isotopes of all the natural elements have been produced by artificial transmutation. In addition, production of technetium and promethium by artificial transmutation has filled gaps in the periodic table. Their positions are shown in red in **Figure 2.10.**

Artificial transmutations are also used to produce the transuranium elements. **Transuranium elements are elements with more than 92 protons in their nuclei.** All of these elements are radioactive. The nuclear reactions for the synthesis of several transuranium elements are shown in **Figure 2.9.** Currently, 20 artificially prepared transuranium elements have been named. Others have been reported, but not confirmed. Their positions in the periodic table are shown in blue in **Figure 2.10.**

SECTION 2 FORMATIVE ASSESSMENT

Reviewing Main Ideas

1. Define *radioactive decay.*
2. a. What are the different types of common radioactive decay?
   b. List the types of radioactive decay that convert one nuclide into another.
3. What fraction of a given sample of a radioactive nuclide remains after four half-lives?
4. When does a decay series end?

Critical Thinking

5. **INTERPRETING CONCEPTS** Distinguish between natural and artificial radioactive nuclides.

Answers to Section Assessment

1. the spontaneous disintegration of a nucleus into a lighter, more stable nucleus, accompanied by the emission of particles, radiation, or both
2. a. alpha emission, beta emission, positron emission, gamma emission, and electron capture
   b. beta emission, positron emission, electron capture
3. 1/16
4. when a stable nuclide has been produced
5. Natural radioactive nuclides are found naturally on Earth, and artificial nuclides are not. They are made by bombarding nuclides with particles.

Nuclear Radiation

SECTION 3

Main Ideas

- Ionizing radiation can harm living tissues.
- Film and electronic methods can detect radiation.
- Radioactivity has surprising applications.
- Storage and disposal of nuclear waste pose important concerns.

Key Terms

roentgen
rem
film badge
Geiger-Müller counter
scintillation counter
radioactive dating
radioactive tracer
nuclear waste

In Becquerel's experiment, nuclear radiation from the uranium compound penetrated the lightproof covering and exposed the film. Different types of nuclear radiation have different penetrating abilities. Nuclear radiation includes alpha particles, beta particles, and gamma rays.

Alpha particles can travel only a few centimeters in air and have a low penetrating ability due to their large mass and charge. They cannot penetrate skin. However, they can cause damage if ingested or inhaled. Beta particles, which are emitted electrons, travel at speeds close to the speed of light and have a penetrating ability about 100 times greater than that of alpha particles. Beta particles can travel a few meters in air. Gamma rays have the greatest penetrating ability. **Figure 3.1** gives the penetrating abilities and shielding requirements of some types of nuclear radiation.

MAIN IDEA

Ionizing radiation can harm living tissues.

Nuclear radiation can transfer the energy from nuclear decay to the electrons of atoms or molecules and cause ionization. The **roentgen** (R) is a unit used to measure nuclear radiation exposure; it is equal to the amount of gamma and X ray radiation that produces 2×10^9 ion pairs when it passes through 1 cm^3 of dry air. Ionization can damage living tissue. Radiation damage to human tissue is measured in rems (roentgen equivalent in man). A **rem** is a unit used to measure the dose of any type of ionizing radiation that factors in the effect that the radiation has on human tissue. Long-term exposure to radiation can cause DNA mutations that result in cancer and other genetic defects. DNA can be mutated directly by interaction with radiation or indirectly by interaction with previously ionized molecules.

FIGURE 3.1

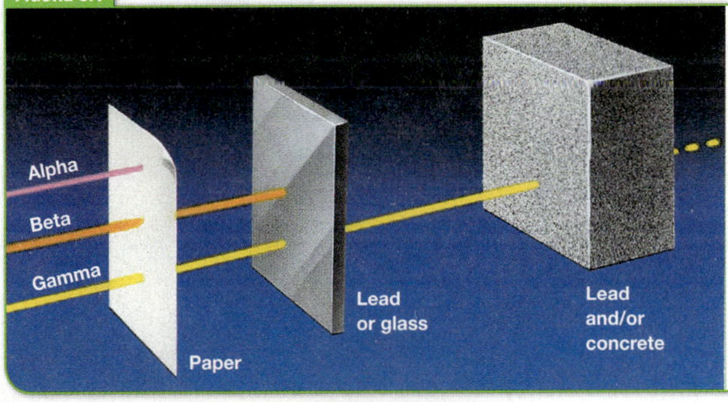

Radiation Energy The different penetrating abilities of alpha particles, beta particles, and gamma rays require different levels of shielding. Alpha particles can be shielded with just a sheet of paper. Lead or glass is often used to shield beta particles. Gamma rays are the most penetrating and require shielding with thick layers of lead or concrete, or both.

Differentiated Instruction

INCLUSION

Help students understand the dangers of radiation exposure by asking a dental hygienist or a radiation technician to make a brief presentation. Prepare for the visit by having the class list questions for the guest speaker to answer. Possible questions include: What radioactive isotopes are used in the diagnostic or treatment equipment? What steps does the hygienist or technician take to minimize radiation exposure? What technological advances they have seen since working in the field?

SECTION 3

Plan and Prepare ▼

Objectives

Upon completion of this section, students should be able to do the following:

- Compare the penetrating ability and shielding requirements of alpha particles, beta particles, and gamma rays.
- Define the terms *roentgen* and *rem*, and distinguish between them.
- Describe three devices used in radiation detection.
- Discuss applications of radioactive nuclides.

Classroom Catalyst

Use a radon detection kit to test the air in your classroom. Radon detection kits for mail-in laboratory analysis can be found at some hardware stores or local health departments. Be sure students understand that the amount of radon in homes depends on the underlying geologic conditions.

Teach ▼

ChemisTrivia

People's exposure to radiation increases when they are at high altitude. What does that say about one of the useful functions of our atmosphere?

READING TOOLKIT

READING RESPONSE LOGS Have students draw a vertical line on a sheet of paper. In the left-hand column, have them write questions, thoughts, or reactions to material in this section. In the right-hand column, have them write responses to these questions or thoughts. Ask volunteers to share some of their passages and responses.

▼ Teach *continued*

Demonstration

DETECTING AND MEASURING BETA RADIATION

This shows how distance and shielding affect beta radiation.

1. Obtain a **beta source** in a sealed container from a scientific supply house.
2. Read the background radiation with a **Geiger-Müller counter.**
3. Measure the radiation by placing the Geiger-Müller tube 5 cm away from the beta source.
4. Repeat step 3 at 10 cm, 30 cm, and 1 m from the beta source.
5. Repeat step 3, but place a **piece of paper** between the source and the Geiger-Müller tube.
6. Repeat step 3 using a **plywood board 1 cm thick** and then using a piece of **aluminum 1 cm thick.** Other types of shielding, for example **Plexiglas,** may also be used.

Safety **Safety goggles,** a **lab apron,** and **gloves** must be worn. Students must be 10 ft or more from the demonstration. Obtain isotopes from scientific supply houses in quantities that do not require licensing. Use only sources in sealed containers.

Do not allow students to handle the sources or the Geiger-Müller counter. Be sure to follow the manufacturer's directions for using the Geiger-Müller counter.

No Disposal Save all materials for future use.

Everyone is exposed to background radiation. The estimated average exposure for people living in the United States is thought to be about 0.1 rem per year. However, actual exposure varies. The maximum permissible dose of radiation exposure for a person in the general population is 0.5 rem per year. Airline crews and those who live at high altitudes have increased exposure levels because of increased cosmic ray levels at high altitudes. Radon-222 trapped inside homes also causes increased exposure. Because it is a gas, radon released from certain rocks can move up through the soil into homes through holes in the foundation. Radon trapped in homes increases the risk of lung cancer, especially among smokers.

MAIN IDEA

Film and electronic methods can detect radiation.

Film badges, Geiger-Müller counters, and scintillation counters are three devices commonly used to detect and measure nuclear radiation. A film badge and a Geiger-Müller counter are shown in **Figure 3.2.** As previously mentioned, nuclear radiation exposes film just as visible light does. This property is used in film badges. **Film badges** use exposure of film to measure the approximate radiation exposure of people working with radiation. **Geiger-Müller counters** are instruments that detect radiation by counting electric pulses carried by gas ionized by radiation. Geiger-Müller counters are typically used to detect beta-particles, X rays, and gamma radiation. Radiation can also be detected when it transfers its energy to substances that *scintillate,* or absorb ionizing radiation and emit visible light. **Scintillation counters** are instruments that convert scintillating light to an electric signal for detecting radiation.

FIGURE 3.2

Radiation Detectors Film badges and Geiger-Müller counters are two methods used to detect nuclear radiation.

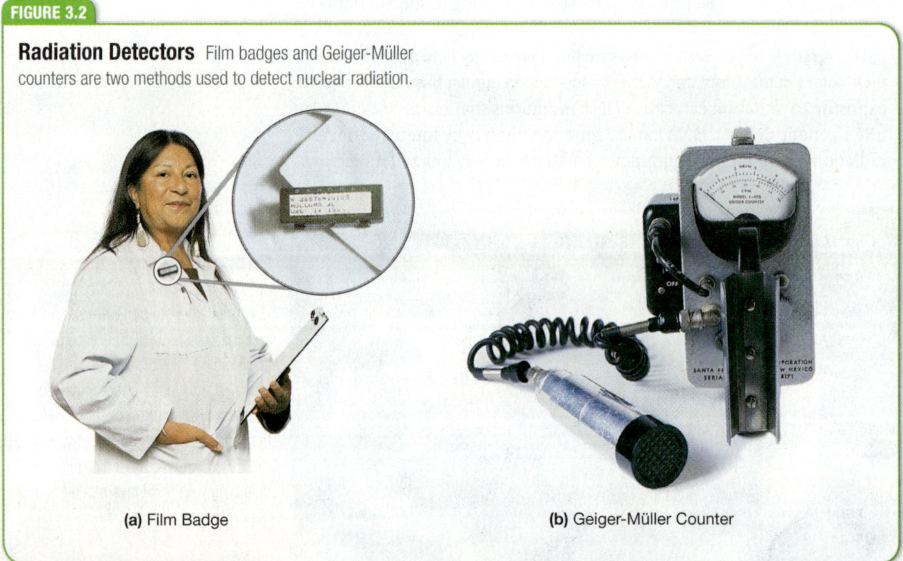

(a) Film Badge

(b) Geiger-Müller Counter

Differentiated Instruction

PRE-AP

Have students prepare a brief report on scintillating light. Have them explain how scintillating light is converted into an electric signal to detect radiation. Also ask students to report on a practical application of scintillating light. For example, scintillation detectors are used in a wide array of applications, including fundamental research in particle and nuclear physics, oil exploration, container and baggage scanning, health physics, and medical diagnostics and therapy.

MAIN IDEA

Radioactivity has surprising applications.

Many applications use the fact that the physical and chemical properties of stable isotopes are similar to those of radioactive isotopes of the same element. A few uses of radioactive nuclides are discussed below.

Radioactive Dating

Radioactive dating is the process by which the approximate age of an object is determined based on the amount of certain radioactive nuclides present. Such an estimate is based on the fact that radioactive substances decay with known half-lives. Age is estimated by measuring either the accumulation of a daughter nuclide or the disappearance of the parent nuclide.

Carbon-14 is radioactive and has a half-life of approximately 5715 years. It can be used to estimate the age of organic material up to about 50 000 years old. Nuclides with longer half-lives are used to estimate the age of older objects; methods using nuclides with long half-lives have been used to date minerals and lunar rocks more than 4 billion years old.

Radioactive Nuclides in Medicine

In medicine, radioactive nuclides, such as the artificial radioactive nuclide cobalt-60, are used to destroy certain types of cancer cells. Many radioactive nuclides are also used as **radioactive tracers,** which are radioactive atoms that are incorporated into substances so that movement of the substances can be followed by radiation detectors. Detection of radiation from radioactive tracers can be used to diagnose cancer and other diseases. See **Figure 3.3.**

Radioactive Nuclides in Agriculture

In agriculture, radioactive tracers in fertilizers are used to determine the effectiveness of the fertilizer. The amount of radioactive tracer absorbed by a plant indicates the amount of fertilizer absorbed. Nuclear radiation is also used to prolong the shelf life of food. For example, gamma rays from cobalt-60 can be used to kill bacteria and insects that spoil and infest food.

FIGURE 3.3

Radioactive Tracers

Radioactive nuclides, such as technetium-99, can be used to detect bone cancer. In this procedure, technetium-99 accumulates in areas of abnormal bone metabolism. Detection of the nuclear radiation then shows the location of bone cancer.

CRITICAL THINKING

Recall What would be the dangers of using radioactivity in medicine? In agriculture?

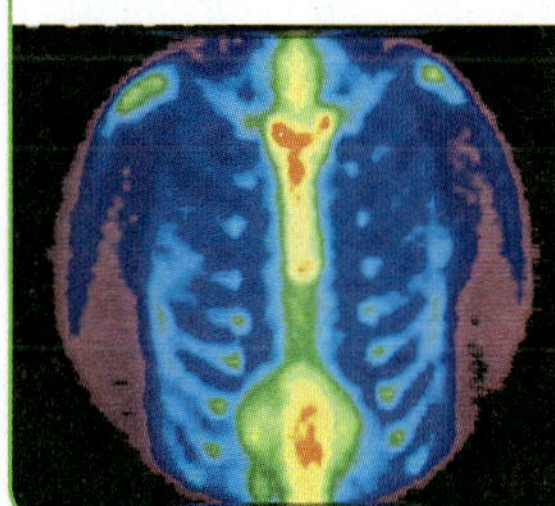

MAIN IDEA

Storage and disposal of nuclear waste pose important concerns.

In nuclear fission, the nucleus of a very heavy atom, such as uranium, is split into two or more lighter nuclei. The products include the nuclei as well as the nucleons formed from the fragments' radioactive decay. Fission is the process that powers nuclear reactors, including those on nuclear-powered submarines and aircraft carriers.

Fusion is the opposite process. In fusion, very high temperatures and pressures combine light atoms, such as hydrogen, to make heavier atoms, such as helium. Fusion is the primary process that fuels the stars. Creating and maintaining a fusion reaction is very complex.

Problem Solving

TAKE IT FURTHER

Many students get confused about why scientists use so many different radioactive elements for dating rocks. Ask students to think of the approximate age of a rock, in thousands, millions, or billions of years. Assume the rock contains a mineral with a suitable isotope.

Have students take a look at **Figure 2.7** again. U-238 has a half-life of 4.5 billion years, and U-234 has a half-life of 250 000 years. They would need to use a U-238/Th system to calculate the age of a rock that is billions of years old, whereas they might use a U-234/Th system to calculate the age of a rock that is millions of years old. There are other systems as well: K-40/Ar, U-235/Pa, and C-14.

Note that Carbon-14 only works for dating something that was once living. The half-life of C-14 is 5 730 years, so it is not used for dating rocks. Geologists use the ratio of C-14 to C-12 to determine the age of what was once living. Ask students what assumptions are made.

ChemisTrivia

Smoke detectors contain small radioactive samples. Artificially produced americium-241 is often used for this purpose. The radiation ionizes air molecules, and the ions conduct a small electric current. When this current is reduced by the presence of smoke particles, an alarm sounds.

Classroom Discussion

Never before has there been a discovery in science that offered such potential for both destruction and progress as the discovery of radioactivity. Discuss both the benefits and hazards of using radioactivity. To prepare for the discussion, have the students bring to class newspaper and magazine articles that refer to topics such as food preservation, CAT scanners, PET scanners, radiation diagnosis and therapy, tracer studies, radioactive dating, particle accelerators, nuclear power plants, disposal of nuclear wastes, nuclear armaments, and the lasting effects of nuclear disasters.

Teaching Tip

The next section gives much more detailed information about fission and fusion. Let students know that this is just a brief introduction while focusing their attention on the issue of containment.

Critical Thinking

Answer: Radioactivity can damage living tissue. Radioactivity damages the atoms in the cell of plants and animals.

▼ Teach *continued*

Classroom Discussion

Discuss why the issue of dealing with nuclear waste can be an emotionally charged topic. Ask students the advantages and disadvantages of putting nuclear waste in the Yucca Mountain site. You may want to include the topic of the transportation of the nuclear waste by trucks or trains in your discussion.

Teaching Tip

To strengthen their understanding of the issues involved in the containment and disposal of nuclear waste, students may want to check out the Web sites of government agencies such as the Nuclear Regulatory Commission and the Department of Energy Office of Civilian Radioactive Waste Management. These agencies share the responsibility of developing a safe nuclear waste disposal program.

▼ Assess and Reteach

Assess Use the Formative Assessment on this page to evaluate student mastery of the section.

Reteach For students who need additional instruction, download the Section Study Guide.

Response to Intervention To reassess students' mastery, use the Section Quiz, available to print or to take directly online at **HMDScience.com**.

Both fission and fusion release enormous amounts of energy that can be converted into energy as heat and electrical energy. **Energy-producing nuclear processes, however, also produce nuclear waste or unusable end materials that contain radioisotopes.** Fission produces more waste than fusion. As new processes are developed to use energy from fission and fusion, a more vexing question arises: how to contain, store, and dispose of nuclear waste.

Containment and Storage of Nuclear Waste

Every radioactive substance has a half-life, which is the amount of time needed for half of a given material to decay. Radioactive waste from medical research, for example, usually has a half-life that is a few months or less. Some of the waste that is produced in a nuclear reactor will take hundreds of thousands of years to decay, and it needs to be contained so that living organisms can be shielded from radioactivity. There are two main types of containment: on-site storage and off-site disposal.

The most common form of nuclear waste is spent fuel rods from nuclear power plants. These fuel rods can be contained above the ground by placing them in water pools or in dry casks. Each nuclear reactor in the United States has large pools of water where spent rods can be stored, and some of the radioactive materials will decay. When these pools are full, the rods are moved to dry casks, which are usually made of concrete and steel. Both storage pools and casks are meant for only temporary storage before moving the waste to permanent underground facilities.

Disposal of Nuclear Waste

Disposal of nuclear waste is done with the intention of never retrieving the materials. Because of this, building disposal sites takes careful planning. Currently, there are 131 disposal sites in 39 states around the United States. Plans to find a permanent disposal site for all the nation's nuclear waste are still not fully realized. Any proposed site has to contend with the concerns of nearby residents regarding the potential environmental and human impacts. Some have suggested either blowing up the waste or sending it into space, but such solutions are still speculative.

SECTION 3 FORMATIVE ASSESSMENT

Reviewing Main Ideas

1. What is required to shield alpha particles? Why are these materials effective?
2. a. What is the average exposure of people living in the United States to environmental background radiation?
   b. How does this relate to the maximum permissible dose?
3. What device is used to measure the radiation exposure of people working with radiation?
4. Explain why nuclear radiation can be used to preserve food.

Critical Thinking

5. **INFERRING CONCLUSIONS** Explain how nuclear waste is contained, stored, and disposed of, and how each method affects the environment.

Answers to Section Assessment

1. Very little material is required as a shield from alpha particles, because the particles have large mass.
2. a. about 0.1 rem per year
   b. The average exposure is about one-fifth of the maximum permissible dose.
3. film badges
4. Radiation kills bacteria and insects that can spoil and infest food.
5. Nuclear waste from power plants is contained temporarily in on-site water pools or dry casks. Nuclear waste is disposed of in 131 disposal sites in the United States. Because some nuclear waste can take thousands of years to decay, the disposal sites are built so that the surroundings are shielded from the radiation. Answers about the environmental impact may vary.

Nuclear Fission and Nuclear Fusion

SECTION 4

Main Ideas

- In fission, atoms split into nearly equal parts.
- Nuclei combine in nuclear fusion.

Key Terms

nuclear fission, chain reaction, critical mass, nuclear reactor, nuclear power plant, shielding, control rod, moderator, nuclear fusion

MAIN IDEA

In fission, atoms split into nearly equal parts.

Recall that nuclei of intermediate mass are the most stable. In **nuclear fission,** a very heavy nucleus splits into more-stable nuclei of intermediate mass. This process releases enormous amounts of energy. Nuclear fission may occur spontaneously or when nuclei are bombarded by particles. When uranium-235 is bombarded with slow neutrons, a uranium nucleus can capture one of the neutrons, making it very unstable. The nucleus splits into medium-mass nuclei with the emission of more neutrons. The mass of the products is less than the mass of the reactants. The missing mass is converted to energy.

Nuclear Chain Reaction

When fission of an atom bombarded by neutrons produces more neutrons, a chain reaction can occur. A **chain reaction** is a reaction in which the material that starts the reaction is also one of the products and can start another reaction. As shown in **Figure 4.1,** two or three neutrons can be given off when uranium-235 fission occurs. These neutrons can cause the fission of other uranium-235 nuclei. Again neutrons are emitted, which can cause the fission of still other uranium-235 nuclei.

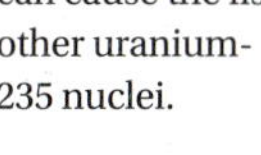

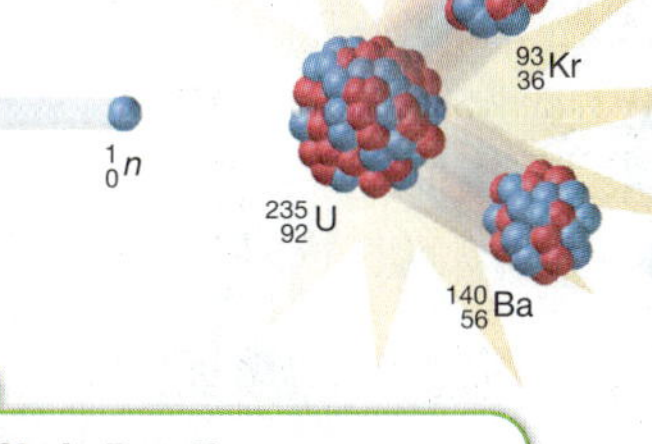

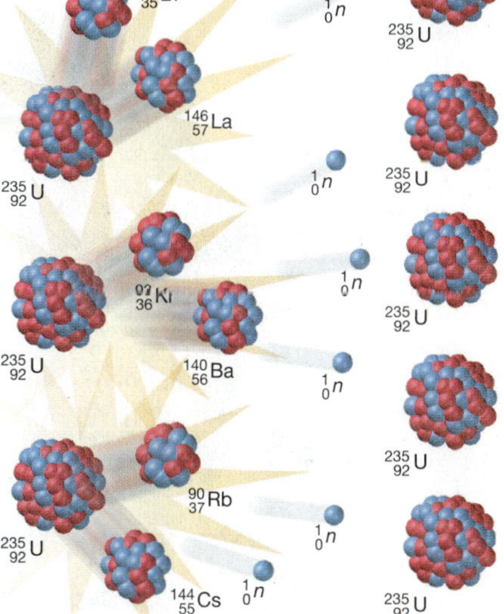

FIGURE 4.1

Nuclear Chain Reactions Fission induction of uranium-235 by bombardment with neutrons can lead to a chain reaction when a critical mass of uranium-235 is present.

SECTION 4

Plan and Prepare ▼

Objectives

Upon completion of this section, students should be able to do the following:

- Define *nuclear fission*, *chain reaction*, and *nuclear fusion*, and distinguish among them.
- Explain how a fission reaction is used to generate power.
- Discuss the possible benefits of fusion reactions and the current difficulty of controlling them.

Classroom Catalyst

Fission and fusion can be explained by looking at **Figure 1.1** in Section 1 of this chapter. For elements lighter than iron, fusion of two smaller elements into a larger element emits energy. For elements larger than iron, fission of a larger element into two smaller elements emits energy.

Teach ▼

Demonstration

MODELING A CHAIN REACTION

A fission chain reaction can be modeled in the following way: set out a series of **mousetraps** with a **table tennis ball** on each one, and throw another table tennis ball into the group of traps. The first ball will spring one trap, then those two balls will spring two traps, then those four balls will spring four traps, and so on. The effect is most dramatic with a large number of traps.

TEACH FROM VISUALS

FIGURE 4.1 Make sure students realize that this figure has been simplified for easier study. The escaping neutrons will bombard more atoms unless they are absorbed by neutron-absorbing materials, such as the control rods used in nuclear reactors.

Differentiated Instruction

BELOW LEVEL

Certain students may have difficulty in understanding the sequence of events occurring in a chain reaction. Have students work in groups of four. Ask each team to think of a model that demonstrates the concept of a chain reaction. Suggest that they think about using dominoes or books to represent the radioactive nuclides. For example, toppling one book could cause two other books to topple, which cause still other books to topple. Show the class a video of one domino setting off a whole series of other dominoes toppling.

▼ Teach *continued*

ChemisTrivia

- Nuclear power provides about 20% of the electrical power in the United States and about 80% of electrical power in France. However, because the United States is larger, it produces more nuclear power than France does.
- The Chernobyl accident occurred shortly after technicians briefly removed most of the control rods—which act as neutron absorbers—during a test.
- Canada has an abundant supply of natural uranium but no facilities for enriching it. Canada has specialized in heavy water, or D_2O, reactors. The heavy water is used both as a coolant and as a moderator.

READING TOOLKIT

K/W/L Students probably have preconceptions about nuclear reactions and the energy they release. Have students list what they know about nuclear fission and fusion. Then have them list what they want to know about these reactions. After reading Section 4, students should determine whether their questions have been answered, noting any unanswered questions as well as new questions they may have.

Critical Thinking

Answer: In both kinds of power plants, heat is generated to produce steam that powers a turbine that makes the electricity. Wastes from fossil fuel plants are dangerous because they enter the atmosphere, causing things like acid rain, which in turn can harm people, animals, and plants. Nuclear waste is dangerous because, if not contained properly, it can enter water supplies or go into the air. Nuclear radiation can cause cancer and mutations in DNA. However, nuclear waste doesn't pollute the air or increase greenhouse gases that play a role in climate change.

A chain reaction continues until all of the uranium-235 atoms have split or until the neutrons fail to strike other uranium-235 nuclei. If the mass of the uranium-235 sample is below a certain minimum, too many neutrons escape without striking other nuclei, and the chain reaction stops. The minimum amount of nuclide that provides the number of neutrons needed to sustain a chain reaction is called the **critical mass.** Uncontrolled chain reactions give the explosive energy to atomic bombs. **Nuclear reactors** use controlled-fission chain reactions to produce energy and radioactive nuclides.

Nuclear Power Plants

Nuclear power plants use energy as heat from nuclear reactors to produce electrical energy. They have five main components: shielding, fuel, control rods, moderator, and coolant. The components, shown in **Figure 4.2,** are surrounded by shielding. **Shielding** is radiation-absorbing material that is used to decrease exposure to radiation, especially gamma rays, from nuclear reactors. Uranium-235 is typically used as the fissile fuel to produce energy as heat, which is absorbed by the coolant. **Control rods** are neutron-absorbing rods that help control the reaction by limiting the number of free neutrons. Because fission of uranium-235 is more efficiently induced by slow neutrons, a **moderator** is used to slow down the fast neutrons produced by fission. Nuclear power plants can provide competitively priced electricity without emitting greenhouse gases or particulates. Concerns about nuclear power include storage and disposal of spent radioactive fuel, as well as public perception.

FIGURE 4.2

Nuclear Power Plant In this model of a nuclear power plant, pressurized water is heated by fission of uranium-235. This water is circulated to a steam generator. The steam drives a turbine to produce electricity. Cool water from a lake or river is then used to condense the steam into water. The warm water from the condenser may be cooled in cooling towers before being reused or returned to the lake or river.

CRITICAL THINKING

Defend How is a nuclear power plant similar to a fossil fuel plant? Which do you believe has more dangerous wastes? Support your opinion with at least three facts.

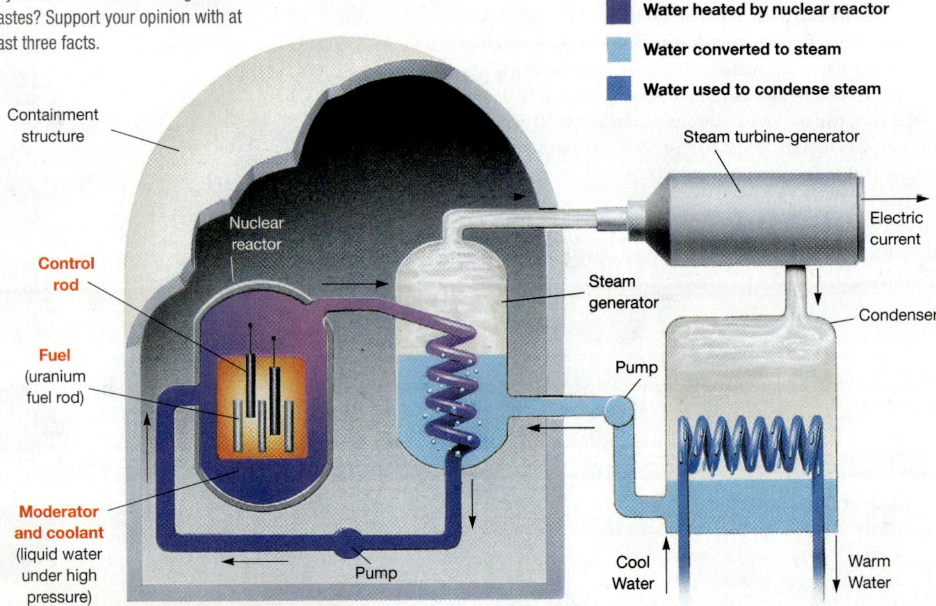

Differentiated Instruction

INCLUSION

Help students with learning disabilities to understand the operation of a nuclear reactor by having them create a poster, bulletin board, or computer sketch of the nuclear reactor shown in **Figure 4.2.** Students can label each part of the reactor. Students may include information about a nuclear reactor in your state or a nearby state. If possible, include a picture of the local reactor in the display.

FIGURE 4.3

Nuclear Fusion Fusion of hydrogen nuclei into more-stable helium nuclei provides the energy of our sun and other stars.

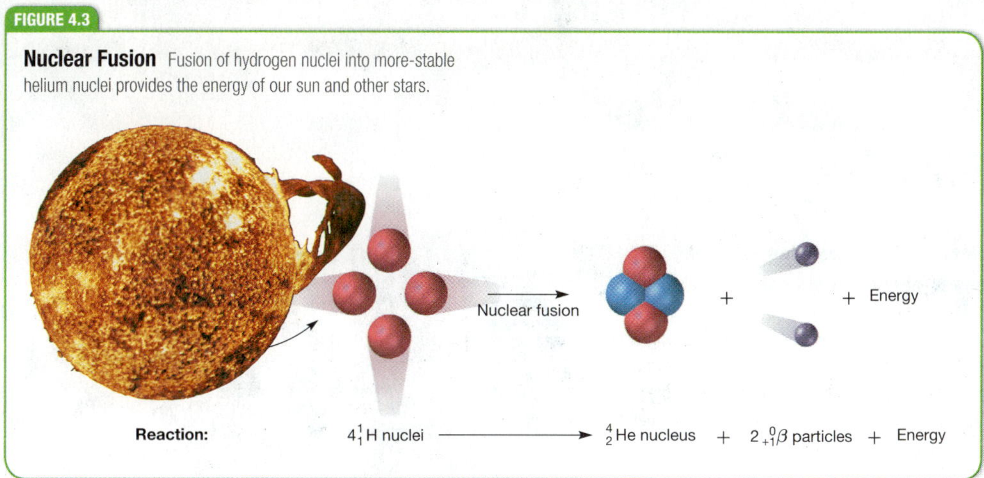

Reaction: $4\,^{1}_{1}H$ nuclei → $^{4}_{2}He$ nucleus + $2\,^{0}_{+1}\beta$ particles + Energy

MAIN IDEA

Nuclei combine in nuclear fusion.

The high stability of nuclei with intermediate masses can also be used to explain nuclear fusion. **In nuclear fusion, low-mass nuclei combine to form a heavier, more stable nucleus.** Nuclear fusion releases even more energy per gram of fuel than nuclear fission. In our sun and stars that are similar to the sun, hydrogen nuclei combine at extremely high temperature and pressure to form a helium nucleus with a loss of mass and release of energy. The net reaction is illustrated in **Figure 4.3.**

If fusion reactions can be controlled, they could be used for energy generation. Researchers are currently studying ways to contain the reacting plasma that is required for fusion. A plasma is an extremely hot mixture of positive nuclei and electrons. There is no known material that can withstand the initial temperatures, about 10^8 K, required to induce fusion. Scientists use strong magnetic fields to suspend the charged plasma inside a container but away from the walls. Additionally, a large amount of energy is needed to initiate fusion reactions. For fusion to be a practical energy source, more energy needs to be generated by the reaction than is put into the reaction.

CHECK FOR UNDERSTANDING

Compare How is nuclear fusion different from nuclear fission?

SECTION 4 FORMATIVE ASSESSMENT

Reviewing Main Ideas

1. Distinguish between nuclear fission and nuclear fusion.
2. Define *chain reaction.*
3. List the five main components of a nuclear power plant.

Critical Thinking

4. **RELATING IDEAS** Explain how fusion is one of our sources of energy.

Answers to Section Assessment

1. Nuclear fission releases energy when large nuclei are broken up; nuclear fusion releases energy when small nuclei are fused together.
2. A chain reaction is a reaction in which the material that starts the reaction is also one of the products. The products of one reaction can then begin other reactions.
3. shielding, control rods, moderator, fuel, and coolant
4. Fusion is the energy source of the sun.

Teaching Tip

Hydrogen nuclei combine through a process known as the proton-proton cycle. This fusion process has multiple steps and is more complicated than what is illustrated in **Figure 4.3.**

Check for Understanding

Answer: Atomic nuclei combine in fusion. Atomic nuclei break apart in fission.

Assess and Reteach

Assess Use the Formative Assessment on this page to evaluate student mastery of the section.

Reteach For students who need additional instruction, download the Section Study Guide.

Response to Intervention To reassess students' mastery, use the Section Quiz, available to print or to take directly online at **HMDScience.com**.

CHEMISTRY EXPLORERS

Teaching Tip

Drawing the sequence of events in picture form on the board may help some students follow the logic of this story.

Classroom Discussion

Have students identify researchers in this article who were affected by discrimination or national politics. Discuss how history plays an important role in scientific research. Some people feel that war is a prime motivator for major discoveries. Does war seem to drive the discoveries in this story?

Chemistry EXPLORERS

An Unexpected Finding

Historical Perspective

The discovery of the artificial transmutation of uranium in 1934 triggered great excitement in science. Chemists who were preoccupied with identifying what they thought were the final missing elements of the periodic table suddenly had to consider the existence of elements beyond atomic number 92. Physicists began to probe the stability of the nucleus more deeply. By 1939, nuclear investigators in both fields had collaborated to provide a stunning explanation for the mysterious results of uranium's forced transformation.

This apparatus from Otto Hahn's lab was used to produce fission reactions.

Neutrons in Italy

In 1934, the element with the most known protons was uranium, with 92. But that year, Italian physicist Enrico Fermi thought he had synthesized elements with higher atomic numbers. After bombarding a sample of uranium with neutrons, Fermi and his co-workers recorded measurements that seemed to indicate that some uranium nuclei had absorbed neutrons and then undergone beta decay:

$$^{238}_{92}\text{U} + ^{1}_{0}n \longrightarrow ^{239}_{92}\text{U} \longrightarrow ^{239}_{93}? + ^{0}_{-1}\beta$$

His report noted further subsequent beta decays, by which he hypothesized the existence of a whole new series of "transuranic" elements, now called *transuranes:*

$$^{238}_{92}\text{U} \longrightarrow ^{238}_{93}? + ^{0}_{-1}\beta \longrightarrow ^{238}_{94}?? + ^{0}_{-1}\beta \longrightarrow ^{238}_{95}??? + ^{0}_{-1}\beta$$

Unfortunately, Fermi and his group of scientists could not verify the existence of the transuranes because, according to Fermi, "We did not know enough chemistry to separate the products of uranium disintegration from one another."

Curiosity in Berlin

Fermi's experiments caught the attention of a physicist in Berlin, Lise Meitner. Knowing that she could not perform the difficult task of chemically separating radionuclides either, Meitner persuaded a colleague, radiochemist Otto Hahn, to help her explain Fermi's results. Joined by expert chemical analyst Fritz Strassman, Meitner's team began investigating neutron-induced uranium decay at the end of 1934.

From the onset, Meitner's team, as well as all other scientists at the time, operated under two false assumptions. The first involved the makeup of the bombarded nuclei. In every nuclear reaction that had been observed, the resulting nucleus had never differed from the original by more than a few protons or neutrons. Thus, scientists assumed that the products of neutron bombardment were radioisotopes of elements that were at most a few places in the periodic table before or beyond the atoms being bombarded (as Fermi had presumed in hypothesizing the transuranes).

The second assumption concerned the periodicity of the transuranes. Because the elements Ac, Th, Pa, and U chemically resemble the transition elements in the third row of the periodic table, La, Hf, Ta, and W, scientists thought that elements beyond U would correspondingly resemble those following W. Thus, the transuranes were thought to be homologues of Re, Os, Ir, Pt, and the other transition elements in the third row. This belief was generally unquestioned and seemed to be confirmed. In fact, by 1937 Hahn was sure that the chemical evidence of transuranes confirmed their location in the periodic table.

Meitner's Exile

By 1938, the political situation in Germany had become dangerous for Meitner. Because she was of Jewish descent, she was targeted by the Nazis and fled to Sweden to escape persecution. Meanwhile in Berlin, Hahn and Strassman, who were critical of the Nazis, had to be careful.

Despite being censored by the Nazis, Meitner's team continued to communicate through letters. Meitner could not formulate a satisfying physical explanation for the chemical results of Hahn and Strassman, and she insisted that her partners reexamine their findings. Because of her colleagues' great respect for her talent and expertise, they quickly performed control experiments to test their results.

A Shocking Discovery

Prompted by Meitner, Hahn and Strassman realized they had been looking in the wrong place to find the cause of their results. In analyzing a fraction of a solution assay that they had previously ignored, they found the critical evidence they had been seeking.

The analysis indicated that barium appeared to be a result of neutron bombardment of uranium. Suspecting the spectacular truth but lacking confidence, Hahn wrote to Meitner for an explanation. After consultation with her nephew, Otto Frisch, Meitner proposed that the uranium nuclei had been broken apart into elemental fragments, one of which was barium, Ba. On January 3, 1939, she wrote to Hahn to congratulate him on the ground-breaking result.

Thus, the "transuranes" turned out to be merely radioisotopes of known elements—atomic fragments of uranium atoms that had burst apart when struck by neutrons.

The politics of World War II prevented Lise Meitner from receiving the Nobel Prize in physics for explaining nuclear fission.

For the discovery of this unexpected phenomenon, which Meitner named nuclear fission, the talented Hahn was awarded the 1944 Nobel Prize in chemistry. Because of wartime politics, however, Lise Meitner did not receive the corresponding award in physics. She was not properly recognized until well after her death in 1968 for her role in clarifying the process that she first explained and named.

Questions

1. What type of element did Fermi expect to find when uranium absorbed a neutron and then ejected a beta particle?
2. What were the products of uranium disintegrations?

Answers

1. Fermi thought transuranic elements would form, because beta decay results when a neutron is changed to a proton.
2. The products were isotopes of known elements that resulted from the splitting of the uranium nucleus.

Answers

1. 1.4×10^{-6} g chromium-51
2. 8 half-lives or 420 000 years (expressed with 2 significant figures)

Math Tutor | Calculating with Half-Life

The rate at which a sample of a radioactive nuclide decays is expressed in terms of half-life. This quantity is the time required for half of the atoms of a sample of a given nuclide to decay. For example, it takes 37.2 min for half of the nuclei of chlorine-38 to decay to argon-38. After 37.2 min, 0.50 g of a 1.0 g sample of chlorine-38 will remain, and there will be 0.50 g of argon-38. After two half-lives (74.4 min), the fraction of chlorine-38 that remains will be $\frac{1}{2}$ of $\frac{1}{2}$, or $\frac{1}{4}$.

After n half-lives, the fraction of a radioactive nuclide that remains is $\left(\frac{1}{2}\right)^n$, or 2^{-n}.

If you know the amount of nuclide that was present initially and the amount of nuclide that remains, you can determine the number of half-lives that have passed.

Problem-Solving TIPS

- **Familiarize yourself with the values of some common powers of two (2^n, $n = 1, 2, 3, 4, 5, 6$, etc). This will allow you to determine the number of half-lives quickly.**

Sample Problem

The half-life of polonium-218 is 3.04 min. A sample of polonium contains 0.00558 g of $^{218}_{84}$Po. What mass of $^{218}_{84}$Po will remain after 18.24 min?

First, you must determine the number of half-lives that have passed in 18.24 min.

$$\text{number of half-lives} = \frac{\text{time elapsed}}{\text{half-life}} = \frac{18.24 \text{ min}}{3.04 \text{ min}} = 6.00 \text{ half-lives}$$

Then, to determine the mass of polonium-218 remaining, apply the following relationship:

$$\text{mass remaining} = \text{starting mass} \times \text{fraction remaining}$$

$$\text{mass } ^{218}_{84}\text{Po remaining} = 0.00558 \text{ g} \times \left(\frac{1}{2}\right)^6 = 0.00558 \text{ g} \times \frac{1}{64} = 8.72 \times 10^{-5} \text{ g } ^{218}_{84}\text{Po}$$

The half-life of potassium-40 is 1.3×10^9 years. A volcanic rock contains $\frac{1}{8}$ of the amount of potassium-40 found in newly formed rocks. When was the rock formed?

First, determine the number of half-lives that have passed.

$$\text{fraction remaining} = \frac{1}{8} = \left(\frac{1}{2}\right) \times \left(\frac{1}{2}\right) \times \left(\frac{1}{2}\right)$$

Therefore, three half-lives have passed. The time since the rock was formed is

$$3 \text{ half-lives} \times \left(1.3 \times 10^9 \frac{\text{y}}{\text{half-life}}\right) = 3.9 \times 10^9 \text{ y.}$$

Practice

1. A sample of chromium contains 8.9×10^{-5} g of the radioactive nuclide chromium-51, which has a half-life of 28 days. What mass of chromium-51 will remain in the sample after 168 days?
2. The half-life of lead-202 is 53 000 years. A sample of lead contains only $\frac{1}{256}$ of the expected amount of lead-202. How old is the lead sample?

662 Chapter 21

CHAPTER 21 Summary

PREMIUM CONTENT
Interactive Review HMDScience.com
Review Games
Concept Maps

SECTION 1 The Nucleus

- The difference between the sum of the masses of the nucleons and electrons in an atom and the actual mass of an atom is the mass defect, or nuclear binding energy.
- Nuclear stability tends to be greatest when nucleons are paired, when there are magic numbers of nucleons, and when there are certain neutron-proton ratios.
- Nuclear reactions, which are represented by nuclear equations, can involve the transmutation of nuclides.

KEY TERMS

- nucleon
- nuclide
- mass defect
- nuclear binding energy
- nuclear shell model
- magic number
- nuclear reaction
- transmutation

SECTION 2 Radioactive Decay

- Radioactive nuclides become more stable by radioactive decay.
- Alpha, beta, positron, and gamma emissions are types of radioactive decay. Electron capture is also a type of radioactive decay. The type of decay is related to the nucleon content and the energy level of the nucleus.
- The half-life of a radioactive nuclide is the length of time that it takes for half of a given number of atoms of the nuclide to decay.
- Artificial transmutations are used to produce artificial radioactive nuclides, which include the transuranium elements.

KEY TERMS

- radioactive decay
- nuclear radiation
- radioactive nuclide
- alpha particle
- beta particle
- positron
- electron capture
- gamma ray
- half-life
- decay series
- parent nuclide
- daughter nuclide
- artificial transmutation
- transuranium element

SECTION 3 Nuclear Radiation

- Alpha particles, beta particles, and gamma rays have different penetrating abilities and shielding requirements.
- Film badges, Geiger-Müller counters, and scintillation detectors are used to detect radiation.
- Everyone is exposed to environmental background radiation.
- Radioactive nuclides have many uses, including radioactive dating, disease detection, and therapy.
- Nuclear waste must be contained, stored, and disposed of in a way that minimizes harm to people or the environment.

KEY TERMS

- roentgen
- rem
- film badge
- Geiger-Müller counter
- scintillation counter
- radioactive dating
- radioactive tracer
- nuclear waste

SECTION 4 Nuclear Fission and Nuclear Fusion

- Nuclear fission and nuclear fusion are nuclear reactions in which the splitting and fusing of nuclei produce more stable nuclei and release enormous amounts of energy.
- Controlled fission reactions produce energy and radioactive nuclides.
- Fusion reactions produce the sun's energy in the form of heat and light. If fusion reactions could be controlled, they would produce more usable energy per gram of fuel than fission reactions.

KEY TERMS

- nuclear fission
- chain reaction
- critical mass
- nuclear reactor
- nuclear power plant
- shielding
- control rod
- moderator
- nuclear fusion

Review Answers

1. a. Mass defect is the mass equivalent of binding energy in the equation $E = mc^2$.
   b. Binding energy per nucleon increases as the mass number increases, until the binding energy reaches a maximum for intermediate mass nuclei (iron); then it decreases as the mass number increases.
   c. The higher the binding energy per nucleon is, the more tightly the nucleons are held together.
2. Certain ratios of neutrons to protons, even numbers of nucleons, and magic numbers of nucleons are the most stable.
3. 0.172 46 u per atom
4. 0.042 13 u per atom
5. 5.2×10^{-12} J
6. a. 4.47×10^{-11} J
   b. 2.99×10^{-11} J
   (a) releases more energy
7. a. K-35: 1.28×10^{-12} J/nucleon Na-23: 1.30×10^{-12} J/nucleon
   b. Na-23
8. 9.00×10^{-13} J/nucleon
9. a. 1 : 1 c. 1.51 : 1
   b. 2 : 1 d. 1.68 : 1
10. a. a, c
    b. (a) is close to the 1 : 1 ratio; (c) is close to the 1.5 : 1 ratio
11. a. $^{0}_{-1}\beta$ c. $^{0}_{-1}e$
    b. $^{4}_{2}He$ d. $^{13}_{6}C$
12. $^{210}_{84}Po \longrightarrow ^{4}_{2}He + ^{206}_{82}Pb$
13. $^{210}_{82}Pb \longrightarrow ^{0}_{-1}\beta + ^{210}_{83}Bi$
14. atomic number 83 and beyond
15. a. mass number decreases by four and atomic number by two
    b. increases the atomic number by one but does not change the mass number
    c. decreases the atomic number by one but does not change the mass number
    d. decreases the atomic number by one but does not change the mass number
16. alpha decay, beta decay, positron emission, and electron capture
17. Beta emission decreases the neutron-proton ratio. Positron emission and electron capture both increase the neutron-proton ratio.
18. a. $^{1}_{0}n \longrightarrow ^{1}_{1}p + ^{0}_{-1}\beta$
    b. $^{1}_{1}p \longrightarrow ^{1}_{0}n + ^{0}_{+1}\beta$
    c. $^{0}_{-1}e + ^{1}_{1}p \longrightarrow ^{1}_{0}n$
19. Beta particles are electrons that originate in the nucleus. Positrons have masses equal to those of electrons, but they are positively charged.
20. a. high-energy electromagnetic radiation
    b. Scientists think that gamma rays are produced when nuclear particles in an excited state lose energy.
21. The longer the half-life is, the greater the stability is.

CHAPTER 21 Review

SECTION 1

The Nucleus

REVIEWING MAIN IDEAS

1. a. How does mass defect relate to nuclear binding energy?
   b. How does binding energy per nucleon vary with mass number?
   c. How does binding energy per nucleon affect the stability of a nucleus?
2. Describe three ways in which the number of protons and the number of neutrons in a nucleus affect the stability of the nucleus.

PRACTICE PROBLEMS

3. The mass of a $^{20}_{10}Ne$ atom is 19.992 44 u. Calculate the atom's mass defect.
4. The mass of a $^{7}_{3}Li$ atom is 7.016 00 u. Calculate the atom's mass defect.
5. Calculate the nuclear binding energy of one lithium-6 atom. The measured atomic mass of lithium-6 is 6.015 u.
6. Calculate the binding energies of the following two nuclei, and indicate which nucleus releases more energy when formed. You will need information from the periodic table and the text.
   a. atomic mass 34.988011 u, $^{35}_{19}K$
   b. atomic mass 22.989767 u, $^{23}_{11}Na$
7. a. What is the binding energy per nucleon for each nucleus in the previous problem?
   b. Which nucleus is more stable?
8. The mass of $^{7}_{3}Li$ is 7.016 00 u. Calculate the binding energy per nucleon for $^{7}_{3}Li$.
9. Calculate the neutron-proton ratios for the following nuclides:
   a. $^{12}_{6}C$ c. $^{206}_{82}Pb$
   b. $^{3}_{1}H$ d. $^{134}_{50}Sn$
10. a. Locate the nuclides in problem 9 on the graph in **Figure 1.2**. Which ones lie within the band of stability?
    b. For the stable nuclides, determine whether their neutron-proton ratio tends toward 1:1 or 1.5:1.
11. Balance the following nuclear equations. (Hint: See Sample Problem A.)
    a. $^{43}_{19}K \longrightarrow ^{43}_{20}Ca + \underline{?}$
    b. $^{233}_{92}U \longrightarrow ^{229}_{90}Th + \underline{?}$
    c. $^{11}_{6}C + \underline{?} \longrightarrow ^{11}_{5}B$
    d. $^{13}_{7}N \longrightarrow + ^{1}_{0}\beta + \underline{?}$
12. Write the nuclear equation for the release of an alpha particle by $^{210}_{84}Po$.
13. Write the nuclear equation for the release of a beta particle by $^{210}_{82}Pb$.

SECTION 2

Radioactive Decay

REVIEWING MAIN IDEAS

14. Where on the periodic table are most of the natural radioactive nuclides located?
15. What changes in atomic number and mass number occur in each of the following types of radioactive decay?
    a. alpha emission
    b. beta emission
    c. positron emission
    d. electron capture
16. Which types of radioactive decay cause the transmutation of a nuclide? (Hint: Review the definition of *transmutation*.)
17. Explain how beta emission, positron emission, and electron capture affect the neutron-proton ratio.
18. Write the nuclear reactions that show particle conversion for the following types of radioactive decay:
    a. beta emission
    b. positron emission
    c. electron capture
19. Compare electrons, beta particles, and positrons.
20. a. What are gamma rays?
    b. How do scientists think gamma rays are produced?
21. How does the half-life of a nuclide relate to the stability of the nuclide?

664 Chapter 21

22. List the three parent nuclides of the natural decay series.

23. How are artificial radioactive isotopes produced?

24. Neutrons are more effective for bombarding atomic nuclei than protons or alpha particles are. Why?

25. Why are all of the transuranium elements radioactive? (Hint: See Section 1.)

PRACTICE PROBLEMS

26. The half-life of plutonium-239 is 24 110 years. Of an original mass of 100.g, how much plutonium-239 remains after 96 440 years? (Hint: See Sample Problem B.)

27. The half-life of thorium-227 is 18.72 days. How many days are required for three-fourths of a given amount of thorium-227 to decay?

28. Exactly $\frac{1}{16}$ of a given amount of protactinium-234 remains after 26.76 hours. What is the half-life of protactinium-234?

29. How many milligrams of a 15.0 mg sample of radium-226 remain after 6396 years? The half-life of radium-226 is 1599 years.

SECTION 3

Nuclear Radiation

REVIEWING MAIN IDEAS

30. Why can a radioactive material affect photographic film even though the film is completely wrapped in black paper?

31. How does the penetrating ability of gamma rays compare with that of alpha particles and beta particles?

32. How does nuclear radiation damage biological tissue?

33. Explain how film badges, Geiger-Müller counters, and scintillation detectors are used to detect radiation and measure radiation exposure.

34. How is the age of an object that contains a radioactive nuclide estimated?

SECTION 4

Nuclear Fission and Nuclear Fusion

REVIEWING MAIN IDEAS

35. How is the fission of a uranium-235 nucleus induced?

36. How does the fission of uranium-235 produce a chain reaction?

37. Describe the purposes of the five major components of a nuclear power plant.

38. Describe the reaction that produces the sun's energy.

39. What is one problem that must be overcome before controlled fusion reactions that produce energy are a reality?

Mixed Review

REVIEWING MAIN IDEAS

40. Balance the following nuclear reactions:
    a. $^{239}_{93}\text{Np} \longrightarrow ^{0}_{-1}\beta + \underline{?}$
    b. $^{9}_{4}\text{Be} + ^{4}_{2}\text{He} \longrightarrow \underline{?}$
    c. $^{32}_{15}\text{P} + \underline{?} \longrightarrow ^{33}_{15}\text{P}$
    d. $^{236}_{92}\text{U} \longrightarrow ^{94}_{36}\text{Kr} + \underline{?} + 3\,^{1}_{0}n$

41. After 4797 years, how much of the original 0.250 g of radium-226 remains? The half-life of radium-226 is 1599 years.

42. The parent nuclide of the thorium decay series is $^{232}_{90}\text{Th}$. The first four decays are as follows: alpha emission, beta emission, beta emission, and alpha emission. Write the nuclear equations for this series of emissions.

43. The half-life of radium-224 is 3.66 days. What was the original mass of radium-224 if 0.0500 g remains after 7.32 days?

44. Calculate the neutron-proton ratios for the following nuclides, and determine where they lie in relation to the band of stability.
    a. $^{235}_{92}\text{U}$
    b. $^{16}_{8}\text{O}$
    c. $^{56}_{26}\text{Fe}$
    d. $^{156}_{60}\text{Nd}$

45. Calculate the binding energy per nucleon of $^{238}_{92}\text{U}$ in joules. The atomic mass of a $^{238}_{92}\text{U}$ nucleus is 238.050 784 u.

CHAPTER REVIEW

22. U-238, U-235, Th-232

23. by bombarding nuclei with charged and uncharged particles

24. Neutrons do not carry any charge.

25. The repulsive force of the protons is too great for a stable nuclide to exist.

26. 6.25 g

27. 37.44 days

28. 6.69 h

29. 0.938 mg

30. Radiation can penetrate paper.

31. Gamma rays have a much greater penetrating ability.

32. It can ionize the atoms and molecules in the tissue.

33. Film badges use the exposure of film; Geiger-Müller counters count electric pulses from gas molecules ionized by the radiation; and scintillation counters convert scintillating light, which comes from substances that absorb ionizing energy and then emit visible light, to an electric signal for detection.

34. by measuring the accumulation of a daughter nuclide or the disappearance of a parent nuclide and correlating this information with the half-life of the parent nuclide

35. by bombarding the nucleus with slow neutrons

36. When slow neutrons are absorbed by uranium-235, the atom splits and emits more neutrons than were absorbed. These neutrons bombard more uranium atoms, and the process continues.

37. The fuel contains fissile material. The coolant absorbs energy as heat. The moderator slows neutrons produced by fission. Shielding keeps radiation from escaping. Control rods absorb free neutrons.

38. Hydrogen nuclei combine at an extremely high temperature and at extremely high pressure to form a helium nucleus with loss of mass and the resulting release of energy.

39. No material tolerates the temperatures required to induce fusion.

40. a. $^{239}_{94}\text{Pu}$ **c.** $^{1}_{0}n$
b. $^{13}_{6}\text{C}$ **d.** $^{139}_{56}\text{Ba}$

41. 0.0313 g

42. $^{232}_{90}\text{Th} \longrightarrow ^{4}_{2}\text{He} + ^{228}_{88}\text{Ra}$
$^{228}_{88}\text{Ra} \longrightarrow ^{0}_{-1}\beta + ^{228}_{89}\text{Ac}$
$^{228}_{89}\text{Ac} \longrightarrow ^{0}_{-1}\beta + ^{228}_{90}\text{Th}$
$^{228}_{90}\text{Th} \longrightarrow ^{4}_{2}\text{He} + ^{229}_{88}\text{Ra}$

43. 0.200 g

44. a. 1.55 : 1; outside
b. 1 : 1; within
c. 1.15 : 1; within
d. 1.60 : 1; outside

45. 1.21×10^{-12} J/nucleon

46. 8.77×10^{-28} kg

47. 2.24×10^{11} J/mol

48. Binding energy per nuclear particle is a more accurate measure of stability than total binding energy.

49. If the rate of decay varied, the length of time could not be determined from the amount of decay.

50. b; Its neutron-proton ratio is 1 : 1, and it has an even number of protons and neutrons.

51. a; It has an even number of protons and neutrons.

52. a. Potassium-40 and uranium-238 would be good choices for dating because of their long half-lives.

b. Potassium-42 and uranium-239 would be good choices for tracers because of their short half-lives.

53. The Manhattan Project started at the University of Chicago and other locations during WW II and resulted in the development of the atomic bomb.

54. The Chernobyl accident was caused partly by an unsafe test on a reactor that had an old design and few safeguards.

55. Various fusion energy projects involve the use of lasers or electromagnetic "bottles" to contain the hot fusion material. Containing this material long enough to produce a net gain in energy is still the major obstacle.

56. Benefits include noninvasiveness, the ability to image both bone and soft tissue, and the ability to pinpoint concentrations. Risks include radiation and chemical toxicity.

CHAPTER REVIEW

46. The energy released by the formation of a nucleus of $^{56}_{26}$Fe is 7.89×10^{-11} J. Use Einstein's equation, $E = mc^2$, to determine how much mass (in kilograms) is lost in this process.

47. Calculate the binding energy for one mole of deuterium atoms. The measured mass of deuterium is 2.0140 u.

CRITICAL THINKING

48. Why do we compare binding energy per nuclear particle of different nuclides instead of the total binding energy per nucleus of different nuclides?

49. Why is the constant rate of decay of radioactive nuclei so important in radioactive dating?

50. Which of the following nuclides of carbon is more likely to be stable? State reasons for your answer.

a. $^{11}_{6}$C **b.** $^{12}_{6}$C

51. Which of the following nuclides of iron is more likely to be stable? State reasons for your answer.

a. $^{56}_{26}$Fe **b.** $^{59}_{26}$Fe

52. Use the data shown below to determine the following:

a. the isotopes that would be best for dating ancient rocks

b. the isotopes that could be used as tracers

State reasons for your answers.

Element	Half-Life
potassium-40	1.28×10^9 y
potassium-42	12.36 h
uranium-238	4.468×10^9 y
uranium-239	23.47 min

RESEARCH AND WRITING

53. Investigate the history of the Manhattan Project.

54. Research the 1986 nuclear reactor accident at Chernobyl, Ukraine. What factors combined to cause the accident?

55. Find out about the various fusion-energy research projects that are being conducted in the United States and other parts of the world. What obstacles in finding an economical method of producing energy must still be overcome?

ALTERNATIVE ASSESSMENT

56. Using the library, research the medical uses of radioactive isotopes such as cobalt-60 and technetium-99. Evaluate the benefits and risks of using radioisotopes in the diagnosis and treatment of medical conditions. Report your findings to the class.

666 Chapter 21

Standards-Based Assessment

Answer the following items on a piece of paper.

MULTIPLE CHOICE

1. Complete the following nuclear equation: $? \rightarrow {}^{187}_{76}Os + {}^{0}_{-1}\beta$
   A. ${}^{187}_{77}Os$
   B. ${}^{187}_{75}Os$
   C. ${}^{187}_{77}Ir$
   D. ${}^{187}_{75}Re$

2. The mass of the nucleus is
   A. greater than the mass of the protons and neutrons that make up the nucleus.
   B. equal to the mass of the protons and neutrons that make up the nucleus.
   C. less than the mass of the protons and neutrons that make up the nucleus.
   D. converted to energy.

3. Which type of radiation has the most penetrating ability?
   A. an alpha particle
   B. a beta particle
   C. a gamma ray
   D. a neutron

4. Which two particles have the same mass but opposite charge?
   A. a beta particle and a positron
   B. a neutron and a proton
   C. a proton and an electron
   D. an alpha particle and a proton

5. Which of the following nuclear equations is correctly balanced?
   A. ${}^{37}_{18}Ar + {}^{0}_{-1}e \rightarrow {}^{37}_{17}Cl$
   B. ${}^{6}_{3}Li + 2{}^{1}_{0}n \rightarrow {}^{4}_{2}He + {}^{3}_{1}H$
   C. ${}^{254}_{99}Es + {}^{4}_{2}He \rightarrow {}^{258}_{101}Md + 2{}^{1}_{0}n$
   D. ${}^{14}_{7}N + {}^{4}_{2}He \rightarrow {}^{17}_{8}O + {}^{2}_{1}H$

6. Gamma rays
   A. have the same energy as beta particles do.
   B. are visible light.
   C. have no charge and no mass.
   D. are not a form of electromagnetic radiation.

7. Which of the following nuclides is radioactive?
   A. ${}^{40}_{20}Ca$
   B. ${}^{226}_{88}Ra$
   C. ${}^{12}_{6}C$
   D. ${}^{206}_{82}Pb$

8. The half-life of thorium-234 is 24 days. If you have a 42.0 g sample of thorium-24, how much will remain after 72 days?
   A. 42.0 g
   B. 21.0 g
   C. 10.5 g
   D. 5.25 g

9. It takes 5.2 min for a 4.0 g sample of francium-210 to decay until only 1.0 g is left. What is the half-life of francium-210?
   A. 1.3 min
   B. 2.6 min
   C. 5.2 min
   D. 7.8 min

SHORT ANSWER

10. Write the nuclear equation that represents the process in which a neutron in the nucleus is changed to a proton with the emission of a beta particle.

11. Describe a positron, and write its nuclear symbol.

EXTENDED RESPONSE

12. Explain the difference between nuclear fission and nuclear fusion, and explain the energy changes that accompany each process.

13. What is meant by the term *mass defect*?

Test Tip

Keeping a positive attitude during any test will help you focus on the test and likely improve your score.

STANDARDS-BASED ASSESSMENT

To give students practice under more realistic testing conditions, give them 60 minutes to answer all of the questions in this Standardized Test Preparation.

Test Answers

1. D
2. C
3. C
4. A
5. A
6. C
7. B
8. D
9. B
10. ${}^{1}_{0}n \longrightarrow {}^{1}_{1}p + {}^{0}_{-1}\beta$
11. A positron is a positively charged particle with the same mass as a beta particle, ${}^{0}_{+1}\beta$
12. Fission occurs when a heavy nuclide is bombarded with nucleons, such as neutrons and disintegrates into two smaller nuclides producing more neutrons and energy. Fusion occurs when two light nuclides combine to form a heavier nuclide and energy.
13. A nuclide is made of a certain number of protons, neutrons, and electrons. The mass of a nuclide is less than the mass of the nuclide's constituent protons, neutrons, and electrons. The difference in mass is the mass defect, and the difference in mass represents the binding energy of the nucleus.

Organic Chemistry

① Core Instruction

Chapter Resources

- The Teacher's Edition wrap has extensive teaching support for every lesson, including Misconception Alerts, Teach from Visuals, Demonstrations, Teaching Tips, Differentiated Instruction, and Problem Solving support.
- Several additional presentation tools are available online for every chapter, including Animated Chemistry features and Visual Concepts.
- You can open your lesson with the Why It Matters Video: Organic Chemistry.

Section	Instruction	Labs and Demonstrations Go Online for Materials Lists and Solutions Lists.
22.1	■ **Textbook:** Organic Compounds **Teaching Visuals:** Types of Molecular Models • Allotropes of Carbon • Representations of Methane • The Tetrahedron • Properties of Diamond and Graphite **PowerPresentations**	■ **Demonstration:** Isomers of Pentane and Hexane ■ **Lab:** Carbon (Core Skill)
22.2	■ **Textbook:** Hydrocarbons **Animated Chemistry:** Functional Groups **Teaching Visuals:** Bonding in Ethene • Alkanes • Alkenes • Resonance Structures of Benzene • Carbon Atom Chain Prefixes • Names of Alkanes • Straight-Chain Alkane Nomenclature **PowerPresentations**	■ **Lab:** Cleaning Up Oil Spills (STEM)
22.3	■ **Textbook:** Functional Groups **Teaching Visuals:** Alcohol: Glycerol • Alkyl Halide: Teflon • Aldehydes and Ketones • Carboxylic Acid: Citric Acid • Ester • Amine • Common Flavors and Odors of Esters • Some Classes of Organic Compounds • Comparing Classes of Organic Compounds • Common Organic Functional Groups • Carboxylic Acids Found in Plants and Animals • Naming Compounds with Functional Groups **PowerPresentations**	■ **Lab:** A Cloth of Many Colors
22.4	■ **Textbook:** Organic Reactions **Teaching Visuals:** Hydrogenation of Fatty Acid • Fatty Acid Composition of Dietary Fats • Forms of Polyethylene • Comparing Structures of Saturated and Unsaturated Fatty Acids • Addition Polymers • Recycling Codes for Plastic Products **PowerPresentations**	■ **Demonstration:** Testing for Double Bonds ■ **Lab:** Polymers and Toy Balls ■ **Lab:** Polymers (Core Skill) ■ **Lab:** The Slime Challenge

Find all of your resources online at HMDScience.com.

② Support and Intervention

- **Interactive Reader** (English and Spanish)
- **Study Guide**
- **Interactive Review:** Review Games, Concept Maps, and Section Self-Checks
- **Scientific Reasoning Skill Builder**
- **Learn It! Videos**
- **Solve It! Cards**
- **Interactive Demos**
- **Sample Problem Sets**

③ Specialized Support

- **Chapter Summary Audio Files**
- **Interactive Reader Audio Files**
- **Differentiated Instruction:** Inclusion, Below Level, and English Learners (TE wrap)

Enrichment and Challenge

- **Differentiated Instruction:** Pre-AP (TE wrap)
- **Chemistry Explorers:** The Beginnings of Organic Chemistry (SE)
- **WebLinks**

Assessment

- **Section Formative Assessments** (SE)
- **Section Quizzes**
- **Chapter Review** (SE)
- **Chapter Tests A and B**
- **Alternative Assessment** (TE wrap)
- **Online Assessment and Remediation**
- **ExamView Banks**

Where do I find it?

	Resource	PRINT	DVD	ONLINE
1	Animated Chemistry		■	■
1	Demonstrations (TE wrap)	■		■
1	Interactive Whiteboard		■	■
1	Labs		■	■
1	PowerPresentations		■	■
1	QuickLabs	■	■	■
1	Teaching Visuals		■	■
1	Textbook	■	■	■
1	Visual Concepts		■	■
1	Why It Matters Videos		■	■
2	Interactive Demos		■	■
2	Interactive Reader	■	■	■
2	Interactive Reviews		■	■
2	Learn It! Videos		■	■
2	Sample Problem Sets		■	■
2	Scientific Reasoning Skill Builder		■	■
2	Smart Grapher Tool		■	■
2	Solve It! Cards		■	■
2	Study Guide		■	■
3	Chapter Summary Audio Files		■	■
3	Differentiated Instruction (TE wrap)	■		
3	Interactive Reader Audio Files		■	■

CHAPTER 22

Chapter Overview

Section 1 describes carbon bonding as the key to the diversity of organic compounds and introduces structural formulas and isomers.

Section 2 discusses formulas, structures, properties, and naming of hydrocarbons (alkanes, alkenes, alkynes, and aromatic hydrocarbons).

Section 3 introduces functional groups and classes of organic compounds and emphasizes properties and uses of each class.

Section 4 summarizes some types of organic reactions and discusses the main classes of polymers.

▼ Focus and Motivate

Activate Prior Knowledge

Students may need a review of the following concepts:

- electron configurations
- hybridization and covalent bonding
- intermolecular attraction with liquids and solids

About the Image

Nanotubes and buckminsterfullerene balls are molecules that contain repeated hexagons of carbon atoms. Before the discovery of these molecules, the only other known carbon allotropes were graphite and diamond. In graphite, carbon atoms are arranged in a hexagonal pattern, and in diamond, they are arranged in a tetrahedral pattern. The rainbow pattern in the image is a graph of the electron distribution around the molecules of a nanotube.

Why It Matters

Students can access the video online and find other helpful resources at **HMDScience.com**.

CHAPTER 22
Organic Chemistry

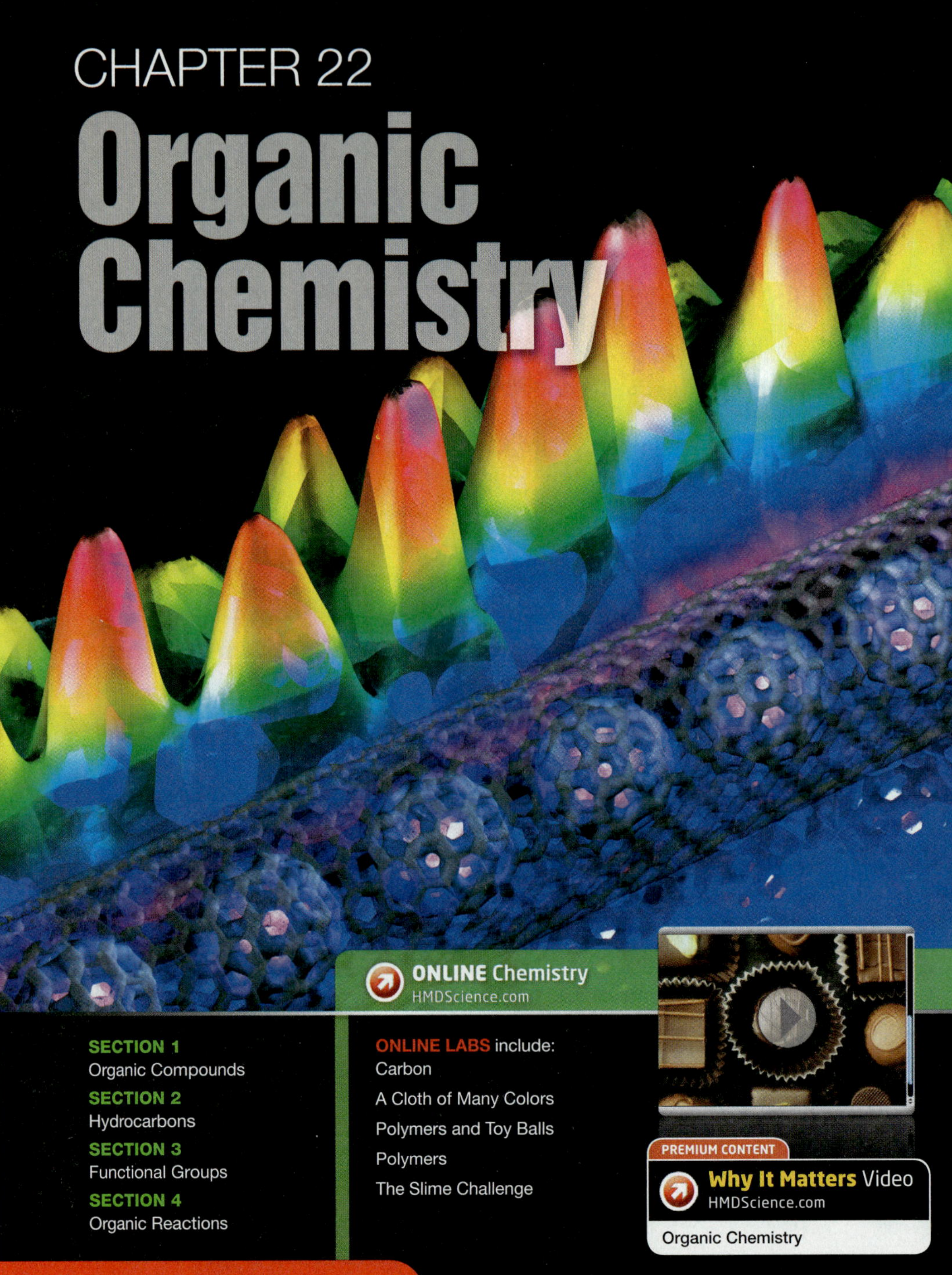

ONLINE Chemistry
HMDScience.com

SECTION 1
Organic Compounds

SECTION 2
Hydrocarbons

SECTION 3
Functional Groups

SECTION 4
Organic Reactions

ONLINE LABS include:
Carbon
A Cloth of Many Colors
Polymers and Toy Balls
Polymers
The Slime Challenge

PREMIUM CONTENT
Why It Matters Video
HMDScience.com
Organic Chemistry

Lab Preview

The following labs and demonstrations support the concepts presented in this chapter.

LABS

Carbon (Core Skill)
A Cloth of Many Colors
Polymers and Toy Balls
Polymers (Core Skill)
The Slime Challenge
Cleaning Up Oil Spills (STEM)

DEMONSTRATIONS

Isomers of Pentane and Hexane
Testing for Double Bonds

Organic Compounds

Key Terms

organic compound
catenation
hydrocarbon
isomer
structural formula
structural isomer
geometric isomer

SECTION 1

Main Ideas

- The uniqueness of carbon bonding results in many organic compounds.
- Structural formulas show the numbers, types, and arrangement of the atoms in a molecule.
- Isomers can be structural or geometric.

All organic compounds contain carbon atoms. However, not all carbon-containing compounds are classified as organic. There are a few exceptions, such as Na_2CO_3, CO, and CO_2, that are considered inorganic. **We can define organic compounds as covalently bonded compounds containing carbon, excluding carbonates and oxides. Figure 1.1** shows a few familiar items that contain organic compounds.

MAIN IDEA

The uniqueness of carbon bonding results in many organic compounds.

The diversity of organic compounds results from the uniqueness of carbon's structure and bonding. Carbon's electronic structure allows it to bind to itself to form chains and rings, to bind covalently to other elements, and to bind to itself and other elements in different arrangements.

FIGURE 1.1

Organic Compounds Aspirin, polyethylene in plastic bags, citric acid in fruit, and amino acids in animals are all examples of organic compounds.

Differentiated Instruction

BELOW LEVEL

Help students understand how carbon's structure and bonding enable it to create such a diversity of molecular compounds. Have one student stand and stretch out his or her arms. Tell the class that the student represents an oxygen atom, and the outstretched arms represent the two covalent bonds that an oxygen atom can form.

Then ask two more students to stand back-to-back and stretch out their arms. Tell the class that these two students represent a carbon atom, and their arms represent the four covalent bonds that a carbon atom can form. Have students explain why the carbon atom can form a greater variety of compounds.

SECTION 1

Plan and Prepare

Objectives

Upon completion of this section, students should be able to do the following:

- Explain how the structure and bonding of carbon lead to the diversity of organic compounds.
- Compare the use of molecular and structural formulas to represent organic compounds.
- Compare structural and geometric isomers of organic compounds.

Classroom Catalyst

Begin this lesson with a group-puzzle exercise. Before class, draw twenty 1.5 × 1.5 in. boxes on a sheet of paper. Draw a circle in each box. Write the letter *C* inside six of these circles, and add four lines from each circle to the sides of its box to represent four bonds. Write the letter *H* inside the remaining 14 circles, and add a single line from the circle to one side of the square for one bond.

Divide students into groups of three. Provide each group with a copy of the puzzle and a pair of scissors. Ask them to develop as many different molecules as possible in five minutes using all of the atoms and all of the bonds. Compare the results. Ask the students how they could do this exercise three-dimensionally. Would anything change? How would it be different?

Teach

Teaching Tip

Using models will help students visualize the structures of the molecules covered in this chapter. Many commercial ball-and-stick and space-filling models are available. It is a good idea to have at least one of these for demonstration purposes.

▼ Teach *continued*

Teaching Tip

- The structural formula of ethanol:

$$\begin{array}{c} \text{H}\quad\text{H} \\ |\quad\;| \\ \text{H}-\text{C}-\text{C}-\text{OH} \\ |\quad\;| \\ \text{H}\quad\text{H} \end{array}$$

- The structural formula of dimethyl ether:

$$\begin{array}{c} \text{H}\qquad\;\text{H} \\ |\qquad\;\;| \\ \text{H}-\text{C}-\text{O}-\text{C}-\text{H} \\ |\qquad\;\;| \\ \text{H}\qquad\;\text{H} \end{array}$$

- Be sure students recognize the difference between a two-dimensional representation and a three-dimensional representation. A two-dimensional representation of CH_4 appears to have 90° angles between hydrocarbon bonds. A three-dimensional representation shows the more realistic 109° angle. As students write and use structural formulas, constantly remind them that even as they write a two-dimensional representation, they should be thinking in three dimensions.

READING TOOLKIT

INTERPRETING VOCABULARY

Explain that the word *catenation* comes from the Latin word *catena*, which means "chain." Tell students that carbon is one of just a few elements capable of forming chains and rings by bonding to other atoms of the same element. Silicon, for example, also exhibits some catenation, but carbon exhibits catenation more than any other element.

FIGURE 1.2

Carbon-Carbon Bonds Compare the shape of a fatty acid found in cream with that of fructose, found in fruit. In the fatty acid, the carbon atoms are in chains. In fructose, carbon atoms form a ring.

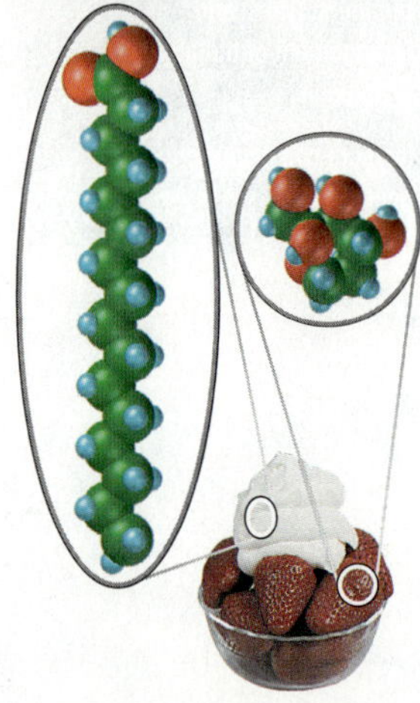

FIGURE 1.3

Carbon and Other Elements In firefly luciferin, carbon atoms bind to hydrogen, oxygen, nitrogen, and sulfur. Luciferin is responsible for the light emitted from the tail of a firefly.

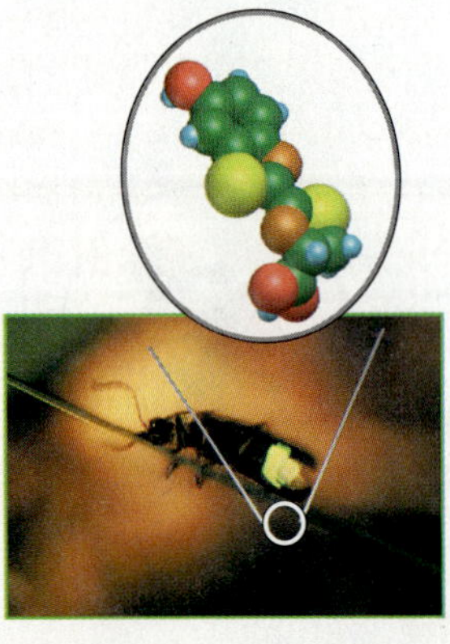

Carbon-Carbon Bonding

Carbon atoms are unique in their ability to form long chains and rings of covalently bonded atoms. **This type of bonding is known as catenation, the covalent bonding of an element to itself to form chains or rings.** In addition, carbon atoms in these structures can be linked by single, double, or triple covalent bonds. Examples of molecules containing carbon-atom rings and chains are shown in **Figure 1.2.**

Carbon Bonding to Other Elements

Besides being able to bind to each other, carbon atoms bind readily to elements with similar electronegativities. Organic compounds consist of carbon and these other elements. **Hydrocarbons are composed of only carbon and hydrogen; they are the simplest organic compounds.** Other organic compounds contain hydrocarbon backbones to which other elements, primarily O, N, S, and the halogens, are attached. **Figure 1.3** shows a molecule in which carbon atoms are bound to other elements.

Arrangement of Atoms

The bonding capabilities of carbon also allow for different arrangements of atoms. This means that some compounds may contain the same atoms but have different properties because the atoms are arranged differently. For example, the molecular formula C_2H_6O represents both ethanol and dimethyl ether. **Compounds that have the same molecular formula but different structures are called isomers.**

MAIN IDEA

Structural formulas show the numbers, types, and arrangement of the atoms in a molecule.

Organic chemists use structural formulas to represent organic compounds. This is necessary in order to show the difference between isomers of a compound. **A structural formula indicates the number and types of atoms present in a molecule and also shows the bonding arrangement of the atoms.** An example of a structural formula for an isomer of C_4H_{10} is the following.

$$\begin{array}{ccccc} \text{H} & & \text{H} & & \text{H} \\ | & & | & & | \\ \text{H}-\text{C} & - & \text{C} & - & \text{C}-\text{H} \\ | & & | & & | \\ \text{H} & & \text{H}-\text{C}-\text{H} & & \text{H} \\ & & | & & \\ & & \text{H} & & \end{array}$$

Structural formulas are sometimes condensed so they are easier to read. In one type, the hydrogen single covalent bonds are not shown. The atoms are understood to bind to the atom they are written beside.

Differentiated Instruction

INCLUSION

Help tactile and visual learners understand the concepts of structural formulas and isomers. Give pairs of students molecular model kits. Tell them that they will use four carbon atoms and ten hydrogen atoms to construct two different molecules. First, ask students to build the isomer whose structural formula is shown on this page. Also have them write the compound's molecular formula. C_4H_{10} Next, have students build another isomer of the molecule and explain why the structure represents an isomer.

ENGLISH LEARNERS

The prefix *iso-* means "equal" in Greek. Ask students about the term *isotope* and its meaning. Isotopes have the same number of protons but varying numbers of neutrons. Isotope means "same element." Tell students that the term *isomers* has a related meaning. It refers to two molecules that have the same chemical composition (same number and type of atoms) but are arranged differently.

The following structural and condensed structural formulas represent the same molecule.

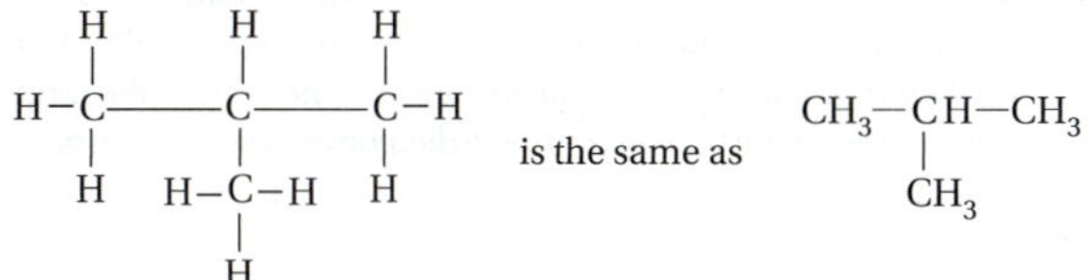

is the same as

$CH_3-CH-CH_3$ (with CH_3 attached to the central carbon)

Remember that the structural formula does not accurately show the three-dimensional shape of the molecule. Three-dimensional shape is depicted with drawings or models, as shown for ethanol in **Figure 1.4.**

MAIN IDEA

Isomers can be structural or geometric.

You have learned that isomers are compounds that have the same molecular formula but different structural formulas. Isomers can be further classified by structure and geometry.

Structural Isomers

Structural isomers, also called "constitutional isomers," are isomers in which the atoms are bonded together in different orders. For example, the atoms of the molecular formula C_4H_{10} can be arranged in two different ways.

```
  H H H H        H       H       H
  | | | |        |       |       |
H-C-C-C-C-H    H-C-------C-------C-H
  | | | |        |       |       |
  H H H H        H     H-C-H     H
                         |
                         H
```

butane — 2-methylpropane

Notice that the formula for butane shows a continuous chain of four carbon atoms, but the formula of 2-methylpropane shows a continuous chain of three carbon atoms, with the fourth carbon atom attached to the second carbon atom of the chain. Structural isomers can have different properties. For example, butane and 2-methylpropane have different melting points, boiling points, and densities, as shown in **Figure 1.5.**

FIGURE 1.5

PHYSICAL PROPERTIES OF THE STRUCTURAL ISOMERS BUTANE AND 2-METHYLPROPANE

	Melting point (°C)	Boiling point (°C)	Density at 20°C (g/mL)
butane	−138.4	−0.5	0.5788
2-methylpropane	−159.4	−11.633	0.549

FIGURE 1.4

Structural and Condensed Formulas The structure of ethanol can be represented in different ways. Ball-and-stick and space-filling models represent the three-dimensional shape of the molecule.

```
  H  OH
  |  |
H-C--C-H
  |  |
  H  H
```

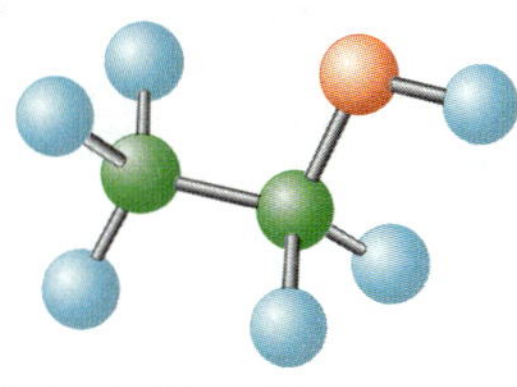

Ball-and-stick model

Space-filling model

CHECK FOR UNDERSTANDING

Explain Why would using structural formulas help chemists understand the shapes of geometric isomers?

TEACH FROM VISUALS

FIGURE 1.4 Have students make a ball-and-stick model for ethanol using gumdrops and toothpicks. Use large gumdrops of one color for C and another color for O. Use small gumdrops for H. After the students have finished the model, have them push the gumdrops together into a compact form to approximate the space-filling model.

Teaching Tip

Some students may have difficulty recognizing whether two molecules are isomers or actually the same molecule from a different perspective. This visual reasoning is quite different from the reasoning required to solve problems. Look for students who can easily determine whether formulas represent isomers. This may be an opportunity to acknowledge students who do not do well in the mathematics-heavy portions of the course.

Demonstration

ISOMERS OF PENTANE AND HEXANE

Have students use **models** to construct the isomers of C_5H_{12} (pentane) and C_6H_{14} (hexane). Have them draw the structural formulas for each isomer they build. How does the number of possible pentane isomers compare with the number of possible hexane isomers? There are many more hexane isomers than pentane isomers.

TEACH FROM TABLES

FIGURE 1.5 Point out the differences in melting and boiling points for the two butane isomers, and then explain the difference in terms of intermolecular attraction.

Check for Understanding

Answer: Structural formulas show the geometry of the compound.

PRE-AP

Have students research optical isomers. Optical isomers are two compounds that contain the same number and kinds of atoms and bonds, but different spatial arrangements of the atoms, resulting in non-superimposable mirror images. Each non-superimposable mirror image structure is called an *enantiomer*. Molecules or ions that exist as optical isomers are called *chiral*. Chiral molecules are important in the pharmaceutical industry, because the correct optical isomer of a drug must be developed so that it can fit properly into its target within the body.

Optical isomers get their name because the plane of plane-polarized light that is passed through a sample of a pure enantiomer is rotated. The plane is rotated in the opposite direction, but with the same magnitude, when plane-polarized light is passed through a pure sample containing the other enantiomer of a pair.

▼ Teach *continued*

Teaching Tip

Students can determine whether two molecules that have double bonds are geometric isomers by trying to superimpose three-dimensional models on top of one another. Simplify the models by representing each group attached to a carbon atom in the double bond with a single ball of a different color. If students cannot turn or twist one molecule so that it matches the other exactly, then the two molecules are geometric isomers.

▼ Assess and Reteach

Assess Use the Formative Assessment on this page to evaluate student mastery of the section.

Reteach For students who need additional instruction, download the Section Study Guide.

Response to Intervention To reassess students' mastery, use the Section Quiz, available to print or to take directly online at **HMDScience.com**.

FIGURE 1.6

Geometric Isomers in Nature Males of the Iowa strain of the European corn borer respond most strongly to mixtures of the female sex attractant pheromone that are 96% *cis* isomer. But males of the New York strain respond most strongly to mixtures containing 97% *trans* isomer.

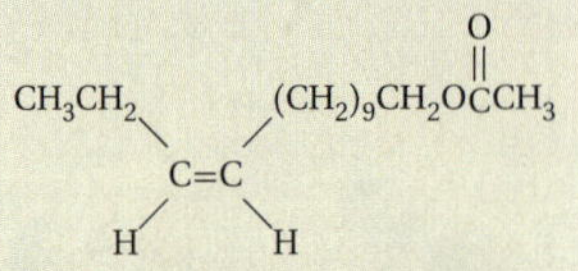

$$\begin{array}{ccc} CH_3CH_2 & & (CH_2)_9CH_2O\overset{O}{\overset{\|}{C}}CH_3 \\ & \diagdown \; \diagup & \\ & C{=}C & \\ & \diagup \; \diagdown & \\ H & & H \end{array}$$

cis-11-tetradecenyl acetate

$$\begin{array}{ccc} H & & (CH_2)_9CH_2O\overset{O}{\overset{\|}{C}}CH_3 \\ & \diagdown \; \diagup & \\ & C{=}C & \\ & \diagup \; \diagdown & \\ CH_3CH_2 & & H \end{array}$$

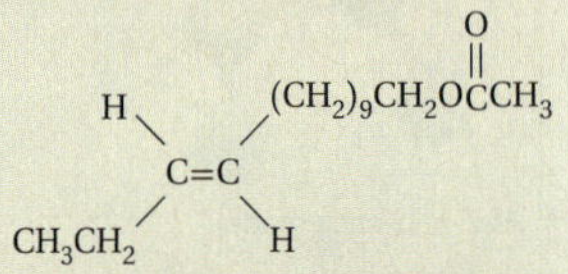

trans-11-tetradecenyl acetate

Geometric Isomers

Geometric isomers are isomers in which the order of atom bonding is the same but the arrangement of atoms in space is different. Consider the molecule 1,2-dichloroethene, which contains a double bond. The double bond prevents free rotation and holds groups to either side of the molecule. This means there can be two different 1,2-dichloroethene geometric isomers, as shown below.

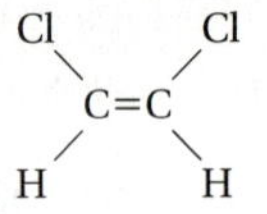

$$\begin{array}{ccc} Cl & & Cl \\ & \diagdown \; \diagup & \\ & C{=}C & \\ & \diagup \; \diagdown & \\ H & & H \end{array} \qquad\qquad \begin{array}{ccc} H & & Cl \\ & \diagdown \; \diagup & \\ & C{=}C & \\ & \diagup \; \diagdown & \\ Cl & & H \end{array}$$

cis 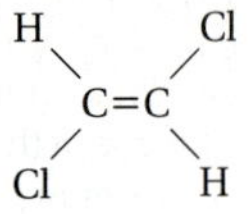   *trans*

The geometric isomer with the two chlorine atoms on the same side of the molecule is called *cis*. The isomer with the chlorine atoms on opposite sides of the molecule is called *trans*. This particular form has been in the news a great deal in recent years, due to research showing the harmfulness of trans fats in the human diet. **Figure 1.6** shows an example of geometric isomers that occur in nature.

The difference in properties between two geometric isomers can be very small or very large, depending on the type of bonding in them. Sometimes, the arrangement of the atoms in the *trans* formation enables the molecules to pack together more easily, and so increases the melting point of the isomer. Similarly, if the arrangement increases the intramolecular forces between two molecules, as a consequence of the polarity of the bonds, the boiling point of that isomer will be higher, because the molecules are held together more strongly.

SECTION 1 FORMATIVE ASSESSMENT

Reviewing Main Ideas

1. Which of the following represent the same molecule?

a. 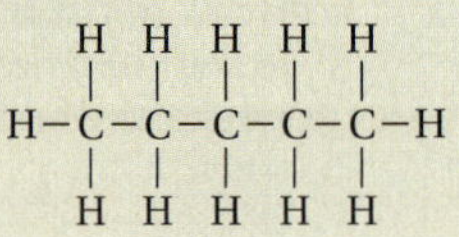
$$\begin{array}{c} H\ \ H\ \ H\ \ H\ \ H \\ |\ \ \ |\ \ \ |\ \ \ |\ \ \ | \\ H-C-C-C-C-C-H \\ |\ \ \ |\ \ \ |\ \ \ |\ \ \ | \\ H\ \ H\ \ H\ \ H\ \ H \end{array}$$

b. $CH_3-CH_2-CH_2-CH_3$

c. 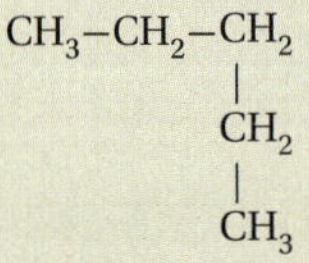
$$\begin{array}{l} CH_3-CH_2-CH_2 \\ \qquad\qquad\quad | \\ \qquad\qquad CH_2 \\ \qquad\qquad\quad | \\ \qquad\qquad CH_3 \end{array}$$

d. C_5H_{12}

2. What are three characteristics of carbon that contribute to the diversity of organic compounds?

3. Define the term *isomer*, and distinguish between structural and geometric isomers.

4. Which of the following types of molecular representations can be used to show differences between isomers? Explain why each can or cannot.
   - **a.** molecular formula
   - **b.** structural formula
   - **c.** three-dimensional drawing or model

Critical Thinking

5. **INTERPRETING CONCEPTS** Can molecules that have molecular formulas C_4H_{10} and $C_4H_{10}O$ be isomers of one another? Why or why not?

Answers to Section Assessment

1. **a, c,** and **d**
2. its ability to bind to itself to form chains and rings, its ability to bind with other elements, and its ability to bind to itself and other elements in different arrangements
3. Compounds that have the same molecular formula but different structures are isomers. Structural isomers have atoms bonded together in a different order. Geometric isomers have atoms bonded in the same order, but the arrangement of atoms in space is different.
4. **a.** A molecular formula cannot show the difference between isomers because it shows only the ratio of atoms involved. It does not show how the atoms are arranged.
   b. and **c.** A structural formula and a three-dimensional drawing or model can be used to show differences between isomers because they can show the order in which atoms are bonded together and arranged in space.
5. They cannot be isomers because they have different chemical compositions.

Chemistry EXPLORERS

The Beginnings of Organic Chemistry

Today, "organic chemistry" refers to the study of carbon compounds. However, organic chemistry was originally thought of as unique among all chemical sciences, because it emphasized the study of compounds that came from living organisms. Chemists of the early 19th century viewed organic compounds as fundamentally different from inorganic compounds, such as rocks and minerals, because organic compounds seemed to come only from living things. But because living organisms are built from carbon-containing molecules, organic chemistry later came to mean the study of carbon compounds, including those that are manufactured artificially.

Like modern researchers, early chemists were interested in the workings of the body. They tried to characterize the chemicals in blood, tissue, and urine. Urea, the molecule that the human body excretes to get rid of ammonia waste, was first isolated from urine in 1773. Although scientists could successfully isolate urea and other organic compounds, they did not know how to synthesize—that is, make from other, simpler chemicals—organic compounds. This tended to confirm a commonly-held belief, called *vitalism*, that organic compounds could only be made inside living organisms with the help of a special life force known as the "vital force."

In 1828, the young German chemist Friedrich Wöhler announced that he had been able to make urea from inorganic chemicals. Wöhler had been attempting to prepare ammonium cyanate, NH_4OCN, from inorganic compounds, such as silver cyanate and ammonium chloride. But Wöhler unintentionally synthesized urea as a byproduct of the reactions that he carried out! Wöhler made an exciting discovery—the first example of organic synthesis—by using the same principles of qualitative analysis used by chemists today.

The remainder of the 19th century saw the syntheses of many other organic compounds. In 1845, acetic acid was prepared in several steps from charcoal. Many other organic molecules, such as dyes and glucose (blood sugar), were synthesized in the last half of the 19th century. Gradually, as more natural products were prepared in chemistry laboratories, the concept of vitalism was abandoned.

Friedrich Wöhler was the first person to synthesize an organic compound from inorganic chemicals.

Interestingly, the newly synthesized, organic compounds made their biggest "splash," you might say, in the dye industry. When he was only 18 years old, the chemist William Perkin discovered that an extraction from coal tar produced a very dark purple color. He found that the color would not wash out of clothing, and so he realized that it could be used as a practical synthetic dye. The discovery, coming as it did in the mid-19th century, coincided with advances in textile manufacturing. Perkin's color, called *mauveine* or *mauve*, became an instant hit. Purple had long been a color associated with aristocracy, and one not easily captured and held in a cloth for any length of time. Perkin's dye brought this color to everyone.

Today, urea, acetic acid, and many other organic chemicals are produced in huge quantities. Organic chemists can synthesize complex drug molecules, such as penicillin and taxol, which were once available only from natural sources. Using methods of organic synthesis, chemists can also prepare completely new drugs, polymers, flavors, and dyes that are not present in nature.

Questions

1. What do people usually mean by the term *organic* when they use it to describe food, such as fruits and vegetables?
2. Think of three things that you use in your everyday life and that an organic chemist might be able to make.

ChemisTrivia

Wöhler actually did make his target molecule, ammonium cyanate, during his accidental preparation of urea. However, when he tried to dry this product by heating it, the ammonium cyanate was converted into urea.

Answers

1. The use of the term *organic* to describe certain foods closely reflects the original definition of the term, in that only chemicals that are naturally present are used to grow these foods (no pesticides or additives). Carbon-containing compounds are present in all foods!
2. Answers will vary. Possibilities include medications (aspirin), clothing (polyester and nylon), cosmetics, and items made out of plastics.

SECTION 2

▼ Plan and Prepare

Objectives

Upon completion of this section, students should be able to do the following:

- Distinguish between the structures of alkanes, alkenes, alkynes, and aromatic hydrocarbons.
- Write structural formulas and names for alkanes, alkenes, and alkynes.
- Relate properties of different types of hydrocarbons to their structures.

Classroom Catalyst

Write the structural formulas of methane, ethane, propane, and butane on the board. Ask students to predict the formula for the next hydrocarbon in the series. Use these structures to introduce the alkane homologous series. Have students confirm that each formula follows the C_nH_{2n+2} rule for saturated alkanes. Have students predict the molecular formula for the alkane with 15 carbon atoms.

▼ Teach

READING TOOLKIT

READING ORGANIZER Have students read Section 2 and organize the information in a table titled "Organic Compounds." Students should include the following information about saturated hydrocarbons: basic structural characteristics, rules for naming, properties, uses, and examples. Students should also list any subcategories that exist, such as alkanes and cycloalkanes. Finally, students should draw condensed structural formulas for representative examples and correctly name them. Tell students to keep their tables so they can add to them as they learn more about organic compounds.

SECTION 2

Main Ideas

- Alkanes contain only single bonds.
- Cycloalkanes have a ringed structure.
- Organic compounds have systematic names.
- The properties of alkanes are related to the lengths of their carbon chains.
- Unsaturated hydrocarbons have at least one carbon-carbon double bond.

Hydrocarbons

Key Terms

saturated hydrocarbon
alkane
cycloalkane
alkyl group
natural gas
petroleum
unsaturated hydrocarbon
alkene
alkyne
aromatic hydrocarbon
benzene

Hydrocarbons are compounds that contain only carbon and hydrogen. They make up the simplest class of organic compounds. All other organic compounds can be viewed as hydrocarbons in which one or more hydrogen atoms have been replaced by other atoms or groups of atoms.

Hydrocarbons are grouped mainly by the type of bonding between carbon atoms. **Saturated hydrocarbons** **are hydrocarbons in which each carbon atom in the molecule forms four single covalent bonds with other atoms.**

MAIN IDEA

Alkanes contain only single bonds.

Hydrocarbons that contain only single bonds are alkanes. In **Figure 2.1,** the molecular formulas, structural formulas, and space-filling models are given for alkanes with one to four carbon atoms. If you examine the molecular formulas for successive alkanes in **Figure 2.1,** you will see a clear pattern. Each member of the series differs from the preceding one by one carbon atom and two hydrogen atoms. For example, propane, C_3H_8, differs from ethane, C_2H_6, by one carbon atom and two hydrogen atoms, a —CH_2— group.

```
    H  H             H  H  H
    |  |             |  |  |
 H−C−C−H         H−C−C−C−H
    |  |             |  |  |
    H  H             H  H  H
   ethane           propane
```

Compounds that differ in this fashion belong to a *homologous series*. A homologous series is one in which adjacent members differ by a constant unit. It is not necessary to remember the molecular formulas for all members of a homologous series. Instead, a general molecular formula can be used to determine the formulas. Look at the molecular formulas for ethane and propane, C_2H_6 and C_3H_8. They both fit the formula C_nH_{2n+2}. For ethane, $n = 2$, so there are two carbon atoms and $(2 \times 2) + 2 = 6$ hydrogen atoms. For propane, $n = 3$, so there are three carbon atoms and $(2 \times 3) + 2 = 8$ hydrogen atoms. Now consider a molecule for which we do not know the molecular formula. Suppose a member of this series has 30 carbon atoms in its molecules. Then $n = 30$, and there are $(2 \times 30) + 2 = 62$ hydrogen atoms. The formula is $C_{30}H_{62}$. Incidentally, an alkane with this formula, known as *squalane*, does exist and is a component in some moisturizers.

Differentiated Instruction

ENGLISH LEARNERS

Relate the term *saturated* to what students read on nutrition labels. Fats come in saturated and unsaturated varieties. Ask students to explain saturation in their own words. thoroughly full or soaked; can absorb no more. Emphasize that *saturated hydrocarbons* refers to molecules that cannot absorb any more hydrogen atoms.

FIGURE 2.1

ALKANES WITH ONE TO FOUR CARBON ATOMS

Molecular formulas	Structural formulas	Space-filling models
CH_4	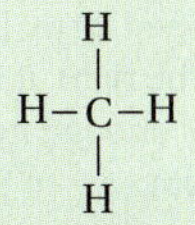 methane	
C_2H_6	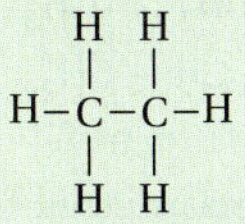 ethane	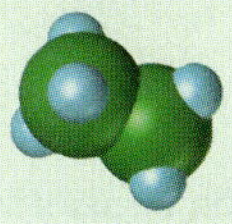
C_3H_8	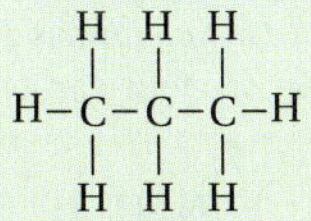 propane	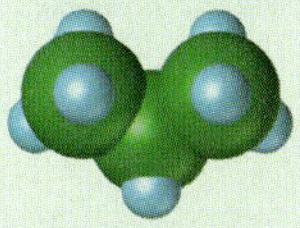
C_4H_{10}	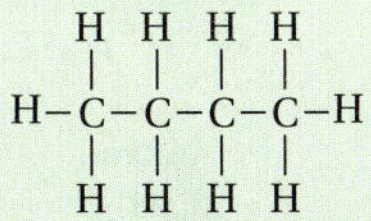 butane	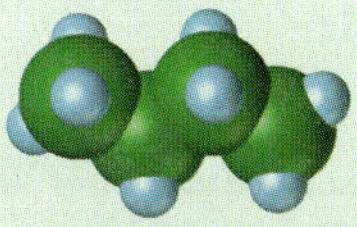
	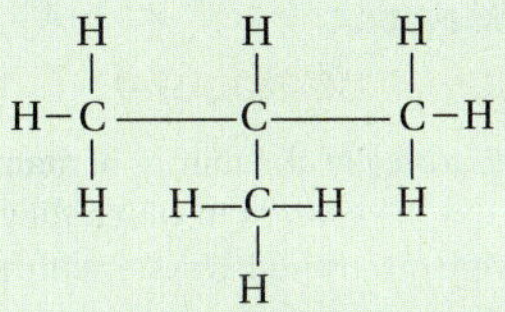 2-methylpropane	

Notice that for alkanes with three or fewer carbon atoms, only one molecular structure is possible. However, in alkanes with more than three carbon atoms, the chains can be straight or branched. Thus, alkanes with four or more carbon atoms have structural isomers. There are two possible structural isomers for alkanes with four carbon atoms, butane and 2-methylpropane.

The number of structural isomers increases greatly as the number of carbon atoms in alkanes increases. There are three isomeric C_5H_{12} alkanes, five isomeric C_6H_{14} alkanes, and nine isomeric C_7H_{16} alkanes. There are nearly 37 million possible isomers of $C_{25}H_{52}$, although most have never been prepared or isolated.

TEACH FROM TABLES

FIGURE 2.1 Point out that each of the formulas is part of a homologous series—they differ by a constant unit. Ask students why there are no isomers listed for the hydrocarbons with only one, two, or three carbon atoms.

Teaching Tip

Help students understand the concept that all alkanes are saturated hydrocarbons. Have students use molecular model kits to build butane. Point out that there are four carbon atoms. Students should use the generalized formula for an alkane to determine the number of hydrogen atoms present. Students should then assemble the molecule, showing only single bonds between all the atoms. Have students explain why the model represents a saturated hydrocarbon.

PRE-AP

Have students draw all five isomers of hexane. Some will argue that additional structures are possible because they will not realize that putting a methyl group on the second carbon is the same as putting it on the fifth carbon. Show students that they are equivalent by flipping the molecule.

▼ Teach *continued*

Teaching Tip

- If hydrocarbon molecules do not follow the C_nH_{2n+2} rule, then they must either be cyclic hydrocarbons or have multiple bonds. Hydrocarbons with double and triple bonds are called *unsaturated* because the carbon atoms are not saturated with hydrogen to the greatest extent possible.
- The IUPAC nomenclature used in this text is an international standard. However, older common names, such as *ethylene* for *ethene*, *propylene* for *propene*, *acetylene* for *ethyne*, and *ethyl alcohol* for *ethanol*, are still in use. These common names can also be found in *The Merck Index*.

TEACH FROM TABLES

FIGURE 2.2 Have students think of common terms that use the same prefixes as those in this table. Some examples include *pentagon*, *octopus*, and *decade*.

Check for Understanding

Answer: Cycloalkanes contain only hydrogen and carbon, and only single bonds.

MAIN IDEA

Cycloalkanes have a ringed structure.

Cycloalkanes are alkanes in which the carbon atoms are arranged in a ring, or cyclic, structure. The structural formulas for cycloalkanes are often drawn in a simplified form. In these skeletal representations, such as the one below on the right, it is understood that there is a carbon atom at each corner and enough hydrogen atoms to complete the four bonds to each carbon atom.

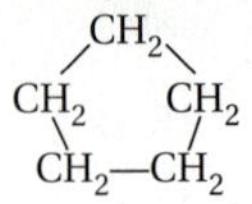

cyclopentane

or

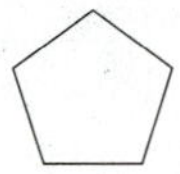

cyclopentane

CHECK FOR UNDERSTANDING
Infer Even though they don't follow the general formula C_nH_{2n+2}, why are cycloalkanes still alkanes?

The general structure for cycloalkanes, C_nH_{2n}, shows that they have $2 \times n$ hydrogen atoms, two fewer hydrogen atoms than noncyclic alkanes, C_nH_{2n+2}, have. This is because cycloalkanes have no free ends where a carbon atom is attached to three hydrogen atoms. Another example, of a four-carbon alkane and cycloalkane, is shown below.

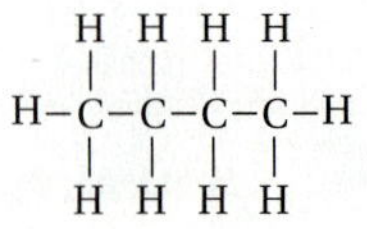

butane
C_4H_{10}

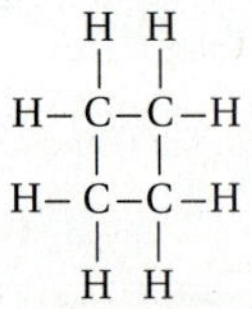

cyclobutane
C_4H_8

FIGURE 2.2

CARBON-ATOM CHAIN PREFIXES

Number of carbon atoms	Prefix
1	meth-
2	eth-
3	prop-
4	but-
5	pent-
6	hex-
7	hept-
8	oct-
9	non-
10	dec-

MAIN IDEA

Organic compounds have systematic names.

Historically, the names of many organic compounds were derived from the sources in which they were found. As more organic compounds were discovered, a systematic naming method became necessary. The systematic method used primarily in this book was developed by the International Union of Pure and Applied Chemistry, IUPAC.

Unbranched-Chain Alkane Nomenclature

To name an unbranched alkane, find the prefix in **Figure 2.2** that corresponds to the number of carbon atoms in the chain of the hydrocarbon. Then add the suffix *-ane* to the prefix. An example is shown below.

$$\overset{1}{CH_3}-\overset{2}{CH_2}-\overset{3}{CH_2}-\overset{4}{CH_2}-\overset{5}{CH_2}-\overset{6}{CH_2}-\overset{7}{CH_3}$$

heptane

The molecule has a chain seven carbon atoms long, so the prefix *hept-* is added to the suffix *-ane* to form *heptane*.

Differentiated Instruction

INCLUSION

Have visual and tactile learners use molecular model kits to build butane and cyclobutane. Have them use the models to describe similarities and differences between the two molecules. Students should recognize that both molecules are saturated hydrocarbons. Butane consists of a carbon backbone chain, while cyclobutane has a ring structure. Molecular model kits are also helpful for understanding chemical nomenclature. Ask students to work in pairs to rearrange the saturated hydrocarbon shown on the next page so that the longest chain is the straight chain. Students should remove carbons 1 and 2, attach carbon 2 to the end of the straight chain, and adjust the number of hydrogen atoms bonded to each carbon atom. In effect, they are building 2,6,7-trimethyldecane.

FIGURE 2.3

Alkane	Name	Alkyl group	Name
SOME STRAIGHT-CHAIN ALKYL GROUPS			
CH_4	methane	$-CH_3$	methyl
CH_3-CH_3	ethane	$-CH_2-CH_3$	ethyl
$CH_3-CH_2-CH_3$	propane	$-CH_2-CH_2-CH_3$	propyl
$CH_3-CH_2-CH_2-CH_3$	butane	$-CH_2-CH_2-CH_2-CH_3$	butyl
$CH_3-CH_2-CH_2-CH_2-CH_3$	pentane	$-CH_2-CH_2-CH_2-CH_2-CH_3$	pentyl

Branched-Chain Alkane Nomenclature

The naming of branched-chain alkanes also follows a systematic method. The hydrocarbon branches of alkanes are alkyl groups. **Alkyl groups** are groups of atoms that are formed when one hydrogen atom is removed from an alkane molecule. Alkyl groups are named by replacing the suffix *-ane* of the parent alkane with the suffix *-yl.* Some examples of alkyl groups are shown in **Figure 2.3.** Alkyl group names are used when naming branched-chain alkanes. We will present only the method for naming simple branched-chain alkanes with only straight-chain alkyl groups. Consider the following molecule.

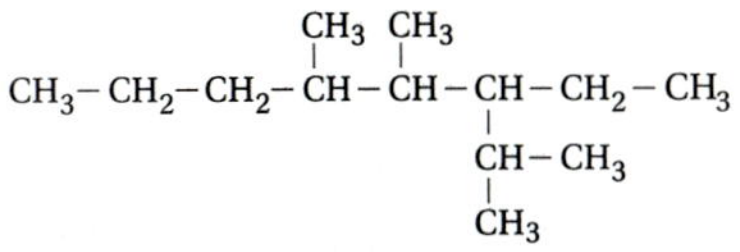

```
                    CH3  CH3
                     |    |
CH3- CH2- CH2- CH - CH - CH - CH2 - CH3
                          |
                          CH- CH3
                          |
                          CH3
```

To name this molecule, locate the parent hydrocarbon. The parent hydrocarbon is the longest continuous chain that contains the most straight-chain branches. In this molecule, there are two chains that are eight carbon atoms long. The parent hydrocarbon is the chain that contains the most straight-chain branches. Do not be tricked by the way the molecule is drawn. The longest chain may be shown bent.

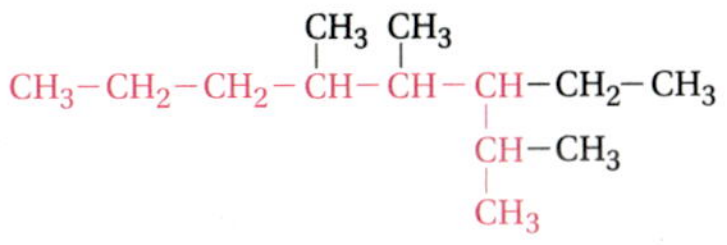

```
                    CH3  CH3
                     |    |
CH3- CH2- CH2- CH - CH - CH - CH2- CH3
                          |
                          CH- CH3
                          |
                          CH3
```

NOT

```
                    CH3  CH3
                     |    |
CH3- CH2- CH2- CH - CH - CH - CH2 - CH3
                          |
                          CH- CH3
                          |
                          CH3
```

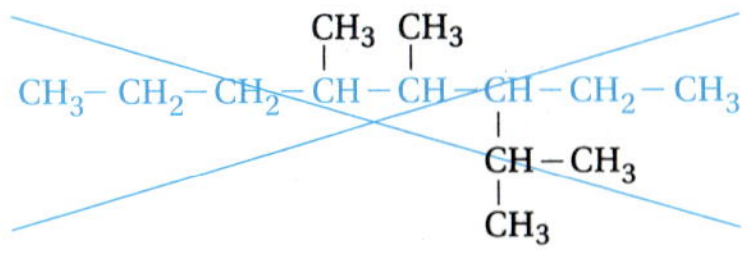

TEACH FROM TABLES

FIGURE 2.3 Write the structures of 3-ethyl-2,4,5-trimethyloctane and 5-butyl-2,2-dimethylnonane on the board. Have students identify all of the alkyl groups.

Teaching Tip

Point out that when drawing a structural formula, it is important to write the longest hydrocarbon sequence first. When given a structural formula, students should remember that the longest chain might not be represented by a straight line.

▼ Teach *continued*

Teaching Tip

Have students notice that all alkanes end with the suffix *-ane*. This signifies that there are no double bonds.

To name the parent hydrocarbon, add the suffix *-ane* to the prefix *oct-* (for a carbon-atom chain with eight carbon atoms) to form *octane.* Now identify and name the alkyl groups.

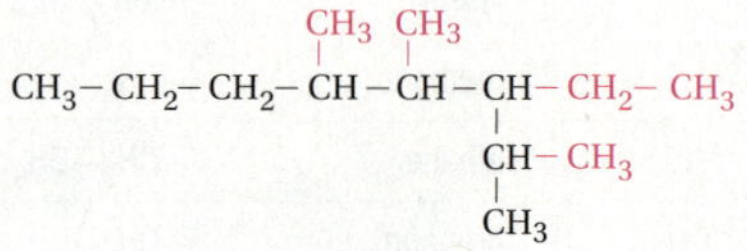

$$\begin{array}{l} \qquad\qquad\qquad\quad CH_3\ \ CH_3 \\ CH_3-CH_2-CH_2-CH-CH-CH-CH_2-CH_3 \\ \qquad\qquad\qquad\qquad\qquad\quad CH-CH_3 \\ \qquad\qquad\qquad\qquad\qquad\quad CH_3 \end{array}$$

The three $-CH_3$ groups are methyl groups. The $-CH_2-CH_3$ group is an ethyl group. Arrange the names in alphabetical order in front of the name of the parent hydrocarbon.

ethyl methyloctane

To show that there are three methyl groups present, attach the prefix *tri-* to the name *methyl* to form *trimethyl*.

ethyl **tri**methyloctane

Now, we need to show the locations of the alkyl groups on the parent hydrocarbon. Number the octane chain so that the alkyl groups have the lowest numbers possible.

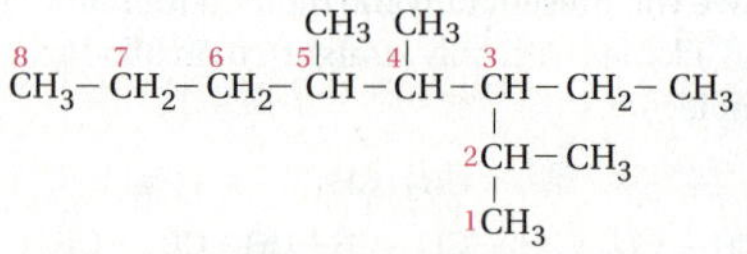

$$\begin{array}{l} \qquad\qquad\qquad\quad CH_3\ \ CH_3 \\ \overset{8}{C}H_3-\overset{7}{C}H_2-\overset{6}{C}H_2-\overset{5}{C}H-\overset{4}{C}H-\overset{3}{C}H-CH_2-CH_3 \\ \qquad\qquad\qquad\qquad\qquad\quad {}^{2}CH-CH_3 \\ \qquad\qquad\qquad\qquad\qquad\quad {}^{1}CH_3 \end{array}$$

NOT

$$\begin{array}{l} \qquad\qquad\qquad\quad CH_3\ \ CH_3 \\ \overset{1}{C}H_3-\overset{2}{C}H_2-\overset{3}{C}H_2-\overset{4}{C}H-\overset{5}{C}H-\overset{6}{C}H-CH_2-CH_3 \\ \qquad\qquad\qquad\qquad\qquad\quad {}^{7}CH-CH_3 \\ \qquad\qquad\qquad\qquad\qquad\quad {}^{8}CH_3 \end{array}$$

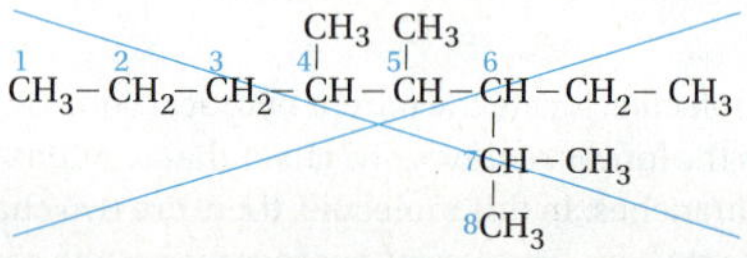

Place the location number of *each* of the alkyl groups in front of its name. Separate the numbers from the names of the alkyl groups with hyphens. The ethyl group is on carbon 3.

3-ethyl trimethyloctane

Because there are three methyl groups, there will be three numbers, separated by commas, in front of *trimethyl.*

3-ethyl-**2,4,5**-trimethyloctane

The full name is 3-ethyl-2,4,5-trimethyloctane.

The procedure for naming simple branched-chain alkanes can be summarized as shown in the list on the next page.

CAREERS IN CHEMISTRY

Petroleum Engineer S.T.E.M.

Petroleum engineers search for underground reservoirs of oil or natural gas. They then work with other scientists and engineers to develop and oversee drilling and production operations. Petroleum engineers are also responsible for developing technology and methods to increase the amount of oil or gas obtained and to lower the cost of drilling and production operations. In addition to possessing a broad range of engineering expertise (chemical, mechanical, or electrical) a petroleum engineer must also apply the basic sciences of chemistry, geology, physics, and mathematics.

Differentiated Instruction

BELOW LEVEL

Tell the class that they will write questions for a new quiz called "The Name Game." Have students work in pairs to write a structural formula for a saturated hydrocarbon. Encourage them to include branches. Have each team write their structure on the board, and challenge the rest of the class to name the molecule.

Alkane Nomenclature

1. **Name the parent hydrocarbon.** Find the longest continuous chain of carbon atoms that have straight-chain branches. Add the suffix *-ane* to the prefix corresponding to the number of carbon atoms in the chain.
2. **Add the names of the alkyl groups.** Add the names of the alkyl groups in front of the name of the parent hydrocarbon in alphabetical order. When there is more than one branch of the same alkyl group present, attach the appropriate numerical prefix to the name: *di* = 2, *tri* = 3, *tetra* = 4, and so on. Do so after the names have been put in alphabetical order.
3. **Number the carbon atoms in the parent hydrocarbon.** If one or more alkyl groups are present, number the carbon atoms in the continuous chain to give the lowest numbers possible in the name. If there are two equivalent lowest positions with two different alkyl groups, give the lowest number to the alkyl group that comes first in the name. (This will be the alkyl group that is first in alphabetical order, *before* any prefixes are attached.)
4. **Insert position numbers.** Put the position numbers of each alkyl group in front of the name of that alkyl group.
5. **Punctuate the name.** Use hyphens to separate the position numbers from the names. If there is more than one number in front of a name, use commas to separate the numbers.

Naming Alkanes

Sample Problem A **Name the following simple branched-chain alkane:**

$CH_3-CH-CH_2-CH-CH-CH_3$
(with CH_3 groups attached to carbons 2, 4, and 5)

SOLVE

1. Identify and name the parent hydrocarbon.

$CH_3-CH-CH_2-CH-CH-CH_3$
(with CH_3 groups attached to carbons 2, 4, and 5)

Because the longest continuous chain contains six carbon atoms, the parent hydrocarbon is *hexane*.

2. Identify and name the alkyl groups attached to the chain.

$CH_3-CH-CH_2-CH-CH-CH_3$
(with CH_3 groups attached to carbons 2, 4, and 5)

There is only one type of alkyl group, with one carbon atom. Alkyl groups with one carbon atom are methyl groups. Add the name *methyl* in front of the name of the continuous chain. Add the prefix *tri-* to show that there are three methyl groups present.

trimethylhexane

Classroom Practice

A-1 Draw the condensed structural formula for each of the following molecules:

a. 2,4-dimethylpentane

$CH_3-CH-CH_2-CH-CH_3$
(with CH_3 on carbons 2 and 4)

b. 4-ethyl-3-methylheptane

$CH_3-CH_2-CH-CH-CH_2-CH_2-CH_3$
(with CH_3 on carbon 3 and CH_2-CH_3 on carbon 4)

c. methylpropane

$CH_3-CH-CH_3$
(with CH_3 on carbon 2)

A-2 Draw the condensed structural formula for 3,3,4-triethyl-4-methylhexane.

$CH_3-CH_2-C-C-CH_2-CH_3$
(with CH_3-CH_2 above and CH_3-CH_2 below carbon 3; CH_2-CH_3 above and CH_3 below carbon 4)

A-3 Draw the structural formulas for two structural isomers of C_7H_{16}.

$CH_3-CH_2-CH-CH_2-CH_2-CH_3$
(with CH_3 on carbon 3)

$CH_3-CH_2-CH_2-CH_2-CH_2-CH_2-CH_3$

(Other structures are also possible.)

A-4 Draw the condensed structural formula for 3-ethyl-2,2-dimethylpentane.

$CH_3-C-CH-CH_2-CH_3$
(with CH_3 above and CH_3 below carbon 2; CH_2-CH_3 on carbon 3)

Problem Solving

ALTERNATIVE APPROACHES

Point out that students can work backward to check to see if their name is correct. In this case, students must decode the name and use the clues to draw the structural formula. Be sure that students understand that the result may not have the same orientation as the original structural formula.

▼ Teach continued

Answers

Practice A

1. methylbutane
2. 3-ethyl-4-methylhexane

TEACH FROM TABLES

FIGURE 2.4 Be sure students recognize that the boiling point of an alkane increases as the number of carbon atoms increases. This is also reflected in the state of the alkane at room temperature. Have students think about pulling apart two strips of hook and loop contact fasteners. The longer the strips, the more difficult it is to separate them. Similarly, the longer a straight-chain alkane is, the greater its intermolecular attractions and the higher its boiling point.

Naming Alkanes (continued)

3. Number the carbon atoms in the continuous chain so that the alkyl groups have the lowest numbers possible.

$$\overset{6}{CH_3}-\overset{5}{\underset{|\atop CH_3}{CH}}-\overset{4}{CH_2}-\overset{3}{\underset{|\atop CH_3}{CH}}-\overset{2}{\underset{|\atop CH_3}{CH}}-\overset{1}{CH_3}$$

4. The methyl groups are on the carbon atoms numbered *2, 3,* and *5.* Put the numbers of the positions of the alkyl groups, separated by commas, in front of the name of the alkyl group. Separate the numbers from the name with a hyphen.

2,3,5-trimethylhexane

Practice Answers in Appendix E

Name the following molecules:

1. $CH_3-\underset{|\atop CH_3}{CH}-CH_2-CH_3$

2. $CH_3-CH_2-\underset{|\atop {CH_2 \atop {|\atop CH_3}}}{CH}-\overset{CH_3\atop |}{CH}-CH_2-CH_3$

The properties of alkanes are related to the lengths of their carbon chains.

Properties for some straight-chain alkanes are listed in **Figure 2.4.** The trends in these properties can be explained by examining the structure of alkanes. The carbon-hydrogen bonds of alkanes are nonpolar. The only forces of attraction between nonpolar molecules are weak intermolecular forces, or London dispersion forces. The strength of London dispersion forces increases as the mass of a molecule increases.

FIGURE 2.4

PROPERTIES OF STRAIGHT-CHAIN ALKANES

Molecular formula	IUPAC name	Boiling point (°C)	State at room temperature
CH_4	methane	−164	gas
C_2H_6	ethane	−88.6	
C_3H_8	propane	−42.1	
C_4H_{10}	butane	−0.5	
C_5H_{12}	pentane	36.1	liquid
C_8H_{18}	octane	125.7	
$C_{10}H_{22}$	decane	174.1	
$C_{17}H_{36}$	heptadecane	301.8	solid
$C_{20}H_{42}$	eicosane	343.	

Problem Solving

TAKE IT FURTHER

Have students draw two isomers of 2,3,5-trimethylhexane and give the correct name for each structure they draw. Ask students to explain why their structures represent isomers even though each compound has a unique name.

Physical States

The physical states at which some alkanes exist at room temperature and atmospheric pressure are found in **Figure 2.4.** Alkanes that have the lowest molecular mass—those with one to four carbon atoms—are gases. **Natural gas** is a fossil fuel composed primarily of alkanes containing one to four carbon atoms. These alkanes are gases because they are very small molecules. Therefore, they have weak London dispersion forces between them and are not held together tightly. Larger alkanes are liquids. Gasoline and kerosene consist mostly of liquid alkanes. Stronger London dispersion forces hold these molecules close enough together to form liquids. Alkanes that have a very high molecular mass are solids, corresponding to a greater increase in London dispersion forces. Paraffin wax contains solid alkanes. It can be used in candles, as shown in **Figure 2.5.**

Boiling Points

The boiling points of alkanes, also shown in **Figure 2.4,** increase with molecular mass. As London dispersion forces increase, more energy is required to pull the molecules apart. This property is used in the separation of petroleum, a major source of alkanes. **Petroleum** is a complex mixture of different hydrocarbons that varies greatly in composition. The hydrocarbon molecules in petroleum contain from 1 to more than 50 carbon atoms. This range allows the separation of petroleum into different portions that have different boiling point ranges, as shown in **Figure 2.6.** In *fractional distillation,* components of a mixture are separated on the basis of boiling point, by condensation of vapor in a fractionating column. **Figure 2.7** shows an example of refinery towers in which the process takes place. During its fractional distillation, petroleum is heated to about 370°C. Nearly all components of the petroleum are vaporized at this temperature. As the vapors rise in the fractionating column, or tower, they are gradually cooled. Alkanes that have higher boiling points have higher condensation temperatures and condense for collection lower in the tower. For example, lubricating oils, which have higher condensation temperatures than gasoline has, are collected lower in the fractionating tower.

FIGURE 2.6

PETROLEUM FRACTIONS

Fraction	Size range of molecules	Boiling-point range (°C)
Gasoline	C_4–C_{12}	up to 200
Kerosene	C_{10}–C_{14}	180–290
Middle distillate, such as heating oil, gas-turbine fuel, diesel	C_{12}–C_{20}	185–345
Wide-cut gas oil, such as lubricating oil, waxes	C_{20}–C_{36}	345–540
Asphalt	above C_{36}	residues

FIGURE 2.5

Solid Alkanes Paraffin wax, used in candles, contains solid alkanes. Molecules of paraffin wax contain 26 to 30 carbon atoms.

FIGURE 2.7

Fractional Distillation
Fractional distillation takes place in petroleum refinery towers.

Misconception Alert!

Many students might think that oil was formed from decayed dinosaurs. Although some of the organic material that makes up existing oil reserves may have come from dinosaur tissue, the vast majority has come from plants and bacteria.

ChemisTrivia

In some cases, the boiling points of two substances are so close together that a fractionating tower does not work well to separate them. In such cases a fractionating column is used to create a multistage process. The column is packed with a material, such as glass beads, that the gases must travel through. The gases first rise through the column and then partially condense on the surfaces of the beads. The condensed liquid flows back down and is revaporized by the rising gases from below. Eventually, the more-volatile substance is concentrated at the top of the column, and the less-volatile substance is concentrated at the bottom.

Differentiated Instruction

BELOW LEVEL

Have students construct a poster to show how fractional distillation works. Ask them to compare a laboratory fractional distillation apparatus with an industrial apparatus. Be sure that students point out both the similarities and the differences.

▼ Teach continued

Teaching Tip

Double bonds are stronger than single bonds, but not twice as strong. The initial single bond is much stronger and therefore has a higher bond energy than each additional bond.

READING TOOLKIT

COMPARING AND CONTRASTING Have students complete another section of their table for unsaturated hydrocarbons, including basic structural characteristics, rules for naming, properties, uses, formulas, and examples of alkenes, alkynes, and aromatic hydrocarbons. Then have them use their tables to compare and contrast saturated and unsaturated hydrocarbons.

Check for Understanding

Answer: It is not possible to know for sure. $C_{10}H_{20}$ fits the general formula for an alkene, but it could be a cycloalkane.

MAIN IDEA

Unsaturated hydrocarbons have at least one carbon-carbon double bond.

Hydrocarbons that do not contain the maximum amount of hydrogen are referred to as *unsaturated*. **Unsaturated hydrocarbons** are hydrocarbons in which not all carbon atoms have four single covalent bonds. An unsaturated hydrocarbon has one or more double bonds or triple bonds. Carbon atoms can easily form double and triple bonds to other carbon atoms, so multiple bonds between carbon atoms are common in organic compounds.

Alkenes

Alkenes are hydrocarbons that contain double covalent bonds. Some examples of alkenes are given in **Figure 2.8**. Notice that because alkenes have a double bond, the simplest alkene, ethene, has two carbon atoms.

Carbon atoms linked by double bonds cannot bind as many atoms as those that are linked by only single bonds. An alkene with one double bond has two fewer hydrogen atoms than the corresponding alkane.

H H H / H–C–C–C–H / H H H — C_3H_8

H / H–C=C–C–H / H H H — C_3H_6

Thus, the general formula for noncyclic alkenes with one double bond is C_nH_{2n}.

Because alkenes have a double bond, they can have geometric isomers, as shown in the examples below.

CHECK FOR UNDERSTANDING
Identify Is the compound $C_{10}H_{20}$ an alkene or an alkane? Can you know for sure?

H, H / C=C / CH_3, CH_3 — *cis*-2-butene

H, CH_3 / C=C / CH_3, H — *trans*-2-butene

FIGURE 2.8

STRUCTURES OF ALKENES

	ethene	propene	*trans*-2-butene	*cis*-2-butene
Structural formula	H, H / C=C / H, H	H, H / C=C / CH_3, H	H, CH_3 / C=C / CH_3, H	H, H / C=C / CH_3, CH_3
Ball-and-stick model				

Differentiated Instruction

PRE-AP

Write the following equations on the board.

ethane + bromine + water ⟶ no reaction

ethene + bromine + water ⟶ 1,2-dibromoethane

Tell students that bromine water has a brown color. Ask students to use this information to explain how bromine water can test for the presence of an unsaturated hydrocarbon. Students should recognize that if the brown color remains, then the hydrocarbon has to be saturated, because no bonds could be broken to add bromine atoms to the hydrocarbon chain. However, the brown color disappears if bromine water is added to an unsaturated hydrocarbon because the bromine atoms are added to the hydrocarbon chain. The degree to which the brown color disappears depends on the degree of unsaturation of the hydrocarbon and the amount of bromine in solution.

Systematic Names of Alkenes

The rules for naming a simple alkene are similar to those for naming an alkane. The parent hydrocarbon is the longest continuous chain of carbon atoms *that contains the double bond.*

$$\underset{\textbf{pentene}}{CH_2{=}\overset{\overset{CH_2-CH_3}{|}}{C}-CH_2-CH_2-CH_3} \quad \textbf{\textit{NOT}} \quad \underset{\text{hexene}}{CH_2{=}\overset{\overset{CH_2-CH_3}{|}}{C}-CH_2-CH_2-CH_3}$$

The carbon atoms in the chain are numbered so that the first carbon atom in the double bond has the lowest number.

$$\overset{1}{C}H_2{=}\overset{2}{\overset{\overset{CH_2-CH_3}{|}}{C}}-\overset{3}{C}H_2-\overset{4}{C}H_2-\overset{5}{C}H_3$$

1-pentene

The position number and name of the alkyl group are placed in front of the double-bond position number. This alkyl group has two carbon atoms, an ethyl group. It is on the second carbon atom of the parent hydrocarbon.

2-ethyl-1-pentene

If there is more than one double bond, the suffix is modified to indicate the number of double bonds: 2 = *-adiene*, 3 = *-atriene*, and so on.

$$CH_2{=}CH-CH_2-CH{=}CH_2$$

1,4-pentadiene

The procedure for naming alkenes can be summarized as follows.

Alkene Nomenclature

Use the rules for alkane nomenclature listed earlier in this section, with the following exceptions.

1. **Name the parent hydrocarbon.** Locate the longest continuous chain that *contains the double bond(s).* If there is only one double bond, add the suffix *-ene* to the prefix corresponding to the number of carbon atoms in this chain. If there is more than one double bond, modify the suffix to indicate the number of double bonds. For example, 2 = *-adiene*, 3 = *-atriene*, and so on.
2. **Add the names of the alkyl groups.**
3. **Number the carbon atoms in the parent hydrocarbon.** Number the carbon atoms in the chain so that the first carbon atom in the double bond nearest the end of the chain has the lowest number. If numbering from both ends gives equivalent positions for two double bonds, then number from the end nearest the first alkyl group.
4. **Insert position numbers.** Place double-bond position numbers immediately before the name of the parent hydrocarbon alkene. Place alkyl group position numbers immediately before the name of the corresponding alkyl group.
5. **Punctuate the name.**

WHY IT MATTERS

Carbon Allotropes S.T.E.M.

Carbon occurs in several different bonding patterns, called *allotropes*, which have very different properties. Diamond is a colorless, crystalline solid form of carbon, in which each atom is tetrahedrally bonded to four others in a network fashion. This three-dimensional bonding makes diamond the hardest material known.

Graphite is a soft, black, crystalline form of carbon that is a fair conductor of electricity. The carbon atoms in graphite are bonded together in layers. Within each layer, each atom is bonded to three other carbon atoms. But because adjacent layers are held together only by very weak London dispersion forces, graphite is very soft.

Diamond and graphite have been known for thousands of years. In the mid-1980s, a new solid allotropic form of carbon known as a *fullerene*, or, informally, "buckyball," was discovered in the soot that forms when carbon-containing materials are burned with limited oxygen. The structure of a fullerene consists of a near-spherical cage of carbon atoms. The most stable fullerene is C_{60}, the structure of which resembles the design of a soccer ball.

Teaching Tip

- Many students will have trouble determining whether an alkene has geometric isomers. Have them draw and examine the structural formulas of each molecule in geometric-isomer form.
- An alkene is numbered so that the double bonds are closest to the carbon atoms with the lowest numbers. Have students compare the structures of 2-pentene and 3-pentene. They are the same molecule. Which is the correct name? 2-pentene, the name that has the double bond closest to the lowest-numbered carbon

BELOW LEVEL

Have students prepare a table with two columns, labeled "Alkane Nomenclature" and "Alkene Nomenclature." Have students write the appropriate rules under both columns and compare them by identifying the similarities and differences. They should notice that the five main rules are the same. The differences include taking into account the position of the double bond when numbering the carbon atoms and using the suffix *-ane* versus the suffix *-ene*.

▼ Teach *continued*

Teaching Tip

Ask students to interchange the methyl and ethyl groups in 2-ethyl-3-methyl-1-butene and then name the resulting alkene. The longest chain contains five carbon atoms, and the name is 2,3-dimethyl-1-pentene.

Misconception Alert!

People often read the names of chemicals in their food and cosmetics and wince because they are intimidated by the IUPAC names that are sometimes used. Some are afraid to buy products that list ingredients using IUPAC names. They do not understand that any organic compound, no matter how "natural," can be expressed using an IUPAC name.

Classroom Practice

B-1 Name the following alkenes:

a.

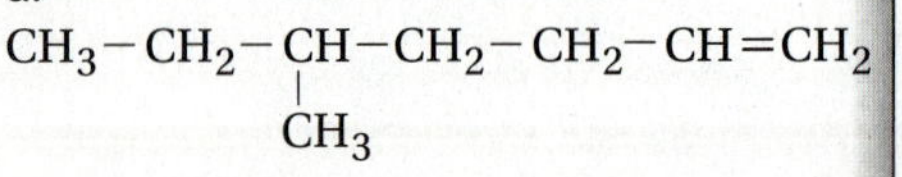

$$CH_3-CH_2-\underset{\displaystyle CH_3}{\underset{|}{CH}}-CH_2-CH_2-CH=CH_2$$

b. $CH_3-CH=CH-CH=CH-CH_3$

c.

$$CH_3-\underset{\displaystyle CH_3}{\underset{|}{CH}}-CH=CH-CH_2-CH_2-CH_3$$

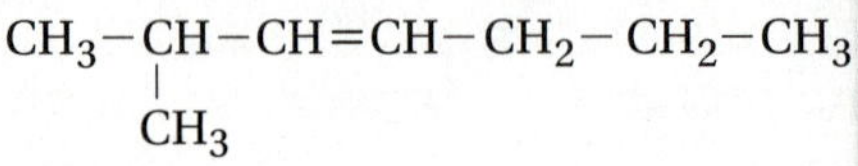

Answers

a. 5-methyl-1-heptene
b. 2,4-hexadiene
c. 2-methyl-3-heptene

Answers

Practice B

1. 2-hexene
2. 2-methyl-2-butene *or* methyl-2-butene
3. 2-methyl-3-hexene
4. 2,5-dimethyl-2,5-heptadiene

Naming Alkenes

Sample Problem B **Name the following alkene.**

$$CH_3-\overset{\displaystyle CH_3}{\overset{|}{CH}}-\underset{\displaystyle CH_2-CH_3}{\underset{|}{C}}=CH_2$$

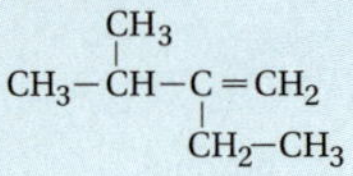

1 ANALYZE

1. Identify and name the parent hydrocarbon.

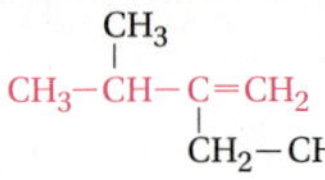

$$CH_3-\overset{\displaystyle CH_3}{\overset{|}{CH}}-\underset{\displaystyle CH_2-CH_3}{\underset{|}{C}}=CH_2$$

The parent hydrocarbon has four carbon atoms and one double bond, so it is named *butene*.

2. Identify and name the alkyl groups.

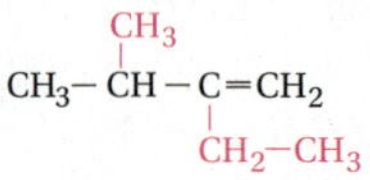

$$CH_3-\overset{\displaystyle CH_3}{\overset{|}{CH}}-\underset{\displaystyle CH_2-CH_3}{\underset{|}{C}}=CH_2$$

The alkyl groups are *ethyl* and *methyl*.
Place their names in front of the name of the parent hydrocarbon in alphabetical order.

ethyl methyl butene

3. Number the carbon chain to give the double bond the lowest position.

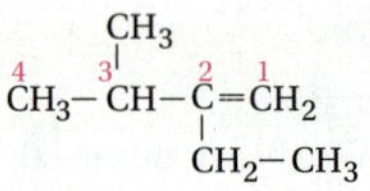

$$\overset{4}{C}H_3-\overset{\displaystyle CH_3}{\overset{3|}{CH}}-\underset{\displaystyle CH_2-CH_3}{\underset{|}{\overset{2}{C}}}=\overset{1}{C}H_2$$

2 SOLVE

Place the position number of the double bond in front of butene. Place the position numbers of the alkyl groups in front of each alkyl group. Separate the numbers from the name with hyphens. The full name is
2-ethyl-3-methyl-1-butene.

Practice Answers in Appendix E

Name the following alkenes:

1. $CH_3-CH_2-CH_2-CH=CH-CH_3$

2. 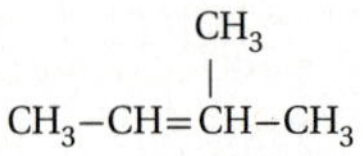 $CH_3-CH=\overset{\displaystyle CH_3}{\overset{|}{C}H}-CH_3$

3. $CH_3-\overset{\displaystyle CH_3}{\overset{|}{CH}}-CH=CH-CH_2-CH_3$

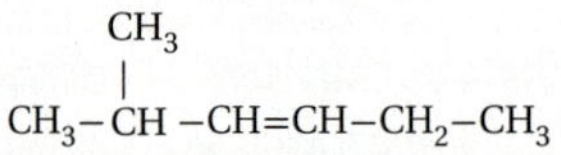

4. 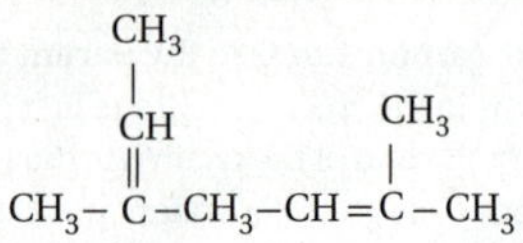 $CH_3-\overset{\displaystyle CH_3}{\overset{|}{\overset{\displaystyle CH}{\overset{||}{C}}}}-CH_3-CH=\overset{\displaystyle CH_3}{\overset{|}{C}}-CH_3$

Problem Solving

TAKE IT FURTHER

Have students work in pairs and use molecular model kits to build two isomers of 2-ethyl-3-methyl-1-butene. Have students use the rules for alkene nomenclature to name each isomer.

FIGURE 2.9

Alkenes in Nature α-farnesene is a solid alkene found in the natural wax covering of apples. Can you determine the IUPAC name for this large alkene?

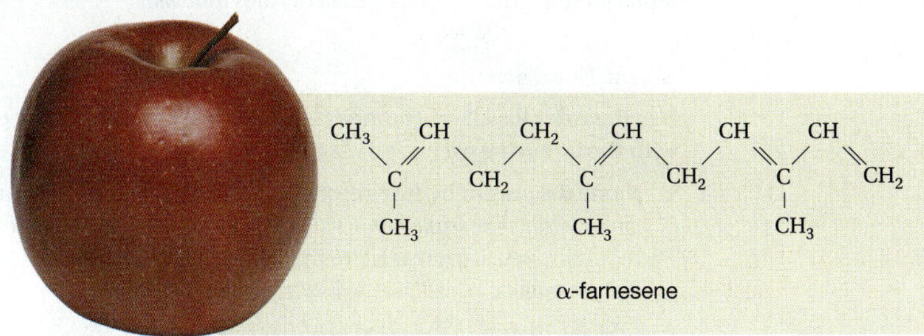

Properties and Uses of Alkenes

Alkenes are nonpolar and show trends in properties similar to those of alkanes in boiling points and physical states. For example, α-farnesene has 15 carbon atoms and 4 double bonds, as shown in **Figure 2.9.** This large alkene is a solid at room temperature and atmospheric pressure. It is found in the natural wax covering of apples. Ethene, the smallest alkene, is a gas. Ethene is commonly called *ethylene*.

Ethene is the hydrocarbon commercially produced in the greatest quantity in the United States. It is used in the synthesis of many plastics and commercially important alcohols. Ethene is also an important plant hormone. Induction of flowering and the ripening of fruit, as shown in **Figure 2.10,** are effects of ethene hormone action that can be manipulated by commercial growers.

Alkynes

Hydrocarbons with triple covalent bonds are alkynes. Like the double bond of alkenes, the triple bond of alkynes requires that the simplest alkyne have two carbon atoms.

$$H{-}C{\equiv}C{-}H$$

ethyne

The general formula for the alkynes is C_nH_{2n-2}. Alkynes have four fewer hydrogen atoms than the corresponding alkanes and two fewer hydrogen atoms than the corresponding alkenes. The simplest alkyne is ethyne, more commonly known as *acetylene*.

$H_3C{-}CH_3$ (H–C–C–H with three H on each C)	$H_2C{=}CH_2$	$H{-}C{\equiv}C{-}H$
C_2H_6 ethane	C_2H_4 ethene	C_2H_2 ethyne

FIGURE 2.10

Fruit Ripening Ethene is a plant hormone that triggers fruit ripening. At ordinary conditions, ethene is a gas.

↓

$$H_2C{=}CH_2$$

↓

Application

The smallest alkene, ethene, is responsible for stimulating fruit to ripen. A feedback loop occurs as ripening fruit produces more ethene. Tomatoes and avocados will ripen more quickly in a bag because the ethene is retained, and one bad apple may indeed spoil the bunch because of this. Fruit growers take advantage of ethene's properties by picking fruit before it is ripe and then exposing it to ethene before it goes to the market.

TEACH FROM VISUALS

FIGURE 2.9 The IUPAC name of α-farnesene is 3,7,11-trimethyl-1,3,6,10-dodecatetraene.

Differentiated Instruction

PRE-AP

Have students draw structures for cyclic alkenes, such as cyclopentene, 1,3-cyclopentadiene, 1,3-cyclohexene, and 1,3,5-cyclohexatriene (benzene). Explain that the orientation of the *p*-orbitals gives rise to aromatic compounds, so named because many of these compounds have pleasing aromas. Many aromatics are biologically essential, such as vitamins, proteins, and hormones. Some are toxic, such as those found in exhaust from gasoline fumes.

▼ Teach *continued*

Demo Problem

1. Name each of the following:

a. $CH_3{-}CH_2{-}C{\equiv}CH$

b.
$$CH_3{-}C{\equiv}C{-}CH_2{-}\underset{}{\overset{\displaystyle CH_3}{\overset{|}{CH}}}{-}CH_3$$

c.
$$CH{\equiv}C{-}\underset{\underset{\displaystyle CH_3}{|}}{\overset{\overset{\displaystyle CH_3}{|}}{CH}}{-}CH_3$$

Answers: **a.** 1-butyne
b. 5-methyl-2-hexyne
c. 3,3-dimethyl-1-butyne

2. Draw the structural formula for each of the following:

a. 2-butyne

b. 3-methyl-1-pentyne

Answers: **a.** $CH_3{-}C{\equiv}C{-}CH_3$

b.
$$CH{\equiv}C{-}\overset{\overset{\displaystyle CH_3}{|}}{CH}{-}CH_2{-}CH_3$$

Systematic Naming of Alkynes

Alkyne nomenclature is almost the same as alkene nomenclature. The only difference is that the *-ene* suffix of the corresponding alkene is replaced with *-yne*. A complete list of rules follows.

Alkyne Nomenclature

Use the rules for alkane nomenclature listed earlier in this section, with the following exceptions.

1. **Name the parent hydrocarbon**. Locate the longest continuous chain that *contains the triple bond(s)*. If there is only one triple bond, add the suffix *-yne*. If there is more than one triple bond, modify the suffix. For example, 2 = *-adiyne*, 3 = *-atriyne*, and so on.
2. **Add the names of the alkyl groups.**
3. **Number the carbon atoms in the parent hydrocarbon.** Number the carbon atoms in the chain so that the first carbon atom in the triple bond nearest the end of the chain has the lowest number.
4. **Insert position numbers.** Place the position numbers of the triple bond immediately before the name of the parent hydrocarbon alkyne. Place alkyl group position numbers immediately before the name of the corresponding alkyl group.
5. **Punctuate the name.**

Two examples of correctly named alkynes are given below.

$$CH_3{-}CH_2{-}CH_2{-}C{\equiv}CH$$

1-pentyne

$$CH{\equiv}C{-}\underset{\underset{\displaystyle CH_3}{|}}{CH}{-}CH_3$$

3-methyl-1-butyne

Properties and Uses of Alkynes

Alkynes are nonpolar and exhibit the same trends in boiling points and physical states as other hydrocarbons. The smallest alkyne, ethyne, is a gas. The combustion of ethyne when it is mixed with pure oxygen produces the intense heat of welding torches, as shown in **Figure 2.11.** As mentioned, the common name of ethyne is acetylene, so these welding torches are commonly called *oxyacetylene torches*.

FIGURE 2.11

Alkynes Ethyne is the fuel used in oxyacetylene torches. Oxyacetylene torches can reach temperatures of over 3000°C.

Differentiated Instruction

INCLUSION

Help students understand the similarities and differences between the three types of hydrocarbons by creating a bulletin board display or poster. Students should identify each type of hydrocarbon, describe what makes it a hydrocarbon and give examples of each type. Students may also research acetylene as a hydrocarbon and the uses of acetylene.

Aromatic Hydrocarbons

Aromatic hydrocarbons are hydrocarbons that have six-membered carbon rings and delocalized electrons. Benzene is the primary aromatic hydrocarbon. The molecular formula of benzene is C_6H_6. One possible structural formula is a six-carbon atom ring with three double bonds.

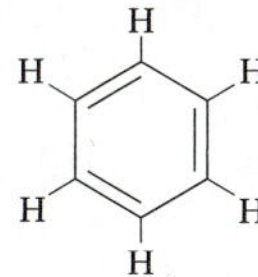

However, benzene does not behave chemically like an alkene. The entire molecule lies in the same plane, as shown in **Figure 2.12.** Benzene contains resonance hybrid bonds, and the structure of the benzene ring allows electrons to be spread through delocalized *p*-orbitals over the whole ring. The structural and skeletal formulas below show benzene as a resonance hybrid, representing the delocalization of electrons.

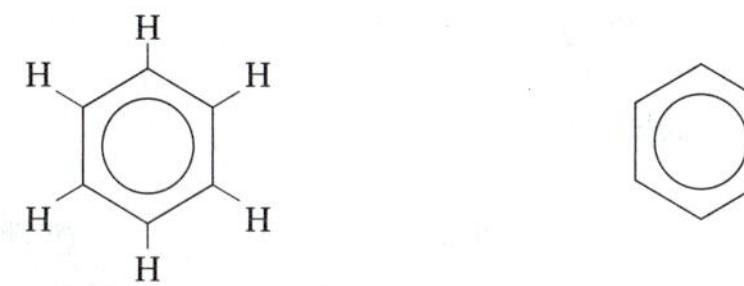

Aromatic hydrocarbons can be thought of as derivatives of benzene. The simplest have one benzene ring, as shown in the following example.

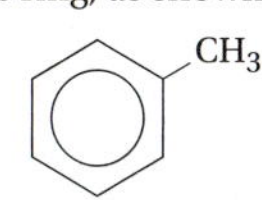

methylbenzene

FIGURE 2.12

Aromatic Hydrocarbons Electron orbitals in benzene overlap to form continuous *p*-orbitals that allow the delocalized electrons to spread uniformly over the entire ring.

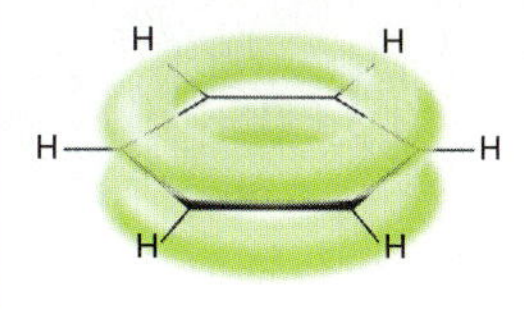

CHECK FOR UNDERSTANDING

Defend How does the circle in the middle of the benzene ring better represent the type of bonding in benzene?

SECTION 2 FORMATIVE ASSESSMENT

Reviewing Main Ideas

1. List the basic structural features that characterize each of the following hydrocarbons:
   a. alkanes
   b. alkenes
   c. alkynes
   d. aromatic hydrocarbons
2. Draw all of the condensed structural formulas that can represent C_5H_{12}.
3. Give the systematic name for each compound in your answers to item 2.
4. Give examples of a property or use of three hydrocarbons.
5. Name the following compounds:
   a. $CH_3-CH_2-CH_3$ (attached to the second carbon of) $CH_3-CH-CH-CH_2-CH_3$
   b. $CH_2{=}CH-CH{=}CH_2$
   c. $CH_3-C{\equiv}C-CH_2-CH_3$

Critical Thinking

6. **ANALYZING INFORMATION** Write the structural formulas for an alkane, an alkene, and an alkyne that have five carbon atoms each. Why are these three hydrocarbons not considered isomers?

ChemisTrivia

Friedrich August Kekulé claimed that his structure of benzene came from a dream in which he saw snakelike chains of carbon atoms. One of the snakes had grabbed hold of its own tail with its mouth. Kekulé realized that the carbon atoms must line up in the same cyclic manner as the snake in his dream.

Teaching Tip

Each carbon atom in benzene is sp^2 hybridized. To draw an accurate Lewis dot structure, one must show two resonance structures, with each showing alternating double bonds.

Check for Understanding

Answer: The circle shows that the bonding between the carbons in the ring is neither single nor double, but a mixture, or resonance, of the two.

Assess and Reteach

Assess Use the Formative Assessment on this page to evaluate student mastery of the section.

Reteach For students who need additional instruction, download the Section Study Guide.

Response to Intervention To reassess students' mastery, use the Section Quiz, available to print or to take directly online at **HMDScience.com**.

Answers to Section Assessment

1. a. all single bonds
   b. one or more double bonds
   c. one or more triple bonds
   d. benzene rings
2. $CH_3-C(CH_3)_2-CH_3$ (central C bearing CH_3 above and CH_3 below)

   $CH_3-CH_2-CH_2-CH_2-CH_3$

   $CH_3-CH(CH_3)-CH_2-CH_2-CH_3$
3. 2,2-dimethylpropane, pentane, and 2-methylbutane
4. Answers may vary.
5. a. 2-ethyl-3-methylpentane
   b. 1,3-butadiene
   c. 2-pentyne
6. One possible set of structures:

   $CH_3-CH_2-CH_2-CH_2-CH_3$
   $CH_3-CH{=}CH-CH_2-CH_3$
   $CH_3-C{\equiv}C-CH_2-CH_3$

   These compounds have different chemical formulas, so they cannot be isomers.

SECTION 3

▼ Plan and Prepare

Objectives

Upon completion of this section, students should be able to do the following:

- Define *functional group* and explain why functional groups are important.
- Identify alcohols, alkyl halides, ethers, aldehydes, ketones, carboxylic acids, esters, and amines based on the functional group present in each.
- Explain the relationships between the properties and structures of compounds with various functional groups.

Classroom Catalyst

Provide groups of students with toothpicks and two different colors of gumdrops. Ask them to make as many different molecules as they can using only four carbon atoms and ten hydrogen atoms. Remind students that carbon atoms can have single bonds, double bonds or triple bonds. Hydrogen atoms can have only single bonds. Repeat this activity after adding two gumdrops of a third color to represent two oxygen atoms, which can each have two single bonds or one double bond. Have students compare their results.

Safety Do not allow students to eat materials used in the laboratory.

▼ Teach

Teaching Tip

Bring household items for students to look at and, when appropriate, smell. Possible items include rubbing alcohol, nail polish remover (acetone), perfume (esters), vanilla beans (aldehyde), and asparagus (amine). Prepare a list on the board indicating the substance and its chemical nature. Have students add to the list and start categorizing the items as they study this section.

SECTION 3

Main Idea

Functional groups can classify organic compounds.

Functional Groups

Key Terms

functional group
alcohol
alkyl halide
ether
aldehyde
ketone
amine
carboxylic acid
ester

MAIN IDEA

Functional groups can classify organic compounds.

A functional group is an atom or group of atoms that is responsible for the specific properties of an organic compound. A functional group undergoes the same types of chemical reactions in every molecule in which it is found. Therefore, compounds with similar groups are classified together.

The compounds in **Figure 3.1** have four carbon atoms, but they have very different physical properties due to their different functional groups. Some functional groups and their characteristic general formulas are shown in **Figure 3.2.** Many of the names may be familiar to you.

FIGURE 3.1

<table>
<tr><th colspan="5">COMPARING CLASSES OF ORGANIC COMPOUNDS</th></tr>
<tr><th>Name</th><th>Structural formula</th><th>Melting point (°C)</th><th>Boiling point (°C)</th><th>Density (g/mol)</th></tr>
<tr><td>Butane</td><td>H H H H
| | | |
H-C-C-C-C-H
| | | |
H H H H</td><td>−138.4</td><td>−0.5</td><td>0.5788</td></tr>
<tr><td>1-Butanol</td><td>H H H H
| | | |
HO-C-C-C-C-H
| | | |
H H H H</td><td>−89.5</td><td>117.2</td><td>0.8098</td></tr>
<tr><td>Butanoic acid</td><td>O H H H
‖ | | |
HO-C-C-C-C-H
| | |
H H H</td><td>−4.5</td><td>163.5</td><td>0.9577</td></tr>
<tr><td>2-Butanone</td><td>H O H H
| ‖ | |
H-C-C-C-C-H
| | |
H H H</td><td>−86.3</td><td>79.6</td><td>0.8054</td></tr>
<tr><td>Diethyl ether</td><td>H H H H
| | | |
H-C-C-O-C-C-H
| | | |
H H H H</td><td>−116.2</td><td>34.5</td><td>0.7138</td></tr>
</table>

Differentiated Instruction

INCLUSION

Have visual and tactile learners use molecular model kits to construct the compounds in **Figure 3.1.** Have students work in groups, and assign each group a model to construct. When all the groups have finished, have two groups compare their models and describe the similarities and differences. Be sure that all students get a chance to evaluate each molecular model.

FIGURE 3.2

CLASSES OF ORGANIC COMPOUNDS

Class	Functional group	General formula
alcohol	$-OH$	$R-OH$
alkyl halide	$-X (X = F, Cl, Br, I)$	$R-X$
ether	$-O-$	$R-O-R'$
aldehyde	$-\overset{O}{\overset{\|}{C}}-H$	$R-\overset{O}{\overset{\|}{C}}-H$
ketone	$-\overset{O}{\overset{\|}{C}}-$	$R-\overset{O}{\overset{\|}{C}}-R'$
amine	$-\underset{\|}{N}-$	$R-\underset{\underset{R'}{\|}}{N}-R''$
carboxylic acid	$-\overset{O}{\overset{\|}{C}}-OH$	$R-\overset{O}{\overset{\|}{C}}-OH$
ester	$-\overset{O}{\overset{\|}{C}}-O-$	$R-\overset{O}{\overset{\|}{C}}-O-R'$

Functional Groups

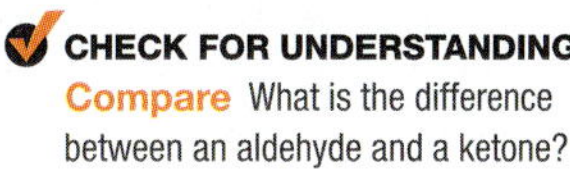

CHECK FOR UNDERSTANDING
Compare What is the difference between an aldehyde and a ketone?

Alcohols

Alcohols are organic compounds that contain one or more hydroxyl groups. The general formula for a class of organic compounds consists of the functional group and the letter *R*, which stands for the rest of the molecule. The general formula for alcohols is $R-OH$. Customarily, alcohols get their names by appending the suffix *-ol* to the hydrocarbon. For example, *butane* becomes *butanol*.

Hydrogen bonding in alcohols explains some of their properties and uses. Cold creams, lipsticks, body lotions, and similar products generally include the alcohol 1,2,3-propanetriol, commonly called *glycerol*, to keep them moist. A model for glycerol is shown in **Figure 3.3.** Multiple hydroxyl groups allow glycerol to form many hydrogen bonds with water molecules.

Alcohols are sometimes used today as alternative fuels and as octane enhancers in fuel for automobiles. Ethanol is combined with gasoline, for example, in a one-to-nine ratio to produce gasohol. Some experts have promoted the use of gasohol as a fuel for automobiles because it burns more cleanly and efficiently. However, there are also disadvantages. The combustion of ethanol produces only about 60% as much energy per gram as the combustion of gasoline does. The presence of ethanol also causes increased water absorption in the fuel.

FIGURE 3.3

Alcohols Glycerol contains three hydroxyl groups. This structure allows it to form multiple hydrogen bonds with water. Glycerol is added to skin products as a moisturizer.

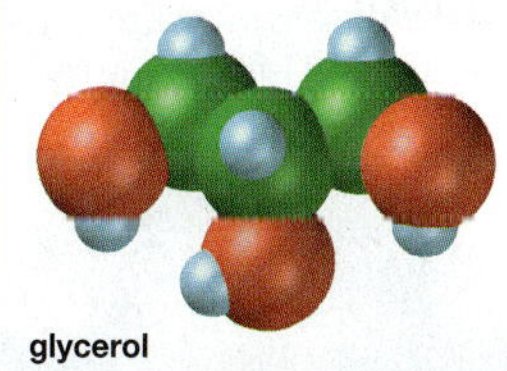
glycerol

Alternative Assessment

Have students identify items at home or in a store that contain alcohol. Tell them to read product labels and look for the *-ol* ending, which is found in IUPAC names and some common names, and the word *alcohol*, which is found in some common names. Examples include windshield-cleaning fluid (methanol or methyl alcohol), liquid medicines (ethanol or ethyl alcohol), and hand lotion (1,2,3-propanetriol or glycerol).

Teaching Tip

Though they have similar symbols, be sure that students understand that the hydroxyl group, —OH, and the hydroxide ion, OH^-, are not the same.

Check for Understanding

Answer: In an aldehyde, the carbon that is double-bonded to the oxygen always has a single hydrogen for one of its remaining bonds. The same carbon in a ketone has two alkyl groups bonded to it.

ENGLISH LEARNERS

Have students recognize that although there are thousands of different compounds, the trick is to look at the endings of the names to classify them properly. For example, alcohols end with *-ol*, as in *methanol*. Have students prepare a table to help them recognize functional groups as they study this section. They should recognize that ketones have *-one* in their endings, as in *acetone*, while aldehydes have *-hyde* in their endings, as in *formaldehyde*.

Organic Chemistry 689

▼ Teach *continued*

Classroom Discussion

Ask students to draw on their understanding of chemical equilibria to suggest factors that might affect the equilibrium between monatomic oxygen, diatomic oxygen, and ozone that exists in the stratosphere.

Application

Because of ozone depletion, CFCs are being replaced as refrigerants by hydrochlorofluorocarbons (HCFCs) and hydrofluorocarbons (HFCs). HCFCs and HFCs contain at least one hydrogen atom, whereas CFCs contain no hydrogen atoms. HCFCs and HFCs break down in the atmosphere, just as CFCs do, but they are much less stable and remain in the atmosphere for a much shorter period of time.

Misconception Alert!

Students may think that ozone exists in large amounts in the stratosphere. Actually, if all the ozone in the atmosphere could be transported to Earth's surface, it would form a layer that is only a few millimeters thick, due to atmospheric pressure.

Teaching Tip

The solubilities of ethers and alcohols in water are similar. This similarity can be explained by the fact that ethers, like alcohols, can form hydrogen bonds with water molecules. Their similarity to water in this respect is part of what makes ethers good solvents.

Alkyl Halides

Alkyl halides are organic compounds in which one or more halogen atoms—fluorine, chlorine, bromine, or iodine—are substituted for one or more hydrogen atoms in a hydrocarbon. Because —*X* is often used to represent any halogen, an alkyl halide may be represented by the general formula *R*—*X*.

Alkyl halides are some of the most widely used organic chemicals. A family of alkyl halides that has received widespread attention in recent years is the chlorofluorocarbons, or CFCs. CFCs are alkyl halides that contain both chlorine and fluorine. The formulas for two widely used CFCs, Freon-11 and Freon-12, are shown below.

```
      Cl                    F
      |                     |
   F— C —Cl             Cl— C —F
      |                     |
      Cl                    Cl
```

trichlorofluoromethane (Freon-11)   dichlorodifluoromethane (Freon-12)

CFCs, which have been used as liquid refrigerants, contribute to the destruction of ozone in the upper atmosphere. When released into the atmosphere, CFCs can break down and release free chlorine atoms.

$$CCl_2F_2 \xrightarrow{\text{solar radiation}} Cl + CClF_2$$

The released chlorine atoms attack molecules of ozone, O_3, found in the upper atmosphere. The ozone is converted to diatomic oxygen.

$$Cl + O_3 \longrightarrow ClO + O_2$$

Chlorine atoms are eventually regenerated in various ways, including the reaction of ClO with O.

$$ClO + O \longrightarrow Cl + O_2$$

This makes it possible for a single chlorine atom to destroy thousands of ozone molecules. Because CFCs are a major cause of ozone depletion, more than 100 nations signed an agreement in 1987 to reduce the amount of CFCs produced.

Another alkyl halide is tetrafluoroethene, C_2F_4. It is joined in long chains to make a material with the trade name Teflon®. Because of the unreactive carbon-fluorine bond, Teflon is inactive and stable to about 325°C. It also has a low coefficient of friction, which means that other objects slide smoothly over its surface. These properties enable Teflon to be used in heat-resistant machine parts that cannot be lubricated. It is also used in making utensils with "nonstick" surfaces, such as the frying pan in **Figure 3.4.**

FIGURE 3.4

Alkyl Halides The nonstick coating on this pan is made of Teflon, an alkyl halide.

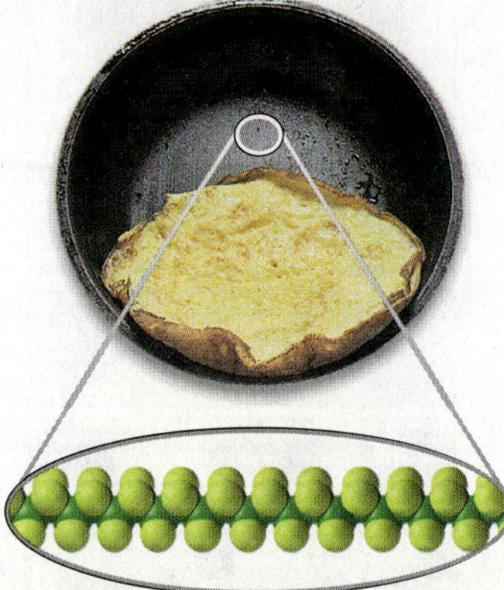

Ethers

Ethers are organic compounds in which two hydrocarbon groups are bonded to the same atom of oxygen. They can be represented by the general formula *R*—O—*R′*. In this formula, *R′* may be the same hydrocarbon group as *R* or a different one. Like alkanes, ethers are not very reactive compounds, so they are commonly used as solvents.

Differentiated Instruction

PRE-AP

Have students make a molecular model of diethyl ether. Ask students to explain its molecular geometry on the basis of VSEPR theory. Tell students that ethers can also be cyclic. Have them make a model of the smallest cyclic ether, ethylene oxide. Point out that this molecule is highly reactive and is used as the basis for epoxy resins and adhesives.

FIGURE 3.5

Aldehydes and Ketones Many common odors and flavors come from aldehydes and ketones.

✔ **CRITICAL THINKING**

Infer Why do you need structural formulas in order to be sure what kind of compound a substance is?

Aldehydes and Ketones

Aldehydes and ketones contain the *carbonyl group*, shown below.

$$-\overset{O}{\overset{\|}{C}}-$$

The difference between aldehydes and ketones is the location of the carbonyl group. **Aldehydes** are organic compounds in which the carbonyl group is attached to a carbon atom at the end of a carbon-atom chain. **Ketones** are organic compounds in which the carbonyl group is attached to carbon atoms within the chain. These differences can be seen in their general formulas, shown below.

$$R-\overset{O}{\overset{\|}{C}}-H \qquad\qquad R-\overset{O}{\overset{\|}{C}}-R'$$

aldehyde   ketone

Aldehydes and ketones are often responsible for odors and flavors. **Figure 3.5** gives some examples.

Amines

Amines are organic compounds that can be considered to be derivatives of ammonia, NH_3. Amines are common in nature. They often form during the breakdown of proteins in animal cells.

The unshared electron pair on the nitrogen atom makes amines act as weak bases in aqueous solutions, as shown below.

$$R-\underset{\underset{R'}{|}}{\ddot{N}}-R'' + H-O-H \rightleftharpoons R-\underset{\underset{R'}{|}}{\overset{\overset{H^+}{|}}{N}}-R'' + OH^-$$

TEACH FROM VISUALS

FIGURE 3.5 Have students identify the carbonyl group in each of the structural formulas and classify each compound as either an aldehyde or a ketone.

Classroom Discussion

Ask students to find examples in this chapter in which common names rather than IUPAC names have been used. Point out to students that many widely used organic compounds are known by their common names rather than by their IUPAC names. For example, ethanoic acid is commonly known as *acetic acid*, and the compound referred to as *ether* is really diethyl ether. One reason for the use of common names is that many compounds have been known for a long time, and their common names have become widely established among chemists.

Critical Thinking

Answer: Structural formulas better represent the bonding in the molecule. They show the functional groups the molecule contains. C_2H_6O, for example, could be an alcohol or an ether.

ENGLISH LEARNERS

One way to help students remember amines is to point out that most amines have unpleasant odors. The stench of decaying proteins can be traced to compounds such as putrescine and cadaverine, whose names come from the words *putrid* and *cadaver*. Ask students to look up the definitions of these two words.

Organic Chemistry 691

▼ Teach *continued*

ChemisTrivia

The common names of many carboxylic acids come from the Latin names of the organisms or products in which they occur.

Acid	Source	Latin name for source
formic	ants	*formica*
acetic	vinegar	*acetum*
butyric or butanoic	butter	*butyrum*
caproic, caprylic, or capric	goats	*caprum*

Teaching Tip

Students may think that the properties of carboxylic acids differ from the properties of inorganic acids. Write ionization equations that illustrate how a carboxylic acid, such as acetic acid, takes part in the same kinds of chemical reactions as does an inorganic acid, such as hydrochloric acid.

▼ Assess and Reteach

Assess Use the Formative Assessment on this page to evaluate student mastery of the section.

Reteach For students who need additional instruction, download the Section Study Guide.

Response to Intervention To reassess students' mastery, use the Section Quiz, available to print or to take directly online at **HMDScience.com**.

FIGURE 3.6

Carboxylic Acids Citric acid, found in citrus fruits, contains three carboxylic acid groups, shown in red on the structural formula.

$$HO-\overset{\overset{\large O}{||}}{C}-CH_2-\overset{\overset{\large OH}{|}}{\underset{\underset{\underset{\large OH}{|}}{\underset{C=O}{|}}}{C}}-CH_2-\overset{\overset{\large O}{||}}{C}-OH$$

citric acid

Carboxylic Acids

Carboxylic acids are organic compounds that contain the carboxyl functional group. A member of this class of organic compounds can be represented by the general formula shown below.

$$R-\overset{\overset{\large O}{||}}{C}-OH$$

Carboxylic acids, like inorganic acids, react to lose a hydrogen ion and become a negatively charged ion in water.

$$R-\overset{\overset{\large O}{||}}{C}-OH \overset{H_2O}{\rightleftarrows} R-\overset{\overset{\large O}{||}}{C}-O^- + H^+$$

Carboxylic acids are much weaker than many inorganic acids, such as hydrochloric, sulfuric, and nitric acids. Acetic acid, the weak acid in vinegar, is a carboxylic acid.

A number of carboxylic acids occur naturally in plants and animals. For example, citrus fruits, shown in **Figure 3.6**, contain citric acid. Benzoic, propanoic, and sorbic acids are used as preservatives. All three acids kill microorganisms that cause foods to spoil.

Esters

Esters are organic compounds that have carboxylic acid groups in which the hydrogen of the hydroxyl group has been replaced by an alkyl group. Esters are considered *derivatives* of carboxylic acids because of their structural similarity to carboxylic acids. The general formula for an ester is given below.

$$R-\overset{\overset{\large O}{||}}{C}-O-R'$$

✔ SECTION 3 FORMATIVE ASSESSMENT

Reviewing Main Ideas

1. Give the general formula and class of organic compounds for each of the following:
   a. CH_3-OH
   b. CH_3-O-CH_3
   c. $Br-CH_2-CH_2-CH_3$
   d. $CH_3-CH_2-\overset{\overset{\large O}{||}}{C}-OH$
   e. $CH_3-\overset{\overset{\large O}{||}}{C}-H$
   f. $CH_3-CH_2-NH_2$
   g. $CH_3-\overset{\overset{\large O}{||}}{C}-O-CH_2-CH_3$
   h. $CH_3-\overset{\overset{\large O}{||}}{C}-CH_3$
2. Compare the boiling points of alcohols, ethers, and alkanes, and explain one reason for the differences.
3. How are aldehydes and ketones alike? How are they different?
4. How do the strengths of organic acids compare with the strengths of most inorganic acids?

✔ Critical Thinking

5. **APPLYING MODELS** Identify the functional groups in vanillin, shown in **Figure 3.5**.

Answers to Section Assessment

1. **a.** alcohol; $R-OH$
   b. ether; $R-O-R'$
   c. alkyl halide; $R-X$
   d. carboxylic acid **e.** aldehyde

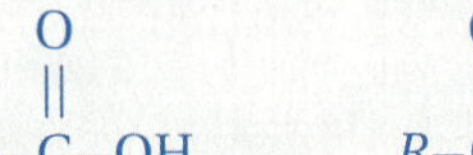

   $R-\overset{\overset{\large O}{||}}{C}-OH$ $R-\overset{\overset{\large O}{||}}{C}-H$

   f. amine; $R-NH_2$
   g. ester **h.** ketone

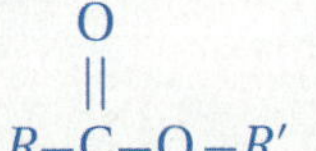

   $R-\overset{\overset{\large O}{||}}{C}-O-R'$ $R-\overset{\overset{\large O}{||}}{C}-R'$

2. The boiling points of alcohols are higher than those of alkanes and ethers of the same molar mass because hydrogen bonds must be broken in alcohols before they are able to boil.
3. Both contain the carbonyl group. The carbonyl group is at the end of a carbon chain in an aldehyde and within a carbon chain in a ketone.
4. Organic acids are weaker.
5. aldehyde, alcohol, and ether

SECTION 4

Organic Reactions

Key Terms

substitution reaction
addition reaction
condensation reaction
elimination reaction
polymer
monomer
copolymer

Main Ideas

- Atoms replace one another in substitution reactions.
- Addition reactions increase a molecule's saturation.
- Molecules combine in condensation reactions.
- A smaller molecule breaks off from a larger one in an elimination reaction.
- Polymers are large molecules made of smaller units.
- Addition reactions produce addition polymers.
- Condensation reactions often make polymers.

MAIN IDEA

Atoms replace one another in substitution reactions.

A **substitution reaction** is one in which one or more atoms replace another atom or group of atoms in a molecule. The reaction between an alkane, such as methane, and a halogen, such as chlorine, to form an alkyl halide is an example of a substitution reaction. Notice that in this reaction, a chlorine atom replaces a hydrogen atom on the methane molecule.

$$\underset{\text{methane}}{H_3C{-}H} + \underset{\text{chlorine}}{Cl{-}Cl} \longrightarrow \underset{\text{chloromethane}}{H_3C{-}Cl} + \underset{\text{hydrogen chloride}}{H{-}Cl}$$

Additional compounds can be formed by replacing the other hydrogen atoms remaining in the methane molecule. The products are dichloromethane, trichloromethane, and tetrachloromethane. Trichloromethane is also known as chloroform, and tetrachloromethane is also known as carbon tetrachloride. CFCs are formed by further substitution reactions between chloroalkanes and HF.

$$Cl{-}CCl_2{-}Cl + H{-}F \xrightarrow{SbF_5} Cl{-}CCl_2{-}F + H{-}Cl$$

$$Cl{-}C(Cl)(Cl){-}F + H{-}F \xrightarrow{SbF_5} Cl{-}C(F)(Cl){-}F + H{-}Cl$$

MAIN IDEA

Addition reactions increase a molecule's saturation.

An **addition reaction** is one in which two parts of a molecule are added to an unsaturated molecule, increasing the saturation of the molecule. A common type of addition reaction is hydrogenation. In *hydrogenation*, hydrogen atoms are added to an unsaturated molecule. Vegetable oils are triesters of unsaturated fatty acids, long chains of carbon atoms that have many double bonds. When hydrogen gas is blown through an oil, hydrogen atoms may add to the double bonds in the oil molecule. Remember, saturation refers to a carbon molecule's number of double bonds. The fewer the double bonds, the less the saturation.

Differentiated Instruction

BELOW LEVEL

Some students may confuse the different types of reactions that occur. For instance, in the examples given above, a substitution reaction looks similar to an addition reaction. In both cases, a chlorine atom is being moved. Explain the difference by using molecular models. In the substitution reaction, a chlorine replaces a hydrogen. There is no change in bonding. It is a simple swap.

Show that in an addition reaction, a double bond is broken, and two chlorine atoms are then added.

Ask students what kind of reaction it would be if two hydrogen atoms were added instead of two chlorine atoms. a hydrogenation reaction

SECTION 4

Plan and Prepare ▼

Objectives

Upon completion of this section, students should be able to do the following:

- Describe and distinguish between the organic reactions: substitution, addition, condensation, and elimination.
- Relate some functional groups to some characteristic reactions.
- Identify the two main types of polymers and the basic reaction mechanisms by which they are made.

Classroom Catalyst

Bring in a banana, an orange, and a pear. Have students smell each fruit. Tell them that the aromas come from esters. Esters can be made in the lab by an acid-catalyzed condensation reaction between an alcohol and an acid. An example is the reaction that occurs between methanol and acetic acid to produce methyl acetate. Identify the esters responsible for each fruit's smell. Banana smell is caused by *n*-amyl acetate. Orange smell is emitted by *n*-octyl acetate. Pear smell is from isoamyl butryate.

Teach ▼

READING TOOLKIT

READING ORGANIZER Have students read the section and then organize what they have learned in a concept map. Concept maps should start with *Types of Organic Reactions.* Students should list each type of reaction, describe it, and provide examples.

Application

Hydrogenation can be controlled to produce a product of almost any consistency, from a liquid to a brittle solid. Hydrogenation of vegetable oils produces products such as margarine and cooking fats, which are easy to package and store. Research indicates, however, that there are health problems associated with diets high in saturated fats.

Organic Chemistry 693

▼ Teach *continued*

Demonstration

TESTING FOR DOUBLE BONDS

This is a demonstration of an addition reaction that tests for double bonds in oils. Using a **fume hood,** prepare an iodine solution by dissolving **1.5 g of iodine** in **50 mL of mineral oil.** Pour **10 mL of cooking oil** into a **50-mL beaker.** Place the beaker on an **overhead projector,** and project the image onto a **screen.** Add 3 mL of the iodine solution to the oil, and stir thoroughly. The color will disappear, indicating the addition of the iodine to the double bonds of the oil. This shows that cooking oil has double bonds and thus is an unsaturated fat.

$$\begin{array}{l} CH_2-O-\overset{O}{\overset{\|}{C}}-(CH_2)_7CH{=}CH(CH_2)_7CH_3 \\ | \\ CH-O-\overset{O}{\overset{\|}{C}}-(CH_2)_7CH{=}CH(CH_2)_5CH_3 + 3I_2 \longrightarrow \\ | \\ CH_2-O-\overset{O}{\overset{\|}{C}}-(CH_2)_7CH{=}CH(CH_2)_7CH_3 \end{array}$$

$$\begin{array}{l} CH_2-O-\overset{O}{\overset{\|}{C}}-(CH_2)_7-\overset{I}{\overset{|}{C}H}-\overset{I}{\overset{|}{C}H}-(CH_2)_7CH_3 \\ | \\ CH-O-\overset{O}{\overset{\|}{C}}-(CH_2)_7-\overset{I}{\overset{|}{C}H}-\overset{I}{\overset{|}{C}H}-(CH_2)_5CH_3 \\ | \\ CH_2-O-\overset{O}{\overset{\|}{C}}-(CH_2)_7-\overset{I}{\overset{|}{C}H}-\overset{I}{\overset{|}{C}H}-(CH_2)_7CH_3 \end{array}$$

Safety Wear **safety goggles, gloves,** and a **lab coat.**

Disposal Add sufficient unsaturated cooking oil to the saturated cooking oil and iodine mixture to react with the iodine. Combine all liquids, and store them in a **labeled container** for disposal by the school waste contractor.

Teaching Tip

Elimination reactions can occur with groups other than the hydroxyl group. For example, the elimination of a hydrogen halide from an alkyl halide is a common and important industrial reaction.

FIGURE 4.1

Hydrogenated Fats The fatty acid shown in the model for vegetable oil contains a double bond. During hydrogenation, which is used to produce margarine and vegetable shortening, addition of hydrogen atoms removes double bonds from fatty acids.

$$\left(\begin{array}{c} \text{H H H H H H H} \\ | \;\; | \;\; | \;\; | \;\; | \;\; | \;\; | \\ -\text{C}-\text{C}{=}\text{C}-\text{C}-\text{C}{=}\text{C}-\text{C}- \\ | \quad\quad\; | \quad\quad\; | \\ \text{H} \quad\quad \text{H} \quad\quad \text{H} \end{array} \right) + H_2 \xrightarrow{\text{catalyst}} \left(\begin{array}{c} \text{H H H H H H H} \\ | \;\; | \;\; | \;\; | \;\; | \;\; | \;\; | \\ -\text{C}-\text{C}{=}\text{C}-\text{C}-\text{C}-\text{C}-\text{C}- \\ | \quad\quad\; | \;\; | \;\; | \;\; | \\ \text{H} \quad\quad \text{H H H H} \end{array} \right)$$

An example of hydrogen addition is shown above. You see, the molecule still consists of long chains of carbon atoms, but it contains far fewer double bonds. This changes the material from an oil, which is a liquid, into a fat, which is a solid. When you see the word *hydrogenated* on a food product, you know that an oil has been converted to a fat by this process. Examples of an oil and hydrogenated fats are shown in **Figure 4.1.**

MAIN IDEA

Molecules combine in condensation reactions.

A **condensation reaction** is one in which two molecules or parts of the same molecule combine. A small molecule, such as water, is usually removed during the reaction. An example is the reaction between two amino acids, which contain both amine and carboxyl groups. One hydrogen from the amine group of one amino acid combines with the hydroxyl from the carboxyl group of the other amino acid to form a molecule of water. When repeated many times, this reaction forms a protein molecule.

$$\underset{\text{amino acid}}{\text{H}-\overset{\text{H}}{\overset{|}{\text{N}}}-\underset{R}{\underset{|}{\overset{\text{H}}{\overset{|}{\text{C}}}}}-\overset{\text{O}}{\overset{\|}{\text{C}}}-\text{OH}} + \underset{\text{amino acid}}{\text{H}-\overset{\text{H}}{\overset{|}{\text{N}}}-\underset{R'}{\underset{|}{\overset{\text{H}}{\overset{|}{\text{C}}}}}-\overset{\text{O}}{\overset{\|}{\text{C}}}-\text{OH}} \longrightarrow \underset{\text{dipeptide}}{\text{H}-\overset{\text{H}}{\overset{|}{\text{N}}}-\underset{R}{\underset{|}{\overset{\text{H}}{\overset{|}{\text{C}}}}}-\overset{\text{O}}{\overset{\|}{\text{C}}}-\overset{\text{H}}{\overset{|}{\text{N}}}-\underset{R'}{\underset{|}{\overset{\text{H}}{\overset{|}{\text{C}}}}}-\overset{\text{O}}{\overset{\|}{\text{C}}}-\text{OH}} + \underset{\text{water}}{H_2O}$$

Differentiated Instruction

INCLUSION

Use molecular models to help students understand what happens during an elimination reaction. Have students work in pairs to build a model of the amino acid glycine. Draw the structural formula on the board for students to use as a guide for building their model. Point out that if there is an excess of proteins in the body, the liver changes the amino acids in the proteins in a process that involves the elimination of ammonia. This process is referred to as *deamination.* Help students identify which part of their amino acid model contributes to the ammonia being eliminated. Students should identify the amino group. Point out that three amino acids—glycine, serine, and glutamic acid—can undergo deamination directly. In these cases, water reacts with the amino acid. The H^+ ion combines with the amino group to form ammonia, while the —OH group replaces the amino group.

FIGURE 4.2

Elimination Reaction Sucrose is dehydrated when it reacts with concentrated sulfuric acid. Elimination of water produces a compound that is mostly carbon.

MAIN IDEA

A smaller molecule breaks off from a larger one in an elimination reaction.

An **elimination reaction** is one in which a simple molecule, such as water or ammonia, is formed from adjacent carbon atoms of a larger molecule. A simple example of an elimination reaction is the heating of ethanol in the presence of concentrated sulfuric acid. Under these conditions, a hydrogen atom bonded to one carbon atom and a hydroxyl group bonded to the second carbon atom are removed from the ethanol molecule. A molecule of water is formed as a result.

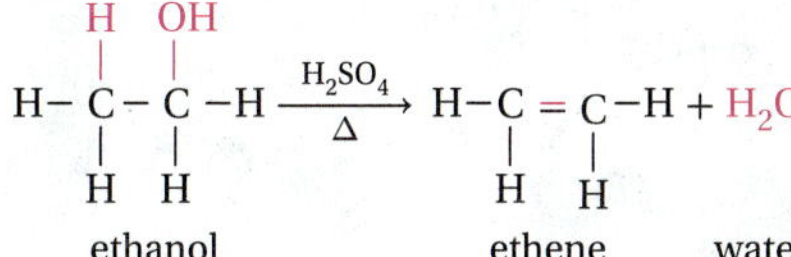

$$\text{ethanol} \xrightarrow[\Delta]{H_2SO_4} \text{ethene} + H_2O \text{ (water)}$$

Another example of an elimination reaction is the dehydration of sucrose with concentrated sulfuric acid, shown in **Figure 4.2.**

CHECK FOR UNDERSTANDING

Distinguish How is an elimination reaction different from a condensation reaction?

MAIN IDEA

Polymers are large molecules made of smaller units.

Polymers are large molecules made of many small units joined to each other through organic reactions. The small units are **monomers.** A polymer can be made from identical or different monomers. A polymer made from two or more different monomers is a **copolymer.**

Polymers are all around us. The foods we eat and the clothes we wear are made of polymers. Some of the most common natural polymers include starch, cellulose, and proteins. Some synthetic polymers may be familiar to you as plastics and synthetic fibers.

Teaching Tip

The uses of H_2SO_4 as a dehydrating agent are also discussed with Group 16 of the *Elements Handbook* (Appendix A).

Teaching Tip

Many students confuse condensation reactions and elimination reactions because water is the side product of both. Using models, show where the water molecule comes from. In a condensation reaction, the water molecule comes from both reactants, and the two molecules are joined by a double bond. In an elimination reaction, the water molecule comes from the same molecule, and the result is a double bond. An example of an elimination reaction occurs between ethyl chloride and potassium hydroxide, as shown by the following formula.

$$C_2H_5Cl + KOH \longrightarrow C_2H_4 + KCl + H_2O$$

The result is the same in both types of reactions—a double bond is formed between adjacent carbon atoms.

Check for Understanding

Answer: In an elimination reaction, a smaller molecule breaks off from a larger molecule. In a combination reaction, two molecules or parts of a molecule combine.

▼ Teach *continued*

Teaching Tip

Ask students to identify the critical feature of the ethene molecule that makes addition polymerization possible. the double bond Point out that in this polymerization reaction, ethene molecules are added to the double bond of other ethene molecules. It might help to show a hypothetical polymerization-reaction equation with only two molecules. (The actual reaction involves radicals.)

$$CH_2{=}CH_2 + CH_2{=}CH_2 \longrightarrow \,\left(CH_2{-}CH_2{-}CH_2{-}CH_2\right)$$

TEACH FROM VISUALS

FIGURE 4.3 Show students an opaque juice bottle like the one shown in the figure. Have them look on the bottom to note the recycling symbol with the number 2 in it and the letters *HDPE* below it. Type-2 plastics are commonly recycled. Have students hypothesize as to why this type of polymer is more easily recycled than other types, such as cross-linked polyethylene (cPE).

▶ MAIN IDEA

Addition reactions produce addition polymers.

An *addition polymer* is a polymer formed by addition reactions between monomers that contain a double bond. For example, molecules of ethene can polymerize with each other to form polyethene, commonly called polyethylene.

$$\underset{\text{ethene}}{nCH_2{=}CH_2} \xrightarrow{\text{catalyst}} \underset{\text{polyethylene}}{\left(CH_2{-}CH_2\right)_n}$$

The letter *n* shows that the addition reaction can be repeated multiple times to form a polymer *n* monomers long. In fact, this reaction can be repeated hundreds or thousands of times.

Various forms of polyethylene, shown in **Figure 4.3**, have different molecular structures. High-density polyethylene (HDPE) is a linear polymer. It has a high density because linear molecules can pack together closely. One use of HDPE is in plastic containers such as milk and juice bottles, because HDPE tends to remain stiff and rigid.

▶ MAIN IDEA

Condensation reactions often make polymers.

A *condensation polymer* is a polymer formed by condensation reactions. Monomers of condensation polymers must contain two functional groups. This allows each monomer to link with two other monomers by condensation reactions. Condensation polymers are usually copolymers with two monomers in an alternating order.

FIGURE 4.3

Polyethylene Properties of the different forms of polyethylene are reflected in their uses. Linear molecules of polyethylene can pack together very closely, as shown in the model of high-density polyethylene (HDPE). The branches of branched polyethylene keep the molecules from packing tightly, as shown in the low-density polyethylene (LDPE) structure. The cross-links of cross-linked polyethylene (cPE) make it very strong.

Differentiated Instruction

PRE-AP

Bring in a collection of erasers. Explain that the erasers are made of synthetic rubber. Interested students can research the history of rubber and present their findings to the class. Point out that a natural polymer made of isoprene units was originally used to rub out pencil marks. Inform students that natural rubber got soft and sticky in the summer and hard and brittle in the winter. The process of vulcanization solved the problem.

Polyamides and Polyesters

One example of a condensation polymer is shown below. A carboxylic acid with two carboxyl groups, adipic acid, and an amine with two amine groups, hexanediamine, react with each other to form water.

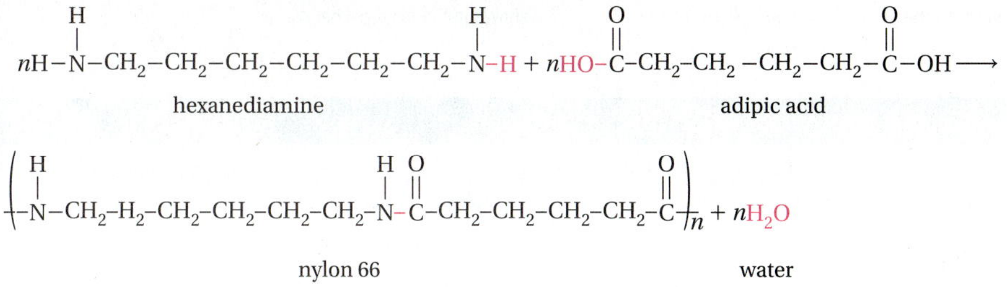

$$n\text{H-N(H)-CH}_2\text{-CH}_2\text{-CH}_2\text{-CH}_2\text{-CH}_2\text{-CH}_2\text{-N(H)-H} + n\text{HO-C(=O)-CH}_2\text{-CH}_2\text{-CH}_2\text{-CH}_2\text{-C(=O)-OH} \longrightarrow$$

hexanediamine adipic acid

$$\left(\text{-N(H)-CH}_2\text{-H}_2\text{-CH}_2\text{-CH}_2\text{-CH}_2\text{-CH}_2\text{-N(H)-C(=O)-CH}_2\text{-CH}_2\text{-CH}_2\text{-CH}_2\text{-C(=O)-}\right)_n + n\text{H}_2\text{O}$$

nylon 66 water

The product contains two kinds of monomers, the adipic acid monomer and the hexanediamine monomer. This copolymer is known as nylon 66 because each of the monomers contains six carbon atoms. Nylon 66 is one of the most widely used of all synthetic polymers.

Polyesters are another common type of condensation polymer. They are formed from dialcohols and dicarboxylic acids, which undergo a condensation reaction to form an ester group, linking the alcohol end of a monomer to the acid end of a monomer. Polyesters have many uses, such as in tires, in food packaging, and as fibers in permanent-press fabrics.

Chemists have synthesized many unique polymers, using reactions that take advantage of the chemistry associated with the functional groups on the monomers. And they have managed to craft materials containing certain desired properties by doing so.

ChemisTrivia

- The strength of nylon and other polymers can be increased by cold drawing, the stretching of cold fibers. Cold drawing aligns the polymer molecules.
- Silk and proteins are both natural polyamides. (See the paragraph on condensation reactions earlier in this section.)

Assess and Reteach ▼

Assess Use the Formative Assessment on this page to evaluate student mastery of the section.

Reteach For students who need additional instruction, download the Section Study Guide.

Response to Intervention To reassess students' mastery, use the Section Quiz, available to print or to take directly online at **HMDScience.com**.

SECTION 4 FORMATIVE ASSESSMENT

Reviewing Main Ideas

1. Can an addition reaction occur between chlorine and ethane? Why or why not?
2. Does an addition reaction increase or decrease the saturation of a molecule?
3. What functional groups does the molecule of water that results in the condensation reaction between two amino acids come from?
4. Explain how elimination reactions could be considered the opposite of addition reactions.
5. Why can a molecule that has only one functional group *not* undergo a condensation reaction to form a polymer?
6. Would it be possible to have an addition polymer synthesized from a monomer that has only single bonds? Why or why not?

Critical Thinking

7. **APPLYING MODELS** Polyvinyl chloride (PVC) is a polymer that is widely used in pipes and flooring. It is an addition polymer made from chloroethene, commonly known as *vinyl chloride*.
   a. Draw the structure of vinyl chloride. Then, look up the structure or check it with your teacher.
   b. Write the reaction for the polymerization of vinyl chloride to form polyvinyl chloride (PVC).

Answers to Section Assessment

1. No; addition can occur only on a double or triple bond. Ethane is a saturated hydrocarbon with neither.
2. increase
3. The water molecule comes from a hydrogen atom on the amine group and a hydroxyl group on the carboxyl group of the acid.
4. An elimination reaction results in the formation of double bonds (a decrease in saturation), while an addition reaction results in the loss of double bonds (an increase in saturation).
5. When a molecule that has a single functional group takes part in the first step of a condensation reaction, no functional groups remain in the product to continue the reaction.
6. No; double or triple bonds are required for addition reactions.
7. a. (H)(H)C=C(H)(Cl) — H and H on the left carbon, H and Cl on the right carbon.

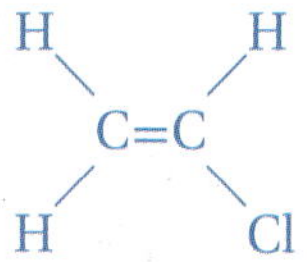

   Students might need to review the nomenclature of alkenes in Section 2. The Cl and H atoms can appear in any of the four positions.

   b. $n\text{CH}_2\text{= CHCl} \longrightarrow (\text{CH}_2\text{-CHCl})_n$
   vinyl chloride polyvinyl chloride (PVC)

Answers

1. CH_4N_2O (which is also the molecular formula of urea)
2. C_3H_5Br
3. CH_2O

Math Tutor — Calculating Empirical Formulas

An empirical formula shows the simplest whole-number ratio among the elements in a compound. For example, the simplest ratio among the atoms in benzene, C_6H_6, can be expressed by the empirical formula CH (or C_1H_1). Empirical formulas may be calculated from simple analytical data, as shown in the example below.

Problem-Solving TIPS

- Sometimes, you can deduce the mole ratios of the elements in a compound just by examining the moles of each element. If not, divide the moles of each element by the moles of the least abundant element in the compound.

Sample Problem

Find the empirical formula of acetone, a common organic solvent, the composition by mass of which is 62.04% carbon, 10.41% hydrogen, and 27.55% oxygen.

The easiest way to calculate an empirical formula from percentage composition is to consider a 100.00 g sample of the compound. In this case, a 100.00 g sample would contain 62.04 g of carbon, 10.41 g of hydrogen, and 27.55 g of oxygen. Convert each mass to moles so that you can compare the mole ratio of the three elements.

$$62.04 \text{ g C} \times \frac{1 \text{ mol C}}{12.01 \text{ g C}} = 5.166 \text{ mol C}$$

$$10.41 \text{ g H} \times \frac{1 \text{ mol H}}{1.008 \text{ g H}} = 10.33 \text{ mol H}$$

$$27.55 \text{ g O} \times \frac{1 \text{ mol O}}{16.00 \text{ g O}} = 1.722 \text{ mol O}$$

$$\frac{5.166 \text{ mol C}}{1.722} : \frac{10.33 \text{ mol H}}{1.722} : \frac{1.722 \text{ mol O}}{1.722}$$

$$3.000 \text{ mol C} : 5.999 \text{ mol H} : 1.000 \text{ mol O}$$

As you can see, the empirical formula of this compound is C_3H_6O.

Practice

1. Urea was the first organic compound to be synthesized in the laboratory. Urea's composition by mass is 20.00% carbon, 6.71% hydrogen, 46.65% nitrogen, and 26.64% oxygen. What is the empirical formula of urea?
2. An organic compound sometimes used in the manufacture of perfumes is 29.78% carbon, 4.17% hydrogen, and 66.05% bromine, by mass. What is the empirical formula of this compound?
3. The composition by mass of lactic acid is 40.00% carbon, 6.71% hydrogen, and 53.28% oxygen. What is the empirical formula of lactic acid?

CHAPTER 22 Summary

PREMIUM CONTENT
Interactive Review
HMDScience.com
Review Games
Concept Maps

SECTION 1 Organic Compounds

- The ability of carbon to bond to other elements and to allow different arrangements of atoms contributes to the diversity of carbon compounds.
- Isomers are compounds that have the same molecular formula but different structures. In structural isomers, the atoms are bonded together in different orders. In geometric isomers, the order of atom bonding is the same, but the atoms are oriented differently in space.

KEY TERMS

organic compound
catenation
hydrocarbon
isomer
structural formula
structural isomer
geometric isomer

SECTION 2 Hydrocarbons

- Alkanes are saturated hydrocarbons; they contain only single bonds. Physical trends in alkanes correspond to trends in alkane size and amount of branching.
- Organic compounds are named according to a systematic method.
- Unsaturated hydrocarbons have one or more multiple carbon-carbon bonds: these include alkenes, alkynes, and aromatic hydrocarbons.

KEY TERMS

saturated hydrocarbon
alkane
cycloalkane
alkyl group
natural gas
petroleum
unsaturated hydrocarbon
alkene
alkyne
aromatic hydrocarbon
benzene

SECTION 3 Functional Groups

- Functional groups are responsible for the properties of the organic compound that contains the functional group.
- Alcohols contain the hydroxyl functional group.
- Alkyl halides contain one or more halogen atoms.
- Two alkyl groups are joined to an oxygen atom in ethers.
- Both aldehydes and ketones contain the carbonyl group.
- Amines are derivatives of ammonia.
- Carboxylic acids contain carboxyl groups.
- In esters, the hydrogen atom of a carboxylic acid group has been replaced with an alkyl group.

KEY TERMS

functional group
alcohol
alkyl halide
ether
aldehyde
ketone
amine
carboxylic acid
ester

SECTION 4 Organic Reactions

- In substitution reactions, an atom or group of atoms is replaced. In addition reactions, an atom or group of atoms is added to a double or triple bond.
- In a condensation reaction, two molecules combine. In an elimination reaction, a small molecule forms from a large molecule.
- Polymers are large molecules made of many repeating units called *monomers*. A copolymer consists of two or more different monomers.

KEY TERMS

substitution reaction
addition reaction
condensation reaction
elimination reaction
polymer
monomer
copolymer

CHAPTER REVIEW

Review Answers

1. **a.** Catenation is the covalent binding of an element to itself to form chains or rings.
   b. Catenation contributes to the diversity of organic compounds by allowing carbon atoms to bond together in many possible arrangements.
2. **a.** the exact number and types of atoms in a molecule and the order in which they are bonded together
   b. to show the structure of a molecule and distinguish one isomer from another
3. no; they have different formulas.
4. no; they do not have rigid structures.
5. Hydrocarbons are molecules composed of hydrogen and carbon. They are important because they form the backbones of other organic compounds.
6. **a.** A *saturated* hydrocarbon has as many hydrogen atoms as possible, with only single covalent bonds to every carbon atom. An *unsaturated* hydrocarbon does not have as many hydrogen atoms because not all carbon atoms have four single covalent bonds.
   b. whether or not a solution contains the maximum amount of dissolved solute possible
   c. Alkanes are saturated. Alkenes, alkynes, and aromatic hydrocarbons are unsaturated.
7. **a.** aromatic hydrocarbon
   b. alkene
   c. alkyne
   d. alkane
8. **a.** C_nH_{2n+2}
   b. C_nH_{2n}
   c. C_nH_{2n-2}
9. **a.** a series in which adjacent members differ by a constant unit
   b. Add the suffix *-ane* to the prefix that corresponds to the number of carbon atoms in the chain.
   c. decane
10. saturated hydrocarbons that contain ring structures
11. **a.** As the number of carbon atoms in an alkane increases, so does its boiling point.
    b. The increased boiling point in larger alkanes is due to greater intermolecular attraction (dispersion forces).
    c. Petroleum products are distilled in various fractions divided by similar boiling points. In a distillation tower, the products with lower boiling points condense near the top, where it is cooler. The larger fractions with higher boiling points condense and are removed nearer the bottom.
12. to ripen fruit, to induce flowering, and to make plastics and commercially important alcohols
13. combustion in welding torches
14. benzene
15. **a.** heptane
    b. 2,2,4-trimethylhexane
    c. 5-butyl-2,2-dimethylnonane

CHAPTER 22 Review

SECTION 1

Organic Compounds

REVIEWING MAIN IDEAS

1. **a.** What is catenation?
   b. How does catenation contribute to the diversity of organic compounds?
2. **a.** What information about a compound is provided by a structural formula?
   b. How are structural formulas used in organic chemistry?
3. Can molecules with the molecular formulas C_4H_{10} and $C_4H_{10}O$ be structural isomers of one another? Why or why not?
4. Can molecules with only single bonds (and no rings) have geometric isomers? Why or why not?

SECTION 2

Hydrocarbons

REVIEWING MAIN IDEAS

5. What are hydrocarbons, and what is their importance?
6. **a.** What do the terms *saturated* and *unsaturated* mean when applied to hydrocarbons?
   b. What other meanings do these terms have in chemistry?
   c. Classify alkenes, alkanes, alkynes, and aromatic hydrocarbons as either saturated or unsaturated.
7. Classify each of the following as an alkane, alkene, alkyne, or aromatic hydrocarbon.
   a. 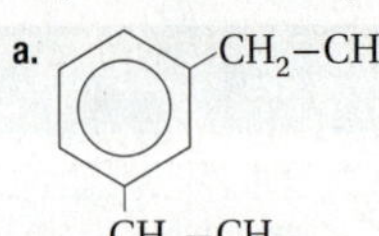

   b. $CH_3-CH{=}CH_2$
   c. $CH{\equiv}C-CH(CH_3)-CH_2-CH_3$
   d. $CH_3-CH(CH_3)-CH_2-CH_2-CH_2-CH_2-CH_3$
8. Give the general formula for the members of the following:
   a. alkane series
   b. alkene series
   c. alkyne series
9. **a.** What is a homologous series?
   b. By what method are straight-chain hydrocarbons named?
   c. Name the straight-chain alkane with the molecular formula $C_{10}H_{22}$.
10. What are cycloalkanes?
11. **a.** What trend occurs in the boiling points of alkanes?
    b. How would you explain this trend?
    c. How is the trend in alkane boiling points used in petroleum fractional distillation?
12. Give examples of ethene's commercial uses.
13. Give one use for ethyne.
14. What is the name of the parent hydrocarbon of simple aromatic hydrocarbons?

PRACTICE PROBLEMS

15. Name the following molecules. (Hint: See Sample Problem A.)
    a. $CH_3-CH_2-CH_2-CH_2-CH_2-CH_2-CH_3$
    b. $CH_3-C(CH_3)_2-CH_2-CH(CH_3)-CH_3$
    c. $CH_3-C(CH_3)_2-CH_2-CH_2-CH(CH_2-CH_2-CH_2-CH_3)-CH_2-CH_2-CH_2-CH_3$
16. Give the complete, uncondensed, structural formula for each of the following alkanes. (Hint: See Sample Problem A.)
    a. decane
    b. 3,3-dimethylpentane
17. Give the condensed structural formula for 2,2,4,4-tetramethylpentane.

700 Chapter 22

18. For each of the following, determine whether the alkane is named correctly. If it is not, give the correct name.

a. 1-methylpropane
b. nonane
c. 4-methylhexane
d. 4-ethyl-2-methylhexane

19. Name the following alkenes. (Hint: See Sample Problem B.)

a. $CH_2{=}CH{-}CH_2{-}CH_2{-}CH_3$

b. 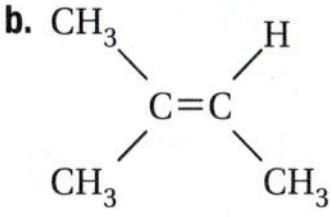

c. 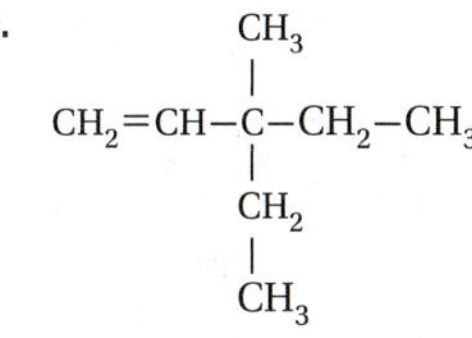

d.
```
CH=C–CH2–CH2–CH=CH2
   |
   CH3
```

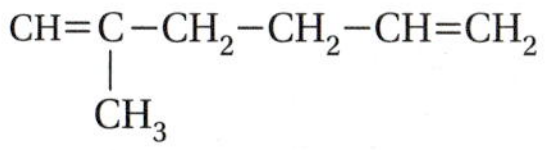

20. Name the following alkynes:

a. $CH{\equiv}C{-}CH_3$

b.
```
CH3–C≡C–CH–CH3
        |
        CH3
```

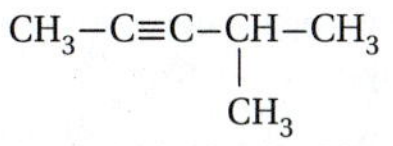

c.
```
CH3–CH–C≡C–CH–CH3
    |       |
    CH3     CH3
```

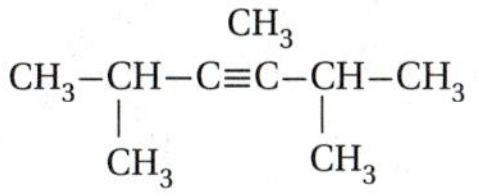

d. $CH{\equiv}C{-}CH_2{-}CH_2{-}CH_2{-}C{\equiv}CH$

SECTION 3

Functional Groups

REVIEWING MAIN IDEAS

21. Write the general formula for each of the following:

a. alcohol
b. ether
c. alkyl halide

22. Based on the boiling points of water and methanol, in which would you expect to observe a greater degree of hydrogen bonding? Explain your answer.

23. a. Why is glycerol used in moisturizing skin lotions?
b. How does this relate to the chemical structure of glycerol?

24. Write the general formula for each of the following:

a. aldehyde
b. ketone
c. carboxylic acid
d. ester
e. amine

25. Aldehydes and ketones both contain the same functional group. Why are they classified as separate classes of organic compounds?

26. How are esters related to carboxylic acids?

27. What element do amines contain besides carbon and hydrogen?

28. Explain why an amine acts as a base.

29. What classes of organic compounds contain oxygen?

SECTION 4

Organic Reactions

REVIEWING MAIN IDEAS

30. What type of chemical reaction would you expect to occur between 2-octene and hydrogen bromide, HBr?

31. How many molecules of chlorine, Cl_2, can be added to a molecule of 1-propene? a molecule of 1-propyne?

32. Compare substitution and addition reactions.

33. In a chemical reaction, two small molecules are joined, and a water molecule is produced. What type of reaction took place?

34. What are two reactions by which polymers can be formed?

35. What is the structural requirement for a molecule to be a monomer in an addition polymer?

36. Which of the following reactions is a substitution reaction?

a. $CH_2{=}CH_2 + Cl_2 \longrightarrow Cl{-}CH_2{-}CH_2{-}Cl$

b. $CH_3{-}CH_2{-}CH_2{-}CH_3 + Cl_2 \longrightarrow Cl{-}CH_2{-}CH_2{-}CH_2{-}CH_3 + HCl$

c.
```
              O
              ||
CH3–OH + CH3–C–OH ⟶

              O
              ||
         CH3–C–O–CH3 + H2O
```


CHAPTER REVIEW

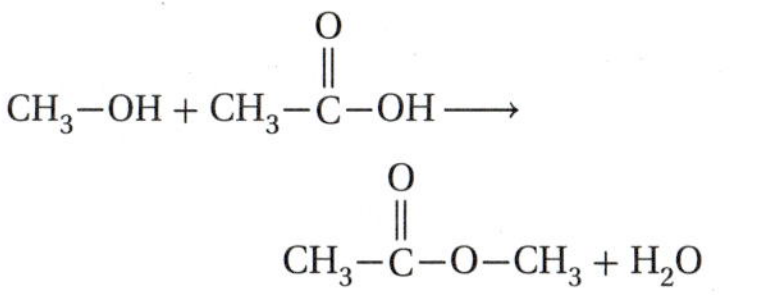

16. a.
```
  H H H H H H H H H H
  | | | | | | | | | |
H–C–C–C–C–C–C–C–C–C–C–H
  | | | | | | | | | |
  H H H H H H H H H H
```

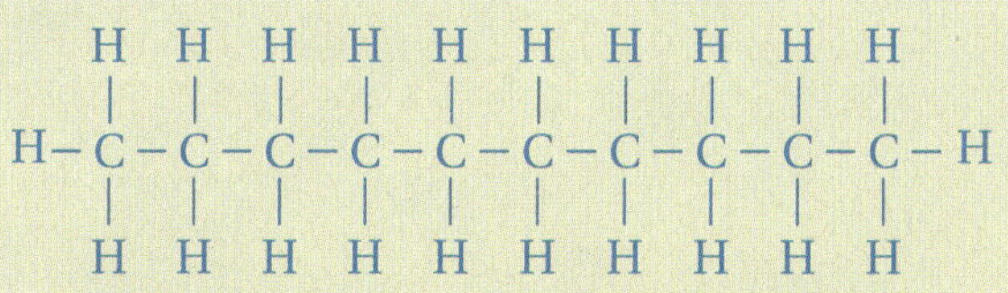

b.
```
           H
           |
         H–C–H
         |    |
  H  H   |    H  H
  |  |   |    |  |
H–C––C––C–––C––C–H
  |  |   |    |  |
  H  H   |    H  H
         |    |
         H–C–H
           |
           H
```

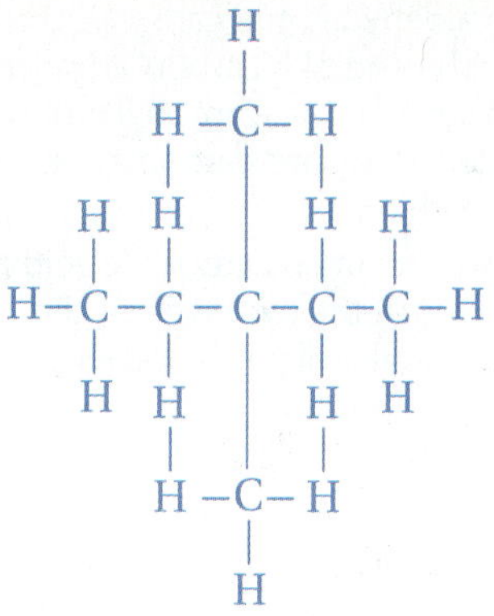

17. 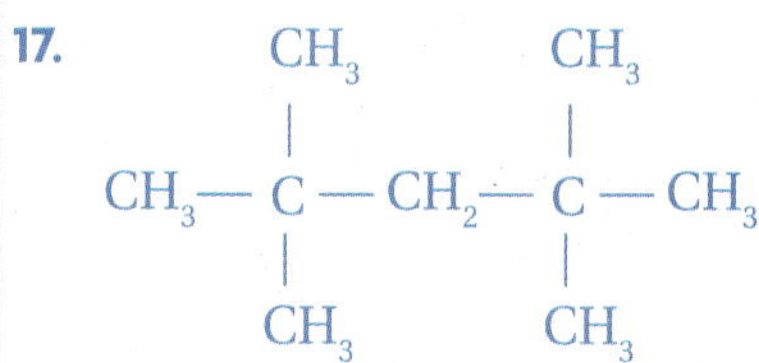

18. a. butane
b. correct
c. 3-methylhexane
d. correct

19. a. 1-pentene
b. 2-methyl-2-butene
c. 3-ethyl-3-methyl-1-pentene
d. 2-methyl-1,5-hexadiene

20. a. propyne
b. 4-methyl-2-pentyne
c. 2,5-dimethyl-3-hexyne
d. 1,6-heptadiyne

21. a. $R{-}OH$
b. $R{-}O{-}R'$
c. $R{-}X$

22. Water; its higher boiling point indicates that it has more hydrogen bonds that must be broken for the liquid to boil.

23. a. It tends to absorb water.
b. It has three hydroxyl groups that can each form a hydrogen bond with water.

24. a.
```
  O
  ||
R–C–H
```

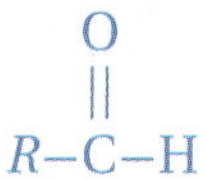

b.
```
  O
  ||
R–C–R'
```

c.
```
  O
  ||
R–C–OH
```

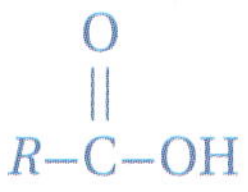

d. 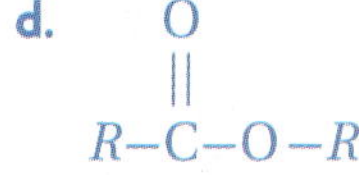

e.
```
R–N–R"
  |
  R'
```

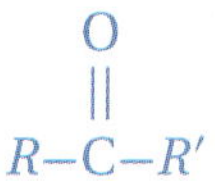

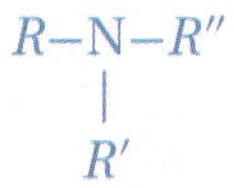

CHAPTER REVIEW

25. In aldehydes, the carbonyl group is at the end of a carbon-atom chain. In ketones, the carbonyl group is bonded to two carbon atoms within the chain.

26. Esters contain carboxylic acid groups in which the hydrogen of the hydroxyl group has been replaced by an alkyl group.

27. nitrogen

28. The unshared pair of electrons on the nitrogen atom in an amine attracts protons from water molecules, leaving OH^- ions in solution.

29. alcohols, ethers, aldehydes, ketones, carboxylic acids, and esters

30. addition

31. one; two

32. In a substitution reaction, an atom or group of atoms replaces a hydrogen atom in a molecule. In an addition reaction, an atom or group of atoms adds to a double or triple bond, forming single bonds.

33. condensation

34. addition and condensation

35. It must contain a double bond or a triple bond.

36. b

37. a

38. c

39. b

40. a. elimination
b. elimination
c. condensation
d. condensation

41. a. substitution
b. addition
c. addition
d. addition

37. Which of the following reactions is an addition reaction?

a. $CH_3{-}CH_2{-}CH{=}CH_2 + Br_2 \longrightarrow CH_3{-}CH_2{-}CH(Br){-}CH_2{-}Br$

b. 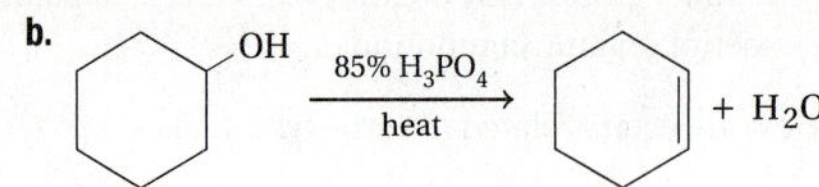

c. 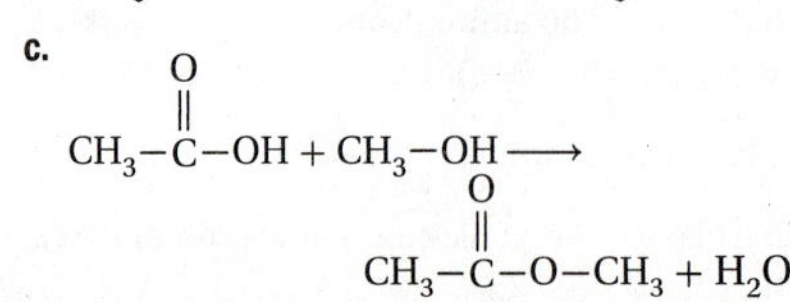

38. Which of the following reactions is a condensation reaction?

a. $CH_3C{\equiv}CH + HBr \xrightarrow{\text{ether}} CH_3{-}C(Br){=}CH_2$

b. 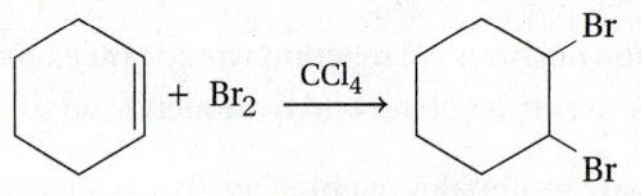 cyclohexene $+ Br_2 \xrightarrow{CCl_4}$ 1,2-dibromocyclohexane (Br, Br)

c. $CH_3{-}CH_2{-}OH + CH_3{-}CH_2{-}OH \xrightarrow{H_2SO_4} CH_3{-}CH_2{-}O{-}CH_2{-}CH_3 + H_2O$

39. Which of the following reactions is an elimination reaction?

a. $CH_2{=}CH{-}CH_2{-}CH_3 + Cl_2 \longrightarrow Cl{-}CH_2{-}CH(Cl){-}CH_2{-}CH_3$

b. $CH_3{-}CH(OH){-}CH_3 \xrightarrow{H_3O^+} CH_3{-}CH{=}CH_2 + H_2O$

c. $CH_3CH_3 + Cl_2 \xrightarrow[\text{heat}]{\text{light or}} CH_3CH_2Cl + HCl$

Mixed Review

REVIEWING MAIN IDEAS

40. Classify each of the following reactions as an elimination reaction or a condensation reaction:

a. $CH_3{-}C(Br){=}CH_2 + NaNH_2 \longrightarrow CH_3C{\equiv}CH + NaBr + NH_3$

b. $CH_3{-}CH_2{-}CH(OH){-}CH_3 \xrightarrow[\text{heat}]{85\%\ H_3PO_4} CH_3{-}CH{=}CH{-}CH_3 + H_2O$

c. $CH_3{-}CH_2{-}OH + CH_3{-}C(=O){-}OH \longrightarrow CH_3{-}CH_2{-}O{-}C(=O){-}CH_3 + H_2O$

d. 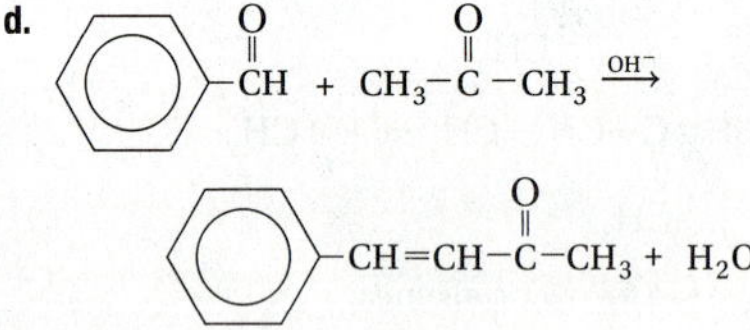

41. Classify each of the following reactions as a substitution reaction or an addition reaction:

a. $CH_3{-}CH_2{-}CH_2{-}CH_2{-}OH + HCl \xrightarrow[\text{heat}]{ZnCl_2} CH_3{-}CH_2{-}CH_2{-}CH_2{-}Cl + H_2O$

b. $CH_2{=}CH_2 + HBr \xrightarrow[25°C]{\text{ether}} CH_3{-}CH_2{+}Br$

c. $CH{\equiv}CH + HCl \xrightarrow{HgCl_2} CH_2{=}CH{-}Cl$

d. 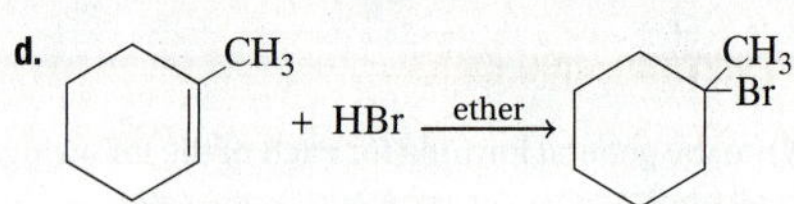

42. Identify each of the following reactions as an addition, substitution, elimination, or condensation reaction:

a. $CH_3-\overset{\overset{O}{\|}}{C}-OH + CH_3-\underset{}{\overset{\overset{OH}{|}}{CH}}-CH_3 \longrightarrow CH_3-\overset{\overset{O}{\|}}{C}-O-\overset{\overset{CH_3}{|}}{CH}-CH_3 + H_2O$

b. $CH_2{=}CH-CH_3 + Cl_2 \longrightarrow Cl-CH_2-\underset{\underset{Cl}{|}}{CH}-CH_3$

c. cyclohexane $+ Cl_2 \xrightarrow[\text{heat}]{\text{light or}}$ chlorocyclohexane $+ HCl$

d. 1-methylcyclohexanol (CH3, OH) $\xrightarrow[50°C]{H_3O^+,\ THF}$ 1-methylcyclohexene (CH3) $+ H_2O$

43. Give the molecular formula for each type of hydrocarbon. Assume each contains seven carbon atoms.
   a. an alkane
   b. an alkene
   c. an alkyne

44. a. Alkyne nomenclature is very similar to the nomenclature of what other group of hydrocarbons?
   b. How do these nomenclatures differ?

45. a. What are delocalized electrons?
   b. What is their effect on the reactivity of aromatic hydrocarbons?

CRITICAL THINKING

46. **Inferring Conclusions** Why are organic compounds with covalent bonds usually less stable when heated than inorganic compounds with ionic bonds?

47. **Inferring Relationships** The element that appears in the greatest number of compounds is hydrogen. The element found in the second greatest number of compounds is carbon. Why are there more hydrogen compounds than carbon compounds?

48. **Relating Ideas** As the number of carbon atoms in an alkane molecule increases, does the percentage by mass of hydrogen increase, decrease, or remain the same?

49. **Applying Ideas** How does ethylene glycol protect radiator fluid in an automobile from both freezing in the winter and boiling over in the summer?

USING THE HANDBOOK

50. The top 10 chemicals produced in the United States are listed in Table 7B of the *Elements Handbook* (Appendix A). Review this material, and answer the following:
   a. Which of the top ten compounds are organic?
   b. Write structural formulas for the compounds you listed in item (a).
   c. To what homologous series do each of these compounds belong?

51. The reaction of methane with oxygen produces two different oxides of carbon. Review this material in the *Elements Handbook* (Appendix A), and answer the following:
   a. What condition determines whether the product of the methane reaction is CO_2 or CO?
   b. If a home heating system is fueled by natural gas, what difference does it make if the combustion produces CO_2 or CO?

52. Silicon is similar to carbon in forming long-chain compounds. Review the material on silicon in the *Elements Handbook* (Appendix A), and answer the following.
   a. How does a long-chain silicon compound differ in composition from a long-chain carbon compound?
   b. The simplest alkane is methane. Methyl groups are found in all alkanes. What is a common subunit of a silicate? What is the geometry of that subunit?

53. Mercury in the environment poses a hazard to living organisms. Review the section on mercury poisoning in the *Elements Handbook* (Appendix A).
   a. Draw a structural formula for the organic mercury compound described in that section.
   b. What is the IUPAC name for this compound?

CHAPTER REVIEW

42. a. condensation
b. addition
c. substitution
d. elimination

43. a. C_7H_{16}
b. C_7H_{14}
c. C_7H_{12}

44. a. alkenes
b. The names of alkenes end with *-ene*. The names of alkynes end with *-yne*.

45. a. electrons that are shared between more than two atoms
b. Delocalized electrons contribute to the stability of aromatic hydrocarbons.

46. Ionic bonds are usually stronger than covalent bonds; more energy is needed to break ionic bonds.

47. Almost all carbon compounds contain hydrogen. In addition, hydrogen is contained in acids, hydroxides, ammonium compounds, and many other inorganic compounds.

48. The percentage of hydrogen decreases as the number of carbon atoms in an alkane increases.

49. The presence of ethylene glycol raises the boiling point and lowers the freezing point of the water in the radiator.

50. a. ethylene and propylene
b. $CH_2{=}CH_2$ (ethylene) $CH_2{=}CH-CH_3$ (propylene)
c. Both are alkenes.

51. a. the amount of oxygen present
b. CO is a deadly poison that binds more readily with heme in the blood than O_2 does. Cells die from a lack of O_2.

52. a. Silicon bonds to oxygen rather than to other silicon atoms. Carbon bonds directly to other carbon atoms.
b. SiO_4; tetrahedral

53. a.

$$H-\underset{\underset{H}{|}}{\overset{\overset{H}{|}}{C}}-Hg-\underset{\underset{H}{|}}{\overset{\overset{H}{|}}{C}}-H$$

b. dimethyl mercury

54. The actual list of compounds will vary from year to year.

55. Student lists may vary. Be sure students are considering petroleum products, such as certain clothes and foods, that may not be immediately obvious.

56. Answers may vary. Students should mention the nonbiodegradability of plastics and the need for recycling or for biodegradable materials.

57. Try not to model large molecules with this method; it becomes very difficult for the models to keep their shapes.

58. This activity will focus on the different groups on both sides of the double bond. The gumdrop models will easily show how there can be free rotation around a single bond. When two toothpicks are used to make the double bond, they will prevent rotation.

59. Approve all student experiment designs before they are carried out, and be sure that appropriate safety precautions are taken.

60. Approve all student experiment designs before they are carried out, and be sure that appropriate safety precautions are taken.

61. Answers may vary. In order to identify functional groups present in organic compounds, particular attention should be given to suffixes in IUPAC names. For example, *-one* indicates a ketone, *-ol* indicates an alcohol, and *-ate* indicates the ionized form of a carboxylic acid, often combined with either an alkali metal cation or ammonium cation as a salt.

62. Student suggestions may vary. Be sure proposed experimental designs have appropriate controls and safety precautions.

CHAPTER REVIEW

RESEARCH AND WRITING

54. *Chemical and Engineering News* publishes a list once a year of the top 50 chemicals. Find out which chemicals on the current year's list are hydrocarbons, and report your findings to the class.

55. Consult reference materials at the library, and read about products made from hydrocarbons. Keep a list of the number of petroleum-related products you use in a single day.

56. The widespread use of synthetic polymers in modern society has led to a number of new environmental problems. Find out what some of these problems are and what can be done to reduce them.

ALTERNATIVE ASSESSMENT

57. **Performance** Models are often used to visualize the three-dimensional shape of molecules. Using gumdrops as atoms and toothpicks to bond them together, construct models of different hydrocarbons. Use large gumdrops for carbon and smaller gumdrops for hydrogen.

58. **Performance** Using your gumdrop models, demonstrate why alkenes can have geometric isomers, while alkanes (except cycloalkanes) cannot.

59. **Performance** Devise a set of experiments to study how well biodegradable plastics break down. If your teacher approves your plan, conduct an experiment to test the procedure on products labeled "biodegradable."

60. **Performance** Your teacher will make available unlabeled samples of benzoic acid, ethyl alcohol, and hexanediamine. Develop an experiment to identify each. If your teacher approves your plan, identify the unknown substances.

61. Keep a list of the food you consume in a single day. Compare the content labels from those foods, and then list the most commonly used chemicals in them. With the aid of your teacher and some reference books, try to classify the organic chemicals by their functional groups.

62. As a class or small group, research the preservatives used in various foods. Examine their chemical structures. Determine a way to test for organic functional groups of possibly hazardous preservatives.

704 Chapter 22

Standards-Based Assessment

Answer the following items on a separate piece of paper.

MULTIPLE CHOICE

1. Which of the following hydrocarbons must be an alkane?
   - **A.** C_2H_2
   - **B.** C_5H_{10}
   - **C.** C_7H_{12}
   - **D.** $C_{14}H_{30}$

2. A hydrocarbon with the formula C_8H_{18} is called
   - **A.** octene.
   - **B.** octyne.
   - **C.** octane.
   - **D.** propane.

3. During a condensation polymerization reaction,
   - **A.** single bonds replace all double bonds that are present in the monomer.
   - **B.** water is often produced.
   - **C.** alcohol groups are formed.
   - **D.** an aldehyde group is changed to a ketone group.

4. In naming an organic compound, we
   - **A.** should remember that naming the locations of all functional groups is optional.
   - **B.** do not consider the number of carbon atoms in the molecule as a factor.
   - **C.** begin by identifying and naming the longest hydrocarbon chain.
   - **D.** ignore side chains when we name the molecule.

5. Which of the following compounds cannot have different isomers?
   - **A.** C_7H_{16}
   - **B.** C_5H_{10}
   - **C.** C_3H_8
   - **D.** $C_6H_{12}O_6$

6. Compounds that differ only in the order in which the atoms are bonded together are called
   - **A.** condensation polymers.
   - **B.** addition polymers.
   - **C.** structural isomers.
   - **D.** geometric isomers.

7. Examine the following structural formula:

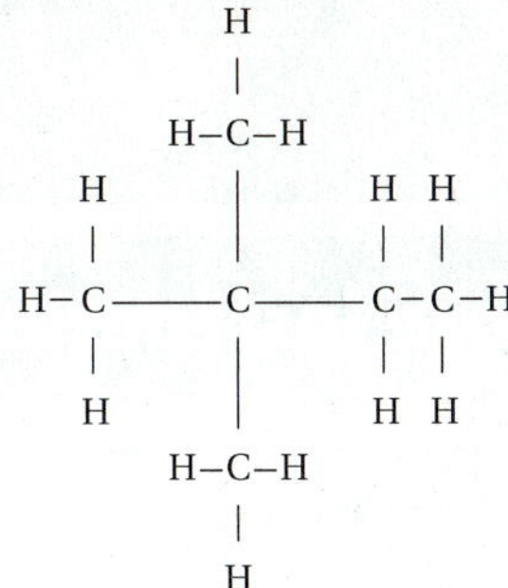

   The correct name for this compound is
   - **A.** 2,2-dimethylbutane.
   - **B.** 1,1,1-trimethylpropane.
   - **C.** 2-ethyl-2-methylpropane.
   - **D.** 3,3-dimethylbutane.

8. Organic functional groups
   - **A.** give characteristic properties to compounds that contain them.
   - **B.** always contain oxygen.
   - **C.** always contain a double or triple bond.
   - **D.** are present in every organic compound.

SHORT ANSWER

9. What feature must be present in a compound for it to undergo an addition reaction?

10. Organic compounds of what class contain only two elements?

EXTENDED RESPONSE

11. Describe the difference between substitution and addition reactions. Your answer should mention the degree of saturation of the organic compound.

12. Explain why some alkanes are gases, others are liquids, and still others are solids at room temperature.

Test Tip
If you become short on time, quickly scan the unanswered questions to see which might be easiest to answer.

STANDARDS-BASED ASSESSMENT

To give students practice under more realistic testing conditions, give them 60 minutes to answer all of the questions in this Standardized Test Preparation.

Test Answers

1. D
2. C
3. B
4. C
5. C
6. C
7. A
8. A
9. The compound must be unsaturated; that is, it must contain at least one double or triple bond.
10. hydrocarbons, which contain only carbon and hydrogen
11. In a substitution reaction, one or more atoms replace(s) an atom or group of atoms in a molecule, so the degree of saturation of the organic molecule is unchanged. In an addition reaction, additional atoms are added to a double or triple bond, so the degree of saturation increases.
12. Very small alkane molecules have very weak London dispersion forces between them, so they are not held together tightly; these low-mass alkanes are gases. Somewhat larger hydrocarbon molecules, such as those in gasoline and kerosene, have stronger London dispersion forces, so these molecules are held together in liquids. Alkanes that have very high molecular mass have much stronger London dispersion forces, so these compounds are solids.

Biological Chemistry

① Core Instruction

Chapter Resources

- The Teacher's Edition wrap has extensive teaching support for every lesson, including Misconception Alerts, Teach from Visuals, Demonstrations, Teaching Tips, Differentiated Instruction, and Problem Solving support.
- Several additional presentation tools are available online for every chapter, including Animated Chemistry features and Visual Concepts.
- You can open your lesson with the Why It Matters Video: Biological Chemistry.

Section	Instruction	Labs and Demonstrations Go Online for Materials Lists and Solutions Lists.
23.1	■ **Textbook:** Carbohydrates and Lipids **Animated Chemistry:** Four Major Biochemical Compounds **Teaching Visuals:** Types of Carbohydrates • Structures of Carbohydrates **PowerPresentations**	■ **Demonstration:** Testing for Simple Sugars ■ **Lab:** All Fats Are Not Equal (Core Skill) ■ **Lab:** Identifying Organic Compounds in Foods (Forensics) ■ **Lab:** Measuring the Release of Energy from Sucrose (Forensics)
23.2	■ **Textbook:** Amino Acids and Proteins **Teaching Visuals:** Levels of Protein Structure • Enzyme Mechanism • Activation Energy With and Without an Enzyme • Structures of Amino Acids • Structures and Roles of Several Amino Acids **PowerPresentations**	■ **Demonstration:** Denaturation of Protein ■ **Lab:** Casein Glue ■ **Lab:** Blood Typing (Forensics) ■ **Lab:** The Neighborhood Burglaries (Forensics)
23.3	■ **Textbook:** Metabolism **Teaching Visuals:** ATP/ADP Cycle • Catabolic Pathways • Hydrolysis of ATP **PowerPresentations**	■ **Lab:** Measuring the Iron Content of Cereal (Core Skill) ■ **Lab:** Measuring the Release of Energy from Sucrose (Forensics)
23.4	■ **Textbook:** Nucleic Acids **Teaching Visuals:** Hydrogen Bonding in DNA • Structure of DNA • DNA Replication • Structural Components of DNA and RNA • Using the Genetic Code • Photosynthesis and Respiration • Nitrogenous Bases of Nucleic Acids **PowerPresentations**	■ **Demonstration:** DNA Strands ■ **Lab:** The Murder and the Blood Sample (Forensics)

2 Support and Intervention

- **Interactive Reader** (English and Spanish)
- **Study Guide**
- **Interactive Review:** Review Games, Concept Maps, and Section Self-Checks
- **Scientific Reasoning Skill Builder**

3 Specialized Support

- **Chapter Summary Audio Files**
- **Interactive Reader Audio Files**
- **Differentiated Instruction:** Inclusion, Below Level, and English Learners (TE wrap)

Enrichment and Challenge

- **Differentiated Instruction:** Pre-AP (TE wrap)
- **Chemistry Explorers:** Dr. Charles Drew and Blood Transfusions (SE)
- **WebLinks**

Assessment

- **Section Formative Assessments** (SE)
- **Section Quizzes**
- **Chapter Review** (SE)
- **Chapter Tests A and B**
- **Alternative Assessment** (TE wrap)
- **Online Assessment and Remediation**
- **ExamView Banks**

Where do I find it?

		PRINT	DVD	ONLINE
1	Animated Chemistry		■	■
	Demonstrations (TE wrap)	■		■
	Interactive Whiteboard		■	■
	Labs		■	■
	PowerPresentations		■	■
	QuickLabs	■	■	■
	Teaching Visuals		■	■
	Textbook	■	■	■
	Visual Concepts		■	■
	Why It Matters Videos		■	■
2	Interactive Demos		■	■
	Interactive Reader	■	■	■
	Interactive Reviews		■	■
	Learn It! Videos		■	■
	Sample Problem Sets		■	■
	Scientific Reasoning Skill Builder		■	■
	Smart Grapher Tool		■	■
	Solve It! Cards		■	■
	Study Guide		■	■
3	Chapter Summary Audio Files		■	■
	Differentiated Instruction (TE wrap)	■		
	Interactive Reader Audio Files		■	■

CHAPTER 23

Chapter Overview

Section 1 discusses the properties and functions of carbohydrates and lipids.

Section 2 describes amino acids and polypeptides and explains how amino acid side chains influence protein structure and function.

Section 3 discusses how ATP is used as an energy source for making new molecules.

Section 4 describes the structure and replication of DNA and discusses how proteins are made.

▼ Focus and Motivate

Activate Prior Knowledge

Students may need a review of the following concepts:

- hydrogen bonds
- chemical reactions
- organic functional groups
- polymerization

About the Image

Chemical reactions occur in all living organisms, including the honeybee shown pollinating a poppy. Chemical reactions also occur in the poppy, providing substances upon which almost all living organisms depend. The study of chemical reactions in living organisms is known as biological chemistry, or simply biochemistry.

Why It Matters

Students can access the video online and find other helpful resources at **HMDScience.com**.

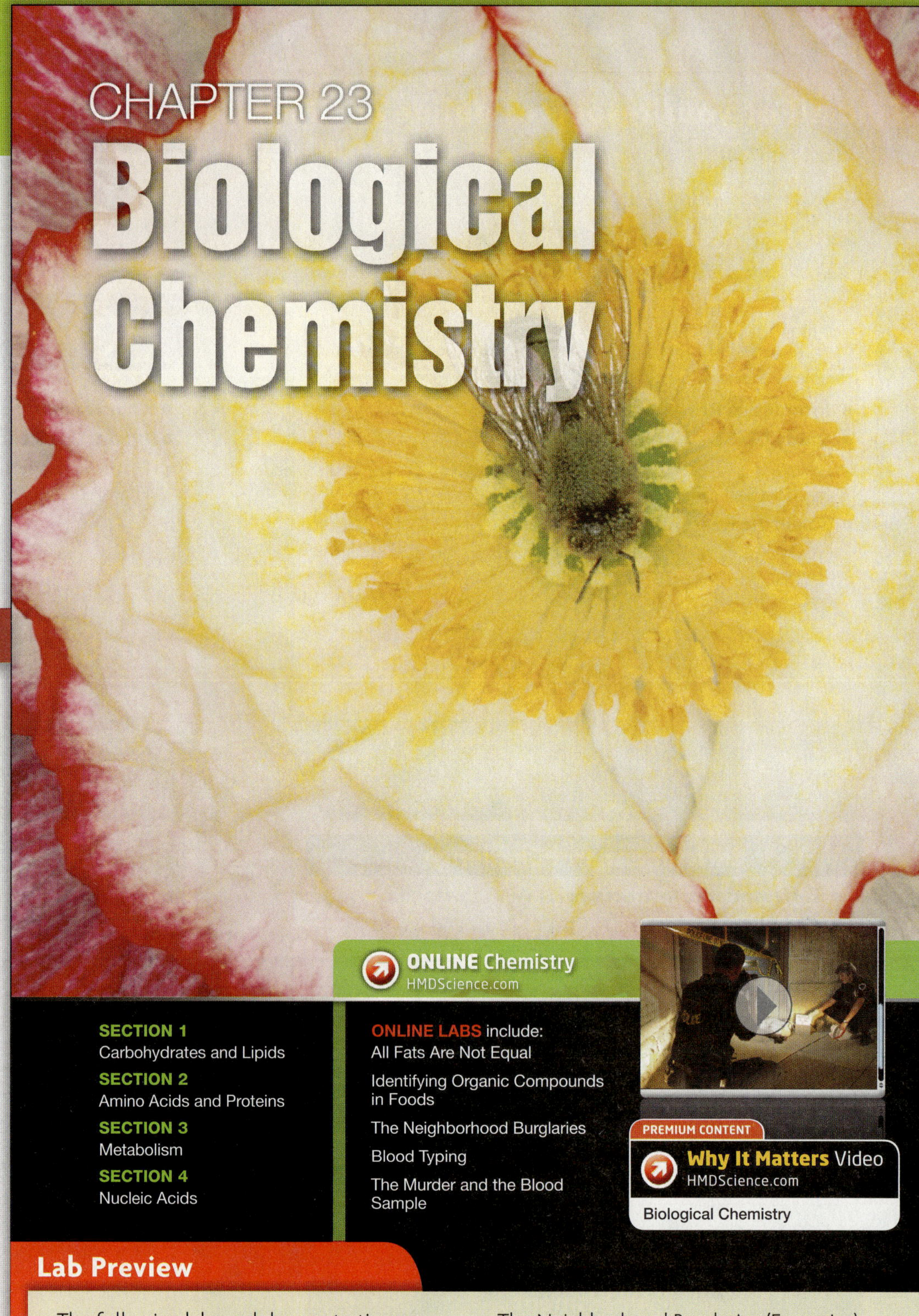

ONLINE Chemistry
HMDScience.com

SECTION 1
Carbohydrates and Lipids

SECTION 2
Amino Acids and Proteins

SECTION 3
Metabolism

SECTION 4
Nucleic Acids

ONLINE LABS include:

All Fats Are Not Equal

Identifying Organic Compounds in Foods

The Neighborhood Burglaries

Blood Typing

The Murder and the Blood Sample

PREMIUM CONTENT

Why It Matters Video
HMDScience.com

Biological Chemistry

Lab Preview

The following labs and demonstrations support the concepts presented in this chapter.

LABS

All Fats Are Not Equal (Core Skill)

Identifying Organic Compounds in Foods (Forensics)

Measuring the Release of Energy from Sucrose (Forensics)

Casein Glue

Blood Typing (Forensics)

The Neighborhood Burglaries (Forensics)

Measuring the Iron Content of Cereal (Core Skill)

Measuring the Release of Energy from Sucrose (Forensics)

The Murder and the Blood Sample (Forensics)

DEMONSTRATIONS

Testing for Simple Sugars

Denaturation of Protein

DNA Strands

Carbohydrates and Lipids

SECTION 1

Main Ideas

- Carbohydrates contain carbon, hydrogen, and oxygen atoms.
- Lipids have a high percentage of carbon and hydrogen atoms.

Key Terms

carbohydrate
monosaccharide
disaccharide
condensation reaction
hydrolysis
polysaccharide
lipid
fatty acid
saponification

Biochemistry is the study of the chemicals and reactions that occur in living organisms. Biochemical compounds are often large and complex organic molecules, but their chemistry is similar to that of the smaller organic molecules. In this chapter, you will study many important biochemical molecules and learn why they are needed to stay healthy. Two of the most common types of molecules that you may know about are *carbohydrates* and *lipids*. These molecules are important parts of the food that you eat and provide most of the energy that your body needs.

MAIN IDEA

Carbohydrates contain carbon, hydrogen, and oxygen atoms.

Sugars, starches, and *cellulose* belong to the large group of biochemical molecules called carbohydrates. **Carbohydrates** are molecules, composed of carbon, hydrogen, and oxygen atoms in a 1:2:1 ratio, that provide nutrients to the cells of living organisms. Their general formula is $C_m(H_2O)_n$. They are produced by plants through a process called *photosynthesis*. Cellulose provides structure and support for plants, and starch stores energy in plants. Because animals cannot make their own carbohydrates, they must get them from food. Carbohydrates provide nearly all of the energy that is available in most plant-derived food. Carbohydrates are also referred to as saccharides. This comes from the Greek word for sugar. It is also the basis for the name *saccharin*, a popular artificial sweetener.

Monosaccharides

A **monosaccharide** is a simple sugar that is the basic subunit of a carbohydrate. A single monosaccharide molecule contains three to seven carbon atoms. Monosaccharide compounds are typically sweet-tasting, white solids at room temperature. Because they have polar, hydroxyl (—OH) groups in their molecular structures, they are very soluble in water. The most common monosaccharides are *glucose* (also called *dextrose*) and *fructose*. Although both of these monosaccharides have the formula $C_6(H_2O)_6$, their structural formulas differ. As **Figure 1.1** shows, glucose in a water solution forms a ring made up of five carbon atoms and one oxygen atom, and fructose in a water solution forms a ring made up of four carbon atoms and one oxygen atom. Notice that both compounds have five —OH groups in their structures.

FIGURE 1.1

Monosaccharides Glucose and fructose both have 6 C, 12 H, and 6 O atoms. The arrangement of the C, H, and O atoms determines the shape and properties of each sugar.

CH_2OH, C, O, H, C, H, C, OH, H, C, OH, OH, C, H, OH

glucose

CH_2OH, O, H, C, H, OH, C, HO, C, C, CH_2OH, OH, H

fructose

Differentiated Instruction

BELOW LEVEL

Students can quickly fall behind if they do not understand the structure of a glucose molecule, so it is important that all students spend some time drawing and building models of glucose and fructose. Make sure they orient the hydroxyl groups correctly. The structural formula shown in **Figure 1.1** represents D-glucose, known commonly in the food industry as *dextrose*.

PRE-AP

Have students build both ring and open-chain structures. Explain that in the open-chain structure, glucose has an aldehyde moiety and fructose has a ketone. Show how the molecule transitions from a ring to an open structure. Also, tell students that there are 16 possible optical isomers of glucose, the most important being D-glucose, or *dextrose*.

SECTION 1

Plan and Prepare ▼

Objectives

Upon completion of this section, students should be able to do the following:

- Describe the structural characteristics of simple and complex carbohydrates.
- Explain the role of carbohydrates in living systems.
- Describe the structural characteristics of lipid molecules.
- Identify the functions of lipids in living cells.

Classroom Catalyst

Place a can of a regular soft drink and a can of a diet soft drink in a tub of water. Ask students to speculate why one can floats and the other does not. Explain to students that aspartame, the artificial sweetener most commonly used in diet soft drinks, is about 200 times as sweet as sucrose. The regular soft drink is denser than the diet soft drink, because there is such a large amount of sugar in the regular soft drink, and only a small amount of sweetener in the diet soft drink.

Teach ▼

READING TOOLKIT

CLASSIFYING INFORMATION Ask students to define the basic nutrient groups. As students proceed through the chapter, they should list the major sources of these nutrients and describe how the nutrients are metabolized.

Application

Helen and Alfred Free's work in diagnostic chemistry led to the development of many tests used in urine testing. The Frees advanced diabetes testing with the first one-minute test for blood glucose, CLINISTIX®, introduced in 1956. This test pioneered the concept of self-testing for people who have diabetes. The Frees were inducted into the National Inventors Hall of Fame in 2000.

▼ Teach *continued*

ChemisTrivia

The average adult's blood contains 5 to 6 g of glucose. However, this quantity is only enough to supply the energy an adult needs for about 15 min. The human body continuously replaces the glucose used by breaking down compounds stored in the liver.

Demonstration

TESTING FOR SIMPLE SUGARS

Use **Benedict's solution** to test for simple sugars in **several types of juice.** Benedict's solution, an **alkaline solution of copper(II) sulfate,** changes color in the presence of monosaccharides, such as glucose and fructose. (More complex sugars, such as the disaccharides sucrose and lactose, cannot be identified by using this test.)

1. Add **4 mL of white grape juice** and **1 mL of Benedict's solution** to a **test tube,** and swirl the liquids to mix them.
2. Repeat step 1 two more times, but use **lime juice** and then **apple juice** in place of the white grape juice.
3. Place all three test tubes in a **boiling water bath.**
4. Wait several minutes to see if color changes occur. Use a **Benedict's solution reference color sheet** to determine the concentration of sugar in each test tube.

Safety Wear **safety goggles** and a **lab apron.**

Disposal All of the solutions can be rinsed down the drain with excess water.

Critical Thinking

Answer: A molecule of water results from the combining of the two. Just as in dehydration, water, in a sense, is taken away.

FIGURE 1.2

Sugar Beets Most of the sugar produced throughout the world comes from sugar beets, such as those shown here, or from sugar cane.

Glucose is the most abundant monosaccharide in nature. It is also the most important monosaccharide nutritionally because glucose provides energy for cellular activities. The carbohydrates we eat are broken down into glucose, which may be used immediately by cells or stored in the liver, as glycogen, for later use.

Fructose, also called *fruit sugar,* is found in most fruits, honey, and corn syrup. The sweetest naturally occurring sugar, fructose is sweeter than table sugar. Because fructose is not regulated by insulin, as glucose is, it does not trigger the release of the hormone *leptin* that causes us to feel "full." Some research links fructose consumption to unhealthy weight gain.

Disaccharides

Generally, when someone asks for "sugar," the person is asking for the disaccharide *sucrose,* $C_{12}H_{22}O_{11}$. A **disaccharide** is a sugar that consists of two monosaccharide units that are joined together. Like monosaccharides, disaccharides have polar hydroxyl groups in their molecular structures and therefore are water soluble. Sucrose forms when a glucose molecule bonds to a fructose molecule. Commercially available sugar comes from sugar cane or sugar beets (see **Figure 1.2**). Another important disaccharide is *lactose.* Lactose is made up of a sugar called *galactose* and glucose. Human milk is 7% to 8% lactose, but cow's milk is only 4% to 5% lactose. Infant formula is enriched with lactose to simulate human milk.

Carbohydrate Reactions

Carbohydrates undergo two important kinds of reactions: condensation reactions and hydrolysis reactions. A **condensation reaction** is a reaction in which two molecules or parts of the same molecule combine. **Figure 1.3** shows a condensation reaction in which a molecule of glucose combines with a molecule of fructose to yield a molecule of sucrose and a molecule of water.

Disaccharides and longer-chain polysaccharides can be broken down into smaller sugar units by hydrolysis. **Hydrolysis** is a chemical reaction between water and another substance to form two or more new substances. Sucrose will undergo a hydrolysis reaction with water to form glucose and fructose. This hydrolysis reaction occurs in many common processes.

FIGURE 1.3

Condensation Reaction The disaccharide sucrose is formed by a condensation reaction between glucose and fructose.

CRITICAL THINKING

Infer Why could this reaction also be called a dehydration synthesis reaction?

glucose + fructose → sucrose + water

Differentiated Instruction

ENGLISH LEARNERS

Students may have difficulty keeping track of the terminology introduced in this chapter. Remind them of the various root words in each. For example, *condensation* comes from "condense," or to combine or join. Review the condensation reactions and the importance of the orientation of the hydroxyl group by writing the following equations on the board:

glucose + glucose (alpha 1⟶4 linkage) ⟶ maltose (malt sugar)

galactose + glucose (beta 1⟶4 linkage) ⟶ lactose (milk sugar)

Whenever students see a word with the suffix *-lysis,* they can be sure it will mean breaking or splitting apart something. The term *hydrolysis* means splitting apart water. The term *lipolysis* means the breaking apart of a lipid into its component parts.

Cooking sucrose with high-acid foods, such as berries and fruits, causes it to break down into a mixture of equal parts glucose and fructose. This new mixture provides the sweet taste in jams and jellies, which is sweeter than the starting sugar. When lactose is broken down, glucose and galactose are formed. Some people do not produce the enzyme needed to break down the milk sugar in dairy products. This condition is called *lactose intolerance*. People who have this may feel ill when they drink milk or eat foods that have milk in them.

Polysaccharides

When many monosaccharides or disaccharides combine in a series of condensation reactions, they form a polysaccharide. **A polysaccharide is a carbohydrate made up of long chains of simple sugars.** Cellulose, starch, and glycogen are *polymers* of glucose, or polysaccharides, that contain many glucose monomer units.

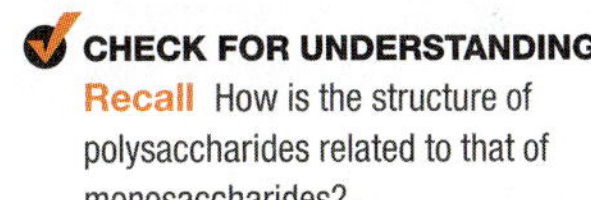

CHECK FOR UNDERSTANDING
Recall How is the structure of polysaccharides related to that of monosaccharides?

As shown in **Figure 1.4**, the glucose molecules in cellulose chains are arranged in such a way that hydrogen bonds link the hydroxyl groups of adjacent glucose molecules to form insoluble fibrous sheets. These sheets of cellulose make up plant cell walls. More than 50% of the total organic matter in the world is cellulose. People cannot digest cellulose, but when we eat fiber, which is cellulose, it speeds the movement of food through the digestive tract. Microorganisms that can digest cellulose are present in the digestive tracts of some animals. Cows and other herbivores have extra stomachs that hold the plants they eat for long periods of time, during which these microorganisms can break down the cellulose.

Starch is the storage form of glucose in plants. Starch from foods such as potatoes and cereal grains makes up about two-thirds of the food eaten by people throughout the world. Starch in food is broken down into glucose during digestion. Glucose is broken down further in metabolic reactions.

FIGURE 1.4

Glucose Monomers Glucose is the monosaccharide subunit for glycogen, cellulose, and starch. Notice that these three polymers differ in their arrangement of glucose monomers.

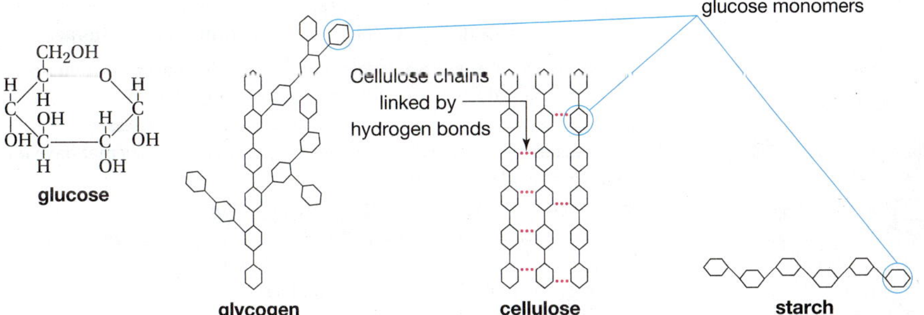

INCLUSION

Have students who are tactile learners make a paper or three-dimensional model with at least six subunits of glucose. Show them what a difference it makes whether the last hydroxyl group on the right is pointing up or down. In alpha-D-glucose, shown in **Figure 1.4**, the hydroxyl group is pointing down. When these glucose molecules make a chain (1⟶4 linkage), starch is formed. Have students look closely at their structures and at the one drawn above. Starch tends to coil in a helical structure, with the polar hydroxyl groups pointing outward.

In beta-D-glucose, the hydroxyl group on the glucose is pointing up. When these glucose molecules make a chain (1⟶4 linkage), cellulose is formed. Again, have students look at their models and at the structure drawn above. Cellulose forms linear chains with the adjacent glucose molecules being "upside down" relative to each other. Separate chains are connected by hydrogen bonding. Tell students that this is what gives wood, which is 50% cellulose, its strength.

Application

Starch is found in granules in the leaves, roots, and seeds of plants. These granules are insoluble in cold water, but will break open in hot water to produce a colloidal suspension that thickens as the temperature increases. This phenomenon allows cornstarch to be used as a thickening agent in cooking.

Teaching Tip

Explain to students that glucose powers the cells of the body. Excess glucose is converted by a condensation reaction into glycogen, a substance that animals can store in their bodies. Glycogen makes up about 5% of the weight of the liver and about 0.5% of the weight of muscle tissue in mammals. Hydrolysis of glycogen stored in the liver and muscles can provide glucose to cells for about 15 hours during normal activity. Strenuous exercise depletes the available glucose and glycogen rapidly in a body, which is why many marathon runners eat a lot of starch the day before their race. This "carbohydrate loading" builds up the glycogen reserves of the runners.

Check for Understanding

Answer: Polysaccharides are several monosaccharides combined together, *mono-* = one and *poly-* = many.

Biological Chemistry 709

▼ Teach *continued*

ChemisTrivia

Detergents are used in laundry instead of soap because of hard water, which contains significant concentrations of calcium and magnesium ions. When soaps come in contact with hard water, calcium and magnesium ions in the water replace sodium ions in soap molecules. The result is an insoluble compound. This white, chalky compound is responsible for "bathtub rings" and lessens the cleaning effectiveness of the soap. Detergents have a sulfonic acid functional group instead of a carboxylic acid group. The sulfonic acid salts of calcium and magnesium are soluble, so detergents keep their cleaning power even in hard water.

Teaching Tip

Explain to students that the terms *hydrophilic* and *hydrophobic* describe how molecules interact with water or other solvents. Hydrophilic refers to something that "likes water" and hydrophobic refers to something that "fears water." A hydrophilic molecule or a hydrophilic portion of a molecule is polar, and therefore capable of forming hydrogen bonds with water or other polar molecules. Hydrophilic molecules can dissolve more readily in water than in oil or other nonpolar solvents. Hydrophobic molecules or portions of molecules tend to be neutral and nonpolar, and prefer other nonpolar solvents or molecular environments. Examples of hydrophobic molecules include alkanes, and molecules that make up oils and fats.

Check for Understanding

Answer: Saturated fatty acids have only single bonds. They are saturated because, in a sense, they don't have room to add another bond. Unsaturated fatty acids contain at least one double bond between two atoms. They have "spaces" available to add another bond.

MAIN IDEA

Lipids have a high percentage of carbon and hydrogen atoms.

Lipids are another important class of nutrients in our diet. They are found in dairy products, grains, meats, and oils. **A lipid is a type of biochemical that does not dissolve in water, has a high percentage of C and H atoms, and is soluble in nonpolar solvents.** As a class, lipids are not nearly as similar to each other as carbohydrates are. Long-chain fatty acids, phospholipids, steroids, and cholesterol are lipids.

Fatty Acids and Triglycerides

Fatty acids consist of a long, nonpolar hydrocarbon "tail" and a polar carboxylic acid functional group at the "head." Fatty acids are the simplest lipid molecules. They have *hydrophilic* polar heads, but their hydrocarbon chains make them insoluble in water. Fatty acids can also be saturated or unsaturated. *Saturated fatty acids* have no carbon–carbon double bonds, while *unsaturated fatty acids* have one or more double bonds in the hydrocarbon chain. The lipid shown below is oleic acid, which is found in animal fat.

CHECK FOR UNDERSTANDING
Distinguish What is the difference between saturated and unsaturated fatty acids?

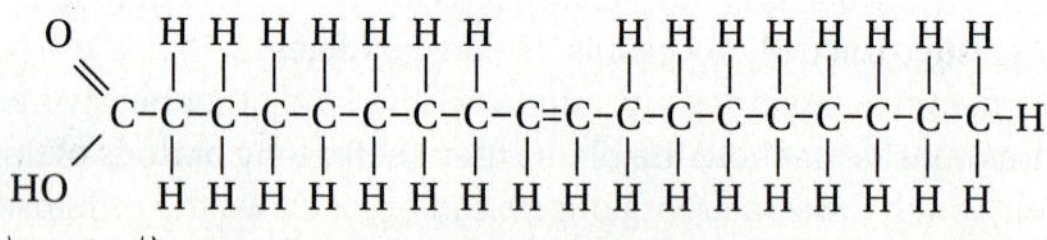

Fats and oils make up the most common group of lipids in your diet. These molecules are known as *triglycerides*. They are formed by condensation reactions in which three fatty acid molecules bond to one glycerol (a type of alcohol) molecule. Fats, such as butter and lard, come from animals, while oils come from plant sources, such as coconuts, peanuts, corn, and olives, as shown in **Figure 1.5**. Because they have a large amount of saturated fatty acids, fats are solids at room temperature. Oils have more unsaturated fatty acids than fats, so they are liquids. Like other animals, humans make fat, which is stored in *adipose* tissue until it is needed as an energy source. Fat has about twice as much energy per gram as carbohydrates or proteins do. Thus, fat is an efficient form of energy storage.

Fats have another important commercial value based on their ability to react with sodium hydroxide, NaOH, commonly known as *lye*. **When a fat combines with NaOH, an acid-base reaction called saponification occurs, and a salt and water form.** This salt is made up of molecules that have long carboxylic acid chains and is called *soap*. A molecule of soap has a charged ionic head and a nonpolar hydrocarbon tail. This structure allows the ionic head of a soap molecule to dissolve in water and the nonpolar tail to dissolve in nonpolar greases. This property gives the soap its cleaning ability. The chemistry of this reaction is also used as a way of classifying lipids. Lipids that react with a base to form soap are called *saponifiable lipids*, which include fats, oils, and fatty acids.

FIGURE 1.5

Foods High in Fats and Oils Fats, such as lard and butter, are obtained from animals. Oils are found in many different plants.

Differentiated Instruction

INCLUSION

Have tactile and visual learners use a molecular model kit to build a small, unsaturated fatty acid. For example, their model may consist of only a four-carbon chain. However, their model must have a multiple bond. Have students explain why the fatty acid is unsaturated. Then ask students to change the unsaturated molecule into a saturated one. Students should replace any multiple bonds with single bonds and add the appropriate number of hydrogen atoms.

Other Important Lipids

Compound saponifiable lipids play an important role in biochemical processes. These lipids are structurally similar to triglycerides in that at least one fatty acid is bonded to the central glycerol or glycerol-like unit. These molecules may also have phosphate groups, sugar units, or nitrogen-containing groups. Phospholipids, shown in **Figure 1.6,** are compound saponifiable lipids and are the main structural component of cell membranes. Phospholipids are arranged in a *bilayer*, or double layer, at the surface of the cell. As **Figure 1.6** shows, the hydrophilic heads of the phospholipids are on the outside surfaces of the bilayer. The heads are in contact with water-containing solutions inside the cell and surrounding the cell. The hydrophobic tails point toward the interior of the membrane, away from water-containing solutions. The cell membrane forms a boundary between the cell and its external environment. Only certain substances may pass through the cell membrane. This enables the cell to maintain a stable internal environment.

Nonsaponifiable lipids are nonpolar compounds that do not form soap. They include *steroids*, many *vitamins*, and *bile acids*. *Cholesterol* is a steroid present in animal cell membranes and is a precursor of many hormones.

FIGURE 1.6

Phospholipids

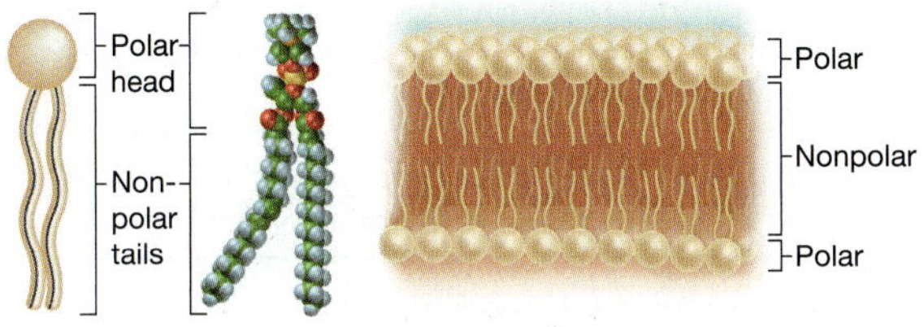

A phospholipid's "head" is polar, and its two fatty "tails" are nonpolar.

Phospholipids are arranged in a bilayer, with the hydrophilic heads pointing outward and the hydrophobic tails pointing inward.

SECTION 1 FORMATIVE ASSESSMENT

Reviewing Main Ideas

1. Describe two functions of carbohydrates in living systems.
2. Carbohydrates make up about 2% of the mass of the human body, yet we need about 1 tsp of glucose every 15 min to maintain energy for our cells. Where does all of this glucose come from?
3. What is the difference between saponifiable and nonsaponifiable lipids?

Critical Thinking

4. **ANALYZING RELATIONSHIPS** Glucose is soluble in water. Why is cellulose, which is made up of glucose, insoluble in water?
5. **EVALUATING IDEAS** Carbohydrates make up 75% of the mass of dried plant material. Cotton is at least 95% carbohydrate. Why do humans not include cotton in their diet?

Answers to Section Assessment

1. structure (in plants) and energy storage (in plants and animals)
2. Carbohydrates from food that is eaten and glycogen stored in the liver are converted into glucose.
3. Saponifiable lipids react with NaOH to form salts of fatty acids, commonly called *soaps*. Nonsaponifiable lipids do not react to form soaps.
4. Because hydrogen bonds form between the hydroxy groups on the glucose molecules that make up cellulose chains, the hydroxy groups are not exposed to water. As a result, rigid, insoluble cellulose sheets form. The hydroxy groups on glucose monomers however, are exposed. So, they are attracted to water, making glucose soluble in water.
5. The carbohydrate in cotton is cellulose, which humans cannot digest.

Classroom Discussion

On the board, draw models to represent the chemical structures of fats and oils. Then remind students that they learned about the flexibility of C—C single bonds and the rigidity of C=C double bonds in the previous chapter. Make sure students understand that the zigzag chains of C—C bonds allow saturated fatty acids to pack together tightly, which maximizes the interactions between molecules, forming a solid. Thus, high temperatures are required to overcome these interactions and allow the sample to melt. In oils, the C=C bonds in the unsaturated fatty acids create a rigid, bent orientation that does not permit the fatty acid units to pack together as closely. The weaker interactions between molecules are easier to overcome, so oils exist as liquids at room temperature.

Assess and Reteach ▼

Assess Use the Formative Assessment on this page to evaluate student mastery of the section.

Reteach For students who need additional instruction, download the Section Study Guide.

Response to Intervention To reassess students' mastery, use the Section Quiz, available to print or to take directly online at **HMDScience.com**.

SECTION 2

▼ Plan and Prepare

Objectives

Upon completion of this section, students should be able to do the following:

- Describe the basic structure of amino acids and the formation of polypeptides.
- Determine the significance of amino acid side chains to the three-dimensional structure and function of a protein.
- Describe the functions of proteins in cells.
- Identify the effects of enzymes on biological molecules.

Classroom Catalyst

Begin this section by reviewing carboxylic acids and amines. Show how the formation of a peptide bond is similar to an acid-base reaction that forms a "salt" (the dipeptide) and water. Another analogy is the formation of a disaccharide. Review the formation of disaccharides from monosaccharides, and note that these reactions are also condensation reactions. Polypeptides and proteins are large molecules that result from many condensation reactions of amino acid monomers.

▼ Teach

Application

Phenylketonuria, PKU, is an inherited disorder that causes irreversible brain damage and leads to mental retardation. The disease is caused by abnormally high levels of the amino acid phenylalanine in the blood. The affected person cannot make the enzyme needed for its initial breakdown, so phenylalanine accumulates. As the artificial sweetener aspartame hydrolyzes, its amino acid components, aspartic acid and phenylalanine, form. For this reason, all aspartame products must have a warning label such as "PHENYLKETONURICS: CONTAINS PHENYLALANINE." Have your class check the labels of diet soft drinks and other foods containing aspartame for this warning.

SECTION 2

Main Ideas

- Amino acids contain an amino and an acid group.
- Proteins are made of 50 or more amino acids.
- Enzymes are biological catalysts.

Amino Acids and Proteins

Key Terms

amino acid	enzyme
protein	denaturation

Proteins are polymers made up of smaller monomers known as *amino acids*. Although only 20 types of amino acids are found in human proteins, more than 700 types of amino acids occur in nature. Combinations of these 20 amino acids make up the more than 9000 different proteins found in the human body. However, our bodies can synthesize only 11 of the 20 amino acids that we need. The other nine, called the *essential amino acids,* have to be supplied by the food that we eat. A deficiency of these can cause illness and in some cases, death.

MAIN IDEA

Amino acids contain an amino and an acid group.

Amino acids are organic molecules that contain two functional groups: a basic $-NH_2$ amino group and an acidic $-COOH$ carboxylic acid group. All of the 20 amino acids have the general structure shown in **Figure 2.1.** The "R" represents a side chain that is different for each amino acid. The *R*-groups of the amino acids present in a protein determine the protein's biological activity. The structures of four amino acids—cysteine, valine, glutamic acid, and histidine—are shown below.

FIGURE 2.1

Amino Acid Structure Amino acids have the same basic structure. The *R* represents a side chain.

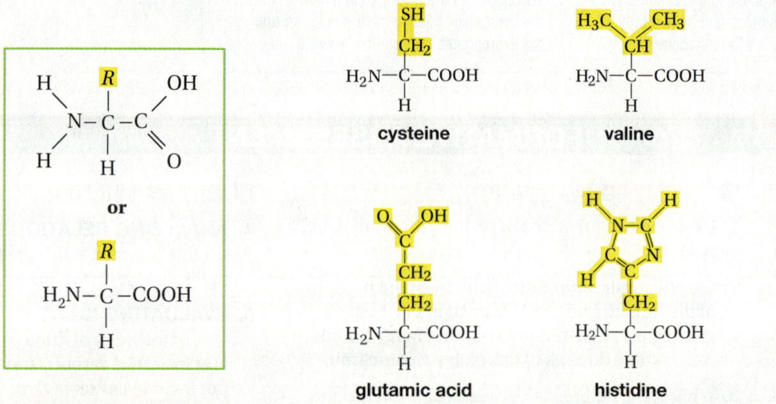

Differentiated Instruction

PRE-AP

Have students write the structures of the 20 different amino acids and classify them into four groups:

1. nonpolar and neutral (ex. alanine, isoleucine)
2. polar and neutral (ex. glutamine, serine)
3. acidic and polar (ex. aspartic acid, glutamic acid)
4. basic and polar (ex. arginine, lysine)

You can also give students a list of five amino acids and have them rank them in order of increasing polarity. Explain to students how an acid group is more polar than an alcohol group, and how even an extra methyl group can decrease polarity.

Amino Acid Reactions

Two amino acids can react with each other in an acid-base type of reaction. The basic amino group of one amino acid reacts with the acidic carboxylic acid group of another amino acid to form a *peptide*, and a molecule of water is lost. This reaction, shown below, is classified as a condensation reaction, or a *dehydration synthesis*, and the two amino acid molecules join together. The bond formed is called a *peptide bond*, and the product is a *dipeptide* because it is made up of two amino acid units. Longer chains are called *polypeptides*, and chains of 50 or more amino acids are called *proteins*.

$$H_2N{-}CHR{-}C({=}O){-}OH + H{-}NH{-}CHR{-}C({=}O){-}OH \rightarrow H_2N{-}CHR{-}C({=}O){-}NH{-}CHR{-}C({=}O){-}OH + H_2O$$

peptide bond

dipeptide

Peptide bonds can be broken by enzymes called *proteases*. These enzymes are found in cells and tissues where they aid in the digestion of proteins from food, or where they degrade unneeded or damaged proteins.

MAIN IDEA

Proteins are made of 50 or more amino acids.

Proteins are found in all living cells and are the most complex and varied class of biochemical molecules. **A protein is an organic biological polymer, made up of polypeptide chains of 50 or more amino acids, that is an important building block of all cells.** These chains may be branched and cross-linked as well. The name *protein* comes from the Greek *proteios*, which means "of first importance." This name was chosen to show the importance of proteins in living organisms.

Proteins are the second most common molecules found in the body (after water) and make up about 10% to 20% of the mass of a cell. Made up of specific sequences of amino acids, proteins have molecular masses that range from 6000 to more than 9 million unified atomic mass units. Nitrogen accounts for about 15% of the mass of a protein molecule, which makes the structure of a protein quite different from that of a carbohydrate or lipid. Most proteins also contain sulfur, phosphorus, or other elements, such as iron, zinc, and copper.

CHECK FOR UNDERSTANDING
Recognize What makes the structures of proteins quite different from those of carbohydrates?

The importance of proteins in living organisms comes from their many different functions. Besides being the body's main food source for nitrogen and sulfur, proteins have many important catalytic, structural, regulatory, and antibody defense functions. Some examples of proteins are *keratin*, which is the main component of hair and fingernails; *enzymes*, which catalyze biochemical reactions; *hemoglobin*, which carries oxygen in the blood; *insulin*, which regulates glucose levels; and *antibodies*, which protect the body from foreign substances. Many genetic disorders, such as cystic fibrosis and sickle-cell anemia (discussed later in this section), result from malformed or missing proteins.

INCLUSION

Help developmentally-delayed and attention-deficit-disorder students understand how a polypeptide forms. Ask students to work in pairs and copy the structural formulas for the four amino acids shown in **Figure 2.1** on the previous page. Instruct one student to indicate the order of the four amino acids found in a polypeptide. The other student should then redraw the structural formulas to show how the peptide bonds form.

Once they successfully complete the exercise, have students reverse roles and repeat the process using a different sequence for the same four amino acids.

ChemisTrivia

Infants and children lack the ability to synthesize arginine. So, arginine is an essential amino acid for children.

Teaching Tip

Proteins and polypeptides, as well as amino acids, exist as charged molecules in biological systems. Their properties and structural features depend on their charge characteristics.

Teaching Tip

Often, amino acids do not have a definite melting point. Instead, in a process called *decomposition*, they start to break down into smaller molecules when heated.

Application

Peptides called *endorphins* act as painkillers by binding to chemical receptor sites in the brain that send pain signals to the body. The sensation of pain is blocked because the chemical receptor sites cannot bind with the molecules that cause pain. The simple pentapeptide made up of the amino acids tyrosine, glycine, phenylalanine, and methionine, Tyr–Gly–Gly–Phe–Met, is a natural endorphin. The prescription drug morphine acts as a painkiller because it binds at the same site that the natural endorphin does.

Check for Understanding

Answer: Because proteins contain nitrogen—about 15% by mass—their structures are quite different from those of carbohydrates.

▼ Teach continued

Application

Hair "permanents" are all about chemistry. First, the hair is treated with a reducing agent, which breaks the S—S bonds holding two cysteine side chains together in hair protein and converts the S—S bonds into two —SH (thiol) functional groups. Because the hair is stretched around a curler while the treatment is taking place, the two —SH groups from any S—S bridge are pulled far away from each other. Later in the process, an oxidizing reagent is added, which allows the S—S bonds to reform but not with the original —SH groups. Instead, the —SH groups react with the closest thiol group to form new disulfide bridges. Thus, the hair proteins are refolded in a new way such that the hair has curl.

Demo Problem

Ask students to write the five isomers of the tripeptide Val–Asp–His.

Answer: Val–His–Asp, Asp–Val–His, Asp–His–Val, His–Asp–Val, His–Val–Asp

FIGURE 2.2

Dipeptide A scanning electron micrograph showing crystals of the amino acid glycine, one of the building blocks of proteins.

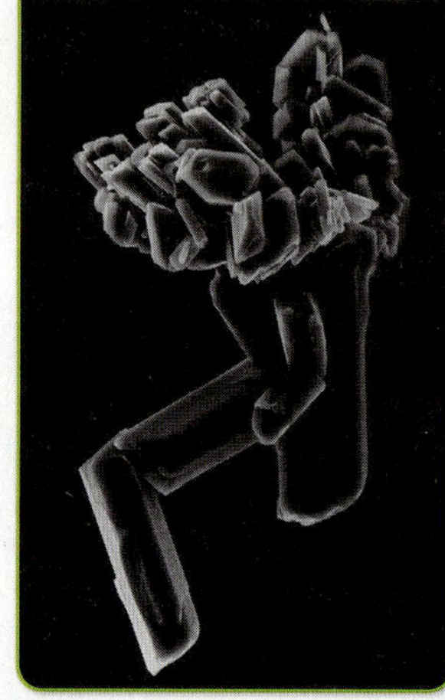

Arrangement of Amino Acids in Peptides and Proteins

Each peptide, polypeptide, or protein is made up of a special sequence of amino acids. A simple set of three-letter abbreviations is used to represent each amino acid in these kinds of molecules. For example, the dipeptide from glycine, shown in **Figure 2.2**, and glutamic acid would be written as Gly-Glu. The dipeptide Glu-Gly is an isomer of Gly-Glu. Both have the same numbers of C, H, O, and N atoms, but in a different order. For the tripeptide Val-Asp-His, made up of valine, asparagine, and histidine, there are five isomers. There are 120 possible isomers for a pentapeptide of five different amino acids. Even though there are only 20 types of amino acids in proteins found in the human body, an incredibly large number of polypeptide and protein molecules are possible. Even for a small protein made up of 100 amino acids, the number of possible combinations of the 20 amino acids is 20^{100}! Polypeptide and protein function depend not only on the kinds and number of amino acids but also on their order. Later, you will see that even the difference of only one amino acid in a polypeptide or protein chain can cause a big change in a protein's activity in a cell.

Amino Acid Side-Chain Reactions

The properties of amino acids—and ultimately polypeptides and proteins—depend on the properties of the side chains present. For example, the side chain of *glutamic acid* is acidic, and the side chain of *histidine* is basic. The side chains of *asparagine* and several other amino acids are polar. In addition, both glutamic acid and asparagine can form hydrogen bonds, shown in **Figure 2.3.** Some amino acid side chains can form ionic or covalent bonds with other side chains. *Cysteine* is a unique amino acid, because the —SH group in cysteine can form a covalent bond with another cysteine side chain. **Figure 2.3** shows that two cysteine units—at different points on a protein molecule—can bond to form a *disulfide bridge.* Such bonding can link two separate polypeptides or can cause one long protein to bond onto itself to form a loop. In fact, curly hair is a result of the presence of many disulfide bridges in hair protein.

FIGURE 2.3

Disulfide Bridge Three kinds of interactions between side chains on a polypeptide molecule are shown here. These interactions help determine the shape of a protein.

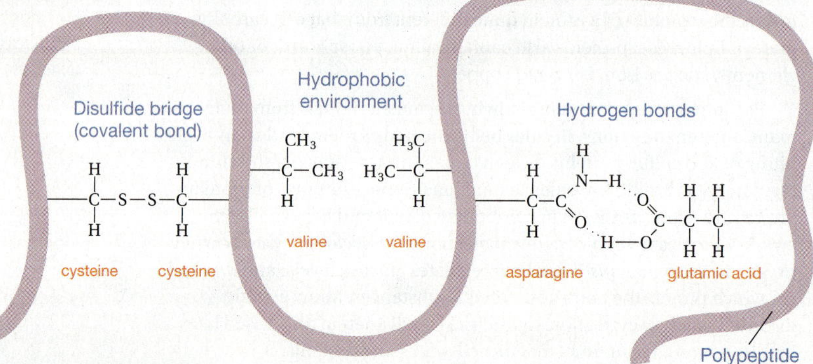

Problem Solving

ALTERNATIVE APPROACHES

Have students make a chart of all the different kinds of interactions that can occur with the side chains that stabilize protein structure. Their chart can include any or all of the following interactions.

1. covalent bond that forms a disulfide bridge
2. hydrophobic interactions between amino acids, such as alanine, valine, and leucine
3. stacking between aromatic ring structures
4. salt bridge between any acidic or amine moiety in close proximity
5. hydrogen bonding

Shape and Structure of Protein Molecules

The interaction of amino-acid side chains determines the shape and structure of proteins, which in turn are important to the proteins' biological functions. In a polypeptide chain or protein, the sequence of the amino acids is called the *primary* (1°) *structure*. The *secondary* (2°) *structure* describes how the chain is coiled or otherwise arranged in space. For example, the alpha (α) helix is a secondary structure that resembles a coiled spring. Another type of secondary structure is the beta (β) pleated sheet, which has accordion-like folds. These secondary structures form because hydrogen bonding occurs between a hydrogen atom attached to the nitrogen atom in one peptide bond and the oxygen atom of another peptide bond farther down the backbone of the protein.

In a protein, the amino-acid side chains project out in such a way that they often interact with other side chains located at various positions along the protein backbone. These interactions give the protein its characteristic three-dimensional shape, which is called its *tertiary* (3°) *structure*. The side-chain interactions can include hydrogen bonding, salt bridges, and cysteine–cysteine disulfide bonds. Hydrophobic interactions that occur between nonpolar side chains also contribute to a protein's tertiary structure. Because nonpolar side groups are repulsed by the water found in cells and body fluids, these groups tend to be found in the interior of the protein, where contact with water is minimal. Polar and ionic side chains tend to be on the protein surface, where they are in contact with water. In some proteins, different polypeptides, each of which has its own 3° structure, come together. In the case of hemoglobin, four different polypeptides make up the *quaternary* (4°) *structure*. The four structural levels of proteins are shown in **Figure 2.4**.

CRITICAL THINKING

Predict Why might a protein's environment have a great effect on its structure?

FIGURE 2.4

The Four Structural Levels of Proteins The functions of proteins are determined by their complex structures.

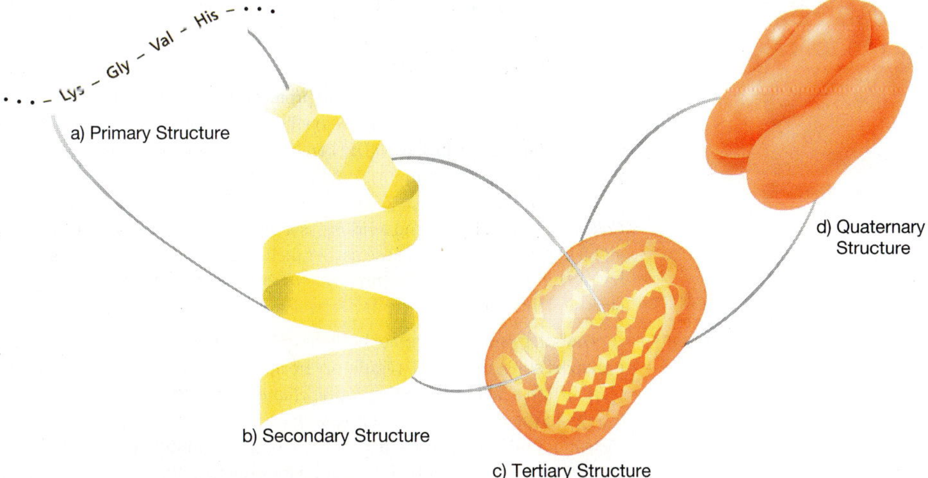

Differentiated Instruction

PRE-AP

Tell students that hundreds of proteins have been crystallized and their structures entered into databases. Explain that crystallography is one of the last steps in determining structure because it takes a large amount of protein in extremely pure form. Have students identify a protein whose structure is known and write a brief report explaining the steps used to determine its structure. Procedures that may have been used include separating the protein from others using electrophoresis, size-exclusion chromatography, or precipitation.

Teaching Tip

The large size of proteins gives them colloidal properties in solution. For example, when solutions containing proteins are poured through a semi-permeable membrane, the proteins do not pass through the membrane. The presence of proteins in urine can warn doctors of possible damage to kidney membranes.

ChemisTrivia

Linus Pauling (1901–1994) won the 1954 Nobel Prize in Chemistry for discovering the alpha helix. He also received the Nobel Peace Prize in 1962. He is the only person to be awarded two individual Nobel Prizes.

Analogy

A coiled cord from a corded landline telephone can serve as an analogy for the primary, secondary, tertiary, and quaternary structures in proteins. When the cord is stretched tight from end to end, it illustrates its primary structure. When allowed to coil, the cord models its secondary structure. When the cord twists around itself, it has a tertiary structure. If two or more cords are tangled together, they have a quaternary structure.

Critical Thinking

Answer: Environment is important because proteins have secondary, tertiary, and even quaternary structures. Changes in the environment, such as a change in pH, can influence the intramolecular forces that produce these structures.

▼ Teach *continued*

ChemisTrivia

The eyeball membrane, which is made of fibrous protein, can withstand a pressure of 400 lb/in^2, four times the pressure of a high-pressure bicycle tire.

Class Discussion

A good exercise in dimensional analysis is to have students calculate the rate of growth of hair (based on 6 in. per year) in terms of the number of turns of the alpha helix of a hair protein per second. Students will have to research the distance of one turn of the alpha helix, which is 5.4 Å (0.54 nm). The result is about nine turns of the alpha helix per second.

FIGURE 2.5

BIOLOGICAL FUNCTIONS OF PROTEINS

Type of protein	Function	Examples
Storage	storage of amino acids	*Casein* protein in milk supplies amino acids for baby mammals. Egg white protein, or *ovalbumin*, is a source of amino acids for developing embryos. Plants store proteins in seeds.
Transport	transport of substances	Proteins transport molecules across cell membranes. *Hemoglobin* in blood transports oxygen.
Structural	support	Spiders produce silk fibers, which are proteins, to make webs. *Collagen* and *elastin* give connective tissues strength and flexibility. *Keratin* is found in hair, feathers, horns, hooves, and nails.
Contractile	movement	*Actin* and *myosin* fibers cause movement in muscles. Contractile fibers in cilia and flagella help propel single-celled organisms.
Enzymatic	catalysis of chemical reactions	Enzymes break down large molecules in food within the digestive system.
Hormonal	coordination of processes in an organism	Pancreatic insulin helps regulate blood-sugar levels.
Receptor	response of cell to chemical stimuli	Nerve-cell membranes have chemical receptors that detect chemical signals released by other nerve cells.
Defensive	protection against disease	Antibodies attack pathogenic viruses and bacteria.

Biological Functions of Proteins

From **Figure 2.5**, you can see that almost everything that occurs in a living organism depends on one or more proteins. Scientists have discovered that the specific function of a protein is related to the protein's shape. The shape of a protein can generally be described as fibrous or globular. *Fibrous proteins* are insoluble in water and are long, thin, and physically strong. *Globular proteins* are generally soluble in water and are twisted and folded into a globe-like shape.

Fibrous proteins give strength and protection to structures in living organisms. *Keratin* is a fibrous protein whose secondary structure is almost entirely alpha helical in shape. The keratin in nails and hooves is much stiffer than the keratin in fur or wool because of the large number of side-chain interactions that occur between the nail and hoof proteins. *Collagen*, found in bone and tendons, is a triple helix of three intertwined alpha helices, which gives these tissues their strength. *Fibrin* found in silk has a beta-pleated sheet structure. *Elastins* in blood tissue, *fibrins* in blood clots, and *myosins* found in muscle tissue are other kinds of fibrous proteins.

Globular proteins regulate body functions, catalyze reactions, and transport substances. The regulatory hormone *insulin* is a small protein of 51 amino acids in two polypeptide chains. *Myoglobin* transports oxygen in the muscles, and *hemoglobin* transports oxygen in the blood. *Casein*, found in milk and used for food, is also a globular protein. It contains phosphorus, which is needed for bone growth.

Problem Solving

DECONSTRUCTING PROBLEMS

Ask students if they can predict the structure or function of a protein molecule, given its sequence. For instance, if there is a sequence of 20–25 nonpolar amino acids, the protein might make an alpha helix and span a membrane. A membrane protein that does not contain many hydrophobic amino acids in a row may be an ion channel. Knowing which cell fraction was the source of the protein provides a clue to its function. For example, membrane proteins are usually receptors that transmit information, or they are transporters.

Amino Acid Substitution

A protein's amino acid sequence determines its three-dimensional structure, which in turn determines its function. Even a single substitution of one amino acid for another can change the shape and function of a protein. For example, the genetic disease sickle-cell anemia can happen when one amino acid—glutamic acid—is replaced by a molecule of valine. This change in only 1 of 146 amino acids in one of the two protein chains in the hemoglobin molecule causes a major change in the shape of the molecule. This change in the shape of the hemoglobin molecule causes the red blood cells to sickle when oxygen levels are relatively low (as is the case in most body tissues). The sickle cells tend to clog small blood vessels, which prevents the transport of enough oxygen to tissue cells. As a result, people who have sickle-cell anemia suffer from shortness of breath. **Figure 2.6** shows the shape of normal red blood cells and sickle cells. The sickle cell gene is more common in some groups of people than it is in others. In areas where the disease malaria is common, scientists have discovered that sickle cells are more resistant to malarial infection than other cells are. So, people who have sickle-cell anemia are more resistant to malaria than other people are.

FIGURE 2.6

Sickle Cell Anemia

(a) The round, flat shape of healthy red blood cells shows they have normal hemoglobin molecules.

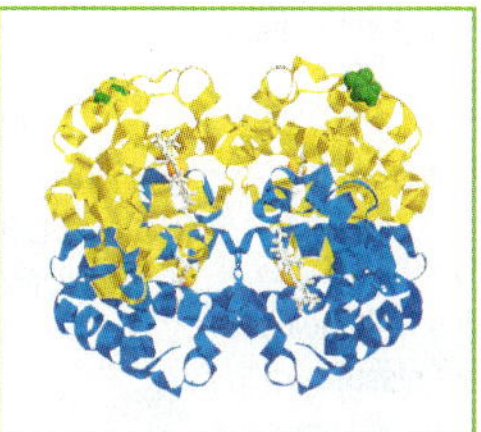

(b) Hemoglobin consists of four polypeptide chains; a fragment of one chain is shown in green.

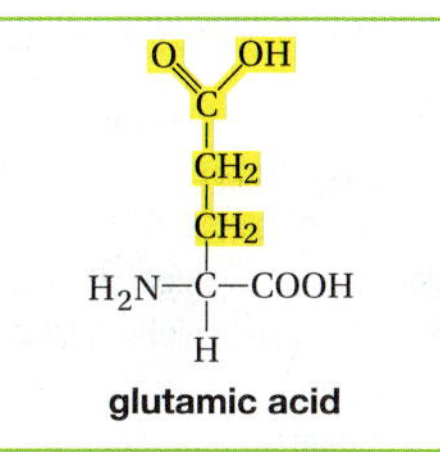

(c) Each of the chains is a polymer of 141 or 146 amino acid units, such as the glutamic acid monomer shown here.

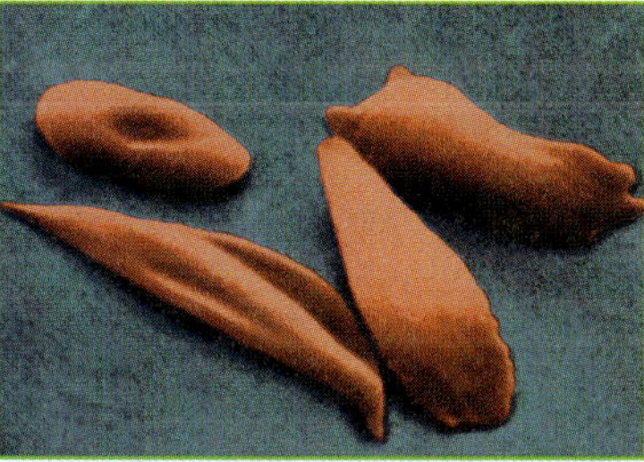

(d) Because of their shape, sickle cells clog small blood vessels.

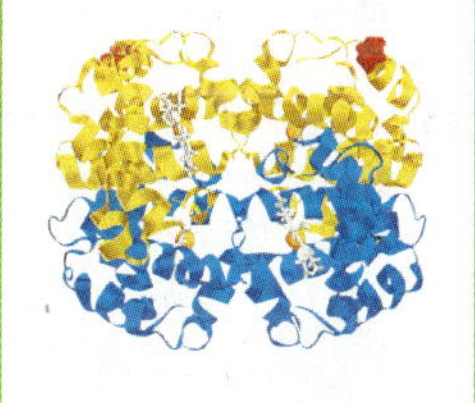

(e) A genetic mutation causes one glutamic acid to be replaced by valine in the hemoglobin molecules, as shown in red.

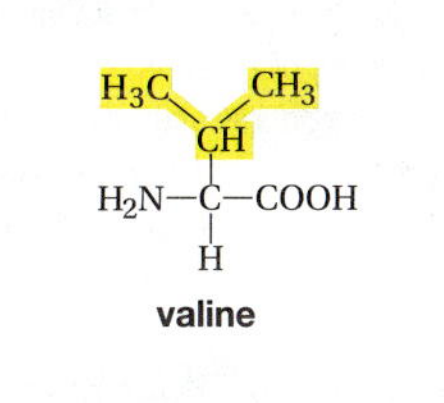

(f) The sickle shape of the cell comes from the different shape of the hemoglobin caused by the substitution of valine for glutamic acid.

ChemisTrivia

Dr. Vernon Ingram could be called the "Father of Molecular Medicine." He demonstrated that conversion of glutamic acid to valine at position 6 of the β-chain was the sole abnormality in hemoglobin produced by people who have sickle-cell anemia. This seminal observation demonstrated that a protein abnormality in which a single amino acid is altered can produce a complex clinical disorder. Today, many diseases, such as hemophilia and cystic fibrosis, are known to result from alterations in a single gene.

Differentiated Instruction

PRE-AP

Have students draw the structure of the porphyrin ring and show how iron is essential for carrying oxygen. Explain that this structure also occurs in chlorophyll, the green pigment in plants that is responsible for photosynthesis—except that in chlorophyll, the coordinating atom is magnesium.

ChemisTrivia

Dr. Drew set up the first American Red Cross unit for the collection of blood. He was also the first director of the program to establish blood donor stations for the American Red Cross. A United States postage stamp was issued in 1981 to honor Dr. Drew's accomplishments.

ChemisTrivia

Modified bovine blood and outdated human blood are being investigated as blood substitutes. While bovine (cow) blood is readily available from slaughter-houses, it is not completely compatible with human blood. Using outdated human blood prevents wasting the blood, but a supply problem still exists, as the amount depends on donations.

Answers

1. Dr. Drew developed the procedures for blood transfusion and for using blood plasma in transfusions.
2. Scientists are searching for blood substitutes in order to reduce the chance of transmitting blood-borne diseases during transfusions and to have an adequate supply of a blood substitute if real blood is not readily available.

Chemistry EXPLORERS

Dr. Charles Drew and Blood Transfusions

Prior to the 1900s, severe bleeding often resulted in death. But today blood is stored at blood banks, where people "deposit" blood so that they or others can "withdraw" it when needed. Charles Drew was a pioneer in the work of blood transfusions, especially in the use of plasma and the development of blood banks.

Charles Drew was a pioneer in the development of blood banks.

The Need for Blood

While in medical school, Drew realized that many lives could be saved if blood could be stored for transfusions. Before 1937, most patients needing blood received it directly from a donor at the time it was needed. In 1938, Drew and physician John Scudder from Britain studied the chemistry of blood to try to find a way to preserve blood. Drew recognized that extracting blood plasma could help solve the problems of storing blood.

There are two main components of blood: blood cells and plasma. Red blood cells, white blood cells, and platelets make up 45% of the volume of blood, while plasma makes up 55% of blood. Plasma is amber colored and is about 90% water. It has more than 100 solutes, including nutrients, antibodies, hormones, and proteins. Drew discovered that plasma could be used as an emergency substitute for blood without testing for blood type, because the ABO blood types are removed with the red blood cells. He also found that plasma could be dehydrated and stored.

During World War II, Drew was the medical supervisor for the "Blood for Britain" program. He also coordinated the American blood storage program by setting up collection centers, standardizing blood bank equipment, and establishing record-keeping procedures and criteria to ensure the safety of blood products. When the United States entered the war, the blood supply was ready, and stored blood and plasma saved several thousand lives.

A Safer Blood Supply

With the emergence of HIV and AIDS in the 1980s, the methods of blood transfusion needed to be modified. Some transfused blood was found to carry HIV in a number of people. Before modifications were put into place, as many as 50% of hemophiliacs in the United States could have been infected with HIV because of their frequent transfusions. Although current screening procedures to detect HIV, hepatitis, and other diseases have almost completely removed the risk of transfusing infected blood, some people choose to bank their own blood before undergoing surgery.

Blood Substitutes

The AIDS epidemic has sped up attempts to find an artificial blood substitute. Perfluorocarbons (PFCs), which are made by replacing the hydrogen atoms of hydrocarbons with fluorine atoms, are possible substitutes. Oxygen binds to PFCs 10 to 20 times more readily than it binds to plasma or water, and products using PFCs have a shelf life of up to two years. Another substitute is a hemoglobin-based oxygen carrier (HBOC). HBOCs may be able to transport oxygen until a body is able to replenish its red blood cells. If these products are successful, they could provide a supply of blood substitutes that do not require typing and do not depend on donors.

Questions

1. What was Dr. Drew's contribution to medicine?
2. Why are scientists searching for blood substitutes?

MAIN IDEA

Enzymes are biological catalysts.

An **enzyme** is a protein that catalyzes a biochemical reaction. Enzymes make up the largest and most highly specialized class of proteins. All living organisms have enzymes; as many as 3000 enzymes can be found in a single cell. Most enzymes are water-soluble, globular proteins. Remember, catalysts speed up a reaction by lowering the activation energy and are not changed in the reaction. An enzyme also does not change the amount of product that is formed in a reaction. Enzymes catalyze both decomposition and synthesis reactions.

Enzymes are also very efficient. For example, the enzyme *carbonic anhydrase* acts on carbonic acid to break down as many as 36 million molecules in 1 minute! Carbon dioxide is carried from all the parts of the body to the lungs as carbonic acid in the blood. In the lungs, carbonic anhydrase breaks down carbonic acid into CO_2 and water vapor, which then exit the lungs as a person exhales.

Enzyme Specificity

In addition to being highly efficient, enzymes are very specific. For example, the enzyme peroxidase is responsible only for the decomposition of hydrogen peroxide to water and oxygen. Hydrogen peroxide is fairly stable in the bottle, but when you put it on a minor cut, the peroxidase enzyme in the blood catalyzes its decomposition. Bubbling occurs as a result of the gaseous oxygen from the decomposing hydrogen peroxide. As you can see in **Figure 2.7**, enzymes act by binding to a specific *substrate* molecule. Hydrogen peroxide is the substrate in the reaction just discussed. The shape of the enzyme is such that a molecule of hydrogen peroxide can fit into the enzyme at a specific part of the enzyme molecule, called the *active site*. The resulting compound is called the *enzyme-substrate complex*. In this complex, hydrogen-oxygen bonds break, and oxygen-oxygen bonds form. Then the enzyme releases the products and is ready to react with another substrate molecule. This model of enzyme action is called the *lock-and-key model*.

FIGURE 2.7

Lock-and-Key Enzyme Model

(a) The substrate comes into contact with the active site.

(b) The activated complex forms and a reaction occurs.

(c) The products form, but the enzyme remains unchanged.

Teach continued

Application

Meat tenderizer contains the enzyme *papain*, which can catalyze the breakdown of peptide bonds in meat protein. Papain is extracted from the fruit and leaves of the papaya plant. For centuries, South Americans have wrapped meat in papaya leaves to tenderize it. An interesting patent has been issued for tenderizing beef by injecting papain directly into the blood of living cattle. Papain is also used in cleaning solutions for contact lenses and in the treatment of insect and jellyfish stings.

Differentiated Instruction

BELOW LEVEL

Have students work in pairs to write the formulas for water (H_2O) and hydrogen peroxide (H_2O_2). You may want to tell students that hydrogen peroxide can also be called *dihydrogen dioxide*. Be sure that students take the necessary safety precautions when performing the following activity.

Have them fill one test tube halfway with water, and a second test tube halfway with 3% hydrogen peroxide. Then have students place a small piece of fresh liver or potato in both test tubes and observe what happens. Have students explain their observations in terms of enzyme specificity. Students should recognize that the liver and potato contain an enzyme that works specifically on hydrogen peroxide, which is the substrate.

▼ Teach continued

Teaching Tip

When discussing activation energy, use the analogy that lowering the activation energy is somewhat like using a tunnel to get from one side of a mountain to the other instead of driving up the mountain and down the other side.

Misconception Alert!

Students may think that each time two reacting molecules collide, a reaction occurs. However, this is not the case. Only molecules that collide with enough energy to exceed the reaction's activation energy and that collide in the proper orientation form products. Baseball is a good analogy. Hank Aaron did not hit a home run every time his bat hit the ball. But when he hit the ball with enough energy and at the proper place on his bat, he was able to "knock it out of the park."

Critical Thinking

Answer: You can tell because the reactants and products are in the same positions on the graph, regardless of the path taken.

FIGURE 2.8

Activation Energy and Enzymes Enzymes decrease the activation energy of a chemical reaction.

CRITICAL THINKING

Interpret In **Figure 2.8**, how can you tell that the enzyme does not change the total amount of energy required for or released by the reaction?

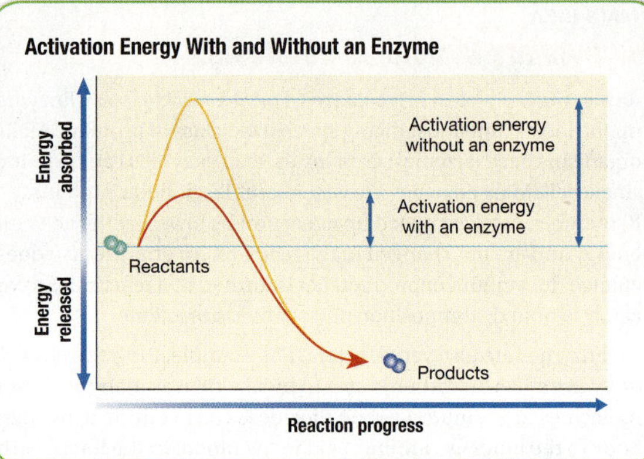

Enzymes and Reaction Rates

The presence of an enzyme in a chemical reaction can increase the rate of a reaction by a factor of up to 10^{20}. Recall that a reaction can only occur when two atoms or molecules collide with enough energy to overcome the *activation energy* and have the proper orientation to change reactants into products. As you can see from the graph in **Figure 2.8**, an enzyme that catalyzes a chemical reaction causes an increase in the rate of the reaction by reducing the activation energy. The enzyme lowers the activation energy by forming the enzyme–substrate complex, which makes breaking bonds in the reactants and forming new bonds in the products easier. The net amount of energy required for the reaction or released by the reaction is not changed by the action of an enzyme.

FIGURE 2.9

Temperature and Enzyme Activity Enzymes have maximum activity within a narrow temperature range. Denaturation occurs at temperatures above 50°C and causes a decrease in activity.

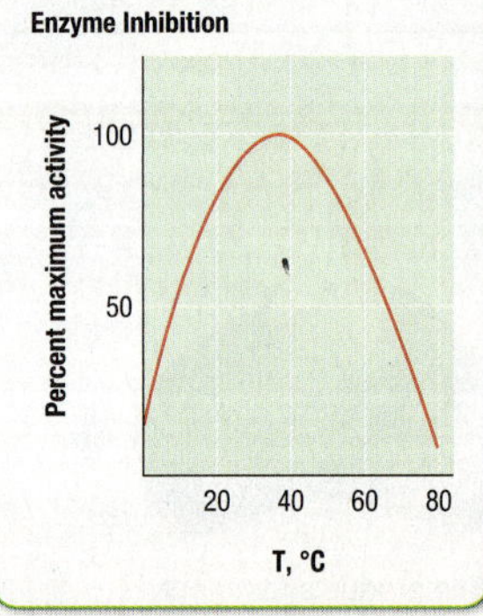

Temperature and Enzyme Activity

Proteins, including enzymes, are also affected by changes in temperature. The graph in **Figure 2.9** shows the relatively narrow range of temperatures within which enzymes typically have maximum activity. Enzymes in the human body work optimally at the normal body temperature of 37°C (98.6°F). At temperatures above 50°C to 60°C, enzymes typically show a decline in activity. High heat can denature, or alter, the shape of a protein, which in turn alters the protein's function. **Denaturation** **is a change in a protein's characteristic three-dimensional shape due to changes in its secondary, tertiary, and quaternary structure.** If you have ever cooked an egg, you have caused protein denaturation. The white of an egg is a solution of the protein albumin. When the egg is placed in a hot frying pan, a dramatic change takes place and the semitransparent solution turns into a white solid. Because the primary structure is retained in denaturation, the nutritional value of the egg white is not affected. The process is not reversible, however, cooling a fried egg does not reverse the denaturation. When food is cooked, the three-dimensional structure of the protein is altered, making the food easier to digest.

Differentiated Instruction

BELOW LEVEL

Have students use modeling clay to build a model of an enzyme. Students can refer to **Figure 2.7** on the previous page as a guide for building their model.

Next, ask students to use modeling clay of a different color to build a model of a substrate.

Students should then use their models to demonstrate the lock-and-key model of enzyme action.

Finally, ask students to use their models to demonstrate how an increase in temperature affects enzyme activity. Students should change the shape of the enzyme model so that the substrate model can no longer fit into the enzyme.

pH and Enzyme Activity

Enzymes also typically have maximum activity within a relatively narrow range of pH. The optimal pH for normal cell enzyme functions is almost neutral, about 7.3 to 7.4. Changes in pH can cause changes in protein structure and shape. For example, adding acid or base can interfere with the side-chain interactions and thus change the shape of a protein. Most enzymes become *inactivated,* or no longer work, because of denaturation when the pH changes. When milk sours (because lactic acid has formed), it curdles, and curds of the protein casein form. Yogurt is made by growing acid-producing bacteria in skim milk, which causes the casein to denature, which in turn gives yogurt its consistency.

The digestion of dietary protein by enzymes begins in the stomach. When food is swallowed, the stomach lining produces HCl and *pre-enzymes,* inactive forms of protein-digesting enzymes. These pre-enzymes travel from the stomach lining into the stomach before they become activated by the stomach's low pH of 1.5 to 2.0. This process is important because it prevents the active form of the enzymes from digesting the stomach lining. A layer of mucus protects the lining of the stomach from the enzymes it contains. Once activated, the enzymes catalyze the breakdown of the proteins in food into shorter polypeptide segments. *Pepsin* is a stomach enzyme found in adults. The partially digested protein in food travels into the small intestine, where the pH is 7 to 8. Under these conditions, the enzyme *trypsin* becomes active. It catalyzes the hydrolysis of the polypeptide segments into amino acids, which are absorbed through the intestinal wall and enter the bloodstream. The body uses these newly acquired amino acids to make new protein molecules. **Figure 2.10** shows how the protein in raw fish looks before and after it is soaked in acidic lime juice. Because the acidic lime juice denatures protein in the fish, the acid-treated fish looks very different. Marinades made with wine or vinegar are also used to flavor meats. As a result, many of the proteins in the meat are denatured, making it more tender.

CHECK FOR UNDERSTANDING

Conclude Why might highly-acidic foods cause problems in digestion?

FIGURE 2.10

Acid Denaturation of Protein

The fish treated with lime has turned white because the acidic lime juice denatures the protein in raw fish.

SECTION 2 FORMATIVE ASSESSMENT

Reviewing Main Ideas

1. Which elements do amino acids and proteins have in common with carbohydrates and lipids?
2. What is the difference between an amino acid and a protein?
3. Explain the difference between fibrous proteins and globular proteins.
4. Why are only small amounts of enzymes found in the body?

Critical Thinking

5. **RELATING IDEAS** Explain how the ball-like structure of globular proteins allows them to be water soluble.
6. **INFERRING CONCLUSIONS** If an essential amino acid is in short supply in the diet, it can become a limiting reactant in building any protein that contains the amino acid. Explain why, under these conditions, the only way that the body could make that protein would be to destroy one of its proteins that contain the limiting amino acid.

Answers to Section Assessment

1. carbon, hydrogen, and oxygen
2. An amino acid is a monomer. A protein is made up of 50 or more amino acid monomer units.
3. Fibrous proteins tend to have helical structures, more strength, and less solubility in water. Globular proteins are tangled into ball-like shapes and tend to be more soluble in water.
4. Enzymes are catalysts. Thus, they are not used up in reactions and can be used over and over again.
5. The nonpolar groups are in the interior, away from the water, and the polar/ionic groups are on the outer surface. Thus, the polar, hydrophilic groups are in contact with water molecules.
6. The body cannot synthesize essential amino acids.

Demonstration

DENATURATION OF PROTEIN

You may want to show a dramatic safety demonstration. Wearing **eye protection** and keeping students at a safe distance, crack a **raw egg** in a **crystallizing dish** or a **beaker** and place it on an **overhead projector.** The yolk will block the light, but the egg white will allow some light to pass through. Then, pour **6 M HCl** onto the egg. The albumin is immediately denatured just as it is when it is heated. You can tell students that protein is an important component of the cornea, which can become clouded if it is exposed to laboratory chemicals. Thus, it is important to wear eye protection in the laboratory. Do NOT pass the egg around unless you rinse it thoroughly to remove residual HCl.

ChemisTrivia

Rennin, the enzyme that coagulates milk protein, is present in the stomachs of infants.

Check for Understanding

Answer: Acidic foods can disrupt the pH of the stomach, thus influencing digestion.

Assess and Reteach ▼

Assess Use the Formative Assessment on this page to evaluate student mastery of the section.

Reteach For students who need additional instruction, download the Section Study Guide.

Response to Intervention To reassess students' mastery, use the Section Quiz, available to print or to take directly online at **HMDScience.com**.

SECTION 3

▼ Plan and Prepare

Objectives

Upon completion of this section, students should be able to do the following:

- Describe the role of ATP in cells.
- Explain how energy is released by metabolic reactions.
- Summarize the relationship between anabolism and catabolism.

Classroom Catalyst

Students may have heard the term "metabolism" used before. Ask them what they think metabolism is and how they believe their bodies obtain energy. Then explain to students that metabolism consists of all chemical reactions that occur within an organism. Tell students that some of these reactions are still not well understood. However, what is known about metabolism is so extensive that not all of it can be covered in this section. Instead, this section will only discuss how our bodies get needed energy from the food that we eat and how cells manufacture the molecules necessary to sustain life.

▼ Teach

Teaching Tip

Explain to students that what an organism uses as a food source depends on its metabolism. For most living organisms, hydrogen sulfide is a poison. But for some types of bacteria, hydrogen sulfide is a source of energy. As chemoautotrophs, these bacteria can manufacture their nutrients using chemical substances, such as hydrogen sulfide.

SECTION 3

Main Ideas

- ATP is an energy source for cells.
- Complex compounds get broken down and energy gets released in catabolism.
- Smaller compounds get converted to larger ones during anabolism.

Metabolism

Key Terms

metabolism
autotroph
adenosine triphosphate (ATP)
heterotroph
adenosine diphosphate (ADP)
catabolism
anabolism

Metabolism is the sum of all the chemical processes that occur in an organism. Complex molecules are broken down into smaller ones through *catabolism,* and simple molecules are used to build bigger ones through a process called *anabolism.* A *metabolic pathway* is a series of linked chemical reactions that occur within a cell and result in a specific product. The major metabolic pathways for most organisms are very similar. So, one can study the metabolic pathways in simple organisms to get information about the reactions in organisms that are more complex, including humans.

MAIN IDEA

ATP is an energy source for cells.

Cells require energy to make the proteins, carbohydrates, lipids, and nucleic acids that are necessary for life. In addition, the body needs energy as heat to keep warm, mechanical energy to move muscles and pump blood, and electrical energy to move ions across cell membranes. The original source for almost all of the energy needed by living systems is the sun. **Autotrophs are living organisms that use sunlight, water, and CO_2 to make carbon-containing biomolecules, including carbohydrates.** The most common form of this process, called *photosynthesis,* occurs in the cells of plants and algae, such as those shown in **Figure 3.1,** within structures called *chloroplasts.* Chloroplasts contain *chlorophyll,* an organic molecule that absorbs solar energy. This energy is captured in two compounds, one of which is adenosine triphosphate (ATP). **ATP (adenosine triphosphate) is a high energy molecule that plant cells use to make carbohydrates.** The other compound, *NADPH,* is also used in carbohydrate-forming reactions.

FIGURE 3.1

Chlorophyll The cells of algae and green plants contain chlorophyll, the green pigment that absorbs light energy from the sun.

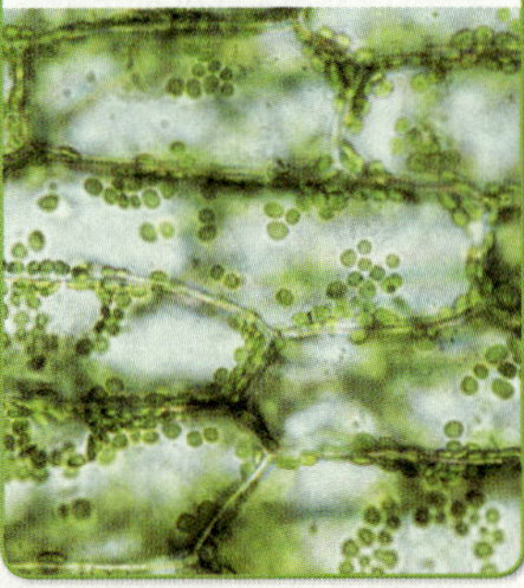

A less-common type of autotrophic metabolism, called *chemosynthesis,* is found in microbes living around deep-sea hydrothermal vents. These organisms obtain nutrients in the absence of sunlight by metabolizing nitrogen and sulfur compounds produced by geothermal activity beneath the oceans.

Animals, however, cannot use the sun's energy to convert CO_2 into food. Animals must get the energy that they need to sustain life by consuming plants and other animals. **Living organisms, including most microorganisms, which depend on plants or other animals for food, are called heterotrophs.** Heterotrophs use the energy obtained in the breakdown of complex molecules to drive chemical reactions in cells. The carbohydrates, lipids, and amino acids that heterotrophs consume undergo several energy-yielding reactions as they break down into simpler molecules. Some of this energy is stored in ATP molecules, which cells use to drive a wide variety of metabolic reactions.

Differentiated Instruction

BELOW LEVEL

Help students understand the role of ATP in cellular metabolism. Point out that ATP can be considered an energy currency. Just as people need money to make purchases, a cell needs ATP to do work.

Have students work in pairs to make a list of ten activities they do that involve metabolic reactions and therefore require ATP. Students are likely to include activities involving motion, such as riding a bicycle, running, and throwing a ball.

Compile a list of all activities on the board. Be sure students recognize that not all metabolic activities that require ATP may be obvious. For example, the active transport of materials into and out of cells depends on ATP.

FIGURE 3.2

The ATP Cycle ATP is formed by photosynthesis or catabolism. Cell activities that require energy are powered by ATP hydrolysis. The "P_i" represents a phosphate.

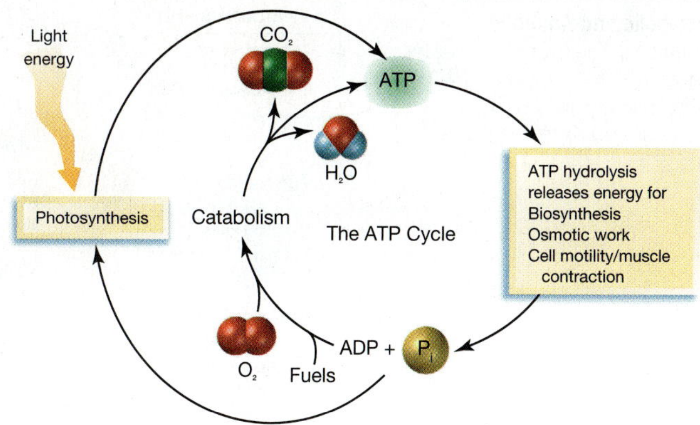

The ATP Cycle

Adenosine diphosphate (ADP) is the molecular building block from which ATP is made. The cycle between ATP and ADP is the primary energy exchange mechanism in the body. **Figure 3.2** provides an overview of the ATP cycle in cells. In this cycle, ATP carries energy from energy-storing molecules, carbohydrates, lipids, and proteins to specific energy-requiring processes in cells. When ATP is hydrolyzed to ADP, in a process called *phosphorylation,* energy is released to power the cell's activities. The molecular structures of ATP and ADP are closely related, as shown in **Figure 3.3.**

The difference in the number of phosphate groups between ATP and ADP molecules is the key to the energy exchange in metabolic reactions. The chemical equation below shows the hydrolysis reaction by which ATP is converted into ADP and a phosphate group (represented by the gold-colored ball in **Figure 3.2**). The free energy for this reaction is –31 kJ, which is the amount of energy available to do work.

$$ATP^{4-}(aq) + H_2O(l) \longrightarrow ADP^{3-}(aq) + H_2PO_4^-(aq)\ \Delta G = -31\ kJ$$

CHECK FOR UNDERSTANDING
Identify What is the primary difference between an ATP and an ADP molecule?

FIGURE 3.3

Hydrolysis of ATP The hydrolysis of ATP produces ADP and releases energy.

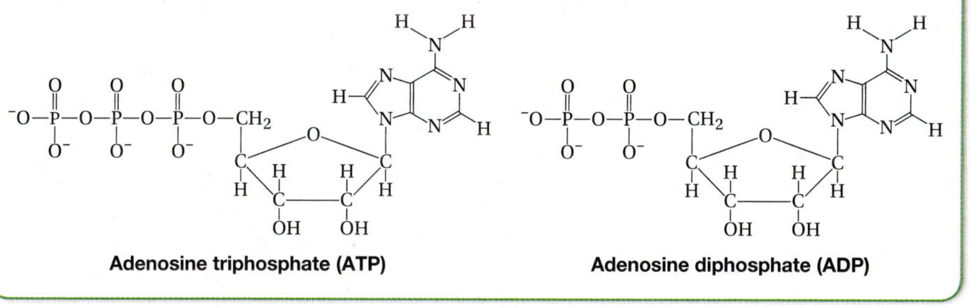

Adenosine triphosphate (ATP)

Adenosine diphosphate (ADP)

Misconception Alert!

The bond that is broken when ATP is converted to ADP is often referred to as a *high-energy bond,* which is misleading. It is better to refer to ATP as a *high-energy compound,* because more energy is released when the hydrolysis of ATP occurs than when most other hydrolysis reactions occur. The energy needed to break the bond in ATP is actually lower than the energy needed to break most covalent bonds.

Teaching Tip

ATP and ADP exist in their ionic form in the body. Therefore, they are shown as ions in **Figure 3.3.**

Check for Understanding

Answer: ATP is a triphosphate and ADP is a diphosphate. The difference between them is one phosphate (PO_3^{-4}) group.

INCLUSION

Help kinesthetic learners understand the relationship between ATP, ADP, and AMP (*adenosine monophosphate*). Have a student join hands with three students of the opposite sex. Inform the class that the one student represents an adenosine molecule while the three students represent phosphate groups. Have the four students act out what happens when ATP is converted to ADP. Be sure that they explain why this reaction is considered a hydrolysis process.

Next, ask students to demonstrate how AMP forms. If students are unsure of how to show this, suggest that they consider the prefix *mono-* and its meaning. Emphasize that a great quantity of energy is released only during the conversion from ATP to ADP.

Biological Chemistry 723

▼ Teach *continued*

ChemisTrivia

The average human brain requires more than 120 g of glucose, delivered by the blood, per day. Glucose that is not used immediately by the brain or other body tissues is converted to glycogen for storage by the liver and skeletal muscles. Glycogen is gradually broken down into glucose and is released into the blood by the liver between meals. Excess glucose is also converted to triglycerides for energy storage. The major hormones regulating glucose concentration in the body are insulin and glucagon. Other hormones, such as epinephrine and cortisol, also affect glucose concentration in the body.

Teaching Tip

The calculation that 36 molecules of ATP are produced by 1 glucose molecule is based on the metabolism of glucose in skeletal tissue cells, where most ATP is generated. However, if the same glucose is metabolized in the heart or liver, two additional ATP molecules are made, which increases the total to 38 ATP. Also note that glucose is not the only monosaccharide that can produce ATP. Galactose and fructose can also be used to generate ATP; they also yield 36 ATP each.

Check for Understanding

Answer: Digestion of carbohydrates begins in the mouth. Fat digestion occurs only in the small intestine. Protein digestion starts in the stomach.

FIGURE 3.4

Catabolic and Anabolic Pathways Catabolic pathways release free energy in the form of ATP and NADH. Anabolic pathways consume energy released by catabolic pathways.

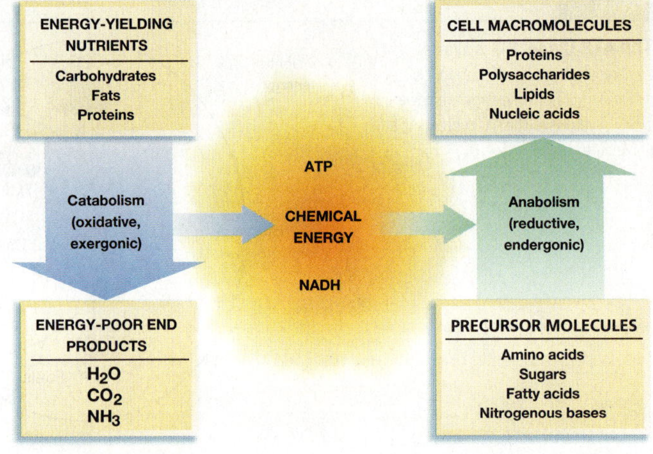

MAIN IDEA

Complex compounds get broken down and energy gets released in catabolism.

The energy that your body needs to maintain its temperature and drive its biochemical reactions is provided through *catabolic* processes, or *cellular respiration*. **Figure 3.4** illustrates the relationship between the pathways of catabolism and anabolism. **Catabolism is the part of metabolism in which complex compounds break down into simpler ones and is accompanied by the release of energy.** First, enzymes break down the complex compounds in food—carbohydrates, fats, and proteins—into simpler molecules, releasing the energy stored in their carbon-carbon bonds.

CHECK FOR UNDERSTANDING
Distinguish Where does digestion begin for carbohydrates? Fats? Proteins?

Carbohydrate digestion begins in the mouth, where the enzyme *amylase* in saliva begins to break down polysaccharides. The food then passes through the esophagus, then the stomach, and into the small intestine. Here, more enzymes are secreted to complete the hydrolysis of carbohydrates to form glucose and other monosaccharides.

Digestion of fats occurs only in the small intestine. Protein digestion begins in the stomach and is completed in the small intestine. During digestion, fats are broken down into fatty acids and glycerol. Proteins are broken down into amino acids.

These products are absorbed across the wall of the small intestine into the blood and are transported to cells. Once in the cells, glucose and other monosaccharides, fatty acids, some amino acids, and glycerol enter the mitochondria and feed into a complex series of reactions called the *citric acid cycle*, or *Krebs cycle*. The citric acid cycle produces carbon dioxide and other molecules, such as NADH (not to be confused with NADPH) and ATP. This NADH and ATP then move through another set of reactions to produce more ATP and water.

Differentiated Instruction

INCLUSION

Help visual learners understand catabolism by constructing a flow chart to show how glucose is processed in cells. As they read the last paragraph, have them start with a single glucose molecule that undergoes glycolysis to produce two pyruvate molecules that then enter the Krebs cycle. Three products of the Krebs cycle should be shown: carbon dioxide, NADH, and ATP. The flow chart should continue by showing the NADH entering through "another set of reactions" (the electron transport chain) to produce even more ATP.

The amount of energy released in catabolism depends on the amount of ATP that is made as the products of digestion are oxidized. The catabolism of 1 glucose molecule generally produces a total of 36 ATP molecules. This accounts for about 40% of the energy released by the complete oxidation of glucose. Most of the energy not converted to ATP is lost by the body as energy in the form of heat. **Figure 3.5** shows how much ATP is needed for some daily activities.

FIGURE 3.5

APPROXIMATE "COST" OF DAILY ACTIVITIES

Activity	Energy required (kJ)	ATP required (mol)
Running	1120	56
Swimming	840	42
Bicycling	1400	70
Walking	560	28

MAIN IDEA

Smaller compounds get converted to larger ones during anabolism.

Cells use the simple molecules that result from the breakdown of food to make larger, more complex molecules. Energy released during catabolism powers the synthesis of new molecules as well as the active transport of ions and molecules across cell membranes. *Anabolic* processes are the energy-consuming pathways by which cells produce the molecules that they need for sustaining life and for growth and repair. The conversion of small biomolecules into larger ones is called **anabolism.**

In an anabolic pathway, small precursor molecules are converted into complex molecules, including lipids, polysaccharides, proteins, and nucleic acids. Energy from ATP and NADH is necessary for these biosynthesis reactions to occur. **Figure 3.4** illustrates that catabolism and anabolism occur simultaneously and that ATP and NADH serve as chemical "links" between the two processes.

One important anabolic pathway that is common to animals, plants, fungi, and microorganisms is *gluconeogenesis*. As the name implies, glucose is synthesized in this pathway from noncarbohydrate substances, including lactate, pyruvate, glycerol, and most of the amino acids. In mammals, glucose from the blood is the fuel source for the brain and nervous system as well as for the kidney, red blood cells, and embryonic tissues.

SECTION 3 FORMATIVE ASSESSMENT

Reviewing Main Ideas

1. List four ways in which the body uses energy.
2. What is the total energy (in kilojoules) stored in the 36 ATP molecules that are made from the metabolism of 1 molecule of glucose in skeletal tissue?
3. The teeth break large pieces of food into smaller ones. However, this process is not considered part of digestion. Explain why.
4. How does the digestion of fat in a strip of ham differ from the digestion of starch in a piece of toast?
5. Why are diets that are severely restrictive in carbohydrate intake potentially dangerous to a person's health?

Critical Thinking

6. **RELATING CONCEPTS** When a molecule of glucose is oxidized, only about 40% of the energy is captured in ATP molecules, and the rest is lost as energy in the form of heat. What do you think would happen if this energy remained in the body as heat?

Biological Chemistry 725

Answers to Section Assessment

1. The body uses energy to make compounds and carry out biochemical reactions. In addition, the body uses energy to keep warm. Mechanical energy is used to move muscles and pump blood, and electrical energy is used to move ions across cell membranes.
2. 1116 kJ
3. Breaking food into small pieces is a physical change and does not involve any chemical reactions.
4. Digestion of starch begins in the mouth and continues in the stomach and small intestine. The digestion of fat does not begin until the fat reaches the small intestine.
5. Carbohydrates are the main source of energy for the body. If carbohydrates are restricted, proteins will be used for energy instead of for other important biological functions.
6. Enzymes and proteins could become denatured, so cells would not function properly.

ChemisTrivia

For invertebrates, about 50 percent of the energy needed by the liver, kidneys, heart, and muscles comes from the oxidation of fatty acids. For hibernating animals and migrating birds, fat is the only source of energy.

Application

The minimum amount of energy required per day to maintain a stable physiological condition (homeostasis) in the body is the basal metabolism rate, BMR. It is about 1400 kcal per day for a 55 kg (121 lb) female and 1600 kcal per day for a 65 kg (143 lb) male. Excess kilocalories are used to supply energy needed to do work or are stored in fat. It takes 3500 excess kilocalories to produce 0.45 kg (1 lb) of fat.

Assess and Reteach

Assess Use the Formative Assessment on this page to evaluate student mastery of the section.

Reteach For students who need additional instruction, download the Section Study Guide.

Response to Intervention To reassess students' mastery, use the Section Quiz, available to print or to take directly online at **HMDScience.com**.

SECTION 4

▼ Plan and Prepare

Objectives

Upon completion of this section, students should be able to do the following:

- Describe the structure of the nucleic acids DNA and RNA.
- Explain the functions of DNA and RNA in the cell.
- Describe applications of modern gene technology.

Classroom Catalyst

DNA is the molecule of heredity. To understand how DNA replicates and passes genetic information to RNA to make proteins, students need to understand hydrogen bonding. It will be helpful to show the structures of the base pairs and the hydrogen bonds that form the links between the two strands of DNA. Make sure that the students understand that DNA replicates by unfolding its two strands, which then pair up with complementary nucleotides. The new nucleotides are then linked together. Each DNA molecule has one "new" strand and one "original" strand that are complementary.

▼ Teach

ChemisTrivia

In humans and other animals, white blood cells contain DNA, and mature red blood cells do not. In bacterial cells, the DNA is not contained within a nuclear membrane but floats freely in the cytosol as a single chromosome or, in some cases, as plasmids.

TEACH FROM VISUALS

FIGURE 4.1 Thymine, cytosine, and uracil have a six-member ring containing two nitrogen atoms and are classified as *pyrimidine* bases. Adenine and guanine are classified as *purine* bases because they contain a six-member ring connected to a five-member ring, with each ring containing two nitrogen atoms.

SECTION 4

Main Ideas

- Nucleic acids are chains of nucleotides containing a sugar bonded to a phosphate and an organic base.
- RNA molecules synthesize proteins.
- Genetic engineers manipulate genetic material.

Nucleic Acids

Key Terms

nucleic acid DNA replication cloning

Nucleic acids contain all the genetic information of an organism. They are the means by which a living organism stores and conveys instructional information for all its activities. They are also the means by which an organism can reproduce. The two major nucleic acids found in organisms are *deoxyribonucleic acid (DNA)* and *ribonucleic acid (RNA)*.

MAIN IDEA

Nucleic acids are chains of nucleotides containing a sugar bonded to a phosphate and an organic base.

A nucleic acid is an organic compound, either RNA or DNA, whose molecules carry genetic information and which is made up of one or two chains of monomer units called nucleotides. However, unlike the monomer units in polysaccharides and polypeptides, each nucleotide monomer can be further hydrolyzed into three different molecules. A nucleotide molecule is composed of a five-carbon sugar unit that is bonded to both a phosphate group and a cyclic, organic base that contains nitrogen.

The sugar unit in DNA is deoxyribose, and the sugar unit in RNA is ribose. The diagram below shows the sugar-phosphate arrangement in three nucleotides.

```
—phosphate— sugar—phosphate—sugar—phosphate—sugar—
              |                 |                 |
             base              base              base
```

The five nitrogenous bases found in nucleic acids are shown in Figure 4.1. *Adenine* (A), *guanine* (G), and *cytosine* (C) are found in both DNA and RNA. *Thymine* (T) is found only in DNA, and *uracil* (U) is found only in RNA.

FIGURE 4.1

Bases in Nucleic Acid There are five common nitrogenous bases. Thymine (T), cytosine (C), and uracil (U) have a single six-member ring. Adenine (A) and guanine (G) have a six-member ring connected to a five-member ring.

adenine guanine cytosine thymine uracil

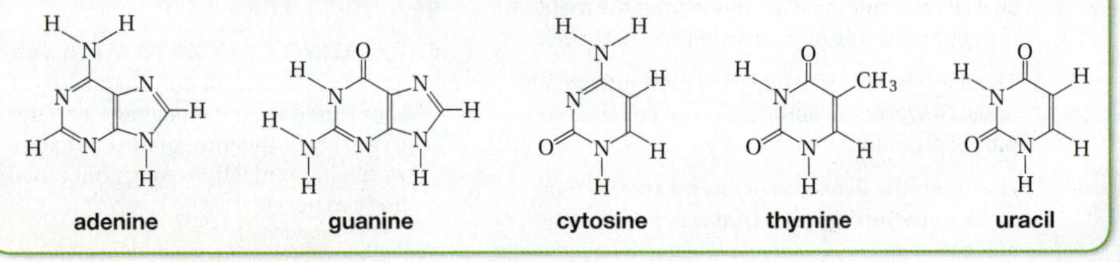

Differentiated Instruction

BELOW LEVEL

Have students write a sequence of ten nitrogenous bases found in DNA, using the letter abbreviations, A, T, C, and G. Have them draw the sugar-phosphate backbone using the letters S and P. Have them refer to the diagram on this page to see how the phosphate, sugar, and nitrogenous bases are bonded to each other. Later, have them return to their drawings and add the complementary strand.

DNA: Deoxyribonucleic Acid

Every single instruction for all the traits that you have inherited and all the life processes that occur in your cells is contained in your DNA. It is no wonder then that DNA molecules are the largest molecules found in cells. Living organisms vary widely in the size and number of DNA molecules in their cells. Some bacterial cells contain only 1 DNA molecule, while human cells contain 23 pairs of relatively large DNA molecules. Each human cell contains about 2 m of DNA, which is divided and packed into the cell's 46 *chromosomes*. An average cell is only about 6 μm in diameter and contains many organelles and structures. To fit in a cell, DNA must undergo extensive twisting, coiling, folding, and wrapping.

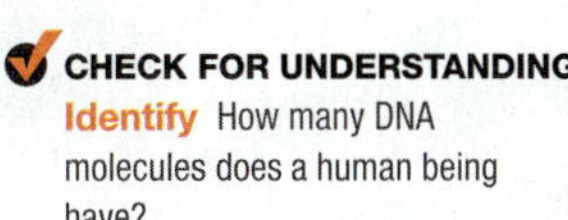

CHECK FOR UNDERSTANDING
Identify How many DNA molecules does a human being have?

The Swedish scientist Friedrich Miescher first extracted DNA from cells in 1868, but its three-dimensional structure was not discovered until 1953. Using the X-ray data of Maurice Wilkins and Rosalind Franklin, James Watson of the United States and Francis Crick of England proposed that DNA was a double helix. In this structure, which has been confirmed by numerous methods, two strands of the sugar-phosphate backbone are wound around each other, and the nitrogenous bases point inward, as shown in **Figure 4.2.** The sequence of these nitrogenous bases along the phosphate-sugar backbone in DNA forms the code responsible for transferring genetic information. The three-dimensional DNA molecule is similar to a twisted ladder. The sides of the ladder are the sugar-phosphate backbone, and the rungs are base pairs of A—T (adenine-thymine) or G—C (guanine-cytosine) bases extending between the two backbones. Hydrogen bonding between these pairs of nitrogenous bases holds the rungs of the ladder together.

FIGURE 4.2

The DNA Double Helix Structure Hydrogen bonding between base pairs makes the three-dimensional structure of DNA stable. Base pairing occurs between adenine and thymine or guanine and cytosine, keeping the distance between the strands constant.

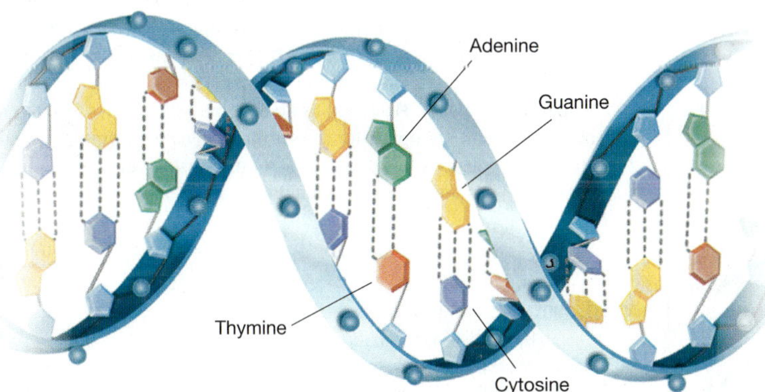

ENGLISH LEARNERS

Write the words *complimentary* and *complementary* on the board. Explain that these two words are frequently confused, even by educated adults for whom English is a first language. Review the meanings. *Complimentary* means either something that praises (a compliment) or something that is free of charge (a complimentary gift). *Complementary* means something that completes another thing, or that provides something the other thing lacks (complementary skills among players on a team, for example). Ask students which word is appropriate when discussing nucleotides and DNA, and why. Complementary, because the two strands within a DNA molecule complete each other.

ChemisTrivia

In 1950, before the structure of DNA was known, Erwin Chargaff analyzed the amounts of nitrogenous bases in cells from different organisms. He was surprised to find that in each organism, the amount of adenine matched the amount of thymine and the amount of cytosine matched the amount of guanine. Chargaff's findings reflect what would be expected if the nitrogenous bases were always paired G—C and A—T in DNA. DNA base pairing would be discovered later by James Watson and Francis Crick.

Demonstration

DNA STRANDS

1. Cut a piece of **thick string** that is **1 m long,** and tie its ends together to form a large loop. Tell students that two strands of the string represent the sugar-phosphate "backbone" of DNA.
2. Hang the loop from a **doorknob,** and then insert **toothpicks** into opposite sides of the loop at 5-cm intervals. The toothpicks represent the base pairs that link the two complementary strands together. For added detail, the base pair toothpicks may be color coded and assembled in the proper sequence.
3. Twist the bottom end of the loop around the axis of the DNA model, and instruct students to observe the resulting characteristic double-helix shape.

Check for Understanding

Answer: Human cells contain 46 relatively large DNA molecules.

▼ Teach *continued*

Application

Methods of determining the sequence of base pairs of DNA were first developed in the 1970s. These techniques were very time consuming and could analyze only small fragments of DNA at one time. By the late 1980s, improvements in DNA sequencing technology enabled scientists to sequence large portions of DNA at one time and at a much faster rate. In 1992, the first complete sequencing of the genetic information possessed by an organism was completed for the fruit fly. The sequence of the 3 billion bases that make up human DNA was completed in July 2000 by the United States Human Genome Project.

ChemisTrivia

The total length of DNA in the human genome is 1.8 m. The longest single piece of human DNA is about 10 cm. The total volume of the DNA double helix is so small that the DNA can be packed in individual cells with plenty of space left over. But this packing is very organized and allows the DNA both to function and to be exactly duplicated when the cell divides.

TEACH FROM VISUALS

FIGURE 4.4 Have students discuss the zipper analogy as it applies to the DNA double helix. In which ways is the zipper analogy a good model? What are the limitations of this model?

Critical Thinking

Answer: Answers may vary. Hydrogen bonds can be easily broken. Therefore, the DNA molecule can easily break apart and "unfold" so it can replicate. If held together by chemical bonds, something stronger would be needed to take the DNA molecule apart, replication might not be as easy, and life may never have developed.

FIGURE 4.3

STM Image of DNA Structure The double helix of DNA can be seen by using scanning tunneling microscopy (STM).

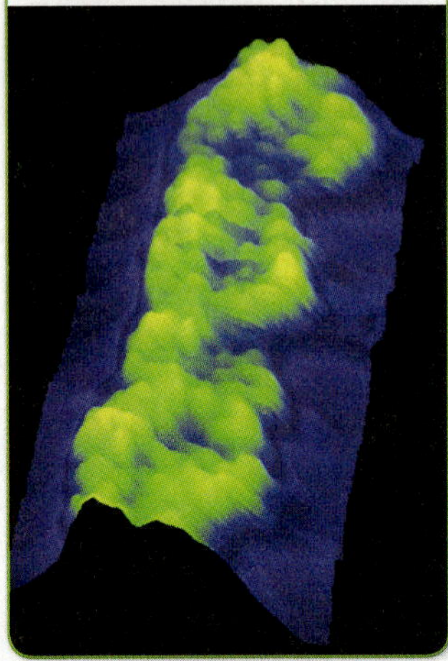

Nitrogenous Base Pairs

In the DNA double helix, base pairing exists only between A—T and between C—G, as you saw in **Figure 4.2.** The reason is that the pairing between one single-ringed base and one double-ringed base provides the correct orientation for the hydrogen bonds to form between the two sides of the DNA ladder. One thymine and one adenine form a link between the two strands of a DNA molecule that is exactly the same size as the link formed by one cytosine and one guanine.

The double-helix configuration of DNA, shown in **Figure 4.3,** can be seen by using a scanning tunneling microscope (STM). The discovery of the relative quantities of the nitrogenous bases A, T, G, and C present in DNA was the key to determining the three-dimensional molecular structure. Analysis of DNA from different organisms reveals that the amounts of A and T are the same and that the amounts of G and C are the same for all members of the same species. In humans, DNA is about 30% A, 30% T, 20% G, and 20% C.

The interaction between base pairs accounts for the ability of DNA to replicate, as you will learn below. Just as combinations of the 26 letters of the alphabet form words that tell a story in a novel, combinations of the four-letter alphabet of A, T, G, and C form the *genes* that define our heredity. Each gene is a section of DNA that contains a specific sequence of four bases (A, G, T, and C) and typically contains about 1000 to 2000 base pairs. As of 2004, researchers with the Human Genome Project had discovered that the human body contains about 20 000 to 25 000 genes.

FIGURE 4.4

DNA Replication DNA replicates when its double helix unwinds and becomes single stranded. The single strands are used as a template for the formation of new complementary strands.

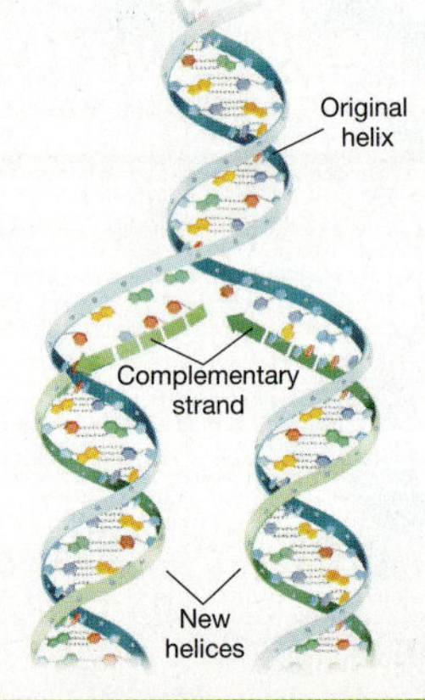

DNA Replication

Like the two sides of a zipper, the two strands of the double helix of DNA are not identical. Instead, the two strands are complements of each other. Thus, a base on one strand is paired through hydrogen bonding to its complementary base on the other strand. For example, if one strand sequence is AGCTC, the complementary strand sequence will be TCGAG.

Each time a cell divides, an exact copy of the DNA of the parent cell is reproduced for the daughter cells. **The process by which an identical copy of the original DNA is formed is called DNA replication.** As replication begins, a portion of the two strands of the original DNA is uncoiled and "unzipped," as shown in **Figure 4.4,** by an enzyme called *helicase.* Each strand can then act as a template for the synthesis of a new, complementary strand. The result is two daughter DNA molecules, which have the same base pair sequence as the original double helix.

✓ CRITICAL THINKING

Predict Hydrogen bonds hold DNA strands together. What would be the implication for life if DNA strands were held together by chemical bonds?

Differentiated Instruction

ENGLISH LEARNERS

Help students understand the concept of replication. Point out that replication occurs when you ask for 100 copies of a chemistry test you prepared.

Have students explain how this replication is a valid analogy to what happens in DNA replication. Students should point out that in both cases, exact copies are made of the original form.

Be sure to emphasize, however, that the two DNA strands separate before replication so that a new DNA molecule consists of one new strand and one old strand. This would be similar to tearing a test in half, making a copy of each half, and then taping a copy to a complementary original half so that you have two complete tests.

MAIN IDEA

RNA molecules synthesize proteins.

Molecules of RNA make up about 5% to 10% of the mass of a cell. RNA molecules are responsible for the synthesis of proteins, which in turn control the operation and function of the cell. RNA differs from DNA in four basic ways: (1) the sugar unit in the backbone of RNA is ribose rather than deoxyribose, (2) RNA contains the base uracil, U, instead of thymine, which occurs in DNA, (3) RNA is a single-stranded molecule rather than a double-stranded helix like DNA, and (4) RNA molecules typically consist of 75 to a few thousand nucleotide units rather than the millions that exist in DNA. Even though RNA is much smaller than DNA, RNA can still twist, coil, bend, and fold back onto itself. In fact, it is not uncommon for up to 50% of an RNA molecule to have a double-helix structure. The reason is that the base sequences along the helical regions of the RNA strand are complementary, making hydrogen bonding possible.

Synthesis of RNA

RNA is synthesized in the nucleus of the cell, where DNA and protein molecules actually help synthesize specific RNA molecules. RNA can be seen by STM, as shown in **Figure 4.5.** As RNA is synthesized, information contained in the DNA is transferred to the RNA molecules. Like the genetic information of DNA, the genetic information of RNA is carried in its nucleotide sequence. One type of RNA molecule is called *messenger RNA* (mRNA) because it carries the instructions for making proteins out into the cytosol, where proteins are produced on ribosomes. A *ribosome* is a cell organelle composed of RNA and protein. Ribosomes are the main site of protein production in cells. The DNA template is also used to make two other types of RNA molecules: *ribosomal RNA* (rRNA) and *transfer RNA* (tRNA). Both of these types of RNA also leave the nucleus and come together in the ribosome where they help synthesize proteins. Ribosomal RNA becomes part of the structure of the ribosome, and tRNA is used to transfer amino acids to the ribosome. Only mRNA carries the coded genetic information that is translated into proteins.

DNA supplies all the information necessary for RNA to make the proteins needed by the body. The portion of DNA that holds the genetic code for a single mRNA molecule is a gene. Each gene codes for a specific mRNA molecule, which produces a specific protein that has a specific function.

FIGURE 4.5

STM Image of RNA Scanning tunneling micrograph of RNA strands being transcribed in a cell.

RNA and Protein Synthesis

RNA is made from DNA in a process that is similar to the way in which DNA replicates itself. A portion of DNA is uncoiled by helicase and RNA is assembled along the unzipped strands of DNA, using the same complementary base pairs as DNA, except that uracil replaces the thymine. As in DNA replication, the RNA sequence that forms has the complementary base pairs of the DNA gene. The DNA sequence on the next page would form the complementary RNA sequence shown.

BELOW LEVEL

Have students use their drawings of the DNA ten-base sequence to show how RNA is synthesized. Be sure that whenever the base A appears in the DNA sequence, students insert the base U into the RNA sequence.

ChemisTrivia

The 1968 Nobel Prize in Physiology or Medicine was awarded to Robert Holley, Har Khorana, and Marshall Nirenberg for their interpretation of the genetic code and its function in protein synthesis.

Teaching Tip

Be sure students are clear on the different kinds of RNA. Most students can remember that mRNA is the messenger, coming directly from DNA. Remind them that rRNA is part of the ribosomal machinery itself. The tRNA, or transfer RNA, is the adapter molecule that is the bridge between the mRNA and the growing polypeptide chain. Review the degrees of structures with tRNA by drawing schematics. tRNA has a sequence (the primary structure), a cloverleaf shape (secondary structure), and an L shape (tertiary structure).

▼ Teach *continued*

Teaching Tip

Explain to students that cells use the RNA strands produced from genes within DNA molecules to build their proteins. Amino acids line up according to the three-base codes, or codons, in RNA. The amino acids form a polypeptide chain by adding one amino acid at a time.

Teaching Tip

Have students look at the table of genetic codes based on mRNA codons that is in the Math Tutor following this section. Explain to students how to use the information in the table to decipher the code. Then have them identify the five amino acids that would be encoded by the DNA strand segment shown on this page. Remind students that they must use the RNA strand (mRNA) to figure out which amino acids would be made.

Answer: glycine, valine, glycine, cysteine, histidine

Check for Understanding

Answer: DNA does not just need to code for specific amino acids. It also needs to code for when to stop, otherwise it might continue to code indefinitely.

CHECK FOR UNDERSTANDING
Decode What do you think is significant about the three "stop" codes?

CAREERS IN CHEMISTRY

Forensic Chemist S.T.E.M.

A forensic chemist applies scientific methodology to physical evidence. Forensic chemists focus on analyzing evidence that has been collected at a crime scene. They then report any conclusions that they can draw from the analysis. Understanding evidence requires knowledge of biology, materials science, and genetics in addition to chemistry. Because forensic chemists are often asked to testify in court, they need to be comfortable speaking in public and be able to give clear and concise explanations to those who do not have a background in science.

DNA strand: C C C C A C C C T A C G G T G
RNA strand: G G G G U G G G A U G C C A C

A sequence of three bases in mRNA, called *triplets*, or *codons*, code for specific amino acids. Thus, the sequence CAG codes for glutamic acid, and GUC codes for valine. There are 64 (4^3) unique combinations of three-base sequences made from four bases. Some amino acids have more than one code. For example, leucine is coded for by six different codons: UUA, UUG, CUU, CUC, CUA, and CUG. Methionine and tryptophan are the only amino acids that are coded by only one codon each. The same three-base sequence always codes for the same amino acid regardless of whether the organism is a bacterium or a human.

Once mRNA forms from DNA, it leaves the nucleus of the cell and attaches to a ribosome. tRNA molecules, each containing three *anticodons* that complement the nitrogen-base sequences found in mRNA, bring amino acids from the cell's cytoplasm to the ribosome, where they are joined to form proteins. The process always begins with the "start" triplet AUG, which codes for methionine and signals the ribosome to begin making a protein. The process ends with the "stop" signals: UAG, UAA, or UGA.

Proteins are absolutely essential to the proper functioning of living organisms. Errors that occur during protein synthesis are known as *mutations*. There are a number of different ways that mutations can occur, such as the insertion or deletion of a nitrogen base, or a triplet being reversed as it is inserted. Mutations caused by incorrect sequencing can lead to many types of genetic disorders and diseases, including cancer.

FIGURE 4.6

DNA Autoradiograph A DNA autoradiograph shows the pattern of an organism's DNA fragments after they have been separated from each other by electrophoresis.

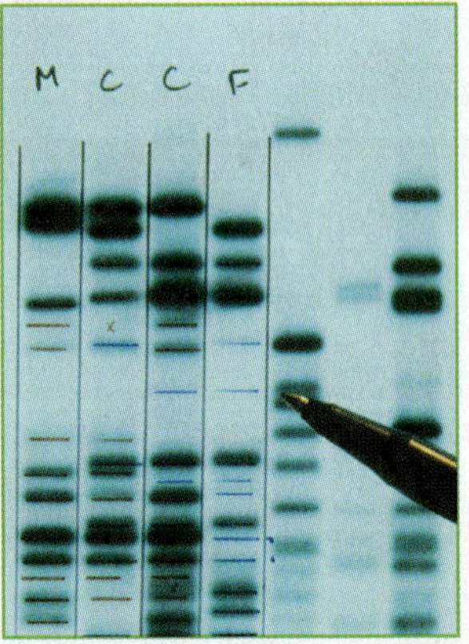

MAIN IDEA

Genetic engineers manipulate genetic material.

Genetic engineers study how the manipulation of an organism's genetic material can modify the proteins that are produced, and the changes that result in the organism. This provides new options for the production of food, medical diagnosis and treatments, and increased understanding of genetic disorders. Although selective breeding of organisms has been done for thousands of years, these scientists use recombinant DNA technology to adapt or clone existing life forms, which is controversial.

DNA Fingerprinting

One visible use of molecular technology is DNA fingerprinting. DNA is unique to an individual except for identical twins. This technology is used in forensic investigations, paternity testing, and victim identification. Often, there are only very small samples available, such as a single drop of blood or one strand of hair. A technique called *polymerase chain reaction* (PCR) may be used to copy a DNA sample to supply sufficient DNA for identification. Electrophoresis and autoradiography are processes used to compare DNA from a sample with the DNA of a known individual to confirm identification, as **Figure 4.6** shows.

Differentiated Instruction

INCLUSION

Understanding the individual roles of the RNAs can be difficult for many students. Help developmentally-delayed students understand this process by using students as models. Give one student a sign labeled *DNA: ATG*; a second student a sign labeled *mRNA: UAC*; a third student a sign labeled *ribosome (rRNA)*; and a fourth student a sign labeled *tRNA: ATG/amino acid.* Orchestrate what happens during RNA synthesis and protein synthesis by directing students to move as the process unfolds. For example, the student holding the mRNA sign should join hands with the student holding the DNA sign and then leave to join the student holding the ribosome sign. Finally, the fourth student should join the mRNA/ribosome students to show how tRNA brings the amino acid for insertion into the growing polypeptide chain. Repeat the process, but this time make only one sign showing a different three-base sequence in DNA. Ask students to make the other signs and direct the sequence of events.

Cloning

Cloning is the process of making an exact copy of an organism. One example of a natural occurrence of cloning is the formation of identical twins, which is the result of a chance splitting of the embryonic cells very early in development. Artificial cloning, mainly used with microbes, can produce identical replicas of the parent cells or, under specialized conditions, a complete organism that is identical to the original organism. The orchid shown in **Figure 4.7** is a clone of its parent plant. Cloning of plants may hold promise for increasing the yields of crops.

The first animal to be cloned, a sheep named Dolly, was born in 1997 in Scotland. The process of cloning higher organisms is so difficult that it took 200 tries to produce Dolly. Due to lung disease, Dolly was euthanized in 2003. She had also been diagnosed with arthritis. Both diseases are normally found in sheep older than Dolly was, so Dolly's early death may be related to the fact that she was cloned from cells obtained from a seven-year-old ewe. More recently, a number of vertebrates have been cloned, including dogs, cats, monkeys, and an endangered Asian oxen.

Therapeutic cloning of human tissues and organs may eventually provide significant advances in health care, but cloning an entire human remains science fiction.

FIGURE 4.7

Orchid Cloning Growers can produce many orchids by artificial cloning of the meristem tissue of a single orchid plant.

Recombinant DNA Technology

Recombinant DNA technology has been used to insert DNA from one organism into another. The technique splices a gene from one organism's DNA into a molecule of DNA from another organism. The genes in *Escherichia coli,* a bacterium found in human and animal intestinal tracts, are often used to obtain spliced segments of genetic material. When the spliced *E. coli* DNA is inserted into a cell, the cell is able to make the protein that is coded by the spliced gene.

One of the first applications of genetic engineering was the synthesis of human insulin. Previously, diabetics usually had to use either pig or cow insulin, which is not exactly the same as human insulin. Today, most insulin used is produced using *E.coli.* Human growth hormone is also commercially produced by using recombinant DNA technology.

SECTION 4 FORMATIVE ASSESSMENT

Reviewing Main Ideas

1. What sugar is present in DNA? What sugar is present in RNA?
2. Explain why the two strands of the DNA double helix are said to be complementary instead of identical.
3. Describe how DNA uses the genetic code to control the synthesis of proteins.
4. Why is a very small trace of blood enough for DNA fingerprinting?

Critical Thinking

5. **INTERPRET AND APPLY** Is it possible to specify 20 amino acids by using only two base pairs instead of three for coding?
6. **DRAWING CONCLUSIONS** Why is the arrangement of base pairs that is found in DNA ideal for holding the double helix of DNA together?

ChemisTrivia

It took 15 years for cloned human growth hormone to be developed, tested, and approved for human use.

Assess and Reteach ▼

Assess Use the Formative Assessment on this page to evaluate student mastery of the section.

Reteach For students who need additional instruction, download the Section Study Guide.

Response to Intervention To reassess students' mastery, use the Section Quiz, available to print or to take directly online at **HMDScience.com**.

Answers to Section Assessment

1. deoxyribose; ribose
2. The base on one chain is not identical to the base on the adjoining chain; instead, the base on one strand is complementary to the base on the other strand.
3. A sequence of three-base codes in DNA is transcribed into a sequence of RNA codes. The three-base code sequences in RNA code for specific amino acids. Proteins are synthesized using RNA according to the sequence of amino acids dictated by the coding of the gene on the DNA molecule. A single gene can code for several proteins.
4. A small amount of DNA can be copied many times by the PCR method.
5. No. The number of two-code bases is $4^2 = 16$, so a maximum of 16 amino acids could be coded.
6. These molecules are ideal because hydrogen bonding can exist between them and their geometry allows the DNA helix structure to form.

Teaching Strategy

Remind students that each amino acid is designated by a sequence of three nucleotides called a *codon*. Explain to students that the table shows the correspondence between the codons and the amino acids.

Answers

1. leucine–histidine–aspartic acid–tyrosine–asparagine–tryptophan
2. leucine–threonine–glycine; The codon UGA is a stop codon, so no more amino acids will be added.

Math Tutor

Interpretation of the Genetic Code

In protein synthesis, the DNA sequence of bases is transcribed onto messenger RNA (mRNA). The mRNA base sequence is the complement of the DNA sequence, except that uracil takes the place of thymine as the complement of adenine.

Problem-Solving TIPS

- Find the first base of the mRNA triplet along the left side of the table.
- Follow that row to the right until you are beneath the second base of the triplet.
- Move up or down in the square that corresponds to the second base until you are even with the third base of the triplet on the right side of the chart.

The Genetic Code (mRNA)

First base	Second base: U	Second base: C	Second base: A	Second base: G	Third base
U	UUU, UUC Phenylalanine UUA, UUG Leucine	UCU, UCC, UCA, UCG Serine	UAU, UAC Tyrosine UAA, UAG Stop	UGU, UGC Cysteine UGA—Stop UGG—Tryptophan	U C A G
C	CUU, CUC, CUA, CUG Leucine	CCU, CCC, CCA, CCG Proline	CAU, CAC Histidine CAA, CAG Glutamine	CGU, CGC, CGA, CGG Arginine	U C A G
A	AUU, AUC, AUA Isoleucine AUG—Start	ACU, ACC, ACA, ACG Threonine	AAU, AAC Asparagine AAA, AAG Lysine	AGU, AGC Serine AGA, AGG Arginine	U C A G
G	GUU, GUC, GUA, GUG Valine	GCU, GCC, GCA, GCG Alanine	GAU, GAC Aspartic acid GAA, GAG Glutamic acid	GGU, GGC, GGA, GGG Glycine	U C A G

Sample Problem

What sequence of amino acids will be incorporated into protein as a result of the mRNA sequence UUACCCGAGAAGUCC?

Divide the sequence into groups of three to clearly see the separate codons.

UUACCCGAGAAGUCC = UUA | CCC | GAG | AAG | UCC

Now, use the table to determine the match between codons and amino acids.

UUA	CCC	GAG	AAG	UCC
leucine	proline	glutamic acid	lysine	serine

Practice

1. What amino acid sequence will be added to a protein as a result of the mRNA sequence UUACACGACUAUAAUUGG?
2. What amino acid sequence will be added to a protein as a result of the mRNA sequence CUAACCGGGUGAGCUUCU?

732 Chapter 23

CHAPTER 23 Summary

Review Games
Concept Maps

SECTION 1 Carbohydrates and Lipids

- Carbohydrates are nutrients that are produced by plants and are made up of carbon, oxygen, and hydrogen.
- Monosaccharides are the simplest carbohydrates. Carbohydrates made of two monosaccharides are called *disaccharides*, and carbohydrates made of more than two monosaccharides are called *polysaccharides*.
- Carbohydrates undergo condensation reactions and hydrolysis reactions.
- Lipids are a varied group of biochemical molecules that have a high percentage of C and H atoms.

KEY TERMS

carbohydrate
monosaccharide
disaccharide
condensation reaction
hydrolysis
polysaccharide
lipid
fatty acid
saponification

SECTION 2 Amino Acids and Proteins

- Amino acid molecules are the basic building blocks of proteins.
- Proteins are biological polymers, each of which has a unique sequence of amino acid monomer molecules.
- The specific function of a protein is related to the shape of the protein.
- Side-chain interactions between amino acids result in secondary, tertiary, and quaternary protein structures.

KEY TERMS

amino acid
protein
enzyme
denaturation

SECTION 3 Metabolism

- ATP is a high-energy storage compound that the body uses to store and provide energy for life.
- The metabolic pathways involve both the conversion of ATP to ADP and the conversion of ADP to ATP.
- Metabolic pathways are classified as two types: catabolism and anabolism.
- Catabolism includes reactions in which large molecules are changed into simpler molecules. These reactions release energy.
- Anabolic processes are energy-consuming pathways by which cells produce the molecules needed for growth and repair.

KEY TERMS

metabolism
autotroph
adenosine triphosphate (ATP)
heterotroph
adenosine diphosphate (ADP)
catabolism
anabolism

SECTION 4 Nucleic Acids

- Deoxyribonucleic acid (DNA) and ribonucleic acid (RNA) are nucleic acids, the compounds by which living organisms can reproduce themselves.
- Nucleic acids are polymers of monomer units called *nucleotides*.
- The two strands of the double helix of DNA are complementary to each other, not identical. These strands are held together by hydrogen bonding of the base pairs.
- RNA is used to produce proteins in the cell.

KEY TERMS

nucleic acid
DNA replication
cloning

Review Answers

1. Carbohydrates consist of carbon, hydrogen, and oxygen molecules in a 1:2:1 ratio.
2. Sample answers: monosaccharides: glucose, fructose, ribose; disaccharides: sucrose, maltose, lactose; polysaccharides: starch, cellulose, glycogen
3. Starch is present for long-term energy storage. Cellulose provides support and structure.
4. unsaturated
5. Liquid triglycerides have large amounts of unsaturated fatty acids, while solid triglycerides have large amounts of saturated fatty acids.
6. triglycerides and a strong base, such as NaOH or KOH

7. [structural formula of glucose: ring of C atoms and O, with CH_2OH, H, OH groups]

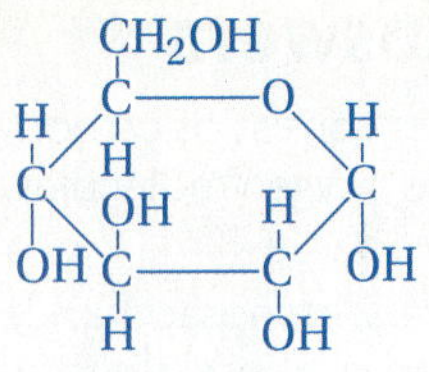

glucose

8. [structural formula: glucose + glucose ⟶ maltose]

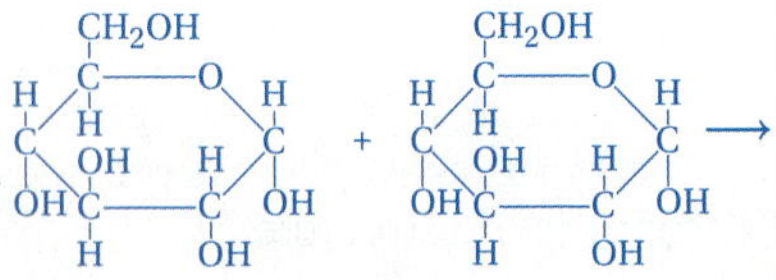

glucose + glucose ⟶

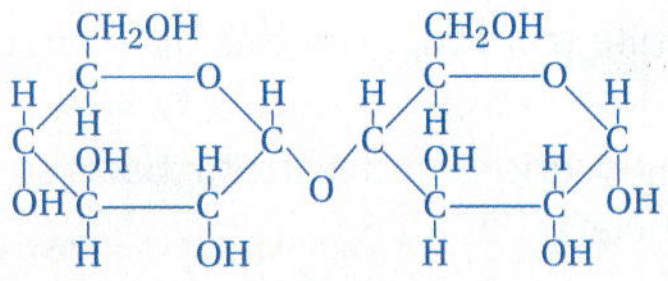

maltose

9. $C_{17}H_{35}COOH + NaOH \longrightarrow C_{17}H_{35}COONa + H_2O$

10. The basic structure of an amino acid consists of an amino group, a carboxylic acid group, and an *R* group. The *R* group is different for each amino acid. When two amino acids combine, the amino group of one amino acid reacts with the carboxylic acid group of the other, forming a peptide bond.

11. [molecule from question 11 with groups circled and labeled: amino (NH_2), carboxylic acid ($COOH$), carboxylic acid ($COOH$), amino (NH_2)]

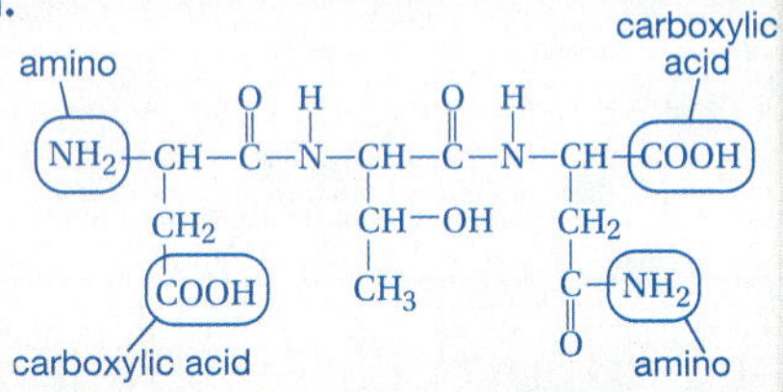

12. Yes they can, but the order of the amino acids would have to be different. As a result, the secondary and tertiary structures would also differ.

13. The secondary, tertiary, and quaternary structures are disrupted.

14. The substitution of one amino acid for another in the primary structure causes a change in the shape of the hemoglobin protein.

15. Nonpolar parts of globular proteins are not exposed to water, but the nonpolar parts of fibrous proteins are. Therefore, globular proteins are soluble in water, but fibrous proteins are not.

CHAPTER 23 Review

SECTION 1

Carbohydrates and Lipids

REVIEWING MAIN IDEAS

1. Describe the general chemical formula of carbohydrates.
2. Name two examples from each of the following classes of carbohydrates: monosaccharides, disaccharides, and polysaccharides.
3. What different roles do the polysaccharides starch and cellulose play in plant systems?
4. What word is used to describe fatty acids that contain at least one double bond?
5. Why are some triglycerides liquid, while others are solid?
6. What reagents are used to make soaps?

PRACTICE PROBLEMS

7. Draw the structural formula for glucose.
8. Using structural formulas, write the equation showing the formation of maltose, which is the disaccharide made of two glucose units.
9. Write the equation representing the formation of a soap molecule from stearic acid, $C_{17}H_{35}COOH$, and sodium hydroxide.

SECTION 2

Amino Acids and Proteins

REVIEWING MAIN IDEAS

10. Describe the structure of an amino acid. Then, explain how amino acids become linked together to form a protein.
11. Circle and identify the carboxylic acid groups and the amino groups in the following molecule:

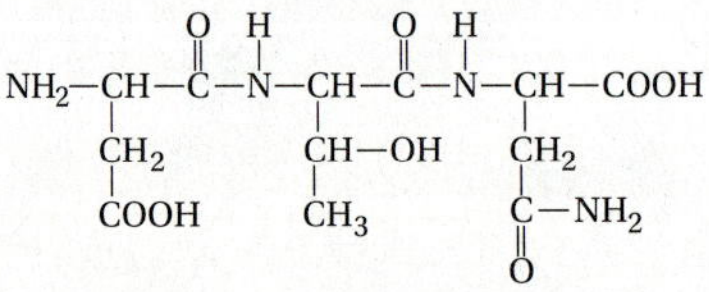

$$NH_2-CH(CH_2COOH)-C(=O)-NH-CH(CH(OH)CH_3)-C(=O)-NH-CH(CH_2C(=O)NH_2)-COOH$$

12. Can two types of enzymes contain the same number and kinds of amino acids? Explain.
13. What happens when a protein is denatured?
14. Explain the cause of the genetic disease sickle cell anemia.
15. Why is the water solubility of fibrous proteins so different from that of globular proteins?

PRACTICE PROBLEMS

16. Draw the structures of two dipeptides made up of glycine and valine.
17. How many different tripeptides can be formed from two molecules of glycine and one molecule of cysteine? Write all the structures by using the three-letter codes Gly and Cys.

SECTION 3

Metabolism

REVIEWING MAIN IDEAS

18. What chemical gains the metabolic energy that is released as glucose is broken down in the body?
19. What does *ATP* stand for? What is the role of ATP in living organisms?
20. Describe the steps that occur in the digestion of fats.
21. Review the following diagram of catabolism.

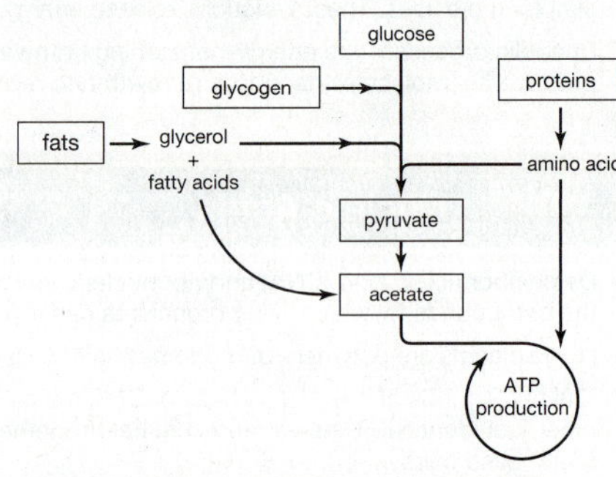

According to the diagram, what could happen in the cell when glucose and glycogen reserves are nearly gone?

16. $H_2N-CH_2-C(=O)-NH-CH(CH(CH_3)_2)-C(=O)-OH$

$NH_2-CH(CH(CH_3)_2)-C(=O)-NH-CH_2-C(=O)-OH$

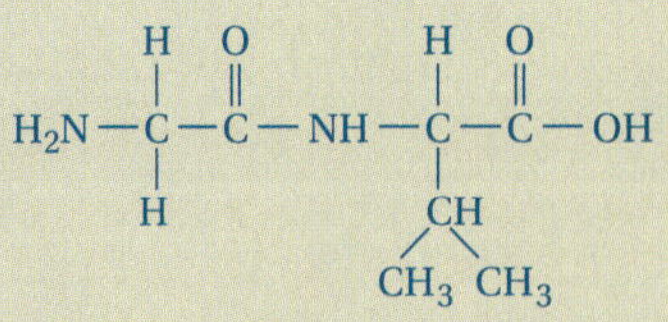

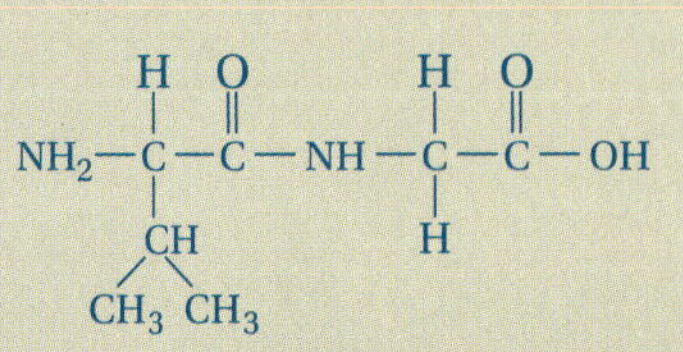

17. three; Gly—Gly—Cys, Gly—Cys—Gly, Cys—Gly—Gly

18. ATP

19. ATP stands for *adenosine triphosphate.* ATP is the molecule that provides the immediate energy to fuel all of life's processes.

20. Fats are hydrolyzed into fatty acids and glycerol in the small intestine.

21. Fats and proteins would be broken down into smaller molecules to produce energy.

PRACTICE PROBLEMS

22. Write the structural formula of ATP. Circle the bond that breaks when ADP forms.

SECTION 4

Nucleic Acids

REVIEWING MAIN IDEAS

23. What are the three components of a nucleotide?

24. How are the two chains of DNA held together?

25. Describe in general terms the process of DNA replication.

26. What are the main differences between DNA and RNA?

27. Describe the similarities and differences between the three kinds of RNA molecules.

28. What is a ribosome? What is the function of a ribosome in a cell?

PRACTICE PROBLEMS

29. The following sequence of bases might be found on the gene that codes for oxytocin, the human pituitary hormone:

TACACAATGTAAGTTTTGACGGGGGACCCTATC

a. What is the base sequence of the complementary strand of DNA?

b. What is the base sequence that would occur on a strand of mRNA transcribed from the oxytocin DNA sequence?

Mixed Review

REVIEWING MAIN IDEAS

30. Name the four main elements that make up compounds found in living organisms.

31. In each of the following groups, one of the items does not belong in the group. Identify the odd item in the group and explain why it is different. Explain how the other items are related.

a. glycogen, starch, fructose, and cellulose

b. amino acids, dipeptides, polypeptides, and proteins

c. fats, oils, and fatty acids

d. cytosine, adenine, and uracil

32. What is the human body's *storage* form of each of the following?

a. glucose

b. lipids

c. protein

33. Is each of the following statements about proteins and triglycerides true or false?

a. Both contain the amide functional group.

b. Both are a part of a major class of biochemical molecules.

c. Both hydrolyze in order to enter the metabolic pathway in humans.

34. Circle the hydrophobic part in each of the figures shown below.

a. 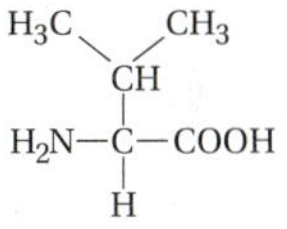 H_3C, CH_3 bonded to CH; CH bonded to C in $H_2N-C-COOH$, with H below C

b. 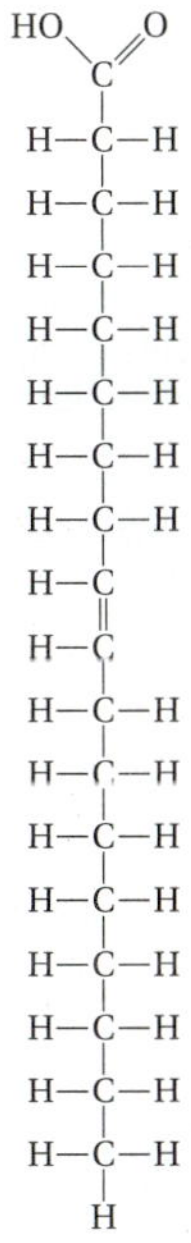 HO–C(=O) (carboxyl C) followed by chain: H–C–H, H–C–H, H–C–H, H–C–H, H–C–H, H–C–H, H–C–H, H–C, ‖ H–C, H–C–H, H–C–H, H–C–H, H–C–H, H–C–H, H–C–H, H–C–H, H–C–H, H

22. 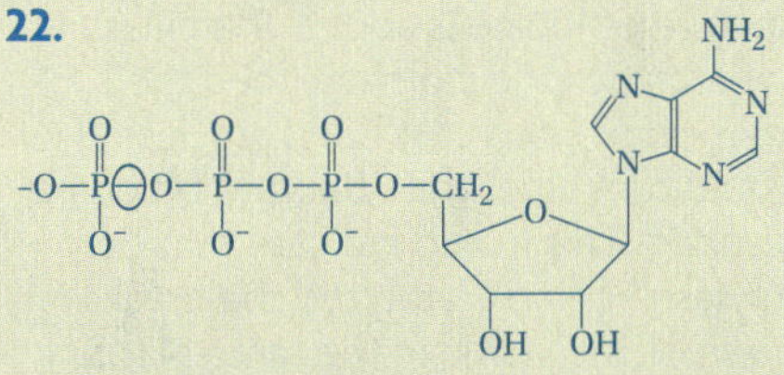 ATP structure: $^{-}O-P(=O)(O^{-})-O-P(=O)(O^{-})-O-P(=O)(O^{-})-O-CH_2$–ribose (OH, OH)–adenine (NH_2); bond between first and second phosphate circled

23. a five-carbon sugar unit, a phosphate group, and a nitrogenous base

24. hydrogen bonds

25. The two complementary DNA chains unwind and act as templates for the synthesis of two new strands. The result is the formation of two DNA molecules for each original molecule.

26. DNA has the sugar deoxyribose, and RNA has ribose; DNA is a double helix, and RNA is a single strand; DNA contains the base thymine, and RNA contains uracil.

27. Messenger RNA carries the genetic code from DNA. Ribosomal RNA and transfer RNA do not carry the genetic code but play a role in the synthesis of proteins.

28. A ribosome is a cell organelle made up of RNA and protein. Ribosomes are the site of protein production in the cell.

CHAPTER REVIEW

29. **a.** ATGTGTTAGATTCAAAACTGC-CCCCTGGGATAG

b. AUGUGUUAGAUUCAAAACUGC-CCCCUGGGAUAG

30. C, H, O, and N

31. **a.** Fructose is a monosaccharide, but the others are polysaccharides.

b. The amino acids have no peptide bonds, but the others have a peptide bond.

c. Fatty acids are not triglycerides; fats and oils are triglycerides.

d. Cytosine is a pyrimidine base; adenine and guanine are purine bases.

32. **a.** glycogen

b. fat in the adipose tissue

c. none

33. **a.** false

b. true

c. true

34. **a.** 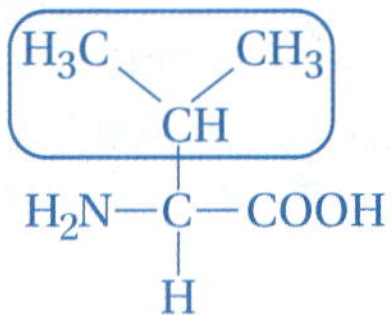 H_3C, CH_3, CH circled; $H_2N-C-COOH$, H

b. 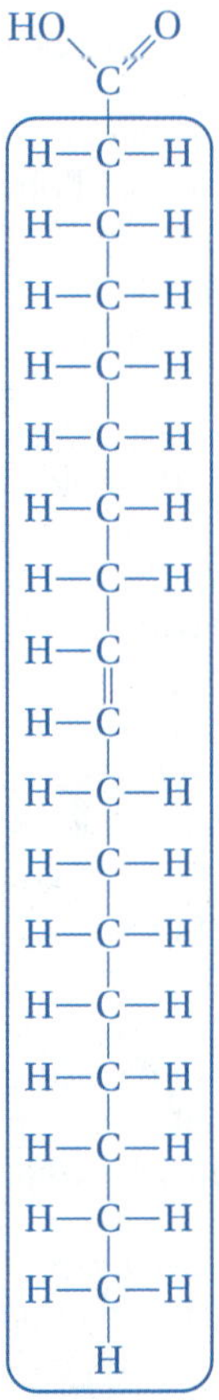 HO–C(=O); hydrocarbon chain (H–C–H ... H) circled

35. Cellulose is not digestible, but the starch in potato chips is and can add to the excess food intake, which is stored as fat in the adipose tissue. Potato chips are also fried in oil, which increases the caloric content.

36. a. carbohydrates

b. proteins

c. fats

37. The cell membrane is made up of a double layer of phospholipids. The nonpolar tails of the phospholipids repel water and make up the interior of the lipid bilayer. The polar heads of the phospholipids face the inside of the cell and the outer environment of the cell, both of which are mostly water. The cell membrane's main function is to control what substances pass into and out of the cell, in order to maintain a stable internal environment.

38. Corn protein does not contain all of the essential amino acids.

39. The same reaction is used to link the units in all three compounds: condensation with the creation of a water molecule.

40. Carbohydrates are the main source of energy in the diet. Energy is readily available after carbohydrates are eaten, or the energy can be stored for later use. If carbohydrates are unavailable, the body must use protein in the body tissues or fat in the adipose tissue for energy.

41. The "lock and key" model of enzyme activity refers to the specificity of an enzyme to a substrate molecule in the same way that a key will only open a specific lock. The enzyme does not become part of the product just as a key does not remain part of the lock.

42. Students' answers will vary. Answers should discuss Olestra and its structure. Answers should also reveal advantages and disadvantages of Olestra in food products.

43. Students' answers will vary. Summaries should include information about the basic molecular structure of each compound, where and how each compound is produced, where each compound is found in the body, and how each compound is used.

35. Both celery and potato chips are composed of molecules that are polymers of glucose. Explain why celery is a good snack for people on a diet while potato chips are not.

36. Carbohydrates, fats, and proteins can produce energy for an organism.

a. Which class of substances most rapidly provides energy?

b. Which class can be used as a building material in the human body?

c. Which is the most efficient as an energy storage system?

37. Describe the basic structure of the cell membrane. What is the cell membrane's main function?

CRITICAL THINKING

38. Interpreting Concepts A diet that consists primarily of corn can result in a protein-deficiency disease called *kwashiorkor*. What does this information indicate about the protein content of corn?

39. Inferring Relationships Explain how a similar reaction forms three kinds of biological polymers: polysaccharides, polypeptides, and nucleic acids.

40. Evaluating Ideas Some diets recommend severely restricting or eliminating the intake of carbohydrates. Why is it not a good idea to eliminate all carbohydrates from the diet?

41. Using Analogies Explain why the model of enzyme action is called the lock-and-key model.

RESEARCH AND WRITING

42. Conduct library research about how Olestra® decreases fat and caloric content of potato chips. What are the advantages and disadvantages of Olestra® in food products?

43. Write a summary discussing what you have learned about the four major classes of organic compounds found in living organisms—carbohydrates, lipids, proteins, and nucleic acids. Include a description of how these organic molecules are used by the body.

ALTERNATIVE ASSESSMENT

44. Amylase, the enzyme present in the mouth, catalyzes the digestion of starch. The pH of the mouth is almost neutral.

a. Do you think that amylase is active in the stomach after you swallow the food? Why or why not?

b. Design an experiment you could perform to test your answer to item a. Note: A common test for the presence of starch is the addition of tincture of iodine, which will produce a blue color if starch is present.

44. a. It is not active in a low pH environment because it becomes denatured.

b. Students' answers will vary. One possible way to test a hypothesis would be to test a starch solution to which some tincture of iodine has been added (the control), and then test a starch solution to which some tincture of iodine, a small amount of HCl solution, and then some amylase have been added. The solution of starch and HCl should have about the same pH that stomach acid does. The starch solution (control) will turn blue when tincture of iodine is added. If amylase is not active in the stomach, then the solution of starch, HCl, and amylase would turn blue when tincture of iodine is added. This would indicate that the amylase had not catalyzed the breakdown of the starch in the same pH as that of the stomach.

Standards-Based Assessment

Answer the following items on a separate piece of paper.

MULTIPLE CHOICE

1. Which of the following statements about enzymes is true?
   A. Enzymes can be biological catalysts.
   B. Enzymes increase the speed of a chemical reaction.
   C. Enzymes are highly specific.
   D. All of the above

2. Which of the following statements about denaturing is true?
   A. Denaturing occurs when a protein unfolds.
   B. Denaturing occurs when a carbohydrate is heated.
   C. Denaturing does not affect the tertiary structure of an enzyme.
   D. Denaturing increases the rate of a chemical reaction.

3. The process in which molecules in a cell break down to produce smaller molecules and energy is called
   A. glycogenesis.
   B. biosynthesis.
   C. catabolism.
   D. metabolism.

4. Which of the following is partially digested by saliva in the mouth?
   A. glucose
   B. starch
   C. fat
   D. protein

5. In the human body, the storage form of
   A. glucose is maltose.
   B. triglycerides is protein.
   C. carbohydrates is glycogen.
   D. nucleic acids is amino acids.

6. The purpose of insulin is to
   A. regulate glucose levels in the body.
   B. catalyze the oxidation of fatty acids.
   C. stimulate RNA production.
   D. initiate DNA replication.

7. Which of the following statements about fats is true?
   A. Fats serve as a reserve supply of energy.
   B. Fats are stored in the adipose tissue.
   C. Fats act as insulators.
   D. All of the above

8. When carbohydrates are unavailable or unable to provide the energy needs of the body,
   A. glucose is converted to glycogen.
   B. proteins or fats are used for energy.
   C. amino acids form proteins.
   D. All of the above

9. Which of the following statements is true?
   A. RNA contains the base uracil rather than thymine, which occurs in DNA.
   B. Both RNA and DNA are double-stranded helices.
   C. The ribose sugar unit is in the backbone of DNA.
   D. None of the above

SHORT ANSWER

10. Draw a simple dipeptide, and label the functional groups and peptide linkage.

11. Describe the shape of the DNA molecule, and discuss how the DNA molecule is held in this shape.

EXTENDED RESPONSE

12. The body has numerous energy reserves. What are they, and where are they found in the body? Which of these reserves provides the greatest source of quick energy?

13. Explain how it is possible to denature a protein without breaking the polypeptide chain.

Test Tip
If a question or an answer choice contains an unfamiliar term, try to break the word into parts to determine its meaning.

STANDARDS-BASED ASSESSMENT

To give students practice under more realistic testing conditions, give them 60 minutes to answer all of the questions in this Standardized Test Preparation.

Test Answers

1. D
2. A
3. C
4. B
5. C
6. A
7. D
8. B
9. A
10. Answers will vary. The $-NH_2$ amino group and a $-COOH$ carboxylic acid group should be labeled. Also, the peptide bond should be labeled.
11. DNA is shaped like a twisted ladder. The double-stranded helix of DNA is held together by hydrogen bonding between the base pairs.
12. The body stores energy in the form of fat in adipose tissue, glycogen in the liver, and protein in muscle and fibrous tissue. The greatest source of quick energy is the glucose in the blood. Glucose comes from the stored glycogen in the liver. All types of proteins (structural, enzymatic, regulator, and others) can also provide energy to the body.
13. The properties of a protein relate to the protein's secondary, tertiary, and quaternary structures, which can be changed (denatured) without affecting the primary structure.

Reference Section

Contents

APPENDIX A
Elements Handbook R2
- Group 1 Alkali Metals
- Group 2 Alkaline-Earth Metals
- Groups 3–12 Transition Metals
- Group 13 Boron Family
- Group 14 Carbon Family
- Group 15 Nitrogen Family
- Group 16 Oxygen Family
- Group 17 Halogen Family

APPENDIX B
Reference Tables R58
- Table B-1 SI Measurement
- Table B-2 Unit Symbols
- Table B-3 Symbols
- Table B-4 Physical Constants
- Table B-5 Enthalpy of Combustion
- Table B-6 The Elements: Symbols, Atomic Numbers, and Atomic Masses
- Table B-7 Common Ions
- Table B-8 Water-Vapor Pressure
- Table B-9 Densities of Gases at STP
- Table B-10 Density of Water
- Table B-11 Solubilities of Gases in Water
- Table B-12 Solubility Chart
- Table B-13 Solubility of Compounds
- Table B-14 Enthalpy of Formation
- Table B-15 Properties of Common Elements

APPENDIX C
Math Skills Handbook and Chemistry Equations R68

APPENDIX D
Problem Bank R84

APPENDIX E
Selected Answers R119

GLOSSARY R127

INDEX R148

PERIODIC TABLE OF THE ELEMENTS . . Inside Back Cover

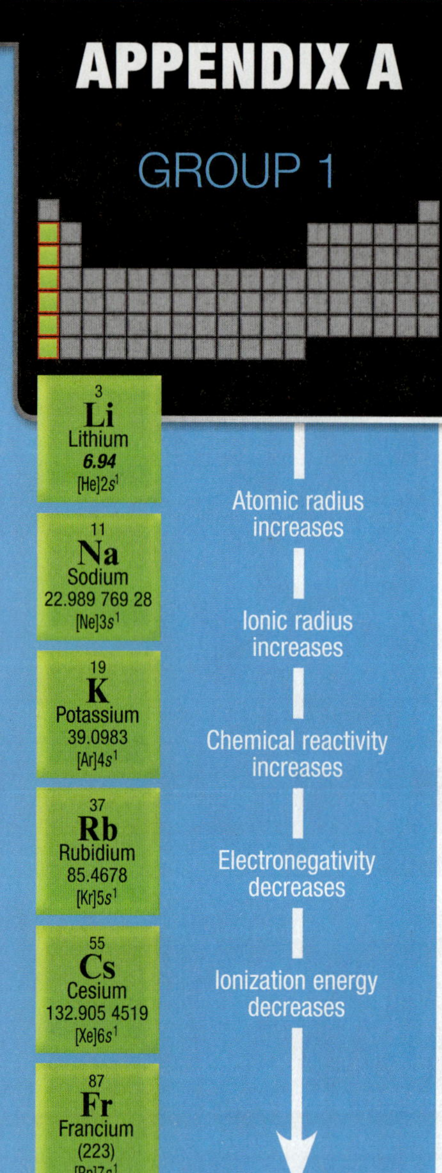

Alkali Metals

Characteristics

- do not occur in nature as free elements
- are reactive metals and are obtained by reducing the 1+ ions in their natural compounds
- are stored under kerosene or other hydrocarbon solvent because they react with water vapor or oxygen in air
- consist of atoms with one electron in the outermost energy level
- form colorless ions in solution, each of which has a 1+ charge
- form ionic compounds
- form water-soluble bases
- are strong reducing agents
- consist of atoms that have low ionization energies
- are good heat and electrical conductors
- are ductile, malleable, and soft enough to be cut with a knife
- have a silvery luster, low density, and low melting point

▲ Lithium was discovered in 1817. It is found in most igneous rocks and is used in batteries as an anode because it has a very low reduction potential. Lithium is soft and is stored in oil or kerosene to prevent it from reacting with the air.

▲ Sodium derives its name from the word soda. It was first isolated in 1807 from the electrolysis of caustic soda, NaOH. Sodium is soft enough to be cut with a knife. It is shiny until it reacts with oxygen, which causes the surface to lose its luster.

▲ Potassium was first isolated in 1807 from the electrolysis of caustic potash, KOH.

Common Reactions

With Water to Form Bases and Hydrogen Gas

Example: $2Na(s) + 2H_2O(l) \longrightarrow 2NaOH(aq) + H_2(g)$

Li, K, Rb, and Cs also follow this pattern.

With Acids to Form Salts and Hydrogen Gas

Example: $2Na(s) + 2HCl(aq) \longrightarrow 2NaCl(aq) + H_2(g)$

Li, K, Rb, and Cs also follow this pattern.

With Halogens to Form Salts

Example: $2Na(s) + F_2(g) \longrightarrow 2NaF(s)$

Li, K, Rb, and Cs also follow this pattern in reacting with F_2, Cl_2, Br_2, and I_2.

With Oxygen to Form Oxides, Peroxides, or Superoxides

Lithium forms an oxide.

$4Li(s) + O_2(g) \longrightarrow 2Li_2O(s)$

Sodium also forms a peroxide.

$2Na(s) + O_2(g) \longrightarrow Na_2O_2(s)$

Alkali metals with higher molecular masses can also form superoxides.

$K(s) + O_2(g) \longrightarrow KO_2(s)$

Rb and Cs also follow this pattern.

Alkali-Metal Oxides with Water to Form Bases

Oxides of Na, K, Rb, and Cs can be prepared indirectly. These basic anhydrides form hydroxides in water.

Example: $K_2O(s) + H_2O(l) \longrightarrow 2KOH(aq)$

Li, Na, Rb, and Cs also follow this pattern.

Analytical Test

Alkali metals are easily detected by flame tests because each metal imparts a characteristic color to a flame.

When sodium and potassium are both present in a sample, the yellow color of the sodium masks the violet color of the potassium. The violet color can be seen only when the combined sodium-potassium flame is viewed through a cobalt-blue glass. The glass blocks the yellow flame of sodium and makes it possible to see the violet flame of potassium.

▲ A small piece of potassium dropped into water will react explosively, releasing H_2 to form a strongly basic hydroxide solution. The energy of the reaction ignites the hydrogen gas that is produced.

▲ Sodium reacts vigorously with chlorine to produce NaCl. Most salts of Group 1 metals are white crystalline compounds.

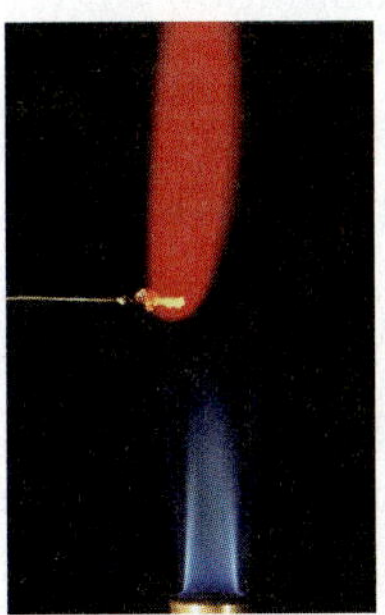

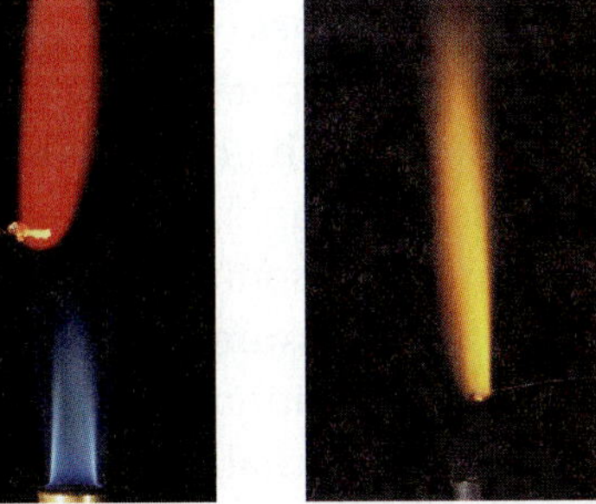

Lithium

Sodium

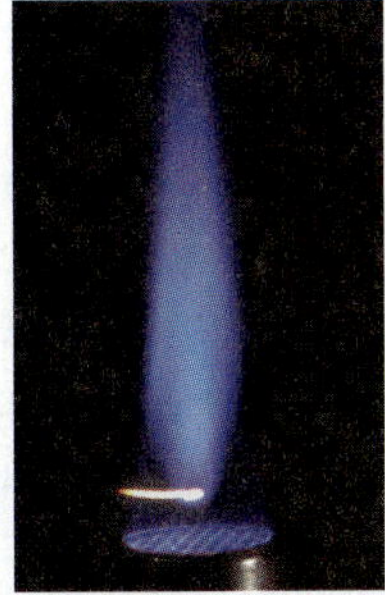

Potassium

Cesium

Properties

GROUP 1 ELEMENTS						
Quantity	Li	Na	K	Rb	Cs	Fr
Melting point (°C)	180.5	97.8	63.25	38.89	28.5	27
Boiling point (°C)	1342	882.9	760	691	668	677
Density (g/cm^3)	0.534	0.971	0.862	1.53	1.87	—
Ionization energy (kJ/mol)	520	496	419	403	376	—
Atomic radius (pm)	152	186	227	248	265	270
Ionic radius (pm)	76	102	138	152	167	180
Common oxidation number in compounds	+1	+1	+1	+1	+1	—
Crystal structure	bcc*	bcc	bcc	bcc	bcc	—
Hardness (Mohs' scale)	0.6	0.4	0.5	0.3	0.2	—

* body-centered cubic

S.T.E.M.

Application *Technology*

Sodium Vapor Lighting

The flame test for sodium shows two bright lines at 589.0 and 589.6 nm, which is the yellow range of the emission spectrum. Sodium can be vaporized at high temperatures in a sealed tube and made to give off light using two electrodes connected to a power source. Sodium vapor lighting is often used along highways and in parking lots because it provides good illumination while using less energy than other types of lighting.

Sodium vapor lighting comes in both low-pressure and high-pressure bulbs. Low-pressure lamps reach an internal temperature of 270°C to vaporize the sodium under a pressure of about 1 Pa. High-pressure lamps contain mercury and xenon in addition to sodium. These substances reach an internal temperature of 1100°C under a pressure of about 100 000 Pa. The high-pressure lamp provides a higher light intensity. The design of both types of lamps must take into account the high reactivity of sodium, which increases at high temperatures. Because ordinary glass will react with sodium at 250°C, a special sodium-resistant glass is used for low-pressure lamps. High-pressure lamps use an aluminum oxide material for the column containing the sodium, mercury, and xenon. Both types of lamps contain tungsten electrodes.

The light intensity per watt for sodium vapor lamps far exceeds that of fluorescent lamps, high-pressure mercury vapor lamps, tungsten halogen lamps, and incandescent bulbs.

S.T.E.M.

Application *Health*

Electrolyte Balance in the Body

The elements of Group 1 are important to a person's diet and body maintenance because they form ionic compounds. These compounds are present in the body as solutions of the ions. All ions carry an electric charge, so they are electrolyte solutes. Two of the most important electrolyte solutes found in the body are K^+ and Na^+ ions. Both ions facilitate the transmission of nerve impulses and control the amount of water retained by cells.

▲ During situations where the body is losing water rapidly through intense sweating or diarrhea for a prolonged period (more than 5 hours), a sports drink can hydrate the body and restore electrolyte balance. However, using sports drinks regularly when not exercising can have a negative effect on electrolyte balance in the body. (See Table 1B)

TABLE 1A

SODIUM-POTASSIUM CONCENTRATION IN BODY FLUIDS

Cation	Inside cells (mmol/L)	Outside cells or in plasma (mmol/L)
Na^+	12	145
K^+	140	4

The sodium and potassium ion concentrations in body fluids are shown in Table 1A. Sodium ions are found primarily in the fluid outside cells, while potassium ions are largely found in the fluid inside cells. Anions are present in the fluids to balance the electrical charge of the Na^+ and K^+ cations.

Abnormal electrolyte concentrations in blood serum can indicate the presence of disease. The ion concentrations that vary as a result of disease are Na^+, K^+, Cl^-, and HCO_3^-. Sodium ion concentration is a good indicator of the water balance between blood and tissue cells. Unusual potassium ion levels can indicate kidney or gastrointestinal problems. Chloride ion is the anion that balances the positive charge of the sodium ion in the fluid outside the cells. It also diffuses into a cell to maintain normal electrolyte balance when hydrogen carbonate ions diffuse out of the cell into the blood. Table 1B shows medical conditions associated with electrolyte imbalances.

TABLE 1B

ELECTROLYTE IMBALANCES

Electrolyte	Normal Range (mmol/L)	Causes of Imbalance	
		Excess	Deficiency
Sodium, Na^+	135–145	hypernatremia (increased urine excretion; excess water loss)	hyponatremia (dehydration; diabetes-related low blood pH; vomiting; diarrhea)
Potassium, K^+	3.5–5.0	hyperkalemia (renal failure; low blood pH)	hypokalemia (gastrointestinal conditions)
Hydrogen carbonate, HCO_3^-	24–30	hypercapnia (high blood pH; hypoventilation)	hypocapnia (low blood pH; hyperventilation; dehydration)
Chloride, Cl^-	100–106	hyperchloremia (anemia; heart conditions; dehydration)	hypochloremia (acute infection; burns; hypoventilation)

Sodium-Potassium Pump in the Cell Membrane
The process of active transport allows a cell to maintain its proper electrolyte balance. To keep the ion concentrations at the proper levels shown in Table 1B, a sodium-potassium pump embedded in the cell membrane shuttles sodium ions out of the cell across the cell membrane. A model for the action of the sodium-potassium pump is shown in the figure below.

Nerve Impulses and Ion Concentration
The difference in Na^+ and K^+ concentrations inside and outside nerve cell membranes is essential for the operation of the nervous system. This unequal concentration of ions creates a voltage across nerve cell membranes. When a nerve cell is stimulated, sodium ions diffuse into the cell from the surrounding fluid, raising voltage across the nerve cell membrane from −70 mV to nearly +60 mV. Potassium ions then diffuse out of the cell into the surrounding fluid, restoring the voltage across the nerve cell membrane to −70 mV. This voltage fluctuation initiates the transmission of a nerve impulse. The amount of Na^+ inside the cell has increased slightly, and the amount of K^+ outside the cell has decreased. But the sodium-potassium pump will restore these ions to their proper concentrations.

Sodium-Potassium Pump

The sodium-potassium pump is a protein embedded within the cell membrane that allows the passage of Na^+ and K^+ into and out of the cell. Each figure depicts the action of a single protein.

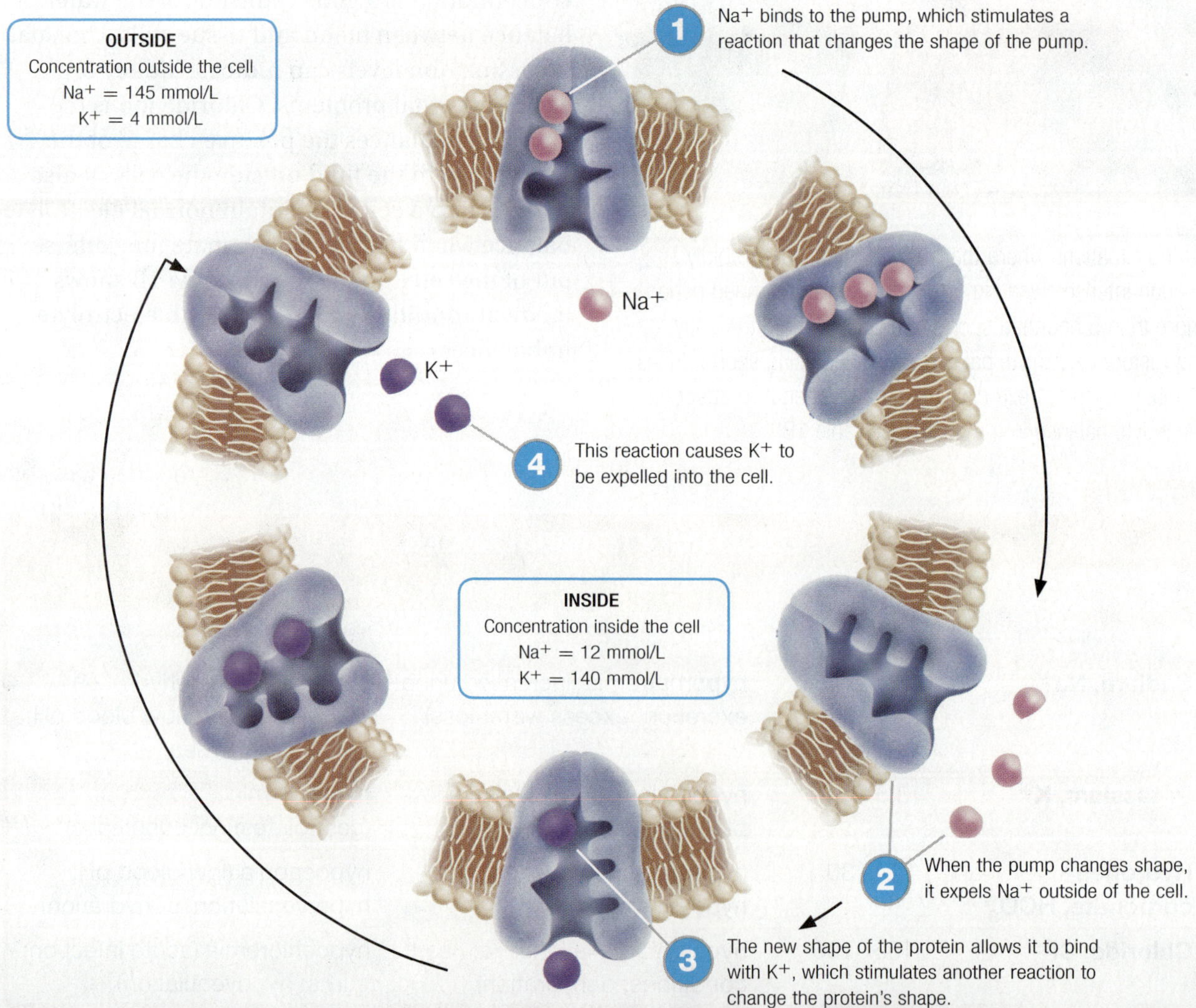

What's Your Sodium IQ?

Though sodium is an important mineral in your body, a diet that is high in sodium is one of several factors linked to high blood pressure, also known as hypertension. High Na^+ levels cause water retention, which results in increased blood pressure. Sodium is not the direct cause of all hypertension, but reducing sodium levels in the diet can affect individuals with a condition known as salt-sensitive hypertension. Therefore, the Dietary Guidelines for Americans recommend consuming salt and sodium in moderation. Test your knowledge about sodium in foods with the questions below.

1. Which of the following condiments do you think has the lowest salt content?
   a. mustard **c.** catsup **e.** vinegar
   b. steak sauce **d.** pickles

2. One-fourth of a teaspoon of salt contains about _______ of sodium.
   a. 10 mg **c.** 500 mg **e.** 1 kg
   b. 100 g **d.** 500 g

3. According to FDA regulations for food product labels, a food labeled *salt-free* must contain less than _______ mg of sodium ion per serving.
   a. 100 **c.** 0.001 **e.** 0.00005
   b. 5 **d.** 0.005

4. The Nutrition Facts label for a particular food reads "Sodium 15 mg." This is the amount of sodium ions per _______.
   a. package **c.** serving **e.** RDA
   b. teaspoon **d.** ounce

5. The recommended average daily intake of sodium ion for adults is 1500 mg. For a low-sodium diet the intake should be _______.
   a. 200 mg **c.** 750 mg **e.** 150 mg
   b. 2000 mg **d.** 500 mg

6. Each of the following ingredients can be found in the ingredients lists for some common food products. Which ones indicate that the product contains sodium?
   a. trisodium phosphate **d.** sodium sulfate
   b. sodium bicarbonate **e.** MSG
   c. sodium benzoate **f.** baking soda

7. Which of the following spices is NOT a salt substitute?
   a. caraway seeds **c.** ginger
   b. dill **d.** onion salt

8. Most salt in the average American diet comes from salting foods too heavily at the dinner table.
   a. true **b.** false

9. Which of the following foods are high in sodium?
   a. potato chips **c.** doughnuts **e.** figs
   b. pizza **d.** banana

10. Your body requires about 200 mg of sodium ion, or 500 mg of salt, per day. Why do these numbers differ?

Answers 1. e; 2. c; 3. b; 4. c; 5. c; 6. all of them; 7. d; 8. b, processed foods can contain very high levels of sodium; 9. a, b, c; 10. Salt is not pure sodium.

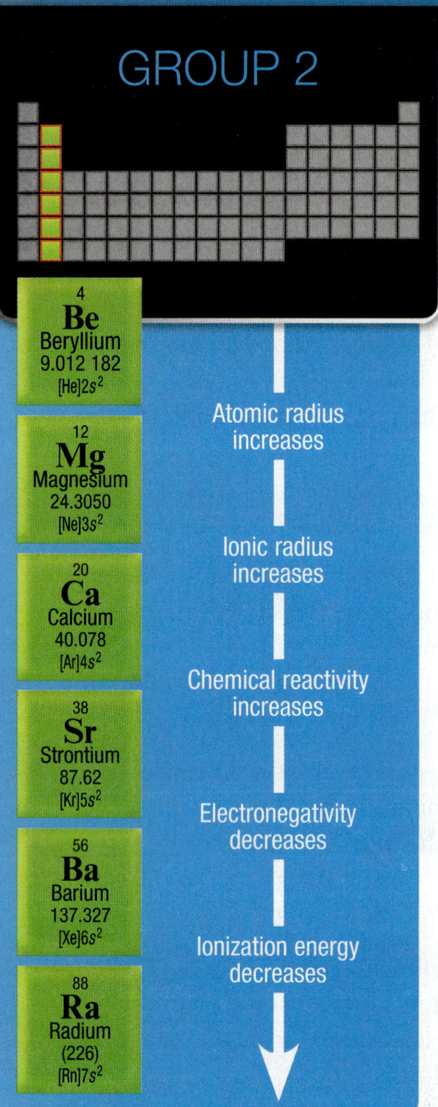

Alkaline-Earth Metals

Characteristics

- do not occur naturally as free elements
- occur most commonly as the carbonates, phosphates, silicates, and sulfates
- occur naturally as compounds that are either insoluble or only slightly soluble in water
- consist of atoms that contain two electrons in their outermost energy level
- consist of atoms that tend to lose two electrons per atom, forming ions with a 2+ charge
- are less reactive than alkali metals
- form ionic compounds primarily
- react with water to form bases and hydrogen gas
- are good heat and electrical conductors
- are ductile and malleable
- have a silvery luster
- include the naturally radioactive element radium

Calcium carbonate is a major component of marble.

Beryllium is found in the mineral compound beryl. Beryl crystals include the dark green emerald and the blue-green aquamarine. The colors of these gems come from other metal impurities.

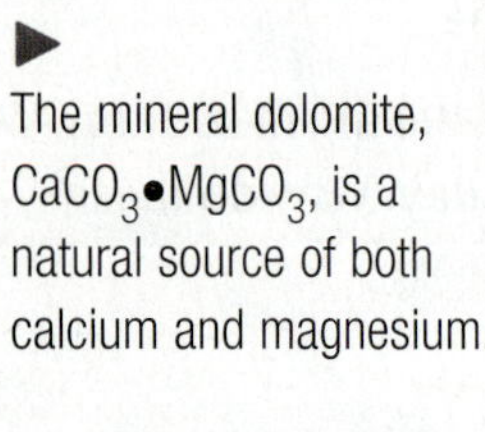

The mineral dolomite, $CaCO_3 \bullet MgCO_3$, is a natural source of both calcium and magnesium.

Common Reactions

▲ Calcium reacts with water to form hydrogen gas.

With Water to Form Bases and Hydrogen Gas

Example: $Mg(s) + 2H_2O(l) \longrightarrow Mg(OH)_2(aq) + H_2(g)$
Ca, Sr, and Ba also follow this pattern.

With Acids to Form Salts and Hydrogen Gas

Example: $Mg(s) + 2HCl(aq) \longrightarrow MgCl_2(aq) + H_2(g)$
Be, Ca, Sr, and Ba also follow this pattern.

With Halogens to Form Salts

Example: $Mg(s) + F_2(g) \longrightarrow MgF_2(s)$
Ca, Sr, and Ba also follow this pattern in reacting with F_2, Cl_2, Br_2, and I_2.

With Oxygen to Form Oxides or Peroxides

Magnesium forms an oxide.
$2Mg(s) + O_2(g) \longrightarrow 2MgO(s)$
Be and Ca also follow this pattern.

Strontium also forms a peroxide.
$Sr(s) + O_2(g) \longrightarrow SrO_2(s)$
Ba also reacts in this way.

With Hydrogen to Form Hydrides

Example: $Mg(s) + H_2(g) \longrightarrow MgH_2(s)$
Ca, Sr, and Ba also follow this pattern.

With Nitrogen to Form Nitrides

Example: $3Mg(s) + N_2(g) \longrightarrow Mg_3N_2(s)$
Be and Ca also follow this pattern.

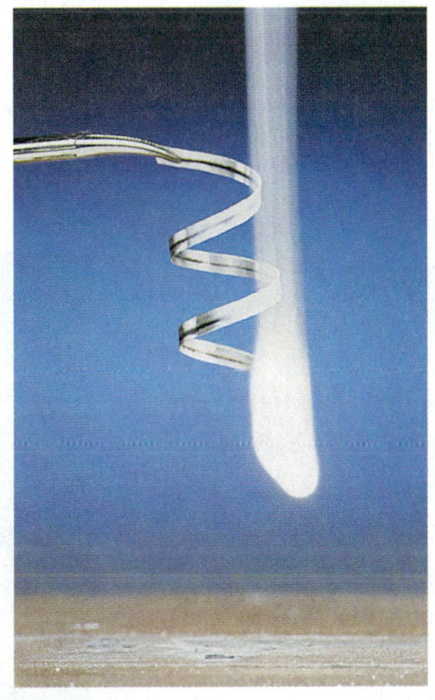

▲ Magnesium burns in air to form MgO and Mg_3N_2.

▲ Magnesium reacts with HCl to produce $MgCl_2(aq)$.

Analytical Test

Flame tests can be used to identify three of the alkaline-earth elements. The colors of both calcium and strontium can be masked by the presence of barium, which produces a green flame.

Calcium

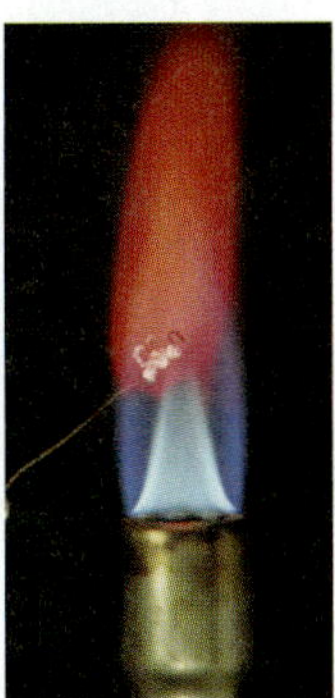

Strontium

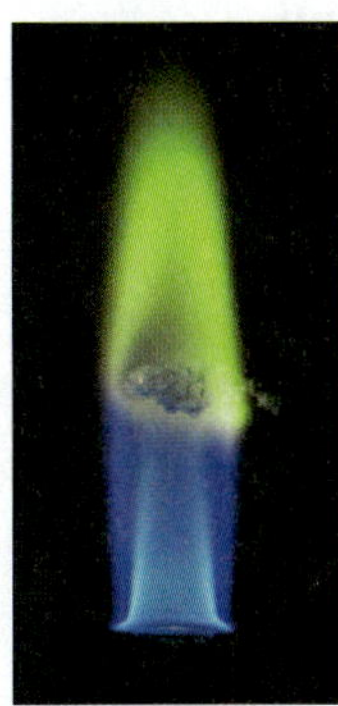

Barium

Properties

GROUP 2 ELEMENTS						
Quantity	Be	Mg	Ca	Sr	Ba	Ra
Melting point (°C)	1278 ± 5	649	839 ± 2	769	725	700
Boiling point (°C)	2467	1090	1484	1384	1640	1140
Density (g/cm^3)	1.85	1.74	1.54	2.6	3.51	5
Ionization energy (kJ/mol)	900	738	590	550	503	509
Atomic radius (pm)	112	160	197	215	222	220
Ionic radius (pm)	45	72	100	118	136	148
Common oxidation number in compounds	+2	+2	+2	+2	+2	+2
Crystal structure	hcp*	hcp	fcc**	fcc	bcc	bcc
Hardness (Mohs' scale)	4.0	2.0	1.5	1.8	1.5	—

* hexagonal close-packed   ** face-centered cubic

S.T.E.M.
Application *Technology*

Fireworks

Fireworks are made from pyrotechnics—chemical substances that produce light and smoke when they are ignited. Pyrotechnics are also used in flares, smoke bombs, explosives, and matches. An aerial fireworks device is a rocket made of a cylinder, chemicals inside the cylinder, and fuses attached to the cylinder. The illustration on the right shows how the device works. The lift charge at the bottom of the cylinder consists of a small amount of black gunpowder. When the side fuse ignites the gunpowder, it explodes like a small bomb. The gunpowder consists of potassium nitrate, charcoal, and sulfur. When these three chemicals react with one another, they produce gases. In this case, the gases produced are carbon monoxide, carbon dioxide, sulfur dioxide, and nitrogen monoxide. These hot gases expand very rapidly, providing the thrust that lifts the rocket into the sky.

About the time the shell reaches its maximum altitude and minimum speed, the time fuse ignites the chemicals contained in the cylinder. The chemicals inside the cylinder determine the color of the burst.

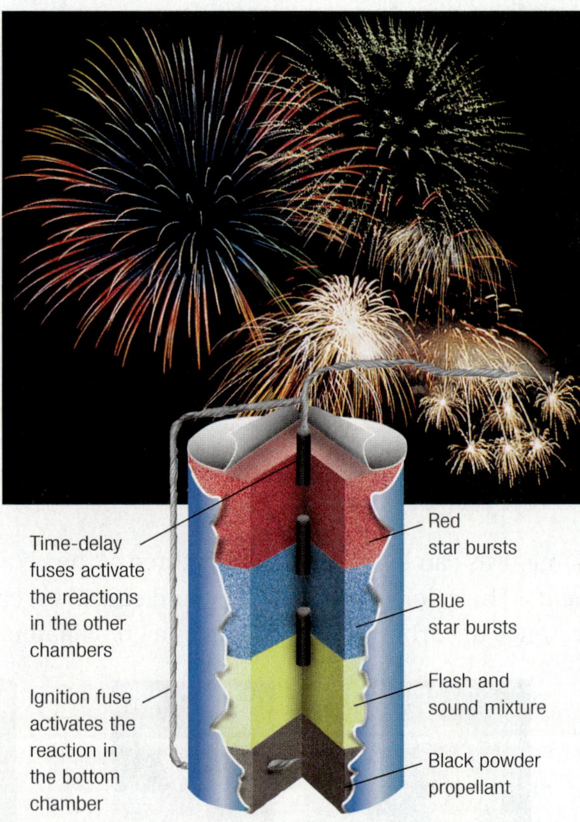

▲ The cylinder of a multiple-burst rocket contains separate reaction chambers connected by fuses. A common fuse ignites the propellant and the time-delay fuse in the first reaction chamber.

Chemical Composition and Color

One of the characteristics of fireworks that we enjoy most is their variety of rich colors. These colors are created in much the same way as the colors produced during a flame test. In a fireworks device, the chloride salt is heated to a high temperature, causing the excited atoms to give off a burst of light. The color of light produced depends on the metal used. The decomposition of barium chloride, $BaCl_2$, for example, produces a burst of green light, whereas strontium chloride, $SrCl_2$, releases red light.

People who design fireworks combine artistry with a technical knowledge of chemical properties. They have found ways to combine different colors within a single cylinder and to make parts of the cylinder explode at different times. Fireworks designers have a technical knowledge of projectile motion that is used to determine the height, direction, and angle at which a fireworks device will explode to produce a fan, fountain, flower, stream, comet, spider, star, or other shape.

Strontium and the Visible Spectrum

When heated, some metallic elements and their compounds emit light at specific wavelengths that are characteristic of the element or compound. Visible light includes wavelengths between about 400 and 700 nanometers. The figure below shows the emission spectrum for strontium. When heated, strontium gives off the maximum amount of visible light at about 700 nanometers, which falls in the red-light region of the visible spectrum.

▶ The emission spectrum for strontium shows strong bands in the red region of the visible light spectrum.

Flares

Flares operate on a chemical principle that is different from that of fireworks. A typical flare consists of finely divided magnesium metal and an oxidizing agent. When the flare is ignited, the oxidizing agent reacts with the magnesium metal to produce magnesium oxide. This reaction releases so much energy that it produces a glow like that of the filaments in a light bulb. The brilliant white light produced by the flare is caused by billions of tiny particles of magnesium that glow when they react. If slightly larger particles of magnesium metal are used in the flare, the system glows for a longer period of time because the particles' reaction with the oxidizing agent is slower.

A colored flare can be thought of as a combination of a white flare and a chemical that produces colored light when burned. For example, a red flare can be made from magnesium metal, an oxidizing agent, and a compound of strontium. When the flare is ignited, the oxidizing agent and magnesium metal react, heating the magnesium to white-hot temperatures. The energy from this reaction causes the strontium compound to give off its characteristic red color.

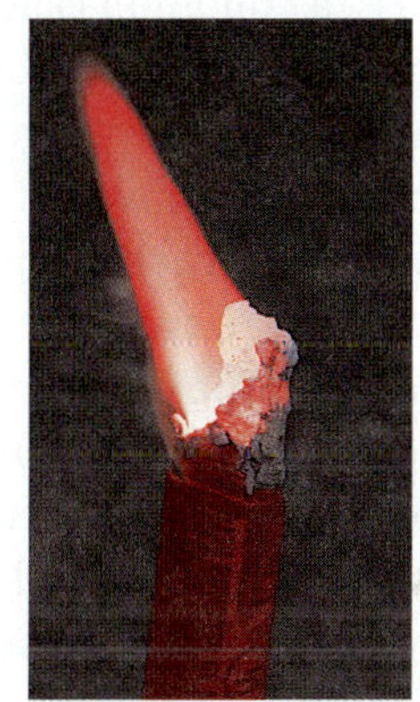

▲ A flare is made up of billions of reacting magnesium particles.

For safety reasons, some fireworks manufacturers store their products in metal sheds separated by sand banks. Also, people who work with fireworks are advised to wear cotton clothing because cotton is less likely than other fabrics to develop a static charge, which can cause a spark and accidentally ignite fireworks.

S.T.E.M.

Application *Health*

Calcium: An Essential Mineral in the Diet

Calcium is the most abundant mineral in the body. It is the mineral that makes up a good portion of the teeth and the bone mass of the body. A small percentage of calcium in the body is used in the reactions by which cells communicate and in the regulation of certain body processes. Calcium is so important to normal body functioning that if the calcium level of the blood falls far below normal, hormones signal the release of calcium from bone and signal the gastrointestinal tract to absorb more calcium during the digestion process.

A prolonged diet that is low in calcium is linked to a disease characterized by a decrease in bone mass, a condition called osteoporosis. Reduced bone mass results in brittle bones that fracture easily. Osteoporosis generally occurs later in life and is more prevalent in females. However, because you achieve peak bone mass during the late teens or early twenties, it is critical that your diet meet the recommended requirements to increase your peak bone mass. The recommended dietary intake for calcium is 1000 mg per day. Maintaining that level in the diet along with regular exercise through adulthood are thought to reduce the rate of bone loss later in life. Excess calcium in the diet (consuming more than 2500 mg daily) can interfere with the absorption of other minerals.

▲ Dairy products are generally good sources of calcium.

Magnesium: An Essential Mineral in the Diet

Though magnesium has several functions in the body, one of the more important functions is its role in the absorption of calcium by cells. Magnesium, like sodium and potassium, is involved in the transmission of nerve impulses. Like calcium, magnesium is a component of bone.

A major source of magnesium in the diet is plants. Magnesium is the central atom in the green plant pigment chlorophyll. The structure of chlorophyll in plants is somewhat similar to the structure of heme—the oxygen-carrying molecule in animals.

TABLE 2A

GOOD SOURCES OF CALCIUM IN THE DIET

Food	Serving size	Calcium present (mg)
Broccoli	6.3 oz	82
Cheddar cheese	1 oz	204
Cheese pizza, frozen	pizza for one	375
Milk, low-fat 1%	8 oz	300
Tofu, regular	4 oz	130
Vegetable pizza, frozen	pizza for one	500
Yogurt, low-fat	8 oz	415
Yogurt, plain whole milk	8 oz	274

▲ Spinach is a good source of magnesium. Magnesium is the central atom in the green plant pigment chlorophyll. The chlorophyll structure is shown on the right.

The recommended dietary intake of magnesium is 400 mg per day for men and 315 mg per day for women. This is equivalent to just 4 oz of bran cereal. Because magnesium levels are easily maintained by a normal diet, it is unusual for anyone to have a magnesium deficiency. Most magnesium deficiencies are the result of factors that decrease magnesium absorption. People with gastrointestinal disorders, alcohol abusers, and the critically ill are most likely to have these types of absorption problems.

Excess magnesium in the diet is excreted by the kidneys, so there are no cumulative toxic effects.

Chlorophyll *a*

TABLE 2B

GOOD SOURCES OF MAGNESIUM IN THE DIET		
Food	**Serving size**	**Magnesium present (mg)**
Barley, raw	1 cup	244
Beef, broiled sirloin	4 oz	36
Cabbage, raw	1 med. head	134
Cashews, dry-roasted	1 oz	74
Chicken, roasted breast	4 oz	31
Lima beans, boiled	1/2 cup	63
Oatmeal	1 oz	39
Potato, baked	7.1 oz	115
Prunes, dried	4 oz	51
Rice bran	8 oz	648
Salmon, canned	4 oz	39
Spinach, raw	10 oz	161

GROUPS 3–12

Transition Metals

Characteristics

- consist of metals in Groups 3 through 12
- contain one or two electrons in their outermost energy level
- are usually harder and more brittle than metals in Groups 1 and 2
- have higher melting and boiling points than metals in Groups 1 and 2
- are good heat and electrical conductors
- are malleable and ductile
- have a silvery luster, except copper and gold
- include radioactive elements with numbers 89 through 112
- include mercury, the only liquid metal at room temperature
- have chemical properties that differ from each other
- tend to have two or more common oxidation states
- often form colored compounds
- may form complex ions

▲ Iron ore is obtained from surface mines. Hematite, Fe_2O_3, is the most common iron ore.

▲ Gold, silver, platinum, palladium, iridium, rhodium, ruthenium, and osmium are sometimes referred to as the noble metals because they are not very reactive. These metals are found in coins, jewelry, and metal sculptures.

▲ Copper ores are also obtained from surface mines. Copper ore is shown here.

Common Reactions

Because this region of the periodic table is so large, you would expect great variety in the types of reaction characteristics of transition metals. For example, copper oxidizes in air to form the green patina you see on the Statue of Liberty. Copper reacts with concentrated HNO_3 but not with dilute HNO_3. Zinc, on the other hand, reacts readily with dilute HCl. Iron oxidizes in air to form rust, but chromium is generally unreactive in air. Some common reactions for transition elements are shown by the following:

May form two or more different ions

Example: $Fe(s) \longrightarrow Fe^{2+}(aq) + 2e^-$
Example: $Fe(s) \longrightarrow Fe^{3+}(aq) + 3e^-$

May react with oxygen to form oxides

Example: $4Cr(s) + 3O_2(g) \longrightarrow 2Cr_2O_3(s)$
Example: $2Cu(s) + O_2(g) \longrightarrow 2CuO(s)$

May react with halogens to form halides

Example: $Ni(s) + Cl_2(g) \longrightarrow NiCl_2(s)$

May form complex ions

See examples in the lower right.

▲ Copper reacts with oxygen in air.

▲ Copper reacts with concentrated nitric acid.

▲ Zinc reacts with dilute hydrochloric acid.

▲ Soluble iron(III) salts form insoluble $Fe(OH)_3$ when they are reacted with a hydroxide base.

▲ Chromium has several common oxidation states, represented here by aqueous solutions of its compounds. The violet and green solutions contain chromium in the +3 state, and the yellow and orange solutions contain chromium in the +6 oxidation state.

$Cu[(CH_3)_2SO]_2Cl_2$ $Cu(NH_3)_4SO_4 \bullet H_2O$

$[Co(NH_3)_4CO_3]NO_3$

$[Co(NH_3)_5(NO_2)]Cl_2$ $K_3[Fe(C_2O_4)_3]$

▲ Complex ions belong to a class of compounds called coordination compounds. Coordination compounds show great variety in colors. Several transition-metal coordination compounds are shown.

Analytical Test

Flame tests are not commonly used to identify transition metals. The presence of a certain transition-metal ion in a solution is sometimes obvious from the solution's color. Some transition-metal ions can be more accurately identified using a procedure called qualitative analysis. **Qualitative analysis** *is the identification of ions by their characteristic reactions.* The transition-metal ions most often identified through qualitative analysis include copper, nickel, zinc, chromium, iron, cobalt, cadmium, manganese, and tin. Most tests to identify the presence of an ion in a mixture involve causing the ion to precipitate out of solution. Some of the more dramatic precipitation reactions for transition metals are shown.

▲ Some transition metal ions can be identified by characteristic colors of their salt solutions.

▲ Copper (formation of $[Cu(NH_3)_4](OH)_2$)

▲ Cadmium (formation of CdS)

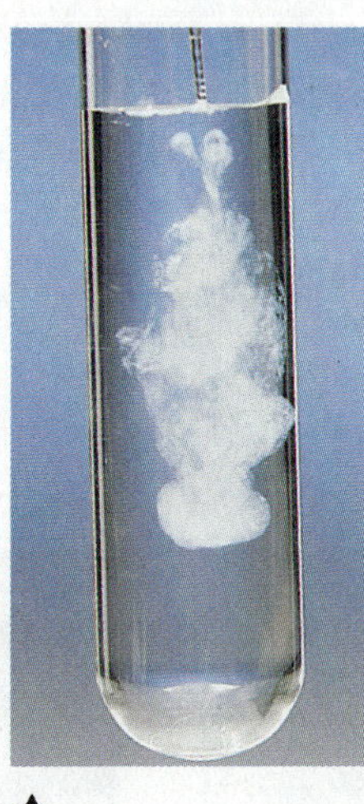

▲ Zinc (formation of ZnS)

▲ Chromium (formation of $PbCrO_4$)

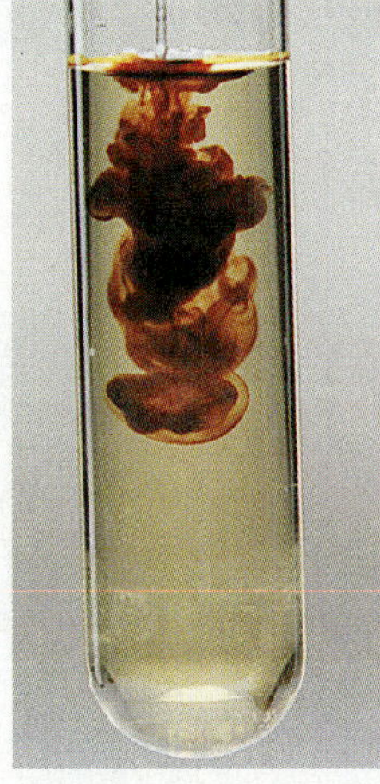

▲ Iron (formation of $[Fe(SCN)]^{2+}$)

▲ Manganese (formation of MnO_4^-)

▲ Nickel (formation of a nickel dimethylglyoxime complex)

Properties

SELECTED TRANSITION METALS									
Quantity	Cr	Fe	Co	Ni	Cu	Zn	Ag	Au	Hg
Melting point (°C)	1857 ± 20	1535	1495	1455	1083	420	962	1064	−38.8
Boiling point (°C)	2672	2750	2870	2732	2567	907	2212	2808 ± 2	356.6
Density (g/cm^3)	7.20	7.86	8.9	8.92	8.96	7.14	10.5	19.3	13.5
Ionization energy (kJ/mol)	653	762	760	737	746	906	731	890	1007
Atomic radius (pm)	128	126	125	124	128	134	144	144	151
Common oxidation numbers	+2, +3, +6	+2, +3	+2, +3	+2	+1, +2	+2	+1	+1, +3	+1, +2

S.T.E.M.
Application *Geology*

Gemstones and Color

A gemstone is a mineral that can be cut and polished to make gems for an ornament or piece of jewelry. At one time, all gemstones were naturally occurring minerals mined from Earth's crust. Today, however, chemists can duplicate natural processes to produce artificial gemstones. Amethyst, emerald, jade, opal, ruby, sapphire, and topaz occur naturally and can also be produced synthetically.

The color of a gemstone is determined by the presence of small amounts of one or more transition metals. For example, aluminum oxide, Al_2O_3, often occurs naturally as corundum—a clear, colorless mineral. However, if as few as 1 to 2% of the aluminum ions, Al^{3+}, are replaced by chromium ions, Cr^{3+}, the corundum takes on a reddish color and is known as the gemstone ruby. If a small fraction of aluminum ions in corundum are replaced by Fe^{3+} and Ti^{3+}, the corundum has a greenish color and is known as emerald. In another variation, if vanadium ions, V^{3+}, replace a few Al^{3+} ions in corundum, the result is a gemstone known as alexandrite. This gemstone appears green in reflected natural light and red in transmitted or artificial light.

Table 3A on the next page lists transition metals that are responsible for the colors of various gemstones. The table provides only a general overview, however, as most naturally occurring gemstones occur in a range of hues, depending on the exact composition of the stone.

Artificial Gemstones

In 1902, the French chemist Auguste Verneuil found a way to melt a mixture of aluminum oxide and chromium salts and then cool the mixture very slowly to produce large crystals of reddish aluminum oxide—rubies.

Sapphire

Ruby

Peridot

Garnet

TABLE 3A

TRANSITION METALS AND GEMSTONE COLORS		
Gemstone	**Color**	**Element**
Amethyst	purple	iron
Aquamarine	blue	iron
Emerald	green	iron/titanium
Garnet	red	iron
Peridot	yellow-green	iron
Ruby	red	chromium
Sapphire	blue	iron/titanium
Spinel	colorless to red to black	varies
Turquoise	blue	copper

Verneuil's method, although somewhat modified, is still widely used today for the manufacture of colored gemstones. When magnesium oxide is substituted for aluminum oxide, a colorless spinel-like product is formed. The addition of various transition metals then adds a tint to the spinel that results in the formation of synthetic emerald, aquamarine, tourmaline, or other gemstones. Synthetic gems look very much like their natural counterparts.

Synthetic sapphire

Synthetic ruby

S.T.E.M.

Application *Technology*

Alloys

An alloy is a mixture of a metal and one or more other elements. In most cases, the second component of the mixture is also a metal. Table 3B lists the composition and uses of some common alloys.

Alloys are desirable because mixtures of elements usually have properties different from and often superior to the properties of individual metals. For example, many alloys that contain iron are harder, stronger, and more resistant to oxidation than iron itself.

Amalgams are alloys that contain mercury. They are soft and pliable when first produced, but later become solid and hard. Dental fillings were once made of an amalgam of mercury and silver. Concerns about the possible toxicity of mercury led to the development of other filling materials.

Cast Iron and Steel

The term *steel* applies to any alloy consisting of iron and less than 1.5% carbon, and often other elements. When iron ore is treated with carbon in the form of coke to extract pure iron metal, some of the carbon also reacts with the iron to produce a form of iron carbide known as cementite. The reaction can be represented by the following equation:

$$3Fe + C \longrightarrow Fe_3C$$

Cast iron is a mixture that consists of some pure iron, known as ferrite, some cementite, and some carbon atoms trapped within the crystalline structure of the iron and cementite. The rate at which cast iron is cooled changes the proportion of these three components. If the cast iron is cooled slowly, the ferrite and cementite tend to separate from each other, forming a banded product that is tough but not very hard. However, if the cast iron is cooled quickly, the components of the original mixture cannot separate from each other, forming a product that is both tough and hard.

▲ Stainless steel, which is hard and resists corrosion, is made of iron and chromium (12–30%). The properties of stainless steel make it a suitable alloy for making cutlery and utensils.

TABLE 3B

COMPOSITION AND USES OF SOME ALLOYS

Name of alloy	Composition	Uses
Brass	copper with up to 50% zinc, some lead, and a small amount of tin	inexpensive jewelry; hose nozzles and couplings; piping; stamping dies
Bronze	copper with up to 12% tin	coins and medals; heavy gears; tools; electrical hardware
Coin metal	copper: 75% nickel: 25%	United States coins
Duralumin	aluminum: 95%; copper: 4%; magnesium: 0.5%; manganese: <1%	aircraft, boats, railroad cars, and machinery because of its high strength and resistance to corrosion
Nichrome	nickel: 80–85% chromium: 15–20%	heating elements in toasters, electric heaters, etc.
Phosphor bronze	bronze with a small amount of phosphorus	springs, electrical springs, boat propellers
Solder	lead: 50%; tin: 50% or tin: 98%; silver: 2% blue	joining two metals to each other joining copper pipes
Sterling silver	silver: 92.5%; copper: 7.5%	jewelry, art objects, flatware
Type metal	lead: 75–95%; antimony: 2–18%; tin: trace	used to make type for printing because it expands as it cools

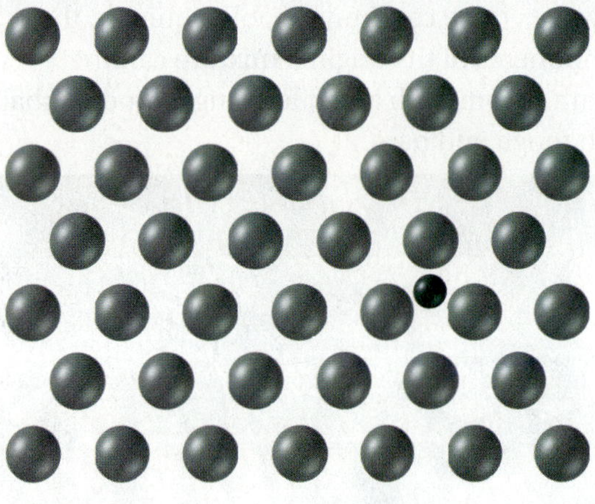

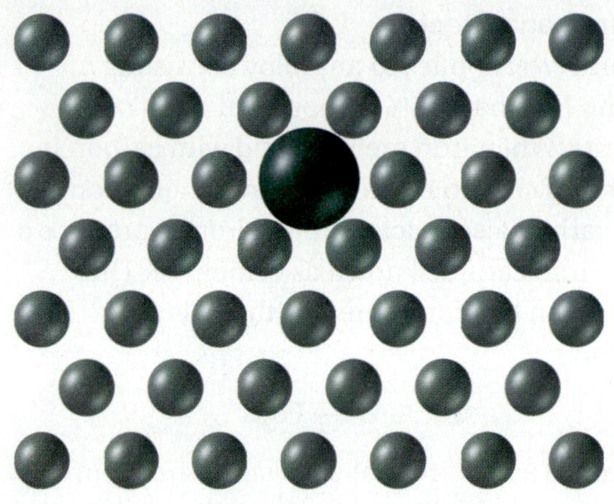

▲ **Interstitial crystal** A smaller atom or ion fits into a small space between particles in the array.

▲ **Substitutional crystal** A larger atom or ion is substituted for a particle in the array.

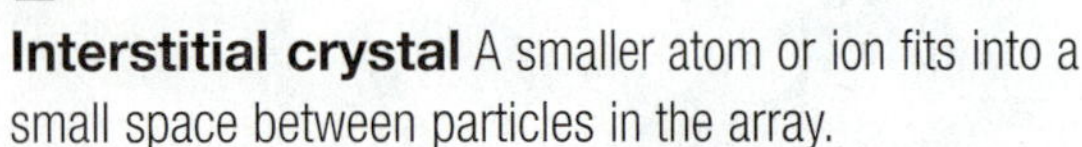

Structures and Preparation of Alloys

Alloys generally crystallize in one of two ways, depending on relative sizes of atoms. If the atoms of one of the metals present are small enough to fit into the spaces between the atoms of the second metal, they form an alloy with an interstitial structure (*inter* means "between," and *stitial* means "to stand"). If atoms of the two metals are of similar size or if one is larger, the atoms of one metal can substitute for the atoms of the second metal in its crystalline structure. Such alloys are substitutional alloys. Models for both types of crystals are shown above.

Techniques for making alloys depend on the metals used in the mixture. In some cases, the two metals can simply be melted together to form a mixture. The composition of the mixture often varies within a range, evidence that the final product is indeed a mixture and not a compound. In other cases, one metal may be melted first and the second dissolved in it. Brass is prepared in this way. If copper and zinc were heated together to a high temperature, zinc (bp 907°C) would evaporate before copper (mp 1084°C) melted. Therefore, the copper is melted first, and the zinc is added to it.

▲ Brass has a high luster and resembles gold when cleaned and polished. A brass object can be coated with a varnish to prevent reactions of the alloy with air and water.

▲ Sterling silver is more widely used than pure silver because it is stronger and more durable.

S.T.E.M.

Application *The Environment*

Mercury Poisoning

Mercury is the only metal that is liquid at room temperature. It has a very high density compared with most other common transition metals and has a very large surface tension and high vapor pressure. Mercury and many of its compounds must be handled with extreme care because they are highly toxic. Mercury spills are especially hazardous because the droplets scatter easily and are often undetected during cleanup. These droplets release toxic vapors into the air.

Overexposure to mercury vapor or its compounds can occur by absorption through the skin, respiratory tract, or digestive tract. Mercury is a cumulative poison, which means that its concentration in the body increases as exposure increases.

Mercury that enters the body damages the kidneys, heart, and brain. The action of mercury on the brain affects the nervous system. Symptoms of mercury poisoning include numbness, tunnel vision, garbled speech, bleeding and inflammation of the gums, muscle spasms, anemia, and emotional disorders, such as depression, irritability, and personality changes. The saying "mad as a hatter" probably came about because of mercury poisoning. Mercury salts were once routinely used to process the felt used in hats. Hatters often displayed the nerve and mental impairments associated with overexposure to mercury.

Methylmercury in Freshwater Ecosystems

Mercury, Hg, can be found in our environment and in our food supply. Fortunately, the body has some protective mechanisms to deal with trace amounts of mercury. However, levels of mercury and of methylmercury, $(CH_3)Hg^+$, are increasing in the environment due to mercury mining operations and runoff from the application of pesticides and fungicides.

Mercury is easily converted to methylmercury by bacteria. Methylmercury is more readily absorbed by cells than mercury itself. As a result, methylmercury accumulates in the food chain as shown in the diagram below. A serious incident of methylmercury poisoning occurred in Japan in the 1950s. People living in Minamata, Japan, were exposed to high levels of methylmercury from eating shellfish.

In the United States, there is concern about mercury levels in fish from some freshwater lakes. Though environmental regulations have reduced the level of lake pollutants, it takes time to see a reduction in the concentration of an accumulated poison.

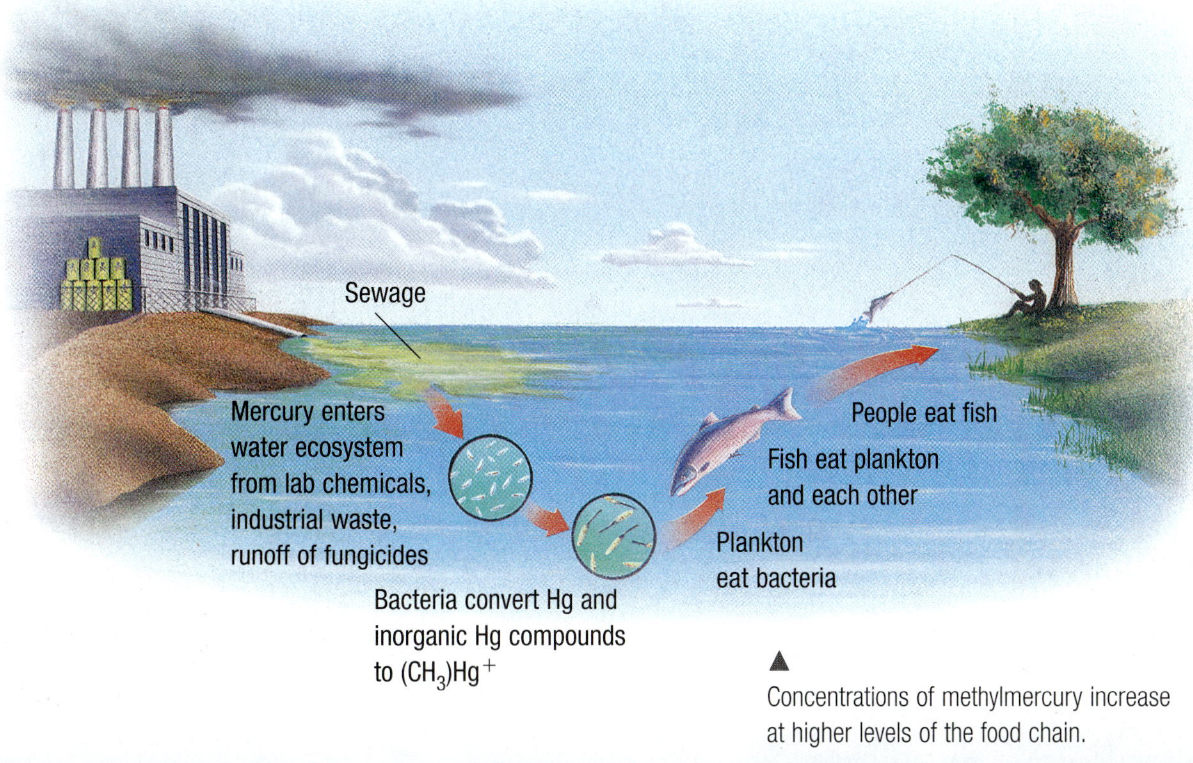

▲ Concentrations of methylmercury increase at higher levels of the food chain.

S.T.E.M.

Application *Health*

Elements in the Body

The four most abundant elements in the body (oxygen, carbon, hydrogen, and nitrogen) are the major components of organic biomolecules, such as carbohydrates, proteins, fats, and nucleic acids. Other elements compose a dietary category of compounds called minerals. Minerals are considered the inorganic elements of the body. Minerals fall into two categories—the major minerals and the trace minerals, or trace elements, as they are sometimes called. Notice in the periodic table below that most elements in the trace elements category of minerals are transition metals.

Trace elements are minerals with dietary daily requirements of 100 mg or less. They are found in foods derived from both plants and animals. Though these elements are present in very small quantities, they perform a variety of essential functions in the body, as shown in Table 3C on the next page.

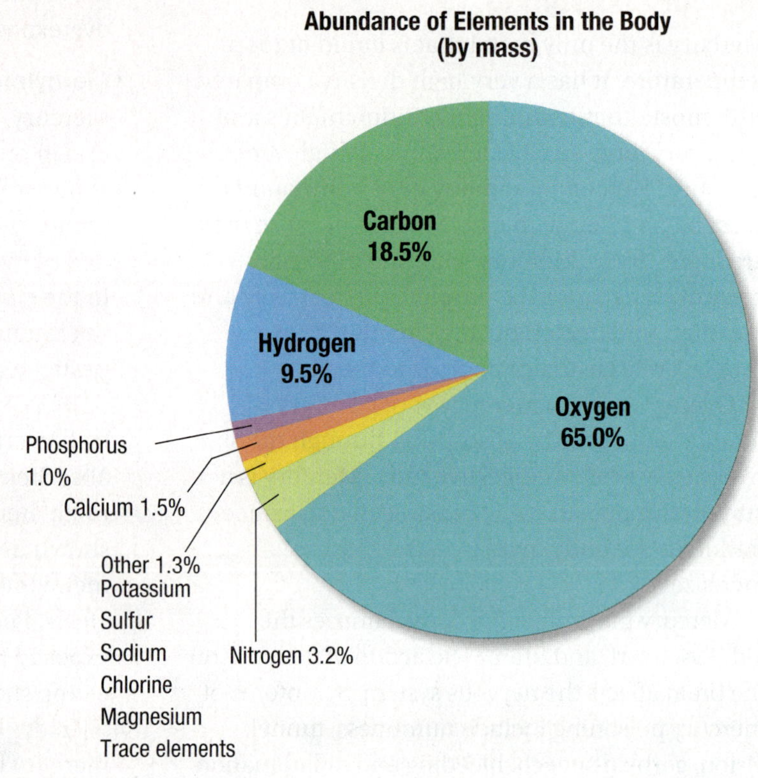

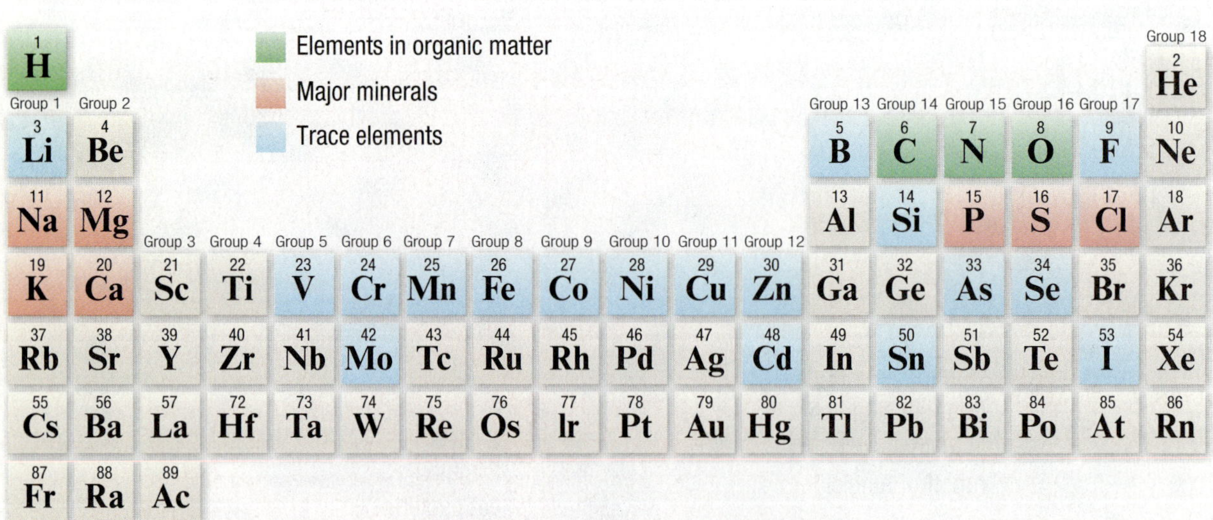

TABLE 3C

TRANSITION METAL TRACE ELEMENTS	
Transition metal	**Function**
Vanadium, Cadmium	function not fully determined, but linked to a reduced growth rate and impaired reproduction
Chromium	needed for glucose transport to cells
Manganese	used in the enzyme reactions that synthesize cholesterol and metabolize carbohydrates
Iron	central atom in the heme molecule—a component of hemoglobin, which binds oxygen in the blood for transport to cells
Cobalt	a component of vitamin B_{12}
Nickel	enzyme cofactor in the metabolism of fatty acids and amino acids
Copper	a major component of an enzyme that functions to protect cells from damage
Zinc	needed for tissue growth and repair and as an enzyme cofactor
Molybdenum	enzyme cofactor in the production of uric acid

Role of Iron

Most iron in the body is in hemoglobin. Fe^{3+} is the central ion in the heme molecule, which is a component of the proteins hemoglobin and myoglobin. Hemoglobin in red blood cells transports oxygen to cells and picks up carbon dioxide as waste. Myoglobin is a protein that stores oxygen to be used in muscle contraction. Iron is also in the proteins of the electron transport system and the immune system.

Mechanisms of the body control the rate of iron absorption from food in the diet. When iron reserves are low, chemical signals stimulate cells of the intestines to absorb more iron during digestion. If the diet is low in iron, causing a deficiency, hemoglobin production stops and a condition called iron-deficiency anemia results. The blood cells produced during this state are stunted and unable to deliver adequate oxygen to cells. As a result, a person with iron-deficiency anemia feels tired and weak and has difficulty maintaining normal body temperature. The recommended daily intake of iron is 8 mg for men and 18 mg for women. The recommended level doubles for pregnant women. Iron supplements are for people who do not get enough iron in their daily diets. Table 3D lists some foods that are good sources of iron in the diet. Too much iron can be toxic because the body stores iron once it is absorbed. Abusing iron supplements can cause severe liver and heart damage.

TABLE 3D

SOURCES OF IRON IN FOODS		
Food	**Serving size**	**Iron present (mg)**
Beef roast (lean cut)	4 oz	3.55
Beef, T-bone steak (lean cut)	4 oz	3.40
Beef, ground (hamburger)	4 oz	2.78
Broccoli	6.3 oz	1.50
Chicken, breast	4 oz	1.35
Chicken, giblets	4 oz	7.30
Oatmeal, instant enriched	1 pkg	8.35
Pita bread, white enriched	6 1/2 in. diameter	1.40
Pork roast	4 oz	1.15
Prunes	4 oz	2.00
Raisins	4 oz	1.88

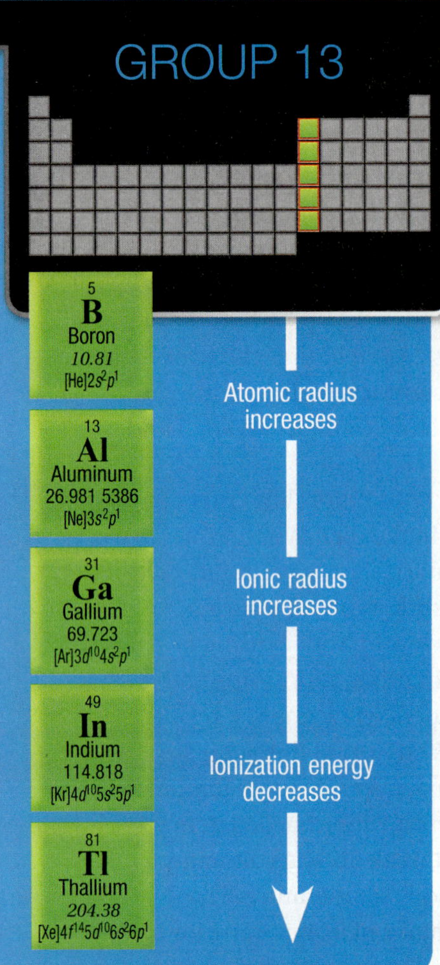

Boron Family

Characteristics

- do not occur in nature as free elements
- are scarce in nature (except aluminum, which is the most abundant metallic element)
- consist of atoms that have three electrons in their outer energy level
- are metallic solids (except boron, which is a solid metalloid)
- are soft and have low melting points (except boron, which is hard and has a high melting point)
- are chemically reactive at moderate temperatures (except boron)

▲ Boron is a covalent solid. Other members of the family are metallic solids.

▶ The warmth of a person's hand will melt gallium. Gallium metal has the lowest melting point (29.77°C) of any metal except mercury.

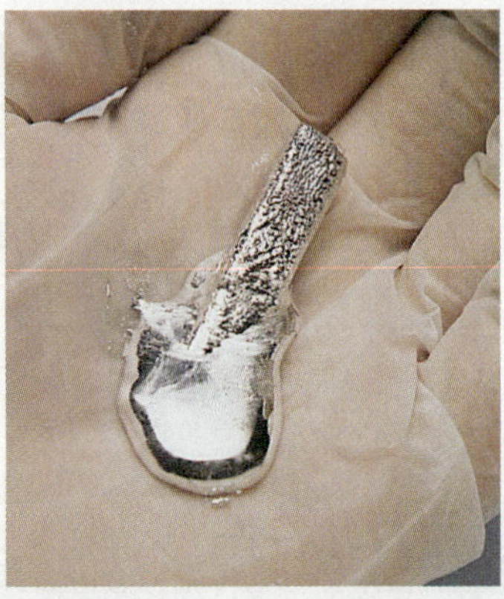

▲ Aluminum is the most abundant metal in Earth's crust. It exists in nature as an ore called bauxite.

Common Reactions

The reaction chemistry of boron differs greatly from that of the other members of this family. Pure boron is a covalent network solid, whereas the other members of the family are metallic crystals in pure form. Boron resembles silicon more closely than it resembles the other members of its family.

With Strong Bases to Form Hydrogen Gas and a Salt

Example: $2Al(s) + 2NaOH(aq) + 2H_2O(l) \longrightarrow 2NaAlO_2(aq) + 3H_2(g)$

Ga also follows this pattern.

With Dilute Acids to Form Hydrogen Gas and a Salt

Example: $2Al(s) + 6HCl(aq) \longrightarrow 2AlCl_3(aq) + 3H_2(g)$

Ga, In, and Tl follow this pattern in reacting with dilute HF, HCl, HBr, and HI.

With Halogens to Form Halides

Example: $2Al(s) + 3Cl_2(g) \longrightarrow 2AlCl_3(s)$

B, Al, Ga, In, and Tl also follow this pattern in reacting with F_2, Cl_2, Br_2, and I_2 (except BF_3).

With Oxygen to Form Oxides

Example: $4Al(s) + 3O_2(g) \longrightarrow 2Al_2O_3(s)$

Ga, In, and Tl also follow this pattern.

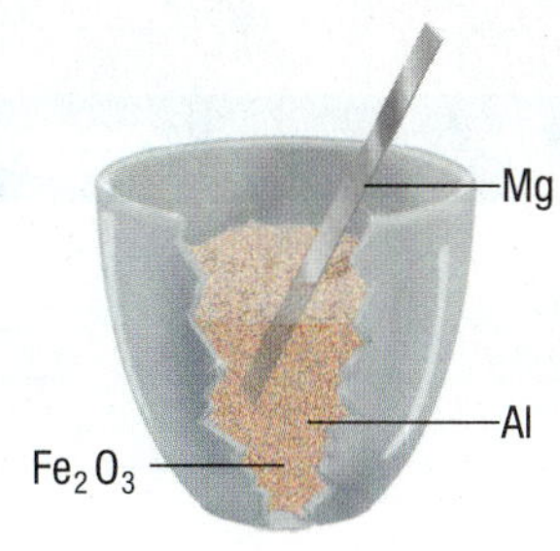

▶ A mixture of powdered aluminum and iron(III) oxide is called thermite. Al reacts with Fe_2O_3 using Mg ribbon as a fuse to provide activation energy. The energy produced by the thermite reaction is sufficient to produce molten iron as a product.

Analytical Test

Other than atomic absorption spectroscopy, there is no simple analytical test for all the members of the boron family.

▶ The confirmatory test for the presence of aluminum in qualitative analysis is the red color formed by aluminum and the organic compound aluminon, $C_{22}H_{23}N_3O_9$.

▲ Aluminum forms a thin layer of Al_2O_3, which protects the metal from oxidation and makes it suitable for outdoor use.

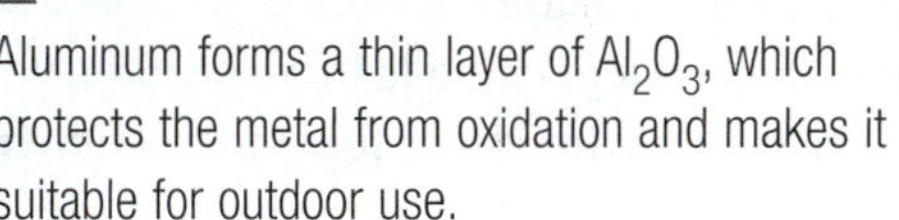

Properties

GROUP 13 ELEMENTS	B	Al	Ga	In	Tl
Melting point (°C)	2300	660.37	29.77	156.61	303.5
Boiling point (°C)	2550	2467	2403	2080	1457
Density (g/cm^3)	2.34	2.702	5.904	7.31	11.85
Ionization energy (kJ/mol)	801	578	579	558	589
Atomic radius (pm)	85	143	135	167	170
Ionic radius (pm)	—	54	62	80	89
Common oxidation number in compounds	+3	+3	+1, +3	+1, +3	+1, +3
Crystal structure	monoclinic	fcc	orthorhombic	fcc	hcp
Hardness (Mohs' scale)	9.3	2.75	1.5	1.2	1.2

S.T.E.M.

Application *Technology*

Aluminum

Chemically, aluminum is much more active than copper, and it belongs to the category of *self-protecting metals*. These metals are oxidized when exposed to oxygen in the air and form a hard, protective metal oxide on the surface. The oxidation of aluminum is shown by the following reaction:

$$4Al(s) + 3O_2(g) \longrightarrow 2Al_2O_3(s)$$

This oxide coating protects the underlying metal from further reaction with oxygen or other substances. Self-protecting metals are valuable in themselves or when used to coat iron and steel to keep them from corroding.

Aluminum is a very good conductor of electric current. Many years ago, most high-voltage electric power lines were made of copper. Although copper is a better conductor of electricity than aluminum, copper is heavier and more expensive. Today more than 90% of high-voltage transmission lines are made of relatively pure aluminum. The aluminum wire does not have to be self-supporting because steel cable is incorporated to bear the weight of the wire in the long spans between towers.

In the 1960s, aluminum electric wiring was used in many houses and other buildings. Over time, however, the aluminum oxidized and so the electrical resistance increased where wires connected to outlets, switches, and other metals. As current flowed through the extra resistance, enough energy as heat was generated to cause a fire. Though some homes have been rewired, aluminum wiring is still prevalent in many homes.

▲ These high-voltage transmission lines are made of aluminum supported with steel cables.

Aluminum Alloys

Because aluminum has a low density and is inexpensive, it is used to construct aircraft, boats, sports equipment, and other lightweight, high-strength objects. The pure metal is not strong, so it is mixed with small quantities of other metals—usually manganese, copper, magnesium, zinc, or silicon—to produce strong low-density alloys. Typically, 80% of a modern aircraft frame consists of aluminum alloy.

Aluminum and its alloys are good heat conductors. An alloy of aluminum and manganese is used to make cookware. High-quality pots and pans made of stainless steel may have a plate of aluminum on the bottom to help conduct energy as heat quickly to the interior.

Automobile radiators made of aluminum conduct energy as heat as hot coolant from the engine enters the bottom of the radiator. The coolant is deflected into several channels. These channels are covered by thin vanes of aluminum, which conduct energy away from the coolant and transfer it to the cooler air rushing past. By the time the coolant reaches the top of the radiator, its temperature has dropped so that when it flows back into the engine it can absorb more energy as heat. To keep the process efficient, the outside of a radiator should be kept unobstructed and free of dirt buildup. Table 4A lists some aluminum alloying agents.

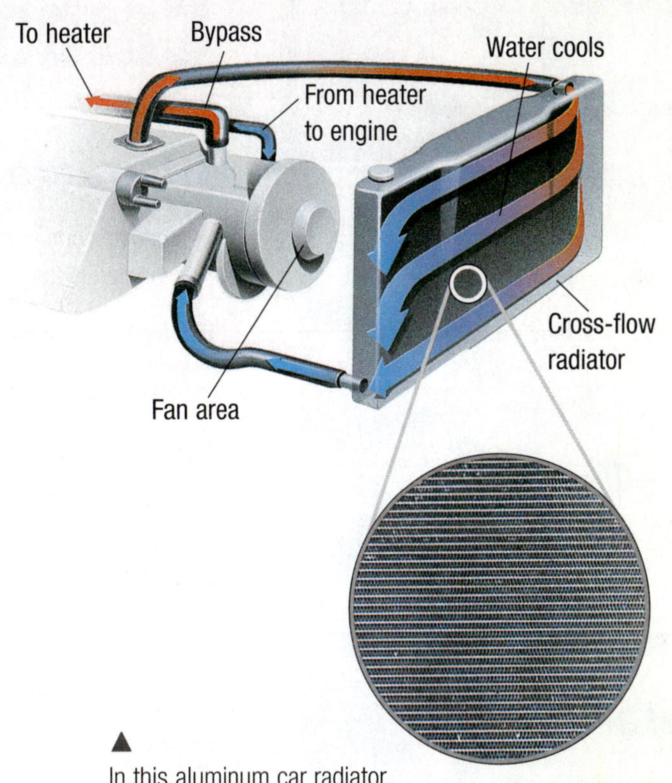

▲ In this aluminum car radiator, many thin vanes of aluminum conduct energy as heat, transferring it from the coolant to the air. Coolant is cycled from the hot engine through the radiator and back to the engine.

TABLE 4A

ALLOYS OF ALUMINUM AND THEIR USES

Principal alloying element(s)*	Characteristics	Application examples
Manganese	moderately strong, easily worked	cookware, roofing, storage tanks, lawn furniture
Copper	strong, easily formed	aircraft structural parts; large, thin structural panels
Magnesium	strong, resists corrosion, easy to weld	parts for boats and ships, outdoor decorative objects, tall poles
Zinc and magnesium	very strong, resists corrosion	aircraft structural parts, vehicle parts, anything that needs high strength and low weight
Silicon	expands little on heating and cooling	aluminum castings
Magnesium and silicon	resists corrosion, easily formed	exposed parts of buildings, bridges

* All these alloys have small amounts of other elements.

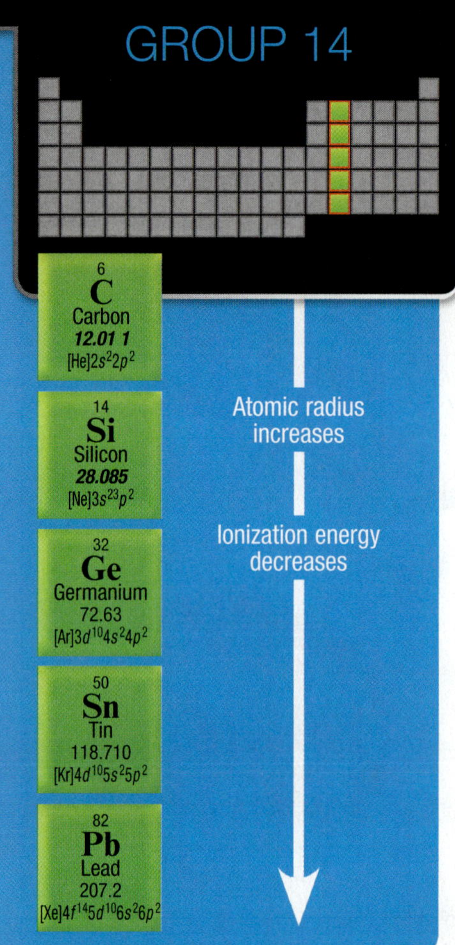

Carbon Family

Characteristics

- include a nonmetal (carbon), two metalloids (silicon and germanium), and two metals (tin and lead)
- vary greatly in both physical and chemical properties
- occur in nature in both combined and elemental forms
- consist of atoms that contain four electrons in the outermost energy level
- are relatively unreactive
- tend to form covalent compounds (tin and lead also form ionic compounds)

Lead has a low reactivity and is resistant to corrosion. It is very soft, highly ductile, and malleable. Lead is toxic and, like mercury, it is a cumulative poison.

Silicon has a luster but does not exhibit metallic properties. Most silicon in nature is a silicon oxide, which occurs in sand and quartz, which is shown here.

Tin, which is shown on the right, is a self-protecting metal like lead, but unlike lead it has a high luster. Tin occurs in nature in cassiterite ore, which is shown above.

Common Reactions

With Oxygen to Form Oxides

Example: $Sn(s) + O_2(g) \rightarrow SnO_2(s)$
Pb follows this pattern, as do C, Si, and Ge at high temperatures.

With Acids to Form Salts and Hydrogen Gas

Only the metallic elements of this group react slowly with aqueous acids.

Example: $Sn(s) + 2HCl(aq) \rightarrow SnCl_2(aq) + H_2(g)$
Both Sn and Pb can also react to form tin(IV) and lead(IV) salts, respectively.

With Halogens to Form Halides

Example: $Sn(s) + 2Cl_2(g) \rightarrow SnCl_4(s)$
Si, Ge, and Pb follow this pattern, reacting with F_2, Cl_2, Br_2, and I_2.

Analytical Test

Ionic compounds of tin and lead can be identified in aqueous solutions by adding a solution containing sulfide ions. The formation of a yellow precipitate indicates the presence of Sn^{4+}, and the formation of a black precipitate indicates the presence of Pb^{2+}.

$$Sn^{4+}(aq) + 2S^{2-}(aq) \rightarrow SnS_2(s)$$
$$Pb^{2+}(aq) + S^{2-}(aq) \rightarrow PbS(s)$$

PbS SnS$_2$

Properties

GROUP 14 ELEMENTS					
Quantity	**C**	**Si**	**Ge**	**Sn**	**Pb**
Melting point (°C)	3500/3652*	1410	937.4	231.88	327.502
Boiling point (°C)	4827	2355	2830	2260	1740
Density (g/cm^3)	3.51/2.25*	2.33 ± 0.01	5.323	7.28	11.343
Ionization energy (kJ/mol)	1086	787	762	709	716
Atomic radius (pm)	77	118	122	140	175
Ionic radius (pm)	260 (C^{4-} ion)	—	—	118 (Sn^{2+} ion)	119 (Pb^{2+} ion)
Common oxidation number in compounds	+4, −4	+4	+2, +4	+2, +4	+2, +4
Crystal structure	cubic/hexagonal*	cubic	cubic	tetragonal	fcc
Hardness (Mohs' scale)	10/0.5*	6.5	6.0	1.5	1.5

* The data are for two allotropic forms: diamond/graphite.

S.T.E.M.

Application *Chemical Industry*

Carbon and the Reduction of Iron Ore

Some metals, especially iron, are separated from their ores through reduction reactions in a blast furnace. The blast furnace gets its name from the fact that air or pure oxygen is blown into the furnace, where it oxidizes carbon to form carbon monoxide, CO. Carbon and its compounds are important reactants in this process.

What happens inside the blast furnace to recover the iron from its ore? The actual chemical changes that occur are complex. A simplified explanation begins with the reaction of oxygen in hot air with coke, a form of carbon. Some of the coke burns to form carbon dioxide.

$$C(s) + O_2(g) \rightarrow CO_2(g)$$

As the concentration of oxygen is decreased, the carbon dioxide comes in contact with pieces of hot coke and is reduced to carbon monoxide.

$$CO_2(g) + C(s) \rightarrow 2CO(g)$$

The carbon monoxide now acts as a reducing agent to reduce the iron oxides in the ore to metallic iron.

$$Fe_2O_3(s) + 3CO(g) \rightarrow 2Fe(l) + 3CO_2(g)$$

The reduction is thought to occur in steps as the temperature in the furnace increases. The following are some of the possible steps.

$$Fe_2O_3 \rightarrow Fe_3O_4 \rightarrow FeO \rightarrow Fe$$

The white-hot liquid iron collects in the bottom of the furnace and is removed every four or five hours. The iron may be cast in molds or converted to steel in another process.

Limestone, present in the center of the furnace, decomposes to form calcium oxide and carbon dioxide.

$$CaCO_3(s) \rightarrow CaO(s) + CO_2(g)$$

The calcium oxide then combines with silica, a silicon compound, to form calcium silicate slag.

The relatively high carbon content of iron produced in a blast furnace makes the metal hard but brittle. It also has other impurities, like sulfur and phosphorus, that cause the recovered iron to be brittle. The conversion of iron to steel is essentially a purification process in which impurities are removed by oxidation. This purification process is carried out in another kind of furnace at very high temperatures. All steel contains 0.02 to 1.5% carbon. In fact, steels are graded by their carbon content. Low-carbon steels typically contain 0.02 to 0.3% carbon. Medium-carbon steels typically contain 0.03 to 0.7% carbon. High-carbon steels contain 0.7 to 1.5% carbon.

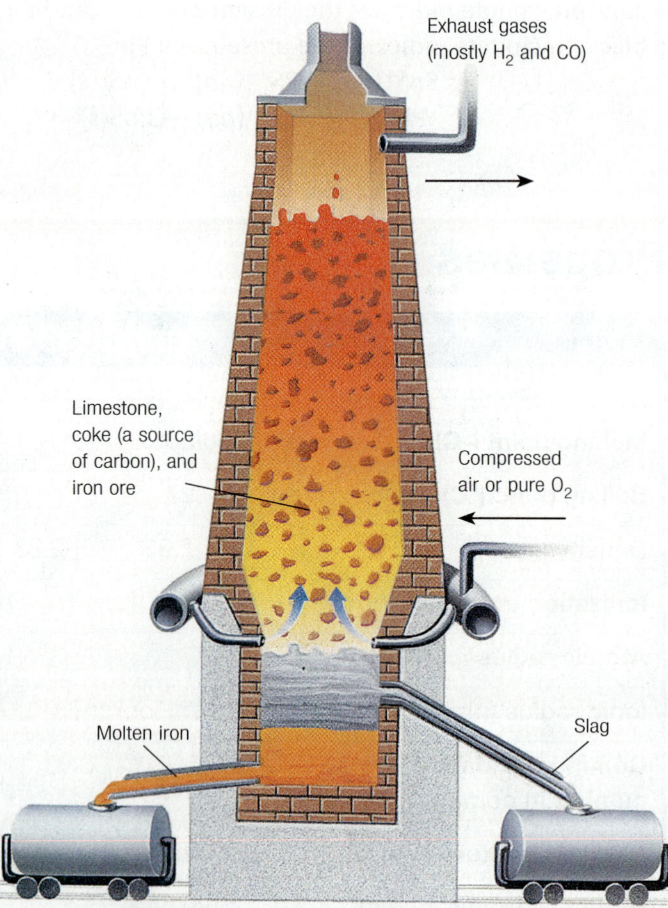

▲ Molten iron flowing from the bottom of a blast furnace has been reduced from its ore through a series of reactions at high temperatures in different regions of the furnace.

Carbon Dioxide

Carbon dioxide is a colorless gas with a faintly irritating odor and a slightly sour taste. The sour taste is the result of the formation of carbonic acid when CO_2 dissolves in the water in saliva. It is a stable gas that does not burn or support combustion. At temperatures lower than 31°C and at pressures higher than 72.9 atm, CO_2 condenses to the liquid form. At normal atmospheric pressure, solid CO_2 (dry ice) sublimes at −78.5°C. The linear carbon dioxide molecules is nonpolar.

CO_2 is produced by the burning of organic fuels and from respiration processes in most living things. Most CO_2 released into the atmosphere is used by plants during photosynthesis, the process by which green plants and some forms of algae and bacteria make food. During photosynthesis, CO_2 reacts with H_2O, using the energy from sunlight. The relationships among the various processes on Earth that convert carbon to carbon dioxide are summarized in the diagram of the carbon cycle, which is pictured below.

Carbon Monoxide

Carbon monoxide is a poisonous gas produced naturally by decaying plants, certain types of algae, volcanic eruptions, and the oxidation of methane in the atmosphere.

Because CO is colorless, odorless, and tasteless, it is difficult to detect. It is slightly less dense than air and slightly soluble in water. Its main chemical uses are in the reduction of iron, described on page R30, and the production of organic compounds, such as methanol.

$$CO(g) + 2H_2(g) \rightarrow CH_3OH(l)$$

Carbon monoxide is also produced during the incomplete combustion of organic fuels. Incomplete combustion of methane occurs when the supply of oxygen is limited.

$$2CH_4(g) + 3O_2(g) \rightarrow 2CO(g) + 4H_2O(g)$$

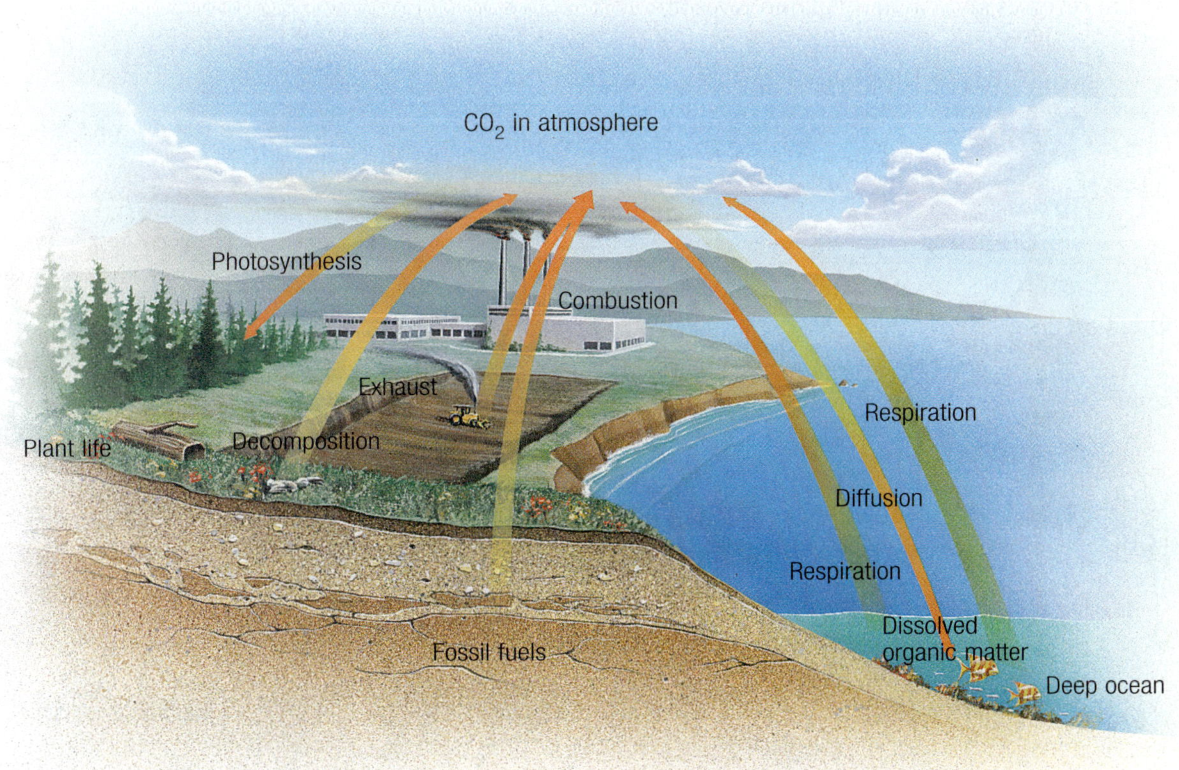

▲ The processes that recycle CO_2 are collectively called the carbon cycle.

S.T.E.M.

Application *Biochemistry*

Carbon Dioxide and Respiration

Many organisms, including humans, carry out cellular respiration. In this process, cells break down food molecules and release the energy used to build those molecules during photosynthesis. Glucose, $C_6H_{12}O_6$, is a common substance broken down in respiration. The following chemical equation expresses this process.

$$C_6H_{12}O_6 + 6O_2 \rightarrow 6CO_2 + 6H_2O + \text{energy}$$

In humans and most other vertebrate animals, the oxygen needed for this reaction is delivered to cells by hemoglobin found in red blood cells. Oxygen binds with hemoglobin as blood passes through capillaries in the lungs, as represented by the following reaction:

$$Hb + O_2 \rightarrow HbO_2$$

Hb represents the hemoglobin molecule, and HbO_2 represents oxyhemoglobin, which is hemoglobin with bound oxygen. When the red blood cells pass through capillaries near cells that have depleted their oxygen supply through respiration, the reaction reverses and oxyhemoglobin gives up its oxygen.

$$HbO_2 \rightarrow Hb + O_2$$

Carbon dioxide produced during respiration is a waste product that must be expelled from an organism. Various things happen when CO_2 enters the blood; 7% dissolves in the plasma, about 23% binds loosely to hemoglobin, and the remaining 70% reacts reversibly with water in plasma to form hydrogen carbonate, HCO_3^- ions. To form HCO_3^- ions, CO_2 first combines with H_2O to form carbonic acid, H_2CO_3, in a reversible reaction.

$$CO_2(aq) + H_2O(l) \rightleftharpoons H_2CO_3(aq)$$

The dissolved carbonic acid ionizes to HCO_3^- ions and aqueous H^+ ions in the form of H_3O^+.

$$H_2CO_3(aq) + H_2O \rightleftharpoons H_3O^+(aq) + HCO_3^-(aq)$$

The combined equilibrium reaction follows:

$$CO_2(aq) + 2H_2O(l) \rightleftharpoons H_3O^+(aq) + HCO_3^-(aq)$$

When the blood reaches the lungs, the reaction reverses and the blood releases CO_2, which is then exhaled to the surroundings.

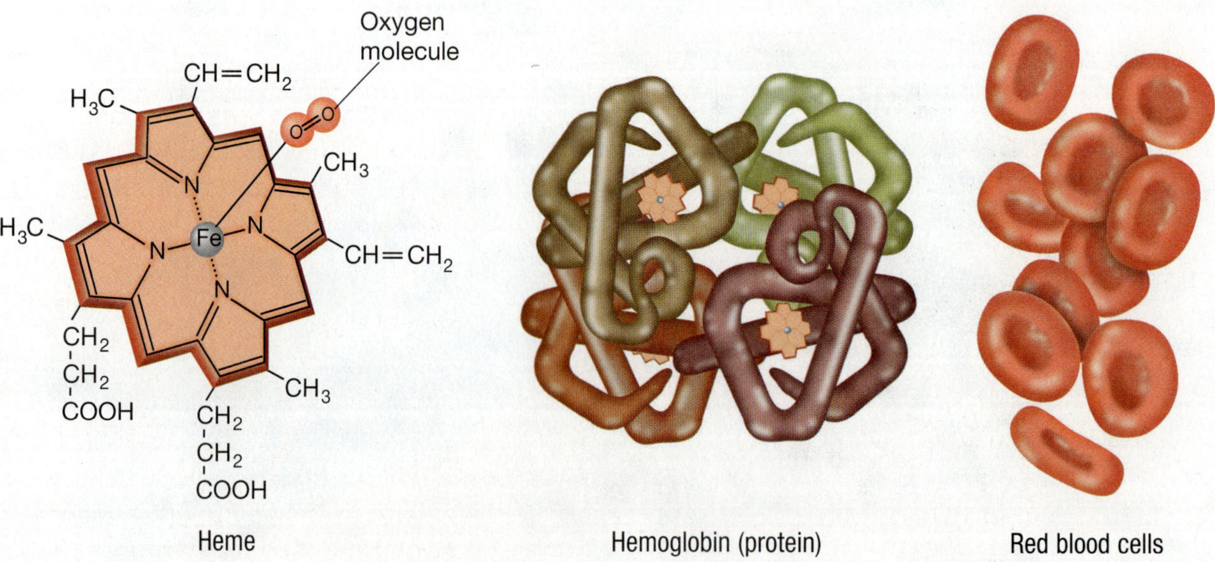

▲ The oxygen carrier molecule, heme, is a component of the more-complex protein hemoglobin. Note that each hemoglobin molecule has four heme subunits. Hemoglobin is a component of red blood cells.

Exchange of CO_2 and O_2 in the Lungs

Why does CO_2 leave the blood as it passes through the lung's capillaries, and why does O_2 enter the blood? The exchange is caused by the difference in concentrations of CO_2 and O_2 in the blood and in the atmosphere. Oxygen is 21% of the atmosphere. Although the amount of CO_2 varies from place to place, it averages about 0.033% of the atmosphere. Thus, O_2 is about 640 times more concentrated in the atmosphere than is CO_2.

Substances tend to diffuse from regions of higher concentration toward regions of lower concentration. Thus, when blood reaches the capillaries of the lung, O_2 from the air diffuses into the blood, where its pressure is only 40 mm Hg, while CO_2 diffuses out of the blood, where its pressure is 45 mm Hg, and into the air. The diagram below summarizes the process.

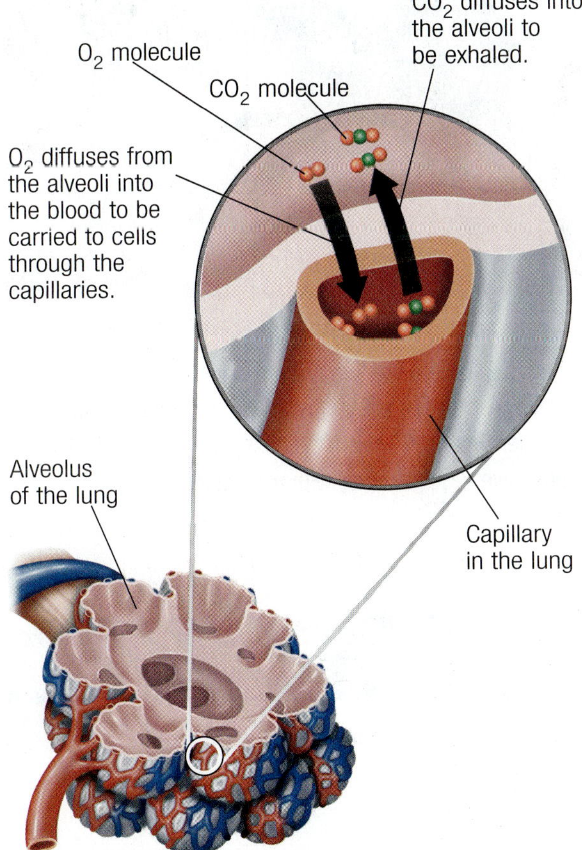

▲ The pressure of O_2 in the blood entering the lung is much lower than it is in the atmosphere. As a result, O_2 diffuses into the blood. The opposite situation exists for CO_2, so it diffuses from the blood into the air. Note that blood leaving the lung still contains a significant concentration of CO_2.

Acidosis and Alkalosis

In humans, blood is maintained between pH 7.3 and 7.5. The pH of blood is dependent on the concentration of CO_2 in the blood. Look again at this equilibrium system.

$$CO_2(aq) + 2H_2O(l) \rightleftharpoons H_3O^+(aq) + HCO_3^-(aq)$$

Notice that the right side of the equation contains the H_3O^+ ion, which determines the pH of the blood. If excess H_3O^+ enters the blood from tissues, the reverse reaction is favored. Excess H_3O^+ combines with HCO_3^- to produce more CO_2 and H_2O. If the H_3O^+ concentration begins to fall, the forward reaction is favored, producing additional H_3O^+ and HCO_3^-. To keep H_3O^+ in balance, adequate amounts of both CO_2 and HCO_3^- must be present. If something occurs that changes these conditions, a person can become very ill and can even die.

Hyperventilation occurs when a person breathes too rapidly for an extended time. Too much CO_2 is eliminated, causing the reverse reaction to be favored, and H_3O^+ and HCO_3^- are used up. As a result, the person develops a condition known as alkalosis because the pH of the blood rises to an abnormal alkaline level. The person begins to feel lightheaded and faint, and, unless treatment is provided, he or she may fall into a coma. Alkalosis is treated by having the victim breathe air that is rich in CO_2. One way to accomplish this is to have the person breathe with a bag held tightly over the nose and mouth. Alkalosis is also caused by fever, infection, intoxication, hysteria, and prolonged vomiting.

The reverse of alkalosis is a condition known as acidosis. This condition is often caused by a depletion of HCO_3^- ions from the blood, which can occur as a result of kidney dysfunction. The kidney controls the excretion of HCO_3^- ions. If there are too few HCO_3^- ions in solution, the forward reaction is favored and H_3O^+ ions accumulate, which lowers the blood's pH. Acidosis can also result from the body's inability to expel CO_2, which can occur during pneumonia, emphysema, and other respiratory disorders. Perhaps the single most common cause of acidosis is uncontrolled diabetes, in which acids normally excreted in the urinary system are instead retained by the body.

S.T.E.M.

Application *The Environment*

Carbon Monoxide Poisoning

Standing on a street corner in any major city exposes a person to above-normal concentrations of carbon monoxide from automobile exhaust. Carbon monoxide also reacts with hemoglobin. The following reaction takes place in the capillaries of the lung.

$$Hb + CO \rightarrow HbCO$$

Unlike CO_2 or O_2, CO binds strongly to hemoglobin. Carboxyhemoglobin, HbCO, is 200 times more stable than oxyhemoglobin, HbO_2. So as blood circulates, more and more CO molecules bind to hemoglobin, reducing the amount of O_2 bond sites available for transport. Eventually, CO occupies so many hemoglobin binding sites that cells die from lack of oxygen. Symptoms of carbon monoxide poisoning include headache, mental confusion, dizziness, weakness, nausea, loss of muscular control, and decreased heart rate and respiratory rate. The victim loses consciousness and will die without treatment.

If the condition is caught in time, a victim of carbon monoxide poisoning can be revived by breathing pure oxygen. This treatment causes carboxyhemoglobin to be converted slowly to oxyhemoglobin according to the following chemical equation.

$$O_2 + HbCO \rightarrow CO + HbO_2$$

Mild carbon monoxide poisoning usually does not have long-term effects. In severe cases, cells are destroyed. Damage to brain cells is irreversible. The level of danger posed by carbon monoxide depends on two factors: the concentration of the gas in the air and the amount of time that a person is exposed to the gas. Table 5A shows the effects of increasing levels of carbon monoxide in the bloodstream. These effects vary considerably depending on a person's activity level and metabolic rate.

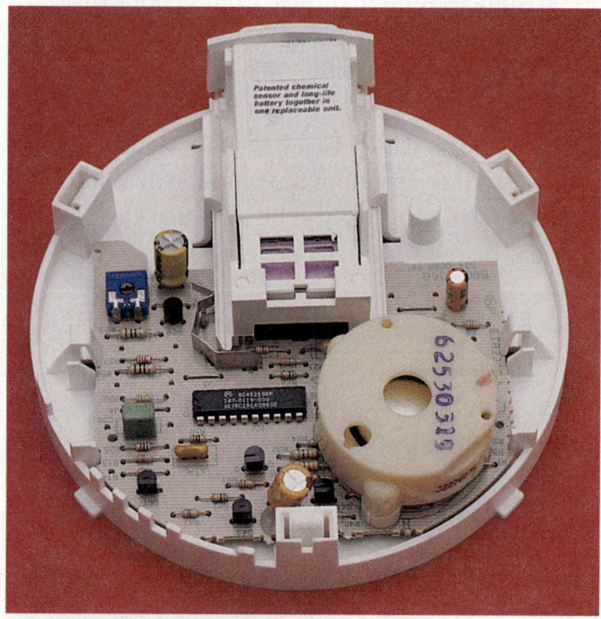

▲ Carbon monoxide detectors are now available to reduce the risk of poisoning from defective home heating systems. The Consumer Products Safety Commission recommends that all homes have a CO detector with a UL label.

TABLE 5A

SYMPTOMS OF CO POISONING AT INCREASING LEVELS OF CO EXPOSURE AND CONCENTRATION

Concentration of CO in air (ppm)*	Hemoglobin molecules as HbCO	Visible effects
100 for 1 hour or less	10% or less	no visible symptoms
500 for 1 hour or less	20%	mild to throbbing headache, some dizziness, impaired perception
500 for an extended period of time	30–50%	headache, confusion, nausea, dizziness, muscular weakness, fainting
1000 for 1 hour or less	50–80%	coma, convulsions, respiratory failure, death

* ppm is parts per million.

S.T.E.M.

Application *Biochemistry*

Macromolecules

Large organic polymers are called macromolecules (the prefix *macro* means "large"). Macromolecules play important roles in living systems. Most macromolecules essential to life belong to four main classes, three of which we know as nutrients in food:

1. **Proteins** Hair, tendons, ligaments, and silk are made of protein. Other proteins act as hormones, transport substances throughout the body, and fight infections. Enzymes are proteins that control the body's chemical reactions. Proteins provide energy, yielding 17 kJ/g.
2. **Carbohydrates** Sugars, starches, and cellulose are carbohydrates. Carbohydrates are sources of energy, yielding 17 kJ/g.
3. **Lipids** Fats, oils, waxes, and steroids are lipids, nonpolar substances that do not dissolve in water. Fats are sources of energy, yielding 38 kJ/g.
4. **Nucleic acids** DNA and RNA are nucleic acids. In most organisms, DNA is used to store hereditary information and RNA helps to assemble proteins.

Proteins

Proteins are macromolecules formed by condensation reactions between amino acid monomers. Proteins contain carbon, oxygen, hydrogen, nitrogen, and usually some sulfur. Some of the amino acids that form proteins are shown below.

All amino acids have a carboxyl group, —COOH, and an amino group, —NH_2, attached to a central carbon atom, which is also attached to hydrogen, —H. Amino acids differ from one another at the fourth bond site of the central carbon, which is attached to a group of atoms (called an *R* group). *R* groups differ from one amino acid to another, as shown in the structures for several amino acids below. The proteins of all organisms contain a set of 20 common amino acids. Amino acids link together with condensation reactions.

There are 22 standard amino acids. Each protein has its own unique sequence of amino acids. A complex organism has at least several thousand different proteins, each with a special structure and function. There can be so many proteins because, just as the 26 letters of the English alphabet give us thousands of words, 22 amino acids arranged in different ways can create a similar number of proteins.

◀ Amino acids have the same general structure. These examples show some of the variations within this class of compounds.

General structure: *R*–C(NH_2)(H)–C(=O)OH

Alanine: CH_3–C(NH_2)(H)–C(=O)OH

Asparagine: H_2N–C(=O)–CH_2–C(NH_2)(H)–C(=O)OH

Glutamine: H_2N–C(=O)–CH_2–CH_2–C(NH_2)(H)–C(=O)OH

Isoleucine: CH_3CH_2–C(H)(CH_3)–C(NH_2)(H)–C(=O)OH

Leucine: H–C(CH_3)(CH_3)–CH_2–C(NH_2)(H)–C(=O)OH

Methionine: CH_3–S–CH_2–CH_2–C(NH_2)(H)–C(=O)OH

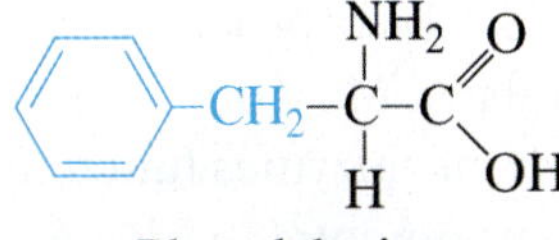

Phenylalanine: C_6H_5–CH_2–C(NH_2)(H)–C(=O)OH

Threonine: CH_3–CH(OH)–C(NH_2)(H)–C(=O)OH

Tyrosine: HO–C_6H_4–CH_2–C(NH_2)(H)–C(=O)OH

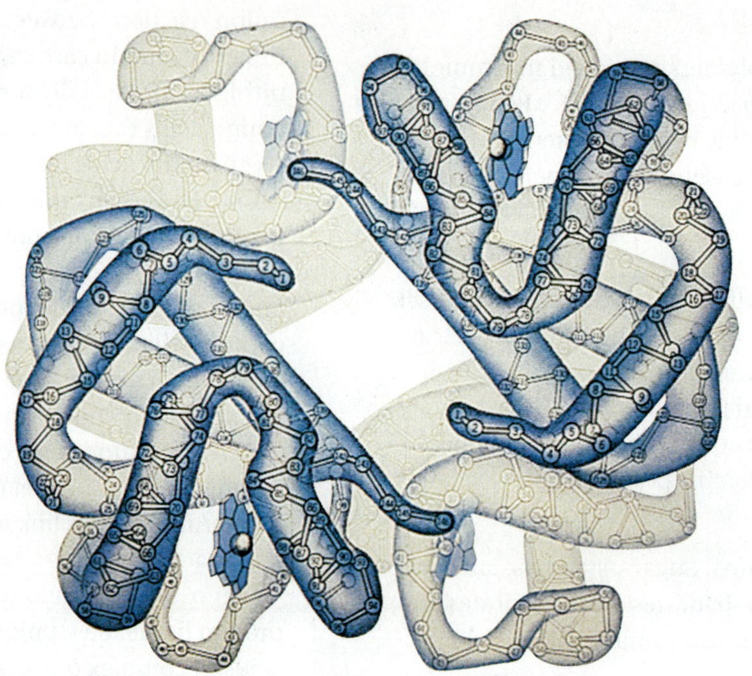

Hemoglobin is a complex protein made of hundreds of amino acids. Its 3-dimensional shape is called a tertiary structure. Tertiary structures break down when a protein is denatured.

For instance, *insulin*, a hormone that helps the body regulate the level of sugar in the blood, is made up of two linked chains. The chains are held together by S—S bonds between sulfur atoms in two cysteine amino acids. Insulin is one of the smaller proteins, containing only 51 amino acids. In contrast, hemoglobin, which carries oxygen in the blood, is a large protein consisting of four long chains with the complicated three-dimensional structures shown above. Proteins can lose their shape with increases in temperature or changes in the pH of their environment.

Changing even one amino acid can change a protein's structure and function. For example, the difference between normal hemoglobin and the hemoglobin that causes sickle cell anemia is just one amino acid substituted for another.

Enzymes

Enzymes are catalysts that alter reaction rates in the body. Some enzymes cannot bind to their substrates without the help of additional molecules. These may be *minerals,* such as calcium or iron ions, or helper molecules called *coenzymes* that play accessory roles in enzyme-catalyzed reactions. Many vitamins are coenzymes or parts of coenzymes.

Vitamin C, $C_6H_8O_6$
Water-soluble

Vitamin A, $C_{20}H_{30}O$
Fat-soluble

Vitamins are organic molecules that we cannot manufacture and hence need to get from our diets. We need vitamins and minerals to enable our enzymes to work. We need only small amounts of them, however, because they are not destroyed in biochemical reactions. Like enzymes, coenzymes and minerals can be used over and over again.

Temperature and pH have the most significant effects on the rates of reactions catalyzed by enzymes. Most enzymes work best in a solution of approximately neutral pH. Most body cells have a pH of 7.4. However, some enzymes function only in acidic or basic environments.

▲ The protein in fish is denatured by the low pH of lime juice. Notice that the flesh shown with the limes has turned white compared with the flesh at normal pH.

For example, pepsin, the collective term for the digestive enzymes found in the human stomach, works best at a very acidic pH of about 1.5. Cells that line the stomach secrete hydrochloric acid to produce this low pH environment. When food travels down the digestive tract, to the intestine, it carries these enzymes with it. In the intestine, stomach enzymes stop working because sodium bicarbonate in the intestine raises the surroundings to a pH of 8. Intestinal enzymes are formed by the pancreas and work best at pH 8.

Most chemical reactions, speed up with increases in temperature. However, high temperatures (above about 60°C) destroy, or denature, proteins by breaking up their 3-D structure. For example, the protein in an egg or a piece of meat denatures when the egg or meat is cooked. Heating can preserve food by denaturing the enzymes of organisms that cause decay. In milk pasteurization, the milk is heated to denature enzymes that would turn it sour. Refrigeration and freezing also help preserve food by slowing the enzyme reactions that cause decay. The protein in the fish in the above photo has been denatured by the lime juice to be more tasty.

Carbohydrates

Carbohydrates are sugars, starches, and related compounds. The monomers of carbohydrates are monosaccharides, or simple sugars, such as fructose and glucose, shown at the top right. A monosaccharide contains carbon, hydrogen, and oxygen in about a 1:2:1 ratio, respectively.

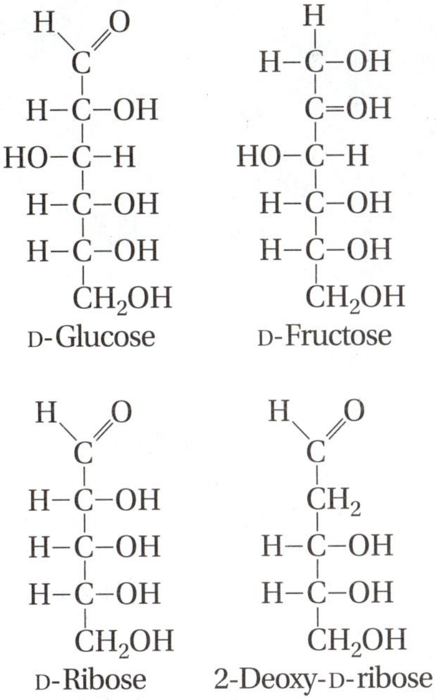

D-Glucose: H–C(=O)–, H–C–OH, HO–C–H, H–C–OH, H–C–OH, CH_2OH

D-Fructose: H–C–OH (with H), C=OH, HO–C–H, H–C–OH, H–C–OH, CH_2OH

D-Ribose: H–C(=O)–, H–C–OH, H–C–OH, H–C–OH, CH_2OH

2-Deoxy-D-ribose: H–C(=O)–, CH_2, H–C–OH, H–C–OH, CH_2OH

Monosaccharides chain representation

Two monosaccharides may be joined together to form a disaccharide. Sucrose, shown below, is a disaccharide. A disaccharide can be hydrolyzed to produce the monosaccharides that formed it. By a series of condensation reactions, many monosaccharides can be joined to form a polymer called a polysaccharide (commonly known as a complex carbohydrate).

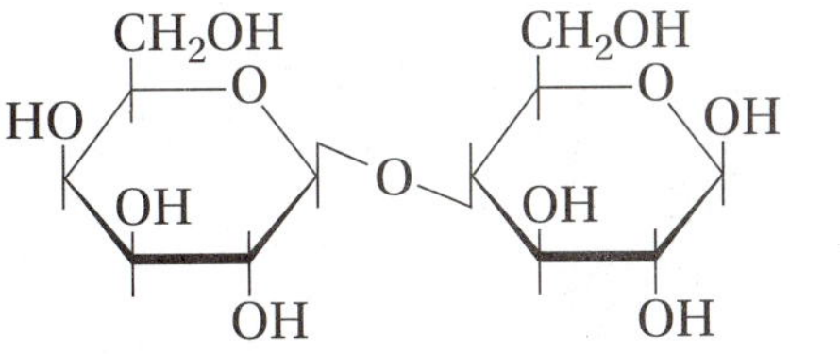

Lactose—made from glucose and galactose

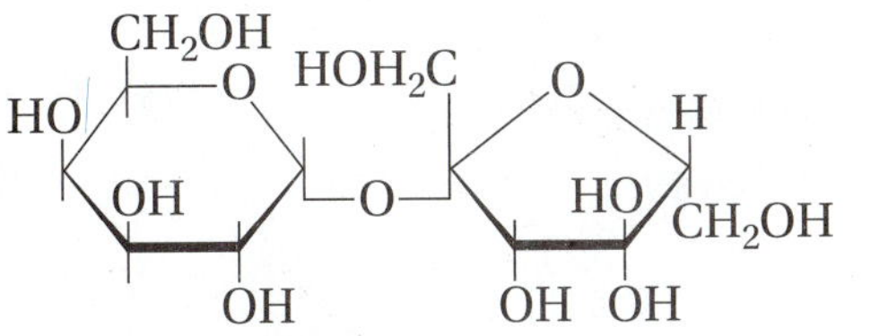

Sucrose—made from glucose and fructose

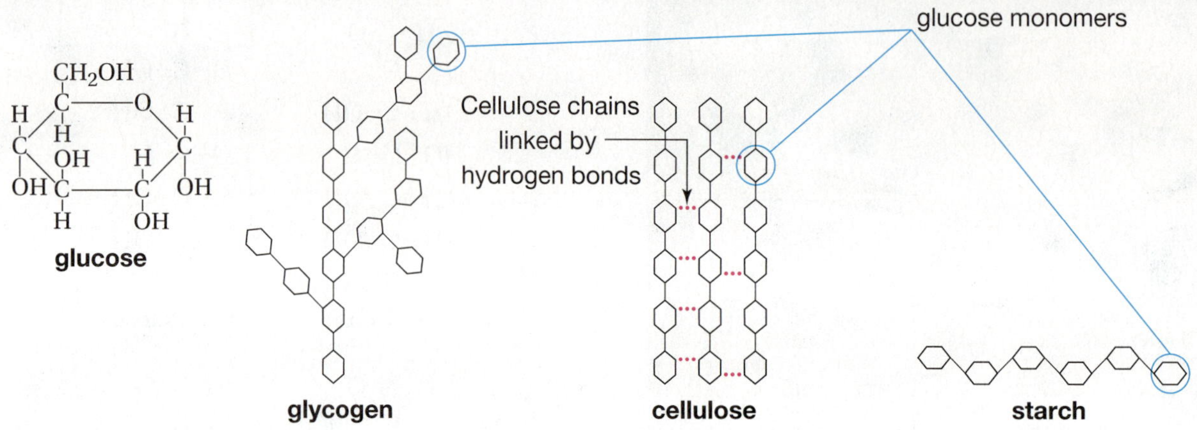

glucose monomers

Cellulose chains linked by hydrogen bonds

glucose

glycogen

cellulose

starch

▲ Glucose is the structural unit for glycogen, cellulose, and starch. Notice that these three polymers differ in the arrangement of glucose monomers.

Three important polysaccharides made of glucose monomers are glycogen, starch, and cellulose. The liver and muscles of animals remove glucose from the blood and condense it into glycogen, which can later be hydrolyzed back into glucose and used to supply energy as needed.

Starch consists of two kinds of glucose polymers. It is hydrolyzed in plants to form glucose for energy and for building material to produce more cells. The structural polysaccharide cellulose is probably the most common organic compound on Earth. Glucose monomers link cellulose chains together at the hydroxyl groups to form cellulose fibers. Cotton fibers consist almost entirely of cellulose.

Lipids

Lipids are a varied group of organic compounds that share one property: they are not very soluble in water. Lipids contain a high proportion of C—H bonds, and they dissolve in nonpolar organic solvents, such as ether, chloroform, and benzene.

Fatty acids, such as the ones shown below, are the simplest lipids. A fatty acid consists of an unbranched chain of carbon and hydrogen atoms with a carboxyl group at one end. Bonding within the carbon chain gives both saturated and unsaturated fatty acids, just as the simple hydrocarbons can be saturated or unsaturated.

The bonds in a carboxyl group are polar, and so the carboxyl end of a fatty acid attracts water molecules.

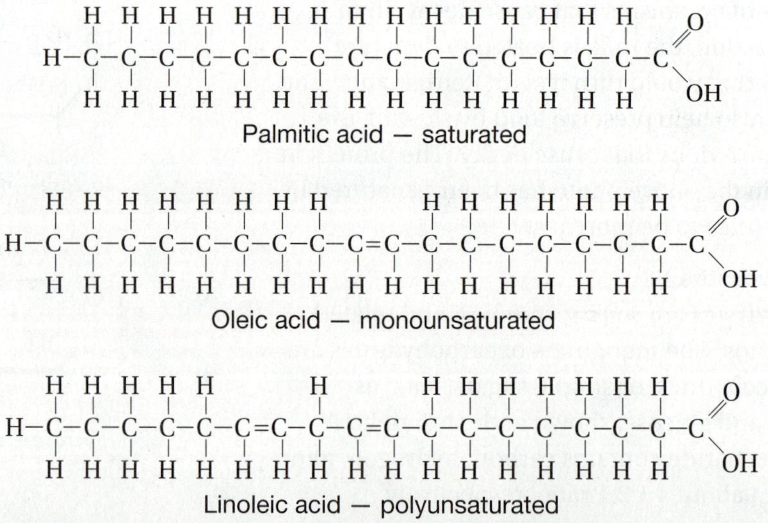

Palmitic acid — saturated

Oleic acid — monounsaturated

Linoleic acid — polyunsaturated

▶ These examples of common fatty acids show the differences in saturation level.

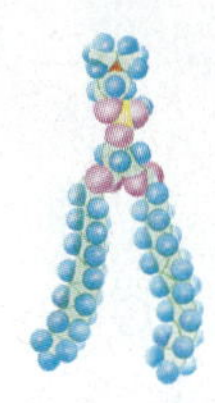

This phospholipid molecule contains two fatty-acid chains.

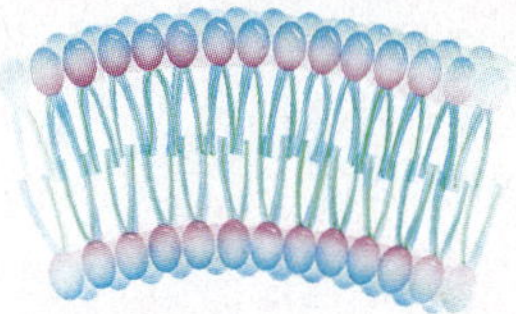

The lipid bilayer is the framework of the cell membrane.

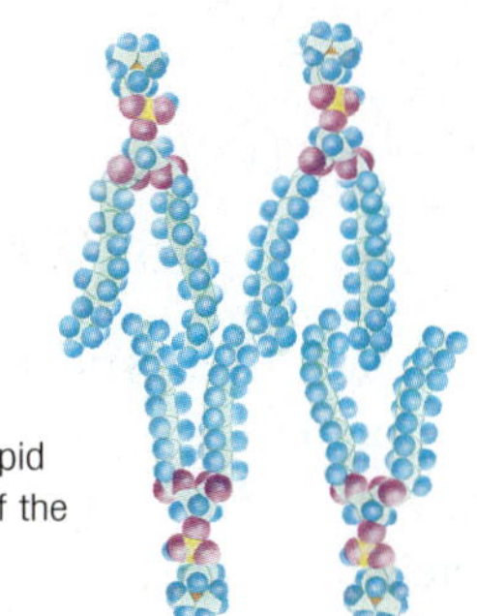

This phospholipid chain is part of the lipid bilayer.

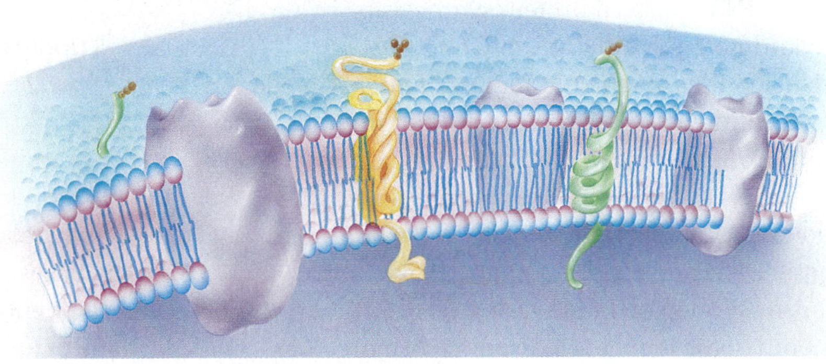

The fatty acids are oriented toward the interior of the bilayer because they have a low attraction for water.

The carbon-hydrogen bonds of a lipid's hydrocarbon chain are nonpolar, however. The polar end will dissolve in water, and the other end will dissolve in nonpolar organic compounds. This behavior enables fatty acids to form membranes when they are dropped into water. It also gives soaps and detergents their cleaning power. The dual solubility of the lipids enables water to "wash away" what it normally could not.

Lipids are the main compounds in biological membranes, such as the cell membrane. Because lipids are insoluble, the lipid bilayer of a cell membrane is adapted to keep the contents of the cell inside separated from the outer environment of the cell.

The structural component of a cell membrane is a phospholipid. The "head" of the phospholipid is polar, and the fatty acid tails are nonpolar, as shown in the model above.

Most fatty acids found in foods and soaps belong to a class of compounds called triglycerides. The fat content shown on a nutrition label for packaged food represents a mixture of the triglycerides in the food. Triglycerides have the general structure shown below.

Fatty acids are usually combined with other molecules to form classes of biomolecules called glycolipids (made from a carbohydrate and a lipid) or lipoproteins (made from a lipid and a protein). These compounds are also parts of more-complex lipids found in the body.

▶ Triglycerides are made from three long-chain fatty acids bonded to a glycerol backbone.

$$\begin{array}{c} \mathrm{H{-}\overset{H}{\underset{H}{C}}{-}(C_nH_{2n}){-}C\overset{\textstyle{/\!/}O}{\underset{\textstyle{\backslash}OH}{}}} \\ \mathrm{H{-}\overset{H}{\underset{H}{C}}{-}(C_nH_{2n}){-}C\overset{\textstyle{/\!/}O}{\underset{\textstyle{\backslash}OH}{}}} \end{array} + \begin{array}{c} \mathrm{H} \\ \mathrm{HO{-}C{-}H} \\ \mathrm{HO{-}C{-}H} \\ \mathrm{HO{-}C{-}H} \\ \mathrm{H} \end{array} \longrightarrow \begin{array}{c} \mathrm{H{-}\overset{H}{\underset{H}{C}}{-}(C_nH_{2n}){-}\overset{O}{\overset{\|}{C}}{-}O{-}\overset{H}{C}{-}H} \\ \mathrm{H{-}\overset{H}{\underset{H}{C}}{-}(C_nH_{2n}){-}\overset{O}{\overset{\|}{C}}{-}O{-}C{-}H} \\ \mathrm{H{-}\overset{H}{\underset{H}{C}}{-}(C_nH_{2n}){-}\overset{O}{\overset{\|}{C}}{-}O{-}\underset{H}{C}{-}H} \end{array}$$

Saturated fatty acids + Glycerol ⟶ Triglyceride

Nucleic Acids

Nucleic acids are macromolecules that transmit genetic information. Deoxyribonucleic acid (DNA) is the material that contains the genetic information that all organisms pass on to their offspring during reproduction. This information includes instructions for making proteins as well as for making the other nucleic acid, ribonucleic acid (RNA). RNA assists in protein synthesis by helping to coordinate protein assembly.

Nucleotides are the monomers of nucleic acids. A nucleotide has three parts: one or more phosphate groups, a sugar containing five carbon atoms, and a ring-shaped nitrogen base, as shown below. RNA nucleotides contain the simple sugar ribose. DNA nucleotides contain deoxyribose (ribose stripped of one oxygen atom). Structures for both of these sugars are shown on a previous page. Cells contain nucleotides with one, two, or three phosphate groups attached. Besides being the monomers of nucleic acids, several nucleotides play other roles.

ATP structure

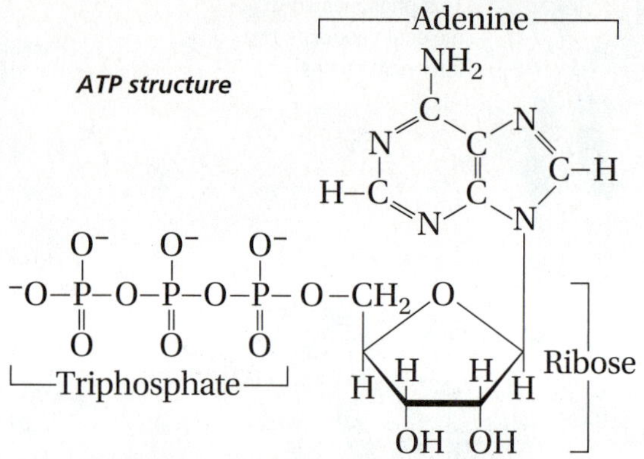

Adenine

Triphosphate

Ribose

For example, adenosine triphosphate (ATP) is the nucleotide that supplies the energy for many metabolic reactions. ATP is shown above.

The bases in nucleic acids attract each other in pairs, a phenomenon known as base-pairing. DNA is made of four different nucleotides—those containing the bases adenine (A), thymine (T), guanine (G), and cytosine (C). The attraction between base pairs is hydrogen bonding. Adenine forms hydrogen bonds with thymine. Similarly, cytosine bonds to guanine. This base-pairing holds strands of DNA together.

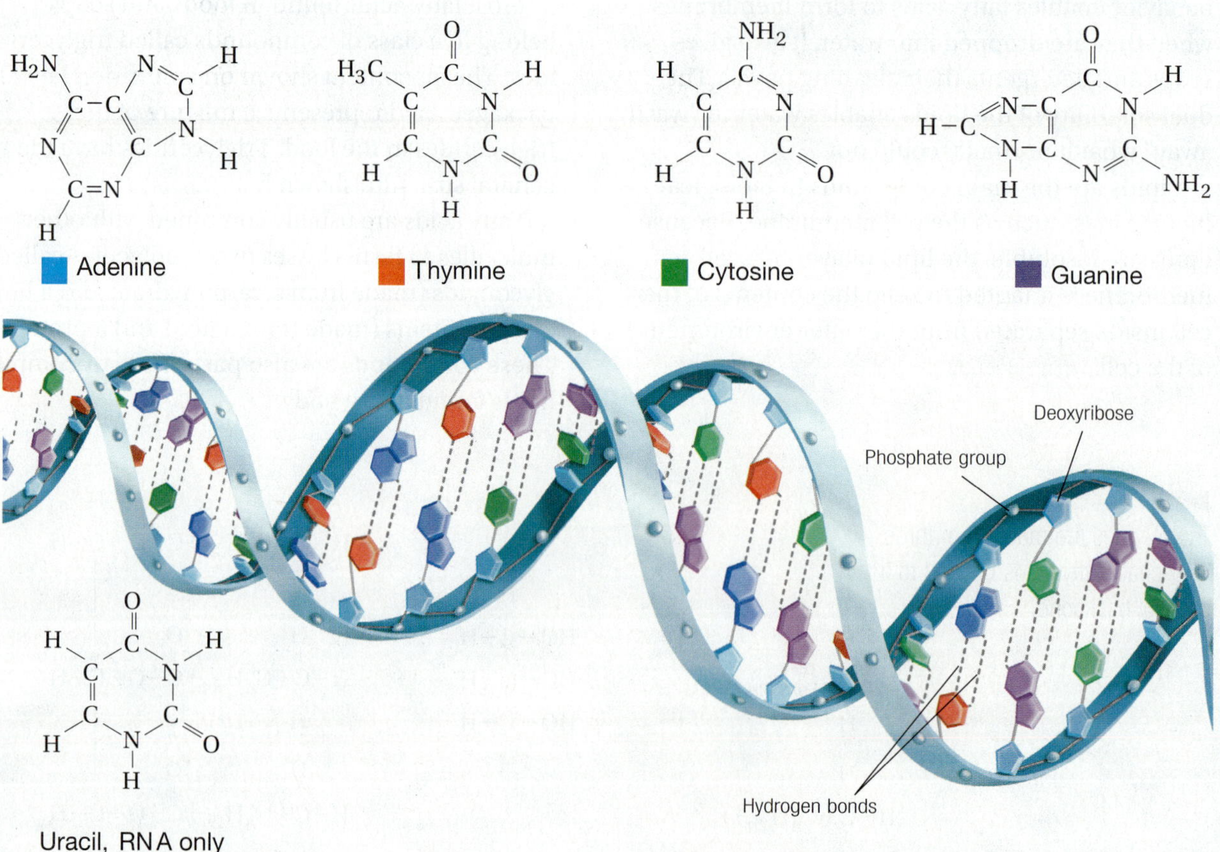

S.T.E.M.
Application *Chemical Industry*

Silicon and Silicates

Silicon is as important in the mineral world as carbon is in living systems. Silicon dioxide and silicates make up about 87% of Earth's crust. Silicates are a class of compounds containing silicon, oxygen, one or more metals, and possibly hydrogen. Many mineral compounds are silicates. Sand is probably the most familiar silicate.

Glasses consist of 75% silicate. Borosilicate glass is the special heat-resistant glass used in making laboratory beakers and flasks. The addition of 5% boron oxide to the glass increases the softening temperature of the glass. Because boron and silicon atoms have roughly similar radii, these atoms can be substituted for one another to make borosilicate glass.

Asbestos is the name given to a class of fibrous magnesium silicate minerals. Asbestos is very strong and flexible, and it does not burn, so it was widely used as a heat-insulating material.

It is now known that asbestos is a carcinogen. When handled, asbestos releases dust particles that are easily inhaled and can cause lung cancer. Asbestos materials found in older homes and buildings should be removed by firms licensed by the Environmental Protection Agency (EPA).

Silicones

Silicones are a class of organic silicon polymers composed of silicon, carbon, oxygen, and hydrogen. The silicon chain is held together by bonding with the oxygen atoms. Each silicon atom is also bonded to different hydrocarbon groups to create a variety of silicone structures.

Silicones are widely used for their adhesive and protective properties. They have good electric insulating properties and are water-repellent. Some silicones have the character of oils or greases, so they are used as lubricants. Silicones are also used in automobile and furniture polishes as protective agents.

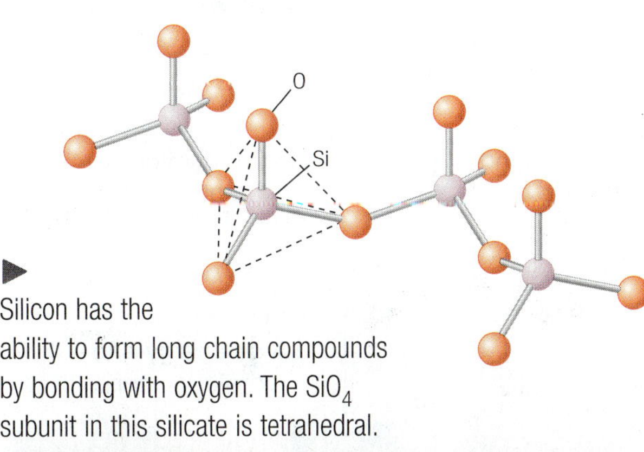

Silicon has the ability to form long chain compounds by bonding with oxygen. The SiO_4 subunit in this silicate is tetrahedral.

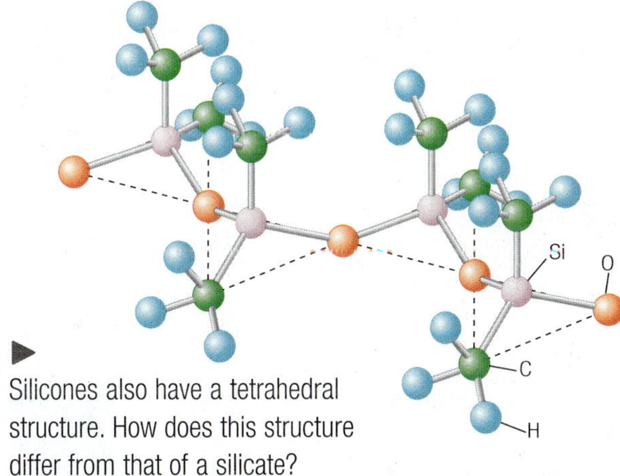

Silicones also have a tetrahedral structure. How does this structure differ from that of a silicate?

Silicates exist in a variety of mineral forms, including mica.

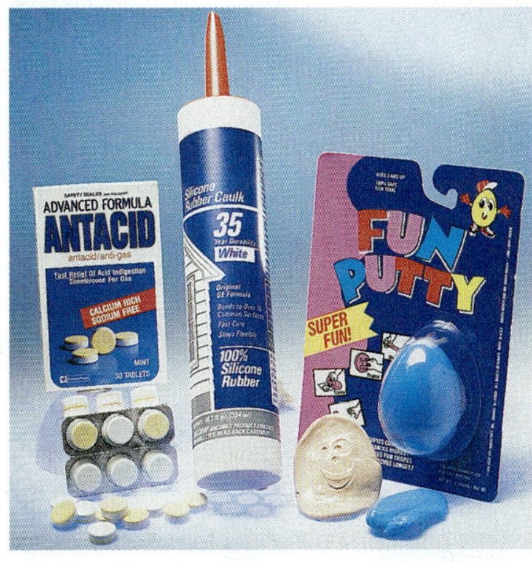

Because of their protective properties, silicones are used in a number of consumer products, from cosmetics to caulkings.

S.T.E.M.

Application Technology

Semiconductors

When electrons can move freely through a material, the material is a conductor. The electrons in metals are loosely held and require little additional energy to move from one vacant orbital to the next. A set of overlapping orbitals is called a *conduction band*. Because electrons can easily jump to the conduction band, metals conduct electricity when only a very small voltage is applied.

Semiconductors conduct a current if the voltage applied is large enough to excite the outer-level electrons of their atoms into the higher energy levels. With semiconductors, more energy, and so a higher voltage, is required to cause conduction. By contrast, nonmetals are insulators because they do not conduct at ordinary voltages. The model below shows the energy required to excite electrons in metals, semiconductors, and insulators.

Semiconductor devices include transistors; diodes, including light-emitting diodes (LEDs); some lasers; and photovoltaic cells ("solar" cells). Though silicon is the basis of most semiconductor devices in the computer industry, pure silicon has little use as a semiconductor. Instead, small amounts of impurities are added to increase its conductive properties. Adding impurities to silicon is called *doping*, and the substances added are *dopants*. The dopant is usually incorporated into just the surface layer of a silicon chip. Typical dopants include the Group 15 elements phosphorus and arsenic and the Group 13 elements boron, aluminum, gallium, and indium.

A silicon atom has four electrons in its outer energy level. Group 13 atoms have three and Group 15 atoms have five. Adding boron to silicon creates a mix of atoms having four valence electrons and atoms having three valence electrons. Boron atoms form only three bonds with silicon, whereas silicon forms four bonds with other silicon atoms.

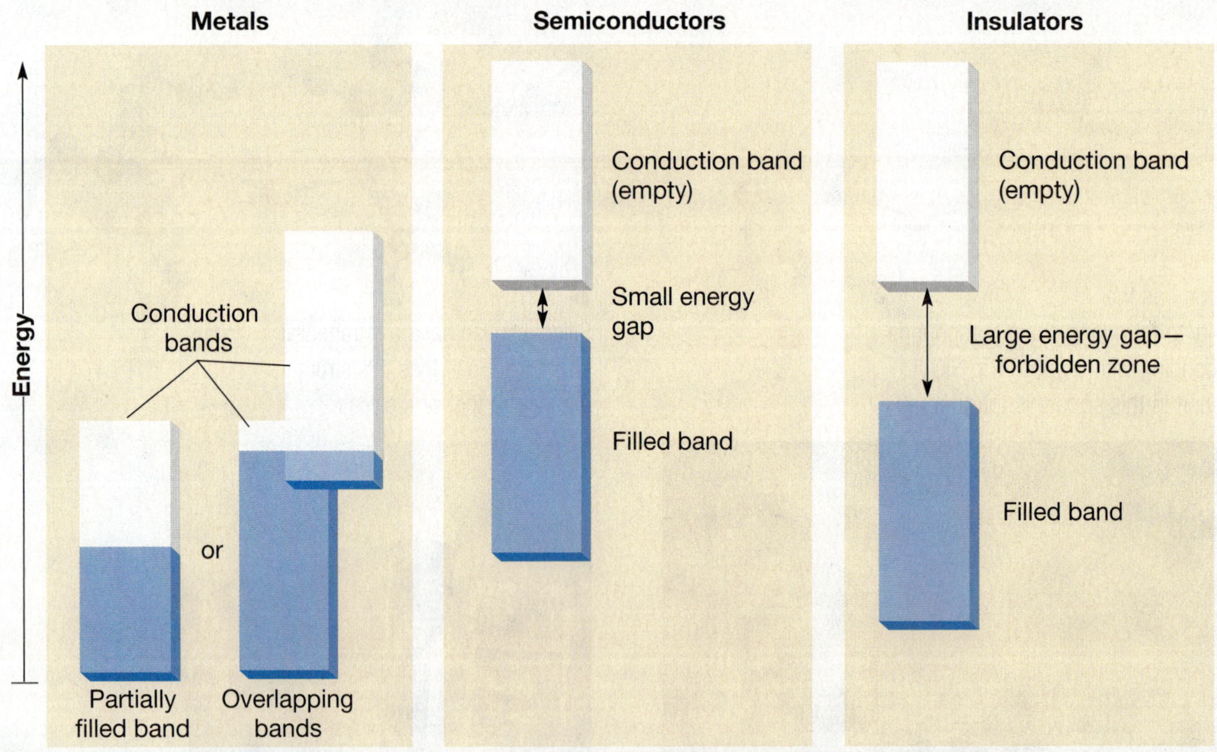

▲ This model shows the difference in the levels of energy required to excite electrons into the conduction band in metals, semiconductors, and insulators. The forbidden zone is too great an energy gap in insulators for these elements to function as conductors. The energy gap for semiconductors is small enough that it can be crossed under certain conditions.

- Dopants
- Semiconductor elements
- Forms semiconductor compounds

Group 1	Group 2	Group 3	Group 4	Group 5	Group 6	Group 7	Group 8	Group 9	Group 10	Group 11	Group 12	Group 13	Group 14	Group 15	Group 16	Group 17	Group 18
1 H																	2 He
3 Li	4 Be											5 B	6 C	7 N	8 O	9 F	10 Ne
11 Na	12 Mg											13 Al	14 Si	15 P	16 S	17 Cl	18 Ar
19 K	20 Ca	21 Sc	22 Ti	23 V	24 Cr	25 Mn	26 Fe	27 Co	28 Ni	29 Cu	30 Zn	31 Ga	32 Ge	33 As	34 Se	35 Br	36 Kr
37 Rb	38 Sr	39 Y	40 Zr	41 Nb	42 Mo	43 Tc	44 Ru	45 Rh	46 Pd	47 Ag	48 Cd	49 In	50 Sn	51 Sb	52 Te	53 I	54 Xe
55 Cs	56 Ba	57 La	72 Hf	73 Ta	74 W	75 Re	76 Os	77 Ir	78 Pt	79 Au	80 Hg	81 Tl	82 Pb	83 Bi	84 Po	85 At	86 Rn
87 Fr	88 Ra	89 Ac															

▲ Semiconductor elements and dopants fall in the metalloid region of the periodic table. Semiconductor compounds often contain metals.

The unbonded spot between a silicon atom and a boron atom is a hole that a free electron can occupy. Because this hole "attracts" an electron, it is viewed as if it were positively charged. Semiconductors that are doped with boron, aluminum, or gallium are *p-type semiconductors*, the *p* standing for "positive." P-type semiconductors conduct electricity better than pure silicon because they provide spaces that moving electrons can occupy as they flow through the material.

Doping silicon with phosphorus or arsenic produces the opposite effect. When phosphorus is added to silicon, it forms four bonds to silicon atoms and has a nonbonding electron left over. This extra electron is free to move through the material when a voltage is applied, thus increasing its conductivity compared with pure silicon. These extra electrons have a negative charge. Therefore, the material is an *n-type semiconductor*. The model below compares these two types of semiconductors.

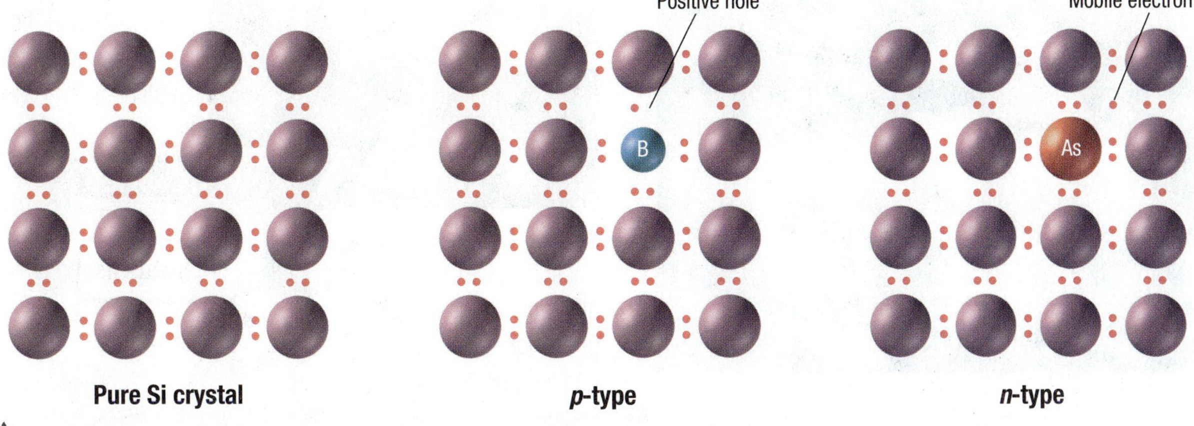

▲ Each silicon atom in the pure crystal is surrounded by four pairs of electrons. The *p*-type semiconductor model contains an atom of boron with a hole that an electron can occupy. The *n*-type semiconductor model contains an atom of arsenic, which provides the extra electron that can move through the crystal.

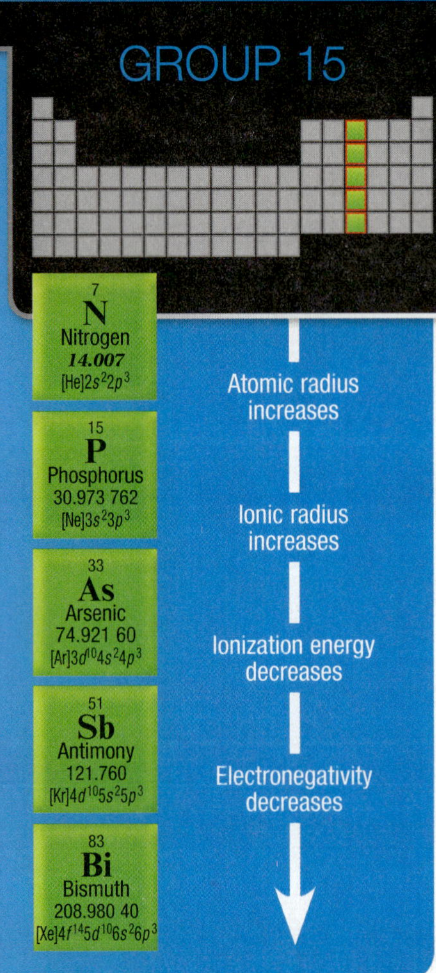

Nitrogen Family

Characteristics

- consist of two nonmetals (nitrogen and phosphorus), two metalloids (arsenic and antimony), and one metal (bismuth)
- Nitrogen is most commonly found as atmospheric N_2; phosphorus as phosphate rock; and arsenic, antimony, and bismuth as sulfides or oxides. Antimony and bismuth are also found as free elements.
- range from very abundant elements (nitrogen and phosphorus) to relatively rare elements (arsenic, antimony, and bismuth)
- consist of atoms that contain five electrons in their outermost energy level
- tend to form covalent compounds, most commonly with oxidation numbers of +3 or +5
- exist in two or more allotropic forms, except nitrogen and bismuth
- are solids at room temperature, except nitrogen

You can see the contrast in physical properties among the elements of this family. Arsenic, antimony, and bismuth are shown.

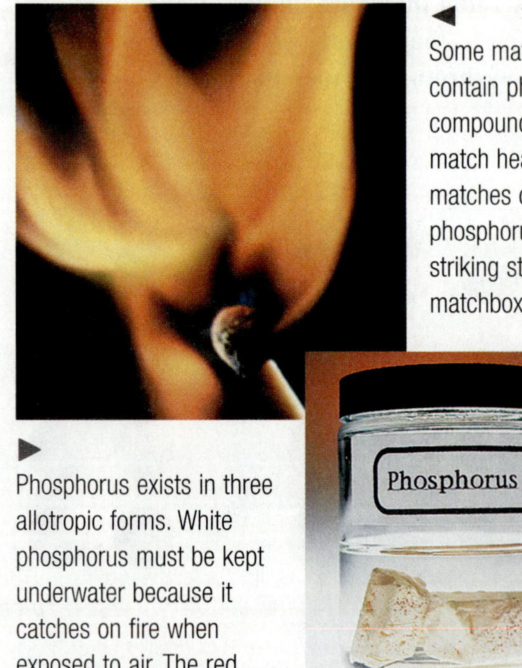

Some matches contain phosphorus compounds in the match head. Safety matches contain phosphorus in the striking strip on the matchbox.

Phosphorus exists in three allotropic forms. White phosphorus must be kept underwater because it catches on fire when exposed to air. The red and black forms are stable in air.

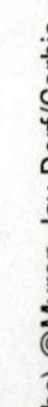

Common Reactions

With Oxygen to Form Oxides

Example: $P_4(s) + 5O_2(g) \longrightarrow P_4O_{10}(s)$
As, Sb, and Bi follow this reaction pattern, but as monatomic elements. N reacts to form NO and NO_2. It also reacts as N_2 to form N_2O_3 and N_2O_5.

With Metals to Form Binary Compounds

Example: $3Mg(s) + N_2(g) \longrightarrow Mg_3N_2(s)$

Analytical Test

There are no simple analytical tests for the presence of nitrogen or phosphorus compounds in a sample. Antimony produces a pale green color in a flame test, and arsenic produces a light blue color. Arsenic, antimony, and bismuth are recognized in qualitative analyses by their characteristic sulfide colors.

Arsenic flame test

Antimony flame test

▲
Formation of sulfides is the confirmatory qualitative analysis test for the presence of bismuth, antimony, and arsenic.

Properties

GROUP 15 ELEMENTS

Quantity	N	P*	As	Sb	Bi
Melting point (°C)	−209.86	44.1	817 (28 atm)	630.5	271.3
Boiling point (°C)	−195.8	280	613 (sublimes)	1750	1560 ± 5
Density (g/cm³)	1.25×10^{-3}	1.82	5.727	6.684	9.80
Ionization energy (kJ/mol)	1402	1012	947	834	703
Atomic radius (pm)	75	110	120	140	150
Ionic radius (pm)	146 (N^{3-})	212 (P^{3-})	—	76 (Sb^{3+})	103 (Bi^{3+})
Common oxidation number in compounds	−3, +3, +5	−3, +3, +5	+3, +5	+3, +5	+3
Crystal structure†	cubic (as a solid)	cubic	rhombohedral	hcp	rhombohedral
Hardness (Mohs' scale)	none (gas)	—	3.5	3.0	2.25

* Data given apply to white phosphorus.
† Crystal structures are for the most common allotropes.

S.T.E.M.

Application *Biology*

Plants and Nitrogen

All organisms require certain elements to survive and grow. These elements include carbon, hydrogen, oxygen, nitrogen, phosphorus, potassium, sulfur, and several other elements needed in small amounts. An organism needs nitrogen to synthesize structural proteins, enzymes, and the nucleic acids DNA and RNA.

Carbon, hydrogen, and oxygen are available to plants from carbon dioxide in the air and from water in the air and the soil. Nitrogen is necessary for plants' survival. Nitrogen gas, N_2, makes up 78% of air, but most plants cannot take nitrogen out of the air and into their cells, because the triple covalent bond in N_2 is not easily broken. Plants need nitrogen in the form of a compound that they can take in and use. The process of using atmospheric N_2 to make NH_3 is called *nitrogen fixation.*

Several kinds of nitrogen-fixing bacteria live in the soil and in the root nodules of plants called legumes. Legumes obtain the nitrogen they need through a symbiotic relationship with nitrogen-fixing bacteria. Legumes include peas, beans, clover, alfalfa, and locust trees. The bacteria convert nitrogen into ammonia, NH_3, which is then absorbed by the host plants.

Because wheat, rice, corn, and potatoes cannot perform the same feat as legumes, these plants depend on nitrogen-fixing bacteria in the soil. Soil bacteria convert NH_3 into nitrate ions, NO_3^-, the form of nitrogen that can be absorbed and used by plants. These plants also often need nitrogen fertilizers to supplement the work of the bacteria. Besides supplying nitrogen, fertilizers are manufactured to contain phosphorus, potassium, and trace minerals.

▲ Nitrogen-fixing bacteria, Rhizobium, live in these small nodules that grow on the roots of soybeans.

▲ Soybeans are legumes that live in a symbiotic relationship with nitrogen-fixing bacteria.

S.T.E.M.

Application *Chemical Industry*

Fertilizers

Fertilizers can supply nitrogen to plants in the form of ammonium sulfate, ammonium nitrate, and urea, all of which are made from NH_3. Now you know why there is such a demand for ammonia. Though some soils contain sufficient concentrations of phosphorus and potassium, most soils need additional nitrogen for adequate plant growth. Ammonia, ammonium nitrate, or urea can fill that need.

Most fertilizers contain all three major plant nutrients N, P, and K, and are called *complete fertilizers.* A typical complete fertilizer might contain ammonium nitrate or sodium nitrate to provide nitrogen. Calcium dihydrogen phosphate, $Ca(H_2PO_4)_2$, or the anhydrous form of phosphoric acid, P_4O_{10}, can provide phosphorus. Potassium chloride, KCl, or potassium oxide, K_2O, can provide potassium.

The proportion of each major nutrient in a fertilizer is indicated by a set of three numbers. These numbers are the N-P-K formula of the fertilizer and indicate the percentage of N, P, and K, respectively. A fertilizer graded as 6-12-6, for example, contains 6% nitrogen, 12% phosphorus, and 6% potassium by weight.

Nitrogen stimulates overall plant growth. Phosphorus promotes root growth and flowering. Potassium regulates the structures in leaves that allow CO_2 to enter the leaf and O_2 and H_2O to exit. Fertilizers are available in N-P-K formulas best suited for their intended use. For example, plants that produce large amounts of carbohydrates (sugars) need more potassium than most other types of plants. Grain crops need more phosphorus. Lawn fertilizers applied in the spring are generally high in nitrogen to stimulate shoot growth in grasses. Lawn fertilizers applied in the fall of the year should have a higher phosphorus content to stimulate root growth during the winter. Common fertilizer types are listed in Table 6A.

TABLE 6A

SOME COMMERCIAL FERTILIZERS AND USES

Fertilizer composition (N-P-K)	Uses
1-2-1 ratio 10-20-10 15-30-15	early-spring application for trees and shrubs with flowers and fruit; general-purpose feedings of the following: cucumbers, peppers, tomatoes
3-1-2 ratio 12-4-8 15-5-10 21-7-4 16-4-8 20-5-10	lawns and general-purpose feedings of the following: trees, shrubs, most berries, apple trees, grapes, vines, walnut trees, broccoli, cabbage, carrots, onions
High nitrogen 33-0-0 21-0-0 40-4-4 36-6-6	pecan trees, lawns, early feedings of corn
Balanced 13-13-13	general purpose feeding of the following: broccoli, cabbage, melons, potatoes
Special purpose: acid-loving flowering shrubs 12-10-4	azaleas, rhododendrons, camellias, gardenias
Special purpose 18-24-16	roses
Special purpose: flowering 12-55-6	flowering plants and shrubs (annuals and perennials)
Special purpose: root growth 5-20-10	starter fertilizer for transplants

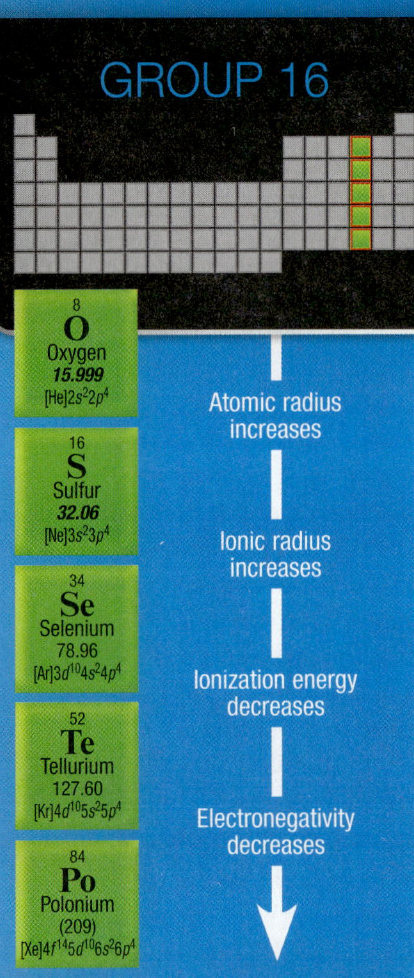

Oxygen Family

Characteristics

- occur naturally as free elements and in combined states
- consist of three nonmetals (oxygen, sulfur, and selenium), one metalloid (tellurium), and one metal (polonium)
- consist of atoms that have six electrons in their outermost energy level
- tend to form covalent compounds with other elements
- exist in several allotropic forms
- tend to exist as diatomic and polyatomic molecules, such as O_2, O_3, S_6, S_8, and Se_8
- commonly exist in compounds with the −2 oxidation state but often exhibit other oxidation states

▶ Sulfur is found naturally in underground deposits and in the steam vents near volcanoes.

▲ Sulfur exists in combined forms in many minerals. Iron pyrite, FeS_2, black galena, PbS, and yellow orpiment, As_2S_3, are shown.

Orthorhombic

▶ Two allotropic forms of sulfur are orthorhombic and mownoclinic. Each has a different crystal structure.

Monoclinic

(cr) ©Charles D. Winters/Photo Researchers, Inc; (b) ©Andrew Lambert Photography/Photo Researchers, Inc; (cl) ©Victor Englebert/Photo Researchers, Inc

Common Reactions

With Metals to Form Binary Compounds

Example: $8Mg(s) + S_8(l) \longrightarrow 8MgS(s)$

O_2, Se, and Te follow this pattern in reacting with Na, K, Ca, Mg, and Al.

With Oxygen to Form Oxides

Example: $Se(s) + O_2(g) \longrightarrow SeO_2(s)$

S, Te, and Po follow this pattern. S, Se, and Te can form SO_3, SeO_3, and TeO_3.

With Halogens to Form Binary Compounds

Example: $S_8(l) + 8Cl_2(g) \longrightarrow 8SCl_2(l)$

O, Se, Te, and Po follow this pattern in reacting with F_2, Cl_2, Br_2, and I_2.

With Hydrogen to Form Binary Compounds

$2H_2(g) + O_2(g) \longrightarrow 2H_2O(l)$

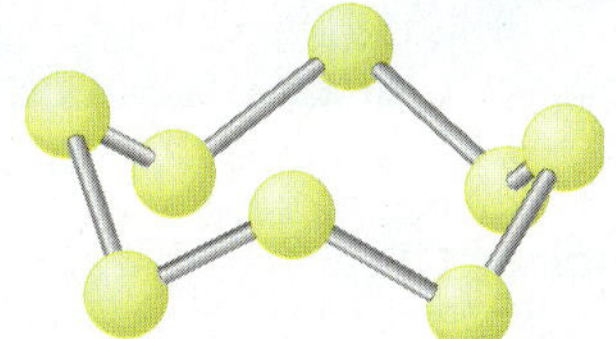

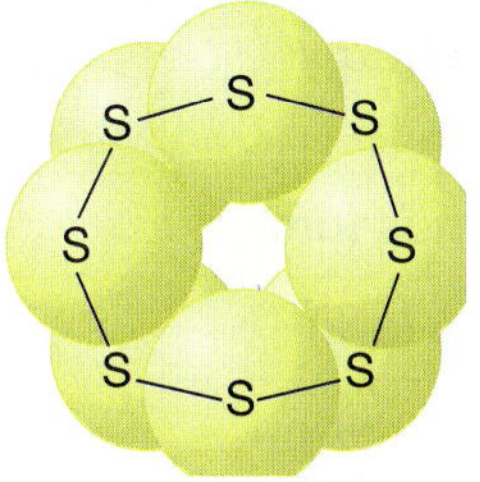

▲ Sulfur exists as S_8 molecules in which the atoms are bonded in a ring, as shown by the ball-and-stick and space-filling models.

Analytical Test

There is no simple analytical test to identify all elements of this family. Selenium and tellurium can be identified by flame tests. A light blue flame is characteristic of selenium, and a green flame is characteristic of tellurium. Oxygen can be identified by the splint test, in which a glowing splint bursts into flame when thrust into oxygen. Elemental sulfur is typically identified by its physical characteristics, especially its color and its properties when heated. It melts to form a viscous brown liquid and burns with a blue flame.

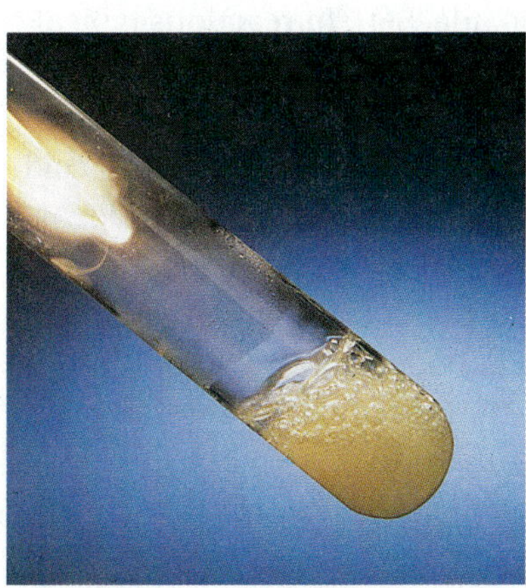

▲ A glowing splint thrust into oxygen bursts into a bright flame.

▲ Sulfur burns with a characteristically deep blue flame.

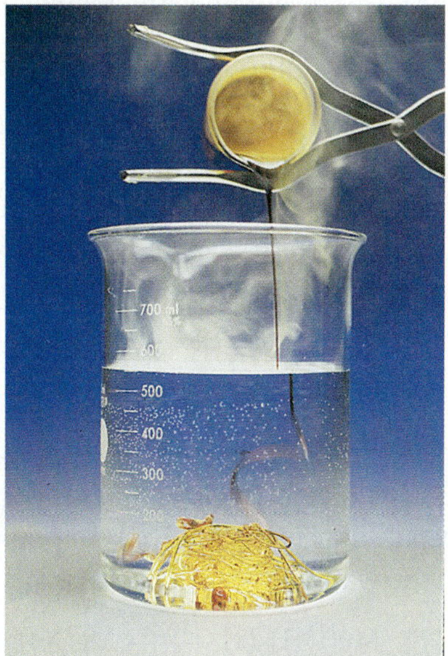

▲ Molten sulfur returns to its orthorhombic form upon cooling.

Properties

GROUP 16 ELEMENTS					
	O	S	Se	Te	Po
Melting point (°C)	−218.4	119.0	217	449.8	254
Boiling point (°C)	−182.962	444.674	685	989.9	962
Density (g/cm^3)	1.429×10^{-3}	1.96	4.82	6.24	9.4
Ionization energy (kJ/mol)	1314	1000	941	869	812
Atomic radius (pm)	73	103	119	142	168
Ionic radius (pm)	140	184	198	221	–
Common oxidation number in compounds	−2	−2, +4, +6	−2, +2, +4, +6	−2, +2, +4, +6	−2, +2, +4, +6
Crystal structure*	orthorhombic, rhombohedral, cubic (when solid)	orthorhombic, monoclinic	hexagonal	hexagonal	cubic, rhombohedral
Hardness (Mohs' scale)	none (gas)	2.0	2.0	2.3	–

* Most elements of this family can have more than one crystal structure.

S.T.E.M.

Application *Chemical Industry*

Oxides

Oxides of the reactive metals are ionic compounds. The oxide ion from any soluble oxide reacts immediately with water to form hydroxide ions as represented by the following equation:

$$O^{2-}(aq) + H_2O(l) \longrightarrow 2OH^-(aq)$$

The reactive metal oxides of Groups 1 and 2 react vigorously with water and release a large amount of energy as heat. The product of the reaction is a metal hydroxide. The following equation is an example of this reaction:

$$Na_2O(s) + H_2O(l) \longrightarrow 2NaOH(aq)$$

A basic oxide can be thought of as the dehydrated form of a hydroxide base. Oxides of the less reactive metals, such as magnesium, can be prepared by using thermal decomposition to drive off the water.

$$Mg(OH)_2(s) \xrightarrow{\text{heat}} MgO(s) + H_2O(g)$$

Hydroxides of the reactive metals of Group 1 are too stable to decompose in this manner.

If a hydroxide formed by a metal oxide is water-soluble, it dissolves to form a basic solution. An oxide that reacts with water to form a basic solution is called a basic oxide or a basic anhydride. Table 7A on the next page lists oxides that form basic solutions with water.

Molecular Oxides

Nonmetals, located on the right side of the periodic table, form molecular oxides. For example, sulfur forms two gaseous oxides: sulfur dioxide, SO_2, and sulfur trioxide, SO_3. In reactions typical of nonmetal oxides, each of the sulfur oxides reacts with water to form an oxyacid.

An oxide that reacts with water to form an acid is called an acidic oxide or an acid anhydride. As with the basic anhydrides, each acid anhydride can be thought of as the dehydrated form of the appropriate oxyacid. For example, when sulfuric acid decomposes, the loss of H_2O leaves the oxide SO_3, which is an anhydride.

$$H_2SO_4(aq) \xrightarrow{\text{heat}} H_2O(g) + SO_3(g)$$

Amphoteric Oxides

Table 7A lists some common oxides of main-group elements. You can see that the active metal oxides are basic and that the nonmetal oxides are acidic. Between these lies a group of oxides, the *amphoteric oxides*. The bonding in amphoteric oxides is intermediate between ionic and covalent bonding. As a result, oxides of this type show behavior intermediate between that of acidic oxides and basic oxides, and react as both acids and bases.

Aluminum oxide, Al_2O_3, is a typical amphoteric oxide. With hydrochloric acid, aluminum oxide acts as a base. The reaction produces a salt and water.

$$Al_2O_3(s) + 6HCl(aq) \longrightarrow 2AlCl_3(aq) + 3H_2O(l)$$

With aqueous sodium hydroxide, aluminum oxide acts as an acid. The reaction forms a soluble ionic compound and water. That compound contains aluminate ions, AlO_2^-. (The AlO_2^- formula is used here rather than the more precise hydrated aluminate formula, $Al(OH)_4^-$.)

$$Al_2O_3(s) + 2NaOH(aq) \longrightarrow 2NaAlO_2(aq) + H_2O(l)$$

Reactions of Oxides

In the reaction between an acid and a metal oxide, the products are a salt and water—the same as the products in a neutralization reaction. For example, when magnesium oxide reacts with dilute sulfuric acid, magnesium sulfate and water are produced.

$$MgO(s) + H_2SO_4(dil.\ aq) \longrightarrow MgSO_4(aq) + H_2O(l)$$

The reaction between a basic metal oxide, such as MgO, and an acidic nonmetal oxide, such as CO_2, tends to produce an oxygen-containing salt. The dry oxides are mixed and heated without water. Salts such as metal carbonates, phosphates, and sulfates can be made by this synthesis reaction.

$$MgO(s) + CO_2(g) \longrightarrow MgCO_3(s)$$
$$6CaO(s) + P_4O_{10}(s) \longrightarrow 2Ca_3(PO_4)_2(s)$$
$$CaO(s) + SO_3(g) \longrightarrow CaSO_4(s)$$

Reactions of Hydroxides with Nonmetal Oxides

Nonmetal oxides tend to be acid anhydrides. The reaction of a hydroxide base with a nonmetal oxide is an acid-base reaction. The product is either a salt or a salt and water, depending on the identities and relative quantities of reactants. For example, 2 mol of the hydroxide base sodium hydroxide and 1 mol of the nonmetal oxide carbon dioxide form sodium carbonate, which is a salt, and water.

$$CO_2(g) + 2NaOH(aq) \longrightarrow Na_2CO_3(aq) + H_2O(l)$$

However, if sodium hydroxide is limited, only sodium hydrogen carbonate is produced.

$$CO_2(g) + NaOH(aq) \longrightarrow NaHCO_3(aq)$$

TABLE 7A

PERIODICITY OF ACIDIC AND BASIC OXIDES OF MAIN-GROUP ELEMENTS

Group Number						
1	2	13	14	15	16	17
Li_2O basic	BeO amphoteric	B_2O_3 acidic	CO_2 acidic	N_2O_5 acidic		
Na_2O basic	MgO basic	Al_2O_3 amphoteric	SiO_2 acidic	P_4O_{10} acidic	SO_3 acidic	Cl_2O acidic
K_2O basic	CaO basic	Ga_2O_3 amphoteric	GeO_2 amphoteric	As_4O_6 amphoteric	SeO_3 acidic	
Rb_2O basic	SrO basic	In_2O_3 basic	SnO_2 amphoteric	Sb_4O_6 amphoteric	TeO_3 acidic	I_2O_5 acidic
Cs_2O basic	BaO basic	Tl_2O_3 basic	PbO_2 amphoteric	Bi_2O_3 basic		

S.T.E.M.

Application *The Environment*

Ozone

Ozone, O_3, is an allotrope of oxygen that is important for life on Earth. Like O_2, O_3 is a gas at room temperature. However, unlike O_2, O_3 is a poisonous bluish gas with an irritating odor at high concentrations. The triatomic ozone molecule is angular (bent) with a bond angle of about 116.5°. The O—O bonds in ozone are shorter and stronger than a single bond, but longer and weaker than a double bond. The ozone molecule is best represented by two resonance hybrid structures.

$$:\ddot{O}=\ddot{O}-\ddot{O}: \longleftrightarrow :\ddot{O}-\ddot{O}=\ddot{O}:$$

Ozone forms naturally in Earth's atmosphere more than 24 km above the Earth's surface in a layer called the stratosphere. There, O_2 molecules absorb energy from ultraviolet light and split into free oxygen atoms.

$$O_2(g) \xrightarrow{\text{ultraviolet light}} 2O$$

A free oxygen atom has an unpaired electron and is highly reactive. A chemical species that has one or more unpaired or unshared electrons is referred to as a *free radical*. A free radical is a short-lived fragment of a molecule. The oxygen free radical can react with a molecule of O_2 to produce an ozone molecule.

$$O + O_2(g) \longrightarrow O_3(g)$$

A molecule of O_3 can then absorb ultraviolet light and split to produce O_2 and a free oxygen atom.

$$O_3(g) \xrightarrow{\text{ultraviolet light}} O_2(g) + O$$

The production and breakdown of ozone in the stratosphere are examples of *photochemical* processes, in which light causes a chemical reaction.

In this way, O_3 is constantly formed and destroyed in the stratosphere, and its concentration is determined by the balance among these reactions. The breakdown of ozone absorbs the sun's intense ultraviolet light in the range of wavelengths between 290 nm and 320 nm. Light of these wavelengths damages and kills living cells, so if these wavelengths were to reach Earth's surface in large amounts, life would be impossible. Even now, the normal amount of ultraviolet light reaching Earth's surface is a major cause of skin cancer and the damage to DNA molecules that causes mutations. One life-form that is very sensitive to ultraviolet radiation is the phytoplankton in the oceans. These organisms carry out photosynthesis and are the first level of oceanic food webs.

Ozone and Air Pollution

Ozone in the lower atmosphere is a harmful pollutant. Ozone is highly reactive and can oxidize organic compounds. The products of these reactions are harmful substances that, when mixed with air, water vapor, and dust, make up *photochemical smog*. This mixture is the smog typically found in cities.

Typically, ozone is produced in a complex series of reactions involving unburned hydrocarbons and nitrogen oxides given off from engines in the form of exhaust and from fuel-burning power plants. When fuel burns explosively in the cylinder of an internal-combustion engine, some of the nitrogen in the cylinder also combines with oxygen to form NO, a very reactive nitrogen oxide free radical.

$$N_2(g) + O_2(g) \longrightarrow 2NO$$

When the free radical reaches the air, it reacts with oxygen to produce NO_2 radicals, which react with water in the air to produce HNO_3.

$$2NO + O_2(g) \longrightarrow 2NO_2$$
$$3NO_2 + H_2O(l) \longrightarrow NO + 2HNO_3(aq)$$

In sunlight, nitrogen dioxide decomposes to give nitric oxide and an atom of oxygen. Note that the NO produced is free to undergo the previous reaction once more.

$$NO_2 \xrightarrow{\text{sunlight}} NO + O$$

Just as it is in the stratosphere, a free oxygen atom in the lower atmosphere is highly reactive and reacts with a molecule of diatomic oxygen to form ozone.

$$O + O_2(g) \longrightarrow O_3(g)$$

S.T.E.M.

Application *Chemical Industry*

Sulfuric Acid

Sulfuric acid is the so-called "king of chemicals" because it is produced in the largest volume in the United States. It is produced by the contact process. This process starts with the production of SO_2 by burning sulfur or roasting iron pyrite, FeS_2. The purified sulfur dioxide is mixed with air and passed through hot iron pipes containing a catalyst. The contact between the catalyst, SO_2, and O_2 produces sulfur trioxide, SO_3, and gives the contact process its name. SO_3 is dissolved in concentrated H_2SO_4 to produce pyrosulfuric acid, $H_2S_2O_7$.

$$SO_3(g) + H_2SO_4(aq) \longrightarrow H_2S_2O_7(aq)$$

The pyrosulfuric acid is then diluted with water to produce sulfuric acid.

$$H_2S_2O_7(aq) + H_2O(l) \longrightarrow 2H_2SO_4(aq)$$

Properties and Uses of Sulfuric Acid

Concentrated sulfuric acid is a good oxidizing agent. During the oxidation process, sulfur is reduced from +6 to +4 or −2. The change in oxidation state for a reaction depends on the concentration of the acid and on the nature of the reducing agent used in the reaction.

Sulfuric acid is also an important dehydrating agent. Gases that do not react with H_2SO_4 can be dried by being bubbled through concentrated sulfuric acid. Organic compounds, like sucrose, are dehydrated to leave carbon, as shown by the following reaction.

$$C_{12}H_{22}O_{11}(s) + 11H_2SO_4(aq) \longrightarrow 12C(s) + 11H_2SO_4 \longrightarrow H_2O(l)$$

The decomposition of sucrose proceeds rapidly and can be quite dramatic looking.

About 60% of the sulfuric acid produced in this country is used to make superphosphate, which is a mixture of phosphate compounds used in fertilizers.

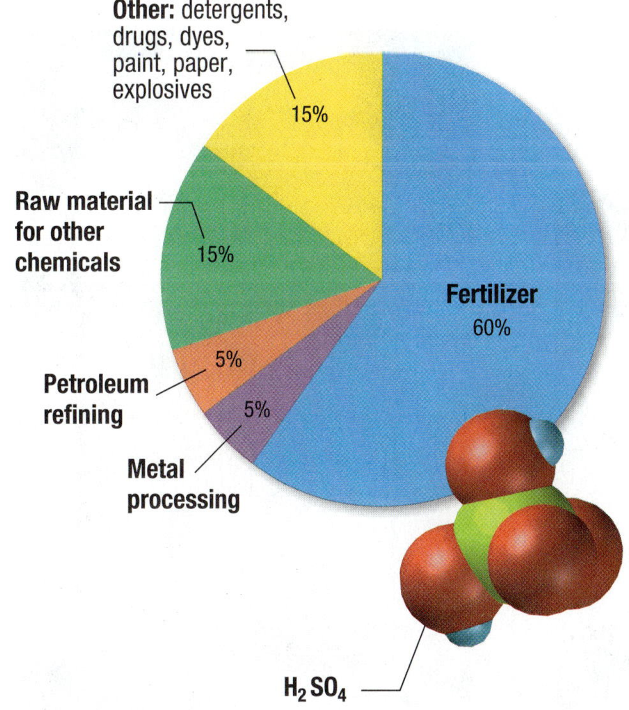

Important uses of the U.S. supply of sulfuric acid

TABLE 7B

TOP TEN CHEMICALS PRODUCED IN THE U.S.

Rank	Chemical	Physical state	Formula
1	sulfuric acid	*l*	H_2SO_4
2	nitrogen	*g*	N_2
3	oxygen	*g*	O_2
4	ethylene	*g*	C_2H_4
5	calcium oxide (lime)	*s*	CaO
6	ammonia	*g*	NH_3
7	phosphoric acid	*l*	H_3PO_4
8	sodium hydroxide	*s*	NaOH
9	propylene	*g*	C_3H_6
10	chlorine	*g*	Cl_2

GROUP 17

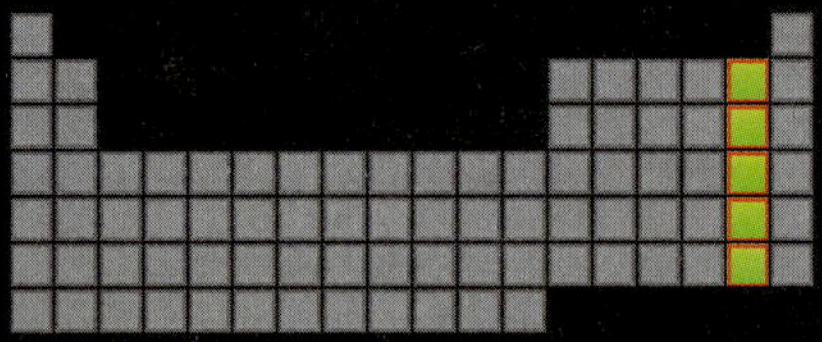

9
F
Fluorine
18.998 4032
$[He]2s^22p^5$

17
Cl
Chlorine
35.45
$[Ne]3s^23p^5$

35
Br
Bromine
79.904
$[Ar]3d^{10}4s^24p^5$

53
I
Iodine
126.904 47
$[Kr]4d^{10}5s^25p^5$

85
At
Astatine
(210)
$[Xe]4f^{14}5d^{10}6s^26p^5$

Atomic radius increases

Ionic radius increases

Ionization energy decreases

Electronegativity decreases

Halogen Family

Characteristics

- are all nonmetals and occur in combined form in nature, mainly as metal halides
- are found in the rocks of Earth's crust and dissolved in sea water
- range from fluorine, the 13th most abundant element, to astatine, which is one of the rarest elements
- exist at room temperature as a gas (F_2 and Cl_2), a liquid (Br_2), and a solid (I_2 and At)
- consist of atoms that have seven electrons in their outermost energy level
- tend to gain one electron to form a halide, X^- ion, but also share electrons and have positive oxidation states
- are reactive, with fluorine being the most reactive of all nonmetals

▲ Halogens are the only family that contains elements representing all three states of matter at room temperature. Chlorine is a yellowish green gas; bromine is a reddish brown liquid; and iodine is a purple-black solid.

▲ Iodine sublimes to produce a violet vapor that recrystallizes on the bottom of the flask filled with ice.

Common Reactions*

With Metals to Form Halides

Example: $Mg(s) + Cl_2(g) \longrightarrow MgCl_2(s)$
Example: $Sn(s) + 2F_2(g) \longrightarrow SnF4(s)$
The halide formula depends on the oxidation state of the metal.

With Hydrogen to Form Hydrogen Halides

Example: $H_2(g) + F_2(g) \longrightarrow 2HF(g)$
Cl_2, Br_2, and I_2 also follow this pattern.

With Nonmetals and Metalloids to Form Halides

Example: $Si(s) + 2Cl_2(g) \longrightarrow SiCl_4(s)$
Example: $N_2(g) + 3F_2(g) \longrightarrow 2NF_3(g)$
Example: $P_4(s) + 6Br_2(l) \longrightarrow 4PBr_3(s)$
The formula of the halide depends on the oxidation state of the metalloid or nonmetal.

With Other Halogens to Form Interhalogen Compounds

Example: $Br_2(l) + 3F_2(g) \longrightarrow 2BrF_3(l)$

* Chemists assume that astatine undergoes similar reactions, but few chemical tests have been made.

▲ Chlorine combines readily with iron wool, which ignites in chlorine gas to form $FeCl_3$.

▲ Hydrofluoric acid is used to etch patterns into glass.

▲ Shown here from left to right are precipitates of AgCl, AgBr, and AgI.

Analytical Test

As with most elements, the presence of each of the halogens can be determined by atomic absorption spectroscopy. Fluorides react with concentrated sulfuric acid, H_2SO_4, to release hydrogen fluoride gas. Three of the halide ions can be identified in solution by their reactions with silver nitrate.

$$Cl^-(aq) + Ag^+(aq) \longrightarrow AgCl(s)$$
$$Br^-(aq) + Ag^+(aq) \longrightarrow AgBr(s)$$
$$I^-(aq) + Ag^+(aq) \longrightarrow AgI(s)$$

Properties

GROUP 17 ELEMENTS					
	F	Cl	Br	I	At
Melting point (°C)	−219.62	−100.98	−7.2	113.5	302
Boiling point (°C)	−188.14	−34.6	58.78	184.35	337
Density (g/cm^3)	1.69×10^{-3}	3.214×10^{-3}	3.119	4.93	not known
Ionization energy (kJ/mol)	1681	1251	1140	1008	—
Atomic radius (pm)	72	100	114	133	140
Ionic radius (pm)	133	181	196	220	—
Common oxidation number in compounds	−1	−1, +1, +3, +5, +7	−1, +1, +3, +5, +7	−1, +1, +3, +5, +7	−1, +5
Crystal structure	cubic	orthorhombic	orthorhombic	orthorhombic	not known

S.T.E.M.

Application *The Environment*

Chlorine in Water Treatment

For more than a century, communities have treated their water to prevent disease. A treatment process widely used in the United States is chlorination. All halogens kill bacteria and other microorganisms. Chlorine, however, is the only halogen acceptable for large-scale treatment of public water supplies.

When chlorine is added to water, the following reaction produces HCl and hypochlorous acid, HOCl:

$$Cl_2(g) + H_2O(l) \longrightarrow HCl(aq) + HOCl(aq)$$

Hypochlorous acid is a weak acid that ionizes to give hydrogen ions and hypochlorite ions, OCl^-.

$$HOCl(aq) + H_2O(l) \longrightarrow H_3O^+(aq) + OCl^-(aq)$$

▲ Swimming pools are routinely tested to be sure the chlorine level is safe.

▲ The "chlorine" used in swimming pools is really one of these compounds and not pure chlorine.

The OCl^- ions are strong oxidizing agents that can destroy microorganisms.

In some water-treatment plants, calcium hypochlorite, $Ca(ClO)_2$, a salt of hypochlorous acid, is added to water to provide OCl^- ions. Similar treatments are used in swimming pools.

Nearly a hundred cities in the United States and thousands of communities in Europe use chlorine in the form of chlorine dioxide, ClO_2, as their primary means of disinfecting water. The main drawback to the use of ClO_2 is that it is unstable and cannot be stored. Instead, ClO_2 must be prepared on location by one of the following reactions involving sodium chlorite, $NaClO_2$.

$$10NaClO_2(aq) + 5H_2SO_4(aq) \longrightarrow 8ClO_2(g) + 5Na_2SO_4(aq) + 2HCl(aq) + 4H_2O(l)$$

$$2NaClO_2(aq) + Cl_2(g) \longrightarrow 2ClO_2(g) + 2NaCl(aq)$$

The expense of using ClO_2 makes it less desirable than Cl_2 in water-treatment systems unless there are other considerations. For example, the use of ClO_2 is likely to result in purified water with less of the aftertaste and odor associated with water purified by Cl_2.

Fluoride and Tooth Decay

In the 1940s, scientists noticed that people living in communities that have natural water supplies with high concentrations of fluoride ions, F^-, have significantly lower rates of dental caries (tooth decay) than most of the population.

In June 1944, a study on the effects of water fluoridation began in two Michigan cities, Muskegon and Grand Rapids, where the natural level of fluoride in drinking water was low (about 0.05 ppm). In Grand Rapids, sodium fluoride, NaF, was added to the drinking water to raise levels to 1.0 ppm. In Muskegon, no fluoride was added.

Also included in the study was Aurora, Illinois, a city that was similar to Grand Rapids and Muskegon, except that it had a natural F^- concentration of 1.2 ppm in the water supply. After 10 years, the rate of tooth decay in Grand Rapids had dropped far below that in Muskegon and was about the same as it was in Aurora.

Tooth enamel is a strong, rocklike material consisting mostly of calcium hydroxyphosphate, $Ca_5(PO_4)_3(OH)$, also known as apatite. Apatite is an insoluble and very hard compound—ideal for tooth enamel. Sometimes, however, saliva becomes more acidic, particularly after a person eats a high-sugar meal. Acids ionize to produce hydronium ions, which react with the hydroxide ion, OH^-, in the apatite to form water. The loss of OH^- causes the apatite to dissolve.

$$Ca_5(PO_4)_3(OH)(s) + H_3O^+(aq) \longrightarrow 5Ca^{2+}(aq) + 3PO_4^{3-}(aq) + 2H_2O(l)$$

Saliva supplies more OH^- ions, and new apatite is formed, but slowly.

If fluoride ions are present in saliva, some fluorapatite, $Ca_5(PO_4)_3F$, also forms.

$$5Ca^{2+}(aq) + 3PO_4^{3-}(aq) + F^-(aq) \longrightarrow Ca_5(PO_4)_3F(s)$$

Fluorapatite resists attack by acids, so the tooth enamel resists decay better than enamel containing no fluoride.

When the beneficial effect of fluoride had been established, public health authorities proposed that fluoride compounds be added to water supplies in low-fluoride communities. Fluoridation started in the 1950s, and by 1965, nearly every medical and dental association in the United States had endorsed fluoridation of water supplies. In the past decade, however, that trend slowed as opposition to fluoridation grew.

APPENDIX B

Reference Tables

TABLE B-1

SI MEASUREMENT

Metric Prefixes		
Prefix	**Symbol**	**Factor of Base Unit**
giga	G	1 000 000 000
mega	M	1 000 000
kilo	k	1 000
hecto	h	100
deka	da	10
deci	d	0.1
centi	c	0.01
milli	m	0.001
micro	μ	0.000 001
nano	n	0.000 000 001
pico	p	0.000 000 000 001

Mass	
1 kilogram (kg)	= SI base unit of mass
1 gram (g)	= 0.001 kg
1 milligram (mg)	= 0.000 001 kg
1 microgram (μg)	= 0.000 000 001 kg

Length	
1 kilometer (km)	= 1 000 m
1 meter (m)	= SI base unit of length
1 centimeter (cm)	= 0.01 m
1 millimeter (mm)	= 0.001 m
1 micrometer (μm)	= 0.000 001 m
1 nanometer (nm)	= 0.000 000 001 m
1 picometer (pm)	= 0.000 000 000 001 m

Area	
1 square kilometer (km^2)	= 100 hectares (ha)
1 hectare (ha)	= 10 000 square meters (m^2)
1 square meter (m^2)	= 10 000 square centimeters (cm^2)
1 square centimeter (cm^2)	= 100 square millimeters (mm^2)

Volume	
1 liter (L)	= common unit for liquid volume (not SI)
1 cubic meter (m^3)	= 1000 L
1 kiloliter (kL)	= 1000 L
1 milliliter (mL)	= 0.001 L
1 milliliter (mL)	= 1 cubic centimeter (cm^3)

TABLE B-2

UNIT SYMBOLS

atm	= atmosphere (pressure, non-SI)
Bq	= becquerel (nuclear activity)
°C	= degree Celsius (temperature)
J	= joule (energy)
K	= kelvin (temperature, thermodynamic)
mol	= mole (quantity)
M	= molarity (concentration)
N	= newton (force)
Pa	= pascal (pressure)
s	= second (time)
u	= unified atomic mass unit (mass)
V	= volt (electric potential difference)

TABLE B-3

SYMBOLS

Symbol	Meaning
α	= helium nucleus (also $^{4}_{2}He$) emission from radioactive materials
β	= electron (also $^{0}_{-1}e$) emission from radioactive materials
γ	= high-energy photon emission from radioactive materials
Δ	= change in a given quantity (e.g., ΔH for change in enthalpy)
c	= speed of light in vacuum
c_p	= specific heat capacity (at constant pressure)
D	= density
E_a	= activation energy
E^0	= standard electrode potential
E^0 cell	= standard potential of an electrochemical cell
G	= Gibbs free energy
ΔG^0	= standard free energy of reaction
ΔG^0_f	= standard molar free energy of formation
H	= enthalpy
ΔH^0	= standard enthalpy of reaction
ΔH^0_f	= standard molar enthalpy of formation
K_a	= ionization constant (acid)
K_b	= dissociation constant (base)
K_{eq}	= equilibrium constant
K_{sp}	= solubility-product constant
KE	= kinetic energy
m	= mass
N_A	= Avogadro's number
n	= number of moles
p	= pressure
pH	= measure of acidity ($-\log[H_3O^+]$)
R	= ideal gas law constant
S	= entropy
S^0	= standard molar entropy
T	= temperature (thermodynamic, in kelvins)
t	= temperature (± degrees Celslus)
V	= volume
v	= velocity

TABLE B-4

PHYSICAL CONSTANTS

Quantity	Symbol	Value
Unified atomic mass unit	u	$1.660\ 5402(10) \times 10^{-27}$kg
Avogadro's number	N_A	$6.022\ 142 \times 10^{23}$/mol
Electron rest mass	m_e	$9.109\ 3826 \times 10^{-31}$ kg; 5.4858×10^{-4} u
Ideal gas law constant	R	8.314 L • kPa/(mol • K); 0.0821 L • atm/(mol • K)
Molar volume of ideal gas at STP	V_M	22.414 10 L/mol
Neutron rest mass	m_n	$1.674\ 9273 \times 10^{-27}$ kg; 1.008 665 u
Normal boiling point of water	T_b	373.15 K = 100.0°C
Normal freezing point of water	T_f	273.15 K = 0.00°C
Planck's constant	h	$6.626\ 069 \times 10^{-34}$ J • s
Proton rest mass	m_p	$1.672\ 6217 \times 10^{-27}$ kg; 1.007 276 u
Speed of light in a vacuum	c	$2.997\ 924\ 58 \times 10^{8}$ m/s
Temperature of triple point of water	*(none)*	273.16 K = 0.01°C

TABLE B-5

ENTHALPY OF COMBUSTION

Substance	Formula	State	ΔH_c	Substance	Formula	State	ΔH_c
hydrogen	H_2	*g*	–285.8	**benzene**	C_6H_6	*l*	–3267.6
graphite	C	*s*	–393.5	**toluene**	C_7H_8	*l*	–3910.3
carbon monoxide	CO	*g*	–283.0	**naphthalene**	$C_{10}H_8$	*s*	–5156.3
methane	CH_4	*g*	–890.8	**anthracene**	$C_{14}H_{10}$	*s*	–7163.0
ethane	C_2H_6	*g*	–1560.7	**methanol**	CH_3OH	*l*	–726.1
propane	C_3H_8	*g*	–2219.2	**ethanol**	C_2H_5OH	*l*	–1366.8
butane	C_4H_{10}	*g*	–2877.6	**ether**	$(C_2H_5)_2O$	*l*	–2751.1
pentane	C_5H_{12}	*g*	–3535.6	**formaldehyde**	CH_2O	*g*	–570.7
hexane	C_6H_{14}	*l*	–4163.2	**glucose**	$C_6H_{12}O_6$	*s*	–2803.0
heptane	C_7H_{16}	*l*	–4817.0	**sucrose**	$C_{12}H_{22}O_{11}$	*s*	–5640.9
octane	C_8H_{18}	*l*	–5470.5				
ethene (ethylene)	C_2H_4	*g*	–1411.2				
propene (propylene)	C_3H_6	*g*	–2058.0				
ethyne (acetylene)	C_2H_2	*g*	–1301.1				

ΔH_c = enthalpy of combustion of the given substance. All values of ΔH_c are expressed as kJ/mol of substance oxidized to $H_2O(l)$ and/or $CO_2(g)$ at constant pressure and 25°C.
s = solid, *l* = liquid, *g* = gas

TABLE B-6

THE ELEMENTS: SYMBOLS, ATOMIC NUMBERS, AND ATOMIC MASSES

Name of element	Symbol	Atomic number	Atomic masses	Name of element	Symbol	Atomic number	Atomic masses
actinium	Ac	89	[227]	**copernicium**	Cn	112	[285]
aluminum	Al	13	26.981 5386	**copper**	Cu	29	63.546
americium	Am	95	[243]	**curium**	Cm	96	[247]
antimony	Sb	51	121.760	**darmstadtium**	Ds	110	[271]
argon	Ar	18	39.948	**dubnium**	Db	105	[262]
arsenic	As	33	74.921 60	**dysprosium**	Dy	66	162.500
astatine	At	85	[210]	**einsteinium**	Es	99	[252]
barium	Ba	56	137.327	**erbium**	Er	68	167.259
berkelium	Bk	97	[247]	**europium**	Eu	63	151.964
beryllium	Be	4	9.012 182	**fermium**	Fm	100	[257]
bismuth	Bi	83	208.980 40	**fluorine**	F	9	18.998 4032
bohrium	Bh	107	[264]	**francium**	Fr	87	[223]
boron	B	5	***10.81***	**gadolinium**	Gd	64	157.25
bromine	Br	35	79.904	**gallium**	Ga	31	69.723
cadmium	Cd	48	112.411	**germanium**	Ge	32	72.63
calcium	Ca	20	40.078	**gold**	Au	79	196.966 569
californium	Cf	98	[251]	**hafnium**	Hf	72	178.49
carbon	C	6	***12.01 1***	**hassium**	Hs	108	[277]
cerium	Ce	58	140.116	**helium**	He	2	4.002 60
cesium	Cs	55	132.905 4519	**holmium**	Ho	67	164.930 32
chlorine	Cl	17	***35.45***	**hydrogen**	H	1	***1.008***
chromium	Cr	24	51.9961	**indium**	In	49	114.818
cobalt	Co	27	58.933 195	**iodine**	I	53	126.904 47

TABLE B-6

THE ELEMENTS — *CONTINUED*

Name of element	Symbol	Atomic number	Atomic masses
iridium	Ir	77	192.217
iron	Fe	26	55.845
krypton	Kr	36	83.798
lanthanum	La	57	138.905 47
lawrencium	Lr	103	[262]
lead	Pb	82	207.2
lithium	Li	3	***6.94***
lutetium	Lu	71	174.967
magnesium	Mg	12	24.3050
manganese	Mn	25	54.938 045
meitnerium	Mt	109	[268]
mendelevium	Md	101	[258]
mercury	Hg	80	200.59
molybdenum	Mo	42	95.94
neodymium	Nd	60	144.242
neon	Ne	10	20.1797
neptunium	Np	93	[237]
nickel	Ni	28	58.6934
niobium	Nb	41	92.906 38
nitrogen	N	7	***14.007***
nobelium	No	102	[259]
osmium	Os	76	190.23
oxygen	O	8	***15.999***
palladium	Pd	46	106.42
phosphorus	P	15	30.973 762
platinum	Pt	78	195.084
plutonium	Pu	94	[244]
polonium	Po	84	[209]
potassium	K	19	39.0983
praseodymium	Pr	59	140.907 65
promethium	Pm	61	[145]
protactinium	Pa	91	231.035 88
radium	Ra	88	[226]
radon	Rn	86	[222]
rhenium	Re	75	186.207

Name of element	Symbol	Atomic number	Atomic masses
rhodium	Rh	45	102.905 50
roentgenium	Rg	111	[272]
rubidium	Rb	37	85.4678
ruthenium	Ru	44	101.07
rutherfordium	Rf	104	[261]
samarium	Sm	62	150.36
scandium	Sc	21	44.955 912
seaborgium	Sg	106	[266]
selenium	Se	34	78.96
silicon	Si	14	***28.085***
silver	Ag	47	107.8682
sodium	Na	11	22.989 769 28
strontium	Sr	38	87.62
sulfur	S	16	***32.06***
tantalum	Ta	73	180.947 88
technetium	Tc	43	[98]
tellurium	Te	52	127.60
terbium	Tb	65	158.925 35
thallium	Tl	81	***204.38***
thorium	Th	90	232.038 06
thulium	Tm	69	168.934 21
tin	Sn	50	118.710
titanium	Ti	22	47.867
tungsten	W	74	183.84
uranium	U	92	238.028 91
vanadium	V	23	50.9415
xenon	Xe	54	131.293
ytterbium	Yb	70	173.04
yttrium	Y	39	88.905 85
zinc	Zn	30	65.409
zirconium	Zr	40	91.224

Values in brackets denote the mass number of the most stable or common isotope. These atomic masses are believed to have an error no greater than ±1 in the last digit given. Atomic masses that are bold and italicized are considered representative of the range of masses found in nature for that element.

TABLE B-7

COMMON IONS

Cation	Symbol	Anion	Symbol
aluminum	Al^{3+}	acetate	CH_3COO^-
ammonium	NH_4^+	bromide	Br^-
arsenic(III)	As^{3+}	carbonate	CO_3^{2-}
barium	Ba^{2+}	chlorate	ClO_3^-
calcium	Ca^{2+}	chloride	Cl^-
chromium(II)	Cr^{2+}	chlorite	ClO_2^-
chromium(III)	Cr^{3+}	chromate	CrO_4^{2-}
cobalt(II)	Co^{2+}	cyanide	CN^-
cobalt(III)	Co^{3+}	dichromate	$Cr_2O_7^{2-}$
copper(I)	Cu^+	fluoride	F^-
copper(II)	Cu^{2+}	hexacyanoferrate(II)	$Fe(CN)_6^{4-}$
hydronium	H_3O^+	hexacyanoferrate(III)	$Fe(CN)_6^{3-}$
iron(II)	Fe^{2+}	hydride	H^-
iron(III)	Fe^{3+}	hydrogen carbonate	HCO_3^-
lead(II)	Pb^{2+}	hydrogen sulfate	HSO_4^-
magnesium	Mg^{2+}	hydroxide	OH^-
mercury(I)	Hg_2^{2+}	hypochlorite	ClO^-
mercury(II)	Hg^{2+}	iodide	I^-
nickel(II)	Ni^{2+}	nitrate	NO_3^-
potassium	K^+	nitrite	NO_2^-
silver	Ag^+	oxide	O^{2-}
sodium	Na^+	perchlorate	ClO_4^-
strontium	Sr^{2+}	permanganate	MnO_4^-
tin(II)	Sn^{2+}	peroxide	O_2^{2-}
tin(IV)	Sn^{4+}	phosphate	PO_4^{3-}
titanium(III)	Ti^{3+}	sulfate	SO_4^{2-}
titanium(IV)	Ti^{4+}	sulfide	S^{2-}
zinc	Zn^{2+}	sulfite	SO_3^{2-}

TABLE B-8

WATER-VAPOR PRESSURE

Temperature (°C)	Pressure (mm Hg)	Pressure (kPa)	Temperature (°C)	Pressure (mm Hg)	Pressure (kPa)
0.0	4.6	0.61	**23.0**	21.1	2.81
5.0	6.5	0.87	**23.5**	21.7	2.90
10.0	9.2	1.23	**24.0**	22.4	2.98
15.0	12.8	1.71	**24.5**	23.1	3.10
15.5	13.2	1.76	**25.0**	23.8	3.17
16.0	13.6	1.82	**26.0**	25.2	3.36
16.5	14.1	1.88	**27.0**	26.7	3.57
17.0	14.5	1.94	**28.0**	28.3	3.78
17.5	15.0	2.00	**29.0**	30.0	4.01
18.0	15.5	2.06	**30.0**	31.8	4.25
18.5	16.0	2.13	**35.0**	42.2	5.63
19.0	16.5	2.19	**40.0**	55.3	7.38
19.5	17.0	2.27	**50.0**	92.5	12.34
20.0	17.5	2.34	**60.0**	149.4	19.93
20.5	18.1	2.41	**70.0**	233.7	31.18
21.0	18.6	2.49	**80.0**	355.1	47.37
21.5	19.2	2.57	**90.0**	525.8	70.12
22.0	19.8	2.64	**95.0**	633.9	84.53
22.5	20.4	2.72	**100.0**	760.0	101.32

TABLE B-9

DENSITIES OF GASES AT STP

Gas	Density (g/L)
air, dry	1.293
ammonia	0.771
carbon dioxide	1.997
carbon monoxide	1.250
chlorine	3.214
dinitrogen monoxide	1.977
ethyne (acetylene)	1.165
helium	0.1785
hydrogen	0.0899
hydrogen chloride	1.639
hydrogen sulfide	1.539
methane	0.7168
nitrogen	1.2506
nitrogen monoxide (at 10°C)	1.340
oxygen	1.429
sulfur dioxide	2.927

TABLE B-10

DENSITY OF WATER

Temperature (°C)	Density (g/cm^3)
0	0.999 84
2	0.999 94
3.98 (maximum)	0.999 973
4	0.999 97
6	0.999 94
8	0.999 85
10	0.999 70
14	0.999 24
16	0.998 94
20	0.998 20
25	0.997 05
30	0.995 65
40	0.992 22
50	0.988 04
60	0.983 20
70	0.977 77
80	0.971 79
90	0.965 31
100	0.958 36

TABLE B-11

SOLUBILITIES OF GASES IN WATER

Volume of gas (in liters) at STP that can be dissolved in 1 L of water at the temperature (°C) indicated.

Gas	0°C	10°C	20°C	60°C
air	0.029 18	0.022 84	0.018 68	0.012 16
ammonia	1130	870	680	200
carbon dioxide	1.713	1.194	0.878	0.359
carbon monoxide	0.035 37	0.028 16	0.023 19	0.014 88
chlorine	—	3.148	2.299	1.023
hydrogen	0.021 48	0.019 55	0.018 19	0.016 00
hydrogen chloride	512	475	442	339
hydrogen sulfide	4.670	3.399	2.582	1.190
methane	0.055 63	0.041 77	0.033 08	0.019 54
nitrogen*	0.023 54	0.018 61	0.015 45	0.010 23
nitrogen monoxide	0.073 81	0.057 09	0.047 06	0.029 54
oxygen	0.048 89	0.038 02	0.031 02	0.019 46
sulfur dioxide	79.789	56.647	39.374	—

*Atmospheric nitrogen–98.815% N_2, 1.185% inert gases

TABLE B-12

SOLUBILITY CHART

	acetate	bromide	carbonate	chlorate	chloride	chromate	hydroxide	iodine	nitrate	oxide	phosphate	silicate	sulfate	sulfide
aluminum	S	S	—	S	S	—	A	S	S	a	A	I	S	d
ammonium	S	S	S	S	S	S	S	S	S	—	S	—	S	S
barium	S	S	P	S	S	A	S	S	S	S	A	S	a	d
calcium	S	S	P	S	S	S	S	S	S	P	P	P	S	S
copper(II)	S	S	—	S	S	—	A	—	S	A	A	A	S	A
hydrogen	S	S	—	S	S	—	—	S	S	S	S	I	S	S
iron(II)	—	S	P	S	S	—	A	S	S	A	A	—	S	A
iron(III)	—	S	—	S	S	A	A	S	S	A	P	—	P	d
lead(II)	S	S	A	S	S	A	P	P	S	P	A	A	P	A
magnesium	S	S	P	S	S	S	A	S	S	A	P	A	S	d
manganese(II)	S	S	P	S	S	—	A	S	S	A	P	I	S	A
mercury(I)	P	A	A	S	a	P	—	A	S	A	A	—	P	I
mercury(II)	S	S	—	S	S	P	A	P	S	P	A	—	d	I
potassium	S	S	S	S	S	S	S	S	S	S	S	S	S	S
silver	P	a	A	S	a	P	—	I	S	P	A	—	P	A
sodium	S	S	S	S	S	S	S	S	S	d	S	S	S	S
strontium	S	S	P	S	S	P	S	S	S	S	A	A	P	S
tin(II)	d	S	—	S	S	A	A	S	d	A	A	—	S	A
tin(IV)	S	S	—	—	S	S	P	d	—	A	—	—	S	A
zinc	S	S	P	S	S	P	A	S	S	P	A	A	S	A

S = soluble in water. A = soluble in acids, insoluble in water. P = partially soluble in water, soluble in dilute acids.
I = insoluble in dilute acids and in water. a = slightly soluble in acids, insoluble in water. d = decomposes in water.

TABLE B-13

SOLUBILITY OF COMPOUNDS

Solubilities are given in grams of solute that can be dissolved in 100 g of water at the temperature (°C) indicated.

Compound	Formula	0°C	20°C	60°C	100°C
aluminum sulfate	$Al_2(SO_4)_3$	31.2	36.4	59.2	89.0
ammonium chloride	NH_4Cl	29.4	37.2	55.3	77.3
ammonium nitrate	NH_4NO_3	118	192	421	871
ammonium sulfate	$(NH_4)_2SO_4$	70.6	75.4	88	103
barium carbonate	$BaCO_3$	—*	$0.0022^{18°}$	—*	0.0065
barium chloride dihydrate	$BaCl_2 \bullet 2H_2O$	31.2	35.8	46.2	59.4
barium hydroxide	$Ba(OH)_2$	1.67	3.89	20.94	$101.40^{80°}$
barium nitrate	$Ba(NO_3)_2$	4.95	9.02	20.4	34.4
barium sulfate	$BaSO_4$	—*	$0.000\,246^{25°}$	—*	0.000 413
calcium carbonate	$CaCO_3$	—*	$0.0014^{25°}$	—*	$0.0018^{75°}$
calcium fluoride	CaF_2	$0.0016^{18°}$	$0.0017^{26°}$	—*	—*
calcium hydrogen carbonate	$Ca(HCO_3)_2$	16.15	16.60	17.50	18.40
calcium hydroxide	$Ca(OH)_2$	0.189	0.173	0.121	0.076
calcium sulfate	$CaSO_4$	—*	$0.209^{30°}$	—*	0.1619
copper(II) chloride	$CuCl_2$	68.6	73.0	96.5	120
copper(II) sulfate pentahydrate	$CuSO_4 \bullet 5H_2O$	23.1	32.0	61.8	114
lead(II) chloride	$PbCl_2$	0.67	1.00	1.94	3.20
lead(II) nitrate	$Pb(NO_3)_2$	37.5	54.3	91.6	133.
lithium chloride	$LiCl$	69.2	83.5	98.4	128.
lithium sulfate	Li_2SO_4	36.1	34.8	32.6	$30.9^{90°}$
magnesium hydroxide	$Mg(OH)_2$	—*	$0.0009^{18°}$	—*	0.004
magnesium sulfate	$MgSO_4$	22.0	33.7	54.6	68.3
mercury(I) chloride	Hg_2Cl_2	—*	$0.000\,20^{25°}$	$0.001^{43°}$	—*
mercury(II) chloride	$HgCl_2$	3.63	6.57	16.3	61.3
potassium bromide	KBr	53.6	65.3	85.5	104
potassium chlorate	$KClO_3$	3.3	7.3	23.8	56.3
potassium chloride	KCl	28.0	34.2	45.8	56.3
potassium chromate	K_2CrO_4	56.3	63.7	70.1	$74.5^{90°}$
potassium iodide	KI	128	144	176	206
potassium nitrate	KNO_3	13.9	31.6	106	245
potassium permanganate	$KMnO_4$	2.83	6.34	22.1	—*
potassium sulfate	K_2SO_4	7.4	11.1	18.2	24.1
silver acetate	$AgC_2H_3O_2$	0.73	1.05	1.93	$2.59^{80°}$
silver chloride	$AgCl$	$0.000\,089^{10°}$	—*	—*	0.0021
silver nitrate	$AgNO_3$	122	216	440	733
sodium acetate	$NaC_2H_3O_2$	36.2	46.4	139	170
sodium chlorate	$NaClO_3$	79.6	95.9	137.	204.
sodium chloride	$NaCl$	35.7	35.9	37.1	39.2
sodium nitrate	$NaNO_3$	73.0	87.6	122	180
sucrose	$C_{12}H_{22}O_{11}$	179.2	203.9	287.3	487.2

*Dashes indicate that values are not available.

TABLE B-14

ENTHALPY OF FORMATION

Substance	State	ΔH_f
ammonia	*g*	−45.9
ammonium chloride	*s*	−314.4
ammonium sulfate	*s*	−1180.9
barium chloride	*s*	−858.6
barium nitrate	*s*	−768.2
barium sulfate	*s*	−1473.2
benzene	*g*	+82.88
benzene	*l*	+49.080
calcium carbonate	*s*	−1207.6
calcium chloride	*s*	−795.4
calcium hydroxide	*s*	−983.2
calcium nitrate	*s*	−938.2
calcium oxide	*s*	−634.9
calcium sulfate	*s*	−1434.5
carbon (diamond)	*s*	+1.9
carbon (graphite)	*s*	0.00
carbon dioxide	*g*	−393.5
carbon monoxide	*g*	−110.5
copper(II) nitrate	*s*	−302.9
copper(II) oxide	*s*	−157.3
copper(II) sulfate	*s*	−771.4
ethane	*g*	−83.8
ethyne (acetylene)	*g*	+228.2
hydrogen (H_2)	*g*	0.00
hydrogen bromide	*g*	−36.29
hydrogen chloride	*g*	−92.3
hydrogen fluoride	*g*	−273.3
hydrogen iodide	*g*	+26.5
hydrogen oxide (water)	*g*	−241.8
hydrogen oxide (water)	*l*	−285.8
hydrogen peroxide	*g*	−136.3
hydrogen peroxide	*l*	−187.8
hydrogen sulfide	*g*	−20.6
iodine (I_2)	*s*	0.00
iodine (I_2)	*g*	+62.4
iron(II) chloride	*s*	−399.4
iron(II) oxide	*s*	−272.0
iron(III) oxide	*s*	−824.2
iron(II) sulfate	*s*	−928.4
iron(II) sulfide	*s*	−100.0
lead(II) oxide	*s*	−217.3

Substance	State	ΔH_f
lead(IV) oxide	*s*	−274.5
lead(II) nitrate	*s*	−451.9
lead(II) sulfate	*s*	−919.94
lithium chloride	*s*	−408.6
lithium nitrate	*s*	−483.1
magnesium chloride	*s*	−641.5
magnesium oxide	*s*	−601.6
magnesium sulfate	*s*	−1261.79
manganese(IV) oxide	*s*	−520.0
manganese(II) sulfate	*s*	−1065.3
mercury(I) chloride	*s*	−264.2
mercury(II) chloride	*s*	−230.0
mercury(II) oxide (red)	*s*	−90.8
methane	*g*	−74.9
nitrogen dioxide	*g*	+33.2
nitrogen monoxide	*g*	+90.29
dinitrogen monoxide	*g*	+82.1
dinitrogen tetroxide	*g*	+9.2
oxygen (O_2)	*g*	0.00
ozone (O_3)	*g*	+142.7
tetraphosphorus decoxide	*s*	−3009.9
potassium bromide	*s*	−393.8
potassium chloride	*s*	−436.49
potassium hydroxide	*s*	−424.58
potassium nitrate	*s*	−494.6
potassium sulfate	*s*	−1437.8
silicon dioxide (quartz)	*s*	−910.7
silver chloride	*s*	−127.01 ± 0.5
silver nitrate	*s*	−120.5
silver sulfide	*s*	−32.59
sodium bromide	*s*	−361.8
sodium chloride	*s*	−385.9
sodium hydroxide	*s*	−425.9
sodium nitrate	*s*	−467.9
sodium sulfate	*l*	−1387.1
sulfur dioxide	*g*	−296.8
sulfur trioxide	*g*	−395.7
tin(IV) chloride	*l*	−511.3
zinc nitrate	*s*	−483.7
zinc oxide	*s*	−350.5
zinc sulfate	*s*	−980.14

ΔH_f is enthalpy of formation of the given substance from its elements. All values of ΔH_f are expressed as kJ/mol at 25°C. Negative values of ΔH_f indicate exothermic reactions. *s* = solid, *l* = liquid, *g* = gas

TABLE B-15

PROPERTIES OF COMMON ELEMENTS

Name	Form/color at room temperature	Density (g/cm^3)†	Melting point (°C)	Boiling point (°C)	Common oxidation states
aluminum	silver metal	2.702	660.37	2467	3+
arsenic	gray metalloid	5.727^{14}	817 (28 atm)	613 *(sublimes)*	3–, 3+, 5+
barium	bluish white metal	3.51	725	1640	2+
bromine	red-brown liquid	3.119	–7.2	58.78	1–, 1+, 3+, 5+, 7+
calcium	silver metal	1.54	839 ± 2	1484	2+
carbon	diamond graphite	3.51 2.25	3500 (63.5 atm) 3652 *(sublimes)*	3930 —	2+, 4+
chlorine	green-yellow gas	3.214*	–100.98	–34.6	1–, 1+, 3+, 5+, 7+
chromium	gray metal	7.2028	1857 ± 20	2672	2+, 3+, 6+
cobalt	gray metal	8.9	1495	2870	2+, 3+
copper	red metal	8.92	1083.4 ± 0.2	2567	1+, 2+
fluorine	yellow gas	1.69‡	–219.62	–188.14	1–
germanium	gray metalloid	5.323^{25}	937.4	2830	4+
gold	yellow metal	19.31	1064.43	2808 ± 2	1+, 3+
helium	colorless gas	0.1785*	–272.2 (26 atm)	–268.9	0
hydrogen	colorless gas	0.0899*	–259.14	–252.8	1–, 1+
iodine	blue-black solid	4.93	113.5	184.35	1–, 1+, 3+, 5+, 7+
iron	silver metal	7.86	1535	2750	2+, 3+
lead	bluish white metal	11.343716	327.502	1740	2+, 4+
lithium	silver metal	0.534	180.54	1342	1+
magnesium	silver metal	1.745	648.8	1107	2+
manganese	gray-white metal	7.20	1244 ± 3	1962	2+, 3+, 4+, 6+, 7+
mercury	silver liquid metal	13.5462	–38.87	356.58	1+, 2+
neon	colorless gas	0.9002*	+248.67	–245.9	0
nickel	silver metal	8.90	1455	2732	2+, 3+
nitrogen	colorless gas	1.2506*	–209.86	–195.8	3–, 3+, 5+
oxygen	colorless gas	1.429*	–218.4	–182.962	2–
phosphorus	yellow solid	1.82	44.1	280	3–, 3+, 5+
platinum	silver metal	21.45	1772	3827 ± 100	2+, 4+
potassium	silver metal	0.86	63.25	760	1+
silicon	gray metalloid	2.33 ± 0.01	1410	2355	2+, 4+
silver	white metal	10.5	961.93	2212	1+
sodium	silver metal	0.97	97.8	882.9	1+
strontium	silver metal	2.6	769	1384	2+
sulfur	yellow solid	1.96	119.0	444.674	2–, 4+, 6+
tin	white metal	7.28	231.88	2260	2+, 4+
titanium	white metal	4.5	1660 ± 10	3287	2+, 3+, 4+
uranium	silver metal	19.05 ± 0.02^{25}	1132.3 ± 0.8	3818	3+, 4+, 6+
zinc	blue-white metal	7.14	419.58	907	2+

† Densities obtained at 20°C unless otherwise noted (superscript)
‡ Density of fluorine given in g/L at 1 atm and 15°C
* Densities of gases given in g/L at STP

APPENDIX C

Math Skills Handbook and Chemistry Equations

Scientific Notation

Positive exponents Many quantities that scientists deal with often have very large or very small values. For example, the speed of light is about 300 000 000 m/s, and the ink required to make the dot over an *i* in this textbook has a mass of about 0.000 000 001 kg. Obviously, it is cumbersome to work with numbers such as these. We avoid this problem by using a method based on powers of the number 10.

$$10^0 = 1$$

$$10^1 = 10$$

$$10^2 = 10 \times 10 = 100$$

$$10^3 = 10 \times 10 \times 10 = 1000$$

$$10^4 = 10 \times 10 \times 10 \times 10 = 10\,000$$

$$10^5 = 10 \times 10 \times 10 \times 10 \times 10 = 100\,000$$

The number of zeros determines the power to which 10 is raised, or the *exponent* of 10. For example, the speed of light, 300 000 000 m/s, can be expressed as 3×10^8 m/s. In this case, the exponent of 10 is 8.

Negative exponents For numbers less than one, we note the following:

$$10^{-1} = \frac{1}{10} = 0.1$$

$$10^{-2} = \frac{1}{10 \times 10} = 0.01$$

$$10^{-3} = \frac{1}{10 \times 10 \times 10} = 0.001$$

$$10^{-4} = \frac{1}{10 \times 10 \times 10 \times 10} = 0.0001$$

$$10^{-5} = \frac{1}{10 \times 10 \times 10 \times 10 \times 10} = 0.000\,01$$

The value of the negative exponent equals the number of places the decimal point must be moved to be to the right of the first nonzero digit (in these cases, the digit 1). Numbers that are expressed as a number between 1 and 10 multiplied by a power of 10 are said to be in *scientific notation*. For example, 5 943 000 000 is 5.943×10^9 when expressed in scientific notation, and 0.000 083 2 is 8.32×10^{-5} when expressed in scientific notation.

Multiplication and division in scientific notation When numbers expressed in scientific notation are being multiplied, the following general rule is very useful:

$$10^n \times 10^m = 10^{(n+m)}$$

Note that n and m can be any numbers; they are not necessarily integers. For example, $10^2 \times 10^5 = 10^7$, and $10^{1/4} \times 10^{1/2} = 10^{3/4}$. The rule also applies to negative exponents. For example, $10^3 \times 10^{-8} = 10^{-5}$. When dividing numbers expressed in scientific notation, note the following:

$$\frac{10^n}{10^m} = 10^n \times 10^{-m} = 10^{(n-m)}$$

For example, $\frac{10^3}{10^2} = 10^{(3-2)} = 10^1$.

Fractions

The rules for multiplying, dividing, adding, and subtracting fractions are summarized in **Table C-1,** where a, b, c, and d are four numbers.

TABLE C-1

BASIC OPERATIONS FOR FRACTIONS

Operation	Rule	Example
Multiplication	$\left(\frac{a}{b}\right)\left(\frac{c}{d}\right) = \frac{ac}{bd}$	$\left(\frac{2}{3}\right)\left(\frac{4}{5}\right) = \frac{(2)(4)}{(3)(5)} = \frac{8}{15}$
Division	$\frac{\left(\frac{a}{b}\right)}{\left(\frac{c}{d}\right)} = \frac{ad}{bc}$	$\frac{\left(\frac{2}{3}\right)}{\left(\frac{4}{5}\right)} = \frac{(2)(5)}{(3)(4)} = \frac{10}{12} = \frac{5}{6}$
Addition and Subtraction	$\frac{a}{b} \pm \frac{c}{d} = \frac{ad \pm bc}{bd}$	$\frac{2}{3} - \frac{4}{5} = \frac{(2)(5) - (3)(4)}{(3)(5)} = -\frac{2}{15}$

Powers

Rules of exponents When powers of a given quantity, x, are multiplied, the rule used for scientific notation applies:

$$(x^n)(x^m) = x^{(n+m)}$$

For example, $(x^2)(x^4) = x^{(2+4)} = x^6$.

When dividing the powers of a given quantity, note the following:

$$\frac{x^n}{x^m} = x^{(n-m)}$$

For example, $\frac{x^8}{x^2} = x^{(8-2)} = x^6$.

A power that is a fraction, such as $\frac{1}{3}$, corresponds to a root as follows:

$$x^{1/n} = \sqrt[n]{x}$$

For example, $4^{1/3} = \sqrt[3]{4} = 1.5874$. (A scientific calculator is useful for such calculations.)

Finally, any quantity, x^n, that is raised to the mth power is as follows:

$$(x^n)^m = x^{nm}$$

For example, $(x^2)^3 = x^{(2)(3)} = x^6$.

The basic rules of exponents are summarized in **Table C-2.**

TABLE C-2

RULES OF EXPONENTS

$x^0 = 1$	$x^1 = x$	$(x^n)(x^m) = x^{(n+m)}$
$\frac{x^n}{x^m} = x^{(n-m)}$	$x^{(1/n)} = \sqrt[n]{x}$	$(x^n)^m = x^{(nm)}$

Algebra

Solving for unknowns When algebraic operations are performed, the laws of arithmetic apply. Symbols such as x, y, and z are usually used to represent quantities that are not specified. Such unspecified quantities are called *unknowns*.

First, consider the following equation:

$$8x = 32$$

If we wish to solve for x, we can divide each side of the equation by the same factor without disturbing the equality. In this case, if we divide both sides by 8, we have the following:

$$\frac{8x}{8} = \frac{32}{8}$$

$$x = 4$$

Next, consider the following equation:

$$x + 2 = 8$$

In this type of expression, we can add or subtract the same quantity from each side. If we subtract 2 from each side, we get the following:

$$x + 2 - 2 = 8 - 2$$

$$x = 6$$

In general, if $x + a = b$, then $x = b - a$.

Now, consider the following equation:

$$\frac{x}{5} = 9$$

If we multiply each side by 5, we are left with x isolated on the left and a value of 45 on the right.

$$(5)\left(\frac{x}{5}\right) = (9)(5)$$

$$x = 45$$

In all cases, *whatever operation is performed on the left side of the equation must also be performed on the right side.*

Factoring

Some useful formulas for factoring an equation are given in **Table C-3**. As an example of a common factor, consider the equation $5x + 5y + 5z = 0$. This equation can be expressed as $5(x + y + z) = 0$. The expression $a^2 + 2ab + b^2$, which is an example of a perfect square, is equivalent to the expression $(a + b)^2$. For example, if $a = 2$ and $b = 3$, then $2^2 + (2)(2)(3) + 3^2 = (2 + 3)^2$, or $(4 + 12 + 9) = 5^2 = 25$. Finally, for an example of the difference of two squares, let $a = 6$ and $b = 3$. In this case, $(6^2 - 3^2) = (6 + 3)(6 - 3)$, or $(36 - 9) = (9)(3) = 27$.

TABLE C-3

FACTORING EQUATIONS	
$ax + ay + az = a(x + y + z)$	common factor
$a^2 + 2ab + b^2 = (a + b)^2$	perfect square
$a^2 - b^2 = (a + b)(a - b)$	difference of two squares

Quadratic Equations

The general form of a quadratic equation is as follows:

$$ax^2 + bx + c = 0$$

In this equation, x is the unknown quantity and a, b, and c are numerical factors known as *coefficients*. This equation has two roots, given by the following:

$$x = \frac{-b \pm \sqrt{b^2 - 4ac}}{2a}$$

If $b^2 \geq 4ac$, the value inside the square-root symbol will be positive or zero and the roots will be real. If $b^2 < 4ac$, the value inside the square-root symbol will be negative and the roots will be imaginary numbers. In chemistry, equilibrium calculations may result in a quadratic equation that needs to be solved.

Example

Find the solutions for the equation $x^2 + 5x + 4 = 0$.

SOLUTION

The given equation can be expressed as $(1)x^2 + (5)x + (4) = 0$. In other words, $a = 1$, $b = 5$, and $c = 4$. The two roots of this equation can be found by substituting these values into the quadratic equation, as follows:

$$x = \frac{-b \pm \sqrt{b^2 - 4ac}}{2a} = \frac{-5 \pm \sqrt{5^2 - (4)(1)(4)}}{(2)(1)} = \frac{-5 \pm \sqrt{9}}{2} = \frac{-5 \pm 3}{2}$$

The two roots are $x = \frac{-5 + 3}{2} = -1$ and $x = \frac{-5 - 3}{2} = -4$.

$\boxed{x = -1 \text{ and } x = -4}$

We can evaluate these answers by substituting them into the given equation and verifying that the result is zero.

$$x^2 + 5x + 4 = 0$$

For $x = -1$, $(-1)^2 + 5(-1) + 4 = 1 - 5 + 4 = 0$.

For $x = -4$, $(-4)^2 + 5(-4) + 4 = 16 - 20 + 4 = 0$.

Example

Factor the equation $2x^2 - 3x - 4 = 0$.

SOLUTION

The given equation can be expressed as $(2)x^2 + (-3)x + (-4) = 0$. Thus, $a = 2$, $b = -3$, and $c = -4$. Substitute these values into the quadratic equation to factor the given equation.

$$x = \frac{-b \pm \sqrt{b^2 - 4ac}}{2a} = \frac{3 \pm \sqrt{(-3)^2 - (4)(2)(-4)}}{(2)(2)} = \frac{3 \pm \sqrt{41}}{(2)(2)} = \frac{3 \pm 6.403}{(2)(2)}$$

The two roots are $x = \frac{3 + 6.403}{4} = 2.351$ and $x = \frac{3 - 6.403}{4} = -0.851$.

$\boxed{x = 2.351 \text{ and } x = -0.851}$

Again, evaluate these answers by substituting them into the given equation.

$$2x^2 - 5x - 4 = 0$$

For $x = 2.351$, $2\,(2.351)^2 - 3(2.351) - 4 = 11.054 - 7.053 - 4 \approx 0$.

For $x = -0.851$, $2(-0.851)^2 - 3(-0.851) - 4 = 1.448 + 2.553 - 4 \approx 0$.

Linear Equations

A linear equation has the following general form:

$$y = ax + b$$

In this equation, a and b are constants. This equation is called linear because the graph of y versus x is a straight line, as shown in **Figure 1.** The constant b, called the *intercept*, represents the value of y where the straight line intersects the y-axis. The constant a is equal to the *slope* of the straight line and is also equal to the tangent of the angle that the line makes with the x-axis (θ). If any two points on the straight line are specified by the coordinates (x_1, y_1) and (x_2, y_2), as in **Figure 1,** then the slope of the straight line can be expressed as follows:

$$\text{slope} = \frac{y_2 - y_1}{x_2 - x_1} = \frac{\Delta y}{\Delta x}$$

FIGURE 1

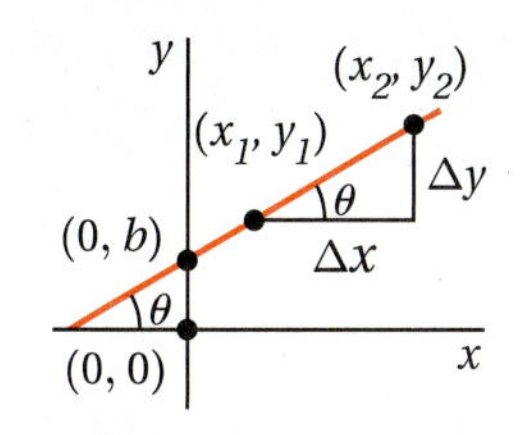

For example, if the two points shown in **Figure 1** are (2, 4) and (6, 9), then the slope of the line is as follows:

$$\text{slope} = \frac{(9-4)}{(6-2)} = \frac{5}{4}$$

FIGURE 2

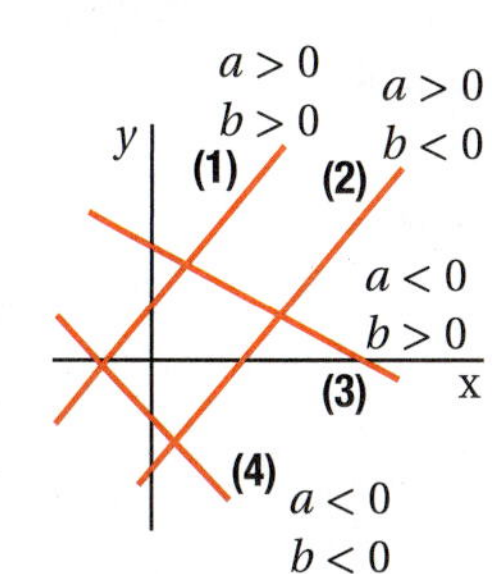

Note that a and b can have either positive or negative values. If $a > 0$, the straight line has a *positive* slope, as in **Figure 1.** If $a < 0$, the straight line has a *negative* slope. Furthermore, if $b > 0$, the y intercept is positive (above the x-axis), while if $b < 0$, the y intercept is negative (below the x-axis). **Figure 2** gives an example of each of these four possible cases, which are summarized in **Table C-4.**

TABLE C-4

LINEAR EQUATIONS

Constants	Slope	y intercept
$a > 0, b > 0$	positive slope	positive *y* intercept
$a > 0, b < 0$	positive slope	negative *y* intercept
$a < 0, b > 0$	negative slope	positive *y* intercept
$a < 0, b < 0$	negative slope	negative *y* intercept

Solving Simultaneous Linear Equations

Consider the following equations:

$$3x + 5y = 15$$

This equation has two unknowns, x and y. Such an equation does not have a unique solution. That is, $(x = 0, y = 3)$, and $(x = 5, y = 0)$, and $(x = 2, y = \frac{9}{5})$ are all solutions to this equation.

If a problem has two unknowns, a unique solution is possible only if there are two independent equations. In general, if a problem has n unknowns, its solution requires n independent equations. There are three basic methods that can be used to solve simultaneous equations. Each of these methods is discussed below, and an example is given for each.

First method: substitution One way to solve two simultaneous equations involving two unknowns, x and y, is to solve one of the equations for one of the unknown values in terms of the other unknown value. In other words, either solve one equation for x in terms of y or solve one equation for y in terms of x. Once you have an expression for either x or y, substitute this expression into the other original equation. At this point, the equation has only one unknown quantity. This unknown can be found through algebraic manipulations and then can be used to determine the other unknown.

Example

Solve the following two simultaneous equations:

1. $5x + y = -8$
2. $2x - 2y = 4$

SOLUTION

First solve for either x or y in one of the equations. We'll begin by solving equation 2 for x.

2. $2x - 2y = 4$

$2x = 4 + 2y$

$x = \frac{4 + 2y}{2} = 2 + y$

Next, we substitute this equation for x into equation 1 and solve for y.

1. $5x + y = -8$

$5(2 + y) + y = -8$

$10 + 5y + y = -8$

$6y = -18$

$\boxed{y = -3}$

To find x, substitute this value for y into the equation for x derived from equation 2.

$x = 2 + y = 2 - 3$

$\boxed{x = -1}$

There is always more than one way to solve simultaneous equations by substitution. In this example, we first solved equation 2 for x. However, we could have begun by solving equation 2 for y or equation 1 for x or y. Any of these processes would result in the same answer.

Second method: canceling one term Simultaneous equations can also be solved by multiplying both sides of one of the equations by a value that will make either the x value or the y value in that equation equal to and opposite the corresponding value in the second equation. When the two equations are added together, that unknown value drops out and only one of the unknown values remains. This unknown can be found through algebraic manipulations and then can be used to determine the other unknown.

Example

Solve the following two simultaneous equations:

1. $3x + y = -6$
2. $-4x - 2y = 6$

SOLUTION

First, multiply each term of one of the equations by a factor that will make either the x or the y values cancel when the two equations are added together. In this case, we can multiply each term in equation 1 by the factor 2. The positive $2y$ in equation 1 will then cancel the negative $2y$ in equation 2.

1. $3x + y = -6$
$2(3x) + (2)(y) = -(2)(6)$
$6x + 2y = -12$

Next, add the two equations together and solve for x.

2. $-4x - 2y = 6$

1. $6x + 2y = -12$
$2x = -6$

$\boxed{x = -3}$

Then, substitute this value of x into either equation to find y.

1. $3x + y = -6$
$y = -6 - 3x = -6 - (3)(-3) = -6 + 9$

$\boxed{y = 3}$

In this example, we multiplied both sides of equation 1 by 2 so that the y terms would cancel when the two equations were added together. As with substitution, this is only one of many possible ways to solve the equations. For example, we could have multiplied both sides of equation 2 by $\frac{3}{4}$ so that the x terms would cancel when the two equations were added together.

Third method: graphing the equations Two linear equations with two unknowns can also be solved by a graphical method. If the straight lines corresponding to the two equations are plotted in a conventional coordinate system, the intersection of the two lines represents the solution.

Example

Solve the following two simultaneous equations:

1. $x - y = 2$
2. $x - 2y = -1$

SOLUTION

These two equations are plotted in **Figure 3.** To plot an equation, rewrite the equation in the form $y = ax + b$, where a is the slope and b is the y intercept. In this example, the equations can be rewritten as follows:

$$y = x - 2$$

$$y = \frac{1}{2}x + \frac{1}{2}$$

FIGURE 3

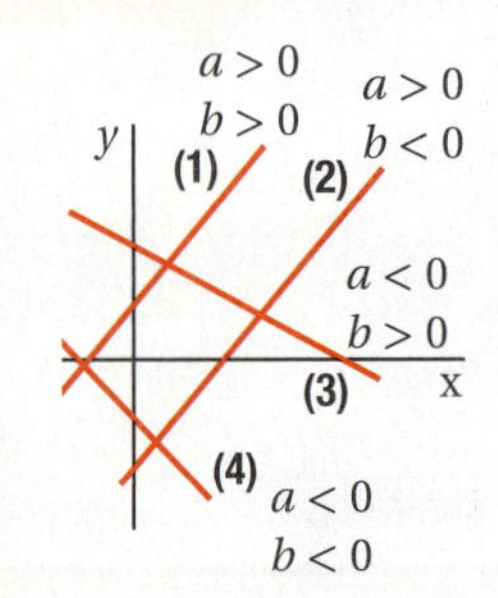

Once one point of a line is known, any other point on that line can be found with the slope of the line. For example, the slope of the first line is 1, and we know that $(0, -2)$ is a point on this line. If we choose the point $x = 2$, we have $(2, y_2)$. The coordinate y_2 can be found as follows:

$$\text{slope} = \frac{y_2 - y_1}{x_2 - x_1} = \frac{y_2 - (-2)}{2 - 0} = 1$$

$$y_2 = 0$$

Connecting the two known coordinates, $(0, -2)$ and $(2, 0)$, results in a graph of the line. The second line can be plotted with the same method.

As shown in **Figure 3,** the intersection of the two lines has the coordinates $x = 5, y = 3$. This intersection represents the solution to the equations. You should check this solution using either of the analytical techniques discussed above.

Logarithms

Suppose that a quantity, x, is expressed as a power of another quantity, a.

$$x = a^y$$

The number a is called the base number. The logarithm of x with respect to the base, a, is equal to the exponent to which a must be raised in order to satisfy the expression $x = a^y$.

$$y = \log_a x$$

Conversely, the *antilogarithm* of y is the number x.

$$x = \text{antilog}_a y$$

In chemistry, pH is calculated using a logarithm.

Common and natural bases In practice, the two bases most often used are base 10, called the *common* logarithm base, and base $e = 2.718...$, called the *natural* logarithm base. When common logarithms are used, y and x are related as follows:

$$y = \log_{10} x, \text{ or } x = 10^y$$

When natural logarithms are used, the symbol ln is used to signify that the logarithm has a base of e; in other words, $\log_e x = \ln x$.

$$y = \ln x, \text{ or } x = e^y$$

For example, $\log_{10} 52 = 1.716$, so $\text{antilog}_{10}\ 1.716 = 10^{1.716} = 52$. Likewise, $\ln 52 = 3.951$, so $\text{antiln}\ 3.951 = e^{3.951} = 52$.

Note that you can convert between base 10 and base e with the equality

$$\ln x = (2.302\ 585)\log_{10} x.$$

Some useful properties of logarithms are summarized in **Table C-5.**

TABLE C-5

PROPERTIES OF LOGARITHMS	
$\log(ab) = \log a + \log b$	$\log(2)(5) = \log 2 + \log 5$
$\log\left(\frac{a}{b}\right) = \log a - \log b$	$\log \frac{3}{4} = \log 3 - \log 4$
$\log(a^n) = n \log a$	$\log 7^3 = 3 \log 7$
$\ln e = 1$	
$\ln e^a = a$	$\ln e^5 = 5$
$\ln\left(\frac{1}{a}\right) = -\ln a$	$\ln \frac{1}{8} = -\ln 8$

Calculating Mean

The **mean** of a data set is the average: the sum of the values divided by the number of values. In chemistry, average atomic masses are calculated in a similar way to mean.

EXAMPLE

To find the mean of the data set {14, 6, 10, 8, 4, 11, 6, 3, 5, 13}, add the values and then divide the sum by the number of values.

ANSWER $\frac{14 + 6 + 10 + 8 + 4 + 11 + 6 + 3 + 5 + 13}{10} = \frac{80}{10} = 8$

Calculating Median

The **median** of a data set is the middle value when the values are ranked in numerical order. Half of the values fall above the median value, half below. If a data set has an even number of values, the median is the mean of the two middle values.

EXAMPLE

To find the median value of the data set {582, 133, 207, 87, 164, 290, 98, 155, 196, 278}, arrange the values in order from least to greatest. The median is the middle value.

87, 98, 133, 155, 164, 196, 207, 278, 290, 582

ANSWER The median is the mean of the two middle values, $\frac{164 + 196}{2} = 180$.

Finding Mode

The **mode** of a data set is the value that occurs most often. A data set can have more than one mode if two or more values are repeated the same number of times. A data set can have no mode if no values are repeated.

EXAMPLE

To find the mode of the data set {6, 7, 6, 4, 4, 4, 3, 6, 4, 6}, arrange the values in order from least to greatest and determine the value that occurs most often:

3, 4, 4, 4, 4, 6, 6, 6, 6, 7

ANSWER There are two modes, 4 and 6.

Constructing Graphs

After finishing an experiment, scientists often illustrate experimental data in graphs. There are three main types of graphs: line graphs, bar graphs, and pie graphs. Organizing data visually helps us identify relationships between variables—factors that change.

The data table on the next page shows data collected by a researcher who has hypothesized that increased salt intake will cause an increase in blood pressure. In this experiment, the independent variable was daily salt intake. Recall that the **independent variable** is the one that is changed by the researcher. You can see in the data table that the researcher varied daily salt intake between 0 and 30 g.

Recall that the **dependent variable** is the one that is observed to determine if it is affected by changes in the independent variable. The dependent variable in this experiment was systolic pressure. You can see that in this case, an increase in salt intake corresponds to an increase in systolic pressure. These data support the hypothesis that increases in salt intake cause a rise in blood pressure.

DATA TABLE	
Systolic pressure (mm Hg)	Daily salt intake (g)
110	0
120	10
140	20
165	30

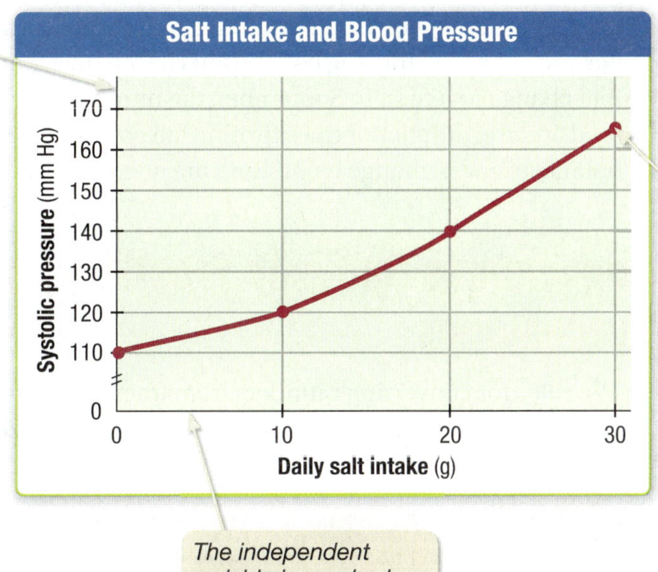

The dependent variable is graphed on the vertical (y) axis.

This last data pair is plotted here on the graph.

The independent variable is graphed on the horizontal (x) axis.

Line Graphs

Line graphs, such as the one shown above, are most often used to compare or relate one or more sets of data that show continuous change. Each set of data—the independent variable and its corresponding dependent variables— is called a *data pair*.

To make a line graph, draw the horizontal (x) and vertical (y) axes of your graph. Label the y-axis with the independent variable and the x-axis with the dependent variable. (Refer to your data table to determine the scale and appropriate units for each axis). Plot each data pair, and then connect the data points to make a line, or curve. Finally, give the graph a title that clearly indicates the relationship between the data shown by the graph.

Sometimes, line graphs can be more complex than the one shown. When a line graph has more than one line, each extra line illustrates another dependent variable. A key must accompany the graph so that the data plotted on the two or more lines are clear. Line graphs can also have data presented on two y-axes, which may have different units. In these graphs, the effect of the independent variable can be observed on two dependent variables.

Using Graphs to Make Predictions

Graphs show trends in data that allow us to make predictions. For example, how might taking in 40 g of salt per day affect blood pressure? Referring to the graph of blood pressure and salt intake, you might estimate that systolic pressure could be 190 mm Hg or more. Using a trend in a range of data to estimate values beyond that range is called **extrapolation.**

Likewise, we can use graphs to estimate values that are untested but that lie *within* the range of our data. How might taking in 15 g of salt per day affect blood pressure? You might use the graph to estimate that blood pressure would be about 130 mm Hg. Using a trend in a range of data to estimate values missing from that range is called **interpolation.**

Some data, such as the values for salt intake and blood pressure, interact in an expected way and seem to indicate a causal relationship. But beware of hastily drawing conclusions based on a graph of two variables that change together. In September, the number of school buses on the road and the number of trees turning fall colors rise. But school buses do not make leaves change color! Both are affected by the time of year.

Conversions Between Fractions, Decimals, and Percentages

The rules for converting numbers from fractions to decimals and percentages and from percentages to decimals are summarized in **Table C-6.**

TABLE C-6

CONVERSIONS

Conversions	Rule	Example
Fraction to Decimal	divide numerator by denominator	$\frac{31}{45} = 0.69$
Fraction to Percentage	convert to decimal, then multiply by 100%	$\frac{31}{45} = (0.69)(100\%)$ $= 69\%$
Percentage to Decimal	move decimal point two decimal places to the left, and remove the percent sign	$69\% = 0.69$

Equations

Chapter 2 Measurements and Calculations

DENSITY

$$density = \frac{mass}{volume} \text{ or } D = \frac{m}{V}$$

PERCENTAGE ERROR

$$\% \text{ error} = \frac{\text{accepted value} - \text{experimental value}}{\text{accepted value}} \times 100$$

Chapter 3 Atoms: The Building Blocks of Matter

ATOMIC MASS NUMBER

Mass number = # of protons + # of neutrons

Chapter 7 Chemical Formulas and Chemical Compounds

PERCENTAGE COMPOSITION BY MASS

$$\% \text{ of element in compound} = \frac{\text{mass of element in the sample}}{\text{mass of the whole sample}}$$

Chapter 9 Stoichiometry

PERCENTAGE YIELD

$$\% \text{ yield} = \frac{\text{actual yield}}{\text{theoretical yield}} \times 100$$

Chapter 10 States of Matter

KINETIC ENERGY

$$\text{Kinetic energy} = \frac{1}{2}\text{ mass} \times \text{velocity}^2 \text{ or } KE = \frac{1}{2}(mv^2)$$

Chapter 11 Gases

PARTIAL PRESSURE

Total pressure of a gas mixture = the sum of the partial pressures of the component gases.

$$P_T = P_1 + P_2 + P_3 + \ldots$$

BOYLE'S LAW

The volume of a fixed mass of gas varies inversely with the pressure at constant temperature.

$$P_1V_1 = P_2V_2$$

CHARLES'S LAW

The pressure of a fixed mass of gas at constant volume varies directly with the Kelvin temperature.

$$\frac{P_1}{T_1} = \frac{P_2}{T_2}$$

COMBINED GAS LAW

This law expresses the relationship between pressure, volume, and the temperature of a fixed amount of gas.

$$\frac{P_1V_1}{T_1} = \frac{P_2V_2}{T_2} \text{ or } \frac{P_1V_1}{n_1T_1} = \frac{P_2V_2}{n_2T_2}$$

AVOGADRO'S LAW

The law states that equal volumes of gases at the same temperature and pressure contain equal numbers of particles.

$$V = kn$$

IDEAL GAS LAW

This law expresses the mathematical relationship among pressure, volume, temperature, and the number of moles of a gas.

$$PV = nRT$$

GRAHAM'S LAW OF EFFUSION

The rates of effusion of gases at the same temperature and pressure are inversely proportional to the square roots of their molar masses.

$$\frac{\text{rate of effusion of A}}{\text{rate of effusion of B}} = \frac{\sqrt{M_B}}{\sqrt{M_A}}$$

Chapter 12 Solutions

MOLARITY

A measure of concentration, relates the number of moles to the volume of solution.

$$\text{molarity} = \frac{\text{moles of solute}}{\text{liter of solution}}$$

MOLALITY

A measure of concentration, relates the number of moles to the mass of the solvent.

$$\text{molality} = \frac{\text{moles of solute}}{\text{mass of solvent (kg)}}$$

Chapter 13 Ions in Aqueous Solutions and Colligative Properties

FREEZING POINT DEPRESSION

The difference between the freezing points of the pure solvent and the solution of a nonelectrolyte.

$$\Delta t_f = K_f m$$

BOILING POINT ELEVATION

The difference between the boiling points of the pure solvent and the solution of a nonelectrolyte.

$$\Delta t_b = K_b m$$

Chapter 15 Acid-Base Titration and pH

pH $pH = -\log[H_3O^+]$

pOH $pOH = -\log[OH^-]$

Chapter 16 Reaction Energy

HEAT GAIN OR LOSS $Q = mc_p\Delta t$

CHANGE IN ENTHALPY $\Delta H = H_{products} - H_{reactants}$

FREE-ENERGY CHANGE $\Delta G^0 = \Delta H^0 - T\Delta S^0$

Chapter 18 Chemical Equilibrium

CHEMICAL EQUILIBRIUM $K = \frac{[C]^x[D]^y}{[A]^n[B]^m}$

Chapter 20 Electrochemistry

ELECTRODE POTENTIAL $E^0_{cell} = E^0_{cathode} - E^0_{anode}$

Chapter 21 Nuclear Chemistry

ENERGY-MASS EQUIVALENCE Energy = mass × [speed of light]^2

$E = mc^2$

Math Skills Handbook and Chemistry Equations

1. a. 52 mm
   b. 49 g
   c. 1600 μL
   d. 2500 μg
   e. 20 000 mg
   f. 3000 L
2. a. 0.15 g
   b. 2.5 L
   c. 0.0005 kg
   d. 0.055 kL
   e. 3.5 cm
   f. 8.74 km
   g. 0.000 209 mm
   h. 0.0005 kg
3. 152 000 Mm
4. 130 mL
5. 1500 mm; 30 segments
6. 76 ladlefuls
7. a. 0.31 m^3
   b. 65 000 cm^2
   c. 35 000 cm^3
   d. 49 mm^2
   e. 1.2 m^3
   f. 0.0875 cm^3
   g. 25 m^2
8. 68 027 cells
9. a. 12 750 km
   b. 2.77 m
   c. 3.056 hectares
   d. 0.008 19 m^2
   e. 300 Mm
10. a. 620 m
    b. 3 875 000 mg
    c. 3.6 μL
    d. 342 kg
    e. 68 710 L
11. a. 0.000 856 kg
    b. 0.001 21 kg
    c. 6.598 cm^3
    d. 0.0806 mm
    e. 0.010 74 L
12. a. 7930 cm^3
    b. 590 cm
    c. 4.19 dm^3
    d. 74 800 cm^2
    e. 197 L
13. 1 L
14. 370 μL
15. 6 L
16. 0.876 L of water per year; 876 kg of water

APPENDIX D

Problem Bank

Conversions: Chap. 2, Sec. 2

CONVERTING SIMPLE SI UNITS

1. State the following measured quantities in the units indicated.
   a. 5.2 cm of magnesium ribbon in millimeters
   b. 0.049 kg of sulfur in grams
   c. 1.60 mL of ethanol in microliters
   d. 0.0025 g of vitamin A in micrograms
   e. 0.020 kg of tin in milligrams
   f. 3 kL of saline solution in liters
2. State the following measured quantities in the units indicated.
   a. 150 mg of aspirin in grams
   b. 2500 mL of hydrochloric acid in liters
   c. 0.5 g of sodium in kilograms
   d. 55 L of carbon dioxide gas in kiloliters
   e. 35 mm in centimeters
   f. 8740 m in kilometers
   g. 209 nm in millimeters
   h. 500 000 μg in kilograms
3. The greatest distance between Earth and the sun during Earth's revolution is 152 million kilometers. What is this distance in megameters?
4. How many milliliters of water will it take to fill a 2.00 L bottle that already contains 1.87 L of water?
5. A piece of copper wire is 150 cm long. How long is the wire in millimeters? How many 50 mm segments of wire can be cut from the length?
6. The ladle at an iron foundry can hold 8500 kg of molten iron; 646 metric tons of iron are needed to make rails. How many ladles full of iron will it take to make 646 metric tons of iron? (1 metric ton = 1000 kg)

CONVERTING DERIVED SI UNITS

7. State the following measured quantities in the units indicated.
   a. 310 000 cm^3 of concrete in cubic meters
   b. 6.5 m^2 of steel sheet in square centimeters
   c. 0.035 m^3 of chlorine gas in cubic centimeters
   d. 0.49 cm^2 of copper in square millimeters
   e. 1200 dm^3 of acetic acid solution in cubic meters
   f. 87.5 mm^3 of actinium in cubic centimeters
   g. 250 000 cm^2 of polyethylene sheet in square meters
8. How many palisade cells from plant leaves would fit in a volume of 1.0 cm^3 of cells if the average volume of a palisade cell is 0.0147 mm^3?

MIXED REVIEW

9. Convert each of the following quantities to the required unit.
   a. 12.75 Mm to kilometers
   b. 277 cm to meters
   c. 30 560 m^2 to hectares (1 ha = 10 000 m^2)
   d. 81.9 cm^2 to square meters
   e. 300 000 km to megameters
10. Convert each of the following quantities to the required unit.
    a. 0.62 km to meters
    b. 3857 g to milligrams
    c. 0.0036 mL to microliters
    d. 0.342 metric tons to kg (1 metric ton = 1000 kg)
    e. 68.71 kL to liters
11. Convert each of the following quantities to the required unit.
    a. 856 mg to kilograms
    b. 1 210 000 μg to kilograms
    c. 6598 μL to cubic centimeters (1 mL = 1 cm^3)
    d. 80 600 nm to millimeters
    e. 10.74 cm^3 to liters
12. Convert each of the following quantities to the required unit.
    a. 7.93 L to cubic centimeters
    b. 0.0059 km to centimeters
    c. 4.19 L to cubic decimeters
    d. 7.48 m^2 to square centimeters
    e. 0.197 m^3 to liters
13. An automobile uses 0.05 mL of oil for each kilometer it is driven. How much oil in liters is consumed if the automobile is driven 20 000 km?
14. How many microliters are there in a volume of 370 mm^3 of cobra venom?
15. A baker uses 1.5 tsp of vanilla extract in each cake. How much vanilla extract in liters should the baker order to make 800 cakes? (1 tsp = 5 mL)
16. A person drinks eight glasses of water each day, and each glass contains 300 mL. How many liters of water will that person consume in a year? What is the mass of this volume of water in kilograms? (Assume one year has 365 days and the density of water is 1.00 kg/L.)
17. At the equator Earth rotates with a velocity of about 465 m/s.
    a. What is this velocity in kilometers per hour?
    b. What is this velocity in kilometers per day?
18. A chemistry teacher needs to determine what quantity of sodium hydroxide to order. If each student will use 130 g and there are 60 students, how many kilograms of sodium hydroxide should the teacher order?

R84 Appendix D: Problem Bank

17. a. 1674 km/h
    b. 40 176 km/day
18. 7.8 kg of sodium hydroxide

19. The teacher in item 18 also needs to order plastic tubing. If each of the 60 students needs 750 mm of tubing, what length of tubing in meters should the teacher order?

20. Convert the following to the required units.
   a. 550 μL/h to milliliters per day
   b. 9.00 metric tons/h to kilograms per minute
   c. 3.72 L/h to cubic centimeters per minute
   d. 6.12 km/h to meters per second

21. Express the following in the units indicated.
   a. 2.97 kg/L as grams per cubic centimeter
   b. 4128 g/dm^2 as kilograms per square centimeter
   c. 5.27 g/cm^3 as kilograms per cubic decimeter
   d. 6.91 kg/m^3 as milligrams per cubic millimeter

22. A gas has a density of 5.56 g/L.
   a. What volume in milliliters would 4.17 g of this gas occupy?
   b. What would be the mass in kilograms of 1 m^3 of this gas?

23. The average density of living matter on Earth's land areas is 0.10 g/cm^2. What mass of living matter in kilograms would occupy an area of 0.125 ha?

24. A textbook measures 250 mm long, 224 mm wide, and 50.0 mm thick. It has a mass of 2.94 kg.
   a. What is the volume of the book in cubic meters?
   b. What is the density of the book in grams per cubic centimeter?
   c. What is the area of one cover in square meters?

25. A glass dropper delivers liquid so that 25 drops equal 1.00 mL.
   a. What is the volume of one drop in milliliters?
   b. How many milliliters are in 37 drops?
   c. How many drops would be required to get 0.68 L?

26. Express each of the following in kilograms and grams.
   a. 504 700 mg
   b. 9 200 000 μg
   c. 122 mg
   d. 7195 cg

27. Express each of the following in liters and milliliters.
   a. 582 cm^3
   b. 0.0025 m^3
   c. 1.18 dm^3
   d. 32 900 μL

28. Express each of the following in grams per liter and kilograms per cubic meter.
   a. 1.37 g/cm^3
   b. 0.692 kg/dm^3
   c. 5.2 kg/L
   d. 38 000 g/m^3
   e. 5.79 mg/mm^3
   f. 1.1 μg/mL

29. An industrial chemical reaction is run for 30.0 h and produces 648.0 kg of product. What is the average rate of product production in the stated units?
   a. grams per minute
   b. kilograms per day
   c. milligrams per millisecond

30. What is the speed of a car in meters per second when it is moving at 100 km/h?

31. A heater gives off energy as heat at a rate of 330 kJ/min. What is the rate of energy output in kilocalories per hour? (1 cal = 4.184 J)

32. The instructions on a package of fertilizer tell you to apply it at the rate of 62 g/m^2. How much fertilizer in kilograms would you need to apply to 1.0 ha? (1 ha = 10 000 m^2)

33. A water tank leaks water at the rate of 3.9 mL/h. If the tank is not repaired, what volume of water in liters will it leak in a year? Show your setup for solving this. Hint: Use one conversion factor to convert hours to days and another to convert days to years, and assume that one year has 365 days.

34. A nurse plans to give flu injections of 50 μL each from a bottle containing 2.0 mL of vaccine. How many doses are in the bottle?

Significant Figures: Chap. 2, Sec. 2

35. Determine the number of significant figures in the following measurements.
   a. 640 cm^3
   b. 200.0 mL
   c. 0.5200 g
   d. 1.005 kg
   e. 10 000 L
   f. 20.900 cm
   g. 0.000 000 56 g/L
   h. 0.040 02 kg/m^3
   i. 790 001 cm^2
   j. 665.000 kg•m/s^2

36. Perform the following calculations, and express the result in the correct units and number of significant figures.
   a. 47.0 m ÷ 2.2 s
   b. 140 cm × 35 cm
   c. 5.88 kg ÷ 200 m^3
   d. 0.0050 m^2 × 0.042 m
   e. 300.3 L ÷ 180 s
   f. 33.00 cm^2 × 2.70 cm
   g. 35 000 kJ ÷ 0.250 min

37. Perform the following calculations and express the results in the correct units and number of significant figures.
   a. 22.0 m + 5.28 m + 15.5 m
   b. 0.042 kg + 1.229 kg + 0.502 kg
   c. 170 cm^2 + 3.5 cm^2 − 28 cm^2
   d. 0.003 L + 0.0048 L + 0.100 L
   e. 24.50 dL + 4.30 dL + 10.2 dL
   f. 3200 mg + 325 mg − 688 mg
   g. 14 000 kg + 8000 kg + 590 kg

MIXED REVIEW

38. Determine the number of significant figures in the following measurements.
   a. 0.0120 m
   b. 100.5 mL
   c. 101 g
   d. 350 cm^2
   e. 0.97 km
   f. 1000 kg
   g. 180. mm
   h. 0.4936 L
   i. 0.020 700 s

Problem Bank

ANSWERS

19. 45 m of plastic tubing
20. a. 13.2 mL/day
   b. 150 kg/min
   c. 62 cm^3/min
   d. 1.7 m/s
21. a. 2.97 g/cm^3
   b. 0.041 28 kg/cm^2
   c. 5.27 kg/dm^3
   d. 0.006 91 mg/mm^3
22. a. 750 mL
   b. 5.56 kg
23. 1250 kg
24. a. 0.0028 m^3
   b. 1.05 g/cm^3
   c. 0.056 m^2
25. a. 0.04 mL per drop
   b. 1.48 mL
   c. 17 000 drops
26. a. 0.5047 kg; 504.7 g
   b. 0.0092 kg; 9.2 g
   c. 0.000 122 kg; 0.122 g
   d. 0.071 95 kg; 71.95 g
27. a. 0.582 L; 582 mL
   b. 2.5 L; 2500 mL
   c. 1.18 L; 1180 mL
   d. 0.0329 L; 32.9 mL
28. a. 1370 g/L; 1370 kg/m^3
   b. 692 g/L; 692 kg/m^3
   c. 5200 g/L; 5200 kg/m^3
   d. 38 g/L; 38 kg/m^3
   e. 5790 g/L; 5790 kg/m^3
   f. 0.0011 g/L; 0.0011 kg/m^3
29. a. 360 g/min
   b. 518.4 kg/day
   c. 6 mg/ms
30. 27.8 m/s
31. 4732 kcal/h
32. 620 kg
33. 34.164 L/year = $\frac{3.9\ \text{mL}}{\text{h}} \times \frac{1\ \text{L}}{1000\ \text{mL}} \times \frac{24\ \text{h}}{1\ \text{day}} \times \frac{365\ \text{days}}{1\ \text{year}}$
34. 40 doses
35. a. 2
   b. 4
   c. 4
   d. 4
   e. 1
   f. 5
   g. 2
   h. 4
   i. 6
   j. 6
36. a. 21 m/s
   b. 4900 cm^2
   c. 0.03 kg/m^3
   d. 0.000 21 m^3
   e. 1.67 L/s
   f. 89.1 cm^3
   g. 140 000 kJ/min
37. a. 42.8 m
   b. 1.773 kg
   c. 150 cm^2
   d. 0.108 L
   e. 39.0 dL
   f. 2800 mg
   g. 23 000 kg
38. a. 3
   b. 4
   c. 3
   d. 2
   e. 2
   f. 1
   g. 3
   h. 4
   i. 5

39. a. 5 490 000 m
b. 0.013 479 3 mL
c. 31 950 cm^2
d. 192.67 m^2
e. 790 cm
f. 389 278 000 J
g. 225 834.8 cm^3

40. a. 49 000 cm^2
b. 3.1 kg/L
c. 12.3 L/s
d. 170 000 cm^3
e. 41 m^3
f. 3.129 g/cm^3

41. a. 90.2 J
b. 0.0006 m
c. 900 g
d. 31.1 kPa
e. 278 dL
f. 1790 kg

42. a. 307 cm^2
b. 30 700 mm^2
c. 0.0307 m^2

43. a. 1800 cm^3
b. 0.0018 m^3
c. 1 800 000 mm^3

44. a. 1300 kg/m^3
b. 1.3 g/mL
c. 1.3 kg/dm^3

45. a. 130 mm^3
b. 430 cm^3
c. 5.0 m
d. 4000 m^3

46. 26 000 000 m^3

47. a. 13.38 g
b. 100. mg
c. 0.015 L
d. 315 cm^2
e. 14.47 kg
f. 353 mL

48. 1.09 kg/L

49. 0.43 g/m; 2.3 m

50. 2000 m^2

51. 26 300 kJ/min; 439 kJ/s

52. a. 15.8 m^3
b. 9800 L/min
c. 590 m^3/h

39. Round the following quantities to the specified number of significant figures.
- **a.** 5 487 129 m to three significant figures
- **b.** 0.013 479 265 mL to six significant figures
- **c.** 31 947.972 cm^2 to four significant figures
- **d.** 192.6739 m^2 to five significant figures
- **e.** 786.9164 cm to two significant figures
- **f.** 389 277 600 J to six significant figures
- **g.** 225 834.762 cm^3 to seven significant figures

40. Perform the following calculations, and express the answer in the correct units and number of significant figures.
- **a.** 651 cm × 75 cm
- **b.** 7.835 kg ÷ 2.5 L
- **c.** 14.75 L ÷ 1.20 s
- **d.** 360 cm × 51 cm × 9.07 cm
- **e.** 5.18 m × 0.77 m × 10.22 m
- **f.** 34.95 g ÷ 11.169 cm^3

41. Perform the following calculations, and express the answer in the correct units and number of significant figures.
- **a.** 7.945 J + 82.3 J − 0.02 J
- **b.** 0.0012 m − 0.000 45 m − 0.000 11 m
- **c.** 500 g + 432 g + 2 g
- **d.** 31.2 kPa + 0.0035 kPa − 0.147 kPa
- **e.** 312 dL − 31.2 dL − 3.12 dL
- **f.** 1701 kg + 50 kg + 43 kg

42. A rectangle measures 87.59 cm by 35.1 mm. Express its area with the proper number of significant figures in the specified unit.
- **a.** in cm^2
- **b.** in mm^2
- **c.** in m^2

43. A box measures 900 mm by 31.5 mm by 6.3 cm. State its volume with the proper number of significant figures in the specified unit.
- **a.** in cm^3
- **b.** in m^3
- **c.** in mm^3

44. A 125 mL sample of liquid has a mass of 0.16 kg. What is the density of the liquid in the following measurements?
- **a.** kg/m^3
- **b.** g/mL
- **c.** kg/dm^3

45. Perform the following calculations, and express the results in the correct units and with the proper number of significant figures.
- **a.** 13.75 mm × 10.1 mm × 0.91 mm
- **b.** 89.4 cm^2 × 4.8 cm
- **c.** 14.9 m^3 ÷ 3.0 m^2
- **d.** 6.975 m × 30 m × 21.5 m

46. What is the volume of a region of space that measures 752 m × 319 m × 110 m? Give your answer in the correct unit and with the proper number of significant figures.

47. Perform the following calculations, and express the results in the correct units and with the proper number of significant figures.
- **a.** 7.382 g + 1.21 g + 4.7923 g
- **b.** 51.3 mg + 83 mg − 34.2 mg
- **c.** 0.007 L − 0.0037 L + 0.012 L
- **d.** 253.05 cm^2 + 33.9 cm^2 + 28 cm^2
- **e.** 14.77 kg + 0.086 kg − 0.391 kg
- **f.** 319 mL + 13.75 mL + 20. mL

48. A container measures 30.5 mm × 202 mm × 153 mm. When it is full of a liquid, it has a mass of 1.33 kg. When it is empty, it has a mass of 0.30 kg. What is the density of the liquid in kilograms per liter?

49. If 7.76 km of wire has a mass of 3.3 kg, what is the mass of the wire in g/m? What length in meters would have a mass of 1.0 g?

50. A container of plant food recommends an application rate of 52 kg/ha. If the container holds 10 kg of plant food, how many square meters will it cover? (1 ha = 10 000 m^2)

51. A chemical process produces 974 550 kJ of energy as heat in 37.0 min. What is the rate in kilojoules per minute? What is the rate in kilojoules per second?

52. A water pipe fills a container that measures 189 cm × 307 cm × 272 cm in 97 s.
- **a.** What is the volume of the container in cubic meters?
- **b.** What is the rate of flow in the pipe in liters per minute?
- **c.** What is the rate of flow in cubic meters per hour?

53. Perform the following calculations, and express the results in the correct units and with the proper number of significant figures. Note, in problems with multiple steps, it is better to perform the entire calculation and then round to significant figures.
- **a.** (0.054 kg + 1.33 kg) × 5.4 m^2
- **b.** 67.35 cm^2 ÷ (1.401 cm − 0.399 cm)
- **c.** 4.198 kg × (1019 m^2 − 40 m^2) ÷ (54.2 s × 31.3 s)
- **d.** 3.14159 m × (4.17 m + 2.150 m)
- **e.** 690 000 m ÷ (5.022 h − 4.31 h)
- **f.** (6.23 cm + 3.111 cm − 0.05 cm) × 14.99 cm

Scientific Notation: Chap. 2, Sec. 3

CONVERTING QUANTITIES TO SCIENTIFIC NOTATION

54. Express the following quantities in scientific notation.
- **a.** 8 800 000 000 m
- **b.** 0.0015 kg
- **c.** 0.000 000 000 06 kg/m^3
- **d.** 8 002 000 Hz
- **e.** 0.009 003 A
- **f.** 70 000 000 000 000 000 km
- **g.** 6028 L
- **h.** 0.2105 g
- **i.** 600 005 000 kJ/h
- **j.** 33.8 m^2

53. a. 7.5 kg•m^2
b. 67.22 cm
c. 2.4 kg•m^2/s^2
d. 19.9 m^2
e. 970 000 m/h
f. 139 cm^2

54. a. 8.8×10^9 m
b. 1.5×10^{-3} kg
c. 6×10^{-11} kg/m^3
d. 8.002×10^6 Hz
e. 9.003×10^{-3} A
f. 7×10^{16} km
g. 6.028×10^3 L
h. 2.105×10^{-1} g
i. $6.000\ 05 \times 10^8$ kJ/h
j. 3.38×10^1 m^2

CALCULATING WITH QUANTITIES IN SCIENTIFIC NOTATION

55. Carry out the following calculations. Express the results in scientific notation and with the correct number of significant figures.

a. 4.74×10^4 km + 7.71×10^3 km + 1.05×10^3 km
b. 2.75×10^{-4} m + 8.03×10^{-5} m + 2.122×10^{-3} m
c. 4.0×10^{-5} m^3 + 6.85×10^{-6} m^3 − 1.05×10^{-5} m^3
d. 3.15×10^2 mg + 3.15×10^3 mg + 3.15×10^4 mg
e. 3.01×10^{22} atoms + 1.19×10^{23} atoms + 9.80×10^{21} atoms
f. 6.85×10^7 nm + 4.0229×10^8 nm − 8.38×10^6 nm

56. Carry out the following computations, and express the result in scientific notation.

a. 7.20×10^3 cm × 8.08×10^3 cm
b. 3.7×10^4 mm × 6.6×10^4 mm × 9.89×10^3 mm
c. 8.27×10^2 m × 2.5×10^{-3} m × 3.00×10^{-4} m
d. 4.44×10^{-35} m × 5.55×10^{19} m × 7.69×10^{-12} kg
e. 6.55×10^4 dm × 7.89×10^9 dm × 4.01893×10^5 dm

57. Carry out the following computations, and express the result in scientific notation.

a. 2.290×10^7 cm ÷ 4.33×10^3 s
b. 1.788×10^{-5} L ÷ 7.111×10^{-3} m^2
c. 5.515×10^4 L ÷ 6.04×10^3 km
d. 3.29×10^{-4} km ÷ 1.48×10^{-2} min
e. 4.73×10^{-4} g ÷ (2.08×10^{-3} km × 5.60×10^{-4} km)

MIXED REVIEW

58. Express the following quantities in scientific notation.

a. 158 000 km
b. 0.000 009 782 L
c. 837 100 000 cm^3
d. 6 500 000 000 mm^2
e. 0.005 93 g
f. 0.000 000 006 13 m
g. 12 552 000 J
h. 0.000 008 004 g/L
i. 0.010 995 kg
j. 1 050 000 000 Hz

59. Perform the following calculations, and express the result in scientific notation with the correct number of significant figures.

a. 2.48×10^2 kg + 9.17×10^3 kg + 7.2×10^1 kg
b. 4.07×10^{-5} mg + 3.966×10^{-4} mg + 7.1×10^{-2} mg
c. 1.39×10^4 m^3 + 6.52×10^2 m^3 − 4.8×103 m^3
d. 7.70×10^{-9} m − 3.95×10^{-8} m + 1.88×10^{-7} m
e. 1.111×10^5 J + 5.82×10^4 J + 3.01×10^6 J
f. 9.81×10^{27} molecules + 3.18×10^{25} molecules − 2.09×10^{26} molecules
g. 1.36×10^7 cm + 3.456×10^6 cm − 1.01×10^7 cm + 5.122×10^5 cm

60. Perform the following computations, and express the result in scientific notation with the correct number of significant figures.

a. 1.54×10^{-1} L ÷ 2.36×10^{-4} s
b. 3.890×10^4 mm × 4.71×10^2 mm^2
c. 9.571×10^3 kg ÷ 3.82×10^{-1} m^2
d. 8.33×10^3 km ÷ 1.97×10^2 s
e. 9.36×10^2 m × 3.82×10^3 m × 9.01×10^{-1} m
f. 6.377×10^4 J ÷ 7.35×10^{-3} s

61. Your electric company charges you for the electric energy you use, measured in kilowatt-hours (kWh). One kWh is equivalent to 3 600 000 J. Express this quantity in scientific notation.

62. The pressure in the deepest part of the ocean is 11 200 000 Pa. Express this pressure in scientific notation.

63. Convert 1.5 km to millimeters, and express the result in scientific notation.

64. Light travels at a speed of about 300 000 km/s.

a. Express this value in scientific notation.
b. Convert this value to meters per hour.
c. What distance in centimeters does light travel in 1 μs?

65. There are 7.11×10^{24} molecules in 100.0 cm^3 of a certain substance.

a. What is the number of molecules in 1.09 cm^3 of the substance?
b. What would be the number of molecules in 2.24×10^4 cm^3 of the substance?
c. What number of molecules are in 9.01×10^{-6} cm^3 of the substance?

66. The number of transistors on a particular integrated circuit is 3 578 000, and the integrated circuit measures 9.5 mm × 8.2 mm.

a. What is the area occupied by each transistor?
b. Using your answer from (a), how many transistors could be formed on a silicon sheet that measures 353 mm × 265 mm?

67. A solution has 0.0501 g of a substance in 1.00 L. Express this concentration in grams per microliter.

68. Cesium atoms are the largest of the naturally occurring elements. They have a diameter of 5.30×10^{-10} m. Calculate the number of cesium atoms that would have to be lined up to give a row of cesium atoms 2.54 cm (1 in.) long.

69. The neutron has a volume of approximately 1.4×10^{-44} m^3 and a mass of 1.675×10^{-24} g. Calculate the density of the neutron in g/m^3. What is the mass of 1.0 cm^3 of neutrons in kilograms?

70. The pits in a compact disc are some of the smallest things ever mass-produced mechanically by humans. These pits represent the 1s and 0s of digital information on a compact disc. These pits are only 1.6×10^{-8} m deep (1/4 the wavelength of red laser light). How many of these pits would have to be stacked on top of each other to make a hole 0.305 m deep?

71. 22 400 mL of oxygen gas contains 6.022×10^{23} oxygen molecules at 0°C and standard atmospheric pressure.

a. How many oxygen molecules are in 0.100 mL of gas?
b. How many oxygen molecules are in 1.00 L of gas?
c. What is the average space in milliliters occupied by one oxygen molecule?

ANSWERS

55. a. 5.62×10^4 km
b. 2.477×10^{-3} m
c. 3.6×10^{-5} m^3
d. 3.50×10^4 mg
e. 1.59×10^{23} atoms
f. 4.624×10^8 nm

56. a. 5.82×10^7 cm^2
b. 2.4×10^{13} mm^3
c. 6.2×10^{-4} m^3
d. 1.89×10^{-26} kg•m^2
e. 2.08×10^{20} dm^3

57. a. 5.29×10^3 cm/s
b. 2.514×10^{-3} L/m^2
c. 9.13 L/km
d. 2.22×10^{-2} km/min
e. 4.06×10^2 g/km^2

58. a. 1.58×10^5 km
b. 9.782×10^{-6} L
c. 8.371×10^8 cm^3
d. 6.5×10^9 mm^2
e. 5.93×10^{-3} g
f. 6.13×10^{-9} m
g. 1.2552×10^7 J
h. 8.004×10^{-6} g/L
i. 1.0995×10^{-2} kg
j. 1.05×10^9 Hz

59. a. 9.49×10^3 kg
b. 7.1×10^{-2} mg
c. 9.8×10^3 m^3
d. 1.56×10^{-7} m
e. 3.18×10^6 J
f. 9.63×10^{27} molecules
g. 7.47×10^6 cm

60. a. 6.53×10^2 L/s
b. 1.83×10^7 mm^3
c. 2.51×10^4 kg/m^2
d. 4.23×10^1 km/s
e. 3.22×10^6 m^3
f. 8.68×10^6 J/s

61. 3.6×10^6 J

62. 1.12×10^7 Pa

63. 1.5×10^6 mm

64. a. 3×10^5 km/s
b. 1×10^{12} m/h
c. 3×10^4 cm

65. a. 7.75×10^{22} molecules
b. 1.59×10^{27} molecules
c. 6.41×10^{17} molecules

66. a. 2.2×10^{-5} mm^2
b. 4.3×10^9 transistors

67. 5.01×10^{-8} g/μL

68. 4.79×10^7 cesium atoms

69. 1.2×10^{20} g/m^3; 1.2×10^{14} kg

70. 1.9×10^7 pits

71. a. 2.69×10^{18} molecules of oxygen
b. 2.69×10^{22} molecules of oxygen
c. 3.72×10^{-20} mL

ANSWERS

72. a. 7.9×10^8 kg/person
b. 7.9×10^5 metric tons/person
c. 5.4×10^8 kg/person
73. 3.329×10^5 Earths
74. a. 4.8×10^{-1} km^3
b. 4.8×10^8 m^3
c. 32 years
75. 1.0×10^7 J/day
76. 47 L
77. 55 metric tons
78. 0.11 kg/L
79. 0.026 mm
80. 3.21 L
81. 0.80 g/cm^3
82. 21.4 g/cm^3
83. 30 boxes
84. a. 1.73 L; 0.120 m × 0.120 m × 0.120 m
b. 9.2 g; 5.0 cm^3
c. 60.4 kg; 1.88×10^4 dm^3
d. 0.94 g/cm^3; 5.3×10^{-4} m^3
e. 2.5×10^3 kg; 2.7×10^6 cm^3
85. 2.8 g/cm^3
86. a. 0.72 μm
b. 2.5×10^3 atoms
87. 1300 L/min
88. 1.3×10^6 cal/h
89. 5.44 g/cm^3
90. 2.24×10^4 cm^3
91. 32 000 uses

72. The mass of the atmosphere is calculated to be 5.136×10^{18} kg, and there are 6 500 000 000 people living on Earth. Calculate the following values.
a. The mass of atmosphere in kilograms per person.
b. The mass of atmosphere in metric tons per person.
c. If the number of people increases to 9 500 000 000, what is the mass in kilograms per person?

73. The mass of the sun is 1.989×10^{30} kg, and the mass of Earth is 5.974×10^{24} kilograms. How many Earths would be needed to equal the mass of the sun?

74. A new landfill has dimensions of 2.3 km × 1.4 km × 0.15 km.
a. What is the volume in cubic kilometers?
b. What is the volume in cubic meters?
c. If 250 000 000 objects averaging 0.060 m^3 each are placed into the landfill each year, how many years will it take to fill the landfill?

75. A dietary calorie (C) is exactly equal to 1000 cal. If your daily intake of food gives you 2400 C, what is your intake in joules per day? (1 cal = 4.184 J)

Four Steps for Solving Quantitative Problems: Chap. 2, Sec. 3

76. Gasoline has a density of 0.73 g/cm^3. How many liters of gasoline would be required to increase the mass of an automobile from 1271 kg to 1305 kg?

77. A swimming pool measures 9.0 m long by 3.5 m wide by 1.75 m deep. What mass of water in metric tons (1 metric ton = 1000 kg) does the pool contain when filled? The density of the water in the pool is 0.997 g/cm^3.

78. A tightly packed box of crackers contains 250 g of crackers and measures 7.0 cm × 17.0 cm × 19.0 cm. What is the average density in kilograms per liter of the crackers in the package? Assume that the unused volume is negligible.

MIXED REVIEW

Solve these problems by using the Four Steps for Solving Quantitative Problems.

79. The aluminum foil on a certain roll has a total area of 18.5 m^2 and a mass of 1275 g. Using a density of 2.7 g per cubic centimeter for aluminum, determine the thickness in millimeters of the aluminum foil.

80. If a liquid has a density of 1.17 g/cm^3, how many liters of the liquid have a mass of 3.75 kg?

81. A stack of 500 sheets of paper measuring 28 cm × 21 cm is 44.5 mm high and has a mass of 2090 g. What is the density of the paper in grams per cubic centimeter?

82. A triangular-shaped piece of a metal has a mass of 6.58 g. The triangle is 0.560 mm thick and measures 36.4 mm on the base and 30.1 mm in height. What is the density of the metal in grams per cubic centimeter?

83. A packing crate measures 0.40 m × 3 0.40 m × 3 0.25 m. You must fill the crate with boxes of cookies that each measure 22.0 cm × 12.0 cm × 5.0 cm. How many boxes of cookies can fit into the crate?

84. Calculate the unknown quantities in the following table. Use the following relationships for volumes of the various shapes.

Volume of a cube = $\ell \times \ell \times \ell$
Volume of a rectangle = $\ell \times w \times h$
Volume of a sphere = $4/3\pi r^3$
Volume of a cylinder = $\pi r^2 \times h$

	D	*m*	*V*	*Shape*	*Dimensions*
a.	2.27 g/cm^3	3.93 kg	? L	cube	? m × ? m × ? m
b.	1.85 g/cm^3	? g	? cm^3	rectangle	33 mm × 21 mm × 7.2 mm
c.	3.21 g/L	? kg	? dm^3	sphere	3.30 m diameter
d.	? g/cm^3	497 g	? m^3	cylinder	7.5 cm diameter × 12 cm
e.	0.92 g/cm^3	? kg	? cm^3	rectangle	3.5 m × 1.2 m × 6.5 m

85. When a sample of a metal alloy that has a mass of 9.65 g is placed into a graduated cylinder containing water, the volume reading in the cylinder increases from 16.0 mL to 19.5 mL. What is the density of the alloy sample in grams per cubic centimeter?

86. Pure gold can be made into extremely thin sheets called gold leaf. Suppose that 50. kg of gold is made into gold leaf having an area of 3620 m^2. The density of gold is 19.3 g/cm^3.
a. How thick in micrometers is the gold leaf?
b. A gold atom has a radius of 1.44×10^{-10} m. How many atoms thick is the gold leaf?

87. A chemical plant process requires that a cylindrical reaction tank be filled with a certain liquid in 238 s. The tank is 1.2 m in diameter and 4.6 m high. What flow rate in liters per minute is required to fill the reaction tank in the specified time?

88. The radioactive decay of 2.8 g of plutonium-238 generates 1.0 joule of energy as heat every second. Plutonium has a density of 19.86 g/cm^3. How many calories (1 cal = 4.184 J) of energy as heat will a rectangular piece of plutonium that is 4.5 cm × 3.05 cm × 15 cm generate per hour?

89. The mass of Earth is 5.974×10^{24} kg. Assume that Earth is a sphere of diameter 1.28×10^4 km and calculate the average density of Earth in g/cm^3.

90. What volume of magnesium in cubic centimeters would have the same mass as 1.82 dm^3 of platinum? The density of magnesium is 1.74 g/cm^3, and the density of platinum is 21.45 g/cm^3.

91. A roll of transparent tape has 66 m of tape on it. If an average of 5.0 cm of tape is needed each time the tape is used, how many uses can you get from a case of tape containing 24 rolls?

92. An automobile can travel 38 km on 4.0 L of gasoline. If the automobile is driven 75% of the days in a year and the average distance traveled each day is 86 km, how many liters of gasoline will be consumed in one year (assume the year has 365 days)?

93. A hose delivers water to a swimming pool that measures 9.0 m long by 3.5 m wide by 1.75 m deep. It requires 97 h to fill the pool. At what rate in liters per minute will the hose fill the pool?

94. Automobile batteries are filled with a solution of sulfuric acid, which has a density of 1.285 g/cm^3. The solution used to fill the battery is 38% (by mass) sulfuric acid. How many grams of sulfuric acid are present in 500 mL of battery acid?

Mole Concept: Chap. 3, Sec. 3; Chap. 7, Sec. 3

PROBLEMS INVOLVING ATOMS AND ELEMENTS

95. Calculate the number of moles in each of the following masses.
   a. 64.1 g of aluminum
   b. 28.1 g of silicon
   c. 0.255 g of sulfur
   d. 850.5 g of zinc

96. Calculate the mass of each of the following amounts.
   a. 1.22 mol sodium
   b. 14.5 mol copper
   c. 0.275 mol mercury
   d. 9.37 × 10^{-3} mol magnesium

97. Calculate the amount in moles in each of the following quantities.
   a. 3.01 × 10^{23} atoms of rubidium
   b. 8.08 × 10^{22} atoms of krypton
   c. 5 700 000 000 atoms of lead
   d. 2.997 × 10^{25} atoms of vanadium

98. Calculate the number of atoms in each of the following amounts.
   a. 1.004 mol bismuth
   b. 2.5 mol manganese
   c. 0.000 0002 mol helium
   d. 32.6 mol strontium

99. Calculate the number of atoms in each of the following masses.
   a. 54.0 g of aluminum
   b. 69.45 g of lanthanum
   c. 0.697 g of gallium
   d. 0.000 000 020 g beryllium

100. Calculate the mass of the following numbers of atoms.
   a. 6.022 × 10^{24} atoms of tantalum
   b. 3.01 × 10^{21} atoms of cobalt
   c. 1.506 × 10^{24} atoms of argon
   d. 1.20 × 10^{25} atoms of helium

PROBLEMS INVOLVING MOLECULES, FORMULA UNITS, AND IONS

101. Calculate the number of moles in each of the following masses.
   a. 3.00 g of boron tribromide, BBr_3
   b. 0.472 g of sodium fluoride, NaF
   c. 7.50 × 10^2 g of methanol, CH_3OH
   d. 50.0 g of calcium chlorate, $Ca(ClO_3)_2$

102. Determine the mass of each of the following amounts.
   a. 1.366 mol of NH_3
   b. 0.120 mol of glucose, $C_6H_{12}O_6$
   c. 6.94 mol barium chloride, $BaCl_2$
   d. 0.005 mol of propane, C_3H_8

103. Calculate the number of molecules in each of the following amounts.
   a. 4.99 mol of methane, CH_4
   b. 0.005 20 mol of nitrogen gas, N_2
   c. 1.05 mol of phosphorus trichloride, PCl_3
   d. 3.5 × 10^{-5} mol of vitamin C, ascorbic acid, $C_6H_8O_6$

104. Calculate the number of formula units in the following amounts.
   a. 1.25 mol of potassium bromide, KBr
   b. 5.00 mol of magnesium chloride, $MgCl_2$
   c. 0.025 mol of sodium carbonate, Na_2CO_3
   d. 6.82 × 10^{-6} mol of lead(II) nitrate, $Pb(NO_3)_2$

105. Calculate the amount in moles of the following numbers of molecules or formula units.
   a. 3.34 × 10^{34} formula units of $Cu(OH)_2$
   b. 1.17 × 10^{16} molecules of H_2S
   c. 5.47 × 10^{21} formula units of nickel(II) sulfate, $NiSO_4$
   d. 7.66 × 10^{19} molecules of hydrogen peroxide, H_2O_2

106. Calculate the mass of each of the following quantities.
   a. 2.41 × 10^{24} molecules of hydrogen, H_2
   b. 5.00 × 10^{21} formula units of aluminum hydroxide, $Al(OH)_3$
   c. 8.25 × 10^{22} molecules of bromine pentafluoride, BrF_5
   d. 1.20 × 10^{23} formula units of sodium oxalate, $Na_2C_2O_4$

107. Calculate the number of molecules or formula units in each of the following masses.
   a. 22.9 g of sodium sulfide, Na_2S
   b. 0.272 g of nickel(II) nitrate, $Ni(NO_3)_2$
   c. 260 mg of acrylonitrile, CH_2CHCN

MIXED REVIEW

108. Calculate the number of moles in each of the following masses.
   a. 0.039 g of palladium
   b. 8200 g of iron
   c. 0.0073 kg of tantalum
   d. 0.006 55 g of antimony
   e. 5.64 kg of barium

Problem Bank

ANSWERS

92. 2500 L

93. 9.5 L/min

94. 244.15 g H_2SO_4

95. a. 2.38 mol Al
   b. 1.00 mol Si
   c. 7.95 × 10^{-3} mol S
   d. 13.01 mol Zn

96. a. 28.0 g Na c. 55.2 g Hg
   b. 921 g Cu d. 0.228 Mg

97. a. 0.500 mol Rb
   b. 0.134 mol Kr
   c. 9.5 × 10^{-15} mol Pb
   d. 49.77 mol V

98. a. 6.046 × 10^{23} atoms Bi
   b. 1.5 × 10^{24} atoms Mn
   c. 1 × 10^{17} atoms He
   d. 1.96 × 10^{25} atoms Sr

99. a. 1.21 × 10^{24} atoms Al
   b. 3.011 × 10^{23} atoms La
   c. 6.02 × 10^{21} atoms Ga
   d. 1.3 × 10^{15} atoms Be

100. a. 1810 g Ta c. 99.91 g Ar
   b. 0.295 g Co d. 79.7 g He

101. a. 0.0120 mol BBr_3
   b. 0.0112 mol NaF
   c. 23.4 mol CH_3OH
   d. 0.242 mol $Ca(ClO_3)_2$

102. a. 23.28 g NH_3
   b. 21.6 g $C_6H_{12}O_6$
   c. 1.45 × 10^3 g or 1.45 kg $BaCl_2$
   d. 0.2 g C_3H_8

103. a. 3.00 × 10^{24} molecules CH_4
   b. 3.13 × 10^{21} molecules N_2
   c. 6.32 × 10^{23} molecules PCl_3
   d. 2.1 × 10^{19} molecules $C_6H_8O_6$

104. a. 7.53 × 10^{23} formula units KBr
   b. 3.01 × 10^{24} formula units $MgCl_2$
   c. 1.5 × 10^{22} formula units Na_2CO_3
   d. 4.11 × 10^{18} formula units $Pb(NO_3)_2$

105. a. 5.55 × 10^{10} mol $Cu(OH)_2$
   b. 1.94 × 10^{-8} mol H_2S
   c. 9.08 × 10^{-3} mol $NiSO_4$
   d. 1.27 × 10^{-4} mol H_2O_2

106. a. 8.08 g H_2
   b. 0.648 g $Al(OH)_3$
   c. 24.0 g BrF_5
   d. 26.7 g $Na_2C_2O_4$

107. a. 1.77 × 10^{23} formula units Na_2S
   b. 8.96 × 10^{20} formula units $Ni(NO_3)_2$
   c. 3.0 × 10^{21} molecules CH_2CHCN

108. a. 3.7 × 10^{24} mol Pd
   b. 150 mol Fe
   c. 0.040 mol Ta
   d. 5.38 × 10^{-5} mol Sb
   e. 41.1 mol Ba

109. a. 52.10 g Cr
b. 1.5×10^4 g or 15 kg Al
c. 8.23×10^{-7} g Ne
d. 3×10^2 g or 0.3 kg Ti
e. 1.1 g Xe
f. 2.28×10^5 g or 228 kg Li

110. a. 1.02×10^{25} atoms Ge
b. 3.700×10^{23} atoms Cu
c. 1.82×10^{24} atoms Sn
d. 1.2×10^{30} atoms C
e. 1.1×10^{21} atoms Zr
f. 1.943×10^{14} atoms K

111. a. 10.00 mol Co
b. 0.176 mol W
c. 4.995×10^{-5} mol Ag
d. 1.6×10^{-15} mol Pu
e. 7.66×10^{-7} mol Rn
f. 1×10^{-11} mol Ce

112. a. 2.5×10^{19} atoms Au
b. 5.10×10^{24} atoms Mo
c. 4.96×10^{20} atoms Am
d. 3.011×10^{26} atoms Ne
e. 2.03×10^{18} atoms Bi
f. 9.4×10^{16} atoms U

113. a. 117 g Rb
b. 223 g Mn
c. 2.11×10^5 g Te
d. 2.6×10^{-3} g Rh
e. 3.31×10^{-8} g Ra
f. 8.71×10^{-5} g Hf

114. a. 0.749 mol CH_3COOH
b. 0.0213 mol $Pb(NO_3)_2$
c. 3×10^4 mol Fe_2O_3
d. 2.66×10^{-4} mol $C_2H_5NH_2$
e. 1.13×10^{-5} mol $C_{17}H_{35}COOH$
f. 378 mol $(NH_4)_2SO_4$

115. a. 764 g $SeOBr_2$
b. 4.88×10^4 g $CaCO_3$
c. 2.7 g $C_{20}H_{28}O_2$
d. 9.74×10^{-6} g $C_{10}H_{14}N_2$
e. 529 g $Sr(NO_3)_2$
f. 1.23×10^{-3} g UF_6

116. a. 2.57×10^{24} formula units WO_3
b. 1.81×10^{21} formula units $Sr(NO_3)_2$
c. 4.37×10^{25} molecules $C_6H_5CH_3$
d. 3.08×10^{17} molecules $C_{29}H_{50}O_2$
e. 9.0×10^{26} molecules N_2H_4
f. 5.96×10^{23} molecules $C_6H_5NO_2$

109. Calculate the mass in grams of each of the following amounts.
a. 1.002 mol of chromium
b. 550 mol of aluminum
c. 4.08×10^{-8} mol of neon
d. 7 mol of titanium
e. 0.0086 mol of xenon
f. 3.29×10^4 mol of lithium

110. Calculate the number of atoms in each of the following amounts.
a. 17.0 mol of germanium
b. 0.6144 mol of copper
c. 3.02 mol of tin
d. 2.0×10^6 mol of carbon
e. 0.0019 mol of zirconium
f. 3.227×10^{-10} mol of potassium

111. Calculate the number of moles in each of the following quantities.
a. 6.022×10^{24} atoms of cobalt
b. 1.06×10^{23} atoms of tungsten
c. 3.008×10^{19} atoms of silver
d. 950 000 000 atoms of plutonium
e. 4.61×10^{17} atoms of radon
f. 8 trillion atoms of cerium

112. Calculate the number of atoms in each of the following masses.
a. 0.0082 g of gold
b. 812 g of molybdenum
c. 2.00×10^2 mg of americium
d. 10.09 kg of neon
e. 0.705 mg of bismuth
f. 37 µg of uranium

113. Calculate the mass of each of the following.
a. 8.22×10^{23} atoms of rubidium
b. 4.05 Avogadro's constants of manganese atoms
c. 9.96×10^{26} atoms of tellurium
d. 0.000 025 Avogadro's constants of rhodium atoms
e. 88 300 000 000 000 atoms of radium
f. 2.94×10^{17} atoms of hafnium

114. Calculate the number of moles in each of the following masses.
a. 45.0 g of acetic acid, CH_3COOH
b. 7.04 g of lead(II) nitrate, $Pb(NO_3)_2$
c. 5000 kg of iron(III) oxide, Fe_2O_3
d. 12.0 mg of ethylamine, $C_2H_5NH_2$
e. 0.003 22 g of stearic acid, $C_{17}H_{35}COOH$
f. 50.0 kg of ammonium sulfate, $(NH_4)_2SO_4$

115. Calculate the mass of each of the following amounts.
a. 3.00 mol of selenium oxybromide, $SeOBr_2$
b. 488 mol of calcium carbonate, $CaCO_3$
c. 0.0091 mol of retinoic acid, $C_{20}H_{28}O_2$
d. 6.00×10^{-8} mol of nicotine, $C_{10}H_{14}N_2$
e. 2.50 mol of strontium nitrate, $Sr(NO_3)_2$
f. 3.50×10^{-6} mol of uranium hexafluoride, UF_6

116. Calculate the number of molecules or formula units in each of the following amounts.
a. 4.27 mol of tungsten(VI) oxide, WO_3
b. 0.003 00 mol of strontium nitrate, $Sr(NO_3)_2$
c. 72.5 mol of toluene, $C_6H_5CH_3$
d. 5.11×10^{-7} mol of α-tocopherol (vitamin E), $C_{29}H_{50}O_2$
e. 1500 mol of hydrazine, N_2H_4
f. 0.989 mol of nitrobenzene $C_6H_5NO_2$

117. Calculate the number of molecules or formula units in each of the following masses.
a. 285 g of iron(III) phosphate, $FePO_4$
b. 0.0084 g of C_5H_5N
c. 85 mg of 2-methyl-1-propanol, $(CH_3)_2CHCH_2OH$
d. 4.6×10^{-4} g of mercury(II) acetate, $Hg(C_2H_3O_2)_2$
e. 0.0067 g of lithium carbonate, Li_2CO_3

118. Calculate the mass of each of the following quantities.
a. 8.39×10^{23} molecules of fluorine, F_2
b. 6.82×10^{24} formula units of beryllium sulfate, $BeSO_4$
c. 7.004×10^{26} molecules of chloroform, $CHCl_3$
d. 31 billion formula units of chromium(III) formate, $Cr(CHO_2)_3$
e. 6.3×10^{18} molecules of nitric acid, HNO_3
f. 8.37×10^{25} molecules of freon 114, $C_2Cl_2F_4$

119. Precious metals are commonly measured in troy ounces. A troy ounce is equivalent to 31.1 g. How many moles are in a troy ounce of gold? How many moles are in a troy ounce of platinum? of silver?

120. A chemist needs 22.0 g of phenol, C_6H_5OH, for an experiment. How many moles of phenol is this?

121. A student needs 0.015 mol of iodine crystals, I_2, for an experiment. What mass of iodine crystals should the student obtain?

122. The weight of a diamond is given in carats. One carat is equivalent to 200. mg. A pure diamond is made up entirely of carbon atoms. How many carbon atoms make up a 1.00 carat diamond?

123. 8.00 g of calcium chloride, $CaCl_2$, is dissolved in 1.000 kg of water.
a. How many moles of $CaCl_2$ are in solution? How many moles of water are present?
b. Assume that the ionic compound, $CaCl_2$, separates completely into Ca^{2+} and Cl^- ions when it dissolves in water. How many moles of each ion are present in the solution?

124. How many moles are in each of the following masses?
a. 453.6 g (1.000 pound) of sucrose (table sugar), $C_{12}H_{22}O_{11}$
b. 1.000 pound of table salt, NaCl

125. When the ionic compound NH_4Cl dissolves in water, it breaks into one ammonium ion, NH_4^+, and one chloride ion, Cl^-. If you dissolved 10.7 g of NH_4Cl in water, how many moles of ions would be in solution?

R90 Appendix D: Problem Bank

117. a. 1.14×10^{24} formula units $FePO_4$
b. 6.4×10^{19} molecules C_5H_5N
c. 6.9×10^{20} molecules $(CH_3)_2CHCH_2OH$
d. 8.7×10^{17} formula units $Hg(C_2H_3O_2)_2$
e. 5.5×10^{19} formula units Li_2CO_3

118. a. 52.9 g F_2
b. 1.19×10^3 g or 1.19 kg $BeSO_4$
c. 1.388×10^5 g or 138.8 kg $CHCl_3$
d. 9.6×10^{-12} g $Cr(CHO_2)_3$
e. 6.6×10^{-4} g HNO_3
f. 2.38×10^4 g or 23.8 kg $C_2Cl_2F_4$

119. 0.158 mol Au
0.159 mol Pt
0.288 mol Ag

120. 0.234 mol C_6H_5OH

121. 3.8 g I_2

122. 1.00×10^{22} atoms C

123. a. 0.0721 mol $CaCl_2$
55.49 mol H_2O
b. 0.0721 mol Ca^{2+}
0.144 mol Cl^-

124. a. 1.325 mol $C_{12}H_{22}O_{11}$
b. 7.762 mol NaCl

125. 0.400 mol ions

126. What is the total amount in moles of atoms in a jar that contains 2.41×10^{24} atoms of chromium, 1.51×10^{23} atoms of nickel, and 3.01×10^{23} atoms of copper?

127. The density of liquid water is 0.997 g/mL at 25°C.
   a. Calculate the mass of 250.0 mL (about a cupful) of water.
   b. How many moles of water are in 250.0 mL of water? Hint: Use the result of (a).
   c. Calculate the volume that would be occupied by 2.000 mol of water at 25°C.
   d. What mass of water is 2.000 mol of water?

128. An Avogadro's constant (1 mol) of sugar molecules has a mass of 342 g, but an Avogadro's constant (1 mol) of water molecules has a mass of only 18 g. Explain why there is such a difference between the mass of 1 mol of sugar and the mass of 1 mol of water.

129. Calculate the mass of aluminum that would have the same number of atoms as 6.35 g of cadmium.

130. A chemist weighs a steel cylinder of compressed oxygen, O_2, and finds that it has a mass of 1027.8 g. After some of the oxygen is used in an experiment, the cylinder has a mass of 1023.2 g. How many moles of oxygen gas are used in the experiment?

131. Suppose that you could decompose 0.250 mol of Ag_2S into its elements.
   a. How many moles of silver would you have? How many moles of sulfur would you have?
   b. How many moles of Ag_2S are there in 38.8 g of Ag_2S? How many moles of silver and sulfur would be produced from this amount of Ag_2S?
   c. Calculate the masses of silver and sulfur produced in (b).

Percentage Composition: Chap. 7, Sec. 3

132. Determine the percentage composition of each of the following compounds.
   a. sodium oxalate, $Na_2C_2O_4$
   b. ethanol, C_2H_5OH
   c. aluminum oxide, Al_2O_3
   d. potassium sulfate, K_2SO_4

133. Suppose that a laboratory analysis of white powder showed 42.59% Na, 12.02% C, and 44.99% O. Would you report that the compound is sodium oxalate or sodium carbonate? (Use 43.38% Na, 11.33% C, and 45.29% O for sodium carbonate, and 34.31% Na, 17.93% C, and 47.76% O for sodium oxalate.)

134. Calculate the mass of the given element in each of the following compounds.
   a. bromine in 50.0 g potassium bromide, KBr
   b. chromium in 1.00 kg sodium dichromate, $Na_2Cr_2O_7$
   c. nitrogen in 85.0 mg of the amino acid lysine, $C_6H_{14}N_2O_2$
   d. cobalt in 2.84 g cobalt(II) acetate, $Co(C_2H_3O_2)_2$

HYDRATES

135. Calculate the percentage of water in each of the following hydrates.
   a. sodium carbonate decahydrate, $Na_2CO_3 \bullet 10H_2O$
   b. nickel(II) iodide hexahydrate, $NiI_2 \bullet 6H_2O$
   c. ammonium hexacyanoferrate(III) trihydrate (commonly called ammonium ferricyanide), $(NH_4)_2Fe(CN)_6 \bullet 3H_2O$
   d. aluminum bromide hexahydrate, $AlBr_3 \bullet 6H_2O$

MIXED REVIEW

136. Write formulas for the following compounds and determine the percentage composition of each.
   a. nitric acid
   b. ammonia
   c. mercury(II) sulfate
   d. antimony(V) fluoride

137. Calculate the percentage composition of the following compounds.
   a. lithium bromide, LiBr
   b. anthracene, $C_{14}H_{10}$
   c. ammonium nitrate, NH_4NO_3
   d. nitrous acid, HNO_2
   e. silver sulfide, Ag_2S
   f. iron(II) thiocyanate, $Fe(SCN)_2$
   g. lithium acetate
   h. nickel(II) formate

138. Calculate the percentage of the given element in each of the following compounds.
   a. nitrogen in urea, NH_2CONH_2
   b. sulfur in sulfuryl chloride, SO_2Cl_2
   c. thallium in thallium(III) oxide, Tl_2O_3
   d. oxygen in potassium chlorate, $KClO_3$
   e. bromine in calcium bromide, $CaBr_2$
   f. tin in tin(IV) oxide, SnO_2

139. Calculate the mass of the given element in each of the following quantities.
   a. oxygen in 4.00 g of manganese dioxide, MnO_2
   b. aluminum in 50.0 metric tons of aluminum oxide, Al_2O_3
   c. silver in 325 g silver cyanide, AgCN
   d. gold in 0.780 g of gold(III) selenide, Au_2Se_3
   e. selenium in 683 g sodium selenite, Na_2SeO_3
   f. chlorine in 5.0×10^4 g of 1,1-dichloropropane, $CHCl_2CH_2CH_3$

140. Calculate the percentage of water in each of the following hydrates.
   a. strontium chloride hexahydrate, $SrCl_2 \bullet 6H_2O$
   b. zinc sulfate heptahydrate, $ZnSO_4 \bullet 7H_2O$
   c. calcium fluorophosphate dihydrate, $CaFPO_3 \bullet 2H_2O$
   d. beryllium nitrate trihydrate, $Be(NO_3)_2 \bullet 3H_2O$

ANSWERS

126. 4.75 mol atoms

127. a. 249 g H_2O c. 36.1 mL H_2O
   b. 13.8 mol H_2O d. 36.0 g H_2O

128. The mass of a sugar molecule is much greater than the mass of a water molecule. Therefore, the mass of 1 mol of sugar molecules is much greater than the mass of 1 mol of water molecules.

129. 1.52 g Al

130. 0.14 mol O_2

131. a. 0.500 mol Ag
   0.250 mol S
   b. 0.157 mol Ag_2S
   0.313 mol Ag
   0.157 mol S
   c. 33.8 g Ag
   5.03 g S

132. a. 34.31% Na, 17.93% C, 47.76% O
   b. 52.13% C, 13.15% H, 34.72% O
   c. 52.92% Al, 47.08% O
   d. 44.87% K, 18.40% S, 36.72% O

133. sodium carbonate

134. a. 33.6 g Br c. 16.3 mg N
   b. 397 g Cr d. 0.945 g Co

135. a. 62.97% H_2O in $Na_2CO_3 \bullet 10H_2O$
   b. 25.71% H_2O in $NiI_2 \bullet 6H_2O$
   c. 17.89% H_2O in $(NH_4)_2Fe(CN)_6 \bullet 3H_2O$
   d. 28.85% H_2O in $AlBr_3 \bullet 6H_2O$

136. a. HNO_3
   1.60% H
   22.23% N
   76.17% O
   b. NH_3
   82.22% N
   17.78% H
   c. $HgSO_4$
   67.616% Hg
   10.81% S
   21.57% O
   d. SbF_5
   56.173% Sb
   43.83% F

137. a. 7.99% Li
   92.01% Br
   b. 94.33% C
   5.67% H
   c. 35.00% N
   5.05% H
   59.96% O
   d. 2.15% H
   29.80% N
   68.06% O
   e. 87.059% Ag
   12.94% S
   f. 32.47% Fe
   13.96% C
   16.29% N
   37.28% S
   g. $LiC_2H_3O_2$
   10.52% Li
   36.40% C
   4.59% H
   48.49% O
   h. $Ni(CHO_2)_2$
   39.46% Ni
   16.15% C
   1.36% H
   43.03% O

138. a. 46.65% N d. 39.17% O
   b. 23.76% S e. 79.95% Br
   c. 89.491% Tl f. 78.767% Sn

139. a. 1.47 g O d. 0.487 g Au
   b. 26.5 metric tons Al e. 312 g Se
   c. 262 g Ag f. 3.1×10^4 g Cl

140. a. 40.55% H_2O c. 20.70% H_2O
   b. 43.86% H_2O d. 28.90% H_2O

141. a. $Ni(C_2H_3O_2)_2 \bullet 4H_2O$
23.58% Ni
b. $Na_2CrO_4 \bullet 4H_2O$
22.22% Cr
c. $Ce(SO_4)_2 \bullet 4H_2O$
34.65% Ce

142. 43.1 kg Hg

143. malachite: 5.75×10^2 kg Cu; chalcopyrite: 3.46×10^2 kg Cu; Malachite has a greater Cu content.

144. a. 25.59% V
b. 39.71% Sn
c. 22.22% Cl

145. 319.6 g anhydrous $CuSO_4$

146. 1.57 g $AgNO_3$

147. 54.3 g Ag; 8.08 g S

148. 23.1 g $MgSO_4 \bullet 7H_2O$

149. 3.27×10^2 g S

150. a. $CuBr_2$
b. $KHCO_3$
c. Ag_3PO_4
d. HIO_3

151. a. Al_2S_3
b. Nb_5O_2
c. $Sr_3P_2O_8$ or $Sr_3(PO_4)_2$
d. $Fe_2S_3O_{12}$ or $Fe_2(SO_4)_3$

152. a. C_2H_4
b. B_4H_{10}
c. $C_6H_3Cl_3$
d. $C_{18}H_{24}O_3$
e. $C_{12}H_8O_4$

153. a. $BaCl_2$
b. BiO_3H_3 or $Bi(OH)_3$
c. AlN_3O_9 or $Al(NO_3)_3$
d. $ZnC_4H_6O_4$ or $Zn(CH_3COO)_2$
e. $NiN_2S_2H_8O_8$ or $Ni(NH_4)_2(SO_4)_2$
f. $C_2HBr_3O_2$ or CBr_3COOH

154. a. CuF_2
b. $Ba(CN)_2$
c. $MnSO_4$

141. Calculate the percentage of the given element in each of the following hydrates. You must first determine the formulas of the hydrates.
a. nickel in nickel(II) acetate tetrahydrate
b. chromium in sodium chromate tetrahydrate
c. cerium in cerium(IV) sulfate tetrahydrate

142. Cinnabar is a mineral that is mined in order to produce mercury. Cinnabar is mercury(II) sulfide, HgS. What mass of mercury can be obtained from 50.0 kg of cinnabar?

143. The minerals malachite, $Cu_2(OH)_2CO_3$, and chalcopyrite, $CuFeS_2$, can be mined to obtain copper metal. How much copper could be obtained from 1.00×10^3 kg of each? Which of the two has the greater copper content?

144. Calculate the percentage of the given element in each of the following hydrates.
a. vanadium in vanadium oxysulfate dihydrate, $VOSO_4 \bullet 2H_2O$
b. tin in potassium stannate trihydrate, $K_2SnO_3 \bullet 3H_2O$
c. chlorine in calcium chlorate dihydrate, $CaClO_3 \bullet 2H_2O$

145. Heating copper sulfate pentahydrate will evaporate the water from the crystals, leaving anhydrous copper sulfate, a white powder. *Anhydrous* means "without water." What mass of anhydrous $CuSO_4$ would be produced by heating 500.0 g of $CuSO_4 \bullet 5H_2O$?

146. Silver metal may be precipitated from a solution of silver nitrate by placing a copper strip into the solution. What mass of $AgNO_3$ would you dissolve in water in order to get 1.00 g of silver?

147. A sample of Ag_2S has a mass of 62.4 g. What mass of each element could be obtained by decomposing this sample?

148. A quantity of epsom salts, magnesium sulfate heptahydrate, $MgSO_4 \bullet 7H_2O$, is heated until all the water is driven off. The sample loses 11.8 g in the process. What was the mass of the original sample?

149. The process of manufacturing sulfuric acid begins with the burning of sulfur. What mass of sulfur would have to be burned in order to produce 1.00 kg of H_2SO_4? Assume that all of the sulfur ends up in the sulfuric acid.

Empirical Formulas: Chap. 7, Sec. 4

150. Determine the empirical formula for compounds that have the following analyses.
a. 28.4% copper, 71.6% bromine
b. 39.0% potassium, 12.0% carbon, 1.01% hydrogen, and 47.9% oxygen
c. 77.3% silver, 7.4% phosphorus, 15.3% oxygen
d. 0.57% hydrogen, 72.1% iodine, 27.3% oxygen

151. Determine the simplest formula for compounds that have the following analyses. The data may not be exact.
a. 36.2% aluminum and 63.8% sulfur
b. 93.5% niobium and 6.50% oxygen
c. 57.6% strontium, 13.8% phosphorus, and 28.6% oxygen
d. 28.5% iron, 48.6% oxygen, and 22.9% sulfur

152. Determine the molecular formula of each of the following unknown substances.
a. empirical formula CH_2
experimental molar mass 28 g/mol
b. empirical formula B_2H_5
experimental molar mass 54 g/mol
c. empirical formula C_2HCl
experimental molar mass 179 g/mol
d. empirical formula C_6H_8O
experimental molar mass 290 g/mol
e. empirical formula C_3H_2O
experimental molar mass 216 g/mol

MIXED REVIEW

153. Determine the empirical formula for compounds that have the following analyses.
a. 66.0% barium and 34.0% chlorine
b. 80.38% bismuth, 18.46% oxygen, and 1.16% hydrogen
c. 12.67% aluminum, 19.73% nitrogen, and 67.60% oxygen
d. 35.64% zinc, 26.18% carbon, 34.88% oxygen, and 3.30% hydrogen
e. 2.8% hydrogen, 9.8% nitrogen, 20.5% nickel, 44.5% oxygen, and 22.4% sulfur
f. 8.09% carbon, 0.34% hydrogen, 10.78% oxygen, and 80.78% bromine

154. Sometimes, instead of percentage composition, you will have the composition of a sample by mass. Using the actual mass of the sample, determine the empirical formula for compounds that have the following analyses.
a. a 0.858 g sample of an unknown substance is composed of 0.537 g of copper and 0.321 g of fluorine
b. a 13.07 g sample of an unknown substance is composed of 9.48 g of barium, 1.66 g of carbon, and 1.93 g of nitrogen
c. a 0.025 g sample of an unknown substance is composed of 0.0091 g manganese, 0.0106 g oxygen, and 0.0053 g sulfur

155. Determine the empirical formula for compounds that have the following analyses.
a. a 0.0082 g sample contains 0.0015 g of nickel and 0.0067 g of iodine
b. a 0.470 g sample contains 0.144 g of manganese, 0.074 g of nitrogen, and 0.252 g of oxygen
c. a 3.880 g sample contains 0.691 g of magnesium, 1.824 g of sulfur, and 1.365 g of oxygen
d. a 46.25 g sample contains 14.77 g of potassium, 9.06 g of oxygen, and 22.42 g of tin

156. Determine the empirical formula for compounds that have the following analyses:
a. 60.9% As and 39.1% S
b. 76.89% Re and 23.12% O
c. 5.04% H, 35.00% N, and 59.96% O
d. 24.3% Fe, 33.9% Cr, and 41.8% O
e. 54.03% C, 37.81% N, and 8.16% H
f. 55.81% C, 3.90% H, 29.43% F, and 10.85% N

155. a. NiI_2
b. MnN_2O_6 or $Mn(NO_3)_2$
c. MgS_2O_3
d. K_2SnO_3

156. a. As_2S_3
b. Re_2O_7
c. $N_2H_4O_3$ or NH_4NO_3
d. $Fe_2Cr_3O_{12}$ or $Fe_2(CrO_4)_3$
e. $C_5H_9N_3$
f. $C_6H_5F_2N$ or $C_6H_3F_2NH_2$

157. Determine the molecular formulas for compounds having the following empirical formulas and molar masses.

a. C_2H_4S; experimental molar mass 179
b. C_2H_4O; experimental molar mass 176
c. $C_2H_3O_2$; experimental molar mass 119
d. C_2H_2O; experimental molar mass 254

158. Use the experimental molar mass to determine the molecular formula for compounds having the following analyses.

a. 41.39% carbon, 3.47% hydrogen, and 55.14% oxygen; experimental molar mass 116.07
b. 54.53% carbon, 9.15% hydrogen, and 36.32% oxygen; experimental molar mass 88
c. 64.27% carbon, 7.19% hydrogen, and 28.54% oxygen; experimental molar mass 168.19

159. A 0.400 g sample of a white powder contains 0.141 g of potassium, 0.115 g of sulfur, and 0.144 g of oxygen. What is the empirical formula for the compound?

160. A 10.64 g sample of a lead compound is analyzed and found to be made up of 9.65 g of lead and 0.99 g of oxygen. Determine the empirical formula for this compound.

161. A 2.65 g sample of a salmon-colored powder contains 0.70 g of chromium, 0.65 g of sulfur, and 1.30 g of oxygen. The molar mass is 392.2. What is the formula of the compound?

162. Ninhydrin is a compound that reacts with amino acids and proteins to produce a dark-colored complex. It is used by forensic chemists and detectives to see fingerprints that might otherwise be invisible. Ninhydrin's composition is 60.68% carbon, 3.40% hydrogen, and 35.92% oxygen. What is the empirical formula for ninhydrin?

163. Histamine is a substance that is released by cells in response to injury, infection, stings, and materials that cause allergic responses, such as pollen. Histamine causes dilation of blood vessels and swelling due to accumulation of fluid in the tissues. People sometimes take *anti*histamine drugs to counteract the effects of histamine. A sample of histamine having a mass of 385 mg is composed of 208 mg of carbon, 31 mg of hydrogen, and 146 mg of nitrogen. The molar mass of histamine is 111 g/mol. What is the molecular formula for histamine?

164. You analyze two substances in the laboratory and discover that each has the empirical formula CH_2O. You can easily see that they are different substances because one is a liquid with a sharp, biting odor and the other is an odorless, crystalline solid. How can you account for the fact that both have the same empirical formula?

Stoichiometry: Chap. 9, Sec. 1–2

165. How many moles of sodium will react with water to produce 4.0 mol of hydrogen in the following reaction?

$$2Na(s) + 2H_2O(l) \longrightarrow 2NaOH(aq) + H_2(g)$$

166. How many moles of lithium chloride will be formed by the reaction of chlorine with 0.046 mol of lithium bromide in the following reaction?

$$2LiBr(aq) + Cl_2(g) \longrightarrow 2LiCl(aq) + Br_2(l)$$

167. Aluminum will react with sulfuric acid in the following reaction.

$$2Al(s) + 3H_2SO_4(l) \longrightarrow Al_2(SO_4)_3(aq) + 3H_2(g)$$

a. How many moles of H_2SO_4 will react with 18 mol Al?
b. How many moles of each product will be produced?

168. Propane burns in excess oxygen according to the following reaction.

$$C_3H_8 + 5O_2 \longrightarrow 3CO_2 + 4H_2O$$

a. How many moles each of CO_2 and H_2O are formed from 3.85 mol of propane?
b. If 0.647 mol of oxygen are used in the burning of propane, how many moles each of CO_2 and H_2O are produced? How many moles of C_3H_8 are consumed?

169. Phosphorus burns in air to produce a phosphorus oxide in the following reaction:

$$4P(s) + 5O_2(g) \longrightarrow P_4O_{10}(s)$$

a. What mass of phosphorus will be needed to produce 3.25 mol of P_4O_{10}?
b. If 0.489 mol of phosphorus burns, what mass of oxygen is used? What mass of P_4O_{10} is produced?

170. Hydrogen peroxide breaks down, releasing oxygen, in the following reaction.

$$2H_2O_2(aq) \longrightarrow 2H_2O(l) + O_2(g)$$

a. What mass of oxygen is produced when 1.840 mol of H_2O_2 decompose?
b. What mass of water is produced when 5.0 mol O_2 is produced by this reaction?

171. Sodium carbonate reacts with nitric acid according to the following equation:

$$Na_2CO_3(s) + 2HNO_3 \longrightarrow 2NaNO_3 + CO_2 + H_2O$$

a. How many moles of Na_2CO_3 are required to produce 100.0 g of $NaNO_3$?
b. If 7.50 g of Na_2CO_3 reacts, how many moles of CO_2 are produced?

172. Hydrogen is generated by passing hot steam over iron, which oxidizes to form Fe_3O_4, in the following equation:

$$3Fe(s) + 4H_2O(g) \longrightarrow 4H_2(g) + Fe_3O_4(s)$$

a. If 625 g of Fe_3O_4 is produced in the reaction, how many moles of hydrogen are produced at the same time?
b. How many moles of iron would be needed to generate 27 g of hydrogen?

173. Calculate the mass of silver bromide produced from 22.5 g of silver nitrate in the following reaction:

$$2AgNO_3(aq) + MgBr_2(aq) \longrightarrow 2AgBr(s) + Mg(NO_3)_2(aq)$$

174. What mass of acetylene, C_2H_2, will be produced from the reaction of 90. g of calcium carbide, CaC_2, with water in the following reaction?

$$CaC_2(s) + 2H_2O(l) \longrightarrow C_2H_2(g) + Ca(OH)_2(s)$$

Problem Bank

ANSWERS

157. a. $C_6H_{12}S_3$
b. $C_8H_{16}O_4$
c. $C_4H_6O_4$
d. $C_{12}H_{12}O_6$

158. a. $C_4H_4O_4$
b. $C_4H_8O_2$
c. $C_9H_{12}O_3$

159. $K_2S_2O_5$

160. Pb_3O_4

161. $Cr_2S_3O_{12}$ or $Cr_2(SO_4)_3$

162. $C_9H_6O_4$

163. $C_5H_9N_3$ (the empirical formula and the molecular formula are the same)

164. The molecular formulas of the compounds are different multiples of the same empirical formula. (FYI: The first could be acetic acid, $C_2H_4O_2$, and the second could be glucose, $C_6H_{12}O_6$, or some other simple sugar.)

165. 8.0 mol Na

166. 0.046 mol LiCl

167. a. 27 mol H_2SO_4
b. 27 mol H_2
9 mol $Al_2(SO_4)_3$

168. a. 11.6 mol CO_2, 15.4 mol H_2O
b. 0.388 mol CO_2
0.518 mol H_2O
0.129 mol C_3H_8

169. a. 403 g P
b. 19.6 g O_2, 34.7 g P_4O_{10}

170. a. 29.44 g O_2
b. 180 g H_2O

171. a. 0.5882 mol Na_2CO_3
b. 0.0708 mol CO_2

172. a. 10.8 mol H_2
b. 10. mol Fe

173. 24.9 g AgBr

174. 37 g C_2H_2

175. a. 30.7 g MnO_2

b. 0.16 g $MnCl_2$

176. 15 mol $(NH_4)_2SO_4$

177. a. 51 g Al

b. 101 g Fe

c. 1.83 mol Fe_2O_3

178. 0.303 g H_2

179. 1.11 g H_2SO_4 ($H_2SO_4 + 2KOH \longrightarrow K_2SO_4 + 2H_2O$)

180. a. $H_3PO_4 + 2NH_3 \longrightarrow (NH_4)_2HPO_4$

b. 0.293 mol $(NH_4)_2HPO_4$

c. 970 kg NH_3

181. a. 90.0 mol $ZnCO_3$, 60.0 mol $C_6H_8O_7$

b. 13.5 kg H_2O, 33.0 kg CO_2

182. a. 60.9 g methyl butanoate

b. 3261 g H_2O

183. a. 0.450 mol N_2

b. 294 g NH_4NO_3

184. 0.751 mg KNO_3 ($Pb(NO_3)_2 + 2KI \longrightarrow PbI_2 + 2KNO_3$)

185. 3.3 mol $PbSO_4$

186. 360 g H_2O ($2LiOH + CO_2 \longrightarrow H_2O + Li_2CO_3$)

187. a. 38.1 g H_2O

b. 40.1 g H_3PO_4

c. 0.392 mol H_2O

188. 81.0 g C_2H_5OH ($C_2H_5OH + 3O_2 \longrightarrow 2CO_2 + 3H_2O$)

189. 76.5 g H_2SO_4; 12.5 g O_2

190. 1.31 g CO_2 ($2\,NaHCO_3 \longrightarrow Na_2CO_3 + H_2O + CO_2$)

---

175. Chlorine gas can be produced in the laboratory by adding concentrated hydrochloric acid to manganese(IV) oxide in the following reaction:

$$MnO_2(s) + 4HCl(aq) \longrightarrow MnCl_2(aq) + 2H_2O(l) + Cl_2(g)$$

a. Calculate the mass of MnO_2 needed to produce 25.0 g of Cl_2.

b. What mass of $MnCl_2$ is produced when 0.091 g of Cl_2 is generated?

MIXED REVIEW

176. How many moles of ammonium sulfate can be made from the reaction of 30.0 mol of NH_3 with H_2SO_4 according to the following equation:

$$2NH_3 + H_2SO_4 \longrightarrow (NH_4)_2SO_4$$

177. In a very violent reaction called a thermite reaction, aluminum metal reacts with iron(III) oxide to form iron metal and aluminum oxide according to the following equation:

$$Fe_2O_3 + 2Al \longrightarrow 2Fe + Al_2O_3$$

a. What mass of Al will react with 150 g of Fe_2O_3?

b. If 0.905 mol Al_2O_3 is produced in the reaction, what mass of Fe is produced?

c. How many moles of Fe_2O_3 will react with 99.0 g of Al?

178. The reaction $N_2(g) + 3H_2(g) \longrightarrow 2NH_3(g)$ is used to produce ammonia commercially. If 1.40 g of N_2 are used in the reaction, how many grams of H_2 will be needed?

179. What mass of sulfuric acid, H_2SO_4, is required to react with 1.27 g of potassium hydroxide, KOH? The products of this reaction are potassium sulfate and water.

180. Ammonium hydrogen phosphate, $(NH_4)_2HPO_4$, a common fertilizer; is made from reacting phosphoric acid, H_3PO_4, with ammonia.

a. Write the equation for this reaction.

b. If 10.00 g of ammonia react, how many moles of fertilizer will be produced?

c. What mass of ammonia will react with 2800 kg of H_3PO_4?

181. The following reaction shows the synthesis of zinc citrate, an ingredient in toothpaste, from zinc carbonate and citric acid:

$$3ZnCO_3(s) + 2C_6H_8O_7(aq) \longrightarrow Zn_3(C_6H_5O_7)_2(aq) + 3H_2O(l) + 3CO_2(g)$$

a. How many moles of $ZnCO_3$ and $C_6H_8O_7$ are required to produce 30.0 mol of $Zn_3(C_6H_5O_7)_2$?

b. What quantities, in kilograms, of H_2O and CO_2 are produced by the reaction of 500. mol of citric acid?

182. Methyl butanoate, an oily substance with a strong fruity fragrance can be made by reacting butanoic acid with methanol according to the following equation:

$$C_3H_7COOH + CH_3OH \longrightarrow C_3H_7COOCH_3 + H_2O$$

a. What mass of methyl butanoate is produced from the reaction of 52.5 g of butanoic acid?

b. In order to purify methyl butanoate, water must be removed. What mass of water is produced from the reaction of 5800. g of methanol?

183. Ammonium nitrate decomposes to yield nitrogen gas, water, and oxygen gas in the following reaction:

$$2NH_4NO_3 \longrightarrow 2N_2 + O_2 + 4H_2O$$

a. How many moles of nitrogen gas are produced when 36.0 g of NH_4NO_3 reacts?

b. If 7.35 mol of H_2O are produced in this reaction, what mass of NH_4NO_3 reacted?

184. Lead(II) nitrate reacts with potassium iodide to produce lead(II) iodide and potassium nitrate. If 1.23 mg of lead nitrate are consumed, what is the mass of the potassium nitrate produced?

185. A car battery produces electrical energy with the following chemical reaction:

$$Pb(s) + PbO_2(s) + 2H_2SO_4(aq) \longrightarrow 2PbSO_4(s) + 2H_2O(l)$$

If the battery loses 0.34 kg of lead in this reaction, how many moles of lead(II) sulfate are produced?

186. In a space shuttle, the CO_2 that the crew exhales is removed from the air by a reaction within canisters of lithium hydroxide. On average, each astronaut exhales about 20.0 mol of CO_2 daily. What mass of water will be produced when this amount reacts with LiOH? The other product of the reaction is Li_2CO_3.

187. Water is sometimes removed from the products of a reaction by placing them in a closed container with excess P_4O_{10}. Water is absorbed by the following reaction:

$$P_4O_{10} + 6H_2O \longrightarrow 4H_3PO_4$$

a. What mass of water can be absorbed by 1.00×10^2 g of P_4O_{10}?

b. If the P_4O_{10} in the container absorbs 0.614 mol of water, what mass of H_3PO_4 is produced?

c. If the mass of the container of P_4O_{10} increases from 56.64 g to 63.70 g, how many moles of water are absorbed?

188. Ethanol, C_2H_5OH, is considered a clean fuel because it burns in oxygen to produce carbon dioxide and water with few trace pollutants. If 95.0 g of H_2O are produced during the combustion of ethanol, how many grams of ethanol were present at the beginning of the reaction?

189. Sulfur dioxide is one of the major contributors to acid rain. Sulfur dioxide can react with oxygen and water in the atmosphere to form sulfuric acid, as shown in the following equation:

$$2H_2O(l) + O_2(g) + 2SO_2(g) \longrightarrow 2H_2SO_4(aq)$$

If 50.0 g of sulfur dioxide from pollutants reacts with water and oxygen found in the air, how many grams of sulfuric acid can be produced? How many grams of oxygen are used in the process?

190. When heated, sodium bicarbonate, $NaHCO_3$, decomposes into sodium carbonate, Na_2CO_3, water, and carbon dioxide. If 5.00 g of $NaHCO_3$ decomposes, what is the mass of the carbon dioxide produced?

191. A reaction between hydrazine, N_2H_4, and dinitrogen tetroxide, N_2O_4, has been used to launch rockets into space. The reaction produces nitrogen gas and water vapor.
   a. Write a balanced chemical equation for this reaction.
   b. What is the mole ratio of N_2O_4 to N_2?
   c. How many moles of N_2 will be produced if 20 000 mol of N_2H_4 are used by a rocket?
   d. How many grams of H_2O are made when 450. kg of N_2O_4 are consumed?

192. Joseph Priestley is credited with the discovery of oxygen. He produced O_2 by heating mercury(II) oxide, HgO, to decompose it into its elements. How many moles of oxygen could Priestley have produced if he had decomposed 517.84 g of mercury oxide?

193. Iron(III) chloride, $FeCl_3$, can be made by the reaction of iron with chlorine gas. How much iron, in grams, will be needed to completely react with 58.0 g of Cl_2?

194. Sodium sulfide and cadmium nitrate undergo a double-displacement reaction as shown by the following equation:

$$Na_2S + Cd(NO_3)_2 \longrightarrow 2NaNO_3 + CdS$$

What is the mass, in milligrams, of cadmium sulfide that can be made from 5.00 mg of sodium sulfide?

195. Potassium permanganate and glycerin react explosively according to the following equation:

$$14KMnO_4 + 4C_3H_5(OH)_3 \longrightarrow 7K_2CO_3 + 7Mn_2O_3 + 5CO_2 + 16H_2O$$

   a. How many moles of carbon dioxide can be produced from 4.44 mol of $KMnO_4$?
   b. If 5.21 g of H_2O are produced, how many moles of glycerin, $C_3H_5(OH)_3$, were used?
   c. If 3.39 mol of potassium carbonate are made, how many grams of manganese(III) oxide are also made?
   d. How many grams of glycerin will be needed to react with 50.0 g of $KMnO_4$? How many grams of CO_2 will be produced in the same reaction?

196. Calcium carbonate found in limestone and marble reacts with hydrochloric acid to form calcium chloride, carbon dioxide, and water according to the following equation:

$$CaCO_3(s) + 2HCl(aq) \longrightarrow CaCl_2(aq) + CO_2(g) + H_2O(l)$$

   a. What mass of HCl will be needed to produce 5.00×10^3 kg of $CaCl_2$?
   b. What mass of CO_2 could be produced from the reaction of 750 g of $CaCO_3$?

197. The fuel used to power the booster rockets on the space shuttle is a mixture of aluminum metal and ammonium perchlorate. The following balanced equation represents the reaction of these two ingredients:

$$3Al(s) + 3NH_4ClO_4(s) \longrightarrow Al_2O_3(s) + AlCl_3(g) + 3NO(g) + 6H_2O(g)$$

   a. If 1.50×10^5 g of Al react, what mass of NH_4ClO_4, in grams, is required?
   b. If aluminum reacts with 620 kg of NH_4ClO_4, what mass of nitrogen monoxide is produced?

198. Phosphoric acid is typically produced by the action of sulfuric acid on rock that has a high content of calcium phosphate according to the following equation:

$$3H_2SO_4 + Ca_3(PO_4)_2 + 6H_2O \longrightarrow 3[CaSO_4{\bullet}2H_2O] + 2H_3PO_4$$

   a. If 2.50×10^5 kg of H_2SO_4 react, how many moles of H_3PO_4 can be made?
   b. What mass of calcium sulfate dihydrate is produced by the reaction of 400. kg of calcium phosphate?
   c. If the rock being used contains 78.8% $Ca_3(PO_4)_2$, how many metric tons of H_3PO_4 can be produced from 68 metric tons of rock?

199. Rusting of iron occurs in the presence of moisture according to the following equation:

$$4Fe(s) + 3O_2(g) \longrightarrow 2Fe_2O_3(s)$$

Suppose that 3.19% of a heap of steel scrap with a mass of 1650 kg rusts in a year. What mass will the heap have after one year of rusting?

Limiting Reactants: Chap. 9, Sec. 3

200. Aluminum oxidizes according to the following equation:

$$4Al + 3O_2 \longrightarrow 2Al_2O_3$$

Powdered Al (0.048 mol) is placed into a container containing 0.030 mol O_2. What is the limiting reactant?

201. A process by which zirconium metal can be produced from the mineral zirconium(IV) orthosilicate, $ZrSiO_4$, starts by reacting it with chlorine gas to form zirconium(IV) chloride:

$$ZrSiO_4 + 2Cl_2 \longrightarrow ZrCl_4 + SiO_2 + O_2$$

What mass of $ZrCl_4$ can be produced if 862 g of $ZrSiO_4$ and 950. g of Cl_2 are available? You must first determine the limiting reactant.

MIXED REVIEW

202. Heating zinc sulfide in the presence of oxygen yields the following:

$$ZnS + O_2 \longrightarrow ZnO + SO_2$$

If 1.72 mol of ZnS is heated in the presence of 3.04 mol of O_2, which reactant will be used up? Balance the equation first.

203. Use the following equation for the oxidation of aluminum in the following problems:

$$4Al + 3O_2 \longrightarrow 2Al_2O_3$$

   a. Which reactant is limiting if 0.32 mol Al and 0.26 mol O_2 are available?
   b. How many moles of Al_2O_3 are formed from the reaction of 6.38×10^{-3} mol of O_2 and 9.15×10^{-3} mol of Al?
   c. If 3.17 g of Al and 2.55 g of O_2 are available, which reactant is limiting?

ANSWERS

191. a. $2N_2H_4 + N_2O_4 \longrightarrow 3N_2 + 4H_2O$
b. 1 mol N_2O_4 to 3 mol N_2
c. 30 000 mol N_2
d. 3.52×10^5 g H_2O
192. 1.1954 mol O_2 [$2HgO(s) \longrightarrow 2Hg(l) + O_2(g)$]
193. 30.5 g Fe ($2Fe + 3Cl_2 \longrightarrow 2FeCl_3$)
194. 9.26 mg CdS
195. a. 1.59 mol CO_2
b. 0.0723 mol $C_3H_5(OH)_3$
c. 535 g Mn_2O_3
d. 8.33 g $C_3H_5(OH)_3$; 4.97 g CO_2
196. a. 3.29×10^3 kg HCl
b. 330 g $CO_2(s)$
197. a. 6.53×10^5 g NH_4ClO_4
b. 160 kg NO(*g*)
198. a. 1.70×10^6 mol H_3PO_4
b. 666 kg $CaSO_4{\bullet}2H_2O$
c. 34 metric tons H_3PO_4
199. 1670 kg
200. O_2
201. $ZrSiO_4$; 1.10×10^3 g $ZrCl_4$
202. $2ZnS + 3O_2 \longrightarrow 2ZnO + 2SO_2$; ZnS is limiting
203. a. Al is limiting
b. 4.25×10^{-3} mol Al_2O_3
c. O_2 is limiting

R95

ANSWERS

204. a. CuS is limiting
b. 15.6 g CuO
205. Fe is limiting; 0.14 mol Cu
206. 54 g $Ba(NO_3)_2$
207. a. 38 g Br_2
b. 510 g I_2
208. a. Ni is in excess
b. 60.2 g $Ni(NO_3)_2$
209. 0.80 mol O_2 remain [$CS_2(g) + 3O_2(g) \longrightarrow 2SO_2(g) + CO_2(g)$]
210. a. 0.84 g $Hg(NH_2)Cl$
b. 0.84 g $Hg(NH_2)Cl$
211. a. $2Al(s) + 2NaOH(aq) + 2H_2O(l) \longrightarrow 2NaAlO_2(aq) + 3H_2(g)$
b. 0.56 mol H_2 (NaOH is limiting)
c. Al should be limiting because you would not want aluminum metal remaining in the drain.
212. a. 0.0422 mol Cu, 0.169 mol HNO_3
b. Cu is in excess
213. a. 2.90 mol NO, 4.35 mol H_2O
b. NH_3 is limiting
c. 1.53×10^3 kg NO (NH_3 is limiting)
214. 565 g CH_3CHO; 29 g CH_3CH_2OH remains
215. 630 g HBr
216. 12.7 g SO_2
217. a. 18.4 g Tb
b. 2.4 g TbF_3

204. In the production of copper from ore containing copper(II) sulfide, the ore is first roasted to change it to the oxide according to the following equation:

$$2CuS + 3O_2 \longrightarrow 2CuO + 2SO_2$$

a. If 100 g of CuS and 56 g of O_2 are available, which reactant is limiting?
b. What mass of CuO can be formed from the reaction of 18.7 g of CuS and 12.0 g of O_2?

205. A reaction such as the one shown here is often used to demonstrate a single-displacement reaction:

$$3CuSO_4(aq) + 2Fe(s) \longrightarrow 3Cu(s) + Fe_2(SO_4)_3(aq)$$

If you place 0.092 mol of iron filings in a solution containing 0.158 mol of $CuSO_4$, what is the limiting reactant? How many moles of Cu will be formed?

206. In the reaction $BaCO_3 + 2HNO_3 \longrightarrow Ba(NO_3)_2 + CO_2 + H_2O$, what mass of $Ba(NO_3)_2$ can be formed by combining 55 g $BaCO_3$ and 26 g HNO_3?

207. Bromine replaces iodine in magnesium iodide by the following process:

$$MgI_2 + Br_2 \longrightarrow MgBr_2 + I_2$$

a. Which is the excess reactant when 560 g of MgI_2 and 360 g of Br_2 react, and what mass remains?
b. What mass of I_2 is formed in the same process?

208. Nickel replaces silver from silver nitrate in solution according to the following equation:

$$2AgNO_3 + Ni \longrightarrow 2Ag + Ni(NO_3)_2$$

a. If you have 22.9 g of Ni and 112 g of $AgNO_3$, which reactant is in excess?
b. What mass of nickel(II) nitrate would be produced given the quantities above?

209. Carbon disulfide, CS_2, is an important industrial substance. Its fumes can burn explosively in air to form sulfur dioxide and carbon dioxide:

$$CS_2(g) + O_2(g) \longrightarrow SO_2(g) + CO_2(g)$$

If 1.60 mol of CS_2 burns with 5.60 mol of O_2, how many moles of the excess reactant will still be present when the reaction is over?

210. Although poisonous, mercury compounds were once used to kill bacteria in wounds and on the skin. One was called "ammoniated mercury" and is made from mercury(II) chloride according to the following equation:

$$HgCl_2(aq) + 2NH_3(aq) \longrightarrow Hg(NH_2)Cl(s) + NH_4Cl(aq)$$

a. What mass of $Hg(NH_2)Cl$ could be produced from 0.91 g of $HgCl_2$ assuming plenty of ammonia is available?
b. What mass of $Hg(NH_2)Cl$ could be produced from 0.91 g of $HgCl_2$ and 0.15 g of NH_3 in solution?

211. Aluminum chips are sometimes added to sodium hydroxide-based drain cleaners because they react to generate hydrogen gas which bubbles and helps loosen material in the drain. The equation follows:

$$Al(s) + NaOH(aq) + H_2O(l) \longrightarrow NaAlO_2(aq) + H_2(g)$$

a. Balance the equation.
b. How many moles of H_2 can be generated from 0.57 mol Al and 0.37 mol NaOH in excess water?
c. Which reactant should be limiting in order for the mixture to be most effective as a drain cleaner? Explain your choice.

212. Copper is changed to copper(II) ions by nitric acid according to the following equation:

$$4HNO_3 + Cu \longrightarrow Cu(NO_3)_2 + 2NO_2 + 2H_2O$$

a. How many moles each of HNO_3 and Cu must react in order to produce 0.0845 mol of NO_2?
b. If 5.94 g of Cu and 23.23 g of HNO_3 are combined, which reactant is in excess?

213. One industrial process for producing nitric acid begins with the following reaction:

$$4NH_3 + 5O_2 \longrightarrow 4NO + 6H_2O$$

a. If 2.90 mol NH_3 and 3.75 mol O_2 are available, how many moles of each product are formed?
b. Which reactant is limiting if 4.20×10^4 g of NH_3 and 1.31×10^5 g of O_2 are available?
c. What mass of NO is formed in the reaction of 869 kg of NH_3 and 2480 kg O_2?

214. Acetaldehyde, CH_3CHO, is manufactured by the reaction of ethanol with copper(II) oxide according to the following equation:

$$CH_3CH_2OH + CuO \longrightarrow CH_3CHO + H_2O + Cu$$

What mass of acetaldehyde can be produced by the reaction between 620 g of ethanol and 1020 g of CuO? What mass of which reactant will be left over?

215. Hydrogen bromide can be produced by a reaction among bromine, sulfur dioxide, and water as follows:

$$SO_2 + Br_2 + H_2O \longrightarrow 2HBr + H_2SO_4$$

If 250 g of SO_2 and 650 g of Br_2 react in the presence of excess water, what mass of HBr will be formed?

216. Sulfur dioxide can be produced in the laboratory by the reaction of hydrochloric acid and a sulfite salt such as sodium sulfite:

$$Na_2SO_3 + 2HCl \longrightarrow 2NaCl + SO_2 + H_2O$$

What mass of SO_2 can be made from 25.0 g of Na_2SO_3 and 22.0 g of HCl?

217. The rare-earth metal terbium is produced from terbium(III) fluoride and calcium metal by the following single-displacement reaction:

$$2TbF_3 + 3Ca \longrightarrow 3CaF_2 + 2Tb$$

a. Given 27.5 g of TbF_3 and 6.96 g of Ca, how many grams of terbium could be produced?
b. How many grams of the excess reactant is left over?

Percentage Yield: Chap. 9, Sec. 3

218. Calculate the percentage yield in each of the following cases.

a. theoretical yield is 50.0 g of product; actual yield is 41.9 g

b. theoretical yield is 290 kg of product; actual yield is 270 kg

c. theoretical yield is 6.05×10^4 kg of product; actual yield is 4.18×10^4 kg

d. theoretical yield is 0.001 92 g of product; actual yield is 0.000 89 g

219. In the commercial production of the element arsenic, arsenic(III) oxide is heated with carbon, which reduces the oxide to the metal according to the following equation:

$$2As_2O_3 + 3C \longrightarrow 3CO_2 + 4As$$

a. If 8.87 g of As_2O_3 is used in the reaction and 5.33 g of As is produced, what is the percentage yield?

b. If 67 g of carbon is used up in a different reaction and 425 g of As is produced, calculate the percentage yield of this reaction.

MIXED REVIEW

220. Ethyl acetate is a sweet-smelling solvent used in varnishes and fingernail-polish remover. It is produced industrially by heating acetic acid and ethanol together in the presence of sulfuric acid, which is added to speed up the reaction. The ethyl acetate is distilled off as it is formed. The equation for the process is as follows:

$$\underset{\text{acetic acid}}{CH_3COOH} + \underset{\text{ethanol}}{CH_3CH_2OH} \xrightarrow{H_2SO_4} \underset{\text{ethyl acetate}}{CH_3COOCH_2CH_3} + H_2O$$

Determine the percentage yield in the following cases.

a. 68.3 g of ethyl acetate should be produced but only 43.9 g is recovered.

b. 0.0419 mol of ethyl acetate is produced but 0.0722 mol is expected. (Hint: Percentage yield can also be calculated by dividing the actual yield in moles by the theoretical yield in moles.)

c. 4.29 mol of ethanol is reacted with excess acetic acid, but only 2.98 mol of ethyl acetate is produced.

d. A mixture of 0.58 mol ethanol and 0.82 mol acetic acid is reacted and 0.46 mol ethyl acetate is produced. (Hint: What is the limiting reactant?)

221. Assume the following hypothetical reaction takes place:

$$2A + 7B \longrightarrow 4C + 3D$$

Calculate the percentage yield in each of the following cases.

a. The reaction of 0.0251 mol of A gives 0.0349 mol of C.

b. The reaction of 1.19 mol of A produces 1.41 mol of D.

c. The reaction of 189 mol of B produces 39 mol of D.

d. The reaction of 3500 mol of B produces 1700 mol of C.

222. Elemental phosphorus can be produced by heating calcium phosphate from rocks with silica sand (SiO_2) and carbon in the form of coke (a fuel resulting from distilling coal). The following reaction takes place:

$$Ca_3(PO_4)_2 + 3SiO_2 + 5C \longrightarrow 3CaSiO_3 + 2P + 5CO$$

a. If 57 mol of $Ca_3(PO_4)_2$ is used and 101 mol of $CaSiO_3$ is obtained, what is the percentage yield?

b. Determine the percentage yield obtained if 1280 mol of carbon is consumed and 622 mol of $CaSiO_3$ is produced.

c. The engineer in charge of this process expects a yield of 81.5%. If 1.4×10^5 mol of $Ca_3(PO_4)_2$ is used, how many moles of phosphorus will be produced?

223. Tungsten (W) can be produced from its oxide by reacting the oxide with hydrogen at a high temperature according to the following equation:

$$WO_3 + 3H_2 \longrightarrow W + 3H_2O$$

a. What is the percentage yield if 56.9 g of WO_3 yields 41.4 g of tungsten?

b. How many moles of tungsten will be produced from 3.72 g of WO_3 if the yield is 92.0%?

c. A chemist carries out this reaction and obtains 11.4 g of tungsten. If the percentage yield is 89.4%, what mass of WO_3 was used?

224. Carbon tetrachloride, CCl_4, is a solvent that was once used in large quantities in dry cleaning. Because it is a dense liquid that does not burn, it was also used in fire extinguishers. Unfortunately, its use was discontinued because it was found to be a carcinogen. It was manufactured by the following reaction:

$$CS_2 + 3Cl_2 \longrightarrow CCl_4 + S_2Cl_2$$

The reaction was economical because the byproduct disulfur dichloride, S_2Cl_2, could be used by industry in the manufacture of rubber products and other materials.

a. What is the percentage yield of CCl_4 if 719 kg is produced from the reaction of 410. kg of CS_2?

b. If 67.5 g of Cl_2 are used in the reaction and 39.5 g of S_2Cl_2 is produced, what is the percentage yield?

c. If the percentage yield of the industrial process is 83.3%, how many kilograms of CS_2 should be reacted to obtain 5.00×10^4 kg of CCl_4? How many kilograms of S_2Cl_2 will be produced, assuming the same yield for that product?

225. Nitrogen dioxide, NO_2, can be converted to dinitrogen pentoxide, N_2O_5, by reacting it with ozone, O_3. The reaction of NO_2 takes place according to the following equation:

$$2NO_2(g) + O_3(g) \longrightarrow N_2O_5(s \text{ or } g) + O_2(g)$$

a. Calculate the percentage yield for a reaction in which 0.38 g of NO_2 reacts and 0.36 g of N_2O_5 is recovered.

b. What mass of N_2O_5 will result from the reaction of 6.0 mol of NO_2 if there is a 61.1% yield in the reaction?

226. In the past, hydrogen chloride, HCl, was made using the *salt-cake* method as shown in the following equation:

$$2NaCl(s) + H_2SO_4(aq) \longrightarrow Na_2SO_4(s) + 2HCl(g)$$

If 30.0 g of NaCl and 0.250 mol of H_2SO_4 are available, and 14.6 g of HCl is made, what is the percentage yield?

Problem Bank

ANSWERS

218. a. 83.8% yield
b. 93% yield
c. 69.1% yield
d. 46% yield

219. a. 79.3% yield
b. 76% yield

220. a. 64.3% yield
b. 58.0% yield
c. 69.5% yield
d. CH_3CH_2OH is limiting; 79% yield

221. a. 69.5% yield
b. 79.0% yield
c. 48% yield
d. 85% yield

222. a. 59% yield
b. 81.0% yield
c. 2.3×10^5 mol P

223. a. 91.8% yield
b. 0.0148 mol W
c. 16.1 g WO_3

224. a. 86.8% yield
b. 92.2% yield
c. 2.97×10^4 kg CS_2; 4.39×10^4 kg S_2Cl_2

225. a. 81% yield
b. 2.0×10^2 g N_2O_5

226. 80.1% yield

ANSWERS

227. a. 95% yield
b. 9.10×10^2 g Au
c. 9×10^4 kg ore

228. a. 87.5% yield
b. 0.25 g CO

229. a. 71% yield
b. 26 metric tons
c. 47.8 g NaCl
d. 500 kg NaOH/h

230. a. $2Mg + O_2 \longrightarrow 2MgO$
b. 87.7% yield
c. $3Mg + N_2 \longrightarrow Mg_3N_2$
d. 84% yield

231. a. 80.% yield
b. 66.2% yield
c. 57.1% yield

232. $2C_3H_6(g) + 2NH_3(g) + 3O_2(g) \longrightarrow 2C_3H_3N(g) + 6H_2O(g)$ 91.0% yield

233. a. 3.41×10^3 kg CH_3OH ($CO + 2H_2 \longrightarrow CH_3OH$)
b. 91.5% yield

234. 96.9% yield

235. $6CO_2 + 6H_2O \longrightarrow C_6H_{12}O_6 + 6O_2$; 6.32×10^3 g O_2

227. Cyanide compounds such as sodium cyanide, NaCN, are especially useful in gold refining because they will react with gold to form a stable compound that can then be separated and broken down to retrieve the gold. Ore containing only small quantities of gold can be used in this form of "chemical mining." The equation for the reaction follows:

$$4Au + 8NaCN + 2H_2O + O_2 \longrightarrow 4NaAu(CN)_2 + 4NaOH$$

a. What percentage yield is obtained if 410 g of gold produces 540 g of $NaAu(CN)_2$?

b. Assuming a 79.6% yield in the conversion of gold to $NaAu(CN)_2$, what mass of gold would produce 1.00 kg of $NaAu(CN)_2$?

c. Given the conditions in (b), what mass of gold ore that is 0.001% gold would be needed to produce 1.00 kg of $NaAu(CN)_2$?

228. Diiodine pentoxide is useful in devices such as respirators because it reacts with the dangerous gas carbon monoxide, CO, to produce relatively harmless CO_2 according to the following equation:

$$I_2O_5 + 5CO \longrightarrow I_2 + 5CO_2$$

a. In testing a respirator, 2.00 g of carbon monoxide gas is passed through diiodine pentoxide. Upon analyzing the results, it is found that 3.17 g of I_2 was produced. Calculate the percentage yield of the reaction.

b. Assuming that the yield in (a) resulted because some of the CO did not react, calculate the mass of CO that passed through.

229. Sodium hypochlorite, NaClO, the main ingredient in household bleach, is produced by bubbling chlorine gas through a strong lye (sodium hydroxide, NaOH) solution. The following equation shows the reaction that occurs:

$$2NaOH(aq) + Cl_2(g) \longrightarrow NaCl(aq) + NaClO(aq) + H_2O(l)$$

a. What is the percentage yield of the reaction if 1.2 kg of Cl_2 reacts to form 0.90 kg of NaClO?

b. If a plant operator wants to make 25 metric tons of NaClO per day at a yield of 91.8%, how many metric tons of chlorine gas must be on hand each day?

c. What mass of NaCl is formed per mole of chlorine gas at a yield of 81.8%?

d. At what rate in kg per hour must NaOH be replenished if the reaction produces 370 kg/h of NaClO at a yield of 79.5%? Assume that all of the NaOH reacts to produce this yield.

230. Magnesium burns in oxygen to form magnesium oxide. However, when magnesium burns in air, which is only about one-fifth oxygen, side reactions form other products, such as magnesium nitride, Mg_3N_2.

a. Write a balanced equation for the burning of magnesium in oxygen.

b. If enough magnesium burns in air to produce 2.04 g of magnesium oxide but only 1.79 g is obtained, what is the percentage yield?

c. Magnesium will react with pure nitrogen to form the nitride, Mg_3N_2. Write a balanced equation for this reaction.

d. If 0.097 mol of Mg react with nitrogen and 0.027 mol of Mg_3N_2 is produced, what is the percentage yield of the reaction?

231. Some alcohols can be converted to organic acids by using sodium dichromate and sulfuric acid. The following equation shows the reaction of 1-propanol to propanoic acid:

$$3CH_3CH_2CH_2OH + 2Na_2Cr_2O_7 + 8H_2SO_4 \longrightarrow 3CH_3CH_2COOH + 2Cr_2(SO_4)_3 + 2Na_2SO_4 + 11H_2O$$

a. If 0.89 g of 1-propanol reacts and 0.88 g of propanoic acid is produced, what is the percentage yield?

b. A chemist uses this reaction to obtain 1.50 mol of propanoic acid. The reaction consumes 136 g of propanol. Calculate the percentage yield.

c. Some 1-propanol of uncertain purity is used in the reaction. If 116 g of $Na_2Cr_2O_7$ are consumed in the reaction and 28.1 g of propanoic acid are produced, what is the percentage yield?

232. Acrylonitrile, $C_3H_3N(g)$, is an important ingredient in the production of various fibers and plastics. Acrylonitrile is produced from the following reaction:

$$C_3H_6(g) + NH_3(g) + O_2(g) \longrightarrow C_3H_3N(g) + H_2O(g)$$

If 850. g of C_3H_6 is mixed with 300. g of NH_3 and unlimited O_2, to produce 850. g of acrylonitrile, what is the percentage yield? You must first balance the equation.

233. Methanol, CH_3OH, is frequently used in race cars as fuel. It is produced as the sole product of the combination of carbon monoxide gas and hydrogen gas.

a. If 430. kg of hydrogen react, what mass of methanol could be produced?

b. If 3.12×10^3 kg of methanol are actually produced, what is the percentage yield?

234. The compound, $C_6H_{16}N_2$, is one of the starting materials in the production of nylon. It can be prepared from the following reaction involving adipic acid, $C_6H_{10}O_4$:

$$C_6H_{10}O_4(l) + 2NH_3(g) + 4H_2(g) \longrightarrow C_6H_{16}N_2(l) + 4H_2O$$

What is the percentage yield if 750. g of adipic acid results in the production of 578 g of $C_6H_{16}N_2$?

235. Plants convert carbon dioxide to oxygen during photosynthesis according to the following equation:

$$CO_2 + H_2O \longrightarrow C_6H_{12}O_6 + O_2$$

Balance this equation, and calculate how much oxygen would be produced if 1.37×10^4 g of carbon dioxide reacts with a percentage yield of 63.4%.

236. Lime, CaO, is frequently added to streams and lakes which have been polluted by acid rain. The calcium oxide reacts with the water to form a base that can neutralize the acid as shown in the following reaction:

$$CaO(s) + H_2O(l) \longrightarrow Ca(OH)_2(s)$$

If 2.67×10^2 mol of base are needed to neutralize the acid in a lake, and the above reaction has a percentage yield of 54.3%, what is the mass, in kilograms, of lime that must be added to the lake?

Gas Laws: Chap. 11, Sec. 2

BOYLE'S LAW

In each of the following problems, assume that the temperature and molar quantity of gas do not change.

237. Calculate the unknown quantity in each of the following measurements of gases.

	P_1	V_1	P_2	V_2
a.	3.0 atm	25 mL	6.0 atm	? mL
b.	99.97 kPa	550. mL	? kPa	275 mL
c.	0.89 atm	? L	3.56 atm	20.0 L
d.	? kPa	800. mL	500. kPa	160. mL
e.	0.040 atm	? L	250 atm	1.0×10^{-2} L

238. A sample of neon gas occupies a volume of 2.8 L at 1.8 atm. What will its volume be at 1.2 atm?

239. To what pressure would you have to compress 48.0 L of oxygen gas at 99.3 kPa in order to reduce its volume to 16.0 L?

240. A chemist collects 59.0 mL of sulfur dioxide gas on a day when the atmospheric pressure is 0.989 atm. On the next day, the pressure has changed to 0.967 atm. What will the volume of the SO_2 gas be on the second day?

241. 2.2 L of hydrogen at 6.5 atm pressure is used to fill a balloon at a final pressure of 1.15 atm. What is its final volume?

CHARLES'S LAW

In each of the following problems, assume that the pressure and molar quantity of gas do not change.

242. Calculate the unknown quantity in each of the following measurements of gases:

	V_1	T_1	V_2	T_2
a.	40.0 mL	280. K	? mL	350. K
b.	0.606 L	300. K	0.404 L	? K
c.	? mL	292 K	250. mL	365 K
d.	100. mL	? K	125 mL	305 K
e.	0.0024 L	22°C	? L	−14°C

243. A balloon full of air has a volume of 2.75 L at a temperature of 18°C. What is the balloon's volume at 45°C?

244. A sample of argon has a volume of 0.43 mL at 24°C. At what temperature in degrees Celsius will it have a volume of 0.57 mL?

GAY-LUSSAC'S LAW

In each of the following problems, assume that the volume and molar quantity of gas do not change.

245. Calculate the unknown quantity in each of the following measurements of gases.

	P_1	T_1	P_2	T_2
a.	1.50 atm	273 K	? atm	410 K
b.	0.208 atm	300. K	0.156 atm	? K
c.	? kPa	52°C	99.7 kPa	77°C
d.	5.20 atm	?°C	4.16 atm	−13°C
e.	8.33×10^{-4} atm	−84°C	3.92×10^{-3} atm	? °C

246. A cylinder of compressed gas has a pressure of 4.882 atm on one day. The next day, the same cylinder of gas has a pressure of 4.690 atm, and its temperature is 8°C. What was the temperature on the previous day in °C?

247. A mylar balloon is filled with helium gas to a pressure of 107 kPa when the temperature is 22°C. If the temperature changes to 45°C, what will be the pressure of the helium in the balloon?

THE COMBINED GAS LAW

In each of the following problems, it is assumed that the molar quantity of gas does not change.

248. Calculate the unknown quantity in each of the following measurements of gases.

	P_1	V_1	T_1	P_2	V_2	T_2
a.	99.3 kPa	225 mL	15°C	102.8 kPa	? mL	24°C
b.	0.959 atm	3.50 L	45°C	? atm	3.70 L	37°C
c.	0.0036 atm	62 mL	373 K	0.0029 atm	64 mL	? K
d.	100. kPa	43.2 mL	19°C	101.3 kPa	? mL	0°C

249. A student collects 450. mL of HCl(*g*) hydrogen chloride gas at a pressure of 100. kPa and a temperature of 17°C. What is the volume of the HCl at 0°C and 101.3 kPa?

DALTON'S LAW OF PARTIAL PRESSURES

250. A chemist collects a sample of $H_2S(g)$ over water at a temperature of 27°C. The total pressure of the gas that has displaced a volume of 15 mL of water is 207.33 kPa. What is the pressure of the H_2S gas collected?

In each of the following problems, assume that the molar quantity of gas does not change.

251. Some hydrogen is collected over water at 10°C and 105.5 kPa pressure. The total volume of the sample was 1.93 L. Calculate the volume of the hydrogen corrected to STP.

252. One student carries out a reaction that gives off methane gas and obtains a total volume by water displacement of 338 mL at a temperature of 19°C and a pressure of 0.9566 atm. Another student does the identical experiment on another day at a temperature of 26°C and a pressure of 0.989 atm. Which student collected more CH_4?

ANSWERS

236. 27.6 kg CaO
237. a. 13 mL
b. 200. kPa
c. 80. L
d. 100. kPa
e. 63 L
238. 4.2 L
239. 298 kPa
240. 60.3 mL
241. 12 L
242. a. 50.0 mL
b. 200. K
c. 200. mL
d. 244 K
e. 0.0021 L
243. 3.01 L
244. 121°C
245. a. 2.25 atm
b. 225 K
c. 92.6 kPa
d. 52°C
e. 616°C
246. 20.°C
247. 115 kPa
248. a. 224 mL
b. 0.884 atm
c. 310 K
d. 39.9 mL
249. 418 mL
250. 203.76 kPa
251. 1.92 L
252. The second student collected more CH_4.

ANSWERS

253. a. 105 kPa
b. 5.0 mL
c. 42.4 kPa
d. 6.78×10^{-3} dm^3
e. 1.24 atm
f. 1.5 m^3
254. 8.0 m^3
255. 0.0258 atm
256. 8.01×10^{-2} dm^3
257. a. 234 K
b. 1.0 dm^3
c. –269.17°C
d. 8.10×10^{-2} L
e. 487 cm^3
f. 67.9 m^3
258. 1.45 cm^3
259. –40.°C
260. a. –208.6°C
b. 5.5 kPa
c. 2.61 atm
d. 297°C
e. 35.6 atm
f. 39 K
261. 0.899 atm
262. 2.23 atm
263. 7.98 K
264. a. 2.02 L
b. 75.8 kPa
c. 110 K
d. 4.69×10^3 mm^3
e. –72°C
f. 2.25 atm
265. 379 cm^3
266. 98 kPa
267. 1.00 atm (Use Boyle's law to find the pressure of each gas in the whole space; add the partial pressures of both gases when they occupy the whole space.)
268. 285 mL
269. 89 cm^3 (The pressure in the bottle on top of the mountain is the sum of P_{O_2} dry at the temperature of the mountaintop and $P_{H_2O\ vapor}$ at the temperature on top of the mountain.)

MIXED REVIEW

In each of the following problems, assume that the molar quantity of gas does not change.

253. Calculate the unknown quantity in each of the following measurements of gases.

	P_1	V_1	P_2	V_2
a.	127.3 kPa	796 cm^3	? kPa	965 cm^3
b.	7.1×10^2 atm	? mL	9.6×10^{-1} atm	3.7×10^3 mL
c.	? kPa	1.77 L	30.79 kPa	2.44 L
d.	114 kPa	2.93 dm^3	4.93×10^4 kPa	? dm^3
e.	1.00 atm	120. mL	? atm	97.0 mL
f.	0.77 atm	3.6 m^3	1.90 atm	? m^3

254. A gas cylinder contains 0.722 m^3 of hydrogen gas at a pressure of 10.6 atm. If the gas is used to fill a balloon at a pressure of 0.96 atm, what is the volume in m^3 of the filled balloon?

255. A weather balloon has a maximum volume of 7.50×10^3 L. The balloon contains 195 L of helium gas at a pressure of 0.993 atm. What will be the pressure when the balloon is at maximum volume?

256. A rubber ball contains 5.70×10^{-1} dm^3 of gas at a pressure of 1.05 atm. What volume will the gas occupy at 7.47 atm?

257. Calculate the unknown quantity in each of the following measurements of gases.

	V_1	T_1	V_2	T_2
a.	26.5 mL	? K	32.9 mL	290. K
b.	? dm^3	100.°C	0.83 dm^3	29°C
c.	7.44×10^4 mm^3	870.°C	2.59×10^2 mm^3	? °C
d.	5.63×10^{-2} L	132 K	? L	190. K
e.	? cm^3	243 K	819 cm^3	409 K
f.	679 m^3	–3°C	? m^3	–246°C

258. A bubble of carbon dioxide gas in some unbaked bread dough has a volume of 1.15 cm^3 at a temperature of 22°C. What volume will the bubble have when the bread is baked and the bubble reaches a temperature of 99°C?

259. A perfectly elastic balloon contains 6.75 dm^3 of air at a temperature of 40.°C. What is the temperature if the balloon has a volume of 5.03 dm^3?

260. Calculate the unknown quantity in each of the following measurements of gases.

	P_1	T_1	P_2	T_2
a.	0.777 atm	?°C	5.6 atm	192°C
b.	152 kPa	302 K	? kPa	11 K
c.	? atm	–76°C	3.97 atm	27°C
d.	395 atm	46°C	706 atm	?°C
e.	? atm	–37°C	350. atm	2050°C
f.	0.39 atm	263 K	0.058 atm	? K

261. A 2 L bottle containing only air is sealed at a temperature of 22°C and a pressure of 0.982 atm. The bottle is placed in a freezer and allowed to cool to –3°C. What is the pressure in the bottle?

262. The pressure in a car tire is 2.50 atm at a temperature of 33°C . What would the pressure be if the tire were allowed to cool to 0°C? Assume that the tire does not change volume.

263. A container filled with helium gas has a pressure of 127.5 kPa at a temperature of 290. K. What is the temperature when the pressure is 3.51 kPa?

264. Calculate the unknown quantity in each of the following measurements of gases.

	P_1	V_1	T_1	P_2	V_2	T_2
a.	1.03 atm	1.65 L	19°C	0.920 atm	? L	46°C
b.	107.0 kPa	3.79 dm^3	73°C	? kPa	7.58 dm^3	217°C
c.	0.029 atm	249 mL	? K	0.098 atm	197 mL	293 K
d.	113 kPa	? mm^3	12°C	149 kPa	3.18×10^3 mm^3	–18°C
e.	1.15 atm	0.93 m^3	–22°C	1.01 atm	0.85 m^3	?°C
f.	? atm	156 cm^3	195 K	2.25 atm	468 cm^3	585 K

265. A scientist has a sample of gas that was collected several days earlier. The sample has a volume of 392 cm^3 at a pressure of 0.987 atm and a temperature of 21°C. On the day the gas was collected, the temperature was 13°C and the pressure was 0.992 atm. What volume did the gas have on the day it was collected?

266. Hydrogen gas is collected by water displacement. Total volume collected is 0.461 L at a temperature of 17°C and a pressure of 0.989 atm. What is the pressure of dry hydrogen gas collected?

267. One container with a volume of 1.00 L contains argon at a pressure of 1.77 atm, and a second container of 1.50 L volume contains argon at a pressure of 0.487 atm. They are then connected to each other so that the pressure can become equal in both containers. What is the equalized pressure? Hint: Each sample of gas now occupies the total space. Dalton's law of partial pressures applies here.

268. Oxygen gas is collected over water at a temperature of 10.°C and a pressure of 1.02 atm. The volume of gas plus water vapor collected is 293 mL. What volume of oxygen at STP was collected?

269. A 500 mL bottle is partially filled with water so that the total volume of gases (water vapor and air) remaining in the bottle is 325 cm^3, measured at 20.°C and 101.3 kPa. The bottle is sealed and taken to a mountaintop where the pressure is 76.24 kPa and the temperature is 10°C. If the bottle is upside down and the seal leaks, how much water will leak out? The key to this problem is to determine the pressure in the 325 cm^3 space when the bottle is at the top of the mountain.

270. An air thermometer can be constructed by using a glass bubble attached to a piece of small-diameter glass tubing. The tubing contains a small amount of colored water that rises when the temperature increases and the trapped air expands. You want a 0.20 cm^3 change in volume to equal a 1°C change in temperature. What total volume of air at 20.°C should be trapped in the apparatus below the liquid?

271. A sample of nitrogen gas is collected over water, yielding a total volume of 62.25 mL at a temperature of 22°C and a total pressure of 97.7 kPa. At what pressure will the nitrogen alone occupy a volume of 50.00 mL at the same temperature?

272. The theoretical yield of a reaction that gives off nitrogen trifluoride gas is 844 mL at STP. What total volume of NF_3 plus water vapor will be collected over water at 25°C and a total pressure of 1.017 atm?

273. A weather balloon is inflated with 2.94 kL of helium at a location where the pressure is 1.06 atm and the temperature is 32°C. What will be the volume of the balloon at an altitude where the pressure is 0.092 atm and the temperature is 235°C?

274. The safety limit for a certain can of aerosol spray is 95°C. If the pressure of the gas in the can is 2.96 atm when it is 17°C, what will the pressure be at the safety limit?

275. A chemistry student collects a sample of ammonia gas at a temperature of 39°C. Later, the student measures the volume of the ammonia as 108 mL, but its temperature is now 21°C. What was the volume of the ammonia when it was collected?

276. A quantity of CO_2 gas occupies a volume of 624 L at a pressure of 1.40 atm. If this CO_2 is pumped into a gas cylinder that has a volume of 80.0 L, what pressure will the CO_2 exert on the cylinder?

The Ideal Gas Law: Chap. 11, Sec. 3

277. Use the ideal-gas-law equation to calculate the unknown quantity in each of the following sets of measurements. You will need to convert Celsius temperatures to Kelvin temperatures and volume units to liters.

	P	V	n	T
a.	1.09 atm	? L	0.0881 mol	302 K
b.	94.9 kPa	0.0350 L	? mol	55°C
c.	? kPa	15.7 L	0.815 mol	−20.°C
d.	0.500 atm	629 mL	0.0337 mol	? K
e.	0.950 atm	? L	0.0818 mol	19°C
f.	107 kPa	39.0 mL	? mol	27°C

278. A student collects 425 mL of oxygen at a temperature of 24°C and a pressure of 0.899 atm. How many moles of oxygen did the student collect?

APPLICATIONS OF THE IDEAL GAS LAW

279. A sample of an unknown gas has a mass of 0.116 g. It occupies a volume of 25.0 mL at a temperature of 127°C and has a pressure of 155.3 kPa. Calculate the molar mass of the gas.

280. Determine the mass of CO_2 gas that has a volume of 7.10 L at a pressure of 1.11 atm and a temperature of 31°C. Hint: Solve the equation for *m*, and calculate the molar mass using the chemical formula and the periodic table.

281. What is the density of silicon tetrafluoride gas at 72°C and a pressure of 144.5 kPa?

282. At what temperature will nitrogen gas have a density of 1.13 g/L at a pressure of 1.09 atm?

MIXED REVIEW

283. Use the ideal-gas-law equation to calculate the unknown quantity in each of the following sets of measurements.

	P	V	n	t
a.	0.0477 atm	15 200 L	? mol	−15°C
b.	? kPa	0.119 mL	0.000 350 mol	0°C
c.	500.0 kPa	250. mL	0.120 mol	?°C
d.	19.5 atm	?	4.7×10^4 mol	300.°C

284. Use the ideal-gas-law equation to calculate the unknown quantity in each of the following sets of measurements.

	P	V	m	M	t
a.	0.955 atm	3.77 L	8.23 g	? g/mol	25°C
b.	105.0 kPa	50.0 mL	? g	48.02 g/mol	0°C
c.	0.782 atm	? L	3.20×10^{-3} g	2.02 g/mol	−5°C
d.	? atm	2.00 L	7.19 g	159.8 g/mol	185°C
e.	107.2 kPa	26.1 mL	0.414 g	? g/mol	45°C

285. Determine the volume of one mole of an ideal gas at 25°C and 0.915 kPa.

286. Calculate the unknown quantity in each of the following sets of measurements.

	P	Molar Mass	Density	t
a.	1.12 atm	? g/mol	2.40 g/L	2°C
b.	7.50 atm	30.07 g/mol	? g/L	20.°C
c.	97.4 kPa	104.09 g/mol	4.37 g/L	? °C
d.	? atm	77.95 g/mol	6.27 g/L	66°C

287. What pressure in atmospheres will 1.36 kg of N_2O gas exert when it is compressed in a 25.0 L cylinder and is stored in an outdoor shed where the temperature can reach 59°C during the summer?

288. Aluminum chloride sublimes at high temperatures. What density will the vapor have at 225°C and 0.939 atm pressure?

ANSWERS

270. 59 cm^3
(Solve the equation: $V_{total}/293\ K = (V_{total} + 0.20\ cm^3)/294\ K$)

271. 118 kPa

272. 935 mL

273. 26.4 kL

274. 3.76 atm

275. 115 mL

276. 10.9 atm

277. a. 2.00 L
b. 1.22×10^{-3} mol
c. 109 kPa
d. 114 K
e. 2.06 L
f. 1.67×10^{-3} mol

278. 1.57×10^{-2} mol O_2

279. 99.4 g/mol

280. 13.9 g

281. 5.24 g/L

282. 329 K or 56°C

283. a. 34.2 mol
b. 6.68×10^3 kPa
c. −148°C
d. 1.1×10^5 L

284. a. 55.9 g/mol
b. 0.111 g
c. 4.46×10^{-2} L
d. 0.846 atm
e. 391 g/mol

285. 2.71×10^3 L

286. a. 48.4 g/mol
b. 9.38 g/L
c. 6°C
d. 2.24 atm

287. 33.7 atm

288. 3.06 g/L

289. 663 g/mol
290. 204 L
291. 0.0101 mol ethane
292. 5.16 g NO
293. 77.0% yield
294. 10.5 g/mol
295. 171 g/mol
296. 6.55 atm
297. 326 kPa
298. 479 K or 206°C
299. 1210 L at −75°C; 1620 L at −8°C
300. 1.11×10^4 kPa
301. 168 mL
302. 3.85×10^3 L
303. 4.05×10^3 L
304. 29.0 g/mol
305. 3500 L O_2 2800 L NO
306. 1.20×10^4 mL O_3 7.20×10^4 mL HF
307. 73.3 mL CO_2
308. 7.02 L NO_2
309. **a.** 1.80 L Cl_2
b. 24.2 L Cl_2
c. 2.21×10^3 L Cl_2
d. 3.65×10^3 g $AlCl_3$
e. 3.71×10^{-3} g Al
f. 8.02×10^2 m^3 Cl_2

289. An unknown gas has a density of 0.0262 g/mL at a pressure of 0.918 atm and a temperature of 10.°C. What is the molar mass of the gas?

290. A large balloon contains 11.7 g of helium. What volume will the helium occupy at an altitude of 10 000 m, where the atmospheric pressure is 0.262 atm and the temperature is −50.°C?

291. A student collects ethane by water displacement at a temperature of 15°C (vapor pressure of water is 1.5988 kPa) and a total pressure of 100.0 kPa. The volume of the collection bottle is 245 mL. How many moles of ethane are in the bottle?

292. A reaction yields 3.75 L of nitrogen monoxide. The volume is measured at 19°C and at a pressure of 1.10 atm. What mass of NO was produced by the reaction?

293. A reaction has a theoretical yield of 8.83 g of ammonia. The reaction gives off 10.24 L of ammonia measured at 52°C and 105.3 kPa. What was the percent yield of the reaction?

294. An unknown gas has a density of 0.405 g/L at a pressure of 0.889 atm and a temperature of 7°C. Calculate its molar mass.

295. A paper label has been lost from an old tank of compressed gas. To help identify the unknown gas, you must calculate its molar mass. It is known that the tank has a capacity of 90.0 L and weighs 39.2 kg when empty. You find its current mass to be 50.5 kg. The gauge shows a pressure of 1780 kPa when the temperature is 18°C. What is the molar mass of the gas in the cylinder?

296. What is the pressure inside a tank that has a volume of 1.20×10^3 L and contains 12.0 kg of HCl gas at a temperature of 18°C?

297. What pressure in kPa is exerted at a temperature of 20.°C by compressed neon gas that has a density of 2.70 g/L?

298. A tank with a volume of 658 mL contains 1.50 g of neon gas. The maximum safe pressure that the tank can withstand is 4.50×10^2 kPa. At what temperature will the tank have that pressure?

299. The atmospheric pressure on Mars is about 6.75 millibars (1 bar = 100 kPa = 0.9869 atm), and the nighttime temperature can be about −75°C on the same day that the daytime temperature goes up to −8°C. What volume would a bag containing 1.00 g of H_2 gas have at both the daytime and nighttime temperatures?

300. What is the pressure in kPa of 3.95 mol of Cl_2 gas if it is compressed in a cylinder with a volume of 850. mL at a temperature of 15°C?

301. What volume in mL will 0.006 60 mol of hydrogen gas occupy at a pressure of 0.907 atm and a temperature of 9°C?

302. What volume will 8.47 kg of sulfur dioxide gas occupy at a pressure of 89.4 kPa and a temperature of 40.°C?

303. A cylinder contains 908 g of compressed helium. It is to be used to inflate a balloon to a final pressure of 128.3 kPa at a temperature of 2°C. What will the volume of the balloon be under these conditions?

304. The density of dry air at 27°C and 100.0 kPa is 1.162 g/L. Use this information to calculate the molar mass of air (calculate as if air were a pure substance).

Stoichiometry of Gases: Chap. 11, Sec. 3

305. In one method of manufacturing nitric acid, ammonia is oxidized to nitrogen monoxide and water:

$$4NH_3(g) + 5O_2(g) \longrightarrow 4NO(g) + 6H_2O(l)$$

What volume of oxygen will be used in a reaction of 2800 L of NH_3? What volume of NO will be produced? All volumes are measured under the same conditions.

306. Fluorine gas reacts violently with water to produce hydrogen fluoride and ozone according to the following equation:

$$3F_2(g) + 3H_2O(l) \longrightarrow 6HF(g) + O_3(g)$$

What volumes of O_3 and HF gas would be produced by the complete reaction of 3.60×10^4 mL of fluorine gas? All gases are measured under the same conditions.

307. A sample of ethanol burns in O_2 to form CO_2 and H_2O according to the following equation:

$$C_2H_5OH + 3O_2 \longrightarrow 2CO_2 + 3H_2O$$

If the combustion uses 55.8 mL of oxygen measured at 2.26 atm and 40.°C, what volume of CO_2 is produced when measured at STP?

308. Dinitrogen pentoxide decomposes into nitrogen dioxide and oxygen. If 5.00 L of N_2O_5 reacts at STP, what volume of NO_2 is produced when measured at 64.5°C and 1.76 atm?

309. Complete the table below using the following equation, which represents a reaction that produces aluminum chloride:

$$2Al(s) + 3Cl_2(g) \longrightarrow 2AlCl_3(s)$$

	Mass Al	*Volume Cl_2*	*Conditions*	*Mass $AlCl_3$*
a.	excess	? L	STP	7.15 g
b.	19.4 g	? L	STP	NA
c.	1.559 kg	? L	20.°C and 0.945 atm	NA
d.	excess	920. L	STP	? g
e.	? g	1.049 mL	37°C and 5.00 atm	NA
f.	500.00 kg	? m^3	15°C and 83.0 kPa	NA

MIXED REVIEW

310. The industrial production of ammonia proceeds according to the following equation:

$N_2(g) + 3H_2(g) \longrightarrow 2NH_3(g)$

a. What volume of nitrogen at STP is needed to react with 57.0 mL of hydrogen measured at STP?

b. What volume of NH_3 at STP can be produced from the complete reaction of 6.39×10^4 L of hydrogen?

c. If 20.0 mol of nitrogen is available, what volume of NH_3 at STP can be produced?

d. What volume of H_2 at STP will be needed to produce 800. L of ammonia, measured at 55°C and 0.900 atm?

311. Propane burns according to the following equation:

$C_3H_8(g) + 5O_2(g) \longrightarrow 3CO_2(g) + 4H_2O(g)$

a. What volume of water vapor measured at 250.°C and 1.00 atm is produced when 3.0 L of propane at STP is burned?

b. What volume of oxygen at 20.°C and 102.6 kPa is used if 640. L of CO_2 is produced? The CO_2 is also measured at 20.°C and 102.6 kPa.

c. If 465 mL of oxygen at STP is used in the reaction, what volume of CO_2, measured at 37°C and 0.973 atm, is produced?

d. When 2.50 L of C_3H_8 at STP burns, what total volume of gaseous products is formed? The volume of the products is measured at 175°C and 1.14 atm.

312. Carbon monoxide will burn in air to produce CO_2 according to the following equation:

$2CO(g) + O_2(g) \longrightarrow 2CO_2(g)$

What volume of oxygen at STP will be needed to react with 3500. L of CO measured at 20.°C and a pressure of 0.953 atm?

313. Silicon tetrafluoride gas can be produced by the action of HF on silica according to the following equation:

$SiO_2(s) + 4HF(g) \longrightarrow SiF_4(g) + 2H_2O(l)$

1.00 L of HF gas under pressure at 3.48 atm and a temperature of 25°C reacts completely with SiO_2 to form SiF_4. What volume of SiF_4, measured at 15°C and 0.940 atm, is produced by this reaction?

314. One method used in the eighteenth century to generate hydrogen was to pass steam through red-hot steel tubes. The following reaction takes place:

$3Fe(s) + 4H_2O(g) \longrightarrow Fe_3O_4(s) + 4H_2(g)$

a. What volume of hydrogen at STP can be produced by the reaction of 6.28 g of iron?

b. What mass of iron will react with 500. L of steam at 250.°C and 1.00 atm pressure?

c. If 285 g of Fe_3O_4 are formed, what volume of hydrogen, measured at 20.°C and 1.06 atm, is produced?

315. Sodium reacts vigorously with water to produce hydrogen and sodium hydroxide according to the following equation:

$2Na(s) + 2H_2O(l) \longrightarrow 2NaOH(aq) + H_2(g)$

If 0.027 g of sodium reacts with excess water, what volume of hydrogen at STP is formed?

316. Diethyl ether burns in air according to the following equation:

$C_4H_{10}O(l) + 6O_2(g) \longrightarrow 4CO_2(g) + 5H_2O(l)$

If 7.15 L of CO_2 is produced at a temperature of 125°C and a pressure of 1.02 atm, what volume of oxygen, measured at STP, was consumed and what mass of diethyl ether was burned?

317. When nitroglycerin detonates, it produces large volumes of hot gases almost instantly according to the following equation:

$4C_3H_5N_3O_9(l) \longrightarrow 6N_2(g) + 12CO_2(g) + 10H_2O(g) + O_2(g)$

a. When 0.100 mol of nitroglycerin explodes, what volume of each gas measured at STP is produced?

b. What total volume of gases is produced at 300.°C and 1.00 atm when 10.0 g of nitroglycerin explodes?

318. Dinitrogen monoxide can be prepared by heating ammonium nitrate, which decomposes according to the following equation:

$NH_4NO_3(s) \longrightarrow N_2O(g) + 2H_2O(l)$

What mass of ammonium nitrate should be decomposed in order to produce 250. mL of N_2O, measured at STP?

319. Phosphine, PH_3, is the phosphorus analogue to ammonia, NH_3. It can be produced by the reaction between calcium phosphide and water according to the following equation:

$Ca_3P_2(s) + 6H_2O(l) \longrightarrow 3Ca(OH)_2(s \text{ and } aq) + 2PH_3(g)$

What volume of phosphine, measured at 18°C and 102.4 kPa, is produced by the reaction of 8.46 g of Ca_3P_2?

320. In one method of producing aluminum chloride, HCl gas is passed over aluminum and the following reaction takes place:

$2Al(s) + 6HCl(g) \longrightarrow 2AlCl_3(g) + 3H_2(g)$

What mass of Al should be on hand in order to produce 6.0×10^3 kg of $AlCl_3$? What volume of compressed HCl at 4.71 atm and a temperature of 43°C should be on hand at the same time?

321. Urea, $(NH_2)_2CO$, is an important fertilizer that is manufactured by the following reaction:

$2NH_3(g) + CO_2(g) \longrightarrow (NH_2)_2CO(s) + H_2O(g)$

What volume of NH_3 at STP will be needed to produce 8.50×10^4 kg of urea if there is an 89.5% yield in the process?

322. An obsolete method of generating oxygen in the laboratory involves the decomposition of barium peroxide by the following equation:

$2BaO_2(s) \longrightarrow 2BaO(s) + O_2(g)$

What mass of BaO_2 reacted if 265 mL of O_2 is collected by water displacement at 0.975 atm and 10.°C?

Problem Bank

ANSWERS

310. a. 19.0 mL N_2

b. 4.26×10^4 L NH_3

c. 896 L NH_3

d. 899 L H_2

311. a. 23 L H_2O

b. 1070 L O_2

c. 326 mL CO_2

d. 25.2 L gaseous products

312. 1550 L O_2

313. 0.894 L SiF_4

314. a. 3.36 L H_2

b. 488 g Fe

c. 112 L H_2

315. 0.013 L H_2 or 13 mL H_2

316. 7.50 L O_2;
4.14 g diethyl ether

317. a. 3.36 L N_2, 6.72 L CO_2, 5.60 L H_2O, 0.560 L O_2

b. 15.0 L total volume all gases

318. 0.894 g NH_4NO_3

319. 2.19 L PH_3

320. 1.2×10^3 kg Al;
7.4×10^5 L HCl

321. 7.08×10^7 L NH^3

322. 3.77 g BaO_2

ANSWERS

323. 5.85 L Cl_2
324. 28.0 kL NH_3; 28.0 kL NO_2 (overall reaction is: $4NH_3 + 7O_2 \longrightarrow 4NO_2 + 6H_2O$)
325. 18.2 g $KClO_3$
326. a. 38 000 L NH_3
b. 1.30×10^5 g $NaHCO_3$
c. 12.3 kL NH_3
d. 5.60×10^3 L CO_2
327. a. 9.93 L CO_2
b. 1.63 L O_2
c. 26.0 L CO_2
d. 3.29×10^3 g H_2O
328. 13.0% ethanol
329. 0.430% KIO_3; 0.765% KOH
330. 7.16 g H_2O
331. 6.59 g $LiNO_3$
332. 0.2106 M
333. 2.40 M
334. 6.494 M
335. 1.94×10^5 g $C_6H_{12}O_6$
336. 12.4 g $MgBr_2$
337. 14.0 g NH_4Cl
338. 16 *m*
339. 2.31 *m*
340. 1.50 mol 2-butanol; 111 g 2-butanol

323. It is possible to generate chlorine gas by dripping concentrated HCl solution onto solid potassium permanganate according to the following equation:

$$2KMnO_4(aq) + 16HCl(aq) \longrightarrow 2KCl(aq) + 2MnCl_2(aq) + 8H_2O(l) + 5Cl_2(g)$$

If excess HCl is dripped onto 15.0 g of $KMnO_4$, what volume of Cl_2 will be produced? The Cl_2 is measured at 15°C and 0.959 atm.

324. Ammonia can be oxidized in the presence of a platinum catalyst according to the following equation:

$$4NH_3(g) + 5O_2(g) \longrightarrow 4NO(g) + 6H_2O(l)$$

The NO that is produced reacts almost immediately with additional oxygen according to the following equation:

$$2NO(g) + O_2(g) \longrightarrow 2NO_2(g)$$

If 35.0 kL of oxygen at STP react in the first reaction, what volume of NH_3 at STP reacts with it? What volume of NO_2 at STP will be formed in the second reaction, assuming there is excess oxygen that was not used up in the first reaction?

325. Oxygen can be generated in the laboratory by heating potassium chlorate. The reaction is represented by the following equation:

$$2KClO_3(s) \longrightarrow 2KCl(s) + 3O_2(g)$$

What mass of $KClO_3$ must be used in order to generate 5.00 L of O_2, measured at STP?

326. One of the reactions in the Solvay process is used to make sodium hydrogen carbonate. It occurs when carbon dioxide and ammonia are passed through concentrated salt brine. The following equation represents the reaction:

$$NaCl(aq) + H_2O(l) + CO_2(g) + NH_3(g) \longrightarrow NaHCO_3(s) + NH_4Cl(aq)$$

a. What volume of NH_3 at 25°C and 1.00 atm pressure will be required if 38 000 L of CO_2, measured under the same conditions, react to form $NaHCO_3$?

b. What mass of $NaHCO_3$ can be formed when the gases in (a) react with NaCl?

c. If this reaction forms 46.0 kg of $NaHCO_3$, what volume of NH_3, measured at STP, reacted?

d. What volume of CO_2, compressed in a tank at 5.50 atm and a temperature of 42°C, will be needed to produce 100.00 kg of $NaHCO_3$?

327. The combustion of butane is represented in the following equation:

$$2C_4H_{10}(g) + 13O_2(g) \longrightarrow 8CO_2(g) + 10H_2O(l)$$

a. If 4.74 g of butane react with excess oxygen, what volume of CO_2, measured at 150.°C and 1.14 atm, will be formed?

b. What volume of oxygen, measured at 0.980 atm and 75°C, will be consumed by the complete combustion of 0.500 g of butane?

c. A butane-fueled torch has a mass of 876.2 g. After burning for some time, the torch has a mass of 859.3 g. What volume of CO_2, at STP, was formed while the torch burned?

d. What mass of H_2O is produced when butane burns and produces 3720 L of CO_2, measured at 35°C and 0.993 atm pressure?

Concentration of Solutions: Chap. 12, Sec. 3

PERCENTAGE CONCENTRATION

328. What is the percentage concentration of 75.0 g of ethanol dissolved in 500.0 g of water?

329. A chemist dissolves 3.50 g of potassium iodate and 6.23 g of potassium hydroxide in 805.05 g of water. What is the percentage concentration of each solute in the solution?

330. A student wants to make a 5.00% solution of rubidium chloride using 0.377 g of the substance. What mass of water will be needed to make the solution?

331. What mass of lithium nitrate would have to be dissolved in 30.0 g of water in order to make an 18.0% solution?

MOLARITY

332. Determine the molarity of a solution prepared by dissolving 141.6 g of citric acid, $C_3H_5O(COOH)_3$, in water and then diluting the resulting solution to 3500.0 mL.

333. What is the molarity of a salt solution made by dissolving 280.0 mg of NaCl in 2.00 mL of water? Assume the final volume is the same as the volume of the water.

334. What is the molarity of a solution that contains 390.0 g of acetic acid, CH_3COOH, dissolved in enough acetone to make 1000.0 mL of solution?

335. What mass of glucose, $C_6H_{12}O_6$, would be required to prepare 5.000×10^3 L of a 0.215 M solution?

336. What mass of magnesium bromide would be required to prepare 720. mL of a 0.0939 M aqueous solution?

337. What mass of ammonium chloride is dissolved in 300. mL of a 0.875 M solution?

MOLALITY

338. Determine the molality of a solution of 560 g of acetone, CH_3COCH_3, in 620 g of water.

339. What is the molality of a solution of 12.9 g of fructose, $C_6H_{12}O_6$, in 31.0 g of water?

340. How many moles of 2-butanol, $CH_3CHOHCH_2CH_3$, must be dissolved in 125 g of ethanol in order to produce a 12.0 *m* 2-butanol solution? What mass of 2-butanol is this?

MIXED REVIEW

341. Complete the table below by determining the missing quantity in each example. All solutions are aqueous. Any quantity that is not applicable to a given solution is marked NA.

Solution Made	*Mass of Solute Used*	*Quantity of Solution Made*	*Quantity of Solvent Used*
a. 12.0% $KMnO_4$	? g $KMnO_4$	500.0 g	? g H_2O
b. 0.60 M $BaCl_2$	? g $BaCl_2$	1.750 L	NA
c. 6.20 *m* glycerol, $HOCH_2CHOHCH_2OH$	? g glycerol	NA	800.0 g H_2O
d. ? M $K_2Cr_2O_7$	12.27 g $K_2Cr_2O_7$	650. mL	NA
e. ? *m* $CaCl_2$	288 g $CaCl_2$	NA	2.04 kg H_2O
f. 0.160 M NaCl	? g NaCl	25.0 mL	NA
g. 2.00 *m* glucose, $C_6H_{12}O_6$	? g glucose	? g solution	1.50 kg H_2O

342. How many moles of H_2SO_4 are in 2.50 L of a 4.25 M aqueous solution?

343. Determine the molal concentration of 71.5 g of linoleic acid, $C_{18}H_{32}O_2$, in 525 g of hexane, C_6H_{14}.

344. You have a solution that is 16.2% sodium thiosulfate, $Na_2S_2O_3$, by mass.
- **a.** What mass of sodium thiosulfate is in 80.0 g of solution?
- **b.** How many moles of sodium thiosulfate are in 80.0 g of solution?
- **c.** If 80.0 g of the sodium thiosulfate solution is diluted to 250.0 mL with water, what is the molarity of the resulting solution?

345. What mass of anhydrous cobalt(II) chloride would be needed in order to make 650.00 mL of a 4.00 M cobalt(II) chloride solution?

346. A student wants to make a 0.150 M aqueous solution of silver nitrate, $AgNO_3$, and has a bottle containing 11.27 g of silver nitrate. What should be the final volume of the solution?

347. What mass of urea, NH_2CONH_2, must be dissolved in 2250 g of water in order to prepare a 1.50 *m* solution?

348. What mass of barium nitrate is dissolved in 21.29 mL of a 3.38 M solution?

349. Describe what you would do to prepare 100.0 g of a 3.5% solution of ammonium sulfate in water.

350. What mass of anhydrous calcium chloride should be dissolved in 590.0 g of water in order to produce a 0.82 *m* solution?

351. How many moles of ammonia are in 0.250 L of a 5.00 M aqueous ammonia solution? If this solution were diluted to 1.000 L, what would be the molarity of the resulting solution?

352. What is the molar mass of a solute if 62.0 g of the solute in 125 g of water produce a 5.3 *m* solution?

353. A saline solution is 0.9% NaCl. What masses of NaCl and water would be required to prepare 50. L of this saline solution? Assume that the density of water is 1.000 g/mL and that the NaCl does not add to the volume of the solution.

354. A student weighs an empty beaker on a balance and finds its mass to be 68.60 g. The student weighs the beaker again after adding water and finds the new mass to be 115.12 g. A mass of 4.08 g of glucose is then dissolved in the water. What is the percentage concentration of glucose in the solution?

355. The density of ethyl acetate at 20°C is 0.902 g/mL. What volume of ethyl acetate at 20°C would be required to prepare a 2.0% solution of cellulose nitrate using 25 g of cellulose nitrate?

356. Aqueous cadmium chloride reacts with sodium sulfide to produce bright-yellow cadmium sulfide. Write the balanced equation for this reaction and answer the following questions.
- **a.** How many moles of $CdCl_2$ are in 50.00 mL of a 3.91 M solution?
- **b.** If the solution in (a) reacted with excess sodium sulfide, how many moles of CdS would be formed?
- **c.** What mass of CdS would be formed?

357. What mass of H_2SO_4 is contained in 60.00 mL of a 5.85 M solution of sulfuric acid?

358. A truck carrying 22.5 kL of 6.83 M aqueous hydrochloric acid used to clean brick and masonry has overturned. The authorities plan to neutralize the acid with sodium carbonate. How many moles of HCl will have to be neutralized?

359. A chemist wants to produce 12.00 g of barium sulfate by reacting a 0.600 M $BaCl_2$ solution with excess H_2SO_4, as shown in the reaction below. What volume of the $BaCl_2$ solution should be used?

$$BaCl_2 + H_2SO_4 \rightarrow BaSO_4 + 2HCl$$

360. Many substances are hydrates. Whenever you make a solution, it is important to know whether or not the solute you are using is a hydrate and, if it is a hydrate, how many molecules of water are present per formula unit of the substance. This water must be taken into account when weighing out the solute. Something else to remember when making aqueous solutions from hydrates is that once the hydrate is dissolved, the water of hydration is considered to be part of the solvent. A common hydrate used in the chemistry laboratory is copper sulfate pentahydrate, $CuSO_4{\cdot}5H_2O$. Describe how you would make each of the following solutions using $CuSO_4{\cdot}5H_2O$. Specify masses and volumes as needed.
- **a.** 100. g of a 6.00% solution of $CuSO_4$
- **b.** 1.00 L of a 0.800 M solution of $CuSO_4$
- **c.** a 3.5 *m* solution of $CuSO_4$ in 1.0 kg of water

ANSWERS

341. a. 60.0 g $KMnO_4$; 440.0 g H_2O
b. 220 g $BaCl_2$
c. 457 g glycerol
d. 0.0642 M $K_2Cr_2O_7$
e. 1.27 *m* $CaCl_2$
f. 0.234 g NaCl
g. 541 g glucose; 2040 g solution

342. 10.6 mol H_2SO_4

343. 0.486 *m* linoleic acid

344. a. 13.0 g $Na_2S_2O_3$
b. 0.0820 mol $Na_2S_2O_3$
c. 0.328 M

345. 338 g $CoCl_2$

346. 0.442 L

347. 203 g urea

348. 18.8 g $Ba(NO_3)_2$

349. add 3.5 g $(NH_4)_2SO_4$ to 96.5 g H_2O

350. 54 g $CaCl_2$

351. 1.25 mol NH_3; 1.25 M

352. 93.6 g/mol

353. 49.6 kg water, 0.5 kg NaCl

354. 8.06%

355. 1.4 L ethyl acetate

356. $CdCl_2(aq) + Na_2S(aq) \longrightarrow CdS(s) + 2\ NaCl(aq)$
a. 0.196 mol $CdCl_2$
b. 0.196 mol CdS
c. 28.3 g CdS

357. 34.4 g H_2SO_4

358. 1.54×10^5 mol HCl

359. 85.7 mL $BaCl_2$ solution

360. a. Measure out 9.39 g $CuSO_4{\bullet}5H_2O$ and add 90.61 g H_2O to make 100. g of solution. The 9.39 g of $CuSO_4{\bullet}5H_2O$ contributes the 6.00 g of $CuSO_4$ needed.
b. Measure out 200. g $CuSO_4{\bullet}5H_2O$, dissolve in water, then add water to make 1.00 L. Water of hydration does not have to be considered here as long as the molar mass of the hydrate is used in determining the mass to weigh out.
c. Measure out 870 g $CuSO_4{\bullet}5H_2O$ and add 685 g H_2O. The hydrate contributes 315 g of H_2O, so only 685 g H_2O must be added.

ANSWERS

361. 383 g $CaCl_2•6H_2O$

362. 0.446 g $C_6H_{14}N_4O_2$

363. 3254 g H_2O (the hydrate contributes 987.9 g H_2O)

364. 9.646 g $KAl(SO_4)_2•12H_2O$; 25.35 g H_2O

365. **a.** 0.100 M KBr

b. 38 mL

c. 0.986 M HI

d. 1.7 L

e. 50 mL

366. 50.6 mL H_2O

367. 0.0948 M NH_4Cl

368. 2.3 mL

369. **a.** 3.0 M H_2SO_4

b. 0.83 L

c. 1.5×10^3 g H_2SO_4

370. 6.35 mL

371. 348 mL

372. 0.558 M NH_4NO_3

373. **a.** 850 mL; 2.4 mL; 86 mL

b. 1.3 L concentrated HNO_3

c. 1.16 L concentrated HCl

374. 0.48 M $FeSO_4$

375. 2.72 M $K_2Cr_2O_7$

376. Dilute 4.73 mL of the 6.45 M acetic acid to 25 mL. This means adding 20.27 mL of water.

377. 39.7 g/mol

378. 0.27 M I_2

379. 1.9×10^2 g H_3PO_4

361. What mass of calcium chloride hexahydrate is required in order to make 700.0 mL of a 2.50 M solution?

362. What mass of the amino acid arginine, $C_6H_{14}N_4O_2$, would be required to make 1.250 L of a 0.002 05 M solution?

363. How much water would you have to add to 2.402 kg of nickel(II) sulfate hexahydrate in order to prepare a 25.00% solution?

364. What mass of potassium aluminum sulfate dodecahydrate, $KAl(SO_4)_2•12H_2O$, would be needed to prepare 35.00 g of a 15.00% $KAl(SO_4)_2$ solution? What mass of water would be added to make this solution?

Dilutions: Chap. 12, Sec. 3

365. Complete the table below by calculating the missing value in each row.

Molarity of Stock Solution	*Volume of Stock Solution*	*Molarity of Dilute Solution*	*Volume of Dilute Solution*
a. 0.500 M KBr	20.00 mL	? M KBr	100.00 mL
b. 1.00 M LiOH	? mL	0.075 M LiOH	500.00 mL
c. ? M HI	5.00 mL	0.0493 M HI	100.00 mL
d. 12.0 M HCl	0.250 L	1.8 M HCl	? L
e. 7.44 M NH_3	? mL	0.093 M NH_3	4.00 L

366. What volume of water would be added to 16.5 mL of a 0.0813 M solution of sodium borate in order to get a 0.0200 M solution?

MIXED REVIEW

367. What is the molarity of a solution of ammonium chloride prepared by diluting 50.00 mL of a 3.79 M NH_4Cl solution to 2.00 L?

368. A student takes a sample of KOH solution and dilutes it with 100.00 mL of water. The student determines that the diluted solution is 0.046 M KOH, but has forgotten to record the volume of the original sample. The concentration of the original solution is 2.09 M. What was the volume of the original sample?

369. A chemist wants to prepare a stock solution of H_2SO_4 so that samples of 20.00 mL will produce a solution with a concentration of 0.50 M when added to 100.0 mL of water.

a. What should the molarity of the stock solution be?

b. If the chemist wants to prepare 5.00 L of the stock solution from concentrated H_2SO_4, which is 18.0 M, what volume of concentrated acid should be used?

c. The density of 18.0 M H_2SO_4 is 1.84 g/mL. What mass of concentrated H_2SO_4 should be used to make the stock solution in (b)?

370. To what volume should 1.19 mL of an 8.00 M acetic acid solution be diluted in order to obtain a final solution that is 1.50 M?

371. What volume of a 5.75 M formic acid solution should be used to prepare 2.00 L of a 1.00 M formic acid solution?

372. A 25.00 mL sample of ammonium nitrate solution produces a 0.186 M solution when diluted with 50.00 mL of water. What is the molarity of the stock solution?

373. Given a solution of known percentage concentration by mass, a laboratory worker can often measure out a calculated mass of the solution in order to obtain a certain mass of solute. Sometimes, though, it is impractical to use the mass of a solution, especially with fuming solutions, such as concentrated HCl and concentrated HNO_3. Measuring these solutions by volume is much more practical. In order to determine the volume that should be measured, a worker would need to know the density of the solution. This information usually appears on the label of the solution bottle.

a. Concentrated hydrochloric acid is 36% HCl by mass and has a density of 1.18 g/mL. What is the volume of 1.0 kg of this HCl solution? What volume contains 1.0 g of HCl? What volume contains 1.0 mol of HCl?

b. The density of concentrated nitric acid is 1.42 g/mL, and its concentration is 71% HNO_3 by mass. What volume of concentrated HNO_3 would be needed to prepare 10.0 L of a 2.00 M solution of HNO_3?

c. What volume of concentrated HCl solution would be needed to prepare 4.50 L of 3.0 M HCl? See (a) for data.

374. A 3.8 M solution of $FeSO_4$ solution is diluted to eight times its original volume. What is the molarity of the diluted solution?

375. A chemist prepares 480. mL of a 2.50 M solution of $K_2Cr_2O_7$ in water. A week later, the chemist wants to use the solution, but the stopper has been left off the flask and 39 mL of water has evaporated. What is the new molarity of the solution?

376. You must write out procedures for a group of lab technicians. One test they will perform requires 25.00 mL of a 1.22 M solution of acetic acid. You decide to use a 6.45 M acetic acid solution that you have on hand. What procedure should the technicians use in order to get the solution they need?

377. A chemical test has determined the concentration of a solution of an unknown substance to be 2.41 M. A 100.0 mL volume of the solution is evaporated to dryness, leaving 9.56 g of crystals of the unknown solute. Calculate the molar mass of the unknown substance.

378. Tincture of iodine can be prepared by dissolving 34 g of I_2 and 25 g of KI in 25 mL of distilled water and diluting the solution to 500. mL with ethanol. What is the molarity of I_2 in the solution?

379. Phosphoric acid is commonly supplied as an 85% solution. What mass of this solution would be required to prepare 600.0 mL of a 2.80 M phosphoric acid solution?

380. Commercially available concentrated sulfuric acid is 18.0 M H_2SO_4. What volume of concentrated H_2SO_4 would you use in order to make 3.00 L of a 4.0 M stock solution?

381. Describe how to prepare 1.00 L of a 0.495 M solution of urea, NH_2CONH_2, starting with a 3.07 M stock solution.

382. Honey is a solution consisting almost entirely of a mixture of the hexose sugars fructose and glucose; both sugars have the formula $C_6H_{12}O_6$, but they differ in molecular structure.
   a. A sample of honey is found to be 76.2% $C_6H_{12}O_6$ by mass. What is the molality of the hexose sugars in honey? Consider the sugars to be equivalent.
   b. The density of the honey sample is 1.42 g/mL. What mass of hexose sugars are in 1.00 L of honey? What is the molarity of the mixed hexose sugars in honey?

383. Industrial chemicals used in manufacturing are almost never pure, and the content of the material may vary from one batch to the next. For these reasons, a sample is taken from each shipment and sent to a laboratory, where its makeup is determined. This procedure is called assaying. Once the content of a material is known, engineers adjust the manufacturing process to account for the degree of purity of the starting chemicals.

Suppose you have just received a shipment of sodium carbonate, Na_2CO_3. You weigh out 50.00 g of the material, dissolve it in water, and dilute the solution to 1.000 L. You remove 10.00 mL from the solution and dilute it to 50.00 mL. By measuring the amount of a second substance that reacts with Na_2CO_3, you determine that the concentration of sodium carbonate in the diluted solution is 0.0890 M. Calculate the percentage of Na_2CO_3 in the original batch of material. The molar mass of Na_2CO_3 is 105.99 g. (Hint: Determine the number of moles in the original solution and convert to mass of Na_2CO_3.)

384. A student wants to prepare 0.600 L of a stock solution of copper(II) chloride so that 20.0 mL of the stock solution diluted by adding 130.0 mL of water will yield a 0.250 M solution. What mass of $CuCl_2$ should be used to make the stock solution?

385. You have a bottle containing a 2.15 M $BaCl_2$ solution. You must tell other students how to dilute this solution to get various volumes of a 0.65 M $BaCl_2$ solution. By what factor will you tell them to dilute the stock solution? In other words, when a student removes any volume, V, of the stock solution, how many times V of water should be added to dilute to 0.65 M?

386. You have a bottle containing an 18.2% solution of strontium nitrate (density = 1.02 g/mL).
   a. What mass of strontium nitrate is dissolved in 80.0 mL of this solution?
   b. How many moles of strontium nitrate are dissolved in 80.0 mL of the solution?
   c. If 80.0 mL of this solution is diluted with 420.0 mL of water, what is the molarity of the solution?

Colligative Properties: Chap. 13, Sec. 2

387. Determine the freezing point of a solution of 60.0 g of glucose, $C_6H_{12}O_6$, dissolved in 80.0 g of water.

388. What is the freezing point of a solution of 645 g of urea, H_2NCONH_2, dissolved in 980. g of water?

389. What is the expected boiling point of a brine solution containing 30.00 g of KBr dissolved in 100.00 g of water?

390. What is the expected boiling point of a $CaCl_2$ solution containing 385 g of $CaCl_2$ dissolved in 1.230×10^3 g of water?

391. A solution of 0.827 g of an unknown non-electrolyte compound in 2.500 g of water has a freezing point of −10.18°C. Calculate the molar mass of the compound.

392. A 0.171 g sample of an unknown organic compound is dissolved in ether. The solution has a total mass of 2.470 g. The boiling point of the solution is found to be 36.43°C. What is the molar mass of the organic compound?

MIXED REVIEW

In each of the following problems, assume that the solute is a nonelectrolyte unless otherwise stated.

393. Calculate the freezing point and boiling point of a solution of 383 g of glucose dissolved in 400. g of water.

394. Determine the boiling point of a solution of 72.4 g of glycerol dissolved in 122.5 g of water.

395. What is the boiling point of a solution of 30.20 g of ethylene glycol, $HOCH_2CH_2OH$, in 88.40 g of phenol?

396. What mass of ethanol, CH_3CH_2OH, should be dissolved in 450. g of water to obtain a freezing point of −4.5°C?

397. Calculate the molar mass of a nonelectrolyte that lowers the freezing point of 25.00 g of water to 23.9°C when 4.27 g of the substance is dissolved in the water.

398. What is the freezing point of a solution of 1.17 g of 1-naphthol, $C_{10}H_8O$, dissolved in 2.00 mL of benzene at 20°C? The density of benzene at 20°C is 0.876 g/mL. K_f for benzene is 25.12°C/m, and benzene's normal freezing point is 5.53°C.

399. The boiling point of a solution containing 10.44 g of an unknown nonelectrolyte in 50.00 g of acetic acid is 159.2°C. What is the molar mass of the solute?

400. A 0.0355 g sample of an unknown molecular compound is dissolved in 1.000 g of liquid camphor at 200.0°C. Upon cooling, the camphor freezes at 157.7°C. Calculate the molar mass of the unknown compound.

401. Determine the boiling point of a solution of 22.5 g of fructose, $C_6H_{12}O_6$, in 294 g of phenol.

ANSWERS

380. 0.667 L

381. For 1.00 L of 0.495 M urea solution, take 161 mL of 3.07 M stock solution of urea and dilute with water (839 mL of water) to make 1.00 L.

382. a. 17.8 m
   b. 1080 g, 6.01 M hexose sugars

383. 47.17 g Na_2CO_3 per 50.00 g sample = 94.3% Na_2CO_3

384. 151 g $CuCl_2$

385. Add 2.3 volumes of H_2O per volume of stock solution.

386. a. 14.9 g
   b. 7.02×10^{-2} mol
   c. 0.140 M

387. −7.74°C

388. −20.4°C

389. 102.6°C

390. 104.3°C

391. 60.4 g/mol

392. 82.1 g/mol

393. −9.88°C, 102.7°C

394. 103.3°C

395. 201.6°C

396. 50 g ethanol

397. 82 g/mol

398. −18.2°C

399. 15.5 g/mol

400. 66.8 g/mol

401. 183.3°C

ANSWERS

402. a. −29.9°C
b. 108.2°C
403. 292 g/mol
404. −47.0°C
405. 190 g/mol
406. 107.2°C
407. −27.9°C
408. 204.4 g/mol; $C_{16}H_{10}$
409. 9.9 g $CaCl_2$; 49 g glucose
410. $C_3H_6O_3$
411. −40.9°C
412. 2.71 kg ethylene glycol; 104.9°C
413. a. 2.2 *m*
b. 1.7 *m*
414. 92.0 g H_2O
415. 150 g/mol; $C_5H_{10}O_5$
416. 124 g/mol; $C_6H_6O_3$
417. 1.6×10^{-10} M
418. $[H_3O^+] = 7.50 \times 10^{-4}$ M
$[OH^-] = 1.33 \times 10^{-11}$ M
419. 2.928
420. a. 0.00
b. −0.30
c. −1.00
421. a. 9.0
b. 6.7
c. 3.46
422. pOH = 5.08
$[OH^-] = 8.3 \times 10^{-6}$ M
423. a. 1.40
b. 11.6
c. 8.96
d. 12.8
424. $[OH^-] = 0.0350$ M
$[H_3O^+] = 2.86 \times 10^{-13}$ M
425. 13.20
426. a. $[OH^-] = 0.05$ M, $[H_3O^+] = 2 \times 10^{-13}$ M
b. $[OH^-] = 2.0 \times 10^{-12}$ M, $[H_3O^+] = 5.0 \times 10^{-3}$ M
c. $[OH^-] = 0.013$ M, $[H_3O^+] = 7.7 \times 10^{-13}$ M
d. $[OH^-] = 6.67 \times 10^{-14}$ M, $[H_3O^+] = 0.150$ M
e. $[OH^-] = 0.0400$ M, $[H_3O^+] = 2.50 \times 10^{-13}$ M
f. $[OH^-] = 2.56 \times 10^{-14}$ M, $[H_3O^+] = 0.390$ M

402. Ethylene glycol, $HOCH_2CH_2OH$, is effective as an antifreeze, but it also raises the boiling temperature of automobile coolant, which helps prevent loss of coolant when the weather is hot.
a. What is the freezing point of a 50.0% solution of ethylene glycol in water?
b. What is the boiling point of the same 50.0% solution?

403. The value of K_f for cyclohexane is −20.0°C/*m*, and its normal freezing point is 6.6°C. A mass of 1.604 g of a waxy solid dissolved in 10.000 g of cyclohexane results in a freezing point of −4.4°C. Calculate the molar mass of the solid.

404. What is the expected freezing point of an aqueous solution of 2.62 kg of nitric acid, HNO_3, in a solution with a total mass of 5.91 kg? Assume that the nitric acid is completely ionized.

405. An unknown organic compound is mixed with 0.5190 g of naphthalene crystals to give a mixture having a total mass of 0.5959 g. The mixture is heated until the naphthalene melts and the unknown substance dissolves. Upon cooling, the solution freezes at a temperature of 74.8°C. What is the molar mass of the unknown compound?

406. What is the boiling point of a solution of 8.69 g of the electrolyte sodium acetate, $NaCH_3COO$, dissolved in 15.00 g of water?

407. What is the expected freezing point of a solution of 110.5 g of H_2SO_4 in 225 g of water? Assume sulfuric acid completely dissociates in water.

408. A compound called pyrene has the empirical formula C_8H_5. When 4.04 g of pyrene is dissolved in 10.00 g of benzene, the boiling point of the solution is 85.1°C. Calculate the molar mass of pyrene and determine its molecular formula. The molal boiling-point constant for benzene is 2.53°C/*m*. Its normal boiling point is 80.1°C.

409. What mass of $CaCl_2$ (which is ionic), when dissolved in 100.00 g of water, gives a freezing point of −5.0°C? What mass of glucose would give the same result?

410. A compound has the empirical formula CH_2O. When 0.0866 g is dissolved in 1.000 g of ether, the solution's boiling point is 36.5°C. Determine the molecular formula of this substance.

411. What is the freezing point of a 28.6% (by mass) aqueous solution of HCl? Assume the HCl is 100% ionized.

412. What mass of ethylene glycol, $HOCH_2CH_2OH$, must be dissolved in 4.510 kg of water to result in a freezing point of −18.0°C? What is the boiling point of the same solution?

413. A water solution containing 2.00 g of an unknown molecular substance dissolved in 10.00 g of water has a freezing point of −4.0°C.
a. Calculate the molality of the solution.
b. When 2.00 g of the substance is dissolved in acetone instead of in water, the boiling point of the solution is 58.9°C. The normal boiling point of acetone is 56.00°C, and its K_b is 1.71°C/*m*. Calculate the molality of the solution from this data.

414. A chemist wants to prepare a solution with a freezing point of −22.0°C and has 100.00 g of glycerol on hand. What mass of water should the chemist mix with the glycerol?

415. An unknown carbohydrate compound has the empirical formula CH_2O. A solution consisting of 0.515 g of the carbohydrate dissolved in 1.717 g of acetic acid freezes at 8.8°C. What is the molar mass of the carbohydrate? What is its molecular formula?

416. An unknown organic compound has the empirical formula C_2H_2O. A solution of 3.775 g of the unknown compound dissolved in 12.00 g of water is cooled until it freezes at a temperature of −4.72°C. Determine the molar mass and the molecular formula of the compound.

pH: Chap. 15, Sec. 1

417. The hydroxide ion concentration of an aqueous solution is 6.4×10^{-5} M. What is the hydronium ion concentration?

418. Calculate the H_3O^+ and OH^- concentrations in a 7.50×10^{-4} M solution of HNO_3, a strong acid.

419. Determine the pH of a 0.001 18 M solution of HBr.

420. a. What is the pH of a solution that has a hydronium ion concentration of 1.0 M?
b. What is the pH of a 2.0 M solution of HCl, assuming the acid remains 100% ionized?
c. What is the theoretical pH of a 10. M solution of HCl?

421. What is the pH of a solution with the following hydroxide ion concentrations?
a. 1×10^{-5} M
b. 5×10^{-8} M
c. 2.90×10^{-11} M

422. What are the pOH and hydroxide ion concentrations of a solution with a pH of 8.92?

423. What are the pOH values of solutions with the following hydronium ion concentrations?
a. 2.51×10^{-13} M
b. 4.3×10^{-3} M
c. 9.1×10^{-6} M
d. 0.070 M

424. A solution is prepared by dissolving 3.50 g of sodium hydroxide in water and adding water until the total volume of the solution is 2.50 L. What are the OH^- and H_3O^+ concentrations?

425. If 1.00 L of a potassium hydroxide solution with a pH of 12.90 is diluted to 2.00 L, what is the pH of the resulting solution?

MIXED REVIEW

426. Calculate the H_3O^+ and OH^- concentrations in the following solutions. Each is either a strong acid or a strong base.
a. 0.05 M sodium hydroxide
b. 0.0025 M sulfuric acid
c. 0.013 M lithium hydroxide
d. 0.150 M nitric acid

e. 0.0200 M calcium hydroxide
f. 0.390 M perchloric acid

427. What is the pH of each solution in item 426?

428. Calculate $[H_3O^+]$ and $[OH^-]$ in a 0.160 M solution of potassium hydroxide. Assume that the solute is 100% dissociated at this concentration.

429. The pH of an aqueous solution of NaOH is 12.9. What is the molarity of the solution?

430. What is the pH of a 0.001 25 M HBr solution? If 175 mL of this solution is diluted to a total volume of 3.00 L, what is the pH of the diluted solution?

431. What is the pH of a 0.0001 M solution of NaOH? What is the pH of a 0.0005 M solution of NaOH?

432. A solution is prepared using 15.0 mL of 1.0 M HCl and 20.0 mL of 0.50 M HNO_3. The final volume of the solution is 1.25 L. Answer the following questions:
a. What are the $[H_3O^+]$ and $[OH^-]$ in the final solution?
b. What is the pH of the final solution?

433. A container is labeled 500.0 mL of 0.001 57 M nitric acid solution. A chemist finds that the container was not sealed and that some evaporation has taken place. The volume of solution is now 447.0 mL.
a. What was the original pH of the solution?
b. What is the pH of the solution now?

434. Calculate the hydroxide ion concentration in an aqueous solution that has a 0.000 35 M hydronium ion concentration.

435. A solution of sodium hydroxide has a pH of 12.14. If 50.00 mL of the solution is diluted to 2.000 L with water, what is the pH of the diluted solution?

436. An acetic acid solution has a pH of 4.0. What are the $[H_3O^+]$ and $[OH^-]$ in this solution?

437. What is the pH of a 0.000 460 M solution of $Ca(OH)_2$?

438. A solution of strontium hydroxide with a pH of 11.4 is to be prepared. What mass of strontium hydroxide would be required to make 1.00 L of this solution?

439. A solution of NH_3 has a pH of 11.00. What are the concentrations of hydronium and hydroxide ions in this solution?

440. Acetic acid does not completely ionize in solution. Percent ionization of a substance dissolved in water is equal to the moles of ions produced as a percentage of the moles of ions that would be produced if the substance were completely ionized. Calculate the percent ionization of acetic acid in the following solutions.
a. 1.0 M acetic acid solution with a pH of 2.40
b. 0.10 M acetic acid solution with a pH of 2.90
c. 0.010 M acetic acid solution with a pH of 3.40

441. Calculate the pH of a solution that contains 5.00 g of HNO_3 in 2.00 L of solution.

442. A solution of HCl has a pH of 1.50. Determine the pH of the solutions made in each of the following ways.
a. 1.00 mL of the solution is diluted to 1000. mL with water.
b. 25.00 mL is diluted to 200. mL with distilled water.
c. 18.83 mL of the solution is diluted to 4.000 L with distilled water.
d. 1.50 L is diluted to 20.0 kL with distilled water.

443. An aqueous solution contains 10 000 times more hydronium ions than hydroxide ions. What is the concentration of each ion?

444. A potassium hydroxide solution has a pH of 12.90. Enough acid is added to react with half of the OH^- ions present. What is the pH of the resulting solution? Assume that the products of the neutralization have no effect on pH and that the amount of additional water produced is negligible.

445. A hydrochloric acid solution has a pH of 1.70. What is the $[H_3O^+]$ in this solution? Considering that HCl is a strong acid, what is the HCl concentration of the solution?

446. What is the molarity of a solution of the strong base $Ca(OH)_2$ in a solution that has a pH of 10.80?

447. You have a 1.00 M solution of the strong acid, HCl. What is the pH of this solution? You need a solution of pH 4.00. To what volume would you dilute 1.00 L of the HCl solution to get this pH? To what volume would you dilute 1.00 L of the pH 4.00 solution to get a solution of pH 6.00? To what volume would you dilute 1.00 L of the pH 4.00 solution to get a solution of pH 8.00?

448. A solution of chloric acid, $HClO_3$, a strong acid, has a pH of 1.28. How many moles of NaOH would be required to react completely with the $HClO_3$ in 1.00 L of the solution? What mass of NaOH is required?

449. A solution of the weak base NH_3 has a pH of 11.90. How many moles of HCl would have to be added to 1.00 L of the ammonia to react with all of the OH^- ions present at pH 11.90?

450. The pH of a citric acid solution is 3.15. What are the $[H_3O^+]$ and $[OH^-]$ in this solution?

Titrations: Chap. 15, Sec. 2

In each of the following problems, the acids and bases react in a mole ratio of 1 mol base : 1 mol acid.

451. A student titrates a 20.00 mL sample of a solution of HBr with unknown molarity. The titration requires 20.05 mL of a 0.1819 M solution of NaOH. What is the molarity of the HBr solution?

452. Vinegar can be assayed to determine its acetic acid content. Determine the molarity of acetic acid in a 15.00 mL sample of vinegar that requires 22.70 mL of a 0.550 M solution of NaOH to reach the equivalence point.

453. A 20.00 mL sample of a solution of $Sr(OH)_2$ is titrated to the equivalence point with 43.03 mL of 0.1159 M HCl. What is the molarity of the $Sr(OH)_2$ solution?

Problem Bank

ANSWERS

427. **a.** 12.7
b. 2.3
c. 12.11
d. 0.824
e. 12.602
f. 0.409

428. $[OH^-] = 0.160$ M
$[H_3O^+] = 6.25 \times 10^{-14}$ M

429. 0.08 M

430. 2.903; 4.137

431. 10.0; 10.7

432. **a.** $[H_3O^+] = 0.020$ M, $[OH^-] = 5.0 \times 10^{-13}$ M
b. 1.7

433. **a.** 2.804
b. 2.755

434. 2.9×10^{-11} M

435. 10.54

436. $[H_3O^+] = 1 \times 10^{-4}$ M
$[OH^-] = 1 \times 10^{-10}$ M

437. 10.96

438. 0.2 g

439. $[H_3O^+] = 1.0 \times 10^{-11}$ M
$[OH^-] = 1.0 \times 10^{-3}$ M

440. **a.** 0.40%
b. 1.3%
c. 4.0%

441. 1.402

442. **a.** 4.50
b. 2.40
c. 3.83
d. 5.63

443. $[H_3O^+] = 1 \times 10^{-5}$ M
$[OH^-] = 1 \times 10^{-9}$ M

444. 12.60

445. $[H_3O^+] = 0.020$ M
$[HCl] = 0.020$ M

446. 3.2×10^{-4} M

447. pH = 0.000
10. kL
1.0×10^2 L
10 kL

448. 0.052 mol NaOH
2.1 g NaOH

449. 7.9×10^{-3} mol

450. $[H_3O^+] = 7.1 \times 10^{-4}$ M
$[OH^-] = 1.4 \times 10^{-11}$ M

451. 0.1824 M HBr

452. 0.832 M

453. 0.1247 M $Sr(OH)_2$

454. 1.26 M NH_3
455. 92.5% acetic acid
456. 94.28% Na_2CO_3
457. 0.4563 M KOH
458. 2.262 M CH_3COOH
459. 2.433 M NH_3
460. **a.** 20.00 mL
b. 10.00 mL
c. 80.00 mL
461. 5.066 M HF
462. 0.2216 M oxalic acid
463. 1.022 M H_2SO_4
464. 0.1705 M KOH
465. 0.5748 M citric acid
466. 0.3437 M KOH
467. 43.2 mL NaOH
468. 23.56 mL H_2SO_4
469. 0.06996 mol KOH; 3.926 g KOH; 98.02% KOH
470. 51.7 g $Mg(OH)_2$
471. 0.514 M NH_3
472. 20.85 mL oxalic acid

454. A 35.00 mL sample of ammonia solution is titrated to the equivalence point with 54.95 mL of a 0.400 M sulfuric acid solution. What is the molarity of the ammonia solution?

In the problems below, assume that impurities are not acidic or basic and that they do not react in an acid-base titration.

455. A supply of glacial acetic acid has absorbed water from the air. It must be assayed to determine the actual percentage of acetic acid. 2.000 g of the acid is diluted to 100.00 mL, and 20.00 mL is titrated with a solution of sodium hydroxide. The base solution has a concentration of 0.218 M, and 28.25 mL is used in the titration. Calculate the percentage of acetic acid in the original sample. Write the titration equation to get the mole ratio.

456. A shipment of crude sodium carbonate must be assayed for its Na_2CO_3 content. You receive a small jar containing a sample from the shipment and weigh out 9.709 g into a flask, where it is dissolved in water and diluted to 1.0000 L with distilled water. A 10.00 mL sample is taken from the flask and titrated to the equivalence point with 16.90 mL of a 0.1022 M HCl solution. Determine the percentage of Na_2CO_3 in the sample. Write the titration equation to get the mole ratio.

MIXED REVIEW

457. A 50.00 mL sample of a potassium hydroxide is titrated with a 0.8186 M HCl solution. The titration requires 27.87 mL of the HCl solution to reach the equivalence point. What is the molarity of the KOH solution?

458. A 15.00 mL sample of acetic acid is titrated with 34.13 mL of 0.9940 M NaOH. Determine the molarity of the acetic acid.

459. A 12.00 mL sample of an ammonia solution is titrated with 1.499 M HNO_3 solution. A total of 19.48 mL of acid is required to reach the equivalence point. What is the molarity of the ammonia solution?

460. A certain acid and base react in a 1:1 ratio.

a. If the acid and base solutions are of equal concentration, what volume of acid will titrate a 20.00 mL sample of the base?

b. If the acid is twice as concentrated as the base, what volume of acid will be required to titrate 20.00 mL of the base?

c. How much acid will be required if the base is four times as concentrated as the acid, and 20.00 mL of base is used?

461. A 10.00 mL sample of a solution of hydrofluoric acid, HF, is diluted to 500.00 mL. A 20.00 mL sample of the diluted solution requires 13.51 mL of a 0.1500 M NaOH solution to be titrated to the equivalence point. What is the molarity of the original HF solution?

462. A solution of oxalic acid, a diprotic acid, is used to titrate a 16.22 mL sample of a 0.5030 M KOH solution. If the titration requires 18.41 mL of the oxalic acid solution, what is its molarity?

463. A H_2SO_4 solution of unknown molarity is titrated with a 1.209 M NaOH solution. The titration requires 42.27 mL of the NaOH solution to reach the equivalence point with 25.00 mL of the H_2SO_4 solution. What is the molarity of the acid solution?

464. Potassium hydrogen phthalate, $KHC_8H_4O_4$, is a solid acidic substance that reacts in a 1:1 mole ratio with bases that have one hydroxide ion. Suppose that 0.7025 g of potassium hydrogen phthalate is titrated to the equivalence point by 20.18 mL of a KOH solution. What is the molarity of the KOH solution?

465. A solution of citric acid, a triprotic acid, is titrated with a sodium hydroxide solution. A 20.00 mL sample of the citric acid solution requires 17.03 mL of a 2.025 M solution of NaOH to reach the equivalence point. What is the molarity of the acid solution?

466. A flask contains 41.04 mL of a solution of potassium hydroxide. The solution is titrated and reaches an equivalence point when 21.65 mL of a 0.6515 M solution of HNO_3 is added. Calculate the molarity of the base solution.

467. A bottle is labeled 2.00 M H_2SO_4. You decide to titrate a 20.00 mL sample with a 1.85 M NaOH solution. What volume of NaOH solution would you expect to use if the label is correct?

468. What volume of a 0.5200 M solution of H_2SO_4 would be needed to titrate 100.00 mL of a 0.1225 M solution of $Sr(OH)_2$?

469. A sample of a crude grade of KOH is sent to the lab to be tested for KOH content. A 4.005 g sample is dissolved and diluted to 200.00 mL with water. A 25.00 mL sample of the solution is titrated with a 0.4388 M HCl solution and requires 19.93 mL to reach the equivalence point. How many moles of KOH were in the 4.005 g sample? What mass of KOH is this? What is the percent of KOH in the crude material?

470. What mass of magnesium hydroxide would be required for the magnesium hydroxide to react to the equivalence point with 558 mL of 3.18 M hydrochloric acid?

471. An ammonia solution of unknown concentration is titrated with a solution of hydrochloric acid. The HCl solution is 1.25 M, and 5.19 mL are required to titrate 12.61 mL of the ammonia solution. What is the molarity of the ammonia solution?

472. What volume of 2.811 M oxalic acid solution is needed to react to the equivalence point with a 5.090 g sample of material that is 92.10% NaOH? Oxalic acid is a diprotic acid.

473. Standard solutions of accurately known concentration are available in most laboratories. These solutions are used to titrate other solutions to determine their concentrations. Once the concentration of the other solutions are accurately known, they may be used to titrate solutions of unknowns.

The molarity of a solution of HCl is determined by titrating the solution with an accurately known solution of $Ba(OH)_2$, which has a molar concentration of 0.1529 M. A volume of 43.09 mL of the $Ba(OH)_2$ solution titrates 26.06 mL of the acid solution. The acid solution is in turn used to titrate 15.00 mL of a solution of rubidium hydroxide. The titration requires 27.05 mL of the acid.

a. What is the molarity of the HCl solution?

b. What is the molarity of the RbOH solution?

474. A truck containing 2800 kg of a 6.0 M hydrochloric acid has been in an accident and is in danger of spilling its load. What mass of $Ca(OH)_2$ should be sent to the scene in order to neutralize all of the acid in case the tank bursts? The density of the 6.0 M HCl solution is 1.10 g/mL.

475. A 1.00 mL sample of a fairly concentrated nitric acid solution is diluted to 200.00 mL. A 10.00 mL sample of the diluted solution requires 23.94 mL of a 0.0177 M solution of $Ba(OH)_2$ to be titrated to the equivalence point. Determine the molarity of the original nitric acid solution.

476. What volume of 4.494 M H_2SO_4 solution would be required to react to the equivalence point with 7.2280 g of $LiOH(s)$?

Thermochemistry: Chap. 16, Sec. 1

477. Calculate the reaction enthalpy for the following reaction:

$$5CO_2(g) + Si_3N_4(s) \longrightarrow 3SiO(s) + 2N_2O(g) + 5CO(g)$$

Use the following equations and data:

(1) $CO(g) + SiO_2(s) \longrightarrow SiO(g) + CO_2(g)$

(2) $8CO_2(g) + Si_3N_4(s) \longrightarrow 3SiO_2(s) + 2N_2O(g) + 8CO(g)$

$\Delta H_{reaction\ 1} = +520.9$ kJ

$\Delta H_{reaction\ 2} = +461.05$ kJ

Determine ΔH for each of the following three reactions.

478. The following reaction is used to make CaO from limestone:

$$CaCO_3(s) \longrightarrow CaO(s) + CO_2(g)$$

479. The following reaction represents the oxidation of FeO to Fe_2O_3:

$$2FeO(s) + O2(g) \longrightarrow Fe_2O_3(s)$$

480. The following reaction of ammonia and hydrogen fluoride produces ammonium fluoride:

$$NH_3(g) + HF(g) \longrightarrow NH_4F(s)$$

481. Calculate the free energy change, ΔG, for the combustion of hydrogen sulfide according to the following chemical equation. Assume reactants and products are at 25°C:

$$H_2S(g) + O_2(g) \longrightarrow H_2O(l) + SO_2(g)$$

$\Delta H_{reaction} = -562.1$ kJ/mol

$\Delta S_{reaction} = -0.092\ 78$ kJ/mol•K

482. Calculate the free energy change for the decomposition of sodium chlorate. Assume reactants and products are at 25°C:

$$NaClO_3(s) \longrightarrow NaCl(s) + O_2(g)$$

$\Delta H_{reaction} = -19.1$ kJ/mol

$\Delta S_{reaction} = -0.1768$ kJ/mol•K

483. Calculate the free energy change for the combustion of 1 mol of ethane. Assume reactants and products are at 25°C:

$$C_2H_6(g) + O_2(g) \longrightarrow 2CO_2(g) + 3H_2O(l)$$

$\Delta H_{reaction} = -1561$ kJ/mol

$\Delta S_{reaction} = -0.4084$ kJ/mol•K

MIXED REVIEW

484. Calculate ΔH for the reaction of fluorine with water:

$$F_2(g) + H_2O(l) \longrightarrow 2HF(g) + O_2(g)$$

485. Calculate ΔH for the reaction of calcium oxide and sulfur trioxide:

$$CaO(s) + SO_3(g) \longrightarrow CaSO_4(s)$$

Use the following equations and data:

$H_2O(l) + SO_3(g) \longrightarrow H_2SO_4(l)$

$\Delta H = -132.5$ kJ/mol

$H_2SO_4(l) + Ca(s) \longrightarrow CaSO_4(s) + H_2(g)$

$\Delta H = -602.5$ kJ/mol

$Ca(s) + O_2(g) \longrightarrow CaO(s)$

$\Delta H = -634.9$ kJ/mol

$H_2(g) + O_2(g) \longrightarrow H_2O(l)$

$\Delta H = -285.8$ kJ/mol

486. Calculate ΔH for the reaction of sodium oxide with sulfur dioxide:

$$Na_2O(s) + SO_2(g) \longrightarrow Na_2SO_3(s)$$

487. Use enthalpies of combustion to calculate ΔH for the oxidation of 1-butanol to make butanoic acid:

$$C_4H_9OH(l) + O_2(g) \longrightarrow C_3H_7COOH(l) + H_2O(l)$$

Combustion of butanol:

$C_4H_9OH(l) + 6O_2(g) \longrightarrow 4CO_2(g) + 5H_2O(l)$

$\Delta H_c = -2675.9$ kJ/mol

Combustion of butanoic acid:

$C_3H_7COOH(l) + 5O_2(g) \longrightarrow 4CO_2(g) + 4H_2O(l)$

$\Delta H_c = -2183.6$ kJ/mol

488. Determine the free energy change for the reduction of CuO with hydrogen. Products and reactants are at 25°C.

$$CuO(s) + H_2(g) \longrightarrow Cu(s) + H_2O(l)$$

$\Delta H = -128.5$ kJ/mol

$\Delta S = -70.1$ J/mol•K

489. Calculate the enthalpy change at 25°C for the reaction of sodium iodide and chlorine. Use only the data given.

$$NaI(s) + Cl_2(g) \longrightarrow NaCl(s) + I_2(l)$$

$\Delta S = -79.9$ J/mol•K

$\Delta G = -98.0$ kJ/mol

Problem Bank

ANSWERS

473. a. 0.5056 M HCl

b. 0.9118 M RbOH

474. 570 kg $Ca(OH)_2$

475. 16.9 M HNO_3

476. 33.58 mL

477. 2024 kJ

478. 179.2 kJ/mol

479. 533 kJ/mol

480. 194 kJ/mol

481. −534.5 kJ/mol

482. −71.8 kJ/mol

483. −1683 kJ/mol

484. −260.8 kJ/mol

485. −385.9 kJ/mol

486. −390 kJ/mol

487. −492.3 kJ/mol

488. −107.6 kJ/mol

489. −121.8 kJ/mol

490. −384.9 kJ/mol
491. 74.2 kJ/mol
492. −169.0 kJ/mol
493. a. $CH_4(g) + 2O_2(g) \longrightarrow CO_2(g) + 2H_2O(g)$
$C_3H_8(g) + 5O_2(g) \longrightarrow 3CO_2(g) + 4H_2O(g)$
b. for methane: $\Delta H = -802.2$ kJ/mol
for propane: $\Delta H = -2043$ kJ/mol
c. $\text{output}_{\text{methane}} = -4.998 \times 10^4$ kJ/kg
$\text{output}_{\text{propane}} = -4.632 \times 10^4$ kJ/kg
Methane yields more energy per unit mass.
494. −132.7 kJ/mol
495. −7171.4 kJ/mol
496. −141.1 kJ/mol
497. 20.2 kJ/mol
498. −285 J/mol•K
499. a. 786.8 kJ/mol
b. −36 kJ/mol
c. 2154 kJ/mol
d. −496 kJ/mol
e. 1346.4 kJ/mol
500. a. $K = 1.83 \times 10^{-3}$
b. $K = 1.55 \times 10^5$
c. $K = 9.47$
d. $K = 7.71 \times 10^{-2}$
e. $K = 5.88 \times 10^{-3}$
f. $K = 1.53 \times 10^3$

490. The element bromine can be produced by the reaction of hydrogen bromide and manganese(IV) oxide: $4HBr(g) + MnO_2(s) \longrightarrow MnBr_2(s) + 2H_2O(l) + Br_2(l)$. ΔH for the reaction is −291.3 kJ/mol at 25°C. Use this value and the following values of ΔH_f^0 to calculate ΔH_f^0 of $MnBr_2(s)$.

$\Delta H^0_{fHBr} = -36.29$ kJ/mol
$\Delta H^0_{fMnO_2} = -520.0$ kJ/mol
$\Delta H^0_{fH_2O} = -285.8$ kJ/mol
$\Delta H^0_{fBr_2} = 0.00$ kJ/mol

491. Calculate the change in entropy, ΔS, at 25°C for the reaction of calcium carbide with water to produce acetylene gas:

$CaC_2(s) + 2H_2O(l) \longrightarrow C_2H_2(g) + Ca(OH)_2(s)$
$\Delta G = -147.7$ kJ/mol
$\Delta H = -125.6$ kJ/mol

492. Calculate the free energy change for the explosive decomposition of ammonium nitrate at 25°C. Note that H_2O is a gas in this reaction:

$NH_4NO_3(s) \longrightarrow N_2O(g) + 2H_2O(g)$
$\Delta S = 446.4$ J/mol•K

493. In locations where natural gas, which is mostly methane, is not available, many people burn propane, which is delivered by truck and stored in a tank under pressure.

a. Write the chemical equations for the complete combustion of 1 mol of methane, CH_4, and 1 mol of propane, C_3H_8.
b. Calculate the enthalpy change for each reaction to determine the amount of energy as heat evolved by burning 1 mol of each fuel.
c. Using the molar enthalpies of combustion you calculated, determine the energy output per kilogram of each fuel. Which fuel yields more energy per unit mass?

494. The hydration of acetylene to form acetaldehyde is shown in the following equation:

$C_2H_2(g) + H_2O(l) \longrightarrow CH_3CHO(l)$

Use enthalpies of combustion for C_2H_2 and CH_3CHO to compute the enthalpy of the above reaction.

$C_2H_2(g) + 2O_2(g) \longrightarrow 2CO_2(g) + H_2O(l)$
$\Delta H = -1299.6$ kJ/mol
$CH_3CHO(l) + 2O_2(g) \longrightarrow 2CO_2(g) + 2H_2O(l)$
$\Delta H = -1166.9$ kJ/mol

495. Calculate the enthalpy for the combustion of decane. ΔH_f^0 for liquid decane is −300.9 kJ/mol.

$C_{10}H_{22}(l) + 15O_2(g) \longrightarrow 10CO_2(g) + 11H_2O(l)$

496. Find the enthalpy of the reaction of magnesium oxide with hydrogen chloride:

$MgO(s) + 2HCl(g) \longrightarrow MgCl_2(s) + H_2O(l)$

Use the following equations and data.

$Mg(s) + 2HCl(g) \longrightarrow MgCl_2(s) + H_2(g)$
$\Delta H = -456.9$ kJ/mol
$Mg(s) + O_2(g) \longrightarrow MgO(s)$
$\Delta H = -601.6$ kJ/mol
$H_2O(l) \longrightarrow H_2(g) + O_2(g)$
$\Delta H = +285.8$ kJ/mol

497. What is the free energy change for the following reaction at 25°C?

$2NaOH(s) + 2Na(s) \xrightarrow{\Delta} 2Na_2O(s) + H_2(g)$
$\Delta S = 10.6$ J/mol•K $\quad \Delta H^0_{fNaOH} = -425.9$ kJ/mol

498. The following equation represents the reaction between gaseous HCl and gaseous ammonia to form solid ammonium chloride:

$NH_3(g) + HCl(g) \longrightarrow NH_4Cl(s)$

Calculate the entropy change in J/mol•K for the reaction of hydrogen chloride and ammonia at 25°C using the following data and the table following item 499.

$\Delta G = -91.2$ kJ/mol

499. The production of steel from iron involves the removal of many impurities in the iron ore. The following equations show some of the purifying reactions. Calculate the enthalpy for each reaction. Use the table and the data given below.

a. $3C(s) + Fe_2O_3(s) \longrightarrow 3CO(g) + 2Fe(s)$
$\Delta H^0_{fCO(g)} = -110.53$ kJ/mol
b. $3Mn(s) + Fe_2O_3(s) \longrightarrow 3MnO(s) + 2Fe(s)$
$\Delta H^0_{fMnO(s)} = -384.9$ kJ/mol
c. $12P(s) + 10Fe_2O_3(s) \longrightarrow 3P_4O_{10}(s) + 20Fe(s)$
$\Delta H^0_{fP_4O_{10}(s)} = -3009.9$ kJ/mol
d. $3Si(s) + 2Fe_2O_3(s) \longrightarrow 3SiO_2(s) + 4Fe(s)$
$\Delta H^0_{fSiO_2(s)} = -910.9$ kJ/mol
e. $3S(s) + 2Fe_2O_3(s) \longrightarrow 3SO_2(g) + 4Fe(s)$

For problems 498–499

Substance	ΔH_f^0 *(kJ/mol)*	*Substance*	ΔH_f^0 *(kJ/mol)*
$NH_3(g)$	−45.9	$HF(g)$	−273.3
$NH_4Cl(s)$	−314.4	$H_2O(g)$	−241.82
$NH_4F(s)$	−125	$H_2O(l)$	−285.8
$NH_4NO_3(s)$	−365.56	$H_2O_2(l)$	−187.8
$Br_2(l)$	0.00	$H_2SO_4(l)$	−813.989
$CaCO_3(s)$	−1207.6	$FeO(s)$	−825.5
$CaO(s)$	−634.9	$Fe_2O_3(s)$	−1118.4
$CH_4(g)$	−74.9	$MnO_2(s)$	−520.0
$C_3H_8(g)$	−104.7	$N_2O(g)$	+82.1
$CO_2(g)$	−393.5	$O_2(g)$	0.00
$F_2(g)$	0.00	$Na_2O(s)$	−414.2
$H_2(g)$	0.00	$Na_2SO_3(s)$	−1101
$HBr(g)$	−36.29	$SO_2(g)$	−296.8
$HCl(g)$	−92.3	$SO_3(g)$	−395.7

Equilibrium: Chap. 18, Sec. 1

500. Calculate the equilibrium constants for the following hypothetical reactions. Assume that all components of the reactions are gaseous.

a. $A \rightleftharpoons C + D$
At equilibrium, the concentration of A is 2.24×10^{-2} M and the concentrations of both C and D are 6.41×10^{-3} M.

b. A + B ⇌ C + D
At equilibrium, the concentrations of both A and B are 3.23×10^{-5} M and the concentrations of both C and D are 1.27×10^{-2} M.

c. A + B ⇌ 2C
At equilibrium, the concentrations of both A and B are 7.02×10^{-3} M and the concentration of C is 2.16×10^{-2} M.

d. 2A ⇌ 2C + D
At equilibrium, the concentration of A is 6.59×10^{-4} M. The concentration of C is 4.06×10^{-3} M, and the concentration of D is 2.03×10^{-3} M.

e. A + B ⇌ C + D + E
At equilibrium, the concentrations of both A and B are 3.73×10^{-4} M and the concentrations of C, D, and E are 9.35×10^{-4} M.

f. 2A + B ⇌ 2C
At equilibrium, the concentration of A is 5.50×10^{-3} M, the concentration of B is 2.25×10^{-3}, and the concentration of C is 1.02×10^{-2} M.

501. Calculate the concentration of product D in the following hypothetical reaction:

2A(*g*) ⇌ 2C(*g*) + D(*g*)

At equilibrium, the concentration of A is 1.88×10^{-1} M, the concentration of C is 6.56 M, and the equilibrium constant is 2.403×10^{2}.

502. At a temperature of 700 K, the equilibrium constant is 3.164×10^{3} for the following reaction system for the hydrogenation of ethene, C_2H_4, to ethane, C_2H_6:

$C_2H_4(g) + H_2(g) \rightleftharpoons C_2H_6(g)$

What will be the equilibrium concentration of ethene if the concentration of H_2 is 0.0619 M and the concentration of C_2H_6 is 1.055 M?

MIXED REVIEW

503. Using the reaction A + 2B ⇌ C + 2D, determine the equilibrium constant if the following equilibrium concentrations are found. All components are gases.

[A] = 0.0567 M
[B] = 0.1171 M
[C] = 0.000 3378 M
[D] = 0.000 6756 M

504. In the reaction 2A ⇌ 2C + 2D, determine the equilibrium constant when the following equilibrium concentrations are found. All components are gases.

[A] = 0.1077 M
[C] = 0.000 4104 M
[D] = 0.000 4104 M

505. Calculate the equilibrium constant for the following reaction. Note the phases of the components.

2A(*g*) + B(*s*) ⇌ C(*g*) + D(*g*)

The equilibrium concentrations of the components are

[A] = 0.0922 M
[C] = 4.11×10^{-4} M
[D] = 8.22×10^{-4} M

506. The equilibrium constant of the following reaction for the decomposition of phosgene at 25°C is 4.282×10^{-2}.

$COCl_2(g) \rightleftharpoons CO(g) + Cl_2(g)$

a. What is the concentration of $COCl_2$ when the concentrations of both CO and Cl_2 are 5.90×10^{-3} M?

b. When the equilibrium concentration of $COCl_2$ is 0.003 70 M, what are the concentrations of CO and Cl_2? Assume the concentrations are equal.

507. Consider the following hypothetical reaction.

A(*g*) + B(*s*) ⇌ C(*g*) + D(*s*)

a. If *K* = 1 for this reaction at 500 K, what can you say about the concentrations of A and C at equilibrium?

b. If raising the temperature of the reaction results in an equilibrium with a higher concentration of C than A, how will the value of *K* change?

508. The following reaction occurs when steam is passed over hot carbon. The mixture of gases it generates is called *water* gas and is useful as an industrial fuel and as a source of hydrogen for the production of ammonia.

$C(s) + H_2O(g) \rightleftharpoons CO(g) + H_2(g)$

The equilibrium constant for this reaction is 4.251×10^{-2} at 800 K. If the equilibrium concentration of $H_2O(g)$ is 0.1990 M, what concentrations of CO and H_2 would you expect to find?

509. When nitrogen monoxide gas comes in contact with air, it oxidizes to the brown gas nitrogen dioxide according to the following equation:

$2NO(g) + O_2(g) \rightleftharpoons 2NO_2(g)$

a. The equilibrium constant for this reaction at 500 K is 1.671×10^{4}. What concentration of NO_2 is present at equilibrium if [NO] = 6.200×10^{-2} M and [O_2] = 8.305×10^{-3} M?

b. At 1000 K, the equilibrium constant, *K*, for the same reaction is 1.315×10^{-2}. What will be the concentration of NO_2 at 1000 K given the same concentrations of NO and O_2 as were in (a)?

510. Consider the following hypothetical reaction, for which *K* = 1 at 300 K:

A(*g*) + B(*g*) ⇌ 2C(*g*)

a. If the reaction begins with equal concentrations of A and B and a zero concentration of C, what can you say about the relative concentrations of the components at equilibrium?

b. Additional C is introduced at equilibrium, and the temperature remains constant. When equilibrium is restored, how will the concentrations of all components have changed? How will *K* have changed?

ANSWERS

501. 0.197 M
502. 5.39×10^{-3} M
503. 1.98×10^{-7}
504. 2.446×10^{-12}
505. 3.97×10^{-5}
506. a. 8.13×10^{-4} M
b. 0.0126 M
507. a. The concentrations are equal.
b. *K* will increase.
508. 0.09198 M
509. a. 0.7304 M
b. 6.479×10^{-4} M
510. a. $[A] = [B] = [C] = 1/2[A]_{initial}$
b. [A], [B], and [C] will have increased equally. *K* will have remained the same.

511. a. $K = \frac{[HBr]^2}{[H_2][Br_2]}$

b. 2.11×10^{-10} M

c. Br_2 and H_2 will still have the same concentration. HBr will have a much higher concentration than the two reactants; at equilibrium, essentially only HBr will be present.

512. 1.281×10^{-6}

513. 4.61×10^{-3}

514. a. $K = \frac{[HCN]}{[HCl]}$

b. 3.725×10^{-7} M

515. a. The reaction yields essentially no products at 298 K; as a result, the equilibrium constant is very small. At 1100 K, the reaction proceeds to some extent.

b. 2.51 M

516. 0.0424

517. 0.0390

518. $K_a = 1.8 \times 10^{-4}$

519. $K_a = 0.167$

520. $K_a = 5.2 \times 10^{-9}$

521. pH = 11.573
$K_b = 4.0 \times 10^{-4}$

522. 4.4×10^{-3} M

523. pH = 2.857
$K_a = 1.92 \times 10^{-5}$

524. pH = 1.717
$K_a = 2.04 \times 10^{-3}$

525. a. $[H_3O^+] = 3.70 \times 10^{-11}$ M
pH = 10.431
$K_b = 1.82 \times 10^{-7}$

b. $[B] = 4.66 \times 10^{-3}$ M
$K_b = 1.53 \times 10^{-4}$
pH = 10.93

c. $[OH^-] = 1.9 \times 10^{-3}$ M
$[H_3O^+] = 5.3 \times 10^{-12}$ M
[B] = 0.0331 M
$K_b = 1.1 \times 10^{-4}$

d. $[B]_{initial} = 7.20 \times 10^{-3}$ M
$K_b = 1.35 \times 10^{-4}$
pH = 10.96

511. The equilibrium constant for the following reaction of hydrogen gas and bromine gas at 25°C is 5.628×10^{18}:

$$H_2(g) + Br_2(g) \rightleftarrows 2HBr(g)$$

a. Write the equilibrium expression for this reaction.

b. Assume that equimolar amounts of H_2 and Br_2 were present at the beginning. Calculate the equilibrium concentration of H_2 if the concentration of HBr is 0.500 M.

c. If equal amounts of H_2 and Br_2 react, which reaction component will be present in the greatest concentration at equilibrium? Explain your reasoning.

512. The following reaction reaches an equilibrium state:

$$N_2F_4(g) \rightleftarrows 2NF_2(g)$$

At equilibrium at 25°C, the concentration of N_2F_4 is found to be 0.9989 M and the concentration of NF_2 is 1.131×10^{-3} M. Calculate the equilibrium constant of the reaction.

513. The equilibrium between dinitrogen tetroxide and nitrogen dioxide is represented by the following equation:

$$N_2O_4(g) \rightleftarrows 2NO_2(g)$$

A student places a mixture of the two gases into a closed gas tube and allows the reaction to reach equilibrium at 25°C. At equilibrium, the concentration of N_2O_4 is found to be 5.95×10^{-1} M and the concentration of NO_2 is found to be 5.24×10^{-2} M. What is the equilibrium constant of the reaction?

514. Consider the following equilibrium system:

$$NaCN(s) + HCl(g) \rightleftarrows HCN(g) + NaCl(s)$$

a. Write a complete expression for the equilibrium constant of this system.

b. The equilibrium constant for this reaction is 2.405×10^6. What is the concentration of HCl remaining when the concentration of HCN is 0.8959 M?

515. The following reaction is used in the industrial production of hydrogen gas:

$$CH_4(g) + H_2O(g) \rightleftarrows CO(g) + 3H_2(g)$$

The equilibrium constant of this reaction at 298 K (25°C) is 3.896×10^{-27}, but at 1100 K the constant is 3.112×10^2.

a. What do these equilibrium constants tell you about the progress of the reaction at the two temperatures?

b. Suppose the reaction mixture is sampled at 1100 K and found to contain 1.56 M of hydrogen, 3.70×10^{-2} M of methane, and 8.27×10^{-1} M of gaseous H_2O. What concentration of carbon monoxide would you expect to find?

516. Dinitrogen tetroxide, N_2O_4, is soluble in cyclohexane, a common nonpolar solvent. While in solution, N_2O_4 can break down into NO_2 according to the following equation:

$$N_2O_4(cyclohexane) \rightleftarrows NO_2(cyclohexane)$$

At 20°C, the following concentrations were observed for this equilibrium reaction:

$[N_2O_4] = 2.55 \times 10^{-3}$ M
$[NO_2] = 10.4 \times 10^{-3}$ M

What is the value of the equilibrium constant for this reaction? Note: the chemical equation must be balanced first.

517. The reaction given in item 516 also occurs when the dinitrogen tetroxide and nitrogen dioxide are dissolved in carbon tetrachloride, CCl_4, another nonpolar solvent.

$$N_2O_4(CCl_4) \rightleftarrows NO_2(CCl_4)$$

The following experimental data were obtained at 20°C:

$[N_2O_4] = 2.67 \times 10^{-3}$ M
$[NO_2] = 10.2 \times 10^{-3}$ M

Calculate the value of the equilibrium constant for this reaction occurring in carbon tetrachloride.

Equilibrium of Acids and Bases K_a and K_b: Chap. 18, Sec. 3

518. At 25°C, a 0.025 M solution of formic acid, HCOOH, is found to have a hydronium ion concentration of 2.03×10^{-3} M. Calculate the ionization constant of formic acid.

519. The pH of a 0.400 M solution of iodic acid, HIO_3, is 0.726 at 25°C. What is the K_a at this temperature?

520. The pH of a 0.150 M solution of hypochlorous acid, HClO, is found to be 4.55 at 25°C. Calculate the K_a for HClO at this temperature.

521. The compound propylamine, $CH_3CH_2CH_2NH_2$, is a weak base. At equilibrium, a 0.039 M solution of propylamine has an OH^- concentration of 3.74×10^{-3} M. Calculate the pH of this solution and K_b for propylamine.

522. The K_a of nitrous acid is 4.6×10^{-4} at 25°C. Calculate the $[H_3O^+]$ of a 0.0450 M nitrous acid solution.

MIXED REVIEW

523. Hydrazoic acid, HN_3, is a weak acid. The $[H_3O^-]$ of a 0.102 M solution of hydrazoic acid is 1.39×10^{-3} M. Determine the pH of this solution, and calculate K_a at 25°C for HN_3.

524. Bromoacetic acid, $BrCH_2COOH$, is a moderately weak acid. A 0.200 M solution of bromoacetic acid has a H_3O^+ concentration of 0.0192 M. Determine the pH of this solution and the K_a of bromoacetic acid at 25°C.

525. A base, B, dissociates in water according to the following equation:

$$B + H_2O \rightleftarrows BH^+ + OH^-$$

Complete the following table for base solutions with the characteristics given.

Initial [B]	*[B] at Equilibrium*	*[OH−]*	*Kb*	*[H3O+]*	*pH*
a. 0.400 M	NA	2.70×10^{-4} M	?	? M	?
b. 0.005 50 M	? M	8.45×10^{-4} M	?	NA	?
c. 0.0350 M	? M	? M	?	? M	11.29
d. ? M	0.006 28 M	0.000 92 M	?	NA	?

526. The solubility of benzoic acid, C_6H_5COOH, in water at 25°C is 2.9 g/L. The pH of this saturated solution is 2.92. Determine K_a at 25°C for benzoic acid. (Hint: first calculate the initial concentration of benzoic acid.)

527. A 0.006 50 M solution of ethanolamine, $H_2NCH_2CH_2OH$, has a pH of 10.64 at 25°C. Calculate the K_b of ethanolamine. What concentration of undissociated ethanolamine remains at equilibrium?

528. The weak acid hydrogen selenide, H_2Se, has two hydrogen atoms that can form hydronium ions. The second ionization is so small that the concentration of the resulting H_3O^+ is insignificant. If the $[H_3O^+]$ of a 0.060 M solution of H_2Se is 2.72×10^{-3} M at 25°C, what is the K_a of the first ionization?

529. Pyridine, C_5H_5N, is a very weak base. Its K_b at 25°C is 1.78×10^{-9}. Calculate the $[OH^-]$ and pH of a 0.140 M solution. Assume that the concentration of pyridine at equilibrium is equal to its initial concentration because so little pyridine is dissociated.

530. A solution of a monoprotic acid, HA, at equilibrium is found to have a 0.0208 M concentration of nonionized acid. The pH of the acid solution is 2.17. Calculate the initial acid concentration and K_a for this acid.

531. Pyruvic acid, $CH_3COCOOH$, is an important intermediate in the metabolism of carbohydrates in the cells of the body. A solution made by dissolving 438 mg of pyruvic acid in 10.00 mL of water is found to have a pH of 1.34 at 25°C. Calculate K_a for pyruvic acid.

532. The $[H_3O^+]$ of a solution of acetoacetic acid, CH_3COCH_2COOH, is 4.38×10^{-3} M at 25°C. The concentration of nonionized acid is 0.0731 M at equilibrium. Calculate K_a for acetoacetic acid at 25°C.

533. The K_a of 2-chloropropanoic acid, $CH_3CHClCOOH$, is 1.48×10^{-3}. Calculate the $[H_3O^+]$ and the pH of a 0.116 M solution of 2-chloropropionic acid. Let $x = [H_3O^+]$. The degree of ionization of the acid is too large to ignore. If your setup is correct, you will have a quadratic equation to solve.

534. Sulfuric acid ionizes in two steps in water solution. For the first ionization shown in the following equation, the K_a is so large that in moderately dilute solution the ionization can be considered 100%.

$$H_2SO_4 + H_2O \longrightarrow H_3O^+ + HSO_4^-$$

The second ionization is fairly strong, and $Ka = 1.3 \times 10^{-2}$:

$$HSO_4^- + H_2O \rightleftarrows H_3O^+ + SO_4^{2-}$$

Calculate the total $[H_3O^+]$ and pH of a 0.0788 M H_2SO_4 solution. Hint: If the first ionization is 100%, what will $[HSO_4^-]$ and $[H_3O^+]$ be? Remember to account for the already existing concentration of H_3O^+ in the second ionization. Let $x = [+ SO_4^{2-}]$.

535. The hydronium ion concentration of a 0.100 M solution of cyanic acid, HOCN, is found to be 5.74×10^{-3} M at 25°C. Calculate the ionization constant of cyanic acid. What is the pH of this solution?

536. A solution of hydrogen cyanide, HCN, has a 0.025 M concentration. The cyanide ion concentration is found to be 3.16×10^{-6} M.

a. What is the hydronium ion concentration of this solution?

b. What is the pH of this solution?

c. What is the concentration of nonionized HCN in the solution? Be sure to use the correct number of significant figures.

d. Calculate the ionization constant of HCN.

e. How would you characterize the strength of HCN as an acid?

f. Determine the $[H_3O^+]$ for a 0.085 M solution of HCN.

537. A 1.20 M solution of dichloroacetic acid, CCl_2HCOOH, at 25°C has a hydronium ion concentration of 0.182 M.

a. What is the pH of this solution?

b. What is the K_a of dichloroacetic acid at 25°C?

c. What is the concentration of nonionized dichloroacetic acid in this solution?

d. What can you say about the strength of dichloroacetic acid?

538. Phenol, C_6H_5OH, is a very weak acid. The pH of a 0.215 M solution of phenol at 25°C is found to be 5.61. Calculate the K_a for phenol.

539. A solution of the simplest amino acid, glycine (NH_2CH_2COOH), is prepared by dissolving 3.75 g in 250.0 mL of water at 25°C. The pH of this solution is found to be 0.890.

a. Calculate the molarity of the glycine solution.

b. Calculate the K_a for glycine.

540. Trimethylamine, $(CH_3)_3N$, dissociates in water the same way that NH_3 does—by accepting a proton from a water molecule. The $[OH^-]$ of a 0.0750 M solution of trimethylamine at 25°C is 2.32×10^{-3} M. Calculate the pH of this solution and the K_b of trimethylamine.

541. Dimethylamine, $(CH_3)_2NH$, is a weak base similar to the trimethylamine in item 540. A 5.00×10^{-3} M solution of dimethylamine has a pH of 11.20 at 25°C. Calculate the K_b of dimethylamine. Compare this K_b with the K_b for trimethylamine that you calculated in item 540. Which substance is the stronger base?

Problem Bank

ANSWERS

526. 6.4×10^{-5}

527. $K_b = 3.1 \times 10^{-5}$
$[H_2NCH_2CH_2OH] = 6.06 \times 10^{-3}$ M

528. 1.3×10^{-4}

529. $[OH^-] = 1.58 \times 10^{-5}$ M
pH = 9.20

530. $K_a = 2.2 \times 10^{-3}$
$[HB]_{initial} = 0.0276$ M

531. 4.63×10^{-3}

532. 2.62×10^{-4}

533. $[H_3O^+] = 0.0124$ M
pH = 1.907

534. $[H_3O^+] = 0.0888$ M
pH = 1.05

535. $K_a = 3.50 \times 10^{-4}$
pH = 2.241

536. **a.** 3.16×10^{-6} M
b. 5.500
c. 0.025 M
d. 4.0×10^{-10}
e. HCN is a fairly weak acid.
f. 5.8×10^{-6} M

537. **a.** 0.740
b. 0.0325
c. 1.02 M
d. It is moderately weak.

538. 2.80×10^{-11}

539. **a.** 0.200 M
b. 0.233

540. pH = 11.37
$K_b = 7.41 \times 10^{-5}$

541. 7.36×10^{-4}; Dimethylamine is the stronger base.

542. a. 8.3×10^{-7}
b. 1.3×10^{-4} M
c. 10.11

543. $K_{sp} = 6.09 \times 10^{-5}$

544. $K_{sp} = 4.20 \times 10^{-11}$

545. 3.0×10^{-3} M

546. a. $[X_2Y] = 4.74 \times 10^{-3}$ M
b. $[AZ] = 6.52 \times 10^{-4}$ M

547. ion product $= 1.9 \times 10^{-5}$
precipitation occurs

548. ion product $= 8.1 \times 10^{-4}$
no precipitate

549. ion product $= 1.5 \times 10^{-5}$
no precipitate

550. ion product $= 1.1 \times 10^{-13}$
no precipitate

551. 1.0×10^{-4}

552. 1.51×10^{-7}

553. a. 1.6×10^{-11}
b. 0.49 g

554. 2.000×10^{-7}

555. a. 8.9×10^{-4} M
b. 0.097 g

556. 0.036 M

557. a. 1.1×10^{-4} M
b. 4.6 L

558. a. 5.7×10^{-4} M
b. 2.1 g

559. 0.83 g remains

560. 2.8×10^{-3} M

561. a. 1.2×10^{-5}
b. yes

562. a. 1.1×10^{-8}
b. no

563. a. $Mg(OH)_2 \rightleftharpoons Mg^{2+} + 2OH^-$
b. 11 L
c. A suspension contains undissolved $Mg(OH)_2$ suspended in a saturated solution of $Mg(OH)_2$. As hydroxide ions are depleted by titration, the dissociation equilibrium continues to replenish them until all of the $Mg(OH)_2$ is used up.

564. a. 0.184 M
b. 46.8 g

565. 5.040×10^{-3}

566. a. 1.0
b. 0.25
c. 0.01
d. 1×10^{-6}

567. 4×10^{-4}; 3×10^{-5}; 3×10^{-5}; 4×10^{-6}; 3×10^{-7}

568. 7.1×10^{-7} M; 1.3×10^{-3} g

569. a. 0.011 M
b. 0.022 M
c. 12.35

570. 0.063 g

571. $2Fe + 3SnCl_4 \longrightarrow 2FeCl_3 + 3SnCl_2$

572. $H_2O_2 + 2FeSO_4 + H_2SO_4 \longrightarrow Fe_2(SO_4)_3 + 2H_2O$

573. $3CuS + 8HNO_3 \longrightarrow 3Cu(NO_3)_2 + 2NO + 3S + 4H_2O$

574. $K_2Cr_2O_7 + 14\,HI \longrightarrow 2CrI_3 + 2KI + 3I_2 + 7H_2O$

575. $CO_2 + 2NH_2OH \longrightarrow CO + N_2 + 3H_2O$

576. $2Bi(OH)_3 + 3K_2SnO_2 \longrightarrow 2Bi + 3K_2SnO_3 + 3H_2O$

577. $3Mg + N_2 \longrightarrow Mg_3N_2$

578. $SO_2 + Br_2 + 2H_2O \longrightarrow 2HBr + H_2SO_4$

579. $H_2S + Cl_2 \longrightarrow S + 2HCl$

580. $PbO_2 + 4HBr \longrightarrow PbBr_2 + Br_2 + 2H_2O$

581. $S + 6HNO_3 \longrightarrow 6NO_2 + H_2SO_4 + 2H_2O$

542. Hydrazine dissociates in water solution according to the following equations:

$$H_2NNH_2 + H_2O(l) \rightleftharpoons H_2NNH_3^+(aq) + OH^-(aq)$$
$$H_2NNH_3^+(aq) + H_2O(l) \rightleftharpoons H_3NNH_3^{2+}(aq) + OH^-(aq)$$

The K_b of this second dissociation is 8.9×10^{-16}, so it contributes almost no hydroxide ions in solution and can be ignored here.

a. The pH of a 0.120 M solution of hydrazine at 25°C is 10.50. Calculate K_b for the first ionization of hydrazine. Assume that the original concentration of H_2NNH_2 does not change.
b. Make the same assumption as you did in (a) and calculate the $[OH^-]$ of a 0.020 M solution.
c. Calculate the pH of the solution in (b).

Equilibrium of Salts, K_{sp}: Chap. 18, Sec. 4

543. Silver bromate, $AgBrO_3$, is slightly soluble in water. A saturated solution is found to contain 0.276 g $AgBrO_3$ dissolved in 150.0 mL of water. Calculate Ksp for silver bromate.

544. 2.50 L of a saturated solution of calcium fluoride leaves a residue of 0.0427 g of CaF_2 when evaporated to dryness. Calculate the K_{sp} of CaF_2.

545. The K_{sp} of calcium sulfate, $CaSO_4$, is 9.1×10^{-6}. What is the molar concentration of $CaSO_4$ in a saturated solution?

546. A salt has the formula X_2Y, and its K_{sp} is 4.25×10^{-7}.
a. What is the molarity of a saturated solution of the salt?
b. What is the molarity of a solution of AZ if its K_{sp} is the same value?

In each of the following problems, include the calculated ion product with your answer.

547. Will a precipitate of $Ca(OH)_2$ form when 320. mL of a 0.046 M solution of NaOH mixes with 400. mL of a 0.085 M $CaCl_2$ solution? K_{sp} of $Ca(OH)_2$ is 5.5×10^{-6}.

548. 20.00 mL of a 0.077 M solution of silver nitrate, $AgNO_3$, is mixed with 30.00 mL of a 0.043 M solution of sodium acetate, $NaC_2H_3O_2$. Does a precipitate form? The K_{sp} of $AgC_2H_3O_2$ is 2.5×10^{-3}.

549. If you mix 100. mL of 0.036 M $Pb(C_2H_3O_2)_2$ with 50. mL of 0.074 M NaCl, will a precipitate of $PbCl_2$ form? The K_{sp} of $PbCl_2$ is 1.9×10^{-4}.

550. If 20.00 mL of a 0.0090 M solution of $(NH_4)_2S$ is mixed with 120.00 mL of a 0.0082 M solution of $Al(NO_3)_3$, does a precipitate form? The K_{sp} of Al_2S_3 is 2.00×10^{-7}.

MIXED REVIEW

551. The molar concentration of a saturated calcium chromate, $CaCrO_4$, solution is 0.010 M at 25°C. What is the K_{sp} of calcium chromate?

552. A 10.00 mL sample of a saturated lead selenate solution is found to contain 0.00136 g of dissolved $PbSeO_4$ at 25°C. Determine the K_{sp} of lead selenate.

553. A 22.50 mL sample of a saturated copper(I) thiocyanate, CuSCN, solution at 25°C is found to have a 4.0×10^{-6} M concentration.
a. Determine the K_{sp} of CuSCN.
b. What mass of CuSCN would be dissolved in 1.0×10^3 L of solution?

554. A saturated solution of silver dichromate, $Ag_2Cr_2O_7$, has a concentration of 3.684×10^{-3} M. Calculate the K_{sp} of silver dichromate.

555. The K_{sp} of barium sulfite, $BaSO_3$, at 25°C is 8.0×10^{-7}.
a. What is the molar concentration of a saturated solution of $BaSO_3$?
b. What mass of $BaSO_3$ would dissolve in 500. mL of water?

556. The K_{sp} of lead(II) chloride at 25°C is 1.9×10^{-4}. What is the molar concentration of a saturated solution at 25°C?

557. The K_{sp} of barium carbonate at 25°C is 1.2×10^{-8}.
a. What is the molar concentration of a saturated solution of $BaCO_3$ at 25°C?
b. What volume of water would be needed to dissolve 0.10 g of barium carbonate?

558. The K_{sp} of $SrSO_4$ is 3.2×10^{-7} at 25°C.
a. What is the molar concentration of a saturated $SrSO_4$ solution?
b. If 20.0 L of a saturated solution of $SrSO_4$ were evaporated to dryness, what mass of $SrSO_4$ would remain?

559. The K_{sp} of strontium sulfite, $SrSO_3$, is 4.0×10^{-8} at 25°C. If 1.0000 g of $SrSO_3$ is stirred in 5.0 L of water until the solution is saturated and then filtered, what mass of $SrSO_3$ would remain?

560. The K_{sp} of manganese(II) arsenate is 1.9×10^{-11} at 25°C. What is the molar concentration of $Mn_3(AsO_4)_2$ in a saturated solution? Note that five ions are produced from the dissociation of $Mn_3(AsO_4)_2$.

561. Suppose that 30.0 mL of a 0.0050 M solution of $Sr(NO_3)_2$ is mixed with 20.0 mL of a 0.010 M solution of K_2SO_4 at 25°C. The K_{sp} of $SrSO_4$ is 3.2×10^{-7}.
a. What is the ion product of the ions that can potentially form a precipitate?
b. Does a precipitate form?

562. Lead(II) bromide, $PbBr_2$, is slightly soluble in water. Its K_{sp} is 6.3×10^{-6} at 25°C. Suppose that 120. mL of a 0.0035 M solution of $MgBr_2$ is mixed with 180. mL of a 0.0024 M $Pb(C_2H_3O_2)_2$ solution at 25°C.
a. What is the ion product of Br_2 and Pb^{2+} in the mixed solution?
b. Does a precipitate form?

563. The K_{sp} of $Mg(OH)_2$ at 25°C is 1.5×10^{-11}.

a. Write the equilibrium equation for the dissociation of $Mg(OH)_2$.

b. What volume of water would be required to dissolve 0.10 g of $Mg(OH)_2$?

c. Considering that magnesium hydroxide is essentially insoluble, why is it possible to titrate a suspension of $Mg(OH)_2$ to an equivalence point with a strong acid such as HCl?

564. Lithium carbonate is somewhat soluble in water; its K_{sp} at 25°C is 2.51×10^{-2}.

a. What is the molar concentration of a saturated Li_2CO_3 solution?

b. What mass of Li_2CO_3 would you dissolve in order to make 3440 mL of saturated solution?

565. A 50.00 mL sample of a saturated solution of barium hydroxide, $Ba(OH)_2$, is titrated to the equivalence point by 31.61 mL of a 0.3417 M solution of HCl. Determine the K_{sp} of $Ba(OH)_2$.

566. Calculate the K_{sp} for salts represented by QR that dissociate into two ions, Q^+ and R^-, in each of the following solutions:

a. saturated solution of QR is 1.0 M

b. saturated solution of QR is 0.50 M

c. saturated solution of QR is 0.1 M

d. saturated solution of QR is 0.001 M

567. Suppose that salts QR, X_2Y, KL_2, A_3Z, and D_2E_3 form saturated solutions that are 0.02 M in concentration. Calculate K_{sp} for each of these salts.

568. The K_{sp} at 25°C of silver bromide is 5.0×10^{-13}. What is the molar concentration of a saturated AgBr solution? What mass of silver bromide would dissolve in 10.0 L of saturated solution at 25°C?

569. The K_{sp} at 25°C for calcium hydroxide is 5.5×10^{-6}.

a. Calculate the molarity of a saturated $Ca(OH)_2$ solution.

b. What is the OH^- concentration of this solution?

c. What is the pH of the saturated solution?

570. The K_{sp} of magnesium carbonate is 3.5×10^{-8} at 25°C. What mass of $MgCO_3$ would dissolve in 4.00 L of water at 25°C?

Redox Equations: Chap. 19, Sec. 2

REACTIONS IN ACIDIC SOLUTION

Balance the following redox equations. Assume that all reactions take place in an acid environment where H^+ and H_2O are readily available.

571. $Fe + SnCl_4 \longrightarrow FeCl_3 + SnCl_2$

572. $H_2O_2 + FeSO_4 + H_2SO_4 \longrightarrow Fe_2(SO_4)_3 + H_2O$

573. $CuS + HNO_3 \longrightarrow Cu(NO_3)_2 + NO + S + H_2O$

574. $K_2Cr_2O_7 + HI \longrightarrow CrI_3 + KI + I_2 + H_2O$

REACTIONS IN BASIC SOLUTION

Balance the following redox equations. Assume that all reactions take place in a basic environment where OH^- and H_2O are readily available.

575. $CO_2 + NH_2OH \longrightarrow CO + N_2 + H_2O$

576. $Bi(OH)_3 + K_2SnO_2 \longrightarrow Bi + K_2SnO_3$

(Both of the potassium-tin-oxygen compounds dissociate into potassium ions and tin-oxygen ions.)

MIXED REVIEW

Balance each of the following redox equations. Unless stated otherwise, assume that the reaction occurs in acidic solution.

577. $Mg + N_2 \longrightarrow Mg_3N_2$

578. $SO_2 + Br_2 + H_2O \longrightarrow HBr + H_2SO_4$

579. $H_2S + Cl_2 \longrightarrow S + HCl$

580. $PbO_2 + HBr \longrightarrow PbBr_2 + Br_2 + H_2O$

581. $S + HNO_3 \longrightarrow NO_2 + H_2SO_4 + H_2O$

582. $NaIO_3 + N_2H_4 + HCl \longrightarrow N_2 + NaICl_2 + H_2O$ (N_2H_4 is hydrazine; do not separate it into ions.)

583. $MnO_2 + H_2O_2 + HCl \longrightarrow MnCl_2 + O_2 + H_2O$

584. $AsH_3 + NaClO_3 \longrightarrow H_3AsO_4 + NaCl$ (AsH_3 is arsine, the arsenic analogue of ammonia, NH_3.)

585. $K_2Cr_2O_7 + H_2C_2O_4 + HCl \longrightarrow CrCl_3 + CO_2 + KCl + H_2O$ ($H_2C_2O_4$ is oxalic acid; it can be treated as $2H^+ + C_2O_4^{2-}$.)

586. $Hg(NO_3)_2 \xrightarrow{heat} HgO + NO_2 + O_2$ (The reaction is not in solution.)

587. $HAuCl_4 + N_2H_4 \longrightarrow Au + N_2 + HCl$ ($HAuCl_4$ can be considered as $H^+ + AuCl_4^-$.)

588. $Sb_2(SO_4)_3 + KMnO_4 + H_2O \longrightarrow H_3SbO_4 + K_2SO_4 + MnSO_4 + H_2SO_4$

589. $Mn(NO_3)_2 + NaBiO_3 + HNO_3 \longrightarrow Bi(NO_3)_2 + HMnO_4 + NaNO_3 + H_2O$

590. $H_3AsO_4 + Zn + HCl \longrightarrow AsH_3 + ZnCl_2 + H_2O$

591. $KClO_3 + HCl \longrightarrow Cl_2 + H_2O + KCl$

592. The same reactants as in item 591 can combine in the following way when more $KClO_3$ is present. Balance the equation.

$KClO_3 + HCl \longrightarrow Cl_2 + ClO_2 + H_2O + KCl$

593. $MnCl_3 + H_2O \longrightarrow MnCl_2 + MnO_2 + HCl$

594. $NaOH + H_2O + Al \longrightarrow NaAl(OH)_4 + H_2$ in basic solution

595. $Br_2 + Ca(OH)_2 \longrightarrow CaBr_2 + Ca(BrO_3)_2 + H_2O$ in basic solution

596. $N_2O + NaClO + NaOH \longrightarrow NaCl + NaNO_2 + H_2O$ in basic solution

597. Balance the following reaction, which can be used to prepare bromine in the laboratory:

$HBr + MnO_2 \longrightarrow MnBr_2 + H_2O + Br_2$

598. The following reaction occurs when gold is dissolved in *aqua regia*. Balance the equation.

$Au + HCl + HNO_3 \longrightarrow HAuCl_4 + NO + H_2O$

ANSWERS

582. $NaIO_3 + N_2H_4 + 2HCl \longrightarrow N_2 + NaICl_2 + 3H_2O$

583. $MnO_2 + H_2O_2 + 2HCl \longrightarrow MnCl_2 + O_2 + 2H_2O$

584. $3AsH_3 + 4NaClO_3 \longrightarrow 3H_3AsO_4 + 4NaCl$

585. $K_2Cr_2O_7 + 3H_2C_2O_4 + 8HCl \longrightarrow 2CrCl_3 + 6CO_2 + 2KCl + 7H_2O$

586. $2Hg(NO_3)_2 \longrightarrow 2HgO + 4NO_2 + O_2$

587. $4HAuCl_4 + 3N_2H_4 \longrightarrow 4Au + 3N_2 + 16HCl$

588. $5Sb_2(SO_4)_3 + 4KMnO_4 + 24H_2O \longrightarrow 10H_3SbO_4 + 2K_2SO_4 + 4MnSO_4 + 9H_2SO_4$

589. $3Mn(NO_3)_2 + 5NaBiO_3 + 9HNO_3 \longrightarrow 5Bi(NO_3)_2 + 3HMnO_4 + 5NaNO_3 + 3H_2O$

590. $H_3AsO_4 + 4Zn + 8HCl \longrightarrow AsH_3 + 4ZnCl_2 + 4H_2O$

591. $KClO_3 + 6HCl \longrightarrow 3Cl_2 + 3H_2O + KCl$

592. $2KClO_3 + 4HCl \longrightarrow Cl_2 + 2ClO_2 + 2H_2O + 2KCl$

593. $2MnCl_3 + 2H_2O \longrightarrow MnCl_2 + MnO_2 + 4HCl$

594. $2NaOH + 6H_2O + 2Al \longrightarrow 2NaAl(OH)_4 + 3H_2$

595. $6Br_2 + 6Ca(OH)_2 \longrightarrow 5CaBr_2 + Ca(BrO_3)_2 + 6H_2O$

596. $N_2O + 2NaClO + 2NaOH \longrightarrow 2NaCl + 2NaNO_2 + H_2O$

597. $4HBr + MnO_2 \longrightarrow MnBr_2 + 2H_2O + Br_2$

598. $Au + 4HCl + HNO_3 \longrightarrow HAuCl_4 + NO + 2H_2O$

599. +0.79 V; spontaneous

600. −0.90 V; nonspontaneous

601. −1.64 V; nonspontaneous

602. +0.80 V; spontaneous

603. +0.24 V; spontaneous

604. −2.91 V; nonspontaneous

605. −0.29 V; nonspontaneous

606. −1.02 V; nonspontaneous

607. cathode: $Fe^{3+} + 3e^- \longrightarrow Fe$
anode: $Ca \longrightarrow Ca^{2+} + 2e^-$
$E^0_{cell} = +2.83$ V

608. cathode: $Ag^+ + e^- \longrightarrow Ag$
anode: $H_2S \longrightarrow S + 2H^+ + 2e^-$
$E^0_{cell} = +0.66$ V

609. cathode: $Fe^{3+} + e^- \longrightarrow Fe^{2+}$
anode: $Sn \longrightarrow Sn^{2+} + 2e^-$
$E^0_{cell} = +0.91$ V

610. cathode: $Au^{3+} + 3e^- \longrightarrow Au$
anode: $Cu \longrightarrow Cu^{2+} + 2e^-$
$E^0_{cell} = +1.16$ V

611. $E^0 = +2.77$ V; spontaneous

612. $E^0 = +1.11$ V; spontaneous

613. $E^0 = -0.46$ V; not spontaneous

614. $E^0 = +1.50$ V; spontaneous

615. $E^0 = +2.46$ V; spontaneous

616. $E^0 = +1.28$ V; spontaneous

617. $E^0 = +3.71$ V; spontaneous

618. $E^0 = -3.41$ V; not spontaneous

619. $E^0 = +1.32$ V; spontaneous

620. $E^0 = -3.60$ V; not spontaneous

621. Overall reaction:
$Cl_2 + Ni \longrightarrow Ni^{2+} + 2Cl_2$
Cathode reaction:
$Cl_2 + 2e^- \longrightarrow 2Cl_2$
Anode reaction: $Ni \longrightarrow Ni^{2+} + 2e^-$
Cell voltage: +1.62 V

622. Overall reaction:
$3Hg^{2+} + 2Fe \longrightarrow 3Hg + 2Fe^{3+}$
Cathode reaction:
$Hg^{2+} + 2e^- \longrightarrow Hg$
Anode reaction: $Fe \longrightarrow Fe^{3+} + 3e^-$
Cell voltage: +0.89 V

623. Overall reaction:
$3MnO_4^- + Al \longrightarrow 3MnO_4^{2-} + Al^{3+}$
Cathode reaction:
$MnO_4^- + e^- \longrightarrow MnO_4^{2-}$
Anode reaction: $Al \longrightarrow Al^{3+} + 3e^-$
Cell voltage: +2.22 V

624. Overall reaction:
$2MnO_4^- + 6H^+ + 5H_2S \longrightarrow 2Mn^{2+} + 8H_2O + 5S$
Cathode reaction:
$MnO_4^- + 8H^+ + 5e^- \longrightarrow Mn^{2+} + 4H_2O$
Anode reaction: $H_2S \longrightarrow S + 2H^+ + 2e^-$
Cell voltage: +1.36 V

625. Overall reaction:
$Ca^{2+} + 2Li \longrightarrow Ca + 2Li^+$
Cathode reaction: $Ca^{2+} + 2e^- \longrightarrow Ca$
Anode reaction: $Li \longrightarrow Li^+ + e^-$
Cell voltage: +0.17 V

626. Overall reaction:
$2MnO_4^- + 16H^+ + 10Br^- \longrightarrow 2Mn^{2+} + 8H_2O + 5Br_2$
Cathode reaction: $MnO_4^- + 8H^+ + 5e^- \longrightarrow Mn^{2+} + 4H_2O$
Anode reaction: $2Br^- \longrightarrow Br_2 + 2e^-$
Cell voltage: +0.43 V

627. Overall reaction:
$2Fe^{3+} + Sn \longrightarrow 2Fe^{2+} + Sn^{2+}$
Cathode reaction: $Fe^{3+} + e^- \longrightarrow Fe^{2+}$
Anode reaction: $Sn \longrightarrow Sn^{2+} + 2e^-$
Cell voltage: +0.91 V

628. Overall reaction:
$Cr_2O_7^{2-} + 14H^+ + 3Zn \longrightarrow 2Cr^{3+} + 7H_2O + 3Zn^{2+}$
Cathode reaction:
$Cr_2O_7^{2-} + 14H^+ + 6e^- \longrightarrow 2Cr^{3+} + 7H_2O$
Anode reaction: $Zn \longrightarrow Zn^{2+} + 2e^-$
Cell voltage: +1.99 V

Electrochemistry: Chap. 20, Sec. 2

Use the reduction potentials in the table below to determine whether the following reactions are spontaneous as written. Report the E^0_{cell} for the reactions.

599. $Cu^{2+} + Fe \longrightarrow Fe^{2+} + Cu$
600. $Pb^{2+} + Fe^{2+} \longrightarrow Fe^{3+} + Pb$
601. $Mn^{2+} + 4H_2O + Sn^{2+} \longrightarrow MnO_4^- + 8H^+ + Sn$
602. $MnO_4^{2-} + Cl_2 \longrightarrow MnO_4^- + 2Cl^-$
603. $Hg_2^{2+} + 2MnO_4^{2-} \longrightarrow 2Hg + 2MnO_4^-$
604. $2Li^+ + Pb \longrightarrow 2Li + Pb^{2+}$
605. $Br_2 + 2Cl^- \longrightarrow 2Br^- + Cl_2$
606. $S + 2I^- \longrightarrow S^{2-} + I_2$

For Problems 599–606

Reduction Half-reaction	*Standard Electrode Potential, E^0 (in volts)*	*Reduction Half-reaction*	*Standard Electrode Potential, E^0 (in volts)*
$MnO_4^- + 8H^+ + 5e^- \rightleftharpoons Mn^{2+} + 4H_2O$	+1.50	$Fe^{3+} + 3e^- \rightleftharpoons Fe$	−0.04
$Au^{3+} + 3e^- \rightleftharpoons Au$	+1.50	$Pb^{2+} + 2e^- \rightleftharpoons Pb$	−0.13
$Cl_2 + 2e^- \rightleftharpoons 2Cl^-$	+1.36	$Sn^{2+} + 2e^- \rightleftharpoons Sn$	−0.14
$Cr_2O_7^{2-} + 14H^+ + 6e^- \rightleftharpoons 2Cr^{3+} + 7H_2O$	+1.23	$Ni^{2+} + 2e^- \rightleftharpoons Ni$	−0.26
$MnO_2 + 4H^+ + 2e^- \rightleftharpoons Mn^{2+} + 2H_2O$	+1.22	$Cd^{2+} + 2e^- \rightleftharpoons Cd$	−0.40
$Br_2 + 2e^- \rightleftharpoons 2Br^-$	+1.07	$Fe^{2+} + 2e^- \rightleftharpoons Fe$	−0.45
$Hg^{2+} + 2e^- \rightleftharpoons Hg$	+0.85	$S + 2e^- \rightleftharpoons S^{2-}$	−0.48
$Ag^+ + e^- \rightleftharpoons Ag$	+0.80	$Zn^{2+} + 2e^- \rightleftharpoons Zn$	−0.76
$Hg_2^{2+} + 2e^- \rightleftharpoons 2Hg$	+0.80	$Al^{3+} + 3e^- \rightleftharpoons Al$	−1.66
$Fe^{3+} + e^- \rightleftharpoons Fe^{2+}$	+0.77	$Mg^{2+} + 2e^- \rightleftharpoons Mg$	−2.37
$MnO_4^- + e^- \rightleftharpoons MnO_4^{2-}$	+0.56	$Na^+ + e^- \rightleftharpoons Na$	−2.71
$I_2 + 2e^- \rightleftharpoons 2I^-$	+0.54	$Ca^{2+} + 2e^- \rightleftharpoons Ca$	−2.87
$Cu^{2+} + 2e^- \rightleftharpoons Cu$	+0.34	$Ba^{2+} + 2e^- \rightleftharpoons Ba$	−2.91
$S + 2H^+(aq) + 2e^- \rightleftharpoons H_2S(aq)$	+0.14	$K^+ + e^- \rightleftharpoons K$	−2.93
$2H^+(aq) + 2e^- \rightleftharpoons H_2$	0.00	$Li^+ + e^- \rightleftharpoons Li$	−3.04

If a cell is constructed in which the following pairs of reactions are possible, what would be the cathode reaction, the anode reaction, and the overall cell voltage?

607. $Ca^{2+} + 2e^- \rightleftharpoons Ca$
$Fe^{3+} + 3e^- \rightleftharpoons Fe$
608. $Ag^+ + e^- \rightleftharpoons Ag$
$S + 2H^+ + 2e^- \rightleftharpoons H_2S$
609. $Fe^{3+} + e^- \rightleftharpoons Fe^{2+}$
$Sn^{2+} + 2e^- \rightleftharpoons Sn$
610. $Cu^{2+} + 2e^- \rightleftharpoons Cu$
$Au^{3+} + 3e^- \rightleftharpoons Au$

MIXED REVIEW

Use reduction potentials to determine whether the reactions in the following 10 problems are spontaneous.

611. $Ba + Sn^{2+} \longrightarrow Ba^{2+} + Sn$
612. $Ni + Hg^{2+} \longrightarrow Ni^{2+} + Hg$
613. $2Cr^{3+} + 7H_2O + 6Fe^{3+} \longrightarrow Cr_2O_7^{2-} + 14H^+ + 6Fe^{2+}$
614. $Cl_2 + Sn \longrightarrow 2Cl^- + Sn^{2+}$
615. $Al + 3Ag^+ \longrightarrow Al^{3+} + 3Ag$
616. $Hg_2^{2+} + S^{2-} \longrightarrow 2Hg + S$
617. $Ba + 2Ag^+ \longrightarrow Ba^{2+} + 2Ag$
618. $2I^- + Ca^{2+} \longrightarrow I_2 + Ca$
619. $Zn + 2MnO_4^- \longrightarrow Zn^{2+} + 2MnO_4^{2-}$
620. $2Cr^{3+} + 3Mg^{2+} + 7H_2O \longrightarrow Cr_2O_7^{2-} + 14H^+ + 3Mg$

In the following problems, you are given a pair of reduction half-reactions. If a cell were constructed in which the pairs of half-reactions were possible, what would be the balanced equation for the overall cell reaction that would occur? Write the half-reactions that occur at the cathode and anode, and calculate the cell voltage.

621. $Cl_2 + 2e^- \rightleftharpoons 2Cl^-$
$Ni^{2+} + 2e^- \rightleftharpoons Ni$
622. $Fe^{3+} + 3e^- \rightleftharpoons Fe$
$Hg^{2+} + 2e^- \rightleftharpoons Hg$
623. $MnO_4^- + e^- \rightleftharpoons MnO_4^{2-}$
$Al^{3+} + 3e^- \rightleftharpoons Al$
624. $MnO_4^- + 8H^+ + 5e^- \rightleftharpoons Mn^{2+} + 4H_2O$
$S + 2H^+ + 2e^- \rightleftharpoons H_2S$
625. $Ca^{2+} + 2e^- \rightleftharpoons Ca$
$Li^+ + e^- \rightleftharpoons Li$
626. $Br_2 + 2e^- \rightleftharpoons 2Br^-$
$MnO_4^- + 8H^+ + 5e^- \rightleftharpoons Mn^{2+} + 4H_2O$
627. $Sn^{2+} + 2e^- \rightleftharpoons Sn$
$Fe^{3+} + e^- \rightleftharpoons Fe^{2+}$
628. $Zn^{2+} + 2e^- \rightleftharpoons Zn$
$Cr_2O_7^{2-} + 14H^+ + 6e^- \rightleftharpoons 2Cr^{3+} + 7H_2O$
629. $Ba^{2+} + 2e^- \rightleftharpoons Ba$
$Ca^{2+} + 2e^- \rightleftharpoons Ca$
630. $Hg_2^{2+} + 2e^- \rightleftharpoons 2Hg$
$Cd^{2+} + 2e^- \rightleftharpoons Cd$

629. Overall reaction:
$Ba + Ca^{2+} \longrightarrow Ba^{2+} + Ca$
Cathode reaction: $Ca^{2+} + 2e^- \longrightarrow Ca$
Anode reaction: $Ba \longrightarrow Ba^{2+} + 2e^-$
Cell voltage: +0.04 V

630. Overall reaction:
$Cd + Hg_2^{2+} \longrightarrow Cd^{2+} + 2Hg$
Cathode reaction: $Hg_2^{2+} + 2e^- \longrightarrow 2Hg$
Anode reaction: $Cd \longrightarrow Cd^{2+} + 2e^-$
Cell voltage: +1.25 V

APPENDIX E

Selected Answers

Matter and Change

MATH TUTOR PRACTICE

1. **a.** 5 significant features
   b. 4 significant features
2. **a.** 4.21 g/cm^3
   b. 16.5 g

Measurements and Calculations

PRACTICE PROBLEMS A

1. 2.75 g/cm^3
2. 1.14 g
3. 5.60 mL

PRACTICE PROBLEMS B

1. 1645 cm, 0.01645 km
2. 0.000 014 g

PRACTICE PROBLEMS C

1. −17%
2. 2.7%

PRACTICE PROBLEMS D

1. **a.** 5
   b. 6
   c. 4
   d. 1
   e. 5
   f. 6
2. **a.** 7000 cm
   b. 7000. cm
   c. 7000.00 cm

PRACTICE PROBLEM E

1. 2.156 g
2. 85.6 cm
3. 1.00 μm^2
4. 440 g

PRACTICE PROBLEMS F

1. 9.69 mL
2. 1.67 g/cm^3
3. 5.12×10^{11} mm
4. 5.2×10^3 s

MATH TUTOR PRACTICE

1. **a.** 7.45×10^{-5} g
   b. $5.984\,102 \times 10^6$ nm
2. **a.** -9.11×10^3
   b. 8.25×10^{-2}

Atoms: The Building Blocks of Matter

PRACTICE PROBLEMS A

1. 35 protons, 35 electrons, 45 neutrons
2. ${}^{13}_{6}C$
3. phosphorus-30

PRACTICE PROBLEMS B

1. 126 g Fe
2. 14.7 g K
3. 0.310 g Na
4. 957 g Ni

PRACTICE PROBLEMS C

1. 0.125 mol Ca
2. 1.83×10^{-7} mol Au
3. 8.18×10^{-3}

PRACTICE PROBLEMS D

1. 2.49×10^{-12} mol Pb
2. 4.2×10^{-21} mol Sn
3. 1.66×10^{24} atoms Al

PRACTICE PROBLEMS E

1. 7.3×10^{-7} g Ni
2. 7.51×10^{22} atoms S
3. 66 g Au

MATH TUTOR PRACTICE

1. **a.** 2.25 g
   b. 59 300 L
2. **a.** 7.2×10^1 μg
   b. 3.98×10^3 km

Arrangement of Electrons in Atoms

PRACTICE PROBLEMS A

1. 7, 7, $\underset{1s}{\uparrow\downarrow}$ $\underset{2s}{\uparrow\downarrow}$ $\underbrace{\uparrow\ \uparrow\ \uparrow}_{2p}$
2. 9, 2

PRACTICE PROBLEMS B

1. **a.** $1s^22s^22p^63s^23p^6 3d^{10}4s^24p^64d^{10}5s^25p^5$, $[Kr]4d^{10}5s^25p^5$, 46
   b. 27, 26, 1
2. **a.** $[Kr]4d^{10}5s^25p^2$, 2
   b. 10, germanium

3. a. $1s^22s^22p^63s^23p^63d^54s^2$
   b. manganese
4. a. 9, $1s^22s^22p^63s^23p^6$
   b. argon

PRACTICE PROBLEMS C

1. a. $1s^22s^22p^63s^23p^63d^{10}4s^2$ $4p^64d^{10}5s^25p^66s^2$, [Xe]$6s^2$
   b. Be, Mg, Ca, Sr
2. a. [Xe]$4f^{14}5d^{10}6s^1$
   b. Au, Cs, Pt

MATH TUTOR PRACTICE

1. 85.47 u
2. 28.1 u

The Periodic Law

PRACTICE PROBLEMS A

1. Group 1, fifth period, *s* block
2. a. ns^2
   b. $1s^22s^22p^63s^23p^64s^2$
   c. Ca, [Ar]$4s^2$

PRACTICE PROBLEMS B

1. fourth period, *d* block, Group 10
2. $4d^{10}5s^2$

PRACTICE PROBLEMS C

1. a. $3s^23p^5$
   b. chlorine, nonmetal
2. a. fourth period, *p* block, Group 15
   b. arsenic, metalloid

PRACTICE PROBLEMS D

1. a. *p* block, second period, Group 17, halogens, fluorine, nonmetal, high reactivity
   b. *d* block, fourth period, Group 11, transition elements, copper, metal, low reactivity

PRACTICE PROBLEMS E

1. Li; F
2. All of the elements are in Group 2. Of the four, barium has the highest atomic number and is farthest down the group. Therefore, barium has the largest atomic radius because atomic radii increase down a group.
3. All of the elements are in Period 3. Of the four, silicon has the largest atomic number and therefore is the farthest to the right on the periodic table. Therefore, silicon has the smallest atomic radius because atomic radii decrease from *left to right* across a period.

PRACTICE PROBLEMS F

1. a. Q is in the *p* block, R is in the *s* block, T is in the *p* block, and X is in the *p* block.
   b. Q and R, and X and T are in the same period. Q and T are in the same group.
   c. Q would have the highest ionization energy, and R would have the lowest.
   d. R
   e. R

PRACTICE PROBLEMS G

1. a. All are in the *p* block. E, J, and M are in the same period, and E, G, and L are in the same group.
   b. E should have the highest electron affinity; E, G, and L are most likely to form 1– ions; E should have the highest electronegativity.
   c. The ionic radius would be larger.
   d. E, G, and L

MATH TUTOR PRACTICE

1. a. $1s^22s^22p^63s^23p^1$
   b. $1s^22s^22p^6$
   c. $1s^22s^22p^63s^23p^63d^{10}4s^24p^6$ $4d^{10}5s^25p^2$
   d. $1s^22s^22p^63s^23p^64s^1$
2. a. [Ne]$3s^23p^2$
   b. [Kr]$5s^1$
   c. [Kr]$4d^{10}5s^25p^3$
   d. [Ar]$3d^{10}4s^24p^3$

Chemical Bonding

PRACTICE PROBLEMS A

See table below.

PRACTICE PROBLEMS C

1. $\text{H:}\underset{\ddot{\text{H}}}{\ddot{\text{N}}}\text{:H}$ or $\text{H}-\underset{\underset{\text{H}}{|}}{\ddot{\text{N}}}-\text{H}$
2. $\text{H:}\underset{\cdot\cdot}{\ddot{\text{S}}}\text{:H}$ or $\text{H}-\underset{\cdot\cdot}{\ddot{\text{S}}}-\text{H}$

BONDING BETWEEN CHLORINE AND	ELECTRONEGATIVITY DIFFERENCE	BOND TYPE	MORE-NEGATIVE ATOM
calcium	3.0 – 1.0 = 2.0	ionic	chlorine
oxygen	3.5 – 3.0 = 0.5	polar-covalent	oxygen
bromine	3.0 – 2.8 = 0.2	nonpolar- covalent	chlorine

3. $H:\ddot{\underset{..}{Si}}:H$ or $H-\underset{H}{\overset{H}{Si}}-H$

4. $:\ddot{F}:\ddot{P}:\ddot{F}:$ with $:\ddot{F}:$ below P, or $:\ddot{F}-\ddot{P}-\ddot{F}:$ with $:\ddot{F}:$ below P

PRACTICE PROBLEMS D

1. $\ddot{O}=C=\ddot{O}$
2. $H-C\equiv N:$

PRACTICE PROBLEMS E

1. **a.** linear
   b. tetrahedral
   c. tetrahedral

PRACTICE PROBLEMS F

1. **a.** bent or angular
   b. trigonal-pyramidal

MATH TUTOR PRACTICE

1. **a.** $\cdot\dot{\underset{\cdot}{Si}}\cdot$
   b. $\dot{S}r\cdot$
2. **a.** $H:\underset{..}{\overset{H}{Si}}:$
   b. $H:\overset{:O:}{C}:\ddot{\underset{..}{O}}:H$

Chemical Formulas and Chemical Compounds

PRACTICE PROBLEMS A

1. **a.** KI
   b. $MgCl_2$
   c. Na_2S
   d. Al_2S_3
   e. AlN
2. **a.** silver chloride
   b. zinc oxide
   c. calcium bromide
   d. strontium fluoride
   e. barium oxide
   f. calcium chloride

PRACTICE PROBLEMS B

1. **a.** $CuBr_2$, copper(II) bromide
   b. FeO, iron(II) oxide
   c. $PbCl_2$, lead(II) chloride
   d. HgS, mercury(II) sulfide
   e. SnF_2, tin(II) fluoride
   f. Fe_2O_3, iron(III) oxide
2. **a.** copper(II) oxide
   b. cobalt(III) fluoride
   c. tin(IV) iodide
   d. iron(II) sulfide

PRACTICE PROBLEMS C

1. **a.** NaI   **e.** $CuSO_4$
   b. $CaCl_2$ **f.** Na_2CO_3
   c. K_2S **g.** $Ca(NO_2)_2$
   d. $LiNO_3$ **h.** $KClO_4$
2. **a.** silver oxide
   b. calcium hydroxide
   c. potassium chlorate
   d. ammonium hydroxide
   e. iron(III) chromate
   f. potassium hypochlorite

PRACTICE PROBLEMS D

1. **a.** sulfur trioxide
   b. iodine trichloride
   c. phosphorus pentabromide
2. **a.** CI_4
   b. PCl_3
   c. N_2O_3

PRACTICE PROBLEM E

a. +1, −1   **f.** +1, −1
b. +4, −1   **g.** +5, −2
c. +3, −1   **h.** +1, +5, −2
d. +4, −2   **i.** +5, −2
e. +1, +5, −2   **j.** +2, −1

PRACTICE PROBLEM F

a. 98.09 u
b. 164.10 u
c. 94.97 u
d. 95.21 u

PRACTICE PROBLEMS G

1. **a.** 2 mol Al, 3 mol S
   b. 1 mol Na, 1 mol N, 3 mol O
   c. 1 mol Ba, 2 mol O, 2 mol H
2. **a.** 150.17 g/mol
   b. 85.00 g/mol
   c. 171.35 g/mol

PRACTICE PROBLEMS I

1. **a.** 0.0499 mol
   b. 61 mol
2. **a.** 1.53×10^{23} molecules
   b. 2.20×10^{23} molecules
3. 1170 g

PRACTICE PROBLEMS K

1. **a.** 74.51% Pb, 25.49% Cl
   b. 52.55% Ba, 10.72% N, 36.73% O
2. 43.85% H_2O
3. 96.0 g O; 6.00 mol O

PRACTICE PROBLEMS M

1. FeS
2. $K_2Cr_2O_7$
3. $CaBr_2$

PRACTICE PROBLEMS N

1. C_6H_6
2. H_2O_2

MATH TUTOR PRACTICE

1. 43.38% Na, 11.33% C, 45.29% O
2. 61.13% I

Chemical Equations and Reactions

PRACTICE PROBLEMS B

1. a. calcium + sulfur ⟶ calcium sulfide; $8Ca(s) + S_8(s) \longrightarrow 8CaS(s)$
   b. hydrogen + fluorine ⟶ hydrogen fluoride; $H_2(g) + F_2(g) \longrightarrow 2HF(g)$
   c. aluminum + zinc chloride ⟶ zinc + aluminum chloride; $2Al(s) + 3ZnCl_2(aq) \longrightarrow 3Zn(s) + 2AlCl_3(aq)$
2. a. Liquid carbon disulfide reacts with oxygen gas to produce carbon dioxide gas and sulfur dioxide gas.
   b. Aqueous solutions of sodium chloride and silver nitrate react to produce aqueous sodium nitrate and a precipitate of silver chloride.
3. $N_2H_4(l) + O_2(g) \longrightarrow N_2(g) + 2H_2O(l)$

PRACTICE PROBLEMS C

1. a. Word: magnesium + hydrochloric acid ⟶ magnesium chloride + hydrogen
   Formula: $Mg(s) + HCl(aq) \longrightarrow MgCl_2(aq) + H_2(g)$
   Balanced: $Mg(s) + 2HCl(aq) \longrightarrow MgCl_2(aq) + H_2(g)$
   b. Word: nitric acid + magnesium hydroxide ⟶ magnesium nitrate + water
   Formula: $HNO_3(aq) + Mg(OH)_2(s) \longrightarrow Mg(NO_3)_2(aq) + H_2O(l)$
   Balanced: $2HNO_3(aq) + Mg(OH)_2(s) \longrightarrow Mg(NO_3)_2(aq) + 2H_2O(l)$
2. $Ca(s) + 2H_2O(l) \longrightarrow Ca(OH)_2(aq) + H_2(g)$

PRACTICE PROBLEMS E

1. a. $2Na(s) + Cl_2(g) \longrightarrow 2NaCl(s)$
   b. $Cu(s) + 2AgNO_3(aq) \longrightarrow Cu(NO_3)_2(aq) + 2Ag(s)$
   c. $Fe_2O_3(s) + 3CO(g) \longrightarrow 2Fe(s) + 3CO_2(g)$

PRACTICE PROBLEMS F

1. a. no
   b. no
   c. yes; $Cd(s) + 2HBr(aq) \longrightarrow CdBr_2(aq) + H_2(g)$
   d. yes; $Mg(s) + 2H_2O(g) \longrightarrow Mg(OH)_2(aq) + H_2(g)$
2. Pb
3. Mn

MATH TUTOR PRACTICE

1. $C_3H_8 + 5O_2 \longrightarrow 3CO_2 + 4H_2O$
2. a. $2KI(aq) + Cl_2(g) \longrightarrow 2KCl(aq) + I_2(s)$
   b. $2Al(s) + 3H_2SO_4(aq) \longrightarrow Al_2(SO_4)_3(aq) + 3H_2(g)$

Stoichiometry

PRACTICE PROBLEMS A

1. 4 mol NH_3
2. 10. mol $KClO_3$

PRACTICE PROBLEMS C

1. 80.6 g MgO
2. 300 g $C_6H_{12}O_6$

PRACTICE PROBLEMS D

1. 7.81 mol HgO
2. 7.81 mol Hg

PRACTICE PROBLEMS E

1. a. 60.0 g NH_4NO_3
   b. 27.0 g H_2O
2. 339 g Ag
3. 2.6 kg Al

PRACTICE PROBLEMS F

1. a. H_2O_2
   b. 0.500 mol N_2H_4
   c. 0.250 mol N_2, 1.00 mol H_2O

PRACTICE PROBLEMS G

1. a. Zn
   b. 0.75 mol S_8 remains
   c. 2.00 mol ZnS
2. a. carbon
   b. 2.40 mol H_2 and 2.40 mol CO
   c. 4.85 g H_2 and 67.2 g CO

PRACTICE PROBLEMS H

1. 79.7%
2. 3.70 g Cu

MATH TUTOR PRACTICE

1. 24.48 mol SO_3
2. 30.75 g O_2

States of Matter

PRACTICE PROBLEMS A

1. 169 kJ
2. 2.19×10^5 g

MATH TUTOR PRACTICE

1. 11.65 kJ/mol
2. 74.7 kJ

Gases

PRACTICE PROBLEMS A

1. 177 kPa, 1330 mm Hg
2. 7.37×10^6 Pa

PRACTICE PROBLEMS B

1. 760.0 torr

PRACTICE PROBLEMS C

1. 1000 mL He

PRACTICE PROBLEMS D

1. 941 mL
2. 91°C

PRACTICE PROBLEMS E

1. 1.30 atm
2. 1.29 atm
3. 219°C

PRACTICE PROBLEMS F

1. 26.3 mL
2. 3.94×10^5 Pa; or 394 kPa

PRACTICE PROBLEMS G

1. 159 L N_2
2. 0.629 mol H_2

PRACTICE PROBLEMS H

1. 9.10 L H_2
2. 0.313 L O_2
3. 236 L NO

PRACTICE PROBLEMS I

1. 2.01 atm
2. 3.98 atm

PRACTICE PROBLEMS J

1. CO_2 will effuse about 0.9 times as fast as HCl
2. 160 g/mol
3. about 235 m/s

MATH TUTOR PRACTICE

1. $T_2 = \frac{P_2 T_1}{P_1}$
2. 694 mL

Solutions

PRACTICE PROBLEMS A–C

1. 0.282 M KI
2. 0.0750 mol
3. 0.834 L

PRACTICE PROBLEMS D

1. 22.0 *m* acetone
2. 3.13 g CH_3OH

MATH TUTOR PRACTICE

1. 0.700 M Na_2SO_4
2. 0.4758 M $Cd(NO_3)_2$

Ions in Aqueous Solutions and Colligative Properties

PRACTICE PROBLEMS A

1. **a.** $NH_4Cl(s) \xrightarrow{H_2O} NH_4^+(aq) + Cl^-(aq)$; 1 mol NH_4^+, 1 mol Cl^-, 2 mol ions

   b. $Na_2S(s) \xrightarrow{H_2O} 2Na^+(aq) + S^{2-}(aq)$; 2 mol Na^+, 1 mol S^{2-}, 3 mol ions

   c. $Ba(NO_3)_2(s) \xrightarrow{H_2O} Ba^+(aq) + 2NO_3^-(aq)$; 0.5 mol Ba^{2+}, 1 mol NO_3^-, 1.5 mol ions

PRACTICE PROBLEMS B

1. Yes; $Ba^{2+}(aq) + SO_4^{2-}(aq) \longrightarrow BaSO_4(s)$
2. No
3. Yes; Na^+ and Cl^-; $Ba^{2+}(aq) + SO_4^{2-}(aq) \longrightarrow BaSO_4(s)$
4. $Ni_2(aq) + S^{2-}(aq) \longrightarrow NiS(s)$

PRACTICE PROBLEMS C AND D

1. −0.426°C
2. 0.175 *m*
3. −118.1°C
4. **a.** −9.0°C
   b. 4.8 *m*

PRACTICE PROBLEMS E

1. 0.15°C
2. 102.7°C
3. 2.0 *m*
4. **a.** 0.75°C
   b. 1.5 *m*

PRACTICE PROBLEMS F

1. −7.4°C
2. 2.6°C
3. 0.054 *m* NaCl

MATH TUTOR PRACTICE

1. −4.77°C
2. 106.3°C

Acids and Bases

MATH TUTOR PRACTICE

1. Formula equation:
   $CuSO_4(aq) + Na_2S(aq) \longrightarrow Na_2SO_4(aq) + CuS(s)$
   Full ionic equation:
   $Cu^{2+}(aq) + SO_4^{2-}(aq) + 2Na^+(aq) + S^{2-}(aq) \longrightarrow 2Na^+(aq) + SO_4^{2-}(aq) + CuS(s)$
   Net ionic equation:
   $Cu^{2+}(aq) + S^{2-}(aq) \longrightarrow CuS(s)$
2. Full ionic equation:
   $Cd^{2+}(aq) + 2Cl^-(aq) + 2Na^+(aq) + CO_3^{2-}(aq) \longrightarrow 2Na^+(aq) + 2Cl^-(aq) + CdCO_3(s)$
   Net ionic equation:
   $Cd^{2+}(aq) + CO_3^{2-}(aq) \longrightarrow CdCO_3(s)$

Acid-Base Titration and pH

PRACTICE PROBLEMS A

1. $[H_3O^+] = 1 \times 10^{-4}$ M; $[OH^-] = 1 \times 10^{-10}$ M
2. $[H_3O^+] = 1.0 \times 10^{-3}$ M; $[OH^-] = 1.0 \times 10^{-11}$ M
3. $[H_3O^+] = 3.3 \times 10^{-13}$ M; $[OH^-] = 3.0 \times 10^{-2}$ M
4. $[H_3O^+] = 5.0 \times 10^{-11}$ M; $[OH^-] = 2.0 \times 10^{-4}$ M

PRACTICE PROBLEMS B

1. **a.** pH = 3.0
   b. pH = 5.00
   c. pH = 10.0
   d. pH = 12.00

PRACTICE PROBLEMS C

1. pH = 3.17
2. pH = 1.60
3. pH = 5.60
4. pH = 12.60

PRACTICE PROBLEMS E

1. $[H_3O^+] = 1 \times 10^{-5}$ M
2. $[H_3O^+] = 1 \times 10^{-12}$ M
3. $[H_3O^+] = 3.2 \times 10^{-2}$ M; $[OH^-] = 3.2 \times 10^{-13}$ M
4. $[H_3O^+] = 2.1 \times 10^{-4}$ M

PRACTICE PROBLEMS F

1. 0.157 M CH_3COOH
2. 0.0128 M H_2SO_4

MATH TUTOR PRACTICE

1. pH = 3.07
2. 8.9×10^{-5} M OH^-

Reaction Energy

PRACTICE PROBLEMS A

1. 0.14 J/(g•K)
2. 329 K

PRACTICE PROBLEMS B

1. −890.8 kJ
2. 2 kJ

PRACTICE PROBLEMS C

1. −125.4 kJ
2. +66.4 kJ
3. −296.1 kJ

PRACTICE PROBLEMS D

1. above 333 K

MATH TUTOR PRACTICE

1. $\Delta H^0 = -396.0$ kJ
2. $\Delta H^0 = -441.8$ kJ

Reaction Kinetics

PRACTICE PROBLEMS A

1. **a.** See figure below
   $\Delta E_{forward} = -150$ kJ/mol
   $\Delta E_{reverse} = +150$ kJ/mol
   $E_a = 100$ kJ/mol
   $E_a' = 250$ kJ/mol

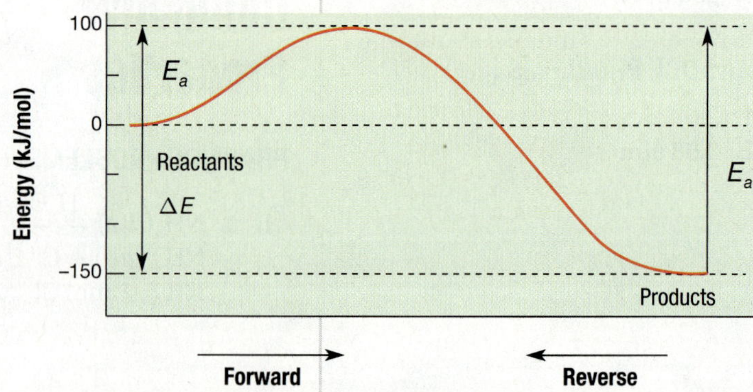

b. exothermic, because the energy of the reactants is greater than the energy of the products.

2. a.

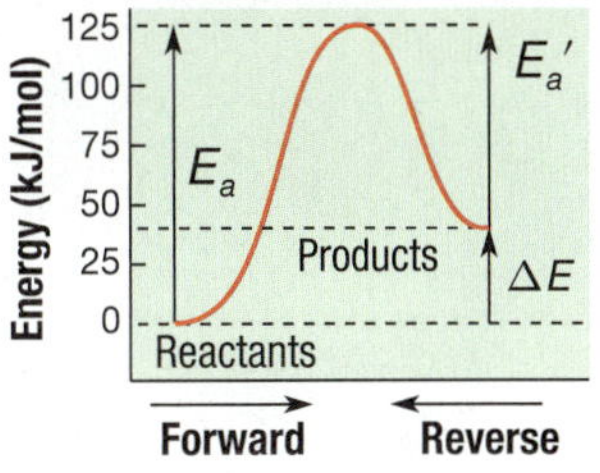

b. $\Delta E_{forward} = 39$ kJ/mol
$\Delta E_{reverse} = -39$ kJ/mol

c. endothermic; The energy of the products is greater than the energy of the products

3. a.

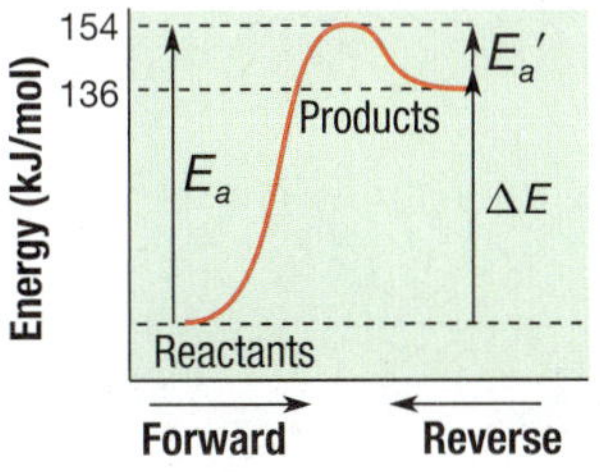

b. E_a (reverse) = 18 kJ/mol

PRACTICE PROBLEMS B

1. rate = $k[A]^2$
2. 27

PRACTICE PROBLEMS E

1. $R = k[L][M]^2$
2. $R = k[NO_2]^2$

MATH TUTOR PRACTICE

1. $R = k[O_2][NO]_2$
2. $R = k[H_2]$; Students should observe that changing the concentration of C_2H_2 has no effect on the rate. The rate depends on only the concentration of hydrogen.

Chemical Equilibrium

PRACTICE PROBLEMS A

1. 0.286
2. 4.9×10^{-3}
3. 4.36

PRACTICE PROBLEMS B

1. 1.9×10^{-4}
2. 1.6×10^{-5}

PRACTICE PROBLEMS C

1. 8.9×10^{-14} mol/L
2. 5.7×10^{-4} mol/L

PRACTICE PROBLEMS D

1. AgBr precipitates.
2. $PbCl_2$ does *not* precipitate.

MATH TUTOR PRACTICE

1. **a.** $K = \dfrac{[AB_2]}{[A][B]^2}$

   b. $K = \dfrac{[D_2][E_2]^2}{[DE_2]^2}$

2. $K = 2.6 \times 10^{-9}$

Oxidation-Reduction Reactions

PRACTICE PROBLEMS A

1. $Cu + 2H_2SO_4 \longrightarrow CuSO_4 + SO_2 + 2H_2O$
2. $8HNO_3 + 6KI \longrightarrow 6KNO_3 + 3I_2 + 2NO + 4H_2O$

MATH TUTOR PRACTICE

1. $2MnO_2 + NaClO_3 + 2NaOH \longrightarrow 2NaMnO_4 + NaCl + H_2O$
2. $N_2O + 2KClO + 2KOH \longrightarrow 2KCl + 2KNO_2 + H_2O$

Electrochemistry

PRACTICE PROBLEMS A

1. **a.** $Cr_2O_7^{2-} + 14H^+ + 3Ni \longrightarrow 2Cr^{3+} + 3Ni^{2+} + 7H_2O$;
   $E^0 = 1.33 - (-0.23) = 1.56$ V

   b. $2Fe^{3+} + H_2 \longrightarrow 2Fe^{2+} + 2H^+$;
   $E^0 = 0.77 - 0.0 = 0.77$ V

MATH TUTOR PRACTICE

1. $E^0 = 1.82$ V
2. $E^0 = 1.20$ V

Nuclear Chemistry

PRACTICE PROBLEMS A

1. ${}^{253}_{99}Es + {}^{4}_{2}He \longrightarrow {}^{1}_{0}n + {}^{256}_{101}Md$
2. ${}^{142}_{61}Pm + {}^{0}_{-1}e \longrightarrow {}^{142}_{60}Nd$

PRACTICE PROBLEMS B

1. 0.25 mg
2. 6396 years
3. 7.648 days
4. 0.009 77 mg
5. 4.46×10^9 years

MATH TUTOR PRACTICE

1. 1.4×10^{-6} g chromium-51
2. 8 half-lives or 420 000 years (expressed with 2 significant figures)

Organic Chemistry

PRACTICE PROBLEMS A

1. methylbutane
2. 3-ethyl-4-methylhexane

PRACTICE PROBLEMS B

1. 2-hexene
2. 2-methyl-2-butene *or* methyl-2-butene
3. 2-methyl-3-hexene
4. 2,5-dimethyl-2,5-heptadiene

MATH TUTOR PRACTICE

1. CH_4N_2O
2. C_3H_5Br
3. CH_2O

Biological Chemistry

MATH TUTOR PRACTICE

1. leucine–histidine–aspartic acid–tyrosine–asparagine–tryptophan
2. leucine–threonine–glycine; The codon UGA is a stop codon, so no more amino acids will be added.

absolute zero the temperature at which all molecular motion stops (0 K on the Kelvin scale or –273.16°C on the Celsius scale)
cero absoluto temperatura a la que se detiene todo movimiento molecular (0 K en la escala de Kelvin o –273.16 °C en la escala de Celsius)

accuracy a description of how close a measurement is to the true value of the quantity measured
exactitud término que describe qué tanto se aproxima una medida al valor verdadero de la cantidad medida

acid-base indicator a substance that changes in color depending on the pH of the solution that the substance is in
indicador ácido-base sustancia que cambia de color dependiendo del pH de la solución en la que se encuentra

acid ionization constant an equilibrium constant for the dissociation of an acid at a specific temperature; denoted by the term K_a
constante de ionización ácida constante de equilibrio en la separación de un ácido a una temperatura específica; se indica con el término K_a

actinide any of the elements of the actinide series, which have atomic numbers from 89 (actinium, Ac) through 103 (lawrencium, Lr)
actínido cualquiera de los elementos del grupo de los actínidos, cuyo número atómico está comprendido entre el 89 (actinio, Ac) y el 103 (lawrencio, Lr)

activated complex a molecule in an unstable state intermediate to the reactants and the products in the chemical reaction
complejo activado molécula que está en un estado inestable, intermedio entre los reactivos y los productos de la reacción química

activation energy the minimum amount of energy required to start a chemical reaction
energía de activación cantidad mínima de energía que se requiere para iniciar una reacción química

activity series a series of elements that have similar properties and that are arranged in descending order of chemical activity; examples of activity series include metals and halogens
serie de actividad serie de elementos que tienen propiedades similares y que están ordenados en orden descendiente respecto a su actividad química; algunos ejemplos de series de actividad incluyen a los metales y los halógenos

actual yield the measured amount of a product of a reaction
rendimiento real cantidad medida del producto de una reacción

addition reaction a reaction in which an atom or molecule is added to an unsaturated molecule
reacción de adición reacción en la que se añade un átomo o una molécula a una molécula insaturada

adenosine diphosphate (ADP) an organic molecule that is involved in energy metabolism; composed of a nitrogenous base, a sugar, and two phosphate groups
adenosín difosfato (ADP) molécula orgánica que participa en el metabolismo de energía; formada por una base nitrogenada, un azúcar y dos grupos fosfato

adenosine triphosphate (ATP) an organic molecule that acts as the main energy source for cell processes; composed of a nitrogenous base, a sugar, and three phosphate groups
adenosín trifosfato (ATP) molécula orgánica que funciona como la fuente principal de energía para los procesos celulares; formada por una base nitrogenada, un azúcar y tres grupos fosfato

alcohol an organic compound that contains one or more hydroxyl groups attached to carbon atoms
alcohol compuesto orgánico que contiene uno o más grupos hidroxilo unidos a los átomos de carbono

aldehyde an organic compound that contains the carbonyl group, —CHO
aldehído compuesto orgánico que contiene el grupo carbonilo —CHO

alkali metal one of the elements of Group 1 of the periodic table (lithium, sodium, potassium, rubidium, cesium, and francium)
metal alcalino uno de los elementos del Grupo 1 de la tabla periódica (litio, sodio, potasio, rubidio, cesio y francio)

alkaline-earth metal one of the elements of Group 2 of the periodic table (beryllium, magnesium, calcium, strontium, barium, and radium)
metal alcalinotérreo uno de los elementos del Grupo 2 de la tabla periódica (berilio, magnesio, calcio, estroncio, bario y radio)

alkane a hydrocarbon characterized by a straight or branched carbon chain that contains only single bonds
alcano hidrocarburo formado por una cadena simple o ramificada de carbonos que únicamente contiene enlaces simples

alkene a hydrocarbon that contains one or more double bonds
alqueno hidrocarburo que contiene uno o más enlaces dobles

alkyl group a group of atoms that forms when one hydrogen atom is removed from an alkane molecule
grupo alquilo grupo de átomos que se forma cuando se elimina un átomo de hidrógeno de la molécula de un alcano

alkyl halide a compound formed from an alkyl group and a halogen (fluorine, chlorine, bromine, or iodine)
halogenuro de alquilo compuesto formado por un grupo alquilo y un halógeno (flúor, cloro, bromo o yodo)

alkyne a hydrocarbon that contains one or more triple bonds
alquino hidrocarburo que contiene uno o más enlaces triples

alpha particle a positively charged atom that is released in the disintegration of radioactive elements and that consists of two protons and two neutrons
partícula alfa átomo con carga positiva que se emite durante la desintegración de elementos radiactivos y que consiste en dos protones y dos neutrones

amine an organic compound that can be considered to be a derivative of ammonia
amina un compuesto orgánico que se puede considerar como un derivado del amoniaco

amine an organic compound that can be considered to be a derivative of ammonia
amina un compuesto orgánico que se puede considerar como un derivado del amoniaco

amino acid any one of 20 different organic molecules that contain a carboxyl and an amino group and that combine to form proteins
aminoácido una de las 20 moléculas orgánicas diferentes que contienen un grupo carboxilo y un grupo amino y que al combinarse forman proteínas

amorphous solid a solid in which the particles are not arranged with periodicity or order
sólido amorfo un sólido en el que las partículas no están dispuestas periódicamente ni en orden

amphoteric describes a substance, such as water, that has the properties of an acid and the properties of a base
anfotérico término que describe una sustancia, como el agua, que tiene propiedades tanto de ácido como de base

anabolism the metabolic synthesis of proteins, fats, and other large biomolecules from smaller molecules; requires energy in the form of ATP
anabolismo la síntesis metabólica de proteínas, grasas y otras biomoléculas grandes a partir de moléculas más pequeñas; requiere de energía en forma de ATP

angular momentum quantum number the quantum number that indicates the shape of an orbital
número cuántico del momento angular el número cuántico que indica la forma de un orbital

anion an ion that has a negative charge
anión un ion que tiene carga negativa

anode the electrode on whose surface oxidation takes place; anions migrate toward the anode, and electrons leave the system from the anode
ánodo el electrodo en cuya superficie ocurre la oxidación; los aniones migran hacia el ánodo y los electrones se alejan del sistema por el ánodo

aromatic hydrocarbon a member of the class of hydrocarbons (of which benzene is the first member) that consists of assemblages of cyclic conjugated carbon atoms and that is characterized by large resonance energies
hidrocarburo aromático un miembro de la clase de hidrocarburos (de la cual el primer miembro es el benceno) que consiste en conjuntos de átomos de carbono cíclicos conjugados y se caracteriza por grandes energías de resonancia

Arrhenius acid a substance that increases the concentration of hydronium ions in aqueous solution
ácido de Arrhenius una sustancia que aumenta la concentración de iones hidrógeno en solución acuosa

Arrhenius base a substance that increases the concentration of hydroxide ions in aqueous solution
base de Arrhenius una sustancia que aumenta la concentración de iones hidroxilo en solución acuosa

artificial transmutation the transformation of atoms of one element into atoms of another element as a result of a nuclear reaction, such as bombardment with neutrons
transmutación artificial la transformación de los átomos de un elemento en los átomos de otro elemento como resultado de una reacción nuclear, tal como el bombardeo con neutrones

atmosphere of pressure the pressure of Earth's atmosphere at sea level; exactly equivalent to 760 mm Hg
atmósfera de presión la presión de la atmósfera de la Tierra al nivel del mar, que equivale exactamente a 760 mm de Hg

atom the smallest unit of an element that maintains the chemical properties of that element
átomo la unidad más pequeña de un elemento que conserva las propiedades químicas de ese elemento

atomic number the number of protons in the nucleus of an atom; the atomic number is the same for all atoms of an element
número atómico el número de protones presentes en el núcleo de un átomo; el número atómico es el mismo para todos los átomos de un elemento

atomic radius one-half of the distance between the center of identical atoms that are not bonded together
radio atómico la mitad de la distancia entre el centro de dos átomos idénticos que no están enlazados

Aufbau principle the principle that states that the structure of each successive element is obtained by adding one proton to the nucleus of the atom and one electron to the lowest-energy orbital that is available
principio de Aufbau el principio que establece que la estructura de cada elemento sucesivo se obtiene añadiendo un protón al núcleo del átomo y un electrón al orbital de menor energía que se encuentre disponible

autotroph an organism that produces its own nutrients from inorganic substances or from the environment instead of consuming other organisms
autótrofo un organismo que produce sus propios nutrientes a partir de sustancias inorgánicas o del ambiente, en lugar de consumir otros organismos

average atomic mass the weighted average of the masses of all naturally occurring isotopes of an element
masa atómica promedio el promedio ponderado de las masas de todos los isótopos de un elemento que se encuentran en la naturaleza

Avogadro's law the law that states that equal volumes of gases at the same temperature and pressure contain equal numbers of molecules
ley de Avogadro la ley que establece que volúmenes iguales de gases a la misma temperatura y presión contienen el mismo número de moléculas

Avogadro's number 6.02×10^{23}, the number of atoms or molecules in 1 mol
número de Avogadro 6.02×10^{23}, el número de átomos o moléculas que hay en 1 mol

barometer an instrument that measures atmospheric pressure
barómetro instrumento que mide la presión atmosférica

benzene the simplest aromatic hydrocarbon
benceno el hidrocarburo aromático más sencillo

beta particle a charged electron emitted during certain types of radioactive decay, such as beta decay
partícula beta electrón con carga que se emite durante ciertos tipos de desintegración radiactiva, tal como la desintegración beta

binary acid an acid that contains only two different elements: hydrogen and one of the more electronegative elements
ácido binario ácido que contiene solo dos elementos: hidrógeno y uno de los elementos más electronegativos

binary compound a compound composed of two different elements
compuesto binario compuesto formado por dos elementos diferentes

boiling the conversion of a liquid to a vapor within the liquid as well as at the surface of the liquid at a specific temperature and pressure; occurs when the vapor pressure of the liquid equals the atmospheric pressure
ebullición conversión de un líquido a vapor, tanto dentro del líquido como en la superficie del líquido a una presión y temperatura determinadas; ocurre cuando la presión de vapor del líquido es igual a la presión atmosférica

boiling point the temperature and pressure at which a liquid and a gas are in equilibrium
punto de ebullición temperatura y presión a las que un líquido y un gas están en equilibrio

boiling-point elevation the difference between the boiling point of a liquid in pure state and the boiling point of the liquid in solution; the increase depends on the amount of solute particles present
elevación del punto de ebullición diferencia entre el punto de ebullición de un líquido en estado puro y el punto de ebullición del líquido en solución; el aumento depende de la cantidad de partículas de soluto presentes

bond energy the energy required to break a chemical bond and form neutral isolated atoms
energía de enlace energía requerida para romper un enlace químico y formar átomos neutros aislados

Boyle's law the law that states that for a fixed amount of gas at a constant temperature, the volume of the gas increases as the pressure of the gas decreases and the volume of the gas decreases as the pressure of the gas increases
ley de Boyle ley que establece que para una cantidad fija de un gas que está a una temperatura constante, el volumen del gas aumenta a medida que la presión del gas disminuye y el volumen del gas disminuye a medida que la presión del gas aumenta

Brønsted-Lowry acid a substance that donates a proton to another substance
ácido de Brønsted-Lowry sustancia que le dona un protón a otra sustancia

Brønsted-Lowry acid-base reaction the transfer of protons from one reactant (the acid) to another (the base)
reacción ácido-base de Brønsted-Lowry transferencia de protones de un reactivo (el ácido) a otro (la base)

Brønsted-Lowry base a substance that accepts a proton
base de Brønsted-Lowry sustancia que acepta un protón

buffered solution a solution that can resist changes in pH when an acid or a base is added to it; a buffer
solución amortiguadora solución que resiste los cambios en el pH cuando se le añade un ácido o una base; búfer o tampón químico

calorimeter a device used to measure the energy as heat absorbed or released in a chemical or physical change
calorímetro aparato que se usa para medir la cantidad de energía en forma de calor absorbido o liberado en un cambio físico o químico

capillary action the attraction of the surface of a liquid to the surface of a solid, which causes the liquid to rise or fall
acción capilar atracción entre la superficie de un líquido y la superficie de un sólido que hace que el líquido se eleve o descienda

carbohydrate any organic compound that is made of carbon, hydrogen, and oxygen and that provides nutrients to the cells of living things
carbohidrato cualquier compuesto orgánico que esté formado por carbono, hidrógeno y oxígeno y que proporcione nutrientes a las células de los seres vivos

carboxylic acid an organic acid that contains the carboxyl functional group
ácido carboxílico ácido orgánico que contiene el grupo funcional carboxilo

catabolism the chemical decomposition of complex biological substances, such as carbohydrates, proteins, and glycogen, accompanied by the release of energy
catabolismo descomposición química de sustancias biológicas complejas, tales como los carbohidratos, las proteínas y el glucógeno, acompañada por la liberación de energía

catalysis the acceleration of a chemical reaction by a catalyst
catálisis aceleración de una reacción química mediante un catalizador

catalyst a substance that changes the rate of a chemical reaction without being consumed or changed significantly
catalizador sustancia que cambia la tasa de una reacción química sin ser consumida ni cambiar significativamente

catenation the binding of an element to itself to form chains or rings
catenación enlace de un elemento consigo mismo para formar cadenas o anillos

cathode the electrode on whose surface reduction takes place
cátodo electrodo en cuya superficie ocurre la reducción

cation an ion that has a positive charge
catión ion que tiene carga positiva

chain reaction a continuous series of nuclear fission reactions
reacción en cadena serie continua de reacciones de fisión nuclear

change of state the change of a substance from one physical state to another
cambio de estado cambio de una sustancia de un estado físico a otro

Charles's law the law that states that for a fixed amount of gas at a constant pressure, the volume of the gas increases as the temperature of the gas increases and the volume of the gas decreases as the temperature of the gas decreases
ley de Charles ley que establece que para una cantidad fija de un gas que está a una presión constante, el volumen del gas aumenta a medida que la temperatura del gas aumenta y el volumen del gas disminuye a medida que la temperatura del gas disminuye

chemical any substance that has a defined composition
sustancia química cualquier sustancia que tiene una composición definida

chemical bond the attractive force that holds atoms or ions together
enlace químico fuerza de atracción que mantiene unidos a los átomos o iones

chemical change a change that occurs when one or more substances change into entirely new substances with different properties
cambio químico cambio que ocurre cuando una o más sustancias se transforman en sustancias totalmente nuevas con propiedades diferentes

chemical equation a representation of a chemical reaction that uses symbols to show the relationship between the reactants and the products
ecuación química representación de una reacción química que usa símbolos para mostrar la relación entre los reactivos y los productos

chemical equilibrium a state of balance in which the rate of a forward reaction equals the rate of the reverse reaction and the concentrations of products and reactants remain unchanged
equilibrio químico estado de equilibrio en el que la tasa de la reacción directa es igual a la tasa de la reacción inversa y las concentraciones de los productos y reactivos no sufren cambios

chemical equilibrium expression the equation for the equilibrium constant, K_{eq}
expresión de equilibrio químico ecuación para la constante de equilibrio, K_{eq}

chemical formula a combination of chemical symbols and numbers to represent a substance
fórmula química combinación de símbolos químicos y números que se usan para representar una sustancia

chemical kinetics the area of chemistry that is the study of reaction rates and reaction mechanisms
cinética química área de la química que se ocupa del estudio de las tasas de reacción y de los mecanismos de reacción

chemical property a property of matter that describes a substance's ability to participate in chemical reactions
propiedad química propiedad de la materia que describe la capacidad de una sustancia de participar en reacciones químicas

chemical reaction the process by which one or more substances change to produce one or more different substances
reacción química proceso por medio del cual una o más sustancias cambian para producir una o más sustancias distintas

chemistry the scientific study of the composition, structure, and properties of matter and the changes that matter undergoes
química estudio científico de la composición, estructura y propiedades de la materia y los cambios por los que pasa la materia

cloning the process of producing a genetically identical copy of an organism
clonación proceso mediante el cual se produce una copia genéticamente idéntica de un organismo

coefficient a small whole number that appears as a factor in front of a formula in a chemical equation
coeficiente número entero pequeño que aparece como un factor frente a una fórmula en una ecuación química

colligative property a property that is determined by the number of particles present in a system but that is independent of the properties of the particles themselves
propiedad coligativa propiedad que se determina por el número de partículas presentes en un sistema, pero que es independiente de las propiedades de las partículas mismas

collision theory the theory that states that, in order for a chemical reaction to occur, collisions between particles must have sufficient energy and correct orientation
teoría de colisión teoría que establece que, para que ocurra una reacción química, las colisiones entre las partículas deben tener suficiente energía y la orientación correcta

colloid a mixture consisting of tiny particles that are intermediate in size between those in solutions and those in suspensions and that are suspended in a liquid, solid, or gas
coloide mezcla formada por partículas diminutas que son de tamaño intermedio entre las partículas de las soluciones y las de las suspensiones y que se encuentran suspendidas en un líquido, un sólido o un gas

combined gas law the relationship between the pressure, volume, and temperature of a fixed amount of gas
ley combinada de los gases relación entre la presión, el volumen y la temperatura de una cantidad fija de gas

combustion reaction the oxidation reaction of an element or compound, in which energy as heat is released
reacción de combustión reacción de oxidación de un elemento o compuesto durante la cual se libera energía en forma de calor

common-ion effect the phenomenon in which the addition of an ion common to two solutes brings about precipitation or reduces ionization
efecto del ion común fenómeno en el que la adición de un ion común a dos solutos produce precipitación o reduce la ionización

composition stoichiometry calculations involving the mass relationships of elements in compounds
estequiometría de composición cálculos que involucran las relaciones entre las masas de los elementos presentes en los compuestos

compound a substance made up of atoms of two or more different elements joined by chemical bonds
compuesto sustancia formada por átomos de dos o más elementos diferentes unidos por enlaces químicos

concentration the amount of a particular substance in a given quantity of a mixture, solution, or ore
concentración cantidad de una cierta sustancia en una cantidad determinada de mezcla, solución o mena

condensation the change of state from a gas to a liquid
condensación cambio de estado de gas a líquido

condensation reaction a chemical reaction in which two or more molecules combine to produce water or another simple molecule
reacción de condensación reacción química en la que dos o más moléculas se combinan para producir agua u otra molécula simple

conjugate acid an acid that forms when a base gains a proton
ácido conjugado ácido que se forma cuando una base gana un protón

conjugate base a base that forms when an acid loses a proton
base conjugada base que se forma cuando un ácido pierde un protón

continuous spectrum an unbroken sequence of frequencies or wavelengths of electromagnetic radiation, often emitted by an incandescent source
espectro continuo secuencia ininterrumpida de frecuencias o longitudes de onda de una radiación electromagnética, por lo general emitidas por una fuente incandescente

control rod a neutron-absorbing rod that helps control a nuclear reaction by limiting the number of free neutrons
barra de control barra que absorbe neutrones y que ayuda a controlar las reacciones nucleares al limitar el número de neutrones libres

conversion factor a ratio that is derived from the equality of two different units and that can be used to convert from one unit to the other
factor de conversión razón que se deriva de la igualdad entre dos unidades diferentes y que se puede usar para convertir una unidad en otra

copolymer a polymer made from two different monomers
copolímero polímero formado por dos monómeros distintos

covalent bond a bond formed when atoms share one or more pairs of electrons
enlace covalente enlace formado cuando los átomos comparten uno o más pares de electrones

critical mass the minimum mass of a fissionable isotope that provides the number of neutrons needed to sustain a chain reaction
masa crítica cantidad mínima de masa de un isótopo fisionable que proporciona el número de neutrones que se requieren para sostener una reacción en cadena

critical point the temperature and pressure at which the gas and liquid states of a substance become identical and form one phase
punto crítico temperatura y presión a la que los estados líquido y gaseoso de una sustancia se vuelven idénticos y forman una fase

critical pressure the lowest pressure at which a substance can exist as a liquid at the critical temperature
presión crítica presión más baja a la que una sustancia puede existir en estado líquido a la temperatura crítica

critical temperature the temperature above which a substance cannot exist in the liquid state
temperatura crítica temperatura por encima de la cual una sustancia no puede existir en estado líquido

crystal a solid whose atoms, ions, or molecules are arranged in a definite pattern
cristal sólido cuyos átomos, iones o moléculas están ordenados en un patrón definido

crystal structure the arrangement of atoms, ions, or molecules in a regular way to form a crystal
estructura cristalina ordenamiento de átomos, iones o moléculas en un patrón regular para formar un cristal

crystalline solid a solid that consists of crystals
sólido cristalino sólido formado por cristales

cycloalkane a saturated carbon chain that forms a loop or a ring
cicloalcano cadena saturada de carbonos que forma un circuito o anillo

D

Dalton's law of partial pressures the law that states that the total pressure of a mixture of gases is equal to the sum of the partial pressures of the component gases
ley de Dalton de las presiones parciales ley que establece que la presión total de una mezcla de gases es igual a la suma de las presiones parciales de los gases que la componen

daughter nuclide a nuclide produced by the radioactive decay of another nuclide
nucleido hijo nucleido producido por la desintegración radiactiva de otro nucleido

decay series a series of radioactive nuclides produced by successive radioactive decay until a stable nuclide is reached
serie de desintegración serie de nucleidos radiactivos producidos por un proceso de desintegración radiactiva sucesiva hasta que se obtiene un nucleido estable

decomposition reaction a reaction in which a single compound breaks down to form two or more simpler substances
reacción de descomposición reacción en la que un solo compuesto se descompone y forma dos o más sustancias más simples

denature to change irreversibly the structure or shape—and thus the solubility and other properties—of a protein by heating, shaking, or treating the protein with acid, alkali, or other species
desnaturalizar cambiar de forma irreversible la estructura o forma (y, por lo tanto, la solubilidad y otras propiedades) de una proteína mediante calentamiento, agitación o haciendo reaccionar a la proteína con ácidos, bases u otros compuestos

density the ratio of the mass of a substance to the volume of the substance; often expressed as grams per cubic centimeter for solids and liquids and as grams per liter for gases
densidad relación entre la masa de una sustancia y su volumen; frecuentemente se expresa en gramos por centímetro cúbico para los sólidos y líquidos, y como gramos por litro para los gases

deposition the change of state from a gas directly to a solid
deposición cambio de estado directo de gas a sólido

derived unit a unit of measure that is a combination of other measurements
unidad derivada unidad de medida que es una combinación de otras medidas

diffusion the movement of particles from regions of higher density to regions of lower density
difusión movimiento de partículas de regiones de mayor densidad a regiones de menor densidad

dimensional analysis a mathematical technique that allows one to use units to solve problems involving measurements
análisis dimensional técnica matemática que permite usar unidades para resolver problemas que incluyen unidades

dipole a molecule or a part of a molecule that contains both positively and negatively charged regions
dipolo molécula o parte de una molécula que contiene regiones con cargas tanto positivas como negativas

diprotic acid an acid that has two ionizable hydrogen atoms in each molecule, such as sulfuric acid
ácido diprótico ácido que tiene dos átomos de hidrógeno ionizables en cada molécula, como el ácido sulfúrico

direct proportion the relationship between two variables whose ratio is a constant value
proporción directa relación entre dos variables cuya razón es un valor constante

disaccharide a sugar formed from two monosaccharides
disacárido azúcar formado a partir de dos monosacáridos

disproportionation the process by which a substance is transformed into two or more dissimilar substances, usually by simultaneous oxidation and reduction
dismutación proceso mediante el cual una sustancia se transforma en dos o más sustancias distintas, usualmente mediante oxidación y reducción simultáneas

dissociation the separating of a molecule into simpler molecules, atoms, radicals, or ions
disociación separación de una molécula en moléculas más simples, átomos, radicales o iones

DNA replication the process of making a copy of DNA
replicación del ADN proceso de hacer una copia del ADN

double-displacement reaction a reaction in which the ions of two compounds exchange places in an aqueous solution to form two new compounds
reacción de doble desplazamiento reacción en la dos iones de dos compuestos intercambian lugares en una solución acuosa y forman dos compuestos nuevos

ductility the ability of a substance to be hammered thin or drawn out into a wire
ductilidad capacidad de una sustancia de formar láminas delgadas o alambres

effervescence a bubbling of a liquid caused by the rapid escape of a gas rather than by boiling
efervescencia burbujeo de un líquido producido por el escape rápido de gas en lugar de por ebullición

effusion the passage of a gas under pressure through a tiny opening
efusión paso de un gas bajo presión a través de una abertura diminuta

elastic collision a collision between ideally elastic bodies in which the final and initial kinetic energies are the same
colisión elástica colisión entre cuerpos elásticos ideales, en la que las energías cinéticas inicial y final son iguales

electrochemistry the branch of chemistry that is the study of the relationship between electric forces and chemical reactions
electroquímica rama de la química que se ocupa del estudio de la relación entre las fuerzas eléctricas y las reacciones químicas

electrode a conductor used to establish electrical contact with a nonmetallic part of a circuit, such as an electrolyte
electrodo conductor que se usa para establecer contacto eléctrico con una parte no metálica de un circuito, tal como un electrolito

electrode potential the difference in potential between an electrode and its solution
potencial del electrodo diferencia de potencial entre un electrodo y su solución

electrolysis the process in which an electric current is used to produce a chemical reaction, such as the decomposition of water
electrólisis proceso por medio del cual se utiliza una corriente eléctrica para producir una reacción química, como por ejemplo, la descomposición del agua

electrolyte a substance that dissolves in water to give a solution that conducts an electric current
electrolito sustancia que se disuelve en agua y crea una solución que conduce la corriente eléctrica

electrolytic cell an electrochemical device in which electrolysis takes place when an electric current is in the device
celda electrolítica aparato electroquímico en el que se da lugar la electrólisis cuando hay una corriente eléctrica en el aparato

electromagnetic radiation the radiation associated with an electric and magnetic field; it varies periodically and travels at the speed of light
radiación electromagnética radiación asociada con un campo eléctrico y magnético; varía periódicamente y se desplaza a la velocidad de la luz

electromagnetic spectrum all of the frequencies or wavelengths of electromagnetic radiation
espectro electromagnético todas las frecuencias o longitudes de onda de la radiación electromagnética

electron affinity the energy change that occurs when an electron is acquired by a neutral atom
afinidad electrónica cambio de energía que ocurre cuando un átomo neutro adquiere un electrón

electron capture the process in which an inner orbital electron is captured by the nucleus of the atom that contains the electron
captura electrónica proceso por medio del cual un electrón del orbital interno es capturado por el núcleo del átomo que contiene el electrón

electron configuration the arrangement of electrons in an atom
configuración electrónica ordenamiento de los electrones en un átomo

electron-dot notation an electron-configuration notation in which only the valence electrons of an atom of a particular element are shown, indicated by dots placed around the element's symbol
notación electrónica de punto notación de la configuración electrónica en la cual solamente se muestran los electrones de valencia de un átomo de un elemento en particular, indicados por puntos ubicados alrededor del símbolo del elemento

electronegativity a measure of the ability of an atom in a chemical compound to attract electrons
electronegatividad medida de la capacidad de un átomo de un compuesto químico de atraer electrones

electroplating the electrolytic process of plating or coating an object with a metal
electrochapado proceso electrolítico de recubrir o aplicar una capa de un metal a un objeto

element a substance that cannot be separated or broken down into simpler substances by chemical means; all atoms of an element have the same atomic number
elemento sustancia que no se puede separar o descomponer en sustancias más simples por medio de métodos químicos; todos los átomos de un elemento tienen el mismo número atómico

elimination reaction a reaction in which a simple molecule, such as water or ammonia, is removed and a new compound is produced
reacción de eliminación reacción en la que se quita una molécula simple, como el agua o el amoniaco, y se produce un nuevo compuesto

emission-line spectrum a series of specific wavelengths of electromagnetic radiation emitted by electrons as they move from higher to lower energy states
espectro de la línea de emisión serie de longitudes de onda específicas de radiación electromagnética emitida por electrones a medida que se desplazan de estados de energía superiores a inferiores

empirical formula a chemical formula that shows the composition of a compound in terms of the relative numbers and kinds of atoms in the simplest ratio
fórmula empírica fórmula química que muestra la composición de un compuesto en función del número relativo y el tipo de átomos que hay en la proporción más simple

end point the point in a titration at which a marked color change takes place
punto final punto en una titulación en el que ocurre un cambio marcado de color

enthalpy change the amount of energy released or absorbed as heat by a system during a process at constant pressure
cambio de entalpía cantidad de energía que un sistema libera o absorbe en forma de calor durante un proceso a presión constante

enthalpy of combustion the energy released as heat by the complete combustion of a specific amount of a substance at constant pressure or constant volume
entalpía de combustión energía que libera en forma de calor la combustión completa de una cantidad determinada de una sustancia, a presión constante o con un volumen constante

enthalpy of reaction the amount of energy released or absorbed as heat during a chemical reaction
entalpia de reacción cantidad de energía que se libera o se absorbe en forma de calor durante una reacción química

enthalpy of solution the amount of energy released or absorbed as heat when a specific amount of solute dissolves in a solvent
entalpía de solución cantidad de energía que se libera o se absorbe en forma de calor cuando una cantidad determinada de soluto se disuelve en un solvente

entropy a measure of the randomness or disorder of a system
entropía medida del grado de aleatoriedad o desorden de un sistema

enzyme a type of protein that acts as a catalyst and speeds up metabolic reactions in plants and animals without being permanently changed or destroyed
enzima tipo de proteína que actúa como catalizador y acelera las reacciones metabólicas en plantas y animales sin cambiar permanentemente ni resultar destruida

equilibrium in chemistry, the state in which a chemical reaction and the reverse chemical reaction occur at the same rate such that the concentrations of reactants and products do not change
equilibrio en química, estado en el que una reacción química y la reacción química inversa ocurren a la misma tasa de modo que las concentraciones de los reactivos y los productos no cambian

equilibrium constant a number that relates the concentrations of starting materials and products of a reversible chemical reaction to one another at a given temperature
constante de equilibrio número que relaciona las concentraciones de los materiales de inicio y los productos de una reacción química reversible a una temperatura dada

equilibrium vapor pressure the vapor pressure of a system at equilibrium
presión de vapor en equilibrio presión de vapor en un sistema cuando éste está en equilibrio

equivalence point the point at which the two solutions used in a titration are present in chemically equivalent amounts
punto de equivalencia punto en el que dos soluciones usadas en una titulación están presentes en cantidades químicas equivalentes

ester an organic compound formed by combining an organic acid with an alcohol such that water is eliminated
éster compuesto orgánico que se forma al combinar un ácido orgánico con un alcohol de modo que se elimine agua

ether an organic compound in which two carbon atoms bond to the same oxygen atom
éter compuesto orgánico en el que dos átomos de carbono se unen al mismo átomo de oxígeno

evaporation the change of a substance from a liquid to a gas
evaporación cambio de estado de una sustancia de líquido a gas

excess reactant the substance that is not used up completely in a reaction
reactivo en exceso sustancia que no se usa por completo en una reacción

excited state a state in which an atom has more energy than it does at its ground state
estado de excitación estado en el que un átomo tiene más energía que en su estado fundamental

extensive property a property that depends on the extent or size of a system
propiedad extensiva propiedad de un sistema que depende de la extensión o tamaño del sistema

F

family a vertical column of the periodic table
familia columna vertical de la tabla periódica

fatty acid an organic acid that is contained in lipids, such as fats or oils
ácido graso ácido orgánico contenido en lípidos como las grasas o los aceites

film badge a device that measures the approximate amount of radiation received in a given period of time by people who work with radiation
lector de película aparato que mide la cantidad aproximada de radiación que las personas que trabajan con radiación reciben en un período de tiempo determinado

fluid a nonsolid state of matter in which the atoms or molecules are free to move past each other, as in a gas or liquid
fluido estado no sólido de la materia en el que los átomos o las moléculas tienen libertad de movimiento, como en el caso de un gas o un líquido

formula equation a representation of the reactants and products of a chemical reaction by their symbols or formulas
ecuación de una fórmula representación de los reactivos y los productos de una reacción química por medio de sus símbolos o fórmulas

formula mass the sum of the average atomic masses of all atoms represented in the formula of any molecule, formula unit, or ion
masa de la fórmula suma de las masas atómicas promedio de todos los átomos representados en la fórmula de una molécula, unidad de la fórmula o ion

formula unit the simplest collection of atoms from which an ionic compound's formula can be written
unidad de la fórmula el conjunto más simple de átomos a partir del cual puede escribirse la fórmula de un compuesto iónico

free energy the energy in a system that is available for work; a system's capacity to do useful work
energía libre energía de un sistema disponible para realizar un trabajo; capacidad de un sistema para realizar un trabajo útil

free-energy change the difference between the change in enthalpy, ΔH, and the product of the Kelvin temperature and the entropy change, which is defined as $T\Delta S$, at a constant pressure and temperature
cambio de energía libre diferencia entre el cambio de entalpía, ΔH, y el producto de la temperatura en Kelvin por el cambio de entropía, que se define como $T\Delta S$, a presión y temperatura constantes

freezing the change of state in which a liquid becomes a solid as energy as heat is removed
congelación cambio de estado en el cual un líquido se convierte en sólido al eliminar energía en forma de calor

freezing point the temperature at which a solid and liquid are in equilibrium at 1 atm pressure; the temperature at which a liquid substance freezes
punto de congelación temperatura a la que un sólido y un líquido están en equilibrio a 1 atm de presión; temperatura a la que una sustancia en estado líquido se congela

freezing-point depression the difference between the freezing points of a pure solvent and a solution, which is directly proportional to the amount of solute present
depresión del punto de congelación diferencia entre los puntos de congelación de un solvente puro y una solución, que es directamente proporcional a la cantidad de soluto presente

frequency the number of cycles or vibrations per unit of time; also the number of waves produced in a given amount of time
frecuencia número de ciclos o vibraciones por unidad de tiempo; también, número de ondas producidas en una cantidad de tiempo determinada

functional group the portion of a molecule that is active in a chemical reaction and that determines the properties of many organic compounds
grupo funcional la porción de una molécula que está involucrada en una reacción química y que determina las propiedades de muchos compuestos orgánicos

G

gamma ray the high-energy photon emitted by a nucleus during fission and radioactive decay
rayo gamma el fotón de alta energía emitido por un núcleo durante la fisión y la desintegración radiactiva

gas a form of matter that does not have a definite volume or shape
gas un estado de la materia que no tiene volumen ni forma definidos

Gay-Lussac's law the law that states that the volume occupied by a gas at a constant pressure is directly proportional to the absolute temperature
ley de Gay-Lussac la ley que establece que el volumen ocupado por un gas a presión constante es directamente proporcional a la temperatura absoluta

Gay-Lussac's law of combining volumes of gases the law that states that the volumes of gases involved in a chemical change can be represented by a ratio of small whole numbers
ley de combinación de los volúmenes de los gases de Gay-Lussac la ley que establece que los volúmenes de los gases que participan en un cambio químico se pueden representar mediante una razón de números enteros pequeños

Geiger-Müller counter an instrument that detects and measures the intensity of radiation by counting the number of electric pulses that pass between the anode and the cathode in a tube filled with gas
contador de Geiger-Müller un instrumento que detecta y mide la intensidad de la radiación contando el número de pulsos eléctricos que pasan entre el ánodo y el cátodo en un tubo lleno de gas

geometric isomer a compound that exists in two or more geometrically different configurations
isómero geométrico un compuesto que existe en dos o más configuraciones geométricamente diferentes

Graham's law of effusion the law that states that the rate of effusion of a gas is inversely proportional to the square root of the gas's density
ley de efusión de Graham la ley que establece que la tasa de efusión de un gas es inversamente proporcional a la raíz cuadrada de su densidad

ground state the lowest energy state of a quantized system
estado fundamental el estado de energía más bajo de un sistema cuantizado

group a vertical column of elements in the periodic table; elements in a group share chemical properties
grupo una columna vertical de elementos de la tabla periódica; los elementos de un grupo comparten propiedades químicas

half-cell a single electrode immersed in a solution of its ions
media celda un solo electrodo sumergido en una solución de sus iones

half-life the time required for half of a sample of a radioactive substance to disintegrate by radioactive decay or by natural processes
vida media el tiempo que se requiere para que la mitad de una muestra de una sustancia radiactiva se descomponga por desintegración radiactiva o por procesos naturales

half-reaction the part of a reaction that involves only oxidation or reduction
media reacción la parte de una reacción que solo involucra oxidación o reducción

halogen one of the elements of Group 17 (fluorine, chlorine, bromine, iodine, and astatine); halogens combine with most metals to form salts
halógeno uno de los elementos del Grupo 17 (flúor, cloro, bromo, yodo y ástato); los halógenos se combinan con la mayoría de los metales para formar sales

heat the energy transferred between objects that are at different temperatures; energy is always transferred from higher-temperature objects to lower-temperature objects until thermal equilibrium is reached
calor la energía que se transfiere entre objetos que están a temperaturas diferentes; la energía siempre se transfiere de los objetos que están a la temperatura más alta a los objetos que están a una temperatura más baja, hasta que se llega a un equilibrio térmico

Heisenberg uncertainty principle the principle that states that determining both the position and velocity of an electron or any other particle simultaneously is impossible
principio de incertidumbre de Heisenberg el principio que establece que es imposible determinar simultáneamente la posición y la velocidad de un electrón o cualquier otra partícula

Henry's law the law that states that at constant temperature, the solubility of a gas in a liquid is directly proportional to the partial pressure of the gas on the surface of the liquid
ley de Henry la ley que establece que a una temperatura constante, la solubilidad de un gas en un líquido es directamente proporcional a la presión parcial del gas en la superficie del líquido

Hess's law the overall enthalpy change in a reaction is equal to the sum of the enthalpy changes for the individual steps in the process
ley de Hess el cambio total de entalpía en una reacción es igual a la suma de los cambios de entalpía ocurridos en los pasos individuales del proceso

heterogeneous composed of dissimilar components
heterogéneo compuesto de componentes que no son iguales

heterogeneous catalyst a catalyst that is in a different phase from the phase of the reactants
catalizador heterogéneo un catalizador que está en una fase distinta de la fase de los reactivos

heterogeneous reaction a reaction in which the reactants are in two different phases
reacción heterogénea una reacción en la que los reactivos están en dos fases diferentes

heterotroph an organism that obtains organic food molecules by other organisms or their byproducts and that cannot synthesize organic compounds from inorganic materials
heterótrofo organismo que obtiene moléculas orgánicas de alimento a través de otros organismos o sus productos secundarios y que no puede sintetizar compuestos orgánicos a partir de materiales inorgánicos

homogeneous describes something that has a uniform structure or composition throughout
homogéneo término que describe algo que tiene una estructura o composición global uniforme

homogeneous catalyst a catalyst that is in the same phase as the reactants are
catalizador homogéneo catalizador que está en la misma fase que los reactivos

homogeneous reaction a reaction in which all of the reactants and products are in the same phase
reacción homogénea reacción en la que todos los reactivos y los productos están en la misma fase

Hund's rule the rule that states that for an atom in the ground state, the number of unpaired electrons is the maximum possible and these unpaired electrons have the same spin
regla de Hund regla que establece que para un átomo en estado fundamental, el número de electrones no apareados es el máximo posible y que estos electrones no apareados tienen el mismo espín

hybrid orbitals orbitals of equal energy produced by the combination of two or more orbitals on the same atom
orbitales híbridos orbitales con la misma energía producidos por la combinación de dos o más orbitales del mimo átomo

hybridization the mixing of two or more atomic orbitals of the same atom to produce new orbitals; hybridization represents the mixing of higher- and lower-energy orbitals to form orbitals of intermediate energy
hibridación mezcla de dos o más orbitales atómicos del mismo átomo para producir orbitales nuevos; esta hibridación representa la mezcla de orbitales de energía superior e inferior para formar orbitales de energía intermedia

hydration the strong affinity of water molecules for particles of dissolved or suspended substances that causes electrolytic dissociation
hidratación fuerte afinidad de las moléculas del agua para con las partículas de sustancias disueltas o suspendidas que causan disociación electrolítica

hydrocarbon an organic compound composed only of carbon and hydrogen
hidrocarburo compuesto orgánico compuesto únicamente por carbono e hidrógeno

hydrogen bond the intermolecular force occurring when a hydrogen atom that is bonded to a highly electronegative atom of one molecule is attracted to two unshared electrons of another molecule
enlace de hidrógeno fuerza intermolecular que se produce cuando un átomo de hidrógeno que está unido a un átomo muy electronegativo de una molécula se ve atraído por dos electrones no compartidos de otra molécula

hydrolysis a chemical reaction between water and another substance to form two or more new substances; a reaction between water and a salt to create an acid or a base
hidrólisis reacción química entre el agua y otras sustancias para formar dos o más sustancias nuevas; reacción entre el agua y una sal para crear un ácido o una base

hydronium ion an ion consisting of a proton combined with a molecule of water; H_3O^+
ion hidronio ion formado por un protón combinado con una molécula de agua; H_3O^+

hypothesis an explanation that is based on prior scientific research or observations and that can be tested
hipótesis explicación que está basada en investigaciones u observaciones científicas previas y que puede ponerse a prueba

ideal gas an imaginary gas whose particles are infinitely small and do not interact with each other
gas ideal gas imaginario con partículas que son infinitamente pequeñas y que no interactúan unas con otras

ideal gas constant the proportionality constant that appears in the equation of state for 1 mol of an ideal gas; $R = 0.082\ 057\ 84\ \text{L} \bullet \text{atm/mol} \bullet \text{K}$
constante de los gases ideales constante de proporcionalidad que aparece en la ecuación de estado para 1 mol de un gas ideal; $R = 0.082\ 057\ 84\ \text{L} \bullet \text{atm/mol} \bullet \text{K}$

ideal gas law the law that states the mathematical relationship of pressure (P), volume (V), temperature (T), the gas constant (R), and the number of moles of a gas (n); $PV = nRT$
ley de los gases ideales ley que establece la relación matemática entre la presión (P), el volumen (V), la temperatura (T), la constante de los gases (R) y el número de moles de un gas (n); $PV = nRT$

immiscible describes two or more liquids that do not mix with each other
inmiscible término que describe dos o más líquidos que no se mezclan uno con otro

intensive property a property that does not depend on the amount of matter present, such as pressure, temperature, or density
propiedad intensiva propiedad que no depende de la cantidad de materia presente, como por ejemplo, la presión, la temperatura o la densidad

intermediate a substance that forms in a middle stage of a chemical reaction and is considered a stepping stone between the parent substance and the final product
intermediario sustancia que se forma en un estado medio de una reacción química y que se considera un paso importante entre la sustancia original y el producto final

inverse proportion the relationship between two variables whose product is constant
proporción inversa relación entre dos variables cuyo producto es constante

ion an atom, radical, or molecule that has gained or lost one or more electrons and has a negative or positive charge
ion átomo, radical o molécula que ha ganado o perdido uno o más electrones y que tiene una carga negativa o positiva

ionic bond a force that attracts electrons from one atom to another, which transforms a neutral atom into an ion
enlace iónico fuerza que atrae electrones de un átomo a otro, lo cual transforma un átomo neutro en un ion

ionic compound a compound composed of ions bound together by electrostatic attraction
compuesto iónico compuesto formado por iones unidos por atracción electrostática

ionization the process of adding or removing electrons from an atom or molecule, which gives the atom or molecule a net charge
ionización proceso de añadir o quitar electrones de un átomo o molécula, lo cual da al átomo o molécula una carga neta

ionization energy the energy required to remove an electron from an atom or ion (abbreviation, IE)
energía de ionización energía que se requiere para quitar un electrón de un átomo o ion (abreviatura: EI)

isomer one of two or more compounds that have the same chemical composition but different structures
isómero uno de dos o más compuestos que tienen la misma composición química pero diferentes estructuras

isotope an atom that has the same number of protons (or the same atomic number) as other atoms of the same element but that has a different number of neutrons (and thus a different atomic mass)
isótopo átomo que tiene el mismo número de protones (o el mismo número atómico) que otros átomos del mismo elemento, pero tiene un número diferente de neutrones (y, por lo tanto, una masa atómica diferente)

joule the unit used to express energy; equivalent to the amount of work done by a force of 1 N acting through a distance of 1 m in the direction of the force (abbreviation, J)
joule unidad que se usa para expresar energía; equivale a la cantidad de trabajo realizado por una fuerza de 1 N que actúa a través de una distancia de 1 m en la dirección de la fuerza (abreviatura: J)

ketone an organic compound in which a carbonyl group is attached to two alkyl groups; obtained by the oxidation of secondary alcohols
cetona compuesto orgánico en el que el grupo carbonilo está unido a dos grupos alquilo; se obtiene por medio de la oxidación de alcoholes secundarios

kinetic-molecular theory a theory that explains that the behavior of physical systems depends on the combined actions of the molecules constituting the system
teoría cinética molecular teoría que explica que el comportamiento de los sistemas físicos depende de las acciones combinadas de las moléculas que constituyen el sistema

lanthanide a member of the rare-earth series of elements, whose atomic numbers range from 58 (cerium) to 71 (lutetium)
lantánido miembro de la serie de elementos de tierras raras, cuyos números atómicos van del 58 (cerio) al 71 (lutecio)

lattice energy the energy released when one mole of an ionic crystalline compound is formed from gaseous ions
energía de la red cristalina energía liberada cuando se forma un mol de un compuesto iónico cristalino a partir de iones gaseosos

law of conservation of mass the law that states that mass cannot be created or destroyed in ordinary chemical and physical changes
ley de la conservación de la masa ley que establece que la masa no se crea ni se destruye por cambios químicos o físicos comunes

law of definite proportions the law that states that a chemical compound always contains the same elements in exactly the same proportions by weight or mass
ley de las proporciones definidas ley que establece que un compuesto químico siempre contiene los mismos elementos en exactamente las mismas proporciones de peso o masa

law of multiple proportions the law that states that when two elements combine to form two or more compounds, the mass of one element that combines with a given mass of the other is in the ratio of small whole numbers
ley de las proporciones múltiples ley que establece que cuando dos elementos se combinan para formar dos o más compuestos, la masa de un elemento que se combina con una cantidad determinada de masa de otro elemento es en la proporción de número enteros pequeños

Lewis acid an atom, ion, or molecule that accepts a pair of electrons
ácido de Lewis átomo, ion o molécula que acepta un par de electrones

Lewis acid-base reaction the formation of one or more covalent bonds between an electron-pair donor and an electron-pair acceptor
reacción ácido-base de Lewis formación de uno o más enlaces covalentes entre un donante de un par de electrones y un receptor de un par de electrones

Lewis base an atom, ion, or molecule that donates a pair of electrons
base de Lewis átomo, ion o molécula que dona un par de electrones

Lewis structure a structural formula in which electrons are represented by dots; dot pairs or dashes between two atomic symbols represent pairs in covalent bonds
estructura de Lewis fórmula estructural en la que los electrones se representan por medio de puntos; pares de puntos o líneas entre dos símbolos atómicos representan pares en los enlaces covalentes

limiting reactant the substance that controls the quantity of product that can form in a chemical reaction
reactivo limitante sustancia que controla la cantidad de producto que se puede formar en una reacción química

lipid a type of biochemical that does not dissolve in water, including fats and steroids; lipids store energy and make up cell membranes
lípido tipo de bioquimico que no se disuelve en agua, como las grasas y los esteroides; los lípidos almacenan energía y forman membranas celulares

liquid the state of matter that has a definite volume but not a definite shape
líquido estado de la materia que tiene un volumen definido, pero no una forma definida

London dispersion force the intermolecular attraction resulting from the uneven distribution of electrons and the creation of temporary dipoles
fuerza de dispersión de London atracción intermolecular que se produce como resultado de la distribución desigual de los electrones y la creación de dipolos temporales

magic numbers the numbers (2, 8, 20, 28, 50, 82, and 126) that represent the number of particles in an extra stable atomic nucleus that has completed shells of protons and neutrons
números mágicos números (2, 8, 20, 28, 50, 82 y 126) que representan el número de partículas que existen en un núcleo atómico extraestable que tiene los orbitales de protones y neutrones completos

magnetic quantum number the quantum number that indicates the orientation of an orbital around the nucleus; symbolized by *m*
número cuántico magnético número cuántico que indica la orientación de un orbital alrededor del núcleo; su símbolo es *m*

main-group element an element in the *s*-block or *p*-block of the periodic table
elemento de grupo principal elemento que está en el bloque *s* o *p* de la tabla periódica

malleability the ability of a substance to be hammered or beaten into a sheet
maleabilidad capacidad de una sustancia de formar láminas al ser martillada o golpeada

mass a measure of the amount of matter in an object
masa medida de la cantidad de materia que tiene un objeto

mass defect the difference between the mass of an atom and the sum of the masses of the atom's protons, neutrons, and electrons
defecto de masa diferencia entre la masa de un átomo y la suma de la masa de los protones, neutrones y electrones del átomo

mass number the sum of the numbers of protons and neutrons that make up the nucleus of an atom
número de masa suma de los números de protones y neutrones que componen el núcleo de un átomo

matter anything that has mass and takes up space
materia cualquier cosa que tiene masa y ocupa un lugar en el espacio

melting the change of state in which a solid becomes a liquid by adding energy as heat or changing pressure
fusión cambio de estado en el que un sólido se convierte en líquido al añadir calor o al cambiar la presión

melting point the temperature and pressure at which a solid becomes a liquid
punto de fusión temperatura y presión a la cual un sólido se convierte en líquido

metabolism the sum of all chemical processes that occur in an organism
metabolismo suma de todos los procesos químicos que ocurren en un organismo

metal an element that is shiny and that conducts heat and electricity well
metal elemento que es brillante y conduce bien el calor y la electricidad

metallic bond a bond formed by the attraction between positively charged metal ions and the electrons around them
enlace metálico enlace formado por la atracción entre iones metálicos con carga positiva y los electrones que los rodean

metalloid an element that has properties of both metals and nonmetals; sometimes referred to as a semiconductor
metaloide elemento que tiene propiedades tanto de metal como de no metal; a veces se denomina semiconductor

millimeters of mercury a unit of pressure
milímetros de mercurio unidad de presión

miscible describes two or more liquids that can dissolve into each other in various proportions
miscible término que describe a dos o más líquidos que son capaces de disolverse uno en el otro en varias proporciones

mixture a combination of two or more substances that are not chemically combined
mezcla combinación de dos o más sustancias que no están combinadas químicamente

model a pattern, plan, representation, or description designed to show the structure or workings of an object, system, or concept
modelo diseño, plan, representación o descripción cuyo objetivo es mostrar la estructura o funcionamiento de un objeto, sistema o concepto

moderator a material that slows the velocity of neutrons so that they may be absorbed by the nuclei
moderador material que disminuye la velocidad de los neutrones de modo que estos puedan ser absorbidos por los núcleos

molal boiling-point constant a quantity calculated to represent the boiling-point elevation of a 1-molal solution of a nonvolatile, nonelectrolyte solution
constante molal del punto de ebullición cantidad que se calcula para representar la elevación en el punto de ebullición de una solución 1 molal de un soluto no-volátil, no-electrolito

molal freezing-point constant a quantity calculated to represent the freezing-point depression of a 1-molal solution of a nonvolatile, nonelectrolyte solute
constante molal del punto de congelación cantidad que se calcula para representar la disminución en el punto de congelación de una solución 1 molal de una solución no volátil, no-electrolito

molality the concentration of a solution expressed in moles of solute per kilogram of solvent
molalidad concentración de una solución expresada en moles de soluto por kilogramo de solvente

molar enthalpy of formation the amount of energy as heat resulting from the formation of 1 mol of a substance at constant pressure
entalpía molar de formación cantidad de energía en forma de calor que resulta debido a la formación de 1 mol de una sustancia a presión constante

molar enthalpy of fusion the amount of energy as heat required to change 1 mol of a substance from solid to liquid at constant temperature and pressure
entalpía molar de fusión cantidad de energía en forma de calor que se requiere para que 1 mol de una sustancia pase de sólido a líquido a una temperatura y presión constantes

molar enthalpy of vaporization the amount of energy as heat required to evaporate 1 mol of a liquid at constant pressure and temperature
entalpía molar de vaporización cantidad de energía en forma de calor que se requiere para que 1 mol de un líquido se evapore a una temperatura y presión constantes

molar mass the mass in grams of 1 mol of a substance
masa molar masa en gramos de 1 mol de una sustancia

molarity a concentration unit of a solution expressed as moles of solute dissolved per liter of solution
molaridad unidad de concentración de una solución, expresada en moles de soluto disuelto por litro de solución

mole the SI base unit used to measure the amount of a substance whose number of particles is the same as the number of atoms of carbon in exactly 12 g of carbon-12
mol unidad fundamental del Sistema Internacional de Unidades que se usa para medir la cantidad de una sustancia cuyo número de partículas es el mismo que el número de átomos de carbono en exactamente 12 g de carbono-12

mole ratio a conversion factor that relates the amounts in moles of any two substances involved in a chemical reaction
razón molar factor de conversión que relaciona las cantidades en moles de dos sustancias cualesquiera que participen en una reacción química

molecular compound a chemical compound whose simplest units are molecules
compuesto molecular compuesto químico cuyas unidades más simples son moléculas

molecular formula a chemical formula that shows the number and kinds of atoms in a molecule, but not the arrangement of the atoms
fórmula molecular fórmula química que muestra el número y los tipos de átomos que hay en una molécula, pero que no muestra cómo están distribuidos los átomos

molecule a neutral group of atoms that are held together by covalent bonds
molécula grupo de átomos neutros que se unen mediante enlaces covalentes

monatomic ion an ion formed from a single atom
ion monoatómico ion que se formó a partir de un solo átomo

monomer a simple molecule that can combine with other like or unlike molecules to make a polymer
monómero molécula simple que se puede combinar con otras moléculas parecidas o diferentes y formar un polímero

monoprotic acid an acid that can donate only one proton to a base
ácido monoprótico ácido que solamente puede donar un protón a una base

monosaccharide a simple sugar that is the basic subunit of a carbohydrate
monosacárido azúcar simple que es la subunidad fundamental de un carbohidrato

multiple bond a bond in which the atoms share more than one pair of electrons, such as a double bond or a triple bond
enlace múltiple enlace en el que los átomos comparten más de un par de electrones, como un doble enlace o un triple enlace

natural gas a mixture of gaseous hydrocarbons located under the surface of Earth, often near petroleum deposits; used as a fuel
gas natural mezcla de hidrocarburos gaseosos que se encuentran debajo de la superficie de la Tierra, normalmente cerca de los depósitos de petróleo; se usa como combustible

net ionic equation an equation that includes only those compounds and ions that undergo a chemical change in a reaction in an aqueous solution
ecuación iónica neta ecuación que incluye solamente aquellos compuestos y iones que experimentan un cambio químico durante una reacción en una solución acuosa

neutralization the reaction of the ions that characterize acids (hydronium ions) and the ions that characterize bases (hydroxide ions) to form water molecules and a salt
neutralización reacción de los iones que caracterizan a los ácidos (iones hidronio) y de los iones que caracterizan a las bases (iones hidróxido) al formar moléculas de agua y una sal

newton the SI unit for force; the force that will increase the speed of a 1 kg mass by 1 m/s each second that the force is applied (abbreviation, N)
newton unidad de fuerza del Sistema Internacional de Unidades; la fuerza que aumentará la rapidez de un 1 kg de masa en 1 m/s cada segundo que se aplique la fuerza (abreviatura: N)

noble gas one of the elements of Group 18 of the periodic table (helium, neon, argon, krypton, xenon, and radon); noble gases are unreactive
gas noble uno de los elementos del Grupo 18 de la tabla periódica (helio, neón, argón, criptón, xenón y radón); los gases nobles son no reactivos

noble-gas configuration an outer main energy level fully occupied, in most cases, by eight electrons
configuración de gas noble nivel de energía principal externo totalmente ocupado, en la mayoría de los casos, por ocho electrones

nomenclature a naming system
nomenclatura sistema para nombrar algo

nonelectrolyte a substance that dissolves in water to give a solution that does not conduct an electric current
no-electrolito sustancia que se disuelve en agua y da una solución que no conduce corriente eléctrica

nonmetal an element that conducts heat and electricity poorly and that does not form positive ions in an electrolytic solution
no metal elemento que es mal conductor del calor y la electricidad y que no forma iones positivos en una solución de electrolitos

nonpolar covalent bond a covalent bond in which the bonding electrons are equally attracted to both bonded atoms
enlace covalente no polar enlace covalente en el que los electrones de enlace tienen la misma atracción por los dos átomos enlazados

nonvolatile substance a substance that has little tendency to become a gas under existing conditions
sustancia no volátil sustancia que tiene poca tendencia a convertirse en un gas bajo las condiciones existentes

nuclear binding energy the energy released when a nucleus is formed from nucleons
energía de enlace nuclear energía que se libera cuando se forma un núcleo a partir de nucleones

nuclear fission the splitting of the nucleus of a large atom into two or more fragments; releases additional neutrons and energy
fisión nuclear división del núcleo de un átomo grande en dos o más fragmentos; libera neutrones y energía adicionales

nuclear forces the interaction that binds protons and neutrons, protons and protons, and neutrons and neutrons together in a nucleus
fuerzas nucleares interacción que mantiene unidos a protones y neutrones, protones y protones, y neutrones y neutrones en un núcleo

nuclear fusion the combination of the nuclei of small atoms to form a larger nucleus; releases energy
fusión nuclear combinación de los núcleos de átomos pequeños para formar un núcleo más grande; libera energía

nuclear power plant a facility that uses heat from nuclear reactors to produce electrical energy
central nuclear instalación que usa el calor de los reactores nucleares para producir energía eléctrica

nuclear radiation the particles that are released from the nucleus during radioactive decay, such as neutrons, electrons, and photons
radiación nuclear partículas que el núcleo libera durante la desintegración radiactiva, tales como neutrones, electrones y fotones

nuclear reaction a reaction that affects the nucleus of an atom
reacción nuclear reacción que afecta al núcleo de un átomo

nuclear reactor a device that uses controlled nuclear reactions to produce energy or nuclides
reactor nuclear aparato que usa reacciones nucleares controladas para producir energía o nucleidos

nuclear shell model a model which represents nucleons as existing in different energy levels, or shells, in the nucleus
modelo de orbital nuclear modelo que representa los nucleones presentes en los diferentes niveles de energía, u orbitales, del núcleo

nuclear waste waste that contains radioisotopes
desechos nucleares desechos que contienen radioisótopos

nucleic acid an organic compound, either RNA or DNA, whose molecules are made up of one or two chains of nucleotides and carry genetic information
ácido nucleico compuesto orgánico, ya sea ARN o ADN, cuyas moléculas están formadas por una o dos cadenas de nucleótidos y que contiene información genética

nucleon a proton or neutron
nucleón protón o neutrón

nuclide an atom that is identified by the number of protons and neutrons in its nucleus
nucleido átomo que se identifica por el número de protones y neutrones que hay en su núcleo

O

orbital a region in an atom where there is a high probability of finding electrons
orbital región de un átomo donde hay una alta probabilidad de encontrar electrones

order in chemistry, a classification of chemical reactions that depends on the number of molecules that appear to enter into the reaction
orden en química, clasificación de reacciones químicas que depende del número de moléculas que parecen entrar en la reacción

organic compound a covalently bonded compound that contains carbon, excluding carbonates and oxides
compuesto orgánico compuesto enlazado de manera covalente que contiene carbono, excluyendo a los carbonatos y óxidos

osmosis the diffusion of water or another solvent from a more dilute solution (of a solute) to a more concentrated solution (of the solute) through a membrane that is permeable to the solvent
ósmosis difusión de agua u otro solvente de una solución más diluida (de un soluto) a una solución más concentrada (del soluto) a través de una membrana que es permeable al solvente

osmotic pressure the external pressure that must be applied to stop osmosis
presión osmótica presión externa que se debe ejercer para detener la ósmosis

oxidation a reaction that removes one or more electrons from a substance such that the substance's valence or oxidation state increases
oxidación reacción en la que se quitan uno o más electrones de una sustancia de tal manera que aumenta la valencia o el estado de oxidación de la sustancia

oxidation number the number of electrons that must be added to or removed from an atom in a combined state to convert the atom into the elemental form
número de oxidación número de electrones que se deben añadir o remover de un átomo en estado de combinación para convertirlo a su forma elemental

oxidation state the condition of an atom expressed by the number of electrons that the atom needs to reach its elemental form
estado de oxidación estado de un átomo expresado por el número de electrones que necesita para llegar a su forma elemental

oxidation-reduction reaction any chemical change in which one species is oxidized (loses electrons) and another species is reduced (gains electrons); also called redox reaction
reacción de óxido-reducción cualquier cambio químico en el que una especie se oxida (pierde electrones) y otra especie se reduce (gana electrones); también se denomina reacción redox

oxidized describes an element that has lost electrons and that has increased its oxidation number
oxidado término que describe a un elemento que ha perdido electrones y que ha aumentado su número de oxidación

oxidizing agent the substance that gains electrons in an oxidation-reduction reaction and that is reduced
agente oxidante sustancia que gana electrones en una reacción de óxido-reducción y que es reducida

oxyacid an acid that is a compound of hydrogen, oxygen, and a third element, usually a nonmetal
oxácido ácido que es un compuesto de hidrógeno, oxígeno y un tercer elemento, usualmente un no metal

oxyanion a polyatomic ion that contains oxygen
oxoanión ion poliatómico que contiene oxígeno

parent nuclide a radionuclide that yields a specific daughter nuclide as a later member of a radioactive series
nucleido padre radionucleido que produce un nucleido hijo específico en forma de un miembro posterior de una serie radiactiva

partial pressure the pressure of each gas in a mixture
presión parcial presión de cada gas en una mezcla

pascal the SI unit of pressure; equal to the force of 1 N exerted over an area of 1 m^2 (abbreviation, Pa)
pascal unidad de presión del Sistema Internacional de Unidades; es igual a la fuerza de 1 N ejercida sobre un área de 1 m^2 (abreviatura: Pa)

Pauli exclusion principle the principle that states that two particles of a certain class cannot be in exactly the same energy state
principio de exclusión de Pauli principio que establece que dos partículas de una cierta clase no pueden estar en exactamente el mismo estado de energía

percentage composition the percentage by mass of each element in a compound
composición porcentual porcentaje en masa de cada elemento que forma un compuesto

percentage error a qualitative comparison of the average experimental value to the correct or accepted value; it is calculated by subtracting the accepted value from the experimental value, dividing the difference by the accepted value, and then multiplying by 100
error porcentual comparación cualitativa del promedio del valor experimental con el valor correcto o aceptado; se calcula restando el valor aceptado del valor experimental, dividiendo la diferencia entre el valor aceptado y luego multiplicando por 100

percentage yield the ratio of the actual yield to the theoretical yield, multiplied by 100
rendimiento porcentual razón del rendimiento real al rendimiento teórico, multiplicado por 100

period in chemistry, a horizontal row of elements in the periodic table
período en química, hilera horizontal de elementos en la tabla periódica

periodic law the law that states that the repeating chemical and physical properties of elements change periodically with the atomic numbers of the elements
ley periódica ley que establece que las propiedades químicas y físicas repetitivas de los elementos cambian periódicamente en función del número atómico de los elementos

periodic table an arrangement of the elements in order of their atomic numbers such that elements with similar properties fall in the same column, or group
tabla periódica arreglo de los elementos ordenados en función de su número atómico de modo que los elementos que tienen propiedades similares se encuentran en la misma columna, o grupo

petroleum a liquid mixture of complex hydrocarbon compounds; used widely as a fuel source
petróleo mezcla líquida de compuestos de hidrocarburos complejos; se usa ampliamente como una fuente de combustible

pH a value that is used to express the acidity or alkalinity (basicity) of a system; each whole number on the scale indicates a tenfold change in acidity; a pH of 7 is neutral, a pH of less than 7 is acidic, and a pH of greater than 7 is basic
pH valor que expresa la acidez o la alcalinidad (basicidad) de un sistema; cada número entero de la escala indica un cambio de 10 veces en la acidez; un pH de 7 es neutro, un pH de menos de 7 es ácido y un pH de más de 7 es básico

pH meter a device used to determine the pH of a solution by measuring the voltage between the two electrodes that are placed in the solution
pH-metro aparato que se usa para determinar el pH de una solución al medir el voltaje entre los dos electrodos que están inmersos en la solución

phase in chemistry, one of the four states or conditions in which a substance can exist: solid, liquid, gas, or plasma; a part of matter that is uniform
fase en química, uno de los cuatro estados o condiciones en los que puede existir una sustancia: sólido, líquido, gas o plasma; parte de la materia que es uniforme

phase diagram a graph of the relationship between the physical state of a substance and the temperature and pressure of the substance
diagrama de fases gráfica de la relación entre el estado físico de una sustancia y la temperatura y presión de la sustancia

photoelectric effect the emission of electrons from a material when light of certain frequencies shines on the surface of the material
efecto fotoeléctrico la emisión de electrones de un material cuando luz de ciertas frecuencias se refleja en la superficie del material

photon a unit or quantum of light; a particle of electromagnetic radiation that has zero rest mass and carries a quantum of energy
fotón una unidad o quantum de luz; una partícula de radiación electromagnética que tiene una masa de reposo de cero y que lleva un quantum de energía

physical change a change of matter from one form to another without a change in chemical properties
cambio físico un cambio de materia de una forma a otra sin que ocurra un cambio en sus propiedades químicas

physical property a characteristic of a substance that does not involve a chemical change, such as density, color, or hardness
propiedad física una característica de una sustancia que no implica un cambio químico, tal como la densidad, el color o la dureza

plasma in physical science, a state of matter that starts as a gas and then becomes ionized; it consists of free-moving ions and electrons, it takes on an electric charge, and its properties differ from those of a solid, liquid, or gas
plasma en ciencias físicas, un estado de la materia que comienza como un gas y luego se ioniza; consiste en iones y electrones que se mueven libremente, tiene una carga eléctrica y sus propiedades son distintas de las propiedades de un sólido, de un líquido o de un gas

pOH the negative of the common logarithm of the hydroxide ion concentration of a solution
pOH el logaritmo común negativo de la concentración de iones hidroxilo de una solución

polar describes a molecule in which the positive and negative charges are separated
polar término que describe una molécula en la que las cargas positivas y negativas están separadas

polar covalent bond a covalent bond in which a pair of electrons shared by two atoms is held more closely by one atom
enlace covalente polar un enlace covalente en el que un par de electrones que es compartido por dos átomos se mantiene más unido a uno de los átomos

polyatomic ion an ion made of two or more atoms
ion poliatómico un ion formado por dos o más átomos

polymer a large molecule that is formed by more than five monomers, or small units
polímero una molécula grande que está formada por más de cinco monómeros, o unidades pequeñas

polyprotic acid an acid that can donate more than one proton per molecule
ácido poliprótico un ácido que puede donar más de un protón por molécula

polysaccharide one of the carbohydrates made up of long chains of simple sugars; polysaccharides include starch, cellulose, and glycogen
polisacárido uno de los carbohidratos formados por cadenas largas de azúcares simples; algunos ejemplos de polisacáridos incluyen al almidón, celulosa y glucógeno

positron a particle that has the same mass and spin as an electron but that has a positive charge
positrón una partícula que tiene la misma masa y el mismo espín que un electrón, pero que tiene carga positiva

precipitate a solid that is produced as a result of a chemical reaction in solution
precipitado un sólido que se produce como resultado de una reacción química en una solución

precision the exactness of a measurement
precisión la exactitud de una medición

pressure the amount of force exerted per unit area of a surface
presión la cantidad de fuerza ejercida en una superficie por unidad de área

primary standard a highly purified solid compound used to check the concentration of a known solution in a titration
patrón primario un compuesto sólido altamente purificado que se utiliza para comprobar la concentración de una solución conocida durante una titulación

principal quantum number the quantum number that indicates the energy and orbital of an electron in an atom
número cuántico principal el número cuántico que indica la energía y el orbital de un electrón en un átomo

product a substance that forms in a chemical reaction
producto una sustancia que se forma en una reacción química

protein an organic compound that is made of one or more chains of amino acids and that is a principal component of all cells
proteína un compuesto orgánico que está hecho de una o más cadenas de aminoácidos y que es el principal componente de todas las células

pure substance a sample of matter, either a single element or a single compound, that has definite chemical and physical properties
sustancia pura una muestra de materia, ya sea un solo elemento o un solo compuesto, que tiene propiedades químicas y físicas definidas

quantity something that has magnitude, size, or amount
cantidad algo que tiene magnitud o tamaño

quantum the basic unit of electromagnetic energy; it characterizes the wave properties of electrons
quantum la unidad fundamental de la energía electromagnética; caracteriza las propiedades de onda de los electrones

quantum number a number that specifies certain properties of electrons
número cuántico un número que especifica ciertas propiedades de los electrones

quantum theory the study of the structure and behavior of the atom and of subatomic particles from the view that all energy comes in tiny, indivisible bundles
teoría cuántica estudio de la estructura y comportamiento del átomo y de las partículas subatómicas desde el punto de vista de que toda la energía existe en paquetes diminutos e indivisibles

radioactive dating the process by which the approximate age of an object is determined based on the amount of certain radioactive nuclides present
datación radiactiva proceso por el cual se determina la edad aproximada de un objeto sobre la base de la cantidad presente de ciertos nucleidos radiactivos

radioactive decay the disintegration of an unstable atomic nucleus into one or more different nuclides, accompanied by the emission of radiation, the nuclear capture or ejection of electrons, or fission
desintegración radiactiva desintegración de un núcleo atómico inestable para formar uno o más nucleidos diferentes, lo cual va acompañado de emisión de radiación, captura o expulsión nuclear de electrones o fisión

radioactive nuclide a nuclide that contains isotopes that decay and that emit radiation
nucleido radiactivo nucleido que contiene isótopos que se desintegran y emiten radiación

radioactive tracer a radioactive material that is added to a substance so that its distribution can be detected later
trazador radiactivo material radiactivo que se añade a una sustancia de modo que su distribución pueda ser detectada posteriormente

rate law an equation that relates reaction rate and concentrations of reactants for a particular reaction
ley de la tasa ecuación que relaciona la tasa de reacción y las concentraciones de reactivos en una reacción en particular

rate-determining step in a multistep chemical reaction, the step that has the lowest velocity, which determines the rate of the overall reaction
paso determinante de la tasa en una reacción química de varios pasos, paso que tiene la velocidad más baja, la cual determina la tasa global de la reacción

reactant a substance or molecule that participates in a chemical reaction
reactivo sustancia o molécula que participa en una reacción química

reaction mechanism the way in which a chemical reaction takes place; expressed in a series of chemical equations
mecanismo de reacción manera en la que ocurre una reacción química; se expresa por medio de una serie de ecuaciones químicas

reaction rate the rate at which a chemical reaction takes place; measured by the rate of formation of the product or the rate of disappearance of the reactants
tasa de reacción tasa a la que ocurre una reacción química; se mide por la tasa de formación del producto o por la tasa de desaparición de los reactivos

reaction stoichiometry calculations involving the mass relationships between reactants and products in a chemical reaction
estequiometría de la reacción cálculos referidos a las relaciones cuantitativas entre los reactivos y los productos durante una reacción química

real gas a gas that does not behave completely like a hypothetical ideal gas because of the interactions between the gas molecules
gas real gas que no se comporta totalmente como un gas ideal hipotético debido a las interacciones entre las moléculas del gas

redox reaction [see *oxidation-reduction reaction*]
reacción redox [ver *reacción de óxido-reducción*]

reduced describes a substance that has gained electrons, lost an oxygen atom, or gained a hydrogen atom
reducido término que describe a una sustancia que ha ganado electrones, perdido un átomo de oxígeno o ganado un átomo de hidrógeno

reducing agent a substance that has the potential to reduce another substance
agente reductor sustancia que tiene el potencial de reducir otra sustancia

reduction a chemical change in which electrons are gained, either by the removal of oxygen, the addition of hydrogen, or the addition of electrons
reducción cambio químico en el que se ganan electrones, ya sea por la remoción de oxígeno, la adición de hidrógeno o la adición de electrones

reduction potential the decrease in voltage that takes place when a positive ion becomes less positive or neutral or when a neutral atom becomes a negative ion
potencial de reducción disminución de voltaje que tiene lugar cuando un ion positivo se vuelve menos positivo o neutro o cuando un átomo neutro se convierte en un ion negativo

rem the quantity of ionizing radiation that does as much damage to human tissue as 1 roentgen of high-voltage X rays does
rem cantidad de radiación ionizante que produce el mismo daño a los tejidos humanos que 1 roentgen de rayos X de alto voltaje

resonance the bonding in molecules or ions that cannot be correctly represented by a single Lewis structure
resonancia enlace de moléculas o iones que no se puede representar correctamente mediante una única estructura de Lewis

reversible reaction a chemical reaction in which the products re-form the original reactants
reacción inversa reacción química en la que los productos vuelven a formar los reactivos originales

roentgen a unit of radiation dose of X-rays or gamma rays that is equal to the amount of radiation that will produce 2.58×10^{-4} of ions per kilogram of air at atmospheric pressure
roentgen unidad de dosis de radiación de rayos X o de rayos gamma que es igual a la cantidad de radiación que producirán 2.58×10^{-4} iones por kilogramo de aire a presión atmosférica

salt an ionic compound that forms when a metal atom or a positive radical replaces the hydrogen of an acid
sal un compuesto iónico que se forma cuando el átomo de un metal o un radical positivo reemplaza el hidrógeno de un ácido

saponification a chemical reaction in which esters of fatty acids react with a strong base to produce glycerol and a fatty acid salt; the process that is used to make soap
saponificación una reacción química en la cual los ésteres de ácidos grasos reaccionan con una base fuerte para producir glicerol y una sal del ácido graso; el proceso que se utiliza para fabricar jabón

saturated hydrocarbon an organic compound formed only by carbon and hydrogen linked by single bonds
hidrocarburo saturado un compuesto orgánico formado solamente por carbono e hidrógeno unidos por enlaces simples

saturated solution a solution that cannot dissolve any more solute under the given conditions
solución saturada una solución que no puede disolver más soluto bajo las condiciones dadas

scientific method a series of steps followed to solve problems, including collecting data, formulating a hypothesis, testing the hypothesis, and stating conclusions
método científico una serie de pasos que se siguen para resolver problemas y que incluyen reunir datos, formular una hipótesis, poner a prueba la hipótesis y plantear conclusiones

scientific notation a method of expressing a quantity as a number multiplied by 10 to the appropriate power
notación científica un método para expresar una cantidad en forma de un número multiplicado por 10 a la potencia adecuada

scintillation counter an instrument that converts scintillating light into an electrical signal for detecting and measuring radiation
contador de centelleo un instrumento que convierte la luz de centelleo en una señal eléctrica para detectar y medir la radiación

self-ionization of water a process in which two water molecules produce a hydronium ion and a hydroxide ion by transfer of a proton
auto-ionización del agua un proceso por el cual dos moléculas de agua producen un ion hidronio y un ion hidroxilo al transferir un protón

semipermeable membrane a membrane that permits the passage of only certain molecules
membrana semipermeable una membrana que únicamente permite el paso de ciertas moléculas

shielding a radiation-absorbing material that is used to decrease radiation leakage from nuclear reactors
pantalla un material que absorbe la radiación, usado para disminuir las fugas de radiación de los reactores nucleares

SI Le Système International d'Unités, or the International System of Units, which is the measurement system that is accepted worldwide
SI Le Système International d'Unités, o el Sistema Internacional de Unidades, que es el sistema de medición que se acepta en todo el mundo

significant figure a prescribed decimal place that determines the amount of rounding off to be done based on the precision of the measurement
cifra significativa un lugar decimal prescrito que determina la cantidad de redondeo que se hará con base en la precisión de la medición

single bond a covalent bond in which two atoms share one pair of electrons
enlace simple un enlace covalente en el que dos átomos comparten un par de electrones

single-displacement reaction a reaction in which one element or radical takes the place of another element or radical in a compound
reacción de sustitución simple una reacción en la que un elemento o radical toma el lugar de otro elemento o radical en un compuesto

solid the state of matter in which the volume and shape of a substance are fixed
sólido el estado de la materia en el cual el volumen y la forma de una sustancia están fijos

solubility the ability of one substance to dissolve in another at a given temperature and pressure; expressed in terms of the amount of solute that will dissolve in a given amount of solvent to produce a saturated solution
solubilidad la capacidad de una sustancia de disolverse en otra a una temperatura y presión dadas; se expresa en términos de la cantidad de soluto que se disolverá en una cantidad determinada de solvente para producir una solución saturada

solubility product constant the equilibrium constant for a solid that is in equilibrium with the solid's dissolved ions
constante del producto de solubilidad la constante de equilibrio de un sólido que está en equilibrio con los iones disueltos del sólido

soluble capable of dissolving in a particular solvent
soluble capaz de disolverse en un solvente determinado

solute in a solution, the substance that dissolves in the solvent
soluto en una solución, la sustancia que se disuelve en el solvente

solution a homogeneous mixture of two or more substances uniformly dispersed throughout a single phase
solución una mezcla homogénea de dos o más sustancias que se dispersan de manera uniforme en una sola fase

solution equilibrium the physical state in which the opposing processes of dissolution and crystallization of a solute occur at equal rates
equilibrio de la solución la condición física en la cual los procesos opuestos de disolución y cristalización de un soluto ocurren a la misma tasa

solvated describes a solute molecule that is surrounded by solvent molecules
solvatado término que describe a una molécula de soluto que está rodeada por moléculas de solvente

solvent in a solution, the substance in which the solute dissolves
solvente en una solución, la sustancia en la que se disuelve el soluto

specific heat the quantity of heat required to raise a unit mass of homogeneous material 1 K or 1°C in a specified way given constant pressure and volume
calor específico la cantidad de calor que se requiere para aumentar una unidad de masa de un material homogéneo 1 K ó 1 °C de una manera especificada, dados un volumen y una presión constantes

spectator ions ions that are present in a solution in which a reaction is taking place but that do not participate in the reaction
iones espectadores iones que están presentes en una solución en la que está ocurriendo una reacción, pero que no participan en la reacción

spin quantum number the quantum number that describes the intrinsic angular momentum of a particle
número cuántico de espín el número cuántico que describe el ímpetu angular intrínseco de una partícula

standard electrode potential the potential developed by a metal or other material immersed in an electrolyte solution relative to the potential of the hydrogen electrode, which is set at zero
potencial estándar del electrodo el potencial que desarrolla un metal u otro material que se encuentre sumergido en una solución de electrolitos respecto al potencial del electrodo de hidrógeno, al cual se le da un valor de cero

standard solution a solution of known concentration, expressed in terms of the amount of solute in a given amount of solvent or solution
solución estándar una solución de concentración conocida, expresada en términos de la cantidad de soluto que se encuentra en una cantidad determinada de solvente o solución

standard temperature and pressure for a gas, the temperature of 0°C and the pressure 1.00 atm
temperatura y presión estándar para un gas, la temperatura de 0 °C y la presión de 1.00 atm

strong acid an acid that ionizes completely in a solvent
ácido fuerte un ácido que se ioniza completamente en un solvente

strong electrolyte a compound that completely or largely dissociates in an aqueous solution, such as soluble mineral salts
electrolito fuerte un compuesto que se disocia completamente o en gran medida en una solución acuosa, como las sales minerales solubles

structural formula a formula that indicates the location of the atoms, groups, or ions relative to one another in a molecule and that indicates the number and location of chemical bonds
fórmula estructural una fórmula que indica la ubicación de los átomos, grupos o iones, unos respecto a otros en una molécula, y que indica el número y la ubicación de los enlaces químicos

structural isomers two or more compounds that have the same number and kinds of atoms and the same molecular weight but that differ in the order in which the atoms are attached to one another
isómeros estructurales dos o más compuestos que tienen el mismo número y tipos de átomos y el mismo peso molecular, pero que se diferencian en el orden en el que los átomos están unidos unos a otros

sublimation the process in which a solid changes directly into a gas (the term is sometimes also used for the reverse process)
sublimación el proceso por medio del cual un sólido se transforma directamente en un gas (en ocasiones, este término también se usa para describir el proceso inverso)

substitution reaction a reaction in which one or more atoms replace another atom or group of atoms in a molecule
reacción de sustitución una reacción en la cual uno o más átomos reemplazan otro átomo o grupo de átomos en una molécula

supercooled liquid a liquid that is cooled below its normal freezing point without solidifying
líquido superenfriado un líquido que se enfría por debajo de su punto normal de congelación sin que se solidifique

supersaturated solution a solution that holds more dissolved solute than is required to reach equilibrium at a given temperature
solución sobresaturada una solución que contiene más soluto disuelto que el que se requiere para llegar al equilibro a una temperatura dada

surface tension the force that acts on the surface of a liquid and that tends to minimize the area of the surface
tensión superficial la fuerza que actúa en la superficie de un líquido y que tiende a minimizar el área de la superficie

suspension a mixture in which particles of a material are more or less evenly dispersed throughout a liquid or gas
suspensión una mezcla en la que las partículas de un material se encuentran dispersas de manera más o menos uniforme a través de un líquido o de un gas

synthesis reaction a reaction in which two or more substances combine to form a new compound
reacción de síntesis una reacción en la que dos o más sustancias se combinan para formar un compuesto nuevo

system a set of particles or interacting components considered to be a distinct physical entity for the purpose of study
sistema un conjunto de partículas o componentes que interactúan unos con otros, el cual se considera una entidad física independiente para fines de estudio

temperature a measure of how hot (or cold) something is; specifically, a measure of the average kinetic energy of the particles in an object
temperatura una medida de qué tan caliente (o frío) está algo; específicamente, una medida de la energía cinética promedio de las partículas de un objeto

theoretical yield the maximum amount of product that can be produced from a given amount of reactant
rendimiento teórico la cantidad máxima de producto que se puede producir con una cantidad dada de reactivo

theory an explanation for some phenomenon that is based on observation, experimentation, and reasoning
teoría una explicación de algunos fenómenos que está basada en la observación, la experimentación y el razonamiento

thermochemical equation an equation that includes the quantity of energy as heat released or absorbed during the reaction as written
ecuación termoquímica una ecuación que incluye la cantidad de energía en forma de calor que se libera o absorbe durante la reacción como se expresa

thermochemistry the branch of chemistry that is the study of the energy changes that accompany chemical reactions and changes of state
termoquímica la rama de la química que se ocupa del estudio de los cambios de energía que acompañan las reacciones químicas y los cambios de estado

titration a method to determine the concentration of a substance in solution by adding a solution of known volume and concentration until the reaction is completed, which is usually indicated by a change in color
titulación un método para determinar la concentración de una sustancia en una solución al añadir una solución de volumen y concentración conocidos hasta que se completa la reacción, lo cual normalmente es indicado por un cambio de color

transition element one of the metals that can use the inner shell before using the outer shell to bond
elemento de transición uno de los metales que tienen la capacidad de usar su orbital interno antes de usar su orbital externo para formar un enlace

transition interval the range in concentration over which a variation in a chemical indicator can be observed
intervalo de transición el rango de concentración en el cual se puede observar una variación en un indicador químico

transmutation the transformation of atoms of one element into atoms of a different element as a result of a nuclear reaction
transmutación la transformación de los átomos de un elemento en átomos de un elemento diferente como resultado de una reacción nuclear

transuranium element a synthetic element whose atomic number is greater than that of uranium (atomic number 92)
elemento transuranio un elemento sintético cuyo número atómico es mayor que el del uranio (número atómico 92)

triple point the temperature and pressure conditions at which the solid, liquid, and gaseous phases of a substance coexist at equilibrium
punto triple las condiciones de temperatura y presión en las que las fases sólida, líquida y gaseosa de una sustancia coexisten en equilibrio

triprotic acid an acid that has three ionizable protons per molecule, such as phosphoric acid
ácido triprótico un ácido que tiene tres protones ionizables por molécula, como por ejemplo, el ácido fosfórico

unified atomic mass unit a unit of mass that describes the mass of an atom or molecule; it is exactly 1/12 of the mass of a carbon atom with mass number 12 (abbreviation, u)
unidad de masa atómica unificada una unidad de masa que describe la masa de un átomo o molécula; es exactamente 1/12 de la masa de un átomo de carbono con un número de masa de 12 (abreviatura: u)

unit cell the smallest portion of a crystal lattice that shows the three-dimensional pattern of the entire lattice
celda unitaria la porción más pequeña de una red cristalina, la que muestra el patrón tridimensional de la red completa

unsaturated hydrocarbon a hydrocarbon that has available valence bonds, usually from double or triple bonds with carbon
hidrocarburo no saturado un hidrocarburo que tiene enlaces de valencia disponibles, normalmente de enlaces dobles o triples con carbono

unsaturated solution a solution that contains less solute than a saturated solution does and that is able to dissolve additional solute
solución no saturada una solución que contiene menos soluto que una solución saturada, y que tiene la capacidad de disolver más soluto

valence electron an electron that is found in the outermost shell of an atom and that determines the atom's chemical properties
electrón de valencia un electrón que se encuentra en el orbital más externo de un átomo y que determina las propiedades químicas del átomo

vaporization the process by which a liquid or solid changes to a gas
vaporización el proceso por el cual un líquido o un sólido se transforma en un gas

volatile liquid a liquid that evaporates readily or at a low temperature
líquido volátil un líquido que se evapora rápidamente o a una baja temperatura

voltaic cell a primary cell that consists of two electrodes made of different metals immersed in an electrolyte; used to generate voltage
pila voltaica una celda primaria formada por dos electrodos hechos de diferentes metales sumergidos en un electrolito; se usa para generar voltaje

volume a measure of the size of a body or region in three-dimensional space
volumen una medida del tamaño de un cuerpo o región en un espacio de tres dimensiones

VSEPR theory a theory that predicts some molecular shapes based on the idea that pairs of valence electrons surrounding an atom repel each other
teoría VSEPR una teoría que predice algunas formas moleculares con base en la idea de que los pares de electrones de valencia que rodean un átomo se repelen unos a otros

wavelength the distance from any point on a wave to an identical point on the next wave
longitud de onda la distancia entre cualquier punto de una onda y un punto idéntico ubicado en la onda siguiente

weak acid an acid that releases few hydrogen ions in aqueous solution
ácido débil un ácido que libera pocos iones de hidrógeno en una solución acuosa

weak electrolyte a compound that dissociates only to a small extent in aqueous solution
electrolito débil un compuesto que se disocia solamente en una pequeña medida en solución acuosa

weight a measure of the gravitational force exerted on an object; its value can change with the location of the object in the universe
peso una medida de la fuerza gravitacional ejercida sobre un objeto; su valor puede cambiar en función de la ubicación del objeto en el universo

word equation an equation in which the reactants and products in a chemical reaction are represented by words
ecuación verbal una ecuación en la cual los reactivos y los productos de una reacción química están representados con palabras

INDEX

Page references followed by *f* refer to figures. Page references followed by *t* refer to tables.

absolute zero, 351
absorption, 96, 96*f*
accuracy, 42–44, 43*f*
acetic acid
as buffer, 572–573, 572*t*
common-ion effect in, 569–570, 570*f*
hydrolysis of ions in, 576*f*, 577
ionization constant, 571–573, 572*t*
properties, 445
strength of, 448–449, 448*t*, 449*f*, 458
acetone, 698
acetylene, 685
acid-base indicators
colors of, 472*f*, 484*f*, 485*t*
equivalence point, 488–489, 488*f*, 489*f*
function of, 483–484, 483*f*
pH paper, 442, 442*f*, 445*f*, 484, 487*f*
in titrations, 487–493, 487*f*, 488*f*, 489*f*, 490*f*–491*f*
acid ionization constants, 571–572, 572*t*
acidosis, R33
acid rain, 265, 463, 463*f*, 482
acids, 440–463. *See also* **pH**
amphoteric compounds, 460-461, 460*f*
Arrhenius, 447–448, 447*f*, 448*t*, 456*t*
Brønsted-Lowry, 452–455, 453*f*, 456*t*
conjugate, 457–459, 459*t*, 574–575
decomposition of, 266
displacement reactions in, 267
household, 446
hydrolysis of salts, 574–578, 574*f*, 576*f*, 577*f*
hydronium and hydroxide ions in, 473–474
industrial, 444–445
ionization constants, 571–572, 572*t*
Lewis, 455–456, 456*t*
monoprotic and polyprotic, 453–455, 454*f*
neutralization reactions, 442, 446, 461–463, 462*f*, 489–493
nomenclature, 218–219, 218*t*, 442–443, 442*t*, 443*t*
organic, 448–449
properties, 442
strength of, 448–449, 448*t*, 458–459, 459*t*, 473*t*, 481
actinides, 128, 140, 149*t*
activated complexes, 533–535, 533*f*
activation energy, 532- 535, 532*f*, 533*f*, 720, 720*f*
active sites, 719
activity series, 271–273, 272*t*
actual yield, 301-302
addition polymers, 696-697, 696*f*
addition reactions, 693–694
adenine, 726, 726*f*, R40*f*
adenosine diphosphate (ADP), 723, 723*f*
adenosine triphosphate (ATP), 722–725, 723*f*, 725*t*, R40*f*
AIDS/HIV infection, 718
air bags, 360
air pollution, R52
alcohols, 689, 689*f*, 689*t*
aldehydes, 689*t*, 691, 691*f*
alkali metals, 134, 134*f*, R2–R7, R2*f*, R4*t*
alkaline batteries, 621, 621*f*
alkaline-earth metals, 134, 134*f*, R8–R13, R8*f*, R10*t*
alkanes, 674–681, 675*t*, 676*t*, 677*t*, 680*t*, 681*t*
alkenes, 682–685, 682*t*, 685*f*
alkyl groups, 677–680, 677*t*
alkyl halides, 689*t*, 690, 693
alkynes, 685–686, 686*f*
allotropes, 683
alloys, 380–381, 380*t*, 381*f*, R18–R20, R19*t*, R20*f*, R27, R27*t*
alpha particles, 70, 70*f*, 71*f*, 645*t*, 646, 646*f*, 650*f*, 653, 653*f*
aluminum
alloys, R27, R27*t*
electron configuration, 112*t*
industrial production of, 633
oxides, R51, R51*t*
properties, 18*f*, R24–R25, R24*f*, R25*f*, R26*t*
in water purification, 259–260
amalgams, 380*t*, R18*f*
amines, 689*t*, 691
amino acids
chemical structures of, 712, 712*f*, R35, R35*f*
in the genetic code, 732
in peptides and proteins, 713–714, 714*f*
synthesis of, 729-730
ammonia
in amines, 691
as base, 449, 449*t*, 456
oxidation of, 293
polarity of, 195, 195*f*
production of, 563, 564–566
structure of, 189, 189*f*, 192
ammonium ions, 184, 184*f*, 576–578, 577*f*
amorphous solids, 320, 323
amphoteric compounds, 460–461
amphoteric oxides, R51
anabolism, 725
angular momentum quantum number, 102, 102*t*
anhydrides, R50
anions
hydrolysis of, 574–575, 574*f*
ionic radii, 151–152, 151*t*
nomenclature, 208–209, 209*f*, 209*t*
oxyanions, 213–214, 214*t*
anodes, 68*f*, 618, 618*f*
antibodies, 713, 716*t*
aqueous solutions, 410–432
attraction between dissociated ions, 432
boiling-point elevation, 426–427
calculating hydronium and hydroxide ion concentration of, 473–474
dissociation in, 411–415, 411*f*, 414*f*
electrolysis, 420–421, 420*f*
freezing-point depression, 424–426, 424*t*, 430–432, 431*t*
ionization, 417, 417*f*
net ionic equations, 415–416
osmotic pressure, 428–429, 428*f*
precipitation reactions, 413–416, 413*t*, 414*f*
standard solutions, 489
strong and weak electrolytes, 418–419, 418*f*
vapor-pressure lowering, 422–423, 422*f*, 423*f*
area, units of, R58*t*
argon, 108–109, 111, 112*t*
Aristotle, 41, 63
aromatic hydrocarbons, 687
Arrhenius, Svante 447
Arrhenius acids and bases, 447–450, 447*f*, 448*t*, 449*t*, 450*f*, 456*t*
arsenic, 113*t*, 131, 217, R44–R45, R45*t*
artificial transmutations, 651–652, 651*f*, 652*f*, 652*t*
asbestos, R41
atmospheres (units), 344–345, 344*t*
atmospheric pressure, 342–343, 342*f*, 343*f*, 345
atomic masses, 77–78, 78*t*, 117, 125, R60*t*–R61*t*
atomic mass unit, unified (u), 72*t*, 76, R59*t*
atomic number, 73, R60*t*–R61*t*
atomic radii, 142–144, 143*f*, 144*f*, 155
atoms, 62–83
in ancient science, 41, 63
atomic number, 73, R60*t*–R61*t*
atomic theory, 63–65, 65*f*
average atomic masses, 77–78, 78*t*
Bohr model, 96–97, 96*f*, 97*f*
definition, 6, 6*f*, 68
isotopes, 73–76, 74*f*, 74*t*, 75*t*
mass numbers, 74, 74*t*
orbitals, 100–104, 101*f*, 102*t*, 103*f*, 104*t*
plum pudding model, 69
quantum model, 98–104, 101*f*, 102*t*, 103*f*, 104*t*
relative atomic masses, 76–77
sizes of, 72
structure of, 68–72, 71*f*, 72*t*, 104*t*
subatomic particles, 642
ATP (adenosine triphosphate), 722–725, 723*f*, 724*f*, 725*t*, R40*f*
Aufbau principle, 105, 110, 110*f*
automobiles, 360, 547, 628, 631, 631*f*, 689, R27, R27*f*
average atomic masses, 77–78, 78*t*, 117
Avogadro's law, 359–360, 359*f*, 360*f*
Avogadro's number, 79, 82, R59*t*

balancing equations
formula equations, 250–251, 253
by inspection, 256–260, 275
redox equations, 601–605, 610
using models, 270
ball-and-stick models, 187–188, 187*f*, 188f, 671*f*
Balmer spectral series, 97, 97*f*
band of stability, 642–643, 643*f*
barium, 115, 584–586, R8–R9, R9*f*, R10*t*
barometers, 343, 343*f*, 356
base dissociation constants, 576
base-pairing, 727–728, 727*f*, R40

bases, 445–453, 455–463. *See also* **pH**
amphoteric compounds, 460–461
Arrhenius, 447, 449–450, 449*t*, 456*t*
Brønsted-Lowry, 452–455, 454*f*, 456*t*
calculating hydronium and hydroxide ion concentration in, 473–474
conjugate, 457–459, 459*t*, 574–575
dissociation constants, 576
household, 446
hydrolysis of salts, 574–578, 574*f*, 576*f*, 577*f*
Lewis, 455–456, 456*t*
neutralization reactions, 461–463, 462*f*
properties, 445–446
strength of, 449–450, 449*t*, 450*f*, 458–459, 459*t*
batteries, 621–622, 621*f*, 622*f*, 631, 631*f*
Becquerel, Henri, 645, 653
benzene, 687, 687*f*
beryllium, 110, 111t, R8–R9, R8*f*, R10*t*
Berzelius, Jöns Jacob, 420
beta particles, 645*t*, 646, 646*f*, 653, 653*f*
binary acids, 218–219, 218*t*, 442–443, 442*t*. *See also* **acids**
binary compounds, 210, 265
binary molecular compounds, 215–217, 216*t*, 217*t*
binding energy per nucleon, 642, 642*f*
biochemistry, 706–731, R35–R40
amino acids, 712, 712*f*, 713–714, R35, R35*f*
carbohydrates, 707–709, 708*f*, 709*f*, 722, R37–R38
DNA, 727–728, 727*f*, 728*f*
genetic engineering, 730–731, 730*f*
lipids, 710–711, 710*f*, 711*f*, R38–R39
metabolism, 722–725, 723*f*, 724*f*, 725*t*
nucleic acid structure, 726, 726*f*
proteins, 713–721, 715*f*, 716*t*,
RNA, 729–730, 729*f*
bioluminescence, 96
blocks, of elements, 130–131, 131*f*
blood. *See also* **hemoglobin**
artificial, 395, 395*f*, 718
buffers in, 575
carbon dioxide in, R32–R33, R33*f*
sickle cell anemia, 717, 717*f*
transfusions, 718
Bohr, Niels, 95*f*, 96–97, 96*f*, 97*f*
boiling, 318, 326–327, 326*f*, 327*f*
boiling-point elevation, 426–427, 433
boiling points, 7*f*
bonding types and, 193, 194*t*
of crystalline solids, 322*t*
determining, 433
of liquids, 326–327, 326*f*, 327*f*
of organic compounds, 680*t*, 681, 681*t*, 688*t*
of water, 326, 326*f*, 333, R59*t*
bond angles, 189–191, 189*f*, 190*t*, 332
bond energy, 171, 172*t*, 177*t*
bonding. *See* **chemical bonding**
bond length, 171, 172*t*, 177*t*
bond strength, 186
boron, 107, 110, 111*t*, 173, R24–R25, R24*f*, R26*t*
boron family elements, R24–R27, R24*f*, R26*t*, R27*t*
boron trifluoride, 188, 188*f*, 193
Bosch, Karl, 563
Boyle, Robert, 349, 356–357
Boyle's law, 349–350, 349*f*, 350*f*, 369
bromine, 113t, 138–139, 153*t*, 155, 223*t*, R54–R55, R54*f*, R55*f*, R56*t*
bromthymol blue, 485*t*, 488
Brønsted-Lowry acids and bases, 452–455, 453*f*, 456*t*
Brownian motion, 382
Buckyballs, 683
buffers, 572–573, 572*f*, 575
butane, 671, 671*t*, 675*t*

caffeine, 458
calcium
dietary, R12, R12*t*
electron configuration, 112, 113*t*
properties, R8–R9, R8*f*, R9*f*, R10*t*
reactivity, 134, 134*f*, R9, R9*f*
calorimeters, 501, 509, 509*f*
Cannizzaro, Stanislao, 125
capillary action, 317, 317*f*
carbohydrates
chemical structure, R37–R38, R37*f*, R38*f*
condensation reactions, 708–709, 708*f*
digestion of, 724
disaccharides, 708, 708*f*, R37, R37*f*
monosaccharides, 707–708, 707*f*, R37, R37*f*
polysaccharides, 709, 709*f*
carbon
allotropes, 683
in aromatic hydrocarbons, 687, 687*f*
Buckyballs, 683
carbon cycle, R31, R31*f*
covalent bonding in, 176–178, 177*t*
electron configuration, 111*t*, 140, 192, 192*f*
forms of, 512
in iron ore reduction, R30, R30*f*
isotopes, 78*t*, 655
oxidation numbers, 223*t*
properties, R28–R29, R29*t*
carbonated beverages, 391, 391*f*
carbon-14 dating, 655. *See also* **radioactive dating**
carbon dioxide
in the carbon cycle, R31, R31*f*
molecular geometry of, 191
nonpolarity of, 195*f*
properties, R31
in respiration, R32–R33, R33*f*
carbon family of elements, R28–R43. *See also under names of individual elements*
carbon monoxide, 261, R31, R34, R34*t*
carbonyl groups, 691
carboxyl groups, 692, 692*f*
carboxylic acids, 689*t*, 692, 692*f*
careers in chemistry
analytical chemist, 488
chemical technician, 284
computational chemist, 194
environmental chemist, 386
forensic chemist, 730
materials scientist, 137
petroleum engineer, 678
pharmacist, 210
casein, 716, 716*t*
catabolism, 724–725, 724*f*, 725*t*
catalysis, 538, 538*f*, 539*f*
catalysts
catalytic converters, 547
in chemical equations, 252
enzymes as, 719–720, 719*f*, 720*f*
heterogeneous vs. homogeneous, 538
reaction rate and, 538, 538*f*, 539*f*
catalytic converters, 547
catenation, 670, 670*f*
cathode rays, 68–69, 68*f*, 69*f*
cathodes, 68*f*, 618, 618*f*
cathodic protection, 624, 624*f*
cations
hydrolysis of, 575–576
ionic radii, 151–152, 151*t*, 156
nomenclature, 208, 209*t*, 212–213, 212*f*
cellulose, 709, 709*f*, R38*f*
Celsius temperature scale, 501
centrifuge, 12, 12*f*
cesium, 78*t*, 115, 167, R2–R3, R2*f*, R3*f*, R4*t*
chain reactions, 657–658, 657*f*
changes of state, 324–330
boiling, 318, 326–327, 326*f*, 327*f*
chemical, 8–11, 10*f*
equilibrium and, 324–325, 324*t*, 325*f*
freezing, 318, 324*t*, 327–328, 333
melting, 320, 324*t*, 328–329
phase diagrams, 329–330, 329*f*, 330*f*
Charles, Jacques, 351
Charles's law, 352, 352*f*, 369
chemical bonding, 164–197
carbon, 669–670, 670*f*
covalent, 168–179
definition, 165
electronegativity and, 166–167, 166*f*, 167*f*
enthalpy of vaporization, 186, 186*t*, 327, 327*f*, 333
intermolecular forces, 193–197, 194*t*, 195*f*, 196*f*, 197*f*
ionic, 180–184
metallic, 185–186, 185*f*, 186*t*, 194*t*
types of, 165–167, 166*f*, 167*f*
VSEPR theory, 187–191, 188*f*, 189*f*, 190*t*
chemical changes, 9–10, 10*f*
chemical equations, 248–260
balancing, 250–253, 256–260, 270, 275, 601–605, 610
coefficients in, 249, 251, 254–255
elements in elemental state, 248–249, 249*t*
net ionic equation, 415–416
requirements of, 248–249
symbols in, 251–253, 252*t*
thermochemical, 505
word, 249–250, 254
chemical equilibrium, 554–586
acid ionization constants, 571–572, 572*t*

base dissociation constants, 576
buffers, 572–573, 572f, 573*f*
calcium-carbonate system, 566-567
common-ion effect, 569–570, 570*f*
determining equilibrium constants, 558, 587
equilibrium expression, 557–561, 557*f*, 559*t*
factors in, 564–567, 565*f*, 567*f*
hydrogen-iodine system, 558–560, 559*t*
ionization constant of water, 472, 472*t*, 565, 573
precipitation calculations, 584–586
reactions that go to completion, 567–569, 568*f*
reversible reactions and, 555–557
salt hydrolysis, 574–578, 574*f*, 576*f*, 577*f*
solubility products, 579–586, 581*t*

chemical equilibrium expression, 558, 587
chemical formulas, 168
calculation of, 233–237
for covalent-network compounds, 218
empirical, 233–235, 698
formula masses, 225–226
for ionic compounds, 210
molar masses, 79, 79*f*, 226–230, 228*f*
for molecular compounds, 215–217, 216*t*, 217*t*
for monatomic ions, 208–209, 209*t*
oxidation numbers, 220–223, 223*t*
for polyatomic ions, 213–215, 214*t*
significance of, 207–208
structural, 670–671, 671*f*

chemical kinetics, 536. *See also* **kinetics of reactions**
chemical properties, 9–10, 9*f*
chemical purity, 14, 14*f*, 14*t*
chemical reactions, 246–274. *See also* **chemical equations; chemical equilibrium; kinetics of reactions; oxidation-reduction reactions**
acid-base, 457–463, 459*t*, 460*f*, 461*f*, 462*f*
activated complexes, 533–535, 533*f*
activation energy, 532–535, 532*f*, 533*f*, 538, 720, 720*f*
activity series, 271–273, 272*t*
addition, 693–694, 694*f*
amino acid, 713
collision theory, 530–531, 531*f*, 537
combustion, 269, 269*f*, 508–509, 509*f*, R60*t*
combustion synthesis, 274, 274*f*
condensation, 694, 708–709, 708*f*, 713
decomposition, 265–266, 266*f*
definition, 247
double-displacement, 268–269, 268*f*, 414–415, 414*f*, 416
driving force of, 516–520, 518*f*, 519*t*
elimination, 695, 695*f*
endothermic, 505–507, 507*f*, 516, 519*t*
enthalpy of, 504–513, 506*f*, 507*f*, 513*f*
exothermic, 393–394, 505–506, 506*f*, 519*t*, 532
half-reactions, 597–599
indications of, 247–248, 248*f*
limiting vs. excess reactants, 296–300, 296*f*
mechanisms of, 529–530, 529*f*
neutralization, 442, 446, 461–463, 462*f*, 489–493
nuclear, 644, 657–658, 657*f*
percentage yield, 301–302
precipitation, 413–415, 414*f*
rate laws, 539–546, 548
reactions that go to completion, 567–569, 568*f*
reversible, 252–253, 252*t*, 255, 255*f*, 555–556, 555*f*
single-displacement, 267–268, 267*f*, 271
substitution, 693
synthesis, 262–265, 263*f*, 274

chemicals, definition of, 4
chemistry, science of, 3–5. *See also* **history of chemistry**
chlorine
chemical bonding, 167, 167*f*, 173, 173*f*
electron configuration, 112*t*
isotopes, 75–76
oxidation numbers, 223*t*, 598–599
oxyacids of, 460*f*, 461
properties, R54–R55, R55*f*, R56*t*
size of, 143*f*
water treatment by, R56–R57, R56*f*

chlorofluorocarbons (CFCs), 690, 693
chlorophyll, 722, 722*f*, R13*f*
cholesterol, 711
chromium, 112, 113*t*, 596*f*, R15–R16, R15*f*, R16*f*, R17*t*
cis isomers, 672, 682*t*
citric acid cycle, 724
cloning, 731, 731*f*
cobalt, 113*t*, 113, R14–R16, R15*f*, R16*f*, R17*t*, R23*t*
coefficients, equation, 249, 251, 254–255, 507
collagen, 716, 716*t*
colligative properties, 422–432
boiling-point elevation, 426–427, 433
electrolytes and, 429–431, 429*f*, 431*t*
freezing-point depression, 424–426, 424*t*, 430–432, 431*t*, 433
of nonvolatile substances, 422–423, 422*f*, 423*f*
osmotic pressure, 428–429, 428*f*
vapor-pressure lowering, 422–423, 422*f*, 423*f*

collision theory, 530–531, 531*f*, 537
colloids, 381–383, 382*f*, 382*t*
combined gas law, 354–355, 369
combustion reactions, 269, 269*f*, 508–509, 509*f*, R60*t*
combustion synthesis, 274, 274*f*
common-ion effect, 569–570, 570*f*
composition stoichiometry, 283
compounds
amphoteric, 460–461, 460*f*, 461*f*
binary, 210–211, 265
definition, 7
enthalpy of formation, 507–508, 512–514, 513*f*
ionic, 180–184, 181*f*, 182*f*, 183*t*, 208–215
molecular, 168–169, 183, 215–217, 417
nomenclature, 208–213
organic, 669
oxidation numbers, 220–223, 223*t*, 598–599
percentage composition, 230–232, 238
polyatomic ions in, 213–214, 214*t*
solubility of, R65*t*

compressibility, 313, 316, 320, 356
concentration, 396–402
chemical equilibrium and, 565–566, 565*f*
molality, 400–402, 400*f*, 430
molarity, 396–399, 397*f*, 403, 471, 489–493, 490*f*–491*f*
reaction rates and, 537–538, 537*f*, 538*f*, 548
titration and, 489–493, 490*f*–491*f*

condensation, 324, 324*t*
condensation polymers, 697
condensation reactions, 694, 708–709, 708*f*, 713
conduction bands, R42, R42*f*
conductivity, electrical, 7, 18
conjugate acids and bases, 457–459, 459*t*, 574–575
conservation of mass, 64–65, 65*f*, 287
contact theory, 420
continuous spectrum, 95
control rods, 658, 658*f*
conversion factors
molar mass, 228–230, 228*f*, 285
mole ratios, 233–235, 284–285, 288–294, 303
SI units, 38–40, 48, 84
using, 38–40, 48, 84

copolymers, 695, 697
copper
in the body, R23*t*
in electrochemical cells, 617–622, 617*f*, 618*f*, 619*f*, 620*f*
electron configuration, 113, 113*t*
ion formation, 156
isotopes, 78, 78*t*
oxidation and reduction of, 607, 607*f*, 607*t*
in photochromic lenses, 598
properties, 18f, 19, R14–R16, R15*f*, R16*f*, R17*t*
reactivity, R15, R15*f*
in tap water, 451

corrosion, 515, 623–624, 623*f*, 624*f*
cosmic rays, 654
covalent bonding, 168–179
compared to ionic, 183, 183*f*
electron-dot notation, 174–176, 174*f*
electronegativity and, 165–167, 166*f*, 167*f*
hybridization, 191–193, 192*f*, 193*t*
intermolecular forces, 193–197, 194*t*, 195*f*, 196*f*, 197*f*
Lewis structures, 174–178, 203
nomenclature, 215–217, 216*t*, 217*t*
octet rule, 172–173, 173*f*
polyatomic ions, 184, 189–190, 218, 218*f*, 275
redox reactions and, 598
resonance structures, 179
VSEPR theory, 187–191, 188*f*, 189*f*, 190*t*

covalent molecular crystals, 322*t*, 323

covalent-network bonding, 179, 218, 322, 323f
covalent network crystals, 322, 322t, 323f
Crick, Francis, 727
critical mass, 658
critical point, 329, 329f
critical temperature, 329, 329f
Crookes, William, 562
crystalline solids, 320
- binding forces in, 322–323, 322t, 323f
- breakage and, 183, 183f
- hydrates, 389, 389f
- ionic bonding in, 181–182, 181f, 182f
- substitutions in, R20, R20f
- types of, 321–323, 321f, 322t

Curie, Marie and Pierre, 645
cycloalkanes, 676
cysteine, 712f, 714, 714f
cytosine, 726, 726f, R40f

Dalton's atomic theory, 64–65
Dalton's law of partial pressures, 345–348, 346f
Daniell Cells, 619, 619f
data collection, 27–28
daughter nuclides, 650
Davy, Humphry, 420
d-block elements, 136, 138, 136f, 155–156
de Broglie, Louis, 98
Debye, Peter, 432
decay series, 650–651, 650f
decomposition reactions, 265–266, 266f
decompression sickness, 348
delocalized electrons, 185, 323, 687, 687f
Democritus, 41, 63
denaturation, 720–721, 720f, 721f, R37, R37f
density
- calculation of, 37
- of familiar materials, 36t, 37
- of gases, 36, 313, R63t
- of liquids, 315, 315f
- of organic compounds, 688t
- of solids, 320
- units of, 34t, 36–37, 36t
- of water, 332, R63t

deposition, 324t, 328
derived units, 34–37, 34t, 36t
deuterium, 74, 74f, 75t
diamonds, 512, 683
diatomic molecules, 168, 187–188, 187f, 249t, 360
diffraction, 98, 99f
diffusion
- of gases, 313, 313f, 318f, 366–368, 366f
- of liquids, 316, 316f
- of solids, 321

digestion, 721, 724–725, 724f
dimensional analysis, 38–39
dipeptides, 713
dipoles, 194–196, 195f, 196f
diprotic acids, 454, 454f
directly proportional quantities, 53–54, 53f, 53t
disaccharides, 708, 708f, R37, R37f
dispersed phase, 381
displacement reactions, 267–269, 267f, 268f
disproportionation, 609, 609f
dissociation, 411–415, 411f, 414f
dissolution, 385–386, 385f, 517–518, 518f. *See also* **solubility**
disulfide bridges, 714, 714f
DNA (deoxyribonucleic acid), 727–728, 727f, 728f
DNA fingerprinting, 730, 730f
DNA replication, 728, 728f
doping, R42–R43
Dorn, Ernst, 109, 127
double bonds, 176–178, 177t, 682–683
double-displacement reactions, 268–269, 268f, 414–415, 414f, 416
Downs Cells, 633
Drew, Charles, 718
dry cells, 621–622, 621f, 622f
dry ice, 472f
ductility, 18, 186

E

effervescence, 391, 391f
effusion, 313–314, 366–368
Einstein, Albert, 93–94, 641
Einstein's equation, 641
elastic collisions, 311
elastins, 716
electrical potential, 624–627, 625f, 626t, 634
electric charge, 69, 71
electric circuits, 618
electric current, 32t, 383–384, 384f, 442, 446
electrochemical cells, 617–619, 617f, 618f, 619f
electrochemistry, 616–633
- corrosion, 623–624, 623f, 624f
- definition, 617
- electrical potentials, 624–627, 625f, 626t, 634
- electrochemical cells, 617–619, 617f, 618f, 619f
- electrolysis, 265, 632–633, 632f
- electrolytic cells, 629–633, 629f, 630f, 631f, 632f
- rechargeable cells, 631, 631f
- voltaic cells, 620–628, 620f, 621f, 622f

electrode potentials, 624–627, 625f, 626t, 634
electrodes, 618, 618f, 625, 625f
electrolysis, 265, 420–421, 420f, 421f, 632–633, 632f
electrolytes, 383–384, 384f
- balance of, R5, R5f
- colligative properties and, 429–432, 429f, 431t
- in electrochemical cells, 618, 618f
- strong vs. weak, 418–419, 418f

electrolytic cells, 629–633, 629f, 630f, 631f, 632f
electromagnetic radiation, 91–94, 647, 647f. *See also* **light**
electromagnetic spectrum, 91–93, 92f
electron affinity, 149–151, 149f, 150f
electron capture, 647
electron configurations, 105–116
- atomic radii and, 142–144, 143f, 143t, 144f, 155
- of d-block elements, 136, 138, 136f
- electron-dot notation, 174–176, 174f
- notation of, 106–107
- period number and, 110–115, 111t, 112t, 113t, 114t
- of s-block elements, 134, 134f
- summary of, 105–106, 105f, 106f, 130–131, 139t, 157
- valence electrons, 152, 152t
- writing, 157

electron-dot notation, 174–176, 174f, 180–181
electronegativity
- acid strength and, 461
- chemical bonding and, 166–167, 166f, 167f
- dipole-dipole forces, 194–196, 195f, 196f
- period trends, 153–156, 153f, 154f

electrons, 90–116
- in Bohr model, 96–97, 96f, 97f
- charge of, 69
- in covalent bonds, 169, 169f, 171–172, 171f, 172f
- delocalized, 185, 323, 687, 687f
- discovery of, 68–69, 68f, 69f
- in electrochemical cells, 617–622, 617f, 618f, 619f, 620f
- Heisenberg uncertainty principle, 99
- in Lewis acids and bases, 455–456, 456t
- line-emission spectrum, 94–95, 94f, 95f
- mass of, 69, 72t, R59t
- in metallic bonding, 185–186, 185f
- orbitals, 101–104, 101f, 102t, 103f, 104t
- photoelectric effect, 93–94, 93f
- properties, 72t
- unshared pairs, 175, 189–190, 189f, 190t
- valence, 152, 152t
- as waves, 98–100, 99f

electroplating, 630, 630f
elements, 16–20. *See also* **families**
- activity series, 271–273, 272t
- alkali metals, 134, 134f, R2–R7, R2f, R4t
- in ancient science, 41
- artificial transmutations, 651–652, 652f, 652t
- atomic masses, 77–78, 78t, 117, 125, R60t–R61t
- atomic numbers, 73, 77–78, 78t, R60t–R61t
- in the body, R22–R23, R22f, R23t
- definition, 6
- Elements Handbook, R2–R57
- enthalpy of formation, 508
- molar mass, 79, 79f, 226–230, 228f
- periodic table of, 132f–133f
- symbols for, 16, 16t, R60t–R61t
- transmutation of, 644, 651–652, 652f
- transuranic, 652, 652f, 652t, 660–661
- types of, 18–20, 18f, 19f

elimination reactions, 695, 695f
emission, 96, 96f
emission-line spectrum, 94–95, 94f, 95f
Empedokles, 41
empirical formulas, 233–235, 698
emulsions, 381, 382t
endothermic reactions, 505–507, 507f, 516, 519t, 532f

end point, 488, 488*f*
energy, 500–520
activation, 532–535, 532*f*, 533*f*, 538, 720, 720*f*
ATP, 722–725, 723*f*, 725*t*, R40*f*
boiling and, 326–327, 327*f*
bond, 171–172, 172*t*, 177*t*
catalysts and, 538, 539*f*
changes of state and, 10–11, 326–335, 327*f*
electron affinity, 149–151, 149*t*, 150*f*
electron configuration and, 105–106, 105*f*
of electrons, 94–97, 95*f*, 96*f*, 97*f*
enthalpy of combustion, 508–509, 509*f*, R60*t*
enthalpy of formation, 507–508, 512–514, 513*f*
enthalpy of reaction, 505–507, 506*f*, 507*f*
enthalpy of solution, 393–394, 393*f*, 394*t*
entropy, 516–518, 517*f*, 518*f*, 519*t*
free, 518–520, 519*t*
in hydrogen bonding, 169, 169*f*
ionization, 145–148, 145*t*, 146*f*, 147*t*, 156
kinetic, 311–312, 366
lattice, 182, 183*t*
nuclear binding, 641–642, 642*f*
of photons, 94–95
quantum, 93
specific heat, 502–504, 503*t*
units of, 501
enthalpy
activation energy and, 532–535, 532*f*, 533*f*
calculating, 509–512, 521
of combustion, 508–509, 509*f*, R60*t*
of formation, 507–508, 512–514, 513*f*, R66*t*
in free energy, 519–520, 519*t*
of fusion, 328, 334
Hess's law, 509–512, 521
of reaction, 504–507, 506*f*, 507*f*, 513*f*, 516
in reversed equations, 510
of solution, 393–394, 393*f*, 394*t*
of vaporization, 186, 186*t*, 327, 333
enthalpy changes, 504
entropy, 516–520, 517*f*, 518*f*, 519*t*
enzymes, 719–721
coenzymes, R36
pH and, 721, R36–R37
as proteins, 712
specificity of, 719–720, 719*f*
temperature and, 720, 720*f*
enzyme-substrate complexes, 719, 719*f*
equations. *See* **chemical equations**
equilibrium. *See* **chemical equilibrium**
equilibrium, in state changes, 325
equilibrium constants, 558. *See also* **chemical equilibrium**
acid ionization, 571–572, 572*t*
base dissociation, 576
determining, 587
ionization constant of water, 472–473, 472*t*, 565, 573
solubility products, 579–586, 581*t*
equilibrium vapor pressure, 325, 325*f*
equivalence point, 488–489, 489*f*
error, 43–44
esters, 689*t*, 692
ethane, 674, 675*t*
ethanol, 326*f*, 390, 671*f*, 689
ethene, 685, 685*f*
ethers, 689*t*, 690
ethyne, 685
evaporation, 317–318, 318*f*, 324–325, 325*f*
excess reactants, 296, 296*f*
excited state, 94
exothermic reactions
activation energy in, 532, 532*f*
enthalpies of solution and, 393–394, 394*t*, 519*t*
thermochemical equations for, 505–506, 506*f*
expansion of gases, 312
explosives, 540, 563
exponents, 48–50
extensive properties, 7

families, R24–R57
alkali metals, 134, 134*f*, R2–R7, R2*f*, R4*t*
alkaline-earth metals, 134, 134*f*, R8–R13, R8*f*, R10*t*
boron, R24–R27, R24*f*, R26*t*, R27*t*
carbon, R28–R43
halogens, R54–R57, R56*t*
nitrogen, R44–R47, R45*t*, R47*t*
oxygen, R48–R53, R50*t*, R51*t*
transition metals, 136, R14–R23, R17*t*
Faraday, Michael, 420–421, 421*f*
fats. *See* **lipids**
fatty acids, 710, R38–R39, R38*f*
***f*-block elements,** 128, 140–141, 155–156
Fermi, Enrico, 660
fertilizer production, 562–563, R47, R47*t*
fibrous proteins, 716, 716*t*
fifth-period elements, 114, 114*t*
film badges, 654, 654*f*
filtration, 12, 12*f*
fireworks, R10–R11, R10*f*
fission, 657–658, 657*f*, 658*f*, 660–661
flame tests, R3, R3*f*, R9, R9*f*, R45, R45*f*, R49, R49*f*
flavorings, 691*f*
fluids, 312–313, 315
fluoridation, 269*f*, R57
fluorine
covalent bonding, 173, 173*f*
electron configuration, 111*t*
electronegativity, 153, 153*t*
properties, R54–R55, R56*t*
reactions, 264, 268
tooth decay and, 269, R57
forces
intermolecular, 193–197, 194*t*, 195*f*, 196*f*, 197*f*
nuclear, 71, 641–643, 643*f*
pressure and, 341–342, 341*f*, 342*f*
units of, 342
forensic chemists, 730
formula equations, 250. *See also* **chemical equations**
formula masses, 225–226, 236–237
formula units, 180
fossil fuels, 681, 681*t*
fourth-period elements, 112–113, 113*t*
fractional distillation, 681, 681*f*
Franklin, Rosalind, 727
free energy, 518–520, 519*t*
free radicals, R52
freezing, 318, 324*t*, 327–328, 333
freezing-point depression, 424–426, 424*t*, 430–432, 431*t*, 433
freezing points, 327–329, 433, R59*t*
freons, 690
frequency, 92–93, 92*f*
fructose, 707–709, 708*f*, R37*f*
fuel cells, 622, 622*f*, 628
fullerene, 683
functional groups, 688–692, 689*t*
fusion, 655–656, 659, 659*f*

gallium, 113*t*, R24–R25, R24*f*, R26*t*
galvanic cells. *See* **voltaic cells**
galvanizing, 624
gamma rays, 645*t*, 647, 647*f*, 653, 653*f*
gas constant, 364–365, 364*t*, R59*t*
gases, 340–368
Avogadro's law, 359–360, 359*f*, 360*f*
Boyle's law, 349–350, 349*f*, 350*f*, 369
Charles's law, 351–352, 351*f*, 352*f*, 369
from chemical reactions, 248, 248*f*, 268–269, 568
combined gas law, 354–355, 369
density of, 36, 313, R63*t*
deviations from ideal behavior, 314, 314*f*
Gay-Lussac's law, 353–354, 353*f*, 369
Gay-Lussac's law of combining volumes of gases, 358
Graham's law of effusion, 366–368, 366*f*
Henry's law, 348, 391–393, 391*f*, 392*f*
ideal gas law, 363, 363*f*
kinetic-molecular theory of, 311–314, 312*f*, 313*f*, 314*f*
molar volumes, 360–361
noble, 20, 20*f*, 127–128, 127*f*, 314
partial pressures, 345–348, 346*f*, 565
pressure, 341–347, 341*f*, 342*f*, 343*f*, 344*t*
properties, 9
solubility in water, R64*t*
stoichiometry of reactions, 361–362
gasohol, 689
gasoline, 390, 681*t*
Gay-Lussac, Joseph, 353
Gay-Lussac's law, 353–354, 353*f*, 369
Gay-Lussac's law of combining volumes of gases, 358
Geiger, Hans, 70, 70*f*
Geiger-Müller counters, 654, 654*f*
genes, 729
genetic code, 729, 732

genetic engineering, 730–731, 730*f*
geometric isomers, 672, 672*f*
glacial acetic acid, 445
glass, 320, R41
globular proteins, 716, 716*t*
gluconeogenesis, 725
glucose, 707–709, 708*f*, 709*f*, R32, R37*f*
glutamic acid, 712*f*, 714, 714*f*, 717*f*
glycerol, 689, 689*f*
glycogen, 709, 709*f*, R38*f*
glycolipids, R39
gold, 18*f*, 380–381, 381*f*, R14, R17*t*
Graham's law of effusion, 366–368, 366*f*
gram/mole conversions, 80
graphite, 512, 683
graphs, 28*f*, 53*f*, 55*f*
greenhouse gases, 547
ground state, 94, 96, 97*f*
ground-state electron configuration, 105
groups, 17. *See also* **families**
guanine, 726, 726*f*, R40*f*

Haber, Fritz, 563
Haber process, 563, 564–566
Hahn, Otto, 660–661, 660*f*
half-cells, 618–619, 618*f*, 624–627, 625*f*, 626*t*
half-life, 648–649, 648*f*, 648*t*, 662
half-reaction method of balancing equations, 601–605, 610
half-reactions, 597–599
Hall-Héroult process, 633
halogens, R54–R57
activity series, 271–272, 272*t*
in alkyl halides, 689*t*, 690, 690*f*, 693
properties, 139, 139*f*, R54–R55, R54*f*, R55*f*, R56*t*
reactions, 264, 268
hazard labels, xxvi-xxvii
heat, 247, 247*f*, 501–504, 502*f*, 503*t*
Heisenberg uncertainty principle, 99
helium, 75*t*, 109, 127, 135
hemoglobin
in carbon monoxide poisoning, 261, R34, R34*t*
heme molecule in, R32, R32*f*
iron in, R23, R23*t*
in sickle cell anemia, 717, 717*f*
structure of, 715, R36, R36*f*
Henry's law, 348, 391–393, 391*f*, 392*f*
hertz, 92
Hess's law, 509–512, 521
heterogeneous catalysts, 538, 547
heterogeneous mixtures, 11*f*, 12, 379*f*
heterogeneous reactions, 536–537
heterotrophs, 722
highest-occupied energy level, 110
history of chemistry
air pressure, 356–357, 357*f*
ancient Greek science, 41
combustion, 286–287, 287*f*
electrolysis, 420–421, 420*f*, 421*f*
nitrogen fertilizer production, 562–563
nuclear fission, 660–661
organic chemistry, 673
periodic table, 108–109, 109*f*, 125–127, 126*f*
homogeneous catalysts, 538
homogeneous mixtures, 11*f*, 12, 379*f*. *See also* **solutions**
homogeneous reactions, 530
homologous series, 674
Hooke, Robert, 356
hormones, 716*t*
Hückel, Erich, 432
Human Genome Project, 728
human growth hormone, 731
Hund's rule, 106, 106*f*
hybridization, 191–193, 192*f*, 193*t*
hybrid orbitals, 192, 192*f*
hydrates, 231–232, 389, 389*f*
hydration, 389, 389*f*, 417
hydrocarbons, 674–687
alkanes, 674–682, 675*t*, 676*t*, 677*t*, 680*t*, 682*t*
alkenes, 682–685, 682*t*, 685*f*
alkynes, 685–686, 686*f*
aromatic, 687, 687*f*
cycloalkanes, 676
functional groups, 688–692, 688*t*, 689*t*
isomers, 671–672
nomenclature, 676–680, 676*t*, 677*t*, 683, 686
saturated, 674
structural formulas, 670–671
unsaturated, 682–687, 682*t*
hydrochloric acid, 417, 417*f*, 445, 458, 462–463, 462*f*
hydrogen
Bohr model of, 96–97, 96*f*, 97*f*
electron configuration, 135
in fuel-cell cars, 628
fusion of, 659, 659*f*
hydronium ions, 417, 447– 448, 447*f*, 448*t*, 459, 459*t*
isotopes, 73–74, 74*f*, 74*t*, 75*t*, 78*t*
line-emission spectrum, 94–95, 94*f*, 95*f*
reactions with, 442, 558–560
solid, 320
hydrogenation, 693–694, 694*f*
hydrogen bonding
bond length and energy, 171–172, 171*f*, 172*t*
covalent bonding in, 166, 167*f*, 169*f*
dipole-dipole forces in, 196, 196*f*
in DNA, 727, 727*f*, R40*f*
in water, 331–332, 331*f*, 332*f*
hydrogen peroxide, 608–609, 719
hydrolysis, 574–578, 574*f*, 576*f*, 577*f*, 708–709, 723, 723*f*
hydronium ions
in acid solutions, 447–448, 447*f*, 448*t*, 459
calculating concentration of, 473–474
ionization and, 417
pH scale and, 475–476, 475*f*
hydroxide ions, 472
hydroxides, 266, 450, 450*f*
hydroxyl groups, 461, 689, 689*t*
hyphen notation, 75
hypotheses (singular, *hypothesis*), 28–29, 29*f*

ibuprofen, 229–230
ice, 324*t*, 328–329
ideal conditions, 288
ideal gas constant, 364–365, 364*t*, R59*t*
ideal gases, 311–314, 312*f*, 313*f*, 314*f*, 363, 363*f*
ideal gas law, 363, 363*f*
immiscibility, 390, 390*f*
indicators. *See* **acid-base indicators**
induced dipoles, 195–196, 196*f*
inner-shell electrons, 110
insoluble substances, 579
insulin, 713, 716, 716*t*, 731, R36
intensive properties, 7
interference, 98, 99*f*, 100
intermediates, 530
intermolecular forces, 193–197, 195*f*, 196*f*, 197*f*
interstitial crystals, R20, R20*f*
inversely proportional quantities, 54, 54*t*, 55*f*
iodine, 114*t*, 223*t*, 558–560, 559*t*, R54–R55, R54*f*, R55*f*, R56*t*
ionic bonding, 180–184
boiling points and, 194*t*
covalent bonding compared with, 183
electronegativity and, 165–167, 166*f*
ionic compounds
crystals, 322, 322*t*
dissociation, 411–415, 411*f*, 413*f*, 414*f*
formation of, 180–184, 181*f*, 182*f*, 183*f*, 183*t*
nomenclature, 210–211, 213–214
salts as, 219
ionic radii, 151–152, 151*t*, 156
ionization
of aqueous solutions, 417, 417*f*
chemical equilibrium and, 569
energy, 145–148, 145*t*, 146*f*, 147*t*, 156
self-ionization of water, 471–472, 471*f*, 472*t*, 565–566
ionization constants, 472–473, 472*t*, 566, 571–573, 572*t*
ionization energy (IE), 145–148, 145*f*, 146*f*, 147*t*, 156
ions, 145
hydronium, 417, 447–448, 447*f*, 448*t*, 459, 459*t*
ionization and, 417, 417*f*
monatomic, 208–209, 209*t*
names of common, R62*t*
polyatomic, 184, 190, 218, 218*t*, 275
iron
alloys, R18–R19, R19*f*
blast furnace reduction, R30, R30*f*
in the body, R23, R23*t*
corrosion of, 623–624, 623*f*, 624*f*
electron configuration, 113, 113*t*,
ionization energy, 156
nomenclature, 212
oxidation of, 263, 263*f*, 298–299
properties, R14–R16, R14*f*, R15*f*, R16*f*, R17*t*
isomers, 670, 671–672, 671*t*, 672*f*

isotopes, 73–76, 74*f*, 74*t*, 75*t*, 78*t*
IUPAC nomenclature, 676

joules, 501

Kelvin temperature scale, 351, 501
ketones, 691, 691*f*
kinetic energy, 311–312, 366
kinetic-molecular theory
Boyle's law, 349, 349*f*
Dalton's law, 346, 346*f*
of gases, 311–314, 312*f*, 313*f*, 314*f*
of liquids, 315–318, 316*f*, 317*f*, 318*f*
of solids, 319–323, 319*f*, 320*f*, 321*f*, 322*t*, 323*f*
kinetics of reactions, 528–546
enzymes and, 720, 720*f*
rate-determining steps, 544–545
rate-influencing factors, 536–538, 537*f*, 538*f*, 539*f*, 546
rate laws, 539–546, 548
reaction process, 529–535, 531*f*, 532*f*, 533*f*
specific rate constant, 541–543
Krebs cycle, 724
krypton, 109, 113t, 129

lactose, 708–709, R37*f*
lanthanides, 128, 140–141, 149*t*
lattice energy, 182, 183*t*
Lavoisier, Antoine, 287, 287*f*
law of conservation of mass, 64–65, 65*f*, 287
law of definite proportions, 64
law of multiple proportions, 65, 65*f*
law of partial pressures, 345–348, 346*f*
lead
in car batteries, 631, 631*f*
nomenclature, 212, 212*f*
poisoning, 451
properties, R28–R29, R28*f*, R29*t*
LeChâtelier, Henri Louis, 564
LeChâtelier's principle, 564, 569–570
length, 32*t*, 33*t*, 34, 34*f*, R58*t*
leptons, 642
Lewis, G. N., 455
Lewis acid-base reaction, 456
Lewis acids and bases, 455–456, 456*t*
Lewis structures, 174–178
light
from chemical reactions, 247, 247*f*
diffraction and interference, 98, 99*f*, 100
as particles, 93–94
photoelectric effect, 93–94, 93*f*
speed of, R59*t*
as waves, 91–93, 92*f*
lime, 264, 482
limiting reactants, 296–300
lipids
digestion of, 724
fatty acids, 710, R38–R39, R38*f*
hydrogenation, 693–694, 694*f*
phospholipids, 711, 711*f*, R39, R39*f*
structure of, R38–R39, R38*f*, R39*f*
liquids
boiling, 326–327, 326*f*, 327*f*
equilibrium vapor pressure, 325, 325*f*
freezing, 318, 324*t*, 327–328, 333
miscibility of, 390, 390*f*
properties, 9, 315–318, 316*f*, 317*f*, 318*f*
supercooled, 320
volatile, 325
liters, 35, 35*f*
lithium, 111, 111*t*, 147–148, 147*t*, R2–R3, R2*f*, R3*f*, R4*t*
litmus paper, 488
lock and key model, 719
logarithms, 477–480, 494
London dispersion forces, 197, 197*f*, 680
lone pairs, 175, 189–191, 190*t*
luster, 18
lye, 710
Lyman spectral series, 97, 97*f*

macromolecules, R35. *See also* **biochemistry**
magic numbers, 643
magnesium
in chlorophyll, R13, R13*f*
dietary, R12–R13, R13*t*
electron configuration, 112*t*
properties, R8–R9, R8*f*, R10*t*
reactivity, 263*f*, R9, R9*f*
magnetic quantum number, 102–103
magnetite, 298–299
main-group elements, 138–140, 139*t*
MALDI mass spectrometry, 224
malleability, 18, 186
Malthus, Thomas, 562
manganese, 112*t*, 113, R16, R16*f*, R23*t*
manometers, 343, 343*f*
margarine, 694, 694*f*
Marsden, Ernest, 70, 70*f*
mass, 6
atomic, 77–78, 78*t*, 117, 125, R60*t*–R61*t*
conservation of, 64–65, 65*f*, 287
conversion to moles, 292–294
critical, 658
of electrons, 69, 72*t*, R59*t*
formula, 225–226, 236–237
molar, 37, 79, 79*f*, 226–228, 227*f*, 228*f*, 236–237
molecular, 225–226, 236–237
of neutrons, 72*t*
numbers of atoms and, 78–80
percentage composition, 230–232, 238
of protons, 71, 72*t*, R59*t*
relative atomic, 76–77
units of, 32–33, 32*t*, R58*t*
mass defect, 641
mass number, 74, 74*t*
mass spectrometry, 224, 224*f*
Material Data Safety Sheets (MSDS), xxvi–xxvii
materials scientists, 137
matter, 2–20. *See also* **states of matter**
building blocks of, 6–7
chemical properties and changes, 8–10, 10*f*
classical ideas about, 41
classification, 11–14, 11*f*, 12*f*, 13*f*
definition, 6
kinetic-molecular theory of, 311–314, 312*f*, 313*f*, 314*f*
particle theory of, 63
physical properties and changes, 7–8, 8*f*
measurements, 26–55
accuracy and precision in, 42–44, 43*f*
direct proportions, 53–54, 53*f*, 53*t*
inverse proportions, 54, 54*t*, 55*f*
scientific method, 27–29, 28*f*, 29*f*
scientific notation, 49–52, 56
significant figures, 21, 44–48, 45*t*, 46*t*, 477
SI units, 31–40
Meitner, Lise, 660–661, 661*f*
melting, 320, 324*t*, 328–329
melting points, 320, 322*t*, 688*t*
Mendeleev, Dmitri, 108, 125–127, 126*f*
meniscus, 317
mercaptans, 600
mercury
amalgams, R18*f*
poisoning, R21, R21*f*
properties, 10*f*, 136*f*, R14, R17*t*
reversible reactions, 555–556, 555*f*
mercury batteries, 622, 622*f*
messenger RNA (mRNA), 729, 732
metabolic pathways, 722
metabolism, 722–725, 723*f*, 724*f*, 725*t*
metallic bonding, 185–186, 185*f*, 186*t*, 194*t*
metallic crystals, 322–323, 322*t*
metalloids, 19–20, 138–139
metals. *See also* **transition metals**
activity series, 271–273, 272*t*
alkali, 134, 134*f*, R2–R7, R2*f*, R4*t*
alkaline-earth, 134, 134*f*, R8–R13, R8*f*, R10*t*
alloys, 380–381, 380*t*, 381*f*, R18–R20, R19*t*, R20*f*
as catalysts, 547
corrosion, 515, 623–624, 623*f*, 624*f*
decomposition reactions, 265–266, 266*f*
displacement reactions, 267–268
metallic bonding, 185–186, 185*f*, 186*t*
as oxidizing and reducing agents, 606–607, 607*t*
properties, 7, 18–19, 18*f*, 185–186, 186*t*
reaction with acids, 442
self-protecting, R26
synthesis reactions, 262–265, 263*f*
transition, 136, 136*f*, 138, R14–R23
methane, 188, 188*f*, 192, 192*f*, 675*t*
methyl orange, 485*t*, 488
metric units, R58*t*

Miescher, Friedrich, 727
Millikan, Robert A., 69
millimeters of mercury, 344–345, 344*t*
miscibility, 390, 390*f*
mixtures, 11–12, 11*f*
colloids, 381–383, 382*f*, 382*t*
solutions, 379–381, 379*f*, 380*f*, 380*t*, 381*f*
suspensions, 381
models, 29
ball-and-stick, 187–188, 187*f*, 188*f*, 189*f*, 195*f*, 671*f*
Bohr, 96–97, 96*f*, 97*f*
constructing, 67
lock and key, 719, 719*f*
nuclear shell, 643, 647
space-filling, 671*f*
moderators, 658, 658*f*
molal boiling-point constants, 424*t*, 426–427
molal freezing-point constants, 424, 424*t*
molality, 400–402, 400*f*, 430
molar enthalpy of formation, 507–508
molar enthalpy of fusion, 328, 334
molar enthalpy of vaporization, 327, 327*f*, 333
molarity, 396–399, 397*f*, 403, 489–493, 490*f*–491*f*
molar masses, 79, 79*f*, 226–230, 228*f*, 236–237, 285, 290–294, 291*f*
molar volumes, 360–361, R59*t*
molecular compounds, 168. *See also* **covalent bonding**
ionization of, 417, 417*f*
nomenclature, 215–217, 216*t*, 217*t*
properties, 183, 183*f*
molecular formulas, 168, 233, 236–237
molecular geometry, 187–197
hybridization, 191–193, 192*f*, 193*t*
intermolecular forces, 193–197, 194*t*, 195*f*, 196*f*, 197*f*
VSEPR theory, 187–191, 188*f*, 189*f*, 190*t*
molecular masses, 225–226, 236–237
molecules, 7, 168
mole ratios, 233–235, 284–285, 288–294, 288*f*, 291*f*, 294*f*, 303
moles, 79–80, 288–294
monatomic ions, 208–209, 209*t*
monomers, 695–697
monoprotic acids, 453
monosaccharides, 707–708, 707*f*, R37, R37*f*
Moseley, Henry, 127
multiple bonds, 177–178, 177*f*, 177*t*
muriatic acid. *See* **hydrochloric acid**

NADPH, 722
names. *See* **nomenclature**
nanotubes, 668*f*
National Institute of Standards and Technology (NIST), 31
natural gas, 681
Nernst, Walther, 563
net ionic equations, 415–416, 569
neutralization reactions, 461–463, 462*f*
hydrolysis and, 576–578, 576*f*, 577*f*
salts from, 442, 446
in titrations, 487–493, 488*f*, 490*f*–491*f*
neutrons, 68, 72*t*, R59*t*
newtons, 342
nickel
in the body, R23*t*
electron configuration, 113, 113*t*, 136*f*
properties, R14–R16, R16*f*, R17*t*
nitric acid, 293, 444, 444*f*
nitrogen
covalent bonds in, 177, 177*f*, 177*t*
fertilizers, 562–563, R47, R47*t*
fixation, 562, R46, R46*f*
nomenclature, 217, 217*t*
oxidation reactions, 223*t*, 511–512, 560–561, 566–567, 567*f*
properties, R44–R45, R45*t*
nitrogen-containing bases, 726, 726*f*, 728
nitrogen family elements, R44–R47, R45*t*, R47*t*
nitrogen narcosis, 348
nitrous oxide, 547
noble gases, 20, 20*f*
discovery of, 108–109, 109*f*
as ideal gases, 314
in the periodic table, 127, 127*f*
noble gas notation, 111, 112*t*
nomenclature. *See also* **notation**
for acids, 218–219, 218*t*, 442–443, 442*t*, 443*t*
for covalent-network compounds, 218
for ionic compounds, 210–211
for molecular compounds, 215–217, 216*t*, 217*t*
for monatomic ions, 208–209, 209*t*
for organic compounds, 676–680, 676*t*, 677*t*, 683, 686
oxidation numbers and, 223, 223*t*, 606*t*
for oxyanions, 213–214, 214*t*, 443*t*
for salts, 219
Stock system, 209, 212–213, 223
nonelectrolytes, 384, 384*f*, 423
nonmetals, 19, 19*f*, 138
nonpolar-covalent bonds, 166–167, 167*f*, 194*t*
nonvolatile substances, 422–423, 422*f*, 423*f*
normal boiling point, 326, 326*f*, 329*f*
normal freezing point, 328, 329*f*
notation. *See also* **nomenclature**
for aqueous solutions, 411, 471
for cycloalkanes, 676
for electrochemical cells, 619
for electron configuration, 106–107, 111, 111*t*
electron-dot, 174–176, 174*t*, 180–181
for isotopes, 75, 75*t*
for nuclides, 651
for proportionality, 540
for reversible reactions, 556
nuclear binding energy, 641–642, 642*f*
nuclear chemistry, 640–662
applications, 655
artificial transmutations, 651–652, 651*f*, 652*f*, 652*t*
band of stability, 642–643, 643*f*
chain reactions, 657–658, 657*f*
decay series, 650–651, 650*f*
fission, 655–658, 657*f*, 658*f*, 660–661
fusion, 655–656, 659, 659*f*
half-life, 648–649, 648*f*, 648*t*, 662
mass defect, 641
nuclear binding energy, 641–642, 642*f*
nuclear radiation, 645, 653–656, 653*f*, 654*f*, 655*f*
nuclear waste, 655–656
radiation detection, 654, 654*f*
types of decay, 645–647, 645*t*, 646*f*, 647*f*
nuclear forces, 71, 642–644, 643*f*
nuclear power plants, 658, 658*f*
nuclear reactions, 644, 657–658, 657*f*
nuclear reactors, 658
nuclear shell model, 643, 647
nuclear symbol, 75, 75*t*
nucleic acids, 726–731
DNA, 727–728, 727*f*, 728*f*
genetic engineering, 730–731, 730*f*
RNA, 729–730, 729*f*
structure of, 726, 726*f*, R40, R40*f*
nucleons, 641–642, 642*f*
nucleus, atomic, 68–72, 71*f*, 72*t*, 642–644, 643*f*
nuclides, 75, 641, 645, 651–652
nylon, 697

Occupational Safety and Health Administration (OSHA), xxvi–xxvii
octet rule, 172–173, 173*f*
oleic acid, 710, R38*f*
orbitals, 101–104. *See also* **electron configurations**
in covalent bonding, 171–172, 171*f*
hybridization, 191–193, 192*f*, 193*t*
models, 100, 100*f*
notation, 107
order of filling, 110*f*
quantum numbers and, 101–104, 102*t*, 103*f*, 104*t*
order of reaction, 540–541
organic acids, 448–449, 692, 692*f*
organic chemistry, 668–697
alcohols, 689, 689*f*, 689*t*
aldehydes, 689*t*, 691, 691*f*
alkanes, 674–681, 675*t*, 676*t*, 677*t*, 680*t*, 681*t*
alkenes, 682–685, 682*t*, 685*f*
alkyl halides, 689*t*, 690, 690*f*, 693
alkynes, 685–686, 686*f*
amines, 689*t*, 691
carbon bonding, 669–670, 669*f*, 670*f*
carboxylic acids, 689*t*, 692, 692*f*
esters, 689*t*, 692
ethers, 689*t*, 690
functional groups, 688–692, 688*t*, 689*t*
history of, 673, 673*f*
hydrocarbons, 670, 670*f*, 674–687
isomers, 670–672, 671*t*, 672*f*

ketones, 689*t*, 691, 691*f*
organic reactions, 693–697, 694*f*, 695*f*, 696*f*
polymers, 695–697, 696*f*
structural formulas, 670–671, 671*f*
unsaturated hydrocarbons, 682–687, 682*t*
organic reactions, 693–697, 694*f*, 695*f*, 696*f*
osmotic pressure, 428–429, 428*f*
oxidation, 596
oxidation numbers, 220–223, 223*t*, 595–596, 595*t*, 598–599
oxidation-reduction reactions, 594–609
balancing equations for, 601–605, 608, 610
in blast furnaces, R30, R30*f*
covalent bonds and, 598
disproportionation, 609, 609*f*
in electrochemical cells, 617–619
half-reactions, 597
nomenclature, 606*t*
oxidation number rules, 595*t*
oxidation states, 220–223, 223*t*, 595–596, 596*t*
oxidizing and reducing agents, 606–609, 606*t*, 607*t*
in photochromic lenses, 598
oxidation states, 220–223, 223*t*, 595–596, 596*t*
oxides, 264–265, R50–R51, R51*t*
oxidizing agents, 606–609, 606*t*, 607*t*
oxyacetylene torches, 686, 686*f*
oxyacids, 218–219, 218*t*, 443, 443*f*, 443*t*, 460*f*, 461
oxyanions, 213–215, 214*t*, 218, 443*t*
oxygen
discovery of, 287
electron configuration, 110*t*, 111
isotopes, 78*t*
molar mass, 228–229
ozone, 179, 547, 690, R52
properties, 10*f*, R48–R49, R50*t*
reactions with, 262–263, 263*f*, 269, 286–287
resonance structures in, 179
ozone, 179, 547, 690, R52

paper chromatography
capillary action in, 317, 317*f*
in mixture separation, 12, 12*f*
parent nuclides, 650
partial pressures, 345–348, 346*f*, 565
particle accelerators, 651, 651*f*
particles
alpha, 70, 71*f*, 645t, 646, 653, 653*f*
beta, 645*t*, 646, 646*f*
colloids, 381–383, 382*f*, 382*t*
positrons, 645*t*, 646–647
solvated, 393, 393*f*
subatomic, 68, 642
pascals, 344–345, 344*t*
Paschen spectral series, 97*f*
Pauli exclusion principle, 106, 106*f*
Pauling, Linus, 153, 153*t*
***p*-block elements,** 138–140, 139*t*
pepsin, 721
peptide bonds, 713
percentage composition, 230–232, 238
percentage error, 43
percentage yield, 301–302
perchloric acid, 458
perfluorocarbons, 395, 395*f*, 718
periodic law, 124–127, 126*f*. *See also* **periodic table of the elements**
periodic table of atomic radii, 143*f*
periodic table of electron affinities, 149*f*
periodic table of electronegativities, 153*f*
periodic table of ionization energies, 145*f*
periodic table of the elements, 132*f*–133*f*
artificial nuclides in, 652, 652*f*, 652*t*
designing, 129
electron configuration and, 110–116, 111*t*, 112*t*, 113*t*, 114*t*
groups in, 127–128, 127*f*, 135 (*see also* families)
history of, 125–127, 126*f*
new elements in, 108–109
organization of, 16–17, 17*f*
periodicity in, 129, 129*f*
periods and blocks of, 130–136, 131*f*, 136*f*, 138–141, 155–156
periodic trends
acidic and basic oxides, R51, R51*t*
atomic radii, 142–144, 143*f*, 144*f*, 155
of *d*- and *f*-block elements, 155–156
electron affinity, 149–151, 149*t*, 150*f*
electronegativity, 153–156, 153*t*, 154*f*
ionic radii, 151–152, 151*t*, 156
ionization energy, 145–148, 145*t*, 146*f*, 147*t*, 156
valence electrons, 152, 152*t*
periods, of elements, 17, 130–131, 130*t*
peroxide ions, 608–609
petroleum, 681, 681*t*
petroleum engineers, 678
pH, 470–493
acid and base strength and, 481, 481*t*
buffered solutions, 572–573, 572*f*
calculations involving, 477–481, 481*t*, 494
of common materials, 476*t*
definition, 475
enzyme activity and, 721
hydrolysis of salts and, 574–578, 574*f*, 576*f*, 577*f*
indicators, 483–484 (*see also* acid-base indicators)
liming of streams, 482, 482f
of neutral, acidic, and basic solutions, 472, 476*t*
pH scale, 475–476, 475*f*, 476*t*
proteins and, 721
of rain water, 486
self-ionization of water and, 471–472, 471*f*, 472*t*, 565–566
of tap water, 451
titration, 487–493, 487*f*, 488*f*, 489*f*, 490*f*–491*f*
phase diagrams, 329–330, 329*f*, 330*f*
phases, 324, 324*t*
phenolphthalein, 485*t*, 488, 488*f*
pH indicators. *See* **acid-base indicators**
pH meters, 484, 484*f*
phospholipids, 711, 711*f*, R39, R39*f*
phosphoric acid, 443*f*, 443*t*, 445, 454–455
phosphorus
electron configuration, 111*t*
fertilizers, R47, R47*t*
oxidation numbers, 223*t*
properties, 19, R44–R45, R44*f*, R45*t*
radioactive decay, 648*f*, 649
photochemical processes, R52
photochemical smog, R52
photochromic lenses, 598
photoelectric effect, 93–94, 93*f*
photons, 94
photosynthesis, 290, 707, 722, 722*f*
pH paper, 9*f*, 442, 442*f*, 445*f*, 484*f*, 487*f*
physical changes, 8, 8*f*
physical chemistry, 4, 66, 421
physical chemists, 66
physical constants, R59*t*
physical properties, 7–8, 8*f*
pickling, 445
picometers (pm), 72
Planck, Max, 93
Planck's constant, 93, R59*t*
plasma (blood), 718
plasma (state of matter), 9, 640*f*
platinum, 136
Plunkett, Roy, 4
pOH, 475
polar bonds, 166–167, 166*f*, 167*f*, 194*t*
polar-covalent bonds, 166–167, 166*f*, 167*f*, 194*t*
polarity
acid strength and, 448
in crystals, 322–323, 322*t*
dipole-dipole forces, 194–196, 195*f*, 196*f*
dissolution and, 389, 389*f*
of hydroxyl groups, 461
ideal gas behavior and, 314
London dispersion forces and, 197, 197*f*
in phospholipids, 711, 711*f*, R39, R39*f*
polar bonds, 166–167, 166*f*, 167*f*, 194*t*
polonium, 645, 662, R48, R50*t*
polyamides, 697
polyatomic ions, 184, 190, 218, 275
polyesters, 697
polyethylene, 696, 696*f*
polymerase chain reaction (PCR), 730
polymer products, 137
polymers, 695–697, 696*f*
polypeptides, 713
polyprotic acids, 454–455, 454*f*
polysaccharides, 709, 709*f*
porous barriers, 618–619, 618*f*
positrons, 645*t*, 646–647
potassium
in electrolyte balance, R5–R6, R5*t*, R6*f*
electron configuration, 113, 113*t*

fertilizers, R47, R47*t*
properties, R2–R3, R2*f*, R3*f*, R4*t*
reactivity of, 134*f*
potential difference, 624–626, 634
potential energy, 169, 169*f*
pounds per square inch (psi), 344*t*
precipitates
from chemical reactions, 248, 248*f*, 568, 568*f*
from double-displacement reactions, 268, 268*f*, 414–416, 414*f*
precipitation calculations, 584–586
precipitation reactions, 413–415, 413*t*, 414*f*
precision, 42–44, 43*f*
preenzymes, 721
prefixes
acids, 219
carbon-atom chain, 676*t*
molecular compounds, 215–217, 216*t*, 217*t*
oxyanions, 214
Stock system and, 223
units, 32, 33*t*, R58*t*
pressure, 341, 341*f*
atmospheric, 342–343, 342*f*, 343*f*, 345
Boyle's law, 350, 350*f*
combined gas law, 354–355
critical, 329*f*, 330
effect on chemical equilibrium, 564–565
force and, 341–342, 341*f*, 342*f*
Gay-Lussac's law, 353–354, 353*f*
measuring, 343, 343*f*
osmotic, 428–429, 428*f*
partial, 345–348, 346*f*, 565
solubility and, 391
units of, 35, 344–345, 344*t*
vapor, 325–326, 325*f*, 326*f*, 346, 422–423
water-vapor, R63*f*
Priestley, Joseph, 265, 286
primary standards, 489
primary structure, 715
principal quantum number, 101, 101*f*
products, 9, 247
propane, 362, 674, 675*t*
properties, chemical and physical, 7–10, 7*f*, 9*f*
proportionality, 53–55, 53*f*, 53*t*, 54*t*, 55*f*, 540
proteins, 713–721
amino acids in, 713, 717, 717*f*
biological functions, 716, 716*t*
denaturation, 720, 720*f*
digestion of, 721, 724
as enzymes, 520, 716*t*, 719–721, 719*f*, 720*f*
pH and, 721, R37
as polypeptides, 713
shape and structure, 715, 715*f*
side-chain reactions, 714, 714*f*
synthesis, 694, 729–730, 732
protium, 74, 74*f*, 75*t*
proton-exchange membrane (PEM fuel cells), 628
protons, 68
atomic number and, 73
nuclear binding energy and, 642–643, 643*f*
properties, 71, 72*t*, R59*t*
p-type semiconductors, R43, R43*f*
pure substances, 11*f*, 13–14, 13*f*, 14*f*, 14*t*
purine bases, 726
purity of reagents, 14, 14*f*, 14*t*
pyrimidine bases, 726

Q

qualitative analysis, R16, R16*f*
qualitative information, 27
quantitative information, 27
quantity, 31
quantum, 93
quantum numbers, 101–104, 101*f*, 102*f*, 102*t*, 103*f*, 104*t*. *See also* **electron configurations**
quantum theory, 94–95, 99
quarks, 642
quaternary structure, 715

R

radiation, 645, 653–656, 653*f*, 654*f*, 655*f*
radiation exposure, 653–654, 654*f*
radioactive dating, 655
radioactive decay, 645–652
decay series, 650–651, 650*f*
half-life, 648–649, 648*f*, 648*t*, 662
types of, 645–647, 645*t*, 646*f*, 647*f*
radioactive tracers, 655, 655*f*
radioactive wastes, 655–656
radium, 645, 648, 648*f*, R8, R10*t*
radon, 109, 129, 654
Ramsay, William, 108–109, 109*f*, 127
rate-determining steps, 544–545
rate laws for reactions, 540–546, 548
Rayleigh, Lord (John William Strutt), 108, 108*f*, 127
reactants, 9, 247, 296–300, 296*f*
reaction mechanisms, 529–530, 529*f*
reaction rates, 536, 557, 557*f*. *See also* **kinetics of reactions**
reaction stoichiometry, 283–285. *See also* **stoichiometry**
reaction waves, 274, 274*f*
real gases, 314, 314*f*
rechargeable cells, 631, 631*f*
recombinant DNA technology, 731
redox reactions, 597–599, 608. *See also* **oxidation-reduction reactions**
reducing agents, 606–609, 606*t*, 607*t*
reduction, 597. *See also* **oxidation-reduction reactions**
reduction potential, 624
relative atomic masses, 76–77
rems, 653
resonance structures, 179, 687, 687*f*
respiration, R32–R33, R32*f*, R33*f*
reverse osmosis, 429
reversible reactions, 252*t*, 253, 555–556
ribosomal RNA (rRNA), 729
RNA (ribonucleic acid), 729–730, 729*f*
roentgens, 653
rounding numbers, 46, 46*t*
rubidium, 114*t*, 116, R2–R3, R2*f*, R4*t*
Rutherford, Ernest, 70, 71*f*

S

sacrificial anodes, 624
salt bridges, 618–619, 618*f*
salts, 463
as electrolytes, 383–384, 384*f*
on freezing roads, 432*f*
hydrates, 231–232, 389, 389*f*
hydrolysis of, 574–578, 574*f*, 576*f*, 577*f*
from neutralization reactions, 442, 446, 462–463, 462*f*
nomenclature, 219
solubility product constants, 579–586, 581*t*, 586
sample problems approach, 50–52
saponification, 710
saturated hydrocarbons, 674. *See also* **alkanes**
saturated solutions, 387, 387*f*
scanning electron microscope (SEM), 3–4, 3*f*
scanning tunneling microscope (STM), 3*f*, 66, 728*f*, 729*f*
Schrödinger wave equation, 99–100, 101*f*
scientific method, 27–29, 29*f*
scientific notation, 48–50, 56
scintillation counters, 654
scuba diving, 348
secondary structure, 715
second ionization energy, 147–148, 147*t*
second-period elements, 110–111, 110*t*
self-ionization of water, 471–472, 471*f*, 472*t*, 565
self-oxidation, 609
self-reduction, 609
semiconductors, 322–323, R42–R43, R42*f*, R43*f*
semipermeable membranes, 428–429, 428*f*
shielding, 658
significant figures, 21, 44–48, 45*t*, 46*t*, 477
silicon, 111*t*, 218, R28–R29, R28*f*, R29*t*
silver
alloys, R19*t*, R20*f*
electron configuration, 114*t*
in photochromic lenses, 598
properties, R14, R15*f*, R17*t*
solubility, 579–580
single-displacement reactions, 267–268, 267*f*, 271
SI units, 31–40, R58*t*
base units, 32–34, 32*t*
conversion factors, 38–40, 48, 84
derived units, 34–37, 34*t*, 36*t*
prefixes in, 32, 33*t*
sodium
in electrolyte balance, R5, R5*t*
electron configuration, 111, 111*t*
industrial production of, 633
oxidation state, 596, 596*f*
properties, R2–R3, R2*f*, R3*f*, R4*t*

sodium chloride
crystal structure, 181–182, 181*f*, 182*f*, 320*f*
dissociation of, 411–412, 411*f*, 574*f*
as electrolyte, 383–384, 384*f*
ionic bonding in, 180–181, 180*f*, 181*f*
lattice energy, 182, 183*t*
sodium hydroxide, 462–463, 462*f*, 710
sodium-potassium pump, R6, R6*f*
solids, 8, 319–323, 320*f*, 321*f*, 322*t*, 323*f*
sols, 382*t*. *See also* **colloids**
solubility, 386–388
calculating, 583–586
definition, 582
dissociation, 411–415, 411*f*, 413*f*, 413*t*, 414*f*
of gases in water, R64*t*
precipitation calculations, 584–586
precipitation reactions, 413–415, 413*t*, 414*f*
pressure and, 391
saturation, 387, 387*f*
solubility charts, R64*t*, R65*t*
solubility products, 579–582, 581*t*
temperature and, 388*t*, 392–393, 392*f*
solubility product constants, 580–586, 581*t*
soluble substances, 379
solutes
dissolution rate, 385–386, 385*f*
electrolytes, 383–384, 384*f*, 418–419
solubility, 386–388, 386*f*, 387*f*, 388*t*
solute-solvent interactions, 388–393, 389*f*, 390*f*, 391*f*, 392*f*
types of, 380, 380*t*
solution equilibrium, 386–387, 386*f*
solutions, 378–402. *See also* **aqueous solutions**
buffered, 572–573, 572*f*
components of, 380, 380*f*
dissolution rate, 385–386, 385*f*
enthalpies of, 393–394, 393*f*, 394*t*
entropy in, 517–518, 518*f*
in Henry's law, 348, 391–393, 391*f*, 392*f*
liquid-liquid miscibility, 390, 390*f*
molality, 400–402, 400*f*
molarity, 396–399, 397*f*, 403
nonelectrolytes in, 383–384, 384*f*
observing, 383
pressure and, 391
properties, 379*f*, 382*t*
saturated vs. unsaturated, 387, 387*f*
solubility, 386–388, 386*f*, 387*f*, 388*t*
solute-solvent interactions, 388–393, 389*f*, 390*f*, 391*f*, 392*f*
standard, 489
supersaturated, 387
types of, 380–381, 380*t*
solvated particles, 393, 393*f*
solvents, 380, 380*f*, 389
specific heat, 502–504, 503*t*
specific rate constant, 541–543
spectator ions, 415, 463, 464
speed, 35*f*
speed of light, R59*t*
spin quantum number, 104, 106
stainless steel, R19, R19*f*
standard electrode potential, 625–626, 625*f*, 626*t*
standard hydrogen electrode (SHE), 625, 625*f*
standard molar volume of a gas, 360–361
standard solutions, 489
standard temperature and pressure (STP), 344
starch, 709, 709*f*, R38, R38*f*
states of matter, 310–335
changes of state, 324–330, 324*t*, 326*f*, 327*f*, 329*f*, 330*f*
gas properties, 311–314, 312*f*, 313*f*, 314*f*
liquid properties, 315–318, 316*f*, 317*f*, 318*f*
solid properties, 319–323, 319*f*, 320*f*, 321*f*, 322*t*, 323*f*
steel, R19, R19*f*, R30
steroids, 711
Stock system, 209, 212–213, 223, 223*t*
stoichiometry, 282–302
composition vs. reaction, 283
gas, 361–362
limiting reactants, 296–300
mass-mass calculations, 294–295
mass-mole conversions, 290–294
molar mass and, 285
mole conversions, 288–290
mole ratios and, 284–285, 303
percentage yield, 301–302
Strassman, Fritz, 660–661
strong acids, 448–449, 448*t*, 458–459, 459*t*, 473*t*, 481
strong bases, 449–450, 449*t*, 450*f*, 458–459, 459*t*
strong electrolytes, 418, 418*f*
strontium, 114*t*, R8–R9, R8*f*, R10*t*, R11, R11*f*
structural formulas, 175
structural isomers, 671, 671*f*
subatomic particles, 68, 642
sublimation, 324*t*, 328–329
substitution reactions, 693
substrate molecules, 719–720, 719*f*
sucrose, 708–709
chemical reactions, 695, 695*f*, 708–709, 708*f*, 709*f*
chemical structure, 168*f*, 708*f*, R37*f*
vapor pressure and, 423, 423*f*
suffixes
hydrocarbons, 678, 683, 686
molecular compounds, 216
oxyanions, 214–215
sugars, 384, 384*f*, 707–709, 708*f*
sulfur
chemical bonding, 167
crystalline forms, R48*f*
electron configuration, 111*t*
oxidation numbers, 223, 223*t*
properties, R48–R49, R48*f*, R49*f*, R50*t*
sulfuric acid, 444
in acid rain, 463, 463*f*
in car batteries, 631, 631*f*
as diprotic acid, 454, 454*f*
nomenclature, 443*t*
production and uses of, 444, R53, R53*f*, R53*t*
structure of, 443*f*
superconductors, 18
supercooled liquids, 320
supersaturated solutions, 387
surface area, 385, 385*f*, 536–537
surface melting, 328
surface tension, 317, 317*f*
surfactants, 395
suspensions, 381, 382*t*, 383
symbols, unit R58*t*
symbols used in equations, 251–253, 252*t*, R59*t*
synthesis reactions, 262–265, 263*f*, 274

temperature
absolute zero, 351
Charles's law, 351–352, 351*f*, 352*f*
combined gas law, 354–355
critical, 329, 329*f*
dissolution rate and, 386
effect on chemical equilibrium, 566–567, 567*f*
enzyme activity and, 720, 720*f*
of gases, 312
Gay-Lussac's law, 353–354, 353*f*
heat and, 501–502, 502*f*
reaction rate and, 537
scales, 351–352, 501
SI units of, 32*t*
solubility and, 388t, 392–393, 392*f*
tensile strength, 18
tertiary structure, 715
Thales of Miletus, 41
theoretical yield, 301
theories, 29, 29*f*
thermite reaction, 528*f*, R25*f*
thermochemical equations, 505
thermochemistry, 501–520
calorimeters, 501, 509, 509*f*
definition, 501
enthalpy of combustion, 508–509, 509*f*, R60*t*
enthalpy of formation, 507–508, 512–514, 513*f*
enthalpy of reaction, 505–507, 506*f*, 507*f*
entropy, 516–518, 517*f*, 518*f*
free energy, 518–520, 519*t*
heat and temperature, 501–502, 502*f*
Hess's law, 509–512, 521
specific heat, 502–504, 503*t*
stability and, 508
third ionization energy, 147, 147*t*
third-period elements, 111–112, 112*t*
Thomson, Joseph John, 69
thymine, 726, 726*f*, R40*f*
time, units of, 32*t*
titanium, 113, 113*t*
titration, 487–493
acid-base, 487–489, 488*f*, 489*f*
balancing equations for, 603–605
end point, 488
equivalence point, 488
procedures, 489–493, 490*f*- 491*f*
redox, 603–605
Torricelli, Evangelista, 343, 343*f*, 356, 356*f*
torr, 344, 344*t*
trace elements, R22–R23, R22*f*, R23*t*. *See also* **transition metals**
transfer RNA (tRNA), 729
***trans* isomers,** 672, 682*f*, 682*t*

- **transition intervals,** 484, 485*t*
- **transition metals,** 136, 137, R14–R23
  - alloys, R18–R20, R19*t*, R20*f*
  - in the body, R22–R23, R22*f*, R23*t*
  - gemstones, R17–R18, R17*f*, R18*t*
  - mercury poisoning, R21, R21*f*
  - properties, 136, 136*f*, R14–R16, R15*f*, R16*f*, R17*t*
- **transmutation,** 644, 651–652, 651*f*, 652*f*, 652*t*
- **transuranic elements,** 652, 652*f*, 652*t*, 660–661
- **triglycerides,** 710, R39, R39*f*
- **triple bonds,** 177, 177*f*, 177*t*, 685–686
- **triple point,** 329, 329*f*, R59*t*
- **triprotic acids,** 455
- **tritium,** 74–75, 74*f*, 75*t*
- **trypsin,** 721
- **tungsten,** 112, 136*f*
- **Tyndall effect,** 382, 382*f*

- **uncertainty principle,** 99
- **unified atomic mass unit** (u), 72*t*, 76, R59*t*
- **unit cells,** 321
- **units.** *See* **SI units**
- **unsaturated hydrocarbons,** 682–687, 682*t*
- **unsaturated solutions,** 387, 387*f*
- **uracil,** 726, 726*f*, 729, R40*f*
- **uranium**
  - chain reaction, 657–658, 657*f*
  - decay series, 650–651, 650*f*
  - discovery of, 660
  - isotopes, 75, 78*t*
  - oxidation numbers, 221–222

- **vacuums,** 356–357
- **valence electrons,** 152, 152*t*
- **vaporization,** 186, 317–318, 318*f*, 324*t*, 327
- **vapor pressure,** 325–326, 325*f*, 326*f*, 346
- **vapor-pressure lowering,** 422–423, 422*f*, 423*f*
- **variables,** 28
- **Verneuil, Auguste,** R17–R18
- **visible spectrum,** 92*f*
- **vitamins,** 711, R36, R36*f*
- **volatile liquids,** 325
- **Volta, Alessandro,** 420
- **voltage** (potential difference), 624–627, 634
- **voltaic cells,** 620–628
  - corrosion in, 623–624, 623*f*, 624*f*
  - electrode potentials, 624–627, 625*f*, 626*t*, 634
  - electrolytic cells compared with, 629–630, 629*f*
  - examples of, 621–622, 621*f*, 622*f*
  - operation of, 620, 620*f*
- **volume**
  - Boyle's law, 349–350, 349*f*, 350*f*
  - Charles's law, 351–352, 351*f*, 352*f*
  - combined gas law, 354–355
  - molar, 360–361
  - units of, 34*t*, 35, 35*f*, R58*t*
- **VSEPR theory,** 187–191, 188*f*, 189*f*, 190*t*

- **water,** 331–333
  - as amphoteric substance, 460
  - boiling point, 326, 326*f*, 333, R59*t*
  - as Brønsted-Lowry acid, 452
  - changes of state in, 8*f*, 9
  - density, 332, R63*t*
  - dipole interactions, 195–196, 196*f*
  - from double-displacement reactions, 269
  - electrolysis of, 632, 632*f*
  - freezing point, R59*t*
  - hydrogen bonding in, 196, 196*f*
  - ice, 324*t*, 328–329, 331–332, 332*f*
  - ionization constant, 472–473, 472*t*, 566, 573
  - molecular geometry, 189, 189*f*, 192, 192*f*
  - phase diagram, 329–330, 329*f*
  - as pure substance, 13, 13*f*
  - self-ionization, 471–472, 471*f*, 472*t*, 565–566
  - structure of, 331–332, 331*f*
  - tap, 451
  - triple point, 329, 329*t*, R59*t*
  - water-vapor pressure, R63*t*
- **water purification,** 259–260, 429
- **water treatment,** R56–R57, R56*f*
- **Watson, James,** 727
- **wavelength,** 91–93, 92*f*
- **waves**
  - diffraction and interference, 98, 99*f*, 100
  - electrons as, 98, 99*f*
  - light as, 91–93, 92*f*
  - Schrödinger wave equation, 99, 101
- **weak acids,** 448–449, 448*t*, 571–572, 572*t*
- **weak bases,** 449–450, 449*t*
- **weak electrolytes,** 418*f*, 419
- **weight,** 33
- **weighted averages,** 77, 117
- **Wilkins, Maurice,** 727
- **Wöhler, Friedrich,** 673, 673*f*
- **word equations,** 249, 254

- **X-rays,** 4, 91, 92*f*, 645, 647, 647*f*, 654

- **Ytterbium,** R61

- **zinc**
  - in the body, R23*t*
  - in cathodic protection, 624, 624*f*
  - in dry cells, 621, 621*f*
  - in electrochemical cells, 617–622, 617*f*, 618*f*, 619*f*, 620*f*
  - electron configuration, 113, 113*t*,
  - properties, R14–R16, R15*f*, R16*f*, R17*t*
  - as reducing agent, 607, 607*f*, 607*t*
- **zinc-carbon dry cells,** 621, 621*f*

Periodic Table of the Elements

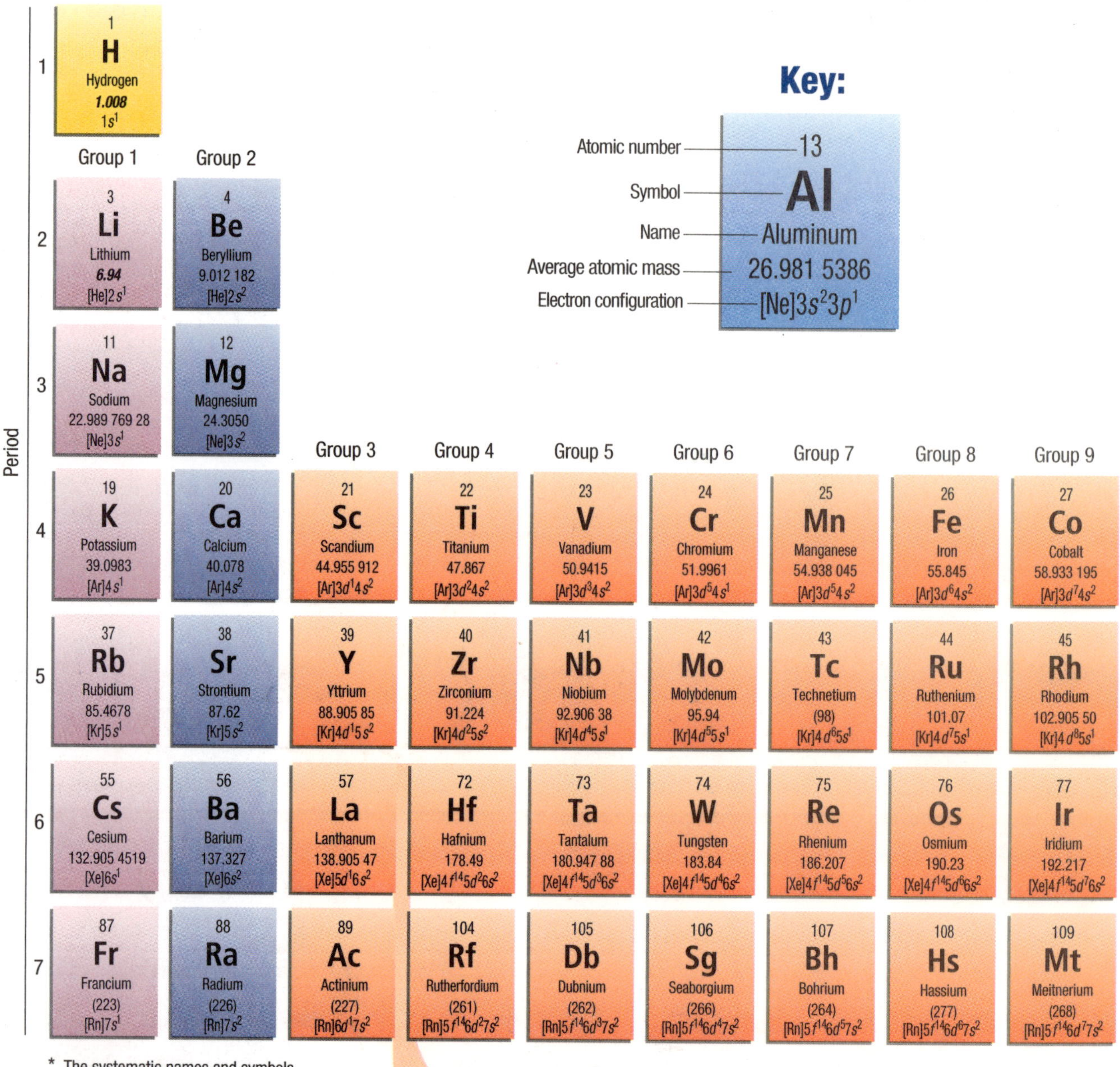

Period	Group 1	Group 2	Group 3	Group 4	Group 5	Group 6	Group 7	Group 8	Group 9
1	1 **H** Hydrogen ***1.008*** $1s^{1}$								
2	3 **Li** Lithium ***6.94*** [He]$2s^{1}$	4 **Be** Beryllium 9.012 182 [He]$2s^{2}$							
3	11 **Na** Sodium 22.989 769 28 [Ne]$3s^{1}$	12 **Mg** Magnesium 24.3050 [Ne]$3s^{2}$							
4	19 **K** Potassium 39.0983 [Ar]$4s^{1}$	20 **Ca** Calcium 40.078 [Ar]$4s^{2}$	21 **Sc** Scandium 44.955 912 [Ar]$3d^{1}4s^{2}$	22 **Ti** Titanium 47.867 [Ar]$3d^{2}4s^{2}$	23 **V** Vanadium 50.9415 [Ar]$3d^{3}4s^{2}$	24 **Cr** Chromium 51.9961 [Ar]$3d^{5}4s^{1}$	25 **Mn** Manganese 54.938 045 [Ar]$3d^{5}4s^{2}$	26 **Fe** Iron 55.845 [Ar]$3d^{6}4s^{2}$	27 **Co** Cobalt 58.933 195 [Ar]$3d^{7}4s^{2}$
5	37 **Rb** Rubidium 85.4678 [Kr]$5s^{1}$	38 **Sr** Strontium 87.62 [Kr]$5s^{2}$	39 **Y** Yttrium 88.905 85 [Kr]$4d^{1}5s^{2}$	40 **Zr** Zirconium 91.224 [Kr]$4d^{2}5s^{2}$	41 **Nb** Niobium 92.906 38 [Kr]$4d^{4}5s^{1}$	42 **Mo** Molybdenum 95.94 [Kr]$4d^{5}5s^{1}$	43 **Tc** Technetium (98) [Kr]$4d^{6}5s^{1}$	44 **Ru** Ruthenium 101.07 [Kr]$4d^{7}5s^{1}$	45 **Rh** Rhodium 102.905 50 [Kr]$4d^{8}5s^{1}$
6	55 **Cs** Cesium 132.905 4519 [Xe]$6s^{1}$	56 **Ba** Barium 137.327 [Xe]$6s^{2}$	57 **La** Lanthanum 138.905 47 [Xe]$5d^{1}6s^{2}$	72 **Hf** Hafnium 178.49 [Xe]$4f^{14}5d^{2}6s^{2}$	73 **Ta** Tantalum 180.947 88 [Xe]$4f^{14}5d^{3}6s^{2}$	74 **W** Tungsten 183.84 [Xe]$4f^{14}5d^{4}6s^{2}$	75 **Re** Rhenium 186.207 [Xe]$4f^{14}5d^{5}6s^{2}$	76 **Os** Osmium 190.23 [Xe]$4f^{14}5d^{6}6s^{2}$	77 **Ir** Iridium 192.217 [Xe]$4f^{14}5d^{7}6s^{2}$
7	87 **Fr** Francium (223) [Rn]$7s^{1}$	88 **Ra** Radium (226) [Rn]$7s^{2}$	89 **Ac** Actinium (227) [Rn]$6d^{1}7s^{2}$	104 **Rf** Rutherfordium (261) [Rn]$5f^{14}6d^{2}7s^{2}$	105 **Db** Dubnium (262) [Rn]$5f^{14}6d^{3}7s^{2}$	106 **Sg** Seaborgium (266) [Rn]$5f^{14}6d^{4}7s^{2}$	107 **Bh** Bohrium (264) [Rn]$5f^{14}6d^{5}7s^{2}$	108 **Hs** Hassium (277) [Rn]$5f^{14}6d^{6}7s^{2}$	109 **Mt** Meitnerium (268) [Rn]$5f^{14}6d^{7}7s^{2}$

58 **Ce** Cerium 140.116 [Xe]$4f^{1}5d^{1}6s^{2}$	59 **Pr** Praseodymium 140.907 65 [Xe]$4f^{3}6s^{2}$	60 **Nd** Neodymium 144.242 [Xe]$4f^{4}6s^{2}$	61 **Pm** Promethium (145) [Xe]$4f^{5}6s^{2}$	62 **Sm** Samarium 150.36 [Xe]$4f^{6}6s^{2}$
90 **Th** Thorium 232.038 06 [Rn]$6d^{2}7s^{2}$	91 **Pa** Protactinium 231.035 88 [Rn]$5f^{2}6d^{1}7s^{2}$	92 **U** Uranium 238.028 91 [Rn]$5f^{3}6d^{1}7s^{2}$	93 **Np** Neptunium (237) [Rn]$5f^{4}6d^{1}7s^{2}$	94 **Pu** Plutonium (244) [Rn]$5f^{6}7s^{2}$

* The systematic names and symbols for elements greater than 112 will be used until the approval of trivial names by IUPAC.

Elements whose average atomic masses appear bolded and italicized are recognized by the International Union of Pure and Applied Chemistry (IUPAC) to have several stable isotopes. Thus, the average atomic mass for each of these elements is officially expressed as a range of values. A range of values expresses that the average atomic mass of a sample of one of these elements is not a constant in nature but varies depending on the physical, chemical, and nuclear history of the material in which the sample is found. However, the values in this table are appropriate for everyday calculations. A value given in parentheses is not an average atomic mass but is the mass number of that element's most stable or most common isotope.